Individualized Intervention with Young Multiple Offenders

Current Issues in Criminal Justice

Michael B. Blankenship, *General Editor*

Stranger Violence
A Theoretical Inquiry
by Marc Riedel

Crimes of Style
Urban Graffiti and the Politics of Criminality
by Jeff Ferrell

Understanding Corporate Criminality
edited by Michael B. Blankenship

Political Crime in Contemporary America
A Critical Approach
edited by Kenneth D. Tunnell

The Management of Correctional Institutions
by Marilyn D. McShane and
    Frank P. Williams III

Academic Professionalism in Law
    Enforcement
by Bernadette Jones Palombo

Controlling State Crime
An Introduction
edited by Jeffrey Ian Ross

The Winds of Injustice
American Indians and the U.S. Government
by Laurence French

African-American Organized Crime
A Social History
by Rufus Schatzberg and Robert J. Kelly

Media, Process, and the Social Construction
    of Crime
Studies in Newsmaking Criminology
edited by Gregg Barak

Altered States of Mind
Critical Observations of the Drug War
edited by Peter Kraska

The Contours of Psychiatric Justice
*A Postmodern Critique of Mental Illness,
    Criminal Insanity, and the Law*
by Bruce A. Arrigo

Innovative Trends and Specialized Strategies
    in Community-Based Corrections
edited by Charles B. Fields

African Americans and the Criminal Justice
    System
by Marvin D. Free, Jr.

Policing Change, Changing Police
Internal Perspectives
edited by Otwin Marenin

Environmental Crime and Criminality
Theoretical and Practical Issues
edited by Sally M. Edwards, Terry D.
    Edwards, and Charles B. Fields

Individualized Intervention with Young Multiple Offenders

Ted Palmer

ROUTLEDGE
New York & London

Published in 2002 by
Routledge
29 West 35th Street
New York, NY 10001

Published in Great Britain by
Routledge
11 New Fetter Lane
London EC4P 4EE

Routledge is an imprint of the Taylor and Francis Group.

10   9   8   7   6   5   4   3   2   1

Printed on acid-free, 250-year-life paper.
Manufactured in the United States of America.

Library of Congress Cataloging-in-Publication Data

Palmer, Ted.
   Individualized intervention with young multiple offenders / Ted Palmer.
      p. cm. — (Garland reference library of social science; vol. 1054. Current issues in
   criminal justice; vol. 27)
   Includes bibliographical references and index.
   ISBN 0-8153-2122-8 (alk. paper)
   1. Juvenile delinquency—Prevention. 2. Juvenile delinquents—Mental health services.
   3. Juvenile delinquents—Mental health. 4. Juvenile delinquents—Rehabilitation. I. Title.
   II. Garland reference library of social science; v. 1054. III. Garland reference library of
   social science. Current issues in criminal justice; v. 27.

RJ506.J88 P35 2000
364.36—dc21
                                                                              00-02963

Contents

Foreword   **xi**
Francis T. Cullen
Patricia Van Voorhis

Preface   **xv**

Acknowledgments   **xxi**

Introduction   **xxv**

VOLUME 1   **CALIFORNIA'S COMMUNITY TREATMENT
                  PROJECT**

PART I   AN EXPERIMENT IN INDIVIDUALIZED
                  INTERVENTION

Chapter 1   Background and Overview   **3**
Chapter 2   Organization, Intake, and Assumptions   **11**
Chapter 3   Program Elements   **29**
Chapter 4   The Youths: Background and I-Level   **47**
Chapter 5   Personality Types and Case Illustrations   **55**
Chapter 6   Methods of Intervention   **69**

PART II   PROGRAM EFFECTIVENESS AND MATCHING

Chapter 7   Research Questions and Measures of Impact   **89**
Chapter 8   Program Effectiveness for Valley Youths   **95**
Chapter 9   Program Effectiveness for San Francisco Youths   **109**
Chapter 10   Social Risk, Pre/Post Change, Age, and Costs   **125**
Chapter 11   Matching of Worker and Youth   **159**

PART III   REVIEW, PHASE 3, IMPLICATIONS, AND KEY
                  FACTORS

Chapter 12   Review of Findings   **197**
Chapter 13   The Phase 3 Experiment: Adding an Institutional   **213**
                  Component
Chapter 14   Program Review and General Implications   **231**
Chapter 15   Key Factors in Performance   **245**

Chapter 16   Additional Observations Regarding Key Factors   **275**

PART IV   THE FEASIBILITY OF COMMUNITY-BASED,
                  INDIVIDUALIZED INTERVENTION

Chapter 17   Social Agency and Parent Organization Factors   **291**
Chapter 18   Staff, Unit Functioning, and Supervisory Factors   **305**
Chapter 19   Case Processing, Maintenance, and Other Operational **323**
                  Factors
Chapter 20   Review and Discussion of Feasibility   **353**

VOLUME 2   **ISSUES, THEORY, AND PERSPECTIVES**

PART I   ISSUES AND DEVELOPMENTS

Chapter 21   Validity of the Research Findings   **397**
Chapter 22   Further Validity and Related Issues   **461**
Chapter 23   Selected Individualized Programs   **645**

PART II   RATIONALES, THEORY, ETHICS, AND TRENDS

Chapter 24   Intervention—Its Rationales and the Needs-Centered   **697**
                  Approach
Chapter 25   Theory, Goals, and Stances toward Intervention   **733**
Chapter 26   Content Effects, and Conclusions Regarding Rationales **777**
                  for Intervention
Chapter 27   Selected Trends and a Habilitation/Developmental   **817**
                  Framework

PART III   PERSPECTIVES ON COMMUNITY-BASED,
                  INDIVIDUALIZED INTERVENTION

Chapter 28   Benefits and Underlying Beliefs   **843**
Chapter 29   Differing Perspectives on Offenders   **855**
Chapter 30   Individualization, Offender Needs, and Related Issues **895**

APPENDICES

Appendix 1   Details Regarding the Phase 2 Objectives   **925**
Appendix 2   Initial Staffing Guide   **926**
Appendix 3   Parole Agreement Used throughout CYA during Phases 1 and 2 **927**
Appendix 4   Sacramento Community Center Floor Plan   **928**
Appendix 5   Background Characteristics of Youths   **929**
Appendix 6   Details Concerning I-Level Theory and Personality Types **936**
Appendix 7   Rare Types of Youths   **944**
Appendix 8   Number of Contacts per Month between Agent and   **952**
                  Youth during First Year on Parole
Appendix 9   Criteria for Favorable and Unfavorable Discharge, Used **953**
                  throughout the Youth Authority during Phases 1 and 2
Appendix 10   Community Treatment Project Severity-of-Offense Scale   **955**
Appendix 11   Comparisons on Background Characteristics of Experimental **958**
                  and Control Valley Males in Phase 1 and 2 Parole and
                  Post-Discharge Follow-ups

Appendix 12	Comparisons between Regular Controls and Directly Paroled Controls on Selected Background Variables	**962**
Appendix 13	Performance of Valley Males in Areas of School and Paid Employment	**963**
Appendix 14	Monthly Rate of Offending for Favorable Dischargees	**966**
Appendix 15	Method for Computing the Number of Arrests per 100 Youths during a Nine-Year Follow-Up	**969**
Appendix 16	Rate of Arrest during Each of 11 Years Prior to Youth Authority Commitment, for Valley Boys	**974**
Appendix 17	Rate of Arrest for Moderate Plus Severe Offenses during Each of 11 Years Prior to Youth Authority Commitment, for Valley Boys—by Age	**976**
Appendix 18	Number of Offenses per 1,000 Months at Risk during Three-Year Precommitment and Three-Year Postcommitment (Parole) Periods, for Valley Males— by Age	**978**
Appendix 19	Number and Severity of Prior Arrests among Valley Boys—by Age	**980**
Appendix 20	Computation of Youth Authority Career Costs	**982**
Appendix 21	Computation of Post-Discharge Costs for Other Correctional and Law Enforcement Experiences, Separate for Experimentals and Controls	**988**
Appendix 22	Developments and Issues in Matching during Early Years of CTP	**990**
Appendix 23	Selected Questions Used with Candidates for CTP	**993**
Appendix 24	Factors Contributing to "Branching Out" by Workers	**995**
Appendix 25	Number of Contacts between Matched Agents, Unmatched Agents, and Two Groups of Conflicted and Power-Oriented Youths throughout Youth Authority Career	**999**
Appendix 26	Rate of Offending during Parole for Specified Youth Types	**1001**
Appendix 27	Rate of Offending during Post-Discharge and during Parole Plus Post-Discharge Periods, for Specified Youth Types	**1006**
Appendix 28	Five Groups of Status 1 Youths	**1009**
Appendix 29	Comparisons on Background Characteristics of Selected Youth Groupings, for Phase 3 Males in Parole Follow-Up Analysis	**1012**
Appendix 30	Number of Arrests per 1,000 Months at Risk during a Four-Year Post-Discharge Follow-Up, for Phase 3 Males	**1014**
Appendix 31	Approaches Used to Identify CTP's Key Factors	**1015**
Appendix 32	I-Level Diagnosis and Ethnicity Issues	**1021**
Appendix 33	Basic Features of Classification for Treatment: An Overview	**1036**
Appendix 34	Offense-Centered Justice, Differential Sentencing/ Assignment, and Strategy 2	**1041**
Appendix 35	Relationships between Classification Systems and Intervention-Centered Factors	**1044**
Appendix 36	Issues Relating to Privately Operated CTP Programs	**1046**
Appendix 37	Factors Responsible for Discrepancies between Suspension Documents and Rapsheets	**1051**
Appendix 38	Factors and Weights Used in Computation of Base Expectancy Scores	**1055**
Appendix 39	Paroled-Out-of-Area Youths and Non-Interviewed Controls	**1057**

Appendix 40   Information Bases for Descriptions and Concepts   **1062**
               Relating to Precommitment Years and to Selected
               Developments among Nonoffenders
Appendix 41   Technical Details Concerning Three-Level Series, and   **1066**
               Predictability of Illegal Behavior
Appendix 42   The A/R Cycle, Long-Standing Difficulties, and   **1071**
               Motivation
Appendix 43   Skill Deficits and Experiential versus Genetic Factors   **1083**
Appendix 44   Factors Bearing on the Crystallization of the Illegal-   **1086**
               Behavior Pattern
Appendix 45   Structural Factors and Their Relationship to   **1096**
               Emotional/Dynamic Factors
Appendix 46   Common Contributors to Recidivism in Selected Types of   **1102**
               Offenders
Appendix 47   Elements Used in Seven Programs that Focused on   **1110**
               Various Targets
Appendix 48   General Guidelines and Specific Information in   **1112**
               Intervention Planning
Appendix 49   Further Discussion and Notes to Chapter 22   **1118**

Bibliography   **1133**

Individualized Intervention with Young Multiple Offenders

Foreword

For the past two decades, American corrections has been descending steadily into an ideological and policy abyss. This descent has been hastened by the forfeiture in many high quarters of the rehabilitative ideal and by the politics of what Todd Clear calls "penal harm"—the idea that the central goal of corrections should be to inflict harm on offenders. The most obvious manifestation of the penal harm movement has been the fivefold increase in prison populations since the early 1970s. More disquieting, however, have been the crass, mean-spirited, and often politically opportunistic attempts to make inmates suffer by eliminating educational programs, reintroducing chain gangs, and stripping away amenities that help to dull the deprivations inherent in institutional life.

Amidst this mean season in corrections, many of those who work with offenders have tried to rise above the prevailing political rhetoric. Each day in agencies across the nation, there are genuine efforts by sincere practitioners to improve offenders' lives and to make communities safer. Within the field of academic criminology, there has been similar opposition to the penal harm movement. Our fellow research criminologists have provided a valuable service in showing the limits of punitive policies and interventions. Too often, however, they have not moved beyond the role of critic to engage the more difficult task of illuminating how we might achieve a better correctional future.

In this context, Ted Palmer has been, and remains, a beacon whose work frames the pathway to more effective correctional intervention. As someone whose career has not been in the ivory tower of academia but in a correctional agency, he understands the difficulty of changing offenders but, nonetheless, the importance of practitioners remaining steadfast in their embrace of rehabilitation as the goal of the correctional enterprise. As a meticulous researcher, Ted is firmly committed to the proposition that science—not hunches, custom, or political ideology—should be the basis for deciding how to intervene with offenders.

Indeed, Ted's writings, career, and person reflect this duality: his fundamental humaneness, which leads him to reject needlessly harmful penal policies and to believe that offenders are not beyond reform, and his rigor as a researcher, which leads him to respect data, to subject his views to empirical test, and to endorse those interventions that are shown to be effective. Ted's correctional message, whether in print or in lecture, is informed by a strong sense of social justice. For over two decades—including his courageous rebuttal of Robert Martinson's "nothing works" doctrine—he has debated the antitreatment forces. Unrelentingly, he has put forward the conclusion that offender rehabilitation "works," and that the current state of correctional programming can be made more effective. He has never stated this message as mere conjecture, but rather has worked assiduously to support his assertions with some of the most well-respected findings that social science could offer. *Individualized Intervention with Young Multiple Offenders* (hereinafter *Individualized Intervention*) thoroughly reflects the optimism that offenders can change if subjected to effective programming, and the belief that hard data are needed to discern the principles of effective correctional intervention. This magisterial work, which evaluates California's Community Treatment Project (CTP), is the crowning achievement of Ted's career. Initiated in 1974, this project occupied his attention off and on for twenty-five years. The result is a book accessible to practitioners and academics alike, rich in detail, and poignant in its conclusions. Most important, *Individualized Intervention* provides a firm rebuttal to the many naysayers who cling to the increasingly indefensible claim that "nothing works" to reform the wayward. In this fashion, it contributes to the growing body of revisionist research, which is building a persuasive theoretical and empirical case for reaffirming rehabilitation.

The Community Treatment Project was one of the most successful and intensive correctional interventions in history. It also was intensively investigated; its experimental study design is one of the most scientifically sound research models available. Unfortunately, very few programs have used such designs as successfully as the CTP. More often, social service agencies view the experimental approach as too difficult to implement and monitor; as a result, the validity of their findings is compromised. This was not the case with the CTP.

Even though the CTP admitted its first clients more than thirty-five years ago, many scholars continue to view it as a state-of-the-art program. Because the CTP was far ahead of its time in terms of its treatment technology, the findings Ted reports are far from outdated. The CTP's use of a "differential treatment" approach, which matched types of youths to types of case managers, is recommended by today's leading experts on rehabilitation. In particular, this approach makes it possible to identify key intervention strategies for each type of youthful offender. It also furnishes a basis for understanding not only *if* a treatment modality is effective but also *why* it might work. Notably, as Chapter 23 reveals, the principles informing the CTP have been used successfully in more recent treatment programs conducted in other settings.

The first parts of *Individualized Intervention* describe in detail the theory informing the CTP, the nature of the intervention, and the project's assessment. This detail is essential, because too often academic evaluations of programs are so sparse in presentation that practitioners cannot reasonably determine what specifically an intervention involves. Because the recipe for the treatment is not supplied, the replication of quality programs becomes virtually impossible. As a result, potentially valuable interventions that might be applied in a number of agencies go unused or even misused. *Individualized Intervention* is an exception to this situation. For policymakers and practitioners who need to know how to run another program like CTP, this book is crucial: It provides the knowledge base to facilitate program design and replication.

The book also furnishes a wonderful analysis of the feasibility of implementing a treatment program such as the CTP. Most commentary on program implementation is sterile and wedded to showing why current knowledge on "what works" in correctional intervention is not feasible to put into place in the "real world." Ted's analysis, however, reveals that the feasibility of program implementation is not an "either-or" phenomenon, but rather a matter of degree and contingent on a number of factors that may be within the control of many correctional agencies.

As its title suggests, the book makes a strong case for *individualizing* treatment interventions. Many critics dismiss individualization by claiming that it is impractical for a bureaucratic correctional agency to give every offender a unique treatment. Ted shows, however, that this critique is flawed both empirically and theoretically.

We would be remiss if we did not note that *Individualized Intervention* contains an important rejoinder to Paul Lerman's *Community Treatment and Social Control,* which claimed that the CTP was ineffective and replete with unintended consequences that subverted the program's treatment goals. Widely read and much praised, Lerman's conclusions have been accepted by many criminologists as the final word on the CTP. *Individualizing Intervention,* however, supplies a persuasive response to Lerman, demonstrating how his plausible criticisms of the CTP ultimately prove empirically vacuous. This rebuttal serves the important function of correcting a distorted view that has been repeatedly cited as showing that well-intentioned community rehabilitation programs are destined to fail.

This book also serves as a fine testimony to the staff of the CTP, to Marguerite Warren, who was its principal investigator during 1961–1967, and to numerous highly skilled case managers and researchers. Their judiciousness, hard work, resilience, and dedication to the youths they served were integral to the CTP's success and, ultimately, have made possible the significant contribution conveyed in the pages ahead.

Much, much more could be said about *Individualized Intervention,* but doing so is beyond the strictures of a foreword. We trust, however, that we have said enough to convince readers that this work is rich, perhaps uniquely so, in the wisdom it imparts. We hope that readers will embark on the lengthy, but ultimately rewarding, journey through its pages.

In closing, we will take the opportunity to pay tribute to Ted Palmer. He is one of the true giants in the field. As a full-time researcher for the California Youth Authority for decades, he intensively studied numerous correctional programs. Indeed, to our knowledge, no other scholar has enjoyed such uninterrupted investigation of the correctional client and correctional intervention. Equally important, Ted has done the immense service of *reporting* the results of his labors. His writings—and *Individualized Intervention* is no exception—stand out for their analytical brilliance. They reflect not only a thorough grasp of the existing knowledge base but also an invaluable wealth of understanding garnered through years of his own highly disciplined research and experience.

Underneath it all, as we stated earlier, is Ted Palmer's sense of decency and caring. It is perhaps these personal qualities that sustained his career-long search to find ways to reform offenders and make communities safer. Through his research, writing, and personal touch, he has made the world a better place. It is a legacy that all of us should hope to achieve.

Francis T. Cullen
Patricia Van Voorhis
University of Cincinnati

Preface

In the late 1950s and early 1960s two of corrections' main unanswered questions were: (1) Can serious offenders be worked with in the open community in lieu of being institutionalized? and (2) Even if the answer to that is yes, that is, even if such programming is acceptable to the community and is operationally feasible, how does its effectiveness compare with that of institutional programming? The latter programming was central to corrections' standard approach, as it still is today. Effectiveness mainly referred to less recidivism, for example, fewer arrests and convictions.

Those questions reflected the fact that because the number of commitments to correctional agencies was rising, many administrators had become increasingly concerned about eventual overcrowding in institutions, and, with that, about the costs and timing of building new facilities. Given those concerns, and because many academicians and others were increasingly documenting "criminogenic" influences of various institutional environments and were drawing attention to the negative effects of "banishment" from the community and to the difficulties of returning to that environment ("reintegrating") after being institutionalized, those administrators, and other correctional professionals, began to consider the possibility of using alternatives to lockup. Nevertheless, as of 1960, questions (1) and (2) had not been systematically and empirically examined for any sizable range of serious offenders, and the thought of *actually* trying to rehabilitate such individuals in the community, rather than in institutions, was still very new. At any rate, to many practitioners and decision makers, the prospects of such an undertaking seemed, understandably, risky.

Starting in 1961, and despite that recognized risk, the California Youth Authority and the National Institute of Mental Health began to address those and related questions via a three-year scientific experiment. As it turned out, this study, because of its findings, was directly extended for another five years, and, after that, for yet another five. During the first eight years of this experiment, young multiple offenders who had been committed to the Youth Authority (the state correctional agency for juveniles) from their local communities were randomly assigned to either an intensive, low caseload, newly established, in lieu program known as the Community Treatment Project, or else to a standard institutional program that was followed by regular parole.

By the mid-1960s this program—"CTP"—had become corrections' most closely watched rehabilitation effort. This was so for two broad reasons. First, and mainly, the YA/NIMH experiment—of which CTP was the principal component and main focus—appeared to have answered question (1) with a definite "yes," and question (2) with a moderately strong "It sometimes is *more* effective." These answers, given their major policy implications with respect to the above concerns and areas of growing awareness, excited correctional professionals and academicians alike. Second, the experiment, which had now begun to focus still further on the nature of CTP itself, seemed well on its way to obtaining answers or at least strong leads regarding two related, practical questions: (3) To which types of offenders do those effectiveness results apply, and not apply? and (4) What main factors are responsible for the program's comparative success? The experiment used an innovative youth-classification system to determine "type."

This book describes, for the first time in detail, the experiment that answered those first two questions in that manner, and which thereby helped launch the deinstitutionalization movement within corrections. Volume 1 focuses on the Community Treatment Project in particular: its place in the experiment; its assumptions, principles, and structure; its case processing and other operational as well as organizational functions; its program elements and other visible factors; its main strategies and interaction techniques, separately for differing youth types; its staff; and its effectiveness or impact as compared to the standard Youth Authority program. This volume also describes the answers that emerged to *questions (3) and (4)*. Regarding (4), in particular, it singles out what appear to be the key ingredients and conditions associated with CTP's comparative success. Separately, it describes a modification that was made in that program and which was explored during the experiment's ninth through twelfth years. This change was designed to address five groups of offenders who, in the first eight years, were unresponsive to or rejecting of the CTP and standard programs alike.

During the 1960s other questions arose about community-based intervention in general and regarding the California CTP model specifically. Is it costlier than standard programming? Does it apply to a range of environments, including the highly urbanized? Is it effective only with older, presumably more mature, adolescents? Beyond those questions, still others arose—especially after the 1960s. These reflected highly significant issues that were neither limited to nor necessarily focused on community-based programming, but to which the experiment's findings were relevant: Can correctional programming reduce violent offending—without, that is, using physically and/or psychologically destructive approaches (e.g., the *Clockwise Orange*), and without imposing extremely harsh conditions of confinement that border on cruel and inhumane? Is incapacitation, per se, necessarily the best way, or even only the best available way, to protect society against serious offenders, whether they are violent or not? Related to that, do not *more controlling* approaches almost always produce less illegal behavior than *less controlling* approaches—whether or not the former occur in the context of *lockup* or else involve high levels of *community* supervision? And, level of external control aside, would not public protection be better served if certain individuals—whether or not violent—were incarcerated prior to participating in community-located intervention? These questions are still very much alive.

Regarding some of these questions, and others as well, the YA/NIMH experiment found that the rate of violent offending for males was about half as much in the Community Treatment Project as in the standard program. It also found that, even allowing for the crime-free periods that occur during lockup, that is, factoring in incapacitation, long-term protection was greater in the community-based than in the institutional program, with a large majority of youths. The study, based on much converging evidence, also obtained a combination of answers and strong leads to questions (3) and (4), that is, "What works for whom, and why or how?" It further showed that intensive intervention in the community can be implemented in a humane, albeit not anxiety-free, way.

Obtaining a highly individualized understanding of the youths' needs and situation was a basic operational requirement at the Community Treatment Project, and individualized programming that occurred in accordance with that understanding was a key ingredient of success. As Chapters 17–20 of Volume 1 were being completed (1981–1984), the author drew three linked conclusions about intervention with most young multiple offenders: (1) If correctional personnel wish to achieve public protection that will continue well after an agency's jurisdiction ends, and long after its external controls and supports cease, they must help those youths generate or increase their internal controls and develop in other personal and interpersonal ways as well. (2) To substantially raise the chances that those changes will occur, it is essential, though not sufficient, for the correctional program to achieve and maintain considerable individualization with respect to understanding and implementation alike. (3) Individualization, in concert with other factors and features, is critical to helping those youths become internally motivated enough to relinquish or markedly reduce their illegal behavior and to seriously try to move toward a better overall future. "Other . . . features" are ones that can help provide support, can reduce negative pressures, and can help increase self-confidence as well as practical skills. Individualized understanding can position staff to (1) focus on relevant issues and needs, (2) concentrate on significant, realistic, and timely activities and goals, and (3) carry out (1) and (2) in ways to which the youths can respond constructively.

Though Volume 2 ranges across several topics, it revolves mainly around the nature of, and issues relating to, *individualization* in correctional intervention with serious offenders. In so doing, it also highlights the "other . . . features" with which that factor acts in concert, and which can even allow it to occur. The volume describes what "considerable individualization" *means*—entails—in such a correctional context. It reviews various practical benefits associated with individualization, ones that were reflected in CTP's results but which can apply, and in many cases have applied, elsewhere. The volume describes a number of individualized programs that existed in the United States and Canada during the past 30 years, programs that drew heavily from the California operation and which usually lasted about 15 years. (Some still exist.) It describes, at length, major connections between commonly observed contributors to illegal behavior and to related risky/excessive behaviors, on the one hand, and the relevance of individualized intervention and the in-concert factors and features, on the other. In this context, and with main emphasis on addressing legitimate youth needs and community needs, the volume indicates why individualized intervention is ethically appropriate. Volume 2 also describes and discusses negative implications of viewing youths in certain stereotyped or overly simplified ways—"negative" with regard to the goal of achieving *long*-term public protection. Finally, it summarizes why and in what respects it is operationally possible for a correctional agency to simultaneously implement an individualized intervention plan for each of its many youths, assuming it can develop such a plan in the first place.

This book is very much about, but not only about, community-based intervention. It also emphasizes, but does not solely emphasize, *intensive* intervention—especially, but not just, in that particular setting. Further, it is about "differential" intervention (DI), that is, differing kinds of treatment and control for differing categories ("types") of youth. Yet even here, the book involves something more: It emphasizes a level of DI that goes beyond the given categories. At this level, called "individualized" intervention, important differences and similarities can exist across any two youths regardless of the categories—one per youth—into which they best fit.

For instance, differences in life circumstances, skills, interests, and attitudes can be found among any two youths who fall within the *same* typological category, and similarities with respect to those areas can exist among any two youngsters who best fit into *differing* categories. Of special importance, any given category, although it can provide very useful information and predictions about most or all youths who fall within it, may not contain certain items that are needed and that must soon be integrated with each other in order to plan a sufficiently realistic, highly relevant, and well-timed intervention for any *particular* youth. As implied above, such a plan would be needed in order to focus not only on changes which address that individual's immediate management and short-term control issues, but on those which can specifically promote his or her long-term positive adjustment.

Consistent with that type and level of planning, and supporting it in several ways, is a developmental theme that runs throughout the book. Here, youths are seen as moving through various stages that can lead to the involvements and roles commonly associated with adulthood. In this regard, the dozen years' experience with the YA/NIMH experiment, especially the direct observations and behavioral follow-ups that were made of several hundred serious offenders in the Community Treatment Project, indicated the following: Despite their pre-program records of repeat offending and their in-program resistance at various points, a large percentage of these individuals are open to substantial positive change even early in their program; or, they can begin opening to it before long. Their frequent facades to the contrary notwithstanding, these youths have not entirely closed their minds and come to believe they have set their course forever. They can change and develop, and, under certain circumstances, they do.

Individualization, and constructive staff/youth relationships, are among the key factors that can promote, accelerate, and help maintain the process of long-term change and development. These factors, together with others, can raise staff's chances of successfully drawing upon the youths' wishes for enjoyment and their need for greater emotional security. In this regard, a developmental perspective can help staff better understand and work with these individuals' ongoing and upcoming psychological and social challenges. It can help them not only be more sensitive to these youths' felt vulnerabilities and areas of ambivalence—often key sources of resistance—but, as implied, better tap into, facilitate, redirect, and enhance their more constructive motivations and interests. Chapter 27 describes one such developmental perspective, one that reflects information and observations from the experiment's first six years.

Besides reflecting intensive intervention (e.g., frequent contacts), the book illustrates *extensive* intervention (e.g., the addressing of several areas of the youths' life). For instance, when intervening with any typical youth, the Community Treatment Project usually focused on several of the following areas; it did so during one or more substantially overlapping, immediately successive, or else substantially separated time periods: educational, vocational, and/or interpersonal *skill/capacity deficits;* family, peer, and/or societal *pressures/disadvantages;* conflicts, defenses, and/or attitudes that mainly reflect *internal difficulties* (Chapter 27). Focusing on those several areas—"targets"—was considered essential not just because the youth had sizable problems or major unmet needs in each, and not just because these problems or needs were usually interwoven, often mutually reinforcing, and substantial obstacles to future adjustment—important though these reasons were. Instead, it was considered essential also because those problems and needs—individually and/or collectively, directly and indirectly—helped trigger and maintain much of the illegal behavior itself.

The book illustrates program scope in one other way, namely, in connection with *inputs.* For instance, since CTP staff assumed that no single component—such as academic tutoring, socializing experiences, pragmatically oriented discussions, collateral contacts, out-of-home placement, material aid, limit-setting, or counseling—could adequately address or even significantly pertain to most of the above target areas, a *number* of those components ("program elements" and "approaches") were utilized. Also, whether or not several *target areas* were addressed at essentially the same time as each other, and especially if they *were,* several of these *program components (inputs)* were usually used during the same period. As a result, this multiple-targets, multiple-components strategy had to be implemented in a coordinated, often complex way. Key issues and challenges of operational feasibility are discussed in Chapters 17–20.

The Community Treatment Project experience, and that of several other programs which were scientifically studied in recent decades, strongly suggested that programs which utilize combinations of components in ways that realistically address relevant target areas can succeed with many multiply problemmed, multiple offenders. The CTP experience also indicated that program operations must be flexible. This quality is needed not only to help the program adapt to sometimes shifting *organizational ("parent agency") resources* and to *agency policies and practices* that are occasionally at odds with those of the program. More specifically, it is essential not just in order to keep implementing, to better implement, or to even begin implementing certain components and combinations, given those external realities and conditions. Instead, flexibility is needed—in fact, most often needed—in order to accommodate and constructively utilize changes that occur in the *youths* and their *life situations,* and to do so in ways that maintain individualization. Given these youth changes and this related aim, particular combinations of components that were previously used with those offenders sometimes have to be modified, even if overall goals and strategies remain the same. At another level, flexibility—as program policy— allows and may even encourage staff to address given objectives and unusual circumstances in differing ways; it can help them utilize emerging opportunities and their own particular skills in order to explore new strategies and techniques.

All in all, programs such as California's CTP are far from simple, unidimensional operations, structurally as well as dynamically. Moreover, regarding dynamics, the following applies: Although each component that is found in such programs makes its own direct contribution to that operation's overall outcome, that component—for instance, an element such as academic tutoring or else counseling—often helps generate a joint, enhanced, nonlinear effect as well. It does so when it interacts with certain other components, for example, as part of a relevant combination, and with the staff/youth-relationship factor as well. For this and related reasons, such programs, like many others, should be viewed mainly as interacting wholes, not primarily or only as linear aggregates of readily observable, mutually independent elements and approaches. This applies even if one or two such elements seem to quantitatively dominate most or all others combined, and are perhaps used to characterize or label the program as a whole.

In summary, the experiment indicated that combinations of program components, together with particular staff/youth relationships and other factors or dimensions, can do the following: They can motivate, induce, and otherwise activate many serious multiple offenders to deal with key challenges, frustrations, and urgencies in ways that can help them move toward a constructive rather than increasingly troubled future. To be sure, the sailing is far from smooth—at various points, and for all parties concerned.[1]

I hope this book will give many practitioners, policymakers, academicians, researchers, and others a detailed picture of one scientifically studied, humane correctional program that, for many years, made large and long-lasting differences in recidivism with serious multiple offenders. I hope it will also provide useful information as to how and why intervention, particularly the individualized, can succeed with those youths—not with all, to be sure, but with many, including several "types." On the constructive or forward-moving side, such detail and information can provide leads, encouragement, direction, and cautions to correctional professionals who might want to establish comparable or very similar programs, who may wish to modify existing ones along those lines, or who may chiefly want to incorporate various concepts, principles, and methods that proved useful into their own operations and plans. On the defensive or "holding" side, this detail and information can help the above individuals challenge assertions and implications to the following effect: (1) that no large-scale, scientifically well designed and implemented correctional intervention program has been shown to work for serious offenders—that no such efforts perhaps even *can* work, especially when their main focus is individual youths; and, (2) that even if glimmers of success have occasionally appeared, no knowledge or even strong leads exist as to *how* or *why* anything works, whether with specified types of youth or across several such groupings. Finally, I hope this book will increase knowledge about the nature of young multiple offenders themselves, about key contributors to their delinquency and related adjustment patterns, and about ethical bases for intervention, particularly the individualized.

Most chapters of this book, especially those in Volume 1, were written with all the above audiences in mind. In such cases, technical details and other clarifications appear in footnotes and appendices wherever possible. Other chapters, whose subjects will interest some audiences more than others, often contain many details and technical points within themselves; yet even here, the chapters are supplemented by footnotes and perhaps appendices. In any event, I hope these latter sections, which sometimes also include discussions of issues that could be only briefly touched on in the chapters, will prove useful to readers whose interests and questions lead them in those directions.

The Youth Authority/NIMH experiment showed it is possible to make a large dent in the illegal behaviors of serious multiple offenders. For instance, the approximately 45 percent drop that was observed in such activities meant that for every 1,000 mixed offenses which would have occurred during a lengthy follow-up period in the community in connection with the standard YA program of institutionalization plus parole, some 550—(1,000–450)—would have occurred with the CTP. Though CTP-type programs can thus play a major role with respect to public protection, a no less important one—in fact, a broader one—can be played by effective *delinquency prevention* efforts, at least for youths in general. Nevertheless, prevention, in its usual meaning, should be pursued not instead of CTP programs and qualitatively adequate modifications thereof, but in parallel with them. One basic reason for this is as follows. Though prevention, in the long run, can indeed have the largest overall impact on society, mainly by virtue of the extremely large number of youths it may address, it does not focus on multiple offenders in particular, or do so in ways that are needed.

Programs such as the Community Treatment Project should be supported in connection with youths whose illegal behaviors have not been and will not be prevented or kept to a bare minimum by delinquency prevention efforts, by extant first-line correctional operations such as probation, and by available intermediate sanctions. In addition, these are youths whose illegal behaviors are not reduced as much—as much as by the CTP—via other correctional means, such as approaches that include but are not limited to institutionalization. In contrast to most prevention efforts, it is programs which are extensive and/or intensive and whose efforts are organized in terms of a realistic plan that can have a sizable impact on repeat offenders. More precisely, it is those—the CTP variety and others—which can focus-in enough to have a large, long-term effect on individuals who are *already* recognized as multiple offenders and whose illegal behaviors are already of much concern to society. Without appropriate intervention, the behaviors of these particular youths are likely to continue for a long time—even while concurrent prevention efforts are successfully carrying out their roles not only with individuals who are nonoffenders and unrecognized offenders but with some of the youths who, absent such efforts, would undoubtedly continue to offend.

Note

1. For instance, when intervention begins, and when major difficulties later arise, staff's immediate tasks are often comparable to those of dealing with a boat that has several large leaks: While (1) moving that boat (i.e., youth) into slower and calmer waters, those individuals must also try to (2) seal, constrict, or isolate its most dangerous leaks (i.e., address the above-mentioned targets) fairly quickly—if only with temporary or partial coverings and plugs. Often, the second task can be accomplished by utilizing certain combinations of the above-mentioned elements and approaches, together with other factors. Carrying out the first task often requires the external-controls element, in particular. In both cases, if staff use inappropriate or ineffectual "sealants," "coverings," "plugs," and controls; if they utilize too few of each; or if ones that they use are qualitatively appropriate and quantitatively adequate yet are applied neither well enough, rapidly enough, nor in a useful sequence, water will fill the boat too fast and will cause it to founder, even if the *calmer* waters have been reached. On the other hand, if and when the main leaks are sealed or greatly diminished, the vessel can begin to be reinforced with further and perhaps better or more complete sealants, coverings, and so on. In particular, it can be strengthened to where it may eventually move ahead on its own, in currents it can handle and on a course that involves few if any serious collisions. Even if some of the boat's own, preexisting strengths eventually emerge and are built upon—and this may happen once the initial leaks are reduced—the challenges and difficulties will remain large all around.

Acknowledgments

First, I want to thank Dr. Frank P. Williams III, though I cannot thank him enough. I can only say that his liaison with Garland Publishing on behalf of this book, and his technical as well as editorial assistance, have been invaluable in helping it see the light of day.

Second, I would like to highlight the foundational nature of Dr. Marguerite Warren's contribution to the Community Treatment Project, the in-lieu-of-institutionalization program on which much of this book focuses. It was she who, in 1960, helped conceptualize this then-new parole program and who gave it its essentially novel feature: the providing of different types of intervention to differing types of young multiple offenders. Warren's belief that at least some such youths can be safely worked with in the community, and her conviction that no one intervention shoe "fits all," inspired and gave direction to that project's operations (parole) staff throughout her six years (1961–1967) as principal investigator of the experiment whose main component *was* the CTP.

Also invaluable was Dr. Stuart Adams' 1960 suggestion—itself novel at the time—to scientifically study the feasibility and effectiveness of treating and controlling serious young offenders in the community rather than in an institution.

Next, I am grateful for the support given to the experiment by the National Institute of Mental Health. In 1961, Dr. David Twain, Chief of its Center for Studies in Crime and Delinquency, supported the original proposal for the experiment. In 1964, he supported the proposal for its second phase. During subsequent years, continued support was given by Drs. Saleem Shah and George Weber, the then-chief and assistant chief of the Center. The NIMH fully funded the research that was done throughout this long-term experiment; and, in a strong psychological sense, I basically, and happily, felt I worked for that Institute. More specifically, during my years of directly researching the experiment (coinvestigator, 1963–1967; principal investigator, 1967–1974), my sense of professional responsibility was, first, to the NIMH and the scientific discipline it embraced. Secondly, and directly related, it involved the sharing of that experiment's findings with the field of corrections in general, especially with its practitioners and policy makers. That, it seemed clear, was integral to the NIMH's own objectives, and this was reflected in the ample "printing," "postage," and so on, allotments within the experiment's research budget. These, in effect, were my main "loyalties" and perceived responsibilities, even though I was, in fact, then employed by a particular state correctional agency, for which I also had respect.

Within that agency—namely, the California Youth Authority—the Community Treatment Project was established, in 1961, as a new organizational entity. It was located within that agency's Division of Parole and it was to be part of a recently proposed experiment for which research funding, and some operational monies, had just then been approved by the NIMH. (See Director Stark, below). In 1960–1961, Dr. Keith Griffiths, chief of the YA's Division of Research, played an important role in obtaining the YA director's approval to undertake that experiment—this being a study that would involve relatively complex operations and whose community based, in lieu component would be new to the agency and not without risk. After the study began, Griffiths gladly and adeptly provided whatever administrative support and liaison its research team needed from time to time. His interest in this Youth Authority/NIMH experiment as a source of possibly useful information for corrections overall, including the YA, remained steady throughout its life.

Regarding Herman G. Stark, his contribution was critical in a different, even more basic way. He, as director of the Youth Authority when the experiment was originally proposed, approved of it in principle—thus, by fiat (as it were), immediately making the Community Treatment Project an organizational possibility. Soon afterward, when the YA's research proposal was approved by the NIMH, he officially established the first CTP parole units themselves, thereby making the concept a reality. In addition, once those CTP operations got underway, Stark, as was his style, "made it clear" to the Youth Authority's relevant administrators and middle managers that (1) the YA/NIMH experiment, overall, and (2) the new, in lieu parole operation (CTP), in particular, were to be taken seriously and given genuine support. The director was a man to whom everyone in the agency always listened—very closely. His instructions regarding (1) and (2) were, in fact, followed, and they were reflected in the YA's yearly operational budgets and their statements of the agency's priorities. Allen Breed, who followed Stark as YA director beginning in 1968, also supported the Community Treatment Project, until its final year.

I would like to acknowledge the *research personnel* who, besides Marguerite Warren and myself, helped implement the experiment: Dennis Johns (1967–1970), Virginia Neto (1965–1968), John Pearson (1969–1971), James Turner (1962–1973), Martin Warren (1961–1963, 1966–1967), and Eric Werner (1969–1973). In this study's early years (1961–1964), a total of three full-time researchers were present at any given time; after that, the number varied between four and five, including, from 1969, the "rotational" staff mentioned shortly. Present during the experiment's middle and later years was the sure hand and steady eye of Alice Herrera, the statistical clerk; and, ably performing its main clerical tasks for the researchers' final nine years was Barbara Penfield (formerly Osborn). Together, the above individuals comprised—to coin a phrase—"a good team," in that everyone understood what had to be done and then did it, professionally. During 1969–1973, three former CTP parole agents and one Youth Authority social worker performed supplementary as well as essential research tasks for either one year or two years each, via "rotational training assignments" designed by the agency for purposes of staff development. These individuals were John Helm, Fred Lippins, Estelle Turner (formerly Basore), and Dudley Sams, respectively, and they were effectively part of the team.

Besides their work with youths, several CTP *parole agents* made special, direct contributions to the experiment's knowledge-building objective. They did do in such contexts as personal interviews with researchers; supervisory case conferences; large-scale, multiagent conferences; and, in some cases, their own writing. They were: Ronald Ackerman, Wesley Beyer, Otto Broady, Frank Bumps, Sharlene Haire, Marvin Litke, Peter Marchi, Vivian Miller, Joel Mitchell, William Nesbit, Nicholas Osa, John Pearson (same as above), Louie Rasmussen, John Riggs, Jack Robberson, Joseph Salas, Estelle Turner (same as above), and William Underwood. Most of these individuals worked at the Community Treatment Project for at least four years. Seven other such contributors, who later became CTP treatment supervisors, are among the individuals mentioned next.

Chief among CTP's treatment supervisors during its many years of existence were: Glen Avery, Louis Baber, Jerry Darling, Dean Dixon, Arthur Dorsey, George Howard, Joseph Kleine, James McHale, and King Morris. Though the nature and significance of these individuals' role is discussed in Chapter 18, it can be said here that the supervisors were a critical part of the operation; and, each of the above individuals did his job well. Similarly, Walter Friesen sensitively supervised the youth counselors and group supervisors who implemented the institutional component that was added for the CTP's final phase.

During 1961–1968, the Community Treatment Project's administrative supervisors were, chronologically: Thomas McGee, Joseph Kleine (same as above), Loren Look, Doyle Roberts, and, in San Francisco, William McCord. In 1969–1973, William Haynes performed this function.

From 1964 to 1973, the CTP's main *education staff* were (also chronologically, but with overlap across the differing parole offices): John McDonald, Stanley White, Margaret Bush, Barbara Whitesel, Rene Barrios, Charles Kirk, and William Hart. These individuals met their many major challenges intelligently, often creatively, and usually with good cheer. The vast majority of youths appreciated them and their efforts.

I wish to thank all staff who served as parole agents for youngsters who were in the Youth Authority's standard program, that is, for those who were control subjects for the boys and girls in the CTP (the experimentals). These agents cooperated with the researchers in all necessary ways: record keeping, information sharing, personal interviews, and so on. I would like to also thank those hundreds of *youths*—controls and experimentals alike—who shared important information and feelings about themselves and their YA experiences. I hope they eventually had a much better life than they were having when they were first sent to that agency.

During 1995, the virtually finalized manuscript—less Chapters 24–26, which were begun soon afterward—was reviewed by Marguerite Warren, George Howard, and James McHale. Their many valuable comments and suggestions are great appreciated and were incorporated. The latter individuals had had long, varied, and in-depth experience with the operations end of the YA/NIMH experiment. Howard was a parole agent at the Sacramento Community Treatment Project office from 1962 to 1965, at which point he became the treatment supervisor of San Francisco's then newly established CTP. He remained in that role until 1967, and from that point through the early 1970s he served as training associate and acting director of the Center for Training in Differential Treatment (CTDT; see Chapter 17). This Center taught the concepts and methods that were used in the various CTP offices. McHale had himself been a parole agent at the Sacramento CTP, from 1962 to 1964. He then became its treatment supervisor and continued in that role until 1970, the second year of the experiment's final phase. At that point he became a training associate at CTDT, while maintaining close information-sharing ties with the ongoing CTP operation. Both Howard and McHale were viewed, by almost all parole agents, by other treatment supervisors, and by the administrative supervisors, not only as knowledgeable, articulate individuals and as effective agents, but—while supervisors—as playing key roles in giving their parole units an atmosphere conducive to productive, humane interactions with and among youths, and to emotional as well as intellectual stimulation and professional growth among staff.

When the chapters (1–9) that describe the basics of the experiment, of CTP, and of the findings on comparative effectiveness were written (mid-1970s), they were reviewed by Dr. Griffiths and Robert Kenney. The latter individual served on the Youth Authority Board (Chapter 2) and in other central office, administrative capacities, throughout the experiment. He was knowledgeable about most aspects of the agency, including its intake and decision-making procedures and roles, and about the CTP itself. The valuable comments and suggestions of these individuals are reflected in the completed document. I also thank Dr. James Bonta, Chief of Corrections Research (Ministry of the Solicitor General, Canada), for his 1994 review of the manuscript and for his valuable observations.

Finally, many thanks to the staff of Garland Publishing, who provided excellent assistance and judgment throughout this lengthy project. I especially appreciate the professionalism, steady hand, and patience of Maria Zamora (Assistant Editor, Humanities and Social Sciences) and Andrea Johnson (Production Editor).

Introduction

This book focuses on individualized intervention with serious juvenile offenders. It describes how such intervention was carried out in a complex, community-based correctional program, with considerable success. This program was operated by a large, state agency: the California Youth Authority. It began in the very early 1960s and ended in the 1970s. Throughout that period it was scientifically studied as part of a controlled experiment, via federal funds. The program was implemented in three separate parole units; these operated in Sacramento (1961–1973), Stockton (1961–1968), and San Francisco (1965–1968).

During those years, collectively, several hundred boys and girls were randomly assigned to either that program, within its given city, or else to the Youth Authority's standard program (whose youths comprised the experiment's control group). The YA's standard program involved institutionalization followed by "regular," large-caseload parole, again within the given city. In contrast, the community-based program was *in lieu of* institutionalization (even though it was called parole), and it was intensive as well as low-caseload. This program contained several components and involved considerable individualization.

The in lieu program operated as a demonstration project, and because all three of its parole units were integral parts of the research study, they were also considered experimental in nature. The overall, in lieu program was experimental in a different sense as well: When it began, it was innovative—in many ways a "first"—within corrections. This intensive, low-caseload program was called the Community Treatment Project (sometimes simply "the Project"), as was the federally funded experiment as a whole. Its line staff were selected to work closely with juveniles who had been committed to the state-level agency, the Youth Authority, after having recently "failed" in their home communities, that is, on probation. CTP staff members—experienced parole agents—each carried a caseload which, when the experiment began, had no more than eight youths; this number became eleven a few years later, and it then remained at that level. The YA's large-caseload parole units had entirely separate parole agents and were located in different facilities. (In California, probation was, and still is, operated entirely at the county level, i.e., "locally," not by the state. The term "parole" is used only in connection with state-level operations, and that of "probation" always refers to the local context, never that of the state.)

Legally, the youngsters whom parole agents supervised were called Youth Authority wards. In California overall, the YA had jurisdiction over some 6,000 wards in its institutions, and another 11,000 on parole (called "aftercare" in many states). Being an integral part of this statewide agency, and being a demonstration effort in particular, the Project's principal task during its early years (1961–1964) was to answer the following question: Can some of these serious offenders be supervised safely in their own communities, without first being locked up for several months or perhaps over a year? In 1961, this was a rather new and, at any rate, a scientifically unanswered question, not just in California but throughout corrections. Few policymakers, and probably no more than a small portion of the general public, took it for granted that the answer might be yes, at least for more than a small fraction of those youths.

Today, community-based operations are far from novel, and the above question is no longer new. Even by the mid-1970s, dozens of community-located, in lieu programs had emerged in the United States and abroad; presently there are hundreds. Such programs began appearing in the mid- to later-1960s, and their numbers grew even during the years (1975–1981) in which the effectiveness and/or legitimacy of almost all correctional treatment was being most strongly questioned and challenged. Many of these community programs were designed to supervise multiple offenders, youths with a sizable record of illegal behavior; few, however, were as individualized in their approach as the California Community Treatment Project (CTP), and very few were experimentally studied. In any case, all such programs rested on the premise that the answer to the above question was that lengthy incarceration *can* be avoided or at least significantly reduced, for some, or many, such offenders.

It was in 1963–1965 that this "answer" first began to emerge within corrections, with some scientific backup. It was in relation to the California CTP that most of this evidence was first obtained, and quickly gained the attention and interest of many practitioners, policymakers, and academicians. Over the next several years, this experiment's research component continued to be a steady source, possibly the largest single source other than professional journals, of detailed empirical information regarding the merits and limits of intensive, in lieu intervention.

Throughout this book, "intervention" refers to the combination of *treatment* and *external controls,* as these terms are broadly used. From literally the start of the in lieu program, its parole staff believed that each of these was an essential dimension and that the two had to operate jointly, to one degree or another, whenever multiple offenders were worked with. To the experiment's researchers, that belief was viewed as a reasonable hypothesis—to be examined, like any other. At any rate, both dimensions and modalities were part and parcel of essentially all aspects of the in lieu program, that is, of the Community Treatment Project.

CTP, as a parole operation and demonstration program, was fortunate in that it did not simply "come and go," within, say, three or four years. Instead, by the time its final case file was closed, what had begun as a modest-sized unit in Sacramento had expanded in size; the program had been tried, in this expanded mode, in other cities; and the overall operation ended up as the longest research project in the history of corrections: CTP had run nonstop for almost twelve years. During that time, it was possible for staff and researchers to observe many consistencies and differences in the responses of hundreds of diagnosed-and-classified youths to a range of interventions, including various combinations of methods and program elements. Because of the Project's duration, there was also enough time to then explore modifications of those interventions.

By the mid- to later 1960s, and especially the early 1970s, the Community Treatment Project's influence within juvenile corrections had become widespread in the United States and parts of Canada. Many of the then-existing, individual community programs had drawn directly from its operational experiences, especially in their planning stages. Even a number of major statewide reforms, such as the deinstitutionalization or related efforts in Massachusetts, Florida, and Colorado, drew a good deal of their original encouragement and direction from the experiences and ongoing findings of the California experiment.

The main reasons CTP had such influence during those years were as follows. This was the program in which community-located intervention with serious multiple offenders, an almost untried approach in 1961, (1) accumulated its first set of detailed, scientifically controlled research results, many of which were positive with respect to recidivism, and were therefore encouraging; (2) underwent its first large-scale and long-term operational "trials by fire," and had widely shared the results of those experiences;[1] and (3) first operated under a youth-classification system and a social/developmental frame of reference that helped many practitioners and policymakers think more sharply or systematically than before about rehabilitation needs and approaches that might be appropriate and effective for a wide range of defined offenders. In addition, (4) fiscal analyses suggested, from an early point on, that the in lieu approach could be less expensive than building and operating large-scale institutions, even if the in lieu program was costlier than regular parole.

Thus, it was not simply that the Community Treatment Project, as a parole operation, had the "in lieu field" largely to itself, except for the also well-known Provo and Essexfield programs, mentioned shortly. Instead, many correctional personnel considered experiences and findings such as the above important to their planning needs and overall policies, and to their everyday practice. They felt it gave them a new and in some ways better alternative than institutionalization alone, or at least another option. The project's influence was increased and accelerated when its methods and first five years of results were summarized and recommended in a widely distributed, media-highlighted, President's Commission Report (President's Commission, 1967a, 1967b, 1967c). After the early 1970s, many programs that CTP had helped set in motion began to generate offshoots of their own, and several of its concepts and principles had already been adopted in various institutional operations as well.

As indicated, when CTP began, the idea of community-based alternatives to incarceration was just starting to be explored with respect to youths whom correctional personnel considered either strong or unquestioned candidates for long-term removal from the community. Specifically, that idea was being implemented in only two, fairly small yet carefully operated, correctional programs: the Provo (Utah) experiment, which began in 1959, and the Essexfields (New Jersey) study, which got into full swing in 1961.[2] These programs focused exclusively on boys in their middle teens. They operated on the assumption that, by using a close-knit, "positive peer-group culture" to reorient the youths' norms and attitudes, future delinquency could be avoided. To achieve that goal, one method or approach—"guided group interaction"—was utilized and was central with all youths, regardless of their differing personalities and life circumstances. As to program elements, a daytime school and/or work component existed in the local community. Members of the youths' families were almost never worked with, and personalized relationships between staff and youths were not encouraged; both strategies were designed largely to maximize the peer group's influence. The main treatment phase averaged four to five months, though subsequent contacts could occur between the youths and the program. During the 1960s and 1970s many community-based programs evolved, with variations, along these lines.

In contrast to those programs, California's Community Treatment Project was designed to use and emphasize any of *several* methods and combinations of program elements—guided group interaction being only one. The methods and elements that were used depended on the youngsters' personal characteristics, major needs, maturity-level classification, overall life situation, and related factors. This, in essence, meant differing approaches with differing youths: "differential treatment," as it was named in the mid-1960s. In 1961, this strategy or intervention principle (absent that later label) was still surprisingly new to corrections—a field which then also lacked any systematic, widely tested classification of youths that might help practitioners sort out which approaches might be emphasized with which youths.

In CTP, the parole agents, who were variously called "workers," "change agents," "community agents," or "treaters," could work with each youngster for two to three years, even longer if necessary. They could interact directly with his or her family and friends, and personalized relationships between themselves and the youths were usually considered quite important. Several direct and/or indirect contacts each week were considered important, with respect to most youths, and in this regard the program was viewed as intensive. The age range of newly admitted CTP youths was considerably broader than at Provo and Essexfields, and the Sacramento, Stockton, and San Francisco units were each housed in their own community center building.

In planning the experiment, staff responsible for the CTP component's nature and scope chose to explore a wide range of methods. This reflected their working assumption that delinquency has various causes and that a range of interventions is needed in order to successfully address them. To implement these views and to initiate CTP, they adopted and adapted a number of methods, such as individual counseling and activity group therapy, from various correctional and noncorrectional settings. By itself, no one of these methods had much resemblance to what the "assembled" Community Treatment Project would involve, namely, various combinations of those methods, or various program elements. In any event, no one of these methods, or even program elements, would likely be applied on an across-the-board basis to every type of CTP-assigned youth, even though some methods and elements would be very common. In addition, more than one method and element could be used with any *one* CTP youth simultaneously or successively, and it often was. Basically, no other such program for serious multiple offenders existed, even until 1965.

With few exceptions, the way those methods and elements were applied was consistent with three principles and objectives that were heavily emphasized throughout, and throughout the life of, that Project. These were:

1. to promote humane interaction between staff and youths, thereby reducing the degree of impersonal ("system-to-object") processing of the offender, and perhaps modifying his negative image of authority figures;
2. to facilitate the youth's personal involvement in the process of change as a way of tapping and building upon his internal motivation—thereby reducing the need to impose decisions on a largely involuntary basis; and
3. to facilitate individualized justice and minimize rigid, undifferentiated solutions ("frontier justice")—thereby integrating, wherever possible, the multiple needs, resources, and professed ideals of society with needs and resources of the growing youth.

Few correctional programs have had the unusual opportunities that the Community Treatment Project received, for instance, the chance to carefully examine a range of interventions for several years, to modify them if necessary, and to then observe the modifications and their effects. This Project's rare opportunity was a direct result of three consecutive research grants from the National Institute of Mental Health (NIMH). Also crucial was the very sizable support provided by the Youth Authority, and the high percentage of parole staff who remained with the CTP—and researchers who stayed with the experiment of which it was a part—for several years or more. It would be highly desirable if many of today's and tomorrow's correctional experiments could have not just a random allocation design as did CTP, but even half the opportunity and continuity that existed in this study.

This unbroken, long-term funding and support made it possible not only to sort out methods and concepts that seemed counterproductive, inadequate, or largely superfluous, and to continue using—in effect, to replicate—others that seemed worthwhile for given youths. Rather, it also allowed for a wide range of detailed data collection and quantitative as well as qualitative analyses. Among the statistical analyses was one that, in the 1970s, was one of corrections' then-longest follow-ups (almost seven years) of individual offenders' arrests and convictions. This follow-up was based on official, California Department of Justice records, and is central to the recidivism results summarized below for Phases 1 and 2 (1961–1968) of the experiment. This and other analyses made it possible to compare the effectiveness—with respect to public protection—of the intense, low-caseload, differential intervention operation known as the CTP with that of the Youth Authority's standard program. This comparison covered the period in which those programs' respective youths were *under* the YA's jurisdiction, and several years after they were *discharged* from that agency. (CTP was also called the

E, or experimental, program. The standard program was also called the C, or control. The Sacramento and Stockton operations combined were the "Valley" units.)

Chief among the findings were the following:

A. For all Valley males combined, CTP youths had far (38% to 50%) fewer arrests and convictions than their matched controls; that is, their rates were much lower. This finding was especially strong in connection with (1) severe offenses (e.g., burglary, felony drug violations, and felonies against persons), and, focusing *within* the severe-offenses category, with (2) violent offenses in particular (e.g., assault with a deadly weapon, forcible rape, robbery, and murder). The results for severe and violent offenses pertained to Valley and San Francisco youths alike. They were especially strong with regard to individuals described as "conflicted"—a youth-group that comprised about 60 percent of all males within the two settings combined. On the other hand, the Community Treatment Project was *less* effective than the traditional program with "power oriented" males, at least with those described as "manipulative." In addition, CTP was neither more nor less effective with females, again with respect to arrests and convictions.

B. The Youth Authority's traditional program clearly provided the community with more short-term protection than did CTP, since traditional-program youths (controls) were first locked up for approximately nine months before being paroled. However, once they were released from the institution, controls soon began committing offenses at a much higher rate than Community Treatment Project youths—none of whom had been initially institutionalized. As a result, beginning about four years from initial commitment to the YA and continuing at least several more years—thereby extending well beyond YA discharge—traditional-program youths had accumulated substantially more offenses than those on CTP. (Within less than two years from initial commitment, the number of accumulated offenses was already *equal* across the two programs.) In effect, the numerous arrests that were chalked up by controls while they were at risk in the community were not offset by the *absence* of arrests while they were in lockup. Thus, incapacitation notwithstanding, CTP ended up providing more long-term protection to the community than did the traditional program, particularly with respect to conflicted, though not power oriented, youths. This finding (and finding D, below) pertains to Valley males, and it would probably have remained much the same even if controls had initially been locked up twice as long as they were.

C. Youths in the traditional and the CTP program *both* had less overall recidivism during a sizable *post*-intake period than in a similar *pre*-intake period, these being three years in the community immediately before and immediately after intake or institutionalization. (This finding, like those in A and B, applied to the "total group," i.e., to all youth groups combined, in the respective programs.) However, this pre-to-post reduction, sometimes explained as a "suppression effect," was moderate (16%) for the traditional program and substantial (59%) for CTP; that is, it was considerably larger in the latter program. As to violent offenses, in particular, these markedly *increased* in the traditional program from pre to post, and they held fairly even in CTP, again for the total group. In the case of Conflicted youths—these being the largest single group—violent offending rose 225 percent in the traditional and dropped 14 percent in the CTP.

D. During the most recent price-period analyzed (1971–1972), Youth Authority career costs were $1,049 lower per CTP youth than per control. When non-YA costs (county expenses for arrests, detentions, and adjudications; prison and parole costs subsequent to YA discharge; etc.) were added in, the overall savings to society was estimated at $4,545 per CTP youth. This cost difference between controls and CTP youths mainly resulted from the larger number of arrests on the part of controls and from these individuals' greater tendency to commit violent offenses—acts that often resulted in long periods of lockup. The estimated overall savings would probably have been about twice as large by the early 1980s, and three times larger as of the early 1990s. These estimated increases mainly reflected the fact that incarceration costs more than doubled since the early 1970s; that, in turn, was apart from the fact that *length* of incarceration itself increased for violent offenses.

E. Results from Phase 3 (1969–1973) indicated that: (1) most juvenile and adult court first commitments who should *not* be directly released to the community can be accurately identified at intake; (2) when these individuals begin their treatment/control in a short-term institutional setting that is operated on CTP principles and by CTP staff, their rate of offending can be sharply (over 50%) reduced in relation to that of similar individuals who *are* directly released to the community; (3) youths and young adults with seriously assaultive committing offenses do not necessarily require long periods of incarceration; (4) the concepts, intervention methods, and program operations that were used during Phases 1 and 2 (Valley as well as San Francisco) were also applicable to older, often very seriously delinquent, adult court commitments. At any rate, although many seriously delinquent youths and young adults can begin their treatment/control in the community, many others would best begin within given institutional settings.

Key factors: For conflicted, passive conformist, and group conformist youth groups combined (together, some 80% of all youths studied), the three most important factors in accounting for the reduced or comparable illegal behavior of CTP cases as compared to their controls were: *small caseloads; intensive (frequent) and/or extensive (multiple-area) contacts; individualization and flexible programming.* Each such factor made a major contribution with respect to all or almost all of those youth groups. Small caseloads were a prerequisite not only to the second and, to a lesser extent, the third of those factors, but to the appropriate utilization of other factors as well. Next in importance were: *personal characteristics and professional orientation of agent; specific abilities and overall perceptiveness of agent; explicit, detailed guidelines (intervention strategies).* Each such factor made either substantial or major contributions to the above youth groups. *Long-term contacts* and three global program features were important as well. Individually and collectively, the key factors also helped implement the three, earlier-mentioned principles and objectives that were emphasized in CTP. With all youth groups, program integrity or qualitative adequacy was essential. For instance, some key factors had to operate to a sufficient degree or for at least a minimum time; others had to be expressed appropriately; still others simply had to "exist"—albeit continuously; and, in all cases, the simultaneous, integrated operation or presence of various key factors was needed.

Program elements (e.g. accredited school program at the community center, recreational and cultural enrichment activities, and out-of-home placement) functioned as content bases *for* given factors. (Not all youths received all such elements, but almost all youths received more than one.) As with those key factors, no single element or even *intervention method* (e.g., counseling) seemed powerful or flexible enough to address the youths' complex problems or situation in ways that entirely accounted for CTP's reduced or comparable levels of arrest and conviction. In this respect, no program element and no single intervention method provided, by itself, a guaranteed "answer" regarding any one youth group, let alone all groups combined. Instead, a number of key factors, program elements, and intervention methods had to operate in concert.

The core procedures of the Community Treatment Project as an operation designed to effect long-term reduction of illegal behavior in serious multiple offenders, mainly through personal growth, were: (1) a careful diagnostic or highly individualized understanding of the youth and his or her situation; (2) a relevant, detailed, and integrated intervention plan, based on that diagnosis/understanding; and (3) implementation of that plan in terms of (a) CTP's key factors—especially, individualized, flexible programming and intensive and/or extensive contacts within a small caseload context—and with (b) program integrity and qualitative adequacy. We have called programming or programs that rely centrally on this set of procedures "individualized intervention" or "differential intervention": differing approaches for differing youths. Such individualization can exist even though the approach used with each youth is not 100 percent unique to him or her. That is, differential intervention, including patterns of intervention that *are* distinctive and individualized, can exist for any given youth even though there are also important *similarities* in the approach used for that youth and approaches used for others. These commonalities in approach reflect similarities that exist across youths with respect to their needs, their life situation, and so on.

Individualization comes, in effect, in differing shapes and sizes, and any two programs can be individualized along differing lines and to different degrees. For staff of a hypothetical program to individualize intervention in the way, and to the large degree, that it existed at CTP, they would first have to get an idea of the youth's interests, expectations, goals, skills, strengths, weaknesses, attitudes, self-image, major adjustment techniques, and key motivations or dynamics, among other things.[3] They would then have to (1) interrelate those factors and (2) also integrate the resulting picture of the youth with similarly interrelated information about his or her personal history, offense pattern, family, external environment, living arrangement, specific pressures and supports, likely crises, and other factors. The overall understanding which then emerges can form the basis of an intervention plan that can concretely and realistically indicate how to proceed with that specific youth, at least initially. A plan that taps an individual's interests, skills, and so on, has more chance than otherwise of being considered relevant by him or her, and less chance of being strongly resisted.

This level of individualization or differentiation allows for more than the providing of (1) *differing* approaches for *differing* categories of youth, and, nevertheless, also the providing of (2) much the *same* approach for most or all individuals who fall *within* any of those categories or classifications. Instead, it allows for (3) differentiations *within* any such category; more precisely, it does so to a sizable degree, if and when the category is utilized in the first place. Within the Community Treatment Project, individualization existed at a level that allowed for intervention based on a picture of the person as a human being, not as a stereotype—a human being who acts and develops within his or her concrete setting. In future programs, this level of individualization would probably have a greater chance of yielding the level of positive results that were obtained at CTP than would a substantially lesser degree of individualization. Nevertheless, programs that might be somewhat less individualized in their diagnostic understanding, in their intervention plans, and in their implementation of those plans, could still produce results that at least approach those of CTP, provided the earlier-mentioned conditions are met.

Differential intervention (DI) in the community is complex and challenging, when it is seriously directed at the long-term goal mentioned above. To achieve results similar to those in the California Community Treatment Project, DI programs which had that goal would require (1) excellent and motivated staff, including the supervisor; (2) considerable material resources (e.g., various program elements), especially if a wide range of youths were involved; and (3) strong support from their parent agency, unless they were independently operated. Such programs would remain complex even if no formal youth-classification system were used, and, *if* used, even if it were simple.

Though hard to implement, such differential or individualized intervention programs would be feasible within and outside North America today, either unmodified relative to California's CTP or, more often, in modified form. However, because of their relatively heavy staff-and-material resource requirements, these programs, though feasible, probably could not be implemented in most local probation departments within the near future, in the United States. There, their prospects might be somewhat better under state-agency auspices. This assessment applies not simply to any and all departments and agencies (i.e., to every single one) but to those which would be *interested* in DI approaches in particular and that would have enough community *support* for an in lieu effort (DI or non-DI) in the first place.

With community support and departmental interest in differential or individualized intervention, today's chances of adequately implementing a DI program that is focused heavily on achieving the long-term goal, with multiple offenders, would probably range from small (20% of the above departments, in the United States), to moderate (35% to 40%), depending mainly on whether various modifications (Chapter 20) were made. Although these odds indicate that most such departments could probably implement neither a full-scale nor a reduced-size DI operation (five to seven and three or four caseloads, respectively), they also suggest that *many* could probably do so and that this group would not be insignificant. Those estimates aside, the following would apply to still other departments, and to state-level agencies: Even if they could not implement a full-scale, a reduced-size, or an otherwise modified *program,* these organizations could probably implement key features of differential intervention in the context of *individual caseloads,* for example, one or two specialized caseloads within a given community or field office. Individually and/or collectively, such caseloads could provide relevant intervention for a sizable percentage of serious multiple offenders within given cities and other geographic areas.

The findings and experiences of the 12-year California Youth Authority/NIMH experiment have several general implications:

1. Community-based programming, in this case individualized intervention, can substantially reduce a wide range of illegal activities on the part of numerous multiple offenders. Given today's high crime rate, this finding, which includes moderate as well as severe offenses, means that such intervention can play a valuable role with respect to the criminal justice system and society overall. It contradicts the view that intervention which focuses on individuals makes no difference.
2. Community-based programming can substantially reduce *violence* among these same, male offenders. Given today's ongoing atmosphere of violence, and the public's continued feeling of vulnerability in this regard, this finding is especially timely. It means that long-term lockup is not the only way to address violent crimes.
3. The above reductions in illegal activities can occur in highly as well as moderately urbanized environments, and with each major ethnic group. Together with point 8, below, this suggests that individualized intervention has relevance to a wide spectrum of society.
4. The reductions mentioned in points 1 and 2 can be achieved at a long-term savings of several thousand dollars per youth, using traditional-program costs plus non Youth Authority and post-discharge costs as the basis of comparison. Given today's increasing financial constraints, the importance of these savings is self-evident. Such savings would be even larger if length-of-incarceration were increased, for instance, for purposes of greater incapacitation or in response to today's pressure for ever-harsher punishment.
5. The above-mentioned reductions and savings would be increased if power oriented youths were excluded from, or deemphasized in, CTP-type programs. This does not mean that few such individuals can profit from such programs; instead, it reflects the fact that traditional programming is somewhat more effective than CTP's approach in reducing the illegal behaviors of this group, and is less expensive as well. These youths probably comprise 15 percent to 25 percent of all young, multiple offenders, whether in probation or on parole, in the United States.
6. Community-based programming can be implemented in a humane way and can reflect substantial youth involvement in the process of change. If society's need for protection is not jeopardized by such programming, the implementation and expression of these principles and/or social ideals might more easily be accepted as a "plus." In addition, such principles might then be judged, at least primarily, as something other than means to practical ends. The same might apply to the fact that, with rare exceptions, multiple offenders apparently prefer the CTP's type of programming to traditional, institutionalization.
7. The reductions in illegal behavior mentioned in points 1 and 2 can be achieved in community settings without increasing—in fact, while decreasing—the intermediate- and long-term risk to those communities. In this respect, long-term lockup need not be viewed as the only viable approach, perhaps not even the best overall approach, to community protection, in connection with numerous multiple offenders. This applies regardless of how humane the institutional environment might be and despite, say, the proportionality, consistency, general balance, and—in those respects—overall fairness/equality that may be involved in each individual's sentence. At base, the above reductions mean that specified types of community programming can be more effective than, not just *as* effective as, traditional programming.
8. Multiple offenders under 16 years of age at intake are just as amenable to a community-based, differential intervention approach as those 16 and over. This and other findings

suggest that "maturation" or "simply growing up" is not, in itself, the critical or even primary ingredient in reducing the illegal behavior of these particular youths—individuals whose arrest rates rapidly accelerated during the two years preceding commitment to the state agency. Insofar as that is true, it would probably be ill-advised to "wait these individuals out" and simply hope their behavior patterns will decisively change within a few years, without considerable input from given individuals. Although a "hands off" or perhaps "minimal involvement" policy might be appropriate for certain individuals (e.g., many first-time offenders), such a policy would probably be inadequate for almost all multiple offenders, with respect to the goal of reducing illegal behavior. In sum, whatever the age of these adolescents, intensive and/or extensive intervention seems much more likely to produce substantial reductions in illegal behavior than does maturation alone, within a two- or three-year period. At the very least, individualized intervention can accelerate or facilitate such change.

9. Many multiple offenders require at least several months of institutionalization prior to being paroled. Most such offenders can be identified at intake; and, when many such youths are first worked with in an individually oriented facility and are *then* released to an intensive/extensive community program, their rate of offending can be markedly reduced. At any rate, a "pure" community approach, that is, no initial institutionalization, is not appropriate for all multiple offenders. This includes many individuals whose records contain no seriously assaultive offenses, and many who are not classified as Power Oriented.

10. A *more* controlling approach (e.g., long-term lockup) does not always result in less illegal behavior than a *less* controlling approach (e.g., community-based intervention such as the Community Treatment Project). Instead, the effectiveness of one such approach as compared to another will vary depending on the overall "power" of the *specific* programs involved and on the specific goal or goals in question. For example, as shown in Phases 1 and 2 of the experiment, a heavily controlling, traditional approach can be less powerful than a moderately controlling, CTP-type community approach, with respect to reducing the illegal behavior of particular youth types. Given this finding, it would seem appropriate for criminal justice personnel, among others, to reassess and specifically address a view that has been common since the late 1970s: The heavier and/or stricter the external controls, the greater the deterrence—at any rate, the better the outcome in terms of reduced illegal behavior.

11. If parole were abolished as a criminal justice tool, institutions and local detention facilities would probably be expected to assume an even larger role than they already have, with regard to protecting society. However, if parole were retained, an expanded role would not be necessary—in fact, a reduced role might be possible—*if* effective community alternatives were indeed available. More specifically, such expansion would be unnecessary for numerous multiple offenders, with respect to the goal of intermediate- and long-term community protection.

12. Community-based programming can involve less labeling and stigmatization, and less external control, than traditional programming. Thus, it can bear on offender-centered goals, not only societal-centered goals. More specifically, it can successfully address objectives and values other than those of community protection and cost reduction alone.

13. Reduced illegal behavior is not always associated with better school and work adjustment during parole, at least with certain youths. For instance, while Passive Conformists in the CTP had less illegal behavior than their Controls, their school and work adjustment was somewhat worse than that of the latter. Thus, the achievement of long-term societal goals, such as greater community protection, is not always paralleled by that of specific offender-centered goals. By the same token, positive attitude change is not always accompanied by reduced illegal behavior.

Volume 1 of this book deals exclusively with the 12-year experiment, and it focuses on the Community Treatment Project in particular. Part I describes CTP's background, organization, intake procedures, assumptions, and program elements. It then describes the CTP and traditional program youths—first their background characteristics and then their groupings with respect to the

Warren Maturity Level Classification, a system that reflects the Sullivan, Grant, and Grant (Warren) Theory of Interpersonal Development. It concludes with a description of CTP's intervention methods. Part II mainly describes the behavioral and other outcomes of the experiment's first two phases (1961–1968): It focuses on program effectiveness, separately for Valley and San Francisco youths; on comparative risk to the community, taking incapacitation into account; on changes from a preintake period to postintake; and on age as well as comparative costs. This section also discusses the matching of workers and youths. Part III first focuses on the experiment's third phase (1969–1973), one in which the Community Treatment Project added a short-term, differential-intervention-oriented institutional component for specified groups of youth. It then describes and discusses ten key factors contributing to the successful performance of CTP's youth groups. The section also discusses female offenders in the CTP and traditional programs, and it reviews as well as summarizes the experiment's Phase 1 and 2 program and overall research findings. Part IV focuses on the feasibility of the Community Treatment Project—mainly its Phase 1 and 2 ("pure community") operation. It then discusses the implications of this situation and of the Phase 3 experience for other community-based, individualized intervention operations. Regarding CTP's own feasibility, this section reviews (1) social agency (law enforcement; probation), school, and parent organization factors; (2) staff, unit functioning, and supervisory factors; (3) case processing, case maintenance, and other operational factors; and (4) the Phase 3 operation itself. This review leads to conclusions regarding what is needed in order to appropriately operate and maintain such a program, and modifications of it as well.

Regarding *Volume 2*, which has four parts or sections, the focus on California's Community Treatment Project continues in Part I and most of II. The rest of Part II details several other individualized intervention programs; and in III and IV, the volume further broadens its scope by discussing general issues, theory, and perspectives that bear on such intervention and on multiple offenders overall. Prior to this broadening, the book, including Volume 1, centers on objective descriptions and quantitative analyses of empirical data that were collected as part of the experiment; however, with the broadening, and especially after Chapter 23, the presentation moves beyond such descriptions and analyses: It involves considerable interpretation, plus conceptual integration of numerous qualitative observations as well as converging information, evidence, and experiences.

Part I (Chapters 21–23) begins with a detailed review and analysis of Paul Lerman's 1975 critique of the YA/NIMH experiment's Phase 1 and 2 findings. It demonstrates that the critique, although based on a plausible hypothesis, was in fact unsupportable and spurious once empirical tests were made. Next, the section presents additional information regarding the experiment's findings and concerning issues such as the rater-reliability as well as the construct validity, of maturity level classifications. The section closes with a description of five North American programs for serious juvenile offenders that drew heavily on the experiences of California's CTP—in some cases, CTP's combined institutional and community-located approach (the Phase 3 operation). These programs are the Shawbridge Youth Centers (Quebec), the St. Francis Boys' Homes (Kansas), the Baltimore Differential Treatment Project (Maryland), the Ormsby Village Treatment Center (Kentucky), and the Craigwood-Bridgeway Program (Ontario). Also described is one statewide and one provincewide application of differential intervention: Colorado's Division of Youth Services and the Manitoba Probation Service.

Part II begins by focusing on rationales for intervention, especially one called the "needs-centered." Here, as with most other rationales, the ultimate goal is the protection of society against illegal behavior. However, in order to achieve *long*-term protection, with multiple offenders in particular, careful, well-coordinated, individualized intervention is required. Such intervention is necessary in order to realistically help these individuals meet their long-term social and personal adaptation needs, not just (1) so that they, like other adolescents, can establish a viable future, hopefully in the free community, but (2) in ways that can help them become *internally* motivated to relinquish their illegal behavior and closely related adjustment patterns. The section continues by focusing on theory: It reviews basic youth needs and dynamics that contribute to the development and reinforcement of illegal behavior, and it details several related dynamics of intervention itself. Also discussed is a seldom emphasized rationale for providing at least some degree of intervention with multiple offenders: the intrinsic, ethical value of trying to assist them because they are human beings. Cutting across this as well as the needs-centered context, the section reviews differing perspectives on *merit*—the question, here, being whether the present individuals "deserve" sizable amounts of assistance, given their records of crime.

The section closes with (1) comments on selected developments within corrections since the 1970s, particularly the Justice Model and Risk Assessment, and (2) the description of a "Habilitation/Developmental" (H/D) framework for conceptualizing needs, challenges, and issues that apparently must be addressed in order for young multiple offenders to substantially, and fairly permanently, change their illegal adjustment patterns. The main dimensions of this framework are *skill/capacity deficits, external pressures/disadvantages,* and *internal difficulties.*[4] Accompanying this description of H/D is a theory of psychosocial growth and change that was developed for use in Phase 3. It was applied in conjunction with the Maturity Level classification as part of operation staff's intervention planning for each individual youth, and it would be applicable to other programs on its own.

Part III provides further perspective on community-based, individualized/differential intervention. It first reviews several benefits of this intervention, based on the California experiment, and it then presents fundamental assumptions and beliefs regarding multiple offenders that were strongly supported by that experiment. The section then compares "intensive supervision," this being a generic approach widely used in the United States since the mid-1980s, with the intervention described in this book.

As Part III continues, two broad views of offenders are described and compared, views commonly held by the public and many correctional professionals. Implications of these views for intervention are mentioned. Next, the public's fears of offenders are discussed, as is many adults' increased sensitivity to crime. After that, significant changes that have occurred among youths in recent decades are examined, as are adults' responses to those individuals. The section then describes certain overly simplified and relatively static views of offenders that have been prominent since the 1970s, and it mentions implications of those views for individualized intervention. Following that, key aspects of corrections' presently dominant approach—one that might be called "strong external controls" (SEC)—are specified. SEC largely incorporates those overly simplified and relatively static views; it addresses the public's fears of offenders mainly on a short-term basis; and it minimally focuses on various personal/developmental needs that bear on long-term public protection.

Part III next discusses the implications, for intervention, of those overly simplified and static views of offenders; it also focuses on these individuals' interest in growth and change, and their resistance to it as well. The section then further specifies or elaborates on a range of practical and theoretical matters: the feasibility of an agency's or organization's simultaneously implementing many individualized intervention plans; the complementary roles of "core" and "as-needed" program features; the structural distinction between individualized and differential intervention. Next, self-fulfilling prophecies are discussed, as is their possible avoidance. After that, the section reviews the role that an emphasis on offender need and long-term *community* needs can play in reducing specified implementation problems. Finally, a few words are said about (1) the validity and utilitarian significance of viewing offenders as individuals with important needs and features in common with *non*offenders, and, again, about (2) various beliefs regarding the likelihood and extent of change in the troubled and/or troublesome youths.

The book ends with a few general thoughts.

The book was written over a period of 25 years, with several brief and lengthy interruptions.[5] Chapters 1–9 (CTP program description and outcomes) were written in 1974–1976, with updated recidivism-follow-ups in 1977–1978. Chapters 10–11 (social risk, pre/post change, costs, matching) were written in 1980–1981; Chapters 12–14 (reviews, implications; Phase 3) in 1981; Chapters 15–16 (key factors) in 1981–1982; Chapters 17–20 (feasibility) in 1983–1984; Chapter 21 (analysis of critique) in 1986; Chapter 22 (further validity, issues) partly in 1986 but mostly in the late 1990s; Chapter 23 (other individualized programs) in 1995; Chapters 24–26 (rationales for intervention; theory; ethics) in 1996–1997 and 2000; Chapters 27–28 (developments; benefits, beliefs) in 1989–1990; Chapters 29–30 (further perspectives; individualization, need) in 1991 and 1995.

The book draws from several sources that were part of the experiment, during most or all of its existence. Included are 12 years of direct observations, by on-site researchers, of CTP program operations and of staff/youth interactions; "rapsheets," from the state's centralized Department of Justice files, which list all known arrests and dispositions that occurred before, during, and after each individual's Youth Authority career; pre/post psychological testing of youths; detailed case files ("chronos," quarterly summaries, suspension reports, personal histories, etc.) on all Experimental and Control youths; approximately 2,000 taped interviews (intake; follow-ups; discharge) between youths and researchers; records of some 1,000 supervisory case conferences (diagnosis and intervention planning; follow-ups; crises; discharge) on individual youths; questionnaires and psychometric tests of parole agents and other Project staff; taped, depth interviews with all parole agents; 65 taped, half-day conferences that focused on eight types of youth (one type per conference, each conference being attended by several parole staff and one or more researchers); written accounts of intervention strategies, by parole agents and their supervisors. From 1963 to 1973, the author was one of the on-site researchers, and he, like the others, always had direct, personal, and immediate access to all staff and virtually all operations.

Some final comments, ones that mainly reflect those years of observations, the many interviews with staff and youths by the research team, and the half-day conferences: The Community Treatment Project was not a place where combinations of program elements, intervention methods, and strategies were, in fact, applied in various individualized ways—yet, say, in a *mechanical,* generally indifferent manner. Instead, it was a place where staff had a strong interest in helping youths improve their lives, and in protecting society by that means. Staff consistently believed that, when these youths first came to the Project, they were at least partly open to, or could soon be opened to, important positive change and growth, and that their lives could eventually be happier than they were. Through time, they conveyed this belief to those youths in many implicit and explicit ways—seldom, however, downplaying to those individuals the challenges and work that would often be involved.

With few exceptions, CTP staff felt that their *own* work at the Project was the most challenging, yet stimulating and rewarding, of their professional lives. Together, their above interest and beliefs, their feelings about their work, and their attitudes in other respects, helped generate a positive, upbeat atmosphere at each CTP office (community center). All in all, it was their energy and drive that helped make this complex program "gel": These factors, together with the individuals' interest, attitudes, and so on, also made the application of CTP's elements, methods, and strategies something far from perfunctory or even boilerplate. In short, staff gave the program "life," considerable variety, and an optimistic, albeit serious, human face. These qualities were sustained for over a decade. Most Project youths believed their parole agents (as they called them) "really tried," even when they disagreed with what those agents were doing. None of this could have been learned by researchers who collected data only at (i.e., from) a distant office, or who seldom visited the Project—the operations program—itself.

The YA/NIMH experiment showed the importance of human relationships and of humane interactions. To most youths, such relationships and exchanges—or their level of consistency and their overall quality—were a new or largely new experience. Partly by themselves, but especially in conjunction with the program's elements and approaches, these relationships and exchanges helped modify and expand the individuals' picture of their world, of how other persons can feel about them and respond to them, and of their own overall potential. In addition, such relationships made it easier for most youths to accept being in an intensive program; they helped these individuals become increasingly comfortable with and involved in, or at least more tolerant or accepting of, various aspects of the intervention plan; and, together with other factors, they often supported these youths during personal crises.

Thus, the experiment indicated that relationships and interactions of a concerned and humane nature can help a program utilize its visible resources and concrete opportunities—ones that can help many of its clients better deal with the practical necessities of their lives. It indicated that these factors, especially in the context of an intervention plan that seems to hold realistic hope for the near and intermediate future, can motivate a wide range of youths to "try" and to "keep trying." It could be helpful if, in future years, the value and potential of such relationships were increasingly appreciated within corrections.

Notes

1. Before as well as after the mid-1960s, the Community Treatment Project was accessible to North American and other correctional professionals who wished to personally visit the Sacramento, Stockton, and San Francisco operations. The Youth Authority's offshoots, for example, "Community Delinquency Control Projects" that were located in Los Angeles and Oakland, were available as well. For individuals who could not visit, many of CTP's experiences, operations, principles, and findings were reflected in the pages of its numerous, periodic project reports, and, to a lesser extent, in journal articles. During most of the 1960s and in the early 1970s, most such reports, and related documents, were widely and regularly distributed—each one to some 1500 individuals, agencies, organizations, university departments, and libraries, mostly in the United States (Palmer, 1970c, p. 23). (About 10 percent of these went to Canada, the United Kingdom, Western Europe, and elsewhere.) They became a principal source, within and outside corrections, of specific information concerning intensive, individualized, community-based intervention with juvenile offenders. In 1967, a center for training in diagnostic and treatment/control methods used at CTP was started, and during the next five years, this resource further disseminated knowledge about the CTP approach, via direct training and personal contacts.

2. Both programs modeled themselves after the well-known Highfields project, an institution-based operation that had existed in New Jersey since 1949.

3. These are among the major factors in terms of which, and the dimensions along which, people *can* be, and usually *are,* "individualized" in the first place—in particular, are (1) objectively distinguishable from one another and are (2) recognized, by various other individuals, as specific persons in their own right. It was assumed, from early on, that these factors and dimensions would be relevant to intervention planning and to subsequent implementation—agent/youth interactions included. This would apply especially, but not only, when those factors/dimensions were combined with each other, and with other information, in order to form a picture of the youths as functioning wholes.

4. Although the 12-year experiment was not explicitly organized with these specific dimensions in mind, they entered into most CTP operations staff's thinking and planning regarding each individual youth.

5. The latter occurred partly because of work pressures and mainly so that the author could write other books that seemed important or urgent at particular points. This especially applied to *Correctional Intervention and Research: Current Issues and Future Prospects* (1978), an analysis of the "nothing works" position which was then at its height; to *The Re-emergence of Correctional Intervention* (1992), a subject that seemed likely to have value to the field at that particular time; and to *A Profile and Correctional Effectiveness and New Directions for Research* (1994), since the time seemed ripe not only for a broad summary and integration of correctional intervention's research to date, but—especially— for suggestions regarding new research approaches that could help pinpoint effective and ineffective interventions.

Volume I

California's Community Treatment Project

PART I

An Experiment in Individualized Intervention

1 BACKGROUND AND OVERVIEW

The Community Treatment Project began in 1961 and ended in 1973. During those years its job was to work with individuals who were typical Youth Authority wards.

Most YA wards were no strangers to delinquency. For instance, during 1961–1965 four out of every five juvenile probationers successfully completed their term of probation and were never sent to the Youth Authority. The one remaining youth did continue to get in trouble with the law and eventually was sent ("committed") to the Youth Authority. The YA, with its large-sized institutions, was "the end of the line" as far as juvenile offenders were concerned. After that came the adult correctional system itself.

Around 1967 the Youth Authority began to receive a still more restricted population: one of every eight probationers (Davis et al., 1975). This narrowing of the population was largely a result of Probation Subsidy, a statewide program that had gotten underway in mid-1965 (Smith, 1965). By 1970 the ratio was one out of fifteen, and by 1973 it was one out of nineteen. In addition, between the early 1960s and early 1970s there was a 49 percent increase in the average number of police arrests these youths had accumulated by the time they were first committed to the YA. The increase was from 5.3 to 7.9 such arrests. The proportion of boys with assaultive or violent committing offenses had also increased, from 15 percent to 32 percent. By 1974 it was 44 percent (Davis et al., 1974). These figures exclude cases of dependency and neglect; they also exclude common traffic citations and traffic-related arrests. Clearly, as the 1960s unrolled, individuals who were sent to the Youth Authority had been increasingly in-

volved in delinquency. It was not just that a smaller number and percentage of the total population was being "sent up" by the courts.

Even in 1961 most correctional personnel seemed to agree that YA wards were among California's most seriously involved juvenile offenders. However, that fact by itself did not settle the following question: Must these youths be removed from their home community for the protection and peace of mind of society? Many people within corrections said yes; others answered no. Those who said no were in the weaker position, since they were running counter to tradition and deep-seated emotion, with virtually no evidence to back their claim.

As for the average citizen, he or she seemed to take it for granted that almost everybody who *was* committed to the YA probably *had* to be committed and "sent up." Although the average citizen probably gave it little thought, he or she did seem to assume that most correctional agencies were doing about the only thing that could be done with respect to repeat offenders ("recidivists"). In terms of what was felt and known at the time, within corrections, it is entirely possible that they were.

Basically, what *was* the Youth Authority doing at the time? What was the nature of its standard program?

In essence, the YA's program had two distinct phases—incarceration, and then parole. Incarceration consisted of the following:

After four to six weeks in a reception center, boys and girls who were committed to the Youth Authority were almost certain to be locked up in one or another of the YA's institutions, each of which housed an average of over 400 youths. The average duration of lockup was nine months (three-fourths of all lockups lasted between five and 13 months). During that period, youths were likely to be involved in regular academic schooling or else vocational training. In addition, they were likely to participate in weekly community counseling sessions, and/or weekly or twice-weekly small group meetings—or else in some form of individual counseling or informal "man-to-man" discussions (Cook and Johns, 1965; Davis and Pike, 1969; Golden, 1968; Johns, 1967).

Eighty-one percent of all juvenile court commitments were between the ages of 14 and 17 at the time of first commitment. The average age was $15\frac{1}{2}$. When interviewed shortly after being released to parole, most youths described their institution as being dreary, oppressive, or both. Many considered it somewhat frightening, as well. Seldom did they regard it as actually inhumane, but equally seldom did they describe it as having many redeeming features. They often referred to the institution as "the joint," and they made it clear they never wanted to return.

The Youth Authority operated several institutions throughout the state, separate for boys and girls. It also operated four small forestry camps for boys; however, these were able to accommodate no more than 6 percent of all boys. (In 1961, girls comprised 18 percent of all juvenile court commitments. In 1973 they accounted for 11 percent.) (Braithwaite et al., 1962; Braithwaite et al., 1963; Davis et al., 1973; Walters, Brown, and Logan, 1961.)

When a boy was released from an institution or camp he was assigned to a Youth Authority parole agent whose caseload averaged 70 youngsters at any one time. Caseloads for girls were slightly smaller. The agent was required to contact the youth at least once a month. Given the pressure of time, this contact usually lasted 15 to 20 minutes, except at times of crisis. Judging from almost 200 follow-up interviews with YA parolees on standard caseloads during 1962–1965, many youths preferred this amount of contact; about as many wished there were more.

The average parole agent harbored few illusions about being able to seriously address, and resolve, long-standing difficulties on the part of youths and their families. Instead, he or she generally tried to provide (1) at least a bare minimum of actual surveillance, or authority-based control; (2) occasional material aid plus a very infrequent collateral contact with employers, teachers, or public agencies; and (3) a few carefully chosen words of encouragement, support, practical advice, disapproval, and/or warning.

Under the circumstances, it was physically impossible for the parole agent to cover more ground than that, at least with more than a handful of particularly receptive and/or unusually disturbed, vulnerable youths. Yet, even then, there was seldom time for detailed case planning and systematic follow-through. In short, most youths were largely on their own. Parole generally lasted about 20 months in the case of youngsters who stayed out of serious trouble and were not reinstitutionalized.

This combination of incarceration and parole was known as the "traditional YA program."

The Beginnings of CTP

In 1960–1961 most people who had access to pertinent statistics realized that the traditional program was not eliminating delinquent behavior in a large proportion of cases. They also knew it was not accomplishing as much as the average citizen probably assumed it was, despite its relatively straightforward, commonsense approach. The facts were that within 15 months after first release to parole, 52 percent of all male juvenile court commitments had "failed" as a result of continued trouble with the law. At 24 months the figure was almost 65 percent. For girls, the figures were approximately 30 percent and 40 percent, respectively. "Parole failures" were returned to an institution, usually for nine more months. In many cases this cycle repeated itself at least one more time.

Youth Authority researchers were quite aware of these statistics. Among them were Drs. Stuart Adams and Marguerite Grant (Warren, after 1963),[1] each of whom had already carried out large-scale research on offenders during the 1950s. They believed there might be considerable room for improvement, not only in the rate of parole success but in the overall approach to working with juvenile offenders. They spoke, for example, of a delinquent environment that often seemed to exist within state training schools, and they implied that this might be an important contributor to the observed rates of parole failure:

> Clearly, incarceration does not "cure" all delinquents. [Youth Authority researchers], in sequential interviews with wards through their period of incarceration, . . . found boys reporting more delinquent than nondelinquent knowledge gained in the institution. [In work done outside the YA] there appears to be a general consensus that institutional experience is not necessarily rehabilitative and that, in fact, its influence may, in part, be criminogenic. A disconcertingly large percentage of former juvenile offenders recidivate and eventually graduate to adult correctional institutions. In large training schools there is, of necessity, some contact between naive delinquents and those whose pattern of delinquency is well established. (Adams and Grant, 1961, p. 14)

They also suggested that "banishment" from the community might, in itself, add to the difficulty that offenders often have, in terms of achieving parole success. Along this line, Adams and Grant hypothesized that there might be considerable payoff in helping the youth learn to identify and directly deal with his problems and environmental pressures. Such an approach would be in contrast to physically removing him from the situation for a long period of time and placing him into a training school where much of his energy would be focused on coping with a new and rather different set of issues, or perhaps on learning how to bide his time.

> Several factors suggest the desirability of developing a new approach to the rehabilitation of many juvenile offenders who are now being committed to the Youth Authority: . . . [One of these is] a belief that maintaining the offender as an integral part of the community is often preferable to "banishment" followed by attempted reintegration into the community. [This is related to] the possibility that the incarcerated youth, removed from family tensions and school and community pressures, may be able to perceive himself as problem-free and that the same youth, kept facing these tensions, may more willingly make use of offered help in meeting his problems. (Adams and Grant, 1961, pp. 1–2)

Thus, in the view of these researchers, banishment from the community was a specific factor to be dealt with. It was separate from that of negative institutional atmosphere. These thoughts were expressed in their original YA proposal to the National Institute of Mental Health (NIMH), for the creation of what was to become the Community Treatment Project (CTP).

Adams and Grant also suggested that a range of intervention strategies might be desirable, since certain methods might work better with some types of individuals than others. Here, they referred to several investigations which suggested that "differential effectiveness of treatment programs over kinds of delinquents can be shown, and that treatment strategies should be built to meet the needs and problems of a particular type of delinquent" (Adams and Grant, 1961, p. 2). In principle, this idea would have been equally valid within and outside an institutional setting. However, these researchers did not believe that most institutions were organized to deal with delinquent youths at such a level of individualization. "Many criticisms have been made of large institutions where an impersonal, formal and complicated organization is unavoidable, where individual initiative is discouraged, simple conformity is adaptive, and the 'well-institutionalized' inmate is developed." (Adams and Grant, 1961, p. 14)

Those were the main factors, hypotheses, and beliefs that then led Adams and Grant to formulate, for the first time, their basic concept of community-based intervention:

> An alternative procedure suggested by these considerations is the use of a plan which would combine individualized treatment and supervision of wards in their own communities rather than in state institutions. *This procedure would, in short, substitute intensive treatment-control in the community for commitment to a training school.* (Adams and Grant, 1961, p. 2)

This concept involved a particular kind of community approach, one which emphasized intensive and individualized treatment and supervision. Given this concept, the Adams and Grant proposal then focused on the substitution of one type of setting for another. Thus, in combination, two factors represented the essence of the proposed new approach: (1) intensive/individualized treatment control and (2) a community-based setting. In effect, the California researchers were saying, "Let's scientifically find out if serious offenders actually need to be incarcerated if, instead, they are provided with certain forms of treatment and control in the community." This line of inquiry received strong support from Dr. Keith Griffiths, chief of YA research.

(Before continuing, it might be noted that the term "individualized" did not refer to the vehicle or context of intervention, for example, a one-to-one approach as opposed to a group approach. Instead, it referred to the principle of developing a set of strategies that could "meet the needs and problems of a particular type of delinquent," or of the delinquent as an individual.)

These originators and supporters of the CTP were very concerned with reducing the rate of return to institutions, and with avoiding the development of delinquent careers. However, their most immediate concern related to ways of reducing the need for institutionalization in the first place. This concern was also stimulated by financial considerations that had begun to appear on the horizon:

[Through this research] it may be found, for example, that a significant proportion of wards can be more effectively treated, and at lower costs, in a community setting than in a training school milieu.[2] The need to construct additional correctional facilities for youths in the future might be appreciably reduced. California Youth Authority population projections show a doubling of institutional wards within the next ten years if present trends continue. This rate of growth is markedly higher than that of the population base from which the juveniles are drawn. Unless effective new approaches to ward rehabilitation are found, the problem of coping with the youthful offender in our society will grow correspondingly. (Adams and Grant, 1961, p. 12)

They hoped that the proposed research would be one way to develop the approaches in question:

The Community Treatment Program . . . is representative of a growing emphasis on utilizing a variety of treatment approaches to meet a variety of treatment and management problems posed by juvenile offenders. . . . In facing the complexities of defining suitable treatment plans for varieties of delinquents under varieties of conditions, new knowledge may be accumulated which will contribute to the social science of understanding and treating delinquents. (Adams and Grant, 1961, pp. 12–13)

Thus, the specific aims of CTP Phase 1 were formally stated as follows:

The aims of the proposed project are threefold: (1) To *determine the feasibility* of releasing selected California Youth Authority wards directly from the reception center to a treatment program in the community; to see whether communities are willing to accept the return under treatment conditions of members who have just been banished as no longer tolerable in the community; (2) To *compare the effectiveness* of a period of community treatment with a period of incarceration as measured by parole performance and attitudinal and behavioral changes in the ward; and (3) To *develop hypotheses* regarding treatment plans for defined types of delinquents in specified kinds of settings. (Adams and Grant, 1961, p. 2)

In sum, the overall goal was to develop an intensive, individualized program in the community, one that could serve as a substitute for long-term commitment to a state training school. It was hoped that this approach would be more humane, less impersonal, less expensive, and at least as effective as the traditional approach.

The most immediate and pressing need would be to see if a community-based parole unit could in fact be established and maintained—that is, to see if a novel operation such as this would be workable and at least minimally acceptable in the first place. The long-range research objective was to figure out *which approaches* would be effective for *which "types"* of youth.[3] It was recognized that this broad objective would not be achieved within the span of time that was allotted for the program: 1961 to 1964.

During the course of its development, the research proposal was carefully reviewed by the YA's Division of Parole—which contributed several important ideas. Its basic objectives and plan received strong backing from Heman Stark, then director of the Youth Authority. To facilitate project operations, a close working relationship was established between the Divisions of Research and Parole.

Overview of Program Developments

The Adams-Grant proposal was accepted by the NIMH, and project operations began in October 1961. CTP's headquarters unit was located in Sacramento. A smaller, satellite office was established in Stockton, 45 miles to the south.

CTP's target population included first commitments to the Youth Authority from local juvenile courts. Certain categories of youth were declared "ineligible" for the program, on an a priori basis. These were mostly individuals (1) whose commitment offense had been of a violent or assaultive nature, or (2) whom the community emphatically did not want returned directly to the streets, for an offense-related reason. All remaining youths were "eligible" and were assigned on a random basis to either CTP or the traditional YA program. The former individuals were called experimentals; the latter were controls. (Details are provided in Chapter 2.)

By mid-1962 the Sacramento and Stockton units had gained considerable acceptance within the community. Support had been expressed by local welfare councils, citizens groups, recreation and youth agencies, and, to a lesser extent, the school system. Local police and probation departments seemed generally accepting of the program, and positive press coverage had been received as well.

During 1963 the first research results came in. These showed that CTP youths were "failing on parole" at half the rate that was observed for youths in the traditional program. (It was not until 1968 that serious questions were raised concerning the relevance

and adequacy of "parole failure" as a measure of comparative effectiveness. This and other measures are reviewed in Chapter 7.) Psychological tests soon suggested that CTP youths were also ahead of traditional program youths in terms of positive attitude change. In addition, a preliminary analysis had indicated that monthly per capita costs were about two-thirds as much in CTP as in Youth Authority institutions, not counting the cost of building new institutions. Per capita costs were not highlighted for the *parole* portion of the YA's traditional program; instead, emphasis was placed on the comparison between CTP and YA *institutions,* since the latter were the basic settings or programs for which CTP was viewed as a possible substitute (Community Treatment Project staff, 1963; Grant, Warren, and Turner, 1963; Warren, Palmer, and Turner, 1964b).

Although tentative, the 1963 results suggested that institutionalization might not be necessary after all, at least for a sizable percentage of youths. It was felt that if these early findings held up—especially those relating to rate of failure—CTP would have achieved a major breakthrough for the field of corrections. The parent agency was understandably pleased with these developments and prospects:

> The Youth Authority's satisfaction with the Project is clearly evidenced in its plans to continue substituting community programs for traditional institutional programs and, also, in its plans to immediately expand the CTP program itself into two full units in Sacramento and Stockton and to gradually expand this program to other communities in California as trained staff becomes available to move out from the original units. (Warren, Palmer, and Turner, 1964b, p. 24)

From several sources, news of CTP's positive results spread rapidly, often in unqualified, enthusiastic terms. Local, national, and international visitors soon filed in to look at the YA's unusual program.

Because of the early findings, plus the interest as well as acceptance that was expressed, Youth Authority researchers (Warren, Palmer, and Turner) decided to propose a second phase of CTP. Their rationale and main objectives were as follows:

The several findings of Phase 1 suggest that a more efficient program for the rehabilitation of juvenile offenders has been developed—that is, a program which has a higher rate of success at a reduced cost.[4] Furthermore, an important step has been taken in defining effective treatment strategies for defined subtypes of delinquents.

If, as part of Phase 2, the Community Treatment program were to expand into other communities, a better estimate of the *generalized applicability* of the findings could be provided. If, in addition, this program, which utilizes a differential treatment model, were to be compared with an alternative program, *elements of community programs related to success* could then be highlighted. (Warren, Palmer, and Turner, 1964a, p. 5; emphases added)

To address the issue of generalized applicability, a CTP parole unit was to be established in San Francisco. The Sacramento/Stockton units were to be continued for purposes of overall comparison with the new San Francisco unit (which would have its own specific comparison group), and to help determine if the Phase 1 findings would hold up under changing conditions.

The second objective would be approached in a number of ways. One would be "to compare the effectiveness of a community-located program based on the CTP differential treatment model with a community-located program modeled after Empey's Provo Experiment" (Warren, Palmer, and Turner, 1964a, p. 2). Both programs would be located in San Francisco. The latter, a Guided Group Interaction program, would, by design, *not* contain certain elements that the CTP program would contain (and which its Sacramento/Stockton units had contained during 1961–1964)—elements that seemed to play an important part in the CTP's particular type of intervention. (Further details are found in Appendix 1.)

Another major aim was to "describe in elaborate detail the program elements of the present CTP operation in order to create a research base for expansion of Community Treatment programs, for training relevant staff, and for comparisons with alternate community programs" (Warren, Palmer, and

Turner, 1964a, p. 2). Here, the experiences of all CTP units would be drawn upon, particularly those in Sacramento and Stockton. The main concern was that if a community-based approach did work, correctional staff would want to know how they might design similar programs within their own agency.

When the Phase 2 proposal was submitted to the NIMH, CTP was still the only correctional project in the United States that was in a position to scientifically focus on questions that many people had begun to consider important. For example: Can the Phase 1 approach be used in other settings? What are the key elements of an intensive, community-based program? A scientific or systematic approach to these questions was possible only because of the Youth Authority's willingness and ability to support the experimental-control designs that were proposed by its researchers. These designs ultimately depended on the use of random assignment procedures, and on agency willingness to support the integrity and special requirements of the study/programs for relatively long periods of time. For similar reasons, CTP was in a position to continue collecting detailed information on large numbers of carefully diagnosed groups of youth. All things considered, the project held promise of working toward its immediate and long-range goals from a reasonably solid base.

The NIMH accepted the research proposal, and Phase 2 soon got underway. It ran from mid-1964 to mid-1969, although the San Francisco units first began operating in 1965. Eligibility criteria and random assignment procedures were the same as in Phase 1. Several interesting findings emerged from Phase 2.

One basic finding was that most of the Phase 1 results held up. However, as new measures of program impact were introduced (i.e., different *kinds* of measures), the previously reported performance differences in favor of CTP no longer seemed as sharp. In the case of one measure, no difference was found at all, except for specific types of youth. Nevertheless, CTP boys continued to perform better than boys in the traditional program on most standard measures of effectiveness. On the other hand, CTP girls performed no better than those in the traditional program (Palmer, 1971a).

When the low operating costs of *regular parole* were added to the picture that had been presented in 1964, the results suggested that CTP was about as expensive as the traditional program. However, CTP seemed less expensive when one considered the fact that (1) most large-sized institutions would cost several million dollars to build, and (2) construction costs of this type could largely be avoided through the use of community-based intervention (Palmer, 1971a).

The basic concepts that had been used in Sacramento/Stockton during Phase 1 did seem applicable to the large-sized urban setting, in this case San Francisco. (The concepts in question were used during Phase 2 as well, with revisions.) This also applied to the CTP's treatment-control strategies. However, certain important differences emerged as to the types of youth that were present within the two settings, and the methods of intervention that were emphasized (Palmer et al., 1968; Palmer, 1971a).

Several factors emerged as probable contributors to the effectiveness of the CTP as compared with that of the traditional program.[5] Included were (1) matching of given types of parole agents with certain types of youth; (2) individualized programming and, if necessary, intervention in several areas of the youth's life (e.g., family, school, peers); and (3) "discretionary" and "treatment-relevant" decision-making.[6] Other factors seemed unrelated to the CTP's comparative effectiveness. These included (4) mere avoidance of institutionalization, (5) type and amount of education and experience on the parole agent's part, and (6) ethnic background of the parole agent in relation to ethnic background of the youth (Palmer, 1968c; 1971a).[7]

During the first half of Phase 2, CTP staff revised and refined their earlier descriptions of various youth types, and of the methods that seemed appropriate for them. This effort served as a basis for the establishment, in mid-1967, of a Center for Training in Differential Treatment. This center was largely a response to the growing interest in community treatment on the part of county probation departments and state agencies, within and outside California. It operated from Sacramento and was directed by Dr. Warren, principal investigator of CTP during 1961–1967.[8]

Finally, as the number of youths who had been studied continued to accumulate, and as their length of follow-up continued to grow, it was possible to get increasingly reliable estimates as to which youth types were performing better in the traditional program and which ones were doing better in CTP. More reliable estimates of program cost also became available.

Although the last Phase 2 youths were assigned to their respective programs in 1969, research follow-up of all Phase 1 and Phase 2 youths was continued through most of 1974. During 1973–1974 several major analyses were updated and refined. New and more widely acceptable measures of program impact were brought into the picture as well. The final results for Phases 1 and 2 combined are presented in Chapters 8 through 12.

Developments Leading to CTP Phase 3

By 1967–1968 it was the consensus of CTP staff that the difficulties and delinquent orientation of 25 percent to 35 percent of all CTP boys were hardly being reduced by the community-based program. This was despite the CTP's generally positive results as compared with the traditional program. It was noted, for example, that at least one-third of this 25 percent to 35 percent group were rearrested within a few weeks or months after having entered the CTP. Much the same was observed with similar types of youth who had been released to regular parole after having spent several months in an institution.

These observations led to the following question: Would many of these individuals become less delinquently oriented if they began their Youth Authority career *not within the community*, but in a small-sized setting that was operated by CTP personnel? Phase 3 was mainly designed to answer that question. A somewhat different goal was to find out if the CTP approach could be successfully applied to a wider range of offenders than had been worked with during 1961–1969—for instance, individuals who, starting in mid-1969, would be committed to the Youth Authority from *adult courts* and/or for *seriously assaultive offenses* (Palmer, 1969a).

Phase 3, research again funded by the NIMH, was to operate within the greater Sacramento area, for a four-year period beginning in mid-1969. Chapter 13 contains a more complete account of this aspect of CTP.

Before describing the structures, procedures, and operating assumptions of the Community Treatment Project, it might be useful to review Table 1–1. This table shows the location of CTP's differential treatment units during Phases 1, 2, and 3. Other information is summarized as well.

TABLE I–I

Facts Concerning Differential Treatment Units

Location of Unit	Local Population	Year of Operation	Phase of CTP
Sacramento	275,000[a]	1961–1973	1, 2, 3
Stockton	100,000	1961–1969	1, 2
Modesto[b]	55,000	1967–1969	2
San Francisco	750,000	1965–1969	2

[a]The Phase 3 study area encompassed approximately 400,000.

[b]Serviced by the Stockton office, 30 miles distant.

Notes

1. Marguerite Grant codeveloped the theory of interpersonal maturity (Sullivan, Grant, and Grant, 1957). Unless otherwise specified, all references to "Warren," "Warren, M.," and "Warren, M.Q.," relate to the same individual— formerly "Grant, M." (Marguerite). In the 1961 proposal to NIMH (Adams and Grant; see text), it was Dr. Warren who translated the idea of community treatment in lieu of institutionalization into an actual scientific experiment, one that would also make sense to operations staff and top administrators.

2. In the original proposal it was "estimated that the average annual per capita cost of operating the Community Treatment Program is [i.e., will be] approximately one-third of the per capita cost of institutionalization plus parole" (Adams and Grant, 1961, p. 12). At the end of Phase 1, the average monthly per capita cost of operating CTP was less than one-half that of institutionalization (Kenney et al., 1965).

3. "The long-range goal of this project will be the development of a theoretical model relating classifications of treatment operations to classifications of delinquents studied" (Adams and Grant, 1961, p. 11).

4. This analysis had serious limitations, some of which were recognized at the time (Grant, Warren, and Turner, 1963; Warren, Palmer, and Turner, 1964b; Kenney et al.,1965b). The main difficulty was that very few CTP and traditional program youths had been discharged from the Youth Authority as of 1964. Because of this it was not possible to carry out a meaningful "career cost analysis." Had such an analysis been available, CTP would not have appeared far less costly than the traditional program—which, of course, included institutionalization *and* parole. In any event, the monthly per capita analysis did not take into account the low costs of regular parole.

5. At this point (1964), rate of success was thought of largely in relation to recidivism data on 15 months' parole follow-up. This was the measure that had traditionally been used in correctional research.

6. For example, "treatment-relevant decision-making as an expression of differential treatment prescriptions, maximum utilization of augmented program resources, sufficient flexibility to shift treatment directions [during times of crisis], and accumulated knowledge of given youth subtypes' patterns of acting out" (Palmer, 1971a, p. 89).

7. The contribution of the first three factors would remain unchanged despite the fact that, during 1968–1970, critics began questioning CTP's earlier assertions to the effect that the community-based program was more successful than the traditional YA program, as judged in large part by the widely differing rates of parole failure. (See Chapter 21 for details.)

8. Phase 1 of CTDT ran from 1967 to 1970. It was jointly operated by the Youth Authority and the American Justice Institute, and was mainly funded by NIMH (MH 10893). Phase 2 ran from 1970 to 1974 (Howard, 1974).

2 ORGANIZATION, INTAKE, AND ASSUMPTIONS

We now turn to the following questions: How was the Community Treatment Project organized? How were youths brought into it? What were its main operating assumptions?

First, it should be understood that CTP was not a static program. During its 12-year existence it went through three phases of development and operated in two distinct environments. Thus, it is not a simple, easily described entity. To present the project in an accurate yet manageable way, we must first focus on the Sacramento/Stockton (i.e., California Central Valley) parole units as they existed during 1961–1969. Except as specified, the Phase 3 (1969–1973) operation will be described in Chapter 13 only. The Sacramento/Stockton operations—that is, the Phase 1 and 2 Valley units—represent CTP as it came to be known within corrections, during the 1960s. In this sense they may be considered prototypes of the program. The San Francisco CTP unit (1965–1969) was similar to the Phase 2 Valley units in terms of structure, organization, intake, and program components. As a result, this unit will be singled out in the present chapter only when notable differences exist between it and the latter units. The San Francisco Guided Group Interaction unit will be reviewed in Chapter 9.

Organization of CTP Valley Units
Caseload Size and Related Issues
During Phase 1 the question of caseload size was interwoven with issues that are still of relevance to corrections. These include community acceptance, use of external controls, and operating costs. To facilitate later discussion of such issues, considerable background material will now be presented. This material will also highlight certain factors that helped determine CTP's final structure during Phase 2.

During the first two and a half years of Phase 1, each CTP agent worked with no more than seven or eight youths at any one time. Larger caseloads had been allowed for in the Phase 1 proposal; yet, by most standards, even these were rather small[1] (Adams and Grant, 1961; Palmer, 1973c). CTP administrative staff operations and research personnel alike—always considered small caseloads an indispensable part of the program. These were seen as a way of facilitating intensive (i.e., frequent) contact between agent and youth, and of implementing the principles of personalized interaction and client involvement in the process of change.

To a lesser extent, CTP's small caseloads were also a response to external pressures and concerns. Chief among these was the need to assure the public, and local police/probation departments in particular, that Youth Authority staff would have the ability to exercise close surveillance and control, if necessary. In this respect small caseloads were one way of addressing the question of whether local communities would get "torn apart" by delinquents who were being returned to the streets without first spending several months in a locked setting.

Eighteen months after the project got underway, the Sacramento and Stockton communities seemed largely satisfied that CTP youths were not going to run roughshod over their neighborhoods. This relieved some, but not most, of the external pressure for close surveillance and control.

At about this time (mid-1963) CTP administrative staff began to feel an increasing confidence in many of the treatment-control approaches that were being tested:

> The original proposal suggested that both the [youth] subtype definitions and the treatment plans be considered tentative and incomplete because they were primarily theoretically derived and largely clinically untested. . . . In the first year and a half of the Project, usefulness and the relative adequacy of the original definitions have been demonstrated. The assumptions regarding the etiology of delinquency for each subtype, and therefore the goals of treatment for each of the subtypes, have received further support. Further, the effectiveness of the general treatment-control approaches with each of the delinquent types has been shown. (Grant, Warren, and Turner, 1963, p. 53)

Staff began to think that most CTP agents might be able to implement these approaches not just with seven or eight, but with approximately ten youths at any one time. Such a caseload could, for example, consist of youths who (collectively) might be located at any one or more of the three "stages of intervention" that had been outlined in the Phase 1 proposal: intensive, intermediate, and light (see endnote 2). However, staff were reluctant to consider any number higher than 10. This reflected the fact that, by 1963, *internal* pressure (i.e., CTP administrative staff pressure) to implement the concept of *treatment*—intensive treatment in particular—was as heavy as, if not heavier than, it had been in 1961. In terms of its implications for caseload size, this internal pressure counterbalanced the effects of the above-mentioned drop in external pressure for close surveillance and control.

This counterbalancing took place somewhat independently of the strong internal (CTP) pressure that also existed in connection with *control*. To most CTP staff, a good deal of this pressure, or concern, related to the ongoing realities of community-based treatment, at least for Youth Authority offenders in general:

> The need for establishing control over the behavior of delinquents is paramount, if they are to be treated in the free community, for it is clear that they cannot be treated while they are in the process of acting-out in that setting. . . . [Many of] these youths do not at first believe in the ability of any agency to control their behavior in the community. . . . Even though they have previously [i.e., prior to their YA commitment] been apprehended and punished a number of times, their predominant experiences tell them that most of the time people either do not know what they are doing or do not care, and often, if they do know and do care, they are too busy or too weak to do anything about it. For this reason, establishing control over the ward must occur in the earliest contacts, and minor evidences of delinquency must be treated as seriously as if they were major incidents, if the ward is to become convinced that the controls are real. (Grant, Warren, and Turner, 1963, p. 46)

In short, surveillance and control were looked upon as ways of preventing given youths from maintaining patterns of delinquent behavior that could easily lead to their removal from CTP, and to their physical unavailability for intensive treatment. Apart from this, most staff believed that externally imposed controls could sometimes be of direct therapeutic value. In any event, staff were not sure that large caseloads would allow for adequate control. This was apart from what the public itself might have wished, in terms of surveillance and control.

Meanwhile, other developments were taking place elsewhere in the YA. Middle managers and upper administrators were beginning to focus on two interrelated facts: (1) average caseload size was smaller than originally planned, and (2) many CTP youths were moving through, or being moved through, the program more slowly than expected. Taken together, these facts meant that operating costs would end up being higher than originally expected.[2] This was quite apart from the then-recognized fact that monthly per capita costs were lower in CTP than in YA institutions. To be sure, this comparison reflected only part of the overall cost picture.

By simple administrative fiat CTP could have forced itself to, or been forced to, bring about rapid *case turnover*. Such action would have kept costs down, while at the same time making it possible to maintain small caseloads. As an alternative, operating costs could have been reduced by greatly increasing average *caseload size*. However, project staff believed that both alternatives would markedly affect overall project quality and might preclude the achievement of basic research goals.

Moreover, by the fall of 1963 it was their belief that operating costs were, in themselves, no longer a crucial or high-priority issue. This view was largely based on the favorable cost comparison between CTP and institutionalization, and the large savings that were beginning to seem possible in terms of avoiding the construction of new institutions—a direct outgrowth of the community-based approach. Seen in this context, CTP appeared to be more than paying for itself. This, of course, was apart from the fact that operating costs were indeed higher than originally expected.

In short, CTP staff felt that the achievement of all *remaining* project objectives was of greater importance than the reduction of operating costs. This especially applied to the long-range goal of developing appropriate intervention strategies for various types of youth.

To achieve this long-range goal, staff felt a need for considerable freedom to follow up on promising leads. This principle had been stated, and agreed upon, as part of the original proposal. In their opinion, freedom to explore would be seriously impaired by arbitrary, irrevocable, across-the-board decisions to reduce the overall length of treatment control by, say, an average of 25 percent to 50 percent. Staff felt strongly about this point, especially in light of the earlier-mentioned findings which suggested that their efforts were beginning to pay off. Since promising leads were a rarity within corrections, the idea of changing directions in midstream seemed inappropriate.

For similar reasons project staff were opposed to any marked, a priori reduction in average frequency of contact. These and other considerations were reflected in the following:

> Often, the ward will react to a lessening of treatment intensity by seeking out the Agent and requesting directly or indirectly a continuation of frequent contact. If he is in one of the group programs, he is likely to reject the suggestion that he no longer need attend meetings. The operations staff have not been willing to force a youth to discontinue any program in which he strongly desires to participate, even if he is reclassified [from "Stage A," which usually involved several contacts a week] to Stage

> B [originally set at one contact a week] or to Stage C. . . . [Regarding Stage C, which was originally set at one contact a month,] operations staff reject the idea of any restriction on the number of case contacts, entirely apart from meeting case crises, and insist upon an individual approach to the matter of frequency of contact. . . . [In short,] experience has shown two errors in the early thinking about stages. First, the three stages cannot be defined in terms of frequency of contact alone, despite the inherent relationship between frequency and intensity. Second, because of differences in treatment goals and change criteria between the institutions and the Project, it is fallacious to assume comparability between length of stay in institutions and appropriate length of stay in any of the Project stages [e.g., Stage A]. (Grant, Warren, and Turner, 1963, pp. 23–26)

YA administrators accepted the validity of CTP's position but believed that costs still had to be reduced. They felt sure that legislative reviewers would not be willing to indefinitely support a rather expensive program—experimental or otherwise, scientifically productive or otherwise—even though that program may have helped save the state considerable money in a number of respects. All things considered, the best long-range solution seemed to be an increase in caseload size, perhaps to 15 or 16 youths per worker.

Project staff believed this number was definitely too high to allow for continued implementation of the intervention strategies that were being tested. A compromise was quickly reached; caseloads would be raised to 12 youths per worker.[3] This decision was soon incorporated into the proposal for Phase 2 of CTP (February 1964);[4] and, about two months later its implementation began.[5] As a result, from mid-1964 to mid-1969 caseloads averaged 11.3 youths per worker. By 1966, project staff believed this number was just about right, from a treatment/control standpoint. YA administrators and legislative reviewers seemed fairly satisfied as well.

In view of these developments the first 32 months of program operation can be called the *buildup,* or *formative,* stage. The subsequent 63 months (June 1964 to August 1969) can be called the *full operation* stage; this includes the final few months of Phase 1 and all of Phase 2.

Frequency of agent/youth contact, and amount of surveillance/control, were both at their height during the formative stage. This was due to the very small caseloads that existed at the time. As suggested earlier, it was also an expression of the need to supply concrete assurance to the public regarding the safety of what was then a novel and possibly risky approach.

Structure and Organization

Throughout CTP's formative stage, one administrative supervisor, one casework supervisor, and a maximum of six case-carrying parole agents (five men, one woman) were responsible for both the Sacramento and Stockton communities. Complete CTP units—one in each community—were first established during the period of full operation. Throughout this period each unit contained one casework supervisor and seven parole agents (six men, one woman). One administrative supervisor was responsible for both units combined (see Figure 2–1).

During the full operation stage each CTP unit was to work with approximately 84 youths (72 boys, 12 girls) at any one time. The actual figure turned out to be 78.

Throughout the formative and full operation stages, the administrative supervisor of CTP operations and the principal investigator of the CTP experiment were coequal in terms of decision-making responsibilities. Together, they directed the project in accordance with agency policies and the basic research plan. Operational decisions that were made by the administrative supervisor and his staff had to be compatible with the CTP research design and objectives, as interpreted and administered by the principal investigator. At the same time, decisions that were made by the latter individual and his staff had to be compatible with YA operating policies and procedures as interpreted and administered by the supervisor of CTP operations, and by administrators to whom he reported.

The administrative supervisor and principal investigator were housed in the same building; they coordinated their efforts whenever necessary. They were each part of separate YA divisions and reported only to the chief, or main deputies, of their division[6] (Figure 2–2). This concept of joint decision-making by coequal, organizationally independent yet functionally interdependent section heads proved to be an efficient and effective

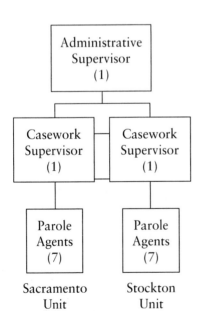

Figure 2–1 CTP unit structure during full operation stage[a].

[a]Excludes clerical and auxiliary positions. All positions are full-time. Unit structure was identical for San Francisco CTP.

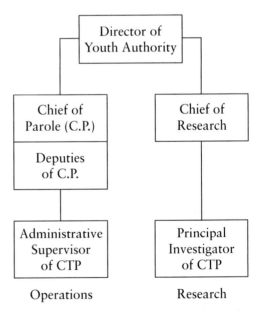

Figure 2–2 Organization of CTP within the Youth Authority.[*]

[*]This organizational structure was identical for San Francisco CTP.

way of coordinating the operational and research needs of CTP. This applied throughout Phases 1, 2, and 3.

Role and Responsibility of Agent

Because of specific research goals, and in light of staffing patterns specified in the proposals to the NIMH, the CTP parole agent was to be the central project member with whom the youth interacted—the individual who provided nearly all treatment and control inputs during Phases 1 and 2 (Adams and Grant, 1961; Warren, Palmer, and Turner, 1964a). All casework coordination and major decision-making responsibility was to remain squarely on the shoulders of this individual, not on other personnel. This also applied to the bulk of everyday activities themselves. In short, the parole agent was to be the principal worker and actual "doer" in terms of direct interactions with youths. He was not to be simply a manager or coordinator of other personnel—individuals who, for example, might carry out much, possibly most, of the day-to-day work.

For these reasons, and to help ensure that (1) lines of communication and responsibility would remain as clear and simple as possible and (2) prescribed treatment and control strategies would be carried out, CTP administrative staff (operations and research) decided, in the mid-1960s, not to add community volunteers and various paraprofessionals to the project. This decision was implemented despite the contribution these individuals might have made, and independent of the fact that such individuals, especially the former, were increasingly available to the Youth Authority beginning in 1966.

For identical reasons the Community Treatment Project never attempted to use a "grandparent program," which became increasingly active within YA institutions, and to a lesser extent parole, after 1966. This program drew upon middle-aged and older volunteers who were willing to spend up to several hours a month with Youth Authority wards, often on a long-term basis. Nor did CTP assign specific youths to "case aides"—paid YA parolees who were not part of the project's study sample. The few case aides who were employed at CTP were used, almost exclusively, to help provide transportation; they were not made responsible for counseling, setting of limits, and so on. (Case aides were neither experimentals nor controls. They had

been selected by institutions' staff based on their relative maturity and expressed willingness to provide assistance to other YA wards, in a community setting. On release to parole they were given partial responsibility, by regular parole staff, for three or four parolees each. More specifically, while assigned to regular parole, case aides were sometimes used to help non-CTP agents supply basic as well as auxiliary services to selected parolees. This practice began in the mid-1960s and, like the volunteer effort itself, remained in effect beyond the close of Phase 2. Generally speaking, it increased the amount of service that would otherwise have been available to the parolees in question.)

Intake and Assignment

Number and Selected Characteristics of Youths

As indicated, some youths (mainly assaultive individuals) were not allowed to participate in the project. These youths, 475 in all, were called "ineligibles." The remaining boys and girls—1,014 "eligibles"—represented a wide range of personalities, and included individuals whose behavior patterns are often considered serious or unacceptable. For instance, characteristics or patterns such as the following did not prevent youths from participating in the program: marked drug involvement, occasional psychotic episodes, apparent suicidal tendencies, homosexuality, and chronic or severe neurosis. In short, none of these features constituted grounds for ineligibility.

During Phases 1 and 2 the total number of eligible youths was as follows: CTP Valley units—396 (338 boys, 58 girls);[7] San Francisco CTP unit—125 (89 boys, 36 girls). The remaining 493 eligibles ("controls," and Guided Group Interaction youths) are mainly described in Chapter 9. (Figures for eligibles and ineligibles refer to all Valley and San Francisco units.)

During most of the formative period, youths who were 11 to 19 years of age at "intake" (point of YA commitment) were eligible for the project. However, beginning in March 1964 those under 13 were no longer accepted.[8] This was mainly because administrative staff felt they "required such a specialized program in the Project that treatment [resources were being] inappropriately diverted from the majority [92 percent] of cases" (Warren and Palmer, 1965). During 1964–1969, intake was therefore limited to boys and girls whose ages were 13 through 19 at intake.[9]

Eligible youths had usually been sent to the YA for property-related offenses such as burglary or auto theft. Except for San Francisco, they were about evenly divided as to the number of Caucasians and non-Caucasians. The large majority came from lower socioeconomic environments. Thus, for Valley boys, the figures were as follows (these figures represent percentages of the total eligible sample; except for commitment offense, they change only slightly when girls are added):

- *Type of YA commitment offense:* property-related—71 percent; person-related (e.g., statutory rape; purse snatch)—5 percent; all others (e. g., incorrigible; runaway)—23 percent.
- *Race:* Caucasian—53 percent; Mexican-American—23 percent; black—20 percent; all others—4 percent.
- *Socioeconomic status of family ("social class"):[10]* lower—81 percent; middle—18 percent; upper—1 percent.[11]

We will now describe the procedure for bringing youths into the project—CTP and the traditional YA program included. As shown in Figure 2–3, five main steps were involved: preeligibility screening, random assignment, diagnostic interviewing, staffing, Youth Authority Board hearing and program assignment. These steps are outlined in Figures 2–4, 2–5, and 2–6.

Preeligibility Screening

Screening for preeligibility was carried out by project research staff. It was done on all youths who, in the opinion of the Youth Authority's central intake and classification (I & C) office, appeared to be "appropriate referrals" for the project. (I & C screening was preliminary or unofficial; it was based on a brief review of selected documents.)[12] An "appropriate referral" was defined by research staff as any individual who:

(1) resided within the Sacramento-Stockton geographic boundaries;[13] (2) was within the preestablished age limits; (3) had never been incarcerated in a state or federal correctional facility within or outside California; and (4) had been committed to the YA from a juvenile court, for the first time. During Phases 1 and 2, 70 percent of all Valley boys and 89 percent of all Valley girls who were appropriate referrals in terms of these criteria were declared eligible for the project by the Youth Authority Board (see below); as seen later, these youths became either "experimentals" or "controls." All remaining youths were "ineligibles," because of either their committing offense, their offense history, strong objections from community agencies, or other reasons.

Preeligibility screening by research staff was based on a review of court reports and related documents that were sent by the local probation department to central I & C, located in Sacramento. Its main object was to verify I & C's unofficial judgment that the youngster was an appropriate referral (AR), and to separate out all AR's whose committing offense made them ineligible for the project. As indicated, this group of ineligibles was to include all appropriate referrals who had been committed to the YA for seriously assaultive behavior or major sex offenses. These "criteria for ineligibility"—and, conversely, criteria for eligibility—were established and agreed upon by the Division of Research, the Division of Parole, and the Youth Authority Board, prior to the start of Phase 1.

Appropriate referrals who were not screened out on the basis of their committing offense were called "preeligibles." (See Figure 2–4.)

Random Assignment

Once the screening was completed the research team made a random drawing on each pre-eligible youth. Its purpose was to determine in an unbiased manner whether that youth would be assigned to CTP or to the traditional program. This drawing, or "random assignment," could be put into effect (i.e., could actually

Figure 2–3 Main steps from intake to program assignment.

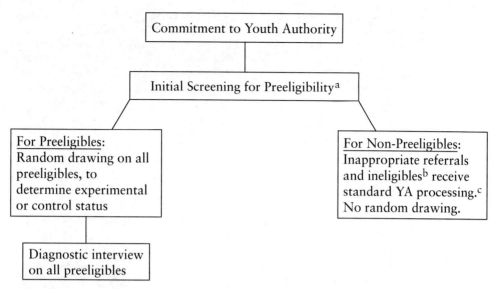

Commitment to Youth Authority		

Initial Screening for Preeligibility[a]

For Preeligibles:
Random drawing on all preeligibles, to determine experimental or control status

For Non-Preeligibles:
Inappropriate referrals and ineligibles[b] receive standard YA processing.[c] No random drawing.

Diagnostic interview on all preeligibles

[a]Preeligibles were appropriate referrals who met the preestablished, offense-based criteria for eligibility. Individuals who did not meet these criteria were ineligible. See text regarding inappropriate referrals.

[b]That is, ineligible on the basis of Youth Authority committing offense alone.

[c]Includes: diagnostic workup by NRCC personnel; Youth Authority Board appearance; etc. (See Figures 2–5 and 2–6.)

Figure 2–4 Steps from Youth Authority commitment to diagnostic interview.

become operative) only if the Youth Authority Board decided that the youngster was indeed "eligible." The board made this decision at the end of the youth's Northern Reception Center and Clinic (NRCC) stay. This was about five weeks after the random drawing had occurred. Thus, prior to the board's official decision on eligibility, the youth was only considered preeligible for the project.

In deciding that a given youth was eligible, the board was officially committing itself to assign that individual to the YA program that had been determined by the random drawing—whichever program that happened to be. More specifically, an eligible youth was one whom the board was willing to send directly to the community program (CTP) without a period of prior institutionalization, if that (namely, assignment to CTP) was indeed the placement indicated by his random drawing.

Prior to stating its decision as to eligibility, the board did not know the outcome of the random drawing. That is, it did not know whether the youth was to be assigned to CTP or to the traditional program in the event it *were* to declare him eligible.

If the board stated that the youth should *not* be eligible, that individual automatically became "ineligible." Whenever this took place, the random drawing did not go into effect. To maintain the necessary scientific control, all such "board ineligibles" were then excluded from the project: They were not assigned to CTP, nor were they counted as "controls" despite their automatic assignment, by the board, to the traditional program.

Thus, despite the preestablished criteria for youths in general, the YA Board always retained the final word and full legal responsibility when it came to determining the actual eligibility or ineligibility of each youngster. Nevertheless, in arriving at its decisions, the board stuck close to the preestablished criteria during Phases 1 and 2, especially in relation to the Sacramento/Stockton units.

In sum, as soon as the board declared a preeligible youth to be eligible, the random drawing came into play and determined whether that youth would be assigned to CTP or the traditional program. If the youth was assigned to the traditional YA program, the board decided which specific institution or camp he would be sent to; it established minimum conditions for his release to parole as well (e.g., minimum amount of time served).

Diagnostic Interviewing

A few days after screening was completed all preeligibles were interviewed by a project researcher.[14] This was the first contact between the youths and any individuals associated with the project.[15] During this contact the youths were told that, at the end of their four- to six-week stay at NRCC, the YA Board would decide whether they would be sent to an institution or a camp, to regular parole, or to CTP. (Almost all youths had heard of the YA Board; half of them knew about CTP.) Their questions, usually few in number, were then answered briefly and objectively. (See Figure 2–5.)

The interview itself was designed to obtain information that would serve as a basis for classifying the youths in terms of the "I-level"

system of interpersonal maturity (Chapter 4), and that might ultimately help the parole agent and casework supervisor develop a relatively individualized treatment-control plan for each youth.[16] As indicated in the Phase 1 proposal, classification was seen as a potential contributor to individualized case planning: "Treatment plans will be made for each case, making use of environmental information, classification information, and treatment suggestions based on both. Revisions will continue to be made as appropriate." (Adams and Grant, 1961, p. 7)

To a large extent the I-level "subtype" classifications were, themselves, shorthand accounts of various patterns and etiologies of delinquency (Chapter 4). For this reason they seemed to provide a rationale for the selection of particular intervention strategies, with specific types of youth. Again, this process was seen as one step in the direction of individualized case planning:

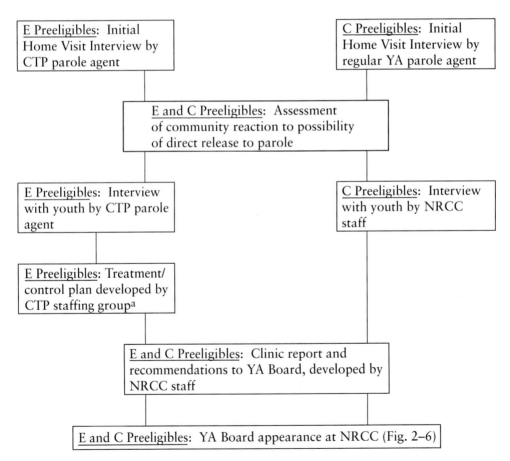

[a]Includes selected information from researcher/youth interview.

Figure 2–5 Diagnostic workup and staffing of experimental (E) and control (C) preeligibles.

Treatment goals will vary from ward to ward but, in each case, will represent an attempt to intervene in the ward's delinquent pattern. For example, in one ward the etiology of the delinquency may lie in the acting-out of some internal conflict, while in another the cause may lie in over-dependence on the approval of delinquent peers. In the first case, an appropriate intervention might consist, in part, of intensive individual psychotherapy sessions. In the second, individual contacts might be contraindicated . . . [etc.]. (Adams and Grant, 1961, p. 7)

To obtain the information that was considered necessary for classification and individualized planning, the diagnostic interview covered such areas as the following:

reasons for being in trouble with the law; type of YA program and type of parole agent that the youth would prefer and not prefer; youth's view of family situation, individual family members, peers, significant others, immediate social environment, school and employment; preferred living arrangement in the community,[17] if directly released to the community from NRCC, and if institutionalized for several months prior to release; view of self and life-situation (e.g.: likes and dislikes; assets and liabilities; influential persons or models; "how would you describe yourself?"; "how would others, who know you fairly well, describe you?"; view of early years/childhood; goals for near future and distant future; ways of achieving those goals).

Staffing

We now turn to the case conference staffing (initial staffing) of youths assigned to the Community Treatment Project.[18] This planning conference was a concrete expression of the underlying goals and assumptions of CTP, and of the principles on which it was based. It usually made a large contribution to the youth's involvement in the program, mainly by helping to determine the level and direction of his relationship with CTP. In view of its importance, this staffing will be reviewed in some detail. First, we will present its underlying rationale; then we will describe the process itself. (The Initial Staffing Guide is shown in Appendix 2.)

Rationale

Broadly stated, the main goal of the initial staffing was to develop an intervention plan that might ultimately help the youth cope with life in a less delinquent, hopefully non-delinquent, way. As indicated by Warren, this behavior change was to extend beyond the period of YA jurisdiction:

The Project [CTP] staff has always viewed its mandate as that of changing delinquents into nondelinquents. This mandate not only involves a *management* function; i.e., control over the behavior of delinquents during the period of agency responsibility for him or her, so that further law violations are not committed. The mandate also involves a *treatment* function; i.e., attempts to change the individual delinquent or the relevant aspects of his environment in such a way that long-term (beyond the period of direct agency responsibility for the offender) nonviolation behavior is assured. (Warren et al., 1966, p. 22)

Despite its broad scope, this mandate was largely accepted by staff from the early days of CTP.[19] At base, it meant that the youth would have to develop new ways—at least some new ways—of dealing with his immediate environment, and of meeting his personal needs and desires. It did not mean he would have to "change completely," as an individual, or that he had to be considered "different" (in a negative sense) or "sick," until such change took place.

The management objective in CTP's mandate reflected three basic facts: (1) some of the youth's behavior was illegal; (2) this behavior was almost certain to *remain* illegal no matter what kind of individual he happened to be and no matter who or what might ultimately have been responsible for his difficulties with the law; and (3) if his behavior was neither modified, redirected, nor eliminated, he might well spend a large portion of his adolescence behind institution walls. To minimize or deny these facts was futile, for it seemed rather certain that society was not going to radically or rapidly alter its views as to what constituted illegal (unacceptable) and punishable behavior. This was apart from the fact that society's response to that same behavior sometimes varied across time and place.

CTP staff assumed that these management and treatment objectives would best be achieved by efforts that emphasized the more immediate causes—the apparent triggering and perhaps sustaining conditions—of the youth's illegal behavior. This view was closely related to yet another assumption, one which concerned the longer-standing, cultural/historical factors that might ultimately have been responsible for the overall conditions within the youngster's social environment, and that may have helped set the stage for his legal and personal difficulties in particular.[20] This assumption was that—within most segments of contemporary American society—most such factors, and related social conditions, could not be changed or improved rapidly enough to make any decisive difference in the youngster's immediate future, or to substantially modify his already established, often self-reinforcing pattern of delinquency. It was therefore taken for granted that most of the changing or adapting would have to come from the individual himself, and from influential members of his immediate environment.

CTP staff also assumed that long-lasting changes would usually require considerable effort on the part of several individuals, certainly the youth. It was believed that most of these changes would not occur within a couple of months. Taken together, these considerations seemed to imply the following. To generate the level of effort that would be called for, and to sustain that effort for a rather long time, a good deal of internal motivation would probably have to exist on the part of the youth. Considerable external support and, in some cases, external direction or guidance might have to be supplied as well, by the parole agent and others. As to external controls (e.g., short-term lockup and various restrictions), these did not seem capable of helping the youth discover any *new* patterns of behavior, *new* sets of goals, or alternate systems of reward. Thus, despite their probable importance in various other respects, external controls, like other factors (e.g., external support and external direction), did not in themselves seem capable of accomplishing the overall goals set forth by staff.

In sum, it appeared that CTP staff would have to place considerable emphasis on tapping into the youth's system of internal motivation, *and* on supplying external support or direction.[21] The exact balance would depend on the individuals involved.

It was assumed that internal motivation could be tapped and sustained more easily if the youth were to associate his program with immediate personal gain—that is, if he could directly experience "personal payoff" that might (1) make the project seem more relevant to his interests and wishes, (2) help compensate for illegal yet gratifying or profitable behavior patterns that he might tentatively relinquish, and (3) offset anxieties, perhaps even crises, that would be likely to arise. It was assumed that some of these factors might also make external support and guidance easier to understand and accept.

In short, personal payoff was likely to mean increased tolerance of, and perhaps active involvement in, the CTP intervention plan. Involvement, in turn, was seen as an important component of long-term, internal motivation. Finally, to accomplish the goals in question it seemed better for staff to build on motives that were associated with "hope," and with conscious satisfaction, than on others that elicited feelings of fear, or deprivation.

Issues of felt relevance, felt payoff, and personal involvement in the process of change were part of the reason for asking the youth to describe some of his present difficulties or concerns, his preferences as to type of parole program and parole agent, and his personal goals for the future. This was done during the researcher/youth, and parole agent/youth, interviews. (See below.)

These issues were also related to the concept of starting from where the client is "at." This widely accepted clinical principle was considered important at CTP. In fact, it was one of the main reasons for asking the youngster, and others who knew him, to describe the following: his likes and dislikes, skills, and hobbies; things he might want to change about himself, and things with which he is satisfied; family and environmental pressures and supports he is feeling, or has experienced in recent years; types of people he likes and dislikes; and situations that make him uncomfortable.

Such information helped provide an initial picture of where the individual was "at" both psychologically and socially, a picture of various things he wanted and of factors that seemed to be working for and against him.

Singly and in combination, the preceding questions and topics were used for purposes which extended beyond that of diagnosis and treatment planning. One usage involved certain aspects of the individual's eventual relationship to the Youth Authority in general, and CTP in particular. For example, it was assumed that a serious, albeit brief, discussion (between agent and youth) of these topics might help the youth begin to see that YA staff were interested not just in his delinquent behavior, but in him as a person, and in his specific wishes and goals.

That, in turn, related to further assumptions on the part of staff, and to other objectives as well. For instance, it was considered important for the parole agent, and project personnel in general, to interact with the youth in ways that might help make selected aspects of his environment, and adulthood, appear less threatening and more attractive than in the past. This was seen as one way to provide the youngster with an increased sense of direction and, in some cases, to help him reexperience or reaffirm some of his previous, infrequent or brief, yet generally positive relationships with adults—this time with a happier ending. In other cases it was seen mainly as a way to provide the youth with an increased sense of power or legitimacy, for example, by making it easier for him to observe and partially identify with self-confident, interesting, respected, or accomplished adults. For such reasons, the agent/youth relationship, and the person-to-person attitudes that were expressed in the project as a whole, were seen as potential contributors to the overall intervention.[22]

Thus, even the early stage of initial staffing was seen as one step in the process of establishing a generally positive, project/youth relationship. It was designed, at the same time, to help figure out which specific type of agent/youth relationship might prove both useful and rewarding. These "relationship goals" were seen as one way of tapping into, and building on, the youth's drive to expand or profit from his present abilities to cope with life, and to reduce his felt deficiencies. That, in turn, was seen as one way of addressing some of the immediate causes or triggering conditions of the delinquent behavior itself.

Procedures

The sequence of events that led to the initial staffing of CTP pre-eligibles was outlined in Figure 2–3 (page 16). Preparations for this staffing began immediately upon completion of the random drawing. As mentioned earlier, information relating to classification and intervention was first gathered by a project researcher, via an interview with the youth. This resulted in an I-level and subtype classification—that is, an I-level diagnosis—which was made by research staff, regarding the given youth. (I-level concepts are described in Chapter 4.)

Once the diagnosis was completed the casework supervisor assigned the youth to a parole agent. This agent was selected because of his skill in working with that particular *type* of youth—that is, "youth subtype," in I-level terminology. Within a few days the agent visited NRCC, where he interviewed the youngster for the first time. This interview covered many of the same areas that were touched on by the researcher; additional areas were discussed as well. This allowed the agent to form his own opinion of the youth as an individual.[23] It helped the youth form an opinion of the agent, and the YA, as well.

During the following week the parole agent usually met with the youth's parents or guardians, in their home; he sometimes spoke with other family members as well. The agent attempted to get their views, and basic information, regarding the youngster's:

- physical, social, and emotional development;
- relationship with the family, peers, and community (neighbors, police, school, employment, etc.); and
- present and past involvement with delinquent behavior.

The agent also attempted to gain a picture of the parents':

- past and present feelings about the youth as an individual;
- expectations of the youth, plus demands that they felt should be made upon him by themselves and others; and
- feelings about his being returned home, either within a few weeks (if no institutionalization were to occur) or else after several months in an institution.

During this contact the agent also obtained and/or verified basic family background information. This entire exchange was called the Initial Home Visit Interview (IHVI).

The initial staffing, or case conference, usually took place a few days after the IHVI. Present at this conference were the researcher who had interviewed the youth, the parole agent who was assigned to work with him, and the casework supervisor. A second parole agent, and the CTP school teacher, were sometimes present as well.[24]

Two main areas were discussed: "Background and Diagnosis," and "Treatment-Control Plan." Background and diagnosis was mainly covered by the researcher and the assigned parole agent. It included such topics as committing offense and offense history (official record; youth's view and interpretation; view by others); characteristics of youth (self-perception; family perception; staff perception); characteristics of family (youth perception; staff perception; family as source of support and stress); youth's attitude toward authority figures; and community as support and stress (peers; school; employment; other). For each topic, the researcher and parole agent described, compared, and discussed their information, most of which had been derived from their respective interviews.[25] The agent usually presented facts and impressions based on probation documents and other sources. The researcher and agent then integrated this information to the extent possible, and concluded each topic by recording, in dictation, their respective or collective summary impressions.

The casework supervisor participated in the summary and recording of impressions, relative to several topics. However, his main contribution usually occurred toward the end of the background and diagnosis area, that is, during the "diagnostic summary section." This included nature of the problem (main dynamics; etiology of delinquent attitudes and behavior; present situation—opportunities and limitations); staff diagnosis (I-level and subtype); and other issues, observations, and remarks.

The treatment/control plan was mainly worked out by the parole agent and casework supervisor. It included such topics as immediate and long-range objectives; placement (home; foster home; other); family treatment; community resources; job and/or school; leisure time activities; peer relations and interactions; controls; type of agent and agent stance; main treatment modalities (individual counseling; small group discussion; other); suggested techniques for achieving the objectives, crucial ques-

tions and case problems; additional assistance for parole agent (outside consultation; specific training; other); predictions; and theoretical diagnostic and treatment-control issues.

The "Background and Diagnostic" section usually took three hours to complete. The "Treatment/Control Plan" usually took two hours. Throughout Phases 1 and 2 this time investment was considered necessary and worthwhile. From the *research* point of view it was necessary mainly in order to document the youth/environmental characteristics and the treatment/control plan in a detailed way. This was regarded as the most direct way of working toward the project's long-range goal of developing "a theoretical model [which relates] classifications of treatment operations to classifications of delinquents studied," and of discovering "to what extent treatment plans are a function of delinquent type and to what extent they are a function of the ward plus his environmental stresses and supports" (Adams and Grant, 1961, p. 11). From the *operations* point of view, the heavy investment of time was considered worthwhile in order to develop an individualized and realistic treatment/control plan, one that would be based on the large amount of information available.[26] Such a plan was seen as having a greater chance of achieving the broad objective of reducing or eliminating delinquent behavior, during and subsequent to the period of YA jurisdiction.

YA Board Hearing and Program Assignment

The Youth Authority Board hearing for project preeligibles took place at the end of each youngster's four- to six-week stay at NRCC. Its basic purpose was to determine which program the individual would be sent to after leaving NRCC—either the traditional YA program, or CTP.[27] The board was the legally designated body that made this determination and assignment for all YA wards. The main steps in the board decision-making and assignment process are shown in Figure 2–6.

In the case of CTP preeligibles (i.e., experimental or "E preeligibles") the board hearing occurred a few days after completion of the initial case conference, described earlier. In the case of traditional program preeligibles (control or "C preeligibles") it occurred a few days after completion of the "Clinic Report and Recommendations" (clinic report) by NRCC staff. Prior to this hearing, NRCC staff completed a

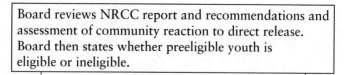

Board reviews NRCC report and recommendations and assessment of community reaction to direct release. Board then states whether preeligible youth is eligible or ineligible.

For Eligible Youths: Research staff informs board of youth's random assignment to E (CTP) or C (traditional) program.

For Board-Ineligibles: Random assignment is canceled, by research. Board assigns youth to traditional YA program. Research excludes youth from experiment.

Board talks with eligible youths, and (1) officially assigns E's to CTP; (2) officially assigns C's to specific YA institution or camp.[a]

[a]See text regarding assignment to direct parole.

Figure 2–6 Youth Authority Board hearing and program assignment for experimental (E) and control (C) preeligibles.

clinic report on all CTP preeligibles as well.[28] (During Phases 1 and 2 it was the clinic report, not the CTP case conference report, that was presented to the board.)

The board made its determination and assignment after reviewing the clinic report plus an "assessment of community reaction" (see below). It sometimes reviewed selected probation documents as well. Both E and C preeligibles were likely to be considered during any board hearing.

For any E or C preeligible, the board made its placement decision (program assignment) within the framework of the preestablished eligibility criteria, and random assignment, as described earlier. That is, it first made a decision regarding the youngster's eligibility or ineligibility for the project. Once that decision was made, it turned to the question of specific program assignment.

Prior to making the decision on eligibility or ineligibility, the board did not know whether the youngster would become an E or a C in the event it were to declare him eligible. If the board were to declare the youth eligible for the project, it was then obliged to assign him to whichever program had been determined by the random drawing: the traditional program or CTP. (As mentioned earlier, the board learned the outcome of this drawing

only after it had stated its decision on eligibility or ineligibility.) However, if it were to declare the youth ineligible, its next step involved automatic assignment to the traditional program. The board always indicated which institution or camp a "traditional program youth" would be sent to, regardless of whether it declared him eligible or ineligible.

The following persons were present throughout the hearing: one or two members of the YA Board; an NRCC staff member; a CTP operations person; and a project researcher. The NRCC staff member was available mainly to answer questions from the board that related to the clinic report and the "Initial Home Visit Interview." The CTP operations person (usually the casework supervisor) was available to present the treatment-control plan for youths who (as it turned out) were declared eligible for the Community Treatment Project.[29] The researcher's role is described below.

The following took place immediately after the board made its decision on eligibility: (1) If the youth was declared *ineligible,* the researcher asked the board to state its main reason(s) for that decision. (The board occasionally reversed its decision at this point, if, on further reflection, it felt that its reason was not very strong.) The board then assigned the ineligible youngster to a specific YA program.[30]

(2) If the youngster was declared *eligible,* the researcher then told the board whether the youth randomly fell "experimental" (CTP) or "control" (traditional program).

If the eligible youth fell experimental, the CTP operations person then presented the treatment/control plan to the board. After the board reviewed this plan it spoke with the youth, who had been waiting outside the hearing room. It asked the youth if the Community Treatment Project had been described to him and discussed with him as a possible (yet not definite) placement. After the youngster responded in the affirmative, the board explained that it was going to assign him to CTP rather than send him to an institution, unless he felt unable or unwilling to handle his situation in a program such as CTP. At this point most youngsters said one of three things: "It's OK with me . . . I'll give it a try"; "I think I can make it at CTP . . . that's where I want to go"; "I'd rather go there than to an institution."

During 1961–1969, one out of 397 eligible Valley youths rejected the opportunity to go to CTP.[31]

If the eligible youth fell control, the NRCC staff member presented the "Initial Home Visit Interview" material to the board. After reviewing this material and the clinic recommendations, the board decided which specific institution or camp the youngster would be sent to. (Members sometimes spoke with the youngster prior to making this placement decision.) After the decision was made, the board presented its basic conditions to the youth—for example, minimum amount of time to be served—together with some ideas as to how the youngster might use that time to his advantage. A small proportion (17%) of youths were assigned directly to parole.

Most individuals were released to CTP, or were sent to a YA institution/camp, a few hours after the board hearing—or one or two days thereafter. Youths who were assigned to CTP or to direct parole sometimes spent an extra week or two at NRCC until their specific living arrangement (e.g., with relatives or a foster home), was finalized. In the case of direct parolees, this process sometimes took three to five weeks. (The conditions of parole that were agreed to by all Youth Authority wards—CTP youths, direct parolees, institutional releasees, and all others—are shown in Appendix 3.)

What main factors entered into the eligibility decision? In determining eligibility, the board placed heavy emphasis on the individual's committing offense. It looked on this as the most important factor, by far. However, it also took into account the reaction, by specific community agencies, to the idea of releasing the youth directly to the streets, from NRCC. The board was told about this "community reaction" immediately after it completed its review of the clinic report. It might be useful to say a few words about this assessment of community reaction.

A *community assessment* was completed for each E and C preeligible, about one week after his arrival at NRCC. It was done by a YA operations staff member on the basis of direct conversations with designated individuals (agency representatives) from two or more local justice system agencies. These were the probation department (in all cases), plus the police and/or sheriff's departments whenever possible.[32] The goal of this assessment was to find out how each agency would feel—for instance, would it object?—if the Youth Authority were to release the youngster, directly from NRCC, to a "special," low-caseload program within the local community. It was made clear to the agency representatives that, in contrast to standard parole, this YA program would involve an intensive, treatment/control approach.

The representatives were advised that direct release from NRCC was not necessarily going to happen, but that if the YA Board found the individual eligible for the program, it *might* happen. They were not told whether the youth had fallen experimental or control. (Agency representatives were already familiar with the implications of random assignment, and with the project experiment in general. As a result, they realized that their opinion—positive, negative, or neutral—could have some influence on the eligibility decision.)

In most cases the agencies voiced no major concerns or strong objections. However, when these *were* voiced, they generally focused on one or both of the following:[33] (1) the nature or perhaps unusual circumstances of the committing offense, or of a previous offense or group of offenses; and (2) doubts, by the agency, as to the ability of the special program to adequately work with, and/or control, the youth—without a period of prior YA incarceration. Although the former, offense-related concerns were taken into account by the YA Board, the latter concerns were not. This was mainly due to the exploratory mission and experimental design of the project.

If the offense-related concerns or objections[34] were unanimous (i.e., across agencies), very strong, or (especially) both, the YA Board then seriously considered declaring the youth ineligible. When this degree and/or intensity of outside-agency concern was present, the chances became very high that the youth would be declared ineligible if, based on its earlier review of the clinic report or probation documents, the board had independently concluded that the circumstances which surrounded the committing offense were considerably more serious than most (e.g., unrecovered stolen weapons or highly vitriolic threats of revenge by the youth). It should of course be kept in mind that the committing offense would not in itself constitute grounds for ineligibility, since it did not fall within the seriously assaultive or major sex offense category. Had it fallen into either category, the youth would not have been pre-eligible in the first place.

Ineligibility was also a rather likely outcome if, in addition to agency concerns, the committing offense had been followed by considerable *negative publicity*. These two factors were often interrelated. Basically, such publicity consisted of fairly widespread newspaper or television coverage in which the youth may have been singled out by name, and which was of a harsh, fear-arousing, or "sensational" nature. Negative publicity of this type was uncommon. However, when present, it sometimes did lead to ineligibility, even apart from factors that related to outside-agency reaction, or prior offense history. Media coverage was routinely checked as part of the overall community assessment.

Prior offense history (prior record) was another factor that the board reviewed. Two main aspects were considered: the assaultive component and total length. Records that contained one or more seriously assaultive offenses sometimes led to a decision of ineligibility, especially if the offense(s) had occurred within a year or two of the YA committing offense. Also, unusually long histories occasionally resulted in ineligibility even if no assaultive offenses were involved.[35]

On the whole, prior offense history was given much less weight, by the board, than committing offense. It was given somewhat less weight than community reaction, as well.[36] This was in accordance with the preestablished agreement between project and board, in which primary emphasis was to be placed on the committing offense and community reaction.

Notes

1. "It is hoped that approximately 50 wards can be handled [by six agents in all] concurrently in the Unit on an *intensive* basis. As an agent begins to reduce case contacts to once a week, he will pick up new intensive cases. The exact timing will be governed by operational experience, but it is estimated that one hundred cases a year will enter the program" (Adams and Grant, 1961, p. 8; emphasis added). As described in note 2, youths were expected to remain in CTP for an average of two years. This meant that each agent's turnover would be 33 cases every two years (100 cases/6 agents, times 2 years = 33 cases per agent per two-year period). This number was far higher than turned out to be the case.

2. Average stay had been figured at two years, relative to individuals who would successfully complete the program (program failures were not discussed in this context):

   The ward will enter an intensive contact period [Stage A], which will vary in length according to his needs but which will average seven to eight months. . . . During the second half of the first year in the Unit, the number of agent contacts will gradually be reduced to one a week [Stage B]. The ward will be maintained in the Unit during a second year, at least on a "paper-work" basis [Stage C]. The average number of case contacts during the second year will not exceed the average in a regular parole caseload; i.e., approximately one contact every three weeks. . . . In order to maximize the therapeutic value of the agent-ward relationship, each agent will be responsible for his wards over a two-year period (with the goal of no transfers between agents). (Adams and Grant, 1961, pp. 7–8. No mention was made of a third or fourth year on the project.)

   Thus, with respect to operating costs: (1) by 1963, youths were remaining in

Stage A or B longer than originally expected; (2) contrary to what was indicated in the Phase 1 proposal, agents were not receiving a new case as soon as a currently active case had moved out of Stage A, or, for that matter, Stage B. Agents were given a new case only after a youth was completely removed from their caseload. For these reasons, overall case turnover, and average caseload size, remained substantially below the rate and level that was originally suggested. This difference was directly reflected in CTP's operating costs.

3. It was never specifically decided whether this would be the *average* or the *maximum* number of cases. YA administrators wanted it to be the former; CTP staff preferred the latter. The tacit understanding was that the number would be as close to 12 as possible.

4. As indicated, 12 youths per worker was the basic understanding between CTP staff and YA administration. It is interesting to note how the various factors and concerns that entered into this compromise were reflected in the Phase 2 proposal: "Each agent would be assigned eight to ten intensive treatment cases and might carry, in addition, up to five cases which had moved on to a minimal supervision stage" (Warren, Palmer, and Turner, 1964a, p. 7).

5. Implementation began soon after the Phase 2 proposal was accepted by the NIMH.

6. The administrative supervisor of CTP usually reported to the chief of parole through two administrators, for example, a regional supervisor and an assistant chief of parole. The principal investigator of CTP reported directly to the chief of research.

7. These figures include Modesto youths as well (28 boys). During the formative stage, 92 youths (80 boys, 12 girls) entered the Community Treatment Project. During full operation the figure was 304 (258 boys, 46 girls)—also for Valley CTP. As indicated, the former stage involved a maximum of six parole agents at any one time and lasted a total of 32 months. The latter involved a maximum of 14 agents at any one time in the Valley units combined, and it lasted 63 months.

8. This applied to "controls" as well.

9. Nineteen-year-olds accounted for 0.2 percent of all eligibles.

10. Reiss, A.J., Jr., and A.L. Rhodes (1961). "The distribution of juvenile delinquency in the social class structure," *American Sociological Review,* 26: 720–732.

11. Figures for San Francisco boys (CTP, GGI, and "control" combined) were: (1) Type of YA commitment offense: property-related—79 percent; person-related—3 percent; all others—19 percent. (2) Race: Caucasian—25 percent; Mexican American—2 percent; black—68 percent; all others—5 percent. (3) Socioeconomic status of family ("social class"): lower—84 percent; middle—15 percent; upper—0 percent.

Except for commitment offense, these figures change only slightly when girls are added. Eighty-one percent of all girls were committed in connection with an "other" offense—incorrigibility, runaway, and so on. For these individuals, prostitution was very often part of the picture; however, it was not singled out and specified as such in connection with the official Youth Authority commitment offense, namely, incorrigibility, and so on.

12. For any given youth, preeligibility screening was set into motion by a phone call from Intake and Classification direct to the research team. A project researcher then went to I & C and carried out the official screening.

13. Project boundary lines were drawn very specifically, for each city.

14. Youths who were *not* preeligible were not interviewed by research staff. They were sent through the standard YA intake and diagnostic process instead. This included: interviews by NRCC personnel; an "initial home visit interview" with the youths' parents or guardians, conducted by a regular (non-CTP) parole agent (Bohnstedt and Beverly, 1960; Gould and Beverly, 1963); case staffing by NRCC personnel; board appearance at NRCC. These youths were not included in the project; that is, they became neither experimentals nor controls.

15. During Phases 1 and 2 the interviewer identified himself to the youth as a member of the YA Division of Research, not as someone specifically associated with CTP, regular parole, or any YA institution. This interview took place either at

the local juvenile hall or in the YA's Northern Reception Center and Clinic. Interviews in juvenile hall occurred a couple of days after the individual had been committed to the Youth Authority, and about three days prior to his physical transfer from the hall to the NRCC.

16. The diagnostic interview usually lasted between 40 and 75 minutes, and 90 minutes was not rare. Its average was just under an hour.

17. For example, return to own home (natural or adoptive parents), foster home, relatives, or independent placement.

18. This staffing was conducted for all preeligibles whose random assignment was CTP, and who were later declared eligible by the board. (Actually, *all* CTP preeligibles were staffed in the manner described in the text. The operating assumption was that all such youths would be declared eligible by the board.) Staffing—that is, the planning conference—was, in many respects, different for CTP youths than for those randomly assigned to the traditional program: The latter individuals were not staffed by personnel associated with the Community Treatment Project; and, on the whole, their staffing was much less extensive than the one for CTP preeligibles. Further details are not needed; however, see Figure 2–5.

19. Two points might be noted: (1) The goal of *post-CYA* nondelinquency was not mentioned in the Phase 1 proposal; in this sense it was essentially a self-imposed (i.e., CTP-imposed), later derived "mandate" (Adams and Grant, 1961). (2) Even in relation to the period of CYA jurisdiction alone, it was the reduction, not the complete elimination, of delinquent behavior that received major emphasis.

20. Without actually "triggering" or releasing his specific, illegal actions.

21. An example of support (indirect support) would be: relieving or neutralizing undue external stress, including (1) parental treatment of an openly rejecting or brutalizing nature, and (2) strong peer-generated pressures.

22. For the most part, the attitudes in question were to be expressed implicitly, or by direct example.

23. Although the researcher/youth interview was always tape-recorded, it was not made available to the parole agent.

24. On rare occasions the second agent was present in the role of a possible alternate worker. That is, it was understood by all participants that this individual would probably be assigned to the case if, after the conclusion of the "Background and Diagnostic" portion of the conference, it seemed likely that the originally assigned agent would not be appropriately matched with the youth. (Matching is discussed in Chapter 11.) The second agent was sometimes present because the originally assigned agent had received a promotion and was scheduled to leave the project.

25. The researcher sometimes presented supplementary information and impressions based on psychological tests such as the Jesness Inventory and the California Psychological Inventory. Results from a standard set of "sentence completion" items were also occasionally used.

26. Nevertheless, were it not for the specific *research* needs, the initial staffing might have been shortened by approximately two hours.

27. There were three alternatives within the traditional program: institution, camp, and direct parole (i.e., parole without any prior institutionalization).

28. The clinic report was worked up independently of CTP's initial case conference; and, entirely different YA staff members were involved in its workup. However, in connection with the areas that were covered—for example, commitment offense, offense history, personal development, family background—the clinic report was similar to the CTP case conference report in several respects. (During Phases 1 and 2 the latter report was used for CTP's internal purposes only. See below.) Because of the project's research design and related documentation requirements, it was difficult to avoid this CTP/NRCC duplication of effort. During Phase 3 the duplication was largely eliminated: CTP staff prepared most of the clinic reports, based on their initial case conference. During Phases 1 and 2 the CTP case conference report, which was usually more detailed

than the NRCC clinic report ("Clinic Report and Recommendations"), was not made available to clinic staff. Nor were any parts of the CTP report included as a supplement to the NRCC clinic report that was reviewed by the board prior to its decision regarding eligibility/ineligibility. As a result, the type and quantity of information/impressions on which the board based its decision was essentially the same for E and C preeligibles.

29. Much of the "Initial Home Visit Interview" material was incorporated into this plan.

30. This assignment was made in the manner that is described for eligible youths who fell into the control group.

31. During 1965–1969, none of the 125 eligible San Francisco (SF) youths turned down the chance to participate in CTP, the Community Treatment Project (called DTU—Differential Treatment Unit—in SF). One out of 166 eligible youngsters rejected GGI, the Guided Group Interaction program (in SF).

32. One or both of the latter agencies was sometimes unfamiliar with a given youth. In such cases it was unable to officially respond. (The agency response was mainly derived from its own files and its direct experiences with the youth. It was not based on information obtained by Youth Authority staff subsequent to the youngster's commitment to the YA.)

33. Agencies were routinely asked to state the reason(s) for their concern or objection. These reasons were recorded and made available for board review during the eligibility hearing.

34. Especially those that focused on the commitment offense rather than the prior history alone.

35. During Phases 1 and 2 an "unusually long offense history" generally consisted of 10 or more arrests and convictions—minor traffic offenses and all status offenses excluded. *Status offenses* mainly consisted of "incorrigibility," "beyond parental control," "runaway," "placement (e.g., foster home) failure," "truancy," and "curfew violations." They were, or involved, behaviors for which an adult would not be arrested, charged, or otherwise sanctioned.

36. That is, it was given less weight than either the outside-agency response or the news coverage component, taken by itself. However, if considerable agency objection and negative publicity were both present, a great deal of influence was then exerted on the board.

3 PROGRAM ELEMENTS

We will now review the main program elements that were used at the Community Treatment Project during 1961–1969. We will also present the factors that influenced the selection of specific elements that were used with individual youths. These elements will be further described in Chapter 6.

Program Elements

The main program elements available at CTP were as follows:

#1. Counseling—individual, group, and family-centered.

#2. Pragmatically oriented discussion and decision-making (e.g., job openings, school transfers, driver's license, court procedures).

#3. Limit-setting, establishment of rules, and checking up on youth by parole agent.

#4. Accredited school program located at the CTP office (community center)—including individual and small group tutoring.

#5. Recreational opportunities and socializing experiences (dayroom activities, outings, cultural activities—coeducational and otherwise), within and outside the community center.

#6. Out-of-home placements (foster homes, group homes, relatives, independent) on temporary or longer-term basis.

#7. Short-term detention (control-oriented and/or treatment-oriented) at NRCC or local juvenile hall.[1]

For any given youth, approximately four of these elements were likely to be in operation at any one time. (Elements #1, #2, and/or #3 were always present to some degree.) This use of several program elements at the same time might be referred to as "extensive intervention." It was part of the general strategy of strengthening the youngster's ties with his community,[2] by providing assistance in areas that seemed crucial to his everyday, and longer-range, adjustment. Insofar as it concentrated on the individual from several directions at once, extensive intervention was an expression of intensive intervention as well (though the latter term basically refers to a high *rate* of contact).

Two additional elements may be mentioned in connection with this strategy:

#8. Collateral contacts by parole agent on behalf of youth, with public and private agencies or individuals.

#9. Material aid (cash assistance, clothing, transportation).

In the present chapter these elements will be reviewed separately from the rest, even though they were commonly used.

Counseling

Counseling was the most frequently used program element at CTP. It involved meetings and discussions whose main focus related to matters such as the following:

> Discussion of the youth's (or family's) current difficulties, interests, or needs—personal and social; offering advice or encouragement regarding same, or helping youth/family identify possible solutions . . . or helping them choose among acceptable alternatives; increasing the

youth's/family's awareness of the concerns and points of view of significant others; helping youth understand the expectations and limitations of society in general; giving ego support: building on youth's present abilities and nondestructive defenses, rather than seriously challenging them; emphasizing current functioning and adaptation; using youth's/family's present resources; reviewing current experiences, to determine what might have "gone awry," and what "turned out ok"; supplying information about—and discussing—the opposite sex, and/or adulthood in general. (Palmer, 1975a)

There were three types of counseling: individual, group, and family-centered. Some youths were involved in more than one type at any given time. However, with most youths, one of these approaches usually received primary emphasis. This was in accordance with their treatment/control plan, which specified the main form of counseling that was to be used. Individual counseling was usually given primary emphasis.

As suggested earlier, the three forms of counseling were sometimes used to supplement each other. For instance, most youths who were involved in group counseling were also involved in individual counseling to some degree;[3] the reverse was less often the case. This applied to many youths involved in family counseling as well.[4]

The parole agent was present at all counseling sessions. Individual meetings and discussions usually lasted 40 to 75 minutes. Group and family-centered meetings generally lasted 1½ to 2 hours.

How often was counseling used? To provide a meaningful answer, this question will be dealt with separately for (1) "participants" and (2) all youths combined—as defined below.

Youths who were involved with a given program element will be called participants. (This definition applies to any program element, not just counseling.) For example, to qualify as a "group counseling participant" in the analyses that follow, youngsters had to be involved in *at least one* session of this type during their CTP program. However, the average participant took part in far more sessions than that.

For *participants*, the average number of sessions per month was as follows: individual counseling—5.2; group counseling—1.7; family counseling—0.6. (The number of monthly sessions—and, in the case of other program elements, monthly contacts and interactions—is shown in Table 3–1, separate for participants and nonparticipants. See below, regarding nonparticipants.) These individuals took part in a total of 6.0 counseling sessions each month (72 a year), of one form or another. By most correctional standards this would be considered intensive. (Since most individuals did not participate in all three forms of counseling, 6.0 is not simply the sum of 5.2, 1.7, and 0.6.)

As indicated, some youths were never involved with certain program elements—individual or family counseling, for example. They were exposed to other elements instead, for example, "pragmatically oriented discussion" or "limit-setting." When these youngsters ("nonparticipants," relative to individual or family counseling) are added to those who *were* exposed to the given program elements ("participants," relative to individual or family counseling), the resulting group would then include all CTP youths—that is, the total CTP sample.[5] Individuals who comprise this total sample can be thought of as typical or "average" CTP youths: Collectively, they represent *all* participants and nonparticipants combined, with respect to the given program

---

TABLE 3–1

Number of Contacts per Month between Agent and Youth, throughout Youth Authority Career

	Sample of Youths	
Type of Contact	Participants	Typical Youths[a]
Counseling		
Individual	5.2	2.5
Group	1.7	0.9
Family	0.6	0.3
Pragmatically Oriented Interactions	0.9	0.5
Limit-Setting	1.6	1.0
Collateral Contacts	0.8	0.4

[a]Refers to all CTP youths combined—i.e., the total sample (participants + nonparticipants).

elements. It should of course be kept in mind that the "average" youth is, strictly speaking, a statistical reality only.

Now then, for *typical CTP youths* (i.e., participants and nonparticipants combined), the average number of counseling sessions per month was: individual counseling—2.5; group counseling—0.9; family counseling—0.3. These youngsters took part in *3.3* counseling sessions a month (40 a year) during the course of their CTP program. This can perhaps be considered moderately intensive.

Twelve to 15 percent of all counseling sessions could have been termed *psychotherapy*. During these sessions the principal focus was on: "self-understanding; recognizing the extent, intensity, and/or roots of one's feelings about self, and toward specified others; understanding the nature of one's relationship or conflicts with significant others, and some of the reasons for—and difficulties that are created by—one's major defense mechanisms" (Palmer, 1975a).

To simplify our presentation, and in view of the moderate overlap that often exists between counseling and psychotherapy, it seems reasonable to treat the latter as one aspect of counseling.[6] Thus, the psychotherapy sessions in question have already been included in the figures presented earlier, for the particular type of counseling that was involved—individual, group, or family.

It might also be mentioned that several forms of group counseling were used at CTP. The main ones were discussion group, activity group, role playing, and Guided Group Interaction; however, the latter approach was rarely used after 1965. Transactional analysis with small numbers of youth entered the picture during the mid-1960s but was used to a somewhat limited degree. Extended group meetings (e.g., four- to six-hour "minimarathons") were rarely used; and, "sensitivity training" (T or encounter groups) as such was never attempted, irrespective of length. As to alternate forms of *individual* counseling and therapy, behavior modification was seldom used and transcendental meditation was not used during 1961–1969. (See note 56.)

Two final points before proceeding. (1) Unless otherwise indicated, all figures (above and below) refer to the youths' entire CTP program, starting from first release to parole. In most cases this period lasted a number of years. (2) The figures refer to all youth sub-types combined. As seen in Chapter 8, the findings vary a great deal, depending on the type of youth involved.

Pragmatically Oriented Interactions

These sessions, between agent and youth, focused on:

> exchange of information and review of plans concerning various "business items"—as, e.g.: employment opportunities and agencies; possibilities of/procedures for returning to public school system, or for transferring from school to school; out of home placement; joining given organizations (e.g., YMCA); budgeting and bank accounts; driver's license; legal arrangements (e.g., child support), and court procedures. Agent and youth may then go out and take care of these matters together. (Palmer, 1975a)

For participants, there was approximately one (0.9) such session a month. For the "typical" CTP youth, there was one such session every *two* months (0.5 a month) (see Table 3–1).

Limit-Setting and Surveillance

Here, primary focus was on one or more of the following:

> Agent (A) and youth (Y) review the Do's and Don'ts, the Must's and May's that apply to Y in connection with Time (curfew), Place (off limit "hangouts"), Persons, and selected Activities. A tells Y that he is expected to abide by the written conditions of parole, and by verbal agreements which the two of them have made. A and Y may discuss the possible, probable or definite consequences of Y's not abiding by same; they may establish, reaffirm or modify various ground rules regarding these and other subjects, activities and consequences. Agent may investigate known or suspected offenses/infractions. . . .
>
> In the case of surveillance, A checks [either in person or by phone] on whether Y is sticking to his agreements, . . . is showing up at school, is getting to work. He personally surveys the scene (streets, hangouts) to see whether, when, or with whom Y shows up. (Palmer, 1975a)

For participants, this program element was used an average of 1.6 times a month. For typical CTP youths—participants plus non-participants—it was used 1.0 times a month (see Table 3–1).

CTP School Program

This element was used mainly for individuals who had been expelled, excluded, or repeatedly suspended from public school in connection with behavioral, social, or academic difficulties. It was sometimes used for individuals who had dropped out on their own, but then had second thoughts on the matter. On occasion, it was also used (1) for older adolescents who were employed during weekdays or evenings, (2) for others who were finding it difficult to obtain employment, and (3) to supplement the credits of those who *were* attending public school at the time.[7]

Primary emphasis was on academic instruction: social studies, English, directed reading, math, and science. After that came remedial reading and arts and crafts, in that order. All school activities were conducted on an individualized or small group basis, within the CTP community center. Late afternoon and early evening classes were held for those who either worked or attended public school during the day.[8] Most youths attended one or more scheduled classes several times a week, depending on their course of study. To earn class credits, they did not have to complete their course work within a certain length of time, or by the close of the regular public school semester.[9]

Concerning the entire project period, 1961–1969, one-fifth (22 percent) of all CTP youths were likely to be enrolled in the school program at any given time. This was a majority of all individuals who were "readily available" to participate: Youths who could not readily take part, or who had other arrangements and commitments at the time, were those enrolled in public school, those employed, and so on. For example, on the average, (1) 33 percent of all CTP youths were enrolled in public school; (2) 30 percent were employed on a full-time or part-time basis,[10] or were participating in Neighborhood Youth Corps and Manpower Training and Development programs;[11] and, (3) 4 percent were "whereabouts unknown," while another 4 percent were serving jail sentences of 60 days or more. Thus, most of the remaining—that is, readily available—individ-uals were likely to be enrolled in CTP's school program at any given time.[12] This figure, and the 22 percent mentioned earlier, was somewhat lower during Phase 1, the period that preceded full operation.

One-third (35 percent) of all youths—availables plus nonavailables—were enrolled in the CTP school program at some point during their entire CTP experience.[13] Most of these individuals were in their earlier teens when they first came to CTP. If one divides the total caseload into younger and older individuals at the point of YA intake, the figures are 54 percent (under 16) and 21 percent (16 and older) as to degree of participation.[14] The overall degree of participation rises to 40 percent if one excludes youngsters who (1) had already completed high school when first released to parole and (2) were fairly steadily employed prior to YA intake or shortly after first release to parole, after having dropped out of public school with no intention of returning.

In sum, the CTP school program was utilized fairly extensively in the case of available youths, especially during Phase 2.[15]

Recreational Opportunities and Socializing Experiences

The CTP Community Center

Beginning in 1965 approximately 13 youths came to the community center on any given day for reasons other than appointments with their agent, or a brief "hello." (Prior to 1965 the average was nine.) This figure excludes friends who may have accompanied the CTP youths, and approximately eight or ten local, non-CTP neighborhood youngsters who generally stopped by each afternoon.

About 30 percent of the total parole caseload lived within one and a half miles of CTP.[16] More than half the youngsters who frequented the community center resided within this area. When CTP youths stopped by they usually spent between 20 minutes and 2 hours in the building, mainly within the dayroom and around the clerical area. The average was about 40 minutes. This figure excludes time that was used for counseling, discussion of business items, limit-setting, and school. It also excludes the half day that was spent at the center by a "core" of five or six youths, three or four times a week.[17] The presence of the latter individuals was in accordance with their treatment-control plan; and for any given youth, this arrangement was likely to last several months.[18]

With few exceptions, participation in center activities was voluntary (see endnote 18). It was largely unscheduled as well, except when youths established meeting times among themselves.

CTP Dayroom

The dayroom was the focal point of most social and recreational activities at the Community Treatment Project. It was a large, multipurpose area within the CTP center itself. (A floor plan of the Sacramento office is shown in Appendix 4.[19]) Next to just "shooting the breeze," the most popular activities and items were ping pong, pool, record player, radio, free coffee, and occasional snacks. After that came popular magazines, cards, dominoes, TV, and weight lifting.[20]

Youth interactions were mostly with their peers. However, considerable interchange occurred with professional and clerical workers as well.[21] In either case there was usually

> a range of spontaneous and informal discussions among many different participants . . . at nearly any time of the day. . . . For instance, there were discussions concerning sports, movies, cars, making money, the draft, and the war. Other discussions dealt with problems encountered in connection with narcotics usage, ideas and misconceptions regarding sex and contraception, the police, the pros and cons of the Black Panther and Brown Beret movements. . . . Certain wards . . . focused upon home problems, delinquent behavior in general, specific fears, etc. (Johns and Palmer, 1970, pp. 16–17)

Parole agents generally looked upon ward/staff contacts as a chance to slowly "break down the stereotypes which youths have of adults and authority figures." For this and other reasons the dayroom never had "an officer of the day whose assignment included that of watching the youths—whether from behind a glass partition or otherwise." All in all, considerable effort was made to "maintain a workable balance between relative permissiveness, flexibility and spontaneity, on the one hand, and definite structure/predictability, on the other" (Johns and Palmer, 1970, p. 8).

The dayroom was open to all CTP youths, five days a week, eight or nine hours a day. However, no more than about 25 percent of the caseload made use of it in the sense described above, during any given year. (The figure was closer to 35 percent for the community center as a whole.) Most of the remaining youths felt that "other settings, and other activities, were of greater relevance to their current interests. As a result, they quietly sidestepped any serious involvement in dayroom activities." (Johns and Palmer, 1970, p. 29)

Nevertheless,

> many wards practically lived in the dayroom for several months at a time. Usually, these were individuals who (1) had no other nondelinquent and nondestructive place to hang their hat, and who, in many cases, (2) were—on a long-standing basis—conspicuously unable to function adequately or acceptably on a job and/or in an ordinary school setting. . . . [It was hoped that the] fears, defenses, and anxieties [of many such youths might] be expressed, *not on the streets,* at home or in the school setting, but in a place where their underlying thoughts and feelings might remain available and might be worked with in a therapeutic manner rather than simply be reacted against, suppressed, denied or repressed. (Johns and Palmer, 1970, pp. 8, 28)

In sum, while most staff did not regard the center and dayroom as something that was "absolutely essential to the treatment of every one (or even a large majority) of their wards . . . [they did view it as] having been virtually indispensable at certain critical periods, in the case of a number of their wards" (Johns and Palmer, 1970, p. 29). Indispensable or not, the center as a whole was regarded as a place in which these and other participants could have pleasurable or self-enhancing experiences, and could develop some rewarding, possibly stable relationships.

Large-scale get-togethers and parties usually took place during Thanksgiving, Christmas, or New Year's holidays. These lasted for several hours and were organized largely around the dayroom. They involved music, dancing, general socializing, and, above all, food. Sixty to 80 people usually showed up, including as many as 20 or 30 CTP youths and their friends. Staff and their families, people from the local community, and others participated as well. These events were quite cheerful and generally well received. They seemed to make many staff and youths feel part of "one large CTP family," at least for a couple of weeks.

Activities outside the Center
Basically, these included outdoor activities, sports, sightseeing, and cultural/educational events. One or more of these activities were quite popular with 25 percent to 35 percent of the total caseload. The remaining youths seldom if ever took part.

Local outdoor activities usually occurred twice a month. Here, one, two, or three parole agents and two or three youths from each of their caseloads would go on a half-day or day-long trip, anywhere from 15 to 50 miles outside of town. Main activities were swimming, fishing, boating or rafting, and hiking. Most agents took part in these activities several times a year. However, only about one-third of their caseload was likely to participate.

Overnight camping, and one- or two-day backpacking trips, occurred five or six times a year. The individuals who participated were often the same as those mentioned earlier. However, from the caseloads collectively, fewer youths were likely to take part on any one occasion.

Larger-scale trips took place about four times a year. The most common "targets" were Lake Tahoe and its nearby ski areas, the ocean, Yosemite, and Mount Lassen National Park. A surprising number of youths had never visited these places—the ocean included—although they had lived in the local area all their lives. These trips lasted two or three days, were usually coeducational, and called for considerable planning and effort. Four or five parole agents, the casework supervisor, one or two teachers and assistants, and ten to twelve CTP youngsters generally participated in each trip. However, on some trips no more than two agents and four or five youths took part. Group meetings were sometimes held during trips of this kind. All in all, these experiences seemed to give most participants a sizable lift, and draw them together in a constructive way.

Local sporting events were a favorite among many agents and youths. About once a month, one or two agents and two or three youths from each of their caseloads would attend at least one of the following events: baseball, auto racing, basketball, boxing, or football.[22] Many of these youngsters occasionally participated in bowling, roller skating, and indoor ice skating, usually without their agent. (Until 1966, parole agents personally furnished transportation and general supervision for these events. After that, "group supervisors" and other auxiliary personnel often performed these functions.)

Equally popular were one-day trips to San Francisco and Oakland, to attend major league sports events.[23] These usually involved two to four staff members and a total of five to ten youths, drawn from each of several caseloads. They occurred about three times a year and were sometimes tied in with the sightseeing activities mentioned below.

One-day sightseeing trips occurred three or four times a year, though on a somewhat smaller scale than for major sports events. The most common trips were to San Francisco, the Feather River canyon, and various Gold Rush sites. These events were sometimes coeducational. Again, many participants had rarely if ever visited these places.

Local cultural/educational activities took place several times a year. No more than three to five youths were likely to participate on any one occasion. Involved were local theater productions, visits to manufacturing and production plants, Sutter's Fort, and so on. Evenings at nearby movies received the same level of participation, but were much more popular. Visits to San Francisco museums, art galleries, and theaters were also considered interesting. These sometimes occurred as part of the sightseeing trips mentioned earlier.

Out-of-Home Placement
Out-of-home living arrangements were quite common during 1961–1969. For instance, at any point in time, 46 percent of all CTP youths were likely to be residing in the following types of settings (collectively): independent placement (15%);[24] relatives (4%); foster home (18%); group home (9%). The remaining 54 percent were residing either with parents or guardians—that is, at home—(39%), or were in some "other" type of setting (15%). "Other" settings included jail (4%), short-term detention in YA (7%), and whereabouts unknown (4%).

Life away from home was not always a new experience for these youths. For instance, of all individuals who were placed out of home during their first year on parole, nearly half (46 percent) had lived in a foster home prior to being committed to the Youth Authority.[25] Another 12 percent had lived with relatives, or on their own.

The subject of out-of-home placement was introduced by the youth, or his parents, at least as often as by the agent himself. Regardless of who initiated these discussions, actual change of placement seldom occurred without careful examination of the advantages and disadvantages, and without general agreement on the part of the main participants.[26] This applied to all placement changes, not just removal from home.

Operations staff recognized that their own feelings concerning the appropriate or optimal placement of a youth could not serve as the sole basis for proceeding with a particular move. This was despite their legal mandate to remove the youth from any placement that they considered destructive or undesirable. In part, their thinking was based on the following:[27]

(1) During 1961–1963, parole agents observed that if they tried to remove an individual from his home without his clear consent, or if they tried to "pressure" or rush him into accepting a placement, the chances were great that he would soon undermine or openly reject whatever placement might be made.[28] This applied regardless of whether his parents had accepted—possibly even promoted—the proposed removal and placement. (2) Parents who expressed considerable dissatisfaction with a proposed placement (e.g., foster home) sometimes made concerted, often successful efforts to undermine that placement if it did come to pass. This occurred despite their apparent acceptance of the proposal that the youth be removed from their home.

Because of these complex feelings and serious implications, agent/youth/parent discussions often continued for weeks or months, in this area. At base, staff believed that the main participants had to be fairly satisfied, or "ready," before a proposed move would have a good chance of success.[29] This was the case with initial out-of-home placements in particular.[30]

The process of discussion, which led to psychological preparation and to the obtaining of clear consent (especially from the youth), probably contributed to the following outcomes: (1) most youths came to regard their foster or group home placement as a sort of "home," in a positive sense of the term; and (2) parents and guardians seldom made concerted efforts to undermine living arrangements that had been developed on such a basis, independent placements included.

Out-of-home placements were almost as common in the traditional YA program as in CTP: Thirty-seven percent of the regular parole caseload was likely to be living away from home at any point in time. The main thing that differed was the type of placement. For instance, independent placements (21%) and relatives (10%) were used more often in the traditional program than in CTP;[31] on the other hand, foster homes (5%) and group homes (1%) were hardly used at all. The number of regular parolees who were living at home (43 percent) was roughly the same as in CTP.[32]

During their *entire* parole experience no less than 67 percent of all CTP youths lived away from home at one time or another.[33] For youngsters in the traditional YA program the figure (53 percent) was not a great deal lower.[34] These rather high figures are partly due to the fact that (1) most individuals remained in the Youth Authority for a number of years, (2) more than half of them were 18 or older at point of YA discharge, and (3) independent living arrangements contributed a good deal to the total.

A few words should be said about the relatively heavy use of foster homes at CTP. In part, this resulted from the "close attention which the . . . agents . . . give to the [parents' home, when] evaluating the ward's chances of becoming or remaining nondelinquent in that setting." Apparently, on close inspection, chances often seemed poor and alternate living arrangements were therefore considered. This process occurred despite "the bias of staff . . . toward leaving a youth in his own home if there is any strength or support available to him there." For the most part, this "bias" remained in effect throughout Phases 1 and 2 (Grant, Warren, and Turner, 1963, p. 36).

An additional but related factor was the agents' small-sized caseload. This gave them more time to seek alternate placements, and to maintain positive working relations with foster parents. This probably contributed to the fact that out-of-home arrangements (foster homes especially) were used to a somewhat larger extent during Phase 1—the period of very small caseloads—than Phase 2.[35]

Group homes were used throughout Phases 1 and 2 in Sacramento and Stockton alike; however, relatively few were used prior to mid-1966. With few exceptions, they consisted of large, private dwellings located in lower-middle or lower income areas, well within the city limits. They usually housed four youths at any one time, but allowed for a maximum of six. They were not coeducational.[36]

Group homes were neither owned nor administered by private agencies. Each was owned and operated by a nonprofessional, husband-wife combination known as "group home parents"—individuals who had entered into a formal contract with the Youth Authority. Supplementary personnel (e.g., culinary, domestic, or relief) were not used. Nor were volunteers and paraprofessionals.

Two or three CTP agents usually made use of a given home at the same time. When it came to group home policies, procedures, and activities, they often worked with the group home parents on a coequal or team basis. However, each agent remained legally responsible for the behavior of his particular youth(s), within and outside the home.

There were two main types of home: long-term and temporary placement. Youngsters remained in these homes for an average of 6 months and 24 days, respectively.

Beginning in 1966 four *types* of long-term group homes ("models") were developed, each for a particular kind of youth. The homes were called protective, containment, boarding, and individualized. Each was operated by group home parents who were selected to interact with the type of youth—for example, higher maturity youths—in question. These homes were developed in connection with the Differential Treatment Environments for Delinquents project (DTED), a jointly sponsored NIMH-CYA effort that focused on CTP youngsters alone.[37] In 1966, the establishment of specific group home environments for specified types of offenders was rather novel within corrections.

Most, but not all, models proved useful. This was related to, and somewhat in spite of, the following. Of all youths who seemed to benefit from given homes, "possibly one-third

... might have done about equally well within adequately staffed, individual foster homes. However, with few exceptions, individual foster homes were not available at the time of maximal placement need; nor were they likely to be available within the near future." In addition, many of these youths did not seem ready for an independent placement, at the time of "maximal need"[38] (Palmer, 1972b, p. 11).

A different type of home was established in the later 1960s: the temporary care home. Operations staff considered this home particularly useful in connection with periods of crisis, and with related placement problems within the youth's own home or foster home. In this and other contexts it was often used as an alternate to short-term detention at NRCC or juvenile hall. On other occasions it was used to shorten the length of stay in those facilities. Unlike NRCC and juvenile hall, the temporary care home was an open, not locked environment.[39]

Short-Term Detention

Short-term detention ("detention") took place at NRCC. It was initiated by parole agents for one of the following reasons or combinations of reasons: therapeutic and/or behavior control, investigation and situational; response to a minor offense.

Detention for therapeutic purposes and/or behavior control involved the following areas, as described in a Youth Authority Task Force report that focused on this program element. (In this report all such areas, e.g., behavior control, were included under the general heading of "treatment"):

a. As a means of controlling behavior. b. To impress ward with his responsibilities to the program [e.g., participation in group meetings]. c. To establish, emphasize, or refine a treatment relationship. d. To handle, in a residential setting, anxieties arising from therapy [mainly counseling, in our terms]. e. To prevent acting out in reaction to internal stress. f. To prevent acting out in reaction to external stress. (Scott et al., 1966, p. 2)

Investigative and situational detention involved three areas. (In the task force report "investigative" was included under the term "adjudicative."):

a. To hold in custody pending decisions by Youth Authority Board, e.g., following arrest on a new offense where it is felt that the ward constitutes a threat to the community, to himself, or would flee the jurisdiction of the Youth Authority [during agent's investigation of the arrest charge]. b. To allow time to develop a placement in the community [e.g., a foster home]. c. To accommodate community reactions to the ward. d. Medical (psychiatric observation; illness). (Scott et al., 1966, p. 2)

In our own account of detention (immediately below), minor offenses are divided into three general categories: (1) *juvenile status plus welfare and institutions code offenses* (curfew; runaway, whereabouts unknown; drinking, possession of alcohol); (2) *technical violations and program infractions* (uncooperative attitude; missed group meeting; home adjustment; poor school adjustment); (3) *specified penal code violations* (malicious mischief, disturbing the peace; unlawful assembly; fighting, no weapons; begging; loitering, trespassing).

Amount of Detention

The following relates to the youth's entire YA career, and to all types of detention combined.[40] As shown in Table 3–2, the average number of detentions per youth was 2.4, that is, one detention for every 14 months on parole. The average detention lasted 19 days and the number of agent/youth contacts during each detention was 2.5—about one a week. The total number of days in detention was 47 (1½ months)—again, during the youth's entire YA career. This NRCC time may be compared with the 270 days (9 months) that were usually spent in a Youth Authority institution, prior to first parole, by non-CTP youths assigned to the traditional YA program. Finally, 46 percent of all detentions were initiated for therapeutic and/or behavior-control reasons; 19 percent related to investigation and situational reasons; and the remaining 35 percent were in response to a minor offense. (The figures in Table 3–2 are broken down by type of—i.e., reason for—detention. Thus, of the 47 detention days for all reasons combined, 21 related to therapeutic goals and/or behav-

TABLE 3–2

Amount of Short-term Detention throughout Youth Authority Career[a]

| | Purpose of Detention | | | |
Variable	Therapeutic and/or Behavior Control	Investigation and Situational	Response to Minor Offense	Total or Average[b]
Number of Detentions per Youth	1.2	0.5	0.7	2.4
Number of Days in Detention per Youth	21	12	14	47
Number of Days in Detention per Detention	17	24	21	19
Number of Agent/ Youth Contacts per Detention	2.6	2.2	2.7	2.5
Percentage Distribution of Detentions	46	19	35	100

[a]Includes participants and nonparticipants. Excludes detentions that resulted from arrests—almost always by law enforcement agencies—that related to fairly serious or quite serious offenses, e.g., those of severity levels 3 through 10. Most such detentions took place in a city or county jail.

[b]*Total* relates to *Number of Detentions per Youth, Number of Days in Detention per Youth*, and *Percentage Distribution of Detention*. *Average* applies to the remaining variables.

ior control, whereas the remaining 26 involved investigations and situational reasons plus agent response to a minor offense.)

The preceding figures refer to all youths combined. However, as described in Chapter 6, there were marked differences in the extent to which detention was used from one group of youths to the next. For instance, the largest single group—"conflicted" individuals—had a total of 1.4 detentions per youth, and 31 days in detention per youth, during their entire YA career. In contrast, "power-oriented" individuals had 6.0 detentions and 75 days in detention during their YA career. (Length of career was approximately equal for both groups. These youth groups are described in Chapters 4 and 5.) These variations reflected not only the different intervention strategies that were generally prescribed for members of the differing groups, but differences in the number of offenses with which individuals in those groups were actually charged.

Additional Observations

From the earliest days of CTP, short-term detention for other than situational, investigative, or penal code reasons was viewed by most agents as a composite of treatment and external control. Seldom did these individuals believe that *only* treatment, or only control, was involved. Nevertheless, on any given occasion one of these factors, for example, treatment, was generally viewed as predominant even though the presence of the second factor was recognized as well. These views or assessments were essentially independent of the *youths'* thoughts and feelings concerning detention. (See below, regarding the latter's perspective.)

Throughout Phases 1 and 2, some form of detention was often required by law in connection with particular charges or known offenses; many periods of detention were the result of this specific circumstance. Partly related to this, both CTP and regular parole agents were occasionally able to use short-term lockup at NRCC not only (1) in lieu of detention within local jails, but (2) as an alternative to the usual nine months of incarceration in a Youth Authority institution—incarceration that might have resulted from revocation associated with a given conviction. However, the latter alternative was infrequently requested by the parole agent and seldom permitted by the Youth Authority Board; and, in any event, *most*

short-term detentions that were "in response to a minor offense" related to violations that, in themselves, involved little risk of directly resulting in revocation by the board and, therefore, in long-term institutionalization.

The use of short-term detention changed considerably through time. For instance, during CTP's formative period—its first two and a half years—detention in response to juvenile status plus welfare and institutions code offenses was used at a rate 2.7 times greater than during its period of full operation (Palmer, 1973c). (These and other changes were only partially due to the increased availability of group homes—for example, as an alternative to NRCC—beginning in mid-1966.) Similarly, detention in response to technical violations and program infractions was used at a rate 1.8 times greater during the formative period than during full operation. (This was especially true in the case of "uncooperative attitude," "missed group meeting," and "poor school adjustment.") Thus, in these two areas, the relatively strict program controls that characterized the early years of CTP were later relaxed to a substantial degree, especially for youths described as passive conformist and power-oriented.[41] Nevertheless, short-term detention continued to play a substantial role at CTP in these and other areas. For example, detention in response to the penal code violations listed above occurred at essentially the same rate during CTP's formative and full operation stages, for these and other youths (Palmer, 1973c). At any rate, the potential role of group homes in reducing the usage of short-term detention at NRCC (for non–penal code violations) was clearly recognized by mid-1963—long before the end of CTP's formative period: "In examining the reasons for placing youths in temporary custody ["in the Reception Center"], it is readily apparent [to "operations staff"] that between 30 percent and 50 percent of the confinement would have been obviated by a suitable live-in facility in the community, without custody" (Grant, Warren, and Turner, 1963, p. 37).

Youths' Perspective

The youths' perspective on short-term detention was summarized and interpreted by the Youth Authority Task Force, based on its interviews with 31 CTP wards who had been detained on at least one occasion.[42] (These detentions mainly related to treatment and/or behavior control, not to situational reasons as mentioned earlier.):

> a. Within the sample interviewed, the wards knew precisely why they were locked up. Beyond this, the majority of cases also had considerable insight into what effect the parole agent was trying to achieve by imposing temporary detention. . . .
>
> b. One of the questions asked was, "How did you respond the instant you found out you were going to be detained?" The varied answers dealt with every emotion from anger to relief, but never did we discover that any sort of physical force had to be used to induce a ward to go into temporary detention. When asked why it was never necessary to physically restrain a ward en route to temporary detention, the wards in effect told us that increased rapport and a feeling of loyalty towards the parole agent and towards the Community Treatment Project held them in a kind of emotional restraint that was stronger than physical restraint. They felt the anger, the frustrations, or the relief as the case may be, but accepted the responsibility or at least behaved in a nonviolent way. . . .
>
> c. The fact that all wards interviewed time and again refrained from any condemnatory remarks about the parole agent, we interpreted as being simply more evidence of a heightened working relationship between the ward and the agent. The wards did not like temporary detention, they did not like the lack of program available to them at the Clinic (NRCC), but they were supportive of the action of the parole agent in every case.
>
> d. The response to the question, "Was this a good experience for you?" varied from an emphatic "No" to a rather mild "Yes," but further questioning led us to the conclusion that the wards viewed temporary detention as a very positive experience. Perhaps the foremost reason cited by the wards relative to this . . . experience is the fact that removal from the community removes most of the external pressure from the detainee. This is best typified by one ward who stated, "My being at the Clinic took all the heat off." Secondly, many of the wards felt that the

> temporary controls afforded them prevented further or continued misbehavior of a more serious nature which would have led to complete failure in the community and perhaps return [i.e., transfer] to a Youth Authority institution. (Scott et al., 1966, pp. 21–22)

Collateral Contacts

Collateral contacts involved person-to-person or telephone and written communications between the parole agent and the following agencies or individuals:

> police, sheriff, probation, Court personnel; school; employment agency; past, present, or prospective employer; Welfare Department; prospective placement (foster home, group home, etc.); Armed Forces; natural parents, relatives; foster or group home parents, etc.; friends, peers, girl [boy] friend; spouse—common-law or otherwise; other (specify). (Palmer, 1975a)

Such contacts often involved direct follow-up on—for instance, initial implementation of—tentative decisions and plans that were made during counseling and pragmatically oriented sessions between the agent and youth. Their purpose was not that of limit-setting, surveillance, or control.

For participants, there was approximately *one* (0.8) collateral contact per month. For the typical CTP youth there was one such contact every two and a half months (0.4 a month) (see Table 3–1). Collateral contacts were provided for 64 percent of all youths at some point in their YA career. Of these contacts, 17 percent were with the juvenile or criminal justice system (police, probation, etc.); 16 percent were with schools, employers, and welfare; and 68 percent were with the remaining categories listed earlier. Two-thirds of all contacts were person-to-person rather than by telephone or letter.

Material Aid

Material aid was provided directly to the youth by CTP staff. It mostly included (1) cash assistance for meals or clothing, and (2) transportation to and from the CTP office, between the youth's home and school, between home and place of employment, and so on.[43] In some cases food itself, rather than cash for food, was provided at the CTP office, that is, the community center.[44]

Nearly all youths received one or more forms of material aid at some point in their YA career. An estimated 35 percent were assisted at least twice a month, and another 35 percent obtained assistance about once every two months. Nearly one-third of the former group—10 percent of all youths—received assistance (mainly transportation) three or more times a week, for periods lasting several months or more.[45] Most of the remaining youths requested and obtained assistance on a sporadic basis only, for example, two or three times a year. For the average youth—that is, all individuals combined—the number of assists was therefore close to two per month.[46] Most recorded assists (79%) related to transportation; 15 percent involved meals or clothing (mainly the former); and the remaining 6 percent were classified as "other."

Additional Activities

The preceding review focused on what might be called primary program elements. It did not deal with such interactions as the following:

Phone Calls

Phone conversations between parole agents and the typical youth occurred once or twice a month; they varied in length from a few minutes to more than a half-hour.[47] These conversations were not restricted as to subject matter. Instead, any given call may have dealt with the same issues that were being considered in ongoing counseling sessions, in pragmatically oriented interactions, or in limit-setting discussions. Nevertheless, since phone conversations between agent and youth were often fairly brief, and were not face to face, they were seen as rather different than the latter types of interaction.

Drop-ins

Here, the agent may have visited the youth's home, school, or place of employment for a brief conversation specifically with the youth—the object of this visit being other than surveillance. In addition, the *youth* may have stopped off at CTP for a brief (e.g., 10-minute) conversation with the agent. The combined number of recorded visits and stop-offs was relatively small: one per six months for participants, that is, youths who were visited or who stopped by, and one per 12 months for all CTP youths

combined (participants plus nonparticipants). While many drop-in activities may not have been mentioned in the written records of parole agents, those that did get mentioned (and that are reflected in the above figures) were usually made by agents, not by youths.[48]

Consultation and Referral

Diagnostic service was occasionally requested, by the agent, at times of particular stress for the youth. This service was furnished by YA and non-YA consultants, usually psychiatrists. On other, generally less stressful occasions, agents sometimes referred the youth to public or private agencies for supplementary counseling or other direct service; however, such referrals were very infrequent. Together, all forms of consultation and referral occurred less than once every 140 months. More concretely, one of every nine youths received such service at some point in their YA career; and of those who were served, the average number of consultation plus referral sessions was 2.5. The vast majority of these sessions (92 percent) involved diagnostic consultation rather than referral for supplementary counseling or other direct service.

Selecting the Program Elements

For each youth, the particular combination of program elements that was selected was determined by three main factors:

Factor A: Youth As an Individual—e.g., specific life circumstances of the youth, together with his current interests, motivations, skills, and personal limitations.[49]

Factor B: Youth As a Certain Type of Individual—e.g., youngster's level of interpersonal maturity, and specific I-level diagnosis.

Factor C: Parole Agent—e.g., preferred treatment approaches and particular skills of the assigned agent.[50]

At any point—for instance, during the initial case conference—Factors A and B each carried more weight than Factor C in determining which combination of elements, that is, which pattern of intervention, would be used.

Several patterns of intervention were used at CTP. This variety existed mainly because of the *differences* that were present from one youth to another, and one parole agent to another. However, the number of patterns was not unlimited; moreover, some were used considerably more often than others. This "limited variety" was partly the result of *similarities* that existed among many of the youngsters, or "youth types"—similarities that existed together with the above-mentioned differences.[51] It was also a result of various practical considerations. The most frequently used patterns are described in Chapter 6.

Factor A (Youth As an Individual)

Factor A had a great deal to do with the specific treatment-control plans that were drawn up relative to the following program elements (the program-element number is shown in parentheses): surveillance (#3), CTP school program (#4), CTP community center activities (#5), out-of-home placement (#6).[52] For instance, in order to respond realistically to the youth as an individual, the agent and supervisor first had to answer such questions as the following:

- How strong are the peer and/or sibling pressures for continued delinquent behavior (#3)?
- How much tolerance do the neighbors and local justice system agencies have for the youth (#3)?
- Has the youth been permanently expelled from the school system (or, has he perhaps dropped out . . . or already graduated) (#4)?
- Does his age (under 16) and/or level of education make it extra difficult for him to obtain employment (#4, #5)?
- Are there few or many resources and outlets available to him in the local community (#5)?
- Are one or both parents in serious difficulty (e.g., alcoholic; addicted to hard drugs; assaultive; psychotic) (#6)?
- Do the parents usually allow him to wander the streets at will, especially during late evening hours (#3, #6)?
- Are his parents opposed to having him return home (#6)?

These questions related to the youth's *specific life circumstances*. Their answers had direct implications for the choices and decisions that were at stake in program areas #2 through #7. They were of relevance to areas #8 and #9 as well.

In developing a specific treatment/control plan the next step was to focus on the individual's *current interests, motivations, skills, and personal limitations*. This was considered important in terms of assessing the practical reality of the choices and decisions that were being considered in light of the individual's specific life circumstances. Thus, to reach a final decision regarding program elements #2 through #7, the agent and supervisor usually addressed such questions as the following:

- Does the youth have much drive or ability to resist peer pressures for continued delinquent involvement?
- Is he strongly opposed to returning to school?
- Is he unusually slow in learning specific kinds of academic material?
- Does he feel that work—or "living a straight life"—is "completely for the birds"?
- Is there strong pressure from parents (pressure that the youth tries to oppose) for him to quit school and start bringing in money for the family?
- Is the youngster interested in earning his own living and perhaps getting married in the near future?
- Is he unwilling to consider living in a foster or group home at this time, even though he may be in continuous, even violent conflict with his parents, and is unprepared or too young for an independent placement?

It was assumed that the answers to these questions were important from the standpoint of developing a plan in which the individual might feel personally involved, one that he might feel had relevance and payoff. It was further assumed that any such plan—any set of program choices—would probably contain some areas of difficulty or continued conflict, again from the youth's point of view. Practically speaking, it was not considered possible to bridge all gaps or close all "wounds" at once. In any event, the choice, or policy, of "letting things remain as they are" was also given consideration.

Factor B (Youth Type)

By design, some elements and combinations of elements were recommended more often for certain types of youth than for others, for example, for higher I-level as compared to lower I-level youths. This aspect of treatment/control planning was known as "differential programming" based on type of youth. It formed an integral part of the Phase 1 proposal:[53]

> [For any youth, the initial treatment/control plan was to contain] lists of tentative suggestions . . . with regard to goals and techniques of treatment and strategies of control for each defined type of delinquent in the community setting. . . . [In part, these lists were to be] based on present thinking about the most effective procedures for identified kinds of delinquents. (Adams and Grant, 1961, pp. 5–6)

Throughout Phases 1 and 2, differential programming was very important in terms of the specific treatment modality—for example, individual therapy (#1), and short-term detention (#7)—that would be used. Thus, for certain kinds of youth, individual counseling was commonly

> listed among the tentative suggestions. In the case of others, it was usually contraindicated. For still others, a group-centered peer-pressure approach was likely to be recommended; in other cases it was never recommended. In some instances, strict external controls and possible short-term detention were almost invariably suggested; in others, an "internal" (youth centered) or relationship-based (agent-youth centered) mode of control was likely to be prescribed. (Palmer, 1973c)

Thus, the influence of Factor B was quite substantial. In fact, the distinctive patterns of intervention[54] that were repeatedly used with certain types of youth could be traced largely to this factor. These patterns are presented in some detail in Chapter 6.

Nevertheless, the influence of other factors on overall case planning should not be underestimated. In this connection, the joint contribution of Factors A *and* B was pointed out as early as 1962: "Treatment intervention plans are now being formed on a case by case basis. An attempt is being made, at the same time, to classify these boys and girls into certain types, which [are] directly related to the types of treatment intervention prescribed" (Grant, 1962b, p. 2). The joint contribution of these factors continued to be strong throughout Phases 1 and 2. In fact, they were the primary basis for all case planning at CTP, for every type of youth. Together, they produced an *individualized* intervention plan.

Factor C (Agent's Preferences and Skills)

Factor C—the parole agent's preferences and skills—also helped determine the pattern of intervention. As described in Chapter 11, CTP agents came to the project with considerable experience in corrections. For instance, they were familiar with basic techniques of counseling and limit-setting, and were fairly skilled in the use of one or both. However, they were often more familiar or comfortable with some of CTP's seven main program elements than with others; and they often believed more strongly in the value of those particular elements than of others, at least for their assigned youths. Largely for these reasons, CTP agents sometimes gave more emphasis to those elements than did other agents who worked with the same types of youth. In short, prior experience and present skills notwithstanding, some agents were only moderately familiar with, comfortable with, and/or accepting of particular program elements during, say, their first three to twelve months at CTP; and for these or related reasons, they and other agents sometimes preferred to deemphasize or even avoid those elements.

Despite their *preferences,* and despite the earlier-mentioned differences in emphasis from one agent to another, CTP agents were not free to greatly minimize or largely ignore many or most program elements. That is, no agent was free to operate in this manner, with his caseload as a whole, simply on grounds that he or she (1) was particularly interested in or perhaps rather comfortable and skilled with one or two other elements instead, or (2) believed that the latter elements could probably "do the job" by themselves. Instead, each CTP agent was expected to utilize whatever program elements seemed to directly bear on *each youth's* personal needs, interests, skills, limitations, and life circumstances. (As mentioned earlier, these needs and circumstances were initially determined by the CTP staffing group; on later occasions they were usually determined by the agent and casework supervisor.) The program elements in question—both their presence and their relative emphasis—were also expected to reflect CTP's preestablished, differential programming recommendations wherever feasible and appropriate. (For details and further discussion, see Chapters 6 and 11.) Thus, Factors A and B were to be the principal determinants of both the *elements* (i.e., their presence or absence) and their *emphasis* or interrelationships; ultimately, it was the supervisor's job to see that this requirement was met. Here, as elsewhere, agents could not simply "do their own thing," with any or all youths.

Within the limits set by this requirement, Factor C made an important contribution. More specifically, since preferences and skills could themselves be instrumental in meeting this requirement and in achieving the project's long-range goal, formal and informal efforts were made to support and encourage the agents' interests, work-centered motivations, and sometimes innovative ideas. This applied in all program areas, including counseling, recreational, and socializing experiences.

For example, some agents seemed especially interested in and skilled at using particular, albeit standard (standard at CTP), approaches—say, *group* rather than individual counseling. If the supervisor agreed that the former approach (e.g., standard, "discussion group" meetings) was probably appropriate for many or most youths on such an agent's caseload (youths who presently received individual counseling)[55] and if that particular approach was not contraindicated by CTP's differential programming document for the youth type(s) in question (Grant, 1961c; Warren et al., 1966b) and seemed likely to add important dimensions to the latter's experiences, the supervisor would then encourage the agent to establish discussion group meetings for those prospective youths, if and as feasible.

In addition, some agents expressed interest in what, at the time, were nonstandard methods. Generally speaking, these techniques or approaches differed from but were not antithetical to those recommended in CTP's then-current (1961 or 1966) differential programming document, or implied in its descriptions (1961, 1963, or 1966) of specific youth types. Nor did they seriously clash with the results of practical experience, or ignore typical community and professional concerns. If an agent arrived at the project with such interests and with related skills, he was encouraged to use these methods,

consistent, of course, with Factor A. That is, he was encouraged to do so if CTP administrative staff—the casework supervisor included—considered those methods (1) appropriate, (2) at least somewhat promising, and (3) not in conflict with the overall research design.[56] Yet, even then, such techniques and approaches could be tried only on a case-by-case, not an across-the-board, basis, and largely, though not exclusively, with fairly new—or else floundering—cases. In any event, these approaches were phased in gradually, relative to most caseloads.

Finally, many agents *later* showed interest in a given program element or particular approach, for example, showed definite interest only after having worked in the project for a year. In such cases the agent was almost always encouraged by the casework supervisor, and often by peers, to seek training or consultation in that particular area and to begin using the method or approach as soon as he felt prepared and had an appropriate youth in mind. Meanwhile, of course, he was to continue using other—for him, more standard—elements or approaches.

Having reviewed CTP's structure, policies, procedures, and program elements, we will now describe its youths—the immediate subjects of all this effort.

Notes

1. The latter was sometimes used for Stockton youths.
2. Program elements #3 and #7 were not, in themselves, designed to achieve this objective. They were, among other things, designed to help the individual remain *available* for community-based intervention.
3. The latter was sometimes used on a co-equal rather than a supplementary basis.
4. However, only a small proportion of youths who were involved in group counseling also took part in *family* counseling, at any point in time.
5. In short, all individuals were either participants or nonparticipants, with respect to each program element.
6. This overlap exists not only conceptually, but in practice. Moreover, using case records alone it was not always possible to tell with certainty which of these approaches was in fact being emphasized. This is the reason for the "12 to 15 per-

cent" finding that is reported, as opposed to one specific figure.

7. Accreditation for the CTP school program began in 1965. Until mid-1964 the schoolteacher was available on approximately a quarter-time basis for each Valley CTP unit. During the 1964–1965 school term he worked half-time for each unit. In 1965 he was assisted in each unit by one or more teacher trainees from local colleges. Beginning in 1966, a full-time teacher was made available to each unit, for academic classes.

These individuals were assisted by a half-time arts-and-crafts teacher in Sacramento and a quarter-time remedial reading teacher in Stockton. The latter, in turn, were soon assisted by a number of part-time teacher trainees and senior students on fieldwork assignments.

8. This aspect of the program was mainly used in the Stockton CTP unit.
9. For further details see Warren and Palmer (1965, pp. 48–55), Palmer and Warren (1967, pp. 31–37), and Palmer et al., (1968, pp. 23–25).
10. Many of these youths had already completed high school, or else dropped out with no apparent intention of returning.
11. There was relatively little overlap between youths who attended public school and those who were employed.
12. As indicated, some youths who were attending public school, or were employed, nevertheless participated in CTP's school program at the same point in time. In this and other respects, the precise nature of "availability" is somewhat difficult to pin down in actual practice.
13. That is, they were enrolled during their first, second, or third year in the program. This contrasted to being enrolled at any one point in time, for example, during their twentieth week on the program. In short, many individuals who were not readily available most of the time were nevertheless available some of the time.
14. During their first 12 months at CTP, 30 percent of all youths participated in the school program. The figures for younger and older individuals are 46 percent and 18 percent, respectively.

15. It was used to a much larger extent in Stockton than in Sacramento.
16. In San Francisco the figure was closer to 15 percent.
17. This feature began around 1965. The specific youths who comprised this "core" slowly changed, through time. (See note 18.) However, the total number remained about the same.
18. For some of these youths attendance was compulsory, especially if they were participating in the CTP school program. Participation in this program did not in itself mean these individuals would have to participate in any specific *dayroom* activities. Nevertheless, they and other individuals often did participate in these activities, especially since both program components were housed in the same building.
19. Floor plans were more or less the same for the Stockton office, beginning in 1965. In the San Francisco CTP office, much less space was available for activities of all kinds.
20. Other activities, for instance, basketball, were available immediately outside of, or fairly close to, the center. This was not the case in San Francisco, where space was at a premium.
21. This was also true within the community center as a whole.
22. Only sporadically did CTP develop a baseball or basketball team of its own, that is, an agent/youth or all-youth team.
23. These cities were a 70- to 90-minute drive from the Sacramento and Stockton units.
24. For example, hotel room, apartment, or boarding home. These youths were not necessarily living alone.
25. Some of these youths were living away from home at the time of their YA commitment.
26. Detailed discussion of placement change was involved to a somewhat lesser extent during than subsequent to 1961–1963, at least in relation to lower and middle maturity youths. It was almost always carried out in the case of higher maturity youths.
27. This did not apply only to the youth's first out-of-home placement.
28. In cases of agent/youth disagreement, it was the youths who usually preferred to

remain at home, in contrast to an alternate placement. However, it was often the agent who preferred that the youth remain at home, at least for the time being. Here, the agent usually felt that the youngster could work on certain problems more effectively and efficiently in that environment, despite known discomforts and risks.

29. "Complete satisfaction" was seldom achieved; risks were often taken if the out-of-home placement still seemed necessary.

30. Placements of this type related to youths who had not previously lived away from home.

31. This partly reflected the fact that individuals in the standard YA program were, on the average, several months older than those in CTP when first released to parole. That, in turn, was due to the former's period of incarceration.

32. The "other" category (20 percent) broke down as follows: jail—9 percent; short-term detention in YA—2 percent; whereabouts unknown—9 percent.

33. For these individuals the average number of separate placements was 2.4. However, for the *total* group—youths who had been placed, plus those who had never been placed—the average number was 1.6. (One-third of the former individuals were returned to their own home on one or more occasions, successfully or otherwise.) For regular parolees who had been placed out of home, the average number of separate placements was 1.8. For the total group—all regular parolees combined—it was 0.9. (One-seventh of those who had been placed out of home were later returned to their home.)

34. Two points might be noted. (1) The figures of 67 percent and 53 percent are both substantially higher than those mentioned earlier. This is because the earlier figures covered a much smaller time span than the present set. The earlier set referred to any *one* point in time, and a "point" generally meant a period of one to four weeks. (2) In both sets of figures, all "other" placements (e.g., short-term detention) were excluded.

35. Although this change was not radical, it was noted as early as 1965 in a departmental task force report: "The proportion of project wards in out of home placements has varied considerably during the length of the project, with a tendency to decrease over time" (Kenney et al., 1965, p. 6). As of November 1965 about 15 percent of all boys were in foster homes, as compared with 25 percent in August 1963; and only 20 percent (an unusually low figure for CTP) were in out-of-home placements of *all* types, as compared with roughly 50 percent in 1963.

36. Group homes were never established in San Francisco.

37. As with CTP itself, all research for this project was funded by NIMH's Center for Studies of Crime and Delinquency.

38. It might be mentioned that a long-term home for girls was operated in Stockton during the later 1960s. This was CTP's only group home for girls; it was considered very successful (Turner and Palmer, 1973).

39. This home was established in Stockton alone, partly because of the limited scope and resources of DTED.

40. This information was obtained in 1973 through a systematic review of case folders, suspension documents, and so forth, on 108 Phase 1 and 2 males. These individuals were selected on a stratified random basis, in order to (1) represent, in precisely equal numbers, individuals who entered CTP during its earlier and subsequent years of operation, respectively, (2) reflect the number of Sacramento as compared to Stockton youths within the total CTP sample, and (3) represent the full range of youth groups and "delinquent subtypes" found in CTP.

41. Relatively speaking, these particular program controls were not very strict in the first place with respect to conflicted youths (Chapter 6). Thus, there was less room for change with this group of individuals.

42. Sixteen of these youths were from Sacramento; the remainder were from Stockton. Eighty-one percent were males and 26 percent had entered CTP during its formative period. All youth groups and delinquent subtypes found in CTP were represented within the sample of males.

43. Beginning in 1966 a "group supervisor" was hired in each Valley unit. This individual worked under the direction of the casework supervisor, and one of his or her duties was that of supplying transportation to individuals who were unable to provide this by themselves, relative to CTP concerns. Parole agents and auxiliary personnel (for instance, teacher trainees) also assisted in this regard.

44. Here we refer to entire meals, mainly lunches, not to snacks alone. Snacks—for example, candy, fruit, soft drinks, coffee, or milk (often available to individuals who dropped in at the community center, generally after lunch or school)—were not counted as material aid, relative to figures shown in the text.

45. For these and other youths, round trips were counted as one assist, as were other multistop trips that occurred within a single day. Transportation that occurred (and meals that were supplied) in connection with "activities outside the center" (see "Recreational Opportunities and Socializing Experiences," in this chapter)—for example, sports, sightseeing, and cultural/educational events—was not counted as an assist. This also applied to transportation of youths to and from (1) jail and (2) NRCC, for example, in connection with short-term detention.

46. Standard foster home and group home expenses were excluded from the definition of material aid. These expenditures and/or subsidies mainly related to room and board, normal clothing replacement, and incidental spending allowance (laundry, haircuts, etc.). Emergency medical, dental, and psychiatric care was considered an assist.

47. The exact number of phone conversations is unknown, since many if not most calls were never referred to in the parole agents' written records. Where these conversations were mentioned, their general content and/or purpose was usually indicated.

48. Drop-ins by the youth were distinguished from instances in which the youngster appeared to have visited CTP mainly (1) for purposes of recreation, for example, games or physical activities within the dayroom, or (2) to receive material aid, for example, meals or transportation.

49. As can be seen, this factor contained two main components or subfactors.

50. The skills in question were those perceived by the casework supervisor and the agent himself (herself).

51. "Limited variety" also resulted from similarities among parole agents.

52. Factor A was also relevant to the *specific treatment modality* that was selected, for instance, group counseling (in program element #1). However, this element will be dealt with in connection with Factor B.

53. It was an integral part of the Phase 2 and 3 proposals as well.

54. Or specific components of those patterns, for instance, program elements #1 and #7.

55. Such agreement did not necessarily mean that the supervisor considered the latter approach inappropriate.

56. During 1963–1966, it was largely through such support and encouragement that conjoint family therapy, psychodrama, transactional analysis, and behavior modification (i.e., simple agreements or mini-contracts, not token economies) became part of the project. By 1967, the first two approaches were no longer moderately common, but were still far from rare within CTP (Berne, 1961, 1964, 1966; Corsini, 1957; Harris, 1967; Haskell, 1961, 1975; Holland and Skinner, 1961; McKee, 1964; Moreno, 1953, 1959; Satir, 1967). (Like the latter two, they never were—nor became—frequent and/or routine.) Sometimes, new approaches were first brought to the project's attention by individuals other than parole agents, for example, by the casework supervisor or other staff. By mid-1966, supervisors and/or one or two agents per unit *informally* introduced most CTP agents to various principles of reality therapy (RT) (Glasser, 1965); however, they did not try to give RT special emphasis, top priority, and so on. By 1967, several newly hired CTP workers brought an RT perspective (more precisely, selected components thereof) with them—without, at the same time, being closed to other perspectives, principles, and approaches. (During Phase 3, a few CTP agents first used sensitivity training—though quite infrequently. This also applied to transcendental meditation—"TM"—but even less often.)

4 THE YOUTHS: BACKGROUND AND I-LEVEL

In working with any population of youths it is appropriate to ask: What are most of these individuals like? What outstanding needs or problems do they have? What is the typical youngster like?

These questions focus on the major *similarities* that exist within the particular population. As such, their answers can play an important part in determining the general features of any correctional program that one might wish to develop, for most such youths.

A further set of questions is equally appropriate: What are the important *differences* that exist within this population of youths? Can the total population be divided into meaningful subgroups? Answers to these questions can serve as a basis for establishing subprograms, or alternate program patterns, for groups of youth within the total population.

In short, information regarding the similarities and differences among youths can, and should, have direct bearing on the focus, scope, and specific content of given correctional programs. Given this premise, we will now present a fairly specific picture of the Youth Authority wards who have been discussed thus far. This should result in a better understanding of the problems and needs that the Community Treatment Project tried to address, and of the various approaches it employed.

First, we will review several background characteristics of the Phase 1 and 2 sample. As before, this includes all Sacramento and Stockton males, experimentals plus controls. This will provide a picture of the youngsters as a whole—a profile of what might be called the average or typical individual at the time of his Youth Authority commitment. After that we will review the widely known I-level classi-

fication system. Together, this information will help us focus on some of the outstanding similarities and differences among youths, for example, their level of social-emotional development and their characteristic ways of responding to others. As indicated in Chapter 3, these features played a major role in determining the type of intervention used at CTP. As described in Chapter 8, they were related to program effectiveness as well.

Background Characteristics

Background characteristics will be summarized in relation to four areas: general factors, family characteristics, personal situation and characteristics, and school situation. Details regarding each area can be found in Appendix 5.

Overview of Background Characteristics
General Factors

The average or typical Phase 1 and 2 youth was: 15½ years old at YA intake; from a lower income family; equally likely to be Caucasian or non-Caucasian; slightly below the normal IQ range; committed to the YA for a property-related offense; not likely to have had a history of violence.

Family Characteristics

Most youngsters came from homes that were broken by divorce, separation, or death. Nearly three of every ten youths had a father or father substitute with a police record; and, four of every ten had one or more delinquent or previously delinquent siblings. CTP and regular parole agents rated most homes—that is, homes in which the youths were living at point of YA intake—as undesirable or less than acceptable for eventual parole placement. Three of every 10 families were receiving welfare payments at the time of the youth's commitment. One family in four had changed its place of residence once every two years during the (average of) 15 years since the youngster was born.

Personal Situation and Characteristics
Most youths had lived away from home on one or more occasions, and many had done so before they were five years old. For the total sample, the first law contact was likely to have occurred at age 13. About half the time, the youngsters' YA commitment offense involved one or more co-offenders. Relatively few individuals were known to have used dangerous drugs or opiates. Histories of persistent nail biting or temper tantrums were noted about one-third of the time; persistent bed-wetting was slightly less frequent. Close to one-third of all youths had seen a psychiatrist or psychologist, for example, while at juvenile hall.

School Situation
Half of the sample were not attending public school, at intake. (Less than 1 percent of all youths had completed high school.) Nine out of every 10 youths had had serious or frequent scholastic, truancy, authority, or peer-related problems at one or more points. The figure remained high—six out of ten—when scholastic difficulties were excluded. "Serious or persistent school misbehavior" usually began at age 12. Regarding overall academic achievement, the average youth was functioning three grade levels below the school grade in which he was enrolled, or last enrolled.

I-Level Classification
Before describing the I-level system, a word about classification itself. Any classification, however sophisticated, can lead to rigidified and limited views of what, in the final analysis, are complex individuals. This is especially true if the labels or diagnoses that are given to those youths are looked at, by staff, as containing virtually all the information that is needed in order to decide what "should" be done. This danger was recognized at an early date, within CTP. As a result, classification came to be regarded not as the "final word," but as one important step in figuring out relevant objectives, and practical ways to achieve

those objectives, for each youth. Given its emphasis on each person's expectations, attitudes, abilities, and concerns, the I-level system, in particular, seemed theoretically consistent with the goal of promoting maximally individualized and personally relevant intervention.

Classification can thus be viewed as one way of implementing the concept of individualized intervention. It is not a fundamental ingredient of *community-based* intervention, as such, since intervention within community settings can occur either with or without the aid of a classification system. Nor is it a fundamental ingredient of intensive intervention, since this, too, can be implemented without any formal classification.

The I-Level System
The I-level classification system is one way of thinking about the many similarities and differences that exist among individuals, especially in relation to attitudes, expectations, and behavior. It consists of two separable, yet interrelated bodies of information: (1) a theory of social-emotional development ("interpersonal maturity") that relates to individuals in general, that is, children, youths, and adults—offenders and nonoffenders alike; (2) a description of several personality types ("subtypes" or "response styles") that can be observed within any large group of offenders. Each body of information will be taken up in turn. First, however, it might be useful to briefly review the concept of "similarities and differences."

On Being Similar yet Different
Ultimately, each youth is a unique individual, made up of many characteristics or traits, combined in particular ways. Equally true is the concept that any *group* of individuals can and do share some of these characteristics in common. Information about shared characteristics can be useful in predicting the responses, of group members, to particular situations and methods of intervention.

One such characteristic or set of characteristics has been called level of interpersonal maturity; its alternate name is level of integration, or I-level. For instance, of every 100 adolescents, 40 may have developed to the level of "average maturity." (For this hypothetical example, a specific definition of terms is not necessary.) These 40 youths would thus be similar to one another when it comes to level of maturity, regardless of how different they might be in other respects.

A second major characteristic that a group of individuals may hold in common is type of personality. For present purposes, personality can be thought of as (1) the blended-together product (i.e., the combination or integration) and (2) the visible expression, of an individual's main beliefs, attitudes, traits, and patterns of behavior.

For instance, of the 40 average maturity youths, 12 might be described as dependent personalities, 20 might be seen as relatively independent, and 8 might be seen as a fairly even mixture of each. It should be added that many components of personality—character traits and items of behavior—can be found at more than one level of maturity. Thus, traits such as persistence and impulsivity are often observed at the "low," "average," and "high" levels of maturity alike. This is seen in connection with certain personality types (e.g., dependent personalities) as well, though in a much more limited sense.[1]

Social-Emotional Development
(Interpersonal Maturity)

The theory of interpersonal maturity was first presented in the mid-1950s, by Sullivan, Grant, and Grant (1957). It was first applied in a military setting and, soon afterwards, within the California Adult Corrections system (Havel, 1960, 1963, 1965; Havel and Sulka, 1962). However, its first large-scale, comprehensive application was in the California Youth Authority's Community Treatment Project, throughout Phases 1 and 2. This, in fact, is where it came to be widely known within corrections.

The I-level theory is a description and attempted explanation of certain ways in which individuals think about themselves and interpret their social environment, at various points in their growth from infancy to adulthood. These thoughts and interpretations become organized (integrated), by each individual, in terms of a relatively stable or long-lasting set of concepts, expectations, and attitudes. This organized "set" is called the "core structure of personality" (Sullivan, Grant, and Grant, 1957). (The next two paragraphs are somewhat technical in nature; the main flow will continue with the subsequent paragraph.)

According to this theory, the preceding concepts, expectations, and attitudes can be organized into seven basic "integrations"—that is, groupings or distinguishable patterns of thought. Almost any pattern that develops *later* in an individual's life will be more complex or structurally articulated than any pattern(s) that developed before it: It will involve the blending together of greater amounts of information and the integration of an increased number of needs, expectations, and areas of potential conflict.[2] As a result, this series of changes—seven patterns, taken as a whole—is described in terms of seven levels of increasing ability or achievement, that is, levels of maturity. The ability in question relates largely to the individual's capacity to conceptualize himself and his environment in an increasingly complex or discriminating way.

Each maturity level relates to three broad areas of ability or achievement: (1) ability to recognize one's own needs; (2) ability to understand the realities of one's social environment; and (3) the blending together of[3] these separate needs and expectations, on the part of self and environment. Each maturity level refers to particular *types* of awareness, understanding, and integration.

The theory of interpersonal maturity distinguishes seven levels of development, ranging from lowest to highest. The following will briefly illustrate this scale of development.

Level 1 represents the least amount of understanding and integration of personal as well as social needs and realities, on the part of the individual. It is found in the newborn infant and very young child, in whom there exist few concepts of self and environment. Intermediate levels of maturity, for instance, level 4 or 5, are found in persons who are much better able to recognize not only some of their own needs, but several needs, feelings, and goals on the part of others. This also applies to their awareness of the formal rules, the role expectations, and the stated ideals, of society. These individuals can also recognize many of the differences in personality, motivation, and role behavior that exist between themselves and others, and among others as well. Finally, compared to individuals of lower maturity, they are better able to organize these thoughts and perceptions into a relatively consistent concept of self.

Levels 6 and 7 are rare. They occur only in adults who have an unusually broad social and psychological perspective on themselves, on others,[4] and on their environment. In addition, they have considerable awareness of (1) the types and levels of interaction that exist,[5] sometimes simultaneously, between self, others, and society, and (2) the differing interpretations[6] that can be given to various interpersonal events. In short, they are "cognitively complex" to an unusual degree.

The vast majority of adults are located at level 3, 4, or 5.[7] Most adolescents—nonoffenders and offenders—are at level 3 or 4. Ninety-nine percent of the Phase 1 and 2 sample of juvenile offenders were located at level 2, 3, or 4 at point of intake. These levels are defined as follows (see note 8 regarding level 5):

Maturity level 2 (I₂): An individual whose overall development has reached this level, but has not gone beyond it, views events and objects mainly as sources of short-term pleasure, or else frustration. He distinguishes among people largely in terms of their being either "givers" or "withholders," and seems to have few ideas of interpersonal refinement beyond this. He has a very low level of frustration-tolerance and a very limited awareness of the basic reasons for the behavior or attitudes of others, toward him. Five percent of the CTP sample were classified as I₂.

Maturity level 3 (I₃): More than the I₂, an individual at this level recognizes that certain aspects of his own behavior have a good deal to do with whether or not he will get what he wants from others. Such an individual interacts mainly in terms of oversimplified rules and formulas rather than from a set of relatively firm and generally more complex, internalized standards or ideals. He understands few of the feelings and motives of individuals whose personalities are rather different than his own. More often than the I₄, he assumes that people operate mostly on a rule-oriented or intimidation/manipulation basis. Thirty-five percent of the CTP sample were classified as I₃.

Maturity level 4 (I₄): More than the I₃, an individual at this level has internalized one or more "sets" of standards that he frequently uses as a basis for either accepting or rejecting the behavior and attitudes not only of himself, but of others as

well. (These standards are not always mutually consistent, or consistently applied.) He recognizes interpersonal interactions in which people attempt to influence one another by means other than compliance, manipulation, promises of hedonistic or monetary reward, and so on. He has a fair ability to understand underlying reasons for behavior and is able to respond, on a fairly long-term basis, to moderately complex expectations on the part of other individuals. Sixty percent of the CTP sample were seen as I₄s. (See Appendix 6, section I, for further details regarding levels 2, 3, and 4.)

Thus, each maturity classification is designed to provide a capsule account of the central attitudes, expectations, and modes of interacting on the part of individuals who are currently functioning at that level. It is a summary account of (1) the extent to which those individuals discriminate (i.e., recognize or "perceive" differences) among the events that occur within themselves and their environment and (2) the ways in which they understand, or generally interpret, their perceived environment.[9]

Before we turn to the earlier-mentioned personality types, three additional points might be mentioned. First, the social-emotional distance that exists between any one maturity level and the next most advanced level is rather considerable. As a result, it is hardly possible for an individual to move through any given level within just a short period of time, say, a couple of months. This was seen in Phases 1 and 2 of CTP. There, youngsters who progressed from level 2 to level 3 did so after an average of 29 months on parole. For those who moved from I₃ to I₄ the figure was also 29 months; for I₄ to I₅ movement, it was 23 months (Palmer, 1968c). Thus, in the long view, social-emotional development might best be thought of as a continuous process, not a series of rapid or sudden jumps from level to level. For this reason, the seven maturity levels might be regarded as important benchmarks, or readily distinguishable points along an unbroken continuum that ranges from very low to very high.

Next, details regarding the basic concepts of I-level can be found in Appendix 6, section II. These relate to the interaction between self and society; the expanding nature of social stimuli; the "integrative [selecting and reject-ing, combining and recombining] character of the human mind"; "core structure of person-ality"; fixed ("invariant") sequence of devel-opmental changes; and fixation.

Finally, I-level theory is, itself, a blend or integration of several closely related lines of thought. Chief among these are the concepts and theories of Mead, Piaget, Sullivan, Lewin, Erickson, Bloch, and Sarbin. (See Appendix 6, section III.)

Personality Types (Delinquent Subtypes)

During the later 1950s it became clear that sizable personality differences existed among offenders who fell within the boundaries of any one maturity level, for example, level 3. As a result, in 1960–1961 certain distinctions were made among individuals who fell within level 2, 3, or 4. These distinctions were made largely by Dr. Warren, in preparation for CTP operations and research. (The nature and background of these developments and dis-tinctions is further reviewed in Appendix 6, section IV.)

Each such distinction represented an identifiable type of juvenile offender, and was called a delinquent subtype. As mentioned earlier, maturity levels were descriptions of the general population—nonoffenders and of-fenders combined. However, the present dis-tinctions (subtypes) were accounts of the offender population in particular; still, they were presumed to be of relevance to many nonoffender groups as well. In any event ma-turity level related to the individual's way of perceiving and interpreting his environment, whereas "subtype" focused on his usual ways of overtly *responding* to that environment.

The main distinction that was made among offenders who were located at level 2 related to the factors of passivity/compliance versus activity/assertiveness. This applied to individuals at level 3 as well. However, at level 4, the primary distinction related to "neuro-sis" (e.g., severe, debilitating, and long-standing internal conflict) versus lack of neurosis; and, secondary distinctions were then made within each such category.

It was thought that these primary and secondary distinctions—for example, compli-ance, assertiveness, neurosis, and traumatic situational reaction—often played a signifi-cant role in the development of delinquent be-havior. For this reason it was assumed they

might have important implications for the treatment and control strategies that were being developed with respect to the Community Treatment Project.[10]

The result of this effort was a description of nine distinct subtypes, across maturity lev-els 2 through 4. They were labeled and sum-marized as follows (Warren, 1967a):

I_2 subtypes: (1) Asocial, Aggressive (Aa)—responds with active demands and open hostility when frus-trated. (2) Asocial, Passive (Ap)—responds with whining, complaining, and withdrawal when frustrated.

I_3 subtypes: (3) Immature Conformist (Cfm)—responds with immedi-ate compliance to whoever seems to have the power at the moment. (4) Cultural Conformist (Cfc)—responds with conformity to specific ref-erence group: delinquent peers. (5) Manipulator (Mp)—oper-ates by attempting to undermine the power of authority figures, and/or usurp the power role for himself.

I_4 subtypes: (6) Neurotic, Acting-out (Na)—responds to underlying guilt [feelings] with attempts to "out-run" or avoid conscious anxiety and condemnation of self. (7) Neurotic, Anxious (Nx)—re-sponds with symptoms of emo-tional disturbance to conflict produced by feelings of inade-quacy and guilt. (8) Situational-Emotional Reaction (Se)—responds to immediate family or personal crisis by act-ing out. (9) Cultural Identifier (Ci)—responds to identification with a deviant value system by living out his delinquent beliefs.

Subtypes (3) through (7) are described in greater detail in the next chapter. (For various reasons—empirical, theoretical, and practi-cal—new names have been suggested for most subtypes, beginning in 1970.[11] These names, which will be used for the remainder of this book (except in parts of Chapter 22), are pre-sented in Table 4–1 (col. 2), together with the original labels (col. 1). Also shown is the degree of representation on the part of each subtype, within the Phase 1 and 2 sample.)

In 1961, the CTP personality groupings were not something new to corrections. During the previous 17 years nearly every one had been described relative to one or more offender populations. The following were among the better known authors and classifications: Jenkins and Hewitt (unsocialized aggressive; overinhibited; socialized); McCord (conformist; aggressive psychopath; neurotic); Schrag ("Outlaw"/asocial; "Politician"/pseudo-social; "Square John"/prosocial; "Right Guy"/antisocial).[12] Lesser known—but perhaps equally influential in the development of CTP's subtypes—were: Abramson (infantile prepsychotic; cultural; neurotic; manipulative psychopath; passive dependent) and Studt (isolate; receiver; manipulator; love-seeker; learner).[13]

Combining of Subtypes
In 1973, subtypes (6) and (7)—assertive-denier and anxious-confused (formerly, neurotic, acting-out and neurotic, anxious, respectively)—were combined, by the author, into a single group, which was then named *conflicted* youths. This combining of subtypes was possible, and plausible, because of repeated observations regarding the following: (1) similarities that existed in the personality makeup and backgrounds of each individual subtype, some of which distinguished the latter from most remaining subtypes as well; (2) similarities in treatment/control approaches that were used with each of the two subtypes, some of which (as before) distinguished them from several remaining subtypes; and (3) similarities in their respective levels of parole performance. At the same time, and for essentially the same reasons, subtypes (4) and (5)—group conformist (formerly cultural conformist) and manipulator—were also combined into a single group. This group was named *power-oriented* youths. The reduction of these four subtypes into two broader "subtype groupings" was soon found to simplify the presentation of CTP's data and experiences.

Conflicted youths comprise slightly over half—53 percent—of the total Phase 1 and 2 sample. Power-oriented individuals comprise 21 percent. When *passive-conformists* (14 percent) are added to the picture, these groups, taken together, account for 88 percent of the total sample—seven of every eight eligible males.

In light of these similarities, advantages, and figures, the remainder of this book will be organized largely around these three youth groups. The remaining individuals—12 percent of the total sample—consist of subtypes (1), (2), (8), and (9). None of these subtypes account for more than 5 percent of the sample. They are referred to, collectively, as *rare types* or *all others*,[14] and will be described whenever necessary. (See Appendix 7 for brief description.)

TABLE 4-1

Delinquent Subtypes in Phase 1 and 2 Sample

Warren Subtype Label	Palmer Subtype Label	Percentage of Sample
Asocial, Aggressive	Assertive-Asocial	1
Asocial, Passive	Passive-Asocial	4
Immature Conformist	Passive-Conformist	14
Cultural Conformist	Group Conformist	11
Manipulator	Manipulator	10
Neurotic, Acting-out	Assertive-Denier	21
Neurotic, Anxious	Anxious-Confused	32
Situational-Emotional Reaction	Stress Reaction; Adjustment Reaction to Adolescence[a]	2
Cultural Identifier	Delinquent Identifier	5

[a]Here, the original Situational-Emotional Reaction category is divided into two separate groups.

Notes

1. To pursue this further would require considerable technical detail, precise definition of terms, and subsequent discussion. (For instance, "What, if any, are the major differences between I_2, I_3, and I_4 dependency?") This would add little that is essential to the present discussion.

2. For example, conflict among and across the differing needs and expectations. Many such conflicts are first made possible by the individual's increased awareness of differences that exist between himself and other people, and *among* other people as well.

3. That is, the (1) resolution/joint-satisfying of, or the (2) adaptation/accommodation/readjustment to. This integration occurs in terms of a "set" or pattern of expectations, attitudes, and resulting behaviors. It is sometimes called the "core structure of personality," for that particular integration level.

4. For example, they have considerable perspective on or understanding of (1) the nature and reasons for their development as particular individuals, (2) the differing ways in which they interpret and adapt to their social environment or personal needs/limitations, and (3) appropriate ways of interacting with them as individuals (not as stereotypes), in various social contexts.

5. Exist, for example, on the part of several individuals whose backgrounds, social obligations, personal needs, or range of information are different than one's own, and different from one another's as well.

6. For example, differing interpretations of formal (role-prescribed) as well as informal interactions and of "surface" as well as "below the surface" interactions.

7. Most people who have used the I-level system for several years estimate this to be about 95 percent of all adults. However, no formal study has been carried out in this regard.

8. A person at this level is quite aware of himself as a changing and developing individual. He recognizes many similarities ("continuities") between his past and present attitudes and/or behavior; he can see several patterns in his relationships with other individuals as well. He is relatively aware of and accepting of the differences that exist between his own value system and the values or priorities of others; he can also see that many people are complex, interpersonally flexible individuals who may prefer not to be dealt with on the basis of simple rules of thumb. An individual at the I_5 level can establish a number of roles for himself (herself), roles that allow him to interact fairly comfortably with a variety of people in a wide range of situations. Compared to persons who are at lower levels of maturity, the I_5 is less concerned with what he can "get" from others in the areas of material aid, sharing of power, loyalty, emotional support, and recognition. This allows him to interact with them more freely, or at least around a different set of themes. It allows him to enjoy them more as individuals (e.g., for who *they* are, apart from their relationship with him), and to not be greatly upset by the fact that they, like himself, may change.

9. Integration levels were originally described as "modal patterns of cognitive organization" (Sullivan, Grant, and Grant, 1955). Also see Sullivan, Grant, and Grant, 1957.

10. CTP was in its original planning stage at the time of this development (1960–1961).

11. The reasons for these suggested changes vary from one subtype to another, and need not be specified here.

12. In general, the Schrag groupings correspond to the following Warren subtypes, respectively: asocial, aggressive or passive; manipulator; neurotic, anxious; cultural-identifier (Schrag, 1944, 1954, 1961, 1971). Also see Jenkins and Hewitt (1944) and McCord, McCord, and Zola (1959).

13. In general, the Studt groups correspond to the following Warren subtypes, respectively: asocial, aggressive or passive; immature-conformist; manipulator; neurotic (Anxious); cultural-identifier (Studt, 1960). Also see Abramson (1957).

14. These groups, certainly subtype (8), would be more common in—and proportionately more frequent within—local probation samples than among individuals committed to a state-level agency, such as the Youth Authority.

5 PERSONALITY TYPES AND CASE ILLUSTRATIONS

Conflicted, power-oriented, and passive-conformist youths will now be presented in more detail. For each group there will be a generalized description followed by an actual, though abbreviated, case illustration.

Each generalized description will emphasize (1) personal and background characteristics that are commonly observed in most individuals who fall within the given group (e.g., the passive-conformist group) and (2) characteristics that distinguish the group from most or all remaining groups.[1] In the case of any *single* youth, most of the "commonly observed" characteristics *would* probably be reflected in a detailed case illustration. (Almost all distinguishing characteristics would be reflected.) However, some features that would be found as part of the generalized description would, in all likelihood, be absent or, in certain cases, contraindicated.[2] Basically, the reason for this is as follows.

As mentioned earlier, each individual is ultimately unique; as a result, he is bound to vary from the norm in some respects. This variation is directly reflected in the fact that a few discrepancies will be observed between the generalized description of a subtype, on the one hand, and any case illustration, on the other. At the same time, the statistical realities are such that, for any group (subtype), the greater the number of case illustrations, the less frequent (proportionately speaking) would be the occurrence of any particular discrepancy.[3] In any event, occasional discrepancies of this type do not negate the general accuracy, or representativeness, of the subtype description itself.

Before proceeding, the following might be kept in mind relative to the five cases that are presented:

1. All five youths were experimentals; that is, they were assigned to the Community Treatment Project. All were committed to the Youth Authority during the same year: 1965. Four youths resided in Stockton; four were Caucasian.

2. Each description is based on information that was gathered as of the same point in time: the conclusion of the case conference staffing.[4] This was prior to the individual's first release to parole. Except for a few statements that are obviously from staff, or the individual's parent, all quotes are those from the youngster himself. Also, all names and other possible identifying information have been changed.

3. The prior offense histories of these individuals are, in most cases, on the slightly mild side when compared to the Phase 1 and 2 sample as a whole, and to the youngster's personality group in particular. For instance, they contain slightly fewer entries than average; and of these entries, a relatively large proportion are status offenses. Generally speaking, these histories resemble those of many youths who are currently worked with in local probation settings, at least within California, and who were no longer sent to the Youth Authority beginning around 1973–1974, and especially by 1977.[5]

Conflicted Youths
Anxious-Confused (General Description)

For anxious-confused youths, most interpersonal relationships are filled with tension, hassles, loyalty binds, and eventual disappointment. These individuals are in considerable conflict as to "who they are" and what sort of person they wish to become; however, they do not wish to think of themselves as becoming criminals. Most people see them as laden with anxiety and, to a lesser extent, feelings of guilt.

Anxious-confused youths sometimes feel as if there were three different parts to themselves: an unalterably "bad" part, a potentially worthwhile but largely unavailable part, and a socially acceptable yet personally unacceptable and phony-seeming part. These differing views of themselves are a major source, as well as product, of their frequent confusion.

These youths often come from a setting in which there have been (1) long years of family strife, with the anxious-confused individuals frequently ending up "in the middle," and/or (2) an early and traumatic death of one parent, a series of separations or marriages, or an early divorce followed by no remarriage.

Anxious-confused individuals hesitate to blame or confront individuals toward whom they may feel considerable resentment or anger. They are accustomed to taking most of the blame, and to blaming themselves, for binds which they and others are in. Generally speaking, they are not adept at concealing their personal distress from themselves and others. In fact, they often make it a point to accentuate the "negative" and virtually eliminate the "positive" when describing their feelings and situation to others.

Most anxious-confused youths initially try to interact with adults on a relatively egalitarian, adolescent-to-adult basis, or even an adult-to-adult basis. However, they allow their numerous dependency strivings to become fairly evident before long. This applies to their mixed feelings about adulthood as well.

There is considerable variation among individuals who fall within this grouping. They vary, for example, in the extent of their withdrawal, their active fantasy life, their anger, and their depression. They also vary in their ability to develop realistic plans for the future, and in their preference for a formalized and somewhat distant relationship with the parole

agent as opposed to one that is rather informal and close.

Despite these differences, and despite the high degree of discomfort they ordinarily feel, most anxious-confused youths are afraid of trying to make major changes in their way of adjusting to life. All in all, their level of self-confidence and optimism is rather low—despite what they may sometimes say.

Anxious-Confused (Case Illustration)

Jim is age 16½, 5'9" tall, and 184 pounds. Birthplace: Ellensburg, Washington. Lives with mother and two sisters in garage apartment, in rural setting at outskirts of Stockton. This is a low delinquency, lower middle-class area. The apartment is close to a small business that is operated by Jim's mother.

Prior Record

Age 12—threatened a minor while pointing a shotgun at him. Age 14—petty theft. Age 14—lewd phone calls. Age 15—beyond parental control (theft of money from mother; forgery on mother's bank account; sexual molestation of 11-year-old sister). Because of these charges Jim was committed to a state mental hospital for a standard 90-day observation. He was released from the hospital as nonpsychotic, and sent directly to the probation department's county boys camp.

YA Committing Offense

Boys camp failure (refusal to accept work assignments; frequent fighting with peers; exposed switchblade knife several times and once threatened a peer with same).

Family Situation

His natural father died at age 48, after 23 years of marriage (see below). Jim was nine at the time. His mother, now age 50, did not remarry. Jim is sixth of seven children: two sons, age 31 and 26, live on their own; two daughters, age 24 (Arlene) and 20 (JoAnn), also live on their own; the two remaining daughters—Lily, age 19, and Susan, age 12—live with their mother and Jim. The family has never been on welfare.

While his father was alive, the family moved from state to state throughout the West and Northwest, every year or two. When Jim was nine and the family was living in a remote area of New Mexico, JoAnn (then 14) told her mother that the father was sexually molesting her. At the same time, Arlene (then 18) said that she too had been molested by her father over a long period of time. A heated argument ensued; and that evening, while the mother and children were packing to leave, their father went into a bedroom and shot himself between the eyes, dying almost immediately. Jim saw his father laying dead, a few moments afterward. Until recent months he refused to consider it a suicide. Instead, he blamed his mother and older sisters for the death, and figured his mother may have pulled the trigger. Most family members have been tense and somewhat gloomy ever since. Sister Lily was recently released from a mental hospital after having a "nervous breakdown" following her divorce.

School, Paid Employment, Etc.
School problems began at age 11 and have continued to the present. Jim is currently on expelled status due to frequent truancy, "recalcitrant behavior," and poor grades. He says he's now ready to "try to do better in school," and wants to complete high school. His IQ scores fall within normal range (mid-90s).[6] Jim has never had a job. He is fairly well accepted within the neighborhood.

Youth's View of Self and Others
"I cry at the least thing. The least things get me all nervous. . . . Until last year I would always feel sorry for myself. I'd get depressed so much that I'd not want to live. . . . I tried to kill myself two or three times. Deep inside me I wanted to live but I was thinking, 'I just don't care.'" One suicide attempt (slashed wrists) occurred when he and his girlfriend got into a fight; another (pills) occurred "when my girl broke up with me." Other attempts also followed arguments with girlfriend and mother: "Once I went up to the hills and tried to drive over a horseshoe curve" (Jim was with another fellow at the time, also interested in suicide).

Jim feels he was "happy-go-lucky" prior to his father's death, but that since then he's been "a very cruel person." He says that he's now beginning to "get over it" and can "forgive" his mother, since he thinks his father actually did commit suicide:

"Until recently I hated my mother. I did everything I could against her"—for example, run up large phone bills, have fist fights with her, steal cash and checks from her, and refuse to do chores. "I tried to hurt her pride and spirit . . . and hurt her physically, too. I know that was wrong." Jim says he wouldn't have been in trouble during recent years "if I'd listened to my mother."

No matter how the father may have died, Jim still feels there would have been *other* reasons for "being mean to her [mother] and refusing to obey her": He believes that, prior to his father's death, "she didn't care enough about us" [family members] . . . and "didn't love" Jim and his father, in particular. He recalls "lots of arguments between mom and dad. Like about his paycheck or about how late he was staying out, or about how he treats some of his kids and stuff like that . . . [and about his] sleeping around with other women."

Jim still has "nightmares" about his family: (1) mother pulls trigger on gun and kills the father; (2) mother "turns into a monster and hurts me"; and (3) Jim fights mother, hurts her badly, and sees her die.

Jim says he always thought of his father as "the greatest man on earth . . . like God." The only thing he "hated" about his father was that he "whipped me too much when he caught me smoking or something like that . . . [or] sometimes he'd give me a cheap Christmas present." Jim thinks his father did not entirely initiate the sexual incidents with Arlene and JoAnn. He says that this—joint involvement—also applied to his (Jim's) sexual interaction with sister Susan, two years ago, and to a sexual incident with JoAnn at about the same time. He says there was nothing seriously wrong with this, but does not intend to repeat either event.

Jim readily acknowledges that he often picks on weaker peers (he was seen as enjoying the role of "duke," while in the state mental hospital): "Sure I push my way around a little bit, if I want. But I'm trying to overcome this." He feels his strongest point is his ability to help a friend in need. He wants to eventually get married and have kids: "I want to be respectable instead of an ex-con. I don't want my kids to be disgraced."

View of Family and Youth, by Other
Mother feels the family moved around so much because Jim's father "just wasn't able to

settle down," for reasons unrelated to his work. She describes him as having had a severe drinking problem. She states she had no feeling of closeness to him during most of the marriage, and that she remained with him for the children's sake alone. She feels partly responsible for his death, since she had "threatened to leave him" as a result of the sexual molestations. (She adds that Jim and the younger daughters soon learned about these incidents.) She also says that she may have been partly responsible for the molestations, since she had "long since locked him out" of her sexual life.

Mother thinks an institutional stay would probably help bring Jim under control—something that she, herself, has been unable to do. Since age 14, Jim would often rage and threaten to get his way; he would come and go whenever he wished, and would return "only for meals or money." Mother thinks Jim likes to associate with older, delinquently oriented men who "drive around until all hours," drink, and are probably on the fringes of illegal activity. She is willing to have Jim live with her and the two younger daughters, but feels she would need considerable help from a parole agent in the area of control.

View of Youth, by Staff
NRCC living unit staff describe Jim as "calm and friendly . . . responds well to encouragement . . . can operate with normal supervision and instruction . . . seeks no attention nor does he demand attention. Jim is an above average worker." Other NRCC staff view him as "almost entirely self-centered. . . . He sees women as hostile and domineering, and has a fair amount of violence potential."

CTP staff describe him as a severely traumatized adolescent, one who is easily depressed, self-condemning, and uses suicidal gestures to express anger toward self and others. They note that—as with his father's suicide—Jim's own attempts occur shortly after arguments with a woman. Staff believe Jim (1) is identifying with his father and indirectly taking revenge on the mother, for him, and (2) is still trying to punish the mother for somehow taking away the individual who was the main source of his childhood security and sense of power or adequacy. Both factors result in considerable guilt and anxiety on Jim's part.

Assertive-Denier (General Description)
Like anxious-confused youths, these individuals have numerous personal conflicts; and they, too, are far from satisfied with themselves. However, in some contrast to the former youths, assertive-deniers are not very aware of the focus, or at least the scope, of their conflicts. In addition, they are not likely to *remain* confused, depressed, self-condemning, or desirous of being taken care of—that is, to remain that way for more than a short time, in connection with any one crisis. In line with this, they have a strong tendency to deny the possibility that their difficulties are seriously influencing their ability to function in specified social settings.

Assertive-deniers are often described as (1) impulsive and "constantly on-the-go" and (2) perceptive, aloof, and sometimes quite cutting. Their emphasis on activity (often vigorous physical activity), and their self-image of adequacy or autonomy, frequently helps them reduce or avoid various tensions and anxieties. This applies to questions of possible inadequacy, or "badness," as well. These feelings and topics are very difficult for most such youths to put up with, or keep their attention focused on, for very long.

In many respects their home life has been similar to that of anxious-confused youths. However, they have learned to "bear up" or even "fight back" to a greater degree. In addition, they are less willing to accept the idea that happiness is far beyond their grasp.

Assertive-deniers try to give the impression that (1) any difficulties they may have are either under pretty good control or are temporary and situational in nature, and that (2) there is no real need for them to do much talking, or thinking, in connection with such matters, anyway. They seldom care to reveal much about themselves or their family and especially wish to conceal the fact that they are not in tight control of certain interpersonal situations that they would like to change, and may still be trying to change.

These youths want people to notice and mainly respond to their areas of greatest strength, and to delve only superficially into areas in which difficulties, personal problems, or shortcomings may have been acknowledged. They show little interest in such things as heart-to-heart discussions, and they are quite squeamish about the possibility, or prospect, of being "pitied." They are quite touchy about psychological and psychiatric "explanations" of their difficulties, since they often associate these with such topics as inadequacy, guilt, mental illness, or lack of complete control over their own destiny. Together with "head shrinkers" in general, these are topics they hate to think about, and often enjoy ridiculing.

When first placed on parole, assertive-deniers usually hope the parole agent (1) will agree to establish an externally oriented, relatively formalized working arrangement with them, and (2) will generally allow them to handle everything by themselves, from that point forward. Together with this hope, they are prepared to struggle rather vigorously, perhaps openly, to maintain their stance of autonomy. This stance, or general attitude, has been rather central to their way of coping with individuals around them, and with various personal feelings as well. Together with its "defensive" function, it has helped them maintain a feeling of hope, in contrast to one of defeat.

Thus, it is quite common for assertive-deniers to quickly move away from commitments or personal relationships that threaten to bring to the surface, or foreground of consciousness, some of their long-held, very strong feelings about not being wanted, or of being inadequate. This includes feelings of not having "what it takes" to be liked or loved by others.

Personal experience has led them to be very careful about depending a great deal on other individuals, at least when it comes to seeking happiness. As a result, seemingly minor feelings of interpersonal discomfort can serve as signals for them to (1) verbally "shine others on," (2) verbally "wound" or otherwise try to antagonize and reject the individual who may have triggered their anxiety, or (3) begin engaging in various physical activities, distractions, or compensations—legal and otherwise.

Assertive-Denier (Case Illustration)
Tom is age 15.8, 5'3" tall, and 122 lbs. Birthplace: Vallejo, California. He lives in a low delinquency, middle-class residential tract in Stockton. The family residence is well kept.

Prior Record
Age 7—battery and several bicycle thefts. Age 8—runaway from foster home. Age 8—petty theft. Age 12—beyond parental control. Age 13—beyond parental control (drinking; verbally abusive; refusal to obey; chasing two-year-old half-sibling with knife; . . . was then placed into probation department's county boys camp). Age 15—beyond parental control (drunkenness; forging checks on stepfather's bank account; refusal to obey; . . . was placed into boys camp for second time).

YA Committing Offense
Boys camp failure, after one month of placement: (1) Tom was involved with two boys in aborted runaway plan; knives had been prepared as part of the plan. (2) Was previously involved in frequent belligerent behavior toward peers (shoving; tripping), and defiance toward camp staff and regulations (refusal to participate in work assignments; possession of contraband).

Family Situation
Natural father, age 34, is whereabouts unknown. Tom lives with stepfather, age 31, and mother, age 34; neither has a record of delinquency. Also in home are one natural sister, age 14, and two half-siblings, ages four and two.

Tom was four years old when mother and natural father were legally married. Natural father had juvenile and adult record that included petty theft, grand theft, drunk driving, and child molestation. Was institutionalized at least once, for forcible rape. Mother and natural father separated when Tom was six; divorce finalized when he was eight. Mother married Tom's present stepfather one month later. She states that her divorce from Tom's natural father was due to latter's drinking and abuse of their children. When Tom was about seven, mother received treatment for "emotional instability." She still experiences minor physical aftereffects of lengthy childhood polio.

At age six, after a series of school problems, Tom was placed into the first of three foster homes. Mother married Tom's present stepfather while Tom was in the third such home; and, when Tom came to live with them at age nine, severe conflict quickly broke out between him and stepfather. The latter, then age 24, seemed to resent Tom from the start; he and Tom's mother could not agree on how the boy should be handled.

Tom's relationship with his 14-year-old sister has been occasionally volatile, but is largely positive. Sister's relationship with mother has been very strained, for years.

School, Paid Employment, Etc.
School difficulties began in the second grade and included stealing, fighting with peers, and defiance toward teachers. They continued through junior high school, with irregular attendance and poor grades being added to the rest. Tom's IQ scores are in the high 80s, but most people consider him well within normal range. Tom has never had a job.

Youth's View of Self and Others
Tom says that, when he was about six through eight, "I was a little brat, I guess. I was ornery, and I didn't think about things until I did them. . . . I was out of control, that's what I was, because I didn't have no father. I didn't do anything my mother told me to do."

When first placed at the ranch (age 13), "I was just a little runt. . . . I was self-conscious of my size. . . . I used to fight a lot." During that eleven-month placement, "I learned not to be so loud, and always talking and spitting all the time." Tom ran away "a few years ago," because "I was trying to pretend like I was 18. Being out on my own." He says that he's "been changing for the better" in the past year, in that "I've got a little more respect for my parents . . . and I can control my temper a little more." Now, "I guess I'm an ordinary kid except I don't think about things before I do it. I don't think about how it'll hurt my parents." Tom says that being locked up is a "disgrace. . . . As soon as I get out everybody's gonna start bugging me about it. I'll get over it!"

Tom's main interests are track, skin diving, rocket engineering, dances, and parties. He considers himself pretty "big" with girls: "Yeah, I got two of 'em [girlfriends]. But I gotta write a letter tonight and get rid of one of 'em." His happiest moment was when, after "only a week" at the boys camp, he "won a Gold Shirt for physical fitness." Tom feels he can "take [bear up under] anything," no matter how difficult or painful it might be. He also feels good about his persistence: "I mean I'll never quit on anything if I want it. Until I die, I'll make it!" In his favorite dreams, "I'm in a Western or something. I'm one of those big guys, fastest gun you know. But it's a funny thing, it's always the slowest guy that

kills me! . . . Or I'm captain of a space ship and I'm going out there to meet a creature that I have to fight. [But again] I usually get killed by some puny guy with a little gun."

Regarding his natural father: "I remember him, all right! I don't like him. He was mean. He was always mean to my mother. He was always threatening her." Tom claims he once hit his father "because I didn't like him to do those things to my mother." According to Tom he once forced her out of the car, threatened to run over her, shot bullets around her feet to scare her, and made her walk home. "Sometimes he'd lock me and my sister out of our rooms or out of the house," usually when drunk. He often threatened to "beat me up. . . . Other boys, you know, are proud of their father. I'm *not* proud of him!"

Tom thinks his mother "worries a lot about me getting in trouble with my friends, and I try to get her not to worry too much. . . . She's always thinking about us kids and just wants us to show respect and everything." Tom considers her "a good mother" and sometimes wonders if she might be getting "fed up with me. . . . She always *knew* if you did something wrong. I don't know how, but she just knew!" Tom recalls a scene when he was about six, in which "my mother was chasing me with a switch and she almost fell into the water" near the end of a low cliff. "I'll remember that for the rest of my life. I'd told her 'No,' I wasn't going to take the garbage out." He felt frightened, ashamed, and angry at the time.

Tom believes his stepfather has gotten "fed up" with him in the past two years. "I never liked him at first, but he's a nice guy once you get to know him. . . . You won't believe this but my stepfather is really important to me. We don't get along so well but I know you're supposed to show a lot of respect to your parents."

View of Youth, by Others
Stepfather sees little hope for Tom. States that, in matters of discipline and guidance, he usually leaves things up to the mother, since he's learned that Tom automatically objects to his own attempts.

Mother says Tom "was a difficult child from the start" (violent temper tantrums; frequent fights with natural sister; bed-wetting until age six), and that the present family difficulties are nearly all his fault. States that she and her own mother had "nervous break-downs" because of him. Believes that, for years, there's been a constant battle between Tom and stepfather, and that she's had to act as liaison between the two. However, she feels squashed between them: Whichever one she tries to please, the other gets unhappy. She's sure there is something "eating at Tom," but feels unable to eliminate it, even though Tom is "an intelligent boy," is "quite close" to her, and can talk with her a good deal. Still, unless one is "very strict" with Tom, things just "go in one ear and out the other." Mother feels she can't carry through on this role very well, and that Tom's stepfather no longer wants to try. As a result, Tom often ends up being able to "pull the wool over our eyes." Despite this, she and Tom's stepfather prefer that he be returned home, once he is paroled. She attributes Tom's poor school performance to "goofing off."

According to NRCC living unit staff, Tom is "a fiery competitor, and can't take too much constructive criticism before lashing out with a tirade of defensive statements. . . . Leadership ability is there, but is not seen until he is on the athletic field. . . . Good responses are obtained [from Tom] through encouragement and compliments."

CTP staff describe Tom as attention-seeking, constantly on the go, quick-tempered, self-conscious of his size, friendly, yet often sarcastic. He has a lively sense of humor but often seems rather pessimistic and tense. Tom was badly frightened during early childhood, mainly by his natural father; yet he has copied some of the latter's aggressive traits and seems to temporarily feel in better control when he expresses these in his interactions with others. His mother tries to "make up to him" not only for the early foster home placements, but for the stepfather's rejection and open preference for his own children as compared to Tom. (These children were born when Tom was 11 and 13.) Staff also believe Tom has increasingly played mother's feelings against those of stepfather, and increasingly feels responsible for the related turmoil that keeps surfacing within the family. Feelings of being disapproved by others are easily triggered in Tom; and, partly to overcome these feelings, he tries to impress peers with his physical prowess and overall daring. However, his aggressive or herd-riding ways of obtaining attention and maintaining control often bring about rejec-tion rather than acceptance or admiration. This places Tom in a bind regarding how to act, for he seems to assume that if he does not act at all, the presumed negative opinions of him will be maintained.

Power-Oriented Youths
Manipulator (General Description)
These youths often appear indifferent, brash, and unconcerned about others. They seldom show signs of "guilt," or of being bothered by their actions, even though these actions may be contrary to widely held social norms. Except toward certain members of their family, they show few if any strong loyalties to individuals as well as groups. All in all, they are markedly opportunistic, and they take special pleasure in the thought of being able to outsmart or dominate others.

Manipulators usually try to maintain a front of "invincibility" or "toughness," that is, a power-based stance that they believe will help them get what they want. This "front" may also serve as a major defense against long-standing fears that often center around an emasculating, abusive, or even manipulative parent figure whom they may have learned to adjust to via bluff or deceit, and to whom they nevertheless maintain a highly ambivalent form of loyalty.

Manipulators often try to give the impression that they are very pleased with themselves, especially with their ability to "take others or leave them" and to defend themselves physically as well as verbally. They can be forceful and direct in their resistance to authority figures who may be trying to clamp down on their illegal behavior or on their exploitive mode of interacting; however, their methods of resistance can be fairly subtle as well.

It is very difficult for these individuals to put themselves into other peoples' shoes. Only rarely do they attempt to do so, in the first place. Largely for this reason, they are seldom aware of, let alone concerned with, the emotional impact of their behavior on others. In addition, they often find it hard to understand *why* others disapprove so vigorously of certain things they do, and why others may become enraged at their unabashed manipulations.

Thus, with few exceptions, these individuals are extremely self-centered. Yet, despite this, they are sometimes seen as "likable," "charming," or "quite delightful," especially when things seem to be going their way. Still, in numerous contexts, manipulators are likely to become openly angry, resentful, and persistently annoying. The latter response is sometimes observed in connection with their struggles to assume a leadership role or to gain center stage. Apart from this, they can become highly suspicious and verbally or physically abusive in the presence of authority figures whom they actually fear.

Although they often describe themselves as "hot tempered," they also speak of themselves as being able to "keep their cool." They are generally unaware of the contradictory nature of these two descriptions, partly because of the positive value they place on both characteristics.

In sum, these individuals like to think of themselves as having both the right and the ability to get what they want, more or less when they want it. Largely because of this, they are often surprised and upset when others refuse to go along with their expressed wishes, or seem to resist the direct and indirect manipulations on which they rely so heavily.

Manipulator (Case Illustration)

Carl is age 17, 5'5" tall, 142 pounds, and has one tattoo—a small cross—on his right arm. Birthplace: Galveston, Texas. The family lives in low delinquency, middle-income neighborhood in suburban section of Stockton.

Prior Record

Age 14—petty theft. Age 16—beyond parental control. Age 16—loitering. Age 17—beyond parental control.

YA Committing Offense

Beyond parental control (runaway). According to Carl, his father angrily said, "Look, I've had enough of you!," and then told him he'd kick him out of the house if he didn't get a job within a week. So, Carl left home that same day and didn't return. He was arrested two weeks later in the Sacramento area, after his father reported him missing.

Carl says his father had claimed that he (Carl) wasn't making much effort to get a job, whereas he (father) could have gotten a job "at the snap of his fingers" when he was Carl's age. (This quote is from Carl's account of what the father told him during the earlier-mentioned confrontation.) Carl feels it would be "embarrassing" to do the kind of work his father (still according to Carl) claims he, Carl, could have found—that of assistant gardener—and that Carl should be proud of doing. Carl thinks men should do other kinds of work instead. Carl's father stated, during the Initial Home Visit Interview, that a 17-year-old boy should either contribute to the family financially or leave the home and be self-supporting.

Family Situation

Natural father, age 54, and natural mother, age 47, live with their children in a six-room flat that is part of a large apartment house complex for which father has worked, as a gardener, ever since he moved the family from Texas to Stockton, four years ago. The flat is well kept. Carl is fifth of twelve children: four are ages 20–25; four are 12–16; three are 7–11. Five still live with the family, Carl being second oldest of this group. Other siblings are married or self-supporting; and the remaining group live in foster homes, an orphanage, or with relatives. Two brothers, ages 15 and 13, are on probation—one for assault, the other (currently a runaway) for "beyond parental control."

Carl's mother has been described by various social agencies as a severe mental defective or, possibly, simple schizophrenic. She was hospitalized for a "nervous breakdown" when Carl was 10, at which point six of her children (Carl included) were placed in an orphanage. Most of them remained there for three years; the parents were considered unfit for youths to be returned home. Carl ran away from orphanage three times during that period.

During the Initial Home Visit Interview the mother did not speak a word; she was unkempt and often just smiled. Carl's father and oldest daughter (Maria) generally spoke as if she were not in the room. Maria, age 22, handles most of the mother's functions within the home. Carl's father appears to be of average intelligence. He had one minor arrest at age 22 and was recently acquitted on a charge of molesting a 12-year-old girl.

School, Paid Employment, Etc.

Carl has had numerous school difficulties since grade 2 (general classroom disruption; belligerence or defiance toward teachers; fighting with peers; very low grades). IQ scores are substantially below normal range (high 70s and low 80s). During preteens Carl delivered newspapers for a while. He's been deaf in left ear since age 4, following a severe infection. He has never shown signs of organic impairment. (Lack of organicity was further confirmed by EEG test while on parole.)

Youth's View of Self and Others

"I had a rotten life. That's all I gotta say. I've just had a bad time! Everything happened to me. Sometimes I'll get mad and I ain't done nothing. If somebody tries to pick on me then, they're gonna have a hard time! . . . What the hell, I shouldn't be in here. I didn't steal nothing. . . . I had a rotten PO [probation officer]. I had a rotten judge. I tell you I felt like hitting the judge when he said YA." Carl feels that "everyone" is against him: father doesn't want him back home; people often wrongly accuse him; police make it a point to hassle him. Despite this, and because of it, "nobody ever gets me nervous. I control myself!" "I don't try to be rough. I don't try to scare nobody. . . . The only guys I beat up are liars."

"On the 'outs' I'm really somethin' big. That's what the cops think. But in here I act normal. I act stupid, like I'm a punk. . . . I can fool the cops any time. They're not so smart. This one cop keeps trying to nail me for a *long* time. He's always around when I'm driving around. But he can't get anything on me." On the outs, "I walk down the street in my black shirt—sometimes black, sometimes red— black Levi's, shoes, socks. That's my favorite color: black. . . . I like to look like a hood."

Carl says that, "just like that!" [at snap of fingers], he can get his friends to help him escape from juvenile hall or YA. "About that tape [tape recording of interview, at juvenile hall] . . . If I don't get a foster home in six weeks [i.e., after going to board at NRCC], it's going to be real bad! I wouldn't feel—something would happen! . . . That judge lied to me. He said he would recommend me for the community. . . . I ain't going to get sent to Preston [large YA institution]. It's a rotten place. I know lots of guys that's been there. . . . I'm going to work my way out of [going] there. I gotta get out [of juvenile hall] and see somebody [to arrange about not going to Preston]!"

As to preadolescence, "I always remember me as a punk. I was nothin!" Starting around age 10, "my father was kinda' rotten, so we started stealing. After that I just wouldn't take no stuff [i.e., orders] from anyone. There was somethin' that was bothering me . . . somethin' that was telling me 'Don't do it.

Don't take no stuff from anyone.' . . . When it tells me 'Don't do it,' you ain't gonna make me do it. I'll never do it!"

Carl feels that, prior to age 10, some of his troubles started because he was kicked out of school after fighting with a teacher who had "shoved me"—and "nobody does that to me!" However, he believes his "real troubles got started when I wouldn't do anything my father would tell me. 'Cause there's somethin' that happened between my mother and father when we were real small [Carl was around 10] . . . somethin' real bad. I'll never tell anyone what it was but it was somethin' I saw done quite a bit. I don't know why he did it. . . . He did it in front of us kids. I don't know why. Well, he thought my mom was goin' out on him or somethin' like that. I don't think so. It wasn't true! . . . But ever since then I just won't listen to him."

Around that time "he [father] left us. . . . We worked like dogs to get some money. I gave my money to my mom. Then he came back and asked my mom for another chance. I told her not to give him a chance, but she did. That's how all my troubles started. I couldn't take anything from anybody. . . . When people ask me if he's my father, sometimes I say No, sometimes I say Yes. If you think I'm ashamed of my father, I *am*! . . . He hates my guts. There's always somethin' bothering him. He's always jumping on me. Nobody else but *me*, Carl!" Carl feels it was his father's fault that he and his siblings were "sent away" to an orphanage when he was 10; Carl says "that shows he's no good."

Carl describes his mother as "real nice. She's real quiet. She's always doing somethin' for us. . . . If anyone touches her, I'll kill them!"

"I always dream about something that pisses me off. I wake up from my dreams and go Bam [demonstrates act of smashing his clenched fist into wall]! . . . Sometimes I dream that somebody is killing somebody, or somebody is beating up on somebody—slapping somebody. I don't know who it is—who is slapping or who is hit. And I wake up, you know, all like that [demonstrates bodily tension, and readiness to spring], and ready to kill somebody, ready to beat up somebody."

Carl likes dancing ("I'm the dirtiest dancer"), guitar playing, and staying out late. He says, "I can get any girl I want, if I really want her!" He also says that the happiest time of his life was "when I had my girlfriend. I'll marry her someday unless she does somethin' wrong. I don't think she will. She's not that kind of girl." Carl wants to eventually become a pipe layer or construction worker. He likes work that "makes me sweat," and considers this the opposite of his father's type of work.

View of Youth, by Others
The father states that Carl, for years, has taken pleasure in doing things he shouldn't do (e.g., stay out overnight without permission; not return home for several days), and has often threatened to leave home if the family tries to stand in his way. The father and Maria are seldom able to learn anything about Carl's friends, his activities, or his whereabouts, even though they've tried. Neither of them object to his YA commitment.

The father feels that Carl, when paroled, should not be returned home since he "would only run away" and his general behavior might cost the father his job. Maria is often embarrassed—personally and for the family—by Carl's behavior, clothes, and mannerisms. She, too, feels he probably would not succeed at home.

NRCC staff see Carl as "a somewhat retarded . . . distrustful, boastful adolescent. . . . His manipulations and/or fabrications were flimsy and somewhat immature." CTP staff describe him as being "of dull-normal intellect. . . . A very angry boy, but, more frequently than not, capable of handling his anger. He doesn't like people to control him and defends against probable realization of some of his inadequacies by extensive boasting, denial and projection. He sees the world as a basically hostile place and states an awareness that his family, particularly his father but not necessarily his mother, has rejected him."

Group Conformist (General Description)
These youths usually gravitate toward delinquency-oriented individuals and groups of individuals of their own age. As a result, they are sometimes called "gang kids." They often derive satisfaction from the thought of being seen, by peers, as one who is skilled at "outguessing the cops" and is "loyal to the guys." With many such youths, much of their energy is spent on maintaining this delinquent image, and self-image. With the remaining youths, the illegal activities *are*

enjoyed, but the individuals do not wish to think of themselves as "real" delinquents; in fact, they are far from completely dependent on their delinquent friends for approval or recognition.

Group conformists often wish to be seen, by delinquent peers, as "hard," "cool," and "tough." Unlike manipulators, they seldom try to be leaders; moreover, they seldom try to "con" or ride herd over their peers. They are usually content with the thought of being accepted as "one of the boys."

When interacting with correctional personnel, group conformists generally state that they are fairly satisfied with themselves, and that they have few if any unmanageable problems. Troubles with the law, yes; difficulties, perhaps; but serious problems, no. They generally blame people in authority, or the environment in general, for difficulties that may be glaringly obvious or that they feel there would be no point in trying to deny. But, even as they do this, they attempt to avoid any open confrontation with "the man" (authority figure) to whom they may be speaking. For one thing, they are not that confident they can "win" if they candidly express their attitudes concerning delinquency. So, in situations of this type, their usual approach is to just "cool it."

Many people describe these youths in terms that range from "polite" and "enjoyable to talk with," on the one hand, to "emotionally uninvolved," "indifferent," "shallow," passive-aggressive, implacable, and undependable, on the other. Only occasionally are they described as callous, cruel, or extremely hostile. People rarely become angered or incensed by their actions, for they rarely feel these individuals have tried to "use" them or harm them in a calculated or personalized way, as opposed to a stereotype-based manner. (See Chapter 15 for related description.)

In sum, group conformists usually go along with the rules that people in authority have established. Whether inside or outside of lockup, their conformity is often a way of either "cooling the situation," "outsmarting the man" in the presence of valued peers, avoiding loss of face, or forestalling possible punishment. Their compliance usually comes to an end soon after the authority figures try to reduce their involvement in illegal behavior, whether in relation to transient delinquent groups or well-established gangs.

Group Conformist (Case Illustration)

Art is age 14.8, 5'6" tall, and 136 pounds. Birthplace: Redding, California. Lives in racially mixed, lower middle-class area of Sacramento, one that is average in terms of crime rate. Resides in low-rent, dilapidated, extremely unkempt home.

Prior Record

Age 12—grand theft, auto. Age 13—beyond parental control. Age 14—truancy (at this point Art was placed into county boys camp).

YA Committing Offense

Boys camp runaway two weeks after arrival, combined with auto theft and burglary. Among the co-offenders were Art's older brother, already on parole, and a second YA parolee. Art believes his actions were justified: "I wouldn't have stole a car if I didn't escape from the Ranch. . . . I wouldn't have escaped if they hadn't sent me there. . . . They shouldn't have sent me there anyway. I just wanted to drop out [of school] and get a job."

Family Situation

Art's parents are separated, possibly divorced. The mother, age 36, gives contradictory stories as to whether the divorce has been finalized. The father, age 41, lives locally. All children live with Art's mother. The oldest, a boy of 18, is unemployed, out of school, and on probation for auto theft. A boy of 17, co-offender in YA committing offense, was on parole but is not being reinstitutionalized. A girl of 16 is on probation for frequent truancy. Another girl, age 13, has no record of delinquency. (Fifteen months after Art's YA commitment, this girl committed suicide.) Art's remaining sibling is three months old, and of uncertain paternity.

The family is on welfare and has experienced considerable financial difficulty for several years. It has made over 20 moves during the past two years, all within California. Mother says this is because she never seems to "feel settled anywhere." Art thinks it's because they usually can't pay the rent.

Mother states that she and Art's father separated two years ago, after years of conflict caused by his being an "alcoholic." One year later, Art and his sisters were placed with their father, by court order. Two months after that, the court removed them from the father's home—and returned them to the mother's home—because of his excessive drinking. The father, who has a short police record (disturbing the peace; fighting), believes he provided an adequate environment for the youngsters during that time.

School, Paid Employment, Etc.

Art's school difficulties emerged at age nine (very poor grades; fights with peers; verbal abuse of teacher, and resulting suspensions), and have continued to the present in greater or lesser degree. His IQ scores are somewhat below normal (high 80s). Art has never had a job.

Youth's View of Self and Others

Art considers himself to be rather "cool," and the opposite of "a punk." He is especially pleased with his ability to defend himself physically, and to stick with a decision once he's made up his mind. He gets nervous only when locked up or is faced with the possibility of lockup. He says he's never liked school, has never done well in it, and simply does not want to continue. He likes to "shoot pool," drink a little, smoke a lot, and "hang around with my friends."

Art's friends are "mostly parolees—just guys you meet downtown. . . . The dudes [police] don't bother with us too much, . . . [but still] most all my friends get in a little trouble. . . . I'm one of them—but I don't follow nobody! . . . I don't take nothin' unless I can use it—or I'll need it. Like when I took that car." Art describes himself as very loyal to friends and always ready to cover up for them. He likes friends "who can fight real good." He, himself, greatly enjoys fighting. Art says that his 18-year-old brother used to beat him up almost every day and sometimes still does, in half-friendly, half-angry fighting. "I'd get *him* a few times, too!" Art adds that this brother, whom he likes a lot, really likes him, and often loans him his driver's license.

Art feels his mom is "a good mother . . . she takes care of the kids." He states it's nobody's business to know more about her than that. He feels his father is also "OK," and that he would be glad to live with him again. He figures the court returned him (Art) to the home of his mother, last year, because his father "used our money" for liquor, then began pawning household items to buy more liquor, and finally "went on a three-day binge." Art didn't like this but figures that's the way his father is when it comes to drinking. Art feels it won't make much difference where he lives once he's on parole, since "I don't spend lots of time at home anyway."

As to the CTP program, "Well, I guess I'd be out [of an institution] at least." However, if he is sent to an institution rather than CTP, he believes he'll be able to manage it: "It didn't hurt my brother too much. I mean it didn't bother him too much."

View of Family and Youth, by Others
His father says that all the youngster's troubles are the fault of Art's mother. (Earlier this year he told probation staff that his own inability to support the wife and children was the cause of his family's problems.) He believes she can't control them as well as he can, and that she seldom tries to do so. The father would like Art to live with him again, someday, and has visited him a number of times at NRCC.

Art's mother believes his troubles are the fault of the father: "It just seems to make them [all the boys] get picked up more often," when they stay with him. She feels that, because he's been a serious "alcoholic" for years, the father has never tried to control their behavior, but, instead, just "lets them roam around." She believes some of Art's troubles were also caused by his dislike for school, and recalls no difficulties with the law prior to his first problems at school (age nine). His mother does not think Art's problems relate to any of his friends; also, she states she knows nothing about who his friends are or what he and they do together.

View of Family and Youth, by Staff
CTP staff see Art's parents as having let him and his brothers fend for themselves, for several years. In large part, the parents seem to "look the other way" when the boys get in trouble, and to cover up for them as needed. Apart from this, Art's mother seems to be rejecting or at least avoiding him at the present time: She did not visit him at NRCC, nor did she tell him, earlier in the year, about her summer trip to Los Angeles with Art's three younger siblings. During the Initial Home Visit Interview, the mother did not suggest that Art be returned to her home, when he is paroled. CTP staff feel "this is probably due to the fact that she did not even consider it a possibility," in view of the

family's history of delinquency and physical instability. She has no idea of where he might live—relatives included.

Probation staff viewed Art as "delinquently oriented, aggressive, and showing little or no remorse." NRCC living unit staff saw him as "very withdrawn . . . appears calm and unemotional . . . no leadership quality. . . . Relationship with staff is good, but seldom. . . . Becomes somewhat confused at encouragement or compliments."

CTP staff see him as extremely guarded but not openly hostile. Talks very little, but, when he does, he tries to convey impression of being wily and difficult to deceive. Seems "totally nonchalant" toward—and accepting of—delinquent behavior on the part of his friends, his brothers, and himself. Except for his belief that his father is against his dropping out of school, Art seems to feel little if any pressure from parents to do anything other than what he's already doing. He appears to assume that they disapprove of neither his friends, his brothers, nor himself.

Passive-Conformist Youths
Passive-Conformist (General Description)
These youths see themselves as being much less adequate than the vast majority of their peers. They also view themselves as "low man on the totem pole" among siblings, and of little value in the eyes of one or both parents. They usually prefer to remain in the background or on the fringes of things; and, most often, they are rather quiet and fairly easy to get along with. Still, they are often quite worried and afraid, and are not infrequently described as "scared rabbits."

Passive-conformists are largely dominated by a need for social or "external" approval, and for related forms of reassurance and acceptance. They try to obtain this via an almost total, unquestioning compliance with the rules and standards of various individuals or groups of individuals. These may include nondelinquent adults and peers, or else delinquently oriented peers; it seldom seems to matter *which*, as far as the youths are concerned. Yet, no matter how compliant they feel they have been, passive-conformists usually continue to believe that adults and peers may be on the verge of rejecting, humiliating, punishing, or somehow exploiting them.

Despite their constant attempts to be

accepted, and viewed as an "OK guy," they usually remain lonely and depressed. As a result, they are often described as "pathetic" and "lacking in any feeling of belonging or support." Along similar lines they are often described as lacking, for the most part, a set of "internalized standards" or ideals to which they feel committed, and in terms of which they might evaluate themselves, guide their behavior, and derive a sense of personal satisfaction or accomplishment.

In sum, passive-conformists usually interact with adults on a child-to-parent basis, not on an adolescent-to-adult basis. They have few intellectual defenses against disapproval or rejection by others. They are often prepared to "run"—that is, physically get away from—situations in which they anticipate disapproval, punishment, or rejection. This is especially true if they reach the conclusion that such reactions, by others, will result from their own inability to satisfy what they, the youths, regard as the overly stringent or perhaps conflicting demands of others—demands that the youths also feel unable to alter.

Passive-Conformist (Case Illustration)
Bill is age 17.7, 5'7" tall, and 155 pounds. Birthplace: Philadelphia, Pennsylvania. He lives in semirural, lower-income area of Sacramento, in which there is occasional gang warfare between rival youth groups. Bill sides with one such group but manages to keep clear of burglaries and most fights.

Prior Record
Age 15—drunkenness. Age 15—petty theft. Age 17—glue sniffing. Age 17—beyond parental control.

YA Committing Offense
Beyond parental control (frequently stayed out until midnight; often sniffed glue). Bill feels there is nothing wrong with someone his age remaining out until midnight. Says he sniffed glue "cause I can't drink . . . and it's fun. . . . It makes me feel braver. . . . I once beat up someone when I was on glue. . . . My friends do it [sniff glue], and if I don't do it they call me chicken." "I don't think that what I did was bad because I did not do a burglary."

Family Situation
His natural father, age 42, is whereabouts un-
known. His stepfather, age 41, and natural mother, age 37, live with Bill, his 15-year old natural brother, and his five half-siblings, ages 4 through 13. The siblings have no record of delinquency. The family has never been on welfare. The home is adequately kept up, physically.

His natural father deserted Bill's mother shortly after she first became pregnant (with Bill). He briefly returned about two years later and again deserted her after she became pregnant a second time; this time he did not return. They divorced when Bill was just under two years of age. Bill has no memory of his natural father. His mother and stepfather were married when Bill was four; neither one has a record of delinquency.

School, Paid Employment, Etc.
Except for physical education and art, Bill received poor grades in school since age nine. He often seemed apathetic and indifferent, and would "play around a lot in class." Bill has been on indefinite suspension status for several months. His IQ scores are noticeably, but not markedly, below normal (low 80s).

According to mother, when Bill realized he would not be allowed to return to school, he cried a great deal, became depressed, and soon afterward began staying out late. He also started to associate with local gangs and began sniffing glue for perhaps the first time. Bill has held a few jobs, but only briefly. He was once laid off because he could not add up the cost of customer purchases.

Youth's View of Self and Others
"I guess I'm normal . . . guess I'm OK." He does not consider himself a delinquent; for example, he can't imagine himself ever stealing a car even though some of his friends do steal, and he feels that friends are very important. He sometimes wonders why *he* gets caught for sniffing glue, whereas his friends, who do some "real *bad* things," "hardly ever get caught" for anything. Bill gets upset when people, mostly adults, disapprove of him after he's tried to please them. He says he can get along OK as long as he knows what people expect of him. However, he believes he'd be happier if his parents let him do more things on his own. He feels his mother shouldn't keep telling him which clothes to wear, what kind of haircut to get, and how to comb his hair.

He describes his mother as "nice . . . just like other mothers . . . [except that] she don't let my friends visit the house . . . and she gets real mad when we don't obey her." "She wants to keep me out of trouble. . . . She blames my friends when I get in trouble." Bill likes the fact that his stepfather is less strict than his mother. He and his stepfather "don't get mad at each other."

View of Youth, by Others
His mother believes Bill's friends are the entire cause of his troubles. She states they are all older than him, that "they come and get Bill . . . take him out with them . . . [and] they all don't get back 'til early morning." "I don't know what to do with Bill because he just doesn't listen to me anymore. I hope they don't turn him loose again right away, because he needs some kind of help."

Until a year ago Bill preferred to play outdoors with individuals much younger than himself. He would also spend much time in his room, either by himself or with his younger brother and half-siblings. He is reported to have enjoyed playing marbles until age 15 or 16.

View of Family and Youth, by Staff
CTP staff note that, according to the mother, Bill can do almost nothing right by himself. The mother appears to involve herself in minute details of his life, as though he were an extension of her—not just a "social invalid"—with few rights to his own ideas and decisions. Also, she does not feel he can be trusted to go to dances. She is quite harsh when speaking with him in presence of staff, and rarely asks him for his opinion. His stepfather generally remains in the background. His mother is eager, and his stepfather would be happy, to have him returned home whenever he is paroled.

In juvenile hall (shortly before coming to NRCC), Bill actively sought staff approval and was "compliant and ingratiating." During periods of staff/youth conflict he "consistently sided with staff against the peer group." He stated, "You be good to them [staff] and they'll be good to you. You do something wrong, and they'll lock you up." NRCC living unit staff feel he has "accepted our program . . . relates well with the staff but prefers to stay away from them . . . is well-mannered and polite . . . responds favorably to encouragement."

CTP staff describe Bill as a kind of "puppy dog" who is eternally falling all over himself to get on their good side, and who seems to genuinely admire a number of them. To look at his face one would think he was almost a preadolescent, certainly "no older than 14." They believe he considers the peer group a place where he can act independently of his mother and where conformity or passivity is a small, not unpleasant, and not unfamiliar price to pay for acceptance and continued participation.

Having described the main youth types that were worked with at the Community Treatment Project, we may now ask: What approaches were used with these individuals? How did CTP attempt to intervene in their lives?

Notes
1. As it turns out, in the present descriptions the commonly observed (i.e., within-group) characteristics outnumber the distinguishing (between-group) characteristics. Largely for this reason, these descriptions need not be thought of as ideal types that are seldom observed in real life.
2. For example, Jim, the anxious-confused youth, is a good deal more confrontive than most individuals within this subtype. Similarly, Bill, the passive-conformist, is considerably more optimistic than most youngsters within this group—that is, more optimistic regarding the anticipated, short-term outcome of his interactions with authority figures and peers.
3. This is one expression of "regression toward the mean."
4. It was gathered by essentially the same techniques as well.
5. The offense history of the "average" individual who was sent to the YA after Phases 1 and 2 (1961–1969)—for example, sent during Phase 3 (1969–1974)— was substantially longer than that of the earlier-mentioned youths. (This was partly a function of increasing age at commitment.) In addition, it contained a much lower percentage of status offenses and a substantially higher percentage of assaultive offenses. Beginning in 1977, status offenses could no longer be the basis for a YA commitment.
6. Normal range is usually defined as 90 to 110, on standard tests of intellectual ability.

6 METHODS OF INTERVENTION

This chapter will focus on the following question: What methods of intervention were used at the Community Treatment Project during Phases 1 and 2? The question will be answered separately for conflicted, power-oriented, and passive-conformist youths, since the methods used were rather different for each. That is, the differences among these methods outweighed the similarities.[1]

For each group of youths, the method in question will be described from three different angles. First there will be a condensed account of the overall pattern of intervention, as used with the typical youth.[2] This description will focus on goals, treatment methods, controls, placement, and so on. It is derived from daily observations of agents and youths plus hundreds of interviews of youths by on-site researchers, extending over several years.[3] These data sources, in turn, are supported by (1) detailed case files on each individual youth and by (2) formal interviews (and more frequent informal discussions), by researchers, with those agents. This account of intervention will be presented in the form of *plans and prescriptions* (e.g., parole agent should "place youth at home initially, if parents are willing to accept his return and if he himself is willing"), even though it reflects the approach that was in fact *used*—not simply planned or prescribed for use.

Next will come a brief account of intervention as further expressed by CTP agents. This will relate to areas of major focus (e.g., goals), agent/youth relationship, personal involvement and decision-making by youth, and so on. This account is based on the agent's response to a 200-item opinion questionnaire.[4]

Agent opinions will be presented as a series of statements (actually, specific questionnaire items), each of which they clearly endorsed.[5] That is, agents regarded each statement as an accurate reflection of how they interacted, and felt they should interact, with the youths in question. Other statements will also be presented; these represent approaches the agents did not use, and which they specifically rejected. (See endnote 6 regarding *endorsement* and *rejection*.) When responding to the questionnaire, agents were instructed to "bear in mind, we are not asking you what should be held as ideal, but rather what *you do* with this type of youth." Their responses were to focus on, without being limited to, the youths' first eight to fifteen months on parole. As will be described, there was considerable agreement between the research observations plus interviews and discussions, mentioned earlier, and the views expressed by parole agents. Together, these accounts provide a converging, fairly comprehensive description of the overall approach that was used; that is, they provide an integrated and reasonably complete account of the major features of each such approach. Mainly due to space limitations, no attempt has been made to describe the many intricacies and particulars of intervention, as practiced at CTP.

Finally, there will be a brief review of five program elements that were presented in Chapter 3: counseling, pragmatically oriented discussion and planning, limit-setting, collateral contacts, and short-term detention. Here the question will be: How *often* were these elements used in the case of (1) participants and (2) the "typical" youth (participants and nonparticipants combined)?[7] The answer will be stated in terms of the number of agent/youth contacts per month, and the time period that is covered will be the individual's entire YA career. (Supplementary information is presented in Appendix 8, with respect to their first 12 months on parole.) This quantitative perspective can add an important element of reality to the preceding accounts. The information in question was obtained from a systematic review of case folders on 207 stratified, randomly selected youths. (See Chapter 11, endnote 45.)

After these accounts have been presented we will mention a number of approaches that were used with all three groups. The chapter will conclude with a review of selected issues: personalized versus impersonal interaction between agent and youth; caring versus neutrality or indifference; use of internal motivation and personal initiative versus use of external structure, surveillance, and demand; development of youth's own values versus imposition of agent's/society's values alone; focus on "strengths" versus focus on "sickness" or defect. Some of these issues were approached in different ways with differing groups of youth.

Intervention with Conflicted Youths
Overall Pattern of Intervention
Goals

Long-range goals include elimination of delinquent behavior; increased level of functioning in school, job, family, and related areas; and reduction or resolution of internal conflicts. Major subgoals include changed self-image in direction of capacity for enjoyment, sense of personal worth, and sense of basic acceptability to others as a maturing individual; and greater awareness of personal limitations and needs. Other goals include increased feeling as to the legitimacy of own needs and reduced use of defense mechanisms in ways that are harmful to self and others.

Stance and Strategies

Strong or primary emphasis on symptoms of underlying conflict (including delinquent behavior) is largely useless, and may be counterproductive. Instead, the agent should concentrate on underlying feelings and problems. This should not preclude his introducing a realistic initial structure.

Encourage youth to explore the social or interpersonal environment; allow him to experience the consequences of his exploratory actions. Give him time to integrate new roles

and tentative decisions with other aspects of his overall pattern of adjustment, for example, his areas of strength or limitation, and his changing standards or ideals. The agent should provide clear emotional support while conflicts are being resolved, especially at times of crisis. Emotional support should be offered in ways that avoid or minimize serious threat to the youth's conscious self-image (e.g., image of autonomy or masculinity).

Treatment Methods

Major methods are individual, group, and/or family counseling—or psychotherapy—with emphasis on the development of insight into personal conflicts and family problems, and improved social functioning. Initial structure, activity groups, school tutoring, and/or environmental manipulation may also be appropriate as ways of achieving long-range goals or major subgoals.

Controls

Although the major focus should be on utilization or development of internal, psychological controls, external, agent-imposed controls may be necessary, especially in the beginning. The content of external controls should be consistent with the youth's expectations, to the extent possible. By deliberately challenging the agent's rules or controls, the youth may raise issues that relate to trust, personal acceptance, dependency, counterdependency, or the impact of his impulses. Any of these issues may provide a forum for discussing various relationship patterns, for helping the youth understand his defenses and modes of adjustment, and for communicating the agent's support and concern.

Related or Additional Approaches

May use formal family counseling or therapy if (1) mother and father figures, and other relevant family members, are available, (2) all family members agree to participate, and (3) individual contacts between agent and youth seem largely unnecessary. Informal family counseling or conferences may occur if these conditions cannot be met. In this case, individual and/or group methods may also be used.

Placement

Place youth at home initially, if parents are willing to accept his return and if he himself is willing.[8] However, if the youth's family is unavailable, clearly rejecting of the youth, or unwilling/unable to modify major problem-producing interactions, the youth may be placed in a foster or group home on a temporary or permanent basis. Psychological emancipation from the parents' home will begin when the youth recognizes why this is the best or the only realistic solution to his placement needs. Some such recognition must usually precede the actual placement. Independent placement, or placement with relatives, may also be a viable alternative.

The characteristics of an appropriate out-of-home placement (foster home or group home) include: a substitute home that will provide a base from which youth may work on resolution of internal conflicts; it will offer initial and continued emphasis on open communication and explanation of motives, to head off or eliminate misinterpretations; substitute parents who will permit youth to take much of the initiative in determining the nature and extent of their relationship; they can relate flexibly to the youth on the closeness/distance dimension; they must be permissive regarding the youth's continued relationship with his own family. Since the youth may reenact parts of his family problem within the foster or group home setting, the agent should offer interpretation and support to the substitute parents, as needed.

School and Employment

Since the major issues relate to the youth's underlying personal or interpersonal conflicts, school and employment, as such, may be viewed as secondary factors in the beginning. However, they may become important in their own right as a way of developing the youngster's overall potential, and ability to function, especially as he begins to deal successfully with his underlying difficulties. In any event, the significance of school and employment will vary from youth to youth and from one phase of his program to the next.

Peer Group

If the intervention plan is largely focused on individual counseling or psychotherapy, the youth may still be encouraged to participate in social activities with an I_4 peer group in order to increase his fund of interpersonal skills and satisfactions. Alternately, he may be asked to assist with lower maturity youths as a way of enhancing his self-concept and sense of value to others.

Leisure Time

Project-sponsored activities may be used as a supplement to specific methods of intervention. The parole agent may offer activities that can be satisfying to the youth and which may meet his status needs in ways that are acceptable to the larger culture. He may involve the youth in sports, especially those in which the youth can compete with himself (e.g., golf, weight lifting, track). Team responsibility is very difficult for some conflicted youths to handle, especially at intake.

Community Supports

These are usually not too relevant to the individual's delinquent behavior problems, at intake. The parole agent may obtain information for the youth, and may encourage participation in community activities, as progress is made in other areas.

Agent's Description of Intervention with Conflicted Youths

In the following, statements that are followed by the word "*Rejected*"—in parentheses—were specifically rejected, that is, the agents disagreed with them. All other statements (i.e., views) were clearly endorsed by the agents.

Areas of Major Focus

- My main goal of treatment is to clear up internal conflicts.
- I am a "sounding board" or "listening post," as a major role.
- I ask questions which lead the youth to evaluate his feelings and goals.
- I try to help the youth learn "who" and "what" he is—that is, resolve identity and adequacy problems.
- I help the youth see that his behavior is related to his conflicts and feelings of guilt, generated within the family.[9]
- I work primarily with *feelings,* more than with performance.

Agent/Youth Relationship

- I spend much time developing a relationship with the youth . . . as a bridge to helping him learn how to have better relationships elsewhere.

- I stress the help of a relationship rather than the help of such things as money, transportation, or clothes.
- I keep communications clear by clarifying feelings about what is happening between me and the youth.
- I try to communicate that I understand the feelings and emotional investments of the youth.
- I often have to define the limits of my availability to the youth—as, for example, by telling him when I can, and will, see him. (*Rejected*)
- I try to relate to the youth by giving respect as an equal, and by respecting his values.
- I talk with the youth in a direct way about how we are relating to one another.
- I often share my personal values, and other things about myself, with the youth.

Personal Involvement, Decision-Making, and Conformity[10]
- I let the youth take responsibility for his own life pattern, and allow him to help determine the [original] treatment plan.
- I give the youth alternatives and make him decide things for himself.
- I avoid giving the youth a dependent child role—for example, I let him enroll himself in school, or look for a job on his own.
- I use the youth's acting-out behavior to point out how he is self-defeating.
- I point out how the youth is not meeting his own expectations, and I use this (in discussions) to get at underlying reasons.
- I present my standards, but do not punish the youth for nonconformance with them.
- I have the job of convincing the youth that societal prescriptions are the way. (*Rejected*)

Agent Stance, and Selected Activities
- I play a protective role, such as getting the youth out of a jam and making sure he knows it. (*Rejected*)
- I try to find a job situation where the youth can work with little interpersonal demand. (*Rejected*)
- Treatment in group (e.g., counseling group) is the method of first choice, for this youth. (*Rejected*)

- Group meetings with the youth are more activity-oriented than discussion-oriented. (*Rejected*)
- I directly discuss and review the progress of the treatment process, with the youth.

Behavior Control, Surveillance, and Sanctions
- I try to use the youth's internal values to get him to control his behavior.
- I set clear and controlling limits, for example, regarding curfew and delinquent activities. (*Rejected*)
- I use the project peer group to put pressure on the youth to control himself. (*Rejected*)
- I avoid doing things that are checking-up type behavior. I avoid looking like a "cop."
- I take action quickly and decisively when the youth misbehaves. (*Rejected*)
- I make the youth responsible for failure to follow through on his agreements to perform, by taking privileges or freedom away from him. (*Rejected*)

Selected Program Elements Used with Conflicted Youths
Counseling
For participants, the average number of sessions per month was: individual counseling—6.2; group counseling—1.6; family counseling—0.6. Participants took part in a total of 6.8 counseling sessions a month (82 a year), in one form or another.[11] Thirty to 35 percent of all counseling sessions involved psychotherapy, as defined in Chapter 3.

For the typical youth (participants plus nonparticipants), the number of sessions per month was: individual counseling—2.5; group counseling—0.6; family counseling—0.3. These youths were involved in a total of 2.7 counseling sessions a month (32 a year), of one form or another. (See Tables 6–1 and 6–2.)

Pragmatically Oriented Interactions
For participants, there was one such session a month. For the "typical" youth, there was one every two months.

Limit-Setting
For participants, limit-setting was used once a month. For the typical youth it was used once every two months.

TABLE 6–1

Number of Contacts per Month between Agent and Youth, throughout Youth Authority Career

Sample and Type of Contact	Type of Youth		
	Conflicted	Power-Oriented	Passive-Conformist
I. Participants Only			
Counseling			
Individual	6.2	4.1	4.4
Group	1.6	1.5	2.4
Family	0.6	0.2	0.8
Pragmatically Oriented			
Interactions	1.0	0.9	0.9
Limit-Setting	1.0	3.1	1.9
Collateral Contacts	0.8	0.7	0.9
II. Typical Youths*			
Counseling			
Individual	2.5	2.8	2.6
Group	0.6	1.4	1.6
Family	0.3	0.1	0.3
Pragmatically Oriented			
Interactions	0.5	0.7	0.6
Limit-Setting	0.5	2.4	1.2
Collateral Contacts	0.3	0.5	0.5

*Includes participants and nonparticipants, that is, the total sample.

Collateral Contacts
For participants, there was slightly less than one such contact a month. For the typical youth there was one every three or four months.

Short-term Detention
The following information covers the youth's entire YA career. The average number of detentions per youth was 1.4—one detention for every 17 months on parole. The average number of days per detention was 22. (If one unduly long detention had not occurred, the average would drop to 19 days.) The number of agent/youth contacts during each detention was 3. The total number of days in detention was 31—again, during the youth's entire YA career.

Intervention with Power-Oriented Youths
Overall Pattern of Intervention
Goals
Long-range goals include elimination of delinquent behavior; increased level of functioning in school, family, and related areas; changed self-definition in direction of nondelinquency, and greater recognition of the legitimacy of efforts by authority figures; and clear recognition that satisfying interactions with peers and adults can take place on an honest, caring basis rather than a deceptive, exploitive, or self-centered basis.

Major subgoals include increasing youth's social perceptiveness and helping him form a more accurate cause-and-effect connection between his own behavior and the feelings or responses of others; reducing his fear of close, meaningful relationships with others, and of more direct expression of dependency needs; reducing his need to maintain a compensatory image of self as invincible or expertly elusive; and reducing his negative stereotypes of adults and authority figures, and his defensive use of projection and displacement.

Other goals include reducing his feeling that being controlled by others (i.e., by a concerned parole agent) is equivalent to "being destroyed" or emasculated; helping him learn that most adult males are neither "weak, pathetic,

TABLE 6–2

Amount of Specified Short-Term Detention throughout
Youth Authority Career, for Three Youth Types[a]

Youth Type and Variable	Purpose of Detention			
	Therapeutic and/or Behavior Control	Investigation and Situational[b]	Response to Minor Offense[c]	Total or Average[d]
I. Conflicted				
Number of Detentions per Youth	0.6	0.1	0.7	1.4
Number of Days in Detention per Youth	8	3	20	31
Number of Days in Detention per Detention	14	34[e]	30	23
Number of Agent/Youth Contacts per Detention	3.8	2.0	2.7	3.1
II. Power-Oriented				
Number of Detentions per Youth	4.2	0.9	0.9	6.0
Number of Days in Detention per Youth	34	30	11	75
Number of Days in Detention per Detention	8	34	12	13
Number of Agent/Youth Contacts per Detention	2.0	5.8	2.5	2.7
III. Passive-Conformist				
Number of Detentions per Youth	1.0	0.6	0.6	2.2
Number of Days in Detention per Youth	23	12	10	45
Number of Days in Detention per Detention	23	21	17	21
Number of Agent/Youth Contacts per Detention	2.4	1.5	2.5	2.2

[a]Includes participants and nonparticipants.
[b]See text for definition.
[c]See text for definition.
[d]*Total* relates to *Number of Detentions per Youth* and to *Number of Days in Detention per Youth. Average* applies to the remaining variables.
[e]One such detention was extremely long: 61 days. If this entry were excluded, the average number of days in detention per detention (for investigation and situational purposes) would be 18, not 34. Similarly, for all types of detention combined (col. 4), the average number of days in detention would be 20, not 23.

and contemptible," nor "dangerous, destructive, and phony."

Stance and Strategies
The agent should create situations in which honest views and genuine feelings can be expressed by the youth and rewarded by the agent. He should also create situations that do the following: Encourage the youth to try new activities; reward him for efforts made, not just for things accomplished; directly meet some of his dependency needs in order to reduce his reliance on compensatory mechanisms such as denial of need or automatic rejection of others as potential need gratifiers; demonstrate concern for the youth's future by being willing to control his delinquent or destructive behavior *before* his future is seriously

jeopardized; convey a message that he is *worth* controlling rather than rejecting—and "sending up"—as one who is apparently hopeless; demonstrate that real understanding (by agent, of youth) need not lead to dislike, exploitation, hurt feelings, or rejection (by agent); via direct interaction, demonstrate that he (agent) can cope with destructive or deceptive parent(s) without being "done in," and without responding in kind.

Treatment Methods

Use mixture of group treatment and individual contacts, if possible. Scheduled individual contacts should initially center around school, employment, or family arrangements/problems. Unscheduled individual contacts can occur around any of several crisis situations; here, agent will often play role of buffer between youth and other individuals. Attendance and participation in group sessions should initially occur two or three times a week if possible, on a mandatory basis. Role-training sessions may be included as part of the group. In individual and group contacts alike, emphasis should be on current interpersonal problems and realities, not on past history and underlying dynamics.

Controls

Use of external controls and explicit limit-setting cannot be avoided with these youths, at least initially. The agent's expectations and rules should be very clear, as should the fact that penalties will occur if the rules are not followed. A communications network should be set up, one that will provide the agent with information regarding the youth's fringe delinquency, and regarding his school, employment, and/or family situation.

The youth must learn that someone can and will control several aspects of his life—for the express purpose of preventing him from committing "social suicide" (e.g., being institutionalized for many months or years as a result of continued delinquent behavior). The youth should repeatedly be shown that the agent is concerned enough to spend large amounts of time in an effort to keep him from getting into trouble or getting further and further "behind the eight ball." Controls are also useful in helping the agent gain the youngster's attention as someone to be reckoned with, especially during initial phase of his program. Unannounced drop-ins by the agent

may be useful in this regard. Ultimately, internal controls should replace external controls.

Related or Additional Approaches

Family counseling, formal or otherwise, is rarely agreed to by the youth's parents. The agent should nevertheless discuss and define the "good parent" image—with the youth's parents (or substitutes)—as one that involves demonstration of concern in terms of their placing clear external structure on the youth, and establishing clear, consistent guidelines for him. In discussing this, the agent should bear in mind that a marked laissez-faire attitude on the parents' part (1) may be a cover-up for indifference toward, or long-standing rejection of, the youth, and (2) is likely to be rationalized on grounds of "letting him (the youth) be independent." The agent should nevertheless encourage parents to handle the youth's behavior directly and immediately, in a firm, realistic, and warm manner. When possible, he should try to enhance, in the youth's eyes, the role or value of the same-sex parent, provided that the individual is available and at all motivated. Ultimately, however, a major confrontation between agent and parents may be unavoidable and essential, if youth is to survive in the community.

The agent may reduce stereotyping, on the part of youth, via peer-group feedback, role-playing, purposely responding in unexpected ways, and rewarding rather than punishing honest expressions and interactions by the youth.

Placement

Group conformists can often be placed with their own family or relatives, without great difficulty.[12] However, in the case of manipulators, initial placement with their own family is usually a major calculated risk. Characteristics of an acceptable home placement include: (1) parents are willing to go along with the agent's overall strategy, or at least will not undermine it; (2) parents neither encourage, reward, nor tacitly agree to the youth's delinquent or manipulative behavior; (3) parents are willing to communicate with the agent in a forthright manner, regarding the youth's infringement of agreements, or destructive behavior; and (4) clear, consistent external structure is usually present in the home. Because of their very strong—albeit mixed—feelings toward the natural parent(s), power-oriented youths (manipulators in particular) may have to be placed in their own home initially, even though few if any of these characteristics are present. Under such conditions, eventual emancipation from the home must be a major subgoal.

School and Employment

Initially, most power-oriented youths have great difficulty in public school and employment situations; in this respect they are likely to require a highly structured setting. For example: (1) careful planning will be needed to gear the school program or job to the individual's present level of ability and interest, if rejection (by youth or others) or probable failure are to be avoided; (2) the agent must give frequent support or interpretation to school personnel or employer, at least initially; and (3) consistent communication between the agent and school personnel or employer will be needed in order to independently verify the youth's attendance, behavior, or performance. If the youth cannot satisfy minimum standards of regular public school, continuation school or a CTP community center program may be substituted, or the public school program may itself be temporarily delayed, for example, for a semester or remainder of semester. The agent should give clear support to the youth for sincere job-hunting efforts.

Peer Group

The group conformist is usually acquainted with several delinquent peers, individuals with whom he is comfortable but not close. The agent should build a project peer group (composed mainly of I_3's) that will increasingly support nondelinquent attitudes and activities, and may eventually serve as an alternate or even primary source of satisfaction and status. At intake, the manipulator is seldom trusted by peers and is seldom a long-term member of any natural peer group. Here, the agent should try to build a peer group (again, largely I_3's) that (1) will point out the youth's phony or "conning" behavior, but will not reject him as an individual, and (2) will support him during crises.

Leisure Time

When the youth begins to view the agent and other project staff as "safe," accepting, or willing and able to meet some of his needs, he may start to spend more time at the community center. The agent should clearly support this; however, he should also encourage the youth's participation in outside activities that show promise of helping to build a reality-based sense of adequacy or worth. Project-sponsored recreational activities may sometimes be directed at alleviating cultural deprivation.

Community Supports

At the point of YA commitment, the power-oriented youth has little involvement in the official, local community structure. This is largely because he has preferred to engage in unsupervised and informal activities, or has been turned away by various organizations as a result of his comfort with delinquent behavior. The agent should nevertheless encourage the youth to participate in any community organization that might support his abilities or interests—recreational, athletic, or artistic—in nondestructive, nonexploitive ways. The agent should provide active help in this regard, by interacting on the youth's behalf, if necessary. The youth's family should be offered help in locating and utilizing community resources for itself as a *family;* and, the agent should be ready to personally follow through with the community or social agencies in question.

Agent's Description of Intervention with Power-Oriented Youths
Areas of Major Focus
- I must help the youth change his view of the world as a power struggle.
- I try to support the idea that the world will allow the youth to achieve.
- I try to help the youth reduce his stereotyped behavior and role.
- I explain reality and the consequences of his behavior to the youth, as a major activity.
- I have to deal in terms of external problems (e.g., school and employment), due to the youth's denial of internal problems.
- I help the youth see that his behavior is related to his conflicts and feelings of guilt, generated within the family. (Rejected)

Agent/Youth Relationship
- The youth is allowed a lot of psychological distance, until he is ready to trust me to be closer.
- I stress the help of a relationship rather than the help of such things as money, transportation, or clothes. (Rejected)
- I try to be very nonthreatening during

the early months of the relationship. (*Rejected*)

- I try to relate to the youth by giving respect as an equal, and by respecting his values. (*Rejected*)
- I make myself very available at virtually all times.
- When the youth begins to ask "why" I keep helping and giving, . . . *that* is when I interpret my "care" and concern for him.[13]

Personal Involvement and Decision-Making

- I convey the idea that I expect acceptable behavior, by setting limits and goals for the youth.[14]
- I let the youth take responsibility for his own life pattern, and allow him to help determine the (original) treatment plan. (*Rejected*)
- I give the youth alternatives and make him decide things for himself. (*Rejected*. This rejection mainly applies to the initial stages.)

Agent Stance and Selected Activities

- I play a protective role, such as getting the youth out of a jam and making sure he knows it. (*Rejected*)
- I help the youth locate and obtain jobs.
- I try to help employers, teachers, or other persons (e.g., foster parents) give supportive help toward the youth's development.
- Group meetings with the youth are more activity-oriented than discussion-oriented. (*Rejected*)
- I try to get the whole family engaged in family therapy or counseling. (*Rejected*)
- I make casual, nonformal-type contacts with the youth, as the best context of interaction. (*Rejected*)
- I try to be very alert to reward any acceptable behavior.

Behavior Control, Surveillance, and Sanctions

- I try to use the youth's internal values to get him to control his behavior. (*Rejected*)
- I set clear and controlling limits, for example, regarding curfew and delinquent activities.
- I check up on the youth's behavior to see

for sure what he's doing. I use all available resources, to do so.

- I show the youth that I know what's going on in his daily life, by relating and reviewing reports from others around him.
- I keep the youth uncertain as to what will happen by way of discipline, if he misbehaves.[15]
- I take action quickly and decisively when the youth misbehaves.
- I never give up the assurance that I will control the youth by locking him up if necessary.
- I make the youth responsible for failure to follow through on his agreements to perform, by taking privileges or freedom away from him.
- I do not necessarily do something about a missed meeting or interview: I don't insist on regular meetings/interviews. (*Rejected*)[16]

Selected Program Elements Used with Power-Oriented Youths

Counseling

For participants, the number of sessions per month was: individual counseling—4.1; group counseling—1.5; family counseling—0.2. These youths took part in a total of 4.9 counseling sessions a month (59 a year), of one form or another. Five to 10 percent of these sessions involved psychotherapy.

For typical youths (participants plus non-participants), the number of sessions was: individual counseling—2.8; group counseling—1.4; family counseling—0.1. They were involved in 3.4 counseling sessions a month (41 a year), of one form or another. (See Tables 6–1 and 6–2, on pages 73 and 74.)

Pragmatically Oriented Interactions

For participants, there was about one such session a month. For the "typical" youth there was about one every six weeks.

Limit-Setting

For participants, limit-setting was used three times a month. For the typical youth, it was used twice (2.4 times) a month.

Collateral Contacts

For participants, there was about one such contact every six weeks. For the typical youth there was one every two months.

Short-Term Detention
Relative to the youth's entire YA career, the average number of detentions was six—approximately two per year during parole. Each detention lasted an average of 13 days. There were about three agent/youth contacts per detention. The total number of days in detention per youth was 75—again, during the youth's entire YA career.

Intervention with Passive-Conformist Youths
Overall Pattern of Intervention
Goals
Long-range goals include elimination of delinquent behavior; increased level of functioning in school, job, family, and related areas; shift in loyalty from delinquent peers to nondelinquent peers and adults; and increased feelings of personal worth and of ability to recognize and stand up for his rights.

Major subgoals include marked decrease in fear of decision-making; increased sense of belonging relative to nondelinquent peers, and adults; increased recognition of, and differentiation among, his personal feelings; greater awareness of the legitimacy of his needs as a growing individual, not as an appendage to others; and increased awareness of how he is viewed by peers and adults, and of their social-emotional impact on him.

Other goals include developing the image of parole agent as a nonthreatening, caring individual, and encouraging identification with one or more adequate male adults (e.g., agent, foster parent, or schoolteacher).

Stance and Strategies
The agent should demonstrate support and concern for the youth, while minimizing the formidable threat that he (youth) perceives in the power of adults. The agent should not push for rapid change or "commitment" on the youth's part. He should label the youth's positive and negative feelings and frustrations as they occur, and should give frequent, concrete explanations as to what is happening between the youth and others.

During early phases of the program, the agent must often "nurture"; however, he should not try to make most of the decisions for the youth. To clearly demonstrate support and concern, he should rely heavily on actions, not just words: The agent may often

have to provide material things (food, clothing, transportation), and he should be prepared to give *large* quantities of time and personal attention to the youth.[17] The agent should often highlight and discuss, in concrete and specific terms, actions that the youth has taken on his own—again, without pushing for rapid change or commitment. He should reward the youth for participation and intention, not for level of performance or end product alone.

Treatment Methods
A combination of individual and group contacts should be used, with initial emphasis on the latter.[18] Emphasis should be on current pressures, interests, and feelings. Past history and underlying dynamics should be played down, as should all forms of intensive confrontation. Individual contacts should be frequent, with allowance for unplanned, on-the-spot discussions regarding emergent needs that are expressed by the youth. The treatment group should consist almost entirely of passive-conformists. Initially, it may resemble a large family, with the agent acting as parent and several youths interacting (though not by design) as siblings; group decision-making should nevertheless be encouraged, both initially and later on. Low-pressure activity group meetings can be quite useful in creating (1) a fund of pleasurable, nondelinquent social experiences, and (2) feelings of acceptance and personal worth.[19] Role-playing sessions can help the youth gain additional information as to how he is viewed by peers and adults, and alternative ways of interacting with them.

Controls
Controls should relate directly to behavior standards presented to the youth, by the agent, and to basic conditions of parole (Appendix 3). Standards and expectations should be specific and readily understandable—for instance, "I want you to go to school beginning next month." However, the agent should not necessarily punish or restrict the youth if these and related verbal agreements are not followed to the letter. In discussing program infractions and law violations, the agent should make every effort to communicate concern, not threat, and to inspect with the youth alternate ways of handling the situation. "Chewing-out" techniques

are appropriate only after the agent/youth relationship is fairly well established and the agent is not seen as "frightening," "unfair," or "mean." Heavy controls, restrictions, or punishments are inappropriate and counterproductive. Frequent periods of detention may seriously interfere with achievement of basic goals.

Related or Additional Approaches

The agent should help the youth's natural or foster family provide a nonthreatening or, at least, minimally confusing environment. Informal conferences between the agent and individual family members are necessary and often productive in specific areas or during crisis situations. However, formal family group counseling is almost always rejected by the natural parents. Major change in the family's pattern of interaction is uncommon and very difficult to achieve. Emotional emancipation of the youth from his family thus remains a serious concern, despite resolution of specific difficulties.

Placement

Initial placement should be in his own home unless the youth requests removal or his parents clearly reject him. Temporary foster care may be needed during times of crisis, especially with younger individuals who are prone to run from stress. Foster or group home parents should be able to accept open expressions of dependency by the youth—older adolescents included. The foster or group home father should be able to "give"—and share—as well as control, and to accept youths who emotionally cling to the substitute mother.

School and Employment

Many passive-conformists are good students and require no special attention. With others, it is impossible for the regular public school setting to provide the necessary attention and support. Individual or small group tutoring may be the only viable alternative. Conferences with school personnel can give the agent an opportunity to interpret problem behavior and to suggest methods of interacting that might help the youth stay in school.

Passive-conformists are typically very fearful when it comes to job hunting. Role-playing techniques that focus on employment situations can help the youth prepare for "hunting" as well as "keeping." However, the

agent's expectations should not be high in connection with the youth's ability to retain his first few jobs for very long. Agent/youth discussions can nevertheless help the youngster profit from job experiences or seeming failures, rather than withdraw from future attempts. Neighborhood Youth Corps and related programs can be useful if they are relatively undemanding from an interpersonal point of view.[20]

Peer Group

During the youth's early months on the project, the agent may have to directly prohibit his involvement with nonproject, delinquent peers. To help shift a youngster's loyalty, an agent may develop a project peer group that can offer him personal acceptance, stability, and a sense of belonging, within a nondelinquent framework. This group should consist almost exclusively of passive-conformists in order to minimize the youngster's tendency to adopt the role of "low man on the totem pole" and to eventually withdraw or be rejected. The group should not be "intense," for instance, highly confrontive and demanding.

Leisure Time

The agent should encourage the youngster to make frequent use of the CTP community center. When the youth shows increasing self-confidence, the agent may gradually encourage him to interact with individuals other than passive-conformists.[21] Still later, when the youth can accept it (the following) as a sign of confidence rather than rejection, the agent should help him spend increasing amounts of time in nonproject activities and settings. This should not mean the "door" at the CTP center will then be closed for good, relative to leisure time activities; rather, the youth should feel he can be a welcome part of the center for as long as he wishes. This in itself can contribute to eventual independence, more than dependence.

Community Supports

Although initial and continued emphasis may be on project activities, the agent should also try to utilize existing neighborhood recreation programs. However, these must be oriented toward nonexploitive interactions and should contain some degree of responsible supervision. After some strong emotional relationships are established between the youth and project personnel, the agent should search for and promote outside relationships with secure adults. Here, the main goal is to preclude long-term overdependence on the agent or other project personnel, and to expand the individual's social horizons. Outside relationships can initially be used as a supplement to, rather than a substitute for, those that exist between the youth and members of the project.

Agent's Description of Intervention with Passive-Conformist Youths
Areas of Major Focus
- I am interested in guiding the growth of the youth—educating and socializing him. This is my main role.
- I support or back the youth in getting his age-appropriate rights recognized at home.
- I encourage the youth to be more assertive and to defend himself.
- I try to reduce the feelings of pressure which preoccupy the youth.
- I spend much time helping the youth "label" various events in his life, and then connect those labels with his feelings.
- I give repeated clarification about how other people feel and react, in order to reduce the youth's stereotypes.
- My main goal of treatment is to clear up internal conflicts. (*Rejected*)
- I help the youth see that his behavior is related to his conflicts and feelings of guilt, generated within the family. (*Rejected*)
- I must help the youth change his view of the world as a power struggle. (*Rejected*)

Agent/Youth Relationship
- I spend much time developing a relationship with the youth . . . as a bridge to helping him learn how to have better relationships elsewhere.
- I build a relationship by very frequent contacts during which I talk and "make noise" in a positive tone, to develop a good feeling in the youth at my presence.
- I often use physical stimuli to encourage the development of a relationship, such as patting the youth on the back, physically taking hold of him, or nudging him.
- I use rewards such as trips, movies, clothes, or books to help build a relationship with the youth.

- I make every effort to portray myself as someone who is adequate, dependable, and caring.
- I often share my personal values, and other things about myself, with the youth.
- I offer more of a friend relationship than a treatment relationship.
- I make myself very available at all times.

Personal Involvement and Decision-Making
- Since the youth takes little or no initiative, I have to reach out to overcome his minimal involvement.[22]
- I let the youth take responsibility for his own life pattern, and allow him to help determine the [original] treatment plan. (*Rejected*)

Agent Stance and Selected Activities
- I make casual, nonformal-type contacts with the youth, as the best context of interaction.
- I try to be very nonthreatening during early months of the relationship.
- This type of youth needs a group setting in order to have opportunities to socialize, and to learn techniques of interaction.
- Group meetings with the youth are more activity-oriented than discussion-oriented.
- I try to protect the youth from peer behavior that would be harmful.
- I find people and situations who will accept and partially shelter the youth, so that he can practice functioning on his immature level.
- I create situations in which the youth will "win"—such as games [at the community center].
- I help the youth locate and obtain jobs.
- I try to help employers, teachers, or other persons [e.g., foster parents] give supportive help toward the youth's development.
- I get other persons to give some positive feedback to the youth, in order to bolster his self-esteem.
- I support positive aspects of job experience such as money earned, and what the youth learned or did, even if he loses the job.
- I interpret the youth's fears about adequacy by telling him he's got problems in growing, rather than being "sick."[23]

Behavior Control, Surveillance,
and Sanctions

- I set clear and controlling limits, for example, regarding curfew and delinquent activities.
- I check up on the youth's behavior to see for sure what he's doing. I use all available resources, to do so.
- I do not initially set limits for the youth, such as curfew, employment, or going to school. (*Rejected*)
- I use the project peer group to put pressure on the youth to control himself. (*Rejected*)
- I make the youth responsible for failure to follow through on his agreements to perform, by taking privileges or freedom away from him. (*Rejected*)
- I keep the youth uncertain as to what will happen by way of discipline, if he misbehaves. (*Rejected*)

Selected Program Elements Used with Passive-Conformist Youths
Counseling
For participants, the number of sessions per month was: individual counseling—4.4; group counseling—2.4; family counseling—0.8. These youths took part in a total of 6.2 counseling sessions a month (74 a year), of one form or another. About 10 percent of these sessions involved psychotherapy.

For typical youths (participants plus non-participants), the number of sessions per month was: individual counseling—2.6; group counseling—1.6; family counseling—0.3. These youths took part in 3.6 counseling sessions a month (43 a year), of one form or another. (See Tables 6–1 and 6–2, on pages 73 and 74.)

Pragmatically Oriented Interactions
For participants, there was about one such session a month. For the typical youth, there was one every two months.

Limit-Setting
For participants, limit-setting was used twice a month. For the typical youth it was used once a month.

Collateral Contacts
For participants, there was about one such contact a month. For the typical youth there was one every two months.

Short-Term Detention
Relative to the youth's entire YA career, the average number of detentions was 2.2—one detention for every 12 months on parole. Each detention lasted an average of 21 days. There were about two agent/youth contacts per detention. The total number of days in detention per youth was 45.

Goals and Techniques Used with All Three Youth Types
Certain goals and techniques had very wide applicability. They were used and endorsed by agents who worked with power-oriented, passive-conformist, and conflicted individuals alike.[24] In this sense they were fundamental to CTP's approach with middle and higher maturity youths. These goals and techniques were as follows:

- I try to make the youth aware of what is happening in his home and community life.
- I use current life experiences to help the youth learn the reactions of others to things he does.
- I try not to dominate during interviews or discussions, and [I try] to encourage free expression by the youth.
- I try to help the youth with specific needs and problems, in order to demonstrate my helpfulness or concern.
- I make an effort to point out "good self" qualities in the youth.
- I try to "confirm" the youth as a capable and worthwhile person, by showing positive regard for his abilities.
- I work closely with foster parents, giving them much support.

Underlying Principles and Treatment Methods
In the introduction to this book, it was stated that: "With few exceptions, the way [in which CTP's methods were applied was consistent with certain] principles and objectives that were emphasized throughout, and throughout the life of, [the] project." These included:

1. Promote humane interaction between staff and youth, thereby reducing the degree of impersonal ("system-to- object")

processing of the offender, and perhaps modifying his negative image of authority figures;

2. Facilitate the youth's personal involvement in the process of change as a way of tapping and building upon his internal motivation—thereby reducing the need to impose decisions on a largely involuntary basis.[25]

Questionnaire items that were endorsed or rejected by CTP agents may illustrate the specific areas in which these principles were and were not followed or approached.

Humane Interaction between Staff and Youth
Personalized versus Impersonal Interaction
This aspect of humane interaction may be reflected along such lines as informality versus formality, closeness versus distance, and sharing versus nonsharing. From this perspective, a personalized approach was clearly used with conflicted and passive-conformist youths. For example: "I try to relate to the youth by giving respect as an equal, and by respecting his values." "I make casual, nonformal-type contacts with the youth, as the best context of interaction." "I stress the help of a relationship rather than the help of such things as money, transportation, or clothes." "I often use physical stimuli to encourage the development of a relationship, such as patting the youth on the back . . . " "I offer more of a friend relationship than a treatment relationship."

A personalized approach was not used with power-oriented youths, at least not during the initial months of intervention. Most of the preceding descriptions (questionnaire items) were rejected by agents who worked with these individuals. The remaining items were neither endorsed nor rejected.

Expressing Concern for the Youth's Feelings and Needs versus Nonconcern, Neutrality, or Indifference
Concern for, and responsiveness to, the individual's feelings and needs were part of the picture with all types of youth: "I try to communicate that I understand the feelings and emotional investments of the youth." "I make every effort to portray myself as someone who is adequate, dependable, and caring." "I am a 'sounding board' or 'listening post,' as a major role." "I try to help the youth with specific needs and problems, in order to demon-

strate my helpfulness or concern." However, in the case of power-oriented youths, open or direct expression of concern seemed to enter the picture only after a certain point was reached: "When the youth begins to ask '*why*' I keep helping and giving, . . . *that* is when I interpret my 'care' and concern for him." (It does not follow that nonconcern, neutrality, or indifference were being expressed prior to that time.) This is consistent with the following account, one that was rejected in relation to power-oriented youths: "I try to be very nonthreatening during the early months of the relationship."

Agent's Availability versus Nonavailability
Agents considered it important to be available *almost always*—this, as distinct from having frequent contacts per se: "I make myself very available at virtually all times." (The average rating was 3.7, 3.6, and 3.4 for passive-conformist, power-oriented, and conflicted youths, respectively.)

Youth's Involvement in the Process of Change
Source of Direction and Control
This aspect of youth involvement would mainly relate to the use of internal motivation and personal initiative or responsibility, versus the use of external structure, surveillance, and demand. Use of internal motivation and personal initiative, relative to major decisions, was clearly preferred in the case of conflicted youths:[26] "I let the youth take responsibility for his own life pattern, and allow him to help determine the [original] treatment plan." "I give the youth alternatives and make him decide things for himself." "I point out how the youth is not meeting his own expectations. . . . " "I use the youth's acting-out behavior to point out how he is self-defeating." However, in the case of power-oriented and passive-conformist youths the first two of these items were rejected or, in one instance, simply not endorsed. The third and fourth items were not endorsed, though not specifically rejected.

Internal control of behavior was preferred in relation to conflicted youths, and external control was rejected: "I try to use the youth's internal values to get him to control his behavior."[27] "I set clear and controlling limits, for example, regarding curfew and delinquent activities" (*Rejected*). "I make the youth responsible for failure to follow through on his agreements to perform, by taking privileges or freedom away from him" (*Rejected*). "I use the project peer group to put pressure on the youth to control himself" (*Rejected*).

External control of behavior was clearly preferred relative to power-oriented youths. For example, agents took an opposite stance on almost all items mentioned in the preceding paragraph.[28] In addition, they endorsed such items as the following: "I convey that I expect acceptable behavior . . . by setting limits and goals for the youth." "I show the youth that I know what's going on in his daily life, by relating and reviewing reports from others around him." "I never give up the assurance that I will control the youth by locking him up if necessary." (These items were rejected relative to conflicted youths.)

External controls were also preferred in the case of passive-conformists, but to a lesser degree than with power-oriented youths. This is also supported by the number of limit-setting contacts per month, and by the amount of temporary detention as well. (See Tables 6–1 and 6–2, on pages 73 and 74.)

Development of Own Identity
versus Forced Conformity
Agents tried to help conflicted youths develop their personal values, together with a sense of self. They did not try to force these youths into accepting or espousing the values of others: "I ask questions which lead the youth to evaluate his feelings and goals." "I try to help the youth learn 'who' and 'what' he is—that is, resolve identity and adequacy problems." "I present my standards, but do not punish the youth for nonconformance with them." "I have the job of convincing the youth that societal prescriptions are the way" (*Rejected*).

With power-oriented youths, agents did focus on conformity, at least behavioral conformity: "I try to be very alert to reward any acceptable behavior."[29] "I take action quickly and decisively when the youth misbehaves." At the same time, agents appeared to leave room for possible growth or development along the lines of the youngster's own interests or abilities: "I try to support the idea that the world will allow the youth to achieve." Nevertheless, their primary concern seemed to involve social conformity in general, and the reduction or elimination of illegal behavior in particular: "I explain reality and the consequences of his behavior to the youth, as a major activity."

With passive-conformists, agents focused on social-emotional growth, for example, the development of practical and interpersonal skills: "I am interested in guiding the growth of the youth—educating and socializing him. This is my main role." "I support or back the youth in getting his age-appropriate rights recognized at home." "I support positive aspects of job experience—such as money earned, and what the youth learned . . ." Within this framework, conformity and nonconformity were not regarded as central, in and of themselves. Thus, if passive-conformists chose to identify with given social values and modes of interacting, as part of their social-emotional development, CTP agents were not likely to stand in their way or attempt to dissuade them from doing so.

A final point relates to the type of identity that the agents tried to support or reinforce. Rather than focus on "sickness" or defect, CTP agents tried to help youths feel increasingly good, or at least not too badly, about themselves: "I try to 'confirm' the youth as a capable and worthwhile person, by showing positive regard for his abilities." "I make an effort to point out the 'good self' qualities in the youth." Although there were occasions on which the agents confronted youths with the fact of their "unacceptable behavior," this, in itself, did not prevent them from stating, on other occasions, that they recognized and valued specific positive qualities within them. This applied to all groups of youths.

With passive-conformists, agents used the following approach as well: "I get other persons to give some positive feedback to the youth, in order to bolster his self-esteem." "I interpret the youth's fears about adequacy, by telling him he's got problems in growing, rather than being 'sick.'"

Notes

1. Space limitations preclude a review of the approaches that were used with the "rare types" of youth, that is, the remaining 12 percent of the sample. This also applies to variations in approach that were used *within* the conflicted and power-oriented categories, respectively—specifically, with assertive-deniers as compared to anxious-confused individuals, and with group conformists compared to manipulators. However, at the

present level of description, the within-group similarities outweighed the *differences;* as a result, it was possible to combine the differing approaches.

2. Participants and nonparticipants combined.

3. Many of these observations and interviews were gathered and conducted during 1961–1966. They were summarized and reported by Warren et al. (1966b). Descriptions of the "overall pattern of intervention" that appears in the present chapter are taken almost entirely from this report; however, statements from the 1966 report have been rearranged and generally rephrased to fit the present context and style. The approaches described in this chapter remained largely unchanged during 1966–1969, although certain important shifts took place relative to power-oriented and conflicted youths. Some of these changes are reflected in the present account, by omission and commission. However, a full or focused account is precluded by space limitations and the need for ease of presentation relative to an already complex topic. (Brief comments appear in Chapter 11, in the section titled "Matching and Youth Behavior.")

4. The sample for this substudy (Grenny, 1971; Palmer and Grenny, 1971) consisted of 34 male parole agents—94 percent of all respondents who could still be contacted. These individuals had either worked at CTP at some point during 1961–1970 or were active on the project at the time of the questionnaire (1971). They were all "matched" with the specific youth type on whom they focused, in the questionnaire. It was coincidental that this parole-agent substudy ended up with the same number of respondents, that is, 34, as did an earlier substudy of male CTP agents (Palmer, 1967a). In the 1967 substudy (see "The Workers" section in Chapter 11 of this volume), complete data were available and used for all male agents (N=34) who had ever worked at CTP's Valley and San Francisco units (excluding Guided Group Interaction and all control units), between 1961 and early 1967. Between 1967 and the time of the present (1971) substudy, many new CTP workers had

been hired, including several for Phase 3. In this 1971 substudy, 80 percent of all workers—36 of 45, hired between 1961 and 1970—whose selection and matching had been appropriate for CTP could be located and contacted. Of these 36, 94 percent (34 individuals) responded to the questionnaire.

5. A few statements were slightly reworded (e.g., substitution of "youth" for "ward"; minor grammatical changes). However, no substantive changes were made.

6. A 5-point scale was used throughout the questionnaire: 1—disagree; 2—slightly agree; 3—moderately agree; 4—definitely agree; 5—highly agree. "Clear endorsement" meant that the item received an average rating of 4.0 or higher, across the various raters (agents). "Rejection" referred to an average rating of 1.7 or lower—again, by whichever group of agents is specified (e.g., those whose questionnaire responses refer to passive-conformists).

7. The remaining program elements (e.g., recreational opportunities and socializing experiences) could not easily and efficiently be presented relative to this question. Here, the figures presented in Chapter 3, for the sample as a whole, must suffice.

8. Placement at home is essential if formal family counseling or family therapy is to be the primary method.

9. Also: "Increase the youth's understanding of the role he has played in his family and the particular ways in which this might have influenced his life."

10. This area might also be labeled, "Responsibility, initiative, and source of direction."

11. Since most individuals did not participate in all three forms of counseling, 6.8 is less than the sum of 6.2, 1.6, and 0.6. This situation was observed among power-oriented and passive-conformist youths as well.

12. This is despite the frequent lack of conditions (3) and (4), listed in the same paragraph within the text.

13. For example, "Show the youth that there are many adults whom he can trust and look up to." Agents attempted to integrate the "giving" and "helping" features with their strategy of frustrating

and restricting the youth in certain respects. Thus, they rejected the following description: "I try to establish a consistent picture of myself, in the youth's view, as a nonfrustrating person."

14. For example, regarding curfew, off-limits places, school, or employment.

15. That is, uncertain as to *which* sanction will occur, not as to whether there will be a sanction.

16. The following are further reflections of the approach used with power-oriented individuals: "Teach the youth how to take care of himself and how to meet his needs on a practical basis." "Work primarily with performance (e.g., school, employment, living arrangements) rather than with emotions and psychological factors." "Maintain a regular schedule of frequent contact with the youth." "Intentionally relate to the youth in ways which will not readily fit into his usual manner of perceiving and interpreting others." "Be verbally forceful, even harsh, when having to confront the youth." "Make sure the youth sees you as the main source of power with whom he must deal when making decisions and plans."

17. For example, in terms of community center activities and outings, not just counseling or limit-setting.

18. Later emphasis would be on individual contacts.

19. These meetings have been described as follows: "One of the activity groups has consisted entirely of [I_2's and I_3's], engaging in simple and unstructured activities, often resembling parallel play, in which some members build models, some paint, some draw, or some may merely watch. Occasionally, the activity has involved a trip or picnic. Always, some kind of food or refreshment has played an important role at the meetings. . . . [Another group] meets at the Agent's home, where the boys work on individual creative projects" (Grant, Warren, and Turner, 1963, p. 33).

20. During the early 1970s, Neighborhood Youth Corps was called the Manpower Youth Program.

21. However, most of the youth's close friends may continue to be passive-conformists, until they move to the I_4 level of maturity.

22. The following are also related to the youngster's general lack of initiative, and fear of decision-making: "I encourage the youth to more actively care about what happens to him"; "I try to get the youth to be more reactive [responsive] to the events in his life, to take a more active stance in determining what happens to him."

23. Also: I "help the youth feel that [I] do not see him as someone who is 'sick,' 'weird,' or 'undesirable.'"

24. When responding to the 200-item questionnaire, each agent focused on one, and only one, of the three youth types. All agents completed only one questionnaire.

25. A third principle or objective was mentioned:
    3. Facilitate individualized justice and minimize rigid, undifferentiated solutions . . . [thereby integrating] the multiple needs, resources, and professed ideals of society with needs and resources of the growing youth.
    The manner in which this was implemented at CTP may be seen, in part, in Chapters 2 and 3. The former describes the intake, diagnostic, and case conference procedures; the latter reviews the main program elements.

26. Here, emphasis was on the establishment of long-term objectives and on the handling of more immediate social-emotional needs. It was not on the control of *behavior* (e.g., illegal behavior) as such. The latter is briefly reviewed in subsequent paragraphs of the text.

27. The following may have been related to internal control of behavior; however, its main purpose was not stated, and therefore remains unclear: "I work with feelings, more than with performance."

28. That is, previously rejected items were endorsed, and previously endorsed items were rejected. One item was neither endorsed nor rejected.

29. Most agents interpreted "acceptable" to mean one or more of the following: conforming, constructive, nonexploitive, or nondestructive.

PART II

Program Effectiveness and Matching

7 RESEARCH QUESTIONS AND MEASURES OF IMPACT

Evaluation of the Community Treatment Project centered around two main issues: feasibility and program impact. Feasibility relates to several organizational and administrative questions. For example, one might ask if a particular approach—say, the CTP approach—is too unwieldy, inefficient, or controversial. Each question might be asked separately in connection with the program's community-based feature, its differential intervention feature, and its classification system. Similarly, one might ask if the given approach is too costly or perhaps too complex from a personnel management standpoint. These questions will be reviewed in Chapters 17 through 20.

Program impact (effectiveness) can be thought of in several ways. However, in each case it must be based on measures (criteria) that make sense and are generally accepted—in this instance, within corrections. Three such measures will be described in this chapter. First, however, the background of CTP's evaluation will be briefly reviewed.

Background

In the early 1960s, community treatment was a subject of serious and widespread discussion within corrections. In a way, it was like an idea whose time had finally arrived. However, it was something more, since at CTP it was actually being implemented, and critical issues were being directly addressed.

One issue was the following: Can serious delinquents be handled safely in a community program alone? Can they be controlled without using lengthy periods of lockup? These questions were fairly new at the time; however, since community treatment was itself quite new, they had never been tackled systematically. As a result, no objective answer was available. What existed were intuitions and educated guesses—basically the product of theory and informal observation, not scientific evaluation.

At about this time, administrators, practitioners, and others began to take increasing note of these persistent questions. They sensed that a reliable answer would soon be in demand, one based on more than theory or feelings alone. They realized that factual information could help them decide whether to endorse or reject the concept of community treatment, that is, decide on a more objective and responsible basis than might otherwise be the case. Perhaps on a more defensible basis as well.

One thing seemed clear. Any such answer would have to be rather convincing, especially if it were yes—that is, "Yes, delinquents *can* be handled safely in a community program alone." The reason for this was simple: most correctional personnel believed the average citizen's answer was no, or mostly no. They believed he was only minimally tolerant of youths who had been "sent up," and that he would be skeptical of programs that did not involve traditional lockup or something very much like it. Experience suggested to them that what the average citizen wanted most was public safety and peace of mind—that he wanted the social behavior of delinquents to be pretty much controlled from the start. At base, this meant offenders were to commit no more public offenses. In short, "Rehabilitation, OK—but first, control." To most people control meant institutionalization, and institutionalization generally meant adequate control. Experience also suggested that this was the view of most public officials as well.

Most administrators, judges, and practitioners interpreted these persistent questions as the expression of a strong, widely held concern: that without "hard lockup," delinquents might simply "go their merry way"; that without institutionalization, even a strict and resourceful program might fail to achieve tight control. Given this genuine concern, an answer of "yes" would have to be very clear indeed, and the supporting evidence would have to be substantial. After all, community treatment seemed very different than any form of long-term lockup.

Thus, in the early 1960s the first major question to be answered was: Will a community-located treatment program be tolerated by the general public, and by criminal justice agencies in particular? Will the program be *feasible* or acceptable in this respect? This boiled down to: Will such a program adequately control behavior?

To obtain factual answers it was necessary to develop a community program and to run an actual test. There was no possible way to get around this. To find out if the community-based approach could actually work, the test program would have to contain ingredients that seemed essential for success. In a way, this would be like trying to prove that a new type of airplane could actually get off the ground: To give the designers' idea a fair test, all major components must be present; in addition, adequate fuel must be supplied and the mechanism as a whole must be in decent working order.

These were some of the basic reasons for establishing CTP as a "demonstration program"—specifically, a program that would (1) have the wherewithal to give the concept of community treatment an adequate test and (2) supply the first systematic information regarding the feasibility of this approach.

It was recognized that no single demonstration could reduce every last doubt that the interested citizen might have, not even if the answer it produced was clearly yes. Nevertheless, an adequate demonstration *could* make a basic difference to the concept of community treatment—the difference between general rejection, on the one hand, and tolerance, acceptance, or even strong approval, on the other.

Comparative Effectiveness

Community acceptance was the overriding concern when CTP began. Yet, if community treatment *were* found to be acceptable, other issues would be sure to arise. Chief among these was "comparative effectiveness." For example: Is the community approach *as good as* the traditional approach? Do CTP youths perform as well as those who—instead—would experience hard lockup? In terms of social policy, the implications of these questions seemed far-reaching.

A team of researchers was available to work on this issue. Its main strategy was to compare the performance of CTP youths ("experimentals," or E's) with that of non-CTP youths ("controls," or C's), that is, individuals who would experience the traditional YA program.

Controls were sent to the Youth Authority for the same reasons that experimentals were sent. They had arrived at the same points in time and had come from the same geographic areas. They, too, spent approximately five weeks at the Northern Reception Center and Clinic (Davis et al., 1965). C's and E's were also very similar on factors such as age, IQ, socioeconomic status of family, race, and type of committing offense. As a result, these groups of youths were said to be "equated," or "comparable." Comparability was exactly what the research team wanted to have in connection with these background factors, and it had been achieved by a routine scientific procedure known as random assignment.

However, controls and experimentals differed from one another in two crucial ways. First, controls had been locked up in a YA institution before being returned to their home community;[1] experimentals had not. Secondly, when controls returned from the institution, they were routinely assigned to the YA's regular parole unit, never to CTP.[2] Controls—that is, institution and regular parole youths—were always supervised by regular YA parole agents, never by CTP agents. CTP youths were always supervised by CTP agents. These experimental/control differences were planned; in fact, they formed the basis of what was called "the experimental design." The concrete steps or events that made it possible to implement this design are shown in Figure 7–1.

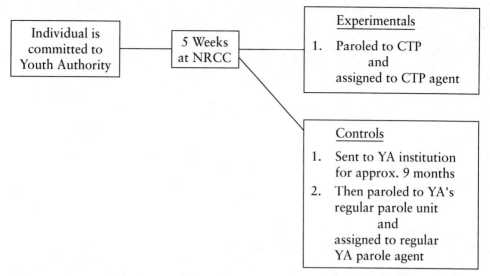

Figure 7–1. Intake, flow, and assignment of study sample.

Because of the systematic comparisons that were made between E's and C's, the project, viewed in toto, was described as "an experimental program." This feature was independent of the fact that each CTP *unit* (whether in Sacramento, Stockton, or San Francisco) amounted to "a demonstration program" in itself.[3]

There were several ways to approach the question of whether E's performed as well as C's. However, the basic strategy was much the same in each:

1. Collect information on the youths' performance over a specified amount of time known as the *follow-up period.*
2. Inspect that information to see how many E's and C's were involved in illegal activities during the follow-up period, and/or how many performed satisfactorily according to preestablished standards.
3. Translate the raw numbers into percentages or other statistics in order to make the E/C comparisons more meaningful.[4]

The following are examples of how this strategy was actually carried out, using three well-known measures of performance. These examples will make it easier to understand the findings presented in Chapter 8. They may also show that program impact on youths can

be evaluated by methods that are straightforward and manageable.

Parole Failure (Removal from Parole)[5]

Say that the performance of 100 parolees is monitored for a period of 24 months, starting from the day of their first release to parole. This procedure is followed for each youth, individually. Next, say that 35 of these youths are found to have committed an offense at some point during those 24 months—specifically, an offense that led to their being removed from parole (revoked) by the Youth Authority Board, and sent to a large-sized institution for several months or more (institutionalized).

(Before continuing, it should be kept in mind that a "revocation offense" is distinct from one that, say, leads to one or more of the following: (1) several stormy sessions with the parole agent, but few repercussions beyond that; (2) an appearance in court, climaxed by a stern warning from the judge, possibly a $100 fine, and then release to the streets; (3) several days in the local jail, or a short-term detention at NRCC; (4) dismissal of all charges. None of these outcomes involves removal from parole.)

Under these circumstances the "failure rate" for the 100 parolees would be 35/100, or *35 percent.* Conversely, the "success rate" would be 65/100, or *65 percent.* This procedure would be carried out separately for E's and C's, and the resulting failure rate for the former group would be compared with that for the latter.

In this example, the performance indicator was parole failure—removal from parole within a stated period of time. When all such failures are added together and averaged out, this index can provide a clear picture of how likely or unlikely it is for a sample of youths to be removed from parole within a specified length of time. Also, it can help provide a picture of how many months the average E and C youths have spent in an institution, on "revoked status." Yet, as a performance indicator, parole failure has serious limitations.

For instance, whereas one youngster may be removed from parole immediately after his second offense, a different youth, for various reasons, may not be removed until his fourth offense. (Say that all six offenses involved the same type of act—petty theft—and that each youth was being removed for the first time.) However, both individuals may have committed their offenses within the same span of time, say, 26 months in the community, counting from the day of their first release to parole. Thus, the second youth was committing offenses twice as often as the first, a fact that would not be reflected in the parole failure index alone. Actually, neither of these youths would have been counted as a "parole failure" in the first place, since the offense that led to their removal did not occur until their *26th* month on parole, two months after the "cutoff date" for the 24-month follow-up. In other words, they would be "successes" on a 24-month follow-up.

Thus, by using the parole failure index alone, a good deal of information concerning offense behavior would remain untapped; and at best, important differences that exist among youths would remain below the surface. For such reasons it is important to ask: *How often* do youths commit an offense? This question brings us to our second measure.

Rate of Offending

To answer the question of *How often?*, the research team first added up the number of days each experimental and control youth spent in the community. This count ran from the individual's first release to parole until the day of his discharge from the Youth Authority; time spent in lockup of any type was subtracted. Next, they counted the offenses that each

youth was involved in during that same time period. (Separate counts were made for [1] all arrests, and [2] arrests with convictions. The present example could refer to either type of count.) With this information they were ready to compute the rate of offending.

Say that a group of 100 parolees accumulates a total of 120,000 days in the community during their entire YA career. This comes to roughly 4,000 months during which they can commit a public offense. (This amounts to 40 months per career, for each youth: 4,000 months divided by 100 youths.) Months spent in the community will be called "months at risk," or "risk months."

Next, say that this group accumulates a total of 200 offenses during those 4,000 months. Under these circumstances the monthly rate of offending is 200 divided by 4,000, or *0.050*. This is equivalent to 50 offenses for every 1,000 months at risk. This of course equals 20 months at risk for every one offense: 1,000 months divided by 50 offenses.

Rate of Discharge from YA

To help round out the picture on comparative effectiveness, still another question was asked: How many individuals received a favorable (or perhaps unfavorable) discharge from the Youth Authority, within a stated period of time? This question was important because discharge from the YA was in some ways different than monthly rate of offending. It was somewhat different than failure on parole, as well. In a sense it represented the individual's final outcome or disposition relative to the Youth Authority as a whole.

For instance, a youth could have received a favorable discharge even though he (1) had previously chalked up six or eight offenses while on parole and (2) had previously been removed from parole and subsequently institutionalized on one or more occasions. The latter, in fact, was not uncommon. It was observed among youths who had eventually "straightened out"—for instance, had committed no offenses for a year or more, starting from the time they were last released from a YA institution.

There was also the following situation. A youth may have ended up with an *unfavorable* discharge from the Youth Authority even though, for example, his first 20 or more months on parole were devoid of offenses. This sometimes happened when an otherwise delinquency-free parolee suddenly and perhaps surprisingly committed a severe offense. (It should be kept in mind that the decision to discharge a YA parolee, either favorably or unfavorably, was made on the basis of preestablished, written standards that were identical for all YA "wards," whether in CTP or regular parole. The decision was always made by the Youth Authority Board.)[6] This brings us to the third measure of comparative effectiveness: rate of discharge.

Say that 200 parolees had been monitored for a total of five years, as of mid-1972.[7] Next, say that the following eventually took place at some point during the five-year follow-up: (1) 140 of the 200 youths received a favorable discharge from the YA; (2) 40 of the 200 youths received an unfavorable discharge; and (3) the remaining 20 had not yet been discharged—that is, they were still somewhere in the Youth Authority, either on parole or in an institution. Under these circumstances, the rate of favorable discharge on five-year YA follow-up would be 140/200, or *70 percent*. The rate of unfavorable discharge would be 40/200, or *20 percent*. The combined total for favorable plus unfavorable discharge is less than 100 percent because of the individuals (20 youths—10 percent of the 200 parolees) who were still in the Youth Authority. Such rates would be computed separately for experimental and control parolees, and a comparison would then be made between the two.

Differential Effectiveness

As these examples show, comparative effectiveness was evaluated by means of a fairly simple strategy. However, in order to deal with a second question, this strategy had to be carried out in a more detailed way. The latter question involved the issue of "differential effectiveness." For instance: Is the community approach as good as the traditional approach for certain *kinds* of youth, but not for others? Do conflicted CTP youths perform as well as conflicted, non-CTP youths? An answer to such questions could be useful to administrators and practitioners who were interested in figuring out the best possible, or best available, placement for each individual youth.

To deal with this issue, separate analyses were needed for each type of youth: Conflicted E's had to be compared with conflicted C's,

passive-conformist E's had to be compared with passive-conformist C's, and so on.

No less important, this type of analysis was necessary in order to avoid what might be called "The Case of the Buried Findings"—a pitfall that can easily cause an entire research project to be sold short or seriously misrepresented.

For instance, say that the E and C groups each consist of two kinds of youths—"independent" and "dependent." Specifically, say there are 100 experimentals in all, 50 of whom are independent and the other 50 dependent. Say the control group is made up in exactly the same way: 50 independent and 50 dependent youths. Now, if the independent E's perform *better* than the independent C's (say, "five points" better), and the dependent E's perform *worse* than the dependent C's (say, "five points" worse), there will end up being no difference at all in the performance of the total group of experimentals as compared with the total group of controls. Indeed, E's and C's *are* performing exactly the same if one merely compares all 100 E's with all 100 C's. The reason of course is that the +5 difference that exists for the 50 independent E's is counterbalanced by the −5 difference that exists for the 50 dependent E's. Unfortunately, both of these experimental/control differences would remain buried if nothing other than a "total group analysis" had been carried out.

Thus, it is very risky to simply ask whether "experimentals" perform as well as "controls." Instead, wherever possible, it is important to check into which *kind* of experimentals perform either better than, the same as, or perhaps worse than, which kind of controls.

This type of analysis is also important for a related reason. It is always possible for a small-sized group of youths to tip the overall balance in a way that obscures the findings as a whole. For instance: Say the experimental group is comprised of 20 independent youths and 80 dependent youths; and say the control group is also comprised of 20 independent and dependent youths. Next, say that the 20 independent E's perform, on the average, *eight points better* than the 20 independent C's, and say that the 80 dependent E's perform *two points worse* than the 80 dependent C's. Under these circumstances the overall difference between the *100* E's and *100* C's would again be zero, since 20 × 8 equals 80 × 2.

Thus, as before, there would end up being no difference in outcome between the total group of E's and the total group of C's if the independent and dependent youths were simply added together and analyzed as a single group. In short, if nothing other than a total group analysis had been made, the markedly positive performance of a relatively small group of experimentals (the 20 percent, independent group) would have obscured the fact that a large majority of individuals (the 80 percent, dependent group) were actually performing somewhat better within one of the two programs, in this case the control program. The erroneous conclusion might have then been drawn that it makes no difference which program an individual is in. However, if one had divided both the E's and C's into specific categories it would have been possible to determine which types of youth performed better in one program than in the other.

We now turn to the main effectiveness findings of Phases 1 and 2.

Notes

1. There were some exceptions to this—known as "direct parolees" (see Chapter 2).
2. Except for the San Francisco office, regular parole (Sacramento and Stockton) was usually located within a mile of CTP, and in a similar socioeconomic setting.
3. Thus, by focusing on each CTP unit, it would have been possible to explore the question of feasibility without delving into that of comparative effectiveness. It was the latter issue, not the former, that called for an experimental design—including a control group in particular.
4. A fourth step is usually distinguished. This involves carrying out statistical tests to see if the experimental/control differences are stable, not due to chance fluctuations.
5. In almost all cases, parole failure results in immediate institutionalization. See Chapter 8 regarding "revocation, recommitment . . . [and] unfavorable discharge"—the three aspects of parole failure.
6. The criteria for favorable and unfavorable discharge are shown in Appendix 9.
7. As with other types of follow-up, the present one would be carried out for each youth individually. Therefore, each of the 200 counts would probably have been started at different points in time between 1961 and mid-1967—depending on the exact day each youth was first released to parole. No youth would be followed up for more than five years, regardless of his starting date on parole. (Mid-1967 is five years prior to the data-cutoff point of mid-1972.)

8   PROGRAM EFFECTIVENESS FOR VALLEY YOUTHS

Did CTP youths and those in the traditional program perform equally well, or did one outperform the other? If differences in performance were present, which youth group(s) accounted for them? These questions will be answered for two separate time periods: (1) parole, that is, the individuals' entire "YA career"; and (2) a four-year span beginning with discharge from the YA. Both periods will refer to time spent in the community—time at risk, not in lockup.

The questions will first be answered for eligible boys from the Sacramento-Stockton-Modesto areas, also known as the Valley. This group represents 72 percent of all males who were studied during 1961–1969; the rest were from San Francisco. Valley girls will be focused on in the final section of this chapter. Findings for San Francisco youths will be presented in Chapter 9.

Level of performance—program effectiveness—will be measured in several ways. However, the most important single measure will be *rate of offending* (r.o.o.), as described in Chapter 7. This index is based on information from centralized records known as Bureau of Criminal Investigation (BCI) rapsheets. These are standardized documents compiled by the Department of Justice, a state agency that gathers information independently of the YA.[1] Most correctional researchers and academicians consider rate of offending, as derived from such documents, the most unbiased, comprehensive, and relevant measure of performance, particularly if one is interested in the impact of a program on the *behavior* of youths. An index that focuses on youth behavior is different in important respects from one that places considerable emphasis on staff decisions that occur subsequent to those same behaviors— for instance, decisions by the YA Board to either revoke or not revoke parole, in response to the act of auto theft. Such decisions and dispositions can be influenced by a variety of factors and policies; however, by way of contrast, the *youths' behavior,* which has already occurred, remains a fact whatever those decisions may be.

Two additional points before proceeding:

1. Three separate levels of offense severity have been distinguished: minor, moderate, and severe. *Minor* offenses, technical violations, and infractions include: routine traffic citations (noninjury/nonfelony), runaway, incorrigibility, curfew, loitering, possession of alcohol, taking specific actions without prior approval of parole agents, missed group meeting, and so on. This severity level thus includes (1) misdemeanors, (2) juvenile status offenses, that is, actions for which an adult would not be charged, and (3) non-penal-code technical violations of parole (see Appendix 3), together with infractions that relate to specific program requirements (e.g., nonattendance).

   Moderate offenses include: petty theft, auto theft, possession of concealed weapons, possession of narcotics paraphernalia, resisting arrest, perjury, pimping, altering or counterfeiting documents for profit, and so on.

   Severe offenses include: narcotics addiction, sale of narcotics, grand theft (planned), first-degree burglary, drunk driving, willful arson, and so on. This category also contains the subgroup known as *violent* offenses. The latter include: armed robbery, forcible and attempted rape, assault with deadly weapon, aggravated assault, kidnapping, voluntary manslaughter, and murder. The vast majority of severe offenses are felonies. By and large, they correspond to the index offenses widely reported by the FBI on a yearly basis, for the United States as a whole.

The Severity of Offense Scale that was used when analyzing Community Treatment Project offense data is shown in Appendix 10.

Minor offenses, non-penal-code technical violations, and infractions are purposely excluded from the rates of offending that are presented. This will help focus on behaviors of particular concern to most people, and will help reduce the total amount of detail. However, it might be mentioned that when offenses of minor severity are included, the overall results are essentially unchanged.

2. Conflicted youths are by far the largest single group. They account for 53 percent of all Valley boys who were studied during 1961–1969. Passive-conformists and power-oriented youths account for 14 percent and 21 percent, respectively. Taken together, these personality groupings thus account for 88 percent of all eligible boys. The remaining individuals (12 percent) consist of four rather infrequent groupings. Together, these four groups are referred to as rare types, and are described in Appendix 7 (Palmer, 1974b).

The results will now be presented, separately for the three main personality groupings. This will allow us to address the issue of differential effectiveness. After that, all groups—rare types included—will be combined into one all-inclusive category known as the total group. Here, our presentation will focus on the question of overall program effectiveness, or comparative effectiveness. Both sets of findings must be presented in detail because the subject matter is itself complex. A summary of these findings, and of those in Chapters 9 through 11, appears in Chapter 12.

Program Impact during Parole
Conflicted Youths

It will be recalled that this category consists of two separate personality types that share certain characteristics with one another. The first type often shows symptoms of emotional disturbance, for example, chronic or intense depression, or psychosomatic complaints. The youths' tensions and conscious fears usually result from conflicts produced by feelings of failure, inadequacy, or guilt. The second type of youths often attempt to deny, to themselves and others, their conscious feelings of inadequacy, rejection, or self-condemnation. Not infrequently, they do this by verbally attacking others or by using boisterous distractions and various interpersonal "games."

As indicated in the top row of Table 8–1, conflicted youths who were handled in the traditional YA program had more than twice as many moderate plus severe *arrests* as CTP youths, for each month in the community: Monthly rates of offending were 0.080 for controls (C's) and 0.034 for experimentals (E's)—that is, 80 offenses for every 1,000 months at risk, as against 34 offenses per 1,000 months. (This is equivalent to one offense per 12.5 and per 29.4 months at risk, respectively. Naturally, no individuals literally had 1,000 months on parole. One thousand is simply a time-standardized amount that involves a multiplier, and it is used strictly for ease of presentation. The actual numbers—still standardized—are 0.34 arrests per 10 months for E's and 0.80 for C's.) Controls had twice the rate of *convictions* as well: 50 convictions per 1,000 months for C's and 22 per 1,000 months for E's. Each set of figures relates to all moderate plus severe offenses combined, throughout the period of parole.

For *severe* offenses alone, arrest and conviction rates were again two times higher among controls than among experimentals. Of special interest is the fact that, for *violent* offenses, arrest and conviction rates were 2.2 and 2.5 times higher among C's than among E's.

These experimental/control differences were sizable. Statisticians would describe them as "significant," which means, in essence, that they were stable and almost certainly not due to chance fluctuations in rates or scores. (When the conflicted category was subdivided into its two components, similar—in fact, stronger—E/C differences were found for assertive-deniers and, to a much lesser de-

TABLE 8–1

Number of Offenses per 1,000 Months at Risk during Parole, for Valley Boys

	Youth Type and Number of Offenses[a]							
Type of Offense and	Conflicted		Passive-Conformist		Power-Oriented		Total Group[b]	
Outcome Measure	Exp.	Control	Exp.	Control	Exp.	Control	Exp.	Control
Moderate + Severe Offenses								
All arrests	34	80	32	86	55	66	38	76
Arrests with convictions	22	50	15	61	39	39	24	48
Severe Offenses								
All arrests	14	28	11	25	21	34	15	28
Arrests with convictions	9	17	6	18	15	21	9	17
Violent Offenses[c]								
All arrests	6	13	8	11	12	16	7	13
Arrests with convictions	4	10	4	7	8	10	5	8

[a]Sample sizes are as follows: Conflicted, E-99, C-64; Passive-Conformist, E-16, C-29; Power-Oriented, E-36, C-39; Total Group, E-173, C-157.

[b]*Total Group* includes all Conflicted + Passive-Conformist + Power-Oriented + Rare Types.

[c]Includes: armed robbery, rape (attempted or actual), assault with deadly weapon, aggravated assault, kidnapping, murder (attempted or actual), etc. These offenses are part of the broader category labeled *Severe Offenses* (sale of narcotics, grand theft auto, first-degree burglary, drunk driving, etc.).

gree, anxious-confused youths. See Appendix 26, section I.)

The above findings apply to all conflicted males who were favorably or unfavorably discharged from the Youth Authority as of September 1974.[2] These E/C differences cannot be explained on the basis of extraneous factors, for instance, preexisting E versus C differences in age, IQ, race, level of parole risk, and so on.[3] This is because conflicted E and C youths were almost identical to one another on each of these factors or dimensions (Appendix 11).

The experimental/control differences also held up when the control group was subdivided into (1) *regular controls*—individuals institutionalized prior to parole—and (2) *direct parolees*—youths released directly from NRCC to a standard-sized caseload (regular parole), without having first been institutionalized. (See Appendix 12. Direct parolees accounted for 17 percent of the 1961–1969 sample of control boys.)[4]

How did conflicted E and C youths compare on other measures of effectiveness?

Parole Failure

On 24-months parole follow-up, 45 percent of the E's and 66 percent of the C's had failed

on parole—that is, they were revoked or recommitted on one or more occasions. This difference was statistically significant, in favor of E's. As before, the conflicted E and C groups were very similar to one another on age, IQ, level of parole risk, and so on. (Throughout Phases 1 and 2 of the experiment, parole failure referred to "any of the following actions: revocation, recommitment by the courts, unfavorable discharge from the Youth Authority" (Palmer, 1970b, p. 27). The preponderance of all such failures involved either revocation or recommitment (R or R), and these were coded as such. Unfavorable discharges (UD's) that had *not* been preceded by one or more R or R's comprised 14 percent of all UD's among E's and 18 percent among C's.)

Rate of Discharge from YA

Within five years from their first release to parole, 77 percent of the experimentals and 40 percent of the controls were given a favorable discharge from the Youth Authority, by the YA Board. During that same time, 17 percent of the E's and 40 percent of the C's received an unfavorable discharge, whether or not they had ever been revoked or recommitted. Again these were nonchance differences, and the E and C samples of conflicted youth were almost identical to each other on all relevant background characteristics.

In sum, conflicted CTP youths performed considerably better than their non-CTP counterparts, during parole. This was true for all three major, traditional indices of effectiveness, indices that—collectively—focused on youth behavior and staff decisions alike.

How did conflicted experimentals and controls compare in the areas of *school* and *paid employment?* On balance, conflicted E's performed a little better than C's in terms of school adjustment. E's and C's performed about equally well in the area of paid employment during their first year on parole; however, during the second year E's were somewhat ahead. Details are presented in Appendix 13.

Another type of effectiveness index was that of *attitude change,* as measured by the California Psychological Inventory (CPI). To determine the amount of change, experimentals and controls were tested at two points in time—pretest and posttest. Before we summarize the findings it should be noted that this index, as used during 1961–1969, was of limited value relative to the question of, "How did E's and C's compare with one another during parole?"[5] Nevertheless, the results were as follows:

In the area of "social adjustment," conflicted E's and conflicted C's showed essentially equal amounts of positive change from pretest to posttest. That is, neither group outperformed the other. What happened was that one of the two categories of conflicted youths—the assertive-deniers—did show significantly more positive change in the case of experimentals. However, this outcome was counterbalanced by the anxious-confused group—conflicted youths, who came out significantly ahead in the case of controls. No experimental/control differences were found in a second area that was assessed—"personal adjustment" (social and personal adjustment were defined and rated by the author of the CPI[6]) (Palmer, 1970b).

Passive-Conformist Youths

It will be recalled that this type of youth usually fears, and responds with strong compliance to, peers and adults whom he thinks have the upper hand at the moment, or who appear more adequate and assertive than himself. He considers himself lacking in social "know-how," and usually expects to be rejected by others despite his efforts to please them.

As shown in Table 8–1 (page 97), passive-conformists in CTP were arrested less than half as often, and were convicted four times less often, than those in the traditional program. These findings applied to moderate plus severe offenses combined.

Looking at severe offenses alone, experimentals again outperformed controls: On arrests, rates of offending were 11 per 1,000 months at risk (E's) and 25 per 1,000 months (C's). This was a 56 percent reduction in delinquent behavior for CTP as compared to traditional program youths. On convictions, the rates were 6 and 18 per 1,000 months at risk, a reduction of 67 percent. These results held up for violent offenses as well, but to a lesser degree.

Except for violent offenses these experimental/control differences in rate of offending were statistically reliable. E's and C's were comparable on most background variables as well. However, when one looks at other measures of effectiveness, the differences were less clear-cut; yet E's managed to retain their lead.

Parole Failure
On 24-months parole follow-up, 59 percent of the controls and 51 percent of the experimentals were revoked at least once.

Rate of Discharge
On five-year follow-up from first release to parole, 54 percent of the controls and 78 percent of the experimentals received a favorable discharge from the Youth Authority. Fourteen percent of the C's and 6 percent of the E's received an unfavorable discharge.

How did passive-conformists perform in the areas of school and paid employment? On balance, these individuals performed somewhat better in the *traditional* program than in CTP, relative to school. They performed better than E's in the area of paid employment as well. This applied to both their first and second year on parole. (See Appendix 13 for details.)

Were there any experimental/control differences in attitude change, as measured by the California Psychological Inventory? Essentially, no: E's and C's *each* showed positive change from pretest to posttest, with respect to personal and social adjustment. However, both groups improved to about the same degree.

Power-Oriented Youths

As described earlier, this category consists of two somewhat different groups of individuals—youths who nevertheless share several important features with one another. The first group (manipulators) often attempts to undermine or circumvent the efforts, suggestions, and directions of authority figures. Typically, they do not wish to conform to peers or adults; and, not infrequently, they try to assume a leading power role for themselves. The second group (group conformists) wishes to think of themselves as delinquent and tough. They are often more than willing to "go along with" others, or with a gang, in order to obtain status and acceptance and to later maintain their reputation.

As shown in Table 8–1 (page 97), power-oriented experimentals were arrested 17 percent less often than controls: rates of offending were 55 and 66 per 1,000 months at risk, for E's and C's, respectively. This finding relates to moderate plus severe offenses combined and could, however, have been accounted for by chance. On convictions, the rates were identical for E's and C's.

Focusing on severe offenses, experimentals performed noticeably better than controls. Arrest rates were 21 per 1,000 months (E's) and 34 per 1,000 months (C's), a reduction in delinquent behavior of 38 percent. Rates of conviction were 15 and 21 per 1,000 months, respectively, a reduction of 29 percent. However, because the sample sizes were not very large, only the first of these substantial differences was statistically reliable. At any rate, the findings for severe offenses also held up to a certain extent for violent offenses, in particular. Here, the experimental/control reductions in delinquency were 25 percent (arrests) and 20 percent (convictions), respectively—both in favor of E's. (See Appendix 26, section I, regarding the parole performance of group conformists and manipulators, respectively.)

When one inspects other measures of effectiveness the picture becomes rather mixed: On 24-months follow-up the rate of *parole failure* was 40 percent for experimentals and 66 percent for controls. This is consistent with the findings on rate of offending. However, results of a different nature were observed for rate of *discharge*. Within five years from date of first parole, 43 percent of the experimentals and 53 percent of the controls had received a favorable discharge; figures for unfavorable discharge were 23 percent (E's) and 15 percent (C's).

Thus, if one focuses on illegal behavior alone, power-oriented youths performed somewhat but not significantly better in CTP than in the traditional program, during their Youth Authority career. However, if one looks at measures that reflect the interaction between illegal behavior and staff decisions in response to that behavior, the results are conflicting. Moreover, as seen below, a rather different picture emerges when one inspects the *post*–Youth Authority behavior of these youths.

How did these individuals perform in connection with school and paid employment? On balance, power-oriented youths performed slightly worse in the traditional program than in CTP, in relation to school. On the other hand, power-oriented controls were slightly ahead of experimentals in the area of paid employment. (See Appendix 13.)

Were there any significant experimental/control differences in attitude change, as measured by the CPI? Yes: Power-oriented experimentals outperformed controls in terms of social adjustment, and results on personal adjustment were similar. In both cases E's showed significantly more positive change than C's from pretest to posttest. This was apart from the fact that controls had shown considerable improvement from the pretest to the posttest, themselves.

The Total Group (All Youths Combined)

As shown in Table 8–1 (page 97), monthly arrest rates for the total group were 76 per 1,000 months at risk among controls and 38 per 1,000 months among experimentals. Rates of conviction were 48 and 24 per 1,000 months for controls and experimentals, respectively. Thus, youths in the traditional program were involved in offense behavior twice as often as those in CTP. This represented a 50 percent reduction in delinquency for CTP as compared to traditional program youths, in the case of arrests and convictions alike. These findings applied to moderate plus severe offenses combined.

Results were essentially the same for severe offenses alone: Experimentals were arrested 46 percent less often, and were convicted 47 percent less often, than controls. The number of arrests per 1,000 months at risk were 15 (E's) and 28 (C's); the number of convictions were 9 and 17. Much the same was observed for violent offenses: Experimentals were arrested 46 percent less often than controls, and were convicted 38 percent less often.

These experimental/control differences were all statistically reliable. Furthermore, they could not be attributed to differing background characteristics, since the total group of E's and C's were very similar to one another on age, IQ, socioeconomic status of the family, race, and level of parole risk (Appendix 11). Thus, with respect to arrests and convictions during parole, CTP youths clearly outperformed comparable individuals who participated in the traditional program. Similar results were also observed on most additional measures of performance.

Parole Failure
On 24-months parole follow-up, 63 percent of the controls and 44 percent of the experimentals had been revoked.

Rate of Discharge
On five-year follow-up, 50 percent of the controls and 69 percent of the experimentals received a favorable discharge from the Youth Authority; 23 percent of the C's and 16 percent of the E's received an unfavorable discharge.

Other Measures
How did the total group of experimentals and controls compare with respect to school and paid employment? In general, E's performed slightly better than C's in the area of school. However, no consistent or substantial differences were found in connection with paid employment. (See Appendix 13.)

Were there any significant differences in amount of positive attitude change, as measured by the California Psychological Inventory? Yes: Experimentals outperformed controls in the area of social adjustment. This applied to personal adjustment as well, but to a slightly lesser degree (Palmer, 1970b).

Program Impact after Discharge
Thus far we have described program impact during parole. But what happened *after* parole—that is, after the youths were discharged from the Youth Authority? Before answering this question three points might be kept in mind. (1) Findings that will be presented once again relate to our main index of effectiveness: rate of offending, based on BCI rap-

sheets. (2) All youths, favorable plus unfavorable dischargees combined, were followed up for four years in the community, counting from the day of their YA discharge; 79 percent of these individuals had received a favorable discharge, and the remaining 21 percent received an unfavorable discharge. (3) These youths are from the same sample that was involved in the rate-of-offending analysis that has just been described, in connection with Youth Authority careers.[7]

As shown in Table 8-2, the results of this postdischarge analysis are as follows.

Conflicted Youths
On four-year post-YA follow-up, conflicted experimentals were arrested 45 percent less often and convicted 39 percent less often than conflicted controls. The rates of offending on which these percentage differences are based were: (1) 32 arrests per 1,000 months at risk for E's and 58 arrests per 1,000 months for C's, and (2) 19 and 31 convictions per 1,000 months at risk for E's and C's, respectively. This refers to moderate plus severe offenses combined, and both findings were statistically reliable. (When the conflicted category was subdivided into its two components, similar results were found for assertive-denier and, to a lesser degree, anxious-confused youths. See Appendix 27.)

Results were similar for *severe* offenses alone. Experimentals were arrested 36 percent less often and convicted 33 percent less often than controls. For violent offenses they were arrested 38 percent less often than controls; however, their rates of conviction were identical to those of controls. Other than this last one, these findings tended to be significant.

Thus, after being discharged from the Youth Authority, conflicted experimentals continued to outperform conflicted controls. It is important to note that this result or finding cannot be explained as a product of differential decision-making across the CTP and traditional programs, or of discretionary decisions by staff, since the youths were no longer under YA jurisdiction. Moreover, the finding (especially on arrests) relates to youth behavior as this term is ordinarily understood, not to revocation or rate of discharge (policy-influenced—albeit behavior-based—measures). Finally, this finding cannot be accounted for in terms of E/C differences in background characteristics, since the conflicted experimentals

TABLE 8–2

Number of Offenses per 1,000 Months at Risk for Valley Boys, Subsequent to Discharge from Youth Authority

Type of Offense and Outcome Measure	Conflicted		Passive-Conformist		Power-Oriented		Total Group[b]	
	Exp.	Control	Exp.	Control	Exp.	Control	Exp.	Control
Moderate + Severe Offenses								
All arrests	32	58	35	38	68	43	39	45
Arrests with convictions	19	31	26	15	43	33	24	27
Severe Offenses								
All arrests	14	22	12	6	37	17	19	16
Arrests with convictions	8	12	7	1	16	11	10	9
Violent Offenses[c]								
All arrests	5	8	7	2	13	8	7	6
Arrests with convictions	3	3	3	0	5	3	4	2

Youth Type and Number of Offenses[a]

[a]Sample sizes are as follows: Conflicted, E-70, C-38; Passive-Conformist, E-12, C-17; Power-Oriented, E-25, C-33; Total Group, E-125, C-109.
[b]See Table 8–1, note b.
[c]See Table 8–1, note c.

and controls who were discharged and followed up for four years in the community were very similar to one another on age, race, level of parole risk, and so on. (See Appendix 11.)

Passive-Conformist Youths

During parole, passive-conformist experimentals had, as indicated, outperformed controls on arrests and convictions alike. However, on four-year postdischarge this was true only for moderate plus severe *arrests* combined; and here, the rates favored E's by only 8 percent, a chance difference. In contrast, rates of conviction favored C's by 42 percent. For severe offenses, arrest and conviction rates also favored controls. Finally, C's outperformed E's on arrests and convictions for violent offenses as well.

All in all, passive-conformist controls who were followed up for four years after discharge had an edge over experimentals during that time. However, because of the findings on moderate plus severe arrests, the overall findings might also be described as mixed.

Power-Oriented Youths

As with passive-conformists, results for the postdischarge period were different than those for the parole period—in this case, very different: On four-year postdischarge follow-up, power-oriented controls were arrested 37 per-

cent less often and convicted 23 percent less often than power-oriented experimentals. The figures on which these percentage differences are based were: (1) 43 arrests per 1,000 months at risk for controls and 68 per 1,000 for experimentals, and (2) 33 versus 43 convictions per 1,000 months for C's and E's, respectively. Looking at severe offenses alone, the results favored controls by 54 percent on arrests and 31 percent on convictions. In the case of violent offenses, the E/C percentage differences were fairly similar to those for severe offenses as a whole. In sum, power-oriented controls who were followed for four years after YA discharge clearly outperformed experimentals during that time period. (See Appendix 27 regarding the postdischarge performance of group conformists and manipulators.)

The Total Group

When all youths are analyzed as a single group, experimentals were arrested 13 percent less often than controls and were convicted 11 percent less often, for moderate plus severe offenses combined. However, there were no really sharp E/C differences in rate of offending, regardless of either severity level or the distinction between arrests and convictions. The reason was rather simple: Postdischarge results that favored conflicted *experimentals* were counterbalanced and essentially canceled by those that favored power-oriented and, on a smaller scale, passive-conformist *controls*.[8] This was much like combining a +1 and a –1: the net result is 0. Specifically, the rather sizable postdischarge difference between E and C power-oriented youths (in favor of controls) more or less evened things out—that, combined with the fact that the sample of discharged controls contained a high proportion of power-oriented individuals in the first place. This again illustrates the value of carrying out more than total group analyses alone.

Before proceeding to the next major analysis it might be recalled that the present findings related to favorable and unfavorable dischargees combined. Most *unfavorable* dischargees had spent a good deal of time in prison and/or jail, after receiving their YA discharge.[9] As a result, they received considerable input from justice system agencies other than the Youth Authority itself. (They experienced these inputs during the time they were accumulating their four years of postdischarge community time, that is, non-lockup time.) Because of this input, there existed a certain degree of ambiguity in the answer to the following question: What were the effects of *Youth Authority* programs—traditional and CTP alike—on the sample of YA dischargees?

To remove this ambiguity, or nearly all of it, a supplementary analysis was carried out. This analysis involved favorable dischargees alone—individuals who, collectively, had experienced little input from justice system agencies other than the YA. Also, it might be recalled that favorable dischargees had already satisfied the Youth Authority's preestablished behavioral requirements for honorable or acceptable discharge.[10] In this respect they represented "the best" that the traditional and CTP programs had produced. Thus, in addition to addressing the above ambiguity, the supplementary analysis focused directly on the following: How did experimental and control *program successes* compare with each other after their discharge from the Youth Authority?

Results of this favorable-dischargees analysis are shown in Appendix 14, section I. Basically, the findings were almost identical to those described earlier, for favorable and unfavorable dischargees combined. This was especially true of conflicted and power-oriented youths, and of the total group as well:

Conflicted experimentals who were program successes outperformed conflicted controls who were also program successes; the reverse was found among power-oriented individuals; and so on.[11] In short, the postdischarge, non-YA experiences of unfavorable dischargees had little practical impact on answers that were obtained to the fundamental questions of differential and comparative effectiveness, for favorable and unfavorable dischargees *combined*: Results were essentially the same whether or not unfavorable dischargees were included.

Program Impact over a Seven-Year Period

What happened when all arrest and conviction data were brought together—that is, when parole and postdischarge periods were combined? Here, the average follow-up was 6.8 years per youth, counting from (1) first release to parole and continuing straight through to (2) 48 months after YA discharge, excluding all lockup time. As shown in Table 8–3, results of this analysis are essentially as follows.

Conflicted experimentals clearly outperformed conflicted controls on arrests as well as convictions. This applied to moderate plus severe, severe, and violent offenses alike. These performance differences could not be accounted for by chance.

Passive-conformist experimentals clearly outperformed their controls on arrests as well as convictions, for moderate plus severe offenses combined; this tended to apply to severe arrests and convictions as well. However, there were no E/C differences on violent offenses, in particular.

Power-oriented controls performed somewhat better than experimentals on arrests as well as convictions in connection with moderate plus severe offenses combined, and severe arrests (but not convictions) as well. These differences could have been accounted for by chance. There were no substantial E/C differences in the case of violent offenses.

For the total group, experimentals outperformed controls by 38 percent on arrests and 35 percent on convictions: Rates of offending were (1) 38 arrests per 1,000 months at risk for E's and 61 per 1,000 months for C's, and (2) 24 versus 37 convictions per 1,000 months for E's and C's, respectively. Findings were generally the same for severe as well as violent offenses; here, however, the experimental/control differ-

TABLE 8–3

Number of Offenses per 1,000 Months at Risk for Valley Boys, for Parole and Postdischarge Periods Combined[a]

| | Youth Type and Number of Offenses[b] | | | | | | | |
| Type of Offense and Outcome Measure | Conflicted | | Passive-Conformist | | Power-Oriented | | Total Group[c] | |
	Exp.	Control	Exp.	Control	Exp.	Control	Exp.	Control
Moderate + Severe Offenses								
All arrests	33	69	33	66	61	53	38	61
Arrests with convictions	20	41	21	42	41	35	24	37
Severe Offenses								
All arrests	14	26	12	18	28	24	17	22
Arrests with convictions	9	15	6	11	15	15	10	13
Violent Offenses[d]								
All arrests	5	11	7	7	13	11	7	10
Arrests with convictions	3	7	4	4	7	6	4	5

[a]*Parole* refers to the entire Youth Authority career, as in Table 8–1. *Postdischarge* refers to the four-year, post-YA follow-up, as in Table 8–2.

[b]Sample sizes are as follows: Conflicted, E-70, C-38; Passive-Conformist, E-12, C-17; Power-Oriented, E-25, C-33; Total Group, E-125, C-109.

[c]See Table 8–1, note b.

[d]See Table 8–1, note c.

ences were not really striking. At any rate, with respect to the present, *combined* parole plus post-YA analysis, the postdischarge performance of power-oriented controls did not carry enough weight to counterbalance and cancel the post-YA and parole performance of conflicted experimentals.

This seven-year follow-up related to favorable and unfavorable dischargees combined. The results for favorable dischargees alone can be found in Appendix 14, section II. Basically, these findings were rather similar to those reported in the present analysis, for favorable and unfavorable dischargees combined.

Program Effectiveness for Valley Females

In general, experimental and control girls performed about equally well with respect to rate of offending. That is, except for the postdischarge period, few statistically significant differences were found between the total group of E's and the total group of C's on this effectiveness index. However, some suggestive findings were obtained for particular youth types. This related not only to the parole period, but to postdischarge as well.

These and other results will be reviewed below.

Before proceeding, two points might be noted: (1) Rates of offending (r.o.o.) for Valley control girls were generally three times lower than those already noted for Valley control boys. Moreover, Valley control girls had a low r.o.o. in absolute terms as well, not just in comparison to boys. Given this situation, there was, from the outset, less opportunity for (a) *experimental* girls to show a statistically significant *reduction* or even a substantial percentage reduction in rate of offending over *control* girls than there had been for (b) experimental boys in relation to control boys. (2) No statistically significant (reliable) differences were found between experimental and control girls in the areas of school and paid employment. A similar result was obtained on attitude change as measured by the California Psychological Inventory. Since these findings were obtained for all three youth groups and for the total group as well, these measures of effectiveness need not be further reviewed. (One exception regarding attitude change is mentioned below.)

Program Impact during Parole
Conflicted Girls

As shown in Table 8–4, conflicted girls in CTP performed the same as (or slightly worse than) those in the traditional program. On arrests, rates of offending were 24 per 1,000 months at risk for experimentals and 23 per 1,000 months for controls. On convictions, conflicted E's tended to perform worse than their controls: 12 versus 9 offenses per 1,000 months, respectively. These findings related to moderate plus severe offenses combined.

Focusing on *severe* offenses alone, rate of arrest was the same for experimental girls as compared to control girls, though convictions were slightly higher for the former. (For E's and C's alike—conflicted and otherwise—one-third of all such arrests involved prostitution.) For violent offenses alone, the same results were observed: There were no statistically reliable differences between experimental and control girls. In fact, violent offenses were almost nonexistent within both groups.

On 24-months *parole follow-up*, 43 percent of the conflicted experimentals and 55 percent of their controls had failed on parole; that is, in almost all cases these individuals were revoked or recommitted and were then sent to a Youth Authority institution for several months. However, this difference in failure rates between E's and C's could have been accounted for by chance; in other words, it was not statistically reliable.

Within five years from their first release to parole, 67 percent of the conflicted experimental girls and 53 percent of their controls were given a *favorable discharge* from the Youth Authority, by the YA Board. During that same time an additional 27 percent of the experimentals and 26 percent of their controls received an unfavorable discharge. These E/C differences could all be accounted for by chance. (Conflicted E's had more positive attitude change than C's, from pretest to posttest [Palmer, 1970b].)

Passive-Conformist Girls

As shown in Table 8–4, passive-conformist experimentals performed substantially better than controls during their Youth Authority career, regarding rate of offending. For arrests, the rates were 23 and 55 per 1,000 months at risk for E's and C's, respectively; for convictions, they were 20 and 41. However, since very few passive-conformist girls were present within the E and (especially)

TABLE 8–4

Number of Offenses per 1,000 Months at Risk during Parole, for Valley Girls

Type of Offense and Outcome Measure	Youth Type and Number of Offenses[a]							
	Conflicted		Passive-Conformist		Power-Oriented		Total Group[b]	
	Exp.	Control	Exp.	Control	Exp.	Control	Exp.	Control
Moderate + Severe Offenses								
All arrests	24	23	23	55	28	18	24	22
Arrests with convictions	12	9	20	41	14	6	13	9
Severe Offenses								
All arrests	12	12	3	27	9	3	10	10
Arrests with convictions	7	4	0	27	7	0	6	4
Violent Offenses[c]								
All arrests	3	1	0	27	5	0	3	1
Arrests with convictions	2	1	0	27	4	0	2	1

[a]Sample sizes are as follows: Conflicted, E-34, C-52; Passive-Conformist, E-7, C-4; Power-Oriented, E-11, C-12; Total Group, E-55, C-72.

[b]*Total Group* includes all Conflicted + Passive-Conformist + Power-Oriented + Rare Types.

[c]Includes: armed robbery, rape (attempted or actual), assault with deadly weapon, aggravated assault, kidnapping, murder (attempted or actual), etc. These offenses are part of the broader category labeled *Severe Offenses* (sale of narcotics, grand theft auto, first-degree burglary, drunk driving, etc.).

C samples, these differences did not reach statistical significance and must be considered highly tenuous at best.

The preceding findings related to moderate plus severe offenses combined. However, for severe—and violent—offenses by themselves, the E/C differences in rate of offending were so sharp that statistical significance *was* obtained (in favor of E's), despite the small number of youths. Even so, the findings must be regarded as highly tentative.

On 24-months parole follow-up, 43 percent of the experimentals and 25 percent of the controls had failed on parole. In this case, the difference in question—though substantial—was not large enough to be statistically reliable.

On five-year follow-up from first release to parole, 71 percent of the passive-conformist experimentals and 100 percent of their controls received a favorable discharge from the Youth Authority. An additional 14 percent of the E's and, of course, 0 percent of the C's received an unfavorable discharge. These differences, like those for the 24-months parole follow-up, could have been accounted for by chance.

Power-Oriented Girls
For moderate plus severe offenses combined, power-oriented *control* girls had substantially lower rates of offending than experimentals. Specifically, for arrests, rates of offending were 18 and 28 per 1,000 months at risk for C's and E's, respectively; for convictions, they were 6 and 14 (Table 8–4). Although these differences were not statistically significant, they might well have been if the sample were twice as large as it was.

Focusing on severe offenses, power-oriented controls did perform significantly better than experimentals in connection with convictions, though not arrests. They tended to perform better than E's with respect to violent offenses as well—arrests and convictions alike. This was despite the low absolute rate of violent offenses among experimental girls.

On 24-months parole follow-up, 9 percent of the experimentals and 42 percent of the controls had failed on parole. This difference tended to be significant, in favor of E's.

Within five years from date of first parole, 78 percent of the power-oriented E's and 100 percent of their C's had received a favorable discharge; however, this was not a reliable difference. Figures for unfavorable discharge were 0 percent and 0 percent, respectively.

The Total Group
As shown in Table 8–4, no substantial or statistically reliable differences were observed in rate of offending between the total group of experimental and control girls. This was mostly due to the lack of substantial differences between conflicted E's and conflicted C's—by far the largest youth groups. However, it also related to the fact that differences which favored passive-conformist E's were counterbalanced by those which favored power-oriented C's. The lack of overall E/C differences in rate of offending, and the presence of counterbalancing in particular, was observed for all levels and types of analysis: moderate plus severe, severe, and violent.

On 24-months parole follow-up, 34 percent of the experimental girls and 49 percent of their controls had failed on parole. This difference tended to be significant, in favor of E's.

On five-year follow-up from first release to parole, 71 percent of the experimentals and 68 percent of their controls received a favorable discharge from the Youth Authority. An additional 19 percent of the E's and 18 percent of the C's received an unfavorable discharge. These differences could have been accounted for by chance.

Program Impact after Discharge
Conflicted Girls
As shown in Table 8–5, conflicted experimental girls were arrested and convicted at about the same rate as conflicted controls, on four-year post-YA follow-up. This related to moderate plus severe, severe, and violent offenses alike.

Passive-Conformist Girls
Passive-conformist E's were arrested and convicted more often than their controls, on moderate plus severe offenses combined. This was the opposite of what had occurred during their YA career. However, as before, these findings are based on a very small sample and are therefore very tenuous. For *severe*—and violent—offenses only, results were again the opposite of those that related to parole. However, in the present case, E/C differences were not statistically reliable.

The pattern of findings for passive-conformist girls was generally similar to that observed for passive-conformist boys: Relative to their controls, passive-conformist E's performed better during parole than subsequent to YA discharge.

TABLE 8–5

Number of Offenses per 1,000 Months at Risk for Valley Girls, Subsequent to Discharge from Youth Authority

| | Conflicted | | Passive-Conformist | | Power-Oriented | | Total Group[b] | |
Type of Offense and Outcome Measure	Exp.	Control	Exp.	Control	Exp.	Control	Exp.	Control
Moderate + Severe Offenses								
All arrests	10	12	21	0	0	29	8	15
Arrests with convictions	6	8	14	0	0	25	5	11
Severe Offenses								
All arrests	1	3	14	0	0	15	3	6
Arrests with convictions	0	3	7	0	0	10	1	5
Violent Offenses[c]								
All arrests	0	0	14	0	0	8	2	4
Arrests with convictions	0	0	7	0	0	6	1	2

Youth Type and Number of Offenses[a]

[a]Sample sizes are as follows: Conflicted, E-15, C-19; Passive-Conformist, E-3, C-3; Power-Oriented, E-5, C-10; Total Group, E-25, C-36.
[b]See Table 8–4, note b.
[c]See Table 8–4, note c.

Power-Oriented Girls

On four-year postdischarge follow-up, power-oriented experimentals performed much better than controls on arrests and convictions alike. These findings related to moderate plus severe offenses combined, and to severe offenses by themselves. (Similar, but weaker, results were observed for violent offenses.) These E/C differences were essentially the opposite of those found for the parole period, and they were statistically reliable despite the small number of youths involved.

The Total Group

On four-year postdischarge follow-up, experimental girls had 55 percent fewer convictions than their controls, for moderate plus severe offenses combined. The rates of offending on which this figure was based were 5 and 11 per 1,000 months at risk, for E's and C's, respectively (Table 8–5). This difference, although fairly small in absolute terms, could not be accounted for by chance. On moderate plus severe *arrests*, the E/C difference was *not* reliable even though it was fairly substantial in terms of percentage reduction.

Experimentals tended to perform better than controls in relation to severe offenses, but not on violent offenses taken by them-

selves. However, the E/C differences in question (for severe offenses) were quite small in absolute terms—three arrests, and four convictions, per 1,000 months at risk, respectively. In addition, the absolute rate of severe arrests and convictions was very low for E's and C's alike.

Program Impact over a 6½-Year Period

As shown in Table 8–6, conflicted experimentals and controls performed about equally well when parole and postdischarge periods were combined (6½-year follow-up).[12] This was true of passive-conformist and (to a slightly lesser extent) of power-oriented girls as well, mainly because their results for the parole period were counterbalanced by their opposite results on postdischarge (see Tables 8–4 and 8–5). For all three youth groups, these findings applied to each level and type of offense: moderate plus severe, severe, and violent.

Finally, for the total group, experimental girls were arrested 26 percent less often and convicted 30 percent less often than control girls, for moderate plus severe offenses combined. However, these differences could have been accounted for by chance. Chance differences were also found for severe and violent offenses—arrests and convictions alike.

TABLE 8–6

Number of Offenses per 1,000 Months at Risk for Valley Girls, for Parole and Postdischarge Periods Combined[a]

Type of Offense and Outcome Measure	Youth Type and Number of Offenses[b]							
	Conflicted		Passive-Conformist		Power-Oriented		Total Group[c]	
	Exp.	Control	Exp.	Control	Exp.	Control	Exp.	Control
Moderate + Severe Offenses								
All arrests	15	18	22	18	17	23	14	19
Arrests with convictions	8	9	18	14	8	16	7	10
Severe Offenses								
All arrests	6	10	12	9	6	10	6	9
Arrests with convictions	3	4	4	9	4	6	3	5
Violent Offenses[d]								
All arrests	4	1	6	9	6	5	4	2
Arrests with convictions	3	1	4	9	4	4	3	2

[a]*Parole* refers to the entire Youth Authority career, as in Table 8–1. *Postdischarge* refers to the four-year, post-YA follow-up, as in Table 8–2.
[b]Sample sizes are as follows: Conflicted, E-15, C-19; Passive-Conformist, E-3, C-3; Power-Oriented, E-5, C-10; Total Group, E-25, C-36.
[c]See Table 8–4, note b.
[d]See Table 8–4, note c.

Notes

1. Bureau of Criminal Investigation information is directly and routinely received by the Department of Justice from police, probation, and sheriffs' departments throughout California. Virtually all rapsheet entries refer to arrests initiated by one or another of these departments, that is, to "law-initiated arrests." These entries are easily distinguished from suspensions of parole, which are initiated by Youth Authority staff (parole agents) exclusively. The latter entries are known as "agent-initiated suspensions" and are, themselves, easily distinguished from actual revocations of parole. Each rapsheet also contains information regarding the disposition of specific acts (charges) for which the individual was arrested. For many years, BCI documents were known as Criminal Identification and Investigation ("C.I. I.") rapsheets.

2. When one adds to this group all conflicted youths who had not been discharged as of September 1974, the results remain much the same, and statistically significant as well. Nondischargees account for approximately the same percentage of all conflicted E's and all conflicted C's who were first released to parole during 1961–1969.

3. Throughout Phases 1 and 2 of the experiment, nine variables and factors were used to compute each individual's parole risk score—also called a "base expectancy" or "B.E." score: age at first admission to YA, age at first release to parole, prior delinquent record, number of offense partners, current attitude toward school, number of foster home placements, truancy, self-respect of family, and "race" (ethnicity) (Beverly, 1964; Warren and Palmer, 1965, pp. 41, 89). In Phase 3, five variables and factors were used: age at first admission to YA, number of prior commitments to YA, school misbehavior, number of prior escapes, and number of offense partners (Beverly, 1968; Palmer, 1970b, pp. 17, 69).

4. The YA Board did not think these individuals needed to be institutionalized. Eighty-one percent of all direct paroles occurred prior to 1966; 88 percent were prior to 1967.

5. This question was not fully and specifically addressed in relation to attitude change. This was because the California Psychological Inventory comparisons related to (1) the period of initial institutionalization, not that of institutionalization plus regular parole, in the case of controls (C's were usually posttested two or three weeks after first release to parole), and (2) approximately the first 12 months on parole, in the case of experimentals. Thus, with respect to attitude change, the impact of traditional institutionalization was compared with that of CTP parole. (In the case of all E's and C's, composite test scores were rated by Dr. Gough, author of the CPI. This was done separately, randomly, and "blindly" for each youth's pretest and posttest profile. The profile was a representation of all 18 scales of the CPI [Gough, 1960; Warren and Palmer, 1965, pp. 87–88].)

6. Definitions were as follows. *Social adjustment:* "The general capacity to adapt to the demands of normal life in the community, including adequate adjustment to family, school, peers, work, etc., and the ability to cope with authority in a realistic and appropriate manner." *Personal adjustment:* "A realistic degree of self-awareness and self-acceptance, ability to cope with internal and external problems with a minimum of distress and anxiety, and an understanding of the determinants of one's own feelings and behavior" (Warren and Palmer, 1965, p. 30).

7. In the case of experimentals, the *YA career analysis* (i.e., the analysis of program impact up to the point of discharge) related to 134 favorable discharges and 39 unfavorable discharges. Of these individuals, 78 percent (105) of the favorable discharges and 51 percent (20) of the unfavorable discharges accumulated at least 48 months in the community (as of the data-cutoff point) after receiving their discharge from the Youth Authority. These were the 125 individuals who therefore comprised the experimental sample in the present, *postdischarge* analysis. In the case of controls, the YA career analysis included 98 favorable discharges and 59 unfavorable discharges. Of these youths, 81 percent (79) of the former and 51 percent

(30) of the latter accumulated at least 48 months in the community between the time of discharge and that of data cutoff. These were the 109 individuals who comprised the control sample in the present, postdischarge analysis.

8. Counterbalancing and canceling relate, of course, to the total group analysis alone. They do not apply to the youth groups that comprise the total group itself. That is, findings for individual youth groups remain unchanged, regardless of their impact on the total group analysis.

9. More than three-fourths of all unfavorable dischargees (UD's) had been discharged—from the YA—directly to a state prison, federal prison, or local jail. Many UD's later went to prison or jail, and/or returned to prison or jail, on one or more occasions while they were accumulating their four years of postdischarge community risk time. For a very similar account of the post-YA prison and jail record of 3,617 male dischargees, see Davis et al., 1973. Also compare Davis and Pike (1983).

10. As shown in Appendix 9, favorable discharge was a direct product of the youths' behavior in the community. By law, minimum standards of behavior—agencywide standards—had to be met before the Youth Authority Board was free to release an individual from the YA on the basis of what was technically known as an honorable or acceptable discharge. As a result, favorable discharge was not something that could be achieved, as it were, "by mirrors" and manipulation—or, for instance, by discretionary decision-making on the part of program staff (traditional as well as CTP), board members, or both.

11. As with the results for the *combined* favorable plus unfavorable discharge analysis, these findings cannot be accounted for in terms of E/C differences in background characteristics, since the E's and C's who were discharged and then followed up for four years in the community were very similar to each other on age, race, level of parole risk, and so on. (See Appendix 11.)

12. The average follow-up time for parole and postdischarge periods combined was slightly shorter among girls than boys.

PROGRAM EFFECTIVENESS FOR SAN FRANCISCO YOUTHS

The San Francisco experiment focused on two main questions: Could the Community Treatment Project's concepts and operations be applied to large-sized, urban settings? What factors accounted for CTP's relative success during Phase 1?

To address these questions two new parole units—a CTP and a Guided Group Interaction (GGI) unit—were established in central San Francisco. These units got underway in 1965 and operated through mid-1969. They were evaluated by the same research team that had studied the Valley units in 1961–1964 (Phase 1), and via the same methods that were used during those years. To compare CTP and GGI with the traditional Youth Authority program, a regular parole unit (SF control) was studied as well.

Throughout this experiment all eligible youths were randomly assigned to either CTP, GGI, or control, via the procedures described in Chapter 2. Eligibility criteria were identical to those used during Phase 1. These criteria were continued in the Phase 2 Valley units as well (Warren, Palmer, and Turner, 1964a).

Overview of Programs and Sample

The San Francisco CTP unit closely resembled the Phase 1 and 2 Valley units with respect to structure, organization, intake procedures, case assignment, caseload size, and program components. However, as to actual operations, out-of-home placements were more difficult to locate in San Francisco than in Sacramento/Stockton, and short-term detention at the Northern Reception Center and Clinic (90 miles distant) was not readily available. Moreover, due to relatively cramped

quarters within the parole office itself, recreational activities were limited in scope and the CTP school program was less elaborately developed than in the Valley (Turner et al., 1967; Palmer et al., 1968).

The Guided Group Interaction unit was modeled after the Provo operation (Empey and Rabow, 1961; Empey and Erickson, 1972; Turner et al., 1967, Warren, Palmer, and Turner, 1964a). Staff were selected on the basis of their expressed interest in the guided group approach and their probable ability to carry out its techniques. Treatment and control were implemented mainly through youth/youth interactions—that is, direct peer influences within a structured group setting.

During full operations the GGI unit usually contained three active groups at any one time—an older boys, a younger boys, and a girls group. Eight to 12 youths participated in each group, and each group went through two distinct phases. Phase A usually lasted six to eight months and involved 1- to 1½-hour-long meetings five days a week, on a mandatory basis. Phase B usually lasted 9 to 12 months and involved twice-a-month "alumni group" meetings for individuals who had successfully completed Phase A. Phase B also included pragmatically oriented interactions between the parole agent and youth. For details, see Turner et al. (1967, pp. 21–26).

Within GGI, no attempt was made to match youths and parole agents (see Chapter 11). I-level information, though available, was not considered relevant to the guided group approach. Thus, it was not used for assigning youths to particular groups, for determining individual treatment goals, and for formulating individual or group strategies and techniques.

Though GGI caseloads averaged 15 youths per worker, the agent/youth relationship usually remained undeveloped; more precisely, its formal and informal role was minimized wherever possible. Also by design, individual counseling was extremely rare and family counseling was nonexistent. Finally, little placement planning was carried out, initially or otherwise, and very few collateral contacts were made during Phase A. Further information regarding this peer-centered program appears in Youth Authority reports (Turner et al., 1967; Palmer et al., 1968). In turn, GGI approaches were not used in the CTP unit.

During the experiment (1965–1969), 51 percent of all boys and 76 percent of all girls who were appropriate referrals (defined as in Chapter 2) were declared eligible by the YA Board and were randomly assigned to either CTP, GGI, or control. Thus, for boys in particular, the eligibility percentage was noticeably lower than that in the Valley. This was mainly because specific board members who regularly handled San Francisco (SF) cases consciously reflected, in their eligibility decisions, (1) the generalized fear of street crime that was rapidly crystallizing in SF by mid-1965, (2) public fear or outrage over very recent, well-publicized, violent crimes within but not necessarily limited to SF, by individuals or groups other than the preeligible youths themselves, and (3) their personal views concerning the seriousness and implications of specific, not necessarily violent or assaultive, commitment offenses and of particular offense histories, as well. As a result, these board members sometimes declared, as *ineligible,* youths who should have been declared *eligible* and thus been allowed into the experiment based strictly on the preestablished, agreed-upon criteria regarding "project-acceptable" commitment offenses, and so on.

Except for an underrepresentation of violent offenders, the individuals assigned to CTP, GGI, and control were typical of most juvenile court commitments to the Youth Authority from San Francisco.[1] However, these individuals—the eligible sample—differed from *Valley* youths in certain respects.[2] First, the SF sample contained a much higher percentage and a very different distribution of minority individuals: 3 percent Mexican American, 67 percent black, and 5 percent all others; figures for Valley eligibles were 23 percent, 20 percent, and 4 percent. Second, it

contained a somewhat lower percentage of males—70 percent as compared to 83 percent. Third, San Francisco youths were typically six months older than Valley youths at point of YA intake.[3] Finally, SF youths were slightly worse parole risks as judged by a standardized base expectancy formula (Beverly, 1964; Palmer et al., 1968; Turner et al., 1967; Warren and Palmer, 1965).[4]

Despite these differences, approximately the same percentage of San Francisco and Valley youths came from lower socioeconomic backgrounds—84 percent and 81 percent, respectively. Moreover, the samples were similar with regard to YA commitment offense, IQ, and percentage of passive-conformist, power-oriented, and conflicted individuals, respectively.[5]

Program Effectiveness for San Francisco Boys

The San Francisco research effort mainly focused on a comparison between two alternate community-based programs: CTP and GGI. This emphasis reflected the central questions of Phase 2 (Chapter 1). Answers to the first such question—which centered on CTP's generalized applicability—will be reviewed at the close of this chapter; answers to the second—which involved the key elements of its success—will be discussed in Chapter 15.

Our immediate purpose extends beyond the Phase 2 issues: It involves the question of CTP's effectiveness relative to the *traditional* Youth Authority program as well. As in Chapter 8, this question will be addressed by comparing the local CTP program with regular parole, in this case SF control (C). Main results for boys as well as girls are summarized in Chapter 12.

Since the San Francisco experiment originally focused on a comparison between CTP and GGI, it was these particular programs that received top priority during 1965–1969, when youths were being assigned to either CTP, GGI, or control. (This priority was implemented by means of stratified random assignment.) Because fewer San Francisco youths were available for assignment than had been originally expected, this meant that relatively few individuals could be assigned to control (Turner et al., 1967). Because a high percentage of all available youths were falling within the conflicted group, it also meant that very few passive-conformist and power-oriented individuals could be assigned to control. Given the small number of youths that ended up in those two categories, the presentation which follows will include no comparisons between CTP and control with respect to those particular groups. Despite this limitation, passive-conformist and power-oriented individuals will of course be included in the total group.

(For the sake of completeness, Tables 9–1 through 9–6 contain the sample sizes and rates of offending for passive-conformist and power-oriented controls; however, these particular rates of offending should not be considered reliable. It might be mentioned that information concerning GGI is also found in these tables, and is reviewed in the text.)

Before we turn to the main findings, four technical points will be mentioned. These points relate to the specific youth samples that were compared with one another in order to assess CTP's effectiveness during parole, using rate of offending as the principal index of effectiveness. Basically, these points indicate that the differences in rate of offending which were found between the youths who were compared (namely, CTP and control; also, CTP and GGI) can hardly be attributed to preexisting (pre-program) differences in the background characteristics of these youths. This is because such differences were almost nonexistent in the first place, mainly due to the stratified randomization procedure that was used throughout the experiment. The background characteristics or variables that were studied are: level of parole risk, age, IQ, ethnicity, socioeconomic status, and type of committing offense.

1. When conflicted CTP boys were compared with conflicted control boys on each background variable, only one significant (nonchance) difference was found: Individuals in CTP had a slightly lower IQ. This applied to the total group as well. Due to the small number of passive-conformist controls (see Table 9–1, note a), the CTP and control boys were not compared with each other on this category. The same applied to power-oriented boys.
2. When the total group of CTP girls were compared with their controls, only one significant difference was found: Individuals in CTP were slightly worse

parole risks. This did not apply to conflicted girls, taken by themselves. For the reason mentioned above, no comparisons were made between CTP and control in the case of passive-conformist and power-oriented girls.

3. When the total group of CTP boys were compared with the total group of GGI boys, no significant differences were found on any background variables. With the following exception this was also true for passive-conformist, power-oriented, and conflicted youths, respectively: among passive-conformists, a higher percentage of property offenders was found in CTP than in GGI; among power-oriented youths, a lower percentage was found in CTP.
4. With one exception, no significant differences were found when the total group of CTP girls were compared with the total group of GGI girls: CTP youths had a somewhat higher percentage of commitment offenses that were directed against persons (12 percent, versus 0 percent for GGI), and a lower percentage of those that related to property (6 percent, versus 16 percent for GGI). Essentially the same results were obtained for conflicted youths.

Impact during Parole
Conflicted Youths
As shown in Table 9–1, conflicted experimental youths performed somewhat better than their controls on moderate plus severe offenses combined. However, the differences in question were not statistically significant, possibly because of the small number of controls that were present. Specifically, for arrests during parole, rates of offending were 70 and 92 per 1,000 months at risk for E's and C's, respectively, a reduction of 24 percent using controls as the base. For convictions, the rates were 38 and 56 per 1,000 months, a reduction of 32 percent.

For severe offenses, conflicted experimentals were arrested 56 percent and convicted 59 percent less often than controls. Here, rates of offending were 12(E) versus 27(C) and 7(E) versus 17(C) per 1,000 months at risk, for arrests and convictions, respectively. These differences were statistically reliable.

For violent offenses (a subcategory within the severe group), experimentals continued to outperform controls. Here, too, the E/C differences—75 percent reduction in arrests and 80 percent in convictions—could not be accounted for by chance.

Also shown in Table 9–1, comparisons between conflicted CTP and GGI youths yielded fairly similar results: For moderate plus severe offenses combined, no significant differences were found on arrests and convictions alike. However, for severe—and violent—offenses alone, substantial as well as statistically reliable differences were observed on arrests and convictions alike. Here, rates of offending were generally two to three times lower in CTP than in GGI. (For information regarding the two components of the conflicted category—assertive-deniers and anxious-confused youths—see Appendix 26, section IV.)

Passive-Conformist Youths
As suggested earlier, meaningful comparisons could not be made between passive-conformist experimentals and their controls due to the very small number of controls within this category. (At best, the results would be highly tenuous.) However, in the case of experimentals (CTP youths) and GGI, comparisons could be made. Here, for moderate plus severe arrests combined, essentially no difference was observed; this was true for convictions as well. Yet, for severe convictions, substantial and statistically reliable differences were observed between CTP and GGI, in favor of the former. For severe arrests and violent convictions, these differences tended to be significant. Specifically, for severe offenses, rates of offending were 12 versus 29 (arrests) and 8 versus 29 (convictions) for CTP and GGI youths, respectively. For violent offenses they were 8 versus 14 and 4 versus 14. (See Table 9–1.)

Power-Oriented Youths
No meaningful comparisons could be made between power-oriented CTP and control youths, again due to the very small number of controls. When CTP and GGI youths were compared, no reliable differences were observed. This was true for both arrests and convictions—moderate plus severe, severe, and violent offenses alike. (See Table 9–1.)

The Total Group (All Youths Combined)
Here, results were similar to those obtained for conflicted youths alone. Experimental

boys performed somewhat better than controls on moderate plus severe offenses combined; however, these differences were not statistically reliable. Specifically, for arrests during parole, rates of offending were 75 and 98 per 1,000 months at risk for E's and C's, respectively, a reduction of 23 percent using controls as the base. For convictions, the rates were 43 and 61 per 1,000 months, a reduction of 30 percent. (See Table 9–1.)

For severe offenses, experimentals were arrested 57 percent and convicted 54 percent less often than controls. Here, rates of offending were 15(E) versus 35(C) and 11(E) versus 24(C) for arrests and convictions, respectively, These differences were statistically reliable. For violent offenses, experimentals again outperformed controls; and here again, the E/C differences (74 percent reduction in arrests and 70 percent in convictions) could not be accounted for by chance. (See Table 9–1.)

Comparisons between CTP and GGI yielded similar results: For moderate plus severe offenses combined, no reliable differences were found on arrests and convictions alike. However, for severe—and violent—offenses alone, substantial as well as reliable differences were observed on both arrests and convictions. Here, rates of offending were half as much in CTP as in GGI. (See Table 9–1.)

Supplementary Findings
Thus far we have focused on impact during parole, as judged in terms of rate of offending. Before we turn to impact *after* parole (postdischarge analyses), we will briefly review three additional indices of effectiveness: rate of parole failure, rate of discharge, and attitude change.[6] Before proceeding with these indices, six technical details may be noted; these apply to boys and girls alike.

1. In the San Francisco experiment, virtually all instances of parole failure (97 percent) involved a revocation or recommitment; rarely did they consist of an unfavorable discharge.

2. The *rate-of-discharge* analysis was based on a three-year follow-up from first *release to parole*. This was two years less than the Valley follow-up and was a direct result of the December 1969 cutoff that had to be established relative to San Francisco operations.

TABLE 9–1

Number of Offenses per 1,000 Months at Risk during Parole, for San Francisco Boys

Type of Offense and Outcome Measure	Youth Type and Number of Offenses[a]											
	Conflicted			Passive-Conformist			Power-Oriented			Total Group[b]		
	Exp.	Control	GGI	Exp.	Control	GGI	Exp.	Control	GGI	Exp.	Control	GGI
Moderate + Severe Offenses												
All arrests	70	92	71	65	60	58	108	225	96	75	98	78
Arrests with convictions	38	56	51	49	37	43	65	150	77	43	61	57
Severe Offenses												
All arrests	12	27	25	12	23	29	32	75	48	15	35	31
Arrests with convictions	7	17	19	8	23	29	32	50	41	11	24	24
Violent Offenses[c]												
All arrests	6	24	13	8	23	14	22	50	30	8	31	18
Arrests with convictions	3	15	11	4	23	14	22	25	26	6	20	14

[a]Sample sizes are as follows: Conflicted, E-57, C-12, GGI-67; Passive-Conformist, E-13, C-4, GGI-12; Power-Oriented, E-11, C-2, GGI-24; Total Group, E-89, C-19, GGI-113.
[b]Total Group includes all Conflicted + Passive-Conformist + Power-Oriented + Rare Types.
[c]Includes: armed robbery, rape (attempted or actual), assault with deadly weapon, aggravated assault, kidnapping, murder (attempted or actual), etc. These offenses are part of the broader category labeled Severe Offenses (sale of narcotics, grand theft auto, first-degree burglary, drunk driving, etc.).

This cutoff reflected the fact that, with the conclusion of Phase 2, the SF experiment had come to an end and the CTP as well as the GGI *programs* were soon reorganized.[7] Given this cutoff, the only youths who could be monitored for three full years were those who had *entered* their programs—CTP, GGI, or traditional—no later than December 1966. Since the San Francisco operation began in 1965, this meant that the discharge analysis could relate only to youths who had entered their program during the first year of the experiment. (Full operations lasted 3.7 years.)

3. Due to limited resources and overall research priorities, pre/post psychological testing was curtailed in San Francisco beginning in 1967. As with the rate-of-discharge analysis, the analysis of attitude change was therefore limited in scope since it largely focused on individuals who had entered their program during the first year or so of operation. No such time restriction existed relative to the rate-of-offending analyses reported in this chapter.

4. Given the relatively few controls who were available for this experiment, and given the factors noted earlier, reliable comparisons could not be made between the following controls and their counterparts in CTP: (a) *recidivism analysis*—passive-conformist and power-oriented males; all females; (b) *discharge analysis*—all youth groups and total group as well, males and females alike; (c) *attitude change*—passive-conformist and power-oriented males; all females. Similarly, reliable comparisons could not always be made between CTP and GGI with respect to (a), (b), and (c); in fact, for passive-conformist and power-oriented girls, this was always the case.

5. The restrictions mentioned in points 2 and 3 do not apply to postdischarge—and parole plus postdischarge—analyses. In these analyses, all youths who received a favorable or unfavorable discharge at any point during the experiment were followed up for 48 months from date of discharge. As mentioned in Chapter 8, this follow-up related to illegal behavior as recorded on Bureau of Criminal Investigation rap-

sheets; and once again, rate of offending was used as the index of effectiveness.

6. Relative to the six background characteristics (age, IQ, etc.), no significant differences were found when comparing CTP with control youths—specifically, those who comprised the rate-of-recidivism and attitude-change samples, respectively. This applied to boys and girls separately, not only for conflicted youths but for the total group as well. For reasons suggested in point 4, no comparisons were made between CTP and control in the case of passive-conformist and power-oriented youths who were part of these samples. For the same reasons, no comparisons were made between CTP and control relative to any group (total group included) that comprised the rate-of-discharge sample. One significant difference was found when comparing CTP with GGI youths who comprised the rate-of-recidivism, rate-of-discharge, and attitude-change samples, respectively: Conflicted CTP boys within the rate-of-recidivism sample were slightly worse parole risks than their counterparts in GGI; this applied to the total group as well.

We now turn to the supplementary findings.

Conflicted Boys

On 24-months follow-up, 42 percent of the experimentals and 67 percent of the controls had failed on parole. This difference was not statistically reliable, possibly due to the small number of controls. On attitude change as measured by the California Psychological Inventory, conflicted E's outperformed controls. Specifically, they showed greater positive change from pretest to posttest on seven CPI scales, whereas controls showed greater positive change than experimentals on one scale only. (No reliable E/C differences were found on the remaining scales.)[8]

Comparing CTP and GGI youths, 42 percent of the former and 62 percent of the latter failed on parole within 24 months. However, 29 percent of the CTP youths and 53 percent of those in GGI received a favorable discharge. (As indicated in Chapter 7, parole failures who are revoked or recommitted may eventually receive a favorable discharge from the Youth Authority. However, in the present case, the seeming discrepancy between rate of parole failure and rate of discharge among GGI youths was mainly a reflection of the partially different follow-up cohorts—that is, specific individuals—that were involved in the two analyses.) Although substantial, these differences in rate of parole failure and favorable discharge were not statistically reliable. Rates of unfavorable discharge were 8 percent and 7 percent, respectively.

Regarding attitudes, conflicted CTP and GGI youths showed equal amounts of positive change from pretest to posttest. However, a more detailed analysis revealed significant differences among the two subtypes that comprised this category. Specifically, assertive-deniers within CTP showed more positive change than their counterparts in GGI; on the other hand, anxious-confused youths within GGI outperformed those in CTP. As will be recalled, the same type of results were obtained for these two subtypes when E and C groups were compared in connection with the Sacramento/Stockton experiment (Chapter 8).[9] As a result, a similar masking effect was also observed in that experiment, relative to conflicted youths as a whole.

Passive-Conformist Boys
Forty-six percent of the passive-conformist experimentals (CTP youths) and 75 percent of their counterparts in GGI failed on parole within 24 months (not statistically reliable; possible reason: small samples).

Power-Oriented Boys
Fifty percent of the power-oriented experimentals and 67 percent of those in GGI failed on parole within 24 months (not reliable; small samples).

Total Group of Boys
On 24-months follow-up, 46 percent of the experimentals and 64 percent of the controls had failed on parole; this difference approached but did not attain statistical significance. As to attitude change, E's outperformed C's on six CPI scales; the reverse—C over E—was true for one scale.

Comparing CTP and GGI, 46 percent of the former and 66 percent of the latter failed on parole within 24 months—a reliable difference. In addition, 24 percent of the CTP and 43 percent of the GGI youths were favorably

discharged within three years from first release to parole (difference not reliable); figures for unfavorable discharge were 8 percent and 4 percent, respectively. Finally, with regard to attitudes, CTP and GGI youths had essentially the same amounts of positive change from pretest to posttest.[10]

We will now address the question of impact after parole, as measured by our main index: rate of offending.

Impact after Discharge[11]
Conflicted Youths
As shown in Table 9–2, no substantial or reliable differences were found between experimentals and controls on moderate plus severe offenses combined. This applied to severe—and violent—offenses as well. However, since very few conflicted controls were involved in this 48 months post-YA follow-up, these findings (actually, lack of significant findings) should be regarded as highly tentative.

When comparing CTP (E) youths with those from GGI, sizable and reliable differences were found on convictions, though not arrests, for each type and level of offense. Specifically, the rates of offending for CTP versus GGI were 16 versus 25, 6 versus 13, and 5 versus 11 per 1,000 months at risk for moderate plus severe, severe, and violent offenses, respectively.

Passive-Conformist and
Power-Oriented Youths
For passive-conformist and power-oriented youths alike, meaningful comparisons could not be made between experimentals and controls due to the extremely small sample sizes within these categories. This applied to comparisons between CTP and GGI as well.

Total Group
As shown in Table 9–2, four substantial but—in three of these cases—statistically unreliable differences were found between CTP youths and the small number of controls who were followed up for 48 months subsequent to YA discharge. Here, regarding the substantial differences, rates of offending for CTP and control were 44 versus 65 (arrests) and 17 versus 26 (convictions) for moderate plus severe offenses combined—differences of 32 percent and 35 percent, respectively. In addition, for severe offenses, one statistical trend (on arrests) and one reliable difference (on convictions)

TABLE 9–2

Number of Offenses per 1,000 Months at Risk for San Francisco Boys, Subsequent to Discharge from Youth Authority[a]

Type of Offense and Outcome Measure	Conflicted			Passive-Conformist			Power-Oriented			Total Group[b]		
	Exp.	Control	GGI	Exp.	Control	GGI	Exp.	Control	GGI	Exp.	Control	GGI
Moderate + Severe Offenses												
All arrests	47	54	50	83	104	125	0	63	115	44	65	63
Arrests with convictions	16	17	25	63	42	104	0	21	73	17	26	37
Severe Offenses												
All arrests	17	17	25	0	42	21	0	21	31	15	23	25
Arrests with convictions	6	8	13	0	0	0	0	21	21	5	13	14
Violent Offenses[c]												
All arrests	11	8	16	0	21	21	0	0	31	9	10	19
Arrests with convictions	5	4	11	0	0	0	0	0	21	4	5	12

[a]Sample sizes are as follows: Conflicted, E-17, C-5, GGI-17; Passive-Conformist, E-1, C-1, GGI-1; Power-Oriented, E-2, C-1, GGI-2; Total Group, E-21, C-8, GGI-23.
[b]See Table 9–1, note b.
[c]See Table 9–1, note c.

was found; here, rates of offending were 35 percent (arrests) and 62 percent (convictions) lower among E's than C's. In the two remaining analyses, that is, regarding violent offenses, no trends or reliable differences were observed.

Comparisons between CTP and GGI usually yielded sharper differences than were found between CTP and controls. More specifically, with one exception, CTP boys outperformed GGI on arrests as well as convictions, for moderate plus severe, severe, and violent offenses alike;[12] and these differences were both substantial and reliable.

Impact over a Six-Year Period
As shown in Table 9–3, when parole and post-discharge periods were combined, no reliable differences were found between conflicted experimentals and controls. For reasons already stated, meaningful analyses could not be carried out with passive-conformist and power-oriented youths. For the *total group*, experimentals had 30 percent fewer arrests and 41 percent fewer convictions than controls on moderate plus severe offenses combined; nevertheless, these differences were statistically unreliable, possibly due to the small number of discharged controls who were subsequently followed up for 48 months. For severe—and violent—offenses, experimental boys clearly outperformed controls on arrests and convictions alike. Here, the differences were reliable, but still regarded as tentative.

Results were fairly similar when CTP was compared with GGI. As shown in Table 9–3, one reliable difference was found between conflicted CTP and GGI boys: On severe offenses, the former individuals had 50 percent fewer convictions than the latter. However, for the total group, reliable differences were found on severe and violent offenses alike, and on moderate plus severe convictions as well. Here, rates of offending were generally twice as high for GGI as for CTP.

Program Effectiveness for San Francisco Girls
Impact during Parole
Conflicted Girls
As shown in Table 9–4, with one exception there were no reliable differences between conflicted experimental girls and their controls. The exception was that control girls performed significantly better than experimentals

(E's) on moderate plus severe arrests combined. Here, rates of offending were 16 and 44 per 1,000 months at risk, respectively. Since few controls were involved, these results should be regarded as tentative only.

With one exception, there were no reliable differences between CTP (E's) and GGI, despite the reasonable-sized samples that comprised both groups. The exception was that CTP outperformed GGI on moderate plus severe convictions. Here, the rates were 15 and 34 per 1,000 months at risk.

Passive-Conformist and
Power-Oriented Girls
For passive-conformist and power-oriented girls, no meaningful comparisons could be made between experimentals and controls, and between CTP and GGI as well. This was due to the very small samples involved.

The Total Group
One reliable difference was found between the total group of E's and C's: Experimental girls were outperformed by controls on moderate plus severe arrests. Rates of offending were 38 and 19 per 1,000 months at risk. All remaining E/C differences could be accounted for by chance. (See Table 9–4.)

CTP outperformed GGI on arrests and convictions. This applied not only to moderate plus severe offenses combined, but to severe offenses by themselves. These differences in performance were reliable as well as substantial.

Supplementary Findings
Conflicted Girls
On 24-months follow-up, 32 percent of the CTP girls and 64 percent of those in GGI had failed on parole; this difference was both substantial and reliable. On rate of discharge, neither CTP nor GGI outperformed the other (31 percent versus 31 percent for favorable dischargees and 0 percent versus 8 percent for unfavorable dischargees, respectively). Too few youths were available for a meaningful analysis of attitude change.

Total Group of Girls
Here, results were similar to those obtained for conflicted youths alone. On 24-months follow-up, 33 percent of the CTP and 59 percent of the GGI girls had failed on parole. Rates of discharge were 33 percent versus 41 percent (favorable) and 0 percent versus

TABLE 9-3

Number of Offenses per 1,000 Months at Risk for San Francisco Boys, Parole and Postdischarge Periods Combined[a]

Type of Offense and Outcome Measure	Youth Type and Number of Offenses[b]											
	Conflicted			Passive-Conformist			Power-Oriented			Total Group[c]		
	Exp.	Control	GGI	Exp.	Control	GGI	Exp.	Control	GGI	Exp.	Control	GGI
Moderate + Severe Offenses												
All arrests	58	62	55	63	82	123	0	135	102	52	74	67
Arrests with convictions	24	27	28	47	41	82	0	94	64	22	37	39
Severe Offenses												
All arrests	15	20	23	0	27	27	0	42	38	13	31	25
Arrests with convictions	6	10	12	0	0	14	0	42	32	5	18	15
Violent Offenses[d]												
All arrests	10	15	14	0	0	27	0	31	19	8	22	16
Arrests with convictions	4	7	9	0	0	14	0	31	19	3	14	10

[a]*Parole* refers to the entire Youth Authority career, as in Table 9–1. *Postdischarge* refers to the four-year, post-YA follow-up, as in Table 9–2.

[b]Sample sizes are as follows: Conflicted, E-17, C-5, GGI-17; Passive-Conformist, E-1, C-1, GGI-1; Power-Oriented, E-2, C-1, GGI-2; Total Group, E-21, C-8, GGI-23.

[c]See Table 9–1, note b.

[d]See Table 9–1, note c.

TABLE 9–4

Number of Offenses per 1,000 Months at Risk during Parole, for San Francisco Girls

Type of Offense and Outcome Measure	Youth Type and Number of Offenses[a]											
	Conflicted			Passive-Conformist			Power-Oriented			Total Group[b]		
	Exp.	Control	GGI	Exp.	Control	GGI	Exp.	Control	GGI	Exp.	Control	GGI
Moderate + Severe Offenses												
All arrests	44	16	55	0	33	0	54	0	174	38	19	57
Arrests with convictions	15	12	34	0	22	0	54	0	174	15	13	35
Severe Offenses												
All arrests	7	12	12	0	11	0	0	0	174	6	11	17
Arrests with convictions	4	8	8	0	11	0	0	0	174	3	8	13
Violent Offenses[c]												
All arrests	7	8	4	0	0	0	0	0	87	6	5	7
Arrests with convictions	4	4	2	0	0	0	0	0	87	3	3	5

[a]Sample sizes are as follows: Conflicted, E-27, C-6, GGI-37; Passive-Conformist, E-2, C-2, GGI-1; Power-Oriented, E-4, C-1, GGI-3; Total Group, E-34, C-9, GGI-43.

[b]Total Group includes all Conflicted + Passive-Conformist + Power-Oriented + Rare Types.

[c]Includes: armed robbery, rape (attempted or actual), assault with deadly weapon, aggravated assault, kidnapping, murder (attempted or actual), etc. These offenses are part of the broader category labeled Severe Offenses (sale of narcotics, grand theft auto, first-degree burglary, drunk driving, etc.).

6 percent (unfavorable) for CTP and GGI, respectively. None of these differences was statistically reliable. Regarding attitude change, CTP girls outperformed those in GGI: They had significantly more positive change on six CPI scales, whereas GGI girls had more such change on one scale.[13] Given the small number of individuals that were tested, these findings should be regarded as highly tentative.

Impact after Discharge

No meaningful comparisons could be made between experimental and control girls. This was due to the very small number of conflicted, passive-conformist, and power-oriented controls that were followed up for 48 months subsequent to discharge (Table 9–5).

With one exception, no reliable differences were found between conflicted experimental (CTP) and GGI girls: Experimentals outperformed GGI on moderate plus severe arrests combined. For all girls combined, that is, the total group, no reliable differences were found between CTP and GGI.

Impact over a Six-Year Period

Sample sizes were too small to allow for meaningful comparisons between CTP and control girls, for the parole and postdischarge periods combined. However, conflicted CTP girls outperformed their counterparts in GGI on moderate plus severe arrests combined: 22 versus 39 arrests per 1,000 months at risk. No other reliable differences were found between CTP and GGI for these and other youth-groups; this applied to the total group as well. (See Table 9–6.)

General Observations

Despite various changes and refinements that occurred during Phases 1 and 2, the concepts, the approaches to youths, and the program operations that were used or existed in Sacramento/Stockton (the Valley) proved applicable to San Francisco. We will briefly review this situation relative to the respective CTP units.

Concepts

The subtype descriptions that were used in the Valley during Phases 1 and 2 seemed equally applicable in San Francisco. This was especially true for passive-conformist, power-oriented, and "rare type" youths, and it applied despite

substantial differences in the ethnic makeup of project youths from the respective geographic areas. At the same time, important differences were observed in the personality structure and character traits of many black, conflicted youths—mainly assertive-deniers—when Valley and San Francisco males were compared. (With the latter individuals, cultural conflicts often reinforced, then magnified, preexisting feelings of unworthiness; specific compensatory reactions then evolved [Neto and Palmer, 1969].) However, *similarities* that were observed far outweighed the preceding differences among these as well as other conflicted youths, especially for any one ethnic group.

Approach to Youths

Most goals and methods that were considered appropriate for Valley youths also seemed appropriate in San Francisco. However, specific modifications were made relative to the conflicted individuals mentioned earlier; and, in general, external controls and pragmatically oriented interactions received more emphasis in SF than in the Valley, for each individual subtype. This increased emphasis was in response not only to greater peer involvement on the part of project youths and to the heavier, negative peer pressures that were felt by those youths, but to the more delinquent and somewhat less supportive social environment that seemed to exist in San Francisco as a whole.[14] Nevertheless, the overall approach to youths, one that included substantial emphasis on counseling and on the agent/youth relationship, was more similar than different across the SF and Valley CTP units. In San Francisco, as in the Valley, this approach seemed relevant with respect to reducing severe and violent arrests and convictions for the male sample as a whole and for conflicted males in particular (Neto and Palmer, 1969; Palmer et al., 1968).

Program Operations

The Valley and San Francisco CTP units operated in a very similar manner, despite physical advantages that existed in the Valley units (e.g., larger, better-equipped, and better-situated dayroom and classroom) and despite various conditions that were more common within SF (e.g., difficulty in locating appropriate foster homes) (Turner et al., 1967; Palmer et al., 1968). More specifically, the Valley operation was "transferred" to San Francisco

TABLE 9-5

Number of Offenses per 1,000 Months at Risk for San Francisco Girls, Subsequent to Discharge from Youth Authority

Type of Offense and Outcome Measure	Youth Type and Number of Offenses[a]											
	Conflicted			Passive-Conformist			Power-Oriented			Total Group[b]		
	Exp.	Control	GGI	Exp.	Control	GGI	Exp.	Control	GGI	Exp.	Control	GGI
Moderate + Severe Offenses												
All arrests	19	10	40	52	0	0	—	0	—	30	5	34
Arrests with convictions	12	0	17	21	0	0	—	0	—	14	0	14
Severe Offenses												
All arrests	12	10	13	31	0	0	—	0	—	15	5	10
Arrests with convictions	7	0	6	10	0	0	—	0	—	8	0	5
Violent Offenses[c]												
All arrests	6	10	1	0	0	0	—	0	—	6	5	1
Arrests with convictions	1	0	0	0	0	0	—	0	—	1	0	0

[a]Sample sizes are as follows: Conflicted, E-14, C-2, GGI-15; Passive-Conformist, E-2, C-1, GGI-1; Power-Oriented, E-0, C-1, GGI-0; Total Group, E-18, C-4, GGI-18.
[b]See Table 9–4, note b.
[c]See Table 9–4, note c.

TABLE 9–6

Number of Offenses per 1,000 Months at Risk for San Francisco Girls, Parole and Postdischarge Periods Combined[a]

Type of Offense and Outcome Measure	Youth Type and Number of Offenses[b]											
	Conflicted			Passive-Conformist			Power-Oriented			Total Group[c]		
	Exp.	Control	GGI	Exp.	Control	GGI	Exp.	Control	GGI	Exp.	Control	GGI
Moderate + Severe Offenses												
All arrests	22	12	39	32	12	0	—	0	—	26	9	34
Arrests with convictions	11	6	17	13	12	0	—	0	—	11	6	14
Severe Offenses												
All arrests	8	12	11	19	0	0	—	0	—	10	6	9
Arrests with convictions	5	6	5	6	0	0	—	0	—	6	3	4
Violent Offenses[d]												
All arrests	5	12	2	0	0	0	—	0	—	4	6	2
Arrests with convictions	2	6	0	0	0	0	—	0	—	1	3	0

[a]*Parole* refers to the entire Youth Authority career, as in Table 9–4. *Postdischarge* refers to the four-year, post-YA follow-up, as in Table 9–5.
[b]Sample sizes are as follows: Conflicted, E-14, C-2, GGI-15; Passive-Conformist, E-2, C-1, GGI-1; Power-Oriented, E-0, C-1, GGI-0; Total Group, E-18, C-4, GGI-18.
[c]See Table 9–4, note b.
[d]See Table 9–4, note c.

virtually en bloc with regard to organizational structure, intake procedures, diagnostic staffings, caseload composition, and other major features or components. Also, like the Valley units, San Francisco's CTP unit received considerable support from upper administration, though sometimes less from middle management; and it too was accepted by the local community in principle as well as practice.[15]

Basically, then, CTP—which was proving effective and operationally feasible in the Valley—seemed about as effective and workable within a large, heavily urbanized setting as well.

Notes

1. Beginning in 1967, parole violators were included in the San Francisco experiment, mainly because of lower-than-expected intake and a higher-than-expected ineligibility rate with regard to YA first commitments (Turner et al., 1967). Parole violators (PV's) were individuals who had been revoked or recommitted while in the traditional Youth Authority program; by design, none of these individuals had been part of the CTP, GGI, or control sample prior to their inclusion as PV's. These youths, who eventually accounted for 18 percent of all San Francisco eligibles (18 percent males, 16 percent females), are included in the CTP, GGI, and control samples to which Tables 9–1 through 9–6 apply. When these youths are excluded from the preceding samples, figures shown in those tables remain essentially the same. For example, in the case of moderate plus severe arrests, rates of offending during parole are reduced by approximately 3 percent for males and are increased by 4 percent for females. Similarly, for moderate plus severe arrests, rates of offending during postdischarge are reduced by 3 percent for males and 12 percent for females.

2. Unless otherwise specified, figures that follow refer to males only.

3. When parole violators are excluded, the age difference drops to four months. PV's aside, it might be noted that the figures for Valley youth relate to 1961–1969, whereas those for San Francisco cover 1965–1969 only. This

difference bears on age in the following way. From 1966 through 1969 the mean and median ages of Youth Authority first commitments slowly increased (Davis et al., 1971; Wright, 1969). This change mainly reflected the statewide Probation Subsidy program, which had the effect of retaining youthful offenders in the community for a longer period than before, prior to their initial YA commitment. This change accounted for the slightly older age of San Francisco youths—CTP, GGI, and control alike.

4. This difference between San Francisco and Valley youths was largely due to the much higher percentage of blacks within the San Francisco sample. (In YA's base expectancy formula, blacks were weighted differently than the remaining groups.) When parole violators were excluded, the difference in question remained largely unchanged.

5. Among eligible San Francisco males, these youth groups were represented as follows (to account for the entire sample, rare types have been included): passive-conformist—13 percent; power-oriented—17 percent; conflicted—61 percent; rare types—9 percent. Among eligible Valley males the figures were: 14 percent, 21 percent, 53 percent, and 12 percent, respectively. For eligible San Francisco *females* the figures were: passive-conformist—4 percent; power-oriented—9 percent; conflicted—83 percent; rare types—3 percent. For eligible Valley females the figures were: 8 percent, 18 percent, 66 percent, and 6 percent, respectively. (The total is 98% due to rounding.) Thus, regarding gross personality type, the chief difference between eligible San Francisco and Valley youths involved the lower percentage of power-oriented girls and the higher percentage of conflicted girls within the San Francisco sample.

6. No analyses were made in connection with school adjustment and paid employment.

7. Twice as many youths could have been included in the discharge analysis if the follow-up period had been two rather than three years. However, a two-year follow-up would barely have been adequate given (a) the standard Youth

Authority policies on favorable discharge (e.g., minimum required time of 18 months from first release to parole, except in unusual circumstances), and (b) the relatively long-term nature of the GGI and especially the CTP program. In addition, a two-year follow-up would have provided little basis for comparison with the five-year Sacramento/Stockton follow-up. Discharge aside, it might be kept in mind that the December 1969 cutoff was used with regard to the 24-months parole follow-up as well, that is, the *rate-of-parole-failure* index.

8. Throughout the San Francisco experiment, a scale-by-scale analysis of the CPI was substituted for the Q-sort analysis that was used relative to Valley youths. This was mainly due to Dr. Gough's increasing time constraints in connection with the performance of Q-sorts. Regarding the scale-by-scale analysis, conflicted experimentals outperformed their controls on capacity for status, social presence, responsibility, tolerance, achievement via independence, intellectual efficiency, and flexibility. Controls outperformed experimentals on communality. See Warren and Palmer (1965, pp. 87–88) for a brief account of these scales.

9. Similar comparisons could not be made in San Francisco, since too few conflicted controls were available.

10. CTP outperformed GGI on achievement via independence, intellectual efficiency, and flexibility. GGI outperformed CTP on dominance, socialization, and communality.

11. As with rate of offending *during* parole, differences in rate of offending *after* parole can hardly be attributed to preprogram differences in the six background characteristics of individuals who comprised the three postdischarge samples—CTP, GGI, and control. This is because the latter differences were relatively infrequent and fairly small in the first place. Specifically: (1) When the total group of CTP boys was compared to its controls, two significant (nonchance) differences were observed: Individuals in CTP were slightly (five months) younger and had a somewhat (nine points) higher IQ. The latter finding also applied to conflicted boys, taken by themselves. Due to the small number of youths involved, no comparisons were made between CTP and control in the case of passive-conformist and power-oriented boys. (2) When conflicted CTP boys were compared with conflicted GGI boys, one significant difference was observed: A higher percentage of property offenders was found in CTP than in GGI. This applied to the total group as well. (3) Due to the small number of individuals involved, no comparisons were made regarding the background characteristics of experimental and control girls. (4) When the total group of CTP girls was compared with the total group of GGI girls, two significant differences were found: Individuals in CTP were slightly (four months) older and slightly better parole risks. The former finding applied to conflicted girls as well.

12. The exception was as follows. Though CTP youths performed substantially (30 percent) better than GGI youths on moderate plus severe arrests, this difference was not statistically reliable.

13. CTP outperformed GGI on capacity for status, sociability, social presence, communality, intellectual efficiency, and psychological-mindedness. GGI outperformed CTP on femininity.

14. In 1967, midway through the San Francisco experiment, juvenile arrest rates per 100,000 population were as follows: *San Francisco,* total arrests (felonies, misdemeanors, delinquent tendencies)—1,679; felonies against persons—85; felonies against property (burglary, auto theft, other theft)—263; felony drug violations—49. For the *Valley* (Sacramento and San Joaquin counties, weighted by population), the figures were 1,425, 26, 204, and 28, respectively. For adults, the arrest rates were: *San Francisco,* total felonies—1,358; felonies against persons—306; felonies against property—644; felony drug violations—307. For the *Valley,* the figures were 512, 109, 275, and 61, respectively (California Department of Justice, 1977).

15. For a discussion of *differences* between the Valley and San Francisco units, see Palmer et al. (1968, pp. 73–77).

10 SOCIAL RISK, PRE/POST CHANGE, AGE, AND COSTS

In this chapter we will present supplementary yet important findings regarding (1) the social risk of CTP versus the traditional approach, (2) changes in rate of offending from pre–Youth Authority years to the YA plus post-YA years, (3) program impact as a function of age, and (4) program costs. Most of these findings will be summarized in Chapter 12, together with those from Chapters 8 and 9. They will relate to Valley males only, since space limitations preclude a similar presentation for San Francisco males and for females from both locations.

Social Risk of CTP
Background and Overview

Our first set of findings relate to community protection. Here, the basic question was: Did CTP or the traditional YA program provide more protection against illegal behavior? Protection was measured in terms of arrests: The fewer the arrests, the more the protection. Relatively minor offenses (severity levels 1 and 2) were not considered.

As discussed in Chapter 8, most CTP youths had a lower arrest rate than controls, during parole. (Parole was a period in which E's and C's were under Youth Authority jurisdiction yet not locked up; i.e., they were "free," in the community.) But what about the fact that most controls were locked up for about nine months *prior* to being paroled, whereas CTP youths were not locked up during those same months (except for short-term detention which averaged about two weeks during that time period). Didn't those extra months of lockup—plus all subsequent lockup—mean that the traditional program

actually provided more protection to the community than did CTP? After all, while individuals were locked up, they were not committing offenses against the community. In short, did the picture change when lockup time was added to the non-lockup time described in Chapter 8?

To answer these questions we conducted an analysis in which all lockup time and all non-lockup time (free time) was taken into account, starting from each youth's first commitment to the YA. This lockup time was not simply the nine months mentioned earlier. It included all jail time, prison time, short-term detention, and so on; and, like free time itself, it could have occurred during Youth Authority (predischarge) and postdischarge years alike. When this lockup time was added to the YA and post-YA periods described in Chapter 8, the total follow-up time came to about nine years per youth.

Our research questions were as follows: Using the arrest rates reported in Chapter 8 for moderate plus severe offenses combined, did the traditional program provide more protection than CTP, when lockup and non-lockup time were considered together? That is, did C's or E's engage in less illegal behavior during a specified period of *time,* whether or not they were locked up? In dealing with these questions we focused, of course, on the same youths that were analyzed in Chapter 8. (See Tables 8–1 through 8–3, on pages 97–103, regarding samples and rates.) In brief, our findings were as follows.

The traditional program *did* provide more protection to the community when lockup time was added to the picture. In fact, its advantage over CTP lasted approximately one year, counting from first commitment to the Youth Authority. Once that year had passed, CTP "caught up" with the traditional program in terms of protecting the community; and once it caught up, it began to pull ahead and develop an increasing advantage. It retained this advantage for the remainder of the nine-year follow-up. This pattern was observed among conflicted youths, passive-conformist youths, and the total group.

To restate and amplify, the traditional program started out with a clear advantage over CTP, simply because most controls were initially institutionalized, whereas CTP youths were not. This "social-risk advantage" over CTP faded away about four months after the controls were released from their initial, nine-month stay in a Youth Authority institution. At that point, CTP not only caught up with the traditional program, it began to pull increasingly ahead. This rather rapid change from the situation that existed at nine months occurred largely because controls began committing offenses at a substantially higher rate than experimentals, soon after their initial release from an institution. The change would have been slightly less rapid if no controls had been directly paroled.[1]

As discussed in Chapter 8, C's produced more offenses than E's *throughout* the predischarge period, and their higher rate of production was maintained well beyond the point of YA discharge. Because of this continued rate differential, at the end of nine years (in fact, even after four) controls had accumulated substantially more arrests than experimentals, despite the fact that they also accumulated more lockup time. Thus, in the long run (four to nine-years follow-up), the traditional program provided considerably less protection to the community than did CTP: The numerous arrests that were chalked up by controls, while these individuals were at risk in the community, had not been sufficiently compensated for by their arrest-free periods in lockup.

Specific details will now follow.

Conflicted Youths

Before proceeding to the findings, certain technical points might be noted. Although these are presented in connection with conflicted youths, they apply to each remaining youth type and to the total group as well.

For conflicted *controls,* the approximately 6½-year parole plus postdischarge period that was analyzed in Chapter 8—and used through out the present analysis—did not occur over an *actual* span of 6½ years. It occurred over a substantially longer period instead: roughly nine years. This was because the 6½ years referred to non-lockup time only. Specifically, it did not include the 2½ years (30.9 months) average lockup time that was accumulated by conflicted controls during the overall period in which the 6½ years of *non*-lockup time were being accumulated.

In other words, both during and after their involvement with the Youth Authority, many controls had lockup time interspersed with their non-lockup time (community time). Because of these lockups—in YA institutions, state prisons, and/or county jails—nine years of actual time had to elapse before these individuals could accumulate 6½ years of community time (YA institution time applies to the YA period, i.e., to predischarge, only. State prison time applies to the postdischarge period, i.e., post-YA, only). As mentioned in Chapter 8, the 6½ years referred to all time on parole plus a four-year postdischarge period (all of which was in the community). This applied to E's and C's alike.

For conflicted *experimentals,* the 6½-year parole plus postdischarge period (also analyzed in Chapter 8) did not include the 13.6 months of average lockup time that was accumulated while the 6½ years of non-lockup time were themselves being accumulated. However, as with controls, all such lockup time was included in the present, nine-year follow-up. This is further discussed below.

The basic research questions were: How many arrests did conflicted controls accumulate during the nine-year follow-up, and how did this number compare with that of conflicted experimentals? For E's and C's alike, arrests—reported on BCI rapsheets—were used as the basic index of community protection, or, rather, lack thereof. As discussed in Chapter 8, if convictions had been used instead of arrests, results would have been essentially the same as those reported below, except for passive-conformists.

As indicated in Figure 10–1, the 30.9 months of lockup that were accumulated by conflicted *controls* included 15.1 months prior to YA discharge and 15.8 subsequent to discharge. The 13.6 months of lockup that were accumulated by conflicted *experimentals* included 6.2 months prior to YA discharge and 7.4 subsequent to discharge. The 6.2 figure mainly involved revocation time; however, 16 percent was accounted for by short-term detention. For experimentals as well as controls, lockup prior to YA discharge included all institution, jail, and NRCC (short-term detention; pre- and post-board stays) time.[2] Lockup time subsequent to discharge related to prison and jail.

Two additional points might be noted: (1) By comparing the 30.9 with the 13.6 months figure, it can be seen that conflicted controls accumulated considerably more lockup time than conflicted experimentals during the nine-year follow-up. (Figures for the total group were 28.6 and 14.4, respectively.) These figures reflect the relative amounts of external control—physical restraint or loss of freedom—experienced by C's and E's. As such, they also relate to the issue of comparative *community protection*, at least insofar as our earlier questions may be rephrased as follows: Did the 17.3 months of lockup (30.9 – 13.6) that were experienced by controls over and above those that were experienced by experimentals translate into greater amounts of protection for the community in the long run, not just while these individuals were locked up? We will answer this question later.

Obviously, the extra amount of lockup resulted in greater protection during the 17.3 months themselves. Yet, society is not just concerned with being protected while individuals are locked up; in this connection it is also not interested in either punishment or justice alone, at least insofar as these concepts and activities center on lockup alone. Instead, society is also concerned with how individuals act when they are on the *streets,* assuming they eventually will be returned to the streets. Thus, when focusing on community protection, it is essential to look beyond lockup alone—in this case, to consider the nine-year period as a whole.

(2) If no statistical adjustments had been made, the total follow-up period (lockup time plus non-lockup time) would have been shorter for experimentals than for controls, except with power-oriented youths. Basically, this would have reflected the difference in lockup time between E's and C's. Given this situation, we statistically extended the experimentals' follow-up period so that the E and C follow-ups would be identical in length, for example, 108 months (nine years) in the case

of conflicted youths. (One-hundred and eight months represented all YA and post-YA lockup plus non-lockup time, in the case of conflicted *controls*.) We then added hypothetical arrests accordingly (to the E's' "unextended" number of arrests), using straight-line projections based on the experimentals' rate of arrest during their actual, that is, *unextended, months of community follow-up. Lockup time was also added accordingly, all within the follow-up period under consideration.[3] (For instance, with conflicted youths this period was the 108 months of lockup plus non-lockup accumulated by controls. See Figure 10–1, note e.).[4]

Results

As shown in Figure 10–1, conflicted controls had relatively few arrests during their first 9.4 months in the Youth Authority, since the vast majority were institutionalized during most of that time.[5] In contrast, about 30 arrests were accumulated by every 100 experimentals, almost *all* of whom were on parole during most of that time. Clearly, the traditional YA program gave more protection to the community than did CTP, during those months. (Note: The term "every 100" is used—here and subsequently—in order to facilitate the presentation, even though it means "any *given* 100" or any *"unselected"* 100, and although "100," in particular, is used for purposes of standardization.)

Once the controls were released from an institution and initially placed on parole, the picture changed. Almost immediately, they began to accumulate moderate plus severe arrests at a rate which more than doubled that of experimentals (Table 8–1, page 97; see 80 versus 34 such arrests). As a result, the following occurred within 13 months after their first commitment to the YA, that is, four months after they (i.e., controls in general) released at 9.4 months average) were first paroled: Conflicted E's and C's had accumulated an equal number of arrests—about 40 for every 100 youths. (See the intersection, i.e., the "catch-up point," between the broken and solid lines in Figure 10–1.) If "direct parolees" had not existed, that is, if all male controls (not just the present 83 percent) had been initially institutionalized, the 13-months figure would have been approximately 15 months.[6]

After the controls "caught up" with experimentals in terms of accumulated arrests,

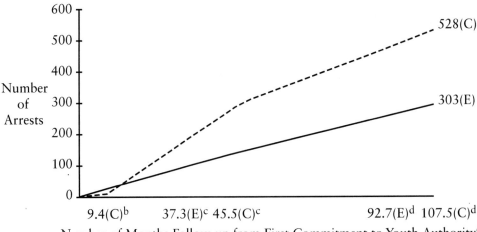

Figure 10–1. Number of arrests accumulated per 100 conflicted experimentals and 100 conflicted controls during 108-months follow-up.[a]

C = Control   E = Experimental

[a]Phase 1 and 2 Valley males.

[b]Average months of initial institutionalization (controls only). Some controls were not institutionalized prior to first parole; all analyses nevertheless include these "direct parolees."

[c]Average months to YA discharge (includes all lockup + non-lockup time).

[d]Average months of follow-up (includes all YA and post-YA lockup + non-lockup time).

[e]For each *experimental*, an average of 6.2 months were spent in lockup prior to YA discharge and 7.4 months were spent in lockup subsequent to YA discharge. These periods of lockup are included in the 92.7 months average follow-up shown for experimentals. An additional 14.8 months of follow-up (including 2.6 months of lockup) were extrapolated beyond the 92.7 months, in order to make the follow-up for experimentals equal to that for controls (107.5 months). For each *control*, an average of 15.1 months were spent in lockup prior to YA discharge, and 15.8 months were spent in lockup subsequent to discharge. These periods of lockup are included in the 107.5 months average follow-up shown for controls. For E's as well as C's, lockup prior to YA discharge includes institutionalization + jail + NRCC time (short-term detention; pre- and post-board stays); lockup subsequent to YA discharge includes jail + prison time.

their higher arrest rate continued (see broken line in Figure 10–1). As a result, conflicted controls began to represent more of a threat to the community than conflicted E's. By the time C's were favorably or unfavorably discharged from the YA—on an average of 45.5 months after their initial commitment (Figure 10–1)—they, that is, every 100 controls, had accumulated about 300 moderate plus severe arrests. In contrast, at 45.5 months the figure for experimentals was approximately 140. Thus, after about four years from initial commitment, for every 100 E's and 100 C's, the latter had accumulated some 160 more arrests than the former (300 compared to 140). This was despite the fact that controls had accumulated 15.1 months of lockup during those years, whereas experimentals had accumu-

lated about half that amount and thus had more opportunity to *commit* offenses (Figure 10–1, note e).

The difference between E's and C's in number of arrests at 45.5 months was, therefore, entirely due to the higher arrest rate on the part of controls, while these individuals were in the community. It can be deduced, from column 2 of Table 8–1 (page 97), that approximately 25 of the 160 control arrests were for violent offenses. Whether one focuses on violent, severe, or moderate plus severe offenses combined, conflicted controls represented a substantially greater threat to the community than conflicted experimentals, during the predischarge period.

As shown in Figure 10–1, once conflicted controls were discharged, their rate of arrest dropped noticeably, compared to their rate during parole (compare Tables 8–1 [page 97] and 8–2 [page 101]). In contrast, after conflicted experimentals were discharged, their rate of arrest dropped only slightly, also compared to parole. Nevertheless, since the postdischarge rate for controls remained higher than the postdischarge rate for *experimentals* (Table 8–2), C's represented a greater threat to the community than E's during the *post*discharge period, not just the predischarge period described earlier.

Thus, the following applied when the Youth Authority and postdischarge periods were combined, that is, when one counted for nine years (108 months) from initial commitment to the YA: For every 100 conflicted E's and conflicted C's who were followed up—favorable and unfavorable dischargees combined—controls had accumulated 225 more arrests than experimentals (528 to 303). This was despite the fact that C's had spent two and a half years in institutions, jails, and/or prisons during those years, whereas E's had been incarcerated for slightly over a year and thus had more opportunity to commit offenses (Figure 10–1, note e). (See Appendix 15 regarding computations.)

Would the findings have changed if controls had been initially locked up much longer than they were, say, twice as long? *Yes,* but not a great deal, and not in terms of final outcome. This answer, and the details that follow, are based on the assumption that the preceding arrest rates would have remained essentially unchanged if lockup were extended. This "constancy" assumption—understandably open to question—was made simply because we had no data to suggest that the rates might be either higher or lower if initial lockup were extended, for conflicted or other types of youth.

Specifically, then, if conflicted controls had been initially locked up for 18.8 rather than 9.4 months, their production of moderate plus severe arrests would have "caught up" with that of experimentals at about 26 rather than 13 months, all things being equal (another assumption). That is, the traditional program would have provided better protection to the community for two years rather than one. Nevertheless, within five years from first commitment, controls (i.e., every 100 C's) would have accumulated about 150 more arrests (330 compared to 180) than experimen-

tals (every 100 E's); and after nine years the E/C difference would have been about 205 (508 to 303)—again, all factors being equal or at least holding one another in check.

In sum, if one had doubled the period of initial institutionalization for controls, one would probably have extended the catch-up process by about a year. However, the final outcome would have changed only slightly. (If initial institutionalization had been doubled *and* if no controls were directly paroled, the catch-up point would have been about 32 months from initial commitment. Nevertheless, after nine years every 100 conflicted C's would have accumulated about 175 more arrests than every 100 E's—again, given the constancy assumption, and all things being equal or mutually canceled out. See endnote 7 regarding the projected effect, on community protection, of 36 months of initial lockup.)

Passive-Conformist Youths

As shown in Figure 10–2, essentially the same results were obtained with passive-conformist as with conflicted youths. Here, in fact, the catch-up point was somewhat earlier than before—a finding that mainly reflected the slightly greater difference between passive-conformist E's and C's than between conflicted E's and C's in rate of arrests during parole (Table 8–1, page 97). At any rate, at 45.5 months from initial commitment the difference between passive-conformist experimentals and controls in number of accumulated arrests was approximately 175 (290 to 115), for every 100 E's and 100 C's (45.5 rather than 49.2 is used to highlight the comparison with conflicted youths).

As with conflicted controls, the arrest rate for passive-conformist controls dropped substantially subsequent to discharge. During this same period, the rate for passive-conformist experimentals increased slightly, again compared to *pre*discharge (Tables 8–1 [page 97] and 8–2 [page 101]). However, since the postdischarge rate was slightly higher for C's than for E's, the traditional program provided less protection than CTP during the *post*discharge period, not just during predischarge. As a result, after nine years of follow-up, passive-conformist controls (i.e., every 100 C's) had accumulated 222 more arrests than experimentals (527 to 305).

If we had focused on convictions rather than arrests, the following would have been particularly relevant. Passive-conformist controls had a substantially lower postdischarge rate than experimentals, even though their predischarge rate was much higher (Tables 8–1 and 8–2). As a result, although controls accumulated more convictions than experimentals on nine-year follow-up—mainly because the E/C predischarge difference outweighed that of postdischarge—they eventually would have had *fewer* convictions than experimentals if their postdischarge rate, and that of E's, had been maintained beyond the nine-year point. (Whether this occurred, we do not know.)

Power-Oriented Youths

With power-oriented individuals both the short-range and long-range outcomes differed from those of conflicted and passive-conformist youths. First, as shown in Figure 10–3, the traditional program provided more protection than did CTP during the first *two* years of the Youth Authority (i.e., predischarge) period. However, for the remainder of that period, and even somewhat beyond discharge, the situation was reversed: Due to the slightly higher arrest rate among C's than among E's (Table 8–1, page 97; see 66 versus 55 moderate plus severe arrests), the for-

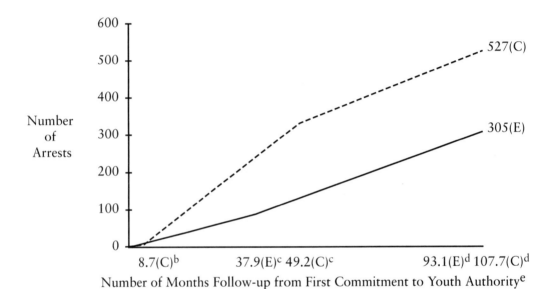

Figure 10–2. Number of arrests accumulated per 100 passive-conformist experimentals and 100 passive-conformist controls during 108-months follow-up.[a]

C = Control   E = Experimental

[a]Phase 1 and 2 Valley males.

[b]Average months of initial institutionalization (controls only). Some controls were not institutionalized prior to first parole; all analyses nevertheless include these "direct parolees."

[c]Average months to YA discharge (includes all lockup + non-lockup time).

[d]Average months of follow-up (includes all YA and post-YA lockup + non-lockup time).

[e]For each *experimental*, an average of 6.1 months were spent in lockup prior to YA discharge and 7.2 months were spent in lockup subsequent to YA discharge. These periods of lockup are included in the 93.1 months average follow-up shown for experimentals. An additional 14.6 months of follow-up (including 2.5 months of lockup) were extrapolated beyond the 93.1 months, in order to make the follow-up for experimentals equal to that for controls (107.7 months). For each *control*, an average of 14.6 months were spent in lockup prior to YA discharge, and 12.5 months were spent in lockup subsequent to discharge. These periods of lockup are included in the 107.7 months average follow-up shown for controls. For E's as well as C's, lockup prior to YA discharge includes institutionalization + jail + NRCC time (short-term detention; pre- and post-board stays); lockup subsequent to YA discharge includes jail + prison time.

mer's number of accumulated arrests eventually caught up with, then slightly surpassed, that of E's. About five years from initial commitment, further change occurred. The number of accumulated arrests was again the same for E's and C's, and, beginning about one year later, the traditional program clearly began to provide more protection than CTP. This change reflected the substantially lower arrest rate among power-oriented C's than E's, subsequent to YA discharge (Table 8–2, page 101).

Thus, after about nine years from initial commitment, power-oriented controls (i.e.,

every 100 C's) had accumulated 105 fewer arrests than experimentals (538 to 433). In the long run, as in the short run, the traditional program therefore provided more protection to the community with respect to these youths. (It might be noted that controls spent 25 percent more time in lockup than experimentals, during the nine-year follow-up. See Figure 10–3, note e.)

Total Group of Youths
For all youths combined (rare types included), the results were similar to, though not as striking as, those described for conflicted

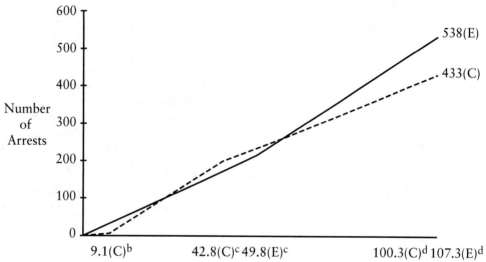

Figure 10-3. Number of arrests accumulated per 100 power-oriented experimentals and 100 power-oriented controls during 107-months follow-up.[a]

C = Control   E = Experimental

[a]Phase 1 and 2 Valley males.

[b]Average months of initial institutionalization (controls only). Some controls were not institutionalized prior to first parole; all analyses nevertheless include these "direct parolees."

[c]Average months to YA discharge (includes all lockup + non-lockup time).

[d]Average months of follow-up (includes all YA and post-YA lockup + non-lockup time).

[e]For each *experimental*, an average of 9.6 months were spent in lockup prior to YA discharge and 9.5 months were spent in lockup subsequent to YA discharge. These periods of lockup are included in the 107.3 months average follow-up shown for experimentals. For each *control*, an average of 12.8 months were spent in lockup prior to YA discharge, and 11.3 months were spent in lockup subsequent to YA discharge. An additional 7.0 months of follow-up (including 1.2 months of lockup) were extrapolated beyond the 100.3 months, in order to make the follow-up for controls equal to that for experimentals (107.3 months). These periods of lockup are included in the 100.3 months average follow-up shown for controls. For E's as well as C's, lockup prior to YA discharge includes institutionalization + jail + NRCC time (short-term detention; pre- and post-board stays); lockup subsequent to YA discharge includes jail + prison time.

individuals. As shown in Figure 10–4, the traditional program provided more protection to the community during the first 13 months after initial commitment to the Youth Authority.[8] After that, CTP provided more protection: Within about three and a half years from initial commitment—this being the average point at which E's and C's received their discharge—every 100 controls had accumulated about 100 more arrests than experimentals (230 to 130). Since controls had a slightly higher arrest rate than experimentals *after* discharge (Table 8–2), the predischarge difference continued to grow during the postdischarge years. This was independent of the fact that controls had a lower arrest rate during postdischarge than during predischarge, whereas experimentals had virtually identical rates during both periods of time.

Thus, after nine years from initial commitment to the YA, the E/C difference had grown to 127 arrests (470 to 343) for every 100 E's and 100 C's. This outcome would have been similar if convictions had been focused on rather than arrests. Of course, in that event, the E/C difference would have been reduced in scale. If, as some authors claim, approximately 10 offenses are committed for every one that is detected (and not all of the latter involve an arrest), the E/C differences mentioned earlier (e.g., 127 arrests) would take on truly major significance relative to arrests and convictions alike (Empey, 1978; Binder, Geis, and Bruce, 1988; Siegel and Senna, 1981).

Finally, if the period of initial institutionalization had been doubled for controls (18.4 rather than 9.2 months), these youths would have accumulated about 100 more arrests than experimentals (444 to 343) after nine years from initial commitment to the YA.[9] This estimate is based on the assumptions mentioned above.

Conclusion Regarding Social Risk

The conclusion seems clear. The traditional program—more specifically, lockup alone—provided more protection than CTP, in the short run. This applied to all youth types, individually and collectively. However, for the traditional program to maintain this short-term advantage, youths would have to remain locked up for a very long time, and/or the program's parole component would have to be substantially improved. This is because con- trols, once initially released to parole, soon become a greater risk to the community than individuals who are being worked with in a program such as CTP. This, at least, applies to conflicted and passive-conformist youths, though not to power-oriented individuals. It also applies to severe and violent offenses in particular, not just moderate plus severe offenses combined.

In sum, in both the intermediate and long run, CTP provided considerably more protection to the community than did the traditional approach. For the latter approach to provide as much protection as a CTP-type program, one would not only have to "lock the (institutional) door," but one would also have to "throw away the key" for a very long time (possibly two and a half years), costs and other factors notwithstanding. The main alternative would be to substantially improve parole.

Starting in the mid-1970s, there have been strong efforts to eliminate or greatly curtail parole (Cole and Logan, 1977; Fogel, 1975, 1976; Jackson, 1983; Stanley, 1976; von Hirsch and Hanrahan, 1978, 1979), not just to seriously reform it and improve its common usage (Citizen's Inquiry on Parole and Criminal Justice, 1975; Foote, 1978; Miller, 1977; Report on the Criminal Code Reform Act, 1978; Twentieth Century Fund, 1978). Yet, barring other alternatives, if regular and intensive parole were eliminated or curtailed, the burden of community protection would fall upon incarceration alone. As suggested earlier, this might well require the use of long-term institutionalization in response to moderate and severe offenses alike. That, at least, is what might be required if one wished to see traditional approaches "break even" with programs such as CTP—that is, provide an equal amount of intermediate- and, certainly, long-range protection against moderate, severe, and violent offenses alike. (For additional discussion regarding the elimination, curtailment, or reform of parole, see Bennett and Ziegler, 1975; Rubin, 1979; Sigler, 1975; Star, 1979.)

A rather different approach would be for society and government to *accept*, or decide to tolerate, present-day rates of offending, and to simply not develop programs that showed promise of reducing those rates. If society were concerned with punishment and justice (narrowly defined) alone, irrespective of their

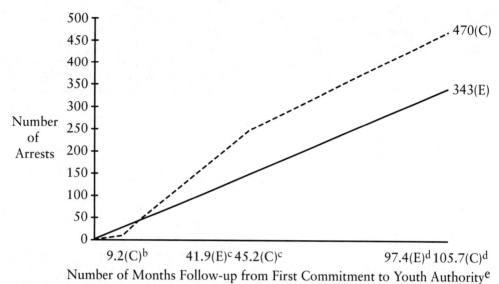

Figure 10–4. Number of arrests accumulated per 100 experimentals and 100 controls (total group) during 106-months follow-up.[a]

C = Control   E = Experimental

[a]Phase 1 and 2 Valley males.

[b]Average months of initial institutionalization (controls only). Some controls—under 20 percent—were not institutionalized prior to first parole; all analyses nevertheless include these "direct parolees."

[c]Average months to YA discharge (includes all lockup + non-lockup time).

[d]Average months of follow-up (includes all YA and post-YA lockup + non-lockup time).

[e]For each *experimental*, an average of 6.9 months were spent in lockup prior to YA discharge and 7.5 months were spent in lockup subsequent to YA discharge. These periods of lockup are included in the 97.4 months average follow-up shown for experimentals. An additional 8.3 months of follow-up (including 1.5 months of lockup) were extrapolated beyond the 97.4 months, in order to make the follow-up for experimentals equal to that for controls (105.7 months). For each *control* (direct parolees included), an average of 14.8 months were spent in lockup prior to YA discharge and 13.8 months were spent in lockup subsequent to YA discharge. These periods of lockup are included in the 105.7 months average follow-up shown for controls. For E's as well as C's, lockup prior to YA discharge includes institutionalization + jail + NRCC time (short-term detention; pre- and post-board stays); lockup subsequent to YA discharge includes jail + prison time.

potential for reducing future offending, this would perhaps be a plausible or at least a logically consistent approach. However, as stated earlier, society *is* concerned with reducing crime, not just with punishment and abstract justice as ends in themselves.

Change from Pre–Youth Authority Period

Thus far, our analyses have focused on the performance of experimentals and controls during periods that began with their first release to parole. We have not considered their behavior prior to that point, that is, prior to YA commitment. (Periods of institutionalization and other secure confinement will now be excluded from consideration, since the present section focuses on risk time only.) In short, we have not asked:

Did CTP and the traditional program reduce their respective youths' rates of offending in comparison to the time period that *preceded* commitment, that is, the pre-YA period?

This question is important because, although one program (say, CTP) may outperform a *comparison* program with respect to a postcommitment period (say, parole plus postdischarge), it is possible that *neither* program has reduced illegal behavior when one compares the performance of program youths (say, E's) during the postcommitment period to the performance of those same youths during specified precommitment years.

Thus, to focus on the present question we would not compare experimentals with controls. We would compare E's with themselves, across the pre- and postcommitment periods;

separately, we would do the same with C's. For example, we would compare the pre-YA performance of either such group (say, E's) with the parole plus postdischarge performance of that very same group. If we wished to obtain additional perspectives on "pre/post" change, we would make supplementary comparisons and analyses (say, ones involving differing *amounts* of pretime and/or posttime). It is these basic and supplementary analyses that will be reported in the present section.

Together with these analyses we asked additional questions that also involve a pre-YA period as the basis of comparison: Did the traditional YA program reduce offending more than CTP, in the postcommitment as compared with the pre-YA years? Did the two programs reduce offending for all youth groups? Did they do so for all *offense groups,* that is, moderate plus severe, severe, and violent offenses?

Method

To address these issues we first traced the official record of each youth as far back as it went. Since a few youths had committed offenses as early as 11 years prior to their YA commitment, we recorded and analyzed the prior records of all youths for 11 years. We included in this analysis all police and probation contacts other than those of a dependency-and-neglect nature, modification hearings (e.g., changes of placement), and the like. All information concerning these pre-YA offenses was obtained from the Youth Authority Clinic Report and Recommendations prepared by NRCC staff (Chapter 2). Clinic staff had obtained this information directly from probation and other court documents that routinely accompanied each individual committed to the Youth Authority.[10] (Eighty-five percent of all moderate plus severe offenses that were listed on these summaries had included a referral to probation, a "finding," and/or a conviction. For severe arrests, the figure was 92 percent.)

We next compared the rate at which these prior offenses occurred with the post-commitment rate reported in Chapter 8. For the pre-YA period, rate of offending was computed exactly as in Chapter 8: The number of offenses was divided by the number of months at risk. When computing this rate for the specific year in which a youth was committed, we naturally included that individual's YA commitment offense. This particular time period will be called the precommitment year, the

first precommitment year, or the year that preceded commitment.

To obtain a broader-based answer to the question of precommitment versus postcommitment offense rates, we made *two* somewhat different, yet partly overlapping comparisons: (1) The rate of offending (r.o.o.) for the precommitment year—that is, for the 12-month period that ended with the individual's YA commitment offense—was compared with the r.o.o. for the 6.8-year parole plus post-discharge period (the latter r.o.o. is found in Table 8–3, page 103). (2) The r.o.o. for the three-year period that ended with the individual's commitment offense was compared with the r.o.o. for the approximately three-year parole period alone (the latter r.o.o. is found in Table 8–1, page 97). These will be called the *basic* and *supplementary* time comparisons (analyses), respectively. Together, they provide somewhat different perspectives on—and bases for answering—the question at hand. Moreover, they reflect the inescapable fact that "precommitment" and "postcommitment" can each be defined in several ways. The sample of youths that was used in our analyses was identical to that described in either Table 8–3 or 8–1 (pages 103 and 97, respectively, depending on whether the basic or supplementary comparison was involved.

In both the basic and supplementary analysis we computed an arrest rate for each of the 11 pre-YA years noted earlier, ending with the year in which the commitment offense occurred. Thus, if a youth's commitment offense occurred on September 1, 1967, that individual's first precommitment year extended from September 2, 1966, through September 1, 1967, and a rate of offending was computed for that particular year. (The r.o.o. that is reported for the precommitment year refers, of course, to all youths collectively, regardless of the exact date of their commitment offense.)[11] The individual's second precommitment year extended from September 2, 1965, through September 1, 1966, and a separate rate was computed for that year. (As before, the reported rate refers to all youths collectively.) Rates for these and each of the nine remaining years are reflected or specified in the figures and/or appendices that accompany this chapter.[12] These year-by-year rates allowed us to detect changes over time.

Overview of Findings

Basically, the answers to our questions are as follows:

1. For moderate plus severe arrests combined, both the traditional program and CTP reduced illegal behavior, using a pre-YA period as the basis of comparison. Specifically, when comparing the precommitment year with the parole plus postdischarge years combined (the basic time comparison), the reduction for both programs was quite marked: 66 percent and 78 percent, respectively, with regard to the total group. When comparing the three-year period that immediately preceded commitment with the approximately three-year period of parole (the supplementary time comparison), the reductions were 16 percent for the traditional program and 59 percent for CTP, again with respect to the total group.

2. For conflicted and passive-conformist youths, CTP reduced moderate plus severe arrests to a greater degree than did the traditional program. This applied in both the basic and, especially, the supplementary time comparison. However, for power-oriented youths, the opposite was true with regard to the basic comparison. For the *total* group, the traditional program and CTP reduced moderate plus severe arrests by similar amounts, in the basic comparison; in the supplementary analysis, CTP outperformed the traditional program.

3. The traditional program and CTP each reduced illegal behavior for all three youth groups, but only when moderate and severe arrests were combined. The traditional program was associated with increased violent behavior among conflicted youths, and CTP was associated with increased severe behavior among power-oriented youths; this applied in the basic and supplementary comparisons alike.

Findings for the *basic* time comparison are shown graphically in Figures 10–5 through 10–16; and, the rates on which the precommitment component is based appear in Appendix 16. Figures for the *supplementary* comparison are shown in Table 10–2 (page 139).

Findings

Before we review the specific findings a few observations might be made. These points refer to the total group, but apply to specific youth groups as well.

For the present sample, offending was neither a "one-shot" nor a narrowly time-restricted affair. As can be seen in and deduced from Table 10–1, prior to his Youth Authority commitment offense, the typical youth had accumulated approximately three moderate plus severe arrests (severity levels 3 through 10) and two arrests of a relatively minor nature (severity levels 1 and 2). As shown in Figure 10–14 (page 144) and Appendix 16 (part IV), moderate plus severe arrests often occurred four or more years prior to commitment, and those that occurred six years prior to that date were not rare.[13] Despite this relatively long history, the rate of offending rose precipitously during the three or four years that preceded commitment: It roughly doubled from one such year to the next.

Thus, during the year that ended with the youth's commitment—the precommitment year—the typical picture was that of an individual whose behavior was rapidly "getting out of control." Compounding this picture was the growing severity of that behavior. For instance, among conflicted, passive-conformist, power-oriented, and the total group of experimentals, the average severity of all offenses prior to the commitment offense was 3.15, 3.09, 3.22, and 3.19, respectively (Table 10–1). However, the severity of their commitment offense was 3.86, 4.00, 3.53, and 3.87.[14] Given the already growing *frequency* of offending, the commitment offense was apparently "the last straw" from the court's perspective. It was this rapidly developing pattern—certainly, the high rate of offending during the commitment year—that was to be curbed and, if possible, eliminated, by sending the individual to the Youth Authority.

The findings for each youth group, and for the total group, will now be reviewed.

Conflicted Youths

As shown in Figure 10–5, conflicted experimentals and controls were arrested for moderate plus severe (m plus s) offenses at essentially the same rate during their precommitment year: 165 and 162 arrests per 1,000

Table 10–1

Number and Severity of Prior Arrests among Valley Boys[a]

| Youth Type | Offense Group | Prior Arrests[b] | | | |
| | | Average Number of Arrests | | Average Severity of Arrests[c] | |
		Exper.	Control	Exper.	Control
Conflicted	1–10[d]	5.17	4.83	3.15	3.24
	3–10	2.93	2.81		
	6–10	0.53	0.51		
	Violent	0.27	0.11		
Passive-Conformist	1–10[d]	4.88	4.36	3.09	3.52
	3–10	3.00	2.96		
	6–10	0.19	0.61		
	Violent	0.13	0.18		
Power-Oriented	1–10[d]	5.78	5.15	3.22	3.17
	3–10	3.64	3.05		
	6–10	0.58	0.51		
	Violent	0.39	0.26		
Total Group	1–10[d]	5.10	4.59	3.19	3.30
	3–10	3.06	2.82		
	6–10	0.49	0.46		
	Violent	0.27	0.15		

[a]Includes all good + poor dischargees described in Table 8–3 (page 103).

[b]Includes all offenses prior to the commitment offense. Excludes all dependency-and-neglect contacts, all modification hearings (e.g., change of status or placement), etc.

[c]Refers to all arrests—severities 1–10 inclusive. Average severity was not computed for the 3–10, 6–10, and Violent offense groups, since these are range-restricted categories.

[d]Includes offenses of a relatively minor nature (severity levels 1–2), in addition to those of levels 3–10.

months at risk, respectively. (All rates are specified in Appendix 16, for this and other pre-YA years.) Moreover, as shown in Table 10–1, E's and C's had accumulated an approximately equal *number* of m plus s arrests during all pre-YA years combined: 2.93 and 2.81, respectively. Thus, at point of YA commitment, these individuals were quite comparable to one another on their level of delinquent involvement.

Basic Time Comparison
During the 6.8-year parole plus postdischarge (p plus p) follow-up, *both* the traditional program and CTP clearly checked, and reversed, the precipitous rise in moderate plus severe arrests that was apparent during the precommitment year (Figure 10–5). For conflicted controls, the decrease from that particular year to the p plus p years amounted to 93 arrests per 1,000 months at risk (162 to 69 arrests; the latter figure is shown in Table 8–3,

page 103); for conflicted experimentals it was 132 arrests per 1,000 months (165 to 33). These were reductions of 57 percent and 80 percent, respectively; they amounted to a decrease of one arrest for every 11 months (controls), and one for every eight months (experimentals), at risk.

The following can be seen by viewing these same findings from a slightly different angle. As shown in Figure 10–5, during the parole plus postdischarge years conflicted controls returned to about the same level of offending that they had exhibited between their first and second years prior to commitment. (This can be seen by extending the broken line horizontally to the left, until it intersects the pre-YA curve for controls.) Conflicted experimentals returned to the level they had shown during their third year prior to commitment. (Extend the solid line in Figure 10–5.) From this perspective, CTP had a stronger impact than the traditional program

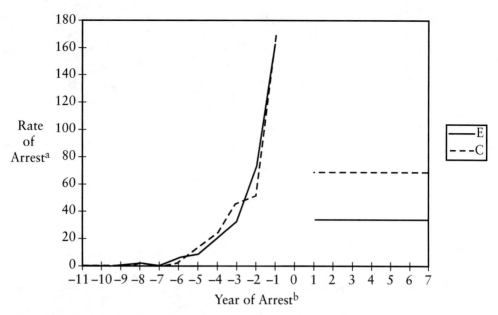

Figure 10–5. Rate of arrest for moderate plus severe offenses before and after commitment to Youth Authority, for conflicted youths.

[a]Specifically, number of arrests per 1,000 months at risk—as in Tables 8–1 through 8–3 (pages 97–103).
[b]Years that are preceded by a *minus* sign are those prior to Youth Authority commitment. For example, "–2" refers to the entire second year prior to commitment; accordingly, the data point that appears in the –2 column represents the rate of arrest for that particular year. For the 11 years at risk prior to commitment, rate of arrest is shown separately for each year. (Note: The YA commitment offense is reflected in the –1 column, since it is the "–1 year" that extends to point of commitment.) Years that are preceded by a *plus* sign are those subsequent to YA commitment. For the seven-year risk period beginning at point of commitment, a single—average—rate of arrest is shown for all years combined. This rate is identical to that shown in Table 8–3 for the parole + postdischarge (p+p) periods combined. Youths who comprise the present sample are identical to those used for the p+p follow-up (Table 8–3). All remaining technical/methodological procedures used in the present analysis are also identical to those followed in the p+p analysis (e.g., dependency contacts and modification hearings are excluded).

in terms of checking and partly undoing the behavior pattern that had developed prior to commitment.

As to severe offenses, both the traditional program and CTP were able to check, and reverse, the rapidly rising pre-YA arrest rate (Figure 10–6). For conflicted controls, the drop in arrests was 19 percent $[(32 - 26) \div 32]$, relative to the precommitment year; for experimentals it was 53 percent $[(30 - 14) \div 30]$. (Figures are shown in Table 8–3 [page 103] and Appendix 16.) Viewed from another angle, the traditional program returned the youths' arrest rate to where it had been during the precommitment year; CTP pushed it back one year more.

With regard to violent offenses, the traditional program did not reverse the pre-YA

trend (Figure 10–7). In fact, the parole plus postdischarge arrest rate for controls was 36 percent higher than that observed during the pre-YA years—the precommitment year included. In contrast, CTP did reduce violence among conflicted youths. As shown in Figure 10–7, it decreased the level of this behavior to where it had been two years prior to YA commitment. This was a 62 percent reduction, using the precommitment year as base.

Supplementary Time Comparison
As shown in Table 10–2, when the three-year period that immediately preceded commitment was compared with the approximately three-year period of parole (36 months of risk time), the reduction in moderate plus severe arrests from the former period to the latter

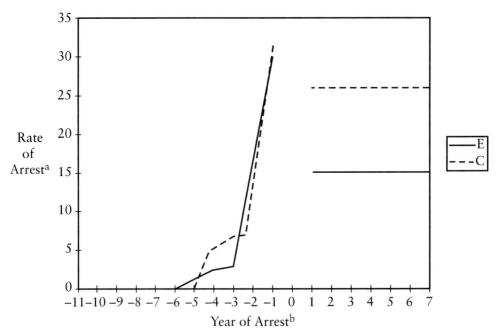

Figure 10–6. Rate of arrest for severe offenses before and after commitment to Youth Authority, for conflicted youths.

[a]See Figure 10–5 (page 137), note a.
[b]See Figure 10–5, note b.

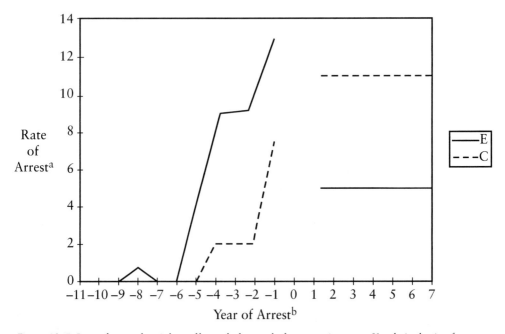

Figure 10–7. Rate of arrest for violent offenses before and after commitment to Youth Authority, for conflicted youths.

[a]See Figure 10–5 (page 137), note a.
[b]See Figure 10–5, note b.

was 10 percent among conflicted controls and 62 percent among conflicted experimentals. For severe offenses, the rate of arrest *rose* 75 percent among C's and dropped 7 percent among E's; for violent offenses, similar results were obtained. (See endnote 15 regarding all offenses combined, i.e., severity levels 1–10, inclusive.)

Thus, for moderate plus severe offenses, findings from the supplementary analysis lent support to those from the basic analysis, particularly among experimentals. However, with severe offenses, the findings were rather different than in the basic analysis, at least among controls. This difference indicates that, although the traditional program substantially reduced offending in relation to the precommitment year (see the basic analysis), it did not reduce the *longer-term* tendency of controls with respect to severe offending (see present analysis). For experimentals, the findings on severe (and violent) offenses were similar to those observed in the basic analysis; more specifically, although reductions were obtained in the present analysis, they were not as strong as before.

In sum, despite substantial differences in direction and/or degree, results from the pre-

sent analysis were moderately supportive of those in the basic analysis—more so for experimentals than controls.

Passive-Conformists

As shown in Figure 10–8, passive-conformist experimentals and controls were arrested for moderate plus severe offenses at essentially the same rate during their precommitment year. (As shown in Table 10–1 [page 136], they had an essentially equal *number* of m plus s priors, as well: 3.00 and 2.96, respectively.) This rate—about 205 arrests per 1,000 months at risk (one offense every five months)—was noticeably higher than that of other E and C groups (Appendix 16), except power-oriented controls.

Basic Time Comparison

Despite the high level of offending during the precommitment year, the arrest rate for passive-conformists dropped dramatically during the parole plus postdischarge period, in the traditional and CTP programs alike (Figure 10–8). The reduction was 69 percent and 84 percent among controls and experimentals, respectively. Specifically, there was a drop of 145 arrests per 1,000 months at risk

TABLE 10–2

Number of Offenses per 1,000 Months at Risk during a Three-Year Precommitment Period and an Approximately Three-Year Parole Period, for Valley Boys

| Offense Group and Follow-up | Youth Type and Number of Offenses[a] | | | | | | | |
| | Conflicted | | Passive-Conformist | | Power-Oriented | | Total Group | |
	Exp.	Control	Exp.	Control	Exp.	Control	Exp.	Control
Moderate + Severe Offenses								
Precommitment period	90	89	102	101	99	94	93	91
Parole period	34	80	32	86	55	66	38	76
% difference[b]	–62	–10	–69	–15	–44	–30	–59	–16
Severe Offenses								
Precommitment period	15	16	7	18	14	14	14	15
Parole period	14	28	11	25	21	34	15	28
% difference[b]	–7	+75	+57	+39	+50	+143	+7	+87
Violent Offenses								
Precommitment period	7	4	5	5	8	9	7	5
Parole period	6	13	8	11	12	16	7	13
% difference[b]	–14	+225	+60	+120	+50	+78	0	+160

[a]See Table 8–1 (page 97) regarding sample sizes.
[b]A minus sign signifies a reduction in rate of arrest from the precommitment to the postcommitment period. A plus sign signifies an increase in rate from precommitment to postcommitment.

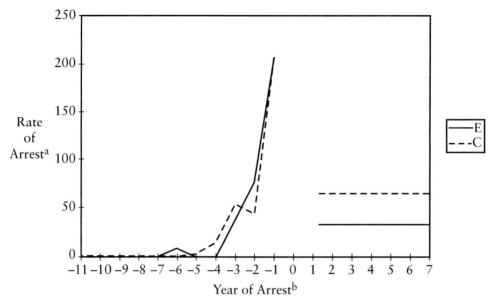

Figure 10–8. Rate of arrest for moderate plus severe offenses before and after commitment to Youth Authority, for passive-conformist youths.

[a]See Figure 10–5 (page 137), note a.
[b]See Figure 10–5, note b.

among C's (211 minus 66 arrests), and 168 arrests per 1,000 months among E's (201 minus 33). In this regard, the YA had a powerful impact on the behavior of these youths.

As to severe offenses, both the traditional program and CTP substantially lowered the precommitment arrest rate of passive-conformists (Figure 10–9). The reduction was 47 percent among C's and 43 percent among E's (Table 8–3 [page 103] and Appendix 16). Nevertheless, this decrease was not as dramatic as in the case of moderate plus severe offenses combined—a fact which suggests that, quantitatively speaking, the YA's main behavioral impact related to moderate rather than severe offenses.

Regarding violent offenses the traditional program produced a 30 percent reduction relative to the precommitment rate (Figure 10–10). For CTP, the reduction was 67 percent. The difference between these percentage changes should be interpreted with caution, given the fairly low base rate for violent offenses, and the sample sizes in question.

Supplementary Time Comparison
As shown in Table 10–2, when the three-year precommitment and three-year postcommitment periods were compared, the reduction in

moderate plus severe arrests from the former to the latter was 15 percent among passive-conformist controls and 69 percent among experimentals. For severe offenses, there was a 39 percent rise among C's and a 57 percent rise among E's. Increases were observed for violent offenses as well. (See endnote 15 for further details.)

Thus, findings from the supplementary analysis lent support to the basic analysis in the case of moderate plus severe offenses combined, particularly among experimentals. However, they differed from that analysis with respect to severe and violent offenses, for E's and C's alike. This difference indicates that, although the traditional program and CTP substantially reduced the rate of severe and violent offending that was observed for the "precipitous" precommitment year (thereby bringing such offenses under some control), neither program reduced the *longer-term* tendencies of passive-conformists in this regard.

Power-Oriented Youths
As shown in Figure 10–11, power-oriented controls were arrested for moderate plus severe offenses at a slightly higher rate than experimentals during their precommitment year: 189 versus 163 arrests per 1,000 months.

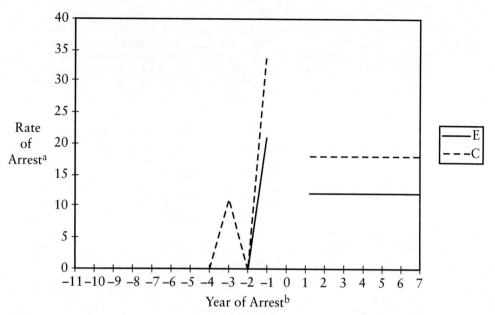

Figure 10–9. *Rate of arrest for severe offenses before and after commitment to Youth Authority, for passive-conformist youths.*

[a]See Figure 10–5 (page 137), note a.
[b]See Figure 10–5, note b.

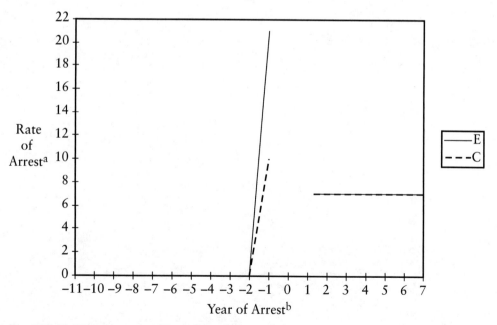

Figure 10–10. *Rate of arrest for violent offenses before and after commitment to Youth Authority, for passive-conformist youths.*

[a]See Figure 10–5 (page 137), note a.
[b]See Figure 10–5, note b.

However, for all pre-YA years combined, their number of m plus s arrests was somewhat less: 3.05 versus 3.64 (Table 10–1, page 136). Thus, on balance, power-oriented C's and E's were *fairly* similar to one another relative to their overall delinquent involvement at point of commitment.

Basic Time Comparison
During the parole plus postdischarge follow-up, the arrest rate for power-oriented youths dropped sharply in the traditional and CTP programs alike, using the precommitment year as base (Figure 10–11). The reduction was 72 percent and 63 percent among controls and experimentals, respectively—a decrease of 136 arrests per 1,000 months among C's (189 minus 53 arrests) and 102 per 1,000 among E's (163 minus 61). Thus, the traditional program had a stronger impact than CTP on these particular youths, even though both programs had an overall positive effect.

As to severe offenses, the traditional program produced a substantial decrease in arrests (37 percent); CTP, on the other hand, produced a 65 percent *rise* (Figure 10–12). With regard to violent offenses the outcome was somewhat different: Although the traditional program

produced a 45 percent drop in arrests, CTP also produced a drop—24 percent (Figure 10–13). Further analyses indicated that the preceding rise in severe arrests, for CTP, was largely due to burglary and drunk driving offenses, not to violent offenses (e.g., robbery or rape) within the severe category.

Supplementary Time Comparison
As shown in Table 10–2, when the three-year precommitment and postcommitment periods were compared, the reduction in moderate plus severe arrests from the former to the latter was 30 percent among power-oriented controls and 44 percent among experimentals. For severe and violent offenses, there was a substantial *rise* among C's and E's alike. (See endnote 15 for further details.)

These findings supported the basic analysis in the case of moderate plus severe offenses combined; however, in the present analysis, CTP had a slightly stronger impact than the traditional program. As to severe and violent offenses, results for power-oriented controls clearly differed from those in the basic analysis. This difference indicates that although the traditional program reduced offending relative to the precommitment year, it did not reduce the

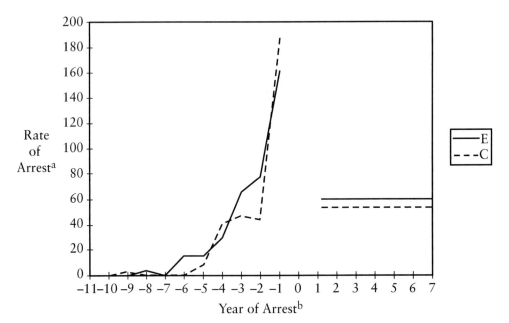

Figure 10–11. Rate of arrest for moderate plus severe offenses before and after commitment to Youth Authority, for power-oriented youths.

[a]See Figure 10–5 (page 137), note a.
[b]See Figure 10–5, note b.

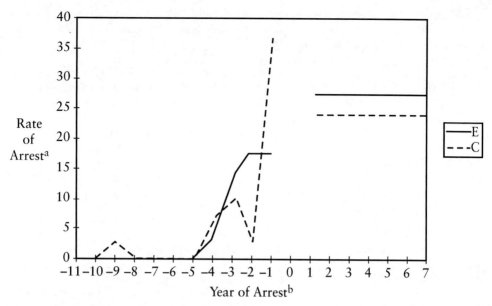

Figure 10–12. Rate of arrest for severe offenses before and after commitment to Youth Authority, for power-oriented youths.

[a]See Figure 10–5 (page 137), note a.
[b]See Figure 10–5, note b.

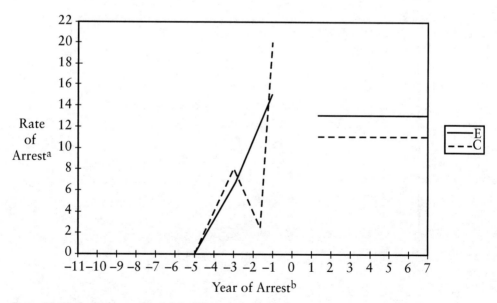

Figure 10–13. Rate of arrest for violent offenses before and after commitment to Youth Authority, for power-oriented youths.

[a]See Figure 10–5 (page 137), note a.
[b]See Figure 10–5, note b.

longer-term tendency of controls in this regard. As to experimentals, the findings supported those from the basic time comparison, but only for severe offenses: In both analyses, there was a rise from the precommitment to the postcommitment years. For violent offenses, results were different in the two analyses.

Taken together, results from the basic and supplementary analyses therefore indicate that neither the traditional program nor CTP was able to check, let alone reverse, the longer-term tendency of power-oriented individuals to commit severe and violent offenses. Nevertheless, the findings also indicate that both programs affected the *overall* offense pattern of these youths, insofar as they substantially reduced moderate plus severe offenses combined. This effect applied to shorter- as well as longer-term tendencies.

Total Group

During their precommitment year, experimentals and controls were arrested for moderate plus severe offenses at about the same rate: 169 and 181 per 1,000 months (Figure 10–14). They had a fairly equal number of m plus s offenses for all pre-YA years combined: 3.06 and 2.82, respectively (Table 10–1, page 136). Thus, at point of commitment, E's and C's were generally similar to one another with respect to their overall delinquent involvement.

Basic Time Comparison
Regarding program impact, the findings were similar to those observed for conflicted youths. During the parole plus postdischarge follow-up, both the traditional program and CTP clearly checked, and reversed, the sharp rise in moderate plus severe arrests that occurred during the precommitment year: For controls, the decrease was 120 arrests per 1,000 months at risk; for experimentals, it was 131 arrests per 1,000 months (Figure 10–14 and Appendix 16). These were reductions of 66 percent and 78 percent, respectively. In effect, controls returned to the same level of offending that they had exhibited toward the start of their precommitment year; experimentals returned to the level they had shown during their third year prior to commitment.

With regard to severe offenses, the traditional program and CTP reduced arrests by fairly similar amounts: 31 percent and 37 percent, respectively. However, for violent offenses, the former program decreased arrests by 17 percent, whereas the latter reduced them by 56 percent (Figures 10–15 and 10–16; see also Table 8–3 [page 103] and Appendix 16).

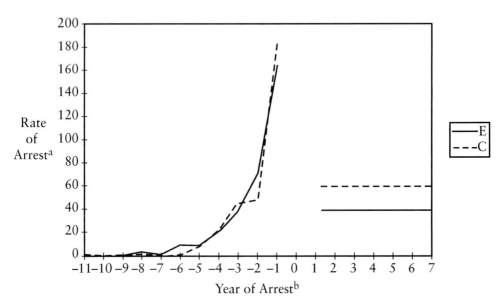

Figure 10–14. Rate of arrest for moderate plus severe offenses before and after commitment to Youth Authority, for total group of youths.

[a]See Figure 10–5 (page 137), note a.
[b]See Figure 10–5, note b.

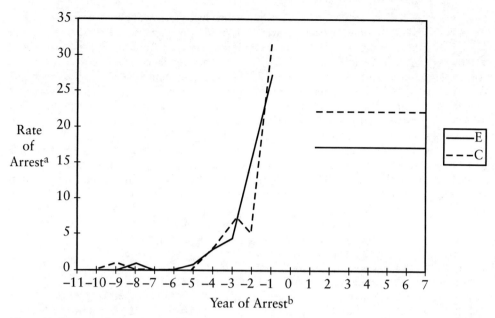

Figure 10-15. Rate of arrest for severe offenses before and after commitment to Youth Authority, for total group of youths.

[a]See Figure 10-5 (page 137), note a.
[b]See Figure 10-5, note b.

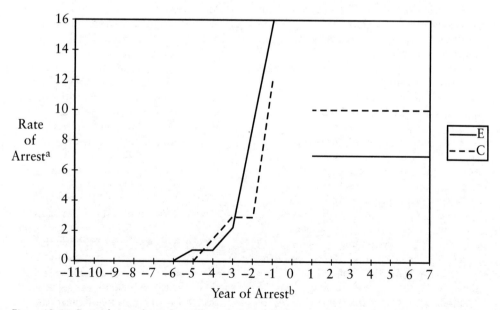

Figure 10-16. Rate of arrest for violent offenses before and after commitment to Youth Authority, for total group of youths.

[a]See Figure 10-5 (page 137), note a.
[b]See Figure 10-5, note b.

Supplementary Time Comparison
In general, findings for the total group were similar to those observed for conflicted youths. As shown in Table 10–2 (page 139), when the three-year precommitment and postcommitment periods were compared, the reduction in moderate plus severe arrests was 16 percent among controls and 59 percent among experimentals. For severe offenses, there was a sharp rise among C's (87 percent) and a slight rise for E's (7 percent). In the case of violent offenses, there was again a sharp rise for C's, but no change for E's. (See endnote 15 for further details.)

These findings supported the basic analysis in the case of moderate plus severe offenses combined, particularly among experimentals. However, they differed from that analysis with respect to severe and violent offenses, especially (though not exclusively) among controls. This difference indicates that although the traditional program and CTP reduced the rate of severe and violent offending that was observed for the somewhat "precipitous" precommitment year, they did not reduce the longer-term tendencies in question. Nevertheless, CTP did at least check these tendencies; that is, it held them fairly constant. This, of course, largely reflected its performance with respect to conflicted youths.

On balance, then, CTP had a somewhat greater impact than the traditional program in terms of reducing or at least curbing the rate of arrest from specified pre-YA periods to various postcommitment periods, for the total group of youths. This applied to moderate plus severe arrests combined and, to a lesser extent, to severe and violent offenses in particular.

Conclusions Regarding Pre/Post Change
The traditional program produced a marked drop in moderate plus severe arrests, mainly when the parole plus postdischarge period was compared to the precommitment year (the basic time comparison). However, this effect—in fact, a stronger effect—was also achieved through intensive community programming, regardless of the time period used for comparison. This, at least, was true for conflicted youths and, to a lesser extent, passive-conformists. It was particularly true for severe and/or violent offenses, at least in connection with the basic time comparison. Nevertheless, the opposite applied for power-oriented youths, regardless of offense group. With these

individuals, the traditional program outperformed CTP except in the three-year precommitment/three-year postcommitment analysis.

These findings (1) indicate that traditional programming is not necessarily superior to community programming, whether for reversing or simply holding in check various patterns of precommitment behavior. They also (2) highlight the need to distinguish between different youth groups and between different offense severities, prior to generalizing about the impact of traditional and community programs. In neither respect do they support the overall, blanket conclusions of Murray and Cox (1979), based on their Unified Delinquency Intervention Services (UDIS) study.

The Factor of Age
The E/C differences that have been reviewed apply to younger and older individuals alike. This may be illustrated by the following results (these results relate to the total group and to moderate plus severe arrests combined, except as specified):

1. When the precommitment year was compared to the parole plus postdischarge years, the reduction in arrest rate was 77 percent for younger experimentals and 68 percent for younger controls; it was 79 percent and 65 percent for older E's and older C's, respectively. (Younger = under 16; older = 16 and over. Tables containing specific details are not presented, due to space limitations and overall priorities; however, see Appendix 17 regarding arrest rates—by age—for the years preceding commitment. Data in this appendix are for moderate plus severe offenses only, again for reasons mentioned earlier.) These reductions were very similar to those of 78 percent (E's) and 66 percent (C's)—that is, those observed for younger and older individuals combined.

2. As shown in Appendix 18, when the three-year precommitment and three-year postcommitment periods were compared, the reduction in moderate and severe arrests was 67 percent for younger experimentals and 10 percent for younger controls; it was 55 percent for older E's and 25 percent for older C's. These reductions were comparable to those of 59

percent for younger plus older *E's* combined, and 16 percent for younger plus older *C's* combined. As to severe—and violent—offenses by themselves, the same pattern of findings was observed for the younger and older groups, individually, as was found for these same two groups combined (compare Appendix 18 and Table 10–2, page 139).

3. Essentially the same findings as those mentioned in item 2 were observed for each youth group individually, regarding moderate plus severe arrests. For instance, among conflicted youths, when the three-year precommitment and three-year postcommitment periods were compared, the reduction in arrests was 72 percent among younger experimentals and 5 percent among younger controls; it was 59 percent and 13 percent among older *E's* and older *C's*, respectively (see Appendix 18). These figures were comparable to those of 62 percent and 10 percent, respectively, for conflicted *E's* and *C's* of the same two age groups combined (Table 10–2). For conflicted and power-oriented youths, similar results (i.e., similar to those in Table 10–2) were usually obtained relative to *severe* and *violent* offenses as well. However, among passive-conformists, the results for these offenses were somewhat varied in the case of each age group; that is, they were mixed or varied when compared to those for the two age groups combined (Table 10–2).[16]

4. The E/C differences described in items 2 and 3 cannot be attributed to certain factors that might conceivably have distinguished younger experimentals from younger controls (and, separately, older *E's* from older *C's*); included, for example, would be preexisting differences in the number or severity of prior arrests. Thus, with respect to prior arrests (Appendix 19), most such differences were found to be relatively small, particularly for moderate plus severe "priors" combined. (E/C comparisons aside, it might be noted that, for experimentals and controls alike, older individuals had accumulated approximately 0.5 more prior arrests than younger individuals. However, since most such arrests—that is, additional priors—were of severity levels 1 and 2, that is, were of a rela-

tively minor nature, younger and older individuals had about the same number of *moderate plus severe* arrests combined, prior to their YA commitment.)

Nor were substantial, preexisting differences found between younger experimentals and younger controls (and, separately, between older E's and older C's) as to their representation on race, socioeconomic status (SES), and other background factors. For instance, the following distributions were observed among youths under 16: (1) *Caucasian* and *non-Caucasian*: E's—50 percent and 50 percent, respectively; C's—51 percent and 49 percent, respectively; (2) *lower SES* and *middle plus upper SES*: E's—81 percent and 19 percent, respectively; C's—82 percent and 18 percent, respectively; (3) *lower IQ (under 90)* and *higher IQ (90 and over)*: E's—47 percent and 53 percent, respectively; C's—48 percent and 52 percent, respectively. (Tables relating to these and other factors are not presented, for reasons mentioned earlier.)

In the next section, we will continue to examine age. Here, the performance (arrest rate) of experimentals and controls will be compared with regard to specified postcommitment years, that is, for a period *subsequent* to YA intake. This analysis will differ from the present one, in which the performance (reduction in arrest rate) of E's and C's was compared for the precommitment *versus* postcommitment years.

Age and Outcome

Did experimentals perform better than controls, regardless of age? Did controls of certain age groups outperform experimentals? Did older E's perform better than younger E's? These and related questions will now be reviewed, albeit in an elementary way.

Briefly, the method used was as follows. First, all dischargees were placed in either a younger or older group—*under 16* or *16 and over*, at point of YA commitment (intake). All youths were followed up from intake to discharge, a period we will call their *YA career*. The study sample was identical to that described in Chapter 8 (Table 8–1, page 97), as was the data source (rapsheets) and the method used for computing the rate of offending (r.o.o.). Each youth was classified as having had either a *lower* or *higher* r.o.o. during his YA career—that is, less than one arrest for every ten months at risk, or at least one arrest per ten months. Given these definitions, distinctions, and procedures, age and r.o.o. were then analyzed in relation to one another, separately for the traditional program and CTP. As shown in Table 10–3, the results were as follows for moderate plus severe arrests combined.

Traditional Program versus CTP

Conflicted experimentals who were under 16 at intake performed better than their controls: Ninety-one percent of the E's and 62 percent of the C's had a lower rate of offending during their YA career. E's who were 16 or over also performed better than their C's; here, the figures for lower r.o.o. were 88 percent and 63 percent, respectively. Both E/C differences were statistically reliable.[17]

Passive-conformist experimentals who were under 16 performed better than their controls: Ninety percent of the E's and 56 percent of the C's had a lower rate of offending. For individuals who were 16 or over, the E/C difference in r.o.o. was not statistically reliable.

Power-oriented experimentals who were under 16 tended to perform better than their controls: Seventy-six percent of the E's and 55 percent of the C's had a lower rate of offending. For youths who were 16 or over, 75 percent of the E's and *91 percent* of the C's had a lower r.o.o.; however, this difference was not reliable.

Experimentals (the total group) who were under 16 performed better than their controls: Eighty-nine percent of the E's and 59 percent of the C's had a lower rate of offending during their YA career. E's who were 16 or over also performed better than C's; here, the figures were 86 percent and 71 percent, respectively.

Thus, in general, experimentals performed significantly better than controls regardless of age. Among individuals under 16, this was true for all three youth types and for the total group as well. However, among those 16 or over it was true for conflicted youths and for the total group only. All in all, the advantage that was held by E's over C's was somewhat larger and certainly more widespread among younger than among older individuals. Finally, controls did not outperform experimentals—at least not significantly so—relative to any combination of age group and youth type.

The Traditional Program

As shown in Table 10–3, conflicted controls who were under 16 performed neither better nor worse than those 16 or over: Sixty-two percent of the younger group and 63 percent of the older individuals had a lower rate of offending during their YA career. Similar results were obtained for passive-conformists: For youths under 16 and those 16 or over, the figures were 56 percent and 71 percent, respectively—a statistically unreliable difference.

TABLE 10–3

Percentage of Younger and Older Offenders with Lower or Higher Rate of Arrest

		Age Group and Rate of Arrests[a]			
		Under 16		16 and Over	
Youth Type	Program	Lower Rate[b]	Higher Rate[c]	Lower Rate[b]	Higher Rate[c]
Conflicted	Traditional	62	38	63	38
	CTP	91	9	88	12
Passive-Conformist	Traditional	56	44	71	29
	CTP	90	10	89	11
Power-Oriented	Traditional	55	45	91	9
	CTP	76	24	75	25
Total Group[d]	Traditional	59	41	71	29
	CTP	89	11	86	14

[a]Sample sizes are shown in Table 8–1, page 97. Percentages shown in the present table are based on the number of moderate + severe arrests per month at risk, during parole.

[b]Less than one arrest per 10 months at risk.

[c]One or more arrest per 10 months at risk.

[d]Defined as: Conflicted + Passive-Conformist + Power-Oriented + Rare Types.

However, among power-oriented controls, the older group did outperform the younger individuals: Fifty-five percent of those under 16 and 91 percent of those 16 or over had a lower r.o.o. This difference was reliable. A similar finding was obtained for the total group: Fifty-nine percent of those under 16 and 71 percent of those 16 or over had a lower r.o.o. This difference was reliable partly because of the much larger sample size than existed among passive-conformists alone. In general, then, older individuals performed somewhat though not strikingly better than those who were younger.

CTP

There were no substantial or statistically reliable differences in the rate of offending among younger as compared to older CTP youths; this applied to all youth types and to the total group as well. The largest single difference was three percentage points (Table 10–3). Apparently, age was not a significant or at least not a distinguishing factor in CTP, with respect to r.o.o.

Conclusions Regarding Age

Viewed in toto, these findings indicate that age is a more important factor within the traditional program than in CTP; moreover, they suggest that the difference in question is centered on middle-maturity, not higher-maturity, youths. In contrast to the traditional program, CTP apparently "overcame" the commonly observed effect or correlate of age, namely, that younger offenders perform worse than older offenders. This was true for middle- *and* higher-maturity youths, in that—within both maturity levels—younger individuals had a rate of offending which was very similar to that of older individuals, in CTP. Thus, the present findings suggest it may be necessary to question the widely accepted view that, among juveniles, older offenders can almost certainly be expected to outperform those who are younger, regardless of the program to which they are exposed.

Costs
Youth Authority Costs
Background and Approach
How much did the CTP and traditional programs cost per youth? Was either program less expensive than the other? Were some youth groups less costly than others? Before answer-

ing, it should be noted that the CTP experiment lasted 12 years—years that were marked by continual, nationwide increases in living costs, salaries, and construction costs. These changes produced large cost increases throughout the Youth Authority; in fact, YA operating expenses virtually doubled during 1961–1973, relative to traditional and special services alike (Davis, 1971; Davis et al., 1971, 1973; Governor's Budget, 1962–1963, 1963–1964, 1966–1967, 1971–1972).

To reflect these changes, the 12-year span was divided into three distinct "price periods," and separate costs were developed for each. This approach was used not only to derive time-specific dollar amounts, but to detect possible shifts in the relative costs of CTP and the traditional program from one period to the next. The price periods and their corresponding youth samples were as follows:

For youths who first entered their program during the early years of the experiment, or *early period,* 1963 prices were used. For those entering during the *middle period,* 1966–1967 prices were used. For individuals who entered during the final years—the *later period*—1971–1972 prices were used.[18] For the three periods combined, the overall sample was almost identical to that described in Chapter 8 (Table 8–1, page 97).

Relative to these price periods, average Youth Authority career costs are shown in Table 10–4, separately for the traditional program (C's) and CTP (E's). (The procedure for computing these costs is shown in Appendix 20.) Also shown is the *difference* between costs for C's and E's. These costs relate to all institutional, parole, and NRCC time, counting from the day of first commitment to the point of favorable or unfavorable discharge. The following, then, is a summary of relative and absolute costs for each youth group, and for the total group as well.

Conflicted Youths
During each price period, costs per youth were lower for conflicted experimentals than for conflicted controls. The E's *cost difference* was $99 per career for the early period and $1,894 for the later period. This was equivalent to eight cents a day, and $1.50 a day, respectively. During the later period, the *absolute dollar amounts* (total career costs) were $12,377 for experimentals and $14,271 for controls.

TABLE 10–4

Youth Authority Career Costs and Cost Differences during Three Price Periods, for Traditional and CTP Programs

| Youth Type | Program[b] | Price Period and Costs[a] | | |
		Early (1963)	Middle (1966–1967)	Later (1971–1972)
Conflicted	Traditional	$6,279	$8,764	$14,271
	CTP	6,180	8,366	12,377
	Cost diff.	$ 99 (E)	$ 398 (E)	$ 1,894 (E)
Passive-Conformist	Traditional	6,223	9,360	14,812
	CTP	6,231	8,595	12,107
	Cost diff.	$ 8 (C)	$ 765 (E)	$ 2,705 (E)
Power-Oriented	Traditional	5,660	7,617	13,180
	CTP	8,676	11,803	16,889
	Cost diff.	$3,016 (C)	$4,186 (C)	$ 3,709 (C)
Total Group[c]	Traditional	6,052	8,459	14,076
	CTP	7,060	9,289	13,027
	Cost diff.	$1,008 (C)	$ 830 (C)	$ 1,049 (E)

[a]The less expensive program is indicated in parentheses: (C) = Traditional; (E) = CTP.
[b]Includes all institutional, parole, and NRCC costs from initial commitment to point of discharge. Costs for camp stays are also included. (See Appendix 20 for details.)
[c]Includes rare types.

Passive-Conformists
Among passive-conformists, experimental and control costs were virtually identical during the early period: The cost difference was $8 per career, or one cent a day. For the later period, the difference was $2,705 ($2.04 a day), in favor of E's. Thus, compared to controls, passive-conformist experimentals eventually became the least expensive youth group. During the later price period, the total career costs were $12,107 for E's and $14,812 for C's.

Power-Oriented Youths
For all three price periods, costs were considerably higher among power-oriented experimentals than among their controls. Cost differences were $3,016 and $3,709 ($2.14 and $2.63 a day) for the early and later periods, respectively. Compared to their controls, and to the remaining E's as well, power-oriented experimentals were by far the most expensive youth group. During the later price period, the total career costs were $16,889 for E's and $13,180 for C's. (Compared to other C's, these controls were somewhat less expensive.)

Total Group
For the total group, YA costs were lower among controls than among experimentals during the early and middle price periods: E/C differences were $1,008 (76 cents a day) for the early period and $830 (63 cents a day) for the middle period. However, by the early 1970s—the later period—costs were lower among experimentals than controls. Here, the difference was $1,049 per career, or 79 cents a day. During the later price period, the absolute dollar amounts (total career costs) were $13,027 for E's and $14,076 for C's.

Obviously, between the 1963 and 1971–1972 periods there was a greater price increase among controls than among experimentals. (For C's, the increase was $8,024; for E's it was $5,967. This applied to the total group.) Although several factors contributed to this situation, most derived from the fact that C's, compared to E's, were spending more and more time in the Youth Authority's increasingly expensive institutions, especially during the middle and later 1960s. Related to this, but extending beyond it, was the fact that controls were more likely to be revoked and institutionalized than experimentals for the 1961–1973 period *as a whole* (Chapter 8); this applied to favorable and unfavorable dischargees alike. (It might be kept in mind that revocation-based periods of lockup were separate and apart from the controls' initial—

preparole—institutionalization, an experience not shared by CTP youths.) These facts and conditions were in turn independent of the following: Starting in 1966, direct parole was used less often, by the YA Board, than during the previous four years; this change in practice added further costs, mainly institutional costs, to the traditional program.

At any rate, the differential price rise that occurred between the early and later period was partly accounted for by individuals—specifically, controls—who eventually became unfavorable dischargees after years of bouncing back and forth between institutions, NRCC, and parole. These youths comprised a slightly larger proportion of the later than of the middle and early price-period samples. This situation was compounded by the fact that the rate of unfavorable discharge itself increased (again slightly)—and that it did so more rapidly among C's than E's, beginning in the later 1960s. In this connection, it can be seen from Table A20–2 (Appendix 20) that the average career cost of unfavorable dischargees was substantially larger than that of favorable dischargees. (Findings that will be reviewed in Chapters 15 and 20 suggest that CTP may have been better equipped than the traditional program to work with the seemingly more troubled and/or resistive individuals who were sent to the Youth Authority beginning in the later 1960s.)[19]

As implied earlier, the absolute as well as differential price rise was also accounted for by *favorable* dischargees. This was a direct result of the greater absolute costs—per youth—associated with the later as compared to the early and middle price periods. For example, whereas a one month's difference between E's and C's in accumulated institutional time would have produced a $313 cost differential during the early price period, that same difference (one month) would have produced a $617 differential, if it had been accumulated during the later period (Table A20–1, Appendix 20). Thus, to obtain a differential price rise in total expenditures there did not have to be a larger absolute amount of lockup within either the C or E program during the later as compared to the early years; nor did there have to be a larger *relative* amount of lockup within the C as compared to the E program, in the later as against the early years. This situation applied to "initial" (pre-parole) and revocation-based periods of institutionalization alike, regardless

of the price period in question. Finally, it applied to unfavorable dischargees as well, entirely aside from the factors just mentioned with respect to these youths.

Non–Youth Authority Costs
Costs during YA Career
The figures shown in Table 10–4 include capital outlay.[20] However, they involve YA expenses alone and do not include certain other costs or losses to society (figures that follow apply to the total group, for the 1971–1972 price period):

1. *Non-YA processing and adjudication costs for individuals who were arrested and detained in local city or county facilities, prior to court hearing (these detentions were generally under 72 hours):* As mentioned earlier in this chapter, every 100 controls accumulated about 100 more moderate plus severe arrests than every 100 experimentals, from initial commitment to YA discharge; this equaled 1.0 additional arrests per control per career. At an estimated $200 per arrest and $200 per court hearing (Glaser, 1973a), this cost was therefore about $400 per youth per career. (The actual dollar amounts for *all* moderate plus severe arrests committed during a 3½-year period that began with initial commitment were $92,000 per 100 C's and $52,000 per 100 E's. This involved 230 and 130 arrests, respectively.) We have, of course, excluded all minor arrests—severity levels 1 and 2.

2. *Replacement costs for damaged, destroyed, or stolen property (also included are medical costs for, and lost earnings of, victims):* Relative to the one additional arrest mentioned in item 1 (i.e., one arrest per control), these costs are estimated to have been $489 more for each control than for each experimental.[21] (Dollar amounts for replacement costs associated with the *230* and *130* arrests were $112,470 and $63,570, for C's and E's, respectively.)

3. *Taxes that could have been paid on money earned while in the community:* These are estimated to have been $15 more for experimentals than for controls; that is, wage-earning E's could have paid, or did pay, slightly more taxes than C's.[22]

4. *Welfare payments for spouse and/or children of youths who were incarcerated*

during their YA career: These are estimated to have been $65 more per C than per E.[23]

As shown in Table 10–5, items 1 through 4 total $969 per youth. If this C/E difference is added to that obtained for YA costs—$1,049—the overall savings to society for the average CTP youth was approximately $2,018 per career, relative to the 1971–1972 price period.[24]

Costs after YA Career
Items 1 through 4 also apply to the post-YA period, since some individuals were arrested and incarcerated after their YA discharge. By analyzing these items relative to a specific post-YA period—namely, the amount of time that was needed in order to accumulate four years of risk time (see Figure 10–4, page 133)—the following C/E cost differences were obtained (all figures again relate to the total group and the later price period).

1. *Processing and adjudication of arrested youths:* Every 100 C's accumulated about 27 more moderate plus severe arrests than every 100 E's, during the *post*-YA

period.[25] This equals 0.27 arrests per youth or young adult. Thus, based on figures of $200 per arrest and $200 per court hearing, the present cost—that is, the C/E cost difference—is estimated to have been $108 per individual (0.27 × $400). (The dollar amounts for all moderate plus severe arrests committed during the post-YA period were $96,000 per 100 C's and $85,200 per 100 E's.)[26]

2. *Replacement:* For the 0.27 arrests, these costs are estimated to have been $167 more for each control than for each experimental.[27] (Dollar amounts for replacement costs associated with *all* preceding arrests—240 for C's and 213 for E's—were $148,800 and $132,060, respectively.)[28]

3. *Taxes:* $88 more per individual, in favor of E's.[29]

4. *Welfare:* $79 more per C than per E.[30]

5. *Other correctional and law enforcement costs:* As discussed in Chapter 8, the traditional program produced a higher percentage of unfavorable dischargees (UD's) than did CTP; this fact has cost implications that spring from the following

---

TABLE 10–5

Non–Youth Authority Cost Differences between Controls and Experimentals, during and after YA Career

Cost Item	C/E Cost Difference per Youth[a]		
	During YA Career	*After YA Career*	*Total*
Processing and adjudication	$ 400	$ 108	$ 508
Replacement	489	167	656
Taxes	15	88	103
Welfare	65	79	144
Other correctional and law enforcement[b]	—[c]	2,085	2,085
Total	$ 969	$2,527	$3,496

[a]All costs relate to the 1971–1972 price period. *C/E Cost Difference* means: Per-youth expenses (or losses to society) were larger for controls than for experimentals, by the amount shown. See text regarding: (1) basis for each cost estimate; (2) definition of the post-YA follow-up ("After YA Career"), and of specified cost items.

[b]Includes: prison, jail, adult parole, and probation—minus the *processing and adjudication* item shown above. No capital outlay costs are included. Prison, adult parole, and probation do not apply during YA career (i.e., during predischarge period). In the present category, jail refers to lockup over and beyond the approximately 72-hour detention period associated with processing and adjudication.

[c]Per-youth jail costs over and beyond those associated with processing and adjudication were minimal during the YA period (predischarge); therefore, C/E cost differences were not estimated for this subcategory. See note b regarding the nonjail subcategories of the *Other correctional and law enforcement* item.

events. First, about 50 percent of all UD's (both C's and E's) were transferred directly from the YA to a state or federal prison for adults, at point of discharge. This event or action usually stemmed from a violent or otherwise serious offense, and it often resulted in two or more years of imprisonment. Other UD's remained in a local jail for several months, after being discharged from the YA at the *start* of their sentence.[31] Still other UD's were *not* discharged directly to prison, or while in jail: Their first incarceration occurred some time after discharge. Like the preceding dischargees, these individuals sometimes returned to prison or jail on one or more later occasions. UD's were usually placed on (1) adult parole and/or (2) either juvenile and/or adult probation, in connection with their offenses (violent and otherwise). The former placement or disposition occurred subsequent to their imprisonment; the latter occurred in connection with, or in lieu of, their placement in jail. (It might be kept in mind that several *favorable* dischargees also accumulated prison and/or jail time; they, too, were later placed on adult parole and/or probation.) Each such correctional and law enforcement experience had a price tag of its own.

When prison, jail, adult parole, and probation were analyzed with respect to the total group and later price period, the expenditures for each control were found to be $2,085 more than those for each experimental. (See Appendix 21 for details, including total expenditures for the present cost item.) This post-YA C/E difference excluded item 1 above (processing and adjudication) and capital outlay as well. It was primarily accounted for by the costs of long-term imprisonment among unfavorable dischargees. Since a higher percentage of C's than E's were unfavorably discharged in connection with severe and, especially, violent offenses, the former individuals were more likely than the latter to be imprisoned on a long-term basis.

As shown in Table 10–5 ("After YA Career"), when this cost difference was added to the preceding four, the overall savings to society during the post-YA follow-up was $2,527 per CTP youth.[32] Together with non-

YA expenses and losses that accrued *prior* to discharge ("During YA Career"), the total for all non-YA cost items was therefore $3,496. Finally, as shown in Table 10–6, by adding the preceding figures to the C/E cost-difference obtained for each individual's YA career ($1,049), the overall savings to society is estimated to have been $4,545 per CTP youth, for the YA and post-YA periods combined. As can be deduced from earlier findings, this savings was largely produced by conflicted individuals.

Although these savings are already substantial, they would probably have been about twice as large as of the early 1980s and three times larger by the early 1990s. This is mainly because incarceration (not to mention YA capital outlay) more than doubled in cost between the early 1970s and early 1980s, and increased by approximately 50 percent to 65 percent from the early 1980s to the early 1990s (Governor's Budget, 1982–1983, 1992–1993; Saylor, 1993; Youth Authority Budget Office, 1982, 1994; Youth Authority Facilities Planning Division, 1995; Youth Authority Information Systems Section, 1980, 1984).[33]

TABLE 10–6

Summary of Youth Authority and Non–Youth Authority Cost Differences between Controls and Experimentals, before and after YA Discharge

Type of Cost	C/E Cost Difference per Youth[a]
Youth Authority	
Predischarge (YA Career)[b]	$1,049
Non–Youth Authority[c]	
Predischarge	969
Postdischarge	2,527
Total	$4,545

[a]Applies to total group, for 1971–1972 price period. C/E cost difference means: Per-youth expenses (or losses to society) were larger for controls than for experimentals, by the amount shown.
[b]See Table 10–4 (page 150), note b.
[c]Predischarge and postdischarge correspond to the "During YA Career" and "After YA Career" categories, respectively (Table 10–5).

Notes

1. Thus, the rapid change was partly due to the presence of direct parolees as well. These individuals comprised about 17 percent of all male controls. (See note 5 for related details.)

2. NRCC stays sometimes included one or both of the following: (1) awaiting assignment to YA institution, to direct parole, or to CTP; (2) awaiting placement with relatives, in a foster home, and so on. The former occurred prior to each individual's appearance before the board, and was a routine matter. The latter—a not uncommon occurrence—took place after the board had already assigned the youth to either regular parole or CTP.

3. For conflicted youths, the number of additional lockup months was 2.6, using straight-line projections based on the proportion of time these individuals (E's) had spent in lockup during their actual, post discharge years.

4. The same types of adjustments were made for power-oriented controls, using identical procedures. (See Figure 10–3, note e, page 131.)

5. The few arrests in question were accounted for by Controls who (1) had been directly released to parole ("direct parolees"), without prior institutionalization, and (2) were released prior to 9.4 months. (The figure of 9.4 was an *average*.) It might be mentioned here that offenses committed while in YA institutions were not included in the present analysis, whether they involved staff, other adults, and/or other youths.

6. This estimate resulted from a straight-line projection based on the actual arrest rate of controls.

7. For C's and E's to end up with the same number of arrests after nine years, conflicted controls would have to be initially locked up for at least 36 months—with (1) none having been directly paroled, and (2) regardless of the nature or severity of their committing offense. (For the total group, the corresponding figure would be 31 months.) Again, this estimate involves the "constancy" assumption plus the increasingly shaky requirement that all factors will remain essentially equal or will at least counterbalance each other.

8. If direct parolees had not existed, the catch-up point would have been about 15 months.

9. Also, the catch-up point would have been about 27 rather than 13 months from initial commitment.

10. Throughout Phases 1 and 2 this information was recorded on the summaries in a simple and uniform manner, and was displayed in terms of a standardized format. Not surprisingly, a reliability check, involving all 161 Phase 3 summaries and over 1,000 offense entries, therefore yielded 98 percent agreement between two coders, with respect to offenses and their dispositions. A second check, involving over 200 summaries on Phase 1 and 2 girls (from the CTP, GGI, and control units), yielded almost identical results.

11. For instance, if 100 passive-conformists collectively committed 200 offenses during their first precommitment year, the r.o.o. for these individuals—for that year—would be 0.167 per month at risk, or 167 offenses per 1,000 months. (0.167 = 200 offenses ÷ 1,200 months. 1,200 = 100 youths × 12 months per youth per year.)

12. Results reported in the present chapter changed only slightly when pre-YA camp and ranch time was excluded from the denominator; when this was done (in supplementary analyses not reported here), the results in question changed to an equal degree for E's and C's. We counted such placement time in the present analyses for two main reasons: (1) Nearly all camps and ranches were minimum security sites—for example, no perimeter fences or posted guards—from which youths could, and often did, walk away. (Thirteen percent of all placements finally terminated with an official "runaway.") In this respect, they resembled community placements more than institutional settings. (2) The vast majority of these placements (81% to 90%) were located no more than 45 minutes from one or more large communities, including the individual's home community. (Twenty-eight percent of all camp runaways were accompanied by a community offense; these offenses were distributed as follows: auto theft—58 percent; burglary—27 percent; other—15 percent.

Ninety-two percent of these offenses were committed during the precommitment year. When all camp/ranch placement time was considered, not just the precommitment year, the rate of offending was 18 arrests per 1,000 months—not much lower than that observed within the community itself.) Youths who were located in such sites were, in a fairly substantial sense, therefore at risk in the community. A few additional facts might be noted: The average camp/ranch placement lasted 5.4 months (median = 4.6). For all youths combined (those with and without placements), 9 percent of their precommitment year (1.1 months) was spent in a camp or ranch. For the three years that preceded commitment, the figure was 5 percent.

13. However, as seen in Figure 10–8 (page 140), such offenses *were* rare among passive-conformists.

14. Increasing severity ("escalation") is also reflected in the following comparisons between the commitment offense (c.o.) and the offense that occurred immediately prior to the c.o. (the p.o.): C.o. was more severe than p.o. 47 percent of the time; c.o. and p.o. were equally severe 21 percent of the time; p.o. was more severe than c.o. 31 percent of the time. The remaining 1 percent were uncodable, since the youths in question had been committed on their first offense.

15. When the three-year precommitment and three-year postcommitment periods were compared, the reductions in all arrests combined (severity levels 1–10), from the former period to the latter, were 28 percent among conflicted controls (C) and 69 percent among conflicted experimentals (E). The reductions in *number* of arrests per 1,000 months at risk were 40 and 103, respectively. For passive-conformists the reductions were: C—31 percent; E—71 percent. The reductions in number of arrests per 1,000 months were 43 and 111, respectively. For power-oriented youths the reductions were: C—40 percent; E—54 percent. The reductions in number of arrests were 57 and 85, respectively. For the total group the reductions were: C—31 percent; E—66 percent. The reductions in number of arrests were 42 and 97, respectively.

16. The findings presented in items 2 and 3 centered on a comparison between two age levels: under 16, and 16 and over. These findings suggested that there were few E/C differences from one such level to the next. Broadly comparable results were also observed from one age level (group) to the next when the sample was divided into *three* such groups: 11–14, 15–16, and 17 and over.

17. Mann-Whitney U-tests were used in all analyses.

18. Regarding the *later* period, the main question was: Based on early-1970s prices, what would be the career costs for youths who actually entered CTP or the traditional program during the latter part of the 1961–1969 effort?

19. In the Sacramento/Stockton area this situation first developed around 1966–1967. It seemed closely related to changes in commitment practices on the part of local probation, beginning about the time of California's Probation Subsidy Program.

20. In this context, capital outlay basically refers to construction costs, and it is distinguished from ongoing operating costs. As of the early 1970s, the cost of building and equipping a complete, new, non-satellite, 400-bed institution (with its planning, land acquisition, and environmental expenses included) would have been $12 million to $15 million. By 1980, the figure was $35 million to $45 million, and by the early 1990s it was $50 million to $65 million (Youth Authority Facilities Planning Division, 1995). Thus, capital outlay per youth would presently be much larger than it was in 1971–1972.

21. This estimate reflects Glaser's distinctions among types of offense: "Damages done by known or inferred offenses [are estimated at] $50 per misdemeanor or incorrigible act, $300 per non-violent felony and $2,000 per violent felony (even if adjudicated delinquency rather than felony)" (Glaser, 1973a, p. 42). Of the present 3–10 severity-level offenses, about 40 percent were misdemeanors and 43 percent were nonviolent felonies; as seen in Table 8–1 (page 97, columns 1–2), the remaining 17 percent were violent felonies. The present estimate was derived by using

Glaser's figures in conjunction with the preceding percentages (transformed into proportions). Thus, $489 per typical (composite) offense = [($50 × 0.40) + ($300 × 0.43) + ($2,000 × 0.17)].

22. During their YA career, the average E and C worked about six hours per day during a total of 171 and 151 days, respectively. (*Average* includes all youths who worked for any length of time, plus those who did not work at all. *Six hours* represents a weighted average of all full-time, part-time, and intermittent paid employment.) At approximately $3 an hour, E's and C's thus earned $3,078 and $2,718, respectively (6 × $171 × $3; and, 6 × $151 × $3). Thus, at an estimated 15 percent overall tax rate, each E and C could theoretically have reimbursed the federal and state government about $462 and $408, respectively—a difference of $54 per youth. However, only about one-third of these individuals earned enough money during any given predischarge year to be required to pay taxes. When this factor is considered, together with various deductions, the overall C/E difference reduces to about $15 per youth per career.

23. During parole—predischarge years—approximately 11 percent of the E's and 11 percent of the C's were married; 9 percent of each group had a known child or two. As seen in Figure 10–4 (page 133), controls spent 7.9 more months in lockup than experimentals during their YA career; and, in families that were eligible for welfare and that applied for it, payments were received for an estimated 75 percent (or 0.75) of all lockup months. (Thus, 7.9 × 0.75 = 5.93 more months of welfare payments for C's than E's.) At $200 per month for payments, the C/E difference in welfare received was, theoretically, $1,186 ($200 × 5.93). That is, if a control spent 7.9 more months in lockup than an experimental, the spouse and/or children (family) of the former (assuming he had a family) might have received an estimated $1,186 more than the family of the latter. Since (1) 89 percent of all E's and C's did not have dependent families, (2) only the families of an estimated one-half of the remaining *11 percent* drew welfare, and since (3) half of 11 percent is *5.5 percent* (or 0.055), the C/E differ-

ence in payments is estimated to be $65 per youth—that is, per family—per career ($65 = $1,186 × 0.055). (Note: A reanalysis indicated that close to *20* percent of all male E's as well as C's either were or had been married as of—that is, at the point of—*discharge*. [Married or not, slightly under *20* percent had a child by that point.] However, relatively few of these and other males had been married *throughout* their YA career; and, partly in consequence, 'eligibility-for-family-welfare' did not exist throughout that period.)

24. Not included in these estimates is "production . . . foregone" (by youths), for time in lockup or while unemployed (Glaser, 1973a, p. 42). Nor have we included estimates for the following: "private guards, security devices, and insurance . . . [plus] the less tangible costs of the effect of fear of crime on the lifestyle of city dwellers and the deterioration of city services due to loss of taxes from those industries and citizens who move from the city primarily because of crime" (Fishman, 1977, p. 91).

25. 27 = [(470 − 343) − (230 − 130)].

26. During the post-YA period, every 100 C's accumulated about 240 arrests (470 minus 230); for E's, the figure was 213 (343 minus 130). See Figure 10–4 (page 133). $96,000 = $400 × 240. $85,200 = $400 × 213.

27. For adults, damages are estimated at "$50 per misdemeanor, $500 per nonviolent felony and $2,500 per violent felony" (Glaser, 1973a, p. 38). Of the present, 3 through 10 severity-level postdischarge arrests, about 40 percent were misdemeanors, 45 percent were nonviolent felonies, and 15 percent were violent felonies. Thus, $167 = (0.27) × [($50 × 0.40) + ($500 × 0.45) + ($2,500 × 0.15)].

28. $148,800 = $620 × 240. $132,060 = $620 × 213. *$620* = [($50 × 0.40) + ($500 × 0.45) + ($2,500 × 0.15)].

29. Lacking real data, we assumed that each individual—being an average of 19 years old at discharge, as against 15½ at intake—accumulated about twice as many days of paid employment during the postdischarge follow-up than during the predischarge years (e.g., 342 rather than 171 days, among E's). We also assumed

that (1) his average workday was still six hours, (2) his hourly pay rate was slightly higher than before ($3.50 rather than $3.00), (3) his overall tax rate was essentially the same as before (15 percent of earnings), and (4) about 70 percent (or 0.70) of all wage earners received enough money during any given postdischarge year to be required to pay taxes. Thus, $88 = [(0.15) \times (0.70)] \times [(6 \times 342 \times \$3.50) - (6 \times 302 \times \$3.50)]$.

30. Lacking real data, we assumed that 15 percent of the E's and C's were married and that about 12 percent had one or more children, during the *post*discharge period (these estimates should have been approximately 75 percent higher). As shown in Figure 10–4 (page 133), controls spent 6.3 more months in lockup than experimentals, during the postdischarge (post-YA) period; and we again assumed that welfare payments were received for about 75 percent of all lockup time. (Thus, $6.3 \times 0.75 =$ approximately 4.73—this being the E/C differential, in months of welfare payments.) At $200 per month for payments, the E/C difference in amount of welfare received could theoretically have been $946 ($200 \times 4.73$). However, since the families of an estimated *55 percent* of the above *15 percent* of all E's and C's drew welfare, and since 55 percent times $0.15 = 8.3$ percent, the E/C difference in payments is very roughly estimated to be $79 per individual (i.e., per family), during the postdischarge years ($79 = \$946 \times 8.3$ percent).

31. At time of discharge, it was known that this sentence would extend beyond the preestablished termination date of the Youth Authority's jurisdiction. These sentences usually related to a serious felony.

32. As before, we did not include Glaser's "production . . . foregone." Nor did we include various items—and other, "less tangible costs"—mentioned by Fishman. (See endnote 24.)

33. For instance, by 1978–1979 alone, the per-ward per-year cost of YA institutionalization (camps included) reached $20,100; this compares to about $8,200 in 1971–1972. It might be added that, by 1978–1979, the per-ward per-year cost of regular parole was $2,300, compared to about $600 in the early 1970s (Youth Authority Information Systems Section, 1980). Thus, costs were increasing throughout the YA, not just in institutions.

11 MATCHING OF WORKER AND YOUTH

When one thinks of matching, one might easily imagine two or more individuals who interact harmoniously, who may share mutual interests, and who probably complement each other in various ways. To some extent this picture would accurately represent many worker/youth relationships at the Community Treatment Project during the 1960s. Yet, for the most part, matching within that setting had a different and more specialized meaning.

Basically, matching at CTP referred to the assignment of certain youth types, for example, passive-conformists, to certain kinds of parole agents. These agents, or workers, were individuals (1) whose methods and style of intervention were, in theory, appropriate for those particular youths, and (2) toward whom those youths were predicted to respond fairly well. This type of assignment was called a *worker/youth match,* and matches of this type were not necessarily marked by continual "harmony" and the frequent sharing of mutual interests.

Broadly speaking, matching was seen as one way to increase the chances that youths would have a constructive experience at CTP, one that would be worthwhile from their own perspective as well. Here, it was assumed that many experiences that are useful to certain youth types, for example, conflicted individuals, are not particularly useful to others. It was also assumed that certain workers would be more likely than others to *provide* those experiences to the former youths; similarly, other workers would be more likely to provide useful input to the latter individuals, for example, power-oriented youths.

Since the late 1960s matching has begun to take root within corrections; in fact, since the early 1970s it has been defined in different ways and used in many settings. For instance, some projects, agencies, and scholars have emphasized what might be called a *settings* or *environments* match, for example, the use of structured classrooms or living units for certain youths (not necessarily classified by I-level) and unstructured classes or units for others. Others have focused on a *program components* match, for example, group counseling for some youths and individual counseling for others. In both forms of matching, the main assumptions are essentially the same as before: Different youths will respond differently—and better—to certain kinds of stimuli or input, for example, structured settings or group counseling; accordingly, to promote a maximally constructive experience, one should emphasize certain inputs with specified youths and rather different inputs with others. In program-components matching, neither the worker's style of interaction nor his personal characteristics are considered especially important; what matters is the program component itself. It is also assumed that all workers who are responsible for implementing the program component can present this input about equally well, or at least well enough. "Program component" and "program element" are synonymous. (Alexander and Parsons, 1973, 1982; Andrews and Kiessling, 1980; Brill, 1978; Empey, Newland, and Lubeck, 1965; Gibbons, 1965; Hunt, 1971; Kobrin and Klein, 1982; Lee and Haynes, 1980; Reitsma-Street, 1984, 1988; Sealy and Banks, 1971.)

The concepts and methods of matching—especially worker/youth matching—were first spelled out and extensively tested at the

Community Treatment Project (Palmer, 1965, 1967a, 1968b; Warren et al., 1966b). In fact, it was mainly CTP's research documents that first introduced matching to the field of corrections and helped determine the latter's initial and perhaps current area of focus in this regard. That is, partly because of CTP's emphasis on *worker/youth* interactions, many if not most correctional efforts have thus far emphasized this specific aspect of matching. Here, some of the broad factors that underlie a positive match appear to be the workers' sensitivity to certain issues and feelings, their style of interaction, and their personal characteristics or qualities. (Each such factor would consist of several specific items.) These factors are expressed in, yet are partly independent of, the particular treatment and control techniques that are used.

In the present chapter we will review CTP's use of matching and will briefly describe its impact on youth behavior. To simplify the presentation our account will mainly reflect matching as it existed during Phase 2. Moreover, many of the basic concepts and practices that will be described either existed or were rapidly taking shape during Phase 1. Some, in fact, existed from the start of the experiment (late 1961), though to a lesser degree or in simpler form. (See Appendix 22 for details.) As always, statistical findings will refer to Phases 1 and 2 combined.

Setting, Rationale, and Goal

As discussed in Chapter 1, a central assumption of Youth Authority researchers was that young offenders differed from each other in several ways, their response to intervention strategies included. Given this view, a long-range goal of the experiment was that of testing and improving the strategies that were hypothesized to be appropriate for—likely to elicit constructive responses from—specified youths, for example, passive-conformists (Adams and Grant, 1961; Warren, Palmer, and Turner, 1964a). Collectively, these strategies or approaches—"treatment-control prescriptions"—later became known as the "differential treatment model." (Warren et al., 1966b)

(Examples of treatment-control prescriptions that were utilized during Phase 2 are found in Chapter 6, in sections titled "Overall Pattern of Intervention" [pages 70–71 and pages 78–80]. While still some-

what general, these prescriptions could probably be described—relative to most standards—as *semi*-individualized intervention plans. In any event, they were much more elaborate than the strategies that were hypothesized at the start of Phase 1 and utilized during 1961–1964.)

To test and refine the differential treatment model it was necessary to employ parole agents who each seemed able to implement one or more approaches. Agents selected for this purpose were called matched workers. Specifically, male agents who were selected for CTP during Phases 1 and 2 were hired to implement at least one major approach that was considered appropriate for at least one type of youth. (Details of selection for CTP are reviewed below.[1] As implied in Chapter 3 and described below, agents were hired to do more than simply apply a hypothesized or "preestablished" approach.)

Agents who were employed in *regular,* that is, non-CTP, parole were not selected to work with specific youth types. Instead, they were hired to work with all non-CTP parolees who lived in given geographic areas. These agents were hired via standard civil service and Youth Authority procedures; they were not selected by researchers or by CTP staff. All non-CTP parolees were assigned to those agents by the latter's unit supervisor, and the agents' methods of intervention included whatever seemed appropriate and feasible to them and the supervisor. In short, in these and other respects, the work situation and overall operation of non-CTP agents were different than and administratively independent from that of CTP.

At base, then, "matched workers" referred to *CTP* agents—individuals who, at point of selection, seemed willing and able to utilize a particular, prescribed approach within that specific setting. It did not mean that they and the youths who would be assigned to them had the same type of personality or were at the same level of social-emotional development. Nor did it mean that the agents—and individuals who were *not* selected for CTP—might not be able to utilize somewhat different approaches when working in settings that may have had different priorities or rather limited resources; in such settings, for example, standard probation, the latter approaches might have been considered appropriate or at least acceptable. Finally, "matched workers" meant that the given agents—again at point of selection—seemed to have a manner of expression, and/or a personality, that would help make their interactions both believable and genuine from the standpoint of assigned youths. At any rate, it seemed probable that most such youths would take these workers seriously and view them as individuals to be reckoned with (Palmer, 1967b, 1968b).

Yet neither a genuine concern for youths, a formidable or "arresting" manner, nor a serious interest in crime reduction were the fundamental determiners of an agent's (candidate's) appropriateness for CTP. Nor were such factors as dedication, integrity, persistence, reliability, and the like. Instead, these factors were considered *necessary* but not sufficient with respect to CTP; moreover, they characterized CTP and non-CTP agents alike. What, then, *did* play the central role in selection and matching?

Selection and Matching: Key Issues

As discussed in Chapters 3 and 6, CTP's treatment-control prescriptions often called for fairly intensive and extensive interactions (relationships) with youths, usually over a long period of time (Warren et al., 1966b; Palmer and Grenny, 1971; Palmer, 1983). Given this requirement, it was necessary to select candidates whose motivations would probably allow them to develop such relationships in the first place and whose system of personal and professional rewards would help or allow them to then maintain those relationships under various conditions. It was recognized, for example, that long-term or intensive interactions might require numerous readjustments and might involve complex personal challenges, frequent uncertainties, occasional setbacks, and even major crises for parole agents. Many candidates were not interested in such interactions with youthful offenders; others were personally or philosophically opposed to them. This, despite their overall concern for youths, their dedication, and the like.

At CTP, matching thus included but went beyond the matter of *selection*—a process that focused on the candidate's motivations and appropriateness for long-term, potentially intensive relationships with fairly serious offenders. Matching came into focus relative to the question of which particular youth types, if any, would be appropriate for candidates who *did* seem interested in and able to sustain such relationships and to utilize prescribed approaches (at least in a general way) as well.

But how, in fact, was the question of matching—and even selection—approached? (Space limitations preclude a detailed answer; a general picture will be presented instead.)

Based on prior research, it was first assumed that very few workers—regardless of professional orientation—would interact equally well with all nine youth types (Grant and Grant, 1959; Palmer, 1963, 1965). This and other research suggested that even workers with fairly *similar* professional orientations might differ considerably not only as to their interest in certain clients, but in their ability to interact effectively with them (Adams, 1961; Holt and Luborsky, 1952; McNair, Callahan, and Lorr, 1962; Strupp, 1960; Sundland and Barker, 1962; Truax, 1963; Whitehorn and Betz, 1954, 1960). Supported by the Santa Monica study, it also suggested that these differences might be based, in part, on the personality characteristics and styles of interaction of those workers (Barrett-Lennard, 1962; Cohen, 1956; Lundy, 1956; Parloff, 1956; Van Krevelen, 1958; Vogel, 1959). It was this study that provided several clues as to *which* characteristics, styles, and orientations were likely to elicit relatively positive responses from, and help avoid negative reactions by, various youths and types of youth (Palmer, 1963, 1973a).

(In the Santa Monica study and in CTP's subsequent research, *professional orientations* basically referred to the workers' assumptions about delinquency causation, main goals of intervention [e.g., behavior control, increased practical skills, self-understanding], main areas of focus, and preferred modes of operation. *Personality characteristics* (style of interaction included) were reflected in higher or lower scores on such scales as socially desirable qualities [e.g., resourceful, patient, unaffected, sensitive to meanings, interesting, self-confident]; sharpness/alertness [e.g., intellectually flexible, inquisitive]; attributes that most adolescents would probably like [e.g., is "up on things" in youths' world and can talk their language, enjoys youths' activities, is enthusiastic, has a sense of humor, has "been around"]; strength of feelings, expressions, and opinions; past personal difficulties, felt as such; satisfaction with world around one.)[2]

All in all, it appeared that workers who had certain combinations of professional orientations and personality characteristics might work out particularly well in terms of forming constructive relationships with given youths. More specifically, workers with some combinations seemed promising for certain youths; those with other combinations showed promise, or more promise, for others.[3] To appropriately select and match individuals for CTP, it therefore seemed important to evaluate them in relation to those orientations and characteristics, and to see which combinations they had. Theoretically, this would help determine the type or types of youth for which they might be best, and least, suited.

Thus, using these clues from the earlier-mentioned studies and given CTP's emphasis on long-term, potentially intensive relationships, the Youth Authority researchers tried to answer three broad questions and corollary questions (given the long-range goal of the experiment, the first question required an affirmative answer regardless of the response to the corollary questions that were associated with the remaining two; the corollaries appear in brackets, as separate sentences).[4]

1. Will either the professional orientation or the so-called natural style of interaction of the candidate permit him to operate within the framework of at least one of the . . . strategies which are prescribed in the differential treatment model for given types of youth?
2. Will the candidate's personality and style [of interaction] be likely to elicit, over time, a positive response from—that is, the general acceptance of, or interest of—given types of youth, and not be overly threatening to them? [If so, *which* youth types?]
3. Will particular kinds of youth be likely to provide types of interpersonal feedback or [to] manifest types of growth which would not only be visible to the particular candidate, but would be personally or professionally rewarding to him? [If so, *which* youth types?]. (Palmer, 1968b, p. 2)

The methods used to answer these questions will be mentioned shortly. First, however, five points might be kept in mind.

1. The main *goal* of worker/youth matching was the establishment and maintenance of relationships that would be of in-creased relevance to the long-term difficulties and capacities of given youths, and which—from the standpoint of those youths—could be of increased relevance to their more immediate investments, preoccupations, and preferred modes of interaction (Palmer, 1965, 1968b). In this respect, matching represented a form of "relevant caseload assignment"; at least, it was directed toward that end.

2. The main *assumption* in worker/youth matching was as follows: At given points in their personal and professional development, workers (in this case candidates) will have areas of greater and lesser ability, and differential interest, relative to interactions they might have with the full range of clients (youths). From this perspective, matching was viewed as one way to capitalize on the special talents, sensitivities, and areas of greater concern on the part of candidates, and to minimize the possible effects of their areas of lesser sensitivity, talent, and/or relative disinterest in certain kinds of problems or personalities (Palmer, 1965, 1971a). These concepts, and the preceding goal statement, largely evolved from the research mentioned earlier (Palmer, 1963). They were independent of CTP's particular intervention strategies and could be applied to different settings as well as differing classification systems.

3. The preceding goal and concepts translated into the following operational definition: Worker/youth matching refers to the exclusive or preferential assignment of certain types of youths to specific types of workers (Palmer, 1971a). At CTP, such assignments resulted in "homogeneous caseloads"; that is, each worker was given responsibility for the one, two, or occasionally three types of youth with whom he seemed well matched. (Thus, they were not always *entirely* homogeneous.) At any rate, he was not assigned the full range of offenders—all nine youth types. As noted below, practical limitations and other problems sometimes made it impossible to provide a theoretically optimal or even adequate match.

4. Matching was closely related to individualized planning and intervention, a fact that had implications for the selection of

workers. To understand this relationship we will briefly focus on these broad aspects of individualization.

CTP workers were not simply expected to apply a preestablished approach (generalized strategy) to all youths who fell within a given classification; instead, they were to adapt that strategy to the needs and circumstances of each youth as an individual. Specifically, they were required to (1) develop an individualized plan for each and every youth, and, at the same time, to (2) utilize the given strategy, or components thereof, with each such youth. In effect, they were to build a specific intervention plan within the *framework* that was to be provided by the preestablished strategy. If the strategy seemed inappropriate or inadequate relative to an individual's needs and circumstances, it was to be modified accordingly. Thus, it was to be used whenever feasible and to the extent possible, given the needs of the individual. (The reasons for this two-pronged mandate are reviewed in Appendix 22.)

As indicated in Chapter 2, individualized intervention (planning included) was viewed as one way to involve youths in the process of change—one way to help them recognize the potential relevance of CTP to their ongoing interests, personal feelings, and current concerns. Such involvement was regarded as the main way to tap and build upon their internal motivations—"personal payoff" included. It was assumed that strong, internal motivation was essential in order to (1) sustain long-term, often difficult efforts on the individuals' part, and, regardless of time and effort, to (2) produce major or lasting changes in their life with a minimum of externally imposed control.

Emphasis on the individuals' current concerns and personal feelings reflected CTP's further assumption regarding its ultimate goal of helping youths "cope with life in a less delinquent, hopefully nondelinquent, way." And, as mentioned in Chapter 2, This goal would best be achieved by efforts that emphasized the more *immediate* causes—the apparent triggering and perhaps sustaining conditions—of the youth's illegal behavior. (In 1961, it was taken for granted by the researchers—then amply verified throughout Phases 1 and 2—that the individuals' current interests, feelings, and concerns had considerable bearing on both their illegal and "legal" behavior.) Given its emphasis on both the "long-term difficulties and capacities" of youths and their "more immediate investments, preoccupations, and preferred modes of interaction," the main goal of *matching* was thus consistent with those of individualized intervention and CTP as a whole. In fact, by Phase 2, matching was viewed as one way to implement, and maximize the opportunities inherent in, the individualized approach. What were the immediate implications of this relationship for worker selection?

To develop and implement personalized plans and to maximize the preceding opportunities, workers, it was believed, could not be individuals who had essentially "made up their mind" about youths and therefore felt little need to listen to them. They could not, for instance, operate on the assumption that all offenders—even those within given subtype classifications—were essentially alike with regard to (1) the causes of their personal/legal difficulties, (2) the ways in which they might best deal with those difficulties and work toward their goals, (3) the major issues and personal challenges that they faced, and (4) the types of worker/youth interactions that might be most useful to them. In these respects CTP workers could be neither dogmatic nor narrow-minded.

Instead, these workers had to operate on the assumption that substantial differences existed within those areas, regardless of similarities that may have existed as well. Accordingly, they had to elicit considerable information from youths about their specific life circumstances (opportunities, pressures, limitations), and they had to remain alert to the youths' beliefs and feelings regarding a wide range of issues. Only with such "data," it was believed, could workers have an adequate basis for consistently dealing with the individuals' current interests and needs, and for anticipating future problems. Besides having the necessary "data base" for individualized intervention, CTP workers needed the skill to actually *respond* with respect to that data, that is, respond in different ways to differing situations and individuals. These factors—particularly the worker's assumptions about youths—were therefore evaluated during the selection and matching ("assessment") interview described below. (Factors such as information-gathering ability and response skills could not be assessed as carefully during this interview.)

Finally, individualized intervention was consistent with the researchers' view that all preestablished approaches were "tentative only" and would doubtlessly be revised or refined as a result of practical experience with diverse individuals and situations (Adams and Grant, 1961). This view mainly reflected the assumption that generalized strategies—which basically related to *idealized* descriptions of youth—could not be adequately responsive to the life circumstances and immediate concerns of specific individuals. (For instance, these strategies would inevitably provide too little detail, even if—amazingly—they never provided inappropriate direction.) Nor could they provide or comprise a formula for handling the frequent intricacies of long-term, worker/youth relationships. Although these prescriptions could indeed serve as guidelines—perhaps very valuable guidelines—the *workers* would have to supply critical details, based on current information and feelings that they would obtain from the youths, from other individuals, and from themselves. Again, this meant they would need the motivation and ability to elicit, then deal with, such material.

5. Given its basic goal, worker/youth matching had immediate relevance to the principle of promoting more humane, less impersonal interaction between individuals and the justice system. At the same time, it was part and parcel of CTP's more specific goal of, as mentioned in Chapter 2, interacting with the youth in ways that might help make selected aspects of his environment, and adulthood, appear less threatening and more attractive than in the past. This was seen as one way to provide the

youngster with an increased sense of direction and, in some cases, with an increased sense of power or legitimacy, for example, by making it easier for him to observe and partially identify with self-confident, interesting, respected, or accomplished adults. These "relationship goals" were seen as one way of tapping into, and building on, the youth's drive to expand or profit from his present abilities to cope with life, and to reduce his felt deficiencies. That, in turn, was seen as one way of addressing some of the immediate causes or triggering conditions of the delinquent behavior itself. Given this principle and these theoretically interrelated processes, the workers' personal characteristics and interactional skills were considered particularly important. These, too, were therefore evaluated in the assessment interview, to the extent possible.

Implementation

The Assessment Interview

To evaluate candidates for the Community Treatment Project, an assessment interview was conducted. This lengthy, "depth" interview included several standard, open-ended questions and was carried out on an essentially projective basis.[5] It was conducted separately by one researcher and one operations person—the casework supervisor.[6] (Thus, there were actually two such interviews, each about two hours long.)[7] These individuals then discussed the candidate and made a joint decision regarding his appropriateness for CTP and for working with particular youth types within that setting. Based on this decision, the candidate, if considered appropriate, was assigned to the youths in question.[8]

This approach to assessment, decision-making, and assignment was used (1) with female as well as male candidates, (2) in San Francisco and Valley units alike, and (3) during Phase 3 of the experiment as well. (Females, of course, were assigned to work with all youth groups.) Beginning in 1967, rating scales were used by the researcher to supplement his assessment interview; however, they were not a primary basis for decision-making.[9]

By examining topics such as the following, the assessment interview helped answer the three earlier-mentioned questions (space limitations preclude a presentation of the complete interview schedule; however, see Appendix 23 regarding representative questions asked by the researcher that bore on professional orientations and interactional skills[10]).

1. General and specific professional orientations—e.g., intellectual convictions which [the candidate] may have with regard to (a) factors underlying delinquency causation, (b) principles and prerequisites of effective treatment of delinquents, etc.
2. The candidates' detailed description and interpretation of working relationships which they have had with each of [several] differing types of youth or adults—together with an indication of the major, or many, personal satisfactions and frustrations which they, together with their clients, appear to have felt in connection with particular relationships.
3. The candidates': (a) sensitivity to, and attitude toward, issues and concerns of particular importance to most youths who fall within given subtype classifications; (b) ability to involve those youths in the process of change and to constructively respond to their preferred modes of interaction and typical defenses.[11]
4. The candidates' description . . . of themes or events which, for whatever reason, they regard as having played a fairly significant part in their personal life, (and, the possible bearing these might have had on their work with youths). (Palmer, 1965, 1968b, 1969c)

Most candidates provided considerable information about the first three topics and a moderate amount regarding the fourth. (See Background Characteristics, below, regarding their prior training and work experience—from which they had drawn much of this information.)

Based on the assessment interviews (viewed collectively), one of every four or five candidates was accepted and was offered a position at CTP. In all cases, these individuals accepted the offer.[12] An additional group—one of every eight or nine candidates—could not be offered a position (caseload) even though they were considered appropriate for the project.[13] The remaining individuals did not meet CTP's requirements, and it seemed unlikely that the training and supervisory resources that were available could help them meet those requirements within a fairly short time span. This fact aside, there were many more candidates than positions, at any given time.

The selection and matching process produced satisfactory results; at least, relatively few decisions proved incorrect. Specifically, about 8 percent of all male agents hired for CTP turned out to be inappropriate *selections*: Despite impressions from the assessment interview, these individuals were unable and/or unwilling to work intensively or extensively with juvenile offenders, at least in terms of CTP's expectations. An additional 5 percent were inappropriately *matched*: Although these agents *were* prepared to implement CTP's approaches and principles, they had been incorrectly placed in terms of their specific caseload assignment (e.g., they should have been assigned to passive-conformist rather than conflicted youths). These figures were based on converging views of the casework supervisor, the agents' coworkers, research staff, CTP youths, and, in some cases, the agents themselves. The time period during which these particular workers had been observed was usually 9 to 15 months. At any rate, the vast majority of selections and matches were appropriate.[14]

Caseload Assignment and Subsequent Developments

Most agents were assigned to one of the four caseloads listed below. Together, these caseloads covered the five most commonly observed youth groups (in the list that follows, standard subtype symbols are used in conjunction with the more recent youth labels [Chapter 4]).

#1. *Cfm*—Passive-Conformist
#2. *Cfc and Mp*—Power-Oriented
#3. *Na, Nx, and Cfm*—Conflicted and Passive-Conformist
#4. *Na and Nx*—Conflicted

Including the relatively rare groups (I_2's, Se's, and Ci's), most agents were therefore originally assigned to work with about three subtypes: two rather common groups (e.g., Cfc's and Mp's) and one rather rare group. Thus, 85 percent to 90 percent of their caseload was usually comprised of two youth groups (subtypes) alone.[15] Agents who worked with conflicted individuals (caseloads #3 and #4) usually had a predominance of *either* Na's *or* Nx's, since they were generally seen as more promising or appropriate for one group than the other. However, a modest percentage of agents were assigned to *only,* or almost only, Na's or Nx's.[16] In effect, this comprised a fifth and sixth type of caseload.

Branching Out

Agents mostly continued to work with the originally assigned subtypes throughout their CTP experience—usually three or four years. However, after their first year or two some 40 percent to 50 percent became interested in and seemed prepared to work with at least one additional subtype, particularly one of the five common groups. This development was called branching out across subtypes.[17] Shortly thereafter, the subtype(s) in question was usually added to their caseload, and occasionally, where feasible, one of the original subtypes was then dropped. Thus, caseload assignment was not a closed issue once the agent began working at CTP.

Some types of branching out were far more common than others. For instance, it was not uncommon for workers originally assigned to caseload #1 (passive-conformists only) to eventually relate well with a sizable range of conflicted youths, that is, to develop a caseload #3 pattern. In contrast, workers originally assigned to caseload #4 (conflicted youths only) seldom branched out to include passive-conformists.[18] (For a discussion of factors that contributed to branching out, see Appendix 24.)

Training

Regardless of whether they branched out, most workers sought and received considerable training while at the Community Treatment Project. For example, a time study conducted during Phase 2 indicated that each CTP worker spent an average of 11 hours per month in activities categorized as *professional development* ("consultation—didactic or seminar," four hours; "training" [e.g., transactional analysis, or psychodrama], three hours; "non-case-related discussion with CTP staff," four hours).[19] This was apart from an additional 18 hours spent with various staff members on *case planning regarding individual youths* ("agent with supervisor," six hours;

"agent with other CTP staff," nine hours; "group staffing," two hours; all others, one hour) (Palmer, 1968c).[20] In contrast, regular parole agents participated in an estimated one-half as much professional development and one-third as much case planning.[21] Even aside from this comparison, the picture of CTP that emerged from the Phase 2 study was one of frequent opportunity—perhaps also pressure—for professional growth. This and the preceding results seemed very similar to those that would have been obtained during Phase 1, or, for that matter, at almost any time during 1961–1969 (Grant, Warren, and Turner, 1963; Warren and Palmer, 1965; Kenney et al., 1965).[22]

As described below, agents hired for CTP had considerable prior experience with youths. In fact, they were hired only if they seemed prepared to begin working at the project *without* first receiving any extra, or at least much extra, initial training or supervision. Thus, these individuals arrived at CTP with what was believed to be, and almost always turned out to be, a rather full complement of basic skills, at least in relation to their assigned youth groups (see Chapter 18 for related details). As a result, professional development (i.e., training) activities were primarily designed to *enhance* their already adequate skills—more specifically, to increase their (1) range of techniques, strategies, and resources, (2) understanding of various youth groups (their own and/or others), (3) sensitivity to particular issues, feelings, and behaviors (e.g., increase their ability to recognize various feelings and interpret given cues), and (4) awareness of how they themselves were viewed and responded to by youths. These activities were also designed to help them work effectively with a wider range of individuals— for example, the more unusual or particularly disturbed youths—within the subtypes to which they were currently assigned. (As described in Appendix 24, training or professional development could have come from various sources, formal as well as informal.)

Together with CTP's relatively heavy emphasis on case planning, this type and degree of professional training was considered appropriate in light of the project's expectations regarding the extent and intensity of worker involvement with youths.[23] In addition, these activities were essential in order to help workers learn, and appropriately apply, new approaches—thereby implementing the experiment's hypothesis-development and knowledge-building goals. This was also true with respect to applying their *present* approaches to a wider range of youths.

The Workers[24]

At the time of their assessment interviews, about 80 percent of all candidates were Youth Authority parole agents who worked in regular parole units. The rest were mostly YA social workers, group supervisors from YA institutions, probation officers, and youth workers from private agencies. These individuals came from throughout California, and in most cases each had personally initiated his contact with CTP. For the most part, they viewed CTP as an interesting and challenging program. What, in general, were CTP agents—accepted candidates—like?

Background Characteristics

On average, Community Treatment agents were 32 years old when they began working at the project, and their ethnic breakdown was as follows: Caucasian—79 percent; black—18 percent; Mexican American—3 percent; other—0 percent. All agents were college graduates (four years or equivalent), and, as undergraduates, their major area had been: corrections—26 percent; psychology—26 percent; sociology—12 percent; social work—9 percent; social sciences—6 percent; other[25]—21 percent. Nine percent had a master's degree and 15 percent had a master's of social work degree (Palmer, 1967a).

CTP agents had accumulated nearly seven years of experience within the helping professions prior to working at the project.[26] Five of these years were in the Youth Authority,[27] and of these years, two and a half had been spent specifically as a parole agent (field supervision of youths). Combining YA and non-YA experiences, these individuals had accumulated four years of counseling and treatment (Palmer, 1967a).[28] Background information was also collected regarding regular parole agents.[29]

Salient Features

What did matched workers look and act like, mainly though not exclusively when interacting with youths? More specifically, what were their salient and relatively permanent features? The answers—descriptions that will be presented below—are based on years of observation and contact by on-site researchers, and on results from systematic ratings as well (Palmer, 1967a, 1967b; Warren et al., 1966b). Through these long-term, literally daily observations, the research team became very familiar with all CTP workers as individuals, and could easily see their similarities and differences.

The descriptions in question will be presented regarding workers who were matched with assertive-denier, anxious-confused, passive-conformist, and power-oriented youths, respectively. Each such "worker group" was first described during Phase 2, and each group will be labeled according to the classification of youths with whom it was matched. Thus, agents who were matched with anxious-confused youths will be called anxious-confused workers, though this does not mean they were anxious or confused, themselves.

Three points before proceeding: (1) The assertive-denier (A-D) workers who will be described below represent about one-half of all agents who were primarily matched with A-D youths. However, for ease of presentation, and since they were by far the most common (the "dominant") group, these workers will be discussed as if they comprised the total group of A-D agents. One-fourth of all A-D agents were characterized by a combination of (a) several A-D features—that is, features which will be described for the dominant group—*and* (b) several features that will be described for *anxious-confused* (A-C) workers. (The vast majority of *A-C* workers looked very much like those who will also be described below. The remaining one-fourth of all assertive-denier workers looked much like anxious-confused workers themselves; in fact, they interacted with A-D and A-C youths almost equally well and were "officially" matched with both. These similarities among A-D and A-C workers paralleled the fact that most assertive-denier and anxious-confused *youths* shared several major characteristics; in fact, about 10 percent to 15 percent of all A-D and A-C youths were more similar than not.)

Despite this overlap among assertive-denier and anxious-confused youths, the A-D and A-C *workers* who are described on the following pages were, indeed, quite different from one another as functioning ("whole," or dynamic) personalities, that is, in an integrated global sense. These workers (worker groups) did not represent respective ends of any single continuum; and—specified continua or possible underlying dimensions aside—each such group was neither (a) an "idealized" type (e.g., a "pure" or even a "modal" group, and seldom observed in real life), nor (b) simply a "statistical average/composite" (but somewhat unreal, in a literal and integrated sense). In short, the workers in question were real-life individuals, not hypothetical or essentially statistical constructs. This applied to passive-conformist and power-oriented workers as well.

(2) The personality features, role-centered behavior, and background characteristics that will be described for power-oriented workers related to individuals assigned to group conformist and manipulator youths alike; that is, most workers who had these features, and so on, were matched with both groups of youth. However, generally speaking, power-oriented workers used a somewhat "softer"—for example, less confrontive and more yielding—approach with group conformists than with manipulators. Basically, this difference reflected various changes in the treatment prescriptions that developed during Phase 2.

(3) The worker descriptions that follow involve a combination of personality characteristics, roles, interpersonal styles, and professional orientations. These multiple-dimension descriptions evolved from the Santa Monica study and the earlier-mentioned CTP observations. They are different and far more detailed than the brief accounts that were available at CTP starting in the second half of Phase 1. (Toward the end of 1961, when this experimental project began, the sole distinction that had been made among workers was that of "internally oriented" versus "externally oriented." [Grant, 1961c].) These brief accounts (termed "worker styles") were formulated in mid-1963 and were as follows (the applicable worker groups are shown in parentheses):

a. Wise, accepting, understanding, warm, interpretive, questioning. Internally oriented. (conflicted [assertive-denier and anxious-confused combined])
b. Tolerant, supportive, protective, instructive, dependable. Externally oriented. (passive-conformist)
c. Firm, "con-wise," alert, powerful, self-assured, honest, willing to punish. Externally oriented. (power-oriented) (Grant, Warren, and Turner, 1963.)

These succinct descriptions were designed and used as an aid in treatment planning. As it turned out, they were also used as guides in matching, despite their somewhat global nature and the substantial overlap between (a) and (b). By themselves, they were of moderate use in agent *selection*. At any rate, much more detail was needed—as were additional dimensions—in order to increase not only the precision of matching (e.g., to better distinguish between possible assertive-denier and anxious-confused assignments, or between anxious-confused and passive-conformist assignments), but to facilitate accurate selection decisions themselves (e.g., to distinguish between questionable and promising candidates).

We will now present the detailed descriptions.

Assertive-Denier Workers
Assertive-denier (A-D) workers were quick-thinking, alert, rather forceful individuals. Compared to most adults, they were quite resourceful—often having several "irons in the fire" and usually figuring out "one more place" to turn. They were aware of current trends and events within the adolescent world and were familiar with its latest terms and phrases. During their own adolescence or early adulthood they had generally "kicked around" more than most people and were thus exposed to a good deal of "life." In some respects they had been self-reliant from an early age.

A-D workers were seldom reticent about describing or evaluating events around them. When interacting with peers their remarks were often pointed and critical, and they took many things with a large grain of salt. When interacting with youths, they had few qualms about displaying impatience, irritation, and even exasperation over the latter's actions, especially when these were exploitive, "obnoxious," or impulsive.[30] Yet they were not rejecting; rather, they tried to express concern over what the youths seemed to be doing with their life in a long-term sense.

For instance, assertive-denier agents often expressed concern over what the youths' present actions (binges, evasions, or psychological wounding of others) might mean with respect to their long-term adjustment—apart from its more *immediate* impact on self and others. This concern, or expression of care, was not communicated in an enveloping, protective (sometimes called "mothering," or autonomy-discouraging) manner. Instead, it was predominantly "masculine," affirmative, even challenging (e.g., "Look, I *know* you've got more brains—more cools—than that!" "You *can* do it."). At any rate, despite their frequently confrontive stance and often brusque manner, these agents did not try to make the youths feel worthless, hopeless, sick, or inadequate—or, for that matter, "crushed," in the sense of thoroughly vanquished and/or humiliated. Moreover, they sometimes described themselves to peers or researchers as purposely having "more bark than bite."

For the most part, A-D workers seemed quite satisfied with themselves and with their accomplishments. They were generally ready to let youths "take a good look" at who they, the workers, *are,* and to share with them, through anecdotes and other communications, who they *have been.*[31] Though coworkers and others sometimes considered these agents fairly opinionated and even "hard to take," youths often viewed them as individuals with interesting things to say about (1) what late adolescence, and adulthood, can be like, and (2) how various people have managed to move from adolescence to adulthood in personally satisfying ways, without compromising their principles or becoming a "square." In this connection, youths often described these agents as being "with it" (i.e., sensitive to key issues or needs), and as having new or different ways of looking at things.[32]

Before proceeding, it will be recalled that assertive-denier workers were careful not to seriously threaten A-D youths' strong need to maintain a sense of autonomy and self-reliance. They realized that these factors played a central role in the youths' definition of self as adequate, strong, or accomplished, and in helping them maintain a feeling of hope despite their moments of self-doubt and the pressures of rejection by others. In this respect, the workers were sensitive to the special significance that both *coercion* (as described since the mid-1970s) and *external control* had to these individuals, and to the latter's particular discomfort with anything resembling "brainwashing" or "mind trips."[33] The following can be better understood with this in mind.

A-D workers did not see themselves primarily in the role of therapist, parole officer, policeman, or father figure. Instead, they viewed themselves as a combination of (1) the concerned, skeptical, and somewhat stern uncle or much older brother, and, to a lesser extent, (2) the advice-giving, trustworthy old friend. They seemed to consider this role an efficient, moderately personalized, yet also relatively formalized vehicle through which emergent issues could be candidly discussed, and decisions arrived at, without using either a "heavy-handed" (autonomy-depriving) or a "highly psychological" ("mind trip") approach.

To expand somewhat, this role allowed assertive-denier workers to provide support, advice, and direction, without, in effect, having to say: "I'm going to help you; after all, you really *need* assistance and it's my responsibility to see that you get it." Together with their self-reliant yet fairly sociable qualities, this stern-uncle/older-brother role allowed the agents to act as partial ego-models without their actually having to say: "Check me out and you might see some traits and values that could make sense for you, and some ways in which you could interact more honestly and enjoyably with people." In short, it allowed the youths to (1) pick up potentially useful information and gain exposure to the personal qualities, personal values, and interpersonal skills of generally accomplished individuals, *without* requiring that they (2) relinquish their stance of independence and strength (as *they* defined these concepts), or that they acknowledge the existence of major "needs."

As these youths increasingly felt that the workers had something worthwhile to say or offer and would not be overly threatening or controlling, more time was spent dealing with feelings and events that—previously—the youths had seldom wished to think about, let alone discuss.

Anxious-Confused Workers

Relevant personality characteristics of anxious-confused (A-C) workers are perhaps best understood in the context of these agents' relationship, or role, with youths. We will first review this role and the main factors that shaped it.

Most A-C workers saw themselves in at least two of the following roles, besides that of parole agent:[34] counselor or therapist, interested or concerned friend, father figure. With most youths, the primary role sometimes shifted back and forth; however, after several months, one role usually became dominant.

The nature of these shifts and of the dominant role was largely determined by an interaction between (1) the personality and, especially, the professional orientation of the worker, on the one hand, and (2) the youth's amount of ability to (a) cope with his immediate environment and develop satisfying social relationships, (b) verbalize his feelings and concerns, and (c) tolerate an examination of his typical defenses and interactions, on the other. As seen below, this worker/youth interaction occurred largely within the framework of stated treatment prescriptions, that is, suggested intervention plans. The dominant role was usually that of counselor.

Despite the shared nature of the preceding roles, that is, shared across most anxious-confused workers, differing approaches or emphases existed within each caseload. More specifically, mainly in response to the preceding differences among *youths* (differences that were often substantial), workers gave differing levels of emphasis to certain major techniques and strategies (these should be distinguished from roles, as such). For instance, at any one time they placed either heavy *or* moderate emphasis on the verbalizing of feelings and exploring of defenses (both levels were considered a "thinking-and-introspecting" approach), and either moderate *or* light emphasis on structure, advice, or external control. These differences cut across individual, group, and family counseling.

Yet regardless of these differences, certain broad goals and related areas of focus applied to almost every youth. These shared—in effect, "standard"—features mainly derived from the prescribed treatment approaches outlined in Chapter 6, especially in combination with the workers' professional orientation. Moreover, it was largely these prescriptions that led—through the goals and loci in question—to striking consistencies or similarities in the worker/youth relationship, that is, similarities across most workers and youths (see below). This sequence is illustrated in Figure 11–1.

Thus, for example, the prescriptions in question clearly suggested that anxious-confused youths should gain more understanding of (1) their feelings about themselves and their future, (2) their attitudes toward and interactions with other people (illegal behavior included), and (3) relationships between (1) and (2). Accordingly, almost all A-C workers focused primarily on "thinking and introspecting"; and, for reasons suggested below, they did so via the counselor or therapist, the friend, and/or the father-figure role. At the same time, they deemphasized those role components, for example, components of the *friend* role, which could conceivably have expressed themselves in terms of "acting and doing" (passive-conformist workers did not deemphasize these components).[35]

This emphasis on, and particular approach to, thinking and introspecting was consistent with the workers' professional orientation. It also reflected their following belief (item 1) and implicit assumptions (item 2) about the earlier-mentioned roles: (1) These roles could provide a more appropriate vehicle than *other* roles, for example, policeman or Big Brother, for working toward prescribed goals. (2) When expressed in a relatively for-

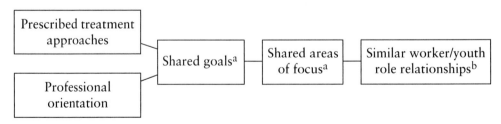

Figure 11–1. Influence of treatment prescriptions and professional orientation on worker/youth relationships.

"—" means: led to.
[a]Shared across workers and youths.
[b]Includes: counselor or therapist; friend; father figure.

mal manner and structured setting, the dominant role could provide a stable, generally acceptable (to most A-C youths) basis for discussing key issues, for communicating and interpreting information, and for conveying or displaying attitudes and traits that some youths might wish to emulate.

Given these views, given the workers' professional orientation, and given the treatment prescriptions as a whole, anxious-confused workers saw little advantage in expressing themselves spontaneously (emotionally or otherwise) and in letting most youths get a very close or detailed look at them apart from their dominant work role. On the contrary, they considered it best to (1) establish and maintain a somewhat formal, though generally relaxed, stance—in effect, to interact on a somewhat calculated, relatively controlled, role-prescribed basis; (2) reveal only those parts of their personal life and value system that they believed would be least distracting, minimally confusing, and potentially useful to the youths. This stance, they assumed, would also make it easier for them, the workers, to focus on major issues, including the youths' "bad" me, "potentially worthwhile" me, and "phony" me self-images.

To implement this stance or role relationship, most A-C workers deemphasized many of their non-job-centered personality characteristics, that is, many aspects of their individuality. This tended to make these agents seem fairly similar to one another within the office setting, especially in terms of being restrained, methodical, attentive, analytical, and introspective. Despite these shared characteristics—which, collectively, resulted in a somewhat serious demeanor—these individuals were friendly and generally, though not highly, outgoing. They also had what their peers, and many youths, considered a good—often wry—sense of humor. At any rate they seldom appeared, especially to youths, to be ill-tempered, impatient, or intimidating; at the same time, they rarely seemed frivolous, indifferent, flamboyant, or impulsive.

As indicated, the prominence of their shared, job-centered characteristics tended to eclipse or partly conceal their underlying spontaneity and individuality. Yet these shared characteristics were not, in themselves, inconsistent with major components of these individuals' self-image and overall personality. For example, most A-C workers *were* fairly restrained, serious-minded, and introspective outside their work role. (To be sure, they were considerably more "fun-loving" than was apparent to youths.) Somewhat related to this, many saw themselves as having experienced considerable personal struggle during their own adolescence or early adulthood, and as having successfully overcome most such struggles.[36] In addition most A-C workers believed they were still growing as persons, and that, for them, growth was a rather important, fairly complex, and somewhat difficult process. In general, they saw little benefit—for youths—in sharing the specifics of these and other complexities or difficulties.

Three final points might be noted:

(1) If one focuses on the typically personalized and sometimes highly sensitive content of the worker/youth (w/y) discussions, the w/y relationship could well be described as "close." However, if one emphasizes the *form* of most such interactions, for example, their largely role-prescribed nature or the relatively little spontaneity and detailed sharing on the part of workers, the relationship might then be described as not very close. Since this relationship could hardly be described as distant (except occasionally), it might best be characterized as formal but relaxed (thus, in a sense, familiar), at least with most youths.

(2) Anxious-Confused workers had at least three of the following skills or characteristics: (a) an ability to accept and not be frightened by whatever these youths believe to be their greatest personal liabilities, their so-called "unforgivable" behavior, or their "secret and bad thoughts"; (b) an ability to not be "taken in" or thrown off the track by those verbalizations, actions, or traits which—while socially acceptable—are regarded by the youths themselves as a cover-up for their more conscious feelings of frustration, inadequacy, or fear; (c) an ability to recognize as *valid* the personal strivings, strengths, and actual accomplishments which the youths already do respect in themselves, and upon which they lean heavily for comfort or reassurance; (d) modelling qualities [with which the youths] . . . might attempt to identify. These qualities include a true respect for self and others plus a striving for continued personal growth—particularly

if this striving is found in the context of an already existing sense of well-being and an apparent enjoyment of adulthood as it *already is* experienced, and includes a degree of satisfaction with one's present accomplishments (Palmer, 1967b, p. 11). (3) A-C workers believed that the most important step these youths could take toward (a) recognizing their legitimate needs, (b) better controlling and directing their lives, (c) reducing their anxiety or confusion, (d) increasing their level of satisfaction, and (e) altering illegal patterns, was to inspect their thoughts, motives, and behavior more carefully than before—perhaps even for the first time. Most agents wanted youths to feel that, during this process, they, the youths, had at least partially confronted the task or issue of assuming personal responsibility for areas of their life that they (a) realistically *could* control (illegal behavior included), and (b) felt an interest in controlling, or some obligation to direct. (This issue was to be approached mainly in terms of specific problems and choices that faced the youths, not through abstract discussions.) A-C workers usually believed that increased self-respect and psychological strength—products that were especially important to often guilt-ridden and emotionally vulnerable youths—could result from having honestly confronted or struggled with this and related issues. This belief reflected their professional orientation and, quite often, their personal experiences.[37]

Passive-Conformist Workers

Passive-conformist (P-C) workers were generally reticent as opposed to outspoken. Their interactions had a quality of leisureliness and calm—rarely haste, impatience, or urgency. Their pace of speech was slow. Rather than convey a quality of forcefulness or ardor, they displayed a mildness that others sometimes described as passivity. They underplayed rather than overdramatized the emotional aspects of most situations, and they displayed few emotional ups and downs.

Besides being unusually even-tempered and rather predictable, P-C workers were quite unaffected and noncompetitive. Their central beliefs about how people should interact were reflected in such phrases as "common courtesy comes first," "meet others more

than halfway," and "kindly or encouraging words at just the right time can't be substituted for." In a sense, their views reflected what was sometimes called a "friendly neighbors" philosophy. Although these agents were not "up" on the jargon of—and on many current trends and events in—the adolescent world, most youths considered them sympathetic to their interests and activities as adolescents.

When interacting with youths, passive-conformist workers expressed firm opposition to illegal, suspicious, or potentially harmful activities. However, they took pains to avoid sharp confrontations, such as blunt and forceful challenges to the youngsters' intentions, integrity, or veracity. They felt that sharp confrontation was usually inappropriate for, and unnecessarily embarrassing or frightening to, these individuals. Such characteristics, beliefs, and sympathies, plus those mentioned earlier, helped make these workers relatively nonthreatening—for example, not forbidding, overwhelming, confusing, or unapproachable—to most passive-conformists.

Compared to most CTP workers these agents had had a generally secure and moderately sheltered upbringing. They felt their adolescence and early adulthood were not marked by (1) debilitating or very intense personal struggles, (2) long periods of social isolation, (3) little opportunity to express rebellion—or gain independence from parents—via socially accepted or generally "tolerated" means, and (4) major restrictions on their ability to enjoy and experiment with life. Their experiences seemed to have given them a generally optimistic view regarding the degree of satisfaction that most adolescents—passive-conformists included—can experience. However, they believed that such satisfaction was possible only if those individuals had access to socially acceptable—not conspicuously deviant—forms of enjoyment and experimentation, for example, were not prevented from *participating* by parents, peers, or others (see items 3 and 4 above). Passive-conformist workers believed that such forms or channels were available not only to most youths who had acquired at least a moderate amount of self-confidence, but to those who had learned—perhaps through the support and encouragement of others (agent, teachers, coaches, or peers)—that one can recoup one's forces despite clear-cut, even major setbacks.

Throughout their relationship with passive-conformists, these workers saw themselves in more of a Big Brother role than in that of any other, for example, therapist, father figure, parole officer, or policeman. They believed that many months of slow, careful work were required to reduce the fears and gain the trust of these youths. In this connection they regarded a "dependency" relationship—for instance, an openly supportive, guiding, even protective relationship—as a temporary yet important prelude to the youths' eventual independence from both worker and others.[38]

Power-Oriented Workers

Most power-oriented (P-O) workers were forceful, energetic, and outspoken; a few were "strong and silent." They had a quick, sharp mentality and often responded rapidly and decisively rather than mulling things over and, even then, acting hesitantly. In this respect they fit the everyday picture of a leader.[39]

These workers were almost always seen, by power-oriented youths, as parole agents or policemen, which was essentially how they wished to be seen. As parole agents, they were usually blunt, businesslike, and to the point; however, they often lightened their tone, and the overall atmosphere, by adding a moderate amount of humor. Still, they spoke with "authority" and acted as if they could neither be ignored, dismissed, conned, nor intimidated. Given these and the preceding features, P-O youths considered them a force to be reckoned with—that is, individuals who made their expectations and demands (their "presence") known in no uncertain terms, and who were sure bets to follow through on what they said. In short, youths regarded them as assertive, persistent, *insistent* individuals, whose recurring message was, "Actions, not words."[40]

This view squared with that of the research team. For instance, researchers viewed power-oriented workers as individuals who, compared to all remaining CTP workers (collectively), "were more likely to demand certainty or closure (in contrast to tolerating ambiguity or much unfinished business); . . . were more likely to set the pace of the relationship rather than let youths set the pace; . . . were less likely to be concerned with *explaining why* they either were or were not doing the things they either had done [or] were in the process of doing" (Palmer, 1967a, p. 45). Thus, researchers saw them as individuals who dominated and controlled the relationship by providing specific structure and expectations, by holding youths closely accountable, and by having the final word in numerous practical decisions. This stance directly reflected the treatment prescription for power-oriented youths.

Despite their emphasis on behavior and accountability, these agents were also concerned with feelings. However, most power-oriented youths had little apparent ability, and even less desire, to concentrate on feelings, especially during early stages—the first 6 to 12 months—of the relationship. (This was independent of the workers' heavy emphasis on behavior.) It was equally difficult for P-O youths to acknowledge *concern*, itself, again during early stages. This reflected their general unwillingness to trust most adults and to attribute constructive motives to them.

Though most youths regarded these workers as "hard-nosed," stubborn, restrictive, and sometimes depriving, they rarely considered them malicious, heartless, totally immovable, or dead-set against kids/delinquents.[41] Nor did they feel that power-oriented workers considered them hopeless, worthless, "disgusting," or "evil." Nevertheless, P-O youths almost always felt on the defensive around these workers, and they usually believed their behavior was being scrutinized. This, to be sure, was essentially what the workers *wanted* them to believe, particularly during early stages. In this regard, youths sometimes described their interaction with agents as a cat-and-mouse game.[42]

Most power-oriented youths did not stereotype these workers as "stupid adults," or simply dismiss them as "lousy agents." (A substantial minority did do so, throughout most of the relationship.) This was despite the fact that P-O workers sometimes expressed marked impatience and acted—by calculation—quite unpleasantly when these individuals broke their promises or engaged in illegal and interpersonally destructive behavior. Thus, for example, when such youths compared these agents to other adults and authority figures they had known, they considered the agents not "stupid" or worthless, but (1) relatively understanding of their world (e.g., able to talk the youths' language; "up on things"—peer culture and street life included) and (2) somewhat interesting as individuals (e.g., someone they might want to know better, especially if they were not one's parole agent). However, from the youngsters' perspective, these positive features also served to make the agents more formidable; and, despite point (2), few workers tried to routinely interact with power-oriented youths as anything other than parole agents (and, on occasion, policemen), except during later stages of the relationship.[43]

Two rather different background patterns were common among power-oriented workers.[44] In the first, and most common, workers came from a highly structured and generally demanding setting. Parents or other caring adults had placed fairly clear, consistent, and strong demands on them; they expected the youths (now workers) to satisfy those demands, to definitely measure up to given standards, and to not "stray very far from the mark"—typical adolescent experimentation, and later "sowing of wild oats," excepted. The parents usually rewarded the youths, emotionally or materially, for fulfilling their obligations, and they punished them—again in standard, socially acceptable ways—for failing to do so. As youths, these workers felt wanted and basically appreciated within this relatively close-knit setting—one which, however, was not entirely without family conflict, family loss, or economic pressures and resulting heavy or early responsibilities.

In effect, these workers re-created certain elements of this experience when interacting with youths: Backed by CTP's treatment prescriptions, they believed that external structure, achievable tasks, firmly enforced standards, and concrete incentives could provide an effective framework for altering not only the youths' behavior but their *view* of the nonpeer environment as largely indifferent, unorganized, hostile, or junglelike.

In the second pattern, workers came from a strained social setting and had personally—or (via close friends) vicariously—been involved in considerable fringe delinquency or in serious illegal activities. Through what they described as (1) "force of will," (2) actual or near encounters with the law, or a period of probation, (3) fear of possible imprisonment and a bleak future thereafter, (4) "dislike of the misery [social environment] around me," (5) "sudden realization of what I *was* [i.e., was *like,* or was becoming, as a person]," and/or (6) the assistance or urging of concerned adults (probation officers included), these individuals eventually broke from this setting and pattern of adjustment. Based on this experience, they felt they knew how to

help many youths "see the light" and pull away from presumably similar settings, pressures, temptations, and patterns.

Given the bleak future they visualized for most power-oriented youths who had reached the Youth Authority, these workers believed that a hard-hitting, uncompromising approach was both necessary and justified. More specifically, they felt that only such an approach could penetrate the youths' defenses, could force them to control long-standing tendencies or reactions, and could help them resist external pressures. Finally, they believed that if this pattern was not broken during adolescence, little change would occur later on. As a result, an urgent, almost missionary tone sometimes characterized their work.

Number of Contacts

In the next section we will review performance differences that were associated with matched versus unmatched assignments. A matched assignment was defined as one in which the youth had been placed on a matched worker's caseload from his first day on parole, and remained with that worker for at least the next 12½ months *or* until he failed on parole (defined as before)—whichever came first. (The former was far more often the case.) An unmatched assignment (UA) included all remaining possibilities—of which there were three broad categories.

1. The youth was originally assigned to an unmatched worker and either remained with that worker, was transferred to a matched worker, or was transferred to another unmatched worker. (Collectively, these comprised the most common UA category or situation.)
2. The youth was originally assigned to a matched worker but, for whatever reason, was transferred to a second—an unmatched—worker during his first 12½ months on parole.
3. The youth had more than one matched worker during his first months on parole. (This was the least common UA situation.)

Thus, in this and all other "matched versus unmatched" analyses, our definition of a matched assignment—therefore, our definition of a *matched worker*—was fairly strict. Specifically, the requirement that a youth be assigned to a *single* matched agent from the *start* of his CTP experience was designed to highlight the relationship component of the worker/youth interaction, not just to eliminate confounding elements in the analysis. (See notes 45–47 for technical details regarding the matched and unmatched samples, matched workers, and unmatched assignments.)

Before we turn to performance, that is, "output," we will briefly focus on agent/youth *contacts*—one aspect of "input." Here, our question will be: Did matched and unmatched workers have the same number of contacts with youngsters throughout the latter's Youth Authority career? This question will be answered with respect to counseling, pragmatically oriented interactions, limit-setting, and collateral contacts, and it will be addressed separately for conflicted, passive-conformist, power-oriented, and the total group of youths. Answers to this question will assume added significance when we turn to rates of arrest and conviction, that is, to "outcome." (Findings presented in the text will refer to "participants only," as defined in Chapter 3; however, with a few exceptions, similar trends were observed for "typical youths," albeit on a smaller scale. Figures for typical youths are shown in the same table and appendix as those for participants.)

Conflicted Youths

As shown in Table 11–1, matched workers conducted slightly more counseling sessions per month with conflicted youths than did unmatched workers: 6.6, 2.4, and 0.8 (matched) versus 5.9, 1.0, and 0.5 (unmatched) for individual, group, and family counseling, respectively. They had slightly fewer pragmatically oriented interactions and limit-setting contacts, and slightly more collateral contacts, than unmatched workers. All in all, these differences were not very large.

When the conflicted group was subdivided into its two components (Appendix 25), substantial differences emerged: (1) Matched workers conducted far more group counseling sessions with *assertive-deniers* than did unmatched workers (4.6 vs. 0.6 per month); also, they placed substantially less emphasis on pragmatically oriented interactions and on limit-setting contacts than did the latter. (In sharp contrast to unmatched workers, matched agents had just as many group as individual counseling sessions with these youths.) (2) Matched workers conducted

more individual counseling sessions with *anxious-confused* youths than did unmatched workers (8.0 vs. 6.1 per month). It might be noted that matched workers conducted far more individual counseling sessions with anxious-confused youths than with assertive-deniers (8.0 vs. 4.5); the opposite applied to group counseling (1.0 vs. 4.6).

Passive-Conformist Youths

As shown in Table 11–1, matched workers conducted more individual and fewer group counseling sessions with passive-conformist youths than did unmatched workers. In addition, they had more pragmatically oriented interactions and fewer limit-setting contacts than the latter.

Power-Oriented Youths

Matched workers conducted a somewhat larger number of individual counseling sessions with power-oriented youths than did unmatched workers; the opposite was true for group counseling. Matched workers also had substantially more limit-setting contacts: 5.6 versus 2.3 per month (Table 11–1).

When the power-oriented group was subdivided into its two components (Appendix 25), sizable differences were found: (1) Matched workers had noticeably more limit-setting contacts with *group conformists* than did unmatched workers (4.7 vs. 2.7 per month). (2) With *manipulators,* matched workers had more individual counseling, fewer group counseling, and far more limit-setting sessions/contacts than did unmatched workers. In the case of limit-setting, the figures were 6.7 versus 1.9 per month.

General Observations

Broadly speaking, matched (M) workers seemed to implement CTP's prescribed treatment plans more closely than unmatched (UM) workers. This, at least, was true in terms of the relatively greater or lesser emphasis they gave to certain modes of intervention, with particular groups of youth. Specifically, it applied to their input within the following areas:

1. *Counseling* (M workers had more contacts—individual, group, and family counseling combined—than UM workers, with conflicted youths. This applied to assertive-deniers and anxious-confused

TABLE 11-1

Number of Contacts per Month between Matched Agents, Unmatched Agents, and Youths, throughout Youth Authority Career

Youth Sample and Type of Contact[a]	Type of Youth and Agent, and Number of Contacts							
	Conflicted		Passive-Conformist		Power-Oriented		Total Group	
	Matched	Unmatched	Matched	Unmatched	Matched	Unmatched	Matched	Unmatched
I. Participants only								
Counseling								
Individual	6.6	5.9	5.2	3.5	5.1	3.7	6.0	4.7
Group	2.4	1.0	1.8	3.0	0.8	1.8	2.1	1.4
Family	0.8	0.5	0.6	1.0	0.3	0.2	0.6	0.5
Pragmatically oriented								
interactions	0.7	1.1	1.3	0.4	1.0	0.8	0.9	0.9
Limit-setting	0.7	1.3	1.2	2.6	5.6	2.3	1.6	1.6
Collateral contacts	1.0	0.6	0.8	1.1	0.5	0.7	0.9	0.7
II. Typical youths[b]								
Counseling								
Individual	2.3	2.7	2.6	2.6	4.0	2.3	2.6	2.5
Group	0.8	0.5	0.8	2.4	0.8	1.6	0.9	0.9
Family	0.3	0.3	0.1	0.4	0.2	0.1	0.2	0.3
Pragmatically oriented								
interactions	0.3	0.6	0.9	0.3	1.0	0.5	0.5	0.5
Limit-setting	0.3	0.6	0.8	1.7	5.6	1.3	1.2	0.9
Collateral contacts	0.3	0.3	0.4	0.7	0.4	0.5	0.4	0.4

[a]Sample sizes are as follows: *Matched:* Conflicted–47; Power-Oriented–11; Passive-Conformist–13; Total Group–73. *Unmatched:* Conflicted–70; Power-Oriented–31; Passive-Conformist–12; Total Group–134. (Total Group also includes Rare Types.)

[b]Includes participants and nonparticipants, i.e., the total sample as defined in Chapter 3.

individuals alike. Among power-oriented youths, a similar result was observed for manipulators but not group conformists); and

2. *Limit-setting* (M workers gave less emphasis than UM workers, with conflicted and passive-conformist youths; they gave more emphasis than UM workers with power-oriented youths. The results for conflicted youths applied especially to assertive-deniers; for power-oriented youths they applied to group conformists and manipulators alike, but especially to the latter).

Matching and Youth Behavior

Did matched CTP youths outperform unmatched CTP youths? Did matched and unmatched CTP youths each outperform controls? As described below, the answer to the first question is yes for some groups, no for others. As before, performance was measured by rates of arrest and conviction (using BCI rapsheets), at three levels of offense severity. *Matched* and *unmatched* youths were those assigned to "matched" and "unmatched" workers, respectively, as defined earlier and in note 46.[48] The youth sample—all matched and unmatched individuals combined—was identical to that used in Chapter 8, relative to the individuals' Youth Authority career (parole). Matched and unmatched youths were very similar to each other on five of the six standard background variables and factors (note 45, part 2). Too few matched individuals were present in most youth groups to allow for a meaningful postdischarge follow-up. Specific results are as follows, regarding parole. (The second question is addressed after the following section. Main results for both questions are summarized in Chapter 12.)

Matched E's versus Unmatched E's
Conflicted Youths
As shown in Tables 11–2 (arrests) and 11–3 (convictions), matched and unmatched conflicted youths performed about equally well during parole: They had 36 and 33 moderate plus severe *arrests* per 1,000 months at risk, respectively, and their rates for severe—and violent—offenses showed a similar trend. Unmatched youths tended to have fewer *convictions* than matched youths for severe as well as violent offenses, but not for moderate

plus severe offenses combined. Possible reasons for the former findings are mentioned below. (As always, "tendency" means $p < .10 > .05$; "significant" means $p < .05 > .01$; and "very significant" means $p < .01$—when used in a statistical context.)[49]

When the conflicted group was subdivided into its two components, important differences emerged: (1) Matched *assertive-deniers* performed much better than their UM counterparts on arrests and convictions alike, relative to all three severity groupings. For instance, the rates of moderate plus severe (m plus s) arrests were 18(M) and 47(UM) per 1,000 months at risk, respectively; those for convictions were 8 and 31. (2) Opposite results were obtained for *anxious-confused* youths. Here, unmatched youths outperformed their matched counterparts relative to all severity groupings. For instance, the rates for m plus s arrests were 24(UM) and 45(M) per 1,000 months at risk, respectively; for m plus s convictions, they were 15 and 30. Statistically, all but one of these results (assertive-deniers: convictions for violent offenses) were significant or very significant. (See note 50 regarding background characteristics of matched versus unmatched A-D and A-C youths.)

A supplementary analysis suggested that the results for anxious-confused youths were at least partly due to the conscious, preferential assignment that was made of particularly disturbed and/or resistant CTP youths to workers who seemed—to the treatment supervisor and others who were sometimes consulted—best able to work with those youths. (During Phase 3 of CTP, these were called "Status 1" youths—individuals who were diagnosed as requiring a period of institutionalization prior to being released to the community. See Chapter 13.) In short, it was generally assumed that only those agents—matched workers, as characterized above—might have a fairly good chance of succeeding with such youths, and temporary initial assignments to nonmatched or questionably matched workers were avoided wherever possible. Because of the resulting assignments, these seemingly poor community-risk youths were, indeed, proportionately more often handled by matched, anxious-confused agents than by "unmatched" agents who, for various reasons (note 47), sometimes handled A-C youths. (As it turned out, the youths in question did have higher rates of arrest and conviction than other

TABLE 11-2

Number of Arrests per 1,000 Months at Risk during Parole, for Matched and Unmatched Valley Males

| | Number of Arrests | | | | | |
| Type of Youth[a] | Moderate + Severe Offenses | | Severe Offenses | | Violent Offenses | |
	Matched	Unmatched	Matched	Unmatched	Matched	Unmatched
Conflicted	36	33	16	13	7	5
Assertive-Denier	18	47	6	18	2	9
Anxious-Confused	45	24	21	9	10	3
Passive-Conformist	11	42	0	17	0	11
Power-Oriented	46	60	20	22	6	16
Group Conformist	66	50	26	15	5	9
Manipulator	33	68	16	28	7	22
Total Group[b]	35	39	15	15	7	9

[a]The sample used in this analysis is identical to that in Table 8–1 (page 97). This sample is broken down as follows, separate for matched (M) and unmatched (UM) youths. Conflicted: M–46, UM–53. Assertive-Denier: M–16, UM–21. Anxious-Confused: M–30, UM–32. Passive-Conformist: M–12, UM–24. Group Conformist: M–6, UM–10. Power-Oriented: M–6, UM–12, UM–24. Group Conformist: M–6, UM–12. Manipulator: M–6, UM–12. Total Group: M–81, UM–92.

[b]*Total Group* includes all Conflicted + Passive-Conformist + Power-Oriented + Rare Types. When two of the four Rare Types (Stress Reaction [etc.] and Delinquent Identifier) are excluded, the six figures shown in this row remain unchanged. The sample sizes become: M–66, UM–92. (All Rare Types were matched.)

TABLE 11–3

Number of Convictions per 1,000 Months at Risk during Parole, for Matched and Unmatched Valley Males

Type of Youth[a]	Number of Convictions					
	Moderate + Severe Offenses		Severe Offenses		Violent Offenses	
	Matched	Unmatched	Matched	Unmatched	Matched	Unmatched
Conflicted	23	21	12	7	6	2
Assertive-Denier	8	31	4	9	2	5
Anxious-Confused	30	15	16	6	8	1
Passive-Conformist	11	17	0	8	0	6
Power-Oriented	34	41	18	13	6	9
Group Conformist	41	28	20	2	5	0
Manipulator	30	52	16	22	7	17
Total Group[b]	24	25	12	8	6	4

[a]The sample used in this analysis is identical to that in Table 8–1. See Table 11–2 (page 178), note "a", for details.

[b]See Table 11–2, note "b". When Stress Reaction (etc.) and Delinquent Identifier youths are excluded from among the Rare Types, the figures of 24, 25, 12, 8, 6, and 4 become 24, 25, 11, 8, 6, and 4, respectively. The sample-sizes become: M–66, UM–92.

A-C youths. Moreover, matched workers did not easily "give up" on these youths: They tolerated more acting-out behavior than usual, at least during Phase 1.) As suggested below, other factors—CTP's general intervention strategy included—may have also contributed to the results in question.

Finally, the following might be kept in mind regarding the fact that, for the conflicted group as an entity (that is, A-C and A-D individuals combined), matched youths had slightly but not significantly higher rates of arrest and conviction than unmatched youths: Since (1) the strength of the M/UM difference was about the same for the anxious-confused and assertive-denier groups, and since (2) there were considerably more A-C than A-D youths in the *study sample* (62 vs. 37), the "negative" results for matched A-C youths outweighed the "positive" results for matched A-D youths. If the sample sizes had been reversed for these two groups, matched conflicted youths would have had slightly lower rates than UM youths. (This particular reversal would have produced lower rates for the total group as well.)

Passive-Conformist Youths

As shown in Tables 11–2 and 11–3, matched passive-conformists had fewer moderate plus severe—and severe—arrests than their unmatched counterparts. (Matched youths tended to have fewer violent arrests and fewer moderate plus severe convictions, as well.) Though these differences were statistically reliable, the sample of youths was fairly small.

Power-Oriented Youths

Matched power-oriented youths had somewhat but not significantly fewer moderate plus severe arrests than their unmatched counterparts: 46 versus 60 per 1,000 months at risk. They had significantly fewer violent arrests—that is, arrests for violent offenses—than the UM group. No M/UM differences were found with respect to convictions. (See Tables 11–2 and 11–3.)

When the power-oriented group was divided into its two components, several differences emerged:

1. Matched *group conformists* had *more*—that is, a higher rate—of severe convictions than their unmatched counterparts.

They also had somewhat but not significantly more moderate plus severe arrests, and they tended to have more such convictions: 66 versus 50 (arrests) and 41 versus 28 (convictions) per 1,000 months at risk, respectively. All in all, matched group conformists thus performed somewhat worse than their unmatched counterparts. Here, too, the sample was fairly small.

2. Opposite results were obtained for *manipulators* (Mp's). Matched Mp's performed significantly better than unmatched Mp's on arrests, and they tended to do so on convictions: 33 versus 68 (arrests) and 30 versus 52 (convictions) per 1,000 months at risk, respectively, for moderate plus severe offenses. A similar, significant result was obtained for violent arrests. Again, the sample was fairly small. (See note 51 regarding background characteristics of M versus UM group conformists and manipulators.)

Thus, different outcomes were associated with matching in the case of group conformists as compared to manipulators. Supplementary analyses indicated that these differences were not accounted for, to any substantial degree, by the factor that seemed to operate with respect to conflicted individuals: the especially careful assignment of "Status 1" youths to agents who seemed best *matched*—and also most likely to "stick with" these youths through behavioral and other crises. Regarding the power-oriented group as an entity—group conformists and manipulators combined—the "negative" findings for matched group conformists were essentially counterbalanced, and even slightly outweighed, by the "positive" findings for matched manipulators.[52]

Total Group

For all youths combined, there were no significant differences between matched and unmatched individuals in rates of arrest and conviction, relative to any severity grouping. This was mainly because the "positive" findings for matched assertive-deniers, passive-conformists, and manipulators were counterbalanced and canceled by the "negative" findings for matched anxious-confused and group conformist youths. (See Tables 11–2 and 11–3.)

In sum, matched and unmatched CTP youths performed about equally well in the aggregate. Yet, matched passive-conformists outperformed their unmatched counterparts, and substantial M/UM differences were found between individual subtypes that comprised the conflicted and power-oriented categories, respectively. Some of these differences favored matched youths—others, unmatched youths.

Additional Observations: Inputs and Performance

The fact that matched *assertive-deniers* performed better than their unmatched counterparts *may* have resulted from their having received far more group counseling than the latter youths (Appendix 25). However, various other factors may have also contributed to this performance difference, and in the present analysis, no one factor could be singled out as most important. For example, (1) among matched A-D's, individual and group counseling were given substantial but equal emphasis, and limit-setting received little individual attention; at the same time, (2) among *un*matched A-D's, individual counseling occurred far more often than group counseling, and limit-setting was given moderate attention. These differences between matched and unmatched youths ("M/UM input differences") suggest that at least the following factors and mixture may be particularly valuable to assertive-deniers, singly or in various combinations: a matched agent; group counseling; a relatively equal mixture of individual and group counseling.[53] (While a minimization of limit-setting may also be important, matched A-D workers may have deemphasized this element partly *because* their youths were performing rather well. This interpretation received indirect empirical support.[54] As seen below, matched and unmatched assertive-deniers *both* outperformed their controls, and from this perspective, the precise sources of the M/UM performance difference—that is, the output difference among *experimentals*—becomes slightly less crucial.

The fact that matched *anxious-confused* youths performed worse than their unmatched counterparts may have partly resulted from their having received more individual counseling than the latter; in effect, they may have been given more than they needed or could handle (Appendix 25). Given the fact that matched A-C workers were assigned more

Status 1 youths than were unmatched workers, the former agents may have provided more individual counseling, and more counseling overall, partly *because* their youths (1) seemed more disturbed or difficult to reach, and/or (2) were engaging in more borderline activities or having greater difficulty with the law. (The second interpretation of the M/UM input difference is weakened by the fact that matched A-C workers engaged in less limit-setting than unmatched workers.) Yet, interpretations aside—and however plausible the workers' rationale may have been—the quantity or type of counseling may still have been "too much" for Status 1 and other anxious-confused youths.

Alternatively, the input from matched agents may not have been inappropriate, or it may have been only slightly inappropriate. In comparison, *un*matched A-C workers may have had a *more* appropriate (or even less inappropriate) overall stance with anxious-confused youths in general, or with Status 1 A-C's in particular. At any rate, unmatched agents—while conducting fewer counseling sessions (Appendix 25)—were somewhat less formal, less focused on feelings, and less "nondirective" than matched workers, and in these respects, they were similar to many assertive-denier workers. Of course, this difference in stance and input may have partly reflected the presence of fewer Status 1 youths on their respective caseloads.

The relative merits of these alternate interpretations of the matched youth/unmatched youth performance difference could not be adequately tested in the present analysis. However, results from Phase 3 of CTP strongly suggest that a somewhat structured or directive approach is quite important with Status 1 youths (the anxious-confused included), at least initially. In this connection it might also be noted that unmatched Phase 1 and 2 A-C's outperformed their controls, whereas matched A-C's did not (Appendix 26). Finally, the preceding interpretations are neither mutually exclusive nor exhaustive. (Phase 3 is reviewed in Chapter 13.)

Matched *group conformists* (G-C's) performed *worse* than their unmatched counterparts even though their workers gave added emphasis to limit-setting. This additional emphasis (1) may have been given partly because the matched youths were engaging in more technical violations of parole or in more socially unacceptable behavior from early in their program, (2) may have been present throughout the parole relationship, regardless of the presence or degree of infractions and unacceptable behavior, or (3) may have involved a combination of (1) and (2). (The first interpretation received the most support.)[55] At any rate, even apart from limit-setting (viewed not only as a response to youth behavior, but as a preestablished input), various interpretations are possible regarding the M/UM performance difference. This is because several factors, such as the workers' overall style or personality, may have differentially contributed to outcome, and it is despite the fact that matched workers used individual as well as group counseling about as often as unmatched workers, with G-C youths.

In contrast, matched *manipulators* performed much *better* than their unmatched counterparts, though their workers, like matched G-C workers, also provided more limit-setting than unmatched workers (Appendix 25). However, matched Mp workers provided more individual and less group counseling as well. Apparently, the preceding factors, singly or in combination, influenced manipulators differently than group conformists; moreover, these and other factors may have contributed to the matched-Mp/unmatched-Mp performance difference itself. At any rate, increased limit-setting was not, in itself, invariably associated with either better or worse performance across the power-oriented subtypes, namely, group conformist and manipulator. These findings assume added significance in light of the fact that matched Mp's outperformed their controls (see below).

Matched and Unmatched E's versus C's

Did matched and unmatched CTP youths each outperform controls during parole? To address this question, the same methods were used as those outlined earlier. As to sample comparability, matched and unmatched E's were each quite similar to C's with regard to the earlier-mentioned background characteristics.[56] (Controls could not be subdivided into M and UM groups. For further details, see Appendix 26.) Results are as follows.

Conflicted Youths

As shown in Table 11–4, *matched* conflicted youths had significantly fewer moderate plus severe arrests and convictions than their con-

trols: 36 versus 80 and 23 versus 50 per 1,000 months at risk, respectively. They had significantly fewer severe arrests and tended to have fewer violent arrests, as well. *Unmatched* conflicted youths also had significantly fewer moderate plus severe arrests and convictions than their controls: 33 versus 80 and 21 versus 50 per 1,000 months at risk, respectively. They had significantly fewer severe arrests and convictions (and fewer violent convictions), and tended to have fewer violent arrests.

Passive-Conformist Youths

Matched passive-conformist (P-C) youths had significantly fewer arrests than their controls, relative to all severity groupings; they had fewer moderate plus severe, and severe, convictions as well. Unmatched P-C youths had significantly fewer moderate plus severe arrests and convictions and tended to have fewer severe convictions than controls. However, no significant E/C differences or tendencies were found in connection with violent offenses (Table 11–4).

Power-Oriented Youths

Matched power-oriented (P-O) youths tended to have fewer moderate plus severe—and severe—arrests (but not convictions) than controls. They had significantly fewer violent arrests, as well. Unmatched P-O youths tended to have fewer severe arrests than controls; however, no E/C differences were found relative to moderate plus severe—and violent—offenses (Table 11–4).

Total Group

Matched experimentals had significantly fewer moderate plus severe arrests and convictions than their controls: 35 versus 76 and 24 versus 48 per 1,000 months at risk, respectively. They also had significantly fewer severe and violent arrests and tended to have fewer severe convictions. *Unmatched* E's had significantly fewer moderate plus severe—and severe—arrests and convictions than controls. They tended to have fewer violent convictions, as well (Table 11–4).

On balance, then, matched and unmatched youths outperformed the controls, during parole. These results, for each group individually, closely paralleled those for both groups combined (Table 8–1, page 97). (Rate of offending during the *postdischarge* and the

TABLE 11-4

Number of Offenses per 1,000 Months at Risk during Parole, for Matched and Unmatched Experimental Boys and for Control Boys[a]

Type of Offense and Outcome Measure	Conflicted			Passive-Conformist			Power-Oriented			Total Group[c]		
	Matched Exp.	Unmat. Exp.	Control	Matched Exp.	Unmat. Exp.	Control	Matched Exp.	Unmat. Exp.	Control	Matched Exp.	Unmat. Exp.	Control
Moderate + Severe Offenses												
All arrests	36	33	80	11	42	86	46	60	66	35	39	76
Arrests with convictions	23	21	50	11	17	61	34	41	39	24	25	48
Severe Offenses												
All arrests	16	13	28	0	17	25	20	22	34	15	15	28
Arrests with convictions	12	7	17	0	8	18	18	13	21	12	8	17
Violent Offenses[d]												
All arrests	7	5	13	0	11	11	6	16	16	7	9	13
Arrests with convictions	6	2	10	0	6	7	6	9	10	6	4	8

[a]*Parole* refers to the entire Youth Authority career, as in Table 8-1 (page 97).

[b]Sample sizes are as follows (E_m = Matched E's; E_{um} = Unmatched E's; C = Controls): Conflicted, E_m–46, E_{um}–53, C–64; Passive-Conformist, E_m–6, E_{um}–10, C–29; Power-Oriented, E_m–12, E_{um}–24, C–39; Total Group, E_m–81, E_{um}–92, C–157.

[c]See Table 8–1, note b.

[d]See Table 8–1, note c.

parole plus postdischarge periods is shown in Appendix 27, for specified types of youth.)

Notes

1. Since relatively few females were committed to the Youth Authority from any one area, each parole unit, for example, the Sacramento unit, contained only one female parole agent (Chapter 2). Since female parolees were not assigned to male agents during Phases 1 and 2, all such youths were assigned to the one female agent. Thus, in any given CTP parole unit, this particular agent worked with the full range of subtypes, whether closely matched or not.

2. Each scale consisted of several items, for example, resourcefulness, patience, and others. For an individual to obtain a scale score, each item was first rated and the ratings for all such items were then summed. These scales—23 in all—contained an average of six items and their mean reliability was as follows: upper-bound estimate, .95 (σ = .02); lower-bound estimate, .67 (σ = .06); average of upper- and lower-bound estimates, .81 (σ = .03). (The latter figure probably represents the best, or most generally acceptable, estimate.) The most reliable items from these scales were used to construct the "Form 3" worker rating instrument (see endnote 9). For further details see Palmer, 1963, 1967a, 1968b, 1968c, 1970b; Palmer and Warren, 1967.

3. Several combinations seemed to occur repeatedly, and each such combination (pattern) was comprised of several professional orientation—and personality characteristics—scales. The resulting characterizations of workers—that is, each pattern (and all patterns collectively)—were therefore more complex and much more specific than those from previous research. Almost without exception, the latter had involved simple dichotomies such as the "A" versus "B," "autonomy-oriented" versus "restriction-oriented," and "internalist" versus "externalist" breakdowns. In addition, nearly all such descriptions had focused on professional orientations alone (Betz, 1963; Eze, 1959; Grant and Grant, 1959; Havel, 1963; Pownall, 1963; Sundland and Barker, 1962; Whitehorn and Betz, 1954, 1960).

4. An affirmative answer to the first question was usually followed by a similar answer to the second and third. Affirmative answers to the latter questions (questions that were occasionally settled prior to the first) were almost invariably accompanied by a similar answer to the first.

5. For example, the interview was characterized by the following: essentially no pressure, direction, or "leading" by the interviewer; a minimum of follow-up questioning; no interpreting of the candidate's statements and no adding of concepts to his presentation, or "putting words into his mouth"; a neutral attitude on the part of the interviewer (therefore no clues as to what his personal views or preferences might be, what a "good" answer might be, and what he might consider significant or revealing).

6. During Phase 1 the researcher was almost always Marguerite Warren; during Phase 2 (and 3) it was the author.

7. A third interview was often conducted by the CTP administrative supervisor; however, this interview was relatively brief—30 to 45 minutes—and much less personal. It mainly involved a review of the candidate's work experience, his career plans, his present job status, *when* he would be available for CTP (if accepted), and other practical or technical matters. For any given candidate, all interviews were conducted on the same day.

8. If the decision was to "hire," the casework supervisor assigned actual individuals, that is, specific youths, to each accepted candidate, though not necessarily all at once. (All such youths were to be members of the agreed-upon youth type or types.) Before finalizing a "caseload assignment," the supervisor sometimes consulted with one or more researchers and/or with fellow operations personnel, regarding the a priori (i.e, subtype) appropriateness of the match, and/or the operational necessity (unavoidability) of the assignment.

9. All rating scales consisted of items that had emerged from the Santa Monica study, and all ratings were based on the assessment interview alone. These items

(variables) statistically distinguished (1) specified groups of CTP agents (e.g., those working with passive-conformists) from other groups of CTP agents, and (2) CTP agents from non-CTP agents (Palmer, 1967a). Prior to 1967, assessment personnel (chiefly the researcher) had often utilized many of these variables when forming their impression of candidates; however, they did so in an informal and unsystematic way. In addition, they had combined many such variables with each other in a rather intuitive manner and had weighted them on an essentially subjective basis. (The results, however, were not unsatisfactory.) In contrast, by utilizing the *scales,* assessment personnel were able to focus on all variables systematically, to combine specified variables in a consistent way, and to weight those variables on a relatively objective basis (Palmer, 1967a, 1968c, 1969c). By the late 1960s all variables that comprised these scales were used outside CTP in the form of a 105-item rating instrument—the "Form 3" (Palmer, 1970b, 1971a; Warren et al., 1974). Based on direct feedback, independent checks, statistical analyses, and experiences within CTP itself, it was concluded that valid ratings of Form 3 items could generally be made by the following individuals ("knowledgeable others"): (1) supervisors and peers who had extensive contact with the candidates; (2) other trained individuals who had conducted nondirective, depth interviews with candidates and agents. (A self-report instrument—the "Form 4"—was developed for use by candidates themselves; however, it worked out only minimally well.) Once the ratings were completed on all 105 items, they were used, in specified *combinations* and with predetermined weights, to derive the candidates' overall score for each of five "worker styles": *asocial* (Aa, Ap); *passive-conformist* (Cfm); *power-oriented* (Cfc, Mp); *assertive-denier* (Na); *anxious-confused* (Nx). Each style referred to a youth group, or youth groups, with whom the candidates would be predicted to interact appropriately and to elicit a constructive response *if* their score equaled or exceeded a minimum cutoff. The cutoff for each youth group had been established specifically for CTP but could be adjusted for other settings and situations. No scales were developed for "non-conflicted, higher maturity youths," since it was believed that almost all CTP workers could relate well with *Se's* and that nearly all "power-oriented workers" could interact appropriately/constructively with most *Ci's* (Palmer, 1967a, 1968b, 1968c). In sum, the Form 3 added considerable uniformity and objectivity to the process of worker/youth matching, even though it was not relied on heavily at CTP (given the already extensive experience—and the resulting, preferred approaches—on the part of the assessment personnel). Its contribution mainly centered on the final phases of matching: the integration and interpretation of data (in this case *ratings*) regarding the candidates' professional orientations, personality characteristics, and so on. Though the Form 3 showed considerable promise and was often used outside CTP, its validity remained dependent on the presence of high-quality data—specifically (1) information from skillful, nondirective interviewing, and (2) ratings (based on that information) that reflected a careful assessment of the orientations and characteristics in question. This applied whether or not the interviewer and rater were one and the same.

10. The casework supervisor seldom asked these identical questions; however, his interview covered essentially the same topics. The schedule from which the researcher's questions were excerpted was developed, by the author, in 1964. Although a formal interview schedule did not exist before then, the topics in question were also covered during the Phase 1 *research* interviews. However, this coverage varied a good deal, depending on the specific topic involved.

11. Item 3a involved the candidates' recognition of the youths' typical ways of interpreting the actions and demands of others. Item 3b involved their recognition of the youths' typical strengths and limitations, and an awareness of stimuli to which these individuals often felt, or at least *were,* especially vulnerable.

12. These individuals usually began working at CTP two to four weeks after their interviews.

13. These individuals could not be offered a position (caseload) at CTP for one, or occasionally both, of the following reasons: (1) A *different* candidate was seen as more appropriate for the caseload that was to be filled; therefore, once the latter candidate had been offered and had accepted that caseload, no position was available. (2) These candidates seemed appropriate for a caseload (e.g., passive-conformist youths) that was *already* fully covered at the time of the interviews. This was apart from the caseload (e.g., conflicted youths) for which they had originally been interviewed—one for which they may or may not have been considered appropriate (and, *if* appropriate, had not been chosen because of reason [1] above). About two-thirds of the present individuals—"appropriate candidates" who had not been offered a position—did not reapply for CTP when an appropriate caseload later became available. For the most part they had become, or remained, involved in other activities. In some cases they had received a substantial promotion, and in rare instances they were simply lost track of. The remaining one-third did reapply and later *were* hired when an appropriate caseload became available (in whatever geographic area); this usually occurred 6 to 15 months after their original interviews.

14. Nearly all incorrect decisions related to individuals who were hired to work with group conformists, manipulators, and, separately, anxious-confused youths. These agents routinely engaged in, or were characterized by, at least three or four of the following: they avoided close or extensive involvement with youths, when such involvement seemed appropriate; they only minimally "listened" to youths; they seemed unable or unwilling to "individualize" their approach in accordance with the youths' specific needs and circumstances; they were unwilling to utilize CTP's "preestablished" approaches on other than a token basis, and they often relied on techniques that seemed inappropriate instead. Thus, in general, (1) these workers interacted with most youths in ways that were inconsistent with or at least tangential to certain underlying principles of CTP, and/or (2) they did not adequately include, in their overall approach, techniques and strategies that were considered essential to the hypothesis-testing goal of the experiment. (Regarding "underlying principles of CTP," since most such workers did not adequately listen to youths and did not seem particularly responsive to their more immediate investments, preoccupations, and preferred modes of interaction, they generally failed to "facilitate the [youths'] personal involvement in the process of change." Perhaps related to this, they often seemed to inadvertently reinforce the youths' "negative image of authority figures," rather than modify that image in a positive direction.) Neither intensive supervision, peer influence, nor other types of input substantially altered their approach.

15. The *Cfm* caseload often included an occasional I_2 and Se, or, in a few instances, several I_2's. The *Cfc and Mp* caseload often included one or two Ci's. The *Na, Nx, and Cfm* caseload sometimes included an occasional I_2 and/or Se. The *Na and Nx* caseload sometimes included an occasional Se and/or Ci.

16. Plus an occasional Se or Ci.

17. Most remaining agents branched out at a considerably slower rate or to a lesser degree. Many of these individuals continued to work exclusively or almost exclusively with the originally assigned subtypes. In such cases, developments within the agents' overall approach usually consisted of one or more of the following (it might be kept in mind that, through time, these agents worked with an increasingly wide range of personalities and problems, even *within* a given subtype): (1) an increased scope of involvement by agents, that is, involvement in more areas of the individuals' life (family, peers, school, employment, or additional social agencies); (2) a greater degree of flexibility on the agents' part, especially in terms of utilizing more techniques for interacting with youths; (3) a somewhat greater intensity in the relationship between agents and selected youths (i.e., greater intensity where

seemingly appropriate). Thus, like agents who branched out across subtypes, the present individuals also added certain dimensions to their approach—but essentially *within* the original classifications. They usually appeared quite satisfied with these developments.

18. Workers originally assigned to caseload #1 (passive-conformists) never branched out to include Mp's, though they occasionally worked with Cfc's; conversely, agents assigned to work primarily with Mp's never branched out to work with Cfm's (passive-conformists). It was uncommon but not rare for individuals assigned to caseload #2 (power-oriented youths) to branch out in the direction of Na's and Nx's (Conflicted youths). Also, individuals assigned to caseloads #3 or #4 (conflicted youths, plus passive-conformists) rarely branched out to include both Mp's and Cfc's.

19. Professional development was defined exactly as in an earlier Youth Authority time study: "Time spent in learning about the job or the correctional field, not related to individual cases. Includes training sessions, both formal and informal; may include training given by supervisor or co-worker" (Johnson, 1960, p. 56). Professional development did not include time that the agent may have spent *as* a trainer; nor did it include training courses he may have attended on his own time.

20. This study was conducted in 1966 and included all Sacramento and Stockton agents.

21. Estimates regarding regular parole agents (RPAs) were derived from (1) an earlier Youth Authority analysis that used categories identical to those in the Phase 2 study, and (2) two 1960s analyses that used very similar categories. Time-study results for RPAs remained largely unchanged into the mid-1970s (Davis, 1970; Johnson, 1960; Seckel and Davis, 1975).

22. Basically, these results applied to all CTP agents, regardless of whether they (1) branched out across subtypes or (2) added new dimensions to their approach with *originally* assigned subtypes instead.

23. In this connection it might be kept in mind that this level of involvement was rather different than that which the workers had previously experienced, at least in relation to a full caseload. Also, it was obviously different than that experienced—and expected—in regular parole, given the latter's standard-sized caseloads.

24. The statistics presented in this section relate to all male agents (34 CTP, 16 regular parole) who were responsible for experimental or control cases during 1961–1967 (Palmer, 1967a). These statistics would change only slightly if one added agents who were hired after 1967 to work with Phase 1 and 2 youths.

25. For example, English, history, philosophy, and physical education.

26. Prior work experience mainly occurred in the following areas: (1) the Youth Authority; (2) juvenile probation; (3) parole and probation combined (found outside California); (4) county welfare; (5) state hospital, private hospital, or other institution; (6) youth recreation, or youth camp.

27. Prior Youth Authority experience included any of the following roles: "(a) field supervision of wards [while a parole agent]; (b) caseworker, counselor, or therapist in specialized or psychiatric treatment program; (c) institutional group supervisor primarily responsible for care and custody of wards; (d) liaison officer between institutions and parole; institutional classification officer" (Palmer, 1967a, p. 18). It might be mentioned that 37 percent of the individuals' prior work experience had been as a parole agent and 25 percent had been as an institutional group supervisor. However, as indicated, their most recent job was usually that of parole agent.

28. "Counseling and treatment" was associated with the following roles: YA parole agent; YA caseworker or counselor in a specialized program; probation officer responsible for field supervision; counselor or therapist in a state or private hospital or other institution.

29. The following relates to regular parole agents (RPAs)—those responsible for Valley controls. (1) On average, RPAs were 33 years old when interviewed by research staff. Twenty-five percent were under 30 and 13 percent were over 40;

for CTP agents, the figures were 35 percent and 9 percent, respectively.

(2) Ethnically, RPAs were distributed as follows: Caucasian—69 percent; black—13 percent; Mexican American—6 percent; other—13 percent. (3) All RPAs were college graduates (or equivalent), and their major area had been: corrections—25 percent; psychology—19 percent; sociology—19 percent; social work—0 percent; social sciences—25 percent; other—13 percent. Six percent had a master's degree. (4) Regular parole agents had accumulated nearly seven years of experience within the helping professions at the time of their interview. Nearly six of these years were within the Youth Authority, and, of these years, three had been spent as a parole agent (field supervision). Combining YA and non-YA experiences, these individuals had accumulated three and a half years of counseling and treatment. When comparing CTP and regular parole agents on items (3) and (4), the following therefore applied:

The two agent-groups were quite similar to one another with respect to type and amount of education at the undergraduate level. As compared with regular agents [RPAs], a somewhat—but not significantly—higher percentage of community [CTP] agents had taken part in courses at the graduate level and had, in addition, obtained advanced degrees. The type and amount of prior work experience in help-related occupations or functions—such as counseling, casework, and the like—was, in most respects, very similar for the two agent groups. All in all, the two groups showed a far greater number of similarities than differences with reference to the above types of general background characteristics. No major differences were found in this area (Palmer, 1967a, pp. 3, 15–22).

(Excluded from items (1) and (4) is one individual who was far older than anyone else—namely, 69—and who had accumulated nine years more experience than any other RPA.) See Chapter 16, section on "Parole Agent's Background Characteristics," regarding CTP/RPA dif-ferences between "PA [parole agent] I's" and "PA II's" during Phase 1 of the experiment.

30. In this connection, such a phrase as "he's a bastard, but he's ok" (i.e., he gets real nasty or sticky, but he knows his stuff, probably means well, and treats you fairly) was not rare, on the part of youths.

31. Partly for this reason, and given the preceding features, such descriptions as "he's a kick" and "he's a character" were by no means rare, on the part of youths. These descriptions were usually presented in a positive—partly amused, partly admiring—tone; they were seldom used in connection with other workers by these and other youth types.

32. A-D workers appeared assertive and self-reliant (in this respect "strong") to the point where, in the youths' view, they could probably "take people or leave them," depending on their—the workers'—choice. However, most youths sensed that these workers had elected to "take them," and to become, in fact, quite interested in constructively interacting with them. Though the workers seemed to have become "committed" to people and to adulthood, they apparently had not (again, in the youths' view) "sold themselves out," "bought the whole package," "become a square," lost their ability to both assert themselves and control their own life, and—in general—to remain master of difficult situations. This seemed to help many youths feel it is possible to be rather autonomous without largely rejecting social norms, and to be an "individual" without being generally disliked, isolated, or rejected.

33. Many of these youths seem to have transferred or projected various fears or doubts concerning their mind and personality (e.g., fear of learning something "terrible" about themselves, or underlying doubts as to their adequacy and likability) into such beliefs as the following: The *agent* might (1) try to pry into their mind, (2) succeed in uncovering something "terrible" or embarrassing, (3) try to "brainwash" them, and (4) try to change their personality. At one level, these actions and outcomes could signify,

to these youths, possible rejection by one more adult. At another level, outcomes (3) and (4) could signify a potential loss of self-control and personal autonomy. The thoughts and projections in question seldom acquired the scope, intensity, and overall role or significance generally associated with paranoid adjustments.

34. The parole agent role was always present—if only in the background—however much the workers deemphasized external controls. Like other agents, anxious-confused workers fully realized that they *were* in fact parole agents—acting on behalf of society as a whole, not just of youths. Though they basically accepted the need for this role, they believed it complicated some aspects of their job.

35. Acting and doing centered on agent intervention with key individuals/agencies in the youth's environment; recreational events and socializing experiences; and so on.

36. The fact that introspection played a large role in producing this outcome—as did identification with supportive and respected others—had direct implications for the agents' work with youths. See endnote 37.

37. When interacting with youths, A-C workers often built on their professional training and experience *plus* their awareness of personal satisfactions and "victories" that they, largely as adults, had derived through their own introspection, feelings of increased self-acceptance, pride of accomplishment, and respect from valued others. They tried to help A-C youths eventually experience similar feelings of gratification, of triumph over uncertainty or frustration, and of recognition by others. Toward such ends—and through the vehicle of their role relationship—they tried to help youths experience feelings of being appreciated and valued by another individual (namely, the worker), and, in turn, to eventually experience feelings of increased respect for self. Hopefully, this relationship would provide a bridge to, and a partial model for, other relationships and experiences.

38. This, hopefully, would not be an "independence" (in effect, an *isolation*) that mainly reflected a denial/abandonment of one's interpersonal needs or desires, or a feeling of being unwanted or undeserving. Nor would it largely reflect a desire to escape the controls, domination, exploitation, or intimidation of various individuals. Instead, it would primarily be based on the youths' sense of confidence in self and others, plus their feeling of being accepted, supported, and liked. In effect, it would reflect their personal desire to move forward in socially accepted ways, plus permission and encouragement from others to do so.

39. Within a few years after leaving CTP almost every power-oriented worker had obtained an administrative or a supervisory position inside or outside the Youth Authority.

40. Youths sometimes responded to the workers' *insistence* and apparent *self-assurance* as follows: "He thinks he's God"; "He thinks he's always right!" Together with the agents' (1) assertiveness, (2) frequent use of examples from their own past, and (3) heavy emphasis on behavior, these characteristics sometimes produced negative emotional reactions in coworkers and other adults. For instance, these individuals occasionally viewed such characteristics as a reflection of arrogance, smugness, immodesty, egocentricity, or a lack of concern for the feelings of others. In short, unless one knew most power-oriented workers rather well (a condition that was often unmet), it was sometimes difficult to tell *where* role-related expressions left off and other aspects or reflections of personality began.

41. This was reflected in, yet went beyond, their willingness to acknowledge that workers often provided concrete, practical assistance.

42. At the start of the relationship most power-oriented workers had let youths know that although they (youths) had several good points and considerable potential, they (workers) presently regarded them (youths) as something less than angels. Thus, most youths realized they would have to "win" or "earn" the workers' confidence before specific restrictions would be removed, and in order to obtain increased privileges and

decision-making power. Given this general situation, youths viewed P-O workers almost exclusively as parole agents (or policemen)—individuals mainly concerned with performance, rewards, and punishments. Only later in the worker/youth relationship—if and when the earlier-mentioned confidence developed, and if the situation regarding restrictions, privileges, and so on, underwent substantial change—did some youths regard these workers as *friends* to any large degree. Even then, power-oriented youths did not come to view these agents as counselors, therapists, or Big Brothers; and only occasionally did they regard them as stern father figures—in addition to, but not instead of, parole agents.

43. During various stages of the relationship, most agents occasionally "let their hair down." They did this mainly to demonstrate that (1) parole agents *were* people after all, that is, they enjoyed situations and activities that most people liked, and (2) they, as "people," accepted and could enjoy the *youths* as "people" (their positive attributes in particular), business and illegal behavior notwithstanding. (From the agents' standpoint, the latter reason was uppermost.) Yet even in these situations, workers usually tried to maintain their image of strength and self-assurance.

44. The section that follows (in text) is based on research interviews with workers.

45. (1) The number-of-contacts analysis was based on a systematic review and detailed coding, in 1973, of stratified, randomly selected case folders on 207 Valley males—61 percent of the total male sample. As in the amount-of-detention analysis (Chapter 3), stratification focused on *location, project stage,* and *youth subtype,* and it achieved its goal. That is, as shown by the following percentages, the resulting "contacts-analysis" (CA) sample ($N = 207$) was highly representative of the *total* sample on all three dimensions (CA percentages are shown first; total sample, second): Sacramento vs. Stockton—59/41; 55/45. Formative stage vs. full-operations stage of CTP—24/76; 26/74. I-level subtypes (Warren labels:

I_2's, Cfm, Cfc, Mp, Na, Nx, Se, and Ci, respectively)—3, 12, 11, 10, 23, 34, 3, 5 (CA sample); 5, 14, 11, 10, 21, 32, 2, 5 (total sample). The randomization was successful for all variables that were used: (a) For conflicted individuals and the total group, there were no statistically significant differences between matched (M) and unmatched (UM) youths on age, race, socioeconomic status, IQ, base expectancy (parole risk), and type of commitment offense. (b) For passive-conformist (P-C) and power-oriented (P-O) individuals there was one statistically significant—though quantitatively small—difference each: Matched P-C youths tended to have a lower IQ than UM youths (eight points difference; $p < .10 > .05$), and matched P-O youths tended to be better parole risks than UM youths (11 points difference; $p < .10 > .05$). Finally, in line with the earlier-mentioned similarities on individual I-level subtypes, there were no statistically significant differences between M and UM youths on subtype groupings (passive-conformist, power-oriented, conflicted) and I-level (I_2, I_3, I_4). In sum, the contacts-analysis sample was highly representative of all Phase 1 and Phase 2 Valley males, combined. (2) In the *matched-E's-versus-unmatched-E's-performance analysis* (see text below), all youths who comprised the earlier-mentioned Valley analysis (Table 8–1, page 97) were included. Here, too, M and UM groups were very similar to each other on five of the six variables and factors. Specifically, only 3 of 24 possible statistically significant differences were found between these groups relative to the passive-conformist, power-oriented, conflicted, and total group categories, respectively (all differences were at the $p < .10 > .05$ level): (a) Matched passive-conformists tended to be worse parole risks than their UM counterparts. The means and standard deviations were as follows: matched, M = 372, σ = 45; unmatched, M = 442, σ = 76. (b) Compared to matched individuals, unmatched power-oriented youths were overrepresented in the "property offenses" category and underrepresented in the "all other offenses" category. (c) Matched conflicted youths tended to be worse parole risks than their UM counterparts; however, the M/UM difference (23 points) was quite small in relation to the means as well as standard deviations: matched, M = 486, σ = 105; unmatched, M = 463, σ = 123.

46. Entirely apart from the analytic requirement that youths remain with their originally assigned, "matched" worker for at least the first 12½ months, on what basis were workers considered *matched* rather than unmatched in the first place? The answer is that, for purposes of all M versus UM analyses, matched workers were those who met the following criteria (these analytic criteria were given essentially equal weight): (1) They implemented CTP's broadly defined treatment-control plans, as these were described—in expanded and revised form—by the end of CTP's formative stage (Grant, Warren, and Turner, 1963; Riggs, Underwood, and Warren, 1964; Warren et al., 1966b). (Full implementation required an ability to individualize these broadly stated plans, and to work intensively or extensively with youths as needed.) Basically, this represented a *process* (specifically, an input) requirement, not a *product* (output) requirement. That is, it focused on whether agents made the "called for" moves—on whether they supplied what was defined, toward the end of Phase 1, as the appropriate overall input for specified youth types. It did not refer to the products of that input, namely, to the relative success or failure of youths on parole. This analytic criterion referred to whether the agents *carried out* prescribed plans, not just whether they were hired to do so; as such, it was distinguished from the hiring criteria described in the text. As indicated, of all agents hired, about 8 percent turned out to be inappropriate selections; an additional 5 percent were inappropriately matched. None of these individuals were considered matched workers in the present analyses. (2) They displayed many personality characteristics, interpersonal styles, and/or professional orientations that seemed—based primarily on the Santa Monica study— likely to produce positive responses in specified youth types. (By 1965, relationships between the Santa Monica youth types—eight "empirical clusters"—and the various I-level subtypes had been determined.) No workers who essentially implemented the treatment-control plans were considered unmatched, when judged by this criterion; only if their characteristics, and so forth, were clearly antithetical to those in question would they have been considered unmatched. At the same time, a few workers who deviated somewhat from the treatment prescriptions *were* considered matched, as a result of this criterion. (Some of the characteristics in question are mentioned on page 161 and the vast majority were incorporated into the *Form 3* rating instrument [endnote 9]. For a list of items and scales that comprised these characteristics, and so on, see Palmer, 1967a; Palmer and Warren, 1967.)

47. Most unmatched assignments resulted from conditions (1) and (2), mentioned next; and each of these, in turn, related to the other factors and conditions mentioned earlier in the chapter. (1) *Limited caseload openings.* Some youths first arrived at CTP during a period in which their potential matched worker(s) had no caseload opening. This sometimes occurred during the full operations stage; however, it was more common during the formative stage. During the formative stage, Sacramento and—especially— Stockton had an incomplete contingent of agents. The relatively few agents who covered these areas, particularly Stockton, were—collectively—simply not matched with the full range of youths, at any one time. (2) *Worker turnover.* This usually occurred in connection with promotions and was relevant to the present analysis for youths who had not accumulated the earlier-mentioned 12½ months. Also, of course, it bore on condition #1, above. Other, quantitatively less influential conditions or reasons were: (3) *Inappropriate selections.* This referred to workers who turned out not to meet criterion #1 and/or #2 in endnote 46, with regard to assigned youths. (4) *Incorrect matching.* This usually referred to agents whose respective caseloads included one youth subtype, say,

passive-conformists, for whom the agent did not implement the prescribed treatment plan. (5) *Retrospective mismatch.* A few workers were seen—in retrospect only—to have been unmatched with one or more subtypes. That is, *after* CTP had refined its understanding of given youths, it was recognized that the workers to whom these youths had been assigned had not provided what "now" was considered the appropriate input. This occurred relative to the formative period only, and for passive-conformist youths particularly. (Prior to 1964, these youths were conceptualized as being quite similar to group conformists; accordingly, the prescribed treatment plans for these groups were very similar [Grant, 1961c, pp. 6–11].)

48. These categories of youth and worker were each inclusive. That is, no other categories existed, and as a result, no youths who appeared in Table 8–1 (page 97) were omitted from the present analyses.

49. Mann-Whitney U-tests (corrected for ties) were used throughout the matched versus unmatched analyses.

50. For assertive-deniers, no significant M/UM differences were found on the six background variables and factors: age, race, socioeconomic status, IQ, type of commitment offense, and base expectancy. For anxious-confused youths, two differences were found. (1) Matched individuals had a significantly higher IQ than UM youths; however, this difference amounted to only four points; (2) as compared to UM youths, matched individuals tended to be overrepresented in the "property offenses" category and underrepresented in the "other offenses" category.

51. For manipulators, no significant M/UM differences were found on the six background variables and factors. For group conformists, two differences were found: (1) Matched individuals tended to have a lower IQ than UM youths; however, this difference was only five points; (2) regarding race, matched youths were highly overrepresented in the Caucasian and black categories.

52. In general, the results for manipulators were countered but not outweighed by those for group conformists. (Compare the results for assertive-deniers and anxious-confused youths.) This was mainly because the sample size was the same for both groups. However, sample sizes aside, M/UM performance differences were generally sharper among manipulators than among group conformists, with respect to moderate plus severe arrests. As a result, matched *power-oriented* individuals came out slightly though not significantly ahead of their unmatched counterparts, in this respect. For the same reason, they were significantly ahead, that is, performed better, on violent arrests.

53. Assertive-deniers received this "relatively equal mixture" as a *group,* that is, collectively. However, it does not necessarily follow that the mixture (amount) in question was received by each *individual* A-D, or even by most of them. In reality, a roughly equal amount of individual and group counseling was received by no more than 35 percent of all A-D's, during their YA career; the remaining 65 percent received substantially more of one (either one) such input than of the other. As to the roughly equal inputs themselves, these were not necessarily received at every single "point" in time, for example, during the youths' (the 35 percent groups') first three months on the project, during their second three months, and so on.

54. The interpretation was supported by at least the following facts: (1) With matched workers, amount of limit-setting during the youths' fourth through twelfth months (second through fourth "quarters") on the project decreased by 45 percent as compared to their first three months (first quarter) on the project; with unmatched workers it increased by 2 percent. (2) With matched workers, limit-setting subsequent to the youths' first year (first four quarters) on the project decreased by 42 percent as compared to their first year on the project; with unmatched workers it decreased by 16 percent. No corresponding determination was made of the youths' rate of *offending* (r.o.o.) during either their first quarter or their second through fourth quarters on the project. Nor was

r.o.o. (Table 11–2) broken down separately for their first year as compared to all subsequent years.

55. Interpretation #1 received some support from the following fact. With matched workers, amount of limit-setting during the youths' fourth through twelfth months on the project increased by 66 percent as compared to their first three months on the project; with unmatched workers it decreased by 18 percent. (With matched workers, limit-setting subsequent to the youths' first year on the project increased by 4 percent as compared to their first year on the project; with unmatched workers it increased by 3 percent. This neither supported nor opposed interpretation #1.) Interpretation #2 received little support from the following fact. During their first quarter on the project, youths assigned to matched workers experienced only 8 percent more limit-setting than those assigned to unmatched workers. As in endnote 54, no additional analyses were made with regard to rate of offending, separate for the first quarter, the second through fourth quarters, the first year, and all subsequent years on the project.

56. *Matched* experimentals were very similar to their controls on five of the six background characteristics. Specifically, only two statistically significant differences or tendencies were found between these groups relative to the passive-conformist, power-oriented, conflicted, and total group categories, respectively: (1) matched conflicted E's tended to be older than C's (by four months); (2) matched E's (total group) were older than C's (by four months). *Unmatched* experimentals were also similar to their controls, except as follows: (1) unmatched passive-conformist E's were more likely to be Caucasian and less likely to be black than C's, and they tended to come from middle socioeconomic backgrounds more often than controls; (2) unmatched conflicted E's tended to be committed to the Youth Authority for slightly more "other" offenses and slightly fewer property offenses than C's; (3) unmatched E's (total group) came from middle socioeconomic backgrounds more often than their C's. (As in all background-characteristics analyses, chi-square tests were used.)

PART III

Review, Phase 3, Implications, and Key Factors

12 REVIEW OF FINDINGS

We will now summarize and review the main results from Chapters 8 through 11. Specifically, we will present an overview of the Phase 1 and 2 findings and a summary of results for conflicted, passive-conformist, power-oriented, and all youths combined (the total group). Males and females will be presented separately, and primary focus will be on Valley youths. Arrests and convictions will receive heavy emphasis in the overviews, but additional outcome measures will be noted as well. A more detailed summary of main results will then follow.

Overview for Males
Performance during and after Parole

Conflicted Valley boys in the Community Treatment Project performed much better than their controls on several measures of effectiveness, rates of arrest and conviction included. These latter rates referred not only to their time on parole—about three years average—but to a total of seven years follow-up in the community, including four years of post–Youth Authority time ("postdischarge" follow-up). Moreover, they referred not only to moderate plus severe offenses combined but to violent offenses in particular. (Moderate, severe, and violent offenses are defined in Chapter 8. Results are unchanged when minor offenses, e.g., runaway, "incorrigibility," and traffic, are included.) In general, rates of offending were 40 percent to 60 percent lower for experimentals than for controls. Fairly similar results were obtained in San Francisco, but mainly during parole, especially for severe and violent offenses. Essentially the same results were obtained for these offenses when San Francisco CTP boys were compared to those in the Guided Group Interaction (GGI) program. (A 40 percent reduction means that instead of 100 or 1,000 offenses being committed, 60 or 600 are committed. Practically speaking, this represents a large drop in illegal behavior.)

Thus, regardless of setting—medium-sized and moderately urbanized (Valley), or large-sized and highly urbanized (San Francisco)—conflicted experimental boys outperformed their controls in the short run as well as the long run, particularly on severe and violent offenses. Conflicted youths accounted for 53 percent of all Valley males and 61 percent of all San Francisco males.

During parole, *passive-conformist* Valley boys in CTP had much lower rates of arrest and conviction than their controls, for moderate plus severe offenses and for severe offenses alone. However, during the four-year post-YA follow-up ("postdischarge") their performance was in some ways worse than that of controls. When the parole and postdischarge periods were combined (seven-year total follow-up), passive-conformist Valley boys retained a definite edge over their controls on arrests and convictions. In the San Francisco study, reliable comparisons could not be made between passive-conformist E's and C's because there were too few C's.

Thus, passive-conformist boys in CTP performed somewhat better, in the long run, than those in the traditional program; this at least was true for Valley youths. These individuals accounted for 14 percent of all Valley males.

During parole, *power-oriented* Valley experimentals performed slightly better than controls. However, subsequent to Youth Authority discharge they were arrested and convicted substantially more often than controls. Thus, when the two time periods were combined (i.e., "in the long run"), power-oriented experimental boys performed slightly though not significantly worse than controls. In San Francisco, reliable comparisons could not be made between power-oriented E's and C's because there were too few C's.

In sum, power-oriented controls performed as well as or slightly better than those in CTP, in the long run. This at least applied to Valley youths. Power-oriented individuals accounted for 21 percent of all Valley males.

During parole, experimental Valley boys (the *total group*) performed better than controls on several measures of program impact. They were arrested and convicted 38 percent to 50 percent less often, in particular; these rates referred to violent offenses as well as those of lesser severity. During the postdischarge period neither E's nor C's significantly outperformed the other on five of the six analyses; this occurred mainly because the performance of conflicted E's was counterbalanced by that of power-oriented C's. For the parole and postdischarge periods *combined,* experimentals were arrested and convicted substantially less often than controls. In San Francisco, similar results were obtained for parole, postdischarge, and both time periods combined, despite the presence of relatively few controls. This applied not only to moderate plus severe offenses combined but to severe offenses in particular. For instance, in the case of parole and postdischarge combined, experimentals had about 35 percent fewer moderate plus severe offenses and over 58 percent fewer severe (and violent) offenses than controls, per month at risk in the community. Similar results were obtained when CTP was compared to GGI.

Clearly, then, the total group of CTP boys outperformed its controls, regardless of setting. It might be kept in mind that Valley boys were primarily Caucasian (53 percent) and secondarily Mexican American (23 percent), whereas San Francisco boys were predominantly black (68 percent) and secondarily Caucasian (25 percent). Also, the total group included not only conflicted, passive-conformist, and power-oriented youths, but all four "rare types."

Supplementary Findings
Social Risk of CTP
While youths are locked up, they are not committing offenses against the community. Given this fact, we asked: Did the traditional program protect the community better than CTP, when lockup time (institutional, jail, prison, and NRCC) was added to the non-lockup time considered thus far? Results were as follows: The traditional program provided more protection than CTP for about 13 months, counting from the day of each youth's commitment to the YA; basically, this was because most controls were institutionalized during much of that time, whereas CTP youths were not. Soon after their initial release from YA lockup, controls began to commit offenses at a substantially higher rate than experimentals, and they continued to do so for the next several years. As a result, about one year after initial commitment, CTP "caught up" with the traditional program in terms of protecting the community; and once it caught up, it pulled increasingly ahead. After approximately three and a half years from initial commitment to the YA (still counting all lockup and non-lockup time), every 100 experimentals had produced about 100 fewer moderate plus severe arrests than every 100 controls, on the average. After nine years the E/C difference was 127 arrests, even though C's had accumulated substantially more lockup time than E's during that period, and therefore had less time at risk. Although the latter figure applied to the total group, a substantially larger E/C difference was observed for conflicted and passive-conformist youths. In contrast, among power-oriented individuals, the traditional program provided more protection than CTP. These findings would have been similar, though reduced in scale, if convictions had been focused on rather than arrests.

Change from Pre-YA Period
The traditional program produced a sizable drop in moderate plus severe arrests, mainly when the parole plus postdischarge years were compared with the year that preceded commitment (this was called the basic time comparison). However, sizable reductions—in fact, larger reductions than in the traditional program—were also achieved within *CTP,* regardless of the time periods that were compared. This was true for the total group, for

conflicted youths, and, to a lesser extent, for passive-conformists. It was particularly true with respect to severe and/or violent offenses, at least in the basic time comparison. However, the opposite applied for power-oriented youths, regardless of offense group: With these individuals, the traditional program outperformed CTP except when the three-year period that preceded commitment was compared with the approximately three-year period of parole. (See endnote 1 regarding "suppression effect.")

Costs
Because of continuous, nationwide inflation during 1961–1973, separate analyses were made for three representative price periods: 1963 (early period), 1966–1967 (middle period), and 1971–1972 (later period). From one period to the next, costs for experimentals grew steadily less when compared to those for controls. For instance, among youths handled during the early and middle periods, respectively, *YA career costs* were higher for E's than for C's: For each youth, the E/C cost difference was $1,008 in connection with the early period and $830 relative to the middle period; these, and all figures below, refer to the total group. However, among youths handled during the later price period, career costs were $1,049 lower per experimental than per control; the specific costs were $13,027 for E's and $14,076 for C's. This change from previous periods reflected the fact that controls, compared to experimentals, were spending more and more time within the YA's increasingly expensive institutions, beginning in the later 1960s. *Non-YA costs* (e.g., county expenses for arrests, detentions, and adjudication; prison and parole costs subsequent to YA discharge; "replacement costs" for stolen property and for medical services) were also lower among experimentals than controls: During the period prior to YA discharge they were $969 less per E than per C; after discharge—that is, while four years of post-YA risk time were being accumulated—they were $2,527 less per E than per C.

When these YA and non-YA figures for the later price period were combined, the overall savings to society was $4,545 per CTP youth. (Net savings—roughly $750 and $1,500—would also have been obtained for CTP youths relative to the 1963 and

1966–1967 price periods, respectively, if non-YA costs had been added to YA career costs.) This savings was largely produced by conflicted youths and it mainly reflected the fact that (1) more YA institution time was accumulated by C's than E's, (2) more prison and jail time was accumulated by unfavorably discharged C's than E's, and (3) more replacement costs were attributable to C's than E's, especially prior to YA discharge. In general, these E/C differences directly resulted from the larger number of arrests on the part of controls and from the greater tendency of these individuals to commit violent offenses. While already substantial, the savings of $4,545 would probably have been about twice as large by the early 1980s and three times larger as of the early 1990s. This change is mainly due to increased incarceration (operating) costs, not to mention those for capital outlay.

Matching of Worker and Youth
In answer to the question, Did matched and unmatched experimentals each outperform controls? the results were as follows: For the total group (all youths combined), matched and unmatched E's each had fewer moderate plus severe arrests and convictions than C's, and fewer severe or violent offenses as well. Similar results were obtained for conflicted and passive-conformist youths and, to a much lesser extent, matched power-oriented youths. (Controls could not be divided into matched and unmatched groups.) In answer to the question, Did matched E's outperform unmatched E's? the following was observed: For the total group there were no significant differences between matched and unmatched youths in rates of arrest and conviction, relative to any severity grouping (i.e., offense group). This was mainly because the positive findings—meaning, "matched outperformed unmatched"—for three of the five main youth types were canceled by negative findings for the remaining two. For both questions, all findings referred to parole only, since too few matched or unmatched youths were present among most "types" to allow for meaningful postdischarge breakdowns.

Overview for Females
Performance during and after Parole
During parole, *conflicted* Valley girls in CTP

tended to have more convictions than their controls, for moderate plus severe offenses combined. Except for this difference, Valley E's and C's performed about equally well during parole, postdischarge, and these two time periods combined; this applied to severe and violent offenses as well. During parole, conflicted San Francisco experimentals had more (i.e., a higher rate of) moderate plus severe arrests, but somewhat fewer *severe* arrests, than their rather small number of controls. Because of an even smaller sample size, reliable analyses could not be carried out with respect to the postdischarge period, and, therefore, the two time periods combined.

Thus, for conflicted girls in general—that is, in the Valley and San Francisco settings combined—the findings were inconclusive regarding *long-term* impact. This was despite evidence that controls performed somewhat better than experimentals during parole, that is, in the short run. Conflicted girls accounted for 66 percent of all Valley females and 83 percent of all San Francisco females. (See Chapters 8 and 9 regarding additional outcome measures for these and other youth groups.)

Passive-conformist Valley girls in CTP performed better than their controls during parole but worse during postdischarge, in terms of arrests and convictions. For both time periods combined, E's and C's performed about equally well. However, these findings were highly tenuous—in fact, the latter were of questionable validity—because of the very few youths involved. Since meaningful analyses were not possible with regard to the even smaller number of youths in San Francisco, nothing can be said about program effectiveness for passive-conformist girls in general. Beyond this, there is no clear evidence that these individuals performed better in CTP than in the traditional program within *any* setting. This lack of differential program impact (at any level of generality) was more the result of insufficient data than of inconclusive, negative, or contradictory findings. Passive-conformist girls accounted for 8 percent of all Valley females and 4 percent of all San Francisco females.

In contrast to the passive-conformists, *power-oriented* Valley experimentals performed worse than their controls during pa-role but much better after discharge. For both time periods combined, neither group clearly outperformed the other, despite some evidence of lower offense rates among experimentals. Since meaningful tests could not be performed with regard to the San Francisco samples (again because of the very few youths involved), nothing can be said about program impact for power-oriented girls in general. As to differential program effectiveness at a less general level, the relatively meager evidence at hand suggests that CTP and the traditional program had about equal long-term impact for the one group of youths that was analyzed: the Valley sample. Power-oriented girls accounted for 18 percent of all Valley females and 9 percent of all San Francisco females.

During parole, Valley experimental and control girls (the *total group*) performed about equally well in terms of arrests and convictions. However, during postdischarge, experimentals generally outperformed controls. In San Francisco, essentially the opposite was found relative to parole: Controls outperformed experimentals in terms of moderate plus severe offenses combined (but not severe offenses alone). Results for the postdischarge period were similar to those for parole; however, they were highly tenuous because of the very small sample involved.

Since mixed results were obtained within the Valley setting and since contrasting results were found across the Valley and San Francisco settings, little can be concluded about the relative effectiveness of CTP and the traditional programs for the female sample—that is, the total group—in general. Perhaps the only conclusion to draw is that youths from neither program clearly outperformed the other, either in the short run or the long run.

Findings on comparative effectiveness for both the Valley and San Francisco programs—E's versus C's—are summarized in Table 12–1, separately for males and females. These findings focus on rates of arrest per month at risk in the community, and they are further described in the remaining sections of this chapter. (As then indicated, results are very similar for rates of conviction.) Additional findings regarding effectiveness are summarized in Table 12–2, for E versus C Valley males. These, too, are described in the pages that follow.

TABLE 12-1

Summary of Findings on Comparative Effectiveness of Experimental and Control Programs, Based on Rate of Arrest per 1,000 Months at Risk

Sex, Setting, and Severity Group	Conflicted			Passive-Conformist			Power-Oriented			Total Group		
	YA	Post-YA	Total	YA	Post-YA	Total	YA	Post-YA	Total	YA	Post-YA	Total
MALES												
Valley — Moderate + Severe	E^{**}_{58}	E^{*}_{45}	E^{**}_{52}	E^{*b}_{63}	—	E^{*}_{50}	—	C^{*}_{37}	—	E^{**}_{50}	—	E^{*}_{38}
Severe	E^{*}_{50}	E_{36}	E^{**}_{46}	E_{56}	C_{50}	E_{33}	E_{38}	C^{*}_{54}	—	E^{**}_{46}	—	—
Violent	E^{*}_{54}	—	E^{*}_{55}	—	C_{71}	—	—	C_{38}	—	E^{*}_{46}	—	—
San Francisco — Moderate + Severe	—	—	—	a	a	a	a	a	a	—	—	—
Severe	E^{*}_{56}	—	—	a	a	a	a	a	a	E^{*}_{57}	E_{35}	E^{**}_{58}
Violent	E^{*}_{75}	—	—	a	a	a	a	a	a	E^{**}_{74}	—	E^{**}_{64}
Valley — Moderate + Severe	—	—	—	—	a	a	—	E^{**}_{100}	—	—	—	—
Severe	—	—	—	E^{*}_{b}	a	a	—	E^{*}_{100}	—	—	E_{50}	—
Violent	—	—	—	E^{*}_{b}	a	a	C_{100}	E_{100}	—	—	—	—
FEMALES												
San Francisco — Moderate + Severe	C^{*}_{64}	a	a	a	a	a	a	a	a	C^{*}_{50}	a	a
Severe	—	a	a	a	a	a	a	a	a	—	a	a
Violent	—	a	a	a	a	a	a	a	a	—	a	a

E or C refers to lower arrest rate by Experimentals or Controls (whichever is specified), at the following probability level (p-level): E or C = $p < .10 > .05$. E* or C* = $p < .05 > .01$. E** or C** = $p < .01$.

Percentage differences are shown, where appropriate, together with the E or C symbol. Thus, "C^{*}_{50}" would mean: Controls had a lower arrest rate than experimentals at or below the .01 p-level, and their arrest rate was 50 percent lower than that of E's. In computing each percentage difference, the higher arrest rate is used as base. All figures are derived from Tables 8-1 through 8-6, and 9-1 through 9-6.

"a" = E and/or C sample was too small for meaningful statistical test.

"b" = E and/or C sample was too small for computing meaningful percentage change.

"—" means: no statistically significant difference ($p < .05$, or $p < .01$) or statistical trend ($p < .10 > .05$) was found. This is despite possible existence of substantial E/C percentage difference in arrest rates.

TABLE 12–2

Supplementary Findings Regarding Impact and Utility of Experimental versus Control Programs, for Valley Males

Type/Index of Impact or Utility	Youth Type and Sample/Program[a]			Total Group[b]
	Conflicted	Passive-Conformist	Power-Oriented	
24-Months Recidivism	E	—	E	E
Favorable Discharge from Youth Authority[c]	E	E	(C)	E
School Adjustment	(E)	C	(E)	(E)
Paid Employment	(E)	C	(C)	—
Attitude Change from Pretest to Posttest[d]	—	—	E	E
Social Risk (community protection)[e]	E	E	C	E
Offending Compared to pre-YA Period[f]	E	(E)	(C)	(E)
Youth Authority Career Costs[g]	E	E	C	E

[a]The sample/program that is shown—either E or C—performed better or had greater utility than its counterpart, on the specified index of impact or utility. If either E or C is shown in *parentheses,* that sample/program was only slightly ahead of its counterpart relative to the given index. "—" means: no significant, substantial, or otherwise noteworthy overall difference in performance or utility between E and C (this would also include: positive findings from within the E total group and negative findings from within the C total group [or vice versa] counterbalance each other).

[b]Includes Conflicted + Passive-Conformist + Power-Oriented + Rare Types.

[c]Within 60 months from initial commitment to the YA.

[d]Based on the California Psychological Inventory.

[e]Based on all community risk time plus all lockup time over a nine-year period, beginning with each youth's initial commitment to the YA and extending beyond YA discharge. The E or C sample/program that is shown represented less of a risk than its counterpart, during that period as a whole.

[f]Combines results from one-year and three-year pre-YA time comparisons. The E or C sample/program that is shown had a larger overall reduction in offending than its counterpart, relative to pre-YA offending.

[g]Based on the most recent price period (1971–1972)—this being (1) the best available indicator of prices and institutional cost trends, and (2) more representative than other price periods of (a) CTP during its full-operations stage (organizationally and programmatically) and (b) the Youth Authority's (and corrections') policies and practices. If non-YA costs were included, results would be unchanged regardless of the price period used.

Main Results for Males
Conflicted Valley Boys
Parole Period

During parole, conflicted Valley (Sacramento plus Stockton) youths who were handled in the traditional Youth Authority program—that is, controls—had at least twice as many arrests and convictions as CTP youths, per month at risk in the community. This applied to all three offense groups: moderate plus severe offenses combined, severe offenses alone, and violent offenses in particular. ("Offense groups" and "severity groupings" are synonymous. As described in Chapter 8, violent offenses were a large subgroup within the severe offenses category.) These E/C differences could not be explained in terms of such factors as age, race, level of parole risk, and so on, since conflicted experimentals and controls were nearly identical to one another on each such factor or dimension. As to related measures, CTP youths outperformed their controls on 24-months *parole follow-up (recidivism rate, or "24-months recidivism")* and on *rate of favorable discharge* from the Youth Authority within five years from their first release to parole. Thus, during parole, conflicted experimentals performed considerably better than controls on three traditional measures of effectiveness, measures that—collectively—focused on illegal behavior *and* on staff decisions relating to that behavior.

Conflicted experimentals performed somewhat better than controls in relation to *school adjustment*. E's and C's performed about equally well in the area of *paid employment* during their first year on parole; however, E's were somewhat ahead of C's during their second year. Regarding *attitude change* (personal and social adjustment) as measured by the California Psychological Inventory (CPI), experimentals and controls showed equal amounts of positive change from pretest to posttest. (Specifically, experimentals classified as assertive-deniers showed more positive change than their controls; however, this finding was counterbalanced by the fact that those described as anxious-confused showed less positive change than controls.) Thus, on three supplementary measures of impact, the findings generally favored experimentals; however, they were neither clear-cut nor strong.

Postdischarge Period
On four-years postdischarge (i.e., post–Youth Authority) follow-up, conflicted Valley experimentals were arrested about 40 percent less often than conflicted controls, on moderate plus severe, severe, and violent offenses alike. Except for violent offenses, essentially the same results were found with respect to rates of conviction. Thus, after being discharged from the Youth Authority, conflicted experimentals continued to outperform their controls. This finding related to *youth behavior* as the term is ordinarily understood, not to revocation or rate of discharge (policy influenced—albeit behavior-based—measures). The finding could not be explained as a product of differential decision-making across the CTP and traditional programs, or of discretionary decisions by staff, since the youths were no longer under Youth Authority jurisdiction. Nor could it be attributed to E/C differences in background characteristics.

Parole Plus Postdischarge Combined
Conflicted experimentals clearly outperformed conflicted controls on arrests as well as convictions, when the parole and postdischarge periods were combined. This applied to all severity groupings—moderate plus severe, severe, and violent offenses. These performance differences could not be accounted for by chance. Here, as with passive-conformist and power-oriented youths, the average follow-up was about seven years in the community, counting from each youth's first release to parole and continuing for 48 months after YA discharge. The seven years included no lockup time.

Supplementary Findings
1. *Social risk.* For a 13-month period that started on the day of each youth's commitment to the YA, the traditional program provided more protection to the community than did CTP. Basically, this was because most conflicted controls were locked up (therefore incapacitated) during the first nine months of that period, whereas CTP youths were not. About four months after the controls were first paroled, CTP "caught up" with the traditional program in terms of protecting the community; that is, C's and E's had by then accumulated, or produced, an equal number of offenses per youth. This change occurred because controls—once released to the community—were soon committing offenses at a substantially higher rate than E's, and because they then continued to do so. Thus, after about four years from initial commitment (counting all lockup and non-lockup time), every 100 C's had produced 160 more moderate plus severe offenses than every 100 E's, on the average; after nine years the number had grown to 225. This happened despite the fact that conflicted C's had accumulated more lockup time than conflicted E's during both periods, and therefore had less risk time in each. In sum, even when lockup time was added to the risk time already reviewed (Chapter 8), CTP provided considerably more protection to the community than the traditional program, except in the short run. This finding would have been the same, though reduced in scale, if convictions rather than arrests had been focused on. In addition, it probably would have remained much the same even if conflicted controls

had initially been locked up twice as long as they were.

2. *Change from pre-YA period.* Supplementary analyses also focused on such questions as the following: Did the traditional program and CTP each produce a rate of offending that was lower than the rate observed during the time period that preceded commitment, that is, during the pre-YA years? Did the traditional program reduce offending more than CTP, from precommitment to postcommitment? *Findings:* During the parole plus postdischarge follow-up, both the traditional program and CTP clearly checked, and reversed, the precipitous rise in moderate plus severe arrests that was observed during the year that preceded commitment. For conflicted controls and experimentals, the reductions were 57 percent and 80 percent, respectively. For severe offenses, they were 19 percent for C's and 53 percent for E's. However, with violent offenses, the parole plus postdischarge arrest rate for controls was higher than that observed during pre-YA years. In contrast, CTP produced a 62 percent reduction, also using the precommitment year as the basis of comparison. Additional analyses, in which an approximately three-year postcommitment (parole) period was compared with a three-year precommitment period, generally supported these findings—mainly for moderate plus severe offenses combined, and more so for E's than C's. These findings applied to younger (under 16) and older (16 and up) individuals alike, not just to both age groups combined.

3. *Costs.* Since the CTP experiment lasted 12 years—years marked by rising prices nationwide—separate analyses were made for three "price periods": 1963 (early period), 1966–1967 (middle period), and 1971–1972 (later period). During each period, YA career costs were lower for conflicted experimentals than for conflicted controls. The E/C cost difference was $99 per career for the early period and $1,894 for the later period. This was equal to 8 cents a day, and $1.50 a day, respectively. During the later period, total career costs (i.e., absolute dollar amounts, not the E/C cost difference) were $12,377 for experimentals and $14,271 for controls.

4. *Matching of worker and youth.* During parole, matched conflicted experimentals had about half as many moderate plus severe offenses as controls: 36 versus 80 arrests and 23 versus 50 convictions per 1,000 months at risk, respectively. They had fewer severe arrests and tended to have fewer violent arrests (i.e., arrests for violent offenses), as well. Similarly, *un*matched conflicted experimentals had fewer moderate plus severe offenses than controls: 33 versus 80 arrests and 21 versus 50 convictions per 1,000 months at risk. They also had fewer severe arrests and convictions, and tended to have fewer violent arrests. Thus, both the matched and unmatched E's outperformed controls, during parole. Focusing on experimentals only, matched and unmatched youths performed about equally well—that is, compared to each other. However, when these conflicted E's were subdivided into their two components, sizable differences emerged: (1) Matched *assertive-deniers* performed much better than their unmatched counterparts on arrests and convictions alike, with respect to all severity groupings (moderate plus severe, severe, and violent). (2) Unmatched *anxious-confused* youths outperformed their matched counterparts relative to all severity groupings.

Conflicted San Francisco Boys
Parole Period

During parole, conflicted San Francisco experimentals (CTP youths) were arrested 24 percent less often and convicted 32 percent less often than their controls, on moderate plus severe offenses combined. However, these differences—while substantial in terms of percentage reductions—were not statistically significant (reliable), possibly because of the small number of controls. For severe and violent offenses, Conflicted E's performed 56 percent to 80 percent better than C's on arrests and convictions; these differences were statistically reliable. (Comparisons between conflicted experimentals and conflicted Guided Group Interaction (GGI) youths yielded results that were fairly similar to those mentioned immediately above, for each severity grouping.)

Other Time Periods
On four-year postdischarge, no substantial or reliable differences were found between conflicted San Francisco experimentals and controls, for any severity grouping. However, the postdischarge analysis operated under heavy constraints due to the very small number of controls. Though identical constraints existed relative to the *parole plus postdischarge* (six-year) follow-up, the results that were obtained for this combined time period were similar to those for Valley males: Experimentals had, in general, substantially fewer arrests and convictions than controls, for severe and violent offenses. (For Valley but not San Francisco males, the E/C differences were also reliable.)

Passive-Conformist Valley Boys
Parole Period
During parole, passive-conformist Valley controls had at least twice as many arrests and convictions as CTP youths, per month at risk, on moderate plus severe and severe offenses alike. For violent offenses the differences continued to favor experimentals, but were not as large. On 24-months recidivism, E's and C's performed about equally well. However, on rate of discharge from the Youth Authority, E's performed better than C's.

Regarding school and paid employment, passive-conformist controls performed somewhat better than those in CTP. (This finding suggests that better performance in these areas is not necessarily associated with, or an essential precondition of, less illegal behavior.) As to attitude change (CPI), E's and C's showed approximately equal amounts of improvement from pretest to posttest. In general, then, the results on supplementary measures of impact during parole tended to favor controls.

Postdischarge Period
On four-year postdischarge follow-up, passive-conformist Valley experimentals performed about the same as controls on moderate plus severe arrests combined. However, they had more arrests for severe and violent offenses, and more *convictions* in the case of all severity groupings. On close inspection, then, passive-conformist controls had an edge over experimentals subsequent to YA discharge, despite their essentially equal performance on moderate plus severe arrests and the generally mixed nature of the results.

Parole Plus Postdischarge Combined
Despite the postdischarge findings, experimentals outperformed controls when parole and postdischarge were combined. This reflected their far better performance than controls during parole; that is, their performance during this time period outweighed their performance after parole. More specifically, on parole plus postdischarge combined, passive-conformist experimentals outperformed their controls on moderate plus severe arrests and convictions, and they tended to do so for severe offenses as well. However, there were no differences on violent offenses.

For the San Francisco sample, meaningful comparisons could not be made between passive-conformist experimentals and controls, due to the very small number of controls.

Supplementary Findings
1. *Social risk.* For a 10-month period that started with each youth's initial commitment, the traditional program provided more protection to the community than did CTP. However, after about four years of follow-up (counting all lockup and non-lockup time), every 100 C's had produced 175 more moderate plus severe offenses than every 100 E's, on the average; after nine years the number had grown to 222. This occurred despite the fact that passive-conformist controls had accumulated more lockup time than experimentals during both follow-ups, and therefore had less risk time in each. Thus, even when lockup time was added to the risk time already reviewed, CTP provided considerably more protection to the community than the traditional program, except in the short run. This finding would probably have remained much the same even if controls had initially been locked up twice as long as they were. In addition, it would have been fairly similar, though reduced in scale, if convictions had been examined rather than arrests. However, since passive-conformist controls had substantially fewer *postdischarge* convictions than experimentals, C's eventually would have had fewer total convictions than E's if their postdischarge rate, and that of E's, had been maintained beyond the nine-year point.
2. *Change from pre-YA period.* Compared

to the arrest rate during the year that preceded commitment, the arrest rate of passive-conformist C's and E's showed a sharp drop during the parole plus post-discharge years: For moderate plus severe offenses combined, the reduction was 69 percent among controls and 84 percent among experimentals. For severe offenses the reduction was 47 percent among C's and 43 percent among E's, and for violent offenses it was 30 percent and 67 percent, respectively. Additional analyses (three-year postcommitment versus three-year precommitment) supported these findings for moderate plus severe offenses combined, particularly among experimentals. However, they indicated that although both the traditional program and CTP substantially reduced the rate of *severe* and *violent* offending observed for the "precipitous" precommitment year, neither program reduced the *longer-term* tendency of passive-conformists to commit such offenses.

3. *Costs.* Among passive-conformists, experimental and control career costs were virtually identical during the early period (1963): The cost-difference was eight dollars per career, or one cent a day. For the later period (1971–1972), the difference was $2,705 ($2.04 a day), in favor of E's. Thus, compared to controls, passive-conformist experimentals eventually became the least expensive youth group with respect to *YA career costs.* During the later price period, total career costs were $12,107 for E's and $14,812 for C's.

4. *Matching of worker and youth.* During parole, matched passive-conformist (P-C) experimentals had fewer arrests than controls, relative to all severity groupings; they had fewer moderate plus severe, and severe, convictions as well. *Un*matched P-C experimentals had fewer moderate plus severe arrests and convictions and tended to have fewer severe convictions than controls; however, no E/C differences or statistical tendencies were found regarding violent offenses. Focusing on experimentals only, matched passive-conformists had fewer moderate plus severe—and severe—arrests than their unmatched counterparts. They tended to have fewer moderate plus severe convictions, and fewer violent arrests, as well.

Power-Oriented Valley Boys
Parole Period
During parole, power-oriented Valley experimentals performed slightly but not significantly better than controls on moderate plus severe arrests combined. However, neither group outperformed the other in terms of convictions. Power-oriented E's performed significantly better than C's on severe arrests and substantially (29 percent) but not significantly better on convictions; these results held up for violent offenses, but were not as strong. With other measures of effectiveness, the findings were mixed: On 24-months recidivism, E's outperformed C's; however, on rate of discharge, C's performed somewhat better than E's.

Thus, if one focuses on illegal behavior alone (i.e., rates of arrest and conviction), power-oriented experimentals performed somewhat but not significantly better than controls—except for severe arrests. However, if one focuses on measures that reflect the interaction between illegal behavior and staff decisions in response to that behavior (i.e., on rates of recidivism and discharge), conflicting results are obtained. (The findings on staff decisions suggest that "differential," "policy-related," or "discretionary" decision-making—insofar as they exist in any given case and happen to favor one group of youths over another—may sometimes favor controls over experimentals.)

With respect to school, power-oriented youths performed slightly worse in the traditional program than in CTP. On paid employment, the opposite was observed; here, controls were slightly ahead of experimentals. As to attitude change, experimentals showed more gain than controls from pretest to posttest. Thus, on supplementary measures of impact the findings were again mixed, with respect to parole.

Postdischarge Period
On four-year postdischarge follow-up, power-oriented Valley controls were arrested and convicted substantially less often than power-oriented experimentals. This applied to all severity groupings: moderate plus severe, severe, and violent.

Parole Plus Postdischarge Combined
When both time periods were combined,

power-oriented controls performed somewhat but not significantly better than experimentals on moderate plus severe arrests and convictions, and on severe arrests (but not convictions) as well. No substantial E/C differences were found relative to violent offenses.

For the San Francisco sample, meaningful comparisons could not be made between power-oriented E's and C's, due to the very small number of controls.

Supplementary Findings

1. *Social risk.* During the first two years of the Youth Authority (predischarge) period, the traditional program provided more protection to the community than did CTP. For the remainder of that period, and even somewhat beyond discharge, the situation was reversed: Due to a slightly higher arrest rate among controls than among experimentals, the former's number of accumulated arrests per youth caught up with, then slightly surpassed, that of E's. About five years from initial commitment (again counting all lockup and non-lockup time), further change occurred: Power-oriented C's and E's again had an equal number of arrests; and, beginning about one year later, the traditional program clearly began to provide more protection than CTP. After about 9 years from initial commitment, every 100 C's had accumulated 105 fewer arrests than every 100 E's, on the average. Thus, in the long run—as in the short run—the traditional program provided more protection to the community with regard to these youths. This was aside from the fact that controls had spent 25 percent more time in lockup than experimentals, during the nine-year follow-up.

2. *Change from pre-YA period.* Compared to the arrest rate during the year that preceded commitment, the arrest rate of power-oriented C's and E's showed a marked decline during the parole plus postdischarge years: For moderate plus severe offenses combined, the reduction was 72 percent among controls and 63 percent among experimentals. For severe offenses there was a 37 percent reduction for C's and a 65 percent rise among E's. With regard to violent offenses, both the traditional program and CTP produced a reduction in arrests. Additional analyses indicated that both programs reduced the *longer-term*, not just the shorter-term, tendency of power-oriented C's and E's to commit moderate plus severe offenses combined. However, the traditional program did not reduce the longer-term tendency of controls to commit *severe* and *violent* offenses in particular. Within CTP, violent offenses were reduced on a shorter- as well as longer-term basis, when the postcommitment and precommitment periods were compared; however, for severe offenses the findings were mixed.

3. *Costs.* For all three price periods, YA career costs were considerably higher among power-oriented experimentals than among their controls: Cost differences were $3,016 and $3,709 ($2.14 and $2.63 a day) for the early and later periods, respectively. Compared to their controls (and to remaining E's as well), power-oriented experimentals were by far the most expensive youth group. During the 1971–1972 price period, total career costs were $16,889 for E's and $13,180 for C's. (Compared to other C's, these controls were somewhat less expensive.)

4. *Matching of worker and youth.* During parole, matched power-oriented experimentals tended to have fewer moderate plus severe—and severe—arrests than controls; they had fewer violent arrests as well. *Un*matched power-oriented experimentals tended to have fewer severe arrests than controls; however, no E/C differences were found in connection with moderate plus severe—and violent—offenses. Focusing on experimentals only, matched (M) power-oriented youths had somewhat but not significantly fewer moderate plus severe arrests than their unmatched (UM) counterparts; however, they had significantly fewer violent arrests. No M/UM differences were found with respect to convictions. When power-oriented E's were subdivided into their two components, matched *group conformists* were found to be performing somewhat worse than their unmatched counterparts; however, matched *manipulators* (Mp's) were performing significantly better than unmatched Mp's.

Total Group of Valley Boys (All Youths Combined)

Parole Period

During parole, Valley boys in the traditional program had twice as many arrests and convictions as those in CTP, per month at risk. This represented a 50 percent reduction in illegal behavior for experimentals as compared to controls. These results, which involved moderate plus severe offenses combined, were essentially the same for severe as well as violent offenses. All such findings were statistically reliable, and none could be accounted for by differences in the background characteristics of E's and C's. Similar results were obtained with most other measures: On 24-months recidivism, substantially fewer experimentals than controls were revoked. On five-years follow-up from first release to parole, more E's than C's received a favorable discharge from the Youth Authority and fewer received an unfavorable discharge. Experimentals performed slightly better than controls in connection with school; however, no consistent or substantial differences were found relative to paid employment. Finally, E's showed more positive attitude change than C's from pretest to posttest.

Postdischarge Period

On postdischarge follow-up, although Valley experimentals were arrested and convicted less often than controls for moderate plus severe offenses combined, there were no really sharp or substantial E/C differences for this and other severity groupings. Basically, this was because the results that favored conflicted experimentals were counterbalanced and canceled by those which favored power-oriented and, to a lesser extent, passive-conformist controls. (The results were mathematically "canceled" relative to the total group analysis only; they were entirely unaffected in connection with the individual youth groups, e.g., conflicted E's versus conflicted C's.)

Parole Plus Postdischarge Combined

Experimentals performed substantially (about 35 percent) better than controls on arrests and convictions, for moderate plus severe offenses combined. (Findings were generally similar, but not really striking, with regard to severe and violent offenses.) Thus, when the two time periods were analyzed together, the postdischarge performance of power-oriented controls did not carry enough weight to counterbalance and mathematically cancel the post-YA *and* parole performance of conflicted experimentals, with regard to all youths *combined* (i.e., the total group).

Supplementary Findings

1. *Social risk.* For a 13-month period that started with each youth's initial commitment, the traditional program provided more protection to the community than did CTP. However, after about three and a half years of follow-up (counting all lockup and non-lockup time), every 100 Controls had produced approximately 100 more moderate plus severe offenses than every 100 Experimentals, on the average; after nine years the number had grown to 127. This occurred despite the fact that controls had accumulated more lockup time than experimentals during both follow-ups, and therefore had less risk time in each. Thus, even when lockup time was added to the risk time already reviewed (Chapter 8), CTP provided considerably more protection to the community than did the traditional program, except in the short run. (In effect, the numerous arrests that were chalked-up by controls, while they were at risk in the community, were not offset by their arrest-free periods in lockup.) This finding would have been the same, though reduced in scale, if convictions rather than arrests had been focused on. Also, it probably would have remained much the same even if controls had initially been locked up twice as long as they were.

2. *Change from pre-YA period.* During the parole plus postdischarge follow-up, both the traditional program and CTP clearly checked, and reversed, the precipitous rise in moderate plus severe arrests that was observed during the year that preceded commitment. For controls and experimentals, the reductions were 66 percent and 78 percent, respectively. For severe offenses, they were 31 percent for C's and 37 percent for E's, and for violent offenses, they were 17 percent and 56 percent. Additional analyses (three-year postcommitment versus three-year precommitment) indicated that both the traditional program and—especially—CTP reduced the longer-term, not just

the shorter-term, tendency of C's and E's to commit moderate plus severe offenses combined. However, they also indicated that, although both programs reduced the rate of *severe* and *violent* offending that was observed for the somewhat precipitous precommitment year, they did not reduce the longer-term tendencies in question. Nevertheless, CTP did at least check these tendencies; that is, it held them fairly constant. These findings applied to younger (under 16) and older (16 and up) individuals alike, not just to both age groups combined.

3. *Costs.* For the total group, *YA career costs* were lower among controls than among experimentals during the early and middle price periods: E/C differences were $1,008 and $830 for the early and middle periods, respectively. However, by the early 1970s—the later period—career costs were $1,049 lower among E's than C's; the specific costs were $13,027 for E's and $14,076 for C's. *Non-YA costs* (e.g., county expenses for arrests and adjudication; prison costs) were $3,496 less per E than per C, for the YA and post-YA periods combined. Thus, when YA career costs and non-YA costs were combined, the overall savings to society was $4,545 per CTP youth, for the later price period. Net savings ($750 to $1,500) would also have been obtained for CTP youths with respect to the 1963 and 1966–1967 price periods, if non-YA costs had been added to YA career costs. Most savings directly resulted from the larger number of arrests on the part of controls and from the greater tendency of these individuals to commit violent offenses—and to be locked up as a result. The estimated savings to society of $4,545 would probably have been about twice as large by the early 1980s and three times larger by the early 1990s. These changes would have mainly reflected the major increases that occurred in incarceration costs (operating expenses such as salaries and maintenance of physical plant), not to mention the increased California Youth Authority or even California Department of Corrections (adult authority) capital outlay costs of building new facilities.

4. *Matching of worker and youth.* During parole, matched experimentals had fewer moderate plus severe offenses than controls: 35 versus 76 arrests and 24 versus 48 convictions per 1,000 months at risk, respectively. They also had fewer severe and violent arrests and tended to have fewer severe convictions. *Un*matched E's had fewer moderate plus severe—and severe—arrests and convictions than controls; they tended to have fewer violent convictions as well. Thus, both the matched and unmatched E's outperformed controls, during parole. Focusing on experimentals only, there were no statistically significant differences between matched and unmatched youths in rates of arrest and conviction, in connection with any severity grouping. This was mainly because the "positive" findings (meaning, "matched outperformed unmatched") for matched assertive-deniers, passive-conformists, and manipulators were counterbalanced and canceled by the "negative" findings for matched anxious-confused and group conformist youths. (As before, the "canceling" in question had meaning only in the total group analysis.)

Total Group of San Francisco Boys (All Youths Combined)
Parole Period
During parole, results for all San Francisco boys combined were very similar to those obtained for conflicted youths alone, mainly because the latter comprised most of the sample: Experimentals performed somewhat (23% to 30%) but not significantly better than controls on moderate plus severe arrests and convictions. However, for severe and violent offenses, they had 54 percent to 74 percent fewer arrests and convictions than controls; these differences were reliable. (Comparisons between experimentals and GGI yielded results that were generally similar to, though not as sharp as, those relating to controls.)

Postdischarge Period
On postdischarge follow-up, San Francisco CTP youths were arrested and convicted substantially (over 30%) less often than controls, for moderate plus severe offenses combined; however, these differences were not statistically reliable. For severe but not violent offenses,

one statistical trend ($p < .10$) and one reliable difference ($p < .05$) *was* found; these favored experimentals. (Comparisons between CTP and GGI usually yielded stronger results across the severity groupings.)

Parole Plus Postdischarge Combined
For the two time periods combined, San Francisco experimentals performed substantially (30% to 40%) better than controls relative to moderate plus severe offenses; however, this difference was not statistically reliable. For severe and violent offenses the E/C differences, which still favored experimentals, were reliable. Nevertheless, given the very small number of controls, these findings should be regarded as tentative. (Results were fairly similar when CTP was compared with GGI. However, these findings were statistically stronger than the former, since the GGI sample was somewhat larger than that of controls.)

Main Results for Females
Conflicted Valley Girls
Parole Period
During parole, conflicted Valley experimental girls tended to have more (i.e., a higher rate of) convictions than their controls for moderate plus severe offenses combined. However, there were no significant E/C differences in *arrests* for any severity grouping (moderate plus severe, severe, or violent). Nor were there any significant differences on 24-months recidivism and five-year rate of discharge.

Other Time Periods
For the four-year postdischarge period, no significant differences were found between Valley E's and C's with regard to any severity grouping. Similar results were obtained for the parole plus postdischarge periods combined (average of six and a half years). Thus, except for moderate plus severe convictions during parole, conflicted experimental girls performed essentially the same as their controls regardless of the time period and severity grouping that was analyzed.

Conflicted San Francisco Girls
Parole Period
During parole, conflicted San Francisco control girls had significantly fewer moderate plus severe arrests than conflicted experimentals. Though E's had fewer *severe* arrests and convictions than controls, these differences were not statistically significant. No substantial E/C differences were found for violent offenses, in particular. Given the very small number of controls, these findings should be regarded as tentative. Meaningful tests could not be performed relative to the postdischarge time period and, thus, for the parole plus postdischarge periods combined.

Passive-Conformist Valley Girls
Parole Period
During parole, passive-conformist Valley experimental girls had far fewer arrests and convictions than their controls, for all severity groupings. However, these results were highly tentative because of the very small number of controls. Passive-conformist experimentals performed worse than controls on 24-months recidivism and on five-year rate of discharge; these E/C differences were substantial but not statistically reliable.

Other Time Periods
During the four-year postdischarge period, passive-conformist experimentals performed much worse than controls relative to all severity groupings. This contrasted with their performance during parole. The present results were highly tenuous, in fact of questionable validity, because of the very small sample involved. On balance, for the parole plus postdischarge periods *combined*, E's and C's performed about equally well; that is, neither group outperformed the other. This was probably because their respective results for postdischarge were counterbalanced by those for parole. Thus, in general, no clear findings emerged for passive-conformist girls, partly because of the small sample involved.

Meaningful analyses could not be made relative to the very few passive-conformist girls in the San Francisco programs.

Power-Oriented Valley Girls
Parole Period
During parole, power-oriented Valley control girls had substantially fewer arrests and convictions than experimentals, for all offense groups. On other indices the results were mixed: E's performed better than C's on 24-months recidivism, but the opposite was true on five-year rate of discharge (as with power-oriented males). Since rates of arrest and conviction were the primary measures of effectiveness, it should

be concluded that—mixed findings on other indices notwithstanding—power-oriented controls outperformed their counterparts in CTP during parole.

Other Time Periods

During the four-year postdischarge period, experimentals performed much better than controls, particularly on moderate plus severe—and severe—arrests and convictions. These results, which were statistically reliable, contrasted with those for the parole period. Given these opposing results and given the rather small sample involved, it is understandable that no statistically significant differences were found between power-oriented E's and C's with respect to the parole plus postdischarge periods *combined*. This was despite the substantially lower arrest and/or conviction rates that were found among experimentals than among controls, for moderate plus severe, and severe, offenses.

No meaningful analyses could be carried out relative to the very few power-oriented girls in the San Francisco programs.

Total Group of Valley Girls (All Youths Combined)
Parole Period

During parole, no significant differences were found between Valley experimental and control girls on arrests and convictions, for any severity grouping. Although E's performed somewhat better than C's on 24-months recidivism, no differences were found on rate of discharge from the Youth Authority.

Other Time Periods

During the postdischarge period, experimentals had substantially fewer moderate plus severe arrests and convictions than controls. They also tended to have fewer severe offenses—though not violent offenses in partic-

ular. However, the E/C difference on severe offenses was quite small in absolute terms, and the rate of offending was very low for E's and C's alike. During the parole plus postdischarge periods combined, experimentals were arrested and convicted less often than controls for moderate plus severe offenses combined. However, these differences, like those found for severe offenses, were not statistically reliable.

Total Group of San Francisco Girls (All Youths Combined)

Results for all San Francisco girls combined were almost identical to those mentioned for conflicted SF girls, since the latter comprised over 80 percent of all females studied in that city.

We have now completed the description of CTP Phases 1 and 2, and the presentation of its main results. Next, we will briefly describe Phase 3—a substantially different approach to groups of youth who had not responded well during 1961–1969.

Note

1. All in all, findings for the total group, for conflicted individuals, and for passive-conformists contradict the Murray and Cox (1979) view that institutionalization generates more positive pre-to-post change in youth behavior than does community-based intervention, supposedly because the latter exerts less control than the former. More specifically, in those authors' view, the presumed (though here unobserved) larger impact of institutionalization reflects such facilities' hypothesized greater ability to suppress—to therein deter—future illegal behavior. Thus, the concept of "greater suppression effect" on the part of institutions.

13 THE PHASE 3 EXPERIMENT: ADDING AN INSTITUTIONAL COMPONENT

By 1966–1967 the Community Treatment Project had shown definite promise with some groups of youth. Yet, there was much room for improvement with these and *other* groups. For example, by mid-1967 it was clear that about one-third of the latter groups had been rearrested for delinquent behavior within a few weeks or months after having entered CTP. Another portion had remained singularly untouched by the program, and after several months on parole they too had become involved in delinquent activities. Almost identical patterns were observed among similar non-CTP youths who had spent several months in an institution prior to being paroled, that is, among youths who otherwise resembled those on CTP but who had been assigned to the traditional YA program. Nearly half of these difficult-to-reach individuals seemed headed for long-term crime careers and lengthy periods of imprisonment regardless of what CTP and the traditional Youth Authority program tried to offer, and despite their respective methods of control.

Could anything be done with this rather sizable group of youths, especially but not exclusively the earlier-mentioned one-third? Research and operations staff believed the answer was *probably yes,* at least for some portion of that group. The central issue seemed to be: *What* could be done?

The staff's main answer was implied in the following question: Would many of these youths become less delinquently oriented if they began their Youth Authority career *not* within the community itself, but in a special kind of institutional setting (described below)? The implied answer, or hypothesis, was based on numerous clues that had accumulated during the early and middle 1960s.[1] This answer formed the basis of CTP Phase 3.

In 1968 a specific research plan was designed, by the author, to scientifically test this hypothesis (Palmer, 1969a). Guidelines for identifying the earlier-mentioned youths at intake were also established (see Groups A through E, below). The research proposal called for four years of program operation plus one year of analysis and wrap-up. It was accepted by NIMH, and project operations began in August 1969.

The idea of using an institutional setting, on a fairly long-term basis if necessary, involved a definite and, at the time, novel departure from the "straight community approach" that had been increasingly utilized during 1961–1969 at the local and national levels[2] (Empey, 1967, 1978; Harlow, Weber, and Wilkins, 1971; Lillyquist, 1980; National Advisory Commission, 1973a, 1973b; President's Commission, 1967a, 1967b, 1967c). Nevertheless, this departure was viewed by research and operations staff as a justifiable and plausible alternative for the sizable group of youths who continued to engage in illegal activities and were largely uninfluenced by the intensive community as well as standard institutional programs.

Sample, Procedures, and Underlying Concepts
The Sample
The Phase 3 experiment obtained its basic sample (Category A youths) from the greater Sacramento area alone. This sample consisted entirely of males who were 13 to 21 years old at intake, and were either juvenile or adult court

first commitments. In short, it was a somewhat older and—except for sex—a broader sample than that which was studied during Phases 1 and 2.[3] (For practical reasons, a separate institutional setting—a secure residential unit—could not be established for the relatively few Sacramento area females who were being committed to the Youth Authority by 1969.) All remaining eligibility criteria were the same as in Phases 1 and 2, except for the following.

Under certain conditions it was possible to include other Sacramento youngsters (*Category B youths*) who, during 1961–1969, would have been excluded on the basis of (1) commitment offenses relating to armed robbery, assault with a deadly weapon, forcible rape, and so on, or (2) offense histories of a particularly disturbed or aggressive-appearing nature. These individuals were analyzed both separate from and together with the basic sample.

A total of 161 youths (134 Category A, 27 Category B) participated in Phase 3.[4] This represented 65 percent of all Category A *referrals* (i.e., 65 percent were declared eligible by the YA Board) and 64 percent of all appropriate Category B referrals who were not excluded due to lack of dormitory space. (See endnote 31.) Combining Categories A and B, and omitting the dormitory-space exclusions, the eligibility figure for all referrals was 61 percent. This was slightly lower than in Phases 1 and 2 (70 percent for Valley boys), probably because of the more severe committing offenses and longer offense histories on the part of Phase 3 youths. (Category A and B youths had almost identical offense histories, but different *commitment* offenses.) Further details regarding the sample are presented in sections dealing with research design and main results.

Procedures and Underlying Concepts

To test the Phase 3 hypothesis, the following question was asked by operations staff regarding each newly committed youth who met the preceding eligibility criteria: Within *which* setting would it probably be best to initiate the treatment and control of this individual? The choice was between the following.

1. Initial assignment to a CTP-staffed-and-operated *institutional* program, later followed by release to the regular CTP community program (staffed and operated as in Phase 2).

2. Direct release to the CTP *community* program (in accordance with the Phase 2 pattern, as above).

The project staffing team approached this question by making a careful study of the individual's interests, limitations, immediate pressures, and underlying motivations. Here, the main object was to identify the most appropriate yet practical goals and techniques for working with the youth.

This diagnostic evaluation also allowed staff to determine whether the youth matched up with any of the descriptions shown below. These descriptions or guidelines were designed to focus staff's attention on the question of *where* the individual's treatment and control might best be started. They were a summary account of five relatively distinct categories of youth—specifically, youths who were unusually difficult or seemingly impossible to "reach" during 1961–1969.

These categories or groups did not simply correspond to the five main I-level subtypes discussed in preceding chapters. Instead, the groups (except Group D, below) *cut across* a number of subtypes, including certain "rare" ones. Specifically, they usually corresponded to the following youth types and/or maturity levels: Group A—conflicted; lower maturity. Group B—power-oriented. Group C—conflicted. Group D—delinquent identifier. Group E—conflicted.[5] These, at least, were how the groups were predicted to break down, at the start of Phase 3.

Thus, it was expected that Groups A through E, collectively, would largely consist of conflicted youths. This was mainly due to the sizable percentage (53 percent) of these individuals within the Phase 1 and 2 sample, and despite the more positive performance of conflicted experimentals than conflicted controls during those phases. (Any one group of youths may perform better than another, even though a sizable portion of both groups may not perform well.)

The five groups may be summarized as follows (a more complete account appears in Appendix 28).

Group A. Youths who are quite disturbed and openly disorganized relative to overall, everyday functioning, and who sometimes become highly agitated or even delusional under the pressures of everyday life.

Group B. Youths who have an intensive drive to prevent other persons from exerting controls upon them, or from substantially influencing the direction of their life. They are prepared to use virtually "everything" in their power—runaway, physical resistance, and so on—to avoid ongoing confrontation by concerned authority figures, and to avoid involvement in nonexploitive relationships with adults in general.

Group C. Youths who are unable to recognize or who vigorously try to deny the existence and influence of the unusually destructive relationships and loyalty binds in which they are involved, at home and in the community. If these youngsters were to be released directly to the community, these conditions would undermine the youth/parole agent relationship at a time when this would still be in its formative stage. The same conditions would very probably lead them into delinquent acting-out of a frequency or magnitude sufficient to result in their early revocation and removal from the community setting.

Group D. Youths who, though nonneurotic and of a relatively high level of maturity, need to personally experience the fact that their freedom will be withdrawn if they persist in their delinquent patterns. These individuals regard themselves as very skilled at "getting away with" illegal activities; and in many respects this self-assessment is accurate.

Group E. Youths who—operating from underlying motives of a self-defeating nature—have become increasingly committed to the use of drugs and/or a drug-using subculture. These youths have reached the point of feeling little interest in coping with long-range social expectations or pressures, or in inter-

acting with others on a nonexploitive basis (Palmer, 1969a, paraphrased).

Individuals who appeared to fit any of these descriptions were called *Status 1* youths. According to the basic hypothesis of Phase 3, these youths would need an initial period of institutionalization prior to being ready for parole. Individuals who did not match these descriptions were called *Status 2;* these youths were seen as *not* needing an initial period of institutionalization.

Once the staffing team completed its study of the individual and finalized his status, a random drawing was made to determine whether his community-based initial placement would be in "Dorm 3" *or* within CTP's community-based component.[6] Dorm 3 was the CTP-operated institutional ("residential") component, or living unit, located at the Northern Reception Center and Clinic. It was CTP's, and the Youth Authority's, first such unit. (Because of the YA Board's requirement, all Category B youths had to begin their program in Dorm 3, despite the random drawing.)[7]

By means of the drawing, four separate youth groups were formed (as in Phases 1 and 2, the YA Board gave the final, legal approval regarding each youth's eligibility for the *program;* it made this decision immediately prior to being told the outcome of the random drawing):

RR. Status 1 youths who were *appropriately placed:* These individuals were diagnosed as needing to begin their program within a ṟesidential, that is, institutional, setting. Their program *did* begin in a ṟesidential setting, namely, Dorm 3.

RC. Status 1 youths who were *inappropriately placed:* Diagnosed as needing to begin in a ṟesidential setting; however, their program was initiated within a ꜿommunity setting, as in 1961–1969.

CR. Status 2 youths who were *inappropriately placed:* Diagnosed as being able to begin their program in a ꜿommunity setting; however, their program was initiated within a ṟesidential setting (Dorm 3).

CC. Status 2 youths who were *appropriately placed:* Diagnosed as being able to begin their program in a ꜿommunity setting.

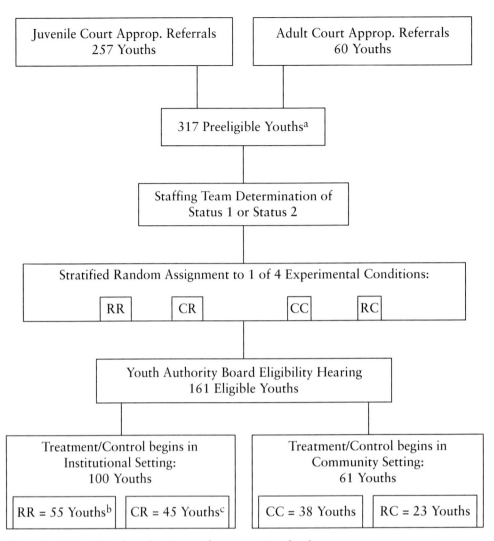

Figure 13–1. Phase 3 intake and assignment for appropriate referrals.

[a]Includes not only Category A youths, but serious/violent offenders who were referred before and after the May, 1971 YA Board policy-change that first allowed such individuals into CTP (see notes 4, 30, and 31). Excluding pre-April 1971 serious/violent offenders, the number of appropriate referrals is 264.
[b]Includes 19 Category B youths.
[c]Includes 8 Category B youths.

Their program *did* begin within a community setting, as in 1961–1969 (Palmer, 1969a, pp. 12-14).

The Phase 3 intake and assignment sequence is reviewed in Figure 13–1. The number of youths who were involved at each stage is also shown.

All parole agents who participated in Phase 3 had caseloads that contained youths from both the institutional and community segments of CTP.[8] Any agent who was originally assigned to work with a given individual remained assigned to that youth whether or not the youth's program centered on the institutional or community section of CTP, at any point in time. This approach—known as "continuity-of-worker"—helped promote a continuity-of-effort within and across settings, relative to the long-range goals for each youth.[9] As in Phases 1 and 2, average caseload size was 11 youths per agent, and the basic principles of worker/youth matching (Chapter 11) were followed throughout the Phase 3 experiment.

Throughout Phase 3, the community segment of CTP—that is, the community center—remained in the same physical structure it had occupied since 1965.

The CTP Institutional Unit (Dorm 3)
Physical and Organizational Aspects
Dorm 3 was located at NRCC, a 10-minute drive from CTP's community center in Sacramento. It had been built to house up to 50 youths at any given time, one per room. However, for purposes of Phase 3 it usually housed between 23 and 25—CTP youths exclusively—and it rarely exceeded 30. Most YA dorms housed 45 youths at any one time.

NRCC was a minimum security facility. It had no walls, towers, perimeter guards, or patrols; it was surrounded by a 10-foot high, nonelectrified, chain link fence that was easy to scale. As in Phases 1 and 2, its population (usually 200) consisted mainly of youths who were awaiting a board hearing and who would then be sent to a Youth Authority institution or camp for long-term placement.

Dorm 3 was physically separated by fences from each of NRCC's remaining living units. However, CTP youths had access to all standard facilities and activities of NRCC: dining room, swimming pool, Friday evening movies, and so on.[10] A school classroom, located about 75 feet from the dorm, was available for the exclusive use of CTP and was staffed by CTP personnel. A combination woodshop and workshop was also available, as was a small darkroom and photography lab. A large field opened onto one side of the dorm and was used by CTP youths for sports, relaxation, and related purposes.

The dorm had a large, centrally located activity area (dayroom) that was often described as having a moderately "homey" appearance during much of Phase 3. More specifically, "lamps, coffee tables, end tables, and chairs were either donated or purchased and were placed in such a way as to minimize the [otherwise] sterile appearance of the dayroom" (Beyer, 1974, p. 18). A ping pong table and pool table were also present in the dayroom. As to each youth's room, considerable latitude was given regarding the exact manner

in which this could be decorated and furnished. However, in almost all other respects, for example, size, design, and building material, all rooms were "standard" with reference to NRCC.[11] The policy of having one youth per room was maintained throughout Phase 3; that is, there was no "double-bunking."

Dorm 3 was staffed by carefully selected individuals, known as youth counselors and group supervisors, and by one senior youth counselor. After the second year of Phase 3, the "y.c.'s" and "g.s.'s" were individually paired to work with one or two CTP agents each. This produced better dorm/agent and dorm/dorm coordination-of-effort, with respect to implementing the goals that were established for youths during their initial staffing conference. Throughout Phase 3, the senior youth counselor and/or a member of his staff participated in all initial conferences.

During Phase 3, half the dorm staff were non-Caucasian at any point in time. Of these minority members, the majority (three-fourths) were black and the remainder were Mexican American. All youth counselors and group supervisors worked specifically for CTP. They were selected by the project and were primarily responsible for implementing its particular goals and approaches, not those of NRCC as a whole.

Although the senior youth counselor (s.y.c.) reported directly to the CTP administrative supervisor, not to NRCC administrators, that supervisor, the s.y.c., and the CTP casework supervisor coordinated their efforts directly with NRCC administrators whenever possible. Coordination and mutual cooperation were essential, since the two organizational entities—CTP/Dorm 3 and NRCC—(1) followed different policies regarding such matters as day passes and response to escapes, and (2) had different standards and levels of tolerance regarding the youths' personal appearance (haircuts, clothing), allowable personal possessions, noise levels, and so on. These and other differences reflected the fact that Dorm 3, as an integral part of CTP, was designed to be "treatment-oriented" at an individual level and that its youths generally had to live in the dorm for five or more months. In contrast, all other NRCC living units were basically part of a four- to six-week, "custody-oriented," processing and rerouting operation. Because of this cooperation, each organizational entity proceeded essentially on its own and rarely interfered with the other.

Though all youth counselors and group supervisors were males, females were often present on the dorm: Among the female *visitors* were (1) friends and relatives of Dorm 3 youths, (2) Phase 2 girls who were still on parole, and (3) the latters' female parole agent. *Other* females included a full-time secretary, a teacher who regularly conducted afternoon arts-and-crafts sessions, and a succession of student volunteers (usually college graduates) (Turner, 1971).

Dorm 3 was readily accessible to all CTP personnel at any hour of the day or night—weekends included. Related to this, two to four parole agents usually had their office within the dorm itself. During Phase 3 there were 10 or 11 agents working in *CTP* at any one time, dorm and community combined. To further familiarize themselves with dorm operations, needs, and perspectives, and to enhance communication and coordination in general, each agent had "at least one 40-hour shift working on Dorm 3 as a youth counselor" (Turner, 1971) and subsequently worked "a regular five-hour shift on the Dorm every two weeks" (Kenney et al., 1970).

Activities and Atmosphere

In working with Dorm 3 youths an individualized approach was used to the extent possible. For instance, considerable flexibility was allowed regarding the scheduling of each youngster's time, thereby giving the agent access to the youth at almost any hour. This reflected an underlying policy that agent/youth contacts were to have priority over all other activities and routines, consistent with the earlier-mentioned goals. To be sure, in actual practice agents tried to coordinate their plans with ongoing dorm activities; seldom did they "barge right in."

Given this flexibility and coordination it was relatively easy for agents and youth counselors to arrange for youths to participate in activities such as the following, sometimes on less than a day's notice: family counseling sessions conducted close to the dorm; small group counseling sessions at the CTP community center; half-day field trips; brief day passes with agent or youth counselor, for example, to check out possible foster homes or job opportunities; car washing and minor auto repair work, carried out on or near the grounds of NRCC. These activities were either substituted for or were "worked around"

the individual's usual routine. Since Dorm 3 was not isolated from the community, staff and youths were in a relatively good position to take advantage of off-grounds opportunities and resources.

No attempt was made to develop one all-encompassing program in which every youth would have to participate—one program that would comprise, for example, the total content or central focus of their institutional experience. Instead, considerable effort was made to develop a program that would implement the long-term objectives that were established for each youth as an individual; this, in effect, meant relatively separate programming or somewhat different patterns of activity for the respective individuals. With most youths it was possible to actually implement this policy of individualized programming, at least to a substantial degree. The resulting approach stood in contrast to others in which a youth's interests and needs may, for the most part, routinely be overshadowed by those of "the larger group," or by the principle of "running a good (e.g., uneventful, yet smoothly operating) program." In this respect the present approach made it possible to implement individualized—and certainly differential—intervention to a substantial degree, within an institutional setting. Further details regarding Dorm 3's activities and atmosphere, as well as its physical and organizational aspects, appear in Beyer (1974), from the CTP parole agents' perspective, and in Turner (1971), from that of a dorm-housed researcher.

A summary of the main program elements and activities that applied to youths who resided on the dorm is found in Table 13–1 (all numbers in this table are averages, unless otherwise indicated):[12]

Dorm 3 youths, though institutionalized, obviously had considerable access to the community, for example, in the form of day passes with parole agents and in order to attend CTP's community center school or even regular public school.[13] A further expression of this access was the fact that, during their period of assigned residence on the dorm, some 70 percent of all Category A RR's and CR's (combined) had at least one furlough. This usually occurred toward the end of their approximately 25-week stay (see below), and its average duration was two weeks (Palmer and Werner, 1972b). Thus, it would be best to think of the CTP dorm as having an

TABLE 13-1

Program Elements and Activities in and around Dorm 3

Element and Activity	Amount of Participation
1. Visits to Youth	
By parole agent	3.4 visits a week, per youth
By family	1 visit every 2.5 weeks, per youth
By friends	1 visit every 3.6 weeks, per youth
2. Counseling with Parole Agent	
Individual	2.6 hours a week, per youth
	85% of the youths had one or more hours of individual counseling per week. 45% had three or more hours per week
Group	0.7 hours a week, per youth
	61% of the youths had one or more hours of group counseling per week
Family	0.2 hours a week, per youth
	10% of the youths had one or more hours of family counseling per week
3. School	47% of the youths regularly attended CTP's NRCC classroom
	27% attended CTP's community center school
	13% attended public school[a]
	13% did not attend school[b]
4. Arts and Crafts	0.9 hours a week, per youth; 24% participated
5. Informal Activity on Dorm/at NRCC	
Athletics	5 hours a week, per youth; 53% participated
Table sports[c]	7 hours a week, per youth; 80% participated
"Quiet activities"[d]	2 hours a week, per youth; 40% participated
6. Formal Activity off Dorm/away from NRCC[e]	5.1 activities per week, for total dorm[f]
	19% of the youths attended one or more activities per week
7. Day Passes with Staff[g]	1.4 per week, per youth
	62% of the youths had one or more day passes per week, with staff

[a]By means of day passes.

[b]Most such individuals were working part-time, away from NRCC. This was made possible by means of day passes; two-way transportation was usually provided by parole agent or group supervisor.

[c]Mainly pool and ping pong.

[d]E.g., cards, dominoes, or checkers.

[e]Usually athletic, musical, or cultural and educational events (theater; visits to community, state, or federal offices; presentations to college classes).

[f]That is, for all youths (collectively) who resided on the dorm at the time.

[g]For example, for shopping, lunch, checking out possible foster homes. Excludes day passes to attend school at CTP community center. Passes ranged from 45 minutes to several hours.

institution-based rather than strictly institutional program.

Based on the Moos Social Climate Questionnaire, words that best described the Dorm 3 atmosphere were Support, Affiliation, and Spontaneity.[14] Briefly, these were defined as follows:

- *Support.* An atmosphere in which youths are frequently given encouragement.

Dorm staff can be counted on for assistance or advice regarding problems, complaints, and so forth.

- *Affiliation.* Staff/youngster relationships are close and amiable, and there is an emphasis on group social activities. A friendly atmosphere in which dorm staff take pains to integrate youngsters into the program.

- *Spontaneity.* An atmosphere that allows

and contributes to the free expression of the youths' feelings, both negative and positive. Youngsters feel free to speak their mind to dorm staff and to engage in activities of their own choosing without guidance from them.

Words that least described the dorm were Submission, Practicality, and Variety:

- *Submission.* A more authoritarian atmosphere, in which dorm staff expect rigid conformance. Staff are in full control of the program. The program tends to be somewhat inflexible and lacking in egalitarian procedures.
- *Practicality.* An atmosphere with an emphasis on preparing youngsters to capably manage their lives. Youngsters are expected to formulate definite plans for the immediate future and to set up certain realistic goals to be achieved.
- *Variety.* The atmosphere does not appear to be static. Activities, topics of discussion, even mode of dress, often change. New approaches are occasionally tried out (Moos, 1975; Palmer, 1970b).

In addition, the following may highlight certain differences in atmosphere between Dorm 3 and many or perhaps most institutional living units of the late 1960s and early 1970s, within, and undoubtedly outside, California. During its 3.8 years of operation, Dorm 3 experienced no racial clashes, small-scale or otherwise. All youths mixed freely, and there were no "gangs" and dominance-seeking groups, ethnically organized or otherwise. Staff carried no weapons, no chemicals (e.g., Mace), and no "panic buttons." There was one minor assault on staff (fisticuffs, one-on-one) and one incident of homosexuality (multiple participation, partly consensual). No grievances were filed, by youths, against staff or administration.

This atmosphere existed during a period in which the following applied to California's Youth Authority and Adult Authority facilities alike: (1) Serious racial clashes occurred several times a year within many institutions, and small-scale incidents occurred almost monthly in most such facilities;[15] (2) "gangs" and dominance-seeking groups were part and parcel of everyday life within many or possibly most institutions; (3) staff in almost every

living unit carried Mace or its equivalent, and, in many such units, they utilized it several times a month; (4) "panic buttons" were routinely carried and often used by most living unit staff; (5) minor assaults on staff occurred several times a year in many or perhaps most living units, and assaults that involved weapons were not uncommon; (6) homosexual activity involving an unwilling participant was conservatively estimated to occur at least once a month in most living units; (7) the filing of grievances was a common and increasingly frequent practice in almost every unit.

Length of Stay

For Status 1 individuals who had been appropriately placed—RR youths—the average number of months spent in Dorm 3 prior to release (i.e., parole) was 7.6. For Status 2 individuals who had been *in*appropriately placed—CR youths—the figure was 5.3.[16] During the second half of Phase 3 operations, months spent in the dorm had decreased by 26 percent per youth for both groups combined. To place these figures and this trend in perspective, it might be noted that during 1969–1973 the average number of months spent by non-CTP males (first commitments) in regular Youth Authority institutions was 10.2, and steadily rising—reaching 12.0 months during 1973–1974 (Davis et al., 1974). This excludes all Reception Center time; and institutionalized youths were quite similar to those placed in CTP, relative to the previously described background characteristics.

Main Results

Before presenting the main results it should be noted that 74 percent of the Phase 3 sample fell within the conflicted category alone. Thus, findings that are shown for the total group are much the same as those for conflicted individuals alone. Results will not be presented separately for power-oriented and passive- conformist youths (9 percent and 12 percent of the total group, respectively), since the number of individuals in these categories was rather small.

The results will apply to:

- Juvenile and adult court commitments combined. (Adult court commitments comprised 17 percent of all Phase 3 youths. If one focuses on Juvenile Court commitments alone, the findings are much the same as those for the combined total; in fact, they are generally stronger than those presented. That is, the differences which exist between key comparison groups, for example, RR and RC groups, are larger than those for all commitments combined.)

- Category A and Category B youths combined. (Category B youths comprised 17 percent of all Phase 3 youths. Results are virtually identical if one focuses on Category A youths alone.)
- The period of parole only. (If one adds, to parole time, the months that were spent within Dorm 3—namely, institution time—the results, as before, are virtually unchanged. Youths sometimes committed offenses prior to completion of their dorm program, usually while on escape status or during a day pass.)
- Finally, the results hardly change when one adjusts for the small number of youths who were removed from the dorm, and CTP, itself, without first having been released to parole.[17]

These findings relate to the first 127 consecutive cases that were released to parole between 1969 and the data cutoff relative to parole performance in CTP.[18] Following, then, are the main results for the total group of youths ("total group" was defined exactly as in Chapters 8–11):

Status 1 youths (unusually difficult or troubled individuals) who began their program in the community—that is, were *in*appropriately placed—performed considerably worse than Status 1 youths who began their program in the dorm, that is, were appropriately placed. Ninety percent of these RC's (inappropriately placed) as compared to 50 percent of the RR's (appropriately placed) committed one or more offenses during their first 15 months at risk (non-lockup time within the community).

Rather than present the findings in terms of *whether or not* youngsters committed an offense, we will now present them in relation to rate of offending (r.o.o.), as in Chapters 8–11. Unlike the preceding index, r.o.o. takes all offenses into account, not just the first one; in this respect it reflects more information and is more broadly based. In presenting these findings, "months on parole" will be used

synonymously with "months in the community" and "months at risk"; and, "offense" will refer to an unweighted combination of all known arrests, suspensions, and convictions. Also, "rate of offending" will be synonymous with "number of offenses per 1,000 months at risk," as described in previous chapters.[19]

As shown in Table 13–2, for every 1,000 months at risk there were 117 offenses among RC's and 57 among RR's—that is, one offense for every nine months in the community among inappropriately placed youths and one per 18 months for appropriately placed youths. This 51 percent difference in rate of offending, using RC's as the basis of comparison, could not be explained by "chance" ($p < .01$). Nor could it be accounted for by factors such as level of parole risk (base expectancy), age, IQ, race, socioeconomic status, and type of commitment offense, since the RC and RR samples to which these figures apply were very similar on each such factor (Appendix 29).

TABLE 13–2

Number of Offenses per 1,000 Months at Risk during Parole, for Status 1 and Status 2 Youths

Youth Status and Youth Group		*Offenses and Youths*[a]	
		Total Group[b]	Conflicted Youths Only
Status 1	RC	117	112
	RR	57	59
Status 2	CR	72	83
	CC	68	72
	RC + CR[c]	88[d]	95[d]
	RR + CC[e]	62[f]	55[f]

---

[a]Sample sizes were as follows: *Total Group*, RC–20, RR–36, CR–36, CC–35. (Average base expectancy was: RC–462, RR–472, CR–528, CC–522. Average number of risk months was: RC–15.1, RR–15.2, CR–15.2, CC–20.7. Average number of offenses per youth was: RC–1.54, RR–0.76, CR–0.96, CC–1.28.) *Conflicted youths,* RC–18, RR–25, CR–27, CC–25.
[b]Total Group = Conflicted + Power-Oriented + Passive-Conformist + Rare Types.
[c]RC + CR = Inappropriately assigned youths.
[d]Weighted average—specifically, the rate of offending for RC and CR groups, weighted by the sample size of each respective group.
[e]RR + CC = Appropriately assigned youths.
[f]Weighted average, as in note d.

For conflicted youths alone, there were 112 offenses among RC's and 59 among RR's for every 1,000 months at risk. This 47 percent difference could not be accounted for by chance ($p < .01$), or by the background factors mentioned earlier. It was equivalent to one offense for every nine months in the community among inappropriately placed youths and one per 17 months for appropriately placed youths. (Table 13–3, below, contains separate results for assertive-denier and anxious-confused youths.)[20]

These findings suggest that the delinquent behavior of Status 1 youths may be substantially reduced if these unusually troubled, troublesome, and/or resistive individuals are first worked with in a setting such as Dorm 3. Since Status 1 youths comprised no less than 48 percent of the Phase 3 sample—44 percent if Category B youths are excluded—the relevance of these findings is considerable. These youths probably comprised a very similar proportion of the Youth Authority population as a whole.[21]

What about the remaining 52 percent of the sample—*Status 2* youths? These, it will be recalled, were the less troubled, troublesome, and/or resistive individuals. Here, the findings suggest there is nothing to be gained with regard to parole performance by initially placing these youngsters in an institutional setting such as Dorm 3: For every 1,000 months at risk, there were 72 offenses among CR's (youths placed on the dorm) and 68 among CC's (youths returned directly to the community)—a rather negligible difference in the present context. Similar results were obtained for conflicted youths alone.[22] (See Table 13–2.)

By combining the Phase 3 groups in various ways *irrespective* of status, it was found that inappropriately placed youths (RC's plus CR's) performed worse than appropriately placed youths (RR's plus CC's): For every 1,000 months at risk, there were 88 offenses among "inappropriates" and 62 among "appropriates"—one offense for every 11 months in the community among the former and one per 16 months among the latter. This 30 percent difference can be accounted for neither by chance ($p < .05$) nor by the preceding background factors. (If appropriately rather than inappropriately placed youths were used as the basis of comparison, the 30 percent figure would become 42 percent.) The results also

hold up in connection with conflicted youths, taken by themselves ($p < .01$) (Table 13–2).

These findings bear on a fundamental question, one that—ever since the early 1980s—has been vigorously debated among correctional thinkers: *Which* youths would best be placed into *which* types of setting, or program? In this connection, the following may be relevant:

1. Status 1 youths who were inappropriately placed performed considerably worse on parole than those who were appropriately placed. However, with Status 2 youths no substantial differences were observed between appropriate and inappropriate placements. This raises the possibility that an inappropriate or less than optimal placement makes much more of a difference to Status 1 than Status 2 youths. The former may be less able to cope with, or make the best of, such a placement, even when its atmosphere is neither harsh nor barren.

2. Inappropriately placed Status 1 youths (RC's) performed substantially worse on parole than inappropriately placed Status 2 youths (CR's). However, *appropriately* placed youths (RR's and CC's) performed at roughly the same level as one another irrespective of status. Once again it would appear that an inappropriate or less than optimal placement may accentuate various differences that involve the personal and interpersonal liabilities of Status 1 as compared with Status 2 youths. In contrast, an appropriate or closer to optimal placement may help offset some of their preexisting differences in ability to cope with stress or anxiety.

Postdischarge Follow-up
As of the data cutoff point, a total of 35 youths had accumulated four years of risk time in the community after being favorably or unfavorably discharged from *CTP*.[23] The resulting postdischarge analysis was therefore of limited value and, in the case of RC versus RR comparisons, of questionable reliability. However, since even limited analyses can sometimes suggest possible emerging trends, and since it seemed better to present even heavily qualified results than none at all, postdischarge findings will be briefly reviewed. All methods used in these analyses were identical to those in Chapter 8.

As shown in Appendix 30, results for the total group were similar, as to overall trend, to those involving parole; that is, inappropriate placement seemed more important to *Status 1* than Status 2 youths. Specifically, for inappropriately and appropriately placed Status 1 youths (RC's and RR's) there were 36 and 23 moderate plus severe arrests, respectively, per 1,000 months at risk subsequent to discharge; this was a difference of 36 percent in favor of appropriately placed youths, using RC's as the basis of comparison. However, for inappropriately and appropriately placed *Status 2* youths (CR's and CC's), there were 29 and 27 such arrests, respectively—a difference of 7 percent in favor of appropriately placed youths.[24] (Although meaningful statistical tests could not be performed for RC's versus RR's due to the small number of RC's, the difference between CR's and CC's was easily accounted for by chance.) In the case of (1) severe as well as violent arrests, and also (2) conflicted youths alone (all severity groupings), appropriates (A's) continued to outperform inappropriates (I's); however, the percentage difference between A's and I's was usually *less* for Status 1 than Status 2 youths, and, in any event, no A/I differences were statistically reliable.

When *all* inappropriately placed youths were compared to all appropriately placed youths—that is, when the respective Status 1 and Status 2 groups were combined—the basic pattern or trend remained present: On four-year postdischarge follow-up, appropriates (RR's plus CC's) performed slightly but not significantly better than inappropriates (RC's plus CR's) relative to moderate plus severe, severe, and violent arrests alike. This applied to the total group and to conflicted youths by themselves.[25] (Appendix 30).

Given the questionable reliability of several preceding results from the post-discharge follow-up, the observations that follow are based on findings from the parole period only.

General Observations

Phase 3 was mainly designed to answer the question of whether difficult to reach individuals (Status 1 youths) would become less involved in delinquent behavior if they began their Youth Authority career within a particular kind of institutional setting, rather than in the community itself. For approximately half the individuals in question, the answer turned out to be yes—there *would* be less delinquent involvement: Judging from their marked reduction in rate of offending, 40 percent to 60 percent of all appropriately placed Status 1 youths derived considerable benefit from the Phase 3 approach. The remaining half were still "unreached"—as in 1961–1969. Together with the Phase 1 and 2 findings for Status 2 youths, and despite the still *unreached* Status 1 youths, these results supported the view that careful diagnosis and appropriate placement can lead to a reduction in delinquent behavior—or, conversely, to a higher rate of success—for institution- and community-based programs alike.

The 40 percent to 60 percent figure applied to each of four Status 1 groups: Group *A* (psychologically disorganized), Group *B* (control-resisters), Group *C* (destructive loyalty binds), and Group *E* (heavily drug-involved). Too few Group *D* youths (delinquent identifiers) were studied to allow for a meaningful estimate of how many such youths derived benefit from the Phase 3 approach, in terms of reduced delinquency. Group E youths—relatively few of whom existed during Phases 1 and 2—posed no special problems during Phase 3. They were worked with largely by the same methods used with most other conflicted Status 1 youths (nearly all Group E youths were considered conflicted), and seldom were medical/chemical approaches or adjuncts used with these individuals to any substantial degree.[26]

Phase 3 findings also indicate that the approaches used at CTP are relevant to a broader range of youths than those studied during the 1960s. For example:

1. Prior to Phase 3, adult court commitments (ACC's) had not been studied within the CTP framework; however, during Phase 3 they were found to be very similar to juvenile court commitments (JCC's). Specifically, ACC's presented no diagnostic problems and few if any special operational or administrative problems. In short, it was possible to work with these youths and young adults in essentially the same way as with JCC's. This applied not only to individuals who started their program in the community, but to those who began in an institution-based setting (Dorm 3). In addition, as shown in Table 13–3, rate of offending

for juvenile plus adult court commitments was similar to that for juvenile court commitments alone.[27] This indicates that the performance of Adult Court commitments (though fewer than 20 such youths were in the analysis) was not sufficiently different—from that of JCC's—to substantially change the overall picture.[28]

2. Phases 1 and 2 focused on ages 13 through 18, at Youth Authority intake. During Phase 3, CTP's range of applicability was extended to age 21 at intake. This extension was closely related to that for adult court commitments, since 95 percent of all 19- to 21-year-olds were ACC's and 78 percent of all *ACC's* were 19 or over at intake.

3. The feasibility of working with somewhat violent or relatively aggressive offenders was demonstrated during Phase 3. For example, Table 13–4 indicates that many or most Category B youths—though small in number—had a rate of offending that was similar to, or else lower than, that of Category A youths. (As indicated, Category B youths would have been ineligible during Phases 1 and 2, based on their often violent commitment offense, their offense history, and so on. Category A youths would have been eligible and

would have started their Youth Authority program in the community.) However, since Category B youths began their program in the CTP dorm, it is not known how well they would have performed if they had started their program within the community.[29]

Category B youths whom the board declared eligible and who were therefore placed on the project represented 64 percent of all Category B referrals whom the board *considered,* that is, reviewed, for possible inclusion in the project—not quite two-thirds of all Category B preeligibles.[30] Thus, Category B eligibles were a somewhat selected group. Despite this selection, the proportion of violent or aggressive Youth Authority first commitments (i.e., all such youths from the Sacramento area) who were declared eligible and were adequately handled within CTP's Phase 3 framework remained substantial. In addition, these individuals spent less time in Dorm 3 than they would have spent in a regular YA institution, prior to being paroled (see endnote 16).[31]

4. Finally, Phase 3 demonstrated that the CTP approach can be applied to individuals whose offense history is longer and

TABLE 13–3

Number of Offenses per 1,000 Months at Risk during Parole, for Adult and Juvenile Court Commitments

	Offenses, Youths, and Court of Commitment[a]						
					Conflicted Youths Only		
	Total Group[b]						
Youth Group	*Juvenile + Adult Court*	*Juvenile Court*	*Juvenile + Adult Court*			*Juvenile Court*	
				A–D*	A–C*		A–D*	A–C*
RC	117	114	112	(133)	(94)	109	(140)	(94)
RR	57	44	59	(58)	(60)	53	(50)	(56)
CR	72	82	83	(59)	(91)	77	(59)	(85)
CC	68	71	72	(70)	(74)	78	(88)	(73)

*A–D: Assertive-Denier. A–C: Anxious-Confused.

[a]Sample sizes were as follows: *Total Group, Juvenile + Adult Court,* RC–20, RR–36, CR–36, CC–35. *Total Group, Juvenile Court,* RC–19, RR–32, CR–29, CC–30. *Conflicted youths, Juvenile + Adult Court* (sample sizes for A–D and A–C youths, respectively, are shown in parentheses), RC–18 (9,9), RR–25 (13,12), CR–27 (6,21), CC–25 (8,17). *Conflicted youths, Juvenile Court,* RC–17 (8,9), RR–23 (12,11), CR–23 (6,17), CC–21 (6,15).

[b]Total Group = Conflicted + Power-Oriented + Passive-Conformist + Rare Types.

TABLE 13–4

Number of Offenses per 1,000 Months at Risk during Parole, for Category A and Category B Youths

| | Offenses, Youths, and Youth Category[a] | | | |
| | Total Group[b] | | Conflicted Youths Only | |
Youth Group	Category A	Category B	Category A	Category B
RC	117	—[c]	112	—[c]
RR	56	67	64	32
CR	76	29	87	29
CC	68	—[c]	72	—[c]

[a]Sample sizes were as follows: *Total Group, Category A,* RC–20, RR–27, CR–33, CC–35. *Total Group, Category B,* RC–0, RR–9, CR–3, CC–0. *Conflicted youths, Category A,* RC–18, RR–20, CR–24, CC–25. *Conflicted youths, Category B,* RC–0, RR–5, CR–3, CC–0.

[b]Total Group = Conflicted + Power-Oriented + Passive-Conformist + Rare Types.

[c]Not applicable, since the RC and CC groups—those initially assigned to the community—contained no Category B youths.

more serious than that of Phase 1 and 2 youths. Phase 3 youngsters and young adults had a larger number of pre-CTP arrests (8.1 vs. 5.8) and a higher proportion of level 6 to 10 (severe) committing offenses (39% vs. 23%) than individuals who comprised the 1961–1969 sample. These trends applied to the Phase 3 sample as a whole, not to its adult court commitments, older individuals, or Category B, youths alone. They applied to Status 1 and 2 youths alike.

Notes

1. These often complex clues need not be reviewed here; however, they are reflected in the guidelines for Groups A through E (see text).

2. That is, "straight" or undiluted except for periods of short-term detention that occurred after release to parole.

3. Average age at intake was 16.5 as compared to 15.6 for Phases 1 and 2. Twenty-three percent were 18 or older at intake, compared to 4 percent for Phases 1 and 2. Individuals who began their program in CTP's institutional facility were older still (by about six months), when first released to parole.

4. All 161 were diagnosed, staffed, and randomly drawn upon in the same manner, despite the fact that all Category B youths had to begin their program in the CTP-operated dorm (see text). (This was the basic condition under which the Youth Authority Board would allow Category B youths to be included in the Phase 3 experiment; the remaining condition involved minimum length of stay on the dorm, prior to community release. [See endnote 7.]) The board first allowed Category B youths to be part of CTP 20 months after Phase 3 began (Palmer, 1971b).

5. As indicated in Chapter 4, *conflicted* refers to the anxious-confused and assertive-denier subtypes combined. *Power-oriented* refers to manipulators and group conformists combined. *Delinquent identifiers* are referred to as cultural identifiers in most I-level literature (Palmer, 1971d; Warren et al., 1966b).

6. Because of the random drawing, Status 1 youths sometimes had to begin their program in the community-based component and Status 2 youths sometimes had to start within Dorm 3 (see text). Whenever such theoretically "less than optimal placements" ("inappropriate assignments") were required, operations staff prepared a modified treatment/control plan—one that differed in several respects from the theoretically *optimal* plan that had been prepared immediately before the drawing. The modified plan contained goals that seemed appropriate with respect to the less than optimal setting and the

youth's individual needs as well. It also contained strategies that seemed likely to allow for, and encourage, maximum use of resources available within the given setting.

7. For research purposes, Category B youths were analyzed both separately from and together with the RR, RC, CR, and CC groups described in the text. At the operations level, Category B youths had access to the same program opportunities as Category A youths. However, they were seldom eligible for day passes prior to having spent at least three, sometimes six, months on the dorm. This minimum-time restriction was specified by the YA Board on a case-by-case basis during the eligibility hearing.

8. With certain planned exceptions, all agents had caseloads that contained youths from all four youth groups: RR, RC, CR, and CC. This also applied to Category B cases (Palmer, 1969a, pp. 27–29; 1971b, pp. 9–11). The exceptions were part of a substudy that focused on CR's and CC's, that is, Status 2 cases (individuals diagnosed as appropriate for initial release to the community). This research centered on three caseloads that were handled only by "generalist agents"—workers whose level of skill and perceptiveness was higher than that of regular parole agents ("RPA's," as in Phases 1 and 2), but who were not always adequately matched with youths on their caseloads. Though the sample sizes in this substudy were modest with respect to conflicted youths, results essentially supported those of Phases 1 and 2 regarding the importance of client/worker matching with these individuals. The numbers were too small to draw conclusions regarding the possible significance of matching with other youth groups (Palmer and Werner, 1973, pp. 22, 24–25—Table 10, items 7 and 10). However, the results also suggested that workers need not be *quite* as skilled, and so on, as were CTP's Phase 1 and 2 matched workers, in order to successfully intervene with conflicted Status 2 youths.

9. Beyond this, individuals whose parole was revoked were often placed into, or returned to, Dorm 3—thus allowing them to remain part of CTP. These indi-

viduals also remained with their original parole agent. In addition, RR and CR youths who had completed their dorm stay could later visit the dorm if they wished, for example, to talk with staff whom they had known.

10. They were not required to participate in the given activities.

11. The one exception was as follows. Each room "had a door which opened from the inside as well as from the outside. This enabled the youngsters to go in and out of their rooms at will rather than being automatically locked in when they closed their doors" (Beyer, 1974, p. 18).

12. These figures are based on a 16-week sample of dorm activities: February through May of 1971. This sample was taken during the middle years of dorm operation, immediately prior to the arrival of the first Category B youths (Palmer and Werner, 1972b, pp. 66–67).

13. Phone calls were another common form of contact, albeit one that was less physical or concrete. This and various other community contacts are not reflected in Table 13–1; nor are visits to the dorm by local college students, for example, in connection with their field assignments.

14. This finding was based on 28 consecutive months of rating (February 1971 through May 1973), twice a month, by on-site research staff. The Moos Social Climate Questionnaire involves 12 separate content scales. Only those three scales that received the highest and lowest ratings, respectively, are shown in the text. The remaining scales are: Order, Insight, Involvement, Aggression, Clarity, and Autonomy.

15. During the early 1970s, correctional staff very often speculated as to *when*—based on various rumors or clues—given institutions would "explode," racially. As it turned out, institutionwide racial "explosions" very seldom occurred; however, various conflicts and confrontations (youth/youth, and youth/staff) almost constantly bubbled to the surface.

16. For both groups combined, the average stay was 6.3 months. (All figures exclude Category B youths, individuals whose average stay was 8.2 months.) If one includes the small number of individuals who were removed from CTP without

having been paroled, the figures remain essentially the same: RR youths—7.3 months; CR youths—5.5 months.

17. Most such individuals had been removed by the YA Board because of offenses committed while on escape status or during a day pass. The rest were removed, also by the board, in connection with Dorm 3's homosexual incident.

18. When Phase 3 operations ended (1973), 11 Dorm 3 youths (RR's and CR's) had not yet been released to parole; also, four community-located individuals (RC's and CC's) had only recently entered the project and had accumulated fewer than six weeks on parole before being transferred from CTP. These youths were excluded from the "basic" parole analysis (N = 127). Six additional youths were excluded, by a stratified randomization process, in order to make the RR and RC groups, and, separately, the CR and CC groups, almost precisely equal in terms of base expectancy (Table 13–2, note a). Even without this adjustment, the groups in question, for example, RR and RC, were very similar to each other on base expectancy; and results from the "unadjusted" parole analysis (N = 133) were almost identical to those shown in Table 13–2. Finally, during 1969–1973, six youths (Group "X") were paroled out of the area (POA), and seven others were removed from Dorm 3 and transferred out of CTP by the Youth Authority Board prior to being paroled. These individuals were not included in the basic parole analysis. However, as indicated in endnote 21, when direct analytic adjustments were made for these individuals—for example, when all non-POA time *was* counted for Group X and when comparably offending youths were removed from RC and CC groups to compensate for the Dorm 3 removals and transfers—results were somewhat stronger than in the basic analysis itself. (POA's were youths who—mainly because of family moves or special employment opportunities—had been allowed to reside either permanently or for relatively long time periods outside the greater Sacramento area. As a result, these individuals, who were distributed among the RR, RC, and CR groupings, received either very little or rather sporadic, fragmented, and unintegrated project input.)

19. Two points might be noted. (1) Results that are presented relate to offenses of all severity levels. However, they are virtually unchanged when those of minor severity (levels 1–2)—7 percent of all offenses—are excluded. (2) *Offense* refers to any delinquent act that resulted in one or more of the following: adjudicated court referral to CTP; court recommitment; revocation of parole; suspension of parole; unfavorable transfer from CTP to other YA program; unfavorable discharge from YA (Palmer and Werner, 1972b, 1973).

20. The following might be noted regarding these youth groups. (1) Inappropriately placed Status 1 *assertive-deniers* performed significantly worse than those who were appropriately placed: For juvenile plus adult court commitments (J plus ACC's), rates of offending were 133 and 58 per 1,000 months at risk for the RC and RR groups, respectively ($p < .05$). Similar results were obtained for juvenile court commitments (JCC's), when these individuals were analyzed separately. Inappropriately placed Status 1 *anxious-confused* youths tended to perform worse than those appropriately placed: For J plus ACC's the rates in question were 94 and 60, respectively ($p < .10 > .05$). Again, similar results were obtained for JCC's by themselves. (See endnote 22 for related findings.) (2) *Inappropriately* placed Status 1 assertive-deniers tended to perform worse than inappropriately placed, Status 1 anxious-confused youths; however, opposite results were obtained in connection with Status 2 A-D's as compared to Status 2 A-C's. These results, like those that follow, applied to J plus ACC's and to JCC's by themselves. In contrast, no significant or substantial A-D/A-C differences were found for *appropriately* placed Status 1 and Status 2 youths alike, that is, for RR's and CC's respectively. (See Table 13–3.) (3) Of all RC's (J plus ACC's combined), 50 percent were assertive-deniers and 40 percent were anxious-confused; for RR's, the figures were 36 percent and 33 percent, respectively.

21. Findings that relate to Status 1 youths held up when five analytic adjustments were made, individually and collectively; this applied to Status 2 youths as well. These adjustments relate to offenses that occurred: (1) during the youths' detention on Dorm 3—or during escapes, day passes, or furloughs from the dorm—subsequent to their having *previously* been released to parole either directly or after completion of the dorm program; (2) after having been placed on CTP parole for the second, third, and so on, time—that is, subsequent to release from a Youth Authority institution or camp into which they were placed after being recommitted or revoked while in the CTP community or dorm program. The adjustments also relate to (3) all charges that were dropped by the juvenile or adult court, and (4) all charges or offenses that occurred while the youths were paroled outside the Sacramento area. Also taken into account were (5) RR and CR youths who did not complete the dorm program. When all five adjustments were made, the number of offenses per 1,000 months at risk were as follows for the total group: RR—48, RC—166, CR—70, CC—68. For conflicted youths by themselves, they were: RR—64, RC—126, CR—87, CC—65.

22. In contrast to Status 1 youths, inappropriately placed Status 2 assertive-deniers did not perform significantly worse than those appropriately placed: For juvenile plus adult court commitments, rates of offending were 59 and 70 per 1,000 months at risk for the CR and CC groups, respectively. Contrasting results were also obtained for Status 2 anxious-confused youths: Here, too, no significant performance difference was obtained relative to the CR and CC groups. These findings also applied to juvenile court commitments by themselves, despite a substantial percentage difference in favor of inappropriately placed assertive-deniers. (See Table 13–3.) Of all CR's (J plus ACC's combined), 17 percent were assertive-deniers and 58 percent were anxious-confused; for CC's, the figures were 23 percent and 49 percent, respectively.

23. Several youths had to be placed on regular parole when CTP wound down, starting in 1973. These youths, most of whom received their YA discharge during the subsequent few years, were purposely excluded from the postdischarge follow-up.

24. When minor offenses were included, results were virtually unchanged. Whether or not such offenses were included, results for *convictions* were also essentially the same; here, however, the specific rates of offending were somewhat reduced in scale.

25. Had the sample been substantially larger, significance might have been reached among conflicted youths in the case of moderate plus severe arrests combined.

26. During Phase 3, Status 1 youths were distributed as follows: Group A—12 percent; Group B—15 percent; Group C—56 percent; Group D—4 percent; Group E—12 percent; Other—1 percent. Conflicted youths comprised 78 percent of Group A, 91 percent of Group C, and 89 percent of Group E. (Group A mainly consisted of anxious-confused individuals; Groups C and E were evenly divided between assertive-deniers and anxious-confused youths.) Power-oriented youths comprised 58 percent of Group B, and delinquent identifiers comprised 100 percent of Group D (Palmer and Werner, 1973).

27. Rate of offending for juvenile plus adult court commitments was slightly higher among Status 1 youths and slightly lower among Status 2 youths, when compared to juvenile court commitments alone. This applied not only to the total group but to the RC, RR, and CC conflicted youths as well. The time period in question was 1969–1973, for juvenile as well as adult court commitments.

28. One can speak of general patterns only, when comparing adult and juvenile court commitments for each such group. This is because the sample of adult court commitments was too small to allow for rigorous statistical testing relative to the adult versus juvenile court dichotomy.

29. Seventy percent of all Category B youths were diagnosed as Status 1; the remainder, it was believed, could begin their program in the community. Apart from this, 67 percent of all Category B youths

were committed from juvenile court and the remainder were from adult court.

30. Youths committed for murder, kidnapping, robbery with injury to victim(s), or "major sale of narcotics or dangerous drug" were not reviewed by the board; that is, they were not Category B preeligibles. Almost all other serious cases—purse snatch, willful arson, extortion with threat or force, manslaughter, and so on—were potentially acceptable for CTP (by preestablished board policy); except for individuals who were randomly excluded by research (see endnote 31), they *were* therefore reviewed by the board.

31. During Phase 3, youths who were sent to the YA for a severe or violent offense (robbery without injury to victim(s), robbery with injury, assault with a deadly weapon [ADW], forcible rape, murder, etc.)—specifically, individuals whose commitment offense would have made them ineligible during Phases 1 and 2—comprised 29 percent of all 13–21-year-old male first commitments from juvenile and adult courts in the greater Sacramento area. (Like Category A youths, these individuals were "*appropriate referrals*" to CTP, that is, appropriate in the sense of being first commitments to the YA, being from the Sacramento area, being ages 13–21, and so on—as required by the research design.) Beginning in May 1971, a YA Board policy change—which had been requested by the researchers as well as CTP operations staff—allowed youths with *certain kinds* of severe/violent (s/v) committing offenses (e.g., robbery *without* injury to victims; ADW) to be considered for CTP; and, counting from that point until the end of Phase 3, 27 percent of *all* "s/v youths" (all such individuals being *appropriate referrals* with respect to the research design requirements) were screened out as ineligible, by research, because of their specific committing offense (robbery *with* injury; murder; etc., as in endnote 30). During that same period, an additional 26 percent of all s/v youths were randomly excluded, again by research, because the dorm and/or agent caseloads were sometimes at full capacity relative to the Phase 3 research design. (Random-exclusion cases were never ineligible because of their commitment offense; that is, were it not for the random exclusion, all such s/v youths would have been reviewed by the board for possible inclusion in CTP. Category A cases were not excluded by research during Phase 3, for any reason.) The remaining s/v youths—"Category B preeligibles"—*were* reviewed by the YA Board; and, of these individuals, 64 percent were declared eligible. *Counting* youths whom research had randomly excluded for the preceding reason, 40 percent of *all* severe/violent appropriate referrals were declared eligible for CTP, by the board. Most such eligibles had been committed for robbery without injury to victim(s).

14 PROGRAM REVIEW AND GENERAL IMPLICATIONS

What are the Community Treatment Project's general implications for criminal justice and society overall? To help answer this question we will first review CTP's main features, its assumptions, its program elements, its central findings, and several additional results. We will then briefly relate this information to issues of relevance to criminal justice and society alike. These issues will be further discussed in later chapters.

The Program: A Review
Main Features and Assumptions
Settings and Samples
As shown in Figure 14–1, CTP operated during three phases and in three main settings: Settings A and B focused on 13- to 18-year-old male and female first commitments from juvenile courts (almost no one was age 19). Individuals with seriously assaultive committing offenses were excluded, but most other individuals (e.g., those committed for bur-

glary, auto theft, forgery, drug abuse, prostitution, and homosexuality) were included. Setting C involved males only, but extended the age range to 21 at intake; it also included adult court commitments and individuals with seriously assaultive commitment offenses (e.g., robbery without injury to victim, and assault with deadly weapon). In Setting C, the seriously assaultive individuals were selected for CTP by the Youth Authority Board on a case-by-case basis, and all such offenders began their treatment/control ("intervention") within the small-sized, CTP-operated living unit located at the YA's Northern Reception Center and Clinic. However, in all settings and phases CTP's basic sample consisted of what could be called serious, multiple offenders: During 1961–1969, their average number of pre-CTP offenses was close to six; during 1969–1973 it was eight. In addition, many youths had assaultive or otherwise severe offenses prior to their YA commitment offense.[1]

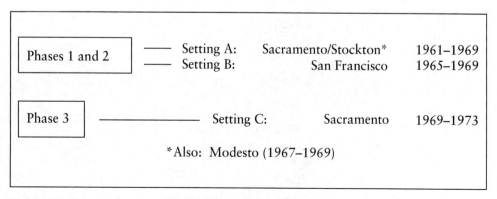

Figure 14–1. *Phases and settings of the Community Treatment Project.*

Goals and Operating Assumptions

Apart from its objectives relative to the Youth Authority–NIMH experiment, CTP's ultimate goal was the long-term protection of society. This goal was to be reached, not primarily through surveillance and external controls, but through the following route or *subgoals:*

1. changes in youth's perception of self and others;
2. expansion or redirection of youth's coping abilities; and
3. reduction of stresses and/or expansion of supports in youth's immediate environment.

Only through such changes, it was believed, could major and relatively permanent effects be obtained; however, it was not assumed that changes had to occur in all three areas. External controls, it was thought, would not in themselves supply new directions, lead to new forms of enjoyment, and result in different patterns of interaction; by themselves, their impact on illegal behavior would probably be short-term only, at least in most cases.

As shown in Figure 14–2, it was assumed that three main conditions or *inputs* ("presumed requirements") were usually needed to achieve the preceding subgoals:

1. long-term interaction between agent and youth;
2. program elements that could bear directly on youth's everyday adjustment and emerging pressures (among these elements were: schooling, pragmatically oriented discussions and decision-making, out-of-home placements); and
3. substantial involvement, by youth, in the process of change.

The latter requirement was considered necessary in order to tap or develop the individual's internal motivation and to avoid, where possible, a primary or heavy emphasis on external controls. Internal motivation and internal controls seemed necessary to sustain long-term efforts, and such efforts were often considered essential to the achievement of *subgoals* (1) and (2).

To help establish, organize, and direct the preceding *inputs,* especially (2) and (3), a careful assessment was made, at intake, of the youth, his life circumstances, and his immediate environment. This assessment resulted in a detailed, individualized intervention plan, one that was later revised if necessary. To facilitate and help maintain each input, particularly (1) and (3), parole agents were carefully matched with youths whenever possible. To implement these conditions in a specific organizational

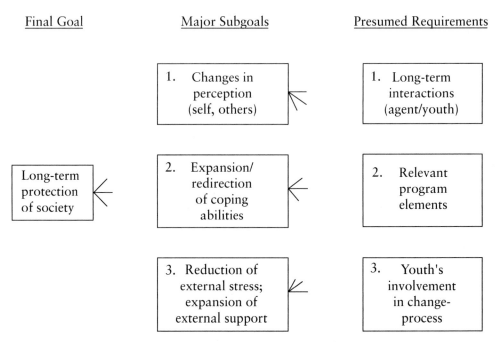

Figure 14–2. Final goal, major subgoals, and presumed requirements of CTP.

context, each CTP parole office consisted of seven case-carrying agents, one casework supervisor, and one administrative supervisor.[2] Since substantial time and effort were considered necessary for implementing the intervention plans, each agent worked with no more than 12 youths at any one time.

Further Assumptions, Classification, and Individualization

CTP's most general, explicit assumption was that youths differ from each other in important ways, for example, in their views of the environment and in their actual as well as desired relationships with others. This general concept had one specific corollary and one related assumption (the latter did not necessarily follow from the general concept, or from the corollary):

1. Illegal behavior and related life-styles may result from a number of factors, operating singly or in combination (e.g., undersocialization/poor impulse control; desire for material gain; subgroup expectations; antisocial or anti-authority family orientation; peer pressures; personal conflicts; long-term overcompensations; family "binds" or pressures; family disorganization; conflicting social values; situational entanglements).[3]
2. A set of youth-specific interventions, either centered around or largely mediated/monitored by adult authority figures, is necessary in order to help most serious, multiple offenders permanently overcome, obviate, or largely circumvent the above factors. (See endnote 4 regarding *subgroup expectations* and *peer pressures*.)

Together, these concepts or assumptions—namely, differential perception and interaction, differential and multiple causation, and differential intervention—were a major, specific source of CTP's stance on individualization. They were consistent with a principle and a tacit goal that also contributed to this stance, though in a more general way: "Facilitate individualized justice and minimize rigid, undifferentiated solutions ("frontier justice")—thereby integrating, wherever possible, the multiple needs, resources, and professed ideals of society with needs and resources of the growing youth." This, in effect, broadly defined one possible role of the justice system with regard to common social ideals and individual needs. (In the review that follows it is recognized that "individualization," "marked," and "moderate" are relative terms and are subject to varied interpretations.)

Extreme individualization in the approach to youths was neither possible nor even attempted at CTP. It was not only precluded by practical considerations, it was somewhat restricted, though not ruled out, by the presence of a classification system that was intrinsic to the research design and which placed each youth into one of nine categories. Each category ("subtype," or youth group) was more closely associated with certain presumed causal factors than were most remaining categories, and each category more often suggested certain broad intervention strategies than did others.

Thus, by dividing "delinquents" into several subtypes—from one perspective, several personality groupings—this classification system ("I-level") itself provided a moderate degree of individualization. More specifically, its subtype descriptions highlighted several features or dimensions that were shared by given youths but which helped distinguish those youths from others. However, by itself, each such description conveyed only some of the unique features of any *specific* individual; that is, it described his or her personality only in part. Moreover, it was not designed to reflect the individual's life circumstances, generally or otherwise.

Throughout 1961–1973 a dynamic balance was maintained between a high or possibly "marked" (but still not extreme) degree of individualization, on the one hand, and I-level's "moderate" individualization on the other. (The typical product of this interaction could be characterized as "considerable" individualization, for example, a large or substantial amount or degree.) More concretely, when intervention plans were developed for each youth, and when everyday decisions were made, classification and underlying I-level theory were usually subordinated to the apparent, specific needs and immediate circumstances of the individual. However, "subordination" was seldom complete, since I-level theory was itself used to help interpret the youth's behavior and to predict his general responses to possible interventions. (I-level theory could be applied somewhat independently of the nine subtype descriptions.)

At any rate, intervention varied greatly *within* each *subtype,* since, in the final analysis, considerable effort was made to address each youth's conscious interests, his actual or emerging skills, his apparent limitations, and his immediate as well as persistent life circumstances. (These factors and conditions could be, and generally were, identified independently of any given classification or theory, I-level and others.) As a result, the specifics of intervention were not primarily determined on an a priori basis, for example, by virtue of the individual's classification. Nevertheless, the broad outlines of intervention often *were* so determined—particularly during initial planning.

Throughout 1961–1973, the value as well as limitations of I-level were increasingly recognized. Although this system remained a major guide—in fact the dominant reference point—in responding to youths, additional and in some respects more refined concepts emerged. For example, during Phase 3 an essentially new set of concepts was used at CTP, together with I-level. These reflected several additional facets of the youth's individuality and psychosocial growth, and they helped address various long-term needs and behavior patterns (Chapter 27).

In sum, as CTP moved through its three phases, considerable individualization existed in the approach to youths. This level of individualization reflected an integration of information that was (1) based on detailed assessment plus continued observation of each youth and (2) already incorporated within given I-level categories and subsequently developed concepts. (The term "considerable" is given concrete meaning in Chapter 6.)

Implicit Assumptions and Related Values
Implicit in the above was the view that project youths were open to substantial and relatively permanent change, under conditions that could be produced and maintained within given communities by a large state agency. (These conditions were the earlier-mentioned, assumed requirements.) It was not assumed that these conditions or inputs would be equally "easy" or "difficult" to provide for all youth groups, and that all youths would be equally responsive to them or others, however adequately provided. As will be recalled, a basic goal of the experiment was to determine *which* individuals would change under *which* conditions (Adams and Grant, 1961).

Thus, it was implicitly assumed that CTP's interventions would be relevant to, but not necessarily have equal impact upon, all major causal factors that impinged on project youths. It was also assumed that these interventions could be, and should be, provided in a minimally coercive context and in a humane as well as nondemeaning way, even though some youths would probably require substantially more external control and direction than others.

Underlying and in some cases complementing the preceding assumptions, it was felt that seriously delinquent youths were neither hopeless, worthless, intractable, nor defective; nor were they "depraved" or basically "evil." Instead, they were seen as having the capacity and, very often, considerable conscious desire to markedly alter or entirely relinquish their socially unacceptable patterns. In these as in other respects they were viewed as neither intrinsically different than nor of lesser potential value than other individuals. This was despite the fact that they were often far more troubled and/or troublesome than most other youths and were seen as having contributed greatly to their own difficulties.[5]

Finally, these individuals were not seen as having forfeited the common right to "improve one's lot in life" and to experience happiness as others might experience it. In this connection, they were not regarded as "undeserving" and as meriting only minimal assistance. This was despite the fact that (1) they were seen as having interfered with the rights of *others* (or, as having often contributed to the latter's unhappiness), (2) they had "worn thin" or even "worn out" the patience of many individuals around them, and (3) many *non*delinquent and *non*troublesome youths and adults were themselves in need of assistance, and sometimes more willing to accept it.

Program Elements and Amount of Intervention
Throughout 1961–1973, several program elements were available for implementing CTP's intervention plans. These elements were "counseling; pragmatically oriented discussions and decision-making; limit-setting sessions and surveillance; recreation and socializing experiences; out-of-home placements; short-term detention." (An accredited school program was also available, beginning in 1965.) Each youth was exposed to an average of four such ele-

ments during any given time period, for example, any three-month interval; and any two or more elements could be used successively rather than simultaneously, for example, across given time periods. This multiple modality approach—referred to as *extensive intervention*—was designed to (1) comprehensively and flexibly address the individual's often complex difficulties or shifting challenges, and (2) substantially improve his "external support versus external stress" ratio and his "coping skills versus coping deficiencies" ratio, in favor of external support and coping skills.[6] Additional elements that contributed to those just mentioned were: "collateral contacts, by parole agent, on behalf of youths; material aid, e.g., clothing and transportation." (Also, starting in 1969, a CTP residential facility—Dorm 3—was available for a wide range of functions, short-term detention included.) By itself, no single element was considered adequate to the task, at least for the preponderance of youths. This mainly reflected the depth or extent of the latter's problems, for example, regarding support versus stress.

The specific combination and/or succession of elements that was used was determined by three main factors: (1) the youth as an individual, for instance, his interests, skills, limitations, and life circumstances; (2) the youth as a certain type of individual, for example, his I-level and subtype; (3) the agent's preferences and skills. Factors (1) and (2) each carried more weight than factor (3); however, (1) and (3) largely determined the *frequency* of contact.

With all subtypes, individual counseling was the most common form of agent/youth interaction; for youths with whom this approach was used ("participants"), there were over five such contacts per month, averaged across their entire parole experience. (For participants and nonparticipants combined, there were 2.5 such contacts per month. See Chapter 3 for definitions.) Group and family counseling were used less often. Limit-setting and surveillance occurred 1.6 times a month, while pragmatically oriented interactions and collateral contacts were each somewhat less frequent. This relatively high rate of interaction was called *intensive intervention*. In all, most Phase 1 and 2 youths had between 150 and 250 face-to-face contacts of one type or another with their agent; many interacted, formally and informally, with other staff as well, such as schoolteachers and secretaries.

Finally, during these same phases, short-term detention totaled 1.5 months during the average individual's parole experience; that is, youths accumulated an average of 47 such days of lockup while on CTP (2.4 lockups, at 19 days each). This contrasted with roughly nine months of initial institutionalization for typical traditional program youths.[7] Thus, external control—in the form of direct, physical restraint—was used in CTP and the traditional program alike; however, its usage was far greater within the latter.

Central Findings: Societal-Centered Outcomes

Findings *A* through *D*, below, summarize the main results from Phases 1 through 3. In reviewing these results the following might be kept in mind. Findings *A* and *B* are based on Bureau of Criminal Identification rapsheets, which list all recorded law enforcement arrests and court convictions—non–Youth Authority actions, in both cases. Thus, the findings reflect *illegal activities* ("youth behavior") plus court actions resulting from those activities; they are not a function of policy-based ("discretionary" or "differential") decision-making by YA staff—CTP, regular parole, board, or other. (Policy-based decision-making, which influenced such actions as parole revocation, reinstitutionalization, and unfavorable discharge from the YA, are dealt with in a separate analysis: the analysis of "parole failure," often referred to as "recidivism.") Also, although minor offenses, status offenses, and technical violations of parole are excluded from these findings, the results are essentially unchanged when such offenses/infractions are included. Finding *D* also reflects youth behavior, not policy-based decision-making; however, see Chapter 13 for details. (Finding *C* focuses on costs only, not youth behavior as such.) The results, then, are as follows.

A. For all Valley males combined, CTP youths had far (38% to 50%) fewer arrests and convictions than their matched controls; that is, their rates were much lower.[8] This finding was especially strong relative to (1) severe offenses (e.g., burglary, felony drug violations, and felonies against persons), and, focusing *within* the severe offenses category, (2) violent offenses in particular (e.g., assault with a deadly weapon, forcible rape, robbery, and murder). The results for severe and violent offenses applied to Valley and San Francisco youths alike, and they were especially strong with respect to individuals described as "conflicted"—youths who comprised about 60 percent of all males within the two settings combined. On the other hand, CTP was *less* effective than the traditional program with "power-oriented" males, at least with those described as "manipulative"; in addition, CTP was neither more nor less effective with females, again with respect to arrests and convictions.[9]

B. The YA's traditional program clearly provided the community with more short-term protection than did CTP, since most traditional program youths (controls) were first locked up for approximately nine months before being paroled. However, once released from the institution, controls soon began committing offenses at a much higher rate than CTP youths—none of whom had been initially institutionalized. As a result, beginning about four years from initial commitment to the YA and continuing for at least several more years—thereby extending well beyond YA discharge—traditional-program youths had accumulated substantially more offenses than those on CTP. (Within less than two years from initial commitment, the number of accumulated offenses was *equal* across the two programs.) In effect, the numerous arrests that were chalked up by these youths while they (controls) were at risk in the community were not offset by the *absence* of arrests while they were in lockup. Thus, incapacitation notwithstanding, CTP ended up providing more long-term protection to the community than did the traditional program, particularly in relation to conflicted, though not power-oriented, youths. This finding (and Finding C, below) pertains to analyses that were made for Valley youths only, specifically, males; it would probably have remained much the same even if controls had initially been locked up twice as long as they were.

C. During the most recent price period analyzed (1971–1972), Youth Authority ca-

reer costs were $1,049 lower per CTP youth than per control. When non-YA costs (county expenses for arrests, detentions, and adjudications; prison and parole costs subsequent to YA discharge; etc.) were added, the overall savings to society was estimated at $4,545 per CTP youth. This cost difference mainly resulted from the larger number of arrests on the part of controls and from their greater tendency to commit violent offenses—acts that often resulted in long periods of lockup. The estimated savings would probably have been about twice as large by the early 1980s and three times larger as of the early 1990s. This change is mainly because incarceration costs have greatly increased since the early 1970s, and that, in turn, is apart from the fact that *length* of incarceration has itself increased for violent offenses—within and, in many cases, outside California.

D. Results from Phase 3 indicated that: (1) most juvenile and adult court first commitments who should *not* be directly released to the community can be accurately identified at intake; (2) when these individuals begin their treatment/ control in a specific type of institutional setting, their rate of offending can be sharply (50% plus) reduced relative to that of similar individuals who *are* directly released to the community; (3) youths and young adults with seriously assaultive committing offenses do not necessarily require long periods of incarceration; (4) the concepts, the intervention methods, and the program operations that were used during Phases 1 and 2 (Valley as well as San Francisco) were also applicable to older, often very seriously delinquent, adult court commitments. At any rate, although many seriously delinquent youths and young adults can begin their treatment/control in the community, many others would best begin within given institutional settings.

Table 14–1 summarizes Findings *A* through *C* for Phase 1 and 2 Valley males, separate by youth group. Together with Phase 3 results, these findings mainly focus on societal-centered goals: community protection and reduced costs. Next, we will compare

TABLE 14-1

Performance or Utility of CTP versus Traditional Program, Relative to Societal Goals[a]

Goals	Youths[b]			Total Group[c]
	Conflicted	Power-Oriented	Passive-Conformist	
More short-term protection[d]	C	C	C	C
More long-term protection[d]	E	C	E	E
Lower costs[e]	E	C	E	E

[a]"C," in table, means: traditional program outperformed CTP. "E" means: CTP outperformed traditional program.
[b]Phase 1 and 2, Valley males.
[c]Includes Rare Types, as defined earlier.
[d]Fewer illegal activities by youths.
[e]Combines short- and long-term costs.

CTP and the traditional program in terms of five *offender-centered* goals that are often distinguished from community protection and costs per se. These relate to reduced labeling, reduced coercion and control, more service and assistance, better school and/or work adjustment, and more positive attitude change.

Additional Results: Offender-Centered Outcomes

Labeling and Stigmatization

The significance of reduced labeling and stigmatization derives from the widely held view that the farther a youth moves into the formal justice system and the longer he is exposed to it, the greater his chance of being negatively labeled by others, of developing a delinquent or criminal self-image (assuming he did not have one before), and of being stigmatized and materially hampered at a later date. In short, according to labeling theorists, the justice system, together with some of the youth's experiences while part of that system, is viewed as a major contributor to the youngster's troubles. Added difficulties can result from or be increased by the youth's official record and by his status as a ward of the court or state. The fact of having been labeled and stigmatized is, itself, thought to further predispose the youth toward delinquency or criminality. Although some components of labeling theory lack strong scientific support, the basic concepts—labeling and stigmatization—merit consideration. In our view they supplement rather than replace other accounts of delin-

quency and criminality (Becker, 1963; Lemert, 1967, 1971; Tannenbaum, 1938).

CTP probably provided less negative labeling and stigmatization than the traditional program. This assessment is not based on specific analytic findings from the present experiment; instead, it reflects the following assumptions: (1) *Not being* institutionalized will usually involve, ipso facto, less social labeling (official or otherwise) and less self-labeling than *being* institutionalized; (2) being worked with in an intensive, justice-system-operated community program will usually involve less labeling than being worked with in an institution; (3) the situations mentioned in (1) and (2) will usually result in less stigmatization as well. In any case, it would be difficult to argue not only the opposite view, for example, that CTP provided more labeling and stigmatization (l/s) than the traditional program, but one that might postulate equal amounts instead, for example, equal l/s across the latter programs.

Coercion and Control

The significance of reducing coercion and control derives from the view that, in general, societal agencies exert too much control over too many people, juvenile offenders being a prime example (Chambliss and Seidman, 1971; Lerman, 1975; Quinney, 1970, 1974; Schur, 1971). For instance, it is widely believed that many offenders should be given neither the type nor amount of control they receive, whether in probation or while under state jurisdiction; to be sure, opposite as well as intermediate views also exist. Our own position is that the goal of reducing external controls, although appropriate in numerous contexts, necessarily coexists with society's need to maintain *sufficient* controls, especially with multiple offenders. At any rate, despite the public's steadily and sometimes sharply growing concern with crime since the later 1960s, and despite its increasing call for strong external controls, interest in reducing social controls and coercion slightly *decreased* among numerous academicians, researchers, and policymakers between the early 1970s and early 1980s; it remained relatively constant, or perhaps slightly increased, during the subsequent decade.

Theories and positions aside, the situation was as follows with regard to the present experiment. (1) Since experimentals and controls had identical legal status while under Youth Authority jurisdiction, *underlying or implicit coercion* was, qualitatively speaking, identical within CTP and the traditional program. At the same time, *direct or explicit coercion* may have differed across these programs, both in type and amount; however, this possible difference was not explored. Finally, prior as well as subsequent to YA discharge, C's experienced a slightly larger "quantity" of implicit coercion than E's, since they remained under state and local jurisdiction for a somewhat longer time; here, all periods of parole, probation, and lockup were combined.

(2) CTP involved less external control than the traditional program. This assessment reflects the widely held view that long-term institutionalization is the quintessence of such control, especially if it occurs in geographically isolated areas and within closely guarded facilities. As described in Chapter 10 (Figure 10–4, page 133), controls spent an average of 14 more months in lockup than experimentals during their YA and post-YA periods combined, and most such lockup occurred in the earlier-mentioned types of areas and/or facilities.

Service and Assistance

Many practitioners and policymakers consider it appropriate to provide direct service and assistance (s/a) to offenders; this is despite often-voiced criticisms regarding the coercive nature of correctional intervention and despite frequently expressed doubts about its effectiveness

(regarding doubts, see Conrad, 1973, 1978, 1982a, 1982b; Greenberg, 1977; Martinson, 1974; Robison and Smith, 1971). (S/a—although recognized as a form of intervention—is not necessarily viewed as a form of "treatment.") In general, they view the providing of service and assistance as a humane and/or pragmatically sound activity that is justified whether or not illegal behavior and short-term costs are thereby reduced (Cullen and Gilbert, 1982; Romig, 1978; Ross and Gendreau, 1980; Warren, 1971). (Here, *providing s/a*, which represents an offender-centered input, is distinguished from *effectiveness* and *reduced costs*, which involve societal-centered outputs.)

No assessment was made regarding the degree to which CTP and the traditional program provided service and assistance inputs. Basically, this was because the results from any such assessment would largely reflect the specific s/a areas that would be analyzed and the particular weights that would be assigned to each. More specifically, the findings would depend on which of the following areas (and other possible areas) would be evaluated and on how many points—in effect, how much relative importance—would be given to each: personal life, family, peers, placement, schooling, and employment. If all such areas were included but more points were given to the first two, CTP would probably have a built-in advantage; however, if more points were allotted to the last two, the opposite might well apply. Even if all areas were given *equal* weight, a central question would remain: How can one measure service and assistance in a way that gives each "input unit" essentially the same meaning in all s/a areas, for example, in both the personal life and employment areas? In short, how can one validly compare different areas with respect to amount of input? This question applies within and across differing programs, and, as implied, differing programs justifiably emphasize different s/a areas in the first place.

Despite the difficulties of comparing E's and C's in this regard, it is clear that both offender groups received considerable service and assistance. E's received s/a input in roughly equal amounts throughout much of their YA career. C's received most of their input while in lockup, not during parole.

School and Work

As indicated in Chapters 8 and 12, experimentals performed slightly better than con-

TABLE 14-2

Performance or Utility of CTP versus Traditional Program, Relative to Offender-Centered Goals[a]

		Youths[b]		
Goals	Conflicted	Power-Oriented	Passive-Conformist	Total Group[c]
Less labeling and stigmatization[d]	E	E	E	E
Less coercion and control	E	E	E	E
More service and assistance	*	*	*	*
Better school and work adjustment	E	—	C	—
Positive attitude change	—	E	—	E

[a]"E," in table, means: CTP outperformed traditional program. "C" means: traditional program outperformed CTP. "*" means: difficult to compare CTP and traditional programs (see text). "—" means: no significant, substantial, or otherwise clear performance difference between CTP and traditional program.
[b]Phase 1 and 2, Valley males.
[c]Includes Rare Types, as defined earlier.
[d]See text regarding assumptions.

trols with respect to school adjustment; however, no consistent or substantial difference was found relative to work adjustment. Thus, E's and C's performed at roughly the same level regarding school and work combined; however, this finding applied to parole only, since no analyses were made relative to post-discharge.[10]

Attitudes
As indicated earlier, E's showed more positive attitude change than C's from pretest to posttest. This change referred to social and personal adjustment as measured by the California Psychological Inventory (youth's self-report); however, as with school and work, post-YA adjustment was not assessed.

Table 14-2 summarizes these offender-centered results for Phase 1 and 2 Valley males, separate by youth group.

General Implications
1. Community-based programming, in this case individualized intervention, can substantially reduce a wide range of moderate and severe illegal activities on the part of numerous multiple offenders. Given today's high crime rate, this finding means that individualized intervention can play a valuable role relative to

criminal justice and society overall. It contradicts the view that intervention which focuses on individuals does not work or makes no difference.
2. Community-based programming can substantially reduce *violence* among these same male offenders. Given today's atmosphere of violence and the public's continued feeling of vulnerability in this regard, this finding is especially timely. It means that long-term lockup is not the only way to address violent crime.
3. These reductions can occur in highly as well as moderately urbanized environments, and with each major ethnic group. Together with point #8, below, this suggests that individualized intervention has relevance to a wide spectrum of society.
4. These reductions can be achieved at a long-term savings of several thousand dollars per youth, using traditional program costs plus non–Youth Authority and postdischarge costs as the basis of comparison. Given today's increasing financial constraints, the importance of these savings is self-evident. Such savings would be even larger if, in response to today's pressure for ever harsher punishment, or for purposes of increased incapacitation, length of incarceration were increased.

5. Community-based programming can be implemented in a humane way and can reflect substantial youth involvement in the process of change. If society's need for protection is not jeopardized by such programming, the implementation and expression of these principles and/or social ideals might more easily be accepted as a "plus"; in addition, such principles might then be judged, at least primarily, as something other than means to practical ends. The same might apply to the fact that, with rare exceptions, multiple offenders apparently prefer CTP's type of community programming to traditional institutionalization.

6. The reductions mentioned in points #1 and #2 *can* be achieved in community settings without increasing—in fact, while decreasing—the intermediate- and long-term risk to those communities. In this respect long-term lockup need not be viewed as the only viable approach, perhaps not even the best overall approach, to community protection, relative to numerous multiple offenders. This applies regardless of how humane the institutional environment might be and despite, say, the proportionality, consistency, general balance, and, in those respects, the overall fairness and equality that may be involved in each individual's sentence. (Also see point #10.) At base, the reductions in question mean that specified types of community programming can be more effective than, not just *as* effective as, traditional programming.

7. The reductions and savings would be increased if power-oriented youths were excluded from or deemphasized in CTP-type programs. This does not mean that few such individuals can profit from such programs; instead, it reflects the fact that traditional programming is somewhat more effective than CTP's community approach in reducing the illegal behaviors of this group, and is less expensive as well. (These youths probably constitute 15 percent to 25 percent of all young multiple offenders, whether in probation or on parole.)

8. Multiple offenders under 16 years of age at intake are just as amenable to a community-based approach as those 16 and over. This and other findings suggest that "maturation" or "simply growing up" is not, in itself, the critical or even primary ingredient in reducing the illegal behavior of these youths. Insofar as this is true, one would probably be ill-advised to "wait these individuals out" and simply hope their behavior patterns will decisively change within a few years, without considerable input from given individuals. (Recall the rapidly accelerating arrest rates on the part of multiple offenders during the two years preceding commitment [Chapter 10]. Moreover, this acceleration occurred with respect to individuals who were younger, middle, or already older adolescents at the time; that is, it occurred regardless of their age.) Thus, although a "hands off" or perhaps "minimal involvement" policy might be appropriate for certain individuals, for example, many first-time offenders, such a policy would probably be inadequate for almost all multiple offenders, with regard to the goal of reducing illegal behavior. In sum, whatever the age of these adolescents may be, intensive and/or extensive intervention seems much more likely to produce substantial reductions in illegal behavior than does maturation alone, within a two- or three-year period. At the very least, individualized intervention can accelerate or facilitate such change.

9. Many multiple offenders require at least several months of institutionalization prior to being paroled. Most such offenders can be identified at intake, and when many such youths are first worked with in an individually oriented facility and are *then* released to an intensive/extensive community program, their rate of offending can be markedly reduced.[11] At any rate, a "pure" community approach—that is, no initial institutionalization—is not appropriate for all multiple offenders. This includes many individuals whose records contain no seriously assaultive offenses and many who are not classified as power-oriented. Institutions are not yet a thing of the past.

10. A *more* controlling approach, for example, long-term lockup, does not always result in less illegal behavior than a *less* controlling approach, for example,

community-based intervention such as CTP. That is, the effectiveness of one such approach as compared to another will vary depending on the overall "power" of the *specific* programs involved and on the specific goal or goals in question. (For example, as shown in Phases 1 and 2, a heavily controlling, traditional approach can be less powerful than a moderately controlling, CTP-type community approach, relative to reducing the illegal behavior of particular youth types.) Given this finding, it would seem appropriate for criminal justice personnel, among others, to reassess and specifically address a view that has been common since the late 1970s: The heavier and/or stricter the external controls, the greater the resulting deterrence—at any rate, the better the outcome in terms of reduced illegal behavior.

11. If parole were abolished as a criminal justice tool, institutions and local detention facilities would probably be expected to assume an even larger role than they already have, with respect to protecting society. However, if parole were retained, an expanded role would not be necessary (in fact, a reduced role might be possible) *if* effective community alternatives were indeed available. More specifically, such expansion would be unnecessary for numerous multiple offenders, relative to the goal of intermediate- and long-term community protection.

12. Community-based programming can involve less labeling and stigmatization, and less external control than traditional programming. Thus, it can bear on offender-centered, not just societal-centered, goals. More specifically, it can successfully address goals other than those of community protection and cost reduction alone.

13. Reduced illegal behavior is not always associated with better school and work adjustment during parole, at least with certain youths. For instance, while passive-conformists in CTP had less illegal behavior than their controls, their school and work adjustment was somewhat worse than that of the latter. Thus, the achievement of long-term societal goals—such as greater community protection—is not always paralleled by that of specific offender-centered goals.[12] By the same token, positive *attitude-change* is not always accompanied by reduced illegal behavior.[13]

14. CTP and the traditional program provided approximately equal community protection in connection with female offenders. That is, relative to long-term arrests and convictions, neither program outperformed the other.

Notes

1. The YA commitment offense is included when counting pre-CTP offenses.

2. The latter individual had overall responsibility for two parole offices or their equivalent—for example, two CTP offices, as in Setting A, or one CTP and one non-CTP office (namely, GGI), as in Setting B.

3. Some combinations seemed more common than others, for example, (1) under-socialization/poor impulse control *plus* desire for material gain, (2) peer pressures plus subgroup expectations (see endnote 4), and (3) personal conflicts plus family binds.

4. In the present context, *subgroup expectations* usually relate to inputs or situations such as the following: (1) slights or insults to the youth's integrity or manhood; (2) insults concerning the youth's girlfriend, date, sister, mother, or friends (e.g., his group or gang); (3) invasions of, or challenges to, the group's or gang's "turf" (geographic or other). More specifically, the youth (delinquent) has directly learned, or has other reasons for believing, that various people he knows—or who may know him—would view him in a positive or at least nonnegative light if his usual responses to such inputs included counter-insults, counter-challenges, and, quite often, physical attacks. Thus, subgroup expectations (as used here), involve selected, essentially predefined inputs or situations that center largely on issues of integrity, honor, and territoriality, and that may result in more or less patterned, overt responses by the youth; the expectations in question focus on these prescribed, patterned responses in particular. Subgroups that hold or are thought to hold such expectations frequently consist of (1) relatively

few, occasionally delinquent, friends and acquaintances or (2) equally few, but often delinquent, gang members. However, such subgroups may also, or alternatively, include (3) numerous, rarely delinquent, friends and acquaintances—peers, and even occasional adults, from more than one ethnic group or socioeconomic class. Thus, although "inputs" and "expectations" are fairly specific and uniform, "subgroups," collectively, are much more general and varied. *Peer pressures* do not focus on patterned responses to predefined inputs. Instead, they involve requests, appeals, exhortations, challenges, and/or direct demands for an individual to participate in various illegal or borderline activities. These requests/demands are often made on the spur of the moment, frequently by members of a group or gang; however, they are often repeated several times and commonly involve one or more of the following: truanting, drinking, smoking marijuana, creating disturbances, fighting, car racing, reckless driving, "malicious mischief", "making out" with any available girls, petty theft, vehicle tampering, and burglary. In addition to "just having a good time," "letting loose," and "killing time," the major though generally unstated goals of these activities often include: (1) demonstrating independence from or rejection of various parental and societal controls and/or values; (2) positively impressing given individuals, usually girls; (3) outsmarting, playing a joke on, or defying "the system"; and/or (4) embarrassing, angering, or turning the tables on adults. Usually implicit is the idea that the individual's participation in one or more such activities will demonstrate not only his "coolness," daring, courage, toughness, masculinity, or overall adequacy and skill, but his reliability, loyalty, and, in a sense, overall value to the given peers—and, thus, the appropriateness of his continued association with those individuals.

5. For example, the following was implicitly assumed: In the final analysis, illegal acts have been—and, by definition, must be—*performed* (executed); they have not been merely *shaped* or "set up" (but still not

executed). Like legal acts themselves, they have been performed by *individuals,* not by social, family, or other external *forces* (conditions). This is literally and specifically true even though these forces may have largely shaped many of the attitudes and perceptions that are expressed in—or have perhaps mediated—the given act, and may even have largely "set up" the individuals in question. Thus, although numerous forces may have helped foster or facilitate a given act, and may in this respect have been partly responsible for its occurrence, the act itself has still been carried out by the actor alone. In carrying out this act, the actor/offender has made an additional—more important, a decisive—contribution of his own. Because of the specific or additional responsibility and social consequences associated with this action, he has greatly contributed to his own difficulties. (This was not the only way in which offenders were often seen as having contributed to their difficulties.) This view was regarded as neither inconsistent with nor negated by the fact that offenders sometimes act—legally and illegally—in response to economic deprivation, short-term or otherwise.

6. Here, in addition to vocational, educational, and general-information dimensions, *coping* also included interpersonal skills, and *deficiencies* also included emotional vulnerabilities.

7. By 1967, few controls were directly released to parole after first being committed to the YA. Almost all were institutionalized, instead.

8. Other indices of effectiveness also favored CTP. These included: (1) 24-months *recidivism,* (2) rate of favorable discharge from YA, (3) school adjustment, (4) attitude change from pretest to posttest, and (5) rate of offending as compared to a pre-YA time period. CTP and the traditional program performed at about the same level with regard to *paid employment.*

9. These results for males and females applied primarily to the parole period, counting all risk time in the community and excluding all lockup time. However, they basically held up during an approximately seven-year parole plus post-YA-discharge period as well, again counting

risk time only. (In Finding *B* [see text that follows], all lockup time was added to all risk time.)

10. School adjustment was largely measured by percentage of youths who advanced in school, number of grades they advanced, percentage of youths who were unfavorably removed from school, and percentage of youths who dropped out. Work adjustment was measured by number of jobs held, number of days worked, and percentage of youths who were unfavorably dismissed from their job. See Appendix 13.

11. The cost savings for these individuals might be smaller than for those who could be directly released to the community. Even so, it would probably remain substantial, considering the reduced institution time that is possible. See Chapter 13.

12. Although this point applies to CTP youths *versus* controls, for example, E's versus C's, we did not have the type and quality of pre-YA data that would allow us to determine definitely if E's and C's *each* had better school and work adjustment after a year or two on parole than at point of *intake*. (In the latter case, E's would be compared with E's and C's would be compared with C's.)

13. Separate from this relationship, E and C youth groups—plus the E and C total groups—*each* showed improved attitudes at posttest as compared to intake. (As to conflicted E's versus conflicted C's in particular, see Chapter 8 regarding the difference in attitude change between assertive-deniers and anxious-confused youths. In brief, the results for these subgroups canceled each other out and, in effect, obscured the specific relationships—one positive, one negative—between attitude change and illegal behavior among conflicted youths.)

15 KEY FACTORS IN PERFORMANCE

What factors seemed responsible for reduced illegal behavior among CTP as compared to traditional program youths? More specifically, what accounted for the better performance of experimentals than controls among particular youth groups? Also, which factors seemed responsible for the roughly equal, that is, comparable, amount of illegal behavior among other E's and C's? As will be seen, the responsible factors were similar but not identical across the several groups.

In addressing these questions we will focus on Phase 1 and 2 males, Valley and San Francisco alike. Phase 3 males—specifically, its Status 1 group (youths whose program should begin in an institutional setting)—will be reviewed in Chapter 16, as will Phase 1 and 2 females. As suggested, *performance* will refer to youth behavior and will involve the same rates of offending that were presented in Chapters 8–14. Thus, "key factors" that will be described relate to the societal-centered goal of community protection, specifically, to reduced illegal behavior. They do not necessarily relate to, and do not directly focus on, the offender-centered goals of reduced labeling and stigmatization, reduced coercion and control, increased service and assistance, better school and/or work adjustment, and more positive attitude change. However, as seen earlier, some of the latter goals are positively related to the former, and given this situation, certain key factors may also bear on offender-centered goals.

Though this and the following chapter focus on performance, they do not assess the feasibility, for example, the operational practicality, of CTP. Feasibility will be addressed in Chapters 17–20 and will take account of

factors that are identified here. Finally, since the present chapter contains numerous details and lengthy descriptions, readers who are chiefly interested in its general conclusions might review Table 15–1 and then skip directly to the "Summary of Key Factors." This summary, and the "General Observations" that follow, largely apply to Chapter 16 as well.

Concepts and Approaches

Concepts

Ten factors made either major or substantial contributions to the reduced or approximately equal illegal behavior of E's as compared to C's. These factors were grouped into four broad areas: conditions of intervention, approaches to intervention, change agents (workers), and global program features. These groupings or areas are shown in Figure 15–1, together with the factors included in each. Some factors consisted of two main subfactors; and, as will be seen, not all factors or subfactors seemed important to every youth group.

(Regarding terminology: In Figure 15–1, "Small caseloads" means approximately 12 youths per worker. "Long-term contacts" means two or more years.[1] "Explicit, detailed guidelines" refers to CTP's preestablished treatment/control prescriptions. "Positive reputation" mainly refers to CTP's then-current "winner image"—in effect, its "aura of success" among most local YA wards and even many probationers. "Positive expectations" refers to the staff's general feeling of confidence in the overall program, and to their typically optimistic outlook regarding almost all youths' chances of succeeding in, or at least

A. *Conditions of Intervention*	B. *Approaches to Intervention*
1. Small caseloads 2. Intensive and/or extensive contacts 3. Long-term contacts	4. Explicit, detailed guidelines 5. Individualization; flexible programming
C. *Change Agents (Workers)*	D. *Global Program Features*
6. Personal characteristics; professional orientation 7. Specific abilities; overall perceptiveness	8. Community setting 9. Substitute for institutionalization 10. Positive reputation; positive expectations

Figure 15–1. Ten key factors, grouped into four areas.

clearly profiting from, the program under various conditions. This feeling and outlook were fairly obvious to most youths. Regarding "Individualization," see endnote 2.)

Each of the four areas reflects a somewhat different kind of influence. For example, "conditions of Intervention" involves what might be called "background" or facilitating (also supportive) factors—characteristics that define and legitimize the range of operational possibilities, and thereby set the stage for particular program activities. In establishing this range and in prescribing general expectations, these factors give organizational, that is, structural and formal, expression to CTP's principles and assumptions, mentioned earlier. "Approaches to Intervention" helps channel and specifically focus (concretize) the broad range of potential, legitimized program activities. Together with "Change Agents (Workers)," it involves what may be described as "foreground" or directive (also motivating) factors; in the case of change agents it involves "modeling" features as well. These broad groupings (areas B and C) thus help determine the scope and nature of most staff/youth and staff/other interactions. Finally, "Global Program Features" refers to aspects of the overall program—CTP as a totality—that can influence a youth's initial and longer-term response to its separate parts, for example, to the intervention plan or even to specific components such as school, short-term detention, and out-of-home placement.

Several factors were interrelated. For instance, small caseloads (factor #1) were, in effect, a prerequisite for factors #2, #3, #4, and #5, at least as implemented in CTP. Specifically,

without such caseloads, intensive and/or extensive (i/e) contacts could not have occurred to the degree they did in CTP. Similarly, given this level of i/e interaction, *long-term* contacts would not have been possible without small caseloads, and without i/e interaction, CTP's preestablished guidelines could have been implemented only sketchily. Finally, irrespective of these or other possible guidelines, individualization, as described in Chapter 14 and earlier, could have only occasionally been implemented within a standard-sized caseload. This, too, was largely a matter of time and logistics.

In later chapters we will touch on such questions as, Would less intensive/extensive contact have been equally effective? and Would less individualization have sufficed? Regardless of the answers that emerge (possible tradeoffs included), small caseloads can, for now, be considered essential to CTP's operation; as a result, this factor will seldom be singled out in the sections that follow. Small caseloads aside, and interrelationships among factors notwithstanding, three or four factors or subfactors usually stood out from the rest in accounting for reduced or comparable illegal behavior. This will be seen relative to specified youths.

Approaches

We will briefly mention several major characteristics of the approaches that were used in assessing the impact of the just-mentioned factors (viewed as "inputs") on any given youth group. Because of the complexity involved in the approaches themselves, specific details have been placed in Appendix 31. Before proceeding, it might be noted that the 10 key factors were not delineated and formally designated as such during Phases 1 and 2, even though several had been hypothesized prior to the end of Phase 1 and although most were discussed in various forms and contexts by researchers and operations staff throughout both phases. In essence, the major characteristics of these approaches are as follows.

Based on several types and sources of information (direct observations, routine documentation, follow-up staffings, informal discussions, and formal interviews), short- and intermediate-term changes in *youth behavior* (performance) were often identified as resulting from specifiable types and levels of *input* (e.g., given intensities of youth/agent contact). Some inputs—more specifically, input changes from one time-period to another—seemed more powerful than others with respect to producing these performance changes. Whatever the former's power, several years of informal observations and comparisons by researchers and others were necessary in order to identify most input/output (performance) sequences with a fair amount of confidence, and to separate causal sequences from mere temporal contiguities.

Together, these sequences or relationships—the more powerful ones and the less powerful ones combined—helped researchers and operations staff form converging impressions regarding: (1) how much impact given factors had on youth behavior and other aspects of adjustment, and (2) the importance of given factors as compared to others. With the partial exception of factors #6 and #7 (change-agent dimensions), these impressions were not the result of quantitative or highly systematized analyses, controlled experimentation included. Nevertheless, they were based on large amounts and a broad range of detailed information—literally thousands of statements, impressions, and reactions—from individuals who were actively and directly involved with respect to the inputs and performance changes in question, namely, parole agents and youths. (Short- and intermediate-term inputs often linked up with long-term outcomes, those derived from BCI rapsheets. The latter outcomes were used in the statistical analysis of change-agent dimensions.)

Despite the above, CTP's study design did not make it possible to focus on each individual factor in a controlled, systematic way. Thus, converging impressions and detailed qualitative information notwithstanding, it was impossible to *quantify* the contribution that individual factors made to various performance changes, and to develop refined distinctions—including, for example, a complete ranking of all factors—with regard to their relative importance. Instead, such impressions centered around, in fact were limited to, three broad distinctions within each of two areas: (1) *overall level of impact* ("very important"; "important"; "of slight importance"); and, (2) *relative impact* ("more important than"; "about as important as"; "less important than"). Perhaps the most systematic observations—those that, in addition, *were* subject to statistical analyses concerning impact on youth behavior—related to factors #6 and #7 (Palmer, 1967a). Results from these analyses (therefore, for these particular factors) served as external reference points against which the remaining factors were partly assessed with respect to those three broad distinctions, relative to each of several youth groups.

Thus, the present approaches to assessing key factors were the outgrowth of a long-term "natural experiment" in which often-repeated, and also often-varying, inputs were studied in relation to various levels of "output" (performance). Although quite different from and vastly better than mere guesswork or speculation, these approaches were not a first-rate substitute for specifically focused and carefully controlled experimentation. Nevertheless, given CTP's study design, they were the only approaches available, and they did seem able to support the distinctions mentioned earlier. As a result, they helped bridge the gap between empirically untested hypotheses, on the one hand, and refined experimental results, on the other.

(In the following, the manipulator subgroup within the power-oriented category is not discussed; this is because the CTP youths who comprised this subgroup performed, on balance, slightly worse than their controls. This outcome applied to the matched plus unmatched youths combined, though the *matched* CTP manipulators [Mp's] generally outperformed the control Mp's [Chapter 11]. Regarding these matched CTP youths, the factors that seemed to make the largest contribution to this positive outcome were #1, #2, #6, and #7 [see Table 15–1]. As with the remaining power-oriented subgroup, namely, the group conformists, factors #3, #4, #5, #8, and #9 also contributed.)

Key Factors
Factors #1 through #7
Conflicted Youths

Besides small caseloads, several factors made substantial contributions to the reduced illegal behavior of conflicted E's. Although these factors spanned all areas mentioned earlier, those categorized as "Global Program Features" will be reviewed later in this chapter. As shown in Table 15–1 and as described below, almost all factors within the first three areas seemed either very important or moderately important for most conflicted E's—assertive-deniers and anxious-confused alike. ("Very important" and "moderately important" [or "important"] will be synonymous with "major contribution" and "substantial (or moderate) contribution," respectively.)

Among *assertive-deniers* (A-D's), intensive/extensive contacts, individualization/flexible programming, and the change agent (both factors) seemed very important in reducing illegal behavior. Other factors, for example, utilization of CTP's preestablished guidelines, were also important, but not as central. Regarding the former factors or areas, extensive contacts, detailed diagnosis, careful staffing, and the agent's personal characteristics plus his specific abilities and overall perceptiveness often stood out above the remaining components or subfactors in terms of importance.[3] (Detailed diagnosis and careful staffing were components of individualization, as was detailed placement planning.) Intensive contacts often seemed more important during the first several months than in subsequent stages.

With most A-D's, the main underlying difficulties or issues addressed, by the preceding factors (#2, #5, #6, and #7), were: personal conflicts, family "binds," long-term overcompensations, and poor impulse control. (Less common, yet occasionally important, were: family disorganization, antisocial or antiauthority family orientation, and subgroup expectations.)[4] Although these issues were seldom fully resolved, they were usually reduced or substantially modified—enough, apparently, to affect illegal behavior. The four factors impacted these issues mainly by helping to achieve two of CTP's three major subgoals or subgoal components, particularly the first: change in perception of self and others (especially others), and expansion of external support. Two such factors—intensive/extensive contacts, and individualization/flexible programming—also helped redirect, though not greatly expand, the individual's already present coping abilities (these abilities were the focus of CTP's second subgoal; see Figure 14–2, page 232).

Changes in the youths' view of others—adults/authority figures, and peers—seemed important in accounting for reduced violence among these often aggressive and sometimes openly hostile individuals. In this regard it generally seemed as if the youths' anger toward others had diminished and as if they considered their surroundings—specific individuals and types of individuals included—less hostile, threatening, arbitrary, "stupid," and/or indifferent. In light of such changes these youths felt less reason to lash out (physically or verbally), ridicule, challenge, defy, intimidate, intrude, domineer, or simply take what they wanted. In this respect, their give-and-take relationship with a nonrejecting change agent appeared to play a large role in reducing not only their negative stereotypes but their highly defensive and often abrasive stance. Their relatively candid and frequently confrontive interactions with peers in their "treatment group" contributed as well, that is, when this program element was in fact used.

All in all, such experiences seemed to help assertive-deniers better understand the attitudes and feelings of others and the impact of their own behavior on those individuals. These reductions and improvements—even when accompanied by only minor behavioral and attitudinal changes in individuals around them—often helped to (1) increase the youths' level of impulse control and (2) either preclude potentially "vicious cycles," for example, mutually escalated aggression among two individuals, or defuse already tense situations.

Among *anxious-confused* (A-C) youths, two of the primary factors mentioned earlier were again central to reduced illegal behavior. These were: intensive/extensive contacts and individualization/flexible programming. The change agent—mainly his abilities/perceptiveness and, to a lesser extent, his professional orientation—was moderately important, as were CTP's preestablished guidelines.[5] (However, the change-agent factor or subfactor—including abilities/perceptiveness and professional orientation—was probably very important with regard to *highly vulnerable or disturbed* A-C's.) These guidelines contained not only a

TABLE 15-1

Factors Contributing to Reduced or Comparable Illegal Behavior among Experimental Males, by Youth Group and Subtype

Area and Factor	Youth Group and Subtype[a]				
	Conflicted		Passive-Conformist	Power-Oriented	
	Assertive-Denier	Anxious-Confused	Passive-Conformist	Group Conformist[b]	Manipulator
Conditions of Intervention					
1. Small caseloads	++	++	++	++	n.a.
2. Intensive and/or extensive contacts	++	++	++	++	n.a.
3. Long-term contacts	o	+	++	+	n.a.
Approaches to Intervention					
4. Explicit, detailed guidelines	+	+	++	+	n.a.
5. Individualization; flexible programming	++	++	++	+	n.a.
Change Agents (Workers)[c]					
6. Personal characteristics; professional orientation	++[d]	+[e]	++	+[e]	n.a.
7. Specific abilities; overall perceptiveness	++	+[f]	+[g]	+	n.a.
Global Program Features					
8. Community setting	+	o	+	+[h]	n.a.
9. Substitute for institutionalization	+	+	+	+[h]	n.a.
10. Positive reputation; positive expectations	o	+	+	o	n.a.

a "++" means: major contribution. "+" means: substantial (or moderate) contribution. "o" means: neither major nor substantial contribution; i.e., no apparently distinctive contribution, or only a slight contribution, to reduced or comparable illegal behavior among E's as compared to C's. "n.a." means: factor not applicable, since E's performed slightly though not significantly worse than C's during parole + postdischarge combined.

b Group conformist E's and C's performed at about the same level during parole + postdischarge combined.

c Factor #6 was the primary basis for agent/youth matching (Chapter 11). Regarding factor #7, see endnote 3.

d Mainly personal characteristics.

e Mainly professional orientation.

f See text, (pp. 177, 181, 248–249) regarding highly vulnerable/disturbed A-C youths.

g Mainly overall perceptiveness, e.g., level of professional sophistication. See Palmer (1967a), regarding notes d, e, and g.

h Applies to "accessible" G-C's only (pp. 253–255).

set of strategies and "opening moves" that were relevant to almost all A-C's, but several useful suggestions and possible alternatives for later on. However, by themselves, they seldom provided adequate individualization and, in this respect, a basis for choosing between various alternatives.

Long-term contacts (factor #3) seemed more important than with most assertive-deniers, at least for the numerous anxious-confused youths who were rather vulnerable interpersonally or were largely unprepared to cope with standard external demands in age-appropriate ways.[6] Yet, a substantial minority (20% to 25%) of A-C's were in reasonably *good* shape both interpersonally and in terms of everyday coping skills; therefore, they often received neither long-term contacts nor the usual intensity and/or range of interactions. In effect, these individuals, although fairly "anxious," were only moderately "confused" and seldom unable to cope.

With most anxious-confused youths—the fairly weak plus the relatively strong—the main underlying difficulties or issues that were addressed by the preceding factors and subfactors (#2, #5, #6, and #7) corresponded to those found among assertive-deniers: personal conflict, family binds, and so on. (Family disorganization and antisocial or anti-authority family orientations sometimes entered the picture as well.) However, impulse control was less often a major issue, and long-term overcompensations—their existence and extent—were often less obvious at intake. Because of the latter, the significance and possible chronicity of various adaptations were sometimes easier to overlook. Nevertheless, with *highly* vulnerable/confused A-C's (10% to 15% of the total), such overcompensations or adaptations *were* apparent and impulse control often was a major concern.[7] Also, with the latter youths, family disorganization was a common underlying issue.

Together, the four factors helped achieve two major subgoals or subgoal components: changes in perception of self and others (especially self), and reduction of external stress. These changes were largely achieved through various combinations of the following elements (this especially applied to the relatively weak as well as highly vulnerable/confused A-C's): counseling, pragmatically oriented interactions, out-of-home placement, collateral contacts, and material aid. To a lesser degree,

two of the main factors—intensive/extensive contacts and individualization—also helped expand, though not so much redirect, the individual's coping abilities, this being CTP's second subgoal. (With psychologically stronger, more independent A-C's, greater emphasis was usually placed on expanding external supports and, especially, on *redirecting* coping abilities that were already present; that is, these objectives received greater emphasis [1] than did reducing external stress and expanding coping abilities, and [2] than with the remaining A-C's.) Despite these efforts and achievements, underlying conflicts and family binds were seldom fully resolved. Nevertheless, they were often substantially reduced or modified.

Passive-Conformists

As shown in Table 15–1, several factors besides small caseloads made major contributions to the reduced illegal behavior of passive-conformists (P-C's): intensive/extensive contacts; long-term contacts; explicit, detailed guidelines; individualization/flexible programming; the change agent's personal characteristics/professional orientation. Among these factors (#2–#6), long-term contacts and CTP's guidelines seemed more important than with most conflicted youths. (For convenience, the term "subfactor" will no longer be distinguished from "factor.")

Before proceeding, the following might be noted. As suggested in Chapter 5, the underlying difficulties of most passive-conformists seemed to originate in negative experiences with parents or guardians; often included were domination, exploitation, overcontrol, marked inconsistency, disinterest, or emotional rejection. These early and usually long-continued experiences led to feelings of unworthiness, powerlessness, and/or inadequacy, and they often set the stage for self-fulfilling prophecies with peers or in school. Usually by the start of adolescence, such experiences and feelings—frequently combined with the youths' tendency to avoid stressful situations—had produced a relative lack of interpersonal skills, and considerable fear or distrust of adults. These early experiences varied in degree among P-C's, as did the youths' resulting view of adults and their (youths') overall optimism versus pessimism (Palmer, 1971e).[8]

By early adolescence, such events and reactions, together with the individual's related interpersonal deficiencies, had produced a strong underlying need for acceptance or at least conditional approval—that is, for acceptance/approval at almost any price. Given the emotional distance of these youths from adults, this need or strong desire made these individuals unusually vulnerable to the expectations, preferences, and demands of peers. It motivated them to readily "go along with the boys" and to prove their loyalty and worthiness in ways primarily determined by whichever group or individuals seemed willing to accept them. As would be true of many other youths in numerous adolescent contexts, the activities in which they engaged, and the "tests" they underwent, sometimes involved acts of daring and defiance, legal and otherwise.

Given (1) the passive-conformists' tendency to associate their possible failure to satisfy with a resulting harshness, ridicule, and eventual punishment or rejection by individuals whom they considered more powerful than themselves or whose approval they sought, and given (2) their strong anxiety over the possibility of ridicule or rejection, the vulnerability mentioned earlier, when operating in relation to the expectations and desires of the youths' *delinquent* peers, constituted the most common and immediate cause of or precondition to their difficulties with the law. By "immediate," we refer to triggering conditions or situations, as distinct from the early/underlying (family) or even intermediate (self-image) conditions mentioned earlier (neither of which, even in combination with each other, necessarily spelled *delinquency*). From this perspective, the following can be better understood.

With most passive-conformists, the main difficulties or issues addressed by factors #2 through #6 were peer pressures, situational entanglements, and family pressures. (Among P-C's, subgroup expectations very often went hand in hand with peer pressures; as a result, this issue will not be singled out.) All three issues were nearly always involved to a considerable degree, and they were often being worked on "simultaneously," for example, during any two- or three-week period. The five factors bore on these issues mainly in terms of, or by helping to achieve, the following subgoals or subgoal components: (1) *reduction of external stress and expansion of external supports;* (2) *expansion of coping abilities;* and (3) *changes in perception of others.* More specifically, intensive/extensive contacts (factor #2) seemed very important relative to the first subgoal; that is, considerable time and effort was usually required, generally in a number of areas, in order to reduce external stress and expand external supports. The same applied to the second subgoal listed immediately above, one which included social/interactions (interpersonal) as well as educational/employment (practical or functional) skills. Here, long-term efforts (factor #3) were also quite important, mainly because interpersonal skills developed fairly slowly in most P-C's and because these individuals had considerable catching-up to do from the start.

In most cases, project input with respect to subgoals (1) and (2), above, was largely shaped by CTP's guidelines (factor #4) for passive-conformists as a group; that is, these guidelines usually seemed appropriate, especially by 1965, and they were used to a considerable extent. In effect, they provided general direction yet also focused the agent's efforts in several respects. At the same time, input and progress relating to the second subgoal—expansion of coping abilities—reflected the influence of individualization/flexible programming (factor #5), in particular. That is, positive developments in this area occurred via a set of program elements that not only reflected *each* youth's life situation, abilities, and so on, but whose pattern was sometimes modified in light of his changing circumstances or personal growth. (These elements included, for example, individual or group counseling, schooling at the CTP center, and recreational or socializing experiences. "Pattern" referred to the specific combination of elements that were used, together with their respective priorities and the sequence in which they were implemented.)

Achievement of subgoal (1), above, centered on, and was relevant to, issues of *peer pressure* and current *family pressure.* If and as this pressure, especially the latter, was reduced or otherwise controlled, the youth was better able to advance with respect to subgoal (2). In turn, movement toward the latter subgoal was directly relevant to the issue of negative *situational entanglements,* peer-related and otherwise. That is, the better the youth's interpersonal skills and defenses, the less his vulnerability in this regard. In effect, though all three subgoals were worked on more or less simultaneously, progress regarding the first usually facilitated movement relative to the rest.

Factor #6, the agent's personal characteristics and professional orientation, helped achieve subgoal (3)'s changes in the youth's view of others, especially adults/authority figures. Here, the main developments were usually as follows. After the youth had been on CTP for a few months, the agent began to seem reasonably safe, predictable, and even fairly enjoyable to him. At any rate, in contrast to key individuals with whom the youth had often interacted or was still interacting, the agent seldom appeared domineering, uninterested, overly critical, or rejecting. Given his close relationship with the youth, he began, in these and other respects, (1) to reduce or at least counter negative stereotypes of adults/authority figures, and, stereotypes aside, (2) to provide a rather new and encouraging picture of what "grown-ups" could be like. In varying degrees, this view, and that which the youth had begun to form of other project staff, slowly generalized to several nonproject adults; at least, the emotional distance between most passive-conformists and adults/authority figures often became much less than before. Together with the generalization process, the latter change was sometimes evident beginning several months after intake.

Factor #6 also modified the youth's view of his *relationship* to others, for example, by helping him feel more accepted, more valued, and, in several respects, no longer powerless or a general "nuisance." Progress in this area had direct bearing on the peer-pressures issue, since, (1) together with the anxiety reduction that related to the youth's increasingly positive view of given adults, (2) the personal satisfactions that were involved in both the present and other project-connected relationships helped shift the youth's attention and primary loyalties from delinquent to nondelinquent individuals. Changes in the youth's view of his relationship to others were also associated with project peers, for example, those with whom the individual had shared various recreational and socializing experiences.

Finally, the agent often served as a model for helping the youth learn various interpersonal skills or modes of relating to others. This modeling was built, for instance, on agent/youth, agent/agent, agent/teacher, and agent/parent interactions. Here, in essence, the youth personally experienced and observed new, apparently effective, often satisfy-ing, or, in some cases, at least not overly threatening ways in which individuals interacted on a short- and long-term basis. To a lesser degree, skills- or relationship-modeling also drew upon individuals other than the agent. That is, it centered around informal interactions between other project staff and the youth or between the given staff themselves, mainly at the CTP center (classroom; dayroom; clerical area) and in connection with outside recreational or socializing events. Together with changes in the youth's view of his relationship to various adults and project peers, these and other modeling inputs also helped change the individual's view of himself, at least to a moderate degree. In addition, they bore directly on his coping abilities with respect to nonproject peers.

Two points before proceeding to the next youths (group conformists): (1) After discharge from the Youth Authority, passive-conformist E's had 35 arrests per 1,000 months at risk as compared to 32 such arrests prior to discharge (Tables 8–1 and 8–2, pages 97 and 101, respectively). Thus, this rate of arrests did not substantially increase once the project's—more broadly, the YA's—controls and/or supports were removed. This finding is independent of the fact that passive-conformist C's performed much better after discharge than during parole (though still not better than E's); here, although controls and/or supports were also removed, arrest rates were 38 and 86 per 1,000 months at risk, respectively. This performance change suggests that, after having engaged in considerable illegal behavior prior to YA discharge (YA's controls and/or supports notwithstanding), P-C controls may have restrained themselves because of the possibility that similar behavior, if occurring subsequent to discharge, would result in lockup within non-YA facilities, specifically, in adult facilities such as a state prison. Within California—as outside—"adult lockup" was generally thought to involve "harder" and perhaps longer "time" than lockup within juvenile facilities, or simply while under YA jurisdiction. Although the idea of adult lockup may have been quite frightening to most P-C's and may have seemed like a more definite possibility to C's than E's (that is, to youths who had compiled a longer record and had already experienced considerable lockup prior to discharge), this is not the only possible explanation for the performance change in question. Nevertheless, prior to YA discharge, passive-conformist controls had a higher arrest rate than conflicted and power-oriented controls, and after discharge, their rate was lower than that of either group.

(2) As mentioned earlier, the following subgoals bore directly on issues of peer pressure and negative situational entanglement: reduction of external stress and expansion of external supports (subgoal 1, as listed earlier); and expansion of coping abilities (subgoal 2). In the San Francisco CTP unit these issues were addressed to a somewhat lesser degree than in the Valley. This occurred mainly because, in the former setting or unit, (a) out-of-home placements were more difficult to locate, (b) short-term detention was less readily available, (c) in-house recreational opportunities were more limited in scope, and (d) the school program was less elaborately developed. Given these conditions, extensive intervention (factor #2) and flexible programming (factor #5) existed to a lesser degree than in the Valley units, and as indicated, these factors bore on subgoals (1) and (2) in the case of passive-conformists. Factors #1, #3, #4, and #6 operated to about the same degree in SF and the Valley, as did intensive intervention and most components of individualization, for example, detailed diagnosis and staffing. Some of these factors bore on subgoals (1) and (2), and, collectively, they partly offset the results of (a) through (d) above, for passive-conformists and others. However, complicating the picture was the fact that the issues at hand were themselves more intense within San Francisco than in the Valley; that is, peer pressures and—especially—opportunities for negative situational entanglements seemed greater or more focused within the "big city," certainly for most P-C's. Moreover, in San Francisco, an individual's coping abilities—interpersonal and practical alike—were particularly important, since the external environment was generally more complex, and competition seemed greater overall.

Group Conformists
As shown in Table 15–1 (page 249), all factors within the first three areas contributed to the essentially equal rates of illegal behavior on the part of group conformist (G-C) experimentals, as compared with their controls. Though most such factors made a moderate and about equal contribution, low caseloads and intensive/extensive contacts (factors #1

and #2) added more than the rest. (As before, factor #1 will not be focused on.)

Before continuing, two groups of G-C's should be distinguished. At point of intake, youths from the first group had generally been involved in illegal behavior for several years—occasionally as "loners," not infrequently with siblings, and most often with a series of delinquent peers (not necessarily gangs). These individuals were personally committed to delinquency and were willing to do almost anything to develop or maintain a reputation as "tough." They rejected and sometimes openly scorned most dominant-culture values and goals relating to education, legitimate employment, personal accountability, and adult responsibility; and, often, their attitudes and life-style were at least passively supported by parents or relatives. Given their broad investment in outsmarting or avoiding the law and given their desire to be free from dominant-culture pressures or from "square"-adult demands, these youths—partly through projection—felt disliked *by* and very distrustful *of* authority figures, and they were often highly defensive or evasive around them.[9]

As of intake, the *remaining* G-C's had likewise enjoyed "messing around" with the boys (drinking, creating disturbances, "making out"), and occasionally "ripping off" prized or expensive items. Like the first group, they too had often obtained status, plus a sense of masculinity and even freedom, from so doing. Yet the present individuals were not strongly attracted to delinquency as a way of life; and, like their parents, they were tolerant to supportive of many if not most dominant-culture goals. For example, though they were not particularly invested in "personal responsibility," they often viewed employment and eventual marriage as an attractive route—in effect, an alternative route—to status, masculinity, or manhood. Also, though they did enjoy various illegal activities and often felt pressure to "stick with" their delinquent friends as well as demonstrate their masculinity, these youths did not wish to see themselves as delinquent and as linked exclusively to those particular individuals. Related to such factors, the present youths usually fell within the normal range in terms of overall self-confidence regarding nondelinquent activities and relationships. In addition, they seldom expected major hassles or basic rejection from adults and nondelinquent peers. For such reasons, they were less defensive and more relaxed than the previous G-C's when interacting with authority figures and nondelinquent peers.[10]

In sum, "messing around" and other illegal activities—while fairly widespread—were not as motivationally deep-seated with the present G- C's; at least, delinquent behavior and the thought of becoming a "real" delinquent were far from central to their self-image and overall adjustment. These youths had other irons in the fire or in the background, including additional, nondelinquent sources of emotional support. As a result, recognition and even acceptance by delinquent peers, while often satisfying, were rarely overriding goals or driving needs.

To simplify communication, the two G-C groups (types) will be called "insulated" and "accessible," respectively, despite the presence of some overlap.

With most G-C's, up to six main issues were addressed by factors #2 through #7, collectively (see Figure 15–1, page 246). These issues were: peer pressures, subgroup expectations, antisocial or antiauthority family orientation, desire for material gain, long-term overcompensations, and family disorganization. Though "material gain" influenced fewer youths than did the first two issues, it was addressed more often than long-term overcompensations and was easier to affect than the latter. Family disorganization, while also influential with fewer youths, was particularly difficult to address and affect, as was antisocial or antiauthority family orientation.

Among "insulated" group conformists, four or five such issues often played or had played a role in connection with illegal behavior. Here, as with "accessible" G-C's, peer pressures and subgroup expectations generally represented the immediate problem or main triggering conditions; in this regard, material gain was a moderately distant "third." With accessible youths, long-term overcompensations, family disorganization, and antisocial or antiauthority family orientation were seldom very influential in setting up or triggering illegal behavior. However, among insulated youths, overcompensations were closely interwoven with peer pressures and subgroup expectations.

Together, factors #2 through #7 related to these issues mainly in terms of four subgoals, that is, subgoal components: (1) *reduction of external stress,* (2) *changes in perception of others,* (3) *expansion of coping abilities,* and (4) *expansion of external support.* More specifically, with both G-C types (insulated and accessible), the following factors seemed important relative to subgoal (1), particularly for dealing with peer pressures: intensive/extensive contacts, CTP's guidelines, the change agent (orientation, abilities, perceptiveness), and, to a lesser degree, long-term contacts. With insulated G-C's, individualization/flexible programming and CTP's guidelines helped pave the way for addressing the issue of material gain.

The following factors seemed important relative to subgoal (2) (changes in perception of others): intensive/extensive contacts and the agent's abilities/perceptiveness. Here, these factors helped address the peer-pressures issue with both G-C types; they bore on long-term overcompensations as well, among insulated youths in particular. Intensive/extensive contacts and the agent's abilities/perceptiveness also helped with regard to subgroup expectations (as did long-term contacts), with both G-C types: They bore on, but only slightly affected, family disorganization and antisocial or antiauthority family orientation as well, in the case of insulated youths.

The following seemed important relative to subgoal (3) (expansion of coping abilities): intensive/extensive contacts and individualization/flexible programming. With insulated youths, these factors—plus long-term contacts—helped set the stage for addressing the material gain and long-term overcompensations issues. Among accessible youths, they bore on material gain and, to a lesser extent, peer pressures as well as subgroup expectations. Relative to these expectations, factor #6—the agent's professional orientation—also contributed.

Finally, with insulated G-C's, three factors seemed important relative to subgoal (4) (expansion of external supports): intensive/extensive contacts, individualization/flexible programming, and CTP's guidelines. Here, the first and second such factors helped set the stage for addressing family disorganization; the second and third bore on material gain. With accessible G-C's, extensive contacts and individualization/flexible programming seemed important relative to subgroup expectations.[11]

In sum, reduction of external stress (subgoal 1, as listed earlier) and change in perception of others (subgoal 2) mainly related to the *peer-pressures* issue and to either *subgroup expectations* or *material gain;* regarding these issues, each such subgoal applied to both G-C types. Expansion of coping abilities (subgoal 3) related to these same three issues, but was achieved mainly with accessible youths. Expansion of external supports (subgoal 4) bore on subgroup expectations and material gain—but, again, it was achieved mainly with accessible youths. Though several factors were brought to bear on most group conformists, the forces or conditions at which they were directed were usually difficult to modify, neutralize, or avoid, via the earlier-mentioned and other subgoals. As a result, only modest progress was made, particularly among insulated youths.

Factors #8 through #10

Factors #8 through #10 ("Global Program Features") refer to three significant characteristics of CTP: its community-based setting; its in-lieu-of-institutionalization nature; its positive reputation ("winner image") combined with the positive expectations apparent to most youths. These characteristics constitute factors #8, #9, and #10, respectively (Figure 15–1, page 246). Though the first two factors were necessarily related, their meaning was somewhat different across differing youth groups. Individually, the three factors were moderately important relative to most or all such groups—that is, especially in accounting for E/C differences in outcome. Collectively, their contribution was usually quite substantial for any one group. Each factor will now be reviewed in turn.

Community Setting

As shown in Table 15–1 (page 249), the community-based setting (factor #8) made a substantial contribution to either the reduced offending or the approximately equal offending of assertive-deniers, passive-conformists, and certain group conformists. Among *assertive-deniers,* this feature made it possible to address various family binds and long-term overcompensations in a direct and continuous manner—for instance, relative to "live," unfolding events—that was hardly possible in the institutional setting.[12] Progress resulting from this approach was difficult to substitute for, despite the fact that other major issues, for example, personal conflicts and poor impulse control, *were* sometimes addressed to a considerable degree within the institution. For instance, without substantial progress regarding family binds and/or long-term overcompensations, insights

and other gains relating to personal conflicts and poor impulse control were likely to be neutralized, or were difficult to achieve in the first place. At any rate, progress relating to family binds and long-term overcompensations—issues of particular importance with most A-D's—was less likely to occur in an institutional than a community setting, partly for the reasons mentioned earlier. (For further discussion, see *anxious-confused* youths, below.)

Similarly, among *passive-conformists,* the youths' presence within the local community made it possible to address family pressures in a direct, continuous, and specific way that could hardly have been implemented within an institution, certainly one that was distant or otherwise isolated from that community. The fact that these pressures were addressed relative to "live," specific events, usually involving parents or guardians themselves, probably raised their chances of being reduced or stabilized. In any event, such efforts increased the chances of producing actual—and to some extent "field tested"—changes in the youth/parent relationship, not just prospective or hoped-for changes. Separate from those efforts, extensive contacts helped reduce external stress and expand external supports in areas outside the family, for example, school; and, as indicated earlier, such efforts and contacts, when successful, often made it easier for the youths to then focus on still other subgoals and issues. At any rate, extensive contacts (factor #2), plus flexible programming (factor #5) that centered on those particular contacts, contributed to the youths' progress. The former factor (#2)—therefore, of course, this particular *combination* of factors (#2 and #5)—could rarely and only minimally have been implemented in most institutions.

Such contacts and programming aside (and, at least partly independent of family pressures), the community setting also made it possible to focus on peer pressures in a context and at a level that differed in important ways from those relating to institutional settings. (Here, "level" simply refers to certain real-life, especially "street scene" or "back alley," situations.) For example, the following situation applied to "context"—in this case, to the overall pattern or combination of inputs and resulting progress.

When combined with (1) inputs and progress within areas other than external stress and support, especially areas relating to coping abilities or perceptions of others, (2) inputs that bore on the peer-pressure issue, for example, external controls by parole agents, seemed to make it easier for most passive-conformist experimentals to not only alter their actual relationship with delinquent peers (street friends, not just institution friends) but to begin shifting their loyalties in the direction of less delinquent and nondelinquent individuals within the community. This and similar patterns of input/progress/loyalty-shifting helped these youths accumulate nondelinquent experiences, satisfactions, and resulting dominant-culture investments. Quantitatively and perhaps qualitatively, these would have been very difficult to accumulate or develop within an institution. Thus, in contrast, passive-conformist *controls*, upon release to parole, often had to "face" various delinquent street friends without having initiated nondelinquent relationships or having accumulated a backlog of reliable, nondelinquent satisfactions. Here, the peer-pressure problems they were likely to face existed somewhat independently of the fact that other major issues, such as subgroup expectations and situational entanglements, sometimes *had* been addressed to a considerable degree within the institution, for instance, via group meetings and role-playing sessions—apart, of course, from any actual "street scene."

With *group conformists,* the community setting made it possible to address peer-pressure and subgroup-expectation issues in a way that was hardly possible within most institutions, and that was especially meaningful to "accessible" youths. For example, such issues were addressed under conditions—specifically, within a community setting—that allowed G-C experimentals to simultaneously participate in a wide range of nondelinquent activities, if they so desired; included were certain hobbies, sports events, travel, and dating. When those key issues were addressed in the context of such activities, accessible youths often developed more incentive—more than they would have developed in an institution—to involve themselves in the change process and to thereby increase their chance of *further* participating in those and related activities. As indicated in note 13, extensive contacts and flexible programming that centered on those contacts contributed to the earlier-mentioned developments, and neither such "input" was particularly feasible within most institutions.

Among "insulated" group conformists, peer interactions within the institution often produced satisfactions that were quite similar to those obtained in the community: acceptance and recognition by delinquency-oriented youths. In this respect, the community therefore had little unique meaning to these youths. In addition, insulated G-C's had little investment in most dominant-culture values and in related short- as well as long-range goals. As a result, extensive contacts and flexible programming—factors that could have helped promote such goals, especially in a community setting—had little distinctive impact in this major area.[14]

With *anxious-confused* youths, the community setting was not a key factor in accounting for reduced or even comparable illegal behavior; at least it did not seem to make a distinctive contribution. For one thing, with most A-C's, the principal issue—personal conflicts—could be substantially addressed in an institutional as well as community setting; that is, changes in self-perception were usually the central consideration when dealing with such conflicts, and progress in this area neither required nor was greatly facilitated by the latter setting per se. In addition, it appeared that other major issues, such as family binds, could similarly be addressed in either such setting, at least to a considerable degree. What mattered, basically, was that most such issues *were* explored or otherwise focused on, even if this had to occur outside the context of "live" relationships (ongoing interactions) between youths, on the one hand, and parents or various friends and authority figures, on the other. Apparently, with most A-C's, such issues could be substantially explored outside that context. In this regard, the following might be noted.

It seemed more important for *assertive-deniers* than for most anxious-confused youths to deal with family binds and long-term overcompensations in the context of live relationships and ongoing social situations, especially those which the former youths considered rather pressing. It was in this context that they, A-D's, were usually best able to recognize and accept the existence, extent, and implications of such issues. At the same time, it was relatively easy for most such youths to minimize or brush aside, for example, during group sessions, numerous interactions and activities that they preferred *not* to discuss.

That is, such avoidance or dismissal could occur unless they (1) felt that staff and/or peers were quite determined to explore those matters, or (2) believed that the nature and implications of those interactions and activities (implications for the youths' immediate well-being or overall interests) were very obvious to staff or peers. For such reasons, and those suggested below, the existence, extent, and significance of various feelings or behavior patterns were easier for assertive-deniers than for anxious-confused youths to deny (not just to others), or to only superficially explore, if and when those feelings or actions were addressed in any of the following contexts: (1) while the youths were in an institution or were otherwise somewhat "distant" from long-standing pressures, triggering events, and perhaps long-term behavior patterns themselves; (2) chiefly in relation to institutional events; and (3) at an abstract or theoretical level alone.[15]

Compared to assertive-deniers, anxious-confused youths were more likely to recognize and accept both the nature and implications of such feelings, activities, or patterns; certainly, they less often required the presence of overpowering evidence, especially in terms of live relationships and ongoing social situations. This was not just because A-C's "denial mechanisms" were less powerful or elaborate in this regard, or because these youths were generally more receptive to the views and interpretations of others (this receptivity was sometimes described as a lesser degree of obstinacy or rigidity). Instead, it also reflected their greater tendency to introspect, and their related, greater acceptance of "psychological realities."[16] Given this tendency and attitude, many such youths were prepared to seriously explore their community relationships and behavior patterns, whether or not they were institutionalized at the time.

Substitute for Institutionalization
As shown in Table 15–1 (page 249), CTP's in-lieu-of-institutionalization nature (factor #9) contributed to the reduced or comparable illegal behavior of each experimental youth group, relative to that of controls. This contribution differed in several ways from group to group, and to better understand it the following might first be noted.

The impact of factor #9 seemed to originate in three main types of "perception,"

more precisely, in one or more areas of feeling or belief on the youths' part. These areas related to (1) the personal meaning of being removed from the community and sent to an institution, (2) the nature of institutions and of long-term lockup, and (3) the postinstitutional consequences of incarceration. How did these feelings and beliefs bear on illegal behavior?

Basically, these perceptions—further described below—seemed to have a deterrent and/or incentive effect when they (1) were considered important, that is, were felt strongly, by youths, and when they (2) then resulted in various youth decisions (see "Area 3," below). Not all youths had such perceptions, and not all who had them felt strongly about them. More specifically, with few exceptions, each youth who felt strongly about one or more such areas also seemed to believe that, as long as he did not "mess up on CTP" and remained in the *community,* he would thereby avoid any or all of the following effects and conditions, that is, whichever were important to him: the unpleasant feelings or negative judgments he associated with removal from the community; the loss of enjoyments, independence, or integrity he associated with long-term lockup; the dreary existence or frightening events he associated with YA institutionalization; and the long-term problems he associated with having been in a YA institution. By avoiding such effects and conditions, he usually hoped to have, or continue having, various positive experiences instead. Thus, avoidance itself was not the only goal. In effect, deterrence and positive incentives largely went hand in hand.

Like other CTP youths, he recognized the following: Since he *was* in fact under YA jurisdiction, albeit in a different sort of program, he could, like any regular parolee, be removed from the community if he broke the law or ignored given parole requirements (Appendix 3). Together with the above, this helped produce the deterrent and/or incentive effect—depending, also, on which decisions (again, see below) he emphasized when responding to his perceptions, and on what other goals he hoped to achieve. The three areas of perception will now be specified.

Area 1 ("personal meaning of being removed from the community . . .") involved at least one of four elements:

a. youth's feeling of "badness," failure, inadequacy, or defeat, in his own eyes, if removed from the community (e.g., removal would constitute evidence or proof, to youth, of his "badness" or failure);

b. youth's feeling that he would be considered "bad" or a failure by friends (mainly nondelinquents), parents, and perhaps others, if removed from the community;

c. youth's belief that institutionalization/long-term lockup would entail a loss of many enjoyable activities and experiences that centered around friends, parents, siblings, and self, even if those individuals did not consider him such things as "bad" or a failure; and,

d. youth's belief that institutionalization/long-term lockup would entail a marked loss of autonomy and might require continual submission to authority figures, or at least marked suppression of one's feelings and views.

As implied, elements "1a," "1b," and so on, reflected what the youth believed *would* be the case if he were removed from the community and sent to a Youth Authority institution, not just to its Northern Reception Center and Clinic (NRCC). To be sure, his YA commitment had itself constituted some evidence of "badness," and his several weeks in NRCC provided a foretaste of long-term lockup. Still, most youths had been convinced, while at NRCC, that the clinic environment was somewhat mild compared to YA institutions, and that since the clinic allowed for frequent contacts with friends and relatives from nearby as well as distant communities, this particular setting did not constitute complete or essential removal, psychologically or otherwise.

Area 2 ("nature of institutions . . .") involved at least one of the following beliefs:

a. The institution is, at best, a dreary and/or oppressive—in that sense, a generally "rotten"—place to live, especially for several months or more.

b. The institution is often frightening or tension-filled, and it is sometimes inhumane as well (e.g., it is dangerous in terms of how some youths or groups of youth behave, and it is sometimes unduly harsh or punitive regarding staff attitudes and behavior); this applied

whether or not it was considered "rotten," in the sense stated in (a).

Unlike elements 1c and 1d these beliefs did not focus on what would presumably be *lost* in the event of removal and institutionalization; instead, they centered on conditions or experiences that would presumably be *faced* if removal, or the like, occurred. Although 2a and 2b could be interrelated not just in reality but in the youth's mind, many such individuals considered only one, and not the other, a really major issue. Finally, though beliefs 2a and 2b were not independent of elements 1c and 1d, these four factors were not considered equally important by all youths.

Area 3 ("postinstitutional consequences . . ."), like Area 2, involved at least one of two beliefs—again, by the youth:

a. Institutionalization would give a person an official record that would adversely affect his job opportunities, his acceptability to the armed services, and so on.

b. Once institutionalized, a person would always be regarded as an "ex-con" by friends, parents, or others, even if he eventually "straightened out."[17]

Individually or collectively, the preceding factors (1a through 3b)—when considered important—contributed to two or three interrelated *decisions* by the youth. As suggested, these decisions were made partly to help him (1) avoid experiencing what he believed would occur if he were removed from the community program and barred from the community itself, and (2) obtain, or continue obtaining, various positive experiences. It was these decisions, which now follow, that directly and indirectly influenced his illegal behavior:

a. restrain one's behavior in various respects, certainly more so than before;

b. "go along with" CTP's overall program—with its goals and general approaches; and

c. become actively involved with the CTP plan, and perhaps try to make major changes in one's life.

"Going along with" did not mean simply pretending to cooperate, that is, pretending fairly often or on many important matters. It meant, from the youth's perspective, doing what CTP required—generally *cooperating* with the parole agent—but seldom doing much more.[18] In effect, and still from the youth's perspective, if one's overall life situation seemed to improve as a result of "going along," so much the better; however, if it did not improve, that might not matter too much so long as one remained in the community and "life" did not get worse. In contrast, "becoming actively involved" implied that the youth would make, at a minimum, a fairly strong and relatively sustained effort with respect to CTP, one that would not easily be curtailed or discontinued if difficulties arose. (The meaning of "restraint"—self-restraint—is self-evident in the present context.)

Of the three decisions, the first ("restrain one's behavior") was the most common, among youths who felt strongly about one or more of these factors. The second was closely related to the first and was also very common. Ordinarily, these decisions were first made shortly after the youth realized he might be placed on CTP; and, like the third decision, which usually developed somewhat later, they often varied through time in terms of strength, scope, and focus. At any rate, such decisions, particularly the third, did not just relate to specific illegal acts, for example, those resulting from emotional reactions to subgroup expectations and to family pressures, or from material desires/needs. Instead, or in addition, they often pertained to long-term and/or complex adjustment patterns, such as the youth's overall approach to school or his mode of interacting with peers and authority figures.[19]

Together with those decisions, this focus on specific acts and/or long-term patterns directly related to CTP's main subgoals. For instance, the youth's decision to "go along with" CTP or to become actively involved with a particular plan usually set the stage for his having at least a moderately tolerant attitude toward, or a fairly open-minded approach regarding, the agent's attempts to *reduce external stress* and *develop or expand given coping abilities;* the agent's efforts, of course, were also (and more fundamentally) directed at specific acts and long-term patterns. More concretely, those decisions raised the chances that the youth would accept various external controls and would seriously consider specific school plans, out-of-home placement, and so on; and, again, such controls, plans, and so forth, were themselves (collectively) directed at illegal acts and harmful adjustment patterns. Thus, in a sense, such decisions predisposed the youth to give CTP the benefit of the doubt regarding the relevance and possible utility of such subgoals, program components, or proposed approaches. This and related predispositions usually continued beyond his initial months on parole. (Once the youth initially decided to "give the program a try," it was up to the program to begin "delivering"; at least, responsibility for various inputs and efforts no longer rested entirely with the youth.)[20]

The preceding events—beginning with youth perceptions and ending with subgoal-relevant decisions—are diagrammed in Figure 15–2.[21]

We will now specify the earlier-mentioned elements (perceptions) that various youths groups considered important, that is, felt strongly about. As indicated, these elements (previously called factors) contributed to decisions that seemed to have substantial impact on youth behavior.

The elements that *assertive-deniers* felt strongly about were as follows, in rough order of priority: (1) institutionalization—involving a loss of autonomy, and so on; (2) institutionalization—involving a loss of enjoyable community activities; and (3) institutions as dreary/oppressive. These were elements 1d, 1c, and 2a. Somewhat less important was: (4) feeling "bad" or "defeated," in his own eyes, if removed from community. A-D's did not seem to feel strongly about the four remaining elements (1b, 2b, 3a, and 3b).

Anxious-confused youths felt strongly about three elements: (1) being considered bad, a failure, or inadequate by various individuals, if removed from the community, (2) institutions as frightening/tension-filled; and (3) adverse effects of lockup on later job and other opportunities. (Assertive-deniers were not particularly concerned with the latter, future-oriented element.) Somewhat less important were: (4) feeling bad, a failure, or inadequate, in his own eyes, if removed from the community; (5) institutionalization—involving a loss of enjoyable community activities; (6) institutions as dreary/oppressive; and (7) "ex-con" image, subsequent to lockup. Apparently, anxious-confused youths felt strongly or moderately strongly about certain elements that were not particularly important to assertive-deniers; however, they did not consider "loss of autonomy"—the A-D's

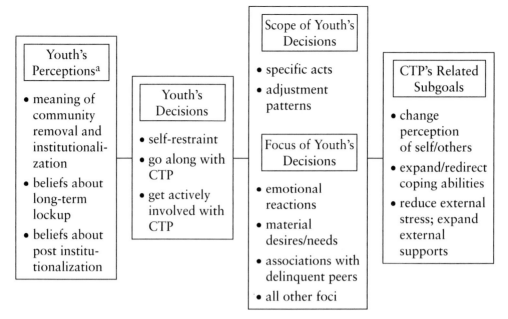

Figure 15–2. *Bases and areas of contribution to reduced or comparable illegal behavior, relative to factor #9.*

[a]See "feelings and beliefs," pp. 257–259.

primary element—especially important in the present context.[22] At any rate, regarding key factor #9, A-C's seemed to be influenced more by an accumulation of certain elements than by any one or two alone.

Passive-conformists felt quite strongly about institutions as being "frightening or tension-filled." For this reason as much as for all others combined, these youths very much wished to avoid such settings. Thus, the following elements, individually and collectively, seemed substantially less important than the former element alone: (1) feeling bad or inadequate, in his own eyes, if removed from the community; (2) being considered bad, a failure, or inadequate by various individuals, if removed from the community; and (3) institutions as dreary/oppressive. As for certain other elements, passive-conformists did not consider "loss of autonomy" particularly important, possibly because they did not try to exercise much autonomy anyway. Their lack of strong feelings about "future job opportunities" was similarly related to their generally dependent stance.

The elements that "accessible" *group-conformists* felt strongly about were: (1) institutionalization—involving a loss of enjoyable community activities—and (2) institutions as

dreary/oppressive. (These were two of the three elements considered important by assertive-deniers.) Less important was: (3) adverse effects of lockup on later job and other opportunities. Accessible G-C's did not consider the remaining elements particularly important.

Finally, it might be noted that the "dreary/oppressive" element was considered important or somewhat important by all four youth groups. However, the "fright/danger" component was emphasized only by the anxious-confused and, especially, by the passive-conformist youths, both of whom had many inadequacy feelings.[23] Also in contrast, the "loss of autonomy" element seemed especially influential with only one group: assertive-deniers. Most remaining elements were considered important or fairly important by two or three groups.

Positive Reputation and Expectations
As shown in Figure 15–1 (page 246), factor #10 had two components (features). The first, "positive reputation," mainly referred to CTP's "'winner image'—in effect, its 'aura of success' among most local YA wards and even many probationers" (youths not [yet] on CTP). The second, "positive expectations," centered on the staff's general feeling of confi-

dence in the overall program, and on their typically optimistic outlook regarding almost all youths' chances of succeeding in, or at least clearly profiting from, the program—given (1) at least a moderate, though often sizable, effort on the youths' part, and although (2) most youths would probably have to face substantial challenges, several difficulties, and some crises. Together, these features helped shape the responses of anxious-confused and passive-conformist youths to the overall program or to components thereof; in so doing, factor #10 added to the earlier-mentioned impact of factors #1 through #9. The following, which focuses on A-C youths, may illustrate the nature of this impact.[24]

Anxious-confused youths usually associated CTP's *positive reputation* with two or three of the following characteristics: helpful, powerful, successful, special, and goal-oriented. (While at NRCC, A-C's had of course only heard about CTP; and, in most cases, they had formed only general, albeit positive, impressions of it. However, after a few months in the program, most such youths had, in their own mind, confirmed or even expanded upon these impressions.) Here, *helpful* meant either "doing good" or trying to do so; in addition, it usually meant working with youths in a fair (even-handed) and reasonable or proper way. *Special,* or different, meant either "above par" (for law-centered operations) or "classy" (skillfully organized and operated). *Goal-oriented* meant "clear and consistent in purpose or direction." Though *power* and *success* differed in meaning, they were both associated with "competence" as well. Additional characteristics, such as "liked" and "respected," were implicit in the concept of positive reputation.

CTP's image influenced not only anxious-confused youths who wished to actively participate in the program, but those who simply wanted to go along with it. For instance, the fact that peers had not portrayed CTP as irrelevant and its workers as arbitrary or irrational often helped reduce both such youths' initial resistance to, and anxieties about, the program; at any rate, it helped obviate several standard excuses for not, at least, going along with it, initially as well as later. In addition, CTP's *positive* reputation, as distinct from its mere lack of a negative one, usually seemed to have one or both of the following effects:

(1) It made A-C's less uncomfortable or embarrassed about being associated with the Youth Authority, that is, less than if CTP had been regarded (based on typical stereotypes) as a "standard" approach to "criminals"—regarded, say, as a heavy-handed or perhaps "dumb" program. Thus, for example, it was easier for these youths to view themselves—and to think of themselves as being viewed by friends and family—as accepting specific controls and general direction or advice from a reputedly high-powered outfit than from "some jerks (agents) who like to play Gang Busters." This applied whether or not the youths sought such direction or advice, and even though CTP *was* still "YA" and its workers *were* parole agents.

(2) It gave many anxious-confused youths a feeling that various intervention plans and related youth/agent discussions were not mere gestures, and that their individual or joint efforts might actually produce concrete results. That is, the program's reputation helped A-C's view CTP as an outfit that not only intended to follow through on given plans, but one that might also have the ability to actually "deliver" in areas that staff and/or youths considered important, areas such as school, placement, and surveillance. In this respect, characteristics such as helpful, powerful, goal-oriented, and so on, added legitimacy *and* credibility to the agents' intervention plans and to their specific efforts regarding those plans. This perception of legitimacy and credibility helped open or keep open the door to the youngsters' use of CTP and its agents as genuine, sometimes major, resources. Of course, at the level of simple or direct deterrence—that is, aside from perceived legitimacy and from utilization-as-resource—CTP's presumed power and apparent goal-directedness also made many youths "think twice" about the possible unpleasant consequences of not restraining their illegal activities or of persistently resisting the program. (As suggested, *self-restraint* and *"going along"* could each exist separately from *active or eager involvement*—that is, could operate, without the presence of the remaining two factors, within given youths as well as across differing youths. [These factors—respectively—were "decisions" (a), (b), and (c), mentioned earlier.] This was the case despite the fact that, with many youths [the same and/or other youths], self-restraint often *coexisted* with both types or levels of involvement.)

CTP's positive image did not always contribute to the outcomes mentioned earlier—in effect, to the following reactions by many A-C's: less difficulty accepting controls, direction, or advice from a YA program; greater chance of viewing the agents' plans and efforts as legitimate and credible; more reason for "thinking twice" about breaking the law or persistently resisting the program. Instead, though sometimes in addition, it activated or helped produce at least one of the following feelings, beliefs, or desires ("responses")[25]—responses that largely centered on the individual's self-image and overall relationship to others:[26]

(1) *A global feeling of self-enhancement or well-being.* Here, anxious-confused youths often felt more vigorous or robust, somehow better as persons,[27] or especially pleased in general, when they viewed themselves as part of a "pretty groovy" outfit (CTP). This feeling, which often contained more than one such component, was based on the youths' relatively simple identification with CTP as a whole—usually viewed as a fairly powerful or somewhat special entity. It occurred at several points during the youths' parole, but it seldom lasted more than a few days or weeks in each instance, and often only a few hours; nevertheless, it was always very satisfying or special to the youths.

The feeling of self-enhancement or well-being thus paralleled and was similar in origin to that experienced by many persons who identify with, or are fans of, a popular and successful sports team or other organized group. (For instance, the group's actual or reputed status directly enhances the self-image of individuals who like to consider themselves part of it—in the case of CTP youths, a generally accepted part.) To experience this heightened or expanded yet rather general feeling, anxious-confused youths did not have to first achieve specified program goals or major subgoals.[28] Instead, they could do so as long as they felt largely supportive of CTP—in a sense, basically loyal to it—and by following its central rules. This did not prevent them from having various reservations or expressing particular dissatisfactions.

Insofar as anxious-confused youths enjoyed this feeling and wished to maintain or reexperience it, they had a reason, aside from other possible reasons, for wanting to *remain* part of CTP—in effect, to remain members in

good or at least acceptable standing. This wish and motive had direct behavioral implications: They predisposed A-C's to be more accepting of the project's overall conditions or expectations, and more willing to give the agents' suggestions or plans a try. Such implications aside, CTP's reputation thus helped these individuals experience a broad, positive feeling more often and perhaps more clearly than might have been the case if that reputation had not existed. Given the overall needs of A-C's, this experience was beneficial despite the fact that simple identification rather than long-term accomplishments had played the central role. This also applied even though the experience in question did not, for example, necessarily help motivate these youths to begin developing themselves along specific lines, or necessarily increase their self-understanding in the first place (see item 3, below).

(2) *A belief that they might be "better" persons, if they achieved specified program goals.* Anxious-confused youths sometimes believed the following: (a) If they satisfied CTP's main expectations, the project would, in effect, give them a stamp of approval. (b) This approval, the tangible expression of which would be a favorable discharge from the YA, would be valid evidence that they, the youths, were "better" than when they began the program or were at least "OK" in some important ways. Here, *CTP's* positive reputation had helped activate the *youths'* wish to be better and/or happier persons than they felt they were. Had they not viewed CTP as worthwhile or perhaps special, its potential stamp of approval would have had little meaning or incentive value with respect to this wish. The presence of this incentive seemed to make A-C's more focused or concerned; for instance, they were somewhat more careful about straying from preestablished program plans and they seemed more likely to give the agents' new suggestions a serious try. At any rate, the hoped-for approval and the subsequent feeling of self-enhancement were to result from the youths' achievement of specified *goals.* This feeling, while similar to that mentioned in item (1),[29] would not be the direct and immediate product of their simple identification with CTP as a whole, and it would probably last much longer.

(3) *A desire to have characteristics that paralleled CTP's.* As indicated, A-C's often viewed the project in terms of two or more of

the following: helpful, powerful, successful, special, and/or goal-oriented. Such images (youth interpretations) of CTP sometimes led these individuals to recognize more clearly *their own wish* to have—that is, to be characterized by—such features, for example, to be more competent or better organized themselves. Together with other inputs, CTP's features—still as interpreted by the youths—also helped A-C's more fully recognize the implications of such wishes (desires).[30] In both cases, relatively specific desires and features were involved (see examples below), not the global reactions (e.g., "feeling pleased in general") or the broad wishes (e.g., "be better as persons") reflected in items (1) and (2).

(Before continuing, two points might be noted. First, the youths' images of CTP reflected at least some objective events, especially during the post-NRCC period. That is, the features or dimensions that these images represented were neither imaginary nor solely reputed. Second, CTP's features should be distinguished from the youths' desires regarding those features, or from their level of attraction to them. For instance, the presence of given features, ones such as CTP's actual as well as reputed "goal orientation," sometimes helped bring those features to the youths' *awareness* for perhaps the first time; however, this was different than increasing the youths' desire to *have* such features—already recognized features.)

For example, the project's apparent "power" or "success" sometimes increased A-C's attraction to such features or dimensions as competence and interpersonal success, or it increased their desire to be "winners" rather than "losers" most of the time. In fact, for some youths, CTP comprised a social-interactional environment in which competence and interpersonal success, together with their constructive implications, were clearly observable for perhaps the first time. Similarly, CTP's relatively focused or efficient mode of operation and its overall "goal orientation" occasionally made *these* characteristics more noticeable and meaningful to youths, and it subsequently helped arouse the youths' often inactive wish to better organize their own daily life or to think more often about their future.[31] Finally the images mentioned earlier helped sharpen many A-C's awareness of what they did *not* want to be, or be like: bad, weak, a failure, below par, disorganized, or aimless.[32]

In sum, CTP sometimes comprised a microcosm or mini-society that helped engender two or more of the following changes in anxious-confused youths (again, "feature" refers to CTP's qualities as interpreted by youths; "desire" centers on youths' wishes regarding those qualities):

1. A-C's became aware of given features for perhaps the first time, that is, aware of qualities or dimensions whose existence or basic nature they had not clearly recognized or been conscious of (this change was less common than those that follow);
2. A-C's became much *more* aware of—more clearly or more often aware of—given features, or the prominence and centrality of those dimensions substantially increased;
3. A-C's more fully recognized the actual or potential significance, for example, the social or personal implications, of certain features or desires; and
4. A-C's developed a greater desire to have certain features, and/or they became more *aware* of their desire for those features.

At any rate, the project (microcosm or not) presented A-C's with several learning inputs and potential modeling inputs, stimuli that sometimes helped motivate the youths to add specified dimensions to their own personality or life, or to emphasize those features more than before. These motives, like others, increased the youths' investment in program goals and specific plans that seemed consistent with those dimensions.

Finally, the preceding motives reflected what might broadly be called a desire for growth and/or for satisfying, constructive interaction with one's environment. In this respect, CTP's actual and reputed features tapped what many anxious-confused youths viewed as the "potentially worthwhile but largely [e.g., very often] unavailable part" of themselves (Chapter 5). A similar "tap" and activation was also reflected in responses (1) and (2) above, that is, in the "global feeling of self-enhancement or well-being" and in the "belief that they [youths] might be 'better' persons" under specified conditions.[33]

CTP's *positive expectations,* which sometimes reflected the preceding features or images (also see below), involved several main "messages." For example, during early discussions with their parole agent, most anxious-confused youths learned that (a) they, like others on CTP, were considered quite capable of profiting from the program, and (b) the agent was fairly confident that the treatment/control (intervention) plan, if followed, could make an important difference in their lives. Implicit in most such discussions was the related message that YA wards were "worth the effort"—mainly because they were human beings, not primarily thorns in people's sides. CTP's general atmosphere, for example, its frequent youth/staff interactions or its hustle and bustle of youth-centered activities, often conveyed a similar idea: Delinquents were neither second-class citizens nor worthy of token aid alone, despite their past behavior.

Supported by, yet separable from the latter message, these and later discussions often helped personalize certain images that A-C's had formed or were forming relative to CTP's positive reputation. For instance, youth/agent discussions concerning given issues—for example, school performance, following-through, self-respect, or control of rage—usually included such underlying though often direct messages as the following: "*You* can be more competent or successful" (interpersonally, pragmatically); "*you* can be better organized and more goal-oriented"; "*you* can be better in various ways, and can respond more constructively (personally, socially)."[34] These messages helped clarify or further specify the somewhat broader communications involved in (a) and (b). That is, they helped concretize such concepts as "profiting from the program" and "important difference"; in fact, they performed this function whether or not CTP's positive reputation was involved. Finally, specific or otherwise, these messages were linked with CTP's main subgoals, such as changing the youths' self-perception and expanding or redirecting their coping abilities; and most youths thought the agent believed these changes were possible under reasonably attainable or even already existing conditions—whether or not substantial attitude change might also be needed, on the youth's part.

Together, these communications and messages involved at least two main, partly overlapping issues: responsibility and support. Responsibility-oriented messages (see [a] and [b] above) indicated to youths that, in the agent's view, there would be good reason for optimism and no solid excuse for failure if the agent and youths worked together or at least not at cross-purposes.[35] Positive change—so the youths understood—had, after all, been achieved by many other individuals, especially those who had "made an effort" and had steered clear of delinquency. In short, the agent's position was: However appropriate the intervention plan might be and whatever the agent might attempt, youths would have to do their share before progress—which would then be likely—could occur. To most A-C's, this view thus represented external pressure even though it also reflected substantial confidence and, in that respect, external support. In any event, responsibility-oriented messages related not just to individuals who were prepared to "get involved," but to those who were interested in only "going along." As suggested earlier, even "going along" meant making some sustained efforts, dealing with certain difficult external circumstances to at least a moderate degree, and responding to the agent's basic requirements or demands.[36]

Support-oriented messages centered on the youths' often largely suppressed (not repressed) desire for personal growth and on their frequent wish for improved, more satisfying interactions with their environment.[37] These messages helped make the agent a partial emotional ally, since they implied not simply that relevant change was *possible* and that the project would offer related assistance, but that there was nothing *wrong* with "changing" and with increasing one's enjoyment of life. This broad suggestion—in effect, a legitimizing of personal needs and nondestructive self-assertion—represented a new and acceptable idea to many depressed, guilt-ridden, or unusually dependent youths; it often had relevance to other A-C's as well. At any rate, when the agent's overall support of the above desire and wish was accompanied by his more specific suggestions or requests to "give it a try" or to perhaps "keep trying" (e.g., relative to handling parental domination or peer pressures), this sometimes helped numerous A-C's counter their frequent tendency to "leave things as is" or to simply "give up." It was under such conditions, for example, that the agent's apparent optimism or general expectation regarding progress helped many A-C's feel safer about "trying," or helped them feel less pessimistic about their future.

Although the present messages focused on support or encouragement, here, too, external pressure was seldom absent. For instance, the agent's "*you* can be" (also meaning: "you *can* be") generally implied: "I'd *like* you to be"— or, at least, "you'd be better off if you *were*." (The implied message did not necessarily include a coercive element in the sense of an "or else," for example, "if you don't do this, such and such will be done to you.")[38] Similarly, his suggestions that youths "give it a try" or "keep trying" were often more than suggestions or even mild requests alone, from his as well as the youths' perspective. Nevertheless, those messages centered on goals or experiences that reflected, or were at least consistent with, the A-C's own needs or desires; and perhaps for this reason, they were considered largely supportive by most such youths.[39]

All in all, support-oriented messages motivated many anxious-confused youths to make extra efforts regarding the intervention plan. In some cases, the agent's apparent confidence in youths helped the latter feel more confidence in themselves; this, in turn, often led to extra efforts. In other instances, youths seemed to try harder in order to be liked by, or approved of as persons by, the agent; here, for example, they wished to be liked by this individual (1) whom *they* usually liked or respected and (2) who believed that youths could succeed, and who usually seemed pleased when they progressed. Still other A-C's were especially responsive to the idea of "working together," whether with a supportive agent alone or with a generally optimistic staff.

Support-oriented messages aside, some A-C's felt an added, largely internal pressure to try somewhat harder than they might otherwise have tried. This occurred when they viewed CTP as a program in which progress and success were the norm, and when they believed that many youths were giving the program a "real try" for that presumed reason (success-as-norm). Here, in making their extra efforts, some such youths were largely concerned with not ending up as "rejects" or feeling way below par when compared to others. In any event, whatever the youths' primary motives, CTP's positive expectations thus posed an added and at least a moderate challenge for these and the remaining individuals to use certain abilities they believed they had.

Finally, some A-C's occasionally felt on-the-spot relative to social responsibility and immediate self-interest alike; that is, they felt an external as well as an internal pressure to exert what, for them, represented extra efforts on behalf of both such interests. This occurred when the agent emphasized to youths that CTP's resources were at their disposal with respect to implementing the intervention plan— emphasized, in effect, that youths were being given a good opportunity to improve their overall situation and that staff were quite willing to assist in this regard.[40] At a minimum— even independently of possible added efforts by youths—this emphasis made it harder for some A-C's to wholly ignore various program resources, particularly when the implication was that such resources, if used, could increase their already reasonable chance of success, and could help them face difficulties as well as crises.

Though factor #10 has been illustrated in relation to anxious-confused youths, several major points that were mentioned also apply to *passive-conformists*. For instance, like the former youths, many P-C's associated CTP's positive reputation with such features as: helpful, powerful, successful, and special. For reasons mentioned in connection with A-C's, these features made it easier for Passive-Conformists to accept the project's direction or advice, and CTP's apparent "power," in particular, gave them substantial reason to "think twice" about breaking the law. Partly because of its reputation, the project also served as a buffer between these individuals and their non-CTP, delinquent peers: In effect, P-C's presence on this project often helped them say "no" to such youths, many of whom were themselves familiar with its operations.

Despite their fear of CTP's power, many passive-conformists enjoyed being associated with it. More specifically, they often liked to identify with a "winning team" for a change, or at least with something special and occasionally exciting. Often, this global identification helped reduce their underlying pessimism, loneliness, self-doubt, and feeling of having little status. Moreover, CTP's positive image plus the staff's overall interest and confidence in youths frequently helped them experience a "global feeling of self-enhancement or well-being," and less anxiety around adults. This repeated reduction of unwanted feelings, and the alternative experiences of more *enjoyable* feelings, had a cumulative effect and usually influenced P-C's behavioral response to the project; this occurred even though the reductions and alternative feelings were, themselves, often short-lived. (The mechanisms involved in these processes were very similar to those observed among A-C's.) For these and other reasons, including CTP's responsibility- and support-oriented messages, factor #10 made a substantial contribution to the reduced illegal behavior of passive-conformists.

On balance, factor #10 had only a slight positive impact on *assertive-deniers* and *group conformists*. More particularly, neither its reputation component nor its expectations component had a large influence through time; and in general, the former seemed less important than the latter. For instance, during their first several months on parole, most such youths viewed CTP's reputation negatively, mainly because they believed the project's "power" and "goal-orientation" would largely be directed at controlling their behavior and otherwise interfering with their life. As suggested, A-D's and G-C's were more sensitive than most youths about their independence and autonomy, especially when authority figures, most of whom they distrusted, were involved. (Group conformists wished to remain largely free from control or direction by authority figures and various conventional pressures; in *that* respect they focused on independence and autonomy.)

Thus, CTP's "winner image"—in this case its "success" feature—provided little comfort to these youths; instead, it reinforced their preexisting belief that any YA program would be more a threat than a support. For instance, despite its having been described by other youths as "helpful," CTP seemed, given that belief, more likely to oppose than support their desired level of autonomy, and various other aspects of their behavior; in fact, from this perspective, the project would probably not be helpful at all. Similarly, to most such individuals, CTP's reputedly "special"—above par or skillfully organized—nature further suggested its probable ability to interfere.

In short, during their first several months on the project, assertive-deniers and group conformists largely judged CTP's reputed and apparent features in relation to their (youths') concern or preoccupation with autonomy and control. Partly for this reason they tried, psychologically, to maintain only minimal involvement with the project; and behaviorally, they made few special efforts with respect to

the intervention plan. Nevertheless, since these individuals viewed CTP as a "threat," they *were* more likely to "think twice" about breaking the law—even though they dismissed the idea that CTP could greatly change their pattern of activities.

At a related level, many such youths took pleasure in acting pointedly unimpressed with CTP's "so-called reputation." Here, the project was resisted partly *because* of this reputation, for example, in order to prove to friends, or to oneself, that one had not quickly or easily "succumbed." In effect, the more one resisted this supposedly formidable project, the stronger and more independent one might seem to be, certainly in relation to authority figures.

After several months on the project, many assertive-deniers and accessible group conformists realized that CTP was somewhat different than they had expected. Usually, in fact, the former individuals no longer viewed it as an overwhelmingly authoritarian "outfit," and the latter no longer considered it little more than a control-focused "enemy." Moreover, many such youths had largely *made* their point about strength and independence. At this juncture, their use of CTP as a resource or at least as a supplement moderately increased, and it became easier for them to regard themselves more or less as part of a "special" (now also a "different," in a positive-status sense) kind of program, without feeling a basic loss of autonomy or a sense of defeat. At any rate, most A-D's and some G-C's no longer interpreted the project's reputation, including its "power" and "goal-orientation," in predominantly negative terms. (Thus, factor #10, like various others, sometimes required at least several months, and a new set of circumstances, before it began taking effect.) Nevertheless, this modified view—and the youths' related, increased involvement—seemed, by itself, to have only a slight effect on reducing illegal behavior.[41]

CTP's positive expectations did affect many assertive-deniers and, once again, accessible group conformists.[42] For instance, after the first few months, support-oriented messages, such as "you *can* respond more constructively toward others" or "you *can* be more successful," were often accepted and appreciated by both youth groups; in this connection they helped increase the youths' investment in given program goals and related plans. Still, the overall influence of CTP's positive expectations on these individuals' behavior—self-restraint included—remained rather modest. For example, although A-D's appreciated and often responded to the above encouragement, they more often acted—and they controlled given behaviors—on the basis of other inputs, for example, long-standing attitudes that again involved autonomy and control. Here, these youths were usually quite invested not just in (1) the idea that they, personally, would be chiefly responsible for any important changes and activities in their life, but in (2) the view that they, in these and other respects, would seldom require help from others. Concrete support and support-oriented messages aside, accessible G-C's were generally receptive to responsibility-oriented messages, especially after the first several months on parole. However, for all group conformists combined—insulated youths included—the overall impact of factor #10 remained slight.

Summary of Key Factors

For assertive-denier, anxious-confused, passive-conformist, and group conformist youth groups combined, the three most important factors in accounting for the reduced or comparable illegal behavior of E's versus C's were: *small caseloads; intensive and/or extensive contacts;* and *individualization and flexible programming.* Each such factor made a major contribution relative to all or almost all four youth groups. Small caseloads were a prerequisite not only to the second and, to a lesser extent, the third such factor, but to other factors as well (Table 15–1, page 249).

Next in importance were: *personal characteristics and professional orientation of agent; specific abilities and overall perceptiveness of agent;* and *explicit, detailed guidelines* (intervention strategies). Each such factor made either substantial or major contributions to the four youth groups, and the latter two factors seemed virtually equal in importance. Individually and collectively, these three factors, and especially the three preceding ones, stood out above the rest (see below) in accounting for reduced or comparable illegal behavior among Valley and San Francisco males—"rare types" included.

Four remaining factors were reviewed. Of these, *long-term contacts* had substantial importance overall, except with passive-conformists (for whom they were very

important); CTP *as a substitute for institutionalization* (SFI) was about equally significant. Collectively, though not individually, *SFI, the community setting,* and CTP's *positive reputation and positive expectations* made a major contribution to most youth groups.

Precise quantitative estimates regarding the relative importance of each such factor were not possible. The general ranking that is summarized above mainly reflects the converging impressions of researchers and operations staff, and it is based not only on several years of on-site observations, routine case documentation, and informal discussions, but on formal interviews between researchers and staff and upon hundreds of interviews with youths. When assessing each factor in connection with each youth group, no *sharp* line could be drawn between "major" (very important) and "substantial" (moderately important) contributions. In short, the present ranking did not result from systematic experimentation and refined statistical analysis, since, with the partial exception of factors #6 and #7 (page 247), such approaches to the analysis of key factors were not possible, given the project's design. Nevertheless, the ranking is probably fairly accurate, especially at its upper end, and no other key factors appear to have been involved.

Some factors, for example, #5, #6, #8, and #10, often required several months—and changes within youths or their circumstances—before they could begin taking effect or full effect.

Finally, it seems clear that most individual factors—averaged over the youths' entire program—were not equally influential across all youth groups. It is equally clear that, for any given youth group, differing factors had different degrees of influence. This is apart from the fact that several factors, collectively, took differing lengths of time to reach their peak and that—once they reached that level—they did not always maintain it. Nevertheless, the key factors regularly provided mutual support and, in that respect, backup.

General Observations

With all youth groups, CTP's observed outcomes depended on the simultaneous, integrated operation or presence of several key factors. Some such factors, for example, intensive/extensive contacts and long-term contacts, had to operate to a sufficient degree or for at least a minimum time. (Here, degree or amount included rate and total number.) Others, such as explicit/detailed guidelines and individualized/flexible programming, had to operate appropriately. Still others, for example, small caseloads and matched agents, simply had to "exist"—albeit continuously. In this respect, what we call "project integrity" or "qualitative adequacy" was essential to CTP. Both terms include not only simultaneous/integrated operation (across factors), but sufficient amount and duration, appropriate implementation, and continued existence (for individual factors).

The 10 key factors should be distinguished from *program elements* and *intervention methods*. Program elements—for example, counseling, recreation, collateral contacts, and out-of-home placement—functioned as content bases *for* given factors. Specifically, at one level, (1) these elements were the vehicle through which, or the context in which, explicit/detailed guidelines were implemented, and (2) the pattern and sequence in which these elements were implemented was the concrete expression of individualized/flexible programming. At another level, such guidelines and programming (therefore, the program elements themselves) were also implemented and expressed in terms of various intervention methods, for example, particular agent stances and activities (Chapter 6). At any rate, all factors other than explicit/detailed guidelines and individualized/flexible programming existed and operated independently of any specific program element and intervention method, and all 10 factors cut across the elements and methods as a whole.

As with key factors, no *one* element or method seemed powerful or flexible enough to address the youths' complex problems or situation in ways that accounted for CTP's outcomes, that is, for its reduced or comparable levels of illegal behavior. In this respect, no individual program element and no single intervention method provided a guaranteed "answer" regarding any one youth group, let alone all groups combined. Nor, for that matter, did it comprise an essential ingredient—a necessary though, again, not a sufficient condition—for all youths *within* any one group. Nevertheless, as with individual factors, that is, key factors, many individual elements and methods did prove useful to most or all youth

groups, and to many or most individual youths regardless of group.[43]

A closing point. Individually and collectively, key factors also proved useful at another level. Specifically, factors #1 through #7 contributed to the three principles and objectives that were emphasized in CTP:

a. promote humane interaction between staff and youths;

b. facilitate youths' personal involvement in the change process; and

c. facilitate individualized justice and minimize rigid, undifferentiated solutions.

Though objectives (b) and (c) varied considerably in theory as well as practice—for example, personal involvement varied from "slight" to "marked," within each youth group—most of these seven factors thus played a role in achieving all objectives. (Factors #4 and #5 were in fact integral to objective [c].) At least, these factors directly contributed to whatever levels of humane interaction, personal involvement, and individualized justice were achieved.[44] Finally, the program elements and intervention methods mentioned above *also* contributed to these principles and objectives; in fact, it was via the integration of selected program elements, specific intervention methods, and key factors that these objectives were "concretely" expressed with respect to individual youths.

Notes

1. Throughout the 1960s and early 1970s, youths seldom spent less than 18 months on parole prior to being favorably discharged from the Youth Authority. This was standard practice in all regular parole units and special programs except for GGI, and it partly reflected YA Board policy (Appendix 9.)

2. "Individualization" was mainly achieved via detailed diagnostic workups and staffings, plus ongoing observations of each youth. It led, presumably, to the utilization of relevant program elements with each such youth, elements such as schooling and/or out-of-home placement. Individualization was viewed as the primary basis of CTP's felt relevance to the youth, and as thereby facilitating his involvement in a change process that encompassed more than illegal behavior

alone. Thus, as used here, individualization does not simply refer to the relatively distinctive pattern of *inputs* received by each CTP youth; instead, it also includes specific operations (e.g., detailed diagnosis) that *produced* those inputs. "Ongoing observations" were largely made possible by intensive/extensive contacts; as a result, they were analytically included within that factor rather than in the present subfactor (individualization).

3. "Specific abilities and overall perceptiveness" mainly referred to the agent's *level of professional sophistication and self-discipline* (LPSS). CTP agents who worked with assertive-deniers, anxious-confused youths, passive-conformists, and power-oriented individuals, respectively, were each statistically distinguished from regular parole agents (RPA's), collectively, regarding this variable; this also applied to CTP agents who worked with lower maturity youths (I_2's) and delinquent identifiers, respectively (Palmer, 1967a). LPSS was partly defined via the following items (here, these items are presented with regard to the "negative" side of the four- and five-point scales in terms of which they were assessed, during and after Phase 2):

1. believes youths need goals, experiences, emotional satisfactions similar to one's own;
2. believes youths need to conquer inner problems similar to one's own;
3. does not differentiate between behavioral and emotional changes in youths;
4. does not differentiate between rejecting the youths' behavior and rejecting the youths as persons;
5. is unaware of own emotional responses to youths; and
6. believes people, including youths, can be taken at face value (almost exclusively) (Palmer, 1967a, p. 69).

Besides being distinguished from RPA's on the LPSS variable as a whole (all items combined), CTP agent groups were different ($p < .05$) on several individual items (four items each, with the majority of groups); for instance, CTP agents who worked with passive-conformists differed from RPA's on items (1), (3), (4), and (5),

above ($p < .02, .05, .05,$ and $.02$, respectively). Finally, specific abilities and overall perceptiveness were also assessed in connection with: (1) the agents' *use of self (past experiences) as a frame of reference for understanding/working with youths* (a five-item variable), plus three final items from an additional scale that bore on professional sophistication, and (2) five items (distributed across two scales) that centered on the agents' *interpersonal sensitivity, overall resourcefulness, grasp of concepts, intellectual flexibility,* and *breadth of perspective.* In some respects, "use of self . . . as a frame of reference" seemed valuable; in others, however, it appeared irrelevant or inappropriate. Given the nature of the five items in (2), immediately above, there was a slight overlap between key factor #7, on the one hand, and the personality characteristics component of #6, on the other. (Factor #6 included a very broad range of personality characteristics.)

4. See Chapter 14, endnote 4, regarding subgroup expectations.

5. Since matched A-C experimentals performed worse than unmatched A-C E's (Chapter 11), it seems likely that the items used as the primary basis for matching CTP staff with A-C's were not, collectively, especially helpful relative to most such youths. To be sure, the effects of this particular matching remain uncertain due to the over-representation of Status 1 youths in the matched-agent group; and, as suggested in the text, matching nevertheless did seem important with respect to highly vulnerable/disturbed A-C's. Although the primary matching items involved personality characteristics and professional orientations, it is possible that *specific skills and overall perceptiveness*—factors common to A-D *and* A-C workers—were still important to most A-C's, that is, even apart from their significance to highly vulnerable/disturbed youths.

6. Though these youths were I_4's ("higher-maturity level"), they sometimes behaved in ways that many staff considered almost childlike and, in this respect, comparable to that of most I_2's ("lower-maturity level"). Here, it should be noted that CTP's I-level diagnosis did not refer

to an individual's *typical* level of functioning or even his response to abnormal stress. Instead, it related to his *highest* level of functioning and perceptiveness, mainly as reflected in his understanding of other individuals. (Though diagnosis related to the individual's highest level of functioning, *treatment planning*—especially regarding concrete or immediate practical matters—generally emphasized his typical functioning.) At any rate, the agent's skills and perceptiveness seemed important when working with the present, behaviorally unstable and often very impulsive youths.

7. In Phase 3, almost all such individuals were classified as Status l, as were many other A-C's. During Phases 1 and 2, the arrest and conviction rates of the former youths were about equal to those of their controls. These rates *might* have been higher if not for matching.

8. For instance, some passive-conformists had experienced considerably less exploitation, marked inconsistency, indifference, or rejection by adults; and, often, they were first exposed to these at a much later age (e.g., 10–11 rather than 3–6). These youths developed fewer or less intense feelings of unworthiness, powerlessness, or resentment than other P-C's, and they entered adolescence with a moderate degree of optimism regarding not only certain types of adults, but their own chances of experiencing interpersonal satisfaction (Palmer, 1971e). Nevertheless, by ages 13–14 they, too, were somewhat deficient in interpersonal skills and were quite dependent on peer approval. Partly for these reasons, their parents or guardians often remained, or increasingly became, rather controlling of and critical toward them.

9. The often exploitive behaviors and/or hostile attitudes of these youths were frequently directed at adolescents and adults from differing ethnic backgrounds, minority or otherwise. This applied whether or not the former (G-C) youths were minority members themselves. In any event, group or gang membership—especially when combined with recognition by their peers as being adequate, or accomplished, delinquents—helped some such youths temporarily

overlook long-standing feelings of inferiority, powerlessness, or rejection. That is, more than all remaining G-C's, these individuals often derived specific satisfaction or relief from viewing themselves as not simply tough or daring, but as *delinquent* in particular and as persons whom their friends recognized as being prepared to actively demonstrate their delinquent loyalties, and to effectively express their antiauthority views.

10. Though these individuals sometimes described the legal system as prejudiced or generally unfair, their illegal activities seldom reflected long-standing anger toward that system or toward authority figures ("cops"; teachers) who represented either that system or broader aspects of society.

11. The following applied to the remaining subgoals, that is, subgoal components: (1) Regarding the *redirection of coping abilities,* individualization/flexible programming, CTP's guidelines, and the agent's orientation/abilities/perceptiveness seemed important. Among both group conformist types, most such factors were relevant to the peer-pressures issue; among insulated youths alone, they applied to long-term overcompensations. (2) Regarding *change in perception of self,* the following seemed important with both G-C types, though neither group showed major changes in this area: intensive/extensive contacts, long-term contacts, individualization/flexible programming, and contact with project youths plus various staff. With accessible G-C's the agent's personal characteristics, specific abilities, and overall perceptiveness also contributed—the former ("characteristics"), largely in terms of skills-and-relationship modeling.

12. With A-D's, long-term overcompensations mainly refer to personality traits and behavior patterns that are central to the youths' definition of self as adequate, strong, or accomplished, and that help overcome not only underlying feelings to the contrary, but the pressures or rejection of others (Chapter 11).

13. As mentioned earlier, CTP's intensive/extensive contacts and its individualization/flexible programming helped achieve various subgoals, mainly among accessible G-C's. These subgoals bore directly

on issues of peer pressure, subgroup expectations, and material gain. Extensive contacts and flexible programming that centered on those contacts not only helped accessible youths expand their practical skills, but they supported these individual's interpersonal development and thus paved the way for a wider range of social satisfactions. Such developments and satisfactions often helped expand these youths' already-existing, dominant-culture investments or areas of tolerance.

14. During Phases 1 and 2, CTP neither reduced nor equalized the illegal behavior of insulated group conformists, in the first place—that is, relative to their controls. During Phase 3, such youths were diagnosed as "Status 1" (Group B, specifically).

15. This does not mean that (1) assertive-deniers' defenses were almost impenetrable under such conditions, that (2) A-D's rarely profited from the discussions or other interactions in question, and that (3) the given contexts applied to A-D's alone.

16. In part, it also reflected their greater readiness to accept or at least listen to "the worst" about themselves, and their greater willingness to tolerate anxiety-producing or personally embarrassing situations.

17. Although this view often represented the youth's extrapolation of belief "1b" into the future, some youths seemed more concerned with this presumed consequence than with "1b" itself.

18. Cooperation included: largely accepting the conditions of parole (Appendix 3); appearing for scheduled meetings; talking with the agent and others about a range of subjects, not just on specific "demand"; and generally working toward agreed-upon goals, such as completion of a school semester.

19. As stated and implied in the text, these decisions were not made in a vacuum, for example, without information/beliefs about YA institutions, CTP as well as YA parole in general, and, to a lesser extent, CTP's emerging intervention plan. At any rate, shortly after the youth's YA commitment, that is, while still at NRCC, the youths' information, among other things, comprised a large part of his "decision-making base." Thus, despite the general

and specific information/beliefs he had about *CTP*, his decisions at that point, and at later points, were partly based on elements 1a plus 3b per se. That is, they reflected his wish to avoid not only being removed from the community but to avoid the experience of YA institutionalization as well—as based on his information and beliefs about removal and long-term lockup, not simply about CTP. These wishes existed independently of his knowledge and assumptions about CTP. In addition, substantial independence existed *subsequent* to his stay at NRCC, despite some interaction between such wishes, on the one hand, and his actual experiences at CTP, on the other.

20. The existence of program responsibilities—especially for inputs outside the area of external controls—was not seen by CTP staff as diminishing the youth's responsibility for exercising self-restraint regarding illegal behavior.

21. Factor #9, as already shown, involved "internal" stimuli and conditions, such as the youth's personal feelings and beliefs.

22. Anxious-confused youths did not simply feel they could more or less "live with" this loss, one that often included integrity. Instead (in some cases, in addition), they had in effect *defined* autonomy and submissiveness somewhat differently than had assertive-deniers, in the first place.

23. This youth-group difference would have substantial implications for "juvenile awareness" programs, especially those of the "tougher," variety, for example, "Scared Straight" (Finkenauer, 1982; Lewis, 1983).

24. Positive reputation and positive expectations were not prerequisites to the beneficial influence of factors #1 through #9 on individual youths and specified youth groups. Nevertheless, "positive reputation," once established, helped maintain the support of public agencies and YA administration for CTP as a whole. (The discussion that follows relates only to direct impact on youths.) As described in Chapter 17, support from particular local agencies, for example, sheriffs' departments, sometimes varied through time; and, within any given community, substantial support from *all* (in contrast to only some) law enforcement plus

justice system agencies was not required in order to operate CTP.

25. That is, CTP's positive image comprised or included various stimuli that in some cases triggered and in other cases helped crystallize these responses.

26. There were three "responses" in all. The first occurred not only among individuals who wanted to be actively involved in the program but among those who wished only to "go along." The second occurred primarily among the former individuals, and the remaining response was seen almost exclusively among the former.

27. But not necessarily in a better *position* than others, for example, advantaged in comparison to non-CTP, delinquent peers.

28. *Enhance* is defined as in *Webster's* (1965): "To make greater (as in value, desirability, or attractiveness): *heighten*." "Heighten suggests a lifting above the ordinary or accustomed." "'*Enhance*' implies a raising or strengthening above the normal in desirability, value, or attractiveness."

29. That is, similar in felt quality and, to a lesser extent, in conscious content.

30. Sometimes they helped still other A-C's *augment* related features that they already believed they had, though perhaps to an insufficient degree.

31. More precisely, the youths' perception of a "feature" that they valued or came to value (e.g., "goal orientation") eventually resulted in their attempt to create or further develop a similar feature within their own personality or life. In general terms, this outcome occurred after the given perception was integrated (combined) with one or more wishes and was processed in terms of established cognitive structures. Thus, CTP's "goal orientation" was not, in itself, an active motivating and processing factor; however, like various other features, it comprised not only a specific stimulus or trigger for those factors, but the central content with which they dealt.

32. At a rather different level but in a related context, CTP's overall positive reputation—whatever its components might have been—helped make the idea of *being liked* or *respected* more concrete, more meaningful (e.g., with regard to social implications), and more personally appealing to some A-C's.

33. At an extremely broad—almost philosophical—level, these responses, like response (3) itself, reflected what might be viewed as the youths' affirmation or endorsement of self and life. (Neither this endorsement nor the "desire for growth" were conceptualized as such by youths. Response (3) was: "a desire to have characteristics that paralleled CTP's".) In any event, activation of the "potentially worthwhile" aspect of self helped A-C's feel less pessimistic, less anxious, and substantially less confused on a short- and sometimes longer-term basis. This occurred partly because the aspect or component in question helped provide an active counterforce to, and/or at least a psychological screen (defense) against, what the youths viewed as the "unalterably 'bad' part" of themselves. In so doing, it reduced their overall sense of futility or level of distress and uncertainty. Again at a very broad level, the major targets of this counterforce were thus the growth- and/or satisfaction-constricting (nonaffirming and disaffirming) aspects of the youths' personality and/or environment. (It might be mentioned that responses [2] and [3] were elicited not just by CTP's positive reputation, but by its positive expectations.)

34. Similar messages were received from CTP teachers and, during group counseling sessions, from various youths.

35. For example, a major though usually implicit message during early discussions was that if youths did their share relative to the intervention plan, important changes would soon occur in their lives, even if difficulties had to be faced.

36. Initially, many individuals were indeed willing to "go along," for example, to generally cooperate and make at least modest or perhaps moderate attempts to follow most of the original, and perhaps already modified, intervention plans. However, these youths were (1) hardly *interested* in facing large (let alone major) challenges at the time and in dealing with various recurring (let alone continuous) difficulties; or, they were (2) largely, though not entirely, *unwilling* to address them. After several months in the program, many such individuals be-

came interested in dealing with these "tougher" issues, or in doing so more actively and more seriously than before—albeit very selectively. In short, they were then willing to do substantially more than just "go along," even though "going along" may itself have often remained difficult for them to do. (Subsequently, even their increased interest/motivation had its ups and downs.)

37. Not all A-C's had equally strong desires/wishes in this area, and, as indicated, A-C's did not conceptualize the first desire as such.

38. With most A-C's the typical implications or underlying messages were: "If you don't do this, it will probably be harder for you to overcome such and such, or to succeed," and "You will probably have to try something else instead."

39. Thus, with most A-C's, support was usually in the foreground and pressure was in the background. The support/pressure ratio often varied through time and, as seen elsewhere, it usually differed for differing youth types.

40. Here, the agent was very likely to add the following, standard message (paraphrased): "If you want to discuss any problems or if difficult situations arise, I *am* readily available and I want you to contact me. If we plan ahead and deal with such matters in time, chances are good that things will work out all right." By itself, that is, independent of any prior or subsequent messages, these instructions and expectations made it easier for some youths to utilize given resources.

41. This slight, albeit positive impact may have reflected the fact that those components (features) of CTP's reputation that the youths increasingly viewed as positive had acquired some personal significance to them. As a result, such features usually engendered the *type of responses* that were seen among anxious-confused and passive-conformist youths, for example, greater investment in various program goals and specified plans. However, since the *degree of significance* in question was considerably less than that observed among A-C's and P-C's, the present *level of response* was also substantially less than that found among those youths. This lower degree of personal significance

reflected the fact that most assertive-deniers and group conformists seemed to have little motivation to identify with CTP's "power" and "success" (now viewed somewhat positively), perhaps because they—particularly the first group, and partly as an overcompensation—already considered themselves sufficiently competent overall. Nor did CTP's "goal orientation" greatly enhance the project's attractiveness (therefore, its identification-potential), possibly because these youths already liked to consider themselves sufficiently "clear and consistent in purpose or direction" (page 261), or were not especially concerned with this dimension in the first place. In short, in these and other respects, assertive-deniers and group conformists did not seem to draw substantially upon CTP's reputed and/or increasingly evident features for ego enhancement and ego support, certainly not to the extent observed among anxious-confused and passive-conformist youths—most of whom were more dependent and less well-defended. (Thus, for example, with many A-C's and P-C's, identification with a powerful, "understanding," or somehow "superior" organization often reflected their desire for acceptance and approval by that entity, and for increased status as well.) Nevertheless, the present youths did utilize these features to some extent, mainly during the middle phase of their program.

42. With relatively insulated G-C's, support-oriented messages were mostly ignored and responsibility-oriented messages were routinely resisted; in addition, CTP's *reputation* had negative connotations even after the first several months on the project.

43. This applied even though alternative program elements and/or intervention methods might have served these same youth groups and individual youths just as well as—conceivably even better than—the present elements and methods. Neither this observation nor the preceding ones contradict the possibility that future research projects may uncover single factors, elements, or methods that *are* powerful or flexible enough to produce, for example, long-term reductions in illegal behavior.

44. In later chapters (see Volume 2) we may review certain implications of the following facts. (1) Some intervention methods that were emphasized with power-oriented youths often seemed less humane than ones that were used with other youths. (2) Many individuals from each youth group did not become actively—in this respect, personally—involved in implementing the intervention plan, even though they had contributed to its *development* and considered it neither inappropriate nor a sizable burden. Despite (1) and (2) above, various key factors did contribute to the achievement of one or more major subgoals, for example, the reduction of external stress. Beyond this (and despite its definite helpfulness), active involvement by the youths during most of their project experience was not invariably—thus, not necessarily—an essential precondition to the achievement of reduced or comparable illegal behavior. That is, with at least *some* youths, or at various points, just "going along"—for example, being no more than moderately active most of the time (and usually being only *slightly* active, or at any rate much more passive)—seemed to suffice. With many more, however, a fairly active involvement, or even concerted efforts, often appeared essential. (Clearly, involvement by youths in the process of change is a complex matter, one that commonly varies through time, across contexts, and in degree, within and across individuals.)

16 ADDITIONAL OBSERVATIONS REGARDING KEY FACTORS

We will now review key factors that relate to Status 1 males who began their program on Dorm 3, and to Phase 1 and 2 females as well. We will then briefly review additional variables or factors that have been considered possible contributors to reduced or almost equal rates of offending among CTP youths: avoidance of institutionalization, type of program and city, parole agents' background characteristics, and differential decision-making.

Status 1 Youths

As described in Chapter 13, Status 1 (S–1) males were those individuals diagnosed in Phase 3 as needing an initial period of institutionalization within a setting such as Dorm 3, prior to being paroled. (Phase 3 was the only period during which CTP's Dorm 3 operation existed.) Though S–1 males were observed among all youth groups, they were mainly found within the conflicted category. Since relatively few nonconflicted S–1 youths began their YA experience within Dorm 3 and since reduced illegal behavior could be statistically examined—and *was* shown—for *conflicted* S–1 youths only, the following comments will be restricted to these particular Dorm 3 individuals (assertive-deniers and anxious-confused) alone.

With Status 1 youths whose program began in Dorm 3, several factors described in Chapter 15 were again important. For example, the personal characteristics, professional orientation, and overall perceptiveness of staff (factors #6 and #7) seemed to make a major contribution. With respect to the dorm setting, specifically, it was quite likely that if youth counselors had not been carefully se-

lected in those respects they would not have provided S–1 youths with the type of atmosphere and experiences to which these individuals seemed responsive. (The role of parole agents has already been described in connection with these general goals; and regarding dorm-assigned youths, this role was coordinated with that of youth counselors.) Closely related to these goals, such staff would probably have found it very difficult to provide the degree of individualized programming and flexibility (factor #5) that was directly and indirectly involved in most youths' intervention plan—a degree not ordinarily obtained, or even sought, in most institutional settings. Since the youths' intervention plan seemed crucial to their overall adjustment and progress and since individualization and flexibility were crucial features of that plan, factor #5, like factors #6 and #7, seemed to make a major contribution with respect to appropriately assigned S–1 youths.

Intensive contacts (factor #2) were part and parcel of the dorm operation. For one thing, numerous informal contacts between staff and youths were almost assured by virtue of the Dorm's physical structure and its daily living arrangements alone; beyond that, frequent formal and informal interactions were specifically prescribed in the intervention plan, and they usually did occur. During the youths' dorm stay, most contacts involved youth counselors, since they (individually or collectively), not parole agents, usually interacted with given S–1 youths several times a day. *Small caseloads* (factor #1) nevertheless made it possible for *parole agents* (individually) to contact their assigned youths three or four times a week, mainly for individual and group counseling (youth counselors usually participated in the latter). In these respects, factors #1 and #2 each made an important contribution to appropriately assigned youths.

Extensive contacts, for example, a combination of counseling, dorm-centered schooling, and off-dorm socializing experiences, were the second component of factor #2. Like intensive contacts, this factor often played a significant role—despite the existence of slightly fewer program elements than in the community setting. For instance, out-of-home placement and certain kinds of material aid either did not specifically apply during the dorm phase of each youth's program or else they were seldom used.

Explicit, detailed guidelines (factor #4) were not available in connection with Status 1 youths; that is, no *separate* guidelines existed with regard to these individuals, whether or not their program began in the dorm. Nevertheless, many principles and strategies that were mentioned in CTP's established guidelines—those that had long been used within the community settings for conflicted youths in general (Warren et al., 1966b)—seemed applicable to, and were regularly used with, the present (S–1) individuals. Yet even so, considerably more firmness and structure was used with S–1 than with S–2 youths within as well as outside the dorm—that is, more than was suggested in the established guidelines. Thus, although these guidelines were noticeably off-target in this important respect, factor #4 remained, on balance, moderately important.

(The main reasons for this difference in firmness and structure were as follows: Compared to Status 2 youths, Status 1 individuals were usually less trusting of adults and more inclined to openly challenge their authority as well as test their sincerity and tolerance; this was not simply a matter of their wishing to avoid close or open relationships with adults. Within these areas—trust, challenge, and even defiance or evasion—the interactions of conflicted S–1 youths thus often resembled those of manipulators and insulated group conformists. At another level, and apart from trust, challenge, and testing per se, the present individuals were simply less interested than S–2 youths in following through on what *staff* considered short- as well as longer-term commitments, whether or not the latter were central to the intervention plan. Here,

compared to S–2's, S–1's were more insistent—in a sense, more self-centered and impulsive—with respect to "wanting *what* they wanted, *when* they wanted it," regardless of possible consequences and of prior agreements with [or even the feelings of] others. These characteristics applied to assertive-deniers and anxious-confused youths alike, whether in or outside the dorm.)

The preceding factors remained important once these youths were released to the community after completing their Dorm 3 program. At this point small caseloads (factor #1) played an even larger role than before, since staff/youth interactions now primarily involved parole agents—*absent* the counselors. Also, long-term contacts (factor #3) entered the picture for the first time, for the following reason: Since the dorm stay had averaged well under a year, this factor had not, by definition, been applicable to that context—insofar as the dorm stay was, or could be, analytically separated from the community phase. Yet, regarding the dorm and community contexts *combined,* factor #3 acquired analytic as well as substantive meaning; and, in this connection, it seemed moderately important to the majority of appropriately assigned conflicted S–1's.

Females
Background Observations

Mainly due to the small number of female controls in San Francisco, especially in the postdischarge analysis, the following remarks will focus on Valley girls, Phases 1 and 2 combined. Two-thirds of these individuals were classified as conflicted, and two-thirds of all conflicted girls were anxious-confused. Very few girls would have been classified as Status 1.

Compared to males, females had substantially fewer arrests and convictions prior to their YA commitment. During the parole and postdischarge periods combined, their rate of moderate plus severe offending (r.o.o.) was 63 percent to 73 percent lower as well (Tables 8–3 and 8–6, pages 103 and 107, respectively). Moreover, 82 percent of their prior law contacts and 66 percent of their YA commitment offenses (therefore, almost 80 percent of all pre-program offenses) involved "status offenses" alone, mainly runaway and beyond control.[1] In these respects, girls seemed less invested than boys in illegal behavior, certainly that which would remain illegal after their eighteenth birthday. Also, females were less likely to have a strong negative attitude toward representatives of the law and a rejecting or indifferent attitude toward middle-class values. Among these values were conventional (as of the 1960s) concepts of femininity, for example, primary emphasis on traditional roles of wife and mother. At point of YA discharge, 42 percent either were or had been married and the majority had at least one child. (For males, the figures were 19 percent [married] and 22 percent [parents], respectively.)[2]

Among females, delinquency usually stemmed from long-standing, discordant family relationships that commonly involved three or more of the following: parental rejection or abandonment; emotional triangles and related loyalty binds between youths and parents; heavy "guilt messages" from, and frequent "put-downs" by, parents (natural, step, or foster); marked parental domination; physical abuse; and intense sibling rivalry. Prior to and continuing into adolescence, these relationships and events had usually produced two or more of the following responses and adjustments: a low self-image, widespread feelings of anger toward one or both parents (natural or other), sharp dependence/independence conflicts, and compensating personality traits or interpersonal stances. Beginning in early adolescence, these relationships, events, and responses—in conjunction with standard, societal inputs—usually led to rapidly increasing desires for acceptance, immediate or short-term gratification, and a sense of status or worth (validation by others). These desires were to be largely satisfied via peer relationships and in the context of nonchild roles—in short, essentially outside the home.

Thus, the illegal behavior in question—often including sexual relationships with boyfriends or casual acquaintances—did not just reflect typical (usual) modes of expression and development within the contemporary society, and seldom did it primarily involve a reaction against then-standard female roles. Instead, it mainly represented an actual or symbolic escape from unpleasant family interactions and, very often, an expression of anger or defiance with respect to specific current events (family, school, etc.). Also, besides the responses and adjustments (e.g., low self-image) mentioned earlier, it occasionally reflected (1) an attempt to divide the family, for example, mother and un-wanted stepfather, or (2) the youths' identification with a promiscuous, angry, or markedly self-destructive mother. Other factors will now be briefly mentioned.

Whether or not status offenses were involved, illegal behavior seldom reflected the following: under-socialization, poor impulse control (as a *long-standing, general* trait), subgroup expectations, antisocial or antiauthority family orientation, and conflicting social values. However, family disorganization and long-term overcompensations were not infrequent contributors, and, on a more immediate basis, peer pressures and situational entanglements usually added to the picture. The latter factors less often centered around gangs or street-corner groups than around one or two male companions, for example, in connection with a runaway episode or a weekend spree. Singly and in combination, these two factors were often decisive in terms of specifically focusing, then triggering or releasing, already existing tendencies and desires.

Finally, "desire for material gain" was a fairly common contributor, usually taking the form of shoplifting and prostitution. However, among Valley girls, the latter behavior generally developed *within* the context of discordant family relationships and subsequent responses by youths, for example, expressions of anger or defiance.[3] In this context the economic motive—while nevertheless significant, especially among runaways—was usually less salient and powerful among conflicted individuals than among passive-conformists and manipulators. Sometimes, with all such groups, prostitution was also a conscious means of ego-boosting, for example, a basis for viewing oneself as acceptable or desirable, or for feeling increased power or control. (In San Francisco, prostitution was very common among all youth groups, for economic and noneconomic reasons alike.)

Key Factors

The comparable illegal behavior of Valley E's and C's (Table 12–1, page 201) partly reflected the low absolute rate of offending by both such groups: less than one moderate plus severe arrest per four years at risk. That is, since neither group engaged in much offending, it was difficult though not impossible for *either* group to outperform the other on tests of statistical reliability, however well that group may have performed. This low absolute r.o.o. reflected not only the youths' lack of heavy investment in moderate plus severe offense behavior, but factors such as the following (these comments are mainly based on [1] extensive, routine case documentation by CTP and non-CTP parole agents; [2] detailed intake and follow-up interviews with numerous, unselected E and C girls; [3] at least one depth interview with each E and C agent; and [4] five taped, half-day conferences during 1966–1969, each attended by female CTP agents from Sacramento, Stockton, and San Francisco and by one or more researchers, and each one focused on girls alone):

With *controls,* given the fact that most females were not very delinquency-oriented from the start, it was probably easier than would otherwise have been the case for their institutional experience to produce a fairly strong "resolve" not to be reincarcerated. Here, institutionalization included not only the counseling, therapy, and/or practical training (schooling; trade classes) that was provided, but—especially—the unpleasantness and frequent dreariness that was felt. In this respect, habilitation and rehabilitation were involved as well as specific deterrence. Regarding deterrence, it might be added that many such youths viewed incarceration as similar to life at home—not just with respect to overall unpleasantness but, specifically, domination by or frequent conflict with a female adult. However, a few seemed to consider it better than home.

Upon the control girls' release to parole, their agents made it clear that illegal behavior—status offenses included—could, and probably would, quickly result in revocation and reinstitutionalization.[4] Agents usually backed this position, often in relation to relatively mild offenses or technical violations of parole. In so doing, they established a reputation for "toughness" that served as an additional deterrent for many girls, under a wide range of conditions. (Fifty-eight percent of all revocations were for such offenses or infractions as beyond control, runaway, whereabouts unknown, foster home failure, and truancy. Forty-two percent were for glue sniffing, drug usage, soliciting [often during a runaway], burglary, possession of dangerous weapons, and so on. Forty-two percent of all revocations were on a first offense, and 88 percent of these revocations were for beyond control, runaway, and so forth.)

This "tough" stance by the control girls' agents often reinforced the resolve mentioned earlier—not just during times of stress or of *weakened* resolve, and not just among youths who were only mildly delinquent. Since (1) many parolees had been returned to their previous community and living environment and to many of the same external pressures that existed prior to institutionalization, and since (2) most parolees were not having their still-existent, already internalized problems or conflicts systematically focused on by the agent, it was largely this stance plus the youths' own resolve that eliminated, curbed, or otherwise greatly reduced given delinquent responses.

Most control girls who *were* later reinstitutionalized because of continued illegal behavior or technical violations developed a greater desire than before to behave in such a way—when back on parole, and when eventually discharged—that they would never reexperience long-term lockup.[5] This applied especially though not exclusively to those whose delinquency orientation was relatively mild, in the first place. Together with the factor reviewed below, namely, marriage, such experiences and desires, plus those already mentioned, helped produce a post-YA rate of offending that was 32 percent lower than that observed during parole, for all control girls combined (Tables 8–4 and 8–5, pages 104 and 106, respectively).

Throughout Phase 1 and part of Phase 2, agents who worked with the vast majority of these controls often encouraged those who were "going steady" to seriously consider marriage; at a minimum, they seldom established major or seemingly unreasonable roadblocks.[6] (These agents seldom discouraged girls from "going steady," in the first place.) For example, on the latter point, they indicated to such youths that they would approve a proposed marriage if the prospective husband showed definite ability to hold a job, was not physically abusive or emotionally disturbed, and, where applicable (which it often was), was probably the father of the girl's child or child-to-be. While paternity was not a precondition, it made approval easier.

The following, which partly reflects the agents' attitude yet also relates to subsequent remarks, might also be noted: Forty percent of all females who received a favorable discharge had gotten married while on parole, 16 months prior to discharge (on average), and almost always with the agents' express consent. Of these girls, 7 *percent* were revoked between the time of their marriage and that of discharge. Thirty-two percent of all females who received an *un*favorable discharge had gotten married while on parole, 14 months prior to discharge, on the average. Almost half of these marriages occurred while the youths were "whereabouts unknown," and did not have the agents' approval. Between the time of their marriage and that of discharge, 83 *percent* of these girls were revoked (usually twice)—this, in addition to their eventual unfavorable discharge. (Months to discharge excludes all lockup time but does not exclude time in marriages that ended in divorce, annulment, or separation, prior to YA discharge.)

Although the following account may seem "old-fashioned" after the 1970s decade of the women's liberation movement, it nevertheless reflects the youths' personal dynamics in conjunction with major social realities of the 1960s. These realities, or characteristics and forces of the times, basically involved numerous stimuli to which almost all females were exposed, independent of their Youth Authority experience. Included were cultural role models, common social expectations of the time, and general ideas as to how one might attain not only the acceptance or affection of others, but a sense of self-worth and overall pleasure plus security. These characteristics and forces were observed or inferred by female as well as male researchers and operations staff.

"Going steady" and, especially, marriage, seemed to help many control girls deal with the earlier-mentioned difficulties and desires in ways that reduced external and internal pressures for continued illegal behavior. Marriage, for example, often helped them physically leave their unpleasant home setting under generally acceptable conditions—legally (e.g., without running away), as well. It also legitimized their desires to make independent decisions, and it frequently helped them resist the long-standing domination of particular adults and peers; as such, it directly bore upon, and obviated, such issues as "incorrigibility" and "beyond control." In addition, marriage sometimes reduced or temporarily resolved their economic problems. For instance, many girls who had been prostituting (like many who had not) were, at point of marriage, still in a weak position with regard to the conventional job market, despite their YA schooling or skills-centered training.

Finally, at a basic psychological level, marriage, with its roles of wife and, often, mother, usually helped supply their long-sought sense of acceptance—including their desire to be wanted, needed, and valued. As long as the marriage held up, these feelings usually served as a powerful, added incentive for remaining "on the good side of the law." This power existed even though several internalized problems or interpersonal difficulties had primarily shifted to the background, without having been largely resolved.

The youths' conscious decision to eliminate or greatly curtail delinquent behavior and to not risk losing what they felt they had gained in connection with marriage—child custody sometimes included—seemed to have made a decisive difference. In this respect the following thus applied despite the individuals' continued self-doubts, their unresolved dependence/independence conflicts, and their relative absence of self-development in nontraditional areas: Marriage seemed to help many such youths "settle down" and act in ways usually considered "more mature," for example, more self-controlled, more considerate, more responsible, and more future oriented.[7] To be sure, several marriages were characterized by considerable turmoil from the start (26 percent of all marriages ended in divorce, annulment, or separation, prior to YA discharge), and they involved little if any settling down. These, however, were in the minority. Finally, the preceding remarks do not imply that girls who did not get married did not settle down or otherwise improve. However, they suggest that most females who did get married *were* likely to do so—often fairly quickly.

With *experimentals,* the previously mentioned "tough stance" was essentially absent. That is, CTP agents rarely revoked females for status offenses alone, even after three or four such offenses. Also, until the second half of Phase 2, these agents usually gave girls "one more chance" subsequent to such offenses as soliciting, possession of drugs, shoplifting, and check passing.[8] (As with controls, E girls were worked with by female agents. Occasionally, however, a male agent served as co-leader in coed group sessions, and assisted during vacations or illnesses.)

Basically, these agents viewed most offenses as the youths' response to internalized conflicts, loyalty binds, and external pressures, often of a crisis nature. (Thus, such offenses were sometimes called "acting-out behavior," though not all acting-out was illegal.) CTP agents believed that (1) these difficulties and issues could be dealt with especially well, or could be constructively brought to a head, when they were uppermost in the youths' mind, and that (2) the latter condition quite often occurred at the time of, and shortly after, the youths' offense, not several months after a resulting revocation. This was the agents' chief rationale for retaining most girls (65 percent) on parole after their first nonstatus offense—provided this was not assaultive or otherwise quite severe—rather than revoking them at that point and recommending, to the board, a long-term lockup.[9]

Thus, like many males, many females were considered especially capable of making progress (1) when they had committed an offense (though, of course, not *only* then), (2) when they returned from or had been returned from a "whereabouts unknown," and (3) at times of crisis or heightened stress, whether or not accompanied by an offense. More specifically, at such times these girls seemed prepared to recognize their problems, needs, and overall situation more clearly than before; often, they were also willing to involve themselves in the program more actively than before, or perhaps for the first time. (To be sure, many other females recognized their problems and made progress without being involved in illegal behavior and without undergoing a serious crisis.) These events, agent beliefs, and actual as well as presumed youth responses occurred within, and might best be understood in relation to, the following context:

From early in most females' CTP experience, agents tried to help them resolve or greatly reduce their internalized problems, neutralize or eliminate various external pressures, and confront as well as modify their counterproductive defenses. To achieve these goals they concentrated on "underlying" (causation-related) issues much more than did control agents, issues that were often quite "loaded." Such an effort was made possible mainly by factor #2 (intensive/extensive contacts), #5 (individualization/flexible programming), #3 (long-term contacts), and #7 (agent's abilities and perceptiveness—not "matching," per se). As with males, factors #2 and #5 required low caseloads (factor #1); and given these factors, so did #3.

This focused effort often aroused tensions and anxieties in youths that might otherwise not have been aroused, at least to the degree that they were. These tensions were seen, by agents, as a sometimes unavoidable part of—and, frequently, a direct consequence of—helping these individuals recognize their internalized problems and begin to deal with or modify their external pressures and counterproductive defenses. However, these intervention-induced or intervention-heightened tensions occasionally led to illegal behavior, for example, runaway followed by soliciting or check passing. (This level of tension was more likely to occur during Phase 2 than Phase 1.)[10]

Because these tensions made it more likely that nonstatus offenses and other illegal behavior would occur among various girls, and because CTP agents were likely to give these girls "one more chance" if and when the former behavior occurred, the following applied (it might be kept in mind that a few girls seemed to think their agent would give them "one *last* chance," if they committed a *second* nonstatus/nonminor offense.[11]). These youths, collectively, accumulated more such offenses during parole than might have been the case if their agents had not been making a concentrated effort, and if they, the youths, had been revoked immediately after their first nonstatus offense. Although relatively few nonstatus/nonminor offenses were thus accumulated, these were enough to prevent experimentals from performing reliably better than controls, since the latter had accumulated few such offenses themselves. In short, given the C's low base rate of arrests and convictions for moderate plus severe offenses, even an occasional nonstatus/ nonminor offense by E's virtually eliminated the chances of their performing significantly better than C's.

Before continuing, it might be emphasized that illegal behavior was not always, and not only, a product of focused efforts, that is, intensive intervention. Nor did it only occur, and invariably occur, at times of heightened stress, whether or not this stress largely resulted from the agents' focused efforts. Illegal behavior also, or alternatively, reflected such factors as a relative lack of deterrence-based (and institution-generated) "resolve" on the part of CTP females (i.e., relative to control girls), focused efforts and added stress aside. This relative lack existed despite the fact that, with the partial exception of assertive-deniers, females in general were more likely than males to regard self-restraint—specifically, restraint of illegal behavior—as a sign of strength or accomplishment than as one of submission or defeat. Finally, as suggested, girls were often given "one more chance" not as a reflection of "softness" or because they were female, but mainly because their agents believed that many youths who had just committed an offense were, at that time, especially open to intervention. The YA Board usually accepted the agents' recommendation ("restore to parole"), in connection with the first nonstatus/nonminor offense.

As implied, CTP agents hoped that, by resolving or greatly reducing the youths' main difficulties, less illegal behavior would occur in the long run. The possible achievement of this goal is suggested by the fact that, with females, postdischarge rates of moderate plus severe offending for E's were 62 percent to 67 percent lower than those during parole. (Such rates were also lower for C's, but to a lesser degree.) Be this as it may, two points might be noted regarding the parole, that is, predischarge, period itself; and, as will be suggested, these points bear on the question of "trade-offs."

(1) Besides its deterrent effects, per se, institutionalization had temporarily removed controls from their family and from other delinquency-related situations. In contrast, CTP had kept experimentals in the midst or proximity of many such interactions and events, and had tried to help them deal with those factors and forces in more acceptable ways than before. Upon release from the institution, and assisted by whatever insights and other gains they had acquired during their stay, *controls* had to deal with their situation largely by themselves—via "inner resolve," and so on—albeit with further backing and/or pressure from their parole agent. This "on-your-own" approach had certain potential advantages over various CTP approaches; for instance, it helped develop the youths' self-reliance more rapidly in certain respects. However, it often led to, or even specifically required, more trial and error than might otherwise have occurred, especially among younger C's. It was also associated with considerably more revocation and long-term lockup than in the case of E's, for example, following given "errors."

(2) Most CTP agents believed in making substantial headway with causation-related issues *before* the youths got married. Given such headway, marriage, they believed, would involve (among other things) less of an escape or attempted escape from problems that might *later* reappear under various conditions, for example, if the marriage were to collapse before the youths developed further strengths and resources. As a result, compared to C's, E's usually got married after they were well into their parole (21 months, on average). This meant that, since the needs and desires mentioned earlier were perhaps not being satisfied to the extent that marriage apparently could often satisfy them, the related "settling down" conditions did not fully come into play until a somewhat later point (controls got married 15 months into their parole, on the average; see figures below, regarding "settling down"). This relative delay, by itself, probably increased the chances of illegal acting-out prior to YA discharge, since many E's could thus have spent a larger portion of their total parole time dealing with unmet or partially satisfied needs and desires that had previously triggered such behavior.[12]

(Of all E's who got married during parole, 86 percent had one or more offenses while in the YA but prior to their marriage ["YA-priors"], and their average number of YA-priors was 2.6. In contrast, of all such E's, 9 percent had one or more offenses *after* marriage but prior to discharge ("YA-subsequents"), and their average number of YA-subsequents was 0.2. Of all C's who got married during parole, 67 percent had one or more YA-priors and their average number of priors was 1.4. In contrast, of all such C's, 15 percent had one or more YA-subsequents and their average number of subsequents was 0.2. [For E's and C's alike, offenses that occurred after a divorce, annulment, or separation—but not remarriage—are excluded from these figures.] For all E's in question, and excluding all lockup time plus divorce, annulment, and separation time but not remarriage time, the before-marriage/after-marriage months at risk were 21 and 13, respectively; for C's, they were 15 and 12. For E's and C's alike, YA-priors and YA-subsequents were predominantly of the *status* variety, yet they also involved many "whereabouts unknown." Among C's, revocations that occurred after marriage mainly centered on the latter offense. For E's and C's alike, 3 percent of all marriages occurred prior to the YA; within one and a half years on the average, all but one had failed.)

Since (1) experimentals had not been institutionalized prior to parole (CTP) and had thus not developed the earlier-mentioned deterrence-based "resolve," and since (2) these individuals remained in the midst or proximity of delinquency-related conditions from the start of their CTP program, the following applied: E's might well have largely maintained their pre-YA behavior patterns if their problems, pressures, and counterproductive defenses had not been focused on from a relatively early point in parole, and if their general interests or specific abilities had not been at least partly tapped. In effect, though intensive, individualized intervention probably helped pave the way for some illegal behavior by bringing troublesome issues to the surface and to a head, such intervention may have been one of the few available ways to avoid a substantially *higher* rate of offending during parole, under the conditions at hand. More specifically, this level of acting-out may have represented a necessary "price," or trade-off, for (1) avoiding the combination of institutionalization plus a relatively "tough" parole stance, while (2) retaining the youths in their home community in order to more directly and comprehensively deal with their delinquency-producing and delinquency-supporting conditions.

For the remainder of this chapter we will focus on Phase 1 and 2 boys, as in Chapter 15.

Additional Variables

Avoidance of Institutionalization

Did E's outperform C's because the former did not experience long-term lockup prior to parole? Based on the following analysis, the answer is no.

As indicated in Chapter 2, 17 percent of all controls did not experience long-term lockup prior to being paroled. Of these youths, 69 percent were paroled directly from NRCC, four to six weeks after being committed to the Youth Authority. The remaining 31 percent stayed either at NRCC or in a YA institution for an additional one to six weeks (3½ weeks average) until placement plans bore fruit, at which point these individuals were immediately paroled. All such youths would have been paroled within the normal period—from NRCC—if a placement, for instance, a foster home, had been available at the time of their original board appearance. Together, these youths will be called *direct and early parolees* (DEP's). Like experimentals, they did not experience long-term lockup (LTL) prior to parole.

To focus on the above question, DEP's were first compared with all remaining controls. (The latter individuals [LTL's] experienced nine months of lockup, on the average, prior to parole.) This comparison, which involved the same methods as those in Chapter 8, indicated that no statistically reliable differences existed in the monthly rates of offending of DEP's and LTL's, with respect to the parole and four-year postdischarge periods combined. Specifically, for direct and early parolees, the rates of arrest per 1,000 months at risk were as follows, for moderate plus severe, severe, and violent offenses, respectively: 54, 20, and 11. For the long-term lockups they were 62, 23, and 10.[13] Next, DEP's and LTL's were each compared with *experimentals,* again using the same methods—for example, definitions, samples, and statistical tests—as mentioned earlier. Here, each such group performed reliably worse than E's with regard to moderate plus severe arrests and convictions (see Table 8–3 [page 103] regarding r.o.o.'s for E's). Although the latter findings (each C versus E), like the former (DEP-C's versus LTL-C's), pertained to the total group, they applied especially to conflicted and passive-conformist youths.

Thus, not only did controls perform about the same whether or not they experienced long-term incarceration, but C's who did not have this experience performed (like those who did have it) significantly worse than E's.[14] The latter finding (DEP's versus E's) highlights the fact that CTP was not only located in the community, that is, did not simply avoid institutionalization, but that it contained features which were essentially absent within, and/or different in degree from, the traditional program, even when *that* program avoided long-term lockup.[15]

Type of Community Program

Two supplementary points might be mentioned. (1) Like CTP, the Guided Group Interaction program avoided long-term lockup. However, unlike CTP (particularly for severe and violent offenses), it did not produce significantly lower rates of offending than the traditional (control) program (Table 9–3, page 118). This suggests that community-based programming does not invariably reduce illegal behavior, even if it involves added resources and is relatively complex or sophisticated. Regarding resources, and so on, it might be noted that, compared to the *control* program, GGI was characterized by small caseloads, intensive contacts, equal program length, and a systematic, theory-based approach. Compared to *CTP*, GGI had slightly larger caseloads, roughly equal intensity of contacts, and an equally systematic (in some respects more systematic) approach, although the latter was not accompanied by detailed, written guidelines and was undifferentiated as to youth type. Overall, GGI placed much greater emphasis on group processes than either control or CTP, and was much less individualized than the latter.

(2) CTP produced significantly lower rates of offending than GGI for the parole and post-discharge periods combined; this involved not only moderate plus severe convictions, but severe and violent arrests and convictions. Together with (1), above, this suggests that not all community-based programs are equally effective in reducing illegal behavior, if and when they reduce it at all. Compared to CTP, GGI involved less extensive contacts with youths and others, less individualization/flexible programming, somewhat shorter program length, and no systematic youth/agent matching. However, GGI and CTP agents were at essentially the same "level" in terms of specific abilities and overall perceptiveness, that is, factor #7.

Type of City
The similarity of findings between the Valley and San Francisco units suggests that *type and/or size of city* was not a significant factor in accounting for the better performance of E's than C's. This conclusion best applies to the specific range of settings that were involved during the experiment and its follow-up period: the modestly and moderately urbanized cities of Stockton and Sacramento, at one end, and the highly urbanized San Francisco, at the other. Including their immediate environs, the former settings spanned the 100,000–275,000 population range and were steadily growing at the time; the latter contained 750,000 and was slowly decreasing in population. Within the Valley, the similarity but by no means identity of findings between Stockton and Sacramento further supports this conclusion (see Palmer and Warren, 1967; Palmer et al., 1968); and, though quantitatively limited, the experience in minimally urbanized or semirural Modesto (pop. 55,000) strengthens and extends the conclusion at the lower end. A direct field test would be needed

to clearly determine whether similar outcomes could occur in cities over 1,000,000 in population, however urbanized they might be. Extrapolating from the present findings, we believe the results would resemble those from San Francisco.

Parole Agents' Background Characteristics
CTP and regular parole agents (RPA's) were quite similar to each other on almost all background characteristics that were measured. As a result, the better performance of E's than C's could only slightly or moderately be attributed to differences in that regard, particularly after Phase 1 (1961–1964). Specifically, as seen in Chapter 11, CTP agents and RPA's were similar on age, racial composition, and amount as well as type of prior work experience within and outside the YA. Regarding experience, for example, they had accumulated, respectively, four years (CTP) and three and a half years (RPA) of "counseling and treatment" combined, and, in each case, seven years total time within the helping professions. (Despite this overall similarity in work experience, no CTP parole agents [PA's] and almost all RPA's were at the entry level ["PA I's"] during Phase 1 of the experiment [1961–1964]. After that point, all newly hired CTP agents were PA I's.)[16] As to level and type of education, all agents had completed four years of college or its equivalent, and their areas of major emphasis were similar (usually corrections, psychology, or sociology) except for heavier emphasis by RPA's in "social sciences" (specific field unstated). A somewhat but not significantly higher percentage of CTP agents had taken graduate courses and obtained an advanced degree, usually a master's of social work. The latter differences may have helped account for their somewhat different professional orientation, for instance, their views regarding needed intervention, and for their generally higher level of professional sophistication—that is, for differences in factor #6 as well as factor #7.

Differential Decision-Making
Prior to 1973, differential decision-making (DDM) by YA staff was described as having contributed to the E/C difference in "rate of recidivism," particularly at 15-months follow-up (Palmer, 1968a, 1968c, 1970c, 1971a). DDM referred to the fact that CTP agents

were more likely than regular parole agents to restore individuals to parole immediately after their first nonminor offense, for example, possession of marijuana (still a felony during Phases 1 and 2), possession of narcotics paraphernalia, drunk driving (noninjury), petty theft, or auto theft (unplanned). This offense had usually occurred prior to 15 months on parole. (A small, statistically nonsignificant E/C difference existed for *certain* nonminor offenses, for instance, glue sniffing, drunkenness, resisting arrest, joyriding, and burglary. That is, CTP and regular parole agents were about equally likely to restore youths for their first such offense. This aside, E as well as C males were seldom revoked for *minor* offenses, that is, severity levels 1 and 2.) At any rate, for this reason, DDM *did* contribute to the E/C recidivism difference at 15 months.[17]

However, recidivism did not literally mean, and specifically reflect, repeat *offending*. Instead, the E/C difference in rate of recidivism meant that a higher percentage of E's than C's had not been *revoked* as of the 15-months follow-up point; that is, they had not been revoked despite their possible, earlier-mentioned offense. (To keep the revocation picture in perspective, *most* youths who were not revoked had accumulated either no offenses or minor offenses only.) In short, youths could have been arrested and convicted for a nonminor offense, say, after several months on parole, and still not have "recidivated" in the specific sense of having been revoked, recommitted, or poorly discharged within 15 months from first release; this, indeed, would have happened if they had been restored with regard to that offense. A few E and C boys, in fact, accumulated two such offenses and restorals without having been revoked. In any event, for E's and C's alike, especially for the former, there were fewer revocations than offenses, since offenses did not always lead to revocation.

"Rate of recidivism" thus reflected revocations, and so on, and—ultimately—frequency of restoral to parole. Restoral, like revocation, was a *staff decision,* not an offense; as such, its occurrence or nonoccurrence depended not just on the nature of given individuals' offense, but on the agents' belief in their ability to assist those individuals while also protecting society. (To be sure, E as well as C agents almost always had parole revoked [see close of endnote 8] subsequent to very severe offenses such as robbery or rape, intervention prospects notwithstanding; given such offenses, DDM was out of the question.) Presumed ability to assist, in turn, largely reflected the agents' assessment of the following: available program resources, current external supports and stresses in the youths' environment, possible new directions or different emphases in the intervention, the youth/agent relationship, and the youths' motivation. Thus, restoral or nonrestoral was often a product of various judgments concerning the youths as individuals—more specifically, individuals within the context of a given program (with *its* particular resources and/or flexibility) and set of forces. For this reason, the agents' act of choosing, and their choice itself, was sometimes described as "information-based" or "treatment-relevant" decision-making, not simply "differential" or "policy-based" decision-making, even though the latter terms were no less valid (Palmer, 1968a, 1971a).

Such decisions and labels notwithstanding, it was clear that (1) "percentage of youths who recidivated" did not adequately reflect known illegal activities, that is, *youth behavior,* and that (2) such behavior provided a better all-around index of program effectiveness than did recidivism, even though the latter had important implications of its own. For these and related reasons, the principal measure of effectiveness that was used in CTP analyses since 1973, and that appears in this book, involves youth behavior itself, not staff decisions in response to that behavior. Once again, *staff decisions* (thus, "recidivism") reflect the percentage of youths revoked, unfavorably discharged, and so on, within specified follow-up periods; in contrast, youth behavior is presented as a "monthly rate of offending" (r.o.o.). The latter index encompasses all known offenses regardless of when they occur; this includes ones for which individuals are restored as well as revoked. (See Chapter 7, page 92.)

As indicated, staff's decision to restore or revoke was necessarily made *after* the given offense to which it referred. Whatever decision was reached, this offense retained its identity; that is, it always remained the same offense ("arrest"), as originally entered on Department of Justice rapsheets.[18] Since this offense occurred during parole, it contributed to the individuals' rate of offending for the parole period specifically, and its contribution to that r.o.o. was identical whether the youths were restored or revoked. All r.o.o.'s that related to the *post-parole* period—specifically, to the four-year postdischarge follow-up—reflected offenses that occurred when the individuals were no longer under the Youth Authority's jurisdiction. That is, they occurred after YA staff could no longer make decisions—differential, information-based, or otherwise—regarding them. Post-parole offenses contributed to r.o.o. in exactly the same way as parole offenses.

In sum, differential decision-making, sometimes called discretionary decision-making, did not account for E/C differences in rate of *offending,* since staff decisions that occurred subsequent to given offenses were obviously not the cause of those offenses and since it was those offenses, not staff decisions, that formed the sole basis of the present r.o.o.'s.

Notes

1. No status offenses fell within the moderate plus severe category. They were all classified as minor.
2. The preceding attitudes were clearly reflected in the girls' initial and follow-up interviews. At point of discharge, 48 percent of all controls were currently married or had been married; another 4 percent were engaged. Among experimentals, the figures were 42 percent and 4 percent. Among C's as well as E's, two-thirds of all girls who were either married or had previously been married had one or more children. Of all C's, whether or not they had been married, 52 percent had at least one child (live birth) and 0 percent were known to be pregnant at the time of discharge. For E's, the figures were 53 percent and 5 percent, respectively.
3. Sometimes, for example, prostitution partly represented the youths' way of trying to punish one or both parents and of saying, in effect, "Look at what you made me do." Similar motives and messages were not uncommon with respect to other forms of behavior.
4. Or, for girls who had been directly paroled, *in*stitutionalization.
5. In this connection, girls were less likely than boys to be institutionalized three or more times during their YA career. This

occurred despite the fact that minor offenses, such as runaway and beyond control, were much more likely to be their basis for revocation.

6. With slight exceptions during the first year of Phase 1, there were two Sacramento-based, female agents throughout Phases 1 and 2—that is, the same two individuals, not simply any two at a time. Since the Stockton regular parole unit never contained many girls, that is, controls, these two agents handled 88 percent of all such Valley girls (Sacramento and Stockton combined).
7. Marriage often seemed to produce similar changes in boys, E's and C's alike.
8. Beginning in 1966–1967, CTP agents were more likely than before to revoke youths in connection with their first non-status offense, for example, burglary or prostitution. This shift was partly due to moderate but steady pressure from Youth Authority administration and the YA Board, segments of which had come to feel that CTP was often "too soft" with repeat offenders. At about the same time, male as well as female *control* agents were becoming "more tolerant." For instance, female agents were less likely than before to revoke girls in connection with their first offense—especially, but not solely, a status offense; moreover, they were less likely to revoke for status offenses at all. This shift seemed largely related to CTP (a development that was widely acknowledged at the time). Specifically, based on their knowledge of CTP's Phase 1 findings and their personal contacts with various operations staff, some control agents—that is, regular parole agents, males and females alike—and their supervisors began to feel they had perhaps been insufficiently individualized in their revocation practices and had not always utilized available options. Utilization of new options soon became especially obvious in the Stockton regular parole unit, where a former CTP parole agent had become supervisor, and then remained in that role until the early 1970s. At any rate, about halfway through Phase 2, CTP and control agents began behaving increasingly alike with respect to revocation practices—especially but not exclusively in

their recommendations regarding moderately serious (levels 3–5), nonstatus offenses. (Regarding *severe* offenses—levels 6 through 10—few CTP/control differences had existed from the start of Phase 1.) Yet, despite substantial convergence during the next two and a half years, modest to moderate differences still existed at the end of Phase 2 with respect to minor and moderately serious offenses. (Two points that applied throughout Phase 1 and 2 might be noted. First, among control boys, over 90 percent of all revocations resulted from nonstatus offenses, moderate plus severe offenses in particular. Second, by law, CTP as well as control agents could only *recommend* revocation ["revoke parole"] or restoration ["restore to parole," i.e., "remove from suspended status"], in connection with any given offense; it was the *YA Board* that actually revoked or restored. To be sure, the board almost never disagreed with CTP and control agents' recommendations concerning revocation; however, it not infrequently disagreed regarding restoral.)

9. For descriptive and analytic purposes, the "nonstatus" category does not include "whereabouts unknown." Usually, this offense was easily distinguished from "runaway," since, in the latter case, the individuals' whereabouts *were* quickly determined by the agent, and the youths, regardless of their age, had not necessarily run away in the first place.
Revocations that followed extended periods of "whereabouts unknown"—for example, 3 to 12 months—were not rare, even among individuals who had accumulated no other nonstatus offenses.

10. With most anxious-confused youths and many assertive-deniers, CTP's Phase 2 female agents concentrated more heavily and more directly than Phase 1 agents on internal problems: personal conflicts, family dynamics, and so on. (Practical issues and external pressures were not ipso facto overlooked or minimized by Phase 2 agents.) This focus, when continued for some 6 to 18 months, seemed closely associated with periods of considerable tension in many girls, and—usually at such times—with occasional illegal behavior.

11. Their belief was not unfounded: Of all E girls who accumulated two or more nonstatus/nonminor offenses (excluding "whereabouts unknown"), 60 percent had not been revoked as of, and were not revoked immediately following, the second such offense.

12. This applied even though the youth/agent relationship partly satisfied many girls' need for acceptance, and their wish to be valued. (The individuals' feeling of being "part of CTP" often served a similar function.) Controls (C's) who got married while on parole were approximately the same age, at that point, as experimentals (E's) who themselves had married during parole. This was despite the fact that E's had been involved in their program for six months longer, on the average, before they got married—that is, longer than C's had been involved in *their* parole program as of that point. Basically, this age similarity reflected the fact that C's were about nine months older than E's when they (C's) were released to parole in the first place. This was the case because institutionalization—during Phases 1 and 2 combined—had averaged 9.3 months for females (8.5 when the direct parolees were included) (Davis et al.,1969).

13. For convictions, the figures were: DEP—34, 14, 6; LTL—38, 13, 5. DEP's and LTL's were similar to each other in terms of age, IQ, race, commitment offense, level of parole risk, I-level, and subtype; however, the former tended to have a higher socioeconomic status ($p < .10 > .05$).

14. The C versus E finding specifically supported that of an earlier-reported analysis which used parole failure—revocation, recommitment, or poor discharge—as the index of effectiveness. The C versus C finding was somewhat different than that of this earlier-reported, *parole only*, C versus C analysis, one whose findings differed in direction:

When the factor of institutionalization (Ins.) is held relatively constant across E and C programs (through a comparison between E youths and C "direct parolees" plus "early releases to parole"), the community-located E program is found to perform better with reference to 24-months follow-up than what may be termed the community-located C program (traditional parole, with prior institutionalization omitted or greatly reduced). At the same time, the direct-parole/early-release group of C's perform slightly but not significantly worse on parole follow-up than C's who have experienced the regular Ins. program. (Palmer, 1971a, p. 90)

Although this recidivism—not r.o.o. per se—analysis included girls as well as boys (and although [for various reasons] 21 percent, not 17 percent, of all C's were DEP's), results were basically the same for boys alone.

15. The latter point is also brought out—albeit less clearly and sharply—by certain differences that emerged regarding two sets of comparisons: (1) In the case of E's, key factor #9 (CTP as a substitute for institutionalization) made, perhaps, a moderate contribution to the reduction of illegal behavior (Chapter 15); here, E's were compared with all C's combined. However, (2) among C's, direct parole (which, like CTP, was a particular type of in-lieu—"substitute"—program) reduced illegal behavior (i.e., rate of offending) marginally if at all; here, specified C's (DEP's) were compared with all remaining C's (LTL's). This slight difference in the contributions of the E and C "substitute" programs suggests the following possibility regarding the reduction of illegal behavior in the present experiment. What may matter is not exclusively or perhaps even *primarily* that which is avoided, namely, long-term lockup, but that which is experienced, for example, a particular form of intensive parole, on the one hand, or standard, nonintensive parole on the other. (This possibility exists not only when the probable role of key factor #8 [the community setting] is also taken into account, but—especially—with respect to Status 2 youths. Moreover, it exists despite the fact that the contribution of factor #9 to reduced illegal behavior may well have been fairly small in compari-

son to that of all remaining factors, collectively [interactions among factors aside].) To be sure, under differing circumstances and perhaps with particular youth groups, that which has been avoided may indeed be the principal factor; this could apply whether or not the substitute program, say, a specific alternative to standard parole, is substantially less powerful than CTP.

16. CTP's Phase 1 male agents comprised about one-fourth of all such agents who worked at CTP in Phases 1 and 2 combined (1961–1969). Recall that, soon after 1964, CTP essentially doubled the number of agents in its Valley (Sacramento and Stockton) units combined, and it established a full-sized parole unit (apart from the GGI unit) in San Francisco as well. In order for CTP to convert its Valley units from PA II's to PA I's in 1965—a change required by the State Personnel Board—an almost complete turnover of CTP's parole staff occurred during that year (Warren et al., 1966a). All San Francisco agents were PA I's from the start.

17. (1) DDM was less influential regarding the 24-months than the 15-months follow-up. Like C's, E's who committed *two* nonminor offenses usually did so prior to 24 months and were very probably revoked as of their second such offense, assuming they were not revoked as of their first. Thus, like C's (who would themselves have been revoked as of their second offense, if not their first), these individuals would have been called "parole failures" in connection with the *24-months* recidivism criterion. This would apply even though E's as well as C's would have been "parole successes" relative to the *15-months* criterion if they had not yet been revoked as of that point, for example, in response to their first nonminor offense. These events and analytic distinctions are independent of the fact that, starting in 1966–1967, most E's were revoked or recommitted after their *first* non-minor offense, especially if it was a felony. Thus, as of mid–Phase 2, DDM became less influential than before with respect to the 15-months follow-up itself. (See

endnote 8.) (2) DDM made relatively little contribution to—that is, it had only modest influence upon—the E/C difference in rate of favorable discharge from the Youth Authority. This was because the decision to discharge, which was always made by the YA Board (based on the agents' recommendation), reflected relatively cut-and-dried standards that were essentially independent of prior revocations and restorals. These standards were uniformly applied to all YA parole units, experimental and otherwise. (See Appendix 9.)

18. Specifically, it remained the most serious charge that was found on the rapsheets for any given episode. Seriousness was determined by the Severity-of-Offense Scale, shown in Appendix 10.

PART IV

The Feasibility of Community-Based, Individualized Intervention

17 SOCIAL AGENCY AND PARENT ORGANIZATION FACTORS

Are programs such as CTP feasible? Are they difficult to implement and maintain? To address these questions we will first focus on Phases 1 and 2, since differing conditions existed during Phase 3. Our answers will refer to CTP as it actually operated—namely, as a complex program that dealt with serious, multiple offenders, not as it might have operated or conceivably should have operated. The question of program modifications will be addressed separately, and that of CTP's justification or lack thereof will be examined in Chapters 24 and 26. Due to its complexity, feasibility will be discussed not only in the present but in the following three chapters. For readers who wish to skip the numerous details, a Review appears in Chapter 20 (pages 360–367).

To better understand the prospects and limitations of programs such as CTP, feasibility will be reviewed with respect to several areas and features. *Areas* include: social agencies, parent organization (the YA), staff, operations, and general conditions. Some of these areas were interrelated. *Features* reflects the fact that CTP was multifaceted. That is, it was community-based, differential-intervention oriented, offender-classification (o-c) centered, operated in terms of a *complex* o-c, and organized around youth/agent matching plus other key factors. As will be indicated, some features were more difficult to implement or maintain than others, within specified areas. Beyond this, it might be kept in mind that some features can exist without others, in given programs. For example, programs can be community-based without being either differential-intervention (d-i) oriented, offender-classification centered, or involved with matching; similarly, they can be d-i oriented and/or o-c centered without including matching and other factors.[1]

Social Agencies

Law Enforcement and Justice System

During most of Phases 1 and 2, CTP was largely accepted and supported by local as well as state agencies and departments with which it interacted, either routinely or occasionally. In this regard, major implementation and maintenance problems did not exist. This applied not only to police, probation, and other agencies and departments such as Welfare, Rehabilitation, and Employment, but in Sacramento, Stockton, and San Francisco alike.

More specifically, each CTP unit found it fairly easy to establish and maintain basic working relationships with law enforcement, with justice system agencies, and so on, from an early point in its existence. In this connection, the attitude and behavior of these agencies and departments (A/D's) toward CTP—as toward the YA overall—usually ranged from (1) cordial but minimal ("strictly business"; "bare essentials"), on the one hand, to (2) definitely accepting or generally accommodating, and even (3) actively supportive, on the other. With police and probation, (1) and (2) were by far the most common responses, and within these A/D's, they were about *equally* common. Among remaining A/D's, for example, Welfare, (2) and (3) were the most frequent responses; within this context, they too were about equally frequent. The one significant exception to this picture of general acceptance is reviewed below.

Regarding acceptance and support of CTP, the central question asked by police and probation was whether this program would protect the community—would adequately substitute for the traditional approach. The fact that CTP was intensive, long-term, and organized around low caseloads—and could thus provide high levels of surveillance, as needed—was of primary importance in reassuring these agencies and departments as to its probable safety. Once they felt reasonably assured—and, to a lesser extent, once they believed that many youths would personally benefit—police and probation were prepared to accept CTP as a "package" and to support it essentially as-is. Once they took this position, they largely maintained it—reservations notwithstanding (see below). Moreover, they seldom focused on, or expressed concern about, CTP's then-special features, such as offender classification and matching; in fact, they often showed only modest interest in these components and in developing an extensive understanding of them. (These and other agencies and departments did understand the program's essential operations, and key supervisory personnel obtained at least a working knowledge of whatever bore on their liaison functions.)

Largely for these reasons, CTP staff did not have to spend much time developing and maintaining the working relationship. In fact, after initial orientation sessions regarding the general nature and goals of the program and research, occasional visits—formal and informal—usually sufficed; these visits largely centered on specific operational issues and emerging trends. Research was seldom discussed, and virtually unanimous support existed for random assignment throughout Phases 1 and 2.[2] Initially as well as later, more time was usually spent with probation than with any remaining agency or department, even though (1) probation, like other A/D's, had neither formal nor informal jurisdiction over YA wards and (2) the YA had no obligation to provide progress reports concerning these youths.

At any rate, police and probation viewed CTP as a legitimate and responsible effort by the Youth Authority, one that, besides protecting the community, would probably assist many youths and harm very few. Still, they believed that an initial period of institutionalization would be *more* appropriate than CTP for specified individuals whom they had known; in this regard, their acceptance and support was not unqualified. The remaining agencies and departments, for instance, Welfare and Employment, were less discriminating (or even aware) with respect to CTP's possible shortcomings and limitations. This reflected not simply their lesser degree of contact with the program but the fact that their principal and immediate focus was the youths' well-being rather than the protection of society per se. In any event, these and the preceding A/D's basically supported and cooperated with CTP despite their occasional differences of opinion and despite underlying reservations.

The one significant exception to this picture of general acceptance occurred in Sacramento, after CTP had been operating for several years. (It might be added, however, that the Sacramento Sheriff's Department had a generally distant, openly skeptical, mildly unfriendly, yet not openly oppositional attitude during much of Phases 1 and 2.) Beginning in 1966, local probation adopted a chilly, sometimes minimally tolerant attitude toward the project, largely due to the latter's continuing practice of giving many youths a second chance prior to revoking their parole. Although this practice had not included assaultive, or otherwise very severe offenses, and although it substantially decreased beginning in 1966–1967, probation's attitude toward CTP only partially thawed between 1967 and the end of Phase 2—at which point it was more or less lukewarm. Despite these developments, the basic working relationship was never seriously jeopardized and all essential communications were maintained.

At base, Sacramento probation had grown dissatisfied, not with everyday, treatment/control decisions, but with particular decisions that were made after given *offenses* had occurred. Specifically, it focused on a four-year accumulation of restorals to parole—actions which, it felt, had often neglected or disregarded the community's need for immediate protection. That is, despite its acceptance of CTP's general approach and its recognition of the latter's numerous "success cases," it increasingly pointed to youths who, during 1961–1966, had *continued* their illegal behavior after being restored to parole. What probation now wanted was simply a tougher policy toward repeat offenders—a direct, physical way (namely, institutionalization) to minimize risk.

Despite probation's pointed objections to these restorals, especially but not exclusively those involving felonies, it did not oppose CTP's differential-intervention approach per se, its classification system, its use of matching, and factors #1 through #5 in general (Chapter 15). Nor did it challenge the concept of community-based intervention as a substitute for traditional programming.

Probation's increasing sensitivity to and specific concern with recidivists was understandable and readily supportable, given society's increasing concern with crime and given probation's own mandate regarding public protection. It was, after all, in the mid-1960s that state and national crime rates, and media coverage of violence, had shown their first conspicuous upswing after years of relative calm. At any rate, seen in perspective, Sacramento probation was a partial though quite substantial exception to the overall picture of external agencies'/departments' support; yet its responses were also an important reflection of the times, and of one approach to crime control.

Schools

During Phase 1 a cooperative working relationship was readily established between Valley CTP units and local public schools. From that point forward this relationship, which was neither difficult nor time-consuming to maintain, was reflected in four main ways: (1) Upon the parole agent's or CTP teacher's request, school staff readily furnished academic information (transcripts, etc.) for use in initial staffings. (2) They and the agent often discussed ways of possibly improving specific youths' school experiences or behavior. (3) School staff routinely assisted agents who wished to "check up" on given youths'—usually group conformists' or manipulators'—attendance and behavior. (4) Though they often ended up disagreeing with the agent, staff usually seemed open-minded when the agent "went to bat" for youths whom he hoped would not be suspended or expelled, those whom he hoped could return to school after months of expulsion, and those whose views or current situation he was trying to convey (here, the issue was often primarily academic or personal, not behavior per se).

All in all, school personnel were glad to know that their troubled, troublesome, and otherwise "different" youths (dropouts, those on suspended or expelled status, etc.) were being worked with intensively and, in many cases, were receiving specialized educational services, supportive and extended tutoring, and so forth. For youths in CTP's school program, responses by school personnel also took concrete form. For instance: "Elementary text and supplemental material appropriate for use in grades 3 through 8 was provided [to the CTP school] by the State Department of Education. Secondary material was, for the most part, obtained on a loan basis from schools, following group or individual conferences with teachers, counselors, vice-principals, and/or principals" (McDonald, 1965, p. 49).

Although CTP agents sometimes asked for what school staff viewed as "special favors for troublemakers" (e.g., for youths who were *not* suspended/expelled, or for those who seemed ready to return to the public schools after being in CTP's school), most such requests were nevertheless handled on an individual-youth rather than fixed-policy or categorical basis. Thus, even when an agent's original request was rejected, an alternative or compromise approach was usually developed; such outcomes both reflected and further reinforced the atmosphere of goodwill and professionalism that generally prevailed. With other requests, similar outcomes also reflected staff's recognition that particular youths were having academic or personal, not necessarily behavioral, difficulties in school—this, irrespective of the youths' problems with the law. At any rate, though CTP and the respective Valley schools were administratively independent entities and had no formal obligation to develop a mutual understanding, each one seemed to respect the other's priorities and limits and to respond rather flexibly on most occasions. (Working relationships that were especially close and positive between CTP and any given school usually resulted either from years of interaction between that school and specific agents or from a preexisting relationship between school personnel and CTP school staff.)

The situation was similar in San Francisco. Here, however, agents spent considerable time "dealing personally with teachers, deans, and principals, because of the high incidence of suspensions from school" (Turner, et al., 1967, p. 17). The San Francisco school system's readiness to suspend or expel "troublemakers" or to transfer them to newly established Guidance Centers was not specifically or primarily focused on YA youths; instead, it was largely a response to the widespread tensions and violence that had rapidly emerged within Bay Area schools during 1966. Thus, given their serious problem of maintaining or even reestablishing a safe learning environment and given their generally limited resources, local school administrators felt that their immediate priorities seldom allowed them to accommodate the individual needs of "acting-out" or seriously troubled youths, or to do so for very long in regular classroom settings. This stance often frustrated parole agents who, for instance, wanted their youths to remain within such settings. Despite resulting disagreements over this and other—for example, non-behavior-centered—issues, San Francisco's schools remained willing to work with CTP agents and youths wherever possible, and an adversary relationship did not develop.

Parent Organization
General Responses
During Phases 1 and 2, CTP produced some problems for its parent organization, the Youth Authority. Few were surprises, none were major, and all were handled without great difficulty and serious repercussions within and outside the YA.[3] Nevertheless, as discussed later, some took on added importance during Phase 3. To help keep all such problems in perspective, the following might first be noted.

The Youth Authority was highly approving of CTP throughout Phase 1 and most of Phase 2; it was also very willing and able to provide necessary support. This stance related not just to CTP as a totality, but to its major features as well—the community-based dimension above all. Chief among these features were its differential-intervention orientation and its use of offender classification in general, as well as its reliance on matching and other key factors.[4]

For example, regarding key factors, the parent organization was quite supportive of CTP's intensive contacts, its use of explicit guidelines, and most aspects of individualized programming; these factors posed neither philosophical nor substantial pragmatic difficulties for the YA. (The "philosophical," for example, policy level, relates to approval or disapproval in principle of given concepts or policies. The pragmatic or operational level primarily relates to the establishment and maintenance, for example, the implementation, of given concepts, policies, and practices, within specified settings. The expansion or transferability of these concepts, and so on, to different settings, is described separately from their implementation within the original settings.) This lack of objections, and the absence of serious problems, applied to other factors as well, such as extensive contacts and flexible programming. To be sure, in the latter cases, pragmatic difficulties were by no means absent.

For instance, with respect to *extensive contacts* the following were difficult to obtain in San Francisco: (1) out-of-home placements and (2) a conveniently located community center that could also house a physically adequate school program and could contain adequate-sized, individual offices. The latter difficulties, which partly yet directly reflected widespread fiscal cutbacks that were ordered by a newly elected state governor (in 1966), did not exist in the Valley parole units; these units had been implemented, and had become relatively well-established, prior to those cuts (Turner et al., 1967). Similarly, regarding *flexible programming*—this being intertwined with individualization—difficulties sometimes arose when, as mentioned earlier, CTP restored given youths to parole in order to try a different or modified approach. (Such restorals partly reflected CTP's mandate as an experimental/developmental program, a setting in which effective approaches could be sought even for youths who had committed a nonminor offense while on parole. This mandate, which was basically accepted by the Youth Authority, was always implemented within the framework of organizational and political realities. That is, youths could not be restored and possibly even re-restored simply for the convenience of an experiment, irrespective of their offense.) Other aspects of flexible programming posed little problem; included, for example, were not only youth/agent contacts at odd hours or outside the office, but, especially, modified approaches that occurred *prior* to minor and nonminor offenses. At any rate, these occasional difficulties regarding extensive contacts and flexible programming were never looked upon as major, or even terribly important, by Youth Authority administrators. Partly because of this general attitude and partly despite it, some such difficulties were—eventually—resolved or reduced, though not to the complete satisfaction of CTP operations staff.

The presence of partly resolved and of unresolved difficulties, especially those relating to extensive contacts, indicated the following with respect to feasibility. CTP was able to operate—albeit less efficiently, and probably less effectively with given youth groups—without having what its staff considered a "full complement" of well-developed program components. This, certainly, was true in San Francisco. As to parole restorals, it has been pointed out that CTP modified its practices considerably during the latter half of Phase 2—again, without dire effects on the overall program. (By the close of Phase 2, relatively few youths were being restored to parole in connection with their first nonminor offense.)[5] Prior to the start of these modifications and also while they were occurring, the parent organization was willing and able to absorb the restoral-related complaints it occasionally received, for instance, by phone or letter, from concerned, local justice system officials.

We now turn to other major features of CTP.

As indicated, the parent organization approved of and supported offender classification throughout Phases 1 and 2—classification not only for ward management, but for differential intervention. However, its stance toward CTP's particular classification system—I-level—was somewhat complex and ambivalent. This was due, primarily, to the system's own complexity, and, secondarily, to other factors mentioned below. The main features of this stance, including its changes through time, will now be reviewed in some detail because of their implications for future programs.

I-Level

By 1966, I-level was fairly well accepted as a useful diagnostic and "treatment planning" tool by numerous Youth Authority administrators, supervisors, and line staff. Together, these individuals represented each type of YA setting: headquarters, reception centers, institutions, and parole. In addition, by the mid-1960s, I-level concepts and selected treatment strategies were often used in (1) special parole units (Community Delinquency Control Projects [CDCPs] and, by 1969, Community Parole Centers [CPCs]) that operated in Los Angeles, Oakland, and San Francisco with caseloads that averaged 25 youths per agent, and within (2) a number of YA institutions

(Andre and Mahan, 1972; Jesness, 1965, 1971, 1971–1972, 1975a, 1978; Pond, 1969, 1970; Pond and Davis, 1971, 1973; Pond et al., 1974; Wedge, White, and Palmer, 1980). For such reasons, and because of CTP's encouraging results as well as national and international reputation (President's Commission, 1967c; Warren, 1969), I-level was designated, in 1969, as the YA's official classification system for parole and institutions alike.

Even before the first special parole units opened, the above-mentioned staff realized that I-level, given its nine youth categories and the relatively complex strategies associated with them, could not be utilized in these and especially in regular parole units either to the same degree or in exactly the same manner as in CTP. This was mainly due to the formers' more limited resources or opportunities and to their (like institutions') partly different goals and priorities. It also reflected staffs' recognition that, within different environmental settings, modified approaches might be advantageous or required. Nevertheless, the use of I-level concepts and strategies—even if the latter were less complex than, or somewhat different from, those in CTP—was often considered a good, an excellent, or even simply the best available way to improve the following: (1) overall treatment planning for, and specific interactions with, youths; (2) the general atmosphere for youth/staff and youth/youth interactions in institutional living units; and (3) staff/staff communications concerning youths. Largely for these reasons, I-level was considered an asset independently of its specific implementation at CTP. It thus remained the YA's official classification system beyond the end of Phase 3—in fact, until almost 1985—despite a major concern that emerged in 1971 (see "Ethnicity Issues," below).

To help utilize I-level and differential treatment concepts to the extent possible, that is, even recognizing the earlier-mentioned limitations and differences, the Youth Authority decided, in 1969, to obtain an *I-level diagnosis* on all newly committed youths—then 4,500 per year, statewide (Davis et al., 1970). (This diagnosis referred specifically to a level and subtype designation, such as "I_4, Na," no more and no less.) This policy, which was implemented at each reception center beginning in 1970, also lasted well beyond Phase 3, even though the resulting diagnosis was seldom used for detailed or elaborate treatment/control planning, especially after 1972. The diagnosis was, nevertheless, often used when reviewing intervention goals and/or strategies, both in institutions and on parole. At any rate, prior to the 1969 decision, the YA, largely assisted by federal funds, had established the Center for Training in Differential Treatment (1967–1974)—this being organized specifically around I-level (Howard, 1974; Tolhurst and CTDT staff, 1970; Warren and CTDT staff, 1972, 1974). CTDT, while Sacramento-based, trained (until 1972) not only YA personnel from throughout the state and interested individuals from other states, but probation staff from numerous (eventually 27 of 58) California counties; in the latter case, it helped implement the state's newly established Probation Subsidy Program (Feeney, Hirschi, and Lemert, 1977; Johns, White, and Berkowitz, 1974; Smith, 1965, 1968). Somewhat later, the YA also established and operated an I-level-based, Differential Education Project (1969–1973) within classrooms of two (and later three) institutions (Andre and Mahan, 1972).

Thus, for several years, the parent organization was willing and able to help establish the I-level system in a variety of settings and to continue supporting it on a rather broad basis. This occurred even though most such years were marked by fairly "tight" fiscal policies, statewide.

During Phases 1 and 2, neither CTP's particular usage of I-level nor the remaining Youth Authority's more varied use of this system posed any external problems for the latter. More specifically, throughout 1961–1969 neither the public, the local justice agencies, nor other public or private agencies and groups objected to I-level classification, for instance, on ethical, theoretical, or pragmatic grounds. This applied not only in each Valley setting, but within the three urban environments (Los Angeles, Oakland, and San Francisco) in which the YA's earlier-mentioned special parole units (CDCPs and CPCs) had been operating since the mid-1960s; the latter were predominantly low-income, ethnic-minority areas, either black or Mexican American.

Lack of objections notwithstanding, the I-level system was complex. As a result, it was often difficult for non-CTP—that is, nontrained or "non-system-experienced"—personnel to thoroughly understand, in the first place, and to

readily explain to other individuals, in the second. Thus, for example, although many YA administrators understood the basics and broad outlines of this system and seemed generally satisfied with its ability to appropriately describe real-life youths, they often felt uncomfortable when non-YA individuals asked them pointed questions about its underlying assumptions and its numerous youth groups; to be sure, they and others would perhaps have had comparable feelings in connection with certain other classification systems. Similarly, but far more important, neither they nor many other YA staff understood the intricacies of, and the current thinking about, I-level well enough to adequately address a specific criticism that emerged in 1971 regarding ethnicity issues (see below). Together with the following, this criticism and its potential implications made top-level administrators increasingly hesitant about openly and vigorously supporting I-level; in fact, by the middle of Phase 3 (1972) they no longer wished to actively promote it (especially its continued expansion) on a department-wide basis. Still, administrators retained it as the YA's official classification system, since (1) its related, treatment-planning concepts and differential intervention strategies *were* being used with apparent satisfaction and usually enthusiasm in several YA and non-YA settings, (2) it did seem useful and generally true to life, and (3) it apparently lacked serious competition from other classification systems. In these respects its status was essentially the same as during the mid-1960s.

After three or four years' experience with the training center (CTDT), YA decision-makers realized the following. To create and maintain a cadre of I-level diagnosticians and treatment personnel and to allow these individuals to act as *trainers* of line staff within their local setting was both time-consuming and expensive, and no guaranteed shortcuts were in sight. (It should be kept in mind that the Youth Authority had over 2,000 nonclerical personnel at any one time, including several hundred supervisors and managers.) The cadre in question were those individuals—usually supervisory staff—who had received five or more weeks of training from CTDT, not only in I-level diagnosis but in treatment planning and methods of differential intervention (Howard, 1974; Warren and CTDT staff, 1974). Their task of training line staff, even in diagnosis alone, would have been less formidable within an organization much smaller than the YA. (In 1972, the Youth Authority included 3 reception centers, 9 large institutions, 5 camps, and 45 parole units. It supervised 17,000 individuals, 75 percent of whom were on parole (Davis et al., 1973a, 1973b).

When the preceding cost factor became clear, these administrators and managers decided the Youth Authority should no longer invest in such a process on a large-scale basis, given the department's overall priorities and limited training budget, and—almost as important—given the availability of an alternative diagnostic tool (see below). Their assessment of costs also reflected the fact that trained staff, who already comprised a basic cadre, were not infrequently being promoted to other positions within a year or two, thus creating a need for *replacements*—CTDT-trained or otherwise. And finally, although some decision-makers recognized that (1) diagnostic skills were often distinguished from intervention (youth/worker interaction) skills per se, and from supervisory abilities in general, and that (2) CTDT had enhanced the latter skills or abilities of many trainees, they and other decision-makers also knew that the *diagnostic* skills of many CTDT trainees—while adequate—were less than had been hoped for (Palmer and Werner, 1972a, 1972b; Warren and CTDT staff, 1972, 1974).[6]

The alternative tool was the Jesness Inventory, a paper-and-pencil questionnaire that was administered to individual youths and that could be used to determine their I-level and subtype fairly inexpensively (Jesness, 1963, 1966). By design, this inventory had no bearing on the training of *differential intervention skills*, for example, the development of individualized treatment/control plans and the implementation of specific approaches. Nevertheless, its availability helped the YA's increasingly budget-conscious decision-makers resolve their problem of how to eventually withdraw support from a time-consuming training process without also eliminating I-level—certainly, I-level diagnosis. (Within CTP, throughout Phases 1, 2, and 3, such diagnosis was based on the interview method rather than an inventory method.)

Several YA researchers, the present author included, felt that this alternative approach yielded less accurate diagnoses than the interview method—the approach used at the training center (CTDT). However, the parent organization believed, and the just-mentioned researchers essentially agreed, that the inventory was sufficiently accurate for *large-scale screening*, particularly if most misdiagnoses could subsequently be detected and corrected within a few weeks by institutional or parole staff. In any event, the *interview* method did not readily lend itself to large-scale screening, mainly because of time constraints on the designated interviewers—namely, basic cadre and/or cadre-trained line staff.[7] Within a smaller agency, large-scale screening would have been unnecessary and fewer interviewers might have sufficed.

Pragmatics, Social Climate, and Ethnicity

In the early 1970s, as CTDT's federal grant wound down, the Youth Authority allowed this training center to "phase out." This occurred despite the center's recognized ability to enhance the treatment-planning skills and differential intervention techniques of supervisory and line personnel, and despite its ability to create a cadre of state and local trainers. The YA's action was not based on its view of CTP's approach to diagnosis, or of the program's overall feasibility; for instance, the interview approach was long recognized by the YA as being readily manageable within both CTP and a number of special parole units (SPUs), and as probably the most accurate technique available. Nor did the YA's action reflect its generally *accepting* attitude toward the vast majority of intervention approaches used in CTP since 1961—especially through Phase 2—and again in various SPUs. Instead, it reflected the following three factors, the first two of which were essentially independent of I-level per se, and all of which had exerted considerable influence prior to 1973 (although the third factor reinforced the others, CTDT would doubtlessly have been phased out even in its absence). These factors are significant even apart from their relevance to the training center.

1. *Agency limitations.* The Youth Authority decided that, given the following developments, it was not pragmatically feasible to establish CTP-type parole units throughout numerous parts of the department, either in toto or in most respects. First of all, continued budget cuts within all state agencies (departments) were making it increasingly difficult to

maintain caseloads of 25 youths per agent in even the Youth Authority's *SPUs* (nevertheless, the YA did so), let alone establish many new caseloads of 12 per agent as in CTP. Secondly, a broader development was involved: During the early 1970s, all additional staff that the YA Parole Division had managed to accrue—chiefly through federal funds—were obtained for the express purpose of reducing its average statewide caseload size from 72 to 50 within all *regular* parole units (RPUs). This reduction, in turn, allowed for a within-unit, structural modification that made it possible to (1) establish or augment various casework activities and (2) redistribute, across specified unit personnel, parole's rapidly increasing investigatory (due process) responsibilities (Pond et al., 1974). Though all seven of the earlier-mentioned Community Parole Centers were retained at the time these changes were made, and although five of these SPUs were maintained throughout most of the 1970s, this modification within its RPUs represented the Youth Authority's statewide response to the following development.

Mainly because of the California Probation Subsidy Program,[8] the YA, by 1969–1970, was receiving an increasing proportion of individuals whom the Parole Division described as having "serious offense histories" and who therefore "required closer supervision and specialized treatment" than youths received before 1968 (Pond et al., 1974, p. 11). (In this context, such treatment or casework activities referred to narcotics counseling and testing, to increased vocational or academic training, and so on—for example, to broad program-level involvements, as needed—but not to *intensive* intervention, as in CTP. The case-planning and case-review approaches that were used to help specify and implement given program involvements for each individual had been largely derived from CTP.)[9] Given this widespread development and perceived need, most YA administrators considered the above-mentioned, department-wide changes within all RPUs more important than the establishment of numerous CTP-type units—units that involved relatively long-term, not just intensive, work with a sizable proportion of their parolees and

which, collectively, could handle only a fraction of the YA's several thousand parolees.

Thus, together with budget constraints, this first factor focused not so much on the merits or feasibility of operating any one CTP unit, or even a few of them, but mainly on the pragmatic difficulty and relative merits of establishing *many* such units within a large agency, across a very large state, and, as indicated below, during a generally stressful time. Within a smaller and perhaps more tightly knit agency, or absent increasingly stringent fiscal constraints, the addition of several low-caseload units might not have seemed largely incompatible with various department-wide changes. Nevertheless, under conditions that existed, even a well-established network of low-caseload units could not, by itself, have handled the YA's large volume of cases.

2. *Broad social/correctional changes.* The Youth Authority, like many correctional agencies nationwide, began to change its emphasis in the early 1970s: By 1973, the "justice model" (or what soon received that name) was given high, possibly even top, priority by the YA director and other key administrators (Fogel, 1975; Morris, 1974; Singer, 1979; van den Haag, 1975; von Hirsch, 1976; Wilson, 1975). This change occurred despite the YA's continued official and public support of the long-dominant "rehabilitation model." Integral to this development, and in the wake of New York's blood-soaked Attica "riot" or rebellion (1971), issues of *wards' rights, due process, grievance procedures,* and *staff security* increasingly occupied center stage. Treatment, in contrast, was steadily shifted to the wings (Serrill, 1975, 1976; Dillingham et al., 1975; Wicker, 1975, 1976).

In part, the latter shift reflected society's increased concern with "law and order." However, it also reflected the fact that, in California and elsewhere, treatment itself was often portrayed in the popular media as little more than "brainwashing"; and in this connection, few if any distinctions were being made between differing types of "treatment," for example, counseling, token economies, sensory deprivation, aversive drug conditioning, and neurosurgery (Davidson and Stuart, 1975; Lovaas and Bucher, 1974; McConnell,

1970; Mitford, 1973; Schwitzgebel, 1972; Stumphauser, 1974). Beyond that, though related to it, almost all forms of intervention were increasingly characterized in correctional writings as a disguised form of "social control," that is, an activity which in fact was not designed to assist offenders (American Friends Service Committee, 1971; Bremner et al., 1971; Chambliss and Seidman, 1971; Lerman, 1975; Platt, 1969, 1974; Quinney, 1970, 1974, 1977; Rothman, 1971; Schur, 1973; Stapleton and Teitelbaum, 1972).

Although social control was not its *predominant* characterization during the early 1970s, correctional intervention was, nevertheless, increasingly portrayed as a major and in some cases unwitting tool of an "establishment" or "ruling class" conspiracy. The essential aim of this presumed conspiracy was to control or repress the economically downtrodden, the sociohistorically disadvantaged (e.g., black and Hispanic minorities), the politically radical, and/or the socially nonconforming. Incarcerated individuals who fell within these categories were said to have commonly found themselves in the justice system for reasons that, at one given point in time, happened to *include* their commission of a crime. At any rate, from one quarter or another—backed by this or somewhat different theories—the following occurred: (a) Treatment (say, counseling or psychotherapy), when combined with almost any degree of external control, was often criticized as an act of unwarranted coercion, a form of overt oppression, or both, and as ipso facto unethical or sometimes inhumane. (b) Treatment efforts that were not accompanied by *strong* external controls were often criticized as "soft" or "indulgent," and therefore surely ineffectual. (c) Treatment, with or without obvious or strong external controls, was still likely to be criticized as "brainwashing" (Mitford, 1974; van den Haag, 1975; von Hirsch, 1976; Wilson, 1975).

Most Youth Authority administrators viewed the preceding characterizations, theories, and criticisms as stereotypes, overgeneralizations, or major exaggerations; however, they considered certain points and underlying concerns valid. Thus, for instance, although these decision-makers largely rejected the specific claims involved in such positions, they did take various concerns into account insofar as these seemed consistent with the justice model's own marked deemphasis upon correctional intervention. In any event, such criticisms and concerns represented one more interacting force that helped restrain these decision-makers from vigorously supporting or independently promoting most forms of intervention. At the same time, they helped these individuals feel justified in primarily focusing on other, seemingly more pressing issues, especially offender rights, due process, and overall institutional atmosphere (staff and ward security included). In many respects, treatment had become a complex and highly controversial issue by 1973, and most administrators felt they already had enough complexities, controversies, and immediate pressures to deal with.

The YA's pressures and resulting responses were directly reflected in its training budget and in the already-limited training time allotted to staff. Specifically, training began to focus almost exclusively on grievance procedures, due process, and institutional security. In short, starting in the early 1970s, the YA began confronting its somewhat new or intensified problems by placing more emphasis than before—especially but not exclusively within institutions—on securing the youth's newly defined or expanded legal rights and on assuring a humane and safe environment. In this context, the possible establishment of numerous CTP parole units seemed not only tangential but a questionable diversion of much-needed funds. Similarly, given the department's decreased emphasis on treatment—especially intensive treatment—CTDT's unique asset as a source of training in specified intervention approaches and differential intervention techniques seemed far from vital.

3. *Ethnicity issues.* The phasing out of CTDT partly reflected, but was basically independent of, (a) specific reservations that administrators had developed regarding CTP's Phase 3 operation, and (b) an increasing hesitation by these same individuals about actively and openly promoting I-level classification. The Phase 3 operations in question are reviewed in Chapter 20; however, the nature and basis of the hesitation was as follows.

Early in 1971, supervisory staff in two of the Youth Authority's northern institutions indicated that I-level classification may have produced a "racial imbalance" in certain standard-sized living-units that housed 45 to 50 youths each. Specifically, staff indicated that (a) units which had been established for group conformists (then called *cultural conformists*) were predominantly comprised of Mexican American youths, and (b) those established for *manipulators* were overrepresented by blacks, especially youths from the Bay Area (San Francisco, Oakland, etc.). To some institutional personnel, this information meant more than "imbalance" alone; it suggested that "racial segregation" (a virtual absence of any ethnic mixing) and "racial discrimination" (especially, reduced privileges and opportunities) would soon appear. However such predictions might turn out, I-level seemed centrally involved in the imbalance, since youths *had* been assigned to these living units after being diagnosed in terms of this system, and since the imbalance had developed after those assignments began. (Like Caucasians, many Mexican Americans and blacks who were neither group conformists nor manipulators were assigned to all other units as well. These units were not considered racially unbalanced.)

Within about four months it became clear that this imbalance was not transitory; it had persisted despite substantial turnover of youths. Although no racial incidents had occurred that seemed related to the imbalance, and although no increased tensions or decreased privileges and opportunities were in fact observed, YA administrators, who were informally monitoring the situation, decided to intervene at this point (mid-1971). Their main reasons were twofold.

First, triggered by the tragic Watts riot of 1965, race relations, chiefly between blacks and Caucasians, had remained a volatile and highly sensitive issue within the United States; it was not just in the background. Accusations and confrontations were still commonplace in several California cities, Sacramento and San Francisco included, and large-scale violence or destructiveness was far from rare. These events, which usually centered on the general theme of "underprivileged and oppressed (minority) versus privileged and oppressor (nonminority)," were reflected to a considerable degree in YA institutions. For one thing, rumors of impending riot or destruction by minority members (e.g., "They say this place will be ashes soon!") were an almost weekly occurrence in one institution or another during the late 1960s. In addition, though neither riots nor major destructiveness actually materialized, racially oriented fights between individuals were common, as were short-lived clashes and long-lasting hostilities between small ethnic groupings; together, these conflicts involved *all* ethnic groups, minority and otherwise. Given this continued social bitterness, these frequent rumors, and these almost daily conflicts, racial issues were understandably a prime concern of the department, and most administrators were wary of any development that might reinforce or intensify the situation and possibly spark a major outburst.

Second, once the living-unit imbalance was recognized as a nontransitory phenomenon, a Mexican American social-action group, some of whose members were Youth Authority employees, contacted YA administrators and expressed its concerns. It objected to whatever "racial segregation" might be occurring, and it suggested that the I-level system, which the YA had recently adopted as its official classification, and which was extensively used in its northern California institutions, might be racially biased. Although similar concerns were not expressed by black organizations, some black staff suggested that occasional misdiagnoses and resulting misassignments were indeed occurring in the case of minority youths, even though I-level theory might itself be unbiased.

YA administrators rapidly responded to these concerns, not only because they considered it appropriate to forestall or eliminate possible harmful effects of any racial imbalance (segregation and discrimination per se, aside), but because the former group was recognized as both vocal and influential. (Administrators did not believe these *possible* effects were in fact occurring, or yet occurring.) The department had no desire to face possible litigation or receive negative publicity from *any* source with respect to racially unbalanced living units. For one thing, this imbalance represented a situation (a) which administrators felt no compulsion to maintain and thus no particular desire or need to defend, (b) whose development and exact causes they only partly understood, and (c) whose existence they had not promoted in the first place. Not only would conditions (b) and especially (c) be difficult or embarrassing for the department to explain, but, given the fact that an imbalance did exist, any charges of *segregation* or even partial segregation could prove difficult to resolve even under the calmest of conditions.

In addition, and in a much more nebulous area, Youth Authority administrators wished to continue improving relations between themselves and *staff*, especially minority staff. In the present context, they did not wish to give various personnel, minority and otherwise, conceivably defensible grounds for accusing the department of "racism" with respect to youths. During 1967–1969, accusations of racism had been both frequent and widespread; however, they were focused, not on youths, but mainly on personnel practices and on the degree of minority staff's participation in departmental decision-making. Though the term "racism" was often indiscriminately applied and not always clearly defined, and although a number of stormy, media-recorded confrontations had occurred between various staff and the YA administration, these accusations and confrontations eventually resulted in considerable change and mutual conciliation. By late 1969, working relations between these staff and "central office" were showing clear signs of improvement, and YA administrators did not want new developments and related accusations to reverse this trend.

The department's response to the preceding concerns was as follows. (a) It acknowledged the existence of an imbalance in specified living units, but maintained that neither segregation nor the above-mentioned harmful effects had occurred. (b) It ordered that *each* living unit be, and remain, balanced. Specifically, each unit was to reflect the department's overall ethnic breakdown to the extent possible, and only insofar as—or after—this condition was met might that unit also be organized by I-level subtype. The YA took this position despite its prior endorsement of research findings which indicated that fewer peer problems, fewer rule infractions, and less use of confinement existed in living units whose youth population was relatively homogeneous with regard to I-level subtype (Jesness, 1969, pp.179–186, 199; 1971, pp. 44-45).[10] At any rate, though some administrators recognized that subtype-oriented living units did not inevitably entail a racial imbalance, the fact remained that, since such an imbalance *had* occurred and doubtlessly could reoccur (and could have serious repercussions), the department's settled position would be that institutional subtype grouping would henceforth exist only if unaccompanied by a racial imbalance. This policy would apply even if complete diagnostic accuracy and lack of I-level bias existed. Once this policy was stated, the social-action group did not challenge the YA's

view that neither segregation nor the earlier-mentioned harmful effects had occurred. (c) The YA did not agree that I-level was racially biased; it felt that other factors, including misdiagnosis, were involved instead. However, as suggested, it was somewhat unclear as to the nature of certain factors and the reasons for misdiagnosis. (The Youth Authority had never encountered bias in its more than nine years of experience with I-level. This applied to parole and institutional settings alike—seven settings in all—and it involved over 3,300 diagnosed youths who had participated in the YA's CTP as well as Jesness studies [Jesness, 1971, 1975b, 1975c]. Another 345 youths had been studied in nine separate, local probation settings [Jesness et al., 1975a, 1975b].)

YA administrators considered it unnecessary to mount a special effort relative to the question of possible racial bias. This was not only because they largely believed in the validity of this system, for example, in its general correspondence to reality, but because, once responses (a) and especially (b) above had been made, the social-action group was essentially satisfied and no longer requested action. In addition, since response (b) (assured racial balance) had already obviated the major immediate stimulus for possible staff accusations of racism, administrators had no desire to have further attention drawn to the general, always potentially volatile subject of race—this time in relation to I-level theory. Moreover, they knew, or believed, that various researchers, supervisory personnel, and others would pursue the question of possible bias on their own, without any official investigation or related pressure.

Although responses (a) through (c) had averted a possible crisis and though external and internal pressures on the department had subsided, many individuals within and outside the YA continued to ask: *Was* the I-level system somehow biased? A detailed review of the entire situation subsequently led to the following conclusions.

(1) The Interpersonal Maturity Theory was not racially biased. Specifically, none of its principles, concepts, descriptive statements, and underlying assumptions indicated or implied that any racial group was inherently more likely to attain any particular, for example, higher, maturity level than any other group. (Cultural conformists and manipulators fell within the I_3—the "middle maturity"—category, as did

passive-conformists.) Instead, each individual's I-level was viewed as essentially a product of social learning and interpersonal dynamics, and (a) since no differential growth-producing factors and no differential growth potentials or capacities were postulated among the various racial groups, and (b) since it was assumed that all necessary and sufficient growth stimuli (social learning, etc.) were available to and operative with all such groups, it followed that individuals from the various groups were considered equally capable of responding to the given stimuli and of progressing from one I-level (I_2, I_3, etc.) to the next at the same rate as each other. Though it was only partially explicit, this position was clear from a reading of any basic I-level document. To grasp it, neither training nor "hands-on" experience with the classification system was required (Sullivan, Grant, and Grant, 1957; Warren et al., 1966b). To miss it, considerable blocking, or at least misunderstanding, was probably involved.

(2) The causes of racial imbalance were centered not on I-level theory or on each individual's I-level per se, but on particular *subtypes* that fell within the I_3 and I_4 levels. (As mentioned earlier, I-level—the core concept of Interpersonal Maturity Theory—refers to ways in which an individual perceives his environment. Subtype, in contrast, reflects his pattern of responses to those perceptions. Though such responses are behavioral, verbal, and intrapsychic, the descriptive material presented in basic I-level documents of the 1960s centered almost exclusively on the first two areas, especially the behavioral.) These causes, discussed at length in Appendix 32, reflected not only diagnostic shortcomings and conceptual or theoretical/descriptive issues but local social-cultural realities.

Briefly, *diagnostic shortcomings* involved information that could have distinguished group conformists and manipulators, respectively, from all remaining subtypes: Often, this information had not been obtained by institutional staff, for example, via a detailed interview; and, in most remaining cases, namely, when such information *had* been obtained, it was largely overridden by other, nondifferentiating data or by given assumptions and stereotypes. (This information, data, and so on, is reviewed in Appendix 32.) *Conceptual issues* centered around the unbalanced or inadequately focused picture of group conformists that was inadvertently conveyed, by omission

and commission combined, in basic I-level documents and descriptions. This picture threw many staff, particularly the less experienced, off the track. *Local social-cultural realities* referred not just to (a) observed relationships among various factors (e.g., lower SES and minority-group status, SES and I-level, age and I-level) and to (b) interactions between some such factors (taken individually), on the one hand, and (c) differential justice-system processing of lower versus higher SES—and, indirectly/inadvertently, younger versus older—individuals, on the other. Instead, it also involved—in fact, it required—an interplay between (a) through (c), collectively, on the one hand, and the earlier-mentioned shortcomings, on the other. Additional factors were also involved.

Given such complexities it was not surprising that few people understood the main reasons for I-level's purported but, in reality, nonexistent racial bias. Nor was it odd that the bias issue had emerged in the first place. Complexities notwithstanding, this issue could have been obviated or reduced by a few basic steps and changes, particularly with regard to diagnostic shortcomings and conceptual issues (see Appendix 32). These actions could have clarified and largely defused the racial issue—one that negatively influenced I-level's acceptability since the early 1970s. Insofar as this classification system is used, and may be used, in present and future CTP-type programs, such improvements would bear directly on the perceived and actual feasibility of these efforts.

Notes

1. In addition—and other features aside—a program can also involve any of several possible classification systems, ranging from the simple to the complex. Finally, such features as differential-intervention orientation, offender-classification focus, and so on, can exist within institutional and community-based programs alike.
2. This support was based mainly on the following. Police and probation believed that CTP youths, collectively, (1) would receive *more* intervention *than,* and, quite possibly, *as effective* intervention *as,* youths who would be assigned to the traditional program, and (2) would be handled responsibly as well as humanely. In addition, these A/D's basically understood why random assignment was

essential to obtaining scientifically definitive results, and why the present research
project could be important.

3. Throughout this section the term "Youth
 Authority" will refer to the following
 groups, collectively, unless otherwise specified: top administrators (YA director and
 deputy director, etc.); top parole administrators and managers (chief and deputy
 chief of parole, regional administrators,
 budget managers); other administrators
 and managers (chiefs and assistant chiefs
 of finance and personnel, etc.). Most such
 people worked at YA headquarters ("central office"), in Sacramento.

4. Some factors, such as #2 and #4 (intensive and/or extensive contacts; explicit,
 detailed guidelines), themselves helped
 implement CTP's differential intervention approach, and/or were aspects of it.

5. This practice continued in Phase 3, during which time only 16 percent of all
 CTP youths who committed a nonminor
 offense were restored to parole in connection with their first such offense. This
 figure was very similar to that found
 within regular parole during the second
 half of Phase 2, for comparable offenses.

6. In its final report, CTDT suggested that
 parent agencies should perhaps be more
 selective than before regarding individuals whom they send to be trained as
 cadre. It offered several suggestions for
 identifying prospective trainees (Warren
 and CTDT staff, 1974).

7. "Scale" aside, for any given youth the *interview* method could yield a relatively
 rapid diagnosis, even if a second rating
 were required. In contrast, the inventory
 had to be computer scored in order to
 yield an I-level diagnosis, and this
 process usually took a week or two.
 Nevertheless, given the YA's overall time
 frame, this delay posed little problem as
 long as the youth was tested fairly early
 in his reception center stay, or at least a
 month prior to his release from an institution. In other settings, such as probation, this delay sometimes posed a
 problem. In general, because "the time
 and inconvenience involved in mailing
 and processing limited the [inventory's]
 use" (Jesness, 1988, pp. 79–80), Jesness
 and Wedge, in the early 1980s, developed a hand-scorable procedure that was

to replace the computer-scored approach
and which was designed to derive modified I-level categories (Jesness and
Wedge, 1983a, 1983b, 1984).

8. Throughout this program, which formally
 began in July 1966, county probation departments were paid $4,000 for each of-
 fender whom they did not send to the
 state, as determined by a preestablished,
 historical baseline (Feeney, Hirschi, and
 Lemert, 1977; Smith, 1965).

9. The Youth Authority's final report on its
 modification of all RPUs contained the
 following, summary observations.

The department . . . was not under the il-
lusion that a simple reduction of caseload
size would necessarily produce better parole services and outcomes. While a reduction in caseload size was regarded as a
necessary ingredient for success, other elements were also deemed to be essential.
Thus, provisions were made for designing
parole unit programs so as to more effectively deploy parole and community resources to meet the needs of individual
parolees. Important program components
included were case planning and review,
differential treatment, closer liaison between parole and institutional staff, and
the development of community alternatives to institutional commitments. . . .
The casework services made possible
under [this program modification]
changed the parole operation from one of
providing only a minimal level of surveillance with little opportunity for "treatment" to a differential treatment system
with planned case services for individual
wards. . . . [These and other services] represent parole functions which would not
have been possible within the constraints
of the previous operational budget (Pond
et al., 1974, pp. ii–iii).

10. Peer problems included "fights and assaults, agitation, and sex activities." Rule
 infractions included "escape attempts,
 stealing, [glue] sniffing, possession of
 contraband, tattooing, self-mutilation,
 and other major rule violations." Living
 units that were involved in this research
 were only partially balanced, relative to
 the department's overall ethnic breakdown at the time (Jesness, 1969, p. 182).

18 STAFF, UNIT FUNCTIONING, AND SUPERVISORY FACTORS

We will now review staff-centered features of CTP's Phase 1 and 2 units, with respect to feasibility. Included will be recruitment and hiring of agents, staff development and unit functioning, and supervision as well as administration.

Recruitment and Hiring of Agents
General Considerations
Recruitment and hiring of matched workers posed little problem. For one thing, many candidates were available and most were relatively skilled. In addition, CTP recruited from throughout—and outside—the department, and only once did Youth Authority administrators veto a project selection.[1] Beyond this, little energy had to be expended on recruitment: Once CTP staff and the Parole Division announced that a caseload position would soon be available, respondents quickly contacted the project and interviews almost always followed. (This announcement/ information was conveyed not only via the Youth Authority's weekly statewide *Staff News* publication, and through the standard, State Personnel Board channels, but—most quickly, and perhaps most effectively—by word of mouth.) The preponderance of contacts and interviews involved respondents from within the YA; the remainder were from probation, social welfare, and so on. Had the YA been much smaller than it was or had major recruitment and hiring restraints existed, this situation would probably have differed. Unlike *recruitment,* hiring (selection and matching) did take time, mainly because of the depth interview and subsequent staff discussion that were required.

On average, there were almost five male, interviewed respondents—candidates—for each male caseload position. Once interviewed, roughly 70 percent to 80 percent remained interested, and a final choice was then made from individuals within this group. The choice usually centered on two such candidates—finalists—both of whom seemed potentially appropriate for the specific caseload. In about 40 percent of all recruitment situations (more so when certain conflicted and/or passive-conformist caseloads were involved), one of the finalists had already been interviewed on a prior occasion, sometimes even in connection with a different type of caseload. Whether or not this individual had seemed well-matched on that occasion (e.g., he may have been a finalist then, too), he had been contacted and was being considered for the present caseload because he seemed quite possibly appropriate.[2]

Such contacts reflected the fact that an informal "pool" of potential matched workers had been developed over the years. Though most such persons were still interested and available when contacted, this might not have been the case under other conditions, for instance, if, during the intervening years, they had found a seemingly better or more interesting job within or outside the agency. At any rate, because of this informal pool, recruitment and hiring for male caseloads would have involved few if any basic problems even if, beginning as early as 1965, half as many individuals had responded to each new position announcement.

There were usually three or four female candidates—and again, two finalists—for each available *female* caseload. Mainly because these caseloads were much fewer and farther between than those for males, a lower number and percentage of previously interviewed candidates was available on later occasions.[3] Despite this smaller pool, recruitment and hiring for female caseloads posed little problem, mainly because the skill level of most respondents/candidates was high and specific matching was not required.

Restrictions and Potential Difficulties

CTP imposed no recruitment and hiring restrictions relative to age, ethnicity, and so on, and no minimum requirements regarding level or type of education, job experience, and (after 1964) job classification.[4] As a result, the project obtained a larger number of respondents—perhaps more important, a wider range of assets among respondents—than would otherwise have been the case. This outcome directly bore on matching, since matching ultimately rests on each person's unique pattern of characteristics (mainly assets)—features that can derive from almost any source. Nevertheless, certain restrictive factors and "realities" existed:

1. Despite their other assets, candidates less than 23 to 25 years of age usually lacked a certain added maturity that often seemed helpful when working with multiple offenders. This situation, though certainly not crucial, would probably still exist today.[5]
2. Agency-wide policies and practices in effect barred females from handling caseloads that were exclusively or even predominantly male; this also applied to males in connection with female caseloads.[6] Possibly for this and other reasons, neither female nor, to a lesser extent, male respondents expressed particular interest in opposite-sex caseloads. Today, the interest level would probably be somewhat greater, not just in agencies that handle less troubled or troublesome youths.
3. Though all YA parole agents had four years of college or its equivalent, many candidates with less education could doubtlessly have handled the job.

Although CTP seemed to function adequately despite these external or non-self-imposed restrictions, the absence of such factors, particularly factor (3), would probably make the operation of many similar projects somewhat easier. However, little could probably be done about factor (1).

Though recruitment/hiring was hardly a problem at CTP, it could prove difficult under other, by no means unlikely conditions. For instance, appropriate matching might well be hard to achieve not only if there are few respondents, but, especially, if most respondents and certainly interviewees are not particularly interested in, that is, motivated to do, CTP-type work. The latter could occur if, for example, most interviewees soon *have* to leave their current position because of agency shrinkage or budget cuts, and if the parent agency then mandates the CTP-type project to select its new workers from those individuals only, regardless of their interest in the project itself. (In this and subsequent chapters the terms "CTP [or CTP-type] project," "CTP program," and "CTP unit" will be used interchangeably.) Though many such persons would, of course, be quite experienced and would have numerous skills plus other assets, this policy would still be troublesome at the individual-candidate/individual-subtype level, for essentially the following reasons. Whereas (1) matched caseloads require workers whose interests lie in certain areas, that is, workers who are personally motivated along given lines, (2) such motivations, in any *particular* candidate, may be largely independent not only of his type and level of skill and experience, but of his other assets as well. Thus, for example, although some individuals may be relatively skilled, they may not be appropriately motivated for the work in question. In addition, whereas (3) matching, for any given subtype, involves not only the given motivation but particular skills and related assets, (4) a candidate who might indeed have numerous skills/assets may still lack the *specific* skills in question, those that seem critical for the subtype at hand. Additionally or alternatively, he may have certain characteristics and professional orientations which contraindicate a match with that subtype—again, even setting motivation aside.

In sum, although specific interests or motivations on the part of candidates did not guarantee "successful performance" at CTP, they, like other factors, doubtlessly increased its chances. Compared to interested and appropriately motivated individuals, persons who are lukewarm or reluctant about working in a CTP-type project are less likely to adequately implement that project's often complex, central strategies; the latter individuals include, for example, many people who "must be placed somewhere," and almost all who mainly view the prospective job as either "treading water" or perhaps even a stepping-stone. Moreover, without considerable motivation, even *critical* skills that do exist would probably be used only sporadically; in addition, the prospective worker might wish to leave the project long before completing the recommended service period of at least two years, certainly no less than one and a half years. (Ideally, the parent agency would support this recommended period.) Mainly for these reasons, a CTP-type project must—as was the case in CTP itself—essentially control its recruitment and hiring. At the very least it should have veto power over "who gets hired," especially if few caseloads exist. Such controls could probably be granted by most agencies under most conditions, and this, in itself, would probably reflect considerable support of the project. To be sure, support or commitment is not "forever"—at least, it sometimes varies. In this case, the strongest and most severe "test" not just of agency support but of its overall priorities and current flexibility would probably come at times of major budget cuts and personnel transfers or reductions.

Appropriate matching could prove difficult under other conditions as well. For instance, however many interested and seemingly motivated candidates existed, skilled interviewers would be needed in order to preclude incorrect hiring decisions or greatly reduce their occurrence. More specifically, though the Form 3 instrument could help synthesize interview-based information and thus help determine the most appropriate match, careful, depth interviewing would still be essential in order to obtain the highly individualized information needed for that determination (Chapter 11). To be sure, if the matches in question were to be relatively crude—for example, if they required no distinction between Na's and Nx's or perhaps even between any "N's" (conflicted youths) and Cfm's (passive-conformists)—somewhat less interviewing skill would probably be needed. Nevertheless, considerable skill would still be required to determine whether given candidates were currently appropriate for *any* intensive, long-term work with caseloads of multiple offenders. Related to the need

for candid, individualized information, if state Personnel Board or even agency policies allowed for relatively superficial or routine questions only, that is, if they specifically prohibited depth interviews, frequent selection-and-matching errors could be expected even if skilled and experienced interviewers were used.

Perhaps the largest potential obstacle to appropriate staff/youth matches would involve certain nonagency-imposed restrictions or preferences regarding hiring priorities. For example, if a caseload opening is to be filled via a state- or region-wide promotional exam, the authorized personnel board may require that the project in question select its worker from the top three scorers or *ranks* of scorers only (unless given individuals voluntarily "waive"). If the board will not allow for the fact that its exam—which, say, is not specific to the CTP-type position—does not focus on staff/youth matching and that this factor is essential to the project, its otherwise understandable requirements, particularly the former (top three scorers), could constitute a major obstacle to appropriate matching. Fortunately, promotional exams may not be the only legitimate and promising source of respondents and candidates. Specifically, in any given instance, lateral transfers and, to a lesser degree, various intra-agency training assignments can overcome the given obstacle. Utilization of such agency-initiated options assumes, of course, that—in the given instance—it is the agency, more than the Personnel Board or perhaps even union, that determines the basis or bases on which its caseload openings will be filled.

Restricting the Range of Workers

Though it was usually possible to obtain satisfactory matches with little difficulty and red tape, it was sometimes fairly time-consuming to locate Mp/Cfc (power-oriented) and, to a lesser extent, Na workers. (This applied during Phases 1 and 2; the following would pertain to other, that is, future, settings.) To be sure, (1) if, hypothetically, relatively few Mp and Cfc youths happened to exist within a YA-type population or if, by policy, few were accepted into a CTP-type project and (2) if, still hypothetically, such youths and/or other possibly uncommon subtypes were then absorbed into, say, the project's conflicted caseloads, there would, from one perspective, no longer be much "need" for the corresponding matched workers. Though such a policy and caseload adjustment could indeed be made— thereby excluding or eliminating certain staff/youth matches—the added effort that would be required to instead *locate* these otherwise excluded/eliminated matched workers would probably seem more than justified under most conditions, certainly with Na's and Mp's. That is, such an effort would probably seem neither inappropriate nor otherwise exorbitant, and, in the latter respect, unfeasible.[7] Under these conditions or from this perspective, there would be no decisive reason for restricting the range of staff/youth matches and for absorbing the given youths into other subtype caseloads.

Staff Development and Unit Functioning
Staff Development

Several facts and issues concerning staff development were reviewed in Chapter 11. Their implications, and those of related factors, will now be summarized relative to feasibility.

At CTP, initial in-service training was not needed, essentially because matched workers arrived on the job with sufficient skills for working with most youths. Nevertheless, staff development—which was based on far more than formal in-service training alone—was very much part of the project's atmosphere and tradition. This condition and history did not just derive from the experiment's long-range goal of determining "which approaches would be effective for [specified] youth." Instead, it mainly reflected the fact that, although most new workers had considerable confidence in their abilities, they also wished to increase their overall skills. In this regard, they often began to seriously express a desire for specialized training after about one and a half years at CTP, even though they usually felt they had already acquired several new skills and insights—largely via other inputs.

During Phases 1 and 2, Youth Authority resources allowed CTP staff to receive specialized training, for example, in conjoint family therapy or psychodrama; most such training occurred off-site. Though specialized training became harder for the YA to maintain as statewide budgets grew tighter beginning in the late 1960s, the agency still supported it for CTP, albeit at a somewhat reduced level. Yet, even when training funds had been relatively plentiful, a limiting condition from CTP's own

standpoint was the workers' availability to youths. More specifically, the project's main decision-makers believed that workers should not leave their caseloads for long periods of time, except for vacation or illness; as a result, since specialized training *was* sometimes lengthy and often *was* held in relatively distant sites, workers, who essentially shared that view, could not simply "take off," for example, either en masse or for five- to ten-day sessions. Therefore, when inconveniently located sites were involved, various schedule adjustments were usually made. Here, for instance, workers (trainees) might be allowed one, possibly two consecutive absent days per week, extended over several weeks. Beyond this, and especially as funds diminished, it was usually possible to send one or two workers and the unit supervisor to a given type of training. Upon completion of this training and quite often an advanced course, these individuals then served as resources to other staff.

The availability of specialized training was rather important to many workers at given junctures in their CTP careers, particularly in augmenting their skills. Such training often helped them (1) work with a wider range of youths ("branch out"), (2) use a broader set of approaches with their present youths, and/or (3) focus more effectively or efficiently on unusually difficult youths and situations. Yet, despite these benefits, specialized training was not, in itself, absolutely essential for achieving basic project goals with most youths. This was true chiefly because—as indicated—most workers were fairly well prepared from the start, and also because the largest and probably most important aspects of staff development usually occurred within the CTP unit itself. (See below, and Appendix 24.)

Whenever possible, then, a CTP-type unit should not depend on specialized, in-service training in order to accomplish its basic goals with most youths—especially, but not only, if such training is distantly located and/or expensive.[8] Instead, regarding these goals, CTP workers should be essentially "ready to go" when first hired. Nevertheless, staff-development, in its broad sense, is important in order to expand the workers' skills, to help maintain or improve individual and unit morale, to improve workers' ability to pool their resources and thus make the unit stronger and more flexible,[9] and to increase workers' future professional opportunities.

Relative to such goals, staff development *may*—but *need* not—include the specific training in question. Though this applies whether or not the workers' immediate or primary goal for such training is that of "branching out" to other youth subtypes, specialized training can be particularly valuable with respect to benefits (2) and (3) above. Moreover, these benefits aside, specialized training or at least consultation could be especially important, even essential, in units that lacked the full range of matched workers—that is, if the available workers were nevertheless expected to know a good deal about youths with whom they were not well-matched, and if many such youths were present.

Unit Functioning and Morale

To facilitate within-CTP sharing and, thus, staff development overall, unit meetings that center on professional issues and even personal feelings can be very useful. These meetings, which can also improve unit morale and overall functioning, would best be regularly scheduled, for example, weekly or twice monthly, and long-term in duration.

Within CTP, there were two types of professional-issues meetings: (1) "group staffings," which focused on individual youth subtypes and were by far the most common, and (2) general intervention and correctional-issues discussions. The latter were occasionally combined with (3) personal-feelings discussions, though this third type of meeting seldom focused on youths. Meetings (1) and (3) were held throughout most of Phase 2; participants in the latter type included almost all unit workers, the unit supervisor, and often the overall CTP administrator. Meetings (1) and (2) sometimes occurred during Phase 1, as well; here, participants usually included several workers, and occasionally the supervisors, from two or more CTP units (i.e., Sacramento, Stockton, and/or—in Phase 2—San Francisco). The parent agency consistently supported these meetings, though somewhat less so—if considerable travel was involved—when budgets grew tighter. Each meeting usually lasted two hours and was almost always held on-site (mainly Sacramento) (Palmer and Warren, 1967, p. 6; Palmer et al., 1968, pp. 10, 66; Turner et al., 1967, p. 15; Warren and Palmer, 1965, p. 2; Warren et al., 1966a, p. 23).

Today, most parent agencies would probably still support such meetings, not only because the latter would seldom require additional funds (substantial or otherwise) but because almost all participants would probably feel positively about them and attribute various benefits to them. Given basic agency support or even passive approval, the actual implementation, the maintenance, and the frequency of any or all such meetings would largely depend on the *unit* (project) supervisor's and/or overall administrator's stance. This stance should, of course, reflect not just these individuals' personal style, needs, and judgments concerning staff development and unit morale, but their assessment of what most project workers prefer. In this connection, for each potential participant—that is, for all staff, the administrator included—initial and continued attendance would best be voluntary, certainly in the case of meeting (3).

As with specialized training, these meetings would not—at least, should not—be absolutely essential for achieving basic or minimum project goals with most youths. Yet even so, if they were maintained for at least several months, such meetings, especially types (1) and (3), could be particularly valuable—often more than specialized training. Specifically, they could often increase goal achievement, job satisfaction, and overall unit functioning beyond the basics or minimum. For these reasons, they should receive agency support whenever possible, even if outside consultants or facilitators are sometimes needed in order to initiate a given type of meeting (almost exclusively meeting [3]), and if added expenses are therefore involved. This justification would be independent of, yet consistent with, given agencies' own commitment to staff development, irrespective of staff's particular assignment at the time.

However valuable, unit meetings—like specialized training—should be kept in perspective. For example, under most conditions, constructive staff interactions also occur *outside* such meetings, usually in a two- or three-person worker/worker or worker/supervisor context; in fact, within most units, such interactions (in offices, over coffee, etc.) seem to occur more often "outside" than "inside." These interactions involve, for instance, an informal exchange of intervention-centered information, of personal feelings, or of both; like "inside" (unit) meetings, they often promote individual staff development and improved unit morale and unit functioning alike.

In addition, such interactions, and the resulting staff and unit growth, often occur *without* the earlier-mentioned meetings, or in conjunction with relatively few.

Nevertheless, growth-producing interactions often do occur—sometimes even originate—within such meetings, for example, inside professional-issues meetings. Moreover, those that occur "inside" are often different in content and somewhat different in outcome than those which occur outside. Beyond this, staff interactions and other events that occur outside such meetings can often be enhanced by those which have taken place within. Specifically, "outside" interactions and related intervention activities may be enhanced in terms of becoming (individually) *more* positive and/or (collectively) *more often* positive than before—quite possibly (judging from staff accounts) because of the overall stimulation and enthusiasm generated by given meetings.[10] Similarly, positive interactions and activities that (collectively) may indeed be occurring within the unit, but only sparingly, sluggishly, or perhaps decreasingly so, can often be resurrected or vitalized by the introduction of type (1), (2), or (3) meetings. Thus, even if "outside" staff interactions are already positive, they and other events may become more positive and more frequent given the introduction of one or more such meetings; moreover, simply "passable" interactions are likely to become increasingly positive. In effect, these unit meetings often help release and focus staff resources that might otherwise remain untapped.

Equally important, meetings (1) through (3) can improve a guarded or perhaps negative atmosphere. For example, type (1) and (2) meetings can sometimes accomplish this goal by showing given staff that valuable information can in fact be exchanged, and by making such exchanges easier or more rewarding than before. Similarly, type (3) meetings can often identify and resolve intrastaff misunderstandings or faulty preconceptions, and they can reveal the existence or extent of otherwise unavailable resources and obscured positive feelings. These processes and outcomes can help overcome sizable difficulties between given individuals; they can also accelerate the resolution of those problems *outside* such meetings.

Standard, that is, "outside," interactions sometimes fail to satisfactorily resolve these problems by themselves, especially if three or more individuals are involved and one is the supervisor or administrator. This limitation was seen most clearly in the San Francisco CTP unit, which did not have type (3) meetings and which was involved in substantially fewer professional-issues meetings than the remaining units (Turner et al., 1967, p. 15; Palmer et al., 1968, p. 66). Yet, in Stockton CTP, nearly all interpersonal difficulties *were* resolved or markedly reduced through standard interactions. To be sure, in Stockton, there were fewer such difficulties from the start, and fewer external complexities and limitations as well. Possibly more important— and, largely independent of such external factors—Stockton's interpersonal problems were less interwoven with sizable philosophical differences than were SF's.[11] Problem resolution aside, such meetings can obviate the *development* of various difficulties and can at least forestall the escalation of others.

Whatever the atmosphere may be, unit meetings can also clarify, not so much the personal difficulties of—and among—staff, but philosophical differences concerning the field of corrections, such as its primary goals and overall scope. The latter issues are often reflected in intrastaff differences within such areas as the following: (1) definitions of *success* with special-project youths, say, CTP youths; (2) justification for recommending restoral to parole; and (3) extent and duration of one's commitment to the youths in question. Such differences, in turn, sometimes influence major aspects of unit functioning, for instance, caseload turnover and resource allocation. Clarification of these issues, especially their underlying factors and assumptions, bears on staff development: It helps many workers see themselves and their beliefs from a broader perspective than before, and it usually helps them become more aware of or receptive to the potential contributions of others.[12] Though it often highlights staff differences, such clarification generally promotes unit morale as well.

In sum, professional-issues and personal-feelings meetings can help maintain and increase already positive unit morale and unit functioning, as well as promote or accelerate staff development. They can also help eliminate low morale and reduce negative interactions. Positive morale and overall functioning can help staff want to remain in the unit for considerable time and continue performing at a high-energy level in their already taxing job. Like staff development, the former factors (positive morale, etc.) thus support the long-term intensive and extensive contacts that are often critical to the achievement of project goals with typical and unusually difficult youths alike. Finally, staff development, positive unit morale, and positive unit functioning often occur in parallel and are mutually reinforcing, especially when staff are neither disinclined nor averse to sharing given information and/or feelings and when they enjoy feedback that suggests they are making valuable contributions to peers and others.

Most agency administrators attach considerable value to positive unit morale and staff development. They often view these factors as subgoals with respect to a broader goal: effective unit functioning. These individuals recognize and usually support various methods, for example, information-sharing meetings, that can help achieve these subgoals. Given the high probability that agency administrators will recognize the relevance of such subgoals to long-term intensive and extensive intervention, and given the relatively minimal costs of methods such as the above, most such individuals are not likely to establish policies that would specifically prevent CTP-type units from thus drawing on their own resources in order to develop and better utilize their strength, both as units and as groups of individuals. In short, key decision-makers are not likely to oppose the meetings in question.

Supervision and Administration
The Casework Supervisor
Before commenting on feasibility aspects of *supervision,* the need for and main features of this activity will be reviewed. Though we will assume that a CTP-type unit would contain one casework supervisor, seven line workers, and roughly twelve youths per worker, both the review and comments would apply even if the latter figures were somewhat different.

Basic Responsibility
A casework supervisor (CWS) who firmly supports the concepts and assumptions of differential intervention, the broad principles and objectives, and the project (unit) goal plus subgoals outlined in Chapter 14, is essential for a well-functioning—even an acceptably functioning—CTP-type unit. Such a CWS would, for example, actively and consistently promote, not just passively allow and casually or hesitantly encourage, the "conditions of intervention" and "approaches to intervention" described in Chapter 15: factors #1, #2, and #3 (small caseloads; intensive and/or extensive contacts; and long-term contacts) and factors #4 and #5 (utilization of explicit, detailed guidelines; individualization/flexible programming), respectively. (The more passive, casual, and hesitant approach might possibly suffice for an acceptably—in this case, barely acceptably—functioning unit.) In these and other respects he would have central responsibility for ensuring that the concepts and methods of differential intervention are appropriately implemented at the individual case level, across all caseloads. This task includes coordination of all unit activities, and it would apply regardless of which youth-classification system is used.

Key Skills
To discharge this responsibility while using the I-level system, it is important for the casework supervisor also to be skilled in I-level diagnosis. As discussed below, it is not just important but virtually essential for him also to be skilled in both worker/youth (individual case) matching and worker selection (hiring) and matching; the latter bears on factors #6 and #7. These diagnostic and matching skills, if not possessed by the CWS, must still exist and be available somewhere (but, as discussed below, not solely among line workers). For instance, if the parent agency maintains a separate organizational unit that, among other services, provides I-level diagnoses, the CTP supervisor could possibly "get by" without this skill. However, his possession of this skill would remain highly desirable, not just to increase the unit's self-sufficiency and overall strength but mainly to improve case supervision itself—even aside from the latter's contribution to staff development. Thus, for example, supervision that focused on a given agent's case (youth) could be improved with respect to factors #2 and #4, if the CWS familiarized himself with both the individual *and* "subtype" aspects of that youth. He could do so largely via an early personal contact, such as a diagnostic interview, or by some other means.

Whether or not personal contact occurred,

such supervision would consist of more than initial case planning, perfunctory case monitoring (however frequent), and implementation of various agency-level responsibilities. It would require considerable understanding of each case, and ongoing interaction with the agent based on that understanding. (Most CTP workers welcomed such supervision, despite their relative competence; this applied especially but not only with unusually difficult cases, during crises [for all cases], and in the absence of assistance from peers.)

The following assumes that neither a separate diagnostic unit nor an equivalent resource is available to the CTP-type operation; this applies to selection and matching resources as well.[13] Whether or not such assistance is available, can CTP *workers* make the necessary diagnostic and matching decisions, thereby eliminating the need for such supervisor skills? Beyond this, *must* such workers possess these skills? (In the following, as mentioned earlier, "diagnosis" refers to I-level/subtype classification only, not to the determination of a youth's (1) specific life situation and (2) personal strengths, interests, limitations, and so on. It is assumed that *either* the worker or supervisor could determine (1) and (2), and that initial case planning—a joint effort by these individuals in any event—would utilize this and subtype information alike. Even if he had not personally interviewed the youth, an experienced CWS could provide considerable assistance to most agents with respect to integrating and interpreting these sets of information prior to as well as during an initial case conference. Based on the information in question—again, without having interviewed the youth—such a supervisor could also finalize the subtype diagnosis.)

Diagnostic and matching skills need *not* be present among line workers, that is, agents (PA I's). However, the former skills often do exist among those who have worked in a CTP unit for two or more years or have received specific I-level training. Yet, agent abilities notwithstanding, and regardless of who conducts the diagnostic interview (supervisor *or* agent), it is important for the *supervisor*—based on *his* diagnostic skills—to (1) finalize each subtype diagnosis and then assign the given youth to an appropriate agent, and, if seemingly necessary, to (2) later rediagnose and perhaps reassign that youth.

Given such skills, the CWS need not act as a rubber stamp, and the earlier-mentioned improved case supervision can be better facilitated. At any rate, agents should not substitute for the supervisor with respect to (1) and (2); this is not simply to maintain clear lines of authority and exclusive areas of responsibility.

As to selection and matching of candidates, most PA I's would require special training in order to adequately perform those functions while in the CTP unit. Yet even if they developed such skills, it would be unwise for them to hire and match given candidates and, ipso facto, to reject others. Basically, such actions would produce serious personnel problems at the unit, and, especially, at the unit/agency level; the unit-level difficulties would be different in content but similar in principle to those that would result from having given agents assign individual *cases* to other agents, newly hired or otherwise. Moreover, even if the agents' and casework supervisor's selection and matching skills were equal, the supervisor would usually be in a better position (and perhaps more strongly motivated) than given agents to select a candidate who would not only increase the unit's overall strength but would personally "mesh" with most staff—in contrast, say, to specified agents alone. For such reasons—certainly in light of the potentially serious problems—responsibility for selection and matching appropriately falls upon the supervisor rather than on line workers.[14] (Under some conditions, this task may be shared with the unit administrator, if such an individual exists; and, in any event, given workers can at least communicate their possible knowledge or impressions of particular candidates to the supervisor.)

General Functions

To actively support and specifically implement the earlier-mentioned concepts, principles, and so on, at the overall unit level, especially with regard to factors #2, #4, and #5, the supervisor must be knowledgeable about the usual dynamics of, and various methods of intervention with, the full range of youth subtypes, certainly those which are other than rare. Given such knowledge, he could provide valuable and in some respects necessary casework assistance and direction to new and seasoned agents alike, regardless of the subtypes with which they work.

The CWS could, for example, (1) help them better think through underlying or current issues and alternatives, (2) suggest ideas or approaches they had not yet considered, (3) help them better utilize their personal assets (e.g., modeling and leadership qualities), (4) alert them to probable dangers or emerging crises, and (5) divert them from probable "dead-end" or even counterproductive approaches. In these respects, especially (1) and (2), his value need not be limited to subtypes with which he himself was, or could have been, well-matched, for example, when he was a parole agent.

At any rate, when focusing on individual youths—especially of given subtypes—such a casework supervisor would not be mainly limited to one or both of the following roles: providing agents with approval or encouragement to do what they already plan to do, are thinking about doing, or have already done; directing agents to other (CTP; non-CTP) sources of assistance, that is, acting as a "resource broker." Though both such roles are often very important, they can usually be performed with little detailed knowledge about given subtypes and with relatively little understanding of the youths as individuals; yet, *given* such knowledge, and so forth, their value can be increased. It might be added that most supervisors who have the earlier-mentioned knowledge would be more confident than the latter CWS's about supporting specified, *nonstandard* intervention methods and prospective case decisions on the part of new and experienced workers alike, whether or not (but especially if) those methods and decisions seemed to involve unusual risk.

A supervisor who is not only knowledgeable about dynamics and intervention but has diagnostic and especially matching skills could perform major functions that extend beyond casework. He could, for instance, help concretize the earlier-mentioned concepts, principles, and subgoals not just when (1) *interacting with agents relative to individual youths,* that is, when performing a casework function, but when (2) *selecting and matching workers plus classifying/assigning youths,* and when (3) *prioritizing and coordinating the unit's activities and resources* on an across-caseloads basis. In so doing, he could spearhead differential intervention within the unit as a whole, a role that is especially important not just during the unit's early stages but

whenever several relatively new workers are present.

Although an understanding of dynamics and intervention would mainly bear on function (1), above, diagnostic and matching skills would primarily relate to function (2). Taken together, this understanding and skill would probably allow the CWS to perform better in function (3) as well.[15] A supervisor who is skilled in all three areas, particularly the first, could help make the difference between a "well-functioning" and an adequately or passably functioning unit. We view the former as one that firmly adheres to principle #2 (Introduction, page xxviii; also see below) and which operates on the assumption that—with serious multiple offenders—achievement of one or more of the preceding subgoals (also see below) is not only crucial but can best be achieved through close work with youths as individuals. Since CTP's findings suggest that this assumption is valid and that individualization bears on increased public protection, "well-functioning" has "outcome" (product) implications, not just "input" or "through-put" (process) meaning.

The principle and subgoals in question are as follows. Principle #2: ". . . facilitate the youth's personal involvement in the process of change as a way of tapping and building upon his internal motivation." Subgoals: "changes in the youth's perception of self and society; expansion or redirection of youth's coping abilities; reduction of stresses and/or expansion of supports in the youth's immediate environment." (These subgoals are particularly focused on the ultimate goal of better protecting society on a long-term basis. If one's exclusive or predominant goal were short-term protection—longer-range outcomes aside—the above assumption could change substantially, not just for serious multiple offenders. More specifically, if one's ultimate goal were no longer long-term protection and if the above subgoals were then modified—for instance, reduced in scope, individually and perhaps collectively—the extent of required *individualization* could itself be affected.)

A casework supervisor who performs not only functions (2) and (3) but especially function (1) could often help agents further individualize the youth/agent interaction, that is, relate it more closely to the youth's needs, interests, current limitations, and so on. Since, as suggested, individualized interaction seems central to implementing the above principle and subgoals with the present youths, and although matched agents usually do individualize their interactions with such youths to a considerable degree even without careful supervision, the following would therefore apply, by definition: "Well-functioning" would not mean that most youths are simply being *classified and matched* efficiently and accurately (*cf.* function [2]), or are just being handled humanely. Nor would it mean that the overall unit is simply operating efficiently and harmoniously with respect, say, to its numerous intra- and extramural *activities* (*cf.* function [3]). At issue, here, are not activities per se, or even their coordinated nature, but rather their bearing on the needs, interests, and so on, of the youths involved (*cf.* function [1]).

Accurate classification, well-coordinated activities, and the like, are nevertheless important components of a well-functioning unit.[16] In effect, they are necessary though not sufficient components, since, as implied, such a unit would, at a minimum, also consist of agents who worked closely with youths as *individuals*. (This would apply whether or not the unit utilized all nine subtype distinctions.) As suggested by the Phase 1 and 2 experience, individualization regarding needs, interests, and so on, is central to concretizing and incorporating principle #2; and it is the youth's personal involvement, plus the motivation that can then be tapped, which substantially raise the chance of effecting the type of changes— namely, the "subgoals" themselves—that can help achieve the *final* goal of increased, long-term public protection. Basically, then, "well-functioning" includes but extends beyond the concept of "appropriately focused." It is defined in relation to major unit operations that seem to substantially increase the likelihood of achieving one's subgoals and final goal. In the present context, these operations are not limited to individualization, for example, as described earlier, even though individual-focused operations do seem especially appropriate.

From this perspective, then, the supervisor must be more than a facilitator and coordinator if the unit is to be considered well-functioning in the present sense—*unless* almost all agents can produce a high degree of individualization by themselves and the CWS therefore needs to add relatively little in this area. Yet even then, a supervisor would be needed with respect to functions (2) and (3), since, as indicated, these too are components of a well-functioning—even an adequately or passably functioning—unit, and since neither (2) nor (3) is a function for which agents should be responsible. Thus, whatever level of unit functioning is involved ("well," "adequate," or "barely passable"), the question is not whether a CWS is needed but which functions, and what primary role, he will perform.[17]

One additional function: A skilled CWS can usually set a tone of seriousness, professionalism, and mutual respect throughout the unit, mainly by words and—especially—actions whose messages to staff are as follows:

> "You've got an important, challenging job to do; therefore, you're here to *work,* not to 'float' or take the easy road." "You each have information and observations from which your fellow workers can often profit, so definitely exchange views and experiences, for example, during unit meetings or group staffings." "Though you already have important skills, you have much to learn and should continue to develop yourselves professionally." "I'll gladly support your requests and actions provided they make sense and seem fairly practical, even though (1) this support may sometimes necessitate my resisting considerable external pressure, and the given action may involve our taking various risks whether or not such pressure exists, and (2) I, personally, might well have used a different approach under similar conditions."

The CWS can further promote mutual respect, in particular, by explicitly indicating to all workers that each worker's skills, characteristics, and approaches are especially important for the types of youth with which he interacts, and that no *group* of workers, such as agents assigned to Cfc/Mp or to Nx youths, is ipso facto "better" or better motivated than any other group. This stance, especially by a CWS, will almost always preclude erroneous beliefs that can otherwise develop among agents (mainly new ones), for instance, morale-lowering beliefs to the effect that I_3 workers are less professional than I_4 workers, or that they need fewer skills in any event. By demonstrating sincerity and determination concerning these messages, the supervisor can substantially add to his or her role as "main focal point" for intervention efforts at the individual-case and unit-activities levels alike. In this connection, he can become an even more-respected and appropriately utilized lead person with regard to ongoing operations, regardless of how self-reliant most staff might be.

Parent-Agency View

Throughout the experiment, the parent agency consistently accepted and supported the need for supervision—one CWS per unit. It recognized that this individual's job involved not simply transplanting agency-wide policies and procedures into the CTP unit but adapting them to that unit's particular operations and long-range goal, wherever possible and appropriate. More generally, agency decision-makers—middle managers and top administrators alike—supported the idea that CTP needed an individual who would be centrally responsible for implementing, not a standard parole operation, but the concepts, principles, and so on, of differential intervention, as defined by unit staff themselves; such implementation involved functions (1) through (3) alike. The agency supported CTP's need for a supervisor even when its (YA's) budget constraints grew tighter and its priorities regarding rehabilitation changed. Under those same conditions the YA also continued to accept the project's one-CWS-per-seven-workers arrangement, a ratio often observed in regular parole units as well.

Since it agreed that the CTP supervisor required, essentially from the start, certain knowledge and perspectives not found in most Youth Authority supervisors, the parent agency also accepted—and supported—the following: First, CTP had to choose its own CWS (and it always *did*); that is, the project's decision-makers were considered the best judges of the specific supervision needed. Thus, at a minimum, the project required veto power over all supervisor candidates (and together with the research team, it always *did* have this power); these candidates included, for example, non-CTP Youth Authority personnel who had been displaced in the wake of budget cuts and whom the agency had to eventually "place." Second, a CTP supervisor needed ample in-service training in order to increase or even maintain his resource value to the unit, especially regarding individual casework, for example, function (1). Here, key agency decision-makers assumed that since matched CTP *workers* were primarily

specialists with respect to this function and since *they* usually continued to develop professionally, a supervisor who was himself professionally advanced and advancing with regard to function (1) would be both appropriate and in some respects essential for such individuals.

Candidates

During all phases, supervisor candidates whose job-related skills and motives seemed to center on two or more of the following (always including the first item) were quite common: implementing standard, agency-wide policies and practices; providing agents with approval or encouragement to do essentially what they wished to do anyway; and acting as a resource broker. Most such individuals also seemed willing and able to support the basic concepts of differential intervention, and they were at least willing to adapt agency policies and procedures to the unit's needs wherever this seemed important. In such respects these candidates had what might be called general supervisory potential; this also included not only the ability to prioritize and coordinate a unit's activities and resources, but moderate to considerable flexibility and the capacity to interact appropriately with outside agencies.

However, many such individuals did not seem particularly skilled regarding functions (1) and (2) above, and, thus, in connection with function (3) as well—at least with respect to a differential intervention context. As a result, had they been hired they would probably have performed only moderately well with regard to (a) supporting the earlier-mentioned principles and subgoals, for instance, actively promoting not only factors #2 through #5 (by helping to translate them into specific actions) but factors #6 and #7 as well, and (b) recognizing *which* policies and procedures required modification under given conditions, or *how* to modify them relative to the principles and subgoals in question. Most such candidates would probably have been able to operate an adequate or, more likely, a barely passable unit only if that unit's workers were already quite skilled and self-sufficient and if outside resources were available regarding function (2). However, even then, much would probably have been lost not only in terms of potential staff development, positive unit morale, and so on, but, most important, with respect to individual youths.

Persons who *were* skilled in functions (1) and (2)—(namely, individual casework; diagnosis and, often to a lesser degree, matching)—were not uncommon. These individuals seemed generally able to perform function (3) as well, at least within a differential intervention context and, as with the preceding functions, for a fairly wide range of youths. Such persons, many of whom eventually received (and, upon so doing, took) the opportunity to become supervisors within and sometimes outside CTP, had almost always "risen through the ranks"; at least, they would have thus "risen" if enough supervisory positions were available. Specifically, prior to receiving this opportunity or at least being considered appropriate for such a position, these individuals had been agents (line workers) for at least two years, almost always at CTP; a few had worked in other intensive supervision units (ISUs), such as a CDCP (Chapter 17). "Through the ranks" also applied to the few individuals who, when hired as CTP supervisors, were already quite skilled in all three functions, with respect to a wide range of youths.

Since "general supervisory potential" is, by itself, insufficient for the job in question and since specialized skills are required, it is not necessarily easy to locate individuals who could probably spearhead a CTP-type unit. The latter are persons who, in effect, would be able to operate such a unit on other than a passable-only, or a possibly adequate, basis, even if most workers were not already quite skilled and self-sufficient and if specific outside resources were unavailable. Nevertheless, as implied, promising CWSs were seldom difficult to locate and hire during the California experiment. This mainly reflected the fact that one or more CTP units usually contained an agent who had the necessary knowledge for the job, who seemed appropriately motivated, and who had scored sufficiently high on the statewide supervisors' exam. The knowledge in question reflected such agents' prior exposure to I-level diagnosis, to individual and subtype dynamics, to methods of intervention, and—usually to a lesser degree—to selection and matching of workers. As implied, some promising candidates had obtained much of their specialized knowledge in other ISUs.

Spearheading a Unit
If, today, an agency wished to start its first CTP-type unit, one of its initial steps should probably be to locate an individual who seems capable of, and interested in, spearheading the operation. In many agencies, this person (the casework supervisor) might well be found in an intensive supervision unit, if such exists; however, he or she might be located *anywhere* within or even outside the agency. Despite the CWS's clear potential, he might not only require but may personally desire specified training in order to be "brought up to speed" and to implement or perhaps better implement certain basic yet critical tasks.

For instance, to help ensure that this individual does a good job of setting up the CTP unit and getting it underway (e.g., hiring staff and establishing procedures for processing cases)—or, to simply help him do a *better* job in these regards—most agencies would probably be wise to take the following step if possible, prior to establishing the unit. Provide the casework supervisor access to an intensive course or consultation program, or combination thereof, that focuses on whichever of the following seem needed or beneficial: diagnosis (I-level and perhaps other); selection and matching of staff; differential dynamics and intervention. Actually, unless the CWS is already unusually knowledgeable, this step should be considered not just wise or prudent but virtually essential, especially if the individual will have primary responsibility not only for finalizing all youth classifications and assignments but for selecting all staff.

Apart from focusing on the casework supervisor, the agency might also try to provide at least one high-level administrator access to a brief, for example, five-day, overview of differential intervention and the main ingredients of a CTP unit. This overview could furnish the agency with a better understanding of the needs, potentials, and limitations of the prospective unit, and it could also promote more effective communication between that unit and the agency (administration) as a whole.

During 1967–1972, such a course and overview were available from the Center for Training in Differential Treatment. For several years afterward they were provided—with primary emphasis on I-level—mainly by certified trainers/consultants.[18] Most such individuals were themselves trained in differential intervention at CTDT or had worked, usually as supervisors, either in the Community Treatment Project or in a CTP-type program (Warren and CTDT staff, 1972, 1974).

Presently, many agencies could probably find and develop appropriate supervisory personnel for a CTP unit, though not without some inconvenience and cost with respect to the earlier-mentioned, or comparable, training. They could do so despite the fact that California's particular "pool" of *past* as well as *potential* CWSs became essentially unavailable to prospective CTP-type units outside the Youth Authority by the early to middle 1980s, that is, unavailable as possible casework supervisors (see comments regarding "IDTA," in Chapter 23). (The pool in question, that is, both groups of casework supervisors, evolved during the days of CTDT and CTP. *Potential* CWSs were those who, despite their apparent skills, never actually became supervisors in a CTP-type unit, at least as far as was known.) In any given state, interested agencies might often be able to recruit appropriate supervisory staff from various specialized and/or intensive intervention programs that have operated in those or other states during the preceding 10 to 15 years.

The Administrative Supervisor

Functions

During the CTP experiment, the administrative supervisor (unit administrator, or UA) performed a unit-centered, an agency-centered, and a unit/agency-centered function. More specifically, he

a. apprised the parent agency of the unit's activities and status, communicated the unit's operational needs to agency managers and administrators, negotiated for the unit's share of standard as well as specialized resources;
b. communicated agency goals, concerns, and options to the unit; ensured that agency policies and regulations were implemented within, or otherwise adapted to, the unit; interacted with Youth Authority Board and with agency regarding legal status of, and casework decisions concerning, individual youths; and
c. presented the unit's policies, plans, and specific decisions to other agencies and institutions, mainly law enforcement, probation, social welfare, and schools; negotiated with those agencies as needed.

In thus representing both the unit and agency, he tried not only to obtain or increase the agency's understanding of and support for the unit, but to help the unit better meet the agency's needs. Similar functions and goals exist in most special supervision units, differential intervention oriented or not. (The UA carried out other functions as well. For instance, he discussed with agency planning bodies both the unit's own needs and the possible implications of its experiences for the agency; he also participated in staff selection and ensured that research requirements were met wherever possible.)

Relationship to CWS

The UA performed functions (a) through (c), above, because they were central to his mandate—one that reflected the following assumptions: A CTP *casework supervisor* usually lacks the time and/or—in some respects or contexts—the specific knowledge and experience needed to effectively implement most such functions; in contrast, most full-time UA's *have* the required time, and so on. As a corollary, it was implicitly assumed—again correctly—that if an experienced CWS were given sufficient time, agency support, and so forth, he could effectively perform most or all components of function (a), the first and last components of (b), and all aspects of (c). Within some CTP units, the casework supervisor did in fact perform these functions; however, even then, the unit administrator retained the basic responsibility and major workload, particularly regarding (a) and (b).

At any rate, throughout 1961–1973, all three functions were not infrequently shared by the CWS and UA; and the degree to which this within-unit sharing occurred seemed to depend more on the CWS's available time than on factors such as emergent or even longer-term circumstances (e.g., the *UA's* special assignments and overall workload), agency preferences (e.g., middle managers' or high-level administrators' views regarding delegation of specified functions, and their personal opinion of the CWS), and the UA/CWS relationship plus the skills and job-centered motivations of each.

Clearly, then, depending on particular circumstances, and except as indicated below, a *UA* is not the only type of person who can perform functions (a) through (c), whether exclusively, primarily, or otherwise. Nor, for that matter, must each CTP unit have a *full-time* UA, even assuming that the person who performs these functions *is* a UA and that this individual must perform them exclusively or at least primarily. Instead, except for unusual circumstances, a full-time UA can probably be shared by two CTP-sized special supervision units. Such sharing, in fact, regularly occurred not only across the two San Francisco units (the Community Treatment Project's Differential Treatment Unit [DTU; Chapter 9] and GGI), where it seemed to work moderately well, but across the Valley CTP units (Sacramento and Stockton), where it appeared to work quite well.

(DTU was differential intervention (DI) oriented, whereas GGI was not; moreover, their operational needs were rather dissimilar. When two "sharing units" differ considerably in orientation as well as operational needs, even-handed treatment by the UA is particularly important but may sometimes prove difficult, as it did during 1967–1968 [Palmer et al., 1968, p. 72]. Both *Valley* units were, of course, DI oriented, and, though their operational needs were slightly different, these units rarely experienced sizable difficulties with respect to UA-sharing and even-handed treatment.)

Regardless of who performs given functions, and of exactly how they are shared within and across units, they should nonetheless be performed. For instance, with respect to function (a), either a UA or a CWS with relevant knowledge, perspective, interpersonal skills, and so on, *should* directly interact with agency administrators regarding the CTP unit's situation and interests. That is, he should explain that particular unit's assumptions and activities (clarifying misunderstandings if necessary), should objectively describe its assets and limitations, and should vigorously as well as consistently try to meet its needs for material resources, organizational support, and particular operating conditions or procedures. Only via such actions, carried out by a knowledgeable and well-prepared individual, can the unit maximize—in some cases, even uphold—its chances of retaining its required integrity and direction. This may be especially true in complex, rapidly moving, and often heavily pressured agencies, whether or not budget cutting is a major factor. The need for such action is independent of the fact that functions (a) through (c) can be rather time-consuming, at least in the aggregate and especially when combined with additional unit- and agency-centered chores.[19]

As suggested, *time*—time devoted to priority activities—is probably the main factor that will limit most casework supervisors' participation in the earlier-mentioned functions.[20] (The UA/CWS relationship, and the skills plus job-centered motivations of each, are likely to be the next main factors.) More specifically, a CWS who is largely involved and invested in individualized casework supervision—typically his highest priority—will often have little if any time to perform functions (a) and (b) in a carefully prepared and integrated way, or with much personal follow-up let alone longer-term continuity of effort. However, to maximize or even uphold the earlier-mentioned chances, an individual who performs (a) through (c) should obviously have opportunities or sufficient latitude to perform them well. Thus, for example, in the case of a CWS, the UA might allow him or perhaps even require him to spend considerable time on activities *other than* individualized casework supervision. Yet by the same token, in order to concretize the unit's basic principles and to help achieve its main subgoals, a unit administrator should, where possible, support and clearly encourage rather than substantially limit or actively encroach upon the CWS's casework priority and investment.

For such reasons, a full-time administrator is highly desirable with respect to the functions in question, even if he must be shared by two units. In addition, within any given unit, this individual, not the casework supervisor, should routinely carry the basic responsibility and major workload, at least for functions (a) and (b) and except as a temporary measure—assuming, of course, that he and the CWS *will* share specified functions.

Relationship to Parent Agency
When performing functions (a) through (c), the unit administrator serves not just CTP but the agency as a whole, and the way he performs these functions helps determine his effectiveness. For instance, when performing function (b) the UA is acting primarily as the agency's direct representative, and to perform this agency-centered function effectively he must gain the confidence of agency administrators and unit staff alike. Moreover, insofar as he gains their confidence he can better serve not just agency goals but *unit* objectives—those he attempts to implement via the unit-

centered function (a). "Confidence" thus emerges as an important factor relative to CTP's unit administrator.

For the UA to obtain and maintain this confidence, three main conditions are probably required. Agency and unit personnel must feel that the UA (1) acts impartially with respect to the agency and *unit,* that is, systematically favors neither one, (2) is nevertheless sympathetic to the goals and major efforts of each, and (3) represents and addresses their concerns and priorities knowledgeably, carefully, and seriously. This feeling would be based more on the UA's collective actions and products than on any one or two efforts alone, unless the latter involved, say, major and virtually irreparable blunders.

To meet the preceding conditions the UA must integrate or at least satisfactorily balance the salient interests of agency and unit, interests that may sometimes diverge in specific situations. In so doing, and possible divergence notwithstanding, he should be guided by a belief that (1) the unit which he represents, namely, CTP, offers (or, if new, potentially offers) specified benefits that are in the *agency's* interests to understand, and that (2) the same applies relative to agency benefits and *CTP's* interests. Under these conditions and given this belief, the UA can serve as "middleman" in a positive sense: He can act as a vehicle through which the agency and unit may benefit each other, not primarily "control" or "fend off" each other. Based on that belief he can also feel in a better position—and perhaps more strongly obliged—to affirm and maintain, rather than negate or dilute, given principles and policies that may be essential to various agency and unit operations. Since agency administration and the CTP unit should each feel that a unit administrator is willing and able to appropriately represent their central interests, each should have a voice—ideally an equal voice—in selecting that individual. At least, they should both have veto power over any given candidate, as was the case in California.

The following applies whether or not the UA is viewed as a "middleman," in the above sense or otherwise; it is mainly based on CTP's experience during 1961–1973: In contrast to that of the UA, the *CWS's* role focuses on the unit itself. That is, it centers not on agency/unit-level relationships and needs but on implementing differential intervention at the individual case level, for example, via interaction with agents and coordination of unit activities. Also in contrast, even when the CWS shares specified functions with the UA, his particular skills, work experiences, and job-related motivations—especially those for which he was hired—will probably result in his dealing with, or at least preferring to deal with, tasks *other than* the following [items (1) and (2) are components of functions (a) and (b), respectively]: (1) negotiating with the agency for given resources and particular operating procedures or conditions; (2) ensuring that agency policies and procedures are implemented within, or otherwise adapted to, the unit; and (3) generally balancing the salient interests of the agency and unit, especially when sizable differences exist or major changes are proposed.

In short, compared to the unit administrator, the casework supervisor will, for valid reasons, be less prepared and less strongly motivated to negotiate, enforce, and balance agency interests with regard to the unit as an entity, at least in the context of shared UA/CWS functions, and beyond the individual-case level in any event. This is independent of the fact that not all agency/unit differences, proposed changes, or specified current policies will require or otherwise lead to negotiation and possible compromise. That is, the agency or unit will generally *accept* such differences, changes, and so on, with little if any question, unless, for instance, (1) those differences, and so forth, are relatively large (e.g., involve major augmentation, curtailment, or redistribution of material resources) or (2) the proposed changes (again by the agency or unit), or even the current policies, seem unduly expensive or unnecessarily awkward if not burdensome. It is also apart from the fact that the CWS, like the agent himself, will of course comply with current agency requirements regarding the processing and supervision of each individual youth.

Background and Orientation

Throughout the CTP experiment, UAs were not difficult to find. Their pre-UA experience was mainly in Youth Authority parole, and it usually extended over approximately ten years. Almost all had been field supervisors, though rarely in special supervision units (CTP included). In addition, most had held a middle management or administrative position inside or outside parole. Within the YA, these individuals were considered quite supportive of innovative approaches, and, generally speaking, it was (1) their orientation and interests relative to youths, (2) their particular work experience, and (3) CTP's reputation as an innovative program that combined to make the unit administrator position attractive to them. Though they were not always very familiar with or entirely uncritical of I-level concepts prior to arriving at CTP (and sometimes even after), these individuals, once they arrived, supported differential intervention whenever possible and almost always worked out well in the job. At base, they believed such intervention made sense and could often benefit the agency—with which they continued to identify despite their positive feelings toward CTP.

For reasons such as the following, UAs did not require the earlier-mentioned specialized training. (1) They did not try to assist in diagnosing of youths. (2) They did not act as casework supervisors, for instance, to partly relieve an overburdened CWS. Also, they rarely tried to substitute for the CWS—for example, in terms of case reviews with line staff—during the supervisor's absence or unavailability, except in emergencies or when legal processing was immediately required. (3) Though UAs participated in all hiring decisions regarding line staff, it was the CWS together with research personnel who made the key hiring recommendations, based on their more detailed understanding of matching; at any rate, UAs rarely exercised their veto power in this area.

Promising UA candidates would probably not be difficult to locate today, in non–Youth Authority agencies that contain individuals with similar orientations, interests, and types or levels of experience. Moreover, these particular features are not likely to be rare, even among persons with lesser *amounts* of experience.

Notes

1. Upper administrators believed the candidate had had some "shady business dealings" in his past and should therefore not be accepted into the Parole Division.
2. This, at least, was true shortly after the close of Phase 1 (1964), by which time a "pool" of candidates had built up (see text). When a new *unit* was opening (San Francisco, 1965), or when an existing unit was substantially expanding (Stockton, 1964–1965), 10 to 20 candidates would be interviewed within a short time span. Since several acceptable candidates could not be immediately accommodated (hired), the pool rapidly expanded on these occasions.
3. Most such candidates would probably have been considered potentially appropriate for the caseloads that were available (open) on these later occasions.
4. From early 1965 to the end of Phase 3, CTP did not require its workers to be "PA II's"—a more advanced grade of *pa*role *a*gent than "PA I's" (the entry-level class). Except for its casework supervisors, who were "PA III's," CTP's first 11 hires had all been PA II's. For further details, see Warren et al., 1966a, p. 22— CTP research report #7. Also see Chapter 16, section on "Parole Agents' Background Characteristics."
5. It might be noted that individuals over 45 rarely expressed interest in CTP.
6. By agency policy, female agents were allowed to work with selected male parolees. However, male agents could not work with female parolees on a permanent, that is, primary worker, basis. They could, nevertheless, supplement a female worker's efforts and could temporarily substitute for her during vacations or illness.
7. Partly independent of the fact that CTP had relatively little difficulty obtaining most matched workers, it was only occasionally necessary for the project to transfer an entire caseload to various temporary, that is, substitute, workers (other CTP staff) for very long. This situation generally occurred when a CTP worker left the program on three or four weeks' notice, for instance, due to a within-YA promotional opportunity, and the new worker (the selected—sometimes the *only*—finalist) could not replace him on equally short notice, for example, could not be hired *and* move to Sacramento.
8. Since many such training sessions are held in or near large metropolitan areas, distance and expense would be reduced if the parole unit were itself located in or near such an area.

9. This and similar benefits could also make it easier for workers to temporarily substitute for each other, for example, during vacations or illnesses, and to complement each other in various activities, such as community center interactions and out-of-town trips.

10. In this context, "stimulating" usually means: (1) information and feelings are being readily, candidly, and perhaps eagerly exchanged; (2) there exists an expectation of *continued* intellectual and emotional challenge and satisfaction in connection with such exchanges and with their related activities; and (3) there exist clear and sometimes increasing feelings of professional understanding and respect among most staff. All in all, staff feel they are sharing in a growth experience—for example, are focusing on critical issues and clarifying important questions, and, as individuals, are functioning closer than before to their maximum potential.

11. In all CTP units, philosophical differences and interpersonal difficulties were often related—usually in more than one way. For instance, with some staff the former occasionally led to the latter; with others, it sometimes heightened difficulties that already existed. With still other staff, the direction of relationship was reversed: Here, interpersonal difficulties heightened preexisting philosophical differences, though this seemed quite infrequent. (To keep this situation in perspective, the following might be noted. The vast majority of philosophical differences neither led to nor heightened interpersonal difficulties. Instead, staff acted rather professionally toward each other even when large differences existed.)

12. This applies regardless of the precise definition of "clarify," and whether or not "clarification" is considered (1) relative or absolute and (2) a condition or outcome that varies in degree.

13. During Phases 1, 2, and 3, no such "service unit" was available to—or, for that matter, sought by—the Community Treatment Project. To be sure, NIMH-funded research personnel served as an "equivalent resource"—though, by the later 1960s, CTP staff could probably have functioned quite well on their own, especially regarding diagnosis.

14. In discharging this responsibility, the CWS would be actively and personally implementing factors #6 and #7 (worker characteristics/orientation/specific abilities/etc.). He would not be simply approving actions proposed by others, for example, workers.

15. A CWS who is not particularly skilled in function (1) will probably have difficulty with functions (2) and (3).

16. In fact, well-coordinated activities are often partial *products* of such a unit.

17. Within a passably functioning unit, the CWS must still consistently support the concept of differential intervention (as one facet of individualization), even if less vigorously than supervisors in other CTP-type units.

18. The course in question was "primarily aimed at the training of supervisors and trainers" (Warren and CTDT Staff, 1974, p. 152; Howard, 1974, p. 9). It was available in a more condensed—and, quite possibly, often more effective—form than during the early years of CTDT (Warren and staff of CTDT, 1972).

19. Also, the required time investment can depend not only on the agency's particular policies and procedures but on its—and the CTP unit's—current circumstances.

20. Here, we assume that CWSs would receive not only agency permission to perform the functions in question but sufficient "official clout" and entrée as well. Under these circumstances, agency permission, among other things, would therefore not comprise a limiting or even preclusive condition.

19 CASE PROCESSING, MAINTENANCE, AND OTHER OPERATIONAL FACTORS

We will now review the feasibility of several operations-centered aspects of CTP's Phase 1 and 2 units. Included will be case processing, case maintenance, and additional factors such as auxiliary staff and teachers. Selected youth characteristics, and physical/structural issues, will also be discussed.

Case Processing
Overview
Case processing posed few problems throughout 1961–1969, both in the Valley and San Francisco. This applied to each of the following steps from YA intake to program assignment, and to all such steps collectively: (1) preeligibility screening; (2) random assignment; (3) diagnostic interviewing;[1] (4) staffing; (5) program assignment. (These steps are described in Chapter 2.) Without the heavy research that was present during this controlled experiment, steps (1) and (5) would have been less complex than they were, steps (3) and (4) would have been briefer, and step (2) would have been absent. (Throughout the experiment, only research personnel were responsible for implementing the nonoperational, that is, exclusively research-centered, components of these steps.)

Neither operations' staff (CTP; regular parole; NRCC) nor the parent agency experienced practical difficulties with the operations-centered components of these steps. The agency recognized the critical nature of these steps (research components included), and it consistently supported them in principle as well as practice; this occurred despite the considerable time required for staffing, and even when agency priorities began changing with regard to intervention. In addition, outside agencies such as police and probation neither questioned these steps nor experienced difficulties with them; in fact, they sometimes seemed pleased with the thoroughness of (3) and (4). Though they accepted the "community assessment" component of step (5) in principle, and though they had no practical problems with it, these agencies still occasionally expressed dissatisfaction with its outcome regarding particular youths.

Given the type of agents and supervisors already described, these steps, (3) and (4) included, would probably present few case-processing problems to most public and private agencies that tried to establish a CTP-type unit. This would apply whether or not, but especially if, heavy research requirements were absent. In any event, without such requirements, these operations' personnel could almost certainly perform the necessary steps by themselves, and could perform them well. However, the following should be noted: These comments focus on case processing—appropriate case processing—per se, not on specified *preconditions* to such processing, for example, staff's (say, the supervisor's) ability to accurately diagnose. Such preconditions, virtually all of which center on step (3), might not always be adequately met within given agencies; this fact, in itself, would therefore complicate the question of overall feasibility. Still, if those preconditions were met, case processing, as outlined above, would probably proceed smoothly and be widely accepted. This "smoothness," and so on, would only partly reflect the fact that steps (1), (3), and (4) might not be entirely new to project staff, that is, the fact that screening, diagnostic interviewing, and staffing were integral to many—possibly most—non-CTP correctional operations to which those individuals were previously exposed (albeit at a lower level of intensity, and in relation to somewhat different concepts, assumptions, and/or goals).

Specific Aspects

For all youths, case processing began with YA intake and involved the five main steps mentioned earlier. Except for complex classification aspects of diagnostic interviewing, discussed below, the essentials of this process could probably be reproduced without specialized training, and would prove feasible, in many agencies today. Random assignment is not essential for CTP operations.

Throughout all phases, case processing proceeded smoothly: It was (1) readily understandable to all relevant personnel, (2) neither cumbersome nor highly complex, and (3) rapid enough to satisfy CTP's and the overall YA's operational needs and commitments. In addition, since some of its components reflected research needs alone, it would have proceeded more rapidly and been even less complex if research had been absent. Yet even with research, neither the board, middle managers, nor various administrators had external (e.g., public relations–centered) or internal (YA-centered) difficulties with case processing; in fact, they raised no questions about it. These individuals recognized the above-average quality of CTP's diagnostic workup and initial treatment/control plan, and they accepted, partly on faith, the idea that such a workup and plan were integral to its case handling approach—research needs aside. Managers and administrators, in particular, accepted the fact that above-average quality, for instance, increased scope and integration of information, required extra time.

Given CTP's rate of intake, sufficient time existed. In this circumstance, operations staff could have produced above-average workups and plans by themselves, without research aid or input. However, if intake had been, say, 100 percent higher than it was, whereas staff size remained unchanged, diagnostic shortcuts/alternatives, treatment-planning shortcuts, or both, would have been required regardless of research participation.

Finally, neither the youths, their parents, nor community groups objected to this process. Even when they recognized that a more-detailed-than-usual process was involved (and they probably seldom did so during Phases 1 and 2),[2] they may have assumed that careful processing might somehow produce better results or simply fewer mistakes. To be sure, some youths seemed fairly indifferent to the diagnostic interviews—that is, to that part of the process which they personally experienced—even though they, like almost all other individuals, hoped they would be assigned to CTP. Other youths would probably have preferred a short and even superficial workup; yet even they neither objected to nor otherwise resisted the process.

Throughout 1961–1973, preeligibility screening was done by research personnel, in line with preestablished criteria that were designed to objectively determine the youths' appropriateness for the experiment and their possible participation in CTP (Chapter 2). Even without experimentation and research, future CTP-type programs, like almost *all* programs, would still require eligibility criteria. Using such criteria, operations staff, located within or outside those programs, could easily perform the screening function by themselves, as they already do in most agencies.

Neither experimentation nor research are crucial to the establishment and operation of CTP-type programs, and random assignment to E versus C programs, or to differing E groups within a *single* program, would, of course, not exist without experimentation. However, when experimentation exists, such assignment should be done by researchers or others whose random drawing reflects, without exception, strictly objective, preestablished procedures alone. Throughout the present experiment, this policy and practice was firmly supported by all decision-makers. In effect, it removed all question that assignments might be made, not randomly, but with various operational, that is, program or agency, interests in mind, or that it might be based on any individual's belief as to whether certain youths or types of youths would best profit from particular approaches, and so on. (In itself, random assignment requires no special technical skills.)

We next focus on diagnosis and planning, with emphasis on the types and levels of information involved.

Diagnosis and Treatment/Control Plans

In CTP, as in non-CTP-type programs, the feasibility of diagnostic interviews depends largely on their scope and depth. In turn, the minimum required scope and depth of these interviews directly depends on such factors as the minimum breadth or complexity of the treatment/control plan to be developed during the initial staffing; and the desired scope and depth of the former (the interviews) depends, for example, on the maximum breadth or complexity of the latter. (For now, we will assume that interviewing and staffing *will* occur in future CTP-type programs. Computer-based alternatives to staffing are mentioned in "Staffing Processes and Products," below, and in Chapter 20.) To better understand the feasibility of particular diagnostic interviews and of related intervention (treatment/control) plans and initial staffings, the following should be kept in mind.

Diagnosis is the process of obtaining, assessing, and integrating information regarding one or more of the following, partly overlapping areas of the individual's life and personality (basically, this information is obtained from youth interviews and case files; it is assessed and integrated mainly in the initial staffing):

1. *Current situation*
   A. Living arrangement and main involvements (home, school, work, peers)
   B. External environment (e.g., neighborhood; city) (These also include specific pressures and supports)
2. *Offense history*
3. *Personal history* (mainly centers on objective events)
4. *Current interests and abilities* (also includes goals, achievements, and special skills)
5. *Major personal limitations* (e.g., physical; intellectual; specific fears)
6. *Personality*
   A. Characteristics (level of development; expectations; self-image and attitudes toward others; modes of adjustment; other traits and features)
   B. Motivations (long-term drives or incentives; dynamics)
7. *Other contributors to crime/delinquency* (Includes any long-standing and/or immediate contributors not covered above).

Some diagnostic efforts address *more* such areas than others. Also, compared with the latter efforts, the former may or may not deal more *comprehensively* with many, or perhaps most, such areas. At CTP, all seven areas were routinely examined, usually in some depth. (The *I-level* diagnosis mainly derived from area 6A, though areas 2, 3, and 7 were usually drawn upon as well; in any event, 6A information was essential. Regarding *subtype* diagnosis, 6B was often crucial.)

When developing a treatment/control plan (TCP), a staffing group may thus have a broader or narrower range of diagnostic information (e.g., more areas) to work with; and, in any one area, their information may range from minimal to detailed and from superficial to deep. However, regardless of the scope, quantity, and quality of available information, the staffing group may concentrate on certain areas and information only; in fact, it may not examine the remainder at all. In addition, the areas/information it focuses on, and from which the TCP is derived, may still be somewhat different, say, broader, than the areas that it addresses in writing and which thus involve the actual (literal) plan. Naturally, some selection is understandable and appropriate, both at the "focusing" and "writing" stage.

Nevertheless, whether such staffing-based selection either is or is not appropriate and either is or is not avoidable—and it often *may* be questionable, or at least avoidable—the treatment/control plan that emerges from the initial staffing may reflect considerably less than was available from diagnostic interviews and case files. For instance, the plan may center almost exclusively on areas 1, 2, 4, 5, and highly selected or perhaps relatively superficial aspects of 6A and 7; this might occur even though considerable diagnostic information was obtained and recorded regarding 1 through 7 inclusive, and although ample time existed for discussion. Such information shrinkage may be fairly routine in given programs; yet even when it is substantial, it need not mean the TCP is largely irrelevant or generally inadequate. (At CTP, the treatment/control plan routinely covered all areas that were examined, again in some depth. Even so, shrinkage often occurred, though what remained was still considerable.)

At any rate, for various, often interrelated reasons—such as limited program resources, limited diagnostic efforts, and staff's specific theoretical views—some treatment/control plans are less comprehensive than others regarding content; for one thing, they may routinely exclude or otherwise downplay certain areas or components thereof. In this respect they may reflect or focus on fewer aspects of the individual's life and personality. Similarly, they may comprise a framework (and provide clues/suggestions) for *intervening* in fewer aspects—relevant aspects—of the individual's life and personality, and for doing so less appropriately, and so on, than might otherwise be possible. Yet, even treatment/control plans that may involve *greater* relevance and *more* appropriateness, efficiency, and/or effectiveness may do so not simply or primarily because they are more comprehensive with respect to content, but mainly because of two features or conditions: (1) crucial themes or factors regarding the individual's life and personality have been identified and highlighted; (2) each plan is well-integrated, for example, logically interrelated and unified, especially but not exclusively with respect to those themes or factors. These features—*centrality* and *integration*—probably compensate to a large extent for various types of shrinkage. Ideally, they are accompanied by balance, practicality, and clarity.

In short, treatment/control plans are potentially relevant to more aspects of the individual's life not only (1) when they cover more areas, but (2) when their information, in any given area, is other than minimal or superficial. In addition, TCPs are potentially even *more* relevant or influential (3) when they are well-integrated, especially with respect to central or overriding themes. Insofar as (1) through (3) exist, TCPs are more individualized as well: They more accurately and more fully reflect and focus on the person's particular situation.

The relative importance of scope, quantity, and quality of information—for example, comprehensiveness of content—on the one hand, and centrality plus integration (C/I), on the other, is difficult to determine. Nevertheless, centrality—the identification and highlighting of crucial themes or factors—and certainly integration *can* occur in connection with limited information; yet, other things being equal (e.g., staff's abilities and efforts), integration and certainly centrality have more chance of occurring when scope, quantity, and, by all means, quality are increased. In any event, C/I, even when present, is likely to be less significant when comprehen-

siveness is absent or substantially reduced. Finally, a less comprehensive plan may still be relatively individualized; but even so, it may be potentially influential, for instance, may provide useful clues/suggestions, in fewer areas—perhaps fewer important areas—of the person's life.

Three additional points are presented here before focusing directly on feasibility:

1. Regarding scope, each new area or successive "layer" of diagnostic information that is tapped, for example, area 6, increases the complexity of the *total*; that is, it adds to whatever areas already exist, such as areas 1 through 3 or perhaps 1 through 5. As indicated: (1) the more areas that are included in this diagnostic "layer cake," the potentially more individualized and influential the treatment/control plan can be, that is, other things, such as quality of information, being equal; and (2) to help actualize this increased potential, centrality and integration must eventually exist. However, whether few or many areas are included, and eventual centrality plus integration aside, the following applies to each such area itself, *individually* (here, we will focus on the diagnostic information—DI—that is originally available to a staffing group, not on the DI as subsequently condensed and integrated by that group and afterward transformed into a TCP):

Some diagnostic areas, for instance, 3 and 6 (6A), are often associated with more detail and/or more potentially sensitive material than others, for example, 2 and 4.[3] However, for most staff, none of these seven areas is intrinsically far more difficult to tap than most remaining areas, especially via interviews but also through case files. (Again, one must distinguish the process of obtaining diagnostic information—tapping the areas—from that of interpreting, condensing, and integrating it [ICI]. Unlike ICI, the former occurs prior to staffing.)

In addition, detail, sensitivity, and other factors aside, the specific information that is sought in connection with any given area, for instance, sought during diagnostic interviews, should be obtained *separately,* say, via separate questions, from information that relates to each remaining area. This is because the former information can only occasionally be deduced or reliably inferred from the latter. (That, in turn, is aside from the fact that minor to moderate content overlap sometimes exists across various areas.) For instance, for any given youth, specific information regarding areas 1 through 3 (*current situation; offense history; personal history*) can seldom be derived with confidence from that concerning area 6 (*personal characteristics/motivations*). By the same token, information regarding area 6 can only partly be inferred or predicted from areas 1 through 3; this would apply even if areas 4 and 5 (*current interests and abilities; major personal limitations*) were added.[4] In this as in other possible examples, much would depend on just how specific and confident one wished to be about the deduced or inferred area(s), for example, area 6. Nevertheless, with few exceptions, diagnostic information should—and, in most cases, must—be directly obtained on an area-by-area basis, not inferred across areas or even from a summary and integration of given information.

On this latter point, even if a staffing group were given a computer-derived *I-level and subtype* (which, if this were a Jesness Inventory diagnosis, would mainly represent a particular integration of questionnaire-based area 6 information), the following would apply: From that informative data alone, the staffing group would still be unable to deduce or infer various important specifics regarding such factors as the youth's current living arrangement and main involvements (home, school, etc.)—that is, area 1A specifics which could be important in developing realistic, future-oriented treatment/control plans. This would apply to his current interests and abilities, that is, to other areas, as well.

2. At CTP, diagnostic information was mainly obtained via three interviews, and, secondarily, through case file material routinely forwarded to the Youth Authority by local probation. Since the quality and scope of case files often varied considerably, especially across counties, extra reliance was placed on interviews, and each interview was designed to cover preestablished areas regardless of those files.

(Case files were, of course, quite thorough and reliable in area 2: *offense history,* at least its descriptive aspects. Also, they generally contained valuable though usually sketchy information regarding areas 1 and, to a lesser extent, 3: *current situation* and *personal history.* Beyond these, and possibly beyond area 5, the quality of their coverage—where coverage did exist—was difficult to predict. [Their quantity of coverage, for example, their detail, was usually minimal unless a psychological or psychiatric assessment existed.] Similar case files would probably exist today, in many or possibly most local agencies. The following thus focuses on the interviews alone, each of which was completed prior to the initial staffing.)

The first interview, conducted by a researcher, was mainly designed to obtain I-level and subtype information. Though it emphasized areas 6 and 7, it routinely dealt with 1 through 4 as well, including both the youth's interpretation of his offenses and his feelings about individuals and events.[5] The second, conducted by a parole agent, focused on practical matters and essentially factual information, for example, areas 1, 2, and, to a lesser extent, 3 and 5; in these and other areas, especially 6A, it partly duplicated the research interview. Finally, the same agent also interviewed the youth's family or relatives; here, primary emphasis was on areas 1A, 3, 5, and 6A, in roughly that order. All three interviews were often moderately deep at several points, even though the interviewee's defense needs were respected and no efforts were made to force the revelation of "dark secrets," compromising material, and so on. Still, he or she was encouraged to be as candid as possible.

In CTP-type programs today, the following would apply. Without research—and, earlier-discussed I-level issues aside—the three interviews could easily be reduced to the latter two. (If this were done, added emphasis on areas 6 and 7 would be useful in the agent/youth interview.) Since valuable information might often be lost if, say, the agent did not discuss immediate and practical matters (areas 1 and 5) as well as personal or developmental issues (area 3) with *parents, guardians, or relatives,* the number of interviews should probably not be reduced to *one*—the agent/youth interview—unless absolutely necessary. More specifically, besides their sharing information not always known to, or reported by, the youth, the latter's family or relatives may often verify, correct, or update material obtained from that and other sources. This information may be valuable quite apart from (1) the possible existence of above-average case file material within the given areas, and (2) intervention-centered advantages of establishing early (pre-staffing) contact and involvement between the program and family/relatives. In addition, with rare exceptions, these individuals must be contacted (though not necessarily interviewed in detail) in *any* event, regarding placement issues and other official or legal matters. Thus, direct contact with the family or relatives may in fact be required by policy, not just regarding minors and nonemancipated juveniles; when such contact occurs, various subjects can usually be broached.[6]

At any rate, if one wished to obtain not just quality information but at least moderate detail and certainly broad coverage, the agent/youth (a/y) interview, like the agent/family interview, would require extra though not inordinate time, compared, for example, to most standard intake interviews.[7] Sixty to 90 minutes would almost always suffice for the a/y interview; however, 40 or so minutes would be quite common if much less detail were desired, say, for use in staffings. Under 40 minutes, major sacrifices would probably have to be made. Apart from helping to accumulate information, per se, "extra time" could promote an unhurried atmosphere and allow for added follow-up questions. This atmosphere and activity could implicitly but directly communicate, to the youth, various useful messages about parole agents' possible stance.

3.   The following would apply to any two or more treatment/control plans that might, theoretically, be developed for a given youth. (1) All such plans might be relevant to the youth's situation, though perhaps not *equally* relevant. (2) All plans might be individualized, though perhaps not *equally* individualized. (3) All plans might be relevant though perhaps not equally *individualized,* and, of course, vice versa. In short, relevance and individualization can vary in degree, and they can do so somewhat independently of each other; thus, each one is relative, and not just to the other.

Still with respect to treatment/control plans, and despite the above independence,

three broad levels of relevance/individualization might be distinguished: high, medium, and borderline or acceptable (most CTP plans were probably high). Regarding these plans, relevance may be considered the main goal, with individualization a means to that end. Finally, centrality and integration (C/I) themselves contribute, not just to individualization, but to relevant plans. As indicated, C/I can occur even when the quantity and quality of information is less than optimal; nevertheless, it is more likely to occur when more and better information is available and used.

Relevance, Individualization, Classification, and Integration

Research needs aside, CTP's initial staffing was designed to produce an individualized, relevant treatment/control plan by carefully assessing and integrating the broad range of information described earlier. Though a researcher participated in each diagnostic effort and initial staffing throughout 1961–1973, operations staff could have obtained, entirely on its own, all the information needed for such a plan. Specifically, a parole agent could have obtained this information via the two interviews plus the standard case file mentioned earlier. After that, he and the casework supervisor could have assessed and integrated this material and thus developed the desired plan. Each such step would probably be feasible in many agencies today, and the product itself could be qualitatively equal to that in CTP.

The following, which again could have occurred in CTP without research participation, could also apply today.

By themselves, most CTP parole agents would probably have been unable to diagnose I-level and subtype (I/S) with a high degree of accuracy. This would apply despite their having obtained adequate information and unless they were unusually skilled, specifically trained, or relatively experienced in an I-level program. In short, they could not have integrated or drawn together I/S-related information, especially from areas 6A and 6B, in the sense of producing that particular diagnostic classification. As suggested, their supervisor could have done so under earlier-mentioned conditions.

However, almost all agents could have integrated that information in other important ways, particularly, though not exclusively, when working with their supervisor during the initial staffing: They could have linked it, not just "internally" or within any one area (e.g., connected various 6A characteristics to each other), but especially "externally," that is, to other types of information (e.g., linked 6A characteristics to 1A and 1B facts). In each case, they could have thereby broadened, sharpened, and/or further clarified its meaning and possible implications.

For instance, the following could have applied to "broadening" and perhaps even "sharpening." Once the agents had (1) recognized various treatment/control implications of one or more of the youth's *personality characteristics* (e.g., communicative or noncommunicative; rigid or flexible; planful or "now-oriented"; independent or dependent [Step 1]), they could have (2) linked those possible or probable implications to others. The latter (Step 2) implications, for example, may have derived from his *current living arrangement and involvements* (e.g., highly demanding or dominating parents, long-standing behavior problems in school, and/or heavy peer pressures toward delinquency), and, perhaps, from his *present goals and skills*. (One might have combined, say, "dependent youth" with "dominating parents," or combined "independent—or hostile—youth" with "demanding parents." These connections, which could have been made in the absence of an I-level and subtype diagnosis per se, and without any other classification system instead, would often have made the implications from each separate area (e.g., area 6A) or even from each individual item (e.g., "now-oriented") more accurate and plausible than before. More important, they would have made the collective (across-areas) implications more meaningful—more relevant, realistic, and predictive—than most individual implications might have been, even if the latter were already accurate and plausible.

(If an accurate I-level/subtype diagnosis or other classification had been present, the overall implications that would have been drawn from, say, area 6A would have been partly *different* from and partly *similar* to, those in Step 1 above, that is, from ones drawn in the absence of that diagnosis. However, if the former ["classification-involved"] implications had then been *combined* with implications from that area and from one or more other areas [as in Step 2 above], the following would probably have occurred: [a] Most such *differences* in

implications would have decreased or become less salient; [b] a few such differences might have increased or remained as-is; and, in any event, [c] almost all *similarities* with respect to implications would have increased or at least remained unchanged. For these reasons, as more and more information had been used and integrated, the overall *classification-involved* [e.g., I-level] implications, on the one hand, and the *non-classification-involved* [as in Steps 1 and 2] implications, on the other, would—appropriately—have probably grown increasingly similar to each other and would have tended to produce similar plans. Nevertheless, each set of implications would—again appropriately—probably have long-retained certain unique features and advantages. [For related discussion, see Appendix 33.])

Even if an accurate diagnosis (classification) were available early in the initial staffing, a highly or even moderately relevant and realistic treatment/control plan could not have been deduced or confidently inferred from that information alone, no matter which classification system or systems had been used and regardless of staff's skill and experience. Such a plan would have to be not only detailed in nature, but *specific* to the youth, as well; by itself, a classification—whether typological or developmental—would supply neither feature. More specifically, a preestablished treatment/control guideline that might accompany the given classification or diagnostic category could only partly fill this need. For instance, a specific classification—say, a diagnosis of passive-conformist (Cfm)—could not, by itself, determine whether the given youth virtually requires an out-of-home placement and should, say, try to remain in school until graduation regardless of his placement. Nevertheless, for this and other Cfm's, the classification could provide valuable clues regarding agent/youth interactions and various external supports or pressures that might help *implement* whatever decisions are made. These clues would reflect features that are shared by many, though not all, Cfm's—and by many non-Cfm's as well.

Whether or not classification is present, the following would thus apply. Though the hypothetical links involved in Steps (1) and (2) *might* eventually have become part of (in fact, might have helped develop) a highly individualized and relevant treatment/control plan, such a plan—even if it did include those links—would not *necessarily* have emerged. For one thing, the links in question—say, four or five valid connections (across three areas), and even the collective implications thereof—would not, by themselves, have automatically eliminated the possibility of a narrowly based plan. Further conditions and links would have been needed in order to reduce that possibility and to help produce a broadly based plan; in fact, without such conditions, a highly individualized and relevant treatment/control plan would probably not develop.

(Further conditions, and so on, would be needed even if centrality were present. Centrality—the identification of crucial themes or factors—would, by itself, preclude superficiality in a treatment/control plan; however, it would not automatically ensure a broadly based and, for that matter, a highly relevant plan. [Here, relevance focuses on the youth's needs alone, not on the plan's overall practicality.] The following might also be noted. Centrality aside, a narrowly based plan need not, in itself, be irrelevant or inappropriate; however, its value, in the sense of power or influence, will often be quite limited, particularly in the long run. Within a long-term program involving intensive contacts or not, such a plan would be more likely than a broader-based plan to require sizable and perhaps frequent revisions in order to maintain—not to mention increase—its overall value. [Other things being equal, broadly based plans, that is, multi-area or "extensive" plans, are more likely than others to be relevant and potentially influential. However, they are not ipso facto more practical. Their practicality, like that of less extensive plans, partly depends on overall program resources; and practicality, of course, can help determine actual as compared to potential influence.])

To raise the chances that integration will be achieved in other than a narrow, spotty, and perhaps even questionable manner, staff must be relatively alert and discriminating. Staff's experience, for example, extensive prior involvement in the given program or similar programs, can be quite helpful, too, especially regarding practicality and power. Like centrality, broadly based integration also requires detailed discussion of the information at hand, and such discussion takes time even for skilled and experienced staff.

However achieved, such integration—which, as indicated, does not require an I-level

or related diagnosis—can help produce a moderately to highly relevant plan. Combined with centrality, it can virtually ensure it. It follows that diagnostic classification—however helpful—is neither the sole basis of, an automatic "road" to, nor even necessarily the principal ingredient in, individualization and relevance. As indicated, treatment/control plans that contain the latter features are the main operational goal of initial staffings.

Staffing Processes and Products
By allowing staff to carefully assess and compare information from differing areas and sources, detailed discussion generates at least two major advantages for the initial staffing (these advantages bear on broadly based plans in general and on relevant, realistic plans in particular): First, this process may reveal, not just inconsistencies in the information pool itself, but, quite often, personal and interpersonal conflicts or potential difficulties—and, perhaps, strengths or supports—that might otherwise go unnoticed. As a result, when staff, for example, has (1) simultaneously assessed and compared, not just "two," but a "third" item from its information pool, and when (2) a significant, otherwise unnoticed conflict has thereby emerged, staff's conclusions and related decisions will sometimes differ from those it would have reached if, say, it had assessed the original two items alone. (The "third," that is, the added, item may have involved the youth's self-image, or his parents' current feelings toward him; the original items may have involved the youth's goals/achievements, and his parents' performance demands. Numbers "two" and "three" are used for illustration only.) In effect, then, the third item may moderate or possibly neutralize key implications from the previous two combined; it may even reverse those implications, or at least alter the conditions under which they apply. Such changes, which are often far from simple refinements, are less likely to occur in staffings that lack detailed discussion.

In short, conclusions and decisions that reflect only the former items—"two" items combined—may often be, not just limited yet otherwise *satisfactory*, but in fact unrealistic or inadequate and in crucial ways misleading. This situation can easily arise with regard to educational or vocational efforts that, though responsive and plausible in themselves, are nevertheless likely to fail or be greatly weakened if, for instance, they are not part of a plan that also assesses the individual's self-image, his family situation, his attitudes toward specified adults, and his general feelings about "growing up" (e.g., assuming responsibility, and standard adult roles) and/or various social values.[8] (The latter group of factors, while often important, need not be addressed in all individuals.)

Secondly, multi-area and across-source comparisons often add important converging or *supporting* evidence. In contrast to the above, this evidence may increase staff's confidence in its previous, albeit tentative conclusions and decisions, that is, those which may have reflected single or at least fewer areas, items, or sources. Moreover, such evidence may not just support or highlight the appropriateness of those decisions; instead, it may begin to suggest their urgency. Especially important, however, is the following: Multi-area comparisons can probably reveal pervasive themes and major issues more accurately and perhaps more effectively than any other process. In thus contributing to centrality, they can provide a firmer basis for the earlier-mentioned confidence and for assessing appropriateness itself.

Thus, the preceding advantages decrease staff's chances of producing a treatment/control plan that, given its errors of omission and commission, will encounter major pitfalls and perhaps essentially fail. They do so mainly by increasing the chances that (1) staff will accurately assess, not just a few, but several important aspects of the individual's possibly complex life situation and personal problems, and that (2) the TCP will adequately and appropriately address those aspects, individually and especially *collectively* (and will thus do so dynamically, interactionally, and in ways that fit together or "cohere,"). Insofar as it accomplishes point 2, the plan may be considered highly or at least moderately relevant and realistic.

For the foreseeable future, a "point 2" plan is not likely to be computer generated and available, say, in the form of a printout alone. This does not just apply to *brief* printouts—those that, for example, might consist of a three- or four-paragraph statement whose content, say, is essentially determined by the individual's particular I-level/subtype, by some other classification, and/or by his response to

given questionnaires. To be sure, such a preestablished statement—in effect, a classification- and/or questionnaire-based treatment/control guideline—might well highlight several distinguishing factors, and in that respect it might be relevant and somewhat individualized; this would also be true if other promising determiners had been used instead, or in addition. Nevertheless, that statement or guideline would not, by itself, adequately reflect—directly or otherwise—the earlier-mentioned, often crucial complexities of the youth and his life situation; nor would it be likely to include alternative approaches and contingency plans.[9] This would also apply to plans that resulted from cursory or perhaps necessarily hurried reviews by staffing groups, especially reviews of limited information. That is, most such plans would, in effect, provide too few details as to what, in fact, the individual probably would and would not respond to, and under what conditions he might do so. (Inadequate specificity is distinct from possibly inaccurate assertion. In the present context, the latter might not be uncommon, either.) In addition, and related to the above, such plans would often fail to reflect specific *urgencies,* serious pressures, or immediate threats in the individual's life.

Staffing Participants

To develop a highly or at least moderately relevant and realistic plan and to prepare for its implementation, at least one parole agent and his casework supervisor (CWS) should attend the initial staffing. The former is the individual whom the CWS has assigned to permanently work with the youth, based on a treatment/control plan that is to emerge from this staffing. If the assigned agent (AA) is not also the one who interviewed the youth and perhaps his family, the latter agent should attend the staffing if possible. If he cannot attend, his interview notes, other written material, and so on—and a tape recording of the youth interview, if extant—should be given to the CWS and AA well before the staffing. (For reasons indicated below, case material might well be reviewed by the CWS in any event, prior to the interview.) In addition, that interviewer (agent) should personally review his impressions with the assigned agent.

To make his agent assignment, the casework supervisor would review all available information, for example, immediately after the youth interview; included would be the case file, other written material, and, again, a tape recording if available. Also, he would briefly discuss the youth with the interviewer. Based on this review and discussion, the CWS might decide that the youth interviewer (YI) will himself become the assigned agent, in which case the YI would also interview the family/relatives. However, if the YI will *not* become the AA, the latter individual should probably conduct this interview if scheduling allows. In either event, it would be useful for the assigned agent, if he were not the youth interviewer, to at least briefly meet the youth prior to the staffing and to review or discuss with him various aspects and possible implications of the above information.

(In the following way, the casework supervisor could increase the chances that the YI will himself become the assigned agent. By reviewing all case material as soon as the youth is assigned or tentatively assigned to the *program,* the CWS could [1] estimate the youth's I-level/subtype and other characteristics and could [2] then assign an agent—one whom he thinks would be appropriately matched to that youth—to do the youth interview. If this "pre-interview assessment" proved correct, the preceding complications, for example, information transfers and related briefings, would be obviated or greatly reduced.)

Whenever possible, the casework supervisor's agent assignment should involve a matching of agent and youth, whether on an I-level or other basis. If I-level is the principal basis of matching, the CWS's earlier-mentioned review—that is, either his pre- or post-interview assessment—of all information is essential in order to reach a subtype diagnosis; a tape recording of the youth interview would be highly desirable in any event (for post-interview assessment). If no recording exists, the detailed interview notes (especially area 6 information) and the CWS/interviewer discussion would be essential; a rating checklist completed by the interviewer could also help.[10]

If the CTP program contains a school component and if further schooling is a definite possibility for the youth in the near future—especially at the community center—CTP's teacher should attend the staffing if possible, at least its treatment-planning section. Unless this individual teaches throughout the day (virtually every day) and has no backup, and unless

the number of staffings is great, the initial staffing can usually be scheduled to meet his or her needs. If the teacher cannot attend, the agent should review the case with him or her prior to the staffing, and, of course, shortly afterward. In addition, the teacher may provide written input to the staffing, for instance, a brief summary of the youth's educational status and prospects.

All in all, the number and type of people who should attend the initial staffing need not present operational/feasibility problems. This applies whether or not the youth interviewer will be the assigned agent, and although at least three hours of meeting time are needed to make the careful assessments and comparisons in question.[11] At base, only the presence of two persons is essential: the CWS and the assigned agent.

As suggested, the teacher's presence is desirable but not essential. In addition, a possible alternative *agent* (not a backup per se) may attend, for example, if major uncertainties exist regarding final assignment and possible agent turnover. Finally, if the program contains a major residential component or is residential-centered, as in CTP Phase 3, the lead youth counselor (YC) should definitely attend. If possible he should attend with the specific YC who may be given special responsibilities for the residence-assigned youth. Since it will usually be difficult to simultaneously assemble *all* these essential plus potential participants, most community-centered (Phase 1 and 2) staffings will in fact include only two people throughout, and most residential- (institutional-) centered staffings will likely include three.

Difficulties would probably arise only if the number of appropriate program referrals (potential cases) remained substantially higher than projected for at least several consecutive weeks—assuming that intake itself could not be temporarily halted or reduced and that, in any event, initial staffings should seldom be delayed more than a few days, for example, to facilitate the assigned agent's or other staff's attendance.

Alternative Staffing Arrangements
Initial staffing arrangements other than those mentioned earlier are both possible and feasible. However, as implied, they would probably produce treatment/control plans whose relevance and individualization is usually bor-

derline acceptable—certainly less integrated than would otherwise be possible, and more limited than might be necessary. Of these alternative staffings, the following might be typical (here, the youth interviewer is not the assigned agent; however, an opposite arrangement might be equally common):

Prior to the initial staffing, the casework supervisor reviews all available information. On this basis, he may derive a tentative I-level/subtype diagnosis; in any event, he decides who the assigned agent will be. Soon afterward, the AA reviews that same information. A few days later, whether or not he has briefly contacted the youth and/or family, the AA and his CWS discuss, that is, officially staff, the case for 30 to 60 minutes. During this discussion they jointly develop a treatment/control plan—one which, barring unforeseen circumstances, will be implemented for at least a few months and then reassessed. Other personnel, such as the teacher, will probably not attend this staffing; however, if they do attend, their contribution to the TCP will probably be significant even if circumscribed. If the youth interviewer attends, his contribution to the assessment-and-comparison segment may be large.[12]

Whatever this staffing may involve by way of information used, persons in attendance, and so on, its brevity would qualitatively limit its final product, namely, the treatment/control plan. This would apply despite the following I-level and matching considerations—ones that, in turn, would apply to lengthier staffings as well.

1. As suggested, the staffing in question could occur, and its treatment/control plan could be developed, whether or not the casework supervisor has derived an I-level/subtype (I/S) diagnosis prior to the staffing and has matched the agent and youth largely on that basis. However, matching would probably be more accurate, and the staffing would be more productive, if that or a similar diagnosis *were* already completed.

2. Though a treatment/control plan that is not accompanied by an accurate I/S diagnosis could still be relevant and realistic in many ways, its relevance would probably be increased if such a diagnosis existed. For one thing, this diagnosis could provide the staffing group with clues as

to how the youth in question might interpret certain important situations or demands/requests, and how he might respond to various individuals (agent included) under those or related conditions. Such information could lead to greater centrality and more complete integration with respect to the TCP. Regarding the TCP and especially its implications, the following might also be noted.

As suggested, I-level/subtype information can help the CWS and assigned agent formulate or refine particular plans and strategies. These approaches may largely focus on interpersonal issues or life circumstances about which the youth might want or need assistance, and perhaps external controls. Yet, regardless of its direct influence on the content of such plans, and whatever the latter's areas of focus may be, I/S information can also help clarify and refine *agent/youth (A/Y) interactions* themselves. In turn, such A/Y interactions or relationships can provide a firmer foundation, such as better communication and increased trust, for implementing those plans and for focusing on the defined issues. (This can happen because important A/Y interactions can occur regardless of—often even prior to, yet in conjunction with—the specific issues at hand, for example, various peer and family relationships.) Even if one's goals and resources were rather limited with respect to the above issues and plans, I-level/subtype information could facilitate a better use of everyone's time by helping to reduce, resolve, or obviate various agent/youth obstacles or misunderstandings; in fact, the more one's resources *are* limited, the more valuable such information could be. (A similar situation exists relative to the initial staffing itself: When less information is available regarding areas 1 through 5, I/S clues—which largely derive from area 6—can be more important than otherwise.)

3. As implied, many salient features of a youth's interactions with others and his attitudes toward others can be identified prior to or during the initial staffing. These interactions, and so on, are often reflected in area-6 items, for example,

"[youth] commonly presents self as help-less," or "[he] has antipathy for [toward] the core culture" (Warren et al., 1966b). Each such item or feature has, in addition to conceptual meaning or specific infor-mational value, a practical value or possi-ble implications. Together, these values comprise what might be called the item's "overall significance," and this signifi-cance exists independently of—and can remain unaffected by—the following two-step process: (1) When pooled with other items, the feature in question can be assessed in a *collective* sense; (2) based on this assessment, such features or items may thereby be "integrated" with each other in terms of an I-level/subtype diag-nosis (classification) per se. Combined, (1) and (2) are simply the standard diag-nostic process itself. (As indicated, I/S di-agnosis often involves the integrating or drawing together mainly of area–6 items.) At any rate, individual features used by staff as evidence for a particular I-level/subtype diagnosis can them-selves—that is, can directly and *individu-ally*—provide TCP-relevant clues (can be significant, in this respect). They can do so whether or not a diagnosis itself (i.e., a classification) is made, and, if it is made, whether or not it is accurate.

If and when an I/S or related diagnosis is made, the following would hopefully apply: To help develop a treatment/control plan, staff would draw, not just from that diagnosis per se (i.e., from its various relevant implications), but also from several individual features by *themselves*. (Staff would, of course, utilize other sources as well.) If this were done, the diagnosis would not only have provided focus and direction to the given features viewed *col-lectively*, for example, direction regarding their shared implications for treatment/control. Instead, it would have provided that focus, among other things, without simultane-ously neglecting or obscuring the possible, *un-shared* or only partly shared implications of those features—implications that may emerge when the latter are considered *individually*.[13] In short, the respective, salient features *would not have lost their individualized, TCP-related values or significance* even if they, the features, had also been (i.e., had simultaneously or later been) integrated with other features, and were

thereby subsumed by a broader or more gen-eralized "reality" (namely, the I/S diagnosis)—a reality that conveyed TCP-related meaning and value of *its* own. "Hope" aside, the pre-ceding probably *could* apply in most CTP-type settings to a substantial degree; and, as implied, the TCP-related meaning and value of the unintegrated, individual features could be utilized even if no diagnosis, that is, classifi-cation, were made.[14]

In sum, CTP's initial staffing is opera-tionally feasible. Individualized, realistic, and, above all, moderately-to-highly relevant treatment/control plans can be developed dur-ing this staffing by agents plus their supervi-sors, even if an I-level/subtype diagnosis and/or other classification is not made. However, to produce such plans, broadly based information and at least three hours of discussion are needed. Alternatives, for example, much shorter staffing arrangements, may be used, again with or without a diagnostic classifica-tion; however, these will probably produce borderline-acceptable plans only. Information, such as specific youth characteristics, that often helps provide the *basis* for an I/S or related di-agnosis can, itself, make a major contribution to relevant TCPs, even in the absence of a diag-nosis per se. Nevertheless, if an I-level/subtype diagnosis exists and is accurate, it can add use-ful focus and/or direction, not only to standard staffings, but to alternative approaches as well—provided the limits and possible pitfalls of classification are recognized.

Other aspects of CTP's case processing, particularly the Youth Authority Board hear-ing and program assignment, have been re-viewed in Chapter 2. These operations were quite manageable from several perspectives, even though they were unavoidably compli-cated due to various research needs. With or without research, they or equivalent opera-tions would doubtlessly be feasible today in CTP-type programs.

Case Maintenance

Case maintenance was fairly straightforward at the Community Treatment Project, and the ap-proach used for this purpose would probably be feasible in most CTP programs today. Basic-ally, CTP's maintenance approach involved (1) a brief, weekly case review, (2) unscheduled discussions and updates, and (3) detailed, peri-odic reviews.

Reviews and Discussions

1. Once a week, the assigned agent verbally reviewed the status of each case with his supervisor.[15] The review and subsequent discussion of any given case was usually brief unless major unfinished business, significant or unexpected developments, or important decisions were involved, or unless the CWS had a special reason for spending extra time (e.g., agent training; possible youth reclassification).[16] Thus, for the most part, the AA and CWS jointly decided which cases should receive added attention. In most CTP-type programs today, this caseload review might satisfactorily occur every two weeks, provided that an hour or more is set aside for all cases collectively (assuming, of course, a low caseload).

2. Whenever necessary, the agent and supervisor discussed any individual case in which changes or fast-breaking events were occurring that seemed important for either the AA or CWS to know about immediately, or regarding which a major decision might be quickly needed. Active involvement by the CWS was, for instance, required in the case of technical violations and known or suspected illegal activities. These unscheduled discussions and updates occurred at either the agent's or the supervisor's initiative. Such discussions, plus any immediate follow-up, were given whatever time was needed and available, whether a few minutes or several hours.

   When major crises occurred, staff members in addition to the agent and supervisor sometimes assisted. This was true at the discussion and/or follow-up stage even if a single youth or a single agent's youths were involved, rather than those from two or more caseloads. Major crises aside, informal, unscheduled, or quickly scheduled discussions and updates also occurred as needed between the assigned agent and other project staff, such as the teacher or fellow agents. Here, the CWS was not necessarily present. Together with their follow-up and any official documentation, unscheduled discussions between the agent and CWS would doubtlessly be needed in most agencies and programs today, whatever the latter's orientation might be.

3. Regardless of #1 and #2 above, for example, irrespective of their content and possible effectiveness, a relatively systematic review and discussion of each case occurred three or four times a year. The exact frequency and timing of this quarterly case conference (QCC) depended mainly on the particular case, the supervisor's preference and work load, and the agent's wishes. Most QCCs lasted about an hour, especially during early phases; usually, just the agent and supervisor attended. During the first QCC, the original treatment/control plan was examined and any necessary changes in direction or emphasis were made, as were desired additions. A similar approach was used in subsequent conferences, taking account, of course, of previous updates. QCCs were typically followed by a quarterly case summary (QCS), sometimes at the supervisor's insistence (occasionally, sections [a] through [c] of this summary [see below] were written shortly before the conference):

The QCS briefly documented the following: (a) youth's current parole status, living arrangement, and family constellation; his work, school, and marital/parental status; (b) each law contact and major technical violation during the given quarter, together with its specific outcomes; (c) nature and frequency of agent/youth contacts during the quarter; focus of agent's efforts; significant case decisions and new approaches by agent; (d) significant changes and developments in the youth and his life circumstances; (e) remaining problems or issues; and (f) immediate needs, alternatives, and plans.[17] Although not absolutely essential for casework purposes, this summary often helped bring the youth's overall situation, and the updated TCP itself, into better perspective and clearer focus. Also, it often served as a point of departure for subsequent discussions, not just between the agent and CWS.

A similar though somewhat shorter case conference was sometimes held in connection with an anticipated favorable discharge decision, depending on when the most recent Conference (QCC) had occurred. In addition, standard QCCs were often advanced a month or two if major crises had recently occurred and a complete reassessment seemed appropriate or imperative.

All in all, QCCs would be highly desirable in any CTP-type program, even if they were not quite "quarterly." Case summaries could be helpful as well, not just to satisfy possible agency requirements. QCCs could be particularly useful if the initial staffing were short and if the resulting treatment/control plan were relatively limited in scope and perhaps of borderline quality.

Together, the preceding reviews and discussions could be very helpful with respect to long-standing difficulties, emergent issues, overall planning, and so on. In fact, they would probably be essential if one wished to address those dimensions, for example, emergent issues, on a timely, carefully considered, and integrated basis. Moreover, besides focusing on already-active issues and perhaps on crises, such reviews/discussions could doubtlessly help staff anticipate and often reduce potential and *incipient* problems. Finally, and again as in CTP, they could help ensure or increase agent accountability and reduce the chances of complacency, perfunctory performance, and simple carelessness.[18]

Yet, if the following preconditions existed, much *less* review and discussion would theoretically be appropriate and required in most CTP programs today (this situation, and the conditions in question, could theoretically have applied in the 1961–1973 program as well; in reality, of course, they did not apply): (1) The youth's external and personal circumstances involved fewer difficulties than they did and were less complex than they were, that is, as compared to those in the 1961–1973 population (though *major* difficulties, and even crises, may be absent or rare, complexity seldom is[19]); (2) the project's involvement in the youth's life was less extensive and perhaps less intensive than it was, again as compared to the original CTP; (3) the project's goal of high or at least moderate degrees of relevance and individualization were absent. However, if conditions (1) and especially (2) applied no more than slightly or moderately in CTP projects today, or assuming that condition (3) applied either negligibly or not at all, there would, instead, often be a good deal for staff to "keep up with" in relation to the youth's life—as was true in the original CTP. As a result, considerable thought, planning, and subsequent adjustment would often be in order, and the preceding reviews/discussions could probably remain essential vehicles in this regard.[20]

In the final analysis, the reviews and discussions in question could help provide relevant, detailed information. They could encourage continuity-of-effort with respect to the youth and his overall situation, regardless of whether many difficulties and complexities are involved. Insofar as this information and effort were considered appropriate and necessary in CTP-type programs today, such reviews/discussions—especially collectively—could play critical roles. As indicated, they would probably be feasible as well.

Program Components

CTP's program components included counseling, recreation, out-of-home placement, and so on. In most settings, most such components were usually not difficult to implement and maintain; this applied not only to youths individually but to unit operations overall. (See endnote 21 regarding certain out-of-home placements.) It also applied despite the frequent complexity of the casework supervisor's and unit administrator's tasks—complexity that, in this context, seemed to reflect not the number of components alone but mainly their frequency of usage. (Here, as elsewhere, difficulty and complexity often varied independently.) Nor were these components—both their type and frequency of usage—questioned or challenged by top administrators, by justice system and other public agencies, or by private citizens; however, see Chapter 26 regarding short-term detention.

This lack of questioning or challenge often seemed to reflect a positive judgment about, a passive acceptance of, or an uncritical faith in the components; yet it probably reflected the following as well. Except for the school program and most recreational/socializing experiences, similar components were present within the standard parole program; in this regard CTP's individual components were not, in themselves, unique or otherwise unusual. The main difference, of course, was that, for any *particular* youth within the standard program, (1) any three or more components were rarely used simultaneously or even in close succession, and (2) any one component was seldom used as often as in CTP, except for limit-setting and out-of-home placement.

Finally, middle managers often noted that some components, for example, "socializing experiences" and "material aid," increased CTP's costs, mainly via their frequency of usage. Though the school program (which was absent in regular parole but not in institutions) increased costs by its very existence, it was operationally feasible; and, as implied earlier, it was generally considered valuable, or was at least accepted, outside CTP.

Other Operational Factors
Auxiliary Staff
Paraprofessionals, Volunteers, and Students
Despite their availability and possible contributions, auxiliary staff such as paraprofessionals and community volunteers (senior citizens; others) were excluded from CTP. (See below, regarding students.) The reasons or factors were threefold, though the first was itself decisive:

1. To implement given research goals which, in effect, required that the parole agent be the central project member with whom the youth interacted—the individual who provided nearly all treatment-and-control input during Phases 1 and 2 (Chapter 2). One such goal, especially during Phase 2 (which is when volunteers, etc., first became available), was to assess the impact of the agent/youth relationship insofar as it could be separated from others. Toward this end, "other" relationships, at least major staff/youth relationships, were avoided, or minimized.
2. To help ensure that lines of communication and responsibility would remain as clear and simple as possible.
3. To help ensure that prescribed treatment-and-control strategies would be carried out (Chapter 2). This factor reflected a central need during all phases of the experiment.

A few case aides—also called group supervisors in Phase 2 (but not 3)—were used after Phase 1 to assist with transportation and to help supervise various dayroom/athletic activities, under the general direction of the CWS. These efforts were not seen as substantially interfering with 1 through 3; in fact, they sometimes helped given agents better focus on 3.

Regarding (2) and (3) above, three interrelated subfactors were involved. First, many project communications, and especially treatment/control strategies, were already fairly complex. In this connection, project decision-makers believed that potential auxiliary staff (volunteers, etc.) would probably add unwarranted complexity to various operations—for instance, often to the point of cumbersomeness or confusion, and not just with respect to (a) the parole agent's peace-officer responsibilities and (b) the auxiliary staff's possible interactions with parents or public agencies. Second, those decision-makers doubted that most auxiliary staff would be able or realistically positioned to engage in long-term, intensive, sometimes complex relationships with CTP's often difficult youths, either in the framework of certain prescribed strategies or at least in parallel with them. This would apply even when those auxiliary staff *wished* to engage in such relationships (however they conceived them), as, presumably, they often would.

Third, regarding such relationships, project decision-makers also doubted that most *agents* had enough time, or should somehow make the time, for either of the following. (a) Coordinate or even largely direct the main efforts of any one or more auxiliary staff, in order for the latter to assume substantial responsibility (as they necessarily would do in the above relationships) for one or more youths from a given agent's caseload. (b) Train such staff to use certain intervention approaches that—at a minimum, and especially in the context of sizable responsibilities—would at least be consistent with the given agent's overall plan for the youth(s) in question and which would definitely be in line with factor 3. In addition, given factor 1—research requirements—these decision-makers recognized that the *casework supervisor* was not the appropriate person to engage in (a), above, in any event; and, factor 1 aside, the CWS seldom had time for (b), whether on an individual or group basis. (Item [a] would have focused on specific youths; item [b] would have involved treatment/control for youths in general and/or for specified subtypes.) Individually and especially collectively, these three subfactors helped operations staff feel they should probably "leave well enough alone," even apart from factor 1 and the CWS's hypothetical roles.

At any rate, throughout Phases 1 and 2, CTP operations proceeded reasonably well without paraprofessionals and community volunteers; and—research requirements aside—several unnecessary complications may in fact have been avoided. To be sure, the benefits and/or losses that might have resulted from the exclusion of these potential auxiliary staff will remain unknown. These include possible decreases or increases in the youths' level of illegal activity.

If the above research requirements were removed, those and other auxiliary staff, such as college-level interns and volunteers, could play several roles in CTP operations today (see below).[22] However, these individuals should be carefully selected, preferably by the CWS, and they should be directly supervised by the agent whose cases they would work with. Such selection would promote *auxiliary-staff/youth compatibility*, while such supervision would promote *relevance-of-staff's-efforts*—factors that would remain important regardless of the type and level of these individuals' involvement with youths.

Thus, in utilizing auxiliary staff the main goal would be to supplement basic program resources without (1) confusing the youth via divergent or incompatible messages and expectations, (2) significantly diluting or otherwise diminishing the agent/youth relationship, and (3) hampering or unnecessarily complicating communications and coordination of efforts within and across caseloads. Toward this end, and to satisfy these conditions, case responsibility and "chain of command" should remain clear, and auxiliary staff should accept project direction rather than largely "do their own thing."

Even if conditions (1) through (3) were met, two possible difficulties would remain. First, compared with regular project staff—usually career employees—auxiliary staff might be less motivated to "stick with a case when the going gets rough" and when youths become resistant, personally rejecting, or openly hostile. This would apply even if staff's skills were generally adequate. (Regular staff could be described as full-time, paid employees—civil service or not. In contrast, auxiliary staff would usually be nonpermanent and/or part-time—paid or otherwise. Individually or collectively, most such differences could often be associated with differing motivational patterns and/or differing degrees of given motiva-

tions for working with youths.) Second, regardless of their motivations and their response to major pressure or resistance, relatively *inexperienced* auxiliary staff—students or others—may simply lack the skills that are needed to carry major casework and decision-making responsibilities, even if they are receiving supervision and support.[23] Careful staff selection would reduce, though not preclude, these difficulties.

Limitations and possible difficulties notwithstanding, auxiliary staff could assist agents and youths in at least three contexts without necessitating major time investments by agents or supervisors, and while satisfying conditions (1) through (3) above (staff's *areas* of assistance and interaction will be mentioned shortly):

1. By helping agents locate or maintain community resources and by relieving them of various "household chores." Auxiliary staff could do this at any point in the youths' project experience, without becoming heavily involved with them as individuals.
2. When the youths and/or their life situation have become much less troubled or volatile than before, and the agent/youth relationship has been largely consolidated. Here, auxiliary staff could personally interact with youths, usually during later stages in their parole.
3. After the youths have left the project, whether or not they and auxiliary staff have interacted during parole.

In short, such staff may provide assistance even if they are neither well-positioned for, well-suited for, nor perhaps even interested in relatively intense, long-term relationships with project youths—or in otherwise assuming major responsibilities for them.

A fourth context—probably the most common of all—will now be used to indicate the main areas of auxiliary staff's input: Besides assisting in contexts (1) through (3), such staff could play significant roles with youths (a) on an ongoing, short- or long-term basis, (b) without engaging in counseling, surveillance, and major limit-setting, and (c) even when the youths and/or their life situations are still quite troubled. They could do so in connection with *arts and crafts, tutoring in specific scholastic or vocational subjects, sharing recreational activities,* and so on. Auxiliary staff—undergraduate and graduate students in particular—played such roles during Phase 3, chiefly within Dorm 3. In so doing, they added relevant elements and variety to the youths' program and they further normalized the institutional environment.

As in the preceding contexts, these individuals could play such roles without creating difficulties with regard to the agent's peace-officer functions (specifically, they would have no such functions) and without interacting with parents and various public agencies in an official capacity, or, if necessary, at all. Nor would auxiliary staff have to be "on-call" apart from their scheduled work hours, for example, to deal with emergent problems and potential or actual crises.[24] Finally, such roles or activities would not necessarily add undue communication and coordination requirements unless numerous auxiliary staff were involved simultaneously or regular project staff began to rely on these individuals extensively.

Teachers

Teacher candidates who had taught delinquents, slow learners, or educationally handicapped youths were fairly easy to locate during the CTP experiment. This would probably be true for most CTP operations today—whether or not the candidates were from the program's parent agency but possibly *not* in the case of low-population areas. In the California program (CTP), most candidates *were* from the parent agency (Youth Authority) and they wished to transfer to CTP. Though their most recent and/or primary teaching experience was in an institution, they preferred to work in a community setting, and certain "special program" features of CTP, for instance, low caseloads for parole agents, and considerable individualization, seemed particularly appealing. However, the I-level system, agent/youth matching, and so on, did not in themselves make much difference.

For CTP programs today, prior teaching experience with delinquents would be very desirable though not essential; this would apply to prior experience with slow learners as well, delinquent or not. Whatever their experience, candidates—to be considered "acceptable"—should show at least the following features: overall teaching skill; some creativity or at

least flexibility as to teaching methods (these could take various forms); open-mindedness; self-reliance yet willingness to work with others; demonstrated or at least probable comfort with delinquents, including an ability to be firm with them if necessary.[25] Modeling characteristics, that is, personality-modeling attributes, would be desirable though not essential; and teachers could be of either sex, whether most project and school-program youths were male or female.

The school program should function as a semi-autonomous entity within CTP, certainly with regard to educational processes and classroom conduct. However, the teacher should be a full-fledged CTP staff member—not a "graft" or second-class citizen, yet *not* an independent entity. More specifically, the school program's efforts regarding any given youth should be integrated with, not just consistent with, the parole agent's overall treatment/control plan for that particular youth. In effect, the relationship between "efforts" and "plan"—as between teacher and total staff itself—should therefore be that of "part" to "whole." In addition, and paralleling this part/whole relationship at a broader level, the school's efforts regarding youths (students) collectively should mesh with the current and anticipated priorities of CTP as a whole.

Toward these ends, coordination of efforts and direct, open communication between the school program and other components of CTP would be essential. Therefore, with regard to individual youths, teaching staff would functionally link with the youths' respective *parole agents;* similarly, in relation to students collectively and to remaining work-centered matters, they would interact with the *casework supervisor.* These formal and informal links would exist even though teaching staff would also have to interact and coordinate with non-CTP personnel, for example, in connection with educational policies, specified funding (state or federal), equipment, and so on. At any rate, to help implement treatment/control plans and overall project priorities, the teacher's willingness to directly work with agents and the CWS—and vice versa—would be particularly important. Though familiarization with the program's specific classification system—I-level or other—would also be valuable, this condition need not exist initially.

To achieve better coordination of efforts, and good communication, program staff should, if possible, control the hiring of teachers in two respects. They should (1) determine which candidates are "acceptable," that is, meet minimum project (as distinct from agency) requirements, and they should (2) have final choice as to which acceptable candidate gets hired. Specifically, with regard to "final choice," if hiring control (1) existed and program staff were to locate two or more acceptable candidates for, say, a CTP unit's *one* available teaching position, the final word as to which of those candidates gets hired should, ideally, not be made by persons, say, education administrators, outside CTP. This reflects the assumption that—given their candidate-based information and the colleague-based input mentioned below (see "optimal decisions")—CTP staff would be in a better position than outside personnel to choose the *most* acceptable candidate, that is, the one who is best suited to the program's current and anticipated needs. In this regard, controls (1) and (2), above, would presumably produce better teacher/agent and teacher/youth matches as well.

If possible, each candidate should be interviewed individually—simultaneously or successively—by both the casework and the administrative supervisor. Again if possible, both such individuals—at least the CWS—should also decide on acceptability and first choice. To reduce unnecessary errors regarding acceptability and to help make *optimal decisions* regarding first choice, these individuals should also obtain specified information from at least one teaching professional ("colleague") who has recently worked with or supervised the given candidate. This information would mainly involve the latter's overall teaching skills, his probable creativity or at least flexibility as to approaches, his comfort with most delinquents or his problems with particular types/groups of youths, and his usual responses to classroom pressures. If the candidate is to replace a present CTP teacher, for instance, one being promoted, the latter individual might try to interview the candidate and, if he or she wishes, convey any resulting impressions to the CWS, and so on.

Staff aside, three general points might be mentioned regarding CTP school programs today.

1. Such programs would be highly desirable, especially but not only if they were accredited. Whether they would be absolutely essential in order to *reduce illegal behavior* to the extent that was observed in California's CTP is unknown. That is, without these programs, illegal behavior could, perhaps, still be substantially reduced; however, this reduction might often be less than in the original CTP and it might or might *not* occur only if relatively few project youths had no viable alternative to some such schooling.[26] In any event, absent a school component, a CTP program need not just barely "exist"; it could, in all likelihood, function at least moderately well with regard to scope, relevance, and coordination/integration of efforts. Also, on balance, it could probably operate about as efficiently without the component as with it. Nevertheless, practically speaking, CTP's overall relevance and flexibility would almost certainly be reduced—perhaps substantially reduced (though still far from low)—if many school-aged, seriously school-troubled youths were present, whereas no *school component* existed or was available. (However, if *alternative* educational opportunities could be developed and tapped, such limitations would be reduced.)

2. Operational advantages would accrue if the CTP school program were housed together with, or adjacent to, the project office (community center), rather than at a fairly distant location. More specifically, the former arrangements could definitely facilitate integration of the school program with remaining components of CTP; at the same time they could raise esprit de corps and obviate or at least reduce minor as well as potentially serious control problems. Nevertheless, despite these significant advantages—plus a savings of agent time and auxiliary staff time—such arrangements are not absolutely essential.

3. Partly due to their apparent practical value and their consistency with traditional cultural beliefs, school programs would usually be easy to justify to administrators, managers, and others, even if they or similar programs had not been scientifically shown to reduce illegal behavior. Moreover, given the necessary

funding, the office space, and so on—and without being exorbitant in any such respect—most school programs would not be especially difficult to establish as well as maintain, at qualitatively satisfactory levels. Nevertheless, ease of justification, of establishment, and of maintenance aside, the chances of obtaining *accreditation,* a *joint/adjacent location,* or *both,* might still depend mainly on local conditions or policies and on overall parent-agency priorities and resources. Also, in many settings, those conditions and priorities may be largely independent of whether the costs for specified components of the actual or proposed school program can somehow be shared by non-parent-agency sources—federal, state, and/or local. These factors and contingencies notwithstanding, concerted efforts should, if necessary, be made to obtain accreditation. Even without such efforts, this goal—like that of joint/adjacent location—may not always be hard to achieve.

Selected Youth Characteristics

Youths who have a sizable and perhaps extended offense history, for example, five "priors" over a four-year span, do not automatically require more intervention than those with relatively few priors and/or a brief, for example, a one- or two-year, history. However, since the number of priors, even by itself, often reflects the extent to which individuals are "serious"—troubled and/or troublesome—offenders, it can often serve as a rough index of the complexity, and perhaps the relative amount, of needed and potentially useful intervention; this, at least, would seem to apply within the range of zero to approximately five priors, duration of offense history aside. Given these observations—which are partly based on CTP's experience with a wide range of youths, some with much longer histories than others—the following seems likely.

Severity

CTP-type programs that handled *less serious* youths than those in the CTP experiment (CTP-E) would probably have fewer operational challenges and problems. For instance, if the former projects handled youths whose average offense history—excluding the instant

offense—consisted of two or three arrests or convictions (all nonviolent), the typical intervention efforts of such projects could probably be somewhat shorter and less complex than those in CTP-E. Those efforts might be somewhat less expensive and would probably generate less pressure from both the public and public agencies, as well.

However, though a need for less complex *intervention efforts* and less overall input[27] might, say, often translate into somewhat less "extensive" and/or "intensive" contacts, it would not, ipso facto, imply a need for substantially fewer staff skills or for a rather different approach to case processing, for example, the omission of detailed diagnosis and staffing. Instead, high-quality efforts, casework supervision, and workers would probably still be needed if one wished to reduce illegal behavior (compared to that in more traditional programs) among the individuals—the less serious offenders—under consideration. If intervention effort were *substantially* less complex and/or were to involve *considerably* less overall input, such high-quality efforts, and so on, might even be needed in order to produce *equal,* not to mention reduced, rates of offending.[28] (It might be added, however, that any decrease in complexity and/or amount of input would not, in turn, call for—or even necessarily allow for—major changes in *project organization or structure,* if one wished to produce the reduced or even equal rates. Nor would it mean that "individualization," "flexible programming," and "explicit, detailed guidelines" are less important than before.)

Quality efforts, casework supervision, and workers, would probably be needed even if all youths who had a severe, for instance, a violent, *instant* offense were excluded from CTP-type projects. This would apply whether or not, but especially if, all nonexcluded youths had numerous and/or serious *priors.* Priors aside, the milder the instant offense the less pressure the project would probably receive from both the public and various public agencies, and the more leeway it would usually have to utilize a wide range of approaches.

At any rate, whether youths had a nonsevere instant offense, a less serious offense history, or both, the *overall* situation regarding feasibility would probably be just slightly different—though, from an operations and organizational standpoint, perhaps significantly different—than at CTP-E. In effect, it would remain very challenging, even if the amount and complexity of program input were less.

Age

The following focuses, not on the less serious offenders just reviewed, but on serious multiple offenders—more precisely, CTP-E's typical clients. Based on observations by numerous operations staff, and by on-site researchers—individuals who, collectively, participated in approximately 1,000 staffings during 1961–1973 (San Francisco included)—it appears that the latter offenders are, on average, about equally troubled and/or troublesome regardless of age, particularly at intake. Given these observations, the following seems likely.

All in all, operational challenges and problems would be only slightly reduced if CTP-type programs were to accept youths who fell within a relatively narrow age range only, for example, 13 to 15 or 16, or else 16 to 18 or 19. In fact, as in the above, the impact on overall feasibility would probably be fairly small, assuming (again as above) that enough youths would be available to maintain the present type and number of caseloads. Given this assumption, the main operational difference from CTP-E would probably center around the extent to which certain program components were used.

For instance, among youths under 16, school, foster care, and possibly recreation might be used to a greater degree than among those 16 or over. In contrast, some forms of "material aid," such as case assistance and clothing but not transportation, might be used less. (See below, regarding external controls.) Nevertheless, most of CTP-E's typically used components, for example, counseling or pragmatically oriented discussion/decision-making, would still receive considerable emphasis regardless of any such changes; and, in any event, the same *range* of components would probably remain appropriate since issues and opportunities concerning school, employment, out of home placement, and so on, would apply to many youths within almost all age groups.[29] Moreover, many individuals who were "younger" (under 16) at intake might well become "older" long before completing the project; during this process, their areas of need, concern, and opportunity might change.

These considerations notwithstanding, CTP operations staff generally believed that their overall intervention task was slightly easier with respect to individuals who were 16 or older at intake. This was partly because these youths required, on the average, somewhat fewer external controls than those under 16 and because they were often "more verbal" regarding their thoughts and plans. Even so, in CTP-type programs today, the same level of staff skill and effort, and essentially the same type of project organization and case processing, would be called for regardless of the age range or average age in question, at intake as well as discharge. Whether greater or less public pressure—or support—would exist in connection with one age group than another is difficult to estimate. In most cases, any such difference would probably be small and would only have modest impact on overall feasibility.

Physical, Structural, and Geographic Issues
Location
Throughout 1961–1973, CTP units were located either in rented space within larger, shared, commercial buildings (Phase 1) or in rented, self-contained, unshared buildings (Phases 2–3).[30] In any given city, the CTP unit was housed separately from federal, state, and local government offices, regardless of where those offices were located.[31] Each unit—known, after Phase 1, as a community center—was also separate from regular parole, which sometimes *was* housed in larger government buildings. For reasons suggested below, similar housing arrangements would probably be appropriate and feasible today, for CTP-type programs in most medium- and large-sized cities.

Separation from government offices and regular parole was not essential to CTP's existence; however, it probably allowed for more operational independence and innovation than would otherwise have been the case. Though separation meant added expense and greater public exposure, its probable role in allowing CTP to establish (1) a distinct identity and (2) particular operating patterns was recognized from the start; and, the need for, that is, positive value of, factors (1) and (2), and for independence itself, was presupposed. This unquestioned acceptance of the need for independence, and so on, remained essentially unchanged throughout the experiment, even though—mainly during Phase 3—several administrators were uncomfortable about the *extent* of CTP's independence, and with various specifics of its operation (Chapter 20).

At any rate, almost all administrators took it for granted that the program's particular operational needs justified the moderately increased expense of separation. Moreover, they seemed to readily accept the fact that CTP, throughout Phases 1 and 2, had to remain physically separate from regular parole anyway—since the research design prohibited a mixing of E's and C's with respect to program activities and operations.[32] In addition, neither administrators, program staff, nor researchers felt that CTP should, for any reason, be hidden or shrouded (say, inconspicuously merged with other YA operations and offices), for example, in order to reduce or minimize its community exposure. Finally, the *self-contained-building arrangement* also allowed for substantially greater operational breadth and flexibility than the *space-within-a-larger-building arrangement*. Not surprisingly, staff and youths preferred the former, though some youths did prefer the latter's greater anonymity. Nevertheless, throughout Phase 1, CTP operated reasonably well under the latter arrangement despite the relative crowding and greater limitations overall. Similar factors and considerations would probably apply to CTP-type programs today, whether or not research were involved.

Within any given city, the CTP center (office; unit) was—by choice—usually located where a sizable portion of its population resided: in a lower- or lower middle-class (m-c) neighborhood. This population-based approach seemed appropriate and worked well throughout the experiment. Usually, for youths who lived, worked, or attended school more than two miles from the center, public or personal (family- or friend-assisted) transportation still provided reasonable access to the office, partly because the office was situated on or near a major thoroughfare. Even when access proved difficult for youths, parole agents almost always had the time and resources to (1) visit them and/or (2) bring them—or (3) perhaps have them brought—to the center. Such agent flexibility—at least alternatives (1) and (2)—is quite important in order to ensure adequate contact, even when a center is optimally located, and socioeconomic factors aside.

If CTP's main populations had remained socioeconomically unchanged, that is, remained "lower-class," most units might well have operated adequately even if they were located in areas within which *fewer* of their youths resided: middle-class or at least borderline m-c/lower m-c neighborhoods. Nevertheless, though a population-based location might not have been indispensable with respect to adequate program operation, its absence would probably have been associated with the following: lower overall efficiency; greater inconvenience, especially for youths; increased costs, for example, for rent and transportation; and less time spent by agent with any given youth, within and perhaps outside the center. In addition, each unit would literally have been less of a *community* center for parolees and others, as described in Chapter 3. Again, similar considerations would probably apply to CTP units today, especially in large cities and if program resources or agent flexibility were rather limited.

Almost all operations staff believed that, because the CTP center had been established on a population basis and was, in effect, therefore located within somewhat "familiar territory," the following applied: (1) Many youths felt more comfortable than they otherwise would, when they visited the center. (2) They and other youths less often regarded the agents and YA as "foreigners." Research personnel largely agreed with these views and also believed the following. Because of the center's location, many agents, like their supervisor, could better assess the youths' environmental situation, that is, their non-family-centered pressures and opportunities. In addition, they could become more familiar with, and could perhaps more easily and even effectively *tap,* various community resources, such as local employment.[33] Along related lines, some youths believed that, since the center was located "closer to the action," their agents probably knew more about various illegal or questionable activities and could keep a better eye on them.

The above-mentioned "comfort" also seemed related to the fact that—physically—the CTP center was neither a part of nor had certain features often associated with government buildings. At any rate, rather than appearing ornate, stark, or somehow imposing and perhaps intimidating, CTP's exterior—and interior—was variously described as undistinguished or humdrum, simple or neat, and homey or inviting. Also, like most buildings around it, the center was open from eight to five or so on Monday through Friday (later, for some group meetings and unusual events). In this as in the preceding respect it largely blended into its surroundings or at least drew little special or negative attention to itself. This feature should be relatively easy to reproduce today.

The center was usually located in a mixed-ethnic area, one in which minority representation was generally large. Because this ethnic mix was usually reflected in the CTP population, especially in youths who visited the center on any given day, the center further blended into and was generally consonant with its surroundings. This probably helped make both the center and the overall project more acceptable to most community members, including those who preferred to have local youths worked with outside of prison whenever possible. Today (as in the past few decades), within the United States, many citizens in many communities would nevertheless dislike or actively resist the idea of having serious offenders "congregating" at a local center or at least outside it, however well supervised it might be. Yet *most* people in most communities would probably accept such a center if local criminal and major "nuisance" activities did not increase and if the number of offenders did not seem great. For this reason, and perhaps under such conditions, the community center concept would probably remain feasible in many or possibly most settings today, whether or not a mixed-ethnic area was involved. However, many middle-class areas might presently (1990s) be less accepting than others.

Structure, Integration, and Atmosphere
Regarding the center itself, that is, the CTP office, the following, among others, were simultaneously housed in this building throughout Phases 1 and 2: (1) all clerical personnel; (2) all parole agents, their supervisor, and (in about half the units) the administrative supervisor; (3) CTP's arts and crafts program and accredited school; and, (4) the dayroom/recreation areas. This "functionally integrated center (FIC)" arrangement, which would probably be feasible in many agencies and cities today, helped pool the unit's resources and coordinate numerous staff/youth activities and interactions.

More specifically, the FIC arrangement doubtlessly helped facilitate the following policies and priority: All center activities were essentially subordinated to, and considered integral parts of, the *treatment/control plan;* to better implement this plan (in effect, CTP's top priority for youths), neither compartmentalization nor possessiveness was encouraged among staff. This was despite the fact that each individual's unique approaches and responsibilities *were* recognized and encouraged, as was the value of personalized, sometimes intense, staff/youth relationships.[34] Almost always, a workable balance was struck. (Interstaff disagreements that occasionally arose, for example, regarding space allocations or other resource allocations within the center, were almost certainly outweighed as to importance, and as to their possible impact on youths, by the relatively efficient coordination that was achieved. In any event they were overshadowed by the broader agreements and by the general sense of unity that existed.)

Regarding compartmentalization-of-efforts or functions, *"casework services"*—activities that might ordinarily be considered the province of parole agents alone—were never even labeled as such, and in this respect never formally or organizationally distinguished from "educational services" and "recreational activities." This reflected the fact that implementation of the treatment/control plan was viewed as virtually requiring or at least being enhanced by a single, coordinated effort, irrespective of that plan's principal focus and regardless of which staff member was in fact responsible for which program element. This view and approach was doubtlessly easier to implement because all operations staff were housed under a single roof, that is, easier than via other possible arrangements. At least, there were fewer chances that poorly communicating and inadequately coordinated domains would develop.

Though CTP could probably have operated if some of the above staff were physically separated from each other, considerable integration and efficiency would likely have been lost and overall costs would have increased. Moreover, differing issues and limitations would doubtlessly have emerged, whatever specific arrangements were made. This, too, would probably apply today.

Numerous interactions took place at the community center, and these were both varied and informal. They mainly occurred in the dayroom and clerical-pool/office-reception areas, and they involved not just agents, clerical personnel, teachers, and the group supervisor (i.e., the case aide, who usually worked in the dayroom/recreational areas), but several combinations of these individuals and the youths themselves. Their frequency and variety were probably due, in part, to the number and variety of participants themselves. Together with the informality and overall program philosophy that existed, these interactions probably helped the center develop its accepting, lively, occasionally challenging, yet largely relaxed atmosphere, one which most youths seemed to like rather than dislike.

An atmosphere that contained most or all such components—variety included—could certainly have existed even with a smaller number and narrower range of staff, especially within a functionally integrated setting. However, CTP's FIC arrangement, like its larger number and wider range of staff, might well have produced *more* variety and challenge than would other possible arrangements and/or smaller staffs. Also, given this and related differences, CTP's interactions could perhaps be more relevant to a wider range of youths and for a longer period of time. Viewed in perspective, these hypothetical differences might have been only moderately important to various youths; nevertheless, they would, presumably, have reflected the center's structure and scope in any event.

Comparisons and hypotheses aside, CTP's atmosphere itself rarely seemed impersonal, compartmentalized, barren, or indifferent. For many youths who frequented the center, this atmosphere (i.e., the climate and feelings that were experienced outside the agent's actual office, and the interactions on which they were largely based) may have helped counteract various negative stereotypes they held of adults or authority figures. Additionally or instead, it may have broadened the previously limited images those youngsters held. In fact, many youths did begin to see, not only *that,* but *how* adults from various ethnic groups and with differing backgrounds and responsibilities could interact in friendly and constructive ways, not just with each other but with they (the youths) themselves (Johns and Palmer, 1970). Such an atmosphere should not be difficult to reproduce today, even with a smaller number and

narrower range of staff, especially in a functionally integrated center.

The FIC arrangement seemed worthwhile with respect to implementing basic, often complex, intervention plans. It proved feasible and practical from a community and agency perspective as well. Moreover, CTP units had a consistently positive "image" within their neighborhoods, and a wide range of individuals considered them a community resource. This perception may have largely accounted for the following. Despite their easy access, their lack of protection, and their known nature as part of the Youth Authority, these centers were neither attacked nor seriously damaged during the several extensive and intensive racial demonstrations and violent incidents that occurred in the general neighborhood and immediate vicinity—literally all along the same street. These occurred during the later 1960s, particularly in Sacramento.

Finally, the fact that each agent had a fully enclosed (not, e.g., simply a partitioned), individual office was very helpful both with respect to his interactions with youths and increased efficiency or overall concentration. Besides being valued by most youths, such privacy was probably essential in order for many of them to reveal, discuss, or ventilate certain information, events, and feelings.

(Most middle managers and upper administrators seemed to believe that these factors, by themselves, justified the greater expense involved. Yet even so, rumors and occasional preliminary discussions about "doubling up" [sharing offices]—or getting partitioned offices—emerged every few years, particularly during statewide financial crunches and when, as in 1967, a new governor took office. This subject, which was almost always initiated outside the YA and which applied to state agencies as a whole, usually faded away in a month or two with respect to CTP.)

Beyond that, individual offices added an element of professionalism, and they probably helped reduce or eliminate various feelings, by youths and others, of impersonal or mass handling. To be sure, many youths seemed indifferent to the factor of privacy: It hardly mattered one way or another. Still other youths would have preferred no privacy—or in any case, less personalized or intense *interaction,* and therefore less risk of personal exposure—especially at first. Nevertheless, the vast majority preferred an enclosed, individual office, whatever the subject might be.

Geographic and Related Issues
Throughout Phases 1 and 2 each CTP unit operated within a geographic area that sent enough serious and/or multiple offenders to the Youth Authority within specified time periods to support a full-scale (five- to seven-youth caseload) program. Had it operated in an area or jurisdiction that sent few offenders—few program-eligible youths—to the YA, no more than a reduced-size program might have been possible. The latter situation, that is, might be especially likely to occur today in geographically small counties, since they—other things being equal—are the ones that have, and that would send to their state agency, fewer (often very few) program-eligible youths from any given area. However, this situation may also arise in geographically large counties that are sparsely populated overall. This could occur whether or not, but especially if, those counties also lack any settings, for example, one or two large cities, in which youths (especially delinquents) are heavily concentrated. Finally, such a situation might arise in counties that—regardless of geographic size—*have* large populations, including heavy youth concentrations, but which nevertheless have low rates of serious and/or multiple offending and, in any event, few commitments to the state.

As indicated in Chapter 20 an appropriate CTP program could probably exist even with three or four caseloads, assuming the standard 10 to 12 youths in each. But whatever the number of caseloads, a precondition of appropriateness is the program's *access* to the youths, and, where necessary, vice versa. For instance, though a county may send numerous eligible youths to a given or proposed program, those individuals might live in areas that are so widespread or scattered relative to the parole office (or even to additional, e.g., "midpoint," locations/suboffices) that frequent program-to-youth and/or youth-to-program contacts would be virtually impossible to achieve and maintain. More specifically, either the agent could seldom travel to, and meet with, the youths and significant others within a reasonable time period and for an adequate duration or the youths could seldom do so with respect to the program (e.g., its school component); that is, insufficient contacts, especially

personal and perhaps crisis contacts, could occur. Other things being equal, this situation is more likely to arise in geographically large counties; however, regardless of size, it could occur whether the county is markedly rural, a mixture of rural and towns or small cities, or mainly the last-mentioned setting. At any rate, *intensive* intervention would be virtually impossible to achieve when access is very limited, even if staff could carefully diagnose the youths and develop relevant and—absent such access problems—realistic treatment/control plans.

In addition, if access were very limited, *extensive* intervention—at least, certain otherwise common patterns thereof—would be quite difficult or impossible to implement, especially in its primary sense: the simultaneous utilization of two or more program components, such as those of the counseling plus pragmatically oriented discussion plus limit-setting plus school program pattern.[35] It would also, but less often, be difficult or impossible in its secondary sense: the successive utilization of those and/or other components; as such, its availability would be greater than would simultaneous utilization. Yet successive utilization, even when available and implemented, would seldom fully compensate for an absence or paucity of simultaneous utilization, mainly for the following reason. With most CTP offenders, successive input from two (especially three) or more components often seems less likely to have immediate positive impact—in fact, less likely to be crucial in terms of eventual positive outcome—than simultaneous input from the same number of, and perhaps even fewer such, components. That is, compared to successive input alone, simultaneous input is much more likely to address, in a sufficiently timely manner, CTP offenders' *interwoven,* mutually and simultaneously interacting, problems, needs, and interests. (In standard CTP operations, these types of inputs are usually combined during most periods in a youth's program. For example, during most three-month intervals, successive input usually occurs not by itself but in addition to simultaneous input—and rarely in its absence. Similarly, simultaneous input is generally accompanied by at least modest amounts of successive input.)

More specifically, if successive input were used because limited access had precluded simultaneous input, the following might therefore occur. An inadequate impact, not just a slightly or even substantially reduced impact, might be made on those youths—of whom there are probably many—who would have responded much better to *simultaneous* input. This would also apply whether or not, but especially if, frequent, for example, twice-weekly, contact was desirable. In addition, it is apart from the fact that, within CTP, frequent contact is more often a key ingredient of simultaneous than of successive input.

In short, though the *successive*-input aspect of extensive intervention may sometimes be feasible or partly feasible in geographic areas that have serious access problems, this input would seldom be an adequate substitute for simultaneous input if the latter were considered important and especially if three or more program components seemed crucial. At any rate, successive input, by itself, would often provide less than extensive intervention's minimum requirements for serious and/or multiple offenders, even in areas that lacked such access problems and if contacts were not infrequent.

Geographically based access problems may also have implications for the overall program, not just for individual youths. For instance, *small caseloads* are needed to implement intensive and extensive intervention, especially simultaneously, and both approaches are critical to CTP. Now then, if an agency has no plans to implement either form of intervention, or cannot do so even if it wishes (except perhaps with respect to successive input), it might have great difficulty justifying small caseloads since the latter—ordinarily—are established almost exclusively to help implement one or both approaches. This difficulty, and related questions regarding the establishment or continuation of a CTP program overall, might well arise with regard to areas in which frequent access is rare or absent, since it is in these locations where intensive and extensive intervention would be difficult or impossible to achieve and since both approaches (the latter in its primary sense) depend heavily on such access. These questions might, at least, arise if a proposed or actual program, or even several caseloads, largely or exclusively focused on such areas.

One last issue will be reviewed, one that relates to agent/youth *matching* in connection with geographically based caseload assignment (GBCA). First, two main forms of GBCA should be noted (both are common within corrections but, by design, neither was used in CTP): In Form 1, all program youths who live in a designated geographic area are assigned to one and only one agent, as long as he or she has caseload openings. In Form 2, all youths from the given area are assigned to two or more agents, usually on an alternating-case or other workload-equalizing basis, until the agents' caseloads are filled. Although we will refer to these *assignment strategies* as the GBCA "models," we will not consider the following *beliefs* regarding matching intrinsic to, and in this respect part of, the models themselves (even though they are quite often associated with the respective models): In Form 1, agent/youth matching is of no concern, and any matches that occur are purely coincidental. In Form 2, matching is either of no concern or of secondary interest only. As implied below, neither belief existed in CTP.

Now then, both forms of GBCA can create serious matching problems regardless of area, for example, type or size of county or other geographic/political entity. However, these problems are particularly likely to arise in an area whose program population is only large enough for one caseload—in CTP, a small caseload—and where, ordinarily, the Form 1 model is therefore used. (In the following discussion, say that only 12 cases—one small caseload—exist within the given, "sparse" area, and that *access* poses only minor problems.) Specifically, since—under these circumstances—one and only one agent (agent "A") would be assigned to the designated area, several youths on "A's" caseload would probably be mismatched because (1) the area in question would almost certainly contain several youth types, whereas (2) few agents ("A" or others) can be matched with all such types, or even with all the common ones.

Still, the following seems likely. By assigning *two or more* agents to an area—specifically, by selecting and combining particular agents so that appropriate assignments seem possible for all or almost all youth types—one can greatly decrease and sometimes entirely eliminate such GBCA matching problems. Thus, for instance, whereas youth "X" might previously have been assigned to—but, say, was mismatched with—agent A (the only one then available), he might now be assigned to, and *matched* with, agent B instead. In short, using the Form 2 model, two or more agents could share a particular—say, a sparse—area;

for instance, agents A, B, and C could each receive four cases from that area (still the 12-case area). At the same time, those agents could share one or more remaining areas; for example, A, B, and C might each receive eight additional cases from these areas combined. If, throughout this two-pronged process, each such agent were assigned as many matched cases as possible, that is, as a matter of policy and as a top priority, he or she might thereby obtain a full caseload (12 cases) of appropriate albeit also geographically designated youths within the sparse as well as remaining areas.

In reality, 100 percent "appropriateness," that is, no mismatches, could perhaps be approached but only occasionally achieved in any given caseload under the preceding conditions, for example, if no more than two or three agents shared each and every area. In addition, and probably of greater concern, is the following. Though perhaps resolving or at least greatly reducing the *matching* problem, the above-mentioned area-sharing approach might sometimes create sizable *access* problems or could substantially increase ones that—however minor—already exist. This difficulty, which could apply to some or all agents and areas, could arise essentially because each agent's sphere of responsibility would have been expanded to include both the sparse (i.e., "original" or "matching-problem") area and the nonsparse (i.e., "main-population" or "remaining") areas. In effect, then, access problems could arise not just in the original area but in main population areas that would otherwise not have had them, that is, in remaining areas. To avoid these new or expanded problems, the time-and-space distribution of each agent's caseload would have to be carefully planned and monitored. At any rate, under some conditions—such as area-sharing by relatively few agents, in the context of a large geographic region—sizable access problems may be generated and may then remain difficult to deal with.[36] This may especially apply to problems that are otherwise low-level and of minor concern.

CTP programs have no intrinsic need for geographically based caseload assignment, certainly no need for one and only one agent to handle all cases from a given area.[37] Ideally, in such programs, all forms of GBCA would be avoided; however, where this is impossible, the area-sharing approach—with purposive, case-by-case matching whenever possible—would be used. Also, where possible, sparsely populated areas would either be excluded—especially if they are distant or extend far from the main area—or they would contribute only a small percentage of youths. For instance, in order to preclude sizable access problems, perhaps only those individuals who live adjacent to the main population area would be accepted into the program.

Nongeographic Factors
Small-caseload programs such as CTP may be precluded even if matching and access pose no problems and if enough youths are available. This could occur in geographically large as well as small counties—even states—in which too few agents are available to support such programs, for example, in addition to, or partly instead of, standard programs or caseloads. This agent shortage could mainly reflect fiscal, ideological (nondepartmental-centered), and/or other nongeographic factors. Given such factors and the resulting shortage, probation departments and even state agencies may be unable to create CTP-type programs, including those with fewer-than-average caseloads.

However, such programs may be barred even if *enough* agents exist. For instance, because of departmental policies or priorities that are largely independent of fiscal and broad ideological issues, key administrators may decide not to reorganize their current units or programs and redeploy staff in order to create a CTP program; that is, they may make this decision mainly for nonfiscal, nonideological, and (again) nongeographic reasons.[38] To be sure, those or other administrators may, for whatever reasons, later alter such policies or priorities and may then reverse the earlier decision if, among other things, enough agents are still available. Agent availability aside, this reversal is more likely to occur if, at the time, fiscal, ideological, and other factors do not constitute a serious or growing problem with respect to CTP approaches.

This brings us to the final chapter on feasibility.

Notes
1. Here, primary emphasis is on diagnostic interviewing as a process, a unit (CTP) task, and a unit/agency responsibility, for example, on its ease, its logistics, and its

acceptability to youths as well as agency administrators. One major *goal* of this process, namely, accurate I-level classification, is reviewed in Chapter 22. Other issues relating to I-level, such as staff training and "ethnic bias," have already been reviewed. These issues, and that of accuracy, are interrelated and bear on the overall feasibility of this classification system—ease and acceptability of processing notwithstanding.

2. Beginning with Phase 3, federal regulations regarding "informed consent" were applied to CTP for the first time. These required a spelling-out, to all youths, of the experiment's major activities, and so on. Even under these conditions, objections by the given individuals and/or their families to involvement in CTP and/or various data-gathering activities occurred in, or relative to, less than 2 percent of the eligible sample. At any rate, because of the informed consent procedure, many youths and families came to realize that a more-detailed-than-usual process existed with respect to tests and interviews.

3. As can be seen in connection with area 5, detail and potential sensitivity are not always directly related.

4. Nor can many specifics of areas 4 and 5 be reliably inferred from areas 1 through 3, and vice versa.

5. During Phase 3, areas 3 through 5 were examined more carefully than before, since a "developmental-adaptation" assessment (Chapter 27) was considered important.

6. Any such contact or interview with parents or relatives would probably be less important, though not necessarily unimportant, with regard to young, unmarried adults. If the youth or young adult were married, the spouse should be interviewed if possible.

7. Even when combined with supplementary activities, the agent/youth interview may, however, require less total time than many standard diagnostic workups, for instance, clinic workups. The latter often involve not just an interview but questionnaires and tests (other than educational/vocational/physical), regardless of whether the latter two items are given much weight with respect to vari-

ous clinic/agency decisions and plans. (In CTP, most questionnaires and tests were given primarily for research purposes even though their findings were often discussed at the intake staffing. Basically, these items were not essential to the CTP operation, that is, apart from research. To be sure, they sometimes helped support, confirm, or refine other information and conclusions.)

8. Here, "likely to fail" means that the educational or vocational efforts are themselves unlikely to be achieved—this, apart from the hoped-for impact of those efforts on future offending.

9. For now, computers cannot, or can only minimally, be programmed to perform key staffing functions such as the following: (1) assess validity of the available information; (2) eliminate seemingly invalid and irrelevant information; (3) give reduced weight to questionable yet relevant data; (4) identify and handle inconsistencies; (5) make often-complex comparisons, inferential and deductive judgments, and other specific assessments or series of assessments; (6) achieve centrality if possible, and draw overall conclusions (adding needed qualifiers); (7) derive the main intervention-centered implications of the findings; (8) integrate those conclusions and implications in terms of a prioritized, sequenced, relatively unified treatment/control plan, taking into account available program resources; and (9) produce the written plan (printout) in a timely manner. Even if staff performed some such steps by itself, such as steps 1 through 4 or perhaps 1 through 7, and fed the resulting information to an on-line computer, substantial difficulties would remain (cf, Palmer, 1984b, p. 259; Palmer, 1992, pp. 104–106).

10. The rating checklist might, for instance, include many items used in the revised I-level manual to define the I-levels and subtypes (Warren et al., 1966b). That aside, a tape recording of the youth interview would probably make the diagnostic process easier and the diagnosis itself somewhat more accurate, unless (1) the interview notes were quite detailed and often relevant to I-level issues

or (2) the interview were conducted by the CWS himself.

11. Occasionally, a late-starting or interrupted staffing must be completed the next day.

12. Regardless of who attends the staffing, the agreed-upon TCP should be formally written up by the assigned agent, within a few days if possible.

13. The differing implications of each such factor should be distinguished from the respective factor's basic, mutual *conceptual* differences as such.

14. The preceding aside, we may now present an earlier point with greater specificity: I-level/subtype information—either the diagnosis itself, the latter's underlying features, or both—can become more important, relatively speaking, the less one uses or integrates *other,* possibly more standard information, for example, mainly from areas 1 through 5.

15. Here, as below, the assistant supervisor substituted if necessary, mainly when the CWS was on vacation.

16. General caseload issues were discussed at these meetings, as well. They and/or broader program issues were also discussed at *unit* meetings.

17. Though all such areas were usually covered, some were occasionally described in minimal detail only—even for a summary. (Agents commonly drew from their "contacts log" for information regarding given areas.)

18. From an agent's perspective, these reviews/discussions could help maintain or increase the supervisor's understanding, input, and support regarding specific cases and issues. The following might also be noted. A CWS's familiarity with given cases could also prove valuable when the assigned agent is temporarily unavailable, mainly due to vacation or extended illness. Here, for example, the CWS might help a substitute agent make better decisions if and when decisions are needed. Moreover, if an originally assigned agent permanently leaves the project, such a supervisor might help a newly hired agent "take over" the caseload with fewer difficulties and greater continuity than might otherwise be possible. Finally, the CWS's familiarity with an open caseload could be valuable with respect to hiring decisions themselves.

19. Four general points might be noted regarding "difficulty" and "complexity" in CTP ("difficulty of intervening," i.e., of project interventions, will be distinguished from "*youths'* difficulties" per se, since their relationship is not invariably close; as seen in context, "complexity" will refer either to project interventions or to the youths' situation—whatever the youths' difficulties may be): (1) Most but not all complex youth-situations were also difficult, or at least challenging, for CTP to deal with; yet, many difficult interventions (and difficult youth-situations) were not, in themselves, very complex. (2) Nevertheless, *most* cases were not just complex per se; they were (whatever their degree of complexity) also fairly difficult, in that the youths had several pre-project—and post-intake—problems. (3) Given these pre-project problems alone, and despite the youths' present strengths and supports, the initial staffing team assumed that the youths' present and future situation would often not work out well on its own, that is, with little or no project planning or intervention. (4) This assumption was borne out by experience, and difficult as well as crucial interventions were required at various points with almost all youths. (While on parole, i.e., during the post-intake period, most youths had one or two major crises and several minor to moderate ones; these events should be distinguished from the above-mentioned, post-intake *problems.* Such problems or difficulties were less intense and more common than crises; in fact, they often existed throughout much of the youths' parole.) For further comments regarding complexity, see endnote 20.

20. The preceding may be stated somewhat differently: To address the youth's difficulties, his complexities, or both, and to do so in a realistic and highly individualized manner, careful consideration and subsequent adjustments would be necessary and appropriate, for example, regarding the original treatment/control plan. This necessity, among other things, would mainly reflect an interaction between the youth's situation, on the one hand, and the project's (staff's) particular commitments and goals, on the other. For

instance, at CTP, the need for, and certainly the appropriateness of, "careful consideration and . . . adjustments" did not simply derive from the youth's often-difficult or at least complex situation per se. Instead, they also—and more actively—reflected staff's *desire* to be involved, not only extensively (when such involvement seemed important), but, very often, intensively as well. Regarding the above-mentioned complexities, the following might also be noted: Complexity may relate, not just to a youth's new or ongoing *problems,* but to his interests, abilities, opportunities, and life circumstances, insofar as these may operate independently or almost independently of those problems. (Individually, these factors—interests, and so on—may not be complex; collectively, however, their interactions and implications often are. And, individually as well as collectively, these same factors sometimes change through time.) At any rate, complexity may involve not just (1) "problem-independent" or nearly independent factors, but (2) interactions between as well as within "problem-independent" factors, on the one hand, and "prob-lemmed" factors or areas, on the other.

21. Foster and group homes were sometimes difficult to establish and maintain. These difficulties would doubtlessly occur today in many settings.

22. Removal of these requirements would not mean that all research must be eliminated.

23. In this connection the following would apply if substantial interactions, say, moderately intensive or extensive relationships, were to occur between auxiliary staff and the present (CTP-type) youths: Any losses or negative effects that might result from one or both such difficulties (see text) would probably be *less*—and less likely to even occur—if the youths in question were much less troubled or troublesome; of course, most CTP-type youths *are* rather troubled, and not just initially. Careful staff selection would substantially reduce the difficulties in question, whatever the youths' level of troubles or troublesomeness, and even if those individuals were probationers (i.e., non-CTP and non-CYA) rather than parolees.

24. Though emergent problems and crises would remain the *agent's* responsibility, auxiliary staff would still have genuine responsibilities and obligations in the areas mentioned.

25. Even when firm, teachers should not be rejecting, repressive, or punitive.

26. For instance, these youths may be unable to function within the public school system, whether or not they have been recently expelled; yet, although unable/unwilling to function (even if not expelled), they may be too young to legally leave school (public or other). Moreover, whether or not these youths plan to leave or perhaps have *already* left (or *have* been expelled), they may, or probably would, have major difficulty obtaining or holding a job, partly because of inadequate schooling. This could apply regardless of their age.

27. "Less overall input" would mean, for example, fewer total contacts and/or a shorter duration of all contacts collectively.

28. More precisely, it is not scientifically known whether a program (a "modified CTP") whose offenders were less serious than those in CTP-E, and which was, accordingly, less complex than the latter but still of high quality, would in fact have an advantage, with respect to reduced illegal behavior, over more traditional (non-CTP) programs. That is, with such offenders, and under such conditions, modified CTPs might be no more effective than non-CTP programs that handled similar offenders. (This suggests that the advantage of *non*modified CTP programs—CTP-Es—over the more traditional and possibly even the modified programs exists and may become apparent mainly in connection with fairly serious and very serious offenders. [Most such individuals may be particularly difficult to handle effectively in traditional and modified programs alike.] However, this, in turn, does not imply that non-modified CTP programs might not also provide more assistance than traditional programs and modified CTP-programs to offenders whose level of seriousness is moderate or less.)

29. Counseling and pragmatically oriented interactions would remain common

partly because they each could be applied to a wide range of issues, and within virtually any area—school, employment, and so forth. In CTP-E, these program components, especially counseling, were commonly utilized at several "points" during the youths' project experience, or else for long blocks of time.

30. The arrangement in which space was rented within a larger commercial building also applied to the Differential Treatment Unit throughout the San Francisco experiment, and to the Guided Group Interaction Unit during its first year.

31. The Youth Authority's main headquarters—"central office"—was in a large state office building in downtown Sacramento. (That city's regular parole unit was located neither in nor near this particular building.)

32. Separation was also maintained throughout Phase 3, even though controls no longer existed in the Phase 1 and 2 sense. All Phase 3 research comparisons were between differing experimentals only.

33. In the case of group and foster homes, this situation applied only to a moderate degree. For instance, there was only a slight, positive relationship between the *center's* location, on the one hand, and the likelihood of locating and establishing (as well as the ease of operating) such *homes,* on the other. This partly reflected the fact that, although most such homes were not very distant from the center, many were relatively far. In any event,

distance, per se, was not a critical factor with respect to establishing and operating such homes.

34. Close personal relationships were not encouraged between clerical staff and youths. Friendly interactions within the center were considered appropriate.

35. By definition, two components are used "simultaneously" if they are applied at any point(s) during the same three-month period in the youth's program. In CTP, three or four components were usually applied during any given three- to four-*week* period; four main components were usually applied "simultaneously."

36. Here, a region is two or more assignment areas combined.

37. An extrinsic or highly contingent need (or requirement) would exist if, first, a CTP program's several workers included only one female, and if, second, the agency within which it operated allowed only female workers to handle all female parolees who lived in the program's designated geographic area(s).

38. Administrators may, of course, make an identical decision because of departmental policies or priorities that largely *depend* on fiscal and/or ideological, yet nongeographic, factors—even if enough agents are available for a CTP program. Alternatively, they may make that decision entirely on fiscal and/or ideological grounds, apart from any such policies or priorities, and—again—even if enough agents exist.

20 REVIEW AND DISCUSSION OF FEASIBILITY

We will first review several feasibility-related aspects of Phase 3, and will describe how these and specific triggering events led to the closing of CTP. We will then review our presentation thus far (Chapters 17–19), and will discuss and summarize the feasibility of operating such programs a number of decades after CTP itself began.

Phase 3

The Institutional Component

During Phases 1 and 2, Youth Authority administration viewed CTP as a complex program, yet one that posed few major problems. In contrast, it soon considered Phase 3 a problem. The latter experiment, which began in August 1969 and operated in Sacramento only, had difficulties that centered almost entirely around CTP's institutional component, Dorm 3. These mainly reflected the interaction between staff's dorm philosophy, summarized below, and administration's rapidly increasing vulnerability to external pressures and criticisms. (Beginning around 1970, these external stimuli were increasing with respect to corrections and the YA as a whole, not just CTP.) Few problems developed around the community-based component of Phase 3, which was essentially a continuation of the Phase 2 operation in Sacramento.

Escapes and AWOLs

Because of its difficulties, reviewed below, Dorm 3 exposed the Youth Authority to various criticisms. At first, these reactions mainly came from probation and police and were usually low-key; however, in 1973, they also came from political figures and were no longer low-key.

Starting in early 1970 (about six months after the program began) and continuing for one and a half years, most criticisms of CTP centered on escapes from Dorm 3 and the failure of many youths to return from day pass on time. More specifically, during this period individuals scaled Dorm 3's fence on 22 occasions (four escaped twice; two escaped three times), that is, about once per month. In addition, Dorm 3 youths were AWOL from day pass on approximately 40 occasions (22 youths were involved, many two or more times), that is, on 1 percent of the nearly 4,000 day passes which occurred during that approximately 550-day period. Day passes were common since, as will be recalled, Dorm 3 was an institution-based—not simply institutional—operation. Specifically, dorm-located youths were, if possible, to have opportunities for contact with their community. Many day passes involved attendance at CTP's community center school (see Table 13–1, item 3, p. 219).

(Before continuing, the following perspective might be useful. Most escapes, and especially AWOLS, were of short duration, and few involved public offenses. Of the 22 *fence escapes,* 9 ended [youth returned or was returned to dorm] within zero to 4 days; 6 others ended in 5 to 10 days, and 3 others ended in 11 to 20 days. Of the 40 *AWOLS,* roughly 30 percent ended [youth returned, usually on his own] within 8 to 24 hours, usually following an afternoon and evening absence or else an overnight absence; another 30 percent ended within 3 days, usually after a weekend; another 20 percent ended within 7 days, and another 10 percent ended in about a month. During all these 62 escapes and AWOLs, six known offenses occurred, mainly auto theft and burglary; no offenses involved violence. Escapes occurred mainly because Dorm 3's side doors were—by design—unlocked during the day and the fence was neither high, barbed, patrolled, nor electrified. To reduce escapes, CTP locked these doors in mid-1971 and barbed wire was soon placed on top of the fence; after these changes, escapes became infrequent. Similarly, by making the consequences more unpleasant than before [e.g., longer room lockups, and withdrawal of privileges], AWOLs were reduced by almost 70 percent.)

Prior to mid-1971, few youths regarded the consequences of escape and especially AWOL as particularly severe. This view was recognized by CTP staff and was, in fact, consistent with their intentions. That is, though staff did not condone escapes and AWOLs, many believed that (1) most such youths, for instance, escapees, had probably "needed" some type—not necessarily *that* type—of psychological "safety valve" at the time, and (2) pressures that had presumably caused the youths' reaction could probably be best worked with—once the individuals were back on the dorm—if the consequences of, that is, punishments for, their escape/AWOL were not so severe as to create additional pressures or complications that would require substantial handling themselves. If the individuals had committed a specific offense during their absence, for example, an auto theft, that of course required separate action.

Though many CTP staff continued to hold those views, they also believed, by 1971, that several dorm youths had responded to this approach in ways that were damaging the overall program. This belief made it easier for them to propose various changes and to accept Youth Authority administration's proposed changes (which were sometimes accompanied by considerable pressure)—even though, in their view, these changes often amounted to substantial compromises between the needs of youths as individuals (which they considered uppermost) and those of youths collectively, or those of the YA itself. To be sure, the actual decision to make these changes was often preceded by considerable debate within CTP and, to a lesser extent, between CTP and administration. Once the changes (e.g., stricter approaches such as

locked doors) were implemented, no major shifts in level of trust or alienation occurred between staff and youth, and significant pressures or issues were still addressed between those individuals. This noticeably relieved staff's anxiety regarding possible adverse impact on individual youths.

At another level, but still related to individual needs, the unlocked doors and low-security-fence policies had been part of staff's attempt to make Dorm 3's atmosphere fairly relaxed and its surroundings less ominous. Seen in this context or perspective, after YA administration had exerted strong pressure on CTP to sharply curtail escapes, the compromises that were reached were, in effect, between a philosophy (CTP's) that emphasized informality plus structural/symbolic expressions of trust and one (administration's) which stressed relatively heavy security. Within even this context, once a compromise was reached dorm activities and staff/youth interactions continued pretty much as before; nevertheless, the overall atmosphere was noticeably heavier or "tighter," particularly in recreational areas outside the dorm but still within the fence. In any event, whatever the context and perspective, most youths seemed to accept staff's decisions concerning locked doors and more secure perimeters. To be sure, many were less accepting of the routine searches for contraband—upon return from day pass and furlough—which had been instituted several months earlier.

Category B Youths

Though escapes and AWOLs greatly decreased beginning in mid-1971, other criticism continued. This mainly involved local probation's across-the-board objection to CTP's newly implemented inclusion of Category B cases on Dorm 3 (Chapter 13); however, it sometimes involved escapes as well.[1] The former objection occurred even though probation knew that the Youth Authority Board had to review and give prior approval for each Category B placement and had—also from the start—been rejecting many *other* potential Category B placements. Local police voiced moderate concern only; moreover, its objections centered largely on specific individuals, not on Category B youths in toto.

Basically, probation wanted all Category B youths sent, not to CTP, but to relatively distant, medium- or high-security institutions, preferably for over a year. Its expressed concern focused less on punishment (and hardly on rehabilitation), per se, than on public protection. That is, it centered on the possibility that these individuals—most of whom were committed for robbery or assault with a deadly weapon—would escape or go AWOL, as, of course, *Category A* youths *had* often done during the preceding 18 months of Phase 3. This concern was not substantially altered by the earlier-mentioned physical changes, such as locked doors, and by the fact that the board (1) expressly required Category *B* youths to remain on the dorm at least six months—often nine months—prior to being paroled and (2) often barred them from day passes or furloughs during their first three to six months. In short, to probation and law enforcement, security—though clearly improved—was still inadequate.

Individually and especially collectively, the issues of *Category B cases, escapes,* and *AWOLs* colored these agencies' attitude toward CTP as a whole. Together with one or two local judges, these agencies sometimes expressed their views concerning this program, especially Dorm 3, directly to YA administrators. Such contacts placed the latter in the uncomfortable position of defending an overall program/experiment (while not defending escapes/AWOLS), an essential component of which they had already found somewhat nettlesome on yet other grounds.

Dorm 3 As "Different"

Almost from the start of Phase 3, Dorm 3 had bothered various administrators and middle managers because it was "too different," or, from some perspectives, "too radical." Some board members were uncomfortable with these differences, as well. Yet the dorm was part of an experiment to which the YA had agreed, and for this reason "difference" was both legitimate and expected, at least within limits. Discomfort notwithstanding, most administrators and others basically accepted this fact. Still, at a practical level, the underlying question was: How different did the dorm have to be? or What kind of differences were important? In short, what *were* the limits? There was, of course, no a priori or otherwise clear answer to this question, and neither CTP nor YA administrators pretended there was. Nevertheless, CTP's approach to this question reflected three explicit views held by its staff (together, these constitute a summary of the dorm's working philosophy):

1. Most Status 1 youths (Chapter 13) had been recommended for the dorm not primarily so they would receive messages of heavy control and punishment but because they needed such a setting to help "get their act together." The former messages could have been provided by standard YA institutions.
2. Dorm 3 was to be seen by both Status 1 and 2 youths as a caring environment in which they would be allowed or encouraged not only to express, and deal with, their feelings and fears but to make their own decisions where possible and to develop new or more constructive ways of interacting with peers and adults.
3. Ideally, Dorm 3's atmosphere and activities would take account of—indeed, take advantage of—the fact that youths and young adults would be residing within that setting not just for a few weeks but, in contrast to all other NRCC wards, for several months, and (especially with Category B youths) for sometimes over a year.

To implement these views and, presumably, to thus promote the individuals' personal and social development, Dorm 3's atmosphere was to be as normal—in effect, as noninstitutionalized—as possible. To help normalize the dorm, to demonstrate respect or concern, and to let youths make their own decisions where possible, staff allowed youths to have long hair and unorthodox hairstyles, to wear some of their street clothes, and to decorate their rooms pretty much as they liked (e.g., with pinups and nonstandard colors/designs/objects). Moreover, they did not insist on spotlessly clean or otherwise neat-and-trim rooms. In short, wherever feasible, they tried to treat Dorm 3 youths like many parents treated many teenagers and young adults who lived at home.

Not surprisingly, unusual hairstyles sometimes appeared and several rooms soon became "sloppy." Within a few months (spring 1970) YA administrators began to express concern over these and related developments. Several non-CTP personnel from the Northern Reception Center and Clinic (the site of Dorm 3) were also dissatisfied, not just because dorm youths seemed to be receiving special privileges relative to other NRCC youths (i.e., the "short-termers") but because they—NRCC personnel—doubted the wisdom of CTP's "soft," minimally regimented, relatively individualized approach itself.

As usual, compromise solutions were developed between CTP and YA administration; however, in this case they were much slower in emerging. In fact, depending on the specific area, compromises did not occur until 6 to 12 months after the differences of opinion first came to a head (late 1970). No less important, they occurred only after many negative feelings had developed on both "sides." Strong feelings were involved because CTP staff believed that basic dorm philosophy and intervention strategies were at stake. However, they also occurred because YA administrators were quite concerned not only with actual and possible external (non-YA) criticism but—regarding the cleanliness issue—with specific health regulations as well. As to CTP's minimally regimented, relatively individualized approach, this continued essentially unchanged.

Though the hair-length, hairstyle, and pinup compromises were essentially acceptable to both parties—and to most youths—and although YA administrators "backed off" with respect to most room decorations and arrangements, the cleanliness issue occasionally resurfaced during the next two years.[2] In fact, despite staff's attempts to maintain what they considered a "reasonable" level of cleanliness and, certainly, a medically safe environment, this particular subject remained a sizable bone of contention. To several YA administrators and NRCC personnel, not only was the overall dorm *still* not clean enough (despite acknowledged improvements), but in 1971–1972, the fact that "gross filth" was occasionally discovered in given youths' rooms cast doubt on CTP supervisors'/administrators' willingness or ability to operate the dorm on a "realistic" basis (intervention strategies notwithstanding) and, in any event, to quickly and consistently resolve particular situations for which the Youth Authority might be taken to task. Beyond this, from a central-office perspective, CTP seemed to be placing itself "above" the YA and was often making the YA adjust to *it*. (As one top administrator later said, "The tail was wagging the dog.") Though the latter view overlooked or down-

played the many areas in which compromises had been reached, it reflected a feeling that—experimentation notwithstanding—CTP was not under enough central-office control. During Phase 3, when YA administrators spoke of control, they almost always meant Dorm 3, not the community component.

Growing Concern and Opposition

In retrospect, though the cleanliness, the hair, and other issues could probably not have been avoided, many of the related negative feelings could theoretically have been precluded or minimized.[3] However, as things turned out, several interactions between CTP staff and YA administrators/managers (and—given those interactions—some of the final *compromises* themselves) instead contributed to a growing central-office concern and, in some cases, resentment: It was felt that CTP's supervisors/administrators were either insensitive to or, more likely, somewhat indifferent toward particular difficulties to which they were potentially exposing the department, in connection with Dorm 3 and under the aegis of experimentation.

Doubts concerning at least the practical judgment of CTP staff had also been fostered by two large-scale outings that occurred in 1970–1971. These events, a three-day trip to Mt. Lassen National Park and a short boat trip near San Francisco, had been turned into carnivals by a handful of dorm youths who decided to "make the most" of their relative freedom. Because of their actions early in one or both trips (e.g., drunkenness, a burglary, and general nuisance behavior), local authorities were notified and the remainder of both trips was canceled. In this regard, CTP had been not simply an internal "bother" but an external embarrassment. Though administration recognized that CTP had provided standard levels of supervision during those trips and that, basically, several youths had taken advantage of the trust placed in them, it nevertheless felt, understandably, that the final responsibility for these "fiascos" (as they were called) rested with staff and that the difficulties partly reflected staff "naivete."[4]

Because of the preceding issues Dorm 3 operated under a cloud during long periods of Phase 3, either with YA administrators, with local probation and police, or with both. This situation existed despite various facts that were recognized by administration, though less so by probation and police: In sharp contrast to numerous living units within standard YA institutions, Dorm 3 had *no* racial confrontations, no "gangs" or other fear-producing/dominance-seeking groups, no grievances filed, no sexual violence, no major or even moderately serious assaults on staff or youths, no use of Mace or other chemical deterrents/suppressors, and so on. Despite these facts—actually, staff accomplishments—a number of non-CTP personnel from NRCC were firmly opposed to the program's nonorthodox approaches. Starting in 1972, some of them began leaking information concerning the dorm's conflicts and occasional "goofups" to non-YA decision-makers and to high-level, YA-related personnel. Some items of information then channeled rapidly into the governor's Cabinet; others moved directly to one or two state senators who had long been critical of Youth Authority and justice system policies in general. Through time, these NRCC personnel thus conveyed the picture, to major decision-makers, of an institutional setting that—while housing "robbers, rapists," and so forth, *close to the community*—was inadequately controlled by YA administration. In this context, the dorm's positive atmosphere and accomplishments went unnoticed or unmentioned; at least, they remained in the background and had relatively little impact.

Termination of CTP
Precipitating Events
Given this background and the markedly increasing, open politicization of corrections throughout the early 1970s, a combination of events that occurred within a four-week period in early 1973 directly precipitated the termination of Dorm 3 (perhaps ironically, these events occurred after the dorm had "settled down"—for about four months—for the first time since early 1970):

1. The dorm failed an unannounced, high-level medical (cleanliness) inspection, thereby reopening an old and only superficially healed wound.[5]
2. The dorm experienced its first and only homosexual incident (youths partly forced a 20-year-old suspected homosexual to perform fellatio).
3. A stabbing murder occurred in Sacramento that involved three CTP youths: the victim, who had recently been paroled; the accused, who was AWOL overnight from a 12-hour day pass; the accused co-conspirator, who had been on escape status from the dorm for two months. The accused's day pass had been of a type (visit to own home) for which he had not received specific board approval.[6]

Though it received no unusual publicity, the latter incident was considered particularly serious by YA administrators not only in itself but because, during the previous three years, several non-CTP wards *had* committed highly publicized acts of murder and/or rape while on furlough or escape status from standard Youth Authority institutions. YA administration wanted no more "bad press" at the time, unusual or otherwise.

These incidents quickly became known to the earlier-mentioned non-YA decision-makers. Although incidents (2) and (3) were first-time occurrences with respect to Phase 3 yet were far from uncommon within the YA, the fact that *three* significant incidents had occurred during a very short time span had two immediate, interrelated effects. First, it made CTP appear especially "bad" (e.g., irresponsibly managed, possibly ineffective, and a potential danger to the community) and—not just in the eyes of its severest critics—it seemed to validate the picture of "poor control." Second, it provided an excellent opportunity for political/ideological opponents of YA administrators' policies to advance their position.

Decision and Phaseout
Given this situation, Youth Authority administrators were quickly confronted and placed under pressure to shut down the dorm, and perhaps even CTP as a whole. More specifically, the YA director was placed under direct, simultaneous pressure by several state senators to close the dorm immediately, "or else." This individual—who, during the previous few years, had become increasingly vulnerable not only to the generally critical or at best lukewarm (toward YA) state administration of then-governor Ronald Reagan but to a leading and vigorous governor-appointed board member who (1) staunchly opposed the director's philosophy and CTP in particular and (2) was widely assumed to be seeking the director's post—agreed to close the dorm as

soon as possible.[7] The actual phaseout lasted three months. Because the Phase 3 research design clearly linked CTP's community-based component to the dorm, the former component was itself phased out (with the concurrence of research staff) a few months after the dorm shut down. Regarding the overall experiment, there was no point in retaining the one without the other.

The Termination in Perspective
Value versus Liability
In perspective, then, CTP was not terminated simply because of three incidents that occurred in early 1973. It was shut down largely because—through time—it was creating more problems and potential problems than it was solving or relieving, not just for the director but mainly for the YA as a whole. Most such problems, including those that were most influential, occurred in the early 1970s; they were associated with the institution-based, Dorm 3 operation in particular, not with the community-based component.

Though its preliminary research results were clearly positive (Palmer and Werner, 1972b, 1973) and of acknowledged strategic relevance to the department, the Phase 3 experiment, by 1973, had simply become "more trouble than it was worth," that is, worth on a short-term basis to departmental administrators who had numerous immediate problems and political pressures to handle. In effect, these administrators, and the YA overall, were having more than enough "headaches" even without Phase 3; and in this connection, the confrontation by several senators that followed the 1973 incidents had, albeit dramatically and forcefully, only reminded them of the generally precarious nature of their positions and various programs. (From this perspective it seems quite possible that a Phase 1 and 2 type of operation could have survived even the intense political pressures and crosscurrents of the times, particularly since it would not have created the types of difficulty that were associated with Phase 3. Its value-versus-liability ratio would have been rather different.) Finally, given the fact that, in early 1973, the operational components of Phase 3 were only six months from their scheduled (NIMH-contracted) data-cutoff point, the further fact that clear positive findings had already emerged made it somewhat easier for YA administrators to

phase out the program when they did. In effect, they could say the experiment was largely completed anyway—in that its likely conclusions seemed to already be known.[8]

Alternative Possibilities
As suggested, the difficulties that created negative feelings toward CTP among top YA administrators did not spring primarily from the external political climate, even though this climate continuously exacerbated and eventually escalated various difficulties. Since the problems in question centered neither on the Phase 3 concept nor on the experiment as a whole, but rather on specific aspects of Dorm 3, and since the resulting negative feelings had much to do with the termination of Dorm 3 and therefore of Phase 3 overall, the following seems quite possible. A Phase 3 type of operation would have remained organizationally viable if three main conditions or practices, which bore directly on the difficulties and feelings in question, had existed from an early point in the experiment. This would apply even if the external political climate had been no more consistent with the YA's general policies than it was, and if YA administrators had therefore been no less sensitive to actual and possible public criticism than they were. These conditions were:

1. Greater concern with security than during 1969–1971 (in effect, more attention to external control).
2. Quicker and/or more frequent removal from the dorm of youths who persisted in acts that clearly threatened the overall program.
3. Stricter adherence to all legally sanctioned administrative requirements (e.g., board specification of earliest allowable parole date), however technical they might seem.

Under these conditions, and given resulting organizational support, it is possible that a Phase 3 type of operation would have also survived the increasingly "heavy" external politics and ideological battles of the 1970s—battles that occurred in both the media-dominated and overall correctional arenas. Yet even so, it seems likely that some of its most critical or even unique elements would only barely have survived these external pressures and that other such elements would not have survived at all.

For instance, community contacts (furloughs; day passes) might well have been substantially reduced. Similarly, given the public's rapidly increasing rejection of violent offenders, all or almost all Category B cases would probably have been ruled ineligible for the dorm by the middle and certainly later 1970s, positive research results notwithstanding.

Even if external politics and the public's attitude toward offenders remained as they were in 1973, that is, became no "tougher," the following would probably have been necessary in order to maintain an organizationally and politically viable dorm operation; this applies especially, but not only, if most Category B youths were to remain eligible (it would probably have been necessary prior to the relatively stringent conditions of the early 1970s, as well): To operate a permanent Dorm 3 program while still retaining staff's earlier-mentioned views/philosophy (regarding the purpose and potential of that setting) and several of the dorm's related "differences" as well, staff would probably have had to (1) further modify some of their Phase 3 approaches to the normalization of institutional life and the expression of trust and (2) adapt more quickly and directly to overall organizational needs if administration seemed unwilling or unable to "budge." Although these changes and adaptations would not necessarily involve hairstyles, clothes, room decorations/ arrangements, various everyday activities and modes of staff/youth interaction, *most* day pass and furlough practices, and so on, they would very probably involve security and cleanliness. Thus, for example, staff would probably have had to adapt more quickly to the fact that, regardless of I-level and subtype, many institutionalized youths often abuse staff's gestures of trust and respond to reduced external control in ways that often harm themselves and others; in a sense, when given a chance to act responsibly, they often choose to act irresponsibly. Here, close scrutiny would thus be needed to determine which individuals, especially Status 1 youths, should, for instance, probably not participate in given off-dorm activities, or under what conditions they could.

Principles and Implications

Reflecting upon the termination of CTP, operations staff felt that certain "principles" were clear. These interrelated principles or guide-lines, outlined below, would be especially important during periods of heavy external stress (CTP's supervisory/administrative staff, having mainly experienced the *less* stressful as well as noninstitutional days of Phases 1 and 2, only partly recognized this situation during most of Phase 3): (1) One's program must periodically demonstrate its ability to "manage"—to fairly quickly gain control of, and bring closure to—difficult and/or potentially embarrassing situations; at least, it must do so, or seem to do so, far more often than it manifests "weakness" or indecision.[9] At a different but related level, (2) regardless of its past or even fairly recent accomplishments within and outside the problem-management area per se, it is the program's *mistakes*—the shortcomings it manifests, and especially the administrative difficulties it creates "right now"—that are generally and most closely attended to by key decision-makers, especially if a program is not relieving current problems for the department, and thus helping it survive. (During Phases 1 and 2, when CTP was clearly helping the YA handle major issues of bed space and capital outlay and was bringing national recognition to the department, this program was understandably viewed with favor. The problems it was creating seemed relatively minor at the time; in any event, they were seldom hard for the department to absorb.)

As a result, (3) a program, like many top administrators themselves, is perpetually vulnerable—almost regardless of its reputation, its specific activities or even broad ideals, and its long-term trends (e.g., clear improvements). Thus, (4) the central maintenance and even survival question for its staff is: "How valuable do key decision-makers consider this program right now?" Here, value is often judged with reference to the importance of the problems (departmental/correctional needs and concerns) that those individuals think it is solving or relieving as compared to the importance of those they think it is creating/maintaining, and actually *is* or may be creating/maintaining.[10] This is somewhat different than asking: "What positive contribution is the program making now and in the long run, irrespective of the perceived and actual difficulties (assuming these are manageable) it may be creating right now?" During Phases 1 and 2, staff were far more oriented toward the latter question and they believed that the difficulties which were present were relatively small. Staff largely maintained this orientation during the first half of Phase 3 (generally speaking, the positive contributions they anticipated were uppermost in their minds, and they believed these would outweigh most short-term difficulties); however, by 1970, that orientation was becoming much less acceptable to *administrators,* probably because the consequences they associated with certain unresolved problems and with possible new problems were more serious than before.

Finally, (5) given the fact that top administrators are neither unlimited in their ability to resist external pressure nor infinitely patient in any event, staff must recognize that even the widely accepted ideals and long-range goals that may characterize their program may not always carry the day, even if those administrators generally support them in principle and have actively supported them in practice. That is, ideals and goals not infrequently bow to other factors, especially during crises and in the face of long-standing doubts or negative feelings. For such reasons, (6) staff must explicitly emphasize the program's strengths and current achievements. That is, they must definitely attend to public (including departmental) relations, especially if theirs is not just a complex but a risk-taking and "different" type of program. They need not do so with fanfare, but they should do so fairly often. Apart from, but not unrelated to, the ongoing intra- and extramural support this "PR" approach may generate, information and other concrete input regarding the nature of the program can help prepare administrators and other decision-makers for certain "bad moments" and crises. However infrequent, such moments *will* almost certainly occur, singly and—perhaps most important—in combination; it makes sense that they not obliterate the many positive events that have, or may have, occurred. Although it may not, in itself, avoid or resolve certain crises, an approach that provides detailed, timely information can at least lead to fewer misunderstandings and perhaps even hasty, unilateral decisions by administrators.

In the case of CTP, these principles would probably have applied even if the project had not been highly visible both with respect to its reputation and its location (headquarters only, or otherwise) within the political nerve-center of California. Regarding the struggles and ultimate fate of Phase 3, in particular, the visibility factor, which necessarily interacted with the overall political climate, probably did exert substantial influence—both positive and, in the final two years, somewhat negative.

The following might also be noted. Within a statewide public agency that operates several large institutions and camps (e.g., 10 or more), that has 20 to 50 parole offices, and that is responsible for several thousand offenders at any one time, *some* extremely negative high profile event or events—for example, the media-highlighted murder or rape of a private citizen, usually by a parolee rather than an escapee—are almost certain to occur several times a year. Especially though not only within given political climates, such events can keep agency heads and division chiefs largely on the defensive or "on edge" and can easily result in their proactively as well as reactively giving much less leeway to many or most programs and operations than they otherwise might. This can apply particularly, though not only, to programs and practices that are experimental and, in substantial respects, "innovative" or "different." That the Youth Authority, which was often faced with precisely such events *somewhere* or other within California, actively and consistently supported the CTP experiment for 12 consecutive years, very likely reflected the following factor at least as much as any other single one: The sizable commitment of its two directors (Stark and Breed), plus that of several high level administrators, to the goal of building practical knowledge—not just for their own agency's use but for that of corrections overall. It also reflected the relative rarity of such events within CTP itself.

Review

Phases 1 and 2, on which the following focuses, covered 1961–1969. Most observations regarding these phases also apply to Phase 3.

Social Agencies
Law Enforcement, Probation, Etc.
During Phases 1 and 2, each CTP unit was largely accepted and supported by local and state agencies/departments with which it interacted. In these and other respects, such as time required by unit staff to develop and maintain a working relationship, major implementation and maintenance problems did not exist. This applied not only to police, probation, welfare, vocational rehabilitation, and

employment, but within each city involved. One probation department was dissatisfied with CTP for several years largely because the project gave many youths a "second chance"—following nonassaultive yet nonminor offenses such as auto theft—rather than immediately revoking their parole. Yet even then, it largely accepted CTP's differential-intervention approach per se, its classification system, its use of matching, and key factors #1 through #5 in general (Chapter 15). All in all, Phases 1, 2, *and* 3 indicated that although CTP could function adequately without the full, simultaneous acceptance of *all* agencies/departments, that is, every single one, the ongoing acceptance of or at least tolerance by most such organizations was very helpful with respect to individual youths; in the long run, it was essential to the overall program.

Schools
Cooperative working relations were readily established between Valley CTP units and local public schools, and these relations were neither difficult nor time-consuming to maintain. Most school personnel were pleased that their troubled, troublesome, and otherwise "different" youths—those who had been suspended/expelled, and those still in the public school—were being worked with intensively or extensively. Though CTP agents sometimes asked for what school staff considered "special favors for troublemakers," most such requests were handled on an individual-youth rather than fixed-policy or categorical basis. Thus, even when an agent's original request was denied, an acceptable alternative or compromise approach usually emerged.

In San Francisco, the CTP/school relationship was moderately strained. This mainly resulted from the widespread tensions and violence that had rapidly emerged within Bay Area schools during 1966, and it was not focused specifically on CTP or other YA wards. Despite their philosophic difference from CTP regarding the handling of "troublemakers," San Francisco's schools remained willing to work with the project, and an adversary relationship was avoided. In fact, relations slowly but steadily improved.

Parent Organization
General Response
During Phases 1 and 2, CTP generated various problems for its parent organization, the Youth Authority. Few such problems were surprises to the YA; none were major, and all were handled without great difficulty and serious repercussions. For these and more positive reasons, the YA was highly approving and supportive of the project. This stance related not just to CTP as a totality, but to its major features as well: differential-intervention orientation; use of offender classification in general; reliance on matching and other key factors, such as extensive contacts and flexible programming; and the community-based dimension above all.

Some practical and interagency difficulties nevertheless existed. For instance, regarding *extensive contacts,* both out-of-home placements and a conveniently located, physically adequate community center were difficult to locate in San Francisco, though not in the Valley. (In San Francisco, rents were high, and at the time, YA budgets were increasingly constrained statewide.) Regarding *flexible programming,* administrator discomfort sometimes occurred when CTP restored given youths to parole in order to try a different or modified approach. However, YA administrators willingly "took the heat" from agencies and individuals—mainly probation and specific judges—who disliked these decisions. Such interactions were uncommon and never became "crises."

The existence of unresolved and partly resolved difficulties, such as those involving extensive contacts, indicated that CTP could operate—albeit less efficiently, and probably less effectively with some youth groups—under less than ideal conditions, for example, without having what its staff considered a full complement of well-developed program components. This would probably apply in CTP programs today.

I-Level
The parent organization approved of and supported offender classification throughout Phases 1 and 2, not only for ward management but for differential intervention. However, its stance toward CTP's particular system—I-level—was somewhat complex and ambivalent. This was due, primarily, to the system's own complexity and, secondarily, to other factors mentioned below. By 1966—four and a half years after CTP began—I-level was generally accepted as a useful diagnostic and treatment-planning tool by numerous

departmental staff. By 1967, the YA—largely via federal funds—established a statewide training center that specifically utilized I-level and also served probation. By 1969, I-level was designated the YA's official classification system for parole and institutions alike.

Throughout 1961–1969, neither the public, justice system agencies, nor other agencies and groups objected to I-level classification, for instance, on pragmatic, ethical, or theoretical grounds. This applied not only in each Valley setting but within the three highly urbanized environments in which YA special parole units (modified CTPs, with caseloads of 25 youths per agent) had operated since the mid-1960s; the latter were predominantly low-income, ethnic minority areas, either black or Mexican American.

Despite this basic acceptance, I-level was often difficult for non-CTP—that is, non-trained or "non-system-experienced"—personnel (most YA administrators included) to thoroughly understand and readily explain to others. In addition, by 1971, YA experience with the training center indicated the following. To create and maintain a cadre of I-level diagnosticians and treatment personnel and to then allow them to act as part-time *trainers* of line staff within their local setting was time-consuming and expensive. This training task, even in diagnosis alone, would have been less formidable on a non-statewide basis or in an organization much smaller than the YA.

Early in 1971, I-level classification seemed to have contributed to a "racial imbalance" in two YA institutions. A careful review of this situation indicated that the I-level system was not racially biased; instead, the imbalance reflected misdiagnoses, conceptual issues, and local social-cultural realities. Though the YA soon resolved this imbalance and took steps to preclude or rapidly handle its recurrence, this experience made top administrators hesitant about openly and vigorously supporting I-level. Nevertheless, they retained it on a low-profile basis as the YA's official classification, because, among other reasons, of its demonstrated utility and its lack of serious competition from other systems. I-level retained this role in the YA into the 1980s. (The Jesness Inventory was used to derive a level and subtype classification, at the YA's reception centers.)

Pragmatics and New Trends

By the late 1960s the Youth Authority decided it was not feasible to establish numerous (as opposed to about a *half-dozen*) CTP-type parole units throughout the state, even with caseloads of 25 youths per worker; budget cuts, among other factors, were making it increasingly difficult to maintain such caseloads within even the YA's few special parole units. (CTP and standard parole caseloads were 12 and 72 youths per worker, respectively.) Starting in 1969, the caseloads of modified CTP units—"Community Parole Centers"—had about 25 parolees per worker, plus seven or eight others in institutions (Pond and Davis, 1973). Starting in the early 1970s the Youth Authority, like many correctional agencies nationwide, began changing its emphasis: The "justice model" (without its often-observed *heavy* emphasis on punishment, however) was given very high, possibly the highest, priority by its top administrators, despite the department's continued support of rehabilitation. Related to this model and to increased U.S. prison disturbances as well as broader social unrest, the issues of wards' rights, due process, grievance procedure, and staff security increasingly occupied center stage and quickly received most training funds. Finally, starting in the late 1960s the YA's population began to increasingly consist of long-troubled/troublesome and/or violent offenders; this was mainly due to the Probation Subsidy Program (Chapter 17).

In the early 1970s, all YA regular parole units (some 25, statewide) were reorganized to reflect these constraints and developments, not to accommodate increased intensive treatment (Pond et al., 1974). However, this reorganization also reflected the department's continued, in fact rapidly growing, interest in establishing some form of *differential* treatment—particularly what it termed "specialized caseloads"—partly in response to its changing population. Yet these caseloads, including the approaches usually used, were rather different than those in CTP in several major respects (Pond et al., 1974, pp. 10–21). At any rate, given the often-volatile or at least fluid and highly demanding context of the late 1960s and early 1970s, CTP's interest-value to many YA administrators began to decrease.

Recruitment and Hiring of Agents (Matched Workers)

General Considerations

Recruitment and hiring (R/H) of matched workers posed little problem during Phases 1 and 2; for one thing, many candidates were available and most were relatively skilled. However, had the YA been much smaller than it was or had major R/H restrictions existed, this situation would probably have differed. Unlike recruitment, hiring (selection and matching) did take time, mainly because of the depth interview and subsequent staff discussion that were required. R/H posed little problem for female caseloads, mainly because the skill level of most respondents/candidates was high and specific matching was not required.

Restrictions and Requirements

CTP imposed no recruitment and hiring restrictions regarding age, ethnicity, and so on, and no minimum requirements regarding level or type of education, job experience, and (after 1964) job classification. This policy worked well. Though YA policy required that parole agents—CTP's and others'—have four years of college or its equivalent, many candidates with less education could doubtlessly have handled the job.

A CTP-type program must essentially control its recruitment and hiring; at least it should have veto power over who gets hired, especially if few caseloads exist. Skilled interviewers are needed in order to preclude incorrect hiring decisions or to greatly reduce their occurrence: Staff/youth matching cannot yet be achieved by written instruments alone—self-reports or others; however, a CTP-developed checklist (the "Form 3") can facilitate this goal once the needed information has been gathered via a careful, depth interview. (Staff must not only be skilled, they must be *motivated* to work in a CTP-type program; a careful interview is needed to assess, among other things, this and related motivations.) Perhaps the largest potential obstacle to appropriate staff/youth matches—that is, to achieving a high percentage of such matches—would be nonagency (e.g., State Personnel Board, or union) imposed restrictions or preferences regarding hiring. Under some conditions, these or related obstacles could prevent effective utilization of the above skills.

Staff Development and Unit Functioning

Staff Development

At CTP, initial in-service training was not needed, essentially because matched agents arrived on the job with enough skills for working with most youths on their caseloads. Nevertheless, staff development—which was based on far more than formal in-service training (initial or otherwise)—was a major part of the project's atmosphere and tradition. Thus, for example, many CTP staff received *specialized training,* usually after one or two years on the project; yet such training, for instance, in conjoint family therapy or in psychodrama, was not in itself absolutely essential for achieving basic project goals with most youths. In CTP programs today, staff development—by this or other means—would nevertheless be important in order to *expand* workers' skills, to help maintain or improve individual and unit morale, to improve workers' ability to pool their resources, and to increase their future professional opportunities.

Unit Functioning

To facilitate within-unit sharing and staff development overall, another useful tool would be unit meetings that center on professional issues, such as intervention with specified youth groups, or even on personal feelings of staff. These meetings, which can also improve unit morale as well as overall functioning and whose cost would usually be minimal, would best be regularly scheduled; those centering on personal feelings would best be voluntary. In CTP programs today, most agency administrators would probably attach considerable value to staff development, unit functioning, and so on; in this connection they would probably support or at least not oppose such meetings, as was true in California. Despite their value, these meetings would not—at least, should not—be absolutely essential for achieving basic or minimum project goals with most youths.

Supervision and Administration

The Casework Supervisor

A casework supervisor is essential for a well-functioning—even acceptably functioning—CTP unit. In such a unit today, this person would have central responsibility for ensuring that the concepts and methods of differential intervention are appropriately implemented at the individual case level, across all caseloads. This includes coordination of all unit activities, and it applies regardless of which youth-classification system is used. To discharge this responsibility while using the I-level system, the casework supervisor (CWS) should be skilled in I-level diagnosis; and, whichever system is used, it is virtually essential for the CWS to be skilled in both worker/youth (individual case) matching and worker selection and matching. These three skills, if not possessed by the CWS, must still be readily available to the unit. In any event, the supervisor must understand the usual dynamics of, and various methods of intervention with, the full range of youth subtypes, certainly those that are other than rare. Under this condition, he or she can provide agents with specific casework assistance, not just with encouragement, support, and approval.

Throughout Phases 1 and 2 the parent agency consistently accepted and supported the need for supervision—one CWS per unit. It recognized that this individual should have the above-mentioned responsibility, and it also accepted and supported the following: (1) CTP had to choose its own casework supervisor; at least, it required veto power over all candidates; and (2) the CWS needed ample in-service, for example, "specialized," training to increase or even maintain his resource value to the unit, especially regarding individual casework. These principles would apply in CTP units today.

Supervisor candidates who were skilled in individual casework, in I-level diagnosis, and, to a lesser extent, in staff/youth matching, were not uncommon during Phases 1 and 2. Most had "risen through the ranks," that is, they had been parole agents for at least two years, almost always at CTP. A few had worked in other intensive supervision units, such as modified CTPs. Presently, many agencies could probably find and develop appropriate supervisory personnel for a CTP unit, though not without some inconvenience and cost with respect to the earlier-mentioned training and, in some cases, even initially being "brought up to speed." Some supervisor candidates might be individuals with experience in intensive treatment-oriented programs that have operated during the past decade or more. However, to access most such individuals, recruitment efforts may sometimes have to extend beyond particular agencies themselves, and perhaps even outside their home states.

The Administrative Supervisor

During Phases 1 and 2 the administrative supervisor (unit administrator, or UA) performed unit-centered, agency-centered, and unit/agency-centered functions. He tried not only to obtain or increase the agency's understanding of and support for the unit, but to help the unit better meet the agency's needs. In CTP units today, a full-time UA would be highly desirable even if he were shared by two parole units—one or both being CTP types. Since agency administration and the CTP unit should each believe the UA is willing and able to represent their central interests appropriately, each should have a voice—ideally an equal voice—in his selection.

During Phases 1 and 2, unit administrators were not difficult to find. Their pre-UA experience was mainly in parole, and it usually extended over several years. Almost all had been field supervisors; most had held a middle-management or administrative position; and almost all were viewed by agency administrators and line staff as quite supportive of innovative approaches to working with youths. Promising UA candidates would probably not be difficult to locate today, even in agencies much smaller than the YA. They need not be very familiar with I-level or any related youth classification prior to arriving at the unit.

Case Processing
Overview
Case processing posed few practical problems for operations' staff and the parent agency during 1961–1969, both in the Valley and in San Francisco. This applied to each major step from YA intake to program assignment: (1) *preeligibility screening;* (2) *random assignment;* (3) *diagnostic interviewing;* (4) *staffing;* and (5) *program assignment.* Neither the youths, their parents, nor community groups objected to the process.

Step (2) may be omitted in nonexperimental programs. Regarding step (3), main emphasis in this chapter's overview is on the task of gathering treatment-relevant information, not on later *integrating* various aspects of that information in order to achieve an accurate I-level diagnosis in particular. The parent agency consistently supported step (4), despite the latter's length.

Given the already described skill level of agents and supervisor, these steps, (3) and (4) included, would probably present few case-processing problems to most agencies that tried to establish a CTP unit. However, a major component of step (3)—namely, staff's (basically, the supervisor's) ability to accurately "I-level" the youth—might not always exist; if so, this, in itself would complicate the question of feasibility. Nevertheless, feasibility need not solely depend on this factor alone, at least as long as accurate youth classification remains but *one* aspect of—and not the only way to achieve—relevant, individualized diagnosis and treatment/control planning.

Diagnosis and Treatment/Control Planning
At CTP, diagnostic and other intervention-relevant information was obtained mainly via three interviews, and, secondarily, through case file material routinely forwarded to the YA by probation. (Each interview was designed to cover most or all of the following areas: youth's current situation, such as living arrangement and external environment; offense history; personal history; current interests and abilities; major personal limitations; personality; and other contributors to crime/delinquency.) The first interview, conducted by a researcher, was mainly designed to obtain I-level/subtype information. The second, conducted by a parole agent, focused on practical matters and essentially factual information, for instance, the youth's current situation and offense history; here and elsewhere, it partly duplicated the first interview. Finally, the same agent interviewed the youth's family or relatives.

In CTP programs today, the latter interviews would suffice. To obtain not just quality (e.g., reasonably accurate and convincing) information but at least moderate detail or depth—and certainly broad coverage—these interviews would require 60 to 90 minutes; however, 40 minutes or so would suffice if considerably less detail was desired. If under 40 minutes, major sacrifices would probably be required, certainly with respect to depth.

CTP's initial staffing was essential. It was designed to produce a relevant, individualized treatment/control (i.e., intervention) plan via a careful assessment of the broadly ranging information mentioned earlier. To develop such a plan and prepare for its implementation, at least one parole agent and his casework supervisor had to attend; this agent was the individual whom the CWS had assigned to permanently work with the youth, based on a plan that was to emerge from the staffing.

Such a staffing would probably be feasible in numerous agencies today. At any rate, plans that reflect the complexities of—and the possible urgencies or serious pressures and threats in—the youth's life *could* be developed within this context by an agent and his supervisor, without assistance from researchers and even without an I-level/subtype diagnosis. Yet, to produce such plans, broadly based information, and at least three hours of discussion, would be needed. Alternative approaches—specifically, much shorter staffings—might be used, again with or without a diagnostic classification; however, such staffings would probably produce borderline-acceptable plans. Regarding other possibilities, present-day computer-generated plans, for example, would probably be even less satisfactory, though they might provide a staffing group with useful information (though not a *plan,* certainly not a comprehensive plan, per se).[11]

Information, for example, regarding specific youth characteristics, that often helps provide key *bases* for an I-level/subtype (I/S) classification or for related diagnosis could make a major contribution to relevant treatment/control planning even in the absence of an I/S classification (or diagnosis) per se. Nevertheless, if such a diagnosis existed and were accurate, it could often provide better focus and direction not only in "standard" initial staffings but in alternative approaches as well—as long as the limits and possible pitfalls of classification were recognized.

Case Maintenance
Reviews and Discussions
Case maintenance was fairly straightforward at the Community Treatment Project, and the approach that was used would probably be feasible in most such programs today. Basically, CTP's maintenance approach involved (1) a brief, weekly case review, (2) unscheduled discussions and updates, and (3) detailed, periodic reviews. This approach helped provide relevant, detailed information, and it encouraged continuity-of-effort with respect to the youth and his overall situation; staff considered such information and efforts important whether or not many difficulties and complexities existed. Insofar as this information and continuity

seemed appropriate and necessary in CTP programs today, such reviews and discussions—especially collectively—could play a critical role.

Program Components
CTP's program components included counseling, recreation, out-of-home placement, and so on. In most settings, especially Valley cities, *most* such components were usually not difficult to implement and maintain; this applied not only to youths individually but to unit operations overall. These components, and their frequency of usage, were essentially accepted by top administrators, by justice system agencies, and by others; however, some concern was expressed, mainly though not entirely from academia, regarding the possible overuse of inappropriate use of short-term detention, primarily during CTP's earlier years. (See Chapter 26.) Some components, for example, "material aid," increased CTP's costs via their greater frequency of usage than in regular parole. In contrast, the school program—which was absent in regular parole but not in institutions—increased costs by its very existence; however, it, too, was generally considered valuable by CTP and non-CTP personnel alike. This cost situation applied to "socializing experiences" (off-site trips, etc.) as well. Without a school component, a CTP program need not just barely "exist"; it could probably function at least moderately well. However, if many school-aged, seriously school-troubled youths were present, its relevance and flexibility would be considerably reduced. Regarding CTP units today, the feasibility of various program components would vary a good deal from one agency and/or setting to the next.

Other Operational Aspects
Auxiliary Staff
Throughout Phases 1 and 2, CTP operations proceeded reasonably well without auxiliary staff such as paraprofessionals and community volunteers (senior citizens, Big Brothers, etc.). This exclusion occurred for research reasons, among others. In CTP programs today, these and other staff, such as college students or interns, could nevertheless play several useful roles. However, such individuals should be carefully selected, preferably by the casework supervisor; also, they should be directly supervised by the parole agent—whose, say, one or two cases they would each work with.[12] At any rate, a *small* complement of auxiliary staff

could assist agents and selected youths without (1) necessitating major time investments by agents or the supervisor, (2) hampering or unnecessarily complicating communications and coordination of efforts within and across caseloads, and (3) significantly diluting the agent/youth relationship. Though these individuals could lessen various agent burdens and could help agents achieve their goals, they are not—and should not become—absolutely essential for the achievement of basic project objectives. That task—like counseling, surveillance, and major limit-setting themselves—should remain the agents' and the supervisor's responsibility.

CTP School and Teacher
The school program should function as a semi-autonomous entity within CTP, in connection with educational *processes*. The teacher should be a full-fledged CTP staff member—not a second-class citizen, yet not a fully independent entity. The school's efforts with respect to each CTP student (e.g., regarding academic content) should be integrated with, not just broadly consistent with, the parole agent's overall intervention plan for that particular youth. In this regard, the functional relationship between its efforts and his plans—as between the teacher and the total staff—should be that of contributing "part" to agreed upon "whole." Similarly, the school's efforts regarding students *collectively* should mesh as closely as possible with the current and anticipated priorities of CTP as a whole.

Selected Youth Characteristics
CTP programs that handled *less serious* offenders than those in the California experiment would probably have fewer operational challenges and problems. However, even if those youths had, say, a nonsevere instant offense, a less serious offense history, or both, the projects' tasks would remain very challenging—whether or not, and perhaps especially if, intervention efforts were less complex and/or were to involve substantially less input. In any event, such reductions in complexity and input would not, ipso facto, imply a need for substantially fewer staff skills or for different types of case processing and major changes in project organization. Similarly, operational challenges and problems would be only slightly reduced if CTP programs ac-

cepted youths who fell within a relatively narrow age range only, for example, 13 to 15–16 or else 16 to 18–19, or whose *average* age was somewhat different (greater or lesser) than that in California.

Location, Community Response, and Structure

In all cities, the CTP center was—by choice—usually located where a sizable portion of its population resided: in a lower- or lower middle-class neighborhood. This population-based approach seemed appropriate and worked well. Though such an approach might not have been indispensable with respect to adequate program operation, its absence would probably have been associated with (1) reduced accessibility by youths and others, (2) lower overall efficiency, (3) increased costs, such as for rent and transportation, and (4) less time spent by agents with youths. In addition, each unit would literally have been less of a *community* center for parolees and others. Similar considerations would probably apply to CTP units today, especially in large cities and if program resources or agent flexibility were rather limited.

During its 12 years of operation, CTP experienced virtually no community resistance, organized or otherwise; some communities, in fact, considered the center a local resource. Today, within the United States, many citizens in many communities would nevertheless dislike or actively resist the idea of having serious offenders "congregating" at a local center or at least outside it, however well-supervised they may be. Yet, *most* people in most communities would probably accept such a center if local criminal and major "nuisance" activities did not increase and if the number of offenders did not seem great. For this reason, and perhaps under such conditions, the community-center concept would probably remain feasible in many or possibly most settings today.

The following were simultaneously housed within the center (unit): all clerical personnel, all parole agents, the casework supervisor, the administrative supervisor (in about half the units), the arts-and-crafts program and accredited school, and the day-room/recreation areas.[13] This "functionally integrated center" arrangement helped pool the unit's resources and coordinate numerous staff/youth activities and interactions; it also

proved feasible and practical from a community and agency perspective and would probably do so in many agencies today. Though CTP could probably have operated if some of the above staff and/or components were physically separated from each other, considerable integration and efficiency would probably have been lost and overall costs would have increased. This, too, would probably apply today.

Throughout Phases 1 and 2 each CTP unit operated within a geographic area that sent enough serious and/or multiple offenders to the Youth Authority to support a full-scale (five- to seven-caseload) program. Had it operated in an area or jurisdiction that sent few offenders—program-eligible youths—to the YA, no more than a reduced-size program might have been possible. The latter situation might be especially likely to occur—today—in, for instance, geographically small counties; this would apply to probation and state-level programs alike.

Even in a reduced-size CTP a precondition of appropriate operations would be the program's access to the youths, and, where necessary, vice versa. Access problems could arise in various counties, for example, the markedly rural and the mixture of rural and towns or small cities. Intensive intervention would be virtually impossible to achieve if access were very limited; similarly, extensive intervention would be quite difficult or impossible to implement, especially in its primary sense: the *simultaneous* utilization of two or more program components. Though the *successive*-input aspect of extensive intervention might sometimes be feasible or partly feasible in areas that have serious access problems, this input would seldom be an adequate substitute for simultaneous input if the latter were considered important and especially if three or more program components seemed crucial, when intervening with given youths.

Where possible, sparsely populated areas would be excluded from CTP programs today, especially if those areas extended far from the main population area. However, if included, they might, by design, contribute only a small percentage of youths; and here, in order to preclude sizable access problems, perhaps only those individuals who lived adjacent to the main population area would be eligible.

Discussion
Community-Based Intervention
Factors Relating to Acceptance
Today, within the United States, many citizens and groups would accept the idea of community-based intervention with young multiple offenders, in lieu of institutionalization. More specifically, many communities, including the large- and medium-sized, would support or at least tolerate this approach, though they would rarely insist on it or protest its absence. This acceptance would exist despite the public's increased concern with victims—mainly of violence—since the mid-1970s. At any rate, sizable portions of today's public still believe that many offenders—some serious—can change or be changed for the better, and that this can often occur outside lockup. In this respect many people in many communities have not "given up" on all repeat and/or nonminor offenders; they usually distinguish among offenders (albeit very broadly)—even among the nonminor—and they consider long-term lockup neither imperative nor even optimal for all. Indeed, during the past few decades, many community-based programs have existed for such individuals.

Nevertheless, these same "publics" or communities would probably want at least three conditions satisfied before they would accept/tolerate a community-based program designed to handle, say, atypical probationers such as third- or fourth-time, and/or nonminor, offenders:

1. Few youths with violent instant offenses could participate in the program; however, many with one or two nonextreme violent *priors* could take part.
2. Like *standard* probation or parole, the program must protect the public by direct, not just indirect, means. In this respect it must "control," not just "treat."
3. Costs could not be unusually high even though policymakers would acknowledge that extra expenses (e.g., compared to standard probation) are probably unavoidable when extra efforts are to be made.

At any rate, within definite yet neither unmanageable nor unrealistic limits, public acceptance/tolerance would exist in many American communities—perhaps about half. Broader acceptance might exist in other places or times.

The public's conditional acceptance—step #1 of feasibility—is usually reflected in the views of many local and even regional or state-level policymakers. In this regard such individuals (county supervisors, legislators, etc.) often crystallize and, in effect, formalize many citizens' nonrejecting (more precisely, their only partly rejecting) attitudes toward given offender groups. Yet, those same decision-makers may instead—or in addition, but on different occasions—express the *rejecting,* that is, rather fully rejecting, attitudes of *other* segments of the public. These differences, shifts, and so on, may thus sometimes reflect, not simply "politics" and efforts to satisfy multiple constituencies, but rather the following situation: (1) Most citizens—as individuals—are often somewhat ambivalent toward given offenders, such as the nonviolent yet nonminor. These feelings may be largely independent of those individuals' possible stance or "official" views—for example, their seemingly definitive and unambivalent views—as group members. (2) For weeks or months, many citizens, like some decision-makers themselves, often react rather negatively to almost *all* nonminor offenders soon after receiving media exposure to a notorious or unusually violent crime, or, especially, to a series of extreme crimes. In short, the public's usual differentiations among offenders, even between the nonminor and others, then temporarily decrease (certainly at an action level).

Still, through time, most of the earlier-mentioned policymakers often legitimize and support the long-standing *principal* attitudes, values, and mixed feelings of most people. They do so in addition to—not instead of—reflecting these and other individuals' immediate fears and frustrations; and in so doing they often help establish or reinforce broadly based and fairly constant policies and directions. In this respect, these policies/directions support the particular community's or region's underlying and sometimes open acceptance, tolerance or rejection, or intolerance of the type of program under consideration.

The public's main attitudes, values, and mixed feelings are reflected, not just in the broad policies of major decision-makers, but in those—and in related specific actions—of many law enforcement and local as well as statewide justice agencies. For instance, if these agencies, say, specified local probation departments, believed that numerous citizens—including given community leaders—would probably accept the given type of program, or would at least "give it a fair trial," *under conditions 1 through 3 above,* such agencies would feel in a much better position to seriously explore that program's feasibility. However, without that probable acceptance or fairly clear interest they would seldom explore the program even if they themselves considered it appropriate and promising. Exploration, of course, would be more frequent and concerted if a strong, explicit mandate, not just "fairly clear interest" (plus considerable ambivalence), were expressed. Such a mandate, however, is rare.

(As implied, many law enforcement [LE] and criminal justice [CJ] agencies are considerably more cautious than their communities [which are usually cautious themselves], and they would, for instance, avoid such programs largely on grounds that they involve too much risk for the public. At the same time, relatively *few* LE and CJ agencies [even if they were not "more cautious than . . ."] are willing to take *more* risks than their local communities. This applies not just if the latter's risk levels happen to be moderately high [which is very uncommon], but especially if those communities seem quite ambivalent about the type of program under consideration [which is common].)

For the rest of this chapter we will focus on the juvenile justice system. Included will be local probation and state-level—in effect, "beyond probation"—agencies such as the Youth Authority; however, emphasis will be on local agencies unless otherwise indicated.

Interest in the above types of programs by individual local justice system agencies would usually reflect not just the *public's* attitude toward community-based intervention but today's moderately accepting, often vacillating, but increasingly positive attitude toward intervention within corrections overall. More specifically, though the "justice model" (Fogel, 1975, 1976; Singer, 1979; van den Haag, 1975)—with its emphasis on punishment and commensurate deserts—has dominated corrections for over two decades, intervention is no longer considered (1) morally or ethically unjustifiable, for instance, intrinsically demeaning and an obstacle to personal freedom; (2) otherwise inappropriate, for example, counterproductive, unduly controlling, and/or inhumane as practiced;[14] or (3) essentially ineffective, for instance, unable to reduce arrests. Those views

were common during the 1970s and the early to middle 1980s. Nor is intervention considered entirely incompatible with the justice model itself, at least with its less narrow and/or less stringent forms. Such views and changes are often reflected in the specific actions of justice agencies.

Differential Intervention
Core Features of CTP

A CTP program for serious offenders would involve not just a community-based approach that satisfied conditions 1 through 3, above. It would involve *differential intervention* (DI), in fact, DI of a particular kind. Specifically, this program—whether local or state, public or private—would have three core features:

First, for each youth, CTP's intervention approach would derive from a very careful diagnosis. This diagnosis would include but extend well beyond any offender classification alone, however valid and sophisticated the latter—I-level or other—might be. More specifically, it would comprise what might be called a highly individualized understanding of the youth and his situation. Achievement of this understanding would require the presence/availability not only of a skilled diagnostician (supervisor or other) but of staff (supervisor and worker) who have sufficient time and ability to *further* analyze the diagnostic information in order to determine its implications for action.

Next, the product of staff's effort, namely, a relevant, detailed, and integrated treatment/control plan, would embody and give practical significance to the individualized (or "trans-classification") understanding in question. As such, it would comprise the second core feature of CTP.

Finally, the treatment/control plan would be implemented in terms of at least two crucial factors: (1) individualized, flexible programming and (2) intensive and/or extensive contacts. (In the diagnostic and planning stages, individualization is achieved via careful analysis and discussion of detailed, usually broad-based information. During the implementation—case-handling or follow-up—stage it is maintained and further achieved via the worker/youth relationship, intensive/extensive contacts, frequent case discussions, and, where necessary, flexible programming and related modifications in approach.) Implementation of these factors would require small caseloads. In addition to these factors, and depending on the particular youth sample, matched, perceptive staff would be very important, as would various methods and strategies used in the California experiment.[15] For many youths, these and other factors would often require long-term contacts. As with careful diagnosis and the development of an appropriate treatment/control plan, implementation of the preceding factors—say, (1) and (2) above—would seldom be easy, let alone quick. For typical CTP youths it would require the availability of considerable resources, such as several program elements. For these and remaining CTP youths, that is, for all eligible offenders combined, it would also require considerable adaptability and persistence on both the operating unit's and the parent agency's part.

These core features would be integral to the type of differential-intervention-oriented, community-based approach that operated during 1961–1969. Other, much less individualized DI approaches currently exist, for example, those centering on the conceptual levels, Minnesota Multiphasic Personality Inventory [MMPI]-based, National Institute of Corrections [Wisconsin], or Quay behavior categories, respectively (Hunt, 1971; Lerner, Arling, and Baird, 1986; Megargee, Bohn, and Sink, 1979; Quay and Parsons, 1971). Such approaches would probably be less effective than that described here, since, for one thing, the categories on which they heavily rely would not, by themselves, be sufficiently relevant and specific to the youth and his situation, and would not, by themselves, often compensate for this lack. Though even I-level categories would usually fail to adequately compensate, they would probably come closer to doing so than those referenced above, for most serious young offenders. Moreover, although they need not serve this function, I-level categories—if and when used—could, in any event, probably (or more often) provide a better point of departure for achieving the required understanding of these youths.[16]

Again, the core features are: a particularly careful diagnosis or highly individualized understanding; a relevant, detailed, and integrated treatment/control plan; implementation of that plan in terms of CTP's "key factors," especially (1) and (2) above, but certainly not all 10. Without all three features, various other aspects would be largely pointless or—at least—much less useful than otherwise, and CTP's particular DI approach could not be adequately implemented. These three features are thus decisive with respect to feasibility.

(One point before continuing. As long as conditions 1 through 3 are satisfied and legal requirements are met, neither the public nor the earlier-mentioned policymakers will often be interested in whether a given program is DI-oriented, or in understanding and approving its *particular* orientation, for example, I-level or conceptual level, if a classification system is used. Instead, the public, and others, will probably entrust such matters to the parent or operating agency. Under this condition, many such agencies, for instance, probation departments, would probably be more interested than otherwise in exploring given differential intervention approaches. This would apply especially if they believed the concept of DI was, simultaneously, receiving at least moderate and fairly steady support within corrections as a whole and if they felt they might be able to implement some such program.)

Key Questions in Feasibility

Given (1) sufficient public acceptance/tolerance of a community-based approach, (2) sufficient support for such an approach by key policymakers, and (3) substantial interest by a specific operating agency, the following would thus become the central questions regarding the feasibility of a proposed CTP-type differential intervention program (unit) for serious offenders—here, young offenders: *Can the given unit obtain the kind of staff required to implement CTP's three core features? Can the operating agency provide the support and material resources needed to implement those features, particularly the third?* In these respects, are CTP units feasible today?

A yes or no answer cannot be given for all local and state organizations, for instance, for all probation departments within a given state or at least within most states, and for all state-level YA-type agencies within the United States. That is, one cannot validly apply either answer to all departments and agencies that exist within given areas or regions, and this would apply to private agencies as well. Instead, each organization's situation and prospects must be assessed individually, even though some areas or regions—and perhaps some types of setting—may be generally better prospects than others.

Thus, for example, say that one asks if probation departments in medium to large cities can meet CTP's first essential requirement—that is, can obtain the type of supervisor and the type and number of workers in question.[17] The answer would be a qualified yes—and no: Many departments *could,* yet many others *could not,* obtain one or both; moreover, one could not tell, without first having considerable information, which specific departments could do so, or even the approximate percentage involved. Similarly, one might ask if those departments that could, in fact, obtain the required staff could then actually implement CTP's key factors. Again, a yes or no answer would not exist for all departments; instead, many doubtlessly could and many certainly could not. (Even after they pondered the question, still other departments would be unsure.) The situation would be similar for state agencies, even though—compared to most local probation departments—these organizations often have more staff as well as material resources, though not always more operational flexibility, to apply to serious offenders.

If the latter assessment is accurate and if other factors are roughly equal, a smaller proportion of local probation departments than state correctional agencies could probably meet the above staffing-and-implementation requirements, within the United States. In addition, the proportion and perhaps number would probably increase where local and state, that is, probation and parole, functions are combined within a single organization—as they are in many states. (This assumes the individual worker's caseload, that is, joint caseload, would remain low.)

Though the preceding answers might not inspire many policymakers and provide them a simple direction, they reflect today's realities and at least would not mislead. The variations among local as well as state organizations are just too large for any universal answer to apply.

Estimates of Feasibility
In the following, we will again focus on probation departments in medium to large cities, in presumably typical regions or states. Though the number of such departments that might adequately operate a program such as CTP would necessarily remain unknown until detailed information were assessed, this number or baseline figure could, under certain conditions, easily be very low. For instance, (1) if 50 percent of all cities/communities were receptive to community-based intervention with serious offenders under the earlier-mentioned conditions, (2) if 50 percent of all probation departments in those receptive locales then felt able and willing to seriously explore such an approach, (3) if 50 percent of the latter departments were much more interested in a CTP-type, *differential intervention* program than in some other community-based approach, (4) if some 50 percent of these "DI-motivated" departments could satisfy CTP's staffing requirements from among their own or other available personnel, and (5) if some 30 percent of the DI-motivated departments could—ignoring, for the moment, item (4)—meet CTP's implementation requirements, only about one probation department in 40 within the given regions or states would be a likely prospect for CTP's highly individualized approach, at any given time ($0.50 \times 0.50 \times 0.50 \times [0.50 \times 0.40]$ departments). These figures reflect estimates 1 through 3, each independently of the other, and 4/5 jointly. (See endnote 18 regarding the latter two figures, particularly that of *0.40* rather than 0.30. For reasons indicated in that endnote we will, except where specified, use 0.40. [Because some area offices within large departments might be better prospects than others, the feasibility situation in those departments might not be "all or none."])

However, if local acceptance of, and departmental interest in, community-based intervention *did* exist—if, say, estimates (1) and (2) were therefore 100 percent for some specific areas—the situation in *those* areas would differ considerably from that overall: Other factors remaining equal, about one department in 10 ($[0.50] \times [0.50 \times 0.40]$ departments) would be a good prospect within the given locales; this figure, of course, is still fairly low. (The multipliers reflect estimates 3 through 5, respectively, with #5 adjusted as per endnote 18.) In addition, if estimate (3) were itself 100 percent for those particular areas, the "odds" would be roughly one in five that a CTP program could be adequately operated. The latter odds are quite different than the baseline figure, and they reflect what typical probation departments might be capable of, given not just external support but their own interest in operating such a program.

As seen below, these odds, like the baseline (one in 40) and subsequent figure (both of which are rough estimates), refer to a full-blown, unmodified or virtually unmodified program.

Changing the Odds

If estimates (1) through (3) were indeed 100 percent each and if one wished to improve the one-in-five odds, one would then focus on estimates (4) and/or (5)—*staff* and *implementation* issues. More specifically, one would explore possible strategies that could bear on these issues. For instance, with regard to *staff*, at least three change strategies could be considered. These deal with (a) the range of matched workers that are required, (b) the range of youths that are served, and (c) the number of caseloads that are present, respectively:

(Before continuing, the following would be useful. In California's typical CTP unit there were six male caseloads at any given time—four main types in all. These four "caseload-types" [A through D, respectively], their composition, and—in parentheses—the number of staff who usually handled each type, were as follows: A—almost exclusively conflicted (2); B—mainly conflicted, but also passive-conformist (2); C—mainly passive-conformist (1); D—almost exclusively power-oriented (1). Most caseloads also contained one or two "other" youths, such as adjustment-reaction-to-adolescence (ARA). This configuration comprised a "standard set" of caseloads, that is, a standard number and range. It included a typical set of matched workers [that is, six—one per caseload], and it directly reflected the usual number and range of project youths. Today, in many *probation* departments, one or more caseload types might differ from the above, since a higher percentage of passive-conformists and ARAs (and also stress reactions) probably exist in those settings than in the Youth Authority's past and present populations. However, despite this likely difference, the same range of youths would probably exist, and worker/youth matching would follow the principles already described [Chapter 11]. In the following discussion, "youth group" refers to power-oriented and conflicted individuals only—whichever is specified. Each such group consists of two "youth types": The power-oriented group contains group conformists and manipulators, whereas the conflicted group contains assertive-deniers and the anxious-confused. For passive-conformists, "youth group" and "youth type" are synonymous.)

Strategy 1. To simplify the task of obtaining a set of matched workers, one could significantly decrease the *range of required matches.* To produce this change one might, for example, not insist on obtaining a worker who is matched with a certain youth group, say, the power-oriented.[19] (Each remaining worker *would* be matched—in this case, to one of the five remaining caseloads among the A through C types.) Thus, the caseload that contains this youth group—here, caseload type D—would continue to exist, but it would remain unmatched with respect to the worker/youth concepts discussed in Chapter 11. Nevertheless, the "unmatched" individual who handles this caseload would be at least moderately effective with its youths. At any rate, by simplifying the task at hand, Strategy 1 might raise estimate (4)'s 50 percent figure at least moderately—perhaps considerably. (It might be mentioned that worker/youth matching at CTP was least effective, and in this regard least important, with power-oriented youths, specifically, group conformists [GCs]. A similar situation might exist, though to a lesser degree, with *probation's GCs*—most of whom are probably less serious than those whom probation commits to the state.)

Strategy 2. By excluding one or more youth groups, for example, the power-oriented, one might decrease the *range of youths.* This would make it easier to obtain a set of workers (collectively), since, if a given youth group were excluded, the corresponding matched worker or workers (individually) would not be needed. As with Strategy 1, this approach would apply not only to youth groups but to any given youth type, such as the group conformist or assertive-denier. At either level, it might raise estimate (4) at least moderately. (See Appendix 34 regarding related, "justice" issues.)

Strategy 3. The number of male caseloads might be reduced, say, from the standard six to four. (If a given locale has relatively few eligible multiple offenders, fewer than six caseloads may be unavoidable anyway.) For instance, a given department might decide to have one Type A and one Type B caseload rather than the standard two of each; yet all four caseload types would be maintained and the full range of youths would remain. (In this example, the standard number of C and D caseloads—one each—would be maintained. Together with the A and B caseloads, this would bring the number of caseload types to four.) This strategy might raise estimate (4) at least moderately; if combined with Strategy 1, it might often raise it considerably.

In all three strategies, certain aspects of CTP would, that is, should, hardly be changed; this applies despite the goal of increasing the 50 percent estimate by obtaining workers more easily. For instance, though less skilled workers could doubtlessly be obtained more easily than others, CTP's need for skilled individuals is, in our view, a virtual "given." Given this presumed need, one could, that is, should, lower the earlier-described (Chapter 11) level of worker skill no more than slightly, even at the expense of the present goal.[20] (See Chapter 13, endnote 8, regarding "generalist agents.")

Use of Strategies 1, 2, or 3 might raise the estimate (4) odds from their present 50 percent level to at least 60 percent. That is, of the five differential-intervention-motivated departments in every ten that "currently" could *not* satisfy CTP's staffing requirements, at least one department might now do so. Given this increase, about six of every ten DI-motivated departments might therefore satisfy those requirements: The five departments that originally could do so and one that originally could not.[21] Use of combined approaches, for example, Strategies 1 *and* 3, might raise the odds to at least 65 percent, again across departments.

We will now turn to the *implementation* dimension.

As suggested by our *30* percent figure for estimate (5), the implementation dimension would probably pose serious difficulties for most organizations; yet, as with the *staff* dimension, certain change strategies may be used to raise the odds. (In discussing implementation, we use the 30 percent rather than the 40 percent figure in order to reflect the independent—that is, the successive—probabilities situation rather than the joint—that is, the simultaneous—probabilities situation described in endnote 18. This is because "successive" centers on *implementation* alone, whereas "simultaneous" combines that and the *staff* dimension.) As with staffing, some aspects of implementation should, however, be

considered virtual givens; for instance, like worker skill, intensive intervention should hardly be reduced. Similarly, few changes should be made regarding individualized diagnosis, detailed staffing and planning, and relatively frequent case review—even within probation. Nevertheless, the situation is different for other aspects of implementation, such as extensive intervention: In many settings, these aspects *may* in fact be substantially changed, thereby raising the odds.

(Before continuing, two additional aspects might be mentioned. As may be inferred from Chapter 15, "long-term contacts" [key factor #3] can be modified somewhat for certain youths, mainly the conflicted. Similarly, slight modifications can be made in the size of "small caseloads" [key factor #1]. Separately and together, these modifications—though important to given departments—would probably produce only slight or perhaps moderate changes in the estimate (5) odds; for instance, they might produce changes from the present 30 percent level to 35 percent or 40 percent, across departments within typical regions or states. That is, of, say, seven DI-motivated departments in every ten that "currently" could *not* satisfy CTP's implementation requirements, approximately one department might now do so. Given this increase, about four of every ten DI-motivated departments might therefore satisfy those requirements: the three departments that originally could do so and one that originally could not. However, since changes in key factor #3, or especially #1, should perhaps be made only as a last resort, the following review and discussion will proceed as if neither such modification were made.)

Since extensive intervention can account for some of the difficulties reflected in the 30 percent estimate—yet can be modified—change strategies relating to this aspect of implementation will now be briefly reviewed.[22] (Local probation will be focused on, though identical considerations would apply to state agencies and perhaps private organizations.) Here, we will deal with neither the *staff* contributors nor certain *departmental* contributors to appropriate or adequate—that is, good quality—implementation. (Specifically, we will assume that with [1] skilled staff plus [2] departmental support/motivation, quality implementation can, but not necessarily will, be achieved. More precisely, if [3] *other* departmental conditions—namely, factors and limitations mentioned below—do not interfere, items [1] and [2] can then make it possible for a program to adequately implement such elements as schooling, counseling, recreation/socializing, and so on.[23] In this respect, items [1] and [2] would be necessary but not sufficient conditions or contributors.) Instead, we will focus on situations in which *practical, resource-centered, and/or policy-based* factors or limitations that are currently beyond the department's control would probably prevent that organization's potential or actual CTP program from implementing the above elements (schooling, etc.) consistently, adequately, or at all. (These factors or limitations are the "*other* departmental conditions," that is, item [3], above.) Thus, worker skill and departmental support/motivation will be regarded as givens, and in this sense we will not focus on (1) and (2) above.

Some probation departments may be unable to implement certain elements of extensive intervention that were often used in California's CTP, program elements that were important to many youths. Included, for example, are the accredited school program and various common forms of recreation as well as socializing experience—whether on- or off-site. Regarding on-site activities, the following applies to the *community center* (CC)—the physical structure that, as in the California program, would house a CTP (as implied below, a CTP unit could theoretically be housed in a *non*-CC setting, such as standard administrative offices; this, however, would be far from ideal): *Neither adequate implementation of the above program elements nor even their very presence within the unit need depend on the existence of a CC;* this is aside from the fact that fewer implementation problems would probably arise if a center did exist.[24]

For instance, (1) some departments that *lack* a community center may nevertheless have few implementation problems regarding any or all such elements, for example, recreation or schooling. This relative absence of problems—in fact, the very presence and utilization of those elements in the first place—may be made possible by various "modifications," that is, planned variations from, or adaptations of, the California program. (Modifications—one type of change strategy—are illustrated below.) Similarly, (2) some departments that *have* an adequate CC may nevertheless have numerous and/or sizable implementation problems regarding one or more such elements.[25] This problem-condition may exist (a) whether or not any modifications have occurred, (b) despite the fact that modifications may often *reduce* the frequency and/or extent of difficulties, and (c) aside from the fact that many such planned variations can occur whether or not a community center exists. At any rate, absence of a CC would not, by itself, preclude the adequate implementation of given elements; nor would its presence guarantee smooth sailing. Finally, item (1), above, is independent of the fact that, if a community center did not exist, all or almost all staff should, if possible, still be housed together or at least quite close to each other so that their efforts and resources could be maximally integrated and shared.

Program elements can be modified with regard to form (e.g., physical/structural aspects or setting), content, scope, and focus, without necessarily compromising their quality or destroying their effect. For instance, without a community center, an appropriate and adequately functioning school program could probably be implemented within small and/or convertible offices, areas, or conference rooms located inside or near a probation department. Such places need not be available full-time; however, when used for CTP's school, they should be sufficiently private and quiet. To be sure, once these or other "formal" changes occur, subsequent modifications may—though not necessarily would—arise. For example, given restricted space, one may have to serve fewer youths and/or scale down, flexibly schedule, or perhaps entirely eliminate some or all constituents of a program element, for instance, arts and crafts or lab science components of accredited schooling. (The latter changes, such as reduced scope or shifted emphasis, may instead occur *without* prior physical/structural—or any other—changes; in such cases they would not be "subsequent modifications." This would apply even within a CC.) Yet, even subsequent modifications need not compromise quality or vitiate an activity.

Sometimes, of course, no modifications can occur; specifically, neither the original (California-style) nor a modified program element can be managed or perhaps even attempted. Moreover, when modifications can be and have been made, they may be unsatisfactory. For instance, without substantial space inside the department's main office areas or building, a modified recreation component may be so restricted as to prove virtually useless. Without a dayroom or convertible conference room, a similar restriction and outcome might easily occur with respect to many or most socializing experiences.

On-site opportunities and limitations aside, *off-site* recreation and socializing experiences would not require a community center.[26] Moreover, whether or not a center existed, most departments that *could* implement these supervised, off-site activities/ elements could probably do so without greatly modifying the California approach (Chapter 3), at least substantively. This applies even though many departments—including some just now referred to—may have as much or even more difficulty implementing off-site than on-site activities that are part of any given element. And that, in turn, is aside from the fact that, in many such departments, off-site recreation and socializing activities may be less often available to youths, and/or available to fewer youths, than similarly categorized on-site activities.[27]

At any rate, various program elements may be consistently and adequately implemented in more than one possible setting (on-site or off-site; community center or standard offices) and via more than one approach. More broadly, even if the implementation of given elements is blocked, curtailed, or discouraged within a particular setting or in connection with one approach, other settings and options may be available and satisfactory. By using either this "program-modification strategy," or else the "admission-policy approach" reviewed below, one might raise the estimate-(5) odds from their present 30 percent level to roughly 40 percent or 50 percent. That is, of the hypothetical seven DI-motivated departments in every ten that "currently" could not satisfy CTP's implementation requirements, about one or two might now do so. Given this increase, approximately four or five of every ten DI-motivated departments might therefore satisfy those requirements: the three departments that originally could do so and one or two that originally could not. If key factors #1 and/or #3 were also modified, these implementation odds would be slightly higher.

If a department *cannot* implement these or other elements—whether consistently, ade-quately, or at all, even on a modified basis—the following approach might be used: Together with CTP staff, it could establish an admission policy that gives low priority to youths who not only seem to need one or more such elements, for instance, schooling, but who seem unlikely to respond well to elements that remain. This strategy would not exclude all such individuals; however, as seen below, it would give them less chance than other youths of entering the program.

In this strategy, a youth's "chance" would not be based on the following:

1. risk of future offending, for example, as estimated by an a priori formula established for offenders in general or for serious offenders in particular;[28]
2. general amenability, for instance, estimated responsiveness to community-based—and perhaps non-community-based—programs overall (intensive or not, and regardless of [1] above); and
3. broad offender classification, such as maturity, moral, or conceptual level.

Instead, it would depend on his overall match, as an individual, with the program's specific resources, such as its available and adequately implemented (AAI) program elements. (Here, "match" means probable responsiveness.) More specifically, for each individual, (a) the degree of *match with* and (b) the apparent *importance of* the AAI elements would be assessed in conjunction with those (at least the "importance" dimension) of other elements— elements that are unavailable or inadequately implemented (UII).[29]

(Overall match, that is, the final, joint assessment, need not involve fine distinctions; four or five broad categories would suffice. Thus, for example, a lower match or priority might ordinarily be given to youths for whom two rather than one important elements are unavailable—though elements that are *available* would also be assessed and would influence the outcome. ["Joint" means that AAI and UII elements would be evaluated together. "Importance" would depend on the youth as an individual.] The resulting, final judgment or prioritization could range—across youths— from very low to very high, and it would reflect more than number counts alone, especially regarding "importance.")

(Individuals who receive a low priority for the community-based program might still be acceptable for CTP if, for instance, that program's operations include an institutional or related residential component—one that has what the youths seem to need. [See CTP Phase 3.] Youths who are not acceptable for CTP may be placed on alternative, yet relatively intensive and/or extensive—or otherwise specialized—caseloads. If the latter are unavailable and still *other* local alternatives seem unavailable or inappropriate, the youths might be sent to the next step in the justice system, perhaps the state agency. This step, or setting, might involve either an institutional or a specialized community-based program.)

As implied, risk-, amenability-, and, to a lesser extent, classification-based approaches would not by themselves highlight the youth's particular interests, limitations, and life circumstances. Nor, in any event, would they directly or substantially relate these youth- and environment-centered factors to the program's specific resources. For these reasons—even the latter alone—a prioritization that might result from such an approach, for example, the risk-based approach, would often differ substantially from one obtained via the present, more individualized strategy. For one thing, the former prioritization—since it would minimally reflect CTP's program-centered factors—might end up the same whether or not all elements were available and adequately implemented, and regardless of which specific elements might be missing.[30] In contrast, the latter prioritization would vary whenever these and the preceding factors, such as youth-centered factors, changed.

Since the present strategy would be a direct response to a situation generated by the absence, and so on, of given elements, the following should be noted:

1. With many youths, few program elements or combinations of elements can fully or adequately substitute for one that is missing, particularly if the latter is important for those youths. For instance, counseling—even combined with recreation and socializing experiences—may seldom substitute for schooling or for out-of-home placement; similarly, schooling and/or recreation may rarely if ever substitute for counseling or for out-of-home placement. Nevertheless, certain types of placement (with or without counseling) or even limit-setting may sometimes substitute for, or reduce the length of, short-term detention—again, depending substantially on the youths as individuals and on their specific situations.

2. For the preponderance of serious offenders, certain elements, such as counseling and limit-setting, seem not only relevant but largely indispensable; as a result, they should always be present in a CTP unit.[31] While this does not mean they should always be in *use* with all such youths, it suggests that a program which lacks one or more such elements will probably function inadequately—assuming it can and will function at all.[32] At any rate, since the elements in question seem particularly important for so many youths, neither the present change strategy nor the related approach mentioned below could effectively deal with their absence. Specifically, if most youths who needed these absent or inadequate elements were excluded in connection with the present or other strategies, very few youths—and very limited operations—would remain.[33]

In a related approach, youths would not simply receive a low/lesser priority yet in some cases enter the program. Instead, *all* individuals who seemed ill-suited to the program for the earlier-mentioned reasons would be excluded.[34] Like the basic approach, this somewhat stricter yet perhaps "cleaner" and operationally simpler strategy would thus reflect a youth/program-elements match; it would not center on risk, amenability, and so on, in the sense described earlier. Also common to both strategies would be the following: (1) A smaller than usual range of youths—that is, range of needs, life-circumstances, and so on—would be accepted into CTP;[35] (2) unless several program elements remained available, extensive intervention, in more than the two- or even three-element sense, might not occur for most accepted youths. Differences between these strategies would include the fact that, in the present approach, various "justice" and "differential sentencing/assignment" issues mentioned in Appendix 34 might arise even though youths would not be excluded largely on the basis of personal/interpersonal characteristics per se.[36] If present, this situation might offset any advantages associated with the earlier-mentioned relative simplicity.

The Modified Odds

By using various staff- and implementation-centered change strategies described thus far, for example, one of each, the number of differential-intervention-motivated probation departments that could probably operate a qualitatively acceptable, modified or unmodified CTP program might well increase from the original one in five to about one in every four or possibly every three. More specifically, whereas the original 20 percent of those departments could continue to operate an unmodified or slightly modified program (or, if they wished, a substantially modified one), an additional 5 percent to 15 percent of those departments might now at least operate a modified one. (The odds might be slightly higher if key factors #1 and #3 were themselves modified.) This again assumes that estimates (1) through (3) were 100 percent each. However, if just estimate (3)—yet therefore estimate (2)—were 100 percent, no more than about one DI-motivated department in seven within typical regions or states would be a good prospect for operating a CTP, modified or not.[37] This is because community acceptance, as reflected in estimate (1), might still occur only about half the time—use of various change strategies notwithstanding. (In general, higher odds would apply to departments that operated several area offices, one or more of which is relatively large. Lower odds would apply to those with one or two offices only, each relatively small.)

As indicated, these modified odds focus on DI-motivated departments (DMDs) that have CTP-appropriate supervisors and workers and can provide or arrange any necessary training. They take account not just of the change strategies already mentioned but of implicit factors such as the following:[38] (1) Due to practical reasons, not legal or philosophical ones, many DMDs may not be in a position to shift or transfer appropriate staff (or enough of them) from their present assignments to a proposed CTP-type program. This situation may be either transitory or fairly long-standing. In either case it may exist even if these departments are already operating specialized programs—or simply individual caseloads—for serious or repeat offenders, and even if most of the respective department's CTP-appropriate staff are already assigned to those programs/caseloads.[39] (2) Practical constraints notwithstanding (or if they and other limiting conditions are sufficiently altered), appropriate staff in DI-motivated departments that do operate special programs or caseloads (these DMDs are called "specialized") may be easier to transfer to a proposed CTP operation than staff in non- or slightly specialized DMDs. Somewhat related is the fact that, other things being equal, appropriate staff may be more likely to exist within the former departments in the first place; theoretically, more such individuals would therefore be available for transfer.

Relatively large departments would often be in a better position to make these staff switches than much smaller ones. This might reflect, not just their often greater quantity of appropriate staff and related resources, but increased organizational flexibility and perhaps greater ability to handle "growth pains," errors, external pressures, and so on. Though such departments might also be more likely than others to operate a specialized program/caseload(s) in the first place, the preceding would apply whether or not they actually did. Staff transfers from one assignment to another might be easier to make within many *state-level* agencies (e.g., the YA) than within many or most probation departments, that is, without adversely affecting everyday operations. The main reasons are: (a) state-agency caseloads usually contain a larger percentage of serious offenders than those of probation; (b) state agencies would often have a higher CTP-appropriate staff-to-ward ratio than probation departments; and (c) daily operations are *already* more likely to center on serious offenders, in most state agencies.

(In the following, "program" and "unit" are used in an organizational sense and are synonymous. Focus is on program-level changes, though parallel approaches would perhaps apply to specialized individual caseloads.)

To shift CTP-appropriate staff within a specialized DMD, two main approaches, that is, alternatives, might be used. In the first, a new type of unit—a DI-specialized program—would in effect *replace* the department's already existing specialized program(s). Specifically, the latter program(s) would be largely or entirely converted to a CTP operation; during this process many or most of its CTP-appropriate staff might be shifted directly into a CTP role. In the second approach, a new type of unit—in fact, a new organizational entity—would be added to the department *without* replacing any currently existing, special program(s). To obtain staff for this added unit (namely, CTP) without hiring new departmental personnel, the DMD's currently existing special program(s)—CESP(s)—might be modified so that some of its CTP-appropriate staff could be shifted to the CTP unit. During this transfer the CESP's or CESPs' newly vacant positions—those which, for example, might now involve differently focused and/or somewhat larger or even less time-consuming caseloads—might be filled by selected staff from standard caseloads. To accommodate the *latter* shift and again maintain appropriate operations, those or other standard caseloads might be reorganized on a differential workload-assignment basis, for instance, a higher- (but rarely "high" in an absolute sense), middle-, and lower-risk and/or need basis.

Such approaches, and the earlier-mentioned odds, are possible without any resource sharing at the interdepartmental level, such as between probation departments in two or three adjacent counties or other regions. However, if sharing were to occur—with respect to staff, program components, and/or training—the odds in question might be further modified, that is, improved. For reasons implied earlier, many state agencies, such as the Youth Authority, might comprise an added resource for local probation departments, for example, in connection with staff transfers or specialized training. Conversely, local probation might sometimes assist state agencies, for instance, regarding selected program components.

Subunits and Specialized Individual Caseloads

Sharing—but not shifting—aside, still other odds might be involved if one focused, not on creating an entire ("full-sized") CTP program, but on establishing either a "*subunit*" or CTP-type ("specialized") *individual caseloads* only. For instance, slightly improved odds might exist if a probation department wished to create, not a full-sized program, for example, five to seven caseloads, but a reduced operation, for example, three or four. Compared to a full-sized program, a reduced operation would involve (1) a somewhat smaller number of youth types, (2) an identical number but narrower range of youth types, or (3) combinations of (1) and (2)—for example, a smaller number and narrower range. Accordingly, a smaller number and/or narrower range of matched staff would be needed for the reduced operation.

Though the latter program might constitute a departmental *subunit,* it could, like a full-sized program, embody CTP's key principles, utilize qualitatively adequate components, be operationally integrated across all caseloads, maintain a distinct identity, and enjoy "equal status" within the department. In so doing, it could probably serve a sizable range of serious offenders on a highly individualized, intensive, and perhaps adequately extensive basis, even if it lacked a community center and possibly one or two additional components for its exclusive or even shared use. Since this subunit would contain fewer caseloads than a full-sized program, the staff transfers that might help create it would—collectively—be easier to implement than in the larger program, and its casework supervisor could be partly shared with other units or caseloads. To help achieve a youth/program-components match and thereby promote extensive intervention, the admission-policy modification described earlier might be used.

(With respect to caseloads, the subunit approach is structurally identical to the reduced-caseload approach, that is, Strategy 3, as briefly described earlier. That description related to a broader discussion of the possible impact, on the "odds," of having to *locate,* that is, find, fewer appropriate workers for a reduced caseload unit than for a full-sized unit. The present review adds to that discussion the possible impact of having to *transfer* fewer workers into a reduced caseload unit once the appropriate individuals have been found, for example, found elsewhere within the department. As such, it introduces a further possible—albeit slight—impact on the odds. Since the "location" impact has been reflected in the earlier-mentioned odds, it is only this further—"transfer"—impact that is considered in the following modified odds.)

By adding such differential treatment subunits to the several approaches described thus far, at least one such approach or alternative—that is, one or more unmodified programs, modified programs, or both—might be feasible for an estimated 35 percent to 40 percent of all DI-motivated departments whose communities would accept or tolerate in-lieu efforts. The odds might be slightly higher for relatively large departments, especially those most likely to have not just a larger than average number of field offices (e.g., one per "standard" city, within an unusually extended yet not overly populated county) but heavier than average *concentrations* of serious offenders and appropriate staff. The 35 percent to 40 percent odds might also apply if those or other probation departments wished to establish not even a differential treatment subunit per se but one or two *specialized individual caseloads* for, say, three or four relatively common youth types (e.g., one caseload for either conflicted youths, passive-conformists, or both, and another caseload for power-oriented youths.) In fact, for many departments, especially the smaller and/or less concentrated, such caseloads might be easier to establish and maintain than differential treatment subunits or full-sized units. (Though specialized individual caseloads might be *easier* to establish in such departments, the latter units—especially differential treatment subunits—might still be feasible; this would apply to larger and/or more concentrated departments as well.)

(The preceding odds would probably show a modest increase if the differential treatment subunits and individual caseloads were organized around a less complex classification system than that described thus far; in this regard, see below. Except for functions such as diagnosis, treatment planning, and case assignment, the one or two individual caseloads in question need not be operationally integrated with each other to the degree that would exist in full-sized units and even differential treatment subunits. Nevertheless, a part-time supervisor could almost always be invaluable with respect to these specialized caseloads, that is, even aside from operational integration.)

Like full-sized units and differential treatment subunits, specialized individual caseloads could embody all or almost all the key factors reviewed in Chapter 15. However, *extensive intervention* would probably be curtailed due to various unavailable program components; this, at least, might occur fairly often, especially in small departments.[40] Since the earlier-mentioned modification might not entirely relieve this problem, the limitation in question would doubtlessly reduce the scope or relevance of the individual-caseloads approach. Still, this approach could have considerable impact on many youths.

A few last comments regarding modified odds. Considerable staff skill is needed to appropriately use a complex youth classification system—unmodified I-level, or other. Together with its related implementation needs, training included, this accounts for some of the difficulties reflected in unmodified estimates (4) and (5). If a less complex system were used, fewer skills would be needed, certainly fewer classification skills on the supervisor's part. As a result, if the original classification skills were the overriding factor involved in the present difficulties, a less complex system could improve—perhaps substantially improve—the unmodified odds.

However, *added* factors play a major role; specifically, estimates (4) and (5) reflect factors other than those which center on classification alone. Prominent among these factors are interpretive and integrative skills that may be used subsequent to, or at any rate largely independent of, classification efforts per se. These skills are used, for instance, not just to determine a youth's particular *classification* (e.g., passive-conformist)—more specifically, to process information which may result in either that or some other categorization. Instead, they are often applied to information—for example, regarding the youth's interests, achievements, limitations, and life situation—which is essential for *intervention planning*.[41] (Though this information seldom if ever provides a crucial distinction between given classifications, for instance, between passive-conformist and power-oriented, it sometimes provides a major clue; in this sense it may, as indicated below, be utilized for classification.) Such planning, that is, specific and concrete planning, is needed irrespective of the youth's particular classification; moreover, it is needed, and the staff skills in question must therefore be applied, whether or not a classification system is used.[42] This situation exists despite the fact that considerable information which is utilized for classification is also—and appropriately—used for planning and decision-making. (Appendix 35 might be reviewed before continuing. It outlines selected characteristics of complex and simplified classification systems, and it suggests various relationships between these characteristics, intervention planning, and needed staff skills.)

Thus, by simplifying one's classification system (CS) one neither eliminates nor necessarily reduces the need for substantial interpretive and integrative skills, since these factors are still required for other immediate tasks. As suggested, it is these skills which, for example, are applied by a staffing team to information that is needed in order to develop detailed, realistic plans. Such planning-centered information goes beyond, or at least often differs from, that which is needed for classification alone. These facts would remain unchanged whether the former information played a large or a small role in determining given youths' classifications, or, for that matter, whether it was even *sought* in connection with the classification system.[43] For such reasons, and since careful planning remains a difficult task regardless of one's CS, the level of staff skill that is needed to interpret and integrate this planning-centered information (whether in itself or together with classification-centered data) would be essentially independent of any simplifications in one's CS. That level or range, we believe, hardly differs from one that is needed in order to utilize a complex CS—as, for example, unmodified I-level.

The following thus seems likely. Even if various classification-relevant dimensions were eliminated or somehow distilled from a complex classification system in order to reduce its complexity, those dimensions (e.g., psychological characteristics such as apathy/uninvolvement, confusion/uncertainty, and defiance/indifference) could still be assessed and utilized for *intervention planning* if staff considered them important. More specifically, whatever role they might be given within a simplified or otherwise *modified* CS—in fact, even if they had no role—these dimensions could still be tapped and appropriately used for planning and decision-making by supervisors and/or other staff who were sufficiently skilled to interpret and integrate them. Nevertheless, detailed and specific planning would continue to depend (1) neither primarily nor exclusively on those or other classification-centered data, but, rather, (2) at least as much on intervention-centered information such as the youth's interests, his life situation, and so on.

In sum, the following would apply whether, or however, those eliminated or modified dimensions, such as psychological characteristics, were used. To maintain a quality CTP operation—modified or not, full-sized or subunit—the level of staff skill would have to remain unchanged from that already described, even if one utilized a less complex classification system than, say, that used in California's CTP. This stability, by itself, would tend to leave the earlier-mentioned odds unchanged. However, although required *staff skills* would remain unchanged, use of the less complex classification system could simplify various program or subunit *operations* and could reduce given training needs; yet even then, this CS would neither obviate nor reduce the preponderance of tasks. As a result, a simplified classification system would—on balance, and in most organizations—probably have only modest impact on the odds in question. In some organizations, its impact might, of course, be large. In this regard its potential value, like that of other possible modifications, should not be overlooked.

Summary and Conclusions
CTP's Basic Operation

Despite some difficulties, the Youth Authority's community-based, differential intervention program was definitely feasible during 1961–1969. This Phase 1 and 2 program—CTP's "basic" operation or approach—was also feasible during 1969–1973 (Phase 3), though it was then coupled with an institution-based component that the YA (parent agency) eventually rejected. During these 12 years, CTP's operation increased in size. Yet the program retained its original principles and most of its early components, and its effects on most youth groups seemed to stem from largely the same factors, that is, the key factors (Chapter 15), throughout.

During the program's first three or four years, CTP's originally formulated intervention strategies (Grant, 1961c) rapidly underwent much fleshing-out, expansion, and/or refinement with respect to each youth type and youth group. By the end of that period, those strategies, together with the description of the youth's characteristics and dynamics, had undergone various specific improvements and/or corrections as well. From the early years of Phase 2 until all operations ended (1973), CTP's thus-refined, improved, and reality-tested intervention strategies—those involving its *community-based* operation—remained much the same in broad outline; with a few notable exceptions they were essentially unchanged in most major, specific respects as well.[44] This, of course, is (1) aside from the *institution-based* component that was added in 1969 for purposes of Phase 3, and (2) apart from several modifications that were made during the latter part of Phase 2 in order to better address particular needs and circumstances of most CTP youths in San Francisco's highly urbanized setting.

CTP's basic operation was manageable in urban and less urban settings, during times of moderate and major social unrest. Throughout all phases, its community-based and differential intervention dimensions were inextricably linked. Both dimensions, certainly the latter, provided ongoing and occasionally major challenges; yet neither one created or experienced insolvable problems or long-standing, severe strains in the following areas (the classification component of differential intervention is considered separately, below):

1. relations with outside agencies/institutions (e.g., law enforcement, probation, schools, local- and state-level departments);
2. the parent agency, especially top and middle management's immediate practical interests (e.g., public protection, political support, positive public image, fiscal responsibility);
3. staff recruitment and hiring;
4. staff development and unit functioning;
5. casework supervision and overall program administration;
6. case processing and maintenance;
7. worker/youth and worker/other (e.g., family, employers) interactions; and,
8. operational aspects (e.g., auxiliary staff, office location, community relations).

More specifically, differential intervention's heavy emphasis on individualization occasionally produced moderate to major, yet generally short-lived, disagreements or other problems in areas 1 and 2, mainly with law enforcement, probation, and middle management; however, much more often, problems within these areas were minor, as were those in 4 and 5. Separate from DI (despite its operational links), the community-based dimension itself occasionally created moderate problems in area 1 and minor difficulties in 2, 5, 7, and 8. (The one

major problem—mentioned next—occurred in area 2, during Phase 3.)

In CTP, differential intervention was linked with a youth-classification system that was very valuable during all phases and that comprised one of the program's main pillars. However, because of its complexity and content—largely in combination—this system sometimes proved difficult in area 2 and, to a lesser extent, 4. The first difficulty mainly centered on ethnic implications of youth classification and especially misclassification; the second involved staff training. Both difficulties emerged within the Youth Authority only after several years; and, though neither centered on *CTP's* daily operations, they each eventually influenced that program's fate and usage within the agency:

The area-2 issue, for example, as reflected in living unit assignment problems (Chapter 17), occurred within YA institutions, not in CTP or other special parole units. The area-4 issue was far less a problem within CTP than for the YA overall: The latter's problem stemmed from its interest—starting around 1966 and rapidly increasing over the next few years—in easily and economically producing and maintaining a cadre of trained diagnosticians and lead treatment staff large enough for its numerous institutions and perhaps parole offices. Nevertheless, because these difficulties were not fully resolved, and thus remained agency-level issues in themselves, and because they were viewed by agency administrators in the context of various state-, national-, and corrections-wide pressures and issues (political, ideological, etc.), they substantially affected the Youth Authority's view of CTP itself, essentially during Phase 3. In general, they helped define and stereotype the *overall* operation, that is, all components combined, as potentially troublesome (e.g., politically) and as largely impractical with respect to any widespread application (let alone detailed replication) within the *agency*.

Other difficulties—specific to the Phase 3 dorm operation but unrelated to the area-2 and area-4 issues—reinforced the "potentially troublesome" view. As to "widespread impracticality," this did not mean that CTP's Phase 1 and 2 operations were, for instance, considered unwieldy. More broadly, YA administrators regarded the "impracticality" view as valid in its own right, that is, at the agency level, even though they also believed

CTP's then-current community-based operation—the Sacramento unit—was, like the Phase 1 and 2 programs, apparently feasible in itself, that is, as a *single,* specialized unit. (Here, as elsewhere, "program," "operation," and "unit" are interchangeable.)

CTP's operational complexity extended well beyond its classification system alone; it was expressed in connection with intensive and extensive intervention as well. Despite this complexity and the preceding problems, CTP's basic, that is, community-centered, operation usually functioned smoothly for months and years at a time and was widely accepted within and outside the agency. This applied especially, but not only, in areas 3 through 8. Staff and others generally assumed that difficulties or issues would soon be resolved and that, in any event, essential operations would remain on course; experience almost always proved them right. All in all, the basic program was considered "upbeat" and appropriate, and from early in Phase 1 until well into Phase 3 its survival was never in question.

Though several years were required, the parent agency largely came to accept CTP's brand of complexity, including the program's often-"different" or nontraditional requests and expectations. From the start, program staff believed—and most agency administrators eventually recognized—that CTP's complexity was often integral to *differential* intervention in the community, not just, or not so much, to community-based intervention per se. In this regard, staff were equally committed to *both* aspects of intervention; moreover, during their ongoing interactions with youths, for instance, when implementing extensive intervention, they were specifically focused on the former aspect (DI). In contrast, most administrators—in line with their agency-level, area-2 interests—were mainly concerned with the community-based feature, and they wished that relatively moderate individualization would suffice. At any rate, (1) throughout Phases 1 and 2, and (2) despite not only this difference in perspective but the program's complexity itself, most administrators regarded CTP as neither unwieldy, potentially troublesome (politically), nor minimally relevant to the agency. With few exceptions they considered it sufficiently productive, at an acceptable "price."

The Phase 3 ("dorm") operation was a different story. Though proving effective with its main target group, this institution-based effort was never quite accepted by the parent agency; ultimately, it collapsed, but probably need not have done so. Political, ideological, and other pressures and crosscurrents notwithstanding, the dorm operation could probably have been maintained if specific program and procedural modifications had been made. These, of course, would have had to occur prior to the events that triggered its demise.

Though *CTP's* particular institution-based effort finally proved unmanageable to its parent agency under the combination of external (political, etc.) and staff-generated conditions that existed, a modified approach might still be feasible and effective for the types of youths who were focused on—individuals who probably should not be returned directly to the community. Nevertheless, any such approach would perhaps have a sizable chance of success only if implemented by skilled and motivated staff—ones who, collectively, are quite experienced with community-based and institutional programs. This reflects not just the difficulty of working with the present youths regardless of setting but the fact that many, possibly most, of the above-mentioned pressures and crosscurrents are essentially as strong and perhaps as widespread within the United States today as they were in California during the early 1970s. At any rate, even with excellent staff and strong agency support, a successful modified (institution-based) approach would require, in a sense, a sophisticated balancing act.

We now return to the basic *community-centered* program.

Feasibility Today
Though CTP's basic program was feasible within the Youth Authority during the 1960s and early 1970s, the important question now is: How feasible would this or similar—that is, unmodified or modified—programs be today, outside the YA?

In the United States today (and this also applies since the mid-1980s), a full-scale, essentially unmodified CTP program would be difficult for most local and state agencies to establish, even if community acceptance existed. The main difficulties would be, first, obtaining the skilled and motivated staff needed to implement CTP's core features (1) through

(3), and, second, obtaining material resources needed to implement feature (3). These core features are: (1) a particularly careful diagnosis or highly individualized understanding of the youth and his situation; (2) a relevant, detailed, and integrated treatment/control (intervention) plan; (3) implementation of that plan in terms of CTP's key factors, especially *individualized, flexible programming* and *intensive and/or extensive contacts* within a small caseload setting. The main challenge in feature (3) would be extensive contacts (extensive intervention).

Because of such difficulties, no more than an estimated one probation department in five would be well-positioned to adequately operate the above-mentioned program for serious offenders; though relatively low, this ratio is not insignificant. Again, this estimate assumes (1) community receptivity to in-lieu approaches and, partly based on that stance, (2) departmental willingness and felt-ability to seriously explore, not just any community-based approach (however promising), but a CTP-type differential intervention approach in particular. An estimated 50 percent of all cities/communities that currently lack either approach would ordinarily accept or tolerate them under conditions mentioned earlier. (This rough estimate, and the one that involves the percentage of probation departments—ones located in receptive settings—which would be interested in seriously exploring a CTP-type differential intervention approach, is based on the author's several decades of observing the American and correctional scenes—their respective trends, variations, and stabilities alike.)

The one-in-five odds refers to all juvenile probation departments combined. Like those that follow, it would probably be somewhat better (1) for relatively large departments, such as those that serve sizable—especially, concentrated—youth populations, (2) for departments that already operate a specialized program or caseloads, (3) in many *state* correctional agencies, most of whose clients have previously been on probation and are already serious offenders, or (4) if relevant staff and/or material resources could be shared across counties and/or between given counties and the state.[45] Presently, item (4) is rare and is reflected in neither the preceding nor the following odds.

As indicated, the odds apply to full-scale, essentially unmodified programs. However, by making certain modifications the number of local and state agencies that might adequately implement a CTP approach could be increased. Major possibilities are as follows (note that despite these program modifications such processes and products as individualized diagnosis, detailed staffing and planning, intensive intervention, and relatively frequent case reviews should remain essentially unchanged, since they directly or indirectly involve CTP's core features):

A. The chances of obtaining adequate *staff* could be somewhat increased by reducing (1) the range (types) of matched workers that are required, (2) the range of youths that are served, or (3) the number of caseloads within a given program. To utilize any such strategy yet maintain needed quality, such as core feature (3), the level of staff skill/motivation should remain unchanged or virtually unchanged. Except for the number-of-caseloads strategy, these and the following modifications could—but need not—occur within a full-sized program.

B. Chances of satisfying CTP's *implementation* requirements could likewise be raised by modifying (1) the form, content, scope, or focus of program elements such as schooling, recreation, and so on, and (2) admission policies involving the match or lack of match between major youth needs and available program elements. If carefully planned, the first modification could probably be made without compromising or vitiating the elements involved; in addition, most such changes could be moderate. At any rate, *if* necessary or desired, many agencies could probably develop creative modifications of, or major and promising alternatives to, the "standard" elements described thus far; also, whether creative or relatively predictable and whether major or perhaps moderate, many such changes could probably be made without a community center. The second modification, changes in admission policies, might be made only if given program elements are entirely unavailable or can be neither adequately implemented nor modified.

Use of such strategies and modifications, particularly two or more at a time, could reduce the program's scope of relevance at least moderately. Most particularly, it could, but need not, involve a narrower range and/or smaller number of youths. Nevertheless, by sacrificing some scope, a CTP approach could become feasible for many departments and agencies to whom it might otherwise be un-reachable; for instance, the number of pro-bation departments that could operate a broadly relevant CTP program would per-haps increase from the previous one in five to roughly one in three or four. (By adding other modifications, these odds might again be im-proved, but only slightly.) As before, such odds would probably be better for typical state agencies than typical probation depart-ments, mainly because of the former's—in our view—higher percentage of CTP-appropriate staff, greater access to needed material resources, and, perhaps, greater or-ganizational flexibility.

By using a less complex classification sys-tem than that employed in California's CTP (even though that system served its treatment function very well), various program opera-tions could be simplified and training needs reduced. Though these changes could be im-portant to numerous agencies, they would, in themselves, seldom be large or broad;[46] nor would they obviate or automatically reduce most other operational issues, for example, those involving extensive intervention. In addi-tion, since (1) activities such as treatment/control planning, worker/youth interactions, and casework supervision would require no fewer skills than those needed for complex classification—moreover, would require some of the same skills—and since (2) treatment/control planning, and so on, remain difficult tasks regardless of one's classification system, high-quality staff would still have to be found. On balance, then, the use of a less complex or even a relatively simple classification system would, directly and indirectly, probably have only modest impact on *overall* feasibility in most departments and agencies; yet it would probably make a critical difference in some. This assessment applies whether or not the preceding strategies and modifications are used and independently of the fact that, given skilled staff, CTP's core features could proba-bly be implemented without any formal youth classification. ("Complex classification system" does not refer to the nine-category, I-level sys-tem alone.)

Finally, some departments and agencies that could establish neither a full-sized (five-to seven-youth caseload) nor a reduced (three-to four-youth caseload) CTP program might nevertheless operate one or two CTP-based individual caseloads that would embody core features (1) through (3). This might often be true of large-sized, not just moderate- and small-sized, organizations. Though such case-loads would not constitute a CTP *program,* they would reflect, and might substantially ex-tend, the differential intervention—and indi-vidualized intervention—approach.

Community Receptivity
We have estimated that about 50 percent of all cities/communities (c/c's) that currently lack an in-lieu approach—and this is the vast majority of c/c's—would ordinarily support them. Given the following, this suggests that many opportunities may exist for changing commu-nities' attitudes and policies, and that such changes—by increasing the pool of depart-ments that might seriously explore a *DI* in-lieu approach—might be no less influential than some of the above *modifications,* with respect to increasing the number of departments that could operate a differential intervention pro-gram. (Moreover, well-conceived *differential* or individualized approaches might, by them-selves, help make *community*-based program-ming itself more acceptable to various communities and departments.)

1. Constituency-building efforts by large probation departments and other correc-tional agencies indicate that community attitudes and policies regarding in-lieu programs for serious offenders can be significantly and sometimes dramatically changed within several months (Cohen and Conklin, 1985). More specifically, they indicate that focused efforts by cor-rectional personnel can generate consid-erable active support by numerous community leaders and ordinary citizens, and that these leaders/citizens, especially collectively, can then affect sizable changes in county policies and priorities.[47] Similar processes may apply to state-level agencies (American Correctional Association, 1981; Center and Cutlip, 1978; Haller and Mullany, 1988; Harlow and Nelson, 1982; McDowell, 1984).

To be sure, some communities may have relatively few correctional and other personnel who are, or feel, in a position to make such efforts or who support in-lieu approaches in the first place. Such factors are reflected in the following estimate, as is the fact that, for various additional reasons, many communities cannot or will not support in-lieu approaches: If, say, constituency building or other public relations efforts were to change the attitudes and policies of about one-fourth to one-third of the presumably nonreceptive 50 percent of cities/communities, the pool of departments that might seriously explore a differential intervention approach would substantially increase. Specifically, for every 100 DI-motivated departments that would exist prior to any such change, an estimated 130 would now be found.[48]

2. Given this larger pool, or base, more departments could implement a differential intervention approach than before, even if the next-mentioned percentages remained constant. For instance, our preceding review suggested that modifications of the "standard" CTP approach might, when combined in various ways, raise the feasibility odds for DI approaches from a 20 percent figure to about 40 percent, that is, from 20 out of every 100 DI-motivated departments to 40 such departments.[49] (One combination, for example, might involve Strategies 1, 3, and various admission-policy changes.) However, by using the new base of *130* while again applying the "20 percent . . . to . . . 40 percent" figures, the number of departments for which a differential intervention approach might be feasible would be approximately 26 and 52 for the pre- and post-modification conditions, respectively. These would not be inconsequential changes from the figures of 20 and 40. Though the preceding estimates are very rough, the principles involved seem valid and could also apply to state agencies, collectively.

Related points: (1) For departments that might wish to explore *non*-DI rather than DI approaches, the newly available community support could again result in changes (increases)—in this case, changes with respect to non-DI approaches. (2) Given community support, whether preexisting or newly available, these or other departments may become receptive or more receptive to a *DI* approach after directly experiencing success with a non-DI approach. (3) Alternatively, such receptivity may develop after the latter departments have observed a nearby or similar department's DI or non-DI operation; this would also apply to departments that are presently uninterested in any community-based approach.

Privately Operated Programs
Regarding privately operated CTP programs, two main models should be noted. In Model 1 all program staff would be private, that is, non-state or noncounty, employees. In Model 2, the casework supervisor would be a justice system, that is, state (parole) or county (probation), employee, and all remaining staff would be private employees. In both models, staff and their employers would be completely responsible for all major operations: (1) staff hiring, matching, case assignment, supervision, and so on; (2) diagnosis, intervention planning, implementation of all plans; (3) establishment of, or at least operation of, most program components and facilities, for example, school and recreation, but not necessarily out-of-home placement and almost certainly neither short- nor longer-term detention. The possible and likely advantages and disadvantages of such programs are discussed in Appendix 36. The results and main implications of that discussion are now summarized:

All in all, it seems unlikely that the possible or even probable advantages of private programs would often outweigh those of justice system programs, or, stated differently, would often compensate enough for the relative disadvantages. In fact, under most conditions, the justice system might just as well hire all staff candidates itself and assume full as well as direct responsibility for all operations, legal functions, and contracting. The reasons for this are twofold: This approach would probably produce fewer substantial problems, such as legal problems, and considerably fewer "hassles," than if the state or county tried to support, intercede for, negotiate with, monitor, and otherwise help establish and maintain an adequate/appropriate Model 1 or 2 program. In addition, a justice system operation might involve no more and quite possibly somewhat less expense.

Despite the above, circumstances doubtlessly exist in which private-agency approaches would be practical and appropriate, and might well be tried. At any rate, if at all possible, a potential source agency (i.e., the private agency's *client* source) should itself operate a CTP or a closely related program before encouraging or allowing a private agency to do so under its auspices. (For further discussion see Mullen, 1985; Robbins, 1986.)

Conclusion

Differential intervention in the community is complex and challenging. To achieve results similar to those in California, DI programs would require excellent and motivated staff, considerable material resources especially if a wide range of youths were involved, and strong agency support. Such programs would remain complex even if no formal youth-classification system were used, and, *if* used, even if it were simple. (Here, we will use the term "differential intervention" with special emphasis on its "carefully individualized" aspect. This aspect goes beyond differing interventions—approaches or interventions—that are based on differing classifications alone or primarily.)

Though hard to implement, differential intervention programs would be feasible within the United States today, either unmodified relative to California's CTP or, more often, in modified form. However, because of their relatively heavy staff requirements and material-resource requirements, these programs, though feasible, probably could not be implemented in *most* local probation departments within the near future; their prospects might be somewhat better at the state-agency level. This assessment applies not simply to all departments and agencies, that is, to every single one, but to those that would be interested in DI approaches in particular and that would have enough community support for an in-lieu effort (DI or non-DI) in the first place. More specifically, the situation is as follows.

First, in-lieu approaches for serious offenders would ordinarily be supported by perhaps no more than 50 percent of all cities/communities that, for whatever reasons, currently lack them (this being the vast majority). This figure could probably be raised some-what by various means. Second, in those communities which would be supportive, many probation departments that would be interested in exploring an in-lieu approach and that would feel able to seriously do so might still not wish to use *differential* intervention. Instead, they might prefer or feel able to use a non-DI approach, that is, essentially the same method, or very few methods, with all youths. Finally, of those departments that *would* be interested in DI, an estimated 20 percent could adequately operate a full-scale program that might closely resemble California's CTP, that is, operate an essentially unmodified program. Through various strategies and modifications, such as program changes, this estimate might be approximately doubled. Whereas these estimates (odds) apply to small, medium, and large probation departments combined, somewhat better odds would probably apply to state-level agencies, at least to most relatively large organizations. Whether at the local or state level, the latter organizations are more likely to have, obtain, and/or be able to deploy the staff and material resources that are needed to implement DI's core features in either an unmodified or modified program.

(Non-DI programs would be easier to implement than their differential counterparts, since the former would have, on average, fewer and less difficult staff-and-resource requirements and would be operationally simpler. However, though "easier," they would not be easy. Also, whether such programs would produce results similar to those in DI programs is unknown, and in our view unlikely.)

At any rate, with community support plus departmental interest in differential intervention, today's chances of adequately implementing a DI program would probably range from small (20%) to moderate (35% to 40%), depending mainly on whether various modifications were made. These odds, of course, refer to the above departments collectively, not individually. Therefore, though they indicate that *most* such departments could probably implement neither a full-scale nor a reduced-size DI operation (five to seven and three to four caseloads, respectively), they also suggest that *many* could probably do so and that this group would not be insignificant. Those estimates aside, the following would apply to still other departments—and to state-level agencies: Even if they could not implement a full-scale, a reduced-size, or an otherwise modified *program*, these organizations could probably implement key features of DI in the context of *individual caseloads*, for example, one or two specialized caseloads within a given community or field office.[50] Individually and/or collectively, such caseloads could provide relevant intervention for a sizable percentage of serious offenders within given cities or other geographic units.

As implied, with little or no community support the chances of implementing in-lieu approaches would be virtually nil; and as indicated, numerous, cities/communities would probably be nonsupportive. Similarly, with little departmental interest in such approaches or in differential intervention as compared to non-DI, chances would again be essentially zero. Here, too, many instances could probably be found even if *community support* existed or could be developed without undue effort. When these "nonsupport," "disinterest," and "other-interest" factors are considered, it seems clear that—if one includes all departments and agencies combined, not just those interested in DI and supported by their communities—those departments/agencies with adequately implemented DI programs would probably remain a minority even if the preceding estimates were each 100 percent.

Finally, in contrast to the community-based programs mentioned earlier, the institution-centered program that was operated during Phase 3 of California's experiment could—unless radically altered—probably be successfully implemented by very few organizations, that is, even among those which are interested in such an approach and that would have community support. These few, and the staff (collectively) involved, would probably need prior experience not just with institutional programs but with a community-based program such as the above. Especially with such experience, sufficient alterations could be made in the institution-centered program to make it accessible to—do-able by—more than just a handful.

Notes

1. Per a May 1971 policy change, Category B cases were first allowed to enter the Phase 3 experiment at the end of April 1971. The first such individual was assigned to the dorm a month later (Palmer, 1971b).

2. Here, the primary stated concern was not with cleanliness per se—though this factor was not considered trivial—but with the possible outbreak of serious disease. However, as it turned out, no outbreaks of disease ever occurred or were believed to be impending. At any rate, in this context cleanliness meant other than simple orderliness or neatness.

3. Minimization of negative feelings could probably have occurred with respect to the escape and AWOL issues as well, even though these feelings were not as strong in the first place.

4. Though staff felt that much of the youths' misbehavior could probably have been avoided through more careful planning and via above-average levels of supervision, and although YA administrators did not adopt a punitive stance, CTP became "gun shy" after these events. As a result, its staff almost entirely eliminated large-scale, relatively distant, off-dorm trips during the remainder of Phase 3. From an intervention standpoint, this was considered a loss.

5. This inspection, the first in several months, occurred immediately after NRCC personnel notified central-office administrators that certain rooms within Dorm 3 were in "filthy" condition. A number of administrators, including the YA director and the chief of institutions, attended the inspection.

6. The Youth Authority Board had given prior approval for this individual—a Category B youth—to attend public school only, until further notice. When CTP was questioned about the dorm's community-contact (day pass; furlough) and community-release (parole) practices in general, it turned out that staff had ignored or cut corners on the board's specific requirements in connection with at least two other dorm youths, during previous months. In these cases, they had released the individuals to parole one or two days prior to the earliest-allowable date, as specified in the original board order. Basically, staff believed that the slightly early release would benefit those particular youths because of given circumstances. This explanation impressed few if any administrators, especially since a specific board order had been

ignored. (The accused co-conspirator had escaped not from the dorm per se, but while being returned to the dorm from a juvenile court hearing in Sacramento.)

7. Of the several state-agency directors appointed by Governor Reagan's predecessor, only two had not been replaced shortly after Reagan took office; the YA director (Allen Breed—an articulate, well-informed, nationally respected, and generally vigorous leader) was one of them. Nevertheless, in 1973, given (1) California's overall politics, (2) the governor's decision-making style plus his known responsiveness to particular legislators, and (3) the overall scrutiny plus the sometimes-exaggerated accusations to which corrections was subjected, it seemed unlikely that even this director would have been retained had he not agreed to close the dorm.

8. As determined in the original Phase 3 proposal (Palmer, 1969a), the research component of the experiment was to continue through September 1974; this was one year after the originally scheduled data cutoff for all *operational* components and, of course, for intake of new cases. Administration's decision to phase out the latter components did not affect the former, which were funded by NIMH. Phase 3 research, in fact, received support from NIMH beyond 1974, via salary savings.

9. In this context, "managerial ability" would not, however, be especially directed at running a low-risk operation, for instance, maintaining a smooth, quiet program and—at almost all costs—"making no waves." This would apply even if the program were not experimental.

10. This concept of value—immediate, palpable, pragmatic value—might thus be operationalized via a crude, qualitative comparison between *problems handled,* on the one hand, and *problems created* (and anticipated), on the other. In this respect, it would parallel the concept of benefit/cost. The weight that would be given to each identified problem would probably vary through time.

11. "Computer-generated plans" does not refer just to *brief* computer printouts— ones that, for example, might consist of a three- or four-paragraph statement whose content, say, is essentially determined by the individual's I-level/subtype, by some other youth classification, and/or by the youth's response to given questionnaires. Though such a preestablished statement might well highlight several distinguishing factors and in this respect may be relevant and somewhat individualized, it would not, by itself, meet the above- (text) suggested standards. In addition, it could be inadvertently misleading in various respects, by commission and especially omission—for example, in terms of marked incompleteness. (In certain non-CTP contexts, such as large institutions, computer-generated plans may, nevertheless, be a leading alternative—given existing staff resources, time and budget constraints, and so on.) At any rate, even Jesness and Wedge (1983a, 1984)—leading advocates, in the 1980s, of computer-generated plans based on I-level subtype classifications— cautioned that "although knowledge of subtype can alert the clinician to important individual differences among delinquents, information about subtype alone is not sufficient for most assessment needs. . . . [It is not] an adequate substitute for more intimate knowledge of the client gleaned from interviews, behavioral ratings, and case history reports" (1984, p. 1009).

12. Under some conditions, auxiliary staff, such as college students, might be supervised by CTP's teacher.

13. One or more on-site researchers were also present in most centers.

14. Most such criticisms—certainly the harshest—focused on institutional treatment or treatment/control.

15. The latter factor is called "explicit, detailed guidelines." (See Chapter 15.)

16. As discussed in Chapter 19, a highly individualized diagnosis can be achieved— especially by a skilled diagnostician— whether or not a classification-based point of departure is used. This would apply to the individualization involved in a relevant, detailed, treatment/control plan as well. (It might be noted that although a diagnosis and treatment plan may each be carefully individualized, the intervention itself may be somewhat or even considerably less so. The latter

situation, for example, can reflect operational and/or resource-related constraints—conditions that may, themselves, exist independently of whether a classification system is used in connection with the diagnosis and treatment plan.)

17. Potential CTP units in these departments (collectively) need not all contain the full range and/or the same number of youths that were present at any given time in California's program. As a result, the type and number of *workers* in some or many such units may themselves differ from those in that program.

18. Like that which immediately precedes it, the estimate of 30 percent refers to departments that were more interested in a CTP-type DI program than in some other community-based approach; as indicated, the former are called DI-motivated departments. Since those DI-motivated departments which could *also* meet CTP's staffing requirements are somewhat different than ones that are simply DI-motivated, our estimate would be higher than 30 percent for those which met such requirements; it might, for example, reach at least 40 percent. (Again, these estimates are only "rough.") Thus, the 50 percent and 30 percent figures shown in the text, for estimates (4) and (5), respectively, apply to DI-motivated departments *simultaneously* (jointly), not successively; therefore, our estimated joint probability that such departments could meet not only the staffing but the implementation requirements is approximately 0.20 (i.e., *0.50 × 0.40*) rather than 0.15 (i.e., *0.50 × 0.30*). Finally, since adequate implementation requires appropriate staff, all departments that meet the implementation requirements would have already met those for staff.

19. Like Strategies 2 and 3, this approach would apply not just to youth groups but to individual youth types.

20. In the Strategy 1 example, though an unmatched worker would be obtained, he would have to be adequate to the task and in this sense sufficiently skilled.

21. This change would, in turn, increase our estimated *joint* probability that DI-motivated departments could meet not only the staffing but the implementa-

tion requirements. Specifically, it would raise those odds from their present 0.20 (i.e., 0.50×0.40) level to about 0.24 (i.e., 0.60×0.40). Regarding joint probabilities, see endnote 18.

22. "Extensive intervention" refers to the simultaneous or successive use of two or more program elements, such as counseling, limit-setting, out-of-home placement, recreation, and so on—depending on the youth's needs, interests, and current life situation. At CTP, four such elements were usually used "simultaneously," for instance (and operationally defined as), within a three-month period. Additional elements—including, for example, collateral contacts and material aid—were often used at various points during the youth's project experience (Chapter 3). Thus, CTP's intervention was indeed extensive; at least it went beyond the basic, *two*-project-element requirement of a "multiple modality"—that is, at least a dual modality—approach.

23. Collectively, "departmental conditions" are components of the implementation rather than of the staff dimension or category. Arbitrarily, these conditions fall within one of two subcategories: *support/motivation* and *others,* that is, all others combined. The latter consists of the "practical, resource-centered, and/or policy based conditions," that is, the factors and limitations mentioned next (text) and focused on in this review.

24. This reduction in implementation problems would probably occur whether or not the *entire* unit (project) were housed within the center.

25. This applies whether or not they try to implement more than one such element at a time.

26. This would apply to an off-site school program as well, though the advantages of an "integrated center" would be lost.

27. In many situations, the relative availability/usage of on-site versus off-site activities may reflect *choice* far more than *difficulty.*

28. Each set of offenders could consist of probationers and/or parolees.

29. The fact that this strategy centers on a youth/program-elements match, not on a priori risk or general amenability, is

reflected in the following: If a different combination of UII elements existed, many youths who, in the present example, received low priority would probably obtain a high or at least higher priority—and vice versa for many who were considered "high."

30. This "static" feature rather than "interactive" feature would apply especially to the risk- and amenability-based approaches.

31. Though counseling can be either individual, group, or family, the first two would probably have the broadest applicability among serious and nonserious offenders. For most youths in a typical serious offender population, pragmatically oriented discussions could probably not replace counseling on an ongoing basis. For rather different reasons, short-term detention could not appropriately substitute for limit-setting/surveillance, except in rare, sharply delimited, legally sanctioned situations.

32. This would relate to the almost certain fact that without such elements—certainly counseling (whether formal or informal)—the potential as well as actual significance and power of "key factors" such as #2, #3, #6, and #7 (Chapter 15) would be greatly reduced. By the same token and at the same time, if such *factors* were not present, the potential and actual value of these *elements* would be greatly reduced.

33. Pragmatically oriented discussion and out-of-home placement are probably crucial to, and nonexchangeable for, somewhat fewer youths than are counseling and limit-setting. Nevertheless, they, too, are so important that it is difficult to imagine an effective, *broadly* relevant community-based program which lacks these particular elements. This includes probation and parole operations that would handle either serious or nonserious offenders, or both.

34. Basically, these reasons centered around the program's missing or inadequate (yet, for the youths, important) elements, combined with the youths' probable negative response to various elements that remained.

35. Given a sufficiently sizable population base, a reduced range need not result in a quantity—a new population number—

that is (operationally) significantly lower than before. Nor, for that matter, need it involve an amount that is reduced at all—let alone reduced proportionately, that is, correspondingly.

36. Also different would be the fact that, depending on the number of youths excluded, fewer caseloads might eventually be unavoidable in the present ("related") approach. This reduction is less likely to occur in connection with the basic strategy.

37. "One in seven" reflects the following calculation: $[(0.50) \times (0.30)]$—or 0.15. The first figure (0.50) refers to estimate (1); the second (0.30) is a probability that involves estimates (4) and (5) combined. The resulting figure of 0.15 is therefore about half of "one in every three or four"—the latter ("one in every. . .") being the second figure itself. Not shown in this calculation is the fact that estimates (2) and (3) are both 1.00. (The latter estimates can vary somewhat independently of estimate [1], and estimate [3] need not be determined by [2]. Nevertheless, when estimate [3] is 1.00, that is, "100 percent," estimate [2] must automatically have been 1.00 as well.)

38. We will continue to assume the following. Though practical, for example, fiscal, constraints may temporarily prevent a department from shifting its present staff, not to mention hiring additional personnel, that same department would nevertheless have the regulatory as well as specific legal and contractual authority (and also the structural/organizational flexibility)—thus, the *theoretical ability*—to shift its present staff from one program/caseload to another, if different practical conditions and/or priorities existed. We also assume the department would have the option to transfer various funds from non-personnel- to personnel-centered budget categories, if necessary.

39. At the same time many departments that *lack* a specialized program, or even specialized individual caseloads only, may nevertheless contain CTP-appropriate staff and may be *able* to shift some such individuals to a proposed CTP unit. (Here, "specialized individual caseloads" are distinguished not only from standard

individual caseloads but from any given *program,* for instance, from several integrated caseloads.)

40. We assume that some of these otherwise unavailable components *could* be made available by small as well as large departments that were willing and able to operate a qualitatively acceptable full-sized program or a differential treatment subunit, that is, in contrast to operating individual caseloads only.

41. These and related interpretive/integrative skills are also used in casework supervision, worker/youth interactions, selection of worker candidates, and specific worker/youth matching. Though matching may be greatly assisted by a formal youth-classification system, skilled, sensitive staff can satisfactorily achieve this goal without it.

42. As implied and suggested in Chapter 19, neither psychometric tests, advanced statistical/computer techniques or models, nor combinations of both, can adequately substitute for interpretive/integrative staff skills if one wishes to develop such plans. This also applies to the foreseeable future.

43. In some systems—simplified or not—planning-centered information (say, about placement) could conceivably play a large role in classification. In the I-level system its role in determining maturity level and subtype is seldom large.

44. The main exception involved power-oriented youths—mostly, but not entirely, group conformists. In general, several "softer" elements were added to, or substituted for, certain approaches and techniques that were previously used. This was not limited to the more "accessible" youths, as compared to those called "insulated." Related to this change, but not restricted to power oriented individuals, was the following. There was, again intentionally, a subtantially lower rate of *parole suspension*—and, with that, less likelihood of *short-term detention* (Chapter 3)—following relatively minor offenses. This change, which became increasingly evident starting in the middle of Phase 2, centered on technical violations, program infractions, and "juvenile

status offenses plus welfare and insitutions code offenses" (Palmer, 1973c, pp. 185–193). It is different than the increased likelihood—starting around 1966—that parole would be *revoked* following the youths' first *moderate severity* offense. This, too, extended beyond the power oriented individuals alone.

45. Simply knowing that such sharing may well occur could increase some departments' "willingness and felt-ability" to seriously explore a CTP approach. That is, it could do so prior to any actual or substantial sharing.

46. Under given conditions, use of a simplified classification system need not involve a loss of information that is critical to relevant, realistic, intervention planning. (See "Relevance, Individualization, Classification, and Integration," in Chapter 19.)

47. Sometimes, community decision-makers, for example, boards of supervisors, may oppose neither the in-lieu strategy/philosophy nor specific in-lieu approaches (actual or proposed); nevertheless, their *support* of both, and occasionally their understanding of one or both, may be weak. Under these conditions, in-lieu approaches may receive such low or mediocre priority that if a choice must be made between those approaches and more strongly supported services, the former may well be bypassed, waived, or rejected. In this regard, relatively weak support—with or without clear understanding—could produce the same result as actual opposition.

48. $130 = 100 + (0.30 \times 100)$. Thirty percent is about midway between the "one-fourth to one-third" estimate.

49. Both figures might be higher if one included departments that wished to explore *any* community-based approach, not just differential intervention.

50. Still other, for instance, large or widespread, organizations might implement a full-scale program in one location and individual caseloads in another. In general, large organizations—widespread or not—would be better positioned than all others to simultaneously operate more than a *single* in-lieu program, DI-oriented or not.

VOLUME 2

Issues, Theory, and Perspectives

PART I

Issues and Developments

VALIDITY OF THE RESEARCH FINDINGS

During and shortly after the California experiment, two main concerns emerged regarding its findings. The first arose in 1968 and focused on the experiment's recidivism index; the second arose in 1973 and centered on its follow-up samples. Both concerns were initiated by the same critic and were then essentially repeated by others. As will be seen, the first concern was fully responded to: A much better index was substituted, as of the early 1970s. The second, although based on a plausible hypothesis, soon proved unfounded once empirical tests were made. However, since these concerns or criticisms were often accepted by reviewers of CTP—invariably without having studied key facts firsthand and in detail—it is essential that the situation be carefully examined. This review should help clarify long-standing misconceptions and unnecessary doubts regarding the experiment's results.

The Phase 1 and 2 Recidivism Measure
Revocation, Recommitment, and Unfavorable Discharge

In 1968, Paul Lerman indicated that the California experiment's principal outcome—rate of recidivism—was unsatisfactory because it focused on revocation, recommitment, and unfavorable discharge. These actions, he emphasized, centered not on *youth behavior*—which would be reflected, especially, in arrests or convictions—but on what he termed "*discretionary reactions to that behavior*" by Youth Authority staff. Particularly important, he believed that such actions or decisions—at least revocation—favored experimentals (E's) over controls (C's) and thereby produced a misleading picture of CTP's effectiveness (Lerman, 1968, pp. 55–58).

Lerman based this conclusion on Youth Authority research reports which indicated that E's—CTP youths—were more likely than C's to receive a "second chance" after committing an offense. That is, for the same type of offense, E's had a better chance than C's of being restored to parole rather than being revoked[1] (Warren and Palmer, 1965; Warren et al., 1966a). These findings applied not only to (1) nonsevere albeit nontrivial offenses, for example, petty theft and intoxication, but to (2) moderately serious offenses (usually felonies) such as auto theft, check passing, and possession of concealed/ illegal weapons. More specifically, they applied—for those offenses and others mentioned below—to *revocations of parole,* though not to recommitments to the YA by probation and not to unfavorable discharges from the YA (see below regarding the latter two). Nevertheless, since (1) nonsevere albeit nontrivial offenses and (2) moderately severe offenses—what we will call "category 1 and 2" offenses, respectively—were, collectively, quite common, and since revocations comprised the bulk of all "failures," Lerman's conclusion (which did not attempt to distinguish revocation from recommitment and unfavorable discharge) remained accurate for *recidivism as a whole* (this being the unweighted sum of all revocations, recommitments, and unfavorable discharges). This applied even though the E/C difference in second chances was somewhat less for category 2—the moderately serious—than for category 1 offenses.

By 1972, following a CTP report on the subject, Lerman used the term "differential decision-making" in connection with differences in *restoral-actions*—and, therefore, in *revocation-actions* (which were the immediate and invariable consequences of *non*-restoral, and only of non-restoral)—between the E and C programs. More specifically, he used it when referring to E/C differences in the likelihood of occurrence of those actions, for identical types of offense. Obviously, staff from the E and C programs often had the option—i.e., the "discretion"—of recommending or not recommending revocation; these individuals used this option to differing degrees (Lerman, 1972, pp. 2–3, 34–37; 1975, 61–67; Palmer, 1968a).

The problem with the experiment's then-principal outcome measure thus sprang not from the concept of recidivism but from the three factors mentioned next. Because of their *joint* operation, these factors made it less likely that E's would become "failures" than C's during the 15- and 24-month parole follow-ups that were used (in reviewing these factors it should be kept in mind that "failure" in the sense of recidivism was *defined* as revocation, recommitment, or unfavorable discharge within either time period,[2] and that nonfailure in this regard was automatically considered "success"):

First, as indicated, an experimental *was* more likely than a control to have been restored rather than revoked for the category 1 or 2 offense in question. Second, assuming this offense did occur, it was likely to have taken place within the first 12 or so months after the youth's release to parole, that is, within one or both of the above follow-up periods. Finally, and of central importance, whereas an E's *restoral* (exactly as with a C's restoral) for the preceding offense may have occurred *within* the 15- or 24-month period, any *revocation* he (or, of course, a C) may eventually have had for a *later* offense may have occurred *after* the follow-up had ended. Given the above-mentioned definitions, this meant that if his restoral offense had occurred within the 15- or 24-month follow-up period but his revocation offense—if any—had occurred after it, he would have been a success rather than a failure with regard to the given follow-up. (He could, of course, have also been a success if he had either no offense at any time or if his offense(s) had occurred only

after the given follow-up had ended, for example, after the 15-month though not necessarily the 24-month follow-up.) In short, because of its delaying effect, his early *restoral*—his "second chance"—may have helped him avoid the 15- and sometimes even the 24-month "failure" category. The latter avoidance, of course, was more difficult to achieve than the former.

Before continuing, certain technical/background matters and operational changes through time might be noted with respect to recidivism follow-ups and category 1 and 2 offenses (nonsevere but nontrivial offenses and moderately serious offenses, respectively):

A. As indicated, most failures had occurred in connection with a *revocation decision*—a YA action that, in the preponderance of cases, had been triggered by a penal code (PC) offense. Considerably fewer failures had involved a *recommitment,* this being a non-YA action (see below) which also typically resulted from a PC offense. Finally, relatively few failures involved an *unfavorable discharge*—a YA action that had usually followed a rather serious PC offense, such as robbery or rape. Revocation decisions and unfavorable discharge decisions were always made by the board, usually, but far from always, based on or consistent with the YA agent's recommendations; this was true for all "restore to parole" decisions as well.[3] Agents recommended; the board decided.

B. Until 1966, CTP's parole agents *were* clearly more likely than regular parole agents (RPAs) to recommend—to the board—restoral to parole rather than revocation of parole, following the youth's first and, to a lesser extent, second category 1 or 2 offense. The board usually accepted this recommendation, at least for the first such offense. This CTP/RPA difference in recommendations began to fade in 1966. By then, not only had RPAs begun to give controls (collectively) more second chances than before, but CTP agents were starting to give experimentals fewer than before (and to give fewer third chances even for minor offenses). Beginning in mid-1967, a sizable E/C difference no longer remained in this regard; however, mainly because of the *already* existing differences, an overall E/C difference remained when all pre-1967 years were analyzed together—and (later) even together with the past. During Phase 3 of the experiment (its operations lasting from 1969 to 1973), second chances were uncommon in connection with even moderately serious offenses.

E's and C's also differed in "second chances" with regard to *minor and status* offenses, such as incorrigibility, runaway, and foster home failure. Specifically, CTP agents almost never recommended revocation for these "category 0" offenses, whereas regular parole agents occasionally did, particularly during Phase 1 (1961–1964). Like most RPAs, CTP agents believed that almost all youths could still be worked with following such behavior; however, unlike most RPAs, the latter agents had enough time and resources to work closely with them and perhaps with their families, and, if necessary, to develop and implement a new or expanded plan. (As with category 1 and 2 offenses, this E/C difference decreased during Phase 2, when several RPAs reduced their use of revocation recommendations for minor and status offenses.)[4] The board recognized these time and resource factors, and most of its members usually believed such factors might make a difference with the given youths. Thus, when these decision-makers—board members—considered a category 0 offender neither "hard core" nor dangerous (based on his prior offenses), and believed he was not "deteriorating attitudinally," they usually gave him "another chance" provided the agent's plan seemed sound.

(As suggested, most *regular parole agents* often recommended [and typically received] second chances for given youths in connection with category 0 offenses—but less often than did CTP agents. Their revocation recommendations partly reflected not just their awareness of having little time and only modest resources but their frequent belief that little or no progress had occurred to date and that, under those combined circumstances, overall prospects were probably mediocre or poor. This applied to category 1 and 2 offenses as well [Palmer, 1968a]. Early in Phase 2, several RPAs began reassessing their chances of succeeding with given youths, despite seemingly limited progress to date.)

At any rate, despite such changes through time and in spite of the differing resources and possibly differing levels of youth progress in question, the concern Lerman expressed in 1968 regarding the researchers' then-principal outcome measure had merit. This was true even though the second-chance factor did not extend to *serious* offenses (invariably felonies), such as robbery, rape, and ADW. For such "*category 3*" offenses, essentially no differential decisions were made between the E and C programs with respect to revocation. This reflected the fact that—(1) on public protection and political grounds alone, and (2) possible treatment considerations, differential program resources, and youth progress notwithstanding (see Chapter 16 regarding differential decision-making)—no discretion or virtually no discretion was available to decision-makers in the first place, and virtually no E's *and* C's therefore received second chances, following such offenses. In effect, within both the CTP and standard YA programs, revocation was essentially a foregone conclusion immediately after the youth's first category 3 offense, and E as well as C agents rarely even requested restoral to parole.

Lerman's concern was also appropriate despite a further restriction. In contrast to revocation, *recommitment*—necessarily (i.e., by law) recommitment to the *Youth Authority*—could be initiated and implemented only by probation, and it was therefore beyond the YA's control. Thus, recommendations and decisions by YA staff that might have given E's more second chances than C's, or even vice versa, were not at issue here; that is, all recommitted youths were, by definition, automatic failures in whichever follow-up cohort (15- or 24-months) they were part of. They could not be restored to parole in connection with the offense for which they had been recommitted; and in this regard the following might be noted. For almost two years during the middle of Phase 2, Sacramento probation (SP) recommitted nearly all (93 percent) CTP males who committed category 2 offenses, for instance, auto theft. This was about triple its previous recommitment rate for similar offenses. (During this period, SP sometimes recommitted E's for category 1 offenses as well, such as petty theft; here, too, it exceeded its previous rate.) SP took this action because it felt that if it simply returned those E s to the YA, for the *YA* to decide the disposition, CTP agents might—as they had done in Phase 1—often recommend restoral; and probation considered CTP too lenient with reoffenders in this regard (though not in connection with category 3 offenses). Thus, by recommitting rather than simply returning such youths, Sacramento probation precluded what it assumed would be the CTP agents' recommendations. In so doing, it applied more direct pressure on the board—more than it believed would otherwise be involved—to remove those youths from CTP and to institutionalize them.[5] (Regardless of the board's subsequent actions, all Phase 1 and 2 recommitments were, as indicated, automatically counted—by research—as *failures* with respect to recidivism, if those recommitments had occurred within the cohort's follow-up period. This automatic-failure rule also applied, of course, to all revocations and unfavorable discharges, if they, too, had occurred within the designated follow-up periods.) During the years in question, this situation markedly favored controls, since Sacramento probation continued to recommit only its "normal," that is, its pre mid-Phase 2, portion (25% to 30%) of male C's who were involved in similar category 2 offenses.[6]

Alternative Measures

Given the preceding concerns, Lerman—in 1968 and again in 1972—indicated that the experimenters should use an outcome measure that reflected not so much discretionary reactions and differential decision-making (DDM) by *YA staff* but *youth behavior* instead—at least, as much as possible. Toward this end, he strongly suggested and implied that *arrests*—particularly for penal code offenses, as distinct from technical violations, and so on—would be appropriate (Lerman, 1968, pp. 57–58; 1972, pp. 33–38, 40; also see Lerman, 1975, pp. 58–67, 229). Other reviewers agreed, though some suggested that *convictions* might be more appropriate and some (e.g. Beker and Heyman, 1972, p. 37) focused especially on important shortcomings of revocation, discharge, and even suspension of parole. In any event, revocation, recommitment, and unfavorable discharge (collectively)—although recognized as having some value and as being widely used and generally "respectable" measures within corrections—were to be dropped as the principal effectiveness index (composite outcome measure).

In the early 1970s the experimenters (researchers) did begin to use youth behavior as their principal outcome measure; from that point forward revocation, recommitment, and unfavorable discharge were, collectively, no longer heavily relied on. (Instead, they were presented as a separate, supplementary index of recidivism, as in Chapters 8 and 9.) Before the 1970s, and in 1970 as well, youth behavior—specifically, suspensions and arrests recorded on all Youth Authority "suspension reports," that is, on its suspension-of-parole reports—had been reported in considerable detail (Warren and Palmer, 1965; Warren et al., 1966a; Palmer 1970b).[7] However, it had never been the central index, mainly because revocation, and so on, were, as suggested, considered appropriate and largely adequate measures of program impact on youths and since they were the YA's standard index as well.

At any rate, youth behavior—together, of course, with any adult behavior (again, arrests/convictions)—was increasingly made central during 1970–1972. This was due not only to the earlier-mentioned concern with discretionary decision-making but in order to focus more directly and heavily on indices of public protection than on measures of program impact that centered on the following: (1) whether youths remained in the community or were (re)institutionalized (due to revocation or recommitment); (2) youths' degree of psychological change; (3) youths' type of termination from YA (specifically, whether they received a favorable or unfavorable discharge[8]). To be sure, measures (1) and (3) were not unrelated to public protection, that is, to some aspects of crime reduction.

Moreover, beginning in 1973, all such youth behavior relating to the experiment was measured solely by Criminal Identification and Investigation (CI&I) rapsheets. This particular change occurred because, in that year, a major problem was recognized with the Youth Authority documents—specifically, in the *suspension-of-parole reports*—that the researchers had previously used when analyzing youth behavior.[9, 10] Details regarding the nature and discovery of that problem are as follows (unless otherwise indicated, all quotations in the rest of this section, and in related endnotes, are from a 1973 report to the National Institute of Mental Health [see Palmer, 1973c]; "YA" and "CYA" are used interchangeably and have identical meaning):

From the start of the experiment (1961) until 1972 the researchers had "taken it for granted that . . . the *CYA suspension reports* were, by themselves, complete or reasonably complete in the case of C and E programs alike—i.e., complete in terms of being a quantitatively unabridged [and a qualitatively accurate] reflection of virtually every arrest which had been made by police [and by sheriffs' departments (and of any resulting recommitments to YA by probation)], and which would have been listed on CI&I rapsheets [that they, the researchers, could have obtained from the Department of Justice (DJ)]. Because of this assumption, only the CYA suspension reports—never the CI&I rapsheets—had therefore been used prior to 1973 to determine the number and rate of suspensions/arrests that had occurred during the youths' *parole*]."[11, 12] Moreover, the researchers knew that suspension reports contained CYA-initiated technical violations and minor infractions that would not appear on rapsheets, since the CYA was not required to notify DJ—which produced the rapsheets—of such behavior. (Palmer, 1973c, p. 68)

However, because of the 1972–1973 developments and findings reviewed in items (1) and (2) below and in related text, the researchers, in 1973, realized it would be best to henceforth base their comparisons of E and C youth and adult behavior—particularly, non-minor (i.e, not-of-minor-severity) offenses—on CI&I rapsheets rather than CYA suspension reports. These developments and findings strongly suggested that the first-mentioned documents provided a much more uniform, and thus fairer, comparison of E and C offense behavior during parole than did the second. This applied to all such documents and reports, that is, beginning in 1961. ("Item (1)"—the first development/finding—was as follows.)

(1) The emergence of various clues which suggested, not just the possible, but the probable existence of *"differential reporting"* [partly based on differential awareness, by parole agents, of offense behavior] across the E and C programs. [See endnote 13.] The apparent existence of an opportunity for differential reporting, plus the fact of its probable operation for some time, was first suggested by results which, e.g., indicated the presence of wide variations in rate of parole suspension as a function of whether the suspension (or arrest) had been CYA-initiated in contrast to non-CYA [i.e., law enforcement] initiated. More particularly [this set of findings—from what is called "Analysis A"—seemed to suggest differences in reporting, and, probably, in awareness of offense behavior in the first place] across the E and C programs (Palmer, 1973c, pp. 68–69). (Data for Analysis A came from suspension reports—alternatively called suspension documents—alone, not from comparisons between those reports and CI&I rapsheets. [All revocation and unfavorable discharge reports were, of course, included in suspension analyses; and recommitments were described in either these or suspension reports per se.] This analysis, conducted in 1972–1973, was a detailed study of youth behavior; as such, it reflected the by-then dominant role of this index in the experiment's outcome-evaluation. This role was further reflected in all Phase 3 analyses: There, revocation, recommitment, and unfavorable discharge were not even utilized.)

For instance, among E's, for each of the three main youth types (conflicted, power-oriented, passive-conformist), a clearly higher rate of agent-initiated suspensions than law-enforcement-initiated suspensions was found on 16-months follow-up.[14] In contrast, among C's, for each of the same youth types a substantially *lower* rate of agent-initiated suspensions than law-enforcement-initiated suspensions was found on 16-months follow-up.[15, 16] Together with the absolute rates involved and the amount of difference in these rates between the respective E and C youth types, these findings "indirectly suggest[ed]" that the former [CTP] agents may be 'more aware and/or more responsive' [in terms of filing suspension, i.e., suspension/arrest, reports] than the latter agents" (Palmer, 1973c, p. 87). Clearer and more specific support for this interpretation was obtained via an analysis of offense listings, for E's and C's, respectively, on CI&I rapsheets as *compared* with those on CYA suspension documents. (See endnote 17, regarding "Analysis B.")

The preceding interpretation was consistent with, and partly drew upon, a long-recognized difference: In accordance with their particular treatment/control philosophies and with their program's need to concretely assure the public and law enforcement of its safety, CTP agents, during 1961–1969, suspended E's for technical violations and minor infractions at a rate (weighted for Phases 1 and 2 combined) that was approximately seven times higher than control agents suspended C's for similar and identical activities;[18] these activities were recorded on suspension documents (Grant, Warren, and Turner, 1963; Palmer, 1973c; Warren et al., 1966a).[19]

Moreover, the following applied to status offenses and to Welfare and Institution Code offenses in particular (curfew; drinking, possession of alcohol; runaway, whereabouts unknown): CTP agents arrested E's at an approximately four times higher rate than *law enforcement* agents arrested E's; in contrast, C agents arrested C's at a slightly lower rate than law enforcement agents arrested C's. (CTP agents arrested E's at approximately 10 times the weighted rate at which C agents arrested C's, for these same offenses. (Palmer, 1973c, pp. 190, 193, 235)

In short, though findings from Analysis A were neither definitive nor highly focused—for instance, they could neither distinguish between occurrence of and awareness of offenses within the E and C programs, respectively, nor between *differential* occurrence, awareness, and reporting of offenses *across* those programs, collectively—they, supported by long-recognized program differences in the handling of minor offenses, alerted the researchers to a possible problem with suspension reports for E's and C's: a lack of comparability between those documents.[20]

Together, the findings next reported convinced the researchers that substantial problems did exist regarding suspension documents and that these problems extended *beyond* minor-severity offenses. These findings, which emerged at about the same time as the above results, were from a Los Angeles county survey (Yockey and Kleine, 1972) and from a resulting CTP/control analysis. Both investi-

gations involved comparisons between suspension reports (and, separately, other field file documents), on the one hand, and CI&I rapsheets, on the other. (The earlier quotation now continues, with "item (2)"—which was as follows.)

(2) Results from an October/November 1972 survey, conducted by CYA administration in Los Angeles county . . . indicated that 28 percent of all CI&I-reported [i.e., rapsheet-based], non-CYA law enforcement arrests (of which the CYA was routinely, and fairly promptly, notified) had remained *unreported* in terms of the set of documents which comprised the official, CYA field folder [file] for each given ward—i.e., unrecorded in terms of suspension reports, special incident reports, chronological entries, etc. (p. 69). [Since these arrests might have been recorded on any one such document but not on the others, the percentage that remained unreported would doubtlessly have been higher with regard to suspension reports alone; this is independent of the fact that more recordings were made on suspension reports, in particular, than on all other documents combined. See quotation in endnote 11 regarding the role of these documents.]

This survey was a first of its kind, certainly in the CYA. (It had been neither planned nor conducted by the Youth Authority's Research Division, and the YA/NIMH researchers first learned of its existence when they heard its results.) Its findings were unexpected and it produced a rapid response: (1) Given the survey's methodological implications with regard to source documents, (2) given the fact that most recorded arrests were nonminor in severity, and (3) although the survey had occurred in a fairly distant location and a somewhat different setting (Los Angeles County), the researchers, early in 1973, then checked to see if a similar discrepancy existed between E and C reports themselves, and if any such discrepancy included nonminor offenses. (Their assumption through the years had been that, at most, a 3 percent to 5 percent discrepancy might exist for such offenses.) Their interest in conducting this 1973 documents analysis (Analysis B) was further stimulated by the then-new findings mentioned in "item (1)" above. These findings had raised questions not only about reporting practices in general but about the interaction between those practices and the particular documents (suspension reports) on which earlier as well as then-recent E/C "youth behavior" analyses of parole-period activities had relied (Palmer, 1973c).

Analysis B produced two main results, the second of which had the more serious implications. Stated generally, these results were as follows. Not only did a reporting problem—one that was quantitatively substantial—indeed exist *within* the E and C programs, respectively (thus, this problem did extend beyond L.A. County), but, this problem (namely, a reporting discrepancy between the same types of documents as those in the L.A. County survey) existed to substantially differing degrees *across* those programs. More specifically (the following quotation is a continuation of "item (2)" above):

> As it turned out, the "suspicions" which we [the researchers] felt in light of the combination of [items] (1) and (2) above were not unfounded: Excluding all offenses of minor severity (i.e., severity-levels 1 and 2), it was found that control agents had filed no suspension report with respect to 43 percent of the CI&I-reported arrests; the figure for CTP agents was no less than 32 percent.[21] [That is, for every 100 nonminor arrests that were reported on the rapsheets of C youths—these being documents obtained from DJ for Analysis B—regular parole agents, from 1961 to the data cutoff for this analysis (12/1972), had filed no suspension/arrest reports on 43. For every 100 nonminor arrests that were reported on the rapsheets of CTP youths, CTP agents—throughout that same period—had filed no suspension/arrest reports on 32. The figure for C's was, thus, one-third higher than that for E's. (As always, arrests leading to revocation, recommitment, and unfavorable discharge were included, regardless of the specific title of the document—such as "Revocation Report"—on which they appeared.)] These figures, which are rather jarring in and of themselves, are of relevance . . . because of the fact that literally all prior Phase 1 and 2, 1961–1969

analyses of individual offenses which occurred throughout the parole period—specifically, all analyses which involved index #2 ["rate of suspension during parole" (p. 66)]—had been based upon the parole agent's *suspension reports* alone [again, regardless of document titles—as in the above]. In short, the information which the research team had previously used as a basis for assessing rate of delinquent behavior (viz., index #2) was quantitatively incomplete—in fact [and most important], differentially incomplete across the C and E programs (pp. 69–70). ("When suspensions of minor severity [levels 1–2] are added to the picture, the figures [of 43 percent and 32 percent] become 52 percent and 39 percent, respectively" [p. 130].)

To view these findings from another angle the researchers then took the following step. They added together all offenses/violations/infractions (o/v/i's), that is, "all known suspensions and arrests," that had been recorded, not just on CI&I rapsheets, but in CYA suspension reports (and, for still further analyses, in field files overall) (Palmer, 1973c). Their main goal was to see (1) what percentage of *all known offenses, etc.*—that is, all CI&I plus all CYA listings combined—had been included on the *suspension documents* (again, document titles were irrelevant), and, especially, (2) whether this percentage was similar for E's and C's. (As in all analyses, any given offense was counted only once.) Results were as follows:

> In the case of E's, 82 percent of all known 3–10 level arrests and suspensions had been documented in CYA files, in the form of suspension reports. A substantially smaller portion—58 percent—had been counted [documented] in the case of Controls. These figures thus represent[ed] the percent of offenses[22] which [on average] were included in any given, 1961–1969 CTP analysis of delinquent behavior [i.e., youth behavior during parole. This also applied to the 1972 suspension analyses that were reported in Palmer, 1973c.]. The difference which is observed in the E versus C figures [and in those mentioned above] suggests that, in any given analysis which related to index #2, (the results had been automatically

and substantially—albeit unknowingly—biased: Of all known non-minor offenses, including those on rapsheets, 18 percent were missing from suspension documents in the case of E's and 42 percent with respect to C's—these figures being the obverse of 82 percent and 58 percent, above).]. (Palmer, 1973c, p. 84)

Given this substantial bias in the recording of nonminor offenses, and apart from the evidence that E agents were considerably more aware of technical violations and minor infractions than were C agents, the following occurred: CI&I rapsheets were recognized, starting in 1973, as the most appropriate data source for use in comparisons of youth behavior—certainly nonminor offenses—across the E and C programs, programs (operations) that were very different from each other.

This conclusion was independent of the fact that rapsheets—unlike suspension documents—could be used for pre- and post-discharge analyses alike and could thus comprise a single and consistent data-source for long-term (pre- plus post-discharge) followup [as was presented in Chapters 8 and 9]. Also, the conclusion was largely but not entirely independent of the long-known fact that "rapsheets" were a type of document very often and perhaps increasingly used by other criminal justice agencies for cross-program comparisons, whether pre- or post-discharge.

Apparently, of the two outcome documents used in the California experiment—rapsheets and suspension reports—only the former seemed able to avoid the earlier-mentioned E/C discrepancies and to provide the uniformity of reporting that was needed for unbiased comparisons between these programs. This applied particularly to offenses that bore most on public protection.

In sum, beginning in the 1970s the California experiment gave central emphasis to the type of outcome index recommended by reviewers and/or critics concerned with eliminating the effects of discretionary and differential decision-making across the E and C programs. That index involved youth behavior, and the specific criterion they had recommended was arrests or convictions; the

experimenters elected to use both such criteria. The optimal type of source document recommended by the reviewers, and others, for E/C parole comparisons was the youth's official rapsheet. This, too, the experimenters then utilized for the given comparisons—but only after they had empirically discovered that this document in fact provided a much more uniform and, thus, a fairer reflection, of youth behavior, especially nonminor behavior, than the one previously used.

The main reasons for the earlier-mentioned omissions from suspension documents are reviewed in Appendix 37. As will be evident, the greater degree of omission in the C than E program was itself a partial expression of discretionary decision-making, and differential awareness, by YA parole agents.

(Correlations between various outcome indices are shown in endnote 103. Among the indices and data sources are 15- and 24-months recidivism, law enforcement initiated arrests [from CI&I rapsheets], law enforcement initiated arrests [from YA files plus CI&I rapsheets], and suspensions plus arrests [from YA files].)

The Phase 1 and 2 Follow-Up Samples
Background
Once the California researchers began focusing more directly and heavily on youth behavior and dropped their former recidivism index as the principal outcome measure, the following occurred. Lerman, apparently in response, no longer focused—as he had from 1968—on the experiment's outcome measure and on discretionary decision-making's impact upon E/C outcome differences involving that measure.[23] Instead, in his 1975 book, *Community Treatment and Social Control* (hereafter called *Social Control*), and in his December 1973 draft of the technical appendix which he included in that book, Lerman turned to certain *youth samples* that the researchers had used when evaluating Phases 1 and 2. That is, he now focused on youths to whom the former—and the more recent—outcome measures were *applied* (Lerman, 1973; 1975).[24] In particular, Lerman suggested that various E's and C's whom the researchers had compared probably differed from each other on certain background characteristics, and that the reported E/C *outcome differences,* particularly those involving suspension rates, might be at-

tributed to these presumed E/C *youth* differ-ences and not to E/C *program* differences. (See endnote 25, point 2, regarding his choice of suspension rates. Also, as mentioned in endnote 32, Lerman—in his December 1973 draft of the technical appendix [pp. 10–11; later, pp. 237 of *Social Control*]—stated that he would not incorporate any further infor-mation [findings, etc.] into *Social Control* [which, as indicated, would include the ap-pendix] as of November 1973. [Though he had only then—in December 1973—provided that appendix for the first time, this position, in effect, pointedly foreclosed any useful re-sponses to it; at any rate, it could have dis-couraged any responses.] He indicated that this decision was necessary in order to facili-tate the publishing of the book—which, how-ever, did not appear until 1975. As described in endnote 32, Dr. Lerman did end up having time to make several changes and additions during 1974, and he did make them. These, however, did not relate to the detailed reply [Palmer, 1974a] he was given to his technical appendix and to other [pre-November 1973], related information as well. This reply and in-formation is discussed in subsequent sections of the present chapter.)

Lerman's suggestions centered on his re-view of, and inferences regarding, two E and C samples from the Phase 1 and 2 Valley units, namely, Sacramento/Stockton. These samples had been used in two particular analyses that the California researchers reported in 1973 (Palmer, 1973c); and it was this report, and these analyses, on which Lerman focused in his technical appendix—also called the "Note." (As indicated, the discussion of CI&I rapsheets and YA suspension documents that appeared in the preceding section of the pre-sent chapter was drawn from this report to NIMH—one sometimes called Palmer's 1973 reply to Lerman.) Lerman, in developing the suggestions he presented in the 1973 Note and repeated in (i.e., transferred verbatim to) his 1975 book, had utilized no specific figures—including no total group and no youth subtype data—regarding what he considered the rele-vant *background characteristics* (e.g., age and IQ) of these 1973-reported E and C samples. (As discussed below, he generally called these "available" or "updated" samples:)

The figures in question, which presum-ably would have involved (a) means and

standard deviations for Base Expectancy (parole risk), age, and IQ, (b) percentages of youths (by category), for race, SES, and commitment offense, and (c) proba-bility levels on significance of E/C differ-ences, for all six of those variables or characteristics—could have been easily obtained on request from the California Youth Authority in 1973; but Lerman did not request them. Though he had indi-cated that he would incorporate no fur-ther information in connection with his book-in-progress (see above), those fig-ures were nevertheless sent to him, to NIMH, and to others, in mid-1974, as part of a detailed report in response to the above-indicated suggestions he had made in his technical appendix, that is, in the December 1973 Note. (See Tables 1, 2, and 6 of Palmer, 1974a.)

Instead, when focusing on the question of whether statistically significant background differences existed between the E's and C's who comprised each set of samples, that is, the 1973-reported samples, he *inferred* what he considered—and termed—a "reasonable" and "likely" answer from information re-ported for *earlier* E/C samples. As will be dis-cussed, it was these inferences on which he based his subsequent conclusion that impor-tant E/C background differences probably ex-isted in the *1973*-reported samples. Lerman's further conclusion—that these presumed background differences could, as he stated, "quite conceivabl[y]" account for the 1973-reported E/C *outcome* differences—was, and remained, untested in *Social Control* (and in Lerman's subsequent writings), and, in effect, amounted to a hypothesis (Lerman, 1973; 1975). We now turn more specifically to the samples.

Of the two samples in question, the first had been used by the California researchers to compare 104 E's with 90 C's on *arrest rates* (not suspension rates) during parole. These 194 subjects consisted of all males who had received either a favorable or an unfavorable discharge from the Youth Authority and who also had four years of community exposure following discharge; *CI&I rapsheets* com-prised the source documents for this analysis. The second sample was used to compare 310 E's with 225 C's on *suspension rates* during parole. These 535 subjects consisted of all males—except those described later in this chapter—who were randomly assigned to the E or C programs during 1961–1969, that is, during Phases 1 and 2.[26, 27] CYA *suspension reports* comprised the source documents for this *second* analysis only, one which Lerman called the "updated suspensions analysis" (UDSA) (Lerman, 1973, 1975; Palmer, 1973c).

Both samples will be discussed in the following pages even though Lerman's suggestions focused heavily on the UDSA. Since these 1973 and 1975 suggestions regarding the possible and conceivable impact of presumably important youth differences on E/C outcome differences were not just substantively identical to each other but appeared in documents (first the technical appendix and later the *Social Control* appendix) that were the same in virtually all respects, they will simply be called the "1973/1975 suggestions."

Lerman's 1973/1975 suggestions will be examined on their own grounds despite the following:

1. The E/C samples on which the *present book's* outcome analyses of Phases 1 and 2 are based are, in fact, highly comparable to each other (see Chapters 8–11 and related appendices). Specifically, when the present E's and C's (total group, 1961–1969) were compared to each other on each of the six background variables studied—Base Expectancy (BE), age, and so on—no substantial differences were found; and none of these E/C differences was statistically significant.[28] This, by itself, indicates that—in direct and sharp contradiction to Lerman's hypothesis about possible bias—the experimentals were neither more nor less predisposed to success than were the controls. Parts 1 and 2 of Appendix 11, of Chapter 8, indicate that similar results also applied to each of the three major subgroups [i.e., youth groups, such as the conflicted].

2. As mentioned in the preceding section, the source documents (CI&I rapsheets) on which the present book's outcome analyses are based are different from and much more appropriate than those (namely, *YA suspension reports*) used in the updated suspensions analysis—those on which Lerman mainly focused in 1973/1975.[29]

3. The UDSA is not simply (a) *less* appropriate than the rapsheets analysis yet is, say, (b) nevertheless appropriate or acceptable *in itself*. Instead, because of the source-document problems already described, it is largely inappropriate in an absolute sense. (Since this point relates to the quality of the *source documents* used, it would apply whether or not the E and C samples were well-matched, that is, statistically comparable to each other, on all background characteristics.)

4. Despite (1) and (3) above, the technical merit of Lerman's suggestions will be examined. As indicated earlier, this is because (though not only because) some reviewers evidently assumed those suggestions were accurate and that they revealed a major and possibly irreparable flaw in the Phase 1 and 2 evaluation—one that confounded, negated, or largely eroded the experiment's main findings. (See, e.g., Wilson, 1980.) It is unclear whether such reviewers knew not just *of the CI&I arrest* results (not *YA suspension* results) presented in earlier-mentioned journal articles (endnote 24) and in related documents (e.g., Palmer, 1978a)—that is, not just of their existence and importance; instead, it is unclear if they knew or accepted that the E and C samples involved in those analyses were highly comparable to each other. (These E and C, *CI&I-analysis* groups were, in Lerman's terms, "available samples"; that is, they comprised all youths available for *follow-up*. They were not simply "eligible samples," that is, all youths who had *entered the programs* but were not necessarily followed up—for instance, by virtue of having been paroled out of area, and so on. See below regarding this distinction.)

Three last points before examining Lerman's approach and position regarding the two E and C samples: (1) In the long run, perhaps the most efficient way to adequately review what might be called the samples issue is to present—as we will—a lengthy excerpt and related material from the 1974 report to NIMH (Palmer, 1974a). (This report, also called Palmer's 1974 reply to Lerman, focused specifically on the samples issue.) Only such a review can include or reflect not just Lerman's approach and position but the researchers' unavoidably detailed response to his observations and inferences. (2) The extensive, *1974 report to NIMH*, which took several months to prepare and which was shared with Lerman in mid-1974, was written in response to his above-mentioned December *1973* draft titled, "A Methodological Note on the CTP Analysis" (Lerman, 1973). This 11-page draft (the "technical appendix"), which later appeared in its entirety as *Appendix A of Social Control* (pp. 229–237), will be called either the "Note" or "Appendix A."[30] (3) In turn, the December 1973 Note—the technical appendix—had been written in response to Palmer's *1973* reply to Lerman's *1972* drafts (to NIMH) of what, after certain modifications, became the text of Lerman's *Social Control* (Palmer, 1973c; Lerman, 1972).[31] As it turned out, Appendix A of *Social Control* was identical in virtually all respects, that is, word-for-word, with the Note.[32] Therefore, it is this Note and Appendix that, individually as well as jointly, contained the earlier-mentioned "1973/1975 suggestions." Excerpts from Palmer's *1973* reply appeared in the "The Phase 1 and 2 Recidivism Measure" section of this chapter.

Excerpts from the California researchers' review of the earlier-mentioned approach and position, that is, from the *1974* report to NIMH, now follow. Unless otherwise indicated, all page references are to that report. (As a partial review, please keep the following in mind. Using Lerman's terminology, [1] all youths who comprised an "available" sample were individuals who could be, and were, *followed up* on parole for specified minimum lengths of time, and the focus of these followup analyses was on those youths' performance. [All analyses that were based on the Department of Justice's *CI&I rapsheets* were followups, though not all parole followups—including all those which were conducted prior to the early 1970s—were based on these rapsheets. After 1972, all followups were based on those rapsheets alone.] [2] The youths who comprised an "eligible" sample were ones who had originally become part of the experiment, *whether or not*—subsequent to their random assignment to E or C—they accumulated enough time to become part of a given "available" [i.e., *followup*] sample. The "eligible" samples upon which Lerman focused in his Note had been analyzed using *CYA*

suspension documents, never CI&I rapsheets, and their primary purpose was that of *describing* the basic pool [i.e., the randomly assigned, original E and C sample], not that of studying performance. [*Rapsheets* were used only for followups—that is, in order to study performance, never to describe the basic pool.])

Specifics and Data

Building upon indirect evidence from [California experiment] research reports of the middle and later 1960s and then proceeding by means of inferences and assumptions, Lerman concludes, in Appendix A [i.e., the December 1973 draft, or Note] that it is a fact or virtual certainty that the "*available*" E and C samples are significantly different from one another on such crucial variables as age [and] IQ[33] . . . [See below regarding this indirect evidence.] His main hypothesis is that these differences will, by themselves, account for the E versus C differences in *parole performance.* [See Palmer, 1973c, the 1973 report to NIMH regarding this analysis.] He does not mention the one variable—Base Expectancy (BE)—that might have *directly* supported his hypothesis, at least if E's had turned out to be substantially and significantly better parole risks than C's. See below. [The main reports from which Lerman obtained his information on age, IQ, and the like, on pre-1972–1973-reported samples (Warren et al., 1966a; Palmer et al., 1968), indicated that *no* significant BE differences—that is, no parole risk differences—existed between E's and C's who comprised the same samples to which that information referred. Thus, his hypothesis was not supported when one focused directly on BE. This applied at the total group as well as subtype levels.] (p. 2)

Lerman's inferences and conclusions are mainly focused on (1) all E's and all C's (i.e., the respective total groups) who entered into the given analysis (more specifically, all individuals who were compared with each other on the particular background characteristics and outcome measure), and on (2) the Na + Nx group (within the total E and C groups). He could have avoided this intricate, scientifically risky, inferential procedure by simply requesting (from YA administration, or from the CTP/NIMH researchers) the actual, E and C background information on the "available" groups' ages, IQs, and so on, in question. When this information *was* sent to him, in mid-1974, he chose to ignore it. Subsequently, he neither acknowledged its specific details nor referred to its existence, in the first place. (Cf. endnote 32.) This included the post–*Social Control* years.

In any event, Lerman sums up as follows: "On the basis of the evidence [see Lerman's four points—later in this chapter] it is quite reasonable to believe that the . . . experimental males are older (and probably brighter) than the . . . controls. [These numbers refer to the updated suspensions analysis. Here, "updated" meant augmented with regard to sample size and modified in terms of singling out males, as compared to the 1965 and 1966 analyses.] The probable difference regarding age is of critical importance, since correctional researchers have known for some time that the older parts of youth and adult correctional populations have tended to be better *parole risks* [emphasis added[34]] than their younger counterparts. Therefore, it seems quite likely that the [E's included in this updated analysis, if they *are* more representative of the "older parts"] are biased toward "success"—prior to being exposed to any particular correctional program. In questioning the reliability and validity [of this as well as the second 1973-reported analysis], there is no intention of inferring that the biased [i.e., the *presumably* biased—in the sense of noncomparable] samples were constructed intentionally. The evaluation literature contains other examples of samples that were unwittingly biased. . . . [In sum], it is quite conceivable that the updated findings [the 1972–1973 suspensions analysis results] are spurious, and could be attributed to age, IQ, or social class." (Palmer, 1974a, pp. 2–3; Lerman, 1975, pp. 234, 236) (See endnote 35 regarding Lerman's emphasis upon terms "probably brighter," "probable difference," and "quite conceivable," in contrast to those such as *actually brighter, actual differences* in age, and so on.)

[Note: Regarding the statement on social class (SES), Lerman had presented no supportive data and had not otherwise discussed this factor. Nor did he subsequently do so. As indicated in a later section of this chapter, in which Table 21–1 appears, neither a numerically substantial nor a statistically significant E/C difference in fact existed in the given sample with regard to social class, whether for Na + Nx (conflicted), Mp + Cfc (power-oriented), Cfm (passive-conformist), or the total group (all subtypes combined, rare types included). Thus, his statement, that is, speculation, regarding social class remained unsupported and *unsupportable,* and he did not pursue it in his Note at a factual level.]

Before returning to Palmer's May 1974 reply, we will present and discuss Lerman's evidence for his following views—Item A, below—and for inferences—Item B—which he related to Item A and to other information discussed below. (The following statements will first summarize and focus those views and inferences; we will then discuss them directly):

A. *Subtype composition.* The total E group ($N = 310$) and the total C group ($N = 225$)—which, together, comprised the *updated suspensions analysis* (UDSA) sample—differed from each other on subtype composition; that is, a significant difference did exist between these E and C groups in their respective percentages of conflicted, power-oriented, passive-conformist, and rare type youths. Lerman's evidence for *this* view was direct, not inferential. It consisted of actual figures.

B. (1) *Total group.* The above-mentioned *subtype-composition* difference that existed between the total E group and total C group in that same updated sample was, according to Lerman, probably linked with E/C differences[36] on particular *background characteristics,* namely, age and IQ—again in that sample. Here, Lerman's inference focused not on the existence of a *subtype-composition* difference but on the idea of probable differences in the background characteristics of the E and C total groups.

(2) *Subtypes.* According to Lerman, particular E and C subtypes[37]—namely, conflicted E and conflicted C youths—

probably differed from each other on the above-mentioned background characteristics (age and IQ). This occurred whether or not (a) a link (correlation) did in fact exist between the E/C subtype-composition difference, on the one hand, and E/C background-characteristic differences, on the other, and whether or not (b) the subtype-composition difference may have been partly *produced* by certain background-characteristic differences (and/or vice versa). Here, Lerman's inference focused not on the possible existence of (a) and/or (b) but on the idea of probable background-characteristic differences *between specified E and C subtypes*.

As discussed below, the inferences involved in Item *B* were based not on actual figures regarding the UDSA sample itself but on information concerning an *earlier* sample (see Palmer et al., 1968). Regarding A and B, Lerman's statements, which are from his Note (1975, p. 233), are as follows.

> *Item A*. [The updated suspensions analysis (E = 310, C = 225), reported in Palmer's 1973 reply] . . . appears to have experimentals and controls that are noncomparable. A secondary analysis of the footnoted data and "new" classifications used in the [1973 reply] reveals the following distribution of available diagnosed personality subtypes: (a) experimental boys had 185 "neurotic" types (Na and Nx subtypes), 57 "power-oriented" types (Cfc and Mp subtypes), 33 "passive-conformists" (Cfm subtypes), and 35 all other [rare] types;[38] (b) control boys contained 103 "neurotic" types, 54 "power-oriented" types, 40 "passive-conformists," and 28 all other types. [Analysis of these figures shows] there is one chance in a hundred that the experimental and control boys were randomly drawn from the same available [subtype] population (chi-square = 11.8, df = 3, and p < .01)."[39] ["'New' classifications" refers to the "power-oriented" and "conflicted" composite categories, that is, to groupings of already existing subtypes, in particular.]
>
> *Item B*. There are very cogent reasons for believing that the diagnostic differences [this refers to the differences in

subtype representation] between the . . . 310 experimentals and 225 controls are linked to two significant population variables—age and intelligence [IQ]. The evidence and reasons are as follows. [Lerman then presents his evidence and reasons in four points.]

Regarding these critical points, which will be specified and discussed below, the following might first be noted: (a) The evidence that Lerman cites in Points 1, 2, and 4 (see below) involves an earlier—that is, an earlier "eligible"—sample. (b) Despite the Item B assertion, above, *IQ* (unlike age), is never mentioned in Points 1 and 4, that is, in connection with possible differences between the updated eligible (that is, the UDSA) E's and C's. Its absence most likely reflects the fact that neither significant nor substantial E/C differences *were* found on IQ (Palmer et al., 1968). (c) Point 1 refers to the *total* group of youths; Point 4 involves *individual subtypes* which comprised that group.[40]

After presenting these four points Lerman concludes: "On the basis of the evidence, it is quite reasonable to believe that the [310] experimental males are older (and probably brighter) than the 225 controls" (Lerman, 1975, p. 234).

We will now discuss Items A and B in turn.

Item A. Here, the lack of comparability mentioned by Lerman involved not the background characteristics of the total E and total C groups but their *subtype composition;* and indeed, noncomparability did exist regarding subtype.[41] That is, as seen in the 1973 reply (Palmer, 1973c) and in Lerman's above-mentioned review of its figures, E's had a different subtype mix than C's, that is, a different ratio of conflicted to power-oriented to passive-conformist youths. More specifically, regarding the updated suspensions analysis sample, the total E group had, proportionately, more conflicted, slightly fewer power-oriented, and substantially fewer passive-conformist youths than did the total C group.

This subtype-composition difference in the updated sample was important not in itself but, according to Lerman, because of its relationship to background characteristics that, traditionally, related to outcome (performance). Specifically, he considered it important for the following series of reasons (namely, [a] through [e] below)—reasons which, except as indicated, he had suggested and implied in connection with Item *B,* below, based on figures from the earlier sample. (Note: (1) Regarding these reasons, subtype composition was not thought of as directly, that is, by itself, influencing outcome; instead, it provided the specific basis of, or precondition for, what Lerman called E/C bias or probable bias. That basis or precondition involved its presumed association with given *background* characteristics. (2) The words "probably" and "likely," in (b), (d), and (e), below, reflect the fact that only inferences, not actual findings, were involved).

Reasons (a) through (e):

a. Since conflicted youths comprised most of the total updated suspension analysis sample (see above-mentioned figures for Item A);
b. since conflicted youths were, in Lerman's view, *probably* older and brighter than youths from all remaining major subtypes;
c. since older and brighter youths were traditionally—that is, in the correctional literature—more likely to outperform younger and less bright youths, that is, were more likely to "succeed"; and
d. since the total group of E's (which, as indicated above, contained proportionately more conflicted youths than did the total group of C's) therefore, in Lerman's view, *probably* contained proportionately more older and brighter youths and, thus (given [c]), probably contained more youths likely to succeed,
e. the *total group* of E's in the given sample *probably* had a preexisting advantage over the total group of C's regarding likelihood of success, and any such advantage was, or would be, a form of bias.

Item B. Together, (a) through (e) comprise the key elements of Item B and, in sequence, constitute its inferential structure. However, before examining that item directly, for example, before reviewing the factual basis and the significance of its four specific points (which precede its conclusion), we will discuss a critical omission in Lerman's approach to the question of subtype-based—and, as reflected in (a) through (e) above, background-characteristics-related—bias. To identify this omission, three preliminary points and several subpoints that would normally be considered self-evident must be stated explicitly and in detail.

Before continuing, note the following: (1) In this discussion, the term "component" will refer to *any individual subtype* within a given sample. Unless its meaning is specifically limited to "any combination of *two or more individual subtypes* within the given—the E or C—sample," the term "composite" will refer to *all such subtypes combined,* within that sample. (2) The validity of this discussion is entirely independent of the fact that, despite Lerman's key *probabilities* (see [b] and [d] above), the actual E/C difference in age as well as IQ turned out to be negligible for both the conflicted group and the total group (of which the conflicted was, of course, a part). See Item B. (3) For related discussion regarding possible pitfalls concerning the nature and context of bias, see endnote 42.

1. Before E and C total groups can differ from each other regarding degree of subtype representation,[43] these groups must—logically—each contain two or more subtypes in the first place; that is, the presence of at least two subtypes is literally required in order to create even the possibility of having E/C subtype *differences.* This requirement is reflected in the following: Throughout the California experiment's data analysis, the very term "total group" meant, qualitatively, that the set of subjects (youths) which was being analyzed as a unit *was* the totality, more specifically, the *composite* of separate—therefore, of at least two—subtypes. "Total group" also meant, quantitatively, that this composite contained *all* subjects who were included in the analysis; and since all such subjects (except for "NICs," as described in Appendix 39) had been subtyped, the composite therefore contained all subtypes. (Note that, throughout the experiment, E and C total groups had the same *kind* of subtypes; that is, they each consisted of conflicted youths, power-oriented youths, and so on. However, as seen in Item A, the suspensions analyses sample contained these subtypes to differing degrees; and it is degree of representation, not specific kind, that is at issue here.) At any rate, the existence of an E/C subtype difference—here, a dif-

ference in the degree of E/C representation across subtypes—logically requires the presence of at least two (the same two) subtypes within the E and C samples, respectively; and the presence of any such subtype *composite* in any given data analysis is the essential ingredient in what is called a "total group."

2. Since (a) a subtype-composition difference between E's and C's can therefore exist only with respect to a total group of E's as compared to a total group of C's, that is, can exist only *between* such composites, and since (b) composition-based *bias* can exist only when a composition difference exists, the following applies. All possibility of *subtype-composition-based* bias necessarily and entirely disappears when E's are compared to C's, not at the total group level, but separately for each component (subtype). That is, since each of these latter—specifically, these separate—comparisons involves only *one* subtype (e.g., conflicted E's versus conflicted C's), literally no E/C *subtype-composition differences* exist in each such comparison (analysis); and—since composition bias requires, in fact is defined in terms of, composition difference in the first place—no composition bias is therefore possible (logically as well as empirically) under the above condition.

Stated differently, when only one subtype is analyzed at a time, no subtype *mix* exists. As a result, any bias that might otherwise have come to exist because of *differential* mix (something that, as indicated, could only have existed at a total group level) is therefore precluded at the outset in any such subtype analysis. Thus, although "*mix*-based" ("composition-based" or "subtype-composition-based") bias may exist at a total group level if and when differing subtype mixes exist across E and C samples, no such bias can exist at an individual subtype level, since—there—no subtype *mix* exists. Obviously, it is only composites, not components, whose subtype representation can differ across E and C samples in the present sense of "representation"—since "representation" refers to "mix" and since only composites, not components, are mixed.

3. As discussed in Chapters 8 through 11, the researchers did not simply make, and present the results of, total group (i.e., composite) comparisons; instead, they focused directly on each of the three major subtypes. Specifically, they made separate comparisons of conflicted E's with conflicted C's, of power-oriented E's with power-oriented C's, and of passive-conformist E's with passive-conformist C's. *After that,* they compared the total E group with the total C group. Similar analyses and reporting were seen in the 1973 reply, to which Lerman's Note referred. By carrying out these separate subtype analyses the researchers directly controlled for subtype; and, in these particular analyses (but, of course, not in the total group analysis, this being the only one whose outcome results Lerman discussed), they thereby precluded all subtype-composition bias.[44]

Since the *total group* findings were solely a mathematical resultant (in effect, a weighted average) of—and, in that sense, necessarily and entirely *subsequent* to—those for the individual subtypes, they could not contribute to, or otherwise influence, those respective subtype findings. As a result, the findings for each separate (individual) subtype analysis, for instance, those for the conflicted E versus conflicted C comparison, were entirely independent of the degree to which each such subtype was represented in the *total* group, and the following therefore applied: The results for each *individual subtype comparison* would have remained entirely unchanged even if the subtype composition of the *total group* had been radically different than it was, for example, even if the total C group had contained far *more* conflicted, slightly *fewer* power-oriented, and slightly *fewer* passive-conformist youths than had the total E group. For instance, for purposes of *conflicted E versus conflicted C* comparisons, it would not have mattered if the *total group* contained 35 percent conflicted E's and 50 percent conflicted C's or if it contained 50 percent conflicted E's and 35 percent conflicted C's: The average rate of offending for any given group—such as conflicted E's or conflicted C's—is independent of *how many* individuals comprise that group, and the group with which it is being compared (if it *is* being compared). Thus, the present rates of offending for each *individual subtype* would also have remained unchanged even if those sub-types had been represented exactly equally within the total group—that is, even if the E and C total groups had each contained 25 percent conflicted, 25 percent power-oriented, 25 percent passive-conformist, and 25 percent all other (rare) types, and even if the underlying, individual categories (Na, Nx, etc.) that comprised the conflicted, and other, groups (respectively) were themselves identically represented.

Separate subtype analyses, that is, individual subtype comparisons, are those which occur between identical youth types, such as conflicted E's and conflicted C's. They are important for two main reasons: (1) In such analyses, the issue of subtype-based composition bias (SBCB) is obviated. This is because the analyses eliminate differential subtype representation itself, and, ipso facto, they preclude all differences (e.g., in age and IQ) that, in given *total group* samples, may happen to be associated with such representation. (2) Separate subtype analyses allow for a more appropriate interpretation and utilization of a study's findings than is possible from a total group analysis alone, that is, from a focus on all subtypes combined. Reason (1) has already been discussed; reason (2) is illustrated by examining two factors: outcome and subtype representation. (For further discussion of SBCB, see endnote 45 and subsequent parts of this chapter.)

Outcome
Say an experimental (E) program and its control (C) each contain—by design—only two subtypes, the conflicted and power-oriented, and that both subtypes contain about the same number of youths within and across those programs. Now then, if E were 30 percent more successful (lower arrest rate) than C with one of those subtypes, say the conflicted, and about 30 percent less successful than C with the other, then, statistically, the E program as a whole—the total E group—would be neither more nor less successful than the total C. However, say that those findings regarding the two subtypes were not actually used, and that the only finding which was used was that for the total E versus total C group, that is, for the conflicted and power-oriented groups *combined*. Under these conditions—since the E and C programs would each have been treated as a homogeneous en-

tity, in that their outcomes were not differentiated by subtype—the E program might simply be considered "just so-so" with respect to outcome, and a decision might then be made to eliminate it and to operate only the C program. (Such a decision could occur even if more than two subtypes were involved. Only two were used in this example in order to simplify the presentation.)

One way to avoid such global decision-making would be to focus directly on the individual subtypes—the total group's actual constituents. By doing so—in this case, by using the above *subtype* findings (arrest-rate differences)—one might, for example, have decided that the E program should *not* be eliminated, and one may, instead, have concluded the following: (1) Continuation of the program might be warranted, particularly if it contained or were to contain a high percentage of conflicted youth; (2) establishment of an additional, similarly operated program might be warranted, for instance, in a new setting, if it, too, emphasized conflicted youths and perhaps deemphasized power-oriented. Thus, conclusions and related policies that are based on individual subtype findings may be rather different than those from the total group alone. (Though the present example involved an approximately equal number of youths in each subtype, such conclusions and policies would apply regardless of numerical equality and the exact number of youths; for example, there could be 50 conflicted E's and 80 conflicted C's or 80 such E's and 50 such C's.)

Two supplementary points: (1) In the above example, the performance of E and C was equal at the total group level. However, if an E program were more successful than its C at that level, decision-makers and others could still benefit from knowing which subtype or subtypes (assuming the program had several) were especially successful, and which, if any, were nevertheless unsuccessful.[46] This principle would also apply if E were less successful than C. (2) Though the outcome for any given youth group may be "negative"—in this example the group happened to be power-oriented—this finding could still provide a stimulus for developing alternative approaches to working with those youths.

Subtype Representation
Subtype representation is the degree to which each subtype is present within a total group,

and this factor can itself impact policy. More specifically, under some conditions, programs may be viewed as either positive, neutral, or negative, depending on whether this factor has been considered. This applies whether the programs, such as those being compared, are E and C or whether they are exclusively E.

Take, for example, two E programs that operate in different settings, and say that the rates of offending (r.o.o.'s) in Program 1 (P1) are consistently but only somewhat lower than those in Program 2 (P2) for each subtype (hypothetical r.o.o.'s are now shown; P2's are in parentheses, immediately following P1's): Conflicted—30 (40); power-oriented—55 (65); passive-conformist—45 (50); rare—45 (50). Here, r.o.o. is the number of arrests per 1,000 months of community exposure. Thus, the unweighted, average percentage-point difference between these subtypes is only 7.5— that is, $(10 + 10 + 5 + 5) \div 4$. Given this overall figure, given the figures for individual subtypes, and noting that P1 and P2 produced roughly similar r.o.o.'s for any given subtype, one might appropriately conclude that Programs 1 and 2 are about *equally* acceptable and can *each* be supported—except, perhaps, for power-oriented youths (whose absolute rates are the highest). Both conclusions presuppose that P1's and P2's overall—total group—arrest rates are not considered unacceptably high in and of themselves, and that r.o.o.'s within and across any control groups that might be added would not alter the picture.

So far, the example has dealt only with outcome; that is, the figure 7.5 has not reflected the relative frequency of each subtype within its program. Therefore 7.5 is "unweighted," since weighting occurs only when relative frequency—here, subtype representation—is used; and this, of course, occurs only with the total group. (This is independent of the fact that one's *eligibility criteria* can substantially affect the degree to which various subtypes are accepted into a given program in the first place, and are thus represented within it.) At any rate, when a weighted figure is used, a substantially different conclusion may be drawn than that presented above. This is true especially if—even when no differential *eligibility* requirements exist, by subtype— some subtypes are rather differently represented in the programs being compared, because they are differentially represented in the

overall offender population or even in the "civilian" population from which the program draws.

For instance, if Program 1 contains 50 percent conflicted, 20 percent power-oriented, 20 percent passive-conformist, and 10 percent rare youths, whereas Program 2 contains 25 percent conflicted, 35 percent power-oriented, 35 percent passive-conformist, and 5 percent rare youths, then, using the above arrest rates, the *overall* rate for Program 1 (i.e., with all subtypes combined) would be 39.5 and that for Program 2 (subtypes again combined) would be 52.8—a *13.3* percentage-point, or 34 percent, difference. Using only these overall, weighted rates—that is, total group figures—one might conclude the following: (1) Although "the program"—viewed generically—produced an acceptable arrest rate in its first setting, it produced an unacceptable one in its second. (2) Other things being equal (setting included), the *program*—still viewed generically—is therefore of questionable effectiveness, especially if one were to emphasize the 52.8 rate; in any event some individuals might conclude that the program is not generalizable ("transportable") or at least should not be used in the second setting. Here, as earlier, P1 and P2 are treated as homogeneous entities.

These conclusions, particularly the second, overlook or downplay the fact that neither program is, in reality, a homogeneous entity, and that, in particular, Program 2's substantially higher arrest rate was mainly produced by one subtype alone: Its power-oriented group not only had the highest rate of all four youth groups in both programs, but—and this was decisive—that group's representation in P2 was considerably higher than in P1.[47] If this information had *not* been overlooked, ignored, or downplayed, that is, if one had instead utilized the rates of offending for individual subtypes, one might have decided to *retain* Program 2 on the assumption that its future r.o.o. could be improved. This goal could presumably be accomplished by appreciably reducing the percentage of power-oriented youths—say, by admitting fewer into the program—and, as feasible, by increasing that of conflicted and perhaps other youths.

It should be mentioned that substantial variations in the subtype representation of total groups are not rare. They can occur in different settings and/or with differing offender populations, for example, (1) rural versus urban; (2) medium-sized city, or suburbs, versus large and highly urbanized city, or ghettos; (3) rather different states, such as Colorado and New York; (4) different countries, provinces, or counties; (5) local probation versus state corrections; or (6) juvenile versus adult corrections. Moreover, some studies that may focus on particular youth groups, for instance, long-established urban gangs, may—by design—contain an unusually high percentage of power-oriented and perhaps passive-conformist youths. Whether or not purposive concentration occurs, some samples—such as those from local juvenile probation—may even contain substantial percentages (say, 20% to 35%) of otherwise "rare types," for example, stress reactions and adjustment reactions to adolescence.

At any rate, by allowing for a fuller interpretation of a study's findings, individual subtype comparisons set the stage for a more valid, appropriately generalizable, yet appropriately qualified set of conclusions than those based on total group comparisons alone. As such, the results from those comparisons can suggest more meaningful directions for practical action and can help avoid undue optimism as well as excessive pessimism.

The Factual Basis of Lerman's Inferences
We now turn directly to the four points on which Lerman based his inferences regarding the existence of bias in the total available E sample. Here, Lerman essentially indicated that (1) since E/C differences on age and IQ had existed in an earlier sample, they probably existed in the later (that is, an "available" 1973) sample, and (2) given the latter differences, this later, E sample was probably biased toward success. Lerman's four points—his "evidence [that makes it] quite reasonable to believe that the available experimental males are older (and probably brighter) than the . . . controls" (1975, p. 234)—will now be discussed in turn.[48] (The general nature of these points, their relationship to Item A, and their role in Lerman's inferences, are summarized in the following material. Also see "Reasons (a) through (e)" above.)

Point 1
Here, Lerman (1975, pp. 233–234) focused on age: ". . . evidence is provided that in

March 1968 the total eligible experimentals and controls [i.e., the "earlier sample" mentioned above] differed significantly on the variables of age and sex. . . . Specifically, the evidence indicates that the experimentals were overrepresented in the seventeen-year-old age category, in comparison to the controls (27 percent versus 17 percent)."[49] (See endnote 50 regarding sex.) Though this statement accurately reflected information from the 1968 report, virtually all professional researchers, including those with relatively little experience, would probably express surprise or even amazement at this singling-out and highlighting of a 10 percentage point difference that was found for a *single* age category—a category which, in fact, was only one of six that had been analyzed in connection with the variable of age.[51] This reaction would probably occur for two main reasons (in the following, the terms *single category* and *individual category* will be used synonymously):

1. In social science data that involves several hundred individuals rather than thousands or tens of thousands, a 10 percentage point difference between E and C groups—indeed, a sometimes larger difference—is not only commonly found in one or more categories (i.e., found for the cases within those categories) in any *one* variable or factor (v/f) that is comprised of several categories. But, when *several* v/f's (e.g., six or even four) have been analyzed, it is, statistically, a virtual certainty (particularly when the respective number of cases *within* given categories is moderate or modest) that *many* such differences—differences that might be called normal or expected fluctuations—will be observed among those v/f's.[52] That is, percentage-point differences of this relatively moderate magnitude—moderate for individual categories—will be observed for many such categories that comprise those variables/factors, collectively. (This is considered basic, common knowledge among statistically oriented social scientists.)

Thus, for example, on three major *variables/factors*—race, SES, and type of committing offense—that, collectively, contained a total of 10 individual *categories*, 26 E/C differences of 10 or more percentage points were found among the 8 I-level subtypes which were analyzed in the eligible sample. (There were 12 such differences on race, 7 on SES, and 7 on offense.) This was 33 percent of the 80 individual-category comparisons that existed.[53] In 10 percent of the comparisons, that is, in eight comparisons, the E/C difference was 20 percentage points or more (Palmer et al., 1968). Moreover, for any given variable/factor, these or even larger differences will occur whether or not a *statistically significant* difference—what might be called an overall difference—exists when all individual categories are considered together.[54] (This fact, like that of the above-mentioned fluctuations, is almost universally recognized by statistically oriented researchers as being entirely common and normal.)

An example was presented by the California researchers in the same section of the 1968 report (p. 6) from which Lerman had drawn the above-mentioned information: "The Experimental and Control groups were equated [i.e., no statistically significant differences were found] with respect to each of the eight subtypes, in connection with the four-way classification [categorization] on *race*. . . . This equality of overall representation was, e.g., seen within the Mp and Cfm classifications [subtypes], in spite of certain percentage differences which were found: Control Mp = 41 percent Caucasians; Experimental Mp = 18 percent Caucasians; Control Mp = 32 percent Negro [then the accepted and usually preferred term, but henceforth called "Black"]; Experimental Black = 53 percent; Control Cfm = 25 percent Mexican-American; Experimental Cfm = 15 percent Mexican-American; Control Cfm = 25 percent Black; Experimental Cfm = 17 percent Black." (Note the magnitudes of these differences: Some are large but none are extreme.)

At this point it will be useful to briefly indicate how statistical *non*significance (NS) can occur despite moderate to sizable percentage-point differences—also called category differences:

For any two groups that are being compared, statistical NS commonly occurs as follows. Though some category differences within a given v/f (say, age) occur in one direction—for example, they "favor" E's over C's with regard to implications for parole risk (say that E's have more 16- and 18-year-olds than C's)—others within that same v/f occur in the *opposite* direction (say that C's have more 15- and 17-year-olds); and, individually and collectively, these other differences are about as large as the former. (Results for any remaining categories, such as ages 13 and 14, may be relatively neutral: Virtually no E/C differences are found.) Thus, unless a particular *category's* E/C difference is extreme (and the frequencies in that category are not comparatively small), various single-category percentage-point differences within the given *variable/factor* will typically counterbalance one another and will thereby cancel or substantially reduce their respective effects. This situation, which usually results in overall nonsignificance or else in a significant but insubstantial E/C difference (e.g., between average ages of 16.4 and 16.7), cannot be seen when focusing on only *one* category difference, that is, when singling out only part of the data, as Lerman did when focusing on "the seventeen-year-old age category." In order to see how much, or how little, difference remains as a result of counterbalancing, one must examine all the data—all the individual categories—together. (Few people would try to draw a conclusion about all adolescents—ages 13 through 18, inclusive—that was based on information regarding, say, 17-year-olds alone, or, for that matter, 14-year-olds alone. Moreover, most people would probably realize that a conclusion or generalization based on 17-year-olds would probably differ in important ways from one based on 14-year-olds.) At any rate, if one wishes to find moderate or larger percentage-point differences at the single-category level, one will almost always have several options to choose from, especially if more than *one* variable/factor (with its *various* categories) is present, and even in overall study samples that—by accepted scientific standards—have been well matched with each other on several v/f's. Essentially for this reason, the following applies (this is the second "main reason" referred to above):

2. What almost all statistically oriented researchers consider appropriate to focus on or at least give primary emphasis to when quantitatively *testing* a hypothesis or when drawing a conclusion is not just one portion—let alone a small portion—of the available data. (Here, in Point 1, this portion was the year-17 category.)

Instead, wherever possible, they routinely emphasize a figure that optimally represents *all* or at least most of the data, that is, all (or most) of the categories combined. (Here, as elsewhere, that figure would commonly be the average or median age—a product of all individual age categories or data points combined.) This approach is considered maximally objective, balanced, or unbiased, since it not only precludes purposive *selection*—such as utilization and presentation of only some (whether supportive or nonsupportive) categories—but it remains unchanged regardless of researcher, subject matter, and particular hypothesis or even ideology. Moreover, that particular figure is more generalizable and more reliable (stable) than any of its components, since it comprises and reflects the full range of events and usually maximizes representativeness.[55] It is thus more predictive as well.

When the California researchers used this standard approach—that is, combined all individual age categories and thus used all available data for the given variable—the resulting age difference between the total E and total C groups (both, of course, being from the 1968-reported sample [p. 7]) was only four months (0.3 years): E's averaged 15.6 years, C's 15.3.[56] Though these maximally reliable, *overall* figures were highlighted in the 1968 report from which the *year-17* information was drawn, they were not, as further described below, mentioned by Lerman.

Few correctional researchers would seriously think of age *15.6* as falling within what Lerman called (1975, p. 234)—(without, it might be added, actually mentioning any specific age figures)—"the older parts of youth and adult correctional populations," or even of the youth population alone. Few would also consider—as Lerman's inference or position required (see quotation below)—age 15.3 as then falling, in contrast to 15.6, within the "*younger*" portions.[57] (These were the averages for C's and E's in the "eligible" as well as "available"—updated—samples.) Not only do *both* ages—by common standards—fall within what might be called the *middle* portion of the juvenile offender age range, or at least not within its older portion, but they are, in any event, essentially indistinguishable

from each other, for example, with regard to parole risk. (Thus, for instance, differential risk predictions are rarely if ever based on differences *within* any one age level, say, within the age-15 category. Differences *across* levels, for example, 14 and under versus 15 and 16 versus 17 and over, are used instead.) Given the above averages, few if any researchers would probably support Lerman's distinction between "older" and "younger," and the conclusion he then drew on that basis:

> On the basis of the evidence [see Points 1 through 4 of this section], it is quite reasonable to believe that the . . . 310 experimental males are older (and probably brighter) than the 225 controls. The probable difference regarding age is of critical importance, since correctional researchers have known for some time that the *older parts* of youth and adult correctional populations have tended to be better parole risks than their younger counterparts. Therefore, it seems quite likely that the . . . updated experimentals . . . are biased toward "success"—before being exposed to any particular correctional program (Lerman, 1975, p. 234; emphasis added).

Had Lerman presented the actual ages of 15.6 and 15.3, his distinction between "older" and "younger" portions of the youth population would have been seen as inapplicable and nonexistent with regard to the given sample, and his argument based on that premise would have collapsed.

Apart from the fact that a four-month age difference—however the respective ages may be labeled—would hardly begin to account for the sizable outcome differences found between E's and C's,[58] three points, not mentioned by Lerman, should be noted (since these items relate to his Point 1, they focus on the "*eligible*" sample; information regarding the "available"—the follow-up—sample, although essentially the same as that for eligibles, is mentioned later):

1. By most standards, the *total E* and *total C* groups, which had been randomly assigned in the first place, were in fact also well matched with each other, for instance, regarding the several variables/factors (excluding sex) that

were studied (included were SES, race, IQ, type of committing offense, etc. [Palmer et al., 1968, p. 4]). Prior correctional research had shown that most of these variables, like age, correlated with recidivism.) This degree of matching was obtained for the eligible E and C groups despite the frequent, within-variable, single-category differences mentioned above. It occurred mainly because, for any given v/f, such differences were typically counterbalanced and/or diluted by other differences and, thereby, were either canceled out or substantially reduced; also, *most* single-category differences were not "jumbo-sized" in the first place.

2. With regard to evaluating *parole risk* and thereby determining whether E/C outcome bias existed in an eligible sample and might, on that basis, also exist in a subsequent sample (whether an expanded—updated—sample or a follow-up/"eligible" sample), most researchers would probably consider the following finding the strongest and most germane of all: no significant E/C difference existed on *Base Expectancy* (BE)(z = 0.29) (Palmer et al., 1968, p. 4). Moreover, considering the range of possible scores on this variable, and the observed standard deviations (σ's) as well, the E/C difference in actual BE scores was very small. (Possible range = 889 points; average σ's for E's and C's = 96; E/C score-difference = 13.) (See Appendix 38.)

The BE formula was derived from extensive, widely accepted research with Youth Authority wards (Beverly, 1959, 1964, 1968; Molof, 1965, 1970). It combined, into a single score for any given individual, weightings on such variables/factors as age, race, prior record, number of offense partners, number of foster home placements, and truancy, and it was shown to predict parole performance moderately-to-fairly well with respect to distinguishing higher from lower scorers on likelihood of recidivism. This composite measure, of course, predicted recidivism better than did *any one component* (variable/factor) alone, such as age or race. Nowhere in his 1973 and 1975 Appendix/Note did Lerman even mention this well-known and critical variable, or any findings relating to it. Instead—as discussed—he chose to focus on one of its components, *age;* and there, he again chose to be selective, singling out individual categories (e.g., year-17), rather than using *average* age. Findings regarding the crucial variable of parole risk had been regularly presented in the main text of California-experiment reports, including those which Lerman especially emphasized in his Note and from which he drew his quoted information about age, race, and IQ. Thus, for example, in the experiment's reports, the following was specified regarding the "eligible" youths, that is, all parole releasees:

a. The *total group* of Experimentals and Controls were equal so far as level of parole risk (Mean Base Expectancy) was concerned (z = 0.32). This finding also held up in the cases of all (Experimental vs. Control) boys separately (z = 0.75) and all girls separately (z = 1.00). It also applied to all (Experimental vs. Control) Sacramento cases only (z = 0.85) and to all Stockton cases only (z = 1.18). . . . Each of the eight Experimental *subtypes* had a level of parole risk (Rank Order of Base Expectancy) which was neither significantly higher nor significantly lower than that of their respective controls (Warren et al., 1966a, pp. 33–34; emphasis added).

b. The *total group* of Experimentals and Controls were equal so far as level of parole risk (Base Expectancy) was concerned (z = 0.29). In addition, no significant differences existed in level of parole risk between seven of the eight Experimental *subtypes* and their respective Controls. . . . [Regarding the eighth subtype,] Control Cfm's tended to be slightly better parole risks than Experimental Cfm's (z = 1.62; p < .20 > .10) (Palmer et al., 1968, p. 4; emphasis added).

Results were also presented in 1967: " . . . with regard to parole risk: no significant differences were found between the Base Expectancies of the 283 Experimentals and the 270 Controls [z = 0.03]. This involves the *total group*. No significant differences in level of parole risk exist between each of the Experimental *subtypes* and their respective Controls" (Palmer and Warren, 1967, p. 9; emphasis added).

Similarly, with regard to the "available" sample—the sample used for a parole followup:

> c. No significant differences in *level of parole risk* (Base Expectancy) existed between each of the Experimental subtypes and their respective Controls: $Ap - z = 0.76$; $Cfm - z = 1.08$; $Cfc - z = 0.46$; $Mp - z = 0.18$; $Na - z = 0.50$; $Nx - z = 0.21$; $Se - z = 0.37$; $Ci - z = 0.69$. U-tests were used in all instances. No significant differences in level of parole risk existed between each of the three Experimental I-levels and their respective Controls ($z = 0.71$, 0.99, and 0.41, in the case of I_2's, I_3's, and I_4's, respectively . . .) (Warren et al., 1966a, p. 52; emphasis in the original).
>
> d. Nor can any differences [in parole follow-up outcome] be accounted for in terms of *level of parole risk* among Experimentals as compared with Controls. For the 15, 24, and 36 month cohort samples, t-tests showed critical ratios of 0.19, 0.05, and 0.35, respectively, with reference to mean Base Expectancy Score" (Palmer et al., 1968, p. 37; emphasis in the original).

Lerman would have had particularly "cogent" and "reasonable" grounds— these being his terms—for *using* Base Expectancy when developing his hypotheses and expectations regarding the relationship between eligible and followup samples, and for even giving BE higher priority than the variables he did use. However, the experiment's findings on Base Expectancy would have directly opposed the position he was taking.

Lerman's selective use of—though here, the complete omission of—information was particularly striking in connection with this *entire* variable, not just regarding any one or two of its categories. For instance, in the opening pages of his Note, he furnished his readers with information about literally every background/demographic variable that the experimenters had analyzed, *except* that of BE:

Besides containing the best indicator of specific youth behavior associated with a police or sheriff arrest, CTP Report No. 7 . . . provided detailed evidence that the total eligible experimental and control samples were comparable regarding sex, socioeconomic status, type of commitment offense, age, and IQ. [Lerman was thus silent about the fact that the report had also specified—on the same page, namely, 33—that the given samples were equal with respect to Base Expectancy, that is, parole risk. See point "a," above.] Regarding race there was a tendency for the two samples to differ, but this was not statistically significant at the .05 level (Lerman 1975, p. 229).

Also, in Research Report No. 9, part one, "there is evidence that . . . while the two eligible samples were comparable on socioeconomic status, race, IQ, and type of commitment offense, they differed significantly on the variables of age and sex" (Lerman 1975, p. 230). (Again, Lerman made no mention of BE—which, however, the 9th Research Report had stated—again on the same page, namely 4—was equal across the E and C samples in question. See point "b," above.)

Regarding both research reports, Lerman thus provided information, plus a format or structure, that undoubtedly made it easy for many readers to assume that the "comparable" variables which he listed were the *only* ones on which the experimentals and controls were statistically comparable. He did not tell or otherwise indicate to the readers that E's and C's were (1) *comparable* on base expectancy but that this fact, in his opinion, was, for example, (2) *unimportant* because—again in his view— BE (as measured) had little or insufficient absolute and/or (compared to age, IQ, and race) relative *value* and already-demonstrated relevance. Instead, he did not supply this information about BE and the given findings at all, and he thereby did not make it possible for readers—from the less experienced and knowledgeable to the highly—to judge for themselves (and, for instance, to compare BE to the other variables). At any rate, whatever the readers' independent or a priori views regarding BE might have been, only those individuals who had themselves read the given reports could have realized that this widely known variable had even been present.

3. Since Lerman examined individual distributions—that is, *single categories* (such as year-17) within given variables/factors—and since he chose to build given inferences upon them, it might be noted that he did not choose to mention the *following* categories, ones which were themselves single (Palmer et al., 1968, p. 5): Regarding *race,* C's, compared to E's, had a slightly higher percentage of whites (60% versus 56%) and a slightly lower percentage of blacks (15% versus 19%).[59] Since minorities (excluding Asians) were known to recidivate somewhat more than nonminorities, and since the preceding E/C differences—collectively, and thereby with respect to their *overall* contribution—were at about the same level of magnitude as that described by Lerman for 17-year-olds (and this is apart from the level of comparability of these race differences to the difference between ages 15.6 and 15.3), this information, if one followed the same reasoning used by Lerman, could have led to the following inference: C's in the *available* (followup) sample were probably better risks than E's, since (judging from the above-mentioned percentage-point difference) that seemed to be the case in the *eligible* sample. This example illustrates the availability of single-category information which—though it likely constituted chance fluctuations, or usually did so—could have been used (albeit with little statistical justification) to construct an opposite side of the picture and to thereby balance or counter the earlier information (based on similar fluctuations) that was offered. See Point 4 for further examples.

Points 2 and 3

Here, Lerman (1975) discussed IQ and age. Regarding *IQ,* he mentioned two points: (1) "[As indicated in the 1968 report,] the CTP personality classifications are significantly associated with . . . IQ.[60] For the total population of *eligible* youth (girls included), the contingency coefficient [is] . . . .225" (p. 234).[61] (2) Given this .225 correlation, given the fact that neurotics fell within the higher I-level category, and given the neurotics' overrepresentation "in the *available* experimental sample . . . , neurotics [in that sample] . . . would be ex-

pected to have more . . . *brighter* youth [than their controls]" (Lerman, 1975, p. 234; emphasis added). Because Lerman jointly used these points to then conclude that the updated, followed up experimental male sample—specifically, the *total group* of 1973c-reported availables—was "probably brighter" than its controls, the following should be noted.

1. As the 1968 report stated, the above-mentioned correlation—though statistically significant (basically because the total group's sample size was several hundred)—was "not very high." In fact, since it accounted for only 5 percent of the total variance it "would hardly allow one to predict I-level" from IQ—and, of course, vice versa (Palmer et al., 1968, p. 8). (A prediction on this basis would hardly have been distinguishable from one that involved a coin flip.) Nor would it have *contributed* substantially to such a prediction, for instance, when combined with other variables, such as age. This would have applied to prediction *within* an "eligible" sample, to prediction *from* an "eligible" to an "available" sample, and so on. (As stated in the 1968 report [p. 8], "the corrected multiple correlation between age *in combination with IQ,* on the one hand, and I-level, on the other, was +.291"—thus accounting for only 8 percent of the total variance. In his 1973 document and in *Social Control,* Lerman mentioned this multiple correlation but did not mention the variance for which it accounted. Nor was variance mentioned for IQ [and age] alone. It is variance that best reflects predictive power.) Lerman apparently hoped or believed that I-level—in the California experiment's study groups—would, or did, have a strong or at least substantial connection to IQ, since (a) the E group in the available, follow-up sample in question (this being one of the 1973c-reported updated samples) *was* overrepresented by neurotics (individuals who were in the higher I-level), since (b) higher IQ *was* traditionally associated with lower recidivism rate—and since (c) E's (total group) therefore *might* be better parole risks than C's.

2. The most direct and reliable way to predict a variable's (e.g., IQ's) *total group*

average (e.g., average score) in an *available* (follow-up) sample would have been to use the *total group's* average (score) in an *eligible* (earlier) sample. These earlier averages—and here the focus is on average IQ's—were presented and highlighted in the 1968 report (pages 6–7). As specified in that report, they were essentially the same for E's and C's (E—88; C—86). They therefore provided no basis for expecting or predicting that the total group of E's in the given follow-up sample would have a *higher* average IQ (higher to any meaningful degree) than its C's.

Experienced correctional researchers and, certainly, psychometricians, would universally or almost universally view the 2-point difference between E's and C's as wholly negligible and chance-based—especially considering the standard deviations that are involved (15 points for E's as well as C's), and the particular test's standard error of measurement (6 points). Under these conditions, even an 8- to 10-point difference would be recognized as usually chance-based.[62] Lerman, however, chose to neither mention nor otherwise refer to or utilize these virtually identical averages in his 1973 and 1975 documents. Instead, his joint use of the above-mentioned significant association and of the neurotic youths' degree of representation sidestepped this direct, germane—in fact critical—finding, and it made the expectation in question seem inferentially plausible. No information or observation was presented that might open that expectation to question, let alone directly eliminate or reduce the need for the given inference itself.

The average score and score difference for total group eligibles did closely resemble those for availables. As shown in Palmer's 1974 reply (p. 73), but not mentioned by Lerman, IQ's for total group *availables* turned out to be: E—87; C—85—again a wholly negligible difference.[63] Together with the finding for age (see average ages, below), this meant that—correlations, possibilities, and inferences notwithstanding—the total group of E availables was not, in fact, brighter than its C's, and was therefore not, on that

basis, likely to be a better risk. Moreover, the Base Expectancy findings had *directly* demonstrated it was not a better risk (and "age," though not IQ, had been one of its specific components).

Regarding *age*, Lerman referred to a correlation—.200—that was presented in the 1968 report (p. 8) for the total population of eligible youths (females again included). He next indicated (exactly as with IQ) that—given this correlation between age and maturity level, given the fact that "neurotics are from the higher interpersonal maturity levels" (p. 234), and given the neurotics' overrepresentation in the E sample—these youths (here, available neurotics) "would be expected to have more *older* . . . youth [than their controls]" (p. 234, emphasis added). Together with Point 1 above and Point 4 below, this evidence—plus the fact that prior correctional research indicated that older age was associated with less recidivism—was then used to conclude that the total *available (follow-up)* E sample was probably a better parole risk than its C's. However, in addition to not using or even mentioning the findings on Base Expectancy itself—these being the most direct and specific measures of parole risk—Lerman omitted the following (cf. discussion of Points 1 and 4):

A. The above correlation between maturity level (I-level) and age accounted for only 4 percent of the total variance. Therefore, the relationship between, say, higher I-level (mainly conflicted youths), on the one hand, and older age, on the other, was in fact quite weak within the given, *eligible* sample, and it could hardly allow one to predict one sample's results from the other's. As indicated, this also applied when age was combined with other variables, such as IQ; and it was independent of the already mentioned situation regarding "older" age.

B. As with IQ, the most direct and reliable way to predict the total group's average ages for E's and C's in the follow-up sample would have been to use the total group's average ages in the eligible (earlier) sample; these "eligible" averages were included in the 1968 report (p. 7), from which Lerman otherwise drew. As mentioned above, they were 15.6 and 15.3 for E's and C's, respectively. As such, they hardly provided a basis for expecting or predicting that the total group of *available* E's would be substantially older than its C's, and, in turn, that sizable or otherwise useful outcome differences would exist between those available E's and C's.

    As was true with IQ, the average age as well as age differences for total group eligibles did predict those for total group availables (Palmer 1974a, p. 73); in fact, the latter were identical with the former (E—15.6 and C—15.3, for availables). Thus, expectations and inferences notwithstanding, the total group of E availables was not substantially older than its C's; therefore, it was not, on that basis, likely to be a better parole risk. Moreover, the four-month age difference between E's and C's hardly began to account for the sizable outcome differences that were observed.

C. Base Expectancy scores for the total group of availables were: E—436; C—444—a negligible difference. (Standard deviations were 85 and 93, respectively.) For neurotic availables, they were: E—438; C—440, with σ's of 85 and 95 (Palmer 1974a, pp. 73–74).

D. In the base expectancy formula that was used throughout phases 1 and 2, age accounted for 38 percent of the total BE score: 341 of 886 possible points. Age plus race accounted for 45 percent, and age plus race plus prior record accounted for 57 percent. Most of the 341 points were specifically allotted to age at release to parole rather than to age at first admission to the Youth Authority (Palmer et al., 1968, p. 101; Warren et al., 1966a, p. 127). Since the control youths had been *institutionalized* for several months prior to their release to parole, whereas the experimental youths had not been, the C's could presumably have been consid-

ered *better* risks than E's on that particular basis, since they would have been older at that point in time. This conclusion would, at least, have reflected the direct relationship that Lerman emphasized between "older age" and better "parole risk": It will be recalled that—regarding the "310 experimental males [and the] 225 controls"—the "probable difference regarding age is of critical importance" with respect to parole risk (Lerman, 1975, p. 234). To be sure, since the phase 1 and 2 E and C males turned out to be *equal* on parole risk (i.e., on total BE score), one or more other variables/factors that entered into the BE formula had counterbalanced or diluted the influence of age. In any event, see endnote 106 regarding the low correlation between E versus C status, on the one hand, and age—as well as base expectancy—on the other. (The following might be noted. Age at first admission accounted for 59 percent of all points that could have been contributed by the six variables and factors that entered into the phase 3 BE formula. Neither age at release nor race were part of this formula. At any rate, as with the phases 1 and 2 formula, age was by far the largest single contributor to the total BE—parole risk—score [Beverly, 1968, p. 9; Palmer, 1970b, p. 69].) This fact, by itself (i.e., even apart from the Youth Authority's empirical findings), would presumably have lent some weight or credibility (e.g., some predictive validity, not to mention construct validity itself) to the BE formula, in Lerman's mind. However, he made no mention of the fact that age was integral to or even part of this formula (let alone dominant within it), and he ignored the base expectancy variable entirely.

Point 4

Here, Lerman dealt exclusively with age; but, whereas in Point 1 he focused on the total group, here he dealt specifically with conflicted ("neurotic") youths:

[In the 1968 report] evidence is presented that . . . the "neurotics" comprising the *eligible* control group were underrepresented within the seventeen-year-old category and overrepresented in the fifteen-year-old category. This finding suggests that the "neurotics" contained in the *updated* [1973-reported, available] experimental sample are even older [compared to C's, and/or by themselves] than what might have been expected by just considering overall trends of the *eligible* population (Lerman, 1975, p. 234: emphasis added).

As with previous expectations regarding neurotic youths (e.g., Point 3),[64] and with both major predictions regarding the *total group* of availables,[65] this expectation was not met. Not only were the absolute age differences for neurotics very small in both the eligible and available samples, but, contrary to Lerman's specific suggestion, the E/C age difference in the latter (available) sample was smaller than that in the former: Whereas the E/C age difference in the eligible sample was six months (average age for E's = 15.9; for C's = 15.4 [Palmer et al., 1968, p. 7]), the difference, as indicated in the 1974 reply to Lerman (pp. 3, 74), was four months (E's = 15.9; C's = 15.6), or 0.3 years (Palmer, 1974a). Moreover, the available (follow-up) E's were not older than the eligible E's; both groups were 15.9. Had Lerman utilized, in *Social Control,* figures from the 1974 reply that reflected *all* the available age information regarding eligible neurotic E's and C's—namely, their average ages, not just their relative representation in *two* of *eight* individual categories—the following would have been clear to his readers: The ages of the eligible *neurotic* E's and C's did not provide a substantive basis for his inference or conclusion that the *total* available E group was probably a better parole risk than its C. Moreover, the following applies even apart from his not having reflected all available information about the given variable/factor—in this case, the information about average ages.

Lerman's above-quoted expectation in Point 4 was based on information regarding two *individual categories*—those for ages 15 and 17—that comprised a particular variable (age) that related to parole risk. As a result, consistent with the principle of "balance" or

at least of utilizing more rather than less data where possible, it would seem appropriate to note a set of information from individual categories within *another* major factor (race), which itself related to risk.[66] This information, which Lerman did not mention, involved the same—the eligible—sample of conflicted youths described in the Point 4 quotation, and it was readily derivable from the 1968 report (p. 99):

The conflicted C group had a higher percentage of Caucasians than the conflicted E group (79% versus 68%), and a lower percentage of blacks (6% versus 13%). Since it was known that minorities (Asians excluded) usually recidivated more than nonminorities, the first of these C/E percentage-point differences, which was the same size as that used by Lerman in connection with Point 1 and for 15-year-olds with respect to Point 4, could have been used—together with the second difference—as a basis for considering C's, not E's, better parole risks. At least, these differences could have been presented, by Lerman, as either mitigating or entirely counterbalancing his expectations regarding age, or for age and IQ combined.

Together with Lerman's items regarding age and IQ, these percentage-point differences for race illustrate that, from any large and complex data set, enough single-category fluctuations may emerge to allow a critic or reviewer to locate and select those which—at least in isolation, or even in particular combinations—will support a given hypothesis. However, if he or she were to use *all* the fluctuations or data, and were to thereby provide a more complete picture, there might be, in many or most cases, no more substantial or even moderate support for than opposition to the hypothesis in question. The statistical equivalent to using all the single-category fluctuations—more precisely, all available information—occurs when one utilizes the above-mentioned *averages,* rather than selects and presents portions or segments of a data set.

The frequency of such single-category fluctuations or "findings" is further illustrated by two additional sets of information derived from the 1968 report (pp. 99–100) for the factors of race and SES. Each set of selective figures involves the *earlier* (eligible) sample and it could, via the inferential process utilized by Lerman, have been used as "evidence" to help support a hypothesis that the *followed up* (available) C's (in the 1973-reported, updated sample), were probably better risks than E's:

a. *Power-Oriented, on Race:* C's = 36 percent Caucasian and 23 percent black; E's = 23 percent Caucasian and 39 percent black.
b. *Power-Oriented, on SES:* C's = 85 percent lower SES and 14 percent middle SES; E's = 94 percent lower SES and 6 percent middle SES.

The actual findings for the follow-up sample were (Palmer, 1974a, p. 75): (1) 28 percent of the power-oriented C's and 19 percent of the E's were Caucasian, and 26 percent and 39 percent of the respective C's and E's were black. (2) 87 percent of the power-oriented C's and 93 percent of the E's were lower SES, and 13 percent and 7 percent of the respective C's and E's were middle SES. Though these figures were in the same direction and of about the same magnitude as those for the earlier (eligible) sample, none of the E/C differences for the given *variables/factors* was statistically significant when all categories were analyzed together; that, of course, was true for the *follow-up* sample as well: In most cases, the single-category differences (fluctuations) within any given v/f were (1) counterbalanced by one or more other (opposite-tending) differences, were (2) generally dampened or diluted by relatively "neutral" (i.e., close-to-the-overall-mean) categories, and/or were—themselves—(3) simply well within the limits of chance, despite the percentage-point differences involved. (Other information that favored C's over E's and was readily derivable from the 1968 report [p. 99], but which was not mentioned by Lerman, included: *conflicted, on race:* E's = 68 percent Caucasian, 13 percent black; C's = 79 percent Caucasian, 6 percent black.) (The fact that the *overall* [1961–1969] sample of Phase 1 and 2 E's and C's were equated on race and SES—also on age and IQ—was indicated in journal articles that appeared in 1971 and 1973 [Palmer, 1971a, p. 77, and 1973a, p. 99], ones that were cited in the bibliography of *Social Control.*)

Background Characteristics and Subtype
Discussion of Points 1 through 4 indicated that the total available E's and C's did not substantially differ from each other on age and IQ, the key variables in Lerman's inferences. It also showed that these groups were essentially identical on Base Expectancy, a widely accepted measure of parole risk. Thus, total group bias, whose existence Lerman considered quite likely on inferential grounds, did not in fact materialize.

Together with remaining sections of the Note, the content and thrust of Points 1 through 4 reflected that author's exclusive focus on the impact of possible bias upon *total group* outcome findings. This concern or perspective was also seen in the fact that he mentioned neither the existence of individual *subtype findings* regarding parole outcome nor the possible value of analyses that might produce such findings. Subtype information, for example, regarding 15- and 17-year-old neurotics, was used only to help draw inferences with respect to possible *total group* bias. In contrast, the California researchers *were* specifically interested in subtype outcomes; and all their reports on the study—one that was uniquely identified as, and widely known as, an *I-level* and *differential* treatment experiment—had therefore emphasized the subtype level (without excluding the total group, i.e., all subtypes combined). For instance, "It is a premise of this project that the most meaningful findings will not be made by overall [i.e., total group] comparisons of the randomly assigned groups but rather by comparisons of change and success within subtypes. While some kinds of wards can best be treated in the community, there may be identifiable kinds of wards for whom a period of institutionalization is necessary or more effective" (Grant, Warren, and Turner, 1963, p. 51). In this connection it might be noted that two of NIMH's independent reviewers of Lerman's December 1972 manuscript and Palmer's 1973 reply, plus related information and reports, touched on this issue; these were the individuals mentioned in endnote 32. The first one stated:

> I [am] convinced that most of Lerman's charges were misleading, and that he neglected the most important message from the Community Treatment Program, the differences in outcome of a given style of treatment for different types of offenders. . . . [Particularly] important, none of the sources of bias with which Lerman is concerned affect the differences in outcome of major types of cases you differentiate

[those "you call 'Neurotic,' 'Power-Oriented,' and 'Passive-Conformist'"] in the experimental-control comparisons of long-run followup data" (Glaser, 1974). (Glaser "c.c.'d" this letter to "Warren, Shah, Weber, Griffiths, Morris, Lerman, Schrag, [and] Moos.")

The second reviewer stated:

Palmer correctly points out that Lerman did not deal with the question of differential effectiveness. This issue has been discussed in several CTP reports and it is an essential aspect of the CTP program. . . . Palmer's newest analysis in terms of three major groups of delinquents, i.e, neurotic, power-oriented, and passive-conformist, is very commendable in that it simplifies the formidable data interpretation problems. This data on differential effectiveness is reasonably convincing although there is the problem of the low numbers in some of the comparisons (Moos, 1973 [November], pp. 23, 26).

The third reviewer, or possible reviewer, was not heard from.

Thus, the following issue is important, even though it was not raised in the Note and although the total available E's were not biased toward success: Did bias—specifically, outcome-relevant E/C differences—exist at the *subtype* level? For instance, assuming—based on prior correctional studies—that older age and higher IQ would correlate positively with better parole performance in the present study, were conflicted E's substantially older and brighter than their C's, and therefore more predisposed toward success? How did such subtypes compare on other variables or factors assumed to correlate positively with parole performance? And, as a *direct* measure of bias (one not involving the above assumption), Were the respective E subtypes better parole risks than their C's, as indicated by their Base Expectancy scores?

To address this issue we return to the excerpt from the 1974 reply, to Lerman, which also summarizes total group findings relating to Points 1 through 4 above:

At this point we are ready to look at data. The main question is: Do Lerman's inferences and conclusions hold water,

that is, actually check out with reality? First we review Table 1 [Table *21–1* in the present book]. All figures in this table refer to the E and C samples described on page 79 of Palmer's 1973 reply to Lerman's [December 1972] draft. These figures are presented separately for the *Total Group* (i.e., all $I_2 + I_3 + I_4$ subjects combined, Rare subtypes included), and [within the Total Group] for the *Na + Nx, Cfc + Mp,* and *Cfm* subtypes [separately, i.e., for the Conflicted, Power-Oriented, and Passive-Conformist youths respectively. Moreover, the figures are presented for the Total Group and for each of these major subtypes within that group] separately for stage 1, stage 2, and stages 1 + 2, respectively. [See endnote 67 for details regarding these stages. Together, the two stages cover the 1961–1969 time period—specifically, the period of *program operations*—that was identical in all respects to that covered by Phases 1 and 2, also collectively. Stage 1 covered a program-operations period that was slightly shorter than Phase 1, and stage 2 therefore covered slightly more such operations than Phase 2. (Aside from program operations, *data-followup* for this analysis went through July 1971.)] All definitions are identical to those used in [Palmer's] 1973 reply to Lerman's December 1972 draft. [The terms "subtype," "youth subtype," and "youth group" are used synonymously in the following.] (p. 3)

Inspection of the critical sections of Table 1—(see especially the final rows—i.e., stages 1 and 2 combined—of Table 21–1, Section A [*Total Group*] and Section B [*Na + Nx*])—reveals an absence of any substantial E versus C differences with regard to each of the six variables in question.[68] Thus, for example, the following *E/C differences* (i.e., entirely insubstantial differences) can be observed in Section B, subsection 3 (*Na + Nx*; stages 1 + 2): *Base Expectancy*—2 points (with average [i.e., joint] mean of 439 points and average σ of 90 points); *Mean Age at Intake*—0.3 years (with average σ of 1.3 years); *Non-Verbal IQ*—0.9 points (with average σ of 15 points); *Race* (C, M, B, O): E—69 percent, 15 percent, 12 percent, 4 percent; C—70 percent, 16 percent, 13 percent, 2 percent. *SES* (lower, middle,

TABLE 21-1

Comparisons between Experimental and Control Males on Selected Background Variables, for an Updated Suspensions Analysis[a]

	BE M	BE σ	Age M	Age σ	IQ M	IQ σ	Race C	Race M	Race B	Race O	SES L	SES M	SES U	Offense Pe	Offense Pr	Offense Ao
A. Total Group																
1. E₁	437	87	14.9	1.7	87.2	15.4	51	14	23	12	75	21	4	5	82	12
vs. C₁	450	99	15.2	1.5	84.5	14.5	54	26	16	4	78	20	1	2	75	23
	30 > 20		50 > 30		50 > 30			30 > 20				70 > 50			20 > 10	
2. E₂	432	85	15.8	1.4	87.2	14.5	57	21	18	3	77	20	2	7	65	28
vs. C₂	435	90	15.3	1.5	85.4	17.2	48	26	25	2	86	14	0	6	72	22
	70 > 50		< 01		30 > 20			20 > 10				05 > 02			50 > 30	
3. E₁₊₂	436	85	15.6	1.5	87.2	15.4	56	20	19	5	77	20	3	6	68	25
vs. C₁₊₂	444	93	15.3	1.5	85.4	16.8	50	26	21	3	84	16	0	4	73	22
	20 > 10		05 > 02		30 > 20			20 > 10				10 > 05			50 > 30	
B. Na + Nx																
1. E₁	438	85	15.8	1.6	90.9	17.2	63	19	13	6	50	44	6	0	88	13
vs. C₁	441	99	15.1	1.5	91.8	13.6	77	14	6	3	66	31	3	0	80	20
	70 > 50		50 > 30		70 > 50			80 > 70				70 > 50			70 > 50	
2. E₂	438	86	16.0	1.3	90.0	14.5	70	14	12	4	70	27	3	6	63	31
vs. C₂	440	94	15.9	1.1	90.9	14.5	66	16	16	1	78	22	0	3	66	31
	70 > 50		30 > 20		70 > 50			70 > 50				30 > 20			70 > 50	
3. E₁₊₂	438	85	15.9	1.3	90.0	15.4	69	15	12	4	69	28	3	5	65	30
vs. C₁₊₂	440	95	15.6	1.3	90.9	14.5	70	16	13	2	74	25	1	2	71	27
	30 > 20		20 > 10		70 > 50			90 > 80				50 > 30			30 > 20	

(continued on next page)

TABLE 21-1 (continued)

	BE		Age		IQ		Race				SES			Offense		
	M	σ	M	σ	M	σ	C	M	B	O	L	M	U	Pe	Pr	Ao
C. Cfc + Mp																
1. E₁	406	91	14.7	1.3	85.4	10.9	24	29	41	6	94	6	0	12	71	18
vs.		70 > 50		20 > 10		05 > 02		50 > 30				50 > 30				70 > 50	
C₁	439	97	15.7	1.1	78.6	11.8	35	42	19	4	85	15	0	4	69	27
2. E₂	422	81	15.5	1.5	84.5	13.6	18	45	38	0	93	7	0	5	78	18
vs.		80 > 70		50 > 30		30 > 20		90 > 80				70 > 50				20 > 10	
C₂	432	90	14.6	1.4	83.6	18.6	21	46	32	0	89	11	0	14	79	7
3. E₁₊₂	417	85	15.2	1.5	84.5	12.7	19	40	39	2	93	7	0	7	75	18
vs.		50 > 30		80 > 70		50 > 30		70 > 50				50 > 30				95 > 90	
C₁₊₂	438	94	15.1	1.4	80.0	15.4	28	44	26	2	87	13		9	74	17
D. Cfm																
1. E₁	478	78	14.7	2.0	90.9	16.3	80	0	10	10	70	30	0	10	90	0
vs.		99 > 98		98 > 95		50 > 30		10 > 05				10 > 05				20 > 10	
C₁	475	79	14.8	2.0	82.7	13.6	38	25	38	0	94	6	0	0	81	19
2. E₂	401	70	15.2	1.2	78.6	10.0	56	26	22	0	100	0	0	13	61	26
vs.		50 > 30		20 > 10		70 > 50		80 > 70				> 99				30 > 20	
C₂	430	83	15.0	1.4	77.2	14.5	42	29	29	0	100	0	0	4	83	13
3. E₁₊₂	425	71	15.1	1.5	81.8	13.6	61	18	18	3	91	9	0	12	70	18
vs.		50 > 30		30 > 20		80 > 70		20 > 10				30 > 20				30 > 20	
C₁₊₂	448	81	14.9	1.6	80.0	14.5	40	28	33	0	98	2	0	3	83	15

aCovers 1961–1969, for Sacramento + Stockton combined. Means and standard deviations are shown for BE, Age, and IQ. Percentages are shown for Race, SES, and Offense. All p-levels are based on the chi-square test. E = Experimentals; C = Controls. "1" (as in E_1) = stage 1; "2" = stage 2. "1+2" = stages 1 + 2 combined. Sample size: E = 309, C = 225.

upper): E—69 percent, 28 percent, 3 percent; C—74 percent, 25 percent, 1 percent. *CYA Commitment Offense* (person, property, all other): E—5 percent, 65 percent, 30 percent; C—2 percent, 71 percent, 27 percent. Very similar results were obtained with respect to the stage 2, Na + Nx group (p. 3). Clearly, conflicted (Na + Nx) E's and C's were very similar to each other on the direct as well as several indirect measures of risk. This applied to the total group as well—and, as discussed below (and in Palmer, 1974a, pp. 75–76), to power-oriented and passive-conformist youths:

For *power-oriented youths* (Cfc + Mp), the E/C differences for stages 1 + 2 were as follows (see Table 21–1, Section C, subsection 3): *Base Expectancy*—21 points (with average mean of 428 and average σ of 90); *Mean Age at Intake*—0.1 years (with average σ of 1.5 years); *Non-Verbal IQ*—4.5 points (with average σ of 14.1 points); *Race* (C, M, B, O): E—19 percent, 40 percent, 39 percent, 2 percent; C—28 percent, 44 percent, 26 percent, 2 percent. *SES* (lower, middle, upper): E—93 percent, 7 percent, 0 percent; C—87 percent, 13 percent, 0 percent; *CYA Commitment Offense* (person, property, all other): E—7 percent, 75 percent, 18 percent; C—9 percent, 74 percent, 17 percent.

For *passive-conformists* (Cfm), the E/C differences for stages 1 + 2 were (see Table 21–1, Section D, subsection 3): *Base Expectancy*—23 points (average mean = 437; average σ = 76); *Mean Age at Intake*—0.2 years (avg. σ = 1.6 years); *Non-Verbal IQ*—1.8 points (avg. σ = 14.1 points); *Race* (C, M, B, O): E—61 percent, 18 percent, 18 percent, 3 percent; C—40 percent, 28 percent, 33 percent, 0 percent; *SES* (lower, middle, upper): E—91 percent, 9 percent, 0 percent; C—98 percent, 2 percent, 0 percent; *CYA Commitment Offense* (person, property, all other): E—12 percent, 70 percent, 18 percent; C—3 percent, 83 percent, 15 percent.

Thus, neither subtype nor total group bias, that is, predisposition to success, existed in the updated sample on which Lerman had focused.

Though the above figures and related discussion were sent to Lerman and others in May 1974 (as Palmer, 1974a), they were neither taken account of nor in any way incorporated into the Note—which appeared as Appendix A of his summer 1975 book, *Social Control*. If nothing else, they could presumably have been alluded to, if not actually addressed, in an addi-

tional appendix, in Appendix A itself, or in a footnote to A, without hindering the book's production schedule. (As is detailed in endnote 32, the main text of *Social Control* incorporated information from various *1974* documents. Included, at times, was considerable material from, and/or discussion regarding, these documents—but virtually nothing that centered on the YA/NIMH experiment.)

(Correlations between BE score, on the one hand, and each of several background/demographic [B/D] variables and factors, on the other, are shown in endnote 104. Intercorrelations among those B/Ds are shown in endnote 105. The relationship between E and C status, on the one hand, and each of those B/D variables/factors (and BE as well), on the other, is presented in endnote 106.)

Sample Sizes

We now turn to additional issues raised in Lerman's Note—issues regarding changes, across specified years, in the sizes of two sets of samples. The first is an *"eligible" (3/68) versus an "updated" (7/71)* set. These are samples discussed in the preceding section of this chapter, and Lerman (p. 232) also called the updated sample the "available" sample and the "postmanuscript analysis." ("[M]anuscript" refers to his December 1972 draft of what later became *Social Control*. The "updated" analyses appeared in Palmer's 1973 reply—written at NIMH's request—to Lerman's 1972 drafts; thus, they were "post-manuscript.") The second set involves the *March 1966 versus March 1968* samples. These, too, were called available (but not updated) samples, since they, like the just-mentioned updated sample, involved parole *follow-up* analyses. In particular, they were used for outcome analyses of only those youths from their respective *eligible* samples (parole release samples) who—prior to the data cutoff for the outcome analyses—had had an opportunity to be followed up for either 15 or 16 months and could therefore be included in the analysis.[69] This terminology and these distinctions are unavoidably complex; moreover, the eligible versus available distinction must be further reviewed below because it is central to the issues in question.

Specifically, Lerman appeared to wonder why the sample sizes in each set had changed and whether these changes were appropriate. Involved were changes among E's and C's alike. His implication was that one or both sets of changes may have been inappropriate and that they may have individually or collectively decreased the validity of results reported for the updated sample in Palmer's 1973 reply to Lerman's 1972 drafts. These issues must be reviewed in turn, and in doing so we will present the three differently focused yet contiguous statements, from Lerman's Note, in which they were raised. Statements 1 and 2 focus on the first and second sample sets, respectively; Statement 3 emphasizes the second set but is more general in nature.

Statement 1: Eligible versus Updated Samples As of 31 March 1968, in *CTP Research Report No. 9,* part 1 (page 2), information is provided that the *eligible* population pool yielded 287 experimental and 296 control males, very close to a 50–50 split. Yet in the CTP post-manuscript analysis [i.e., in an updated analysis that appeared in Palmer's 1973 reply to Lerman's 1972 drafts], presumably written more than four years later, the number of available [updated] experimental boys increased to 310—a gain of 23—while the control boys *decreased* to 225—a loss of 71. This loss may stem from eliminating the categories "parole out of area" (POA) and "Non-Interviewed Controls" (NIC) from the eligible samples (Lerman, 1975, p. 232). [Though reported in 1973, the updated analysis is the 7/71 analysis, because of its data-cutoff point.]

We will first comment on the above-mentioned controls, then on the experimentals; while doing so, we will continue to distinguish between eligible and updated samples. (Though the POA and NIC youth categories are generally described below, see Appendix 39 for details. Again, it should be kept in mind that *follow-up* analyses involve E/C comparisons on a given *outcome* measure, for example, rate of offending, and that *eligible* samples are not, themselves, used for *follow-ups.*)

Controls
The numerical difference between the 296 control males in the eligible sample and the 225 in the updated *did,* in fact, reflect the exclusion of all POAs and NICs. Specifically, although POAs and NICs were present in the *eligible* sample (the pool), they—necessarily and appropriately—never became part of the updated

one.[70] As indicated in CTP reports, these youth categories were routinely excluded from *parole follow-ups*—(and the *updated* sample in question involved a *follow-up*)—for reasons summarized below and further discussed in Appendix 39 (Warren et al., 1966a; Palmer and Warren, 1967; Palmer et al., 1968). However, all POAs and NICs had—per routine—been included in the *eligible sample,* since this, rather than being a follow-up, simply presented the numbers and background/demographic characteristics of *all* youths (again, the pool) released to parole as of a given date (e.g., 3/31/68—or, simply, 3/68).

For inclusion in any given *eligible* sample, it did not matter how much or how little post release time (e.g., 60 months or one month) youths would have eventually accumulated as of the cutoff date that was later chosen for a given follow-up—that is, *available*—sample; it only mattered that they had been *released* during the period which the eligible sample was to cover. (In the present context, postrelease time and follow-up time are synonymous.) Nor did it matter whether they ever had been, or possibly would be, paroled out of area; they, like all other E's and C's, were automatically included in the eligible sample, that is, in the basic subject pool. In effect, then, the eligible sample introduced and described the subjects from which the E and C *follow-up* samples—the "available" samples (of which the "updated" was one)—would be drawn. However, all eligible-sample youths who did not have an opportunity to be followed up after release for a specified minimum time, for example, 16 months, would be automatically excluded from—more precisely, not allowed *into*—those available samples. As will be discussed, POAs and NICs were always excluded, regardless of that opportunity.

"Opportunity," in this context, means mathematical chance; that is, there either was or was not enough elapsed time between given individuals' first release to parole, on the one hand, and the preestablished cutoff date (which applied to all youths) for the given follow-up analysis, on the other. "Opportunity" was therefore only a matter of dates or time intervals, never of performance, experience, program status, and so on.

Eligible and available samples are compared and contrasted in Table 21–2, and the alternative terminology associated with each is shown.

TABLE 21-2

Characteristics of Eligible and Available Samples

Sample	Alternative Terminology	Type of Sample	Main Uses and Content	Does Sample Involve a Parole Follow-up Analysis?	Youths Excluded from Sample	Temporal Basis for Inclusion in Sample[a]
ELIGIBLE	Basic pool; Pool	Parole-release sample; All-releasees sample	Describe/compare E's and C's on background/demographic characteristics; Provide pool of cases for available sample	No (Is a release sample only)	None (All parole releasees are included)	None
AVAILABLE	Updated; Post-manuscript sample or analysis	Follow-up sample or analysis; Parole follow-up; Outcome analysis	Analyze/evaluate parole or post-parole performance (E/C comparison)	Yes (Is used for follow-up only)	1. POAs (Paroled-out of-area) 2. NICs (Non-interviewed controls) 3. Youths without mathematical chance for 15 (or 16[b]) months follow-up[c]	Youth has a mathematical chance for 15 (or 16[b]) months follow-up[c]

[a] Also called parole release time needed for inclusion in sample.
[b] Applies to 7/71 (available) sample only.
[c] From parole release to preestablished data cutoff (the latter is an identical date for all youths).

Thus, specifically, of the 296 control males referred to by Lerman in connection with the *eligible* sample, 71 were POAs and 25 were NICs; other than these two categories, the eligible sample therefore contained 200 diagnosed (i.e., non-NIC), non-POA males (296 − [71 + 25]). In contrast, the *updated* sample—which, as Lerman indicated, consisted of 225 control males—contained none of these POAs and NICs. Instead, it therefore consisted not only of all 200 diagnosed, non-POA males but of 25 additional such males who (1) were released to parole *after* March 1968 (the cutoff date for the *eligible* sample) and who, subsequent to that release, (2) could have been, that is, had a mathematical chance to be, followed up for 16 months prior to the data-cutoff point for the updated ("available") sample.

Basically, then, POAs and NICs were not included in the updated sample because this sample was used for an E/C *follow-up (outcome) analysis* and because—in any such analysis—E's and C's must be as similar to each other as possible with regard to the *categories* of youth included. As specified below, whereas the eligible C sample to which Lerman referred contained numerous POAs as well as NICs, the eligible E sample contained only a sprinkling of POAs and no NICs. This percentage difference did not exist in the E/C *follow-up* (the available sample) since—there—the POA and NIC *categories,* that is, *all* youths in these groups, were excluded in toto. For reasons summarized below, all POAs would have been excluded from this follow-up even if their percentage, that is, their degree, of representation had been identical across the E's and C's. As to NICs, experimentals—by design—could never have been non-interviewed cases in the first place. (See below for details.)

In short, when one moved from the March 1968 *eligible* sample to the July 1971 *updated* sample there was, as would be expected, an *increase* not a decrease in cases that were *appropriate for inclusion* in the follow-up; specifically, there was an increase—from 200 to 225—in the number of diagnosed, non-POA'd controls. That is, since the *eligible* sample *included* all POAs and NICs—cases that the *updated* (the *follow-up*) sample would *exclude*—it therefore, understandably, contained more controls than the latter—296 versus 225. However, when one *excluded* the 71 POAs

and 25 NICs from the eligible sample, this sample had fewer *outcome-appropriate* cases than the updated (200 vs. 225).[71]

Thus, the seeming disparity—the apparent numerical *decrease* from the eligible to the updated sample—that emerges from a first reading of Lerman's statement basically, though only partly, results from his having juxtaposed, without sufficiently describing and differentiating in this context, two different types of samples: the all-parole-*releasees* sample and the parole *follow-up* sample. The former contained youth categories (POAs and NICs) that were excluded from the latter, since *its* purpose—unlike that of the latter sample—did *not* require category-level comparability between E's and C's. (The issue of category-level comparability was independent of whether the percentage of youths *within* a given category, say, the POA category, was identical across E's and C's.) At any rate, cases that were appropriate for the *outcome* analysis were compared, in Lerman's statement, with a broader, *all-releasees* group.

In addition, readers must be familiar with the *experiment,* and especially with the nature and requirements of follow-up analyses, in order to recognize such distinctions and understand the importance of various exclusions. Yet, given an exposure only to the particular numbers presented in Lerman's Note and only to the brief descriptions and comments he provided in connection with those numbers and with the samples in question, readers could—perhaps even if they *were* somewhat familiar—still have missed some of these aspects and not have realized that the exclusions in question strengthened the outcome analysis and its interpretation; they did so by making E's and C's more comparable than these groups would have otherwise been, and by specifically reducing confounding. Only a systematic and integrated presentation in the Note—backed by all the required numbers, definitions, and distinctions—could have (1) made it clear that such exclusions had avoided the substantial confounding which would have otherwise occurred and (2) indicated what the seeming disparity really meant.

Experimentals[72]

The difference between the 287 E males in the eligible sample and the 310 in the updated (follow-up) reflects the following (note that the 287 refers to all E males released to parole as of 3/68): (1) Many males were released to parole between March 1968 and the close of Phase 2 (therefore also Stage 2); (2) after their release, 23 such Sacramento/Stockton males could have been followed for at least 16 months prior to the data cutoff for that "updated" analysis and could therefore have been included, and were included, in that follow-up analysis; (3) 287 + 23 = 310.

Statement 2: The 1966 versus 1968 Parole Follow-Up Samples

Before proceeding it should be noted that the 283 and 381 controls (POA + NIC + *all other*) involved in Lerman's second statement—immediately below—both consisted of males and females combined. They were all such youths released to parole, and they thus comprised eligible, not follow-up, samples.

> . . . in 1968, according to *CTP Research Report No. 9*, part 1 (page 36, note 2) the eligible experimentals lost only 2 youths while the controls lost 84 wards as POA and 22 as NIC.[73] [Here, as below, "lost" did not mean unaccounted for. It meant or would have meant (if clarified in Statement 2) that these youths—all of whom had been part of the *eligible* sample—had automatically been excluded when the *available* sample was created; that is, they had appropriately been excluded from the *follow-up* for reasons mentioned above.] A few years earlier, in *CTP Research Report No. 7*, the loss had been 2 experimentals and 63 controls as POA, with no NIC youth. In 1966, 22 percent (63 of 283) of the controls were dropped from the eligible sample, but in 1969 [this should have read 1968] this increased to 28 percent (106 of 381) (Lerman, 1975, pp. 232–233).

Four aspects of this statement will now be reviewed in order to clarify, not only the E/C differences as of any point in time, for example, March 1968, but various changes through time.

1. *The difference in number of E and C POAs.* Throughout Phases 1 and 2, CTP's policy allowed youths to be paroled out of area only in highly unusual circumstances, not just because such an action seemed likely to be ad-

vantageous for some time or to alleviate undesirable pressures. Moreover, only in this way could E's be fully exposed to the CTP program and not be exposed or substantially exposed to other approaches and policies to which their parole performance might then be partly attributed. (From an operational or treatment/control perspective, full exposure to the program was viewed as what they needed—and what could benefit them the most—in the long run.) In contrast, regular parole used POA more often, and such actions were standard Youth Authority practice statewide. As a result, substantially fewer E's than C's (1% versus 22%) were paroled out of area during the Phase 1 and 2 experiment, and all such youths were routinely excluded from parole follow-ups (outcome analyses).

Basically, these exclusions occurred in order to make the E and C follow-up samples comparable to each other at the youth-category level, that is, comparable with regard to analytic categories. For instance, all POAs were automatically excluded because—among other prime reasons—the environmental conditions that existed in their new settings were often different than or quite possibly different than those to which the non-POA'd controls and experimentals were exposed; on balance, the new conditions might have been harsher or milder—it did not matter which. This also applied to law enforcement and judicial practices in various counties outside the Sacramento/Stockton areas; differing *reporting* practices may have existed as well, that is, in addition to differing arrest, convictions, and/or sentencing practices. In order to reduce any E/C confounding that might have resulted from these actual and possible differences, and to thereby increase the interpretability of findings overall, the entire POA category was therefore excluded from follow-ups. It was not eliminated because of differences in the overall *percentage* of E and C POAs, that is, differences in their degree of representation within any given sample. This factor was irrelevant to the basic methodological issue, namely, that of analytical—categorical—comparability (identity).

2. *The different number of control POAs excluded from the 1966 and 1968 parole follow-ups.* The group or cohort of C parole releasees that—apart from its POAs and NICs—was otherwise appropriate for inclusion in the *March 1968* follow-up analysis contained 21 more POAs than did the group that was otherwise appropriate for the *March 1966* analysis. (*Both* groups of releasees were appropriate by virtue of having had a chance to be followed for at least 15 months prior to the data cutoffs for the respective analyses; individuals were *in*appropriate if they were POAs, and so on.) Since all 63 youths who were excluded from the *March 1966* follow-up analysis because they were POAs were also excluded from the *March 1968* analysis as POAs, the 21 *additional* POAs directly accounted for the difference between the 63 and the 84 cases mentioned by Lerman in connection with the respective analyses. That is, the difference between 63 and 84 reflected a simple accumulation of 21 new POAs during the period between the 1966 and 1968 analyses.

3. *The different number of NICs excluded from the 1966 and 1968 parole follow-ups.* Background: (a) Beginning in mid-1966 and continuing through the end of Phase 2, a random 31 percent (the goal had been 33 percent) of all Sacramento/Stockton controls were—by design—never interviewed by the diagnostic team and were therefore never subtyped. This step was taken by research staff because of added time pressures they were experiencing and because they felt that enough interviewed, and therefore analytically usable, C's could still continue to enter the experiment. The nonsubtyped (nondiagnosed) youths were called NICs—non-interviewed controls; and it was soon recognized that these individuals would have to be excluded from *follow-up* analyses. (b) Meanwhile, all CTP youths (E's) continued to be interviewed and subtyped, since—as always—they had to be assigned to a matched worker whenever such an individual was available, and since subtype was used as a key basis for matching. Therefore, the E group never acquired

NICs. (c) Throughout the experiment, neither case-file reviews nor paper and pencil tests—singly or combined—were considered *sufficiently* revealing and accurate for purposes of subtype diagnosis and resulting assignment. Only interviews were accepted. (d) NICs were first mentioned in CTP's 8th Research Report, in connection with the *March 1967* sample (Warren et al., 1966a; Palmer and Warren, 1967, p. 4).

As is evident in the experiment's reports but is not indicated in the Note (and, of course, in *Social Control*), the reasons that no NICs were present in (rather than being excluded from) the *March 1966* follow-up sample, whereas 22 such non-POA'd males (not 25) were indeed excluded from the *March 1968* follow-up, are as follows: No NICs *existed* as of March 1966 (see point [a], above), whereas 22 such males existed as of March 1968; and, once NICs did exist they had to be excluded because, as indicated, the experiment's key analyses centered on E/C subtype comparisons, and NICs had no subtype (Warren et al., 1966a; Palmer and Warren, 1967, p. 4; Palmer et al., 1968, p. 36). More specifically, since NICs were those individuals who—by design—had not been interviewed, they could not, given the experiment's diagnostic standards (cf. point [c], above), be subtyped with sufficient certainty. Since NICs therefore received no subtype diagnosis and since all such individuals were C's, no such C's could be compared with E's—all of whom *had* been subtyped. Thus the exclusion in question, of all 22 such C's who had accumulated between 1966 and 1968.

4. *The different percentage of C's excluded from the 1966 and 1968 parole follow-ups.* As indicated in Lerman's Note, more C cases (28% versus 22%) were excluded from the 1968 follow-up than from the 1966 follow-up; that is, although these youths existed in the respective (1968 and 1966) *eligible* samples, they were not considered for the respective follow-ups. As can be seen from the above reports, this increase reflected the presence, in March 1968 but not March 1966, of NICs. That is, by 1968 a new category—NIC—existed,

and all such youths were excluded from the 1968 follow-up (Palmer et al., 1968, p. 36). In contrast, as of March 1966 no such category existed, and there were no such youths to exclude (Warren et al., 1966a).

Specifically, the 106 of 381 (28%) mentioned in the Note for 1968 involved 84 POAs and 22 NICs; the 63 of 283 cases (22%) mentioned for 1966 consisted of 63 POAs and 0 NICs. Since 22 = 6 percent of 381—precisely the 1966-to-1968 increase to which the Note refers—the difference in question was accounted for simply by the new category (NICs). This is further reflected in the fact that the percentage of remaining, *non*-NIC exclusions—the POAs—was identical in the 1966 and 1968 samples: 63/283 equals 22 percent (1966), and 84/381 also equals 22 percent (1968) (Palmer et al., 1968, pp. 3, 36, 106–107; Warren et al., 1966a, pp. 39–40).

Statement 3: Attrition and Representation
Following his above statements, Lerman (still 1975) then concluded:

[Whereas the exclusion of controls rose from 22 percent in the 1966 sample to 28 percent in the 1968,] the experimental['s] loss remained at less than 1 percent. This increased attrition of the control youth certainly evokes the doubt of whether the "updated" available samples adequately represent the original pool of 1961–1969 males. (p. 233)

Increased Attrition
As mentioned earlier, paroling out of area was rare among E's; not only were just two experimentals POA'd during 1961–1966, but none were added for the rest of Phase 2. (Several E's, of course, left the area for relatively short periods but did not meet the criteria for "true POA" described in Appendix 39. Several C's also left the area for short, nonqualifying periods.) Thus, together with the fact that E's had no NICs throughout 1961–1969, this continued paucity of POAs explains why the exclusions were, and remained, 1 percent. And, as indicated, the increased exclusions among C's—from 22 percent to 28 percent—referred entirely to NICs.[74]

Representation
Representativeness is not an end in itself, but is one determiner of an experiment's value; and value—an experiment's practical goal—first involves and centers on outcomes. (As previously discussed, outcome was Lerman's main concern in connection with his hypothesis that sample differences gave the total group of E's a greater chance of success than its C's.) The critical element in determining the value of the present study's outcome findings was not whether the E and C follow-up samples ("availables") represented an *original pool* of individuals, in this case youths ("eligibles") released to parole; instead, in the present context, it centered on validity and scope.

Regarding validity, the key aspect was the E and C follow-up samples' similarity to *each other* on such outcome-relevant variables/factors as age, IQ, race, SES, commitment offense, and—certainly—Base Expectancy. In this regard, as shown earlier, E's and C's were well-matched (i.e., statistically similar or "equated"). Other aspects of design, and elements of statistical analysis as well, need not be reviewed here; suffice it to say the experiment met scientific standards.

Regarding scope, Phase 1 and 2 Valley E's and C's comprised 70 percent of all male and 89 percent of all female juvenile court first commitments to the Youth Authority from the catchment areas. In San Francisco, the percentages were 51 and 76, respectively; and during Phase 3, which involved males only and included adult court commitments as well, the percentage for otherwise similar, nonviolent individuals was 61. (Besides those individuals, 40 percent of all violent offenders—who themselves comprised 30 percent of all male first commitments to the YA—were eligible to begin their program in CTP's short-term, Dorm 3 setting.)

Thus, not only were the outcome findings for available E's not confounded or diluted by differential risk and by such factors as age, IQ, and the like, but equally important, they applied to, and had utility for, a broad range of serious offenders, even without POAs. In short, though the exclusion of POAs moderately decreased the overall range of youth types (at least among C's—since only two such E's were excluded during Phases 1 and 2 combined), it affected neither validity for nor applicability to the preponderance of eligible youths; and these eligibles, themselves, represented most YA wards. Nor did it affect the experiment's key analyses: subtype comparisons.

In addition, representativeness and applicability were not influenced by *increased* attrition from 1966 to 1968, since POA exclusions remained constant during those years and since the 6 percentage point rise was due to non-interviewed controls. NICs probably affected neither representativeness nor applicability, since they were randomly derived and, therefore, likely adhered to expected frequencies regarding subtype.

Finally, as seen in the next section, though POAs were excluded from parole follow-ups, they were similar to all remaining (non-POA, non-NIC) controls on the background characteristics emphasized by Lerman (age; IQ) and on parole risk (BE) in particular. This applied not only to the total group but to conflicted, passive-conformist, and—with one exception—power-oriented youths alike. Specifically, POAs were representative of available as well as eligible C's in terms of the main-outcome-relevant—thus, value-relevant—items under discussion. As indicated in the same section, this applied to NICs as well. These youths closely resembled—and in this sense reflected—all remaining C's on age, IQ, and BE; they also resembled C's plus POAs combined. Moreover, the *combination* of POAs and NICs was similar to all remaining C's on age, IQ, and BE.

Paroled-Out-of-Area Youths and Non-interviewed Controls

We now address two questions regarding POAs and NICs: Were these groups better risks than the remaining C's? Would their presence have improved the latter's performance—both in itself and, therefore, relative to that of E's? These questions, as indicated, reflect the underlying, practical issue in Lerman's remarks (cf. Statements 1 through 3), and they will be reviewed in turn. Appendix 39 indicates how POA was operationally defined and why POAs were excluded from follow-ups. Based on case-file reviews it describes related policies, it illustrates how POA often came about, and it details selected factors associated with this action (e.g., main initiators; main reasons/goals; assessments of POA and non-POA placements). It briefly describes NICs, as well.

1. *Risk.* Regarding POA and NIC background features—with emphasis on risk

(BE)—the following appeared in Palmer's 1974 reply (pp. 17–18):

Comparisons between POAs and Remaining Controls

In Table 7 [here, Table 21–3], Control POA's (C_o's) are compared with all *available* Controls (C's), in relation to the six background variables. (As before, "availability" has reference to the updated suspension analysis—just as it does in Dr. Lerman's Appendix A [the Note], itself.) In addition, they are compared with all *eligible* Controls (C_{ae}'s). [The C_o vs. C comparisons are found in subsection 1 of each Section of the Table; the C_o versus C_{ae} are found in subsection 2.][75] The POA/Control differences in means, percentages, etc., which are observed with respect to the former comparisons [C_o versus C], are, in the case of all variables, extremely similar to those found in connection with the latter comparisons [the C_o versus C_{ae}] as well. This is because of the [considerable overlap between] the C and C_{ae} samples, themselves, with regard to the specific youths involved. To avoid repetition we will therefore focus on only one of these comparisons: C_o versus C_{ae}.

Before proceeding, the following might be mentioned. There were no significant differences in *subtype representation* between the POA's [that is, all diagnosed, correctly categorized male POA's] on the one hand, and all remaining eligible C's, on the other ($p < .30 > .20$).[76] Nor were there significant differences between POA's and all eligible E's ($p < .30 > .20$).[77] The same applied with reference to the C's, and, separately, to the E's, who were "available" with respect to the updated suspension analysis ($p < .30 > .20$ and $p < .50 > .30$, respectively). [See endnotes 76 and 77 regarding X^2's.]

The following has reference to the *Total Group:* On Base Expectancy, Age, and I.Q., the observed differences between POA's and eligible Controls ranged from slight to nonexistent. More specifically, C_o's were slightly, but not significantly, worse parole risks than C_{ae}'s;[78] beyond this, the two groups were identical on Age and were less than 1 point apart on I.Q. Yet at the same

TABLE 21-3

Comparisons between Groups of "Paroled-Out-of-Area" Control Males and All Remaining Control Males on Selected Background Characteristics, for Sacramento and Stockton Combined[a]

	BE		Age		IQ		Race				SES			Offense		
	M	σ	M	σ	M	σ	C	M	B	O	L	M	U	Pe	Pr	Ao
A. Total Group																
1. C_o	431	104	15.3	1.5	86.3	16.3	77	13	7	3	70	25	4	13	56	31
vs.																
C	444	93	15.3	1.5	85.4	16.3	50	26	21	3	83	16	0	4	74	22
	20 > 10		90 > 80		20 > 10		< 01				< 01				< 01	
2. C_o	431	104	15.3	1.5	86.3	16.3	77	13	7	3	70	25	4	13	56	31
vs.																
C_{ae}	444	93	15.3	1.6	85.4	16.4	51	26	22	2	81	17	2	5	75	20
	20 > 10		90 > 80		20 > 10		< 01				05 > 02				05 > 02	
B. Na + Nx																
1. C_o	448	70	15.4	1.2	90.0	14.5	86	12	0	2	67	29	5	10	52	38
vs.																
C	442	95	15.6	1.3	90.9	14.5	70	16	13	2	74	25	1	2	71	27
	30 > 20		90 > 80		50 > 30		10 > 05				50 > 30				05 > 02	
2. C_o	448	70	15.4	1.2	90.0	14.5	86	12	0	2	67	29	5	10	52	38
vs.																
C_{ae}	448	92	15.7	1.4	90.9	14.5	69	15	15	2	70	26	4	3	73	25
	70 > 50		50 > 30		50 > 30		05 > 02				95 > 90				05 > 02	

(continued on next page)

TABLE 21-3 (continued)

	BE M	σ	Age M	σ	IQ M	σ	Race C	M	B	O	SES L	M	U	Offense Pe	Pr	Ao
C. Cfc + Mp																
1. Co	440	70	15.1	2.1	87.2	22.7	88	0	12	0	50	38	12	50	25	25
vs.																
C	438	94	15.1	1.4	80.0	15.4	28	44	26	2	87	13	0	9	74	17
	70 > 50		70 > 50		02 > 01		< 01				< 01				< 01	
2. Co	440	70	15.1	2.1	87.2	22.7	88	0	12	0	50	38	12	50	25	25
vs.																
Cae	434	97	15.1	1.4	80.9	15.4	26	46	26	2	89	11	0	9	76	15
	30 > 20		70 > 50		02 > 01		< 01				< 01				10 > 05	
D. Cfm																
1. Co	429	57	15.6	1.7	88.6	11.8	78	0	22	0	78	22	0	0	67	33
vs.																
C	448	84	14.9	1.6	79.6	14.5	40	28	33	0	98	2	0	3	83	15
	50 > 30		95 > 90		30 > 20		10 > 05				02 > 01				50 > 30	
2. Co	429	57	15.6	1.7	88.6	11.8	78	0	22	0	78	22	0	0	67	33
vs.																
Cae	447	82	14.9	1.6	80.9	13.6	43	29	29	0	93	7	0	2	83	14
	70 > 50		90 > 80		30 > 20		20 > 10				20 > 10				50 > 30	

[a] Covers 1961–1969. C_o = Paroled-out-of-area controls ($n = 71$). C = All available controls ($n = 225$). C_{ae} = All eligible controls ($n = 296$).

time, statistically significant differences were found on Race, SES, and Offense, [when all their respective individual categories were *combined*. At the individual-category—the *uncombined* category—level per se,] the POA group contained a substantially higher percentage of Caucasians than did the eligible Controls (77 percent versus 51 percent). It also contained a somewhat higher percentage of middle and upper SES individuals (30 percent versus 19 percent). Finally, it contained a substantially lower percentage of property offenders (56 percent versus 75 percent).

Much the same was observed in connection with the [Conflicted (Na + Nx)] group. Here, however, the above-mentioned difference in SES had disappeared, the difference in Race was somewhat smaller than before,[79] and the difference in Offense was slightly [negligibly] larger than before.[79] Finally, the two groups of Controls were now identical on BE.

After viewing these similarities and differences in toto, it would seem difficult to think of the POA's as being, in a statistical sense, "biased" either toward or away from greater success, when compared with eligible Controls. From a strict technical standpoint it might, in this connection, appear justified to focus directly upon level of parole risk, itself [i.e., on B.E.]: Here, no significant differences were noted. . . . [To be sure,] the *POA* group [did contain] a higher percentage of Caucasian and middle-class youths[80]—i.e., individuals who [in the literature] are found to be somewhat better parole risks, in at least a number of correctional contexts. [Also], the *Control* group contained a higher percentage of property offenders—individuals who are often among the poorer "risks."

Generally speaking, it would probably be appropriate to conclude that there are no decisive, overall POA/Control advantages one way or another. This conclusion at least takes account of all the available facts [including due consideration to the prime parole risk factor, namely, Base Expectancy, itself]. (pp. 17–18)

Comparisons between NICs and Other Groups (C, E, C + E)—with and without POAs

. . . when all male NIC's were compared with all remaining, Non-POA male Controls, there were again no significant differences. The probability levels (based upon the chi square test) were: Age < .30 > .20; I.Q. < .50 > .30; Race < .50 > .30; SES < .90 > .80; Offense < .20 > .10; Base Expectancy < .70 > .50. When all male POA's [then totaling 71] were added to the above Controls, there were still no significant differences: Age < .20 > .10; I.Q. < .80 > .70; Race < .20 > .10; SES < .98 > .95; Offense < .30 > .20; Base Expectancy < .70 > .50.

When the male NIC's were compared with the male Experimentals, there were no significant differences on five of the six background variables: Age < .01; I.Q. < .70 > .50; SES < .95 > .90; Race < .30 > .20; Offense < .50 > .30; Base Expectancy < .50 > .30. In the case of Age, the actual means were: NIC = 15.4; E = 15.6. [Regarding this and the subsequent two findings on age, see "A Note on Age," near the end of this chapter.]

When the male NIC's were compared with all remaining, Non-POA male Controls *plus* all male Experimentals, there were no significant differences on five of the six background variables: Age < .02 > .01; I.Q. < .70 > .50; SES < .98 > .95; Race < .50 > .30; Offense < .30 > .20; Base Expectancy < .70 > .50. In the case of Age, the actual means were: NIC = 15.4; C + E = 15.5.

Finally, when the male NIC's were compared with the above C's plus E's *plus* all male POA's, there were again no significant differences on five of the six background variables: Age < .05 > .02; I.Q. < .80 > .70; SES < .95 > .90; Race < .30 > .20; Offense < .50 > .30; Base Expectancy < .70 > .50. The mean Ages were: NIC = 15.4; C + E + POA = 15.5. (pp. 19–20)

It seems appropriate to conclude that NICs were very similar to non-NIC's on risk and related features.[81]

Comparisons between NICs + POAs Combined and Remaining Controls
When all remaining NICs and POAs were combined into a single group, they were similar to

all remaining male C's on each key risk item: age, IQ, and BE; that is, no significant differences existed between the former group and the latter.[82]

2. *Performance.* The following appeared in the 1974 reply (pp. 22–25):

If the above-mentioned POA's are added to the remaining group of Controls[83]—the latter . . . being those who Lerman has referred to as the "available Control sample"—the resulting, combined group may be referred to as the "*expanded Control sample.*" . . . Once we have added these previously excluded POA's, we may ask: Does the expanded . . . Control sample have an r.o.o. [rate of offending] which differs substantially from that of the available Control sample . . . ? The answer is provided by the following:

[a]. *Updated suspension analysis.*[84] Monthly r.o.o.'s are shown below for the expanded control sample;[85] they are also shown in parentheses for the *available* control sample.[86] Both sets of figures have reference to offenses of 3–10 severity level only [and to suspensions involving possible and alleged such offenses].

- Total Group   0.12 (0.12)
- Neurotic [Conflicted] 0.12 (0.12)
- Power-Oriented   0.12 (0.13)
- Passive-Conformist   .10 (0.10)

Since the figures for the expanded sample are identical or virtually identical to those for the sample [with which Lerman was concerned] (viz., the available sample), it is evident that the inclusion of POA's has made essentially no difference with respect to monthly rates of offending. . . . (pp. 22–25)

[b]. *CI&I rapsheet analysis.*[87] This analysis is entirely analogous to that which was reported in section ["a"], immediately above, with reference to *suspension* data. In both analyses, relevant POA's—together with their relevant followup periods (risk-months) and their related offenses—were simply added to the [given], "available Control sample." This resulted in an "expanded Control sample." Also in both cases, the main purpose was to see if there would be a

substantial change in monthly rates of offending, for Controls, subsequent to the addition of the given Control POA's. . . .

Preliminary findings: When POA's were added to the available Control sample, monthly r.o.o.'s underwent the following changes, from those [presented earlier in the 1974 reply]. [Soon after the 1974 reply was completed and distributed, the *final* results were in. For each analytic group (Total, Neurotic, etc.), these are shown in brackets immediately following the second figure]:[88]

(1) For the Total group, r.o.o. changed from .067 to .064 [.063] . . .[89]

(2) For the Neurotic group, r.o.o. changed from .082 to .079 [.075] . . .

(3) For the Power-Oriented group, r.o.o. changed from .059 to .054 [.052] . . .

(4) For Passive-Conformists, r.o.o. changed from .060 to .058 [.070] . . .

Generally speaking, the amount of change in question—i.e, from available C's to expanded C's—was about the same as that which was observed in connection with the earlier-mentioned, updated suspension analysis; it, too, was very little. (pp. 27–28)

In short, the addition of POAs would have had—and, in the above analysis, *had*—a negligible to slight impact on the E/C, CI&I rapsheet comparison, that is, on Control r.o.o.'s in particular.

For *NICs,* the rates of offending were: updated suspension analysis—0.10; CI&I rapsheet analysis—0.09 (0.093).[90] As with POAs, the first analysis was the 16-months parole follow-up and the second was the CYA career follow-up. The r.o.o.'s, and those shown below, were for the total group, since NICs had no subtype. They involved severity levels 3–10 and referred to all male NICs who—had they *not* been NICs—would have been included in the given analysis or analyses if they met the earlier-mentioned criteria for that analysis (e.g., if they had had an opportunity for sufficient follow-up).

When these NICs were added to the updated suspension analysis—thereby creating a C + NIC sample—the rate of offending, which had been 0.12 for C's alone, remained 0.12. That is, the NICs' rate of 0.10 for this 16-months follow-up (see above) did not alter the rate of 0.12 already reported for the suspensions analysis, for the total group of C's (see above). This lack of change reflected the NICs' much smaller sample size than that of C's, that is, "regular" (non-NIC, non-POA) C's, and also the fact that r.o.o.'s for NICs and C's were fairly similar in the first place. When the NICs were added to the "expanded" C sample—that is, the C + POA sample for the updated suspension analysis—the resulting (C + POA + NIC) rate was still 0.12.

When NICs were added to the CII rap-sheet analysis—thus creating yet another C + NIC sample—the already reported rate of 0.067 (preliminary finding [1] above) became 0.072. That is, the NICs' rate of 0.093 for this CYA career follow-up (see above) slightly increased the rate of 0.067 reported for the total group of C's alone, also for the career follow-up. When the NICs were added to the expanded C sample—the C + POA sample for the career follow-up—the resulting (C + POA + NIC) rate was 0.067; this was similar to the already reported 0.063 for C's + POAs alone.

Thus, the addition of NICs—like that of POAs—had a negligible to slight impact on the earlier-mentioned rates for C's alone, that is, for "regular" C's; this also applied when NICs and POAs were combined. These results generally reflected the NICs' (1) relatively average to somewhat above average r.o.o.'s compared to those of C's, combined with their (2) much smaller sample sizes than those of C's as well as C's + POAs.[91, 92]

We will now briefly review the relationship between (1) *matching* on outcome-relevant background characteristics and (2) *numerical equality or inequality* of sample sizes.

Matching and Numerical Equality

After describing the greater "loss" of cases among C's than E's and after suggesting a possible implication thereof (see "Statement 3," above), Lerman characterized this loss as a quantitative ("numbers") rather than qualitative (categorical—here, an E/C subtypes) problem.[93] Since this combined description, suggestion, and characterization may have led some readers to mistakenly conclude that no two groups can remain adequately matched (i.e., statistically comparable—still equated—) if either group has substantially *fewer cases* than the other—for example, after it has lost (or even failed to gain) more cases—the following should be noted.

Though a group (say, C's) may have lost many cases due to POA, NIC, and/or other reasons, it can, in fact, easily remain well-matched with one (say, E's) that has lost few if any cases and that may now outnumber it.[94, 95] In the present study, this was observed for E's versus C's—groups that, after the latter's reduction in size from the eligible sample, were still well-matched on background characteristics. However, it was also seen *within* the C group—for example, for POAs versus remaining C's and for NICs versus those same C's.[96] (These POAs and NICs had been part of the original—the eligible—C group.) That is, it was observed when comparing each removed group (POA; NIC) with the C group from which it was derived; and as indicated in a later section as well as in related notes, such groups were generally well-matched, particularly on key variables. This match, that is, statistical comparability, was also observed when the removed groups were compared with *available* C's.

In short, having the same number of cases or even close to that number is not a precondition to being adequately matched (equated) on age, IQ, or any other background item. This applies both before and after any removal. Stated differently, E/C comparability on outcome-relevant matching variables neither requires nor, for that matter, is guaranteed by numerical equality or near equality. (Moreover, such equality or near equality does not even make comparability more *likely* to occur. Drawing upon Lerman's suggestion and characterization, statistically unsophisticated readers could easily reach an opposite conclusion.) Thus, for example, in many successful correctional and noncorrectional studies, E's and C's—say, available samples—have been well-matched (well equated; highly comparable) on key background variables (including risk per se), even though those E's and C's differed considerably in size, and regardless of any absolute and relative size reduction (or increase) that may have occurred. Yet in other studies, E's and C's were *poorly* matched despite identical or near-identical sizes, whether in eligible or available samples.

At any rate, in the present study, numerical inequality did not prevent these groups from being well-matched in the sense of having comparable background characteristics individually and collectively, and of thereby being partly interchangeable. Nor did it stop NICs—and, for example, NICs + POAs combined—from adequately representing remaining C's with regard to such characteristics, at least those of primary outcome relevance. Finally, available samples—whether comprised of E's or C's—were quite similar to their respective *eligible* samples on age, IQ, and so on, even though their sizes differed from those of the eligibles.[97]

In sum, by itself, neither size equality nor size inequality produces positive or negative consequences, or inevitable effects of any type, with respect to matching and representativeness. Comparative size—relative number of cases—does not determine such issues; nor do absolute and relative *changes* in sample size.

A Note on Age

We close this chapter by addressing a question that may have puzzled readers: Since the age difference between given samples was so small, why was it sometimes "statistically significant"? For instance, mean ages for *NICs* and *C's + E's + POAs* (all others) were 15.4 and 15.5, respectively, yet the probability level for their chi-squares—the standard tests for analyzing background items—was < .05 > .02. The answer is not that relatively large samples were always involved (though size mattered in some analyses); for example, NICs were hardly numerous, even though "all others" were. Rather, the answer mainly centers on an interaction between the way in which chi-square tests on age were analytically structured and that particular test's statistical properties. This interaction, explained below, did not require large samples; instead, it built and depended on specified differences within *particular* age categories. It did so even when little age difference existed between the samples *as a whole* (all categories combined), for example, between the NIC and the "all others" samples that were being compared.

Regarding analytical structure or approach, the explanation begins with the fact that, when using chi-square to compare given samples on age, the researchers first routinely subdivided (structured) each sample— whether NIC, POA, regular C, E, or combinations thereof—into six or, more often, nine categories. These were either ages 13 and under, 14, 15, through 18 and up (thus, six categories), or ages 11, 12, 13, through 19 (nine categories). (See, e.g., Palmer et al.,

1968, p. 7, regarding control and experimental analyses.)

When this many categories—six or especially nine—are used, rather than the typical two to four as in *race, SES,* and *offense,* the following automatically occurs in any chi-square analysis. (Note: The following is over and beyond, but not entirely independent of, the fact that when dividing a given offender sample—say, one with 100 individuals—into six to nine categories, there will be, on the average, fewer individuals per category than when dividing that 100 into only two to four categories.) (1) The chances of creating several *small-frequency cells,* for example, one such cell for 12-year-old NICs and another for those age 13, are substantially increased. Simultaneously, (2) the chances are increased of obtaining, from among those cells, one or more with an *atypical number of cases,* that is, either substantially more or fewer youths than would be expected anyway (e.g., using a normal curve). Items (1) and especially (2) are more likely to occur for the smaller of the two samples being compared, such as NICs rather than "all others." Since the *proportion* of cases that are atypical is likely to be numerically higher in any given cell that belongs to the smaller than to the larger sample—and partly because of the statistical properties mentioned below—the impact of those cases on chi-square is also likely to be greater for the smaller or small-sized sample.

Especially when they occur in small-frequency cells, atypical frequencies result from what are usually considered either normal fluctuations or an otherwise relatively average number of unusual individuals (i.e., average when they occur in *average*-sized cells). These fluctuations, and so on, would be relatively inconspicuous and would generally make little difference in an average-sized cell. In effect, normal fluctuations, and so forth, are likely to have greater impact in connection with smaller-than-average-sized cells, and these smaller cells are more likely to exist in the first place if one uses a larger-than-average number of analytic categories.

Especially in light of item (2), an atypical numerical "ratio" will not infrequently exist in one or more *sets* of cells, for instance, the cell for 13-year-old NICs (treated as a numerator) compared to that for 13-year-old "all others" (treated as a denominator). Thus, for any given set of cells, that is, two cells from the same age category, a "ratio" is produced by dividing one sample's number of cases in the given category, such as in age 13, by the other sample's number of cases in that same category.[98] An *atypical* ratio—for example, a ratio of 13-year-old NICs to 13-year-old "all others" that differs considerably from the NIC/"all others" ratio in most or all remaining age categories combined—is further illustrated below.

Because of chi-square's statistical properties with respect to integrating the squared deviation from the "expected" number of cases in any given cell, the following sometimes occurs:[99] Atypical numbers of cases within given, small-frequency cells—more specifically, atypical ratios that are produced by those numbers for given *sets* of cells—can yield a statistically significant result for any given variable as a whole (here, age), that is, for its six or nine categories combined. Moreover, and particularly important, even one or two such numbers/ratios can produce this result largely or entirely by themselves. It was precisely this that happened in a number of earlier-mentioned analyses.

Thus, when a more traditional analytic structure was used to supplement those six- or nine-category analyses—that is, when the age distribution was simply trichotomized—statistical significance almost always disappeared. For instance, when three rather than the previous nine age categories were used, none of the NIC-related differences reported earlier remained significant (the three categories were: 11–14; 15–16; 17 and up. This age grouping, one that involved a relatively typical number of categories, eliminated—and would otherwise have precluded—most cells with very small frequencies; it also decreased the degrees of freedom from eight to two): *NIC versus E:* $X^2 = 1.35$; $p < .50 > .30$; *NIC versus C + E:* $X^2 = 0.52$; $p < .80 > .70$; *NIC versus C + E + POA:* $X^2 = 0.41$; $p < .90 > .80$.

Before summarizing, the following might be noted. Small-frequency cells may exist anywhere within a given distribution, regardless of whether many categories have been used. With variables such as age, the more categories that are used—and here we emphasize ungrouped categories—the likelier it is that such cells will occur at or near the ends of the distribution, for example, in the 12- or 13-year categories; this of course is where the smallest cell frequencies usually occur. At any

rate, it is in small-frequency cells/categories—wherever they occur—that otherwise minor or moderate numerical fluctuations more often produce an atypical ratio (cf. proportion) between groups that are being compared, for instance, between NICs and "all others."

Again, "atypical ratio" essentially means "unlike the ratios found in most or all remaining categories combined." For example, it can refer to a set of two cells (one cell for NICs and one for "all others"—together comprising, say, the 16-year category) in which a *1:20* sample-size ratio exists between those cells, rather than, say, the more typical, *1:8* ratio that exists in most or all remaining categories combined. Specifically, in a given chi-square analysis there may be eight NICs versus 160 "all others" in one particular set of cells (the 16-year category)—a 1:20 ratio—and 45 NICs versus 360 "all others" in all remaining sets combined—a 1:8 ratio. Because of chi-square's statistical properties, referred to earlier, the former numbers and resulting ratio would, by themselves, contribute heavily toward any statistical significance that might be obtained. However, if a relatively few more NICs had been part of the *16*-year category—for example, four youths who had instead been in the *15*-year cell—the statistical result might have differed considerably. Specifically, if those four individuals had been merged with the 16-year-olds, the probability level might no longer have been significant. At any rate, by *combining* ages 15 and 16, as in the earlier-mentioned trichotomy, the above situation—for the most part, fluctuation-based significance associated mainly with small-frequency cells—would not usually arise, and the resulting probability levels would be more reliable in the sense of stable.

In sum, when performing chi-square analyses the use of numerous categories not infrequently yields some small- or very small-sized cells.[100] This occurs regardless of overall sample size but is likeliest when at least one of the samples being compared (as, e.g., NICs) is only moderate in size. If a relatively few unusual cases and/or otherwise expected fluctuations happen to fall or occur in these cells, their contribution to the overall chi-square can be disproportionately large. This can produce or greatly contribute to a relatively unreliable picture of the magnitude or significance of differences between the *overall* samples being compared. Grouping of data, that is, combining of categories (this being a very typical practice), such as ages 11 through 14 or ages 15 and 16, generally prevents such cases and/or fluctuations from unduly influencing the overall chi-square. In the present experiment, the fact that data were sometimes ungrouped or hardly grouped in analyses of items such as age largely accounted for the statistical significance that was occasionally observed despite the small to negligible differences between the means of samples being compared.

For age and IQ, the researchers nevertheless did often group the data; specifically they trichotomized them. However, they sometimes did so only to supplement the more detailed, for example, nine-category, breakdowns—that is, to supplement what they had already decided would be the main analyses. And, though they usually showed the actual *means* (e.g., average ages) for the samples that were being compared, the researchers therefore routinely reported *significance levels,* not for the trichotomized supplements but for the more detailed breakdowns only, such as for the ungrouped—the numerous-category—analyses.[101]

In the case of race, SES, and offense, the data neither had to be nor, in effect, appropriately could be grouped or further subdivided. This was because three or four pragmatically useful, intrinsically meaningful, and/or (at least) widely used categories—for instance, lower, middle, and upper SES—existed from the start.[102] Therefore, in contrast to age and IQ, no supplementary analyses—analyses with a smaller number of categories—were performed for these factors, and no additional significance levels existed.

In the next chapter we will conclude our response to Lerman's 1973/1975 critique of the experiment's findings, and will review other issues as well.

Notes

1. E's and C's who were "restored" after committing an offense or alleged offense were continued in their program; those "revoked" were almost always institutionalized. Both such decisions—continuation and institutionalization—were made by the Youth Authority Board. Institutionalization following revocation was a long-standing statewide YA policy, exceptions to which were rare.

2. More precisely, recidivism was measured from the date on which the individual's parole was suspended for the offense that led to any such action; this date corresponded closely to the actual offense date. The 15- and 24-month follow-ups were, of course, two *separate* follow-ups; one was simply nine months longer than the other, and was thus more comprehensive. Fifteen (15.49) months was the YA Research Division's standard parole follow-up period, prior to as well as throughout the California experiment (Davis et al., 1974; Walters, Brown, and Logan, 1961). Six-, 12-, and 24-month follow-ups were commonly used in California's adult corrections research (Conrad, 1965; Dickover, 1970), and the first two of these were widely used throughout corrections.

3. If the board neither revoked nor unfavorably discharged an individual subsequent to his offense, it restored him to parole.

4. Before Phase 2, RPAs made such recommendations proportionately more often for females than for males.

5. Probation decreased this recommitment practice when, by the later 1960s, it fully recognized that CTP agents were, themselves, less likely than before to recommend restoral following the first—certainly the second—such offense.

6. During all preceding and subsequent years, Sacramento probation recommitted an approximately equal percentage of male E's and C's for similar offenses within any category.

7. These formal reports of penal code offenses, of infractions, and of technical violations were written by E and C parole agents regarding youths on their caseloads. They were detailed and specific (often two or more pages, single-spaced), and they followed a standard format that was used, statewide, in all regular and special Youth Authority parole units. Suspension reports were written only by YA staff; in contrast, Criminal Identification and Investigation rapsheets were produced only by Department of Justice staff, entirely independent of the YA. See endnote 10 for related details.

8. That is, *whether* they received any such discharge, regardless of any offenses (or

even revocations, etc.) they may have accumulated at any time *prior* to discharge or prior to the offense that triggered the discharge.

9. It might be noted that all suspension reports were kept in each E and C youth's parole field folder (file); however, no rap-sheets per se, and no copies thereof, were maintained in this or other such files. Since the researchers maintained an up-to-date copy of all relevant documents contained in parole files, suspension reports had always been immediately and easily available for their review and analysis. In contrast, in order to obtain CI&I data for any given follow-up cohort—such as one that involved numerous E's and C's—the researchers had to formally request, from the Department of Justice (DJ), each individual rapsheet; this applied throughout the experiment. Depending on the cohort size and DJ's work load, these documents usually arrived—in batches—over an approximately six week period, beginning about three weeks later.

10. Independent of this problem with YA suspension reports, CI&I rapsheets had the following advantage. They were generated by a source—the Bureau of Criminal Investigation, of the Department of Justice DJ—that was organizationally independent of the YA and was therefore not subject to its decision-making policies/practices and to its other possible influences. (The DJ's head, namely, the state Attorney General, was an elected official. As such, he was directly responsible to the voters and fiscally accountable to the Legislative branch of state government. The YA director, in contrast, was a governor's appointee and, as such, reported to the Executive branch.) DJ routinely received its arrest information directly from the police/sheriff, and its conviction data from the courts. It processed and recorded this information without input from YA staff. (See endnote 12.) As to other information, some data *were* supplied by YA: The YA, by law, routinely notified DJ of its major actions regarding youths—for instance, actions that involved *revocations* as well as *favorable/unfavorable discharges.*

Excluding favorable discharges (these, of course, were never triggered by an arrest), notification by YA occurred after the arrest in question and therefore subsequent to the arrest's independent processing and recording by DJ. (In short, offenses leading to the revocation or unfavorable discharge were routinely reported to CI&I not just by YA but by arresting agencies.) Thus, revocation and unfavorable discharge data appeared on all rapsheets, as did those of the *original commitment* and *all releases to parole*. Only those four types of actions/information *had* to be supplied to DJ by the YA. However, *recommitments* were initiated and implemented by probation, not by the YA, and they almost always resulted in a major YA action: (re)institutionalization. As a result, both probation and YA routinely notified DJ of their occurrence—including their basis and dates. However, YA notification was not *required* in this case. (Note: During the 1960s and 1970s all requests for CI&I rapsheets were made through the DJ's Bureau of Criminal Statistics. As a result, the documents in question were sometimes known as "BCS rapsheets.")

11. Before 1973, the researchers had used rapsheets for only three analyses—each of *post-YA* data (specifically, information on postdischarge arrests) (Palmer and Herrera, 1972a, 1972b; Palmer and Turner, 1970). These documents were used because they were the only reliable, uniform, official, and non-cost-prohibitive source of such arrest data. (Integral to this source issue was the fact that Youth Authority agents no longer had access to, and responsibility for, discharged youths.) They had not been used to analyze *parole-period data,* that is, predischarge arrests, because, as indicated, suspension reports written by YA parole agents—control (C) and CTP (E) agents alike—were assumed to be complete or essentially complete. This assumption was partly based on the critical role these reports had long played in the YA and on their resulting, special status. For instance:

"Together with the agent's recommendations [regarding restoral to parole, revocation of parole, or unfavorable discharge], it was these reports which contained nearly all the key stimuli [agent's recommendations included] to which the Youth Authority Board responded when deciding what to do with a ward [whether E or C] who had gotten into legal difficulties. (The occurrence of 'Special Incident Reports' [note: like the suspension documents, these were written to the board] was relatively infrequent during most of Phases 1 and 2. 'Chronological entries'—[which were generally based on the E and C agents' logbooks]—were rarely focused upon by the Board.)" (Palmer, 1973c: 70) Together with suspension documents and the Special Incident Reports [which were approximately one-tenth as common as suspension documents], these "chronos" were always located in the youth's field file; and although this file was readily available upon Board request, the Board rarely reviewed it in its entirety. At any rate, (1) all information regarding the youth's parole adjustment and behavior that the agent and his/her supervisor considered pertinent was to be reviewed or summarized in the Suspension Report (and in what was sometimes titled Revocation Report and [Unfavorable] Discharge Report), and this included non-trivial, non-moot occurrences and issues also recorded in Special Incident Reports; (2) the Board therefore relied heavily on suspension reports (together with Revocation and Discharge reports) as a source of relevant information regarding the youth. Of all YA documents describing youth behavior, these were the most complete.

Thus, although *rapsheets* contained parole-period data in addition to post-CYA data, no *parole*-period analyses were made using these documents prior to 1973 because, until then, it was believed that such analyses would reveal nothing that analyses of Suspension Reports would themselves reveal (Palmer, 1973c).

12. [Rapsheets] are a compilation of all individual reports-of-arrest—reports which have routinely, and directly, been received *by* DJ from arresting agencies throughout California (specifically, from police, probation, and sheriffs' departments). [DJ is supposed to receive such reports whenever an individual has been *booked and fingerprinted,* irrespective of any decisions that are made thereafter. Almost all its reports do originate this way. (Rapsheets also contain dates of selected background checks in connection with employment applications, and dates of YA actions mentioned in endnote 10.)] Throughout Phases 1 and 2, DJ would routinely send a copy of each individual arrest report [this was a small, "Notice of Arrest" form] to the CYA's central office [i.e., "headquarters"] in Sacramento. (Headquarters then forwarded a copy of the CI&I notice directly to the parole unit to which the youth's agent was assigned.) (Palmer, 1973c, p. 68)

13. These results/clues mainly related to CTP analyses which were carried out between October 1972 and March 1973. They included [among other measures] E versus C comparisons on *law enforcement*-initiated versus *YA agent*-initiated suspensions during parole (as based [in both cases, entirely] upon the standard, YA suspension reports [though some may have been called Revocation Reports, etc.]). . . . The point is that things were not quite adding up . . . : [i.e., results were suggesting that] some type of systematic difference seemed to exist, or remain "left over," which wasn't entirely accounted for by the factor of *who* (YA agent versus law enforcement agent) initiated the arrests. Instead, the data seemed to point—indirectly, in large part—toward the factor of *which program* (C or E) was doing the reporting relative to the given types of arrests (Palmer, 1973c, p. 68).

14. Sixteen months was the longest follow-up in Analysis A; the remaining follow-up was eight months. Like all follow-ups in the California experiment these involved cohorts. The lengths of follow-up were not *average* time periods, for example, with some youths followed for less than 16.00 months and others for more. Thus, except for cases described in this chapter and in Appendix 39, all individuals who had had an opportunity to be followed up for 16 months (or, in the

other analysis, 8.00 months) were included in the analysis. (The eight-months follow-up existed mainly because a reviewer had indicated it would approximate the then-typical duration of initial institutionalization for controls, and would thus constitute a comparable time base for E's and C's. Despite its limitations, this rationale was accepted for exploratory purposes in Analysis A. Sixteen months was selected as the central measure because it was—simultaneously—twice that of the eight-months period yet very close to the standard 15.49-month period.)

15. When an individual's parole was suspended he or she almost always was, or already had been, (1) arrested (and, thus, booked and fingerprinted) and (2) incarcerated in either a jail, juvenile hall, or YA facility. (Thus, the term "suspension" really means "suspension/arrest.") (See endnote 16.) The main exception involved youths on "runaway" or "whereabouts unknown" status. Such offenses, and various technical violations, often did not appear on CI&I rapsheets, especially those of E's. This was not just because the *YA* agents (especially CTP agents), not *law enforcement* personnel, were usually the first to know about these activities and were the ones who initiated these particular suspensions, but because they (especially CTP agents) usually pursued and resolved the situation on their own. Thus, for example, though youths may have been suspended and temporarily detained by a YA agent in a YA facility (mainly the Northern Reception Center and Clinic), they were often not booked and fingerprinted by the police in the process. (The latter actions—which, for instance, would have occurred had the youths gone to jail [whether or not on a YA warrant for parole violation]—*would* have automatically triggered the CI&I notification process.) As indicated, there was no legal requirement that suspensions—when they involved YA (C as well as E) handling and facilities exclusively—be reported to the Department of Justice, and therefore appear on rapsheets. (Such handling was not possible with nonminor offenses, nearly all of which resulted in arrests, booking, and fingerprinting.) Nevertheless, all offenses—even minor infractions or technical violations—that led to revocation or unfavorable discharge in the E or C program *were* reported to DJ, and therefore did appear on rapsheets. (See endnote 10 regarding "major actions," including recommitments.)

16. Arrests are typically but not always followed by a Youth Authority Board action suspending parole. [For instance, a youth may have been arrested by the police and may then have served and completed a jail term before the parole agent became aware of these events. (This was more common in the C than E program, since C agents ordinarily tried to contact youths much less often than did E agents.) Since the term was completed, the E or C agent may have felt there was no point in requesting suspension of parole, particularly if the agent did not plan to conduct a further investigation into the offense.] The term "arrest" applies whenever a parolee is held in custody, regardless of the reason. Board action suspending parole legalizes detention by the Youth Authority pending the gathering of information pertinent to a further decision. Parole is sometimes suspended before an arrest is made, as in [but not limited to] the case of a missing parolee (Warren et al., 1966a, p. 63).

17. As part of Analysis B, information bearing on differential occurrence, awareness, and reporting of youth behavior was obtained by comparing the rapsheets that the researchers requested and analyzed in 1972–1973 with all available *suspension documents.* (In all such document analyses, that is, throughout Analysis B, identical definitions, statistical/analytic approaches, time periods, C/E youth samples, and CI&I as well as YA source documents were used. The documents also included those which, though they described suspensions, happened to be titled Revocation Reports or Discharge Reports.) In this analysis the arrests that were listed on C and E rapsheets, respectively, were used as the base against which to compare the suspensions/arrests (s/a's) that were listed on C and E suspension reports in each youth's field file. The goal

was to see if the arrests reported on rap-sheets were equally or not equally likely to be listed on the suspension reports of E's and C's, respectively. In other words, were E and C suspension documents equally complete, when judged against rapsheets? *Results:* Of all arrests listed on the *rapsheets,* the following was observed. For every *1* such suspension/arrest that was also reported on the suspension documents of control youths, 2.4 such s/a's were reported on those of CTP youths. In short, a much lower ratio or percentage of reporting was found for C's than for E's. In this connection the following might also be noted: Most often, the incidents that were listed on E's suspension reports but which did *not* also appear on CI&I rapsheets were relatively minor (as to severity level) or technical in nature, such as poor school adjustment or missed group meeting. It was mainly but not entirely these severity-level 1 and 2 incidents that accounted for the higher reporting ratio among E's than C's. This was consistent with the fact that far more of these incidents, especially technical violations, occurred and/or were known about in CTP than in the control program. Together with results from Analysis A (see text), this finding suggested that differential "awareness" of violations/infractions, not just differential reporting of such behavior, very probably existed. Moreover, since it was known that CTP agents had far more contacts with their cases than did control agents and that they (especially those working with power-oriented youths) believed in responding to even "minor misbehavior" in order to convey specific treatment/control messages (Grant, Warren, and Turner, 1963; Warren, Palmer, and Turner, 1964b; Warren and Palmer, 1965; Warren et al., 1966a), this finding was not unexpected. Therefore, it seemed appropriate to conclude that, in effect, differential "awareness" often but not entirely reflected differing degrees of "occurrence," in the first place; this applied even though, as suggested, it was not proven by Analysis B itself. Similar findings had been observed elsewhere, by 1973. See, for example, Adams, Chandler, and Neithercutt, 1971; Havel, 1965; Havel and Sulka, 1962; Johnson, 1962; Lohman et al., 1967; Roberts, 1970; Robinson et al., 1969.

18. In Phase 2 as compared to *Phase 1,* E's were suspended at a 45 percent lower rate for the violations/infractions in question, and C's were suspended at a 23 percent lower rate. (The monthly E rates were 0.050 and 0.091, respectively; the C rates were 0.010 and 0.013. [Palmer, 1973c, pp. 185–186]) For this reason, the rate difference between E's and C's was considerably larger in Phase 1 than Phase 2. Thus, in effect, the suspension practices of the CTP and control programs converged in Phase 2. This was only partly because a former CTP agent—mainly a power-oriented worker—became a control-program (Stockton) supervisor in Phase 2.

19. In the control program, some such infractions (e.g., for "missed group meeting") simply did not exist, because given activities (e.g., group meetings) were not part of the parole program. Various other matters (e.g., poor school adjustment; poor attitude toward program) were either known about but largely deemphasized or were simply *not* known about, for instance, due to relatively little contact—and, perhaps, for related reasons—between agents, on the one hand, and youths, parents, and teachers, on the other.

20. Since Analysis A was not made separately for minor and nonminor offenses, it was not known if this cross-program problem included nonminor offenses (severity levels 3–10).

21. [This difference] "was significant at the .06 level ($X^2 = 3.71$). (The E versus C difference remains significant . . . when severity-levels 1–2 are included.) That is, the control agents had made out no suspension report relative to a significantly larger number of public offenses than was the case among CTP agents. Virtually identical figures were obtained in connection with the offenses of a 57 percent subsample of E and C wards who were closely matched on I-level, subtype, location (city), year of entry into their YA program, etc. ($p < .05$).

The figures of 43 percent and 32 percent dropped to 33 percent and 24 percent, respectively, when Special Incident Reports were included (Palmer, 1973c, pp. 69–70).

YA operations staff who were apprised of these findings and who had been administrators and/or middle managers [or parole agents] on the local scene during Phases 1 and/or 2 . . . were readily able to advance a number of "practical" as well as "mechanical/procedural" oriented explanations for the rather high rate of non-reporting [on suspension documents. (See Appendix 37 regarding these explanations.)] They were somewhat surprised in relation to CTP [mainly because they knew its agents made extra efforts to provide detailed documentation to the board and others]. (Palmer, 1973c, p. 69) In this connection it might be noted that the figures of 33 percent and 24 percent for C's and E's, respectively, dropped to 26 percent and 12 percent when "chronos" were included. The drop for E's was larger than that for C's because these documents were more often used and were also more detailed in CTP than in the control program, and, perhaps, because CTP's chronos probably listed most of the technical violations that were known about in that program but which were not elsewhere documented.

22. "Or, at any rate, the *approximate* percent of all 'now-known' offenses [i.e., known as of Analysis B]" (Palmer, 1973c, p. 84). Besides #2, other indices described in the 1973c document (pp. 66–67) were: #1 (24-months parole follow-up), #3 (rate of favorable discharge), #4 (rate of unfavorable discharge), #5 (rate of post-YA arrests), #6 (rate of post-YA convictions), and #7 (rate of arrests during parole, based on CI&I rapsheets). The latter two had been used in types of analysis that were new at the time.

23. As can be seen in the preceding section, the youth behavior on which the researchers now focused was *mainly* reflected in, and operationally consisted of, nonminor, law-enforcement-initiated arrests, and any resulting convictions.

These events had been recorded by the Department of Justice, on CI&I rapsheets. The recidivism index that the researchers dropped as their principal outcome measure had been operationally defined as revocation, recommitment, or unfavorable discharge (collectively), within either 15- or (especially after 1968) 24-months parole follow-up.

24. Despite the California researchers' new outcome measure and Lerman's new focus, the following occurred. During the next several years a number of reviewers reiterated—or, in some cases, independently discovered and agreed with—Lerman's *1968* critique of the experiment's then-current principal *outcome measure*. Some reviewers may have done this without realizing that a different and more appropriate outcome measure was now being emphasized—one which, in effect, had been substituted for the former index. (Theoretically, some such reviews need not have occurred, since the new measure in question had already been highlighted in two major journal articles and was, therefore, generally available to correctional scholars and others (Palmer, 1974b, p. 5; 1975b, p. 146). This availability outweighs or supersedes the fact that, although the new measure was also emphasized in the report (Palmer, 1973c) quoted throughout the first section of this chapter and in a report (Palmer, 1974a) to NIMH, some such individuals may not have seen or closely examined either *document*. (In the text that follows, these two documents or reports are sometimes called "replies to Lerman." Both were fairly widely distributed in the mid-1970s, and their distribution to correctional researchers, to scholars, and to others, continued into the 1980s.)

25. (1) Lerman also implied that this type of situation, that is, a presumed noncomparability, would theoretically apply to *any* E/C samples, whatever outcome measures (e.g., revocation rates) and source documents (e.g., CI&I rapsheets) were used. (2) Lerman focused on *suspension* rates because he considered them a better reflection of youth behavior than were *revocation* rates, and so on, particularly when suspensions centered on

law-enforcement-initiated arrests rather than *YA-agent*-initiated arrests (Lerman, 1968, pp. 56–58; 1972, pp. 34, 39–40; 1973, pp. 1–2; 1975, pp. 59–61, 63–64, 229). For instance:

[For use in *Social Control*], suspension of parole was chosen even though I was aware that suspension, like revocation of parole, could involve elements of discretionary decision making. However, suspensions could arise from the arresting decisions of non-CYA law enforcement officers—and not only from YA parole officer [i.e., parole agent] decisions. The arrest decisions of police and sheriff representatives were deemed to be less biasing than those of interested YA personnel, and a closer approximation of probable youth behavior in the community (Lerman, 1975, p. 229).

The following comments might be made regarding Lerman's observation: Even if one assumes that discretionary decision-making (DDM) existed within and/or outside the YA, it does not follow that "bias"—the *favoring* of any one group over another—also existed, either accidentally or unavoidably. Thus, for example, there is no reason to believe or assume (and Lerman seemed to not assume) that the arrest decisions of law enforcement personnel were at all *biased*—whether or not they happened to involve DDM. Moreover, this issue is independent of whether or not those arrest decisions may have involved not only *less DDM* than may have existed with YA personnel but *less "bias"* as well.

26. As of the early 1970s—the time of the analysis—most of these youths had been discharged; however, many had accumulated less than two years' postdischarge time in the community. Regardless of *post*discharge time, all youths included in this 16-months follow-up had had an *opportunity* for 16 months parole (*pre*-discharge) follow-up in the community. Youths whose parole was *revoked,* and so on, prior to 16 months were still included in the analysis.

27. Virtually all the exceptions in question had been paroled out of area, were non-interviewed controls, or had not had an opportunity (a mathematical chance) to be followed up for 16 months between their date of parole release, on the one hand, and the cutoff point for inclusion in the analysis, on the other.

28. We distinguish between a statistically significant difference (SSD) and a difference that is substantial, for example, substantial in terms of the actual—numerical—difference involved, and/or its (related) practical meaning. For instance, though an SSD may exist between two groups—say, between E's and C's—the actual amount of that difference may be very small, such as 87 IQ versus 85, or 436 points (on an 889-point parole risk scale) versus 444; such relatively minor differences are of neither practical nor predictive significance. An SSD can be obtained between two groups despite the lack of a substantial numerical difference when—though not only when—the sample size of one or both groups is relatively large (especially, but not necessarily, if the standard deviations are relatively small). Many differences are, of course, statistically significant *and* numerically substantial, whatever the sample size; however, the present analyses yielded no such differences.

29. As already indicated, the updated suspensions analysis, which was conducted in the early 1970s and reported in the 1973 reply (Palmer, 1973c), was based on a type of source document—namely, CYA suspension reports—that was soon found to be inappropriate for comparing E's and C's on minor as well as nonminor severity offenses. (This would apply to the 1965 and 1966 suspensions analyses [Warren and Palmer, 1965; Warren et al., 1966a].) Specifically, regarding the latter offenses, control agents were found to have not included, in these documents, far more law-enforcement-initiated arrests (LEIAs) than was the case with CTP agents (Palmer, 1973c, p. 5). (All LEIAs had been recorded on CI&I rapsheets, and it was these documents with which the suspension reports were compared.) In the updated suspensions analysis, the "available" sample involved the "eligible" sample minus all individuals paroled out of area ("POAs"), for example, approximately 70 males in the case of C's; also see discussion of non-

interviewed controls ("NICs"). POAs and NICs are discussed in Appendix 39. ("Available sample" and "eligible sample" are Lerman's terms [1973, 1975], though he left open the question of whether, in his view, a key difference between them often involved POAs.)

30. When it became Appendix A of *Social Control,* this Note retained the same title it had had as a draft (or manuscript), in December 1973.

31. Palmer's 1973 reply (referenced here as 1973c) was written in response to the National Institute of Mental Health's March 1973 formal request for Youth Authority comments on Lerman's 1972 draft (this being a contracted manuscript—dated May 15, 1972, but sent to the YA and CTP, by NIMH, in *March 1973*) regarding (1) the 1961–1969 California experiment and (2) the statewide Probation Subsidy Program (see Feeney, Hirschi, and Lemert, 1977; Johns, White, and Berkowitz, 1974; Smith, 1965). (A revised and expanded version of Lerman's May 1972 manuscript—one dated December 15, 1972— was sent to the YA and CTP, by NIMH, in May 1973 [again with a formal written request for comments to NIMH, and with NIMH's written apologies for its having indvertently sent—in March 1973—the May 1972 version instead of the December 1972 version, and for its lengthy delays] [Shah, 1973a].) In response to *part one* of that request (in regard to Lerman's May and December 1972 drafts, jointly), a 235-page document (Palmer, 1973c) was sent to NIMH in four "installments," during May to September 1973 (cf. endnote 32). NIMH simultaneously forwarded the respective sections to Lerman. Separately, the *Youth Authority's* response to *part two*—which focused on Probation Subsidy—was prepared by YA researchers and others, not directly associated with the 1961–1969 experiment at the time (Breed, 1973b; White and Johns, 1973). In the Fall of 1973, as soon as the final section of the 1973c document was sent to NIMH (Shah and Weber) and its independent reviewers (Glaser, Moos, and Schrag [see endnote 32]), a copy of it—together with Lerman's December 1972 manuscript—

was sent to Jerome Beker, Herbert Cross, Doris Heyman, James Tracy, and David Twain. This procedure was repeated the following May, with the same individuals, but in connection with the *1974a* document (and Lerman's Note). Among *others* who—after NIMH and its reviewers—were first to receive one or both documents (in all cases the 1974a item, plus the Note) were Stuart Adams, John Conrad, Lawrence Kohlberg, and Norval Morris.

32. Thus, unlike the California researchers' 1973 reply—which led to several changes in Lerman's 1972 drafts to NIMH—the *1974* report to NIMH (Palmer, 1974a) produced no changes in Lerman's December 1973 *Note.* In December 1973, Lerman made his Note (also called "Appendix A") available to NIMH, to the editorial staff in charge of the *Social Control* manuscript, and to this author. In the accompanying cover letter (December 4) to the author (Palmer), he stated that, "While 'Appendix A' might be edited prior to publication (as will also occur with the entire manuscript), it is unlikely that the substance of my comments will change." As of September 20, 1973, NIMH was still collecting and beginning to review material from two, possibly three, independent reviewers' (Dan Glaser, Rudolf Moos, and Clarence Schrag) of the author's (Palmer, 1973c), and other YA staff's, written responses to Lerman's December 1972 draft. NIMH hoped that this process would, among other things, help it make a "decision about the possibility of an NIMH publication of the [December 1972] Lerman report" (Shah, 1973a). In early October 1973, the present author learned that Lerman had arranged or was completing arrangements for the publication of that report (as *Social Control*) with the University of Chicago Press. (NIMH ended up publishing neither the report nor any shortened or otherwise modified version of it.)

    Social Control appeared in the Summer of 1975. The following indicates that Lerman had sufficient opportunity to make substantive changes—certainly minor and nonminor additions—between November/December 1973 and the point at which *Social Control*'s editor/publisher could not or would not accommodate them. At various points in that book (though never in the Note itself, i.e., in Appendix A), Lerman presented information from documents and other materials dated *1974*. (See, e.g., pp. 138, 142, 151, and 196.) In addition, he sometimes discussed both that and/or its related implications and information at length. (See, e.g., pp. 171–172 and 201–203.) Even extensive quotes were involved. However, with one possible exception (p. 213), such material and discussion related not to issues bearing on CTP per se, but to California's Probation Subsidy Program (CPSP) in particular— this being the second major subject area of Lerman's book. (In any event, the material in question was basically used to further support or clarify his main and subsidiary points regarding CPSP.) Thus, the 1974 material that had been added was quantitatively substantial and, at times, qualitatively complex—sometimes individually, not just collectively. The presence of such material makes it clear that—subsequent to his stated "cut-off date [of] . . . 12 November 1973" (see *Social Control,* p. 237)—Lerman, had he chosen to do so, (1) could have added information and discussion (not to mention basic reference) concerning Base Expectancy and other matters of particular relevance to *CTP,* and (2) could have done so in addition to having included 1974 material concerning CPSP. He could have done so because no completely inflexible, narrow editorial restrictions evidently existed regarding substantive additions, certainly not as of November/December 1973 and for at least a number of months afterward. The fact that there was still considerable time for changes and additions—not just minor, organizational, and/or stylistic ones—was further supported by the following. In June 1974, the editor and associate editor of the University of Chicago Press series on Studies in Crime and Justice, of which *Social Control* would be one volume, wrote to Palmer, with a "c.c." to Lerman, and stated that "The Press plans to proceed with production, in the hope that the book

[*Social Control*] will be out in the spring of 1975," that is, almost one year in the future (Morris and Wasserman, 1974).

33. Here, "available"—still Lerman's term— refers to samples that were *followed up* (e.g., for 16 months, E = 310; C = 225), and that were used in one of the California experiment's updated analyses. Also in his December 1973 Note, Lerman contrasted available samples with "eligible" samples. The latter referred to all Sacramento/Stockton youths who had *entered* the E and C programs at any time during Phases 1 and 2 (1961–1969); all such youths, of course, had been randomly assigned to one program or the other. (See materials in this chapter and in Appendix 39 regarding "NICs"—randomly assigned C's who had received no I-level/subtype diagnosis. These individuals were present in eligible but not in available samples.)

34. Note that *parole risk* is traditionally determined by a total Base Expectancy score, and that items such as age help *constitute* that score. Maximally reliable and predictive risk estimates are obtained by combining several individual items or variables, age being one of them. Because a combined-variables score is more reliable and predictive than a single-variable score, the former rather than the latter is traditionally used to determine parole risk.

(This does not necessarily mean the combined-variables score, for example, the Base Expectancy score, is a highly powerful predictor of parole risk. However, it may be, and often is, [1] a moderately to fairly good one, and/or [in any event], [2] the best available one. At any rate, the combined- ["composite"] variables score is invariably a better predictor—often a much better one—than any score that is based on any of its *components* [constituents]. Included are such components, that is, such single variables, as age [at first arrest, commitment, and/or release to parole] and number of priors [arrests or convictions]. [IQ is rarely included among parole-risk predictors.]) Thus, to optimally control (i.e., statistically equate) E and C groups on parole risk, it is more appropriate to utilize BE *itself* (i.e., the combined-variables score) than to simply use any one or two of its individual components, or correlates, such as age or "priors." This is apart from the fact that the effects of some variables may be counterbalanced and even outweighed by those of others. As indicated, the findings on parole risk itself—that is, on Base Expectancy—specifically contradicted Lerman's suggestion of an E/C difference in this regard; and Lerman's Note contained literally no direct or even indirect reference to these obviously pertinent and—in the research reports he had utilized—highly visible figures. Yet parole risk, as such, was the principal focus of Lerman's concern and central to his argument, since the variables/factors that he did discuss and highlight (mainly age and IQ) were used specifically to illustrate and serve as proxies for *it*. At any rate, information about Base Expectancy was already available in the 1960s research reports from which Lerman otherwise drew extensively, for example, when discussing age, IQ, and race. As a result, it—or even simply references to it—could easily have been included in his *pre*–November 1973 (i.e., his pre–data cutoff) material—the material that, as in the 1975 Note itself—emphasized age, IQ, and race. Even after Lerman was sent *further* details about Base Expectancy in mid-1974 (Palmer, 1974a), key elements of this information, not to mention simple references to it, could have been added to his Note, especially since this was an appendix.

In *Social Control,* though not in its Appendix, Lerman provided what was apparently his rationale for not using BE: "In California, base expectancy scores are computed by using background variables associated with parole revocation (Beverly, 1965; Molof, 1967) . . . [However,] it is unlikely that base-expectancy scores are very powerful indicators of risk to the community," that is, of "youth behavior" in contrast to "*adult* decisions about youth behavior" (p. 94). (Lerman had earlier indicated that "parole revocation rates may provide an inadequate basis for the measurement of youth behavior," and that "parole suspensions appear to be a more valid indicator of youth behavior"

[pp. 90–91]; he later concluded that the research goal should be "to accurately assess illegal youth behavior" [p. 95].)

Though base expectancy may indeed not be *very* powerful, it can, and does, still have a substantial relationship to illegal behavior. At any rate, there is certainly no total disconnect or even a near disconnect between revocation decisions, on the one hand, and preceding youth behaviors (particularly illegal acts), on the other. (See for instance, points [1] and [2] of endnote 103, regarding the substantial relationship between law enforcement initiated arrests, on the one hand, and recidivism, on the other.) All this is independent of the following: Dr. Lerman, in the above comments and elsewhere, did not mention the fact that "age," a variable he characterized (in the Appendix) as "critical" to the assessment of parole risk and presumably to the prediction of illegal behavior itself (and hence an important or even "powerful" indicator), played the largest single role, by far, in the *BE* formula that was used throughout the California experiment, that is, the YA/NIMH experiment. In addition, revocation—a decision by given "adults"—typically leads to *incarceration,* and the latter does address the "risk to the community" (the need for social protection) with which Lerman is concerned. At any rate, insofar as *age*—BE's chief component—is considered "crucial," *BE* itself can hardly be dismissed.

35. The following may be why—at various points in his Note—Lerman spoke of an *actual* difference and an actual bias, but soon after introducing those terms, would speak of a *probable* difference and probable bias only, and why he then kept alternating in this regard: Since his conclusions with respect to the updated suspensions analysis were based, *not* on actual figures regarding the background characteristics of E's and C's who comprised the samples for that analysis, but instead on inferences built upon an earlier sample, he could not present his conclusions regarding E/C "differences" and "bias" as empirical—i.e., as specifically established—facts (or as based on other than inferences). That is, he could not maintain that they *were* actual rather

than "probable," "quite likely," "quite conceivable," and "quite reasonable" only. This was particularly true for E/C comparisons at the youth subtype level, such as those involving Conflicted E's versus Conflicted C's—the "neurotic" group, in *Social Control*.

36. That is, differences between those same total E and total C groups—which, together, comprised the updated (UDSA) sample.

37. That is, subtypes which were included in the above-mentioned total updated sample.

38. The "rare" grouping contained four separate subtypes (see Appendix 7). The "new classifications" in question referred to "neurotic" (conflicted) and power-oriented groupings; thus, their newness was in their *name*, and in the fact that they combined single subtypes. They were not a new element in—not a brand new component of—the analysis.

39. The percentages of representation were as follows, separately for E's and C's (figures for C's are in parentheses): neurotic = 60 (46); power-oriented = 18 (24); passive-conformist = 11 (18); all other = 11 (12). Lerman's chi-square refers to this information analyzed collectively.

40. Regarding the *total group,* the following appeared in Palmer et al. (1968): "Results of these comparisons [for the eligible sample] indicate that the Total group of Experimentals was equated to the Controls (i.e., was represented in approximately equal proportions) on socioeconomic status, race, IQ, type of committing offense, and Youth Authority Board Order (regarding [specific] institutional placement)" (p. 4). The related statistics on IQ were: $X^2 = 3.50$; $df = 8$; $p < .90 > .80$ (p. 4). Regarding *individual subtypes,* the following appeared: "The Experimental and Control groups were equated with respect to each of the 8 subtypes, on the variable of IQ" (p. 6). Mean IQ's were then shown for each E and C subtype. (The number of IQ points by which E's differed from C's on each of the main subtypes were: Cfm = 1; Cfc = 5; Mp = 1; Na = 1; Nx = 1.) The ninth subtype—asocialized-aggressives—was not analyzed because the E sample contained no such individuals (p. 6).

41. *Item B* focuses directly on background characteristics. The present section emphasizes subtype composition and its *relationship* to those characteristics.

42. As discussed above (text), as well as by Lerman, bias reflects and results from a particular difference *between* the total E group and the total C group. It does not exist *within* either group, since any one group—whether a total E (or C) group or, for that matter, an individual subtype—can only be biased relative to another. Thus, the following statement (labeled, "Context of Bias"), which is descriptively accurate in terms of its various *individual assertions,* is nevertheless misdirected and, in that sense, is invalid or without actual reference. This is because it implicitly assumes that bias exists *within* a given group (i.e., as an attribute of that group) rather than as an expression of certain differences, that is, relationships, *between* two or more groups, and because it therefore focuses on only one group at a time.

Context of Bias. Substantively, that is, regarding its specific sources and analytic origins, any bias that exists within a *total* E or *total* C group—bias with respect to likelihood of success—is literally nothing other than the mathematical resultant of any biases that may exist among that group's components—in the present case, its individual youth subtypes. Specifically, since this total E or C group is in no respects an entity that exists on its own—that is, one with substance or content apart from or beyond that of its particular components, individually and/or collectively—it can, therefore, under no circumstances be either biased or not biased independently of those components. (Here, substance/content is emphasized, since "meaning/significance" is not at issue.)

Again, the error in this "Context of Bias" statement results from the fact that subtype-composition bias cannot exist at the "individual youth subtype" level, in the first place. Instead, the judgment "bias" or "possible bias"—that is, actual or possible "noncomparability" (here, with respect to likelihood of success)—should be based on one or more presumed or actual differences *between* E's and C's. (Here, we are focusing on comparisons between total E and total C groups, not between individual E subtypes and individual C subtypes.) Thus, it is not simply the case that a total E or C group cannot be either biased or not biased *independently* of its components; that group, in addition (or—more precisely—instead), cannot be biased *regardless* of those components. This applies in the sense that it cannot, under any conditions, be biased on its own.

43. And, as mentioned, differential subtype representation supplied the necessary precondition or original basis for the bias proposed by Lerman.

44. Since subtype-composition bias was not literally and entirely *precluded* in the total group analysis, the question of whether such bias in fact existed in the total group remained. It is discussed in the following three paragraphs (text) and in the subsection of this chapter titled "Background Characteristics and Subtype," on page 423.

45. Subtype-based composition bias *may* exist in connection with total group analyses, though it can never exist in individual subtype comparisons. However, whether or not total group, subtype-based composition bias (TG-SBCB) *in fact* exists in any particular study can be determined only empirically, for example, by examining actual scores or averages on the specific variables/factors (say, age and IQ) that are used as evidence of bias. The presence of TG-SBCB can never be conclusively *inferred*, for instance, from information regarding the degree to which various subtypes are represented in each of two total groups that are being compared; that is, its existence or nonexistence cannot be definitively determined from that type of information alone, regarding those subtypes themselves. This is because TG-SBCB is always a *possible,* but never an inevitable, effect or concomitant of subtype representation differences, and is never those differences themselves. For various reasons, differential subtype representation—whether by itself or together with age, IQ, and so on—need not produce bias in a total group; in the simplest case, for example, various differ-

ences associated with one or more subtypes may cancel or otherwise neutralize those associated with one or more other subtypes, *whatever* each subtype's degree of representation within the total group may be. (Bias was defined as preexisting differences in likelihood of success among two total groups that are being compared with each other. In Lerman's discussion, these differences resulted from presumed differences in *ages* and *IQ;* the latter differences, in turn, sprang from *differential subtype representation* across the E and C total groups.)

46. Since this hypothetical total E group outperformed its C's, results from the unsuccessful *subtypes* within the total E group had not been strong enough to cancel or otherwise undo those from the successful ones.

47. The fact that the rather successful *conflicted* subtype was represented much more in P1 than P2 also helped produce the P1/P2 rate difference for the total group.

48. It should be noted that Lerman extrapolated from the eligible to the available sample even though the figures he used for the former were based on an 86 percent male, 14 percent female distribution for the total sample, whereas the figures used for the latter were based on males exclusively. (Given the samples he was comparing, he had no choice but to do so.) Though this, in itself, weakened the basis of his inferences, we will proceed as if it did not matter; and, in fact, it may *not* have mattered much.

49. Unless otherwise stated, all Lerman quotations for Points 1 through 4 refer to Palmer et al. (1968), also called the 1968 report.

50. Because Lerman mentioned sex (gender) when describing E/C background differences that presumably favored *E's* over C's with regard to parole risk, it should be noted that the E/C sex difference instead favored *C's,* not E's: The total eligible C group contained *23 percent* females; the total eligible E, *14 percent*—and, females were known to clearly outperform males with regard to r.o.o.'s. Males were separated from females in the *updated* samples/analyses, by the California researchers (Palmer, 1973c, 1974a).

51. These categories were: 13 and under, 14, 15, 16, 17, 18 and over.
52. In the 1968 report mentioned in the above statement by Lerman, seven variables/factors—race, base expectancy, and so on—were involved when E and C groups were compared. Together, these v/f's, which did not include I-level, subtype, and sex, contained over 25 individual *categories*.
53. $80 = (8 \times 4) + (8 \times 3) + (8 \times 3)$, for race, SES, and committing offense, respectively. SES, for example, contained 3 categories: upper, middle, and lower.
54. This is independent of the earlier-mentioned fact that, when sample sizes are sufficiently large, a statistically significant difference (say, between the average ages of E's and C's) can be very small in absolute amount (e.g., ages 16.4 versus 16.7) and can therefore be of little practical use with respect to predicting differences in the behavior of two groups that are being compared. As will be seen, this was true of age, in the present context.
55. This applies whether or not one conceptualizes the single-category, percentage-point differences between two groups as normal fluctuations—expected deviations—from an overall sample mean.
56. As discussed later, identical ages (15.6 and 15.3) were obtained for the updated, that is, "available," sample. That is, they were found when females were no longer included (they were analyzed separately) and the database was extended more than five years beyond that for the eligible sample—from a March 1966 to a July 1971 cutoff (Palmer, 1973c). Throughout the California experiment, when computing average age (at intake), each youth's specific age was used—for example, down to age nine (these being the youngest wards prior to 1965) and up to age 19 (these being the oldest). The same multicategory approach was used with IQ.
57. This is apart from the fact that the dividing line between younger and older offenders would then have to be age 15.45. Together with the fact that age 15 represents neither the older nor younger portion of typical correctional youth populations (certainly of heterogeneous ones), the finding that "neurotic" (conflicted) C's and E's in the 1968 eligible

sample were *each* age 15 (C's, 15.4 and E's 15.9; see text, p. 420) reduces the predictive significance, suggested by Lerman (1975, p. 234), of the fact that those particular control youths "were overrepresented in the fifteen-year-old-category." That specific age category has—both by itself and in the present overall, that is, C + E, context—little differential predictive significance with respect to parole risk. This would probably apply to the age-16 category, as well—again, particularly if both groups being compared were approximately the same age.
58. This applies, for instance, to the differences presented in Chapter 8 of this book. Also, it applies independently of the fact that many other factors could have counterbalanced any effects of age and/or could have accounted for more of the E/C differences themselves.
59. Figures computed directly from Palmer et al. (1968, Appendix A) are: 61 percent versus 56 percent and 14 percent versus 19 percent.
60. More precisely, the 1968 finding (p. 8) focused on *I-level* (lower, middle, higher) not—as suggested in this quotation—on "personality classifications" (i.e., *subtypes*) per se. The correlation in question was positive: Higher I-level was associated with higher IQ, and the latter accounted for 5 percent of the variance in the former. Separate analyses were not made for females alone. Regarding *age,* the following was noted in the cited report (p. 8): "When the study samples are divided at [ages] 15 and below vs. 16 and above—with this particular dichotomization coming slightly closer to a median split than [one which yielded a .200 correlation]—the results [corrected contingency coefficients (CCCs)] were: E = + .147; C = + .140; E + C = + .145." The figures referred to as "shown above" (above, in the research report) are those—also CCCs—which Lerman cited in his Note (and, of course, in *Social Control*). They are based on a dichotomization at ages 16 and below versus 17 and above, and they indicate that age accounted for 2 percent of all variance in the given sample's I-level.
61. Note that this finding applied to the total group, not just to "neurotics." (Neu-

rotics comprised most of the higher I-level category—which, itself, was one portion of the total group.) This is apart from the fact that the finding applied to males and females combined, whereas the available sample—on which Lerman's conclusions focused—involved males only. Also note that these findings involve no comparisons between E's and C's. Instead, they involve a correlation between I-level, on the one hand, and age or IQ on the other—for the *total* "population of eligible youth," that is, for E's and C's combined. Thus, possible differences between E's and C's, on age and IQ, are not at issue here.

62. The test in question is the California Test of Mental Maturity, Non-Language section (Palmer, 1974a, p. 3).

63. As shown by the following average scores, IQ differences for E and C *neurotics* were also negligible: eligibles = 90.6 and 90.4, respectively; availables = 90.0 and 90.9. Figures for eligible neurotics were readily derivable from the 1968 report; those for available youths were discussed in the 1974 reply (Palmer et al., 1968, pp. 2, 6, 99; Palmer, 1974a, pp. 3–4, 73).

64. Namely, that they would be brighter than their C's.

65. Namely, that they would be older and brighter than their C's, and, therefore, would probably be better risks.

66. Since data from only some rather than all categories are involved, terms such as "information," "selected information," or "single-category data" may be more appropriate than the scientifically more forceful, broader yet pointed, and perhaps consequential term or concept "finding." (See Lerman—Point 4, in the text, regarding his term "finding.")

67. The *eligible* sample in question covered the period from October 1961 to *March 1966;* that is, it "happened to straddle two rather different stages or phases of CTP's development"—stages 1 and 2 (Palmer, 1974a, p. 1). The updated suspension analysis was an expansion of the previous analysis, in that it covered stage 1 as well as the *entire* stage 2. In the updated suspensions analysis—16-months follow-up—there were 57 E's and 93 C's in stage 1 and 252 E's and 132 C's in

stage 2 for the total group. Thus, considering the fact that stage 2 was also twice as long as stage 1 with regard to program operations, it seems clear that stage 2 was much more representative of the overall experiment—particularly of CTP's operations and structure, which had evolved considerably in its early years—than was stage 1. For CTP, stage 1 (10/61 to 3/64) was not just a time in which treatment methods were tried and refined; it was, organizationally, a trial and caseload-buildup period. During this stage, relatively few CTP caseloads existed and their average size was only eight. Because of this and because several large caseloads existed in *regular* parole, far fewer eligible youths could be—and were—assigned (randomly, as always) to the E than the C program. This situation was reversed in stage 2, the full operations period. Here, because considerable expansion occurred not only in the number of E caseloads but in their average size, most eligible cases could be—and were—assigned (still randomly) to CTP. (Random assignment—between any two groups or conditions—on other than a 50/50 basis is achieved simply by establishing, within the Table of Random Numbers, differing ratios for the respective groups/conditions. Thus, if one wishes to randomly assign approximately 70 percent of all eligible youths to the E rather than C group during a given time period, one assigns to the E group all individuals whose randomly drawn number is between 00 and 69; and, one assigns to the C group everyone from 70 to 99, again inclusive. Thus, E and C groups need not be divided on a 50/50 basis to be randomly assigned (and to end up statistically equated). This procedure is useful during periods in which few caseload openings exist, and in order to (re)establish equality across samples that—through chance alone—have become or are becoming unbalanced, for example, regarding age, race, or SES.)

68. As seen in the table, although one of the six E/C total group differences reached the .05 significance level, the actual amount of this difference was virtually nil. (This total group difference, which centered on age, was neither significant

nor substantial for any of the three separate youth groups—that is, [1] for groups [Na + Nx; Cfc + Mp; Cfm] whose samples were considerably smaller than that of the total group, and [2] when type of youth was controlled.) Of the 18 remaining stage 1 + 2 E/C comparisons—six for each of the three youth groups—neither substantial nor statistically significant differences were found (pp. 73–74).

69. The March 1966 and March 1968 follow-ups were 15 (15.49) months; the updated (7/71) analysis was a 16-month follow-up. Each, of course, was an E/C outcome comparison that focused on parole performance. (An eight-month, 7/71 follow-up need not be reviewed here. The 1968 follow-up was, of course, an updating of the 1966 analysis; and since each one *was* a follow-up, it involved an "available" sample.) "7/71" was a cutoff date.

70. It is in this sense that such cases were excluded from the available sample. They had not been literally *removed* from that sample, since, strictly speaking, they had never been part of it. In addition, though they were excluded from entering the available sample, they had not been literally removed from—analytically or otherwise dropped from—the *eligible* (in contrast to what Lerman's statement [1975, p. 232] suggested may have occurred). No cases could be literally or otherwise removed from the eligible sample, since it comprised, that is, it *was,* the basic pool itself. These terminological distinctions are useful only because, without them, inaccurate impressions or preconceptions might arise, or confusion may remain.

71. (1) To avoid a substantial increase in the complexity of this presentation the six male, asocialized-aggressives (Aa's) who were excluded from the *updated* (an available) sample were not mentioned in the preceding discussion. (When these youths are considered, the 25 males in the updated sample who were released after March 1968 and who had an opportunity for sufficient follow-up prior to the cutoff date becomes 31.) These six asocialized-aggressives comprised all male Aa's in the Valley units, for Phases 1 and 2 combined. Like POAs and NICs, this *category* of individuals was excluded

in order to make the E and C available (follow-up) samples more comparable with respect to their analytic categories—since, by chance, no Aa's had been randomly assigned to the E program, that is, to CTP. (2) It might also be noted that the 95 *POAs* mentioned in connection with the March 1968 *eligible* sample should have been slightly less. Also, as of that date, there were 70 diagnosed *male* POAs and 19 such *females,* in addition to several who were NICs. (In various analyses the male POA count is, mistakenly, 71, because one youth was misclassified as a POA.)

72. To simplify this review, the rare E's who were paroled out of area and were therefore excluded from the updated analysis are omitted. Had they been included, (1) certain numbers that are shown would have changed, but only negligibly, and (2) the reasons for the overall numerical change from the eligible E sample to the updated E sample would have remained the same. (See reasons [1] and [2], in the text paragraph that follows.) The fact that one E POA was a female would have further complicated the presentation, at least the account of numerical changes from the eligible to the updated sample. At any rate, the sizable gain in simplification seemed, on balance, to far outweigh the relatively minor loss in precision.

Another point might be mentioned: Since E's were released to the community shortly after their commitment to the Youth Authority, their follow-up began earlier than that of C's (exception: a handful of C's were still directly paroled as of 1968)—individuals who were *committed* at the same time as E's but who spent an average of several months in an institution prior to release. Thus, of all males who became part of the experiment between March 1968 and the close of Phase 2, a slightly higher percentage of E's than C's were included in the updated analysis (i.e., the 16-months parole follow-up) for this reason alone.

73. Some of these NICs were also paroled out of area, and were categorized as *NICs* when parole follow-up cohorts were developed (Palmer et al., 1968, p. 36; Palmer, 1974a, p. 12).

74. Ultimately, two main factors made the paucity of E POAs operationally possible: (1) CTP's line, supervisory, and administrative staff understood and accepted the study—its goals, design, and research needs. (2) As suggested, almost all such individuals also believed youths had a better chance of succeeding, in the long run, if they remained on the project.

75. What is now subsection 2 was subsection 4 of the 1974 table. Subsections 2 and 3 of that table compared POAs with available C's, separately for stage 1 and stage 2, respectively; these comparisons are omitted here.

76. $X^2 = 9.60$; d.f. = 7. The subtype distribution among POAs was: $I_2 = 10$ percent (Aa = 3 percent, Ap = 7 percent), Cfm = 13 percent, Cfc = 5 percent, Mp = 6 percent, Na = 20 percent, Nx = 38 percent, Se = 0 percent, Ci = 6 percent. (For *available* C's, $X^2 = 9.15$; d.f. = 7.)

77. $X^2 = 8.35$; d.f. = 7 (For *available* E's, $X^2 = 8.03$; d.f. = 7.)

78. That is, their BE was only 13 points lower on an 889-point scale; and the average C_o/C_{ae} σ was 99 points—much larger than their difference in means.

79. Though it remained statistically significant.

80. "These . . . are individuals who might ordinarily be in a somewhat better position to move from one geographic area to another—either with or without their parents" (p. 18).

81. This conclusion remains appropriate after, that is, even after, the following adjustments or relatively minor changes. In the analysis on which the preceding probability levels were based (early 1974), several NICs were inadvertently omitted. When these individuals were included (June 1974)—thus bringing the total to 52 males—the results were: (A) *NIC versus non-POA controls:* age = < .50 > .30; IQ = < .30 > .20; race = < .50 > .30; SES = < .05 > .02; offense = < .20 > .10; Base Expectancy = < .90 > .80. (B) *NIC versus non-POA controls + POA controls:* age = < .10 > .05; IQ = < .70 > .50; race = < .20 > .10; SES = < .20 > .10; offense = < .50 > .30; Base Expectancy = < .80 > .70. (C) *NIC versus E's:* age = < .02 > .01; IQ = < .50 > .30; race = < .30 > .20; SES = < .20 > .10; offense = < .50 > . 30; Base Expectancy = < .70 > .50. Mean ages were: NIC = 15.5; E = 15.6. (D) *NIC versus non-POA controls + E's:* age = < .20 > .10; IQ = < .30 > .20; race = < . 50 > .30; SES = < .10 > .05; offense = < .30 > .20; Base Expectancy = < .80 > .70. Mean ages were: NIC = 15.5; C + E = 15.5. (E) *NIC versus non-POA controls + POA C's + E's:* age = < .20 > .10; IQ = < .50 > .30; race = < .30 > .20; SES = < .20 > .10; offense = < .50 > .30; Base Expectancy = < .90 > .80. Mean ages were: NIC = 15.5; C + E + POA = 15.5. Findings (A) through (E) were virtually identical after removing the eight NICs who also happened to be POAs. The following might be mentioned at this point: For NICs, the average IQ was 94.5 ($\sigma = 13.6$) and the average BE was 450 ($\sigma = 118$).

82. Comparing the male NIC + POA groups with the male C group on the key risk items the results were: age = < .90 > .80; IQ = < .95 > .90; Base Expectancy = < .30 > .20. These probability levels, which are based on chi-square tests, are for the total group only, since NICs had no subtype diagnoses. The eight NICs who were also POAs were counted only once.

83. "And if all relevant analytic controls are applied—e.g., those which relate to length of parole followup . . ." (p. 22).

84. As seen earlier, the updated C sample consisted of 225 males. When one added previously excluded POAs who had a mathematical chance to be followed up for sufficient time prior to the data cut-off, the figure became 292 (not 296). As always, total group also included all rare types.

85. . . . these rates include all *out of area, POA experiences* and all *within-local-area, non-POA experiences.* This distinction takes account of the fact that any given POA youth could have accumulated a number of risk months, and a number of offenses, not only outside the Sacramento/Stockton area, but within that area as well. Twenty-four percent of the POA's accumulated only the former 'type' of risk months/experiences (and, where applicable, offenses as well); 76 percent accumulated both types of risk months. (p. 23)

86. "These may be derived from [the separate—stage 1 and 2—findings, and their respective sample sizes, on] page 80 and page 93 of the 1973 reply . . ." (Palmer, 1973c; 1974a, p. 24).

87. CI&I rapsheet findings are detailed in Chapter 8. For present purposes we need only present r.o.o.'s relating to NICs, and mention the following: (1) Without POAs, the sample size for this analysis was: E = 104; C = 90. (2) Whereas the updated suspension analysis involved 16-months follow-up and was based on suspensions recorded in each youth's case file, the present analysis covered the individual's entire YA career and drew exclusively from CI&I rapsheets. In short, these analyses involved indices #2 and #7, respectively, as described in Palmer (1973c, pp. 66–94). Also see Palmer (1974a).

88. "As before, the figures which are given have reference to offenses of 3–10 severity level only. To facilitate various comparisons, r.o.o.'s have been rounded to three significant figures." Here, the main analytic control was inclusion (within the CI&I rapsheet analysis) of only those POAs "who received either a favorable or an unfavorable discharge from YA by the close of the 1961–1969, Phase I and II effort, or shortly thereafter" (Palmer, 1973c, p. 72; 1974a, p. 27).

89. "Thus, the [first] figure (.067) relates to the available Control sample alone; the [second] figure relates to the 'expanded Control sample'—viz., the available C sample plus all appropriate POA's. [The second figure is therefore the preliminary finding, when POA's are added.] The rates which are shown for the available C sample were [those] reported [earlier in the (Palmer) 1974 reply (p. 27)]." The bracketed figure—like the second—refers to the expanded C sample. As indicated, it is the final result for the C + POA group—CI&I rapsheet analysis.

90. These rates, and the remaining NIC rates shown below (in text), resulted from a mid- 1974 analysis of each youth's file and rapsheet(s).

91. "At this point the following may be noted [because of its bearing on E/C performance]: (1) When all *available* E's, on the one hand, were compared with all available C's plus POA's (combined), on the other, no significant [*p* < .05] differences were found on four [this should have said five] of the six background variables in question. The probability-levels (based on chi square) were: Age = < .10 > .05; I.Q. = < .80 > .70; Race = < .30 > .20; SES = < .95 > .90; Offense = < .70 > .50; Base Expectancy = < .02 > .01. The actual Mean Ages were: E = 15.6; C + POA = 15.3. E's turned out to be worse parole risks (cf. Base Expectancy) than the C + POA grouping. However, the actual difference was less than 20 B.E. points [—a negligibly predictive difference]. (2) When NIC's were added to the C + POA grouping, the results which were shown in (1), above, underwent little change. The probability levels were: Age = < .05 > .02; I.Q. = < .80 > .70; Race = < .50 > .30; SES = < .95 > .90; Offense = < .80 > .70; Base Expectancy = < .02 > .01. [As before,] the actual Mean Ages were: E = 15.6; C + POA + NIC = 15.3. Once again, E's were worse, but not substantially worse, parole risks than the composite group with which they were compared. The results shown in (1) and (2) above were virtually unchanged when (3) all *eligible* E's, on the one hand, were compared with all eligible C's plus POA's, on the other. They continued to be essentially unchanged when (4) the NIC's were added to the C + POA grouping which was mentioned in (3), above" (Palmer, 1974a, pp. 23–24).

92. Regarding the generally average performance of *NICs,* the following might be noted: By 15-months follow-up, 54.5 percent of all male NICs had failed on parole (this, as always, meant revocation, recommitment, or unfavorable discharge); by 24-months follow-up, the figure was 63.4 percent. (Eight NICs, who had been POA'd, were excluded from these mid-1974 cohort analyses; therefore, N = 44.) These results were almost identical to those for all remaining, non-POA'd males—for whom the 15- and 24-months figures were 51.1 percent and 62.8 percent, respectively.

For *POAs* on whom complete or essentially complete suspension and discharge data seemed to exist, the 15- and 24-months figures were 50.0 percent and 60.4 percent. (Such information existed for 68 percent of the 71 POAs who were analyzed. For the remaining 32 percent, few or—in most cases—no parole reports were received by research staff once the individual left the Sacramento/Stockton area, whether temporarily/repeatedly or—especially—on a permanent basis; and in all such cases, no discharge document, in particular, was received. For conflicted POAs, the 15- and 24-months figures were 48.4 percent and 58.1 percent.)

93. Lerman's characterization appeared immediately after the description and suggestions, and was as follows: "In addition to the '*numbers*' problem, the second type of population used in the CTP post-manuscript analysis appears to have experimentals and controls that are *noncomparable* [i.e., qualitatively different—different, regarding subtype categories, as Lerman next indicated]" (p. 233, emphasis added).

94. Though this example assumes that the two groups were—originally—about equal in size, this assumption, as will be discussed, is not essential.

95. This is independent of the fact that if the E group had originally been *smaller* than the C, those groups may now be *equal*—and they may also have remained (or even become) well-matched.

96. For present purposes it is immaterial that—in contrast to the situation involving E's versus C's—POAs and NICs were each *smaller* than C's.

97. This similarity can best be summarized by figures for the total group of availables and eligibles. For *experimental* males the average BEs, ages, and IQs were as follows (figures for availables appear first, and those for eligibles are in parentheses; this applies throughout the endnote): BE = 436 (435); age = 15.6 (15.6); IQ = 87.2 (86.6). The percentages on race (Caucasian, Mexican American, black, other), SES (lower, middle, upper), and offense (person, property, other) were: race = 56, 20, 19, 5 (55, 20, 20, 5); SES = 77, 20, 3 (78, 19, 3); offense = 6, 68, 25 (6, 70, 24). For *control* males the figures for availables and eligibles were: BE = 444 (442); age = 15.3 (15.3); IQ = 85.4 (84.5); race = 50, 26, 21, 3 (55, 22, 20, 3); SES = 84, 16, 0 (78, 20, 2); of-

fense = 4, 73, 22 (6, 68, 26). *Note:* (1) Whereas all preceding figures for the available E and C samples (Palmer, 1974a, p. 73) relate to males only, those in Palmer et al. (1968, pp. 3–7) were for males and females combined. (2) Figures for eligible *E's* exclude the 23 males who were part of the available sample. (The eligible figures are for the March 1968 males in the above-mentioned report; the available are for the July 1971 "updated" sample shown in the 1974 reply [pp. 3–5, 73] and also reviewed in the 1973 reply [pp. 66–67, 76–77, 79–87, 91–93, 131].) (3) Figures for eligible *C's include* all male NICs and Aa's (asocialized-aggressives) who were excluded from the March 1968 background characteristics analysis shown in the 1968 report (pages 3–7); thus, those figures usually vary slightly from the ones in that report. They also include all male POAs, as did the March 1968 figures.

98. When two samples are being compared to each other, any given set consists of two cells only. This is because only two cells *can* then exist for any given category, such as the 16-year age category.

99. In this context, the expected number is analogous to a hypothetical *average* of all frequencies that would be obtained for the given cell from numerous independent samples, that is, from all such samples combined. In this sense it can be considered the most "typical"—most likely single—number.

100. This could also occur simply by virtue of using the standard eight or nine *I-level* subtype categories. More particularly, it could occur, for example, even if no more than three or four *age* (or race, or SES, etc.) groupings are being used *in conjunction with* those eight or nine subtype categories, that is, are being used in the context of a χ^2 analysis that involves subtype × age. (Further, when an *uncommon or rare* subtype is distributed across a particular age—or race, etc.—category that is itself relatively infrequent, such as age 13 and under, the chance of obtaining a rather low-frequency cell is considerably greater. This is true even if the total group, that is, all subtypes and all age categories combined, contains several hundred cases.) In short, the "small-cells

condition" can arise from other than the use of detailed age breakdowns alone.

101. The averages in question directly indicated whether a negligible or—in contrast—a substantial and pragmatically meaningful difference existed between the samples in question, on any given variable or factor (e.g., between average ages of 15.3 and 15.6). Like its numerical value, the *interpretation* of any given average remained unchanged regardless of whether grouping had occurred—that is, whatever the number of categories that were used—and despite any differences in significance level.

102. Base Expectancy was always—and only—trichotomized. BE, that is, parole risk, is routinely trichotomized in correctional research (cf. "lower," "middle," and "higher" risk).

103. A. For phase 1 and 2 Valley males (E = 334, C = 236), the following corrected contingency coefficients (CCCs) were obtained between *15-months recidivism,* on the one hand, and the next-specified indices, respectively, on the other (figures for 24-months recidivism are shown in parentheses): (1) law-enforcement-initiated arrests (from CI&I rapsheets only): E—.40 (.41), C—.58 (.58). (2) law-enforcement-initiated arrests (from CI&I rapsheets plus YA casefiles): E—.66 (.62), C—.63 (.60). (3) suspensions plus arrests (YA-agent initiated plus law-enforcement-initiated; from YA casefiles only): E—.67 (.64), C—.59 (.59). B. Other correlations were as follows: (4) law-enforcement-initiated arrests (from CI&I rapsheets plus YA casefiles) versus arrests plus suspensions (law-enforcement-initiated plus YA-agent initiated, from YA casefiles): E—.87, C—.89. For items (1) through (4), ar-

rests and suspensions were analyzed in terms of their monthly rates (as in Chapters 8 and 9), for offenses of severity levels 3 through 10 only. (5) 15-months recidivism versus 24-months recidivism: E—.89, C—.90. (E + C: .90.) (6) 15-months recidivism versus YA discharge: E—.48, C—.32, and (7) 24-months recidivism versus YA discharge: E—.62, C—.48.

104. For phase 1 and 2 Valley males (E = 310, C = 225), the CCCs between *base expectancy,* that is, level of parole risk, on the one hand, and other specified variables and factors, respectively, on the other, were as follows (figures for conflicted youths [Na's plus Nx's] appear in parentheses): age—.41 (.41), IQ—.04 (.04), race—.09 (.07), SES—.02 (.10), offense (type of commitment offense)—.11 (.14).

105. For the same sample used in endnote 104, the following intercorrelations were obtained: *Age* versus IQ—.04, race—.08, SES—.09, and offense—.12. *IQ* versus race—.13, SES—.12, and offense—.05. *Race* versus SES—.29, and offense—.18. *SES* versus offense—.09. For the conflicted youths within this sample, very similar results were obtained.

106. For the same sample that was used in endnote 104, the following were the CCCs between *E versus C status,* on the one hand, and the next-specified background/demographic variables, respectively, on the other (the corresponding percentages of variance accounted for are shown in parentheses): age—.12 (1), IQ—.10 (1), race—.06 (less than 1), SES—.09 (1), offense—.04 (less than 1), and base expectancy (BE)—.09 (1). These findings pertained to the total group. For conflicted individuals within this sample, the results were very similar.

22 FURTHER VALIDITY AND RELATED ISSUES

In Chapter 21 we mainly focused on the updated suspensions analysis (UDSA), which was based on CYA documents. We also indicated that Lerman's Note mentioned a second analysis, one we call "the CI&I parole analysis." This was a substudy of performance, using Criminal Investigation and Identification rapsheets, not CYA documents, as the data base. Like the UDSA, it was presented in the 1973 reply. Because Lerman (1975) questioned the validity of the sample on which this substudy was based, and, especially, given that this same type of sample—only expanded in size—was later used in the present book's follow-up analysis (see Table 8–1), Chapter 22 will review his position, the overall issues, and the evidence involved. Basically, what Lerman questioned was whether the experimental (E) and control (C) youths who comprised the CI&I follow-up sample were similar to each other on variables (background items) related to success, and whether these E's and C's had had an equal opportunity to be included in the sample.

The Chapter then turns to other issues and analyses that bear on the validity of this book's findings regarding the comparative effectiveness of the experimental and control programs, particularly those involving Phase 1 and 2 Valley males. After that, it examines the reliability of the youth-classification approach—the Warren I-Level and subtype system—that has played a major role throughout. The subtype classifications which are reviewed were basic to the book's *differential* analyses, that is, its separate breakdowns for specific kinds of youth. These analyses are distinguished from ones involving all those individuals *collectively* (the "total group"). It might be

kept in mind that the book's differential analyses involved certain *combinations* ("conflicted"; "power oriented") of the individual subtypes whose reliability is reviewed, and that this combining raised interview—based subtype reliability by approximately 15 percent (10 to 12 percentage points), in the CYA/NIMH experiment. It could probably have done so in more other studies.

Finally, the preponderance of this chapter focuses on an extensive review of both the concurrent and construct *validity* of I-Level and subtype. Involved, here, are empirical findings from numerous studies conducted over some 40 years. The chapter closes with a wide-ranging discussion of factors and conditions that bear on the following: (1) *differences* between the "power orientation" which is central to certain youth-subtypes' (Cfc's; Mp's) key perceptions of their environment, on the one hand, and the "control/domination approach" which is often prominent, though not always predominant, among other youths (Na's; Ci's), on the other; and (2) *similarities* that nonetheless exist in various socially learned *behaviors* and *techniques*, on the part of all four subtypes.

The CI&I Parole Analysis[1]
Comparability of E's and C's
In his Note, Lerman indicated that (1) the 109 experimentals and 90 controls who comprised the discharge sample for the 1973 CI&I parole analysis probably differed from each other on "population variables." These PVs were mainly the same background items, not specifically or at least directly the subtype and I-Level factors, that were focused on in Chapter 21.

(We will discuss these two factors later.) He also implied that (2) if the E's and C's were indeed noncomparable on these background items, for instance, were significantly different on IQ, this would reflect differing degrees of *opportunity* that these individuals had had to be included in the sample; that is, persons with, say, a higher IQ would have had a greater chance to be included. Lerman suggested that such a difference in opportunity—specifically, an "[un]equal chance" to be included in (a) the discharge sample, and, hence, in (b) any analysis which utilized that sample—would have been a direct expression and product of differing processes that existed in the E program, on the one hand, and in the C, on the other. He viewed these processes as *screens*, which, in effect, functioned as filters, and he indicated that the differential screening mechanism in question involved the differences in "decision making" that had been discussed in a report on the California experiment (Palmer, 1968a).[2]

In short, Lerman believed that differences in the way the experimental program processed its youths from the way the control program processed *its* youths led these two groups of individuals to have an unequal chance of completing their respective programs. In particular, they led the E's (CTP youths) to have a greater chance of being favorably discharged than the C's. This result or situation, he strongly implied, was evidenced by, and in this specific respect was proven or supported by, differences in the above-mentioned background items (characteristics), such as IQ, on the part of the E's and the C's who comprised the CYA/NIMH—that is, the California—experiment's discharge samples (Lerman, 1975, 232 ff.). The central consequence of differential processing and of such presumed differences in the samples was that the discharged experimentals as a whole, that is, the total group of E's, would have had a different chance of success (not defined simply as *favorable discharge* itself, of course) than would the control sample as a whole. Here, its chances would be greater since—or if—its IQ was higher. This, in turn, was the case because individuals with higher IQs were, based on prior correctional literature outside the California experiment, generally considered somewhat better parole risks than those with lower IQs. (Of course, in order to predict outcome, the best index would have been "BE" [base expectancy]—the standard measure of risk.)

It is in this context, and in this better-risk sense, that Lerman believed discharge samples were "biased"—presumably "unwittingly," and instead due to program screening—in favor of E's. That is, he believed the E's who comprised these samples were biased toward success, as compared to their C's (1975, 231, 234–235). His main point or concern, here, was that because, or insofar as, the discharge samples were thus biased, they should not be used. Utilization of these or any other samples as a basis for analyzing parole performance and/or post-parole (i.e., post-discharge) performance would be justified, he felt, only if the E's and C's who comprised those samples and who were thereby involved in the analysis *were essentially equal to each other in terms of their likelihood of success*. That is, such samples should be used only if they were not biased, in that respect.

Three points before continuing. 1. In the following review, "parole analysis" will mean an examination of the parole performance of individuals who were either *favorably or unfavorably discharged* from the CYA, and who, therefore, were no longer on parole. It is in this sense, and for this reason, that analyses which center on *parole*—here, on the youths' entire parole career, not, say, on only their first 12 or 16 months from initial release to parole—take place in the context of what have been termed *discharge* samples. (To be sure, such samples *can* be separately used to examine a cohort of youths' first "x" number of months on parole. This was done in the updated suspensions analysis—the "UDSA," discussed in Chapter 21.) 2. "Parole performance" will refer not to revocation—this being an outcome that *can* reflect considerable discretionary decision-making by E and C staffs alike, at least with respect to whether or not they recommend this action, rather than restoral, to the YA board. Nor will it reflect the rate of favorable and unfavorable discharge. Instead, it will center on monthly rate of official arrests and/or convictions (A's & C's)—these being the performance measures emphasized in this book. A's & C's occur prior to revocations, and so on, and they are generally the main basis of or trigger for discretionary and nondiscretionary recommendations and decisions alike, in the E as well as C programs. 3. This review will help us address the question of whether the E's and C's who comprised the 1973 CI&I parole analysis sample did differ from each other, and whether this sample was therein biased toward either of these groups with respect to likelihood of success—that is, rate of official arrests and convictions, not rate of revocation, rate of favorable discharge, and the like.

The quotation presented shortly, from Lerman's Note, reflects points (1) and (2) from the start of this section. Regarding this quote and our subsequent discussion, it might be kept in mind that the *1973 CI&I parole analysis sample* consisted of favorable and unfavorable dischargees combined, whereas the *March 1972 sample* that Lerman described in the quote as constituting the basis of his inference about probable differences within this CI&I sample's E and C background items contained favorable dischargees only. Also, Lerman referred to this *CI&I parole analysis,* which appeared in Palmer's 1973 reply (for NIMH) to Lerman's December 1972 draft/manuscript, as the "post-manuscript" analysis. In this context, the *March 1972 analysis* was "pre-manuscript." Given the relative complexity of the present subject, we will partition the Lerman quotation in order to help separate our review of E and C background characteristics, as such, from our discussion of differential opportunity (DO) for inclusion in the E and C discharge samples—ones that can be described via those or any particular characteristics. Because the link between points (1) and (2), above, involves Lerman's implication that background differences in E and C samples would reflect DO across the associated E and C programs, we will examine the given background items before focusing directly on opportunity for inclusion. We will do so despite the following, which Lerman did not point out.

On the one hand, significant E/C *background differences* can exist between an E and a C sample even if differential processing/screening—and any resulting differential opportunity for inclusion—does *not* exist across the associated E and C programs, and never did exist. In other words, such background differences (BDs) can have alternative precursors and causes, ones that have little or no connection with the differentials themselves. At the same time, such *differentials*—again including DO—can exist even if such BDs do *not* exist and never did; that is, the former differences need not produce or otherwise lead to background differences, directly or otherwise. (All this applies whether or not the significant differences in these BDs are also

numerically sizable.) Taken together, the preceding means that (1) the presence of substantial E/C *differences*—inequalities—on any one or more background items (e.g., age and/or race) would no more prove, or even necessarily make it likely, that *inequality* of opportunity for inclusion in the given samples exists or existed than that (2) the presence of striking E/C *similarities*—equalities—on those same background items would prove, or necessarily make it likely, that *equality* of opportunity exists or existed. At any rate, E/C comparability as well as noncomparability on any or all background characteristics can exist independently of any differentials with respect to program processing, and also apart from any related or resulting differences in level of opportunity for inclusion within discharge samples. Even so, a relationship *may* exist in any given instance; yet, it and when it does, it is a contingent relationship, not a necessary or otherwise intrinsic one.

The first part of Lerman's statement now follows.

. . . evidence exists that indicates that the organizationally screened samples [i.e., the differentially program-processed E's and C's] *result in* significant differences [background-characteristic differences] between experimental and control favorable discharge samples (1975, 232; emphasis added).

The favorable dischargees he referred to here, and on which he next focused in this regard (see the conclusion of his statement, below), were the E's and C's from the March 1972 analysis—which was based on what we will call "The 1972 sample." *This* sample is what he believed contained the *evidence,* and the *1973* sample is where he expected to find the significant E/C background differences which paralleled the ones that had been reported (Palmer and Herrera, 1972a) in connection with this *1972* sample. If these differences existed, this, he believed, would back his point about organizational screening. (Regarding results for the *1973* sample, see "The CI&I sample," below. This sample was the basis of the post-manuscript, 1973 CI&I parole *analysis* [PMCPA].)

The 1972 sample. To restate, Lerman's expectation that significant E/C background differences probably existed in the PMCPA sample centered on an inference involving E/C differences among earlier-described youths: the 1972 sample. (The latter sample had been used for a post-discharge analysis, that is, a post-parole analysis.) Specifically, Lerman indicated that because E/C background differences existed in the 1972 sample, one which consisted of favorable dischargees, they probably existed in the 1973, PMCPA sample, which consisted of favorable and unfavorable dischargees. Evidence for the 1972 sample-differences, which was referred to in the above quotation and is specified next, involved E's and C's who were described in the then-recent, March 1972, Palmer/Herrera document (1972a). This pre-manuscript document's description of background differences in E's and C's led Lerman to the below-stated expectation regarding the post-manuscript sample: the 1973 CI&I sample. (The Lerman quotation now concludes.)

> In March 1972, the CTP reported on a 24-months cohort and a 48-months cohort of post-discharge male youth. The 24-months cohort yielded differences on four of ten population characteristics at a probability level of .05 or .01. In both samples experimentals tended to differ significantly [from controls] on two critical population variables: socioeconomic status [SES] and IQ. Experimentals were favored on both characteristics. It seems reasonable to believe that comparable differences are likely to exist in the type of population used in the post-manuscript analysis [the CI&I parole analysis, presented in the 1973 reply].

(Note: Of the ten characteristics, six were the standard background items [age at intake; BE; etc.], two were personality or social-developmental [subtype and I-Level], and two were tailor-made for the discharge analysis [age at discharge; months on parole prior to discharge]. No significant [p ≤ .05] E/C differences existed on the last two items, for either the 24- or the 48-months cohort—referred to as separate samples, in the quotation.)

We will now review the specified differences in this 1972 E/C sample, and will then compare this sample with that used in the post-manuscript, 1973 analysis: "the CI&I sample."

Of the four significant E/C differences mentioned by Lerman in connection with the 24-months CI&I cohort (sample), one related to *subtype* representation and one to *I-Level*: Compared to the C's, the total group of E's had proportionately more I_4's and fewer I_3's (the preponderance of whom were conflicted and power oriented, respectively). The two remaining differences were found among the six standard background items. Of these two, that shown for *SES* was in error. What was reported as a .05 p-level should have been .20 (one degree of freedom had been used instead of two, in connection with the X^2), and the non-significance of this E/C difference was missed by the researchers despite the relatively similar percentage distributions that were present (Palmer and Herrera, 1972a, 2).[3] As shown in Table 22–1, the remaining difference involved *IQ*, with E's averaging 9 points higher than C's (E – 92; C – 83). Though statistically significant, this was not large in absolute terms. Neither it nor one that might have been considerably larger was likely to have accounted for much of the E/C difference in the then—already-reported rate of offending (Palmer, 1973c, 72–74, 92–95), for instance, much more than 5 percent of it. No differences were found on *BE, age, race,* and *offense.*

In sum, on the six standard background characteristics, one significant difference (IQ) was found for the total group. *Within* this group, one E/C difference (age; p < .05) existed for conflicted youths and none was found for the power oriented and passive conformist. Thus, with respect to background items, the March 1972 E's and C's who comprised the 24-months sample were not very different from each other. More specifically, these experimentals and controls were similar to one another in connection with (1) the sample as a whole—that is, regarding the total group, on five of the six items—and with respect to (2) the three major youth-groups as well, including the conflicted. Of particular importance, no significant difference existed on the one item that most observers would probably have considered the most relevant, and perhaps decisive by itself, with respect to *risk*—and, thus, regarding *bias* in the sense of a preexisting, unequal chance of success: base expectancy. (As in the Note's/ Appendix A's discussion of the updated suspensions analysis [also see "UDSA," in Chapter 21], no mention was made of BE, by Lerman,

TABLE 22–I

1972 Post-discharge Analysis—Comparisons between Experimental and Control Males (Favorable Dischargees) on Selected Background Characteristics, for Sacramento and Stockton Combined[a]

	BE		Age		IQ		Race				SES			Pe	Offense	
	M	σ	M	σ	M	σ	C	M	N	O	L	M	U		Pr	Ao
A. Total Group																
E	479	80	16.1	1.2	91.8	17.8	58	16	15	11	73	23	4	11	73	16
vs.																
C	481	87	15.8	1.2	82.7	15.0	51	33	13	3	83	17	0	7	76	17
	50 > 30		30 > 20		< 01		10 > 05				20 > 10				80 > 70	
B. Na + Nx																
E	479	74	16.4	1.0	94.5	17.0	68	16	7	9	59	36	5	16	68	16
vs.																
C	480	83	15.8	1.6	87.2	13.5	75	13	6	6	75	25	0	0	88	12
	50 > 30		05 > 02		70 > 50		98 > 95				50 > 30				20 > 10	
C. Cfc + Mp																
E	426	85	15.8	1.1	85.4	12.2	29	29	36	7	93	7	0	7	64	29
vs.																
C	436	91	15.8	1.0	79.1	13.4	32	52	16	0	84	16	0	12	68	20
	90 > 80		> 99		70 > 50		30 > 20				80 > 70				80 > 70	
D. Cfm																
E	430	82	15.5	1.2	87.2	18.0	75	8	8	8	92	8	0	0	83	17
vs.																
C	464	77	15.7	0.9	80.9	13.4	50	31	19	0	94	6	0	6	88	6
	70 > 50		98 > 95		20 > 10		30 > 20				99 > 98				70 > 50	

[a] E = Experimentals. C = Controls. 24-months follow-up. Sample-sizes are: *Total Group*, E-96, C-70; *Na + Nx (conflicted)*, E-56, C-16; *Cfc + Mp (power oriented)*, E-14, C-25; *Cfm (passive conformist)*, E-12, C-16. (*Rare types*, E-14, C-13.)

in any respect—e.g., as being a "critical" population variable or not. Nor was *age* mentioned in connection with this, the March 1972 analysis [nor was SES, whether as critical or otherwise], even though this variable was the specific focus of his discussion of the updated suspensions analysis [1973 reply to NIMH]: Regarding the UDSA, Lerman indicated that an E/C difference in age, in particular, would be of "critical importance." It would constitute central evidence of differential "risk"—evidence that "older" youths were "biased toward 'success'" [1975, 234]. We have seen, in Chapter 21, what "older" in fact meant.)

Results were generally similar in the 48-months CI&I sample (Palmer and Herrera, 1972a, 3). For instance, for the total group, E's and C's again differed on IQ (by 7 points; p < .05), and they did not differ significantly on SES. Nor did they thus differ on BE (p < .10 > .05), although a .01 difference now appeared on *offense* (proportionately fewer E's and C's were committed to the Youth Authority for a property offense, and proportionately more for a person offense; the first type is generally associated with a somewhat higher risk of reoffending than is the second). As in the 24-months sample no significant E/C difference existed on age and race, and no such difference was found on each of the four remaining features—the personality- or social-developmental-centered ones of subtype and I-Level representation included. (The results on subtype and I-Level—p < .10 > .05, in both cases—thus differed in strength, though not direction, from those in the 24-months sample.) For conflicted youths by themselves, findings were essentially the same as at 24 months, and no analyses were made of power oriented and passive conformist individuals, respectively, because few such youths had at least 48 months of follow-up. (The overall sample-size of the 48-months cohort was 58 percent that of the 24-months.)

The CI&I sample. This is the sample used in the 1973, post-manuscript CI&I parole analysis. As indicated in the preceding quote, Lerman believed that E/C differences which existed in the 1972 sample were likely present in this, the 1973, as well. This may have seemed reasonable to him partly because both samples contained favorable dischargees, and even though the present one, unlike that of 1972, also contained unfavorables.[4] But

were these samples indeed similar to each other on the standard background variables? and were E's and C's *within* the 1973 sample similar to *each other*? Before addressing these questions, and to better understand the analysis, some contextual information now follows.

The 1973 CI&I sample consisted of all males—104 E's and 90 C's—who had received a favorable or unfavorable discharge by the end of Phase 2 or soon afterward. Its youths were not—for purposes of the 1973 report to NIMH—analyzed in connection with *post-CYA*, that is, post-discharge, performance. Instead, they were analyzed and used to provide the Youth Authority experiment's first review of *parole* performance based on *rapsheet* data.[5] As seen in Chapter 21, this approach was part of substituting such CI&I information for the CYA parole *suspensions-document* data, since the latter had recently been found to have substantial shortcomings and the former had definite advantages.

Though rapsheets had not been used before 1973 to analyze *parole* performance, they had recently been utilized to examine the *post-CYA* performance of favorably discharged males; in fact, it was for this specific purpose, and in order to update an *earlier* analysis, that these documents had been obtained, in September 1971 (Palmer and Turner, 1970; Palmer and Herrera, 1972a). Because the rapsheets of almost all favorable dischargees were already available in 1973 (given the 1972 analysis of these documents), and *especially* since time was of the essence in producing the 1973 response for NIMH,[6] the researchers, in mid-1973, decided to utilize these same documents (though now with respect to their *parole* performance information) and to add the ones already in hand for unfavorable dischargees (themselves obtained in September 1971) rather than request rapsheets on the remaining dischargees and then analyze these documents as well.[7] Obtaining and analyzing the latter rapsheets, and especially any additional ones (see next)—and also obtaining information needed to update the *present* documents—all this would have involved a three-months time-span. Also central to the researchers' decision was the fact that a particular objective of this 1973 analysis for the reply to NIMH was to examine, for the first time, each youth's *entire* parole period, not, as in the updated suspensions analysis (the UDSA), just his first 16 months. To achieve this goal, only *dischargees* would suffice.

We now review the findings of this CI&I analysis.

1. Comparisons across samples: As seen by comparing Table 22–2 with 22–1, the sample used for the 1973 CI&I parole analysis had—like that used for the March 1972—very few E/C differences on background characteristics. First, for the total group in the CI&I analysis, as for that in the March 1972, no significant E/C difference was found on five of these six items; and, in both analyses, the one difference involved IQ (in 1973, E's were 6 points higher than C's). For conflicted, power oriented, and passive conformist youths (collectively), still in the CI&I analysis, no significant E/C differences were found among the 18 E/C comparisons that were made (3 youth-groups × 6 background items per group). Only one such E/C difference had been found in the 1972 analysis, among these same youth-groups collectively. In short, E's resembled C's within the 1973 sample—as they had done in the 1972. On this score, then, these samples *were* mutually comparable, as samples.

    Comparing 22–2 and 22–1 from a different angle, E's were very similar to *each other* across the two samples. Separately, this also applied to C's. More specifically, E/E similarity was present across the two samples and C/C comparability existed as well, in each case with regard to (1) average scores on BE (with one exception among C's), age, and IQ, and to (2) percentages-within-categories on race, SES, and offense.

    Thus, the CI&I parole sample and the 1972 sample that were focused on by Lerman were similar to each other not only in that they each contained almost no statistically significant E/C differences on the standard background items at the total group and at the youth-group levels, respectively. Instead, they were also similar numerically, with regard to direct *E* versus *E* and *C* versus *C* comparisons.

2. Comparisons within the CI&I sample: As shown in Table 22–2, and as indicated in the across-samples review, above, E's and C's who comprised the 1973 CI&I sample were similar to each

other on background characteristics. For instance, for the total group only one statistically significant E/C difference existed on these six items, and for conflicted youths by themselves there were none. Moreover, the means and percentages were generally close on their (total groups'; conflicted youths') respective background items—meaning, there were few *substantial* E/C differences, either. No statistically significant E/C differences existed among power oriented and passive conformist individuals, respectively—although, with each of these youth-groups, moderately different means were found on BE and fairly different percentages existed on race.[8]

    In sum, not only were E's similar to E's and C's comparable to C's across the two samples, but—more to the immediate point—E's and C's resembled *one another, within* each sample, on almost all background items. Specifically, since only one statistically reliable E/C difference (and few substantial numerical ones) was found on the six such items collectively, within each respective sample at the total group level, the following was the case. Little support was given to Lerman's view—which, here, he focused exclusively *on* the total group (1975, 232)—that (1) E/C *differences* in background items within the 1972 sample, and (2) similar such *differences* that he believed these first differences implied with respect to the *1973* sample, constituted evidence of organizational screening and of resulting or otherwise unequal opportunity for the E's and their C's to be included in the respective discharge samples. Little support was given on that basis—both for such screening and for other possible precursors—mainly because, as just indicated, hardly any statistically reliable E/C differences *did* exist, when one considered BE, age, IQ, race, SES, and offense together. This applies even apart from the fact that only a small-to-moderate absolute difference in amount existed between E's and C's on the one item—IQ—that did yield a reliable difference. Finally, as can be deduced from the opening portion of the present discussion, this basis of little support exists, and is sufficient, independently of the following (" . . . little" reflects the presence of very few—and, then, fairly small—E/C differences): Even if *several* background differences—SES among them—had been found, this would have (1) no more

TABLE 22-2

CI&I Parole Analysis—Comparisons between Experimental and Control Males (Favorable + Unfavorable Dischargees) on Selected Background Characteristics, for Sacramento and Stockton Combined[a]

A. Total Group

	BE M	BE σ	Age M	Age σ	IQ M	IQ σ	C	Race M	Race N	Race O	Race L	SES M	SES U	SES Pe	Offense Pr	Offense Ao
E	471	75	16.1	1.2	90.9	18.5	57	17	15	11	74	22	4	12	72	16
vs.																
C	468	77	15.8	1.2	84.5	13.6	51	30	16	3	82	17	1	7	76	18
	80 > 70		50 > 30		< 01			10 > 05				50 > 30			70 > 50	

B. Na + Nx

	BE M	BE σ	Age M	Age σ	IQ M	IQ σ	C	Race M	Race N	Race O	Race L	SES M	SES U	SES Pe	Offense Pr	Offense Ao
E	484	69	16.4	1.0	93.6	19.4	68	16	7	9	61	33	5	12	72	16
vs.																
C	463	77	16.0	1.3	87.2	11.8	76	14	7	3	72	24	3	0	83	17
	70 > 50		30 > 20		10 > 05			95 > 90				80 > 70			30 > 20	

C. Cfc + Mp

	BE M	BE σ	Age M	Age σ	IQ M	IQ σ	C	Race M	Race N	Race O	Race L	SES M	SES U	SES Pe	Offense Pr	Offense Ao
E	432	70	15.9	1.2	85.4	11.8	26	32	37	5	95	5	0	11	63	26
vs.																
C	471	71	15.8	1.1	80.0	12.7	28	52	17	3	86	14	0	10	72	17
	10 > 05		> 99		70 > 50			70 > 50				70 > 50			90 > 80	

D. Cfm

	BE M	BE σ	Age M	Age σ	IQ M	IQ σ	C	Race M	Race N	Race O	Race L	SES M	SES U	SES Pe	Offense Pr	Offense Ao
E	430	79	15.5	1.2	87.2	18.0	75	8	8	8	92	8	0	0	83	17
vs.																
C	470	75	15.7	0.9	81.8	13.6	47	29	24	0	94	6	0	6	88	6
	50 > 30		95 > 90		20 > 10			30 > 20				95 > 90			30 > 20	

[a] E = Experimentals. C = Controls. Sample-sizes are: *Total Group*, E-104, C-90; *Na + Nx (conflicted)*, E-57, C-29; *Cfc + Mp (power oriented)*, E-19, C-29; *Cfm (passive conformist)*, E-12, C-17. *(Rare types)*, E-16 , C-15.) This table corresponds to Table 6 of Palmer 1974a—where its title should have included the descriptor "Favorable + Unfavorable Dischargees," instead of only "Favorable Dischargees." Table 6 contained some slight numerical errors, here corrected. Also, one "Rare type" youth was originally misclassified as a Cfm, in connection with the 1974a analysis.

proven or otherwise definitely and necessarily supported the existence of differential opportunity (DO) for inclusion—that is, for such DO in *any* degree (here, particularly based on organizational screening, whether or not any additional factors applied)—than an absence or paucity of any such differences would have (2) proven its *non*-existence. Nor would the presence of background differences have made the existence or non-existence of this DO *highly likely* (as distinct from proven or unequivocal), or, for that matter, even only *probable*.

(For further discussion, including notes, see Appendix 49.)

Other Analyses and Information
Background Factors Examined Jointly
Regarding the updated suspensions analysis sample (Table 21–1) and that of the CI&I parole analysis (Table 22–2), we have seen that the total group of Phase 1 and 2 Valley male E's was similar to its C's on almost all six background items when these were examined one by one, that is, independently of the remaining items. This also applied to the more recent parole and post-discharge samples, which were used for the effectiveness analyses described in Chapter 8 (Tables 8–1 and 8–2, and their corresponding parts I and II of Appendix 11). In all four samples essentially the same overall breadth—that is, across-items scope—of E/C similarity, and much the same general *level* of similarity as well—that is, for each item—was also found for *conflicted* individuals, by themselves.[21] ("Item" is synonymous with "variable" [BE, age, IQ] as well as "factor" [race, SES, and offense]. As such, it applies generically, in the sense of "feature" or "characteristic.")

When each of the six background items was examined in a different manner and within a different analytic framework than that involved in the above—specifically, when the correlation for any given item (e.g., BE) with respect to the youths' E versus C status was obtained after statistically holding all remaining items *constant* (in this example, age, IQ, race, SES, and offense)[22]—the E's and C's were again found to resemble each other.[23] That is, the correlation which was obtained for that item—in effect, the standardized difference between E's and C's on that variable or factor—was not significant; in addition, it seldom accounted for more than 1 (one) per-

cent of the variance. Again, in each of these partial correlation analyses—there being six such (i.e., one per background item) for the total group of youths and six more for conflicted individuals by themselves, for each youth-sample specified shortly—one item was focused on while the five others were held constant. The particular item in question, together with the five that were controlled, was systematically varied from one analysis to the next. Thus, for instance, in the first such analysis, the correlation for BE with respect to the youths' E versus C status was focused upon, for the total group of youths, while *age, IQ, race, and so on* were statistically held constant for those individuals. The goal was to see if the result that would be obtained regarding the statistical significance or nonsignificance of this item's (BE's) correlation would differ from the result which had earlier been obtained when the effects of the five other items had *not* been controlled. In the next such analysis, the correlation for *age* was focused on, again for the total group of E's and C's, but this time with BE, IQ, race, and so on held constant. In turn, the same was done, again separately and independently, regarding each remaining item-of-focus: first with IQ, then with race, next with SES, and finally with *offense*. These analyses, 24 in all (6 × 2 × 2), were carried out with respect to the samples described in Appendix 11. That is, they were conducted only for those which formed the basis of this book's examination of parole and post-discharge effectiveness, for the Phase 1 and 2 Valley males.[24] Given the individual and collective results that were obtained with regard to E versus C status, that is, in light of findings which (1) quantitatively paralleled those already shown in Appendix 11 regarding the nonsignificance versus significance of the six items and which, in particular, (2) involved very low correlations, no higher-order partialling was undertaken. (Regarding "paralleled," also see Tables 21–1 and 22–2.)

Odd/Even Analyses
As a limited check on the reliability—at least, the internal consistency and, in a sense, the stability—of certain major findings from the California experiment, an "odd/even" analysis was carried out, in 1980, regarding the Phase 1 and 2 Valley males who comprised the sample that was used to evaluate E and C

program impact during and after parole (Chapter 8). In this quasi- and ersatz-replication effort—"quasi" in that it did not involve a new sample of youths—the following steps were taken, first with respect to the *parole* sample described in Chapter 8: The 173 experimental males who, collectively, constituted the original, total E group within this sample (Table 8–1) were divided into two groups, based solely on whether the final digit of their Youth Authority identification number was odd or even.[25] The same was then done with the 157 control males—the original, total C group in that same sample. This resulted in two approximately equal-sized groups of E's and two such groups of C's. (For the 173 experimentals—that is, the original, undivided, total group (OUTG) of E's—the percentage of odd-digit and even-digit individuals was 48 and 52, respectively. For the 157 controls—again the OUTG, this time of C's—it was 49 and 51. As always, the total group—whether of E's or of C's—consisted of all youths: the conflicted, the power oriented, the passive conformist, and the rare.) Rates of offending were then derived from the original data, separately for arrests and convictions, for the two E groups and the two C groups—thus, for each of the now-*divided* original groups.

Parole period: As seen in Chapter 8 (Table 8–1), the monthly rates of *arrest* during parole, for the OUTG of *experimentals,* were .038, .015, and .007 in connection with the "moderate + severe," the "severe," and the "violent" offense—categories, respectively. In the 1980—that is, the odd/even—analysis, the rates of arrest for each of the first two categories ("moderate + severe," and "severe") were similar to each other across the odd-numbered E group ("Eo") and the even-numbered one ("Ee"): *.035 and .041 and .018 and .013,* for Eo and Ee, respectively; regarding the third offense-category ("violent") they were *.009 and .004* for the respective divided groups—thus, not particularly alike. In the case of OUTG-*controls,* still during parole, the rates of arrest were .076, .028, and .013 for the three offense-categories (Table 8–1). In the 1980 breakdown the rates for the first two categories were similar to each other across the odd-numbered sample ("Co") and the even-numbered ("Ce"), and they were fairly similar across the third category: *.078 and .074, .026 and .030,* and *.015 and .011* for Co and Ce, respectively.

Regarding the original, undivided group of *conflicted* experimentals (N = 99) within the total parole sample (conflicted individuals being this sample's—and the post-parole sample's—largest single component), the monthly rates of arrest for the three offense-categories were *.034, .014,* and *.006,* respectively (Table 8–1). In the odd/even analysis the rates for these first two categories were fairly similar to each other, and those for the third were identical, across the Eo and Ee groups: *.030 and .037, .016 and .012,* and *.006 and .006* for these divided groups, respectively. For the original, undivided, conflicted C's (N = 64) the rates of arrest were *.080, .028,* and *.013.* In the odd/even breakdown they were similar to each other for the moderate + severe and for the severe offense categories alike, but dissimilar regarding the violence category, across the Co and Ce groups: *.085 and .076, .027 and .028,* and *.008 and .017* for these divided groups.[26]

Essentially the same type of results were obtained in connection with *convictions* ("arrests with convictions"; Table 8–1): Considerable similarity was observed in the rates of conviction for (1) the Eo's compared to the Ee's and, separately, for (2) Co's compared to Ce's, mainly with respect to the moderate + severe and the severe offense-categories. As in the above, this applied to the total group and, within it, to conflicted individuals by themselves.

Regarding arrests and convictions alike, no odd/even breakdown was made of the power oriented group and of the passive conformists. This was essentially because of the sample-sizes that would have been involved if each group were divided roughly in half—even though the power oriented group was borderline in this respect, for purposes of the present-type analysis (Table 8–1).[27]

Post-parole period: As shown in Table 8–2, the monthly rates of *arrest* during post-parole for the original, undivided, total group (OUTG) of experimentals (N = 125) were .039, .019, and .007, in connection with the moderate + severe, the severe, and the violent offense-categories, respectively. In the odd/even analysis, the rates for all three categories were similar to each other across the Eo and Ee groups: *.037 and .041, .016 and .021,* and *.008 and .006.* In the case of OUTG-*controls* (N = 109) arrest rates were *.045, .016,* and

.006 for the three categories, respectively (Table 8–2). In the present breakdown, that is, the odd/even analysis, the rates for Co's and Ce's were moderately similar to each other in the first category of offenses, dissimilar in the second, and similar in the third: *.052 and .039, .021 and .012, and .007 and .005.*

Regarding the original, undivided *conflicted experimentals* (N = 70), the arrest rates during post-parole were *.032, .014,* and *.005* for the three offense-categories, respectively (Table 8–2). In the odd/even analysis the rates for all three categories were quite similar to each other across the Eo and Ee groups: *.031 and .032, .013 and .015,* and *.004 and .005,* respectively. For the original, undivided, *conflicted controls* (N = 38) the rates were *.058, .022,* and *.008.* In the present breakdown they were fairly similar to each other for the first two offense-categories, across the Co's and Ce's, and were similar across the third: *.063 and .054, .025 and .019,* and *.007 and .009.*[28]

Regarding post-parole *convictions,* largely comparable odd/even rates were obtained for the first two offense-categories (mainly the moderate + severe) and also for the third,[29] with respect to the total group and its conflicted individuals alike. This applied to the experimentals (Eo, Ee) and, to a slightly lesser degree, the controls as well (Co, Ce).

To review: (1) For the *total group,* that is, all youth-types combined, *arrest* rates for the *parole* follow-up of the Phase 1 and 2 E and C samples described in Chapter 8 remained largely unchanged—in this respect, "stable"—after each of these samples had been randomly divided into two subsamples and each of the latter had then been compared with the other (Eo with Ee; Co with Ce). (2) This stability applied especially with regard to moderate + severe (m + s) offenses combined and to severe (s) offenses by themselves. Findings regarding the stability of arrest rates for violent (v) offenses (a subset of the s) were mixed (i.e., they were opposed in the Eo/Ee comparison and supported in the Co/Ce)—still in this, the *total group, parole* context. (3) Points (1) and (2), which involved arrest rates for the total group, applied to *conviction* ("arrest with conviction") rates as well, though with slightly less overall strength than for arrests by themselves. (4) Point (1) ("*arrest* rates . . . remained largely unchanged") continued to apply to the total group when *post-parole* was examined; this pertained to the m + s offenses

and, to a lesser extent, the s offenses (more so in connection with Eo versus Ee than with Co versus Ce, particularly for s offenses), (5) Still regarding post-parole, the results for *convictions* were much the same as those for arrests. However, the stability of v offenses was difficult to assess in this, the post-parole, *convictions* context. This mainly reflected the low rate of convictions associated with v offenses during this period, combined with the relatively low base rate of such offenses in the first place.

Points (1) through (5) pertained to the total group; we now focus on the conflicted. (6) For conflicted youths during *parole*, points (1) and (2), above, which had focused on *arrests* during that period, continued to apply with respect to arrests. As in point (3), this finding applied to convictions as well—especially (as in point (2)) regarding m + s offenses combined, and s offenses by themselves. (7) Concerning *post-parole arrests,* results for the conflicted group showed, on balance, at least as much stability as they had shown in connection with parole, and this time they were not "mixed" in the case of violent offenses. As to post-parole *convictions* involving conflicted youths, almost the same level of stability was observed as that seen for arrests, at least with regard to moderate + severe and severe offenses. (For the combination of reasons mentioned in point (5), it was difficult to assess the stability of v offenses in this, the post-parole *convictions* context involving conflicted youths.)

All in all, then, the odd/even breakdown of CI&I rapsheet-data indicated that the following applied to favorably + unfavorably discharged Phase 1 and 2 Valley males: Considerable stability existed in the parole and post-parole arrest and conviction rates of these individuals—total group and conflicted alike—mainly, but not only, for moderate + severe offenses combined and for severe offenses by themselves. (Unlike conflicted youths, the power oriented and passive conformist were not also assessed *independently* of the total group.)

Before continuing, the following might be kept in mind. The odd/even analyses, or assessment, of stability—stability of certain Chapter 8 offense rates—focused on what can be called four separate "areas": (1) the parole period, for the total group of youths, (2) the parole period, for conflicted youths, (3) post-parole, for total group, and (4) post-parole, for conflicted. Each area was examined regarding the *m + s,* the *s,* and the *v* offense categories, and each *combination* of area and category can be called a "set"—whether the analyses focus on arrests, convictions, or both. (For present purposes we need only consider arrests.) For any given set, the findings that were reported in Chapter 8 concerning E versus C arrest rates—in other words, the rates that were reported, regarding that set,[30] in connection with the original, undivided E and C samples—were said, in connection with the *present* analyses (i.e., the odd/even), to be "stable" or fairly stable if the following occurred: The quantitative differences that were observed in arrest rates for *both* of the *divided* samples—more specifically, the differences that existed between Eo and Ee (in connection with the m + s, s, and/or v offenses), and, separately, those which existed between Co and Ce—were either small or no more than moderate. (If the differences were small/moderate with respect to only *one* of these pairs, whether it was the Eo/Ee or the Co/Ce, the original—that is, the Chapter 8—arrest rates were said, in connection with the odd/even analyses, to be "mixed," with regard to stability.) As seen in the above review of these analyses, most of the original, undivided rates *were* found to be stable or fairly stable, in that the arrest rates for neither the Eo/Ee pair nor those for the Ce/Co pair diverged very far from their common baseline,[31] and, hence, from each other, particularly in connection with the moderate + severe category and, separately, with the severe.

In various chapters of this book, program impact itself—as distinct from the just-mentioned stability-of-findings *regarding* impact—was assessed. Because "impact" referred specifically to the comparative effectiveness of the E versus the C program, its assessment centered on comparisons *across* these programs, not within each of them. As a result, comparisons such as those between *Eo* and *Ee,* and those between *Co* and *Ce,* did not have to be made.[32] At any rate, in Chapter 8, as in 9, program impact with respect to each of the four above-mentioned sets was assessed on the basis of (1) an E versus C comparison—more specifically, and of equal importance, on the basis of (2) a *single* such comparison—between the *overall* (the "undivided") E sample and the *overall* (itself undivided) C. This might be called

an "overall-samples" (OS) assessment. In contrast, the present—the odd/even—approach, given its two-way structural breakdown within each sample, made it possible to have not just one but, instead, *four* types of program-impact comparisons per set (still across the E and C programs [hence, samples]): an Eo versus Co, an Eo versus Ce, an Ee versus Co, and an Ee versus Ce. These might be called "split-samples" (SS) assessments, or comparisons. regarding any given set (e.g., *set 1:* parole period, for total group), any one of the four SS comparisons—for instance, that between Eo and Co—involved, of course, only half the number of experimentals and half the number of controls that were present in the original—the *OS*—assessment of that set. As a result, for any given amount of difference in the arrest rates of experimentals, on the one hand, and of controls, on the other—say, a difference in connection with the moderate + severe offenses—the SS comparison was intrinsically weaker, with regard to statistical reliability (without ipso facto being unreliable), than was the OS. Yet, despite this disadvantage, which pertained to each *one* of the four SS comparisons, the following applied when all four—after each *one* had been examined separately—were viewed collectively and could then be seen with respect to the overall pattern they formed and in terms of the evidence they had cumulatively provided: The SS comparisons—in effect, four reduced-size studies rather than a single, considerably larger one—provided results which largely paralleled those found regarding the larger study.[33] (The latter, of course, was the OS analysis or assessment—that is, the basic, overall E versus C analysis, as in Chapter 8.) In this respect, findings from the former supported those from the latter, and they did so in connection with all four *sets* (parole period, total group; parole period, conflicted youths; etc.).

Again, the underlying bases of this support—that is, of the parallel between the SS results and those from the OS analysis—were the several similarities, observed separately for each of those sets, between the following (note: few sizable differences accompanied these similarities): (1) the rates of arrest that were obtained with respect to each of the four *split-samples (SS) analyses* (the Eo versus Co; the Eo versus Ce; etc.), on the one hand, and (2) the rates of arrest that were obtained for the E's versus C's in the overall—the undivided—*OS analysis* of those same respective sets, on the other. (Regarding SS arrest rates, see the "Parole period" and the "Post-parole period" sections, above. Concerning OS rates in the case of parole—and, thus, with respect to sets 1 and 2—see Table 8–1. Regarding post-parole—thus, sets 3 and 4—see Table 8–2.) This overall congruence and correspondence between the SS rates and the OS rates existed even though, as already implied, a minority of the SS comparisons revealed experimental/control differences, with respect to the moderate + severe offense categories, which, for some of the sets, were either somewhat larger than or somewhat smaller than those observed in the OS analysis, and which, in this connection, favored either the experimentals or the controls.[34] One example of a moderately larger difference which favored *experimentals* involved the *Eo* versus *Co* comparison regarding the post-parole total group (this being set 3), with respect to m + s and s offenses: In the m + s category, for instance, the Eo rate was .037 and that for Co was .052, whereas, in the OS analysis, the rates were .039 for E's and .045 for C's. (Parallel results for moderate + severe offenses were obtained in connection with the post-parole, conflicted set [set 4].) Also regarding set 3, results in which the SS's larger-than-OS differences favored *controls,* at least with respect to severe offenses, occurred in the *Ee* versus *Ce* comparison. Here, the arrest rates were .021 and .012 for the Ee's and Ce's, respectively, whereas, in the OS analysis, they were .019 for E's and .016 for C's. (In the first example, SS arrest rates—compared to those in the OS analysis—dropped for E's and rose for C's; in the second, they rose for E's and dropped for C's.)

Analytic Exclusions

Not included among the 173 experimentals and 157 controls who comprised the Valley sample in Table 8–1 were 39 E's and 41 C's— themselves Sacramento/Stockton males. Of the latter youths, 18 E's and 21 C's were in the "conflicted" group and the others (21 E's, 20 C's) constituted all remaining individuals combined.[35] The 39 and 41 youths were not *removals*—for instance, cases withdrawn from a sample of which they were already a part. Instead, they were exclusions from a follow-up sample that was being constructed, and of which they were not a part. These cases had to be excluded in order to establish or retain an equality, between the experimental and control groups, with regard to the categories of individuals who were to be com-

pared with each other. (This is discussed shortly.) At any rate, the exclusions in question did not occur after-the-fact. They did not involve, for example, statistical or other adjustments that take place, in some studies, following the construction of a sample and/or the comparison of E's with C's. As indicated in Chapter 21's "Sample Sizes" discussion, certain kinds of cases, such as the "NICs" (which were present only among *controls*), must be excluded from an "E/C *follow-up (outcome)* analysis . . . because—in any such analysis—E's and C's must be as similar to each other as possible with regard to the *categories* of "youth" that are included. Such preestablished similarity helps preclude the presence of inputs and/or the emergence of conditions that are likely to bear differentially on E's and C's.

Each of the 39 excluded E's and 41 excluded C's belonged to one of the following three categories (the number of individuals appears in parentheses; regarding the reason for category 1 and 2's existence, see n. 36): (1) youth was recommitted to the YA from an adult court (12 E, 15 C); (2) youth was not returned to the E or C program following institutionalization, for a reason other than that of "paroled-out-of-area" (24 E, 24 C); (3) [a] YA's period of legal jurisdiction over the youth ran out, or almost ran out, by the end of his institutional stay; [b] youth was transferred out of his program (Stockton unit only)[37] at the end of Phase 2 (3 E, 2 C). These categories thus accounted for the following percentages of all exclusions, respectively: (1) 31% E, 37% C; (2) 62% E, 59% C; (3) 8% E, 5% C.

The 12 E's and 15 C's who were involved in category 1 constituted *all* the E's and C's who had been thus recommitted, beginning in Phase 2 (1964) of the experiment. This "all who" aspect pertained to the five category 3 youths as well—though here, no start-date was involved. Concerning category 2, the following applied: Except for the 24 E's mentioned above (plus 1 E and 2 C's from category 3), individuals who had been institutionalized for an offense they committed during parole, and regardless of what type it was, were returned to their program after completing that period of lockup.[38] (*Note:* Except for the "direct parolees," described in Chapter 2, all C's who had gone to an institution following a parole offense were, more precisely, "*re*-institutionalized" [REIN'd]; that is, they had already completed an institutional stay—prior to being first paroled. In contrast, E's who went to an institution following a parole offense were "*in*stitutionalized" [IN'd], since this was their *first* such lockup.) However, because those 24 E youths were *not* returned after being IN'd, whereas all REIN'd C's (controls)—and all *other* IN'd E's—*were* returned to their program, it was necessary to equalize the experimental and control sample with regard to this category of exclusions, and to thereby make the evaluation of E versus C program impact more valid than it would otherwise be.

In order to do so, 24 REIN'd C's who were similar to the 24 excluded—from-returning E's would have to be identified, from within the total group of REIN'd C's. These individuals, together with the 24 E's, would then have to be excluded from what would become the E/C follow-up sample. Once this was done, the overall sample would no longer contain a certain category of E's—specifically, a subgroup of the institutionalized E's—whose identical (counterpart) category it otherwise *would* contain in the case of C's. If the 24 REIN'd C's were *not* excluded, the sample would remain unequal in this respect and the E's would have a built-in advantage over the C's that would reflect the following: If individuals who have been sent to an institution after committing an offense while on parole are excluded from subsequent analyses—thus, if that offense, and any other offense they may have committed, is not counted—this automatically lowers the average rate of offending for the overall sample of which they are a part. (This applies to E's and C's alike.) As a result, if—as in the present case—such a subgroup of institutionalized *E's* were not included in given analyses, an identical subgroup of IN'd (i.e., REIN'd) *C's* would have to be excluded as well, in order to preclude that advantage. Moreover, the youths who comprised this E and C subgroup, that is, the analytic category which is to be excluded, should, if possible, be similar to each other in specified respects. (*Note*: The "overall sample" consists of all parole *offenders* [whether or not they were institutionalized in connection with their parole offense] plus all parole *nonoffenders* [none of whom were institutionalized, since none ever committed a parole offense]. Whether or not youths who are sent to an institution in connection with a parole of-fense are later *returned* to their parole program [whether it is the E or the C], these individuals, collectively, have (1) a higher average rate of offending, during parole, than does the composite of individuals who have *not* been sent—especially, and obviously, (2) a rate which is higher than that of the youths who, in particular, have not *offended*. As a result, if these higher-rate individuals were excluded from an overall sample, that sample's average rate would drop.)[39]

The identification-and-exclusion process was carried out via a stratified-random approach that focused on three standard background features generally considered relevant to the prediction of reoffending, and, thus, to the evaluation of program impact and comparative effectiveness. Here, depending on the context, they are also called "dimensions" or "items." These were features of the 24 E's for whom 24 matched C's were to be found from among the total group of reinstitutionalized C's, and for whom, collectively, a statistical equivalence was to be thereby achieved with these 24 C's, themselves collectively. Listed in the order of priority with which the E's and C's were to be matched individually, insofar as possible, and thereby equated collectively, again insofar as possible, these stratification features or dimensions were: *base expectancy* (using four numerical categories, which together ranged from the lowest to the highest BE); *age* (under 15; 15–16; 17 and up); and *race* (caucasian; noncaucasian).

Because the number of reinstitutionalized C's from which to draw was much larger than the 24 C's that were to be identified, and because of the stratification framework as well as the drawing procedure that was established in this context, the random drawing was able to bring about a satisfactory matching-and-equating, and to essentially reflect the given priorities (*note*: drawing occurred after basic stratification-cells were identified and alternative, adjacent cells were then established—all with respect to the three dimensions):[40] (1) Ninety-two percent of the individuals—22 E's and 22 thus-identified C's—were closely matched on BE; that is, 12 of these youths were identical—category (IC) matches and the rest were one category apart. (2) Seventy-three percent of the 22 BE–matched E's were also matched on age *together with* race—higher percentages of these "also-matched-on" individuals being matched on *either* age or race.

(Almost all of the age-matched were IC.) (3) At the "collective" level, no statistically significant (p ≤ .05) difference was found between the 24 E's and 24 C's with respect to BE, age, and race. When the specific differences between these E's and C's were examined, they were found to be 24 points for BE (with a far larger standard deviation) and 0.5 years for age. Regarding the caucasian/noncaucasian breakdown, the percentages were 54 and 46 for E's and 63 and 38 for C's. All in all, then, matching/equating was achieved at the individual and collective levels for the category 2 youths. When category 1 + 3 individuals—15 E's and 17 C's in all—were then added to the thus-matched/equated 24 E's and 24 C's, an analysis of this composite group (the now-39 E's and 41 C's) indicated that the E/C difference mentioned in (3), above, remained nonsignificant (p > .05) for BE, age, and race. The composite group, that is, the matched/equated category 1-through-3 E's and C's together, was then excluded from the follow-up sample and analysis, thereby precluding the inequality or bias that would have otherwise existed, essentially because of category 2.

To see what would have happened if the composite group had been *included* in the follow-up, a supplementary analysis (SA) was carried out: For the SA of the *total group* (i.e., all youth-groups combined), the composite group's 39 E's and 41 C's were added to the *basic sample's* total of 173 E's and 157 C's. For the SA of *conflicted* individuals (youths who were *part* of this total group), the composite group's 18 conflicted E's and 21 conflicted C's were added to the 99 conflicted E's and 64 conflicted C's who, of course, were part of the *basic sample's total* group (173 E's, 157 C's). The following results were obtained regarding moderate + severe, severe, and violent offenses, respectively. A. For *moderate + severe* arrests combined, the monthly rate of offending (r.o.o.) that is shown in Table 8–1 for the *total group* rose 16 percent (not percentage-*points*) for E's and 12 percent for C's. That is, the r.o.o.'s of *.038* and *.076*, for the E's and the C's, respectively, increased to .044 and .085. For *conflicted* youths, the r.o.o. rose 18 percent for E's and 17 percent for C's; that is, the monthly arrest rates of *.034* and *.080*, for the E's and C's, respectively, increased to .040 and .094. (It should be kept in mind that all rates of offending—both the basic ones [Table 8–1] and those from the supplementary

analysis—reflect not just the E's and C's who were *institutionalized* and those who were *re-institutionalized* but also the large percentage of individuals who were never institutionalized and who had committed no offenses—or perhaps no more than one moderate-level offense. Collectively, these latter youths greatly lowered the overall, average r.o.o.'s; or, viewed from a different perspective, they markedly held them down from the start. This influence also applied to *changes*—for instance, to increases, in r.o.o.'s.) Statistically, the E/C differences within each of the just-mentioned pairs of supplementary rates continued to be non-chance; that is, these SA-based differences yielded essentially the same findings, with respect to level of significance, as did the differences that emerged in analyses of the basic sample. Similar results were obtained in connection with *convictions* ("arrests with convictions"): For both the total group and the conflicted youths, the increase in monthly rate of offending was marginally larger than that found for arrests, and the actual difference between the *E* r.o.o.'s, on the one hand, and the *C* r.o.o.'s, on the other, continued to be non-chance. *B.* Regarding arrests in connection with *severe* offenses, the increases in r.o.o. were as follows, when the composite group was added to the basic: *total group* – E, 22%, C, 17%; *conflicted group* – E, 22%; C, 20%. That is, for the E's and C's in the total group, the r.o.o.'s rose from *.015* and *.028*, respectively, to *.018* and *.033*. For the conflicted E's and C's, they increased from *.014* and *.028*, respectively, to *.017* and *.034*. As with moderate + severe offenses combined, the SA-based differences in rate of offending remained statistically significant for both the total group and the conflicted. Regarding *convictions* for severe offenses, these, too, remained non-chance. *C.* As to *violent* offenses, the E/C differences in arrest rates, which were previously significant, now only tended to be non-chance (p < .10 > .05), for both the total group and the conflicted youths. In the case of convictions, the differences were nonsignificant for both groups, though a statistical tendency again existed with respect to the conflicted.[41]

In summary, the stratified-random approach essentially equated the 24 category 2 E's with an equal number of C's on BE, age, and race, in that order of priority. Together, these youths were then made the core of a broader, "composite" group (39 E, 41 C), one whose E's and C's were themselves statistically equivalent on those dimensions. The exclusion of this equated composite from what subsequently became the basic parole follow-up sample (173 E's and 157 C's, not counting the 39 and 41) precluded what would otherwise have been a built-in advantage for the E's over the C's, in the given follow-up analyses. Had this advantage *existed,* it would probably have reduced the amount of E/C difference by about 15 to 20 percent; that is, it would have reduced the difference between the rate of arrest that was obtained for E's, on the one hand, and that found for C's, on the other (Table 8–1), by approximately that amount. In so doing, it would have changed the overall parole follow-up results by what, in context, might be called a modest—small-to-moderate—degree. Because of (1) the sizable percentage-differences that existed at the start between the E's and C's and that would still largely exist after this change, and given (2) the sample-sizes, and so on, that were involved, this reduction would not have, or would seldom have, eliminated statistical significance where this had been found (except with violent offenses); and in fact it did not do so. Together, the preceding pertains to arrest rates for moderate + severe offenses combined and to those for severe offenses alone—in both cases, for the total group and for the conflicted individuals by themselves. It applies to convictions as well. The power oriented, passive conformist, and rare youths were not analyzed one-by-one in this context, but were collectively part of the total.[42]

Background Items × I-Level and Subtype

As already seen, the Warren I-Level system has played a major role in this book, for instance, with respect to youth—groupings ("conflicted," etc.) that reflect its subtypes. As a result, the rest of this chapter will mainly focus on certain issues that involve this system, especially those of concurrent and construct validity. First, by way of related information, the following relationships (e.g., correlations) between this system's three main youth-centered *I-Levels,* and also between the book's *youth-groupings,* on the one hand, and each of the six standard *background items* (BE, age, etc.,) on the other, might be kept in mind (*Note:* Two figures are shown regarding each relationship; the first is the correlation— the corrected contingency coefficient—and the

second [in parenthesis] is the percent of variance accounted for by that correlation. All figures pertain to Phase 1 and 2 Valley males. As elsewhere, $Na + Nx$ = conflicted; $Cfc + Mp$ = power oriented; Cfm = passive conformist; *all others* = rare types):

A. *I-Level (trichotomized:* $I_2/I_3/I_4$) versus *BE:* .05 (0+); versus *age:* .34 (12); versus *IQ:* .24 (6); versus *race:* .27 (7); versus *SES:* .23 (5); versus *offense:* .09 (1). B. *I-Level (dichotomized:* $I_2 + I_3/I_4$) versus *BE:* .10 (1); *age:* .33 (11); *IQ:* .25 (6); *race:* .25 (6); *SES:* .30 (9): *offense:* .11 (1). C. *Four-way youth-grouping* ($Na + Nx$, $Cfc + Mp$, Cfm, *all others*) versus *BE:* .35 (12); *age:* .26 (7); *IQ:* .23 (5); *race:* .33 (11); *SES:* .24 (6); *offense:* .06 (0+).

Like the analyses involved in notes 104 through 106 of Chapter 21, this one was based on the updated suspensions analysis sample (E = 310; C = 225) and was itself conducted in 1975 (Palmer, 1976). All in all, the six background items, individually, accounted for relatively little variance in I-Level as well as the youth-groupings—the average being about 6 percent and 7 percent per item, respectively. In this regard these items—including age, IQ, and SES, not to mention BE—were relatively weak predictors of I-Level and youth-group, even though statistically significant relationships were the rule. This would remain the case even if given background items were combined.[43]

Reliability of Warren Classifications[44]

A. Interview-based Classifications

Using exclusively or preponderantly interview-based information, raters who worked in the same setting as each other had percentages-of-agreement that averaged in the mid-60s (66) with respect to I-Level *subtype* (9 categories) and in the low-80s (82) regarding *I-Level* itself (possible, or at least very likely, levels 2 through 5), for *juvenile* offenders.[45] The specific figures reported in the main studies were:

- 62% – subtype; 81% – level[46] (Palmer and Werner, 1972a);
- 74% – subtype; 86% – level (Harris, 1983); and,
- 63% – subtype; 80% – level (Molof, 1969).[47, 48]

(Regarding *adult* offenders, the percentages of interrater agreement that were reported averaged 51 for subtype and 68 with respect to level. In the two studies involved, the specific figures were:

- 51% – subtype; 63% – level (Heide, 1982);[49]
- 51% – subtype; 74% – level (Van Voorhis, 1994).[50]

See n. 51 regarding three Canadian studies, two of which involved adults.)

Raters who (1) worked in *different* settings from each other yet who (2) each had independently interviewed and rated a particular—an identical—set of juvenile offenders or had independently rated a set of standardized tape recordings of interviews with identical youths, had considerably lower percentages-of-agreement than did the raters, in *above*-mentioned studies, who generally worked within a *single* setting:

- 35% – subtype; 63% – level (Molof, 1969);
- 39% – subtype; 66% – level (Molof, 1969);[52]
- 57% – subtype; 63% – level (Jesness, 1969).[53]

Here, the effects of what can be called 'differing diagnostic cultures' may have been operating (Harris, 1986a; Van Voorhis, 1994; Adlfinger, 1980). In the first two of the just-mentioned studies, one set of raters had been from the Community Treatment Project (CTP) and the second set were from Youth Authority reception centers and clinics (simply called "clinics"). At any rate, agreement was higher among individuals who had worked or were working with each other for some time than among those who (1) had not worked together as long—or at all—and/or whose (2) views regarding certain classifications may have changed substantially through time, e.g., since the individuals had first been trained (cf. "drift").

B. Inventory-based Classifications

Based predominantly or exclusively on the Jesness Inventory, two major studies of reliability yielded percentages-of-agreement that averaged approximately 40 for subtype and 70 for I-level, in the case of *juvenile* offenders. The specific figures, which related to test/retest intervals of 8 to 12 months, were:

- 39% – subtype; 67% – level (Jesness, 1969; Palmer and Werner, 1972a);
- 42% – subtype; 72% – level (Jesness and Wedge, 1970).[54, 55]

For *adult* offenders (County Jail Farm inmates), the test/retest agreement was 58% for subtype, on 3-to-12 months followup. (Jesness, 1974, 1984, 1988; Jesness and Wedge, 1983). No figure was presented for I-Level agreement; however, it would likely be in the 75–80% range.[56, 57] (Jesness, 1999)

C. Agreement between Interview and Inventory Classifications

In the four analyses that addressed the issue of interview/inventory correspondence, the average percentage-of-agreement between these classification tools was 32 in the case of subtype and 62 for I-level. Very little variation was observed across the analyses, in this regard; and, this applied whether (1) the *interviews* had been done by CTP staff, by Center for Training in Differential (CTDT) staff, or by staff (mainly researchers) of the Preston institution study, and whether (2) the *inventory* classifications resulted from the early approach to the Jesness Inventory (JI) or from the later, more quantified ("Sequential") technique (see n. 56 regarding "early" and "later" in the Preston study). For the respective analyses, the specific figures were:

- 32% – subtype; 60% – level (Jesness, 1969, p. 50);
- 32% – subtype; 60% – level (Jesness, 1969, p. 57; Jesness and Wedge, 1970, p. 43);
- 30% – subtype; 57% – level (Jesness et al., 1973; Jesness, 1974);
- 34% – subtype; 70% – level (Jesness et al., 1973; Jesness, 1974).[58]

D. Other Aspects of Interview-based Classification

The earlier-mentioned findings reported by Molof (1969)—viz., those involving (1) a 35% *subtype*- and 63% *level*-agreement, and (2) a 39% subtype- and 66% level-agreement—refer to Youth Authority staff who had received a 3-to-5 week training course at the CTDT in 1967, and/or were trained mainly by individuals who had done so. (Molof, 1969; Warren and CTDT staff, 1972; Howard, 1974).[59] For a *separate* set of individuals—one that received CTDT's later-evolved (1969), more intensive and extensive course, viz., one lasting 9 weeks—the percentages-of-agreement were as follows:

- during their training: 51% – subtype; 74% – level;[60]
- one year after completion of training: 46% – subtype; 66% – level.[61] (Palmer and Werner, 1972a)

Findings from these 'other-aspects' analyses can be viewed as reflecting level-of-*accuracy,* not just agreement. That is, they involve accuracy in that the judgments by given individuals, e.g., the trainees, were assessed against a *standard* (e.g., the CTP or CTDT taped-interview classifications) that were considered maximally correct, i.e., definitive and, in any event, final. This also applied to an analysis that compared ratings which were (1) based on the above-mentioned, abbreviated classification-interviews conducted as part of the Preston study with (2) the Preston staffing teams' *final classification* of the youth, based on all available information (the JI included). Here, the percentages-of-agreement were 57 for subtype and 73 for level.[62] (Jesness, 1969; Jesness and Wedge, 1970). Similarly, when ratings from the initial interview by CTP staff (i.e., by any one individual) were compared with the final CTP classifications (made by a staffing group, based on all information/observations, and usually covering more than a year), the percentage-of-agreement (accuracy) was 74 for subtype and 89 for level.[63] (Palmer and Werner, 1972a) It might be added that, in the Preston study, the level-of-agreement between the Jesness Inventory (using a pre "Sequential-method" of scoring) and staff's final classification (N = 1,656) was 49% for subtype and 70% for level—roughly comparable to that obtained in connection with the abbreviated interview alone. (Harris, 1988; Jesness, 1969, p. 47; Jesness and Wedge, 1970, p. 35) In a subsequent statistical analysis the "provisional" Sequential JI's level of accuracy reached 52% for subtype and 78% for level (Jesness and Wedge, 1970, 47–48). Technical efforts and refinements during the early 1970's, ones that involved augmented as well as differing Youth Authority samples, may have raised the percentages somewhat, though no specific figures were reported (Jesness, 1974, 1999; Jesness and Wedge, 1984).

Validity of I-Levels and Subtypes

In the present context, there are two particularly relevant types or facets of validity: "concurrent" and "construct." The first is sometimes viewed—and reasonably so—as an aspect of the second, or even an integral part of it. For present purposes, we need not focus on either "face" or "predictive" validity. (Terminology: A concept, a group or set of concepts, and/or a system of concepts that is to be validated will be called an "original" concept, and so on. This is to distinguish it from all "other" concepts—those which are used to *validate* the original one. "Concept" and "construct" are sometimes used synonymously.)

Concurrent validity centers on whether or not, or the extent to which, an original concept, a group or set of interrelated original concepts, or an entire system of such concepts—for instance, Warren's collective I-Levels—is (1) comparable to or partly equivalent to, is (2) an extension/expression or other aspect of, and/or has (3) other substantive parallels with, or a statistically significant relationship to, any one or more of the following (note: "concept"— whether "original" or not—can refer to any trait, behavior, attitude, or other feature, stance, disposition, or condition, such as impulsiveness, external directedness [including submissiveness], and hostility/negativism): certain *other* concepts, groups of concepts, or systems of concepts (such as Kohlberg's stages of moral development). These "*other(s)*" are viewed, in particular, as having either an already established, a fairly well established, a mostly presumed, or a comparatively new—but increasing degree of—*credibility, trueness-to-life, and significance* (theory-centered and/or practical import). In those respects, these concepts/systems already have some reality, acceptance or legitimacy, and meaning—in effect, some validity— of their own.

Because of this reality, and so on, any judgment (that is, any finding or decision) to the effect that "concurrent validity exists" is usually taken to mean the following: The original—the to-be-validated—concept or system has received at least a moderate or substantial degree of support (usually direct support) from one or more of those other concepts/systems (C/Ss). In particular, it has been supported by C/Ss that seem to focus on or otherwise substantially involve a similar or identical dimension or dimensions, whether these are somewhat broader or narrower than the original. In effect, these "other" C/Ss have served as a final, or at least a partial and provisional yet frequently recognized, outside criterion or standard for helping to validate—to provide a type of meaning, legitimacy, and reality to—the original concept/group/system.

As suggested, *construct validity* can encompass the above. However, in one of its most salient respects it centers on whether or not—or again on the extent to which—an original concept (and/or elements within a *system*) fits into, helps to complement, or may even help support or promote, the following: a (1) relatively unified (and/or increasingly unified or self-consistent), (2) partially or largely integrated (perhaps causally interrelated), *and* (3) logically meaningful as well as (4) seemingly true-to-life *set or network of concepts/elements*. This set, which may consist of very few elements at first, is sometimes called a "nomological network." In the present context it is a group—or perhaps a closely, even causally, interrelated set—of traits, and so on, that can be predicted to exist *in relation to* the original concept/group/system (CGS)—specifically, predicted to be statistically associated with it. This prediction would usually derive from some aspect or implication of the original CGS (the one to be validated), or of the context in which that CGS often exists. Regarding "context," the prediction could be based, for example, on an explicit theory in which an original concept plays an integral part. Alternatively, it could derive largely from frequently accepted *non-original* (i.e., "other") concepts, from implicit assumptions, or from various empirical findings—(1) none of which is necessarily linked to or limited by any explicit theory, or even by any *further* set of concepts, yet (2) each of which, like an articulated theory itself, *would* link with the *original* CGS itself (Campbell, 1960; Cronbach and Meehl, 1955; Miller, 1972; this Cronbach/Meehl/Campbell position was fully supported by Beker and Heyman [1972, 18–19], as well).

Jesness (1974, 22), in effect, summarized much of the above by simply describing a system's *concurrent* validity as "how well [its variables] agree with [other]variables purporting to measure the same thing." Similarly, he described *construct* validity as how well a concept or system "relates to theoretical concepts that can help one understand its meaning," or as "how [a concept/system] relates to theoretically related concepts." Besides also discussing *predictive* validity, Jesness (p. 38) distinguished one other type or aspect, one with properties of both the concurrent and the construct: the "convergent" (Campbell and Fiske, 1959). This centers on the "agreement between two [or more] maximally different types of measures (e.g., experts' Q-sorts, observers' ratings, and self-ratings, *or* questionnaires, projective tests, and physiological responses] of the same characteristic"—especially, but not only, on any one sample. To generally simplify matters, we will review concurrent and construct validity in turn, but we will not focus separately on the convergent—though examples of it will be seen.

Concurrent Validity of Youth Typologies

Broad Groupings or Bands. In March 1966, the National Institute of Mental Health sponsored a "Conference on Typologies Related to Delinquency" (Rubenfeld, 1967). Most of the conferees had done extensive research and theoretical work in this subject area and eight of them had developed a typological system of his or her own. After describing their systems these individuals (Jesness, Hunt, Hurwitz, MacGregor, Makkay, Quay, Reiss, and Warren), together with three other conferees, then discussed and compared the several typologies. Based on this discussion they essentially agreed that the various subtypes (individual categories or classifications) which comprised these systems could be largely encompassed within—in that sense, fairly adequately represented by—five broad groupings of delinquents: the *Impulse Oriented,* and *Power Oriented,* the *Neurotic,* the *Normative Outsider,* and the *Mentally Ill.* (The Impulse Oriented contained "Aggressive" and "Passive" youths, and the Power Oriented contained Conforming and Controlling individuals.) At any rate, they agreed that these general categories were very common across the several systems and seemed to represent the preponderance of delinquents.

Inspection of Rubenfeld's report on the conference (pp. 8–9) indicates that eight of Warren's nine subtypes are included under the first four of these groups: Her Aa and Ap subtypes fall within the Impulse Oriented category; her Cfm, Cfc, and Mp subtypes fall within the Power Oriented; her Na and Nx are, of course, within the Neurotic; and her Ci (Cultural Identifier) equates to the

Normative Outsider. The report also noted that "a sixth general type, not [included in the overall cross-classification] because it is not present in the other systems here, may be represented by Warren's Situational Emotional Reaction [Se] subtype" (1967, 10).

Soon after the conference, Warren (1966, 1971) added eight typological systems—six already well-known— to the eight which were discussed during that meeting. The additional ones were those of Argyle, Gibbons, Jenkins and Hewitt, McCord, Reckless, Schrag, Studt, and the American Psychiatric Association (APA). Together, these, by themselves, covered most of the broad groups already delineated at the conference; and, based on her cross-classification of all 16 systems/typologies, Warren derived six broad "classification bands": *Asocial (aggressive; passive); Conformist (nondelinquently oriented; delinquently oriented); Antisocial-manipulator; Neurotic (acting-out; anxious); Subcultural-identifier;* and *Situational.* Together, these bands encompassed the vast majority of the specific types (that is, categories/classifications) found in the several systems, collectively. (Included, in this case, was the Situational-Emotional Reaction, a group present in Warren Gibbons, Reckless, and the APA classifications. Excluded, however, was the separate category previously set aside for individuals often labeled mentally ill—for instance, borderline or openly psychotic.)

More recently, Van Voorhis (1994) empirically cross-classified five of the past two decades' most commonly used typology systems: Quay's, Megargee's (MMPI-based), Jesness' (inventory-based), Hunt's, and Warren's. Targeted, in her study, were *male adults*; 48 percent of the sample were imprisoned at the time, 52 percent were in a nearby prison camp, and more than half were ages 30–45 at admission. Based on staff observations, self-reports, a large battery of tests, and so on, and using factor analysis, multiple regression and the like, she derived four broad classifications ("personality types"): *Committed Criminal; Neurotic Anxious/High-Anxiety; Character Disorder;* and *Situational.* (Together, these encompassed the groups seen most often across the systems—that is, not *all* groups but, instead, categories which were most *common* among the given, male offenders.) Warren's I_4 *Ci's* were found in the first of these; her I_4 and I_5

Nx's were present in the second; her I_4 and I_5 *Na's* in the third, and her I_4 and I_5 *Se's* in the fourth. (As discussed later, no I_2 and I_3 groups were obtained via the interview method—the tool used to determine Warren levels and subtypes. Using the *Jesness Inventory* rather than the interview method [to which the just-mentioned findings referred], *Cfc's* were found in the first broad classification [namely, the Committed Criminal], *Nx's* were in the second, *Na's* were in the third, and *Se's* as well as *Ci's* were in the fourth [the Situational]. Using the Jesness Inventory (1962, 1983), I_4 is the highest obtainable level. See below for further discussion.)

It would now be useful to review the research that led to those four broad classifications, particularly because they bear on the I-Level groups themselves.

In the pilot study (N = 52) for the just-mentioned investigation, Van Voorhis (1988) statistically intercorrelated and otherwise analyzed several of the individual groups that were encompassed by the broad categories which were distinguished by Rubenfeld (1967) and/or Warren (1966, 1971)—ones that, on preliminary examination, seemed to exist across some or most of the Hunt, Kohlberg, Megargee, Quay, and Warren (interview-based) systems. She called these hypothesized groups the *Neurotic, Subcultural, Power Oriented, Character Disorder, Situational, Immature Dependent,* and *Manipulative,* respectively. In her analysis, she observed a number of these groups, and continued to focus on them in her main (1994) study. Also based on her pilot findings, she combined the Subcultural and Power Oriented into a single group termed the Committed Criminal; and although Van Voorhis obtained nonsupportive and/or inconclusive results regarding the Situational, Immature Dependent, and Manipulative groups (for whom cell sizes were fairly small) in the pilot, she examined them in the main study as well.[64] This was done on the assumption that they might appear in considerably larger numbers with a sample whose size [N = 350+] would markedly exceed that of the pilot, and that the resulting analysis might therefore better test the groups' validity. As in the pilot, Van Voorhis hypothesized which categories from each typology system would go with—would "converge" with—which ones from each other system, and which ones would *differ* or differ greatly from—"diverge" from—which of the others. Here, again, she studied the Hunt, Megargee, Quay, and Warren systems, but dropped the Kohlberg and substituted the Jesness Inventory-based I-Level system. (As is further discussed below, the latter's categories, that is, its subtypes, were essentially the same as those in the Warren system, except for the Ci.)

In light of the convergences and divergences that emerged in the main study of the relationships that existed between the 32 categories (whether or not they had been called "subtypes") which constituted the five typology systems (Hunt's, and so on), collectively, Van Voorhis found considerable evidence for what she termed the construct validity of several hypothesized groupings. She summarized these findings in the following statements (note: though our basic focus is on the I-Level typology, other systems mentioned by Van Voorhis are included in order to add context, specificity, and perspective, and to better illustrate the interrelationships involved):

> Our cross-classification appears to have produced a convergence of four important personality types: (1) situational, (2) neurotic anxious, (3) committed criminal, and (4) a neurotic acting-out/character disorder type, as typified by Megargee's Able and Delta and by the I_4 and I_5 Na . . . [However,] the manipulative and immature traits are less clear constructs among adults than they may be among juveniles; they may be secondary to the types enumerated above rather than types in themselves . . . Generally, the penitentiary findings support the research hypotheses more strongly [than did those from the prison camp] (pp. 116, 118).

> [More specifically,] in the penitentiary four types appeared common across most of the systems: (1) a committed criminal type, as exemplified by Quay's Asocial Aggressive, [by] Megargee's Charlie and Fox Trot, [by] Jesness' Cultural Conformist (Cfc), and [by] the I-level (interview [i.e., Warren]) I_4 Cultural Identifier; (2) a situational type, as exemplified by Quay's Situational, [by] Megargee's Easy and Item, [by] Jesness' Situational and Ci (adaptive), and [by] the I-level (interview) I_4 and I_5 Situational; (3) a neurotic anxious/high-anxiety type (e.g., Quay's Na, Megargee's George and Jupiter, Jesness' Neurotic Anxious, and the I-level Neurotic Anxious types), a construct which also was observed to converge with type How (disturbed) and immature types; (4) a character-disordered type as shown in Megargee's Able and Delta, and in all of the I-level neurotic acting-out types. These groupings were similar for the prison camp except that the neurotic/high-anxiety convergences were stronger than those for the penitentiary; also, no committed criminal cluster was present in this minimum-security setting . . . Other personality dimensions, such as immaturity/dependency and manipulative tendencies . . . did not converge well . . . [These] were more likely to converge with other dimensions (e.g., with the neurotic and the disturbed for the immature dependent types or with the committed criminal types for the manipulative types) than with similarly defined types in [the five systems studied] (pp. 233–234) . . .

> [At any rate,] overall, approximately four personality types will classify a major portion of the prison population. Beyond those four categories are rare types, transitional types, and types with multiple classifications (p. 268). [65, 66]

In the following sections we will, as usual, not distinguish between $p < .01$ and $< .001$. In addition, unless otherwise specified, the I-Level and subtype categorizations that are used in each study that is reported will have been based on an interview—this being the type of diagnostic tool used throughout the California experiment. Interview-based categorizations have often been called the *Warren* levels and subtypes (LSs), and that is what will be meant here. This designation and meaning is used (cf. Van Voorhis, 1994) to distinguish these interview-based LSs from levels and subtypes derived from the Jesness Inventory. In the studies reviewed below, these inventory-based LSs almost always have identical names as the interview-based ones; and, otherwise, they have similar names. They almost always have identical *meanings* (or, again—in studies of nondelinquents—similar ones [except for the Ci's]), as well.

When reviewing concurrent and construct validity (each one separately), we will first present studies or aspects of studies that involve *I-Level,* and, after that, *subtype.* In each such section and subsection, for example, within the "Construct Validity of Levels" section/subsection, below, we will, wherever possible, first focus on juvenile offenders, then on adult offenders, and finally, on presumed nonoffenders (mainly unselected school samples—sometimes called "general population youths"). Following this review, which comprises sections A through D, below, we will briefly focus on correlations between I-Level, on the one hand, and intelligence, age, SES, and ethnicity, on the other. After that, we will single out two of these variables or factors (first *intelligence,* then *ethnicity*), ones that various authors have highlighted in connection with construct validity.

A. Concurrent Validity of Levels[67]

1. *Hunt and McManus (1968),* studying 53 boys on probation in Syracuse, New York, obtained a correlation of .48 (p < .01) between I-Level and Hunt's Conceptual Level (CL).

2. *France (1968),* studying 199 males, ages 15–19, who were incarcerated in a California Youth Authority (YA) institution (Preston), obtained a correlation of .45 (p < .01) between Jesness Inventory (JI)-based I-Level and Hunt's Conceptual Level.

3. *Jesness (1974) and Jesness et al., (1972),* studying 627 males, ages 15–17, who were incarcerated in two YA institutions (Holton and Close), obtained a correlation of .47 (p < .01) between JI-based I-Level and Loevinger's Ego Level. When age, IQ, and race were partialled out, the correlation was .33[68] (p < .01).

4. *Palmer and Helm (1975),* studying 40 randomly selected males from Phase 3 of the CTP experiment, obtained the following correlations between the interview-based I-Levels (2 through 4), on the one hand, and the levels or stages of six separate developmental systems, on the other (the correlations are shown in parentheses):[69] Hunt's Conceptual Levels (.63); Kohlberg's Moral Judgment levels (.65); Loevinger's Ego Levels (.70); Palmer's Developmental-Adaptation Stages (.57);[70] Schroder's Information Processing Levels .51); and, Van den Daele's Ego-Ideal Levels (.61).[71] These relationships all reached p < .01.[72]

5. *Makkay (1966).* Prior to the NIMH typology conference, discussed earlier, Makkay had grouped the preponderance of delinquents and otherwise behaviorally disturbed youths under six main headings: *Primitive Aggressive; Primitive Passive-Aggressive; Organized Aggressive; Organized Passive-Aggressive; Neurotic Passive-Aggressive;* and, *Subcultural.* (All other groups, such as *Borderline Psychotic and Psychotic,* were relatively rare.) Her Organized, Neurotic, and Subcultural youths, respectively, were all viewed as structurally stabilized and developmentally more advanced than the Primitive; that is, they had reached, and they functioned at, a higher level. In a small cross-classification analysis of 24 randomly selected, behaviorally acting-out and/or adjudicated Judge Baker Guidance Center males from the Boston area in the 1960s, *Palmer (1973b),* in conjunction with Warren and Makkay, found the following. Makkay's *Primitive* groupings were mainly associated with Warren's Aa, Ap, Cfm, and Cfc subtypes, that is, with her lower maturity as well as most middle maturity individuals. Her *Organized and Neurotic* groups were largely related to Warren's Mp, Na, and Nx subtypes, the latter two being higher maturity and the first one being middle. [73, 74] (Further details appear in Palmer, 1973c, 39–40.)

6. *Butler and Adams (1966)* studied 139 psychologically disturbed, acting-out probationers who were consecutive admissions to the Las Palmas School for Girls, in Los Angeles. These youths, ages 13 to 17, entered this residential facility soon after those who had comprised Budnoff's below-mentioned, 1963 sample; and, like Budnoff, the present researchers carried out an inverse (Q) factor analysis of Jesness Inventory items. (For further information about the residents, the facility, and the analytic technique, see the description of Budnoff's study.) From this analysis, and based on information from staff who had observed and worked with the individuals for several months,

> it was evident that two of the Q-types thus derived were equivalent to two of the major [Warren] I-level types; the I-4 Neurotics and the I-2 Immatures. The third Q-type, the Covert Manipulator, may possibly correspond to one of the varieties of the I-3 'middle maturity' subtypes, but the resemblance is not readily obvious (Adams, 1966, 11)[75]

Together, these factors applied to some 73 percent of the sample, and the first two were called Disturbed-Neurotic and Immature-Impulsive, respectively.

It might be added that a separate but contemporaneous study (Childers, 1964) found that Las Palmas cottage staff—counselors—"generally reported [in interviews] behaviors consistent with expectations for [the I_4] level" (Zaidel, 1970). A second study (Palk, 1964) obtained similar results for I_3 girls, as did a third (Wilson, 1964), for I_2's. (Each I-Level was housed in its own Las Palmas cottage—an I_4, I_3, or I_2.)[76]

7. *Van Voorhis (1983; 1985)*, studying 63 probationers who had received an interview-based I-Level diagnosis, obtained a correlation of .34 (p < .01) between I-Level and Kohlberg's Moral Development Level. For 53 individuals who had been *diverted* from probation, the r was .30 (p < .01). Sample characteristics were as follows (those for the diverted group appear in parentheses): Median age − 22.5 (23.0); gender − 83 (79) percent males; ethnicity: white − 40 (60) percent, Black − 5 (2) percent, Hispanic − 55 (34) percent, all others − 0 (4) percent.

8. *Van Voorhis (1994)*, studying 179 male adults in a large, low-maximum or high-medium security federal *penitentiary* in Indiana during 1986–1988, obtained modest though statistically significant correlations between *interview-based I-Level,* on the one hand, and Conceptual level as well as Jesness Inventory-based I-level, on the other: .23 and .29, respectively (p < .01 in both cases).[77] Comparable results had been obtained during the pilot phase of the study (Van Voorhis, 1986, 1988)—which involved 52 newly admitted, randomly selected male adults, median age 31, from the same penitentiary. (The Jesness Inventory was not used in the pilot [1983–1985]; Kohlberg's Moral Judgment [MJ] system *was* used. The correlations were: I-Level and CL: .26 (p < .05); and, I-Level and MJ: .31 (p < .01).)[78]

Weaker, though still theoretically meaningful, correlations were obtained in connection with 190 adult males located in a nearby, minimum security federal *prison camp* at the time: Interview-based I-Level (IBIL) and CL: .14 (p < .10);[79] and, IBIL and JI-based I-Level: .17 (p < .05).[80] Further details appear in this chapter's "Construct Validity of Levels" section, below.

The preceding findings were based on bivariate analyses.[81] Separate, factor analyses

also provided general support for concurrent validity.[82] Whereas Van Voorhis' comprehensive study (further described below) focused on incarcerated male adults in the 1980s, several studies, substudies, and analyses other than those already discussed had involved incarcerated and nonincarcerated male and/or female *youths* in the 1960s and 1970s. These, and others, bear on the concurrent validity of *subtype* classifications and will be reviewed after the following study.

9. *Sullivan, McCullough, and Stager (1970)*, studying *120* 12, 14, and 17 year-old males and females from a general school population in Ontario, Canada, obtained the following correlations (figures in parentheses are correlations with age partialled out, that is, statistically controlled):[83] Conceptual Level and Ego Level: .56 (.23); Conceptual Level and Moral Judgment Level: .62 (.34); Ego Level and Moral Judgment Level: .66 (.40). Each relationship reached p < .01. Though this study did not examine Warren's I-Level system, the general degree of relationship between each of these systems and the Warren system itself are seen elsewhere in this chapter. In the present study, "the extent to which scores [that is, the successively higher developmental levels] increased with age is represented by the correlations with age of .66, .65, and .65, respectively . . . [Such correlations—hence, "developmental trends"] were consistent with the theoretical formulations of all three theories"—Kohlberg's, Loevinger's, and Hunt's (1970, 404–405).

B. Concurrent Validity of Subtypes
1. *Jesness (1965, 1971–1972)*, studying 210 individuals in the institution (Fricot) that housed the California Youth Authority's youngest males, derived eight youth groups in the early 1960s. These empirical groupings so "closely paralleled" several Warren subtypes—that is, the individual groups (types) were so often strikingly similar or virtually identical, descriptively—that Jesness gave some of them the names which Warren had used, and he gave others a name that was very close. Jesness' eight types were as follows (the symbol for the Warren subtype with which each Jesness type was very similar or even essentially identical is shown in parentheses): Immature, Aggressive (Aa); Immature, Passive (Ap); Socialized, Conformist (Cfm); Cultural Delinquent (Cfc); Manipulator (Mp); Neurotic,

Acting-out (Na); Neurotic, Anxious (Nx); and Neurotic, Depressed (Nx). No parallels appeared for Warren's Se's and Ci's.

These types had been derived via a multi-step statistical process that began with a preliminary cluster analysis of a wide range of information which, collectively, was obtained mostly at intake to, and discharge from, the institution.[84] At intake, the youths' average age was 10.8. The study involved random assignment and its experimentals had a mean length of stay in the institution of 18 months; its controls, 15 months.[85]

2. In Palmer's (1973b) earlier-mentioned cross-classification analysis of *Makkay's (1966)* 24 acting-out and/or adjudicated boys, it was found, as hypothesized from theory and from observations at CTP, that "the *aggressive* component described in Makkay's classification system tended to be associated with Warren's Aa (Asocial, Aggressive] and Mp grouping[s], whereas the *passive-aggressive* component was related to the Ap [Asocial, Passive], Cfm, and Cfc grouping[s] (p < .10)"[86] (Palmer, 1973c, 39).

3. In another cross-classification (Palmer, 1973b), three of *Gibbons (1965)* major types of young offenders were found to strongly or substantially correspond to, converge with, or parallel specific Warren subtypes with which they would be expected to correspond, and so on; in addition, they were found to markedly or entirely *differ/diverge* from types which they would be *expected* to be different than, again based on the types' (Gibbons') and subtypes' (Warren's) respective descriptions, and on observations/information regarding the Warren subtypes:[87] Gibbons' *Predatory Gang Delinquent* very strongly resembled Warren's Cfc and had considerable similarity to her Ci as well. It least resembled her Nx and Se subtypes. His *Casual Gang Delinquent* had key similarities to Warren's Cfm and Na, and substantial differences from her Mp, Ci, and Aa. Regarding his *Behavior Problem Delinquent,* the respective Warren subtypes were Nx and Ap, on the one hand (i.e., resemblance), and Ci (again) as well as Cfc, on the other (difference). Other strong convergences and divergences existed with respect to Gibbons' *Casual Delinquent, Nongang Member,* his *Conflict Gang Delinquent,* and his *Overly Aggressive Delinquent.*[88]

In Warren's (1971) cross-classification of 16 typologies or classification systems, Gib-

bons' *Overly Aggressive Delinquents* appeared in her "Asocial Aggressive" group ("Band 1"); his *Gang Offenders* corresponded to her "Conformist, Delinquent-oriented" and her "Subcultural-Identifier" (Bands 2 and 5); his *Behavior Problem Delinquents* resembled her "Neurotics" (Band 4); and, his *Casual Delinquent* was similar to her "Situational" (Band 6). Some of these correspondences and convergences are similar or identical to those independently found in Palmer's just-mentioned analysis.

4. In another analysis, *Palmer* cross-classified (1) each of eight types ("clusters") he had empirically derived from a random sample of 178 juvenile probationers in Los Angeles county against (2) each of Warren's nine subtypes.[89] The clusters were called: Communicative-Alert; Passive-Uncertain; Verbally Hostile-Defensive; Impulsive-Anxious; Dependent-Anxious; Independent-Assertive; Defiant-Indifferent; Wants To Be Helped and Liked (Palmer, 1963, 1965, 1973b). When these clusters (based on the specific characteristics that comprised them [by having been mutually associated]) were rated against those subtypes (based on the features which defined *them*), several of the latter—judging by the highest Palmer × Warren intercorrelations that were obtained—were associated with salient features (as reflected in the just-mentioned labels) which were the ones most expected. For instance, Warren's *Manipulators* were Verbally Hostile-Defensive, Independent-Assertive, and Defiant-Indifferent, and her *Neurotic-Anxious* youths were most associated with the Impulsive-Anxious, the Wants To Be Helped and Liked, and the Dependent-Anxious. Viewed from the opposite direction, some examples are as follows (correlations appear in parentheses): *Communicative-Alert* youths most resemble Warren's Se's (.73) and Ci's (.70), and they were least like Cfm's (−.33). *Passive-Uncertain* individuals most resembled Cfm's (.60), Cfc's (.55), and Ap's (.54), and they were least like Se's (−.54) and Ci's (−.41). *Verbally Hostile-Defensive* youths were most like Na's (.73) and Mp's (.65) and least resembled Se's (.10) and Ci's (.14). *Dependent-Anxious* individuals most resembled Nx's (.50) and were least like Mp's (−.16). *Independent-Assertive* youths were most like Se's (.60), Na's (.59), and Ci's (.55) and they least resembled Cfm's (−.12) and Cfc's (−.06). Finally, *Defiant-Indifferent* youths most resembled Cfc's (.70)

and Ap's (.65) and were least like Se's (−.25), Ci's (−.18), and Nx's (−.15).[90]

The Jesness and Makkay samples discussed above involved males only, as did the Gibbons groups we singled out. Palmer's probationers included males as well as females, and the next two samples contained females only.

5. *Budnoff (1963)* studied 75 "severely disturbed" probationers who were consecutive admissions to the Las Palmas School for Girls, in Los Angeles, and who were ages 13 to 17 at intake. Via (1) an inverse or Q-technique factor analysis of the Jesness Inventory's 155 *items,* administered at intake, and by utilizing (2) JI *scale scores* to help interpret the five final "factor-types" that emerged after several subsequent statistical steps (e.g., rotation to simple structure; item analysis; scale construction), he obtained what might be called substantial albeit mixed and partial support for the Warren typology (note: all youths had received an interview- and staff observation-based I-Level diagnosis during the intake phase, and youths' diagnoses were changed at their six-month review, if deemed appropriate; in all analyses, the final diagnosis was focused on): One factor fairly clearly corresponded to Warren's I_2's, mainly the Aa's. Another closely resembled her Cfc's. A third involved many Nx's and Cfm's (mostly the former), and, possibly, many youths whose personality involved a considerable mixture of both groupings. A fourth factor seemed to mainly consist of many Na's and many Mp's, and perhaps several individuals with key elements common to both. The final factor seemed to center on Mp's, though here, too, many Na's were apparently present.[91]

Thus, although this study did support certain subtypes and/or, at least, subtype-pairings (a broader level of grouping), the following was the case: When analyzed via the Q-technique and by certain subsequent statistical approaches, Jesness *items,* by themselves, largely did not yield factors that differentiated—that is, fairly clearly differentiated—most of the present delinquents from each other at the individual Warren subtype level. However, it did bring out—even highlighted—major *cross*-subtype features, ones that were often or perhaps regularly shared by many youths. One such group of salient features was passivity, relative cooperativeness, and comparative trust in adults/authorities; another was assertiveness/aggressivity, uncooperativeness, distrust, and even open hostility toward such individuals.[92] This situation or picture applied not just to point of intake, but later on as well.[93]

6. *Ferdinand (1978),* studying 234 females committed to a state correctional institution near Chicago,[94] obtained partial—yet, compared to Budnoff, more pointed or subtype-specific—support for Warren's typology. Based substantially on a Q-factor analysis of the youths' responses to Quay's Personal Opinion Survey, but strongly complemented by background data, by extensive interview information, and by a battery of tests, he observed 13 *patterns* among those individuals. Over and above, yet operating together *with* the individuals' personal features, these youths' social and family backgrounds, in particular, were an integral part of each pattern, also called a group or type. As such, these background factors helped to operationally distinguish each group from every other one, and to thereby define the respective groups themselves.[95]

Ferdinand observed a close, content-level correspondence between Warren's Aa, Cfm, Cfc, Mp, Na, and Nx subtypes, on the one hand, and the preponderance of his groups, on the other. Moreover, and more particularly, the second through fifth of these Warren subtypes seemed to each be well represented by *two* of his observed patterns. These four Warren subtypes collectively, were thus covered by a total of eight Ferdinand groups: his two Cfm groups, two Cfc, two Mp, and two Na. The next-listed Warren subtype—the Nx—divided into *three* Ferdinand groups. (Ferdinand also distinguished individuals—called "Normal"—whom he felt were not represented, as such, in the Warren typology. Hence, together with his 12 counterparts to Warren's just-mentioned six subtypes [including the Aa], there were 13 groups or patterns in all, for the particular sample he studied.)

At base, these findings, while supporting Warren's typology overall, indicated, in Ferdinand's view, "the existence of some important subcategories *within* [it]. One of the basic conclusions of this research is that similar personality types [each of which, for instance, is currently considered a single (Warren) subtype] often display distinct behavioral patterns because of sharply different social situations," and that such differences can often have significantly different treatment implications (1978, 33, emphasis added).[96]

Ferdinand did not observe the remaining Warren subtypes, in his sample: Unsocialized Passive (Ap), Cultural Identifier (Ci), and Situational-Emotional (Se). [97] Assuming they were nonetheless real, he hypothesized that this occurred because such youths "are either mildly delinquent and [therefore] dealt with in the community or are relatively rare among girls" (1978, 39).

Interestingly, Ferdinand (1978) and Budnoff (1963), each utilizing a different primary questionnaire for their Q-factor analysis of incarcerated delinquent girls, had independently observed groups that resembled the identical Warren subtypes—Aa, Cfm, Cfc, Mp, Na, and Nx—and neither researcher observed her Ap, Se, and Ci. Ferdinand's analysis, however, separated or more clearly separated some of Warren's groups (e.g., the Nx and Cfm) from *each other*; and, as is evident, he derived more groups or subgroups—more patterns—overall. Both differences may have largely reflected his having utilized a larger amount and wider range of information, in addition to having a larger sample.

Two final, concurrent validity studies involved male adults. The subtype dimension of Van Voorhis' (1994) already-mentioned research on males—this being a third such study—will appear in a later section of this chapter, under *construct* validity. This is despite its *concurrent* aspects.

7. *Gaensbauer and Lazerwitz (1979)* studied 20 randomly selected, court-marshalled young adult males who had been "sent to [a minimum security] Air Force Retraining Group for rehabilitation," in Colorado. Based on unstructured interviews conducted at three points in time (with the initial information mainly involving family, social, educational, and occupational histories), on official records, on psychological test data, and on followup input from treatment staff, a clinical profile—in effect, a pattern of information—was developed for each young adult. Three types or groups of individuals readily emerged from these profiles, groups that "differed consistently [from each other] in almost all characteristics assessed: a neurotic group, an immature yet socially conforming group, and an antisocial group" (p. 44). The authors specified and discussed what they considered strong overall similarities—even fundamental, point by point identities—between these groups and ones that were present in the "six

broad bands of personality types" that Warren had derived in connection with the 1966 NIMH conference on typologies (Warren, 1966, 1971; Rubenfeld, 1967), and which closely reflected her own subtype categories as well. [98]

Specifically, in terms of those bands, Gaensbauer and Lazerwitz' "neurotic" group corresponded closely to Warren's Neurotic and Situational bands. Their "immature, socially conforming" group mainly involved her Conformist—and, for reasons they specified, her Subcultural-Identifier. Finally, their "antisocial" group corresponded closely to her Antisocial-manipulator, and, less often, possibly to the Asocial. (They also found that the three groups, respectively, responded to rehabilitation efforts in much the same ways that were described in CTP-experiment literature.)

8. Based on information regarding 704 newly admitted male adult prisoners in California, *Spencer (1966)* presented one of the first typologies of violent offenders:[99] "The Culturally Violent . . . grew up in a subculture where violence is an accepted way of life; the Criminally Violent will commit violence if necessary to gain some end, as in robbery; the Pathologically Violent offenders . . . are mentally ill or have suffered brain damage; the Situationally violent [are individuals who,] under extreme provocation [have committed] a rare act of violence" (p. 1). (Other groups were the Accidentally Violent and Institutionally Violent.)

Palmer, in the above-mentioned cross-classification research (1973b), analyzed the prior offenses plus the commitment offense of 286 unselected Community Treatment Project youths (86% males) and found the following (results were essentially the same with and without females):[100] *Cultural violence* was observed proportionately most often among Cfc's (Warren's cultural conformists) and next most often among Mp's (manipulators). (In fact, the Cfc and Mp groups in combination—the individuals subsequently labeled "power oriented"—accounted for almost as much such violence, that is, proportionately as much, as did all remaining subtypes combined.) It was observed proportionately least often among Se's and Cfm's (the situational-emotional and immature conformists). *Criminal violence* was observed most often among Mp's (Palmer, 1968c, 15–16; 1973c, 38).[101]

These findings, that is, cross-system convergences, were in general and often specific accord with theoretical expectations—ones that reflected (1) the definitions of the Spencer-Conrad groups, on the one hand, and (2) the preexisting descriptions of the Warren subtypes, on the other. They were also consistent with years of operational experience with, and behavioral followup of, those subtypes.

Before starting the next section, we will restate and further illustrate certain key issues, concepts, and approaches relating to construct validity. As summarized by Miller, who in turn drew from the American Psychological Association's (1954) recommendations regarding test construction, and from Cronbach and Meehl (1955) plus Campbell (1960), construct validation is needed

in circumstances ["such as the present one, with I-level theory"], where an attempt is being made to operationalize a new conceptual system in terms of appropriate criteria or measures. [This situation, according to the APA, arises when one has "no definitive criterion measure of the quality [or characteristic] with which [one] is concerned, and must use indirect [i.e., *other*] measures to validate the theory" (1954, 214).] The task of the investigator is to select a measure which is logically and consistently related to the [system—here, to the I-Level] theory so that the results can be interpreted and can lead to future hypotheses within the same theoretical context . . . The ultimate goal of such a validational procedure is to imbed the new construct [again, the system/theory] in a nomological network, an interlocking system of laws . . . If [when trying to set up such a procedure or test] it is impossible to find a criterion measure which is *equivalent* to [i.e., almost or essentially identical to] the trait or theory being tested, then the investigator can search for other observable behaviors [or for still other reliably measurable factors] which, while not equivalent to the trait, are nonetheless *related* to it. For example, if an investigator has a test of the trait 'depression,' he might be unable to find a criterion which is equivalent to this construct; however, he can make a number of predictions about relevant behaviors [and/or other indices] which are based on his theoretical under-

standing of what is implied by the term 'depression.' Such predictions might include statements to the effect that those scoring high on his test would show a greater incidence of suicides, sleep disorders, crying behavior, psychiatric hospitalizations, pessimism, etc. . . . The verification of a number of hypotheses such as these would lead to increasing confidence in the investigator's theory and instrument [i.e., in the validity/reality/significance of its concepts/elements] (1972, 21–23, emphasis added).

Thus, to help operationalize a group or set of new constructs (such as I-levels 2, 3, and 4, individually and especially collectively), researchers and others should

(1) select known/previously accepted variables or constructs which are . . . related to the [new constructs in question, or to a *theory* that may underlie them (here, the theory of interpersonal maturity). Among them might be] such constructs as: cognitive complexity, differentiation of the psychological field, level of social awareness, impulse control, future time perspective, perceived locus of control over rewards) and to then (2) demonstrate the existence of significant positive correlations between measures of these constructs, on the one hand, and those which reflect or directly represent the theory itself (e.g., the specified levels [—2, 3, and/or 4—] of interpersonal maturity), on the other. {By embedding, for instance, by statistically associating] the new constructs within a nomological net [the contains a number of those previously accepted variables/constructs, one would thus build] a body of findings which could then be said to constitute the empirical basis of, and/or support for, an operationalized or validated theory (Palmer, 1973c, 12).

The preceding concepts, issues, and approaches—ones first focused on by Cronbach, Meehl, and Campbell—were also described and discussed by Nunnally (1967, 83–101), in considerable detail.

C. Construct Validity of Levels
1. *Miller (1972)*, studying 138 delinquents, ages 13 and 21, obtained results that were in line

with theory when she correlated *I-Level* with each of the following (correlations are shown in parentheses; all reached p < .01):[102] *cognitive complexity* (.50); *impulse control* (.37); and *foresight or ability to plan behavior* (.32). In short, the higher the I-Level, the more the cognitive complexity, the more the impulse control, and the more the foresight. When she partialled out verbal and nonverbal IQ, all correlations remained significant at p < .01:[103] cognitive complexity was .25, impulse control was .24, and foresight was .24. (See endnote 103 regarding definition of cognitive complexity.)

At the same time, Miller obtained correlations that did not support theory, that is, were not statistically significant, in two instances (this applied even when verbal and nonverbal IQ were *not* partialled out; also see below, regarding partialling): internal versus external locus of control (−.15); and, internalization of guilt (.05). (Note: If Miller had used a one- rather than two-tailed test—which she could have done since a direction-of-relationship had been predicted—the first of these two correlations would have been statistically significant [p < .05], as predicted from theory.) With IQ partialled out, the relationship with *locus of control* remained nonsignificant (−.13) (except, again, if a one-tailed test had been used; p = .07, a tendency); nor was the correlation with *internalization of guilt* then significant (.04).

(When *cognitive complexity* was partialled out in addition to IQ, I-Level's relationship to *impulse control* continued to be significant [r = .20; p < .05], as did that to *foresight* [r = .22; p < .01].[104] Its correlations with *locus of control* and *internalization of guilt* were −.15 and .05—again nonsignificant, except, in the first case, with a one-tail test. [The possible impact of cognitive complexity had been examined because of its high absolute and relative correlation with IQ—which, in turn, was known, from prior research, to have a statistically significant relationship to I-Level. IQ is reviewed in a later section of this chapter.][105] Further, when age, sex (gender), and ethnicity (race) were partialled out [not in addition to IQ and/or cognitive complexity], the first-mentioned findings remained significant, again at p < .01: cognitive complexity was .40, impulse control use .26, and foresight was .23.)

To measure the preceding constructs, Miller used the following: Hunt's Paragraph Completions, for *cognitive complexity;* Porteus Maze Q-scores, for *impulse control;* Porteus Maze TQ-scores, for *foresight;* Rotter Internal-External Scale, for *locus of control;* and Mosher Guilt Scale, for *internalization of guilt.*

The preceding results were all based on the youths' responses to those *instruments.* In addition, separate statistical analyses of *ratings* that were made by the youths' case worker, cottage counselors, house parents, and others yielded similar results for cognitive complexity (p < .01), even with various types of partialling. Two of the remaining constructs—locus of control, and internalized guilt—were also rated by these individuals; and here, too, positive relationships—usually p < .01—were found with I-Level, again with and without partialling (Miller, 1972, 90, 170).

Discriminant function analyses indicated that—of 11 variables and factors which were examined—instrument-based (not staff-rating-based) cognitive complexity was by far the best single predictor of I-Level. (Involved were the five instrument-based variables/factors just-mentioned, plus staff-rated [SR] cognitive complexity, SR locus of control, SR internalized guilt, SR liking [of the youth], verbal IQ, and nonverbal IQ.) This was the case even though subsequent multiple regression analyses indicated the following: To distinguish between I-Levels 2 and 3, the two strongest predictors were instrument-based cognitive complexity and nonverbal IQ; to distinguish between levels 3 and 4, the two leading items were verbal IQ and staff-rated cognitive complexity; and to differentiate levels 2 and 4, the leading items were verbal and nonverbal IQ. Miller believed that "results [from] the discriminant function and multiple regression analyses substantiated the postulated orderings [i.e., sequence] of the stages of I-level theory . . . [Most of] the predictor variables which were found to best separate these I-level groups also arranged themselves along a linear axis in the same ordering as is presumed by the theory" (1972, 99). For instance, the youths' scores on instrument-based cognitive complexity were 0.55, 1.09, and 1.42 for I_2's, I_3's, and I_4's, respectively.

Regarding this sample (90 males, 48 females), 75 percent were incarcerated in two Colorado correctional institutions, and the rest were in the California Youth Authority's

NRCC. (All females were from Colorado.) As to the I-Level classifications (11 percent of the youths were I_2's, 40 percent I_3's, and 49 percent I_4's), 70 percent were obtained via interview—often by persons trained at CTDT—and the remainder were derived via the Jesness Inventory.

2. *Zaidel (1970, 1973)* studied 110 delinquent females, ages 14–21, whose interview-based I-levels ranged, collectively, from three to five (I_3 – 34 percent; I_4 – 55 percent; I_5 – 12 percent) and who were incarcerated in a California Youth Authority institution (Ventura) at the time.[106] Each youth was administered at least three intelligence tests (Raven's Progressive Matrices; Science Research Associates [SRA], verbal; SRA, nonverbal),[107] and three "affect awareness" tests ("tasks"). Affect awareness was "broadly defined to include cognitive and perceptual awareness of feelings in other people . . . Task A, a cognitive-verbal measure [of it], . . . was concerned with the salience of feelings and other internal attributes in describing others. Task B was concerned with perceptual attention to feelings in others. Task C [, which centered on "judgments" regarding affect], measured ability to identify moods from facial expressions" (1970, 46–47).[108]

Besides obtaining substantial correlations between I-Level and intelligence [109] (.59, .59, and .44 in the just-mentioned IQ tests, respectively—each relationship reaching p < .01), Zaidel found the following. ". . . all three measures indicated that affect awareness increased with I-level. [At the same time, though,] intelligence was an important factor in the I-level differences in awareness of feelings in others" (1973, 54). These overall findings were broken down more specifically: Regarding Task A, "I-level groups differed in the size of their vocabulary for describing other people and in their use of internal constructs in particular. The differences were related to both I-level and verbal intelligence. The positive correlation between verbal intelligence and I-level enhanced the I-level differences in interpersonal vocabulary . . . [Regarding Task B,] the results indicated that under neutral conditions I-level groups differed in their tendency to attend to affect in other people and that the differences were a function of nonverbal intelligence (i.e., SRA nonverbal scores)[110] . . . [As to Task C, pairwise F-tests on IQ-adjusted means] indicated

that the I-3 and I-4 groups did not differ [from each other] in ability to judge affect; however, the I-4 vs. I-5 comparison was significant (p < .05), as was the I-3 vs. I-5 difference (p < .01). Thus, the I-5 subjects showed greater emotional sensitivity even after adjustment for verbal intelligence"[111] (1973, 53–54).

Despite the joint-contribution of intelligence, these findings regarding affect support I-Level's explicit theoretical position that "*the degree to which a person is aware of feelings in other people . . .* increases with increasing maturity" (1973, 49; emphasis in the original); in fact, greater awareness is considered a crucial contributor *to* increased maturity.

At the same time, the findings on intelligence, in themselves, support the strong implication, in basic I-Level literature, that higher maturity is associated with higher degrees of intellectual functioning. Thus, for instance, Zaidel points out that in Warren et al. (1966b), "I-2's are described as having an 'undifferentiated view of others,'" her further point being that a "low-ability to differentiate is generally [, at least *apart* from I-Level theory] considered a characteristic of low intelligence. [Similarly,] I-3's are described as 'cognitively concrete' [another feature which, outside I-Level,] suggests a relatively low level of cognitive functioning. [At the same time, I-4's are described, here *within* I-Level literature, as having] some perception of causal factors and [as having] 'potential for considerable insight into meanings, dynamics, cause and effect.' [To many people, the latter situation] suggests a higher degree of intelligence" (1973, 49).

3. In a small-sample study, *Whitesel (1972)* examined 26 CTP-Phase 3 males, ages 13–19,[112] whose IQ's, collectively, were representative of the larger population and who had each provided two human figure drawings (one male and one female—the "Draw-A-Person" Test) during their routine intake processing. Thirty-eight percent of this sample were I_3's and the remaining 62 percent I_4's. Using the Witkin et al. (1962) Articulation-of-Body-Concept (ABC) Scale, she observed that I_4's were more likely than I_3's to produce drawings which, in ABC terms, contained "articulated elements—alternatively called "sophisticated" features. This finding was consistent with various departmental theories, I-Level among them.

(Via the ABC Scale, each drawing was assessed in three broad areas or respects: Form Level; Identity and Sex Differentiation; and Level of Detail. For each drawing, each area could be rated either "Primitive" or "Sophisticated" on each of the *specific dimensions* that comprised it. In all, 21 such dimensions could be rated per drawing per youth, across the three areas collectively. There were no global [cross-dimension] ratings, whether for an entire area or for the whole drawing.)

In particular, 40 percent of the I_3's as compared to 63 percent of the I_4's had one or more specific-dimension ratings (in whatever area or areas) that reached the Sophisticated (S) level; all remaining individuals, whether I_3's or I_4's, had no such rating on any specific dimension of either drawing. In addition, for *all* youths (N = 26) collectively, not just those with an S rating, the average number of S ratings per youth was 2.3 for I_3's and 4.8 for I_4's. (Regarding the above-mentioned 40 percent and 63 percent of youths, that is, those individuals whose drawings *did* have at least one sophisticated feature, the average number of such features was 5.8 among I_3's and 7.7 for I_4's.) As to Primitive (p) features, the average number per youth—for *all* individuals collectively—was 12.3 for I_3's and 6.8 for I_4's.[113, 114]

Finally, when Whitesel organized her data around certain "Developmental-Adaptation" information—specifically, the level-of-D-A diagnosis that each youth had received at intake (Palmer, 1969b, 1969d)—she continued to observe the above-mentioned trends, in some respects more clearly or specifically: D-A intake information had made it possible for Whitesel to divide the I_3 group into a "low" and a "high" D-A subgroup, and to do the same with I_4's. Given these distinctions it was found, for instance, that 40 percent of the low I_3's as compared to 75 percent of the high I_4's had one or more Sophisticated ratings on the above-mentioned, specific dimensions. (The first of these groups averaged 1.0 such ratings per youth; the second, 7.1.) For all youths collectively, the average number of P features per youth was 14.0, 10.6, 9.3, and 4.3, for the low I_3's, high I_3's, low I_4's, and high I_4's, respectively.[115,116]

4. *Eaks (1972),* studying 117 randomly selected males, average age 17.3, in a California Youth Authority institution (Holton), found a low but significant correlation (.18; p < .05) between Jesness Inventory-based I-Level, on the one hand, and one of three *future time perspective* measures, on the other, when several control variables—verbal and nonverbal IQ, age, socioeconomic status, and length of commitment (sentence)—were simultaneously partialled out.[117] The same applied regarding the correlation between I-Level and the Jesness *Asocial Index* (.21; p < .05). Both findings were predicted from, and in accord with, theory. However, no significant relationship (yet somewhat of a trend) was found between I-Level and Taylor *Manifest Anxiety* (−.13; p < .10 > .05), except when the listed control variables were *not* partialled out (−.17; p < .05) (1972, 101). (As seen later, much the same results were obtained on the first two variables in connection with the Warren *subtype* classifications.)

5. *Cross and Tracy (1971),*[118] studied 73 institutionalized and 46 noninstitutionalized (probation) males—average age 15.0. Regarding these 119 Connecticut delinquents, they found a significant positive relationship—usually at p < .01—between maturity level and *intelligence, age, socioeconomic status (SES),* and *internalized locus of control,* respectively, but not between maturity level and *future time perspective (FTP)* as well as several measures of *felt and/or perceived guilt.*[119] The first, second, and fourth findings supported construct validity; the remaining two did not (though the first of these came close). Concerning Cross and Tracy's analysis and findings separate for Blacks and whites, see endnote 120.)

6. *Jesness (1974), and Molof and Jesness (1973),* studying 123 males at the California Youth Authority's NRCC, found that these youths' scores on Witkin et als' (1971) Embedded Figures Test (EFT) correlated as expected with Jesness Inventory-based I-Level: The higher the EFT score, the higher the youths' level. The correlation was .36 (p < .01)—though, when age, race, and IQ were jointly controlled, it dropped to .14 (p = .06, i.e., "borderline").[121] Age-range in this study was 13 to 21, the average being 17.6.[122] EFT scores reflected degrees of self-differentiation and the complexity of cognition as well as perceptions of the external environment.

7. *Werner (1972, 1975),* studying 934 experimental and control males who participated in California's CTP experiment between 1961 and 1971 and whose mean age was 15.6 at intake, found a significant relationship (phi

= .23; p < .01) between indices of maturity (derived from the California Psychological Inventory), on the one hand, and interview-based I-Level, on the other. That is, the higher the youths' score on the CPI indices, the higher, in general, was their I-Level.[123] (See endnote 124 for details.) Werner summarized his findings as follows.

The major expectation regarding the nature of the relationship between I-level and the CPI configural clusters was confirmed. Variation in three specific aspects of personal and social development was positively related to I-level diagnosis. [These aspects were "Adult-role Socialization," "Ascendant Extroversion," and "Personal Maturity." Findings] were consistent with the considerable emphasis given in I-level theory to the relationship between maturity and each of the following variables: internalization of cultural and sub-cultural values; interpersonal sensitivity and perceptual abilities; empathy; abstractness of cognitive and learning processes; and self-differentiation and development within interpersonal contexts. The overall statistical relationships found [i.e., the percentage of variance accounted for], however, was small and its value theoretical rather than predictive" (1972, 43. [Cf. 1975, 64–65, and Palmer, 1973c, 61]).

8. *Werner (1972)*, analyzing the Jesness Inventory scale—score differences of 900 white and nonwhite males who had participated in the California study, found the following: For each of these groups, the "means of the four I-level categories [I_2, I_3, I_4 Neurotic, and I_4 NonNeurotic, respectively] were ordered almost exactly as one would predict on the basis of the [I-level] theory" (p. 5). In particular, the given means—which reflected degree of maturity—signified less maturity for I_2's than for I_3's, and also less for I_3's than for I_4's. This applied to the Social Maladjustment, Immaturity, Autism, Alienation, and Manifest Aggression scales, respectively (p < .05 for each scale).[125] (Also see Werner, 1975, 52.) Details appear in Palmer and Werner, 1972, pp. 60–63.

9. *Jesness (1974)*, studying 115 youths (93 percent males) in two California Youth Authority Institutions, found that scores on

Rotter's (1966) Internal-External Locus of Control dimension correlated in the expected direction with Jesness Inventory-based I-Level: More internal control was associated with a higher level.[126] The correlation was .38; and when age, race, and IQ were jointly controlled, it was .25 (p < .01 in both cases). The age range in this study was 13 to 21 (average = 16.8).[127] For related details, see Molof and Jesness (1973).

10. *Smith (1974)*. studying 153 males, ages 16–20, in a borstal center near Manchester, England, correlated several scale-scores from Eysenck's Personality Inventory (EPI) with Jesness Inventory-based I-Level and obtained results that mainly accorded with theory: EPI Impulsiveness was negatively related to I-Level—I_2's having the highest scores (the most Impulsivity); EPI Neuroticism correlated positively with I-Level—I_4's having the highest scores; and, EPI Psychoticism was negatively related to level—I_2's having by far the highest scores. Correlations were statistically significant, but modest: .22, .24, and .35 (p < .05 in each case), respectively.[128] Results for the remaining scales—Sociability and Extroversion—were not statistically significant; that is, they did not reliably distinguish any one I-Level from any other.[129]

11. *Van Voorhis (1994)*, studying the earlier-mentioned male adults in a federal penitentiary and its camp (N = 179 and 190, respectively), obtained results which, all in all, supported the construct validity of the "levels" or "stages" aspect—the "developmental" or "cognitive developmental" dimension—of the systems that were assessed:

Inmates classified into the lower developmental stages generally had a more difficult time adjusting to prison. They were more likely to display high stress and fear, and to show poor emotional control. At the same time, they appeared to need more from the prison experience than the inmates diagnosed at higher stages. For example, inmates at lower levels evidenced a higher need for safety, structure, help from others, and programmatic support. In contrast, correlates for the more developed inmates emphasized [these individuals'] social and intellectual skills, such as high initiative, maturity, good emotional control, and ability to learn (178–179).[130]

These findings pertained to the Hunt Conceptual Level, the Jesness Inventory-based I-Level, and the interview-based (Warren) I-Level classification systems collectively, with respect to the penitentiary and prison camp together. In effect, they constituted, themselves collectively an integration—at least, the general thrust and recurring dimensions—of major findings that were obtained across those classification systems and correctional settings. This applied even though important differences existed regarding various individual findings, by omission or commission, from one system and/or setting to another. As seen, that overall set of findings focused on the more *psychological* aspects of the individual's prison experience, for instance, on stress, fear, emotional control, and need for structure. *Behavioral* aspects—those involving disciplinary infractions, interpersonal aggression, and victimization—also provided some construct validity, though less than the psychological. This validation in connection with behavior came especially from official records and staff reports, much more than from inmate self-reports (Van Voorhis, 1994).[131]

Regarding the interview-based (still Warren) I-Level in particular, such correlates—including characteristics, qualities, and/or responses—as the following were found with respect to penitentiary inmates who were at the I_4 level (note: in all analyses, interview-based I_4's comprised the *lower* portion on the developmental scale, even though their classification was neither I_3 nor I_2. This situation is further discussed below): "Institutionalized – high fear – high stress – poor emotional control."[132] (As to the camp setting, interview-based I_4's had "fewer friends" and "poor emotional control.") In considerable contrast, penitentiary inmates classified as I_5's had the following correlates (as implied above, these individuals constituted the *higher* portion of the example on the developmental scale): "need for programmatic support – oriented to rehabilitation goals – high initiative – high ability to learn."[133] The last two correlates were also found in the camp setting, as were: "high fear – will seek help from others – communicates with staff – [seems] mature" (p. 177).

(Before continuing, it should be noted that—using the just-mentioned interview approach to classification—59 percent of the penitentiary sample were I_4's and all remaining individuals—42 percent—were I_5's. Figures for the

camp were 66 percent and 35 percent, regarding these respective levels. In neither setting were any individuals classified, by this approach, as I_2's or I_3's, though some perhaps *could* have been called I_3's.[134] [As a result, I_4's, as indicated above, were analytically and statistically the lower group, since they were compared only with I_5's—who, ipso facto, served as the higher.] In contrast, when the Jesness Inventory method of classification was used, the percentages were 5, 62, and 33 for the penitentiary I_2's, I_3's and I_4's, respectively. [The JI's scoring does not attempt to distinguish I_5's from I_4's; I_4 is the highest available, that is, obtainable, level.] Percentages for the camp were 4, 56, and 39. As elsewhere, rounding accounted for totals of other-than-100 percent.)

Using the JI approach, the following correlates were obtained for the I_4—in this case, the *higher* maturity—penitentiary inmates: "[a] need for emotional feedback – good emotional control – high initiative – high ability to learn" (1994, 175). (No statistically significant findings were obtained regarding the I_4 *camp* sample.) As is evident, some of these characteristics—features associated with the JI's highest possible I-Level classification—are the same as those which, in the *interview-method* classification, were themselves associated with the highest level, in that case I_5 rather than I_4.[135]

12. *Gottfredson and Ballard (1963),* utilizing 141 male adult prisoners in California as a validation sample in an effort to develop a written instrument that might predict I-Level, found the following via a discriminant function analysis: A combination of five California Psychological Inventory scales—Dominance, Responsibility, Tolerance, Good Impression, and Self-Control—differentiated fairly well (correlation = .47) between individuals who had been diagnosed, via an interview, as either I_2's + I_3's (together, a "low maturity" group) or as I_4's + I_5's (a "high" group).[136] Directly related to their *joint*-predictive ability was the fact that *each* such scale, on its own, positively related to level of maturity—in the first three cases at $p < .01$, and in the fourth at $< .05$. This finding was in accord with general developmental theory, since those CPI scales or dimensions, like others, had been previously found to reflect youths' and adults' overall degree of social and intellectual functioning[137] (Gough, 1960). The present findings are also briefly mentioned by Werner (1972, 1975).[138]

13. *Andrews (1974)* studied 112 juvenile and adult probationers (66 percent males) who were referred for psychological testing from an intensive supervision program (ISP) in San Diego, California, because they appeared especially troubled.[139] For each individual—all of whom had obtained an interview-based I-Level diagnosis at ISP intake (8, 44, and 48 percent were I_2's, I_3's, and I_4's, respectively)—she obtained a Performance (P) and a Verbal (V) score on the Wechsler Intelligence Scale (Childrens' or Adults' form), and her overall results (significant at p < .05) were as follows: The mean difference between individuals' P score and their V score was largest among I_2's (18 points), next largest among I_3's (7 points), and smallest for I_4's (4 points). These cross-level differences or changes were consistent with the proposition, or general view, that the tendency for individuals to increasingly utilize or rely on processes which are more cognitive in nature and/or origin and that are more internally mediated, dominated, and verbally facilitated, is a major aspect or element of their personal and interpersonal development. Moreover, the assumption, here, is that these processes are not just (1) *increasingly internal* and reflected in *greater verbal skills,* but that they can also produce (2) measurable reductions in, or a controlling of, *impulsive behaviors and related activities.* These latter may include relatively direct and immediate expressions of raw and/or strong emotions, feelings, and desires (especially irrespective of their consequences—particularly ones that are foreseen). Regarding *subtype,* Andrews' findings are summarized below.

14. *MacKay (1962),* studying 427 males, almost all under age 22, who were entering, first-time students in a California public junior college, found a low but significant correlation between I-Level and *persistence* (. 19; p < .01; when aptitude was held constant, it was .15; p < .01). Persistence was defined as completion of (1) the two consecutive semesters of college that ensued immediately upon enrollment, directly followed by (2) enrollment in the third semester.[140] I-Level was measured via the Student Opinion Survey, which consisted of the I_2 through I_5 scales of the Inventory of Personal Opinions (IPO) that had been developed as part of the original I-Level research at the Camp Elliott Naval Retraining Command (Ives and Grant [Warren], 1956). Aptitude was measured by the College Qualification Tests.

MacKay also found that "the relationship between maturity and persistence is closer at the extremes of the range of aptitude than in the center when aptitude is divided into quarters and maturity [is] dichotomized between the two upper [I_4 and I_5] and two lower [I_2 and I_3] levels" (p. 85).[141] Also, the correlation between maturity and grade point average was not significant when aptitude was held constant.

All in all, MacKay believed his general hypothesis was "fully supported insofar as persistence is a measure of the student's ability to adopt and pursue long range goals which may involve the postponement of immediate satisfactions . . ." (p. 63). His hypothesis, which he derived directly from I-Level theory, was that the higher an individual's maturity, "the more his behavior will show postponement of immediate satisfactions in order to achieve long range goals," and so on (p. 31).

15. *Jesness (1974, 55–56)* found a significant (p < .01) relationship between JI-based I-Level and the presence of teacher-identified behavior problems among 211 boys and girls, mostly ages 12 to 14, in a California junior high school: Of the 107 youths who had *one or more disciplinary problems,* 45 percent were I_2's plus I_3's (combined), and the remaining 54 percent were I_4's—a ratio of about 1 to 1.2. However, of the 104 youths who had *no disciplinary problems,* some 24 percent were I_2's plus I_3's (combined) whereas the remaining 77 percent were I_4's—a ratio of about 1 to 3.1. (Percentages are rounded, as usual.) Thus, within this general school population—one largely comprised of presumed nondelinquents—the *disciplinary*-problem group had a substantially *lower* percentage of *higher* maturity youths than did the nondisciplinary-problem group. Stated alternatively, the ratio of higher maturity youths to middle plus lower maturity youths was substantially *higher* in a *non*disciplinary-problem school sample than in a disciplinary-problem sample. (For related details and discussion, see Harris [1983, 146, 156].) These findings were consistent with the theoretical expectation that, in a general population at least, prosocial behavior will be increasingly likely to occur as individuals move up the social maturity scale, other factors—such as age and IQ—being more or less equal.

D. Construct Validity of Subtypes
1. *Jesness (1969, 1971) and Jesness and Wedge (1983a, 1984), studying 741 males*

who were mostly (88 percent) ages 16 through 18 when first sent to a California Youth Authority Institution (Preston) in the mid- to later-1960s, obtained the following results from a behavior checklist filled out by staff who had observed these youths for an average of 8.4 months: Aa, Mp, and Na youths were "the most hostile, nonconforming, and obtrusive" of the nine subtypes; Cfms, Cfc's, Se's, and Ci's manifested "the most benign behavior"; Nx's (and I_2's collectively) were the "most anxious and easily perturbed"; Cfc's, despite being seen as conforming, "were also rated as [the] most alienated and distant from staff" (1983, 48–49; 1984, 1004–1005). (The Staff Behavior Checklist that was used contained such scales as Conformity, Obtrusiveness, Hostility, and Perturbability.)

2. *Jesness (1974, 46–49) and Jesness et al. (1972, 56–60, 263–271)* studied 319 to 346 males (depending on the specific data set), ages 15 to 17 when first sent to the YA's Northern Youth Center institutions in the late 1960's and very early 1970s. Upon analyzing all 14 scales of the Staff Behavior Checklist (BCL), which was usually filled out some 7 or 8 months after a youth first arrived, the researchers found the following: The more "mature"—that is, higher (I_4) I-level—individuals obtained the "better, more desirable ratings from staff, the most immature behavior being that of the I_2 subjects" (1974, 46). Statistically significant differences were found, across *I-Levels,* on Unobtrusiveness, Friendliness, Independence, Conformity, Communication, and Social Control; they were found, across *subtypes,* on Unobtrusiveness, Friendliness, and Independence, and were in directions consistent with, that is, expected from, theory. For instance, at the subtype level, Cfm's and Nx's were the most unobtrusive; I_2's (collectively), Cfc's and Mp's were the least friendly, and Mp's were the most independent. (Ci's and Se's were not included in these and the following subtype analyses, due to their small, respective numbers.)

When staff responded to the BCL on 276 of the above youths shortly before these individuals left the institutions, analysis revealed statistically significant differences on Considerateness, Independence, Rapport, and Calmness. In particular, Cfc's were rated as having been the least considerate, Mp's as again the most independent, Cfc's as having had the

least rapport with staff (and/or vice versa), and Na's as having been calmer than Nx's. As before, the differences accorded with descriptions in the basic I-Level literature.

When Jesness' (1969) and Jesness and Wedge's (1983a) *Preston* sample described *themselves* (soon after arriving at the institution) on a 136-item Youth Opinion Poll questionnaire, I_2's and Cfc's were particularly unlikely to say they obeyed and/or would obey the rules ("because it is the right thing to do"), and Se's, Nx's, and Cfm's were more likely than the remaining subtypes to "try to talk their friends out of doing something wrong" (1969, 81–84; 1983, 46–47). Also,

analysis of variance . . . showed that subtype means differed [significantly] on virtually all of the variables [studies—including, e.g.,] verbal and numerical aptitude, attitudes toward family, attitudes toward school, self-concept, observer ratings of institutional behavior, self-reported delinquency, and number of subsequent criminal offenses . . . The most distinctive differences were on attitudinal measures . . . Hierarchical multiple-regression analyses with age, aptitude, socioeconomic status, and ethnicity entered first revealed that subtype conveyed much more than could be learned from background information [alone] (Jesness, 1988, 84).

When studying over 1,000 youths—again all males—at the *Northern Youth Center,* Jesness (1974, 48–49) and Jesness et al. (1972, 48–52) found the following, based on youths' self-descriptions from a revised (approximately 40-item) Youth Opinion Poll: Cfc's had had the most gang fights; Cfm's and Nx's were least likely to have used weapons in connection with their delinquency; Se's saw themselves as far better behaved in school than did the remaining subtypes; Aa's and Ap's (i.e., I_2's, collectively) believed that being punished is the best response to failure on their part; Cfc's and Aa's were much less likely than the other subtypes to want to talk about their problems, for instance, in a group counseling setting; very few Nx's believed they were liked by others; and, Ap's and Nx's were particularly likely to express feelings of worthlessness.

In general, I_4 subtypes—and, as a result, the I_4 level overall—felt more need than did the remaining subtypes/levels to change their behavior and/or attitudes, and to talk about their problems in counseling (small group) meetings; they had a greater anticipation of getting along well with teachers and group counselors, and expressed more liking for school. After aggregating these and related findings, Jesness (1974, 49) concluded that "the I$_4$ subjects [i.e., subtypes, overall] perceived themselves as needing to change, whereas other types were more prone to look to changes in others and in their environment. The I$_4$'s also were more inclined to see the cause of their being in trouble as a consequence of their own behavior, rather than resulting from external conditions." This applied even though various specific findings "were no longer [statistically] significant" once age, race, and IQ were partialled out [whereas several others did remain significant].

Still other analyses by Jesness and his colleagues bear on construct validity, even though Jesness used the more specific terms "concurrent" and "convergent" instead, as defined earlier. Regarding the concurrent, he described one analysis in which the I-Level subtypes were correlated with the major scales of Eysenck's Personality Inventory. Of all the subtypes, Cfm's had the lowest score on EPI Impulsiveness, whereas Aa's and Ap's obtained the highest. Nx's were by far the highest on Neuroticism, even well ahead of Na's. Aa's and Ap's were the highest on Psychoticism, whereas Cfm's and Cfc's were the lowest; and, Nx's had the lowest scores on Sociability, again clearly distinguishing themselves even from Na's. In another analysis (N = 618 Youth Center males), Jesness et al. found sizable relationships between two of Loevinger's Ego Level groups, on the one hand, and the two I-Level subtypes, on the other, that, based on theory, *should* have been most closely related to them: Of the 206 youths classified as Loevinger's "Conformist," 69 (that is, 33 percent) were cross-classified (via the JI) as I-Level Cfm's; and, of the 162 youths diagnosed as I-Level Cfm's, 69 (43 percent) were cross-classified as Leovinger's Conformist. Separately, Loevinger's Opportunistic/Self-Protective ("Delta") youths were found most often among the I-Level system's Manipulators: 35 (36 percent) of her 98 Deltas were Mp's; and, correspondingly (though not as strongly), of the 180 Mp's in the Youth Authority sample, 35 (19%) were Loevinger's Delta (Jesness et al., 1972, 47).

As to convergent analyses, Jesness (1974) and Jesness et al. (1972), focusing on approximately 1,000 institutionalized YA males who had received I-Level subtype diagnoses between mid-1969 and early 1971 and who were 15 to 17 years old at the time, statistically compared *observed behaviors* of each such youth with *generalized profiles* that were independently developed for each of the nine I-Level subtypes by seven I-Level experts; these were profiles of behaviors that would be *expected* for the respective subtypes. In so doing, hc found sizable positive correlations between the observed and expected behaviors among seven of the nine subtypes.[142] These correlations, which ranged from .54 to .80 and which averaged .68, all reached the p < .01 level.

Expected behaviors were contained in (and, thus, were operationally defined as) the profile ("pattern") of items which emerged from Q-sort ratings—of 80 Behavior Checklist (BCL, Observer Form) items—that were made by the above-mentioned experts, separately for each subtype.[143] Regarding the *observed* behaviors, data on the diagnosed institution males "had previously [i.e., prior to the Q-sorting/profiling] been obtained from the Youth Center Research Project (Jesness et al., 1972). More than 100 youth counselors, social workers, and teachers [had] rated institution [wards] assigned to their caseloads or unit [that is, had rated the approximately 1,000 youths on the BCL]" (1974, 38). The raters' (usually three) average rating was used as the item raw score, this being the information with which Jesness later statistically compared the respective profiles.

Jesness et al. also found sizable correlations—on six of those seven subtypes (from among the nine possible)—between (1) the *expected* (the profiled) behaviors and the youths' *self-ratings* on the 80-item BCL—Self Appraisal Form. Correlations ranged from .46 to .78, and averaged .62. Similar correlations were obtained, regarding the same six subtypes, between the above-mentioned *observed* behaviors and those same self-ratings. (Range: .52 to .84; average: .72)[144] In addition, and not surprisingly, they found the following by intercorrelating (2) the *expected* (still profiled) behavior patterns of all nine subtypes: For any given subtype, the pattern which was obtained resembled the pattern of *other* subtypes (that is, of each such subtype pattern separately) that—based on the preexisting descriptions of I-Level subtypes—it was expected to resemble in certain significant respects, and, in some cases, to a substantial degree overall. Also, that same obtained pattern substantially *differed* from the pattern of particular subtypes which it was *not* expected to resemble (these were still *other* subtypes).[145] Finally, results that largely resembled the just-mentioned set (set 2: the *expected*) were obtained with regard to intercorrelations among (3) *observed* behavior patterns (again in the case of the respective subtypes). and, separately, among (4) the already-mentioned *self-ratings* by the youths who comprised those given subtypes. For both these sets, the intercorrelations were, however, somewhat lower than those of set 2. (As before, "observed" ratings [here, the set 3 data] were those by institutional staff; the self-ratings [set 4 data] were those by the institutionalized youths.) Technically, all four of the just-mentioned correlation- and intercorrelation-based sets of findings might be viewed as forms or varieties of "convergent" or even "concurrent" validity—in any event, not primarily of *nomological-network-expanding* validity.

3. *Eaks (1972),* in his earlier-mentioned study of 117 institutionalized Youth Authority males, found a low but significant correlation between subtype and one of three *future time perspective* measures (.20 and .18, respectively, with and without the already-listed variables controlled; p < .05 in both cases).[146] Similar findings—ones which were themselves predicted from theory—were obtained in connection with the Jesness *Asocial Index* (–.18 and –.21, with and without the partialling; p < .05 in both instances). In contrast, yet in line with the analysis of I-Level per se, results for subtype were not significant in connection with *Manifest Anxiety*—but this time *whether or not* the control variables were partialled. (For reasons not described by Eaks, but likely centered on small sample sizes, neither Se's nor Ci's were present in the [otherwise] random sample. It is not known how, if at all, their presence would have affected the results. Since Se's and Ci's, when combined, comprised only 7 percent of the institution's overall population at the time, most impacts would probably have been small, except with otherwise borderline findings.)

4. *Andrews (1974),* in the earlier-mentioned study of 112 juvenile and adult offenders, found that "even within the same I-level, some of the sub[types] were characterized by a stronger, weaker, or absent P > V sign" (p. 333), and these cross-subtype differences in direction and/or degree were consistent with theory. (P > V is sometimes considered [1] an "impulsivity index" and a reflection of [2] fewer verbal than performance *skills* and/or of [3] a *preference* for physical over verbal expressions and interactions.) In particular, among the I_3's, manipulators had a slightly better Verbal than Performance score, whereas the remaining I_3's (Cfm's and Cfc's) were each clearly *lower* on V than on P. In addition, the Neurotic-Anxious had essentially the *same* scores on V as on P, whereas Na's—a more acting-out group than an anxious and often introspective one—scored clearly lower on Verbal than on Performance.[147]

Especially related to construct validity (CV), Andrews—though not actually focusing on CV per se—viewed her findings as likely reflections of the following (which she had "inferred" from I-Level literature): Both the Mp's and Nx's "rely upon *verbal ability* to implement their respective defenses: in the case of the 3-MP's, to manipulate; in the case of the 4-NX's, to express emotional distress verbally, rather than to act-out impulsively as the 4-NA might do [or, might, at least, be likelier to do]" (p. 334). Also in this regard, the Mp's and Nx's (when grouped together) were significantly different than all remaining subtypes (themselves combined as one), with respect to their average difference between P and V (p < .01). Specifically, they had much less of a difference.

5. *Grant (1961b),* in a controlled laboratory setting that involved perceived group pressure and group norms, studied the "yielding behavior" and "independence behavior" of 104 male adults in a California state prison. For these individuals, whose developmental levels ranged from I_2 to I_5, the main findings were as follows: I_3 conformists[148] had "significantly higher [p < .01] yielding scores than all other subgroups . . . In yielding [, these subjects] considered the achievement of personal success . . . subordinate to the achievement or retention of social approval, or the avoidance of social disapproval." I_3 manipulators "made up the lowest yielding group of subjects. Many . . . offenders in this group not only did not yield,

but actually moved in a direction opposite to the pressure." Finally, higher maturity subjects—I_4's and I_5's—"yielded significantly less than the I_3 Conformists" (Fosen and Grant, 1961, 5–6).

6. As indicated, *Van Voorhis (1994)* conducted a detailed analysis of (1) disciplinary-related penitentiary (prison) behaviors and (2) psychological correlates of treatment-related prison outcomes, for male adults. Disciplinary data were based on staff ratings, self reports, and official records. The staff ratings centered on each individual's relationships with other prisoners and with prison authorities, on aggressiveness, on cooperativeness, on need for supervision, and on responses to supervision. The self-reports focused on aggressive and nonaggressive behaviors toward others and on victimization by others. The official data centered on disciplinary incidents, use of drugs/alcohol, and insubordination. Psychological data, which was followup in nature, involved such areas as institutional victimization, support networks, utilization of programming, stress, and self-reported disciplinary actions; and, each area consisted of subareas.

Regarding the construct validity of the Warren (interview-based) subtypes, Van Voorhis obtained such findings as the following (again note: When the interview method was used, no individuals in the sample were classified as I_2's or I_3's;[149] for this reason, there were no Warren-centered results for subtypes within these levels):

[*Na—Neurotic Acting-out*:] . . . High stress scores [were not observed]. I_4 Na's were high on self-report aggressive behaviors, but the relationship was not significant. Staff-ratings of relations with authority, emotional control, ability to learn, and need for supervision were unfavorable . . . [*Nx—Neurotic Anxious*:] . . . These inmates . . . showed some adjustment difficulties (e.g., high stress and poor emotional control). Their interviews showed a need for emotional feedback; their surveys showed that they were participating in prison programs. They scored relatively low on staff ratings of their need for supervision . . . [*Se—Situational*:] . . . These inmates appear to be inexperienced in coping with prison life. At intake, they indicated a need for safety

and emotional feedback, and felt that others would be willing to help. Upon follow-up their surveys indicated high scores on fear and stress measures and a reluctance to participate. They showed the highest rates of official citations for insubordination; yet staff ratings were favorable . . . [It is possible that they] simply do not know how to do time (i.e., to stay out of trouble and to cope with prison life) . . . [*Ci—Cultural Identifier*:][150] . . . Ci's had high overall disciplinary rates and significantly more citations for insubordination than other inmates. Staff reported that this group needed more supervision than other inmates. They showed high stress and fear scores and communicated with staff, but also showed a greater tendency to be institutionalized than other types. The latter finding was not [statistically] significant, however"[151, 152]

Many of the findings for these subtypes were in accordance—in general and/or specific ways—with preexisting descriptions (of *juveniles*) in the literature and with related expectations from theory. (All in all, the differences that existed *between* given subtypes were somewhat *more* in line, as were certain similarities.)

Results for these four I_4 subtypes were largely—but far from entirely—paralleled by those for their respective, I_5 counterparts.[153]

When Van Voorhis analyzed the same types and ranges of data as the above for the identical sample of offenders (N = 179), but this time according to these individuals' Jesness Inventory-based classification rather than their just-reviewed interview-based classification, considerable construct validity was again observed.[154] (This is despite the fact that the inventory-based and the interview-based classifications have been found—in this and other research—to have a far from perfect [in fact—at the subtype level—an only fair, though statistically very significant and positive] correlation with each other.)[155] These observations, it would appear, were consistent with the following (Van Voorhis, 1994, 35, 37): "Jesness has reported numerous expected correspondences between subtype and relevant differences in attitudes, self-concept, influence of delinquent peers, responsibility, and confidence [as distinct from the "conformity," which appeared on a different instrument . . . [Also, but still in the various research studies reviewed in the present chapter,] over several tests of the validity of the Jesness Inventory I-level subtypes, Jesness reports that subtype differentiates youths consistently on such factors as observers' ratings of institutional behavior, self-reported delinquency, disciplinary referrals, classroom disturbance, and subsequent offenses and probation referrals" (Jesness, 1988 [pp. 84–85]). Whereas Van Voorhis' sample consisted of adults, Jesness', as indicated, involved juveniles.

7. *Jesness (1986) and Jesness and Wedge (1983a)*, studying an unselected population of some 1,600 8th grade boys and girls in California, obtained several significant findings regarding individuals who—based on their Jesness Inventory scores and profiles—were placed into the specific Warren subtype they most resembled (best fit): Overall, many of these youths (1) expressed given views and attitudes, (2) reported having had certain experiences, and (3) had been involved in a given behaviors (ones already recorded in official record) which were similar to those observed in prior research with *delinquents*—individuals who fell within the same specific subtypes as the 8th graders.[156] Those characteristics were similar to, and/or paralleled, ones expected from theory and regularly described in the literature—again, for delinquents of the given subtypes.[157] ("Subtype" will also be called "group" or "grouping.")

Salient among these findings were the following: (1) Aa's, Ap's, Cfc's, and Na's (which, together, included two of Harris' three predicted—most-delinquent subtypes [see below]) were the ones most likely to report having delinquent friends and as having been "picked up by the police." Se's and Ci's were those least likely to do so.[158] (2) Individuals who comprised the same four groups were also likely to report having engaged in the largest amount of minor and major delinquent behavior, and Se's as well as Ci's—this time together with Cfm's and Nx's—reported far less such behavior. (3) Similarly, Aa's and Ap's (henceforth simply "I$_2$'s," when jointly present) were the individuals who said they received the most by way of scolding from their teacher, for (as the question put it) "a variety of classroom misdeeds"; here, too, Se's and Ci's, followed by Cfm's, reported receiving the least.

Findings (1) through (3) held up when the joint effects of age, sex, ethnicity, socioeconomic status, and achievement-test score were statistically controlled. That is, the I-Level subtypes contributed substantially and significantly (p < .01) to those particular findings, over and beyond the joint contributions of such background/demographic (B/D) factors.[159] Similarly, (4) I$_2$'s, Cfc's, and Na's were the youths most likely to have received disciplinary referrals to the vice-principal's office (Se's and Ci's, followed by Cfm's and Nx's, were the least likely); and, (5) Cfc's, Na's, Mp's, and then Aa's were those most likely to have had a referral to *probation* during the post-test followup, which covered 1978–1982 (Se's, Ci's and Nx's were the least likely).[160] However, findings (4) and (5), unlike the first three, *were* largely accounted for by those B/D factors combined. More specifically, when all nine subtypes were considered jointly, *subtype*, per se, added relatively little to that combination with respect to accounting for the findings on these particular measures (cf. Jesness, 1988, 85–86).[161] Because (4) and (5)—though important in their own right—comprised a minority of the total, and especially in light of results obtained from the Scheffe multiple-comparison procedure (which evaluated numerous findings *collectively*), it seemed reasonable for Jesness to nevertheless conclude that the various "differences among subtypes were [very] consistent with expectations based on previous studies with *delinquents*" (Jesness, 1988, emphasis added). This was separate from Jesness' finding that there was a "very close correspondence [i.e., *similarity*] between the scores achieved on [the nine JI subtype] scales by . . . presumably *non*delinquents [i.e., the 8th graders] as compared with those of the delinquents [a Preston population]" (1983, 61, emphasis added). This correspondence was reflected in the mean T-scores, on the 11 Jesness scales, for the two different youth groups.

8. *Harris (1977, 1979, 1983, 1988)* studied 133 white males, ages 13 to 15,[162] who comprised a stratified ransom sample drawn from a school list that covered a city (Schenectady, population 78,000) in upstate New York.[163] Each received an interview-based Warren level and subtype classification and was rated on numerous scales derived from I-Level theory. Self-reported delinquency information was also obtained, as were school- and achievement-centered data and police

contact information. Because I_2's and I_5's were rare, the analysis and discussion focused on I_3's and I_4's.[164] Harris reported that

> All youths in the sample [—a "general population"—] were successfully classified according to integration *level* (I-Level). Only 35 percent fit any of [Warren's] nine delinquent *subtypes,* however. The remaining 65 percent [were] unclassified [26 percent at I_3, and 39 percent at I_4 . . . In other words,] the I-level delinquent *subtypes* [, in contrast to the levels themselves,] appear to fit only a minority (approximately one-third) of the general adolescent population . . . The remaining two-thirds most often have personality characteristics that are usually seen as healthy and are less involved in delinquent behavior than are those fitting the I-level subtypes (1983, 149–151, 160; emphases added).

In this regard Harris' primary conclusion concerning the Warren classification system was:

> While the developmental levels of I-level were found to apply descriptively to the population studied, the subtypes did not describe a large proportion of the male adolescent population. Based on official records of delinquent behavior, . . . the I-level subtypes [appear to] describe *delinquent* youth better than they describe nondelinquent youth (1978, 7, emphasis added).

> Collectively, the I_3's who did *not* fit any delinquent subtype, that is, any Warren subtype, were subsequently divided, by Harris, into two nondelinquent groups, and the I_4's who did not fit became—via the same statistical technique—three such groups. The former were called Conventional Conformist (Cvc) and Reorienter (Ro); the latter—the I_4's—were termed Adolescent Anxiety (Ax), Adolescent Autonomy-Seeking (Aas), the Care-Free (CF), respectively (Harris, 1977, 1979).[165]

> Youths who were called I_3U (Unclassified) were very similar to [Warren's] I_3 Cfm subtype in that they expressed positive feelings about parents, teachers, and

school; they were generally seen as conforming to rules. They differed from the Cfm youths in several ways, however [: . . .] The I_3U subgroup was less fearful and more independent than the Cfm subgroup, and more capable of making realistic plans for the future. The Cfm youths, on the other hand, were considerably more conforming with adult authority and more likely to express low self-esteem . . . Characteristics that most distinguished the I_4U [from Warren's] I_4N center around a positive self-image, self-confidence, positive relationships with adults, and high aspirations (Harris, 1983, 152, 156, emphasis added).

Further,

The relationship between I-level and age was strongest among the youths who did *not* fit the I-level subtypes and very weak among those who did. This supports the contention that several of the I-level subtypes . . . represent ways in which personality becomes blocked (1983, 161; emphasis added).

Finally, and bearing on the preceding:

Although I-level was found not to be related to either police-reported or self-reported delinquency measures for the *total* sample [this, essentially, involving only I_3's and I_4's], for the *older half* of the sample, a much greater proportion of youths classified at I_3 than at I_4 had official records of delinquency. This [suggested, for instance, that . . .] as the immaturity of the I_3 level becomes less appropriate because of expectations related to age, coming to the attention of legal authorities becomes more likely . . . [At any rate, three Warren subtypes] emerged as highly delinquent compared with the other subtypes: the Cfc, Mp, and Na . . . These [particular] subtypes are [the ones] most associated with the characteristics [found, in the literature,] to be related to delinquency (1983, 161, emphasis added). [In this regard, Harris cites several factors often mentioned as distinguishing delinquents from non-delinquents. Among them are] less abstract in their thinking, . . . less accepting of authority, less compliant, . . . deficient in role taking ability, less future oriented, . . . less socially mature, . . . and more impulsive (1983, 147) (Another feature—"more anxious"—would apply to Nx's, and *more* compliance would pertain to Cfm's.)

E. Relationships between Selected Variables and I-Level Intelligence ("IQ"). Among delinquents, correlations ("r's") between IQ and I-Level have ranged between the .20s—more often .30s—and the .50s; as such, IQ has accounted for some 5 or 10 percent to approximately 30 percent of the total variance in this construct. Regarding the specific correlations, those most often and widely cited are the following: Jesness (1974) and Jesness and Wedge (1984), in their analyses of various institutional samples and subsamples within the California Youth Authority—for instance, at Preston and the Northern Youth Center—reported r's of .29, .33, .36, and .59. Other researchers, focusing on different samples, within and outside California and the YA (but, almost always, still institutional), reported r's of .32, .33, .37, .54, .58, and .59 (Cross and Tracy; Sealy and Banks; Beverly; Eaks; Miller; and Zaidel, respectively).[166] Finally, regarding the YA/NIMH experiment (that is, "CTP"), Palmer et al. (1968) and Palmer (1976) obtained correlations between .22 and .24, and Werner (1975) reported an r of .27.[167, 168, 169] (A large majority of the preceding studies focused entirely or almost entirely on males. In general, studies of delinquents that involved a sizable or very large percentage of females produced somewhat higher r's between IQ and I-Level; however, there were few such studies, and this relationship is therefore tenuous.)

(Endnote #169 not only further details IQ in relation to I-Level, it discusses the near-absence of Cronbach/Meehl/Campbell-type construct validity studies during Phases 1 and 2 of the California experiment. [This low priority was not limited to analyses involving intelligence.] In addition, #169 extensively reviews the nature and reasons for that experiment's *high*—or top—analytic priorities during those phases.)

When a report or reports regarding any of the preceding studies included a correlation concerning nonverbal *and* verbal intelligence (sometimes called "nonlanguage" and "language" IQ), the first type of correlation was likely to be 15 percent to 25 percent lower than the second. Thus, in Sealy and Banks, in Eaks, in Zaidel, and in Miller, respectively, r's between *nonverbal* IQ and I-Level were as follows (r's that involved the *verbal* [these particular ones were shown above] appear in the corresponding parentheses): .28 (.33), .40 (.54), .44 (.59), and .53 (.58).[170]

Regarding correlations between IQ and developmental systems other than I-Level—in effect, for added perspective on this relationship—see endnote #171. This material also includes information about *non*delinquents.

Finally, compared to the several correlations just presented regarding IQ and I-Level, a considerably smaller number are shown in the sections on *age, socioeconomic status (SES),* and *ethnicity,* immediately below. This difference reflects the fact that fewer analyses were carried out and/or reported regarding the relationship between each of these three variables/factors, on the one hand, and I-Level, on the other—fewer, that is, than for IQ.[172]

Age. Regarding delinquents, correlations between age and I-Level were, on average, noticeably lower than those involving IQ. In particular, in the just-mentioned studies by Jesness, Eaks, Palmer, Zaidel, and Cross/Tracy, they were .11, .19, .20, .23, and .31, respectively.[173] Also for offenders (but this time young adults, in the military), Ives and Grant earlier reported an r of .24. Among *non*delinquents, Harris obtained an r of .45.[174]

SES. For delinquents, correlations between SES and I-Level were roughly the same as those with age:[175] (1) Regarding the Preston sample, Jesness and Wedge (1984, 1003) reported a .22.[176] (2) For wards at Holton, Eaks (1972, 96) reported an r of .18.[177] (3) Concerning Phases 1 and 2 of CTP, Palmer obtained a .23, and for Phase 3 he obtained a .25 (1976). (4) Regarding their partly institutional, partly probation sample, Cross and Tracy obtained a correlation of .31 (Tracy, 1969, 14, 16; Beker and Heyman, 1971, 29; 1972, 28).[178] Among *non*delinquents, Harris obtained an r of .19. In each of these studies the sample involved—and/or the analyses focused on—males only.

Ethnicity. Among delinquents (particularly males), correlations between ethnicity and I-Level were, on average, a little lower than those with IQ and a little higher than those involving age—and SES as well: (1) For the Preston sample, Jesness and Wedge obtained an r of .28.[179] (2) Regarding his

Northern Youth Center sample, Jesness (1974, 27) reported a .38.[180] (3) For Phases 1 and 2 of CTP, Palmer obtained a .27, and for Phase 3 he obtained a .30 (1976). (4) From data presented by Werner also regarding CTP (1972, 12; 1975, 53), a correlation (ø) of .25 was derived. (5) Zaidel (1970, 38–39; 1973, 55), whose study focused on females, reported an r of .51.[181] Finally, (6) from data presented by Cross and Tracy (1969, 18; 1971, 18), a correlation of .34 was derived. All these analyses, except Palmer's, involved a Caucasian/nonCaucasian breakdown.[182] No correlations were available concerning nondelinquents. For perspective involving two other developmental systems, see endnote 183.

Combinations of IQ, Age, SES, and Ethnicity. Regarding the preceding variables and factors, researchers have uniformly concluded that an individual's I-Level and subtype are each more than products, functions, or other expressions of IQ, age, SES, and ethnicity, whether individually or in given combinations. This applies even though—as just seen—I-Level and subtype *are* often statistically and otherwise related to each of the latter.

Before we specify the conclusions of various researchers and then present interpretations of the connection between I-Level and *intelligence* in particular, the following might be kept in mind concerning the *extent* (and, paralleling or commensurate with that, the *limits*) of the statistical relationship between I-Level (and/or subtype), on the one hand, and various combinations of IQ, age, and so on, on the other. These "multiple correlations" ("R's") were obtained in some of the just-mentioned studies. Together, they reflect the range as well as thrust of the *R's* that have been found with respect to delinquents.

1. Palmer et al. (1968) reported an R of .29 between I-level and *IQ + age.*
2. Tracy (1969) obtained an R of .48 between I-Level and *IQ + age + SES.*[184]
3. Cross and Tracy (1971) reported a .52 between subtype and *IQ + age + SES.*
4. Jesness (1974) obtained a .52 between I-Level and *IQ + age + ethnicity.*
5. Zaidel (1973) reported a .66 between I-Level and *IQ + ethnicity* and a .73 between I-Level and *IQ + ethnicity + verbal fluency regarding persons.*
6. Eaks (1972) did not present a specific fig-

ure for the *R* between I-Level (as well as subtype), on the one hand, and IQ + age + SES, on the other. However, based on (a) the intercorrelations among the latter three, (b) the simple r's between each of these three and I-Level (as well as subtype), and (c) the stepwise multiple correlations involving those three (not entered first) plus other variables/factors as well, which he did present, the *R's* between I-Level (and subtype), on the one hand, and *IQ + age + SES,* on the other, would have been close to .60 (and .45 for subtype).

Thus, combinations of IQ, age, SES, and ethnicity—but, in almost all of the above studies, that of at least IQ and age—have jointly accounted for some 10 percent to 50 or so percent (usually for some 25 percent to 35 percent) of the total variance in I-Level and/or subtype, thereby leaving most (usually two-thirds or more) of the variance unaccounted for by those particular features.

We now turn to the given conclusions.

1. Harris (1988, 72), after reviewing several studies of delinquents, concluded that "the developmental component of I-level is clearly more than age and intelligence, although both of these variables are related to I-level."
2. Jesness and Wedge (1984, 1007–1008), after reviewing "the results of [our (i.e., their)] regressions on selected dependent variables that represent several attitudinal/behavioral domains," and after removing the effects of "background variables" such as intelligence, SES, and ethnicity, "conclud[ed] that subtype conveys more about the person than can be learned from knowledge of the youth's age, ethnicity, intelligence, and socioeconomic status." As these researchers later restated, and further specified, "hierarchical multi-regression analysis with age, aptitude, socioeconomic status, and ethnicity entered first revealed that subtype conveyed much more than could be learned from [that] background information" (1988, 84). Involved were about 1,000 males in the Youth Authority's Preston institution.
3. Jesness (1974). given his already-mentioned R of .52 for Northern Youth Center (NYC) males, stated:

One can conclude that there is a moderate relationship among [Jesness Inventory] I-Level, IQ, and Race. However, it is clear from the partial correlations and prediction problem that Sequential [JI] I-Level is, indeed, something more than Age, Race, and IQ. It is also clear that we cannot distinguish some of these relationships, such as whether I-Level is in part a function of IQ, or if it is more accurate to say that IQ is in part a function of maturity level . . . (p. 28)[185, 186]

4. Miller (1972), referring to her study of delinquents (65 percent boys, 35 percent girls), concluded that

the data . . . clearly indicate that when the effects of both verbal and nonverbal intelligence are removed from the dependent variables, there still remains a significant relationship [between] the instrument measured constructs of cognitive complexity, foresight, and impulse control [on the one hand, and also between each of those] three constructs measured by behavioral ratings [still on the one hand, and] *I-level classification* [, on the other]. The same results are true when Hunt's cognitive complexity is also removed (p. 91; emphasis added).

5. Zaidel (1973), whose study of delinquent girls yielded the highest correlation between I-Level and intelligence and the largest multiple correlation with that plus other features, herself observed that although

[1] verbal fluency regarding people, [2] verbal intelligence, and [3] race . . . together account[ed] for approximately 54 percent of the variance [in I-Level, "mainly on I-3 and I-4 . . . delinquents and a small group of I-5's"] , . . . it is certainly possible that the attitudes and values described as aspects of 'interpersonal maturity' account for the remaining [46 percent of the] variance in I-level classification. In fact, it is likely that differences in personality and social attitudes are involved in the various subtypes of delinquency within each I-level (pp. 57–58).

6. Finally, Jesness and Wedge (1983), in their study of *non*delinquents (boys and girls), stated that

a discriminant function analysis was . . . run to determine how successfully the youths could be classified as to subtype from knowledge of demographic and background characteristics. The results show that, of the 1,146 youths . . . , [only] 22.8% could be correctly classified from age, sex, ethnicity, achievement test score [a measure of intelligence], and socioeconomic status. As was true for delinquents [specifically, the Preston sample], we conclude that subtype classification tells us that although subtype is not completely unrelated to background characteristics, it is more than just a measure of them (p. 80).

Moreover, regarding the *extent* of its difference from these characteristics—its difference in specified areas—Jesness later pointed out the following:

[Because] subtype differences were found . . . for age, ethnicity, achievement test scores, and socioeconomic status [,] the question arises as to whether these differences might account for apparent subtype personality differences on . . . other variables [and factors. These differences had been found with respect to school achievement, school attitudes, classroom misbehavior, family cohesion, home misbehavior, self-appraisal dimensions (e.g., Responsibility, delinquent peers, and self-reported delinquency.]. To answer this question, regressions were run in which age, sex, ethnicity, socioeconomic status, and achievement test scores were partialled prior to entering subtype (as dummy variables). The results indicated that subtype contributed to the variance of all variables (p < .001). In most instances, subtype was by far the largest contributor . . . (1988, 85–86).

Connections between I-level and Intelligence. Several researchers have focused on the statistically significant, positive correlations found between I-Level and intelligence during the 1960s (Beverly [1965]) Cross and Tracy [1969]; Palmer et al. [1968]) and in their own as well as others' subsequent studies. In the following, observations and interpretations by seven such individuals—Zaidel, Werner, Eaks, Miller, Molof and Jesness, and Harris—will be briefly presented.

(Note: [1] It was Zaidel [1970] who first focused specifically on the nature, possible implications, and certain limitations of the I-Level/IQ relationship. [2] Because Werner's research first appeared in Spring, 1972, *Eaks,* whose study appeared in June of that year, had no opportunity to reflect the former's findings and thoughts. Similarly, Miller, whose work appeared two months later, had no chance to utilize *Eaks'* findings and thoughts, though she did draw on Werner's. All three, however, drew not only from their own statistical findings but from ones reported in the 1960s [in all cases, Cross and Tracy's], and in 1970 as well [specifically, Zaidel's]. In addition, neither Werner nor Eaks had an opportunity to utilize *Molof and Jesness'* early 1972 observations.)[187]

1. *Zaidel (1970),* in discussing the results of her study, and the I-Level/IQ relationship in general, indicated that

> [although] intelligence would not [i.e., probably does not] account for differences in attitudes, values, or quality of interpersonal relationships, it could account for the degree of differentiation with which persons at different I-levels describe themselves, others, and their environment. The low degree of perceptual differentiation typical of lower level persons may be viewed as one manifestation of low cognitive functioning which would limit their ability to function at [certain] academic and vocational levels as well as socially (p. 76).

Regarding the latter point, she had earlier suggested that

> I-level diagnosis [, other than that derived from a Jesness Inventory,] is based on interview behavior, which is largely a function of verbal skills. It is likely that intelligence would be manifested in the person's ability to express his attitudes, thoughts, and feelings. An inarticulate person would be more likely judged low in 'maturity' because he would appear relatively unaware of other people's personalities, feelings, and so on. A highly articulate intelligent person would more likely be judged high in 'maturity' because of his extensive descriptions of other people (p. 10).

2. *Werner (1972)* drew the following conclusions:

> It seems quite clear that intelligence is a component of I-level. All ... studies which considered this factor have found positive though varying correlations between the two. Moreover, with the exception of Beverly, this relationship has been at least as strong as those found between I-level and any personality variables considered. It seems reasonable that intelligence may affect the extent to which persons are able to accurately perceive and effectively react to individual differences in the needs, motives, values, and styles of verbal as well as nonverbal expressions of others. Since these latter qualities of interpersonal functioning undoubtedly help determine the nature of the interpersonal relations developed by an individual (and perhaps also the extent of growth—conducive social opportunities available to him), the moderate correlation between I-level and intelligence [that has been found in a number of studies] is understandable.[188] It is possible that this correlation will be found to be larger in samples diagnosed by methods or by interviewers overly reliant upon Ss' verbal skills, reasoning ability, or simple willingness to talk about themselves or others (p. 47).

3. *Eaks (1972),* highlighting earlier, more theoretical works per se, pointed out the following, and then drew the stated conclusion:

> Intelligence was not indicated in the concept of interpersonal maturity (Sullivan, Grant, and Grant, 1957) or in the descriptions of the various I-levels (Warren, 1966 [i.e., Warren et al., 1966a ... Yet,]) Piaget's (1969) theories of cognitive development suggest that intelligence could account for the degree of differentiation with which persons at different I-levels describe themselves, others, and their environment. It seems plausible that the low degree of perceptual differentiation typical of lower I-level persons may [, as indicated by Zaidel, "be viewed as one manifestation of low cognitive functioning"] ... The I-level system was originally based theoretically upon a developmental model in which the subject saw himself in

relation to others and the world—not upon a measure of intellectual development. However, in support of Piaget, it seems that intellectual development cannot be divorced from interpersonal maturity. The fact that future time perspective and asociality in [the] present study were not significantly related to *IQ,* but that future time perspective and asociality [nevertheless] helped to predict *I-level* [and subtype] classification, suggests that interpersonal maturity consists of an array of complex and interrelated factors . . . (141–142; emphasis added).

4. *Miller (1972),* who (1) concurred with Molof and Jesness' early 1972 position[189] (see below regarding their *final*—1973—statement), (2) fully endorsed Werner's view (see above) as well, and (3) concluded that "I-level [evidently] *does* involve something more than intelligence" (p. 104), also provided the following observations, perspectives, and interpretations concerning I-Level in general and the I-Level/intelligence connection in particular.

The cognitive-developmental approach to socialization makes the assumption that social development is cognitively based since any description of shape or pattern of a structure of social responses necessarily entails some cognitive dimensions. A description of the organization [including the basis] of the child's social responses involves [information about how] he perceives, or conceives, the social world, and [how] he conceives himself. This last sentence is [tantamount to a statement of the basic thrust of I-level theory itself—this being a set of constructs that focus] upon the ways in which the individual is able to see himself and the world, and the ways he is able to interpret what is happening between himself and others. [Thus, in these respects, I-level theory is itself a cognitive-developmental approach.]

A major diagnostic indica[tor] within the I-level interview is the sophistication of youths in ability to perceptually [that is, conceptually] differentiate between people in their environment. Questions such as 'How is your Mother different from other mothers?' and 'What kind of people do you prefer as friends?' are asked

the interviewees in order to determine the extent to which they differentiate what they see in their world. Within the cognitive-developmental model, constructs such as 'differentiation' are regarded as structural components of development and as such are [viewed as] characteriz[ing and otherwise reflecting and involving] every aspect of the personality: the social-emotional, the perceptual, and the intellectual.

There is research which indicates that differentiation is quite highly correlated with standard psychometric measures of intelligence as well as with a variety of social attitudes and traits . . . If differentiation is a basic structural component common to the development of both intelligence (cognition) and social traits (affect), then it does not seem unreasonable to suggest . . . , not that I-level stages are cognitive, but rather that interpersonal development also has a basic structural component. In other words, in the same way in which the development of cognition and affect were said [elsewhere] to have a common structural base, so it is suggested that the development of interpersonal maturity (which has both cognitive and affective aspects) also has a basic underlying structural component . . . The correlations cited in the literature between I-level and intelligence, ranging from .30 to .59, indicate that interpersonal maturity has [that is, *does* have] a cognitive base, but is not simply general verbal intelligence applied to social situations or relationships . . . [Given the above,] cognitive complexity [which intrinsically involves and requires *differentiation (DF),* and in those respects is structurally *based on* DF,] is a necessary, but not a sufficient, condition for interpersonal maturity [itself] (pp. 104–110).

Thus, from Miller's perspective, an individual's cognitive complexity (CC) goes hand-in-hand with his ability to differentiate, and is both a product and aspect of it. This ability is a major contributor to, or basis of, his performance on many standard intelligence tests; and CC—in this case as a product—is often considered a direct and/or indirect sign of intelligence itself, even apart from such tests.

The (1) role of differentiation in the process of *personal growth* and the (2) bearing that DF has to *intelligence-as-measured-by-tests,* can be further gauged as well as inferred from observations—first by Eaks, and then by Zaidel—that appear in endnote 190. These observations, which briefly present Sullivan, Grant, and Grant's (I-Level) position on *emotional-social* development (including the key factor of differentiation), which next outline Piaget's stages of *intellectual* development, and which then summarize O'Sullivan. Guilford, and de Mille's (1965) concept of social intelligence, can provide added perspective on Miller's views themselves—including her concept of "structural component" (see quotation above). In short, they can help identify and clarify not only certain relationships between differentiation and personal as well as social development, but ones that exist between differentiation and cognitive skills per se—of which, measured IQ is one major, direct reflection.

5. *Molof and Jesness (1973),* emphasizing the relatively high correlations found by Zaidel (1970), Miller (1972), and Eaks (1972), but also supported by (1) Cross and Tracy's I-Level/IQ correlation for their total sample (whites + Blacks combined) and by (2) research of their own, drew the following conclusion:

> [There is clearly a] similarity, *in certain respects,* between the abilities which make up an individual's I-level and abilities which are part of the construct of intelligence. I-level may be considered . . . an ability concept: as one's frame of reference matures, certain abilities develop. They include ability to conceptualize, social awareness, information processing capacity, and the abstraction and manipulation of social symbols in a culturally prescribed manner. It appears that in order to develop to a higher level of integration one must possess some of these abilities, which are also the abilities measured by tests of intelligence (23; emphasis in the original).

6. *Harris (1983, 151)* indicated that "one would expect I-level and IQ to overlap, since both connote a perceptual complexity, social awareness, and the ability to conceptualize." Nevertheless, in view of specific correlations

(.24, .27, .36, .37, and .59) that have been reported in various studies, one can conclude that—any such overlap or communality notwithstanding—"I-level and IQ are far from synonymous."

(Endnote 191 describes the main views of Community Treatment Project parole agents ["workers"] regarding intelligence. In so doing, it briefly mentions certain functional parallels between this factor and several others, such as attitudes and interests, and it reviews its general role in intervention.)

Connections between I-Level and Ethnicity. Very few studies exist in which differing ethnic groups were compared with each other on variables relating to the construct validity of I-Level—more particularly, variables that constituted hypothesized correlates of this construct. In these studies, the question—a two-parter—was: Did ethnic group(s) "x" differ significantly from group(s) "y" (1) on the given variables or factors (V/Fs)—differ, not "in general," but, specifically, (2) in connection with either any one *I-Level* or with all such levels combined? The V/Fs may have been personal/interpersonal characteristics, stances, or modes of adjustment, such as "social presence," "responsibility," or "achievement via independence"—each of these presumably having a positive correlation with I-Level.[192] Or, they might have been other constructs/dimensions, such as internal (versus external) locus of control, or else future time perspective—these, too, being associated with maturity. (The I-levels were 2, 3, and 4, except in Zaidel's sample.) If the ethnic groups did differ from each other, particularly on a number of relevant V/Fs, this would raise questions about the I-Level construct's meaning and utility. If they did not differ, this would support its stated meaning as a description of personal/social development; it would support the construct's generalizability as well.

Werner (1972) conducted an "ethnic group (White vs. non-White) by I-level (I_2 vs. I_3 vs. I_4 neurotic vs. I_4 nonneurotic) analysis of variance" on the same data used in his 1972 study of 900 California experiment males, and his results were as follows:[193]

> Considering all [11] Jesness scales, there was not a single instance of significant interaction between the two factors

[namely, ethnic group and I-level]. Thus, this study indicated that the Jesness scale correlates of I-level do not differ by racial or ethnic group, as indeed they should not if the [I-level] construct is to have broad applicability and relatively parsimonious interpretation (1972, 5–6; 1975, 65). (Details appear in Palmer and Werner, 1972, 60–64.)[194]

In Werner's second earlier-mentioned study (1972; 1975), this one involving 934 males, analyses were again made separately for Whites and non-Whites, and comparisons were made between these two, by I-Level, on presumed correlates of this construct: Six CPI "person types" (also called "Otypes" or "person clusters" [see endnote 124]), which had been statistically generated from three broad personality clusters that—in turn—had been previously derived from the California Psychological Inventory's (CPI's) 18 individual scales, were analyzed in relation to ethnicity, in terms of a "three factor interaction."[195] This "ethnic status × Otype × I-level" analysis—a 2- by 6- by 4-category analysis—indicated,

> with a probability exceeding .80, . . . that there is no difference between White and non-White groups in [the way that] personal characteristics, as reflected in Otype membership, are related to I-level diagnosis. This result was also obtained through a rather different method of analyzing these CPI data for the two [ethnic] groups . . . : Results for interaction effects in a 2 × 4 (ethnic group by I-level) analysis of variance for each of the 18 CPI scales [indicated that] only for Flexibility and Femininity did the *F* ratios reach conventional levels of significance . . . Confirmation of the prediction of no significant interaction between I-level, CPI Otype, and ethnic status . . . was in accord with I-level theory. There is nothing within written presentations of interpersonal maturity theory which suggests that either the strictly theoretical characterization of the [I-level] construct or its meaning in terms of correlations with other variables should change as a function of ethnic status (Werner, 1972, 36, 45; 1975, 61–65; Palmer and Werner, 1972, 32–41, 68–70).[196]

In the earlier-mentioned study by *Molof and Jesness,* "a decreasing external focus [was observed] across all three levels [, one level at a time] for both Black and Caucasian subjects [groups]" (1973, 19–20). That is, for each group *separately,* each progressively higher I-Level had an less external locus of control.[197] (In this analysis, unlike Werner's, the ethnic groups were not compared with *each other.* As a result, the meaning of these findings with respect to construct validity is somewhat different than those of Werner's. Regarding "earlier-mentioned," see *"Jesness (1974)"* in the "Construct Validity of I-Levels" section of this chapter.)

F. Overview, Discussion, and Conclusions
Concurrent Validity of Levels. The Interpersonal Maturity system received considerable concurrent validation in connection with the several studies that were reviewed: Its levels, collectively, were found to have substantial, statistically significant correlations with a broad range of other developmental systems—ones which, in turn, had substantial and again significant correlations with each other.[198] Based on the extent to which these other systems had been used within and outside corrections and on the number of reviewed studies in which they appeared, the main such systems were Hunt's Conceptual Levels, Loevinger's Ego Levels, and Kohlberg's Moral Development or Moral Judgment Levels. Also present were the Jesness-based I-Levels and the lesser known as well as infrequently studied Makkay Primitive-to-Organized Levels, Palmer Developmental-Adaptation Levels, Schroder Information Processing Levels, and Van den Daele Ego-Ideal Levels.

At any rate, among serious juvenile offenders the unpartialled correlations between I-Level and the respective systems were in the mid- and upper- .40s, and among adult offenders they mainly spanned the mid .20s to low .30s. On average, they thereby accounted for a little over 20 percent and 10 percent of the total variance, for juveniles and adults respectively. Thus, on the one hand, the I-levels—whether for juveniles or adults—seemed to have or involve one or more factors and/or processes in common with some or all of those developmental systems. In that respect they apparently had external connections or a recognizable reality (existence)—one that helped provide, among other things, a "concurrent" meaning, legitimacy, significance, and so on. At the same time, and based on those same correlations, the I-Levels seemed to involve something different as well, such as one or more factors/processes that may have been unique to them and/or were at least uncommon in the given individual systems.[199] This, in short, was something other than or separable from the just-mentioned "external connections" and the related concurrence as well. It involved aspects of reality, and *their* related meanings (including integral as well as contingent connections), which differed in type and/or degree from what was reflected in the variance that was *shared* by many or most of the developmental systems. As such, the factors/processes in question helped give I-Level substantial identity and related implications—and, with those, potential importance—of its own.

Construct Validity of Levels. The I-level system received strong construct validation from numerous studies and analyses, collectively. (1) In those which emphasized certain written and other instruments or scales, the main generic variables or dimensions with which I-level was found to be significantly correlated were as follows: impulse control; locus of control; cognitive complexity; articulation and/or complexity of body-image, of self-concept, and of (perceived) external environment; affect awareness; and—depending on the particular measure and study—what was termed future time perspective, foresight and planning, and persistence-of-efforts regarding long-range goals. (2) In studies or analyses that centered on widely used psychological questionnaires (California Psychological Inventory [CPI]; Eysenck Personality Inventory [EPI]; Jesness Inventory [JI]), I-Level had significant correlations, again in the expected direction, with still other dimensions or types of factors. Chief among these were not only interpersonal attitudes and modes of adjustment, such as Tolerance, Responsibility, and Alienation, but personal characteristics and psychological conditions, such as Self-Control (CPI) or (non)Impulsiveness (EPI), Manifest Aggression, Immaturity, and Autism (JI) or Psychoticism (EPI). (3) Also consonant with theory, and again statistically significant, was the relationship between I-level and certain *combinations* of individual dimensions—specifically, Werner's carefully derived, CPI-based Adult-role social-

ization, Ascendant Extroversion, and Personal Maturity clusters, respectively. (Each of these "configural clusters" may have included dimensions that often operated jointly in real-life settings and that, in this regard, constituted and actively involved adjustment patterns, stances, and/or life-styles that were more encompassing than those reflected in most of the individual items mentioned in (2), above. At any rate, certain individual dimensions [for instance, interpersonal factors—such as Tolerance—and/or psychological features—say, Self-Control] may have been important contributors to one or more of these presumably broad adjustments or stances.) (4) Sometimes in the already-referred-to studies and sometimes in different ones (at any rate, especially in research that utilized rater-observations, self-reports, and/or official records), still further, though not unrelated, individual factors and variables (F/V's) were found. That is, statistically significant correlations were obtained between I-Level and these respective F/Vs, in a direction that was consistent with and/or specifically predicted from theory. Salient among these F/Vs were initiative, ability to learn (and/or—perhaps—psychological readiness/willingness to do so), orientation to rehabilitation goals, emotional control, level of stress, and—whether in adult prison, youth institution, or public school settings—disciplinary problems.[200]

Concurrent Validity of Subtypes. Six of the nine Warren subtypes within levels 2 through 4 received considerably concurrent validation. This resulted not just from all studies collectively (though, of course, not every one individually), but from a particular group of them by itself. In each study within this subset (Jesness, 1965, 1971–1972; Ferdinand, 1978; Gaensbauer and Lazerwitz, 1979), cluster analysis, factor analysis, and/or other methods were used to integrate information from varied sources, such as questionnaires, personal interviews, observer ratings, and/or personal/social histories. (Most of the remaining studies were less detailed or elaborate in these respects.) The three remaining subtypes, specified below, received moderate concurrent validation, though not from that subset as a whole. Unless otherwise indicated, all findings in this section, including those from the subset, involved subtype diagnoses that were interview-based.

Focusing on all studies collectively, these—to restate—found a sizable majority of the subtypes pretty much as they had been originally described in 1961 or revised—mainly refined—in the mid-1960s (Grant, 1961; Warren et al., 1966b).[201] More specifically, their authors observed, derived, or otherwise found (1) most of the original/revised *individual features* that were key descriptive ingredients of those subtypes—that is, were attributes central to the definition (the core conceptual meaning) of those categories. These features mainly involved personal characteristics, interpersonal styles/adjustments/defenses, and attitudes/opinions regarding self and others. For the respective subtypes in question, the studies—still collectively—also found (2) much the same *combinations of certain individual features*. Here, as a result, they generally obtained what could be called similar "patterns" of features, and (based on given features' higher- or lower-than-average score, rating, or intensity) sometimes similar "profiles," in particular. Finally, also found were (3) what seemed to be similar or identical (a) *dynamics and/or major personal issues* and (b) *influential external factors or conditions*—these latter centering on family, peers, and/or social environment. Item (3a), however, and to a lesser extent (3b), emerged mainly in the subset, since the types and/or range of information needed in order to reflect, infer, or deduce those dynamics and so on were largely absent in most remaining studies. (In the following, (1), (2), and (3), above, will be called items, areas, or criteria, depending on the context.)

Still in all studies collectively, the conclusion regarding "considerable concurrent validation" pertained primarily to the *Aa, Cfm, Cfc, Mp, Na,* and *Nx* subtypes. (It did so most clearly with respect to areas or criteria (1) and (2).) This was mainly because the *Ap, Se,* and *Ci* groups were not found in connection with some studies—when, at least, there were no essentially methodological reasons for their absence.[202] ("Absence" applied even in area (1)—that of basic description.) Nonetheless, as indicated earlier, and again below, these groups did receive more than just slight or weak concurrent validation.

In only one study (Budnoff, 1963) were certain combinations of *two* Warren subtypes clearly suggested, namely those of Cfm/Nx and Mp/Na. Thus, in the studies collectively,

it was *individual* subtypes that were found—that is, were identified in terms of the original/revised descriptions (in effect, were largely matched with them), and were distinguished from each other as well. This was true not only when—as in the above-mentioned subset—several types of information had been used.

Certain "constellations," and two "dimensions" or factors, will now be discussed; they bear not only on the content of Warren's subtypes, but on their concurrent validity: Three very broad groupings (constellations) of offenders—the *conforming, antisocial,* and *neurotic*—have long been mentioned by correctional typologists, as has the personal/interpersonal dimension of passivity versus activity (sometimes viewed as compliance, or even submissiveness, versus assertiveness, domination, controlling, or even aggressivity).[203] When the *passive* pole and the *active/assertive* pole of this dimension are each separately blended with the *antisocial* and *neurotic* constellations—themselves separately—the following occurs (see below regarding the *conforming* constellation): (a) Major aspects or outlines of various Warren subtypes—particularly the Cfc, Mp, Na, Nx, and even Ci—appear, each individually; that is, key similarities or correspondences to the original/revised descriptions of those subtypes—though not every important aspect of them—become recognizable.[204] Simultaneously, (b) some of these subtypes, for instance, the Cfc and Mp, begin to be distinguished from *each other.* as do the Na's and Nx's. In addition, (c) when each of these first two is compared with one or both of the latter two—for example, when the Cfc is compared with the Na in terms of its (and the Na's) particular blend of dimension and constellation ("its" being passive and antisocial, and the Na's being active/assertive and neurotic, as indicated in endnote 161)—important mutual distinctions again appear. Other such comparisons would be Cfc with Nx, Mp with Nx, and Ci with Nx.

(Two points before continuing: First, regarding various concurrent and construct validity studies reviewed in this chapter, points (a) through (c), immediately above, applied or would have applied even when certain "dynamics [and] . . . external factors and conditions"—items (3a) and (3b), mentioned earlier—were not, or would not have been, clearly known. [To simplify matters, we will generally use the present tense.] That is, the initial *recognizability* and *mutual differentiation* which were focused on in (a) through (c) occurred in terms of items or criteria (*1*) and (*2*), by themselves. They did so, it might be noted, absent any developmental component per se, such as Makkay's primitive versus organized levels, Hunt's cognitive complexity levels, or Warren's own maturity levels [I_2 through I_4]. That is, the degree of recognizability and differentiation [R & D] in question could and did occur without there being a link between the following: (1) any combination [blend] of either pole of the *dimension* under consideration with any given *constellation* [for instance, a blend of the passive pole with the antisocial constellation, or a blend of the active/assertive pole with the neurotic], on the one hand, and (2) any given developmental level, on the other.[205] As indicated and implied, this degree of R & D—although substantial and important—was nevertheless only partial. Second, the passive versus active/ assertive (P/A) dimension does not apply to the first-mentioned constellation [the "conforming"] with respect to the blending under discussion. This is because passivity—one pole of that dimension—is *already integral* to the conformity constellation. [The P/A dimension's inapplicability is independent of the fact that "conforming" youths who fit the revised description of Warren's *Cfm* subtype are—essentially from the start—distinguishable from the Mp, Na, and Ci subtypes, thought not from the Cfc and Nx.])

When a certain *further dimension* (see *gangs,* below) is added to the already described pictures—more specifically, when it is added to respective blends of given constellations, on the one hand, and a pole of the P/A dimension ("dimension one"), on the other—the following occurs: Some subtypes mentioned in point (*a*), above, especially the Cfc and Ci groups (which we will now emphasize), become further recognizable as such. That is, their key similarities to the original/revised descriptions become substantially clearer than before, in fact, sometimes *much* clearer or sharper; this also applies to Cfm's. Simultaneously, once each of these subtypes, and any others, obtains this increased recognizability, and—with that—a more particular and distinct "identity," it becomes better differentiated from the other such

subtypes, that is, better differentiated than before; in this, it further develops with respect to point (*b*). In addition, any or all of these groups may become more differentiated from still *other* subtypes, that is, more differentiated from *them* than before;[206] and in this connection, it constitutes a further development with regard to point (*c*). At any rate, as this particular dimension is added to the already described information-blend, they types of outcomes mentioned in points (a), (b), and (c) continue to occur. Broadly speaking, these center on increased recognizability and identity, on better—for instance, deeper and perhaps more integrated—overall differentiation, and on expanded/branching differentiation, respectively.

Specifically, the "further" dimension or factor in question ("dimension two") involves certain *types of relationships between youths and "gangs,"* the latter being delinquent groups that may or may not be relatively large, well-organized, and/or long-lived. Regarding these gangs, and concerning the youths collectively, three main types or patterns of relationships—outlined below—have long-been described by typologists, collectively. (Most typologists, individually, have described at least one of the three patterns, almost always the first or second.) With respect to Warren's subtypes, the first pattern ("A") is, as it turns out, closely associated with Cfc's;[207] the second ("B"), particularly with Cfm's; and the third ("C"), most notably with Ci's. In this respect these patterns, when combined with the already existing blends of constellations and dimension one, play the following roles: Regarding the three respective youth-groups, they further identify and particularize; concerning the first and third of these groups (the Cfc and Ci), they increase and sharpen mutual differentiations that began with the distinction between passivity (Cfc) and activity/assertiveness (Ci); and, regarding each of the same three groups, they further differentiate from *other* subtypes—for instance, they distinguish the Cfc from Nx, the Cfm from Mp and Na, and the Ci from Nx.[208] These developments are continuations of outcomes (a), (b), and (c) above, respectively; that is, they are expansions of the "*recognizability* and *mutual differentiation*" [RMD] associated with the initial blends—blends of given constellations with dimension one. As with that RMD—*initial*

RMD—these particular expansions can occur without the presence and assistance of a developmental component, that is, of any developmental-level concepts and categories per se.[209]

Gang-centered. Youth regularly participates in gang's activities, as an enthusiastic follower and core member. He accepts and agrees with other members' antisocial attitudes and has few qualms about supporting the gang's usual illegal activities; in these respects he solidly identifies with the gang.[210] Like *most* of these youths, he considers himself and largely *wants* to consider himself an actual delinquent, not just occasionally "wild," temporarily or perhaps situationally "bad" or "dumb," and so on—but inwardly *dis*approving of illegal activities or quite ambivalent about them.[211] His gang involvement often provides immediate pleasure, gratification, and a sense of status; salient, for instance, are feelings of excitement, power, and independence, frequently capped by thoughts of being considered "cool" and "with it." As a result, many of his everyday thoughts center on recent and desired-future gang activities—legal as well as other—and a high percentage of his illegal and borderline-legal behaviors occur when he is together with other members. Most gang-centered youths have largely rejected not only most conventional life-styles or adjustments (especially but not only those usually associated with mainline-culture *adulthood,*[212] but also certain involvements, social supports, paths, and institutions—often including the educational—that, collectively, could help them move toward those adjustments and maintain some conventional interests that may still exist. Most *remaining* gang-centered youths, although they have *not* largely rejected such adjustments and related means-to-ends interactions, supports, and the like, have nevertheless considerably reduced various activities and involvements that bear on them.[213] Still, despite this reduction, and mainly because they have not largely and inwardly rejected "most conventional life-styles or adjustments," and so on, these particular individuals are not as uncomfortable in most nondelinquent social settings and interactions as are *most* gang-centered youths.[214]

Gang-dependent. Youth regularly "hangs out" with a gang and participates as a fol-

lower in its usual activities. He does so not only to gain its acceptance and approval, and the satisfactions that these in themselves provide, but to *thereby* (1) counter his feelings of being disapproved, unappreciated, mistreated, and/or substantially rejected, by parents, parent-substitutes, and others, and—less consciously—to therein (2) help neutralize, reduce, and/or partly avoid his related feelings of unworthiness, inadequacy, and, quite often, "badness." These feelings, and those in item (1), predate his delinquency.[215] (The youth also participates in order to experience positive *pleasures,* feelings of being *liked* [not just OK'd], and—again less consciously—a sense of place.)[216] Because his needs for acceptance and approval, his item-(1) and -(2) feelings, and his related emotions and desires are strong, and because those needs are only moderately addressed elsewhere and are there largely unmet, the gang has considerable power over him—more than most members realize—and he generally tries hard to satisfy it.

Nevertheless, although the youth often agrees with some of the gang's anti-social stances and its attitudes toward given life-styles, though his actions reflect an acceptance (see below) of its illegal activities, and although he acknowledges that these actions *do* mean he is a delinquent, the following is the case:[217] The youth does not want to become a "*real*"—an avowed and otherwise committed—delinquent and, eventually, criminal. Moreover, if he is presently incarcerated and sees this can last a long time, he does not want to continue being delinquent at all, once he is released. In addition, he still wishes to obtain acceptance and approval from one or both parents and/or from other adults (not to mention delinquent peers), at least more than he feels he has received.[218] Mainly for these and related reasons—for instance, because he never feels sure the gang will continue to accept him, and because he more or less believes acceptance, pleasure, and relaxation can accompany certain *conventional* life-styles (CLSs) anyway, such as those involving marriage—the youth has neither largely nor indiscriminately, let alone sweepingly, repudiated CLSs, or has otherwise abandoned interest in them.[219] Nor has he largely withdrawn (openly, and perhaps emotionally/inwardly) from given activities, interactions, and supports that could help him do the following:

(1) move toward various CLSs that can occur only in the relatively distant future—in any case, move toward certain *nondelinquent* adaptations, even if they are *unconventional* or borderline; and, (2) maintain some aspects of his *existing* conventional involvements.[220] (The preceding applies even though he has openly *reduced* or *toned down* certain activities, and so on, partly in order to be better accepted by the gang.) In this connection the youth remains open to relatively conventional ("square"), or at any rate law-abiding, adults and/or adolescents. In particular, he can be substantially influenced by them and he hopes these individuals will accept or continue to accept him for—among other things—the nondelinquent interests, attitudes, behaviors, and other characteristics he displays, even if they know something about his delinquency.

Thus, notwithstanding his dependence on the gang—this being a type of relationship he generally desires—the youth is not linked to those individuals alone. Moreover, he does not *want* to rely on the gang alone, and he sometimes feels *too* dependent on it—feels, for instance, unable to sufficiently resist or avoid its pressures and even attractions, in given situations. Still, because of his strong needs and desires for acceptance and approval, and due to other factors also specified earlier, the gang can, and frequently does, play a powerful role. Not only is it often uppermost in the youth's mind and a key to how he structures much of his non-school time, and not only does it in fact help him satisfy or partly satisfy some of those needs/desires, and counter given worries, but it provides the main platform and context—together, the immediate basis—for much of his delinquent behavior. (Here, "basis" involves most or all of the following, for any given youth: incentives and justifications; major opportunities and related physical preconditions; active pressures; specific triggers and opening moves.) Nevertheless, (1) despite that role, including what the gang does "deliver" for the youth (that is, helps satisfy and counter), and (2) even if the youth has been part of the gang for a year or more, he is far from firmly committed to most of its antisocial values, attitudes, and stances, let alone to illegal behavior per se.[221] In this respect, his type and level of commitment to the gang (and, of course, the inversely related *limits* of this commitment)[222] has allowed him not only to retain some major alternatives

to it, such as conventional life-styles or presumes components thereof, but to not be wholly or almost wholly dependent on it.

All in all, then, the gang, whose overall pressures and attractions are indeed often large, exerts what can be viewed as considerable, frequently decisive, yet far from *absolute* immediate power over the youth; and it is in this connection that the following applies: The youth's earlier-mentioned "acceptance of . . . illegal behavior" is not, it turns out, as deep, solid, and otherwise ingrained or entrenched as his frequent contacts and often-extensive involvement might lead one to expect.[223] Nevertheless, even though the gang's immediate power is less than complete, the consequences of its antisocial influence can be vast.[224] (For further details regarding "acceptance," see endnote [225].)

Gang-organizer. Youth often plays a key, sometimes lead role in encouraging and organizing gang members regarding many of their illegal, borderline, and other joint activities. Members recognize and accept him as being among the core of individuals who, separately or together, usually activate and often steer the gang, and in various respects dominate it. Through his relationship with the gang, which is a direct and stable one, he (1) experiences physical pleasures, (2) partly satisfies material desires (sometimes illegally, in connection with objects and cash), and (3) obtains what might be called "ego charges" (when, for instance, members consider him "cool" or "sharp," and gladly follow him).[226] Though the youth obtains these particular physical, material, and psychological outcomes in the context of the gang, and although they are often strong and otherwise reinforcing, he does not obtain these *types* of outcomes in the gang setting alone; nor does he try to rely on it alone, with respect to them. (He does, however, often rely on the gang *primarily,* for some of them or at least for certain aspects of them—such as the illegal aspect of (2), or for certain kinds of "charges" or "kicks" within (3).) Instead, the youth obtains some such gratifications, for example, other aspects and/or forms of (2) and (3), in a few nongang, nondelinquent (NGND) settings as well, albeit often to a lesser degree.[227] (Items (1) through (3) will be termed "immediate personal payoffs" [IPP's], whatever their settings might be. Besides the school setting, NGND's commonly include clubs and other formal or informal groups.)[228] Although he (a) regularly participates in these NGND's (which, as such, constitute potential alternatives to the gang), though he (b) adapts himself fairly easily to these nongang settings and—as implied—obtains certain nondelinquent IPP's (gratifications) in connection with them, and, finally, although he (c) is sometimes uncomfortable with the immediate personal risks that given *gang* activities entail, the youth nevertheless maintains his relationship to the gang on a full-scale basis. In effect, he thereby utilizes the *non*gang, *non*delinquent settings and activities in parallel with the gang as separate additions to it, not as substitutes and actual alternatives. (Details appear in endnote 229.)

With all three groups—the gang-centered, -dependent, and -organizer—the individual's gang plays a critical role in his life and is often uppermost in his mind. It comprises the main vehicle and setting for many or most of his delinquent behaviors and it often supplies powerful stimuli and incentives for them; moreover, its post-behavior feedback frequently reinforces those activities.[230] In all three groups, the individual's relationship to the gang is strong and either stable or largely so. "Strength" is seen, for instance, in his sizable commitment and loyalty, in the time and energy he willingly expends, in most other members' view of him as valuable or perhaps essential, and in their readiness to defend him. "Stability"—partly a reflection of strength itself—primarily means the relationship is largely uninterrupted and unbroken for long periods of time (even if moderate ups and downs occur) and is relatively constant in content and tone. For such reasons, and in the ways mentioned, the youth is rather predictable and reliable in connection with major gang activities and its usual interactions. Finally, his and the other members' delinquent behavior, together with the latters' subsequent responses and additional feedback to the youth regarding those behaviors, are central ingredients and activities of the given relationship, including its maintenance and often its expansion; that is, they are fundamental elements, exchanges, and binding factors.[231]

As indicated earlier, the type or pattern of relationship that exists between each youth-group (the "centered," "dependent," and "organized"), on the one hand, and its gang, on the other, helps distinguish or further distinguish Warren's Cfc's, Cfm's (and, to a lesser extent, Nx's), and Ci's from more than just each other. Instead, these three largely different patterns of relationships, including the just-described features they *share* with each other (namely, strength and stability), also help differentiate each such youth-group from the Aa, Ap, Mp, Na, and Ci groups, themselves individually.[232] Regarding features shared among these *five* groups, the following are salient: The youths' interactions with any local gang, including their involvement in its illegal activities, are, collectively, *more*—usually much more—situational, oppotunistic, adventitious, incidental, and even spur-of-the-moment than are most interactions/involvements of the three groups already discussed.[233] In this and other respects their relationship to the gang is—both comparatively speaking and in absolute terms—transitory, largely fluid, sporadic or frequently episodic, and often ad hoc. At any rate, it is rarely strong and stable in ways, and to the various degrees, mentioned above. (In this connection most gang members seldom, or seldom for long, view these youths as full-fledged, reliable, and otherwise solid members, and as individuals who would try to "stick with the gang" through serious difficulties.) All this applies even though many such youths do participate in the gang quite heavily during given, albeit often short, periods or episodes, and although they may contribute substantially in those instances.

In the preceding remarks, as in the following, "Mp" refers to "manipulator." "Na" means "neurotic, acting-out"—this book's "assertive denier."

A further word about two of those five youth-groups, the two who are by far the most common. These groups—*Mp's* and *Na's*—are at or near the active/assertive pole of "dimension one" (as are Aa's), whereas Ap's and Se's are near the passive/compliant.[234] Most Mp's and Na's can sense that many members—the "gang-centered" and "gang-organizer," in our terms—far from entirely trust them, and that others—the "gang-dependent"—are largely uncomfortable when interacting with them, and in many cases are somewhat afraid of them and/or seem to dislike them.[235] However, these Mp's and Na's (1) are usually not bothered, worried, or upset by their awareness of those and related feelings, at least not considerably (and consciously). In addition, they (2) react in a largely unruffled or unperturbed manner to their awareness of the generally unsettled or even marginal status of their *overall relationship to the gang,* that is, to the gang as an entity, operating as such;[236] specifically, they respond much as in (1), but are often somewhat *more* bothered by that awareness. (Prominent among the gang-as-entity operations are its basic and usual expectations of each member—not only the full-fledged/ core—*as* a member. In this respect these operations reflect the gang's dominant ethos, whatever the gang's degree of overall cohesion might be.)

Two points might be emphasized regarding the Mp's and Na's above-mentioned reactions (*note:* the term "youths" will refer to Mp's and Na's only, and "other members" will signify the gang-centered, -dependent, and -organizer groups, collectively): *Point 1.* (a) The interactions between youths and *other members*—interactions that help produce these members' above-mentioned uneasiness with the given youths—and (b) the relationship between these same youths and the *gangs-as-an-entity,* in which the youths were characterized as having an "unsettled . . . status," are each at least passively *compatible and congruous* with these youths' (still Mp's and Na's) dominant wishes and key modes of adaptation, and with central aspects of their respective self-images. In particular, the given interactions and relationship do not contradict them, and they essentially blend with them.[237] *Point 2.* Those interactions, and that relationship, often actively *express, support, and facilitate* the given wishes, adaptations, and so on.[238] Regarding point (2), the Mp's and Na's general absence of substantial worry or upset reflects the fact that these youths do not want to largely fit into a "gang-member" mold or framework anyway, at least not on a fairly permanent basis and not on what they either sense or more explicitly and firmly believe might be very largely the overall *gang's* terms.[239] (Such terms or expectations would be implicitly and/or explicitly communicated to them, by gang-organizers and others.) This directly reflects the next-mentioned factor.

In gangs and other settings, most such youths strongly prefer to have considerable, sometimes even marked, freedom of action and choice, with respect to "timing" and "content" alike. Regarding *timing,* they would like, for instance, to control the playing-out of major activities in which they are directly involved—more specifically, to largely orchestrate their appearance, duration, and points of reappearance along the way. (This includes initiation and termination, insofar as activities are separable from each other.) However, in the gang setting, relatively little such control *can* be ordinarily exercised by any such youth in connection with *major gang-level activities.* As mentioned shortly, it can, nevertheless, be exerted with certain narrower, often one-to-one, *interactions.* (Regarding major gang-level activities, see "joint actions . . ." as well as the "V/GR level," below. As used here, all such activities are joint actions by and for the gang as a whole [the overall gang], and all such actions involve the V/GR level.)

As to *content* (with the focus, here, on freedom of choice), these individuals, again in the gang setting, dislike the following idea or realization—one they nonetheless consider accurate and which *does* bother them: Full-fledged membership would probably entail various expectations—by the gang as a whole, concerning joint actions to be taken by its members for the overall gang—that they, the youths, would (1) be uninterested in and might even consider "dumb" and/or too dangerous, but would (2) be unable to avoid participating in.[240] These feelings—dislike, and so on—contribute substantially to the individuals' not making a strong commitment to the gang, *as* a gang.

Though the youths' feelings of dislike are usually considerable in strength, and not infrequently intense, they can regularly exist despite the following (*note:* regarding joint actions by and for the gang as a whole, this and related feelings or reactions pertain to aspects of the "overall" *youths/gang-as-entity relationship [Y/GR]* described earlier): Various give-and-take interactions between these youths, on the one hand, and any one or more full-fledged members (mainly gang-centered or gang-dependent), on the other, may—even from the youths' own perspective—be tilted substantially in their, the youths', own favor with respect to power or domination. Such interactions need not involve the already-mentioned joint actions—activities that directly reflect broad, gangwide expectations or even virtual requirements, some of which are assumed to also test one's loyalty to the overall gang. Instead, they mainly focus on more personal matters and satisfactions (illegal, borderline, and legal activities, collectively), ones in which, for example, the youths' overall status as a gang member may not even be an issue, let alone possibly at stake.[241] In any event, these somewhat narrower, usually lower-visibility, but not necessarily low-risk interactions can provide the youths (still the Mp's and Na's) substantial opportunity to "call [various] shots." In this respect these individuals can have considerable choice, at least at *this* level of involvement with the gang, as distinct from the Y/GR level or context.[242]

Having briefly mentioned (1) three "very broad groupings (constellations) of offenders" and having described (2) three "types of relationships between youths and 'gangs,'" we will now present an overview of findings from the several validation studies and—especially—from the major, cross-system comparisons. We will also review several reasons for certain subtypes'—particularly the "rare" ones—having received concurrent validation (CV) less often than the rest. After that will come a final summary and discussion of the findings. Here, we will return to points (1) and (2), immediately above, as part of specifying major bases of the observed CV—these bases being substantive dimensions that various typology systems have in common. We will also indicate how some systems, such as Warren's, end up with more categories than others. In summarizing/discussing the CV of subtype *groupings,* as distinguished from *individual* subtypes, we will give extra attention to the Van Voorhis study (1994), since it is the only large-scale cross-classification examination of (a) *adults—most of whom, in addition, were (b) in other than their* 20's.

As already indicated, considerable concurrent validity was obtained, from the already—reviewed *studies,* for Warren's Aa, Cfm, Cfc, Mp, Na, and Nx subtypes.[243] This conclusion reflected three types of evidence or findings, here called "levels of information": (1)*Most* of the "*individual features* that were . . . central to the definition" of *each* such subtype were observed in those studies, taken collectively. Together with that, individual features that had helped define a number of those subtypes were, of course, observed—for instance, they were statistically/analytically identified—in several of the individual studies as well, that is, in *each* such study. These "central" features mainly involved specified

"personal characteristics, interpersonal styles/adjustment/defenses, and attitudes/opinions." (2) Correspondences were found in connection with "*combinations* of . . . individual features"; that is, similarities and/or identities were again observed regarding the basic definitions of those subtypes. More specifically and precisely, particular groups of features—such as small numbers or simple patterns of personal characteristics, interpersonal adjustments, or both—were statistically/analytically derived, and were otherwise observed. These groups largely coincided with those which had (a) helped define and otherwise describe the respective Warren subtypes themselves, and which (b) indicated some of those subtype's common correlates, as well. As with level 1 information, which involved single features only, such findings applied not just to the studies collectively but—again in detail, and again with a number of those subtypes—to several of those studies individually. Finally, (3) in the subset of studies whose information—and methods—was the broadest, the most varied, and/or the most detailed, considerable correspondence existed with respect to "*dynamics and/or major personal issues* and [also to] *influential external factors or conditions.*" That is, strong similarities were derived, and were also often inferred—similarities, once again, to the original or revised subtype descriptions.

(Two points before continuing. First, although level 3 information necessarily involved various combinations of features and though its logical or structural base was therein the same as level 2's, its breadth and variety of *content* extended beyond that of 2. Moreover, level 3 information or description often differed from level 2's in that the former's frequently implied, sometimes directly suggested, and occasionally even specified, *causal relationships* between various contents—for example, among or across given features, dynamics, personal issues, and external factors.[244] As a result, it is called the *depth/breadth* level, and it consists—in the preceding sense—of often-interrelated, relatively integrated, content. Second, although "subtype," "type," and "youth-type" are functionally equivalent in the following discussion, the first term is reserved for Warren's categories—that is, for *her* groups of youth only—and the remaining terms are used for categories described by other typologists only.)

Concurrent validity was evident not only in connection with the above-mentioned studies, but from judgments made by the several *typology experts* (Hunt, Jesness, Quay, Reiss, and so on) who participated in the earlier-described NIMH conference.[245] At that meeting, during which these individuals compared their respective typology systems (one system per expert) with each other, most of Warren's subtypes were found in—specifically, each of them had one or more close correspondences with, and/or analogues within—almost all other systems, when those systems were focused on one by one.[246] In addition, almost all of her subtypes (8 out of 9) were found when these typology systems—seven systems, excluding Warren's—were reviewed collectively.

Regarding these seven typologies collectively, the following also applied. The eight Warren subtypes in question, together with almost every youth-type that comprised each of the seven other expert's respective systems (still one per expert), were readily grouped under four "superordinate categor[ies] or general type[s]," in the NIMH conference report (Rubenfeld, 1967, 7–9).[247] These four were as follows (*note:* for each superordinate category in turn, (a) Warren's corresponding subtype[s] appears in parentheses, as a *subordinate* group—that is, as a constituent of the general type, and, (b) in the conference report, each of the remaining expert's youth-types themselves appear—like Warren's—as subordinates): *Impulse Oriented (Aa, Ap); Power Oriented (Cfm, Cfc, Mp); Neurotic (Na, Nx); and Normative Outsider (Ci).*[248] Each of the superordinate four, including its subordinate, individual subtype[s] and types, was constructed not only from level 2 ("combinations")-type information, but, conspicuously, from that of level 3 ("depth/breadth") as well. In particular, each of these four was an assemblage and integration (A & I) of information from the "cognitive," "motivational-affective," "interpersonal-behavioral," "familial," and "socio-cultural" areas—that is, from almost all such areas collectively (Rubenfeld, 1967, 10–16). In each case, the information- and inferential-base for the A&I consisted of the moderate and strong concurrences and other similarities or even identities—convergences, overlaps per se, and so on—that existed across many or most of the typology systems, with respect to these several areas.

When Warren later added eight typology systems to the eight that were discussed at the NIMH conference, and then examined all 16 together,[249] her own eight *subtypes* were still present and her ninth—the Se (situational-emotional reaction)—now emerged and was added.[250] Though the *substance*—the content and meaning—of those eight subtypes was the same as in the "NIMH" classification (NIC), most of them were now *rearranged*. That is, Warren grouped and/or placed them differently than had the conference participants, collectively. For one thing, the subtypes were no longer subordinates within "NIMH's" four superordinates. In short, structural, not substantive, changes were made (Warren, 1966, 20; 1971, 250).[251]

Warren's changes centered, basically, on the "Power Oriented" group—this, as indicated, being a superordinate category in the NIC (*note:* as implied, "superordinate"—and, thus, "subordinate"—refers only to the *structural position* of a category and to the structural relationship *among* categories, not to its/their substance, relative or absolute value, and so on): (1) Two of the NIMH Power Oriented's three *subordinates*, namely, Warren's Cfm and Cfc subtypes (which were structural constituents of that superordinate, in the NIC) were regrouped, jointly, as one *superordinate*—one simply called "Conformist." (Having made this change, together with that mentioned in point (2), below, Warren did not utilize the term "Power Oriented.")[252] The Cfm and Cfc subtypes, which now became the structural constituents of this *Conformist* category, each retained their separate identities; Warren called the first "non-delinquently oriented" and the second "delinquently oriented." In any case, "Conformist" was now a category of its own: Structurally, it was a superordinate—one composed of two subordinates. (2) The third *subordinate*, that is, structural constituent, of NIMH's Power Oriented superordinate became a *super*ordinate itself. That is, it was made another of Warren's basic categories (each of which she called a "band")—as had the Cfm and Cfc jointly. At any rate, this subordinate, namely, the Mp subtype in Warren's preconference classification system, was made a category of its own and it was no longer a constituent of any other. (In the NIC, this subordinate had been labeled "controlling"; in Warren's classification of all 16 typologies collectively, that is, in her post-conference classification, it became "Antisocial-manipulator.")

Other than those structural changes—which, as can be seen, centered on three subtypes (Cfm, Cfc, and Mp)—little was altered: First, NIMH's "Impulse Oriented" superordinate was changed in name only—to that of "Asocial"; and, its two subordinates (constituents)—the Aa and Ap subtypes—were maintained as such. Second, NIMH's "Neurotic" superordinate remained unchanged, even in name; to be sure, within *Warren's* "Neurotic" superordinate, in contrast to NIMH's, the Na ("Acting-out") and Nx ("Anxious") subtypes were *specified* as constituent categories, and—thereby—as having mutually distinct identities. Third, NIMH's "Normative Outsider" superordinate was altered in name alone—now becoming "Subcultural-identifier." Finally, as indicated, the *Situational* group was added, as a new category. (Like NIC's Normative Outsider, it still had no structural constituents, that is, no specified subordinates.) Thus, Warren's examination of the 16 typology systems, including her own, resulted in six basic categories (bands), three of which (Asocial; Neurotic; Subcultural-identifier) were the same as three of NIMH's superordinates (Impulse Oriented; Neurotic; Normative Outsider), and two of which (Conformist; Antisocial-manipulator) were essentially regroupings of NIMH's fourth superordinate (Power Oriented). Together, the six bands—structurally, superordinates themselves—encompassed all nine of her subtypes, and, of course, essentially all types that comprised the 15 other systems.

The concurrent validity that was found with respect to Warren's subtypes applied across a sizable range of *settings,* and, simultaneously, across the varied youth-samples associated with those settings. This range-of-applicability is evident in connection with the earlier-described empirical studies, viewed collectively. (See section B ["Concurrent Validity of Subtypes"] of this chapter.) It is also reflected in three separable yet mutually supportive points, none of which involves those particular studies: (1) The "NIMH" classification, which integrated eight typology systems including Warren's, was based on samples drawn from public schools, probation intake, psychiatric clinics, and state correctional institutions, among other settings;[253] and, as already seen, the numerous youth-types and subtypes (40 in all) that comprised those eight systems, collectively, converged to four broad categories—each an NIMH "superordinate." Thus, there were 5.0 types/subtypes per system, on average ($40 \div 8$); and since these *five* reduced to the *four* superordinate categories, each of which was represented in each of the eight typology systems, two things are readily apparent or easily deduced:[254] (a) the large amount of overlap (a direct sign of concurrence) that existed across the typologies/subtypes which comprised those systems; and—specifically to the point—(b) the sizable degree of generalizability—in that sense applicability—that existed across the *settings* in which those systems had been used.[255] (The four superordinates exclude NIMH's "Mentally Ill.")

(2) Of those four superordinates, each of which seemed rather clearly distinguished from every other one as a category,[256] three were identical to three of the six "bands" that *Warren* later derived after adding eight typology systems to the NIMH eight. These added systems, collectively, themselves involved a range of settings and youth-samples.

(3) Of the four broad categories that *Van Voorhis* (1994) later derived in connection with imprisoned male adults (this being a further setting and sample), two—called "Neurotic Anxious/High Anxiety" and "Committed Criminal"—largely corresponded to two of the just-mentioned "three [that] were identical" across the *Warren post-conference classification (WPC),* on the one hand, and the *NIMH classification (NIC),* on the other. Those in the WPC had been labeled "Neurotic" and "Subcultural-identifier"; those in the NIC, "Neurotic" and "Normative Outsider." (Van Voorhis' two remaining categories—the "Character Disorder" and "Situational"—appeared quite similar to two categories—the Na and Se—that were present in Warren's classification. The first of those remainders also corresponded to the Na group that was described in connection with NIMH's "Neurotic" superordinate, even though the Na group had not, in the NIMH classification, been explicitly labeled and thereby specifically distinguished from the also-described *Nx* group.)

Though this discussion of settings and samples has focused on superordinate categories per se and on their structural equivalents, such as Warren's bands and Van

Voorhis' broad categories, it also pertains to individual subtypes—the structural and substantive *constituents* of superordinates, and so on. Moreover, it applies whether or not these subtypes existed as *formal subordinates,* especially as constituents which have been (1) made explicit within the structure of the NIMH and/or WPC classification (that is, had been specifically identified and delineated as subcategories), which had also been (2) given a name and perhaps an accompanying symbol, and so forth. Thus, for instance, three such subtypes (Na, Nx, and Ci), *as* individual subtypes, were found within the NIMH, WPC, and Van Voorhis classifications alike— hence, were present across all three systems' settings and the latters' associated samples— irrespective of how these subtypes had been arranged within those systems and of whether, or how fully, they had been formalized. In addition, a fourth Warren subtype—the Se—was present in two of those three classifications, that is, typology systems, as were three subtypes (Cfm, Cfc, and Mp) which, however, were *not* found in Van Voorhis' classification, and which are discussed shortly. Finally, the Na and Nx subtypes were present, and explicit, in most section-B empirical studies in which they *could* have been specifically identified as such, particularly in those by Budnoff, Ferdinand, and Jesness.[257] This applied to the Aa, Cfm, Cfc, and Mp subtypes as well.

Limitations. As seen, evidence supporting the existence of concurrent validity (CV) can accumulate across several studies combined— as, in effect, can findings that suggest little or no CV. Such evidence, and lack thereof, can, of course, also involve any single study. Though results from several studies combined—whether or not they largely support CV—are almost always weightier than those from any one alone,[258] it will be useful to briefly focus on certain solo studies. These investigations, because of their particular samples and/or circumstances, can provide clues as to why certain Warren subtypes are (1) sometimes unlikely—or else less likely than *other subtypes*—to be observed by all, and, when they *are* observed, are (2) sometimes less likely than other subtypes—or else unlikely per se—to be supported by *other typology systems,* that is, by systems whose *own* offender-types have been compared with them. In short, these studies can help identify

certain limitations of concurrent validation and can suggest why it was sometimes not obtained or was relatively weak.

Specifically, lesser degrees of CV, or sometimes its complete absence, were found in certain individual studies, usually regarding two or more subtypes per study. In some cases these findings mainly reflected such factors as *age, gender,* and even *sample-size,* operating either directly and perhaps essentially alone, or else in substantial interaction with the type of setting from which the sample was drawn. In other instances they seemed to mainly reflect the type of *setting per se*—operating apart from some of those factors, yet in line with its parent agency's policies. Such findings (lesser degree and/or complete absence) and each factor (age, gender, and so on) pertained not just to the relatively rare subtypes—the Aa, Ap, Se, and Ci—but to certain common ones as well, specifically, the Cfm, Cfc, and Mp.[259] Three examples of these findings will now be given, the first of which involves the joint effects of age and setting. In particular, it involves the possible role played by these mutually interacting factors in bringing about a lack of concurrent support—in this case, a lack of substantive overlap between some of the just-mentioned subtypes, on the one hand, and various offender-groups from *different* typology systems, such as Hunt's or Quay's, on the other.

1. No concurrent validation was obtained regarding Warren's Cfm, Cfc, and Mp subtypes in Van Voorhis' study (1994), of imprisoned males, in which the Hunt (H), Jesness (J), Megargee (M), and Quay (Q) typologies were compared with one another and with Warren (W) subtypes as well, on each of several behavioral and psychological variables. That is, none of the just-mentioned W subtypes converged with (for instance, correlated positively and significantly with) H, J, M, and/or Q offender-types with which they would be *expected* to converge if they and those types had a moderate or larger degree of substantive commonality. No convergence occurred in connection with Aa's and Ap's, as well. To help understand these findings it should first be recalled that the median age of this all-adult sample—34—was about twice that of most *delinquent* samples—delinquents (youths) being the individuals regarding whom most of Warren's subtypes had been delineated, and to whom they had been chiefly

applied.[260] Next, it should be kept in mind that (1) Cfm's, Cfc's, and Mp's—and they alone—constitute Warren's middle maturity (I_3) level, and that level only, and that (2) Aa's and Ap's—again, alone—comprise the low (I_2) level, and again, that level only. Finally, and decisively, everyone in the sample had been classified, via the Warren interview approach, as either *high* or *very high* (I_4 or I_5) maturity. Thus, there were no middle or low maturity individuals—no Cfm's, no Cfc's, and so on—in the analysis. Ipso facto, there was no possibility of *convergence* between these W subtypes and any H, J, M, and/or Q categories, whether in connection with behavioral, psychological, or any other variables.[261] Absent any cross-system convergence, and given that such convergence or substance—based overlap is integral to the concept of concurrent validity in any cross-classification study, no CV was obtained in this investigation with respect to those middle and low maturity subtypes.[262] To help account for the *absence* of Cfm's, Cfc's, and so on, and even for a *paucity* of them if—instead—a modest percentage actually had been present but were misclassified, Van Voorhis reasonably implied the following: Persons who have not reached the I_4 maturity level may be rare or at least uncommon in most samples that are well past chronological adolescence—for instance, in those which, on average, are well beyond early adulthood, not to mention well into their 30's.[263] Regarding classification issues, and the factor of age as well, see Van Voorhis (1994, 69–70, 99–100, 116, 336).

We now turn to example 2. This centers on the role that (1) certain admission policies which are utilized by specified types of settings (facilities) can play in screening out or deemphasizing particular youth-subtypes, and that (2) "alternative programs/resources" can have in determining whether these same subtypes will seldom even be referred to those facilities. In addition, it further illustrates the impact of age—this time, however, the opposite of *above*-average age. After that, in example 3, we will focus on the role of gender in connection with one particular subtype, and on the collateral effect of sample size in that same context.

2. Neither situational-emotional (Se) nor cultural identifier (Ci) youths were found in the earlier-reviewed studies by Budnoff (1963), Ferdinand (1978), and Jesness (1965,

1971–1972) that took place at Las Palmas, Geneva, and Fricot, respectively—these being secure, justice system facilities.[264] Nor were they present at Shawbridge (Chapter 23)—in this case, *ordinarily* present—for instance, in its secure and its open residential units outside Montreal. Except at Fricot, discussed below, the absence of these Warren subtypes probably reflected the following major factors (*note*: As will become clear from example 3, neither of these factors appears to be the dominant one in the case of female Ci's; nor does it *become* dominant when combined with its counterpart. Nevertheless, each one does seem critical, and may sometimes be decisive by itself, with respect to *male and female Se's and male Ci's*. Moreover, regarding female Ci's themselves, these same factors—namely, #1 and #2 which follow—probably *would* be central if the factors discussed in example 3 did *not* apply):

(#1) *Agency-level policy* that required or otherwise influenced the three secure/residential facilities to routinely exclude, or to seldom admit, youths who were *not* (a) acutely or chronically disturbed and/or (b) physically dangerous to themselves or others—not to mention (c) quite involved in delinquency. Given this policy, and assuming it regularly outweighed whatever counterpressures may have existed, all or almost all Sc's and Ci's would have been or at least should have been rejected by intake staff at those facilities (i.e., rejected if and when these subtypes had in fact been referred to them; however, see factor #2 regarding referral). This rejection would/should have occurred because, as indicated in various places, it is the Se's and Ci's who, among all delinquents, are not only the least disturbed and otherwise personally troubled (especially deeply) and are usually the least "trouble*some*" overall (this, at any rate, pertains to Se's), but who have the most available—accessible—personal and interpersonal strengths/skills.

(#2) The *ability of other programs/ resources,* ones that existed within and/or outside the given agency (sometimes even outside the justice system), to do the following: (a) Adequately work with, and otherwise be productively used for, the preponderance of Se's and Ci's (especially the former)—the result being that (b) these youths, or most of them, were, or may have been, handled successfully via these alternative programs/resources and were not referred to the secure/residential facilities under consideration. In other words, these individuals—or, at least, most of them—were not, or might not have been, sent further into, or sometimes even *to,* these justice system settings.[265] In light of this factor, facilities such as Las Palmas, and so on, would not or might not have had *frequent occasion* to reject Se's and Ci's (as per factor 1), since—ordinarily—such youths would/might not have been often referred to them in the first place.[266] Nevertheless, alternative programs/resources were neither uniformly nor continuously *available* throughout one or more of the given states/regions during the periods in question. For this reason—in other words, even apart, for instance, from the fact that *available* programs/resources do not always *succeed*—referrals to Las Palmas, Geneva, and/or Shawbridge would, at times, have undoubtedly occurred more than just rarely.

Though factors #1 and #2, often even singly, were probably fundamental as well as decisive in accounting for the absence of male and female Se's and male Ci's in the just-mentioned settings, that of *age* was very likely the underlying and critical one—and, by itself, a sufficient one—at Fricot. Before, during, and after Jesness' study of this latter setting, Fricot was *the* California facility officially designated to accept, insofar as feasible, the preponderance of very young male delinquents committed to the state. (Moreover, it—and only it—could accept *just* the very young: maximum age at admission was 14.) This applied even if (a) these youths' degree of personal disturbance and/or (b) the extent of their prior delinquency was less than considerable. (Thus, the following was the case even though (a) and/or (b)—just mentioned—were usually *not* less than considerable [e.g., item (b) usually involved more than 3.0 "prior . . . official police entries" (Jesness, 1965, A–13)]: If the "less than . . ." condition had *not* existed, (a) and (b)—especially, but not just, together—could have largely ruled out Se's and Ci's. However, since Fricot's admissions did *not* have to be rather disturbed, and so on [even though *most* apparently *were*], Se's and Ci's were *not* in fact excluded on those specific grounds; at least, they were not supposed to be.) Fricot youngsters averaged not quite 11 years of age, at admission, and only 5 percent were over 12—1 percent being 13 or more.[267] This particular age-constraint is relevant be-cause typology studies have regularly indicated or strongly suggested that Se's and Ci's (especially the former) who have been committed to the state are seldom under age 13—that, instead, they are among the oldest delinquents (Se's perhaps being *the* oldest).[268] Given this situation, it is very likely that Fricot's low age-ceiling, operating essentially by itself, largely eliminated any realistic chance of this facility's receiving more than a very occasional Se and Ci. Even during any two- or three-year period, little more than a handful of these individuals—none, of course, being over age 14—would likely have arrived.[269] (As indicated in endnotes 30 and 31, there were no Se's and Ci's in *Makkay's* sample as well, where the average age at intake was 12.0 [Palmer, 1973c, 39–40]. Besides age, *setting* [via screening] probably contributed to this absence—given that the sample consisted entirely of behaviorally disturbed individuals [all boys] at a psychiatric clinic.)

3. One factor, namely *gender,* was very likely fundamental in accounting for the absence of female Ci's at Las Palmas, Geneva, and Shawbridge. (As indicated, the first two facilities admitted females only, and Shawbridge—starting in 1976—had females as well as males. At Fricot, however, no opportunity *existed* for females to be "absent," because no such individuals were even referred to it in the first place.) Gender's fundamental influence and status directly reflected the following (*note:* Here, "fundamental" refers not to the fact that gender is an intrinsic attribute, and not *just* to the fact that its impact temporarily preceded that of all other factors, including #1 and #2 above. Instead [and still regarding the "absence of female Ci's . . ."], it emphasizes that gender's influence was very likely *predominant*—that it outweighed the impact of all other factors combined, including #1 and #2): Female Ci's—Ci's particularly with respect to being gang leaders or coleaders, just as with males—are probably an especially rare category of delinquents, one that perhaps accounts for little more than 1 or 2 percent of all nonlightweight female offenders (NLFOs). (See, e.g., endnote 202.) Given this rarity—one that various studies/observations support, and that essentially none oppose—the following would apply: Unusually large numbers of NLFOs—literally several hundred, at least—would likely be needed before enough female

Ci's could be present in order to emerge as a distinct entity (here, a Ci category), particularly via standard quantitative approaches to deriving typologies.[270]

Thus, for instance, if female Ci's constituted 1 percent of an NLFO population, about 1,000 NLFOs would be needed before 10 such Ci's (this being a commonly needed, rough minimum) would likely appear via random drawing. Similarly, if female Ci's comprised 3 percent of such a population, about 333 NLFOs would be needed before 10 Ci's would likely appear, again on unselected grounds. The relevance that these large required numbers have to the conclusion that gender was "very likely fundamental . . ." can be deduced from the fact that (1) the entire study sample at Las Palmas and Geneva involved 75 and 234 individuals, respectively, that (2) at Shawbridge all residential plus community units, taken together, accommodated about 40 females at any one time, and that (3) all three settings *did,* in the first place, consist largely—at Las Palmas, and perhaps Geneva, entirely—of "nonlightweights." (In this context, *sample size*—particularly the need for a very *large* sample—can be viewed as a key collateral factor or condition in accounting for the given absence. It was "key" in the following respect: With *it* and *gender* being functionally inter-woven, as is apparent they were, the latter's influence was not just the predominant one [i.e., very likely primary]; instead, it was very likely the decisive one as well.)

In sum, gender was probably the principal and sufficient source of the absence of female Ci's at Las Palmas, Geneva, and Shawbridge—at least, of their nonemergence as a statistically distinct category via the technical tools at hand.[271] This would have been true even if there had also existed not only (1) admission policies that prevented most or all such individuals who may have been *referred* to those settings from actually *entering* them, but (2) alternative programs/resources that reduced the *referral* of such youths to those facilities in the first place. In short, gender could have adequately accounted for the absence in question, and it very likely did so, even if factors #1 and #2 had reduced the number of female Ci's that would otherwise have been present in those facilities and could therefore have been statistically reflected. Basically, it could have done so because Ci's were not only

unusually rare in the underlying, female delinquent population as a whole, and even among nonlightweights within that population, but because this rarity existed from the start. In particular, it existed—was a reality—*before* the just mentioned policies and programs/resources (PPRs) could have been, and perhaps were, applied to any given youth; in addition, it continued to exist as such.

At any rate, these PPRs, even if they had been fully implemented and successful with respect to their goals, would not have made what was already quite rare, namely, female Ci's, *rarer* to a degree that mattered—mattered, specifically, in terms of making a substantial difference in accounting for these youths' "absence." In effect, then, these admission policies and alternative programs/resources were, or would have been, nonessential with regard to the present context—again, because of the following: Given not just the preexisting, and subsequently continued, underlying rarity of these individuals but the actual sample sizes associated with the particular facilities in question, there were already *few* enough of these youths to preclude their emergence as a statistically distinct category within those settings. That is, there were already few enough prior to and, in any event, independent of, any and all impact by factors #1 and #2. This, we believe, applied to the impact of other possible factors as well.

Concurrent Validity of Subtypes: Final Summary and Discussion. To facilitate this section, the following might be kept in mind. Our review of concurrent validity has drawn from two kinds of *approaches*: multisystem studies and syntheses, and single-system studies and analyses. In addition, it has involved two largely different kinds of *information,* and their often-associated methods of analysis or bases for drawing conclusions: the more quantitative/statistical (QS), and the more qualitative/experts' judgments (QE). Each type of approach—the "multisystem" and "single"—could have involved quantitative and/or qualitative information, though, in fact, it usually rested heavily on one *or* the other.

In any given *multi*system approach, Warren's typology system was compared with at least one other system, such as Quay's; that is, the study or synthesis in question involved at least two systems. Here, the main question was whether any subtypes from Warren's system had any substantive equivalents in that *other* system or systems; that is, Were counterparts of her subtypes present within it/them? In any *single*-system approach, *no* cross-system comparisons were made, since, of course, none *could* be made. Here, the main question was whether any given Warren subtype (e.g., Manipulator) emerged—seemed to be present—*at all,* within the study sample. That is, Did it analytically appear in connection with the sample?—say, Was it derived via factor analysis? Alternatively, Did it simply *not* emerge (even though others perhaps *did*), or perhaps appear only weakly? As is implied, its presence was not a "given" at the start of each single-system study and analysis. More precisely, the subtype was never analytically present at that point (e.g., no youths had an already-existing subtype diagnosis).

In what follows, the first approach–the multisystem—will usually be called a *cross-classification* study or synthesis and the second will often be termed a *one-system* study of analysis. Most of the cross-classifications (i.e., cross-typology comparisons) rested largely or entirely on QS information, the remainder, on QE. We will summarize the leading one of each. In contrast, almost all one-system studies/analyses were chiefly QS; results from several of these will be summarized first—sometimes collectively, sometimes individually. In our view, these two different approaches methodologically supplemented each other, and their joint presence broadened as well as strengthened the basis for drawing generalized conclusions about the concurrent validity of subtypes; so did the "differ[ing] kinds of *information*, . . . [the differing] methods of analysis," and related dimensions. At any rate, these different types of just-mentioned approaches and dimensions [A&D's] provided varied kinds and levels of evidence regarding concurrent validity; in so doing they furnished reasonably robust empirical and logical grounds for drawing overall conclusions. As seen in the summary, which now follows, the results that were obtained in connection with these A&D's constituted—collectively—largely *converging* evidence, evidence that was quite consistent in the case of Warren's major subtypes. Especially but not only in this respect, they led to largely unitary conclusions.

Evidence for the concurrent validity of Warren's typology systems was obtained at two substantively related levels of analysis: the *individual subtype* and the *subtype grouping*. Concerning individual subtypes, consistent and specific evidence was obtained, from the one-system studies, regarding the existence of several types of youth—six of Warren's nine categories: Asocial aggressive (Aa), Immature conformist (Cfm), Cultural conformist (Cfc), Manipulator (Mp), Neurotic, acting out (Na), and Neurotic, anxious (Nx). These studies, particularly Jesness' at Fricot, Budnoff's at Las Palmas, and Ferdinand's at Geneva, were heavily quantitative—deriving/identifying those individual subtypes via factor analysis and the like.

(In this book the Cfm, Cfc, Mp, Na, and Nx are called "passive conformist," "group conformist," "manipulator," "assertive-denier," and "anxious-confused," respectively. At the "subtype grouping" level, the second and third of these are collectively termed "power oriented," whereas the fourth and fifth are called "conflicted." [As may be inferred, any given "grouping" was based on a salient *feature, mode of adjustment, stance,* or even *diagnosis*—such as "conformist," "power oriented," "committed criminal," or "neurotic" ("conflicted")—that characterized two or more subtypes in an important way and that simultaneously distinguished them from the remaining subtypes. That is, the former subtypes were differentiated from the latter on the basis of that same shared feature, mode, or whatever.] Warren's Aa's, together with her Asocial passive (Ap), Situational-emotional (Se), and Cultural identifier (Ci), constitute the book's "rare types"—a label that stems from their infrequency in the California experiment.[272] [In the one-system studies collectively, evidence for the existence of Ap's, Se's, and Ci's was weak.] The remaining subtypes—Cfm, Cfc, Mp, Na, and Nx—are "nonrare.")

Still at the individual subtype level, evidence of concurrent validity was also obtained for (1) four of the five nonrare subtypes, in Gaensbauer and Lazerwitz' partly quantitative, partly qualitative (clinical), one-system study, (2) four of the five nonrare ones (and the Ap, Se, and Ci rare ones), in Palmer's examination of Gibbons' typology, and (3) all five nonrare ones (plus the three just-mentioned rare ones), in the former's comparison of the nine Warren subtypes, on the one hand, with eight empirical clusters of youth from the Santa Monica probation sample, on the other. Palmer's analysis of the (4) Spencer-Conrad typology of violent offenders found strong, specific parallels for the Cfc and Mp subtypes only.[273] (Analyses (2) through (4) were simple, two-system comparisons—as was that of the Makkay sample/system, mentioned later in connection with subtype *groupings*. The cross-classifications summarized shortly were much more comprehensive overall, and they involved several systems each.)

In sum, within the *one-system (non cross-classification)* studies collectively, Cfm's, Cfc's, and Mp's were almost always found, that is, identified; basically, this applied to Na's and Nx's, as well. In the *two-system (simple cross-classification)* studies/analyses, evidence generally appeared for many of these same five subtypes. Also in these two-system comparisons, some evidence emerged for Ap's, Se's, and Ci's; though this support was far from consistent across these studies, there was proportionately much more of it than across the one-system studies. (The latter studies provided substantial support for the existence of Aa's.)

When any of these "rare types"—including Aa's—did not emerge or was nearly absent (in *whatever* type of study/analysis), the reason(s) often centered on the type of setting that had been examined. Chiefly involved, here, seemed to be (1) the setting's eligibility criteria or preferences and/or (2) the low probability or reduced likelihood that certain offenders had been referred to it in the first place.[274] (Conditions (1) and (2) reflected, among their dimensions, the individuals' offense history, type of instant offense, and/or degree of major personal disturbance [Aa, Ap] or relative lack thereof [Se, Ci].) However, "setting" was not always the *central*—the dominant—factor in accounting for the absence or near-absence (ANA) in question, even though it was almost always important. Instead, ANA sometimes chiefly reflected the *age* or *gender* of the sample (youths);[275] and, in its interaction with these factors, *sample-size* sometimes made a decisive difference. At any rate, "absence or near-absence" sometimes mainly reflected the closer relationship that age or gender had to the rare subtypes than did *setting*, that is, conditions (1) and (2). Likeliest of all, however, was the following: The ANA of Aa's, Ap's, Se's, and/or Ci's in the given studies/analyses seemed to mainly result from a *combination* of setting, on the

one hand, and one or more of the subsequently mentioned factors (e.g., age), on the other—with no single factor being almost all-powerful, and each one being important.

(Whereas the four rare subtypes were not infrequently absent from the various studies collectively—more concretely, whereas some were "missing" from certain studies and others were missing from some of the rest—the *remaining* subtypes, that is, the five "nonrare" ones [not just collectively], were seldom absent from those same collective studies—this, *irrespective* of the individual study sample's setting, age, gender, size, and combinations thereof. Given certain assumptions and already-mentioned information, this strongly suggests that a broad range of nonlightweight, juvenile and perhaps young adult offender samples, and possibly their underlying populations, not only (1) consisted mainly of these five nonrare Warren categories but, accordingly, (2) could be fairly well characterized—at the individual subtype level—largely in terms of them, or, of course, their counterparts in other typology systems.[276] Concerning somewhat older adults, see below.)

Regarding the second level of analysis—that of *subtype groupings*—considerable support was obtained, for the existence of groupings specified below, from *major multi-system efforts*, specifically, from large-scale cross-classifications. This support, which constituted evidence of concurrent validity, involved the substantive similarity and/or identity—together, the "overlap"—that was found between the following: (1) the particular *Warren*-system subtypes (categories of offenders)—or, at times, just one of the subtypes—which comprised those respective groupings, on the one hand, and (2) one or more equivalent or similar specific types (again categories of offenders) that constituted each of various *other* classification systems, on the other. (Simultaneously, of course, significant overlap existed, that is, was present, between most or all of these "other" classification systems *themselves*, with respect to various specific types [i.e., individual categories]—from these systems—that were conceptually and/or statistically linked with the just-mentioned Warren-system subtypes.) To facilitate the discussion, "classification system" and "typology system" will be used synonymously.[277]

In the first of these large-scale cross-classifications (CCs)—the one developed at the NIMH conference—the presence or nonpresence of significant substantive overlap, that is, similarity and/or identity with regard to contents and concepts, was decided via consensus judgments by the several experts who had mutually discussed, compared, and contrasted their respective typology systems in that setting. This might be called a chiefly "qualitative" determination. In the second large-scale CC—that by Van Voorhis (below)—the existence of overlap was determined "quantitatively": Operationally, it reflected statistically significant positive correlations and/or other substantial relationships between the relevant categories of the respective typology systems. (In both CCs, the *name* of any given "subtype grouping" [e.g., NIMH's "Power Oriented"; Van Voorhis' "Committed Criminals"] reflected a critical, salient dimension that seemed to be shared in common by the constituents—the overlapping individual categories [subtypes]—of the given grouping.)

Specifically, in the first of those efforts, what happened was basically as follows. The cross-classification that emerged at the NIMH conference, in which the contents and concepts of eight typology systems (Warren's being one) were directly compared and contrasted with each other by the authors of those systems, provided strong support for the existence of three main groupings of individual Warren subtypes (and of one additional, separate and ungrouped, subtype: the Ci). These groupings, which the conferees decided were very common across the eight systems and could therefore be considered "general types," were named "Impulse Oriented," "Power Oriented," and "Neurotic," respectively. Together, they encompassed seven of Warren's nine individual subtypes. For instance, "Impulse Oriented" specifically included her Aa and Ap subtypes jointly, whereas "Power Oriented" encompassed the Cfm, Cfc, and Mp subtypes, themselves collectively. ("Neurotic" accounted for the remaining two.) Impulse orientation or global impulsivity was the critical, salient feature that Aa's and Ap's seemed to have in common and which significantly distinguished them from the remaining groupings—not just, and not even chiefly, in degree. The same applied to power orientation, in the case of Cfm's, Cfc's, and Mp's.

(Warren, who soon afterward examined those eight conference-discussed typology systems together with eight others, derived—herself qualitatively/globally, rather than via statistical correlations per se—essentially the same three groupings.[278] The first one had a name change only, from "Impulse Oriented" to "Asocial"; the second was subdivided—structurally rearranged—and was then given different names, but was not substantively altered; the third was not changed at all. The subjects of (1) the *conference's* synthesis of the various systems' individual categories and of (2) *Warren's* 16-systems synthesis, as well, were preponderantly male offenders—mostly juveniles.)

Considerably later, Van Voorhis' largescale cross-classification study identified four major groups of male prisoners, individuals who were modally in their 30's (*note*: (a) In this study, Warren's Ci's and Se's were common: 17 percent and 24 percent of the sample, respectively; for Jesness' Ci's and Se's the percentages were 3 and 15. (b) In the following, "included" means "included but was not limited to"): (1) *Neurotic anxious/High anxiety* (this included the Warren interview-based Nx); (2) *Committed Criminal* (this largely corresponded to the NIMH conference's Normative Outsider grouping; it included Warren's preconference *Ci*—her postconference "Subcultural-identifier"); (3) *Situational* (included Warren's *Se*—preconference and postconference); and (4) *Character Disorder* (like group (1), this had a counterpart in one of the implicit components of the conference's Neurotic grouping; it included one of the two explicit constituents of Warren's Neurotic group, namely, *Na* [the other being *Nx*]).

Each Van Voorhis (V) group was statistically built on and substantively contained a number of typology systems,[279] not just I-Level. (Regarding I-Level, each V group did not just reflect results associated with *interview*-based subtype diagnoses, to which Warren's system—as distinguished from Jesness' *inventory*-based subtype diagnoses/system—specifically referred, in this study.) Thus, (1) *Neurotic anxious/High anxiety,* which, as indicated, included the *interview*-based Nx, also contained Megargee's "George" and "Jupiter" types, Quay's "Neurotic Anxious" type, and Jesness' (i.e., the *inventory*-based) Nx—as well as his *NA,* to a lesser degree.[280] Similarly, (2) *Committed Criminal* contained not just Warren's interview-based Ci but Megargee's "Charlie" and "Foxtrot" types, Quay's "Asocial Aggressive," and Jesness' inventory-based *Cfc*. In addition, (3) *Situational* included not only the interviewed-based Se but Megargee's "Easy" and "Item," Quay's "Situational," and the inventory-based Se as well as *Ci*. (As will be recalled, Jesness' Ci was the only I-Level subtype whose definition differed from that of Warren's.[281] All others were identical or virtually so.) Finally, (4) *Character Disorder* involved not just the interview- and inventory-based Na (I-Level subtype) but two of Magargee's types. Thus, regarding adult offenders, certain groupings of individual I-Level subtypes received concurrent validation in this study, specifically, from the Megargee and/or Quay systems. As is evident, however, these combinations of subtypes—*Nx and Na, Ci and Cfc*, and *Se and Ci*, in V groups (1), (2), and (3), respectively—existed only when the interview-based results were combined with those from Jesness' inventory. (In each of these combinations, the first-listed subtype emerged from the interview, the second from the inventory.)[282]

Whereas the preceding subtype combinations existed under the just-stated condition, others—ones delineated in earlier syntheses—did not emerge under *any* that was present. ("Condition" still centers on the method of diagnosis—the interview or inventory—that precedes any data analysis and synthesis.) Specifically, Van Voorhis did not find (A) the NIMH conference's and Warren's *Impulse Oriented* (however named), (B) Warren's *Conformist*, and (C) the conference's *Power Oriented*—that is, the *Aa + Ap, Cfm + Cfc*, and *Cfm + Cfc + Mp* combinations, respectively (each of which had been delineated, by the conferees and/or Warren, chiefly with respect to juveniles). Of course, because her sample did not *have* any Aa's, Ap's, Cfm's, and so on in the first place, as diagnosed via *interview,* none of these subtype combinations *could* have emerged in her study. More precisely, none could have even *existed* that involved any one of the given subtypes, as determined by that method.[283] Yet, none of these combinations emerged in connection with *inventory*-based diagnoses either, and in this case two of them—(B) and (C), above—theoretically *could* have emerged. They could have done so because, based on this method, which involved the Jesness Inventory, many Cfm's, Cfc's, and Mp's *were* present. (Very few Aa's and Ap's—the constituents of (A)—existed, even via this method.)[284]

Specifically, the JI-based *Cfm's* did not statistically link with the JI-based *Cfc's*. If they *had* been thus linked—linked particularly because they each had significant positive correlations with one or more of the same, reasonably expected Megargee and/or Quay types—they, in conjunction with those M and/or Q types, would then have constituted the following:[285] (a) a *major Conformist group* (one whose statistically derived typology content [SDTC] would have been broader than the qualitatively determined typologies/categories that comprised (B), above; and, given this context, that is, given the existence of this major group (cross-system cluster), the Cfm's and Cfc's would have simultaneously and automatically constituted (b) the *subtype combination Cfm + Cfc itself.* It would have done so because this combination would, of course, have already been present within the "broader," cross-system cluster.

Besides not linking with Cfc's, the JI-based Cfm's did not statistically link with Mp's. As a result, these three subtypes did not jointly form the following, via the already-mentioned kind of connections with M and/or Q types—and, thereby, also in conjunction with those types: (a) a *major Power Oriented group* (one whose SDTC would have been broader than the "qualitatively determined . . . categories" that constituted (C), above); and, again given such a context, those subtypes ipso facto did *not* constitute the *combination Cfm + Cfc + Mp.* In sum, the subtype combinations that comprised the (B) and (C), respectively, did not emerge in the present study, even when they theoretically could have done so. Basically, this was because the JI-based Cfm's were not linked with the JI Cfc's via Megargee and/or Quay types and were not similarly linked with the JI Mp's either, along lines just described. More concretely, group (B's) two constituent subtypes (CSs) did not each have significant positive correlations with one or more of the *same* M and/or Q types—types with which they would each have been expected to thus correlate if they, the CSs, (1) were similar to each other and (2) had substantial content overlap (substantive commonality) with those types. The same applied to group (C's) three constituent subtypes.[286]

Further discussion regarding "Power Oriented" appears in n. 287. There, similarity and/or overlap—aspects of *concurrence*—between Cfc's and Mp's (absent the *Cfm's* is reviewed. More broadly, however, the discussion moves toward an explicit focus on the following: (1) *differences* between the "power orientation" that is central to *Cfc's* and *Mp's* perceptions of and typical interactions with their environment, on the one hand, and the "control/domination approach" which is often prominent among, though by no means always central and paramount to, *Na's* and *Ci's*, on the other; and (2) *similarities* that nevertheless exist in various socially learned behaviors and modes of interpersonal interaction, on the part of all four subtypes. (In many situations, an Na's and Ci's interpersonal approach can be partly independent of, or even purposely contrary to, his usual values and views regarding interpersonal reciprocity. In this respect, among others, his "approach"—or certain major ones—can differ from his "orientation," even though both of them reflect his overall dynamics.) To deal with this subject matter and with various psychological as well as objective realities and interactions it

entails, n. 287 touches on several areas and issues and is, as a result, wide-ranging and long.Unfortunately, due to an unexpected, externally imposed, short deadline for the completion of this book, our discussion cannot be continued in a step-by-step manner and brought to full closure. (One aspect of its final section does conclude, in n. 288.) For the same reason, the remainder of our "Overview, Discussion, and Conclusions" cannot be completed in any detailed way. This especially applies to (1) our final assessment of the *construct* validity of *subtypes* (CVOS), (2) a presentation of major factors and conditions (FCs) that help account for the main differences between classification systems, especially in the number and kind of youth-types that are identified and used (most of these FCs, however, can be directly inferred from earlier discussion, as can our assessment of CVOS), and (3) our view of *which* main classification categories (e.g., five or six principal groups) can usefully serve a number of major purposes in most—or at least very many—juvenile and/or adult correctional contexts.

Notes

1. In the 1973 reply, the UDSA and CI&I parole analyses were discussed in connection with "criteria #2" and "#7," respectively (Palmer, 1973c, 66–95).

2. These decisions centered on whether to give a youth a second chance or to recommend revocation, particularly for his first non-minor, though non-severe, offense. (For related details, see "The Phase 1 and 2 Recidivism Measures," in Chapter 21.) Receiving a revocation did not mean the youth, whether an E or a C, could not eventually complete his program and obtain a favorable discharge (Chapter 7). At the same time, however, the E's greater likelihood than the C's of receiving a second chance, that is, of being restored if he had committed, say, a moderate-level offense, did give the individual in question an extra opportunity in this respect. (Regarding ". . . in question," it might be kept in mind that other E's and C's obtained a favorable discharge *without* having been arrested and—in that or any other connection—restored.) Whether and how an E or C *used* this opportunity—and it usually was literally *one*, for a non-minor offense—and whether or not he eventually obtained such a discharge, any offense he had committed and for which he had been restored was counted and analyzed in exactly the same way and to exactly the same extent as any one for which he had *not* been restored. (The same applied to any offense for which he had been recommitted to the YA, by probation.) This was the case regardless of its context and outcome, including, for instance, whether or not the individual's arrest (1) had been parole-agent-initiated or law-enforcement-initiated, (2) had resulted in a restoral, in a recommitment, and so on, and/or in any change of status or of parole conditions and requirements. In these and all other respects, arrest and conviction information was handled independently of discretionary and any other actions. That is, it was handled independently of such actions (by experimental- and control-program staff, by the YA board, and/or by anyone else) that took place subsequent to but particularly in connection with the youth's behavior—more specifically, with the illegal activity or alleged illegal activity for which he had been arrested. As implied, the bulk of the discretionary actions/responses centered on (1) the already-mentioned recommendations by parole agents (whether E or C) to either restore given youths to parole or to instead revoke them, and on (2) subsequent decisions by the board regarding those recommendations.

3. The percentage distributions in question—and shown in the 1972 document—were as follows, for lower, middle, and upper SES youths, respectively: E – 72, 24, 4; C – 83, 19, 0. When all distributions and corresponding p-levels for the six standard background variables (age, etc.) were being reviewed in preparation for follow-up analyses to the 1973 reply (whose corresponding discharge analysis was itself then reviewed), the at-*that*-point obvious mismatch appeared. As a result, the raw data were themselves reexamined and a X^2 was recalculated. Though the original X^2 was virtually unchanged, a new p-level was obtained based on the *correct* degrees of freedom. The new SES figures were: E – 73, 23, 4; C – 83, 17, 0, and their associated p-level of $< .20 > .10$ would have applied to the original figures as well. (All that aside, the figure of 19 percent, shown in Table 22–1 for middle SES C's [total group], should have been 17 percent. In addition, slight percentage changes occurred on race as well, but the original p-level stood.)

4. As mentioned in n. 6 (section D), below, Lerman indicated that he first received information about this post-manuscript analysis and its results in October 1973. This information, which appeared in the third section of the California researchers' 1973 reply to NIMH (Palmer, 1973c), had been sent to that agency on September 1, 1973. NIMH probably forwarded it to him a month later—perhaps together with the fourth (the final) section of that reply, which the researchers' had sent to NIMH on September 14. Had Lerman wished to obtain the background-characteristics

information that is presented below, in connection with this analysis (see text, and Table 22–2), and to obtain it quickly, he could have chosen to inquire about its existence and could have then requested it, either directly from those researchers or indirectly through NIMH. Doing so could have obviated his decision to instead hypothesize about the possible or likely similarities between the 1973 CI&I sample and the March 1972 sample.

5. Because this analysis involved parole performance exclusively, none of its E's and C's had to have acquired any at-risk time in the community *after* parole, for instance, a minimum of 24 or 48 months subsequent to favorable or unfavorable discharge from the YA. Instead, each youth only had to have been discharged. In contrast, the sample used in the present book's post-discharge analysis (Chapter 8, Table 8–2) contained only individuals who had accumulated at least 48 months of at-risk time in the community subsequent to their favorable or unfavorable discharge.

6. (A) In March 1973, the National Institute of Mental Health mailed Lerman's manuscript or draft to the California researchers and others, and, with it, requested a written reply from the researchers in 30 days if possible. (Lerman's *Note,* of course, did not yet exist. See below.) In May 1973, NIMH indicated it would extend its original due-date for the report because it recently realized that it had, in March, "foul[ed]-up" by mistakenly sending the researchers an "earlier draft version of the [Lerman] report dated May 15, 1972" instead of "the revised version [dated] (December 15, 1972) . . . ." This extension turned out to be quite modest, given the still remaining tasks perceived by the researchers. Specifically, (1) although, an NIMH indicated in May 1973, "the revised version . . . has been expanded" [over the original one] but would nevertheless have to be reviewed by the California researchers, and (2) although—"in view of our [NIMH's] goof [in mailing the wrong manuscript, and, apparently, in having mailed it late—*it* being dated 12/15/72]—NIMH was "re-

luctant to give you [the researchers] a time deadline," it again requested a 30-day turnaround, starting as of early May (Shah, S., written communications to Palmer, March 13 and May 3, 1973). Thus, pressure remained sizable; and because considerable work already awaited completion, relatively for new and/or expanded analyses or substudies—certainly no lengthy data-collection/analyses—could be undertaken as of May. In this connection it might be mentioned that the 1973 reply was to NIMH, not to Lerman, and that three independent reviewers selected by NIMH were also awaiting this response. As indicated in Chapter 21, NIMH forwarded the reply to Lerman and the reviewers (or in some cases forwarded its four sections as they each reached NIMH), who were then known as such only to it. The first two sections were mailed to that agency on May 2 and June 6, respectively. (B) Lerman's Note, already titled "Appendix A," reached the California researchers in early December 1973 (cover letter from him dated December 4). Palmer's 1974 report was developed for NIMH essentially in response to this December 1973 Note (which—unrevised and verbatim—later became Appendix A of *Social Control).* (C) In late September 1973, the California researchers—whose lengthy 1973 report ("reply") to NIMH had recently been completed, and whose final two sections had been mailed to that agency on September 1 and September 14—first learned, from NIMH, that it was considering "the possibility of an NIMH publication of the Lerman report" (Shah, S., written communication to Palmer, September 20, 1973), presumably or at least possibly contingent upon revisions, by Lerman, that might reflect (1) input from the researchers' now—completed reply to NIMH, and (2) comments from individuals such as the three independent reviewers. (By mid-to-later September, the input from the researchers had been only partly reviewed by NIMH and others; and, of course, no overall input had yet been given to Lerman by the three reviewers, at least not in connection with the researchers' full 1973 reply.) NIMH never did publish the Lerman report, for example, as part of its already-existing *Crime and Delinquency* series. As of October 1973 at the latest, Lerman had taken steps to have it published outside NIMH, as *Social Control* (Palmer, written communication to Philip Jones, Editor-in-Chief, University of Chicago Press, October 19, 1973; Jones, P., written communication to Palmer, October 26, 1973). (D) According to Lerman, it was October when he received that part (section 3) of the California researchers' report to which he responded in the form of his Note. As he stated in the Note, "In October 1973, I was offered a 'new' and 'updated' analysis . . . in response to the analyses contained in the [December 1972] draft manuscript" (Lerman, 1975, 231). As is clear from this statement in combination with the December 4 date of his cover letter (to the researchers) for the by-then-completed appendix, he wrote this Note/appendix during October/ November.

7. (A) Unfavorable dischargees (UDs) were excluded from the 1970 analysis mainly because—as of the cutoff date for initial release to *parole* (October, 1966)—relatively few such males existed for inclusion in a 24-months *post-discharge,* that is, *post*-parole, follow-up (Palmer and Turner, 1970). For the same reason, a 48-months post-discharge follow-up, which would have involved still fewer UDs (cutoff of October 1964 release to parole) was not even considered. (Ordinarily, all Youth Authority wards, in this case whether E's or C's, were expected to be on parole for a minimum of approximately 18 months from their initial release. At *that* point, if their behavior and overall adjustment had been satisfactory, they became eligible—in accordance with standard YA board practice—for a favorable discharge.) Although the publication date of the given analysis was 1970 (*February* 1970), the rapsheet data were received in December 1968 and the analysis itself was carried out during 1969. A similar situation—with the calendar year of publication, however, usually differing by only *one* from the year of data-collection—

applied to some other analyses as well, including the one next-mentioned. (B) Because the 1972 (March 1972) analysis was mainly an updating of the 1970—which, as indicated, involved *favorable-dischargees (FDs)* only—the favorable dischargees were again excluded. This was done even though (1) the rapsheets of the *UDs* had again been obtained, and, thus, were themselves updated, (2) the total number of UDs had substantially increased, and (3) a 48-months cohort—though relatively limited—could now be added. (C) In the 1973 report to NIMH (CI&I rapsheets analysis specifically), only the *parole* period, not a post-discharge period, was examined. As a result, the just-mentioned "updating" factor, which had previously led to the exclusion of UDs, no longer applied, and these individuals were then *included*. This made it possible to analyze (using the CI&I- rather than suspensions-based data) the parole performance of a broader offender group than that which would have been reflected in a favorable dischargees analysis alone, even though FDs still constituted the preponderance of the sample.

8. Given these groups' relatively small sample-sizes, it is important, as elsewhere (see, e.g., Table 22–1), to keep the background items' standard deviations in mind—for instance, when observing the differences in means between E's and C's on BE and IQ.

(See Appendix 49 for notes 9–18.)

21. Much the same breadth and level was found in connection with power oriented and passive conformist E's and C's.

22. This was done based on the raw background-item data on each individual in the two samples specified shortly.

23. One exception was found: E's continued to have a slightly higher IQ than C's (now 5 points; $p < .05$) for the total group, in the post-discharge sample used in Chapter 8 (Appendix 11, part II).

24. The analyses were carried out on the total group and on conflicted individuals, even though certain conditions widely considered important or even es-

sential with respect to using partial regression approaches—mainly in a parametric context—could not be fully and/or clearly met, and although resulting limitations were recognized. Regarding *power oriented* and *passive conformist* youths, the samples were too small for such an approach, especially given, but even separable from, the number of variables and factors that were present and the overall issue of shrinkage. At any rate, the sample-size problem, by itself, would have precluded a fairly reliable such analysis with respect to these two youth-groups even apart from the "conditions" and related issues alluded to above, such as those which involved the following: (1) intermingling of continuous variables (even if they are, say, analytically dichotomized) with categorical factors (here, the analyzing of BE, age, and IQ in conjunction with race, SES, and offense); and (2) frequent absence of clear homoscedasticity, whether or not largely normal distributions are present. Regarding the *Phase 3 experiment* (Chapter 13), sample-size again posed a problem with respect to partial regression. Here, the numbers were too small in each of the main analytic groups (AGs) that would have to have been compared with each other—particularly the "RC" group in comparison to the "RR," and the "CR" group versus the "CC." (Each such AG contained more than one I-Level as well as youth-grouping—that is, subtype-group, such as the conflicted. Together, the four AGs constituted the total group, that is, the full sample of youths—including all subtype-groupings.) As a result, these analyses were not conducted in connection with the Phase 3 sample. (As seen in Appendix 29, when the just-mentioned analytic groups *were* mutually compared—i.e., RC with RR, and, separately, CR with CC—in the basic study, that is, when they were compared via approaches other than the one presently discussed, they were found to be very similar to each other with respect to the six background items individually, at the total group as well as the conflicted-individuals level. This level of similarity reflected the closely monitored, and peri-

odically readjusted-as-needed, stratified-random procedure that was used throughout Phase 3 to determine RC or RR assignment and that of CR or CC as well. (The "other approaches" involved chi square, and so on.)

25. This number was always assigned to each individual by the Youth Authority's central intake and classification (I & C) office, immediately upon its acceptance of the youth into the Department. During all phases of the experiment, such assignment was always and only made on a continuous, consecutive-numbers, statewide basis onten or more youths being accepted and numbered almost every weekday from throughout California. Numerical assignment was made without I&C's knowing if (and caring if) any given, local individual—for instance, one from Sacramento and environs—would or would not be eligible for the experiment. In addition, it was made without the experiment's researchers having yet been notified, by I&C or any other source, of the youth's "existence." For related details regarding eligibility and intake, see Chapter 2.

26. Eo's constituted 47 percent of the conflicted experimentals, and Ee's were the remaining 53 percent. Co's accounted for 47 percent of the conflicted controls, and Ce's made up the rest.

27. If divided roughly in half, the original, *un*divided power oriented group would have probably split into about 18 or 20 youths each, for the E's and C's alike.

28. Regarding the total group of post-parole [TGPP] experimentals (N = 125), 49 percent were Eo's and 51 percent were Ee's. Of the TGPP controls (N = 109), 48 percent were Co's and the rest were Ce's. With respect to the conflicted post-parole [PP] E's (N = 70), 47 percent were Eo's and the rest were Ee's. Of the conflicted PP C's (N = 38), 45 percent were Co's and 55 percent were Ce's.

29. Regarding the third category, that of violent offenses, each "original, undivided" rate was so low, in the first place (Table 8–2), that it could not change very much. That is, its "odd" and "even" components could mutually diverge to only a very limited degree. This applied to E's (thus, to the Eo's versus

the Ee's) and C's (thus, Co's versus Ce's) alike.

30. For example, reported in Table 8–1, in the case of set 1. (This table also contained rates for set 2.)

31. For instance, diverged with regard to percentage-of-*change in rates,* using the original, "undivided," Chapter 8 rate as their mutual baseline—that is, their common denominator or reference point—from which to compute the respective degrees of change.

32. Within-program comparisons were essential in the Phase 3 experiment (Chapter 13). There, the main ones involved the "RC" versus "RR" groups and the "CR" versus "CC" groups.

33. A similar pattern and parallel would probably have been found for the parole *plus* post-parole periods combined (Table 8–3), had this extended time frame been examined in the present context—that of SS comparisons.

34. Because much smaller samples were involved in the SS analyses than in the OS, some of the "larger" arrest-rate differences that were found as a result of the SS comparisons were not associated with a higher degree of statistical reliability than that which applied to the rate-differences that resulted from the OS—the *full* sample—comparisons. (Involved, here, were SS and OS comparisons for the same *set,* for instance, set 1.)

35. The constituents of this combined, "remaining individuals" category—namely, the power oriented (PO), passive conformist (PC), and rare type (RT) youths, respectively—were distributed more or less equally, within the E and C groups alike. Because relatively few of these individuals—that is, few PO's, PC's, and RT's, still *respectively*—helped comprise the 21 "remaining" E's and the 20 such C's, separate analyses were not carried out on each of these youth-groups.

36. Category 1 and 2 exclusions resulted entirely from the need to maintain room for new cases in the E program (CTP), given that each of its agents had a caseload which was not to exceed 12 youths at a time. To be sure, some leeway existed, and this was often used, in part, to make room for those cases. This leeway mainly centered on the fact that a caseload could, and sometimes did, slightly albeit usually briefly exceed the standard *12* if and when an above average number of its youths were nearing discharge at about the same time and if, in this connection, most of them seemed to usually require relatively little attention. (Compare Chapter 2: notes 3 and 4 , and related text.) Nevertheless, in order to (1) more reliably (predictably) allow for new cases, to (2) do so on a uniform as well as broader and longer-term basis, and to (3) all the while avoid or minimize possible negative effects on existing cases, the following step was taken: Operations staff, in conjunction with the experiment's researchers and with approval from YA central administration plus support from the YA board, decided that the two a priori-defined categories of youth which are specified in the text (see: youth has been "recommitted . . . from an adult court," and so on—that is, categories 1 and 2, respectively) would be excluded from returning to, and from thereby and otherwise continuing in, the E program. This differed, of course, from the later exclusion of these individuals from certain *research analyses,* particularly those involving a parole follow-up of youths who had completed their program in the sense of having been favorably or unfavorably discharged from it.

The category 1 and 2 exclusion policy was to be, and always *was,* applied automatically and across-the-board. More specifically, it was applied (1) to all youths who met either criterion, and (2) absent any prioritization and distinctions among any youths. Thus, for instance, no advantages, disadvantages, separations, or differentiations were involved with respect to I-Level, youth-subtype, age, race, type of offense, and so on, and no decisions as well as allowances were made based on any assessment of, and/or anyone's perception regarding, the individuals' particular circumstances, general level of difficulty, degree of motivation, and presumed chances of eventual success or failure. Though the starting date for implementing this policy was April 1964, very few youths met one criterion or the other, and were therefore "excluded from returning . . . ," prior to October. Only by early 1965 had a handful of E's who had entered the program after March 1964 (this being required, with both criteria) been recommitted by an *adult* court, or been institutionalized.

Given the then-usual rate of initial commitment to the YA from the Sacramento and Stockton-area juvenile courts and given the E program's usual turnover time, this policy or approach, supplemented by the caseload-size leeway, generally sufficed. After 1966, however, it was occasionally further supplemented; this was done via the researchers' direct reduction of *overall intake* to the E program, for preestablished blocks of time. Specifically, throughout each such period, which usually lasted two months, a higher- or much higher-than-usual percentage of cases were channeled into the C program, via a temporary modification of the usual random-drawing ratios. For instance, numbers such as *00 through 29* and *30 through 99* were used for assignment to the E and C programs, respectively, instead of, say, the more commonly used *00 through 49* and *50 through 99*, or, perhaps *00 through 44* and *45 through 99*.

(Two points might be added. (1) Between mid-1967 and the end of 1968, intake to the Sacramento as well as Stockton E and C programs was nearly zeroed-out on several brief occasions. [The modified-ratios approach was used, but this time with very one-sided ratios.] This was done in order to deal with exceptional, not just heavy, workload pressures being experienced by operations staff and, especially, the researchers. This near zeroing-out (NZO) occurred (a) over and beyond the "NIC" [non-interviewed controls] situation and its related ratios-approach, described in Chapter 21, and (b) even though the time-periods involved in the respective situations/approaches necessarily intersected on occasion. [When they did, the NZO prevailed.] During these brief periods—usually about two weeks each—in which intake almost entirely closed, nearly all referrals who were otherwise

eligible for E or C assignment became "non-study" cases and were neither further processed nor subsequently followed. Depending on the outcome of the then-heavily-weighted random drawing, they did not even become controls—including [NIC] "analytic ineligibles" [Chapter 21]. (2) Between January and August of 1969, intake of Phase 2 *E* cases was randomly reduced—again almost zeroed-out. This, however, was done in order to prepare and otherwise reserve or retain caseload openings for Phase 3 youths. This phase was scheduled to begin, and it did begin, that August. Once its operation started, the category 1 and 2 exclusions policy ended, and no comparable one had to be substituted for it.)

The category 1, 2, and 3b exclusions policy never applied to the San Francisco component of the CYA/NIMH experiment (1965–1969). Not only were openings almost always available for eligible new cases, but, instead, there was nearly always a substantial shortage of such individuals (Warren et al., 1966a; Turner et al., 1967; Palmer et al., 1968). (Category 3a was again very rare.)

37. This applied to two experimentals.

38. Neither the 24 individuals nor any returnees had been directly *paroled-out-of-area* upon release from the institution. By definition, direct POA's (D-POA's) were not returned to their program; as will be seen, they were therefore irrelevant to the issue at hand. In the present context, namely, that of reinstitutionalization (REIN) (see text that follows), there were only a handful of post-REIN'd D-POA's (all of whom were C's) in any event, since almost all youths who had become direct parolees at *any* time had done so in connection with their *original* period of institutionalization. (Regarding POA's, see Appendix 39.) Direct POA differs, of course, from "direct parole" (Chapter 2).

39. No E's and C's who have been sent to an institution are "parole *nonoffenders*"; restated, no parole nonoffenders have been sent. At the same time, however, although most E's and C's who

have *not* been sent to an institution *are* nonoffenders, all *others* who have not been sent nevertheless have an offense, and therefore are "parole *offenders*." (Thus, the "not sent" group is a composite.) At any rate, youths who have been *sent* to an institution raise the rate of offending for the overall sample (assuming they are included in the analysis), whereas the composite of those who have *not* been sent (and are included) lower it. That is, the former individuals help bring about a higher overall average; the latter, a lower.

40. "Alternative" cells were adjacent to the "basic" one. The latter was the cell that would involve an exact match, for a given E, on all three specific categories that applied to him—say, (1) the numerically "highest" of the four *BE* categories, (2) the 15–16 year *age* group, and (3) the caucasian *race* category. That is, it would involve such a match if one or more REIN'd C's had those same specific features. For any given E, an alternative cell (AC) was to be used only if a match could not be obtained in connection with the basic one; this situation was not infrequent. (Because each basic cell had more than one AC, the particular AC that would end up being used would be (1) determined within the framework of the already-mentioned priorities [and, when this alone did not suffice, via random drawing], and, of course, (2) contingent upon the *presence* of one or more C-youths within the various ACs.) At any rate, if more than one REIN'd control youth—that is, potential match—was available within a basic or alternative cell (*whichever* AC this turned out to be), the one who would become the E's match was determined via random drawing.

41. As in various Chapter 8 and 9 analyses, the Mann-Whitney "U," corrected for ties, was used to test the significance of E/C differences in rate of offending. In Chapter 13 it was applied to "RC"/"RR" differences, to "CR"/ "CC" differences, and so on.

42. As can be inferred, the following applies. Because all E's (N = 12) who had been recommitted from adult court were excluded from the parole follow-up

sample, all C's (N = 15) who were recommitted from that court had to be excluded from it as well, to help equalize the analysis of that sample with respect to the kinds of youths who would be compared with each other. This was the case even though these excluded E's were not returned to their program, whereas the excluded C's *were*. Together, these E's and C's were the category 1 analytic exclusions. Similarly, because all category 2 E's (N = 24) had to be excluded from that sample, the same type of C's (N = 24) had to be excluded from it, for the same reason that pertained to category 1. This, too, applied even though these E's had not been returned to their program, whereas the C's *were* returned to it. Because the just-mentioned category 1 + 2 E's (N = 36) had not completed the E program— (specifically, they could not do so, that is, could not receive a favorable or unfavorable discharge from it, because they could not *return* to it)—they had to be analytically excluded from the *post-discharge* sample, that is, the *post-program* sample, as well (Table 8–2). As a result, and again in order to equalize the analysis in the sense mentioned above, the category 1 + 2 C's (N = 39) had to be excluded from that sample, as well. Thus, no "supplementary analyses"—SAs—were conducted with respect to the post-discharge follow-up. (SAs were ones which—as in the *parole* follow-up—utilized the analytic exclusions.) On the same grounds, these 36 E's and 39 C's were excluded from the *parole + post-discharge (PPD)* sample (Table 8–3), which, of course, was identical to the post-discharge sample.

Regarding the PPD follow-up, however, an SA *was* conducted, even though its value was recognized as limited. (Before continuing, please note: Because category 1 and 2 E's did not complete their E program in the sense of having been discharged from it, it would not have been appropriate to utilize any *post-discharge* offense information concerning them—and, ipso facto, regarding their C's—in the given parole + post-discharge SA. Nevertheless, a supplementary analysis seemed potentially useful even if it would address only the following question: What difference would it make if the *parole* records of these individuals were counted? More specifically, what difference, if any, would it make if the parole arrest or arrests that occurred during the period which preceded these youths' institutionalization or reinstitutionalization were examined? [For purposes of such an SA, it did not matter if the category 1 and 2 E's and C's in question either had or had not each accumulated at least four years of post-YA risk-time. As it turned out, however, 78 percent of the E's and 87 percent of the C's had done so. This made these E's and C's, collectively, at least fairly representative of the INs (E's) and REINs (C's) who were part of the *basic* sample—all of whom *had* accumulated that amount of time.] Thus, the following:) When the (a) pre*institutional parole performance (i.e., any and all arrests shown on CI&I rap-sheets) of the 36 excluded category 1 + 2 E's, and the (b) pre-*reins*titutionalization parole performance (same measure and source) of the 39 excluded category 1 + 2 C's was counted—that is, when it was added to the parole + post-discharge performance of the 125 E's and 109 C's who constituted the basic PPD sample (Table 8–3)—the following results were obtained: (1) For moderate + severe arrests combined, the monthly rate of offending (r.o.o.) that is shown in Table 8–3 for the *total group* rose 18 percent for E's and 17 percent for C's. For *conflicted youths,* the r.o.o. rose 21 percent for E's and 26 percent for C's. (2) Regarding arrests in connection with *severe* offenses, the increases in r.o.o. over those shown in Table 8–3 were as follows, again when the defined parole arrests of the otherwise—analytically—excluded individuals were included: *total group* – E, 23%, C – 23%; *conflicted youths* – E, 24%, C – 29%. No changes occurred regarding level of statistical significance. Specifically, for the total group the .05 level was maintained in connection with moderate plus severe offenses (combined), and the level for severe offenses (as well as that for the violent) remained nonsignificant. For

conflicted youths, the .01 and .05 levels were maintained for $m + s$ offenses and s (as well as v) offenses alike. Thus, the addition of these individuals—at any rate, the inclusion of their parole performance—made no critical difference, or even a substantial difference, with respect to the question of comparative effectiveness.

43. Thus, for example, when a sample of several hundred Phase 1 and 2, E and C Valley males and females was analyzed, a multiple correlation of .29 was obtained "between age in combination with IQ, on the one hand, and I-Level, on the other" (Palmer et al., 1968, 8). Though statistically significant, this correlation accounted for only 8 percent of the variance. The first—order correlation between each of these background variables and I-Level was .20 and .23, respectively. Males comprised 82 percent of the study-sample, and the analysis was not done separately for males and females.

44. Findings refer to United States samples and to males only, unless otherwise specified.

45. Except as indicated (see, e.g., n. 55), findings regarding interview-based reliability refer to ratings made by two or more raters at about the same point in time.

46. For females, the figures were: 70% – subtype; 85% – level. These and other major reliability findings concerning classification at the Community Treatment Project throughout 1961–1969— (see, e.g., section D, in the text, and n. 55 as well as n. 63)—were also presented to the National Institute of Mental Health. (Palmer, 1973c, p. 21)

47. These figures regarding the Molof report are weighted averages of those from three geographically separated Youth Authority Reception Centers and Clinics: Northern (54% subtype- and 75% level-agreement; N = 300); Southern (77% – subtype; 87% – level; N = 296); Ventura (76% – subtype; 90% – level; N = 49). The figures are percentages-of-agreement among raters (staff) who worked within any one of the three, respective settings, i.e., who worked in the *same* setting as each other. As seen shortly, in the text,

the figures are considerably higher than those of raters who worked in *different* settings from each other. (Males comprised 86%, 100%, and 0% of the NRCC, SRCC, and VRCC samples, respectively—about 25% of the 645 total.) Supplementary information about the NRCC portion of Molof's study appears in Hobbes et al. (1969). These authors reported interrater agreements of 57% for subtype and 74% for level—*within* NRCC, that is.

48. The two remaining studies of delinquent boys that are known from the 1960s reported comparatively high interrater agreement:
    • 79% – subtype; 90% – level (Hunt and McManus, 1968);
    • 75% – subtype; 96% – level (Cross and Tracy, 1969, 1971).

    See Beker and Heyman (1971, 1972) regarding possible reasons for such agreement and for why these averages were substantially higher than those reported (Palmer, 1968c) with respect to the Community Treatment Project's first four years of operation, for males and females (approximately 85% and 15% of the sample) combined. Beker and Heyman's main points are quoted in Palmer (1973c, p. 19).

49. 20% of the sample were females.

50. When 9 categories—choices—are involved (as they were), chance alone would be associated with, or would otherwise account for, an 11% agreement-rate between any two raters, assuming they each make one selection. Thus, 51% subtype-agreement is well beyond chance, not just negligibly so—as it *would* be in a '50/50' coin flip (2 categories). As to I-level, when 4 categories—viz., I_2 through I_5—are involved, chance alone would result in 25% agreement. (Since the I_5 level was quite rare in most studies, one could say, however, that *33%* agreement—i.e., the figure associated with 3 categories—would be a more likely expectation regarding chance alone, in those studies.)

51. Results from these early investigations were presented for *I-level* only, and were discussed by Tolhurst (1966): (1) In a study by Pettit (1961), an "inter-judge agreement of .89" [or, 89%] was ob-

tained. (2) In a small-scale study of juvenile offenders by Sydiaha (1964), an intraclass r of .88 was reported. (3) In Tolhurst's investigation, the intraclass r's were: I_2 – .85; I_3 – .83; I_4 – .75; I_5 – .79. For further details and brief discussion regarding these studies, see Palmer (1973c, pp. 22–25). When the Pettit study began, the Warren (then Grant) *subtypes* did not, of course, yet exist; and, for a few years thereafter, emphasis—in Canada—remained on I-level rather than level *and* subtype. – Reasons for using the intraclass r are discussed by Tolhurst (1966), and quoted in Palmer (1973c, pp. 24–25).

52. These figures are an average of the following sets: *NRCC:* 38% – subtype; 65% – level. *SRCC:* 40% – subtype; 67% – level. (No data were obtained from VRCC in this connection.) Figures for this and the preceding study are also found in Jesness (1974).

53. The identity between these figures and those obtained in Heide's (1982) very different study is, of course, coincidental. – The Jesness results involved "a limited sample of 30 subjects who were interviewed twice (due primarily to clerical error). These interviewers were geographically separated and did not communicate prior to recording their diagnoses [classifications]." (Jesness, 1969, p. 36)

54. As described by the researchers, this analysis involved a more objective method of obtaining a subtype and I-level classification—a quantitative, more explicit, and more standardized one—than did the first analysis. (Jesness and Wedge, 1970; Jesness, 1969, 1974). It also involved an expanded sample (still all males): 1,130 versus the previous 525.

55. Regarding the initial versus the routine followup *interviews* that were conducted at *CTP,* the percentages-of-agreement in the diagnoses that were reached—chiefly *based* on those respective interviews—were 75 and 91 for subtype and level, also respectively, in the case of males. For females, the corresponding figures were 78 and 89. The usual time-interval between interviews was estimated as 8 to 12 months. (Palmer and Werner, 1972a, p. 8)

56. In this study (N = 130), the subtype diagnosis was based on a "more objective approach," as mentioned in n. 11. (Jesness, 1974) Jesness and colleagues called this the "Sequential I-level Classification," as distinct from the original discriminant function approach used during the early part of the Preston study.

57. In a separate study, a sample of *nondelinquent youths* was used, in 1977 and 1978, to help develop and validate the Jesness Inventory Classification System (JICS)—the successor to the *Sequential* I-level Classification. Like Warren's system, the JICS had—and still has—9 subtype categories. (Jesness and Wedge, 1983a, 1983b; Jesness, 1988) These more or less paralleled those of Warren, but they were considered more applicable to nondelinquents than to delinquents, and therein more generalizable. For the JICS validation sample, test/retest agreement, at approximately 1-year followup (7th grade to 8th), was 46% for subtype and 68% for level. It might be added that the percentage-of-agreement between the JICS and its immediate *predecessor,* viz., the Sequential I-level Classification (SIC), was 66 for subtype and 81 for I-level. Agreement between the JICS and the *SICS's* predecessor—viz., the subjective combination of information from the Jesness Inventory plus one or two other sources—was 45% for subtype and 68% for I-level. Finally, agreement between the JICS and the original *construction sample*—viz., CTP youths who were classified by CTP researchers—was 35% for subtype and 67% for level. (Jesness and Wedge, 1984).

58. The first analysis (N = 204) compared classifications obtained by CTP interviews with those from the Jesness Inventory (JI). The second (N = 741) compared classifications obtained via Preston staff's brief albeit routine interview, on the one hand, with those obtained from the JI (involving a pre-Sequential scoring approach), on the other. (The sample in both these analyses consisted of youths who were first-time commitments—also called "admissions"—to the Youth Authority.

The first sample was of CTP youths; the second, of youths at the Preston institution. [In the second analysis, when all 899 of Preston's *recommitments* were added to the 741 consecutive first commitments, the new percentages-of-agreement were 31 for subtype and 59 for level. (Jesness, 1969, p. 58).] The fact that identical percentages were obtained in these two independent analyses was coincidental.) The third analysis (N = 68) compared classifications made by CTP interviewers with those based on the later, more quantified JI technique—the Sequential I-level approach. The fourth (N = 122) compared classifications made by the Center for Training in Differential Treatment interviewers—staff—with those obtained via the sequential approach. Jesness (1974, p. 24), it might be noted, believed these latter studies helped provide concurrent validation of the I-level system.

59. The second of these analyses reported by Molof involved, however, only those persons who had received the CTDT training themselves—i.e., individuals who, in turn, initiated the training of various other classification-team members at any given clinic. Of the individuals who received training at CTDT (the "Center") itself, one person from each clinic (NRCC, SRCC, and VRCC) received 5 weeks of training and specialized orientation; these individuals became the I-level *coordinators* at the given clinic. All other clinic staff who had been trained at the Center received its 3-week course (one that coincided with the third-through-fifth week of the course being received by the coordinators, and which was therein part of the earliest one presented by the Center in its several years of operation). Eventually, the Center came to recommend a minimum of 5 weeks training and an optimum of 9 weeks. (Warren and CTDT Staff, 1972; Warren et al., 1974; Howard, 1974).

60. Most ratings occurred during the 4th-through-7th weeks of the training course. Involved were 39 trainees and 313 ratings, mostly of males.

61. Here, the same 39 individuals each rated four standardized tapes that had been selected by CTDT trainers (staff).

62. In this analysis, N = 1,753. When the sample was later expanded to 2,075, the percentages-of-agreement, i.e., accuracy, were 55 for subtype and 73 for level. (Jesness and Wedge, 1970)

63. These figures were for males (N = 535). For females (N = 119), the level of agreement—again accuracy—was 80 in the case of subtype and 92 for I-level. When this sample was expanded along specified lines (Palmer and Werner, 1972a, p. 12), the figures became 81% and 92% for males (N = 765) and 86% and 94% for females (N = 168).

64. In the main study, most of what had been called "Character disorder, psychopathy" in the pilot was added to the already-existing—and continued— "Manipulative."

65. Van Voorhis' following observations might be noted.

[A. Inspection of various intercorrelations] suggests that the [Situational] construct may not be unidimensional . . . [Instead, there may be] higher- and lower-functioning types. [If there are,] we may describe one as an underachieving, perhaps naive individual who becomes involved in criminal activity during periods of adversity or perhaps through attempts to catch up with a perceived notion of where one should be in life (an I_4 notion). Classifications of this type include Easy, Quay Si, Jesness Se, and I_4Se. the other type might pertain to an individual who is functioning and achieving at a higher, perhaps brighter, level (Item, Jesness Ci, and I_5Se), albeit occasionally in a criminal or unethical fashion (pp. 92–94) (Cf. Palmer [1971d], for various, related distinctions within Warren's original situational-emotional subtype.)

[B.] ". . . immature dependent patterns may be secondary to the neurotic anxiety traits evidenced by the neurotic inmates. [And yet, some] inmates may be diagnosed as immature, inadequate, or dependent *instead of* neurotic . . . [The various] findings suggest that it may not be useful to attempt to isolate an immature type among adult inmates.

Although immaturity may appear in connection with other traits, such as psychological disturbance, high anxiety, and low self-esteem, it is likely to be secondary to those traits. It may make sense to characterize *juveniles* as immature and dependent, and this may be the most salient and observable feature of their personality. Adults, however, may evidence such a personality trait not as a global characteristic but rather as one that is complicated by more important psychological factors (pp. 99–100; emphasis added).

[C. Based on the findings,] we might speculate that manipulative types, like the immature/dependent types, are secondary characteristics to the neurotic acting-out and committed-criminal types. Perhaps the utility of a distinct manipulative type among adult male inmates should be questioned (p. 107).

66. Regarding the differing statistical results that were associated with the penitentiary as compared to the camp, and concerning the fact that, overall, "the findings were more likely to support the hypotheses generated by specific type descriptions in our analysis of the penitentiary data than of the camp data" (1994, 227), Van Voorhis' following comments might be noted:

Clearly, the two institutional environments were very different, housed different types of inmates, and produced dramatically different prison experiences . . . The differences across institutions suggest caution regarding the claims to be made for psychological classification. Type descriptions are likely to vary across settings; the classic type descriptions and predictors are most observable in more traditional, maximum-security settings (p. 227).

67. Regarding studies #1, #2, #3, and #8 in this section, additional details appear in Palmer (1973c, 12–14, 30).

68. In another analysis at these institutions (N = 915 males), a correlation of .52 was obtained between the JI-based I-Level and Loevinger's Ego Level, when

age, IQ, and race were partialled out (Jesness et al., 1972). (Physically and operationally, Holton and Close were distinct institutions within the YA's "Northern Youth Center" facility.)

69. All 40 youths, who were ages 13 through 20 at intake, had been stratified in order to proportionately represent the overall Phase 3 sample's (N = 161) various I-Levels and subtypes, and its lower, middle, and higher age categories as well. Each youth had received, per routine at intake, an interview-based Warren classification and a Palmer developmental-adaptation rating (see Chapter 27) as well. His classification or rating on the Hunt, the Loevinger, the Schroder, and the Van den Daele systems, respectively, was based on a review of several information sets in conjunction with the written accounts, by each author, of his or her developmental system. The information sets, which were complete for all subjects, included not only the Jesness Inventory, the California Psychological Inventory, the Thematic Apperception Test (12 cards), the Bender-Gestalt, and a revised Sentence Completion Test, but each of the following: "I and Me Questionnaire" (regarding ideal self-image versus actual self-image); "Checklist of Ward Characteristics and Behaviors" (which tapped dimensions assessed in other studies, by Palmer as well as Quay); and, "Youngster Behavior Inventory" (Palmer, 1970b, 16–17, 52–66). All other materials—background information, pre Youth Authority assessments, court reports, and CTP initial staff workups—were also reviewed.

70. Earlier, Palmer (1973c) examined the relationship between I-Level and developmental-adaptation with regard to all 161 Phase 3 individuals (males) plus 24 randomly selected Phase 1 and 2 males. The correlations, which all reached p < .01, were as follows: I-level and developmental-adaptation (14 phases, collectively dichotomized): .51; I-Level and developmental-adaptation (5 stages): .60. (Uncorrected figures—.61 and .73, respectively—appeared in Palmer [1973c, 15], as did the Cramer's: .68 and .64.) (94 percent of the Phase 3 sample was under age 20, and 0 percent were over 20.)

71. Since the Schroder (Schroder, Driver, and Seufert, 1967) information processing levels are not always distinguished from Hunt's (1966) conceptual levels and because the two systems have sometimes been referred to interchangeably, the following might be noted. Regarding Schroder's system, the levels—"integration indices"—that were used in the present analysis could have ranged, for any given youth, from that of "fixed rule" to "alternative rule" to "comparison rule" to "causal/relativistic rule." Concerning Hunt's (also known as Hunt and Hardt's), the possible levels for any youth were "self-centered, unorganized," "cultural standards, organized," "learning to distinguish self from general rules," "applying self-anchored dimensions to empathic understanding," and ". . . integration of self and empathy forces . . ."

72. Other correlations were as follows (to facilitate matters, only the author's names will be used): *Hunt* and: Kohlberg (.42); Loevinger (.56); Palmer (.62); Schroder (.54); Van den Daele (.54). *Kohlberg* and: Loevinger (.59); Palmer (.41); Schroder (.46); Van den Daele (.50). *Loevinger* and: Palmer (.51); Schroder (.61); Van den Daele (.63). *Palmer* and: Schroder (.48); Van den Daele (.45). *Schroder* and: *Van den Daele* (.57). All correlations reached the .01 level, and, like those which involved Warren's system, those were based on the individual's primary classification—his best fit—alone.

73. No warren Se's (Situational-Emotional reactions) and Ci's (Cultural Identifiers)—both higher maturity youths—were found among the 24 individuals, whose mean age at intake was 12.0 and at discharge 14.0. Baker Center staff, with whom Makkay was closely associated at the time, classified each youth in terms of her system. Palmer, usually in conjunction with a separate rating by Warren, and otherwise with one by Makkay, subsequently (1967) classified the same individuals with respect to the I-Level system.

74. As seen in Warren's cross-classification chart (1966, 1971), *Makkay's* (1) Primitive Aggressive and (2) Primitive Passive-

Aggressive, respectively, theoretically corresponded to *Warren's* Asocial aggressive and Asocial passive, also in turn; her (3) Organized Passive-Aggressive similarly corresponded to the latter's Conformist, non-delinquently oriented. Makkay's (4) Organized Aggressive corresponded to Warren's Antisocial-manipulator; her (5) Neurotic presumably corresponded to the latter's two Neurotic groups, namely, the Acting-out and Anxious; and, her (6) Subcultural theoretically corresponded most closely to Warren's Subcultural-identifier (Ci). In Palmer's (1973b) cross-classification analysis, these *theoretical* correspondences usually held up. It might be added that Baker Center staff had classified none of the 24 individuals as Makkay Subculturals; and, as indicated in endnote 30, none of these 24 were *later* (that is, in Palmer's analysis) categorized as Warren Ci's, either. Finally, and of course apart from the just-mentioned analysis, Makkay's groups (1) and (2), above, had—in connection with the NIMH conference—been categorized by Rubenfeld (1967) as *Impulse Oriented;* her groups (3) and (4), respectively, corresponded to his (and the conference's) *Power Oriented, conforming* and *Power Oriented, controlling,* also in turn; her group (5) corresponded to the Rubenfeld/conference's *Neurotic;* and, her group (6) corresponded to his/its *Normative Outsider.* At any rate, Makkay's Primitive groups—(1) and (2)—corresponded to Warren's lower maturity ("I_2") youths, her Organized groups—(3) and (4)—corresponded to two of Warren's three middle maturity ("I_3") categories, and her remaining major groupings—(5) and (6)—had close parallels to Warren's higher maturity ("I_4") individuals.

75. The correlations between these types were: 1 and 2: –.22; 1 and 3: –.09; 2 and 3: –.60.

76. Because each study had its own set of interview questions, it was not possible to systematically and specifically compare various youth-behaviors—ones reported by the respective staff's of the three different cottages—*across* the three I-Levels.

77. The Conceptual Level figure (.23) is for the average of the respondents' three highest-scored answers to the CL test's six sentence-stems (hence, "CL 3"). When the average of its *five* highest scores ("CL 5") was used, the figure was .17 (p < .05). The correlation between CL 3 and CL 5 was .81; and, in the pilot study (mentioned next), it was .79.

78. For I-Level and CL 5 (rather than the CL 3 of the .26 figure), the correlation was .20 (p < .10). The correlation between Moral Judgment and *CL 3* was .19 (p < .10); regarding *CL 5* it was not reported, because the p-level exceeded .10. Van Voorhis concluded that "the construct validity of the cognitive-developmental measures is strongly supported [by the pilot. Involved were] Kohlberg's Stages of Moral Judgment, I-Level (interview method), and Conceptual Level" (1994, 88). (As indicated, we use the concept of "concurrence" for this type of validity.)

79. In this setting, the correlation between interview-based I-Level and CL 5 was .22 (p < .01).

80. Correlations between *JI-based* I-Level and CL 3 as well as CL 5 were .23 and .20, respectively, in the penitentiary; they were .19 and .29 in the camp (p < .01, in three of these four instances).

81. Van Voorhis summed up these findings as follows:

All of the cognitive-developmental measures [i.e., the interview-based I-Level, the JI-based I-Level, and the Hunt CL, mutually] converged in both the penitentiary and the prison camp. This finding supports earlier research among probationers diagnosed according to I-level and [Kohlberg's] Moral Judgment (Van Voorhis, 1984), and substantiates the findings from the pilot study for this research (Van Voorhis, 1988). [Unlike the present study, the] earlier research, however, did not examine the construct validity of the Jesness Inventory measure of I-level among adults (1994, 114).

Van Voorhis then added the following (note: the term "developmental measure"—sometimes "cognitive-developmental measure"—refers to the levels or stages that comprise the I-Level and Conceptual Level systems; they, the levels, are distinct from the individual *subtypes or groups*—referred to as "personality measures"—that comprise each of the particular *classifications or types* which, in this study, collectively make up the Quay and MMPI systems, respectively):

The developmental measures converged [with each other] more strongly than the personality measures in both samples [that is, in the penitentiary as well as the prison camp. This is consistent with the fact that,] theoretically, the developmental measures are presumed to be 'universal' rather than specific to offender populations. The personality measures emerged empirically from offender populations, and thus are more likely to be sample-specific . . . The personality-based classification systems [may be] more sensitive to setting than their originators envisioned (p. 118).

82. The three "cognitive-developmental measures"—Jesness I-Level, I-Level (interview), [and] CL—were factor analyzed, separately for the penitentiary and camp samples, in each case separately for CL 3 and CL 5. "As expected, one factor was produced for each data set (penitentiary and prison camp) and each measure [i.e., each developmental system] loaded onto each factor. Communalities and proportion of explained variation were low [ranging from 17 percent to 25 percent], although not surprisingly so, in light of theoretical differences pertinent to the type of cognitive complexity being measured" (1994, 116).

83. Males and females were equally divided within each age level, and these respective levels each constituted one-third of the total sample.

84. The preliminary analysis was followed by a canonical factor analysis that involved 103 individual variables and cluster scores and which yielded 15 factors. Next came an inverse or "Q" factor analysis, one that led to the final typology via a further cluster analysis. For all subsequent analyses, each individual was classified—that is, grouped or typed—according to his highest factor coefficient. Data included: ratings from interviews with the youths; behavior ratings by staff; sociometrics; probation reports; the Jesness Inventory; the Wechsler Intelligence Scale for Children (WISC); the Porteus Maze; and, various projective as well as nonprojective tests, such as the Rorschach, Bender-Gestalt, Draw-A-Person, Franck's Drawing Completion Test, Story Completion Test, Thematic Apperception Test, Semantic Differential, and Spiral Aftereffect Test.

85. This was much longer than that of youths in all other YA institutions at the time (Braithwaite et al., 1963; Davis et al., 1965).

86. In Makkay, all Neurotics were classified as passive-aggressive.

87. Related details are found in Palmer (1973c, 40).

88. Gibbons indicated that his typology "was developed through a process of explication, in which existing descriptions of offender patterns in the criminological literature were examined. An effort was made to uncover, by logical analysis, the underlying dimensions or variables that are implicit in these characterizations. In turn, an attempt was made to identify the basic patterns of delinquent conduct that have been discussed by different investigators" (Gibbons, 1965, 75).

89. Sixty-seven percent of the probation sample were males; mean intake age of the overall sample was 15.6; and, there were no "dependent and neglect" cases, with respect to their penal code descriptions. The cross-classification was carried out in the mid-1960s. See Palmer (1973c, 37) regarding technical details, and for further specifics concerning the main findings.

90. Regarding the eight empirical types, selected intercorrelations are as follows: *Communicative-Alert* and: Independent-Assertive (.33); Dependent-Anxious (.04); Defiant-Indifferent (−.36); Passive-Uncertain (−.44). *Dependent-Anxious* and: Passive-Uncertain (.27); Independent-Assertive (−.07); Defiant-Indifferent (−.17). *Independent-Assertive* and: Passive-Uncertain (−.24); Defiant-

Indifferent (−.03). *Passive-Uncertain* and: Defiant-Indifferent (.34). *Wants To Be Helped and Liked* and: Dependent-Anxious (.55); Communicative-Alert (.50); Impulsive-Anxious (.33); Independent-Assertive (−.10); Passive-Uncertain (−.15); Verbally Hostile-Defensive (−.16); Defiant-Indifferent (−.26). The analysis in which these empirical types were statistically correlated with Warren's subtypes—and that in which various Makkay groupings were themselves cross-tabbed with those subtypes—was first referred to in Palmer and Warren (1967, 56), under the heading "Pilot Efforts at a Cross-Classification of I-Level with Other Typologies."

91. Budnoff (pp. 2–3) indicated that Las Palmas staff observed no Ci's in their population. Separate and apart from that, there probably would have been considerable surprise if an *Se* group emerged from Budnoff's analysis, given the following: Girls

who are ordered placed in Las Palmas tend to be youngsters with unstable personalities characterized by hostile, aggressive, impulsive acting-out behavior . . . Most Las Palmas girls have had multiple contact with the police and juvenile authorities. For many there is a history of previous unsuccessful attempts by the Probation department to supervise them in the community either in their own homes, in foster homes, or in other institutions that [are] open, semi-open, or short-term closed. For all of them it was eventually judged necessary that they be placed under 24-hour supervision in a closed institution [namely, Las Palmas] where limits could be set and they could receive long term treatment.

92. In utilizing the Q-technique, Budnoff, like Butler and Adams (1966, 404), who were to themselves study Las Palmas youths, had accepted Guilford's (1954) following view as correct and relevant: "What the Q technique brings out is personality traits or syndromes. Persons having outstanding *combinations* of traits in common [with each other] will show these as factors in the Q tech-

nique. Only when a syndrome is dominated by a single common factor would a Q-technique factor coincide with an R-technique factor" (529). It would seem, then, that "Q" would be quite appropriate—would operate, at least, in a way that allowed for realistic *mixtures*—if, for instance, the following view on the part of W. Somerset Maugham, the storyteller, was largely true to life, and if the content and range of a test's items could adequately reflect relative complexity.

Selfishness and kindliness, idealism and sensuality, vanity, shyness, disinterestedness, courage, laziness, nervousness, obstinacy, and diffidence, they can all exist in a single person and form a plausible harmony. It has taken a long time to persuade readers of the truth of this . . . I suppose it is a natural prepossession of man-kind to take people as though they were homogeneous. It is evidently less trouble to make up one's mind about a man one way or the other and dismiss suspense with the phrase, he's one of the best or he's a dirty dog. It is disconcerting to find that the saviour of his country may be stingy or that the poet who has opened new horizons to our consciousness may be a snob. Our natural egoism leads us to judge people by their relations to ourselves. We want them to be certain things to us, and for us that is what they are; because the rest of them is no good to us, we ignore it (1951, 46–47).

93. Budnoff's overall conclusion was that "the general hypothesis that the Inventory attitude—types are related to the I-level types [that is, the *subtypes,* as distinct from the levels per se] of Sullivan, Grant, and Grant, or to dimensions underlying these types, has been confirmed" (p. 36).

94. Namely, the Illinois Youth Center at Geneva.

95. Particularly important was information about whether, for instance, the youths lived in certain kinds of physical/social environments: the urban ghetto, urban middle-class, or rural. At any rate, it was the combination of personality con-

figurations (derived from the Quay POS, from the interview, and from the test-battery), on the one hand, and the social-family backgrounds (SFBs), on the other, that gave Ferdinand's respective groups what might be called a distinctive operational reality or identity. Absent the SFB dimension or axis, considerably fewer *patterns* would have emerged, and few if any of the below-mentioned distinctions (see text) would have been made *within* various Warren subtypes. Nevertheless, most or all of the subtypes themselves (specifically, at least six or seven of them) would apparently—or quite likely—still have emerged as such. For related discussion, see Ferdinand (1966).

96. With or without the integral contribution that was made by the just-mentioned social and family background factors in particular, the following applies. Several of Ferdinand's groups may have partly or largely corresponded to what might be called the "variations" that had been regularly observed, and recognized as such, within specified Warren subtypes, beginning in the mid-to-later 1960s, within the California experiment's sample. (For one thing, sample-sizes had by then grown large enough for the variations to become evident as such, especially via their frequent occurrence.) Several of these substantive distinctions—often called "subgroupings"—within Warren's original nine-category level-two-through-four typology—were delineated, described, or, in some cases, only listed, by Palmer (1971b, 1971c, 1971d, 1971e).

97. Ferdinand referred to the Se's as "stress reactions" and, separately, as "adjustment reactions" (and felt they should be distinguished from the Normal). These were the two broad categories and terms—called "subgroupings"—that Palmer (1971d) had distinguished within Warren's overall Se category, and which he then named Stress and Adjustment (Sa) Reactions.

98. The authors believed, without qualification, that "the three offender groups [they had observed] can be integrated into these six broad types quite easily" (p. 51). They also believed there were

strong resemblances to the typology developed by Jenkins and Hewitt (1944)—one later supported by Lewis' research in England (1954)—and to that described by Quay and others in connection with juveniles and adults alike (Quay, 1964; Quay and Parsons, 1971).

99. In order to "determine what factors are associated with different kinds of violence prior to imprisonment, . . . information [was collected regarding] early childhood experiences on life history questionnaires, . . . current feelings of aggression—hostility on the Buss-Durkee Inventory, . . . feelings of isolation on an anomie scale, as well as demographic and criminal history data from the inmate's cumulative case summary. On the basis of offense history, subjects [were] classified as non-violent or violent offenders, and violent offenders [were] further classified as to type of violence on the Conrad Aggressive History Profile . . . [Groups were] compared on 30 variables relating to criminal offense careers, occupational-educational achievements, and background characteristics" (Conrad, 1965, 24).

100. Females accounted for 2 percent of all such offenses.

101. Pathological violence was rare in the CTP sample, as was the Situational.

102. To facilitate the presentation, the term and concept of "correlation" will sometimes be used, even though Miller performed analyses of variance—and focused on F-tests as such—in connection with her main hypotheses. She did so—appropriately—because the conformance of "some scores . . . to parametric assumptions [was] questionable" (1972, 48). The symbol "r" will sometimes be used to mean "correlation".

103. This analysis was conducted in light of the strong relationship she had obtained between I-Level and IQ (correlations were .58 and .53, for the verbal and nonverbal aspects, respectively) and because of statistically significant as well as substantial relationships she had observed in the literature (Beverly, 1965; Cross and Tracy, 1971; Molof and Jesness, 1973; Werner, 1972; Zaidel, 1970). (When age, sex, and ethnicity

were partialled out, the just-mentioned relationships remained significant at p < .01. [The correlations were .45 and .41, respectively.]) Two-tailed tests appeared to be used in connection with all main hypotheses, including those involving locus of control and internalization of guilt. This applied whether or not any variables and factors had been partialled out. Operationally, *cognitive complexity (CC)* was literally identical to Hunt's *conceptual level (CL):* As with CL, Miller's CC was determined via the same Paragraph Completion Method that Hunt used to determine CL. It was based on an average of the three highest-scored responses to Hunt's six topic stems ("When someone disagrees with me . . ." "When I am unsure . . ." and so on.) (Miller, 1972, 41–42)

104. Almost identical results were obtained when cognitive complexity was partialled out by itself.

105. The correlations between verbal IQ (WISC, as usual), on the one hand, and cognitive complexity, impulse control, foresight, locus of control, and internalization of guilt, on the other, were .57, –.23, .18, –.15, and .05, respectively. The first three reached p < .05 or beyond; the fourth, p < .10 (two-tailed tests).

106. Three points might be noted. (1) This I_5 percentage was by far the highest obtained as of that time, in I-Level research with juveniles. Previous figures seldom exceeded 2 or 3 percent. (2) Mean age at intake was about 17.1, and 82 percent of the total sample was 16 and up. This above average age likely contributed a modest—but only modest—amount to the above average percentage of I_5's, judging mainly from the fact that the correlation between age and I-Level turned out to be no more than .23. (3) The racial breakdown was: white – 50 percent; Black – 34 percent; Mexican-American (hispanic) – 15 percent; all others – 1 percent.

107. Everyone age 16 and up also received the Revised Beta Examination.

108. The following should be noted regarding Task B. This measure "consisted of twenty-five pictures of people who differed in affect state and a number of ex-ternal characteristics. In the *neutral condition* of administration, *Ss* were simply asked to write good descriptions of the main person in each picture. In the *affect attention condition, Ss* were asked to include the person's feelings or mood in their description" (1970, xi).

109. Ones she summarized as collectively involving "a moderately high positive relationship between I-level and intelligence" (1970, 94). Zaidel also indicated that, "Overall, the partial analyses of variance suggest[ed] that the relationship between I-level and intelligence was independent of race" (1970, 45).

110. At the same time, however, "Affect attention was higher when instructions (see endnote 65] and a previous task made affect salient, and I-level groups did not differ in affect attention under the latter conditions" (1973, 54).

111. Elsewhere, Zaidel stated this last point as follows. ". . . the I-5 group showed superior decoding ability beyond that accounted for by verbal intelligence" (1970, 66). The present, Task C tests were conducted after—and partly because—"covariance analysis with the SRA verbal scores" had reduced the previously significant (p < .01) results for I-level as a whole—namely, that "higher I-level groups show[ed] greater ability to judge affect communications"—"to borderline significance" (p < .10) (1973, 54). Zaidel summarized her Task A through C, affect awareness findings as follows. As predicted, and in the directions expected from theory, "I-level groups differed in size of their vocabulary for describing other people (particularly in number of internal constructs), in their natural set to attend to affect cues, and in their ability to judge affect from facial expression. [That is,] increasing[ly higher] I-level was associated with larger vocabulary, greater attention to affect, and better ability to judge nonverbal affect communications" (1973, 58). ("Natural set" referred to responsiveness under neutral conditions.)

112. Average age = 16.9. For age-ranges 13–15, 16–17, and 18–19, the youth representation was 15 percent, 42 percent, and 42 percent, respectively.

113. As is reflected in these several averages, the number of specific-dimensions that received a rating of Primitive plus those which received a rating of Sophisticated totals less than 21. This is because—with regard to most individuals' drawings—some specific dimensions (1) could not be rated as clearly P or as clearly S, or, for whatever reason, they (2) could not be applied to the particular drawing; they were then left unrated in those instances. All this applied to I_3's and I_4's alike. This 'less-than-21' situation is independent of the fact that, for one or both of their drawings, 38 percent of all individuals received ratings of *Sophisticated* on *some* specific dimensions (more precisely, on one or more) *and* ratings of *Primitive* on *other* such dimensions (again, one or more)—with respect to any one of their drawings, or regarding both of them.

114. Whitesel (1972, 12) reported that a study by McLachlan (1972), which used a modified ABC scale and a Human Figure Drawing test with 87 male and female alcoholic patients in Canada, had obtained a positive correlation (r = .38; p < .01) between Hunt's Conceptual Levels and increased sophistication of body image.

115. All the preceding percentages and averages were recently derived, by the present author, from the raw data presented in Whitesel's study (1972, 42, 48, 57–58, and 67–68). That aside, it was from visual inspection/analysis of her raw data that Whitesel had formed her judgments concerning trends. At any rate, based on all her observations, Whitesel concluded: "(1) A greater incidence of specific graphic features of primitivity was identified in the drawings of youths diagnosed at the lowest level of social maturity [in this study, I_3]; (2) specific graphic features reflecting sophistication became increasingly apparent in the drawings of youths diagnosed at higher levels [i.e., the I_4 level—there being no I_5's] of social maturity" (1972, 77; Palmer, 1973c, 10).

116. The main focus of Whitesel's study was not on construct validity, but on whether human figure drawings by juvenile offenders could help determine (di-agnose) these individuals' level of social maturity—here, their I-Level. From her study, she concluded that professional staff who were knowledgeable and experienced regarding social-developmental theory and its application to young offenders *could* successfully determine if drawings by such individuals—in this case, the present 26 youths—reflected a comparatively low or a comparatively high level of maturity. (All drawings had been rated—sorted—under instructions to determine whether they were "representative of low social maturity . . . [or else] high social maturity.") The correlations she obtained between an unweighted composite of the respective staff's ratings, on the one hand, and the youths' previously determined (but unknown-to-the-raters) diagnosis were: Pearson r = .62; tau = .50; with IQ partialled out they were: r = .56; tau = .47; p < .01 for the first three correlations, and < .05 for the fourth; all two-tailed. In short, staff matched the youths' drawings with those youths' earlier determined I-Level diagnoses to an extent that definitely exceeded chance. The three raters were senior staff of the Center for Training in Differential Treatment, and their level of inter-rater agreement, that is, reliability, with respect to the drawings, was itself significant beyond chance (intraclass r = .65; p < .01).

117. The I-Level breakdown was: I_2 – 20 percent; I_3 – 39 percent; I_4 – 41 percent. The racial composition was: white – 48 percent; Black – 29 percent; Mexican-American – 18 percent; all others – 5 percent. Statistical significance was obtained on the Stein, Sarbin, and Kulik Future Events Test (FET), but not on the Wallace FET and the Ross Time Reference Inventory.

118. To reduce or forestall possible reader-confusion the following night be noted. This 1971 work—whose title, "Personality Factors in Delinquent Boys: Differences Between Blacks and Whites," focuses on *ethnicity*—involves the identical study and analysis that was reported by the same authors, in 1969, under a title—"A Study of Delinquent Boys in Connecticut: Application of the

Interpersonal Level Classification System and Its Relationship to Guilt"—which centered on the Warren's system and *guilt*. The same basic study was presented by Tracy (as his thesis), also in 1969, under a title that focused on *locus of control* (and future time perspective), not on ethnicity and/or guilt. In sum, the titles of these three works/documents collectively spotlighted differing aspects of what was one and the same study, sample (N = 119), and analysis.

119. The specific correlation for *I-Level* were .32, .31, .31, and .24, in the case of IQ, age, socioeconomic status, and locus of control, respectively (Tracy, 1969, as reported in Beker and Heyman, 1971, 29–30). With regard to *subtype* they were .36, .32, .33, and .32 (Cross and Tracy, 1969, 19). In connection with *level*, future item perspective attained p = .07 (Cross and Tracy, 1969, 14), but with subtype it was more than .90—virtually flat-out chance.

120. Because these particular analyses have major shortcomings, the authors' findings and conclusions with respect to them neither add to nor subtract from the present review of construct validity. Nevertheless, they should be discussed. This is not just because they (1) became widely known and somewhat influential in the 1970s and beyond, but especially due to their (2) then-purported implications regarding I-Level's construct validity and generality, given that the analyses in question were assumed to be adequately grounded, scientifically and of course logically. Specifics now follow.

Concerning the relationship between level of maturity, on the one hand, and *locus of control, future time perspective (FTP),* and *felt/perceived guilt,* on the other, Cross and Tracy's statistical comparisons between Blacks and whites (28 percent and 72 percent of the 119-boy sample, respectively) were, in the view of this author as well as that of Werner (1972, 1975), hardly appropriate, and certainly not sound. This was not only because there were literally no more than *two* I_4 Blacks (this being 6 percent of all the Black youths [N = 33] in the entire sample that was statistically analyzed, but because this

number, and the percentage of the total sample's Black youths that it comprised, sharply contrasted with that of I_4 whites (namely, *35* individuals—this being *41* percent of the overall white sample that was analyzed. Thus, when (1) Blacks were compared with Blacks in connection with the statistical relationship between increasingly higher maturity levels, on the one hand, and FTP as well as felt and/or perceived guilt, on the other, I_2's (these [N = 8] being 24% of the overall Black sample [33 youths]) were being compared essentially with I_3's (these [N = 23] being *70* percent of the overall Black sample, and hardly at all with I_4's [N = 2; 6 percent of that sample.])

In short, (1) neither the I_2 Blacks nor the I_3 Blacks—nor both of them combined—were being compared with youths (namely, I_4s) who, in all the writings on I-Level, had been, and still are, considered the only "mature" ones, within the delinquent range from I_2 to I_4. However, in the case of (2) *whites,* that is, when these youths were compared with other whites, Cross and Tracy's analyses could and did meaningfully involve the youths (namely, I_4's) who had been considered "mature." This was because, as indicated, these individuals—35 in all—comprised *41* percent of the overall sample of whites (N = 86). (I_2's and I_3's accounted for the remaining 9 percent and 50 percent of whites.) (3) Obviously, too, statistical tests that compared any 35 individuals (here, the I_4 whites) with any 2 individuals (here, the I_4 Blacks) have essentially no statistical reliability and scientific weight. (This would also apply if the 35 were, instead, 2, 5, 135, 350, or any number whatsoever.) Yet, Black versus white findings such as the following *were* reported, and they became central to extensive interpretation and basic conclusions regarding differences between Blacks and whites: ". . . as Blacks become more mature, they become more external and [they believe they are] more fate-controlled while the reverse is true for whites" (Cross and Tracy, 1971, 20). But, as is evident from the above, "more mature" was not used, in its usual, specific sense, one that focused on the I_4 level as compared to the I_2 *plus* I_3. In fact, it was used in two differing senses within the same analysis: Operationally (hence, analytically) it essentially referred to movement from I_2 to I_3 (since there were only two I_4's) in the case of Blacks, and—again operationally—to movement from I_2 to I_3 to I_4 in the case of *whites*. In short, in this and other separate analyses (including Cross and Tracy's comparisons of Blacks with Blacks), "more mature" referred—to all intents and purposes (that is, by virtue of an operational ratio of 23 to 2)—to I_3's rather than I_2s, the former indeed being more mature than the latter. In the case of whites it referred—and (as was the standard and sole practice in the literature) it was *intended* to refer—to I_4's, as compared to the numerically lower levels.

Given the above, it is no surprise that Cross and Tracy's "more mature" Blacks—being, in fact, almost entirely I_3's—seemed "external" (since this is how I_3's had always been described, in the literature: externally oriented, and far more so than the often self-absorbed I_2's in any event), and that their "more mature" whites seemed the opposite (most particularly, the I_4's were more internally oriented that I_3's—the externally oriented individuals). Cross and Tracy's results on future time perspective are explainable on exactly the same grounds.

In order for the Black versus white comparisons on *locus of control* (1971, 20) to be logically parallel, that is, to be on equal terms and, in that respect, scientifically appropriate, Cross and Tracy would have had to compare the white I_2's with the white I_3's (adding in a 6 percent group comprised of I_4's)—just as they had done when they compared Blacks with each other, that is, when they had examined the difference, on locus of control, between the Black I_2's and the Black I_3's (plus the 6 percent who were I_4's). Because they did not do this, what they referred to as "increased maturity" and as "more cognitively differentiated" signified one thing in the case of Blacks and something essentially different with regard to whites. Among the former individuals, it meant—in operational fact—being I_3 rather than I_2; among the latter, it meant being I_4 rather than I_2 and, especially, I_3. Thus, "mature" Blacks—I_3's in this Cross/Tracy analysis—were *externally* oriented, while "mature" whites—I_4's in the analysis—were *internally* oriented. Both these findings were consistent with and supportive of I-level theory (Sullivan, Grant, and Grant, 1957) and its related literature.

In connection with *future time perspective* and with felt/perceived *guilt* (1971, 20–21), Cross and Tracy had to compare Black I_2's and I_3's with Black I_4's—just as they had done with whites. However, since the entire study sample (N = 119) contained only 2 Black I_4's, the authors still could not meaningfully make this comparison. As a result, what they essentially ended up with was, as before, a comparison between I_2's and I_3's in the case of Blacks and between I_2's plus I_3's and I_4's, among whites. However, they again interpreted their findings as though these comparisons were parallel and equivalent, when, in fact, "maturity" (as well as "more mature") had—as before—different operational meanings across the Black and white groups.

Werner (1972, 7–8) described this general situation as follows:

[Cross and Tracy] conclude that as Blacks become more mature, they (1) become more externally and fate-oriented with regard to locus of control (while just the opposite is true for Whites) and (2) are increasingly characterized by a shorter time perspective and a lesser tendency to view delay of gratification as instrumental to goal attainment (while this is not the case for Whites). Before accepting these conclusions, it should be noted that the sample used by Cross and Tracy contained but two Black I_4's. As a result, their conclusions regarding Blacks really apply to differences between I_2's and I_3's. Yet neither in the original statements of I-level theory nor in subsequent research efforts have persons at the I_3 level been considered to be "mature."

The "Immature Conformist" subtype belongs, for example, within the I_3 level. Moreover, comparisons between mature Blacks and mature Whites are really impossible as a result of the virtual absence of any Black I_4 subsample. [Werner referred to the N of 2 in his 1975 article (p. 66) as well.]

Because this virtual absence of any I_4's within the sample of Blacks was never indicated in Cross and Tracy's journal article (1971), readers, at the time, had no reason to question the Black/white findings, interpretations, and related conclusions, and no grounds for exploring possible alternative explanations on their own. (The numbers in question appeared in Table 5 [p. 17] of Cross and Tracy's 1969, final report on the study.) The authors' only reference to this virtual absence was oblique, was non-specific as to the actual number, the I-Level, and the ethnicity, was characterized as a technical/statistical matter only, and gave no indication that this N-of-2 problem had broad and major implications for the interpretation of findings, even though the authors called their "race by maturity" analyses "supplementary only": ". . . a small number of subjects in one of the six cells precludes meeting the assumption of homogeneity of variance" (1971, 16).

Werner continued:

It should also be pointed out that in their application of multiple regression procedures to predict diagnostic *subtype* on the basis of personality and other measures, Cross and Tracy assume maturity differences among these I-level subtypes (e.g., Cfm vs. Cfc [within the I_3 level]). [Werner's reference is to the fact that Cross and Tracy (1971, 19) had indicated the following. In "the ordered multiple stepwise correlation coefficients predicting to all subcategories [not only for all subjects combined but also according to race,] . . . an assumption of linearity was made for the subcategores [i.e., subtypes] (Aa = 2.0, Ap = 2.3, Cfm = 3.0, Cfc = 3.3, Mp = 3.7, . . . Se = 4.7). This analysis was in some ways a more stringent test than the analysis of vari-

ance because the prediction here is to seven subcategories rather than to only three major I-levels." Again Werner:] No such assumptions have ever been part of I-level theory. [See, "Theory aside," below.]

The linearity issue aside, the following would remain the case. Upon observing the very high multiple R of .86—the number that was obtained for Cross and Tracy's sample of fewer than 35 Black youths—researchers would ordinarily be alerted to the issue of shrinkage. However, Cross and Tracy missed or ignored this point. As indicated by Werner (1972, 8), "no consideration is [was] given to the issue of shrinkage of the ethnic sample multiple *R's* resulting from the stepwise procedure [that they employed] . . . Such reduction is almost inevitable as a result of the application of this least squares method to small samples . . ."

It might be added that the "N of 2 issue" was entirely missed by Beker and Heyman (1971, 29–30; 1972, 28–29) as well—authors who drew from Cross and Tracy's 1969 report and from Tracy's 1969 thesis. In this connection they fully accepted Cross and Tracy's (1969) findings and interpretations regarding differences between more mature and less mature Blacks, between mature Blacks versus mature whites, and so on.

Theory aside, Warren's Mp's were found to be less advanced than Cfc's when Palmer applied his developmental—adaptation framework (see Chapter 27 of this book) to 185 Community Treatment Project youths (1973c, I–L). The mean D-A "phase" scores for the I_3 subtypes were: Cfm – 5.9, Mp – 6.2, and Cfc – 7.1. This sequence differed from that which was assumed to apply in Cross and Tracy's stepwise multiple regression. (Other scores obtained in connection with CTP were: Ap – 3.3, Na – 8.7, Nx – 9.9, Ci – 10.9, and Se – 11.2. No Aa cases existed among CTP experimentals.) These numbers refer to phases—analytically describable as points—along a 14-phase D-A sequence. Phase 5 is less advanced than 6, and 6 is less advanced than 7. (The Cross/Tracy numbers refer to a different type of scale.) These CTP-experiment findings—which were from the only such quantitative analysis that was done—did not exist in 1968–1969, when Tracy (or Cross and Tracy) was preparing his (or their) analysis.

Besides the Mp/Cfc difference between Palmer's developmental-adaptation data and Cross/Tracy's postulated sequence, Loevinger believed that her "Delta Level, Opportunistic—Self-Protective" category—individuals who seemed very similar to Warren's Mp's—were at a lower developmental level than her "Level 3: Conformist"—individuals who were quite similar to Warren's Immature Conformist (Cfm). This, too, constituted a reversal from the above-presented I_3 sequence. Regarding these Ego Levels, see Loevinger (1966; 1976, 17, 24) and Jesness (1974, 29). (Loevinger indicated that the Opportunistic Stage has the following features: "Rules . . . are obeyed in terms of [their] immediate advantage . . . the morality is purely an expedient one. What is bad is to be caught. Interpersonal relations are manipulative and exploitive . . . Conscious preoccupation is with control and advantage, domination, deception, getting the better of, and so on. Life is a zero-sum game; what you win, I lose" (1966, 199) Elsewhere, Loevinger called this the "Self-Protective State (Delta Δ)" (1976, 17, 24).)

121. According to Jesness (1974), it was EFT's fairly high correlation (.54) with IQ—particularly verbal IQ (cf. Molof and Jesness, 1973)—that lowered the original correlation "so markedly." Molof and Jesness, reporting a partial correlation of .13 (p = .08), concluded that they had found "little evidence . . . that the I-level concept adds more information to the idea of psychological differentiation and cognitive organization than [is] supplied by the concept of intelligence" (p. 22). (The mean, unadjusted EFT scores were 117, 81, and 68 for the I_2, I_3, and I_4 levels, respectively. When the contributions of age, race, and IQ were removed, the scores in question were 99, 78, 76.) That conclusion centered on I-Level per se and involved EFT in particular; no separate findings were presented for *subtype* as such. Elsewhere, based on a wide range of other (non-EFT) data on institutionalized delinquent males, Jesness and Wedge (1983, 53; 1984, 1007–1008) concluded that subtype added considerable information—did account for substantial variance—on its own. (Here, no separate findings were reported for *I-Level* per se.) Similar results were obtained with nondelinquents as well (Jesness, 1988, 85–86; Jesness and Wedge, 1983a, 80).

122. The racial breakdown was: white – 47 percent; Black – 29 percent; Mexican-American – 22 percent; all others – 2 percent.

123. Results also suggested that, on average, I_4 NonNeurotics were slightly more mature—with respect to CPI dimensions—than were I_4 Neurotics (1972, 45; 1975, 65).

124. Via successively refined cluster analyses of the CPI's 18 scales, Werner first derived three broad clusters: I – *Adult-Role Socialization (ARS)*; II – *Ascendant-Extroversion (AE)*; III – *Personal Maturity (PM)*. These clusters, as it turned out, were similar to ones that previous investigators had derived—ones whose respective constituents, namely, particular CPI scales (especially in the aggregate), they considered reflective of psychological and/or social maturity (Werner, 1972). Thus, for instance:

Cluster I is clearly a very general factor, having correlations above .63 with the following 10 CPI scales: Well-Being, Responsibility, Socialization, Self-Control, Tolerance, Good Impression, Achievement via Conformity, Achievement via Independence, Intellectual Efficiency, and Capacity for Status. Considered collectively, these scales appear to represent certain normative products of middle-class socialization experiences through which persons are supposed to acquire personal characteristics deemed necessary for adjustment to adult society. These characteristics include social skills, tolerance, acceptable ambitions, methods of self-regulation and cooperation, and internal standards for self-direction and evaluation. As a result, Cluster I was given the label *Adult-Role Socialization (ARS)* ... This cluster is virtually identical to the first factor extracted by Nichols and Schnell [1963] in their analysis of scale intercorrelations presented in the CPI manual. On the basis of their study of both item content and factor score correlates, they conclude that the dimension represents a general psychological maturity as indicated by a concern for values and conformity to conventional standards. The cluster is also nearly identical to the first factor defined by Mitchell and Pierce-Jones [1960] and seems to represent a combination of Gough's second and third scale classes: measures of socialization, maturity, responsibility, and intrapersonal structuring of values; and measures of achievement potential and intellectual efficiency.

Cluster II had its highest correlations with Sociability, Dominance, Capacity for Status, Self-Acceptance, Social Presence, and Intellectual efficiency, suggesting that it be named social ascendancy or *Ascendant Extroversion (AE)* ... [This] dimension seems appropriate in making distinctions among persons in terms of such qualities as leadership potential, persistence, interpersonal sensitivity, versatility, competitiveness, independence, social interest, and poise. From their analysis, Nichols and Schnell ... describe [this cluster's] item content in terms of five areas: comfortableness with others, joy in interpersonal interactions, dominance and leadership, absence of fear and embarrassment, and quickness of response.

Cluster III ... appear[s] to emphasize the qualities of intellectuality, autonomy, confidence, self-differentiation, assertiveness, breadth of interest, and insightfulness. The cluster was accordingly named *Personal Maturity (PM)*. It seems quite similar to Mitchell and Pierce-Jones' fourth factor, which they name Capacity for Independent Thought and Action (19, 21–22).

(The correlation between I and II was .49; between I and III, .70; and between II and III, .34.)

Using each youth's composite score on each of these three clusters ("variable clusters"), Werner next statistically developed six "person clusters [that reflected] similarities and differences among score patterns over the ARS, AE, and PM variable clusters." (These six were derived from 11 that had first emerged, from the given score patterns.) The characteristics that defined person cluster #1 were those—especially collectively—associated with a lesser degree of social/psychological maturity than those of #2; #2's, in turn, involved a lesser degree that #3; and so on through #6. Thus, for example, #1.

is a [statistically] very depressed profile indicative of significant difficulties in interpersonal and social adjustment. Persons in this cluster are particularly weak with respect to Adult-Role Socialization, underscoring their social immaturity, poorly developed value system, lack of interest in achievement, low level of responsibility, and impulsivity. Their below-average status on Personal Maturity suggests a lack of independence and ability to adjust to complexity and change in their lives. The low Ascendant Extroversion dimension illustrates a lack of social interests, skills, and interpersonal sensitivity. Persons of this type are probably nonparticipative and deficient in ability to express themselves acceptably or persuasively in social contexts ...

[Regarding cluster #2,] this profile has no strong or high points although it is not so depressed as is the Type I pattern ... [Its] standing on the Ascendant extroversion scale ... suggests a particularly withdrawn style of social response, a low sense of personal and social worth, ... and an absence of social sensitivity and poise ... [Cluster #5] is characterized by marked elevation of the Ascendant Extroversion dimension ... Adult-Role Socialization, and Personal Maturity, however, are only somewhat above average ... [Relative to all other

Types, the #6] profile is very much elevated across all three dimensions . . . This type represents substantial and balanced strength in all three areas—internalized values of responsibility, self-regulation, achievement, and independence; interpersonal interest, skill, and sensitivity; and personal development in terms of autonomy, breadth of interest, open-mindedness, and flexibility (Werner, 1972, 27–30).

The central point is that the lower-numbered person-clusters were, empirically, more likely to be associated with Warren's lower and middle maturity levels ($I_2 + I_3$) than with her higher (I_4) level; and, the higher-numbered clusters were more often associated with her higher level of maturity. (Though the overall correlation in question was statistically very significant, it was not at all high, in absolute terms. (It would have been considerably stronger if Type I, which contained a great many I_4 Neurotics, were eliminated.) Nevertheless, it supported the expected relationship; it expanded the nomological network regarding I-Level's developmental component; and, it therein added to construct validity. (The Werner study is also—but very briefly—summarized in Harris, 1983.)

125. Subsequently, "an ethnic group (White vs. non-White) by I-level (I_2 vs. I_3 vs. I_4 Neurotic vs. I_4 NonNeurotic) analysis of variance was carried out on [the] same data. Considering all Jesness scales, there was not a single instance of significant interaction between the two factors [namely, race and I-Level]. Thus, this study indicated that the Jesness scale correlates of I-level do not differ by racial or ethnic group, as indeed they should not if the construct is to have broad applicability and relatively parsimonious interpretation" (Werner, 1972, 6–7). That aspect of the study aside, the overall statistical analysis suggested that—as was soon found in Werner's California Psychological Inventory study—I_4 NonNeurotics are, on average, a little more mature than I_4 Neurotics. (This time, of course, maturity centered on dimensions reflected in the

Jesness Inventory.) This, as Werner also indicated, was despite the fact that "I-level theory [Sullivan, Grant, and Grant, 1957] implies no difference in maturity between I_4 nonneurotics and I_4 neurotics" (Werner, 1972, 5). (Warren et als.' [1966b] classification manual *does,* however, strongly imply at least a functional difference in this regard, and perhaps an underlying, intrapsychic one as well. Essentially the same implications also existed in Grant [Warren], 1961c.)

126. The mean, unadjusted external scores were 11.1, 9.1, and 7.3, for the I_2, I_3, and I_4 levels, respectively. When the effects of age, race, and IQ were statistically removed, the scores were 10.3, 9.8, and 7.7. Analysis of covariance indicated that these overall differences in means remained statistically significant ($p < .01$)—still in the predicted direction—following this adjustment.

127. The racial breakdown was: white – 40 percent; Black – 41 percent; Mexican-American – 13 percent; all others – 7 percent.

128. The results regarding Neuroticism were expected not just based on I-Level theory, but because of what had been learned from experience, at least in the United States, about incarcerated male delinquents who were classified as *Neurotic,* in particular (Jesness, 1969, 1971; Jesness et al., 1972; Warren et al., 1966b).

129. Smith (p. 382) suggests that if sizable differences exist among delinquents on one or both of these dimensions, say, on sociability, they do so (largely or entirely) *within,* not across, the respective I-Levels, such as the I_3.

130. As in Van Voorhis' pilot study (1988), all individuals were new admissions, on their first institutional placement. Within the penitentiary (in the main—the *present—* study), the average age was 33 and the median 32; 37 percent of the inmates were ages 19–29, 56 were 30–45, and 7 percent were 46 and up. Thus, at least half were 15 or more years older than the average *juvenile* who had been studied in various correctional research projects, and about one-third were some 20 years older. (In the camp, the average age was 37 and the median 36; the percentage of

individuals in the above age categories was 25, 53, and 22, respectively.) Still in the penitentiary, 50 percent were white, 41 percent Black, 5 percent Hispanic, and 4 percent all others—figures that practically duplicated those in the pilot. (Figures for camp were 80 percent, 16 percent, 3 percent, and 2 percent.)

131. Thus, for example, "if we examine only the official and staff data we observe that the inmates classified in the lower I-level categories tend to be difficult, especially in tests [i.e., on measures] relevant to relationships with others" (p. 169). However, "inmates diagnosed at higher developmental levels appeared to do poorly on self-report measures" (p. 168). Regarding this last, that is, this countersupportive, finding, Van Voorhis speculated that self-report data which involve the present content in particular may reflect something other than or in addition to the individuals' *behavior*. Specifically, those data "may be highly sensitive to idiosyncratic perceptions of what [it is that] constitutes behavior that crosses over the line to qualify as threatening, aggressive, or in violation of the institutional policies. Such perceptions in themselves may vary according to personal and emotional states, and by cognitive complexity" (p. 169). In effect, they may vary—with respect to the Warren system—by I-Level and subtype.

132. For instance, based on self-reports, "significantly more I_4 inmates had high fear scores . . . and high CESD stress scores . . . than the inmates diagnosed as I_5" (1994, 198). CESD = Center for Epidemiological Studies Depression Scale.

133. For example, with regard to staff ratings, "I_5 inmates [especially Se's] generally received higher ratings than I_4 inmates [on initiative and learning ability. In addition, and still regarding the penitentiary setting,] . . . I_4 inmates were more likely to receive lower [staff] ratings on their emotional control, . . . initiative, and learning ability [than were I_5's]. These findings are similar to those observed for inmates classified at lower stages on other developmental measures, [namely,] on Conceptual Level, and on the Jesness Inventory I-Level measures" (1994, 205).

134. Van Voorhis, suggests that, in retrospect, some individuals who were categorized as I_4 by the interview method might best have been viewed as I_3's—that, at any rate, there would have been grounds, including experimental precedents, for doing so. Compared to the pilot study, where 2 percent of the sample was categorized, via the interview method, as I_2's and an additional 8 percent as I_3's (Van Voorhis, 1988), "less conservative criteria [were used in the main study, that is, the present one] for classifying an inmate I_4 rather than I_3"; and, this fact, "may explain why we have inflated our [Warren] level diagnoses over what we would have observed using the latter [the more conservative] criteria" (1994, 100, 336). In any event, the interview-based I_4's, who collectively comprised the developmentally lower 59 percent of the total sample in the main study, were, analytically, almost equivalent to the *Jesness Inventory-based I_2's plus I_3's* in that regard; at least, the latter—themselves collectively—constituted the lower 63 percent of the total, main-study sample in the JI analysis. That is, this analytic comparability existed when interview-based I_4's were compared with interview-based I_5's (i.e., with the remaining part of this analytic sample—the part that served as the developmentally higher group), on the one hand, and the JI-based I_2's plus I_3's were compared with JI-based I_4's (again, the remaining part of this [still-main-study] analytic sample—the part that served as the developmentally higher group in *that* case), on the other. As a result, the correlates that were reported with respect to the interview-based and the inventory-based classification approaches each reflected contrasting or at least mutually differentiated developmental groupings, namely, a *lower* versus a *higher*—that is, regardless of what those groupings were called (e.g., I_3, I_4, or I_5).

135. Using the Jesness Inventory, there were too few I_2's for other-than-very-tentative findings, both in the penitentiary and camp. The only JI-correlate reported in connection with I_3's was: "sees others as willing to help" (Van Voorhis, 1994, 175). (This pertained to the peniten-

tiary.) Regarding this paucity of significant findings for the overall I_3 category—that is, for its three subtypes combined—it is quite possible that correlates which may have existed for, say, Cfm's were diluted or canceled by those for Cfc's and/or Mp's; and, vice versa. (See, for instance, the respective I_3 *subtype* correlates [1994, 175].) Diluting or canceling—in effect, masking—may have operated in other studies described in this chapter, for example, in ones that examined the relationship between *internalization of guilt* and I-Level. Here, results for Na's may have countered those for Nx's—and vice versa—thus reducing the impact of the overall I_4 level (which had few *Ss other than* Na's and Nx's) and thereby producing results which did not attain statistical significance for the I_2's, I_3's, and I_4's *combined* (i.e., for the sample as a totality).

136. When the 141 individuals were combined with an additional 161 male adult prisoners from the same institution who had constituted a *construction* sample in connection with this overall study, the correlation rose to .51. "Construction" centered on first intercorrelating all CPI scales with a previously developed, 48-item instrument—the Interpersonal Personality Inventory (IPI)—and on then determining which combination of CPI scales and scale-weights would best predict the IPI's classification of these 161 individuals into either the "low" or the "high" maturity category. (The IPI had *itself* been previously found to successfully make this distinction [Ballard, 1963].) The results, namely, the five CPI scales and the corresponding weights which had been derived, were then used on the present—the validation—sample of 141 separate individuals.

137. Utilizing *Ballard's IPI* alone, on the validation sample (N = 141), a correlation of .74 was obtained with respect to differentiating low from high maturity individuals. (As seen in endnote 136, the IPI had been previously used with a construction sample of 161 individuals.) Though this true/false paper-and-pencil test had not been originally developed on the basis of *CPI scales,* it had correlations of more than .40 on nine of this

instrument's 18 scales, and of more than .35 on three others. Its correlations with Dominance, Responsibility, Tolerance, Good Impression, and Self-Control were .48, .56, .63, .17, and .14, respectively. Again regarding the validation sample—N = 141—the correlation between the combination of these five scales, on the one hand, and IPI scores, on the other, was .60; as to the earlier, construction sample, it was .53 (Gottfredson and Ballard, 1963, 40).

138. On a historical note, the IPI's item-content drew heavily from scales developed at the Camp Elliott Naval Retraining Command in California, chiefly by Ives and Grant (1956), for the purpose of measuring interpersonal maturity. The nature and development of these scales and of the Inventory of Personal Opinions (IPO), of which they formed the core, is summarized in MacKay (1962, 37–41); also see Gunderson (1956) and Tolhurst (1966, 58–59) regarding these scales and related instruments. Prior to his contributions at the California Department of Corrections (this being the statewide, adult prison system), Ballard was instrumental in Camp Elliott research that utilized the Ives and Grant (later Warren) scales (Gunderson, Ballard, and Huge, 1958; Gunderson and Ballard, 1960). Finally, the role played by theory and research concerning the "authoritarian personality" construct (Adorno et al., 1950) early in the development of these scales is described in the MacKay, the Ives and Grant, and the Tolhurst documents, as is that of CPI and MMPI items in the development of the IPO as a whole.

139. Regarding age, 44 percent of the sample was under 16; 47 percent was 16–24; and 9 percent was 25 and up. As to race, 60 percent were white, 24 percent Black, 12 percent hispanic, and 4 percent all others. The operation was part of California's Probation Subsidy Program (see Chapter 17) and it had elected to utilize the I-Level system as a way of facilitating its intensive component. Its intake/diagnostic staff had been trained in I-Level at the Center for Training in Differential Treatment and/or by one or

more individuals who had themselves been trained there.

140. In this regard, all individuals were assessed via an "examination of the Permanent Record Cards, . . . of registration records," and so on (1962, 42).

141. Even more narrowly, *Martin (1959),* studying a general population of 203 10th grade boys in California, found stronger correlations between I-Level and grade point average among I_2's as well as I_5's, on the one hand, than among I_3's as well as I_4's (again, each individually), on the other. (In this connection, also see MacKay, 1962, 29, 61–62. It is not known if these differences would remain if level of aptitude were held constant.) Though "stronger," the I_2 and I_5 correlations— $-.14$ and $+.16$, respectively (compared to $-.02$ for the I_3's and $-.04$ for the I_4's)—were nevertheless low, in absolute terms. As in MacKay's study, I-Level was determined via the Student Opinion Survey—in effect, via the IPO.

142. The specific correlations were .80, .80, .57, .63, .54, .77, and .68 for the Aa, Ap, Cfc, Mp, Nx, Se, and Ci youths, respectively. Very low correlations— $-.07$ and $-.07$—were obtained for Cfm's and Na's. In Jesness' subsequent factor analysis of the expected behaviors, each of the first seven subtypes were found to have a single-factor structure whereas the latter two each involved two factors. This suggested to Jesness that "the experts had differences of opinions about these subtypes, and [had] described two different kinds of people within both the Cfm and Na subtypes." This possibility is consistent, for example, with the fact that Palmer (1971e) had then-recently distinguished two clear-cut categories of Cfm's and a third group that seemed more transitory, situational, or even transitional. The former were called "Rejection – Failure Avoiders" and "Approval – Participation Seekers." (The third was termed "Transitory or Situational Conformists" and it comprised 26 percent and 11 percent of all male and female conformists, respectively. It was further termed "Incipient Neurotics.") Four of the expert raters were staff of the Center for Training in

Differential Treatment and three were researchers engaged in various Youth Authority I-Level studies. When doing their Q-sorts, several or all of the raters may have been significantly influenced—perhaps differentially so—by the Palmer document, among other things. The same may have occurred regarding Na's, partly because of certain major distinctions made by Neto and Palmer (1969) with respect to higher maturity youths generally placed in this category. As to other subtypes, informal distinctions did exist, but they were not yet in documented or even systematized form. This, for instance, applied to Mp's; and, in general, elaborations or refinements regarding I_2's, Cfc's, and the non-neurotic I_4's were being worked on or nearing completion at the time (Palmer, 1971b, c, d; 1972a).

143. Each rater independently Q-sorted each of the nine subtypes, one at a time. Specifically, he or she first sorted each of the 80 BCL items—into one of the several frequency categories (the preestablished Q-sort slots)—according to his/her judgment of that item's relative frequency-of-occurrence for the given subtype. The rater (expert) then repeated this process for the next subtype, and then did the same, in turn, for every remaining one. To statistically analyze the resulting raw data, Jesness subsequently averaged the ratings—the item-by-item Q-sorts—of all seven experts, and thereby developed a single, overall profile for each subtype.

144. Here, as in the just-mentioned case of *expected* behavior ratings in comparison to the youths' *self-ratings,* an extremely low correlation was obtained in the case of Mp's; this was in addition to the low, nonsignificant correlations that were obtained for Cfm's (except with regard to "observed" versus "self") and Na's, respectively. This, as Jesness indicated, may have reflected the following: "Since the low correlations [on the part of Mp's] are found only for self-ratings, the results suggest that the Mp is less truthful than other subtypes in describing his own behavior, a possibility that fits with I-level theory" (1974, 41). This suggestion, it might be added, is quite consistent with earlier in-

formation and discussion by Budnoff (1963, 11) as well as by Butler and Adams (1966, 405), regarding female delinquents who appeared to be Mp's.

145. Thus, for example,

the expected behavior for Aa's most resembled that for Ap's (correlation = .88). The expected behavior for Aa's least resembled that for Se's (−.76). Ap's expected behavior . . . was least like Ci's. The Cfm's expected behavior was most like Nx's (.51) and least like Ci's (−.51). Cfc's expected behavior was equally like Mp's and Na's (.39) and least like Nx's (−.62). Na's expected behavior was most like Mp's and Ci's (.57), while Nx's was most like Se's (.64) (Jesness, 1974, 41).

All this, of course, was separate from, though not in conflict with, the following. Except with Cfm's and Na's, the correlation between any given subtype's expected behavior and that same subtype's *observed* behavior was higher than the correlation between that subtype's expected behavior and the observed behavior of any *other* subtype. To a lesser extent this also applied with respect to the correlation between *observed* and *self-rated* behavior; and it applied, to a still lesser degree, to *expected* and self-rated behavior—with the most conspicuous additional exception, in these two analyses, involving Mp's (1974, 44–45). (Youths of this particular subtype were, for instance, "rated by observers [staff] as most similar to Aa's and Cfc's, but [they] rate[d] themselves as most like Se's, Na's, and Cfm's" [p. 42]. In effect, they largely portrayed or tried to portray themselves—on the given checklist—as generally cooperative, prosocial, optimistic, and benign; staff, however, viewed them differently.)

146. As in the analysis of I-Level, significance was obtained on the Stein, Sarbin, and Kulik test but not on the remaining time-perspective instruments.

147. Andrews' sample of 112 probationers included no Se's and Ci's—individuals situated at the I_4 level. Nor did it contain Aa's—persons at the I_2 level.

148. This category undoubtedly included not just Cfm's but Cfc's, since these groups

were only minimally distinguished from each other as of 1961 (cf. Fosen and Grant, 1961, 4; Grant, 1961c, 6–8). (Also, in the California CTP experiment, they were no more than moderately distinguished from each other prior to about 1964.

149. For discussion of this point, see Van Voorhis, 1994, 336 (n. 4)—and pp. 84, 100, and 335 (n. 6) as well. Also see endnote 134 of this chapter.

150. Van Voorhis points out that, unlike the Ci's presented by Jesness (1988), those described by Warren et al. (1966b) are considered "subcultural offenders who have a criminal value system and usually a criminal network." In Jesness (p. 82), they have "positive attitudes toward authority, school, parents, and self, [and a] nondelinquent orientation"—and are called "adaptive[s]" (Van Voorhis, 1994, 336).

151. The preceding findings pertain to the penitentiary sample (N = 179) only. For the prison camp sample (N = 190), results for Na's, Nx's, and Se's paralleled those of the penitentiary inmates in several respects, both at the within-subtype and the across-subtypes levels. Important differences were, however, observed as well.

152. A factor analysis was performed "to test the construct validity of the personality measures" (e.g., subtypes), as distinct from that of developmental levels. This analysis was "limited by measurement [parameters] and sample sizes, . . . was constrained to the analysis of dummy variables, . . . was possible only with the penitentiary data," and, nonetheless, produced three "interpretable" albeit "weak factors: (1) a situational . . , (2) a committed criminal . . , and (3) a neurotic." In the initial (the principal-axis) as well as the final (the varimax rotation) solution, Warren's I_4 Se loaded on the first factor (i.e., on the situational), her I_4 Ci loaded on the second, and her I_4 Nx loaded on the third; the same occurred with Quay's Si (i.e., on the situational factor), Megargee's Charlie and Jesness' Cfc (on the committed criminal), and Quay's Na (on the neurotic). Though no other groups appeared in *both* those solutions,

several other Quay, Megargee (MMPI), and Jesness groups loaded on one or the other, particularly in the principal-axis solution. In this, the first solution, the three factors (collectively) nevertheless accounted for only 21% of all variance; in the second, for 14 percent— that is, both relatively small portions of the total (1994, 114, 116).

153. For instance, regarding I_5 Na's, "staff ratings . . . generally were unfavorable. As a group, [these inmates] received lower scores on (a) relations with authorities, (b) aggressiveness, and (c) need for supervision. Adjustment measures showed high fear scores and some learning difficulties, but revealed a willingness to communicate with staff." I_5 Nx's "showed adjustment difficulties in the form of stress, fear, and need for emotional feedback and programmatic support. Followup surveys showed that they were participating in programs." As to I_5 Se's, "difficulties were not observed on disciplinary-related measures; staff rated these inmates quite favorably, as motivated and demonstrating good emotional control and an ability to learn. Nevertheless, these inmates experienced some difficulties, such as high stress, limited participation in programs, and needs for safety and emotional feedback." Finally, I_5 Ci's "incurred a high number of disciplinary citations and significantly higher rates of self-report[ed] nonaggressive infractions. Staff reported a relatively high need for supervision as well as good emotional control and a high ability to learn" (Van Voorhis, 1994, 258–259).

154. For instance, regarding the three I_3 subtypes, the following was found (Van Voorhis, 1994, 251–253). Cfm (Immature Conformist): "Cfm's [were] somewhat difficult to describe. They do not appear to evidence a criminal value system, and would appear somewhat benign on the basis of correlations with situational types; yet [a correlation with the MMPI "How" type] suggests a somewhat troubled, but not troublesome, inmate. Subsequent tests confirm this description. There were no correlates to official or self-disciplinary behaviors. Staff believed, however, that

these inmates were having difficulties in their relationships with other inmates. Prison adjustment measures [indicated they] had few friends and rather high stress scores, but the relationship was not statistically significant. They evidence a strong need for safety and programmatic support and viewed others as willing to help." Cfc (Cultural Conformist): ". . . They were more likely than others to self-report nonaggressive behavioral problems. Staff ratings were unfavorable, finding that Cfc's (a) showed poor relationships with other inmates, (b) were aggressive, (c) were uncooperative, (d) needed supervision, and (e) responded poorly to supervision. Adjustment measures were favorable; these inmates were not loners (according to staff) and formed friendships (according to their surveys). They also expressed a need for safety early in their prison terms and showed few tendencies to participate in prison programs." Mp (Manipulator): "Mp's scored relatively high on self-report nonaggressive infractions and poorly on some of the staff ratings. Staff observed them as (a) having poor relationships with other inmates, (b) aggressive, (c) uncooperative, (d) in need of supervision, (e) responding poorly to supervision, (f) unmotivated, and (g) having poor emotional control. In their interviews they showed a need for safety. Their survey disclosed limited program participation but revealed an ability to form supportive friendships."

155. In the present study, the Jesness levels correlated significantly (p < .01) with the interview-based levels, even though this correlation was only modest (.29) in absolute terms and although the latter's (interview-based) levels involved no I_2's and I_3's whereas the former's necessarily contained no I_5's.

156. Besides the JI and the Jesness Self-Appraisal Behavior Checklist (BCL), all youths—over a three-day period—filled out several questionnaires; together, these tapped their thoughts, feelings, attitudes, and/or behaviors concerning school, parents and home life, peers, police, and involvement in delinquent behavior. School records were obtained regarding achievement scores, official

disciplinary actions, and demographic as well as background information. The youths consisted of 67 percent whites, 16 percent Blacks, 12 percent Mexican-Americans, and 5 percent all others. Most individuals were ages 13 or 14 and they were enrolled in a total of eight junior high schools within the city of Sacramento. The male/female ratio was 52/48.

157. As mentioned, the 8th graders—called "presumed nondelinquents" by Jesness—*best* fit one of the given *Warren categories*. (This was the case even though Jesness substituted the *labels* [i.e., the category names] from his own classification system for those of Warren's categories [subtypes], while retaining Warren's original *symbols* for those same categories [see below].) More precisely, as indicated by Harris (1983, 146), all such youths—by virtue of the Jesness Inventory's available subtype choices and its related scoring methodology—were necessarily placed into one (any one) of Warren's nine I_2 through I_4 categories, these being *preexisting* categories. In effect, the classification question had been, "Which one of these preexisting categories (groupings, subtypes)—preestablished *delinquency* [i.e., delinquent-sample-based] categories in particular—does the individual most resemble?" The answer was determined by statistically comparing (1) his or her scores and profile on the JI with (2) the scores and profiles, on that same inventory, which had earlier been developed and validated with respect to delinquent populations alone, for each of the respective Warren categories. The scores/profile that most resembled each other—in that respect, best matched—were then selected. Though this forced-fit, into the particular preestablished categories that were available, was logically, technically, and otherwise straightforward, meaningful, and correct in itself, it might, as Harris indicated, have nonetheless "give[n] a distorted picture of the nondelinquent population" (p. 146). This could have occurred, for instance, because the available category choices made it literally impossible for a youth to be placed into any *non*delin-

quent category, such as those which he—Harris—has elsewhere observed. This would be the case not only if many "fits" were *close*, but if they were not at all difficult in most respects. (Whether or not preestablished categories are involved [and, in some respects, they almost always are], "forced" fits—that is, best fits—are not ipso facto close, difficult, and so on.)

The issue of forced best-fit aside, the following might be noted. Jesness, as indicated, substituted a set of modified labels for several of Warren's subtype (category) names. He did so—and he had chosen the particular concepts that those labels stood for—in order to reflect and emphasize major *non*delinquent features, adjustments, and other aspects of general—population youths. This substitution seemed worthwhile and appropriate even though nondelinquents shared various significant features with delinquents and although Jesness' 155 item inventory (with which the nondelinquent sample had been tested) had remained unchanged as to content. At any rate, in the classification system that Jesness introduced in the 1980s (Jesness, 1988; Jesness and Wedge, 1983a, 1984), Warren's Unsocialized, aggressive (Aa); Unsocialized, passive (Ap); Immature conformist (Cfm); Cultural conformist (Cfc); Manipulator (Mp); Neurotic, acting-out (Na); Neurotic, anxious (Nx); Situational-emotional reaction (Se); and Cultural identifier (Ci) were renamed as follows, "for use within nondeviant populations" (Jesness and Wedge, 1983, 11): Undersocialized, active; Undersocialized, passive; Conformist; Group-oriented; Pragmatist; Autonomy-oriented; Introspective; Inhibited; and, Adaptive, respectively. (All individuals remained at the same I-Levels as before.) Finally, Jesness' and Jesness and Wedge's above-mentioned findings were not presented separately for the Warren I_2, I_3, and I_4 levels per se. This was because, in his nondelinquent-centered classification system, "subtype rather than level [becomes] the primary focus of classification," since more emphasis is (now) to be placed on behavior than on perception (1983, 11). Jesness did, at any rate, utilize the familiar level and subtype *symbols*—such as "I₃, Cfc," for his own Group-oriented category—in order to "maintain continuity" with those which most researchers would recognize; and, I-Level concepts, as well as their related subtype classifications and characterizations, did continue to substantially channel, and perhaps generally dominate, his system.

158. Related findings were obtained in connection with the individuals' answer(s) to the specific question, "Do you see yourself as a delinquent?" I_2's, Cfc's, and Na's were the youths most likely to say yes. The same groups—I_2's. followed by Cfc's and Na's—expressed the most by way of negative opinions about teachers. (Se's as well as Ci's expressed the least.)

159. A discriminant function analysis indicated that 23 percent of the youths in this general, 8th grade population "could be correctly classified [as to subtype] from age, sex, ethnicity, achievement test score, and socioeconomic status." This indicated that "although subtype is not completely unrelated to background characteristics, it is more than just a measure of them" (1983, 80).

160. This referred to (1) having any one or more referrals and to (2) the average number of referrals, based on probation department records.

161. Essentially the same applied regarding Victimization: Thought Ap's, followed by Aa's and Na's, were the individuals most likely to report 'having had things stolen from them, or having been threatened or attacked by others at school,' and although Se's and Ci's were those least likely to so report, *subtype* per se (i.e., the nine subtypes jointly), added relatively little variance to these findings. This was true even though what it *did* add was statistically significant, mainly due to the large sample-size. (In still other cases subtype did account for considerable variance over and beyond that accounted for by the control variables [CVs] collectively—as it had done with findings (1) through (3). [In fact, with these latter—as with other findings, such as for Behavior Checklist Unobtrusive-

ness, BCL Responsibility, and BCL Confidence—it accounted for substantially *more* total variance than did the several CVs, combined, not just for a good deal of variance *over and beyond* them (1983, 79; 1986, 959; 1988, 86).]) In any event, Aa's and Na's were also the youths most likely to report having been "scolded at home for various misbehaviors," while Se's and Cfm's were those least likely.

Findings that were in a similarly expected direction applied to Aa's, Ap's, Na's, and Cfc's—and the opposite applied to Se's and Ci's—with regard to the self-reported level of overall Delinquency Orientation on the part of the youths and their friends. However, the significance of these findings was greatly limited because of the following. Some of the specific content or general focus of the Delinquency Orientation and the Home Misbehavior items to which the youths responded was very similar, that is, closely related, to various true—false Jesness Inventory items that were used to help distinguish given subtypes from one another in the first place. Examples are items 7, 14, 32, 64, 71, 98, 122, and 147 ("It makes me mad that some crooks get off free." [F] "If the police don't like you, they'll try to get you for anything." "Police stick their noses into a lot of things that are none of their business." "Police usually treat you dirty." "It's fun to get the police to chase you." "It doesn't seem wrong to steal from crooked store owners." "If you're not in with the gang, you may be in for real trouble." "Stealing isn't so bad if it is from a rich person."), items 103 and 107 ("Parents are always nagging and picking on young people." "At home I am punished too much for things I don't do."), and, to a lesser extent, items 9, 33, 44, 51, 59, 70, 81, and 148. In effect, the youths were repeating, in their responses to Delinquency Orientation and Home Misbehavior items, fundamental aspects of their answers to these JI subtype differentiaters and determiners; this created a substantial degree of circularity and a resulting, spuriously inflated relationship in this instance. Regarding the previous findings—(1)

through (5)—although various JI items had addressed a general subject area, such as school or home life, they were not focused on *misbehavior* per se or on other specific content and aspects that were independently tapped by the remaining questions, scales, and so on (that is, on the particular criterion measure in question). Thus, essentially no 'statistical inflation' existed here.

One last finding might be mentioned, one in which circularity did not play a part. Cfc's and I_2's were the individuals lease likely to have "made expected progress in school," as indicated by their average age, whereas Se's and Ci's had made the most progress. Reflecting this was the fact that 72 percent of the Cfc and 67 percent of the I_2 8th graders were 14 or older, whereas 40% of the Se's and 28% of the Ci's were in that age group. However, it is unknown whether given demographics, such as socioeconomic status, substantially or even largely accounted for this finding.

162. At point of selection. A few turned 16 before being interviewed.

163. Though the study mainly bore on construct validity, it related—technically— to concurrent validity as well. *Unrelated* to the issue of validity per se, Harris' operational definition of a *delinquent* required that the youth "have a record of at least two offenses in the last two years, one of those constituting what would be a felony for an adult, or he must have a record of at least three offenses of any kind" (1976, 38).

164. Of all youths within Warren's I_4 subtypes, only one was an Se and none were Ci's. Thus, findings regarding I_4's centered essentially on Na's and Nx's.

165. These five nondelinquent groups make developmental sense to the present author. For one thing, Harris' I3 groups may be viewed as cross-situational—in that sense, broad or even global, and usefully generalizable—adaptations along a path to an I_4 adjustment. Thus, for instance, the Cvc group may later become an Ax or an Aas, and many Ro's may develop into one of the three I_4 groups themselves (especially the Ax and/or—later—the Aas).

166. Two of these studies reported correlations not just for level, but for subtype: In Eaks', the r's between IQ and subtype were .42 and .31 for verbal and nonverbal IQ, respectively. In Cross and Tracy's, the correlation was .36.

167. Palmer's figures were .23 for males plus females as of the mid-1960s, .24 for all Phase 1 and 2 males (1961–1969 intake), and .22 for the entire Phase 3 sample (161 males). Werner (1972, 50) had previously reported phi, Cramer, contingency, tau, and gamma correlations/coefficients of .31, .18, .30, .24, and .34, respectively. His .27 figure (1975, 64) happened to equal as unweighted average of these five.

168. Across the several studies collectively, a wide range of intelligence tests was used. Chief among them were the Wechsler Intelligence Scale for Children (WISC), Wechsler Adult Intelligence Scale (WAIS), General Aptitude Test Battery (GATB), Scholastic Aptitude Test, California Test of Mental Maturity (CTMM), Science Research Associates (SRA), Lorge-Thorndike, Revised Beta Examination, Raven's Progressive Matrices, and Shipley Institute of Living Scale. In many studies, more than one such instrument was involved. Moreover, several of the major tests had verbal *and* nonverbal (language *and* nonlanguage) sections, whereas others contained only one or the other. In the former case, some researchers chose to utilize and analyze only one or the other, for particular purposes.

169. Regarding CTP, the following might be noted. Apart from the IQ/I-Level correlation reported in the just-mentioned work (Palmer et al., 1968, 8), specific information about IQ was presented, separately for each subtype (hence, in effect, for each I-Level), in 1965 (Warren and Palmer, p. 7) and 1966 (Warren et al., p. 35). The identical type and degree of information was also provided in the 1968 document itself (p. 6). By using this information in conjunction with the sample-size data that were also presented, various correlation estimates could have been readily derived. At any rate, detailed information existed prior to 1969 regarding the relationship between intelligence,

on the one hand, and the analytic/intervention categories used in the YA/NIMH experiment, on the other.

In the 1965, 1966, and 1968 documents, the existence of a moderate positive correlation was evident from the subtype figures that were presented. For instance, in the 1966 report (p. 35), average IQs for the I_2 (Ap) and I_3 experimentals were: Ap – 78, Cfm – 86, Cfc – 92, and Mp – 85, whereas for the I_4 subtypes they were: Na – 96, Nx – 98, Se – 106, and Ci – 94. Similarly, IQs for controls were: Ap – 88, Cfm – 86, Cfc – 89, and Mp – 85, on the one hand, whereas they were Na – 96, Nx – 96, Se – 91, and Ci – 87, on the other. (Ap's Se's, and Ci's collectively comprised a small portion of the total, and the preponderance of I_4's were Na's and Nx's.)

Such information notwithstanding, Zaidel (1970, 10; 1973, 49), and Miller soon afterward (1972, 29–32, 104), indicated that Warren, Palmer, and other California researchers involved with I-Level during the 1960s had—throughout that period—written very little about relationships between individuals' intelligence and their I-Level. More precisely, they accurately pointed out that those researchers had not discussed the possibility (and possible nature) of important connections between IQ and the *underlying theory* of interpersonal maturity—in particular, the theory's principles, concepts, and other aspects of ingredients of personal, social, and cognitive growth. (Beker and Heyman [1971; 1972], in the meantime, had extensively criticized them for not focusing on the theory's overall construct validity [CV]—CV in the Cronbach/Meehl/Campbell sense.) Their not having done so—their not, of example, having explored (1) possible *contributions* by higher IQ to higher maturity level, or (2) possible *substantive overlap* (similarity, identity, or other communality) between aspects of intelligence and aspects of maturity—partly reflected the following. (As seen later, it also reflected the experiment's overall priorities and primary mandates.)

Throughout Phases 1 and 2 of the YA/NIMH-sponsored study, its re-

searchers' principal focus with respect to IQ involved the question of whether this variable was statistically equivalent across the experimental (E) and control (C) samples—particularly, though not only, across all E subtypes combined, on the one hand, and all C subtypes combined, on the other. (These combinations constituted the respective, "overall" groups or samples.) The same main focus existed with other variables/factors as well, such as age, commitment offense, base expectancy, and—still in the E versus C context—even SES and ethnicity. In this regard, IQ was simply one of several important background/demographic features. The researchers' analytic goal, here, was to determine if, despite their having utilized a random allocation approach in order to establish each youth's E or C status, substantial threats existed to the internal validity of the study's E/C outcome-comparisons, in connection with those features. Such threats would have existed if large E/C differences (nonequivalences) were present—and, if present, did not counterbalance and cancel each others' effects.

Once it was determined that E/C equivalence did exist, the given features—in this case IQ—were not further focused on as such, particularly regarding their possible bearing on outcome. Thus, for instance, in the 1967 report, once the essential equality of the overall E and C groups was determined with respect to IQ (the specified [p. 35] averages were: E – 92.5; C – 90.8), no correlations were computed to describe the extent of relationship between this feature and *I-Level* (nor with anything *else* in particular), and essentially no discussion ensued in connection with IQ's possible implications for intervention. Moreover, little also ensued partly because—*within* the E sample (as within the C)—the average difference in number of IQ points from any one I-Level, as well as any one subtype, to any other one was fairly small. (This especially applied to the I_3 and I_4 levels/subtypes—which, together, encompassed over 90 percent of the overall sample's youths.) Finally, and still in the within—sample context, because of the (1) relatively limited, main *range* of IQs that were present across and within those levels, and, with that, especially given the (2) very frequent *overlapping* of IQs (even across the I_3 and I_2 levels), there appeared to be no reliable, certainly no sizable or somehow likely, *differential* implications of this factor with respect to intervention. Again, and in particular, the very frequent IQ-overlap also applied at the *subtype* level, that is, "within . . . levels"; and subtype was not only a key focus of intervention strategies/techniques per se, but a fundamental focus of almost all Phase 1 and 2 analyses, including those of outcome.

We now turn to the experiment's priorities and its related, stated goals—the latter, in effect, constituting contractual obligations with the National Institute of Mental Health. As will be seen, the priorities and goals were direct and major contributors to the experiment's relative absence of certain construct validity studies, particularly in the 1960s.

Throughout Phases 1 and 2, the identification and refinement (I&R) of effective intervention approaches was given a much higher priority than the testing and refining of basic I-Level theory, *as* theory. This I&R priority was reflected in the main goals that were stated in the experiment's Phase 1 and 2 proposals to NIMH, and in one of Phase 3's goals as well (Adams and Grant, 1961; Warren, Palmer, and Turner [WPT], 1964; Palmer, 1969). In this regard, and as one aspect of Phase 2's goals in particular, even the researchers' proposed examination of *construct validity* was focused, not on the standard, Cronbach/Meehl/Campbell (CMC) approach or definition, but—as was clear in context—on a more pragmatic matter: the outcome—centered dimension or criterion of successful intervention (treatment):

[The second goal of the proposed study is to] *detail* by example and illustration the *treatment model* developed in Phase 1, and to describe the operationalization of the treatment model, as a form of construct validation of the Development of Interpersonal Maturity theory (WPT, 1964, 2; emphasis in the original).

The implicit assumption in this goal was that if a program's approaches (methods) derive from a given theory, if they actively and substantially reflect that theory, and if they appear successful in terms of outcome, this outcome constitutes evidence that the theory has some validity. Methods which had seemed successful in Phase 1 were to be further and more widely field-tested in Phase 2; and it was those methods, if still successful, that would be formally presented as—would be "describe[d]" as—the "operationaliz[ed] . . . treatment model."

(One point before continuing. Phase 2's (1964–1969) first goal was to "*describe* in elaborate detail the *program elements* of the present CTP operation in order to create a research base for expansion of Community Treatment programs, for training relevant staff, and for comparisons with alternate community programs." Its third and final goal was to "*compare the effectiveness* of a community-located program based on the CTP differential treatment model [that had evolved in Phase I] with a community-located program modeled after Empey's Provo Experiment [that is, the Guided Group Interaction approach]" [WPT, 1964, 2; emphasis in the original.] Phase 1's goals appear in Chapter 1.)

At any rate, consistent with the experiment's overriding emphasis on identifying, refining, and disseminating effective intervention approaches, its researchers, during the 1960s, dealt chiefly with that aspect of validity which is sometimes called "practical" validity—an aspect which, to a large degree, can in turn rest on the "predictive." They gave no particular emphasis to (1) any pointed examination, such as a correlation study, of the Interpersonal Maturity theory's developmental component per se—namely, its I-Level construct—and, in that respect, to (2) directly examining this construct's validity (and, ipso facto, much of the theory's itself), in the CFCM sense.

As implied, specific examination of the developmental component's construct validity—CV in the CMC sense—

was given little consideration during Phase 2 in particular (and none during Phase 1 [see below]). This was not only due to the large amounts of time and effort that were needed in order to carry out the experiment's *top* priority activities alone and to achieve its *central* goals alone, but also because the experiment's main observed I-Level categories—2, 3, and 4—seemed to have made considerable conceptual and practical (intervention-centered) sense as-is, throughout Phase 1. In particular, those levels had each described what appeared to be important aspects of real-life people (not, of course, of any *complete* person); and—collectively—the given descriptions had helped distinguish among individuals, while simultaneously allowing for similarities (hence, for "subtypes").

As a result, when the Phase 2 proposal was being written (1964), and during the subsequent few years as well, little felt-need existed, and certainly no urgency was sensed, with respect to examining specific *correlates* of those I-Levels—in particular, to studying measurable aspects of the respective level's external relationships. Such a Cronbach/Meehl/Campbell-type examination—for example, a set of correlation analyses—could have indicated how strongly or weakly the respective and successive I-Levels were linked to certain *other* constructs or features, that is, to ones with which they, theoretically, *should* have been linked. Among them were cognitive complexity, locus of control, foresight and future time perspective, impulse control, and affect awareness. Findings of this nature could, for one thing, have helped to further characterize and otherwise "flesh out" those levels, and, in that respect, to further specify and otherwise clarify their conceptual meaning. They could have done so even though the levels' *reality* was already evident, and although various areas of their *relevance*—for instance, their bearing on intervention goals, strategies, and techniques—were already becoming known, or seemed fairly clear. ([1] At any rate, they could have done so even though many practi-

tioners, researchers, and others seemed satisfied with the levels' overall utility, and believed that these constructs were already adequately formulated and sufficiently detailed as well as understandable. [2] Regarding "clarify . . . ," one or more Cronbach/Meehl and so on studies might have also helped identify some of those levels' underlying—that is, *internal*—components, forces, and relationships.)

Nevertheless, absent the above-mentioned pressure or felt-need, issues and questions which were reflected in the experiment's central goals seemed much more important than specific analyses of construct validity. In no small part, this difference in perceived importance existed because a rapidly growing number of practitioners and policy makers within and (by 1966–1967) outside the United States (1) considered those issues/questions immediate and fairly pressing, given their broad implications for the field, and because many of those individuals (2) were turning to the California experiment (for example, to its yearly reports, and other publications as well as updates) for scientifically based answers and suggestions, and for field-tested leads. Chief among the questions were: Does community-based intervention (CBI) really reduce recidivism among serious delinquents? If so, For which kinds? and What are its key elements and approaches? Is CBI feasible in large urban setting ? Is it "cheaper" than standard institutionalization? In short, under the circumstances, studies of construct validity in the CMC sense could not compete with the felt need to address such questions, ones whose policy implications seemed—and were—huge. All-in-all, the California researchers believed that any sizable examination of basic theoretical issues such as the above would have to wait, in order for the YA/NIMH experiment to carefully and extensively address or continue addressing those questions—for essentially the first time.

(Two points might be noted before continuing: [1] Levels 2, 3, and 4 made sense as general, successive *categories* or benchmarks, even though it was recognized that important continuities existed between them—that they were not 100 percent distinct from each other. As indicated, those levels also made sense regarding specific *content,* in that—apart from having been described in terms of "ideal types" [see below] (this being intrinsic to—a necessary aspect of—their benchmark nature)—they reflected various concrete and readily recognizable aspects of reality. [2] Even though it was felt that the I-Levels made considerable sense as-is, both as categories and substantively, the following can be inferred from discussion below: (a) Information that was continuously accumulating regarding the experiment's youths, and, in particular, (b) *patterns* and mutual *differences* that were becoming evident among those individuals after the mid-1960s [mainly based on the given information], essentially led the author—starting near the end of Phase 2—to make certain additions and distinctions with respect to levels 3 and 4, and to refine various subtypes as well. However, although these modifications supported and sometimes even advanced the "levels" construct as such [and, with that, the overall theory itself], the efforts which led to them were not CV studies. Instead, they were direct, empirical/clinical syntheses of numerous observations and other sources as well as forms of information. At any rate, the efforts/syntheses in question neither tested nor were designed to test the "levels" construct and/or other central aspects of the Interpersonal Maturity theory, quantitatively or otherwise; not, at least, from the CMC, nomological network perspective. For an informative discussion of construct validity as it related to the California experiment and I-Level during the 1960s, see Beker and Heyman [1971, 18–31; 1972, 18–30].)

Even though the (1) identification and detailing of effective approaches, the (2) identification of key contributors to success, and the (3) ongoing as well as broadened evaluation of comparative effectiveness (E versus C [and GGI]) were, appropriately, the researchers' and Youth Authority's main priorities, tasks,

and actual activities, the following nonetheless applied (in effect, it applied despite the immediate, practical questions the researchers attempted to seriously address—ones with which practitioners/policy makers were especially concerned): In retrospect, it is fair to say that the nomological network aspect—in particular, the specific variables, specific correlation's aspect—of construct validity probably *should* have been given a higher priority than it was, certainly during Phase 2. In the long run, it is scientifically important to establish a sizable degree of CV per se (at least, to substantially examine and test a theory's CV), even if one has already established or is establishing concurrent, practical, and other important forms or aspects. Though one cannot test such validity all at once or in any single analysis, let alone clearly *establish* it under those conditions, it is—obviously—necessary to begin the process. In any event, the following would apply. Because I-Level and personal development have *several* facets and dimensions (however these may be layered and/or sequenced) and because they appear to involve *interactional* processes—and in these respects, collectively, can be viewed as structurally complex as well as "global" or holistic—one would have to study several variables/factors, preferably but not necessarily together, in order to do the following: (1) appropriately test I-Level/personality development (IPD), and, based on IPD's having passed key tests, (2) thereby possibly establish an adequate or perhaps even strong and wide-ranging nomological network.

That having been said, the following might nevertheless be noted. In the California experiment, during the 1960s, the just-mentioned "should" (basically, the substantial examination of CV) would have been a realistic option—that is, logistically and otherwise doable—only under the following conditions: (1) If added staff resources could have been built into Phase 2 for such a purpose (note: existing staff already had a full 'workload' in connection with their basic, proposed tasks); and/or (2) if some of the resources that *were* provided by NIMH in response to the Phase 2 proposal could have been used to a *sizable* rather than a modest degree for validation analyses—in effect, could have been partly redirected, somehow expanded, and/or merged with other activities, in connection with their type of usage. (It might be kept in mind that NIMH, in response to the proposal, *did* provide sufficient resources for purposes of implementing the basic tasks.)

During Phase *1* (1961–1964)—particularly its first half—there was essentially no scientific "call" for construct validity analyses, especially since the theory's relevance for intervention with serious delinquents had only begun to be demonstrated, in the first place. This being the situation, and given the type and amount of Phase 1's tasks/workloads in any event, there was no realistic possibility of condition #1 and/or #2 occurring at any point in that phase.

The upshot is as follows. It is unknown if, and how well, efforts—that is, requests—involving condition #1 would have succeeded, had they been made. In this regard it can be said, however, that when the Phase 2 and 3 proposals were submitted to NIMH, it was believed that the maximum possible amount of resources—for instance, five full-time researchers, for most of Phase 2's five-year duration—were already being requested. (The request was granted.) Nonetheless, efforts relating to condition #2 might well have been possible and manageable during Phase 2, as the existence of certain Phase 3 activities and products imply. (In this regard, see items #4 and #5, directly below.)

At any rate, in the 1960s the researchers' main interests and obligations involved the following: applying the Sullivan, Grant, and Grant (Warren) I-Level theory (1) as it had been originally formulated, and, later, (2) with its revisions from Phase 1; scientifically evaluating the effects of that application, particularly in connection with the nine subtypes Warren had specified at the start of Phase 1; and, building a body of knowledge—detailed, field-tested, practical information—about approaches and

ingredients that seemed effective with those subtypes in specified kinds of settings; and so on. Despite these principal interests and obligations—or the experiment's main goals, priorities, and tasks—the following did occur:

1. As already seen, modest, initial examinations of the *concurrent* validity of I-Levels and subtypes were made—and in some cases initiated—during the middle of Phase 2 (Warren, 1966; Palmer and Warren, 1967). Some of the latter efforts were resumed and completed in the middle of Phase 3 (Palmer, 1973b; Palmer and Helm, 1975).

2. The appropriateness and utility of (1) *adding* an I-Level—for the most part, an identifiable transition phase—between the then—existing, originally formulated, I_3 and I_4 levels, was recognized and described at the close of Phase 2, as was that of (2) *dividing* the originally formulated I_4 level itself, into a less advanced and a more advanced developmental stage (Palmer, 1969d). The addition and distinction (A&D) was pontentially relevant not only to the general scientific and practical objective of increasing diagnostic reliability and accuracy, but—hardly unrelated—to workers' and supervisors' goal of improved intervention planning. Also, the A&D was consistent with, and in that respect it supported, the fundamental position that Interpersonal Maturity theory "describes a *continuum* of development" and defines "ideal types along the scale" (Adams and Grant, 1961, 6; Warren et al., 1966b, 2). (The "ideal types" are the theory's successive *I-Levels,* which serve as benchmarks along the growth continuum—that is, the scale.) In any event, this A&D was considered a potential advance in the understanding and application of I-Level theory, though it neither involved nor resulted from a construct validity study.

3. A "Developmental-Adaptation [D-A] Theory of Youthful Personality" was formulated at the end of Phase 2 (Palmer, 1969b). It was used extensively and regularly throughout Phase 3 in parallel with I-Level, and it directly assisted with intervention planning. As such, D-A theory helped advance the overall

intervention model, even though it—like the above addition and division—was not used to address construct validity in the CMC sense.

4. Better differentiated, more complete, and, in any event, broader-based descriptions of several Warren subtypes were developed in the early years of Phase 3 (Palmer, 1971b, c, d, and e). They seemed relevant to improved understanding and intervention planning within as well as outside the experimental program and community setting. (In all the above respects, also see the Neto and Palmer [1969] report—a later-Phase 2 document that focused on certain I_4–level San Francisco youths.) Over and above the *clarifications* these accounts often provided, the greater accuracy that they involved helped increase the trueness-to-life quality or correspondence to reality—in that respect the overall validity—of the already-existing subtype accounts. This, of course, applied more to the new accounts that were rather detailed than to those (and there were several) which were only sketchy.

5. Partly motivated by Zaidel's (1970) as well as Beker and Heyman's (1971) observations regarding construct validity in the YA/NIMH experiment, and also by those of Gibbons (1970) in addition to Cross and Tracy (1971), one of the experiment's researchers conducted, midway through Phase 3, a detailed examination of construct validity in the Cronbach/Meehl and so on sense, using California Psychological Inventory scales. He also carried out a less extensive analysis, based on Jesness Inventory scales. The first-mentioned effort focused on IQ as well (Werner, 1972; 1975).

170. Youths whose intake classification (diagnosis) was I_5 comprised 1 percent of the 1,014 boys and girls who had been eligible for California's CTP experiment from the Valley and San Francisco areas during 1961–1969. These individuals (N = 12) had an average nonverbal IQ 14 points higher than that of the eligible sample as a whole, and they were one year older as well. Of these youths, 83 percent were classified as Neurotic Anxious and the rest as Cultural Identi-

fiers (Palmer, 1970b, 46–47; 1971a, 78).

171. For delinquent males, Jesness (1974, 27, 31) reported r's of .58 and .06 between verbal and nonverbal IQ (respectively), on the one hand, and *Ego Level* (Loevinger's system), on the other. Concerning *non*delinquents, (1) Hunt (1971, 38), in reference to four studies by himself and/or others, reported correlations of .06, .15, .24, and .29 between IQ and *Conceptual Level*. (Some portion of the differences among these correlations may have reflected the differing combinations of intelligence test and range of school grade that were involved across the four studies. At any rate, the two studies with the larger correlations were also those with the larger grade range [hence, also age range].) (2) Harris (1977, 33) reported an r of .27 between IQ and *I-Level,* for a sample of males. Still regarding nondelinquents, (3) Loevinger's own findings might be noted: "Correlations between our sentence completion test of ego development [Ego level] and IQ have ranged from about .1 to .5 in a series of unpublished studies, the value depending on heterogeneity and the mode of sampling" (1976, 176).

172. Miller (1972, 47), for instance, computed the correlation between I-Level, on the one hand, and age, sex, and ethnicity (respectively), on the other, and then partialled out the effects of the latter (all three combined) on the former. She did not, however, present the three separate correlations—statistical relationships—themselves.

173. Palmer's I-Level figure of .20 involved the YA/NIMH experiment's mid-1960s sample, referred to in endnote 167. Separately, the correlation for all males in Phases 1 and 2 (1961–1969) of that experiment was .34 and for all those in Phase 3 (1969–1973) it was .16. *Subtype* r's, which were reported in the Eaks as well as the Cross and Tracy study, were .10 and .32, respectively.

174. Regarding other developmental systems, (1) Jesness obtained an r of .23 between age and Loevinger's Ego Level, for institutionalized delinquents. (2) Van Voorhis (1983, 52) obtained a correlation of .63

between age, on the one hand, and Kohlberg's Moral Development Level, on the other, for her adult, mostly male, "pre-prosecution diversion" sample. (No such correlation data were available for her "conviction" sample—individuals placed on probation and required to pay restitution.) (3) Among *non*offenders, r's ranged from .07 and .08 in the Hunt (1965) and Cross (1966) studies of Conceptual Level to the already-mentioned mid-.60s in the Sullivan, McCullough, and Stager (1970) research on Moral Development, Ego Level, and Conceptual Level. (It is likely that the overall age-ranges of given samples—and perhaps the *particular* ages that comprised those ranges [e.g., 10–12 rather than 13–15 or 16–18]—had considerable, even differential, impact on the size of obtained correlations. At any rate, Jesness (1972, 42), for instance, indicated that Loevinger had obtained an r of .74 between age and Ego Level, for a sample of boys aged 9 to *18*. In contrast, the above [text] studies of delinquents had not only lower correlations but smaller age ranges as well—often three or four years instead of the nine years just mentioned. [Cf., the age range of the Jesness study (1974, 27, 31) that reported an r of .23 between age and Ego Level; to be sure, IQ and ethnicity were statistically controlled in connection with this correlation, but probably not with Loevinger's.])

175. Fewer r's have been reported between (1) I-Level and *SES* than between (2) I-Level and *age*, and, of course, between I-Level and *intelligence (IQ)*. As seen shortly (text), point (1) also applied to *ethnicity*. Further, few studies presented r's between more than two or three—any two or three—of these four variables/factors. In particular, correlations for SES and ethnicity rarely appeared together—that is, each with respect to I-Level.

176. From Preston data they presented elsewhere (1983, 43), a correlation (ø) of .26 was derived between SES and *subtype*.

177. Regarding subtype, he obtained a .11.

178. As to subtype, they obtained a .33 (Cross and Tracy, 1969, 19).

179. When they partialled out age, IQ, and SES, the correlation became .14 (Jesness and Wedge, 1988, 1003).

180. With age and IQ partialled out, this dropped to .27 (Jesness , 1974, 28).

181. This figure pertained to her Caucasian/nonCaucasian breakdown. When she excluded all Mexican-Americans and focused on the resulting Caucasian/*Black* breakdown in particular, the correlation became .60. (All Mexican-Americans had previously been part of the non-Caucasian category, and, as indicated, they comprised 15 percent of the *total* study sample.)

182. Palmer retained the distinction between white, Black, Mexican-American, and all others, rather than combine any categories. In Cross and Tracy's analysis, "nonCaucasian" necessarily consisted of Blacks only, since the researchers' study sample contained neither Mexican-Americans not "all others," in the first place.

183. Jesness (1974, 27, 31), focusing on the Northern Youth Center sample, obtained an r of .29 between ethnicity and Loevinger's Ego Level. When he partialled out age and IQ, the correlation became .09. Van Voorhis (1983, 52), analyzing her adult, mostly male probationers, obtained an r of .34 between ethnicity and Kohlberg's Moral Development Level.

184. This finding is also mentioned in Beker and Heyman (1972, 28).

185. The partial correlations (p. 28) were: (1) between maturity level and *IQ*, with *age and race* removed: .23; (2) between maturity level and *race (white/non-white)*, with *IQ and age* removed: −.27; and, (3) between maturity level and *age*, with *IQ and race* removed: .07.

186. For perspective, it might be noted that Jesness (1974) found much the same in connection with Loevinger's *Ego Level*, and drew essentially the same conclusion (the sample was again NYC males):

The results of a regression problem in which Ego Level was predicted from Age, Race, and IQ showed that 37 percent of the variance in Ego Level could be accounted for by these variables (multiple correlation = .61). This figure is somewhat higher than that for I-Level (27 percent of the variance [multiple correlation = .52]) . . . Ego Level appears to be somewhat more highly related to Age than is I-Level. The relationship between Ego Level and IQ is higher than that between I-Level and IQ (partial correlations of .47 and .23, respectively), but Ego Level shows a lower correlation with Race [.09]. Ego Level, like I-Level, appears to be something more than a mere function of Age, Race, and IQ, and whatever it is that something is shared by Ego Level and I-Level (p. 31).

Again Jesness (1974), this time for other Youth Authority wards:

While there is a relationship between I-Level and IQ, and between Rotter's I–E [Internal–External Locus of Control] and IQ, after the effects of IQ, Age, and Race are removed there continues to be a significant relationship between I-Level and *Internal-External Locus of Control.* As predicted, the more mature I-Level subtypes show a greater tendency to perceive controls as internal and reinforcement as contingent upon their own behavior (p. 34).

187. We will use only these authors' 1973 study (see text). Unlike their 1972 work, this one incorporated results and observations from Eaks' and Miller's 1972 studies.
188. In his 1975 article, Werner added a reference to Miller's (1972) study.
189. Miller (1972, 30) summarized their view regarding the I-Level/IQ relationship as follows: "[1] The concepts of perceptual development and cognitive differentiation, and [2] the ability to understand and cope with one's inner and outer worlds—(both [1] and [2] being fundamental in the I-Level framework, and hence in I-Level diagnosis)—should theoretically have in common certain of the attributes measured by tests of intelligence." (Quoted from Molof and Jesness, 1972, 68.)
190. Eaks (1972) pointed out the following:

Alluding to Piaget's theories of cognitive development, Sullivan, Grant, and Grant (1957) [stated] that "the normal pattern of emotional-social development follows a trend toward increasing involvement with people, objects, and social institutions. These involvements give rise to new needs, demands, and situations. Inherent in many of these new situations are problems of perceptual *discrimination [differentiation]* with regard to the relationships existing between the self and the external environment. As these discriminations are made and *assimilated,* a cognitive restructuring of experience and expectancy takes place. A new reference scheme is then developed; a new level of integration is achieved." [Quoted from Sullivan, Grant, and Grant, 1957, 374–375; emphasis added.] Piaget (1968) called this process equilibration (19–20).

[Piaget believed] that intellectual development is a chronological progression through four major stages . . . of cognitive development: (1) sensory motor intelligence (0–18 months), (2) preoperational or intuitive intelligence (18 months–7 years), (3) operational or concrete intelligence (7 years–11 years), and (4) formal operational intelligence (11 onward) . . . Thus, I_2 maturity [that is, this level of *integration*] seems to correspond with Piaget's stage of preoperational cognitive development, I_3 with operational (concrete) cognitive development, and I_4 with the beginning of formal (hypothetico-deductive) cognitive development. Both Piaget's theory of child development and the I-level classification system are based on the premise that growth—whether cognitive or behavioral—[involves] progress toward ever more complex and stable levels of organization (33–34; emphasis added).

Also, Zaidel (1970) indicated that

social perception, which is the basis of I-level classification, has been conceptualized in terms of ability. O'Sullivan, Guilford, and deMille [OGD] (1965) defined *social intelligence* as the ability to differentiate social stimuli or to understand complex interpersonal interactions. In Guilford's model of the structure of the intellect, social intelligence refers to cognitive operations on "behavioral contents," which include "feelings, motives, thoughts, intentions, attitudes, or other psychological dispositions which might affect an individual's social behavior" [OGD, 1965, 4]. Since I-level groups supposedly differ in their awareness and understanding of feelings, motives, needs, etc. in others, it could be said that they differ in social intelligence . . . (p. 9; emphasis in the original).

(Cf. Molof and Jesness' view on "abstraction and manipulation of social symbols in a culturally prescribed manner." This follows Miller, as item 5 in the text.)

191. To Community Treatment Project workers, a youth's level of intelligence ("IQ"; see below) was simply one more important factor in an array of varied yet often interacting factors. Among the latter were his attitudes, values, expectations, emotions, major motivations, interests and related desires or goals, and defenses. Like several of these, *IQ,* besides having a generalized bearing on intervention, had a more specific or heightened relevance to *particular* areas or issues, for instance, educational and vocational planning. Nevertheless, CTP workers, (1) aside from assessing and addressing IQ's likely role in connection with those areas/issues, and (2) unless the youth had shown either a substantial deficiency or advantage with respect to this factor, seldom focused on it as such, and did not try to separate it from the rest. "Seldom . . ." applied especially if the youth's IQ score was anywhere near—say, within 10 points from—either end of the normal range (90–110) for the general population. At any rate, workers focused specifically or intelligence itself mainly if—and whenever—a youth had a special learning problem, for instance, a physiologically grounded disability.

(For present purposes, and in simplified form, a youth's IQ score might be viewed as a standardized, quantitative indication of how he compares to others of his age on tested combinations of the following: amount and range of knowledge—that is [chiefly], familiarity with conventional information [*content,* such as facts]; understanding of concepts, principles, and situations—that is, ability to recognize or deduce their meaning, relationships, and implications; usual leaning speed and styles; and, usual information-processing/interrelating speed/styles, for already known material.

As indicated and implied, CTP workers, when addressing a youth's IQ—for example, when stating its likely implications in the initial intervention plan—viewed it as one more factor that could significantly affect his life. It could do so partly on its own ("directly") and partly with or via other factors ("indirectly")—ones, such as emotions, motivations, and defenses, it could often influence and that could frequently affect *it,* for instance, its quality and extent of functioning. (In both the direct and indirect case, the focus is on intelligence in *action,* not as capacity or potential alone.) Given its potential influence—here, its likely effects—IQ, like other active factors or forces (say, certain attitudes and desires), was to be not only worked *with,* that is, utilized essentially as-is (and whenever feasible), insofar as it would probably function as a *positive* force or ability. Instead, it was to be worked *on,* if and as needed—for example, if it was apparently serving as a liability or hindrance, again directly or indirectly. ("His life," above, refers not only to delinquent and delinquency related behaviors per se, but to everyday adjustment in general, to longer-term needs, and to various states of mind.)

Whatever factors, areas, or issues might have been involved (such as: certain *other* attitudes and desires; continuation of schooling; strivings for independence), "working with" and "working on" each applied irrespective of the individual's mode or level of thinking. For example, *both* types of effort could have been considered important not only for a youth who was almost always "concrete" in his thinking, but for one who often grasped and expressed "abstractions" and who may have recognized and utilized distinctions that many other individuals generally missed, or seldom used. "With" and "on" also applied regardless of a youth's usual *speed* of thinking, his amount/ range of information, and so on.

Basically, CTP workers believed that all or virtually all individuals on their respective caseloads had enough mental capacity—intellectual ability—to (1) avoid continued trouble with the law and to (2) participate in the program in ways that could improve their lives. Such capacity, per se, was not in question on either of these scores. (As implied above, for the vast majority of youths collectively, intellectual ability [whether reflected in style, speed, or content] with respect to (1) and (2) ranged from sufficient to easily more than enough, and this applied from the start of their program.) Instead, regarding any given youth, workers essentially believed that the intervention-relevant question centered on how that individual—especially as a result of his dynamics, motivations, and life-situation—was able to *use* the capacity he had and on how he actually *did* use it. More specifically, it centered, in the latter respect, on the particular behavioral choices/ decisions he made. (These decisions were conscious and intentional in one degree or another, that is, insofar as—and in the sense that—the youth could and did control and direct [ultimately and largely direct] the given behavior. This implies that he had at least *largely* resisted external pressures, that he had not been overwhelmed and otherwise largely controlled by his and/or others' emotions, ones he would have preferred to disavow and that were mainly unwanted; and so on. It does not, on the other hand, mean these choices were always unhurried and carefully considered, that they were seldom made under some—perhaps considerable—external pressure, and that they almost always occurred without any ambivalence, doubt, or regret.)

Community Treatment Project workers believed or implicitly assumed that these decisions were more often, or at least more heavily, influenced by the earlier-mentioned factors—especially *combinations* of factors (such as attitudes, interests, and defenses)—than by whether the individual's overall IQ was, say, somewhat below the normal range rather than somewhat above it (for instance, in the 80s instead of 110s). In any event, workers operated on the belief/assumption that such factors/combinations often had a major and primary influence—again a direct or indirect effect—on the individual's attention and judgment. In this regard, these separate or collective factors—operating as forces and conditions—could, for instance, divert or dilute his attention, cloud and confound his judgment, and so on. As a result, they could cause him to overlook and devalue possible choices, and to reject or delay possible decisions, he had the mental capacity, and, say, the realistic opportunity, to make—ones he perhaps *would* otherwise ordinarily make. This applies even when those factors/ combinations do not include strong *desires* and/or *fears,* or are not particularly compounded by them.

At any rate, workers felt that a youth whose IQ was, say, 110–115 or more could ignore/overlook positive opportunities, and make harmful or wasteful decisions, just as easily and often as could an individual whose score was 85–90 or less. That is to say, he could do so not just irrespective of whether his score was above or below average, and of what his particular I-Level and subtype might be, but, specifically, regardless of whether (1) his thinking was relatively quick rather than fairly slow (not just deliberate and cautious), (2) his thoughts and concepts were often differentiated rather than simplistic, and (3) he possessed a large pool of learning skills and a larger rather than smaller amount of culturally shared, practical information. To be sure, the more conceptual skills, accurate information, and so on he had the faster he could ordinarily move in a productive manner with respect to various areas, such as the vocational—move, that is, if and when he was ready, and with other conditions being about equal. Also, the more likely he would be to generate helpful options, approaches, and positive decisions themselves, in situations of heightened complexity or ambiguity.

Finally, workers took it for granted that a youth's *assumptions and stereotypes (A&Ss)* could markedly affect the nature and quality—and, more concretely, the direction and extent—of his intellectual functioning, and that this applied to a wide range of contexts. With that, A&Ss could significantly or decisively affect the chances of his drawing sensible conclusions and could substantially influence his decision-making and decision-avoidance alike. Moreover, the workers assumed this could often occur despite the contrary implications and overall force of other information and inputs (I&Is) the youth possessed or received, and that of new (I&Is) he might receive. (For these reasons, many workers worked *on* certain A&Ss. Here, their efforts were similar to those centering on any other negative "factor," such as certain attitudes, desires, and defenses.)

192. These are measured by the California Psychological Inventory.

193. Regarding that study, see the "Construct Validity of I-Levels" section of this chapter.

194. Empirically, the JI scales—individually and especially collectively—were most directly related to the Warren *subtypes.* As detailed next, their relationship to the *I-Levels* followed automatically from their connection with those subtypes, since each subtype was already an intrinsic constituent of a particular level, and of that level only (examples of JI scales are: Social Maladjustment, Value Orientation, Immaturity, and Denial): Jesness, when developing and validating his inventory, had proceeded by first empirically identifying particular profiles that were each comprised of *scale-scores,* profiles that, respectively, were most closely associated with a given Warren subtype (one profile per subtype, and one subtype per profile). In so doing, his goal was not only to best predict—to therein identify—each youth's subtype, but to reliably distinguish that subtype from all other subtypes, and, in so doing, to optimally classify the individual in this regard.

(Operationally, each individual's profile consisted of—and consisted *only* of—his score on each and every scale;

and, to determine his subtype classification, that profile was compared to each of the just-mentioned, maximally predictive profiles that had already been established and validated for the respective subtypes. [On any profile for any subtype, any scale's score could have been far above, somewhat above, somewhat below, or far below average—or else essentially average. This applied not only to the preestablished, normed and otherwise standardized, profiles for a given subtype, but to the particular profile for each given youth.] The individual's subtype classification—his "diagnosis"—was based on *which* of these preestablished, standardized profiles *his* profile most resembled.)

Because each subtype belonged to a particular I-Level—more specifically, because (given Warren's elaboration [Grant, 1961c] of the basic Interpersonal Maturity theory) a given subtype had helped constitute, and was intrinsic to, a particular level and only that level—the following was the case. A given *scale*—particularly in the context of the preexisting profile that served as the standard for determining each individual's *subtype*—was related (broadly speaking, it was a "correlate") not only to a specific subtype, but, ipso facto, to a particular *level*: Logically and functionally, not by virtue of any separate or further statistical operation(s) that might have occurred, the scale in question was, so to speak, a correlate of that I-Level "one-step-removed." Once the subtype had been determined, so—by definition and, thus, automatically—had the level.

Finally, all of the preceding applies independently of the following. Even apart from various statistical procedures that may be (and had been) used, such as correlation analyses and discriminant function techniques, it is evident that particular Jesness Inventory scales *should* be associated with certain subtypes more than with others. (This applies especially to particular combinations of scales— more precisely, to combinations or patterns of their *above average, below average,* and so on, scores.) It is "evident" in view of the (1) substantive overlap (the direct, content-centered relationship), and/or the (2) logically inferable connections (clear connections, again centered on content) that exist between the explicit definition of those respective scales (that is, the statement of their *meaning* which appears in the inventory's manual), on the one hand, and the definitions as well as descriptions of the given subtypes, on the other. Chief among these scales are Value Orientation, Alienation, Manifest Aggression, Withdrawal-Depression, and Social Anxiety.

195. The three personality clusters—also called "CPI variable clusters"—were "Adult-role Socialization," "Ascendant Extroversion," and "Personal Maturity." They were seen as reflecting broad aspects of social and personal development.

196. Werner then added:

No support can be found in these data for the implications of the Cross and Tracy findings regarding ethnic status as a moderator of I-level meaning. It is, of course, still possible that such interaction effects exist with respect to the particular measures of future time perspective and locus of control employed by these investigators. Also, it should be remembered that [they] compared Whites with Blacks while the present research compared Whites with non-Whites, only 60 percent of whom were Black (1972, 45–46).

In conclusion, Werner noted the following—which bears on the factor of intelligence as well:

Although Cross and Tracy found that Blacks and Whites within their study sample did not differ significantly with respect to intelligence, they did differ markedly with respect to I-level. Thus, although the importance of intelligence to the well-documented I-level/ethnic status relationship has not yet been definit[ively] determined, there is good reason to believe that its role is less than a dominant one. The lack of three-factor interaction together with the presence of the significant I-level/CPI Otype relationship indicates that the I-level/ethnic status relationship is not the result of ethnic status *per se* playing a role in diagnosis.

Were this the case, one would not expect particular I-level groups to appear so similar (in terms of the configurations of CPI cluster scores studied) across ethnic samples (1972, 46; 1975, 66).

(Regarding the I-Level/ethnicity/*intelligence* interaction, findings and a general conclusion by *Zaidel* [1970, 40–45; 1973, 52] might be mentioned:

I-level × Race ANOVAs were carried out for all four intelligence tests [Raven's Progressive Matrices, SRA verbal, SRA nonverbal, and Revised Beta] . . . The overall I-level effect was stronger than the Race effect on all four tests, although Race was significant on three of [them] and approached significance on the fourth . . . Overall, the partial analyses of variance suggest that the relationship between I-level and intelligence was independent of race. [This applied to all four tests.] [1970, 43]

Finally, and still with reference to intelligence, *Cross and Tracy* [1971, 18–19] found no significant difference in verbal IQ between Blacks and Whites, although they neither analyzed and compared each of these groups separately for each I-Level nor carried out an overall analysis of variance on IQ × Race × I-Level.)

197. Molof and Jesness added that Cross and Tracy's "findings that Black I-3 subjects had a greater external perception of control over rewards than Black I-2 subjects . . . were not replicated in the present study . . . [Similarly,] in our sample there was hardly any difference in mean I-E [Internal-External] scores for I-2 and I-3 subjects who were Mexican-American" (1973, 20). (Too few Mexican-American I_4's [N = 2] were present for meaningful analyses. No findings were presented for I-2 vs. I-4 Blacks as well as I-3 versus I-4 Blacks, and none at all were provided for Caucasians.)

It might be noted that *Eaks* (1972), in his earlier-mentioned study, drew the following conclusions regarding ethnicity (race):

Analyzing the [study's] data within racial groupings rather than pooling

Caucasian, Black, and Mexican American together, failed to add much additional information to the hypothesis findings [that is, to those presented earlier in this chapter regarding future time perspective in particular] . . . Differences did occur on the test variables, but the racial differences were more in *magnitude* than in direction. In general, racial differences did not contradict hypothesis findings, thus giving added credence . . . to developmental theory . . . [Related to this was the fact that] for each racial group where significant relationships occurred, future time perspective . . . correlated positively with I-level" (1972, 116, 143, 205).

(It might be kept in mind that Eaks' findings did not reflect comparisons between one ethnic group and another [as in Werner], or between one ethnic group and itself [as in Molof and Jesness, across I-Levels]. Instead, they reflected first-order correlations and partial correlations between each ethnic group and given test variables—here, measures of future time perspective.)

198. Three points might be noted. (1) The levels that were analyzed typically included all I_2's through I_4's, and any I_5's as well. However, in a few studies or analyses, the small percentage—and, almost always, small number—of I_2's and/or I_5's who were present in the main or the eligible sample were excluded, for statistical reasons. (2) Based on separate studies of their own, each of the first four "other . . . systems" that is mentioned next (see text) appeared to have not just concurrent validity (say, mutual substantive overlap), itself, but substantial construct validity as well. (3) Despite their "substantial and . . . significant [inter]correlations," the eight developmental systems that are mentioned in the text are far from duplicates of each other. Again, this is despite the intrinsic and/or extrinsic similarity or connection—sometimes a rather close one—that several of these systems have to each other, in one or more respects.

199. Based on not only the correlation between I-Level and each of the eight other developmental systems, respectively, but also on the intercorrelations among each of the eight themselves (Hunt's, Loevinger's, and so on), these systems, collectively, account for about 55 percent to 60 percent of the variance in I-Level. When one adds intelligence, age, SES, and ethnicity (race) to the picture, the number reaches approximately 70 percent. Similar figures would result if one reversed the analytic procedure, that is, if—still using multiple regression—one began with the background/demographics (starting with "intelligence") and subsequently added the systems.

200. In studies that involved the first types of "instruments or scales," no statistically significant relationships were found between I-Level, on the one hand, and (1) felt/perceived *internalized guilt* as well as (2) *manifest anxiety,* on the other. (See Miller [1972], Eaks [1972], and Cross and Tracy [1971], whose studies focused mainly on "generic variables.") Miller suggested an explanation for the first of these findings—one that could also be applied to the second, that would probably make considerable sense to most practitioners familiar with I-Level subtypes, and that, in any event, centered on

the characteristic response styles of one of the subtypes within Level 4 [:] Labeled Neurotic – Acting-out (NA) youths, a dominant characteristic of this group (who comprise nearly half of the population of I-4 juvenile offenders) is a tendency to deny categorically any feelings of inadequacy or inferiority. The feelings of *guilt, anxiety,* and negative self-image are theoretically present within the I-4 NA, however, an admission of these feelings will not readily be forthcoming. The subtypes within I-level classification (unlike the theory of levels) are said to be empirically derived, and if this characteristic of the NA was indeed operating in the present study, it might help explain the lack of increased internalized guilt as I-level increased (pp. 94–95; emphasis added).

Finally, although one of the reviewed findings that involved (3) *future time perspective* or its related/comparable constucts was not statistically significant, all of the others were.

201. This, of course, does not include the distinctions and other refinements made by the present author during 1969–1971, with regard to several of Warren et al's. mid-1960s revisions.

202. Three points might be mentioned in this respect. (1) The absence in question applied even in area (1). (2) Virtually no female Ci's were ever encountered. Even within the California experiment, none were found in the Valley units (Phases 1 and 2) and only two were observed in San Francisco (Phase 2). (3) Regarding policy-based and resource-based factors that may have contributed to the absence of Warren *Se's,* see the Budnoff study (1963) and that of Ferdinand (1978). These factors existed independently of the fact that, in the 1978 study, many or most youths whom Ferdinand called "normal" could perhaps have been called Se instead.

203. Various typologists have delineated and emphasized all three of these constellations; several others have mentioned two—one usually being the neurotic. At any rate, these particular *three* have long been described by typologists collectively. This is the case whether these individuals have used (a) the specific names in question or (b) ones that differed somewhat—yet, as in (a), that conveyed very similar or identical concepts. These broad groupings, when taken together, have usually been viewed as constituting the preponderance of all adjudicated youths, particularly those other than first-timers.

204. In this regard, each of the following blends is associated with the subtype that appears next to it (again: in any given blend, one pole of a dimension is combined with one constellation): passive antisocial – *Cfc;* active/assertive antisocial – *Mp;* active/assertive neurotic – *Na;* passive neurotic – *Nx;* active/assertive antisocial – *Ci.* As is evident, some subtypes (here, the Mp and Ci) are not yet distinguished from each other when the pole that partly describes them (here, the "active/assertive" pole) is combined with the constellation ("anti-

social") that does likewise. As a result, further information—for instance, a second dimension or factor—is needed before these groups can be mutually distinguished. This information might help differentiate or further distinguish various *other* subtypes as well, mainly from each other.

205. In order to recognize major correspondences between *Aa's* as well as *Ap's,* on the one hand, and the original/revised descriptions of these subtypes, on the other, a developmental component *is* important. (As seen in Rubenfeld [1967, 7–13], the individuals who comprise these two subtypes—and the latters' corresponding, presumed level—have, collectively, been given the following labels by various typologists: "impulse oriented," "primitive," "unsocialized," and "immature"; Warren termed them "asocial" as well as "low maturity" [I_2].) To substantively distinguish each of these subtypes from (a) *specific other subtypes*—as opposed to only distinguishing them from (b) *each and every other presumed level* and its *collective* constituent subtypes (which can be done via a developmental component, operating by itself)—further information is needed. The passive versus active/assertive dimension constitutes one such type of information. When providing this "further information" and thereby contributing to the differentiation in question (that is, to item (a), above), this dimension is operating not only on its own or at least partly on its own (thus, "in its own right"), but also in conjunction with the developmental component. Absent this component it could still provide important differentiating information, but not as much. These same considerations apply to other dimensions as well.

206. Of these *"other* subtypes," some—for instance, the Mp and Nx—may not become substantially more differentiated from *one another* when the "further" (the second) dimension is added. This near-absence or even a complete absence of increased mutual differentiation on their part is separate from whether they had each become more *recognizable* than *before,* in the first place. That is, it

differs from, and can be essentially independent of, whether these respective subtypes had acquired a more particular and distinct identity when dimension two was added. (Certain subtypes, such as the Cfm, *would,* as indicated, have already become more recognizable when that further dimension was added.)

207. These are the relatively "insulated" Cfc's far more often than those characterized as "accessible." (See Chapter 15.)

208. Two points might be noted. (1) Complicating matters somewhat is the fact that pattern B is associated not just with Cfm's in particular (and above all), but also with a modest-to-moderate percentage of all youths classified as *Nx's.* Though this percentage—about 20 to 30—is considerably smaller than that of all Cfm's, the absolute *number* of Nx's and Cfm's in many gangs is about equal. (Most remaining delinquent Nx's spend substantial time with groups of friends, but not with delinquent gangs per se.) (2) The patterns, "when combined with . . . ," also help distinguish the Cfc, Cfm, and Ci groups, respectively, from *Se's.*

209. This, of course, does not mean that the patterns of relationships next described did not *develop*—did not, for instance, evolve from various personal, social, and other inputs.

210. It will be recalled that gang affiliation is not a required element, let alone the decisive factor and the sine qua non, in the definition of Cfc. This is the case even though such affiliation is very common and usually strong among Cfc's, especially the "insulated." As indicated in Appendix 32, the decisive factor is the individual's self-identification as a delinquent, whether or not this identification is prominent and rather strong (therein a conspicuous component of his self-image, not just an important one; the "whether" and the "not" pertain to "insulated" and "accessible" youths, respectively). This point regarding "the decisive factor" applies (1) whatever might be the usual setting for the individual's illegal behavior, and whoever he may be with at the time (gang member or not), and (2) whether or not that particular component of his self-image

seems (a) much more crystallized and strong than (b) formative, unsettled, and perhaps transitory (but is, even in (b), still critical to his *present* delinquency).

211. Though quite willing to engage in frequent and even serious illegal behavior, most gang-centered youths do not believe they would easily commit homicide or a life-threatening offense, and that they are otherwise inclined to do so. Nevertheless, many feel that situations could arise which might, in their view, necessitate such actions. Chief among these situations or circumstances would be the gang's efforts to protect not only its "turf" (geographic and other), but any physically attacked member.

212. This rejection/repudiation—even when only moderately intense—goes beyond disinterest and general indifference.

213. As can be inferred from Chapter 26, such reductions are limited to neither gang-centered youths nor the Cfc category per se. At any rate, regarding Cfc's in particular, they include individuals who are not gang-centered as well as those who are.

214. Of all *youths* who are *gang-centered,* a high percentage correspond to the "insulated" Cfc's described in Chapter 15, and many or most of the rest are the "accessible" Cfc's. Of all *Cfc's* who are *insulated,* a high percentage, though again not nearly all, are gang-centered. (Many insulated Cfc's who are not gang-centered are often considered loners.) However, of all Cfc's who are *accessible,* many are *not* gang-centered—particularly in that they are not solidly identified with it, may or may not want to spend large amounts of their free time with it, and so on. Whether insulated or accessible, Cfc's, like many other youths (gang-centered or not), not infrequently engage in illegal and borderline-legal behavior when in the company of one or two delinquently oriented or delinquency—accepting friends or acquaintances who are *not* known members of a gang. (Throughout this endnote we have, as usual, focused only on serious multiple offenders.

215. Two points might be noted. First, item-(1) feelings, and especially the first two feelings in item (2), when expressed by the youth, are seldom verbalized in

terms of the particular words that appear in the text. (The third item-(2) feeling usually appears as "bad" or "no good.") Second, regarding the individual's *responses* to those feelings—for instances, behavioral responses that involve his dependence on the gang and his related roles within it—the following applies: The youth hardly at all conceptualizes or otherwise grasps the cause/effect relationships that exist between any of the listed feelings (for instance: being "unappreciated"; "inadequacy"), on the one hand, and various such responses to them, on the other. In this regard, those input/output relationships or connections are not part of his focused awareness. Stated differently and more specifically, the existence and (especially) the nature of these connections is largely "outside"—and often "below" (as in: dynamically kept below)—that aspect of his consciousness. (Both their existence and nature, however, are sometimes sensed in a diffuse, global, and—in the case of "nature"—simplified but not necessarily accurate manner.) Given this situation, those relationships are not available for the youth's direct and purposeful inspection (I), evaluation (E), and subsequent modification (M)—that is, M which is based on the results of that I and E. More specifically, the relationships between the youth's feelings and his responses to them are not *yet* available—as of, for example, his first entering a program. In particular, those feelings and responses are not yet focused on *jointly* (in fact, only seldom have they—especially the latter—even been examined individually), and the connections between the two are not recognized as such by the youth, let alone clearly understood with respect to their nature.

216. When with the gang, the youth is in a "place" where he can do each of the following: (1) Often relax more than in most other settings—for example, experience considerably less, and less frequent, interpersonal tension, hassle, and mistrust, and, as a result, be less defensive and on-the-alert; (2) usually feel wanted or mostly wanted; (3) sometimes even feel needed—or, at least, often ap-

preciated and considered helpful; and, largely because of (1) through (3), (4) usually have a sense of at least partial belonging. Item (4) mainly involves, in particular, a feeling that the gang is something he is more or less part of— pretty much fits in with. Finally, and substantially related to all four points, most gang-dependent youths feel they are treated more consistently within that setting than in most others, and usually more fairly as well.

217. Usually, the youth neither minimizes the seriousness of most such actions nor tries hard to conceal their main intent and to justify them—by saying, for instance, such things as, "It was no big deal, and we made sure no one would get hurt anyway," "We were just foolin' around," and, "They [the burglarized store owners] are rich, anyway." In this regard, he generally does not utilize what are many gang-*centered* members' "neutralization techniques" (Matza, 1964) and related approaches to describing and attempting to justify those illegal activities, and their own role in them. To be sure, the fact that the youth usually acknowledges the often-serious as well as deliberate nature of those behaviors *and* provides basic details about them does not mean he *hardly ever* tries to avoid consequences, evade responsibility, withhold information, and so on. Nevertheless, his level of forthrightness regarding the given offenses— essentially the same type of offenses—is higher than that of most gang-centered individuals.

218. Presently, the gang-dependent youths hope that the punishment they receive will lead some of these other adults to forgive them or, in any event, to at least give them a chance to eventually gain or regain their acceptance. At the same time, however, these youths commonly believe and worry that—punishment notwithstanding—their illegal behavior may well have set most of those adults, and perhaps others as well, against them (that is, against them once and for all), or may have confirmed and perhaps even strengthened those individuals' preexisting, negative impressions of them. (Most gang-*centered* youths are less concerned with this possibility.)

Such beliefs, and especially worries, exist more often with respect to parents or parent substitutes.

219. The youth believes in the existence of this pleasure and relaxation, or at least implicitly assumes it, mainly based on general social inputs and specific personal experiences. Chief among these are: media characterizations of marriage and family life; first- and second-hand observations regarding the families of certain friends; and, observations of interactions between other couples or partners, for instance, neighbors or relatives. The individual's view in this matter, and his related positive feelings, largely predates his exposure to the gang's mostly dismissive or otherwise *rejecting* attitudes toward various conventional life-styles; that is, it formed (though may not have entirely *stopped* forming) prior to most such exposure. Whether this belief/assumption exists within, outside, or somewhat below consciousness—(in each case, it is fairly accessible to the youth)—it can, and often does, function rather independently of his knowledge of the gang's attitudes. In effect, it exists and frequently operates in parallel with that awareness, or largely irrespective of it. (This applies whether or not it is largely crystallized, and especially if it is relatively so.) In addition, this belief/assumption sometimes neutralizes and otherwise modifies the results of—for instance, expectations that arise from—various negative personal experiences involving his parents or parent substitutes.

220. Regarding the youth's eventual independence from the family, that is, his physical and economic emancipation from it, this can be a component of highly conventional, less conventional, and unconventional life-styles alike.

221. When talking about his antisocial beliefs with fellow gang members, the youth thinks he is saying things they will welcome. Although, in stating those beliefs (views, positions), he is expressing values and attitudes he actually does accept, and although he is being accurate—is speaking honestly—in that respect, he does not mention certain *other* things he believes and/or accepts.

These are views he knows are rather different than those he talks about with the gang; they are positions and preferences regarding *pro*social values/attitudes— ones that conflict with the former and which are no less significant to him. In this regard, the youth does not tell gang members "the *whole* truth." (The preceding has focused on the content of given views, not on their "level" and "intensity"—which are mentioned next.) Moreover, the youth's actual *commitment* to most of the antisocial views he expresses to those individuals—that is, his level of internal adherence to (true acceptance of) the first-mentioned values/attitudes—is seldom deep and intense; instead, it is somewhat fluid, and open to change. (Compare endnote #225 regarding forms—and strength— of "acceptance.")

(Though the youth knows he can change in that regard, he does not specifically associate this lack of *depth* and *intensity,* per se, with the views he expresses to the gang; he does not actually connect or otherwise ascribe these particular features to those positions. More fundamentally—that is, to add a causal element—he is only vaguely aware of these aspects of commitment, themselves; specifically, he hardly even conceives of them in the first place, and ipso facto can hardly think about them. Moreover, the youth's gang—centered companions do not recognize this absence of strong internal commitment; that is, they are essentially unaware of it in him. As a result, they cannot press him on it and thereby help bring it to his awareness. Most of these companions seldom think about, let along focus on, the internal-strength factor in any event; at least, they seldom do so in connection with verbalizations. Instead, they routinely take members' statements regarding personal beliefs at face value [for instance, without particularly reflecting on them and trying to look beneath the surface]; and what they mainly focus on is these youths' *actions,* much as they do on their own. What counts with them is knowing that these youths do in fact "run with" them and back them up— that they actively participate in the gang's illegal and borderline activities, help protect its members when necessary, and so on.)

The gang-dependent youth does not often focus on the above-mentioned differences, divergences, and conflicts that exist between the views he presents to the gang and those he does not. (The latter, as indicated, involve socially acceptable values and attitudes he expresses to other, largely *non*delinquent peers, and/or to certain adults.) Instead, he mostly compartmentalizes and controls those two sets of views, as follows: (1) He tries to keep them separate from each other, in his mind. (2) He keeps the prosocial views to himself, when interacting with the gang. Regarding (1), the youth tries, for instance, to not compare the two sets of views with each other on various scores, and to not think about their already evident, differing implications for his life. In both respects, particularly that of implications, he tries to avoid making major, zero-sum choices between those sets: For one thing, he especially wants to avoid becoming increasingly and heavily involved with activities that reflect gang-supportive beliefs/positions—more precisely, becoming *so* involved that they might eliminate or greatly reduce and restrict certain prosocial activities and opportunities. At the same time (but to a lesser yet still sizable degree), he does not want to make choices that increase *pro*social involvements to the point of crowding out or precluding the gang-related. At any rate, the youth senses that the two sets of views—each of which has substantial attraction to him, and, in effect, exerts a force—are only marginally compatible, and cannot be fundamentally integrated. Rather than becoming substantively merged they must exist side by side, and separately. The youth realizes this without having given the matter much thought and having made numerous point by point comparisons.

Regarding (2), the youth does not feel significantly disloyal to the gang even though he withholds that prosocial information in question. More particularly, he usually feels loyal *enough,* or more than just enough, when (a) he reminds himself of what—despite his prosocial beliefs, attitudes, and involvements—he in fact *is* willing to do for and with its members, and especially when (b) his actions directly show those individuals that this is the case. In short, when the youth feels he "come[s] through" for the gang to the extent of meeting its main expectations, and when he intends to keep doing so in the future, he considers himself a good member—good enough, at any rate, to be and remain accepted. Because of (a) and (b), he feels little need or obligation to tell its members about his activities and involvements with certain other groups or individuals. He feels further justified in this regard insofar as he believes (which he largely does), or convinces himself, that those interactions—as long as he does not substantially increase them—will hardly affect his ability to meet the gang's main expectations. Nevertheless, despite his awareness of what he does with and for the gang, of what he is willing to continue doing, and so on, the youth hopes its members will not learn much about his prosocial activities, involvements, and related beliefs (AIB's). This is because he is not sure of how those youths would individually and collectively react to such information, even if he tried to assure them that those AIB's pose no threat to the gang, are not as important as his involvements with *them,* and so on.

As implied, the gang-dependent youth regularly makes strong efforts to present two rather different pictures of himself—one to fellow gang members, one to essentially law-abiding peers and adults. (These pictures are disparate—mutually incompatible in key respects—not just divergent yet fairly compatible or ultimately reconcilable.) These efforts, and their main results (namely, the dual pictures), usually create little mental distress (pain) for him, even though they involve ongoing stress (strain). More specifically, (1) the gang-dependent youth easily self-justifies those efforts, and does not feel distressed or otherwise badly about making them. (2) Apart from the general stress involved in his trying to maintain a somewhat double life, the main psychological difficulty he experiences regarding those efforts centers on his worry or fear that if some of his "other" beliefs/activities become known to the "wrong" individuals—whether gang members or the law-abiding—they will seriously undermine the picture he hopes that have of him.

(In general, the gang-dependent youth creates and maintains the respective pictures by highlighting different sides of himself to the differing groups/individuals—by spotlighting, for instance, only certain characteristics, beliefs, and activities while downplaying or omitting others. For many or most other adolescents, and for most adults, such spotlighting, and so on, would involve interpersonal deceptiveness that they would consider unjustified and unacceptable in the vast majority of circumstances with which they are familiar. [This would apply whatever the *content* of the *disparate* pictures might be, and it would especially pertain if the given efforts—the accenting and minimizing—were made to the same large degree that the gang-dependent youths made them.] As a result, if those adolescents and adults were to seriously undertake such efforts—again, particularly but not only to the degree in question—this would cause them considerable distress with regard to the integrity component of their self-image. As can be inferred, this distress would differ in focus from the strain of trying to *maintain* the resulting pictures, that is, from the attempt to manage this major duality in their life. It would also differ from, but be far from unrelated to, the following—which involves the earlier-mentioned aspect of compartmentalization that centers on trying to keep the "two sets of views . . . separate from each other, in [one's] mind": Whether they are law-abiding or not, most adolescents and adults, including most of the above who would feel distress, resemble the gang-dependent youth in (1) frequently believing—often uncritically and based on little evidence—what they have a strong *need,* and a related desire, to believe and accept, and in (2) often rejecting, misinterpreting, or blocking out much of what is simply unwanted by them or which would oppose those beliefs. [Especially among the gang-dependent, the "need" is to gain or maintain acceptance/approval, to avoid or reduce long-standing psychological pain, and so on.] In this regard, they resemble many other delinquents as well.)

Finally, the fact that the present youth's "true acceptance of" most of the *anti*social views he verbalizes is "seldom deep and intense" is closely linked to the coexistence of his substantial commitment to various *pro*social activities/involvements, ones he wants to retain no less than some antisocial. That is to say: (1) because the youth realizes that antisocial and prosocial stances are largely incompatible, especially if they are not kept separate; (2) because he senses that if he becomes heavily and/or rigidly invested in *one* of those stances (not to mention both), and if he generally acts in accordance with such an investment, (a) the two stances will be harder to keep separate from each other and, in any event, (b) the given investment and form of activity could undermine and perhaps largely unravel many of his desired, existing involvements with his *other* stance (say, the prosocial); and, (3) because he does not want to take a sizable chance of precipitating such events and possible loss, the following occurs *(note:* (2a) and (2b) would occur especially but not only if the youth tried to clearly favor one of those stances over the other, when acting "in accordance"): He emotionally holds back—and sometimes partially pulls back—in connection with one or both stances (areas). For instance, the youth especially tries to not let his investment in the *anti*social area become entrenched, unbending, and rather pervasive in the first place; also, in order to facilitate the type and amount of involvement which he *does* have in that area, he may withdraw somewhat—sometimes considerably—from sizable, long-standing interests and active involvements he has maintained in the *pro*social. At any rate, it is for such interrelated reasons as (1) through (3) that the youth's "actual *commitment*" to his verbalized antisocial stance—that is, his "internal adherence" to it—is very often other than deep and intense. (Here, "stance" need not be limited to views that are verbalized, whether to gang members or others.)

Thus, driven and directed mainly by his strong unmet needs, by his wishes, and by his understandings and related expectations, the youth accommodates and adapts the antisocial and prosocial stances to each other and simultaneously prevents each one from developing beyond a given point. In effect, he functionally relates these stances to each other on (1) a mutually impelling (prompting, engaging, prodding) and amending (modifying) basis yet also on (2) a mutually constraining and limiting one. This allows him to retain sizable amounts of *both* stances/investments. By avoiding what to him would be *over*commitment to one or both stances, it also helps him handle, though not eliminate, his fear of substantial undermining, unraveling, and loss.

Although the youth, "when talking about his antisocial beliefs with fellow gang members, . . . is expressing values and attitudes he actually does accept," and although he, like many other individuals, believes and accepts what he has "a strong *need,* and a related desire, to believe and accept," it remains the case that his level of personal commitment to most of those beliefs is often neither deep nor intense. In other words, he holds certain beliefs and accepts given stances or sizable portions thereof even when his internal, emotional commitment to them is not *strong*. This applies even when the content as well as the comparative "strength" (strength usually being less than high) of those respective beliefs/stances is—functionally—fairly stable and predictable at the time. Moreover, and more particularly, even though a *strong need,* and so on, *is* closely associated with the generation and maintenance of the given beliefs, this does not ipso facto mean the youth necessarily has or will have a strong *internal commitment* to them. One reason for this is that other factors, among which may be *different* needs and desires, are also at play. By helping to dilute and otherwise counter various effects of the first-mentioned needs/desire(s), some of these factors, individually and/or collectively, can significantly influence the youth's overall level of commitment—can prevent it, for example, from becoming intense in the first place, or can lead to its reduction later on.

222. Though this emphasizes boundaries per se, it includes *content* which may differ from and/or oppose that of the commitment's, even if often partly restrained by it.

223. Expect, at least, if one considered no information other than these two features—"contents" and "involvements"—alone.

224. Any one or more illegal acts can get an individual into serious, long-lasting difficulty (1) whether or not a gang helped generate the act(s), (2) irrespective of how encompassing and otherwise strong a contributor's—here, a gang's—overall influence and power happened to be and may continue to be, and (3) regardless of whether and how that individual is personally *committed* to illegal behavior. (Regarding "how," see "acceptance," in the endnote which follows.)

225. Among serious juvenile offenders, "acceptance" of illegal behavior and of antisocial values an attributes can range from a *genuine/sincere* form to a largely *opportunistic/convenience-based* one—with the latter, unlike the former, often involving relatively little personal conviction, yet not infrequently moderate amounts. In between (or "alongside") these forms, but generally closer to the first one, is a somewhat separable, relatively *unthinking/uncritical* type, one that often seems passive and in some respects reflexive. Even though the first-mentioned form of acceptance is genuine/sincere (G/S), it can be strongly (S), moderately (M), *or* weakly (W) *felt* by the youths; and, again somewhat separably, the illegal behavior involved—like the given values/attitudes—can be S, M, or W *defended* by them, verbally and/or otherwise. (Together, S, M, and W comprise an "intensity-range." In this connection an individual can, for example, strongly accept [feel] illegal behavior yet only weakly [or, alternatively, strongly] try to defend it.)

Compared to G/S acceptance, the unthinking/uncritical (U/U) and especially the opportunistic/convenience-based (O/C) ones have a narrower intensity-range; in addition, they—particularly the O/C—are much more often associated with its "weaker" than its "stronger" end. Among gang-dependent youths, collectively, the O/C and U/U forms are each a little more common than the G/S. Regarding *gang-centered* individuals, the genuine/sincere is modal. (In all the preceding, G/S, O/C, and U/U are types or products, not *bases* of acceptance.)

226. For reasons related to the following, those "charges" have a different meaning and dynamic than *boosts* which are obtained by the *gang-dependent* youth: With the gang-organizer, in marked contrast to the latter, needs for acceptance, approval, and overall emotional security are seldom largely *unmet*, and, with that, are seldom unusually *strong*. (The listed needs exist, of course, among essentially all adolescents, in one form or another.) In addition, the present individual, again unlike the gang-dependent, does not have a sense of wide-spread inadequacy and of being minimally valued by parents, by certain other significant adults, and even by various peers. Given this situation, and in light of the gang-organizer's positive strengths per se, this youth, obviously, does not have a need to rely on the gang—let alone rely on it heavily—to help him address factors, conditions, and complexities such as the following: (1) strong, unmet needs of those particular types, and (2) feelings that exist, and often become intense, mainly because those needs are largely unmet, and that, in turn, adversely affect various areas of the individual's life.

Directly to the point, the fact that the preceding (specifically, certain unmet needs, a sense of inadequacy, and so on) is essentially a *non*issue for the gang-organizer—that it constitutes neither a problem for him nor even exists—yet *is* an issue for the gang-dependent youth, largely reveals why, and indicates how, the former's "charges" differ from the latter's "boosts": The first (the charge) provides an added pleasure or "kick" to a view of one's self that already regularly involves *average or above average* confidence, respect—(that is, the youth has self-confidence and self-respect)—and a concept of being likable to others. In effect, that "charge" also helps confirm (to the youth), and sometimes temporarily expand, positive thoughts and feelings the individual already has about himself, regarding those dimensions. The second (the boost), in contrast, helps raise a self-image that is *low or very low* with respect to those dimensions. In this connection it, in effect, helps counter and relieve—though often only briefly—negative thoughts and feelings the youth has about himself. It may simultaneously provide at least a modicum of positive feeling per se, ones that can nonetheless matter greatly to him. To be sure, with both types of youth, and with the gang-centered as well, the preceding outcomes and related reinforcements commonly result—within the gang setting—from illegal or borderline behavior, from verbal expressions of antisocial values, and so on.

227. These may be group or individual settings. Also, they may involve peers only or can include some adults. Here, we will focus on peer-centered, group (though not gang) settings.

228. The youth's attempts to obtain these IPP's, particularly but not only in the gang setting, can be distinguished from certain activities and efforts that can occur most fully in *NGND* settings *(note*: besides schools and other social institutions, these settings mainly involve formal and informal organizations, associations, groups, and events; we will emphasize schools): In the non-gang, nondelinquent setting, the present youth, like any other, can familiarize himself with certain *future-oriented* opportunities and/or necessities (FON's) that have broad relevance to adolescents—delinquent and other—and that generally involve or imply adulthood-centered activities such as employment, and roles that relate to marriage, cohabitation, and perhaps parenthood. If and as interested, the youth—like others—can also begin to *work on* these FON's in those settings, say, via vocational-

centered classroom efforts. He can, for instance, try to acquire requisite skills and knowledge and he can learn to adapt, redirect, and perhaps expend certain already-existing abilities, information, and habits. As to the IPP's themselves—specifically, the already-mentioned, *delinquently-involved, gang-centered,* immediate personal payoffs—the following applies. These, like FON's as well, can be distinguished from certain immediate physical pleasures, material satisfactions, and psychological gratifications—in other words, from *other* IPP's—that do *not* rely on delinquent activities, let alone center on them. In this connection the following might also be noted. (1) Though nondelinquent activities and their resulting personal payoffs (rewards/gratifications) are most common and most readily available *outside* the gang, (2) other such activities can occur—and their personal payoffs would be obtained—*within* the gang setting, often even to a sizable degree. Both (1) and (2) apply to all gang members, not just the present youth, and point (2) reflects the fact that not all gang activities are ipso facto delinquent or borderline.

229. Like many other adolescents, most gang-organizers place a premium on eventually having amenities, material objects among them, that are relatively conventional in type and average in amount; and they, too, assume money will be needed to help them reach this goal ("amenities-goal"). By obtaining not only these *comforts, conveniences, and possessions (CCPs),* but related social/interpersonal enjoyments, the latter individuals would be experiencing and satisfying what, in their minds, would be mainly a continuation of certain things they presently obtain, experience, try to experience, and/or partly or very largely *satisfy,* in or via their gang and nongang settings (*note*: in some respects, these contents and feelings would be an expansion or elaboration of them): the already-mentioned *point-2,* immediate "material desires," the *point-(1)* "physical pleasures," and the *point-3* "ego charges." (Of the present gang-organizers—who, as indicated, highly value of the amenities-goal—many want to have well-*above*-average amounts of these CCPs and enjoyments. Such amounts will be termed level 2, whereas the average will be level 1. Regarding these amenities, level 2 youths may seriously speak of hoping to "some day hit it big," financially, and to then—and thereby—"have it made" with respect to enjoying life.) Both the 1 and 2 individuals hope to reach their goal (a) by their early 20's, (b) without working long and, especially, hard (educationally and otherwise, and "from the bottom up"), and (c) without having to engage in any—certainly many—personally *high*-risk and otherwise dangerous activities, whether clearly illegal or not. Though most gang-organizers place a high priority on the conventional-amenities goal, this does not ipso facto mean they also want to pursue and genuinely—inwardly—adopt a largely conventional *life-style* (a CLS). In fact, they seldom want to do so. Moreover, they do not feel they somehow *must* do so, in order to achieve that end. (Those points, and the following, also apply to the adoption and expression of socially standard adulthood roles.) In addition, these individuals do not believe or assume that they need to even *display* a CLS—that is, need to manifest one, though in fact adhere to it *only* outwardly—as part of reaching and perhaps maintaining that goal. At any rate, what these level 1 and 2 youths do believe/assume is that they have or probably have the key personal tools and strengths—for instance, enough brains, general know-how, and drive—needed to somehow reach or closely approach that goal. What they need to figure out, they feel, is exactly *how* to do it—do it, insofar as possible, under conditions (a) through (c) above.

Given their desire to reach that goal, and in line with their wishes regarding these conditions, the present individuals view the gang, criminality, and conventional contexts, respectively, as follows: first, they are not sure that their existing types and amounts of *gang* activities, if continued or even somewhat modified, would help them move far toward that long-term, high-priority goal, even its level 1 alone. In this respect they feel the gang could become largely a dead end for them, and that this could occur even if they and other core members were, for example, able to somehow eventually make its illegal and borderline activities less risky than they presently may be. Second, regarding *criminality* as an eventual way of life—at least, as the critical, dominant source of money and CPPs —this, they usually think, *may or may not* help them reach and maintain the goal in question, whether at level 1 or 2 and whether or not in the context of a gang. (Though "way of life" may mean or often include large-scale "organized crime," it could instead involve "con games" and other fraudulent enterprises that center on *one*- or *two*-person operations.) In this respect most of the present youths sense that they have no clear idea of how much or how little risk they would need to take in order to reach, not to mention maintain, their CCP goal via this route—that is, via the professional, semi-professional, or, in any event, functionally and relatively "committed" (Van Voorhis, 1994) criminal route. In addition, these individuals sense that they may have no way of satisfactorily figuring out that level of risk ahead of time; and risk—certainly the possibility of *high* risk or repeated danger—is, as already implied, a factor they do not want to downplay or ignore. At any rate, depending partly on level of risk, the present youths believe that some forms of systematic criminality can have greater or lesser potential for providing a comparatively quick and easy route to the desired goal; they could therein satisfy conditions (a) and (b), even though the question of maintenance would remain open. Third, gang-organizer youths believe that many *conventional* routes and settings could almost certainly allow them to eventually reach level 1—though perhaps not much beyond it unless they made extra or unusual efforts. (Depending on their degree, such efforts, or course, could clash with condition (b).) In any event, one of the largely unappealing ideas

these individuals associate with the preponderance of these routes is that of working long and possibly hard in order to first reach their goal, and of probably having to then work at least *long*—that is, for a large, unknown number of years—in order to retain what they have gained. (Both aspects of this idea largely lack appeal to gang-organizers, and are sometimes distasteful to them, despite the fact that many or most such youths [1] sense that most adults view persistent and arduous efforts, even when without self-sacrifice, as signs of positive strength, and [2] associate those same types of efforts with considerable masculinity and, perhaps, commendable loyalty.)

Because these youths see neither criminality nor conventionality as providing, by itself, a fairly definite route to the amenities-goal under conditions (a) through (c), they make no broad or otherwise serious commitment to either one, in connection with that goal. Yet, they also *reject* neither one—particularly the former, and especially wholesale. In effect, they keep their options open with respect to each. In so doing, they hope to eventually figure out or come upon a satisfactory variant or aspect of one or both—that is, they hope to find some "angle" or approach—through which they can reach or closely approach their level 1 or 2 goal. (Besides hoping, they largely *believe* this will occur, or at least believe it can.) Given the risks they feel exist in connection with full-blown criminality, and in light of the unwanted requirements and/or constraints they associate with conventional—that is, mainline or traditional, and broadly accepted—routes and life-styles, these youths regularly assume the following: For them to reach their goal without having to first face unacceptable risks and make long, hard efforts, the angle(s) or approach(es) in question may well have to involve *borderline*-legal activities, *borderline*-conventional (or instead quite unconventional) activities/settings, possible some of each, and perhaps even occasionally unscrupulous practices and sporadic, low- or moderate-risk lawbreaking. Thus, this assumption is intertwined with the youths' underlying hope that they will not have to (1) significantly, let alone largely, relinquish some of their desired conditions or strong preferences (for instance, those centering on the early attainment of their goal, and on reaching it without laborious efforts), and/or (2) substantially alter or scale back central aspects of their goal itself (such as the type and amount of material desires, physical pleasures, and interpersonally triggered or reinforced ego satisfactions).

At any rate, these individuals believe they can eventually answer the question of how to reach or closely approach their goal—hopefully without making sizable, unwanted modifications in their key conditions and preferences. As already implied, they sense, and sometimes more specifically believe, that a continuation of their present relationship with the gang might not be critical to that answer, and may not even have to play a significant part. (Regarding interference or incompatibility per se, the youths sense these possibilities as well, but rarely focus on them; this is partly because they have little specific picture of *what* that relationship is likely to clash *with*, in the first place.) Nevertheless, for now, most such individuals gladly, actively, and often enthusiastically "stick with" the gang—feeling that, in and through it, they can not only continue to obtain many immediate satisfactions, but can do so under risk-conditions which—at least for the present—they are willing to accept. (In the present setting, compared to most *non*-gang, *non*delinquent contexts, these and the remaining gang-organizers feel better able to obtain—in fact, to help bring about—the material, physical, and psychological satisfactions in question, particularly on their own terms. [As with many or most other youths, in a wide range of settings, their main focus is on what they might *obtain,* not provide.]) At the same time, however, these individuals remain open to information about *conventionality* and *criminal lifestyles (gang and nongang)* alike—including gray areas and "borders" associated with each—that might bear on the na-

ture and achievement of their long-term goal, under conditions (a) through (c) to the extent possible.

One further matter. if other factors are fairly equal, the more these youths feel *economically and socially disadvantaged* regarding conventional routes to their goal, the more they feel the following would apply if they were to rely almost entirely on those routes (here, "disadvantage" centers on the quality and quantity of mainline opportunities the youths feel are available to them, under conditions they implicitly assume would be usual not only for themselves but for other individuals in their economic and social position, and local physical environment): (1) They would have to work longer and harder than most *non*disadvantaged individuals—long and hard, in any event. (2) Despite those efforts they might still not reach or approximate their goal, essentially due to external constraints; and, even if they reached it, they might not be able to sustain it without undue effort. (3) The longer and harder they would have to work in order to reach level 2, in particular (if they chose to seek it), especially in the absence of considerable assertiveness, maneuvering, and related efforts on their part—and, quite possibly, extra luck.

As implied, points (1) through (3) mainly reflect the present youths' assumed and otherwise perceived difficulty with respect to accessing adequate mainline opportunities, in the first place— that is, aside from problems and challenges that might later emerge. (They also imply, of course, that conventional—mainline—routes/opportunities are not all perceived as equally adequate or helpful.) Partly because of their point-(1) perceptions, these individuals are more likely than most others to think they may well have to utilize—in fact, heavily utilize—borderline and gray-area approaches in order to reach even level 1, especially but not only by their early 20s. This applies all the more regarding level 2; and in *this* context, the present individuals would be more likely than most others, including other gang-organizers, to feel they may need to engage in illegal activities per se. (To simplify the presentation, we have treated "routes" and "opportunities" as functionally equivalent and otherwise interchangeable, even though they are somewhat different aspects—partly overlapping components—of a general means-to-ends process.)

Within most parts of contemporary United States, the socioeconomic disadvantages in question are more likely to be felt and otherwise perceived by various *racial and/or ethnic minorities* than by most other "groupings." These perceptions have substantial roots in external reality. In particular, most of those disadvantages are traceable not only to distant historical factors and forces, but, more concretely and proximally, to the often-still-active expressions of those factors/forces—the direct effects of which, when combined with indirect and further spinoffs, are often large. At any rate, even among gang-organizers who are not *minority members,* the more economically and/or socially disadvantaged they are, and in any event consider themselves, the more they feel they must either work long and hard or take sizable risks—unless, as indicated, they come up with an "angle," and so on. This applies even more if their goal emphasizes level 2.

230. In these respects the gang is a major and specific contributor not only to the youth's behaviors, but, often, to a continuation of them and of closely related activities. As such, it sometimes constitutes a direct causal factor, whether highly proximate or not.

231. The strength, stability, and various other aspects of this youth/gang relationship stems not just from the individual's (1) underlying needs—some of which he is not clearly aware of, yet which, like various others, often exert much force—but (again to a considerable degree) from a number of his (2) wishes and interests— ones that are largely conscious, in fact, often specifically focused and directed. Whichever source(s) is involved (need, wish, other), and whatever degree of consciousness and focus there may be, there is, in effect, essentially nothing haphazard, purely passive and non-

dynamic, and/or largely incidental or accidental about the existence, content, and continuance of his relationship to the gang.

232. As already indicated, the latter subtypes—more precisely, ones that are substantively rather similar to them, despite somewhat different labels—are also found in typologies other than Warren's. Some such typology systems contain one or two of them; others have more—including the rarer groups.

233. At this "collective" level, "more" means proportionately more—here, *more often situational,* and so on. In contrast, any *individual* illegal activity or event can be "more" situational, "more" opportunistic, and so forth, than some *other such activity/event.* In the first case, the comparison is with a different youth-group; in the second, with a different activity/event.

234. Only in juvenile justice populations (JJPs) comprised chiefly of first- and second-time offenders are any of the five groups—specifically, *Se's* ("situational emotional reactions") only—more common than, or at least *as* common as, Mp's and Na's, respectively. Aa's and Ap's are infrequent or rare in almost all JJPs. First- (and second-) time offenders are often called "lightweights" or "minor delinquents," unless their offense(s) is severe. Within the USA, it is *local probation,* and only local probation, whose standard juvenile caseloads are comprised of a large percentage— often even a majority—of lightweights. (Everything in this endnote applies whether or not "status offenders" are included.)

235. Two points—separate and distinct from each other—might be kept in mind. (1) Mp's and Na's do not view gang members, collectively, in terms of these three categories, or, for that matter, any other type and number of delineations or groupings. This is not a question of the particular *words* that are used to describe those members, and/or of possible differential labeling. (2) With few exceptions, the youths we call "gang-dependent" are uncomfortable with individuals who, like many or most Mp's and Na's, have some or all of the

following, interrelated features. They: (a) are verbally and/or otherwise assertive, and seem to often "get their way" as a result; (b) are often willing and able to confront, rebuff, verbally "put down," and reject, various peers; and, (c) often act independently of peers (gang members and/or others, as in (a) and (b)). All in all, gang-dependent youths, who are relatively insecure and are above-average in passivity and unassertiveness, feel unable to keep pace with or hold their own against such individuals—and, especially, to defend themselves against them in most respects. All this applies even though the gang-dependent youths not infrequently wish to be more assertive and independent themselves, within and outside the gang setting.

236. Three points might be noted. (1) Although the Mp's and Na's reactions to the various other members' discomfort, limited trust, and so on, are, collectively, an important and sizable aspect of the former youths' (Mp's and Na's) *overall relationship to the gang,* the specific content and general nature of this relationship includes and involves more than just these reactions. (2) Among the Mp's as well as Na's (each group collectively), the "awareness" in question is about equally often diffuse, on the one hand, and somewhat clear or specific, on the other. That is, approximately as many Mp's have a chiefly diffuse awareness as those who have a somewhat clear one; and, the same applies to Na's. (3) Neither of these two youth-groups uses the particular terms "unsettled" and/or "marginal," or their essential verbal equivalents. Nevertheless, each group is aware, as indicated, that the conditions or statuses in question (namely, "unsettled . . . ") do apply to them—that is, to their, the Mp's and Na's, relationship to the gang.

237. Prominent among the factors that mutually interact to help produce those other members' feelings of uneasiness are the respective youths' and members' major personal needs and personality features. This applies especially—and more recognizably—to overt behaviors, openly expressed attitudes, and overall stances that stem largely *from* those needs and that regularly *reflect* those features. (The mutual interactions occur not just among the given needs and among the given features, but also across these domains.)

238. Though Point 2 basically presupposes *1,* Point 1, by itself, does not necessarily or inevitably generate, trigger, or otherwise lead to 2. Nor is 1 invariably *accompanied* by 2—causation, per se, apart.

239. This "fact," including its exclusionary conditions (such as, "not on a . . . permanent basis"), extends beyond the following, even though it is far from independent of it: In their usual interactions with peers, Mp's and Na's—to a proportionately and substantially larger degree than most other serious offenders—definitely want to be "takers" far more than "givers" or even "equal participants." This applies within most settings or contexts—and, here, with the gang *as* a gang.

240. The youths' reactions of "dislike," and so on, would occur and be strong—though somewhat less so—even if these individuals felt or assumed that the joint activities in question would not *heavily* (1) limit their freedom-of-action, (2) cramp their style, and (3) clash with some of their dominant wishes. Moreover, even if the youths did feel they would not be thus limited, and so on, such reactions would occur particularly, though not only, if they believed that the given gang-level activities—ones they assume are probably unavoidable—would not especially, and perhaps not primarily, benefit *them.*

241. Even when "more personal matters . . ." are involved, the interchanges or interactions between participants occur—as often as not—on a fairly impersonal basis. In addition, even when these interactions are *not* impersonal, they are seldom highly *personalized,* and very seldom intimate. All this applies to the Mp's, and the Na's, in their respective interactions with remaining participants—"mainly [the] gang-dependent."

242. A few final details and clarifications regarding most Mp's and Na's, chiefly in connection with their peers. (1) Whether in gang or nongang settings, these

youths seldom try to engage in honest, relatively straightforward interactions. They have experienced very few trusting, nonexploitive relationships of substantial length during their lives, particularly, though not only, with parents and parent-substitutes. Partly as a result, their level of overall interpersonal comfort has long been low and their degree of wariness as well as self-protection high. Their (a) underlying distrust and overt wariness, especially when combined with (b) related reactions, other defenses, and various adjustments (ones not developed mainly for self-protection), generate, among other things, (c) certain barriers, blind spots, rigidities, and/or artificialities (BBRA's) in their involvements with peers. These BBRA's constitute sizable limitations as well as limiting conditions or factors (ones which, in turn, often lead to *further* limitations and constraints) in the extent to which the youths' individual and collective peer-relationships develop, and in the overall strength or resilience those relationships attain.

(2) Among the youths' defenses and broad interpersonal stances as well as other adjustments, three—simply called "factors"—are particularly salient: (a) These individuals try hard to have *controlled interactions* with their peers—themselves being the controllers and chief beneficiaries (at least, not big "losers" if things do not go their way). Closely associated with that effort among most of these same youths, yet fairly independent of it (and also of its absence) among the rest, is the next factor. (b) Few of these individuals seek *relatively close relationships* with those peers. This applies whether or not, but especially if, these youths believe those relationships would likely include substantial responsibilities and obligations (R&Os) to the given peers—material and/or emotional R&Os. Finally, (c) these youths do not genuinely—inwardly—favor *equal or nearly equal give-and-take* with most or even many peers. This is despite the youths' occasional feelings and verbalizations to the contrary, even in connection with relationships that might have fewer than

usual BBRA's and that might be somewhat closer than most.

(3) The present youths—still the Mp's and Na's—implicitly assume that most relationships have a large zero-sum component. This assumption provides a major starting point for the preponderance of their interactions with peers; after that, its influence continues. (With these youths, "zero-sum" basically means that in order for one or more individuals in an interaction to obtain something they want or need, one or more of the others must lose something of value; and, the amounts or values in question must roughly balance. The youths' assumption regarding the existence of "zero-sum" has strong connections with their past, exploitive relationships.) Given this influence, *and*—although the youths do not see this next connection—because of factors (a) and (c), above, these individuals usually expect eventual clashes with their peers. Together with this expectation, they are primed—sometimes consciously, sometimes not—for possible subsequent sourings, major and abrupt ruptures, and complete terminations in their usual relationships with those peers; at least, they are primed for lengthy, full-scale suspensions. That expectation, and this frame of mind, help give many or most of their interactions and relationships a certain edginess—a fairly constant, above-average tension, and a related tentativeness. The youths' often-high-strung, sometimes-energy-intense qualities, and/or their occasionally evident volatility, themselves contribute to this tension.

(4) Most Mp's and Na's try to control their interactions and involvement's with peers via open assertiveness (including one-upmanship), direct persuasion, and, if they think it necessary, various maneuvers, stratagems, falsifications, and/or hit-and-run tactics. Any one or more of these approaches, or of their related expressions and offshoots, can markedly affect not just (a) the content and quality of these youths' involvements but (b) their outcomes or long-term trends as well. (It can do the latter especially when combined with

other factors.) For instance (regarding "expressions"), these individuals' frequent demandingness and stubbornness (D&S)—say, their insistence on having things very largely their way, and their resistance to substantial compromise—can do more than help *limit* those involvements and *channel* them along certain lines; that is, D&S can do more than narrow their scope, significantly restrict or shape their content, and so on. (This applies whether these involvements are at early, middle, or later stages of development.) Instead, when those expressions of the youths' assertiveness—and, with that, of these individuals' underlying motivation to *control*—are combined with such factors as the already-mentioned lack of substantial trust per se and with the zero-sum perspective itself, the resulting mixture and dynamics can generate serious *difficulties* in the relationship or acquaintanceship. Alternatively or additionally, it can aggravate already-existing problems and vulnerabilities and can thereby contribute—sometimes decisively—to the relationship's eventual undoing and termination.

Such difficulties are not limited to two-person interactions; instead, they can involve several individuals. Here, we will focus on interactions between youths who comprise three mutually distinct categories—the (a) gang-centered and/or gang-dependent, the (b) Mp or Na, and the (c) gang-organizer—thus, between at least *three* individuals. (These will be "a," "b," and "c" youths, to correspond with their category.) For example, some relationship-difficulties can result from conflicts—here, ones felt chiefly by *a-youths*—that have been generated by expectations, requests, and/or demands (ERDs), on the part of *b-youths* (concerning those *a*-youths), that clearly diverge from or at least partly clash with ERDs from certain *c-youths* (regarding those same *a*-youths). More specifically, if *a-youths*, namely, the gang-centered and/or gang-dependent individuals, react to pressures they feel in connection with these ERD-generated conflicts—that is, if they react to the binds they feel themselves in, between the b-youths and

c-youths—by largely siding with or seeming to side with the *c-youths* (namely, the gang-organizers), this could trigger or increase various difficulties between *them* (the a-youths) and the *b-youths* (the Mp's or Na's). These difficulties could result in an eventual or even rapid unraveling of the a-youth/b-youth relationship, or, at least, in a major and permanent shift. They could also reduce many b-youths' motivation to participate in activities involving the gang as a whole. (To clarify: If *a-youths* mainly side with *c*'s instead of *b*'s, this can loosen the *b-youths'* actual or felt control over those *a*'s. In any event, it can reduce the b's present or hoped-for benefits from their relationship with those youths. It can also lessen—still for these Mp's or Na's—the felt- or anticipated-value of the overall gang, especially if a *number* of these relationships are involved.)

(5) All in all, most Mp's and Na's are more conflict- than cooperation-oriented. Partly as a result, and also because of many peers' negative reactions to that and to related features (some less obvious), those youths usually have difficulty being part of any teamlike group, and its teamwork, for long. This, at least, applies if they believe they must very largely, and often, subordinate themselves to its approaches and requirements or to several of its members, instead of being among the persons in charge or at least free to often do things mostly their own way. A major reflection of the just-mentioned feature, difficulty, and belief, and of those youths' (1) below-average trust in others as well as their (2) need to feel "strong" and in control—therein safe, is the following ("activities," "behaviors," and "acts" will be interchangeable): Even after these individuals first become involved with a gang, they (1) carry out many or most of their delinquent activities *apart* from it, and (2) these behaviors can be (that is, can continue to be) reinforced by sources—personal (youth himself) and external ones—*other* than that gang. In any event, the gang is not necessarily the central vehicle and setting for, let alone

the principal generator and sustainer of, all delinquent behaviors on the part of these youths. (This is true even if it does not rely *heavily* on teamwork when—acting *as* a gang—it carries out most of its illegal behaviors.)

Because this point regarding "all" delinquent behaviors focuses on the youths' illegal acts when viewed in the *aggregate* (still starting with these individuals' first involvement with a gang), the following one, although it is implied in preceding remarks, should perhaps be stated explicitly: Regarding various—though, of course, not all—*single* illegal acts by most Mp's and Na's, these individuals (still the b-youths) feel that certain gang members (the a- and c-youths alike), and/or joint gang-actions, can provide otherwise unavailable or difficult-to-obtain opportunities, assistance, and advantages (such as "cover") with respect to successfully carrying out those acts. In short, the present individuals see given gang members (*usually* a-youths), and/or the gang acting *as* a gang, as useful and sometimes even essential in various respects, for whatever periods of time. (The present point, in turn, might help tie down yet another one: In the earlier remarks, the concept, "a major reflection of . . . ," means a major *consequence of* the given "feature, difficulty," and so on, when the youths' delinquency is viewed in a broad, not a narrow, time frame—specifically, a time span that encompasses, and can thereby emphasize, the individuals' aggregate delinquent behavior rather than one or two such acts alone. "Reflection," thus, means neither *antecedent* nor simply *concomitant;* instead, it specifically means *product* or *result,* within that broad temporal framework.)

243. The last five of these were by far the most common of Warren's nine subtypes, during each of the California CTP experiment's three operational phases (1961–1964, 1964–1969, and 1969–1974).

244. The interrelated items—for instance, certain current traits and/or attitudes (T/As), on the one hand, and specified dynamics or issues, on the other—were not always closely connected in *point of time;* instead, they were sometimes mutually distal. Other items, however, such as the preceding T/As themselves, or perhaps other T/As instead, *did* have comparatively close temporal ties with each other, or may have even presently overlapped. (Proximal connections, and overlaps, were often implied in the case of level 2 combinations; however, *causation* per se, in contrast to temporal contiguity/overlap alone, were not usually part of these implications.)

245. The remaining experts were Hurwitz, MacGregor, Makkay, and Warren. In the present discussion, Warren is of course separated from these and the remaining four experts. This is because—as indicated next—it is her typology system which is being compared to theirs.

246. Six of these "other systems"—there being seven in all—were far more psychological ("person") than sociological ("system") in orientation and content. Of these six, three mainly focused on "traits" and the rest largely centered on intrapsychic "dynamics" and "development" (Rubenfeld, 1967, 4–7).

247. By the end of the conference, "there was tentative agreement among these [eight experts/authors] on the proposed categorization across their systems" (Rubenfeld, 1967, 7).

248. A fifth NIMH grouping—Mentally Ill ("Schizophrenic; Psychotic . . .")—has not been focused on in this chapter, mainly because of its youths' relative rarity within juvenile justice and correctional settings. At any rate, according to Rubenfeld (1967, 7), "all [eight typology] systems could be cast fairly clearly into a five-fold categorization"—Mentally Ill being its final one.

249. The eight she added were those of Argyle, Gibbons, Jenkins and Hewitt, McCord, Reckless, Schrag, Studt, and the American Psychiatric Association (APA). Like the previous eight, these mainly focused on delinquent males.

250. Warren considered the Se subtype comparable to Gibbons' "Casual delinquent," Reckless' "Offenders of the moment," and the APA's "Adjustment reaction of adolescence" (Warren, 1966, 20; 1971, 250).

251. As can be seen, these "structural . . . changes" referred to differences between the *NIMH conference* classification system (CS), on the one hand, and *Warren's post-conference* CS, on the other. It is these differences which are specified in the next text-section, in connection with "Warren's changes . . ." Separately, it might be kept in mind that Warren made no changes in the substance of her nine subtypes, from her own *pre*-conference CS to her just-mentioned *post*-conference CS. (The NIMH system, as such, does not enter into this comparison.) For example, she made no changes, from pre-conference to post-conference, in the content as well as meaning of the *Na subtype,* the *Nx subtype,* and so on. (Nor were any name changes made.) The same applied to each of her seven other subtypes.

252. She replaced it with two terms: "Conformist" and, as will be seen, "Antisocial-manipulator."

253. Besides the types of setting that were involved in these eight typology systems, three more types of setting would enter the picture if one also considered settings associated with the studies reviewed in section B. (This is independent of the fact that most of the typology *systems* that were focused on in section B's studies happened to differ from the NIMH eight.) These added types of *setting* would be: field probation (Palmer), probation institution (Budnoff), and military disciplinary facility (Gaensbauer and Lazerwitz). Although three of section B's studies centered, respectively, on the typology systems of three experts who participated in the NIMH conference (namely, Jesness, Makkay, and Warren), those studies were independent of the work done by these individuals in connection with that conference.

254. Actually, the representation was not quite complete: Of the 32 cells in question (four superordinate categories for each of eight typology systems), *31* were filled.

255. The total of 40 types and subtypes, combined, excludes the three youth-types that became NIMH's fifth broad category—that of Mentally Ill. Were these three included, the average number of youth-types/subtypes per system would still be approximately 5.

256. In this connection the following might be noted (also see endnote 204). Rubenfeld, after focusing on (1) clinical and behavioral "differences in subject populations" (and in the settings from which these respective youth-populations were drawn) that existed across the eight typology systems—the systems which were compared with each other at the NIMH conference—and after mentioning (2) "contrasts . . . in ages of [the] subject populations" and differences that existed across the given typologies' "frames of reference," as well (for instance, between MacGregor's and Makkay's "psychiatric-clinical" approaches, on the one hand, and Hunt's as well as Quay's "concepts and methods derived from academic psychology," on the other), commented as follows:

In view of these multiple differences, there appears to be a striking convergence, at least at a descriptive and conceptual level, among the categories of [the eight] typology systems . . . All the systems could be cast fairly clearly into a five-fold classification [when one also included that of "Mentally ill"]. Except for those typologies that had only three subtypes each, each subtype could be associated with [one of the five] superordinate categor[ies] or general type[s] . . . [And,] there are some empirical interrelationships among the typologies represented here which indicate that their similarities are not just verbal. (1967, 7)

During this conference, which was held on March 15–16, 1966, under the auspices of NIMH's Center for the Study of Crime and Delinquency, Rubenfeld served as a consultant to the Center.

257. The Neurotic category was salient in Gaensbauer and Lazerwitz (G&L) as well. Though these researchers did not explicitly and otherwise formally separate Na's from Nx's, they mentioned emotions, interpersonal responses, and other dimensions that have generally been highlighted by typologists and others who *have* formally distinguished these subtypes from each other. G&L's main

emphasis, however, was on factors and forces that are *shared* by most or all individuals in this, "the neurotic group"—these being persons with "internal conflicts around such issues as competitiveness, self-assertion, and dependency" (Gaensbauer and Lazerwitz, 1979, 44).

258. This assumes, of course, that the methodologies used in the respective studies are of acceptable and roughly equal quality, that the sample-sizes are substantial, and so on.

259. Not every possible combination and permutation of these varied findings (lesser degree; complete absence) versus these differing factors (age, sample size, and so on) was observed in connection with each and every subtype just mentioned.

260. The point regarding "delineation" and "application" applies independently of both the following. (1) The individuals in *NIMH's* classification were preponderantly juvenile, across its eight constituent typology systems (CTSs), taken together. (2) The eight CTSs that Warren later added to NIMH's eight—in connection with her *post-conference classification*—contained, themselves collectively, a somewhat lower percentage of juveniles, though still well over a majority. (These same points, it might be noted, also apply to males, and to the combination of juvenile and male.)

261. Because these Warren subtypes were entirely absent from the analysis, no *combinations* of them could have been generated, and could have therefore converged, either. For instance, neither of the following combinations could have converged with any Hunt, Jesness, Megargee, and/or Quay category: (1) NIMH's "Power Oriented" individuals, defined as the Cfm + Cfc + Mp subtypes; (2) Warren's "Conformists," defined, in her post-conference breakdown of that NIMH superordinate, as the Cfm + Cfc subtypes.

262. In this study, overlap and resulting resemblance would have been evidenced in terms of statistically significant correlations, or otherwise substantial relationships, between the W subtypes, on the one hand, and H, J, M, and/or Q categories (offender-types), on the other, with respect to the variables in question.

263. When using Warren's interview approach in Van Voorhis' 1994 study, the first classification decision always centered on whether the interviewee's maturity level was low (I_2), middle (I_3), high (I_4), or quite high (I_5); once his level was decided, the question of subtype was addressed. This two-step procedure was in accordance with traditional practice. As it turned out, step one yielded neither low nor middle maturity individuals, in Van Voorhis' particular sample. As a consequence, all possibility of there being any Aa, Ap, Cfm, Cfc, and Mp subtypes in the subsequent data analysis automatically and immediately disappeared, since those subtypes, by definition, exist within the low and middle levels alone. In contrast, when the *Jesness Inventory* was used, classification focused directly and solely on *subtype;* that is, no prior classification decisions/steps were involved, or even existed (again, as per standard practice). In particular, no pre-subtype-determination was made regarding *maturity level (ML)*. As a result, although—in Warren's typology—all subtypes structurally exist within maturity levels alone, no subtypes could be analytically eliminated from Van Voorhis' sample on grounds that those levels had been *found to not exist.* They could not be ruled out on that basis because, as indicated, no determination of any maturity levels—no "step one," mentioned above—*had* in fact occurred, with respect to the Jesness Inventory. At any rate, when the JI approach (one that might be called "straight-to-the-subtype") was used, many Cfm's, Cfc's, and Mp's—15, 23, and 21 percent of the overall penitentiary + prison camp sample, respectively—were found among Van Voorhis' adults. These percentages were roughly the same as those often obtained when the JI approach was previously applied to samples of serious male *delinquents,* individuals who were predominantly multiple offenders. For information about the limited albeit suggestive convergences between the JI-based *Cfm* and *Mp* subtypes, on the one hand, and the Hunt, the Megargee, and the Quay categories, on the other, see Van Voorhis (1994, 92–113, 121–122, 251–253). Sizable

convergences did exist in connection with the *Cfc* subtype. (Regarding the JI-based Aa's and Ap's, each of these comprised 2 percent of Van Voorhis' adult sample—a figure somewhat lower than in most samples of serious delinquents.)

264. Unlike Van Voorhis' research, none of these was a cross-classification study; in particular, none statistically compared Warren's subtypes with categories that constituted *other* systems/typologies, such as Hunt's, Quay's, or Megargee's. As a result, its findings did not center on, and its conclusions did not mainly reflect, the degrees of cross-system convergence and divergence—each of which could have ranged from very high to very low. Instead, for present purposes, the question of concurrent validation centered on whether specified Warren subtypes were present *at all*—that is, on whether (operationally speaking) they had emerged as distinguishable statistical entities.

In *other* than a cross-classification context, concurrent validation—if one wishes to examine it on broad rather than narrow grounds—should be considered chiefly a function not just, and not even mainly, of (1) any *one* study alone but of (2) whether the categories in question (still youth subtypes) emerge *across* studies, that is, across a number of them (preferably most). This, of course, requires that several studies do exist in which those categories can emerge, and that these studies—and, perhaps, separate and additional observations/information such as systematic records of subtype diagnoses—are of at least acceptable quality. (If several *cross-classification* studies are themselves available, parallel principles and conditions would apply to them.)

265. The "alternative programs/resources" (APRs) may be community-based; they may or may not be administered locally, publicly, and so on; and their clientele/targets may be mainly (or exclusively) local, regional, or statewide. In any event, whether or not a particular APR is a formal component of "the given agency" discussed in the text, its usual case processing, its routine communications (e.g., inter- and intra-agency/ facility exchanges), and the *nature* of the program/resource per se may or may not be closely coordinated with, and largely compatible with, the secure/residential facility in question. This can apply whether or not the APR's main approaches and elements are specialized, intensive, and/or extensive. (The term "agency" is used very broadly, and it can include, for example, "department," "bureau," "ministry," and even "organization.")

266. In various contexts, the following "item," which is italicized, may have a moderate positive relationship to factor #2a, mentioned in the text almost immediately above (*note*: here, in this endnote, #2a's role is that of *input or causal force,* and the item—in this instance, a possible "tendency"—is, in part, a result of it): *Se's and Ci's, especially the former, may ordinarily have a shorter delinquent career than most other subtypes.* If such a tendency in fact exists, it would—on sheer opportunity grounds alone—make the Se's and Ci's (respectively) proportionately less likely than those other subtypes (themselves respectively) to be randomly selected for inclusion within given, unstratified study samples. This would apply particularly if these samples were generated at a fairly specific, single point in time (e.g., right at—or close to—admission, for each youth in turn)—at any rate, were created during a rather delimited time span. Any such tendency would have some bearing on the absence or at least paucity of Se's and Ci's, in given contexts.

267. This was so young, even for a sample of delinquents, that Warren's lowest maturity individuals (I_2's) alone comprised 25 percent ($52 \div 210$) of the study group (Jesness, 1965, 126, A–12)—roughly four times higher than that found in most other researched settings, whether secure/residential or not. (In most such settings—or, at least, in the most common [modal] among them—the average age was within or close to the 15 – 16 range.) Of these I_2's, three-fifths closely resembled Warren's Ap's and the rest were very similar to her Aa's. (See Types 2 and 4 in Jesness, 1965, 129–131, 134–136.) It might be added that the percentage of I_2's was far above average

in *Makkay's* sample as well, where the mean age at intake was 12.0 (Palmer, 1972b, 1973c, 39).

268. For statistical reasons, this age-difference is best observed in minimally or even moderately "age-restricted" study samples—say, ones that span at least four or five years (and whose lowest age category and highest age category each has more than a negligible representation). In contrast, an example of a *substantially* restricted sample of adolescents would be that of the Northern Youth Center Project. There, all wards had to be between 15 and 17 years of age at intake (Jesness, et al., 1972, 17).

269. Even if these subtypes had each comprised, say, 2 percent of Jesness' 210-youth study sample, this would have involved only four such individuals each—too few to emerge as clear categories even via the thorough statistical approach he used. Fricot's overall capacity was about 220 youths. Prior to his study, these individuals had routinely been distributed across four living units that housed 50 boys each, and in another—newer—unit that accommodated 20 more. To implement his research design Jesness used one of these large units for the entire control group (C's) and the small unit for all experimentals (E's). During the study the weighted average length of stay for E's + C's turned out to be 15.7 months per youth. Case intake was continuous, and it went on for several years (Jesness, 1965, 1971–1972).

270. Two points might be noted. (1) The standard approaches mainly involve factor analysis and cluster analysis, whatever the latters' specific variations may be. As seen earlier, one or more such analyses played a central role in the Las Palmas, Geneva, and Fricot derivations of subtypes, respectively. The findings at *Shawbridge,* however, were not based on a statistical "derivation," particularly in the quantitative/analytic sense. Instead, for instance, the absence of Ci's (males and females alike) within this setting was determined directly by staff's review of qualitative case intake plus followup data (as was the *presence* of any given subtype)—especially information that centered on diagnosis and classification themselves. (2) Among the "varieties" or species of analysis used in the first three settings (collectively), there was the inverse factor technique and the canonical factor technique (Budnoff, 1963; Ferdinand, 1978; Jesness, 1965).

271. The predominance of gender in this particular—Ci—context was independent of the fact that the figures of 75, 234, and 40 by no means reflect *small* or at least *very small* samples per se, as these terms are commonly applied in typology research, in correctional effectiveness studies overall, and elsewhere. In this regard it might be noted that the samples of 75, and so on, did not ipso facto—that is, by virtue of size as such—practically rule out the emergence of *other* subtypes (nor did they do so on other grounds): Most subtypes *were* found, in each given study.

272. Aa's, Ap's, Se's, and Ci's accounted for the following percentages of the experimental Phase 1 and 2 Valley samples: 1, 4, 2, and 5, respectively (Chapter 4). They were equally rare in its San Francisco operation, and also during Phase 3. These subtypes turned out to be rare in almost all other study samples as well, within and outside California and not just during the 1960s and 1970s. (The chief exception involved Aa's and Ap's from samples whose youths were very young, for instance. age 11 or 12 on average.) All these findings pertained to interview-based diagnoses, including interviews that were supplemented by clinical information. In studies that relied chiefly on the Jesness Inventory for a subtype diagnosis, the percentage of Aa's and Ap's combined was usually about three times higher than that obtained via the interview-based or -centered method; specifically, it was around 15 percent of the total sample, usually give or take about three or four percentage points. Thus, these individuals were seen as rather uncommon, but not exactly rare. Ss's and Ci's typically did remain rare.

273. Analyses or studies (2), (3), and (4) did not, in themselves, center on such approaches as factor analysis and cluster analysis, although (3)'s basic data in-

cluded a *preexisting* cluster analysis. Instead, those studies—except the one involving Gibbons' typology—centered on simple cross-tabs, on resulting first-order correlations, and so on. This applied to the examination of Makkay's sample/system, as well.

274. Selective referral was very likely the key factor responsible for the virtual absence of Se's and Ci's from a study (Andrews, 1974) not previously mentioned in the present context. The study sample—112 males and females—consisted of every individual, and of only those individuals, whom staff of an intensive probation supervision unit considered sufficiently disturbed to refer for psychological testing, during a 27-month period. However, this sample excluded all individuals from "subtypes [that] contained too few Ss [subjects]"; the total number of these exclusions, across all such subtypes (of which there were three) was *four* (Andrews, p. 332). As can be deduced from Andrews' presentation, at least one of these subtypes must have been Se or Ci, since six others (out of Warren's nine) *were* represented. (See endnotes #139 and #147, regarding study #13 in Section C of this chapter.) Ninety-one percent of the 112 were adolescents and young adults (under age 25).

275. And, simultaneously, the age or gender of the setting's overall population or perhaps subpopulation, from which the sample had been drawn. In the present context, a *sub*population can be thought of as that portion of an agency's or department's total offender population which, in a research study or analysis, (1) consists of a certain category or categories of offenders, and from which (2) all offenders with specified histories or characteristics are excluded. For instance, some research samples—study samples—purposely *consist*, not of an agency's total population, but of one of its following categories alone (*note*: the agency may be local, countrywide, regional, or statewide/province-wide in its scope and responsibility; its population is determined, and the sample is drawn or otherwise created, at a particular point in time or in connection with a specified time-period; category "a," which follows, may exist either on its own or as an added dimension within "(b)," "(c)," or "(d)"; and, again, the sample contains the specific category or categories of individuals *only*): (a) *first-time commitments* (e.g., to any specified *one or more* of the agency's probation or parole units, or perhaps to certain—or even all—of its institutions); (b) *brand new admissions* to designated institutions or to all nonresidential programs of certain types, such as "intensive" and/or "specialized" probation supervision (*note*: new admissions are not necessarily *first-time commitments*; nor are they necessarily equivalent, e.g., in their background and/or personal characteristics, to a cross-section of *all* the individuals currently in those institutions/programs [e.g., the type of persons being admitted may have undergone somewhat recent change]); (c) persons whose *remaining amount of time* in an institution or on probation/parole theoretically allows them to participate in a given program or type of program from its beginning to its end, or in at least certain aspects of it or for a specified percentage of it; (d) *new releases to parole*.

In addition, those respective study samples could purposely *exclude*—say, from among the offenders who fall within an applicable, just-mentioned *inclusion* category (assuming that at least one of those categories *is* used)—all individuals who have one of the following offense histories, and so on (*note*: The history or characteristic [together, "factors"] that is excluded would be specified, and no others would be listed. Alternatively, *all* of these factors—(a) through (e), below— might be listed; in this case one or *more* might be excluded, yet, even so, the particular one[s] in question might or might not be specified as such, and could thus be *any* one or more): (a) a violent instant offense; (b) any seriously assaultive offense in the prior record; (c) a serious or chronic offense history (e.g., two or more felonies of any kind, or else four or more other-than-"status"-offenses of any type; (d) indications of past or present psychosis; (e) any major physical/neurological disability or impairment, or any marked cognitive deficiency. (In an alternative scenario, only the serious/chronic offenders, or, for that matter, only the "violent" or "assaultive" individuals, might be *included*.)

276. Insofar as the range of samples was in fact broad, and insofar as these samples' underlying populations and/or subpopulations were, collectively, fairly representative, the preceding findings, themselves collectively, would reasonably indicate the following: Warren's five nonrare subtypes, or their equivalents within/across other typology systems, may well have collectively constituted the preponderance of all nonlightweight juveniles and perhaps young adults (NJAs) with whom local and state justice/correctional systems (JCSs) were ordinarily called upon to work. More precisely, they may well have comprised (conceptually encompassed) this sizable majority *qualitatively*—specifically, with respect to the range of possible *subtypes* or major personality configurations. However, those same subtypes may or may not have constituted an overwhelming or even a sizable majority of the given NJAs *quantitatively,* that is, such a large proportion of the *individuals*—the total number of persons—within the systems at any particular time. (This situation regarding qualitative and quantitative representation may well apply even today. We might add that [a] the range of samples undoubtedly *was* broad, and would also be so today, and that [b] we think their underlying populations and/or subpopulations *were,* and probably still would be, fairly representative of various JCSs.) This could have been the case even though many *other* NJAs—still collectively—who fell within those same nonrare subtype categories undoubtedly had been sent to *other* local and state JCS settings instead (if these alternatives were available), within and/or outside the given agencies, organizations, and so on. In this connection, however, the following might be noted, even though it does not negate the just-mentioned point concerning qualitative—subtype—representation:

    Although most of these latter—these "other"/"alternative"—settings (especially collectively) may well have been comparable to the former (themselves collectively) in many operational and structural ways, and *non*comparable in many other such ways, these alternative settings had, obviously, not been used for the studies. This situation probably reflected—most often and/or mainly—*practical/logistical factors,* and—not infrequently—the *nature of the offender populations* in question, including but not limited to their legal/jurisdictional status. In any event, it is essentially unknown if, despite their identical subtype categorizations (and, therein, their qualitative equivalence), a large percentage of the individuals who had undoubtedly received the alternative dispositions (ADs) differed greatly from those who were sent to the *present* settings and who were *studied* (and whose subtypes, as indicated, matched up with those of the AD offenders). Our guess is that there could well have been many—and, *as* many—moderate and sizable differences *and* similarities, each in specific as well as global respects and each in content areas that had sizable subtype—centered and *other*-than—subtype-centered treatment/control implications.

277. Typology systems commonly involve classification, insofar as the latter is defined as "systematic arrangement in groups or categories according to established criteria" (Webster, 1965), and insofar as these groups/categories are not restricted with regard to their type or amount of content, the nature of their respective internal structures/relationships (if any), and their type of mutual—*across* categories—relationships. However, typology systems do not *necessarily* involve classification, as defined. This is because their constituents—say, five individual personality configurations that, together, are *referred to* as a "system"—are not, in fact, always arranged "systematic[ally]" (e.g., are not known to be mutually related on the basis of a given criterion or criteria, whether the/these latter are general or specific and whether explicit or implicit). All this applies whether a typology system is psychologically centered, sociologically centered, or involves, for instance, a substantial *mix* of that content and/or of

cognitive-developmental dimensions, of moral development dimensions, and so on.

278. More precisely, *one* group was essentially the same as NIMH's, and the other two were identical to NIMH's in a fairly strict sense. It might be added that Warren found the "one additional"—an individual—*subtype,* as well, namely, NIMH's "Normative Outsider," and called it "Subcultural-identifier." This subtype, which was originally her Ci ("Cultural identifier"), later appeared as a constituent of *Van Voorhis'* "Committed Criminal" *group*; the other constituent among the I-Level subtypes was Jesness' inventory-based Cfc ("Cultural conformist"). (Outside the I-Level framework, two of Megargee's categories and one of Quay's were components.)

279. Hence (1) their being described by Van Voorhis as "clusters" (in addition to "groupings" and "types"), structurally— and, at the same time, therein (2) the basis of her considering them *broad* (cross-system in nature), substantively.

280. Regarding the inventory-based Na's, see correlations and discussions in Van Voorhis (1994, 102, 104–105, 253). In this connection, differences between the penitentiary findings and those involving the prison camp were substantial.

281. Regarding the nature of this difference, see endnote 150.

282. As can be seen, Van Voorhis' study yielded three groupings that each contained two individual I-Level subtypes; these subtypes are specified in the "combinations" just listed. The *first* grouping, that is, subtype combination, corresponded to one that the NIMH conference and Warren had delineated: the Neurotic. Distinguishable from the general subject of groupings (combinations), yet bearing on Van Voorhis' findings regarding the *second* and *third* groupings (V groups (2) and (3)), is the following: During the NIMH conference, which occurred in 1966, Jesness used Warren's definition of Ci; he had made both this and her remaining subtype definitions central aspects of his Preston study (Jesness, 1969, 3–4, 33), which began six months earlier. Jesness

had not yet developed his inventory-based system, in which a *new* definition of that subtype first appeared (Jesness and Wedge, 1983a, 95–96; Jesness, 1988, 82). When Van Voorhis' study was conducted, this new system, which was finalized in the early 1980s, was available for use. In the results from her study, the "Ci" subtype that appeared in *V group (2)* was *interview*-based and thus involved the Warren definition; in contrast, the "Ci" found in *V group (3)* was Jesness Inventory-based and thus involved the new definition. In both the conferees' and Warren's syntheses the Ci subtype (like the Se)—in contrast to Van Voorhis' findings regarding adults—stood alone, in that it was not part of any grouping.

283. Moreover, since none of these particular interview-diagnosed subtypes (Aa, Ap, Cfm, Cfc, and Mp) existed in Van Voorhis' study, no combination emerged that could have included any one such interview-diagnosed subtype (say, the Aa) *plus* any complementary inventory-diagnosed subtype (say, the Ap) either. To be sure, certain combinations *did* emerge that included one interview-diagnosed subtype and one inventory-diagnosed subtype: V groups (1), (2), and (3), respectively. None of these groups, however, included any *interview*-diagnosed Aa, Ap, Cfm, Cfc, or Mp. (Group (B) included the *inventory*-diagnosed Cfc. The interview and the inventory were the only ways used to diagnose subtype.)

284. In the penitentiary the percentage-representation of Cfm's, Cfc's, and Mp's was 13, 28, and 21, respectively. (The figure "28" refers to the 43 of 153 inmates.) In the prison camp it was 16, 19, and 21. For Aa's and Ap's the corresponding percentages were 3, 2, 1, and 3, in those respective settings (Van Voorhis, 1994, 81).

285. In addition, the overall picture that would have resulted from these "positive correlations with . . . [M and/or Q] types" would have been expanded and enhanced if similar correlations existed between some of these Megargee and Quay types *themselves*—that is, if substantial correlations were found between

one or more of these M types, on the one hand, and one or more of these Q types, on the other. This applies to the later-mentioned *Cfm* + Cfc + Mp combination, as well. "Overall picture . . ." refers to the cluster (sometimes called group or grouping) of empirically inter-related, cross-system types and subtypes that would have emerged and been identified.

286. At any rate, in order for a subtype combination to statistically emerge as such, it—given the methodology of this study—would have had to do so as a constituent part of a given cross-system *cluster*. Such clustering, of course, is what would have provided that subtype combination, together with its individual components, some *concurrent validation*. It would have done so whether or not, but more so if, the cluster in question were "expanded and enhanced" (see endnote 285).

287. Although Mp's and Cfc's did not *appear* together in—that is, emerge as joint components of—any Van Voorhis personality group ("V group," such as Committed Criminal), evidence was present, in her study, regarding the existence of some similarity (commonality) between them. This evidence, which collectively neither contradicted nor substantially diluted any of her four V groups, reflected, we believe, at least one important factor shared by Mp's and Cfc's: "Power Orientation." Before proceeding to this evidence of commonality, that is, to relationships #(1) through #(5), below, several points might be noted (all page numbers refer to Van Voorhis, 1994):

(A) as will be seen from the overlapping typological content that is involved in the working definitions of the "Able," "Delta," "Antisocial Aggressive," and "Manipulative" types, below, these relationships jointly constitute a set of substantively interconnected findings. The nature of these connections is further specified, and their general role is explained, in points (E), (F), and (H), below. (B) The numbers ".01," and ".05" will refer to the levels of statistical significance of those relationships; ".10" will refer to a definite tendency: results

accountable for by chance alone in six to 10 cases out of every 100. The specific correlations to which these levels refer appear in Van Voorhis (p. 108 and 111). The letter "p" indicates that the relationship applies to the penitentiary sample; "c," to camp. By "anomaly," Van Voorhis (p. 92) referred to any statistical relationship that was (i) hypothesized to be divergent (e.g., two personality types or constructs, such as the Cfc and Megargee's Able, were predicted to be *negatively* correlated with each other) but which (ii) instead turned out to be "significant and convergent" (*positively* correlated). (C) As already discussed, all Mp's and Cfc's are Jesness Inventory-based. (D) Our focus is on "Power Orientation" as this term (i) has been used throughout the present book, where it refers to the *Mp* + *Cfc* subtypes only, (ii) is defined in connection with the I-Level concept of middle maturity (the developmental stage at which Mp's and Cfc's are located), and (iii) was used by the NIMH conferees—though absent the *Cfm's*. (E) Findings #(1) through #(5) center on (i) the Mp's and Cfc's respective relationships to particular *Megargee and/or Quay types* (more specifically, to the *same* M &/or Q types), on (ii) these M and Q types' relationship to *each other*, and—thereby, indirectly—on (iii) concurrence/similarity/overlap (c/s/o) between the Mp's and Cfc's *themselves*. (F) C/s/o can be empirically assessed *only* indirectly: As with any two categories in any typology system (e.g., Megargee's and Quay's), the Mp and Cfc subtypes cannot be cross-tabulated with *each other*. This is because each individual—whether an Mp, Cfc, Na, or other subtype—within the study sample belongs to only *one* of the categories which comprise that system; nor, for the same reason, can any two categories be involved in a mutual rank-order approach to correlation (and, thereby, to the assessment of c/s/o). As a result, the empirical (as opposed to theoretical) c/s/o between those two categories—here, Mp's and Cfc's—has to be assessed by (i) determining the correlations that those respective categories each have with theoretically and/or empirically *similar* categories from *other* typology systems (here, the Megargee and/or Quay systems); these are categories which, in turn, (ii) might be positively correlated with *each other*. (G) Related information appears immediately after the findings. (H) The following salient features—together, working definitions—were presented by Van Voorhis (pp. 18–20). The first two types are Megargee's; the second two, Quay's.

Ables are described as charming, impulsive, and manipulative. They are achievement-oriented and often adjust well to incarceration. [They have MMPI elevations on scales 4 and 9.] . . .

Deltas are described as amoral, hedonistic, egocentric, manipulative, and bright. They are impulsive sensation seekers who have poor relations with peers and authorities. [Elevation on scale 4.] . . .

Antisocial Aggressive: Gets along with 'hoods.' . . . cannot be trusted, victimizes weaker inmates, . . . quick-tempered, holds grudges, . . . tries to form cliques, . . . stirs up trouble among inmates, . . . defiant, physically aggressive, guiltless, braggart, lack of concern for others. . . .

Manipulative: Continually tries to con staff, doesn't trust staff, complains of unfairness, feels unjustly confined, plays one staff member against another.

Findings. (1) Not only were Mp's positively correlated with Megargee's *Ables* (.01p, .10c) but Cfc's were positively correlated with them as well (.01c). The first of these parallel findings (the one involving Mp's), and the *opposite* of the second (. . . involving Cfc's), had been predicted by Van Voorhis. (2) Not only were Mp's positively correlated with Megargee's *Deltas* (.10p) but Cfc's were so correlated with them as well (.10p). Again, the Mp relationship was predicted, as was the opposite of the Cfc. (See Van Voorhis, p. 108 and 111, regarding the anomalous nature of Cfc findings #(1) and #(2),) These relationships, by themselves and especially

together with the set of three that now follows, suggest the presence of at least moderate similarity—unpredicted similarity—between the Mp's and Cfc's themselves: (3) Cfc's were positively correlated with Quay's *Antisocial Aggressives* (.05p, .05c). (4) Quay's *Antisocial Aggressives*, in turn, were positively correlated with Megargee's *Ables* (.10c) and *Deltas* (.10c)—to which, as seen in findings #(1) and #(2), were the Mp's and Cfc's themselves. (5) Megargee's Deltas were positively correlated with Quay's *Manipulative* (.05c). Findings #(3) and #(5) were predicted, as was the opposite of #(4) with respect to Ables and Deltas alike (p. 111).

Related information. The Cfc subtype, together with the Ci but not Mp, was among the components of the Committed Criminal (CC) group; others were Megargee's Charlie and Foxtrot and Quay's Antisocial Aggressive. Besides the CC, Van Voorhis derived three other main personality groups; that is, she synthesized them from her statistical findings. However, neither the Cfc, the Ci, nor the Mp subtypes were components of any of these three groups—the Situational, the Neurotic, and the Character Disorder.

As is evident, the *Mp* subtype thus did not appear in any of the four main groups that emerged in this study. (These four groupings or clusters, called V groups, were derived after five had been originally hypothesized.) More to the point, however, the Mp's were not expected to appear *together with the Cfc's* (likewise with the Ci's) in any grouping/clustering (p. 91). This was reflected in the fact that Cfc's were expected to *diverge* from certain types, namely, Megargee's Ables and Deltas (p. 111), with which Mp's were expected to *converge* (p. 91 and 108). As it turned out, Mp's—in accordance with those expectations—did *not* end up appearing together with Cfc's (and with Ci's) as components of any V group. Nor did these two subtypes appear together in, or together as, any other group. To be sure, evidence did emerge which indicated that Mp's and Cfc's had meaningful overlap. (See *Findings,* above—which include the fact that the Cfc's and the Mp's, *converged* with the Ables and Deltas.) Nevertheless, for justifiable statistical and other reasons that were presented by Van Voorhis, Cfc's ended up as a core component of a V group—the Committed Criminal—to which Mp's did not seem to firmly or even fairly definitely belong. At any rate, Mp's would not have been a statistically central (e.g., a directly- and multi-connected) constituent of that group; and, still from a statistical standpoint, they would not, in any event, have been part of that group—been uniquely connected to *it*—alone. In the end, this subtype remained structurally unattached to all four V groups.

For the reason indicated in point D, prior to the findings, we did not focus on *Ci's*—particularly on two chains or networks (C/Ns) of correlational connections that indirectly linked this subtype with the *Mp*. (The Ci's were entirely Warren's in the first C/N, and predominantly so within the second. Jesness' "adaptive" Ci [endnotes 150 and 282]—seemingly anomalously—appeared in the second.) In the *first* C/N, the Ci/Mp connection was as follows: The Ci's and Cfc's—which, as already seen, were linked to each other—were each connected with Quay's Antisocial Aggressives; the latter (Quay Aa) was anomalously linked with Megargee's Ables and Deltas—with which, as we have seen, *Mp's* were linked. Depending on one's perspective and approach, that C/N, and the one next mentioned, can be considered a two—or three-step consecutive linkage—collectively, a chain—or, alternately, a mutually converging network. In any event, the first Ci/Mp connection was rather indirect, and, like the following one, it was perhaps considerably weaker than the already-discussed *Cfc*/Mp. In the *second* chain/network, Mp's first had indirect—that is, via-other-system—connections with Na's (both Warren's and Jesness'); and the Na's had indirect relationships with Cfc's as well as *Ci's*. (As in the first C/N, "other-system" mainly involved the Quay and/or the Megargee typology. The *Warren* Na was directly, albeit

anomalously, related to the Jesness Cfc [p. 102]. Regarding the specific correlations that comprised the first and second chains/networks, see p. 108 and 111.) Van Voorhis, in whose study both C/Ns had emerged, pointed out the overall connections between "manipulative types [including but not limited to the given Mp's, on the one hand, and] the neurotic acting-out and committed-criminal types [including . . . the Na's, Cfc's, and Ci's, on the other]" (p. 107).

Discussion. In our view, Van Voorhis' study of adult prisoners suggested "A" and "B," which follow. Related matters, and other implications, are mentioned in "C" through "E."
A. Mp's and Cfc's have substantial commonality—mutual substantive overlap—with respect to important features, such as those in "C," below. They do so even though they also *differ* from each other in important features, and in overall personal dynamics. (In contrast to our judgments regarding features, those concerning *dynamics* do not derive from the study's specific analyses and findings; however, they are consistent with them.)
B. Mp's have important features in common with *Ci's* as well, and—not necessarily to a lesser extent—with *Na's*. Simultaneously, Cfc's have features in common with *Ci's* and—very likely to a lesser extent—with *Na's*. B applies even though Mp's and Cfc's also *differ* from Ci's and Na's in important respects (personal dynamics included). It also applies even though only *some* of the features that Mp's have in common with Na's, and—separately—with Ci's, are the same as those which Cfc's themselves separately share with these respective subtypes.

To facilitate the discussion, certain points might be kept in mind: (1) "Features," that is, individual characteristics, mainly refers to such observables/measurables as *behaviors, styles of interpersonal interaction, attitudes, values,* and *self-images,* but not to "dynamics" itself. (To a larger degree than when identifying and delineating at least these first four types of *features,* processes that involve not only considerable comparison and contrast but also fair amounts of inference and integration or synthesis must be used to determine *dynamics,* particularly the long-term. Van Voorhis' study did not attempt to develop and test hypotheses about any subtype's dynamics—say, its typical combination(s) of personal motivations, desires, and needs, viewed together with external factors and conditions. Given its main goals and priorities, the study did not try to systematically obtain the kinds of personal, life history, and other information that would have been critical in this regard.) (2) Though a given feature may be shared in common by any two subtypes—more specifically, although its content (quality/substance/category, and common meaning) and even its main functions may be identical or quite similar across those groups—it not infrequently differs in *degree* (intensity and/or amount) from one such group to the other, say, from Mp to Cfc. An example would be the extent to which and/or the frequency with which these subtypes ordinarily utilize "force," or else "deception," listed below. At any rate, the shared feature need not be quantitatively identical or even virtually so, across the groups in question. (3) Except where specified, the *Ci's* under consideration are Warren's interview-based, not Jesness' inventory-derived "adaptives." (4) *A* and *B,* above, and the remaining parts of this endnote, apply despite certain substantially *differing* salient features and groups of such features that have been observed among the individuals who (a) nonetheless all fall *within* the same given subtype (i.e., who "belong to" that one—and only that one [albeit *any* one]—of the four such groups under consideration), and who, by themselves, (b) collectively comprise that group. *Some* of these differences—for instance, significant distinctions within the Mp subtype—are specified at the conclusion of this endnote.

C. Salient among the important behaviors and styles of interaction (BSIs) that are often shared by various subtypes (e.g., Mp's and Na's) and are manifested by them in many situations are a number of the following: assertiveness; use of force/fear/intimidation/deception (includ-

ing, e.g., strong demands, ultimata, anger, and/or tactics/maneuvers such as misleading, bluffing, "beating others to the punch," and one-upmanship; conspicuous resistance to or undermining of authority figures; an ignoring or rejecting of usual community standards and/or expectations; and, particularly among youths, early strivings for independence/autonomy. With the partial exception of "strivings . . . ," these BSIs seldom involve the giving of much consideration to the interests and/or feelings of other individuals. Some of these shared behaviors, styles, and/or often-underlying attitudes, values, and self-images are directly reflected, for example, in the form of identical responses, by the given sets of subtypes, to relevant individual Jesness Inventory items (in the following, the item-number is shown; each of the subtypes in question *agrees* with each item [however, each one rejects #21]): *Mp and Cfc* – "I worry about what other people think of me" (21); "Nowadays they make it a big crime to get into a little mischief" (44). *Mp and Na* – "I am smarter than most boys [men] I know" (6; also applies to Ci adaptives); "I'm good at out-smarting others" (138). *Cfc and Na* – "Sometimes it's fun to steal something" (27); "I get a kick out of getting some people angry and all shook up" (43); "I think that someone who is fourteen years old is old enough to smoke" (58) (Jesness and Wedge, 1983, 111; Jesness, 1966, 1988).

In real-life settings, such BSIs and attitudes were observed in connection with Van Voorhis' adult prisoners and were also reported by these individuals themselves: In the penitentiary (pen.), not only were staff ratings of *Cfc's* "unfavorable, finding that [these individuals] (a) showed poor relationships with other inmates, (b) were aggressive, (c) were uncooperative, (d) needed supervision, and (e) responded poorly to supervision," but staff ratings of *Mp's* in that setting were identically unfavorable in all five respects. Within the prison camp, Cfc's had "relatively high rates of official disciplinary citations, and [of] self-reported aggressive behaviors," Mp's had such rates of disciplinary infractions and of self-reported aggression themselves. At the same time, Jesness' *Na's,* (a) individuals whose "self-reports of nonaggressive infractions were relatively high" (pen.), (b) were rated by staff as "aggressive" (pen.), (c) "showed significantly [high] disciplinary citations and citations for insubordination" (camp), and (d) "scored high on self-report measures of aggression" (camps). Warren Na's seemed much the same: "self-report measures of aggression" were high (I_4's and I_5's; pen./camp); staff rated them as "aggressive" and considered their relationships with authorities poor (I_4's and/or I_5's; pen. and/or camp). Finally, in the penitentiary, Warren *Ci's* had "high overall disciplinary rates and significantly more citations for insubordination than other inmates" (I_4's); they "incurred a high number of disciplinary citations and significantly higher rates of self-report, non-aggressive infractions" (I_5's). In the camp, I_4 Ci's showed "no disciplinary-related problems . . . , and staff ratings were favorable." There were too few I_5 Ci's for meaningful analyses, and the same applied to the Jesness adaptives (all I_4's; pen./camp) (Van Voorhis, 1994, 252–253, 257–259).

Regarding a *juvenile probation sample (JPS)* that had been described mainly in terms of eight empirically derived "clusters" which consisted of behaviors, styles of interaction, and so on (Palmer, 1963, 33, 169–173), the following statistical relationships were later found—in the mid-1960s—with respect to the four *subtypes* now under consideration (Palmer, 1973b); the five *remaining* Warren subtypes were examined at the same time as those four; the eight JPS *clusters* had been derived by the author, in 1962, prior to learning about I-Level and its subtypes): Of the three JPS clusters that were found to be most closely associated with—that is, most highly correlated ("r'd") with—the standard, mid-1960s, interview-based descriptions of *Cfc's,* two were the "Defiant-Indifferent" (D-I) and the "Verbally Hostile-Defensive" (VH-D). The three JPS clusters found to be most

closely associated with the standard description of *Mp's* were the VH-D, the "Independent-Assertive" (I-A), and the D-I. Of the three clusters most closely linked with *Na's,* two were the VH-D and the I-A; and, of the three that were closest to *Ci's,* one was the I-A. (For related perspectives, see study #4 in section B of this chapter. Regarding the several cluster/subtype relationships just mentioned, the average r was .58 [σ = .09]—all individual r's being positive. The five *remaining* Palmer clusters— those other than D-I, VH-D, and I-A— were the "Communicative-Alert," "Passive-Uncertain," "Impulsive-Anxious," "Dependent-Anxious," and "Wants To Be Helped and Liked"; their average r with the four specified subtypes was .13. [Note: The only I-Level subtype descriptions that were used in corrections as of the mid-1960s *were* the "standard, . . . interview-based."])

D. Based on findings and information such as the preceding—that is, on Van Voorhis' direct and indirect correlational connections regarding adult prisoners, on the staff ratings of and self-reports by those individuals, on responses to Jesness Inventory items by serious offenders (mostly juveniles), and on correlations regarding less serious offenders (juvenile probationers), collectively—it seems reasonably clear that Mp's share certain important features with Cfc's, and that both subtypes share some of them with Na's and Ci's. Salient among these features are behaviors, styles of interpersonal interaction, and so on, such as: (1) assertiveness that not infrequently involves verbal and/or physical aggression, intimidation, and/or high levels of other force or pressure; (2) tricks and related stratagems or deceptions; (3) active, *un*disguised maneuvering, and (4) frequent and often-strong resistance to authority figures and other adults—for instance, resistance not only to (a) commonly encountered types and levels of *accountability* to those individuals but to (b) other forms of felt and/or actual *control* or partial control by them.

A type of resistance that largely differs from (4a) and (4b) should be mentioned, one associated with many individuals' drive for *independence/autonomy (i/a)* per se. Though this resistance, like (4a) and (4b), always involves the just-mentioned figures/adults, it does not mainly center on *accountability/control* as such. Specifically, in i/a-centered resistance, the chief or even high-priority concern of the present individuals—say, adolescents and young adults—is not that of being ". . . control[led]" by these persons; instead, it involves and directly focuses on *content,* that is, on the specifics of *what* is occurring, or of what might occur. For instance, resistance that accompanies these individuals' independence/autonomy drive often pointedly involves the partial or complete rejection of certain conventional goals, paths, expectations, and perhaps life-styles—in each case, ones that authority figures and/or other adults with whom the individuals interact have begun to urge, perhaps enforce, or even just favor and possibly propose. By the same token, however—and still in contexts where particular content is or might be the key source of the individuals' resistance—the *following* also applies: When—or once—there is an *absence* of sizable differences regarding goals, paths, and so on, between these figures/adults and the given individuals, the latter do not consider those areas or aspects of their i/a strivings in danger; and, given this reality plus perception, they have little, or at least much less, to resist/reject. This usually applies even if the authority figures/adults offer moderate amounts of unsolicited advice/information, express preferences regarding goals or approaches, and—again within limits—indicate that they want to be informed about changes, developments, and difficulties. At any rate, with the presently considered subtypes (and with others), independence/autonomy-centered resistance is relatively common, though not inevitable; and when it occurs, it is not necessarily permanent—irrespective, for example, of changes in the content and quantities involved.

(For related perspective on the preceding points the following might be noted. A. The independence/autonomy drive of given individuals can be (1) more an aspect of (a) normal adolescent or post-adolescent change and development [e.g., reorientation, reorganization, and expansion] than, say, or (b) a deep-seated compensation or—very largely—a related, major repair and/or a critical psychological-security operation. [There are, of course, moderate compensations, and so on.] Moreover, i/a-focused *resistance* can operate with considerable force even when—as occurs among many individual Cfc's, Mp's, and Na's—the i/a drive involves (2) a relatively *equal mix* of (a) and (b), rather than dominance by (a). Finally, i/a resistance can also occur (3) when (b) outweighs (a); and, it can then operate no less *vigorously* than when (1) or (2) apply. Any of the just-mentioned mixes—that is, (1), (2), or (3)—can occur in connection with any given content issue. B. Other subtypes, such as Nx's and Se's, manifest an independence/autonomy drive themselves, during adolescence and early adulthood. In their case, however, this drive—its noncompensatory and compensatory aspects alike, and others already mentioned—is usually less conspicuous and apparently vigorous than it is among the present subtypes, particularly Mp's, Na's, and Ci's. [Among Nx's and some Cfm's, it is often compounded by considerable ambivalence and is intermingled with near-the-surface, often conscious, dependency wishes.] In addition, the resistance these individuals express to control/direction by authority figures/adults—say, express when substantially differing views exist between them and those persons—is usually less sustained than it is with the present subtypes; it is not just less salient, and less-often direct, in various ways.)

When one sets aside the just-discussed independence/autonomy-centered resistance, which involves content such as goals and paths, and when one instead focuses especially on the earlier-mentioned behaviors and styles (i.e., features (1) through (3): "force . . . , decept[iveness] . . . , maneuvering") and also on a largely different type of resistance (feature 4a/4b), the four features in question—ones that Cfc's, Mp's, Na's and Ci's share with each other—can be seen as reflecting, collectively, a *control orientation*. This term refers to a stance or approach that centers on, or otherwise heavily involves, individuals' efforts to achieve or largely achieve goals (a) through (c), which follow, and to sometimes expand them (*note*: (1) whatever their subtype, few of these individuals conceptualize and describe these goals in essentially the terms used here [this and the next points apply to adolescents and adults alike]; (2) the goals, especially the first two, can be considered "intermediate" ["I"], not "primary or basic" in the sense of "extremely long-standing and largely intrinsic" [Chapter 25]; (3) with any given individual, all three goals are usually involved, again especially the first two): (a) interpersonal dominance, (b) situational advantage or mastery, and (c) maintenance of social-image and/or self-image, including relief from associated, near-term fear or anxiety—all via frequent and/or heavy use of actual or feigned power and/or of other, often-associated, methods. (Achievement of (b) is generally followed by a sense of satisfaction, a feeling of comfort, and perhaps of physical pleasure.) These efforts are designed to "achieve . . ." those goals even at what the individuals realize can be a sizable psychological, material, and/or other affront, injury, loss, or related harm to one or more other persons and to know parts of the environment.

Though this control/dominance approach is very often proactive and direct—and often openly forceful—it is also often reactive and indirect. Moreover, it can include the two latter qualities whether or *not* it is forceful (openly or otherwise) rather than, say, apparently mild and perhaps seemingly harmless—as, for instance, when wile and ruses prevail. Separate from that, and exemplifying point 2 of the Discussion, the four across-subtype areas of commonality—that is, of content-overlap—exist despite *differences in degree* that are not infrequently found, from one subtype to the next, within each of these four content-areas (i.e., features (1)

through (4a/4b)). In addition, commonalities exist as such even though important *differences in content* are simultaneously present across those same subtypes—that is, even though significant *non*commonalities/*non*overlaps exist as well. Involved, here, are differences regarding features *other than* the four in question.

E. Preceding sections of this endnote have shown that certain Warren subtypes can be characterized as sharing (1) a *power* orientation or, viewed somewhat differently, (2) goals and methods centering on *control*. This section will explain the distinction between (1) and (2) and will indicate how the latter substantively extends beyond the former. It will also explain why—that is, the sense in which—one can think of the second characterization as referring less to a control *orientation* than to a control, or control/domination, *approach*. This, at least, would apply when focusing on the Cfc, Mp, Na, and Ci subtypes—certainly the last two (the I_4's)—collectively.

In all analytic parts of this book, such as Chapters 8–11, the concept of "power orientation" reflects the following descriptions—found in basic I-Level writings—of middle maturity (MM) individuals (*note*: In these writings, the concepts and quotations next presented referred to and were applied specifically as well as solely to MMs, all of whom, of course, were I_3's and I_3's alone. Except as indicated, these quotations, and the page numbers shown, are from Warren et al., 1966b): Whether he is a Cfm, a Cfc, or an Mp, an I_3 "perceives the world [i.e., his environment] and his role in it on a power dimension. This is his primary interpersonal concern. . . . [He] wants to know exactly what [external structure] to expect, who the power is, etc. . . . [Given that perception—i.e., that assumption or interpretation—and concern, once the individual answers those directly resulting questions he *responds* by trying to] manipulate his environment . . . so that his wishes and/or needs will be met and is fears evaded. [He does this particularly] by conning, conforming, or intimidating." Thus, for example, among the I_3's, a typical *Mp* believes his "conning [will] . . . control others and bring about the desired outcome"—goals he shares with Cfc's. He considers himself "cool, smooth, [and] powerful . . . [—also able to "outsmart others"—and he] sets up a battleground re power and control whenever he perceives the power of another as likely to have an [unwanted] impact on him." Not unrelated, one of the main motives ("reasons") for *delinquency* on the part of *Cfc's* is "defiance of adults" (pp. 2, 9–10, 18, 22–23. Also see: Grand, 1961c, 6, 12–13; Warren, 1969, 53). ("Conforming" especially characterizes *Cfm's* and *Cfc's*—the former in almost *all* settings and the latter among delinquent peers and when such behavior seems "unavoidable" in light of the "authority power structure" (p. 18.)) The key point is that, in those writings, such responses were viewed as fundamentally originating in the following, and as regularly fueled as well as essentially dominated by them: (1) that particular I_3 *perception* of the environment (i.e., the assumption/interpretation that interactions center on power, and that—to achieve one's goals—power is king) and (2) the individuals' directly and closely related principal *focus and concern,* namely, "power fields" (p. 9). Hence the view that—and the specific sense in which—the individuals' basic outlook and the fabric as well as character of their interpersonal behaviors are power-*oriented.*

As used here, individuals' "orientation" thus emphasizes not only their particular type of perception and their related principal concern but certain kinds of *behaviors,* that is, responses— such as those just presented regarding Mp's. More specifically, it refers not just to those persons' fundamental "assumption/interpretation . . ." (i.e., perception) but to behaviors viewed as (1) originating basically and perhaps solely in, as (2) flowing directly and perhaps only from, and, in any event, as (3) dominated wholly or at least chiefly by, that *perception*—and concern. (To simplify the presentation, we will generally omit "concern.") In the case of *Cfc's* and *Mp's* this, of course, is necessarily and

only an I_3 perception, since these subtypes are I_3's only. Regarding *Na's* and *Ci's,* a parallel situation exists: "Orientation" continues to involve behaviors that are "dominated . . . by" the individuals' chief basis for interpreting and understanding their environment. However, with these individuals, this is an I_4 perception, since the subtypes in question are I_4's only.

Insofar as given behaviors ("B's") mainly reflect individuals' principal ("core") perception ("P") regardless of those persons' I-Level—and, in the just-mentioned writings, they *do*—the substantive relationship that exists between B and P (specifically: $B = (f)P$) applies, ipso facto, to the I_3 and I_4 levels alike, and, simultaneously, to each subtype within these levels. Given this (a) across-levels and within-levels *B/P relationship;* given that (b) each orientation involves not just various B's but *a particular P (namely, the core perception);* given that (c) the core perception is what *specifically defines* each respective I-Level (e.g., the I_3) and is what thereby substantively distinguishes it from every other level with regard to orientation; and, in particular as well as obviously, given that (d) the respective I_3 *and* I_4 levels therefore differ from each other substantively with regard to core perception and hence in orientation, and that this same substantive difference also exists between each I_3 *subtype* and each I_4 *subtype,* the following is the case: Although earlier-mentioned *behaviors*—specifically, features "(1) through (4a/4b)"— are shared by Cfc's, Mp's, Na's, and Ci's, the individuals who are *Cfc's* and those who are *Mp's* have, separately and together, a different *overall orientation* (perception of their environment) than those who are *Na's* and those who are *Ci's* (themselves singly and jointly). This is because the first two subtypes are I_3's and the second two are I_4's. In short, each of these sets of subtypes (say, the Cfc + Mp set) has its own particular "B's" [and a] P" *combined*—hence, its own "overall orientation" ("OO")—even though it simultaneously shares certain important B's (behaviors) with the other set (the Na + Ci).

This difference in 00 thus exists despite the following areas of similarity and/or identity. A. *Behaviors* "(1) through (4a/4b)," respectively, involve essentially the same type of content in the Cfc + Mp set as in the Na + Ci set: (1) through (3) focus on individuals' use of force, deception, and maneuvering, respectively, and (4a/4b) centers on their "resistance to . . . control" by authority figures/adults. These behaviors, collectively, are the shared, important ones referred to above. B. The *intermediate ("I") goals* at which these shared behaviors are directed involve essentially the same type of content in both sets of subtypes. That is, as with the behaviors mentioned in A, the substance of each such I-goal is generically the same with Cfc + Mp individuals as with Na + Ci. These goals, as indicated earlier, involve "(a) interpersonal dominance, (b) situational advantage or mastery, and (c) protection of self-image, including relief from associated near-term anxiety or fear."

(Five points before continuing: First, similarities A and B exist despite differences in *degree* that are present in any given type of behavior and type of I-goal, across any two or more of the four subtypes. Second, and regardless of subtype, individuals' behaviors and goals are not the same as their *overall orientations;* in particular, they are neither the conceptual nor functional equivalents or near-equivalents of those 00s, even though they are aspects and reflections of them. This applies whether the four behaviors are viewed individually or collectively, whether the three goals are viewed in either of these ways, and whether as well as how any one or more of those behaviors *and* goals—however viewed—are mutually combined. Third, because (1) *behavior* is considered a function of perception—that is, $B = (f)P$—the relationship between the former and the latter can be called "causal": Specifically, perception plays a role, in fact a key role, in generating the behavior. Similarly, because (2) respective *goals* can be considered functions of (again, products of) perception—that is, $G = (f)P$—this relationship can itself be called causal. Both (1) and (2) apply even though the *behaviors* in question can be viewed as ways of implementing these *goals,* that is, as having a means/ends relationship to them: $B = m/e \rightarrow G$. They also apply even though the goals (I-goals) in question—sometimes called the "present" goals—may have existed *prior to* the behaviors that are used to help achieve them, and although these goals may have played a role in shaping the content of the given behaviors, that is, in determining their character. [*Note:* The present goals—say, interpersonal dominance and situational advantage/mastery—may have been fully, partially, or only slightly developed prior to the existence of these behaviors. Whatever these I-goals' degree of development may have been during that time, these behaviors—once they did develop, and however fully they did so—may or may not have been originally and immediately used to help achieve *them.* At any rate, in contrast to this goals-before-*behaviors* scenario, these behaviors may *have* existed prior to the development/crystallization (D/C) of the present goals: In this behavior-before-*goals* situation the behaviors' role—prior to that D/C—would, of course, have involved other goals instead. Only later (i.e., during and/or after the D/C) would these behaviors have been used—in a modified form or not—to help achieve the present goals. This applies even if this *new* role had been partly or wholly *added* to the prior one instead of being partially or entirely substituted for it, and however fully or rapidly these I-goals (and the behaviors themselves) developed. Finally, and especially in the goals-before-*behaviors* scenario, the overall influence of the present goals in shaping the content of these behaviors may have been large or small. This applies whether that impact (i.e., the effect on content) is mainly general and directional or else relatively specific.] Fourth, the following are a few additional descriptions from I-Level literature's basic classification document, descriptions that bear on the *Na + Ci* set. They illustrate behaviors (3) and (4a/4b) as well as goals (b) and (c). In most cases their generic resemblance to already-specified features that are associated with the $Cfc + Mp$ set is close, despite differences in degree: The typical Na "anticipates a . . . relationship with adult authorities [that is] focused around the issue of control of behavior . . . , [and he] is prepared to challenge [their] ability to shape or limit his everyday activities." He has a "self-image of actual or potential super-adequacy." He wants others to "view him as . . . very nearly autonomous." [He] "consciously attempts to master [e.g., by] direct action," . . . "immediate anxieties and [external] pressures"''; and, he believes he "can manipulate his way out of [difficulties]." The typical Ci considers himself "adequate, capable, independent. . . . [He may have] delinquent or criminal [identification figures. He often] has antipathy for the core culture, [and delinquency is sometimes] a way of attacking [that] culture or the authority system" (Warren et al., 1966b, 32, 33, 46).)

Fifth, the classification document also specifies the main bases on which, and the types of dimensions along which, a *higher maturity* individual—an I_4—orients and focuses his self-concept, often interacts with other persons, and wants to direct many of his near- and longer-term activities. It also mentions major, desired outcomes of those interactions and activities: The I_4—thus, the Na and Ci—

has internalized a set of standards ["ideals, standards, and values"] by which he judges his and others' behaviors . . . . [He] has status and prestige concerns . . . , wants recognition from those he admires . . . , [and wants] to be like them in actions, attitudes, or attributes (p. 2, 29).

In other words, those standards and concerns provide not only a substantive vantage point or perspective from which the I_4 views himself and his surroundings, and a baseline in relation to which he frequently thinks about and gauges them. Instead, complemented by his directly related wishes (e.g., for recognition and certain attributes), they also serve as a stimulus and framework for

various major actions and responses, one that often helps initiate, direct, focus, delimit, sustain, and sometimes even prioritize them. In these respects such standards, concerns, and wishes (SCWs) function, collectively, as a core conceptual and emotional force—a basis of broad influence. Viewed as a set of interconnected though not always mutually consistent factors, these SCWs essentially distinguish him from middle maturity individuals, that is, from I_3's (e.g., Cfc's and Mp's). In addition, the I_4 is differentiated in the degree to which he (1) "perceive[s] feelings and motivations which are not just like his own" (p. 29). Moreover, and again largely unlike I_3's, he (2) "recognizes interpersonal interactions in which people attempt to influence one another by means other than compliance, manipulation, promises of hedonistic or monetary reward, and so on. [Because, as just implied, he can at least partly] understand underlying reasons for behavior [he can] respond, on a fairly long-term basis, to moderately complex expectations [by] other individuals" (Chapter 4). In this regard, and given item (1) directly above, he has "some ability to . . . relate with another person in terms of [both his own and that individual's *particular*] needs, feelings, standards, or ideals" (p. 29)—still in considerable contrast to I_3's.) As indicated, individuals who comprise the Cfc + Mp set ("set 1" or "s-1") differ from those in the Na + Ci ("set 2" or "s-2"), despite their generic similarities and/or identities regarding behaviors (1) through (4a/4b) and concerning intermediate goals (a) through (c): First, and most basic, they distinctly differ in their main assumption about, and overall interpretation and understanding of, their world; that is, s-1 individuals clearly differ from s-2's with respect to their core perceptions of the environment, and regarding their resulting central concerns. Second, s-1's and s-2's differ with respect to the above *behaviors (B's)*, and, simultaneously, those *I-goals (G's)*. This difference, which centers on what can be called "subjective meaning" (see below), reflects the fact that two different *contexts* are involved:

The B's and G's occur in one psychological context for set 1 individuals and in a different such context for set 2's. They do so even though set 1's B's are overtly (observably) very similar to set 2's and although set 1's G's are likewise similar to set 2's.

Specifically, for *s-1* individuals the "context"—the overall content of the core perception (i.e., *what* the "perception" comprises)—is that of *world-as-power centered (a power field)*. This applies not only when these individuals assume or believe that power is often used in an effort to (1) control, thwart, defeat, physically deprive or harm, and/or emotionally hurt them, but also when they think its use, at least by themselves, is (2) the main effective way, perhaps the only effective way, and, in any event, a justified way to obtain what they want or need, and to defend themselves. For *s-2's*, the context is that of *world-as-standards-centered (a standards field)*—more specifically, as a broad social/interpersonal setting or arena that is structured and dominated by widely held values, standards, and ideals (VSIs). These VSIs objectively constitute general or specific social expectations, norms, and so on, and many are personally experienced as such. Among them, some are partly or entirely internalized by the s-2's and may become aspects of their desired self-image; others seem largely impersonal, are basically just accommodated (e.g., "gone along with," as needed), and are not internalized; still others are considered unacceptable and are rejected or resisted. (*Note*: (1) Each context or core perception can be viewed as a psychological reality, in that the thoughts which are involved—that is, the overall content of which the "perception" is comprised—are *internally* [mentally, subjectively], and consciously, experienced. (2) Each core perception, as such, is separable from—and, of course, originally exists prior to—its *consequences,* some of which are mostly external and have a "reality" in *that* respect. [Here, "external" means physical/social/interpersonal, not mainly psychological."] All this is independent of the fact that *interactions*

often occur between a core perception and given consequences, and that some of these interactions can eventually alter the perception itself—and, with that, may modify later consequences. (3) Feelings and emotions, not just thoughts, can enter into (1) and (2)—thus, can be involved with perception [ipso facto with "context"] and consequences alike. (4) For present purposes there is no need to distinguish between "thoughts," "ideas," and "concepts" [Webster, 1965, 171, 412–413]. As elsewhere, "perception" is used as it appears in standard I-Level literature [Sullivan, Grant, and Grant, 1957; Warren et al., 1966b], not in most philosophical and general psychology writings. The I-Level meaning approximates that of "conception" or "concept," with the elements of "assumption" and "interpretation" definitely included, in contrast to simply implied.)

In particular, then, the difference between set 1 and set 2 individuals regarding the "subjective meaning" of *behaviors (1) through (4a/4b)* involves the following (the difference in the meaning of *I-goals (a) through (c)* itself reflects these interrelated points—which culminate in the final [the fifth] one): (1) Insofar as perception (thought/assumption/interpretation [t/a/i]) determines the nature of *context*—more precisely, accounts for it in the sense of substantively constituting it (in short, insofar as a context is—i.e., concretely consists *of*—a core perception's "overall content" [its t/a/i's]); (2) insofar as s-1 and s-2 individuals have mutually *different* perceptions about their physical/social/interpersonal environment; (3) insofar as s-1's and s-2's consciously experience the given behaviors *in connection with* those respective core perceptions (i.e., experience them with regard to, and understand/interpret them largely or entirely in terms of, those differing contexts or frameworks); and (4) insofar as perception (" . . . interpretation") or context—still a subjective ("psychological") reality—is a central or *the* central determiner of *meaning* (e.g., constitutes and therein provides a framework—a set of interrelated factors, categories, and parameters—within which to interpret given actions, and in terms of which to understand them); then (5) those behaviors—their overt, generic similarities/identities notwithstanding—can be said to have mutually different meanings, in the sense of different *referents,* to those s-1's and s-2's. (Because these meanings are subjective [whatever their content], they can be considered "personal" or "psychological"; insofar as they are substantive reflections and functions of given contexts, they can be called "contextual." The *referential* aspect of "meaning" differs from that of *significance* or *importance.* The latter centers, for example, on personal and/or interpersonal implications and related consequences [I's /C's] of one's behavior. One other distinction might be noted: The fact that psychological and contextual meaning can differ for set 1 as compared to set 2 individuals with respect to I's/C's applies whatever the absolute and comparative *effectiveness* of the given behaviors might be—that is, effectiveness in addressing those youths' and adults' respective core perceptions ["assumptions . . ."] and related major concerns. Like points (1) through (5), immediately above, these considerations and distinctions also—and simultaneously [hence, jointly]—pertain to the intermediate goals at which those behaviors are directed.)

Regarding those mutually different psychological/contextual (p/c) meanings—different to s-1's and s-2's—the following would thus apply to the behaviors in question (e.g.: "force"; "maneuvering"), ones used by these individuals to achieve the specified I-goals (e.g.: "interpersonal dominance"; "situational advantage or mastery"): Any such behavior and goal, separately and especially in combination (e.g.: "maneuvering" *and* ". . . dominance"), can have a given, principal p/c meaning to those *s-1* individuals—that is, to youths and adults who would view the achievement of this goal mainly in the context of a surrounding *power field,* and who, accordingly, could regard the given behavior/goal combination as a justified and perhaps necessary way of dealing with

that field. However, in the case of *set 2* individuals, that same type of behavior, occurring in conjunction with the same kind of goal (and again in an implementing role), can have a rather different primary p/c meaning. Many s-2's, for instance, can see this behavior and combination—especially but not only given the *achievement* of this goal—as a way of internally affirming and overtly manifesting (sometimes even trying to promote) certain *values, standards, and/or ideals* they have incorporated. (If these individuals largely ignored these VSIs or acted contrary to them, many would feel "bad," guilty, and/or undeserving [in whatever degree], even if they achieved the desired, intermediate goal—say, "dominance," or perhaps situational mastery. If they largely *followed* these VSIs yet did *not* achieve or approach that goal, many would mainly feel either mistaken [due to personal misjudgment] or misdirected [by others], on the one hand, or else inadequate and/or inferior [again in whatever degree], on the other—though not "bad," and so on [e.g.: disloyal to principles, and perhaps to persons who embody them].)

Similarly, the following would apply to *another* of the earlier-mentioned behaviors ("strong resistance to [control by] authority figures and other adults") and to another I-goal ("maintenance of social-image" [persona]—e.g., as decisive, consistent, persistent, courageous, physically strong, and perhaps quick-thinking, in the case of set 1 individuals [Cfc's, Mp's], and independent as well as "cool," in that of set 2's [Na's, Ci's]): Among many *set 1* individuals, use of this behavior/goal combination can be mainly a way of dealing with their implicit or explicit assumption, and their related concern or fear, that if they are *not* seen in various such ways—that if, in particular, they are often viewed as uncertain, as inconsistent, as easily swayed, fooled, or frightened, and/or as physically or otherwise "weak"—they might well be disliked or despised, frequently opposed or thwarted, and, all in all, often hassled, threatened, or harmed, by aggressive or hostile peers and/or by certain authorities/adults. However, among many *set 2* youths and adults, that same behavior/goal combination can have a different primary psychological/contextual meaning. This meaning, which reflects their perception that "values, standards, and/or ideals" play a key role in interpersonal interactions, can closely relate, for instance, to these I_4 individuals' following, implicit assumptions: When they behave in ways (see below) that other persons (say, certain peers) view as expressions of a commitment to those VSIs, these peers will feel that those I_4 youths and adults favorably measure up, that is, have "good" qualities or traits; in addition, they will enjoy being with those I_4's (s-2's), for instance, talking and sharing activities as friends or acquaintances. In those respects these peers will provide approval and acceptance—aspects of recognition and status (i.e., esteem or regard, not just relative position). (The recipients in question, that is, the I_4 individuals, rarely describe these peer responses—functionally, "inputs" to these I_4 youths and adults—in those particular terms.) For present purposes we can focus on the I_4 *youths*—especially on their behaviors and on most such individuals' related concern regarding the peers' assumed views and resulting inputs. This concern, mentioned shortly, exists despite the fact that these I_4 youths can provide substantial *self-approval* in connection with the values, standards, and/or ideals, even during times of little above input from those peers. Their ability to do so depends largely on the extent to which they have internalized given VSIs, know they are trying to apply them in various contexts (including ones not involving those peers), and feel they are succeeding in this regard.

The behaviors in question bear on two broad movements or objectives that most adults consider legitimate and important to adolescents, as do the present I_4 youths—that is, the same set 2 individuals (adolescents)—themselves: (1) modification of their current or recent, often largely child-role-centered, relationship with their parents, in order to become more emotionally independent and, eventually, physically emancipated; (2) formation of a rather different identity, one that involves, at a minimum but in particular, nonchildhood-centered beliefs, attitudes, interests, and behavior patterns. In both respects *opportunities* for change mainly occur in connection with one's choice of friends, types of relationships with those peers and others, access to new experiences and information, practical preparations for the future, use of free time, habits (e.g.: smoking, drinking), appearance (e.g.: attire, grooming), and so on (e.g.: driving, curfew); and, one's *actual* change with regard to (1) and (2) usually involves several of these areas—sometimes almost simultaneously. (Note, before continuing: As used here, "childhood" emphasizes the period from the start of grade school through the preteen—preadolescent—years. Also, as implied above, the adolescents' identity, including that of the present I_4's, will not be *entirely* different. Specifically, some salient and important individual qualities, traits, and skills [QTSs] will be largely or entirely retained—for instance, ones that these youths already feel are OK about themselves, and that they may think are considered "good' by persons they like. This applies to certain combinations of those characteristics, as well. [The preceding points partly reflect the fact that some major aspects of overall or long-term *motivation* and *dynamics,* and of related "personality," will not change substantially for some time, often a long time. This is the case even though, as reflected shortly, the youths' "identity" as a whole—whether or not it is fairly well integrated—does undergo major change. (Concerning identity, see "*overall pattern*" of QTSs, and so on, below.) Regarding interactions between "motivation, . . . personality, . . . [and] identity," the individuals' conscious, desired self-image and their intended, outwardly projected social-image (persona) are *both* involved in what eventually does and does *not* largely change—involved, substantially, in connection with their content.] Nevertheless, the *overall pattern* of [e.g., relationships among and integration of] the youths' above-mentioned, collective QTSs [say, of their interacting contents] *will* be rather different than before; this also applies to these characteristics' functional capacity and scope, especially, though not only, when these qualities, traits, and skills are combined with others. Finally, both differences are related to but separable from the fact that some of the essentially retained characteristics—various QTSs, individually—will sometimes largely change in degree; and, because of these qualities', traits', and skills' respective, changed capacities and scope—thus, their different, usually increased, potential influence—some will at times be used differently than before.)

In contemporary society, changes or developments regarding the above-mentioned areas, such as "friends," "relationships," "habits," and "appearance," involve *behaviors, thoughts, and attitudes (BTAs)* widely considered rather different than those of childhood. Viewed collectively at any point in time, these BTAs constitute a general stance toward the environment and they help provide a framework for adjusting to what most persons, not just most adults, associate with—and call—the "adolescent years." (In the literature, certain commonly observed sets of BTAs are often said to each comprise, or at least reflect, an "adolescent subculture." That is, each set/subculture contains salient individual B's, T's, and/or A's whose specific content differs significantly from that of each other set's BTAs; and, those respective BTAs may be mutually combined in different ways. In addition, some sets include other types of features, among which are the sociological and environmental.) Given these areas, these features, this societally recognized and reinforced childhood/postchildhood distinction, and these widespread associations between certain BTAs on the one hand and adolescence on the other, the following occurs: When a number of those behaviors, and so on, are observed—usually repeatedly—by, say, the set 2 youths' friends and acquaintances, those observations lead these peers to take it for granted that

those youths are indeed being (are acting and talking/thinking like) *adolescents*—in this respect, are not being "kids." (Here, "kids" refers to individuals who behave like most "children," in the sense of chronological preadolescents.) For those peers to "take [the preceding] for granted" they need not specifically know or assume that the given youths are changing or trying to change their *child-to-parent relationships,* or that they may have already substantially done so. Instead, they can make that assumption mainly by—in effect—(1) comparing their various observations with their already existing picture of what *adolescence*—its salient and relatively distinct behaviors/thoughts/attitudes—is often like, and by (2) sensing that those observations and that picture mostly match. (This process occurs largely intuitively, and often preconsciously.) Only secondarily and sometimes distantly does that assumption/belief reflect their—still the peers'—having assimilated adult society's common, but not entirely correct, view or assumption that a sizable relationship-change between individuals and their parents is a largely necessary precondition to the very existence of certain adolescent-type behaviors, and to their overall maintenance as well.

Given (1) the *specific content* of the youths' (not the peers') observed individual behaviors, thoughts, and attitudes, and, in effect, with reference to (2) the *overall stance* that those BTAs collectively comprise, these youths are commonly and favorably viewed by those peers as "kind of [or "pretty"] independent," as "cool," and as "with it"—which is how I$_4$/s-2 youths often *want* to be viewed by them. (Here, "cool" does not center on "nonchalant," for example, apparent or even genuine indifference or unconcern; but it may include "casual.") Salient among the related words and phrases that those friends and acquaintances (collectively) often use to further describe these individuals along these dimensions are: "can take it or leave it"; "strong" (e.g., can stand firm); "different"; "sometimes real daring" (and "far out"); "does lots of things" ("gets around"); "smooth";

"sharp" or "pretty smart"; "up on things"; and "knows where the action is." Such descriptions and their equivalents are not given only by males, regarding other males.)

The next few paragraphs are mainly a review, but they also add necessary detail and precision: Because of the I$_4$/s-2's behaviors, thought, and attitudes with respect to friends, to new experiences and information, to the use of free time, to personal habits and appearance, and so on, some of these individuals' peers—often may—consider them persons who are fairly "independent" as well as "cool" and "with it"; this perception helps these peers respond positively to them.

In addition, these peers implicitly assume that those youths are persons who see themselves as other than "kids" not only because of their age but especially by virtue of the BTAs—thus, on content-centered grounds. Yet even with that perception and assumption, they do not *always* respond positively: Some youth-behaviors, such as particular forms or expressions of independence, are not especially liked; as a result, they may sooner or later elicit a lukewarm, an indifferent, or even a negative reaction. (Despite that, when youths act or assert themselves independently, this in itself is often viewed *sympathetically* by many peers—that is, almost irrespective of the particulars [the content, and perhaps even issues] involved. Nevertheless, these responses, which are often triggered by an immediate sense of identification with the youths or with their efforts/achievements, and which sometimes convey a message of solidarity as well, may or may not especially contribute to *sustained acceptance/approval* of the youths themselves.) A similar, full range of content-determined reactions occurs with regard to the youths' particular *thoughts* (e.g., expressed beliefs) and *attitudes*.

At any rate, because of the set 2 youths' BTAs in the above-mentioned areas (e.g.: free time; habits; appearance), and given the fact that "independence," "coolness," and the like are widely—societally—considered major facets of adolescence and characteristics of various adolescent subcultures, the following occurs: Those peers, who prefer an adolescence-centered stance to one of childhood in their *own* lives, view these individuals as adolescents rather than as "kids"; this perception provides the overall backdrop or framework for—though not the specific, critical, determinative basis of—almost everything else. In addition, and more to the issue of specific, critical impact, the peers usually accept those youths and approve of them—or, in other instances, do *not*—depending chiefly on the particular content of their overt stance. (This especially applies to acceptance or at least approval that is other than momentary or even moderately short-lived, whether or not this acceptance/approval was ever associated with spontaneous, "immediate," emotional reactions.) Specifically, these peers do not accept/approve chiefly because they consider those individuals *adolescents,* that is, ones who view themselves as such in the "nonchildhood-centered" sense. Nor do they accept/approve largely because of the latters' fairly-to-highly independent behavior per se, for instance, regarding habits and appearance. Instead, it is the nature—the content—of the youths' *specific* behaviors (e.g., their particular habits/appearance, viewed as expressions of independence), their specific thoughts (e.g., expressed beliefs), and their specific attitudes—and even their *types* of BTAs—that usually constitute the key ingredients, particularly regarding acceptance/approval that is other than short-lived. (This also applies to generally known, sometimes societally labeled, adolescent subcultures or groupings—ones with which the peers may associate those youths.) Similarly, not all "daring," "far out," and/or "smooth" behaviors are ipso facto considered "cool," and thereby contribute substantially to approval. This is the case even if, for instance, "daring" behavior, and perhaps its related physical skills, is admired in some respects. The same applies to the youths' being "up on things"; that is, a good deal often depends on just *what* is involved—not only, or sometimes not even, on whether *much* is known.

As is clear, the already-discussed behaviors, and so on, reflect the set 2 youths' overall interest in adolescence, an interest and attraction that largely accords with and complements the societally recognized importance of forming a "rather different identity" than that of childhood, as one moves into and through the teenage years. The youths' expressions of these behaviors, thought, and attitudes not only lets their peers know what *interests* them about adolescence; instead, they also indicate and imply what these s-2's are *un*interested in, are not especially committed to in any event, and/or wish to specifically distance themselves from—such as certain activities and involvement, and, often, particular "subcultures" as a whole. By thus communicating what they do and do not wish to be "like," to participate in, and to be associated with, these set 2 individuals in effect partly define "who" they are, for instance, what they value and believe, and where they stand. Whether directly, indirectly, or both, they convey this picture, that is, this personal information, even though some of its elements may not be entirely clear, may be fairly unstable or perhaps even new, and/or may be mutually inconsistent. At any rate, the content of what these youths convey most often and most *clearly,* and of that which is least unstable, constitutes a major part of what is ordinarily termed these individuals' "identity." This is the part or aspect which involves their social-image, and it is the content of this image that mainly helps the given peers develop *their* image of "who" these s-2's are and of what can usually be expected of them.

(None of the preceding, including the youths' overall interest in adolescence, and even their *commitment* to some of its main aspects, requires that these individuals have little or no ambivalence and/or anxiety about any of the following changes or possible changes relating to it; this applies even if they do not view these changes/actions as having to occur quickly: (1) greatly modifying almost all—or even just many—major aspects of childhood, or

of their child-to-parent relationships in particular; (2) substantially involving themselves in *certain* aspects of adolescence [e.g.: preparing for early adulthood; close relationships with the opposite sex]—again, even when these are of interest and appeal to them, and perhaps to many of their friends; and/or (3) specifically moving into or further into adolescence on a *wide* front, and, in that connection, in a clearly committed way. Item (1) applies especially to aspects the youths have often associated with physical pleasure, psychological satisfaction, overall comfort, and/or relief; (2) and (3) apply even if these individuals believe they have, or can obtain, sufficient information about the given aspects or areas; and, all three items, including their implications, are substantially interrelated. Finally, the youths can have considerable ambivalence and/or anxiety even if their adolescence-centered behaviors and overall stance [ACBOS] is apparently *vigorous;* also, irrespective of items (2) and (3), these individuals can have substantial motivation to develop a nonchildhood-centered identity [self- as well as social-] even if their ACBOS often seems more passive than active.)

Thus, by expressing given behaviors, thoughts, and attitudes, set 2 youths achieve their intermediate ("I") goal of maintaining a particular social-image. The broad aspects of this image are—chiefly—a seeming independence and a general appearance of being "cool" (frequently including "unruffled"). Often by themselves, these aspects (features; components) lead various peers to assume that those youths (1) reject childhood-centered roles, (2) are essentially committed to adolescence, and, in these respects, (3) are much like themselves. The peers' awareness of these features, when operating in conjunction with assumptions (1) and (2), can be considered a largely accurate "perception" of those s-2 youths' readily visible personality and stance. (However, see below regarding its completeness.) By itself, this perception often rapidly elicits (1) a relatively undifferentiated positive feeling—about those youths—within the peers, and, soon thereafter, (2) a closely related, *overt* response by the peers. This response, whether it is mainly verbal or not, is picked up by the s-2 youths and is considered positive by them—for instance, friendly and/or approving, in whatever degree.

The peers' perception of the youths' independence and coolness is largely accurate within its sphere, that is, as far as it goes: On the one hand, it appropriately involves and adequately encompasses these broad aspects or features of the youths' visible personality and stance; on the other, it does not *also* include—explicitly contain—various *specifics,* that is, particular contents which are either intrinsic to those broad features or that often *accompany* them. In short, the peers' perception—the one thus far focused on—reflects and includes *one* important layer or level of content: the "broad." It does not, however, involve or adequately involve another: the "specific." In this regard it is incomplete, and its scope or perhaps depth is less than it would otherwise be.

(Before continuing, the following might be kept in mind: (1) The "specific" features/contents exist within the *youths,* even though they might not be reflected in—included in—some peers' *perceptions* of these individuals. Also in connection with these youths, such f/c's are either intrinsic to or associated with the "broad aspects" [see next]—again independently of the peers' perceptions. (2) As used here, the concept of "layer or level" falls under the category of "structure"; that of "specifics" [as in "particular features"] belongs to "substance"—meaning, content as such. Specifics that "often accompany" the broad aspects—in other words, features which are frequently *associated* with them—are ones whose presence is not (a) absolutely required or forced, whether via logical *necessity* [see point (4), below] or essentially by definition alone. In that connection, such specifics are also—and simultaneously—ones whose *content* [e.g., concrete detail] is not (b) "intrinsic" to those broad aspects, in the sense of being inherent and integral. This means it does not necessarily follow

from those aspects, in the sense of not being derivable from them by deduction alone, and, hence, with certainty and sameness every time. [Basically, (a) and (b) simply refer to that facet or aspect of "association" which involves contingency rather than ironclad linkage and/or underlying mutual identity.] At any rate, in this and the following discussion, "specific" features differ *substantively* from "broad" features. Simultaneously, these specifics exist at, or at least can be represented as existing at, a layer or level of reality which can be conceptualized as differing *structurally* from that of those features. [Categories, such as "structure," can be viewed as constructs that represent aspects of external/physical as well as internal/psychological reality.] (3) "Specificity"—its absence, or else its limited presence—is only one chief dimension along which incompleteness can exist. Another is that of scope, as in range or reach. In the present context, the latter dimension would involve contents [features] which are *other than* those of "independence" and "coolness" and which, if used, would extend an individuals' perception beyond them. (4) As implied in point (2), the substantive dimension of the relationship that exists between any *broad*-aspect "perception" [say, that of independence per se], on the one hand, and any *specific* aspects [say, concrete expressions of independence], on the other, involves what is called "contingency," in that the content of these specific aspects can vary: It can vary, and it often does, when given circumstances arise, and, in any event, as the youths themselves change—change as individuals and/or, collectively, in the sense of samples. In this major respect that broad-aspect/specific-aspect [BA/SE] relationship or association—whatever its *form* or *structure* might be—is neither unalterable in principle nor unchanging in fact. Moreover, being contingent, it neither reflects nor actually involves "necessity," at least in the sense of inevitability. In particular [though not only], this relationship—whichever direction is involved [BA-to-SA, or vice versa]—is not, with respect to its content, a product of *logical necessity.* This is because such necessity, strictly defined, can occur only within the framework of syllogistic logic [SL] or else in relation to "summative induction" [SI] {Von Wright, 1972, 182], and neither of these apply to the present situation. [A logically necessary conclusion—that is, inference—which is drawn via appropriately used SL or SI is one that *has* to be drawn and which, in that connection, *should* be drawn.] Thus, because the broad and specific aspects of the perceptions under consideration are not mutually related via SL or SI, these aspects cannot be derived from each other with literal certainty, and neither of them can in that regard be said to "necessarily follow" from the other; this especially applies to the 'specific-aspects from the *broad*-aspect' derivation. [Specific-from-*broad* certainty would involve deduction and would be based on SL. Broad-from-*specific* certainty would call for SI, that is, the use of *all* items/instances as the basis for drawing a conclusion. "Ampliative induction" (AI; see Von Wright)—use of only *some* items/instances as the basis—would not involve certainty, even though it could yield high probability if these inputs were highly representative. The realities of the present situation allow for AI, nor SI.] Related discussion appears in endnote #288.)

As indicated, the peers' above-described perception focuses on broad features only. It involves little awareness, by those individuals, of "who" the set 2 youths are in specific or detailed respects, such as what they value, believe in, and stand for separate and apart from —distinguished from—those broad aspects. (Here, the concept "distinguished from" centers on given *structure* [layer/level, as in "over and above"], and it differs, for instance, from that of "extend[ing] . . . beyond"—which, here, would involve that of additional types of *substance* [content]. The "broad aspects" in question still center on "independence" vis-á-vis parents/authority-figures, and on "coolness" overall.) As a result, s-2 youths, insofar as they are only or mainly perceived in terms of such broad features/categories, are hardly, or not at all, distinguished from each other; for example, they are not differentiated (1) with regard to the *par-*

ticular expressions (forms) of and/or the *particular circumstances surrounding* their independent behavior, (2) with respect to *ways* of being cool, and so on. To form more personalized or individualized perceptions regarding these areas, the given peers would have to observe, and recognize as such, various specifics/details of the respective youths' BTAs—for instance, *particular* independent behaviors or types of behaviors, and particular thoughts or attitudes concerning this area. This would apply even if these peers had, say, already recognized sizable differences in *degree* among those youths, in connection with the *broad* features (aspects).

Some peers—usually acquaintances—have few if any good opportunities to observe specifics/details (s/d's). Others do have such chances, in that the s/d's *could* be readily observed; yet these peers may hardly "look" for them, and/or they may, no matter what, see (register) only the above-mentioned, broad aspects, and seldom distinguish much else. Still other individuals do distinguish s/d's but only occasionally focus on them, mainly because they seldom care much about them as such. Finally, a remaining group of peers, one that is relatively common, distinguishes specifics/details *and* substantially cares about them; this is the group centered on next: If these peers (1) usually *like* what they see of the s-2 youths at this comparatively detailed or at least concrete level, and if, in this connection, they (2) feel these youths are, in effect, *measuring up* (here viewed as having "good" qualities or traits, and, by implication, as adequately using them), the following is likely to occur: These peers will accept/approve (a/a) the youths based chiefly—at any rate, decisively—on those specifics. In particular, their a/a will *not* rest chiefly/decisively on their (1) awareness that these s-2's behave fairly independently, on their (2) assumption that the youths are committed adolescents, and so on—that is to say, not on these, and any other, "broad aspects" *by themselves* (and, in any event, chiefly/decisively), regardless of the specifics and details (e.g., the "particular expressions [and] circumstances").

("Decisive" features or events—together, "factors"—are those which have effects such as the following [*note*: these factors are conceptualized as forces or as possessing force, and their effects are not invariably dramatic]: tip a balance; alter a condition or direction; push, pull or otherwise move matters beyond a threshold or a minimum standard; trigger a breakthrough or a new phase. They achieve these results, for instance, by (1) overcoming passive or active barriers/resistance essentially by *themselves,* or—indirectly—by (2) mobilizing, focusing, and/or releasing forces *other* than themselves or their own. Both (1) and (2) apply even when various "other" factors/forces have been essential in bringing matters to the point at which the *decisive* ones play their given roles. At any rate, decisive or deciding factors make the *immediate*—the specific, *present*—difference, and they do so whether this difference [also: condition; outcome] centers on the initiation, the modification, or, when viewed from a different perspective, the "completion" of matters. In addition, they make this difference irrespective of any roles they may or may not have previously played, and regardless of their absolute as well as comparative strength in that connection. Finally, such factors often have components and operate as composites; typically involved, for example, are (1) two or more mutually supportive or perhaps enhancing traits and/or attitudes [usually complemented by behavior], or else (2) a substantively complex yet functionally unified "event." A detailed discussion of decisive ["deciding"] factors [DFs] appear in Palmer (1994, 199–203). There, emphasis is on the "completion"-perspective [particularly the end-stage of processes or products, and it is indicated that, "Broadly stated, [a DF] is the one that puts a situation or entity 'over the top' or completes it, and without which that specific outcome, condition, or difference would not occur or be reached."]

As we have seen, set 2 youths, "by expressing given behaviors, thoughts, and attitude, . . . achieve their intermediate ("I") goal of maintaining a particu-lar social-image," one whose "broad aspects . . . are—chiefly—a seeming independence and a general appearance of being 'cool.'" That behavior/goal combination reflects, among other things, the youths' implicit assumption that when they behave in ways that certain peers consider reflections of a commitment to adolescence, those peers (1) will feel that they, the set 2 youths, "favorably measure up," (2) will enjoy being with them, and so on. One of the major behaviors or stances expressed by these s-2's in this regard, and directly observed or otherwise learned about by those peers, is that of "strong resistance to [control by] authority figures and other adults," parents included. Through time, and when taken as an aggregate, this resistance plus others perform various functions. One function is that of directly addressing the youths' I-goal, and other functions—or contexts (see "RC-3," below)—indirectly bear on it.

Among all these resistances (*Rs*), some have considerable temporal overlap with each other, and others occur largely in sequence. Under both temporal conditions, especially the first, content-centered overlaps (substantive commonalities)—that is, subject-matter similarities and/or identities—are common and substantial across respective *Rs*. These commonalities involve not just the direct targets (objects) of the resistance, namely, given adults, but also goals that closely reflect major youth-desires and related developmental issues (YDDIs). Chief among these YDDIs are increasing one's independence, developing/maintaining a personal identity, and the I-goal itself: presenting/maintaining a particular social-image. These YDDIs—here, "content-centered commonalities" (CCCs)—are separate and apart from resistance per se, that is, from this action or effort itself. (Resistance, or "opposition," has a distinct character wherever it appears. In this regard it, too, provides commonality—here, a qualitative similarity or identity—across given contexts.) At any rate, despite the temporal overlap and that CCC, the various *Rs*—more precisely, the "resistance contexts" (*RCs*)—

can be usefully distinguished from each other. Salient among these *RCs* are the following, each of which constitutes a given situation and involves at least one major type of youth-effort or -action.

RC-1. In this situation youths oppose certain efforts, by parents, to either (a) maintain their *personal/emotional relationship* to these youths on a largely preadolescent (parent-to-*child*) basis, and/or—later—on an early adolescent basis, or else to (b) alter the given relationship(s) but to do so chiefly or exclusively on their, the parents', terms and timetable. *RC-1* is designed as and functions as a signal to the parents that the youths want that basis, and so on, to change; in addition and in particular, it involves the latters' active and/or passive efforts to *change* it. (Even so, many youths are ambivalent about given aspects of change, including its degree and pace. Partly as a result, and also depending on the parents' *response* to these individuals' efforts, the extent of the latters' resistance varies.)

RC-2. Here, the youths' resistance/opposition is mainly designed to help create reasonable opportunities to participate in and explore various post-childhood activities, and, if necessary, to establish preconditions for them. That is, its chief goal is to help make it possible or likely for the youths to engage in specific adolescence-centered activities or types of activities that interest them. If successful, these *RC-s* efforts can thereby help these individuals move toward, into, or perhaps even further into "adolescence," in real-life, content-centered respects. (In *new* settings/contexts, or if rather different circumstances arise within the present one, the youths sometimes repeat their resistance/opposition, and may try to reestablish given preconditions. If and when this occurs, these efforts begin to parallel and partly overlap those of *RC-3,* below. The preceding points apply whether or not, when moving "into" or "further into" adolescence, the youths commit themselves to the given activities only moderately, as opposed to seriously.)

RC-3. These resistance/opposition (r/o) efforts are designed to help the youths *maintain* certain choices they

have made and activities they are already engaging in, especially during the early and middle adolescent years. (For these individuals to consider such efforts necessary or important, "new settings/contexts" and/or "rather different circumstances" need not have occurred.) Insofar as the youths achieve this goal, and even while they are working on it, these r/o efforts can help them do the following: test, modify, consolidate, and/or intensify the personal/social identity they are developing or have developed, one that is reflected, for instance, in their choice of certain friends, types of relationships, interests, and habits. Like *RC-4,* below, this resistance/opposition can be directed, not just—not even mainly—at parents, but at any adults/authority-figures whom the youths believe are substantially opposed to their existing choices, activities, or major interests. In any case, *RC-3's* main function may be compared, for example, to that of (a) a barrier behind which, or an enclosure from within which, individuals can reactively defend their choices/activities (c/a's) against actual, presumed, or anticipated opposition/interference, or to that of (b) a line of scrimmage or some other starting point from which they can apply pressure, can maneuver, and can otherwise proactively support those c/a's. Among other things, their r/o thus gains these youths some breathing space. (All the preceding applies—and the reactive and proactive approaches can *both* be used—even if the *RC-1* situation is very much alive, that is, even if the personal/emotional relationship between parents and youths still largely centers on pre- or early-adolescence. *RC-2* efforts are more affected by a highly active *R-1* situation than are the *RC-3's*; nevertheless, they can still occur.)

RC-4. This resistance/opposition is directed at *expanding* already existing choices, activities, and so on—that is, at broadening their nature and/or scope. It can operate whether or not these adolescence-centered c/a's were first established and were subsequently maintained—via *RC-2* and *RC-3,* respectively—(a) in the face of significant and steady resistance from parents and/or other adults, (b) despite only lukewarm and perhaps wavering support from these individuals, and so forth.

It is the set 2 youths' hope, are often their specific intent, that various peers will either observe their acts of resistance or will soon hear about them, usually from the youths themselves. Especially common among these acts are those involved in *RC-1*, which is directed against parents, and *RC-3 and -4*, whether against parents or other adults. The youths' immediate hope is as follows (*note*: see "youths do not formulate this, " below): Those observations (Os), and so on, will lead these peers to view them as having an adolescent-centered identity, or as trying to develop one; this especially applies if those Os are combined with information about some of the youths' "behaviors, thoughts, and attitudes" (hence, about their interests and perhaps involvements). Insofar as the youths' resistance, plus this content-centered information, leads these peers to see them as "independent" and "cool," they, the youths, will have successfully conveyed—and, from their perspective, maintained— (1) the "broad aspects" of the social-image they wish to project, and, in all likelihood, (2) various "specifics/details" of that image, as well. (More precisely, the broad aspects, and any such s/d's, will have been conveyed to some peers, and then registered by them, for the *first* time. Only with respect to *other* peers will those aspects and s/d's have been literally "maintained," in the sense of "continued" and "sustained.") The preceding points apply whether the individuals' interests/involvements (i/a's) are not particularly intense, on the one hand, or are rather strong, on the other—and, in any event, are *viewed* as such by the peers. They also apply whether these i/a's are few or many— and, again, are viewed in either way by the peers. (Concerning the above-mentioned, "immediate hope," the youths do not formulate this in terms of the *framework* [namely, that certain observations and information, functioning as inputs, will lead to the peers' view of

the youths, regarded as output] and via the particular *terminology* [e.g., "adolescent-centered identity"] that is presented. Nor do they explicitly conceptualize it along those lines.)

As implied, all four RCs share or are likely to share "goals that closely reflect major youth desires and related developmental issues." The *desire* that was focused on involves the main hoped-for product of a certain near-term or relatively near-term goal. This goal—here called "G-1"—is that of successfully "presenting/maintaining a particular social-image," and the hoped-for result is "acceptance/approval" (a/a) by peers. (As is clear, G-1 simultaneously functions as a *means*—to this a/a end.) The *developmental issues* that were referred to center on two, generally longer-term goals: "increasing one's independence" ("G-2") and "developing/maintaining a personal identity" ("G-3"). In the discussion, the set-2 youths' *resistance to control by authority-figures and other adults* mainly focused on the hoped-for product—namely, a/a—of that relatively *near-term* goal: G-1. This is despite the fact that the given resistance, and the resistance-contexts (RCs) overall, also help these youths achieve or at least move toward the continually present— that is, the ongoing—yet generally *longer-range* goals: G-2. (increased independence) and G-3 (identity). At any rate, although "resistance to control [RTC] . . . "focused more on the near-term goal (G-1) than on these broader, less tangible and sometimes less evident, longer-range ones (G-2; G-3), RTC still makes an important contribution to these latter, as does resistance overall.

Regarding G-1 (i.e., the successful presenting . . . of a given social-image), the essential target is peers, and its main as well as immediate objective is acceptance/approval by them. In this respect these individuals are "used," by the youths, to obtain *near*-term emotional support, satisfaction, pleasure, and/or ego-enhancement. Though the set 2 youths do not, in this connection, purposely use these peers to mainly assist in what they, or at least certain adults/professionals, might conceptualize as "personal growth and development" (PGD), the peers' approval/acceptance (a/a) of these youths nevertheless *does* often support the latters' efforts regarding "increased independence" and even "identity," per se. At any rate, a/a often helps to confirm as well as highlight (both, in the eyes of these youths) their present status, situation, or position in these respects, and it frequently helps these individuals assume those efforts are justified. (*Note*: (1) Such utilization of peers by youths is much the same as that which occurs in many one-to-one interactions and relationships that most adults consider normal and acceptable, whether between general-population youths or in their own lives. (2) The support in question is especially likely to be experienced as such [by the youths], and it is most likely to be strong, when the peers' apparent acceptance/approval is accompanied by, or is soon followed by, shared *activities* between them and the youths. (3) The points that precede (1) and (2) apply even if these youths do not delineate the concept of PGD as such; also, if these individuals *do* recognize this concept, those points apply even if the youths do not largely associate it with a need for fairly *long*-term efforts on their part. (4) With *G-1,* the acceptance/approval that results from the youths' having successfully presented/maintained their social-image comes, as indicated, essentially from their adolescent-aged peers. In addition, the personal rewards that those set 2 youths experience in connection with that a/a often center largely on near-term "emotional support, satisfaction," and so on. However, regarding the achievement of G-2 [increased independence], and/or when several developments ["changes"] have occurred regarding G-3 [identity]—in short, with respect to these broader and comparatively longer-term goals—the situation is somewhat different: First, the acceptance/approval that (a) largely results from this achievement/change, that (b) may be substantially increased by it, or that (c) is simply associated with it, need not come essentially from the youths' approximately same-aged peers alone—at any rate, from adolescent-aged peers alone, or even principally. Instead, the youths' sources of acceptance, approval, and perhaps other psychological rewards can now be broader as well as older than in connection with G-1 alone—for instance, broader with respect to type and age-range alike. Second, the rewards that these set 2 youths experience with regard to their G-2/G-3 achievement/change, and to some of the G-2's/G-3's major consequences and concomitants [CCs] of that ". . . /change," often extend beyond the psychological alone—say, beyond that which is internally sensed, felt, and recognized. In any event, these rewards involve more than what might be called "directly and immediately experienced" internal events. Regarding those CCs, say, ones that center on social or external matters, these mainly involve issues, needs, expectations, and roles generally associated with later- or even post-adolescence. Among these issues are interpersonal and practical matters alike, and involved are opportunities as well as options. (5) For set 2 youths to achieve goal 1 [G-1], peers must view them as having an interest and investment in gaining relative independence from various adults and in an adolescent-centered identity. G-1 thus involves, in fact pivots on, the same dimensions that are basic to G-2 and G-3: independence and identity, respectively. However, whereas G-1 focuses on the "social-image" aspect of identity, G-3 centers on the more personal. [See (6), below.] As indicated, achievement of goal 1 depends specifically—in fact, depends by definition and therein necessarily—on how the youths are *perceived*. In particular, it rests on whether they are viewed, by the peers in question, as (a) having *reached some level* of independence and identity [I&I], as (b) having *made substantial progress* along these lines, or, at least, as (c) seriously *trying* to attain considerable independence and/or an adolescent identity. [This peer-perceived "identity" centers, essentially, on aspects on the youths' *social*-image, not on these individuals' more personal identity or view of self.] In contrast, achievement of goals 2 and 3, respectively, does not rest on perception—again, by peers. Instead, it centrally reflects changes, progress, and efforts that have in fact occurred or are occurring, irrespective of these individuals' perceptions. At any rate, *G-1* can be achieved if the youths induce or otherwise lead various peers to believe that changes, progress, or efforts [CPEs]—particularly those reflected in (a), (b), or (c), above—have occurred or are taking place in connection with I&I; this applies whether or not substantial CPEs actually *have* occurred [or actually *are* taking place] in that regard. To be sure, the peers in question are more likely to *perceive* CPE's and/or to be brought to believe they exist, if and insofar as they [the changes, etc.] *do* exist—as, indeed, they usually do. Finally, G-2 and G-3 are often substantially built upon changes/progress/efforts that have in fact occurred in the course of achieving G-1, or that may still be occurring with respect to that goal. This fact, and basis of development, is made possible by, and also reflects, the considerable degree of substantive commonality—here, regarding I&I—that exists between goal 1, on the one hand, and goals 2 and 3, on the other. [The latter goals, in short, can each utilize G-1 in this connection even though *actual* changes, progress, or efforts, as opposed to ones that are only perceived, are not the specific, defined bases on which the achievement of G-1 rests—that is, are not its necessary, its required, grounds. "Only perceived" CPEs are those which peers believe exist, whether or not they—unlike the "actual"—in fact *do*.] Nevertheless, the following itself applies: Despite the just-mentioned independence/identity-centered commonality, G-2 and G-3 are not *always* built on changes, progress, and/or efforts associated with the youths' achievement or even partial achievement of a goal 1; specifically, these long-range goals are sometimes reached without it. In particular, G-2 and G-3 can be attained (a) even if these youths do *not* demonstrate the G-1—that is, the I&I-centered—social-image to their peers, and (b) even if these individuals gain

and subsequently maintain little or no peer-acceptance/approval in connection with any I&I they perhaps *do* demonstrate. [Points (a) and (b) apply even if the youths' "demonstration" rests basically on "perceived" changes, progress, or efforts only, rather than on the present, "actual" ones. Separately and in addition, the principal factors or dimensions that underlie the limited or non-acceptance/approval which is involved in point (b) are implied in the items next mentioned (see "*particular* forms . . . .").] Achievement of G-2 and G-3 can also occur irrespective of certain earlier-indicated facts: Depending on the *particular* forms and degrees of independence, of adolescent identity, and of resistance that are expressed by these youths in the context of G-1 and are then perceived by their peers, these individuals may obtain little or no overall acceptance/approval in the first place, if these peers dislike, are uncomfortable with, or are uncertain about what they perceive. Alternatively, the youths may *receive* moderate or substantial a/a, but perhaps not for long. Whatever the case may be, and regarding all preceding points, the following nevertheless applies: If goal 1-centered a/a feedback from peers is positive, is at least fairly strong, and is rather consistent [whether or not it is frequent], it ordinarily provides added incentive—often considerable incentive—for most set 2 youths to continue trying to develop themselves with respect to factors or elements that centrally define G-2 and G-3: given areas and/or levels of *independence*, and certain kinds/degrees of personal or personal/social *identity*, respectively. As implied, however, that acceptance/approval-feedback and its resulting incentives are not the only possible bases of this independence/identity, and, thus, the only ways to reach the long-range goals in question. [Related discussion regarding selected interactions between peer input and youth development appears in Chapter 26—sections titled "Exaggerated, Excessive, or Extreme Reactions," "Broad Effects of Reinforced AASs," and "Critical Junctures and Sequences in Youths' Lives." Its emphasis is on early and subsequent delinquent involvement of youths in general, not of set 2 individuals specifically.] (6) Earlier, it was indicated that "whereas G-1 [goal 1] focuses on the 'social-image' aspect of identity, G-3 centers on the more personal." The latter chiefly consists of often-interrelated thoughts, feelings, and other types or areas of internal awareness. {See "self," in item (7), below.} Here, it might be added that most set 2 youths sometimes sense that this more personal reality or identity differs somewhat—sometimes considerably—from the picture of themselves that they often try to present outwardly and interpersonally, and which they usually believe or implicitly assume the *do* present at the time. This difference coexists with areas of major *similarity* which they usually believe/assume exist, themselves. [The term "reality" and "identity" are not used by youths. Also, whether the differences and similarities are *believed* rather than *assumed* to exist depends mainly on the particular content, feelings, and dynamics involved.] At any rate, the already-discussed social-image—the *G-1* image, which centers on independence and identity and which might not extend much beyond them—is substantively and structurally only part of the youths' *overall* social-image, albeit a very important part. [The overall image (OI) is more often directed at a relatively broad range of individuals than at any comparatively narrow and, in any event, more targeted group only. An example of the latter is the present peers—the principal targets of G-1. The OI, like the G-1, is an *intended* social-image.] Substantively, the OI, in turn, is a particularly major expression of the youths' more personal, *internal reality*—that is, these adolescents' direct awareness/consciousness of their own thoughts, feelings, wishes, attitudes, and so on. Restated, the overall, intended social-image is an outgrowth or consequence of this felt-reality. [For purposes of point (6)—also of (7), which follows—it has sufficed to consider only *wanted* aspects of the social self and the inner reality. Neither point would significantly change in meaning if unwanted

aspects were added.] (7) When set 2 youths focus on certain traits, interests, and/or activities [TIAs] and on various emotions, attitudes, and/or beliefs [EABs]—in particular, when they recognize that these features and factors pertain to themselves—the following often occurs: They realize, whether vaguely and fairly globally [as in "sensing" or "feeling"] or else more clearly and specifically [as in "believing" or "thinking"], that "This is what I am like—what I have and want," that "This is what I am" or, at least, *some* of what "I am" and "am like"; that is, there then occur feelings or beliefs—and, in some contexts, words—to this effect. Substantively, this realization and assertion (a) amounts to a generalization or a summary-conclusion, by the youths, about themselves; structurally, it (b) involves an integration or at least an aggregation of information, by those same individuals, regarding given TIAs and EABs. Both points apply whether or not *all* the features/factors-information available to these individuals during a specified period is *used* by them during that time; in any event, they also apply regardless of which *particular* features and factors, and which *combination* of them, the youths focus on and perhaps end up emphasizing. When viewed collectively, the traits, interests, activities, emotions, attitudes, and/or beliefs that this integration/assemblage encompasses are often considered a "self" and are termed—though not by the youths— "the self." [In the present discussion the youths are *conscious* of these features' and factors'—these TIAs'/EABs'—existence; in this respect the "self" is a self-*representation,* as of a particular time.] As indicated, (a) the youths feel or believe that given "features and factors" [FFs] characterize them; and as can be inferred, (b) it is these FFs—more precisely, the youths' perceptions of them—that these same individuals integrate or aggregate. It is in this context and on this basis that the FFs which mutually share the predicate-to-subject relationship [PSR] that is referred to in (a), immediately above, are the ones that can become the particulars or constituents—

the contents or "whats"—of the youths' self-representation, which is involved in (b), above. [The PSR "referred to in (a)" involves the *perceived youth-characteristics,* as predicates, and those same *youths,* as subjects.] In addition, it is *only* these features and factors, though not necessarily all of them, that in fact *become* constituents—consciously recognized contents—at any given time. As can be further inferred, both the particular content and the overall scope of any integration or assemblage of features and factors—that is, of any self-representation with respect to TIAs/EABs—can *change.* They can do so particularly by virtue of changes in what the youths focus on at differing points in time, and, of course, in what they then respectively attribute to themselves. In this connection the TIAs and EABs they consider more acceptable and desirable than others are the ones more likely to be retained through time, or to reappear after an absence. It is some of these features and factors, taken together, that are likely to constitute what various practitioners and theorists might describe as "central" aspects of the individuals' personality, or, perhaps, as these youths' dynamic, motivating "core" per se. [*Note:* (a) The youths' self-*recognition* mentioned at the start of item (7) occurs particularly, but not only, if the given interests, emotions, and so on seem to be at least fairly strong or otherwise clear, and recent or recurring. (b) All aspects of item (7) apply even if the individuals hardly recognize various *causal links* between and among the TIAs, EABs, and perhaps even certain external conditions. (c) The types of features and factors listed at the start of this item—namely, Ts, Is, As, Es, As, and Bs—are not, collectively, exhaustive. To simplify the presentation we have not included other possible FFs, and, hence, other possible constituents of the youths' self-representation. (d) Though the youths in question rarely use words such as "traits" and only sometimes specify "interests" and "attitudes" as such, they, nonetheless, regularly convey these concepts.])

Some additional comments about resistance by set 2 youths: As seen ear-

lier, this resistance is expressed in a range of contexts, such as R-1 through R-4. Involved in them, collectively, are goals relating to youth–desires and to developmental issues, some of which (e.g., a desire for peer-acceptance) have a heavy near-term emphasis, whereas others (independence; identity) extend well beyond this. Whatever the content and goal, resistance, like many *non-oppositional* youth-efforts, involves an attempt by these individuals to help themselves achieve that goal. In this connection, these efforts thus constitute ways of implementing and otherwise responding to various desires, needs, interests, and issues (DNIIs) that become salient and even predominant at differing points in, and/or stages of, adolescence. As these DNIIs change and mutually realign, the specific content, focus, scope, and sometimes intensity of the individuals' efforts—that is, of their resistance—themselves change and shift. (As seen next, all this applies to resistance directed *outward.*)

Regarding the targets—the *person* targets—of this resistance or opposition, we have focused essentially on what might be called the "external" (as in, say, "other persons"—distinct from "oneself"). Specifically, the main targets were adults, in this case ones whom youths saw as opposing or likely to oppose efforts that they, the youths, considered important with respect to the following: establishing, maintaining, or expanding (a) friendships, opportunities, and, in general, activities as well as involvements—in particular, ones that (b) reflect, implement, and otherwise express the individuals' desired self-image. We did not discuss what might be called "internal" targets of resistance, these being certain elements or aspects (EAs) of the individuals' overall self or psyche (which encompasses more than the youths' *desired* EAs) that are often opposed by *other* EAs within the given youths. In this connection, inward-directed resistance involves these individuals' attempts to minimize, deny, or otherwise weaken, block, avoid, reject, or dissociate themselves from various thoughts, wishes, emotions, and im-

pulses. To the given youths, these particular thoughts, and so on, usually or almost always constitute *un*wanted EAs and attributes. For one thing, they very often conflict with these individuals' *desired* self-image, and perhaps with much of what the youths want as their social-image; in addition, they are sometimes associated with anxiety. As a result, and, for instance, in order to help reduce or avoid that anxiety, those "thoughts . . . and impulses" are common, internal targets of the youths' resistance. (Conflicts between certain wanted and unwanted EAs—*internal* conflicts—are sometimes reflected in, and complicate, these individuals' relationships with peers and adults.) Seen in perspective, most instances of resistance, like many other youth-efforts, ultimately bear on strivings, needs, and/or conditions that are relatively fundamental to these individuals' adjustment and well-being. In particular, these instances involve the following—often to a larger degree (two broad items—"(a)" and "(b)"—will be specified; in (a), the core content involves strivings, needs, and wanted conditions; in (b), it involves unwanted conditions; in both, it is italicized):
(a) attempts to generate, support, and/or increase feelings not only of physical/social/psychological *security* and *enjoyment* but of *self-worth, being accepted by others,* and *control* or perhaps *mastery;* and/or (b) efforts to avoid or minimize feelings of *discomfort, pain, insecurity, anxiety, fear, inadequacy, badness (being "bad"),* and/or *loss of control* or perhaps *mastery.* (*Note*: 1. Though the preceding is considerably more evident in instances of comparatively intense and/or protracted resistance, its applicability is not at all limited to them. Instead, the "bear[s] on"-relationship between resistance, on the one hand, and the just-listed items with their respective contents, on the other, exists for essentially all levels and ranges of resistance. 2. For obvious reasons, those same two items [i.e., (a) and (b)], each with its *collective* contents, apply much less to the earlier-discussed forms of expressions of resistance—that is, to R-1 through R-4—*individually*

[i.e., distributed within each such R] than they apply to these resistances collectively [i.e., distributed across all such Rs, jointly]. 3. As can be inferred, *achievement* of item (a), above, would refer to the *generating, supportive, and/or increasing* of item-(a) contents—specifically, of the item's various listed feelings. In the same respect, achievement of item (b) would signify the *avoiding or minimizing* of *its* contents. As with the item-*(a)* feelings, however, not *all* those listed in *(b)* would have to be included for "achievement" to occur, in the case of any one youth; moreover, some contents may hardly apply to him or her in the first place. 4. Whichever contents/feelings apply and *are* included, achievement of item (a) does not, ipso facto or otherwise, guarantee the same type of outcome—namely, achievement or perhaps near-achievement—for item *(b).* This is true even though achievement of *(a)*—for instance, an increase in feelings of personal security and/or control—often does make an important and sometimes crucial positive difference with regard to the achievement of item (b). Similarly, absence of an automatic guarantee remains the case even though the initial achievement of *(b)*—for example, a reduction of anxiety, fear, and/or feelings of inadequacy—sometimes greatly facilitates that of item (a). For instance, such a reduction [a "minimizing"] can provide enough psychological relief, encouragement, or breathing room to where the youths are more willing and/or able to not only explore new roles and types of relationships but to consider expanding their existing social skills and/or acquiring new pragmatic ones. At any rate, because items (a) and (b) are not simply opposite sides of the same coin, their respective contents are not mutually related [specifically, the item-(a) set or group of feelings is not related to the item-(b)] in a lockstep albeit inverse manner; that is, they do not have a −1.00 correlation. For this reason these groups/sets—substantively, items (a) and (b) themselves—can vary independently of each other. Because of this independence [one that is actual, not just potential, and which usually ranges from moderate to considerable], because of the lack of an automatic guarantee, and also due to often-impinging external conditions, each such item—that is, (a) and (b) separately—must sometimes receive specifically targeted attention in order for *it*—hence, for any or all of its contents—to be "achieved" [e.g., for its feelings/factors to be increased or reduced, as the case may be]. This applies whether or not substantial progress has already been made, and/or is presently occurring, in connection with the *other* item—for instance, with (b) as distinct from (a). 5. The factor termed "control," which is listed in items (a) and (b) alike, does not necessarily refer to or otherwise involve *characteristics of certain interpersonal relationships,* such as the feature termed "domination." Instead, this factor—here, still a "feeling" of control, or of loss thereof—can refer to the *status of particular impulses and emotions,* and it can do so whether or not the just-mentioned relationships are centrally and directly involved. Thus, for instance, "control" can refer to and principally reflect the youths' degree of willingness and/or ability to suppress or moderate some of their outwardly directed impulses or drives [I/Ds], such as the sexual—these I/Ds often being expressed, say, outside the context of non-transitory personal relationships. [The I/Ds in question may or may not be components—major ones or not—of these individuals' *desired* self-image.] Also, "control"—or, again, felt loss thereof—can have an identical type of reference in connection with various self-directed emotions, such as anger. Parallel considerations apply to "mastery." 6. Item (a) centers more on self-development than does (b), and item (b) focuses more on self-defense than does (a). Despite this, and although "development" is commonly and accurately thought of in connection with proactivity whereas "defense" is likewise associated with reactivity, achievement of item (a) as well as (b)—that is, of each one separately—often involves sizable amounts of proactivity *and* reactivity. For related discussion of strivings, needs, and/or conditions, see the "Theo-

retical Perspectives" section of Chapter 25. 7. As indicated, the youths' act or acts of resisting bear on the listed contents of items (a) and (b), that is, on features/factors [FFs] such as "control," "mastery," "anxiety," and "fear." Here, we would add that they often do so not only without direct input from other individuals—a situation termed "by themselves," below—but quickly as well. More specifically, these youth-actions ["instances of resistance"] relate to and effect those FFs prior to and essentially apart from any actual—and often any anticipated—*reactions* to them [the actions] by these youngsters' peers, and, separately, by adults at whom the actions are usually directed. For instance, insofar as these acts of resistance help youths feel somewhat *stronger,* more *courageous,* and/or *freer* [SCF] than they almost always felt before the actions, and perhaps feel a little *better about themselves overall,* the following commonly applies [note: feelings of increased SCF are "effects" that those actions frequently *do* have; they have them not just directly but rapidly]: The actions in question—more precisely, the just-mentioned SCF feelings that they help increase and bring to focus—often, in turn, bear on and directly help generate, support, and/or increase such *item (a)* features/factors as felt *control, mastery, overall psychological security,* and perhaps *self-worth.* Moreover, the acts of resistance, and, hence, the given SCF feelings, have this effect on those item (a) FFs "by themselves," and they do so either immediately or soon thereafter. See point 8, below, for related information. [It should be emphasized that the already-mentioned feelings of increased *strength, courage, freedom, and so forth,* does not, by itself, almost guarantee that any resulting feelings of increased *control, mastery, and so on (CMS)* will do either of the following: (1) subsequently *further* increase (starting, say, in the weeks or months that follow the rapid, initial increase in SCF); and (2) eventually become *relatively crystallized and long-term* (i.e., fairly stable and permanent), especially, but not only, if there *is* little further felt increase in CMS. This situation reflects, for one thing, the fact that the *SCF* features/factors, and the like—ones that, as indicated, helped "generate . . . and/or increase" those of *CMS*—are often far from powerful in an *absolute* sense, and are often sporadic and somewhat transitory in any case; this applies even if many distinct moments of substantial power exist. Moreover, the given situation—that is, the lack of near-"guarantees" or even high probabilities concerning the relationship between CMS, on the one hand, and (1) and (2) above, on the other—exists despite the presence of the following: (a) the SCFs' definite importance to the youths even when they, the SCFs, *are* sporadic and transitory; (b) the SCFs' moments or periods of intensity—in this respect, their considerable temporary power.] Likewise, insofar as the youths' acts of resistance help these individuals feel less *vulnerable* than they almost always felt prior to these actions, or help them feel somewhat less likely to be frustrated, ignored, dominated, and/or even injured in any event, the given actions often bear, for example, on the individuals' efforts to avoid or reduce the *item (b)* feelings of *insecurity, anxiety,* and *loss of control.* [The actions in question often *do* help them feel less vulnerable, and so on.] Nevertheless, in parallel with the *item (a)* situation, above, there is no fairly high probability, let alone any near-certainty, that the following will occur: The feelings of increased strength, courage, and so forth—that is, of SCF—which result from these acts of resistance will, largely by themselves, bring about a *further* decrease in such feelings of insecurity, and so on, or will make the initial decrease relatively permanent in any event. However, although there is no fairly *high* probability that either of these will occur when the given feelings operate largely "by themselves" [i.e., apart from *other* features/factors], there is usually a fair chance it will occur—and always a good chance it can occur—when these feelings of increase SCF, and the like, are joined by various *other* FFs. The latter are usually complemented or supplemented by support from external

sources, and/or by external conditions. [Two points: (1) In the just-mentioned situation, which involves multiple factors (whether internal or external), the feelings of "increased SCF . . . ," collectively, may or may not make the largest overall contribution toward "bring[ing] about [the] *further* decrease" in feelings of insecurity, anxiety, and so on—that is, toward initiating, promoting, and completing it, combined. This applies with respect to making the initial decrease "relatively permanent," as well. (2) The less than ". . . *high* probability," mentioned above, exists despite the following: Insofar as strength, courage, and freedom are valued aspects of the youths' desired self-image, as they almost always are, feelings of *increased* SCF, even by themselves, usually give these individuals psychological boosts or lifts; and these latter, in turn, can become substantially self-reinforcing even absent any clear feedback (particularly the more positive) from *peers* regarding the given acts of resistance. These internal boosts are direct and often rapid. As indicated, they typically involve and emphasize feelings of increased "control" and "mastery" (here, tested and at-least-substantial *ability*). Also, they are frequently accompanied by—and often thereafter have a substrate that consists of—a usually diffuse and somewhat sporadic feeling or sense of self-affirmation, -validation, or, especially, -enhancement (worth).] 8. During the height of the youths' resistance, and during its other critical points or phases, the already-mentioned feelings of increased *strength and courage [SC]* are (a) very often experienced consciously by these individuals, rather than sensed—most often, and otherwise mainly—just preconsciously. When this occurs these feelings are (b) frequently thought of, by the youths, specifically *as* SC, and they are (c) often fairly vivid and/or otherwise prominent—and possibly dominant; (b) and (c) apply even when the feelings are fairly transitory. Characteristics (a) and (c) apply to these SCs' frequently resulting—and themselves already-mentioned—feelings of increased *control and mastery,* as well, though perhaps to a lesser degree and less often than they do to SC. Beyond this, and in substantial contrast to that which applies to feelings regarding control and mastery, not to mention strength and courage, the following is the case; it is also the case *more often than not* [thus, in and of itself], regardless of given contrasts: Feelings of increased *overall psychological security [OPS]* and *self-worth* are (a) largely preconscious [at least OPS is]; in conjunction with this they are (b) not conceptualized by the individuals—not "thought of" by them—specifically *as* OPS, though exceptions sometimes occur with self-worth. In addition, these feelings are therein usually diffuse and are experienced rather globally, except as indicated in (b). Further, they generally occur shortly after the youths' main resistance and their closely/immediately related efforts, not mostly during its peak or otherwise in its midst. [Throughout point 8, the distinction between primarily active resistance and chiefly passive resistance is—albeit sometimes relevant—not crucial.])

Section *E* of this long endnote largely focused on "set 2" (s-2) individuals—I4's labeled Na and Ci. It mainly discussed the fact that the behavior/goal of *resistance, plus maintenance of a particular social-image,* has, for s-2's, a primary "psychological/contextual meaning" (PCM) which differs in a critical way from that seen among "set 1's" (s-1's)—I3's labeled Cfc and Mp. For present purposes, the discussion centered on adolescents. Though both sets of youths often strongly resist heavy, partial, or attempted control by given adults—do so, for instance, in connection with the first and third "resistance contexts" (RC-1; RC-3)—and although both sets hope their intended social-image will greatly help them gain and maintain approval/acceptance (a/a) from peers, the critical difference between these s-2's and s-1's with respect to PCM centers on the following (*note:* to simplify the presentation we will use "belief" instead of "assumption or belief," and "achieve" a/a rather than "gain and maintain" it): Most s-2's, as distinct from s-1's, have a substantial and/or

growing belief that values and approaches (VAs) which are other than power-centered are, and/or should be, of major or central importance in their everyday interactions with most individuals. We will focus on these s-2's peers. Because (1) these non power-centered VAs often generate and involve efforts to elicit *acceptance/approval* from certain peers, and because (2) a key function of these s-2 youths' intended *social-image* is that of triggering and supporting interactions which can help *achieve* this a/a, (3) the non power-centered (NPC) VAs that are reflected in and partly comprise this social-image, and which, in so doing, serve as major bases and elements of the given interactions, can therein function as important *means to that end*—that is, to the goal of achieving peer acceptance/approval. NPC values and approaches involve a good deal of mutual consideration and accommodations between the youths and peers, and they can be characterized as "reciprocity-centered" or "give-and-take oriented." Interactions in which these VAs predominate include few elements of manipulation, trickery, intimidation, and so on. More specifically, they involve few expressions of power in which other persons are to be taken advantage of, especially, but not only, if they might well experience significant personal, social, and/or other hurt, harm, or loss. (This, of course, is aside from sports and other situations known to be intrinsically competitive, mostly "zero-sum," and/or possibly injurious, but which are accepted as such by all parties concerned. The power-centered approaches discussed in this book have an intentionally *negative* character; however, other uses and instances of interpersonal power can be mixed, borderline, neutral, largely constructive, or even entirely positive in their intent and/or impact. At any rate, they need not be chiefly exploitive or purposely demeaning, harmfully zero-sum, and so forth.) In short, within most peer-centered contexts, set 2 youths try to avoid, minimize, or at least substantially curtail the use of power-centered approaches. They do so mainly because they feel psychologically more comfortable with approaches that are essentially *give-and-take* oriented, instead. In particular, they feel the latter are "right"—are socially/ethically appropriate (SEA)—are, in any event, better than the power-centered alternatives. (Though these youths do not use the words "social," "ethical," and "appropriate," and although they do not explicitly distinguish and therein specify "SEA" as such, they nevertheless convey the concept of interpersonal appropriateness.) To be sure, set 2 individuals utilize these give-and-take—non power-centered—approaches for the following reasons as well: (1) They believe these NPCs have a good chance of *working*, that is, of helping to elicit acceptance/ approval; (2) they consider most *power-centered* approaches (even the less conspicuous ones) wrong or largely wrong—unjustified (i.e., not SEA)— in most peer-centered contexts; and (3) they sense, or more explicitly believe, that many such power-centered approaches will often not work—will simply not, or might well not, help achieve a/a. Point (3) applies apart from the issue of interpersonal appropriateness. (*Note*: Showing one's ability to trick, outsmart, rattle, or embarrass various *adults* or other peers, to sometimes "beat the system" or gum it up, and so on, is typically *not* ruled out by many or most s-2 youths. Nor is: *presumed*-harmless [though sometimes *not,* in fact, harmless] attention-getting behavior and words; less-than-harmless, but usually limited [and, in any event, often casually rationalized], situational exploitation of the opposite sex; et cetera. Nor are dominance/submission relationships usually ruled out if, in effect, they are mutually agreed upon and if they seem, to all participants, nonexploitive, noninjurious, and otherwise within frequently observed and generally accepted social norms or bounds—and, thus, can seem, to them, sufficiently SEA in these respects. In this connection, see, for instance, the review of "Gang-centered," "Gang-dependent," and "Gang-organizer" youths in the "Overview, Discussion, and Conclusions" section of the present chapter—subsection titled

"Concurrent Validity of Subtypes." This describes Ci and other delinquents' relationship to gang or group members such as Cfm's and Cfc's.)

As indicated, set 2 individuals utilize *give-and-take* approaches with most peers in most interactions, and they prefer to do so; however, they often use *power-centered* approaches (PCAs) with certain *other* peers, and not just in gang- or group-focused contexts. Basically, s-2's use PCAs because they believe that only these will likely work with the latter peers—that is, will probably help (1) satisfy certain wishes, (2) avoid or reduce unwanted situations or outcomes, and (3) otherwise resolve or relieve problems and worries, regarding those particular individuals. (In contrast, s-1 youths believe PCAs should be used with almost *all* peers, in one degree or another. These approaches are the main ones through which s-1's feel they have obtained frequent satisfaction and relief in matters they consider important.) When using *power-centered* approaches, the s-2's principal goal is, of course, seldom that of obtaining peer acceptance/ approval—an otherwise hoped-for satisfaction (at least primarily, at the conscious level); and, as may be inferred, when s-2's are *not* utilizing these PCAs to mainly obtain *satisfaction* (a/a or other), they are often using them chiefly for defense—as, for instance, in "The best defense is a good offense." (Set 2 individuals utilize power-centered approaches—though not *only* these approaches—in connection with various *adult*-focused contexts as well, such as RC-1 through RC-4.) Beyond this, it might be kept in mind that power-centered approaches need not, and seldom do, constitute significant elements of the "mutually agreed upon . . . ," *dominance/submission relationships* mentioned earlier, in connection with set 2 youths. (As seen in points (1) and (2), below, "significance" refers to extent of presence as well as degree of influence.) That is, although these s-2 youths do utilize power-centered approaches with "*other* peers" (also already mentioned)— do often use elements such as force, trickery, and/or manipulation (F/T/M) with *them*—the following nonetheless applies: (1) Dominance/submission (DS) relationships in which these s-2 individuals are involved—(*note*: it is these youths who dominate them)—seldom contain these and/or other power-centered elements to more than even a moderate degree. (Seen in context, this means that the individuals whom the s-2's dominate in these relationships—dominate, as indicated, on what amounts to an *agreed upon*, albeit unstated, basis—are not, or are seldom, the above-mentioned "*other* peers.") Mainly due to (1), above, that is, to the essentially moderate-at-best presence of those power-centered elements, the following is the case: (2) These DS relationships seldom involve those F/T/M elements in ways that render the latter *effective* against the main forces that hold these dominance/submission relationships (DSRs) together. More specifically, the DSRs essentially do not involve these power-centered elements (F/T/Ms) in a qualitative manner and/or—especially—to a *degree* that would enable them, the F/T/Ms, to significantly counterbalance, neutralize, or otherwise weaken those binding forces and to thereby alter, undermine, and possibly undo the overall relationships. This point applies whether the elements—F/T/Ms and/or others—operate and have their effects within a short time-frame, that is, mainly cross-sectionally, or over a considerably longer period, that is, most longitudinally and cumulatively. It also applied whether or not the peers to whom the set 2 youths provide the F/T/Ms and other power-centered inputs are themselves s-2's.

Points (A) through (C) summarize, further detail, and compare the three types of approaches just-described—those used by set 2 youths with their peers: (A) S-2s' approaches to *most* peers are give-and-take oriented, that is, reciprocity-oriented and distinctly not power-centered. Not only are these inputs nonexploitive, or only seldom and then just moderately the opposite, but the resulting s-2/peer interactions (IAs) are of interest to these peers, and these individuals assume that not only the IAs but the s-2s' approaches themselves are well-intentioned. Mainly for such reasons, type-(A) approaches are essentially accepted by the peers, and resulting interactions between these individuals and s-2's are often actively engaged in by the former. (B) S-2s' approaches to a considerably *smaller* percentage of individuals—called "*other* peers"—are often power-centered. This type of input is almost always reserved for these peers only, especially when its strength—including its frequency—is moderate or greater. Via such approaches s-2's hope to gain or maintain an advantage over these individuals, to preemptively defend against them, and so on. Moreover, mainly because these power-centered approaches are often exploitive and injurious, and are experienced as such by these peers (i.e., the recipients), interactions between the s-2's and these peers that result from this type of input are seldom willingly accepted by the peers, let alone actively or otherwise sought by them. (C) S-2s' approaches to another ". . . *smaller*" percentage of individuals are distinguished by their salient dominance/submission (DS) dimension, or, more broadly, by a clear dominance/compliance (DC) factor (see "submission" and "compliance," below). Nevertheless, s-2s' domination inputs are not essentially *power-centered,* particularly as the latter was described in (B) and earlier. For instance, type-(C) inputs only infrequently include such elements as manipulation and trickery, even at moderate levels of intensity; their frequency is even less in the case of intimidation and physical force, again at the moderate levels. In any event, type-(C) inputs, being dominance-centered rather than power-centered, are not the distinguishing approaches used with "*other* peers." Similarly, these type-(C) inputs—still given their central DS or DC character, but, in this case, instead of one that involves more *give-and-take* and more related or resulting interpersonal equality—are not the distinguishing approaches used with "*most* peers"; nor are they the most common. At any rate, peers who (1) are the principal recipients of type-(C) inputs, that is, of the s-2 youths' dominance-centered approaches, and for whom (2) these inputs *are* the distinguishing ones, usually consider them acceptable (right; good; OK), not basically exploitive/injurious, and so on. This view or reaction, by these C-recipients, differs considerably from the *non*acceptance and dislike that regularly exists among "*other* peers," with respect, however, to type-(*B*) inputs—that is, power-centered approaches. (In the following, the inputters continue to be the s-2 youths and the recipients of those inputs arc still the peers.)

(Regarding type-(*C*) inputs, the recipients' "submission" or "compliance"—especially the latter—can include, as part of itself, an aspect or quality of *consent* that distinguishes it somewhat, yet importantly, from complete or simple acquiescence. Specifically, this peer-response to the s-2s' dominance-centered inputs can involve a degree of initial and/or subsequent *initiative* which, though seldom more than slight or moderate, makes the individuals' consent other than fundamentally or almost wholly passive—and, perhaps, mostly tacit. In any event, and even *apart* from whatever level and cumulative amount of peer-initiative may exist. submission or compliance need not mainly constitute a response or other adjustment to a possible s-2 inputs such as (1) substantial external pressure and (2) either *clear* and present, *implied* and present, or only *presumed* and future personal threat. That is, it need not be an adjustment, whether reactive or proactive, to global or specific elements/inputs frequently found among *power-centered* approaches, in the case of type-(B) inputs.)

A few more points should be made explicit about types (A), (B), and (C)—the reciprocity-, power-, and dominance-centered approaches. The first two focus on the contents (elements; ingredients) that comprise each approach and on the fact that some contents which "belong" to any one approach can sometimes resemble, and thereby be mistaken for, ones of a different approach. The final point is that the main approach, for instance, type-(C), which characterizes a youth's relationship to given peers can change through time. *Point 1.* Each of the three types of approach consists of several mutually distinguishable elements, and each element can vary in degree. However, regardless of the particular *degrees* that are present among the several elements at any given time, it is these specific ingredients—*as ingredients,* and especially in the aggregate—that fundamentally characterize the given approach and which, in that respect, concretely operationalize it. The elements' particular degrees are not what "fundamentally" distinguish the approach from all others, and which, in this regard, define it. (Regardless of its particular degree, no element is part of more than *one* approach's set of fundamental, i.e., defining, ingredients, and, hence, more than that approach's one—and only—operational definition. See below.) In any event, any ingredient which thus helps comprise/define a type-(A), -(B), or -(C) approach can be inputted—by an s-2 youth, to his peer-recipient—to, say, a high, medium, or low *degree of intensity* and, independently, *frequency of usage.* In addition, its *scope of usage*—"scope" with respect to the content involved—can be broad or narrow. (Here, we need focus only on *degree*—specifically, on intensity.) Thus, or instance, any type-(A) element—that is, any *reciprocity*—centered ingredient, such as the sharing of enjoyments and objects, the giving of friendly advice or of practical assistance, or the expressing of interest/concern/support—can be involved to a high, medium, or low degree of intensity. More specifically, it can be thus offered, exerted, or otherwise provided, utilized, or "inputted"; so can the youths' efforts to cooperate and compromise. Similarly, each type-(B) element—that is, each *power*-centered ingredient, such as trickery, one-upmanship, manipulation, and threats or intimidation—can be utilized at differing intensities. Likewise, any type-(C) element—that is, *dominance*-centered feature, such as forcefulness, persistence, persuasiveness, seeming self-confidence, leadership, proprietorship (active possessiveness), and demandingness—can be thus inputted. So can expressions of felt-superiority or other specialness, of felt-privilege, and of related presumptuousness. The commonality that exists between forcefulness and "insistence" will be briefly discussed at the end of Point 2, as will the generic—the cross-approaches—nature of insistence and "force." (As can be inferred, we are using a framework in which all elements—such as trickery and intimidation—are considered intrinsic and otherwise fundamental to only the particular approach—here, type-(B)—under which they are, or would be, listed. In addition, it is these elements alone—that is, *only* these elements—which *define* the given approach, and they do so in the sense of distinguishing it from each of the remaining approaches conceptually and a priori. [This applies even though s-2 youths may sometimes utilize certain of these elements with peers for whom they ordinarily use *different* elements—say, ones that are fundamental to only one of the two remaining approaches (e.g., to type-(C))), and that help define/distinguish only *it*.] Moreover, the elements define the given approach by virtue of their particular, intrinsic or underlying nature alone—at any rate, via their respective, a priori and distinguishing characters. In this regard, they define that approach irrespective of what their various *expressions* and *usages*—for instance, their particular intensities, frequencies, and/or scopes—happen to be on given occasions, or even modally across several occasions and contexts. Thus, this framework distinguishes what might be called an approach's (1) "formal definitional character" [in short, its *definition*]—which builds upon and centers on the approach's *types* of elements, alone and only as such—from (2) its characteristics [individual and collective elements] as these are expressed and otherwise inputted by the s-2 youths during any particular time-period, and in given ways as well as contexts [e.g., inputted at one level of intensity and/or breadth of content ("scope") during time *X*, and at a considerably different level/breadth during *Y*].) When an approach is viewed and integrated *across* time, the following applies: What might

be called the approach's "overall expressed character" can be thought of mainly as an active product of elements that have been the most intensively, frequently, and/or broadly inputted; this includes the approach's defined elements collectively and in mutual interaction. Involved, in particular, are one or more comparatively *long* time-periods [whether or not these periods encompass a *variety* of "occasions and contexts," as distinct from "several" that may closely resemble each other].) We will now continue the focus on intensity—one of the two major aspects of *degree*.

Point 2. Partly because any element of any given approach can be inputted to a high, medium, or low degree, some can be confused, especially by outside observers, with elements that are actually part of a *different* approach. (In the following, recall that the type-(C) and -(B) approaches are the dominance- and power-centered, respectively.) For instance, a high level of *forcefulness* (here, interpersonal assertiveness)—this being an element that helps characterize the (C)-approach—can sometimes be mistaken for a medium or even a low level of *threat/intimidation,* or for these same levels of *physical force*—each of the latter elements being a defined feature of type-(B) only. This and comparable mistakes can occur especially, but by no means only, if type-(C) elements are observed neither for long nor repeatedly. Under such conditions, as compared with their opposites, the contexts in which these elements appear are more easily misinterpreted, and the reasons for their usage may, in any event, be far from clear. In addition, the likelihood of confusion can increase if the type-(C) element—here, individuals' forcefulness—is observed in particular *combinations,* for example, in conjunction with medium or high degrees of certain *other* type-(C) elements, such as *persistence*. These combinations can produce mutually reinforcing and enhancing perceptions. (In various interpersonal contexts, "persistence" can sometimes be channeled, expanded, or otherwise developed into what is viewed/experienced as "stubbornness" or "unyieldingness."

However, these elements are more often regarded, by the given "observers," as forms or aspects of *each other,* from the start. Here, "regarded" means implicitly assumed.) At any rate—and, the combinations-context aside—some type-(C) and -(B) elements, such as assertiveness and intentional intimidation, can be mistaken for each other partly because the degree to which the (C)-element is inputted can give it considerable surface resemblance to the (B)-element, when the *latter* ingredient is itself viewed or conceived at a given, consonant level of intensity. As implied, this mistake can be made even though the elements' respective underlying psychological/contextual meanings are—unlike their surface appearances—in fact dissimilar, and may even differ sharply. (These meanings, of course, closely reflect those of the elements' respective *approaches.*)

Though point 2 has thus far centered on outside observers (OOs), it also applies albeit to a lesser extent, to the actual recipients of the s-2 youths' input, namely, to peers: These individuals, like OOs, can confuse an element which is integral to *one* approach, say, to type-(C), with one that helps define a different approach, say -(B). They can do so partly because they, still like the outside observers, often focus mainly on surface or other external aspects of the s-2s' input—though in their, the peers', case, this emphasis occurs chiefly during the early points or phases of their interactions with s-2's. (. . . "external" involves, for instance, physical aspects of observable behavior, as distinct, say, from the intended and/or underlying meaning of that behavior. "Early points . . ." is irrelevant to OOs because these individuals do not literally "interact" with the s-2's, as distinct from only *observing* their inputs.) Nevertheless, peers can mistakenly equate one element with another even after the early phases. In other words, they can do so even though they have experienced an inputted element—say, one involving the type-(C) approach—for some time, and perhaps also "repeatedly." In this connection they can make the given mistake especially if, and as long as, they neither recognize nor otherwise sense the s-2s'

main, immediate intention regarding the inputted element (i.e., the element's "meaning." in this respect). Here, as elsewhere, "intent" centers on the main role an element is supposed to play in promoting the type of interaction or relationship its inputters have in mind—for example, one that is dominance- rather than power-centered. Absence or slightness of "recognition" can exist even though these peers, *un*like the outside observers, do interact with the s-2's and are otherwise involved with them. (An *involvement,* which is a process and may have various phases, can (a) exist to a slight, moderate, or large degree. Similarly, but partly independently, it can (b) entail a low to high level of awareness of various meanings. Also, dimensions (a) and (b) can each (c) apply cross-sectionally and through time. Given (a) through (c), a participant—here, a peer—can be "involved" with another individual [an s-2] even if the peer hardly recognizes, and may misunderstand, the latter's immediate intentions regarding the role of given elements, especially but not only when these are first inputted.) Finally, the following OO/peer comparisons might be made explicit: Because they are *outside* the peer/s-2 interaction, whereas the peers are not, outside observers are more likely than peers to focus largely on surface aspects of elements that the s-2's "input" to these peers. Together with this, and substantially resulting from it, OOs are *less* likely than peers to recognize the main meanings of those elements, particularly their intended uses by the s-2's. Largely for these reasons, outside observers are more likely than peers to mistakenly equate certain inputted elements that are in fact rather different from each other, and it is especially in this respect that point 2 applies more to OOs than to peers. This is true even though, as indicated, peers themselves confuse various elements. (They do so for cognitive *and* emotional reasons—the latter more so than do OOs.)

The peers' mistaken equating of elements whose respective meanings actually differ from each other has a definite reality base: the physical/behavioral similarity that exists between these ingredients. (The peers recognize this resemblance after focusing on surface aspects of the given elements.) This resemblance is made possible by the fact that the three broad approaches—each consisting of several elements, all of which can be inputted—are not completely different from each other, particularly on the surface. That is, although approaches (A), (B), and (C)—the reciprocity-, power-, and dominance/submission-centered—do differ from each other with regard to *most* of their elements (i.e., the elements' surface aspects), and though they differ *clearly* in this respect, a few elements that belong to given approaches, such as to (B) and (C) respectivley, have a surface resemblance (SR) to each other—and this overt similarity is recognizable to many peers at various points in time. Specifically, the "few" elements have this SR (1) when they—ingredients of the respective approaches—have been expressed in certain *mutually consonant degrees (intensities)*, that is, in particular concrete ways and in those ways only (here, at those intensities only). Alternatively, and sometimes even additionally, such elements have an SR (2) with respect to their and perhaps other ingredients' major *subject matter (content)* or common foci of activity (behavior); that is, they have this second resemblance conceptually (a priori—see below). The first type of resemblance has been illustrated in connection with a medium or low intensity of *approach (B's)* "physical force" and/or its "threat/intimidation," on the one hand, in conjunction with and when compared to a high—and only *then* consonant—level of *approach (C's)* "interpersonal assertiveness" ("forcefulness"), on the other. Concerning the second resemblance, areas of overlap (hence, of similarity) exist and can be recognized between some *contents/behaviors* that are involved in approach (B's) "outsmarting" of others, and even in its "one-upmanship," on the one hand, and certain contents/behaviors that are involved in approach (C's) "leadership," on the other. The same applies to (B's) "one-upmanship" when it is juxtaposed with certain behavioral expressions of (C's) "felt superiority" and "presumptuousness"; likewise with various acts of (B's) "trickery" when in conjunction with (C's) "felt-privilege."

Whether the first or the second type of surface resemblance is involved, the following applies (*note*: the first SR is between "type-(1)" elements, the second is between "type-(2's)"): The contents that comprise the substance of an approach's elements—one such element being, for instance, approach (C's) "leadership," another its "felt-privilege"—can be thought of, in general, as *attributes, qualities,* or *predicates* of those elements. Simultaneously, and particular content, such as a given behavior or even a specific trait, can be considered an *aspect* or *expression* of an approach's element—can be viewed, for example, as an aspect of an individual's "leadership."

(For any two or more of the type-(2) elements, a contents-centered resemblance, that is, a subject matter similarity [SMS], can exist across a *range of intensities*. More precisely, the intensity of *any* such element, say, approach (B's) "one-upmanship," that has an SMS with another element [or with more than one] can vary from low to high or very high [though it usually starts at medium], and the same applies to the latter element, say, to (C's) "leadership." Given these available, respective ranges, several intensity-*combinations* can occur across elements from differing approaches; this can happen whenever any two or more of the above elements are mutually juxtaposed [say, paired] and are then considered in relation to each other. For instance, various peers—including individual ones—can take it for granted or can otherwise implicitly consider any of the following combinations similar to each other, that is, similar in one degree or another (e.g., very similar or only moderately so): *Medium* one-upmanship and *medium* leadership, or, separately, *high* leadership; *high* one-upmanship and *medium* as well as *high* leadership. In any event, because a "contents-centered resemblance . . . can exist across a *range* . . . ," it is possible to consider two elements that have been paired-and-compared similar to one another somewhat or even largely independently of each element's *particular* level of intensity at the time. In this respect the type-(2) resemblance is broader than that described for the type-(1) elements [see the "first type of resemblance," above]: For any two type-(2) paired elements there is almost always more than one resemblance, and there are often three or more; however, for the same number of type-(1) paired elements there is only one resemblance, that is, just one combination of consonant intensities. At any rate, because (a) any element's *intensities* necessarily accompany that element's particular, physical expressions [e.g., a given behavior or a specific trait that is part of an individual's "leadership" must be present to a high, medium, or low degree, at a given time], and because (b) any *element* must, logically, preexist in some respect in order for it to *have* or even potentially have any such concrete expressions [cf. the above-mentioned "attitudes" or "qualities"—in logical terms, ["predicates"], and any range of expressions as well, the following is the case: That same element—at least as, but not only as, a *concept* [see below]—can be said to exist "prior to" and "separate from" those or any of its other concrete expressions, with these expressions occurring, as indicated, at one or another level of intensity. [*Note*: (1) Each "element" is ultimately defined in terms of a specific area or region of content, one it encompasses and emphasizes. (2) As can be inferred, an "expression" is an element's specific, concrete "instance"—one of the element's physical manifestations. (3) Structurally, a "concept" is a definitionally circumscribed entity. Like other entities it can be classified, with respect to standard logic, as a "subject"—one that can have, or be characterized by, various "predicates." Simultaneously, a concept is "an abstract idea generalized from particular instances" (Webster, 1965, 171). In this capacity it can involve other defined entities or subjects, and among them are the present "contents"/"elements" and other various "attributes," whether or not these have been physically manifested. At any rate, it is (a) in the just-mentioned respects and (b) within a subject/predicate framework that a given element—(like a

concept itself: constituting a definitionally circumscribed entity)—can be said to "exist" separately from and prior to ("a priori") any of its concrete expressions. In order for an element to concretely interact with anything else and to be, as a result, physically observed or observable—(to "exist" in this respect)—it must necessarily occur in one *degree* or another: If it is not expressed at *some* level of intensity, on at least one occasion, it can literally not be manifested in the sense of having/involving *concrete content*. Nevertheless, when an element is considered solely as a *concept*—in particular, only as a defined "area or region of content" that encompasses "particular instances" *irrespective* of their specific intensity at the time—(in other words, that involves them only abstractly)—it exists, in that respect and context, "independently" of any physical interaction, of given "expressions" (as defined), and of actual behavioral observations.] None of the preceding requires that any element—any defined area/region of content—is *entirely* different than all other elements, including ones from the same approach; in other words, it need not lack even a modicum of content-overlap. In real life, elements are not wholly isolated from everything else. Instead, at one or more points in time, one or more parts of their respective contents—that is, one or another of their attributes—shade observably [and beyond just conceptually] into some portion or portions of one or more other elements' contents. This occurs however restrictively the given elements may be *defined*.

(When the type-(1) and type-(2) *surface resemblances [SRs]*—considered jointly—are taken together with approach (A's), (B's), and (C's) *surface nonresemblances [SNRs]*, the following, valid impressions can easily form [*note*: the dimensions of "intensity" and "content," which have been discussed in connection with SRs, apply to all SNRs as well]: The three broad approaches—(A) through (C)—can be viewed as having what might be called "partially shared borders" with each other, and also a degree of "content overlap." Simultaneously, however, they can be seen—still validly seen, and seen without contradicting or otherwise weakening the just-mentioned views—as *not* sharing *most* of their borders and substance with each other. By way of analogy, one might visualize the physical contact-points that join regions of France, Switzerland, and Italy to each other, or, alternatively, those which similarly connect parts of Switzerland, Austria, and Italy. In addition, one might think of the cultural commonalities—"mixed" regions, as it were—that exist at and near these boundaries. [The preceding pictures would parallel the first two impressions, above; the next one would represent the third.] Yet each country, even though it would partly border on each of the others, and despite its partial, substantive overlap with them, would remain clearly distinguished from both of them, overall. More specifically, it would remain distinct with respect to *most* of its boundaries and contents [this latter not just quantitatively]. Returning to the approaches themselves: Each one differs from the others not only with regard to (1) the *literal meaning* [say, the more commonly held/assumed referents—in this sense relatively objective ones] of its several respective contents [with each approach's contents taken *as* individual elements, that is, defined one by one]. Instead, each approach also differs from the others regarding (2) the *overall psychological meaning [OPM]* and intent of its contents [still the individual elements], when these are taken *collectively,* and integrated substantively [not, as in (1), only aggregated—and only structurally]. This OPM encompasses and reflects the approach's content similarities *and* differences.)

As seen, the peers' and outside observers' (OOs') emphasis on surface resemblances (SRs) between given elements can lead to their mistakenly equating these elements with each other. This can occur even though the intended *uses* of the respective elements, by s-2 youths, largely differ from each other. (In this regard, the *meanings* of these elements also differ, to these youths.) High among the reasons for the peers' and OOs' emphasis on SRs are the following

two; these can also be called "factors," and they help account for the reduced chances that the s-2s' main intended uses of the elements will be accurately perceived and interpreted by those individuals—hence, also distinguished by them: the type of and/or the relatively limited degree of *involvement,* with these s-2's, by the peers; and, the limited extent of *observation,* of these same youths, by the OOs. Yet, *whichever* reason is involved, and whether an "intensity"-centered or a "contents"-centered type of surface resemblance dominates (see SRs (1) and (2), above), the discussion, thus far, has focused only on *individual elements*—more specifically, on the influence that one such element can have upon another, with regard to bringing about the erroneous equating. There is, however, a further source of influence—a broader type of input—regarding this equating. (*Note:* "Involvement" and "observation" are important background factors in connection with this, the "broader type." This is true even though *meaning* plays a somewhat larger role, within this context, than it did in relation to the preceding context's *physical/behavioral SR.*) This source is the overall approach, namely, (A), (B), and (C), itself; and, as already seen, each approach includes *several* elements. Specifically, the average, modal, or otherwise typical strength of these several elements can substantially affect the peers' and outside observers' interpretation of or implicit assumptions above any individual elements, and even about other approaches as a whole. Involved, as the key inputs for this process, are either *all* the approach's elements or its *most common, actively operating ones* only—with the inputs/elements functioning collectively, in each case. When the strength of these several inputs is combined, for instance, with the degree of directness, consistency, and frequency with which they are used, the product that is particularly relevant here can be called the approach's usual "applied strength." (Here, "approach" is functionally synonymous with "several elements," when the elements are considered not only jointly but with regard to their actual operation. What we have elsewhere called an approach's *structure* mainly signifies the manifest *arrangement* of and relationships among that approach's several elements—usually "*all* [its] elements." As such, this structure can exist prior to and irrespective of how and how well these several elements—the ingredients that constitute the approach's particular contents—jointly *function,* that is, in fact operate.)

As broadly indicated, "applied strength"—active, inputted force—involves both of the following: First, it can substantially affect the degree to which peers and outside observers regard one *approach* as being comparable to *another*—say, approach (C) as being similar to (B); specifically, it can lead to their being erroneously equated. Here, for example, what we might call an "above average" (C)—that is, a *dominance-*centered approach which is, say, stronger than usual in the sense of being inputted, by s-2 youths, more vigorously and perhaps more directly as well as frequently than most—can be mistakenly interpreted, by peers and OOs, as a (*B*)-approach (*power*-centered), particularly, though not necessarily, one that is or would be somewhat "below average" (e.g., weaker than usual, in the sense of being expressed/inputted less energetically and/or less directly, and so on). Similarly, a stronger-than-usual (*A*)-approach (*give-and-take/reciprocity-*centered)—say, one that involves rather clearly and/or comparatively often inputted expectations of reciprocity, by s-2 youths, from various peers to whom they feel they have "given"—can be mistakenly considered, by those peers, a (C)-approach, particularly, but not only, one whose expressions are less energetic than most. In both samples, surface resemblance—insofar as it is separable from specific "meanings" (here, from the s-2s' main intent or purpose)—can play the primary role in accounting for this erroneous equating of *approaches.* To simplify the presentation, and because the "perceptions" and subsequent events that are described next focus chiefly on peers, we will omit outside observers; in addition, "perception" will substitute for "assumption," "implicit assumption," "interpretation," and so on.

Second, an approach's—say, (C's)—applied strength can set the stage for one (or more) of its *individual elements* to seem comparable to a particular *element* (or elements) that belongs to a different approach—say, (B). This mistaken equating, by the s-2s' peers, involves three main steps: *Step 1.* An s-2's approach—due, for instance, to its above or well above average applied strength, for its expressed elements combined—is perceived, by peers, to have a meaning that it does *not* in fact have. (Four items before continuing: (a) An approach's meaning can be called "overall" in that it pertains to that approach's various elements *jointly,* even when there are very few. This is a structural aspect of its meaning and it applies not only to the s-2s' intentions/expressions regarding the elements but to the peers' subsequent perceptions/misinterpretations of them. (b) For present purposes, an approach's "main" meaning will still refer to only the s-2s' intended expressions. This involves substance [content], which differs conceptually from the just-mentioned structure per se. (c) Though substance and structure are separable conceptually, they are inseparable operationally: They necessarily coexist, they are intrinsically interwoven, and they complement each other at all points, in any internal or external—here psychological or physical—process. The perceptions and misinterpretations (misperceptions), mentioned above and immediately below, are themselves interwoven, even though they are not, at base, simply different aspects and/or phases of a single, unitary process. (d) Steps 2 and 3, below, each of which centers on internal peer-processes, take place largely preconsciously—rarely on a consciously thought-out basis, whether quickly or not.) *Step 2.* The peers' perception of an approach's "overall" meaning (see item (a), above) and their misinterpretation of its "main" meaning (see (b), above) become—jointly and at largely the same pace (*pari passu*)—relatively concentrated on the following:

(a) a smaller number of the approach's various element, in fact, often only one; and (b) somewhat narrower substantive aspects of those elements (e.g., of approach (C's) "leadership" and "persistence"), or of even just that one. In short, "meaning," at this step, can be described as having been channeled— channeled (1) from that of the overall approach, (2) *with respect to* the quantitative and qualitative (i.e., the numerical- and substance-centered) dimensions or features (a) and (b), immediately above. In particular, perceived/misinterpreted meaning has been focused, by the peers, on fewer elements than in step 1 and on some or all elements and aspects *more specifically or pointedly* than before. (*Note*: (1) The present step occurs almost simultaneously with step 1. It can do so partly because the s-2 youths' *expressing* of an approach's elements and their peers' subsequent *experiencing* of them—here [in each case], in the aggregate—have considerable temporal and substantive overlap with those same respective individuals' expressing and experiencing of any *one* such element. [As before, subsequent experiencing involves perception/misinterpretation.] (2) As already implied, there may be few or several s-2-expressed/inputted and peer-perceived/misinterpreted elements in connection with any given approach. However, because the present discussion expressly centers on the erroneous equating of *one* such element with another—more specifically, an s-2 inputted element with a peer-perceived one—we can now focus mainly on the relationship between *one* s-2-expressed/inputted element, on the one hand, and the peers' *one*, or main, perception/misinterpretations [P/M] of that element, on the other, not on elements and their P/Ms in the aggregate.) In conjunction with its just-mentioned focusing, and partly because of it, the s-2-expressed, peer-misinterpreted element acquires, in step 2, not just (1) a more circumscribed character (as does its *meaning*, in this example), but often (2) a salience or prominence as well, or perhaps an augmented one. In connection with (1), and, where applicable, (2) ([increased]

salience not being perfectly correlated with "more circumscribed character"), the element acquires, conceptually *and* operationally, what can be called an increased separateness or identity. To partly recap: The s-2 approach, given its here *above*-average strength-of-expression, provides an overall backdrop, context, or milieu that casts the s-2s' inputted element in a light it would not otherwise have, at least not ordinarily. (A different example could involve *below*-average applied strength.) This sets the stage—in effect, makes it easier or easy, though not inevitable—for peers to erroneously interpret the s-2s' intended meaning and for the peers' subsequent, relatively concentrated, step 2 misinterpretation to occur. (*Note*: The concentrating of an element's already erroneously interpreted meaning is different, obviously, than a *broadening* of it—for instance, a simple suffusing or other spreading and diffusing of it into and perhaps throughout various other individual elements, such as those from a different approach. At any rate, step 2—and 3—can occur even if the peers' above-mentioned misinterpretation involves "fewer element*s*" alone [see dimension (a), above]. That is, it need not involve substantively "narrowed" [SN'd] ones—in this sense, "more specifically or pointedly" focused ones—as well [see dimension (b), above]. Nevertheless, other things being equal, SN'd elements from one approach [say, from (C)] are easier to erroneously equate with elements [unmodified—here, unnarrowed—ones] from a different approach [say, (B)] than are (C)-elements which are not substantively narrowed. [This applies especially, but not only, if the narrowing of one or more (C)-elements results—results within what then *remains* of these elements—in a highlighting of certain unusual and therein unrepresentative facets. It does not, however, necessarily apply to (C)-elements whose (1) substance (say, whose normal range of content, or, in effect, whose operating definition) is considerably *broadened,* that is, is expanded and diffused, and that (2) may be rendered partly nondescript based on their resulting substantial commonality with elements from which they were previously well-distinguished.] In addition, and consonant with the general points above, considerable *salience [SAL]*, or augmented SAL, can be acquired without any prior substantive narrowing of the given (C)-elements, as can increased overall separateness/identity [OSI] itself. Specifically, such SAL and OSI can be acquired based on the "smaller number" of (C's) alone, even though SAL/OSI is more likely to exist and to *be* considerable as well as increased if these elements are narrowed. To be sure, when only *one* element is involved in the first place, "substantive narrowing" [dimension (b)] *is* essential, since "fewer elements" [dimension (a)] no longer meaningfully applies. This is also the case regarding steps 2 and 3 as a whole. Finally, an element can acquire SAL and, in any event, an increase OSI even if the approach it is part of has below rather than above average applied strength.) *Step 3*. Here, the peer-misinterpreted (M) element from step 2 is erroneously equated, by these individuals, with one or more elements that belong to the "different" approach; for instance, an M-element from approach (C) can be mistakenly equated with "outsmarting," which is part of (B). As before, "belong to" and "part of" mean: help define; is a central component of; is used chiefly with and for. Taken together, steps 1 through 3, particularly their final outcome, are reflected in the following examples of erroneous (mistaken) equating: (1) When the *dominance*-centered—the (C)—approach's applied strength (AS) is substantially *above* average, an M-element (e.g., "leadership") that is part of it can seem, to peers, to have the following: Not just, and not mainly, a strong *surface resemblance* to an element (e.g., "outsmarting") that helps define the *power*-centered—the (B)—approach, but, in particular (and it is *this* which is erroneous), a substantially similar, perceived *meaning*. (In this example. (*B's*)—the power-centered approach's-—strength would not be above average.) The same can occur—again given above-average AS in approach

(C)—with respect to (C's) "persistence," on the one hand, and (B's) "threat/intimidation," or simply "intimidation" and/or even "manipulation," on the other. (2) In the same vein, certain peer-misinterpreted elements from a *power*-centered approach whose applied strength is *below* average can, after step 2, mistakenly seem similar in meaning to—can, in this respect, be erroneously equated with—given elements that belong to a *dominance*-centered approach. Chief among these power-centered/dominance-centered pairs of elements are the following (*note:* Though the dominance-centered—the (C)—approach's strength can be *average* in these pairs, not necessarily *above* average, the relationship between the (B)-approach's element and the (C)-approach's element, that is, their relationship of mistaken-equivalence, is more likely to exist and be strong if (C's) strength *is* above-average at the time. "~" means "is erroneously equated with."): A below-average (B's) "threat/intimidation" ~ (C's) "forcefulness (interpersonal assertiveness)," or, say, with its "demandingness"; a below-average (B's) "one-upmanship" ~ (C's) "presumptuousness"; such a (B's) "manipulativeness" ~ (C's) "persuasiveness"; and such a (B's) "outsmarting" ~ (C's) "leadership." (3) The same can occur in connection with a peer-misinterpreted element from a substantially *above*-average *give-and-take*—the (A)—approach, on the one hand, in relation to an element form a below-average or even average *dominance*-centered —(C)—approach, on the other. For instance, an above-average (A's) "giving of friendly advice or of practical assistance," or, say, its "expressing of interest/support/concern" [EISC], can be erroneously equated, in step 3, with a below average or even an average (C's) "forcefulness (interpersonal assertiveness)" or even "presumptuousness." (The reverse can occur, as well: An above-average (*C's*) peer-misinterpreted element, such as "presumptuousness," can be thus equated with a below-average (A's) element, such as EISC.) In this context EISC can also be erroneously equated with (C's) "proprietorship."

Regarding steps 1 and 2, jointly, it can be seen that the peers' imbuing of an overall approach's element (element "X") with a mistaken meaning is triggered by that *approach's* other-than-usual—its substantially above or below average—applied strength. In this respect, these individuals' misinterpretation does not originate in the *element* alone, that is, in X by itself—including its *intensity*. Nor is it triggered by, and still in this sense initiated by, X's particular physical/behavioral *characteristics* (PBCs) alone, that is, by these content-centered surface aspects alone. (This applies even apart from X's next-mentioned, surface *overlap* with the PBCs of an element—e.g., "Y"—which belongs to a *different* approach.) As implied, however element X's own content-centered surface aspects do contribute to the peers' misinterpretation of its meaning—"meaning" being a nonsurface dimension. But they do so only after the triggering. (*Note*: X's own surface aspects exist and, of course, preexist, independently of any actual as well as peer-perceived surface *overlap* that this element may have with surface aspects of any *other* element, such as Y. Element X's surface overlap with aspects of Y—thus, X's and Y's mutual resemblance with regard to, say, their PBCs—*can* contribute to the just-mentioned misinterpretation, but, again, only after the indicated triggering occurs.) Whatever the surface overlap's degree of contribution may be in any given case, it is only step 3 that involves the peers' erroneous *equating* of element X, on the one hand, with the presumed meaning of the element—still Y—that belongs to the different approach, on the other. This equating occurs via and specifically with respect to X's misinterpreted meaning, which, as indicated, forms during steps 1 and 2. In any event, "equating," which involves at least two elements (always X and, here, Y), is a qualitatively different process than that of "misinterpreting," which, as used in this brief overview, involves only one (always X). This applies even though both processes involve the erroneous attributing of certain meaning(s) that the peers associate with the element or elements—that is, the content(s)—in question.

A few more specifics and elaborations will now be presented; these may make some previously implicit factors and relationships more explicit: (1) In the case of peers, and starting with step 1 above, an "approach" operationally consists of whichever s-2-inputted elements these individuals are aware of and preconsciously or more consciously associate with each other, however few or many such inputted element this may involve. This implies that, for any given peer, an approach can functionally contain fewer elements than those we mentioned in our general description and working definition of it—more specifically, in our narrative listing of its main elements; and this is indeed the case. Moreover, seldom does any one *s-2 youth* even *utilize* a majority or large majority of the listed elements in the first place, at least those which comprise approaches (B) and (C); and it is only these utilized—inputted—elements which the youth's *peers* become aware of and to which they subsequently respond. (All that, and the following, applies even though—except in unusual circumstances—an s-2 youth uses only one of the three broad approaches with most of his peers, during sizable periods and major stages of his adolescence.) Regarding the respective elements themselves, our categorization of these ingredients as belonging to a given approach—say, to (B)—and as thereby helping to define it substantively is based on what the s-2 youths, collectively, ordinarily use. In particular, it derives from the types of concrete actions (say, tricking, intimidating, outsmarting) these individuals often take or try to take—action/inputs that are sometimes juxtaposed and can support each other—in order to express given attitudes and expectations, to establish and maintain preferred types of relationships with most peers, and to thereby help achieve personal goals and satisfactions. ("Types of relationships" refers to approaches (A), (B), and (C) themselves: give-and-take/reciprocity-centered, power-centered, and dominance-centered, respectively.) Though neither the s-2's nor their peers articulate the approaches as such, or even clearly conceptualize them, both groups of individuals can focus on given *elements*—(s-2's, on elements they utilize/input; *peers,* on inputted ones they are "aware of . . .")—and they *can* sometimes touch on the approaches themselves. To be sure, the s-2s' and peers' references to or actual accounts of these elements, and more so to the approaches per se, are frequently indirect, often only hazy, and, in any event, regularly involve words and phrases that largely differ from those used here. Nevertheless, the meanings in question—in this case, the intended referents of those words and phrases—are evident, even absent extensive context.

(2) The degree of "similarity" peers perceive between two entities, such as two approaches or two elements, sometimes involves *identity* or near-identity, not just moderate or considerable *overlap.* This applies to similarity regarding the entities' *surface resemblance (SR)* and, separately, concerning their *meaning.* It can pertain, for instance, not only to (a) the degree of *SR* these peers perceive between two approaches but also to (b) the degree of *similar meaning* they believe or implicitly assume exists between two elements as such—specifically, between an ingredient from one approach and an ingredient from another. At any rate, in the case of (a), and still with respect to peer-perception, "degree of *SR*" can involve not just substantially *overlapping* surface resemblances but ones that are completely *identical.* Similarly, with respect to (b), and still from the peers' perspective, "degree of *similar meaning*" can involve not only overlapping meaning but again that which is identical. (Identity is the highest level of resemblance. As always, "approaches" are entities that we, not the peers, conceptualize as such.) The preceding applies independently of the following: Regarding the peers' erroneous equating (EE) of two *approaches, surface resemblance* rather than meaning plays the lead role. In particular, it does so whatever degree of perceived similarity is in-

volved, for instance, moderate overlap *or* near-identity. However, with respect to the EE of two *elements, meaning* plays a larger overall role than surface resemblance; and it, too, does so apart from the degree of perceived similarity, for example, overlap *or* identity. (Also, it plays this role even though SR's contribution is nonetheless major—as is *meaning's* itself, in the preceding EE.) In any event, degree of peer-perceived similarity restricts the ability of neither surface resemblance nor meaning to play the principal role with regard to erroneous equating, and this applies whether approaches or single elements are involved. (3) Considerable SR and even substantive overlap (SO)—but not, objectively, identity—exists between *insistence,* on the one hand, and the approach-(C) element *forcefulness* ("interpersonal assertiveness"), on the other. (Considered jointly, SR and SO will simply be called "similarity.") This similarity mainly reflects the fact that both features involve *force* and require that this property or attribute is verbally and/or nonverbally expressed, that is, manifested, to a moderate or higher degree. Regarding insistence, this applies even when the expression is neither loud, otherwise conspicuous, nor rather long-lasting. Given their moderate or greater "force," *insistence* and *forcefulness* have substantial similarity—mainly SR—not only to *persistence* and *demandingness* (both approach-(C) elements) but to *intimidation* (a (B)-element) as well—elements that intrinsically involve such force themselves and that manifest it in one way or another. The same level and type of similarity even applies to a variant of approach (A's) *assistance*—specifically, to some s-2s' expressed eagerness to provide help that certain peers seem to at least partly want. (These peers, for one thing, are ordinarily reluctant to accept offers of "practical assistance" from those youths and from many other individuals—this, largely independent of whether they are more willing to accept various expressions of emotional "concern/support." As a result, those s-2's, acting as friends, and in order to achieve their goal, consider it important or even necessary to (a) "insist," that is, to seriously and earnestly try to provide assistance that the peers will, hopefully, accept, and to (b) perhaps even persevere in their attempts. The following distinction, relationships, and considerations regarding insistence are neither centered on nor limited to approach (A)—and, thus, to the offering of assistance.) Whether or not over an extended period of time, s-2 youths—collectively—can be insistent in at least two main ways (*note*: The second way, or pattern, is the most common one; though both patterns are found in many contexts, not all of their respective aspects apply in every one): First, s-2's can be insistent in a relatively quiet, perhaps somewhat subtle, and not particularly—let alone highly—conspicuous manner; second, they can be insistent in a *hardly* quiet, in a relatively *un*subtle (perhaps even fairly blunt and insensitive), and in a generally open or even prominent, way. Yet the quieter, *non*prominent pattern, though most often associated with approaches (A) and (C)—these being the reciprocity- and dominance-centered—is sometimes used, still be given s-2's (and it is *often* utilized by some *others*), to achieve *power*-centered, that is, approach (B)—ends instead. At the same time, the more open, predominantly direct and conspicuous pattern is more evenly utilized in connection with the three approaches. In any event, *insistence,* as used in this discussion, is not a defining feature of any one approach. As a result, it is not listed under any of the three approach's, that is, among their a priori, distinguishing ingredients. This is the case even though, as indicated, it is commonly *utilized*—in terms of the first and second pattern—in connection with each of these approaches. In contrast, *forcefulness is* presented as a distinguishing feature (ipso facto, of only one approach)—specifically, as a defining element of (C); hence, it *is* listed—in connection with that approach. As to *force,* this is never an element itself, and it is not listed. Nevertheless, it is intrinsic to—is an integral attribute, property, or quality of—all three approaches; in this regard it is expressed to a substantial or greater degree in one or more of these approaches' respective elements, for instance, in forcefulness, persistence, intimidation, and assistance. In the present discussion, force is a property these elements share with "insistence" to a significant degree and which thereby helps account for their substantial mutual *similarity,* that is, their perceived surface resemblance and substantive overlap. The term is not used with regard to its role in *causation,* that is, in the production, alteration, or even maintenance of one entity, event, process, or condition by another entity, and so on. (A cause is "something that produces an effect. [More precisely,] CAUSE applies to any event, circumstance, or condition or combination of these that brings about or helps bring about a result" [Webster, 1965, 133].) In this connection production, alteration, and the like *require* force—manifested or inferred as the application of power, and often including its continuation or reapplication. Thus, still regarding causation, not mutual similarity, "force" constitutes the key active factor in, and provides essential impetus and perhaps reinforcement for, any substantively interrelated chain of occurrences. Together with force, the contents of this chain help trace and explain, for example, entity or event "X's" type and/or degree of influence on "Y," "Y's" subsequent impact on "Z,"perhaps even "Y's" reciprocal influence on "X," and so forth. (4) Though considerable similarity exists between insistence and elements such as forcefulness as well as persistence, overall differences are common. For instance, when being *insistent*—conspicuously or not—s-2 youths, in most contexts, purposely tell their peers what they, the youths, would like to happen, what each person (youth, peer) should do, *why* they think this goal and action is OK and perhaps important for both of them, and so on. They do this in order to obtain these individuals' agreement, cooperation, and perhaps active participation, or at least their passive if even reluctant and wavering compliance. At any rate, they try to engage these peers and to *persuade* them—without intimidating them, preferably without misleading them, and so forth. In substantial contrast, the following applies to *forcefulness*: Those and/or other s-2 youths sometimes try to achieve given goals *without* personally engaging or even seriously trying to engage their peers, and regularly without giving them relevant information, or much such information, of the types just mentioned. Instead, they rely heavily on pushing things through even in the absence of peer-consent, and/or despite the latters' resistance. In this regard they often act quickly, firmly, and not necessarily smoothly and steadily. They frequently try to reach given goals on a "one-shot" basis, as well. In any event, these youths often "rush" their peers in order to (a) preclude or reduce what they consider the latters' possible or likely resistance, (b) disrupt opposition that already exists and which they assume might even increase, and, overall, (c) raise the chances of getting what they want—first and foremost for themselves.

When these s-2's do *not* act rapidly, vigorously, and so on, they still do not mainly rely on persuading their peers. This especially applies when they believe or assume their efforts may negatively affect those individuals or will, in any case, probably not benefit them, and also when they do not try to do much for these peers in the first place. At any rate, the s-2s' forcefulness—their interpersonal assertiveness—is chiefly a proactive stance, not mainly a fallback. Moreover, its expressions are at least as often deliberate in nature, that is, relatively measured in character, as they are somewhat impetuous or otherwise relatively impulsive—therein more immediate and unplanned. (This applies even though the ". . . impulsive" expressions often recur and are, in this respect, habitual.) Given the preceding, the following applies when these youths are being forceful chiefly in order to implement their own priorities (e.g., achieve personal goals) and only secondarily—sometimes fairly distantly—to benefit their peers: From an early point forward, they usually have no more than moderate expectations of obtaining these individuals' genuine consent and cooperation (C&C), let alone their enthusiastic support; in addition, in many cases they are prepared—even entirely willing or "more than" willing—to forgo any *desire* for such peer-C&C. All in all, the preceding essentially constitutes one way of being forceful, and one way in which this feature relates to others. In particular, it involves being forceful without necessarily being *persistent,* in the sense of persevering through time; it also involves being forceful without being *insistent,* in the sense and via the types of input indicated earlier. All this applies even when, on occasion, the youths' interpersonal assertiveness broadens and/or intensifies to where it substantially overlaps *aggressiveness* (e.g., to where the former manifests clear overtones of the latter's frequent combativeness)—which, in the present context, it generally does not do. Moreover, the preceding exemplifies a type, though not necessarily a level, of forcefulness that not infrequently involves aspects of *manipulation* and *deception.* As can be deduced from earlier discussion, these B-elements (both power-centered) are sometimes used—specifically, they are used with particular peers and/or under unusual circumstances—by s-2 youths whose basic and *regularly* utilized approach is the *dominance*-centered, not the power-. (Forcefulness, a (C)-element, belongs to the dominance-centered.) To be sure, a parallel situation exists with forcefulness itself: Under certain conditions, and so forth, this element (feature, ingredient) is used by s-2's whose basic approach is the *power*-centered, not the dominance-. These examples of individual elements being utilized outside their "basic"—their a priori-defined—approach, by youths who do not ordinarily use them and who do not prefer the approach of which they are a part, reemphasizes the following. To obtain an adequate, hopefully an optimal, and, in any event, a relatively accurate understanding of the main *psychological meaning* that given elements have to the youths who are utilizing them at a certain time, it is always important, and usually essential, for these ingredients to be considered not just by themselves and not only on the surface. Instead, insofar as possible, they should be examined as part of, and interpreted in relation to, the context in which they play an active role. "Activity," with regard to this context, includes not only major actions that involve the given ingredients, and clear interactions among these elements, but, in particular, the seeming intentions of the s-2 youths in question.

(*Note to reader*: Because of the suddenly imposed external deadline referred to in the text, we must conclude this endnote with the following, foreshortened section, and therefore without rounding out the endnote's overall discussion by further tracking, and then pulling together, certain of its points. The chapter will conclude with endnotes #288–289, which were written earlier.)

Point 3. In the preceding pages, two points were examined regarding approaches (A), (B), and (C)—the reciprocity-, power-, and dominance-centered. These focused on the elements that comprise each approach and on the fact that some elements which belong to any one approach can sometimes resemble, and thereby be mistaken for, ones of a different approach. The third point is that the main approach which is used to characterize an s-2 youth's relationship to given peers—for instance, to describe it as "dominance/submission"—can change through time. Whether this modification is slow or rapid, it occurs largely because the youth, those peers, or both are undergoing or have already undergone certain changes, mainly in their respective types and/or levels of interest, desire, need, skill, and/or opportunity. More particularly (and in regard to "both"), it occurs largely because key aspects of, say, the *youth's* changing or changed interests and desires (I&Ds) are not as compatible with *present* I&Ds (*themselves* changing or changed I&Ds) on the part of the *peers* as were corresponding or comparable aspects of that s-2 youth's *pre-change* I&Ds; in the same vein and often at the same time, areas of specific *in*compatibility may have emerged, may be increasing, and may even predominate.

Thus, for example, in the dominance/submission pattern (i.e., the (C)-type relationship), matters on which youths and peers had, in effect, implicitly or explicitly agreed—ones that had helped draw these individuals together, largely based on these youngsters' mutual interests, desires, and/or needs—are often no longer considered (a) desirable or *as* desirable by one or both parties, or perhaps even (b) minimally acceptable by them, once these interests, and so on, have changed. Related to this is the following. Various changes in what these youths (the s-2's) and/or peers consider desirable or acceptable often occur because the former, the latter, or both individuals are moving toward or have already moved substantially toward an (*A*)-type pattern, that is, a more reciprocal/give-and-take approach. (This movement involves the youths' and/or peers' interactions or relationships with many of the *other* individuals in their lives, including various peers of these *peers*; also, the movement has been mainly associated with personal satisfactions.) In any event, the following are typical outcomes of substantial personal and interpersonal adaptations, growth, and new directions, and they are neither invariably nor always chiefly caused by movement toward pattern (*A*): (a) Peers who were previously compliant in their relationships with a given s-2 may no longer want to comply, or be dominated per se—either at all or to a degree that might continue to satisfy that s-2. (Here, the latter is an essentially unchanged and unchanging individual.) (b) An s-2 who already *has* changed or who has been recently changing may no longer prefer to be as dominant as before, with most of his peers. He may have made many or most of the former changes, and even the latter one, prior to the occurrence of the peer-changes mentioned in (a). Whenever it takes place, the s-2s' change with respect to dominance satisfies some of those peers but not necessarily all. At any rate, concerning (a) and (b) alike, various inputs, expectations, and related interactions (IEIs) that were previously considered positive or acceptable by at least one of the two parties in this type-(C) relationship begin to seem considerably less so. In many such cases these IEIs have, in effect, become less able to successfully compete with certain relatively recent types and/or levels of experiences or observed IEIs. Prominent among the latter are newly perceived and conceived, personally experienced or anticipated, satisfactions. In many other cases, however, the IEIs have become unwanted mainly on their own.

One other example of point-3 modifications and/or their implications will be given—this in connection with a different major approach: Because of changes in their interests, needs, skills, and so on, other s-2 youths may choose to no longer rely on some or all of the key elements that have jointly constituted their (B)-approach. That is, they may no longer rely on, or perhaps even substantially utilize, *power*-centered ingredients such as force, trickery, and/or manipulation. This change, in itself, may be welcomed by their peers. In contrast, however the s-2's may choose to utilize such ingredients *more* than, not less than, before, and various behavioral expressions of this choice may be resisted by their peers (successfully or not). In both cases (more than before; less than before), the character and direction of the youth/peer relationship shifts, and it does so even if the *peers* have undergone little or no recent personal change. Sometimes, when these individuals *have* thus changed, they are substantially less vulnerable than before to some of those (B)-elements; this is the case even if the s-2's have not chosen to utilize these elements *less* than before, and may instead even use them more than before. Here, too, the youth/peer relationship has qualitatively changed or will noticeably change through time, even though the s-2s' main approach can still be characterized and categorized as power-centered.

In short, a youth/peer relationship can change when various modifications occur within the former's approach, for instance, in parts of his (C)- or perhaps his (B)-approach; these modifications involve the usage, that is, the presence, frequency, and/or intensity, of certain elements (parts; ingredients) which help comprise that approach, or input-pattern. Though they are often major, these and related relationship-changes do not require that the youth's *entire* approach changes to a *different* overall approach—say, that the individual's overall (C)-type changes to the (B)-type. (For present purposes, "approach" = "input-pattern" = "type.") To be sure, a youth/peer relationship almost always does change significantly when the youth's input-pattern changes from that of (C) to (B), or, say, from (C) to (A).

It might be noted that point 3's original focus is not on any youth/peer *relationship (R),* or even on their R-change. Instead, it centers on the youth's *approach,* that is, on his overall input-pattern (but not on this pattern's *individual elements,* as such), including its psychological meaning. Specifically, the basic point is that the main approach which an s-2 utilizes can change to a different approach—through time, and for the type of reasons specified. Moreover, s-2's, viewed collectively, though not at all individually, not infrequently *do* change their approach; and regarding any *individual* s-2 who changes his approach, any such change seldom takes less than a year, and it not infrequently takes two. The most common type of approach-to-approach change—at least the one most likely to occur within, say, an approximately two-year period—is *from* the dominance-centered (i.e., the (C)) approach *to* the reciprocity-centered (the (A)), and, to a somewhat lesser extent, from the (A) to the (C). Other changes, such as from the power-centered (i.e., the (B)) to the (C) and perhaps from the (C) to the (B) as well as from the (B) to the (A), are noticeably less likely to occur within that time frame; nevertheless, except for change from approach (A) to (B), that is, from the reciprocity- to the power-centered, these and other changes or major developments are still far from rare. Whether it is among the most likely (this being what might be called "moderately common," for s-2's viewed collectively) or among the least, such a change in a youth's overall approach almost invariably has, as suggested, substantial implications for the nature and extent of his relationship with his peers. Moreover, and particularly by the middle and later stages of most such approach-to-approach changes, many of these individual s-2's have acquired or are acquiring various *new* peers. That is, they are doing so rather than mainly or only retaining a substantial relationship with their current ones, particularly if this relationship has changed only moderately (unless for the better, from their perspective). Basically, whether these s-2 youths "drop" certain peers or whether given peers "drop" the youths depends largely on (a) the nature and extent of the changes that have occurred or are occurring in their mutual relationships (and on those which have *not* occurred . . .), and on (b) the type, quality, and extent of friendships/acquaintanceships that these respective individuals are maintaining and/or developing with *other* individuals—peers and adults (parents included) alike. Such changes often play an important role in various relationship-patterns mentioned in Chapter 26.

Finally, neither the reality of nor the potential value of the three approaches we have discussed is negated or reduced by the fact that an s-2 can, over time, change the main approach he uses. Nor is this reality and value substantially diminished by the fact that certain elements of these approaches have a significant surface resemblance to, and/or some actual content overlap with, given elements of one of the *remaining* approaches—and, to a lesser extent, to/with some elements of the second. (See below regarding overlap.) Thus, the following applies to approaches (A), (B), and (C), even though these respective input-patterns—each viewed globally—have what can be thought of as stretches of common border or as mutual grey areas, and even though certain elements of these respective approaches share some of their delineated and circumscribed *aspects* ("within-element" features) with one another: (a) Each approach, taken as a whole, largely or very largely *differs* from each of the oth-

ers. In particular, it differs to that extent with respect to the character ("nature") and observed actions of its elements—its contents—considered collectively, both quantitatively and qualitatively. Regarding quantity, the totality of the respective approaches' *un*shared, relatively distinctive contents well exceeds that of their mutual grey areas or common boundary regions plus that of their shared, within-element "aspects." As to quality, this involves not only each approach's unique, overall pattern of elements (a structural factor) but, especially, its actual overall interactions and operation (a dynamic factor). In both respects, all three approaches decidedly differ from each other. (b) Each approach is specifically defined and its main meaning is clear. In these respects it is an entity, albeit also a construct. (c) Each approach, as a functioning entity (here, as an actual stance and pattern of inputs), is important in its own right and its own way *pragmatically*—for example, in its implications for intervention. Separable from items (a) through (c), and of fundamental importance, each approach clearly differs from the other two with regard to its psychological meaning—a dimension that centers particularly on the overall orientation and the main intent of the approach's user (inputter), namely, the s-2 youth. "Meaning," in this respect, is distinct from scope and nature—for instance, distinct from a listing of what is included in an approach and from a description of what is observed about it. Given all the preceding, the three approaches remain essentially and importantly distinguished from each other whether *or not* the youth moves away from one of them and begins to mainly rely on another, and, if he does move away, even if he temporarily returns to the other or occasionally utilizes some of the elements. [*Note:* 1. For a change to occur from one approach to another— say, from the *dominance*-centered to the reciprocity-, or *vice versa,* or perhaps from the *power*-centered to either the reciprocity- or the dominance-centered— the youth's *I-Level* does not necessarily have to first change, or even change at all. However, because (a) it often *does* change (sometimes first, sometimes not), because (b) a change in I-Level and a change in *approach* very often accompany each other (temporarily overlap, in the youth's life), and because, in any event, (c) changes in each of them have various identical *causes* (initiators; generators), it might be useful to mention major content-factors that are involved in the approach/I-level relationship: As already indicated, change in the youth's *approach* and in his relationship with given peers is largely produced by a change in his and/or these peers' "types and/or levels of interest, desire, need, skill [e.g., cognitive/perceptual, social, and/or practical], and/or opportunity." (Thus, on this score alone, a change in these factors within the *peers* sometimes suffices to initiate and further generate a change in the youth/peer relationship, that is, even absent any substantial, accompanying change in the youth's approach and/or I-Level. A change in the youth's approach may or may not soon follow.) At the same time, a change in the youth's *I-Level* is itself closely associated with most of these content factors, such as "interest," "desire," and "skill." In particular, not only does this change in level largely *result* from various combinations of these factors; instead, it—and especially the changed I-Level itself—incorporates, entails, and otherwise directly reflects these factors, and in this respect the latter—the I-Level—is in large part substantively *defined* by them, not just brought about by them. Despite the large, substantive (i.e., specific content-centered) overlap in the causes of I-Level change, on the one hand, and in approach (A), (B), or (C), on the other, there is not, as indicated, a one-to-one connection between change in the former and that in the latter. As seen from items (a) and (b), below, this absence of an inevitable and invariable causal relationship between I-Level change and change in approach is reflected, for instance, in connection with certain *discriminations* (differentiations) made by the s-2 youth. (Related background: In basic I-Level literature, an increase in a youth's differentiations—for example, a sizable increase in the distinctions he draws between other people and/or between himself and these individuals [thus, in aspects of his relationship to them]—is a sine qua non and hallmark of an increase in his I-Level. Compare "change in his . . . levels of [cognitive/perceptual and social] skills," above.) Specifically, a youth's I-Level does not automatically increase (nor *must* his approach change) when, and essentially because, he becomes better able than before to do the following— even just the first item: (a) perceive (here, accurately detect) certain differences that exist between his present approach and another one, for instance, between his dominance-centered approach and the reciprocity-, or, in the case of a different youth, between the power-centered and the reciprocity-; (b) then recognize, and perhaps feel concerned about, various personal and possibly other-person implications of these perceived differences in approach, and perhaps recognize certain implications of the self-to-others-person relationships that are involved in the respective approaches. (For perspective, the following might be kept in mind. Though I-Level indeed does not automatically increase under the conditions just mentioned, the individual's increased ability or sensitivity [IAS] with respect to (a) and (b) nevertheless often *does* help produce an I-Level change, particularly if this IAS is substantial and sustained. In addition, IAS often *does* promote, though it does not be itself almost ensure, a change in *approach*. In both connections, namely, that of I-Level and of approach, IAS plays this facilitating role whether its own underpinnings—the factors which produce and support *it*—are chiefly emotional, mainly cognitive, or a sizable mix of both.) 2. Regarding content overlap, two or more elements that each belong to a different approach but which nonetheless have some substantive commonality (SC) are often involved in similar observable activities and are sometimes used to achieve similar or even identical immediate goals. SC is separable from, though often causally related to and temporally associated with, peer-perceived surface resemblances.]

288. In a later section of endnote #287 we indicated that the "specific" features/contents—when they exist at all in peers' perceptions of set 2 youths—cannot be inferred with absolute certainty from the "broad" aspect of those same peers' perceptions. (Specific features/contents would, for instance, be the "particular expressions (forms)" of the youths' independence; the broad aspect would be "independence per se." See #287 regarding the sense in which a "perception," such as one involving that broad-aspect, is a peer *interpretation* of the set 2 youths' behaviors, traits, and/or attitudes.) This means that the type of substantive association or relationship which exists between a "y" (i.e., specific features/contents) and an "x" (the broad aspect) can be and should be described as one of "contingency" (CT) rather than "logical necessity" (LN)—absolute certainty always being integral to LN but never to CT. (LN and CT are not *polar opposites* with respect to necessity. In particular, although LN does involve "inevitability" and "invariability"—constructs whose central observable facets involve predictability and stability— CT does not ipso facto imply only accident or chance, and near or total *un*predictability/*in*stability. As used here, contingency basically means being "dependent on or conditioned by something else," for example, dependent on "other . . . events for existence or occurrence"; *conditioned,* in turn, means "brought or put into a specified state" [Webster, 1965, 5, 173, 180]). The basic reasons for this inability to infer those specific features/contents with certainty—say, certainty that revolves around invariability—can now be stated in connection with a more familiar context and in perhaps a less abstract way than was done in endnote #287. There, the reasons were presented only with respect to and in terms of the syllogistic/deductive framework that is involved in inferential processes. In that regard they were presented fairly abstractly and, in effect, aside from real-life circumstances, impacts, and causal sequences.

The "basic reasons" for the inability in question center on the following: Some *forces and/or conditions* that ordinarily maintain given "y's"—that is, which support and sustain the *specific features/contents* (these being the "particular expressions . . .")—sometimes vary or else are overcome. When either this "vary"- or this "overcome"-scenario occurs, the effects of given forces/conditions (F/Cs) on the specific features/contents are sometimes substantially different than usual. More precisely, under various circumstances (usually external), certain F/Cs, which we will call the "original" ones, (1) sometimes operate outside their usual quantitative and/or qualitative ranges. (In this connection, the F/Cs' functional capacity—their potential power or influence as inputs—can be said to have changed ["varied"]; this can occur whether or not this change is accompanied by a substantial change in the F/Cs' intrinsic character, that is, their nature.) When these original forces/conditions operate outside their usual ranges they (2) sometimes affect the *specific features/contents* in atypical ways; that is, they bring about "particular expressions"—"forms" or manifestations—of these features/contents that are substantially different than usual. Alternatively, under other circumstances, the original forces/conditions are *overcome*: They are outweighed, diluted, or otherwise functionally checked and neutralized by *other* F/Cs. (Regarding this scenario, which is the second one, these "other" forces/conditions are ones whose collective impact on the given features/contents is comparatively small when the original forces/conditions are operating within their usual ranges and are functioning normally in that respect.) The upshot is that here, as in the first scenario (the "vary"-scenario), the following sometimes occurs: The original forces/conditions—some internal to the individual youths, other external—no longer maintain the specific features/contents (f/c's); these f/c's, of course, are the "y's" that are ordinarily present and which, as such and *as* y's (these being specific content), are integral to any adequate characterization of a typical y/x relationship that emphasizes the relationship's substance (content). At any rate, under various circumstances, specific features/contents may—like the original forces/conditions themselves—no longer retain their original, that is, their "normal," form.

In sum, when key forces/conditions—ordinarily the principal maintainers—operate rather differently than usual or else are largely overcome by other F/Cs, the specific *features/contents* ("f/c's," or "y's") that depend on the usual operation of those forces/conditions sometimes vary (i.e., are modified), whether considerably or not. Given that (1) these *y's* can and do vary, and given that (2) these features/contents are fundamental to the *y/x relationship*, that is, are integral to its composition and hence to determining its character or nature, (3) the nature of this relationship can and does itself vary. The existence of this variation or change ipso facto indicates that this—the y/x relationship or association—is "contingent," within the meaning of this term. It also indicates that, for the reasons given earlier and in endnote #287, y's cannot be derived from an "x" with absolute certainty. (This inability is further reflected in the fact that y's can change even if an "x"—the *broad*-aspect perception—has undergone little or no change.)

289. I wish to thank Carl Jesness for discussing some of his specific methods and findings with me and for thereby confirming and/or clarifying my understanding of them.

23 SELECTED INDIVIDUALIZED PROGRAMS

By the time Phase 2 of the Community Treatment Project ended (1969), several agencies and organizations (a/o's) within and outside California had begun to adopt a number of its major features. This involved more than simply using its broad strategy of intervening in the *community* rather than in institutions, for example, more than, and often other than, the approach that Massachusetts adopted statewide, in early 1972, after observing its feasibility in CTP and elsewhere (Coates, Miller, and Ohlin, 1978; Ohlin, Coates, and Miller, 1974). Instead, those a/o's reorganized their operations, or added new structures, in ways that not only supported but that directly required *increased distinctions among youths*—in short, in ways that specifically promoted a more differentiated treatment and control. In effect, this change individualized intervention to a greater extent than before, thereby targeting it better and presumably increasing its relevance to differing youths' needs, abilities, limitations, and so on.

The features or combinations of features that were adopted—and adapted—varied from one a/o (henceforth called "agency") to another. Nevertheless, these and subsequent agencies almost always used (1) one or more forms of personality, social/developmental, and/or cognitive/developmental *classification* of their youth population, and, slightly less often, (2) a *worker/youth matching*, or at least a more deliberate and explicit selection of workers for particular skills and orientations. In addition, if and as their specific setting and organizational realities allowed, these agencies often used small or at least considerably *reduced caseloads* or else their functional equivalent, for example, small(er)

residential living units and/or a high(er) staff-to-youth ratio in those units. However, regardless of setting and of various realities and limitations, most such agencies also increased the frequency, scope, and—less often—overall duration of direct staff/youth *contacts*. Finally, the agencies usually utilized several *strategies and techniques* that had not only proven useful at CTP and had been described in its literature, but that had, in several instances, been directly taught to their staff either at the Center for Training in Differential Treatment (Chapter 17) or else via consultation with, and/or work-site sessions and seminars with, CTDT's trainers, its graduates, and so on.

The present chapter will mainly describe five programs that drew heavily from the experiences of California's CTP—including, in some cases, the latter's combined institution- and community-located facility, namely, its Phase 3 operation (Chapter 13). These programs emerged and took firm shape in the late 1960s, the early 1970s (two programs), the late 1970s, and the early 1980s, respectively—thus including periods, and, in any event, surviving *through* periods, when treatment and rehabilitation efforts were widely questioned and often openly rejected, mainly but not only in the United States.

Three of the five programs operated in the United States and the rest were in Canada. Though their clients were usually moderately to very seriously delinquent males, and, not infrequently, females, relatively mild or nonserious delinquents were far from rare in a couple of programs. At any rate, many youths had been placed into their program in lieu of being sent to a state- or province-operated training school or else to some other secure or semi-secure facility. Two of the five programs were within a city or county probation department; one was under a Provincial Ministry; the other two were "quasi-private" (e.g., also serving a Ministry) and private, respectively. One program operated in a community setting only; two were in a residential setting almost entirely (though with some community follow-up); and two others involved an integrated residential and community setting, using the continuity-of-intervention strategy that characterized Phase 3. Most programs were relatively modest in size, though not necessarily uncomplicated or easy to run.

The five program operations to be described are as follows: the Shawbridge Youth Centers, the St. Francis Boys' Homes of Kansas, the Baltimore Differential Treatment Program, the Ormsby Village Treatment Center, and the Craigwood-Bridgeway Program. Though each program had features in common with every other one (in fact, there were often several such features), each operation remained unique or distinct, particularly in terms of having its own overall pattern or "gestalt," and emphasis. The individual descriptions of these programs will include information about the several common and basic types of features and issues. However, these same descriptions, collectively, will also include information that reflects each program's individuality and special emphasis. Finally, besides having mutually different *patterns* of features, and differing emphases, the programs—at least some of them—differed from each other in the degree to which they individualized intervention itself. Nevertheless, the degree of individualization was always substantial.

The chapter concludes with a review of one statewide and one provincewide effort and operation.

Shawbridge Youth Centers

Shawbridge Youth Centers (SYC) consists of several residential cottages in one general setting about 50 miles north of Montreal, Quebec, plus a number of community centers and other facilities in and around Montreal itself. During the periods specified below, the SYC agency served two categories of individuals—both delinquents—who had been admitted to it from detention units in that large metropolitan area:

1. *Article 20 Cases.* Youth who have been adjudged delinquent after having been found guilty of an offense under the Criminal Code. [These are individuals who have violated given "articles as defined by the Canadian Criminal Code, the Food and Drug Act, the Narcotic Act, and other related acts."];
2. *Article 15 Cases.* [These youths] are considered to be in need of the protection of the Court, . . . and [they] fall under the Youth Protection Act, usually as a result of some antisocial or self-destructive activity. [They "often have longstanding histories of maladaptive behavior"; and, in the U.S.A., many are called status offenders.] (Girard et al., 1979, p. 9; Wylie, Hanna, and Scully, 1971, p. 31)

Some 85 percent of these youths are male; their average age at intake is 14.7; their mean IQ is about 82 (79 Verbal, 85 Non-Verbal— Lorge-Thorndike), and they (especially youths first placed in the residential cottages) are two to four years below the norm in reading and math (Harvie and Brill, 1977, 1978).

The following summarized this program and its philosophy as of 1979 (Brill, 1979, pp. 2–4). Additional details and subsequent developments are mentioned below.

"Shawbridge Youth Centers (formerly known as The Boys' Farm and Training School) has cared for wayward and delinquent boys for 70 years. In the last eight years, this agency has greatly expanded in size, complexity, and scope of responsibilities. It now [cares] for and treat[s] 250 adolescent clients, of whom 210 are boys and approximately 40 are girls. [It] provides residential, group home, and community services in its 17 treatment units. There are three locked facilities (two short-term, one long-term), five open residential units ["cottages"], six group homes in the Greater Montreal community, two centers ["Community Centers"] for day-care and casework, and one community detention facility." (In 1970 and 1980, the population of Montreal and environs was about 2.5 million and 2.8 million, respectively. This was some 45 percent that of all Quebec Province.)

"On campus [i.e., in the residential facility], there are centralized educational, recreational, food, and maintenance services. Closed and open residential units are staffed by teams [comprised of] child care staff ["Counselors"] and one coordinator. Group homes [i.e., community facilities] are run by one set of full-time and one set of relief houseparents, as well as a coordinator. In the community project centers [also in the Montreal area], social workers and teachers, supervised by a treatment coordinator, provide day-care and casework services.

"In 1968, SYC [began to adopt] a differential placement and treatment philosophy which was drawn from research and experience with Interpersonal Maturity Level [I-level] Theory, [and "the Conceptual Level Matching Model . . . was added in 1973" (*see endnote 1 regarding the "CL" model*)].

[Thus, as indicated by LeBlanc, Hanna, and Brill (1975),] as a quasi-private organization serving all Anglophone [youths] in the Province of Quebec, the Boys' Farm is concerned with providing treatment/change resources to delinquent boys between the ages of 12 and 18 years [at intake], with a minimal functional IQ of 80. Unlike many programs which have followed the trend toward deinstitutionalization, the Boys' Farm believes that different settings and different techniques are necessary at different times for different youth. To support this philosophy the Boys' Farm combines an assessment program [i.e., service], an institutional program, a group home program, and a community-based project-center program. Through the utilization of [various] treatment approaches (e.g., Transactional Analysis, Reality Therapy), different environments are created within settings. The agency then utilizes these resources, as necessary, to meet the particular characteristics of the individual clientele. Although diverse and complex, this diversity of approach is quite deliberate and planned. (p. 8)

"An important organizational feature of this agency is the degree of responsibility given to its program coordinators and treatment staff. [For instance,] the unit coordinator [of each residential cottage (i.e., of the unit itself) has] the primary responsibility for development and maintenance of specialized environments for youth with different treatment needs. A comprehensive statement of

that [unit's] philosophy and [of] procedures [used] by its team to accomplish this task is required in the unit's Action Plan. Within each unit, individual workers are responsible for working out an Individualized Treatment Plan for each youth for whom they are [primarily] responsible. This is expected to be on file within the first few months after the youth enters a program."

A more detailed and structured overview, including a historical/developmental perspective, was provided earlier by Hanna (1977, pp. 6–14).[2] (Information from other individuals is specified as such.)

"The Boys' Farm is [a] . . . residential and community oriented differential treatment program for adolescent, delinquent youth. Utilized in the development of the individual treatment plan are: Interpersonal Maturity, Conceptual Level, learning problems, and family interaction patterns. Although there is a primary focus in the program on treatment in the community, it is a fundamental belief that a wide range of services is necessary to respond to specific clients' needs and [to] produce positive growth. Thus, within the Boys' Farm program, there are: assessment resources, secure residential treatment facilities, cottage oriented residential facilities, holding resources, group homes, group living resources, and intensive counseling services. This approach to treatment encourages internal movement [that is, from the residential facility to the community] based on specific client needs, with a clear responsibility for change invested in only one agency [and with a community-located caseworker, among others, helping to coordinate this movement from one setting to another].

Historical Context
"The Boys' Farm was established in 1907 for the protective care, guidance, and training of boys. It was originally established in the home of the first Director, and when his facility became inadequate, . . . the community allowed it to purchase the present property in the Laurentian mountains. In the late 1930s, the Boys' Farm was a pioneer in Canada with the establishment of a family-group plan of cottage life with small (30-bed) cottage groups living in separate houses with houseparents as the primary staff.

"In the early 1960s it became apparent that to help the numerous acting-out, retarded, delinquent, and/or emotionally disturbed boys who were being referred to the agency, a more intensive treatment program than just group living was required. In 1966 the Board of Directors [asked] three objective professional groups to assess the Boys' Farm program and to make recommendations on program change. These evaluations resulted in the decision to focus the Boys' Farm resources on the acting-out and/or delinquent boy who was between [ages 12 and 18 at intake], had a minimum functioning IQ in the borderline range, was assessed as non-psychotic, and was able to communicate in the English language."

"The three program evaluations, coupled with consultation with the [Quebec Province] Department of Social Affairs, led to the establishment of a policy that The Boys' Farm would accept, for diagnosis and treatment, all [Anglophone] delinquent and/or acting-out children whom it had the resources to treat" [Wylie, 1972, p. 6].

"In March 1969, Ron Wylie was appointed the Executive Director and the change process began [in earnest]. Mr. Wylie had been in contact with the California Community Project, . . . and developed the program utilizing Interpersonal Maturity as a primary classification approach. During the period 1970 to 1972, six Boys' Farm staff members received training in Differential Treatment Classification from the Center for Training in Differential Treatment [located in Sacramento]. Since 1971 all clients referred to the Boys' Farm have been classified [via Warren's] I-level interview method. Utilizing their I-level classification, clients were placed into homogeneous cottage groups, and, since 1973, with the establishment of the Boys' Farm Community Treatment Program, community treatment workers have had caseloads which match the worker and client characteristics.

"In February 1976, the Minister [i.e., Department] of Social Affairs [of Quebec] requested the Boys' Farm to assume responsibility for the female counterpart of its male referrals. As of June 1976, the Boys' Farm extended its admission criteria to include adolescent females with the same other basic admission focus.

". . . Boys' Farm [provides four main types of direct service]:

1. Assessment Services
"As a Greater Montreal residential treatment resource for Anglophone youth, referrals to the Boys' Farm primarily come from the Juvenile Courts in [that] area, although the agency does accept referrals from other Juvenile Courts in the Province of Quebec and, on occasion, has accepted referrals from out-of-province agencies. [Moreover, and more precisely, the Boys' Farm is Quebec's sole equivalent of a U.S.A. *training school,* for Anglophone's throughout the province, not just in the Montreal area.] Referrals are made to a Joint-Admission Committee of the Ville Marie Social Service Center and the Boys' Farm. The individual who fits the broad agency admissions criteria is then referred for assessment. The primary responsibility of the [Boys' Farm] assessment services . . . is to designate the most appropriate placement resource and to assist the initial treatment program in the development of the first treatment plan."

[As may be deduced, the designated 'best' placement/assignment is either a residential program, a Community Center (also called a "Project Center"), or a group home. At any given time, about 30 percent of SYC's total population is in a residential program, 50 percent are supervised at a Community Center (CC), and 20 percent are in a group home—this, despite the fact that most youths are initially sent to SYC's residential facility. (Right after completing their residential stay, many youths are transferred directly to a CC or a group home—these being longer-term settings than the former. The average length of stay/assignment/supervision for individuals assigned to any one of these respective settings is: residence—11 months; Community Center—15 months; group home—26 months. The median lengths are very similar, and the typical ranges are wide.) Most youths remain in the agency 20 to 28 months—usually having been in two of its settings during that time (either residence and CC or residence and group home). Some 15–20 percent of all youths are in a Community Center or group home 36 months after first being assigned to a DYS residential unit by SYC's Referral Committee (see below). Many of these youths were in all three settings (Girard et al., 1979; Hanna, 1977).]

"The assessment process includes: [a tape-recorded] I-level interview, a second rating of the I-level interview, a Jesness Inventory, a Conceptual Level test, IQ testing [Canadian Lorge-Thorndike; Peabody Picture Vocabulary, if needed], educational testing [Gates-MacGinitie, Reading; Stanford Achievement, Arithmetic], and a family assessment. [Also regularly included is a sentence completion test and the Jesness Behavior Checklist—Self-Appraisal Form.] An Assessment Worker is responsible for developing an Assessment Report, which is then submitted to the Boys' Farm Referral Committee [also called the "Client Movement Committee"] for a placement decision. [At any given point, the Boys' Farm—i.e., SYC's—youth population consists of approximately 40 percent to 45 percent Nx's, 25 percent Na's, 25 percent Cfm's, 5 percent Cfc's and Mp's combined, 1 percent to 2 percent I_2's, and no Se's and Ci's. As to Conceptual Level, about 30 percent are at Stage A, 60 percent at Stage B, and 10 percent at Stage B/C.]"

[Once the Assessment Report is complete, . . . [and] the Child Movement Committee [has sent the youth to either the residence or] the community, a *community* worker ["Caseworker"] is assigned at this point in both cases. He/she will work with the youth right up until . . . discharge from the agency. [Thus, . . . contacts will also occur during the *residential* stay, with the youth, with his/her family, and with cottage line staff as well as supervisory staff.] The community worker plays a major role in decision-making around both the transfer of a youth to a different [SYC] program [e.g., from the residential to the community program] and his/her discharge from the agency. These workers are based in . . . Montreal, at a Community Project Center [and they—plus designated residence staff—regularly play an important role in coordinating efforts across settings and in promoting overall continuity of treatment]. [Girard et al., 1979, pp. 3–4; emphasis added]

"The assessment team is also responsible for assessments whenever a client is transferred from one [part of the] agency to another, yet has remained within a specific program for more than three months. Also, when the individual is discharged from the agency, the . . . team is responsible for duplicating the initial assessment process. [Thus, the team initially] integrates . . . information . . . into a statement of client needs [in order] to facilitate treatment planning; and [it later] acts as an internal research group gathering client data and providing analysis of change trends which will have impact on the development of agency resources."

2. Residential Services

"*Residential Cottage Programs.* The Boys' Farm [renamed Shawbridge Youth Centers, in 1977] operates five cottage-based programs. An integration of I-level and Conceptual Level are the primary placement criteria, with the clear goal of placing these young persons into a community-based program as quickly as possible. Individuals with a low Conceptual Level [i.e., Stage A] are generally first placed in a residential cottage.

"The Cottage program I-level orientations are:

1. a female cottage of mixed subtypes;
2. a male cottage for I_2's, primitive Cfm's, and emotionally disturbed I_4N's [neurotics, i.e., conflicted youths];
3. a homogeneously grouped program for Cfm's;
4. a program based upon the more acting-out and/or manipulative person, including Cfc's, Mp's, Na's, and some Nx's with high Na Jesness Inventory scores; and,
5. a program designed principally for Nx's with some higher maturity Cfm's.

"Regardless of the youth's subtype, the cottage staff person ('Counselor') who is assigned the primary responsibility for the care and treatment of that boy or girl develops an individualized treatment plan for him/her. The counselor does so—though he/she may not fully round out the plan for some time—after meeting with the youth, reviewing his/her Assessment Report and other casefile material, assessing the individual's strengths and weaknesses, perhaps meeting with the family, and discussing the youth with the supervisor and other staff. (A very similar approach is used by the *community* workers, in the case of individuals assigned to them in a Project

Center. See below.) [Reitsma and Brill, 1978a, pp. 13–17]

"There is a maximum of sixteen individuals in each cottage group . . . [and an average population of thirteen]. . . . Staffing patterns vary by program, but generally, each team has a Cottage Coordinator [plus "educational and child care" Counselors] from 8:00 A.M. to midnight, and from midnight to 8:00 A.M. there is a Night Supervisor.

"*Short-Term Security Programs.* The Boys' Farm presently operates a Short-Term Security program for twelve boys [and expects], in 1977, to operate a short-term security program for eight girls. These resources are designed as support services to residential cottages. [The goal] is to provide specific intensity during the treatment process by focusing on particular issues with which the individual appears unable to cope in his normal program. Referrals may be made from the residential cottages, the group homes, and from community caseloads. The maximum length of stay in this program is three months and the programs are primarily reality or peer-group oriented. During the individual's stay in one of these programs the worker who made the referral continues to have principal responsibility and to meet regularly with the client. The staffing for the boys' unit is similar to the Detention and Security programs [see below], while the staff from the girls' unit will be prorated to the population."

"*Security Treatment Program.* In 1977, . . . a Security Treatment Program will be established as part of the Boys' Farm resources. This program will be designed primarily to serve individuals who are unwilling to accept the control structures of an open cottage program. A maximum twelve-month stay in this program is conceptualized, with intensive group and individual therapy occurring during [that time]. When the staff . . . believes the individual can profit from a less secure environment, a decision will be made to refer either to the residential program or to a community-based program. [The Security Treatment Program will] accommodate eight boys and four girls and will have a mixed I-level subtype [orientation].

3. Community Treatment Services
"*Project Centers.* The Boys' Farm Project Centers are located in the center of Montreal. . . . Their primary focus is to provide community-based treatment services to those young persons [living in that area. They offer services as follows]:

1. to a direct referral where the initial placement should be either in the individual's own home or in a foster home;
2. when an individual is placed in . . . open residential cottages a community worker is immediately assigned to work with the family while the individual is in the residential program; and,
3. when the residential program has a cottage-based social service position, the community program becomes involved with the individual when a transfer is made from the residential program to the Greater Montreal area. [Two cottages have such a position.]

"The services provided by the Project Centers include: casework, therapy groups, recreational opportunities, remedial academic opportunities, family counseling/therapy, and vocational counseling. Each individual is assigned a primary worker with a maximum of fifteen clients per worker.

"Utilizing the information from the California Community Treatment Project, individuals are assigned a [community] worker who is matched to their individual I-level characteristics [based on] the treater-matching concepts developed by Palmer. After the client has been assigned to a matched worker, the worker meets with the client, reviews the Assessment Report, and develops a treatment plan. The treatment plan includes goals and objectives in the area of education, employment, family, peers, and housing. [It] is developed utilizing I-level information and attempts to provide a coordinated approach to the individual's positive change.

(From the start, "The I-level classification, no matter how impressive or significant, [was viewed, at the Boys' Farm,] as only a section of a comprehensive differential treatment program; the subtype diagnosis is simply the beginning point for the establishment of differential treatment plans for the individual client. The client's individual treatment plan consists of a number of goals, based on the problems identified by his subtype diagnosis, as well as the various treatment techniques, methods, and suggestions that are both applicable to the treatment setting and within the resources of that setting.") [Wylie, Hanna, and Scully 1971, p. 11; the Warren et al. (1966b) document was referred to as a key source of many such techniques, etc.]

"In addition to the Community Treatment Workers there are six program specialists (three in each of the two Project Centers) who coordinate the recreational, educational, and vocational activities of [those] Centers. Although it is preferred that the individual utilize normal recreational and educational facilities of the community, many [youths] associated with the Project Centers require specialized programs in these areas."

"As of October 1976, . . . approximately [20 percent of all youths newly sent to SYC] were *direct* referrals [subsequent to the Assessment Team's workup] to the community program [i.e., to either a Project Center or a group home]. Approximately [three-fifths] were involved with a community worker [CW] *after* a residential stay. [Another 20 percent, in residence, also had a CW.]" (Emphasis added)

"*Reflection Unit.* As the residential program of the Boys' Farm is [located] approximately fifty miles north of Montreal, it was decided to develop a short-term holding resource in the community. . . . The purpose of [this] Unit is to provide an intensive living resource for an individual who is in crisis. The crisis may be related to his normal living resource or it may be a broader issue with which the persons in his normal living environment feel unable to cope. . . . [The Unit] is staffed with two Child Care Counselors [during the day, etc., and its] maximum number of youth (boys and girls) is eight. Although the Reflection Unit is utilized primarily by community treatment workers, it is also a resource to the Group Home [Branch].

"*Group Home Services.* The Boys' Farm and Training School presently operates six group homes. . . . [They are] designed to serve three primary [groups/] purposes:

1. . . . individuals who require a residential [but *noninstitutional*] placement on their initial referral to Boys' Farm, [yet] who appear able to negotiate their way in the *community* system;

2. . . . individuals who have been in the institutional [i.e., SYC's cottage] program and require a residential reentry point into the community; and,

3. as a continuing residential [but noninstitutional] treatment resource to complete the treatment goals within a community setting [e.g., for youths who begin SYC at home]. (Emphasis added)

"Within these three broad categories there is a long-term and a short-term focus. The Group Home represents a living resource which is partially protected but which results in the individual having to negotiate with the 'real world' and allows [him or her] to develop appropriate response patterns to the pressures of community living. The Group Home staffing pattern for eight boys and girls is based upon a parental model with primary Houseparents. For support and relief there is a part-time Child Care position and a relief Houseparent couple. There is a Social Service Worker/Community Treatment Worker for [every sixteen youths] and a Group Home Coordinator who offers staff supervision and coordination."[3]

[All group homes involved largely homogeneous grouping with respect to I-level subtype or compatible subtypes. For instance, during the mid-to-later 1970s, some homes had a preponderance of Nx youths, and the rest consisted of either Na's and Nx's or else Cfm's and N's. (No Power-Oriented and I_2 youths were placed in any group homes.) This situation reflected the fact that "each group home receive[d] the majority of its cases by transfer from specific residential units"; i.e., it had its own given source, and that source had its particular philosophy of placement. Also, group homes were relatively homogeneous regarding Conceptual level—with over 80 percent of the youths being at Stages B and B/C combined. Stage A's representation was about 15–20 percent, despite its substantially higher representation in the residential cottages [Harvie and Brill, 1978, pp. 48, 183–185, 202–204].

4. *Detention Services*
"In June 1975 the Boys' Farm opened, on an emergency basis, a twelve-bed detention unit

for males. In February 1976 the Boys' Farm was requested by the Minister of Social Affairs to assume the mandate for detention services in the Anglophone network of Greater Montreal.... [By July 1976, two detention units—one for boys, one for girls—were in operation.] ... Detention services are viewed as a short-term holding resource for those youths who do not have appropriate living arrangements. ... Boys' Farm believes that open, community-based detention facilities can be appropriately utilized for many youngsters after a relatively brief assessment period in the secure facility [unit].

"A primary focus during the detention period for most youths is the development of a treatment plan which is integrated with appropriate treatment resources. ... [D]etention unit staff, through observation of youths in their unit, [should add] to the development of the treatment plan. Crisis intervention is another important element of the detention period."

Other Aspects of SYC
Hiring
"The Boys' Farm believes that hiring decisions must be directly related to the specific needs of the position. Therefore, although seniority is an important agency concept, the individual's suitability (which includes matching criteria) is given priority in hiring and transfer decisions."

Organization
"The utilization of I-level as the primary classification technique integrated with a variety of treatment methods requires a specific and clearly conceptualized organizational model. It is important that . . . direct-service staff have clear decision-making responsibility. The Boys' Farm has opted for a decentralized structure as the most appropriate integration of leadership and professional objectives, in the pursuit of a differential treatment program. . . . [Within] the Shawbridge [Residential Cottages] Division and the Community Services Division [, respectively, there are work-groups in which] the work-group leader serves [, in turn,] as a 'Linking Pin' between his work-group and the next work-group up in the agency's organizational structure, . . . [eventually ending with] the agency's Management Committee."

"The Boys' Farm . . . believes in managerial responsibilities which effectively integrate external issues with the internal issues of a specific work-group, providing leadership and direction which supports the work-groups' objectives. . . . [Various committees] provide an integration between work-groups and [implement] a specific process for problem-solving and procedures-development. . . . [Present] on the Management Committee are all directors and supervisors of the agency. They meet regularly to discuss agency program issues, to develop modifications or new programs, [etc.]."

Later Developments
The program, procedures, philosophy, and strategies reviewed above continued beyond the 1970s; this applied to SYC's utilization of differential diagnosis/assignment/intervention in its residential and community components alike. Thus, for example, the agency's use of I-level, Conceptual Level, and staff/youth matching was maintained in those settings through at least 1983, as were related aspects of classification for treatment, and still other expressions of individualized intervention. In addition, those features were implemented to the same degree as before, during that period. In short, SYC continued to draw heavily on I-level strategies and techniques and on CL methods as well; and most staff remained—or, through training, continued to become—knowledgeable about the differential intervention approaches that bore directly on their roles.

As of the early 1980s, SYC's main originators had moved to other agencies (or had retired), and several key clinical and supervisory personnel followed during 1983–1985. Related to these departures and to changes in top management, the agency's *staff training* function—a subunit that emphasized differential intervention—was discontinued in the mid-1980s. Given those developments, given the pressures mentioned below, and in light of further personnel turnover (namely, that of residential and community line staff, among others), I-level methods began to be used less and less during the next few years, in staff interactions with youths and even in their treatment plans for them. This decrease was not limited to new or, in a sense, to "untrained" or differently oriented staff.

Despite this decreased usage of given methods, SYC's *intake assessments* were provided until the later 1980s, and youth-classification information remained part of them. These workups, by the Assessment Services Unit (ASU), continued to facilitate the subsequent production of treatment plans by residential and community staff; that is, they still provided part of an information base that staff could then use, if it wished, to help develop individual, needs-related, "case plans." The ASU's workups were continued even though, as implied earlier, some of the integrated and differentiated information they contained was usually *not* used to the same degree and along much the same lines as before. That is, it was generally not used to the same extent, and in the same way, by line staff who were developing and/or implementing the treatment plans in question.

Eventually, the intake assessments themselves became difficult to produce at the same level of detail and integration as before. This mainly resulted from continuously growing work load pressures, ones that—absent an increase in the ASU's staff size, among other things—required faster processing and disposition of new and transfer cases alike. Directly and indirectly contributing to these pressures was a blend of factors such as the following: First, there had been a broad, societal change in attitude toward crime and delinquency; specifically, there was a noticeably "tougher," less tolerant stance toward many offenders and offenses. In this respect, in various parts of Canada, such attitudes and expressions had—by the mid-1980s—started to "catch up with" the similar, though possibly harsher ones that had crystallized in much of the United States, six to eight years earlier. Second, and more decisive, there had been a related increase in the volume of court processing and in subsequent referrals to SYC.

At any rate, after 1985 various aspects of I-level were implemented less and less, even though, as indicated above, subtype information remained part of the Assessment Service Unit's workups, for instance, its intake assessments. Yet, (1) partly because these workups remained available, and (2) especially because the individual case plans—albeit modified—were still being produced, SYC's long-standing *Case Management Approach (CMA)* continued to have a content basis for existing.

A main defining feature of Shawbridge's CMA was the use of agency structures and procedures that helped support and promote given treatment approaches—ones that, in particular, were designed to help implement needs-centered, *individual case plans*. This applied however complex, differentiated, and/or individualized those plans might be. (As implied, after 1985 certain aspects of SYC's treatment plans were usually less complex and differentiated than before. Also, most plans probably addressed a narrower range of youth needs.)

Case management, in this general sense (and apart from the range of needs it involved), remained present at Shawbridge well beyond the mid-1980s; in fact, it existed through at least the early 1990s. This was the case (1) even though the ASU, as such, was eventually phased out, and (2) *because,* among other reasons, some degree of meaningful treatment planning had nevertheless been maintained. This planning had continued not only in spite of item (1), above, but, of course, despite the fact that it now reflected or was based on a partly different set of information inputs.

In conclusion, even though case management—as defined earlier—continued at SYC, the type and degree of differentiated and individualized *intervention* that was spelled out after the mid-1980s in given treatment plans, and which was subsequently implemented in actual interactions with youths and others, was quite different than that of the 1970s and early to middle 1980s.

Shawbridge Youth Centers is one of four Montreal-area, Anglophone-serving agencies and organizations that were regrouped, in the early 1990s, as the *Batshaw Youth Family Centres.* The other three are: Mount St. Patrick Youth Center, Ville Marie Child and Youth Protection Centre, and Youth Horizons.

St. Francis Boys' Homes of Kansas

The St. Francis Boys' Homes (SFBH) of Kansas are two open, privately operated, residential facilities located near the center of that state, some 30 miles apart. The Salina Home is a few miles from the city of that name (pop. 42,000 in 1980 and 43,000 in 1990), and the Ellsworth Home is at the outskirts of Ellsworth (pop. 2,000 in 1980 and in 1990). Each home mainly serves adjudicated delinquents, though some nonadjudicated, behaviorally problemmed, or otherwise troubled youths are accepted as well. As described below, these homes provide an individualized approach and, starting in the late 1970s, their program has drawn heavily from both the Warren I-level classification system and the principles as well as methods of worker/youth matching described in Chapter 11. The first St. Francis Home—Ellsworth—opened in 1945; Salina began in the 1950s. Both homes operate in essentially the same way. (St. Francis Boys' Homes operates a third residential facility—at Lake Placid, in New York State—and a "wilderness-type" program for boys and girls, in Kansas itself.[4])

Most Ellsworth and Salina youths have a court order and were referred by probation, social agencies, parents, guardians, or others, such as ministers. Each home is licensed to serve up to 26 youths at a time, its occupancy rate averages 95 percent, and it is accredited as a psychiatric facility for children and adolescents by the Joint Commission on Accreditation of Hospitals (SFBH, 1979, p. 2).[5] Though intake has been nationwide since the 1950s, the preponderance of referrals—some two-thirds of whom are accepted and become residents—come from Kansas, and most of the rest are from nearby states. Boys from all socioeconomic, regional, cultural, racial, and religious backgrounds are accepted.

At intake, all youths are somewhere between school grades 7 and 12. They are no more than two years behind academically, and, thus, are almost always between ages 11 and 18. In addition, they (1) have scored 85 or above on a recent, standardized IQ test; (2) exhibit no more than "mild to moderate emotional disturbance"; (3) do not have a "primary diagnosis of organicity or specific learning disability"; and (4) express a willingness to participate in the program. Though the youths are not accepted for less than a full school year (nine months), they often remain for an entire calendar year and not infrequently for six months longer (SFBH, 1979; SFBH Operating Manual, 1981/1982).

St. Francis staff and administrators describe their most common—modal—youths as follows:

Our boys upon entrance are typically (a) low in self-regard and so are self-defeating; (b) often insufficiently reared and have been acting with little constraint; (c) father-haters or at least passively against authority; (d) self-centered despite their low self-image, not belong-ing, and . . . mediocre in accomplishment; (e) only weakly controlled by self-direction or future plans; and (f) have been caught in illegal behavior several times and have been unresponsive. But those selected have assets, such as being concerned, still have resilience, some conscience, and [are] able to get along in public school" (SFBH, 1979, p. 12).

Regarding SFBH's correctional tenets, its operating principles, and its general goals:

The boys are not here for punishment. We suppress only that behavior which is unlawful; instead, we accentuate assets as a prominent method. . . . Our goal is to change the boy in such a way that his self-control is buttressed, he has an increasing identification and empathy with authority, and he solves his problems by talking them out instead of attempting to solve them by delinquent behavior.[6] We want the boy to understand and be proud of his own strengths and talents. . . . We want [him] to expect change for the better in himself and to welcome self-understanding from the other boys, staff members, and from objective tests. We lead him to plan and work for his future . . . through regular individual and group counseling and guidance [see below]. We want to [further] develop his conscience"[7] (SFBH, 1979, pp. 11–12).

To determine if a referred youth can benefit from the program and should be accepted, an evaluation committee reviews (1) recent social history material; (2) the most recent psychological assessment that includes a standardized intelligence test and either projective techniques/tests and/or a personality-profile questionnaire; (3) scholastic aptitude and achievement tests; (4) vocational and/or other interest tests; (5) other, specialized tests, for example, ones relating to physical and health factors; and (6) the youth's self-descriptions.[8] The individual's overall physical health history and status is also reviewed. Once the committee—a psychiatrist, clinical psychologist, social workers, residence directors, home treatment coordinators, and others—recommends that, say, a given boy be accepted (admitted), the executive director of St. Francis Boys' Homes makes the final decision, one way or the other.[9]

"Once admitted, [the] boys are classified by I-level and matched with a Primary Counselor [see below] and with a weekly therapy group" (Burnett, 1982). Within two weeks after residency begins, a battery of standard psychological tests is administered, as are tests of audio-visual and speech-language functioning. Together with the information already reviewed by the evaluation committee prior to admission and with early observations made at the home, this material is then used to develop an initial treatment plan, one whose main goal is to "set out the broad directions of treatment, [and] a basic treatment strategy." During the next two weeks a more detailed treatment plan is developed. This plan incorporates direct staffing inputs, and/or other forms of input, from a psychologist, psychiatrist, home treatment coordinator, resident director, and primary counselor, and it is subsequently overseen by the latter individual—being reviewed at least quarterly, and revised as needed (Force, 1986; SFBH Operating Manual, 1981/1982). The main treatment modality (or modalities) to be used or emphasized, if possible, is specified in this plan, subject to later modification. It (or they) is a function of the youth's overall personality and situation, his "fundamental unmet needs," and his I-level and subtype. Examples of possible modalities, general approaches, or broad techniques are "reality therapy, . . . transactional analysis, . . . supportive therapy, . . . intentional role playing, . . . Gestalt therapy, . . . [and] reflective exploratory therapy." Also included is "modification of . . . behavior [via verbal reinforcement/] recognition" (SFBH Operating Manual, 1981/1982).

The Ellsworth and Salina facilities are large, open (i.e., nonsecure), two-story, brick, colonial-style buildings that sleep two youths per room. These "living centers" are situated, respectively, on 190 and 40 acres owned by SFBH. Near each center is an activities center, a chapel, and a horse barn and corral. The Ellsworth activity center includes, for instance, a gymnasium, hobby shop, woodcraft shop, and dark room.

Upon entering the program, each boy has restricted privileges—usually for about a month—and is called a *Supervised Boy.* His next step forward is *Novice Membership,* and his third step—which involves "the highest level of privilege and responsibility"—is that of *Membership.* (Visits from parents/guardians are not encouraged during the first month; after that, visits by appointment are encouraged.)

Regarding the typical range of activities, youths

participat[e] in normal community life under careful supervision. . . . [They] attend local public schools, . . . mingle with local young people, play on local athletic teams, and date local girls. During summer vacations and sometimes after school, [they] may work in town or on neighboring farms.[10] [They] share in the necessary routine maintenance of the buildings and grounds. . . . Daily chores and work projects, such as helping with construction, making improvements on the baseball field, and working around the horse corral, are typically boy's work at St. Francis." During the boy's [stay,] "there are camping trips, public school functions, special interest trips, roller skating, bowling, swimming, . . . and TV. . . . We seek cultural enrichment and give-and-take in personal relationships. [Also, the youths attend religious services.[11]] (SFBH, 1979, pp. 2, 11)

These activities are apart from the youths' participation in weekly group counseling, in individual counseling or therapy, and so on.

Each home is directly staffed and supervised by a resident director, a home treatment coordinator (HTC), a home social worker (HSW), and several home counselors. The HTC, HSW, and others (such as specified home counselors) comprise the given home's treatment team.[12] The HSW, besides being the liaison between boys and their courts, social agencies, parents, schools, and others, may lead or co-lead the weekly group counseling and may also provide individual counseling. In addition, the HSW may conduct intensive weekend workshops for boys and their parents, ones that focus on communication and role-related issues (St. Francis Annual Report, 1981, p. 7; SFBH, 1979, 1981). The resident director of each home is a priest of the Episcopal Church.

"Individualized treatment (a hallmark of the St. Francis program) is further emphasized [and the Treatment Plan's implementation is made more realistic] by the assignment of boys to Primary Counselors"—individuals who also play the above-mentioned role of home counselor. That is, together with his *general* care-and-supervision duties, which are carried out with respect to all youths, the *home counselor* is assigned up to four of those individuals to whom he provides "personal counseling" and for whom he is considered the *primary counselor*. (This counseling is in addition to any that the home social worker may provide. Like, or together with, the HSW, a home counselor may lead or co-lead the earlier-mentioned group counseling sessions [SFBH Annual Report, 1981, p. 5; SFBH Operating Manual, 1981/1982].) "The Primary Counselor does most of the implementing of the Treatment Plan for his counselees," and, as part of that responsibility, he may also counsel the youths' parents. Based on the weekly treatment team meetings, and/or the quarterly progress reviews, the primary counselor updates his counselees' treatment plan and modifies it as needed (SFBH Operating Manual, 1981/1982).[13]

Each home's treatment team is assisted by additional staff, housed at the St. Francis Boys' Homes administrative office (its national headquarters), located in Salina. These individuals—called the clinical staff—are a clinical coordinator, psychiatrist, clinical psychologist, supervising social workers, and others (e.g., dietician). The psychiatrist, for instance, serves as the medical director, helps select referrals, writes evaluations, reviews and certifies treatment plans, helps train home counselors in their role of primary counselor, provides individual therapy to referred boys, and so on. The clinical psychologist provides assessment reports and other information relating to referrals, diagnosis, treatment, and so forth, to the evaluation team, the treatment team, and others. Like the home social worker and supervising social workers, the psychologist may also provide individualized counseling/therapy.

Following are some common interactions and involvements with the community that were not mentioned earlier. (1) "There is liaison with churches and Alcoholics Anonymous, [plus] frequent informal interchange with area residents" regarding the youths' recreational, visiting, and shopping activities, and/or concerning part-time job opportunities. (2) A designated staff member from each home has scheduled, weekly contact with local school personnel; he or she also interacts with those individuals by phone, as needed. If medical, dental, optical, hearing, speech, vocational,

educational, and/or other needs are identified that cannot be adequately met by St. Francis staff, a referral is made to a "local, professionally sanctioned and/or accredited facility," agency, or individual (SFBH Operating Manual, 1981/1982).

In addition, shortly before the youth completes his program, "the Home Social Worker [develops] and implements, with the appropriate community agency [e.g., Probation or Social Services], a follow-up plan [that also has input from] the Treatment Team, including Clinical staff, and [that reflects] the youth's problem, the available resources in [his] community, and the family situation. If [the youth should not return] to his family, or if he has no family available, a plan for his continued care will be designed and implemented, hopefully employing facilities available in [his] community." (Upon completing the program, youths often do return home. Some, however, go to a foster home, to an independent living situation combined with employment, to college or trade school, or to the military. In this regard, St. Francis has operated several licensed foster homes in Kansas [SFBH, 1975, 1979].)

Within 60 days from release, the social work supervisor (1) contacts the youth's "guardian and the person(s) who has referred [him]," (2) indicates to those individuals that "St. Francis Boys' Homes wish[es] to maintain interest [in] the boy," and (3) offers "to be of further service," for example, in terms of continuing to meet for family counseling. "Though our primary leverage is directly with the boy while he is in the [resident] population, an increasing effort is being expended in continuity of aftercare" (SFBH Operating Manual, 1981/1982).

Starting in 1977, St. Francis' staff received training and consultation in the I-level system.[14] This process, which gradually phased in differing staff members, involved I-levels' basic concepts, interviewing, classification by subtype, and treatment strategies. Training was also received in selecting appropriate workers for intensive individualized intervention, and in matching those individuals with given types of youth. Much of this training was received from I-level trainers and consultants who, themselves, had been trained at the California Youth Authority's Center for Training in Differential Treatment and who had subsequently been certified by the

International Differential Treatment Association (IDTA) to conduct the specified types of training.[15] (See endnote 59 regarding IDTA.)

By 1980–1981, most of this training was completed for all relevant staff, and the St. Francis operation at Ellsworth and Salina had been modified to reflect or incorporate the given perspectives on, the elements of, and the particular approaches to, differential and individualized intervention.[16] (In 1981–1982, training was also received in the Conceptual Level system—one that was mainly used to help determine the type and degree of *program structure* that would likely be most helpful to given types of youth [Hunt and Hardt, 1965].) The I-level system was used, for example, "in [determining] primary counselor assignment;[17] in group therapy assignment; in selection of roommates; . . . by the social worker in briefing the school as to the probable reaction of the [youth] to his school environment; . . . in setting therapy and recreational goals for each resident; and as partial criteria for release planning" (Hebison, 1986, pp. 25–26; Hebison and Gustitus, 1982).

SFBH of Kansas still exists—not only having added *on-grounds schooling,* but operating and largely relying on the original concepts, structures, procedures, and philosophy. Included are I-level classification, the home treatment team, the primary counselor model, worker/youth matching, given strategies and techniques, a familylike atmosphere, and so on. This especially applies at Ellsworth, whereas the Salina home now emphasizes a shorter-term, more intensive, more individual counseling/therapy approach.

Mainly to save time, the Jesness Inventory has been substituted for the interview method—at intake—as the means of determining I-level and subtype. However, a standard I-level interview is conducted soon afterward if questions arise regarding the JI classification; it may (also) be conducted at a later point if various indicators suggest a new or different level/subtype exists or is emerging. Conceptual Level (CL) information is also obtained at intake, to indirectly support or otherwise address the I-level classification and—as before—to help determine the type and degree of program structure most appropriate for the youth.

Not unrelated to SFBH's more than 25 years of program continuity is the fact that some of the its original, leading clinical and supervisory staff (e.g., Force, Gustitus, and Rathbun) are still present, and that they either remain in or have advanced to key managerial/administrative positions.

Baltimore Differential Treatment Program

In the early 1970s, the Maryland Department of Juvenile Services developed a community-based program that, by design, utilized several major features of the California Community Treatment Project. Among them were low caseloads, intensive and extensive intervention, and differential intervention. This program was developed

1. as part of Maryland's participation in the federal "High Impact Anti-Crime Program" that began in 1972, as a way to address the growing problem of burglary and "stranger-to-stranger" crime— (together called *impact* or *high impact* offenses)—in large cities;
2. to reduce that state's utilization of waiver as well as institutionalization of juvenile offenders; and
3. in response to, and based upon, a recommendation by the John Howard Association that the department "adopt a system of differential diagnosis and treatment," such as that used in California's CTP.

Baltimore was one of eight American cities chosen by the Law Enforcement Assistance Administration (LEAA) to receive demonstration funds under (1), above.[18]

Maryland's program was to be a three-year effort designed to test the feasibility and practicality of working with serious male offenders in a community rather than institutional setting, and of doing so without using waivers to the adult correctional system. Feasibility/practicality was to include not only community acceptance and cost-reasonableness; instead, it also implied operational and organizational "do-ability," and a reduction in institutional commitments as well.[19] Organizationally, the new program was to be an integral part of the Baltimore Probation Department, and it was to be created or developed by modifying and converting already existing departmental operations and structures, as needed. The program was named the Baltimore City Intensive Probation

Project (IPP), or, simply, the "Community Treatment Project." Its operations began in September 1973, and it reached full capacity in early 1975.

In October 1976, by which time the project's feasibility and general practicality had been satisfactorily demonstrated,[20] the following occurred. The Intensive Probation Project's "funding was completely absorbed by the State, [and the program was at that point] integrated by the Baltimore Regional [Probation] Office"—in which it thereafter operated, in essentially the same manner as during September 1973 to September 1976, as a "specialized division within the Juvenile Services framework in Baltimore city" (Waldman, 1980, p. 16).[21] At the same time, this nominally new but substantively already existing operation became more commonly known as the Differential Treatment Program (DTP). During and after DTP's (i.e., IPP's) demonstration phase, and after it was incorporated into the regional office, the program involved three organizationally separate units, each with its own supervisor and six line workers (probation officers). This unit structure corresponded to that of California's CTP.

In the third year of its LEAA-funded demonstration phase, the project's director provided the following overview and description (Chesley, 1976, p. 4), one whose applicability continued even after that phase ended:

> The basic concept of this program is to match . . . juvenile impact offenders [burglary, robbery, assault, etc.] with an appropriate treatment program and [with] Probation Officers whose personal characteristics are suitable for the selected types of youth. The Probation Officer ["Juvenile Counselor"] has a caseload from 12 to 15 [maximum of 20]. A basic element of the classification of youth is the use of the Interpersonal Maturity scale (I-level scale). Additional testing (Jesness Inventory) is employed as a supplementary measure. Treatment techniques include intensive, differential supervision, family-centered counseling, group and/or individual counseling, the use of residential facilities, and [a] new-career intern project (Port of Baltimore Sea School). . . .
>
> At full capacity, approximately 200 juvenile impact offenders are being served by the Program.[22] These young-

sters [have been] adjudicated delinquent [as a result of] impact offenses, and they are screened [on that basis] by the project prior to Court disposition. At the disposition hearing, Program staff recommend placement on Intensive Probation as an alternative to the normal sanctions imposed by the Court (i.e., traditional probation, institutionalization). . . .

(Cases [were] referred from a number of sources, including the judiciary, probation or aftercare workers, the court medical office, and the assignment unit. . . . Referrals [were] discouraged for those children whose primary problems [were] drug or alcohol abuse,[23] mental retardation, or children already on aftercare supervision [since the latter may not have involved impact offenses, as defined]. However, the latter [that is, aftercare cases, when referred] were accepted quite frequently, as 16.2% [of all project youths had previously] been institutionalized prior to acceptance in [the program, for impact offenses]. Referral sources understood the program to be "a final community alternative," i.e., an alternative to institutionalization for many or most non-aftercare youths [Waldman, 1980, pp. 17, 26].)

Participation in the program is voluntary on the part of the youth. This is done to assure that [his] rights are protected. A youth who comes into the Project must agree to a term of probation that may be longer than he would receive if he were placed on traditional probation by the Court [, and sometimes longer than if he were to be institutionalized]. No youth is encouraged [to enter] the Program if he or his parents object, because both parties are an integral part of the treatment process (Chesley, 1976, p. 4).

All project youths were 14 to 18 years old at intake, with the average being 16.3 and almost everyone being 15 to 17. More than 90 percent had an instant offense of either assault (32%), breaking and entering (attempted or actual burglary) (48%), or robbery (11%), with most others involving purse snatch (8%). Twenty-seven percent had one or two prior offenses and 18% had three or more; for the rest (55%), the instant offense was a first, but serious, one. As indicated, one of every six youths had at least one institutional commitment prior to entering the program. Two-thirds of all youths were classified as conflicted (Na or Nx), and most others were considered passive-conformists (Cfm's) (Sasfy, 1975; Waldman, 1977, 1979, 1980).

In 1977, Waldman (pp. 4–5) provided several other details regarding the program:

> Subsequent to the development of a differential treatment plan for the client, [various] differential treatment techniques, such as group home placement, employment, individual, group, and family counseling [as already mentioned], recreational activities, and tutoring, are employed by the Juvenile Counselor to achieve specific client objectives.

(Also available are "foster care and shelter care." However, "the option of providing therapeutic detention without the youth having to return to the Court system"—as in California's CTP and at the Shawbridge Youth Centers—is not available (Chesley, 1976, pp. 4–5). Nor does the project have its own schoolteacher and classrooms, on-site or otherwise.) "Additional services, such as the provision of clothing, . . . medical, eye, and dental examinations, are offered to *all* clients. [Similarly,] cultural and recreational activities, such as sports, dances, outings, and plays, have been developed to offer [all youths] a variety of experiences" (Waldman, 1977; emphasis added).

(Regarding the earlier-mentioned features, the following might be noted. *Individualized* intervention is expressed in the *particular mix* of program elements/activities that is used with the given youth, a mix that may seldom be found with any other youth. Also, for any given individual, the mix that is initially used may, and often does, vary through time, depending on his changing needs and circumstances. As such, it reflects the factor of flexibility (Chapter 15), which is integral to the maintenance of individualization. *Differential* intervention—which involves the differing approaches used with differing *types* of youth—was expressed, for example, in the types (and combinations) of approaches as well as techniques that were *more likely* to be used with some youth subtypes than with others (e.g., "small group activities" with passive-conformists, and "one-to-one discussions" with the conflicted).[24]

Coexisting with this individualization and differentiation was the fact that "some activities were made available to *all* clients," regardless of their subtype and further individuality. "These included baseball and basketball teams, trips to amusement parks and the Smithsonian [Institution, in nearby Washington, D.C. . . . Any youth could also] obtain private tutoring, . . . and enjoy individual activities with [his] counselor, such as horseback riding or trips" (Waldman, 1980, pp. 18, 24–25; emphasis added).

Also, "The Juvenile Counselor [is] on call 24 hours and is available to his probationers and contacts [them] at such times (evenings and weekends), with such frequency (daily if needed), and in such places (streets, home) as may be required. In addition, he ensures that his probationers observe the conditions of their probation . . . [and] if additional services are needed outside the Program, he refers his clients to the appropriate community agencies. [Regarding referrals and nonreferrals combined, staff] had contact with almost 50 different public and private health and welfare agencies" [between October 1974 and September 1976] (Waldman, 1977, pp. 5, 22).

During the demonstration phase, the average number of monthly contacts was approximately eight. Of these, 4.2 (53%) were "in-person" (with the youth), 2.2 (28%) were "with the family" (the youth almost always being present), and the remaining 1.5 (19%) were "collateral." These figures exclude diagnostic interviews, intake investigations, phone contacts, brief meetings/encounters on the street, "counts of group participation," and office drop-ins initiated by the youth, such as for recreational purposes (Waldman, 1977, pp. 22–25).

> The youth remain in the program for approximately two years. Twenty-two Juvenile Counselors and supervisory staff have been trained in the I-level methodology, with its various treatment methods; classification techniques are utilized, [together] with the necessary technical assistance and [with] monitoring to ensure the integrity of the Program.[25] A Juvenile Counselor whose sensitivity, talents, and interests are compatible [with a given type of youth, i.e., I-level subtype] is matched to [that type of] youth, and a treatment strategy plan is developed . . .

that reflects the youth's overall level of maturity, responses to others, self-image, and various unique features of his personal life-situation.[26] [I-level classification was derived via a taped, second-rated, interview conducted by Project staff. . . . Though that treatment plan] is developed for a two-year period, [it is, as indicated and implied above, revised and refined when necessary and possible] (Waldman, 1977, p. 4).

As also indicated, each of Baltimore DTP's units has a counseling supervisor, one lead worker (a rotating assistant supervisor), and five juvenile counselors. It also has a project director, and consultants are available to all units for use in connection with cases as well as for ongoing, in-service training. Of DTP's treatment staff, "fourteen are matched [to the youths, and the remaining ones] have the propensity to be matched."[27] Finally, two staff members also serve as diagnosticians (Chesley, 1976, p. 5; Waldman, 1977, pp. 5–6).

Though the preceding descriptions focused on the early to middle 1970s, the Differential Treatment Program's structure, procedures, and overall approach remained essentially unchanged during 1977–1987. This was the case even though DTP steadily refined its intervention strategies in order to reflect its past successes and to avoid the questionable or irrelevant (Dolina, 1995; this individual was a DTP supervisor and intake coordinator during the latter period).

Thus, for example, the program still had three organizational units, each with one supervisor and six counselors. Each intake worker—a counselor who also carried cases—still prepared an integrated, albeit provisional, intervention plan. This was basically a detailed treatment framework that addressed needs and issues identified during the taped, diagnostic intake interview. This procedure was applied to all youths who—tentatively—seemed appropriate for the program, based on a brief, preliminary screening. The I-level aspect of this often-lengthy interview was soon second-rated by the youth's assigned counselor; and, over the next few to several months—the length depending on the youth—the provisional plan was adjusted, as needed, to reflect that worker's direct experience with the individual. The courts consistently supported DTP, largely because they believed its

staff understood the cases thoroughly, had realistic plans for them, had many resources with which to implement those plans, and would modify their approach as needed. Besides formal case conferences regarding each youth, the counselor prepared a detailed, quarterly report concerning status and progress, issues, problems, case dynamics, and future goals and directions. Youths continued to be worked with for an average of two years, sometimes through several personal/social crises.

Regarding the youths collectively, DTP's intervention strategies and techniques (STs) continued to vary a great deal from (A) one I-level *subtype* to the next, and especially from the passive-conformist to the conflicted to certain rare types. (Power-oriented youths continued to be uncommon.) This applied not just to the individual STs, that is, the separate STs, that were used (since many of the same STs were used with many or even most subtypes), but, especially, to their pattern, degree, and manner of usage, for example, their particular combinations, intensities, and/or sequences.

Strategies and techniques also varied (B) within any given subtype, depending partly on the youth's more *individual features, needs, and circumstances*. This "Type B" variation often included, but was almost always more detailed and specific than, yet another one: "Type C." The latter type—in a sense, a mid-level variation—was associated with certain major groupings of individuals (called "*subgroups*") that were found within specified I-level subtypes; these subgroups had been described in the California experiment's literature. (See, for example, the "domination-exploitation resister," the "markedly inadequate-frightened," and the "support-approval seeker" subgroups within the overall passive-conformist subtype. Similarly, see the "pro-delinquent identifier" and the "reactive delinquent identifier" within the overall delinquent-identifier subtype [Palmer, 1971b, 1971d, 1971e]).

Regarding *individuals,* but also applying to any youth subtype and youth subgroup, the program elements and techniques that were used often varied through *time*. For instance, though a counselor might, say, begin by emphasizing one-to-one, pragmatically oriented discussions, he or she might (depending on the youth's reactions and progress) later emphasize group-centered approaches. Or, the counselor might start with group meetings/activities and increasingly introduce individual discussions and counseling. Still regarding individual youths, certain types of change were more likely to occur with some youth subtypes/subgroups than with others; but, in any event, these and the earlier-mentioned, planned or semi-planned changes through time reflected the program's flexibility—a key aspect, or at least a major dimension, of individualization. In DTP, flexibility also existed during and after crises, that is, in largely unplanned contexts.

Throughout 1977–1987, Baltimore's program continued to regularly use the California experiment's concepts and methods of staff/youth matching; this also included the hiring, in the first place, of only those individuals who seemed well suited for implementing long-term intensive and/or extensive intervention, in particular (Chapter 11). Regarding the latter point, DTP supervisors successfully resisted external pressures to accept (hire), as program counselors, persons who—though skilled in various important ways—would probably not be suited as counselors in the context of *DTP,* even despite their interest in the program. (Also, the department had sometimes wished to, or needed to, soon place these and/or other individuals *somewhere,* regardless of the latters' interest or relative lack thereof.)

The following development was largely independent of hiring and matching per se, and its utility extended beyond those processes, tasks, and issues. Because DTP's funding for outside training and consultation had dried up when the 1973–1976 LEAA grant ended, the program developed and maintained its own staff-training capacity—implemented, for example, by given supervisors. This training focused mainly on diagnostic issues, treatment planning, and intervention strategies/techniques.

Finally, beginning in the later 1970s, intake was no longer limited to individuals with high-impact offenses, and to males. Instead, any youth who—based on the diagnostic workup—seemed likely, or certainly able, to profit considerably from the program could be recommended to the courts for acceptance. (Also see point 2, below.) However, DTP seldom recommended (and received) "lightweights"—youths who appeared to need relatively little correctional intervention from

any source, or who, at any rate, could probably profit just as much from a less intensive/extensive program than DTP. (This policy, coincidentally, helped to avoid or greatly reduce one major form or aspect of "net widening.") In any event, each DTP caseload typically contained individuals who—collectively—had a wide range of delinquent involvement (e.g., total number of offenses), of severity levels with respect to those offenses, and of personal and/or social problems, difficulties, and needs. All in all, the program's 1977–1987 population, like that of the earlier years, thus consisted of moderately serious to serious offenders.

Youths with conspicuously poor and extremely poor *prognoses,* such as those with high and very high likelihoods of near-future serious offending, and/or of being minimally responsive, were not often recommended for the program. As a result, they—especially the more extreme individuals—comprised only a modest portion of the total caseload. This policy reflected the idea of applying the bulk of DTP's knowledge, skills, and overall resources to youths with whom it seemed likely, or certainly able, to (1) make a considerable positive difference, and to (2) make substantially *more* difference than other available programs, including the institutional. (It is not known if this policy, which applied from the later 1970s, also existed in the earlier years.)

Between 1987 and 1989 the number of available program options in Baltimore's DTP was steadily decreased, even though the program's basic concepts and approaches were maintained where possible. This phasing-out—completed in early 1989—mainly reflected given department administrators' declining interest in differential and individualized intervention, and, in the case of newer administrators, their greater relative interest in other approaches and/or their concern with different issues.

New York City Differential Treatment Unit

Before describing the next main program (Ormsby Village), it might be mentioned that another large East Coast city—New York—operated an intensive, community-based program in the early 1970s. This program or operation, called the Differential Treatment Unit (DTU), existed within the New York City Office of Probation (NYCOP); it was administered by NYCOP's Family East Branch. As described by Brice (1976, pp. 13–16), DTU

> ran from May, 1972 through December, 1975. . . . ["To justify" this program's creation, structure, and type of operation, it was agreed, at the outset, to accept] only the most difficult children, i.e., only those who had been rejected by two or more placement facilities. In other words, the DTU would work intensively in lieu of placement, [with] children on probation. . . . The Unit obtained the cooperation of judges, law guardians, and probation administrators [in this and related matters]

(The family court, for example, specifically committed each youth to the program for "two years in lieu of placement within a Training School"—two years thus being the maximum possible stay in the program, as well.) Of DTU's youths, all of whom were males, about 50 percent turned out to be I_3's—mainly Cfm's and Cfc's—and the other half were I_4's—Na's and Nx's.

As will be clear from the following, this community-based operation was much smaller than Baltimore's; in addition, details regarding its nature are few and sketchy. Nevertheless, it will be useful to briefly review what information *is* available and to describe certain major difficulties that arose. Such difficulties or problems could arise elsewhere, under similar conditions—though, to be sure, not *every* relevant "condition" that existed in the New York operation is known. One thing that is known is that—by most 1970s standards—the program's youths were unusually difficult to work with and their offense histories were particularly severe. Many or most had literally committed a murder prior to entering DTU. At any rate, the difficulties in question were experienced and observed by the individual (Brice) who was DTU's supervisor throughout its relatively brief existence. (All quotations in this section are from Brice [1976].)

In January 1972, a supervisor in NYCOP's Family East Branch was sent to CTDT—the Center for Training in Differential Treatment (Sacramento)—for five weeks of training in the I-level system and in its related treatment strategies for adolescent offenders. Soon after she returned to New York, the Office of Probation decided to utilize her

new information and experiences by provisionally establishing a small DTU operation that she would head. This operation, or Unit, would employ unusually intensive intervention (see, e.g., caseload size, below) with some of NYCOP's most difficult and/or troubled delinquents. (As it turned out, most youths were in the program between 15 and 20 months.) Shortly after that decision was made, the to-be-established Unit—namely, DTU—was staffed.

> [With the cooperation of NYCOP's Director of Training, and of other agency personnel,] the staff . . . was selected from volunteers throughout the agency. After considerable [telephone] dialogue [between the already named DTU supervisor, i.e., the recent CTDT trainee, and the CTDT staff, about the pool of] volunteers, five people were selected from various branch offices. [This group of five, together with the supervisor, then became DTU's complete operational unit.]

Next, the supervisor began to provide these five line staff with essentially all their training in differential intervention—in particular, their training regarding the youth subtypes to which they had been assigned, on a best-match basis. In this capacity, she thus saw herself as a "trainer." At the same time, the supervisor felt it necessary to advance and consolidate her own knowledge in differential intervention; in this respect she considered herself still a "trainee." Throughout this period, she also made all final decisions regarding each youth's I-level and subtype.

To assist this newly established Unit, one which quickly began to supervise cases, the following was done from the start: "Ongoing [, gratis] consultation was provided [to the supervisor] by the Training Center in California, through telephone calls, letters, exchanges of written material, and the interchange of tapes." Additional consultation was provided by CTDT's director, who, by the early 1970s, was often available in New York State itself. Underlying much of this consultation—particularly its large amount and its specific content—were such factors or considerations as the following:

> In spite of the trainer's [supervisor's] knowledge, skills, and experience, five

weeks of intensive training [at CTDT had been] inadequate to absorb all the complex differential program elements. [Also,] because the agency had not sent additional person[s] to the [CTDT] training [both in 1972 and later,] the supervisor [trainer] did not have the advantage of feedback and differing perspectives and interpretation [from others at her work site. In any event, she had to, as indicated,] assume two roles, that of trainee as well as trainer.

Those factors were largely, but not entirely, independent of the following situation, one that involved *program features* as such:

Resources such as short-term detention, foster homes, group homes, [and] meaningful alternative school programs were not available to the probationers as an ongoing service [—a situation that contrasted with what had existed in Sacramento CTP. In addition, the number of youths per caseload was extremely small, that is, three to five (see below regarding implications, for staff, of the latter)].

In summarizing the "areas that [detracted] from the overall effectiveness of the program," that is, areas other than that of certain unavailable program features, three factors were mentioned:

1. By accepting, for probation community treatment, only those youths who had been turned down by at least two placement facilities, worker satisfaction and payoff were, from the beginning, extremely low. It would [have been] far more desirable to provide a mixture of less difficult and more difficult cases. . . .
2. The worker caseload of *3 to 5* proved to be far too small. . . . [This small] number of cases, and the subsequent intensity of involvement [with them, meant that even one or two] "failures" becam[e] extremely personal issues for the workers. A higher caseload size in this situation is recommended. (Emphasis added)

Together, factors 1 and 2, above, "resulted in [line staffs' eventually] being 'burned out,' 'turned off,' and [often] not wanting to continue."

3. [Especially under the above conditions, and prior to such burnout,] the availability of at least one other differential treatment supervisor [in the agency, or of an equivalent individual with closely related experiences] would have been invaluable not only for support but for [case-related as well as supervision-related] input from another perspective. . . .

[At any rate,] in order to maximize effectiveness, [a] supervisor/trainer needs [certain types of professional] outlets [e.g., in order to help handle] the pressures and anxieties that build up. [This is despite the *rewarding* experiences that occur, such as (1) helping to] free [line staff, emotionally and otherwise,] to work more effectively with their clients, [(2) observing clients] improve . . . in their ability to relate to adults in a less threatening fashion, [and (3) seeing an apparent decrease in] the average number of arrests [from the pre-referral period to that of program supervision].

All in all, burnout was probably the principal and decisive factor underlying the program's closure, and its having ended when it did: Though the New York City Office of Probation preferred that DTU not close down, but instead continue if possible (presumably in much the same way), all line staff felt drained and wished to "move on" to different types of assignments. They did not wish to continue working mainly, let alone exclusively, with the unusually difficult types of youth in question, at least—and, in any event, especially—under earlier-mentioned conditions. These included, and probably went beyond, the material-resource limitations that had existed from the start.

For similar reasons (e.g., overall drain; particular external limitations), and because of related ones, the DTU supervisor, who had received her requested transfer to a different NYCOP location as the program ended, did not wish to develop and operate a similar intensive DTU program elsewhere in the city. This was despite the Office of Probation's willingness to support such a program, to make her its supervisor, and to obtain fresh and equally talented staff for it—all as an alternative or heir to the 1972–1975 undertaking.

Ormsby Village Treatment Center

Ormsby Village Treatment Center (OVTC) is a county facility for males and females, located at the outskirts of Louisville, Kentucky, and operated under the auspices of that city's Metropolitan Social Services Department (MSSD).[28] Though it was a relatively traditional institution since its inception in the early 1920s, Ormsby Village acquired a new type of program in the late 1960s, soon after a new superintendent had been hired.[29] The new program is a "combination of the Highfields New Jersey system of Guided Group Interaction and the California [I-level] approach." (Scott and Hissong, 1973, p. 42; except as specified, all quotations in this section are from pp. 42–51 of this reference). The new superintendent had decided to use I-level and its related, differential intervention strategies as a result of attending the Center for Training in Differential Treatment, in Sacramento, in May 1968.[30]

OVTC, also called "the campus" or "Village," consists of eight open cottages and two small security units or areas. It is situated on 400 acres (a former estate that was sold to the county), and it also contains classrooms, a recreation center, a gymnasium, modest vocational training facilities, a chapel, a staff training center, and other general- or special-purpose buildings, such as a small medical/dental clinic (whose upper floor contains the security area for females).

All Village youths, that is, its residents, are referred by the juvenile court and are

> adjudicated delinquents, ranging in age from 13 to 17. Generally, they have IQs of 70 or above. They are children with all types of official records—mild to sophisticated delinquent boys and girls who have committed all types of offenses. Several have been in private institutions and some have already been in state institutions. Perceptually and behaviorally, they include the very immature child who is impulsive and seems more helpless and blundering than criminalistic. Also included is the peer-group oriented youth who is dedicated to delinquent values and is proud of his stance. There are the manipulators and . . . some highly perceptive children who have keen insight but seem unable to put [it] to use.[31]

Shortly before arriving at the Village, youths are evaluated at the County Detention Center (CDC). There, they

> are tested and diagnosed in a few days. They are classified according to the California Interpersonal Maturity Level Classification System (I-level system). . . . This diagnostic system . . . provides treatment goals and treatment agent characteristics. When a youth arrives at [the Village,] a staffing [and classification] committee reevaluates the diagnosis [seldom changing CDC's I-level/subtype classification] and decides the cottage and therapy group to which the child [will be officially] assigned. [A treatment plan is generated within one week, during which time the youth resides in an intake cottage (MSSD Policy Manual, 1968, 1971).] The cottages and therapy groups are homogeneous [mainly by I-level subtype (see below)], with staff members being matched to the type of children with whom they are best able to relate. The social workers and cottage parents are more carefully matched to the children than are other staff [e.g., recreation personnel and work supervisors]. The treatment program is differential and varied according to the needs of each child and the group to which he is assigned."

Program Features, Elements, and Activities
Principles and Assumptions

> All operations are oriented toward treatment. Children are treated first and controlled as a secondary matter. They are permitted . . . to show problems, . . . [and] recreation, religious, and educational programs [i.e., activities and elements] are designed to further the treatment goals while at the same time meeting their own formal professional requirements. . . . [The Village tries to maintain a coordinated,] milieu therapy process, . . . [one in which each person contacting each child knows the treatment prescription and has been advised . . . as to how to relate to the child. [Also see OVTC Policy Manual, 1968.]

> In order to convert a traditional institution program into a treatment program, [the following preconditions, among oth-

ers, must be satisfied:] The contraculture [or counterculture] must be controlled by grouping children homogeneously [e.g., in order to reduce or preclude manipulation, "set-ups," and exploitation by dominant or aggressive individuals or groups], and by forming a communication network of children and staff around those who contribute to the negative social system. A differential treatment program is mandatory [and, as indicated,] staff must be carefully matched to the needs of the specific children they serve . . ." [See endnote 32 regarding related implications for recruitment and hiring of staff.]

Cottage Organization

Cottages are generally distinguished from each other by I-level subtype or relatively compatible subtypes. Thus, of the eight cottages, five are for males—one each, for the I_2's, *passive-conformists, power-oriented* (Cfc's and Mp's), *conflicted* ("N's," or "neurotics"), and *"mixed I_4's* (Na's and Nx's, as just indicated, plus Ci's and Se's). Of the three cottages for females, one is for *power-oriented,* one mainly for *N's,* and one mostly for *mixed I_4's* (again mainly N's, but especially those better suited for individualized than for group counseling/therapy). Cfm girls, and the rare I_2's, are placed within this third cottage.

Counseling/Therapy (c/t)

Partly but not only for purposes of *group* counseling/therapy, which usually occurs five times weekly for 60 or 90 minutes per session, most cottages are organized into two sets of eight or nine youths each. (Any given c/t group—and its group c/t session—involves one such set. It generally meets in the later afternoon or early evening, after academic training and other regularly scheduled activities are completed. In all group sessions, Guided Group Interaction comprises the format and method.) However, in any given cottage, even for purposes of group c/t, youths are not organized, or subdivided, *only* by I-level subtype. This is despite the fact that most c/t groups (across the various cottages) do involve just one such type, or perhaps two compatible types.

For instance, a set of 8 or 9 individuals that comprise a particular counseling/therapy group from a given cottage, and which consists of a specified subtype, may contain mainly the following: (1) The more dominant, verbally assertive youths, or, say, (2) the relatively "street-wise" youths, from that cottage and subtype; or, and again alternatively, it may contain mostly (3) the older—or possibly the younger—individuals from that cottage/ subtype. Simultaneously, the remaining set of 8 or 9 individuals within that same cottage may largely consist of that cottage's and subtype's (say, the Nx subtype's) (1) *less* assertive or less vocal youths, or else its (2) comparatively naive and vulnerable individuals, whatever their (3) average age might be.

Moreover, and group composition aside, the following applies in the case of some cottages, such as those for male I_2's, passive-conformists, and mixed N's, respectively: Only *one* set of eight or nine individuals may be engaged mainly or exclusively in group counseling/therapy, whereas the remaining youths, or most of them, receive *individual* c/t. ("Children not assigned to [group] therapy normally attend school all day [rather than for approximately three hours, . . . and/or for three hours] in a vocational [and/or] work assignment. . . . In addition, several of them receive on-the-job training through a program of individual work assignments" (MSSD Policy Manual 1971, p. 49).

Family counseling occurs occasionally. This method was used more often in the middle and later 1970s.

The following applies in any given cottage, whether or not group c/t is used with almost everyone there: Additional information regarding youths—specifically, information which is distinct from that of subtype, dominance, sophistication, age, and so on is regularly used by, and shared across, various staff. This information, which often comes from social history material and from ongoing observations, makes it possible or easier for those individuals to better address, adjust to, and otherwise utilize some of the youths' more specific, personalized, and sometimes even unusual needs, fears, defenses, strengths, achievements, interests, limitations, and/or life circumstances. In that respect it allows for, and can promote, further individualization and relevance; it can support flexibility, as well. Staffs' actual *responses* to and other uses of this additional information may often take place outside of, not just or not necessarily as part of, the group sessions themselves, or even the individual sessions.

Finally, for any given youth, the duration of group and/or individual c/t is essentially the same as that of his or her entire OVTC program, that is, 6 months on average. This is the case on all cottages. Occasionally, though infrequently, duration is as little as three months and as long as nine. (OVTC is never long-term.)

Education
Since the late-1960s' program changes, youths have been

> assigned to classes based on grade level achievement. A youth is trained from this starting point regardless of the grade to which he was assigned in his school in the community. [Besides the regular classes,] there is a half-day Summer School program, and a General Educational Development program [during evening free-time]. School credits are . . . transferable back to [the] community.

Teachers are employees of the County Board of Education and are not on the institutional staff per se. Related to this, and prior to 1968, communication was [infrequent, except during crises, and] there was considerable conflict in views [between teachers, child care workers, and social workers. However,] after the treatment team concept was developed [see below], this problem was alleviated. [To help implement the team approach,] the school principal and each teacher [receive] at least 20 hours of training in the institution's classification and treatment program, including principles of Guided Group Interaction, [by OVTC's] superintendent. The county school system honors this training by giving teachers in-service credit for pay purposes. This cooperative effort between the Board of Education and the institutional administration helped bridge [former gaps] and has helped teachers relate better to children. Teachers [now act more] in concert and in coordination with the institutional staff, and social workers and child care workers assist teachers by making certain that study times are provided and supervised on the cottages.

Vocational Training
> Vocational assignments [now] correlate with therapy prescriptions. . . . [The present] program amounts to assignments . . . by therapy groups. Vocational train-

ing is never more than 3 hours per day. Those involved also receive 3 hours of academic training. Entire therapy groups usually attend a particular course. The emphasis is not only on developing technical skills but on helping children work together in a common activity. When interpersonal problems develop, this provides "food" for group therapy sessions. At best, this is a prevocational training designed for *short-term residential treatment*. . . . Relationships [can be] reinforced through the [given] vocational activity. . . . The county school system gives academic credit for [some types of training, e.g.,] the auto mechanics program. [Emphasis added.]

As in other program areas, "deliberate matches" are made between staff and youth. Thus, e.g., "two groups of sophisticated, peer-group oriented boys are assigned to the auto mechanics program, [this being] a masculine-type activity in a setting in which [boys] can act-out their masculinity needs. The instructor is a retired U.S. Army sergeant of significant stature. The social worker is an ex-professional football player, [and] the child care worker can "hold her own" with the most sophisticated delinquent. [Also], by grouping these residents together, they cannot dominate weaker children, [e.g., the passive-conformists].

The remaining vocational training (VT) for boys involved "shop" (e.g., furniture repair, and upholstery) and, for a few youths, "grounds" (as distinct from work details and general maintenance). VT for girls centered on home economics and food services.

Recreation
[In contrast to past practices,] the treatment program is much more than a tension-management and social control device. It allows children . . . to plan some of their activities, such as parties, dances, and off-campus trips for bowling, baseball games, movies, plays, and community center activities. [In those as well as on-campus sports, arts-and-crafts, and game room activities, the] children "try out" their treatment measures by mixing with [youths] of different perceptual levels and behavioral subtypes. The recre-

ational activities, including off-campus trips, [also] allow for the mixing of the sexes, and thus, social interaction can be observed by the staff. While these activities are supervised, enough freedom is given to allow children to show problems. These problems do not call for immediate reprimands; they call for group actions. [All of this, plus the youth's response to the group, gives staff a better] index for measuring the child's readiness for return to the community.

Religion

The religious program includes both the traditional Sunday services and occasional, special Sunday evening musical or drama programs. Therapeutically, there is a student chaplain . . . on each cottage, supervised by the institution's Protestant chaplain. . . . Sunday school classes are taught on the cottages [and attended on a voluntary basis. . . . A full-time chaplain counsels the youths at "their level," that is, maturity level, and in relation to their individual feelings and views. Thus,] the religious program [, which is multi-denominational,] becomes more than indoctrinational. [Rather,] it becomes functionally related to the degree of interpersonal maturity the child has achieved . . . [and it can therefore be] integrated into the overall treatment program and [be] reinforcing.

Other

(1) Work details are a regular part of almost all youths' program and are overseen by full-time work supervisors. (2) Parents may visit on any given weekend; however, furloughs, including weekends at home, seldom occur. (Weekend visits by youths increased after 1974.) Community volunteers (individuals and groups) are trained and coordinated by a half-time volunteer coordinator (VC)—who tries to match them to the types of children with whom they will mainly interact, for example, on a given cottage.[33] The VC also acts as "liaison between the campus council (two youths from each cottage), which meets monthly, and the policy committee." In addition, the VC conducts a "social interaction group for [several] very immature children [, . . . one that involves role-playing techniques. She also teaches] a course in sex edu-

cation, working closely with the nurse, the chaplain, and the recreation director." (4) If and as needed, psychologists are available at the County Detention Center, for special testing, additional diagnosis, and so on, after the youths begin their program. For other or related needs and issues concerning youths, a part-time, contracted psychiatrist is used. (5) Chaplain interns voluntarily provide liaison between the Village and persons in the community, to help pave the way for the youths' return. However, this aspect of OVTC, namely, transition and especially aftercare per se, was neither extensive nor systematic in the early 1970s. (It increased considerably, starting in 1975.)

Organization and Implementation

Under the previous (pre-1968) organizational structure,

> there was a basic "line staff" and "professional staff" distinction. . . . While the line personnel had most of the authority and influence in the institution, the professional staff existed to support them and the custodial program. This custodial orientation permeated the institution to the extent that nearly all support services established custody and control rules, regulations, and operations. For example, recreation included fun and games, but was integrated with a high degree of regimentation. The vocational and farm programs were designed to keep children busy and to produce needed products rather than to meet the needs of inner-city children. . . . Custody and control were foremost, while recreation, . . . casework, . . . [and other programs and dimensions] were mechanisms for achieving these goals.
>
> The basic chain of authority and supervision for the line staff was from superintendent, to the assistant superintendent, to the director of cottage life, to the child care worker (known as cottage parents in some systems). The child care workers were evaluated by, and answered to, the director of cottage life, so they did not have to work closely with the social workers, who were only peripheral to the cottage life, [this being] the basic operation of the institution. Child care workers were the *hub* of the custody-control operation,

and the professional staff supplied supportive and ancillary services which reinforced the containment practices of the institution. . . . Social workers were lower in status [and in decision-making power] than the child care workers, even though their official position [might have seemed to] indicate otherwise. . . .

[There was no] policy committee [and] professional committee [see below], and cottage-based treatment teams were nonexistent. There were no comparable coordinating structures that tied all personnel together and created extra networks of communication. Recommendations, communications, directives, and specifications were primarily one way—from the top downward.

[Under the new arrangement,] all social workers have been brought into the line structure, and each cottage of 18 children has its own social worker [now called the "cottage supervisor"]. The line of authority and supervision is from the superintendent, to the assistant superintendent—treatment, to the director of boys' (girls') residential services, to social workers, to child care workers. In this new chain, all social workers possess B.A. degrees, while top and middle management are all social workers with professional graduate school training. The authority hierarchy and the skills hierarchy are synonymous. The professionally educated staff control all the authoritative decisions concerning children and cottage life. This means that the professional values, the ethics, and the practices of the social workers predominate. . . .

Child care workers are now evaluated by and answer to the social worker on the cottage. The social workers are responsible for the performance of the child care workers. In addition, the social workers are responsible for the treatment and care of all the children on their caseload, all of whom have been placed in their cottage. [Thus,] the social workers and child care workers . . . are locked in an interpersonal coalition wherein one cannot succeed without the other [nor] fail without the other one also failing. . . .

In order to tie in staff so that they [are] integral rather than peripheral, treatment teams have been organized. . . .

Each social worker now coordinates a . . . team for each cottage, [one that consists of] all those adults who teach, care for, counsel, or supervise the child on a day-to-day basis. Each child has a treatment team (the cottage team) that monitors and evaluates his progress. The treatment teams include child care workers, chaplains, teachers, work supervisors, and recreation personnel, [and together, they] coordinate and articulate [the given youth's treatment]. . . . The teams advise social workers and inform them of how children are adjusting in each area of the program. In turn, the social worker interprets to team members ways to meet the needs of the children for which his team is responsible. . . . [Thus,] under this system, . . . the cottage social workers are the [initiators], the coordinators, and the facilitators. They also make treatment decisions in joint consultation with team members, . . . [and, in all the above, it is they who are] primarily responsible for [implementing the] Guided Group Interaction, individual counseling, and some family therapy. . . .[34]

Besides the treatment team [there now exists] a policy committee and a professional staff committee. . . . [The policy committee includes the superintendent; assistant superintendent—administration; assistant superintendent—treatment; director of boys residential services; director of girls residential services. It] makes decisions only after consulting with department [e.g., education department] heads and professional staff. The superintendent has veto authority and final responsibility for any decisions made. [The professional committee] meets weekly [regarding] coordination and training. [Besides including policy committee members, it has] all social workers, chaplains, recreation workers, the nurse, and the volunteer coordinator. It makes suggestions to the policy committee and [also] evaluate[s] proposals from [that] committee before they are effected and published.

[Staff training] occurs primarily through treatment teams by the social worker, but at times they are trained by policy committee members. . . . Most staff members receive at least a 20-hour course on I-level, taught by the superintendent. This course is taught to approximately 20 staff members at a time from all segments of the institution. Such mixed groups encourage the sharing of problems, perspectives, and frustrations, and help develop an appreciation for the problems of other staff at differing levels. . . . Training and consultation are continuous activities within the institution. New ideas are interjected into the system [sometimes by "outside experts"], and old ideas [if relatively weak or now incompatible, etc.] are ejected through the constant evaluation and training process. This keeps the system ideologically tight—yet renewed and innovative in an incremental way. . . . The combining of various educational levels, [and of] professional and nonprofessional staff and administrators, in training, helps to limit the gamesmanship associated with specialized knowledge, [and] to reduce the esoteric and unnecessary mystique surrounding treatment concepts and techniques. . . . Most important, it [allows] continuous coordinated therapy to [go] on throughout the system. . . ."

Organizationally and procedurally, the Village continued to operate in essentially the manner described earlier, until the late 1970s. It continued to emphasize differential intervention, as well. Nevertheless, several conspicuous program changes that involved particular treatment modalities and subtype groupings took place in the mid-1970s. For instance, by 1975–1976, one of OVTC's units was being used to focus on "solvent abus[ing]" males. This cottage, which now emphasized *transactional analysis (TA)* rather than Guided Group Interaction, could contain all three I-levels and up to six of their nine aggregated subtypes, including the power-oriented. (Youths who were "actively using hard core drugs" were ineligible for OVTC.) In another unit, one that now—that is, again 1975–1976—consisted of some of OVTC's passive-conformist boys and some of its I_2's (lower maturity youths), *behavior modification (BM)* had been substituted for GGI. Similarly, TA was substituted for GGI in a unit that now contained not just power-oriented males, but conflicted and passive-conformist boys. In short, new treatment modalities existed at OVTC and subtypes

were more widely mixed. BM and TA, respectively, began to be used with females, too—specifically, with the passive-conformists and I_2's, who comprised a first unit, and with conflicted individuals, who constituted a second. Regarding other changes, the age limit was lowered to 12, greater emphasis was placed on status offenders (all females had this legal status), and power-oriented girls were no longer eligible for OVTC.

Because of a growing preference by departmental administrators for community-based approaches over residential programming, the Village operation—though not its differential intervention view—was phased out in 1979. Many youths who were in OVTC during that year were moved to local group homes—some during one month, some during others (especially the final one). Several of these approximately ten homes were homogeneous by I-level subtype or compatible subtypes, and they were generally operated by matched staff who, collectively, had been gradually transferred to them from Village cottages themselves. Largely independent of OVTC's eventual phase-out, group homes had been increasingly used by the department during 1974–1979, for youths who had *completed* their stay at the Village.

Craigwood-Bridgeway Program

The Craigwood-Bridgeway Program is a self-incorporated, nonprofit, residential, and community-located operation that serves delinquent and emotionally disturbed adolescents and which emphasizes differential intervention and a continuum of service across settings. It combines the I-level system and that of Conceptual Level, or "CL," and its continuum-of-care dimension is designed to provide treatment, other direct services, and supervised activities to youths in the community, after they have completed their residential phase of intervention. (See endnote 1 regarding CL and its implications for differing treatment milieus and approaches.) The following description emphasizes Craigwood-Bridgeway's (C-B's) first five years of operation, ending in 1984. Subsequent years will be described later, though some aspects will be mentioned along the way. As will be seen, many features remained the same while others changed significantly.

C-B is located in Ontario Province, Canada. It began its operation as a treatment facility for serious delinquents in 1979, and its differential intervention approach started in 1980. Its residential component is in Ailsa Craig (population 800) and its community-located unit, which opened in 1981, is in London (population 270,000), 20 miles away.[35] Craigwood-Bridgeway draws from a five-county area whose population center is London, Ontario's fourth largest city. Some 90 percent of C-B's youths come from this city and one adjacent county.

As an organizational entity and as functionally interrelated facilities the Ailsa Craig and London components are jointly termed Craigwood Youth Services. Viewed programmatically, however, the overall operation has been simply called *Craigwood, Bridgeway,* or—more often and meaningfully—Craigwood-Bridgeway. Functionally, "Bridgeway" refers, not to an actual place, but to the continuum of service whose goal is to help youths successfully bridge back, or transit, into their community.

From the start, Craigwood-Bridgeway has had its own board of directors and has received all its operating funds from the Ontario Ministry of Community and Social Services (MCSS). It was originally organized to accept only those youths, ages 13 to 16 at intake (admission), "who had been stabilized in," and were about to leave, a Ministry training school,[36] but "who required additional intervention to [help them better adjust] in their home communities" (Leschied and Thomas, 1983, p. 24. Except as specified, all quotations, below, are from pp. 1–27 of this reference). Some 30 percent of all Ministry training school graduates were believed to need such intervention, usually beginning with a transition program, yet not an entirely residential one. Starting in 1979, Craigwood-Bridgeway was used, by MCSS, to provide that service and to thus help implement the given policy. C-B, itself, was not considered a training school.

About one year later, with the Ministry (1) continuing to reduce the number of *training schools* (it closed or realigned seven during 1977–1981), and (2) wishing to maintain more youths in the *community* (all the while continuing its above policy and use of C-B), Craigwood-Bridgeway began to also accept two other groups of youth: young adolescents who were viewed as "*headed* for training school if a major intervention were not to [occur; and, those who had not] benefitted

from programs in other [i.e., non-C-B, non–training school] *residential treatment centres [RTCs]*" (emphasis added). These new subpopulations came from either the open community—mainly foster homes, group homes, or homes of parents/guardians/relatives—or from other *RTCs* in which youths were living, from which they were departing or had recently departed, or from which they had absconded. Collectively, these individuals were sent to Craigwood-Bridgeway either directly from the courts, for instance, following an offense, or via formal referrals by probation officers and child welfare workers.

Like all other referrals to C-B, these new subpopulations were assigned to either C-B's residential program (Ailsa Craig) or its community center component (London). Prior to the 1984–1985 expansion of Craigwood-Bridgeway's *community* component (described later), some 80 percent of all referrals were assigned directly to Ailsa Craig. Upon completing this residential program they were usually transferred directly to the London operation, that is, to the community phase of C-B. (In 1982, the Ministry established an eight-bed, treatment-oriented, coed group home in London. This was chiefly for Ailsa Craig graduates, and was thus designed to broaden the program's scope.) The remaining 20 percent began their C-B program in the community. Usually, they were not transferred to the residential component, after that.

Overview of Program Structure and Approach

Craigwood-Bridgeway's overall population, some 80 percent of which is male, are wards of the Family Court Service, which is funded by the above-mentioned Ministry. By most standards, these individuals—especially but not only those who begin in residence—can be viewed as serious delinquents, as personally troubled to a considerable degree, and/or as multiply-problemmed. (Details are provided below.)

Ailsa Craig, a residential facility exclusively for C-B youths, is on a 52-acre site within a rural setting. It contains three semisecure living units (two during 1979–1982), each housing 10 individuals (males and females) and each using a different overall approach. The first unit provides a "highly structured, behaviorally oriented program tailored for immature, impulse-directed youths [mostly I₃'s. The second offers a] less structured program, with emphasis on peer-to-peer responsibility and the working-through of personal feelings, with a focus on future planning."[37] The third living unit, which was the last to begin and which also houses 10 individuals, resembles the first with regard to program emphasis, degree of overall structure, and the Conceptual Level as well as I-level of most of its youths. Also part of the Ailsa Craig campus is a vocational shop, a gymnasium, an ice skating rink, facilities for horses and other animals, and, through 1981, a school building. (Starting in 1982, all nonvocational classroom facilities were placed into the three living units.) There are no intake and detention units.

Before a youth is released from Ailsa Craig and transferred to the community supervision/support phase, he or she should be able to: (1) function on the basis of fewer external structures than before, with fewer or less frequent external controls, and based on stronger or clearer internalized standards and goals; and (2) handle more complex interpersonal situations and expectations largely on his or her own. These changes are seen as paralleling the individual's growth in CL and/or I-level, among other dimensions. The residential structure and program, guided by CL and I-level concepts, is designed to facilitate the given changes and growth.

As implied earlier, Craigwood-Bridgeway's long-term strategy for Ailsa Craig assignees—viewed as eventual graduates—is to use its *Community Centre*[38] in order to help consolidate and augment gains those youths should make during their residential phase, and to reduce new as well as remaining pressures or weaknesses, and/or their impact. Toward these ends, this postresidential, London operation attempts to "support . . . youths [graduates] in their living situations in the community" (Leschied and Thomas, 1983; Efron, 1984). In a broad sense, and when used for these particular individuals, this operation is thus designed to "facilitate . . . reintegration into the community." For these youths and for those *directly* assigned to it (i.e., without first being in Ailsa Craig), the Community Centre is organized as a "day treatment program."

Youths remain at Ailsa Craig for 9 to 15 months, the average being 12. For graduates

from this facility, the Community Centre (CC) program also lasts about 12 months. Some youths who are adjusting poorly to the CC operation and/or within the community in general may repeat part or all of Craigwood-Bridgeway's residential and/or community program. (Regarding poor adjustment, they may, in particular, be committing public offenses, be openly self-destructive, and so on.) As part of this process, they may, for instance, be transferred back from the latter setting (London) to the former (Ailsa Craig)—or else just be *transferred*, if they had not previously been in residence. Whether or not such repetition occurs, C-B's residential and community programs may each utilize a local facility for the short-term detention of youths who commit various offenses, who abscond, and so on. This facility is not the earlier-mentioned group home—an individual-treatment-oriented operation whose modal length of stay is itself one year.

As an agency that differentially intervenes with serious young offenders and with emotionally disturbed youths, Craigwood-Bridgeway was conceptualized and developed by Ken Thomas, its Executive Director from 1979 to the present. During most of the 1970s, this individual worked at the Shawbridge Youth Centers, where he headed residential services as well as personnel services and resources, and had been a diagnostician as well as teacher. In 1971 he was trained in I-level at California's CTDT.

Youth Characteristics

The delinquency and other difficulties/problems that characterize most C-B youths can be seen from the following (all figures are averages, and they focus on point of first admission to C-B): For all boys and girls combined, the first court contact had occurred at age 10.6. By age 14.8, when these individuals first entered Craigwood-Bridgeway, they had accumulated 6.2 offenses, mainly in the property category. One-third of the youths had at least one violent/assaultive offense in their record, and nearly half had already been in a Ministry training school—the latters' number of stays averaging 1.8.[39] About 85 percent had school attendance problems, 95 percent had been "identified as 'exceptional' and in need of special instruction." Many had been classified by their schools as "learning disabled," in particular, and over 60 percent had repeated at least one grade.

Regarding family, placement history, and so forth, significant difficulties and/or instabilities were common. Among them, and/or reflecting them, were: parental divorce—33 percent of the youths; physical abuse of youth ("extra-familial," e.g., by guardians)—37 percent; parental violence (interspousal, and/or toward youth)—14 percent; incest in the case of girls—40 percent. Over 90 percent of all youths had had at least one out-of-home placement, the first of which occurred at age 10, and over 80 percent of Craigwood-Bridgeway's population had run from pre-C-B placements three or more times.[40] Fifteen percent had attempted suicide and 16 percent—sometimes the same individuals—had purposely injured themselves in other respects (again physically). In all, C-B youths had been assessed by, assisted by, and otherwise contacted and/or supervised by over seven different public agencies and organizations in the years preceding admission.[41]

Given this background, C-B staff and other professionals regarded these youths as "high-risk" for offending and as "hard-to-serve," overall (A.R.A. Consultants, 1981).[42]

Concerning I-level, some 50% of Craigwood-Bridgeway's total youth-population are I_3's (middle maturity) or below, and about 42% are I_4's (higher maturity); the remaining youths' category is unclear. As to Conceptual Level, the percentage of individuals at Stages A, A/B, B, and C—"A" being the least developed ("low CL") in terms of cognitive complexity—is 36, 18, 32, and 3, respectively, with the rest again being unclear.

Though the above figures all relate to *Ailsa Craig* youths in particular, those for individuals directly assigned to London are generally similar. Broadly speaking, the latter youths have largely the same type—and range—of difficulties/problems, but these are somewhat lesser in intensity and duration. Regarding specific differences in degree, these individuals, for example, are less likely to lack an intact family or an available extended one, are less likely to have been assaultive (and were less often assaultive), and are less at risk of offending in the near future. These individuals are also less likely to have a low CL, and, with that, are somewhat more likely to be I_4's.

Specific Procedures and Structures

After a basic screening for eligibility and appropriateness—one largely centering on the youths' having an IQ in at least the high 70s,

and an absence of heavy physical or psychological dependence on drugs—all new referrals to Craigwood-Bridgeway are tested and interviewed by its Assessment Unit (AU). The AU, which consists of four MSWs and is housed in London, also develops a social history and then integrates its test/interview(s) information with that history and with already existing case-file material.[43] Using all such inputs, the responsible AU worker ("diagnostician") determines whether the youth would best be assigned to the residential or community program—and if to the former (Ailsa Craig), then into which of its three living units.

When determining living unit assignment within Ailsa Craig, main weight is given to input information regarding I-level and, especially, Conceptual Level. This is because each unit is characterized by a particular milieu and approach, one designed to help youths of specified CLs—and of I-levels often associated with those CLs—adjust as well as grow. The staff assigned to any given living unit are primarily matched to (1) that unit's particular milieu and approach, and, where possible, to (2) the given unit's most common I-level (e.g., I_4) or levels, and/or the subtypes within a given level—at any rate, to those more likely to be associated with the unit's primary *CL(s)* than with the main CL of another. This applies not just to Counselors in particular but to Social Workers and Teachers as well.

Ailsa Craig's two *highly structured units* have a milieu, approach, and overall program mainly designed for individuals whose Conceptual Level scores are in the Stage A category. (Almost all I_3's, and some I_4's, are in this "low CL" category. Thus, as it turns out, these living units contain mainly I_3's; and, of these individuals, most are Cfm's.) The third unit, that is, the *less structured one*, mainly contains youths at CL's transitional A/B or low Stage B level. Also, these individuals very often turn out to be I_4's; more precisely, this unit usually has a mix of Na's and Nx's, though it may have a few I_3's as well. Even if Conceptual Level were not to have precedence over I-level with regard to unit assignment, considerable mixing of I-level subtypes (some hardly compatible with others) would be essentially unavoidable within at least some living units. This is because there are only three units in all, with no prior exclusion of given subtypes per se. (Whatever the particular mixes may be, the relative compatibility that exists within the respective units by virtue of their youths' similar or identical *CLs* serves as a partial counterweight to subtype- or personality-related incompatibility.)

Heading Ailsa Craig's treatment operations is a director, who supervises the respective heads of that facility's three living units. Each such head—unit director—supervises his or her unit's male and female counselors, one of whom has various lead ("senior") responsibilities. A counselor who personally oversees a given boy's or girl's treatment is that individual's primary counselor (PC). Each living unit also has its own social worker (assigned part-time) and two full-time teachers (one emphasizing remedial/academic areas and the other the vocational). The unit's full treatment team, which reviews each new case before a PC is assigned to it, consists of the unit director, social worker, both teachers, and all counselors.

Shortly after determining the unit assignment, the Assessment Unit's diagnostician (AUD) discusses the case with the living unit's full treatment team. Based on that interaction, the unit director assigns a primary counselor to the youth. The AUD and PC then meet and develop a plan designed to address the youth's particular needs, characteristics, and situation, especially in the context of (1) the living unit's particular milieu and approaches, and (2) the already agreed-upon educational targets and techniques. Postresidential factors are focused on, as well.

At this point in the planning, Conceptual Level prescriptions (ones found in the literature, in manuals, etc.) and I-level concepts/guidelines (e.g., Warren et al., 1966b) often play complementary and supplementary roles, and they partly overlap each other in so doing. Broadly speaking, the CL's are used to supply or suggest various principles and general techniques for interacting with individual youths and groups of youth, and the I-level's are used to furnish several general as well as specific strategies and techniques.

Strategically, that is, beyond their immediate and concrete contributions in terms of specific techniques, etc., the CL and I-level systems are viewed by Craigwood-Bridgeway staff as helping to shape and detail a treatment plan which, if implemented adequately, should accomplish the following: It should help the youth move, and should help others move him or her, "through a *developmental sequence* in which information and external stimulation [is] processed [by the youth] with increasing maturity and greater cognitive complexity. [This information/stimulation is to be provided in classrooms, in one-to-one interactions with staff, via living-unit atmospheres, and so on. Particular] worker styles, unit routines, [and other program features as well as activities, will, hopefully,] facilitate this growth process," as well (Efron, 1984, p. 7; emphasis added).

With various details of the treatment plan filled in, the unit director approves it and Ailsa Craig's treatment director reviews it. From that point forward, the primary counselor is responsible for updating it and for recommending any needed changes. The PC and social worker jointly review the plan at least quarterly, and all proposed major changes in the youth's status, including his transfer to the community component, are decided upon during formal case conferences between the PC and treatment team. When considering these changes, conference participants are to bear in mind the major goals and approaches specified in the plan.

Main Program Elements
Residential Facility

All living units have two group meetings per week; a further meeting, one that centers on broad, unit-level or facilitywide issues, is held once a week. Again across all units, and, thus, regardless of the unit's earlier-mentioned differences in milieu and approach, each youth has two one-to-one counseling sessions per week with his or her PC. These sessions focus, further focus, or follow up on the youth's individual needs, problems, and overall situation, for instance, on needs or worries that were only partly discussed in group. Youth/PC meetings may deal with pending decisions as well. About 10 percent of all youths also meet regularly and/or often with their social workers for generally more intense sessions, again one-to-one. In addition, a consulting psychiatrist meets with—and regarding—certain very complex or otherwise unusual youths. Specialized psychological services are available as well, again on an as-needed basis.

Given that some 70 percent of Ailsa Craig's youths had dropped out of school prior to entering C-B, the campus classes largely function, in effect, as an alternative school. Though one of their overriding goals is, thus, that of arousing/increasing those and other individuals' interest in education, this longer-term objective is separate and apart from the following: the immediate, but also ongoing, job of (1) providing or enhancing basic, practical skills, for example, reading and math, and of (2) supplying generally useful information per se. Since the vast majority of C-B youths are of school age while in residence as well as in the community, essentially all vocationally focused programming they may be involved in is provided as an integral part of their overall educational curriculum, not as a substitute for it. It thus occurs during the individuals' regular school hours and is simply another type of class.

At any rate, youths spend five hours a day, five days a week, involved in education, mostly in the living-unit class setting rather than in the vocational shop. For any particular individual, both the amount of focus and the relative weight that is given to the remedial, academic, and vocational content areas, respectively, is based on the educational and other targets specified in his or her treatment plan. Each youth's primary counselor interacts directly with both teachers assigned to the living unit, in order to help blend that plan with specific issues relating to school and to changes in the youth.

Other program elements and activities include conjoint family therapy, family support groups, visits from parents/relatives, short furloughs to home/relatives, various sports, horse riding, off-campus trips (e.g., camping and Outward Bound events), and so on. Not all youths are involved in *all* these elements during their stay at Ailsa Craig.

Community Centre
The Community Centre program was established in 1981. Between then and 1984 it accommodated up to 30 youths at a time, the bulk being Ailsa Craig graduates and the rest having been directly assigned to it by the Assessment Unit. The type and range of approaches available at the Centre were the same for both groups of youth, as was the average duration of intervention (one year). Regardless of group, that is, graduate or assignee, the ways in which given approaches were *combined* with each other largely reflected the individual's treatment plan; thus, they often varied considerably from one youth to another.

Using four full-time caseworkers, the Centre provided individual counseling, group counseling, family therapy/counseling, and/or, from 1983, a parent support group. I-level and Conceptual Level, among other factors, helped determine which of these approaches—individually and in combination with one or more mentioned next—would be most appropriate at the time, for each given youth. Also in 1983, the Centre added an on-site *school*, which further reflected the Ministry of Community and Social Service's desire to expand community programming in general and Craigwood-Bridgeway's scope in particular. It occurred soon after C-S's already mentioned *group home*, which often functioned as a treatment-oriented halfway house, had been established. The Centre's school was operated by two full-time teachers, and it, like Ailsa Craig's, provided remedial, general academic, and vocation-focused instruction.[44] Other elements available at the Centre were (1) "focus groups" that addressed life-skills issues such as job seeking/interviewing, cooking, and hygiene, and (2) various organized as well as informal activities and events, such as summer programming and year-round, daily lunches.

Key features and procedures already described for Ailsa Craig also existed at, and were paralleled by, the Community Centre (CC). For instance, regarding any direct assignee to CC, an Assessment Unit diagnostician—subsequent to his or her discussion of that youth with CC staff—met with a Centre caseworker and jointly developed an individualized treatment plan. The caseworker was assigned to the youth by the CC's unit director, based on the worker's (1) skill at and comfort with the main counseling approach(es) and/or focus groups that seemed to be needed, and (2) overall suitability to, that is, match with, the individual and type of individual in question. Items (1) and (2) also applied to the Centre's Ailsa Craig graduates; and, as implied above, Conceptual Level and I-level contributed to the individual plan diagnostically as well as prescriptively.

The Community Centre operated five days a week, eight hours a day, and it later expanded into the evenings. In both the earlier and later years, Centre staff, for example, child-care workers (counselors), were on call after hours and on weekends.

Later Developments

From the mid-1980s to the present, most major structures, procedures, and types of programming that existed in 1979–1984 were maintained, especially but not only at Ailsa Craig. For instance, the primary counselor and treatment team models were used throughout, and initial case planning as well as regular follow-up conferences still took place. However, although the three living units were physically/structurally maintained, all assignments to them occurred on a different basis; also, the living unit milieus were themselves altered. These and other changes are reviewed below.

At a broader, more philosophical, yet also operationally critical level, Craigwood-Bridgeway continued to emphasize the view that intervention, especially with hard-to-serve youths, "has to be individualized. It takes time, and you do not give up on them [youths]" (Thomas, 1995). Closely related, the concept of a continuum-of-service across settings remained central and was implemented whenever possible—this, despite major difficulties mentioned later. At any rate, in accordance with that concept, individualized treatment plans—ones that also addressed the youths' postresidential needs and situations—were still developed; in fact, they became more important than before. In addition, the broad, earlier-mentioned criteria for release from the residential setting to the community were unchanged. More precisely, rather than being *criteria,* they became *goals or objectives,* chiefly because determinate sentencing controlled the release date from 1985 forward. Details now follow, starting with the populations served.

Basic Populations

From the mid-1980s to the present, Ailsa Craig and London continued to serve their original types of youth (the delinquent and emotionally disturbed)—their "basic populations." The first-mentioned operation continued to work with 30 individuals at a time, that is, 10 youths in each of three living units. The second, as part of the Ministry's continued interest in expanding community-based services and alternatives to custody, increased to about 50; this number included Ailsa Craig graduates and, especially, direct assignees. This increase was apart from yet another, much larger Community Centre augmenta-

tion. The latter involved a *new* youth-population (described next), one consisting of up to 100 additional individuals. The basic populations continued to have the same background, family, academic, and other characteristics as those indicated earlier.

New Population

In the mid- to later 1980s Ontario's Ministry of Community and Social Services again paved the way for a programmatic expansion of Craigwood-Bridgeway, whose London operation was by then in a different and larger building. In this case, a technically new, relatively different type of population was added, one that reflected MCSS's increased emphasis on *early intervention.* Most individuals who comprised this population had no known offense, and the rest had very few and minor ones; in addition, few such youths were part of the justice system. Nevertheless, because many had been expelled or repeatedly suspended from school, and/or had often exhibited unusual types or amounts of behavior problems (these not being limited to considerable overt aggression) outside school, these individuals were considered "high risks" for delinquency, in particular. Also, their behavior, "if unaddressed," was seen as possibly "result[ing] in the need for more intrusive mental health intervention, child protection, or legal involvement" (Hogan, Johnston, and Liehmann, 1994, p. 12).

Developments Focused on the Centre (London)

By 1988, in order to work with many such youths, the London operation had been geared up to serve as many as 150 individuals at any one time, that is, the basic populations (now about 50 in the community) plus the approximately 100 new youths. Additional staff were hired to facilitate this further Centre expansion. (Ailsa Craig's 30-youth operation remained unchanged in size, though a much smaller percentage of its graduates had been moving on to the Centre program after 1985.)

To focus on this new and sizable population and to do so on a high-priority basis, the London operation became heavily involved with (1) parent support groups, and, especially, with (2) short-term, that is, three- to six-month, family group intervention (FGI) that largely utilized "Cognitive Restructuring" techniques (Ross and Fabiano, 1985)—all still within a day programming, and by now also evening meeting, framework. Though this new initiative, that is, that which involved the new population, was fully underway in 1988 (Hogan, Johnston, and Leihmann, 1994), Cognitive Restructuring had been introduced to C-B in 1986. Regarding its application to short-term FGI in particular, C-B staff and administrators considered Cognitive Restructuring not only relevant but more specific than—and, under the circumstances, generally easier to utilize than—I-level. (Related details appear below.) At the same time, the restructuring approach was viewed as compatible with and even somewhat complementary to the Conceptual Level approach—yet again, more specific and concrete than it. This was true in both London and Ailsa Craig. Nevertheless, short-term FGI was not considered adequate for families with "ongoing psychiatric difficulties, . . . acute marital stress, or . . . histor[ies] of extensive previous treatment" (Hogan, Johnston, and Leihmann, 1994, p. 12).

Craigwood-Bridgeway incorporated these very sizable changes while not only maintaining its individual counseling, group counseling, parent support group, and life-skills approaches with its basic populations, including Ailsa Craig graduates and the direct assignees to the Centre. Instead, it did so after also having added (in the mid-1980s), and having subsequently maintained, such elements or modules as anger management and victim awareness focus groups.

> Again focusing on the Centre operation, *which* boys and girls would be considered appropriate for participating in *which* of these focus groups (or even in neither or both of them) increasingly reflected (1) various details of those youths' individual dynamics and behavior more than it reflected (2) their CL or I-level and subtype per se; this was despite the overlap or positive correlation between (1) and (2). As a result, the focus groups cut-across those levels, etc.
>
> (It might be added that when various expansions and changes of the mid-1980s [further described below] occurred, Craigwood-Bridgeway's larger number of services and approaches provided more options than before for Ailsa Craig graduates who were involved in, or were about to start, the community phase of

their program. At the same time, however, C-B's 8-person *group home* began to be used much more often for the direct-assignees than for Ailsa Craig's graduates. That, in contrast, reduced the latters' options.)

At any rate, in working with some 180 youths at a time, Craigwood-Bridgeway—not just the London component—soon provided, and has continued to provide, various interventions and services to over 300 youths per year, the vast majority via Community Centre programming. The Centre's remedial/academic/vocational component remained intact and continued to focus on C-B's basic populations; however, due to funding limitations, it could not expand in size. To address the increased need for educational programming, especially in connection with new-population youths, local school boards augmented their own remedial and vocational services.

Developments at Ailsa Craig and Beyond
In 1984, the Young Offenders Act was passed in Canada, and in 1985 it became operative. Among its effects, this broad-gauged law immediately eliminated Craigwood-Bridgeway's ability to decide whether youths appropriately referred to it would be assigned to the residential facility (Ailsa Craig) or to the Community Centre (London), and, if to the former, into which living unit. Moreover, because of this law, all three units had to be organized on a new primary basis, that is, in terms of whether they were *open* or *secure*. Specifically, all assignments were now made by judges. In addition, these individuals sentenced youths directly to one or another of Ailsa Craig's units, and they did so based on its designated level of security rather than its potential for assisting in growth.

In short, (1) C-B's Assessment Unit staff no longer determined placement; (2) the living units were no longer systematically and purposively distinguished from each other in terms of their residents' Conceptual Level(s) and their related I-levels/subtypes; (3) because of (1) and (2), youths of all CLs and subtypes could be, and regularly were, fully mixed together in each unit; and, (4) a unit's relative ability to support and promote a given individual's rehabilitation was no longer the principal concern when that person was assigned to that particular unit; nor was it necessarily a major concern.

Also based on the new law, judges sentenced the youths for a specific length of time, one that varied from individual to individual and was not constant by living unit. The amount of time chiefly reflected the punishment or just desert dimension and, presumably, possible risk of future offending, since that amount was largely linked to offense history and related behavior. (These sentences seldom exceeded 12 months at Ailsa Craig, and youths' average stay in that facility dropped to 9 or 10 months—as it did in the Centre.)

In light of such changes—above all, those whose effect was to eliminate the earlier-described unit milieus and their relatively homogeneous/compatible youth groupings, not those involving determinate and/or shorter average sentences per se—Craigwood-Bridgeway took the following step, in its work with each youth. Broadly speaking, this step was an attempt to integrate, to the extent feasible at the time, its still extant philosophy of rehabilitation with that represented by the new, more legalistic reality and resulting limitations: Its Assessment Unit staff, in concert with the youth's assigned primary counselor, developed a treatment plan that was more individualized than before. (Craigwood-Bridgeway did not alter its earlier-mentioned organizational structure, staffing patterns, and post-assignment case-handling procedures, for instance, procedures involving the AU's initial case conference with the unit's Treatment Team, and the Unit Director's subsequent assignment of a matched Primary Counselor.)

This plan continued to reflect various treatment implications of Conceptual Level and I-level—though, in both cases, these implications now involved the youth-*as-individual* (not necessarily the youth-*in-group-setting*) more than before. At the same time, it gave increased emphasis to the following:

1. *one-to-one interactions* between staff (not limited to primary counselor) and youth, for example, ways of interacting, and types of relationships, which, hopefully, would be highly relevant to addressing the latter's immediate and longer-range personal needs and to constructively challenging various modes of adjustment (especially under conditions known to exist in the given living unit); and

2. ways of utilizing the unit's, and the rest of Ailsa Craig's, human and material resources *as a whole,* while, of course, no longer being able to draw upon the particularly relevant—and also across-youth—structures and environments that previously existed.

Various constituents of items 1 and 2 may not have been specifically derived from, or even generally implied in, CL and I-level. Instead, they may have sprung largely from other knowledge bases or experiences.

As may be deduced, the treatment plan in question, with its increased emphasis (and perhaps sharper focus) than before on items 1 and 2, was designed to do more than directly promote personal growth and a more positive environment for intervention, critical though these were. Instead, it was also designed to achieve one or both of the following, and to thereby *indirectly* promote and, in any event, maintain, key personal gains by the youth:

1. partly substitute for, or at least compensate for, given atmospheres and external/structural supports that no longer existed or that had been greatly reduced, once CL was displaced as the principal basis for unit assignment and organization; and

2. help reduce not only normal stresses of residential life but others that had emerged or increased because of the greater mixture of Conceptual Levels as well as certain subtypes, in each unit.

At any rate, by individualizing the treatment plan and the subsequent intervention to a greater degree than before, staff hoped it would be possible to effectively and efficiently address each youth's particular needs, defenses, and so on. More to the point, they hoped it would be possible even if he or she had been assigned to a living unit whose external structures and whose mix of youths might not, by themselves, have been particularly consonant with—let alone specifically or actively useful in the context of—his or her CL and other treatment- or learning-relevant dimensions.

As to major types of approach that Ailsa Craig had provided during 1979–1984, such as generic counseling methods, these remained available. However, a complication arose in

1985: Based on the Young Offenders Act and on its enabling legislation (the Child and Family Services Act of Ontario [see endnote 35]), youths could, for the first time, legally refuse treatment, for example, treatment in the sense or form of, but not limited to, personal psychotherapy. Moreover, they could do so at any point, whether initially or after it began. They could thus serve "dead-time" or partial dead-time; and in this connection, for instance, many youths declined individual, group, and family counseling. (Persons under age 16 could not refuse schooling, a program component that continued as before.)

Despite this new option, semi-structured and often somewhat didactically presented elements or modules such as anger management groups, victim awareness groups, and sexual appropriateness or sexuality awareness groups were commonly used. (These focus groups first appeared at Ailsa Craig in the mid-1980s, and their overall content as well as format was much the same regardless of the participants' CLs and I-levels/subtypes. To be sure, for any potential participant, any or all such elements/modules might have been contraindicated in the first place, as specified in the original and/or revised treatment plan; as a result, they might not have been used at all, or at least at given points. This applied to any type of counseling as well, and to various methods listed below.)

In addition, youths regularly participated in Cognitive Restructuring. In fact, after 1986, this being its point of introduction, CR soon became one of Ailsa Craig's staples, and perhaps even its main generic approach, again regardless of CL and I-level. That aside, all previously available elements and activities—recreation, outings, visits from parents/relatives, brief furloughs ("Temporary Release"), and so on—remained in place.

The new law had one other major effect on Craigwood-Bridgeway: Its determinate sentencing feature greatly diluted the program's continuum-of-care strategy. Specifically, upon completing their Ailsa Craig program—and, in so doing, their determinate sentence—youths could decide to not become involved with the Community Centre; and that is what the vast majority decided. They did so despite the encouragement that Ailsa Craig staff gave them to voluntarily utilize that resource.

Staff provided such encouragement when they believed the Centre could significantly help those youths (1) deal with specific external/environmental conditions that were patently, or even just potentially, harmful or overwhelming, and/or (2) progress and develop in ways that still seemed to be needed at the emotional level, needed with respect to practical skills, and so forth. Both points applied, not to all graduates automatically, but to only those who, as reflected in the Ministry's earlier (pre-1985) concern regarding youths who were to be served by Ailsa Craig, *still* "required additional intervention to [help them better adjust] in their home communities." Given the above option, however, only a small percentage of graduates chose to utilize the Centre's resources. Those who declined any involvement included, but extended beyond, the many individuals who—prior to arriving at Ailsa Craig—had already spent a number of years under relatively continuous supervision, often in one or two training schools.

From 1985 to the present, Craigwood-Bridgeway obtained its basic, hard-to-serve populations from the same catchment areas as before. Its staff were hired mainly for their likely ability to work appropriately with a large portion of these difficult and/or troubled youths—in effect, for their potential as "generalists" for a somewhat specialized yet mixed group. Staff did not have to also, or instead, be specifically matched with one or more subgroups within that overall group, for instance, be highly sensitive to and specially responsive to those types of youth. Though matching in this latter, more restricted yet standard sense was considered a "plus," it was therefore neither an essential precondition for, nor the overriding factor in, hiring.

Also from 1985 to date, *Conceptual Level* was routinely drawn upon regarding its implications for individual treatment planning, for staff/youth and staff/group interactions, and for assessing progress. This was the case despite its no longer being the primary basis of unit assignment and of overall, within-unit structure (applicable across all unit youths), in the first place. Besides being compatible with Cognitive Restructuring and often adding significantly to it, CL—throughout that period—was regarded as neither too time-consuming nor overly costly with respect to (1) the training of new staff in CL's proper usage and (2) its actual *application*, especially the process of obtaining a CL and of subsequently specifying that information's implications with regard to any individual's particular characteristics and situation. Nor was CL considered too difficult in these respects.

By the late 1980s, time and costs were major, general concerns for Craigwood-Bridgeway, and these factors bore significantly on *I-level*. For one thing, considerable time—hence money—was often required to train new staff in this system. Nevertheless, as implied below, these factors, by themselves, did not *automatically* or *intrinsically* constitute problems, let alone major problems, with respect to I-level—ones that might invariably, or even just often, arise independently of external conditions. (In this regard it might be noted that I-level, like CL, had already been used at Craigwood-Bridgeway for almost 10 years without creating major time-and-money problems and/or related, unmanageable challenges.) Still, as discussed next, time and money did become serious issues at C-B largely because of or in connection with broad, external conditions.

Starting in 1989, Craigwood-Bridgeway had to reduce costs and redirect various resources, mainly because of the following: (1) Sizable budget cuts and related constraints were being mandated throughout Ontario's community and social services system, and in its correctional (ages 16 and up) and mental health agencies as well. (2) The Ministry's (MCSS's) continued policies and priorities encouraged C-B to attempt to emphasize early intervention even more than before. However, given the provincewide fiscal situation, and in light of the Ministry's and C-B's *other* longstanding priorities, this new emphasis was supposed to occur (1) without additional funding and (2) while still maintaining the present scope and level of Ailsa Craig's and the Community Centre's service to their basic populations, namely, hard-to-serve youths.

Since cost-reductions, unlike shifted priorities, could not be achieved by simply redirecting existing funds, it was decided that—to achieve those reductions, especially permanent ones—various operational functions or activities would have to be reduced, consolidated, otherwise streamlined/modified, and/or simply phased out, not just delayed or temporarily suspended. For the most part, the functions in question would be those that—given Craigwood-Bridgeway's new realities and requirements—now seemed too costly or

else insufficiently cost-effective. As to phasing-out, in particular, this could occur if, for instance, it was believed that C-B's basic goals would still be adequately met via the functions, resources, and levels of service that would remain.

Given this situation and framework it was decided that the formal and systematic usage of I-level would be permanently discontinued in 1990–1991; and this did occur. The direct cost reduction that would accrue from this action would largely result from Craigwood-Bridgeway's no longer having to train new staff in this system when turnover and other relevant personnel changes occurred, for example, when Assessment Unit diagnosticians and other C-B personnel moved to different assignments or agencies. (Staff turnover had previously posed a challenge with respect to I-level training, but this challenge was considered manageable and the training justified.) Apart from these cost-savings, other benefits would accrue—some marginal, others relatively substantial. This could occur, for instance, by using the staff time-and-energy that would be redirected from the phased-out process of obtaining and integrating the information needed to determine I-level/subtype. In general, the given benefits would involve various C-B functions, program approaches, and different priorities or emphases that could now be better supported, and in some cases initiated.

Further supporting that phase-out decision was the following, which centered on a key aspect of the treatment process, namely, planning: The combination of Conceptual Level information, on the one hand, and treatment plans that were more individualized than before, on the other, was viewed as providing enough detail and scope—that is, even without I-level—to help C-B achieve its main goals with most of its youths, or to at least begin that process with an adequate to firm base. (The treatment plans, of course, included CL information but went beyond it.) Closely related to this was the following experience-based belief regarding several important dimensions that would have been tapped during a formal I-level interview and which would have been subsequently focused on when deriving and finalizing the I-level/subtype itself: These dimensions, that is, types of information regarding the youth and his or her situation,

1. would, or certainly could, be tapped in *other* interview-contexts involving the youths and/or others, especially as part of obtaining those types of information that would be called for in any event, for purposes of developing the now-more-individualized plan; and, they
2. could be incorporated into the subsequently produced plan.

In short, Craigwood-Bridgeway's policymakers believed that even though the I-level interview and the resulting level/subtype classification would provide worthwhile information and could lead to useful integrations and unique perspectives, this procedure and product was no longer *sufficiently* important and uniquely needed for the purposes at hand, and—under the circumstances—it had therein become insufficiently cost-effective.

Statewide and Provincewide Efforts
Before concluding this chapter, the following might be mentioned regarding various efforts designed to increase intervention's degree of individualization and relevance. Unlike those just reviewed, these particular efforts—again outside California, during the 1970s and 1980s—were not made by

1. *single, private or quasi-private programs* that largely controlled their own intake (cf. St. Francis), or else operated in close conjunction with county, state, and/or provincewide public agencies and, for example, received many or all their referrals directly or indirectly from them (cf. Shawbridge);
2. *single, public-agency programs* that were an organizational entity within a *broader* public agency (cf. Baltimore DTU and Ormsby Village), for instance, an agency that contained several relatively traditional programs or approaches that, separately and together, may have made few if any substantial treatment-relevant distinctions among most youths, and/or hardly used them in that context in any event.

Nor were such efforts or programs limited to those of

3. *entire agencies*—more precisely, ones whose jurisdiction did not extend be-

yond a given city or county, however large or populous.

Instead, the given efforts/programs involved

4. *an entire state or province,* and in this regard they were either a primary or an otherwise major aspect of that entity's operation.

Two examples of these broad efforts and operations now follow, one emphasizing institutions and the other the community.

Colorado's Division of Youth Services
Colorado—about 40 percent the size of Texas—is the eighth largest state in the United States, geographically. Its population in 1970 and 1980 was 2.2 million and 2.9 million, respectively, and its largest metropolitan area—Denver and environs—accounted for slightly over half that number.

Beginning in 1970 and completed within the next three to five years, Colorado's entire Department of Institutions, Division of Youth Services (DYS),

> managed to effectively close its traditional training schools. These facilities now [1978] function as treatment centers where treatment units [i.e., individual "cottages," each] provide a total scope of services for a specifically identified youth according to his or her I-level classification. [More particularly, once a] diagnosis and classification [is obtained], in one of [DYS's] six regional [diagnostic and] detention centers, a youth is placed directly into one of approximately fourteen possible treatment programs [each located in its own cottage-style "unit"], according to his unique characteristics and needs [as partially and initially determined by that diagnosis, etc.] (Adlfinger, 1978, p. 26).

(Each center "has Colorado-trained and certified I-level diagnosticians [see below] who . . . also develop a needs assessment statement on each youth" [Adlfinger, 1980, p. 68].)

Once the youth arrives at an institution from a diagnostic/detention center, the information packet and treatment recommendations that accompany him or her is reviewed by a staffing group. This group then develops an individualized intervention plan, one designed to specifically reflect and build upon the diagnostic/detention center's needs assessment, among other items. (The packet also includes family history and social history material, an educational assessment, and, in some cases, a DYS psychological/psychiatric report. Drug and alcohol assessments were added in the 1980s.) Youths can be reinterviewed at this point if, for example, the center's I-level classification seems questionable; they can then be reassigned to a different unit, if necessary.

DYS's institutions are given enough flexibility and overall resources—including a relatively high staff-to-youth ratio—to in fact implement the staffing group's plan, or to at least seriously try to address its main aspects, issues, and goals. In this regard, institutional administrators, managers, and line staff are given the latitude and encouragement to use any of several well-known, lesser-known, relatively new, and/or innovative approaches, if necessary—provided they are humane and "within reason"—in order to address the youth's legitimate needs as an individual, and his or her particular life circumstances as well. The intervention plan can be revised or refined, during scheduled case conferences.

As indicated, the 14 programs are physically housed in the 14 treatment units that, collectively, comprise Colorado's state-level juvenile institutions (also called schools): The *Lookout Mountain School* has eight treatment units (seven for boys); together, these can house 160 boys and girls. DYS's other institution, *Mount View School,* has six such units (four for boys, one for girls, and one coed) and can house 140 boys and girls.[45] Besides these institutions, DYS's two youth camps serve 48 boys each and are also programmatically oriented around I-level concepts and strategies—as is *aftercare (parole),* though to a much lesser degree. (DYS administers aftercare.) Except for the coed unit (see endnote 45), the vast majority of youths remain in the institutions and camps 8 to 11 months, the average being about 9.

During the 1970s and 1980s, the DYS received some 500 to 600 committed youths per year, from the local courts,[46] and most youths in each DYS facility were 16 or 17 years old at admission (Adlfinger, 1978).

The composite picture of the youth we now [1978] have in our [institutional, i.e., treatment center] programs is of an immature [usually I_3] delinquent who has committed a number of serious offenses, has failed in numerous community placements, and often in mental health facilities. We [are] seeing generally more seriously disturbed, more seriously delinquent youth [than in the late 1960s as well as the early to middle 1970s] (Miller, 1978, p. 32).

The conversion of the Division of Youth Services' institutions and camps from traditionally organized and oriented operations to differential intervention facilities largely originated with the training that was received at California's CTDT by DYS's soon-to-be director of institutional treatment (Adlfinger), in 1969. Also facilitating that change was CTDT's training of six other staff, in early 1970. Together, these and subsequent trainees[47] represented a broad range of Colorado's social and correctional services and functions: mental health; probation intake, field services, and administration; and DYS diagnosis, casework, aftercare, and staff training. By 1971, DYS had established a statewide Staff Development and Training Center, one that soon produced a cadre of I-level diagnosticians, that assessed DYS staff for subsequent matching with youths,[48] and that began to train institutional and other staff in differential intervention strategies and techniques. By 1974, the center had developed an extensive program of certification for diagnosticians (Emmick, 1978; Mertz, 1978; Warren and CTDT staff, 1972, pp. 256–260, 280; Warren and CTDT staff, 1974, pp. 164–175, 190–191).

The following briefly illustrates some of DYS's broad programmatic differentiations among *groups (subtypes) of youths*—youths assigned to their respective treatment units, as of the later-1970s. (Some units housed conflicted individuals only, for example, either Na's or Nx's; others contained power-oriented youths only, that is, Mp's and Cfc's; still others—in fact, the majority—housed passive-conformists [a group that, for various reasons, was quite often sent to DYS]. However, homogeneous grouping by subtype did not supersede all other factors.[49] Except as indicated, all quotations from here to the end of this section are from Miller, 1978, pp. 28–32.)

As would be expected from a differential treatment model, there is a great deal of diversity across the various programs in the Division [DYS]. In certain units there are highly structured programs with very tight behavioral controls; in others, the structure is looser, with a significant amount of responsibility put on the residents to determine their own rules and structure. Some programs place a heavy emphasis on groups and have group meetings as often as five times a week; others meet infrequently in groups, perhaps once a week. Expectedly, the groups vary quite a lot [, in other ways]. Some are very problem-solving oriented; some emphasize teaching social and communication skills; others are more insight oriented [—all in accordance with differing I-level/subtype strategies and guidelines]. In some groups the residents are primarily responsible for the running and direction of the group, while in others the counselor takes the most active role. Some counselors . . . take their groups out of the institutions for social activities, while others prefer to keep their group contacts more formal.

[Also,] the variety of treatment *modalities* [continues] to expand as staff become more sophisticated and better trained, and again varies from program to program. [Thus,] going from one unit program to the next, one could witness [the use of Gestalt techniques, Transactional Analysis concepts, assertiveness training groups, role-playing groups, and so on, respectively]." (Emphasis added.)

The implementation and effective coordination of such approaches relative to the *individual youths* within each unit (hence, within each group) was made possible by converting the DYS institutions from their previous, traditional staffing pattern and relatively self-contained program-area structures to one that centered on "treatment teams."

Prior to 1970, Colorado's juvenile correctional programs operated very much within the traditional, 3-way split of custody, treatment, and education, under the respective titles of Group Life, Clinical Services, and Academic-Vocational School. . . . [By 1971, given an infusion of funds from the state legislature,] the staffing pattern in each cottage was [increased] from four to eight full-time staff. In addition, the Clinical Services Department was eliminated as such and the clinical personnel from that department were placed in supervisory positions over the eight staff in each unit. This made a total of nine people in each unit, with the clinical person being called the treatment team coordinator, [and given] the responsibility [of] putting together and supervising a total treatment program in the unit. Group Life and Clinical Services were thus merged, forming the nucleus of the treatment team. [See below regarding education staff.]

[During the next few years, with the expansion of youth-classification and worker/youth matching, there was] a whirlwind of change in the Division. Units were set up to provide programs for homogeneous groups of youth, and a flurry of worker-styling was accomplished with resulting staff reassignments to various units. A rigorous and concerted effort was launched to provide extensive training for the new, as well as the older, staff, and to build the unit teams into cohesive, well-functioning, entities. The [Division's Staff Development and] Training Center conducted and arranged for literally hundreds of classes, not only in I-level but in [numerous] treatment modalities and management approaches.[50] [In 1975, academic and vocational teachers were also integrated into the treatment teams, whereas they had previously functioned as a largely independent entity. At any rate, students no longer] attended academic school and vocational programs during the day with very little integration of their educational and counseling needs, even though these needs would . . . frequently impact one another.

Each boy and girl had a primary counselor. That person served as the overall case manager/coordinator and conducted an average of one to two formally scheduled, individual counseling sessions per week, with the youth. Vocational programming, when prescribed, usually centered on auto repair or printing for boys and on office skills for girls.

In all institution units, visits by parents and other family members were encouraged; and family counseling—involving the parents and youth together—sometimes occurred during those visits. Weekend visits—by youths, to their homes—were common throughout the 1970s but largely discontinued as of the early 1980s.

Many parole agents would visit the institutions to meet with staff and, separately, with the individual youths assigned to them; this was done mainly to discuss major issues and needs and, often, to develop an aftercare plan. It was generally these agents who scheduled and conducted the family counseling, and these sessions sometimes occurred prior to, and/or somewhat apart from, release planning per se.

In 1982 the Division of Youth Services "completed I-level retraining of 153 staff, including all administrators, program supervisors, teachers, community workers, and direct child care staff. Many staff had not had I-level training for a number of years" (Adlfinger, 1983, p. 7). (For further details regarding the DYS's policies and practices concerning staff training, especially that of diagnosticians, see Dreo [1976], Emmick [1978], and Mertz [1978].) All in all, the DYS's statewide differential intervention programming—including its worker/youth matching[51]—remained in full force from the early 1970s until approximately 1984. At that point, DYS began to modify some of its above-mentioned strategies and procedures in order to increasingly utilize risk-level information regarding predicted parole performance. For the next several years risk level coexisted with the more individualized, differential intervention approach, though the former was increasingly emphasized. In 1990, the latter was formally discontinued at the agency level, although some individual staff members continued to use its concepts, strategies, and techniques on a small-scale, independent basis.

Manitoba Probation Services

Canada's province of Manitoba is about two and a half times larger than Colorado,[52] though, in 1970 and 1980, it had less than half as many people. Manitoba's largest metropolitan area—Winnipeg and environs (population somewhat over 500,000 during those years)—contained half its populace.

In 1969–1970, all juvenile probation officers serving the Winnipeg area received training and follow-up in I-level strategies and techniques. This was provided by two individuals who had completed an extensive course at the Center for Training in Differential Treatment, in early 1969. One was a regional director of the Manitoba Probation Services (MPS); the other was named coordinator of I-level training for MPS (hence, the "provincial coordinator"), shortly after his CTDT training.

By early 1976, all 90 Probation Officers who, collectively, covered the *entire* province had received training in those strategies and techniques.[53] Many of these individuals were each responsible not only for supervision and treatment in a given community, in a number of communities, or in portions thereof, but also in a broader, overall "region."[54] When combined with Manitoba Probation's practice of classifying, and developing plans for, all adjudicated youths at point of intake, the training these 90 officers received—training which, itself, focused on juveniles—helped increase the degree of individualization and of relevant intervention throughout MPS. At least, it accomplished these ends when both it and Probation's practice were adequately implemented.

In broad outline, the youth-classification and treatment-planning process was as follows (this summary focuses on the mid-1970s and was written by the above-mentioned coordinator):[55]

> The initial I-level interview is done by the Provincial Coordinator or a Senior Probation Officer, one of thirteen officers who direct regional or community teams. After the initial interview, a second rating is conducted with [1] the Probation Officer who is to carry the case, [2] the Senior Probation Officer, and, in most cases, [3] the [Provincial] Coordinator. At this point [in the process], a treatment plan is worked out and a report is dictated that may be provided to the Court, to a treatment facility, to a training school, or to a Forensic unit [in order] to assist with [a] psychiatric and psychological assessment. The treatment plan becomes part of the case file. The basic strategy worked out by [this] second-rating team is articulated therein, and is expected to be followed.[56]

[If] a child is committed to a training school, . . . a reinterview is conducted [prior to his or her start of active *aftercare,* in order to] evaluate progress in the training school and to articulate new goals and plans, for aftercare (Pritchard, 1976, pp. 6–7; emphasis added).

This process remained essentially unchanged throughout the 1970s. Each treatment plan, whether initial, updated, prerelease, or other, is to present ways of realistically addressing factors, conditions, issues, and opportunities that bear most significantly on the particular youth's delinquent behavior and attitudes, on his or her overall current adjustment and needs, on his or her interests, strengths, and limitations, and on his or her future growth and development. In this respect, the plan is to be individualized—is, moreover, to go well beyond a review or statement of selected strategies and techniques often found useful or even critical with the youth's particular *subtype.* Probation usually lasted one to two years, more often closer to one. For individuals who had gone to a training school, aftercare usually lasted six months.

Worker/youth matching is considered important. As a result, Manitoba's probation officers are assigned to caseloads that have a sizable or high percentage of matched youths whenever this is logistically possible and is otherwise realistic and appropriate.[57] Also, with any given officer, particularly a newly hired one, matching is likely to occur on a gradual and relatively personalized or developmental basis. (For details, see endnote 58.) The matching concepts that are used are those developed in California, mainly during the Phase 1 and 2 experiment.

Together with the individual programs reviewed in this chapter, these just-described statewide/provincewide efforts reflect (1) the operational feasibility and "transferability" of major differential and individualized intervention concepts and approaches. They suggest or indicate the latters' (2) utility or practical validity as well. Both points apply not so much—or, perhaps, not just—to these concepts/approaches insofar as they function on their own or largely on their own, but, instead, as they operate within and contribute to a total "package" or overall program, and sometimes constitute its structural as well as dynamic core. Finally, the concepts/approaches seem applicable to a *variety* of correctional settings and contexts, and under a sizable range of conditions.[60]

Notes

1. This model was described by Brill (1979, pp. 106–112) as follows:

   [In the] Conceptual Level [CL] Matching Model, . . . behavior is a function of both the Person and his Environment. . . . [The] Model describes Person-differences along the dimension of conceptual complexity and related motivational orientations. The aspect of the environment which relates most directly to this Person characteristic is described by Hunt (1971) as *degree of structure,* and by Schroder, Driver, and Struefert (1967) as *degree of complexity.*

   Degree of structure has been used generically to refer to the amount and diversity of informational components present in the environment which the individual could use in evaluating and/or formulating responses to that environment. The higher the structure, the more these elements might be thought of as 'pre-packaged' in some organized, coherent ways. From a treatment-program perspective, structure would refer to the degree of order, organizational clarity, and support which residents/clients experience. The most important feature of degree of structure for the individual treater or treatment team is how much the staff is responsible for the treatment interaction, but variation in specificity and organization of the content of treater-client interactions would appear to be very important as well. Highly structured environments (1) are treater controlled, (2) involve specifically focused content, and (3) involve specific expectations. Environments low in structure would be (1) more determined by the client(s), (2) involve less pre-organization of interactions, and (3) involve mutual staff-client negotiation of expectations. . . .

   Given the conceptually simple, egocentric nature of very low ["Stage A"] CL persons, they should profit more from a highly structured approach. High ["Stage C"] CL persons, on the other

hand, are complex, capable of generating new concepts, and capable of adapting to different or changing environments. Hence, they should profit more from low structure, or be less affected by changes in structure. . . . [It is] necessary to know the CL stage of the person in order to determine what [conditions] would provide a "matched" or optimal environment.
. . . For the conceptually simple, Stage A person, a matched environment is seen to be highly structured, that is, clear, consistent, well-organized. These conditions are seen to induce movement to Stage B by making it possible for the Stage A individual to comprehend the norms and values in the situation and to accept them as guidelines for his own behavior. [Many youths are best classified as "Stage A/B."]

For the Stage B individual, who already has an internalized set of values from which he has been operating, movement to Stage C requires that he begin to generate internally relevant standards and to make decisions based on [them]. Hence, the optimal ["matched"] environment is one which encourages a breaking away from previously accepted standards, and [also] greater decision-making based on self-relevant needs, but still within the overall context of accepted norms. . . .

The optimal environment for the Stage C individual should encourage the work of that stage, i.e., development of self-distinctiveness from the norms he has previously accepted, and therefore should deemphasize normative pressures and emphasize opportunities for independence. An environment which enforced continued compliance to previously accepted norms would block further growth." [Many delinquents and nondelinquents are at "Stage B/C."]

2. Hanna was assistant executive director of the Boys' Farm during most of the 1970s and was the first president of the International Differential Treatment Association. (See endnote 59.)

3. Other community and residential service staff not described or emphasized thus far include "2 full-time and 1 part-time nurse, as well as a part-time doctor."

These individuals staff the campus [i.e., the-site-of-the-cottages'] medical center. Whereas "community and group home youths generally use *community* [i.e., public] health, educational, and recreational services, . . . four [SYC] recreation counselors provide daily classes and evening supervision to campus youth." Also, "on the residential [i.e., cottages'] campus, 20 teachers [not all of whom are full-time, and] some having special education degrees, provide schooling to 60 to 80 youths. In the city, five teachers provide classes four days a week to 20 to 30 youths. In addition, a program specialist [operates] a work training program for six to eight youths" (Reitsma and Brill, 1978b, p. 14; emphasis added).

4. The New York home—called Camelot— serves 26 youths at any given time. It opened in the 1960s and mainly uses behavior modification. The third *Kansas* operation—called Passport for Adventure—serves some 100 youths per year, and began in 1971. It is described as "combining some of the concepts of 'Outward Bound' camping with family counseling. It is for sixth graders . . . who are nominated by their school teachers as their kids most likely to get into trouble." Thus, it is a nonresidential approach, mainly for nonadjudicated youths (SFBH Annual Report, 1981; SFBH, 1975, p. 8).

5. SFBH is also a charter member of the National Association of Homes for Boys and the National Association of Homes for Children.

6. Whether or not the boy has been acting-out in any given instance, "[we may] say 'no' to reinforce his developing ego, but not when we needn't do so. Twenty-four hour a day supervision is available, but we expect each boy to need it less and less." "A boy with serious acting-out problems, or otherwise out of control, no matter what his status [on the 3-step ladder], may [be] briefly restricted to ["sitting in a chair in the living room"— this being "our most severe form of discipline"], or be subjected to a restricted area. . . . He loses privileges and freedoms while re-earning his place in the Home family. This is a period during

which staff persons help him develop his needed inner controls [mainly through personal counseling, etc.]" . . . "Forgiveness and counteralienation take precedence over suppression and regimentation." "We do not use isolation rooms, convulsive shock, surgical, or any physically or mentally risky treatment procedures." "We don't degrade, strip of felt dignity, or disorient (as in brainwashing), and then rebuild" (SFBH Operating Manual, 1981/1982; SFBH, 1979, pp. 3–5, 12).

7. Further, "We aim not only for the absence of disability, but [for] the presence of robust health, maturity, . . . [and for] a person subjectively and objectively appreciating and valuing himself" (SFBH Operating Manual, 1981/1982).

8. These descriptions are from an open-ended "Personal History" and a structured "Biographical and Personality Inventory." Unless a recent psychological evaluation is available, this material is requested prior to admission (SFBH Operating Manual, 1981/1982; SFBH, 1979, p. 9).

9. "After [the] boy is accepted, the Executive Director determines with the parents or other referring persons their fair share amount of payment for the cost of the boy's care. The difference is borne by interested individual contributors over the nation, and this constitutes an awarded 'charity allowance.' . . . [Parents pay for their son] on a 'sliding scale,' and agencies purchase our services. (The Internal Revenue Service has allowed deductions of maintenance payments as a medical expense.) Many medical insurance policies recompense toward purchase of certified clinical services. Our donors [there being several thousand, nationwide] allow us to continue to accept boys whose parents cannot pay the full fee" (SFBH, 1979, p. 7).

Though the homes have always been directly related to the Episcopal Church, they "receive no regular subsidies or grants from [that source]" (SFBH, 1979, p. 7). St. Francis' sources and percentages of funding/income are as follows (figures are averaged for FY 1980/1981 and 1981/1982): governmental funding—41 percent; contributions by individuals, churches, and church organizations—37 percent; legacies—8 percent; private fees from parents—4 percent; grants and other—10 percent. Expenditures are: program (including salaries and wages)—63 percent; clinical services and research—13 percent; administration—12 percent; fund-raising—7 percent; development—5 percent (SFBH Annual Report, 1981, p. 7).

10. Tutorial assistance is available throughout the school year, and volunteer teachers provide remedial services during the summer.

11. "[The] youth has the right to practice a religion with which he has identified. If [he] is able to function unsupervised, he may choose from available local churches. . . . *Attendance* and not interfering [with] or distract[ing] others in worship is [required]; *participation,* [however,] is an option. . . . As in every other area of life, we recognize the right of the youth to make up his own mind about his values and to be free from negative consequences for personal convictions contrary to those of staff and administration" (SFBH Operating Manual, 1981/1982; emphasis added).

12. This team consists of home staff as well as individuals from the St. Francis Boys' Homes administrative office (the "Clinical staff"), and it meets weekly to review individual youths' overall progress, release plans, and so on. It might be mentioned that, besides this and the evaluation team, various other teams, groups, or committees exist at SFBH. Among them, the most influential and integrative with regard to administration, program development and modification, quality control, and so forth, is the Clinical Child Care Committee (CCCC). This is

the staff policy group concerned with client services for all St. Francis Boys Homes operations. . . . [In its capacity as the] Executive Committee for the clinical staff, . . . it reviews and recommends to the Board's Client Services Committee [CSC] policies regarding clinical/professional staff organization, treatment philosophy, and treatment services. It reviews and approves clinical staff appointments, . . . and certifies staff credentials. . . . [It] reviews and recommends to the [CSC] all policies regarding clients' rights [e.g., as prepared by the Human Rights Committee]. . . . At least annually, the Quality Assurance Officer reports to CCCC [and, as a result, the latter] may call for . . . specific Quality Assurance studies. . . . [CCCC also regularly reviews admission policies and practices, and average length of stay; and, in this and related matters, it may] call for the research psychologist or Clinical Coordinator to [conduct] Utilization Review studies. . . . [CCCC may also] initiate or call for specific program evaluation studies, of which the Clinical Coordinator assures implementation. . . . [Finally, it] reviews all patient care policies and may initiate or call for specific patient care studies. . . . [CCCC meets monthly and consists of] the medical director [psychiatrist], Clinical Coordinator, research psychologist, Social Work Supervisors, . . . Home Treatment Coordinators, and a representative of [the CSC]" (SFBH Operating Manual, 1981/1982).

13. The treatment plan, plus its updates and modifications, are reviewed and approved by the home treatment coordinator.
14. Beginning in that year, each newly accepted youth received an interview-based I-level/subtype classification. Soon afterward, all interviews—having been tape-recorded—were second-rated (either within SFBH or by outside consultants).
15. Between 1977 and 1981, various St. Francis staff were trained in central aspects of I-level and matching. Staff received the type or types of training they would be called upon to use. Starting in 1981, ongoing "training and skill development in the I-level method, . . . and quality control of [that] classification strategy, [was mainly provided by] nine I-level classification case conferences per year," at St. Francis. These meetings focused on "I-level classification, diagnostic/interviewing skills, treatment strategy, matching issues, and case progress," and they were available to a wide range of staff (SFBH Operating Manual, 1981/1982).

16. By 1981, the I-level system was "utilize[d] as primary strategy," and its subtype categories were seen as "lead[ing] directly to certain general treatment strategies, and [to] the stance of the Primary Counselor" (SFBH Operating Manual, 1981/1982). Even before 1980, Treatment Plans were partly reflecting the youths' subtype classification, and worker/staff matching was taking place (SFBH Annual Report, 1981, pp. 5–6). These approaches were implemented by various clinical staff who had been trained in those regards.
17. Thus, for instance, the subtype classification "is a direct aid in prescribing the primary counselor best able to have rapport and be effective with clients [of the given subtype]" (Force, 1986, p. 11; Hebison and Gustitus, 1982).
18. Other cities that received LEAA High Impact Program funds at the time were Atlanta, Cleveland, Dallas, Denver, Newark, Portland (Oregon), and St. Louis. In 1970 and 1980, Baltimore City's population was 910,000 and 790,000, respectively. Including the city's immediate surroundings—the "standard metropolitan statistical area"—the population was approximately 2,000,000 during those years.
19. The formal statement of these aims, one which did not expressly mention the operational/organizational "do-ability" factor, was as follows: "The first specific objective [is] to gain community acceptance; the second [is] to show the feasibility of maintaining youth adjudicated of impact offenses in the community, instead of commitment [or "transferring for prosecution"]; and the third [is] to demonstrate that the cost of such a program [is] less in comparison to commitment and/or waiver to the adult correctional system" (Waldman, 1977, pp. 1, 10–11).
20. Even by September 1975, "In its progress summary, . . . the Governor's Commission on Law Enforcement and the Administration of Justice summarily state[d that] . . . the Project appears to be a viable alternative for Baltimore City High Impact Offenders" (Chesley, 1976, pp. 5–6). (Regarding community acceptance, reduced commitments, and

comparative costs in particular, see Waldman, 1977, pp. 10–13, 18–19, 62–63.)

21. When absorbed and integrated, the project maintained essentially the same organizational structure and staffing pattern that existed during the demonstration phase. (See text, below.)

22. Besides working directly with youths, some project staff performed major intake/diagnostic functions. As a result, they carried only partial caseloads at the time.

23. Though these were not considered their primary problem, "moderate" drug abuse was found in the histories of 51 percent of all project youths, and "high" abuse was found among 9 percent. The respective figures for prior alcohol abuse were 55 percent and 10 percent.

24. For a review of other, related differences between individualized and differential intervention, see Chapter 30.

25. As with St. Francis staff, those in Baltimore's DTP were trained by IDTA-certified diagnosticians and treatment consultants. Most such consultants, in turn, had either attended the California Youth Authority's Center for Training in Differential Treatment or had been trained by individuals who, themselves, had attended that Center.

26. The "Form 3" Rating Inventory (Palmer, 1968d) is used as the main basis for matching. (See, however, endnote 27.)

27. According to a MITRE Corporation evaluation of several High Impact programs, the following occurred regarding matching. Because of "State personnel regulations and problems with the experience and training of the officers (juvenile counselors), the matched officer feature of the [Differential Treatment] Project had to be somewhat modified in Baltimore" (Sasfy, 1975, p. 32). This may partly account for DTP's less than complete matching with respect to youth subtype. It might be added at this point that, when they began working at the Differential Treatment Program, staff were an average of almost seven years younger than those at California's CTP. They also had two to three years less counseling plus treatment (e.g., therapy) experience than the latter individuals and

four to five years less work experience overall, within the helping profession (Palmer, 1967a; Sasfy, 1975).

28. Louisville's population in 1970 and 1980 was approximately 300,000. OVTC's specific location is the town of Anchorage, whose population was between 1,500 and 2,000 during those years. Except where specified, the text that follows describes OVTC as it existed in the early 1970s.

29. The preceding superintendent had retired in 1966, after serving in that capacity for four decades. The facility, formerly called Ormsby Village, was renamed Ormsby Village Treatment Center, in 1968.

30. Also present for that training were two staff members from the Diagnostic and Clinical Probation Services of Jefferson County, of which Louisville was, and is, the population hub. The CTDT training received by these individuals and by the new OVTC superintendent (Jerry Hissong) was preceded by similar training obtained by the director of diagnostic services of Jefferson County, in January 1968. Interest in CTP and its classification system had been peaked by the national attention California's Community Treatment Project had received in 1967, soon after it was highlighted in a Presidential Commission report on crime, delinquency, and corrections, and was then discussed in the Commission's supplementary Task Force reports—besides being showcased in television newscasts (President's Commission, 1967a, pp. 170–171; 1967b, pp. 22, 41–42; 1967c, pp. 130, 423). Jerry Hissong initiated and developed the OVTC program beginning in 1968, and directed it from then until 1974. Kay Gunderson was its superintendent/director during 1974–1979.

31. These brief characterizations refer to the Cfm (and/or I$_2$), Cfc, Mp, and Na/Nx subtypes, respectively, as presented in I-level literature (Warren et al., 1966b).

32. "Recruitment . . . entails identifying the vacant staff position and the needs of the specific children a person in that position must meet. Staff are then recruited according to those therapeutic and professional requirements. The professional staff members are easy to recruit because

of the attractiveness of the program. Retention has been easier, too, with the new treatment concepts. The net result is that there are usually several applicants for each professional position, thereby allowing selectivity and matching (staff to children) to be as extensive as desirable."

33. Collectively, volunteers provide the usual range of services, activities, information, interactions, and relationships associated with these individuals.

34. "Chaplains with clinical training may also be involved in family counseling."

35. These census figures are for 1980. London's estimated population in 1990 was 300,000 and Ailsa Craig's was 1,400. The Ailsa Craig component of Craigwood-Bridgeway is located on farmland donated in 1954 to the Menninite Central Committee of Ontario, in order to assist delinquent boys. In 1959, MCC established a board of directors and gave it responsibility for all farm operations, including youth care. In the later 1960s this "Ailsa Craig Boys Farm" (ACBF) served individuals age 16 through 20. During most of the 1970s, a period in which it concentrated on preadolescents instead, ACBF operated under the Ontario Ministry of Health (Children's Services Division); also, from then on, it no longer emphasized farm products to financially support its youths. In 1978, MOH(CSD) was transferred to Ontario's Ministry of Community and Social Services, and "Craigwood" (ACBF's new name as of 1964) has been closely associated with this Ministry, and has operated via its funding, from 1979 to the present. (All farmland except Ailsa Craig's present site was sold in the early 1980s.) In 1983, the board of directors self-incorporated, and the agency's name was changed to Craigwood Youth Services. Since 1984, CYS has been licensed by, and all its programs have fallen under the auspices of, the Child and Family Services Act (CFSA) of Ontario. Also governing CYS's programs is the slightly younger, and more general, Young Offenders Act (YOA) of 1984; this is a federal, that is, nationwide, law, and is discussed later in the text. Ontario Province's enabling legislation for the YOA is contained in the

CFSA, which also establishes and formulates various rights, on the part of youths and parents, that were not covered or spelled out in the federal act (Hogan, Johnston, and Leihmann, 1994, pp. 2–4). Craigwood Youth Services was Ontario's first child mental health center to focus exclusively on a young offender population. It remains the only agency that works with hard-to-serve adolescents in the earlier-mentioned five-county catchment area.

36. Most, but obviously not all, Ontario training schools mainly house youths from *Toronto* and environs (population 2,500,000 in 1980)—this city being 100 miles east of London. Of all training school referrals to Craigwood-Bridgeway, about 90 percent are from one facility and the remainder are almost always from one other.

37. The treatment environments, including their degree of structure, are assessed via the Moos Correctional Institutions Environment Scale (CIES).

38. Also called the "Community-Based Treatment Project Centre," the "Project Centre," and "Craigwood-Bridgeway-Phase II."

39. The average duration per training school stay was eight months.

40. It might be noted that, on one-year follow-up from admission to C-B, 50 percent of all youths had absconded ("unauthorized absence"), whether briefly or not. Of these individuals—not all of whom had been placed in a local detention facility as a result—88 percent "were able to return and re-integrate back to the program, with only minor interruptions in the treatment process" (Leschied and Thomas, 1983, p. 26).

41. Included, for example, were the following (all figures refer to the percentage of youths assessed, assisted, etc.): Probation—94 percent; Family Court Clinic—92 percent; Children's Aid Society—89 percent; Observation and Detention Home—82 percent; Family Counseling Center—55 percent; Residential Treatment Center—40 percent; Psychiatric Placement—27 percent; Hospital Affiliated Counseling Center—21 percent. "Family Court Clinic" mainly involved a clinical assessment

ordered by a family court judge. "Children's Aid Society" generally involved referrals to, or placements into, foster or group homes.

42. As further indicated by Leschied and Thomas (1983), such individuals also seemed comparable to the "impossible" child (Barker, 1978) and to "Ovinnik syndrome" youths (Rae-Grant, 1978).

43. The social history encompasses standard content areas such as health, education, family situation, neighborhood/environment, court contacts and offense history, involvement with community resources, placements, psychiatric evaluations, prior treatment, and so on. Each youth's I-level and CL is determined by standard means, that is, a semi-structured interview (Warren et al., 1966b), in the first case and a semi-structured sentence completion or paragraph completion test (Hunt et al., 1978) in the second. The Jesness Inventory was not used at Craigwood-Bridgeway (nor was it used after 1984), whether for I-level diagnosis or other purposes.

44. School operations in C-B's community as well as residential components were always under the auspices of local boards of education.

45. The coed unit, housing up to 26 youths, is the widely known "Closed Adolescent Treatment Center" for repeat and/or violent offenders who seem particularly disturbed or threatening, and who must usually remain at least a year. About 50 percent are serious (mainly assaultive) sex offenders, and some 25 percent are murderers—there being some overlap between these subpopulations. The differing therapy groups *within* this unit are organized as "homogeneous groupings based on [the I-level "typology"]. Staff are also matched with students [youths] for treatment purposes, using this typology. Therefore, group, individual, family therapy, and all treatment planning are done by matched staff" (Agee, 1986, p. 78; also see Agee, 1979). The matching of staff, however, is of the less differentiated form mentioned in endnote 51, below; and, in any event, "each of [DYS's dozen-plus program] units has a treatment team [comprised of] staff who are worker-matched

to the specific group they handle" (Adlfinger, 1980, p. 68).

46. About 90 percent of these individuals were males; their average age at admission was 17; they were, collectively, about 58 percent Caucasian, 30 percent Mexican American, and 12 percent black; some 75 percent were from the Denver metropolitan area; and approximately 20 percent were in DYS's secure locked units (Adlfinger, 1978, pp. 25–26).

47. Two DYS staff, one a trainer and the other a psychiatric team consultant (see endnote 50) as well as trainer, received extensive differential treatment training at CTDT, in late 1970 and early 1972, respectively. Moreover, Law Enforcement Assistance Administration (LEAA) funds "designed to acquire and implement the I-level methodology on a comprehensive basis in [DYS made it possible for various] CTDT-trained staff [to be] sent back to California, as necessary, to obtain further skills and knowledge from the Probation Subsidy Units, the [YA's] Northern Reception Center [and Clinic], several institutions which were using I-level, and, of course, for refresher work with CTDT" (Mertz, 1978, p. 30; emphasis added).

48. "An I-level Task Force was formed early in 1971 and continues today. [It was] responsible for many aspects of the Division's acquisition of I-level. [It has] provided managerial consultation, diagnostic procedures, pilot treatment projects, certification and other standards, and some research/evaluation efforts" (Mertz, 1978, p. 35).

49. Thus, while we consider the homogeneous grouping of youth according to their I-level diagnosis a very important, key factor in [unit/program] placement, we have also learned that other considerations are sometimes equally important. For instance, many of our youth are learning disabled, some very much so, and consequently, one of our programs at Mount View School was specifically set up to work with [them]. . . . Also, we have designated two units at Lookout [Mountain School] to provide long-term treatment programs for [those "repeat and violent juvenile offenders" who have certain mandatory minimum sentences. The latter individuals, of course, are other than the

ones—also a mix of subtypes—housed in Mount View's Closed Adolescent Treatment Center unit]. (See endnote 45.)

50. Also, individuals from DYS's Psychiatric Consulting Team provided ongoing consultation to each unit, with an emphasis on team-building and program development, often spending 8 to 10 hours a week in single units [within] the Division. Individual agency staff members, caught up in the excitement of being treatment agents rather than jailhouse guards, often attended classes and training sessions outside the system, on their own time and with their own money, in order to increase their treatment knowledge and skills.

51. For the first six or seven years, the fairly detailed approach to matching that was developed in California was used; that is, *several* specific distinctions were made among workers or worker candidates, even though the Form 3 Rating Inventory (Palmer, 1967a, 1968c) was not utilized. Subsequently, however, a less differentiated form of matching was employed; specifically, workers were categorized as either "Expressives" or "Instrumentals," only. As indicated by Miller (1978, p. 30), "it has not been possible, due to state hiring practices and other system limitations, to carry out a 'pure' [this refers to the California] system of matching workers to our youths. . . . As a result, we had to reluctantly discontinue this method [of determining] worker styles." (Regarding Expressives, Instrumentals, and various matching issues and procedures in Colorado, also see Agee [1982, pp. 32–39].)

52. It thus compares in area to Texas.

53. In the early 1970s, all officers who had carried juvenile cases only also began to supervise adults. Thus, some of their training probably affected the latter individuals, as well.

54. Together, these regions comprised Manitoba's entire geographic area, much as counties in the United States collectively cover an entire state.

55. This individual remained in that role until the late 1970s, from which point many line and senior staff whom he had trained continued the process largely on their own. This occurred despite MPS's

no longer requiring an I-level classification and, thus, I-level-centered treatment plans.

56. Through the years, the coordinator's and most other senior staff's impression was that the strategies and overall treatment plans usually *were* followed, and with considerable fidelity.

57. Sometimes, such caseloads are "created," in the sense of being constructed or reconstructed. This may be done, for instance, by reassigning individual *youths,* or, in effect, by exchanging ("switching" or "swapping") certain youths across two or more caseloads. (In all reassignments, the overall benefits must, of course, outweigh any and all drawbacks.) Also, two or more *workers* who supervise overlapping, contiguous, or nearby geographic areas may, under certain circumstances, exchange most or all their youths—or else their areas. (The senior probation officer would usually initiate this process and would, in any event, coordinate it.)

58. Major aspects of the worker/client matching process and strategy were described by Pritchard (1976):

[Because] Probation Officers are hired through a *provincial hiring agency* which is not looking for a specific worker style, *we* [MPS] are not in the position to hire into [, say, a given] Cfm, or Na, or Mp/Cfc, position [caseload]. Rather, staff are taken as they come, [and are] then assigned to teams after the Senior Probation Officers are able to look over [these] new applicants. . . .

Matching follows worker style determination [in a way] that is perhaps different than in [other] jurisdiction[s]: We have taken the position . . . that new officers should be given a broad range of experience initially, and then, after fairly intensive casework supervision [has occurred], and, where possible, [after] seminars on matching in worker style [have occurred], the individual Probation Officer can come to the realization or acceptance of certain strengths and aptitudes that tend towards more effective work with a particular type of probationer. We [have] found this method [is] fairly successful, is palatable to staff, and does not force them into positions of denying their generalist training background. (Emphasis added.)

59. A few years after the Youth Authority's Center for Training in Differential Treatment closed down, a new training and staff development operation was created to replace it. It was housed at the Shawbridge Youth Centers, near Montreal, and it also served to gather and disseminate information on differential treatment programs and concepts as well as to encourage and support related research, chiefly in the United States and Canada. In early 1977 its functions were formalized, consolidated, and broadened via the establishment of the International Differential Treatment Association (IDTA), a non-profit organization incorporated in Canada. Besides publishing biannual newsletters and, by the early 1980s, a full-length yearly journal, IDTA, in conjunction with the Shawbridge operation, (1) provided extensive training and consultation in diagnosis, in treatment planning and methods, in supervision, and in program development/operation, mainly to public and private agencies; (2) certified individuals in differential diagnosis, treatment, supervision, and training; and, starting in 1977, (3) held annual international conferences. By 1980 the Association contained four offender-classification divisions: Interpersonal Maturity (Warren), Conceptual Level (Hunt), Behavior Categories (Quay), and MMPI-based (Megargee). Soon afterward, a Moral Development (Kohlberg) division was added, as was a General division. During its approximately 14 years of existence its presidents were (in sequence): Wayne Hanna, Loren Adlfinger, Philip Harris, and W. Gustitus. At the time, most of these individuals were closely associated with agencies and programs described in this chapter.

60. Mainly in the interests of space we have not reviewed various other programs and operations that drew heavily from the California experiment. However, it would be useful to briefly mention at least one: the Alameda County Probation Department's Differential Treatment Unit (DTU). (The information and quotations that follow are from Neto, 1972 and 1973.) This California operation was a "special unit" established under the Statewide Probation Subsidy Program (see Chapter 17), designed to "implement the I-Level diagnostic and treatment system, modeled after the Community Treatment Project of the California Youth Authority," and largely directed at reducing the number of offenders committed to the state. DTU began operating in January 1968, and it served "all new male wards of the Juvenile Court who reside[d] in [a] designated East Oakland area." Caseloads were limited to 15 youths each in order to "allow enough time for intensive involvement with the ward, his family, and others in the community. In addition, time [was] allotted for [taped] diagnostic interviews, treatment planning, case conferences, and on-going training."

The DTU had two I_2-Cfm caseloads (hence, two workers), one Cfc-Mp, one Na, and one Nx-Cfm. "Se's [were] usually assigned to one of the N workers; Ci's [were] spread across all caseloads." Before being assigned to any caseload, each probation officer had been "interviewed at length," following the protocol used at the YA's Center for Training in Differential Treatment (CTDT). The scoring norms that were developed in the California (YA/NIMH) experiment (Palmer, 1968d) were then applied—the aim being to obtain staff need for good worker/youth matches. Each matched-and-assigned worker was "trained in I-Level theory by the CTDT, either in Sacramento or in Oakland. On-going training in diagnosis, case planning, and treatment [was] provided by consultants and through staff meetings." The DTU also had a supervisor, one who was simultaneously responsible for other Probation Subsidy caseloads as well. Insofar as possible, each DTU staff member "follow[ed] the differential treatment stand" that was generally associated with his given, assigned subtype(s).

By June 1971, three and a half years into the operation, 160 wards had become part of the DTU unit. (The unit, itself, was part of a formal experiment, one called the I-Level Research Project; in this connection, an additional 130 identically eligible wards from the same geographic area had been randomly assigned to Control [C] status—this being standard probation, with caseloads averaging about 50 youths per worker. DTU cases were called Experimentals [E's].) The average age of E's was 15.7 at intake; their racial composition was 86 percent black, 12 percent Caucasian, and 3 percent Mexican American; the preponderance (some 85 percent) were of low or very low socioeconomic status. Before their referral to the experiment/unit, 23 percent had had no referrals to probation (no official prior offenses), 43 percent had had 1 or 2, and 34 percent had had 3 or more; in toto, the offenses involved persons (16 percent), property (42 percent), and other (41 percent—again, of all official priors). The percentage representation by subtype or subtype group was: I_2—9; Cfm—32; Cfc-Mp—13; Na—16; Nx—17; Se—8; Ci—6. (Wards were classified via the interview method; second ratings occurred as needed.) DTU workers saw 66 percent of their wards at least once a week, mainly on a one-to-one basis; they were "involved with [39 percent of] the wards' families in an on-going supportive role, or in family counseling [with 35 percent]"; and, they occasionally contacted school personnel and employers.

The randomization was successful as of June 1971, in that the 160 E's and 130 C's were comparable to each other in age, race, number and type of priors, and so on, and in that the respective subtypes were fairly similar to each other as well. Using five outcome measures regarding offenses (O's) during wardship—number of O's per ward, number of months per O, time to first O, severity of O's, and number of law contacts—it was concluded, with respect to this sample, that overall [i.e., for all subtypes combined], Experimentals are slightly ahead of Controls on three of five dimensions; Controls are slightly ahead on lower average severity ratings. By subtype, Experimentals are ahead in 15 categories, Contols in 9 subgroups, and in 11

there are no differences. Experimental Cfc-Mp's are ahead in all items; Control I_2's and Experimental Nx's are ahead on four out of five items. The data show a slight tendency in favor of the Experimental Unit for Cfm's and in favor of Controls for Se's. For Ci's the trends are mixed. For Na's there are no [E/C] differences (Neto, 1972, page 9).

Based on the experiment's preliminary results and supported by unit staff's operational experiences, DTU, in June 1971, "began expand[ing] its intake to include . . . referrals of active 'difficult' cases from [other] probation units, in San Leandro and East Oakland." As a result, by early 1972, an additional 100 cases had entered DTU—with average caseload size having by then doubled in order to accommodate this rapid increase within the existing five-worker, five-caseload structure.

61. In 1995, confirmatory information, additional details, and/or various clarifications were obtained by the author regarding several programs/operations (p/o's) described in this chapter. It was obtained via personal phone conversations with the following individuals (similar information has already been indicated concerning the *remaining* p/o's): Estelle Turner (Shawbridge Youth Centers); Cheryl Rathbun (St. Francis Boys' Homes of Kansas); Jerry Hissong and Kay Gunderson (Ormsby Village Treatment Center); Loren Adlfinger (Colorado Division of Youth Services); Gibb Pritchard (Manitoba Probation Services). These individuals, who were directly associated with and very knowledgeable about those programs/operations, also provided considerable information about those p/o's more recent and/or final years.

PART II

Rationales, Theory, Ethics, and Trends

24 INTERVENTION—ITS RATIONALES AND THE NEEDS-CENTERED APPROACH

Together, this and the next three chapters cover a wide range of subjects. This section—Part II of the volume—begins by describing four main rationales for intervening with serious multiple offenders. When focusing on what is called "needs-centered intervention," it provides a rationale for individualizing intervention, in particular. The section also discusses theory. Here, it reviews youth needs and dynamics that contribute to the development and reinforcement of illegal behavior; and, during this review, it details related dynamics of intervention. Also discussed in various parts of the section are perspectives on "deservedness"—the main issues being whether, when, or to what extent the present youths merit assistance, given their records of crime. In effect, the following presentation of rationales for intervening, of contributors to delinquency, of dynamics regarding intervention, and of deservedness—each of which involves society's needs and inputs, as well—collectively comprises an examination of the ethical bases or appropriateness of intervention, both in general and in its individualized respect.

The section closes with (1) comments on selected developments within corrections since the 1970s, particularly the Justice Model and Risk Assessment, and with (2) the description of a "habilitation/developmental" (H/D) framework for conceptualizing needs, challenges, and issues that apparently must be addressed in order for young multiple offenders to substantially, and fairly permanently, change their illegal adjustment patterns. Accompanying this description of H/D is a theory of psychosocial growth and change that was developed during the Youth Authority/NIMH experiment and

which was then applied in conjunction with the Maturity Level classification system.

Rationales for Intervention

As already discussed, "intervention" includes not only treatment but external controls. Its treatment component involves planned efforts to help individuals achieve personal growth and development, and, with that, social growth. When appropriately used, its external controls can themselves help youths achieve that growth-centered goal, also called the offender-centered goal. (Whereas "external controls" and "controls" are sometimes used synonymously, "internal controls" are always specified as such. Also, see endnote 1 for more details regarding treatment. The offering or providing of assistance is an integral part of intervention.)

Intervention is directed not just at the offender-centered goal but at the protection of society (POS).[2] In fact, POS is the final goal—and, as such, the principal goal—of intervention. This goal applies to its treatment and control components alike, whether those components operate individually or in concert.[3] Here, intervention is an input or process, and POS an outcome or product. As a product, "protection . . ." generally signifies the avoidance, elimination, or reduction of illegal behavior.

Rationales #1 and #2: Pursue and Achieve Social Protection

Again, given the earlier-mentioned framework, what correctional intervention is mainly supposed to accomplish is the protection of society—this being a fundamental and self-justified need. From this perspective, *the pursuit of this socially centered goal*, that is, the intent and attempt to meet this broad, practical need, is the first justification for intervening—more specifically, for humanely intervening at all. This pursuit or effort is essential and justified (1) whether or not given interventions are subsequently *well*-implemented and (2) however much or little the socially centered goal is then achieved.[4] *Actual or increased achievement of this goal* comprises a further, no less important, albeit after-the-fact rationale. This second justification fulfills or helps fulfill the original intention; and, together with the fourth rationale, below, it gives the overall effort its main practical meaning and value to society as a whole.

Rationale #3: Assist Human Beings

A third justification centers not on the broad, pragmatic value of protecting society but on the intrinsic, ethical value of *attempting to assist offenders because they are human beings.* Like the first rationale, this one is before-the-fact, that is, prior to any goal achievement, and independent of its degree. Such efforts, which seldom stem from and/or comprise staff's *dominant* reason(s) for assisting others,[5] reflect and express a certain level of acceptance, respect, and/or perhaps compassion (ARC) that many human beings have (intellectually) and/or feel (emotionally) for others who are human, simply because they are human.[6] Not unrelated, these three ARC components involve some degree of partial identification.[7] Far from all people have or feel this ARC. (Of those who do not, many, nevertheless, partly or largely accept most offenders. They do so for other reasons, ones that often center on general and specific needs emphasized in the fourth rationale.) The acceptance, respect, and/or compassion in question usually ranges from slight or modest, on the one hand, to moderate or substantial, on the other.[8]

The content of the above-mentioned, attempted assistance—further specified in the fourth rationale—relates to more than offenders' health and safety and to more than assuring an absence of physical/psychological mistreatment/degradation.

The third justification is valid independently of the first-mentioned one (the effort to protect society), even though the two commonly coexist among correctional staff as individuals, and although substantial amounts of attempted humane assistance often do contribute to POS. The third is also valid even when given efforts to protect society leave much to be desired. Finally, and independent of the just-mentioned coexistence, "third-rationale-efforts"—when present at all—generally coexist with, though are almost always surpassed in strength by, interests and concerns that center on the relatively concrete, practical needs associated with the *fourth* rationale. As such, these fourth-rationale-interests and concerns reflect and express factors that are considerably different than—but which, in real life, are often functionally joined with and give palpable support to—the acceptance, respect, and/or compassion in question.

The central, defining component of the third justification for intervening is also called its "core." In this core, assistance, as indicated, is considered an intrinsically appropriate value. In this regard, its presence is not conditioned upon the offender's various activities and/or personality features. Thus, for instance, upon being committed to a correctional agency or department, an individual should be offered at least some assistance without first having *earned* it—for example, without having already come to deserve it by virtue of (1) various positive ("constructive," "useful") activities he or she (hereafter "he") has already engaged in or (2) the type of person he has been or hopes to be.

It might be added that assistance-as-reward (i.e., "earned assistance"), especially for factors such as (1) and (2), can be largely distinguished from assistance-as-intended-inducement, for instance, inducement to constructive actions and changes. In the first case, deservedness in the sense of *merit* is implied; in the second, deservedness focuses only on future utility. Since assistance, *here,* would not be intrinsic in *either* case, this particular distinction—between merit and utility—applies aside from the core of the third rationale; as a result, this rationale's specific meaning and validity, which center on that core, are not at issue.

Finally, the core component of the third rationale for intervention, especially for offering or providing assistance, differs from that rationale's next-mentioned, *supplementary* aspect or component. As will be seen, the latter aspect is one in which assistance is *again* not something earned by virtue of the types of merit or deservedness that are reflected in factors such as (1) and (2) above.

Supplement to Rationale #3: Implications of Positive Features/Potentials

Following is a separate aspect of the third justification (this aspect differs from and supplements that rationale's core/central, defining component, namely, the ethical value stated above): Offenders' illegal behavior, and/or certain undesirable or even destructive personal characteristics they may have, do not, individually and jointly, (1) literally undo, cancel, or otherwise eradicate the fact, value, and results of every personal or interpersonal activity those individuals may have carried out *adequately, effectively, or increasingly well.* (These activities, which may also include responsibilities and obligations, may have occurred in the years preceding and/or following the first such behaviors.) Nor do those illegal behaviors and/or undesirable personal characteristics (2) literally, ipso facto, eliminate every personal characteristic, strength, and/or tendency that many people would consider already *worthwhile, socially desirable, or promising* about those youths. (This is the case whether the youths have engaged in many or few positive/effective activities, referred to in point [1].) Both points apply even if the youths' offenses, and perhaps their closely related problem behaviors, are viewed as having (3) substantially or even markedly *diminished them as persons,* and as having greatly reduced their trustworthiness and perhaps the extent to which they "deserve" assistance on grounds other than their simply being human—grounds such as the kind of persons they are, and their level of need.[9]

Even if point (3) were considered entirely valid, points (1) and (2), taken together, would mean that neither (a) illegal and related *negative* behaviors nor (b) *undesirable* and problem-related personal characteristics, on the one hand (and collectively), would somehow entirely destroy, nullify, or dissolve given individuals' (c) past *positive/effective* activities, and their (d) present, *worthwhile/promising* features, on the other (also collectively). More precisely, and further to the point, the presence of (a) and (b), even in above-average amounts, would not only be unable to literally produce that result itself ("destroy," "nullify," etc.). Instead, simultaneously, it would—by the same token (i.e., again resting mainly on logic)—also be (4) unable to do so any more than the presence of those same *"positives/worthwhiles"* (that is, [c] and [d]) would automatically or necessarily be able to literally eliminate, cancel, or entirely suppress all or even most of those youths' past *negative* activities and present *undesirable* characteristics ([a] and [b]). That is, it would—more precisely, it logically would, and in that respect theoretically should—be unable to do so at all, by itself. (However, see "emotional reasons" in the section "Rationale #3, the Public, and Staff," below.) Offenders, then, despite their negatives, which may be many or few, still have positives.

The supplementary aspect of the third rationale for intervening thus focuses on certain particulars that characterize offenders (O's) as persons, not on the global fact that O's are human beings.[10] More specifically, it involves the four, below-mentioned implications and corollaries of the fact that offenders, including serious multiple offenders, are—or have—more than just a collection of negative features/behaviors.[11]

(Before continuing, certain similarities and differences might be noted. *Non*offenders (NO's) themselves have a mix of positives and negatives; however, among other things, they generally have fewer, less striking, and/or fewer long-standing negative features and defenses than do most O's, at least most other-than-lightweight O's. Also, by definition, NO's have no official, recorded *illegal* negative behaviors, even though they, like O's, may have engaged in undetected unlawful acts. (The latter, obviously, differ from certain *legal* behaviors that NO's, again like O's, sometimes exhibit and which are far from exemplary.) Finally, as with O's, undesirable characteristics/behaviors of NO's—whether the behaviors are legal or not—do not entirely nullify or otherwise literally obliterate *their* positives. Instead, with these individuals, again as with offenders, the positives still remain—to be used or not.[12] In this regard it might be noted that the positives have *already* coexisted with those and/or other negatives for considerable time—during which period they have also been used, in varying degrees.)

The supplement to the third rationale emphasizes the following: If the positive characteristics of O's, for example, certain interests, abilities, personality features, and motives, are carefully tapped, increased, and/or better organized/focused/directed, this can promote the offender-centered and socially centered goals alike.[13] However, even prior to those interventions and, of course, preceding their outcomes, the very fact of those positives, by itself, signifies or implies the following:

1. There is something to build upon. This applies even though that "something," that is, the positives or at least some of them, are often unreliable and, in any event, may be relatively weak, especially at first.[14]

    Given that (a) offenders *have* positives (often a range of them), that (b) O's sometimes purposely express and otherwise constructively act upon some of those positives or strengths, and commonly wish to maintain or expand them, and that (c) offenders therefore need not be considered "totally bad," "without redeeming features" or value, and so on— at any rate, completely characterized by and/or driven by negative features—the following applies:

2. There is reason to believe that these individuals will not necessarily, and not entirely, reject intervention that acknowledges, supports, tries to build upon, and may try to increase their positive features. This includes not only existing features but other positives or strengths they think or hope the program might add. It also applies even though many such O's *will* be generally resistive, and others highly resistive, particularly during early stages or months. (Early resistance will occur partly because the intervention also addresses and often heavily focuses on their negative features, especially those closely linked to illegal behavior and destructive adjustment patterns.)

    More specifically, and despite the just-mentioned resistance, the following applies. Given (a) through (c) above (especially the particulars involved in [a] and [b]), it is likely that most O's will not, over time, largely and fairly consistently, let alone completely and unrelentingly, try to reject most or all attempts by others to assist, control, and/or change them, to utilize and increase their positives in particular (especially ones the youths themselves like), and to help them change themselves. Nor, on this last score (". . . change themselves"), will they probably try to reject all efforts that they, themselves, might recognize as possibly relevant to and supportive of their own interests and desires (say, various constructive ones). Instead, all in all, O's will mainly be *ambivalent* about changing themselves and their adjustment patterns in certain ways—with this response reflecting the dynamic interplay between their positives and negatives, among other factors.

    Moreover, (a) given offenders' various positives and areas of strength (plus their underdeveloped but potential strengths), (b) taking into account Os' commonalities with *non*offenders in general, and (c) despite their *differences* from those NO's, there is reason to believe the following. When these offenders (here again, serious multiple offenders [SMOs]) do resist or try to reject intervention, this does not reflect—either primarily or at all—a literal and relatively permanent *inability* or insufficient capacity to respond to adequately implemented, humane intervention, even if that intervention is not rather individualized. For instance, and in particular, it does not reflect a cognitive or other "hard-wired" incapacity, one that is perhaps considered an "innate," "constitutional," or physical-trauma-based condition, or even an environmentally triggered innate predisposition. It would reflect such conditions/factors no more, for instance, than resistance to *external controls alone* would reflect an innate inability or an insufficient ability to respond to such controls.

Together, points 1 and 2 imply the following:

3. Far from being remote, the chances of obtaining a successful outcome with serious multiple offenders via humane intervention are almost always at least modest, and often moderate to good; at least they *can* be, especially if intervention is appropriately implemented.

This point, while already relatively firm, is further strengthened when (a) considerable potential exists in correctional programs/agencies for constructive working relationships between staff and youths, for example, via matching, and given that (b) a clear majority of many relevant, adequately designed and implemented studies provide quantitative evidence of the point's validity—as they presently do (Lipsey, 1992; Palmer, 1994).

At any rate, given point 3, one that draws considerably from 1 and 2, there are substantial reasons for believing the following (this applies especially when "condition (a)," immediately above, exists; in any event, the reasons, collectively, are logical *and* empirical, and they extend beyond simple plausibility):

4. Well-planned, adequately implemented intervention will not be—certainly need not be—largely or entirely fruitless, with respect to offender growth and, ultimately, social protection.

Points 1 through 4, collectively, thus provide a significant supplement to the third rationale for intervention. This supplement rests on the existence of offenders' positive features/activities/potential, and it centers on the related, reasonable possibility of achieving offender-centered and socially centered goals alike—major behavioral objectives. As such, it builds on certain implications of those features, and so on, and it is outcome-focused as well as pragmatically oriented.

The supplement extends beyond the earlier-mentioned and -implied core aspects of the third rationale, namely, that (1) offenders are human beings, that (2) they should, ipso facto, be seriously offered at least some substantial, relevant assistance as a major part of intervention, and that (3) item (2) should apply despite the individuals' negative personal attributes and their often minimal level of demonstrated achievements and/or apparent abilities.[15] For instance, if one were acting in accordance with only the *core* aspects of the rationale (item 3 in particular), assistance would be justified and should be offered even if (1) offenders—individually—were thought to have many negatives and even very few if any positive attributes/abilities, and, in any event, even if (2) their chances of success were considered essentially nil. However, with respect to the *supplement,* intervention in general and assistance in particular would be justified on grounds that—given the positive characteristics that exist and can be built upon, despite the negatives which themselves exist and may impede change—there is, or at least there can be, a reasonable possibility of success.[16] (With most SMOs, such building usually requires skilled staff who receive adequate and reliable organizational support.)

Rationale #3 and Deservedness

Neither the core of the third rationale nor its supplementary portion requires, or in fact utilizes, the concept of *deservedness.*[17] Here, we refer to "deserve" or "deserving" in its ordinary senses: "[Having] a right, . . . because of acts or qualities; . . . worthy, fit, or suitable for some reward; . . . earned or merited" (Webster, 1965, 1974). Using these meanings, we will briefly mention various aspects of "deserved assistance." In so doing, it will suffice to focus on individuals' actual and/or intended "acts" (activities), and to leave aside those "qualities" (e.g., personality features or traits, such as imaginative, humorous, analytic) that can often be separated from specific actions and deeds or that describe general *ways* of acting (e.g., calmness, alertness).[18] Also, we will emphasize the past and present more than the future, especially when the latter is somewhat distant.

(Again, although the subject is *deserved assistance (D/A),* the third rationale neither depends upon nor draws on deservedness, as this was delineated above and in the context as well as manner discussed below. In addition, the earlier-mentioned type of D/A, which is associated with simply being human, differs—as to its base—from the kind that is summarized below, that is, from that which mainly draws upon certain aspects of individuals' activities and efforts. The earlier type involves the core portion of the rationale.)

As used here, "deserved assistance" refers to any type and level of aid, service, or treatment that would be offered or provided to or for offenders because of the following: constructive or potentially constructive activities or efforts that they (1) have already purposely undertaken or carried out, (2) have seriously *tried* to engage in, (3) plan or wish to presently undertake, and/or (4) hope to eventually engage in. Often, such assistance would amount to an explicit or implicit acknowledgment, by others, of various deeds, achievements, efforts, or intentions by those individuals, or on their parts. In effect, D/A would thereby comprise an earned response to those activities, and so forth. (Condition [1], above, is the one most often associated with deservedness—here, with earned assistance. In that sense, among others, it is the strongest. By the same token, condition [4] is the weakest.)

For offenders' past activities and efforts to have substantial merit, they would not have to have been *completed*, satisfactorily or otherwise. This is despite the fact that completion or near completion, especially when satisfactory, *is* usually associated with greater merit. Also, whether the past, present, or future is involved, the earlier-mentioned points regarding deservedness and deserved assistance are valid and self-sufficient independent of offenders' *needs*.[19] "Need" is central to the *fourth* rationale, and is not required in the third.[20] (Related details concerning "intentions" are briefly mentioned next.)

Some actions, deeds, and/or efforts (ADEs), by offenders, involve direct or indirect benefits to other individuals, whether immediately or later. To be "deserving" to any substantial degree, these ADEs must be carried out with the belief or assumption—in any case, with the hope or intention—that those other persons, for example, nonoffending adults or peers, will, or at least can, (1) benefit from those ADEs materially or otherwise, say, psychologically, or will (2) appreciate them in any event, if they become aware of them. However, instead of being directed outward, for instance, toward the just-mentioned "others," some efforts by offenders can be considered deserving even if they center on the offenders themselves. (Again, the above deservedness is not integral to rationale #3.) (Offenders' efforts may focus, for example, on various challenges or on aspects of self-development. The challenges may be externally or internally initiated and/or triggered; and, if met or partly met, they may be considered personal achievements.) Outward-directed efforts, that is, those mostly centered on other individuals, may be called Type A; inward-directed ones, Type B.

Type B efforts, and resulting changes that soon become manifest in the offenders and that may shortly benefit those youths, sometimes do not, however, soon or simultaneously benefit those other individuals. (The changes in youths may involve, say, new, increased, or decreased "qualities," and modi-

fied patterns of adjustment.) Alternatively, yet again fairly soon after those initial changes have become manifest, various benefits may *indeed* accrue to others; moreover, some may be more than modest, and they or others may not quickly dissipate. In any event, whatever the early or initial value Type B efforts and resulting changes may have to those other persons, that value or benefit may sometimes increase, and also stabilize, through time. This increase may occur, for instance, if and when the youths' overall life-styles—and, perhaps, certain more specific roles, self-concepts, and/or intentions on their parts—have *further* changed, taken shape, or even crystallized, and are now, perhaps, often expressed in different ways and areas than before.

Nevertheless, whatever value the Type B (and Type A) efforts may have to others, and regardless of when that value or benefit is first received by them, the following applies: Various activities or efforts by offenders may be deserving—say, in at least a moderate degree—even if they are undertaken for what might seem to be, and may actually be, largely personal or even "self-serving" reasons, particularly in the short run. This is usually, or especially, the case if those activities/efforts are not knowingly harmful to the broadly defensible interests of others, or knowingly *likely* to harm them. Yet it sometimes applies even if those efforts do seem likely to displease and perhaps interfere with given individuals—for example, with delinquent peers who do not want the youths to change (a desire that, however, is not "broadly defensible")—and even if they may thereby lead to short- or even longer-term conflict and rejection. (The above-mentioned, "personal . . . reasons" may include, say, not only the "pursuit of happiness" in an overall sense, but other recognized ends. Individually and collectively, all such objectives may be pursued by means or via steps such as the following: increasing specific skills; meeting given requirements; reaching conventional benchmarks and arriving at major choice-points (e.g., completing high school); meeting new friends and/or modifying existing adjustment patterns; and, "growing up" in various attitudinal or behavioral ways.[21] These ends and means are ordinarily considered "normal" and even commendable in the case of nonoffenders; and, most such means are seen as opening the door to various opportunities, in particular.) The preceding suggests that the deservedness of given activities/efforts might best be assessed contextually and on balance, not in isolation from the range and mix of factors or issues involved. Nevertheless, the following applies whether deservedness/merit is assessed on relatively broad grounds, such as the contextual, or on fairly narrow ones.

As indicated, in the supplement to the third rationale the appropriateness of providing assistance does not rest on merit-centered grounds. In any event, offenders, in order to receive assistance when first entering a program, are not required (1) to have already engaged in several constructive activities and (2) to have manifested or to manifest several positive personality features—these being common, albeit subjective, bases for assessing merit.[22] If one or both requirements existed, if they were strictly applied, and if they dominated all others that perhaps coexisted, they would preclude assistance for many, though not most, serious multiple offenders.[23]

In the given supplement, the appropriateness of assistance instead rests on the following and on its implications for offender- and socially centered goals: For SMOs collectively, there almost always exists "at least [a] modest, and often [a] moderate-to-good," possibility of achieving success—together called a "reasonable" possibility—especially if intervention proceeds appropriately. As a result, if one were to use and give primary emphasis to that supplement, assistance would be, or at least should be, made available even if those youths do not seem to already *merit* it on grounds such as requirements (1) or (2) above. Moreover, and again from the outset, assistance would/should then be no less available to individuals who might be considered poor *risks* than to those considered fair or good ones—or, more broadly, worse risks rather than better.

In addition, if one used and emphasized the *core* component of the third rationale, for example, used it instead of the supplement, the following would apply. Some assistance would and should be seriously offered to offenders—as human beings—even if their chances of success initially appeared *slight,* that is, did not even seem "at least modest, . . . [let alone] moderate-to-good." (The latter are the somewhat to substantially higher chances associated with the supplement.) At any rate, in accordance with the core, assistance would/should be offered not only irrespective

of the serious multiple offenders' seeming chances of success—that is, their *risk*—but (as with the supplement, when it is used), despite their degree of initial merit, as assessed, say, in relation to (1) and (2) above. Also, assistance should be made available regardless of how little those youths may wish to initially—at or shortly after intake—participate in and contribute to any aspect of society, and even irrespective of whether they then express interest in making a noncoerced contribution in the more distant future. In short, using the core component, at least some initial assistance should be made available independent of deservedness that relates not only to those youths' direct and indirect past contributions to others, but to their expressed interest in presently, soon, and/or eventually contributing. This is apart from the fact that many practitioners have learned, through experience, that many or most such initially uninterested and/or resistive SMOs—when receiving relevant intervention—will eventually express genuine interest in some day participating constructively. (Also, other youths express initial interst that is [a] far from sincere, or else is [b] largely sincere but which later fades away.)

Before continuing, three points will be made more explicit and/or specific than before, and a few general thoughts will then be added regarding deservedness (merit) in relation to society's broad goal of long-term self-protection:

1. From some perspectives, SMOs can also be assessed as poor or questionable *risks* on grounds of their seeming disinterest in undertaking constructive activities, and/or their few apparent positive personality features.[24] Similar grounds have been used when judging initial *merit* to be low.[25] (Here, as above and below, "risk" refers to offenders' chances of success, especially in such respects as nonrecidivism.)
2. The validity of the "supplementary-component view" that assistance should be provided regardless of the youths' initial *merit* depends on neither of the following—these being two sides of essentially the same coin: First, some or many serious multiple offenders who, at intake, would be seen as definitely meriting assistance (based, say, on requirements [1] and/or [2], above), would,

nevertheless, be among the overall group of SMOs who are *less* likely to succeed. Second, and simultaneously, some or many SMOs who may be considered *low* on merit—again at intake—would be among the overall group of SMOs who have a *moderate to good* chance of succeeding. In short, the correlation between merit and risk is far from perfect; and, to state the point directly, the supplementary-component view regarding assistance would be valid even if that correlation were zero. (In this point, as in the following, "assistance" is used as an input, not as an output or product.)

3. Again regarding the supplementary component, the appropriateness of providing assistance to serious multiple offenders reflects the fact that success would be less likely to occur if there were no assistance at all, or if intervention were minimal and perfunctory. Moreover, this applies whether the likelihood of success, for groups of individuals that each consist of SMOs, would, say, be slight, fair, or good, respectively, if the youths within those groups *had* received or were to receive appropriate assistance. Restated, and viewed from a different angle, if assistance were *absent*, the chances of success would be lower than they would otherwise be—not only for worse-risk youths but for better-risks as well, each within the overall category of SMO.

If, via its correctional practices, society were to withhold relevant assistance from serious multiple offenders whom it believed did not sufficiently deserve it, society would, ipso facto, deny itself the degree of long-term protection which that assistance could often have provided relative to those youths.[26] This withholding could occur if deservedness were given precedence over all remaining factors that may be used to determine whether given SMOs should receive assistance, and, if so, what types and amounts. (In this discussion, "society" can refer to any one or more—including all—of its various jurisdictions, regions, and so forth.)

More specifically, if society were to withhold relevant assistance from particular offenders on grounds of insufficient merit, it would simultaneously be subordinating its long-term self-protection—something *it de-*

serves—to the principle of not giving those individuals something it believes they do *not* deserve. It would be subordinating its long-term need, on the one hand, to its interest in implementing and highlighting that particular principle, on the other. (If society chose to interpret that principle literally, to implement it strictly, and to give it top priority, it would, to be self-consistent, have to withhold assistance even if it believed the given offenders probably *needed* such input and might well improve it they received it.[27]) At any rate, society, in effect, would then be curtailing one of its major needs largely because it believed it should respond, in the specified way, (1) primarily or exclusively to the SMOs' negatives rather than positives, and (2) mainly on the basis of a moral/ethical framework whose chief concern, in this context, is deservedness. When responding in terms of (1) and (2), society, as implied, would not be trying to carefully build upon or otherwise substantially reflect and enhance the potential pragmatic value of the individuals' already existing *positive* characteristics and abilities, whether these are many or few, and regardless of their type.

The upshot would be that society, by virtue of its particular deservedness-centered response to those individuals' past and point-of-intake ("present") negatives,[28] would make its own future riskier—less safe—than it otherwise would be. Its response would allow various negative aspects of those individuals to affect society to a larger degree and for a longer time than they otherwise would. This would be true even if none of those past/present negatives were to escalate.

(In proceeding, it might be kept in mind that the curtailment of long-term self-protection would occur even if factors other than *deservedness* were used as the basis or main basis for withholding meaningful assistance. Also, of course, the use of deservedness for *other* purposes need not involve such curtailment.)

Rationale #3, the Public, and Staff
We will conclude the discussion of the supplement to the third rationale with general comments about its validity, or lack thereof, with respect to the general public and correctional staff, or, rather, to a sizable portion of each. The comments involve direct implications of ways in which these groups usually perceive the earlier-mentioned negative and positive

features; they will especially reflect the perceived strengths of the negatives compared to the positives.

N and P Features

As already suggested, each offender can be characterized by negative (N) and positive (P) features, and these fall within various categories. The main categories include, and may be called, not just personality traits and dispositions, particular skills, and general abilities, respectively, but actions, deeds, and other behaviors that reflect or involve the first three and that express related attitudes or values. There are N as well as P personality traits, N and P actions, and, among many offenders, N and P deeds. By themselves, skills and abilities are usually positive; and their absence, shortage, or underdevelopment is not a negative in the sense that applies to various personality traits, even though it is generally a drawback.

As background to the comments that appear below, and to subsequent discussions, two general areas will first be reviewed in connection with negative and positive features. The first involves the varied nature of these features, individually and collectively: Some are typically or highly "conditional" with respect to being N or P; others are much less conditional in that regard; and still others are more "intrinsically" N or P. The second area will focus on ways in which N's and P's can influence each other.

Area 1. Many individual features, such as specific traits, can be generally positive *or* negative. That is, they can be considerably more, or more often, constructive/helpful, or else considerably more, or more often, destructive/harmful. Whether they are one or the other mainly depends on how the individual offenders commonly use or apply them, for instance, for what purposes and in what situations.[29] Examples of such traits are aggression, assertiveness, dominance, passivity, submissiveness, and conformity.

A different set of attributes or qualities, such as attentiveness, resourcefulness, flexibility, and intelligence, are much less conditional with respect to their being appropriately labeled positive or negative. These are often viewed as globally or broadly positive—though, again, not "intrinsically" so in the sense of invariably, almost invariably, or else just by definition (and, thus, necessarily). In any event, such qualities, which are among the individuals' above-listed "general abilities," can be considered functional strengths; and in that regard they are, or can be, instrumental in achieving constructive ends. Nevertheless, even these attributes can be used in ways designed to harm. Even when no harm is intended, their formal *opposites,* for example, inattentiveness and inflexibility, are negatives—again, conditional ones—but mainly in the sense of often being drawbacks.

Regarding the concept of intrinsic positives, this is perhaps most clearly reflected or closely approximated in such traits and dispositions as thoughtfulness, kindness, friendliness, sincerity, and so on, at least if one emphasizes the individuals' main intentions and downplays or discounts any actual and possible harm—specifically, unintended, unforeseen, and/or unforeseeable harm, immediate or otherwise. On the negative side, there is exploitiveness, meanness, hatefulness, viciousness, and the like, irrespective of whether any or all of their known potential effects, their known likely effects, or, in any event, their intended effects, come about. Other, often lesser but still "basic," negatives are unreliability, irresponsibility, *marked* selfishness and self-centeredness, and so forth, at least among chronological adolescents and adults.[30] These features, though often less severe in the sense of usually being less harmful to persons who soon feel their effects, are not necessarily less common or less potentially significant than the just-mentioned negatives ("exploitiveness," etc.)—certainly with regard to *offenders'* overall adjustment, whether short-term or long. The same would apply to thoughtlessness, unkindness, unfriendliness, and so on.

At any rate, traits, individually, do not invariably fall within only the positive or only the negative arena, even though (1) many of them often, or very often, do fall within just one such arena and, thus, can be reasonably and best labeled as belonging there, and although (2) certain others *almost always* fall within just one. (Regarding negatives in particular, some traits and dispositions often have, or are characterized by, considerably more negativity than others; that is, they are much more negative than others.)

(Again, and mainly bearing on point (2), the actions or interpersonal exchanges associated with such traits as "meanness" are, when consciously undertaken, almost always intended to harm or, perhaps, to obtain inappropriate advantage; and, they often achieve their ends to at least some degree. From a process standpoint, this situation parallels that in which still other intentional actions, such as those associated with "kindness," are nearly always designed to help.[31] Finally, both the issue and process are the same regardless of which particular traits [e.g., assertiveness], which functional strengths [e.g., resourcefulness], and/or which specific skills are used when carrying out actions that can be appropriately called N or P.[32])

Area 2. Most traits are expressed during various acts—many of which, but far from all, directly and immediately involve other persons, intentionally or otherwise. Each act or action may be short and simple or longer and more complex. Many are part of offenders' and nonoffenders' everyday life, modes of adjustment, and/or preparations for adulthood; especially in these contexts, they may be considered positive (constructive/helpful) or negative, even though they may be "mixed" in some respects. For present purposes, relatively neutral actions and activities can be ignored.

Some of these trait-and-action combinations, or traits-in-action, can be described as strong behavior patterns—again, whether shorter, longer, and so forth. Since many are also habits, they are—here—jointly called "patterns/habits" (P/Hs). Individually, these combinations are often or routinely repeated, for example, daily, weekly, or monthly, and usually with little variation (hence "strong" and "patterns"). In addition, many are carried out rather automatically, such as with little or no focused thought (hence, in the above context, "habits"). P/Hs can be activated by particular feelings, desires, demands, information, and/or events, and by various external situations.

Through time and via reinforcement—often much of each—two general, mutually independent developments can occur regarding an individual's patterns/habits:[33] First, certain *positive* P/Hs can frequently weaken, divert, suppress, or even figuratively dissolve (functionally eliminate) various *negative* traits, actions, and trait/action combinations (patterns/habits) themselves, temporarily or otherwise. These positive P/Hs would be acting as "stimuli" or inputs that affect or influence the negative traits—these negatives being the "objects" of those positives. Second, given comparable time and reinforcement, some *negative* P/Hs—themselves acting as stimuli—

can often produce similar changes or outcomes in various *positive* traits, behaviors, and so on, and even in specific skills and functional strengths. That is, such negatives can weaken the positives (which, in this case, are the objects of those negatives). Not *all* positive and negative patterns/habits can produce such results, regardless of how much time and reinforcement is involved, let alone under most or all conditions. That aside, the specific P/Hs that *do* produce such results—such changes/outcomes in their objects—can vary considerably in content across individuals and situations, and in that respect can be rather individualized. This is the case whether or not those P/Hs, that is, the producers/stimuli/inputs, are positive or negative.

The following applies to the preponderance of serious multiple offenders, whether a just-mentioned *positive* pattern/habit is affecting (influencing, changing) a negative one or whether a *negative* pattern/habit is affecting a positive one (these two processes relate to the first and second "independent developments" mentioned earlier, respectively; again, any pattern/habit that operates on its object is functioning as a producer/stimulus/input, and this "stimulus-P/H" can be either positive [P] or negative [N]): Neither the positive stimulus nor the negative stimulus (i.e., the first and second sources of influence, respectively) can (1) literally and completely obliterate its given, affected N or P object *very quickly* (a la "matter" and "anti-matter"). Nor can either stimulus-P/H (2) entirely *suppress* its object very soon. More precisely, the stimulus-P/H can seldom accomplish the latter in a way that occurs not only quickly but which will be long-lasting. Nevertheless, it can (3) often begin to *weaken* its object fairly soon.[34] Points (1) and (2) usually reflect the fact that since neither the positive stimulus, the negative stimulus, nor their respective N and P objects exist separately from the rest of the individual, various other aspects of those offenders' life and personality must be modified or "worked through." As implied in the above, points (1) through (3) would apply not just to trait/action combinations—patterns/habits—that act on other combinations, but to those that may act on single features, such as particular traits or dispositions, as well or instead.

(This ends the review of the two areas. For related comments regarding Area 2, see endnote 35. In the following, "general public" and "correctional staff" will refer, respectively, to one large and influential portion of each. In the case of the general public, that portion has been the dominant group during at least the past several decades, with regard to the public's influence on corrections. A detailed description of this and the correctional staff group is provided in Chapter 29. There, a second large and important portion of the general public, and a second among staff, is reviewed as well. Except where specified, these additional portions or groups will not be involved in the *present* chapter, for instance, when "the public" or "the general public," and "staff" or "correctional staff," are mentioned.)

When thus focusing on offenders, both the public and staff emphasize personality traits they frequently associate with illegal and interpersonally harmful or threatening behavior, not limited to violence. Mostly but not only within the general public, this emphasis mainly occurs (1) for *emotional reasons* that are strong, often long-standing, and very often centered on fear and anger, and (2) because of desires for self-protection, anxiety reduction, and relief from frustration that directly relate to those emotions. Especially when combined with these related desires (taken individually or collectively), such emotional reasons (individually but especially collectively) usually have a more powerful hold on *both* the public's and staff's consciousness than do any of the following:

a. a general but largely unfocused realization that some positives exist among many or most offenders;
b. a belief or understanding, or a clear awareness and recognition, that at least some positives often or usually exist among most offenders; the understanding is accompanied by some specifics—usually stereotyped and limited, but still partly accurate; or
c. a clear knowledge of various—sometimes several—specific positives that are common among many offenders and that even distinguish some such individuals from others; here, there is less stereotyping than in (b), above. (This knowledge is in addition to the general recognition that some positives exist among most offenders.)

The first level of awareness/understanding is proportionately more common in the general public than among staff; the third level—level (c)—is more common in staff.

Even when positives are clearly recognized as such and when at least some are believed or known to exist within numerous offenders (see levels [b] and [c]), their *significance* or potential importance is very often downplayed, both in itself and relative to that of the negatives. Such evaluations or judgments, whether delineated or more global, usually reflect, but can be partly independent of, the earlier-mentioned *emphasis* per se; thus, for example, downplaying can occur even if the difference in emphasis between N's and P's is minimal. In any event, it can and does occur (1) even when "significant" refers to the possible practical utility of the features, say, to their bearing on offender growth and reduced recidivism,[36] (2) whether or not the positives are believed/assumed to be many or few, among most individual SMOs, and (3) whether or not the given members of the public, or persons within their families, have been direct victims of crime.

Because of the preceding emphasis on negatives over positives, and also due to the earlier-mentioned views/assumptions regarding the limited significance of offender positives, positive features are often *neutralized and largely obscured.*[37] This outcome (product) does not occur solely in individuals' minds, and then end there; instead, it often has concrete, operational effects on intervention itself. For instance, neutralizing/obscuring—whether viewed as a process or product—eliminates or greatly reduces the chances that positive features will (1) be focused on during the diagnostic and information-gathering stage, (2) be carefully considered and built upon during the initial and subsequent planning stages, (3) help place negative features into a broader context, (4) be available and used during crises, and, all in all, (5) make much difference in the final outcome. In these respects, most—sometimes all—of the positives that staff and the public were, or are, aware of and might have otherwise used are rendered functionally ineffective, and in that sense insubstantial, by the main negatives with which those groups are usually concerned. In short, the positives are disempowered or minimally empowered, and they often end up being largely unused during much or all of the intervention. This occurs even though they have not been literally destroyed/dissolved by the negatives—have not, somehow, been actually eradicated from the offenders' personality, social interactions, and palpable environment.[38]

Entirely separate from those operational effects on intervention would be staff's view regarding the validity of the rationale for intervening *at all*. (We are still focusing on the supplement to the third rationale.) As described below, the view in question would result from those individuals' comparison of (A) the supplement's general premise and central component, on the one hand, with (B) the relevance and strength of positive features, on the other—as judged by those same individuals. Positive features are involved in (A) and (B) alike: They are the supplement's main structural and dynamic component; also, it is they, in particular, that are neutralized and obscured—a fact which reflects their judged ("perceived") significance, that is, their relevance and strength combined.

To better compare (A) and (B), three points will first be made more explicit than before. These relate to the supplement itself, not to the way in which staff perceive it and judge its positive-features components. Point 1 involves the supplement's general premise; 2 and 3 center on its positive features, its line of reasoning, and related facts. (To simplify matters, "rationale" will be substituted for "supplement" and "supplement to the third rationale."):

1. The essence of this rationale or justification is that intervention is worth the effort because it has a reasonable chance of succeeding, along lines important to offenders and society alike.
2. Whereas the actual *achievement* of this success requires that intervention be well-planned and adequately implemented, the very *possibility* of success requires the existence of positive features in the first place, and their eventual directed usage in the second.[39]

    (These positives can include not just certain traits and dispositions but constructive motives and interests. During early stages of intervention, many serious multiple offenders have considerable ambivalence about using the latter two in connection with changing their adjustment patterns and with seriously preparing for their future. In that regard or context, they, themselves, partly obscure and withhold those positives.)

3. Success is not just a "possibility"; nor are its chances of occurring simply remote. Instead, as required in the premise, they are "reasonable," that is, "almost always at least modest, and often moderate to good." This reasonable likelihood, in turn, reflects certain facts and conditions relating to the positive features themselves—facts, and so forth, that are critical to the third rationale: With most SMOs, these features are not numerically rare, whether or not they are readily apparent from the start; in addition, the relevance and strength of these positives is substantial or potentially so; and finally, such features are *available*, for partial or complete use, at least under certain conditions (e.g., less-than-marked resistance or ambivalence).

    ("Strength," while sometimes only moderate for various *individual* features, can be enhanced when—as can occur more readily in extensive intervention contexts—a number of those features operate in a somewhat coordinated, mutually supportive way, for example, as a set of means to identical or closely related ends. Positive features are often *not* viewed in this collective way, and this fact contributes to the frequent overlooking or downplaying of their potential operating, that is, functional, strength. Also, many staff assume that most SMOs are so resistive or recalcitrant that whatever positives they have or may have will not become available in any event. This is an example of functional neutralization by negative features.)

Now then, since the concept of "a reasonable [likelihood] of succeeding" is integral to the present rationale, and since—in this same rationale—that same likelihood critically depends on the relevance, strength, or potential strength of various positive features (not on their existence or sheer number alone, or per se), the following is clear: Individuals (1) who believe that positives, even if common, are *not* particularly relevant and strong (even potentially so), and/or (2) for whom most or all positive features have been neutralized/obscured (or would be unavailable in any event),[40] would reasonably conclude that the rationale's preconditions for a reasonable likelihood of success with SMOs do *not* exist. They would therefore reject that rationale since they would consider it baseless.[41] In short, the supplement to the third rationale for intervening would have little or no validity and force to persons for whom positives have little significance in themselves, and/or for whom negatives seem much stronger or important in any event.

Despite these individuals' views, positive features remain a substantial basis on which to build, and success can still be reasonably likely to occur. In short, those staff's perceptions and conclusions do not alter such realities; and as a result, they neither diminish nor otherwise modify the validity of the rationale, that is, its logical and literal appropriateness. Nevertheless, as indicated, those views would result in such staff's actual *rejection* of that rationale, since these individuals would consider it invalid. A similar position would presumably be taken by that portion of the general public discussed thus far.

Such rejection would be much less likely to occur with two sizable groups briefly mentioned earlier in the chapter.[42] The first mainly consists of numerous practitioners who support or actively promote types of change and growth often associated with rehabilitation or habilitation.[43] The second is a portion of the general public that is more supportive of such change/growth than is the earlier-mentioned, presently dominant part. With these rehabilitation-supportive (R-S) groups, the relevance, strength, and potential strength of positive features is less likely to be downplayed or underestimated than by the staff and public that have been emphasized thus far.[44] (For related discussion, see "Group 'B' Views and Responses" [pp. 29-3–29-6] in Chapter 29, and "Deservedness, Need, and Program Improvement" in Chapter 30.)

Except with these R-S groups, the upshot is that the rationale for intervening on the above-mentioned grounds—namely, that offenders have positive features which can help make success reasonably likely—would be, and is, often unused. This is the case despite its actual validity.

Even when that rationale is used, the *following* one usually plays a larger role. It is accepted not only by R-S groups but—albeit to substantially lesser degrees, and in partly different ways—by groups or persons less supportive or much less supportive of the given change/growth. (The latter groups or persons differ from still others, or from individuals, who are specifically opposed to rehabilitation/habilitation.) This rationale centers on the appropriateness and importance of helping youths address their personal and social needs, ones that have practical implications for their near-term and, especially, long-range adjustment.

Rationale #4: Protect Society by Addressing Growth- and Adjustment-Related Needs
General Points
We will now focus on this needs-centered rationale, still emphasizing serious multiple offenders. We will also discuss various adjustment patterns, related defenses, and views of self and others—factors that can bear on the nature and outcome of intervention. As will be seen, and may be deduced, such factors—more specifically, their potential effects—make it important to develop a detailed understanding of SMOs as individuals and to craft an intervention plan that addresses those factors, their major interactions, and various *other* factors and dynamics. Thus, this section will present not just a fourth rationale for intervening *at all*. Instead, it will discuss features and processes that, collectively, highlight the importance of intervening in a careful, coordinated, and individualized way in particular—in order to reduce or obviate major obstacles to success and to productively tap the youths' strengths and positive motivations. (Here, "adjustment patterns" includes but is not limited to often-repeated behaviors and interactions with others. Many such behaviors and interactions occur in the context of, and may be expressed in terms of, longstanding relationships and roles, for example, with parents and/or peers.)

A basic premise of the fourth rationale is that nearly all serious multiple offenders—at intake and often well beyond—are at a point in their lives where, unlike most nonoffenders, they need considerable assistance and direction. Particularly at intake, they (1) do not *have* and/or (2) do not *utilize* enough internal and/or external resources to successfully address or begin to address various adjustment challenges they will face; this applies especially, but not only, to the major, long-range challenge described below. Item (1), immediately above, mainly refers to SMOs who, for example, are largely unprepared to start moving forward or to keep moving ahead with respect to that long-range challenge; that is, they are not prepared to do so on the basis of their present, normally available resources alone. They are, for instance, seriously deficient in relevant skills or strengths, or they are well below average in external supports. Item (2) focuses on SMOs who usually have insufficient *motivation* to utilize relevant skills/strengths that they already *have,* or external resources that do exist. With many such youths, this situation largely reflects their above-average level of ambivalence about changing and/or moving forward; with others, there is little desire to change/move, and also little ambivalence in this regard. Among still other individuals, items (1) and (2) are fairly equally mixed, at various points starting from intake.

Challenge and Tasks
This rationale for intervening centers largely on a challenge that faces all adolescents, not just known delinquents: that of eventually establishing some kind of "future" for themselves, hopefully one that is viable in the free community. Whereas the *content* of this future, that is, its specific life-styles and activities, can vary considerably from person to person, its *form* or framework would likely involve some kind of independent living, paid employment, and so on—broad modes of adjustment that typify postadolescence in contemporary society. For any given adult, these modes need not exist 100 percent of the time. In addition, though they do not, by themselves, guarantee law-abiding behavior, and although they are not, in that respect, absolute prerequisites for it, they are strongly associated with such behavior (whereas their opposites are less so), and in that sense may be said to facilitate it or help increase its likelihood.

To have a realistic chance of meeting this challenge starting in early adulthood, youths must begin preparing themselves in practical ways by middle or later adolescence. (See Area A, below.)[45] They must also modify some of their personal adjustment patterns and perhaps change or improve their life-circumstances, including, for example, aspects of their relationships with peers and/or parents. (This involves Area B. Here, needed changes can relate not just to unsuccessful, often frustrating, or even harmful behavior patterns and relationships, but to interactions that have been generally appropriate, for instance, age-appropriate, and perhaps largely

satisfying.) More specifically, youths in general, and serious multiple offenders in particular, must readjust, grow, improve, and otherwise change in such ways and areas as the following (for serious multiple offenders as a group, these readjustments, and so on, must often be substantial; for SMOs individually, two or more areas are usually involved):

A. develop or increase practical and interpersonal skills;
B. deal successfully with social-environmental and/or family factors; and,
C. increase one's understanding of self and others, and reduce or resolve personal/psychological difficulties or conflicts.

In the context of establishing a workable future, these ways/areas can each be viewed as a general *task, need,* or even *means to an end.* Since the preponderance of youths in general have no recorded delinquency, they will often be called "nonoffenders." The components of Area B, including peers, are sometimes called "external" factors, as distinct from the "internal" ones found in C and in aspects of A.

Nonoffenders
As indicated, nonoffenders face these same general tasks. However, unlike numerous SMOs, most such individuals have few if any *major,* sometimes debilitating deficits or difficulties in Area A and the second part of C. Moreover, few have become personally and—especially—heavily involved with physically dangerous aspects of Area B, that is, with certain social-environmental or community-life facets in particular. At any rate, with youths in general, the extent of change that is needed in each area, including A, is usually less than with SMOs, and it is generally much less in all three areas combined. In these and related respects, their overall situation regarding the long-term social-adjustment challenge is as follows:

1. Most nonoffenders, when trying to change—to readjust, grow, and/or improve—in any given area (say, A or B), do not, at the same time, have to deal with *unusual* types and/or levels of difficulties/obstacles (D/Os) in connection with that or related areas. More specifically, when addressing the challenge of establishing a viable future, those individuals do not have to deal

with such D/Os before they can move forward at all, or even after they have started to progress. In these respects, most nonoffenders have a less bumpy or winding road to travel, or, in effect, "less far to go," than do most SMOs. The latter individuals—beginning at intake—often do face many uncommon and/or sizable D/Os, together called "unusual" ones. In that absolute sense, not just relative to nonoffenders, they often start out with "a long way to go" in terms of addressing the challenge in question.

(Regarding SMOs' motivation to address that challenge and its related tasks, see various comments below. Point 2, discussed next, will begin by focusing on youths' actual functional abilities, or overall readiness, with respect to resources. *Functional*—and functioning—abilities, that is, ones that can be made available under usual or at least nonextreme conditions and that may then be *used,* also reflect, of course, such factors as willingness and interest, together an expression of motivation.)

2. Even when the changes that are needed by particular nonoffenders in any area (say, B or C) *are* rather large,[46] most such individuals have more internal (personal) resources with which to proceed than do most SMOs; at least, more are readily and reliably available. Also—and this pertains especially to Area B— nonoffenders, compared to SMOs, are likely to have more *external* supports/ resources readily available or otherwise accessible. If necessary, those particular externals can help neutralize or reduce specific negative factors, such as external pressures; or, they can help individuals work on the overall challenge more directly and positively. These external resources may include nondelinquent peers, nonparental/nonguardian adults, and/or public agencies, private organizations, and informal networks.[47]

Because of (1) and (2) combined, the A, B, and C tasks that are faced by most nonoffenders usually are, and feel, less formidable than they do to most serious multiple offenders. In particular, this applies not only to the preponderance of nonoffenders who (a) wish to begin preparing for their future in specific ways and to do so fairly soon, but to those whose (b) approach to that future and to adulthood in general is more passive and less focused.

(The (b) group may be no less accepting of its image of adulthood than the (a) group is of *its* image—one that is similar to the other. However, (b) youths are usually more interested than (a's) in retaining their adolescent activities and satisfactions in their present form and formats, where possible.[48] [To simplify the presentation, we will focus mainly on (a) youths.] The fact that the tasks are usually less formidable and disquieting to the nonoffenders than to most SMOs does not mean the former individuals experience no anxiety and doubt regarding them and about the future itself, or that their readjustment efforts never involve interpersonal confrontation or unpleasantness.)

Moreover, partly because the tasks seem more doable to these nonoffenders than to the SMOs, and in part because the former youths are more likely than the latter to broadly visualize a future they can not only accept but which they largely want and which they assume they can probably manage, those individuals—despite their anxieties and other just-mentioned factors—are also likely to be less *ambivalent* than the SMOs. That is, they are likely to have fewer mixed feelings and major reservations about modifying or slowly relinquishing their present adjustment patterns, or aspects of them, in order to help move toward that future. This even applies to peer- and/or parent-centered interactions (Area B) that have been relatively satisfying and not dysfunctional thus far—ones that, however, may soon become largely incompatible with the type or level of behavioral, emotional, and physical independence those youths consider important.

At any rate, though most nonoffenders who have reached mid-adolescence take it for granted that various difficulties will arise when preparing for their future, they are basically willing to "get going" and to "give it [change] a try" or several "tries."[49] Also, they largely believe their efforts to establish a workable and reasonably satisfying future will probably succeed—eventually. This is the case even if their overall self-confidence is, deep down (i.e., beyond any possible facades), usually no more than average or perhaps somewhat below.

No less significant than these individuals' essentially sanguine attitude about "getting started," and than their readiness to apply themselves, are their non- or minimally self-defeating ways—in fact, their essentially constructive and largely practical ways—of dealing with sizable difficulties or obstacles that arise at various points.[50] That is, they, like most remaining nonoffenders, for instance, the (b) group, respond to such D/Os not only nondestructively but along lines that are, typically, consistent with and supportive of their main needs and objectives, and that are seldom more than moderately antithetical to them. In thus responding, these individuals remain largely "on track" and seldom end up complicating their lives in major, long-lasting ways.[51]

Also significant, most nonoffenders can respond to such D/Os based on the internal and external resources—skills, strengths, and supports—normally and fairly reliably available to them. These include not only those internals and externals that are at-hand and are ordinarily used for different, non-D/O purposes, but other externals—themselves supports—that are likely to be accessible if and as needed. At any rate, these individuals, via their usual and normally available resources alone, can adequately—though often not easily—deal with sizable difficulties/obstacles and can continue to address their long-range challenge. Given their overall level of development and their life situation (personally/emotionally and interpersonally/socially), these youths are at a point at which, and in a position from which, this is possible.[52, 53]

Offenders

In considerable contrast, almost all SMOs—at intake—are at a point where they need planned, sustained assistance and direction in order to move forward and to adequately deal with related D/Os. Specifically, these individuals, by themselves, do *not* then have—and/or do not have or make *available,* and then utilize—sufficient internal and/or external resources (usually both) with which to meet the above-mentioned challenge, or to substantially increase their chances of meeting it, via growth, improvement, and/or readjustment in Areas A, B, and/or C. (See below regarding "availability.") Nor do these SMOs then have, or have/make available and then utilize, enough resources with which to adequately

address the following (the two difficulties/obstacles that follow are distinguished from the long-range challenge per se): sizable *D/Os* that (1) sometimes arise in the normal course of events that occur during the years in which the challenge first emerges as a significant reality for adolescents (even if they are not especially trying to address it); or, also, sizable D/Os that (2) not infrequently arise as an integral part of actually *addressing* that challenge, per se.[54]

(Interwoven with those actual and functional resource shortfalls, and in further contrast to most nonoffenders, many SMOs would soon "dig themselves deeper into a hole" than they have already done.[55] This near-term outcome, whether it results mainly from legal or illegal behavior, would make their task of addressing the long-range, social-adjustment challenge even harder.[56] In the following discussion we will continue to focus mainly on intervention's role vis-à-vis that long-range challenge, not on its more immediate, albeit closely related task of preventing SMOs from making mistakes and of helping them avoid mistakes—ones that, individually or collectively, would "dig [them] deeper" in the near-term, and would also harm other people.)

Regarding resources that do not *exist,* on the one hand, and those which exist but are *unavailable,* on the other, two major but partly overlapping groups of SMOs should be distinguished; together, they comprise the "almost all SMOs" mentioned earlier. In the first group, which includes many youths, there is a literal shortage of various needed resources, though far from a complete absence of them. (Though we are now focusing on these resources individually, "far from a complete absence" also applies to them collectively.) More particularly, and still viewed *individually,* those skills, strengths, and/or supports either do not exist—have never formed or developed—or else they are minimal, for example, have barely begun to form. (With some youths in this group and with a number of other SMOs, various *other* relevant resources exist, but they are somewhat to largely underdeveloped.) In the second group, and with many individuals from the first, the following applies (note: at intake, this second group is at least as large as the first, setting aside all mutual overlap): SMOs often (1) lack sufficient overall motivation, and/or (2) have too much ambivalence, to reliably draw on certain relevant internal and external resources that do exist and which are sufficiently developed.[57] In that sense, and for those reasons, these youths "do not have or make *available,* and then utilize," the given resources. (Most such internal skills/strengths can, however, become available—and many such external supports can be sought and utilized—if intervention proceeds in ways that increase the individuals' trust, that modify their motivation and ambivalence, and so forth.)

At any rate, the upshot is as follows, and it reflects the existence, strength, and/or utilization of the given resources, particularly at intake and soon thereafter: SMOs, as a group, are insufficiently prepared and/or motivated to seriously or at any rate adequately initiate and follow up on various steps that could help them successfully address the long-range *challenge* largely on their own. This insufficient preparation, and so on, also bears on their relatively low likelihood of similarly addressing various sizable or major *difficulties/obstacles* that are associated with those steps and with the overall challenge itself. This certainly applies to D/Os that, collectively, are temporally overlapping during short time spans and which may thus "pile up" or become intense enough to reinforce and perhaps exacerbate each other.

The challenge of establishing a viable future exists regardless of how youths feel about it, and it must be addressed in some way. (1) Given this challenge; (2) given areas of need A, B, and C, which can help youths move forward relative to the challenge; (3) given most SMOs' extensive deficits and/or difficulties regarding those areas of need; and (4) in light of many such youths' strong ambivalence about changing and moving forward even if their deficits are below average or are subsiding, intervention with SMOs can be further justified as follows:[59] *It can provide a context in which and through which, and specific ways in which, those individuals can be helped to move forward relative to that challenge*—move forward by making various changes and improvements regarding A, B, and C, and in connection with other, for instance, more immediate, factors and conditions which themselves bear on that challenge. This needs-centered or life-adjustment-centered function of intervention is its rationale #4.

Needs-Centered Intervention
Role and Assumptions
Here, intervention's assistance, direction, and other aspects, would be designed to ultimately meet the socially centered goal of eliminating or substantially reducing specific offenders' illegal behavior. Toward that end it would try to help them effectively address their long-range, social-adjustment challenge via personal change/growth and through changes in their practical and/or personal/emotional relationships to portions of the environment; also, staff and perhaps others would help them modify parts of that environment itself, if necessary and possible.

Besides addressing long-range goals via A, B, and C (and, as an integral *part* of doing so), intervention, as indicated, would focus on immediate and emergent factors and conditions as such. Some of these factors/conditions, for example, various social opportunities, could facilitate efforts to meet the long-range challenge itself; others, such as negative external or internal pressures, could—absent relevant intervention—seriously hinder it and could promote illegal behavior itself.[60, 61]

Implicit in needs-centered intervention, and, thus, in the fourth rationale, is the assumption that intervention programs need certain broad characteristics and conditions (together called "features") if they are to significantly help serious multiple offenders "meet the socially centered goal [regarding] . . . illegal behavior." That is, not just *any* features—*any* context and approaches—will substantially contribute to success. Instead, particular ones are needed.[62]

For instance, rationale #4 assumes that if a program's process features and organizational features do not include detailed assessment, careful planning, and responsible implementation, most of its SMOs will not receive, or will not have fairly reliable access to, the following, or to enough of it: relevant, interrelated, operationally coordinated *content inputs* (see below) that they need or appear to need in order to productively address their deficits, difficulties, and ambivalence, and to thereby move forward regarding (1) and (2), mentioned earlier.[63] (Careful planning, coordination, and so on, can be considered *broad* process features, ones that are independent of the particular content inputs associated with them, regardless of the latters' relevance. Here, "inputs" generically includes various types or forms of assistance, opportunity, direction, external control, and other features. Compared to ". . . planning, coordination, and so on," any such content input can be considered a relatively *specific* type or level of "feature.")

Rationale #4 involves a second major assumption, one that relates directly and closely to the first and which not only centers on but also explicates the concept of needed input: Most SMOs need the earlier-mentioned inputs—assistance, direction, and so on—mainly because (1) *their own resources* are literally absent, inadequate, or insufficient in key respects, or else because (2) they—usually a second subset of SMOs—seldom want to *use* the more adequate and otherwise sufficient resources that they *have*. More precisely, the latter individuals are, psychologically, unwilling and/or unprepared to often apply those resources to the long-range goals in question, or even to various ongoing issues and needs.[64] This situation exists especially, but not only, at intake, and it applies whether the resources in question are mainly internal or external.

Thus, given this second assumption, the *first* one—namely, that programs need certain broad features rather than others if they are to help youths make significant progress—involves the following, almost self-evident, corollaries (this applies to the relatively specific inputs as well, that is, to the earlier-mentioned content rather than process and organizational features[65]): (1) The program features/inputs that are needed are ones that can help SMOs *develop* their own resources, or can help them want to *use* or more often use ones they already have—or use more of them. (2) During program periods in which those needed youth resources and/or that internal motivation do *not* exist or are insufficient—more specifically, during the main intervention periods in which they are being *developed or increased*—the following is the case. It is those process, organizational, and other features/inputs that can help reduce, resolve, neutralize, preclude, and/or compensate for actual and potential negative *effects* of the youths' (a) not initially having, or using, those needed resources or enough of them, and of their (b) *using* resources in the ways they do.[66] (Each point applies whether its collective resources are personal, environmental, or both.)

For example, *well-planned* intervention and *close monitoring* of youths are among the process features needed in order to help reduce, neutralize, or compensate for such effects as the following:[67] most SMOs' above-average tendency to physically or emotionally withdraw, to curtail their efforts, or to even "give up," when they experience or anticipate various difficulties/obstacles in connection with the long-range challenge and with more immediate problems and issues as well. As implied, this tendency to withdraw, curtail one's efforts, or perhaps give up partly but substantially reflects the status of the individuals' resources, for instance, the extent of the deficit in given areas.[68]

Besides being needed to address the concrete and often immediate effects of that tendency and to do so fairly directly, intervention which is well-planned and at least adequately implemented is also needed in order to focus on factors that contribute to the tendency.[69] (Such planning, and other process features, would operate not by themselves but in conjunction with given content inputs and organizational features. This would also apply to process features that are used to address "the concrete and often immediate effects.") For instance, such intervention is needed to help reduce or possibly resolve some of the youths' *internal pressures,* ones that not only help maintain/support the sizable *potential* for withdrawal (or the strong, ongoing possibility of it) but that can activate, release, or specifically focus that tendency, under certain conditions. As illustrated in the section on "Difficulties and Obstacles" (below), such pressures, and the related or resulting tendency, partly reflect the status or extent of the youths' actual and available resources.[70] (As may be deduced, the practical significance of this entire situation centers on the fact that if the earlier-mentioned program features/inputs are absent or insufficient, various effects associated with those youth resources can impede and weaken the programs' efforts.) In that and in the chapter's closing section ("Youths' Curtailment of Efforts") we will mention various responses by serious multiple offenders to difficulties/obstacles that occur during intervention, especially its early phases. Also, we will describe major contexts in which these D/Os and responses occur, and underlying factors involved. Considerable detail will be provided because these responses have important implications for intervention, for example, regarding the type or level of complexity that is needed in order to effectively address—and keep up with—them.

Complexity and Individualization

Concerning this aspect of intervention, namely, *complexity*, these implications go beyond a need for differing program components (even for any one youth), and for well-coordinated efforts across those components. Instead, they also include, for instance, a need for considerable *individualization*—a dimension that itself involves substantial complexity, whether as a process or product. Before starting the later sections, we will focus on individualization as a prime example of the broader need for complexity, and because it is a key dimension itself.

In this brief description, individualization will be viewed as a product only. As such, it will refer to a substantial level of detail, depth, and integration that is involved in staff's understanding of, and overall approach to, clients, especially when the latter are viewed as functioning, striving, adapting, and self-defending persons. This is a level of detail, and so on, that reflects and is tuned to the clients' particular personality and situation enough to distinguish any one such individual from any other and, hopefully, to thereby better achieve the long-range, socially centered goal. (For further details, see endnote 71.)

Programs that not only try to (1) challenge SMOs to modify some of their key adjustment patterns and interpersonal relationships and to take their future more seriously than before, but that simultaneously try to (2) help those SMOs do so, must become aware of and remain alert to the given youths' feelings about, and behavioral as well as psychological defenses against, those and similar challenges and their related stress points.[72] By itself, staff's awareness of those feelings and defenses constitutes one important portion of the needed individualization. Another part is mentioned shortly.[73]

(As will be discussed, the youth responses under consideration—mainly responses to actual and/or expected difficulties/obstacles—include but are not limited to the just-mentioned feelings and defenses. Also in the present discussion, such responses often center on, yet are not restricted to, D/Os that arise in connection with *long-range* challenges, that is,

those oriented to the youths' relatively distant future. Finally, "individualization"—still as a product—is a relative term; in particular, it can vary in degree. Here, as above, we will focus on at least a *sizable*—a substantial or large—degree.)

To further understand and better anticipate such feelings, defenses, and other responses, and to better recognize their intensity or extent, staff should also individualize youths with respect to the latters' major beliefs, assumptions, and desires, and their longstanding worries as well as fears. Collectively, these five areas comprise a large and important segment of the cognitive and emotional framework that underlies most SMOs' perceptions and interpretations of actual and anticipated interactions and events, and that thereby helps determine many of their near-term, subsequent responses and adjustments.[74]

Individualized Understanding and Responses

Staff should not only recognize and *understand* the nature and major causes of, or at least triggers for, such feelings, defenses, and—more broadly—responses. Instead, they should also develop individualized *responses* to or strategies regarding their respective youths, that is, to/regarding each such individual's feelings, defenses, and other responses in question. Staff should do so by drawing from their overall pool of information about those youths, including material about their actual and perceived life circumstances. (As discussed in Chapter 30, staff can respond to and otherwise work with youths as specific individuals and as certain *types* of persons. Conceptually, and operationally, considerable overlap exists between these levels.) Staff's responses (inputs) should address not only the more immediate effects of each youth's particular responses but, to the extent possible, longer-range implications as well. In any event they should also take account of major reasons for those individuals' responses.[75] Staff inputs that focus on these effects, implications, and reasons, especially collectively, will almost always be individualized to at least the degree mentioned earlier. Obviously, they will also be complex or multifaceted.

If staff (1) have too little of the earlier-mentioned information and understanding to make a substantially individualized response theoretically possible, or if they (2) have *enough* such information and understanding but still do not or cannot address the youths' earlier-mentioned responses in individualized ways, the chances of long-term success will be less or considerably less than would otherwise be the case, especially for those SMOs collectively. This reflects the fact that many such youths would then be much more likely to do one or more of the following: remain only minimally involved with large portions of the program, or eventually disengage from them; avoid important challenges in particular, or make only minor, largely insufficient progress regarding them; otherwise resist or dilute needed change. Also, and directly related to these points, the youths would be less likely to consolidate and perhaps extend their various program gains, or even their already existing strengths; or, they would do so to a lesser or much lesser extent.

When combined with other program features, individualized understanding and response (U&R) can help prevent programs from unnecessarily stumbling and perhaps eventually "losing" many youths, for example, during and partly because of actual or impending crises, or even in connection with seemingly moderate difficulties and pressures. Besides reducing or forestalling such unwanted events, those same individualized U&R aspects of complexity can often promote various "positives." For instance, they can make it easier, and sometimes possible in the first place, to identify and utilize the youths' internal strengths and constructive wishes, in addition to identifying and better utilizing/matching various external supports; they can better consolidate and perhaps reinforce those strengths, and so forth, as well. Individually and, of course, collectively, such developments can often help those youths begin to move forward and/or keep moving ahead, despite certain difficulties and obstacles.

Given this background, the next section will illustrate the relevance and potentially critical contributions of individualized understanding and response. It will do so by describing youth-centered problems that can easily have serious negative effects—problems that can be better addressed, and whose effects can often be forestalled or reduced, via individualized U&R. In light of this role, relevance, and potential as well as actual value, such U&R provides one major basis, or constitutes one important portion, of a general rationale for complex intervention. Other important aspects of intervention that intrinsically involve complexity (whether content-centered or operational complexity) further add to that rationale. These aspects include, for example, the need for several different program components and for well-coordinated efforts among them.

Difficulties and Obstacles

Individually and collectively, large difficulties/obstacles that are not soon overcome or substantially reduced often lead many SMOs to do one or more of the following: (1) withdraw from, or reject, particular aspects of the intervention plan, while remaining involved with the rest; (2) reduce their overall energy investment in, and their enthusiasm about, most or all aspects of the program; (3) increase their current resistance to the overall program; (4) violate technical conditions of the program and agency; (5) abscond; (6) act-out in terms of public offenses. Though neither these nor other such responses are inevitable, they are most likely to occur if those D/Os arise before the youths have seriously invested in the program or have developed substantial trust in staff—conditions which, themselves, most often exist in early stages of intervention.[76]

Whereas those *large* difficulties/obstacles often precipitate a response such as (1) through (6), *lesser* D/Os may likewise frazzle, baffle, and even seriously disrupt many SMOs, and may themselves lead to one or more such reactions. Like the responses to large D/Os, those associated with lesser ones may occur not just when SMOs (a) only barely accept the program anyway, and already have highly mixed feelings about it,[77] but also when they (b) largely want to work *with* it—their mixed, though then usually less intense, feelings notwithstanding. For instance, even in situation (b), where, say, the SMOs initially agree to address Tasks A, B, or C, and do begin to do so, many such individuals nevertheless end up curtailing various efforts (*see* responses [1] and [2] above), and some abscond briefly or otherwise, soon after relatively moderate or seemingly routine difficulties/obstacles emerge.[78]

Whether the D/Os that frequently lead to responses (1) through (6) are large-scale or seemingly moderate ("lesser"), and whether they are single or cumulative, the overall conditions under which those reactions occur are common and the contexts involved are themselves familiar. For instance, curtailment of effort with respect to given D/Os often occurs in connection with the following conditions and contexts (here, it does so despite the coexistence of largely constructive or otherwise socially accepted motives): First, it occurs when the youths regard, and partly accept, their efforts concerning Tasks A, B, or C as mainly involving a preparation for adulthood, and—directly related to that preparation—as ways of addressing the long-range challenge of establishing a viable existence for themselves in the community. Second, curtailment occurs when the youths regard/accept their efforts mainly as ways of better adapting to their more *immediate and near-term,* adolescent-centered life situation, interests, and/or needs.[79] (In contrast to the first context, yet no less common, a curtailment of effort in response to given D/Os also occurs when SMOs do *not* partially accept the idea of moving ahead with respect to adulthood or the long-range challenge, or of beginning those related processes soon. This also applies to forms of withdrawal/resistance/rejection other than curtailment per se; for example, it pertains to responses [3], [4], and [5], above.)

Whether the difficulties/obstacles that activate these youths' tendency to withdraw/resist/reject are large or seemingly moderate, and are unusual or seemingly routine, the tendency or attitude *itself* thus exists in connection with either or both of the following (*both* factors mentioned next are usually involved, especially among SMOs who are early or middle adolescents at intake; also, regardless of chronological age, the distinction between these factors corresponds in various ways to that between the "long-range challenge" and the "more *immediate . . .*" situation mentioned above):

1. *Personal/interpersonal development,* particularly that which involves the SMOs' roles and relationships with parents, guardians, and peers, and which is reflected in self-images that are associated with the given roles/relationships. Here wishes, concerns, conflicts, and/or decisions regarding dependency, independence, social conformity, and/or self-identity are usually central from early or middle adolescence forward. Ones relating to sets of personal principles and values, to reliability and responsibility, and to overall personal/social

priorities, frequently become salient or even dominant soon afterward, though temporal and content overlap usually exists.

Often, serious multiple offenders partly or largely wish to maintain their present relationships, and so on; however, as implied, ambivalence exists about doing so, and its *intensity* is sometimes considerable. Regarding these youths' *dependency* relationship with parents or guardians in particular, substantial ambivalence often continues for long periods as well, unless, for example, those adults have done the following: (a) fairly consistently encouraged, accepted, and otherwise supported the youths' coexistent strivings for *independence,* or else for self-identity; or, on the other hand, (b) rather clearly or repeatedly rejected those youths or long been hostile or indifferent toward them. Comparable issues, including the internal and interpersonal conflicts often associated with them, frequently exist with respect to the youths' peer groups, albeit often in capsule form.

By middle or later adolescence, many SMOs' dominant feelings and wishes regarding their desired types of roles/relationships with adults and peers have largely changed or, more often, are in the midst of changing. This is the case even if no more than mild or moderate rejection by those others has occurred, or no rejection at all. Nevertheless, ambivalence regarding the nature of the youths' desired roles/relationships (a) often remains a significant overall factor, whichever change status ("largely changed"; "midst of changing") is involved; also, in specific situations, such ambivalence may (b) substantially contribute to emotional strain, to volatile reactions or interactions, and to hasty or inconsistent decisions—besides increasing the individuals' sensitivity and vulnerability to difficulties/obstacles in the first place. (Point [b] especially applies if the youths' feelings and wishes regarding those roles/relationships are "in the midst of changing," rather than being already "largely changed.") At any rate, the overall developmental situation often remains fluid in this—the "desired roles/relationships"—and related respects, with parents, guardians, and peers alike. This applies, though to a generally decreasing degree, even as the youths simultaneously grow more aware of, interested in, and/or tolerant of various components of adulthood per se, and perhaps of the long-range challenge as well.

2. *Relatively specific emotions, feelings, and responses,* especially ones involved in failures, disagreements, "hassles," and/or related frustrations that the SMOs consciously and preconsciously assume may occur, or be repeated, in various situations and interactions. (The emotions and feelings [see below] are mainly but not only the youths'. Some *responses* are also the youths', while the rest are those of others. [We will mainly emphasize emotions and feelings on the part of *youths,* and responses to those youths by *others.*] Here, "involved in" means either *resulting from* or *in anticipation of.*) The youths' assumptions or expectations especially center on emotions/feelings such as anger, hostility, fear, inadequacy, confusion, and helplessness, and on responses such as disapproval/condemnation by self or others, and punishment by others. They mainly derive from unpleasant and unwanted personal experiences and related events. These experiences and events almost always did or do occur, though they have sometimes been partly misinterpreted and/or exaggerated. In any case, their occurrence—collectively—was/is temporally distant, recent, and/or current, and they usually involve(d) authority figures, other adults, and peers (siblings included) in home, neighborhood, justice system, or school settings. Besides having their strongest sources, and some of their frequent reinforcers, in such experiences, events, and related memories, the emotions and feelings in question are commonly, but far from always, accompanied by a low self-image and an underlying belief that one is largely "bad." (Such images and beliefs are often obscured to the casual or inexperienced observer by various facades and overcompensations. The images differ from those mentioned in connection with the above roles, relationships, and so on—e.g., those of child-to-parent, or of "teenager.")

Even when such an image and belief hardly exist, various anticipated emotions, feelings, and responses, for instance, ones involving anger, fear, confusion, or punishment, can substantially affect many SMOs' willingness and felt ability to *stick with* given tasks. As implied earlier, this impact often occurs when—as is itself commonly the case—the youths are already experiencing above-average overall pressures or are faced with specific difficulties/obstacles.[80, 81] Such anticipated emotions, feelings, and responses can also negatively influence those or other SMOs' (especially ones *with* a particularly low self-image) desire to seriously *undertake* those tasks or activities in the first place, and to thereby risk later arousing or rearousing the unwanted emotions, and so on. Finally, those emotions/feelings/responses can have such impacts (a) partly independent of, or in spite of, and (b) also at the same time as, those individuals' possible and perhaps growing interest and investment in the *long-range challenge* per se, and despite their overall stance regarding the above-mentioned developmental issues which relate to that challenge. As suggested earlier, these issues may involve, for example, the youths' broad desire to either maintain or modify certain childhood and adolescent roles and behavior patterns. (See Factor 1.)

Before continuing, the following might be noted by way of review and further detail. Factor 1, above, is more directly and specifically linked to future considerations—namely, adulthood and the challenge—than is Factor 2, and its overall scope is broader. However, despite Factor 2's narrower scope, its influence on SMOs is no less than Factor 1's. With both factors, the youths' tendency to curtail or even discontinue various A, B, or C efforts exists—and can be activated by the above range of difficulties/obstacles, emotions, and so on—even when these individuals' overall interest/investment (I/I) in the program is fairly sincere and substantial. Such an I/I may be reflected, for instance, in their general acceptance of its main goals,[82] including (1) the reduction/elimination of illegal behavior and (2) the promotion of overall personal/social growth. Naturally, the tendency to curtail one's efforts can be more easily activated among youths whose I/I in such goals is considerably *less* than the above, not to mention minimal.

(Regarding the second such goal—projected beyond the near future—the following might be added. Hesitancy and mixed feelings about modifying existing relationships and adjustment patterns [Task or Area B] in order to move toward the more distant future are more likely to occur when the individuals do not have a fairly clear, let alone strong, image of a desired future in the first place, or at least one they find acceptable *and* that they assume involves activities and roles within their reach. This also applies to mixed feelings about gaining various practical and interpersonal strengths/skills [Task or Area A] in order to help achieve that end.)[83]

Youths' Curtailment of Efforts
Intervention as Perceived Threat
Briefly, why and how does *Factor 1*—personal/interpersonal development—bear on the tendency for serious multiple offenders to curtail/discontinue their efforts, and on responses (3) through (6) as well? One major part of the answer involves the fact that many SMOs have moderate to serious misgivings about substantially modifying their overall child- or early adolescent-to-parent relationship, as well as certain "carefree," spontaneous/impulsive, "teenage," behavior patterns and roles that may characterize and sometimes be integral to their peer activities and that they may consider important to their acceptance by others. Because of these misgivings, and in spite of the *remaining* portions of their overall ambivalence and desired self-image—for instance, despite their coexisting wishes to modify that relationship, and their strivings for greater independence and perhaps even more "coolness"/consistency/directionality/maturity—such youths consider the program a partial or sizable threat to the given relationship, roles, and so on, under the following combinations of conditions:

1. Insofar as they view program staff as (a) trying to make them "grow up" too fast or change in ways they are only partly interested in at the time, or are even partly opposed to (e.g., thinking more—or much more seriously—about their future; becoming much more reliable and considerate; taking greater personal responsibility for certain actions), and/or as (b) emphasizing the long-range challenge in general (e.g., via involvement in Task A); and,

2. insofar as they assume that modifications in those relationships and roles are—and/or are considered by staff—essential components of growing up and/or of addressing the challenge.

Given this perceived threat, these individuals can soon become wary of, and passively as well as actively resistive to, aspects of the program that definitely seem to bear on those areas. This can occur whether or not the youths' already existing interest or investment in "going with the program" is sizable, and subsequently remains that way, with respect to *other* significant areas and issues, for example, school, physical aggression, and illegal behavior per se. (This entire scenario regarding the youths' desire to maintain rather than modify their existing relationships and roles is called *Context 1*, or *C-1*.)

Modifying versus Maintaining Existing Relationships/Roles
Another large part of the answer to the above question focuses on a different context (*Context 2*, or *C-2*), but it still involves difficulties/obstacles. In Context 2, D/Os mainly interfere with the youths' wish to *move forward*; as such, they differ from those in C-1, where they comprise, or, in any event, are interpreted as comprising, threats to conditions, interactions, or behaviors that the youths mainly wish to *maintain*. Thus, in C-2—that of moving forward—the difficulties/obstacles are ones encountered by youths who largely wish to modify, rather than maintain, their existing relationships and roles (R/Rs) with parents, guardians, and/or peers. More specifically, in C-2, the youths mainly want to change those R/Rs, and they want to do so despite their general ambivalence—their simultaneous misgivings, and hesitancy—in this regard. (As implied, neither "modifying" nor "maintaining" has an all-or-none basis; instead, the youths *mainly* want to do one or the other. Thus, at any given time, one set of forces collectively outweighs or dominates the other. This reflects the youths' general ambivalence.)

In Context 2, as in C-1, the difficulties/ obstacles that the youths encounter—say, the obstacles to modifying those R/Rs—are not just internal. Instead, in C-2, they sometimes also come from parents, and others, for example, from external sources that (in this context *unlike* the youths) try to largely *maintain* the status quo. (In Context *1*, the key external pressure to *change* comes from, and/or is interpreted by the youths as coming from, program staff. Parents and peers may or may not be applying such pressure; that is, they can do either, and they are not the key sources in any event.) With these particular C-2's, those external pressures—collectively—are more influential than the mix of internal pressures/desires, for example, the various personal forces, that, also collectively, produce the youths' ambivalence.

At any rate, in Context 2 these youths often end up substantially curtailing their personal efforts to modify the given relationships/roles, that is, to make changes in that particular respect.[84] They do so more because of those external (parental and/or peer) pressures than due to their own reservations—the latter, as indicated, having already been outweighed/dominated by the youths' desire for change. More specifically, these individuals often end up curtailing their efforts—thus, restricting their dominant wishes—mainly because they do not, at the time, want to continue trying to deal with the tensions, complications, and/or unpleasantness frequently associated with those external difficulties/obstacles. Again, this occurs despite the youths' dominant wish, which is to make substantial changes in the given relationships and roles. (If such external pressures are sufficiently reduced, the overall balance of forces can shift and the youths' dominant wish can be asserted or reasserted.)

In the present, Context-2 situation, which centers on relationships/roles, these youths do not, at the same time, necessarily curtail or resist possible movement toward adulthood in certain *other* areas, mentioned next. However, such curtailing or resisting, in those other areas, often occurs in Context 1. There, for example, youths frequently resist opportunities to acquire or increase *practical and/or interpersonal strengths/skills,* these often being preeminent among the curtailed, resisted areas. They resist, and so on, not primarily because the task of acquiring/increasing those strengths/skills itself seems unduly diffi-

cult (which, in other instances, it *does*), but mainly due to the following. Substantial progress in those areas could or would simultaneously constitute a step toward adulthood, and that step, if other than minor, would, in those individuals' minds, comprise a threat to the relationships/roles that—in this case (C-1)—they themselves mainly want to *retain,* not change. (Implicit in this and the following discussion is the fact that, with many SMOs, substantial movement toward adulthood and regarding the long-range challenge may require changes/developments which are in addition to the modified R/Rs with parents and/or peers. This is despite the fact that the latter changes—like some in other areas—may themselves remain relatively important or crucial. For instance, regarding "other areas," developments such as an increase in practical and interpersonal strengths/skills can be important or critical as well—or, with some individuals, instead.)

Regarding terminology, relationships/roles involve the earlier-mentioned Task, or Area, *B*. The acquiring/increasing of practical strengths, and so on, involves Task, or Area, *A*. Task C centers on increasing one's self-understanding and on reducing/resolving one's psychological difficulties or conflicts. "Task" and "area" are used interchangeably.

We next continue to focus on the role played by difficulties/obstacles in the youths' curtailment/withdrawal of given efforts, such as ones involving Tasks A, B, or C. The observations also apply to youth responses (3) through (6)—which include resistance per se, technical violations, and so on. To simplify the presentation we will not—as before—specifically focus on and discuss Task C.

Even when the youths mainly *want* to modify their present R/Rs and their parents/peers do not substantially resist attempted changes in that area, these SMOs may nevertheless encounter difficulties/ obstacles when also trying to move toward adulthood—say, when attempting to do so by acquiring or increasing their practical/ interpersonal strengths/skills.[85] (These particular D/Os thus center on given *tasks* as such—specifically, on Task-A items—not on various parent or peer *inputs* regarding existing relationships/roles, that is, Task-B items. Because of these Task-A, that is, Area-A, difficulties, and because of possible or anticipated unpleasant personal feelings or external consequences associated with them, many individuals curtail their efforts in that particular area. They do so, as implied, even though they had previously reduced their ambivalence, anxiety, and the like regarding that area to the point where they could at least get started with the task and could do so in the context of moving toward adulthood and/or the long-range challenge per se, not just that of adapting to more immediate, adolescent-centered needs. Under these circumstances, when such youths curtail their efforts in that particular area, they are not, for example, using the D/Os largely as an excuse for avoiding challenges or tasks that, say, they largely do *not* want to undertake in the first place, for whatever reasons. (The same would apply regarding Area/Task C.) Under other conditions and circumstances, for example, some found in Context 1, various difficulties/obstacles *are* sometimes used—even seized upon—as partial or major excuses for curtailing given efforts, or for avoiding them in the first place.

Signaling Distress, Cutting One's Losses, Obscuring Facts and Feelings

With the already mentioned Context-2 youths, the key difficulties/obstacles are mainly "external"; for example, they chiefly reflect parental opposition or the nature of the practical skills to be developed.[86] However, with many other C-2 youths, the principal D/O—that is, the individuals' long-standing *low self-concept*—is more "internal" than external, if one uses parental opposition and skills development as examples of the latter.[87] (D/Os are "key" or "principal" in connection with their impact on youth efforts concerning Tasks A, B, or C.)[88]

Especially because of their low self-concept, such C-2 youths readily anticipate "failure."[89] They have long felt unable to adequately handle various situations and challenges and, in any event, to satisfy parents and other significant adults. Given this self-concept plus those related expectations and feelings, these SMOs are initially reluctant to engage in various intervention efforts. More to the point, once they do decide to engage, and once they *have* become mainly interested in moving ahead, they nevertheless remain primed to curtail those efforts when faced with seemingly moderate difficulties/obstacles, not to mention major ones. More specifically, they long remain conspicuously prone to re-

strict or even abandon what they had decided to do and even what they now largely *want* to do, when such D/Os arise and especially if *they* are not soon reduced, resolved, or otherwise dealt with. These difficulties/obstacles may take the form of direct or indirect opposition, double messages, procedural complications, new/unforeseen challenges, increased demands, and so on.

Here, some D/Os *are* used by these C-2 youths as partial or major "excuses" for backing away from various efforts, or for reducing the attempted rate of change.[90] Yet even then, they are not being utilized to retreat from efforts and changes that the youths did *not* largely want to make or bring about anyway, for example, from ones they had *not* mainly come to want—their initial reluctance or even strong ambivalence about them notwithstanding. This contrasts, for example, with many C-1 individuals' frequent use of D/Os as convenient reasons (yet, often simultaneously, plausible ones) for curtailing various Area-B efforts—more specifically, for thereby making it easier to retain given relationships/roles they did not mainly want to change anyway, in both the early and the following phases of intervention.

The curtailment of interest and effort by these Context-2 youths is seldom designed to signal distress or to only reduce their existing level of anxiety; this is despite the fact that these particular motives often do predominate (especially collectively), and, in any event, are very common. Instead, and not infrequently, such curtailment/withdrawal also comprises the youths' attempt to "cut their losses" psychologically, for instance, to pull back before they feel even worse about themselves and/or their efforts, and before they become more anxious than before. Both of the preceding points apply (1) whether or not the curtailment of interests and efforts (CIE) is intended as a temporary move only, and (2) not just to CIE as such but to other forms or expressions of retreat as well—various technical violations included.

Among somewhat fewer C-2 youths,[91] curtailment, withdrawal, and so on, are ways of *obscuring* more than of signaling; this applies whether or not they are also designed to cut one's losses. In particular, their main and immediate aim is to partly obscure such facts and/or feelings as the following, or to even divert attention from them: The individuals have been—or are being/becoming—seriously thrown off stride; they are frightened about continuing certain Task A, B, or C activities/efforts, let alone increasing them or entering new paths; and/or, they are worried and perhaps confused about how to proceed, even if the activities themselves are not in question.[92]

Often related to such obscuring or diverting, these and numerous other C-2s, including many who abscond, have long been uncomfortable about revealing, let alone seriously discussing and examining, various aspects and characteristics of their self-concept and their frequent state of mind: felt weaknesses; self-doubts; conflicts; confusions; and/or moderate to intense feelings/emotions of anger, hurt, and fear.[93] This discomfort—which is also experienced by many other offenders, albeit often to a lesser degree—especially occurs in interactions between the given youths and the authority figures or other adults whom they know have decision-making power over them and/or have actual or potential emotional power as well (e.g., they can make the youths feel anxious, happier, and better or worse about themselves).

Such offenders believe or implicitly assume that those revelations and discussions would make them vulnerable or more vulnerable to such individuals, and probably more controllable—in particular, substantially controllable—by them. Whether inside or outside of intervention, vulnerability and control are particularly meaningful to these youths if, as is often the case, they believe/assume the above individuals might not accept or like them anyway, might purposely try to "make life difficult" for them, might take advantage of them, and/or might purposely let them down or otherwise harm them.[94] At various points *within* a program, such discomfort and defensiveness can themselves constitute major and potentially crucial obstacles to addressing and reducing factors that may heavily contribute to the youths' no longer wanting (i.e., mainly wanting) to proceed, no longer mainly wanting to keep trying or trying as hard, and so on. As indicated earlier, these unaddressed—often even unexpressed—factors would include the individuals' felt weaknesses and other aspects of their long-standing self-concept; they would also include anger, fear, and other facets of their state of mind.

Regarding *Factor 2* ("relatively specific emotions, feelings, and responses"), we have already indicated how this bears on SMOs' tendency to curtail/discontinue their Task A, B, or C activities, and on their reluctance to seriously undertake them in the first place. Basically, this tendency and reluctance reflects those individuals' desire to reduce or eliminate the chances of experiencing unwanted feelings and emotions, such as anger, fear, anxiety, and confusion, and of generating unwanted responses, such as punishment or rejection, by others. These are feelings and responses that the youths believe or assume could be easily aroused, generated, or increased during, and because of, "failures, disagreements, 'hassles,' and/or related frustrations" that occur or can occur in connection with their A, B, or C activities. (The preceding applies whether or not the youths view progress and success on A, B, or C as possible steps toward adulthood and as ways of addressing the long-range challenge per se, and whether or not they largely want to use them in those ways.)

Thus, these individuals want to preclude the occurrence of, or reduce the frequency and intensity of, various anticipated, emerging, or ongoing experiences of an unpleasant or traumatic nature. Common among them are increased external pressure from or resistance by others, with this producing personal anxiety; angry confrontations, and "scenes"; condemnation by self and/or others; and, feelings of inadequacy or helplessness, and related social embarrassment.

Precluding or Forestalling Disappointment/Rejection

Causally and substantially related to such expectations and to the youths' resulting responses (their preemptive, unilateral actions included[95]) is the following; this applies especially, but not only, in the early phases of intervention: Most such individuals do not expect to receive much useful and reliable assistance from staff—let alone most other adults—during times of difficulty, increasing tension, or crisis. In part, this commonly reflects the youths' implicit assumption that (1) they are not considered important enough to warrant much time and effort, that (2) they are not particularly liked—and, thus, not persons whom others would *want* to help, anyway, or that (3) both (1) and (2) apply. Many also believe that (4) authority figures expect them to eventually "mess up" and will probably give up on them if and when they do, or will otherwise "pull the rug out in order to prevent things from getting worse." Messing up would involve not just substantial but possibly even minor *lawbreaking;* in any event, it would involve behaviors which differ in that respect from others that may arise in connection with A, B, or C.

As may be deduced, many SMOs try to broadly protect themselves against unwanted feelings, emotions, and responses by taking certain steps *before* the difficulties/obstacles arise that, they assume, could bring about those feelings, and so on.[96] In general, these steps or actions involve the youths' attempts to *prevent their program from getting well underway, in the first place.* Two sizable groups of SMOs, discussed below, make these attempts to a well-above-average degree; also, they usually achieve their goal, that is, they succeed (often to such a degree), temporarily or more permanently. In either case, this *level* of success, and sometimes even just that level of effort, often complicates intervention in ways that can adversely affect the individuals' longer-range adjustment.

In itself, the earlier-mentioned *type* of effort, action, self-protection, or resistance is fairly common among SMOs, and in that respect it is normal. When this effort or action is carried out in its usual way—more specifically, to its usual degree rather than a *well-above-average* degree—it is far less likely to have negative effects on certain intervention goals. Restated, when this fairly common type of self-protective action is expressed to no more than its usual—*average*—degree, it can be fairly readily integrated or otherwise balanced with the individuals' broader, and longer-range, needs. (We now turn to the "well-above-average" groups.)

The first such group tries to protect itself in the above manner (". . . prevent [the] program from getting well underway") by directly and strongly resisting staff efforts to involve it in given program elements and activities (collectively called "aspects").[97] It does not, however, reject the program as a whole, particularly its core legal requirements regarding behavioral control. The second group, which itself essentially accepts those requirements, uses a somewhat different approach. For one thing, it does not directly oppose, largely resist, or similarly try to hamper certain specific aspects; in fact, it involves itself in the usual content, such as Tasks A, B,

or C, and in that important respect it accepts or goes along with the program. However, this group's *involvement* in such tasks, areas, or aspects is no more than tenuous and is considerably more provisional than that of most other SMOs; also, it may be only superficial, for at least a number of months.[98]

In effect, these youths greatly restrict not so much the breadth or scope of their involvement—this (a reduced "range") being associated with the first group; instead, they restrict or try to restrict the *degree* ("depth") of their involvement with most or all individual areas/elements, even if there are few. In this respect they try to insulate themselves by markedly reducing the program's chances of gaining a major or serious "hold" on them, initially and often beyond. Consciously or preconsciously, these group-2 youths (still collectively) assume that—without this "hold"—various difficulties/obstacles that they associate with unwanted feelings, emotions, and responses will be less likely to occur in the first place, and that, if they do occur, their intensity will often be less than if such a hold or involvement exists.

In any event, via the earlier-mentioned actions or stances (collectively called "defenses"), both groups of serious multiple offenders try to avoid such things as (1) eventual major upset, and anxiety as well, (2) "getting [new] people mad" at them, and (3) making parents and/or peers angrier at them than before. More broadly, they try to preclude, delay, or weaken anticipated difficulties, obstacles, and related involvements that they believe could otherwise make the overall program a major "hassle." Many hope—also broadly— that their defenses will at least be enough to prevent the program, and related D/Os, from making their general life situation *worse,* that is, worse in their view. Here (as with "preclude . . . a major 'hassle'"), their main focus and concern involves current adjustment patterns and interpersonal relationships.[99]

As suggested earlier, when such preemptive defenses are utilized to the above degree and are successful in the above sense, they often potentially worsen the youths' long-term prospects.[100] They do so by distancing these individuals from otherwise available resources and opportunities and, in many cases, by functionally diluting those resources, by establishing or supporting a negative atmosphere, and by constraining communications. All in all, the situation that surrounds these preemptive or anticipatory defenses thus reflects a major adjustment bind that these individuals are in, one which they themselves have largely generated yet which they are often unaware of as such or else may only moderately care about:[101] On the one hand, these youths wish—usually strongly—to protect themselves against the above-mentioned, anticipated feelings, responses, and so on; and they then attempt to do so. However, because of the *degree* to which they attempt this—and, especially, achieve it—they often, by the same token, end up screening or virtually severing themselves from resources/opportunities that are relevant to adulthood and the long-range challenge per se. This screening/severing—together, "distancing"—then makes it extra difficult to adequately address those longer-range issues and needs, ones that may eventually become important to the youths even if they seem unimportant to them "now." (None of this means that these individuals' wish for near-term protection and relief is seldom important, and never crucial, itself.)

In short, by heavily directing their attention and energy to certain anticipated negatives and to the achievement of near-term protection/relief, these youths, in effect, often work against various longer-range needs, possibilities, and prospects. At any rate, they do so far more, and more often, than they work *for* or *toward* them. This overall situation or process involves commission as well as omission; and, in both cases, its results can also affect the individuals' more immediate needs and prospects themselves. Thus, they can apply to near-term issues that differ from those involving the youths' desired protection and relief alone.

Notes

1. Treatment, and treatment programs, have been described as follows (the external controls dimension is discussed only in the text):

Within the justice system, increased protection of society is the primary or *socially centered* goal of treatment. . . . Attitude change, increased ability to cope, and so forth, comprise the secondary or *offender-centered* goal. . . . Though this [secondary] goal has absolute value in itself, it is, given the justice system's main role in society, chiefly

a means to the socially centered end of public protection. . . . The goal of increased public protection, that is, reduced illegal behavior, is shared by punishment and incapacitation. However, what distinguishes treatment from these social-protection strategies is its manner of focusing not so much on illegal behavior per se but on one or both of the following: factors which have presumably generated or helped maintain the individual's illegal behavior, and factors which may help offset or eliminate those causal, triggering, or sustaining factors. In addition, treatment is more concerned than either punishment or incapacitation with offender-centered goals per se, that is, aside from the latter's role as a means to increased public protection. . . .

Specifically, then, treatment, as a vehicle of rehabilitation or habilitation, usually tries to reach its socially centered and offender-centered goals by focusing on such factors and conditions as the offender's *adjustment techniques, interests, skills, personal limitations, and/or life circumstances*. It does so in order to affect his or her future behavior and adjustment. That is, treatment efforts focus on any of several factors or conditions and are directed at particular future events. These efforts may be called *treatment programs* or *approaches* insofar as they involve specific components and inputs (e.g., counseling or skill development) that are organized, interrelated, and otherwise planned so as to generate changes in the above factors and conditions—changes which, in turn, may help generate the desired future events (e.g., reduced illegal behavior).

Through this set of inputs and sequence of events, treatment attempts to modify the offender's adjustment pattern or techniques, immediate environment, or both. In effect, it tries to modify the relationship between the self and the environment, and/or the relationship which parts of that environment (e.g., peers or family) have to the offender. . . . The distinguishing features of most treatment programs are those designed to change or modify the offender mainly through positive incentives and rewards, subtle and otherwise, or to change or modify his or her life circumstances and improve social opportunities by various pragmatic means. One might call such efforts Positive Treatment Programs (PTPs) or approaches, which apply to juveniles and adults alike.

Consistent with these distinguishing features, PTPs focus on methods that basically utilize, develop, or redirect the powers and mechanisms of the individual's mind and body, not reduce, physically traumatize, disorganize, or devastate them. (Palmer, 1992, pp. 20–24)

2. This applies whether treatment takes place with little or much by way of external controls, particularly those that are explicitly applied rather than being only or mainly covert and/or implicit. Even when external controls are used to aid in treatment, their principal goal is the protection of society. Both points apply whether short-term or long-term protection is involved.

3. We are not referring to 100 percent protection of society, or even to near-perfect protection. To achieve either level would probably require an almost complete police state or its equivalent, with respect to social surveillance, overt or covert intimidation, and so on.

4. Obviously, without the intent and effort, this goal could be neither achieved nor approached. Regarding particular attempts/efforts, these could be justified, at one level, if they seemed to involve or reflect empirically and/or theoretically reasonable and relevant approaches and to be appropriately implemented. However, at a practical level, one could validly question the significance of those efforts—and, in a sense, their justification—if they fairly consistently failed to produce the intended results.

5. Regarding reasons or intentions that usually dominate, see (in text) the first rationale, above, and the fourth one, below.

6. Acceptance often involves a desire to include the other individual. In this regard it is somewhat comparable to wanting or gladly allowing one more individual—someone who is believed to have at least basic, requisite capacities—to be part of what one considers a worthwhile group.

In this case it is the "human" group or team, or the "human race." The individual can be seen and accepted as part of this group even if he or she chooses to not *actively* contribute to it, or to not contribute in socially standard ways.

7. This identification generally involves two main processes and content levels. First, it involves seeing *general* aspects of oneself—oneself-as-a-being-with-human-feelings-and-thoughts—in other persons. (Here, "seeing" includes believing and/or assuming that such feelings and thoughts exist in others.) Simultaneously, but usually to a lesser degree and less consciously, this identification involves the assumption that certain *specific,* desired feelings and thoughts that one considers important in oneself are the same as or similar to those which exist in the other individuals.

8. This range exists *across* the individuals who, collectively, have or feel ARC, at any given time; and, by definition, ARC is always genuine in quality, whatever its degree. Simultaneously, acceptance, respect, and compassion—viewed collectively—commonly differs *within* any one person, again at any given time. (This applies whether its degree is modest or more substantial.) For instance, many people have or feel a degree of ARC for some individuals, including many offenders, which differs from that which they have/feel for others—offenders and nonoffenders alike.

9. Implicit in this last point is the assumption that deservedness is inversely related to the type and/or amount of offending. For instance, in this framework, and other things being equal, the more the offending and/or the worse the offenses, the less one would be thought to deserve assistance.

10. At another level of abstraction, yet also depending on the particulars that are focused on (e.g., the characteristics or qualities), one could say that the supplementary aspect relates to the *kind* or *kinds* of humans they are.

11. These, in combination, help make them distinguishable persons in the sense of separate individuals—apart from their being humans in an *across*-individuals sense, that is, a common-to-all-persons respect.

12. Some positives are harder to use or express when negatives are present, at least in certain degrees and in given combinations. Similarly, various negatives are weakened or harder to use when certain positives are present, are strengthened, and so on, individually or collectively.

13. This assumes the positives will not be largely blocked or undercut by negative features and/or by obstacles, deficits, fears, and the like.

14. Collectively, positives may be overt and/or covert at any time. Also, many such features—individually—may alternate *between* overt and covert, through time.

15. The supplement expands on the core with regard to certain implications of item (3). It takes (1) and (2) for granted and, thus, does not differ in that respect.

16. In itself, the third rationale has meaning and significance independent of (1) how much effort will be needed to produce the given results and of (2) what the absolute and comparative costs of that effort will be per youth per unit of positive-outcome. In real-life, factors (1) and (2) must, of course, be considered; yet, by themselves, they neither alter nor diminish the meaning, etc. of the rationale itself.

17. As indicated, the core of this rationale for intervening in general and for offering assistance in particular involves the fact that offenders are human. The supplementary part centers on certain implications and corollaries, of those individuals' positive features and actions, which are other than merit-centered.

18. These features can be positive or worthy even if they are infrequently expressed in actions and deeds.

19. Regarding the whether or not of deservedness, the quality of individuals' efforts, that is, of their inputs, is seldom considered all-determining.

20. The core and supplementary components of the third rationale have already been described. In the present discussion, one that happens to occur in the context of that rationale, *deservedness,* as delineated in the text above (cf. Webster), is a function only of merit; as with "need," it is not integral to the rationale itself. At any rate, the presently delineated aspects of deservedness differ from that which either does or should automatically accompany the fact of being human; that is, they differ from that which reflects the core component of the third rationale. Compared to those present aspects, this component involves a less common meaning of "deserve." In this latter sense, that is, the third-rationale sense, deservedness exists prior to and separate from whatever an individual (1) may or may not *do,* or have *done,* for others, (2) may have achieved for himself or herself, (3) may hope or plan to do for self or others sooner or later, and (4) may "have" by way of personality features. In any event, regarding the third rationale (also when its supplement is involved), at least *some* meaningful assistance would be offered or provided even if the offenders had not specifically earned it on grounds, say, of either their performance or their expressed intentions to date. Instead, deservedness with respect to receiving some assistance would automatically inhere in and accompany the status—the fact—of being human (Homo sapiens, even if still minimally socialized/civilized and sociable). The goal, here, would be that of trying to significantly increase the chances that individuals will be better able to develop, and *will* eventually develop, the constructive attributes that human beings are known to be capable of having and expressing.

21. The generally accepted "pursuit of happiness" is an endeavor seldom considered ipso facto unduly "selfish," and—necessarily—of no significant, present or future benefit to others. At any rate, to the extent it is viewed as selfish or self-serving but nonetheless acceptable in principle with respect to nonoffenders, it could presumably be viewed the same way for offenders.

22. A more complete and specific statement would refer not just to "constructive activities" but to "constructive or potentially constructive activities or efforts."

23. The first group of serious multiple offenders, that is, the "many," would meet neither condition (1) nor (2), above. This, however, does not mean these youths have done nothing or virtually nothing constructive to date. Nor does it

mean they have, and manifest, few if any positive features. (Here, the distinction between "several" [see conditions (1) and (2) in the text], on the one hand, and "few" or none," on the other, is important. For instance, if no more than "few" of the activities and features were required, the percentage of youths seen as having merit would be considerably higher than if at least several were required.) At any rate, these SMOs include, among others, the following: (a) youths who, at intake, do not readily *manifest* their various positive features and/or abilities because, say, of their (the individuals') open defensiveness or overall ambivalence about changing; and, (b) individuals whose overall positives are largely *obscured, distorted, diverted,* or *diluted* by their (the youths') fears, anger, and/or facade of indifference. At and shortly after program entry, considerable overlap exists between individuals described in (a) and those mentioned in (b).

24. A more detailed and precise statement would be as follows. SMOs can be assessed as poor or questionable risks partly or largely on grounds of their seeming or actual, past and present disinterest in undertaking constructive activities, and/or their few apparent and perhaps actual positive personality features.

25. In both cases—risk and merit—these assessments are likely to involve such broad categories as the number and/or type of constructive activities and positive features. With most practitioners, the judgments, themselves, are likely to remain global and subjective, and to not focus systematically on those categories. This partly reflects the fact that no generally agreed-upon set of categories—thus, standard items—exists regarding *type* of constructive activities and positive features. (For present purposes, it suffices to use "assess" and "judge" on a loosely synonymous basis, even though—under some definitions—the latter process can be considered a product of the former.)

26. Four points might be noted. (1) The correctional practices in question are those that dominate at the time, not necessarily ones with which the entire community, or even its preponderance of adults, fully

agree. (2) Here, society focuses on any jurisdiction or assemblage of jurisdictions, whether or not the latter are substantively related to each other. The term is used in this structural sense for purposes of simplicity alone. (3) If the partial or complete withholding of assistance is to be of sizable import, in fact, if it is to matter at all, that assistance would have to be potentially meaningful in the first place, not simply token or perfunctory. (4) The idea that serious multiple offenders do not sufficiently deserve relevant assistance is much more closely associated with the view that such inputs or efforts are an earned privilege rather than an intrinsic right— something that need *not* be earned by, at least, certain means. At any rate, privilege, much more than intrinsic right, is sometimes associated with the position or the implicit assumption that if an offender has not *already* earned any assistance, say, as of that individual's point of commitment to a given agency, he or she will never do so. That view sometimes reflects a further position or assumption, one especially applied to multiple offenders: The individual has *already* had many opportunities to obtain and/or use such assistance; as a result, he or she either *deserves* no more or, deservedness aside, has amply demonstrated that nothing more will matter.

27. It might be noted that society, by not providing assistance, would not be giving individuals, whom it already considers insufficiently deserving, a potentially effective opportunity to change and improve in ways that might eventually *render* them deserving, or more deserving. The same situation would apply if a society decided to not use assistance that might help reverse unwanted tendencies among youths whom it believes became worse—for whatever reasons (but, in this case, deservedness aside)—during the months or years preceding intake or commitment.

28. And apart from the fact that differing types of deservedness-centered responses might be possible—responses that might have rather different consequences for society.

29. Viewed at another level—one that can be included in, yet is separable from, the

first—some individual features, such as unyieldingness, can be used positively in one specific situation yet negatively in another.

30. These, like "thoughtfulness, kindness," and so on, can occur whether or not the individuals are attentive, resourceful, and so forth, and however many or few skills and abilities they might have.

31. Complicating the matter would be actions that are recognized, ahead of time, as likely to be considered "mean" only in the eyes of the recipient, but which are viewed as necessary for his or her own good. These differ from harsh—and/or "mean"—actions that are taken for revenge, and from those based on a belief that the recipient deserves to be harmed in such ways or to those degrees whether this will or will not eventually help him or her.

32. Obviously, when judging the overall positive or negative quality of actions, as distinct, for example, from traits, skills, and abilities per se, actual consequences can enter the picture even though the main emphasis can remain on *intentions*. To be sure, not all major consequences can be foreseen when the various judgments are made; moreover, the effects of some actions (foreseen or not) that start out negative may later turn out positive, and vice versa. This is apart from the fact that intentions, or motives, may themselves be mixed—not necessarily or not just unclear—from the start, rather than "purely" or firmly positive or negative.

33. These developments can occur either inside the intervention, that is, as part of it, or else aside from it. At any rate, intervention, among other possible inputs, can raise the chances that the first development will occur, and it can reduce the likelihood of the second.

34. The same would apply to nonhabit combinations that are set against *their* counterparts.

35. Nothing can literally undo positive and negative actions and deeds that have already occurred—more precisely, undo the fact, though not necessarily various important effects, of their having existed. Nor, to use an illustration involving positives, can anything literally undo/dilute

the fact that value, and related merit, had been chalked up in connection with some of those actions/deeds, or, separately, with various personal achievements. (If one's example involved negatives, "blame" would substitute for merit and "failed efforts" would substitute for achievements.) Nevertheless, in "real life," that is, within many contemporary societies, individuals' past positives, for example, many of their personal actions/deeds/achievements, *are* often viewed as no longer particularly relevant to present and future decisions, for instance, to certain actions that correctional staff/administrators may wish to take with respect to the given offenders. (To be sure, opposite views are also often held.) The value and merit-centered significance of SMOs' past positive actions is separable from various forms of current *practical utility*, as viewed by many correctional and noncorrectional persons. In any case, and practical utility aside, the past—from some perspectives—can be considered a relevant and major basis for judging individuals' deservedness—not, however, in terms of past negatives alone but also past positives. In this case, when positives (P's) and negatives (N's) are both taken into account, the judgment in question would be more reflective of what might be called *overall* deservedness than if only the P *or* the N actions, deeds, achievements, factors, and/or features had been considered.

36. Here, for instance, significance would not involve the features' actual or possible contribution to judgments regarding offenders' overall *deservedness*. This is separable from the fact that, when thinking about serious offenders' deservedness, many or most individuals focus largely—sometimes almost exclusively—on their negative features.

37. Again, this occurs even though, in reality, various P's and N's usually *coexist* within any offender at any given time, say, at intake.

38. Even if it were possible to achieve, a literal elimination of any given positive would be no more than functionally equivalent to that positive's having simply been (1) *suppressed* within those individu-

als' (here, staff's) minds/consciousness, and (2) *ignored* in connection with various intervention contexts—in effect, equivalent to its having been disallowed after, say, being implicitly or explicitly judged irrelevant or insubstantial.

39. As indicated, this supplement emphasizes the idea that if offenders' positive characteristics, say, certain interests, abilities, personality features, and motives, are carefully tapped, increased, and/or better organized/focused/directed, this can promote the offender-centered and socially centered goals alike.

40. Not just because they are considered weak but because the negatives are considered much stronger and more important.

41. Their rejection would be even more complete if, in the first place, they did not accept the idea that various positives even existed in most SMOs, or if they believed that most or all such features either only *seemed* positive or, in any event, would usually be used negatively (harmfully).

42. This involves both moderate and strong rejection.

43. Collectively, their interest in these goals and processes ranges from moderate to high.

44. That is, the relevance, and so on, of those features is less likely to "be downplayed" to the same degree, or even at all.

45. As discussed later, this preparation can also, or instead, be passive, and in some respects largely permissive.

46. And even if they are not essentially situational or, for whatever reasons, acute.

47. Although the *existence* of these external resources is essentially independent of the individual youth's motivation, their accessibility partly depends on it.

48. Key aspects of the more passive stance are as follows: (1) Remain on relatively conventional or otherwise socially acceptable paths, ones that are broadly consistent with typical forms of adulthood and which seem unlikely to interfere with one's eventually obtaining desired goals. (2) Meanwhile, allow most or all specific preparations, decisions, and any related or strong commitments to be delayed. (Still, various decisions, partial decisions, or their functional equivalents, do end up being made, albeit via acquiescence and/or default.) In

a sense, the present individuals operate on the assumption that—if they simply make a few decisions here and there (with many occurring later on)—their future will eventually fall into place; that is, it will do so without frequent, concerted, fairly early, and, in any event, specifically directed efforts on their part. At any rate, despite their relative passivity, these youths do allow their options to be narrowed. In doing so, they essentially eliminate—partly knowingly—certain unappealing or unwanted futures.

49. Naturally, they prefer to do so at their own pace, in order to avoid or reduce major interference with their current enjoyments. As to minor and occasionally moderate interference and conflict, they take it for granted that these will occur.

50. Even these youths—their optimistic attitude notwithstanding—sometimes find it moderately to rather difficult to "get started" and/or to "keep moving ahead." This is separate from the fact that some difficulties/obstacles which they encounter—largely external ones—may result in disappointments for them and may sometimes lead them to make moderate to sizable shifts in their plans, whether as to means, ends, or both.

51. This is the case as long as several sizable difficulties/obstacles do not occur more or less simultaneously, or in rapid succession.

52. In part, they can continue to address that challenge by using other, already developed aspects of A, B, and/or C themselves, since these are already at a point where they can serve as a base or resource.

53. Implicit, here and below (in text), is the following: Nonoffenders, as a group, would also be more likely than SMOs—ones who do not receive planned intervention—to deal with Tasks A, B, and/or C, via these "usual or normal" means, to an *extent* that would help them eventually meet that challenge.

54. With SMOs, the extent of need is rather different than with relatively nonserious, or "lightweight," offenders. At any rate, the former individuals, in some contrast to the latter, are seldom persons who have had numerous success experiences and who, on those or related grounds, look forward to substantial new challenges.

Along similar lines, they are often far from eager to make major modifications in existing adjustment patterns that help keep them at least partly comfortable. The latter stance exists even though they are usually quite unhappy about, or are otherwise dissatisfied with, certain aspects of their present life circumstances and would like to see *those* change.

55. The functional shortfalls are those involving resources which, though existing and at least reasonably well developed, are not available and utilized because of the individuals' motivation and ambivalence.

56. In this regard *external controls* could help preclude or reduce various such complications; and in this capacity, they would be performing an immediate as well as long-range function. To carry out this role effectively, they would operate in conjunction with the earlier-mentioned "assistance and direction" per se, that is, with other major aspects of intervention.

57. Often, ambivalence itself partly reflects the fact that the level of motivation which is operating at the time is only moderate, for given purposes.

58. Even when considerable motivation exists and ambivalence is perhaps only moderate, the types or levels of external resources that are needed in connection with the challenge may be *unavailable* or not reliably available. Also, those resources—unlike, say, various actual but unavailable internal ones—may often hardly exist, in the first place.

59. This is a "further justifi[cation]" in the sense of being in addition to that of rationales #1, #2, #3, and the supplement to #3.

60. If not focused upon sufficiently, some ongoing needs, fears, and internal or external pressures could soon lead to illegal behavior which could result in the youths' revocation, recommitment, or unfavorable discharge. That, most likely, would reduce their chances of eventually meeting the long-range challenge, particularly as of their early adult years.

61. Insofar as it addressed the range of factors just mentioned, and thereby tried to help the youths eventually live more satisfying, often more productive, lives, needs-centered intervention would be focusing on the offender-centered goal.

62. With any particular youth, a given feature may make a decisive difference between success and little or no success. Regarding any group of youths, viewed as a group, that same feature may *usually* be decisive. At any rate, that feature, especially when operating with others, may make a pivotal difference between overall success and overall failure for a sizable percentage of those individuals.

63. At the same time, "productively address[ing]" those deficits, difficulties, and ambivalence would not, by itself, guarantee success. That is, the features in question, although necessary, may not be enough to achieve the given objective.

64. In some cases they cannot or will not provide these resources *reliably;* in other cases, *at all.* This differs from not knowing *how* to use the resources, when, for example, one largely wants to do so.

65. It applies especially when the constituents of each respective type are combined with other apparently useful constituents. That is, it applies not only when the given *features* are used in conjunction with each other, but when various *inputs* are themselves so combined.

66. Some features that are central to process (1) differ from those which contribute heavily to process (2).

67. As described later, this particular example can involve effects of point (a) as well as (b), in the text immediately above.

68. This tendency is not limited to point of intake and shortly thereafter.

69. Intervention efforts that focus on contributing factors generally take longer to achieve their end, and appear much less direct, than those which center on "immediate effects."

70. Thus, the following applies: (1) Internal pressures help generate, trigger, and maintain the tendency to withdraw. (2) Resource deficits partly cause those internal pressures. (3) These deficits, partly operating through those pressures, themselves help generate that tendency to withdraw. The contributions of such deficits is simply more distal—here, one step removed—than that of the pressures themselves.

71. This detailing, depth of content, and interrelating makes it possible to explicitly represent any given youth's overall per-

sonality and life situation, and to then deliberately address them concretely and as such. Taken together, these same specifics and mutual relationships can convey a useful idea not only of that individual's particular, often unique pattern of personal/emotional *features* but of his or her often-partly-shared *needs, opportunities, and limitations* (NOLs). Even apart from each youth's particular *combination* of those NOLs and of the NOLs' interactions with various *features,* the overall pattern or combination of just those features—say, of the youth's traits, attitudes, and values alone—itself often largely distinguishes the given youngster from most others. In that respect, it begins to individualize him or her in a comparative sense. When one then adds in the NOLs, individualization is even greater.

72. For present purposes, we need not focus on youths' feelings about receiving assistance itself, and on their reactions to doing so.

73. When staff recognize the main, specific factors and conditions that *constitute* stress for each given client, this, in itself, can be helpful.

74. This framework, in turn, relates to major, underlying, and long-standing forces or motives such as the drive or need for (1) physical and emotional security, (2) psychological and physical pleasure (also including activities/excitement), and (3) interpersonally generated as well as self-generated respect or esteem. (The dimension of "acceptance by others" exists in a number of these drives/needs.) These three factors are widespread; that is, they exist across a very high percentage of individuals. (See Chapter 25 regarding items (1) through (3).)

75. "Immediate effects," "longer-range implications," and, especially, "major reasons" cannot always be addressed simultaneously, and, in any event, by essentially the same means. Usually, however, there is considerable overlap, particularly as to means, and especially regarding the first two factors.

76. If staff successfully deal with such difficulties/obstacles or help the youths do so, this, itself, can increase the latter's trust in them.

77. This being a particularly common scenario at and soon after intake.

78. This can occur apart from the fact that *progress* in one area, for example, Area A (greater practical/social strengths/skills), can itself precipitate a threat—a substantial difficulty—within another, such as B (this can include family relationships).

79. In connection with this second context, the individuals may be fairly neutral about whether to accept the *long-range* challenge.

80. In line with given facades, the youths may have undertaken the given tasks with seeming confidence and apparent enthusiasm, and with little apparent uncertainty and reluctance. Underneath, however, many sizable doubts or misgivings may already exist, and these may sometimes surface soon after difficulties and obstacles are encountered. Under these conditions, the youths sometimes exit the situation or substantially reduce their involvement before they begin to "look really bad." Such withdrawal may obscure the main reasons for those individuals' actions.

81. Subjectively or psychologically, the pressures are entirely real; that is, they fully exist and are experienced as such. Objectively or factually, they are again real or at least predominantly—that is, very often and largely—existent, rather than imaginary or substantially exaggerated.

82. For example, a moderate to substantial, and fairly broad, acceptance.

83. This is apart from, or in addition to, using such strengths/skills mainly to handle/address more immediate issues and needs common to adolescence per se.

84. This is apparent from the overall extent to which the youths may nevertheless be ambivalent about moving toward adulthood per se and about addressing the long-range challenge. That is, they may not view various changes in the roles/relationships as worth the effort, relative to those ends.

85. Such difficulties can be encountered even when the youths mainly do *not* want to modify their present R/Rs, regardless of whether parents/peers would strongly resist any attempts to change them.

86. Also, the difficulty level of these skills interacts with the individuals' ability and

opportunity to acquire them—motivation aside.

87. They are more internal—youth-centered—as to (1) the *sources* of their immediate power (this being their triggering-and-sustaining potential/ability) and (2) their past strength as well, that is, that of at least several years past. This is despite the fact that their effects—their impacts—can be internal and external alike.

88. The point regarding the relative power of "internal" versus "external" difficulties/obstacles applies not only if these C-2 individuals, like some C-1 youths, have been trying to develop or improve in Area 1, namely, that of practical and interpersonal strengths/skills. Instead, and in contrast to C-1s, it also pertains if these C-2s have been largely trying to change in Area 2 namely, one that includes, but is not limited to, relationships and roles with parents and/or peers. It also applies whether or not the parents and/or others have substantially tried to oppose those efforts.

89. In a broader sense, their anticipation of failure also reflects underlying causes and effects which involve that self-concept. These have usually related to that concept for at least the preceding several years.

90. This is apart from the fact that these and other youths sometimes need a "breather," and that some need a longer one than others.

91. And also among some individuals from groups already mentioned.

92. This third point also applies to many C-1 youths.

93. Though nonoffenders have some negatives in their self-concept, the latter are usually less intense and far-reaching and they do not render those individuals' view of themselves negative overall, or even low on average.

94. The underlying reasons for such beliefs or assumptions can be complex, and they may involve, for example, one or more of the following factors: The youths' (1) past experiences with other adults, who had in fact acted in one or more such ways; (2) fear of how the present adults might react if they knew about various things the youths were *not*

telling them with respect to their thoughts, feelings, and actions; (3) projections of their own dislike of the given adults and of their willingness to take advantage of *them* (and, e.g., to not give those adults the benefit of the doubt).

95. These actions may involve, for instance, withdrawal/avoidance/rejection *before* one is pressured/punished/rejected, or before certain difficulties/obstacles arise or worsen.

96. With some youths, this defense or form of resistance is also, or instead, an attempt to reduce the chances that *any* D/Os will arise, whether or not they might lead to the above feelings, emotions, and/or responses, in particular.

97. As indicated earlier, difficulties/obstacles can arise that are neither generated by, triggered by, nor substantively centered on Tasks A, B, or C. In any event, SMOs can anticipate and preemptively defend against D/Os whether or not the latter are in fact likely to arise. Like those difficulties/obstacles, the earlier-mentioned feelings, emotions, and responses can arise in connection with situations other than ones that center on A, B, and C per se.

98. These types of involvement differ from simply proceeding cautiously, albeit *with* substantial commitment and sincerity. To be sure, considerable surface resemblance exists between the two.

99. This response has important similarities to the approach taken by a large portion of the public and by many public officials to corrections itself: There is an almost exclusive emphasis on short-term goals and on immediate relief. In this regard, for example, there is relatively little recognition of and/or serious—let alone focused and/or sustained—concern with various implications that this emphasis has for society's longer-term interests, issues, and needs.

100. This worsening involves, but goes beyond, a reduction in the youths' number of options.

101. That is, they have "largely generated . . ." that bind insofar as they have been consciously and/or preconsciously motivated to use those defenses, especially to the above-average degree in question.

25 THEORY, GOALS, AND STANCES TOWARD INTERVENTION

The type and level of support correctional personnel give to particular interventions depends greatly on how well they believe those approaches can achieve goals they consider necessary in order to reduce or eliminate illegal behavior and on whether they think *other* approaches can do an equal or even better job, and/or are more deserved. In each case, the achievement of those goals, and the utilization of approaches that seem able to bring them about, is more likely to be considered important and to receive those individuals' support if that accomplishment occurs together with a reduction or elimination of factors and conditions that help *generate, trigger, and/or maintain* that illegal behavior, in the first place.

While Chapter 26 will describe several such factors and conditions in detail, the present one will set the stage by discussing the following: (1) *goals* whose achievement bears on the reduction of illegal behavior (see "secondary or instrumental goals"); (2) *stances* on the part of various personnel toward those goals and toward the needs-centered approach (here, "content-areas intervention") that can often help achieve them; (3) *why* those individuals' understanding of that approach's potential influence is often inaccurate or incomplete; and, (4) *how* that understanding may be changed in ways that can lead to increased support of that approach.

To facilitate the discussion, considerable time will be spent describing basic yet socially shaped motives, needs, or drives. Also, as will become clear in this and especially the next chapter, the discussion of factors and conditions that help produce and/or sustain illegal behavior—and that of approaches which can

then reduce it—supports the rationales for intervention described in Chapter 24; among those rationales is not just the fourth but the third. In addition, the present chapter broadens the framework for this support; it does so by describing goals, needs, wishes, and efforts that most adults consider legitimate in the case of nonoffenders, and regarding which they often provide encouragement and, not infrequently, assistance. (When *not* focusing on nonoffenders, this chapter, like others, centers on serious multiple offenders [SMOs] in general. It does so without singling out youths who try to prevent their programs from getting well underway.)

Appropriateness and Importance of Given Goals and Efforts

As implied in Chapter 24, if serious multiple offenders are to (1) modify various behavior patterns (especially on a long-term basis), (2) grow personally/emotionally to a considerable degree, or (3) do both (1) and (2), they must, with few exceptions, make concerted and repeated efforts during their programs. Such efforts commonly relate to the earlier-mentioned Area or Task B ("deal successfully with social-environmental and/or family factors") and to the second part of C ("reduce or resolve personal/psychological difficulties or conflicts"). The modifications in behavior, and the personal/emotional growth as well, pertain not only to youths' near-term albeit important adaptations to ongoing or often-recurring situations, pressures, and other factors but to their longer-term challenge of making a workable future both possible and realistic, at even a basic level.[1]

Some important behavior changes, including the control of negative wishes or impulses, can occur with no more than modest psychological/social growth and internalized personal change. Such behavioral changes, however, are less likely than the more growth-based ones to hold up over time, particularly under considerable or new types of stress. However long they hold up, and regardless of the conditions under which they do so, key behavioral changes—like sizable personal/social growth itself—are not necessarily easy to bring about.

In general, the extent of the needed efforts, by SMOs and staff, will depend on *how much* and *what* those youths must overcome, undo, or neutralize, on the one hand, and must achieve in positive or growth-centered respects, on the other. Regarding "how much" effort is needed, this will reflect many factors, including, for example, the *number* of areas or tasks, of difficulties, and of behavior patterns that must be carefully addressed more or less together—more specifically, during time periods, say, three- to six-month intervals, that largely overlap throughout the first year. (Here, the areas/tasks also involve A, above ["develop or increase practical and interpersonal skills"].) As to the "what" aspects of needed effort, these include particular content, such as attempts to "change for the better," that relate to "secondary goals"—described later.

Whether the "how much" dimension or the "what" is involved, the significance of the youths' efforts—and the means-to-ends role of those efforts—can be better understood in the context of certain primary and secondary goals. Equally important, the efforts made by staff and others with respect to offenders depend heavily on the former's main views, and on those of the general public, regarding the *appropriateness and importance* of the goals in question and of the youths' related attempts to achieve them. ("Appropriate," "legitimate," and "justified" will be used interchangeably.)

Before reviewing these goals and salient content associated with them, the following reality might be kept in mind: Often, an important or even essential first step in clearing the way for broad, positive change or for making it realistically possible is the reduction, modification, neutralization, or elimination of various negative factors and conditions.[2] These negatives, obstacles, and so on, often center on

Area/Task-*B* issues such as harmful interactions/relationships with parents, or major socioeconomic and other external/environmental deficits and negative pressures, including those from peers. In contrast, the task or process of developing *positives* or strengths often involves improvements in *A,* and/or *C*. This task, which is one of basic building, expanding, or augmenting, differs from that of redirecting or even just utilizing already existing strengths and, say, potentially constructive motives. Other important *negatives* include, of course, the youths' illegal behaviors per se, though these are independent of any particular area, for instance, *B,* or *C*. Though the reduction of these negatives may be only modest or moderate during early stages of intervention, say, its first six months, this fact, by itself, need not largely block, undermine, or undo significant progress and the "clearing [of] the way." At any rate, these particular negatives will not be among the factors directly focused on in the following review.

To gain a certain perspective on the appropriateness of *serious multiple offenders'* efforts to establish such positives or to even reduce negatives—that is, to gain perspective on the justification of those efforts as based on (1) their need and functional importance; (2) their further and/or broader meaning, purpose, significance, and/or potential results (see primary and secondary goals, below, e.g., item 2[b] under primary goals); and (3) what are commonly viewed as individuals' rights—we will first examine the following: widely held, long-standing, societal attitudes regarding those same types of efforts (e.g., efforts to establish positives) and underlying bases or factors (e.g., need, significance, and rights) on the part of, and in relation to, adolescent *nonoffenders*. These attitudes or views are held by the preponderance of adults who, collectively, comprise the general public—whichever of its earlier-mentioned subgroups is involved, and including its laypersons as well as professionals. They have been held throughout the United States, and perhaps elsewhere, for at least the past several decades, and probably much longer. We will review these positions in relation to "primary goals," "secondary goals," and, finally, "salient dimensions" or particular content associated with the latter. By specifying these goals and dimensions, the intent, significance, and potential significance of the youths' efforts can be made evident; and that, in turn, can help address the issue of justification or appropriateness itself. Later in this chapter we will examine the stances of correctional personnel not only toward those secondary or instrumental goals but regarding what will be called content-areas intervention—in effect, needs-centered intervention—when applied to offenders.

Theoretical Perspectives
Primary or Basic Goals

Decades of direct observation and experience amply indicate the following. Regarding non-offenders, the general public, like numerous scholars, considers each of the next-listed goals fundamental, justified, and important:

A. Physical and emotional security or relative security.
B. Acceptance by others.
C. Physical and psychological pleasure or enjoyment.

For simplicity, these will be called *primary or basic goals.* (For present purposes, pleasure and enjoyment are interchangeable.) Insofar as they are achieved or maintained (e.g., for sizable periods of time), and while they are being experienced even briefly or for fairly limited periods, these goals are "states" and/or "conditions"—in effect, felt realities. For this and related reasons, primary goals A through C are often considered one or more of the following (the first two items are mutually overlapping; the third is an attribute of both):

1. Desired and desirable states of mind and states of being.
2. Legitimate and important conditions, in the sense of (a) end-states in themselves, or even (b) *pre*conditions to, or at least important contributors to, a more meaningful, satisfying, and worthwhile personal and social life.
3. Conscious, or preconscious, strivings or motives.

Thus, in many real-life contexts, goals A through C are viewed as ends per se, and that is how we will mainly consider them. In other contexts, they often serve as either means to or specific preconditions for *other,* relatively abstract or global ends, as in 2(b) above; and these contexts do not necessarily involve broad time frames, such as many years of adulthood.

Finally, and more concretely, some goals are viewed as means to one or more of the others or to certain aspects of them, for example, goal A as a means to, or precondition for, C, and goal B as a means/step/precondition regarding A or C. In the latter contexts, these goals are functional realities, not just felt ones.

Views 1 and 2, above, largely reflect the fact that goals A through C are implicitly or explicitly considered ones that almost all children, adolescents, and young adults would *understandably*—in a sense, or in large degree, would "naturally"—want and strive for. In that respect or to that degree, the desires/strivings in question are often assumed to be ingrained in the sense of deep-seated, and they may be described as basic tendencies. The *objects* of these desires/strivings are the goals themselves, that is, the achievement or experiencing of A through C. To better understand the implications of this situation with respect to rationales for intervention, we will spend some time on theory per se.

Acculturation or Social Learning

In our view, the preceding goals and tendencies can be recognized in very young children, even by age one. At that point, they exist in general forms as well as states of activity ("conditions") that are still minimally channelized and only broadly focused. This implies that neither one—neither the goals (end-states) nor the tendencies (strivings/desires for those goals)—is originally generated by, that is, derived from, substantial acculturation.[3] Instead, both exist prior to any considerable or specific social/interpersonal ("social") learning as well as channeling/focusing—processes that are directed *at* the goals and tendencies in question rather than being responsible *for* them. At any rate, the latter two predate such learning—learning, as well as channeling/focusing, via various kinds of conditioning.[4]

Early acculturation does, nevertheless, greatly affect the way in which those goals and tendencies are eventually expressed: In general terms, it alters their forms and often their states. For instance (regarding "states of activity"), social learning, including experiences that commonly accompany interpersonal interactions, frequently *intensifies* the above goals in the minds of young children (e.g., those between ages two and three), therein making the goals more psychologically salient to them. (More specifically, those experiences—given the conditioning/reinforcement generally associated with them—may, for example, increase the *degree* to which goal B ["acceptance by others"] functions as a *need*. [See below regarding "need."] Similarly, those experiences/inputs may increase the *extent* to which certain aspects of goal C ["physical . . . pleasure"] are *desired*.) In addition (regarding "form"), social learning shapes, crystallizes, and otherwise *organizes* or sometimes even fixates the individuals' preexisting, goal-related strivings/desires—that is, the "original," general tendencies—around given contexts and content, such as particular parent/child or peer-and-sibling/child interactions and outcomes. In this respect it channelizes and focuses those underlying tendencies; and each culture produces its own patterns or forms.

In the above picture, then, (1) goals A through C, themselves, are cardinal, extremely long-standing and largely intrinsic, motives; and, insofar as the child's general adjustment and well-being depend on those goals' being met to at least a moderate degree, they, the goals, function as *needs*. In addition, (2) the original or "underlying" *appropriateness and importance* of A through C and of the individuals' directly related strivings for them have non-, pre-, or perhaps minimally cultural roots. In both respects, particularly the latter, those goals, motives, or needs can be said to have a "natural" or "intrinsic" legitimacy—one that predates any other. "Other," for instance, would include a legitimacy that might be subsequently *earned* on the basis of the youths' socially approved behavior toward various persons. (In the following, except when otherwise apparent, "natural" will signify that which predates substantial acculturation.)

Based on that theoretical perspective, individuals, however young, can be said to have a natural inclination and desire—and, with that, a natural "right" and motivation—to *want* to reach those goals. That is (though this may seem self-evident), they can be thought of as having, at a minimum, a right to "mentally strive" for them, whether or not they, the individuals, think of them as *A, B,* and *C* per se.[5] Further, to accompany that minimum right (with this "right" amounting, in effect, to an acknowledgment/legitimization of desires that would occur naturally anyway), the individu-

als should, logically, also be said to have a right to *act and interact* in ways that may help them achieve and maintain those goals; at least, their dominant society, and, if applicable, their subculture, should accord them such a right.[6] Most people who comprise the general public implicitly assume these individuals do have both "rights": the right to want what is legitimate and needed (in whatever degrees), and the right to act/interact in ways that may help achieve it. They take it for granted that both are justified and supported, with respect to nonoffenders.

To review: If (1) individuals—here, very young persons or children—are predisposed to strive for certain goals (A through C), if (2) those goals or "ends" are considered appropriate and important, and if (3) it is considered appropriate for those particular individuals to want the given goals, those persons, and even ones older than them, should then have a right to so strive; and, given that right, they should be allowed to act in ways that will help them achieve those ends.[7] (With all that granted, the question would then center on *how* the given individuals should, or at least should not, act when attempting to implement those rights.)[8] At any rate, these *original* rights, being minimally culture-rooted, neither would be nor could be originally based on *deeds* that the individuals may have already carried out, or on achievements they may have chalked up. As children, for example, they may not yet have carried out such deeds, or have even had good opportunities to do so.[9]

Views on Legitimacy of Primaries

Notwithstanding the earlier-mentioned perspectives regarding origins and natural appropriateness, the following remains the case, particularly for individuals other than very young children: Most members of the general public implicitly consider goals such as A through C legitimate, not *unconditionally* or carte blanche, but, instead, when those youths seek them and/or achieve/maintain them without intentionally, or otherwise knowingly, harming or being likely to harm other persons in the process.[10] Thus, even granting the existence of a fundamental or original *need* with respect to those goals, and granting a related, underlying *right* to achieve, satisfy, or otherwise meet that need, at least in part, the following applies: Neither that need nor its related right is to be expressed and satisfied in ways that purposely/knowingly harm other persons, certainly to a substantial degree, or that reflect little concern about the impact of one's decisions and actions on those other individuals' own legitimate strivings and needs, especially if that impact can well be serious. As suggested, these social expectations, or general standards, begin to apply even before adolescence, and they are then increasingly insisted upon.[11]

In short, most people implicitly assume that even natural or original tendencies which involve legitimately self-interested wishes are to be limited by societal-centered interests, particularly after early childhood. More specifically, they are to be limited in their manner or extent of behavioral expression and in how individuals should seek their objects—namely, the goals of those strivings/desires. (Even channelized and focused tendencies are to be limited in such ways.) These external, societal interests or concerns have a legitimacy and major importance of their own,[12] one that goes beyond the youths' self-interest and personal needs, however justified and important both may be in their own right. At any rate, those societal interests/concerns set outer limits—often, but not always, broad ones—on the expression of the individuals' own interests and needs.[13] Outer limits, of course, continue into later childhood and then to adolescence.

Expectations in Adolescence

Though limits per se *continue,* and although limits or restrictions are one type (subcategory) of "expectation," various *changes* occur in this broader category, namely, in expectations; these changes, like limits themselves, bear on the youths' self-interest and personal needs. For instance, by early to middle adolescence, expectations that were not applied to those individuals during middle to later childhood or that were less salient or important at that time enter the picture or assume a larger role than before. These expectations are sometimes described as "new realities," and their chief goal is to substantially affect the content, conduct, and direction of the adolescents' lives.

1. the expectations mainly involve preferences, restrictions (including *new* limits), and/or requirements;
2. their main sources are parents, peers, and the general social/cultural environ-

ment (teachers, relatives, other adults and/or authority figures; the media);
3. they mainly focus on (a) *what* activities and relationships those sources believe the youths should and should not engage in during adolescence and perhaps seriously invest in with respect to eventual adulthood, and on (b) *how,* according to those sources, the individuals should and should not act/interact in those regards; and
4. they are usually implemented via incentives, suggestions, directives, pressures, and/or sanctions.

Points (1) and (3) apply even though the sources—including most parents and many authority figures—generally accept the idea that those individuals probably need, and certainly want, substantial leeway to test and explore their environment, options, and relationships. (This acceptance also reflects their realization that new or increased opportunities and challenges occur for most youths anyway, once adolescence arrives, and that they—the parents and others—could only partly control and otherwise influence the youths' actual testing, exploring, and decision-making, even if they tried rather hard to do so.) More precisely, those sources—particularly parents—accept the idea with mixed feelings. This partly reflects their concern that the youths may choose to reject or only halfheartedly accept certain key preferences (whether or not they have carefully explored various alternatives), that they may make serious mistakes (even apart from any such rejection), and that their long-range economic- and emotional-security needs may therefore be jeopardized and inadequately met.

Despite such concerns, parents and most other adults who comprise the general public implicitly assume the following regarding adolescents (together, these beliefs lower the former's anxiety about the youths' eventual adjustment): However much or little the youths explore various alternatives to the earlier-mentioned expectations, and regardless of any reservations they may have about fully accepting those expectations, these youths can seldom if ever entirely ignore or alter them—namely, the parental/societal preferences, external limits, and so on. Instead, they must sooner or later come to terms with them—must, for example, assimilate or at least substantially accommodate some of them, if only in modified form. In addition, most *parents and other adults* believe that—despite any temporary or even lengthy uncertainties, disagreements, and setbacks— most adolescents will probably end up making fairly sensible choices and will do so before it is too late. To be sure, this does not mean that numerous parents do not feel there are good reasons for often worrying about their particular teenagers, and for therefore actively intervening and sometimes taking firm stands. All in all, the picture is thus one of general optimism mixed with considerable concern.

Most parents/adults also implicitly assume the following, or would consider it self-evident (as seen below, this is not limited to the exploring of *alternatives*): Adolescents have a legitimate instrumental need—in that sense, a pragmatic right—to take steps and make choices that may help them come to terms with the expectations or modified expectations in question, and that may also help them make other important adjustments. In effect, they have a need, and right, to be empowered, especially if they are to be held accountable. This pragmatically oriented need/right pertains not just to youth efforts directed at satisfying or accommodating the interests and needs of other individuals and of various components, such as institutions and groups, within society. Instead, it also applies to efforts involving the youths' personal interests and content needs, including ones that differ from what the *other* individuals would prefer.[14, 15] Regarding most youths (nonoffenders in particular), few if any questions arise concerning the existence and legitimacy of this instrumental need and pragmatic right to take various steps that can serve as means to ends, including steps that may involve the seeking of assistance.

The impact of those expectations on the adolescents' adjustment and life directions can be substantial not just if, and as, the expectations are *assimilated/accommodated*, but even if, and as, those youths seriously question, challenge, and perhaps reject them, or some of them.[16] For instance, the content of expectations that are rejected, and the significance or implications that the youths believe those rejected expectations could have for them, may indirectly help determine the main thrust of those individuals' reactions and explorations. More specifically, many adolescents will try to do the opposite of what others want them to do; or, they will try to become a "very different kind of person" than the one they think

they *could* become if they were to fully accept those other individuals' wishes and preferences (more broadly, their expectations). Thus, the specific content of parental/societal wishes/preferences, and their perceived personal meaning as well, can help set the terms of, and much of the agenda for, those youths' efforts, activities, and stances.

Finally, the influence—this time direct influence—of those new realities can be substantial despite the following (here, we focus on expectations that are being largely assimilated or accommodated, *not* rejected or even generally challenged; also, the time period is still adolescence): (1) The youths' original, underlying goals and content needs (A, B, and C), and the strivings/desires that directly relate to them, continue to exist and to function as strong motivators—as major, concurrent sources of action.[17] (2) The youths' *right* to actively address those earlier-mentioned goals and related strivings—that is, their justified instrumental need to do so—itself remains present; and it does so to a sizable degree. It remains present because the goals/strivings themselves still exist and operate (see [1], above). It is still sizable because the goals, needs, and related strivings are no less important than before, not only to the youths but, potentially, to society.[18, 19]

Secondary or Instrumental Goals

Again with respect to nonoffenders, nearly all chronological adults also view a second set or level of goals as legitimate. Moreover, these goals, specified shortly, are implicitly recognized as highly important in their own right, with respect to youths' personal/social functioning. Nevertheless, despite this importance, these goals can be considered *secondary or "instrumental"*; this is because they also serve, individually and collectively, as a means to the attainment or experiencing of primary goals themselves, that is, as a contributor to or precondition of those goals. More particularly, they are—as used here—a major means, though not the only means, to the attainment or experiencing of those primary goals on a relatively stable, longer-lasting basis, rather than on an infrequent, fairly transitory, or perhaps hit-and-miss basis only.

The secondary goals in question can also be considered instrumental even though they are often discussed as ends in themselves, and, more importantly, although certain *primary* goals—such as emotional security, and acceptance by others (even if these exist only partially and are far from stable)—can contribute significantly to the development or consolidation of the secondaries themselves, for instance, to goals C and D, below. At any rate, other key interactions often occur between primary and secondary goals; and in this regard, for example, a relatively stable attainment of the *former* goals often depends heavily on the prior achievement of the *latter,* that is, not just vice versa. The latter—the secondary—goals are as follows (these will soon be called A_{2g} through D_{2g}):

A. Adequate or better adjustment to preexisting, ongoing, and emergent challenges, expectations, requirements, and opportunities that involve typical as well as atypical issues, problems, and/or needs of a personal or interpersonal nature, whether they are substantial or routine. This also includes everyday challenges, unpleasant surprises, and so on.
B. Elimination, substantial reduction, or neutralization of anxieties, stresses, and negative external conditions, especially those associated with preexisting/ongoing/emergent challenges, expectations, requirements, and opportunities. These anxieties, and so on, reduce or limit one's ability to utilize already existing skills and motivations and to move forward in various ways.
C. Eventual adulthood, (1) in psychological/emotional or at least overt behavioral (e.g., role-centered) respects, and (2) regardless of which particular *forms* of adult-centered adjustment are chosen, for instance, type of employment "x" rather than "y" or "z," nonmarriage instead of marriage, and nonparenthood rather than parenthood.
D. Establishment of a viable, post-teenage-years existence for oneself, hopefully outside correctional settings and on an economically self-sufficient basis to the extent feasible, or, in any case, necessary.[20]

Secondary goal A, whose scope is broad, can be characterized as mainly or essentially near-term, immediate, continued/ongoing, and/or "here-and-now" in its tasks and content; goal B as mostly immediate and ongoing;

and goals C and D as long-term, ones that can also become ongoing themselves, for example, once they are partly achieved. Whether transitory or not, none of these goals are states of mind, or feelings, per se; however, as suggested, they can pave the way for those states or feelings. (To differentiate the three primary goals from these four secondaries, these will now be designated A_{1g}, B_{1g}, and C_{1g}, and A_{2g}, B_{2g}, C_{2g}, and D_{2g}, respectively.)

Two final, general observations before we further focus on legitimacy and importance and describe "salient dimensions" that relate to those factors: (1) Though each of the four secondary goals can be viewed as a major end in itself and as a means to the primary goals as well, some can also serve as means to the others; in this latter respect, functional interaction can be said to exist among those secondaries. Above all, A_{2g} and B_{2g} play major, often critical roles in the achievement of C_{2g} (particularly in its psychological/emotional respect) and D_{2g}, especially on relatively stable bases. (2) Since A_{2g} and B_{2g} can thus contribute greatly to C_{2g} and D_{2g}, and since the latter two can each help facilitate the three *primary* goals themselves (viz., A_{1g}, B_{1g}, and C_{1g}) in prosocial/legal contexts, A_{2g} and B_{2g} are particularly important goals on two fundamental fronts: overall social/personal *functioning,* and the tapping of strong, relatively enduring *motivators* (ones that, when satisfied or partly satisfied in given contexts, can reinforce such functioning itself). Moreover, since A_{2g} and B_{2g} can themselves be facilitated by first clearing away obstacles reflected in the original, global "B" and "C" *areas* (Chapter 24)—namely, those involving negative social/environmental forces, and personal difficulties/conflicts/limited understanding, respectively—this dynamic, or reality, highlights the value of making sizable progress in Areas B and C.

Views on Legitimacy of Secondaries
As indicated, most people who comprise the general adult population consider the three primary goals—A_{1g}, B_{1g}, and C_{1g}—legitimate and important with respect to *nonoffending* youths. Almost all people implicitly or explicitly feel the same about the four secondary goals as well, whether these are ends in themselves or means to the primaries. In the case of *offenders* (serious multiple ones), many or most adults consider the *primary*

goals (1) legitimate and important in themselves; also, they probably regard them—this time mostly intuitively (nonverbally and usually preconsciously)—as (2) appropriate products of some interventions themselves. (Point (2) would apply whether these products are planned or unplanned and direct or indirect. In addition, (2) as well as (1) would pertain whether the three primaries are assumed to be short-term or long-term goals.) Though points (1) and (2) pertain most strongly and broadly to goal A_{1g} ("physical or emotional security or relative security"), they also apply substantially to B_{1g} ("acceptance by others") and C_{1g} ("physical and psychological pleasure or enjoyment").[21]

Still regarding offenders, most adults consider the *secondary* goals—A_{2g} through D_{2g}—legitimate and important, both in themselves and as short- or long-term products of intervention per se, again whether they are planned or unplanned. In some contrast, however, many but far from all correctional policymakers and academicians, though proportionately fewer practitioners, believe C_{2g} and D_{2g} should receive no more than slight or moderate emphasis during intervention, or should not even be focused on as such. (Part of the general public believes this as well, but the majority assumes the emphasis should be at least moderate.) More precisely, though these individuals—administrators included—would not be adverse to C_{2g} and D_{2g} as products of intervention, many believe or implicitly assume that the process of achieving these outcomes may sometimes be, and may adequately be, set in motion largely by externally imposed controls, and by resulting self-controls themselves. (Others view those outcomes as often evolving from success with A_{2g} and B_{2g}. See "Group 4 CCRIs," later in this chapter.) More particularly, the latter individuals assume the following regarding these goals, insofar as the goals are to be promoted *at all,* via correctional inputs other than externally imposed controls: Goals C_{2g} and D_{2g} can be adequately supported and implemented either without the agencies'/organizations' having to create and utilize many programmatic resources, or, in any event, via approaches that are far simpler and much less individualized than those emphasized in this book. This is apart from whether those individuals generally consider some skills training an important or at least useful additional component, though not nec-

essarily a crucial component and often not even an essential supplementary one. (Further details are discussed in Chapter 29.)

We now turn to two particularly important content dimensions or subject areas—called "salient dimensions."

Salient Dimensions

Following are two major content dimensions that are each associated with the four *secondary goals* collectively, especially with A_{2g} and B_{2g} (salient dimension A, immediately below, mainly relates to external/environmental conditions; B largely involves the internal/personal):

A: Bettering One's Life Situation or Life Circumstances

This is commonly described as "improving one's life"—occasionally one's "lot" in life—and as generally "changing things for the better." It involves not just conditions, such as living arrangements or peer relationships, that the youths already find acceptable and manageable but which they nevertheless want to improve. Instead—and this is what we will emphasize—it also includes situations and circumstances that those individuals consider unacceptable or intolerable with respect to their being seriously hampering, physically dangerous or unhealthful, anxiety-laden, humiliating, and/or otherwise clearly negative. These are not just conditions the youths view as moderately unpleasant or bothersome, whether or not they also consider them transitory.

Thus, for example, dimension A often involves "leaving behind" actual miseries and/or objective deprivations associated with particularly stressful home/neighborhood conditions or settings, or trying to leave behind, or substantially modify, unstable, confusing, and perhaps psychologically hurtful situations. Such conditions are often, but not necessarily, long-standing or repetitious, and they are essentially not "of one's—the youth's—own doing." Finally, this salient dimension—now designated A_{sd}—may also relate to serious difficulties and complications directly *resulting* from such conditions.

Though A_{sd} is very common among offenders, it is, as implied, also frequent among nonoffenders. More specifically, many of the latter have the identical *types* of social and/or environmental deficits or difficulties (viewing each type individually) as do many of the former; and, both groups of youths wish to better their situation or circumstances in those respects. Nevertheless, despite these broad and important similarities, the following applies. Compared to those of offenders, the deficits/difficulties ("problems") of *non*offenders are usually less numerous and less intensive *collectively* (i.e., all individual types together). On average, they are also less extensive (broad in content), less intensive, and of shorter duration—in each case, *individually*.

Thus, for instance, with any given *offender* compared to nonoffender, there is likely to be a larger number of respective, individual types of problems; in addition, any two of those types are likely to have more temporal overlap with each other, since, among other things, each one is likely to have been of longer duration. This increased overlap and—especially across any three or more types of problems—greater *interweaving*, can, by itself, often heighten the overall impact of those problems (individually and collectively), even if the overall *number* of problems, that is, types of problems, or problem areas, happens to be the same for the nonoffenders and offenders.

B: Undoing, Overcoming, or Reducing Past Personal Mistakes, Shortcomings, Etc., and Their Negative Effects

This is commonly thought of as leaving certain parts of one's "past" behind, that is, as moving beyond them, as partly or entirely repudiating them, or as generally disassociating oneself from them. Involved are acts, activities, behavior patterns, and/or life-styles that the youths now (1) feel dissatisfied with, critical of, or badly about, (2) believe were mainly of "their own doing" and/or their failure to "do," and (3) largely attribute to some aspects of their self or personality, for example, to certain traits, motives, or attitudes. In short, it is such actions, patterns, and so on, that these individuals presently want to undo, overcome, or reduce, and it is those aspects of their personality that they now wish to modify or reject. They may also wish to undo, overcome, or reduce *negative effects* of the given actions, and so forth; and here, "undoing" may include "making up" for those effects upon others as well as self. Regarding the perceived mistakes themselves, these may have involved commission or omission. (As to "reactions," these are implicit in this discussion—as one form, aspect, or phase of "actions.")

Whether the youths are now highly dissatisfied with the given activities/patterns ("behaviors") or are no more than moderately disapproving, they may not have previously recognized some of the main, negative, short- or long-term *implications* of those behaviors. That is, they might not have recognized them (or, possibly, cared much about them) when those behaviors first occurred and—if the behaviors continued—when they were, say, subsequently most active. (In this discussion, the individuals *now*—presently—recognize at least some important implications, and they also care about them.)

Moreover, (1) whether the youths' present degree of recognition is no more than modest, on the one hand, or is fairly large, on the other, and (2) regardless of when that awareness of negative implications began and first reached its current level, the following applies: Salient dimension B remains important—important with respect to intervention, and in its relevance to rationales #3 and #4—even if the youths mainly attribute those presently disapproved activities/patterns to relatively *moderate* factors and motives. These factors/motives, such as thoughtlessness, self-indulgence, exploration or adventure, efforts to impress others, and even some manipulating and "using" or exploiting of others, are comparatively or seemingly benign. (Depending, in part, on their degree and frequency, and also on their impact, they are generally moderate/benign *individually*. However, when combined with one another, and/or in conjunction with still other factors/motives, they—that is, any one or more of them—are often less benign.) Also, most "moderates" are factors/motives with which the individuals may not have originally felt highly dissatisfied, and may still not feel that way. Nevertheless, many such youths are *now* relatively dissatisfied with them and they dislike as well as disapprove some of their negative effects on self and/or others. As a result, these individuals (collectively) often wish to partly or entirely renounce and/or control those factors/motives—or, no less often, to at least reduce them to where they no longer interfere or seriously interfere with various key desires.

(The importance and relevance of dimension B is perhaps easier to see in connection with factors and motives that are more than "moderate"—that are generally considered far from benign, even individually—and with which the youths are now likely to be at least quite dissatisfied. Compared to the more moderate factors and motives, these are also more likely to be ones the youths presently know, and even previously realized, most adults would consider definitely unacceptable and harmful, and less excusable based on situational factors.[22])

As with salient dimension A_{sd} above, the present one—designated B_{sd}—also involves undoing/overcoming various *effects,* that is, reducing or eliminating already existing results of the given actions, behavior patterns, and so on. As such, B_{sd} is not limited to the reduction or elimination of various ongoing or otherwise existing activities, patterns, and features themselves—these being ones the youths no longer want to support, engage in, or identify with, to whatever substantial degree. (To facilitate the remaining discussion, we will neither emphasize nor often specify and single out the "undoing/overcoming [of] various *effects*" in connection with B_{sd}. That aside, it might be noted that whereas external controls/punishment can often help many offenders control their impulses and thereby address B_{sd} it cannot, by itself, largely address A_{sd}, namely, the "bettering [of] one's life situation." It does not, for instance, contain the content needed for *positive* direction and for learning new, practical, and/or interpersonal skills.

Progress on one or both salient dimensions not only reduces or eliminates various negative conditions per se; instead, and for that very reason, it can help clear the way for key behavior change and for growth in other respects. In particular, progress on A_{sd} and B_{sd} ("bettering one's life situation or life circumstances"; "undoing . . . past personal mistakes . . . ") can position youths to focus on and achieve the two near-term yet ongoing secondary goals: A_{2g} ("adequate or better adjustment to preexisting . . . and emergent challenges, expectations . . . ") and parts of B_{2g} ("elimination . . . or neutralization of anxieties, stresses, and negative external conditions").[23] Substantial progress on these goals, or achievement of them, can then help those individuals advance more solidly toward the two *longer-range* secondaries: C_{2g} and D_{2g} ("eventual adulthood . . . "; "establishment of a viable, post-teenage-years existence . . . ").[24]

Views on Legitimacy of Salients

Almost all adults sense or otherwise recognize these integral, often causal connections between the salient dimensions, on the one hand, and the secondary goals, on the other.[25] As a result, and given that they already view those goals as valuable, these adults consider both salients important and they regard youths' efforts to achieve them as appropriate. More specifically, they intuitively or explicitly recognize—as significant—nonoffenders' attempts to better their life-situations/circumstances, to undo/overcome past personal mistakes, and so on. They also believe those youths are justified in trying to change their lives—that they, like adults themselves, have an objectively supportable right to make such efforts. This applies even if the youths' mistakes (like adults') were, say, "of their own doing" and mainly involved commission.

Together with such views by the general public—in effect, *because* most adults believe there is value in making progress on one or both salient dimensions—nonoffenders, during adolescence, (1) receive various forms of *encouragement* to try to overcome/reduce their adverse external conditions or to undo/overcome significant personal mistakes/shortcomings. They are sometimes reminded, for example, that it may take courage or fortitude to initiate and/or sustain such efforts. In addition, these youths (2) are often *commended* and otherwise intentionally reinforced when they make progress along those lines.[26]

As implied, most people assume that nonoffenders, that is, "everyday youths," have a widely accepted right to change/improve—a broad social approval or a generally recognized and strong consent to do so.[27] Moreover, most people assume or at least hope that these individuals will *utilize* this general approval—in particular, will act upon it if and as needed. Of these adults, however, many do not just leave it at that. Instead, they often fault given youths if they believe those individuals (1) realize that change and improvement are probably important and perhaps feasible for them, yet (2) seem to make little effort to change/improve. (The focus is on effort, not outcome.) More precisely, they fault them if, given (1) and (2), these youths also (3) seem *capable* of making substantial effort.[28]

Whether tacit or explicit, this disapproval, though usually mild, implies that those adults assume these individuals have a moderate or larger *obligation*—mainly to themselves—to try to reduce or overcome certain past and present conditions and factors.[29] (The external conditions, for instance, are ones that seem likely to seriously limit, or that already so limit, not only the youths' opportunities to adjust well to life but their chances at happiness per se.[30]) However, whether or not those and/or other adults believe such an obligation exists,[31] the "widely accepted right to change/improve"—mentioned earlier—implies, by itself, the following:[32] To all intents and purposes, most people consider it natural and not overly self-interested—in those overlapping respects, they consider it intrinsic, appropriate, and acceptable—for nonoffenders to (1) want to change their difficult or limiting external conditions and to try to overcome internal "negatives" from the past, in order to (2) move toward a more positive, near-term or longer-term, future. In this regard, most adults—including those who fault given youths—assume, in effect, that a drive or impulse exists which, by itself, ordinarily points or can point those individuals (and can motivate them), irrespective of the possible obligation in question and regardless of whether that obligation is assumed to be either largely intrinsic or mostly socially learned.[33] (Its motive force, however, is not invariably *sufficient* to help them move forward or keep moving forward under given conditions.)

At any rate, regarding nonoffenders who do make substantial efforts to change (soon called Group Y), most adults—whatever they may assume and feel about obligations—take it for granted that many such youths (3) will encounter sizable external *obstacles* along the way, and/or will sometimes feel considerable internal resistance to making substantial changes; and (4) will therefore experience *slowdowns, setbacks, and, possibly, crises*—in any event, may sometimes become frightened and unsure of themselves in connection with their efforts. They also assume that many nonoffenders (5) may need slight-to-considerable *assistance, concrete advice, and/or moral support,* particularly, but not just, from the start, and even apart from crises.

Factor (5) pertains not only to nonoffenders who do *not* prefer to make substantial efforts to alter their adverse conditions, and so on (these youths are called Group X). Instead, it also applies to those who do make such efforts (Group Y), yet for whom most

adults consider factor (3)—especially, "sizable . . . obstacles"—relevant. These adults thus take it for granted that many Y individuals who face such obstacles/conditions may be unable to handle them entirely by themselves. This is true even if—as is generally the case—such youths, individually, are assumed to have (a) a typical range of personal strengths and (b) a generally "positive" attitude and self-concept (features that those adults would also assume could apply to X individuals).

Given factors (3), (4), and, of course, (5)—and whatever *exactly* may apply regarding (a) and (b)—the question of whether it is *in*appropriate to offer nonoffenders (X's and Y's alike) verbal and concrete support/assistance seldom if ever arises. Nor does that of whether harmful or otherwise undue dependency will be fostered, as part of that assistance. Instead, many adults take the following idea, and its subsidiary subject of dependency, for granted; more specifically, they accept it, mostly implicitly: Assistance can be useful and often even critical—in those respects, *appropriate*—in helping given nonoffenders achieve the broad goal of better overall adjustment;[34] and, such assistance can include temporary, partial dependency, at least various forms and degrees of it. In any event, many or most adults assume that nonoffenders, including those with presumed strengths and positive attitudes, will (6) often require *considerable time* to make the needed or desired changes/improvements, that is, to reduce/overcome/eliminate often long-standing obstacles, and/or to undo past personal mistakes.[35] This time factor would apply even if little or no assistance were assumed to be needed regarding the changes/improvements; and, if assistance *were* considered necessary, the factor would pertain whether or not any related, temporary dependency were involved.

In sum, adults in general view nonoffenders' efforts to reduce or eliminate various negative conditions as not only appropriate and important in their own right but as clearing the way for those youths to focus on positive goals per se, especially insofar as such efforts succeed.[36] They have a similar, again-implicit assumption regarding the youths' efforts to undo/overcome certain past mistakes and various shortcomings. Most adults take it for granted that nonoffenders have a *right* to make both such efforts. They assume this rests not only on (1) the intrinsic value of reducing negative conditions and of undoing/overcoming given mistakes/shortcomings (irrespective of a possible obligation to do so), but on (2) the fact that the given efforts can serve as key instrumental means—often essential means—to those positive goals themselves (goals which, moreover, most adults believe *should* be sought and achieved). At any rate, regarding point (2), if such efforts were absent or if little progress occurred in connection with them, it would often be unusually difficult for the youths to achieve the goals in question—in particular, the longer-range secondaries (C_{2g} and D_{2g}). This would apply to the achievement of primary goals as well, for instance, A_{1g}—again on a relatively stable rather than sporadic basis. It would pertain even if those individuals had prosocial attitudes and were not below average with respect to overall strengths.

Thus, although they rarely conceptualize the following as such, most adults assume, in effect, that the processes, targets, and intended results that are collectively involved in reducing negative conditions, and so on, generally consist of the following: (1) The releasing, organizing, directing, and sometimes redirecting of energy, emotion, and motivation, so that (2) the nonoffenders in question can focus or better focus on various tasks and building blocks (TBBs)—ones which, in turn, (3) bear on, and can help produce, better near-term and longer-term functioning. These TBBs directly and indirectly relate to goals A_{2g} through D_{2g}; and, in their relationship to the primary goals, they may also involve a broader "pursuit of happiness."[37] Toward these individually and collectively important ends, namely, the various primary and secondary goals, most such adults take it for granted that there would be nothing intrinsically inappropriate about those youths seeking or receiving assistance from others, particularly if this input seemed relevant and needed.

The preceding sections, and their brief summary, emphasized the views of *adults,* mainly regarding *nonoffenders.* (The rest of this chapter will emphasize *offenders,* even though it sometimes mentions nonoffenders to help bring out meaning. Also, it will increasingly focus on *policymakers and practitioners,* rather than the general adult population ["most adults"].) Those preceding sections indicated that most adults consider

the primary and secondary goals not only legitimate in themselves but important in terms of their influence on the nonoffenders' everyday lives, on the direction of those youths' activities, and on their future adjustment. This legitimacy and importance applies to the adults' view of offenders as well. Moreover, concerning offenders, those adults' again implicitly assume that progress toward one or both types of goals, or the achievement of them, can be an appropriate and important product of *intervention,* in particular.[38, 39]

Apart from as well as within the context of intervention, then, the following applies to the primary and secondary goals (it pertains to them especially, but not just, collectively): These goals define or comprise some of the basic content or subject matter—that is, they comprise major aspects or dimensions of *what* it is—that most adults consider justified and important regarding nonoffenders' and offenders' short-term and long-term activities, their attempted adjustments or adaptations, and their overall strivings; this also applies to what those individuals believe these youths have a right to seek, namely, those same types of goals, among other things. Concerning major content of intervention in particular, many, but far from all, policymakers and practitioners themselves view these goals as justified and important, and they, too, regard the given offenders—SMOs—as having a right to seek them. (The differences that exist among these mostly correctional personnel are often large and important. They will be discussed below, chiefly in connection with secondary goals.[40])

As to *how* the primaries and secondaries might be addressed and approached, most adults take it for granted that efforts centering on one or both "salient dimensions" would be particularly relevant; more specifically, they would be appropriate, important, and probably often essential. This, of course, would apply to progress on those dimensions, as well—that is, to positive results of those efforts.[41] (As indicated, these dimensions involve the bettering of one's life situation/circumstances and the undoing of past personal mistakes or the overcoming of various shortcomings. As a means to ends—the ends being the primary and secondary goals—each dimension comprises a broad line of approach, or a general strategy.) More specifically, those adults would consider such progress (and its underlying efforts) appropriate and often critical—first, to *nonoffenders* who have experienced or are still experiencing sizable difficulties, shortcomings, and the like in their immediate living situation, in their broader social-cultural environment, and/or intrapsychically. In addition, most adults, though they seldom focus their attention on those salient dimensions per se in connection with *offenders,* implicitly assume that progress along one or both such lines would be a significant or perhaps even critical step for *these* youths, as well. That is, they believe it often would be (not occasionally might be) an important means to the above ends (goals), much as it is with nonoffenders. (These views, by most adults, are separate from those individuals' further assumption that such progress could help youths in general meet, or better meet, various social expectations and requirements which are distinct from the primary and secondary goals as such.)

Accordingly, most adults take it for granted that, to help nonoffenders and offenders address those difficulties, shortcomings, and related factors or conditions, it would be useful for them to receive some encouragement and commendation/reinforcement for their efforts—and encouragement *to* make efforts—along those lines, and for making progress as well. Also, many adults consider it natural and not unlikely that—at some point(s)—many nonoffenders and offenders will probably encounter significant external obstacles and internal resistance, will then experience related slowdowns and perhaps setbacks, may need general and specific assistance/advice/support in those regards, and will need considerable time for conditions to change and settle down in any event, that is, even absent those obstacles, setbacks, and the like.

Stances toward Content-Areas Intervention
Background: The Role of Content Areas (A, B, and C)
We have emphasized the important role that (1) movement along the *salient dimensions* can play in overcoming obstacles to the youths' progress toward the shorter-term secondary *goals* (A_{2g} and B_{2g}), and that (2) such progress, especially if sizable, can itself play in opening the way for significant movement toward the longer-range secondaries (C_{2g} and D_{2g}) and toward a fuller, less sporadic attainment of the primaries as well. Together, these points indicate that substantial progress toward A_{2g} and B_{2g} in particular, or the essential achievement of those goals, is especially "important [with regard to] overall social/personal *functioning* [this involves the secondaries], and the tapping of strong, relatively enduring *motivators* [i.e., the primaries as reinforcers]." Basically, progress toward A_{2g} and B_{2g} themselves, and movement along each salient dimension as well, can be facilitated by carefully focusing on the original, global B and/or C *content areas* (Chapter 24); this fact highlights the wide-ranging appropriateness and the cardinal importance of efforts and progress in those domains. In this respect, content-area A is itself relevant and valuable. We will briefly review the nature of these content-areas or subject-matter domains, and the general role they play in the present context.

In this context, Areas B and C refer to negative, that is, *harmful,* "social/environmental forces," and [to] personal difficulties/conflicts/limited understanding, respectively"; Area A centers on practical or interpersonal skill deficits/deficiencies. Since these domains, especially B and C, have considerable substantive overlap with the content of the two salient dimensions, that is, since they have much subject-matter similarity with them, those domains or areas can supply the following: Individually, they can provide basic content *in terms of which* progress can occur on those salient dimensions, and, in turn, on the secondary goals themselves; collectively, they can provide the bulk and main range of intervention's content, that is, its readily visible activities and foci of effort. In the same vein, Areas A through C can often bear on those secondary goals (e.g., A_{2g} and C_{2g}) *directly,* that is, without having to operate via the salients per se.[42]

Structurally, A, B, and C are the major *settings or mediums* in which personal and interpersonal change, growth, and adaptation can occur; functionally, they are the concrete *vehicles* through which these can occur. Substantively, those same areas contain and otherwise involve key *subject matter,* and *foci,* of staff and youth activities, of the youths' progress, and of these offenders' potential progress; that is, they—usually collectively—involve the main content (the "what") that operationally defines many aspects of the above-mentioned change, growth, and often-constructive adaptation.

Except as specified, we will now focus exclusively on serious multiple offenders, still in relation to the three content areas.

Stances of Three Groups of Correctional Personnel

Obviously, for SMOs to make substantial progress in any given content area, that area must first be addressed not only by the youths themselves but, at various points and in varying respects, by a range of correctional and corrections-related individuals—together, "CCRIs." (Here, we will focus on the CCRIs alone. These mainly include various policymakers and legislators, academicians, administrators, supervisors, line staff, and other direct-service professionals plus their assistants.) Moreover, with these offenders, the area(s) in question must be addressed seriously, for example, to a sizable degree and with sustained, directed effort. However, (1) before CCRIs such as policymakers and administrators will even *moderately* support and maintain those areas or will try to obtain area resources in the first place, and (2) before other CCRIs such as line staff will focus and sustain their own efforts, each of the following must occur: First, those individuals must regard efforts and progress that center on A, B, and C as *appropriate* and *important*—here, "appropriate" in the sense of being or probably being quite relevant (not just slightly or tangentially relevant, and not just possibly so), and "important" in having a good deal of actual or potential power (influence, ability) to advance accepted goals. Second, those CCRIs must believe or implicitly assume that the given offenders have—or have *at least*—an *instrumental need* or *pragmatic right* to receive such efforts and services.[43]

In short, correctional and related persons must want to focus on those areas in a committed way; and, a key determiner of such motivation, or even of general acceptance and support, is those individuals' view of the *efforts' and content areas'* likely relevance and influence, and of the *youths* as having a pragmatic right to, or a sufficient means-to-ends need for, the efforts and services themselves. In abridged and simplified form, the existence of serious efforts (SEs) can thus be described as a product or direct function of the CCRIs' particular view (V) of those factors; that is, $SE = (f)V$. (Though "view" includes relevance, influence, and so on, and although it is therefore already complex, even *it* omits—in this abridged formulation—other major factors, such as [1] available resources and [2] external support as well as opposition. Nevertheless, if CCRIs' above-mentioned, positive outlook and their specifically directed efforts were largely absent, even relevant and otherwise quantitatively sufficient external resources, and various [other] potential supports, would likely be unused or else inadequately applied.[44])

As indicated, sizable differences often exist among CCRIs regarding their attitudes toward the primary and secondary *goals,* with respect to intervention. Equally large differences commonly exist in their attitudes toward the three *content areas* and toward the two *salient dimensions,* respectively. Involved, in each case, are differences among those CCRIs in their attitudes of acceptance or nonacceptance of those goals, of those content areas, and so on, again respectively. Such differences, in turn, mainly reflect those individuals' differing views concerning the value of, or need for, those goals, areas, and dimensions, again in the context of intervention.

Beyond the general fact that attitudes reflect views and that the present views largely involve perceived values or needs, the following applies regarding the *relationship* between the content areas (A, B, and C, collectively), on the one hand, and the earlier-mentioned goals (ends), on the other: Differences among CCRIs in their attitudes toward those *content areas* are not necessarily based on—and, thus, do not invariably require—preexisting differences among those same individuals in their attitudes toward the *primary goals,* toward the *secondary goals,* or toward *both.* That is, even though (1) many CCRI differences in acceptance versus nonacceptance of given content areas *are* closely and causally related to preexisting differences among those individuals in their views regarding the value of or need for the given goals, (2) many other such differences regarding those same content areas exist among CCRIs who *agree* with each other as to the value of and need for those goals. (Details are discussed below.) In each pattern, the CCRIs' differences in attitudes toward the content areas often have sizable implications for the level of effort and support those individuals actually—concretely—give to those areas, and, more broadly, for the nature, scope, and focus of intervention overall. Thus, the differences—whether their relationship to the goals follows pattern (1) or pattern (2)—do not just lead to differing types and degrees of support or opposition in *principle,* important though this is.

We will now review the specifics of these varied attitudes and views, and will mention their general implications. Emphasis will be on the three content areas, collectively. As mentioned, these areas are major settings and vehicles in and through which personal and interpersonal change, growth, and adaptation can occur. They also comprise key subject matter, and foci, of staff/youth activities, of the youths' progress, and so on.

As already indicated, efforts involving the *salient dimensions* are closely related to those centering on these content areas. As a result, and to facilitate the discussion, those dimensions will not be focused on as such, though they will sometimes be mentioned. That aside, it will also suffice to emphasize the secondary goals alone.

To proceed, we will first distinguish three major groups of CCRIs that differ from each other in their views of the goals and content areas *combined.* Group 1's attitude toward these goals and content areas, respectively, can be thought of as "plus, plus" (+,+); Group 2's as "minus, minus" (−,−); and Group 3's as "plus, minus" (+,−)—again respectively, in each case. "Plus" means the attitude is mostly accepting; "minus" means it is mainly nonaccepting. Each group has been quite common in the United States since at least the 1960s.

Group 1 (+,+)

These correctional and corrections-related individuals have an accepting view not only of the secondary *goals* but of most or all of the *content areas.* More specifically, they regard both factors as generally to highly valuable—as appropriate and important, not to mention legitimate—with respect to intervention; and, as suggested, their accepting attitude toward those content areas often exists partly *because* they also regard them as valuable means, in fact often necessary means, to the given ends, that is, to the also-valued goals.

At any rate, with respect to the content areas, Group 1 CCRIs consider A, B, and/or C relevant and important. They also believe serious multiple offenders have an instrumental need for correctional efforts and resources that center on or otherwise emphasize at least one such area, for example, Area B (improving external conditions and/or family interactions). (These points concerning relevance and need apply to the salient dimensions, as well.) In sum, the present individuals consider those areas valuable in the sense of being "on-target" and often essential with respect to goals—including reduced illegal behavior—they view as valid and valuable themselves, for SMOs and society alike.

(Content-areas that are considered relevant and important, and for which SMOs are thought to have a pragmatic right based on an instrumental need, can be described—simply—as "needed," even if they are not considered sufficient by themselves. In any event, being needed in these respects helps make them legitimate and appropriate.[45])

Group 2 (−,−)

Other CCRIs do not consider the secondary goals, mainly but not just the long-range ones, particularly relevant and important. This is largely because they believe that progress toward those goals, or even achievement of them, will seldom sufficiently accomplish—and in most cases will not even significantly help accomplish—corrections' task of reducing/eliminating illegal behavior, on at least an immediate basis. This applies whether the correctional system's attempts to achieve those secondary goals, especially via efforts directed at given content areas, constitute the sole intervention approach, the dominant approach, or one that is somewhat subordinate to others, for instance, to punishment-oriented methods.

Further bearing on Group 2's general nonacceptance of those goals is the following. Many such individuals believe the long-range secondaries, in particular, extend beyond or largely beyond what they consider interventions' proper sphere of responsibility and even its sole legitimate task or mandate, namely, the given reduction/elimination. Moreover, even if that sphere were broadened, this mandate, in the view of those individuals, could still seldom be sufficiently (hence "successfully") *implemented* via the main forms of personal change/growth emphasized in this book—ones that place considerable emphasis on those secondaries. In contrast, these same CCRIs consider various standard forms of punishment and external control almost always necessary, often sufficient, and, in any event, the most promising modalities and methods, with respect to reducing/eliminating illegal behavior per se, and essentially apart from long-range growth and development.

In general, then, Group 2 correctional and corrections-related individuals regard sizable progress toward, and even the achievement of, various secondary goals or key ingredients thereof as noncritical or seldom critical, and as a secondary benefit or an acceptable by-product at best; also, many view these changes as somewhat or largely tangential. Thus, even when such goals are *not* considered entirely outside intervention's proper sphere they are still regarded—before the fact—as targets or objectives that should not be specifically focused on as such, that should not warrant substantial priority and careful, systematic efforts even if they *are* addressed, and that are seldom literally needed—are seldom critical or essential—in any event, in order to substantially curtail illegal behavior.[46]

Given these CCRIs' view of what intervention's overarching and perhaps sole legitimate task should be, and given their general view of how that task would best be, and perhaps must be, implemented, these individuals do not believe that efforts which focus on the *content areas* in ways already discussed are particularly meaningful and on target, let alone essential. In this regard, they therefore consider such efforts insufficiently justified.[47]

These nonaccepting or largely rejecting views and attitudes regarding those efforts are neither compromised nor contradicted by the following: Many such individuals believe correctional efforts that focus carefully on certain content areas can often make positive contributions to specific kinds of growth and adaptation that are directly reflected in the secondary goals and which therein involve dimensions and ingredients *other than* the curtailment of illegal behavior. (These contributions, and the various issues just discussed, pertain to efforts involving the salient dimensions as well.)[48]

In sum, Group 2 CCRIs do not consider efforts that focus on the three content areas particularly relevant, important, or critical with respect to the correctional tasks they view as essential. Though these individuals, or most of them, do not reject those areas completely, they are, to all intents and purposes, largely nonsupportive of intervention that

carefully and perhaps intensively centers on them and that, in so doing, tries to emphasize personal/interpersonal change/growth—without downplaying illegal behavior. Most such individuals' general rejection of such intervention largely stems from the fact that they do not consider the secondary goals critical in the first place, even though, as implied, those CCRIs may slightly, or, on occasion, moderately accept one or two. More specifically, that general rejection reflects their view that progress/achievement with respect to those goals is not enough—usually not nearly enough—to largely curb illegal behavior. Chapter 29 further discusses this group, specifically its largest and most influential portion.

Group 3 (+,−)

Like Group 1 and unlike 2, still other CCRIs consider the secondary *goals* relevant and important, and their overall attitude toward them is accepting. Nonetheless, like 2 and unlike 1, these individuals—Group 3—(a) do not essentially support most or all *content areas,* that is, intervention which focuses on them; also, many within this group (b) actively reject those areas. Both (a) and (b) are valid generalizations for Group 3 as a whole, even though many individuals within this group, like many in Group 2, slightly support certain areas, and although some give moderate support to one (usually A).[49]

Key attitudes on the part of Group 3, like those held by Group 2, are especially relevant to observations in the later part of Chapter 26; and since Group 3 is particularly differentiated in ways that bear on those remarks, we will briefly describe its main *subgroups* (SGs). (The first SG is the smallest; the others are of about equal size.)

SG 1

These CCRIs have seldom if ever focused on the following idea, or perhaps even thought about it: To substantially reduce most SMOs' illegal behavior, or to eliminate it, what might be needed are changes and/or improvements that could result from intervention which focuses on the content areas.[50, 51] (This approach will hereafter be called *content-areas intervention,* or *CAI.*) Instead of having focused on that idea and having even moderately incorporated it, most such individuals have taken the following for granted, and their approach has mainly or entirely reflected it: For corrections to reduce/eliminate most SMOs' illegal behavior, it only, or predominantly, needs to provide punishment and heavy external controls (PHEC).[52]

Thus, regarding SMOs, these individuals have seldom if ever thought about or paid serious attention to broad approaches other than PHEC. As a result, they have not actively *considered* those approaches and then specifically rejected them—rejected, in the present case, intervention that involves and often centers on the careful addressing of particular content areas. Given this situation, these individuals can be described not necessarily as *uninterested* in careful, systematic CAI, but as nonaccepting of it mainly by default. In either case, they do not view SMOs as needing the earlier-mentioned "changes and/or improvements," ones that could conceivably result from content-area intervention. The practical effect of that view is that they do not support this approach.

SG 2

These CCRIs believe that most serious multiple offenders, perhaps like some nonoffenders, *may* need the earlier-mentioned changes/ improvements; more specifically, they might or might well need external, interpersonal, and/or personal changes, and to a sizable degree. For instance, these CCRIs recognize, as such, societal- and/or family-centered conditions that could help account for (1) the *existence* of needed changes, that is, which could understandably lead to it, and—beyond that—for (2) the SMOs' wish to *make* those changes.

Despite this recognition, most such individuals believe or assume the following: To achieve corrections' principal goal (see "socially centered mandate," below), few SMOs literally *need* (require) the type of intervention that would carefully target Areas A, B, and/or C for the purpose of (1) generating the given changes/improvements and, as most such CCRIs realize, in order to (2) ultimately reduce/eliminate illegal behavior. Instead, they assume these offenders' *willpower* could be, and usually is, the key to achieving that reduction/elimination; they also assume it could produce this effect largely or entirely by itself—in any case, with little or no support from content-areas intervention. (As just implied, efforts that involve such intervention would be seen as mainly centered on other issues in any event, such as short-range adjustment issues or long-range growth-and-development ones.)[53] At any rate, CAI would be viewed as not literally needed in order to substantially reduce *illegal behavior*. Together with those assumptions, these CCRIs generally take it for granted that correctional punishment, accompanied by related negative sanctions and by external controls, can arouse that willpower and can then help as well as partly force most SMOs to focus it on the immediate task of curbing illegal behavior. (The goal of curbing that behavior is called intervention's "socially centered mandate.")

At any rate, SG 2's recognize practical, interpersonal, and other issues and possible needs that they believe might be productively addressed by focusing on various content areas, and which they realize may not center on or otherwise involve illegal behavior as such. Instead, these issues and needs often involve socially expected, accepted, or even required aspects of any adolescents' life—that is, its legal aspects. Among them are personal and interpersonal growth-and-adjustment, common "teenage" interests/ desires/challenges, and so on. These issues, needs, possible needs, and concerns are immediate and/or long-term in nature; and, regarding either time frame, they are ones these CCRIs realize could understandably become a major focus, or the prime focus, of intervention—over and beyond whatever attention the youths' illegal behavior requires.[54]

Nevertheless, these SG 2's essentially *reject* the idea of concentrating efforts and resources along that line—of heavily emphasizing changes and/or improvements in A, B, and/or C. They do so mainly because they do not consider such changes essential to the reduction/elimination of *illegal behavior* per se; nor do they view them as major or potentially major contributors to such a reduction, at least in the preponderance of cases.[55] In effect, these CCRIs do not view content-areas intervention as particularly likely to produce a satisfactory type of, or an acceptably large degree of, reduction, even if it *were* to productively address, for example, growth-and-adjustment issues. At any rate, many such individuals reject CAI even though they realize that some "issues and possible needs" that it may productively address might well have substantial preintervention *links* to illegal behavior itself, and potential postintervention ones as well.[56]

All in all, then, the preponderance of these CCRIs believe each of the following: (1) If the content areas were emphasized in lieu of punishment and heavy external controls, this might lead to some progress concerning illegal behavior per se and often to considerable progress regarding broader aspects of growth and adaptation. However, that emphasis would seldom generate acceptable amounts of progress in the former domain, namely, that of illegal behavior, even if it made considerable difference in the latter.[57] (2) Since PHEC can often reduce illegal behavior to an acceptable degree and can presumably reduce it considerably more than other such approaches, *it* should comprise virtually the entire content of most correctional efforts; in any event, it should be the predominant focus of those efforts. Seen in this context, the content areas—especially collectively—should receive little or no emphasis, whether absolute or relative, as vehicles for working toward given secondary goals.[58]

Thus, the present individuals believe illegal behavior can be reduced and often eliminated without one's first or simultaneously having addressed and at least partly resolved various issues and needs—emergent and/or long-continued ones. This also applies to the addressing/resolving of long-term, future-oriented growth issues, as distinct from ones centering on more immediate adjustment and adaptation.

SG 3

These CCRIs believe that SMOs, given their history of illegal behavior, either (1) do not *deserve* the types of input and level of effort that would likely be involved in intervention which emphasizes the secondary goals, or (2) they deserve that input/effort only slightly and/or infrequently. This view, which distinguishes SG 3's from the others, exists despite the following:

A. SG 3's believe that most SMOs personally need and could often substantially benefit from the types of change that could result from content-areas intervention. Such changes bear directly on the secondary goals, and these changes could benefit SMOs by substantially improving their chances of adjusting to various immediate and/or long-range social and personal expectations, requirements, and needs. (For present purposes, we need

not include CCRIs who, while believing SMOs do not deserve or only slightly deserve content-areas intervention, also consider them [1] unlikely to benefit from it—say, unlikely due to their unyielding rejection of it—and, in some cases, [2] probably not in need of it, in the first place.)

B. Many CCRIs to whom point A applies believe this intervention, when combined with standard or perhaps added external controls, could substantially, and often, reduce illegal behavior itself. Other such CCRIs believe that, under those same conditions, the amount of reduction (though not the frequency with which it occurs) would usually be less—yet not unimportant.[59]

In general, SG 3's believe that although serious multiple offenders may well have deserved various rights and privileges before they engaged in illegal acts, they lost them or many of them, either largely or entirely, and they did so because of those acts.[60] Involved, in this loss, are not just commonly accorded social opportunities and benefits, but, in particular, various types and degrees of assistance associated with content-areas intervention itself—assistance that could often be available to youths considered deserving (i.e., mainly to non-SMOs). This applies whether the rights and privileges that were lost are viewed as having been (1) originally *earned (merited),* by virtue of one's actions and perhaps related attitudes; (2) "natural" and, in effect, automatically given to, or assumed to exist for, any child or young person in the society (and, thus, as not having been originally earned in connection with approved actions); (3) generosity-based, or perhaps empathy-based, offerings and/or conditions that were provided by particular individuals; or (4) combinations of the above.

As described shortly, many of the present SG 3's consider serious multiple offenders categorically or unconditionally undeserving; all remaining 3's have a conditional or contingent perspective in this regard. This means that SG 3's, collectively, do not support the use of the above-described content-areas intervention with respect to these youths; or, at most, they support it rather minimally. These CCRIs maintain this stance even though, as suggested earlier, they believe that that particular approach—CAI—could help many such offenders make significant progress regarding immediate and/or long-range needs.

Concerning *illegal behavior* itself, most such CCRIs believe that certain types and amounts of punishment and external control ("punishment/control") that are routinely applied to SMOs can—even when essentially unaccompanied by CAI—reduce this behavior at least as much as can a predominantly CAI approach, whether or not the latter actually reduces it a lot. Such reduction aside, many SG 3's believe a punishment/controls approach, unlike a predominantly content-areas one, *would* be deserved (though, of course, not because of past *approved* behavior). It would be deserved mainly as (1) a response to individuals' past negative behavior and in order to deter or otherwise prevent future such behavior, not—or hardly—as (2) an input designed to help offenders work toward a constructive future per se, via progress on various fronts. In this regard, of the two approaches in question, these SG 3's consider only punishment/control appropriate, that is, justified. Many such CCRIs view this approach as justified in its own right, irrespective, moreover, of any limitations that it, like content-areas intervention itself, might have in addressing growth-and-adjustment needs.[61] We now turn to absolute and nonabsolute deservedness.

To many 3's, deservedness is categorical ("absolute") rather than graded and contingent ("nonabsolute"): Offenders either deserve content-areas intervention or they do not; and SMOs, in particular, do not. This applies whatever the circumstances of their offenses and lives, and, in effect, regardless of their expressed hopes—also their recent or ongoing efforts—with respect to the future.

Thus, to these SG 3's, it is not just that serious multiple offenders should squarely face various unpleasant, often quite restrictive, and sometimes even harsh correctional consequences of their past illegal actions—consequences that are partly expressed in, and that purposely flow from, a punishment/controls approach.[62] Instead, even if they *are* facing those consequences, for instance, *are* "paying the price" set forth in their sentences and in related sanctions or requirements, the following applies: These individuals should receive little or no assistance, from corrections, that generally or specifically focuses on building strengths and on reducing external obstacles in order to promote a constructive future. Rather, corrections should use punishment/controls (incapacitation being part of this, as needed), in order to focus almost solely on deterring those offenders from further illegal behavior (and also on *continued* punishment); this task is fundamental, and often difficult, in itself. At any rate, in accordance with these CCRIs' view that SMOs no longer deserve certain types of assistance that are commonly part of content-areas intervention, corrections not only *need* not but it specifically *should* not try to help them build those strengths, and so on. If SMOs wish to develop such strengths and to reduce or overcome various obstacles, they should largely or entirely draw from elsewhere and from themselves.

To many other SG 3's—or, in the past few decades, to perhaps most—deservedness is not absolute; it is not, in this respect, "all or none." Instead, it can vary somewhat in degree, depending, for example, on the offense history, the instant offense, and so on. With serious multiple offenders, however, (1) the variation is *small* and (2) the threshold above which content-areas intervention is considered appropriate, that is, deserved, is only occasionally passed. Both points, in turn, reflect two interrelated, underlying beliefs: The present SG 3's, who hold the just-mentioned views, also believe that (3) SMOs' level of deservedness is seldom more than *low* and that (4) these youths' rights and privileges should be quite limited in scope. Accordingly, that is, in line with (1), (3), and (4), these CCRIs believe that even when content-areas intervention *is* appropriate, its level of effort and degree of input should be generally slight and its *range* of input (scope of content) should be no more than modest.[63] This "slightness" and "modesty" or moderation with respect to CAI also reflects the fact that the attitude of these SG 3s' regarding *youth accountability,* especially the-facing-of-consequences, closely parallels that of the preceding 3's, that is, the "absolute" grouping. A direct relationship also exists between that intervention's relatively low *frequency of usage,* in the first place, and the same underlying attitude.

Thus, regarding SG 3's *overall*—that is, the "absolute" and "nonabsolute" groupings combined—the following generalizations apply: Despite differences that exist across this SG's groupings (specifically, differences in various beliefs about SMOs' deservedness), hardly any SG 3's—that is, regardless of their grouping—give more than slight support to the idea of *extensive* or relatively comprehensive content-areas intervention. Many 3's, however, give some support to that of limited, narrowly gauged CAI.

Nevertheless, despite even this latter support, when SG 3's make concrete choices between CAI on the one hand and punishment/control on the other, that is, when they decide which of these broad approaches to utilize almost exclusively or to give, at least, a clear priority,[64] most take the position that corrections should largely or almost entirely limit its inputs and efforts to punishment/control. They take this stance despite their frequent, concurrent belief that (1) some SMOs, even though they have lost many rights and privileges, still deserve or otherwise warrant a little assistance with respect to the secondary goals, and that (2) most SMOs (apart from having lost the above) *need* assistance, in any event. Again, point (1), immediately above, involves the generalized—composite—attitude of SG 3's toward efforts and inputs that are still viewed as deserved. As indicated earlier, however, many individual 3's believe SMOs deserve *no* content-areas intervention at all, narrowly gauged or otherwise.

Major Path or Steps to Short- and Long-Range Goals

In broad outline, content-areas intervention can help achieve the short- and long-range secondary goals via the following path or steps (this is its commonest path):

1. Careful, sustained focusing on Areas A, B, and/or C can help generate and otherwise promote changes and improvements in external conditions and in personal as well as interpersonal understanding, skills, and attitudes.
2. When sufficient in amount, depth, or breadth, those changes/improvements can reduce or eliminate obstacles to everyday functioning and ongoing adjustment, to rewarding prosocial experiences, and, in general, to achieving the short-term secondary goals (A_{2g} and B_{2g}) or major aspects thereof.
3. When sustained for at least several months—more often for around a year—

such functioning, adjustment, and experiences can engender not only increased self-confidence, greater willingness to face continued challenges, and better feelings about oneself overall, but also less fear of, less anger toward, and/or greater comfort with others. These changes can occur well before the long-range goals (C_{2g} and D_{2g}) are achieved or even approached, and they are often reflected in psychological test-score changes and via other measures.

With most SMOs, short- and long-term reductions in *illegal behavior* are more likely to occur when corrections' direct focus on that behavior takes place not largely in isolation but, instead, as part of a broader context. This context especially centers on steps 1 through 3, and it directly involves content-areas intervention. (For details, see endnote 65.)

4. Utilizing their step 3 gains, such as increased self-confidence and greater comfort with others, SMOs can redirect, expand, further focus, and/or consolidate their efforts and activities. In particular, they can "try themselves out" in new and sometimes more complex situations, can test possible new roles and responsibilities, can further build given skills, and so on. These efforts and activities can increasingly involve preparations for key aspects of adulthood and/or, in any event, for prosocial life-styles. Such developments and involvements would have been less likely to succeed, and—often—would not or could not have even been undertaken, if steps 1 through 3 had not already cleared the way and helped provide sufficient foundation.[66]

For correctional and corrections-related individuals to *want* to engage in careful, sustained, content-areas intervention, they must—understandably—view both *it* and its major intended products, such as various changes, as having considerable intrinsic and/or instrumental value. For instance, regarding CAI's intermediate products, namely, step 1 and 3 *changes/improvements,* CCRIs must believe or assume that these are meaningful and important—or (viewed and described more instrumentally) relevant and needed. In addition, regarding later products, those individuals must feel that some or all of the *secondary goals* toward which many such changes are directed are themselves of value. Finally, though operationally the most basic, they must feel positively about the *content-areas emphasis* that can help generate those changes/improvements in the first place. However, in all three respects, major differences exist among CCRIs concerning their beliefs, assumptions, and/or feelings; that is, they exist regarding those individuals' views and evaluations of the given process (CAI itself) and of its intermediate as well as later products.

Review of Personnel Stances

Specifically, and to briefly review, *Group 1* CCRIs regard the content areas as relevant and important. They also consider the secondary goals of value; and, in sum, they believe serious multiple offenders have an instrumental need for correctional efforts that focus on one or more such areas for the main purpose of generating changes/improvements that can help achieve those goals. In contrast, *Group 2* CCRIs do not consider efforts that focus on Areas A, B, and/or C especially important. More particularly, they do not view them as strong enough and relevant enough to achieve the only goal these individuals consider necessary—and fully justified: substantially reducing illegal behavior, and, where possible, eliminating it. At any rate, though such CCRIs do not entirely reject the content-areas focus, and although they consider it relevant to changes and improvements that involve certain types of growth and/or better adjustment, they nevertheless *largely* reject it: They do not, basically, support efforts that would carefully address those areas, let alone do so on a relatively long-term basis. This is because they do not consider the changes/improvements that could result from such a focus, and the secondary goals that those changes could in turn facilitate, as having enough impact on illegal behavior, either individually or collectively.

Finally, *Group 3* CCRIs, like those of Group 1, do value the secondary goals. Some 3's believe their achievement may, and others believe it will, often reduce or substantially reduce illegal behavior, and sometimes even eliminate it completely. Nevertheless, unlike Group 1 and like Group 2, these individuals are largely nonsupportive of content-areas efforts—though some individuals do support them, if only on a narrow and otherwise limited basis. Although most 3's are similar to each other regarding this general nonsupport—in fact, are similar even though they consider a content-areas focus potentially helpful in some respects—various CCRIs (subgroupings) within this overall group differ from each other as to the main reasons for that attitude:

SG 1's have seldom or never focused on content-areas intervention in the first place, that is, have not specifically thought about its possible role and importance in generating changes that can substantially reduce illegal behavior (and even in generating other changes). They have assumed that a different approach will generally work, and that it will do so largely on its own. Though these individuals have not, therefore, pointedly rejected CAI as such, the net result of their position—this being nonsupport—is the same as if they *had*.

SG 2's believe that content-areas intervention *might* help promote changes/improvements and might thereby help achieve the secondary goals. However, they believe that neither such changes nor such achievement, while important in their own right, would make a sufficient difference in illegal behavior. Also, given their belief that a better—an *alternative*—approach exists for reducing such behavior, these individuals feel that CAI should receive little support at best and that almost all agency resources should be organized around that alternative: one that is punishment/controls-centered. At any rate, these CCRIs do not regard content-areas intervention and the changes/improvements it may generate as being adequate for achieving the "sufficient difference" in question, or even being somehow *essential* but nonetheless inadequate/insufficient contributors. In contrast, they consider punishment/controls sufficient, and in that sense adequate.

SG 3's view content-areas intervention as often able to successfully address the secondary goals—which they, like SG 2's, do consider important. However, many of these individuals do not believe SMOs *deserve* the type and amount of effort that would be involved; and, for that reason (sometimes apart from and sometimes together with the one mentioned below), they do not concretely support CAI. Still other SG 3's, based on a partly different view of SMOs' deservedness, and sometimes despite the reason mentioned below (see "p/c"), often support it slightly. In any event, even though SG 3's, collectively, believe content-areas intervention can often substantially reduce *illegal behavior* as well as successfully address the secondary goals, they prefer a punishment/controls (p/c) approach to CAI. This is not only because they believe p/c can perform as well as or better in that regard, but because they consider it much more in line with *deservedness*—sometimes as defined in a just desert framework.

A Fourth Group—and Stance

We have described three major groups of correctional and corrections-related individuals who differ from each other in their views of the secondary goals and of content-areas intervention combined, and we have described one set of subgroups. However, certain other CCRIs are rather different than the above, despite areas of similarity. Because there are many such "others," because these individuals can be characterized by various important features they share in common, and due to other reasons,[67] these individuals (at least the most typical/modal ones)—called Group 4 or "moderates"—will now be described:

Group 4 CCRIs

This group believes that most serious multiple offenders have moderate to sizable external difficulties and/or personal problems, some of which contribute significantly to their illegal behavior. Group 4 CCRIs also believe these difficulties and/or problems need to be reduced or resolved to where they (1) no longer comprise substantial obstacles to immediate adjustment and ongoing functioning—thus, are reduced or resolved to where the *short-range* secondary goals are approached, achieved, or can soon be achieved; and (2) no longer help generate, trigger, or maintain that illegal behavior and its clearly related adjustment patterns.

Though these CCRIs support content-areas intervention as a means to those important objectives, namely, the short-range secondaries as well as the social protection goal, they mainly do not believe corrections should use CAI to also specifically target the *long-range* secondaries. That is, it should not add and direct resources—and its personnel should not exert substantial or even moderate efforts—in order to help SMOs (1) get clearly established on a path that can lead to the

achievement of the long-range secondaries;[68] and/or (2) *move* substantially along that path, let alone actually achieve those secondary goals.[69]

This rejection or nonsupport of a long-range focus derives from two main sources. First, it reflects these CCRIs' following belief or assumption concerning the achievement or near-achievement of the *short-range* secondary goals, namely, A_{2g} and B_{2g} (note: "near-achievement" goes substantially beyond moderate progress): This achievement can usually be enough to not only (a) help point SMOs "in the right direction" regarding major *long-range* adjustment and needs, namely, C_{2g} and D_{2g}; rather, it can also (b) help reduce/eliminate those youths' *illegal behavior* on a long-term basis and can help preclude, eliminate, or largely dilute related life-styles.

This means that Group 4 CCRIs do not believe that only the *short-range* goals can be accomplished via appropriate content-areas intervention, and that these goals can be achieved via CAI *on its own*. Instead, and more precisely, they feel that if a substantial or at least a moderate amount of well-implemented CAI is used, and is combined with punishment/controls, it can not only help most SMOs achieve or largely achieve those short-range goals, but it can also make contributions (a) and (b), as a direct and intended consequence of that achievement.

Besides the above, these CCRIs believe that CAI—as combined—can set the stage for, and can also help trigger, subsequent long-range efforts and progress by the youths. In this regard, they believe that content-areas intervention need not have a long-range focus *itself*, that is, need not have that focus in order for the long-range goals to have a reasonable chance of being achieved and for ongoing social protection to have a fair chance of occurring. Instead, CAI, combined with p/c, need only set the long-range process in motion.

Group 4 CCRIs implicitly assume that this motion will usually occur if one first builds an adequate foundation, and that *that* can be done by implementing steps 1, 2, and—hopefully—most or all of 3, of the four-step process outlined earlier. More specifically, these individuals assume that if (1) those three steps, or ones comparable to them, are taken, achieved, or mostly achieved, and if (2) the SMOs seem positively motivated when step 3 is well underway or largely achieved, step 4 is likely to occur or largely occur, and it can do so with little or no added correctional input. Such input would otherwise exist mainly to guide, to further support and encourage, and to variously help implement and consolidate additional forward movement. (Most Group 1 CCRIs believe or assume that such added input *is* usually needed.) Thus, short-range CAI can indirectly lead to long-range goals.

Secondly, and just as influential, Group 4's nonsupportive stance regarding a direct, long-range focus reflects its view that most SMOs, because of their illegal acts, are no more than moderately deserving of substantial CAI resources and staff efforts; this also applies to resources/efforts focused on the short range. Given this broadly applicable (long- and short-range-focused) view regarding moderate deservedness, and given the fact that a long-range focus would call for more resources/efforts than a short-range one, these individuals' stance regarding deservedness applies particularly sharply to resources and efforts that would be directed at long-range goals. Nevertheless, despite their view and stance, these individuals also believe those youths *should* be given substantial or, at least, moderate CAI resources—in connection, however, with the short-range goals alone. (SMOs are not considered sufficiently deserving of the resources that would be called for in connection with a direct, *long-range* emphasis.) We will now focus on this point, with main attention given to the short-range goals. ("Substantial" resources, referred to next, are distinguished from the "large" amounts mentioned afterward.)

Group 4 CCRIs consider it justified to give most SMOs those substantial or moderate resources, for two main reasons: First, as a practical matter (and thus, despite the youths' limited merit), specifically in order to benefit society by changing those offenders' stance toward illegal behavior; second, because they believe these individuals are not entirely undeserving of assistance and may not be entirely blameworthy as well.[70] At any rate, these CCRIs do not consider SMOs' partial nondeservedness sufficient justification for withholding all or almost all content-areas intervention and for foregoing that practical interest, especially if this CAI is combined with punishment/controls—all this, as indicated, in connection with the short-range goals.

Still, the idea of limited merit leads these individuals to believe that serious multiple offenders do not deserve a *large* amount of CAI-based assistance; and this of course does not apply only if such input would be directed at the short-range secondaries. Rather, limited merit also leads Group 4 to believe that a large amount of such assistance (as distinct from a moderate amount) would not be deserved in connection with the long-range secondaries as well. The latter point applies independently of these CCRIs' belief that, given the earlier-mentioned foundation, targeted assistance—whether large, substantial, or small—would be unnecessary in any event, with respect to these long-range secondaries.

(What is here called "a *large* amount of . . . assistance" is comparable to intervention that, in this book, involves not just frequent and/or numerous contacts, but which is comprehensive, fairly complex, and usually lengthy, in particular. Often, such intervention is simply called "comprehensive," with this term emphasizing its simultaneous scope, degree and specificity of relevance, and considerable integration.)

The operational implications of Group 4's view that most serious multiple offenders do not deserve a *large* amount of targeted assistance in connection with the long- and even short-range secondaries happen to be consistent with those of its following belief or assumption regarding *need*:[71] Though SMOs have moderate to sizable personal problems and/or external difficulties, they are not *highly* problemmed; and, if they do not have a high degree of problems/difficulties, they do not need a *large* amount of assistance to deal with them.[72] A substantial or at least moderate amount will usually suffice. In particular, it will be enough to not only help most youths achieve or closely approach the short-range secondary goals of substantially improved immediate adjustment and ongoing functioning; instead, it will be enough to also get the long-range process underway. In addition, Group 4 CCRIs will consider this amount appropriate in the sense of deserved—with respect to the short-range goals.[73]

In summary, these CCRIs believe that when a moderate-to-substantial amount of content-areas intervention is combined with standard punishment/controls and is focused directly on the short-range goals, this can lead to outcomes those individuals consider central: a large improvement in most SMOs' immediate and ongoing adjustment (A_{2g} and B_{2g}) and a reduction/elimination of illegal behavior. As a result, although Group 4 CCRIs have sizable reservations about these youths' deservedness, they accept and actively support CAI when it is thus combined and focused. They also support it because they believe the achievement or near-achievement of the short-range goals can set the stage for major movement toward the long-range ones.

Though these individuals believe the long-range goals need not be focused on and otherwise addressed *directly*—in fact, should not be—they consider them important. They believe and implicitly assume[74] that these goals (C_{2g} and D_{2g}) can instead be achieved (1) as later outgrowths of CAI efforts that have led to successful outcomes regarding the *short*-range goals, (2) with little or no targeted program-inputs other than those already used to achieve the latter goals, and (3) essentially by the SMOs acting on their own, subsequent to those inputs and mainly after the program itself. To achieve the short-range goals in the first place, a moderate to substantial amount of CAI will generally suffice, and "comprehensive" CAI—besides being undeserved—is not needed. At any rate, achievement or near-achievement of the *short*-range secondaries, plus sizable reduction of illegal behavior on even a short-term basis, is itself considered sufficient justification for intervention.

(As implied, Group 4 considers punishment and external controls integral to intervention's overall success, including its achievement of the short-range goals. In addition, p/c's presence—particularly punishment's—helps these CCRIs feel better about providing an amount of content-areas intervention which they generally regard as more than some youths deserve; this applies to the short-range goals, and it does so together with the view that these SMOs are not entirely undeserving. Further helping these CCRIs accept and actively support the idea of providing that intervention under those circumstances is their belief that p/c, integral though it is, cannot adequately promote social protection by itself.)

It is clear, from the above, that Group 4 has basic similarities to Group 1 and, to a substantially lesser extent, Group 3. Group 1 is "+,+" and 3 is "+,−" regarding its overall acceptance of (1) the four secondary goals

(collectively) and (2) content-areas intervention (especially but not only careful, systematic CAI), respectively. Group 4 can be considered "moderately or partially +,+" in these same respects.

We have described the views of four major groups of CCRIs concerning the secondary goals and the use of content-areas intervention, combined. We have also mentioned several factors contributing to, or, in some cases, largely responsible for, given group's or groups' accepting/supportive or nonaccepting/nonsupportive attitudes toward them. Regarding those *secondaries,* some of the key contributors were the group's or groups' views of the goals' (1) own value or significance, that is, the importance of improved personal and social functioning, of overall growth, and of long-term adjustment, on the part of the youths; (2) value compared to that of reducing/eliminating illegal behavior (REIS—this being a separate goal); (3) instrumental value as a *means* to REIS; and/or (4) appropriateness as a correctional endeavor in the first place. As to *content-areas intervention,* main contributors included the CCRIs' views or assumptions concerning (1) the need for and value of any such intervention at all, whatever its amount; (2) the effectiveness and adequacy of punishment/controls, this approach being an alternative to content-areas intervention; and (3) SMOs' deservedness with respect to receiving assistance.

Contributors to Non- or Limited Support of CAI

Factors contributing to the support or nonsupport of the secondary goals often differed across the four groups, as did those involved in supporting or not supporting CAI or in supporting it in relatively limited ways. We will now mention other important factors or reasons contributing to the nonsupport, or limited support, of content-areas intervention. For present purposes, there is no need to routinely specify which contributor applies—for instance, applies the most and the least—to each of the four CCRI groups.

Extent of Difficulties/Problems

The first major contributor is the CCRIs' nonrecognition or limited awareness of the *extent* of most SMOs' external difficulties and/or internal problems; extent can involve scope, intensity, interrelatedness, and/or overall complexity. This factor, which most often applies to Group 2 yet whose existence is widespread, has such sources as the following: (1) academic or in-service training/orientation, regarding delinquency causation, that places emphasis on overly simple theories; (2) a long-standing conviction that most youths' illegal behavior largely reflects their "bad attitudes" and "willfulness"—these usually being atheoretical features that are generally considered neither complex nor deep-seated, let alone heavily intertwined with further possible contributors; and/or (3) stereotypes (apart from "willfulness") and narrowly representative views that result from other inputs and impressions, for example, media sources and personal encounters. If these CCRIs more clearly or more fully realized or understood the extent of those difficulties/problems (D/Ps), they would be more likely to recognize the importance of intervention that—whatever its main subject matter or content—is broad, concerted, and persevering enough to address and remain focused on the above-mentioned degree of complexity, of possible intensity, and so on.

An awareness or understanding of the *extent* of most SMOs' difficulties/problems is separable from one that centers on the *substance*—the content and/or dynamics—of those individuals' D/Ps. The latter understanding would make given CCRIs more likely to recognize the appropriateness and value of an intervention (such as CAI) whose main focus and range of efforts, for instance, its focus on content areas A, B, and/or C, directly relates to that particular content and dynamics, or, at least, to the main *accessible* substance. This recognition, like that which involves the extent of the youths' D/Ps, would usually be accompanied by increased support of such CAI. Most CCRIs, though far from all, do recognize the general content or constituents of this "substance," with emphasis on ones that involve external forces and conditions.

The CCRIs' support of that intervention (say, of CAI) would usually be larger still if they recognized its relevance to the youths' *illegal behavior* per se, that is, not just to other important aspects of adaptation and growth. (This relationship—between content-areas intervention and illegal behavior—is focused upon in connection with factors #3, #6, and

#8, below.) To be sure, those CCRIs would be more likely to recognize and accept that relationship between *CAI* and illegal behavior if they already accepted the connection between the youths' *difficulties/problems,* on the one hand, and that same illegal behavior, on the other. (These D/Ps would be ones that, say, they already recognized *CAI itself* as bearing upon.) At any rate, to be more supportive of such intervention (CAI), CCRIs, under the above conditions, would only have to understand the *extent* of this relationship between D/P and illegal behavior. They would not necessarily have to understand the details of its dynamics—more specifically, how and why a substantial reduction of the former could affect the latter.

Temporal Sequences among Factors

The second reason for nonsupport or slight support of CAI centers on CCRIs' nonawareness or limited awareness of certain *temporal sequences*—successive links or connections—that commonly exist across various factors, elements, and/or conditions. ("Factors" will usually be used to cover all three terms, and these factors are specified shortly.) Awareness or increased awareness of such links would help given CCRIs recognize key steps or benchmarks that are involved as youths move forward. In effect, it would help them recognize salient components or defining features of that movement as a whole ("overall movement")—help them see *what* that movement entails and, in a sense, *how* youths can move from one point to another.

(This forward movement can be thought of as progress, and the particular types and areas of progress can also be termed "outputs." The specific steps or features that can be considered outputs—that is, the individual steps that involve particular types and areas of movement [progress] and which, collectively, comprise the *overall* movement—begin with factor #4 and end with #8 of the sequence described shortly. Factors #1 and #2 are background and factor #3 is the key intervention *input*—in effect, the dominant generator of movement—under consideration.)

Relationships among Factors

The third reason centers on CCRIs' view of the *relationship*—specifically, the strength of the connection—that can exist across various individual factors, particularly from factor #3 forward. This applies whether these factors are adjacent to each other in the sequence or are separated by intermediate ones. Like the second reason for nonsupport of CAI, this one can apply, but does not necessarily do so, even among individuals to whom the first reason does not pertain, that is, among persons who do recognize the *extent* of most SMOs' difficulties/problems. (D/Ps are the second of the eight factors that, collectively, comprise the temporal sequence. We will next consider the second and third reasons together, though the third will be emphasized.)

In short, many CCRIs are not aware of certain series of events in the first place, that is, of various temporal sequences among specified factors. For instance, they are unaware or only slightly aware of the one-step sequence from factor #4 to #5, from #5 to #6, and/or from #7 to #8; this is apart from the fact that most CCRIs *do* recognize several sequences, even ones that involve more than two such factors and/or whose two factors are more than one step removed. In addition, when those individuals *are* largely aware of given sequences, they, nevertheless, often do not recognize or accept the idea that a fairly close, that is, a strong and positive, *relationship* can often exist between given factors and certain others that occur subsequent to them in the sequence, for example, between #4, on the one hand, and #5, on the other.[75] (As used here, "relationship" always refers to the amount of influence that one factor has or can have on a subsequent one's existence, nature, and/or degree; for present purposes, later interactions that may involve reciprocity between those factors need not be considered.)[76]

The Eight-Factor Sequence
To focus on these relationships efficiently, we will first list and briefly comment on the entire eight-factor sequence. This particular sequence is best considered very common as-is, even though, as will be described, a number of its factors are sometimes leapfrogged.[77]

#1 Particularly Negative Events and Conditions of Childhood and/or Preadolescence
Individually or collectively, these have directly produced or contributed to adjustment problems and/or to delinquent/illegal behavior per se; or they have indirectly and even distally raised the chances of such problems/behavior.

They have usually done both the former and latter by generating and/or reinforcing (a) given views of and attitudes toward self and others, (b) general or specific desires, expectations, deficiencies, and vulnerabilities, and (c) major defenses against various inputs, types of situations, challenges, deficiencies, and so on.

#2 Sizable, Current, External Difficulties and/or Internal Problems, usually Quite Evident at Intake
These have generally existed during most of adolescence to date, however short or long; and, not infrequently, they started developing earlier. Even when they have not been substantially preceded by factor #1, these D/Ps, by themselves, can generate, trigger, and maintain not only important social and interpersonal problems but illegal behavior itself. At any rate, they constitute a negative force that is sufficient to prevent many SMOs from largely utilizing important opportunities, to discourage or help prevent them from *wanting* to utilize those opportunities and related available supports, and to often prevent them from moving forward, whether slowly or at all. Even when movement occurs, these difficulties/problems commonly act as encumbrances or energy-drains that make such progress slower and less reliable than it otherwise would be. As a result, and because these youths often fail to constructively utilize their already existing strengths and potentials (or sometimes purposely choose to not do so), they steadily fall farther and farther behind most other individuals with respect to overall development.

#3 Content-Areas Intervention
CAI can address factor #2 directly and concretely; in so doing, it can indirectly reduce various negative effects of #1 as well. Insofar as it strongly impacts the former, and even when it does not largely undo or neutralize the latter (which is usually the case), CAI can help generate and maintain factor #4; this is its major and usual, direct and near-term, effect. Sometimes, it can help SMOs move directly to #5, particularly if #2 is less extensive than usual; such movement, however, more often takes place at about the same time as that toward #4. Furthermore, that is, even as it helps achieve #4 and/or #5, CAI—usually in conjunction with punishment and/or external controls—can often help those youths make

major progress regarding #6. However, with most SMOs, content-areas intervention helps achieve #5 and #6 via #4; that is, it does so essentially after, and as a result of, having substantially affected that particular factor. In this respect it does not usually "leapfrog" or otherwise bypass #4—and/or #5—and, for example, in that sense help most SMOs branch directly to #6, let alone to subsequent factors.

#4 Movement along the Salient Dimensions

This involves the bettering of one's life situation and/or the overcoming or reducing of one's past personal mistakes, shortcomings, and so on. Substantial progress on these dimensions can pave the way for factor #5, and—often simultaneously—for #6.

#5 Achievement or Near-Achievement of the Short-Range Secondary Goals

This involves significantly improved overall adjustment and ongoing functioning. Though it centers largely on adaptation to adolescence and on obtaining satisfactions in that context, it can simultaneously lay important groundwork for movement toward adult roles and responsibilities. The adolescence-centered adaptation and satisfactions that are obtained usually draw from and reflect increased social, personal, and interpersonal strengths, together with a more positive self-concept. It is particularly when such increases and/or changes have occurred or are occurring that factor #6 can be generated on other than a largely or exclusively external basis, such as that of external controls.

Though #5 can also help create a direct path to #7, the latter objective is more likely to be achieved on a relatively stable rather than tenuous basis if #6 already exists. Given that factor's existence, #7 will also have a more realistic chance of occurring at all, at least starting from the period immediately following chronological adolescence. In any event, movement from #5 to #7 can occur partly by (1) tapping and helping to direct or redirect the SMOs' motivations, especially those involving the *primary* goals (A_{1g}, etc.), by (2) helping those individuals develop new skills, interests, and understandings, and—given those youths' also-increased confidence and willingness to face certain situations or challenges—by then (3) helping them concretely apply and refine their skills and their

new or growing interests and understandings within everyday settings. This last thus involves direct, experiential learning and reinforcement, generally outside of institutions.

#6 Short-Range, Immediate Reduction and/or Elimination of Illegal Behavior and of Closely Related Adjustment Patterns

External controls, and punishment, can substantially contribute to this reduction/elimination. This especially applies not only when such controls are used carefully and humanely, but when—simultaneously—they are an integral part of the broader input itself, in this case content-areas intervention.

#7 Achievement of, or Approach to, the Long-Range Secondary Goals

Even an *approach* to either such goal can help lay a foundation for factor #8 that is considerably stronger than that which would result from the achievement of #5 and #6 alone. With most SMOs, substantial movement beyond #5 (and, of course, #6) to a relatively stable #8 (not just #7) generally seems to require at least the following: A continued application, with results that are largely rewarding rather than frustrating to the youths, of various skills and interests that helped those individuals achieve #5 itself. At any rate, subsequent to the individuals' reaching #5, those or other skills/interests would have been tested, and sometimes modified, in connection with more adult-oriented contexts and expectations. Also, the changes and progress in question would usually require continued reduction of pre-factor #3 vulnerabilities and of related defenses, including ones that were already substantially lessened as part of achieving #5.

#8 Long-Range, i.e., Relatively Stable, Reduction or Elimination of Illegal Behavior and of Closely Related Adjustment Patterns and Life-Styles

This includes a reduction, in the frequency and severity of illegal behavior, over and beyond that achieved in factor #6.

To most correctional and corrections-related individuals, the relationship of maximum concern or importance is that between factor #3 and its two-steps-removed #6, that is, between "content-areas intervention," as input, and "short-range, immediate reduction . . . of illegal behavior," as an output. The relationship of next largest concern involves factors #3 and #8, that is, CAI and "long-range . . . reduction." With many CCRIs, the #3/#6 relationship is a close second in terms of importance, and with some it is equal or even primary. With many others, however, #3's relationship to #8 is a distant second to that of #6. In line with this view, and usually together with their belief that CAI's influence on overall illegal behavior is only modest anyway, these latter individuals seldom give more than a moderate amount of resources, specific attention, and other active effort to the long-range, law-centered goal (#8), and to content-areas intervention (#3) in particular.

Also, many CCRIs who feel those long-range behavioral goals *are* important, whether as a close second or not, believe or assume the following (this applies whether or not they (a) regard CAI as the principal contributor to the achievement of #6 and perhaps #8 and (b) give that approach [either its less complex or its more comprehensive variety] much specific attention): Most reductions of illegal behavior that occur soon after release to parole, or else early in a community-based, in-lieu-of-lockup program, will adequately or entirely hold up long after that parole or in-lieu intervention ends. More precisely, they will continue to exist after the program is completed if they were maintained for, say, the next six to 12 consecutive months *of* the program (after which point or period most CCRIs would feel those youths could be discharged).[78] As implied earlier, this would apply even if, in those CCRIs' view, that initial reduction, and its subsequent maintenance for those several or many months, had been largely or perhaps even entirely produced by (1) a punishment/controls approach or even via a p/c component that was part of, yet which dominated, some other approach, rather than by (2) content-areas intervention overall, that is, via #3 in concert with, but not dominated by, p/c.[79]

Understanding CAI's Contribution to Selected Factors

Regardless of how some of the above CCRIs view factor #8's importance as compared to #6's, the broader situation regarding *content-areas intervention* is as follows (this is not limited to persons who believe #6 and #8 can be achieved, or only achieved, via input [1], above, that is, essentially by p/c): Many

CCRIs do not realize that CAI—input (2)—can have considerably more influence than they think it can have, on the short-range (#6) as well as long-range (#8) reduction/elimination of illegal behavior.[80] As a result, they give it little attention and their active support of it is no more than slight to moderate. Two broad reasons for their believing one cannot adequately reach #6 or #8 via CAI (factor #3) might be mentioned. First, these individuals are unaware of, or do not understand, the intermediate steps (factors #4, #5, etc.); in this respect, they do not recognize certain major ways in which—in effect, processes by which—one can move from #3 to #6 or #8. Second, although these CCRIs (or some of them) may, instead, *be* aware of those factors and may conceptualize them accurately as well, they do not accept their respective and/or cumulative *ability*—in the context of CAI—to help achieve #6 and #8. That is, regarding this second reason, they do not accept, or are perhaps even unaware of, the degree to which #4 and/or #5—as products of #3 (CAI)—can contribute to the process of helping youths achieve those short- and long-range, law-centered goals.

In sum, this suggests that many CCRIs would be more likely to support CAI or support it more strongly if they could better recognize and understand its bearing on #6 and #8. That recognition would be likelier to occur if, in the first place, they not only had a clearer or fuller picture of the intermediate steps involved in moving from CAI to both those law-centered goals, but if they realized that CAI, in particular, could be a critical force in generating and sustaining those steps, and, therefore, that movement. In this regard, those individuals would have to see it as stronger or potentially stronger than they presently do. This altered, more accurate or complete view of CAI's role and strength would be more likely to exist if those CCRIs recognized most or all of that approach's following contributions regarding factors #2, #4, #5, and #7, collectively.

1. CAI can, and often does, substantially help SMOs deal with *external and/or internal difficulties/problems (factor #2)*—most of which had hampered and would continue to hamper those individuals' everyday functioning and ongoing adjust-

ment, many of which still trigger and/or help maintain their illegal behavior, and many of which do both. Its assistance in this regard can be direct, indirect, or both.

2. As content-areas intervention helps reduce some of the preceding obstacles to prosocial functioning/adjustment, and as it reduces stimuli that help trigger or maintain illegal behavior, substantial movement can and generally does occur along the *salient dimensions (factor #4)*. When this movement or change is largely rewarding to the youths and/or does not overwhelm them with fear of consequences, it, in turn, usually paves the way for *continued* movement. More specifically, the *earlier* movement largely centers on improvement with respect to reducing or neutralizing "negatives," especially various external and internal obstacles, conditions, and resistance. However, the *continued* movement, that is, the further change, involves not only more such movement, namely, more reduction of negatives; instead, it also involves the development, improvement, and/or increased utilization of "positives," such as practical skills. Also involved at this early stage—at least, often involved—are the beginnings of more positive interpersonal relationships, including new and perhaps clearer perceptions of adults. Thus, by helping SMOs reduce/overcome obstacles and by lessening related energy-consuming pressures and concerns,[81] content-areas intervention can, and commonly does, help free SMOs enough to where they begin directing increased attention to prosocial activities and requirements and to related developmental matters.[82]

3. By not only continuing or at least maintaining the earlier-mentioned changes/improvements that involve the reduction of "negatives," but by also building on the progress that involves "positives" (e.g., by helping youths accumulate and then partially consolidate their various gains), CAI can help those individuals reach the point described as the achievement or near-achievement of the *short-range secondary goals (factor #5)*.[83, 84]

4. While helping SMOs maintain, strengthen, and expand various gains involved in the achievement of factor #5,

content-areas intervention can also help those individuals move toward the *long-range secondaries (factor #7)*. Moreover, it can do so increasingly, if and as those youths' ambivalence about relinquishing prior adjustment patterns is decreased or continues to decrease, and if their energy available for moving forward is increased or at least maintained.

If the preceding contributions by the CAI approach were recognized as such by given CCRIs, this, as suggested, would make these individuals more likely to view this approach as strong and relevant enough to help SMOs achieve the *adjustment- and growth-centered goals* (factors #5 and #7).[85] However, before those individuals would be more likely to consider that same approach a major contributor to the *law-centered goals* (factors #6 and #8), that is, to the reduction/elimination of illegal behavior per se, they would have to recognize and accept two relationships:

Relationship A: Some—often many— of the youths' external and/or internal difficulties/problems trigger and/or help maintain those individuals' *illegal behavior,* or much of it. (In those respects, these D/Ps "cause" or help support that behavior; this is the case even when they or their predecessors are not also its main *original* sources or generators.)[86] This applies to the youths' closely related adjustment patterns, as well.

Relationship B: Content-areas intervention can help reduce or neutralize many such *difficulties/problems,* including ones that individually or collectively trigger/maintain the illegal behavior.

Given that recognition and acceptance, the CCRIs in question could more easily draw the following, valid conclusion: Insofar as content-areas intervention helps reduce given *difficulties/problems* and insofar as some of those D/Ps—absent that reduction—play a key role in triggering/maintaining given *illegal behavior,* that *CAI* can reduce not just those difficulties/problems but the illegal behavior itself, or at least much of it. That is, it can do so by impacting the *D/Ps*—these being conditions or stimuli that have previously (especially recently) triggered/maintained such behavior and which either seem quite capable of still doing so or that may well *be* doing so to some degree.[87]

Expressions of CAI's Strength

Thus, if they recognized contributions 1 through 4 (above), and if they accepted relationships A and B, many CCRIs would be more likely to view content-areas intervention as having enough *strength* to move youths toward the goals of (a) personal/social adjustment and growth and (b) reduced illegal behavior, and to often help them reach these goals.[88] (The perceived instrumental and/or intrinsic value of (a) and (b) is what already gives such intervention, and the movement it produces with respect to them, its *relevance* and *importance,* in numerous CCRIs' view.) The nature of contributions 1 through 4 indicates that CAI's strength, that is, its force, helps produce various types of *movement* in SMOs; involved, for example, is these individuals' below-mentioned "release," their subsequent advancement, and their still later consolidation.[89] It is in and through such movement that content-areas intervention produces its main results. These results span three broad areas or domains—specifically, those centering on "*negatives,*" on "*positive[s],*" and on what might be viewed as *further* positives. Each area is mentioned immediately below, together with its type or types of movement. These areas—individually and especially collectively—are integral to goals (a) and (b) themselves.

Initially, CAI's strength results in the release, the diverting, and so on, of SMOs from major *negatives.* As described, these are external and/or internal conditions or stimuli (forces) that—especially collectively—would otherwise disrupt those individuals' overall functioning, would play a key role in their illegal behavior, and would generally lead them to fall farther and farther behind, socially-developmentally.

Next, that strength results in the youths' advancing in *positive* respects per se. With any given individual, this usually involves some of the following changes or gains, most of which are likely to be interrelated: (a) development or augmentation of practical and interpersonal skills; (b) increased self-confidence, self-control, and self-respect; (c) better overall understanding of oneself and one's situation; (d) changed perceptions of and attitudes toward others; (e) increased social and interpersonal supports or utilization of available ones; and, (f) more focused, and/or differently directed, motivation.[90]

Finally, especially in later stages of relatively comprehensive intervention, CAI's strength helps those youths maintain, apply, increase, and/or consolidate the given changes or gains (e.g., [a] through [e], above), helps them add one or more (e.g., [f]), and perhaps helps them reassert or regain any that become weakened or lost (e.g., [b] or [d]). In so doing, this approach helps those individuals move forward, or at least "keep trying" in that regard. Such progress or efforts frequently occur despite new, objectively and/or subjectively difficult challenges faced by the youths. Common among these challenges are ones that may have accentuated or reactivated vulnerabilities or deficiencies which, though having been markedly reduced, still exist. Some of *these,* in turn, may then have revived or reinforced the youths' underlying or residual ambivalence about relinquishing certain adjustment patterns; and/or they may have heightened various reservations about moving ahead.[91] (Some challenges may have involved, or arisen from, changes in the nature or extent of the individuals' external supports, themselves.)

Across these three areas, then, CAI's strength is utilized and expressed in an essentially sequential way. This is the case even though, with many SMOs, movement in the first area has some temporal overlap with that in the second—as is true across the second and third areas as well. In addition, but not unrelated, the latter two areas sometimes have moderate *substantive* overlap; and finally, regarding the three areas collectively, CAI's products are cumulative.

The main elements and the usual sequence that underlie the earlier-mentioned perceptions of strength may be summarized as follows: Starting with its impact on factor #2 (difficulties/problems), content-areas intervention can help SMOs move toward, and achieve, #4, #5, and #7—major adjustment-and-growth objectives. As it does so, it can reduce or eliminate illegal behavior as well, both on an immediate basis (#6) and—later—a long-term basis (#8). It can achieve these latter goals, especially much of #6, partly because it reduces various "negatives" that are integral to, or have resulted from, the factor #2 difficulties/problems themselves; that is, it reduces conditions and forces which often trigger/maintain that behavior itself.[92] In addition, CAI can achieve those goals—namely, #6 and, especially, #8—via the "positive" movement and developments that usually follow its assistance with respect to those negatives.

The Difficulties/Problems Factor and Relationship A

In this sequence, the difficulties/problems factor is particularly critical, for two reasons. First, these D/Ps constitute obstacles that must be dealt with before most SMOs can make substantial progress regarding adjustment and growth.[93] Second, as per relationship A, above, various D/Ps "trigger and/or help maintain those [youths'] *illegal behavior.*" To many correctional and corrections-related individuals, the second reason would be the main one even if they considered the first important. Obviously, however, for those CCRIs to view that second reason as important *at all,* they would already have to consider relationship A *valid,* that is, factually correct; and this view is not one they necessarily, let alone almost always, accept.

These CCRIs would be more likely to accept A as valid, and to then consider its action implications important, if they first regarded those difficulties/problems as "strong," that is, as consequential and substantial in the sense of influential and durable, respectively.[94] The first sense emphasizes D/Ps' capacity as a contributor or causal agent (cf.: "setting the stage for" illegal behavior, and "triggering" it). The second emphasizes their tendency—again, mainly but not only collectively—to remain largely unchanged for long time spans and to keep exerting their negative and sometimes compounding influence throughout those periods (cf.: "maintaining" illegal behavior).

Structural Features Associated with D/Ps' Strength

Those CCRIs would be more likely to consider these difficulties/problems strong in both senses of the term if they realized that, with most individual SMOs, the D/Ps in question are—collectively—almost always characterized by at least the first two, and often by three or all four, of the following structural features (note: "components," below, refers to SMOs' *individual, i.e., respective, difficulties/problems* or to types of D/Ps; "level[s]" refers to differences in scope and/or in locus of operation, for instance, to narrowness versus breadth and/or to overt issues ["up-front" or surfaced issues] versus those operating largely, and often, below the surface):

1. *frequent complexity,* that is, a number of active—often-operating—components (not just potentially active ones), and/or more than one level across those components (note: regardless of level, some components often operate simultaneously and others have moderate to considerable temporal overlap during any given period of days or weeks);

2. *substantial interrelatedness,* that is, content overlap across some such components, and, in any event, mutual interaction and reinforcement among most or all of them (e.g., across and between [a] family pressures, on the one hand, and personal conflicts, on the other, and/or [b] various skill deficits, on the one hand, and low self-esteem, on the other);

3. *considerable overall scope (coverage),* that is, involvement or inclusion of two—often more—significant areas of the youth's life (involved—still—are all components collectively); and

4. *considerable intensity.* With any given individual, this feature exists especially when the first two or more are present to their usual degree ("frequently," "substantially," etc.), and even to a somewhat lesser one. More specifically, this level of intensity is an expression and product of those two or more structural features, operating jointly. However, at this and other levels, intensity in toto (as a whole), including its separable or particular aspects, also reflects certain *content* around which the SMOs' difficulties and problems center. For instance, that aspect of intensity which involves the individuals' strength of feeling can directly reflect and partly result from those youths' level, type of, and/or specific *skill deficits, external pressures, and/or personal conflicts.* In such respects, the content-based portion of overall intensity can thus be viewed as adding to the above-mentioned part, that is, to that which reflects and results from the structural features. ("Adding to" is discussed shortly.)

Even by themselves, structural features (1) and (2), when jointly present, commonly generate what might be described as considerable "entanglement" or "knottiness" across most difficulties/problems, collectively. (Some people compare this type of product or condition to "a can of worms.") This applies whatever the content of those D/Ps may be, for instance, regardless of its type, and even if it is atypical.

In sum, and temporarily setting aside the role and effects of content, it is via an awareness of (1) through (4), or at least (1) and (2), that many correctional and corrections-related individuals could consider SMOs' *difficulties/problems* sufficiently influential and durable to sometimes trigger and maintain illegal behavior; this is in addition to seeing them as hampering those youths' everyday functioning and perhaps slowing or stopping forward movement. By itself, an awareness of those structural features and of their frequent joint presence in any given SMO would not only help these CCRIs accept D/Ps as a force to be reckoned with; instead, it would also allow them to better understand major *bases* of those D/Ps' strength, including key contributors to the D/Ps' durability and, with that, to the continuation of their negative effects. The upshot is that such awareness of structural features would make these CCRIs more likely to accept relationship A as valid.

Content Issues Involved in D/Ps
The chances that this acceptance would occur would be further raised—often considerably so—if those CCRIs also became more aware of the earlier-mentioned *content,* more specifically, of issues involved in the youths' difficulties/problems. This further raising of those chances would be important for reasons such as the following, and in relation to the context then mentioned: Although, as just indicated, many CCRIs would already be "*more* likely to accept relationship A as valid," this "more," in itself, would not necessarily mean they would actually be *likely* or *very likely* to accept it; it would only mean they would be more likely than before. As indicated, this greater likelihood of acceptance—this "more"—would result, or would have resulted, from their having recognized the earlier-mentioned, *structural* features alone.

It is in relation to that context and structural-features baseline that those CCRIs' increased awareness of the content which comprises the youths' difficulties/problems

would, as indicated above, (1) *further* raise the chances in question, that is, would raise them above the "baseline" that resulted or that would result from those CCRIs' earlier-mentioned awareness of structural features alone. (The main content areas that comprise those youths' D/Ps are the already-mentioned *practical and interpersonal skills deficits, family/peer/environmental pressures,* and *personal conflicts.* Various *effects* of these factors, for example, types of complications that arise from them, will be called "content issues" or "content effects" and are discussed in Chapter 26.) Besides being a first step toward that outcome [here, "outcome (1)"], this increased awareness of such content areas—including some of their effects—would (2) simultaneously raise the chances that those CCRIs' acceptance of relationship A's validity *would* be "*likely* or *very likely*" to occur. Increased awareness, of course, would not guarantee these latter levels of acceptance, that is, those associated with "outcome (2)." It would, however, raise the chances of their occurring, if, say, they did not already exist in connection with the CCRIs' awareness of structural features alone.

Though increased awareness of the content areas' existence would be a precondition for outcomes (1) and (2) (more specifically, although such awareness would be needed in order to set the stage), those outcomes could actually occur only if a further condition existed: The CCRIs would have to see the content areas as *stronger and/or larger* than they otherwise would, or, perhaps [particularly regarding outcome (2)], as strong and/or large per se.

Keeping in mind that content issues or content effects are integral to many of the youths' difficulties/problems and that various such D/Ps, in turn, contribute greatly to those individuals' illegal behavior and related adjustment patterns, we now turn to the next chapter. There, such issues and relationships will be focused on and their implications for intervention will be mentioned. We will then return to the rationales for individualized intervention with those serious multiple offenders, particularly in connection with the content-areas or needs-centered approach.

Notes
1. Most SMOs can make important adaptations to various immediate pressures

even if they have achieved only a modest portion of the overall growth they will need in order to make considerable progress relative to establishing the workable, *long*-term future (this being the earlier-mentioned "challenge").

2. In a broad sense, this reduction, modification, and so on, can be considered an integral part of the overall positive change itself, even though it may be functioning as a precondition *to* or precursor *of* that eventual change.

3. To simplify the presentation, parent/child dynamics or psychodynamics and the types of emotional learning often associated with them will be subsumed under "acculturation." Similarly, the former processes and products will not be specifically distinguished from those relating to "social learning," or, equivalently, "social/interpersonal" learning.

4. Later, after the very early years, simple conditioning is increasingly accompanied by various forms of cognitive learning or cognitive restructuring.

5. This right can exist even though the youths may conceptualize neither it nor the related desire, and its objects, as such.

6. Later, the individuals can take steps specifically designed to help themselves develop in ways that will broadly increase their chances of eventually achieving their goals, in various social contexts.

7. Being "predisposed" does not necessarily mean they act, ultimately, as automatons. In particular, they are not driven—not largely or entirely forced (as in "against their wills")—to satisfy any or all such goals, in one way or another, in order, ultimately, to just reduce physiological, psychological, or other tensions. To be sure, such tension reduction does play an important and often dominant role, particularly, but not only, in young children. Nevertheless, the developing individuals' increasingly strong ego, or, say, their desire to self-direct, plays more and more of a prime-determiner role. (This desire is often accompanied by a larger repertoire of constructive choices, of adaptation techniques, and of related information, and by an increased overall ability to *make* many of the given choices and to apply that information.)

8. Regarding those rights, youths should be seen as striving for something that is appropriate and proper, not just "to be tolerated." In this respect, the individuals would *themselves* be considered legitimate and acceptable, not just persons to "tolerate."

9. This being so, the original right to strive for goals A through C would not derive from that particular aspect—the deeds- or achievement-based aspect—of "deservedness." It would, however, relate to considerations that the youths may be said to warrant because they are human—or, for instance, because the goals in question also serve as needs which, if adequately addressed, can contribute to those individuals' basic functioning and personal benefit *as* human beings. In addition, these individuals would be more likely to eventually contribute to society itself if they were to actualize various human potentials rather than *not* develop and/or use them.

All of the preceding applies regardless of the following: (1) Particularly when viewed as preconditions—that is, not as end-states, such as item 2(a) in the text above—goals A through C would often be considered "needs" in the sense of "being needed for," that is, as important or essential *means* to some other end or ends. (2) The goals in question could be considered important/essential means, as in 2(b), even if they are not also viewed as first existing prior to substantial acculturation.

Regarding the right to *seek* those goals—at least the preacculturation, original right to do so—this, itself, would be "natural" in the sense that it would not have to first be earned on the basis of one's social behavior, one's intentions, and/or one's accomplishments. That aside, many people nevertheless implicitly assume that, once individuals reach or approach adolescence, they must behave in ways that earn them the right to *continue* seeking or deserving goals A through C. In other words, their underlying view is mainly that the right—the original, preacculturation right in question (granting that it exists)—does not automatically remain in force, whether largely or entirely.

Moreover, even if those individuals possessed that right "originally" or naturally, they could, from this perspective, still lose it or partly lose it because of what they may or may not have done afterward. In effect, whatever original right may be said or conceded to exist, it may, to all intents and purposes, later no longer do so or entirely do so. Instead, it either is or, at least, legitimately can be essentially suspended, or curtailed, by virtue of new social realities, expectations, limitations, or external demands.

10. More precisely, such goals are viewed as justified when sought, achieved, and/or maintained without intended harm to individuals and/or groups, and without actual harm as well. Moreover, they are considered justified even if they do not specifically *help* other individuals attain those same or related goals. They are, however, implicitly considered even more justified if they do help others or are intended to do so. At any rate, such goals are considered appropriate in principle, that is, as goals in themselves; still, as indicated, they require the above conditions in actual practice, that is, in real life.

11. Some forms and substantial degrees of harm to others, or loss on their parts, are often difficult or impossible to avoid. This, for instance, is the case if one chooses to seriously play certain roles in societies that approve, reinforce, and otherwise support or clearly accept given types of "victory" over others. Involved, for example, are "victories" in various commercial enterprises and related interpersonal exchanges. (Here, the concept of "zero-sum" applies: for one party to "win," another must—or will— "lose.") Thus, in numerous everyday contexts, some principles of fairness are commonly honored in the breach, say, by many nonoffending adults who help comprise the general public within those societies.

12. Namely, that of social well-being or at least relative equilibrium.

13. Individually and collectively, these points do not imply that any one or more of society's interests either are or automatically should be the "final word" when differences of almost any kind arise between society and the youth. Nor does it imply that the society should have complete or otherwise overwhelming moral or other dominion—including, in any event, the power and authority to largely, let alone entirely and unconditionally, determine the individuals' major decisions or directions in life. Both points apply whether one focuses on a society's dominant component or on its various subgroups/subcultures. In turn, all this differs from saying that the overall society should not have a decisive ability and authority to protect individuals and groups against certain injurious acts of other individuals, and groups, toward them.

14. When it is considered appropriate and important for one person to cooperate with others, for example, to help or allow them to meet *their* needs, that person is commonly said to have an "obligation" to do so. (This includes but goes beyond such matters as returning a favor or fulfilling an explicit or implicit contract; it also involves more than or other than simple convenience, and more than a way of furthering one's own concrete ends.) In such contexts, few people would feel there is any question about those youths having a concurrent, instrumental need—and, hence, a right—to take certain steps that would help them meet the obligation. A direct parallel exists regarding the youths' having a right to take steps that are needed in order to address *personal* needs—as well as the earlier-mentioned expectations—that are considered appropriate. At any rate, even when obligations per se are *not* at issue, most people would agree that if certain means or conditions are needed in order to help achieve various important or required ends, individuals have or should have a right to obtain or create the needed means/conditions. To some extent, obligations to others can be separated from certain abstract obligations one might be said to have mainly to oneself. Among the latter, for instance, would be an obligation to actualize one's potentials, to achieve one's goals or strivings, and so on—in each case, to the extent possible and feasible. It can, of course, be maintained that an important aspect of actualizing one's potential—or, say, certain human potentials—is that of

learning to assist *other* humans, and of then trying to do so.

15. The latter's wishes and the former's (youths') needs often coincide or substantially overlap in connection with the concrete steps that may be taken to help establish a practical basis for the youths' long-range economic security or relative security. For instance, they overlap regarding the need for vocational and/or academic training.

16. Challenging them, and so forth, often differs from temporarily ignoring them and from mainly putting them "on hold."

17. Here, "concurrent" means they coexist with other wishes and/or needs, ones that were elaborated after early, middle, and later childhood. (As elsewhere, the overall childhood era is distinguished from those of adolescence and adulthood.)

18. The "original" goals/needs are those which existed in the youths from very early childhood and that were soon channeled, focused, often intensified, and, in effect, organized—via externally initiated and directed social learning, conditioning, and the like. They are not ultimately separate and distinct from goals which those individuals may consciously seek when accommodating *adolescent*-era expectations. At that point, the original goals/needs often exist beneath the surface content of these later ones.

19. For youths, and most adults, one of their broad life challenges is that of blending those underlying, long-standing motivators with some of the content and requirements, for instance, the "what's" and "how's," that comprise the new external realities—the latter being expectations associated with adolescence in the particular culture/subculture.

20. In given marital and other conjoint living arrangements, the economic basis could be alternatively called "constructive interdependence."

21. However, as suggested in Chapter 29, a large and influential part of the public has sizable reservations about whether C_{1g} is a legitimate and/or important goal of intervention for most SMOs. For many people in this subgroup, these reservations partly spring from their feeling that the youths no longer deserve much pleasure or enjoyment. With some of these latter individuals it also partly reflects their implicit assumption that in order to adequately control most SMOs' illegal behavior, program resources need not be directed at achieving that goal, even if the goal—like A_{1g} and B_{1g}—*is* still slightly deserved. With both such groups, that assumption is frequently one they have absorbed—have accepted tacitly, globally, and often without substantial reflection—from TV, newspaper, and other media assertions/quotations by or from various policymakers and other professionals within and outside corrections. Similar reservations, usually ones that are more explicit, exist among a sizable portion of correctional and law enforcement policymakers, administrators, and academicians, and even among many line and supervisory staff.

22. As was the case with "moderates," the issues of "importance and relevance" relate, respectively, to dimension B's (1) intervention-centered implications— say, its actual treatment-planning and treatment-implementation implications— and to its (2) rationales-for-intervention implications or functions. (Following is a restatement and simplification: In the case of more serious factors/motives, "importance" relates to point (1) and "relevance" refers to (2).)

23. In some respects, the salient dimensions, particularly A_{sd}, are integral parts of, not separate from and antecedent to, certain aspects of these secondary goals.

24. C_{2g} and D_{2g} are more directly and concretely "linked" to the *primary* goals than are A_{2g} and B_{2g}. More specifically, they are linked to the two such goals— B_{1g} and C_{1g} ("acceptance by others"; "pleasure/enjoyment")—that are part of one's conscious strivings for happiness. "Acceptance . . ." also includes or merges with status, esteem, recognition, being liked, and being loved—these, as a result of what one has done, is like, values, and does/feels for others. "Pleasure . . ." includes exploration, release, excitement, sex, and so on.

25. This is the case even though they rarely conceptualize the former as such, yet

intuitively do recognize the latter as goals.

26. Both the encouragement and commendation can come from various "live sources," and via general social/cultural messages. (They need not come mainly, or even at all, from parents and/or peers, though they sometimes do.) In contemporary society such messages are transmitted by a wide range of methods and in many contexts; they are often concretized, for the receivers, in terms of well-known persons who overcame hardships, met major challenges, and so on. This general encouragement, still with respect to nonoffenders, is often backed with specific assistance.

27. This general acceptance exists, and youths believe it exists, even when society's concrete support is no more than moderate—that is, when, in that respect, its actions do not match its verbalizations and implied principle of acceptance.

28. Thus, the present adults do not necessarily fault these individuals for being unsuccessful or largely unsuccessful in their efforts. Rather, their focus is on how much the youths *tried*.

29. As to undoing negative impacts of one's actions on other individuals, obligation centers on those others, not on oneself.

30. This applies (1) especially, but not only, if the conditions are seen as being or as having been "unfairly" limiting, and (2) whether or not—not only *if*—"adjust[ing] well to life" involves the individuals' later playing a particularly constructive role in society. (Regarding the given opportunities, these are usually available in wide segments of society and are considered legitimate at least with respect to legality and nondestructiveness.)

31. And, if they do, regardless of its degree and actual or presumed major sources.

32. It implies this prior to any reluctance, on the youths' part, about changing; and in that respect it implies the following (see text), in the first place.

33. This would also apply if the impulse itself were regarded as largely socially learned rather than "natural"—specifically, "natural" in the sense of being inborn and original, or at least existing prior to any substantial acculturation

(whether or not it was eventually intensified or otherwise magnified, through various social and personal inputs).

34. Such adjustment includes physical and emotional emancipation—opposites of dependency or overdependency—whether from parents or negative peers. It also includes sufficient self-reliance.

35. Understandably, most adults would like this change process to take place more rapidly, and it not infrequently does. In any event, of these adults, a sizable subgroup believes, and hopes, that a rapid or sudden change, a "turnaround," or even a seeming conversion *could* in fact occur very often. For instance, the latter assume that such a change could, and would, take place largely via the youths' "force of will"—use of willpower—even if that power might first have to be activated via encouragement or urging from various external sources and individuals. (See Chapters 29 and 30 regarding willpower.)

36. The focus on positive goals often has considerable temporal overlap with the first-mentioned efforts themselves; that is, that focus does not get underway only after the latter have been completed or largely completed. At any rate, progress in dealing with major negatives is often needed before various types and degrees of progress can *set in* with respect to the positives.

37. As implied earlier, this pursuit is usually considered appropriate if it is not largely a self-centered enterprise that knowingly involves actual or likely physical, psychological, or material injury to or loss for others. (To be sure, many youths may have to make parents or peers generally unhappy—temporarily or otherwise—in order to make major progress with respect to their own growth-related needs, for example, to achieve given types/levels of emotional independence.) Yet, certain types and amounts of loss, and of nonphysical injury (among other things), are, in effect, often "allowed," and these dimensions vary across cultures and through time: In some cultures and even subcultures, it is, for instance, more acceptable or at least allowable than in others to "take advantage" of persons with whom one *competes*—say, as part

of advancing one's material interests, of generally pursuing happiness, and so on. At any rate, in what is commonly called the *real* world within those cultures, "appropriate" and "allowable" are often determined or defined quite situationally, besides, of course, consensually; and in both regards, contradictions and logic-tight compartments—as distinct from gray areas and simple ambiguities—frequently exist between, and among, some of those cultures' professed ideals and many of their actual, daily practices.

38. With serious multiple offenders, however, many adults are not sure if the primaries and secondaries can *often* be achieved—and achieved to an adequate degree—apart from intervention. In our view, progress regarding both types of goals is less likely to be sizable and sufficient, and much less likely to be relatively stable in any event, if well-implemented, relevant intervention does not occur. As to the secondary goals in particular, this especially applies to C and D (C_{2g} and D_{2g}).

39. Depending on one's assumptions and perspectives, one could think of the primary goals, especially collectively, in either of the following terms: (1) as essentially impersonal, built-in motivators that—served *by* the individuals' consciousness or ego, and regardless of the cultures' particular content and inputs—largely drive those youths and, for the most part, determine many key aspects of their lives; (2) as states or conditions which those individuals—by focusing and otherwise purposely using their mind and/or ego—mainly *choose* to strive for in one form or another. As implied, sets (1) and (2) can each operate even when postinfancy acculturation has played an important role in shaping and channeling the various strivings (cf. desired states of mind, and conscious or preconscious motives), and in setting their intensity levels as well. Though built-in motivators and self-determined actions can mutually coexist, particularly in the postinfancy individual, and although their overall strength vis-à-vis each other can change from one era to another, such as from childhood to adolescence (and within eras as well), we will emphasize set (2). This does not mean the youths in question always, or almost always, *fully*—not to mention immediately—control their actions and responses, that is, control them via their conscious strivings, decisions, and so on. Nevertheless, it leaves room for substantial, in fact decisive amounts of, self-determined action, especially, but not only, on an accumulative basis.

40. The issues that surround the factors of "justification," "importance," and "right" each relate not only to the youths' social or interpersonal functioning and behavior but to their personal satisfaction/growth as well—in both cases, short-term and long.

41. This does not mean they would necessarily regard those efforts, on their own, as *sufficient* with respect to achieving given goals, or that those efforts would in fact usually suffice.

42. This applies to youths in general and to serious multiple offenders in particular. Regarding the SMOs, it applies whether the intensity and extent of their negative life situation and of their personal difficulties/conflicts are well above or well below average.

43. The second view would be likelier to exist, that is, likelier than otherwise, if those correctional personnel also believed the following: (1) Serious multiple offenders should not only be held closely accountable for eliminating or greatly reducing their negative, illegal, and/or destructive behaviors; rather, they should also be pressed and strongly encouraged to change/improve major elements of their life-style whose contents extend beyond that of the behaviors alone, yet which contribute to them. In this regard, those individuals should have the wherewithal and other means, abilities, and opportunities that are needed in order to *make* the changes for which they would be held accountable. (2) The given efforts and services would significantly raise the chances of producing—for example, of helping those individuals actually achieve—the various reductions, changes, and so on.

44. The existence and/or availability of those and other resources itself reflects policymakers' and administrators' willingness

to create them, to allocate or reallocate them, and to specifically apply them, in the first place. Similarly, line staffs' and supervisors' attitudes regarding the relevance and potential influence of given content areas can largely determine their willingness to persistently *seek* needed resources and conditions, and, in any event, to make the most of what they already have.

45. Again, this emphasizes, but is not limited to, pragmatic appropriateness. It is not anchored in that view of deservedness which centers on such factors as earned privileges and rights.

46. This does not mean they might not strengthen whatever curtailment may have occurred by other means. However, Group 2 CCRIs do not focus on this point.

47. This especially applies insofar as these CCRIs regard those areas as possible means to the above ends, and as little other than that; also, this is how those individuals often *do* regard them.

48. As implied earlier, some Group 2 individuals view the short-term secondaries as moderately to fairly important. In this case, the content areas as well as the salient dimensions are considered more important than they otherwise would be. Yet, even here, their respective priorities are seldom high.

49. That is, the latter individuals moderately support Area A: personal/interpersonal skills development.

50. Though this usually applies to the idea of any change at all, it sometimes pertains to that of substantial change instead.

51. Given their membership in Group 3, these individuals implicitly accept, or otherwise take for granted, the secondary *goals*.

52. Many such youths, they believe, also need credible threats, or fear, of continued or future PHEC. Collectively, the threats may be implicit and/or explicit.

53. This applies whether or not correctional approaches/inputs that those CCRIs have in mind in connection with the youths' subsequent use of willpower chiefly involve forms of punishment and external control that are then considered *standard* in the sense of being common and generally accepted within the field.

54. These individuals do not necessarily assume that most correctional and corrections-related agencies/organizations can successfully mount such an effort, in the first place. However, that is not their concern here. Nor does the present issue center on whether corrections and the juvenile justice system are the best setting for that effort, or are even an appropriate one.

55. Some individuals within the SG 2 group believe that content-areas intervention is somewhat stronger than do others in that subgroup—stronger with respect to addressing growth-and-adaptation issues. (This strength applies to CAI's overall effort, not just that involving Area A.) However, both sets of individuals feel that progress in this regard will usually be no more than modest or perhaps moderate; and, both believe CAI's ability to curb *illegal behavior* is inadequate and/or too slow, in any event.

56. Whether they view the strength of these past, present, and future links as considerable or moderate, they generally do not dwell on their implications or possible implications for correctional intervention.

57. The following might be added regarding the beliefs and assumptions of these CCRIs—SG 2's: Little or no critical difference would be made in curbing illegal behavior—in fact, only a little more such behavior would be curbed—if the external controls and resulting self-controls themselves produced (say, as spinoffs) *other* types of substantial change, such as the earlier-mentioned growth. The latter change could even include and emphasize personal/interpersonal development and adaptation, through which, and in terms of which, the individuals would move toward the longer-range secondaries (C_{2g} and D_{2g}).

58. Area A, however, is often an exception. (See Chapters 29 and 30.)

59. A comparatively small percentage to whom point A applies believes there would be *little or no* reduction in illegal behavior under the given conditions, particularly if there were no extra external controls. These individuals will not be focused on here.

60. To the preponderance of SG 3's, these youths did not forfeit those rights/

privileges because of their overall lifestyles or their related attitudes per se, even if these were generally antisocial, asocial, and/or hostile. Instead, the "forfeiture" resulted from their illegal behavior alone.

61. Many SG 3's believe a punishment-and-external-controls approach is called for not only, or not mainly, because SMOs do not deserve or sufficiently deserve *something else*—in this case, content-areas intervention that seriously focuses on the secondary goals. Rather, they believe it should be given because of what they think SMOs *do* deserve: punishment/control, itself. To these SG 3's, this approach is often considered justified because it implements/expresses a major aspect of deservedness, namely, "just desert." This aspect is often dealt with separately from (1) the role or potential role that a punishment/controls approach can play in implementing/expressing incapacitation and/or deterrence per se, and from (2) whether that p/c approach plays a major or otherwise substantial role in actually reducing individuals' *illegal behavior*—say, to a relatively low level. Though incapacitation, general deterrence, and/or specific deterrence are often kept separate from just desert, and although they are, in any event, neither intrinsic to nor exclusive to that aspect of deservedness, they are, nevertheless, often used as supplementary components of this feature's justification.

62. Most CCRIs from SGs 1 and 2 believe SMOs should face such consequences as well, as do the CCRIs who comprise *Groups* 1 and 2.

63. It does not follow that this degree and scope will be enough to successfully address certain major needs and issues on the part of many SMOs.

64. This, of course, is aside from the fact that each approach can include elements of the other.

65. Together with efforts that center on illegal behavior per se, progress along step 1's personal, interpersonal, and/or other lines (*see* Areas C, B, and A) can very often produce not only a short-term reduction in such behavior. Instead, and especially, when that progress is *followed*

up, as in step 3, it can often lead to—or, at least, substantially pave the way for—relatively long-term reductions as well. With such followups, the chances are often greater that the reductions will involve decreased severity, not just a lowered rate. ("Focusing on" factors that closely relate to the individuals' illegal behavior and that otherwise directly bear on them includes addressing that behavior's main underlying, triggering, and/or sustaining conditions.) With many SMOs who have more serious difficulties than average, the following applies: Relatively *sustained* reductions of illegal behavior almost only occur when (1) considerable personal/interpersonal growth—as against early-progress/consolidation alone—takes place, and when (2) the individual has moved toward the secondary goals or is in a fairly good position to do so.

66. Step 4 movement is more likely to begin, in the first place, and to continue with few major disruptions, in the second, if, during steps 2 and 3, the youths have had some "breathing room" and opportunities to consolidate various gains. At any rate, even when it occurs while elements of step 3 are still active and while various gains are far from consolidated, step 4 can help SMOs socially and psychologically grow and develop in ways that advance them toward, and even begin converging on, the long-range secondaries. (Toward this end, the number and content-range of the step 3 changes that are involved [see "increased self-confidence, . . . less anger toward, and/or greater comfort with others"] is less important than the *relevance* of those and/or other changes to the respective individuals' dynamics and life situations.) In any event, step 4 can help them maintain the realistic possibility or even likelihood of achieving the long-range secondaries within their relatively near future, for example, a few years.

67. Additional reasons are as follows: (1) The shared features, especially when combined with each other, make these individuals different enough from Groups 1, 2, and 3; (2) "moderates," like those three groups respectively, also constitute a sizable "voice" in corrections; and,

(3) moderates' views concerning CAI have—again like those of the preceding groups—implications for the next chapter's final sections.

68. This goes beyond making them aware of such a path, helping arouse their interest in it or their curiosity about it, and getting them generally "pointed" in the given direction or possibly even started in terms of trying themselves out in relation to it and to its usual roles. Thus, it does not get well into step 4.

69. One exception would involve situations in which the individuals are already somewhat established along such a path at point of intake. This is sometimes seen among older and/or more psychosocially advanced offenders. Nevertheless, even these individuals may have considerable difficulty or ambivalence about moving *further* along that path.

70. Both points are largely independent of a further, less influential reason, one that springs from largely implicit assumptions by many such CCRIs: SMOs, as persons living in free society or as ones who will eventually return to it, have legitimate adjustment needs that they should be capable of meeting, and, hence, should have adequate preparation for meeting. These needs and needed capabilities are thought to exist even though the CCRIs believe that most SMOs, because of their illegal behavior, have lost—or have at least had reduced—various *rights* and *privileges*. (Sometimes, those adjustment needs become objectively and/or psychologically larger or more intense and urgent partly *because* other persons feel those rights/privileges have been lost or reduced, and because they then take certain actions based on those and related feelings. This applies whether or not those rights and privileges bear directly on what is needed in order to make the adequate preparations.) Various internal and external *obstacles* to meeting those adjustment needs and to the given preparations can be focused on via the above resources and efforts, as can some preparations themselves. Group 4 individuals, like many in Group 1, believe it makes sense to focus on key obstacles right away, while a reasonable chance to do so exists and when resulting success in this

regard can have considerable overall impact. This applies to "preparations" as well—a focus that includes, for instance, helping the youths build necessary or useful practical and interpersonal skills—as in Area A.

Thus, most Group 4 CCRIs have multiple, even mixed, views concerning the rationale for intervention, both as to its type and amount. In this regard their rationale does not center on a highly dominant core; and it is not based on any single, commonly recognizable ideology or principle alone.

71. This point is independent of these individuals' view that most SMOs do not deserve a relatively *small* amount of such assistance either, in connection with the long-range goal. (In short, they deserve *some*—not very little—but not a *lot*.)

72. Restated with respect to *needs* per se, Group 4 CCRIs believe that *most* SMOs have needs which, (1) while substantial, and though serious in their implications, are (2) usually not *highly* intensive, extensive, and/or complex. This second belief is directly reflected in these CCRIs' assumption that content-areas intervention, itself, need not be similarly intensive, extensive, and so on. At the same time, Group 4 individuals believe a *small* percentage of SMOs have negative attitudes that are deeply entrenched, or that they have "character flaws or 'defects'" which are very deep-seated, possibly unalterable, or barely alterable. Various *other* CCRIs believe these features—though extreme in themselves—characterize *most* SMOs, and that, as a result, only external controls, together with punishment and incapacitation, can adequately address the social protection issue. CAI, they believe, is largely useless with respect to significantly modifying those features.

73. These CCRIs assume that a moderate level of assistance—though it should be coordinated, otherwise carefully implemented, and, of course, relevant—may or may not have to be complex and relatively comprehensive. (From the perspective of this book, the present input is "moderate" in amount. From the perspective of Group 4 CCRIs it is substantial even to the point of "considerable,"

though still not "large.") At any rate, these individuals assume that the assistance in question requires few if any of the additional dimensions and/or further efforts that would be involved in helping most SMOs move substantially toward the *long*-range secondaries, if such movement was regarded as necessary and largely deserved.

Even offenders—say, a small portion of all SMOs—whom these CCRIs might view as *needing* the type and amount of effort generally called for in order to substantially help them move toward those goals would still be seen as far from entirely—or even largely—*deserving* of it. More specifically, these youths would be seen as not meriting the added efforts/dimensions needed to help them move—move beyond their achievement of A_{2g} and B_{2g}—substantially along a path that focuses on, or is at least compatible with, C_{2g} and D_{2g}.

74. Regarding "believe," see point (1) in the text that follows. Concerning "implicitly assume," see (2) and (3).

75. In both cases, "awareness" can be explicit or implicit. Here, "explicit" generally means conscious and focused, whether broadly or narrowly, and however clearly or vaguely the subject matter may be verbalized. "Implicit" can mean or refer to: (1) largely taken for granted or assumed, though rarely if ever thought about as such; (2) an *underlying* assumption, or, also, something that would directly follow from some other thought or assumption; and/or, (3) "intuitively" held or felt.

76. Most CCRIs accept the idea that at least a slight or moderate relationship exists among a number of factors, and that a substantial one exists or can exist among at least a few. (We are referring to the relationship between any two factors at a time; and several such two-factor sets exist, with each involving its own relationship.) Taken as a whole, this view nevertheless differs considerably from one which recognizes that a number of *fairly close* or even *very strong* relationships exist or can exist among those same adjacent or even more distant factors. Insofar as the latter view is more accurate than the former under given

conditions, it can be said that many CCRIs substantially underestimate those particular relationships. This occurs even when they recognize most or all of the eight factors that comprise the temporal sequence, recognize the particular *sequence* of factors in question, or given portions of that overall sequence, and, finally, recognize *which* factors can influence *which*.

As indicated and implied below (in text), many CCRIs *over*estimate the strength of certain relationships. This especially applies to that between (1) punishment/controls—whether this operates as a major component of a broader intervention or as an overall intervention approach itself—and (2) the reduction of illegal behavior on a long-range, that is, long-term, basis.

77. For instance, certain factors may sometimes branch out along additional paths (each one still involving a forward direction) more or less simultaneously—rather than first leading to the usual factor (i.e., the numerically "next higher" one), and only thereafter to the *next* one.

78. After holding up for those several or many months they could be considered "#6-reductions." Those which were maintained for well *beyond* the program—not just during, say, a program that was relatively long, for example, 18 to 24 months or more—would be "#8-reductions." Since #6- and #8-reductions are called short- and long-range ones respectively, reductions that held up during, i.e., throughout, those lengthy programs could be called "intermediates," particularly if post-program outcomes were unknown.

79. This would apply whether or not they saw CAI as almost always linking to #6 via #4 and/or #5, rather than as generating it directly.

80. As indicated and implied, long-range reductions are more likely to occur as a result of the more comprehensive forms of CAI, and they often require considerable progress with respect to factor #7. Even when the given CCRIs have a clear concept regarding the nature of the more comprehensive CAI, they often prefer to believe that, in order to reach #8, #7 can

be largely or entirely omitted and/or will often or usually occur largely automatically if only #5 and #6 occur. In these latter respects, they generally assume that SMOs will, at that or those points (viz., #5 or #6), have much the same motivation, available energy, and perhaps even sense of direction that most *nonoffenders* have, at comparable developmental points. At any rate, they are often unaware of these individuals' vulnerabilities and ambivalence; or, if these CCRIs *are* relatively aware of their existence, scope, and/or general strength, they nevertheless downplay their significance and implications with respect to further progress, and even regarding the maintenance of progress that has already occurred.

81. Collectively, these pressures and concerns are key ingredients of factor #2's and #4's "negatives"—negatives whose respective contents partly overlap.

82. Together with other factors, this reduction, overcoming, and lessening also helps *motivate* many youths to thus direct their attention and energies. This motivation is based more on desire than on fear or anxiety reduction.

83. To use a military or even biological analogy, CAI would first "crack through" or help the youths break down or neutralize given resistances. After that, the individuals would be able or better able to move forward, even though some resistance could and likely would regroup and reemerge.

84. By itself, a punishment/controls approach can seldom help SMOs substantially accumulate and consolidate those gains. This applies even if it induces, forces, or otherwise convinces and motivates those individuals to begin addressing various difficulties, life-styles, and personal attitudes as well as shortcomings. For such accumulation and consolidation to occur—even if *CAI* or other relevant approaches are present—the youths' motivation/willingness to make substantial changes and to stick with them is required (though this drive or stance need not emerge all at once). CAI can help those youths want to make the changes, and then maintain them, or at least make serious efforts along those lines.

85. Here, content-areas intervention—in its various contexts, phases, and capacities, collectively—would be serving as a generating (arousing), triggering (releasing), directing, and binding force. "Binding" would emphasize its role in mutually linking certain factors, processes, and products (e.g., #4 to #5, and #5 to #7) that have been activated, that are in progress, or that are largely achieved, and in thereby sustaining, building upon, and extending *existing* developments and growth. Once such factors, and so on, are fairly well established (individually), they can do the following (they can do so via the *youths' own* inputs/efforts, that is, via efforts that can occur not only together with but also partly over and beyond direct, continuing *CAI* inputs): They can function as new conditions and/or forces (see #4 and #5, respectively) that facilitate or actively contribute to *forward* movement and that help maintain already existing improvements, for example, with respect to overcoming negatives. This—the forward-movement component—can especially occur if staff has tapped and is able to substantially utilize, for instance, channel and help focus or organize, various key motives or motivators, such as primary goals that have helped sustain given factors and processes. (Here, positive staff/youth relationships can assist.)

86. Depending on the circumstances, those difficulties/problems, during adolescence, help bring, allow, and/or propel that illegal behavior to the surface, and can often help keep it there.

87. To be sure, some CCRIs believe the illegal behavior in question—and some related behavior—is mainly or substantially caused by factors other than those difficulties/problems. Many such individuals believe or assume that these latter factors, such as "sheer willfulness," and "malevolence," cannot be effectively or adequately addressed by CAI even if the various difficulties/problems (and perhaps still others, as well) possibly can be.

Such beliefs notwithstanding, the following also applies: The earlier-mentioned (text) reduction of illegal behavior, that is, that which is produced by content-areas intervention overall, will be larger than the reduction which results from that approach's external-controls component alone (granting that—in actual program operations—this component is only partly *separable* from the whole, in the first place). By much the same token, the overall reduction of illegal behavior includes a portion that stems from CAI's staff/youth relationship—with this factor providing a different, more internally based control. In this connection, the effects of that relationship, on the one hand, and of relevant, adequate "content" input (e.g., skills training), on the other, are themselves difficult or impossible to entirely separate from one another. This is largely because the two are usually interdependent when CAI, overall, is intensively and/or extensively implemented—particularly, but not only, within an individualized, needs-centered framework.

88. Stated more fully, these could be described as the interrelated yet separable goals of: (1) constructive or at least nondestructive personal and social functioning/adjustment, including growth; and, (2) eliminated or at least substantially reduced illegal behavior. Though goal (1) includes and requires *improved* functioning/adjustment, its scope extends beyond that.

89. It might be useful to distinguish not only potential and actual force but two broad senses of "relevance." First, regarding any serious multiple offender, content-areas intervention has potential force, broadly defined as an ability to help that individual move or change, and to substantially *move*/change him or her. In general, CAI has this potential if the content—the subject matter—in question satisfies two main conditions: (1) It can center on and help address the youths' major needs, dynamics, and circumstances (more specifically, it can be "on-target" or relevant in that respect); and, (2) it can do so in ways the individual is likely to eventually accept or otherwise constructively handle. (1) and (2) might be called "content relevance"—or even "needs-based relevance"—and "operational relevance," respectively; as such,

they are aspects of appropriateness. Second, when CAI is literally *used by* and/or *applied to* the given youth and begins to influence him or her, the preceding, potential force becomes actual; here, it can be effective with respect to specific objectives and in terms of given outcome measures. Content-centered and operational relevance differ from that which reflects the significance of the intervention's main intended objectives, these being reduced or eliminated illegal behavior, on the one hand, and adjustment/growth, on the other. The latter relevance might be called "instrumental and/or intrinsic," and, as implied, its main focus is outcome-centered value or importance.

90. In effect, CAI's power *functionally increases* even as this approach's frequent presence, as literal input, becomes *less necessary,* that is, becomes decreasingly needed as this approach progressively releases and develops the *SMOs'* strengths. Among the latter's strengths are ones that reflect these individuals' reality-based feelings of value; and here, as with content-areas intervention itself, value can involve "relevance" and "importance," for example, actual significance to given persons.

91. Though their increase in various skills and abilities may have been large, these individuals can still be functioning at a level which is well below that of most same-age youths. This situation can exist if the former were very far behind the latter at the start.

92. These D/Ps largely differ from ones that commonly arise after intervention has gotten well under way.

93. Cf.: "*Starting with* its impact on factor #2 (*difficulties/problems*), content-areas intervention can help SMOs move toward, and achieve . . . major adjustment-and-growth objectives."

94. Here, "strong" or strength involves the difficulties'/problems' level of ability to not only shape and otherwise influence certain conditions and events but to resist being substantially altered *by* various factors and inputs, including given interventions. Both levels are greater when a number of D/Ps act jointly, as they often do.

26 CONTENT EFFECTS, AND CONCLUSIONS REGARDING RATIONALES FOR INTERVENTION

Introduction

As indicated in Chapter 25, a basic task of content-areas intervention is that of reducing, neutralizing, or eliminating difficulties/problems (D/Ps) in broad content areas such as *skill deficits, peer or family pressures,* and *personal conflicts.* Among given youths, D/Ps that persist within or across these areas—D/Ps that are frequently complex, widespread, intense, and/or otherwise sizable—often help produce and maintain various negative "effects"; these are called content-area effects or, simply, *content effects.* (*Types* of content effects, and the types of difficulties/problems that help produce them, are called content issues.) Common among these D/Ps are several that were mentioned in the preceding chapter's eight-factor sequence.

As discussed later, these products or effects—content effects of those underlying, often early-occurring, "first-generation" difficulties/problems—frequently become a source of *further* D/Ps, and, at times, even a concrete form or expression of D/Ps as well. (Much illegal behavior is one such *expression.* For present purposes, "underlying," "early," "first-generation," and "original" will be used synonymously.) That is, these first-generation content effects pave the way for, and/or sometimes constitute, subsequent—second-generation—D/Ps themselves. Salient among the *first-generation effects* are what will be called "risky/trouble-related activities, attitudes, and/or stances." (As explained later, these "risky . . . activities . . ." are a form of third-*level*—not just first-*generation*—content effects.)

Separately and together, the preceding concepts, distinctions, and relationships are not as complex as they may seem at this point; and, they as well as others will be described more fully after this introduction. Meanwhile, it might be kept in mind that illegal behavior, though it comprises and poses a second-generation *difficulty/problem* in the present framework, is obviously also an *effect.* In addition, it is sometimes a direct, *first-*generation effect of given D/Ps, such as particularly intense or traumatic ones. (For present purposes, this chapter needs to focus on illegal behavior only as a second-generation phenomenon.) Finally, and in any event, the salient first-generation effects (FGEs) referred to above are not the only FGEs that generate illegal behavior, even though they are cardinal ones and are extremely common as well.

As indicated, second-generation difficulties/problems, which the salient first-generation effects helped establish and/or activate, frequently include illegal behavior per se. Often, those and/or other FGEs also help produce illegal behavior after they, the FGEs, have evolved into, or else have operated together with, certain behavioral adjustment patterns or even life-styles. Such patterns, operating with or without the just-mentioned "risky . . . activities" and often-associated factors (these being salient FGEs), frequently precede and contribute to reductions in *prosocial interests* or at least active involvements.

Because of such factors, relationships, and added—parallel, or even complementary—developments, content-areas intervention addresses more than first-generation difficulties/problems per se. For instance, it focuses not just on the D/Ps, mentioned earlier, which involve the broad content areas—such as peer and/or family pressures—that may be directly providing inputs or may be similarly creating conditions which interfere with the youths' functioning. Instead, it also addresses various responses and adjustments *to* those difficulties/problems, that is, to those inputs and conditions. Specifically, it focuses on (1) the earlier-mentioned youth responses, and so on, called "content effects," and it addresses (2) further problem-centered adaptations that, in major ways, result *from* those effects. These subsequent responses or adaptations often include illegal behavior as such, not just behavior that is "risky" yet which either falls short of being illegal or else is borderline.

Given that background, the following is the case. For many correctional and corrections-related individuals (CCRIs) to see and accept the relevance or at least potential importance of content-areas intervention, they would have to recognize the following more clearly or fully than they do:

1. The *specific nature* of those content effects. That is, "What *are* they (substantively)?" other than—in general terms—"products" or results of difficulties/problems. In short, "What do they consist of?"
2. *Significant contributions* that early-emerging, that is, first-generation, content effects (such as risky activities and attitudes) frequently make not only to the earlier-mentioned "reduction in prosocial . . . involvements" but, in particular, to the development of illegal behavior per se.

The latter recognition, by those policymakers, administrators, and other CCRIs, would be likelier to occur if these individuals were also more aware of certain sequences of events commonly associated with the major types of content effects. At any rate, many CCRIs would be more likely to value and then support content-areas intervention, or support it more strongly and reliably than otherwise, if they better recognized that it focuses on difficulties/problems which frequently generate/maintain illegal behavior either directly or—as emphasized in this chapter—via certain content effects that those and/or other first-generation D/Ps help produce, maintain, and sometimes increase. (It is, of course, the *youths*—not, somehow, D/Ps themselves—who literally and finally

perform specific acts and in those respects create or generate and trigger them. To be sure, difficulties/problems help set the stage for that "perform[ance]," that is, for those specific actions, and in that sense they fundamentally contribute to the creation/generation in question.)

This chapter will therefore begin by specifying those content effects of such early or original difficulties/problems. In particular, it will describe three *levels* of first-*generation* content effects, with heavy emphasis on the third such level. This level consists of (1) specified emotional and cognitive defenses and (2) certain exaggerated, excessive, or extreme (EEE) reactions to the underlying, first-generation difficulties/problems. (The earlier-mentioned "risky/trouble-related activities, attitudes, and/or stances" epitomize these EEEs.) It is especially, but not only, in connection with level three that the illegal behaviors and closely related adjustment patterns of many SMOs-to-be often take a very serious turn and sometimes assume relatively advanced, for instance, largely self-sustaining, forms. The chapter will also discuss external/environmental factors and internal/personal forces—together, D/Ps—that strengthen and otherwise help support and further develop "defenses and . . . reactions" (1) and (2) above, especially (2). In so doing, it will illustrate important phases or stages in the emergence and establishment of illegal behavior.

The second part of this chapter rounds out the presentation of rationales for intervention, which appeared in Chapter 24. It builds on the premise that if serious multiple offenders (SMOs) are to eventually have a viable existence in the free community, they, like many nonoffenders and minor offenders, first need opportunities to address and reduce existing difficulties/problems in order to better their life situation or life circumstances and undo, overcome, or reduce past personal mistakes, shortcomings, and so on—that is, move forward along the salient dimensions (Chapter 25).

Integral to many needed opportunities are various forms of assistance. The part-two presentation does not focus mainly on what comprises that assistance and on *how* to make it especially relevant, for example, how to individualize it vis-à-vis the youths' present and anticipated circumstances, interests, abilities, and overall needs. Instead, it illustrates the following: Several major aspects of assistance that large segments of the general public and/or the correctional community consider important and legitimate in the case of most *nonoffenders,* for instance, important in order for them to better deal with their lives, are often viewed, by those same groups, as unimportant and/or unjustified in the case of *SMOs,* with respect to that same goal. These differences or discrepancies—that is, the differing beliefs and/or implicit assumptions that are held with regard to assisting nonoffenders as compared to SMOs—have practical and ethical implications, and they shed light on given rationales for intervention.

The chapter concludes by briefly reviewing selected policy and operational issues involved in intervention, ones that also bear on already-mentioned rationales and related ethics. Included are: voluntary versus mandatory participation; societal responsibility for youth development; intervention: justified when "unequal?"; out-of-home placement; use of short-term detention; social control in the community versus institutional program. In some cases the focus is on individualized or even substantially differentiated intervention, for example, the typology-centered; in others it is on any intervention at all.

Supplementing the chapter are appendices that collectively address a broad range of content issues: "Technical Details Concerning Three-Level Series, and Predictability of Illegal Behavior" (Appendix 41); "The A/R Cycle, Long-Standing Difficulties, and Motivation" (Appendix 42); "Skill Deficits and Experiential versus Genetic Factors" (Appendix 43); "Factors Bearing on the Crystallization of the Illegal-Behavior Pattern" (Appendix 44); and "Structural Factors and Their Relationship to Emotional/Dynamic Factors" (Appendix 45).

Descriptions and concepts presented in this chapter regarding serious multiple offenders' *pre*–California Youth Authority development, interactions, and so on, derive from some of the same types and sources of information mentioned in this book's introduction, and from other major sources as well. During most of this pre-CYA time the youths were, of course, still SMOs-*to-be.* The *types* of information mainly involve these individuals' personal development, their interactions with nondelinquent and minor-delinquent friends and acquaintances, and their interactions with parents as well as other adults. The information also encompasses these youths' involvement in conventional activities, their ways of responding to given difficulties/problems (*see* "Content Effects of Difficulties/Problems"—the next section of this chapter), and their growing involvement in delinquency.

As to the *sources* of information, and regarding *non*offenders as well, see Appendix 40. Though this chapter's descriptions of youths center on males, several general concepts and specific aspects of the three-level series also apply to females.

Content Effects of Difficulties/Problems
General Considerations
Together, the three levels of content effects that will soon be presented are also called a three-level series. Each *level,* which might be thought of as a step, is comprised of its own particular "effects"—also called *features.* For example, level one—which is temporally the first—consists of four main features, one of which is "feelings of frustration," and level two itself contains four such features, one of which is "feelings of futility." Though the latter's four are each outgrowths of the former's, they also, as will be further described, significantly differ from them. To facilitate the presentation and to help place in context (1) the given *features,* (2) the respective *levels* that the respective groups of features (e.g., four features for level one) comprise, and (3) the overall *sequence of levels* (three in all), four points, mentioned next, might first be kept in mind. Related points, and further technical description, are discussed in Appendix 41.

(Again, individual features are the specific content—the substance—that, collectively, exclusively, and completely, comprise respective levels or *levels-of-effect,* that is, respective "content effects." No feature that helps comprise any level, such as the first, is also part of any other level. In other words, each level consists of its own features only. In the case of level two, these are evolved forms of level one's features.)

1. Together, levels one, two, and three form a progression, and in this respect they can be called a "series"—a series of levels. Movement, by youths, from one

level to another occurs in terms of each level's features; the features are the content of that movement. Any one of level *one's* four main features (e.g., " . . . frustration") may be directly followed by (1) a level *two* feature (e.g., " . . . futility") that is an evolved form of that first feature. Alternatively, that same level one feature may be directly followed by (2) another level *one* feature (e.g., "worry" or perhaps "self-doubt") before movement to level two occurs. In each case—namely, direct movement from a feature of one level to a feature of another level, or else movement across features that are of the same level *prior to* the movement into that next level— change from any one *feature* to any other feature may be described as a *sequence* of features. In order to distinguish this feature-to-feature movement from change that occurs from one *level* to another *level* per se, movement across levels— even though it always, and only, occurs *in terms of* a sequence of features—will be thought of as a *series* or as part of a series. To recap, movement from one feature to another is a "sequence" of events or is part of a sequence, whether within or across levels. Change from one level to another is part of a "series." (This terminology, and the distinctions in question, can help simplify various aspects of the presentation. Regarding "sequence," also see point D of the appendix.)

2. Concerning level one, the presence of any *one* of the four features that will be listed, for example, "frustration," can suffice in order for a sequence to become active, with any given youth. The same applies to any of the four features, such as "feelings of futility," shown for level two. Nevertheless, it can be said that all *four* features "comprise" each respective level, since that—substantively—is what they do collectively, that is, *across* the present youths; they do so even though they are seldom all present in any *one* youth, especially at about the same time. (Two or three are often present more or less simultaneously.) What these respective groups of features therefore do comprise—collectively—is the main *range* of content for levels one and two, respectively. (With level three, which is struc-

turally more complex and substantively more extensive and varied, both of the broad "categories" of effects that will be listed, namely, "A" and "B," *are* almost always found in each youth, at essentially the same time.)

3. Though each individual feature that is found in level *one* of the present series is very common among youths who will later become serious multiple offenders, these features are not the only ones, that is, not the only contents, that can collectively comprise the first level of a content-effects series. For example, features such as "frustration" or "worry"— two of the present three-level series' four level-one effects—can each differ substantially from any two features that help comprise level one of any *other* three-level series. The same applies to features that comprise level *two* of the present series, as compared to level two of any other, that is, again any different, series. Finally, it pertains to level three features as well—though here, the features that are found differ from each other less often and to a lesser degree, across differing three-level series, than do the respective level one features and the respective level two features of differing series. (See point A of the appendix, regarding "different" series.)

Although three-level series exist whose overall content, that is, all their respective features combined, is therefore slightly, moderately, or largely different than that of the one presented below, the latter series of levels is very widespread and influential among youths who will become SMOs. As a result, it can amply illustrate the issues at hand—those mentioned in the introduction to this chapter. Moreover, level *three* of this series is, in major ways, quite similar to the numerically same level of many other three-level series, even ones whose first two levels are substantively quite different than those of the present one. More specifically, many or most of the individual features that collectively comprise the third level of the present series are, substantively, identical or nearly identical to those which comprise that same level of many other series. This correspondence or overlap goes beyond their simply sharing the same label and conceptual categorization; it particularly applies to features—to various specified "risky activities, attitudes, and stances"—that will be discussed under "Category B" of the present series' third level. This situation regarding level three, whose content refers to ways in which the present youths cope mainly with level two, largely reflects the many key similarities that exist across these individuals with respect to the type, quantity, and persistence of their needs as well as difficulties/problems. (See point B of the appendix.)

4. Whatever content, that is, particular features, may comprise any and all levels of a three-level series, the logical and functional relationship that exists *between* the respective levels is the same as that which exists between the same numbered levels of any other three-level series, that is, of any series which involves different content. Specifically, the content that comprises the *second* level or step of any series always involves a significant expansion, intensification, and so on of that which constitutes its first. In addition, the content that comprises its *third* level always involves or centers on attempts, by the youths, to handle—especially—that series' second-level effects/issues, and, less often, to directly address those of its unexpanded or unintensified first level. (See point C of the appendix.)

We will now specify the features and levels in question, those which would often be observed among youths with earlier-mentioned, persistent difficulties/problems. What has been termed individual "features" will simply be called "effects"—these being the separate components of one or another of the three levels of content effects.

Three Levels of Effect

The first such effects of given difficulties/problems would be feelings and emotions such as *frustration, worry, self-doubt, and anger*—here called "initial" or "first-level" effects or reactions; confusion, and a sense of unfairness, would sometimes exist as well. The more the present CCRIs recognize the specific content, the strength, and the sustained nature of SMOs' *difficulties/problems,* the more clearly they would realize not only how and why such D/Ps could generate those frustrations, worries, and so on, but why those same feelings and emotions, like the D/Ps that generate, trigger, and reinforce them, would often be strong and sustained themselves. This applies whether those difficulties/problems are considered individually or collectively and whether they center on external or internal factors/conditions, such as the social/environmental or the more intrapersonal/psychological.[1]

The second such effects would center on significant outgrowths of those initial feelings and emotions, specifically, on (a) substantial expansions and intensifications of the frustrations, worries, and self-doubts, and on (b) those two dimensions as well as generalizations and/or displacements in the case of anger. Regarding serious multiple offenders collectively, the outgrowths in question—ones whose content is specified next, and which are called "secondary" or "second-level" effects or reactions—would include, but not be limited to, all of the following (as to any SMO *individually,* the outgrowths would involve any one or more of them):

1. *Feelings of futility*—mainly as a deepening of the initial, but subsequently persisting, frustrations.
2. *Broader, more often occurring, and/or often stronger, feelings of anxiety and insecurity*—largely expansions or elaborations of the initial, but still existing, worries.
3. *Broader self-doubts,* (a) sometimes accompanied by a growing and even solidifying sense of inadequacy or inferiority, and, in any event, (b) often together with substantial fears of given situations and of challenges in general. Though these broader doubts are chiefly outgrowths of the earlier ones, they sometimes partly reflect the first-level *worries* as well, whether or not these have subsequently grown.
4. *Intensified, often generalized and sometimes fairly indiscriminate, anger and hostility*—outgrowths of the initial anger.[2, 3]

Types of Level-3 Effects

The "tertiary" or third-level" effects are

primarily outgrowths of the *secondaries* and of related reactions to them.[4] For present purposes, these effects, collectively, can be grouped into two partly overlapping categories: (A) *Emotional and "cognitive" (or mental/intellectual) defenses.* (B) *Exaggerated, excessive, or extreme reactions.* Each category can encompass a wide range of content; more specifically, it can include a large number and variety of content effects. In this regard it can be considered a generic means by which serious multiple offenders commonly adapt to and otherwise deal with any given effect or effects of factor #2 difficulties/problems.[5] (This refers to #2 of the eight-factor sequence [Chapter 25].)

Category A
As indicated and implied earlier, these adaptations and other responses—"third-level effects"—are chiefly outgrowths of second-level rather than of the unelaborated, for instance, unexpanded, first-level effects. Therefore, to illustrate these third-level effects and two generic categories into which they can be placed we need only emphasize certain commonly observed effects—salient outgrowths—of the four earlier-mentioned *secondaries* (since these four can function as proxies for all secondaries) or of reactions closely related to them.[6] For SMOs collectively, then, three examples of Category A effects—third-level effects—are as follows (note: as may be inferred, the youths' adaptations, i.e., responses, do not always prove or remain effective, let alone even entirely satisfying from these individuals' standpoint.[7]):

1. *An overall turning away from or against most adults, including most authority figures.* This stance is often a broad defensive adaptation—at any rate, a response—to more than any one of the four second-level effects, these being the feelings of futility, the increased anxiety, the broader self-doubts, and the increased, perhaps generalized, anger, respectively. Moreover, it is often accompanied by a resistiveness and negativism whose strength, breadth, or both, often go substantially beyond that of most nonoffenders and nonserious offenders. (Like most SMOs, these two groups themselves sometimes verbally challenge and sharply disagree with par-

ents and other adults, commonly on issues involving autonomy, pleasure- and/or status-seeking, anxiety and responsibility avoidance, and related aspects of personal identity.)[8]

2. *A wariness about personal relationships,* one that often includes considerable emotional insulation from the preponderance of adults and even peer-level acquaintances. This wariness may, for example, largely result from a general discomfort with others or from a sizable distrust of them, but it is not invariably accompanied by a large-scale "turning away from or against" them. In any event, this adaptation to such secondaries as *broad self-doubt* or *generalized anger* may reflect the youths' wish to avoid the following, each of which these individuals view as otherwise likely to occur (this listing applies to SMOs collectively, since few individuals expect all such items): major "hassles"; exploitation; undue control by others; arousal of one's own anger or rage; exposure of one's felt inadequacies or blameworthiness; uncomfortable or frightening situations; failure; disappointment; emotional hurt. Finally, this adaptation may sometimes be a response to (a) continued, not significantly expanded or intensified, *first*-level effects (e.g., frustrations and self-doubts) as such, and it may partly result from (b) the youths' projections, onto others, of their own hostility or unfriendliness.

3. *Above-average or well-above-average use of denial, rationalization, displacement, and projection.* These relatively standard "ego defenses" (Freud, 1937) sometimes enter the picture after the fact, for instance, in order to help the youths account for, justify, maintain, and perhaps enhance their already existing, earlier-mentioned stance, wariness, and so on. However, if such mechanisms have already been ongoing features of those individuals' response repertoire, they may have helped generate and trigger those and other adaptations, in the first place. They may have done so, for example, by initially focusing, reinforcing, and/or later expanding the youths' sense of futility and their outwardly directed anger or hostility.

Category B

Collectively, Category B effects, that is, "exaggerated, excessive, or extreme reactions," are another group of responses or adaptations to the second-level reactions to factor #2 difficulties/problems.[9, 10] More specifically, these "B-effects," like "A-effects," consist of several substantively distinct though functionally comparable approaches to avoiding, opposing, or otherwise trying to resist or reduce secondary reactions, such as increased anxiety/insecurity, broader self-doubt, and feelings of futility. (Examples are given below.) The general nature of these approaches, and the principal reason for their use, is essentially the same as that of approaches frequently used by most *non*offenders as well, for instance, used when these individuals pursue routine interests, address standard challenges, and adapt to situational or perhaps even longer-term D/Ps. Though these approaches, collectively, (1) are thus relatively commonplace in some respects, (2) encompass various features that range from the conventional to the unconventional, and (3) are functionally and, in a broad sense, substantively shared with SMOs, many SMOs, but comparatively few nonoffenders, use them (1) in an often exaggerated way and sometimes even to an extreme *degree*, and (2) frequently in contexts that intrinsically include "trouble" or that could easily and knowingly lead to it.[11]

Exaggerated, Excessive, or Extreme Reactions
Reasons for Their Usage

We will now illustrate the general nature of these shared approaches, particularly their usual type and range of content; prior to that, however, we will mention the relatively simple and immediate, primary intent that underlies their use. (Before proceeding, though, the following should be kept in mind: In this section, as in that immediately above and in the presentation of Category A effects, "SMOs" refers to youths who will *become* serious multiple offenders but who are not offenders, or are perhaps relatively minor offenders, when they first use or begin to substantially rely on these third-level approaches [this being the time period now under consideration]. In contrast, "nonoffenders" ["*nonOs*"], as used in this context, are youths who will *remain*

nonOs throughout at least adolescence, or who will become infrequent, minor offenders at most. "Effects," "responses," "reactions," and "adaptations" will be synonymous, as will "B-effects" and "B-responses.")[12]

Gaining Acceptance

Many serious multiple offenders—the present SMOs-to-be—regularly try to gain the acceptance of given peers. They do so not only to help counter and thereby relieve or reduce their own increased anxiety/insecurity, their growing self-doubts, and so on—this being a cardinal motive—but, where possible, to also experience enjoyments with or via those peers. Basically, these individuals hope to obtain that acceptance by pleasing or satisfying those youths, and, in some instances, by impressing them or gaining their admiration. Involved, in the SMOs' efforts, are the same general approaches commonly used by most *nonOs* (see "types of approaches" 1 to 5, below)—used, in their case as well, as part of seeking acceptance and enjoyment. With *nonOs*, however, these approaches are seldom *also* directed, let alone heavily or even chiefly directed, at (1) countering the above-mentioned anxiety, self-doubts, and the like, more specifically, the same *degree* of anxiety, and so on; and, (2) the same degree and complexity of underlying difficulties/problems.

At any rate, the serious multiple offenders, like most nonoffenders, try to obtain and maintain the earlier-mentioned acceptance via some of the following types of approaches, usually most of them: (1) Behaving in certain ways or playing particular roles when around the peers in question; (2) participating in given activities with those youths; (3) anticipating and, in any event, largely conforming to those individuals' wishes; (4) manifesting—behaviorally and/or otherwise—given personal qualities or personality traits; and, (5) adopting particular values and outlooks, ones largely consonant with those of the peers. As is evident, some overlap—often considerable—can exist across various such factors, for instance, (1) and (4).

Underlying Feelings, Fears, and Assumptions

To gain that acceptance from given peers—and, before that, their attention—these SMOs are willing to sometimes act in ways that many observers, and some peers themselves, consider exaggerated, excessive, or extreme.[13]

Examples of these actions, and of related qualities or traits, are presented shortly. (As implied, this is not the only way these individuals behave, whether to obtain that or—especially—other ends. They usually act in more typical or mainstream ways at this stage, and they generally prefer to do so. [As before, "SMO" still means SMO-to-be.]) The SMOs' readiness to thus behave, and to exhibit related features, results from the joint operation of three main factors or conditions. These factors, mentioned next, also help account for the youths' related tendency to sometimes seek out delinquent peers and trouble-ripe situations.

First, and most fundamental, these youths (collectively) consciously or preconsciously want the above acceptance in order to help counter their increased anxiety/insecurity, their now-broader self-doubts, their fear of "missing-out" on various enjoyments, and so on.[14] More specifically, they seek and, in effect, psychologically need this external acceptance as a major source of relief from those sometimes-intense and, in any event, frequent anxieties, insecurities, and the like. Simultaneously, they also seek it as an indirect assurance that they are "OK" and have somewhere to belong, and as a precondition as well as direct channel to enjoyable activities.

Second (and still collectively), these SMOs globally feel, implicitly assume, or specifically believe they are in a weak position with respect to *obtaining* that acceptance from peers; they feel, in particular, that they start out with sizable disadvantages. Fueling their overall feeling or view is the negative aspect of their self-image, together with their related, increased self-doubts; further generating or triggering it are—often—actual and/or felt material disadvantages and/or skill deficits. The immediate product of this self-image component, self-doubt, and, perhaps, of significant disadvantages/deficits—also, sometimes, of strong negative messages from, or direct opposition by, given adults—is the following: these youths' general assumption, and often-strong worry, that they (1) may not be liked by those peers or, at least, may not be particularly interesting to them, and that they (2) lack, or in any event are seen as lacking, certain important features and attractions.[15] This assumption and worry sometimes also reflects input from peers themselves. At any rate, (1) and (2) apply whether or not, but especially if and when, the self-image/self-doubts factor and one or more additional factors, such as perceived material disadvantages, are operating simultaneously. Even apart from added factors, (1) and (2) apply whether or not, but again especially if and when, the self-image/self-doubts factor exists under conditions of high anxiety.

Finally, given the above situation, these SMOs feel or implicitly assume they must do the following if they are to raise their chances of obtaining and maintaining attention and at least basic acceptance. They must make extra, possibly frequent, and otherwise unusual or special efforts to be more interesting, useful, and the like, and to therein become more likable to those peers.[16] (These processes, for instance, feelings, occur even though the youths seldom explicitly think about the above factors and conditions, let alone clearly conceptualize them as such.)

Thus, these individuals' overall willingness to make such efforts, and their sometimes even strong desire to do so, largely results from their strong psychological need for acceptance, as a source of relief and an opening to enjoyment, and from what they feel or assume is their weak position with regard to obtaining that acceptance.[17] It also reflects their broad, often underlying feeling of vulnerability over possibly losing it once they obtain it.

Nature of Unusual or Special Efforts
Activities
These efforts, as indicated, sometimes take the form of ". . . excessive . . ." activities, ones that generally occur in the presence of, and often in concert with, peers whose attention is sought. Many such activities or behaviors are considered "risky" in the sense of daring or dangerous, usually in and of themselves though sometimes partly because of their overall context. Basically, they are viewed as risky because they can have negative personal, interpersonal, and/or physical consequences. In particular, if "something goes wrong" in connection with them, say, if they are discovered or if an accident occurs, the SMOs—especially if they are active or leading participants—can get in trouble with parents, with "the law," and so on. That, in turn, can (not necessarily will) set them back and complicate their lives.

Typical of these risky—in any event, "excessive"—activities/behaviors are: heavy or frequent drinking; use of drugs, especially "hard" ones; sex beyond "petting," especially if frequent; and, fast or reckless driving. As implied, their negative consequences and unwanted complications can be large, particularly, but not only, if the activities occur mainly in "off-limits" places or well after hours—contexts often considered intrinsically risky themselves. Risky activities can occur or begin to occur during, or in connection with, relatively *standard* events or occasions as well, for example, during parentally and otherwise approved outings, sports, concerts, and dating. They may also occur during other leisure times, and shortly before or after school.

Attitudes and Stances
Wherever and whenever they occur, such activities are sometimes preceded or accompanied by attitudes and stances that strike various observers as excessive, exaggerated, and occasionally even extreme themselves.[18] That impression can form if, for instance—regarding any particular SMO—the given attitudes/stances seem *common* and, thus, somehow characteristic, or if they are expressed openly or forcefully. If and when they are thus perceived, those attitudes and stances, like the earlier-mentioned activities themselves, are often considered risky as well, again because of their possible consequences. Common among these attitudes/stances, that is, frequent across the youths, are defiance, obstinacy, impudence, contempt, seeming indifference, and evasiveness.[19] (Some such stances are often accompanied by bravado, cockiness, and loudness—features that sometimes seem exaggerated even on their own, but which are usually considered less risky than the others. At any rate, these, too, usually gain peer attention, and sometimes approval.)

As implied, the earlier-mentioned attitudes are expressed, and the stances are taken, not just in off-limits or unusual contexts, but also in connection with typical or commonplace settings and everyday interactions. For instance, many such expressions occur in school settings, where the SMOs may verbally and otherwise manifest the given attitudes toward particular teachers, students, and/or groups. Many others occur in mundane places such as streets, parks, stores, and auditoriums, during what would otherwise be simple

and relatively neutral interactions with adults/authority figures. In both contexts or settings, the direct "targets" or objects of those youths' expressions are various adults; however, the main intended "audiences" are any on-scene peers with whom those individuals hope to make a positive impression. At any rate, whether the context or setting is unusual or commonplace, and "off-limits" or "on," the attitudes and stances in question would be considered exaggerated, and so on, essentially because of their content, frequency, or degree.[20]

A theme that runs through many of the above *activities, attitudes, and stances (AASs)* involves the resisting or even flouting of given individuals, expectations, and/or rules. That or related themes are often involved in the SMOs' following behaviors as well: deceptiveness or trickiness, though short of illegality; rough, rude, or "gross" language and/or gestures; talking and acting belligerently or otherwise threateningly.[21] (When these behaviors are considered "excessive," this judgment mainly reflects their content per se, though it also involves their above-average frequency or degree; they are often considered "extreme" simply when their *frequency* is higher still.)

Involvement, Features, and Motives of Nonoffenders
Serious multiple offenders, especially when they are clearly manifesting the earlier-mentioned AASs, such as the drinking and defiance, sometimes create certain opportunities for many *nonoffenders* who are then observing those activities, and the like, or else who hear about them. These are opportunities to experience what might be called "psychological and/or emotional outlets," chief among which are vicarious satisfactions, other forms of personal satisfaction, and feelings of release as well as subsequent relief. (Here, "psychological" refers to thoughts or cognitions that may range from simple mental wanderings to more and less focused, purposive, and discrete images and ideas. "Opportunities" may—also—be viewed as "stimuli" and "occasions.") (The SMOs, that is, SMOs-to-be, generally create these opportunities unknowingly, in the sense of not realizing that such an outlet process exists and what their behavior and attitudes may personally mean to the nonOs. Instead, as indicated earlier, what the SMOs immediately hope for is simply to gain attention and acceptance.

In this regard, they neither think nor care about how and why these come about, in terms of the givers'—the nonOs'—perceptions and needs.) As described shortly, the implications of the above situation, particularly of the nonoffenders' actions subsequent to experiencing that outlet, are often critical for the SMOs in question—these individuals being our basic focus. To better understand this situation, including those actions, the following might be kept in mind regarding the psychological/emotional outlet process.

This process has two main facets. First, certain activities, attitudes, and stances on the part of the SMOs are quickly, and usually just briefly, "incorporated" by the nonoffenders who have noticed them, that is, have seen or heard about them. (This applies whether or not the nonOs are acquainted with those SMOs as individuals.) That is, (1) upon being observed or otherwise learned about, such AASs are psychologically approved of by the nonoffenders; and, (2) in conjunction with that approval and at essentially the same time, those same activities, and so on, are added—temporarily, and in a limited way overall—to that portion of the nonOs' self-concept or self-attribution system whose content centers on personally acceptable behaviors, attitudes, and other characteristics. (For further details, see endnote 22.) In the present case, this can apply even if those characteristics are only *situationally* and otherwise conditionally acceptable, and, in any event, when they are only briefly accepted. Second, once that incorporation occurs, the nonoffenders briefly experience thoughts and/or images of a personally satisfying nature—for example, vicarious enjoyments, in which the nonOs may partially identify themselves with specific individuals—and they often experience some immediate emotional release and relief as well.[23] The background of these individuals' need or desire for such psychological/emotional outlet is mentioned next, and the main dynamic follows. Its bearing on the SMOs themselves will become clear.

These nonoffenders, who are well-represented in most youth populations and are considered entirely "normal" by their peers and others, are individuals who, on their own, almost always hesitate to do each of the following; or, they avoid it entirely: (1) Seriously, and fairly directly, try to challenge given adults, expectations, or rules, let alone

flout them. (2) Substantially, and relatively openly, engage in behaviors and interactions that would be nonconforming and which they consider possibly risky. Item (2) applies even when the nonOs believe or implicitly assume that these behaviors and interactions would probably give them some satisfaction if they could be engaged in or expressed without negative consequences.[24]

Given this background, the SMOs' earlier-mentioned activities, attitudes, and stances provide opportunities for these nonoffenders to psychologically, for instance, in imagination and image, experience various thoughts and satisfy given wishes regarding adults, expectations, and rules, and to release some of their emotions and feelings concerning often related matters. Collectively, these thoughts, emotions, and so on, would otherwise remain largely unexpressed, or contained, for a considerable period of time. Common among the issues and related matters involved here are not only strivings for independence and/or autonomy—even for no more than partial and moderate independence/autonomy—but specific frustrations or dissatisfactions. Thus, for example, in providing the above opportunities, the SMOs' observed and otherwise known activities, attitudes, and stances toward given adults, expectations, and rules, often do the following: In effect, they set the stage for, and help trigger, the nonoffenders' wishes to experience more "freedom"—say, to further test or explore it—and to generally partake of apparent adolescent enjoyments.[25]

Some such issues, say, increased freedom, are not necessarily the main ones that the *SMOs* are personally focusing on at the time, in connection with, and via, those AASs. Nevertheless, the contents and targets of those SMOs' activities, and so on, are sufficiently consonant with or readily associated with those involved in the nonOs' *own* current concerns or interests that they can often help trigger or otherwise release them.

(In the following, it might be kept in mind that although the nonoffenders in question are the SMOs' peers, for example, are adolescents whom the SMOs see in class or who commonly see *them* on the school grounds or in the neighborhood, these nonOs are not necessarily the SMOs' personal friends or acquaintances—or even highly comparable in age. This refers to the point in time when they [the nonoffenders]—as described next—"react in [certain ways to] those individuals," or at least react to them initially. Also, this situation is a common one.)

Reinforcement by Nonoffenders

The upshot of this situation is that nonoffenders, soon after experiencing some satisfaction/relief in connection with the SMOs' activities, and so on, react in ways that reinforce those individuals. More specifically,

1. in reinforcing these SMOs, the nonOs are mainly strengthening those individuals' *activities, attitudes, and/or stances* that helped release the nonoffenders' wishes, feelings, and the like, and which, in that respect, provided or comprised the opportunities for psychological/ emotional outlet;
2. that strengthening partly occurs because—and when—(a) the nonOs (peers) show interest in and otherwise *pay attention to* those AASs, and, hence, to the SMOs themselves. It also occurs when (b) they, the peers, openly or tacitly *approve of* or seem (to the SMOs) to approve of some of those noticed AASs. Finally, and in conjunction with (b), the strengthening further occurs when (c) those nonOs explicitly or implicitly *accept* the SMOs themselves, to at least a moderate degree. (The SMOs must, of course, become aware of this attention, and so on.)[26] Though peer response (a), above, often provides considerable reinforcement itself, the overall reinforcement of those activities, attitudes, and/or stances is considerably stronger when the SMOs believe, or take it for granted, that responses (b) and especially (c) also exist;[27] and
3. the nonoffenders often provide this attention, approval, and acceptance while hardly being aware that these responses—functionally, these "inputs"—are, in effect, reinforcing those AASs. At any rate, the nonOs almost always provide those inputs without understanding the immediate personal meanings that the AASs and any such strengthening may have to those individuals, without trying to get those youths "in trouble," and without recognizing or even thinking about the possible implications of any

strengthening for those youths' much longer-term adjustment.

Since (a) peer attention and—ultimately—some measure of peer acceptance are a large part of what the SMOs-to-be had hoped to obtain by expressing given activities, attitudes, and stances, mainly in the presence of various peers, and since (b) those particular peer responses *are* subsequently obtained or apparently obtained by these individuals via those stimuli, (c) the SMOs' use of the stimuli in question, that is, of the AASs, is therefore reinforced. Moreover, it is reinforced by the given peers, though not necessarily just by them. This acceptance helps reduce various fears, frustrations, and anxieties, and it can involve personal satisfactions as well. In these respects its impact is positive. (The events described on the preceding pages can be viewed as an "action/reaction cycle." Its main components and basic sequence are: *"risky activities,* followed by *peer approval,* followed by *personal relief/satisfaction,* and then back to *risky activities,* and so on." See below. To simplify the presentation, the term "behaviors" will now often substitute for "AASs." In addition, "and/or" will usually be dropped from "activities, attitudes, *and/or* stances.")

Negative Implications

Nevertheless, for these same SMOs, this acceptance and reinforcement also has negative implications, ones based on the following situation: What get reinforced are behaviors which—even though they help generate peer acceptance—can also lead to sizable difficulties. These behaviors include, for example, not just borderline or else clearly illegal *activities,* but often-hostile or -alienating *attitudes* and *stances;* in this regard, those strengthened behaviors act as inputs or stimuli that can generate the difficulties in question. Broadly speaking, these difficulties can encompass not just "troubles" and "problems," but, as described below, relatively long-term "distractions" or divergences from given paths, tasks, and opportunities. More concretely, these resulting difficulties include, but are not limited to: troubles or problems that preexisted but which now involve new individuals and public agencies; problems that are essentially new in type; and major distractions or diversions from prosocial activities that are ongoing or prospective.

These SMOs are almost always soon aware of certain difficulties that those reinforced behaviors (activities, attitudes, etc.) have already helped generate, or to which they may lead; at least, they recognize some of those behaviors' more immediate and palpable effects or implications. However, instead of believing or assuming that these fairly immediate difficulties can be largely or entirely avoided, those individuals soon come to view them as a "price" they must probably pay or a "chance" they have to take. More specifically, they see these relatively immediate difficulties as closely linked to those reinforced behaviors—as being, in effect, *part of* obtaining the attention and acceptance they seek from peers, or else a key to maintaining and perhaps increasing the level of acceptance they may have already received from them. Common among these expected problems and troubles—or, at least, among ones that would come as no surprise to most SMOs-to-be—are "hassles" with school officials, with parents, and/or with neighbors, plus occasional encounters with the law.

Broad Effects of Reinforced AASs

Concerning the broad implications of those behaviors—for example, regarding wider, usually long-term effects or impacts of the strengthened activities, attitudes, and stances—these difficulties reflect the following conditions or developments, and they involve the following general content as well (note: for any given youth, the AASs are *new* in terms of type or at least degree; with some youths, major impacts occur soon after these AASs first get reinforced; with others, they emerge more slowly yet can become equally strong later on).

Modification of Attitudes and Investments: Changes, or Phases, A and B

If the youths' new activities, attitudes, and stances continue to be reinforced by peers for many months or more after those AASs first receive peer attention and apparent approval, the SMOs—during that period—begin to change some of their hitherto-existing *attitudes and emotional investments (A/Is)*. They modify these A/Is in a direction, and in ways, that help accommodate the content and intent of those new AASs, that is, of those peer-reinforced, albeit problem-related, behaviors (AASs).

Specifically, the youths in question change the A/Is in order to more easily or often express those AASs, and—especially—to more easily/often experience the peer acceptance associated with those new activities, attitudes, and stances. As to the change itself, this mainly involves a modification of the hitherto-existing, that is, the preexisting, attitudes and emotional investments' content per se (thus, it involves a change in the youths' positions or views), and/or a reduction in their amount of usage. At any rate, the change, at this point, is just that: a modification and/or deemphasis, not a virtual abandonment. Finally, the attitudes and investments in question are ones that have been essentially prosocial in nature and expression, for instance, friendly, accepting, and perhaps helpful; or, they have at least been interpersonally neutral in intent, such as nonhostile and nonalienating. (The latter, in itself, does not mean these youths have rarely been angry, rejecting, standoffish, and so on.)

Once that change ("Change A") occurs in the youths' A/Is, and especially after it has become at least moderate in degree, a further, dual-faceted development ("Change B") takes place: (1) The SMOs soon become less interested in focusing or seriously focusing on certain aspects of their lives. These are generic aspects or areas (see below) that are important to their ongoing and longer-term social adjustment and to that of virtually any contemporary adolescent, as well. (2) Accompanying that decreased interest or motivation and directly reflecting it, there is a reduced likelihood that these SMOs-to-be will actually *try* to make various efforts, particularly serious or sustained ones, in or with respect to those areas. As a result, there is a reduced chance that they in fact *will* focus or seriously focus on them.

Salient among the generic areas are (a) standard skills-building activities, (b) various interpersonal challenges and possible involvements or relationships, and (c) other tasks, interactions, and opportunities. Efforts and progress within these areas ordinarily helps adolescents move toward a future that the dominant society, and usually a dominant subculture (if present), accepts, supports, or at least does not try to substantially oppose. (Thus, the given movement is toward an externally—a socially—"accepted" or "acceptable" future.) This applies whether or not that movement is steady, that future is largely conventional, and those youths eventually *reach* or even closely approach the socially accepted future. Moreover, youth efforts within the generic areas—and, especially, across them collectively—are not just helpful; instead, they are usually essential. This is the case even if, among given individuals, the efforts are largely sporadic and often far from concerted, and even though the various efforts cannot, by themselves, absolutely ensure the above outcome in any event (e.g., even if they *are* steady and concerted).

During the Change-A phase, these SMOs, as indicated earlier, do not entirely or even largely abandon their *preexisting, prosocial* attitudes and emotional investments; this applies to given personality features and traits, as well. As a result, during the B phase, these youths' activities and interactions—collectively—can and do continue to partly reflect those attitudes, investments, and so on; this applies even if these individuals' actual efforts and involvements are usually no more than moderate in degree and intensity. At any rate, some of these youths' B-phase activities and efforts continue to reflect, express, and in these respects remain largely consistent with the youths' preexisting, prosocial positions, views, and characteristics.

External Pressures and Below-Average Supports

Whether many or few prosocial positions and features continue to be expressed soon after Change A has been established and also when B is underway, Change B's existence and extent also reflect the following: Even before Change *A* began, many SMOs-to-be were already having comparative difficulty focusing their attention and efforts on various tasks and challenges involving their near-term, prosocial adjustment and sometimes even their daily functioning; this occurred even when they were largely *interested* in focusing on them. Difficulty focusing also applied to challenges and social expectations that were additionally, mainly, or specifically oriented toward the longer-term future.[28] Whether near-term or longer-term adjustment issues predominated, those individuals' focusing difficulty partly reflected the above-average *external pressures* that commonly comprised a major part of the previously mentioned "factor #2 (difficulties/problems)." Often, both adjustment problems, especially the near-

term, also partly reflected below-average *support* from parents and others—a condition that contributed to the youths' frequency and level of stress and/or anxiety; this applied regardless of whether, but all the more if, above-average external pressures existed.

Such "external pressures" typically involved: (1) inflexible requirements/expectations; (2) unrealistic individual demands; (3) widely divergent, sharply incompatible, and otherwise inconsistent or conflicting *mutual* demands as well as expectations, such as double messages. Also common was (4) a relatively rigid or intense enforcement of (1) and (2). When incessant, and especially when prolonged, (1) through (3)—even individually—helped generate frustration, stress, and/or anxiety. These, in turn, reduced the individuals' ability to function at given levels; and, together with input (4), they sometimes also reduced the youths' motivation to adjust in various prosocial ways. Again, these developments occurred prior to Change A itself, and they helped bring it about.[29]

Regarding "support," this, when present, included general or specific approval, encouragement, guidance, and/or direction. As such, it simultaneously helped determine the amount—and the type—of functional power exerted by the various external *pressures,* that is, their actually available and effective power. More specifically, it helped determine their net amount of influence, within particular areas, after they, the pressures, had been mitigated, partly diverted, diluted, forestalled, or somewhat blunted by that same support. (By the same token, the external pressures reciprocally, and often simultaneously, helped determine the amount of functional *support* from parents and other adults. In short, support and pressure influenced each other.)

During the later part of this pre–Change A ("pre-A") period, and continuing into A itself, the following took place (note: the "later part" occurred after the AASs had first emerged and were reinforced): One aspect or component of support, namely, approval, *was* obtained by SMOs. However, this was obtained from peers, not from the parents/adults in question; also, it was based on the often-risky, earlier-mentioned activities, attitudes, and stances. In addition, and still regarding those peers, this approval was not accompanied by the "encouragement, guidance, and/or direction" components of support, particularly in connection with prosocial activities. At any rate, the SMOs' new or more salient pre-A and A-phase behaviors (AASs) helped generate and maintain the approval component of support, from those peers. It did so even though the pre-existing external *pressures,* from the given adults, had seldom diminished substantially and/or other than temporarily during those same periods, and although they may have even increased on average. This approval aspect substantially influenced the present youths, even absent such other aspects as guidance.[30]

AASs as an Escape Valve
In view of this pre-A situation—one that commonly includes above-average or unusual external pressures, below-average support, and related frustrations as well as stress—the following applies: The behaviors that the youths subsequently continue to focus on as they move from pre-A toward and into the *A-phase* involve a form of "escape valve," or a "bypass," with respect to those external pressures. That is, those AASs act as, and help provide, a partial release from such pressures, or else ways of sidestepping them. ("A-phase" is also "Change A" or "Phase A.") In addition, those behaviors comprise a basis for new hope—hope for what the youths think would be better and generally enjoyable times, though not entirely conventional ones. In this connection the AASs, collectively, provide various paths to those "better" times—at least, to hoped-for happier and lighter ones. This new-hope function, like the "escape valve" and "bypass" function, itself applies to the pre-A period, and, later, to Phase A as well.

Though the youths sense or feel the existence and importance of the preceding AASs' functions, namely, "partial release," "side-stepping," and "new hope," they do not conceptualize them and their outcomes as such, and in essentially those terms. Besides performing those particular functions, the behaviors provide yet other forms of relief. Also, they lead to relatively *immediate,* specific moments of satisfaction and feelings of pleasure, such as those resulting from the already-mentioned, emotionally satisfying responses of certain peers.

Given that the present youths, collectively, are globally and/or emotionally aware of the above functions, given that they sense one or more relationships between the behaviors and those functions, and given that the

youths largely or entirely *want* various products of such relationships, that is, want the outcomes that involve satisfactions, relief, and so on, these activities, attitudes, and stances come to have considerable incentive value to those youths—the individuals who generate them. This felt value first began to form and crystallize when certain peers responded positively to those behaviors and to the individuals in question, during the pre-A period. Because of it, those youths become motivated to maintain, to generally facilitate, and, often, to expand those behaviors—all this despite various risks and costs such AASs are known to entail, even as of pre-A.

Increased Investment in Risky/Trouble-Related Behavior: Phase C

During *Phase A,* that motivation, as mentioned earlier, results in the youths' modifying or deemphasizing various preexisting, essentially prosocial *attitudes and emotional investments (A/Is).* In *Phase B* ("Change B" or "B-phase"), the impact of one or both of the following factors reduces the likelihood that those individuals will seriously address—even try to address—certain areas of broad importance to their *overall social adjustment* (these being the "generic areas"):[31]

1. A continued or sometimes increased
   (a) behavioral deemphasis on, and/or
   (b) modification in the content of, those preexisting prosocial *attitudes/investments.* (The continuation or increase is from Phase A.) This—particularly (a)—applies whether or not the youths have personally grown less *interested* in those A/Is than they usually still were during Phase A.
2. A continued or growing interest and emotional investment in the personally rewarding, hence valued, *AASs* themselves.[32, 33]

More precisely, during Phase B, the youths do commonly begin to focus even less often and/or less seriously than before on the above areas of ongoing or longer-term social adjustment—these being the various tasks, challenges, and so on, that collectively comprise generic areas (1) through (3).[34] Like the "expansion" mentioned next—a change that applies to the activities, attitudes, and stances—this reduction in focusing often occurs if the earlier-mentioned satisfactions, relief, and/or feelings of hope continue to occur for at least several months, at roughly their same level of frequency, or at a higher level. It especially occurs if, for whatever reasons, those outcomes grow psychologically stronger to the individuals, for instance, become more satisfying and otherwise meaningful than before.

However, even when this reduced focusing on "generic[s]" does *not* occur, the preexisting behaviors may expand. Specifically, the youths may still increase the frequency of usage of these often-risky and/or trouble-related AASs; and/or they may apply and express these behaviors in new contexts and in new ways or forms. When such an expansion in these AASs occurs during the course of an already well-established Phase B, and when it is substantial in terms of frequency of usage, new contexts involved, and/or the number of "new ways or forms," the present individuals may be said to have moved to "Phase C": At this point, in other words, these youths have become (1) quite *involved in,* (2) psychologically, that is, dynamically and perhaps "ego-," *invested in,* or, at least, (3) largely *accepting of* many risky/trouble-related behaviors. (The involvement is behavioral and usually active; the investment and acceptance apply whatever the degree of activity.) These are the defining events, conditions, and characteristics of Phase C; all other aspects—such as the commonly reduced focusing on generics—are concomitants, however frequent and important they may be in their own right, and whatever their interaction with the defining features.[35]

Reduced Dependence on Peer Reinforcement
The present youths' movement into Phase C is less dependent upon peer reinforcement, that is, on this external input, than was the case when those individuals had moved into earlier phases, for example, Phase A. This applies to most such youths, and it mainly reflects the following interrelated developments: First, based on their personal experiences during portions of Phase B and even A, these individuals come to realize that if they expand the frequency, intensity and/or scope of some of their existing behaviors, this will sometimes increase the *satisfactions, relief, and/or feelings of hope (SRHs)* they already associate with those AASs. That is, the youths begin to sense that they will sometimes increase the

frequency and/or extent of those *SRHs* or that they will, at least, be more likely to then maintain them at their existing level. Second, during those same phases, especially B, these individuals increasingly find that they (1) *can,* in fact, expand certain AASs, and can thereby increase or at least maintain the prior level of SRH, and that they (2) can bring about that expansion largely—in any event, increasingly—by themselves. As indicated, "expanding" means raising the frequency, altering the intensity (and other expressions) of, and/or broadening the contexts of those behaviors; and it is the expansion of Phase-B behaviors (also including attitudes) that singularly characterizes Phase C.[36]

During the transition from B to C, and continuing beyond it, these same youths (1) feel less overall need than before for peer reinforcement that is fairly rapid, largely direct, at least moderately clear, and, in any case, frequent.[37] To be sure, their (2) felt need for peer-reinforcing inputs (PRIs) *per se* by no means vanishes; nor does their desire for them. These *inputs* comprise one form or another of attention, approval, and/or acceptance, usually to at least a moderate degree. The *objects* (in effect, targets) on which these inputs focus are the youths' risky or trouble-related "behavior," that is, their activities, attitudes, and stances. The *outputs*—the results or products—of these PRIs are the peer reinforcements (PRs) themselves. These outputs involve various feelings of satisfaction and relief—including "hope," or, by now, partially fulfilled hope. (The inputs are the reinforc*ers.*)

Because of item (1), above, and because of as well as despite item (2), the following can occur with respect to those targets or foci, namely, the *AASs* (this is again from the youths' standpoint, but it also applies independently): There can now be lengthier periods during which those peers are *not* directly, clearly, or even *at all* providing PRIs (the inputs) and are not thereby leading to the PRs themselves, that is, to the outputs—the actual reinforc*ements.*[38]

Also contributing to this reduced level of felt need for frequent, for fairly rapid, and so on, PRIs and PR is the following: The present individuals increasingly substitute, for *actual* peer approval, certain *beliefs* or *hopes* regarding approval. In particular, they increasingly draw upon their own expectations—sometimes growing expectations—that the given peers would approve the behaviors in question, simply if and when they had a chance to do so.[39] In this situation, peer approval has not yet occurred; and, the actual or provisional behaviors in question—here, expanded ones—may or may not be very new. (Again to simplify the presentation, peer "approval" will henceforth also encompass "attention" and "acceptance," unless otherwise specified.)

Those beliefs or hopes intuitively seem natural to the present youths, due to either one of these individuals' following perceptions (i.e., presumptions) (note: the youths do not conceptualize these perceptions explicitly and specifically, let alone formulate them in exactly the terms next used; instead, the perceptions are implicit and global):

1. Except for their respective quantities, the *expanded* behaviors (EBs) and the *previous* behaviors (PBs) are essentially the same as each other, particularly regarding their content; that is, the EBs involve, or contain, more of what the PBs involve or contain.

Given this presumed sameness, the youths expect—in effect, they automatically take it for granted—that the EBs would elicit identical or comparable responses from those peers, if and when opportunities arose. That is, they feel peers would respond to the expanded behaviors in essentially the same ways—approvingly— that they already responded to the previous ones. This will be called expectation #1.

2. The content of those expanded behaviors *does* differ substantially from that of the already-approved behaviors (activities, attitudes, and stances); however, the difference is not marked, let alone radical.

Under this slightly different perception, the youths come to expect that the EBs would elicit responses that are at least *roughly* comparable to those of the PBs, again if opportunities to respond arose. This is expectation #2.

(Three points might be noted before continuing. [a] In part, *expectations* #1 and #2 reflect the fact that the expanded and the previous behaviors also share the qualities of *riskiness* and *trouble,* per se. They do so even though these qualities may occur in connection with somewhat different content, or in differing contexts, in the case of EBs com-

pared to PBs. [b] Regardless of *perceptions* 1 and 2, some of the youths' expanded behaviors may *in fact* be markedly different than the previous ones, for instance, different with respect to content; at any rate, those EBs may be quite different to the peers. In particular, the PBs—in "becoming" EBs—may have changed to the point where many of those previously supportive peers would no longer approve of them or would, at most, support them only briefly, mildly, and/or reluctantly. [c] Even aside from the fact that such new peer reactions and possible responses either escape the present youths' notice or are somehow denied by them, these individuals' present beliefs and hopes may be described as largely wish-driven. This applies even though they seem straightforward and realistic to those youths, given that these individuals are centering on perceptions/presumptions 1 and 2 alone.)

Aspects of Self-Reinforcement

To review and briefly elaborate, youths who move to Phase C along the earlier-mentioned path have become more *self-approving* of their risky, trouble-related behaviors than before. This change leads to increased *self-reinforcement* of those behaviors.[40] ("Self"-based approval of behaviors (AASs), which is internally initiated and implemented, is distinguished from approval that is externally based—in this case, *peer-* initiated, and reinforced.) The self-reinforcement process includes, for example, the following: Once the youths internally approve the above AASs they experience—directly feel—the same or similar types of satisfaction, relief, and/or hope (SRH) that they experienced when various *peers* had approved those same or similar AASs, or were assumed to have done so.[41] In this process, the youths' self-approval of those behaviors is the key, immediate input; their resulting feelings and emotions of satisfaction, and so on—their SRHs—are its binding forces, that is, the reinforcements themselves.[42] At any rate, these youths, during the self-reinforcement process, in effect reexperience feelings and emotions they had previously experienced in connection with those same or even similar behaviors—feelings that, however, had then been *externally* triggered or initiated and which had subsequently constituted substantial reinforcement.[43]

As can be inferred, the relationship between self-approval and self-reinforcement, on the one hand, has basic parallels to that which exists between *peer*-approval and peer-based reinforcement, on the other. Specifically, (1) peer-approval had previously helped reinforce the earlier-mentioned behaviors; and, within limits, (2) the more this peer approval had occurred, say, the more frequent or intense it was, the more those behaviors were reinforced. Accordingly, that is, analogously, the youths' (1) *internal* approval of those behaviors helps make these individuals *self*-reinforcing in connection with those same, as well as similar, behaviors; and, again within limits, (2) the more such internal approval occurs, the more those behaviors are reinforced, that is, strengthened. (The earlier-mentioned behaviors had been reinforced mainly by virtue of the fact that the peer-approval had led to satisfactions, relief, and/or hope. More precisely, this had occurred in conjunction with the youths' resulting belief or assumption that they themselves were being accepted by those peers.)

Over and beyond those formal parallels, a *causal* connection exists between the peer-initiated process and the youth-initiated one: The latter partly stems from and reflects the former. Specifically, (1) the youth-initiated process emerges—that is, *exists,* in the first place—partly as an outgrowth of the peer-initiated one; and, (2) the products of the youth-initiated process—in particular, their anticipated (and actual) *characteristics*—partially reflect the youths' prior experiences with peer-initiated approval and with reinforcements that resulted from it. Point (2) refers, for example, to the types and general amounts of *satisfaction/relief/hope* that the youths implicitly assume they may obtain from their self-initiated approval—such SRHs being like reinforcements these individuals had already experienced and had come to associate with their *peers'* approval of the risky, trouble-related activities, attitudes, and stances.

Finally, as the youths' behaviors become increasingly and substantially self-reinforcing, they become increasingly—and often largely—*self-maintaining.* In particular, those behaviors can now be expressed and sustained even when the amounts of *external* input and resulting external reinforcement have been decreasing, and sometimes even small. At any rate, the youths' risky/trouble-related AASs can, and do, now function somewhat independently of those inputs. In this respect they even appear, to many observers, to have acquired "a life of their own" (*see* "seeming independence," below). (In the present context, external inputs, especially peer approval, are not just expected or hoped for; they are actual.)

Nevertheless, the following also applies: (1) External inputs, such as peer approval of the youths' behaviors, continue to be desired by and obtained by those individuals to at least some degree; and, (2) the resulting external reinforcement of those behaviors does augment the youths' self-reinforcement—most often to a moderate degree, itself. As a result, even when the present behaviors *are* characterized by considerable self-maintenance in the sense of actual as well as seeming independence, and even when the overall youth-initiated (YI) process *does* dominate the peer-initiated (PI) one with respect to influencing those AASs, that *PI* process can, and usually does, still exert at least a moderate influence on the YI.[44]

Critical Junctures and Sequences in Youths' Lives

Phase C, and even the transition from B to C, is an important juncture in the present youths' lives. This reflects two main implications of the following developments, especially when two or more of these are combined (of these developments, the first and second have already been described; the third is new, and temporally follows the others):

1. Starting at B/C and C, these individuals' risky, trouble-related activities, attitudes, and/or stances are *expanded* with respect to frequency of usage, forms or ways of expression (including intensity), and/or contexts involved.
2. From those periods forward, especially from Phase C, the youths' AASs can occur on an increasingly, and largely, *self-sustaining, self-reinforcing* basis. In particular, these individuals no longer need considerable, let alone heavy, approval or even attention from the earlier-mentioned peers.
3. As C continues, these youths can—and many do—become resistive or refractory to the following, or they become otherwise defended against it: *dis*approval of given behaviors (AASs) by those same,

previously reinforcing peers, and by other peers/friends as well. This disapproval can be moderate or sometimes even substantial, and it differs from a simple disinterest or growing indifference.

Regarding the implications, these center on the contributions of those developments to the present youths' illegal behavior; that is, they focus on the influence that (1), (2), and (3) have on the emergence, augmentation, and related aspects of that behavior. Concerning the first implication, those developments make an important contribution *in and of themselves,* that is, they help set the stage for illegal behavior, and they later strengthen it, essentially *by* themselves. Here, specifically, various combinations of (1), (2), and/or (3) increase the chances that such behavior will *occur,* if it has not already done so; in addition, some help *expand* and/or *reinforce* illegal activities and related supportive patterns that do already exist. (Expansion/reinforcement also pertains to borderline illegal behaviors—activities that, almost always, have first occurred before the above developments.)

As to the second implication, those developments are important because of how they are often responded to by given individuals— here, by adults—before and/or after any illegal behavior has occurred. (For present purposes, we will mainly focus on the "before.") These responses do not just increase the chances that such behavior will occur at all, that is, in the first place; instead, they can also help accelerate its initial appearance and determine its frequency and severity once it does take place.[45] Preceding those responses, however, are certain important perceptions, judgments, and concerns on the part of those individuals. These perceptions, and so on, usually trigger various responses which, in turn, can set in motion sequences of events (including further responses) that contribute to the existence and nature of illegal behavior.[46]

Perceptions by, Inputs from, and Interactions with Adults

For instance, when various adults, authority figures among them, first become either globally or pointedly aware of (1), (2), and/or (3) above, many begin to view the present youths as "getting out of control," "having gone too far," "serious problems," "jeopar-dizing their own future," and/or "troublemakers" per se. They are more likely to feel that way when any one or more such developments are accompanied by (a) considerable evasiveness or unresponsiveness toward *them,* the adults, or—especially—by (b) frequent open opposition to or rejection of their requests, instructions, and attempts at persuasion.

Such perceptions, judgments, and concerns usually trigger significant action responses by those adults, and they help determine certain "how," "what," and related aspects of those responses. For example, regarding the "how," they provide an impetus for those individuals to respond to the given youths forcefully or very forcefully, emotionally or very emotionally, and even rigidly—or, at any rate, often *more* forcefully and emotionally than before. As to the "what," those perceptions, judgments, and concerns furnish a rationale for the general direction and primary focus of those responses, and they therein help shape their overall individual content. Finally, they help determine the responses' collective scope. Here, although the main, immediate focus (target) of the adults' responses is, of course, the youths' risky activities, attitudes, and/or stances, and although these AASs, in themselves, may be narrow or broad, the adults' responses are not limited to those AASs. Instead, they often include relatively routine, ordinarily nontroubling aspects of the youths' lives and adjustment; moreover, this inclusion is often intentional and even pointed, not coincidental or else mainly "spillover."

Precursors and Reinforcers of Illegal Behavior
Such responses, when followed by the youths' subsequent *reactions* to them, and when next followed by the given adults' responses to those reactions, frequently revive old, often currently inactive or relatively quiescent issues, emotions, and feelings that are nevertheless unresolved; this reactivation is usually moderate or sizable in degree. In addition, or often instead, that "adult response → youth reaction → adult response" (RRR) sequence—or sometimes even just the initial adult response—sometimes broadens and/or intensifies differences and irritations that are *currently active* between those adults and youths. This broadening/ intensifying is in fact very common, and the differences in question are already often siz-

able. Finally, the RRR sequence may generate essentially *new* issues, differences, and irritations.

When the "old," "current," and "new" elements operate in various combinations (including all together), they usually revive, increase, and produce a number of tensions, frustrations, and/or problem-related feelings. (Here, the youths' feelings—though not just theirs—typically include anger, hurt, guilt, resentment, and/or reduced trust.) The new and increased tensions, frustrations, and feelings that result from these old, current, and/or new issues, differences, and so on—that is, that are generated or augmented by them—help make the youths' illegal and other problemmed behavior or harmful acting-out more likely to occur than before, often much more likely. This applies regardless of whether the old, the current, or the new tensions/frustrations/feelings are dominant at the time. As implied, it also applies especially, but not only, when those *older* and *newer* issues, and so forth, operate in given combinations, rather than singly. (For examples of mechanisms and content involved in parts of this sequence, see endnote 47.)

In short, Phase C and the B/C transition are periods in which youth/adult tensions and difficulties substantially increase, as do chances of youth acting-out. They are critical periods because—given those increases—the youths' chances of (1) initial, continued, augmented, and largely self-sustaining involvement in *illegal behavior per se* become considerably higher than before. Though this latter increase is enough to make the B/C and C periods critical by itself, those periods, especially C, are potential turning points also because of the youths' then-increased likelihood of (2) developing an at-least-partial, yet influential, *self-identification as a delinquent,* and of (3) initial or continued involvement in *severe* illegal behavior. Finally, and closely related to point (1), Phase C, in particular, is also crucial because the youths, by the time they reach that phase, *can* be largely beyond the "control" of parents, guardians, and other adults. More specifically, they can already be, or can soon become, relatively impervious or unresponsive to those individuals' usual range of input and reinforcement with regard to relatively conventional or prosocial versus illegal behavior. This applies whether the *old-but-reactivated* issues/emotions/feelings/differences/irritations, the already *active* ones, or else the essentially *new* ones are involved—and, if two or more (say, the already active and the new) are involved (this being typical), irrespective of which one dominates.[48] It also applies even if the parents or guardians had maintained a moderate to considerable overall or selective influence upon those youths, until a fairly recent time.

Critical Junctures Regarding Selected Phase B Youths

Criticality is not limited to the B/C transition and to Phase C; it often occurs in Phase B as well. In B, however, it is associated with largely different individuals than the C-youths described earlier, and it frequently occurs without a rapid and, in any event, a major rise in youth/adult tensions. Moreover, "B-criticality" is chiefly characterized by a substantially *increased* reliance on peer input and approval, not—as in B/C and C—by a decrease. We will next describe most B-youths who become "critical"—"B-criticals"—and will mention features and factors associated with their increased reliance. Though this section goes into considerable depth in order to illustrate certain youth dynamics and their relationship to the development of illegal behavior and, in many cases, of a possible delinquent self-identification, its relevance is not limited to that of B-criticals alone. This also applies to its discussion of the action/reaction cycle.

Major Features and Factors

The B-critical group includes many individuals who, collectively, are well above most adolescents' average on *dependency, vulnerability,* and—even absent those levels—a *tendency to follow* their peers.[49] Together, as implied, these youths comprise the preponderance of the B-criticals being described; and, neither they nor the remaining "criticals" invariably become serious delinquents (some remain only moderate). Fairly common *among* the "preponderance" are individuals previously called "passive-conformist" and "group conformist," respectively, and even "anxious-confused" (Chapters 4 and 5). Among these I-level subtypes, one or more of the earlier-mentioned features, such as the tendency to follow and otherwise comply, are highly characteristic and functionally significant. As may be inferred, youths who, collectively, comprise these three subtypes still do not, by themselves, constitute the vast majority of B-criticals.[50, 51]

In the case of B-criticals, as with B/C and C youths themselves, "criticality," as an attribute or condition, mainly refers to substantially increased chances of "initial, continued, [or] augmented . . . involvement" in illegal behavior. However, with these *B's*, in contrast to those other youths, this involvement neither is nor often becomes "largely self-sustaining." (The latter point applies even though some such B-criticals [most particularly the group conformists] can—*like* the B/C and C youths—develop a fairly strong view of themselves as delinquents or partial delinquents, a view that they largely want.) It might be added that many B-youths, for instance, those who are particularly dependent, who may often feel rather vulnerable, and who include passive-conformists and the anxious-confused, among others, are less resistive and opaque to usual types of adult input than are many C-youths—and the above group conformists as well.

Among the B-criticals, reliance on the earlier-mentioned peer input and approval (I&A)—that is, on I&A regarding risky and trouble-related activities, attitudes, and so forth—reinforces and, in effect, thereby solidifies and partly entrenches those AASs. This reliance and outcome—more specifically, (1) these individuals' relatively heavy reliance on that and similar peer I&A, and (2) the resulting establishment, stabilization, and maintenance of those particular AASs—jointly decreases the chances that substantially *expanded* AASs will occur. Given this decrease, there is also less chance that these youths will soon move to *Phase C*, since substantially expanded AASs are integral to such movement. In any case, (1) and (2), jointly, at least reduce the extent and rate of that expansion and movement; and they sometimes long preclude the movement itself. Further, such reductions, and of course any preclusion, are accompanied by a decreased chance (not necessarily little chance) that various youth/adult *tensions, frustrations, and the like,* will occur to as large a degree as they otherwise would, or will even emerge at all. This, in turn, reflects the fact that those tensions, and so on are closely—though not exclusively—associated with Phase C itself, and also with the B/C transition. (Youth/adult tensions and frustrations occur in Phase B as well; moreover, they

occur among B-criticals, even though these youths do not seem to be moving toward Phase C, or are moving very slowly. At any rate, because of these B-youths' personalities [see "dependency," above] and their overall relationship with most adults, the tensions and frustrations associated with these individuals and with that relationship usually seem, and overtly are, less intense and persistent than those generally seen in connection with the earlier-described, Phase C youths.)

The immediate implications of the preceding situation revolve around the following: In itself, the existence of fewer or lesser tensions—together called "decreased," "lowered," or "lower" tensions—helps reduce the chances that *illegal behavior* will occur. More specifically, decreased youth/adult tensions and frustrations (T/Fs)—say, fewer tensions beginning from early in Phase B—help reduce the likelihood of occurrence of such behaviors and of closely related acting-out. That is, the presence of less or of fewer overall T/Fs reduces the chances that those behaviors and types of acting-out will occur often, intensely (e.g., with violence), or even at all.

Decreased tensions, and so on, can reduce those chances because it is those same T/Fs—when *not* decreased, that is, when not at the lower levels—that ordinarily help generate or otherwise lead toward various illegal behaviors and related acting-out in the first place, and which later help sustain and perhaps augment them. In particular, those tensions/frustrations can begin to generate such behaviors when they, the T/Fs, first reach and maintain a substantial level, not when they exist in just any amount. Though the preceding are general points and pertain to a wide range of youths, they specifically apply to the Phase B individuals presently being focused on, as well: youths for whom movement toward C is either very slow or seemingly absent, and who, it might be added, usually manifest little spontaneous interest in such movement at the time.

Though (1) the present Phase B individuals have generally *lower* levels of youth/adult tensions/frustrations than do Phase C youths, though (2) these B-youths' lower levels of T/F—during Phase B—help reduce, minimize, or even essentially avoid the considerably *higher* T/Fs that would occur among them if they *did* move to Phase C, and although (3) the chances are that related *illegal activities* (those which the higher Phase B and C [potential Phase C] tensions, etc., would have helped produce) might thus be *lower* among these "unmoved" or slowly moving B-youths than among the earlier-described C's, the following is the case:[52] The overall likelihood that illegal activities will occur among these B's—B-criticals in particular—is, nonetheless, *not* lower than in those C-youths. This net result reflects the presence of other factors, ones whose heightening effects with respect to illegal behaviors, or regarding the chances of such behaviors, counter the lowering effects on illegal behaviors of decreased tensions and frustrations.

Chief among these counterbalancers is the already-mentioned reinforcement itself: peer reinforcement of risky, trouble-related activities, attitudes, and stances. This reinforcement, which, as already discussed, first helps *establish* those AASs as part of the youths' repertoire of responses, subsequently plays an equally important role in those individuals' *retaining* them—moreover, in retaining them largely as-is, that is, as when first established.[53] This last point, in other words, means that reinforcement, as an input, acts or functions as follows during the "post-establishment" or "maintenance" stage (note: with B-criticals, this and the establishment stage occur entirely during B, even if some B-to-C transition activity exists): It helps shape, move, and otherwise influence the youths' behaviors in the direction of (1) constancy, sameness, and stability.[54] Involved, here, is constancy, and so on, regarding the content and/or the contexts of usage on the part of those behaviors, though often not with respect to their overall frequency or amount of usage. This direction of influence contrasts with that of (2) variability, expansion, and *change* of content and/or contexts, and even with (3) a mixture of (1) and (2)—the latter one occurring, say, in moderate to substantial amounts.

In thus helping to maintain the youths' risky activities, attitudes, and stances—actions and involvements that can include illegal behaviors even during Phase B—this increase in the "constancy . . . and stability" of those often-trouble-related AASs largely or entirely counters the effects that the B-criticals' *lower level of tensions and frustrations (T/Fs)* have or would have with regard to such AASs. (As implied earlier, this counterbalancing pertains

not only to T/Fs that would exist during Phase C if that phase *were* eventually reached by these individuals. Instead, it also applies to tensions/frustrations that exist during later or fully formed stages of B, and in connection with B/C transition activities per se.) Obviously, the preceding points apply even though the increase in constancy, sameness, and stability operates in a way that helps retard, or can even essentially preclude, these youths' movement toward, and eventual arrival in, C.[55]

In summary, the following are five factors, plus certain motives and a related view, that collectively underlie and support the "establishment" and "maintenance" roles of external reinforcement: (1) Because B-critical youths have more or stronger unmet needs for emotional security than do most adolescents,[56] (2) because such unmet needs often produce considerable anxiety and unhappiness in these B-youths, (3) given the related strength of these individuals' desire for relief and satisfaction (in each case, hopefully soon),[57] (4) because of their particular personalities and adaptations, which highlight features such as above-average dependency and vulnerability, and (5) given their sizable difficulties with key adults, these youths are especially receptive to peer inputs that bear on those needs and desires, even partly.[58] These are inputs that involve peer interest in, and apparent approval of, the youths' risky/trouble-related behaviors. To the youths, this approval often signifies personal acceptance, whether or not the approval is accompanied by explicit, verbal encouragement of the given behaviors. Such peer inputs, plus that assumed or actual acceptance and any related concrete pleasures, help the individuals feel moderately to considerably relieved, less insecure, and more hopeful regarding their immediate and sometimes intermediate future. In so doing, they bear on the above needs and desires, albeit often indirectly.

The Action/Reaction Cycle
B-criticals, having found that (a) their given activities, attitudes, and stances often make a palpable, immediate, desired, and sometimes long-lasting difference in how they feel, and that (b) the "price" they usually pay for those AASs is smaller or much smaller than the emotional gains involved, soon become motivated to retain those AASs largely as-is, to

continue engaging in them or expressing them (often or not), and to be identified or partly identified with them in the eyes of their reinforcing peers. In this regard, they generate and otherwise engage in an action/reaction cycle whose main components and basic sequence are: *risky activities,* followed by *peer approval,* followed by *personal relief/satisfaction,* and then back to *risky activities,* and so on.[59] The youths do not conceptualize this cycle or even sequence as such, though they globally realize that certain inputs, events, and feelings occur in a certain order. (This aspect of the discussion continues in Appendix 42, which, thereafter, extensively describes the role and effects of long-standing difficulties and their interactions with the youths' motivations, and whose applicability extends beyond B-criticals alone.)

Complementing these individuals' (a)- and (b)-centered motivation to maintain their reinforced AASs "largely as-is" is their particular and often strong reluctance to *change* them: These youths soon come to feel or to implicitly assume that if they substantially modify those behaviors they could well lose or largely lose their peers' attention and approval—and, with that, their own felt gains. In short, they believe or sense that by changing step one of the above sequence, they could jeopardize the remaining steps.

That view, and degree of concern, partly reflects the youths' personalities (cf. features such as vulnerability) and other previously mentioned factors, such as (2) and (3). Because of it, these individuals believe that *new kinds* of behaviors should be minimized or avoided whenever possible, unless initiated and apparently supported by given peers; otherwise, the risks and possible losses would be too large. Minimizing or avoiding also applies to expansions or substantial variations of *existing* behaviors, that is, those already integral to the action/reaction cycle; here, too, the youths feel or implicitly assume the risks would be too high. At any rate, factors (1) through (5) help generate and support the B-criticals' heightened receptivity to peer attention and approval of the given behaviors, and they thus pave the way for establishing them. Those same factors, operating in conjunction with specified motives and in the context of related beliefs and assumptions, subsequently help maintain them largely as-is.[60]

In the next section, emphasis is no longer on Phase B youths, especially its B-criticals.

Deeper Involvement: The Illegal Behavior Pattern

Regarding the following discussion, it might be kept in mind that behavior which is specifically illegal is most likely to be found in the category called "trouble-related activities"— one which, in turn, is part of and interwoven with the broader category termed "risky, often trouble-related activities, attitudes, and/or stances (AASs)." (Many *risky* activities are trouble-related, and most of the latter are risky; obviously, the content correspondence between these two is substantial but far from perfect. Moreover, like the trouble-related activities, not all risky ones are illegal per se, or at least quite seriously so;[61] and, as implied, trouble-related activities are more likely to be illegal than are the risky. At any rate, all *illegal activities* involve not only risk, but actual or potential trouble. [The preceding points, and the next one, apply not only to the present individuals, that is, specified B-youths, but to earlier-mentioned youths who move or have moved to Phase C.] Finally, although the present, illegal behaviors are generally minor in severity and low in frequency, particularly at first, such behaviors may slowly increase in both respects, especially the latter. Thus, illegal behaviors are among the AASs that— whether they have been characterized mainly as risky, as trouble-related, or as both—sometimes *do* change to a certain degree, and in content as well, among the B-youths described earlier and among other youths as well.)[62]

As already indicated, many B-youths, and the differing individuals who reach Phase C, have encountered difficult, even critical periods and/or forks in the road in their recent years. However, both groups face what can be their most critical period or juncture yet, if they substantially establish the next-described pattern. This is a pattern of, or method for, obtaining relief and/or satisfactions (R/Ss)—obtaining them, for instance, in response to, or when otherwise dealing with, various long-standing as well as more recent/difficulties, challenges, and even opportunities. Basically, this pattern involves the direct, sometimes increased, use of *illegal behavior per se* (i.e., over and beyond that which is risky and/or trouble-related alone), as one way, albeit an important way, of obtaining that *R/S.*

(The illegal behavior thus serves as input, and the R/S is output. As implied earlier, some or most such behavior may have already been used to obtain relief/satisfactions regarding various conditions and situations. In the present context, however, the youths depend on or have started to depend on that input in a more focused or particularized way—thus giving it, in effect, more weight and often more salience than before. These individuals, especially but not only in light of their overall problems, need engage in this illegal behavior—this input—only occasionally, for it to markedly affect their lives. Appendix 43 briefly expands on these problems and focuses on related skill deficits.)

Conditions and Aspects
More specifically, B-youths during Phase B and C-youths during C reach a major turning point regarding their immediate and long-range adjustment if they have definitely moved toward crystallizing the use of illegal behavior (IB) as a way of achieving relief/satisfactions (R/Ss). From their perspective, this "illegal-behavior-as-a-means-to-R/S" pattern (IBP) involves each of the following conditions and aspects; in fact, absent these features, the youths cannot be said to have moved far toward crystallizing the IBP in the first place, that is, toward substantially establishing it.[63]

1. The relief, the satisfactions, or both, occur fairly *soon* after the youths' behavior takes place—in this case, shortly after their illegal activity. Also, these R/Ss *literally* occur; that is, they are not just or not primarily hoped-for, or are not only thought *likely* to occur, soon or otherwise.

2. The youths have begun to substantially *count on* the relief/satisfactions; that is, they count on them in connection with the IB input (yet not to the exclusion of *non*-IB input). More specifically, these individuals do not only (a) expect the R/Ss to usually *occur;* instead, and in particular, they now also (b) emotionally *depend* on them, to at least a moderate degree. Psychologically and cognitively, reaction 2(b) becomes possible in the first place mainly because these youths have come to view the illegal-behavior input as sufficiently reliable in terms of producing those R/S outputs, and to also see those inputs, themselves, as sufficiently worthwhile. (Feature 1, above, contributes to perception or expectation 2(a); also, it is a precondition to 2(b),

though it does not, by itself, virtually ensure its occurrence. See Appendix 44 regarding the crystallization of the IB pattern, and about "sufficient reliability" and "sufficient worth" in particular.)

It might be noted that the youths have begun to accept the illegal-behavior component not just or not mainly for its own sake but because of its role in the overall IB pattern—in particular, because it (like *non*-IB inputs) helps generate R/Ss. In this regard these individuals have, in effect, accepted the pattern, method, or sequence *as a whole,* not just its separate parts. Also, the youths have begun to substantially rely on that overall IBP even if—still from their perspective—its relief/satisfactions leave something to be desired with regard to scope and/or intensity, though perhaps not frequency.[64]

3. As implied by feature 2(a), the youths, for the most part, *want to* support the illegal-behavior pattern; that is, they largely and willingly accept and try to sustain it. They do not, say, only reluctantly utilize it, let alone feel they must mostly *force* themselves to break the law—must, in effect, engage in, and win, a vigorous internal battle against disinterest in doing so, or against an interest in not doing so. Moreover, these individuals mainly want to and try to support the illegal-behavior pattern in spite of the following (the first-mentioned factor almost always exists; the second is frequent):

    a. their slight, moderate, or considerable ambivalence about engaging in the illegal behavior (included, e.g., are their mixed feelings about participating in activities that—regardless of the relief/satisfactions associated with them—they feel are partly or largely "wrong," in the usual sense of the term); and

    b. their earlier-mentioned, underlying sense that the relief/satisfactions, even though these make a sizable difference to them, are somehow not enough; in short, despite the individuals' sense that something important is absent or insufficient.

At any rate, despite (a) and (b), the youths' level of interest in and resulting support for the IB pattern is—overall—still enough to allow them, and partly impel them, to continue engaging in the given behavior.[65] This is the case even though their support for illegal behavior is, usually, by no means *marked*—even if and when, for example, their ambivalence about engaging in it is only slight. (They are not, at this point, *highly*—firmly, solidly—committed to delinquency, and to "being delinquents.")

Finally, the youths' largely accept and want to sustain the illegal-behavior pattern regardless of the related, increased pressure and/or reduced support they feel from adults, and despite what they, the youths, implicitly or explicitly consider the pattern's immediate and perhaps longer-range "price" in other respects. These responses and perceptions, on the youths' part, often contribute to feature 3(a), though they can also operate in parallel with it.

In sum, the IBP has taken definite shape, and the youths are already substantially involved with it and at least partly invested in it. The critical juncture that exists at this point depends not primarily—or not necessarily *even*—on the earlier-described, "risky activities" (those that are, say, borderline with respect to legality and which, therefore, are commonly "trouble-related" as well). It reflects, instead, mainly the illegal behavior per se, even though—when present—the "borderline," risky activities can add significantly to the IB-generated difficulties and can make them likelier to occur in the first place. At any rate, given the negative implications of the illegal-behavior pattern in particular, for instance, in light of the often-widespread complications and negative consequences largely generated and partly sustained by this pattern, the present period can be more critical than any thus far.

Notes

1. These frustrations, worries, and so on, are responses to life situations and/or personal issues whose content, in some respects, extends beyond that of situations/issues that most youths—most SMOs included—face as a *regular* part of contemporary adolescent, and adolescence-to-adulthood, adjustment. In this regard it involves "more" than and/or other than ordinary pressures, challenges, expectations, and/or demands, ones which themselves sometimes frustrate and worry those youths and that occasionally even generate substantial self-doubt and inner- or outer-directed anger. Nevertheless, among most adolescents, when these or other feelings and emotions reach the level of intensity frequently seen in many *SMOs,* as they occasionally do, they usually subside faster and more fully than they do among the latter youths. In any event, with most SMOs, these feelings and emotions, for example, ones that center on long-standing difficulties/problems, complicate and heighten the "regular[ly]" occurring ones; similarly, the *latter* feelings and emotions, together with their own underlying contributors, simultaneously complicate the former. This mutual compounding pertains to the next-mentioned—the "secondary" or "second-level"—effects, as well.

2. Not infrequently, secondaries 1 through 4, respectively, develop from their four corresponding primaries even if the difficulties/problems that contribute to those primaries remain at about the same level as before. This situation largely reflects the nature and extent of factor #1—the "particularly negative events and conditions" of childhood and/or preadolescence, in Chapter 25's eight-factor sequence; that is, it reflects issues and conditions that existed before the given difficulties/problems (factor #2) operated to a substantial degree. In short, the developments under consideration can largely result from deep-seated—here, long-standing—factors that remain strong in themselves and that are not largely quiescent. Common among them are feelings of being disliked by many or most people one knows, of being considered "no good" by one or both parents or parent figures, and of perhaps being openly rejected and unwanted by them. (For these general reasons, relieving the factor #2 D/Ps does not, by itself, always sufficiently pave the way for substantial forward movement, even though it can be important or essential with respect to better everyday adjustment and can thereby put the indi-

vidual in a better position for such eventual movement.)

3. Still among SMOs collectively, the second and third outgrowths are sometimes accompanied by increased or at least continued confusion. Moreover, whether or not such confusion exists, most of the four outgrowths may be accompanied or soon followed by feelings of depression that are often more than transitory and mild. Like all four outgrowths—these being the second-level content effects—confusion and depression may each result from internal, external, or both types of difficulties/problems. In addition, whichever of those sources predominates, some of these same secondaries, taken individually, may partly result from interactions with *other* individual secondaries. This involves interactions among given *effects* of the internal and/or external difficulties/problems.

4. These reactions occasionally develop directly from the *initial* reactions to D/Ps. (When this occurs, it is to a lesser extent.) In these instances, the secondary reactions—content effects—had not developed, and the tertiaries functionally substitute for them.

5. Among most *non*offenders and many nonserious offenders, "defenses" and "reactions" are usually directed at first- rather than second-level effects. Partly for this reason, these defenses and reactions are not likely to be particularly inflexible or intense (individually) and/or extreme in scope (collectively); and, under most conditions, they *are* in fact somewhat malleable and delimited in those respects. In contrast, most SMOs' defenses and many reactions are usually less flexible and more intensive or extreme (individually), and more extensive in scope (collectively). In general, such characteristics reflect the heavier reliance these youths place on them. This is partly because they, the SMOs, have fewer alternative or additional responses in, or usually available from, their repertoire, and partly due to the larger issues and problems—namely, second-level effects—at which the responses are commonly directed.

6. Though these particular four are emphasized, the underlying concepts would be unchanged even if substantial "confusion" and/or "depression" were added.

7. Despite the shortcomings associated with these defenses and overcompensations, and in spite of negative consequences that often result from them, the following might be kept in mind. At intake, these defenses and overcompensations are usually the main ones these youths are accustomed to using in order to adapt to various situations. From the youths' standpoint, they may reflect the best—the functionally best—these individuals can bring to bear at the time.

8. With all *three* groups, the content of these interactions commonly involves the individuals' wishes and attitudes concerning participation and nonparticipation in various conventional and/or unconventional activities. It is in connection with these contexts that the resistiveness and negativism mainly occurs; and these stances or reactions are often stronger or broader among SMOs than among others.

9. Category B adaptations/responses have some content-overlap with those of Category A, especially in connection with #(l), in the text immediately above, and, to a lesser degree, with #(2), particularly regarding adults. A and B sometimes both involve the use of similar ego defenses as well, e.g., denial and rationalization. Despite this overlap, B's content largely differs from that of A's. In that respect, B can be considered a separate or alternative path to the goal of (1) resisting/reducing secondary reactions (e.g., increased anxiety/insecurity), and yet, often simultaneously, to the goal of (2) dealing with immediate and emerging challenges and opportunities of adolescence. (Items (1) and especially (2) relate to the "secondary goals" described in Chapter 25, particularly to A_{2g} and B_{2g}.) At any rate, *B's* are often used instead of given *A's,* not primarily in addition to them or functionally in conjunction with them. Also, through time, they are sometimes used *subsequent* to them.

10. They sometimes bear directly on first-level effects and on factor #1 events and conditions, as well. For present purposes, these further areas of relevance need not be pursued here.

11. Regarding point (1), these Category B effects differ from the varied, socially accepted adjustments and reactions often seen among nonoffenders and many nonserious offenders to the first-level responses to relatively typical or common difficulties/problems. These first-level responses generally involve moderate amounts of frustration, worry, self-doubt, and/or anger, and, in many cases, some confusion and a sense of unfairness.

12. In the case of nonOs, B-responses are seldom directed at second-level effects, even though such responses—like the "B's" of serious multiple offenders—sometimes do center on first-level effects, such as nonintensive or nonchronic self-doubts and anxieties.

13. From the standpoint of most such peers, for example, most nondelinquents, it may not be necessary for those SMOs to go to extremes.

14. Certain activities in which they now engage, and qualities they display, also help some SMOs express their hostility/anger, usually in a displaced way. Some *nonOs* end up encouraging these expressions when they do not clearly *oppose* them; and, in such situations, they sometimes indirectly express or vicariously release some of their own frustrations.

15. The following is a related, common contributor to many such SMOs' expectations regarding (1) and/or (2): Because these individuals have often considered it difficult to obtain, let alone maintain, substantial or reliable *approval, acceptance,* or perhaps even *attention* from parents or parent figures (and/or siblings), they implicitly assume they will often have comparable difficulty obtaining such responses from many other individuals—in the present case, peers. Involved, here, is a form of preconscious generalization or extrapolation: In effect, past or continued experiences have primed these youths to expect a repeat, unless they make different or extra efforts in the present, or run into different kinds of people. When these youths do find peers—even some adults—who seem to accept them (whether or not with, or because of, "extra efforts"), they are often pleasantly surprised and are sometimes readily drawn to those individuals, and may be easily reinforced by them.

16. Efforts that are "extra . . . and . . . special," for example, with respect to frequency and perhaps overall amount, are also common among *nonoffenders;* thus, they are not unique to serious multiple offenders. Nevertheless, with nonOs compared to SMOs, these efforts, individually and collectively, are likely to be less often "exaggerated" and/or "extreme" with regard to their content, their manner of expression, or both; and, even when they are exaggerated, or excessive, these qualities usually exist to a lesser degree. Beyond that, nonoffenders draw a fairly sharp line against engaging in behaviors they know are *illegal per se* or probably so, particularly but not only if those activities or types of activity also seem likely to physically harm others or cause major property damage. This, however, does not mean these individuals do not occasionally, intentionally, engage in the following (both points are especially relevant or applicable to those youths, but not only those, who are average or somewhat below average in overall conformity): (1) *less* harmful/damaging behaviors, and/or (2) legal or borderline activities which they know most peers and adults would consider "far out" ("wild"), "foolhardy" or excessively "daring," and so on, whether or not these are also physically risky to the participants themselves. (Even here, most such nonOs—especially those of average conformity—prefer to not engage in (1) and/or (2) with peers who are known "troublemakers" or "delinquents." In practice, however, they are often not choosy.)

17. Regarding content and amount, these efforts involve the youths' going farther than most nonoffenders would usually go—and that other nonoffenders would ever go—in order to gain similar acceptance. This difference between SMOs and nonOs is a major reason for characterizing the former's efforts as "exaggerated . . . ," and so on.

18. Some such *stances* amount to a form of behavior themselves, though they are not an "activity" per se.

19. Two points might be noted here. (1) Often, attitudes and stances that are first associated with very few situations

gradually connect with, are triggered by, and/or come to encompass several more. (This can occur with closely related behaviors—activities—as well.) Usually, such attitudes and stances then begin to comprise a larger and larger part of the self, including the individuals' self-concept. Depending on their overall frequency, duration, and cross-context generality, they may eventually be described as traits rather than situational responses only, or mainly. (2) Many nonoffenders sometimes engage in the already-mentioned, excessive, risky, and essentially "unauthorized" *activities*. However, relatively few engage fairly often, let alone increasingly so (except for short time-periods and/or in response to certain crises); and, all in all, few are involved to the same degree as are SMOs. For instance, these individuals are less willing and less likely than the latter to visit or revisit "disreputable places," to often "hang out" with known "troublemakers," to continue drinking heavily (as against having a rare or occasional spree), and/or to experiment with hard drugs—especially, to try them repeatedly. This applies even though many such individuals occasionally manifest some of the *attitudes/stances* that were just mentioned, particularly "obstinacy, . . . seeming indifference, and evasiveness," but, even here, to a lesser overall degree than do most SMOs.

In considerable contrast to these and most other nonOs, some *SMOs* develop a social role and a related self-concept that includes or readily allows for many or most such activities, and perhaps for several of the attitudes/stances, as well. This applies whether or not these individuals' role and self-concept are *centered* upon, dominated by, or otherwise heavily dependent upon such activities, and so on. However, with other SMOs-to-be, for instance, many who later become what have been called "group conformists," and, to a lesser degree, "delinquent identifiers" and also "assertive-deniers," such activities, attitudes, and/or stances are more prominent and often dominant. (The Warren names for these three subtypes are "Cultural Conformists," "Cultural

Identifiers," and "Neurotic, Acting-out," respectively.)

20. This judgment would apply to any given attitude and stance, individually, in connection with any relevant dimension—namely, "content, frequency, or degree"—individually. It would apply more strongly, of course, if—again regarding any given attitude or stance—any *two or more* such dimensions were involved simultaneously, as they often are.

21. Depending on the overall context, these three types of behavior may also be considered "risky," though this dimension applies primarily when the behaviors—unless fairly extreme—are directed at adults rather than peers. (Concerning the earlier-mentioned activities, attitudes, and stances, these apply across SMOs collectively, since virtually no one individual exhibits all or nearly all of them and because few show even most of them, especially at this early stage of their occurrence. This applies regardless of who, and what, they are directed at.)

22. At this point in the overall process, the approval in question occurs only within the nonoffenders; that is, this activity involves them alone. They have not yet indicated their approval externally, that is, to others; at least, they have not purposely tried to do so. In particular, nonoffenders have not knowingly expressed approval, to the serious multiple offenders, of these SMOs' behavior.

Two other points might be mentioned. First, regarding "added" activities (see point [2] in the text), these *nonoffenders* briefly imagine themselves doing or having the given activities, attitudes, and/or stances. More specifically, they see themselves as *wanting* to do them, have them, and feel or express them. (In the present comments, AASs will be called "features.") In this connection, the nonOs briefly identify with the SMOs (SMOs-to-be) whom they observe and whom they assume want to do and have the features that they, the SMOs, are expressing. More precisely, these nonoffenders incorporate only—or identify themselves only with—those particular features, namely, the given AASs alone. That is, they generally do not try to incorporate several of the SMOs' *other* observed or known features; in this and other respects they do not identify with, or otherwise try to "be like" or "be," those individuals as a whole. In short, they generate a temporary emotional and cognitive—or otherwise imagined—equivalence and congruence between some of their own wishes, feelings, and thoughts, on the one hand, and those they assume are involved in the SMOs' behavior, on the other. In this respect they establish a limited bond.

Second, as implied, what might be called the *nonOs'* "active, desired self-concept"—say, those parts or aspects of the recognized self that these individuals knowingly utilize and want to use at the time—involves some content and emotions that have been relatively long-lasting and other aspects (here, in particular, the AAS features) that are usually fairly transitory. Under certain conditions, the latter may reappear and can become more permanent.

23. Watching these SMOs gives many such nonoffenders a form of catharsis. In key respects, this situation parallels one in which the nonOs would, say, be observing a play. There, via the actors' words, expressions, and activities, those nonOs' own feelings would first be aroused; via the play's eventual outcome, the feelings would later be released (Ackrill, 1987). Nonoffenders and others who, at some point, *knowingly* encourage the expression of SMOs' particular AASs may, in effect, be trying to make the "play" go on.

24. This behavior would not be nonconforming and unusual with only them, the nonOs, as the reference frame, that is, only in relation to those individuals—say, their past and present activities. Instead, it would also be nonconforming in comparison to many local, age-attuned, societal standards or expectations, including those of any applicable adult subcultures.

Besides the nonoffenders to whom text points (1) and (2) apply, certain *other* nonOs might be mentioned. These individuals, who partly overlap with the former, hesitate to resist pressures from given peers or groups—in either case, from other *conforming* nonoffenders—to *remain* conforming in major respects, or,

in extreme cases, to become even more conforming and compliant than they already are. These nonOs ("who partly overlap . . .") are not emphasized in the immediate discussion; however, it might be noted that this feature is observed in most passive-conformists, though most individuals *with* the feature are not ipso facto those particular conformists—at, say, a predelinquent stage.

25. Some SMOs' verbal encouragement, and even their overt manner, often makes it easier for various nonoffenders to *actively* "go along with" risky-seeming actions/behaviors, for example, to more openly support them, to physically participate in them, or to later copy them, at least for a while. If these nonoffenders respond in any of those ways to either forms of encouragement, they are not, or are no longer, trying to only or mainly obtain *vicarious* satisfactions/release. Even then, however, they often see and rationalize the given behavior as part of their only occasionally "letting loose" or "letting go," and of not really being invested in such actions. Even very conforming nonOs sometimes act this way.

26. At first, serious multiple offenders may be unclear as to exactly which activities, attitudes, and/or stances are being approved by given peers, even though they implicitly assume these include—and are perhaps mainly—the AASs they *hoped* were being approved, or that seemed to be receiving the most attention. At any rate, their primary overall concern at this early point is that they, the SMOs, are being *accepted*. Insofar as they feel this is occurring, they take it for granted that either their general activities/attitudes/stances or else particular aspects of those AASs are responsible. (At this point, a range of AASs is commonly reinforced; however, this range often extends beyond that which the *peers* have generally or specifically centered on in connection with their *inputs,* that is, with their attention and approval.) After their behaviors have been reinforced for some time—whether by the peers who originally provided this, by new individuals, or by some of each—the SMOs develop a clearer sense as to which particular behaviors, and so on, usually obtain the attention and approval of those peers.

27. Two further points. (1) In the present context, even though the rate and quantity of peer input may be modest during given periods, and perhaps in "all" periods combined, the emotional significance or dynamic meaning (ES/DM) of this input may be considerable. This factor— ES/DM—can provide the main active ingredient or force that usually carries and sufficiently maintains the reinforcement process. Here, "significan[t] . . ." inputs can be thought of as those, or those characteristics, which substantially bear on an individuals' strivings, actual and desired self-image or sense of identity, main fears, and so on. These, in turn, relate to primary goals A, B, and C, in Chapter 25. (2) Initially, most SMOs-to-be will accept reinforcement from essentially any available peers—"straight arrows" (nonoffenders), occasionally "wild" youths, and seemingly committed "troublemakers," alike, even though they are not equally comfortable with all. This situation is paralleled by most *nonOs*' initial, overall indifference as to which of *their* peers, or what "kind" of peers, manifest the activities, attitudes, and stances in question. However, these nonoffenders are usually wary of the more "committed" youths, in particular.

28. At this point, namely, pre-A, such challenges and expectations are much less salient in the individuals' lives, particularly from the youths' own standpoint, than are near-term ones. As a result, they usually generate less overall youth motivation or active effort, not to mention basic interest, than do the near-term challenges.

29. Regarding external pressures, "above average" generally means unusual, or particularly difficult, in amount and/or type—individually or together; *amount* involves frequency, intensity, and/or duration. Prior to the Change-A phase, and often throughout it as well, many of the present youths have a somewhat narrow, albeit still meaningful, experiential base for considering the external pressures they receive "above average"—say, less flexible or more intense than is common. This base involves, for example, comparisons with various peer situations of which they are aware. However, media

inputs, such as news and dramas, often broaden that base, sometimes helpfully, sometimes not; on the latter score, the information or depictions are often misleading by omission or commission. In any event, even apart from most peer comparisons and media inputs, the present youths can often subjectively, and accurately, recognize inflexibility—and especially inconsistency and mutual conflict—as such. They can often sense some of their immediate effects, as well. (Above-average external pressures are not the only sources of frustration, stress, and/or anxiety, whether before, during, or after the Change-A period.)

30. Three points might be mentioned. (1) Often, as of the pre-A and A phases, relatively consistent encouragement, guidance, and/or direction (EGD), by parents and parent figures, was absent from the youths' lives. In such cases, the fact that the youths had not, more *recently*, followed given advice, and so on, was thus neither originally nor necessarily a matter of their simply having never paid much attention to adult-based EGD that had, say, *been* available and adequate. Instead, many youths began "tuning out" partly because, for example, of (a) various inconsistencies in the parents' messages, (b) the nature or content of the parents' advice even absent any inconsistencies, (c) their changing views regarding parents, parent figures, and adults overall, and so on. (2) Increased external pressures by adults usually would have occurred in response to the youths' (a) activities, attitudes, and stances that emerged during the pre-A phase, and/or—somewhat later—to those individuals' (b) modification/ deemphasis of various prosocial attitudes/investments during the Change-A phase itself. However, whether or not the adults' external pressures *had* already increased, were already unusual, and/or *were* already well above average in difficulty—in each case, during the just-mentioned phases—the following applied: The adult-based pressures were likely to continue well into Phase B if those individuals believed the youths' were, at the time, making relatively few serious or sustained efforts—or fewer

than before—regarding generic areas (1) through (3), and if they, the adults, considered such efforts important or increasingly important in the youths' lives. (3) As used thus far, the term "peer approval" mainly focuses on those individuals' responses to the youths' (SMOs-to-be) *behaviors*. However, peer acceptance, or that which the youths believe is the peers' acceptance, centers more on the SMOs *themselves,* that is, on an explicit or implicit judgment of, or feeling about, those individuals as *persons* (e.g., the particular generators/maintainers of the behaviors). This distinction, however, is neither a hard-and-fast one nor a sharp and, in any event, critical one.

31. The reduced likelihood of "seriously address[ing]" these—the generic—areas pertains to the B-period in particular. As indicated later, a subsequent, *additional* reduction in the likelihood of addressing them commonly occurs in Phase C (again see text), and beyond. Yet, the *first* reduction does not *necessarily* occur; and it is neither an essential precondition of Phase C nor one of its defining features. ("Additional" reduction, that is, *further* such change, is distinguished from *continuation* at essentially the same level as before.)

32. Earlier phases, namely, pre-A and A, partly reflected *difficulties* the youths had or were having with various tasks, challenges, and so on, even when these individuals were motivated to address them. Later phases, such as B and beyond, were much more likely to involve and reflect a *disinterest or lessened interest* in such tasks/challenges, for instance, tasks that were part of or increasingly part of generic areas (1) through (3).

33. To review and elaborate: The peer support, the relief, and the often-immediate satisfactions/pleasures that are experienced constitute sizable incentives, even if they are not intense, fairly consistent, and quite frequent. Because of these factors, and despite the increasingly evident risks and hassles associated with the *activities, attitudes, and stances* in question, the present individuals are motivated to maintain or even expand those AASs in one way or another. Partly in order to do so, the youths are willing and sometimes eager to modify and/or deemphasize certain already-existing *attitudes and emotional investments (A/Is)* that seem, or seem likely, to interfere. They are also prepared to deemphasize those A/Is partly because these may now seem less interesting, rewarding, or promising than before. In general, the A/Is in question may seem less important to the youths based on how they compare with emerging *new* interests and activities—in particular, on how they measure up not only to the types and amounts of reward/satisfaction (r/s) that the latter seem likely to produce but to the amount of effort that seems necessary in order to obtain that r/s and to experience relief as well. (The measuring or comparing occurs on an essentially global-intuitive, sometimes even preconscious, basis—at any rate, not in an explicit, specifically thought-out, deliberate manner.)

All this is aside from the fact that, with most of the present SMOs-to-be, many of their external pressures literally continue to exist; moreover, they usually do so at about the same level as before, or else somewhat higher. (This reflects the fact that *relief* from those external pressures is, substantively, mainly a psychological reality, though nonetheless very important in that respect itself.) At any rate, even when the youths resist, delay, or partly ignore those pressures, and whether or not they then often feel considerable relief from them, neither those nor various other youth actions and responses usually alter the actual external pressures more than moderately. This applies, for instance, during the pre-A phase, Phase A, and often even B. In sum, most such pressures continue to exist; parents, other adults, social agencies, and so on can still apply or reapply them at any of several points. This is independent of the fact that many SMOs have partly internalized various such pressures in any event, and therefore sometimes feel them (1) even when little actual external activity is occurring and (2) despite the partial success they may have felt when they "resist[ed] . . . or . . . partly ignore[d]" pressures that *were* being applied.

34. It becomes increasingly easy for these individuals to reduce their focus if and as they learn to better fend off, evade, and otherwise partly or largely resist various external pressures that adults bring to bear regarding those areas. This resisting-of-pressures—and, with it, the experiencing of some relief from internal worries about them—gives those youths further leeway to continue in their Phase-B mode. It also helps open a path to Change C (Phase C).

35. As may be deduced, the Phase C level of involvement and investment can exist even if, as indicated, the youths have not withdrawn from generic areas (1), (2), and/or (3) to a degree over and above that which existed in Phase B. Also, that level can exist even if those individuals have not further withdrawn their emotional investments in prosocial activities that may be closely related to those generic areas. Thus, the following would apply: Though youths who move to Phase C have expanded with respect to certain activities, attitudes, and stances, they have not ipso facto become or remained involved and/or invested in *only* risky or trouble-related behaviors—that is, in only those and comparable AASs. Instead, several prosocial investments can remain alive and substantial, even if they are functionally low in priority or are virtually inactive at the time.

   To be sure, the following also applies: With some SMOs-to-be, prosocially oriented "emotional investments . . ." are, individually and collectively, substantially reduced while the youths are moving into Phase C, that is, during the expansion of the already-existing AASs. Especially in this context, such a reduction can often be an additional forerunner of Phase C and even an important contributor to it. However, as may be deduced, this reduction, like the "withdraw[al] from generic areas (1), (2), and/or (3)" per se, can nevertheless occur without its being an essential precondition or a defining feature of that phase.

   Many Phase C youths who have not substantially reduced their prosocial investments and/or their focus on generic areas (2) and (3) over and beyond the

Phase-B level are sometimes viewed as "living a double life": On the one hand, they seemingly and/or actually manifest and engage in at least some prosocial/generic attitudes, values, and/or activities; on the other, they simultaneously tolerate and perhaps actively engage in trouble-related behavior and in illegal behavior per se. A similar duality sometimes exists during Phase B, albeit usually to a lesser extent.

36. Though still other youths (1) expand their Phase-B AASs only modestly at best (not substantially), and although they may thereby (2) continue to experience their SRHs at the B-level as well, they, too, can maintain those activities, attitudes, and stances increasingly by themselves, that is, in ways that are less dependent upon peer reinforcement than before. (These individuals—"B-criticals"—are soon described in the text.)

37. Here, "frequency" does not just mean the number of peer-reinforcing inputs—that is, PRIs, however counted—or resulting peer reinforcements (PRs), per unit of time. (For purposes of simplification, only "time" will be emphasized in the text. PRIs involve attention, approval, and acceptance, from or by peers.) Instead, it also refers to the *proportion of all activities, attitudes, and/or stances* that have received PRIs or have led to PR itself. Thus, for example, even if the youths' "risky" Phase-B AASs are increased in absolute number during the transition from B to C, the (1) percentage of times that those AASs receive peer-reinforcing inputs, and the (2) overall proportion of actual reinforcements (PRs) that are involved (using the number of AASs as the denominator, in both cases), can still be less than that which previously existed. In the present discussion, "reinforcement" or "reinforcing" need only refer to the actual results—the PRs—of the PRIs.

38. The youths' reduced feeling of need for the given PRIs—and PRs—would exist even if these individuals' emphasis during the B-to-C transition, and beyond, were on maintaining, not expanding, the Phase-B level of *satisfactions, relief, and hope*. One must distinguish, here, between these SRHs, on the one hand, and

the youths' activities, attitudes, and stances, on the other, since the youths can maintain their Phase-B level of SRHs even if they expand their AASs.

39. Five points might be noted. (1) The preceding applies even if that peer reinforcement is already becoming less frequent. (Cf. the earlier-mentioned "lengthier periods.") (2) As elsewhere, the peers in question can be the original ones (e.g., those from pre-A and A), entirely new ones (e.g., from B), or some of each. (3) "*Actual* peer approval," as an input, occurs apart from the SMOs' thoughts/beliefs alone. Its existence, like that of various other phenomena in question, can, for instance, be verified by still other (nonpeer) individuals, in that they can directly observe the inputs called "approval." (4) The peer-attention and peer-interest components of reinforcement first occur prior to any established or other-than-provisional expansion of the youths' Phase-B activities, attitudes, and stances. The peer-approval aspect of reinforcement occurs not only then but after given AASs have occurred or been expressed a number of times. This overall process, particularly its approval aspect, provides general and/or specific encouragement for the maintenance of that expanded behavior. (5) Peer attention, peer encouragement, and related inputs would ordinarily help youths commit themselves to various behaviors that they have begun to explore, say, as part of the B-to-C transition. (This also applies during earlier periods, such as pre-A.) However, such inputs could also exist after the transition is essentially completed, and they could then help *maintain* the given behaviors, that is, support and sustain the now-expanded activities, and so on, during C itself. To be sure, as indicated elsewhere, Phase C youths can increasingly achieve this maintenance objective without substantial input—actual input—from their peers.

40. Phase-C individuals are not the only ones who become more self-approving in these respects. For instance, many youths who have remained in Phase *B* become more self-approving of their existing behaviors; in so doing, they also self-reinforce to some degree, they maintain

those unexpanded behaviors (AASs) essentially as-is, and, of course, they need less peer approval than before with regard to the AASs. ("As-is" involves, for example, not only frequency of occurrence but type and range of content.) To be sure, many other Phase B youths remain quite *dependent* on their peers regarding the reinforcement of their existing activities, attitudes, and stances. Usually, in fact, these individuals will modify those AASs, for instance, will slightly or moderately expand their frequency and/or content, only or chiefly if peers have induced, persuaded, or clearly pressured them to do so. (Common among the salient personality features and interactional styles of these particular B-youths are those seen in most "passive-conformists"; however, P-Cs are not the only Phase-B youths involved.) The peers who provide this input, especially the persuasion and external pressure, are often high risk-taking nonoffenders or even delinquents per se. Given the present B-youths' (not just its P-Cs') above-average desire to please and their felt vulnerability, these peers need not be unusually assertive.

One further point. As discussed later in the chapter, the relative and absolute influence of high risk-taking nonoffenders and of delinquent peers often increases considerably if and when, for example, that of *average* risk-taking nonoffenders (ARNs) *decreases*. This shift in influence is usually precipitated when the ARNs decide to reduce or terminate their support of given behaviors—something they often eventually do. Regarding "personality features and . . . styles" (including level of risk-taking), ARNs are, by far, the modal individuals in everyday youth populations; however, even prior to their just-mentioned decision, they are—whether singly or together—not necessarily the persons with the largest point-in-time and cumulative *influence* on the present youths' behavior. In any event, the overall shift in influence can apply to any youths who are not largely self-reinforcing.

41. Self-initiated approval of AASs is often felt less intensively by the youths than is

the peer-initiated, whether or not the former is more immediate and more sustained. Nevertheless, the self-initiated usually involves more certainty in the sense of more clearly *being* approval, and there is usually more clarity as to what is being approved, as well.

42. This situation does not require that Phase C youths experience *increased* satisfactions, and so on; instead, their level of SRH can remain essentially the same as in Phase B. In other words, if one uses B as the baseline, a key objective associated with C is that of at least maintaining, not necessarily increasing, that B-level of satisfaction, relief, and/or hope, via an expansion of the given activities, attitudes, and/or stances. It is that expansion, not an increase in SRHs, which is critical to Phase C.

43. Early in the self-reinforcement process, these individuals visualize, imagine, or otherwise recall and mentally represent the given behaviors; and, when they do so, they feel essentially *approving* or otherwise accepting of them. In addition, these youths then consider themselves—and want to consider themselves—actively and substantially involved in that process. In this regard, for instance, they believe or take it for granted that it is they, personally, who *bring about* the key outcome of those actions, for example, who generate the satisfaction, relief, and/or increased hope, and that it is they, again personally, though sometimes with assistance, who can later *re-create* or at least take the lead in re-creating such feelings and emotions. The fact that it is even possible for self-reinforcement to result from the earlier-mentioned self-approval reflects the following.
(1) *Approval* is reinforcing, or at least it can be, whether it is externally or internally (i.e., self-) based, in this case peer- or youth-initiated. (2) Satisfactions, relief, and/or hopes are reinforcements, or at least they can be, whether *they* mainly spring from an external or—again—an internal source; and approval can be a key basis and/or ingredient of SRHs, and therefore of given reinforcements, whichever such source is involved. Ultimately, both such points reflect one other: (3) Psychologically, that is, in the

individuals' conscious and/or preconscious experience, feelings of satisfaction usually have a similar to identical quality, or qualities, whether their main, immediate triggers and/or reinforcements (here, *approval* being one) are externally or internally based. Such similarity/identity applies to the emotion of *relief*, as well, and to feelings of *hope*, too—together, with *satisfaction*, the constituents of SRH. The fact that those satisfactions, this relief, and these hopes have at least substantially similar qualities in connection with external and internal contexts helps account for their comparable—at any rate, their substantial—and positive-reinforcement values in those respective contexts.

44. When the youth-initiated process starts to dominate, it does so not only via routes and mechanisms already described, but, of course, despite the earlier-mentioned "*causal* connection" between it and the peer-initiated (PI) process. That connection, in which the *PI* process dominated the YI, was at its peak strength during what amounted to a critical and formative period for the SMOs-to-be. Throughout that period, given peers exerted not only a more direct and more immediate influence than at present (Phase C), but a larger overall influence as well—all with regard to activating and reinforcing the AASs.

45. To be sure, various responses by those individuals may sooner or later *decrease* the chances of illegal behavior or may decelerate given processes. Whether they do depends on various circumstances, not the least of which center on reactions and counterreactions to that first set of responses.

46. The perceptions can trigger the given responses, by the youths, whether or not those perceptions are, say, moderately or highly accurate. In addition, the given perceptions generally help sustain subsequent steps of the process being described.

47. Youth reactions to perceived and/or actual inputs by other individuals, and to various external conditions, can involve any of several mechanisms and sequences of events. Collectively, these reactions encompass a range of content; for instance,

they cut across various issues that may jointly involve the youths and adults. Two examples are as follows: First, youths may displace given feelings that basically relate to parents or parent figures onto other individuals and authority figures instead, or else onto objects, property, and the environment. The release of such feelings can sometimes include or even center on an illegal act, violent or not; the feelings themselves may involve, say, frustrations and/or hostilities that originally revolved around those parents or others and that may have been substantially triggered as well as sustained by these individuals. That overall situation, in turn, may relate to such older and/or newer factors as the youths' (1) perceptions of being disliked or rejected, (2) unsatisfied wishes for attention and acceptance, or for considerably more of each, (3) sibling rivalry, and/or (4) conflicts over the rate at which and the ways or areas in which they, the youths, wish to increase their independence or autonomy, or wish to have given experiences and satisfy particular desires. Second, the youths may turn various feelings, such as anger relating to certain adults, largely against *themselves*. This action, which may partly involve feelings of guilt, is often accompanied or soon followed by (1) withdrawal and a sense of helplessness or hopelessness, (2) counterproductive and sometimes intentionally self-defeating behavior, and/or (3) extra-risky and perhaps physically self-injurious activity. Often, (2) and (3) include illegal behavior and related involvements with peers.

48. As implied earlier, various changes that sometimes increase the chances of illegal behavior can occur even if the "old . . . issues, emotions, and feelings," in particular, have *not* or not yet been largely reactivated, let alone expanded. For instance, these issues, and so on, may have been diverted, held largely in abeyance, or otherwise functionally diminished or contained, since early in Phase A.

49. Regarding vulnerability, many such youths are extra susceptible to stress, external pressure, disapproval, and conflicting messages, and also to efforts, especially by peers, to persuade or entice

them to participate in given activities. In general, this susceptibility reflects considerable insecurity, much of which is conscious.

50. Collectively, the "preponderance" of B-criticals are characterized not just by one or more of the individual features just mentioned—above-average dependency, vulnerability, and a tendency to follow peers—but by various others. In addition, each subtype or subgrouping that was just mentioned, and which is part of the larger, B-critical "predominance," *itself* contains at least one of those three features. Moreover, as indicated in Chapters 4 and 5, these subtypes are defined by *more* than any one of them. Specifically, they each require certain combinations of features, and they involve various dynamic relationships among the features. The present text discussion emphasizes the larger—the B-critical—grouping per se, not just certain subtypes (subgroupings), separately as subtypes, that are important parts of it.

51. As indicated, some members of these respective subtypes remain *moderately* delinquent and a small portion are even "lightweights"; others, of course, are the SMOs. For descriptions of youths who, in most cases, are nondelinquents or no more than minor delinquents with respect to any official records, yet who have individual features and perhaps groups of features identical or quite similar to some found in the given subtypes, see Harris (1983) and Jesness and Wedge (1984). Regarding related, "Situational-Emotional" individuals—youths who, however, *have* been officially involved or more involved in delinquency, see Palmer (1971d).

52. For B-youths—here, B-criticals—the Phase C tensions and frustrations are "potential" in that these individuals may or may not eventually reach that phase. For C-youths—individuals who, by definition, do reach that phase or have already reached it—they obviously are not potential in that respect.

53. With B-criticals, this "as-is" retention of the AASs often but far from always occurs while the external reinforcement continues, as an input, at much the same

level as during the initial stage, that is, during what might be called the "establishment" stage. With most other youths, maintenance of the initial level of input reinforcement plays a *lesser* role in such retention.

54. In short, reinforcement performs this *maintenance* function besides having already helped to (1) shape and strengthen, for instance, crystallize and partly solidify, those behaviors, and/or to (2) refine them. (Some temporal overlap exists between its performance of this function, on the one hand, and its carrying out of the earlier, *establishment* role, on the other.) With many youths, especially SMOs-to-be, the behaviors in question (AASs) were initially put forth by the youths themselves, at least largely so. However, with some individuals they were first introduced by peers, especially by delinquent, near-delinquent, or generally high risk-taking ones. Regarding external (peer-initiated) reinforcement the following comments, which involve but also go beyond maintenance alone, might be noted: Large and important differences can exist in the content of what is being reinforced and in what may thereby result. For instance, if little other than the youths' already-existing (established; original) AASs are being reinforced, that is, are being encouraged by given peers, little if any change may end up occurring in those individuals' collective behaviors. In contrast, if *new* AAS content is being clearly encouraged, moderate or even major change can take place; at least, it will be likelier to do so, whether rapidly or not. This, and the preceding, also applies to individuals viewed singly.

Content change, and lack of change, is usually not an either/or matter, especially when an individual's AASs are viewed in toto, that is, together. Specifically, for any given youth, change may indeed be occurring or have occurred in certain areas even while some of that individual's original unchanged AAS content is being *maintained in others*, for example, while the latter content is remaining in force essentially as-is, partly or largely by virtue of peers' continued active encouragement of it. This dual nature of the overall reinforcement that may be received by an individual is, for instance, sometimes evident during the B-to-C transition. There, overall expansion is occurring, but not total change—for example, not a complete transformation or replacement of all the original, established content (AASs), or even of the contexts in which that content is expressed. This situation reflects the fact that not only is certain *new* content, or even just moderately altered content, then being encouraged/reinforced (this activity being "Input 1"), but, during that same time period, some of the *original,* essentially unchanged or unaltered content is continuing to be encouraged/reinforced ("Input 2"), by the same and/or other peers. (Nevertheless, in many B-to-C transitions, Input 2 substantially decreases in amount. That aside, the youths themselves often become responsive to Input *1* as such; and, whatever may occur regarding both such inputs, these individuals increasingly make AAS choices on their own.)

The preceding comments focus on means by which or conditions under which the *content* of youths' activities, attitudes, and/or stances is likely to change or not change, *as* content. They also indicate how—regarding an individual's AASs, collectively—an area or degree of "sameness" or nonchange can be maintained even while *changes* are occurring in other areas, and/or when still *other* changes may have already occurred. Those matters, particularly the changes in content *as* content, can be distinguished from others, ones that nevertheless involve content themselves, such as given activities or behaviors. For instance, (1) if the intensity, rate, and/or overall quantity of reinforcement (still, peer encouragement) increases during a given period, this augmented input can *strengthen* any given AAS content. More to the point, it can do so irrespective of whether that content is thereby changed in any other ways, for example, substantively (in other words, "as content"— and/or with regard to scope). In addition, (2) if reinforcement—still as input—is directed not just, or not even, at transforming or modifying given content itself (i.e., at changing either its entire nature or else particular aspects alone) but, instead, at increasing or decreasing the *frequency* with which that content takes place, the following can occur: It can result, say, in a higher or lower rate of occurrence on the part of a specific activity which has been receiving that peer encouragement. This would apply whether or not that activity or behavior—and perhaps the social context in which it occurs or is expressed—was substantively and objectively the same as or different than before, that is, again as content. It would also apply whether the quantity of reinforcement had itself remained the same, and whether or not any strengthening (or weakening) of that content had occurred.

55. Four points should be noted: (1) This situation therefore emphasizes the retarding or precluding of substantially, not just slightly or modestly, expanded content and/or contexts of usage, in connection with those individuals' AASs.
(2) Besides referring to constancy and sameness, "stability" or stabilization can mean *more enduring*—in that respect, *stronger*. More specifically, post-establishment reinforcement can make the youths' activities, and so on, more durable and lasting than they would otherwise be, and in that sense stronger than before. The AASs can be stronger in that respect even though they continue to occur, that is, to be expressed and/or observed, in essentially the same *form* as before, namely, their "as-is" form. (3) In the present context, "stronger" and "strengthened" can also, albeit secondarily, refer to increases in the *intensity*, for example, the overall force, with which the AASs are likely to be expressed at any given time, whether or not in their "as-is" form. Increased intensity is often, but far from always, initially or subsequently characterized by a higher frequency—and/or overall amount of usage. (4) Increased strength of expression is often, but not necessarily, preceded, accompanied, and/or soon followed by an increase in the individuals' level of personal commitment to those AASs. In that respect, B-criticals are substantively and functionally comparable to and some-

times identical with Phase C youths, even while largely differing from them regarding the earlier-mentioned expansion of both content and contexts of usage.

56. Two points might be kept in mind. (1) Though B-criticals have rarely conceptualized "unmet needs" and "emotional security" as such, they feel and concretely experience various effects of the latter's being unmet, that is, unmet in major respects. These effects often contribute to many such youths' anxieties—here, especially, to their worries about possibly losing the continued support of peers who reinforce their risky and/or trouble-related behaviors. (2) Unmet needs for emotional security are often less extensive and/or intensive among B-criticals who are called group conformists (G-Cs) than among the remaining subtypes already mentioned in this context; this, at least, applies to the many G-Cs described as "accessible" rather than "insulated" (Chapter 15). Mainly for this reason, the remainder of this summary—insofar as it applies to these subtypes in particular, rather than to B-criticals overall—pertains more to passive-conformists (P-Cs) and the anxious-confused (A-Cs) than to G-Cs as a whole.

57. This involves conscious desires as well as what might be called underlying—generally preconscious—drives. The text will emphasize the conscious desires, even though "drives" focus on the same primary goals and are no less influential.

58. The youths are receptive despite—and partly due to—their fears of rejection. In addition, their "desires for relief" are strong despite frequent feelings of futility. These individuals, like many others, try to relieve and reduce not just (1) general anxieties and overall unhappiness that relates to those and/or other fears and feelings, but (2) particular frustrations and specified external pressures as well.

59. At this point, most such youths are more interested in their immediate emotional gains—the relief, satisfactions, and feelings of hope—than in thinking about various consequences their activities may have for the more distant future. This applies despite their awareness that some consequences may not only be very nega-

tive but can have more than a slight chance of occurring. At any rate, the earlier-mentioned "price" these individuals feel they presently pay is not the only one they realize they may *have* to pay; but they want to avoid thinking about the latter.

60. Though B-criticals are particularly receptive to the earlier-mentioned attention and approval and genuinely welcome it, that same peer input often generates a moderate to considerable worry as well—especially a fear-centered anxiety—in most such youths. (Both the anxiety and its fear element are unintentional on the part of most peers who provide the given input.) This type of anxiety reflects the fact that—collectively—the individuals in question sense, usually preconsciously, the considerable influence or control that those inputs often have over some of their feelings or moods, even including, for example, aspects of their overall, immediate happiness and unhappiness. Such anxiety also involves a form of tension or stress that is more likely to be long-lasting and often-experienced than short-lived and felt only infrequently. At any rate, this anxiety—through time, and in its various aspects combined—(1) sometimes helps increase these individuals' already-present feelings of emotional dependence on those peers, and it (2) thereby raises the chances that the youths will try to "go along with" the actual and presumed wishes, preferences, and so on, of those peers. For any *given* youth, (1) and (2) apply whether or not his or her "sense" regarding the influence of those inputs is more often preconscious than conscious; and in either case, "sense," here, involves global or intuitive recognition.

Entirely apart from the above, the following might be noted: The presence of these peer-centered anxieties indicates that the earlier-mentioned, adult-related ones are not the only externally supported—and, in part, externally generated—anxieties (including tensions and stress) that these youths experience. In this regard it also implies that adult-related anxieties are not the only external ones that contribute to the occurrence and maintenance of the youths' risky or illegal activities themselves.

61. For instance, many risky activities differ substantially from penal code offenses—such as theft, burglary, and major assault—(1) that are widely considered serious breaches of the law, (2) for which the formal sanctions and other consequences are often sizable, and (3) that almost all relatively mainstream adults take quite seriously, whatever the legal sanctions may be. The risky activities in question differ in content and/or degree from the "illegal per se," even though the risky are themselves broadly disapproved and can easily "get [one] in trouble." At any rate, the level of disapproval and the amount of trouble are usually less in connection with the *risky,* even though the resulting complications and consequences may still be large. As indicated and implied, common among these risky behaviors are truancy, curfew violations, frequenting off-limits places (whether "congregating" or not), disturbing the peace (whether or not in a group), drinking certain alcoholic beverages (at least in large amounts), frequent drunkenness (usually well beyond slight tipsiness), and various types of sexual expression and experimentation. To be sure, both categories of behavior—the risky and the illegal per se—are often part of the same overall adjustment pattern and they commonly play similar or identical roles for the given youths, particularly at first. In addition, each type of risky behavior, for instance, truancy or frequenting off-limits places, is usually taken more seriously than otherwise if it occurs together or in close conjunction with other types, and, of course, with activities that are illegal per se.

62. This is the case even though, as indicated, these individuals' activities, attitudes, and stances usually remain—collectively—largely unchanged for considerable time, both qualitatively and quantitatively. Moreover, and particularly relevant to the subsequent text discussion, the following applies when changes do occur: Though the content and perhaps the absolute number of these youths' changes are usually small, some of these changes—individually and collectively—involve an additional factor (and/or, in some cases, an increased aspect) that can nevertheless

make them especially important. That factor involves or consists of *illegal behavior (IB) per se,* as an input. (Penal code listings would exemplify IBs.)

63. The youths neither conceptualize this pattern as such nor describe its "conditions and aspects" in the terms next used. (See features 1 through 3, in the text.)

64. Two points might be kept in mind. (1) Whether by themselves or when combined with the IB pattern, relief/satisfactions that are associated with the non-IB inputs may "leave something to be desired" themselves, still from the youths' perspective. At any rate, it is these individuals' new and/or increased emotional reliance on the *IB* input, not their continued or possibly even augmented dependence on non-IBs, that makes the present period so consequential or potentially fateful. (2) Whatever they may leave to be desired, the R/Ss, nevertheless, also *do* bear on and partly address the youths' immediate life situation, their various near-term desires, and/or long-standing issues, problems, and so on—whether these latter are fairly quiescent or not.

65. This level of support exists not only because actions that are part of the illegal behavior often contribute to the achievement of (1) *"secondary goal"* B: the "elimination, substantial reduction, or neutralization of anxieties, stresses, [and so on,] especially those associated with preexisting/ongoing/emergent challenges, expectations, [etc. of adolescence]." (This also applies to *reactions,* by peers, that are closely related to that illegal behavior and to the overall IB pattern.) Instead, such support also exists because the illegal behavior and IBP in question—again their related "hassles" and risks notwithstanding—sometimes lead to and otherwise link with significant amounts of the following: (2) ". . . emotional security . . . ," "acceptance by others," and/or ". . . pleasure or enjoyment." These are any youths'— SMOs' and nonOs'—three *"primary goals"*; they exist and are active from very early in life, well before any illegal behavior occurs. (See Chapter 25—also regarding secondary goals.)

Given the nature of what is involved, namely, major and even fundamental goals, the achievement or partial achievement of (1) and (2), especially together, helps generate feelings of relief and/or satisfaction—or of partial relief/satisfaction. These feelings, at any rate, pertain not only to immediate and ongoing issues but also to longer-standing drives, motives, desires, pressures, and/or needs. Such R/Ss, which are conscious and/or preconscious in any given youth during certain periods, can help establish and maintain the above level of support for illegal behavior and for the overall IB pattern. They can do so especially if they occur a number of times and are cumulative, and even if— individually—they, the R/Ss, are not intense and may seem brief. Finally, these reliefs/satisfactions can reflect and result from not only *actual* experiences, for example, from already-existing reactions, to given illegal behaviors, by the external—the social—world, but also from experiences that have not yet occurred but which are anticipated and *hoped-for,* concerning those IBs.

The foregoing indicates and implies that reliefs/satisfactions which are involved in (1) and/or (2), above, are also associated with significant aspects of the serious multiple offenders' *overall* life situation, or at least with sizable parts of it. The content of these aspects, viewed in toto, usually extends well beyond that of the illegal behaviors and the IB pattern alone. (Still collectively, that content can often substantially affect the illegal behavior—can even help generate or trigger some of it in the first place—even though, at various times, it can also be influenced by it.) Salient among these aspects of the youths' life situation are, as can be inferred from the preceding, the types of external and internal issues, problems, and needs that comprise items #1 and #2 of the eight-factor sequence in Chapter 25.

For these reasons, and to restate as well as summarize, it can be said that the SMOs' level of support for their illegal behavior exists partly because of the following (these relationships and contributors or sources are over and beyond that which involves the IB alone): First, there is an active link or functional relationship between (a) that *illegal behavior,* on the one hand, and (b) the youths' *primary goals,* and also *secondary goal B,* on the other. In addition, there is such a link, and there is also some causally significant content or substantive overlap, between (a) *and/or B,* on the one hand, and (c)—to wit, aspects of the youths' *overall life situation*—on the other. Individually and collectively, these two points regarding interrelationships and content overlap signify that the illegal behavior and the IB pattern are not the sole producers of relief/satisfaction and of R/S-based *reinforcement* which can bear on that illegal behavior, and which, in so doing, can help establish and maintain the level of support in question. As indicated, much of the youths' *overall* relief/satisfaction is produced by other sources instead and

in addition, ones that are, nevertheless, functionally related to that illegal behavior. This can and does occur partly because the youths' overall life situation is itself substantively and actively linked with that behavior (and vice versa), partly because both that situation and the illegal behavior can bear on the primary goals and major secondary goal in question, and because the achievement or partial achievement of any or all such goals can help produce reinforcing—establishing and maintaining—R/Ss themselves. At any rate, the level of support in question does not exist by virtue of the relief/satisfactions obtained from the illegal behaviors alone; it does not result from the nature of that behavior alone and from the *effects* of that behavior, on its own and on their own. Instead, it reflects and results from the earlier-described contents and relationships, as well.

27 SELECTED TRENDS AND A HABILITATION/ DEVELOPMENTAL FRAMEWORK

From the mid-1970s through the early 1980s rehabilitation, that is, personal-growth-centered intervention, declined in status and usage. This mainly resulted from criticisms and attacks by Martinson (1974, 1976), Mitford (1973, 1974), Fogel (1975), van den Haag (1975), von Hirsch (1976), Wilson (1975), Greenberg (1977), Quinney (1974), Schur (1973), Murray and Cox (1979), and others, regarding its effectiveness, humaneness, utility, and therefore overall appropriateness.[1]

During the 1980s, intervention in general and rehabilitation in particular regained considerable strength and were, in effect, largely re-legitimized. This mainly occurred because of studies, meta-analyses, and literature reviews that, collectively, demonstrated frequent effectiveness, and partly because (1) few programs were in fact inhumane and (2) personal as well as practical assistance was often provided to youths and adults. By the mid-1980s it was generally apparent that the *Clockwork Orange* stereotype of treatment as inhumane and dehumanizing—thus, morally illegitimate—seldom applied and was not intrinsic to intervention. This was despite the fact that abuses did often exist before 1980, as did several questionable approaches (Burgess, 1965; Mitford, 1973, 1974).

Trends since the 1970s
The Justice Model
As suggested, the idea that correctional intervention can help offenders change their lives in ways that also reduce recidivism on a long-term basis reemerged in the 1980s from pre-1975 days. However, given (1) the large volume of often serious crime and (2) the

public's strong concern with safety *now*, the main emphasis in corrections was on short-term behavior control. Though the *justice model* originally emerged in the early 1970s for reasons other than (1) and (2), it seemed directly relevant to those factors and has dominated American corrections since the mid-1970s (Fogel, 1975; Morris, 1974; Morris and Tonry, 1990; Singer, 1979; van den Haag, 1975; von Hirsch, 1976; Wilson, 1975).

Through much of the 1970s and well into the 1980s this model embodied the view that punishment, not rehabilitation, should be corrections' central goal, and that rehabilitation is a public-protection failure. It incorporated a "just desert" perspective that centered on proportionality (make the punishment fit the crime), which downplayed offenders' future needs, and which substituted—for rehabilitation—the hope that punishment or punishment plus external control would greatly deter delinquent and criminal behavior. Together with just desert, the justice model also reflected a widespread concern with indeterminate sentences and sentencing disparity—the former being closely associated with rehabilitation during 1960–1975 (Altschuler, 1978; Frankel, 1973; Gottfredson, 1979a; Hoffman and Beck, 1975; Morris, 1978; National Advisory Commission, 1973a, 1973b, 1973c; O'Leary and Hanrahan, 1976; Thomas, 1977; von Hirsch, 1976; Zimring, 1976).[2]

The contribution of just desert and the justice model to determinate, proportionate, and relatively equal sentencing has been large and lasting; in this regard these approaches mainly achieved their original goals. Yet elsewhere, their achievements have been partial. Included, for example, is the justice model's implied goal of long-term public protection and its explicit goal of short-term protection, via punishment or punishment plus control alone. Through the 1980s it achieved some of the former and a good deal of the latter, but not as much as originally implied or expected. However, whereas the *sentencing* achievements partly existed even as the 1970s were ending, the public-protection shortfalls were not yet clear; still, as indicated, considerable short-term protection was obviously occurring (Andrews et al., 1990; Blumstein, Cohen, and Nagin, 1978; Blumstein et al., 1986; Byrne, 1990; Byrne, Lurigio, and Baird, 1989; Erwin, 1987; Gottfredson and Gottfredson, 1986; Gottfredson, Mitchell-Hersfeld, and Flanagan, 1982; McCarthy, 1987; Murray and Cox, 1979; O'Leary and Clear, 1984; Pearson, 1988; Sechrest, White, and Brown, 1979; Wilson, 1975).

Thus, backed by the justice model, supported by the view or hope that swift and certain punishment would provide an amount of deterrence that rehabilitation presumably could *not,* and, above all, given the large volume of crime and the public's concern with safety now, the 1980s became an era of incapacitation and of anticipated, short-term behavior-control. Not until the closing years of that decade was it clear that swift and sure punishment had not produced the originally assumed, implied, or hoped-for levels of protection, and that rehabilitation could add something in this regard. Moreover, by the end of the 1980s neither justice model proponents nor others had provided convincing arguments to the effect that rehabilitation (1) should be considered intrinsically inappropriate as a major correctional goal, (2) was in fact unimportant or perhaps even harmful (or commonly harmful), and (3) should be secondary to punishment in any event, whether for short- or long-term goals.

Nevertheless, even through the 1990s and quite possibly the following decade, the justice model will probably remain dominant in the United States, and incapacitation, together with intensive supervision (Chapter 28), will likely continue as corrections' preeminent strategy. This is because the latter usually provide considerable short-term protection, which is what the public mainly wants, and because they do so at a cost which, though in-creasingly questioned, is deemed acceptable or at least manageable (though decreasingly so) in most jurisdictions. For further discussion of the justice model see point 2 of the Chapter 29 section titled "Changes in Youth/Staff Relationships."

Risk Assessment

To help facilitate (1) the justice model, incapacitation, and intensive supervision, and to continue assisting in (2) the implementation of determinate sentences and in addressing sentencing disparity, *risk assessment* (RA) will play a major role throughout the 1990s (and beyond), as it did since the mid-1980s. Moreover, by identifying candidates for in-lieu programs and/or early release, RA can play an important and increasing role in helping address institutional crowding—this being partly a product of the incapacitation strategy that RA, itself, often helped implement, while making incarceration more *equitable* (Clear and Gallager, 1985; Gottfredson and Tonry, 1987; Kress, 1980; O'Leary and Clear, 1984; Palmer, 1992; Wilkins et al., 1978).[3]

Though risk assessment will remain important in addressing population management and other system-level issues, it has often been used somewhat uncritically, in that a basic dimension has been overlooked or bypassed. This omission stems from the fact that many policymakers and practitioners have operated almost exclusively on the following assumptions—ones that, throughout the 1980s, were widely promoted in most risk-assessment literature:

1. Higher-risk offenders will, as a group, almost certainly perform worse than medium risks; the latter, in turn, will almost invariably be outperformed by lower risks.

Other things being equal, this assumption seems reasonable in itself on statistical grounds alone. However, it is accompanied by a second, implicit assumption:

2. Assumption 1 applies regardless of external conditions; that is, the previously mentioned outcomes (the relative rankings across risk groups) will occur somewhat like an immutable fact of life. Stated differently, the performance differentials between higher, medium, and

lower risks will almost always occur, except, perhaps, by chance.

Assumption 2 is incorrect; and, as suggested below, this has important implications. Its difficulty relates not simply to the fact that "other things" are often unequal, but to the fact that they *need* not be equal and that differing types of programs can differentially affect risk.

Specifically, though the performance differentials between the respective risk levels are indeed likely to occur and *do* often take place as stated or predicted in assumption 1, they are far from inevitable and they may often—not just rarely or by chance—be eliminated or even reversed. Moreover, this may occur under "routine" operating conditions. For instance, in a large-scale 1984–1989 study of juvenile probationers, several standard, non-experimental camp programs had better recidivism results with higher risks than with medium risks; and in some cases they or other camp programs had equal or better results with medium than with lower risks.[4] (Those were within-program results; the following are across-program.) In addition: (1) many such programs had substantially better results than other standard camp programs when various outcome-related factors, including risk level, were controlled; (2) many of these results were cross-validated for the same set of camps but with an independent sample of offenders; (3) key components of the former programs, that is, the more successful ones, were identified (Gottfredson and Taylor, 1986; Palmer and Wedge, 1989; Wedge and Palmer, 1989, 1994).

In short, particular program features can substantially modify generally expected outcomes; and offender characteristics, which—to date—have comprised the essential basis of standard risk assessments, do not operate alone, unaffected by external conditions. More specifically, certain combinations of program features and offender characteristics can produce, or are at least associated with, better results than others, and some of these results can, in effect, contradict or heavily qualify the above assumptions or undifferentiated views regarding risk-level outcomes. When designing future programs, practitioners and policymakers should not assume an offender's risk level necessitates conclusions that are virtually "foregone," that is, irrespective of a program's features.

Rehabilitation in the 1990s

Though rehabilitation/habilitation regained considerable strength beginning around 1983–1984, and especially by 1986–1988, continued movement into the later 1990s (and early 2000s)—other than at a snail's pace—is far from assured. This applies not just to knowledge building but to growth-centered intervention's (GCI's) possible existence as little more than the following, combined: (1) an appendage to either a management-and-control-centered or a punishment/just-desert-centered strategy; (2) a vehicle for providing—at most—modest services to perhaps most offenders, and somewhat more to those actively seeking them or in obvious need.

The possibility of life-as-appendage partly reflects the presumed impact of several factors outside or independent of rehabilitation, especially surveillance/control techniques, incapacitation, and risk classification. These "external" factors or activities serve important functions and need not be implacable foes of growth-centered intervention. Nevertheless, they comprise major, established movements or forces; and when combined with each other, as they often are, they eclipse and in some respects constrain or dilute GCI. The combination and interaction of these activities *and* GCI itself reflects society's and correction's own mixture of jostling, and in some cases divergent, needs, priorities, and philosophies. Though this broader and somewhat unwieldy mix of forces or activities has often produced false starts, inconsistencies, and inefficiency, it dominated corrections during much of the 1980s and into the 1990s, especially at the adult level and mostly under the broad aegis of the justice model.

Within the United States, surveillance/control, incapacitation, and risk classification (as a key determiner of intervention) seem likely to continue for at least several years at about their present intensity, breadth, and level of acceptance. Under these circumstances, the relative status of growth-centered intervention is not likely to *radically* change during the remainder of the 1990s (and in the early 2000s). Nevertheless, its status as well as usage will probably increase substantially during that time, and important knowledge building can certainly occur. But even so, institutional crowding, overall cost containment, and society's overriding desire for short-term protection will probably influence corrections more than any other forces throughout that period; they will probably absorb most resources as well. As a result, control-centered approaches will probably remain in the forefront even as rehabilitation advances and is increasingly viewed as an important option. At any rate, given such movement, rehabilitation will not be a mere appendage.

Despite growth-centered intervention's reemergence in recent years, its movement during the next several could be sluggish in major respects, for "internal" or scientific reasons alone, that is, even if today's competing and diverging activities somehow lessen and GCI's usage increases. For instance, with respect to *increased discovery of and knowledge about effective programs, and of how to establish and operate them,* slight progress might well occur by year 2005 if, by the late 1990s, fewer than two of the following goals are met—particularly #1, #4, and #5 (any of the five goals listed would be achieved across intervention studies collectively, not via any handful of experiments alone; insofar as they are achieved, a mere-appendage status could be replaced by near-equality, even if usage increases only modestly):

1. A higher percentage of studies than in the past should be well-designed, and many fewer should be of questionable quality. For instance, random assignment is more often needed; and even if this occurs, experimental/control matching on several crucial variables should be virtually assured rather than simply assumed to invariably accompany this procedure.
2. A much higher percentage of studies than in 1960–1995 should be purposely designed as replications or partial replications. The first such studies might be planned repeats or partial repeats of programs that seem promising, feasible, and relevant, for instance, those associated with sizable recidivism reductions, whose designs were at least adequate, which were implemented appropriately, and whose settings or—especially—offender samples seemed common.
3. Purposive variations of earlier studies should be conducted more often than in the past. This could be done (a) especially, but not only, if the earlier ("varied") studies yielded significant and sizable positive results, and (b) regardless

of whether—but particularly if—those studies had been at least partly replicated. Variations could involve age range, setting, intensity, and so on.
4. Wherever possible, each study should describe the main offender subgroups that comprise the overall target sample; and separate outcome analyses should be conducted for each subgroup whose size is not too small. These "differentiated analyses" could be valuable whether or not, but especially if, differing interventions were used with those subgroups.
5. Intervention processes, such as specific techniques, strategies, and program features, should be examined closely and described more often and more fully than before. When this occurs in the context of well-designed studies in which positive outcomes are found, researchers may obtain clues or strong evidence as to which of those factors substantially contribute to growth-centered intervention.

Theoretical Perspectives
Offender Needs, Challenges, and Issues

The following problem has existed since at least the 1960s with respect to serious multiple offenders: Many or most correctional policymakers and numerous practitioners do not recognize or accept the extent and interrelatedness of most such individuals' difficulties. This includes not just personal problems/conflicts, but life- and social-skills deficits and youths' ambivalence about changing their lives. As a result, planners often substantially underestimate (1) the strength and extent of programming, support, and sometimes pressure that is needed to motivate and help such individuals confront, unravel, or overcome those difficulties/deficits, and (2) the amount of time needed to readjust and stabilize their lives. This error is independent of the accurately *recognized,* equally important fact that most such youths simultaneously have various strengths and skills—some already functional, others largely potential.

Thus, for example, the often considerable strength of youths' "willpower" is indeed generally recognized, as is the key role of motivation. Yet, what is often overlooked or minimized is the difficulty of harnessing and *redirecting* those powers/forces—for instance, of helping to (a) substantially detach the youths from activities, interests, desires, and loyalties that sometimes lead to illegal behavior, and to then (b) redirect those individuals—or their "willpower" and motivation—to less troubled paths.

In short, the first thing often overlooked is the fact that—despite workers' initial efforts—the current interests, commitments, feelings, self-image, ambivalence, psychological defenses, and/or unexpressed fears of youths often actively block or divert the socially more-acceptable use of the latter's actual or potential strengths, skills, and even legitimate opportunities.[5] For such reasons, and given the interrelatedness of those difficulties/deficits, it is perhaps overly optimistic to expect fairly short-term programs, such as those lasting eight to ten months, to help most such youths sort out and settle these matters once and for all or even very largely, even when they have substantial motivation to do so.

The preceding applies independently of the following. Because the previously mentioned interplay of forces operates at all socioeconomic levels and for minorities as well as nonminorities, *social, economic, and historical* disadvantages complicate the situation even more. For instance, when youths—during adolescence—recognize their social and/or economic disadvantages as such, this can further impact what may already be their troubled self-image. The youths' awareness of these disadvantages, and the impact of this awareness on their *subsequent* self-labeling and self-image, may then increase or consolidate feelings of bitterness and alienation and may make long-term change more difficult.

With or without such added complexities, individuals with numerous or serious difficulties are not ipso facto "sick" and, for example, walking instances of deep-seated pathology. Yet, although a "medical" model description (*specifically, a "diseased-entity" equivalent*) essentially misses the mark, on the one hand, and though strengths and skills exist, on the other, it remains important to not overlook or minimize the frequent extent and breadth of these individuals' social and/or personal needs—since offenders, like nonoffenders, can have major needs and problems without being "sick."[6] In this regard, if most serious or multiple offenders are to substantially and fairly permanently change their present adjustment patterns, the following combination of needs, challenges, and issues

(or, collectively, factors and subfactors) must be addressed:

A. *Skill/capacity deficits:* Various—often major—developmental challenges, frequently including life- and social-skills deficits, for example, educational and vocational.

B. *External pressures/disadvantages:* Major environmental pressures and/or major social disadvantages, also including comparatively limited or reduced family, community, and other supports or social assistance.

C. *Internal difficulties:* Long-standing or situational feelings, attitudes, and defenses; ambivalence regarding change; particular motivations/desires/personal and interpersonal commitments (Palmer, 1991b, p. 57).

The weight and frequent *interrelatedness* of this combination increases these and other youths' potential vulnerability to failure and helps make intervention difficult. Given this situation, if some of these factors, such as factor C, are only minimally addressed, the focus of many such youths' attention and activities—in effect, of their "willpower" and motivation—may remain prosocial or largely prosocial for only a limited time, during or after intervention. This situation can arise even if substantial change and improvement has occurred in the remaining factors, that is, A and B.

More specifically, if, say, problem-related factor-C items such as negative feelings about self or destructive attitudes toward others are only minimally addressed and resolved during a program, the delinquency-related interests and activities of many seriously troubled youths may reassert themselves. This can happen even if those interests and activities have been controlled, avoided, or reduced for several months. With some youths, this return to earlier adjustment patterns can, for example, be triggered or supported by continued interpersonal fears or by repeated setbacks relating to a still low or confused self-image, by continued ambivalence about change, and by ongoing or growing conflicts with specific individuals or categories of individuals. With other youths it may be supported by a continued sense of superiority and a disdain for standard life-styles. In either case, the former interests, activities, and even loyalties are more likely to reappear if youths become particularly vulnerable, unhappy, or enraged—for instance, to a pre-program degree—because of frequent frustrations, anxieties, or stresses in their daily lives, whether at school, at work, or in closer personal relationships. Under these circumstances, unaddressed or minimally resolved problems and issues, such as the preexisting fears and conflicts mentioned earlier, will have an increased influence on their behavior, especially if few counterbalancing satisfactions exist.

Thus, for example, we would hypothesize that problem-related—more specifically, delinquency-related—interests, loyalties, and adjustment patterns often reasserted themselves in connection with most New Pride and Violent Juvenile Offender programs, despite the following facts: First, these programs, conducted in several cities during the 1980s, were thoughtfully conceived blends of components that reflected a multicausal approach and which focused intensively on factors A and B above. Second, those components impacted A and/or B. For instance, New Pride and VJO improved vocational and/or educational skills, regularly increased job opportunities, and often provided job placements; sometimes they reduced negative peer and family pressures as well. In these respects they often increased "social competence," they improved "social bonds," and they generally promoted community integration (Fagan, Forst, and Vivona, 1988; Fagan and Hartstone, 1986; Gruenewald, Lawrence, and West, 1985). These were no small accomplishments, and they usually utilized the preponderance of time and resources.

However, those programs may not have sufficiently focused on, or effectively dealt with, potentially critical aspects of factor C, such as feelings, attitudes, and/or motivations that involved interpersonal conflicts, long-standing or growing fears, and ambivalence about change. With many youths, these feelings/attitudes/motivations, which may often have contributed to pre-program delinquency, may, during the program itself, have therefore been strong enough to act as follows:

1. substantially undermine progress in factors A and B, and thereby contribute, for example, to recurring academic- or work-adjustment problems despite the

youths' increased educational or vocational skills; they might also have contributed to episodic interpersonal aggression or violence despite the individuals' increased social competence in general; and/or

2. prevent actual progress from being *consolidated* in terms of new priorities, shifted loyalties, and a modified life-style that could theoretically provide youths more satisfaction than frustration or anxiety in their daily lives, during and after the program.

At any rate, to account for the general lack of experimental/control recidivism differences in New Pride and VJO, we believe that many or most youths in those programs had significant personal/interpersonal problems or conflicts that related to delinquency and which needed to be addressed more closely and perhaps more directly than they were. This means that those individuals, at program entry, were, for instance, not *only* educationally or vocationally deficient, socioeconomically disadvantaged, and/or negatively pressured by peers and family, important or vital though these were. Also, it implies that even substantial progress in those and other factor A and B areas was not enough to *indirectly* achieve the following: resolve or greatly and genuinely reduce—as opposed to temporarily divert or superficially contain—the youths' personal difficulties, some of which were presumably self-activating and possibly even growing.[7] Nor could the programs resolve or adequately reduce those difficulties via either a "rising-tide-lifts-all-boats" effect or a "trickle-down" effect. However, with other youths, say, those whose difficulties were somewhat less, such indirect impacts might have been larger and/or more permanent than with more troubled or resistive individuals, that is, even when combined with the program's normal degree of attention to factor C.[8]

The Habilitation/Developmental Perspective
Together, factors A through C may be considered a habilitation—or personal and social growth/development—framework. Basically, this structure would add factor C to the A and B factors emphasized by Elliot, Ageton, and Canter (1979) and by Weis and Hawkins (1981) in their "integrated theory" or "social

development" approach. That approach, which was integrated in the sense that it combined "social control," "strain," and "social learning" theories, was the explicit conceptual basis for the Violent Juvenile Offender experiment; moreover, factors A and B, which are centered in those theories, received main emphasis and, by far, the most resources in the New Pride programs as well.

The habilitation/developmental (H/D) perspective would consider factor C a very serious and often crucial dimension, not just (1) an appendage to A and B, (2) a *moderately* important set of forces at best, or, for that matter, (3) a set that seriously applies to only a modest portion, for instance, 30 percent or less, of most "non-lightweight" samples—each of which is how it actually functions in the "integrated theory." Also, in H/D, factor C's role applies regardless of those samples' modal or even predominant socioeconomic status or ethnicity. The habilitation/developmental perspective would be relevant to other than serious multiple offenders as well.

Though many people might find a habilitation/developmental framework easier to visualize and accept with *youths,* it also applies to adults and it can be a useful organizing tool with respect to program development. Also bearing on its utility, though for other reasons, is the fact that the term "habilitation" remains relatively free of certain stereotypes that generally accompany "*re*habilitation." For instance, "rehabilitation" is much more likely to connote a fairly thorough overhauling or reconstituting of once-developed but then "fallen," "failed," "partly broken," or even "sick" individuals—generally *adults;* and, for example, "fallen" or "failed" individuals are often considered less worthy—sometimes even unworthy—of serious, sustained, sometimes costly assistance. Moreover, it is often erroneously assumed that such individuals, especially the "partly broken" or "sick," may have been left with few internal strengths on which to draw. To be sure, the term or concept "rehabilitation" does channel attention to offenders' often substantial needs, and many such individuals are potentially quite vulnerable or have recently "hit bottom." For this and other reasons, that term should not be avoided. Still, a developmental or habilitation framework, per se, can be particularly useful in the 1990s and beyond, not just because of its intrinsic appropriateness and the above connotations, but because rehabilitation's "name" is not yet *completely* "cleared" (rehabilitated) following its quasi-banishment from American corrections during 1975–1985, and despite its relegitimization since the later 1980s.

As implied, an H/D framework does not suggest that youths—at least many serious multiple offenders—are never manipulative, hurtful, blameworthy, or highly resistive, and that their predicaments and illegal actions may never be considered personal failures, at least in part.[9] This applies whether or not these individuals are seriously troubled or disturbed, and/or often vulnerable and anxious. Nor does this framework suggest that youths may never require substantial external controls while various developmental issues and related anxieties as well as resistance and ambivalence are being addressed.

However, the habilitation/developmental framework, with its emphasis on factor C, does imply that corrections should carefully examine the subject of engaging and redirecting motivations. If individuals' strengths and skills are to be used constructively and if community reintegration is to occur and last, motivation—not just, say, external control—must somehow lead and sustain them, even through frustrations and anxieties. To be sure, external support and specific coping techniques can also assist in this regard.

Psychosocial Development

A motivation-related theory of psychosocial growth and change was developed for, and used in, Phase 3 of California's Community Treatment Project. This approach was called the "developmental/adaptation theory of youthful personality" (Palmer, 1969d, 1978a). Throughout Phase 3, each youth was diagnosed and individualized not only with respect to the areas and dimensions described in Chapter 19 (see "Diagnosis and Treatment/ Control Plans, on pages 325–328"),[10] but, he was evaluated in terms of his position on the continuum reflected in this theory. Such evaluations seemed relevant and proved useful not only when formulating the original intervention plan but in subsequently interpreting change, in tracking progress, and in developing further plans. Together, the individualized diagnosis and the developmental/adaptation evaluation encompassed factors A through C of the H/D framework in considerable detail.

The following illustrates the theory in question, one that focuses on major stages in the establishment of person-society links and which postulates specific forces that help promote those links. The structure and constructs presented below comprise the main features of personal/social change; to facilitate the presentation they will focus on later childhood, on adolescence, and on the transition to early adulthood. However, many of the concepts and dynamics also apply to, and have direct parallels in, adulthood itself.

Basic Concepts and Stages of Development

The basic concepts of this theory, and the relationships among those concepts, are as follows:

1. *Era.* Each era is subdivided into a number of distinguishable stages.
2. *Response-adaptation sequence.* Each sequence is subdivided into a number of separable phases.

Three main eras will be distinguished. Simply labeled, they are:

Era II.   Later Childhood
Era III. Socialized Relationships
          (Adolescence)
Era IV.   Role Establishment, Commitment
          (Early Adulthood).

For contemporary American society it is appropriate to roughly equate Era II with the ages of approximately 5 to 10, to think of Era III as encompassing not only several aspects of preadolescence, but much of what is commonly termed adolescence (ages 10–11 to 16–17), and, finally, to think of Era IV as mainly a period of early adulthood, generally beginning around age 17 or 18.

"Era" is thus used as a generic term. In its reference to later childhood, to preadolescence together with adolescence, and to early adulthood, it signifies a set of actual[11] as well as perceived,[12] interrelated opportunities, expectations, activities, challenges, and themes. Viewed as separate entities, each era usually extends over a period of years and can be distinguished from the others based on differences in the observable content and quantity of social opportunities, expectations, and challenges.

Five *stages* of psychosocial development will now be outlined, stages A through E; together, they encompass Eras II and III. This description largely relates to normal, that is, typical or modal, development in contemporary society.

Era II (Later Childhood)

This era consists of two main stages, both of which have certain parallels in early adolescence and early adulthood. The stages are:

Stage A: Familiarization, Coping. This is a period in which the child learns many new things about what the external world is like and what it expects of him or her. He learns the permissible and nonpermissible ways of expressing a number of feelings and impulses. He is highly involved in coping with external demands and with attempting to master as well as reduce anxieties. He is quite concerned with being able to control the actual and perceived power of "significant others" by whatever methods seem acceptable to those individuals or which at least seem to work (e.g., by his complying, by being "good," by direct or more subtle demanding, and, if necessary, via intimidation).

Stage B: Stabilization, Repetition. This stage is reached when a pattern of activities has been established for and/or by the child, one that brings predictable satisfactions and which the child usually enjoys repeating. He is generally satisfied with his role as child and with the opportunities that seem open to him. His expectations, thoughts, and wishes seldom extend beyond hoping for more of the same or for variations and exciting elaborations thereof.

The shift from later childhood to the era of "socialized relationships" occurs gradually, not overnight. This transition comprises a distinct stage in itself.

Stage C: New Awareness, Suspension, Assessment. The Stage C youth has begun to recognize the existence of a rather extensive new world of expectations, opportunities, different possible activities, and privileges. He associates many of these features with the approaching years of adolescence; that is, he recognizes, if only intuitively, that a person must be of at least adolescent age in order to participate in many such activities. He generally begins to curtail and redirect some of his childhood activities in accordance with his new awareness of "what the bigger guys (or girls) do and don't do," and in relation to skills and traits that seem to be desired (strength, courage, self-control, endurance, etc.), and which he, too, desires in one form or another.

This is generally a period of rising uncertainty, ambivalence, and anxiety, with the youth having neither fully relinquished the most pleasurable aspects of later childhood nor "bought into" the world of adolescence in an intense and involved way, or in much detail.

Era III (Socialized Relationships)

This era consists of two main stages, the second of which is often a transition to Era IV:

Stage D: Reorientation, Assimilation of Social Values. Stage D youths are consciously concerned with acquiring a set of standards or with participating in groups of activities that they recognize as being different than those of later childhood. They seek new people to emulate or new activities to master, largely in order to gain a sense of social or personal status, esteem, or acceptability. This process involves a beginning "redefinition of self" relative to newly recognized sources of potential status, power, and/or pleasure. It also involves a generally conscious repudiation of, or nonconformity toward, previous standards and roles—at least toward some of them. It often involves a propensity toward thinking of many individuals (and of oneself) as being either categorically worthy/good or else unworthy/bad, largely on grounds of whether they live up to certain all-encompassing standards of behavior, or else in terms of the particular beliefs, attitudes, and motives they seem to have. This process usually occurs in the following context:

1. A minimally discriminating conformance to—in fact, often a direct copying or attempted assimilation of—a new set of social expectations, opportunities, or significant others. Though this new level of conformity seems internally directed when compared to Stages A through C, it may be characterized as primarily an "external" approach to reorienting oneself and/or defining one's worth.[13]
2. Relatively little awareness, by the youth, of longer-term implications of many such external standards, that is, implications with regard to his newly emerging personal interests or convictions and to the more individualized needs, personality traits, and personal/social limitations of which he is first becoming aware.[14]

Stage E: Self-Responsibility, Personalization of Attitudes and Values. Individuals at this stage no longer vigorously copy or assimilate the attitudes, traits, or expressed values of people who have usually been their first or second set of post-childhood friends and/or "heroes," people who may have appeared to possess considerable social and interpersonal power, influence, or status.[15] Instead, they are likely to feel that their *own* experiences or beliefs ought to lead them toward interpersonal or personal satisfactions of an ongoing or longer-term nature, and that those experiences/beliefs can also guide their everyday affairs, at least in principle.

These youths have a fairly clear idea of how various people generally view or respond to their expressed attitudes and/or personality traits (though they may not use these terms). They have several definite ideas regarding the apparent differences and similarities between themselves and others. These perceptions and beliefs help give them a clearer picture, and often a stronger feeling, of "who" they are, where they stand, and where they ought to be moving—clearer, that is, than Stage D youths. This development occurs despite the fact that their views and assessments of self and others continue to be characterized by a large segment of stereotyping and overgeneralizing.

Stage E youths feel they have identified many, possibly most, of the major social or personal choices they will need to make in the near and intermediate future. They also feel they have identified the principal, personal implications of the differing choices in question. They generally, though not always consciously, expect to build their life around some of the attitudes, traits, or values they have assimilated subsequent to childhood and have personalized or integrated in the form of a moderately self-consistent self-image, or at least a set of priorities. This does not mean they are free of occasional confusion, uncertainty, or even strong anxiety.

The temporal and formal relationship between Eras II and III, on the one hand, and Stages A through E, on the other, is shown in Figure 27–1. The relationship between the three stages of Era II and the six phases of the Era II adaptation sequence is also shown. The temporal and formal relationship between the two stages of Era III and the eight phases of the Era III adaptation sequence is shown in Figure 27–2. For present purposes, we need not detail the latter phases. (The response-adaptation sequence is described below.)

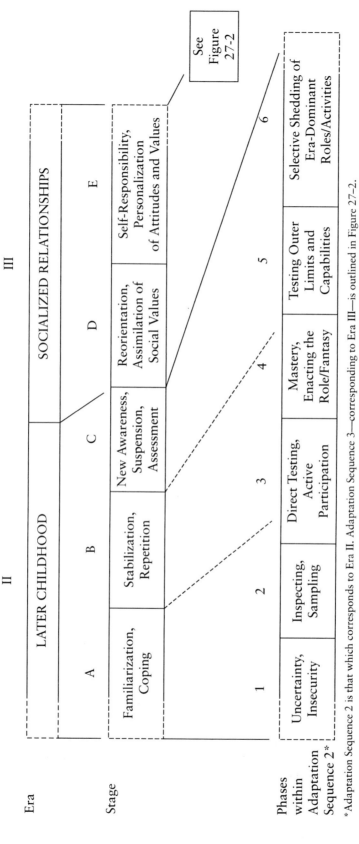

Era   II   III

	LATER CHILDHOOD			SOCIALIZED RELATIONSHIPS	

A	B	C	D	E
Familiarization, Coping	Stabilization, Repetition	New Awareness, Suspension, Assessment	Reorientation, Assimilation of Social Values	Self-Responsibility, Personalization of Attitudes and Values

Stage

See Figure 27-2

1	2	3	4	5	6
Uncertainty, Insecurity	Inspecting, Sampling	Direct Testing, Active Participation	Mastery, Enacting the Role/Fantasy	Testing Outer Limits and Capabilities	Selective Shedding of Era-Dominant Roles/Activities

Phases within Adaptation Sequence 2*

*Adaptation Sequence 2 is that which corresponds to Era II. Adaptation Sequence 3—corresponding to Era III—is outlined in Figure 27-2.

Figure 27-1 Temporal Relationships between Selected Eras, Stages, and Phases (Emphasis on Era II).

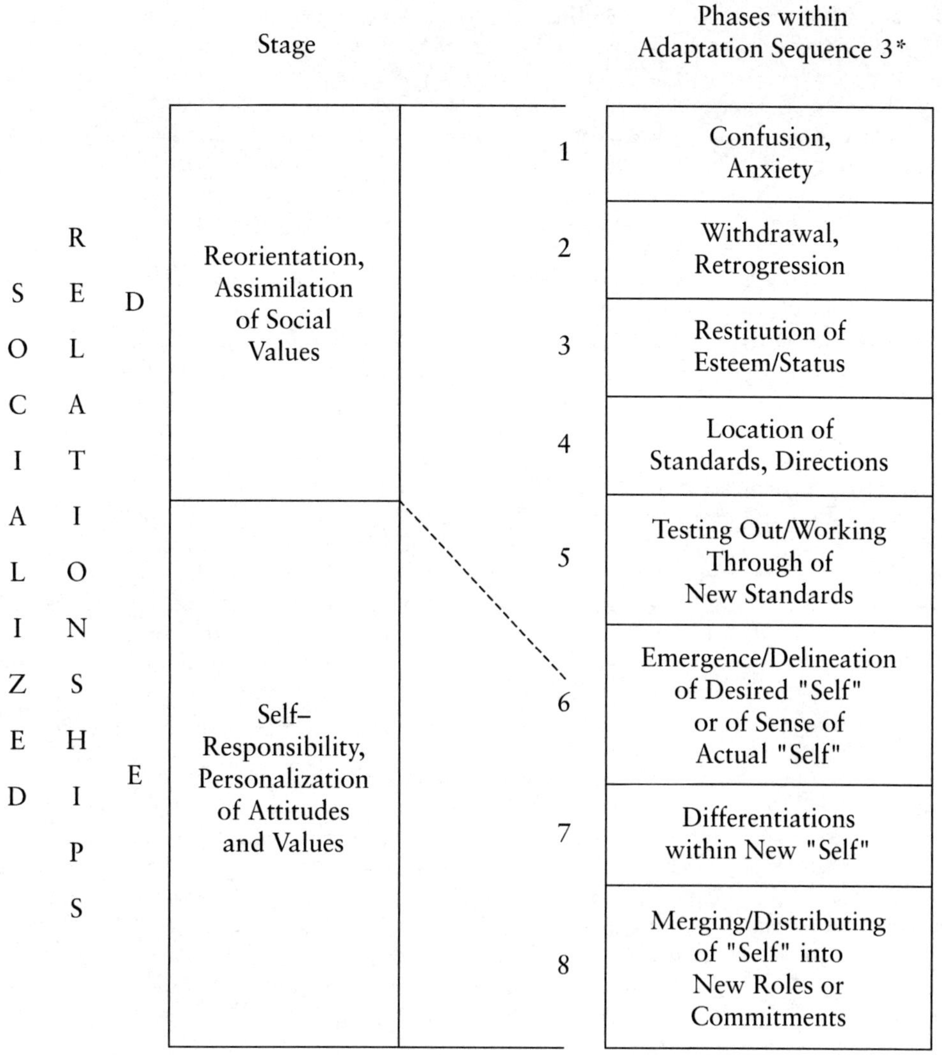

Stage		Phases within Adaptation Sequence 3*
		1 — Confusion, Anxiety
	Reorientation, Assimilation of Social Values (D)	2 — Withdrawal, Retrogression
S O C I A L I Z E D — R E L A T I O N S H I P S		3 — Restitution of Esteem/Status
		4 — Location of Standards, Directions
	Self–Responsibility, Personalization of Attitudes and Values (E)	5 — Testing Out/Working Through of New Standards
		6 — Emergence/Delineation of Desired "Self" or of Sense of Actual "Self"
		7 — Differentiations within New "Self"
		8 — Merging/Distributing of "Self" into New Roles or Commitments

*In part or whole, this adaptation sequence is sometimes repeated a few times during Era III—each time centering on somewhat differing content (e.g., new identification figures and/or shifting social expectations). This is most noticeable in connection with Phases 1 through 5 of Adaptation Sequence 3.

Figure 27–2 Temporal Relationships between Era III Stages and Era III Phases.

Era IV (Role-Establishment, Commitment)

These individuals take on at least one of the more or less positively sanctioned, adult or young adult roles available in the society. Their activities and self-image become centered around role involvements of this nature. For now, we need only note the following regarding this era:

1. In normal development within most present-day societies, Stage E is the main transition between Eras III and IV. Many individuals remain in this stage for several years before entering Era IV.

2. Many individuals move into adult-type roles, such as marriage and/or parenthood, without having reached Stage E[16] in terms of psychosocial development. (See endnote 17 regarding differences between "movement" and "development.") Their involvement in these roles may be largely voluntary or involuntary.

3. The number of conceptual differentiations that are made between self and others,

and among others, does not automatically increase in connection with, or as a precondition to, the transition from Era III to Era IV. Though the number of differentiations is nevertheless *likely* to increase, stereotyping and overgeneralizing are almost as widespread during much of Era IV as during Stages D and E of Era III. At any rate, important differentiations can be added in some areas even when equally significant or influential stereotyping/overgeneralizing continues to exist in others.

We now turn to the concept of the response-adaptation sequence. This sequence is positively though not perfectly correlated with the earlier-mentioned stages.

Response-Adaptation Sequence

Insofar as it involves a set of complex social conditions, each era undergoes very little modification as to content and scope during the life of any individual.[18] Individuals, on the other hand, can usually produce a range of responses and a series of adjustments to the opportunities, expectations, and challenges of the given era. By and large, then, it is the individual who in some fashion responds and adapts to the era, not vice versa. In this connection, the *response-adaptation sequence* describes the changing and developing relationship between the individual and the main stages of any given era, that is, the changing nature of the person/society link. For present purposes we need not review each and every phase of the Era II and III adaptation sequences; however, certain aspects of Phases 4, 5, and 6 of Era II will be described by way of background for later discussion. Again, these phases have various parallels in the transition from adolescence to adulthood, for delinquents and nondelinquents alike. (Later, we will briefly mention Era *III* phases collectively.)

Phase 4: Mastery, Enacting the Role/Fantasy

The Phase 4 child applies some of his abilities or skills to a slowly increasing number of social and/or family-centered contexts. As this phase progresses he becomes increasingly aware of the relationship that generally exists between being strong, powerful, skilled, or "cool," on the one hand, and being able to participate with peers or adults in a number of

known (though, in many instances, not personally experienced) activities, on the other. He often regards these activities as being, actually or potentially, at least as enjoyable or exciting as many of those he already knows. Much of his energy is invested in elaborating upon desired activities or fantasized roles in this area. Thus, in a way that directly bears on his everyday activities, his ongoing interests, and his emerging personality, the youngster begins to form certain ideas about types of people whom he would like to emulate and about areas of participation, that is, ongoing activities, in terms of which his own life differs in fact or fantasy from that of individuals who have become increasingly interesting to him.

Phase 5: Variations, Testing the Outer Limits and Capabilities of One's Present Adaptation/Role

At this point, the youngster begins to express his skills and fantasies in ways that he recognizes may (and, at times, probably do) go beyond previous levels of acceptability to others. He sometimes allows himself to participate in a number of "way out" activities. In so doing, he is (1) checking the limits, and value to self, of his present range of Era II options, alternatives, and priorities, and is comparing these with what he believes to be those of Era III; he is also (2) checking on the interest value, and the level of acceptability to others, of his changing set of primary interests. During this process, he is hardly cognizant of the concepts described in (1) and (2).

Phase 6: Selective Shedding of Era-Dominant Roles or Activities

At this point the youth becomes increasingly reluctant to interact with peers or adults in ways that may be labeled "babyish" or "childish" by those individuals, and which might lower his standing in their eyes. He tries, both personally and vicariously, to see if his emerging areas of skill and information will allow him to participate in what appear to be the more legitimate, available activities of early adolescence. Though he still holds on to several aspects of his Era II adjustment, his explorations relative to Era III are often quite conscious and deliberate. He begins to feel, and often worry, that he might be unable to participate in desired or interesting activities relative to the broader social environment if he lacks the needed skills or does not have certain accoutrements and privileges apparently possessed by others.

Factors Related to Change

We will now review several factors that relate to psychosocial development through all phases of Era II. Era III need not be focused on, since many of these factors operate similarly during that and Era II.

The responses and longer-term activities of Era II youths are chiefly a result of expectations that come from the external environment—mainly parents and (to a lesser extent in most environments) peers, together with relevant others such as siblings, relatives, or teachers. Significant others—primarily parents—usually remain in firm possession of the capacity or power to take a number of critical and sometimes decisive steps in connection with the child's exposure to many opportunities, activities, and challenges of Era II. In broad terms, they may (1) permit, encourage, channelize, and generally support; (2) be largely indifferent or perhaps ambivalent toward; and/or (3) discourage or prohibit much of the preceding exposure or ongoing experience. They can, for instance, be supportive of, indifferent toward, or opposed to the child's attempts to inspect and sample the opportunities and activities of his Era II world (Phase 2). They can do likewise with respect to his later attempts to test the outer limits of the Era II roles he may previously have accepted and enjoyed (Phase 5). Generally speaking, the way in which significant others can effectively use their power varies somewhat from phase to phase.

The Era II child senses that he will need the approval of others if he is to participate fairly regularly in Era II activities and, in a general sense, stand up to its challenges. Particularly during Phases 1, 2, and 3, he will gladly align himself with individuals who seem willing and able to use their strength and authority to help him obtain or gain access to the things he wants. In effect, he would like to participate in, comply with, or even come to possess the external "power" of these individuals. This is so because he assumes, generally and implicitly, that he can benefit from those forms of relationship with this type of strength and authority.

This actual or perceived power on the part of others can be termed "wanted" or "supportive" outer power. Usually, such power or influence is willingly assimilated by, and becomes ego-syntonic to, the Era II youth. On the other hand, environmental influence that markedly discourages, opposes, or oppresses the youngster will be termed "unwanted" or "nonsupportive" outer power. To the Era II youth, this form of influence or perceived influence is often frightening or overwhelming. It is frequently evaded, fought against, and/or unwillingly submitted to.[19]

The environment can exert influence on the Era II youngster in a supportive and/or oppositional direction. Relative to any given youth, it generally exerts influence in both directions. This influence can be thought of in terms of force, that is, quantitatively. Thus, for example, at any given point such influence would consist of, or result in, a specified amount of support as well as a particular quantity of opposition.

Support and opposition comprise two of the eight broad factors that are integrally related to movement along the Era II adaptation sequence. These factors, together with their labels, are as follows:

1. Support/approval from environment (esa)
2. Opposition/disapproval from environment (eod)
3. Individual's own accomplishments/ abilities (iaa)[20]
4. Psychological difficulties/conflicts/ ambivalence (dca)
5. Difficulty of tasks/goals invested in by individual (itg)[21]
6. Individual's interest/motivation level regarding tasks/goals (iim)
7. Difficulty of social requirements/ opportunities (sro)[22]
8. Major or sudden trauma and overwhelming events (ote).[23]

Individually, these factors operate in one of two basic directions. Three factors (*esa, iaa,* and *iim*) can promote or accelerate continued development; the five remaining factors (*eod, dca, itg, sro,* and *ote*) can hinder or decelerate it.

To assess the prospects of continued development or forward movement by a given youth, one must evaluate both the separate contributions and overall product of these factors. This product may be conceptualized in terms of the following general formula (the product would represent *total effective power*

(TEP), for example, developmental power, that may be ascribed to a youth at a given time):

$$TEP = \frac{(esa)(iaa)(iim)}{(eod)(dca)(itg + sro)(ote)}$$

The higher the ratio of numerator to denominator, the greater the chance of continued movement or development through given phases and stages. "TEP", conceived as a force, has meaning relative to the challenges, expectations, and opportunities of each particular society, and it may thus vary accordingly in absolute terms (quantitatively).[24] Similar numerators and denominators operate in Eras III and IV. However, in contemporary American society, the specific content of most such factors is rather different and more complex than in Era II. This applies, for instance, to the individual's overall psychological functioning, which also has a larger relative force than before. In the *habilitation/developmental framework*, psychological functioning is a product of factor C items such as conflicts, ambivalence, and defenses (cf. factor *dca*), on the one hand, and various motives and mental skills (cf. factor *iim* and aspects of *iaa*), on the other. As such, it plays a major and often critical role during and after adolescence.

The differing types of power, ability, and/or positive potential that an Era II youth may come to feel relative to himself can be termed *developmental capacities*. They may be described in terms of several postulated items or general categories. For instance, most of the following have considerable bearing not only on the transition from later childhood to adolescence, but on that from adolescence to early adulthood:

1. A general competence regarding objects and activities, including an ability to adequately utilize one's body, apply one's mind, and/or perform well in physical or social activities often defined as important or good.
2. An ability to influence other individuals.[25]
3. An ability to resist what others define as "bad" activities or individuals, and/or to avoid or neutralize situations that seem physically threatening.
4. An ability to help other individuals.
5. An ability to understand or predict what is happening around one.
6. An expectation that enjoyable activities will occur, and a belief that one can participate in some of them.
7. A feeling of being generally supported in one's desires to try new things and seek varied experiences.

Capacities 1 through 5 are major components of the *iaa* and *iim* factors, whereas 6 and 7 are products of *esa*. Few youths score high on all or nearly all capacities, at least with respect to long time periods. Nor need they do so, since—regarding continued movement or development—some capacities can partly substitute for others. Nevertheless, the more "high" or at least positive scores the better, other things being equal. In any event, capacities 1 through 7 can be important targets of intervention, especially since they mitigate factors *eod*, *sro*, and *ote*, among others, and because they can help individuals through difficult transitions and often assist with factor *dca* itself.[26] (As such, they can reflect, not only "program integrity," but intermediate impact.)[27]

As indicated, most of these capacities are also quite relevant to Eras III and IV. However, several important differences exist in this regard between the latter eras and Era II. These differences relate to (a) specific content and overall complexity; (b) rules that informally govern their application or expression in given situations; (c) significance or implications, for example, consequences of a relative lack or perhaps nonutilization of given capacities. Eras III and IV include other capacities as well, for instance, those which help individuals respond and adapt to challenges and opportunities that rarely exist in Era II, and which include various psychological strengths (and limitations).

For present purposes, these capacities need not be reviewed in detail. However, it might be mentioned that in all eras, *personnel, settings, and program operations* that promote these capacities are those most likely to be seen as useful means to ends that the individuals in question are likely to desire and which can link with factors A, B, and C alike.

As chronological adolescence approaches, many Era II youths begin to feel they may not have enough by way of usable and/or useful accomplishments/abilities (*iaa* factor), or enough by way of support from others (*esa* factor) in connection with developmental capacities 6 and 7. This change in perceptions often occurs because these individuals have, to an increasing degree, begun to compare themselves to, and/or be compared with, new reference groups or new sets of standards. At about this time, many youths experience new or increased pressures with regard to social requirements and opportunities (*sro* factor). Beyond this, they generally begin to recognize new areas of opposition as well as pressure, from parents and/or significant others (*eod* factor).

It is at about this time that the first three phases of Era III get underway, namely, confusion/anxiety, withdrawal/retrogression, and attempted restitution of esteem/status. (One or more such phases often occurs in connection with early, chronological adulthood as well.) It is under the preceding conditions, and during these phases, that a number of significant personal compensations and social adjustments often occur. Developments of this nature are particularly relevant to the formation and/or reinforcement of psychological structures and behavioral/interpersonal response patterns commonly observed among several groups of delinquents. This applies, for example, to passive-conformists and power-oriented individuals.

The central themes and products of Era III's eight phases can be inferred by relating the respective phase names shown in Figure 27–2 to the Stage D and E descriptions presented prior to it. However, the following details might be useful in understanding program implications described below.

In contemporary society, *Stage D* typically or modally involves five main phases:

1. Confusion, Anxiety
2. Withdrawal, Retrogression
3. Restitution of Esteem/Status
4. Location of Standards, Directions
5. Testing Out/Working Through of New Standards

It is during these phases that the earlier-mentioned compensations, adjustments, structures, and response patterns often occur. Parts of this sequence are sometimes repeated during Stage D, each time involving somewhat different content, such as new identification figures or shifting social expectations. This is reflected in the emotional "ups and downs," the behavior shifts, the inconsistencies, the ex-

perimentation, and the temporary "regressions" observed in delinquent and nondelinquent adolescents.

Stage E generally involves three main phases:

1. Emergence/Delineation of Desired "Self" or of Sense of Actual "Self"
2. Differentiations within New "Self"
3. Merging/Distributing of "Self" into New Roles or Commitments

This stage has already been described.

After Stage E comes early adulthood. In the typical developmental pattern Stage E takes two to four years; however, some delinquents and nondelinquents remain in this stage much longer before passing through its three phases and entering early adulthood. Moreover, and sometimes in contrast to the latter rate of speed, many Stage E youths move into adult-type activities and/or roles, for example, jobholder, parent, or spouse, without passing through all three phases. In particular, they do so without experiencing clear feelings of growth or personal/interpersonal improvement and accomplishment, or at least without having considerable emotional satisfaction along the way.

For instance, these individuals may have precipitously moved along given vocational paths or into the adult-type roles while being mostly unsure about wanting to do so. They may have been thrust into those roles or along such paths somewhat involuntarily or at least more than reluctantly, say, by external circumstances or pressures or because they either had or saw no alternatives at the time, or had little confidence that they could "do better."

Not infrequently, other individuals acquire such roles, jobs, and prospective vocations without ever having resolved or greatly reduced the still earlier confusions/anxieties and perhaps even the withdrawal(s)/retrogression(s) of Stage D, and without having then developed and tested-out a set of post-*childhood* standards and values. (In some contrast, still other individuals may have previously *developed* such standards but then rejected them and returned to Phase 1 or 2 of Stage D rather than move toward E. During this return or recycle they may, however, have become involved in the adult-type activities/roles in question, without, for instance, necessarily assuming or wishing to assume various adult responsibilities.)

Under these circumstances, both groups of individuals' first few job-and-role involvements of early chronological adulthood can be tenuous and somewhat easily disrupted. This, in turn, can raise the chances of a return to earlier adjustment patterns, possibly including delinquency. At any rate, the previously described events reflect, in some cases, Stage E youths' ambivalence about the *particular* involvements in question, not so much whether to invest in *any* adult behavior. However, in other cases it largely reflects the fact that individuals, their chronological age notwithstanding, are still largely focused on Stage D issues and involvements. Even if the latter individuals have developed several components of a compensatory self-image (one they may or may not really like), this image may leave little room for serious investment in adult roles and responsibilities; and this situation may place these youths in direct conflict with some programs' principal goals. (For related discussion of "resistance" and "ambivalence regarding change," see "Difficulty of Change and Growth," in Chapter 30; also see "Shared Issues, Dynamics, and Implications," in Appendix 46.)

Selected Program Implications

Many correctional programs do not adequately help serious multiple offenders reduce or resolve personal difficulties that simultaneously bear on growth and delinquency. As suggested, this may sometimes occur largely because planners and staff have underestimated or downplayed major psychological issues in the first place. However, it may especially happen if, while such issues are being underestimated or downplayed, those individuals have placed heavy emphasis on seeing the youths do the following: make major and, from the youths' standpoint, uncomfortably rapid commitments to (1) post-adolescent involvements or responsibilities, or perhaps to (2) heavily structured or lengthy adult *preparatory* activities and training alone, that is, without literally becoming involved in adult life-styles per se.

More precisely, those programs, while indeed promoting the individuals' capacities and skills, and while appropriately helping them break negative peer associations, do not provide the above assistance *to the point*

where many such youths become seriously motivated to modify or relinquish the following: (1) long-standing, anxiety-reducing or security-producing adjustment patterns; and/or, (2) pleasures/excitements closely associated with specific delinquent involvements. This especially applies when (1) and (2) center around either adjustments of later childhood or around Phases 1 through 3 of adolescence—as they often do with serious multiple offenders. Here, for example, many Stage D youths who feel external pressure to make major or rapid strides toward adult involvements and toward much greater personal and social responsibility are neither ready nor willing to relinquish various adjustment patterns or personal compensations they developed during the "restitution of esteem/status" phase of adolescence. With other youths there is less a "battle over relinquishing"—relinquishing given patterns/compensations the youths consider threatened by adult expectations in general—than a need to reduce or resolve conflicts or ambivalence about particular adult involvements.

What may often happen under the above conditions, including the program pressures in question, is the following: The youths' commitment to the earlier-mentioned involvements/responsibilities is weak, superficial, or insincere; or, rather than superficial, and so on, it is strongly opposed by either the youths' specific desire to *not* reduce/relinquish (1) and (2), above. On the other hand, especially if the youths have reached Stage E of development, the involvements/responsibilities may be opposed or undermined by the youths' ambivalence and genuine conflicts about continuing to move forward, and in that respect to change. Such responses and situations may often have occurred in programs such as New Pride and Violent Juvenile Offender, despite important or essential gains in educational as well as vocational skills and perhaps in social bonding as well as reduced peer and family pressures. Thus, although such gains may occur, they may be neither strong, "embedded" in one's self-concept, nor otherwise largely integrated into one's life and major interests.

This suggests the value of determining, not only the era, stage, and phase(s) in which each youth is invested, but both of the following: (1) the main delinquency related activities/involvements he seems unwilling or unable to readily relinquish, and, therefore, (2) the program expectations likely to pose particular threats and to be strongly resisted. At a broader but related level, staff should first determine if their overall program, including its content and goals, relies heavily on the following assumptions, especially with serious multiple offenders over age 16: At or close to intake, the main interests/investments of most clientele already center on a pre- or early *adulthood* stage/phase; and, if they do not, they can usually be brought to that point within several months.

In contrast to those assumptions, the following often occurs: Despite clientele's chronological age, for example, 17 to 21, and even after months of intensive programming, their underlying interests and self-image remain largely centered around adolescent or even pre-adolescent activities, roles, and relationships. With any given individual this may reflect psychological difficulties more than immediate or even long-standing sociocultural forces and related conditions; or, the *reverse* may clearly apply. Regardless of which type of factor dominates, relatively solid change or forward movement will frequently require considerable time and effort, even if the difficulties, forces, and conditions are skillfully addressed. This is largely because they are usually interwoven and may each be strong in itself.

Besides time and effort, rather different emphases, intermediate goals, motivational strategies, and worker/client interactions may be needed within any given program. This is because offenders who (collectively) are at differing stages/phases of psychosocial development often have substantially different interests, limitations, and ways of responding to adults. The need for differing emphases, for differing albeit partly overlapping goals, and so on, would especially exist if, at point of intake, the interests/investments of numerous offenders centered on pre- or early adolescence, whereas those of others mainly involved pre- or early adulthood—or even middle adolescence.

These implications do not just apply to serious multiple offenders or to the goal of investing in adult roles and activities during or soon after the program. They are, however, more likely to be in the forefront with those offenders and goals, and they can often make a larger difference with them.

Notes

1. Earlier opposition and/or pointed challenges to rehabilitation was mainly by Platt (1969), Rothman (1971), and Robison and Smith (1971). Though considerable, their individual and collective impact was much less than that of the later authors.

2. Proportionality is neither unique to nor monopolized by just desert and the justice model, though it was first emphasized in those approaches. Like determinate and equal sentencing, it is compatible with rehabilitation and has been used in that context.

3. Risk assessment can help implement determinate sentencing and address sentencing disparity entirely independent of the justice model and an incapacitation strategy. It can, for example, perform those functions in a rehabilitation context.

4. In addition, recidivism rates of higher risks occasionally equaled or bettered those of lower, not just medium, risks. This occurred, for instance, when lower risks performed worse than usual while higher risks did better than usual.

5. Stated differently, it is mainly the coexistence and interaction of the following that often makes those strengths and skills unavailable or which limits their usage in socially acceptable contexts: (1) the earlier-mentioned deficits plus (2) major external pressures and/or an insufficiency of reliable supports, on the one hand, and (3) particular motivations, feelings, attitudes, defenses, and conflicts, on the other. In this connection, program planners sometimes assume that by substantially reducing factor (1), by addressing and relieving (2), and by also providing legitimate social opportunities, many or most serious multiple offenders can be fairly quickly and perhaps permanently "turned around," that is, within well under a year. Though such change may sometimes occur, it would be far from typical. In any event, though strategy (1) plus (2) plus opportunity may be valuable or even vital as far as it goes, it can overlook or obscure the major interfering/limiting power of factor (3). This factor has considerable relative importance for a high percentage of the youths in question.

6. The medical model characterized in the text has seldom been invoked since the early or mid-1970s as a major or primary factor for any substantial percentage of typical youth populations—serious multiple offenders included. (For a discussion of issues associated with this model and with the concept of "sickness," see Chapter 29, endnote 31.)

7. It is often wrongly assumed that youths' personal difficulties seldom *increase* during given programs, at least when progress is occurring in other important areas. Yet, increased tension and problems do often emerge in one area, say, that of peers or family, *because* of progress in another, such as employment. Similarly, it is sometimes forgotten that progress, unlike a rising tide, may not occur fairly evenly and simultaneously—along an entire "shore," as it were.

8. (a) This discussion does not assume that New Pride and VJO *fully* overcame the factor-A and -B deficits/disadvantages. For instance, though youths may have made marked educational improvements, they may still have finished their program far behind—because they began *very* far behind. This, for example, occurred in New Pride. (b) As implied earlier, it would be surprising if, say, personal stresses and related factor-C difficulties had *not* developed in many such youths prior to program entry, partly as those individuals' response to their presumably self-recognized and unwanted deficits and disadvantages. Regarding other youths, specifically, many who may have had fewer such deficits and disadvantages at program entry, we believe similar difficulties existed (though partly for other reasons), and that they, too, needed close, often direct attention.

9. Though a "rehabilitation"—especially an "overhauling"—perspective or emphasis would more easily or directly connote those features and factors, even this would not justify avoiding the term.

10. These areas/dimensions included, e.g., the youth's: personal history; current interests and abilities; major personal limitations; personality; offense history; current situation (living arrangement and main involvements with peers, family etc.; external environment).

"Personality" included two main dimensions: characteristics and motivations. "Characteristics," for example, included level of development, self-image and attitudes toward others, modes of adjustment, and other traits/features.

11. Related terms are "consensually validated," "external," "objective," or "visually observable."

12. Related terms are "personalized" or "psychologically interpreted," "internal," "subjective," or "verbally reportable."

13. Here, the individual's observable activities, fantasized choices, and self-image are still largely shaped by the standards and expectations of significant others, even though he may say he is following his own conscience. This contrasts with activities and choices that are primarily directed by, and to a self-image that is partly or largely organized around, more carefully selected and more fully personalized or internalized principles and standards (see Stage E).

14. The youth has seldom individualized these external standards, for example, applied them to his specific needs and limitations.

15. However, the earlier emphasis on assimilation does not entirely disappear.

16. This is apart from the fact that Stage E may itself be largely absent in certain societies. That is, Era IV can occur within whole societies—and in subcultures from still other societies—in which Stage E is seldom found.

17. Basically, *movement* involves adding new roles and activities to old ones, and/or substituting the former for the latter. Also, it need not be accompanied by psychosocial development in the sense described below. More specifically, forward movement involves, at a minimum, adding roles and activities that are generally associated with a given era or stage to other roles and activities that are usually associated with, or largely restricted to, an earlier era or stage. (Typically, it also involves the partial or relatively complete relinquishing of selected activities that are associated with the earlier era or stage.) For example, an individual's involvement in parenthood, in the breadwinner role, or in ongoing sexual

relationships can occur without his having experienced, and integrated, most or all phases of the response-adaptation sequence that is usually observed within the given society or subculture prior to the point at which those roles and activities are ordinarily initiated, within that society/subculture. (One major element of an individual's substantial integration would be reflected in his having experienced feelings of growth or of personal/interpersonal improvement, or, at least, of having felt considerable emotional satisfaction during given phases. [Cf. "emergence/delineation of desired 'self' or of sense of actual 'self'"—Phase 6 of Era III].) Nevertheless, it is the experience and at least the partial integration of those particular phases, for example, Phases 3 through 6—and then, jointly and subsequently, Phases 6 through 8—of Era III, that distinguish what we call *psychosocial development* from forward movement itself. In effect, psychosocial development represents one way that forward movement can occur. In this connection it might be noted that many youths become involved in Stage D roles and activities without having developed beyond Stage C (likewise with Stage E roles and Stage D development). Movement that is unaccompanied by psychosocial development and which largely has been thrust upon the individual by external circumstances is not uncommon. Though psychosocial development in the sense of "integration of . . . phases" may not have occurred, this does not automatically preclude a successful or satisfying adjustment. At any rate, an individual may later catch up on psychosocial development, that is, *after* a major role change has occurred. (For convenience, "movement" and "development" will often be used synonymously, despite the preceding distinction.)

18. In this context, terms such as "external conditions" and "external reality" would refer to long-standing, socially sanctioned expectations, opportunities, and roles. By and large, these conditions and realities exist, and continue to exist essentially unchanged, regardless of the wishes and beliefs of particular individuals, say, "ordinary citizens." They do change, but usually over a number of generations.

19. The Era II child becomes differentially sensitized to particular processes in his environment, at differing phases of the adaptation sequence. For example, during Phases 1 and 2 he is largely support- versus nonsupport-oriented. He seeks supportive power from the outer world, that is, from his environment, and he tries to avoid, oppose, or placate nonsupportive power. During Phases 3 and 4 his primary concern relative to significant others lies in the areas of approval/acceptance versus disapproval/rejection. He gravitates toward persons who seem ready to help him feel comfortable, welcome, or competent, and he tries to avoid or ignore others who make him feel anxious, unwanted, or less than adequate. During Phases 5 and 6 he becomes mainly support/acceptance- versus opposition/ rejection-oriented; this adaptation usually combines or integrates his Phase 1 through Phase 4 concerns and perceptions. Thus, in general, the Era II individual implicitly regards the outer world chiefly in terms of such dimensions as *support, indifference/ nonsupport,* and *opposition.*

20. Three levels of accomplishment/ability should be distinguished: (1) objectively verifiable or consensually validated; (2) subjectively (self) evaluated; (3) fantasized and uncritically evaluated by self. These levels are not entirely independent of each other (Palmer, 1969b, 1969d). Also included would be the individual's overall psychological functioning. This, for example, is the product of his psychological strength, on the one hand, and his difficulties and dysfunctional adjustments, on the other. Thus, it relates to factor C of the habilitation/developmental framework. Some psychological defenses may promote or at least allow growth, and in this regard they function as strengths. Other defenses may hinder growth or change.

21. This refers to a scalable difficulty continuum that could help assess the tasks and goals an individual may be pursuing. In contemporary society, the absolute and

relative impact of this factor ordinarily increase to a marked degree as Era III approaches.

22. This refers to a scalable difficulty continuum that could be used to focus on the tasks, standards of performance, and patterns of living that the given society or subculture (environment) more or less requires of nearly all members of the given era or stage. Regarding this scale, *sro* would reflect two separable subfactors: (a) the environment's *minimum demands/tasks/requirements* relative to a composite of all theoretically available tasks, standards, and interaction patterns that bear on the given era; and (b) the environment's *position and attitude* relative to the tasks, standards, and interaction patterns in which the individual has become invested.

23. This refers to four main categories of events: (a) physical assault/injury and major illness (self and/or others), declining health, death (e.g., a parent); (b) first-hand observation of events such as serious accidents, gross physical assault/brutality, or other unmistakable physical/emotional injury or destructiveness; (c) divorce, separation; and (d) family mishaps or misfortunes (financial disaster, loss/destruction of home).

24. For present purposes there is no need to delineate actual reference populations and to postulate numerical amounts or relative weights for the eight factors. Nor is it important to review major interactions within and between factors. Finally, each developmental/adaptation principle that has been described in the text would fully apply even if the relationships among the eight broad factors that enter into the TEP formula—more precisely, among the three numerator factors, on the one hand, and among the five denominator factors, on the other—were viewed as additive rather than multiplicative.

25. For instance, an ability to get other individuals to sometimes or often do what he wants, to attract and hold their attention, and/or to *avoid* their attention or efforts.

26. More so at some stages and phases than at others.

27. Certain findings regarding Phase 3 of the California experiment (Chapter 13) might be relevant here. They are from unpublished analyses prepared for NIMH by the author, John Helm, and Dudley Sams, during 1973–1974.

(1) Regarding the total sample (N = 161), the average correlation among the seven "developmental capacities" was .33 (σ = .16). There were 21 correlations in all.

(2) For the 62 Phase 3 youths whose CTP program began in residence (Dorm 3) and who, as of the data-cutoff, had had a mathematical chance of being followed up for 16 months on parole after being released from the dorm, the following applied: Individuals who had advanced at least one *developmental-adaptation (D-A) "phase"* during their dorm stay were more likely to have a lower than a higher monthly rate of offending (r.o.o.) during that followup than were youths who did not gain a D-A phase during their stay (r = .36; p < .01. For this and for all remaining analyses whose findings are reported in this endnote, one tail-tests of significance were used; and, except as specified in the second part of analysis (5), below, "lower" r.o.o. routinely means "less than 0.10 per month," and "higher" means "0.10 or more"). Specifically, of the individuals who advanced at least one phase while on the dorm prior to release, 81 percent had a lower r.o.o., and, of course, the rest had a higher rate; in contrast, of the youths who did not advance during that time, 49 percent had a lower r.o.o. and the rest had a higher. Similar results were obtained not only for (a) the individuals (still from among those 62 dorm-assignees) who had been *appropriately* assigned to the residential facility (all these were "RR" cases [Chapter 13]; r = .29; p < .05), but for (b) the remaining youths as well—that is, those who had been *inappropriately* assigned to it (the "CR" cases; r = .57; p < .05). In addition, regarding the 40 *conflicted* youths, the just-mentioned findings held up for the individuals who had been *inappropriately* assigned (r = .52; p < .05), but not for those appropriately assigned. ("Conflicted" was the one large subtype [a "sub-grouping": Na's plus Nx's] cate-

gorized within the larger sample of 62 followed-up dorm-assignees. Of *all* dorm releasees as of the data-cutoff, not just the 62 who could be followed-up for 16 months, 21 percent had achieved a one-phase D-A gain as of their point of release; an additional 14 percent had gained two phases, and another 3 percent had gained three. These figures, based on 90 youths, were very similar to those for the 62 per se. Phase-gain or nongain was determined as part of a general reassessment that was made immediately prior to each youth's scheduled release, or which was otherwise focused on that event.)

Close inspection of all outcome data and their interrelationships indicated that the above-mentioned finding (the r = .36) for the *overall* group of 62 followed-up dorm-assignees was accounted for—in no small measure, and perhaps even chiefly—by the *nonconflicted* youths combined, almost all of whom were appropriately assigned I_3's: Of *all* nonconflicted individuals (thus, appropriately and inappropriately assigned—analyzed *jointly*), 91 percent of those who had advanced one or more D-A phases while on the dorm had a lower rate of offending during their 16 months followup; in contrast, of those who had not advanced during their dorm stay, 36 percent had such an r.o.o. (r = .60; p < .01). As just implied, this outcome centered almost entirely on appropriately assigned nonconflicted (NC) youths alone, for whom the separate results were: r = .57; p < .01. Regarding inappropriately assigned NCs (who, as indicated, were part of the combined analysis), there were too few youths for a separate analysis—even, for instance, via a Fisher exact probability test.

(Exept for the use of a few Fisher's, findings (2) through (5) of this endnote were all based on chi square tests [using Yates' correction when needed]; in turn the latters' equivalent *correlations ["r's"]* were routinely based on contingency coefficients. In addition, except for the already-referred-to r.o.o. variable within finding (5), below, all dichotomizations were as close to the analyzed variables' medians as the overall distributions allowed. ["Allowance" greatly reflected the routine, "higher" versus "lower" r.o.o. split that was used, and, hence, (a) the statistical constraint it imposed on the variables with which r.o.o. was cross-tabulated, (b) the basis it provided for standardized comparisons, and, thereby, (c) the basis it also provided for more uniform interpretations—across findings.] Finally, all contingency coefficients were corrected for coarse grouping, in this case, for the joint-dichotomizing of raw data. The correction factor that was used was always halfway between the maximum possible, on the one hand, and none at all [i.e., no correction], on the other. Had the "maximum" been used—that is, the one which would have been appropriate if *exact* median splits had been made in both dichotomized variables [which, of course, they could not be]—each correlation that appears in this endnote would have been about 15 percent larger than it is, for instance, .46 instead of .40.)

(3) Of the seven *D-A capacities,* the three that had the highest first-order correlation with the Status 1 versus Status 2 distinction were combined with one another so that the 161 Phase 3 youths could each be given a single, composite *intake* score on them. These three were "an ability to resist . . . and/or to avoid or neutralize [negative activities/situations]," "an ability to help other individuals," and "an expectation that enjoyable activities will occur, and . . . that one can participate in some of them"; see capacities #3, #4, and #6, in the text. (The correlations in question were .27 in each case, and the average *inter*correlation among the composite's three components—namely, the D-A capacities—was .23 [σ = .16].) Of the 129 youths (dorm-assigned and community-assigned, *together*) who could be followed-up on parole for 16 months as of the data-cutoff, those who had a "higher" score on these capacities combined were more likely to have a lower rate of offending during the followup than individuals who had a "lower" score on them—that is, than youths whose amount of capacity at intake, in the areas tapped by those items, was less than that of the higher-score group.

Specifically, of the youths with the higher D-A capacity score, 66 percent had a lower r.o.o.; of those with a lower score, 49 percent had a lower r.o.o. ($r = .21$; $p < .01$). This finding held up whether the 129 individuals had started their CTP program in an *appropriate* setting (irrespective of whether this setting was Dorm 3 [and the youths were therefore *RR* cases] or the community [and the youths were *CC* cases], or whether they had begun in an *inappropriate* setting (again, either in the dorm [thus, as *CR* cases] or in the community [as *RC's*]) ($r = .23$; $p < .05$, and $r = .21$; $p < .05$, for the 70 appropriate assignees and the 59 inappropriates, respectively). It also held up for *conflicted* youths by themselves: Regarding the 95 appropriately plus inappropriately assigned conflicted individuals combined, that is, for the overall conflicted group (within the total group of 129 youths—*all* subtypes combined), 69 percent of the "higher" D-A scorers had a lower rate of offending, whereas 44 percent of the "lower" D-A scorers had a lower r.o.o. ($r = .29$; $p < .01$). Finally, this finding, in turn, held up for the 50 *appropriately* assigned conflicted youths and for the 45 *inappropriates* as well—that is, for each of these groups analyzed separately ($r = .29$ and $p < .05$, in each case). (Note: Regarding conflicted youths, these correlations were, indeed, .29 in all three cases.)

(4) Another analysis centered on "*support/approval from the environment*" ("*esa*")—one of the eight "factors . . . related to [forward] movement." Here, it was first found that the youths' degree of *esa* at point of intake was *not* significantly related to—predictive of— higher versus lower rate of offending on 16 months parole followup. This applied to *all youths combined,* that is, to the conflicted and nonconflicted individuals analyzed jointly (N = 129; $r = .12$; $p < .20 > .10$). However, for the 95 *conflicted* youths analyzed separately, statistical significance was approached: Of the conflicted youths with a "higher" score on *esa* (i.e., with a larger amount of support/approval [note: these youths constituted 39 percent of the 95]), 62 percent had a lower rate of offending; in moder-

ate contrast, of those individuals with a "lower" *esa,* 48 percent had a lower r.o.o. ($r = .16$; $p < .06$). (For conflicted youths, "lower" r.o.o.'s comprised 54 percent of *all* r.o.o.'s; again, this was as close as possible to a median split. "*Esa*" was selected from among the eight movement-related [m-r] factors because, of all these factors, it had the highest correlation [.29] with the Status 1 versus Status 2 distinction, for the full sample of Phase 3 youths [N = 161]. No other m-r factor was analyzed in connection with r.o.o.)

The preceding findings applied not just to all conflicted and nonconflicted individuals combined, but, *simultaneously,* to the residential facility *plus* the community. In other words, they applied to those youths combined when the two initial *settings* were *combined* (because those settings had not yet been examined separately). When the residential-first and the community-first youths *were* examined separately (i.e., were "disaggregated" in this respect—although the conflicted and nonconflicted *youths* still remained combined, within each of those settings), it was found that the degree of *esa*—support/approval from the environment—was unrelated to rate of offending among individuals who had begun their program in the *residence.* However, among youths who had started directly in the *community,* those with a higher score on *esa*—(i.e., youths with more support/approval from their environment at that point in time)—did have a significantly lower r.o.o. on 16 months followup. Specifically, of the individuals with "higher" *esa* at intake (i.e., start of program), 64 percent had a lower rate of offending during the followup. In contrast, of those with "lower" *esa* at that same point, 38 percent had a lower r.o.o. during followup ($r = .31$; $p < .01$). The picture was essentially unchanged when *conflicted* youths were examined separately. That is, for those who began their program in the residential facility (the dorm), degree of *esa* at intake made no statistically significant difference in r.o.o. However, for those began in the community, it mattered: Of the conflicted youths with higher *esa* at intake, 65 percent had a lower rate of offending; of those with a lower such score, 42 percent had a lower r.o.o. (r = .28; p < .05).

At this point it can be efficiently added that the distinction between residential-first youths and community-first youths also applied to the three *developmental capacities* discussed in analysis (3), above—for the total group (i.e., for conflicted and nonconflicted individuals combined): Whereas the composite intake score ("higher" versus "lower") on those D-C's was unrelated to rate of offending for youths who began their program in the residence, it did matter for those who started in the community: Of the latter individuals, 64 percent who had a higher developmental-capacities score at intake had a lower r.o.o. on 16 months followup (thus, 36 percent had a higher r.o.o.); in contrast, of those with a lower D-C score, 41 percent had a lower r.o.o. (thus, 59 percent had a higher r.o.o.) (r = .28; p < .05).

(5) Finally, youths who had been diagnosed at intake as being "higher" on the *overall developmental-adaptation (D-A) dimension* per se (see below) were no more likely to have a lower monthly rate of offending, on 16 months parole followup, than were those found to be "lower" on that dimension at intake. This applied to the total group *and,* separately, to its conflicted portion alone—

in each case, for residential-first and community-first combined. However, when monthly r.o.o. was divided, not at its usual lower versus higher point, that is, at its near-median-split point, but at *low plus medium* versus *high* (i.e., at 0.00 through *0.16* r.o.o. versus *0.17* and up—with 20 percent of all youths qualifying as "high"), the outcome was different: For the total group, individuals who had a higher overall *D-A* level at intake were less likely to have a *high* rate of offending on 16 months parole followup than were youths with a lower D-A level at intake. Specifically, 10 percent of the higher development-adaptation group had a high r.o.o., compared to 27 percent of the individuals whose initial D-A level was categorized as lower (r = .26; p < .01). Similar results were obtained for conflicted youths alone: 6 percent of those with a higher developmental-adaptation level at intake had a high rate of offending during the followup, while the figure for conflicted youths with a lower D-A level at intake was 28 percent (r = .33; p < .01). No other r.o.o. splits were examined. (Throughout the present analysis, "lower" D-A level ended at the "Restitution of self-esteem" phase, in era III; "higher" began at the next phase: "Location of standards/directions." See Figure 27–2.)

PART III

Perspectives on Community-Based, Individualized Intervention

28 BENEFITS AND UNDERLYING BELIEFS

As discussed in Chapter 20, the core features of California's 12-year experimental program were (1) a careful diagnosis or highly individualized understanding of the youth and his situation; (2) a relevant, detailed, and integrated intervention plan; (3) implementation of that plan in terms of CTP's key factors—especially individualized, flexible programming and intensive and/or extensive contacts within a small caseload context. In this chapter, we will focus on benefits and beliefs associated with community-based approaches that rely centrally on these features and that use appropriate staff; these will be called "individualized intervention" or the "individualized approach." The chapter will also discuss "intensive supervision," a major correctional approach that first emerged, and that then rapidly developed, in the 1980s.

Benefits of Individualized Intervention
Recommending the Approach
Individualized intervention can be recommended for many serious multiple offenders, for reasons mentioned below. These recommendations and reasons apply, not just in California, but very likely in most of the United States. We believe they were applicable not just from the 1960s to, say, the mid-1970s, but from the latter point to the present. They will probably apply well beyond the year 2000 as well. The main reasons—and related benefits—are as follows:

1. Regarding males, individualized intervention in a community setting can produce intermediate- and long-term public protection: It can substantially reduce not only overall recidivism but violent offending in particular, when compared to traditional approaches such as institutionalization plus routine aftercare (parole). These intermediate- and long-term reductions exist even if one counts the crime-free period that occurs during institutionalization as a direct, immediate result of incapacitation. To be sure, if average length of institutionalization were extended to several years, for example, three or more, even long-term reductions would be substantially reduced, though they might still not disappear. (Here, "long-term public protection" refers to the period beginning about five years from first commitment, also called intake, and extending at least three more years. "Intermediate" means three to five years from intake. For this discussion it is assumed that routine parole would *continue*, and would remain largely unchanged, even if institutionalization were extended to several years.) Regarding Power Oriented males in particular, violence reduction can occur, but under relatively limited conditions only.

2. Compared to traditional programming, individualized intervention in a community setting can produce a larger reduction in recidivism from the pre-program period to the post-program period: Though youths in the traditional and individualized programs *both* had less overall recidivism during a sizable post-intake period than in a comparable pre-intake period (three years in the community immediately before and after intake or institutionalization), this pre-to-post reduction,

sometimes considered a "suppression ef-fect" (Murray and Cox, 1979), was mod-erate (16%) for the traditional program and substantial (59%) for the individual-ized. However, violent offending, in par-ticular, markedly increased in the traditional program from pre to post and held fairly even in the individualized. For conflicted youths—the largest single group—violent offending rose 225 per-cent in the former program and dropped 14 percent in the latter.

3. The individualized approach—which avoids institutionalization—can result in less labeling and stigmatization than the traditional. This would apply whether or not, but especially if, the latter involved *long-term* institutionalization (LTI). Regarding youths committed to state correctional agencies, LTI is a highly variable term: In many states it is taken to mean one or more years; in others it signifies two or more years; and for "youthful offenders"—ages 18 to 20 or more, depending on the state—it may mean even longer. Though we therefore leave the term without formal quantita-tive definition, and although no legal or widely accepted definition exists nation-ally, we will generally consider it at least two years in the contemporary United States—again with respect to youths in state training schools.

4. The individualized approach costs less than the traditional. Moreover, if one increased average length of institution-alization to three or more years, for ex-ample, for purposes of just desert or greater incapacitation, costs might favor the individualized approach even more. For instance, in one scenario this increased cost difference would reflect major new system expenses for the tra-ditional approach—particularly capital outlay needed to expand existing facili-ties or to construct, that is, add, en-tirely new ones. Expansion and/or new construction normally occurs when decision-makers respond to increased length of institutionalization by adding "bed space," that is, actual square footage, instead of simply adding "beds" to existing space (thereby often overcrowding the facility)—as in double-bunking.

In a second scenario, overcrowding would be accepted by decision-makers and expansion or new construction might thereby be delayed or avoided. Yet here, too, the cost difference which favors indi-vidualized intervention might—in fact, al-most certainly would—increase. This would reflect the greater total expenses associated with increased length of insti-tutionalization itself, for instance, with the three or more years per youth instead of the previous one, two, or fewer. Greater total expenses would basically re-sult from the higher *per-month* costs of institutionalization than those of the community-based approach—whose av-erage length per youth would not have increased. ("Overcrowding" exists in a facility when that structure's or institu-tion's resident population exceeds its physical "design capacity" at a given point in time. For instance, if, on January 1 of a given year, 110 youths were living in an institution designed for 100 residents—thus, for 100 beds—that facility would be considered 10 percent overcrowded on that day.)

5. Individualized intervention reflects cer-tain principles and goals often valued in themselves, independent of recidivism, violence, and cost reduction. These are: (a) promote humane interaction between staff and youths, thereby reducing the impersonal processing of individuals and perhaps modifying their negative image of authority figures; (b) facilitate youths' personal involvement in the change process as a way of tapping and building upon their internal motivation, thereby reducing the need to impose decisions on a largely involuntary basis; (c) facilitate individualized justice and minimize rigid, undifferentiated solutions, thereby inte-grating, where possible, the multiple needs, resources, and professed ideals of society with needs and resources of growing youths. It is probably easier to implement/achieve most or all such val-ues and goals via individualized interven-tion than in most traditional programs.

Though item (b), immediately above, focuses on involvement, motiva-tion, and decision-making in general, two points might be made regarding con-trols in particular: First, given an appropriate and adequately implemented intervention plan, less overall use of external controls by workers can probably help many youths eventually develop clearer and more consistent internal controls—in those respects, stronger and less situation-vulnerable controls—than would otherwise be the case. (This is likelier to happen if "less overall use" is accompanied by carefully timed reduction in use.) Though traditional and individualized program staff may each be able to decrease their use of external controls if they wish, and although both such programs can, in any event, help youths develop internal controls, less reliance by staff and youths on external controls is probably more likely to occur in the individualized. This is mainly because it lacks the months or years of relative regimentation and daily programming/ structure that often accompany institutionalization.

Second, the possibly greater reliance on external controls in the traditional approach, and the eventual development of clearer and more consistent internal controls in the individualized, occurs independently of the following: Regardless of what program (operations) staff actually do, roughly *equal* amounts of *underlying/implicit* external control and even coercion probably exist in the traditional and individualized approaches alike. This is true simply because both approaches occur, from start to finish, in a correctional setting—ipso facto an externally constraining and always potentially sanctioning or punishing context. That is, this context or ubiquitous background condition exists—and underlying/implicit control therefore exists—regardless of the degree to which staff *openly/explicitly* use surveillance, make demands that are accompanied by actual or conditional sanctions, and allow for genuine choice by youths. In short, it exists regardless of staff's greater or lesser use of specific, concrete controls and their creation of a controlling atmosphere. Nevertheless, underlying/implicit factors need not dominate a program, and that which is open and explicit can decisively distinguish one program from another.

6. Individualized intervention can avoid the often unnecessary removal or lengthy "banishment" of youths from their immediate environments and broader communities. By itself, such removal/rejection can further complicate youths' pre-removal, that is, *already existing,* problems. It can also produce *negative reactions* that are separate from such complications of preexisting problems. One or both impacts—those that involve preexisting problems and/or those that do not—may have yet another effect: They may add to, or complicate, various problems that youths may need to address in any event when they eventually return to, and try to adjust to, their communities and immediate environments. That is, youths must ordinarily address these problems or tasks whether or not (a) removal/rejection has complicated preexisting problems and/or (b) negative reactions to removal/rejection have occurred.

Removal from the community may involve other possible losses. For instance, despite the negative or potentially harmful factors and conditions often found in environments (communities) from which youths have been removed, these settings may contain features or resources that can help those individuals achieve a better overall adjustment—sometimes in those same settings. Individualized diagnosis can play a key role in identifying not only the pitfalls and challenges that exist in those settings, but the opportunities and other positive factors and potentials in question. An integrated intervention plan can then be a critical step in actually avoiding, neutralizing, or counterbalancing the identified negatives and in tapping into the positives in ways that make sense (and have "felt payoff") to the youths. Such a diagnosis and plan are among the core features of community-based, individualized intervention, and they cannot be derived—whether directly, by inference, or by both combined—from needs checklists alone.

Nonremoval can do more than allow staff and youths to access potentially helpful environmental/community features and resources from the start: It can avoid not only the previously mentioned complications (of already existing problems) often associated with removal alone, but it can preclude the need for *reintegration* per se, that is, reintegration into the immediate environment and broader community. Restated, these complications, and this need, would exist whether or not (1) negative reactions to removal had in fact occurred (as indicated, these reactions can be separate and apart from any complications of *pre*-removal problems), (2) institutionalization were long-term and/or involved unusually negative conditions and experiences, and (3) positive community resources were scarce. In addition, readjustment difficulties associated with reintegration might or might not be greater if *parole* did not exist—depending, of course, on what parole would otherwise have offered or produced, for instance, with regard to helping avoid the above negative factors and to tapping into positives.

At any rate, nonremoval would allow energies and sometimes scarce resources that would otherwise be expended on reintegration and other issues to instead be directed elsewhere from the start, by youths, workers, and others. Individualized intervention could help avoid unnecessary removal, and an integrated intervention plan could help mobilize, coordinate, and appropriately direct those energies and resources.

7. Few if any approaches other than the individualized have been experimentally shown to outperform the traditional with serious multiple offenders, as measured by general recidivism and by specific violence reduction on a long-term basis. We believe that individualized intervention would apply, not just in the United States, but within various non-U.S. nations and regions, and that its applicability in those areas would probably be based on many or most of the earlier-mentioned reasons. The nations/regions involved would include, for example, Canada, Great Britain, parts of Europe, and Japan, and not just the more industrialized or urbanized portions thereof.

Underlying Beliefs
Assumptions, Views, and Values

California's 12-year study strongly supported the assumptions and beliefs next described, most of which were implicit or explicit from either its start or its very early years. Though these assumptions and beliefs were never framed as specific hypotheses or tested systematically, their support and validity stem from literally thousands—actually, tens of thousands—of observations and experiences by researchers and program staff.

1. Youths, like other people, differ from each other in their current life circumstances, attitudes toward the environment, types of relationships with others, and views of themselves. Within a correctional setting, these differences have particular implications. For instance, in almost any sizable, random group of offenders—say, 30 or more—many will respond quite differently than others to nearly identical forms of intervention and to even the same agent of intervention (the worker). As their typical or dominant response, some youths will be enthusiastic, fairly accepting, or tolerant; others will be rejecting, passively resistant, or indifferent; still others may be confused, ambivalent, or inconsistent.

These variations largely reflect the youths' differing ways of perceiving and interpreting external events and of relating those events—and the people who produce them—to themselves. The differing responses reflect not only (a) their expectations in general and (b) broad aspects of their personalities (e.g., independence versus dependence; impulsiveness versus caution), but (c) their interests, preferences, values, skills, limitations, fears, and self-image in particular. These "c-items" (interests, etc.) often function as motivating, directing, and/or sustaining factors with regard to immediate and longer-term actions and adjustments. Individually and especially in various combinations (ones that characterize and themselves help define the particular youth), their influence is often major or decisive. At any rate, *en masse* their impact usually equals or exceeds that of a- and b-items (general expectations, etc.) combined—not just with serious multiple offenders.

When developing, implementing, and modifying intervention plans and when matching workers with youths, the following is therefore important if one is to adequately implement the individualized approach. At a very early point, one should identify, carefully consider, and, where possible, tap into not just the broad or general factors mentioned earlier—the a- and b-items—but the c-items in particular. To do so, especially with c-items, the use of neither typological- nor developmental-classification systems will suffice, even if those systems involved, say, 5, 10, or 15 and more validated categories each. Nor will extensive checklists suffice, including those which specify common areas of need (educational; vocational; peers; family relationships; substance abuse; etc.) and various levels of need within each area (none; slight; moderate; marked).

That is, whether singly or together, neither the classification-systems approach nor the checklist approach will directly provide or otherwise encompass and reflect the type and degree of specific information needed to achieve the following: (1) produce a sufficiently integrated understanding of the youth as an individual and of his actual/anticipated life circumstances (crises included), and, therefore, (2) make possible a sufficiently realistic, focused, and responsive plan. Moreover, to literally *integrate* a-, b-, and c-items (plus life circumstances and other material) and to actually produce that plan, staff must discuss and carefully compare the detailed information in question and must identify significant relationships between factors.

Despite the above limitations, typological, developmental, and checklist approaches usually provide valuable information and can represent major steps *toward* adequate understanding and individualization. Nevertheless, their implications for planning, especially specific and integrated planning, are not always clear and differentiated. Unless placed in a broader context, they can not infrequently mislead or misdirect.

2. Among serious multiple offenders, illegal behavior and related life-styles usually stem from or are triggered by at least three factors; they seldom result from one alone. These factors often operate more or less simultaneously, even though—with any youth at any time—one or two generally dominate and have done so for years. Like the dominant factor(s), the specific combination of three or more varies considerably across youths.[1]

In California's Sacramento, Stockton, and San Francisco samples the most often identified factors were as follows (most items listed took several forms and were therefore considered "types" of factors): personal conflicts, family "binds" or pressures; long-term overcompensations; peer pressures; subgroup expectations; situational entanglements; desire for material gain; family disorganization; undersocialization/poor impulse control; conflicting social values; antisocial or antiauthority family orientation. Together with the a-, b-, and c-items mentioned earlier, these social-psychological factors provided the primary basis for understanding most youths' illegal behavior. To almost all program staff and to researchers as well, these items and factors also seemed a *sufficient* basis for understanding—at least initial understanding. Most such factors would probably apply to numerous other samples within and outside the United States.

Besides those factors, definite and suspected physical injuries and impairments were always carefully considered during the 12-year study, whether they were past or present. Their role in the intervention plan was integrated with that of factors such as the above. Few youths had major physical impairments in addition to their other difficulties; those who did had an extreme overall burden. Genetic/hereditary factors and explanations only rarely played a role, even though they were never ruled out a priori with any youth. Major organicity ("brain damage") was rare or at least rarely clear-cut. Minor or moderate organicity was infrequent, that is, neither rare on the one hand nor somewhat common on the other. When it seemed to exist and was reasonably well confirmed, its role in the intervention plan was substantial.

Finally, medical/pharmacological regimens and approaches were used very seldom and to a slight degree, and then only as adjuncts. This partly reflected the social-psychological views that prevailed and the belief that "nonphysiological" interventions would generally suffice, provided they took account of physical injuries, impairments, and the like.

3. To work realistically with youths, one's intervention plan should carefully address the more "immediate" contributors to their recent illegal behavior and adjustment problems. More specifically, it should directly address the apparent triggering and sustaining conditions of those behaviors/problems and should do so in an individualized way. When coupled with an emphasis on the motivating, directing, and sustaining factors mentioned earlier, this plan can realistically focus on two equally important goals—one short-term, the other long: (a) reduce the chances that youths' illegal behavior, especially if it is nonminor, will continue in the immediate future and will thereby cause their removal from the program; (b) help youths change direction in order to permanently cope with life in a nondelinquent or less delinquent way (this change may occur slowly). Selected developments and issues relating to these goals will now be mentioned; after that, we will turn to points 4 through 6.

Intensive Supervision

Since the mid-1980s, "intensive supervision" (IS) has been a common, community-based approach that mainly focuses on the goal of short-term public protection. As described below, it differs from individualized intervention in important respects despite having certain components and features in common. Though chiefly used with adult probationers and/or parolees in lieu of or subsequent to institutionalization, IS has recently been employed in several states as an *alternative* to training schools or other youth incarceration, with respect to comparatively serious offenders/offenses (Byrne, Lurigio, and Baird, 1989; Clear and Hardyman, 1990). Before 1980, the term "intensive supervision" basically referred to staff/client contact, that is, supervision, which occurred two—possibly three—times a month rather than the standard *once*. However, since around 1984–1985 it has generally meant the following (note: we will emphasize its utilization as an alternative to lengthy incarceration. This largely differs from "probation enhancement"[2] for somewhat less serious, but not lightweight, offenders. These are individuals whose likelihood of being incarcerated would, in most jurisdictions, not be rather sizable or high, even absent the probation enhancement, not to mention an alternative program—such as an intensive supervision program—itself):

First, with virtually all program participants (usually multiple offenders), intensive supervision emphasizes close controls, heavy time structuring (scheduling of daily activities), and frequent surveillance. To help implement these features it often relies heavily on electronic monitoring.

Next, IS usually stresses the concept of "holding people accountable for their behavior"—more precisely, holding them very strictly accountable. This emphasis, which relates directly to intensive supervision's primary goal of short-term public protection, is mainly reflected in IS's typically swift and, in any case, "no-nonsense" or relatively severe sanctions for unacceptable behavior. For instance, youths are often automatically and immediately removed from IS programs not simply for their first penal code offense (whether minor or moderate), but for their first or second infraction or technical violation. This may occur not only regardless of the youths' circumstances but despite the fact that, instead of removing the individual from the program, a somewhat different intervention approach or emphasis could perhaps have been substituted for the previous approach (see point [d], below). Though not all intensive supervision programs operate precisely this way or to this degree, the majority do so; and the sanctions mentioned earlier are both typical and modal. In any event, strict and swift sanctions are generally considered the main appropriate response to unacceptable/illegal behavior, and they are often viewed as a *sufficient* response to it. They are almost always considered an essential ingredient in, and a distinguishing feature of, IS.

Finally, though its main public protection goal is to stop immediate illegal behavior, intensive supervision usually tries to achieve the long-term goal—permanent change—as well. Toward this end, the heavy external controls/structuring/surveillance that it uses mainly to achieve the short-term goal is generally accompanied by program elements such as restitution (via community service or other methods) and perhaps substance abuse or other personal/problem-centered counseling. In addition, either employment or continued schooling are almost always required. In many or most IS programs nearly all participants are exposed to the same or almost the same elements, and frequency of contact is also similar. Together, phone and face-to-face contacts usually occur about twice a week, but in a few programs they occur daily.[3]

Intensive supervision therefore often involves extensive and intensive intervention, that is, use of two or more program elements and frequent contact. However, despite this breadth and degree of intervention, it seldom individualizes its approach in certain respects. For instance, IS generally does not:

a. focus thoroughly or heavily on the wide range of motivating, directing, and sustaining factors that often affect youths. For example, though IS often identifies and focuses on a few of the c-items mentioned earlier, it seldom takes careful account of, integrates, and tries to tap into most or all of them *collectively*. (For review, c-items include such factors as interests, preferences, values, skills, limitations, fears, and self-image.)
b. work in depth and detail with, or on, certain environmental pressures and supports—such as family and peers—that may substantially affect youths;
c. match workers and youths, particularly along lines described in Chapter 11; and
d. respond flexibly when unacceptable/illegal (u/i) behavior occurs.

Judging from the present experiment, features (a) through (d) are probably important to many youths.

A few words about feature (d): As indicated, intensive supervision programs commonly remove individuals in response to nonmajor u/i behavior. However, such removal may eliminate the opportunity for youths to examine and directly confront key contributors to their u/i behavior, and to do so with support and guidance from persons with whom they are familiar. For instance, if a given youth had been *retained* in the program,

he might—assisted by staff and others—have identified and successfully examined/confronted a number of "live and active" feelings, pressures, misunderstandings, overcompensations, or fears that directly related to his unacceptable/illegal behavior. Moreover, such feelings, and so on, may have contributed not just to a *single* infraction, technical violation, or nonmajor penal code offense. Instead, they may have triggered, sustained, and even escalated a *set* of u/i behaviors, such as the following (as will be described, it is the connection between these *feelings, pressures,* and so forth, that links the *behaviors* to each other and which sustains and directs them; these interrelated behaviors, or set of events, will be called an "episode" [though the following is a hypothetical example, similar episodes were common during the study]). The youth:

a. skips school (truants) on a given Friday;
b. has major argument with his parents and runs from home the next afternoon;
c. has a drinking spree with friends and, after being insulted or challenged, has a fistfight that same evening (and simultaneously violates curfew); and
d. participates in a "joyride" (unauthorized use of a car), and either returns home or is apprehended the next day (Sunday).

This rapid series of events—which, say, occurred three months into the program—was largely unexpected and constitutes a moderate crisis. Except, say, for a prior truancy and several arguments with parents, none of its components (drinking spree, etc.) had occurred during those months. Also, the youth's adjustment may have been generally satisfactory even though substantial attitude change and increased self-understanding had not been seen.

Not only might this episode's first steps—truancy and runaway—have been difficult or impossible to prevent in almost any program, but its subsequent events might have been difficult to interrupt even in an IS program, that is, under conditions of particularly heavy control. The first steps could have been triggered by recent academic difficulties combined with related pressures at home and with continued anger toward parents, plus an underlying but increasing depression. The school problems, in particular, might have revived long-standing feelings of inadequacy that the youth ordinarily suppressed or denied. Subsequent events could have been directed and sustained by the following factors, in roughly this sequence:

a. internal pressure to undo a loss of self-esteem—more specifically, to psychologically build himself up after having felt "beaten down" or "put down" in school or at home;
b. a wish to directly display not only anger at the parents' increased demands but dissatisfaction with their attempted controls; and a wish to indirectly express hurt feelings—and to hurt his parents' feelings in return—for what he considered partial parental rejection or unwillingness to respect his views (these factors bear on the runaway);
c. a desire to impress peers and thereby gain their reassurance regarding his "coolness," acceptability, and partial autonomy; also, a need or wish to counter his feelings of depression and to divert his thoughts from them (these factors bear on the drinking spree, the fight, and the curfew violation); and
d. an impulse to vent his frustrations and a wish to experience an hour or two of physical release and a sense of freedom, power, control, or escape, before letting the episode end (this bears on the joyride).

The youth would probably have wanted the episode to end at about that point if he felt he had successfully asserted himself, had made his point, was less depressed, and wanted to avoid *really* big trouble."

Rather than remove the youth from the program, staff should try to help him not only examine the specifics of, and reasons for, this episode, but to learn other ways to assert himself, to rebuild his self-esteem, and to "make his point." Given (1) this staff effort and some such learning, and given (2) staff assistance in recognizing, valuing, and increasingly utilizing (or developing) his positive skills, qualities, and potentials, the youth would be less likely to respond similarly in the future to similar stimuli and emotions, particularly those which might revive underlying feelings of inadequacy. (It might be noted that the opportunity for such learning and for developing alternative responses would be lost or greatly reduced even if, instead of program removal, little or no change were made in the intervention plan other than intensifying external controls.)

Though comparable crises or components thereof are experienced by many nonoffenders and minor delinquents as part of "growing up," most such individuals apparently "learn their lessons" from those behaviors or events without having to simultaneously experience major changes in their social environments or living arrangements—long-term lockup included. The present experiment suggests that much the same can often apply to serious multiple offenders.

An individualized intervention program can help such offenders benefit from the above type of crisis by using its overall resources, its staff and supervisory skills plus motivations, and its administrative as well as conceptual flexibility to shift gears and try something new. Of course, the "new" will sometimes be accompanied by something "old" or standard, including, for example (as in this hypothetical case), placement of the youth into short-term—say, 3 to 15 days—detention (here, closer to 15 days, mainly because of the joyriding—a penal code offense.)

In any event, using this flexibility, staff, for example, would reexamine the present intervention plan and modify it as needed. In the above example, this would occur as soon as the episode ended, that is, right after the joyride. Any such modification could be later refined, and still later readjusted. These refinements and readjustments would be based, for instance, not only on early reactions by the youth and others but on the nature as well as outcome of new approaches that the youth might be trying out in connection with school and with family interactions, among other things. Ideally, these new approaches would not be *largely* based on external demands or on the youth's fear of negative consequences such as short- or longer-term lockup; realistically, of course, some such fears are unavoidable and not at all unfounded. Instead, the new approaches could mainly or at least increasingly reflect his own desires and his greater understanding of why certain aspects of the episode occurred, and of how alternative responses would better support his overall needs. Hopefully, these need- or goal-directed behaviors would help produce improvements and satisfactions in his life, and—for those reasons rather than the above fears—they would continue after he completed the program.

Though *intensive supervision* programs show evidence of controlling short-term illegal behavior, careful research is needed to determine their (1) longer-term, post-program impact, (2) short- and intermediate-range impact compared to traditional and other approaches, and (3) areas of greater and lesser impact on their typical range of participants. This research might also address the question of whether IS's heavy external controls/surveillance is appropriate and essential with all youths, at various program stages. The present experiment suggests it is not, at least when other specified elements are operating. Whatever such research may reveal—and especially if serious concerns or shortcomings emerge—it should be remembered that intensive supervision as it currently exists can doubtlessly be modified, that is, toward increased individualization regarding points (a) through (d), made earlier. Until the late 1980s, little carefully controlled (scientific) research existed regarding intensive supervision, and the varied studies that were completed showed—collectively—mixed or largely negative results (Armstrong, 1988; Byrne, Lurigio, and Baird, 1989; Krisberg, Austin, and Steele, 1989; Palmer, 1992). In the few scientific studies that have been completed—mostly since that time—much the same results have been obtained for the respective study samples as a whole. (Seldom have the intensive and comparison samples been subdivided along various lines, programmatically and/or analytically.) The few positive findings that have emerged were associated with (1) programs that combined "treatment" with "control," instead of almost exclusively emphasizing control/surveillance, and with (2) offenders (*within* given programs) who received above-average amounts of counseling. Most intensive supervision research to date, however, has centered on adults (Clear and Hardyman, 1990; Palmer, 1994; Petersilia and Turner, 1992; Turner, Petersilia, and Deschenes, 1992).

Proximal versus Distal Causes

As indicated, a realistic, individualized plan carefully addresses the "immediate" causes of the youths' illegal behavior, that is, the triggering conditions or contributors—sometimes called "near-term" or "proximal" causes. This focus, whose rationale is by now self-evident, also reflects the following belief about certain long-standing cultural/historical factors that might *ultimately* have shaped or heavily contributed to various negative conditions in the youths' social or even family environment (these factors include, e.g., economic, racial, and demographic conditions): *Few such factors ("distant" or "distal" causes) will change or improve quickly enough to make any decisive difference in the youngsters' immediate future or to substantially modify these individuals' already established, often self-reinforcing pattern of delinquency.*[4] From almost the start of the study, program staff considered this belief plausible and probably valid. As a corollary, they believed most changes or adaptations would instead have to come from the youths themselves and from members of their immediate environment. Both beliefs were borne out by the 12 years' experience. (Note: Although given delinquent patterns or acts are "self-reinforcing" or largely so, they may still be triggered by—though, of course, not literally carried out by—immediate external events/conditions; and they may, as described above, be partly directed and/or sustained by those or other such factors.)

In short, it was thought that broad social changes, even structural and/or attitudinal changes in local communities, usually occurred too slowly or seemed too moderate to bear significantly on the major immediate needs and current adjustment patterns of offenders as individuals, and to thereby decisively impact either the short- or long-term goal. (Structural changes involve, for instance, modifications in [1] the nature and degree of governmental/institutional roles and responsibilities, especially those of the state, local communities, schools, and family, and [2] the distribution of political and economic power and opportunity among individuals, groups, de facto social classes, organizations, and/or institutions. Attitudinal changes may for example, focus on race relations and on feelings toward given minority groups.)

These broad and slow social and structural changes should be distinguished from changes and fluctuations that may develop fairly quickly and which are often relatively short-lived. One such change involves general economic improvement that lasts, say, one or two years and is accompanied by substantially increased need for skilled, semiskilled, or unskilled labor. Yet despite this distinction, and although such temporary improvements and increases did occur a number of times during 1961–1973, the following applied: To take advantage of the increased job opportunities associated with this change, many youths still had to improve their employment skills and/or—especially—increase their motivation to obtain and retain a job. In short, although such changes did create a more positive general atmosphere within society, did produce something more concrete for many individuals to work toward, and did immediately improve job prospects for youths who already had requisite skills and motivation, they did not, by themselves, ensure or even begin to ensure that any given individual's delinquent behavior and overall adjustment pattern would automatically change, let alone change substantially. This is apart from the fact that many youths also had to improve their skills and increase their job-centered motivations during periods in which employment opportunities had *not* increased, or during those in which they decreased or returned to their earlier level.

Even when the relatively short-lived improvements had not occurred or no longer existed, and although broad social/structural change occurred too slowly to bear significantly on offenders' immediate needs, this did not mean that *specific resources*—local, state, or federal—were currently nonexistent, unavailable, or unhelpful. Such resources, for example, social, health, and employment services, did in fact exist throughout 1961–1973. Some, such as social services, even increased during given periods in which few short-lived improvements had occurred, or after recent increases, such as those in job opportunities, had subsided. At any rate, though some community resources, or at least increased resources, largely resulted from the temporary changes in question, the majority did not. The latter were generally more stable with regard to level and availability, perhaps because they usually had an ongoing or relatively longstanding local, state, or federal funding base.

Yet whatever the source, the stability, and the extent of community resources, the following applied: To draw on the youths themselves and to work toward the earlier-mentioned short- and especially long-term goals, it was important for staff to (1) engage the youths' conscious motivations and to realistically assess their limitations. This called for (2) the type of individualized understanding already described, particularly of a-, b-, and c-items (expectations, interests, skills, etc.). Both (1) and (2) applied whether or not staff's intervention plan specifically included and emphasized

the subgoal of helping youths become willing and/or better able to make immediate or eventual use of the available community resources.

By the mid-1960s, program staff believed that insofar as an individualized understanding was achieved and the resulting intervention plan proved successful, internal rather than external controls would be more likely to dominate the youths' behavior and overall adjustment in the long run, including, in particular, the period after discharge from the Youth Authority. This belief was probably correct. Internal change was considered more likely to occur if staff took careful account of a-, b-, and c-items.[5]

4. The 12 years of experience also supported the tacit assumption that many of the experimental program's intervention methods *would* appropriately address immediate causal factors or major contributors to illegal behavior. More specifically, most approaches used in approximately the final decade did turn out to be relevant to, and of assistance to, most youths. Yet also as originally expected, others missed the mark; of these, most proved largely inadequate by themselves, and some lost impact when poorly combined.

5. The dozen years' experience clearly supported two explicit, even more basic assumptions: (a) Despite their records as repeat offenders and despite their frequent resistance, many or most youths *are* open to substantial positive change, perhaps fairly permanent change. During their relatively close interactions with youths—usually lasting several months to a few years—program staff often saw sizable changes; these or similar developments were also observed by researchers. How long or how well they lasted beyond the program itself was not fully determined, since contact ended at discharge; however, judging from several years of post-discharge follow-up using Department of Justice rapsheets, many behavioral changes probably did endure with numerous youths, particularly males. Again using rapsheets, these changes seemed larger (in terms of offense severity) and/or more frequent (with respect to offense rate) in the individualized than in the traditional program, across those youths collectively.

(b) The openness to change mentioned in assumption 5(a) depends on certain conditions being generated by a state agency and its program staff, and on their being maintained for a number of years. Included, in particular, is the use of given intervention methods within an accepting or tolerant community. During 1961–1973, the Youth Authority—a state agency—did generate and maintain certain conditions needed to support particular interventions in various communities, and numerous youths seemed responsive to these methods. To be sure, many Phase 1 and 2 (1961–1969) youths did *not* seem open or sufficiently open to initial intervention within the community, at least not to the original CTP approach. In Phase 3 (1969–1973), such youths were first programmed within an institutional setting that operated according to individualized intervention principles, and under this condition many did respond.

6. Finally, throughout the 12 years, program staff retained the following views of the offenders with whom they worked. They did so despite these youths' past and occasional present illegal behavior and/or self-injurious acts, and in spite of some offenders' frequent unpleasantness and resistance. The youths:

   a. are neither hopeless, worthless, intractable, nor defective; nor are they "depraved" or "basically evil";

   b. are able and—before long—are often eager to markedly change the direction of their lives or to change their pattern of adjustment; in these and other ways multiple offenders are neither intrinsically different from nor of lesser potential value than other individuals, even though the former may be more troubled or troublesome in various respects and although, in many cases, their desire to change fluctuates considerably and periodically wanes.

   c. have not forfeited the common "right" to improve their lot; nor have they lost all claim to personal happiness, including the satisfaction of helping or pleasing others; though "paying their price" for certain past behavior, they should be allowed, in fact encouraged, to simultaneously move forward.

At the end of the 12 years, new and "old-time" staff considered or still considered these views valid. Perhaps because of such views, among others, their interactions with youths almost always seemed humane and nondemeaning, even from most youths' perspective.[6] This was true even though firm external controls and direction often seemed necessary with particular individuals (power-oriented and others), and although direct, sometimes heavy confrontation was occasionally used with most.

Such views were supported by the fact that—among other things—initial progress was usually observed by staff within two or three months from intake, and further progress, albeit slow or slight, was often noticed every few months thereafter. Also, staff only occasionally observed an extended (four plus months) impasse or apparent impasse with most youths or had an overall sense of futility about them. To be sure, with other youths—some of whom were soon revoked and institutionalized due to their major illegal behavior—progress either *was* nonexistent, had been neutralized/undone, or, in any event, was difficult to see.

At a related level, views 6(a) through 6(c) were reinforced by experiences and interactions such as the following (descriptions that follow reflect 85 to 100 follow up research interviews with staff, hundreds of research discussions and meetings with staff, hundreds of interviews with CTP youths, and more than daily, informal observations of staff/youth interactions through 1961–1973—a period covering approximately 3,000 work days for any given on-site observer): Confrontations, roadblocks, and setbacks notwithstanding, most staff had many pleasant and calm moments with youths; also, after their first few months, many youths often enjoyed themselves with staff and sometimes shared moments of triumph.[7] In addition, staff and youths did not always consider their interactions a cat-and-mouse game, whether subtle or blatant; though these contacts and discussions frequently *did* involve maneuvering, they were often straightforward and sincere. Moreover, rather than almost always being tense, stark, and humorless, they were often fairly cheerful even though serious underneath. Thus, not surprisingly, friendly small talk—even banter—was far from rare. Most interactions simultaneously involved more than one "level."

Finally, staff believed that almost all youths demonstrated—more than just occasionally—traits and behaviors generally thought to involve everyday positive feelings or to reflect socially desirable values. Youths showed these features, such as thoughtfulness, unselfishness, persistence, and courage, when interacting with staff as well as others. (Not all youths showed all such features.) This was despite many youths' frequent self-absorption or self-centeredness and despite the fact that some such features often faded or temporarily disappeared when youths grew defensive, confused, hostile, or fearful in response to perceived threat or general anxiety.

Together, such experiences and facts supported staff's earlier-mentioned views of youths, and in some cases they *reflected* the views themselves. For instance, insofar as staff's (1) positive expectations regarding youths and (2) implicitly or explicitly encouraging attitudes toward those individuals helped *produce* positive change, those expectations and attitudes themselves helped support or verify the original views, that is, the positive expectations. In this respect staff's input to youths helped produce a self-fulfilling "prophecy." All in all, of course, change depended neither ultimately nor primarily on staff's attitudes and encouragement alone.

Notes

1. The idea that several factors usually interact to produce illegal behavior and related life-styles was not fully recognized at the start of the California experiment; nor was the full range of causal factors that is next mentioned in the text. Both became certain only after years of careful diagnosis and follow-up observations.

2. "Probation enhancement and parole enhancement have generally been described as involving (a) more contacts than in standard supervision (often made possible by reduced caseloads) and/or (b) the addition, to standard supervision, of one or two service or control elements, for example, family and collateral contacts, or, in recent years, electronic monitoring" (Palmer, 1994, p. 30). *Intensive* supervision, since the mid-1980s, has commonly connoted three to ten or more supervision/ surveillance contacts per week, in contrast to "enhancement's" two or three contacts of all types combined, per month.

3. Three other points might be noted: In many IS programs a sizable percentage of staff/youth contacts are by phone rather than face-to-face; the latter contacts usually occur in standard office settings, not in community centers shared by or operated specifically for IS; and few IS programs routinely work with youths well over a year, let alone for two or more.

4. Also, by the mid-1960s it was clear that *most* youths' illegal behavior seldom centered around, or even substantially involved, either an emotional or a calculated reaction to perceived and actual social injustice, to long-standing racial discrimination, and/or (to a lesser extent) to diminished or relatively few economic opportunities. Today, the impact of these factors is probably somewhat larger, on average.

5. The following might be mentioned in connection with, but not limited to, staff's development of intervention plans: When focusing on such factors as offenders' interests and skills, staff were aware, in specific or concrete ways, of the youths' achievements and potential; that is, they centered on various positive features that bear on Underlying Belief #6 (this chapter). When youths' limitations were added to their interests and skills and when, in addition, their personal development was traced from childhood (if only sketchily), a "three-dimensional" or relatively realistic and individualized picture generally emerged, one that was neither a stereotype nor an oversimplification. This picture played a critical and dominant role even though each youth also received a diagnostic label and, in that connection, theoretically *could have been* stereotyped/oversimplified in various respects, particularly by inexperienced staff. (This bears on Underlying Belief #1.)

6. Power-oriented individuals often felt differently, especially during their early months at CTP.

7. Though these interactions frequently occurred when progress had taken place or when certain goals were reached, they were not limited to achievement-centered contexts.

29 DIFFERING PERSPECTIVES ON OFFENDERS

This chapter addresses several interrelated subjects. First, two broad views of offenders are described and compared, views commonly held by the public and many correctional professionals. Implications of these views for intervention are also mentioned. Next, the public's fears of offenders are discussed—as is many adults' increased sensitivity to crime. After that, significant changes in youths are examined, as are adults' responses to those individuals. The chapter then presents certain overly simplified and relatively static views of offenders that have been prominent since the 1970s, and it mentions various implications of those views for individualized intervention. Finally, key aspects of corrections' presently dominant approach—the "strong-external-controls" (SEC) approach—are specified. SEC largely incorporates those overly simplified and relatively static views; it addresses the public's fears of offenders mainly on a short-term basis; and it minimally focuses on various personal/developmental needs that bear on long-term public protection.

Two Major Views and Responses

Group "A" Views and Responses

In the contemporary United States, many people are fairly indifferent to the needs and problems of offenders as individuals. They think mainly of their crimes—sometimes serious crimes—and then focus on the punishment they assume will occur. These individuals will be called Group A, and many of them, possibly most, generally support, accept, or defer to the following view (fewer actively promote it): It is OK for offenders' personal or social lives to remain difficult or less than satisfying long

after the official punishment is completed, that is, more difficult or less satisfying than that of nonoffenders. (A typical, official punishment for nonminor offenders would be lockup followed by probation or parole.)

Though that view or assumption is usually tacit and perhaps less than conscious, it is not infrequently explicit and conscious. It implies that, in major respects, offenders need not expect to receive the same social opportunities as nonoffenders, and that, in any event, they may well be "last in line." This also applies to opportunities as well as other forms of general to concrete aid/assistance *during* the time of official punishment, especially but not only with serious or multiple offenders.

Thus, many Group A individuals go beyond passive disinterest in, or pointed indifference toward, offenders' needs and problems. They, in effect, largely reject offenders as persons of equal intrinsic value or even potentially equal or considerable social value. They support or sometimes promote the view that, with few exceptions, it is all right for offenders to *not* receive certain types or levels of otherwise available, relatively low-risk assistance (over and beyond general opportunities). This might include rather individualized programs or aid that various correctional personnel may consider important for future adjustment. Practically speaking, this de facto, virtual rejection of offenders as persons worthy of specified consideration therefore goes beyond the temporary banishment associated with lockup and beyond the direct curtailment of opportunities and enjoyments that is often associated with various sanctions. It may or may not involve revenge per se. (It does not, however, imply that they should receive no assistance *at all,* particularly during the period of their official punishment.)

This type of rejection is an understandable part of Group A's overall reaction to offenders' past and possible future actions, especially those involving physical threat or injury, and major property loss. In that respect it is largely a defensive move, one which, to a sizable degree, often spreads to less serious offenses and threats. Broadly speaking, Group A's main goal is to maximize near-term personal and public safety by separating offenders from society or by otherwise controlling and/or punishing them in order to prevent or forestall further crime and delinquency. A's secondary goal—not a close second, but still a substantial wish—is to provide long-term safety, mostly via the individual and collective deterrence that it hopes punishment, including lockup, will also provide in the *short* run. Thus, except for lockup, Group A largely relies on the same mechanism—punishment → deterrence—for short- and long-term effects. A second group (discussed below) uses this mechanism as well, but to a lesser extent and together with other approaches, with these approaches being seen as ways to better produce the *long*-term effects.

Though anger is often associated with, and sometimes dominates, A's response to offender behavior, about equally often it neither *is* nor *does.* (Here, dominance means being the largest single influence in determining what one would like to "do" about offenders, that is, do with, for, or to them.) Anger may dominate even if it is largely submerged; and when anger dominates, revenge is more likely to be considered an acceptable part of punishment.

When anger is only slight or moderate and when, in any event, it does *not* dominate, one of the following stances or reactions may prevail (these are more intellectually controlled than anger):

1. a largely pragmatic, seemingly nonpersonalized focus on social defense;
2. disgust or disdain.

In Reaction 1, most non-"lightweight," that is, nonminor, offenders are considered troublesome or undesirable "elements" in society. Here, Group A's main interest is in establishing a "cordon sanitaire" between those individuals and others, until the offenders prove able to behave acceptably. In this reaction,

there may or may not be interest in making them "pay" beyond the time of their official punishment. In fact, it is commonly assumed—tacitly—that as long as society is protected, these offenders can "go their way" and experience whatever satisfactions they may legitimately achieve.

Though Reaction 2 is more emotional than 1, it is—especially when strong—influenced less by anger than by disidentification or psychological/emotional distancing of oneself from offenders. A belief that offenders are "really sick, or else depraved" sometimes accompanies this response, especially in connection with certain compulsive, exploitive, or violent/sadistic offenses. Fear sometimes enters the picture as well, as it often does with other reactions. Disgust or disdain may also be felt toward offenses and offenders *in general*—that is, more broadly, and usually less intensely, than with very serious behaviors or perhaps unusual individuals. This, in fact, is Reaction 2's most common context and level of expression, and it may occur whether or not fear and strong disidentification exist.

Whether anger is marked or slight (or even unseen), rejection, when present, is sometimes marked and enduring. (This refers to a global or general rejection, one that is less specific than the earlier-mentioned "reject[ion] . . . as persons of equal intrinsic value." Also see endnote 22, regarding degrees of rejection.) Moreover, when anger dominates, *empathy* is relatively weak or circumscribed and its impact on decisions about other-than-lightweights is probably slight. Under these circumstances, and whatever the level of rejection, Group A's emphasis remains—by far—on safety and punishment, and relatively little attention is paid to individualized needs other than those involved in legally required, minimal care, safety, and supervision. This applies not just to Reactions 1 and 2 but to the earlier-described disinterest and indifference.

Fear of offenders, or, simply, the experience of past unpleasantness or "hassles" with them, very often underlies, or indirectly contributes to, rejection and anger. However, neither of the latter inevitably springs from, or depends on, the former. Whether or not fear and/or personal encounters have shaped most A's views and reactions, these individuals often regard offenders, at least non-lightweights, as little other than criminals or incipient criminals. In any event, they frequently view them as persons who, with few exceptions, (1) are already sufficiently "understood" for purposes of achieving the primary and perhaps secondary goals mentioned earlier, and who, whether understood or not, (2) deserve only minimal time, effort, and sympathy.

In this connection Group A seldom tries to think of offenders as individuals, or feels much need to do so; the main exception involves many of its care, safety, and supervision members, for example, among correctional personnel. At any rate, Group A feels little if any moral obligation in this regard and generally little humanitarian incentive. One expression of this stance is the following; in fact, it is sometimes a consequence: Only occasionally will A's professionals and nonprofessionals emphasize offenders' post-lockup or post-supervision future, except in relation to the latter's threat potential. For instance, though A's nonprofessionals—say, its members of the public—may sometimes consider offenders' future schooling or employment in connection with intervention, their overriding concern is with reducing future recidivism. That is, no more than modest interest exists in identifying and addressing the specific needs or problems of offenders—in that regard, their needs or problems as individuals—and in helping those individuals live more satisfying or productive lives. Many Group A members may not even consider the latter outcomes important complementary goals. Though most A members have limited sympathy for, and few humanitarian impulses toward, offenders as individuals, they have strong sympathies, and often such impulses, toward society as a whole. In this regard they are usually quite concerned—emotionally, intellectually, or both—with protecting everyday citizens and with helping *them* experience personal and mutual enjoyments.

The Group A position has been the largest single influence on American corrections during much of the latter's history, certainly for the past several decades. Moreover, beginning with the increased salience of violent crime in the early 1970s and continuing with the marked rise of drug-related offenses in the 1980s, A's dominance has increased. Even if it stops increasing in the next several years, it will probably continue for at least 10 to 15 years, whether or not violence and substance abuse plateau or even subside during that period.[1]

Though heavily focused on protecting society, Group A supporters are not devoid of care or concern for offenders. However, such feelings are neither abundant nor strong; and, as implied, more generalized or abstract humanitarian thoughts and sympathies are uncommon with regard to offenders. Moreover, even those feelings may have decreased since the early 1980s, by which point explicit concern for victims, and for "*society*-as-crime-victim," had become prominent.

In addition, dating from the continuing rise and spread of *violence* in the early 1970s, offenders were less often viewed by various segments of the general public—especially persons from Group A—as victims of society themselves. Within a few years even correctional professionals, such as academicians and practitioners, less often spoke of offenders, even those from economically deprived backgrounds, in that context. Not until the early 1980s were some offenders, whatever their backgrounds, widely acknowledged to have experienced serious parental and other interpersonal abuse and to have been victims in *that* regard. But even then, only small to moderate portions of the general (mainly middle-class) public strongly supported or promoted the idea that a great many offenders were mostly victims of *society* and were, for example, either "owed" assistance or—in any case—should receive it, for that reason. This is aside from whether those same portions of the public, when discussing offenders' victim status, were especially or principally concerned with the latter as individuals, for instance, with their future satisfactions and potential contributions.

Group "B" Views and Responses

Despite its long-term dominance, the Group A position, which largely focuses on *safety/punishment*, has not been corrections' only sizable force. This is because of a second set of individuals: Group B. As with A, this set consists of "nonprofessionals" and "professionals." To facilitate the discussion, nonprofessionals in A and B are often called Group A and B "publics," respectively. They are distinguished from A's and B's respective "professionals," such as correctional administrators, practitioners, and academicians. (In the next major section of this chapter, "Decreased Tolerance, Increased Sensitivity, and Changing Images," "public" is redefined slightly.)

Group B supports public protection goals designed mainly to reduce or eliminate not just short- but long-term illegal behavior, primarily by helping offenders change as individuals. Such intervention is usually called rehabilitation or, sometimes, habilitation. Though almost as large as A, B has been much less active and forceful in the past two decades. Following rehabilitation's major decline in 1975–1985, Group B's numbers have slowly but steadily grown, at least among its professionals. B's focus has sharpened as well, and its influence has gradually increased, even though A remains dominant.

Most Group B supporters believe that A's safety/punishment combination, especially its safety component, has considerable relevance under certain conditions. However, they consider A overly narrow and seriously lacking— all in all, an approach that should not predominate. Individuals who articulate this view, that is, B's correctional professionals, also believe A overemphasizes punishment with most offenders. They think the Group A position, viewed in toto, lacks adequate content and direction—that, for example, it says little about how to build skills, change attitudes and self-perceptions, and resolve internal and external problems.

Group B supporters believe that those areas, if adequately addressed, could help most offenders direct their lives along more satisfying and constructive lines. Thus, B usually believes that *safety/change,* or at least safety plus less punishment plus change, would provide more long-term benefit to society and offenders than safety/punishment alone. Though this benefit would involve more than behavior change, the latter, particularly the reduced illegal behavior, would itself be a major or central achievement. Long-term reductions in such behavior usually require internal change plus external control.

Unlike many in A, few in B believe that offenders—by virtue of having offended, or because of particular offenses—henceforth deserve relatively little by way of concrete assistance, not to mention general opportunities. Nor do most B-members assume the following:

1. Offenders have largely forfeited most claims to happiness, for several years or more.
2. Unless punished and perhaps threatened with further sanctions, most offenders may not get seriously interested in addressing their difficulties, in suppressing given impulses, desires, or activities, or in substantially redirecting their lives. Except with "lightweights," the required punishments or "negative consequences" would generally be frequent or heavy.

Thus, most people in B do not believe that actual or threatened punishments/sanctions are a *decisive*—that is, a make-or-break— factor in motivating most offenders to address specific difficulties or to redirect their lives; nor are such punishments, and so on, necessarily considered even the largest single factor. These views contrast with those of many A's; and in that respect the following might be noted. If offenders *have* in some sense "forfeited" most claims to happiness—if, say, they are no longer supposed to really expect it for themselves, at least via conventional means—that in itself could weaken their possible motivation to substantially change the direction of their lives, for instance, to seek socially acceptable forms of happiness, certainly in the absence of sanctions. In short, they could find themselves in a partial but major catch-22, and their chances of failure might well increase.

Group B believes that most offenders often want to change for reasons other than avoiding sanctions, and despite the difficulties and ambivalence involved. Also, it obviously believes offenders have the ability to change, particularly if adequate support and assistance exist. This is apart from the fact that some change can occur without support/assistance or, for that matter, without punishments/sanctions plus external control. Attributing nonpunishment-based interests, motives, and abilities to offenders neither minimizes the difficulties in question nor romanticizes those individuals. Indirectly, it implies that offenders—their troubles and frequent troublesomeness notwithstanding—are more similar to than different from most other individuals; also, it suggests they are neither more nor less human. All in all, this position therefore maintains that offenders are far from "irreparably sick," or, for that matter, "fundamentally different/deviant" in a negative sense. In those respects it links rehabilitation to neither a "diseased entity" type of medical model, on the one hand, nor a pollyannish idealization—a paper-angel view—on the other.

Finally, the above position suggests that even if one accepts the view that offenders are less deserving of happiness, opportunities, and assistance per se than are nonoffenders, the following questions remain: How much less deserving are they? For instance, has their worth presumably diminished to the point where they should be "written off" or provided only minimal, or else token, aid? If they are not completely written off, can they—or, say, can most nonlightweights—*really* be expected to change, that is, to "turn around," in response to minimal aid and/or fleeting or even unrealistic opportunities? On the other hand, if improvement does emerge after some months (whatever the level of aid), should that be taken to mean the individuals are now more deserving than before and are thus eligible for increased support or aid? Merit aside, might not such change or improvement become partly self-reinforcing if accompanied by personal satisfaction? For example, could it not then produce further efforts to change— some of which might need, or simply benefit from, continued support and opportunity?

Viewing offenders as human and not undeserving does not preclude Group B from ever feeling anger toward them, or even fear. Nor does it bar them from considering any offenders destructive, self-destructive, or unpleasant, either in general or situationally. Nevertheless, such feelings and views, when present, neither preclude nor wholly destroy B's empathy or tolerance for offenders, or—perhaps more intellectually—its "interest" in the latter's future, as individuals with needs, potential, and rights.[2] As a result, those feelings/views (anger, etc.) are less likely to produce the considerable rejection that not infrequently occurs in A— where, for example, empathy with offenders is weaker or less common in the first place, and merit often seems decisive.[3]

If, of course, B's were to assume that offenders have little potential for growth and accomplishment, they, like some A's who do make that assumption, might feel justified in withholding or diverting substantial assistance. (This could occur even if they empathized with those offenders' feelings and, say, generally understood their life situation and problems. Empathy and understanding aside, it could also occur if they simply believed those individuals had few, or greatly reduced, legal or moral rights.) Basically, B's reasoning, like that of A's, might be as follows (this focuses on the "little-potential-for-growth" assumption): If offenders are already largely "set in their ways"—except, say, for responding behaviorally to external controls

and to fear of punishment—little can be gained from programs designed *mainly* to increase skills, change attitudes, and so on.[4] This would apply even if those programs also used many external controls, sanctions, and the like, since the skill-building elements, and so on, would be largely superfluous in any event. Under those circumstances, deterrence—via punishment and control, and with few if any growth-centered efforts—might be the only appropriate strategy. However valid or vulnerable that reasoning, it might be noted that a major withholding of assistance could unwittingly promote a negatively oriented self-fulfilling prophecy regarding potential for growth. This is apart from the fact that individuals who comprise Group B—and proportionately more of those who constitute A—seldom in fact assume offenders have little *potential* for growth. (*Motivation* for growth is a separate, and more complex, matter.)

Despite the preceding feelings, views, and possible assumptions, A and B *both* want offenders to change in the sense of reducing or eliminating their illegal behavior. However, A believes this can and should occur mainly via punishment plus external control, or, for instance, via punishment plus contrition. In contrast, B, especially its correctional professionals, believes increased skills, more positive attitudes toward others, and/or greater psychological strengths are needed. Specifically, it considers those factors keys to more permanent or at least longer-term change, whether or not they are partly developed in locked or otherwise restricted settings. From this perspective, B's professionals usually believe—and many of its nonprofessionals intuitively sense—that just desert, and/or control via incapacitation and fear of punishment, is insufficient.

Thus, when interpreting various A/B differences, say, when trying to understand the choice of respective "keys," one might keep in mind that A largely focuses on shorter-term change, especially the behavioral, whereas B mainly centers on longer-term change—behavioral and social-psychological. (With many or most offenders, certainly with lightweights and moderates, heavy punishment plus external controls can doubtlessly produce short-term reductions in illegal behavior. If little more than that is sought, and if one is willing to ignore serious offenders, intervention-centered research could be greatly curtailed since the only essential approaches would be punishment plus control—plus heavier-duty and/ or refined versions thereof.) In addition, many B-professionals and nonprofessionals assume long-term change often takes considerable time, and many of the former think it requires much effort as well. (Though the B public is less clear or convinced about required time, it does not automatically oppose concerted efforts in that regard.) In contrast, Group A believes the most critical change—behavioral change—requires much less effort with respect to diagnosis, planning, personal contact, coordination of effort, and so on. It assumes punishment plus external controls, which can presumably do most or all of the behavior-change job by itself, requires less by way of diagnosis, planning, and so on.

To be sure, some Group A individuals believe many offenders can not only change their behavior but, under various conditions, can improve their social/survival skills and can significantly change certain attitudes.[5] To achieve the latter objectives, something beyond punishment is needed, even though the latter may remain a primary catalyst—frequently the central catalyst—of change, and the most salient program feature. Among these A's, this view is mainly held by many professionals and it primarily relates to non- and moderately serious offenders. Yet even so, A, as a whole, has considerably less tolerance than B with the often slow and laborious process of developing those skills and of changing attitudes; this process *is* often slow and tedious, not just with many moderates, but with most serious multiple offenders. Relatively few A's focus on a third major area: reducing or resolving long-standing personal difficulties. They may consider this an even slower and harder task than the others, and one with less potential payoff. With lightweights and most moderates, they think it is not particularly necessary in the first place.

Even within Group *B,* sizable differences exist in level of tolerance for this process. This occurs not only despite B's support of the reasons for increasing the individuals' social skills and for helping to change various attitudes, but despite their belief that some such process is probably needed in order to produce changes that are largely self-motivated/sustained—changes that most B's, especially its professionals, consider important. At any rate, for both A and B the tolerance factor applies to each of three broad offender severities (non- or low; moderate; high); it is a larger issue for A than

B, especially, but not only, with more serious offenders.

Views Regarding Merit, Time, and Effort
Though many Group A supporters recognize that various changes require other than minimal effort, especially with other-than-lightweights, they nevertheless believe those efforts should be rather limited. Many or most A-professionals do not consider this "should" simply an expedient, such as a temporary adaptation to scarce resources. Instead, they support it mainly on grounds of merit ("deservedness") and, to perhaps a lesser extent, expected outcome ("payoff"). Specifically, they believe that many such offenders *could* improve with respect to social skills and perhaps attitude change, via moderate amounts of support; however, they assume, often implicitly, that many others would require considerably more. (The latter assumption is somewhat difficult to integrate with the belief that—based on merit, and given the hope that punishment can yield powerful effects at least on behavior—input/effort should and hopefully could be rather *limited,* or at least not particularly complex.)

As suggested, most A supporters believe that, with lightweights and most moderates, some types and amounts of change, for example, major psychological change, are not particularly needed, and that behavioral change should suffice. Behavior change, they feel, neither requires nor justifies complex, time-consuming programs, certainly for most such offenders; in contrast, major psychological change could require them. Yet, since psychological change is considered unnecessary in the first place with most moderates, it seems, to those A-supporters, all the more appropriate to waive most such programs. (This position sets aside the more difficult task of addressing serious offenders.) (It should be noted that major psychological change is distinguished from social/survival skills-building and from various attitudinal changes. In general, the former is more complex and difficult to produce than either of the latter, whatever the individuals' severity level. As suggested, some A-supporters view each of the latter as needing some efforts and approaches over and beyond punishment per se. But again, they hope this effort can somehow be modest.)

Furthermore, Group A sometimes maintains that many disadvantaged *non*offenders deserve more of society's time and effort than most offenders. This, they feel, is especially true if the former—unlike the often resistant/ambivalent latter—seem strongly motivated to improve their lives or conditions, for instance, by overcoming personal/physical handicaps or social pressures and hardships. Though B does not try to refute this "relative merit" view it maintains that one should nevertheless provide whatever help seems feasible and that, hopefully, such aid will not just be boilerplate or token. Feasibility might be determined, not a priori or abstractly, but separately for each society or perhaps jurisdiction, based on the latter's overall needs, priorities, and resources—correctional and other.

In any event, Group B maintains that—priorities notwithstanding, and whatever the *relative* merit involved—offenders themselves have rights and needs as citizens and human beings, even while being punished and although some privileges may be temporarily withdrawn or curtailed. It believes these rights and needs justify genuine efforts by society and that those efforts can further society's own long-term interests. This applies not just to serious multiple offenders. It implies that those efforts should address short-term issues in ways that facilitate or enhance—not minimize, unduly complicate, or contradict—long-term, post-punishment adjustments and needs.

Regarding long-term adjustment and major change, many Group B professionals consider it unrealistic to expect that various offenders, not just the very serious, will change or relinquish certain long-standing behaviors or adjustment patterns without resistance, "stops and starts," and "negative acting-out." After all, those behaviors and patterns may have produced or supported satisfactions, relief, or a sense of security—factors that motivate nonoffenders themselves. Nor do those B professionals think these offenders can handle all their environmental obstacles or harmful pressures, perhaps even those from peers or parents alone, without substantial or repeated help—and, quite possibly, external controls and considerable time structuring. As a result, they acknowledge that intervention is often expensive and they emphasize the importance of not, for example, automatically withdrawing support soon after the appearance of sharp resistance, of acting-out, of marked inconsistency, or perhaps even of bizarre, regressive thoughts and

behaviors. They do not think such resistance, and so on, ipso facto proves offenders cannot or will not change and that they deserve little or no further support. Instead, B-professionals often consider it part of a crucial adjustment phase, or, quite possibly, a crisis and potential turning point.

Even the general public—certainly its B-segment—senses that many offenders, especially the more serious, need considerable time to change. This applies not just to various crime-related behavior patterns but to the development of new skills, different attitudes or perceptions, and other changes. Where differences exist between A and B, and sometimes even within each group, is on how *much* time offenders need, how *many* resources they need and/or deserve, and how *best* to use given resources. These differing views exist even regarding offenders of any one seriousness level, such as lightweights. Thus, for instance, they do not necessarily occur because people are discussing different groups of offenders without realizing it—because, for example, A's are stating what they think is needed with lightweights or moderates while B's are emphasizing the more serious.

Factoring in Need

A seldom recognized source of difference between many A's and B's regarding serious multiple offenders is the following tacit assumption about the relationship between *need* and merit (this position is occasionally an explicit rationale rather than a tacit assumption; it is especially but not only found in persons who lean toward A): If certain offenders really need or are said to need (e.g., by B's professionals) extensive resources in order to change substantially,[6] they must already be so "bad" that they hardly *deserve* them.[7] This could apply even if offenders say they want to change.[8] (In this assumption or rationale (whose validity we doubt), allowance could be made for individuals with marked psychological disturbances that involve unusual circumstances beyond their control, and which therefore presumably entail less by way of personal responsibility and "demerit.") Therefore—or so an argument might proceed—such offenders, even if needy, should perhaps receive modest resources at best. Moreover, if they express strong resistance or act-out negatively during intervention, they should perhaps receive one or two "chances" at most. Some Group A supporters would consider this view even more justified when resources are scarce: Especially under those conditions, the lion's share should probably go to moderates—not to the serious—since moderates are presumably more deserving, yet not without need.

In contrast, many in B would maintain that it is precisely the more seriously delinquent and perhaps troubled offenders who, individually, need the following: (1) a relatively *larger* portion of the available resources, even if that portion seems more than modest; (2) extra, not reduced, patience by correctional staff, even in spite of resistance. This is independent of the fact that these B-group persons do not think a need for more resources ipso facto means the offenders in question are quite "bad" in the first place, and/or are necessarily less deserving than others. It is also apart from the fact that if these individuals were treated as undeserving of precisely what—or much of what—they might need in order to help them change or improve, this would comprise a "no-win" situation and could promote a negative self-fulfilling prophecy.

At any rate, these Group B individuals believe that *need* should be a larger determinant than offense-based merit of how many resources are provided, or at least the relative amount; this applies not just for offenders' benefit but for long-term public safety. In addition, they do not think offender-based merit should be *the* decisive—or even *a* decisive—factor with serious, multiple offenders, and they do not believe greater seriousness of problems and needs should necessarily mean that fewer resources should be provided. This, in turn, is apart from the fact that even offense-based merit would not necessarily equate with *overall* merit, for instance, with a "total deservedness" rating that might also reflect the several *other* areas of individuals' lives, including their positive contributions and achievements. The concept of overall merit implicitly reflects what many people accept as the fact that offenders are not *only* offenders—that, instead, their lives have additional facets and meaning.

Overall merit aside, even if the more serious offenders were indeed considered more *blameworthy*, it would not necessarily follow that less time and effort should be spent on them for that reason alone. Similarly, and by the same token, even some individuals who seem *less* blameworthy than others may, for example, need more time and effort than the latter. At any rate, blameworthiness, in itself, is neither directly nor linearly related to needed time and effort, and it can be distinguished from *deservedness*—particularly from offense-based merit as opposed to overall merit—in the first place.

Group B makes a few simple distinctions that have sizable program implications. For instance, like its professionals, its public considers juveniles more open to sizable change than adults, for instance, more responsive, in this respect, to ordinary and specialized programming. It tacitly regards most young offenders as less threatening than their adult counterparts and perhaps less in "need" of long-term lockup—though not necessarily less in need of assistance and meaningful opportunities after, or instead of, lockup. The juvenile/adult distinction also applies to merit, a factor to which the B-public is not indifferent. For example, this group usually considers adolescent offenders more deserving of service than adult offenders who may have comparable records, even though, as with B's professionals, it seldom regards adults as undeserving and—whether with juveniles or adults—it gives merit less overall weight than does A.

Factoring in Seriousness and Threat

In addition, much of the Group B public differentiates among adolescents themselves, not just on age (younger vs. older) but on seriousness. It intuitively distinguishes between *very, moderately,* and *non*serious (or low-seriousness) with respect to personal or social problems and concerning overall threat to others; it makes parallel distinctions regarding level of unmet need. Based on such distinctions this public can generally support a moderate to sizable range of goals, approaches, and/or amounts of effort with differing offenders. That is, it can sense—or accept on explanation—a reasonable connection between differing degrees of *problem/threat/need* (p/t/n) and resulting differences in *goals/approaches/efforts* (g/a/e). Such a connection between p/t/n and g/a/e is not limited to juveniles.

That connection, which may reflect assumptions and values already mentioned, also helps the Group B public respond "pragmatically" more often than "moralistically," and perceive differentially at least as often as uniformly, especially with juveniles. With adult offenders, moralistic considerations or judgments—with which merit is sometimes entwined—play a larger role than with juveniles, especially but not only with the chronic or highly violent. Nevertheless, even with adult offenders, those considerations usually do not outweigh the pragmatic, except, for example, with those who are very violent offenders.

Regarding the more pragmatic approach, a number of steps often occur when the B-public focuses on offenders whom it senses or assumes have moderate or severe personal/social problems but who are neither *chronic*—chronic with serious offenses—nor fairly *violent* in particular (chronic, i.e., very frequent, offenders may be included here if almost all their offenses are relatively minor): First, this public accepts the goal of growth and attitude change. This acceptance might be called Step 1, and it is considerably greater than with the A-public. Next, B focuses not so much on judging the given *offenders,* especially in terms of merit,[9] but on intuitively approving or disapproving given *approaches* (programs). More specifically, the B-public forms a general opinion about the probable safety of existing or proposed approaches that are designed to produce Step 1 change. This global, early, generally quick, and usually informal "safety assessment" might be called Step 2, and it is seldom based on scientific data.

If the programs seem fairly safe, and if they also seem globally relevant in terms of their connection between p/t/n and g/a/e and with respect to common sense, they may well be considered acceptable provided their costs do not seem exorbitant or hard to justify. This broad "relevance or content check" could be called Step 3. Like 2, it occurs quickly, largely intuitively, usually without scientific evidence, and very informally. As suggested, its outcome may partly depend on perceived level of safety itself, such as high versus moderate. (Ordinarily, B's professionals would take Step 4: They, unlike the public, would focus somewhat specifically on feasibility and operational challenges, over and beyond safety needs alone and costs per se.)

Group *A* often rejects the Step 1 goal and therefore may not reach 2 via the earlier-mentioned route. However, when it does directly assess certain approaches, that is, irrespective of that goal, it may quickly reject them for reasons other than their safety or content; in fact, it may have few if any objections or concerns on either score, and it may consider the approaches operationally feasible

or theoretically so. At any rate, Group A may reject the proposed use of those programs or approaches partly or largely because of the intended *target population;* and this may apply to widely recognized approaches as well. Specifically, A may feel that those particular offenders do not deserve the type and/or level of effort in question, mainly because of their offense or offense history, and perhaps—though often to a lesser degree—because they seem unmotivated to change. Group A may feel, for example, that most individuals with given offense histories are not motivated to substantially change as individuals or perhaps even with regard to behavior alone. Whether or not this group considers motivation a large factor in determining merit itself, it may assume that the individuals in question would be uninterested in, and perhaps openly or at any rate strongly resistive to, the given program's particular elements and content.

Those considerations are separable from questions of *relative* merit and relative need. For instance, they can be independent of the fact that A, in principle, may consider most *non*offenders more deserving than most moderately or very serious offenders, on the one hand, and often more needy than most non- and moderately serious offenders, on the other. This principle would apply regardless of the specific approaches involved, including their safety, content, and cost, among other things. It might be noted that in these relative-merit-and-need scenarios, "moderates"—who, collectively, may comprise most offenders—can "lose out" in both comparisons and can therefore receive less assistance than they otherwise might. That is, they can lose opportunities for assistance if decisions in that regard are based largely on Group A judgments of the offenders' merit and need, respectively, as compared with that of *non*offenders (as distinct from serious or very serious ones).

Merit aside, level and seriousness of support for given programs or approaches can interact with perceived level of offender *seriousness,* particularly degree of problem or need. Here, the earlier-mentioned distinctions between high, moderate, and nonserious (or low seriousness) offenders can play substantial roles. For instance, the Group *B* public may moderately support a program or proposed program that focuses on growth and attitude change if it (1) believes the target population can change, (2) assumes it wants to change (at least in part), and (3) feels it probably needs some help in that regard, that is, has at least minimal or modest problems/needs and can make at least some use of the given program's content. However, that same public might lend somewhat *stronger* support to the program if, for instance, whereas conditions (1) and (2) remain the same, a new population seems to have *sizable* rather than minimal or modest problems/needs, and could probably make considerable use of that program's content. As implied, this interaction between program support and offender seriousness can exist independently of offender merit, that is, perceived degree of merit, at least within certain limits, and especially with Group B. (Some limits are mentioned below.) In any event it reflects a needs-centered approach and is consistent with a moderately differentiated, pragmatic framework.

Besides level of problem or need, physical threat often enters the picture. Needs and problems notwithstanding, this can play a critical role in determining how much support may be given to various approaches, such as the community-based; in this regard it can influence both flexibility and direction. For instance, if a potential target population were considered a *serious to extreme* threat, even the Group B public or large parts of it might well withhold or mostly withdraw support for a given rehabilitation program or for some of its components. Moreover, it might prefer to clearly emphasize control/deterrence instead. Both the withholding/withdrawing of support and the switch in emphasis or direction would be even likelier to occur if the offenders seemed strongly opposed to, or likely to persistently oppose, almost any change in their adjustment patterns, especially if they denied having substantial problems (cf. Category B [Group B] cases, among others; Chapter 13).

Yet even the impact of physical threat may be modified—not only by offenders' motivation but by the type of program or program components in question. For example, the above withholding or lessening of support might be precluded or reduced if the B-public considered the target population even moderately motivated to change or if it thought the program's general approach or content might appeal to many offenders and might well develop such motivation in them. This would apply regardless of the offenders' level of problem or need—

provided those individuals would not be likely physical threats, that is, serious such threats, if substantial external controls were used. The A-public is generally less willing than B to take a physical-threat risk with these and other offenders. This especially applies if it questions their "merit" and/or motivation in the first place, or if it is rather unsure of the program's effectiveness for offenders in general. Group B—both its public and professionals—also has limits regarding risk-taking with these offenders, whether or not it has more overall confidence in the program.

At any rate, perceived severity levels of offenders—levels of problem, need, and physical threat—can shape the public's views of the likely impact of various programs, especially if the public thinks it knows something about those programs. Such perceptions can often shape or even produce implicit assumptions about motivation level itself, and these assumptions can then affect the public's support for particular goals, approaches, and amounts of effort associated with the given programs. In short, perceived levels of problem or need, of program strength, and of offender motivation can each influence sizable portions of the public, and together their impact can be large with respect to support or tolerance. Though such impact shrinks substantially in connection with offenders who are serious to extreme physical threats, it nonetheless remains.

The preceding situation is modified by the fact that the Group B public is also influenced by issues other than *offender need,* for instance, by concern with merit and victims. This applies even with less threatening/resistive offenders, however many problems they may have or needy they may be. In short, B's public, like its professionals, does not operate almost exclusively with offenders' problems/needs uppermost in mind, or, for that matter, almost solely on pragmatic grounds and focused almost entirely on long-term goals. Nevertheless, this public, again like B-professionals, usually ranks problems/needs above *merit,* even when the latter plays a substantial role and some safety risk exists. (The latter ranking is essentially independent of the fact that merit is less often decisive for B than for A—especially with moderate and serious offenders—and that, with A and B alike, merit is itself sometimes outweighed by safety—especially with violent offenders.) Finally, the B-public does not rank offender needs above those of society in general, even though A usually believes that B ranks the former too high.

As suggested, with very violent or threatening (VVT) offenders the Group B public might well consider strict and frequent external controls/surveillance—with little or no rehabilitation—the only acceptable in-lieu-of-lockup approach. (VVTs are a subgroup within the broader category of *serious or very serious offenders,* some of whom are violent or very violent.) More specifically, with VVTs, this public may prefer short-term behavior control to long-term, change-oriented intervention, if an in-lieu program is to be used at all. In contrast, most B-professionals would try to maintain rehabilitation and its long-term goals even within such a setting, assuming they considered in-lieu intervention appropriate in the first place. If they did consider it appropriate, say, on a pilot or demonstration basis, they would stress controls/surveillance and immediate public protection much more than otherwise, even in a rehabilitation framework.

If given jurisdictions will not support in-lieu approaches with VVTs, these individuals will instead begin their intervention in locked or otherwise closely structured settings. Though perhaps not optimal in itself, *rehabilitation* programs available to these individuals in at least some such settings may, in the long run, have more to offer than the particular *control/surveillance-only* approaches that might have been used if in-lieu programs had been allowed. The possibility of such an advantage does not mean one should reject all in-lieu programs for VVTs—nor, of course, for all other individuals who are neither lightweights nor moderates.

Regarding those "other individuals," namely, *serious multiple offenders,* the following should be noted: Because A-publics, A-professionals, and even B-publics in many jurisdictions are reluctant to support community-based rehabilitation with most such individuals on grounds of seeming risk, B's professionals may have to lead the way in showing where—and how—this general approach can be viable and advantageous with this group. (Included among the serious multiple offenders would be persons who may have some violence in their records but who are not ipso facto *very violent or threatening.*) More specifically, B-professionals may have to emphasize the following. With many, possibly most, SMOs, change-and-growth objectives

(and their careful implementation) are important in order to substantially—sometimes greatly—increase the chances of long-term improvement; this applies *whatever* the intervention setting may be. With the remaining SMOs, those objectives are important or essential if such improvement is to occur at all; this applies irrespective of whether these individuals, too, have violence in their records.

With *VVTs,* A- and B-publics and professionals alike are understandably more concerned with a particular *similarity*—namely, the individuals' major threat potential—than with the usual differences that might otherwise be salient, such as differences regarding individual problems, needs, interests, and abilities. (With these offenders, the *B-public* takes it for granted that what might be called the assistance-centered aspect of "deservedness" does not outweigh level of physical threat to society—that is, even if individualized intervention must be reduced. The assistance-centered aspect, which we will call called "deserved assistance," relates to the offenders' perceived value or potential value, whether as a member of society or simply as a human being. It contrasts with the payment-for-harmful-activities aspect, that is, with "deserved punishment" [just desert], and with the substantial to marked withholding of opportunities or rewards—either as ends in themselves, as means to public protection, or as both.) Since it can be hard to individualize intervention when one focuses on similarities far more than differences (certainly when the main similarity is major threat potential), the following applies: It is important for both the public and correctional professionals to keep in mind that even VVTs have particular problems and needs, have individualized interests and abilities, and so on. Information about these areas can help preserve a path to individualized intervention and to the achievement of long-term goals, even with VVTs.

Thus, for example, even if one has relatively little concern for VVTs *as individuals*—say, for their eventually experiencing genuine, nondestructive personal satisfactions—a detailed, individualized understanding of these offenders would probably still be critical in order to substantially reduce their illegal behavior on a long-term basis. This applies to the broader category of serious multiple offenders, and to nonserious individuals, as well. (The personal satisfactions in question would be ends in themselves, not means to other ends. This would apply regardless of genuine satisfactions that any such persons might eventually provide to *other* individuals.)

Decreased Tolerance, Increased Sensitivity, and Changed Images

The following discussion pertains to those parts of the overall adult population that, together, have had the largest cumulative influence—in fact, a dominating influence—on juvenile corrections in recent decades. There are two such parts, and—again together—they include most of the adult population. The first part is comprised of Group A's nonprofessionals (NPs); more specifically, it includes the preponderance of these NPs. The second consists of Group B's nonprofessionals (also NPs)—a large minority of them, at least.

These A's and B's are each part of the respective NP "publics" described in the preceding pages; in the case of A's, they are almost all of them. Collectively, the Group A nonprofessionals in question contributed more than their corresponding Group B NPs to the cumulative influence that these A's plus B's have had on juvenile corrections. This was not just because of A's higher proportionate representation—(compare its "preponderance" among all A-NPs with B's "large minority, . . ." among B-NPs)—and not just because A's, on average, were more active and forceful than their corresponding B's, but also because the overall adult population of nonprofessionals contained somewhat more A's than B's in the first place.

To facilitate the discussion these A and B nonprofessionals will be considered a single unit, and in that regard they will be called "the general public" or simply "the public." We will examine certain factors and features these groups share in common with each other, including particulars of A's and B's (1) decreased tolerance for offenders, (2) changed image of those individuals, (3) oversimplified and relatively static views of offenders, (4) actual and preferred responses to those individuals, and so on. Implications of this situation will be mentioned along the way. Though these A and B nonprofessionals share the particulars in question, they—like A and B professionals, themselves—also *differ* from each other in various ways, for instance, ways described in the first section of this chapter, "Two Major Views and Responses." However, it is the nonprofession-

als' *shared* characteristics, including those mentioned in "Two Major Views . . . ," that seem largely responsible for the dominating influence these groups have jointly had in corrections.

Unless otherwise indicated, the discussion will focus on the "serious multiple offender" (SMO) category described throughout this book, not on the "very violent" and/or "highly disturbed" subcategories mentioned above. Regarding these distinctions, recall, for example, that many SMOs have no violent offenses in their official records, even though such offenses are not *uncommon* among the SMOs. At any rate, whether in connection with violence or with other behavior that SMOs (collectively), may exhibit neither the preponderance nor the majority of these individuals are "serious to extreme physical threats" (or even "highly disturbed," psychologically); nor are *most* such youths even moderate physical threats. In short, although most SMOs have sizable personal, interpersonal, and/or environmental *problems*—such as deficits, difficulties, and/or disadvantages—they are not, *ipso facto,* substantial *physical threats* to others. Though this is true whether or not those serious multiple offenders have several arrests or convictions (not just charges or counts) in their records, SMOs *with* numerous such offenses are *often*—but again, not necessarily—a substantial threat, particularly if more than one offense is violent. Yet, in turn, youths who have violent offenses (even more than one) are not ipso facto *VVTs,* that is, *very* violent or threatening offenders, especially in terms of severity. This applies even though VVTs are far from rare within that broader ("violent") category.

Finally, "offenders" will refer not just to lawbreakers who have been apprehended, but, especially, to all others not yet caught.

Decreased Tolerance for Offenders

In most of the United States, the public's tolerance for offenders decreased sharply beginning in the early 1970s. This applied especially to serious multiple offenders (SMOs), some of whom had also been violent, and to violent offenders, not all of whom had multiple offenses. The public's tolerance then continued to drop, and it has remained low since the end of that decade.

Starting mainly in the mid- to later 1970s, public support for *rehabilitation or habilitation,* as distinguished from tolerance for offenders, itself decreased. This drop was moderate and less precipitous than that for offenders, but it was nevertheless significant. It pertained mainly, though far from exclusively, to rehabilitation for the above, overlapping groups: SMOs and violent offenders. Regarding those groups, it applied especially in the context of community-based alternatives to institutionalization. For instance, it pertained to approaches such as CTP (Phases 1 and 2)—though CTP itself had ended—and not just when they emphasized personal changes and growth, as well as related interpersonal improvement. The public's decreased support was considerably less in the case of community-located institutional adjuncts and supplements, such as work furlough and halfway houses, that is, less for "transitional approaches" or program components that were available to selected individuals who had completed much of their institutional stay. Programming *within* many institutions underwent a moderate, though in some cases quantitatively large, drop in support; and within many facilities in which programming was already sparse, even modest-sized cuts had noticeable effects.

The Role of Fear

The public's decreased tolerance for offenders had probably been nurtured, triggered, and then maintained mainly by its increased fear of those individuals, and by its subsequent responses of anger and considerable rejection.[10] (Occasionally, anger came first and fear was less than moderate.) This fear, together with the subsequent responses, frequently involved specific, highly personalized concerns. For example, in all likelihood *fear,* and the responses which followed, often reflected the thought or image of being confronted and possibly injured by violent or potentially violent individuals. To a lesser degree they—at least anger and rejection—were also likely to have reflected the thought of being badly "ripped off" (financially) in connection with a burglary.

From a broader perspective, and viewed through time, the public's increased fear of and anger toward offenders undoubtedly reflected such factors as the following, as well.

1. Widely reported official statistics were indicating that the rate of violence had continuously increased in the preceding several years. Possibly more important, by 1975 it was more than twice as high as in 1965 within the United States as a whole (urban plus rural) and it had risen steadily in medium- and large-sized cities as well (Uniform Crime Reports, 1976).

2. Though still relatively rare, gruesome and bizarre crimes seemed to be increasing; certainly, the major media were reporting them more often, as was the case with violence in general.

3. Besides its increased reporting, the media, together with movies, increasingly highlighted the more shocking or particularly frightening details of violent crimes, whether or not those offenses were gruesome or bizarre. As a result, in many parts of the United States, vividly described murders, assaults, robberies, and other violence soon became a common feature in broad-circulation newspapers, on the radio, and on evening TV news. These reports focused primarily on the readers', listeners', or viewers' own city and environs—especially if it was a large, urbanized center—and secondarily on other cities, suburbs, and/or towns within the state. (Multiple and mass murders, especially by persons who seemed to have "suddenly gone berserk," were regularly reported even if they had occurred in other states. Kidnappings were also highlighted, and were often followed for days or weeks. Both types of crime were particularly upsetting even if they had occurred several hundred miles away, and especially when concrete details were given.)

   Moreover, such reports increasingly appeared as lead stories, thus being further highlighted and easier to access. In addition, harmful or devastating effects that serious crimes had already had or might eventually have on their direct and indirect victims were increasingly discussed; and victimization per se was becoming a prominent issue for the first time (Bureau of Justice Statistics, 1977, 1982; Clements and Kleiman, 1977; Garofalo, 1977, 1979; Hartnagel, 1979; Hindelang, Gottfredson, and Garofalo, 1978; McDonald, 1976; National Advisory Commission, 1973c; National Criminal Justice Information, 1976; President's Commission, 1967c; Schafer, 1976; Skogan and Maxfield, 1981; Stafford and Galle, 1984).

4. Given factors 1 through 3, and given such others as the increased occurrence and

reporting of "gang violence" in urban areas and the greater reporting of certain common crimes (e.g., residential burglary) that were sometimes accompanied by sudden confrontation, by serious injury, or by death, much of the public began to believe that serious crime and danger were definitely and perhaps inexorably approaching their neighborhood, or had perhaps already reached it. Thus, by 1978–1980, large numbers of people had begun to feel vulnerable to serious crime for perhaps the first time, even though many offenses that were especially upsetting had occurred several miles from their neighborhood or city. As implied, many other offenses were upsetting partly because of their growing nearness per se, even if reported details were not shocking. Also disturbing was the sheer quantity of accumulated local crimes, even those which had occurred *anywhere* within, or close to, one's city or town.

During the later 1970s other relevant events were occurring. Public officials were beginning to call for "a war on crime" with increasing frequency. Such high-profile, often dramatic announcements further validated some people's fears or anxieties, and they sometimes seemed to increase them. Those expressions of official concern, when accompanied by political support and pressure (plus financial assistance) for the "war," were themselves often associated with such events and trends as the following (however, in most cases they were probably not the main *causes* of those events, etc.): (1) Prison construction kept increasing, despite its costliness. (2) Several states' legislatures were—increasingly often—lengthening various prison terms, especially for violence. (3) Standards for search and seizure, and for admissibility of evidence, were being loosened. (4) Juveniles were being "bound over" ("remanded"; "transferred") to adult courts at a higher rate than before. (5) Efforts were increasingly being made to lower the age of remand to those courts.

Also, and particularly important, true-life as well as fictional and semifictional police and detective stories had just become mainstays of prime-time TV, and, with that, had become basic parts of evening "entertainment" or "education." Watching these often graphic shows, especially in conjunction with the nightly news or with increasingly violent movies, a sizable portion of the public became almost obsessed with crime, and the rest grew quite familiar with it. Given this and the earlier-mentioned factors and events, adults of all ages—in growing numbers—identified themselves, their family, and their friends with the observed victims (and with potential victims) of crime, and they increasingly wished to defend themselves against it. Under these circumstances and those mentioned next, they turned against offenders more forcefully than before. They directed their attention mainly and increasingly at individuals considered dangerous, potentially dangerous, and/or chronic, even if those offenders were juveniles.

Increased Sensitivity to Crime

Even by the mid- to later 1970s, the previously mentioned fear seemed to be broadly affecting the public's basic image of offenders. This image related not just to the violent and serious multiple offender subgroups; rather, it encompassed offenders in general, even though it emphasized those subgroups. For instance, words such as "offender," "criminal," and "delinquent" were less likely than in the 1960s to be quickly, let alone mainly, associated with petty theft, receiving stolen property, forgery, possession of illegal drugs, and purse snatch, not to mention vandalism, runaway, and beyond control ("incorrigible") in the case of youths. Also, these types of offense were less likely to comprise a major part of the public's informal conversations about offenders, not that they had previously dominated them. (Though auto theft [other than joyriding] was usually viewed as more serious than the above offenses, it was regularly considered less severe than the ones mentioned next.) Instead, in a wide range of cities and towns, including the larger as well as smaller, terms such as "offender" and even "young offender" seemed to increasingly elicit images and conversations regarding murder, robbery, rape, kidnapping, various assaults by gangs, and burglary accompanied by violence. Often associated with these images was the already growing thought that at least a few unapprehended, active offenders might not be far away, even during the day. Adding force and meaning to this picture were the disquieting thoughts that a potentially violent burglar might actually enter *one's own* home/apartment, or that of a friend/relative, and that this possibility was no longer remote.

Because of such concerns, more and more adults began to double-lock their doors, further secure their windows, install home security systems, purchase guns, and participate in "neighborhood watches." Many women, responding to their increased fear of being raped, began carrying either a chemical defense called "Mace," an "electric stunner," or a sound alarm. In addition, self-defense courses soon multiplied and people became generally more guarded in public.

By 1980 it was clear that a great many men and women no longer considered their residential streets, their parks, and especially their city's nonresidential areas particularly safe, certainly after sundown. In fact, for perhaps the first time in several decades, growing segments of society began to anxiously and repeatedly ask, "Can police officers, probation officers, and other safety officials adequately protect us and our families against serious, apparently increasing, outdoor crimes (e.g., robbery and sexual assault), even apart from indoor crimes (e.g., burglary)?" and, "Will the legal system adequately prosecute and punish individuals who *are* arrested for, and found guilty of, those and even less serious offenses?" These concerns and substantial levels of anxiety were not just associated with large cities, though they did exist more often in such settings.

Passing a Threshold[11]

This type and level of anxiety reflected the fact that, as of the later 1970s, a certain threshold had been passed in the United States: Many adults' concerns regarding crime now seemed to be sustained—fueled and maintained—as much by those individuals' fears/anxieties as by the high volume and rate of crime itself. In any case, those fears and anxieties were now stronger and more influential than before, both relatively and absolutely. In addition, during the immediately preceding years, many individuals had become so sensitized to crime, and so concerned with it, that this subject was now often on their minds.

Moreover, crime was no longer just a significant background factor in society itself; nor was it just a sizable "annoyance" to which most people had grown somewhat accustomed. Instead, it had become a prominent part of the social landscape, a type of behavior that often worried many individuals and communities, and about which they definitely wanted something done. These changes from the pre-threshold period, particularly the early and middle 1970s, mainly resulted from the higher volume/rate of crime in general, from the increased frequency of violence in particular, and from the greater media emphasis on serious offenses—increases that occurred in most cities, regions, and states.

Thus, by the later 1970s, crime was a definite foreground factor to many or most individuals, and a widely shared problem. Its prominence reflected not only crimes per se, especially the many serious ones, but the following: Numerous adults, community groups, and others had—individually and collectively—heightened and consolidated the social/psychological significance of crime. They did so by virtue of their increased efforts to draw attention to it in order to better address it or to have it collectively addressed. These efforts, which reflected those individuals' and groups' now-larger concern with crime, thus helped give it a reality and prominence that differed from, that is, went beyond, its basic physical presence and prominence. ("Physical" directly involved and reflected volume and frequent severity, not people's heightened and/or collective social responses.)

As the earlier-mentioned threshold—a reality-based as well as concern-driven threshold—was being passed, a disquieting change seemed to rapidly emerge in much of the United States: The everyday interpersonal tone and the general social atmosphere became noticeably more strained and considerably less trusting than it had been only a few years earlier. (In a sense, this change had "crystallized," much as an ice surface quickly establishes itself as a distinct new presence, where—shortly before—water had prevailed.) A large part of the change seemed to center on and directly link with crime, even though some of its aspects, such as increased tension, reflected other broad factors and conditions, as well (see, e.g., "Adults' Perceptions, Felt Challenges, and Responses," later in this chapter).

The crime-centered portion of this altered tone partly resulted from the fact that crime—particularly serious, worrisome offenses—had become a much larger part of many individuals' everyday world, and especially of their personal awareness. More specifically, *actual crime*—crime in the external, social environment—was more widespread than before; and, *thoughts, images, and feelings* regarding those actual crimes now often entered into many aspects of people's everyday awareness. In effect, when those individuals looked outward, they saw crime as already widespread or somewhat pervasive; when they looked inward, for instance, briefly reflected, they knew it was very often present and that it occurred in (as well as affected) many contexts. Inwardly, crime was particularly meaningful not just because of its frequent and widespread occurrence but due to the specific emotions and general anxiety it aroused. Also, such emotions and anxiety linked it with the external tone and atmosphere.

Both the internal and external aspects of this situation applied especially to the numerous adults—this being most of the overall adult population—who paid substantial attention to television, radio, and/or newspapers. (Other media, such as movies and magazines, were not relevant to the context next discussed.) For instance, looking outward, via the media, these individuals realized that serious crimes were occurring almost every day of the year, somewhere or other within the state or region (if not one's own city), or else close to the state's borders. In addition, they usually learned about those offenses in either a matter of hours or within one to two days. This gave crime an "ongoing" quality and, depending on where they lived in the state, somewhat of a "surrounding" presence.

On any given day, and day after day, the media had accumulated several of the state's, region's, and/or city's specific instances of crime and had brought some of them to the attention of its viewers, listeners, and readers. In effect, it had aggregated and focused those events for such individuals. This process thereby increased the number of specific offenses that those viewers/listeners/readers would otherwise have known about; that is, it functionally multiplied or magnified them. In so doing, it had also assembled the raw material that would help form a global picture in individuals' minds—an integrated image (see below) that could be called an "aggregated, enhanced reality" or picture of crime (i.e., of "crime-reality").

("Enhanced" refers not just to the functionally multiplied aspect but to the increased, collective power of those accumulated, focused offenses when compared to the power of the far fewer crimes that those individuals would otherwise have known about. Here, "power" refers to influence on adults' views, emotions, attitudes, and behavior; and this power had

been increased, by the media, via qualitative, not just quantitative, means, including the interaction between them. For instance, the accumulated, focused offenses had a greater influence on many individuals' emotions not only because there were more such offenses than would otherwise have been known about, but because the media's often detailed and graphic account of many such crimes made it easier for those individuals to be psychologically closer to them, for example, closer in the sense of partly identifying and/or disidentifying with certain police officers, victims, and aggressors who were described. In effect, the sheer increase in the number and variety of specific offenses and circumstances that were available via the media provided more opportunities for individuals to encounter behaviors, emotions, and other responses that would strike particular chords. This is apart from the fact that the sheer rapidity with which the media usually conveyed its sizable amount of information often generated, or increased, a sense of immediacy—sometimes even urgency—and of shared concern.)

These media inputs, and the individuals' subsequent mental assimilation and *integration* of them (with this product then becoming their "view" or provisional picture of crime), was decisive in helping many people reach the earlier-mentioned threshold. When media inputs then continued to occur in the *post-threshold* period (as they invariably did), such inputs—at this point acting in combination with the mental integration that was now present—then further strengthened that very same integration, that is, the individuals' view of crime-reality. Thus, via this continued input and the related interaction, this internalized picture of crime became partly self-reinforcing; and this occurred even though it had rarely been, and would seldom become, entirely static (unchanging). The earlier-mentioned, post-threshold change in tone and atmosphere also contributed to this strengthening.

Accompanying the more stressful, less trusting tone and atmosphere of the post-threshold period, and partly in response to it, were many new decisions by individuals, groups, and communities; at any rate, more such decisions occurred than before, as did their accompanying plans and subsequent actions. These decisions, and so on, centered on how those individuals and others should and would use their resources, and generally organize themselves and their activities, in order to reduce and prevent crime. The main emphasis was on relief, that is, alleviation in terms of reduced offending. This especially applied to the near-term reduction of serious offenses and to any accompanying decrease in fear and anxiety. As to longer-term goals, these mainly involved a greater *degree* of relief.

Beyond relief—critical though this was— few people seemed to expect that the pre-threshold state of affairs, including its less guarded atmosphere, could be largely reestablished within the near-, intermediate-, and perhaps even longer-range future. This seemed to reflect a general pessimism that had begun to prevail regarding the chances of *greatly* reducing the high crime rates, including those of violence. It appeared to reflect other broad changes as well, for instance, those involving increased societal uncertainty regarding the future (see "Adults' Perceptions . . . ," later in this chapter). (Widespread efforts to greatly reduce crime rates and violence by focusing on "career criminals" and via "selective incapacitation" were still a few years in the future. Similarly, increased use of stringent—"intensive"—probation/parole supervision [Chapter 28] was only about to begin, itself with adults.)

The Critical Mass

As implied, the earlier-mentioned sensitization and concern on the part of many individuals was originally triggered and subsequently fostered by the large amount of actual crime that occurred in the early and middle 1970s, especially by violent and otherwise serious crime. However, during that period this sensitization/concern was also—and increasingly—generated by the earlier-mentioned media inputs, on the one hand, and by the individuals' resulting image of and concepts plus feelings about crime, on the other. The latter factor, that is, the image/concepts/feelings, involved the individuals' assimilation and integration not just of those media inputs but of separate information and of their feelings about crime. (This integration—seen as a product, not process—thus had visual, conceptual, and emotional dimensions. It can be considered a composite image, idea, and "sense," one which, as suggested, was never completely finalized and unchangeable, yet which—once it was provisionally formed— was easily reinforced as such and was therefore, and thereafter, far from entirely fluid.)

Collectively, this mixture of actual offenses, functionally multiplied ones, and, ultimately, the individuals' integrated product, served as the crucial determinant in the attainment and surpassing of the earlier-mentioned threshold. As such, it might be called the "critical mass." Specifically, this composite factor decisively increased many individuals' already existing fears/anxieties and it helped trigger a new level of concern about crime. In so doing, it also helped generate or trigger additional phenomena and adjustments, such as the post-threshold changes in tone, atmosphere, and behavior.

As suggested initially, by the later 1970s— after the fear/anxiety threshold had been passed—many adults' concerns regarding crime had become partly "self-sustaining"; at least, the fears and anxieties, collectively, now fed on themselves much more than before. (Recall that these concerns were reflected in the individuals' integrated image of crime-reality, though that image included more than those concerns.) However, they were not *entirely* self-sustaining; instead, a substantial quantity of external input was still needed in order to maintain them at the same level as before (see points [1] and [2], immediately below). Nevertheless, with most individuals, this quantity was considerably less than that which had served as a major precondition to reaching the threshold in the first place. With still other adults, very little external input seemed necessary at all. (1) The needed input was actual crime—mostly, but not entirely, crime that had been functionally multiplied. (2) To sustain the fears/anxieties *less* than fully—say, less than when the threshold was first passed—considerably less such input was probably needed. Whether the fears/anxieties were fully or less than fully sustained, the amount of input (input of all types combined) that was needed in the post-threshold period could be thought of as an "adjusted critical mass."

Indirect evidence that a lesser amount of input sufficed in the post-threshold period included the fact that many individuals' fears/anxieties did not seem to decrease when state, regional, and/or local statistics indicated that crime had declined, for instance, during a preceding 6- or 12-month period. Basically, most people ignored or downplayed such information even when it was generally the same type, from the same sources, and of about the same size (though opposite in direction) as that which they had accepted when those earlier statistics *supported* their growing fears and underlying assumptions. They mainly brushed it aside due to the more compelling, psychological power of the following factors, especially in combination: First, their already existing fears and/or anxieties regarding crime; second, the concrete, often detailed offenses they were still regularly hearing, reading, and otherwise learning about via the media and other sources; and third, their integrated image of crime-reality—with this factor reflecting and summarizing, in a single package (as it were), most of their underlying feelings and assumptions about crime's overall frequency and trends, local and otherwise. In effect, the reinforcement that this combination of internal and external factors had often provided, and was still providing, had substantially reduced those adults' openness to contrary information that was, or that may have been, presented essentially on its own. Thus, for example, these individuals had not rejected the contrary information *mainly* because they (1) considered the reductions only small to moderate, which they usually were, (2) knew that figures often shift back and forth, (3) thought the information might not apply well to *their* particular area or neighborhood, and/or (4) believed crime in their locale was too high even if the information did apply and was reliable.

Simultaneous Reassurance

Even while many media presentations were strengthening or at least helping to maintain many individuals' fears/anxieties regarding continued crime, some of them, and others as well, were also providing reassurance. For instance, various television police dramas, clips of "crime busts," documentaries, and newspaper stories or special reports were partly reassuring to many people when they indicated, implicitly or otherwise, that the main "enemies"—active, unapprehended offenders, and sometimes even parolees—were being seriously challenged, that their challengers (including parole officers) were skilled and determined for the most part, and that crime, overall, was thus being contained. (To be sure, other media inputs sometimes countered this view, as did various personal experiences; and many people still worried that someday there might be too few police and related personnel to maintain control.) These presentations seemed to resonate with many individuals'

underlying—sometimes preconscious or perhaps even unconscious—desire to be told that conditions were at least "not getting worse" and perhaps "won't get worse." With many such adults, it is possible that reassurance was more believable when it involved the idea that conditions were not getting worse than when it suggested—as via the above statistics—that matters might actually be improving. The first such message might, for example, have been more consistent than the second with their integrated image of, and underlying assumptions and feelings about, crime's prevalence, incidence, and overall seriousness.

As indicated and implied, even while many individuals were receiving some reassurance via given media presentations, their fears/anxieties were often being simultaneously *reinforced*. Yet sometimes—in catch-22 fashion—these were not only the same fears and anxieties that those individuals wished could be *reduced* (via decreases in actual crime), albeit to a greater degree than even the largely ignored or doubted statistics may have indicated; but they were often ones that—even despite such wishes or desires—were already *self-reinforcing* to a sizable degree (i.e., partly independent of actual crime). In any event, as implied, many individuals nevertheless wished to receive a "not-getting-worse" message, because they felt the situation was already quite serious or could soon get out of control. This underlying desire may have partly accounted for their seeming hunger to closely and/or often follow police dramas, crime-related docudramas, newspaper accounts of crimes/manhunts/trials, and so on—even though these inputs also helped maintain anxiety.

Changes in Youths, and Adults' Related Responses
Changes in Youths

Before discussing "inadequate differentiations" among offenders, including "oversimplified and static views" of those individuals, the following should be noted: A sizable portion of the total youth population (TYP) that existed in the later 1970s was different than the TYP that existed in the later 1960s. Both TYPs consisted of (a) offenders (O's), many of whom were different in the later 1970s than O's in the later 1960s, and (b) nonoffenders (NO's), a sizable percentage of whom were themselves different in the later 1970s than NO's in the later 1960s. The offenders who were different in the later 1970s than O's in the later 1960s are called Group A. The nonoffenders who were different in the later 1970s than NO's in the later 1960s are called Group B. The particular ways in which Group A and Group B differed from their respective later 1960s counterparts are mentioned next, and these "ways" were the same for both groups. ("Nonoffenders" means individuals with no known law contact.)

Group A (offenders) and Group B (nonoffenders) differed from the later 1960s youths in that they were more prepared to challenge adults, including their parents or guardians. For instance, A and B youths were less likely to unquestioningly or readily comply with adults' requests or directions. In fact, there was more chance that they would often end up only partly accepting the adults' guidance and advice, and that—occasionally—they would almost entirely reject it. In these respects the later-1970s offenders and nonoffenders were, on average, more assertive than their later-1960s counterparts. No less significant, Group A and B youths had a substantially lower threshold for acting and responding assertively—sometimes even aggressively and angrily—with like-aged friends and acquaintances, and occasionally even strangers. Yet, however frequently or infrequently they actually *did* act/react in those ways with similar-aged youths, they resisted the requests, directions, guidance, and advice of various adults/parents more often than did youths of the later 1960s—more precisely, the later 1960s and early 1970s. When present in any given individual, this resistance was likely to be stronger than before; and across the O and NO groups collectively, it was also more often stronger.

The following states the quantitative aspects of these "changes in youths" in a more differentiated way, and it then mentions resulting changes in many adults' view of youths: (1) *Most* offenders and nonoffenders who comprised the total youth population in the later 1970s were essentially the same as the total O and NO youth populations in the later 1960s; that is, they did not differ from the latter youths with respect to the above features (challenge, assertiveness, etc.). (2) The remaining offenders and nonoffenders in the later 1970s—namely, Groups A and B—therefore differed on those same features; that is, they were not the same as youths of the later 1960s. (3) Despite point (1), these remaining youths—Groups A and B—each comprised a *sizable* portion of the total, later-1970s population. (4) Moreover, the A-youths probably comprised a higher percentage of the overall, later-1970s offender subpopulation than B-youths comprised of the overall, later-1970s nonoffender subpopulation.

Given the particular features (challenge, etc.) that were involved in the change from the later 1960s to the later 1970s, this entire situation, including points (3) and (4), was of such a nature as to help create, in many adults, a substantially different image of youths. More precisely, it helped generate two different, albeit overlapping images. These images involved not only youths in general but adolescent offenders in particular—specifically, "juvenile delinquents," considered *as a whole*. That is, by the later 1970s the earlier-mentioned content (features), together with the quantitative aspects involved, helped create certain overlapping images of youths in a large portion of the adult public, images that differed from those of the later 1960s. (The later-1970s images overlapped with each other quantitatively because all juvenile delinquents, who comprised the second image, were, necessarily, part of the larger group that comprised the first image, that is, that of youths in general. More important, however, the later-1970s images overlapped qualitatively, that is, substantively, in that both of these changed images included challenge, assertiveness, and the like, among their several features.) Again, one image involved youths in general and the other consisted of delinquents in particular. The latter image had been formed by broadly generalizing—in effect, extrapolating—the features that distinguished Group A (challenge, etc.), on the one hand, to delinquents *as a whole*, on the other. In effect, these distinguishing or core features were next given primary status, and "juvenile delinquents" were then mainly thought of (and visualized or "imaged") in terms of those and related features.

Regarding the increased resistance to adults by Groups A and B, this largely resulted from the following: Group A and B youths were more likely than individuals in the later 1960s to think of most adults—everyday, "conventional" adults, as well as most authority figures—as individuals whose opinions, advice, requests, and/or directions were often irrelevant, outdated, or inadequate. Though they were also more likely to believe that they, the Group A and B youths, could sometimes change those opinions, directions, and so on, by questioning or challenging them (and they were more likely to think it was not wrong to question), they mainly believed those opinions, and so forth, would usually be difficult—often even impossible—to change significantly. The latter belief especially applied to views held by those adults/figures as to how young people should lead their daily lives, while bearing in mind their future. Under the circumstances, that is, given this situation as the Group A and B youths saw it, many or most such individuals were also more prone to think of those adults/figures as persons to often avoid, evade, and, if necessary, deceive—rather than simply obey or largely agree with.

Adults' Perceptions, Felt Challenges, and Responses

The adults, meanwhile, generally knew this was happening. For one thing, they realized that many youths viewed them as often having little acceptable, let alone highly valuable, advice to offer on matters of major personal concern. (For emotional reasons, many adults then equated "many youths" with *most* youths, in this regard.) Moreover, they assumed that if those adolescents believed they could not obtain the adults' permission or approval for specified activities and involvements, many of them would try to "get their way" by other means. They might, for example, passively oppose or quietly ignore the adults; or they might actively, openly, and strongly resist or confront them, or even directly deceive them. This assumption was largely correct.

Given that situation, which centered on certain views and preconceptions many youths had of adults' opinions, advice, and so on, the following often occurred: Many adults/parents felt unable or only moderately able to obtain the youths' serious attention; or they felt less able to obtain it than they knew other adults had been. (Obtaining attention focused on getting youths to listen to information being provided or to feelings being expressed, or to seriously consider the possible relevance of the adults' views. Usually, "other adults" included not just those from, say, the 1960s or early 1970s, but the present adults' own parents. In this connection, however, the present adults' main reference group seemed to be the individuals from the 1960s and early 1970s.) Moreover, even if the present adults did eventually obtain the youths' attention,

they often felt unable to convince them that their, the adults', views or positions were useful and should be largely accepted, or even given a serious try. This applied whether the discussion topics involved broad life-styles and possible future involvements the adults considered appropriate or inappropriate, or involved specific situations and activities they believed should be avoided or reduced. It also applied even when the youths seemed to believe the adults did mainly have their, the youths', best interests at heart—that is, at least had good *intentions* or unselfish motives.

In addition, most such adults probably recognized that many youths—in order to indicate they do not want to be "treated as children"—would consider it important to oppose most directions or demands, by adults, that rested largely on a "do-it-because-I-say-so" base. That is, they probably realized, and partly accepted the fact, that it would often be counterproductive for them to "pull rank" and try to "get their way" by mainly relying on what was still, presumably, their traditional, socially ascribed status and authority as adults/parents. Moreover, as discussed below, even this traditional status/authority had been somewhat diminished as of the later 1970s, and many parents sensed this was the case.

Such differences and difficulties were commonly assumed to reflect a "generation gap," even though this gap interacted with other broad factors and with the highly personal dynamics of each family member. For present purposes, we will emphasize the generation gap only, even though the other factors and dynamics were always present and helped shape specific ways in which it was expressed.

Within the United States, generation gaps between youths and adults—especially parents—were widespread geographically and occurred quite regularly from one decade, or other time period, to the next. Indeed, they were often considered unavoidable, partly due to rapid cultural changes and partly given the centrality and typical strength of the youth needs involved. On the latter point, generation gaps were broadly viewed as normal expressions of the youngsters' need, and in most cases desire, to gain emotional independence from parents and to develop their own identities by the end of their chronological adolescence. (Most adults, and most parts of society, considered both needs legitimate and important.) For such reasons, the tacit, mainline cultural understanding was that each parent—as parent—should try to accommodate constructive expressions of those needs and should, in that sense or to that degree, essentially accept "the gap." At least, they should try to accommodate the situation (1) insofar as they and the youths could largely agree on what *was* constructive and concretely needed; (2) insofar as such accommodation seemed pragmatically, say, financially and physically, possible and reasonable; and (3) despite the unpleasantness and tensions they might experience, not just in connection with specific challenges that could occur, but because of their broader decrease in control, authority, and power with respect to youths.

Reasonable though this understanding may have been, it was particularly hard for many adults/parents to implement, though obviously not impossible. For one thing, the gap that existed in the later 1970s may well have been somewhat wider than several preceding ones, partly because of the broader range and larger mix of ideas, life-styles, and options that had come to exist or were theoretically available to most youths (notwithstanding the below-mentioned uncertainties regarding the immediate present as well as the future). In addition, this gap, in considerable contrast to its immediate predecessors, was often positively reinforced by the mass media, particularly by movies and television. These influential vehicles frequently supported the youths' general perspective, especially their needs and desires for independence and identity, their picture of many adults as irrelevant and/or rigid (as being, in a sense, somewhat uninformed prisoners of earlier-generation values), and their more challenging/assertive stance in promoting or defending their needs and wishes. To be sure, the media did not always portray the youths' particular ways of *expressing* their stance as being well thought through, without harmful excesses, and considerate of others' feelings. Still, the youths' overall situation and their resulting conflicts were usually portrayed sympathetically, especially as to the given needs' legitimacy. This reinforcement and support, which complemented the media's broader and growing emphasis on youth culture, helped many adolescents consider their stance vis-à-vis adults even more important and appropriate.

As implied, this stance, which involved challenge, assertion, and resistance on the *surface*, had, as its *underlying* theme, expressions of independence and identity. In either case, its context and forms, for example, roles and activities, were ones the *youths* considered important. Often, however, these contexts/forms did not involve *adulthood* in its most typical senses or at least not with respect to the relatively traditional roles and activities many adults/parents had in mind, and in terms of which the latter individuals were generally portrayed in the mass media. (In that media, adults/parents were typically associated with a settled, staid, and relatively restrained/restricted existence. In contrast, youth culture, and youth needs, were associated with change, exploration, self-expression, and expansion.) At any rate, one cumulative effect of the media presentations and images was that of calling into question, and generally diluting, the adults' ascribed as well as experience-based authority and power with regard to addressing youths' independence and identity needs in particular, and to guiding as well as controlling these individuals in general.

Compounding and augmenting those media contributions were other factors, ones that had helped create, and were currently crystallizing or reinforcing, certain perceptions and feelings in wide segments of society. Among the most salient were the (1) post-Vietnam (1960s–1970s) and (2) post-Watergate (1970s) tensions and themes, and the divisiveness associated with the (3) 1960s free speech and (4) 1970s women's liberation movements. (Factor [3] was still lingering, and [4] was expanding. Meanwhile, the backlash against direct, forceful efforts to achieve racial equality for blacks was already strong; and this, too, heightened social tensions.) Though (1) and (2), unlike given movie and television dramas, did not focus on the more specific, familiar areas of youth/adult concern, such as drugs and sex, they—like (3) and (4), and like the media itself—helped generate or reinforce a less trusting, more challenging attitude toward authority figures and "the establishment" in general. More broadly, (1) through (4) raised new questions, for a wide range of youths, about the adult world and adults' behavior overall—at the same time that they helped produce a more strained social/interpersonal world.

As indicated, many adults found the present generation gap especially difficult to handle, even when they tried to accommodate youths' needs for eventual independence and personal identity. As implied, this difficulty did not just reflect, or always primarily reflect, the formers' feelings of diminished control, authority, and relative power; this was true even though that particular combination always *was* a major contributor and was probably often critical by itself. Instead, the difficulty in handling the given generation gap also reflected two other important factors—especially in combination with each other, and partly independent of (1) through (4) above.

The first can be described as broad, ongoing, societal uncertainties and adjustments, ones that, for example, related to the still-recent Mideast oil crisis and the ballooning inflation rate. Though these particular events differed from those which helped generate the heightened distrust of authority (cf. [1] and [2], immediately above), all such events or factors, taken together, created an ongoing sense of anxiety among many adults regarding the immediate present. They also portended an uncertain or at least more constricted and cautious future for adults and youths alike, one that contrasted with the more vigorous, more carefree exploration and self-expression—also known as "freedom"—that most youths preferred to envision. Together with the growing atmosphere of uncertainty, these features and associations thus helped discourage many youths from wanting to think much about the conventional future; in that sense, those features and associations served as an inducement to alienation from mainstream society. This situation made that future a somewhat harder topic for youths and parents to broach, one that was also more tenuous when it eventually was discussed.

The second factor was the substantial sense of responsibility that many adults continued to feel for youths' ongoing well-being, especially given the growing uncertainty about the future, and despite many youths' challenges and resistance. Here, many adults/parents were concerned with what they considered the serious personal consequences of certain choices youths might make regarding drinking and drugs, casual sex, gang membership, and school dropout, in particular. These concerns, which cut across socioeconomic and racial/ethnic lines, were heightened by the following situation, one that produced considerable frustration in many adults: On the one hand, adults generally realized that the preceding activities and involvements were more

available than before and that many youths were interested in exploring one or more of them. At the same time, however, many such individuals sensed that they lacked the overall power to almost certainly prevent youths from engaging or further engaging in the given activities or types of activities, that is, those which the adults knew the youths were interested in or already participating in.

Together with this concern and frustration, the already mentioned factors—for instance, the substantially different image of youths and the increased level of general social/interpersonal tension—heightened many adults' sensitivity to issues of power, control, aggression, hostility, and resistance to authority, and also to clashes with the law. This sensitivity was further increased by the initially mentioned fear of, and/or anger toward, offenders—feelings that often existed prior to and/or independent of the concerns in question.

The adults' heightened awareness of such issues or dimensions helped generate or strengthen the following assumption, called "assumption (a) through (c)" ("[a] through [c]" was almost always implicit and global; that is, the adults in question seldom consciously focused on it, and they rarely delineated it to the extent next specified): Since "juvenile delinquents," on average, are (a) probably *more assertive/aggressive* than most nondelinquents, and since many or most delinquents are (b) even *less under the control of adults* than are most nondelinquents—many of whom are themselves more assertive/aggressive and harder to control than many adults would wish—then (c) a sizable percentage of those delinquents are probably *headstrong and recalcitrant* in particular, that is, probably beyond being simply assertive, and so on. Related to points (a) and (b) (mainly by extrapolation), and even more closely associated with (c), was the further view that many delinquents are probably more—and more often—(d) *hostile, impulsive, deceptive, and/or self-centered* than most nondelinquents, in addition to being more callous and/or (at least) callous more often.

Given the already mentioned concerns, developments, and factors, and given the likelihood that many delinquents—including first-timers—had at least a few (c)- and (d)-features (e.g., recalcitrance and deceptiveness, or hostility and self-centeredness), assumption (a) through (c) had two direct implications, each of which was less often implicit than "(a) through (c)" itself: First, if those youths did not quickly control or reduce such features, not to mention eliminate them, they—the features—might well lead to continued or more serious illegal behavior, especially if they had contributed to the present such behavior. Second, many activities that involved or revolved around those features, for example, around impulsivity and callousness, could seriously damage the youths' own future whether or not they had significantly contributed to prior *illegal* behavior, and apart from problems they could create for other individuals.

Given those implications, assumption (a) through (c) helped generate the following belief (this belief sometimes existed before "[a] through [c]," in which case the latter *reinforced* it; in either case, the belief was consciously held by many adults, though it was usually in the form of a global impression rather than being delineated and specified as follows): If youths who had even a few such features engaged in almost any nonminor offense that lacked sufficient extenuating circumstances, what those individuals probably needed above all were strong and immediate *external controls* by the justice system. That, at least, would be true if current evidence indicated those individuals would not be adequately controlled or redirected by their parents or guardians alone, and even if the system would perhaps try to redirect the individuals' energies and to organize/enhance their skills *as well,* in each case via *rehabilitation-centered* efforts. (As to family courts, these were not often considered serious alternatives to the justice system, in the United States as a whole.)

Most adults assumed the justice system *could* "pull rank" and that, given its presumed power, its controls could not be easily evaded or ignored. In these respects, the system could "pick up" where adults/parents had to partly leave off. If all went well, those justice system controls would make a great many youths "think twice" and would "turn them around" before it was too late; they would presumably do the latter by themselves, though perhaps assisted by standard rehabilitation components. In any event, such controls would *initiate* this overall process and would better protect society in the meantime. That, at least, is what most adults hoped.

This scenario meant that those adults considered external controls essential. They believed that, without such restraints, many or most delinquents would not simply "outgrow" their present modes of adjustment, that is, would not do so without first committing further offenses. Most such adults did not want to risk the occurrence of one or more added offenses while, in a sense, waiting for youths to "finish growing up." Moreover, many also seemed to believe that, with numerous such youths, offending—again, if not directly and firmly reacted to (opposed)—might well escalate in frequency and/or seriousness, rather than decrease and soon disappear. Thus, they wanted the justice system to sharply reduce the risk of continued offending and to prevent escalation, especially with regard to violence.

For such reasons, many adults/parents seemed to want an approach that would quickly gain the youths' attention and virtually force them to take seriously certain social norms, and various adults who support them. This desire, and the strength of the underlying feelings and concerns that helped generate and maintain it, were strikingly reflected in the public's willingness to support the application of verbally abusive, highly coercive, fear-instilling, psychological-shock-oriented programs such as Scared Straight, ones in which adult inmates (often "lifers") served as joint confronters of groups of youths who were required to visit a secure prison setting. More to the point, the public supported their use with relatively *nonserious* offenders (NSOs)—first- or second-timers whose illegal behavior may have been no more than moderate in degree.

(Such support was forthcoming even though this approach lacked reasonable scientific evidence of success. After a few years, however, the public and much of the correctional community grew skeptical of Scared Straight programs, at least as applied to NSOs. [Among other things, America's experience with Scared Straight indicated that wide, albeit implicit, differences existed among adults as to what constituted necessary, sufficient, and justified force, certainly in the case of minor offenders.] This is apart from the fact that the degree of force which many people had accepted in the case of *Scared Straight* far exceeded, in intensity, that which others had regarded as the "unjustified coercion" of various *rehabilitation*-centered programs that required [i.e., partly or largely *because* they required] participation in counseling and other components or activities. Moreover, the latter programs, which were seldom verbally abusive, publicly demeaning, fear-instilling, and so on, were generally applied to relatively *serious* offenders.)

As to serious and very serious delinquents, the strength of the public's underlying feelings and of its desire for immediate protection against violence was reflected in the increasingly frequent efforts of its elected public officials, and others, to remand many of these individuals to adult courts, based on the severity of their offense(s), and to lower the allowable age of remand itself.

Changes in Youth/Staff Relationships
Scared Straight and remand efforts aside, the earlier-mentioned changes in youths and in youth/adult relationships were also reflected in youth/staff relationships. For instance, starting in the mid-1970s and continuing well into the 1980s, progressively fewer correctional staff seemed strongly motivated to establish close or extensive working relationships with many offenders, especially but not only with relatively serious multiple offenders. (Little overall change occurred with first-timers, since—with few exceptions—they were already seen as needing or perhaps needing such relationships only if their offense was violent or otherwise serious.) This change in motivation reflected factors such as those mentioned next, ones that, collectively, involved two different levels of observation—two different settings, at any rate.

First, the change partly stemmed from the somewhat different image that many adults had of *youths in general*—with staff, who were also members of the public, being among those adults. This difference in image—one that was not mainly based on observations made in justice system settings—centered on the dimensions already noted. For example, many adults, including many staff, viewed nonoffenders and offenders (especially the latter) as somewhat more hostile and/or more closely defended than before, and as less receptive in general. Interwoven with this view, they felt—and here we emphasize staff—that youths were less interested in interacting fairly sincerely and openly, let alone closely and extensively, with authority figures in particular. As suggested, these views and impressions mainly originated in everyday life; from there, they diffused into the justice system, to some extent.

Second, the change in motivation, that is, its narrowed scope and reduced degree, reflected the fact that numerous staff had directly observed such changes as increased hostility and greater defensiveness among many *specific individuals* in their facilities or on their caseloads. Among these offenders, the hostility and defensiveness was usually evident early in any given program, as was the decreased interest in interacting fairly genuinely with authority figures. Moreover, with most such youths, these features or stances were not superficial only, or, in effect, veneer. (They were "surface" features only in the sense of being readily visible, not in being insubstantial and/or "mere show.") Instead, each feature was likely to be at least substantial in degree and was designed, as it were, to be taken at face value, and seriously as well.

Nevertheless, even this readily observable hostility, defensiveness, and—all in all—resistance was far from the whole story, strong or at least substantial though they were; that is, other important meanings, and underlying processes, were involved. More specifically, the overall situation and its dynamics was larger, more complex, and even partly different in meaning from that which was, indeed, readily observable, for example, the youths' defensiveness. In short, despite the importance and particular functions that those "surface" features/stances had under the *existing* conditions—such as early-program and early-interaction conditions—those very same features (e.g., resistance to certain types or levels of interaction, and even to change in general) could, under various other conditions, be taken at other than or more than face value, though no less seriously. (Regarding these complexities and different or additional meanings, see the later discussion of "facades," and various comments on "ambivalence.") As will be discussed, the *public* hardly recognized these particular complexities and meanings. Instead, its image of and reactions to offenders centered on (1) what it saw at first glance, (2) what it had directly or personally been confronted with by way of illegal or threatening behavior, (3) what it had been told by friends, relatives, and others about encounters with offenders, and (4) its generalizations/extrapolations from the earlier-mentioned changes in its image of youths in general (cf. later-1970s image versus that of earlier period), and from generation-gap phenomena overall. In no small measure, its image/reactions also stemmed from and centered on the generally simplified and otherwise stereotyped presentations repeatedly emphasized in the mass media.

Factors besides the changed image of youths sometimes contributed to the changed youth/staff interactions. One such factor was the sizable increase in populations and caseload sizes within institutional and community settings, particularly in standard programs. Such increases were likely to have a substantial effect mainly when they occurred without commensurate or compensating increases, improvements, or other changes in: number and skill of line staff, personal creativity and initiative, organizational flexibility, technology, physical plant, and/or material resources.

However, such unrelieved or insufficiently relieved population increases (rises) were not universal; some locales and/or specific settings experienced even little *rise* in the first place. Nevertheless, starting in the mid- to later 1970s, sheer increases were quite common, as were insufficiently relieved/compensated rises. When either of these occurred, especially the latter, it generally reduced the opportunities for unaugmented staff to establish and maintain many close or extensive working relationships (interactions). Yet even so, realistic opportunities for some such interactions often remained. This was true especially when policymakers and administrators provided at least a moderate amount of consistent support for them and as long as staff's motivation to establish them had not conspicuously dropped—based, for instance, on a changed image of offenders. (Though unrelieved increases and/or minimal administrative support in this regard affected all staff, their impact may have been most important—sometimes even decisive—among those whose motivation to establish close and/or extensive working relationships was already relatively low. Finally, as long as enough administrative support, enough material resources, and so on, existed, neither the close nor the extensive youth/staff interactions—each of which could be varied in degree and through time—required indeterminate sentences and/or very long programs.)

A second factor involved the justice model. More specifically, in some settings a decreased interest in establishing close/extensive working relationships partly reflected the increased emphasis upon this framework within corrections as a whole. In particular, the justice model, whose influence in juvenile and especially adult settings grew steadily and substantially during most of the 1970s and whose application to juveniles was quite extensive by the early 1980s, hardly provided encouragement for such interactions. It viewed them as a way to facilitate *rehabilitation,* which it essentially opposed or greatly downplayed, not *punishment,* which the model considered central. In this connection, the justice model influenced policymakers and administrators (PMAs), not just line staff.

For instance, few PMAs who agreed with the model's key tenets made concerted and/or sustained efforts to promote the establishment, maintenance, and/or expansion of various rehabilitation-centered components or activities (RCCAs)—some of which, such as counseling, did directly involve the above interactions, and most others of which could indeed be facilitated and possibly improved by them. To be sure, many such PMAs did not try to directly, actively, and/or strongly *oppose* attempts that were made by others to promote the modest introduction or expansion of those components (though many other PMAs did routinely do so)—particularly when external pressures, say, population and fiscal pressures, were not great. Nevertheless, those policymakers and administrators seldom tried to resist—vigorously or otherwise—the proposed or ongoing reduction or essential dismantling of existing RCCAs, especially but not only when such pressures did mount. At any rate, even when external conditions might have allowed them to do so, those individuals seldom advocated—enthusiastically or otherwise—an investment of many program resources in concerted, sustained efforts to help youths grow and develop. Accordingly, they seldom in fact *provided* substantial, consistent support for staff (viewed as a resource) to assist in that way, via close and/or extensive working relationships in a context of RCCAs. Their support, when not verbal only, was instead usually token and/or sporadic.

All in all, then, the acceptance of basic justice model principles made it easier for policymakers and administrators to downplay youths' growth and development needs, especially but not only when external pressures and constraints were substantial; this often directly limited staff's ability to realistically undertake or maintain the earlier-mentioned interactions. As to those line staff themselves, these individuals sometimes used the same principles as grounds for not personally engaging in efforts that might otherwise have focused on such needs, whether or not via the already-mentioned relationships, and certainly *with* their aid. Moreover, staff who agreed with those principles were able to implement them even if PMAs, and/or population/caseload pressures, had not, by themselves, already significantly reduced the chances of realistically undertaking or maintaining the given relationships.

We will now discuss (1) inadequate differentiations, (2) oversimplifications, and (3) static views that were made or held regarding offenders. Emphasis will be on "oversimplified and static views" that have been held by the public—and, in the case of static views, by some professionals as well. Implications of both the oversimplified and static views will be mentioned.

Inadequate Differentiations, Oversimplifications, and Static Views

Fewer Perceived Differences among Offenders Given its concern with confrontive, bodily-injury crimes, the public, by 1980, no longer focused heavily on what it now viewed as much less serious offenders, such as "petty thieves" and "check passers." In particular, it discussed these individuals less often than before and it no longer considered them high priority, even though most people realized that those offenders, collectively, committed many crimes. Nevertheless, when such offenders and others—including "auto thieves"—were discussed, whether in informal conversations or public forums, it was not uncommon for some of the fear, anger, and/or rejection that many people felt toward the *violent and violence-prone* to be implicitly or explicitly generalized to them. In this connection a large portion of the public often assumed that many or most of these less serious offenders might well be violence-prone or occasionally violent themselves, and that, accordingly, they probably needed and most likely deserved justice system responses which broadly resembled those for known violent offenders.

Thus, in this emotionally charged atmosphere, it often seemed to be taken for granted that almost *no* offenders, including juveniles, were to be spoken of with particular tolerance. In fact, in public forums, if a panelist or audience participant were to ignore or fail to recognize this implicit assumption or even tacit understanding, he or she would generally risk being viewed and perhaps labeled as "soft on crime," indifferent to victims, unrealistic, uninformed, or naive. This would apply unless, say, the offenders who were being discussed had, themselves, been (1) seriously or repeatedly abused in the past (particularly but not only if female) or (2) almost inhumanly brutalized (regardless of gender), and, in many cases (more likely with males), only then if (3) their own current offense—assuming it was not in self-defense and that no past offenses were more severe—was not itself considered heinous.

Partly because of this atmosphere, even relatively few professionals seemed eager to closely address such questions as the following, whether or not in public forums: "Which offenders—say, which types of individuals—seem open to major change and growth, or even more open than others?" "How might such openness or even moderate openness be maintained or increased?" and "How, specifically, might the desired change be accomplished?" This hesitancy, slight or moderate interest, general *dis*interest, or whatever applied, was observed among many correctional researchers, academicians, and, to a lesser extent, practitioners. Of those professionals who *were* interested in such questions, some seemed to assume—often, perhaps accurately—that if they spent much time on them, this might be disapprovingly interpreted to mean they did not strongly support, and perhaps even disagreed with, that which large parts of the public, and many prominent policymakers, seemed to consider the only "really" important, truly justified, approach and goal: (1) respond rather harshly—over and beyond firmly, swiftly, and reliably—to the preponderance of criminal activity, especially the violent, in order to (2) protect the public against immediate dangers.[12] Hopefully, this combination would adequately and automatically address longer-run dangers, as well.

At any rate, for these and other reasons, a large number and growing percentage of professionals paid relatively little attention to (a) various characteristics—for example, several traits and attitudes—of offenders as individuals, that is, as specific persons, and to (b) differences in traits, attitudes, and other features that existed across those offenders, collectively.[13] To be sure, because the Martinson era was then predominant, few programs/approaches—certainly fewer than before—were being viewed as effective in the first place; and directly reflecting this view, it was generally assumed that individualized programming would hardly improve matters. Together with other factors, this assumption made it seem futile and somewhat "academic" to focus on various individual characteristics and differences, especially to a large degree. In any event, such attention was considered unlikely to promote the earlier-mentioned approach and goal (see [1] and [2] in the preceding paragraph); and sometimes, it was viewed as possibly detracting.

Oversimplified and Static Views of Offenders
Oversimplifications
The public, meanwhile, never *had* paid much attention to offenders as individuals, except in broad terms; and it was not disposed to start doing so in the mid- to later 1970s. Indeed, as its fear of offenders increased during those years, its view of them as persons seemed to become narrower, and in that sense less differentiated, than in the 1960s and early 1970s. This applied to offenders overall, not just to the violent and serious multiple offender subgroups (to the extent these did not overlap).

In particular, the public's image and concern seemed to increasingly center on only a few features (here called Group A features)—ones it especially associated with those subgroups. These were *hostility, impulsiveness, and frequent as well as considerable overt— even covert—resistance to changing one's self and one's behavior.* (Those particular features were indeed often conspicuous among violent offenders and SMOs. They were also *more often* obvious in those individuals than in others. Finally, although one or more A-features also existed in many *less* serious offenders [LSOs], each such feature, on average, was present among LSOs [individually] to a substantially lesser *degree;* moreover, it was less *likely* to be present in the first place among LSOs [collectively] than among the violent offender and SMO groups. For these reasons, A-features—individually and collectively— were less obvious as such, within and across "lesser" offenders.)

Yet, simultaneously, the public seemed to essentially overlook or be much less concerned with various *other* significant features (three key ones—together called *Group B features,* which includes "self-doubt"—are specified shortly). Though many of these were less noticeable than the A-features of hostility and impulsiveness, particularly among violent and serious multiple offenders, they existed no less often in many of these same individuals.[14] (In effect, they coexisted with the A-features. Also, like A's themselves, these less obvious ones were not uncommon among LSOs.)

Nevertheless, these overlooked, ignored, or downplayed features, such as self-doubt, were not only (1) less *evident,* but (2) their role in generating and maintaining the individuals' illegal behavior was usually less *direct.* (Point [2] specifically applies to the three Group B features—the "Group B triad"— mentioned below.) In both respects—certainly that of point 2—these features, for example, the B-triad, existed not only at what might be called a "subtler" level of the personality (sometimes because the offenders preferred to downplay or even conceal them), but also in a manner or mode that was less directly engaged with other individuals—or was less action-primed—than were A-features, such as hostility and impulsiveness. See, for instance, "ambivalence," below.

Particularly important among these less noticeable but nonetheless significant features was the Group B triad: *self-doubt, vulnerability,* and *ambivalence regarding change and growth.* Often, the first two were present despite the coexistence of certain frequently used, sometimes long-standing, *facades* (and of related, often quite transitory, and frequently overcompensatory, feelings and attitudes). (These facades involved *considerable* self-confidence, *broad* self-satisfaction, and even *calculated* indifference to others, in the sense of an absence of much need for others. The last of these—indifference—occurred more often, and was usually more convincing [at least at first glance, or to the casual observer], in relation to adult than juvenile offenders. That is, it seemed more real, strong, and not a facade [in that context]. All in all, these facades diverted attention from the individual's self-doubts, vulnerability, and so on, and they partly served to convey an air of power and control instead.)

As to the third B-feature—the ambivalence—this existed very often, usually to at least a moderate degree. Its presence meant that, (1) in contrast to what one might reasonably expect based on the presence of the third A-feature, namely, "considerable . . . resistance to changing one's self and one's behavior," (2) resistance on the part of many offenders was actually neither unalloyed nor even necessarily intense—or, for that matter, almost continual. Point (2), however, did not mean that resistance was commonly weak, token, or even no more than moderate.

Neither the existence of the Group B triad itself nor the fact that the appearance of "considerable self-confidence" was a frequent facade meant that the given offenders actually had *no* substantial strengths and areas of reality-based confidence, for example, no useful skills or accomplishments. Nor, however, did either the facades or the actual/reality-based *strengths/confidence* mean that none of these individuals ever appeared unsure and unhappy to the trained eye, even at first glance.[15]

Given the public's increased focus on—even overemphasis upon—A-features, and given its near-exclusion of, or decreased interest in, others (including B's), its view of offenders, especially the serious multiple and the violent, became not just more incomplete but also more one-sided or unbalanced. In effect, its image of those individuals became more oversimplified and stereotyped. Moreover, insofar as the public generalized that image beyond the SMO and violent—as it appeared to do—both its oversimplification and its related exaggeration of A-features, that is, its added absolute and relative emphasis upon them, applied to a *large portion* of all offenders, possibly even a majority. Its view in this regard already pertained to most SMOs and violent offenders.

In sum, the public seemed largely unaware of, or minimally concerned with, various characteristics of offenders as individuals, and with certain important distinctions across those individuals.[16] (Whereas this point emphasizes features and distinctions per se, the earlier-discussed "B-public"—at least, most of it—did care about those offenders' needs and future.) Instead, what seemed to exist or matter to it were a few *similarities,* especially violence-related ones that involved the A-features of hostility and impulsiveness. More precisely, those features seemed to matter together with certain additional characteristics. The latter were either integral to or direct expressions of A-features (e.g., regarding hostility, they in-

cluded verbal or physical confrontation), or else they were often associated with A-features but were not integral and exclusive to them (e.g., regarding impulsiveness, they included unreliability, unpredictability, and even deceptiveness). These added characteristics reinforced the public's discomfort with serious offenders, even when they were seen among the less serious individuals as well.

Static Views

Together with the preceding developments, not only the public but many professionals and numerous policymakers assumed or believed that offenders, for example, most serious multiple offenders and violent offenders, had already gone about as far as they wished to go in their personal development. In particular, the public assumed, and many professionals, and others, believed, that these individuals were largely satisfied with the kind of persons they were (i.e., with "who" they were), with what they were doing, and with the nature of their usual inputs and responses to others, though often not with the outcomes.[17] For such reasons, it was largely taken for granted—more explicitly by the professionals—that these individuals would be essentially closed to significant personal growth if left on their own or even if exposed to rehabilitation components alone, as these inputs were generally conceived at the time.[18]

Recall, in this regard, that the public and many professionals did not assume that most SMOs and violent offenders were (1) *dissatisfied* with the kind of persons they considered themselves, though they often disliked others, and were (2) *ambivalent* about possible change and growth. Moreover, the public, in particular, hardly recognized these individuals' self-doubt and vulnerability. If anything, it usually observed the opposite (especially in news clips of live arrests and of court appearances); for instance, it saw a facade of self-confidence and imperturbability, or an air of indifference or cockiness.[19] (To be sure, it sometimes also saw possible and genuine regret and remorse, as well as apparent submissiveness.) Yet, the public did not identify these opposite features *as* facades, as mainly facades, or as other types of defense against other individuals and/or self. It thus accepted the self-confidence, and so on, largely at face value.

Given this lack of recognition regarding *SMOs and violent* offenders, given the inaccurate view of these individuals that it promoted, and given that the public did *not* assume (1) and (2) immediately above, the public could have reasonably assumed the following with respect to *less* serious and *nonviolent* offenders: No *less* self-confidence would exist among these "lesser" offenders than presumably existed among the more serious. (Recall that self-*doubt* was not recognized among the SMOs and the violent; or, if it was seen, it may have been heavily outweighed by the facade of self-confidence.) Also, since the public could have assumed that little *ambivalence* existed among these lesser offenders—and that, in this regard, LSOs were no *less* satisfied with their present adjustment than were serious multiple offenders—it would also have been understandable, though again not logically inescapable, for the public to take it for granted that LSOs, like SMOs themselves, would strongly resist attempts to challenge that adjustment. In this way, the public would have been able to generalize—though not entirely accurately—from SMOs and violent offenders to many or most less serious and nonviolent offenders, in connection with resistance to change.

In addition, many professionals believed, and the public seemed to implicitly assume, that this virtual closing off of development was mainly self-imposed. More specifically, they thought it largely reflected the SMOs' and violent offenders' often "impetuous," "willful," and/or "headstrong" rejection of various social opportunities and conventional expectations or pressures; they believed it included, in particular, a refusal to even halfway seriously, and even provisionally, explore "mainstream" roles and life-styles.[20] Also, many professionals thought the closing-off, checking, or halting sometimes reflected a fairly deliberate or at least *less* impetuous avoidance of commitments to traditional or even moderately traditional life-styles—certain preconditions to which, for example, the acquisition of given educational/employment skills, may already have been briefly explored.[21]

Those beliefs by many professionals were partly inconsistent or uncoordinated with a view with which they nevertheless often coexisted: Some individuals' *social milieus*—especially their families, peers, and/or neighborhoods—had contributed significantly to the closing-off or impeding in question, often beginning in early stages of the persons' development. Assuming this view was correct, the closing-off, halting, or curbing of development, when viewed longitudinally and broadly, was not entirely self-imposed. This applied whether the external contributions were mainly ones of commission (cf. family/peer pressures/restrictions) or omission (cf. inadequate neighborhood resources, and, later, limited economic opportunities). Yet, even when the influence of these past external forces was granted, and granting the possibility of their continued influence as well, it was still assumed that the resistance of most SMOs and violent offenders to future change and growth was strong and largely *without* ambivalence. In effect, these individuals were viewed as being largely satisfied with "where" they were (i.e., are), irrespective of how they may have gotten there in connection with their social milieu, and regardless of how aware or unaware they may have been as to the ways in which external forces had helped shape them and were perhaps still shaping and sometimes limiting them.

The Strong-External-Controls Approach

Together, the above beliefs and assumptions thus made it easier for the public to largely accept the following views, ones that were broadly supported by various professionals and policymakers especially from 1975–1977 through 1983–1985 ([a] and [b], below, were explicitly advocated by those individuals; [c] and [d] were implied): The best way to reduce or eliminate future illegal behavior is to (a) rely chiefly or exclusively on *strong external controls* (SECs), ones that (b) focus directly and heavily on illegal behavior. Any given program that would center on these views (c) might or might not include educational, vocational, and/or other components often associated with rehabilitation; if it included them, their priority would not be high. Thus, the (a)/(b) strategy—here called the SEC approach, or SEC—(d) would not necessarily try to address offenders' resistance to personal change and growth; and even if (c)-components were present they would not be extensive and the program would not have to make a resolute and/or repeated effort to provide or increase practical and interpersonal skills.

As suggested, the public largely accepted or deferred to these views, or at least to some of them. In particular, regarding violent offenders and the serious multiple, it tacitly accepted the "rely *chiefly*" part of (a) and the gist of (b). However, according to repeated surveys that generally emphasized serious offenders, most of the public only moderately agreed with (c) and, by inference, with (d). As to nonviolent and less serious offenders, the public's attitude toward (c) and (d) seemed to resemble that which involved violent offenders and SMOs; but even here—and despite the formers' nonviolence, and so on—the (a)/(b) message of "strictness first and foremost" again prevailed.

Regarding its "only moderate agreement" with (c) and (d), most of the public (or simply "the public") seemed to believe that rehabilitation efforts should, whenever feasible, accompany a program and be integral to it. They should not be largely peripheral activities—little more than time-structuring devices, mainly token acknowledgments of or sometimes even concessions to the ethic of humane treatment, or, for that matter, just as easily absent. In that regard, the public evidently assumed offenders should be helped to change *more* than their illegal behavior. This was true even though the reduction/elimination of that particular behavior was indeed their overriding goal, and although any rehabilitation components which were present would mainly serve as a potentially important means to that end (even while the components focused directly on the above-mentioned "*more* than . . . illegal behavior," e.g., on various social/personal needs and problems).

The public's attitude toward (c) and (d) thus implied that offenders should not be perfunctorily offered initial and perhaps even subsequent opportunities to participate in educational, vocational, and/or other possible components, such as counseling and cognitive skills training. Instead, the possible or probable value of participating should presumably be discussed carefully and perhaps repeatedly with them, and in that way emphasized. That is, the public's attitude implied that offenders who have needs/problems which bear on their illegal behavior should at least be genuinely and clearly encouraged to participate, and should, if necessary, be actively helped to address their social and personal needs/problems via those and/or other components. Nevertheless, even from the standpoint of rehabilitation proponents, those efforts would be made

mainly, but not exclusively, because progress with respect to such needs/problems could presumably contribute substantially to the principal goal itself.

The public's view was by no means homogeneous regarding the *degree* of opportunity, encouragement, and active assistance that was appropriate; that is, a substantial range of opinion existed. Still, as implied above, the degree in question was seldom considered small.

Finally, since the public apparently assumed its "more-than-illegal-behavior" stance despite its increased fear of offenders, in spite of its frequent anger toward them, irrespective of the fact that it emotionally distanced itself from most of them, and not without some reluctance/ambivalence of its own, this implied it was not entirely rejecting of or indifferent toward them as persons. This, again, was despite the fact that what mattered most to the public was the offenders' illegal behavior, not their personal well-being or growth.[22]

Besides being considered the *best* approach by SEC proponents, this method and stance—namely, strong external controls—was presented as the *only* one likely to work with most SMOs and violent offenders, that is, with persons regarded as strongly resistive and essentially closed. Moreover, given these individuals' overall "recalcitrance" or "intractability," it was considered important, appropriate, and a particularly strong point that the SEC approach—presumably unlike much of rehabilitation—would not rely on, or at least have to rely on, their genuine cooperation, their *largely* genuine/sincere cooperation, or even their general acceptance of the program.[23] (Such acceptance would not have to be accompanied by much interest in the program, let alone much enthusiasm about it.) In addition, with respect to achieving the basic, behavioral goal, SEC was considered not only essential but often sufficient by itself.[24] Finally, although shorter- versus longer-term behavior change was not often distinguished here, proponents and followers hoped the strong-external-controls approach would produce change that was longer-term or permanent.

Rehabilitation, in contrast, was regarded by SEC proponents as neither essential nor sufficient in that respect. To be sure, its components were often viewed as adjuncts to the strong external controls, that is, viewed as supplements but hardly complements. More specifically, rehabilitation components were mainly considered possible additions that could sometimes help improve the offenders' personal and social adjustment, and that might even occasionally help reduce illegal behavior. Nevertheless, those components were regarded as neither strong enough nor focused appropriately enough to reduce the illegal behavior of most, possibly even many, SMOs and violent offenders, or to reduce it sufficiently in any event. Under the circumstances, SEC proponents basically viewed those components as nonessential—as ones that could probably be reduced or dispensed with prior to various others, if, for instance, budgets became tight.

As advocated by the above policymakers and professionals, the SEC approach would basically rely on actual and threatened punishments, restrictions, and inconveniences. (Though the public seemed to accept this basic reliance, it appeared to envision somewhat less reliance or relative emphasis than that advocated by the policymakers and others—at any rate, far from an almost-exclusive reliance.) Broadly speaking, it would achieve its behavioral goal by convincing offenders to apply their willpower and utilize their already existing strengths/skills, plus whichever ones they might acquire or increase during the program.[25] It would do so via actions more than words, for example, by punishment/restrictions more than counseling/advice. These efforts, particularly the application of willpower, would be made for the express purpose of redirecting and/or better controlling certain desires, impulses, and emotions that led to trouble with the law. (See endnote 26 for further details and discussion.)

As suggested, SEC proponents often assumed—sometimes implicitly, sometimes explicitly—that a role could exist for practical and interpersonal strengths and skills, including strengths other than willpower itself. However, the only factor internal to offenders they seemed to consider *crucial* to *illegal behavior* per se—crucial to determining its future degree or absence—was the application of willpower. In particular, by focusing directly and heavily on illegal behavior, the program's punishments, restrictions, and inconveniences could, theoretically, trigger the reduction/elimination of that behavior; that is, they could do so *if* they were sooner or later followed by the offenders' serious exertion of will, for instance, in the form of

self-control and in rejecting pressures from others. Also theoretically, punishment, and so on, followed by exertion of will, could produce that result whether the individuals' practical and interpersonal strengths/skills were extensive or limited, whether they had been increased or not increased during the program, and whether they were well or poorly used in areas other than those involving illegal behavior.[27]

In theory, then, offenders, via redirection and better self-control, would substantially change their ways of responding to various desires, impulses, and emotions, to specific situational pressures and "temptations," and to given conditions of daily life. Also via redirection and self-control, not only the frequency but the intensity and possibly even the very presence of certain problem-related desires/impulses/emotions might themselves undergo change, in the first place.[28] This change would be apart from the offenders' manner of *responding* to those forces and states of mind.[29]

Except for minor variations in content and focus, the strong-external-controls approach—its overall method and stance—would be essentially the same for the less serious, more serious, nonviolent, and violent. Some variations would involve the "program inputs" that are used. For instance, slight differences would exist in the relative emphasis given to the programs' respective components—assuming those components, such as vocational training and group or individual counseling, do exist. Other variations would relate to the particular areas of the offenders' life that are targeted ("target areas"), such as family or peers. However, SEC could and generally would be applied in differing *degrees*. For example, with less serious offenders and nonviolent offenders there would usually be less actual and threatened punishment, fewer or less severe restrictions, fewer direct contacts, and perhaps fewer areas of focus than with the more serious and the violent individuals; this would apply whatever the program inputs and target areas might be. At the same time, SEC's emphasis and scope would be essentially the same regardless of the following: (1) the broad category or level into which given offenders might fall (e.g., "unsocialized aggressive" or "overinhibited"; lower/middle/higher cognitive complexity or interpersonal maturity); and (2) the more specific personality features (defenses included) of those offenders, as well as their particular skills, needs, interests, problems, and life circumstances. This, too, would apply to inputs as well as targets. In this regard, all clients would receive much the *same* program, and definitely the same overall approach (viz., SEC), despite significant differences in degree.

A few closing remarks. All in all, violent offenders, serious multiple offenders, and other justice system clients were often viewed in a minimally differentiated way from the mid-1970s into the 1980s (and beyond).[30] This fairly homogeneous view related not only to the type of approach considered necessary and often sufficient for all or almost all offenders, but to the description of those offenders as persons. No less important than the oversimplified, markedly incomplete picture of those individuals as persons was the poorly balanced picture of them that resulted from the heavy, albeit understandable, emphasis that was placed upon Group A features, on the one hand, and the virtual omission of no less important B-features, on the other. Together, this oversimplification and imbalance helped reinforce the belief—one shared by the public, and partly accurate—that many offenders, not just numerous SMOs and violent offenders, strongly resist attempts to change them as persons or to help them grow and develop along that line.[31] (Though accurate as far as it went, this belief was incomplete.)

In the view of SEC proponents, however, that particular resistance hardly mattered. Instead, what ultimately counted was the offenders' opposition to modifying or relinquishing their illegal behavior; and this opposition, like the preceding one, was considered quite strong, especially among SMOs and violent offenders. Together, this set of views—views of certain individuals as being "static"—provided a major basis or rationale for the strong-external-controls approach. More precisely, it did so when (1) complemented by the further view that strong offender resistance necessitates even stronger correctional counterforce, and especially when (2) placed in the context of the earlier-mentioned oversimplifications.

Given this situation or scenario, SEC would presumably provide the needed counterforce (and only such force could succeed). In so doing, it would cause offenders to direct their willpower against their illegal behavior in such ways as to reduce/eliminate that behavior. Theoretically, this approach could, and would, be essentially the same for all offenders (other than the most lightweight), regardless of their level of skill, maturity, violence, and overall seriousness, and irrespective of their attitude toward acquiring adult roles and exploring conventional life-styles.[32] It could, and would, also be essentially the same even if the program contained components often associated with rehabilitation. Thus, differentiated and individualized approaches would not be used, except—perhaps—to a minimal degree.

Notes

1. The rate of increase in Group A's dominance probably diminished during 1985–1990, but its degree of dominance over the soon-described Group B has been largely unchanged since the early 1990s.

2. A third group, comprised almost entirely of citizens, that is, "nonprofessionals," is smaller than either the A or B publics and is called Group C. These individuals have fewer strong feelings about most offenders or offenses (O/Os) than does either of those publics; and, they less often give O/Os extensive thought, as well. While not indifferent to crime, they infrequently express themselves about "what should be done with criminals." When they do state opinions they generally, but seldom intensively or fervently, support specific Group A positions. Nevertheless, C's can also accept and support various B views, not just in spirit or principle. As a result, they seldom, for example, oppose rehabilitation sharply and persistently, even when they largely agree with particular aspects of A. Most C's can be fairly easily swayed by well-articulated, sincerely presented A and B arguments.

3. As indicated, this A/B difference in empathy and tolerance is a matter of degree, not an either/or. Though it usually does not involve extreme contrasts, as, for instance, in "bleeding heart" (B's) versus "frozen heart" (A's) caricatures and stereotypes, it is nevertheless sizable and important.

4. The "fear" in question does not just center on given sanctions themselves, such as lockup, and on possible subsequent (and perhaps consequent) difficulties, such as reduced job opportunities. Instead, it also includes the experience of being detected, apprehended, and processed.

5. It is not clear if they usually believe that—under the given conditions—sizable, genuine attitude changes are somewhat less common than significant, increased social/survival skills.

6. Group A, of course, generally disputes the need for such resources, as a means of changing illegal behavior.

7. At the same time—or so another tacit assumption might go—if those offenders are *not* so "bad" as to no longer deserve at least substantial resources, they may, however, not actually *need* them very much. In other words, if they can still deserve such resources, they might not really need them. If this assumption is added to the former, then the "no-win" situation involved in the former becomes a classic catch-22. However, this "22" is probably uncommon in contemporary corrections, while the "no-win" situation is not.

8. That, in turn, sometimes reflects the following: If an individual's "merit" is thought to be solely based on his instant and/or prior offense(s) or on other past behavior(s) which—it might be said—"cannot be undone or diminished," it would presumably follow that the individual, strictly speaking, can become no more deserving in the *future,* no matter what he says or does. (Also, if merit is thought to depend, not solely, but *almost* solely on the offense(s)/behavior(s) in question, future deservedness could presumably change to only a minor, that is, a corresponding, degree.) This framework or logic presents deservedness as being, in principle, essentially "static"—that is, unchangeable, not just unchanging—rather than "dynamic," for example, at least moderately responsive to new events.

9. And, for example, on then making these individuals eligible or ineligible for certain types or amounts of assistance based largely upon the nature of their offenses and records—in effect, on offense-based merit.

10. Though fear, anger, and rejection generally seemed to link with each other, and in that particular order, fear sometimes led directly to rejection, without the intermediate or even subsequent emergence of anger. At any rate, anger and rejection—individually and combined—were not always, and certainly not only, pro-duced by fear; nor were they *invariably* linked to each other, in the first place, whatever their respective degrees. The latter was true even though *intense* anger was almost always associated with at least slight or moderate rejection.

11. The views and inferences in this section stem not from quantitative measurements but from everyday observations, discussions, and so on, that occurred during the time periods covered.

12. Firmness, like swiftness and reliability (certainty), can readily occur in community-based settings, whether or not in connection with in-lieu-of-institution sentences. Harshness can more readily occur in institutional than community settings, and in connection with institutional sentences. Neither of the above means that (1) firmness does not characterize many institutions, even more of them—and more so—than does harshness, (2) harshness rarely occurs in community settings, and (3) firmness and harshness only rarely intermix, in whatever settings.

13. Beginning in the early 1980s the situation regarding point (b) changed somewhat, if only at a broad level. It was at that point, for example, when sustained, focused, and substantially increased correctional attention was first given to sex offenders and substance abusers as such. This situation was reflected in the several more or less distinctive prescriptive packages that began to appear and evolve in connection with those respective groups.

14. Group B features were less noticeable even to various professionals, at least at first glance. As to the public, it seldom took a close initial look at individual offenders during those years, and it rarely seemed to reflect and elaborate upon those initial—essentially surface—impressions. First impressions aside, the public's tendency to overlook or downplay critical features and to generally oversimplify offenders still exists, and to about the same degree as before. In contrast, during the past several years many professionals seem to be revisiting a more differentiated view of offenders, one that is more realistic and better balanced. Whether this trend will continue is, of course, unclear, as is the situation regarding the public's generally *un*differentiated views.

15. The public, itself, sometimes witnessed or personally experienced dissatisfaction or strong displeasure on the part of offenders, as, for example, when the latter's unhappiness toward individual members of the public whom they had encountered was made verbally clear, or was directly implied, in connection with anger they may have directed at those persons. As to the facades themselves, for instance, that of *"considerable self-confidence"* or even a near cockiness, these often reinforced the public's preexisting fears of offenders. This occurred mainly because they made those individuals seem more powerful, less controllable, and potentially more impulsive—thus, more threatening or discomforting overall—than persons who did not seem to purposely accentuate, pointedly highlight, or otherwise draw sharp attention to traits such as self-confidence and indifference, and to the related features of assertiveness and independence. (As implied, an exaggerated form of these traits was sometimes expressed in a context that involved personal confrontation of, or direct observation by, members of the public.)

16. Regarding minimal concern, the public obviously had to recognize those characteristics in the first place—either their actuality or possibility.

17. Despite these offenders' areas of general satisfaction, and despite their facade of considerable self-confidence, the public did not regard most of them as, ipso facto, happy. Nor did it assume they usually acted cheerful around others.

18. Various professionals seemed to believe that both conditions, especially the latter, applied somewhat less to individuals under age 15 or 16 at intake. Many others, however, made no such age distinction.

19. To be sure, these clips usually involved adults.

20. "Refusal" by these individuals did not mainly reflect realistic caution, simple hesitancy, or understandable confusion, say, in the face of something new, seemingly major, and quite likely challenging; at least, those reactions, even collectively, were neither the major nor decisive contributors. Sometimes, however, refusal or considerable resistance in the face of challenge reflected a long-standing self-doubt or low self-image, and a related fear of failure as well as anticipated disapproval or rejection by others. Under such circumstances, offenders sometimes felt it would be better—less personally painful—"not to try" than to "try, and fail." In this situation these individuals often tried to make it seem as if they were "really not interested," in the first place, or as if they were only slightly interested. What the public then saw was an apparent indifference—or else resistance—and it seldom recognized this as a preemptive defense, or avoidance.

21. Thus, even these presumably more deliberate decisions were not assumed to have been, ipso facto, *very* carefully calculated (e.g., as to their immediate and longer-term implications), and without any significant emotional base. This applied especially to youths, but was not limited to them.

22. The present type of rejection by the public might be called general or "global rejection," though not sweeping, full-fledged, and unmitigated rejection; this is to distinguish it from specific aspects of rejection (see immediately below). Though the public's level of global rejection was, on average, substantial, a sizable range existed. Specifically, such rejection was occasionally, but by no means rarely, *complete*; not infrequently *high* (this was more common than complete rejection); not infrequently *moderate*; and occasionally—again not rarely—*slight*. In general, it seemed greater for the more serious and violent than for the less serious and nonviolent. Global rejection should be distinguished from certain of its aspects, for example, rejection of offenders as persons "of equal intrinsic value" or as individuals "worthy of specified consideration"; the latter includes various types and degrees of assistance, as well as basic opportunity or access. Regarding these aspects, see "Two Major Views and Responses: Group 'A' Views and Responses" at the start of this chapter.

23. Nevertheless, many SEC proponents believed that substantial, not just minimal or token, cooperation would often emerge, particularly in the middle or later stages of a well-implemented program. Generally

speaking, it would emerge when offenders began to believe that there was, in a sense, "no escape" for them—say, no avoiding or significantly weakening the program's main requirements and restrictions—and that their immediate and perhaps longer-term interests would be served by at least "going along with" the program and perhaps even "getting with" it. The latter referred, for example, to actively participating in certain skill-building and/or counseling components that might have been present. These, it may be noted, are ordinarily considered rehabilitation or rehabilitation-related features.

24. Only around 1980, soon after the appearance of a major report on deterrence (Blumstein, Cohen, and Nagin, 1978), did many academicians and researchers, though not the general public, begin to realize the following: No body of research even moderately, let alone clearly, supported the idea that a relatively pure deterrence approach, such as the one described here, reduced recidivism—that is, reduced it more than did alternative strategies. No substantial support exists even today (Andrews and Bonta, 1994; Gendreau, 1993, 1994; Gendreau, Cullen, and Bonta, 1994).

25. As implied earlier, SEC proponents often assumed that many of the latter strengths/skills could be generated or increased via the programs' rehabilitation components in particular (assuming these elements existed), for example, by what is now often called cognitive skills training; however, they did not emphasize this point. Those components might also have helped individuals *better utilize* already existing, that is, pre-program, strengths and skills.

26. Basically, SEC proponents assumed that strong external controls could first hamper, dilute, contain, or otherwise weaken/neutralize various defenses. (These defenses—the principal agents of the individuals' resistance to change—were considered strong enough to withstand the possible incentives, inducements, goads, and/or pressures often associated with *rehabilitation* components, such as educational training or group counseling, used separately or together.) Having

weakened/neutralized important defenses, having thereby reduced or eliminated key bases and even specific areas of resistance, having interfered with various trouble-related adjustment patterns per se, and having gained the offenders' serious attention as well, these strong external controls would then (or at least eventually) be ready to achieve the following. They could convince SMOs and violent offenders, among others, that by refraining from future illegal behavior, they—the offenders—could remain free from physical and other legal restraints/constraints and could thereby better pursue their desired *legal* pleasures and inclinations. (If they wished, they could do so even if little else, for instance, other persons' needs, mattered to them.) More precisely, the external controls could achieve those results if (1) they, and obviously their effects, were then somehow *maintained,* and especially, but not only, if (2) they included some actual, not just threatened, *lockup.*

SEC proponents believed this approach could achieve its behavioral goal even if the offenders remained largely unchanged as to their level of self-understanding, their understanding of others, and their underlying or even overt attitudes toward others. Moreover, even without those particular changes, the ability to refrain from illegal behavior and to better manage related desires and/or impulses could directly contribute to an improved—certainly a modified—self-concept and to increased self-confidence as well; in addition, such improvements/increases could be considered important aspects of growth and development itself, or they could help pave the way for it. Theoretically, this would be the case even though—when using the SEC approach—the ability in question would presumably have been brought to the surface and then often reinforced (1) in response to external force and via fear of physical punishment/restrictions, rather than (2) as part of, that is, as an important concomitant or product of, a broader growth and development. (It would thus parallel the type of reward/punishment-based growth/development—or learning—commonly seen with small children.)

27. In the SEC view, (1) even improved and extensive skills—practical and interpersonal skills—could not, by themselves, play a decisive role in preventing illegal acts. (Here, "decisive" contrasts with contributory or supplementary.) Presumably, and strictly speaking, (2) only the exertion of willpower could play that role in the sense of physically and specifically making a person move or not move. (As discussed below, other factors may help *set up* a situation or *relieve* it, but they themselves do not initiate or stop the physical action per se.) Regarding point (2), offenders, for example, must ultimately *decide* to move or not move their arms and legs; and, in the former case, they must then actually *move* those parts in order to carry out an activity. This process may often require several acts or efforts of will—ones that, collectively, are directed, sequential, and more or less coordinated. (Though an impulsive or sudden act may be relatively unplanned and simple, even it requires the above decision and internally directed movement—in short, exertion of will.) Moreover, the willpower and physical effort in question is ultimately the *offenders'*. Neither their peers, parents, nor others make or even *can* make the final decision to move or not move those arms and legs; and none of them can subsequently *move* those parts on a second-by-second basis so as to physically and literally sustain and direct the activity.

Next, a word about point (1), above. Even if one grants this point, the following, which is seldom considered in connection with SEC, is possible; moreover, it can occur independently of any external controls: (a) The utilization of practical and interpersonal skills—especially the efficient, effective, or even improved use of those skills—can help *motivate* many individuals to exert their will or willpower somewhat differently than before. This would apply especially, and perhaps more reliably, if that utilization were (b) followed by rewarding personal experiences. More specifically, the occurrence of (a) and (b), combined, could help motivate those offenders to exert their willpower to a greater *degree* than before (i.e., more strongly and/or more often), or perhaps in different *ways* and *areas*. These different degrees and ways may include the area of illegal behavior itself, among others. Also theoretically possible, if the skills in question were to help those individuals broaden certain positive aspects of their self-concept and increase their self-confidence in one or more practical/interpersonal areas—say, in education (or sports or employment), or in interactions with adults other than their parents—then, by gradual extension, the following might sometimes occur: A new or increased desire may emerge for them to exert their will or exert it differently in *other* contexts as well, for instance, in the face of delinquency-promoting, as well as growth-opposing, messages and harmful external pressures from parents, peers, or others.

Thus, even granting the SEC view that practical and interpersonal skills could not, by themselves, play a *decisive* role in preventing illegal acts—certainly not directly, physically, and specifically— there remains the possibility that they, for example, their utilization, could make *important* albeit indirect contributions, especially though not only if the skills in question (1) soon lead to satisfying moments as well as rewarding overall experiences and if they (2) suggest an other-than-slim chance of future benefits and enjoyments. Moreover, under some conditions or for certain individuals such contributions may be *essential* in the short and/or long run, even if they are not, by themselves, decisive in the above sense and contexts. This could be the case if, for instance, the external controls are not quite strong enough by themselves, for whatever reasons. It might also or alternatively be true once those controls (though already quite strong) have been discontinued, as, for example, after a program has ended or an agency's jurisdiction has terminated. Whatever the time or circumstances, such skills could help relieve pressures that might otherwise make it likelier that individuals will choose to exert their will in favor of illegal acts. In addition, they (plus any related improvements in self-concept) may give those youths more reason to (1) exert it in legal ways—and to regularly (2) retain their *ability* to fully exert it (e.g., by not becoming drunk or otherwise "high," and thereby giving known trouble-related impulses, tendencies, and/or specific desires as well as emotions greater relative power over one's immediate behavior).

28. Ideally, redirection/control would also help offenders modify or relinquish roles, loyalties, close personal relationships, and other adjustments that directly involve or significantly contribute to illegal behavior. (Various rehabilitation programs, themselves, try to affect such changes.)

29. Even in the SEC approach, some worker/offender discussions could presumably generate information about how and where to redirect various wishes, impulses, and so on; this could then be used to help reduce or perhaps even minimize pressures and opportunities to engage in illegal behavior. However, as to specifically precluding that behavior, that is, preventing it from occurring even if important pressures/opportunities *are* greatly decreased, SEC proponents considered the exchange of information, or even of certain feelings, insufficient. In particular, it was not (or they were not) the key factor(s), and this applied irrespective of how practical, enlightening, and supportive it (they) might have been. Instead, as indicated earlier, the only key factor that existed—the only critical or decisive ingredient—was the offenders' exertion of willpower; more precisely, it was that exertion (1) *in response to* the individuals' fear or dislike of physical punishment/restrictions/inconveniences and (2) *in order to* preclude, reduce, or avoid whatever those offenders considered major attendant losses. Yet, if the subject matter of (1) and/or (2)—for example, the "fear or dislike" in question—was indeed a necessary basis for activating and sustaining that critical ingredient, the following would apply (assuming no other factor could adequately compensate for the "lack" in question): If, for whatever reasons, those offenders did *not* have much fear/dislike of the particular punishment/restrictions they were receiving or might receive, or if those individuals were *not* particularly bothered by the attendant losses of or reductions in certain activities, enjoyments, and the like, then SEC, if used by itself, would

theoretically lack the types of leverage or the overall power and focus needed to achieve its basic behavioral goal.

In this connection the following might be noted. At one or more points in their lives, certainly during and soon after their first or second formal correctional experience or program, many offenders do substantially fear/dislike the given punishments/restrictions and they genuinely wish to avoid or reduce the known attendant losses. Partly—sometimes largely—for these reasons, they may refrain from illegal behavior. However, as time passes subsequent to program completion or agency jurisdiction, significant changes may take place (this can also occur after rehabilitation programs): In some cases offenders may grow accustomed to hardships, social limitations, and constraints; or they may feel increasingly defeated and dejected, and might even backslide with respect to interpersonally responsible behavior. They may adapt and harden themselves to other life circumstances and may undergo various attitudinal/personality changes that are not primarily situational and transitory and that may subsequently affect their behavior and outlook in any event—and may lower their expectations/aspirations in particular. Directly related to these changes, many such individuals may no longer fear, feel overwhelmed by, or greatly mind the types of punishment, and so on, that they previously experienced, were threatened with, or only expected. In effect, they may no longer worry or care as much about various correctional inputs and conditions that *were* previously effective, whether to a large degree or only barely. In addition, the losses and delays that were previously experienced, and others which were threatened or potential, may no longer seem as important to them or perhaps as hard to bear. This could apply even if the individuals now have few if any substitutes in mind for the future possible losses of or reductions in given activities, enjoyments, and the like. These changed attitudes toward, and reactions to, correctional punishment and other disincentives may, by themselves, substantially decrease the individuals' previous, that is, program-induced, level of resistance to illegal behavior, and they may thereby raise the chances of recidivism. At about the same time (still post-program), internal incentives to engage in such behavior may *increase,* for whatever reasons, and external incentives may *be* increased. (Both types of increase may occur whether they are contributors to or results of the decreased resistance, or even if they are largely unrelated to it.) Obviously, as this occurs, one or both such incentives can themselves increase the likelihood of near-term recidivism. Still, as implied, the likelihood of recidivism would be greater than before even without these incentives, as long as decreased resistance exists.

By way of summary and implications: (1) The SEC approach may be overly reliant upon a single factor: the exertion of willpower. This applies independently of the fact that if additional factors were to play substantial roles in SEC-oriented programs, this in itself might increase the latters' chances of success. (See point [4], below.) Thus, overreliance may exist not just because other factors, such as utilization of skills, ordinarily play a somewhat small role in SEC, but because the earlier-mentioned conditions that are believed to activate and sustain the exertion of willpower may be weaker than assumed (within individual offenders), however widespread they may be (across those individuals). (2) Once a program has ended, the deterrent value of previously effective punishments and restrictions may substantially decrease through time, as might that of related losses/delays of enjoyable activities. This may result from attitudinal/personality changes within the offenders themselves, for example, in conjunction with various life circumstances. (3) Many such post-program changes, ones that may directly or indirectly increase the chances of recidivism, would—theoretically—be less likely to occur, or would have a less negative impact, if those individuals had undergone considerable growth and development as persons during their original and/or subsequent correctional contacts. For instance, such growth might have prevented or tempered the offenders' earlier-mentioned, post-program decrease in

resistance to illegal behavior, and/or their increased interest in it, per se. (4) The development and utilization of additional factors, such as practical and interpersonal skills, may help many individuals better address important conditions relating to illegal behavior; among those conditions might be pressures from family and peers. Also—*subsequent* to the program—those factors might help offset the decreased deterrent value of given punishments and other disincentives.

30. Not that the *public,* for one, had previously recognized and been interested in more than a handful of distinctions among them.

31. This fact was taken to mean that offenders (O's), especially SMOs and the violent, were substantially different—as *persons*—than most nonoffenders (NO's). Many professionals emphasized this O/NO difference even though "nonoffenders" essentially meant the given individuals had no known *law contacts*—a variable which did *not,* itself, focus on them as persons, for example, on their personalities or their types/levels of adjustment. This gap or discrepancy suggested that the assumed O/NO difference as persons perhaps did *not* simply refer to the O/NO difference in *law contacts,* as such. Instead, the law-contacts difference was apparently an expression of some other difference, one that did directly involve personality or (other) manner of adjustment. To SEC proponents the latter difference seemed to mainly involve particular attitudes or traits, or, more generally, the dimension of *character* (see below). As indicated above, this difference was apparently considered substantial—especially, but not only, when serious and violent offenders were involved.

Despite the size and perhaps the nature of this difference, most proponents did not go so far as to specifically describe most SMOs and violent offenders as "sick," that is, as very disturbed or as having serious problems. (Here, "serious problems" means troubled well beyond [1] being burdened with the usual types or degrees of adolescent difficulties or worries, and even occasional crises, and [2] sometimes being or feeling unable to adequately handle those matters.)

Nonetheless, the implication was that O's and NO's were quite different—in general, characterologically different; and here, one common distinction, though not necessarily the "core" difference if there was one, often seemed to involve the concept of "moral deficiency" in the case of O's. At any rate, most SEC proponents seemed to believe there *was* a deficiency or lack, one that almost always involved poor self-discipline/self-control with respect to given impulses, desires, and emotions; and this lack was usually seen as ranging from moderate to very serious, rather than being somewhat minor—and/or rather transitory—or, in many cases, even largely situational.

(It might be noted that one could view these offenders as "deficient" without ipso facto considering them "defective"—defective, especially in the sense of being generally *inferior* [this, as a relatively permanent condition, not just—say—a temporary state], or else somehow—possibly even intrinsically—*broken* [perhaps from early childhood]. In this regard, "defective" would overlap with "sick," itself. It would do so because both terms, certainly the latter, emphasize the idea of being seriously—especially chronically—problemmed or flawed, and not just in a small or unimportant part of one's self. "Deficient," on the other hand, could be viewed as far short of "sick," and certainly as much less pervasive.)

At any rate, SEC proponents seldom made a point of describing these offenders as "psychologically sick"—especially as being deeply disturbed or even "mentally unbalanced," particularly in the manner often associated with the *medical model* and commonly expressed in terms of various psychiatric diagnoses and/or psychological labels. During those years the medical model was being strongly, almost exclusively, and—in part—validly linked with rehabilitation. However, SEC proponents largely rejected various rehabilitation practices and beliefs and, with them, the medical model. They believed, in any event, that rehabilitation programs—regardless of *differences* among them—were improperly focused, since they did not center directly and almost exclusively on illegal behavior per se.

Moreover, most SEC proponents did not seem to consider most offenders "sick" in the first place, at least not in the manner, and to the extent, implied by psychiatric diagnoses, by various labels, and so on.

As indicated, these proponents distinguished their own approach from rehabilitation. The latter approach, but not the former, emphasized the importance of seriously addressing personal problems/needs, often in an individualized way. Rehabilitation proponents realized that if individuals were indeed troubled, not to mention "sick," their problems could hardly be downplayed let alone ignored; at least they *should* not be, if, for one thing, resources existed. (This position did not imply that most rehabilitation proponents considered most SMOs and violent offenders sick, defective, or mentally unbalanced, as opposed to often being troubled, very troubled, problem-laden, and/or psychologically confused; the distinction in question was important.) SEC proponents, on the other hand, seemed to feel that since the main difficulty that related to illegal behavior centered around a *character* problem—such as a "bad attitude," a willfulness or recalcitrance, an exploitive stance, or a self-centered, hedonistic, short-term outlook—it made sense to mainly emphasize strong external controls. Here, the assumption was that these controls would, in effect, force the given individuals to direct their willpower against impulses, desires, and emotions that were reflected in those attitudes, in the recalcitrance, in the hedonism, and so on. This strategy, which would hopefully produce greater self-control/self-discipline with respect to forces or factors (e.g., impulse) that were involved in illegal behavior per se, required essentially no counseling and no related inputs that would otherwise be focused directly on psychological problems or personal/individualized difficulties and needs. This was not just because willpower, by itself, could be decisive under certain conditions, but because the given offenders presumably did not have very large, or very deep, personal/psychological problems, such as severe internal conflicts, in the first place. (Skills, themselves, could almost always be used, though they, too—like the increased self-insight and sensitivity to others that could result from counseling and/or related inputs—were not considered essential or critical to controlling various impulses, desires, and emotions related to illegal behavior.)

Moreover, if a certain percentage of offenders *did* turn out to have very serious personal problems—for instance, if (1) the earlier-mentioned attitudes/traits were deeply or firmly rooted after all and did not just represent superficial or situational role behavior and defenses, and especially if (2) those offenders were in fact disturbed or "defective" to the point where they "probably could not be repaired anyway" and might often have considerable difficulty controlling themselves, as well—then the following would apply (still from the perspective of SEC proponents): There would be even *more* reason to impose strict *external* controls, to probably highlight this feature above all others, and to make relatively little effort to change those offenders as persons. Thus, the basic approach would remain one of containment, not one that tried to combine control with considerable growth and development.

32. Their frequent resistance against "acquiring . . . and exploring" was not considered apparent only, and it was not, for example, assumed to mainly reflect any of the following factors: (1) A *general passivity*—usually together with a lack of much enthusiasm about most things, including the adolescent-oriented. (2) A *specific disinterest* in adulthood per se, one that stemmed from the individuals' overall immersion in, and generally active interest in, their daily lives as adolescents. Though these youths probably had little or nothing *against* adulthood as they understood it—or nothing special against it—that period or aspect of life, with its more settled adjustment and its overall responsibilities, nevertheless had little drawing power for them. (It had little such power when viewed as a *totality* or overall life-style, even though some individual features and opportunities often did interest them.) As a result, serious preparations for independent living would, in these youths' view, get underway only in the indefinite future—presumably all in good time. This also applied to the initiation of new behavior patterns and lifestyles that related to adult responsibilities and roles. Meanwhile, it was "time" for adolescence—its own pressures and problems notwithstanding. (3) Relatively *little stimulation by,* or *poor/insufficient information from,* one's environment.

If the low interest or actual resistance shown by these individuals to moving forward *had* mainly reflected one or more such factors, then an emphasis on strict external controls—certainly a heavy and principal emphasis—would probably be unnecessary in the first place and would leave those factors and related issues largely untouched. At any rate, SEC would then be less relevant to those factors/issues than would other possible approaches, such as rehabilitation; and, other things being equal, SEC would address them to a much lesser degree and less effectively as well. For instance, if (1), (2), and/or (3) were major contributors to the youths' resistance or to their low interest in moving forward, then, when using certain rehabilitation programs, this situation—theoretically—could be markedly altered by somehow "turning them (the youths) on," by "energizing them," by "cluing them in," or by otherwise activating, focusing, and peaking their interest.

In such programs, individually and collectively, those and related intermediate goals might be achieved by providing some of the following: enjoyable new experiences, appropriate and stimulating challenges, role models, encouragement, general and specific guidance, and better/more/new information about self and others and about opportunities relating to education and employment. However, when using *SEC,* such approaches and techniques would probably be given low priority in the first place, since they would be seen as not directly focused on the reduction/elimination of illegal behavior. As a result, the turning on, the energizing, and so on, would be less likely to occur, or it might not be achieved to the same degree. To be sure, from the standpoint of SEC, this outcome, by itself, would hardly matter—as long as external controls ended up reducing the illegal behavior itself.

INDIVIDUALIZATION, OFFENDER NEEDS, AND RELATED ISSUES

This chapter begins by briefly reviewing issues raised in Chapter 29 regarding overly simplified and static views about offenders. It then discusses implications of these views for intervention and it focuses on offenders' interest in, as well as resistance to, change and growth. The chapter then turns to several issues that, though in some cases touched on earlier, need further specification or elaboration. Among these are the feasibility of an agency's simultaneously implementing many individualized intervention plans, the complementary roles of "core" and "as-needed" program elements, and the structural distinction between individualized and differential intervention. Next, self-fulfilling prophecies are discussed, as is their possible avoidance; after that, the chapter reviews the role that an emphasis on offender needs and on long-term community needs can play in reducing specified implementation problems. Finally, a few words are said about the validity and utilitarian significance of viewing offenders as individuals with important needs and features in common with nonoffenders—and, again, about various beliefs regarding the likelihood and extent of change in troubled youths.

Dominant Views Regarding Offenders: Review and Discussion

The following relates to *delinquents in general*—even more to serious multiple offenders (SMOs). Emphasis will be on that part of the public, and on those professionals, who— jointly—have had the largest overall influence on corrections in recent decades. Together, they will sometimes be called the dominant group.

Highlighted Features

Since the mid-1970s, most members of this group have had an inadequate view of offenders, yet one which has heavily influenced their actions.[1] Though this view highlights features that *are* commonly found among these youths, and which are important in understanding them, it omits or greatly downplays others. While the latter are usually less evident than the former on cursory examination, they are no less real, no less important, and just as common. As a result, the dominant group's view is oversimplified and, for reasons indicated below, misleading in significant ways.

Specifically, the view that this group has held heavily emphasizes offenders' hostility, impulsivity, and often-strong resistance to relinquishing or substantially reducing illegal activities and related adjustment patterns. Closely associated with those features is the belief that these youths are not just more assertive/aggressive than nonoffenders and less under the control of adults, but that they are headstrong and recalcitrant in particular, and, in most cases, self-centered and deceptive. Further, the public largely accepts at face value certain facades often presented by many offenders, particularly those of considerable self-confidence and broad self-satisfaction.

Together, this cluster of features has produced a dominant impression of offenders as "willful" persons—willful in "wanting what they want, *when* they want it," and in their resistance to relinquishing/reducing delinquency. Though these youths are generally considered headstrong, they are not primarily thought of as being oppositional simply for its own sake, or, say, mainly to resist adults on principle. Nor is their resistance mainly viewed as an effort to remain "teenagers" per se, in order, for example, to enjoy its common, socially accepted activities (many of which they do enjoy). Instead, the dominant group associates these youths' willfulness and resistance with a specific interest in maintaining their illegal or borderline-illegal activities and adjustments. Thus, their willfulness/resistance is not viewed as *mainly* reflecting their presumed, active disinterest in, or at least moderate opposition to, moving toward adulthood and increased responsibility per se (a disinterest/opposition which nevertheless does exist to some degree; see "ambivalence," below).

All in all, these offenders are considered other than simply somewhat atypical teenagers or even moderately eccentric ones (or, for that matter, simply rather "testy" and often "impertinent" ones)—individuals who are otherwise "basically social" and "will soon come around on their own." They are assumed to give little thought to other persons, or to their own future. With few exceptions, they are thought to be in what could be called a "static" condition developmentally or psychosocially. Specifically, they are seen by the dominant group as not especially wishing to change or grow as persons, even though they may often wish to alleviate their life circumstances and improve themselves materially. (Many people in the dominant group missed and still miss the following: The fact that numerous adolescents and delinquents [1] often resisted adults' suggestions and [2] showed less interest in traditional adulthood and in assuming more responsibility than most adults would have wished did not mean those youths were almost entirely *uninterested* in growing/changing as persons, and in gaining/improving various skills. Their desire to change—at least in certain ways—existed despite their ambivalence and hesitancy about doing so and about largely relinquishing adjustment patterns that provided them some satisfactions and relief.)

The public/professionals in question do not just regard these youths' hostility, impulsivity, and so on, as distinctive and distinguishing characteristics, but of no special significance beyond that. Instead, they assume—implicitly, in the case of the public—that one or more such features constitutes an active force, often the principal force, that sets the stage for illegal behavior or which directly triggers specific delinquent and destructive

acts themselves. In any event, these features, certainly when aggregated, are viewed as central to the individuals' delinquency—a point which indirectly implies that the *omitted or downplayed* features (mentioned shortly) are not particularly important, let alone central. Moreover, even though factors such as hostility and impulsivity are implicitly—and accurately—assumed to be more easily triggered in certain contexts, as, for example, ones involving delinquent peers or the use of drugs and alcohol, the following also applies: To many people, the omitted features—such as self-doubt—are implicitly assumed to be intrinsically less suited to delinquency than are hostility, impulsivity, and so on, whether in those or other contexts. This is largely because self-doubt and the other omitted features seem directly antithetical to, or at least general impediments to, the self-assertion, aggression, and risk-taking that are commonly associated with the act of committing a crime—especially, but not only, a violent one.

To the dominant group, this picture of delinquents and causation thus places such features as willfulness, aggression, and self-centeredness in the forefront of intervention. In particular, it suggests the following, especially to many of that group's professionals: The correctional system's key task, indeed its only essential one, is that of directly confronting and overcoming the willfulness in particular. This task is to be carried out via actual and threatened punishments, restrictions, and the like—these presumably being the only inputs and conditions that can reliably gain most offenders' serious attention in any event, and the only ones strong enough to force most youths to resist delinquent peers and abstain from drugs and heavy alcohol consumption if necessary. In this intervention paradigm, only *those* inputs/conditions—assuming they are made strong enough and maintained long enough—would eventually make such willful individuals believe it is in their own best interests to control or even reject the impulses, desires, emotions, and situations that steer and thrust them into illegal activities and that are considered integral to their related adjustment patterns.

As to the illegal or destructive expressions of the aggression and self-centeredness, these, too, would be controlled or at least adequately redirected. Basically, this would occur as a natural and important by-product of the earlier-mentioned approach and its resulting control of willfulness. (The factors themselves—aggression, and so on—could thus largely remain; however, their expression would be more socially acceptable.) In any event, successful outcomes would ultimately derive from the power of external controls and from the offenders' subsequent decisions to control their behavior, even in difficult circumstances which they may have been unable to avoid.

Commonly glossed over or else ignored in this paradigm is a major possibility, one that is often borne out in actual life: Illegal behavior, and related adjustment patterns, may reemerge soon after external controls are removed or reduced, for instance, at program termination. At any rate, they may reemerge even if those controls have been *internalized* to a considerable degree, if and when internal or external pressures and difficulties increase. Such increases are common, after program and agency jurisdiction ends. (These pressures and difficulties are more likely to increase if the youths have gained few new emotional strengths, have developed or increased few practical skills, and have obtained few external supports during their program. Under these conditions, the pressures in question are also more likely to have a detrimental *effect* once they occur, even if the increase in pressure is only moderate.)

However, the dominant group's hope is that the previous behaviors and patterns simply will not return, or—across offenders—will seldom return. Basically, it hopes the external controls will have been *sufficiently internalized* to handle whatever pressures, difficulties, impulses, and temptations are likely to arise, increase, or remain. This is the case even though most professionals in the dominant group would probably acknowledge that the sources of those pressures, and other factors, may not have been addressed during the program, and that the pressures probably still exist or may largely exist when it ends. The hope, then, is that those pressures, and so on, will at least be controlled to the point of being neutralized with respect to *crime.*

Though that hope or wish is often fulfilled, it very often is not. Illegal behavior frequently returns within weeks, months, or less than a year after the program terminates, and it does so even when the external controls that were utilized have been internalized to a con-

siderable degree. It often returns because of the pressures—and impulses as well as fears—that are still active, and also due to the youths' related drive to reduce continued anxieties and psychological stress. These broadly stated dynamics exist in many offenders, and the pressures in question are not just external, say, from peers or family. Instead, many have been long-internalized, and are often strong.

For instance, various effects of internalized pressures and problems can be seen in individuals we have called "conflicted" and who are sometimes termed "neurotic." Many such youths compulsively repeat short- or long-term cycles of self-punishment and, in part, self-defeat. This also occurs even after these individuals have completed a standard institutional or community-based program and have, technically, thereby "paid their debt to society"—and perhaps to specific victims—for their previous, official, adjudicated offenses. In brief, many such individuals return to crime partly to set themselves up for further punishment, lockup, and "defeat"—and to relieve anxieties, stress, and fear—once they are caught or turn themselves in.

This situation generally occurs if they have not substantially reduced their underlying conflicts. It may also occur if they continue to live out (1) related, self-defeating life scripts they have not cast off and (2) various partial identifications with "losers" they know or know of, and with friends/relatives who have been involved in crime. In each case it can occur even when these individuals have developed or augmented several practical, interpersonal, and cognitive skills during their program, and even though various observers would likely agree they already have enough general ability, specific skills, and/or external resources to eventually obtain employment and "live a fairly normal life" if they wish.

At any rate, these offenders frequently react in ways the dominant group would not expect, that is, expect in response to strong and credible threats of future punishment, to major restrictions, and so on. In this regard, the offenders often do not seem to fit the above paradigm (viz., external punishment leads to deterrence), and they act contrary to what others would consider "their own best interests." However, as suggested, their "interests" are often mixed and partly self-contradictory, both at the surface and below. (This also applies to other youths, including many passive-conformists.) For a detailed discussion, see Appendix 46.

The following remarks are neither limited to, nor emphasize, conflicted and passive-conformist youths.

Omitted/Downplayed Features

We now turn to the main features or factors that the dominant public/professionals commonly omit or downplay: self-doubt, vulnerability, and ambivalence about changing and growing.[2] Individually and collectively, these features paint a picture quite different than one that highlights (1) willfulness, (2) considerable self-confidence/self-satisfaction, and so on. Yet, the *omitted* features are no less a part of the individual than are (1) and (2), even though (2) is largely facade. Functionally, these omitted features may be thought of as generally operating at different times than the earlier-mentioned ones, and often in differing contexts. Structurally, they may be considered different aspects or levels of the personality than (1) and (2).

(Such differences [or surface disparities] are common, and considered normal, in offenders and nonoffenders alike, both youths and adults. For instance, many nonoffenders consider themselves to be—and are—quite capable and confident in some areas or situations, yet barely capable, quite vulnerable, and routinely anxious in others, or at other times.[3] Similarly, that is, again by virtue of differences in context and time, the existence and operation of self-doubt, vulnerability, and the given ambivalence is not incompatible with the individuals' hostility, impulsiveness, resistance, self-centeredness, and related factors. The presence of these sets of features generally becomes evident in differing contexts or at different times.)

As with the highlighted features (hostility, etc.), the intensity of the omitted/downplayed ones is often considerable rather than slight. However, unlike hostility, and so on, these features (e.g., self-doubt) may not be evident on cursory observation; in any event, they are easily obscured by the earlier-mentioned facades. Most important, however, is the following. When these features are overlooked or downplayed, it is easier to assume that the offenders in question have more—stronger—willpower and self-control than they often do, and that these latter features (e.g., willpower), when present, are more reliable than they are and already apply to a broader range of challenges and situations than they do, for example, employment, continued education, and peer pressure. Moreover, when self-doubt, vulnerability, and ambivalence are not recognized as such or are not considered significant contributors to delinquent behavior or its related adjustment patterns, they are not likely to be considered important aspects of intervention. This would apply, say, to self-doubt and vulnerability mainly as targets of intervention, that is, as problems or conditions for youths to overcome or reduce. It would relate to the third omitted or downplayed factor, namely, ambivalence regarding change and growth, not just as a target but as a *force* that staff might use.

Change, Growth, and Planning

For instance, many people do not see, or they give little weight to, offenders' desire to change and grow—with growth, here, often including the wish to improve in certain ways. To some degree, this desire might be described as "underlying." This is because, although it is sometimes in the forefront of the individuals' consciousness, it is at least as often in the background (though fairly accessible).

At any rate, this desire is one side or "half" of most offenders' overall *ambivalence* about change/growth—a mix of contrasting desires that is not exclusive to conflicted youths.[4] The other half, of course, involves their desire to not change. This reflects, for one thing, their discomfort, anxiety, or fear with respect to relinquishing known sources of security, satisfaction (mental and physical), and relief—even though the type of security, and so on, that they now obtain might often seem minimal, unreliable, and, in a sense, very costly, to most observers. As implied earlier, this second half is not only integral to (1) the youths' resistance to moving toward adulthood per se, it is central to (2) their efforts to maintain given adjustment patterns that bear on delinquency. Point (1) applies whether or not the youths are clearer about what they want to relinquish or reduce—particularly as to behaviors and personality features (and they usually *are* clearer about these)—than about what they would genuinely like to acquire, especially by way of specific life-styles. (In the following, one might keep in mind the differing possible dimensions or areas of change, such as, practical skills life circumstances, attitudes toward and interactions with others, and personality.)

In any case, a large percentage of offenders do often want to change in certain ways—and/or they want changes to occur. When they visualize these personal and/or other changes fairly clearly they often hope these can occur sooner rather than later (as, e.g., in connection with acquiring or improving given practical skills or perhaps modifying their difficult life circumstances—say, their living arrangements or emotional relationship with parents). When their picture is less clear, they generally want the change to occur more slowly and to a modest degree (or sometimes not at all)—as in connection with new relationships and life-styles.[5] At any rate, these individuals, in some respects, want to change only slowly as persons; moreover, like most other adolescents, they can seldom clearly picture themselves making broad personal changes. Yet, in other, much less global ways, they may feel ready "right now"; this is sometimes seen in connection with specific personality features and interactional skills they would like to acquire, including some they may observe in staff.

Even when these youths can visualize certain changes and can understand their significance and potential benefits, those changes are not ensured. Moreover, even when youths initially seem to welcome possible change, caution is generally in order. For instance, regarding plans for offenders to acquire various *practical skills* via vocational and/or educational training, many such youths will show a fair amount of initial enthusiasm or at least interest. However, if their ambivalence about relinquishing certain present roles and adjustment patterns or about moving toward adulthood has not been reduced and remains relatively strong, their follow-up on those plans and on their initial involvement will often become superficial, and their efforts can be easily abandoned. In addition, if their efforts *are* largely abandoned or if they produce little apparent gain, this can sometimes arouse preexisting feelings of inadequacy or inferiority. (These possibilities do not mean such efforts should seldom be undertaken prior to the resolution or substantial reduction of various problems. In fact, even modest progress in areas of practical skills can sometimes make it easier for these youths to begin thinking about personal matters they would otherwise avoid. Moreover, youths can learn from seeming failure.)

Yet, with many other individuals, the efforts are much less likely to be half-hearted, even if substantial ambivalence exists. This, for instance, is often seen in adolescents—usually older ones—who are faced with immediate practical demands and/or unusually adverse circumstances. These offenders often recognize and accept practical skills as a vehicle that can directly help them in these regards. Age and circumstances aside, serious efforts are also seen among youths who have reached or are about to reach "Stage E" of adolescence (Era III) (see Chapter 27)—individuals who presently wish to further consolidate their lives and move forward, step by step (whether slowly or not).

Obviously, the situation with respect to change differs from one youth to the next. Moreover, with any given youth it may be complex and multileveled—whatever the amount of enthusiasm, ambivalence, and reality pressures. Given such differences and complexities—ones whose implications we have only alluded to—it can be seen why detailed information about offenders is regarded by rehabilitation-oriented persons as necessary and appropriate. In particular, a working knowledge of such factors as the youths' main motivations, interests, skills, felt and actual limitations, fears, defense mechanisms, and external supports/pressures is considered highly relevant to realistic planning. Such planning is also assisted by information about the sources, focus, and specific triggers of the offenders' self-doubts, hostility, and so on, not just about the extent to which these features exist. Insofar as information about such factors as "motivations, interests, [and] skills . . . " bears directly on change and growth—and it clearly seems to do so—it could be used to help staff work on both "halves" of the ambivalence. Not unrelated is the fact that some of those factors, for example, "limitations, [and] fears," bear on or involve self-doubt and vulnerability themselves, whereas others can relate to the individuals' hostility and impulsivity.

Knowledge regarding such motivations, interests, features, and the like can help staff figure out what to emphasize and count on, what to avoid and monitor, what is needed sooner rather than later, and what can serve as support as well as backup. It can furnish clues as to how one might generate interest and enthusiasm, or even provide effective encouragement and reduce anxieties early on. Because of this, many youths can experience positive feelings about the program relatively soon, thereby strengthening their attachment to it—and to staff—before various difficulties emerge or increase in their lives. This can help them further see the program as a potential *aid* in dealing with those difficulties when they arise, rather than viewing it as a source of added stress at an already troubled time.

In broader terms, such knowledge can help staff provide not only relevant and well-focused as well as timely direction, but appropriate structure, tactical and strategic support, and useful feedback. When combined with careful planning, with ongoing contacts, and with generally positive communication, it can help them provide this direction, and so on, while simultaneously allowing youths to not only retain as much autonomy as possible (within limits of safety), but to increasingly take the initiative and assume personal responsibility for the direction and content of their lives, not just for controlling their illegal behavior. Under such circumstances, change, on the part of most youths, can be more a product of their clarified and/or developing social desires than of various types of fear and avoidance.

Presumed Irrelevance of Change and Growth
The underlying assumptions in the above are that change which builds upon given motivations, interests, and skills is more likely to involve and produce emotional rewards along the way, and that those rewards will, in turn, put youths in a stronger position to develop new adjustment patterns, to seriously test and sort them out, and to eventually substitute the more workable and satisfying patterns for what would, by then, have become the older, decreasingly rewarding, and seemingly unnecessary ones. Yet, as implied, the dominant group, particularly many of its professionals, has assumed and still assumes the following: Even *if* those youths have a substantial wish to change/grow as persons, for example, to begin substituting various adult-related personality features and roles for certain "childish" or even teen-centered ones, and even *if* a rehabilitation or other program could help them achieve that goal, any and all such change would be of secondary importance only. This would be true because—presumably—that change would not be literally essential to the goal of *public protection,* that is,

not a sine qua non. All that is thought to be needed in order to achieve *this* goal is for (1) the correctional system to "turn off" the offenders' illegal behavior—not to "turn on" anything in particular. Moreover, all that point (1) supposedly requires is for (2) the offenders—using their willpower—to decide to turn it off and to then act on that decision as often as necessary. Point (2), in turn, could presumably be generated entirely by (3) the correctional system's application of strong external force.

From this perspective, all efforts and complications associated with rehabilitation/habilitation are therefore unnecessary and—strictly speaking—irrelevant, even if they help youths make the earlier-mentioned changes. Theoretically, or logically, those nonessential changes would even include improvements in vocational and academic skills. In actual practice, however, many people welcome such gains or simply do not oppose them, even when they consider them secondary. More specifically, except for uncompromising advocates of punishment only, vocational/academic training is largely supported if it is seen as not substantially interfering with efforts directed at the central goal, and if it may even indirectly promote that goal's achievement or enhance it insofar as it is, in fact, achieved. Such training *is* generally seen as not interfering, and it is largely accepted by other than those advocates.

Yet, very often, this same practice—namely, accepting efforts that do not significantly interfere, and whose products could possibly support and enhance—is not extended to the area of personal/psychological change.[6] This even includes change with respect to features that are considered, by strong-external-control (SEC) supporters themselves, to be key aspects of delinquency. (Here, change is distinguished from control, that is, from control of given features but without any *change* in those features.) Thus, from this perspective, one that is not just held by "uncompromising advocates," little or no effort should even be made to identify and reduce various forces and conditions that probably generated, sustained, and/or triggered the youths' major negative features themselves, such as hostility, impulsivity, and self-centeredness. (Our assumption, here, is that the redirection of such forces/conditions would, in turn, produce a change in—for instance, a reduction, elimination, or more acceptable expression of—those negative features, not just control or temporary control over them.) (Given this same premise, no efforts should be made to identify and address possible precursors of willfulness or misdirected willpower, themselves. This would be true even if one or both such features were considered the only ultimate generator[s], or at least a key trigger, of illegal behavior.) The same would apply to the identification and modification of internal and external factors that likely generated and reinforced self-doubt, vulnerability, and even feelings of despair, and to conditions that probably sustained significant family conflicts, overreliance on peer approval, given defenses (e.g., projection and verbal aggression), and so on. This would be especially true since, except perhaps for "overreliance on peer approval," SEC proponents seldom regard such features as key aspects of delinquency.

At any rate, many individuals in the dominant group essentially ignore or downplay the following idea; at least, they seldom wish to reflect it in actual program operations and ingredients: By reducing, modifying, or even diverting *underlying forces and conditions,* one can substantially decrease the intensity of, and sometimes even change the main objects of, various desires, emotions, feelings, and impulses. This includes, but is not limited to, desires, emotions, and so on that may lead to illegal behavior or that are directly involved in it. Instead, these individuals emphasize the view that external force and resulting self-control—control of illegal *products* of those underlying factors and conditions—are not only sufficient and entirely appropriate with the preponderance of offenders, but, all in all, are the only viable approach. As indicated, this view has also been held by SEC supporters who nevertheless consider it useful to increase offenders' practical skills. This applies regardless of whether they consider an absence or paucity of such skills an underlying but significant contributor to these offenders' past and present delinquency.

Difficulty of Change and Growth
Many strong-external-controls proponents have felt that the choice of their approach over rehabilitation is strengthened by the generally accepted view that the latter is difficult and time-consuming. For instance, even by the 1970s, many rehabilitation supporters had

indicated that if one wished to help serious multiple offenders substantially change/grow as individuals, it was not enough to just provide relevant *program components* and to use appropriate strategies and techniques, important though these were. Instead, considerable skill, sensitivity, determination, and time were also needed. In any event, rehabilitation was described as complex, and not just in a structural sense.

At the same time, however, other rehabilitation supporters left the impression that growth-centered intervention, even though it *was* relatively complex both structurally and dynamically, was only moderately difficult with most offender populations. This was the case even if it were implemented by staff who had an average level of prior experience, prior and ongoing training, and current supervision. Though this impression was probably left more by omission than commission, it was the one most widely held regarding rehabilitation until the early 1980s. In addition, its scope included many or most serious multiple offenders, at least by implication. (The view in question did not focus specifically on programs such as CTP, ones that were not just rehabilitation-oriented but which involved an offender typology and differential intervention in particular.) At any rate, SEC supporters essentially ignored this overly sanguine view. They focused—not without justification—on the more formidable difficulties that had been indicated, instead; and in that regard their main concern involved serious offenders, especially but not only the violence-prone, particularly in community-based programs.

Whether or not youths have violent offenses in their records, and whether intervention occurs in a community setting or not, it *is* difficult to successfully address serious offenders' often interrelated problems. For one thing, it requires considerable—though far from rare—skill to help them substantially reduce long-standing and/or powerful factors, such as high levels of self-doubt, vulnerability, and ambivalence.[7] The challenge is further complicated because one must address such factors while also bearing in mind, and often directly dealing with, the same youths' anger, impulsivity, distrust of adults/authority figures, and—at least initially—standard facades.

SEC proponents also generally recognized that considerable time and effort is needed to help many serious multiple offenders even develop various *marketable skills,* not to mention a "work ethic" (e.g., responsibility and reliability) and a level of frustration tolerance that could help those and other individuals retain their jobs. Time/effort was needed because—even here—staff had to initially break through the common barriers involving hostility, distrust, self-doubt, and ambivalence themselves; and often, they had to later revisit those obstacles.

Finally, it was also apparent to SEC supporters that even if various types of growth occurred and several personal-emotional problems were greatly reduced, those advances, by themselves, would not guarantee less crime. This situation, on top of the earlier-mentioned challenges, helped these individuals feel that if there was an easier, quicker, cheaper, and more direct way to reduce crime, one that would also be at least as likely to do so as rehabilitation, then *that* would be the best one to use (assuming it was humane and did not create special problems or buttress existing factors and negative conditions over and beyond what other approaches might have created/buttressed).[8] Indeed, beginning around 1975, many or most people believed rehabilitation might not reduce crime any more than would punishment/restrictions; and soon afterward, they began hearing there were quicker and easier ways, as well.

To rehabilitation supporters in general, the critical policy question has not been whether an intervention—assuming it is humane, and so on—is difficult, time-consuming, "direct," and the like. Instead, it has centered on whether those factors, given the present state of knowledge, are perhaps unavoidable. That is, it centers on whether they are unavoidable if one wishes to achieve results that are substantially better than ones produced by other approaches—more specifically, and wherever possible, results that are better on a long-term basis, and, also, ones that are more cost-effective in that particular context. As indicated, SEC proponents, in general, are satisfied with—or, at least, make few attempts to go beyond—a short-term framework, and with assessing cost-effectiveness in *that* context.

As to absolute or virtual guarantees, no known approaches, including SEC, provide these with respect to any given client. Yet, when one considers an agency's clients as a whole, that is, its collection of individuals, one can safely predict that crime will be reduced or eliminated for some, perhaps even most. Here, again, the issue should therefore center on "Which approach will reduce offending to a greater degree and/or for a higher percentage of clients during a given time period?"—not on whether it will guarantee success in any given case.

Selected Issues
Individualization and Operational Feasibility
Differences and Similarities
Each offender is ultimately unique, for instance, distinct from other individuals in the way he or she has combined various features, or in what might therefore be called a "gestalt" or "configurational" sense. Nevertheless, he or she also shares certain features as well as groups of mutually associated features with various other offenders. These single characteristics, and the often-interrelated groups or clusters of characteristics, include not just personality factors and variables such as those mentioned earlier—for example, impulsivity, vulnerability, and ambivalence about change—but broader needs, interests, and attitudes toward self and others.

Because of these shared features ("similarities") across offenders, the intervention that an agency or operating unit uses with any given client need not be unique in the following respect (as seen later, it *is* unique in a different sense—more specifically, at a different level of detail or abstraction): The intervention need not be totally different than all other interventions that the agency uses, in terms of their respective *components, strategies, and techniques,* in order for it to address the given client's needs, interests, and so on, in a sufficiently individualized way. (The following will emphasize the intervention's readily visible and often-easily-describable major content, and related factors.)

For example, the agency need not use completely different program components ("ingredients") with every client. This is true even though that agency or operating unit may, for example, often use different *combinations* of them (selected from among its full range of ingredients) with many of its clients,[9] or even though it may sometimes vary the order ("sequence") in which those ingredients are introduced, or perhaps their respective durations and intensities—again, across many clients.

Thus, if an agency were working with 50 clients during Year-X, it would not have to use 50 entirely, largely, or even moderately different approaches with them during any or all of that time. (Here, "approach" is used in its broad, commonly understood sense, one that refers to at least the main ingredients, strategies, and techniques, usually in combination.) This content-and-general-operational-*similarity* exists despite the fact that if each of the 50 hypothetical approaches (more concretely, 50 interventions) were examined in sufficient *detail*, for instance, if the sequences, durations, and intensities were compared with each other, each "approach" (since its ingredients, etc., would now collectively involve a particular configuration, combination, and set of interactions), *would* of course be somewhat different than the next; and in that specific sense it would be literally unique.[10] In effect, each approach would be unique when one reached this level of relatively fine detail; and this is the level that the individual client experiences.

Nevertheless, at the practical, functional level (this is where the agency and staff operate; i.e., it is the focus of *their* overall "experience," with clients collectively), there would still be large areas of similarity across the interventions: content similarity, similarity or identity of techniques, and so on. From the standpoint of operational feasibility, these similarities could outweigh the differences, with respect to their importance. As a result, it would be possible for a given agency or unit to collectively implement its numerous individualized plans in partly similar ways at any given time, without this becoming unwieldy let alone virtually unmanageable for the overall agency as well as the individual workers.

Core and As-Needed Elements
Basically, as implied, similarities in the interventions that are used across an agency's many clients would reflect, and take functional advantage of, the following:

1. Many or most clients have a number of critical needs and life circumstances in common with other clients.
2. These shared, critical needs and circumstances can be partly or largely addressed by the same types of program ingredients ("elements" viewed individually) as can some of the shared features (e.g., self-doubt) described earlier.

Such an element, mentioned in item 2, could be called a "core element" (1) if it were used with the *preponderance* of clients (or with every client) during some period or periods in the program—in many cases, during most or all of it—and (2) if its frequency of usage, say, its monthly rate, were substantial during much of the time it *was* used. (At least, it would be among the most often or most steadily used of the program's elements—whatever its absolute rate might be.) Chief among these core elements, at least in many programs, might be group and/or individual counseling, pragmatically oriented discussions, and standard limit-setting. (See endnote 11 for further details and regarding the use of other possible elements, such as the cognitive-behavioral or behavioral.)

As to other needs/circumstances—ones that are no less personal but are sometimes more specific or concrete (e.g., they may involve particular skills/abilities, or perhaps external pressures/disadvantages)—these could be addressed via other elements, such as the vocational, general educational, or placement. These might be called "as-needed" elements. (With any given youth, certain *core* elements, such as counseling or pragmatically oriented discussions, could sometimes focus on various *general issues* that arise in connection with each such area, for instance, the vocational or placement—issues that, in some cases, cut across a number of areas. Simultaneously, a given core element could be addressing one or more *other* areas, as well, such as ones centering on feelings and goals, generally or specifically.) Any one of *these* elements might be needed by anywhere from a small to a large percentage of the total client population. Also, quite often, it might be needed only during a smaller portion of the total program than might core elements (yet *when* it is needed, it would usually be used at a substantial rate—or, say, as often as the core). Besides vocational training, and so on, these ingredients could include remedial education, job counseling and placement, collateral contacts, family counseling, extra limit-setting, and material aid (e.g., clothing and transportation). Any such element would be used only with those clients who clearly needed, or could substantially benefit from, the specific services in question.

Such a "core plus as-needed" arrangement has been used in several successful, scientifically evaluated programs. Among them—besides *CTP*—are the *Winnipeg* (Manitoba), *CREST* (Clinical Regional Support Teams), *Boston* (Vocationally Oriented Psychotherapy), *CaVIC* (Canadian Volunteers in Corrections), *Los Angeles Camps,* and *Danish* programs (Barkwell, 1980; Lee and Haynes, 1980; Shore and Massimo, 1979; Andrews and Kiessling, 1980; Palmer and Wedge, 1989; Palmer, 1994; Wedge and Palmer, 1989; Bernsten and Christiansen, 1965). In virtually all programs the core elements were counseling, pragmatically oriented discussions, and standard limit-setting (external controls). The main as-needed elements were vocational training, academic training (or remedial education), collateral contacts, and material aid. Compared to the core elements, the as-needed were used in somewhat fewer programs and with fewer clients at a time. By using the latter features together with the core, each program was able to develop and implement a relatively individualized plan with each of its clients, even though the degree of individualization varied somewhat, across those programs. Collectively, these operations addressed adolescents as well as young adults; they were used with individuals who ranged from serious multiple offenders to much less serious ones; and they involved community and institutional settings alike. (For further details and discussion, see Appendix 47.)

Differential and Individualized Intervention

Though the following concepts do not focus specifically on those seven operations, they are relevant to them and could pertain to other programs as well. Moreover, they were operationalized in the CTP and Winnipeg programs in particular, especially regarding "differential intervention," as described.

In almost any agency at any given time, interventions that are partly different from each other yet partly similar are needed in order to adequately address the important, corresponding differences and similarities that exist across its clients. In this regard an agency, when working with, say, 50 clients, might use only five *broad types* of intervention ("overall approaches"). These types would have some core and as-needed elements in common with each other, yet each type would still differ from all others globally or configurationally. For instance, major differences across the five broad types might center

around the sequencing and intensity of certain as-needed elements, and perhaps around the presence or absence of one or two such elements. Or, differences might involve the presence/absence of certain *types* of *core* elements, such as group versus individual counseling, or even the presence/absence of particular techniques for interacting with youths (see Chapter 6 regarding techniques). Each of those five overall approaches might be used with, say, 10 clients—more specifically, with a set of individuals who have certain important motivations, needs, views of self/others, and personality characteristics in common with each other, and who might be called a particular "type" (category) of client in that regard. In this example, there would thus be five client types, and any given client would receive one of the five overall approaches, depending on his or her type.

From an individualized intervention perspective, the application of any overall approach to its particular client type can be justified under conditions mentioned shortly. This can occur despite the fact that, notwithstanding the presence of important similarities, significant *differences* also exist among the several youths who fall *within* any one of the five offender categories, say, among the 10 passive-conformists. It can also happen despite the fact that, notwithstanding the presence of important differences, significant *similarities* also exist across various offenders *regardless* of their category, for example, across those passive-conformists and the 10 anxious-confused individuals. Basically, the application (use) of that overall approach can be justified because each individual youth's personal needs, interests, abilities, limitations, life circumstances, and other factors/conditions can be accommodated even in the context of—that is, in *conjunction* with—such a relatively broad approach. More precisely, those needs, and so on can be accommodated, and can even be made to dominate the intervention plan and its implementation, as long as any aspect of the overall approach can be substantially modified or even entirely bypassed if necessary, for any given youth. (For related discussion, including details on individualization and its relationship to overall approaches, see Appendix 48.)

Generally speaking, then, even if one wishes to achieve considerable individualization, the use of an overall approach would be justified as long as, and to the extent that,

(1) a relevant, realistic, and flexible plan were developed and implemented. (Keep in mind that various aspects of the overall approach can themselves contribute to relevance, realism, and individualization.) If and as such a plan is developed and implemented, and is later modified if necessary, then (2) the given individual's more personalized needs, circumstances, and so on, will have been adequately accommodated, reflected, and addressed. This is true by definition, since item (1) is the basic criterion or indicator of item (2). It might be added that the clients' needs, and so forth, can be accommodated to this extent (i.e., at least adequately) by many, though far from all, agencies, depending largely on their respective resources, circumstances, philosophies, and related factors.

By contrasting these five globally different yet—substantively—partly similar approaches with each other, one can say the agency is using *differential intervention* (DI) with its clients. That is, some clients are receiving overall approach A, others are receiving B, and so on—through E. Yet, since each client's overall intervention is largely built around his or her personal needs, interests, and the like, the agency is simultaneously using *individualized intervention*. That is, any given overall approach is also being applied to a given client in a relatively personalized way, regardless of which particular approach—for example, which of the five—it is, and which *type* of client is involved. (Again, even the *common* features that define or distinguish any overall approach are relevant to the offender's personalized/individualized needs, interests, and so on. This is true even though these needs are also commonly found not only in other clients of the same type, such as in other passive-conformists, but among different types of clients as well, say, among the anxious-confused.)

Structurally, the "differential" aspect of intervention thus refers to an agency's across-client operations, whereas the "individualized" focuses on the nature of each client's program and plan. Regarding the intervention plan, "individualization" intrinsically involves more detail than would exist in connection with any overall approach alone, for example, more than with the general approach for passive-conformists as a group. Moreover, beyond its involving more *differentiation* and greater detail per se, but directly related to both, individualization, as we have described it (i.e., with its emphasis on motivations, interests, abilities, life circumstances, etc.), can increase or greatly increase intervention's relevance to the client's immediate and longer-range needs. It can first do so by increasing an intervention plan's accuracy, precision, scope, and timeliness—and, in the final analysis, its *integration* as a meaningful and realistic whole. To be sure, correctional staff and other individuals who believe there is little need for, or practical value in, *differential* intervention would generally see little if any separate—let alone greater—justification for the individualized.

Self-Fulfilling Prophecies
Program Resources
If one assumes offenders have little or no desire to change and grow and if one then establishes or maintains few program ingredients and activities that could help them do so, one sets up a self-fulfilling prophecy. In effect, one provides few vehicles through which those individuals could realistically challenge that assumption—few opportunities for them to display certain growth-related motivations and interests, and to perhaps develop or augment practical and interpersonal skills. Moreover, when program resources are scarce, such individuals will not just have fewer opportunities to change and grow than they otherwise might, and fewer chances to address and improve difficult life circumstances and negative peer relationships; instead, many may also have less *desire* to change than they otherwise might, and they may not try as hard or as often to do so.

In addition, when programming is thus limited, those individuals may have few or at least fewer good opportunities to manifest personal and interpersonal qualities that would be considered positive but which many people assume they have few or little of. They might have less overall motivation to display those features, as well. Partly by default (and thus, motivation aside), these individuals might instead be more likely than would otherwise be the case to manifest some of their *remaining* characteristics—including, in particular, the more "problem-centered" features, such as hostility and impulsiveness. At any rate, their more positive motivations, abilities, and personal features might less often come to the surface, be constructively channeled, and then further reinforced. The likelihood that these youths would change and grow in socially desirable ways would then be less than would otherwise be the case.

Staff/Youth Interactions

Whether or not program resources are scarce, and even if the offenders exhibit little hostility and impulsivity, these individuals may remain defensive in general and emotionally distant in particular. This is more likely to occur if staff mainly exhibit an unmistakably impersonal or distant attitude toward *them,* if they seem (to the youths) to do their job in a perfunctory way, and if, in general, they implicitly or indirectly convey any of the following messages/impressions to those individuals (before continuing, note that these messages/impressions may partly reflect staff's oversimplified and static views of offenders; also, and in any event, these staff inputs—particularly those that involve point 2, below—may be partly in response to the *youths'* initial distance, defensiveness, and distrust):

1. They, the youths, are of little interest to them (staff) as individuals, and are of general interest chiefly in connection with their negative features and their potential for continued illegal behavior.
2. They, the staff—not just in their role as representatives and protectors of society, but personally—very largely distrust them.
3. They, the youths, given the nature of their instant offense or their overall offense history, deserve relatively little time and attention, except for purposes of enforcing controls and in order to discuss crises.

Such messages or impressions—especially insofar as they convey emotional rejection, or dislike—can directly support or "confirm" specific expectations, stereotypes, negative images, and even fears these youths have of many adults/authority figures. Those perceptions, in turn, can then make it easier for many youths to decide to share only "safe" information and feelings with staff, and to be only as truthful as they feel they must. Beyond that, such inputs by staff can generally discourage those and/or other individuals from relaxing to the point where they can more easily display some of their positive, enjoyable qualities. Instead, the youths may largely maintain or heighten their regularly available defenses.

This overall situation may, in turn, help support staff's original assumptions about the youths. It may also reinforce certain early observations and conclusions on their part, for example, regarding those individuals' evasiveness and deceptiveness, and it may help some staff decide to broadly generalize from those observations, and conclusions. At that point, in fact earlier, this series of events can begin to confirm and reinforce messages/impressions 1 and 2 themselves (above), in the minds of offenders.

Whether they are conveyed from the outset or starting later on (i.e., as part of the subsequent staff/youth interactions), messages/impressions 1, 2, and 3 as well would be more than just a disincentive to sharing certain information and feelings. Instead, they would often revive feelings of self-doubt and vulnerability that exist beneath the facades, themselves; and, in general, they would arouse and reinforce some youths' long-standing beliefs that many people dislike them as individuals or would do so—and might also reject them—if they learned more about them. In this respect, those messages/impressions would be discouraging in a broad sense. (Such feelings and beliefs would not be aroused/reinforced in conflicted and passive-conformist youths alone.)

To be sure, many staff, including ones not engaged in comprehensive rehabilitation programs, often recognize that youths' initial defensiveness and emotional distance does not necessarily reflect their main personality features, let alone represent the full range. They also understand and are alert to reactions, misunderstandings, and so on, such as the above, and they can recognize facades as well. In addition, these individuals often realize the following. Among youths who already have limited confidence in themselves, who partly or largely dislike themselves, and who often expect to be rejected (and sometimes test this out), it often helps to feel that "someone important"—in this case, the staff person—has some confidence in them, believes they possess some positive qualities and are not essentially "bad," and is not mainly trying to "make life difficult" for them.

Given these types of awareness and concern, such staff are usually prepared to preclude or defuse negative spirals in their interactions with youths. They can use their knowledge and awareness even when they are engaged in programs that emphasize external controls and that contain (1) few and/or infrequently used core and as-needed rehabilitation-centered elements, and (2) few opportunities for concerted efforts by staff in any event. Nevertheless, it remains the case that many other staff's oversimplified, static views of offenders can, and often do, set the stage for the earlier-mentioned spirals and for negative self-fulfilling prophecies. This is particularly true if anger, impulsiveness, resistance, and so on, on the part of those youths, is regarded as their most important set of features—not just one important set—or if such features are considered the only ones to emphasize in intervention.

Overlooked Factors and Resources
Many people who believe that little other than punishment and strict external controls should be provided, and who think one should focus almost entirely on offenders' negative features, do not seem to recognize, accept, or attach much importance to the following factors, conditions, and resources:

1. Carefully planned, skillfully implemented efforts by staff can bring out the positives in the majority of serious multiple offenders; and, in many though far from all cases, such efforts can produce—usually fairly soon—internalized, relationship-centered controls. (Although these controls can be strong and often dominant, some external controls usually remain important during most of the program.)[12]
2. Sensitive, knowledgeable staff, when implementing a relevant, individualized plan, and when seen by youths as interested in their well-being, have a good chance of making alternative adjustment patterns seem plausible, interesting, or even appealing. At least they can make those patterns, or parts of them, seem worth *considering*—if only because they might help improve the youths' present life situation or be an improvement upon it.[13] Staff's chances of accomplishing this are substantially greater if these offenders consider them "worth listening to" more by virtue of their "brains" and general "know-how" than because of their sanctioning power and, in effect, the keys they hold to freedom. This often applies even in early stages of intervention.

3. Below the surface, and beneath their initial facade of self-satisfaction, many youths *are* interested in certain adults, ones we will call "potential, partial role models" (PPRMs). In effect, these offenders are open to acquiring various things from them—in a sense, certain powers.[14] (With any given youth this process is sometimes conscious; however, it is usually below consciousness, though fairly accessible to it.) More specifically, they often pay extra attention to these PPRMs, and they take them more seriously than other adults; this is due to certain aspects of the PPRM's (1) adjustment patterns or broader life-styles, (2) interpersonal and/or practical skills and abilities, and/or (3) personality features that have become apparent or which they often manifest. Basically, then, the youths are somewhat interested in (1), (2), and/or (3), especially in the latter two. These are aspects or features that the given youths would like to have or have more of, themselves—ones they consider acceptable and sometimes describe as "not so bad" or even "pretty good." Regarding factor (1), such adults—here, staff—can therefore provide guideposts or benchmarks for the future. With respect to (2) and (3), they and/or others can indirectly help youths who, by emulating and identifying with certain of their (staff's) characteristics, can sometimes feel better about themselves "right now," and can feel better liked by others, or potentially more likable—and, all in all, somewhat more hopeful about the future and less worried about new challenges or demands. This applies not only to youths who have comparatively few actual skills and areas of self-confidence at point of intake, but to those who have several of each. In both cases, it pertains to individuals who nevertheless have numerous self-doubts, several areas of vulnerability, and limited frustration-tolerance.
   A. Despite the above, youths' emotional security, their real-life security, and their sense of satisfaction will be stronger and more reliable in the long run if these are ultimately based on actual, tested accomplishments than if they rest or center

largely on a sense of *identification* with given individuals' behavior, attitudes, and perceived qualities—accomplishments included. However, such identification or partial incorporation is often an important step that can help many youths take further steps, ones that can promote and produce the accomplishments themselves. It can, for example, help them feel—or realize—that they do have the power to take such steps, and it can help them want to keep trying when obstacles arise.

B. Many youths pay attention to, and may even come to accept and appreciate, staff who may *not* be partial role models to them, whether in the above or other respects, but who nevertheless do certain things the youths find helpful. Specifically, these staff can help them deal with personal/interpersonal problems or with possible crises that they, the youths, recognize as such but feel or find themselves unable to handle on their own—and which they are willing to discuss with someone who seems interested. If staff have not, as of that point, made youths highly uncomfortable or defensive in general, if they have not conveyed negative messages/impressions such as those mentioned earlier, or if they have been able to overcome or substantially reduce any such messages and various related, preexisting stereotypes, most youths will be likely to consider them sufficiently approachable and trustworthy for those particular purposes. This is despite their recognition of the fact that staff, even if they "want to help" and are often sympathetic, must still be firm, often controlling (besides being basically in control), and always opposed to illegal and destructive behavior.

Finally, many people, not all of whom are SEC supporters, oppose rehabilitation with serious multiple offenders for reasons which—at base—are other than that "it is usually difficult and time-consuming." These reasons, specified next, are not unrelated to the earlier-mentioned stereotypes and oversimplifications. In addition, and *related* to those inadequate views themselves, the opposition (objection) partly reflects those individuals' nonrecognition of, or else skepticism about, point 1 above (namely, the factor of "carefully planned, skillfully implemented efforts").

In particular, the objection in question centers on the individuals' underlying anxieties regarding these offenders' actual or potential violence and on their own related unwillingness to "take a chance" with those youths, especially in community-based settings in lieu of lockup. (Such anxieties have often been considerably reduced by programs that excluded individuals who had an official record of recent, substantial violence—not, for example, occasional, brief fisticuffs with peers.) What these persons do not realize or accept is that, under various operationally feasible albeit challenging conditions, such as those described in this book, the degree of risk is greatly reduced and most youths themselves soon want to show they can progress and be trusted to not break the law. Point 1, above, reflects one such condition; points 2 and 3 provide clues regarding other factors.

Taken together, the several threads of this discussion suggest it is possible to set up *positive* self-fulfilling prophecies, ones to which—as with the negatives—both the staff and the youths actively contribute. Though youths would have ultimate responsibility for carrying through, staff—and agency—must be careful not to short-circuit, derail, undermine, or neglect the process at any point. In particular, they must initiate and maintain it on a constructive basis, one that also makes as much overall sense as possible to the youths, even though the latter might dislike certain restrictions, requirements, and program ingredients that are necessary at the time.

Staff can greatly increase the chances of starting off right if they tap into the youths' motivations, interests, and skills, if—based on clear support from the agency—they make available a program that can allow these individuals to utilize and further develop those positives, and if they actively encourage the youths to do so. For much of this to happen, staff must, from the start, think in terms that extend well beyond the earlier-mentioned stereotypes and restricted as well as static views. They should, in effect, draw on the range of dimensions that constitute offenders not only as self-defending individuals but, simultaneously, as developing persons. The latter aspect would include characteristics that reflect their underlying and sometimes verbalized desires to be happier and better than they often feel they are.

Deservedness, Need, and Program Improvement

Though several aspects of "deservedness" were discussed in Chapter 29, some will now be further considered, mainly in connection with need, program improvement, and the community. Related issues will be examined.

Issues and Problems

Deservedness, or merit, should encompass both punishment *and* assistance, as reflected in the question, "What type and degree of punishment and assistance do offenders merit?" Regarding assistance, one should further ask, "What does the *community* deserve, and need, from the justice system?" (Since some aspects of assistance are found in deservedness as well as need, these two partly overlap each other.) If one wished to integrate these questions, say, around the dimension of *need*, one might further inquire, "How would (1) deservedness as well as need, on the part of offenders, relate to (2) certain needs, on the part of the community—needs that it deserves to have considered?"[15] We will briefly address this question.

When sentencing offenders, judges and juries generally try to address both the deservedness and need dimensions, especially the punishment aspect of deservedness and, to a lesser extent, the assistance component of need. That is, they try to provide a composite but blended response—in a sense, a compromise. This response often reflects other factors as well, such as retribution.[16]

When correctional staff then receive those offenders and soon spell out the terms or implications of their sentences—that is, when they "flesh them out" and partly interpret them in order to develop intervention programs or to apply/adapt already available ones—certain problems often arise. That is, they arise *when* (not primarily and automatically *because*) those staff translate—in effect, transfer and assimilate—the intervention-related meanings or implications of those sentences into their own agency's "reality" and/or "culture," one that has its particular

mix of ideologies, priorities, opportunities, and correspondingly distributed resources.[17]

Those problems, mentioned below, reflect not just the mix itself, and not just the pulls, tugs, and gaps that frequently exist in connection with the above dimensions, for instance, between, or in relation to, deservedness and need. Instead, they also reflect interactions between that mix, on the one hand, and the issues associated with those dimensions, on the other. (For present purposes, it will suffice to mainly focus on the pulls, tugs, and gaps themselves, not on their interactions with the mix.) The problems in question can occur not only with respect to an agency's overall program, for example, its structures or operations that affect many or most clients, but in intervention plans developed for any particular individual. In addition, the intensity of those problems can vary, depending on how staff interpret deservedness and need themselves; this, of course, goes back to the earlier-mentioned *mix,* insofar as this reflects ideologies.

Broadly stated, when pulls, tugs, and/or gaps exist in connection with the earlier-mentioned dimensions, various program elements or activities are not as well coordinated with each other as they could be; or else they are inadequately implemented, singly or in combination. (This does not mean that all coordination/implementation problems result solely from those pulls/tugs/gaps.) More specifically, and focusing largely on the coordination problem, important facets of a program may mutually conflict or otherwise interfere with each other; they may frequently fail to support and utilize one another, as well. Both types of problems—conflict/interference, and failure to support/utilize (or, insufficient support/utilization)—are sometimes observed, for instance, in interactions between the punishment-related expressions of deservedness, on the one hand, and various assistance-related expressions of offender and community-need, on the other. Often, and to a substantial degree, such problems emerge, or are increased, when neither the deservedness dimension nor the need dimension has been given clear and/or consistent operational priority over the other—and, as implied, when they pull in different directions, mainly by virtue of serving substantially different, albeit partly overlapping, goals. The upshot is that, under these circumstances, such programs are less effective than they would otherwise be, say, with regard to reducing recidivism.

Given this issue of priority and that of differing goals, and also given the pulls, tugs, and gaps involved, the existence of some poorly coordinated, mutually divergent, and/or directly conflicting program elements and activities is virtually inevitable—even though it is often minor and nonserious. (Related as well as different problems—again, often nonserious ones—may also occur in connection with inadequately and/or inconsistently utilized *individual* elements/activities, and with components of intervention plans themselves.) Nevertheless, poorly coordinated, mutually divergent, and/or directly conflicting elements frequently *do* involve or result in important missed opportunities, and they often *are* counterproductive to a significant degree. These undesirable outcomes can occur with inadequately/inconsistently used elements and with poorly coordinated intervention plans as well.

Priority and Critical Goal
Because these more substantial losses and difficulties can collectively dilute or even preclude the high levels of program planning and functioning that are needed in order to work effectively with serious multiple offenders, and even with the somewhat less serious, they and related problems should be reduced when possible. Basically, this reduction could be facilitated by prioritizing the earlier-mentioned dimensions in the manner specified next—one that, moreover, could pave the way for much better implementation of a *goal*, and of a closely related *means* (also specified below), that we consider critical when working with those individuals.

In other words, two major factors (one being a particular prioritization, the other a particular goal), plus a related one (a means), could make a sizable difference with respect to avoiding or substantially reducing certain coordination/implementation problems. This third factor could increase the chances of achieving that outcome in the first place, and it could enhance the effect produced by the first two as well. All that is apart from the fact that an even larger effect could be obtained if one were to reduce some of the difficulties associated with the earlier-mentioned mix, and could thereby reflect the broader combination of forces involved in the overall interaction.

Specifically, one of those dimensions—namely, *need,* especially community need—would be given clear priority over the other—*deservedness,* especially offender deservedness with respect to punishment; this could be done despite the partial overlap between those dimensions. In addition, program activities that address need, deservedness, and other dimensions should be mainly oriented around, or otherwise directed at (not just be consistent with), the "critical goal": helping communities better meet their *long-term protection needs* regarding the given clients. Those steps—prioritizing need over deservedness, and emphasizing that particular goal—would allow and substantially help the deservedness and need dimensions involved in inquiry (1)/(2) above (see first paragraph of "Issues and Problems") to be more consistently and frequently coordinated than they often are, and less often in substantial conflict.[18] However, as indicated, one other step is important, one that relates to the type of means—the "intervention focus"—that is involved. As suggested, this particular means could further increase the degree of coordination and could decrease the level as well as frequency of conflict. This is apart from its remaining contributions to the reduction of recidivism.

Intervention Focus and the Needs-Centered Approach
In trying to achieve the critical goal, one would not mainly use just *any* means, such as very long incarceration (thus, lengthy incapacitation), especially but not only if it were accompanied by few concerted attempts to rehabilitate offenders. Instead, one would mainly focus on helping those individuals change and grow, especially in long-lasting ways. This, in particular, would be the "central means" to the earlier-mentioned "end" of long-term community protection, and it might be called "long-term intervention." This "means," when combined with that end and with the earlier-mentioned prioritization, could provide an impetus, an overall direction, and a self-consistent framework for specific action; and it is those factors, particularly the latter two, that would provide a basis for better interrelating and coordinating deservedness, need, and other dimensions. This particular goal/means framework, when combined with that prioritization, could be called a needs-centered approach (NCA), and it could allow for individualized

intervention as well as encompass the need for near-term protection.

As indicated, NCA's long-term intervention would be the central or, certainly, *a* central means to an end; and that end—the critical goal—would emphasize a major, long-term community need. Since deservedness—broadly conceived (i.e., as also including assistance for *offenders*)—would be an important part of that intervention (which includes assistance and external control), deservedness itself (not just its punishment and/or control aspect) would be relevant to the life of the community. This would apply especially but not only insofar as that intervention were to reduce recidivism.

Relevance to the "life of the community," at least most communities in contemporary society, involves more than the critical issue of long-term protection/security. Moreover, it includes but goes beyond the embracing and expressing of certain widespread beliefs, feelings, and/or assumptions about what other people should be accorded, at a minimum. (Also, these beliefs/feelings/assumptions are separable from but not unrelated to those which comprise what is often called humane treatment, not just in its physical sense.) For instance, relevance to the "life of . . ." reflects yet goes beyond the idea that offenders, by virtue of still being humans (albeit ones who have offended, even seriously),

1. have a right or perhaps natural right to be *treated* as humans,[19] even if one is afraid or wary of them (as many people *are* of various *other* individuals—ones not known to be offenders, and who are treated decently despite that fear);[20]
2. have a right to change (not just to wish for it)—change, moreover, in ways that often involve more than controlling/ reducing their illegal or destructive behavior, and which thus go beyond society's minimum requirement regarding type of change; and
3. deserve some reasonable opportunities to change (change regarding the minimum requirement, and beyond); this would include at least having access to relevant means for change.

Instead, "life of . . ." also relates to the fact that if these individuals do change, some of their positive change that goes beyond the minimum may eventually benefit the community in concrete ways. Individually or collectively, some such benefits—including intentional contributions and even assistance per se—might be quantitatively and qualitatively similar to those provided by many nonoffenders themselves, over the course of several years.[21] In short, a community might benefit from offender change in concrete and practical ways that might be other than those involving increased protection alone. These gains would constitute an important part of what could be considered relevant, to the community, about (a) programs that provide direct and indirect assistance that offenders are often thought to need, and about (b) according offenders rights/opportunities such as #1 through #3, above. The latter are rights and opportunities that most *non*offenders are, in fact, allowed or given, by most communities, simply because they are human—ones that offenders themselves are commonly thought to deserve on those same grounds, whether or not the granting of such rights/ opportunities is considered part of humane treatment per se.[22] If (b) were accompanied by considerable (a), the concrete/practical gains to the community would probably be larger and/or more frequent than if it were not.

(Such gains would be independent of other, less tangible ones. The latter include those which may be *felt* by members of a community or society mainly as a result of their individually, and collectively, knowing the following: (1) that they have supported the earlier-mentioned beliefs, ones that include certain standards of fairness, as well; and, (2) that they have done so mainly, though not entirely, apart from what they might thereby obtain, "in return," by way of tangible gain over and beyond increased protection.[23])

Regarding the various practical benefits that needs-centered programs might eventually provide the community as a result of their direct and indirect assistance to offenders (as in point [a], above), these, then, could be partly different than the benefits that may be provided by programs which are instead dominated by, say, the abstract-justice aspect of deservedness (cf. "deserved punishment" or "just desert") and which do not focus heavily on offender need. Whether or not those NCA-based gains should be considered either more or less important to the community than the latter benefits, the following would remain the case:[24] Since the needs-centered approach is so heavily future-oriented and since it also centers on change and growth, neither the type nor amount of punishment and even external controls that offenders would receive during its long-term intervention would be designed to mainly express the justice system's response to those individuals' past offenses (as in just desert), or even to their actuarially derived likelihood of reoffending (as in risk management, etc.). This would also apply to the type and level of assistance those serious multiple offenders would receive via the needs-centered approach.[25] Thus, in long-term intervention, that is, change-and-growth-focused programming, the nature and scope of punishment and assistance (especially in combination) would not be determined chiefly—let alone overwhelmingly—by offense-centered considerations.[26]

In the needs-centered approach, if one were to compare *control* and assistance, program emphasis would be on the latter, for example, on building personal, interpersonal, and practical strengths. In this regard, and given that the needs in question would be those of offenders as well as the community, NCA's overriding programmatic issue would not be, "How can one motivate or force offenders to control their delinquency- and crime-related feelings and impulses?"—critical though it is for staff and offenders to nondestructively control the destructive expression of such feelings/impulses. Instead, it would be, "What do offenders need by way of skills, psychological strengths, understanding of others, feelings and attitudes toward self and others, broad motivations and interests, and satisfactions plus relatively reliable external supports and opportunities in order to function and *want* to function acceptably and productively in the community (including obeying its laws)?"

In this regard, staff's first operational task would be to translate answers to the latter, substantially broader issue into a coordinated and relevant treatment *and* control plan for each individual, a plan that would realistically address need and deservedness alike. Staff's subsequent and ongoing challenge would be to appropriately implement that intervention plan—modifying it as needed. To help them meet the latter challenge they would need (setting aside "deserve") reliable administrative support, among other factors. Though a different context is involved, this

need would have key points in common with the assistance, acceptance, and consideration often needed by offenders themselves, when they face various tasks and challenges.

The needs-centered approach need not oppose, should not oppose, and should not detract from continuous, long-range efforts directed at fundamental delinquency prevention—also called "primary prevention." Such efforts, if serious, and if coordinated locally, regionally, and often beyond, could provide the single best strategy for eventually reducing communities' (and society's) overall volume of crime, and their high crime rates as well. At the same time, however, it is essential to also focus on the *present* offenders, since they—collectively—still account for a sizable portion of all offenses, often very serious ones.

Offenders As Human Beings
Similarities and Challenges
When focusing on offenders (O's), especially the more serious, many people think almost entirely about behaviors and personality features that distinguish them from nonoffenders (NO's).[27] They seldom consider the similarities, and they sometimes forget these even exist or matter. In addition, these individuals often overlook the fact that (1) O's and NO's have many needs, hopes, expectations, and emotions in common, (2) many or most responses by O's and NO's to other people's treatment of them are similar, and (3), at a broader level, the lives that O's and NO's can each live must somehow take account of society's own needs and expectations.

By not recognizing these similarities, or by forgetting them, many people in a sense often overlook or downplay the fact that offenders, particularly serious multiple offenders, are no less human than nonoffenders. They simultaneously overlook the fact that O's, like NO's, are or will be part of society in one way or another, not just physically and in their everyday interactions but with regard to various roles they may eventually play. (This also applies to almost all O's who are presently incarcerated.) At the same time, most people would probably agree that offenders, like nonoffenders—say, other adolescents—should eventually live as independent adults in free society, insofar as possible.

This situation has direct implications for the earlier-mentioned rights and opportunities (r/o's), and with respect to other factors as well. For instance, regarding r/o's, if the large segment of the public in question (see endnote 27) were to focus on, or even briefly think about, the fact that offenders are indeed human, and that (1) through (3), above, do apply, it might be easier for those individuals to recognize and accept the following: These youths and young adults face some of the same types of challenges—or tasks—that are faced by other humans, namely, by nonoffenders. Prominent among these challenges is that of establishing a future for themselves, hopefully a workable one. By recognizing that, first, this broad task must be dealt with in one way or another by all youths and young adults, and by realizing that, second, its accomplishment requires that these individuals change, modify, or even further develop and improve some aspects of their present adjustment patterns, many of the above persons might then find it easier to accept the legitimacy, to young offenders, of rights/opportunities #1 through #3 above (see, e.g., "[having] reasonable opportunities to change").

Moreover, if those rights/opportunities were seen in the context of that broad challenge, they might often be regarded as necessities or needs—needs in the sense of being important or essential preconditions to establishing some type of workable future, or as being one set of means to that justified end. Thus, for instance, if it were recognized that the social and personal challenge of establishing a workable future is common to offenders and nonoffenders and is major in scope and importance, it might be easier for many people to regard factors such as "reasonable opportunities . . ." (#3, above) as being no less legitimate and important to offenders than to nonoffenders.[28]

Still regarding that challenge, even the right to be treated as a human being (#1, above) can have practical importance or instrumental value in a direct, social/utilitarian sense. (This is aside from the more intrinsic, less utilitarian value or appropriateness of that right.) More specifically, being treated as a fellow human can have pragmatic, means-to-an-end value with respect to offenders' efforts to establish a workable future. This value can be seen, for instance, in connection with these individuals' attempts to initiate and/or follow up on contacts with prospective employers: At a very basic level, being treated as human would mean, among other things,

that people (here, job seekers) should not be "constantly ignored, often rudely dismissed, or not even acknowledged to exist" (see endnote 20). At any rate, the instrumental value of treating offenders as human beings might be easier for many people to see and accept if they thought of these individuals, of their situation, and of society's appropriate "move," from the following, basic perspective: These individuals—as humans in society—share or will share certain major social challenges with other youths and young adults; treating those individuals as such, that is, as human, could help them meet those challenges.

A parallel situation exists regarding offenders'/exoffenders' relatively routine, ongoing interactions, including those with various adults and authority figures. (These interactions sometimes occur on an everyday basis and are distinguishable from ones that are more specifically concerned with the individuals' "future"—not necessarily a very distant one.) Here, for instance, it would make instrumental sense for the latter individuals to treat the former decently and with tolerance if they wished to increase the chances that those offenders would, in turn, treat other individuals with consideration and in fewer hurtful ways, and if they wished to perhaps decrease the chances of self-fulfilling prophecies. This "routine . . . interactions" example, like the "workable future" one, does not focus on the more intrinsic appropriateness of treating offenders as human beings—in contrast, that is, to doing so for more social/utilitarian reasons.

Refocusing on the "workable future," the following would apply even if the earlier-mentioned persons doubted that those rights/opportunities (r/o's) would significantly increase the chances of bringing about that future:[29] Many such persons, because they viewed offenders as human, might—despite that doubt—accept the legitimacy and significance of that future; and that legitimacy/significance would stem not just from its possible contribution to society's well-being, but partly from its value to offenders themselves. Moreover—and still given their doubts about the instrumental value of r/o's #1 through #3 in the present ("workable future") context—those individuals might believe that certain other factors could make a significant difference. For instance, and more specifically, if those persons accepted that offenders have a good deal in common with nonoffenders—not just in what they may generally need or face, but in how they often respond to certain inputs—they might then find it easier to also accept the following. The qualitative adequacy with which offenders' critical personal and interpersonal needs and interests are addressed by given programs can substantially shape those individuals' long-term future and improve its prospects. This applies especially during crises and periods of heightened stress; and the program-inputs involved might be called "relevant assistance."[30] (The individuals in question may hold this view even if they are only slightly interested in the personal well-being of offenders as an end in itself, and are instead almost exclusively focused on protecting and otherwise benefitting society.[31])

Finally, by thinking of offenders as also human in the sense of having various desires, feelings, and abilities in common with others, it might be easier for many people to accept the following: Offenders and nonoffenders share not only (1) the broad wish and ability to have satisfying experiences, but (2) the motivation to reduce or avoid anxiety, unhappiness, and various forms of misery—each in the present and near future. In addition, insofar as they accepted (1) and (2) as realities or implicitly took them for granted, and insofar as they also considered them both important, the earlier-mentioned persons might regard various rights and opportunities as themselves important—specifically, important and legitimate preconditions to the offenders' adequately addressing the given wish and implementing that motivation. (Thus, they could consider those rights/opportunities important in this "present and near future" context, whether or not they viewed them as significant in one that involves the more distant future and its related life-styles.) This view, which centers on the influence or possible influence of rights/opportunities, is separate from a parallel one that could focus on the role of "relevant [program] assistance" (e.g., specified elements and activities)—that is, on "other factors" or inputs. Like the former's targets and influence, the latter's could involve near-term issues in addition to the longer-term challenges.

As to the satisfying experiences themselves, these can often be prosocial. In this context, the earlier-mentioned individuals may even consider them potentially helpful in addressing offenders' long-term challenges,

including that of establishing a workable future. In this regard their contribution would be comparable to that of new or increased practical and interpersonal skills: Both they and such skills could serve as "plusses" or "positives" that would accumulate one by one, that could sooner or later boost the individuals' self-confidence, broaden their self-concept, and/or help refocus their energies, and that could collectively strengthen their resistance to negative pressures. In these and other ways they could make a workable future more likely to occur.[32]

Whatever positive potential these near-term satisfactions might have, and however those members of the public might often view them, the pursuit of such experiences need not be mainly an exercise in self-indulgence and/or the "feeding of one's ego."[33] Nor need that pursuit, or even the attainment, preclude or seriously interfere with longer-term efforts on the youths' and young adults' parts, or prevent these offenders from developing or increasing a sense of responsibility to others. That is, they *need* not do so, even though—under some conditions—they might. Those conditions can be largely avoided, controlled, or alleviated in well-planned programs.

Likelihood and Extent of Change
Implicit in all the above is a central point, one that several studies support: Serious multiple offenders can change for the better. This change can range from slight to marked; it can include but go beyond the rejection or controlling of illegal/destructive behavior; and its content as well as strength can probably be much the same as that seen in less serious offenders, and among individuals who may rarely if ever have offended.

Nevertheless, as suggested earlier, many people's beliefs about *whether* offenders, that is, offenders in general, can change and grow, about *how much* they can change, and about *what is needed* for them to do so are incorrect, sometimes markedly so. This is often because those beliefs, that is, those individuals' generalizations and conclusions, are largely based on inaccurate and/or incomplete images and assumptions regarding particular offenders and offender subgroups, or on relatively extreme and, in any event, unrepresentative offenders/offenses. In a sense, the problem is one of faulty generalizing; however, this process interacts with the limited or faulty information base and perceptions just mentioned, say, with the inaccurate views concerning offender characteristics. (Regarding offenders, the qualifiers "in-general," "as a whole," and "collectively" will be synonymous and will distinguish this overall or predominant composite group from its various—usually much smaller—components, for example, from "particular offenders" and "offender subgroups.")

For instance, many people (Group-X) who have certain stereotyped and otherwise partly inaccurate views regarding the personal features and motivations of specified offender subgroups believe or assume the following: The features and motivations on which they focus also apply to—and are probably primary to or decisive among—most or all *other* offenders; that is, they are probably central to the overall, composite group itself (offenders as a whole). If Group-X individuals believe/assume—as they often do—that the first-mentioned offenders, that is, the specified offender subgroups on which they focus, cannot or will not change and grow to a significant degree or in important ways, they will then be more likely to believe that the same inability or unwillingness applies to offenders collectively, that is, to the overall, composite group.[34]

Simultaneously, many such persons are likely to believe or implicitly assume—again in light of their stereotypes regarding the specified subgroups—that if any such change/growth *can* occur for offenders collectively, that change would probably occur, and would *have* to occur, via no more than one main type of approach (or perhaps two). This would be the same approach or intervention they would visualize as possibly having some positive impact on the specified subgroups, that is, the particular offenders, on which they focus.

Another set of individuals (Group-Y) that usually believes few young offenders (mainly "nonminor" ones) will significantly change and improve consists of persons who not only are (1) especially concerned with, and focus heavily upon, offenders who have committed one or more very violent, rather bizarre, or otherwise extreme offenses, but who (2) fear that many or most other nonminor offenders, including most SMOs, have a definite potential for similar, possibly even *as* serious, offending. Because Group-Y believes the more extreme offenders—(1), above—cannot or will not substantially change and grow, and

because its members very often assume that most other nonminor offenders—(2), above—have important negative features in common with them, such as antisocial drives, they usually believe or assume that few of the latter individuals will themselves change and improve very much. This view regarding change/growth as persons is separate from their frequent belief that most individuals' illegal behavior can be *controlled*, a view also common in Group-X.

In addition, many in Group-Y take the position that most or all nonminor offenders, like essentially all very violent ones, *deserve* little programmed assistance in any event.[35] This is true even when they feel the former, again like the latter, should definitely receive more than just the most basic consideration as *human beings,* such as various physical aspects of humane treatment.[36] At any rate, deservedness aside, the offender base—that is, the type of individuals—from which Group-Y usually generalizes[37] is a quantitatively narrow, particularly unrepresentative segment of the total spectrum, even though it is not necessarily stereotyped and descriptively distorted in itself, and is obviously important as well.

The more that Group-X individuals can correct their various stereotypes, can recognize or recall the positive features and drives shared by offenders and nonoffenders, and can thus more easily regard the former as humans too, the more likely they will be to believe or seriously consider the following:[38] Significant change and growth, which Group-X would regard as common in nonoffenders, can be far from rare in offenders (including the nonminor) as well, even if only in well-implemented, non-token programs. Also, the more they realize that almost all offenders will live most of their adult lives in social contexts outside of locked settings, the more they will probably see the relevance, to the community, of seriously addressing the long-term needs and challenges those individuals share with nonoffenders. This relevance, or utilitarian value, involves not only the relinquishing of illegal behavior but the positive contributions offenders may make.

On a related track, the more Group-Y individuals recognize and focus on a broader spectrum of offenders and offenses, for example, on a fuller range of personalities and offense histories, the more likely they will be to believe or seriously consider the following: Not only is substantial change/growth possible after all, at least with many non-minor offenders, but, for it to actually occur, somewhat different approaches may be necessary with differing kinds of offenders, that is, in contrast to only one or two approaches being adequate and in fact essential for the full range. Similarly, the less Group-Y's attention remains focused on very violent, rather bizarre, and otherwise extreme offenses, the less likely many of its members will be to continue believing that "offenders," that is, nonminor offenders in general, *should* not receive much serious programmed assistance. (This "*should* not . . ." would have been applied even if—judging from other known programs, or from various studies—the available assistance seemed to hold reasonable promise of [1] helping those individuals live most or all their lives in free society—doing less harm or no harm to others—and of [2] thereby having substantial utilitarian value.)

In sum, if many people were to draw from a more accurate as well as broader information base, their generalizations or conclusions about the likelihood and extent of change and growth would be more accurate and better justified than they often are, as would their views and assumptions regarding the various interventions that might help generate and sustain it. With Group-X individuals, this would mainly call for information that could help them become more aware of important *similarities* between those offenders, on the one hand, and nonoffenders, on the other, for instance, similarities as to their respective needs or their long-term, underlying drives. With Group-Y, in contrast, more information would be needed regarding *differences*—specifically, those which exist among offenders themselves, much as various differences often exist among nonoffenders. This need would apply not just to Group-Y, but to any group that tends to focus heavily or almost exclusively on a narrow segment of the overall spectrum, whatever the content of that slice may be.[39]

Despite their ability to change, serious multiple offenders—compared, say, to most nonoffenders—commonly do have extra difficulties in modifying their present adjustment patterns.[40] In addition, they are more ambivalent about doing so. These realities, and the offenders' frequent environmental pressures and limitations, should not be downplayed. At the same time, however, substantial and

critical long-term change *can* occur with many such individuals, and this can be achieved via resources that many organizations can assemble and operate—challenges and problems notwithstanding. Moreover, the offenders themselves often bring many positives to the intervention process, especially if their motivation is engaged. It is important for policymakers, practitioners, and others to recognize these latter points, since—absent that awareness and understanding—they could easily believe that the substantial time, effort, skills, and resources which are called for would be largely wasted, that program success would be quite unlikely, and that the programs' cost-benefit ratios would be unsatisfactory.

Notes

1. Though the main features and beliefs emphasized in this view (see text) pre-date the 1970s, the view, on balance, was then less narrow and also less dominant over others.

2. These features are usually below the surface even in most conflicted and passive-conformist youths. However, they are generally closer to it than is the case with most other offenders; that is, they are easier to observe on other than cursory examination. Also, the three features—particularly the first two—are often more intense in the conflicted and passive-conformist than in most remaining individuals, even though their strength is considerable in the latter as well. At any rate, their *frequency*—across individuals—is essentially the same. These remarks emphasize the situation at point of program intake.

3. The scope, frequency, and/or intensity of many offenders' latter feelings—for example, vulnerability—is, on average, greater than that of nonoffenders. Also, the offenders' feelings in question generally extend further back in time at a problem level, and they are now less often defused, reduced, or essentially counterbalanced by the youths' actual accomplishments alone and by increased external support alone, important though these are.

4. With many conflicted individuals, the desire to change and improve—though sometimes strong—is regularly accompanied by an internal countercurrent, one

that can curtail, block, or attenuate, for long periods, much of the progress these youths could otherwise make. Moreover, though many such individuals would like to change/improve, particularly when they view themselves as "bad," disliked, and perhaps not too likeable, it is often at those same times that they especially wonder if they actually *will* change/improve in important ways, such as those which will make them more likeable and lead to happier times.

5. Though many youths (individually) want certain change to occur more slowly and to a modest degree, their desire for the *change itself* is not uncommon. Moreover, it is relatively common *across* those youths (collectively)—again, regardless of the preferred pace and degree.

6. Personal/psychological change is often addressed by, say, counseling and pragmatically oriented interactions between client and staff. In the present discussion, we assume that counseling and such interactions *could* be accurately characterized as neither more nor less of an interference than vocational/educational training—whether operationally or in other important ways.

7. This is true whether one approaches such factors fairly directly, somewhat indirectly, or both directly and indirectly. "Directly" could include, for example, (1) cognitive/interpersonal skills training and (2) focused discussions during group or individual counseling. "Indirectly" could involve helping youths gain practical and "basic survival" skills, offering encouragement and support, and so on.

8. Problems associated with an *absence,* paucity, or major diminution of humane rehabilitation programming have been described by several authors. See, for example, Cullen and Gilbert (1982), relative to institutional settings.

9. For instance, Combination 1 (which, say, consists of ingredients a, b, c, and d) may be used with 10 of an agency's 50 clients; Combination 2 (consisting of a, b, e, and f) may be used with 10 other clients; Combination 3 (a, c, e, and g) may be used with 10 more; and so on. Ingredient "a" might be group counseling and "b" might be vocational training. This same example or paradigm

could be applied to an agency's several *strategies and techniques,* those it might use with various subgroups within its total client population.

10. For example, even within Combination 1, ingredients a, b, c, and d might be introduced in a different sequence (or at somewhat different times) among some of its 10 clients; and, even if those ingredients were always used in the same sequence, they might be used for different lengths of time and/or at differing intensities.

11. (1) Some programs, say, those which follow particular correctional philosophies or perhaps focus on certain types of clients, might use given components, such as restitution or perhaps remedial education, much more often than other programs. Based on criteria (1) and (2) in the text, those components might be "core elements" in the first programs but not in the second. In short, whether a given component, that is, element, should be characterized as either a "core" or an "as-needed" part of a given program will ultimately depend on how it is used in that particular program, not on which element it is. (See text regarding "as-needed.") Nevertheless, in many programs that each address a broad range of serious multiple offenders and that each use a number of elements (specified individual components), some such elements are more likely than others to serve as the "core," particularly if growth-centered goals are emphasized. ("Element," "component," and "*approach*" will now be used synonymously.)

(2) Some cognitive-behavioral, cognitive-emotional, and behavioral approaches that have been used since the 1980s have substantial content overlap with various types of counseling or with certain aspects and phases of that approach, and with aspects of pragmatically oriented discussions (PODs) as well. However, other such approaches have less in common. With that in mind, points (a) and (b), below, together with the subsequent remarks, briefly explore the idea of adding a cognitive or behavioral element to programs that already use counseling and/or PODs (these points would apply whether or not one even distinguished between core and as-needed): (a) In a given program, if no

more than moderate content overlap would exist (and preferably, if *little* would exist), a cognitive or behavioral approach might sometimes be usefully added, in part or whole, either *before* that program's routine counseling element has gotten underway with given clients or else *after* that element has been completed or largely completed with those individuals. (By the same token—but, of course, in a different program—one might reverse the situation: One might usefully add certain forms or aspects of *counseling* either before or after the program's routine cognitive or behavioral element.) (b) Alternatively, certain aspects of the cognitive or behavioral approach might be temporally *interwoven* with the counseling per se (and—again in a different program—vice versa), or perhaps interwoven with ongoing PODs and other elements that may already temporally overlap each other. In (a) and (b), the cognitive or behavioral elements could serve as either supplements or complements to the program's routine elements, including counseling and POD. (However the cognitive or behavioral approaches may function and be classified in that respect, this linking or interweaving of elements that might each contribute substantially could be described as a flexible, multimodular strategy; and, in any given program, it could reinforce or enhance an already existing one. As to the overall wisdom of actually adding a cognitive, behavioral, or other approach in any particular instance, this would mainly depend on such factors as how much that approach would probably contribute, the operational feasibility and implications involved, and so on.)

At any rate, under some conditions, future programs might productively utilize combinations of elements which, to date, have seldom been seriously considered for joint usage in connection with the same specific clients, let alone be actually *used* in that regard. Nonutilization may have occurred for reasons such as the following, among others: (1) The previously unused element—that is, the non-linked or non-interwoven component, such as the cognitive, or, alternatively, the

counseling—was viewed as inadequate or inferior, even if not irrelevant or inappropriate. (2) The program's already existing elements may have seemed sufficient by themselves. In any event, future correctional operations—ones that will often reflect the flexible, multimodular strategy—should allow for the possibility of using new combinations of elements or parts thereof, elements/approaches that may have seldom been combined to date. (All this is apart from the separate possibility of fully *substituting* one such element for another.)

Regarding this possible linking and/or interweaving of approaches, the following might also be kept in mind: Presently, most approaches (A's)—whether cognitive, behavioral, counseling, or other—each exist in several *varieties* (v's). In addition, these approaches (say, A_1 and A_2) and/or their main variants (A_1,v_1 and A_2,v_1) may have considerably more in common with certain other approaches (A_3; A_4) and/or other variants (A_3v_1; A_4v_1) than they have with still others (A_5; A_5v_1; etc.). Linking, and so on, would be theoretically possible even if no more than one such A or v were actually available for possible use in a given program. And, as suggested, the combining in question might make a practical difference if the commonality—specifically, the content overlap—were no more than moderate. (Content overlap should be distinguished from technique, or technical, overlap, that is, from the particular interpersonal means by which staff convey, address, and otherwise work with or on the content. Here, the commonalities could be substantial.) Moderate content overlap can exist even if the two approaches that are combined or linked, say, the cognitive-behavioral and pragmatically oriented interactions (or, alternatively, counseling), are—ordinarily—largely different than one another at a global or gestalt level. They may thus differ overall even if they are similar or very similar with respect to several important *individual features*. As suggested above, the approaches used in this example often do share such features, as do some of their common variants.

12. With some individuals (usually the power-oriented), external controls remain not only important but almost always *dominant* during much of the intervention; nevertheless, even with these youths, relationship controls can become increasingly important and should eventually prevail. With still other youths, relationship controls may take almost a year to develop, rather than occurring "soon," for example, in four to six months.

13. These possible alternative patterns neither relate to nor are discussed with youths mainly with respect to *hypothetical* situations. Nor are they discussed on an essentially impersonal or largely abstract basis, for instance, in connection with their possible or seeming utility and feasibility for *other* offenders under various conditions, and/or with their general value in the eyes of society. Instead, these alternatives arise, and are examined, chiefly in relation to the present youths' current and recent personal experiences, and as possible contrasts to or improvements upon *them*. In this regard, the less satisfied these individuals are with their current life situation the more likely they are to give those alternatives more than passing thought.

14. Broadly speaking, these mainly involve one form or another of social/interpersonal ability, competence, and/or status (plus their hoped-for, attendant enjoyments and positive responses from other individuals). Simultaneously, however, but at a different psychological level (yet itself partly involving competence/power), it could be said that many male offenders—without realizing this as such—are "seeking" different or more acceptable father figures than they have had. This would also apply to many females, with respect to mother figures.

15. When used as a *noun* in this context, "consideration"—which may take various forms—would be part of assistance. In this role, it would be a product, not an activity or process, such as "being considered."

16. Each such dimension or factor may be seen as directly or indirectly bearing on one or both forms of *deterrence*, namely, "general" or "specific." Deterrence,

however, need not always be its ultimate or even sole purpose.

17. For purposes of programming, it is appropriate and unavoidable to translate and flesh out the terms and implications of those sentences.

18. Those steps would therefore have practical significance and would not, instead, produce simply a higher level of formal or technical coordination. Moreover, their applicability would extend beyond the dimensions of need and deservedness.

19. Thus, this right should not be thought of as something that must be earned, say, earned or deserved as a result of personal accomplishments or contributions/assistance to others. This does not imply that individuals who have offended, or have seriously and perhaps repeatedly offended, should ipso facto be assumed to have never accomplished anything, assisted anyone, or made other useful contributions. It does, however, imply that the right is automatic, and presumably permanent. (Regarding "permanence," however, see endnote 20.) Complicating these concepts as well as their application is the fact that rights are often acknowledged, allowed, and respected in differing ways and degrees, by different people.

20. Regarding *which* rights exist, *how far* they extend, and the *conditions* under which they do so, "universal" agreement can seldom be expected, even within a given community or society. This is true even though *widespread* agreement often occurs with respect to some rights. At any rate, just as easily as some members of a community can assert that offenders have lost or "forfeited" a given right, say, that of being treated as a human being, other members can claim they have not lost it, in any significant respect. (There are no a priori grounds for definitively settling this particular difference of opinion.) Much the same would apply to various other rights that many people either believe or implicitly assume offenders, especially serious ones, either have lost or should lose. Among these is the right to have a happy and/or productive future—at least to pursue and earn it, presumably on the same grounds as nonoffenders. Thus, disagreement would often exist as to whether even "the

pursuit of happiness" is an "inalienable" right for everyone—a right that cannot or should not be revoked (1) even in part, (2) even while the offenders are serving their formal sentences, not to mention after they have completed them, and (3) only with offenders who seem to have rehabilitated themselves. (Sizable disagreements would sometimes exist even regarding the following question[s]: What does, and/or should, the "pursuit of happiness" encompass, at a minimum?)

(In everyday interactions, "being treated as a human being" usually includes being given at least simple courtesies or respect; being listened to and given honest consideration; and, in those regards, being treated "decently" and with tolerance. It excludes being constantly ignored, often rudely dismissed, or not even acknowledged to exist; being routinely treated with contempt; being often humiliated, degraded, or made to suffer marked indignities ["treated like dirt" and/or as being generally worthless or even loathsome]. In type and degree, it overlaps but goes beyond being treated as an inferior. In addition, it does not necessarily focus on exploitation, domination, and/or possessive control—though these motives, or at least products, often do loom large, whether or not they are accompanied by physical intimidation, abuse, and/or terrorization.)

21. Contributing to others, or even trying to do so, would go beyond "the pursuit of (personal) happiness"—this pursuit being implicit in points #1–#3, above. In any event, the "pursuit" need not be wholly self-oriented, (a) particularly if its meaning is shifted to emphasize—or at least broadened to include—the attempt to create "a worthwhile life," (b) clearly if point (a) includes being responsive to other persons' needs and expectations (partly for those persons' benefit), and (c) whether or not it is considered an "inalienable" right.

22. Such rights/opportunities (r/o's) would presumably be very broad or even "universal" in scope, certainly within the given community or even society. They would not, in any event, be considered appropriate (i.e., applicable to or valid) only for individuals who seem largely and consistently willing to grant similar r/o's to others. (In most communities/ societies, however, many people would insist on this type and level of willingness.)

23. The community or society, that is, its members collectively, could accurately lay claim to embracing and representing those beliefs and standards to the extent that it expressed and tried to support them with essentially all its members, and other than only verbally and feebly. This would apply especially, though perhaps not solely, if the society did not necessarily seek tangible gains for itself from that expression and support. (As indicated, the community could obtain less tangible or nontangible benefits.) From this perspective, it would therefore be appropriate for the community and its justice or correctional system to allow offenders the given rights and opportunities even if it were far from clear to the community, and justice/correctional system, that those individuals *would* in fact make, or at least probably make, substantial positive contributions to others, whether or not immediately. At any rate, even if this stance were not strongly supported on the direct, pragmatic grounds of "likely, tangible benefit to others" (setting aside the fact that *reduced recidivism* could still be likely and, as such, would itself constitute such gain), it could still receive significant support on grounds of "fairness" in general, for example, equal treatment, or consistency in particular. For instance, regarding offenders, that stance would be consistent with the apparent fact that although a sizable percentage of *non*offenders (1) make few if any contributions (including small ones) to others in their communities during much of adolescence, early adulthood, and perhaps beyond, and may (2) hardly even try to contribute, those communities seldom if ever question the appropriateness of according those individuals the above rights and opportunities, even though they implicitly realize that (1) and (2) do apply to many of their nonoffenders.

24. Moreover, even if one approach had less overall importance or value than the other, or than any other, the former's value could still be substantial on an absolute scale.

25. In short, in the needs-centered approach, the punishment and especially assistance that offenders receive would not be mainly determined by sentencing guidelines or grids, by risk-prediction formulas, and the like. For instance, though these guidelines and formulas are valuable in several ways and although they have reduced various justice system problems, they can play only a limited, albeit not insignificant, positive role in change-and-growth-centered intervention planning. This is mainly because they cannot, by themselves, adequately incorporate and reflect various complex areas—and interactions across those areas—that are often highly relevant to SMOs' long-term adjustment. (These areas, most of which contain several factors themselves, include specific circumstances of the individuals' life and offenses, major changes through time, recent and long-standing motivations, personality features and adjustment techniques, areas of resistance, and so on.) To be sure, guidelines, risk-formulas, and related methods or approaches were not designed to incorporate/reflect these complex areas and especially their interactions—not to mention other, often less complex but important areas such as skills, interests, strengths, vulnerabilities, fears, and impending crises—and to thereby play a large role in developing and later modifying specific, integrated, individualized intervention plans.

This limitation with respect to intervention planning and program follow-up exists regardless of how reasonably and carefully such approaches may express, and even *combine*, various meaningful issues and considerations, such as risk management and just desert, and even though the given approaches may allow for flexibility, say, via overrides. It also exists despite the *partial compatibility* between those approaches (e.g., risk-prediction formulas or even risk/need checklists) as well as issues (e.g., risk management), on the one hand, and the type as well as level of individualization described in this book, on the other. Finally, as one works with increasingly serious offenders, the limitations of those approaches with respect to intervention

planning become increasingly important. This is mainly because such planning is itself more important with those offenders than with the less serious, and because the information on which that planning is largely based should be even more carefully interrelated and integrated. This issue, and the limitation it reflects, is not only important but "live"; this is because guidelines, grids, and formulas—though indeed not *designed* for intervention planning, especially on their own—are nevertheless commonly *used* (often on their own) in ways and contexts that greatly affect it. More specifically, they are sometimes utilized in ways that—while appropriately serving their own primary objectives—may nonetheless preclude or otherwise seriously limit the manner in which various program elements or activities may be (or at least *are*) used; and, as implied earlier, they substantially delimit the amount of individualization—necessary individualization, for purposes of the needs-centered approach—that might otherwise be possible. (This issue and limitation also apply, though to a significantly lesser extent, to problem-area checklists, including the more advanced and detailed ones. Most area checklists, at least, *are* partly or largely designed with intervention and change/growth—change beyond behavior control alone—in mind. But even here, the type and range of needed information—and integration—is insufficient.)

26. Programmatically, the difference between a punishment emphasis and an assistance emphasis could often be substantial rather than slight, even in contexts other than long-term intervention. At any rate, in order for an agency or program to shift from the former emphasis to the relatively comprehensive assistance emphasis described in this book, more would be needed than simply reducing the punishment component and/or adding or else "beefing up" one or two program elements. An overall, *integrated* change would be required, and in this regard the shift would be major.

27. In this section, "many persons" and "many people" will refer predominantly to a large and influential segment of the general public, and secondarily to a

much smaller but not insignificant portion of all correctional staff.

28. Among the characteristics that comprise reasonable are "realistic "and "relevant." (This, in turn, links with the importance of developing relevant, realistic intervention plans.)

29. This applies whether the rights/opportunities would be operating by themselves or in interaction with other factors, such as "relevant assistance" (see text that follows). Rights/opportunities can interact with, and thereby reinforce, those factors. They can even raise the chances that the latters' potential impact will be actualized.

30. In this context, "qualitative adequacy" (e.g., appropriate implementation, or program integrity) should be distinguished from the degree to which relevant assistance and "reasonable opportunities" are made available and/or accessible to offenders. Overlap, however, clearly exists.

31. The fact that they may be only slightly interested in offenders' well-being for its own sake does not ipso facto mean they consider these individuals less than human.

32. Some satisfactions and skills may also interact with, and enhance, each other. With or without such interaction, the "accumulation" (output) in question need not be linear or even based on completely discrete (and/or quantitatively equal) "units" (input)—for example, on entirely separate "satisfying experiences" or individual skills.

33. The "feeding" would be of various aspects of a person's self-concept. It would not, for example, focus on the enhancement of certain functions or coping skills that are a further aspect of the individual's mental activities and awareness. In any event, "ego"—in all its aspects, collectively—need not be viewed as (1) sharply distinguishable from everything else that is mental (or from all other aspects of mental activity, collectively), and, in that respect, as (2) a literal, circumscribed entity—even one that changes and develops through time. This applies whether or not "ego" is viewed

as unitary or composite, and despite the integrations of information that are involved in, and/or result from, various "ego activities."

34. The latter point, which relates to beliefs concerning change/growth in offenders collectively, is unaffected by the fact that the stereotyped views which are held regarding specified subgroups within that overall group contain some *accurate* information in addition to the inaccurate. With any offender subgroup, both types of information usually relate to individuals' personality features, motivations, and so on; and regarding that subgroup, the overall or global picture that is produced by all such information *combined* can easily and often be misleading.

35. Others in Group-Y do not hold this view regarding most nonminor offenders.

36. Neither the "basic-consideration-plus" nor the relatively small amount of programmed assistance that many in Group-Y believe these nonminor offenders deserve would often be able to adequately address the offenders' main problems and needs.

37. This generalization focuses on both the potential for, and the motivation for, substantial change and growth in nonminor offenders collectively.

38. In addition, the more likely they may be to take seriously various scientific studies that support or tend to support the idea of change and growth.

39. This assumes that—given its quantitative narrowness—no one segment or portion could be more than moderately representative of the total spectrum, and that it would often be only slightly representative instead. If a broader segment were used, the situation would of course differ.

40. Though "extra difficulties" involves a comparison with nonoffenders, the typical level of difficulty for these offenders is also high *in itself,* that is, in absolute terms. That aside, even many *non*offenders often have difficulty making the changes in question; and this may occur even if they have not previously experienced sizable, frequent, or sustained personal problems and/or similar environmental pressures and disadvantages.

APPENDICES

1 DETAILS REGARDING THE PHASE 2 OBJECTIVES

In the proposal to NIMH, the purpose and thrust of Phase 2 was stated in the following quotation.

> It is necessary to begin Phase 2 of the program in order to determine which element or combination of elements is responsible for the success of the community program. The following aspects of the program are [those] most often suggested as contributing to the high success rate of the Experimental group [i.e., CTP youths]:
>
> A. The treatment model which defines nine delinquent subtypes and prescribes differential treatment for each;
> B. The extensive impact in all the youth's life areas permitted by low caseloads, including: (1) high surveillance level, (2) careful planning for a placement which allows nondelinquent behavior to occur, (3) concentrated work with families or foster families, (4) work with schools and other community agencies, . . .
> E. Emphasis upon the working through of the ward-agent relationship as a major treatment tool;
>
> F. Choice of the study communities in Phase 1, including: (1) less sophisticated or less gang-oriented delinquents than in larger urban centers. . . .

> It is suggested that research in Phase 2 of the Community Treatment Project represent the initial steps in determining the essential ingredients of a successful community program. (Warren, Palmer and Turner, 1964a, pp. 1–2)

The relative importance of factors A, B, and E would be estimated by comparing a CTP unit with a Guided Group Interaction unit, both of which would be established in San Francisco. Factor F would be evaluated by comparing the Sacramento/Stockton experiences/results with those of San Francisco. Other factors would be studied as well. These would include (1) "avoidance of institutionalization" and (2) "nature of the parole agents"—for instance, their personality characteristics. This part of the study would draw from the Sacramento, Stockton, and San Francisco experiences alike.

2 INITIAL STAFFING GUIDE

YA#: _____ Name: _____ Release Date: _____ Age: _____

I-level: _____ Stage: _____ Agent(s) Present: _____ Supervisor: _____

Researcher: _____ Others: _____ Recorder: _____

Part I. BACKGROUND AND DIAGNOSIS

1. Offense and Offense History (or Recent Misbehavior or Crisis)
2. Frequency and Nature of Contacts
3. Characteristics of Ward
   A. Self-Perception
   B. Staff Perception
4. Characteristics of Family
   A. Ward Perception
   B. Staff Perception
   C. Family as Support and Stress
5. Ward's Attitude toward Authority Figures
   A. Agent
   B. Project
   C. Research Interview
6. Community Support and Stress (school, job, other)
7. Nature of the Problem
8. Staff Diagnosis
9. Misc. Notes and Comments

_____ _____
Kind of Staffing   Date

Part II. TREATMENT/INTERVENTION

1. Goals
2. Placement
3. Family Treatment
4. Community Resources
5. Job and/or School
6. Leisure Time Activities
7. Peer Relations and Intervention
8. Controls
9. Kind of Agent
10. Agent Attitudes
11. Treatment Methods
12. Suggested Techniques for Achieving Goals
13. Crucial Questions and Case Problems
14. Help for Agent (supervision, consultation, resources, etc.)
15. Predictions
16. Theoretical Diagnostic Issues
17. Theoretical Treatment Issues

3 Parole Agreement Used throughout CYA during Phases 1 and 2

DEPARTMENT OF THE
YOUTH AUTHORITY

STATE OF CALIFORNIA

PAROLE AGREEMENT

NAME _____ Y.A. No. _____

It is my understanding that I am being paroled on the condition that I comply with the following rules:

First, I will recognize my parole officer as the official representative of the Youth Authority.

Second, I will not change my address or leave the State of California without obtaining the permission of my parole officer.

Third, I promise to attend school or to secure and maintain regular employment, and I will not change or leave my employment without the approval of my parole officer.

Fourth, I will not drive a motor vehicle without the approval of my parole officer.

Fifth, I will agree to keep in contact with my parole officer in the manner he or she prescribes.

Sixth, I will make a written report to my parole officer on the first of each month.[a]

_____

I HEREBY CERTIFY that I have read the above agreement and that I have been informed that I am being paroled on the condition that I comply with the above rules, and with the laws of the State of California, and that I can be returned immediately to an institution as a parole violator if I fail to do so.

(SIGNATURE) _____

Date _____

YOUTH AUTHORITY

By _____

*Classification Counselor
(Or Parole Officer)*

I agree to act as parole advisor for the above named person.

I have read the Parole Agreement and will do all in my power to help him keep its rules. I will report promptly to this Parole Officer any unnecessary absence from work, drinking, late hours, bad companions or other harmful conditions which may endanger his liberty.

SIGNED_____

DATE _____ *Relationship*_____

_____

[a]In 1964, a seventh condition was added, as follows: "I agree to take medical tests or submit to physical examinations whenever directed to do so by my parole officer."

4 SACRAMENTO COMMUNITY CENTER FLOOR PLAN

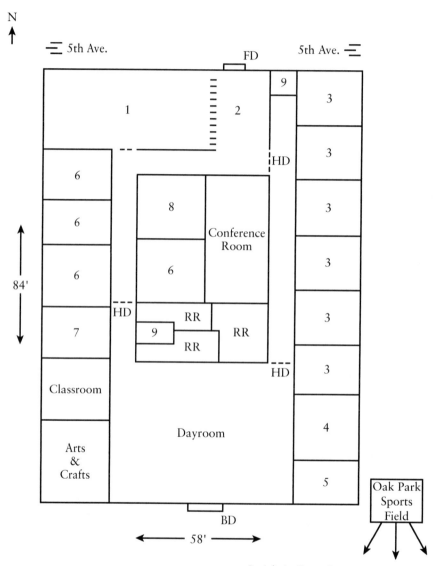

1. Clerical area
2. Reception area
3. Parole agent office
4. Parole agent/group meeting room
5. Storage & study area
6. Research office
7. Casework Supervisor

8. Admin. Supervisor
9. Maintenance

FD = Front door
HD = Hall door
RR = Restroom
BD = Back door

5 BACKGROUND CHARACTERISTICS OF YOUTHS

Background characteristics will be reviewed in relation to four areas: general factors, family characteristics, personal situation and characteristics, and school situation.

General Factors

Average age at intake was 15.5 years (see, e.g., Warren and Palmer, 1965, p. 7; Palmer et al., 1968, p. 7). Three of every four youths were between ages 14 and 17 when first committed. (YA "intake" and "point of first commitment" are synonymous.) The statewide average age during 1961–1969 was 15.6 years. (From this point forward, statewide figures will be found mostly in the notes. These figures indicate that the E plus C youths were similar to the statewide sample on all general factors considered.)[1]

A large majority of youths were from lower income or "lower class" families: lower—81 percent; middle—18 percent; upper—1 percent.[2] (See below for definitions.)

Slightly over half the sample was Caucasian; the remaining individuals were about evenly divided between Mexican American and black: Caucasian—53 percent; Mexican American—23 percent; black—20 percent; all others—4 percent.[3]

The average nonverbal IQ score was 86. This was slightly below the normal range (90–110) for the youth population as a whole, that is, for nonoffenders plus offenders[4] (see, e.g., Warren and Palmer, 1965, p. 7; Palmer et al., 1968, p. 6). (During most of the 1960s the California Test of Mental Maturity was routinely used at NRCC. In the later 1960s the Lorge-Thorndike and, only briefly, the Revised Beta, were used.)

Most commitment offenses were property-related (e.g., auto theft; burglary). Offenses against persons accounted for only a small percentage of the total. This was partly because the Phase 1 and 2 eligibility criteria excluded most such offenses in the first place. "All other" offenses—mainly status offenses (e.g., runaway, incorrigible)—accounted for about one-fourth of the total. The exact breakdown was: property—71 percent; person—5 percent; all others—23 percent.[5]

Fourteen percent of the youths had one or more violent offenses as of their commitment to the YA.[6]

Family Characteristics (Table A5–1)

Fifty-nine percent of the youths' natural parents were not living together at the time of the youngsters' YA commitment. This includes 36 percent divorced, 11 percent separated, and 12 percent broken by death. The statewide figure was 57 percent (34 percent divorced, 10 percent separated, 13 percent broken by death). See endnotes 7, 8, and 9 regarding statewide figures on the next three family-characteristics items. As before, the present sample was similar to the overall YA population.

At intake, the following "parental configuration" was observed:

- 31 percent of all youths were living with their natural mother and natural father;
- 25 percent were living with natural mother and father substitute;
- 26 percent were living with natural mother and no father or substitute;

Selected Family Background Characteristics at Youth Authority Intake[a]

I. Marital Status of Natural Parents	Percent of Parents	II. Parents or Parent Figures with Whom Youth Resides	Percent of Parents
Not married	9	Nat. Mother & Nat. Father	31
Divorced	36	Nat. Mother & Father Sub.	25
Separated	11	Nat. Mother & No Father	26
Broken by death	12	or Substitute	
Unbroken/Discordant	7	Nat. Father & Mother Sub.	4
Unbroken/Congenial	25	All other[b]	14

III. Family Members with Record of Criminality or Delinquency	Percent of Each Type of Family Member[c]	IV. Rating of Home for Youth's Return[d]	Percent of Homes
Father or Substitute	28	Undesirable	57[e]
Mother or Substitute	11	Acceptable	38[f]
Sibling(s)	41	Good or Excellent	5

[a]Relates to all eligible experimental (E) and control (C) males. All information is based on a standardized, Initial Home Visit Schedule. (The IHVS was filled out by a CTP parole agent on each preeligible E, and by a regular parole agent on each such C; standard parole exposure cohort; 335 E's, 236 C's.)
[b]Includes: Natural Father & No Mother or Substitute; Other Relatives; Adoptive Parents; Foster Parents.
[c]For example, 28 percent of all fathers or father substitutes had a record of criminality or delinquency.
[d]On release to parole.
[e]For E's, the percentage was 60; for C's it was 54.
[f]For E's, the percentage was 37; for C's it was 40.

- 4 percent were living with father and mother substitute;
- 14 percent were living in other situations (relatives, foster parents, etc.).[7]

Twenty-eight percent of the fathers or father substitutes had a police record, as did 11 percent of the mothers or mother substitutes. Forty-one percent of the youths had at least one sibling with a delinquent record.[8]

Parole agents answered the following question regarding the home in which the youth was living at the time of his YA commitment: "Would this home be a suitable placement for the youth, upon his release to parole?" The homes were rated as follows: 57 percent were undesirable or less than acceptable; 38 percent were acceptable; 5 percent were good or excellent.[9]

Since the youngster's birth, 52 percent of the families had made five or more "moves," that is, an average of one change of residence every three years. Twenty-five percent had made eight or more moves—one every second year.[10]

Three of every 10 families (30 percent) were receiving some form of public assistance at the time of the youngster's YA commitment: one family in seven (14 percent) received part of its income from this source; an additional one in six (16 percent) obtained all its income from this source.

Personal Situation and Characteristics

Nearly three-fifths of all youths (57 percent) had lived away from home on at least one occasion prior to their YA commitment. Twenty-three percent of this group were less than five years old when they first lived away from home. The figure was 35 percent for youngsters under nine. Foster home placements are included in these figures.

On average, the youth's first official law contact was likely to have occurred at age 13.4. (Compare, e.g., Davis et al., 1965; Gould and Beverly, 1963; Wright, 1969.) Dependency contacts, such as placement changes, are excluded here. Since his YA commitment usually occurred at age 15.5, and since he had accumulated 5.8 law contacts as of that point, he averaged one law contact every five months during the two-year period that began with his first official contact and ended with his YA commitment offense. (Age at time of first law contact and first commitment to YA are very similar to the statewide figures. See Youth Authority Annual Statistical Summaries, 1961 through 1970.)

About two-fifths of the youths (38% to 43%) were involved with one or two co-offenders in connection with their commitment offense. An additional one of every seven or eight (12% to 14%) were involved with three or more co-offenders. (See, e.g., Davis et al., 1965; Gould and Beverly, 1963; Wright, 1969.)

Eight percent of all youths had one or more offenses—prior plus commitment—that involved dangerous drugs or opiates. (This excludes marijuana.) Narcotics usage did not become common among YA first commitments until the later 1960s (see, e.g., Davis et al., 1965).

At point of intake, 31 percent of all youths either had been, or still were, nail biters. Thirty percent had exhibited temper tantrums and 20 percent had had problems with bed-wetting. All three items had been characterized—for individuals (parole agents) who were to provide this information—as "developmental behavior [problems] persistently exhibited." (See Bohnstedt and Beverly, 1960, pp. 19–20; Gould and Beverly, 1963.) In short, these items were not to be thought of as having occurred on little more than an occasional or perhaps normal developmental basis.

At one or more points prior to YA intake, 30 percent of all youths had been "the subject of psychiatric or psychological observation, evaluation, or therapy resulting from definite or suspected psychological disorder." (See Bohnstedt and Beverly, 1960, p. 18; Gould and Beverly, 1963.)

School Situation (Table A5–2)

Ninety percent of all youngsters had one or more *types* of school difficulty listed in their record.[11] More specifically, the following percentages were listed as having had each of the following types of school-related difficulty (together, these numbers total more than 100 percent because most youths had two such listings): scholastic—56 percent; truancy—46 percent; authority—45 percent; peers—22 percent. The "authority" item means that 45 percent of all youths had difficulty getting along with teachers, at one or more points in their school career. The "peers" item usually referred to fighting.

Forty-nine percent of all youths (50 percent E's, 48 percent C's) were not attending public school as of their commitment to the YA. For these individuals the reasons were as follows: dropped out—40 percent; suspended—30 percent; expelled or excluded—26 percent; all other—4 percent.

As to overall academic achievement, the average youngster was operating somewhere between grade levels (GL) 6 and 7, at point of

---

TABLE A5–2

School Problems and School Nonattendance, at Youth Authority Intake[a]

I. Type of School Problems	Percent of Youths[b]	II. Reason for Nonattendance[d]	Percent of Youths[e]
Scholastic	56	Dropped out	40
Truancy	46	Suspended	30
Authority[c]	45	Expelled or Excluded	26
Peers	22	All Other	4
Bizarre Behavior	0+		

[a]All information is based on the Clinic Summary Report, completed by NRCC staff prior to each youth's board hearing. "School" always refers to public school, as distinct, for example, from Probation Camp school (see note d, below).

[b]Figures relate to all eligible experimental and control males—the E and C sample. The total for these figures exceeds 100 percent because some youths had more than one such difficulty.

[c]For example, defiance of teachers.

[d]Fifty-one percent of the E + C sample were attending school at point of Youth Authority intake. Percentages shown in the right-hand column relate to the remaining 49 percent (all nonattenders) less a group of individuals (19% of the E + C sample) who were attending a Probation Camp school shortly before their YA commitment. Excluded from all figures are a 1 percent group who had graduated from high school prior to commitment.

[e]For example, 26 percent of the nonattenders had been expelled or excluded from public school.

intake: He was at GL 6 with regard to mathematical skills and GL 7 in reading comprehension and vocabulary.[12] Since he was enrolled in tenth grade at the time, he was roughly three grade levels behind the average individual of his age (15.5), with respect to overall academic achievement and functioning.

The average age at which "serious or persistent school misbehavior began" was 12.3. For truancy in particular, it was 12.9. Scholastic difficulties are excluded, here.

Following are the guidelines used by research staff during Phases 1, 2, and 3 of CTP to rate socioeconomic status (e.g., lower, middle, and upper "class"), as defined by the occupation of the head of household.

I. Used during Phases 1 and 2 of CTP[13]
    HIGH STATUS
        Manager of insurance company; self-employed plumbing contractor; department manager, Penney's Department Store; head of motor pool, at Army signal depot; chiropractor; general sales manager, Ford dealer; insurance salesman; plant manager, Lead Salvage Company; self-employed buying and selling cattle.
    MIDDLE STATUS
        Instrument repair, Aerojet; self-employed "mercantile" store owner; general repairman for city; full-time painter at air base; accountant at Aerojet [contractor for military]; automotive mechanic for city; aircraft mechanic at air base; civilian employee at air base, at about $8,800; Air Force captain; manager, building materials company; quality control specialist at air base; full-time carpenter; liaison engineer, Aerojet; full-time roofer; metal pattern maker; self-employed, ceramics; equipment specialist, at about $8,800; plasterer; aircraft inspector; fireman; horse trainer; welder; yard foreman; ranch foreman; code clerk, air base; electrician; draftsman; sheet metal worker; machinist, Southern Pacific Railroad; bookkeeper; plumber.
    LOW STATUS
        Laborer at Campbell Soup; owner and operator of lower-class bar, mak-

ing "marginal existence"; dishwasher; mother is part-time nurse's aid; Southern Pacific Shops, presumably unskilled; cook at Chili Parlor; taxi driver; construction worker; wholesale house employee ("employed" is used when exact type of work done is unclear but indications are that it is unskilled labor.); father unemployed-disabled, mother works; car man with Southern Pacific Railroad; father missing, mother earns low income; stepfather bartender plus Aid to Needy Children (ANC) for ward's sister; employed by Rice Grower's Association; Signal Depot employee, at $400 net; ranch laborer; truck driver; storeroom clerk and part-time janitor; floorman at card club; warehouseman; unemployed plumber; stepfather auctioneer plus ANC; maintenance man for city; cannery worker; mechanic; school custodian; machine operator, can company; employed by ice company; longshoreman; employed in bowling alley; father installs burglar alarms; packer at air base; equipment operator for construction firm; mail handler, Southern Pacific Railroad; "tail-off man" for lumber products company; garbage collector; junk dealer; employee at box company; self-employed, low income, hauls trash; employed at drive-in dairy; self-employed trucking contractor and hay hauler on small scale, plus seasonal cannery work and unemployment compensation.

II. Used during Phase 3 of CTP
    HIGH STATUS
        All managers, officials, proprietors and professional workers not included in the middle status category, and sales workers in finance, insurance, and real estate.
    MIDDLE STATUS
        All craftsmen, foremen, and kindred workers, clerical and kindred workers, protective service workers, managers and proprietors of small businesses, sales workers of wholesale and retail stores, and technicians allied to the professional services.

LOW STATUS

    All laborers, including farm laborers, operatives and kindred workers, service workers (except protective service workers), and peddlers and door-to-door salesmen.

VERY LOW STATUS

    1. Receiving welfare aid only (e.g., public assistance; also, receiving pension only);

    2. Currently unemployed (plus indications that *usual* work is of "lower" status type);

    3. Unsteadily employed (plus indications that *usual or current* work is of "lower" status type);

    4. Seasonal only plus unemployment compensation (plus indication that *usual* work is of "lower" status type);

    5. Veteran's pension plus babysitting only.

Notes

1. Unless otherwise indicated, statewide averages will refer to male, first commitments from juvenile court. These categories apply to the present experimental plus control sample as well. In most cases, 1961–1969 statewide figures will represent an unweighted average of Youth Authority data that were reported for 1961, 1965, and 1969, respectively (Walters, Brown, and Logan, 1961; Davis et al., 1965, 1969). In some cases, data for 1961 were not available; this information had not been collected in connection with the 1959 version of the YA's Initial Home Visit Research Schedule (IHVS). For information on variables mentioned in notes 2, 3 and 5, below, and on several other personal, family, and offense-related variables, also see Wright (1969).

2. The categories of lower, middle, and upper income range (or social class) referred to the occupation of the head of the household in which the youngster resided at point of intake. These categories were used in connection with the E plus C sample. On the other hand, statewide data—collected in terms of IHVS categories previously established by the Division of Research—focused ex-clusively on the neighborhood in which the given home was located. On this basis, the results were: below average—65 percent; average—30 percent; above average—6 percent.

3. Statewide figures were: Caucasian—53 percent; Mexican American—19 percent; black—26 percent; all others—2 percent. Here, the percentage of Mexican Americans was slightly lower than in the E plus C sample, while that of blacks was slightly higher. This relatively small difference reflected the fact that statewide figures, unlike those of E plus C, included YA commitments from Los Angeles, San Francisco, and Oakland. Collectively, these areas then had a somewhat lower percentage of Mexican American and an atypically high percentage of black commitments, compared to the state as a whole. They accounted for 48 percent of all male, juvenile court first commitments within California (1961–1969), and they thus had enough weight to lower, and raise, the respective percentages.

4. The E plus C figure was similar to those found statewide, in YA Clinic studies that were based on various group and individually administered instruments (see, e.g., Woodring, 1971). This near-identity, which also applied to verbal scores, is also reflected in the following: "His [male, juvenile court, first commitment's] mental ability was judged normal (60 percent), with eight percent rated above normal and 32 percent rated below normal" (Davis et al., 1965, p. 18). (For scores based on the Lorge-Thorndike, see Davis et al., 1970, 1971.)

5. The 1961–1969 eligibility criteria eliminated youths who had a seriously assaultive YA commitment offense. (All assaultive offenses were classified as ones against persons.) As a result, the overall E plus C sample was of a slightly different type than that found statewide. Despite this difference, statewide figures were fairly similar to those for E plus C with respect to YA commitment offense. The statewide figures were: property—57 percent; person—18 percent; all others—24 percent.

6. Five percent of the total sample had a YA commitment offense that involved some

degree of physical violence; 11 percent of the sample had at least one such offense *prior to* their commitment offense. Some of the former individuals were included in the latter group, that is, included among the 11 percent who had at least one such prior offense. Because of this overlap, the figure for youngsters with either a violent commitment offense or a violent prior offense was somewhat less than 5 percent plus 11 percent; it was 14 percent of the total. As used above, *physical violence* ("actual violence") was defined as "specific acts which have been committed against the victim's will and which have resulted in actual physical harm or which have involved attempted physical harm (shooting and missing, etc.)" (Palmer, 1968c, p. 11). In addition to "actual violence," 6 percent of the total sample had a "potentially violent" YA commitment offense (see below), and 20 percent had at least one such offense prior to their commitment offense. As in the case of actual violence, there was some overlap between the former youths and the latter. As a result, 23 percent of the total sample, not 26 percent, had at least one potentially violent offense at some point, or points—either as the commitment offense, a prior offense, or as both. Potential violence referred to "acts which have involved a threat of bodily harm, except for verbal threats [by themselves]; and, it includes the carrying of concealed weapons" (Palmer, 1968c, pp. 11–26; Spencer, 1966). There was about 65 percent overlap between individuals who had a potentially violent offense and those who had one or more instances of actual violence.

7. Statewide figures were available only for 1961–1962: 35 percent of all youths were living with their natural mother and natural father; 20 percent were living with natural mother and father substitute; 27 percent were living with natural mother and no father or substitute; 6 percent were living with father and mother substitute; 12 percent were living in other situations. (Cf. Gould and Beverly, 1963; Beverly, 1964. Also see Youth Authority Annual Statistical Reports, 1961 through 1970, for selected statistics.)

8. Statewide figures were: 29 percent of the fathers or father substitutes had a police record—as did 6 percent of the mothers or mother substitutes. Thirty-six percent of the youths had one or more siblings with a delinquent record. (See Youth Authority Annual Statistical Reports, 1961 through 1970.)

9. Statewide figures were available for 1961–1962 only: 40 percent of the homes were rated as undesirable or less than acceptable; 52 percent were acceptable; 9 percent were good or excellent. (Cf. Gould and Beverly, 1963.)

10. These are statewide figures, not those of the E plus C sample (Beverly, 1964; Gould and Beverly, 1963; Youth Authority Annual Statistical Reports, 1962 through 1964). E plus C case folders had never been analyzed relative to this particular factor, or area. However, based on the high degree of similarity found between "statewide" and "E plus C" in virtually all areas that *had been* reviewed jointly, it seemed moderately safe to assume that the former figures would be (or might well be) representative or at least fairly representative of the latter, within the present area as well. The same reasoning was applied to the following items (i.e., all figures that appear in the appendix are statewide, and they are only assumed to be *representative* of E plus C): public assistance; percentage of youths who had lived away from home (and age at which their move first occurred); age at first delinquent contact; presence or absence of co-offenders in YA commitment offense; use of narcotics; temper tantrums, nail biting, and bed-wetting; psychiatric/psychological observation, diagnosis, or therapy prior to YA commitment; age at start of serious or persistent school difficulties (and age at start of truancy in particular) level of overall academic functioning (see Youth Authority Annual Statistical Reports, 1961 through 1970).

11. There are no known statewide figures on this subject, that is, at the level of *types* of school difficulties. This applies to the subsequent item—nonattendance—as well. In both cases, E plus C data were obtained via a review of individual case folders. However, see Youth Authority

Annual Statistical Reports (e.g., Davis et al., 1965) for years 1961 through 1970, for general information with respect to "positive," "indifferent," or "negative" attitudes toward school, and regarding prevalence of "school misbehavior." Also see Wright (1969), for 1964 through 1968.

12. These findings were the same as those observed statewide, based on the Gates-MacGinitie Reading Vocabulary and Reading Comprehension tests and on the Comprehensive Test of Basic Skills—Arithmetic. See, for example, Davis et al., (1969).

13. The definitions given for high, middle, and low status are those in Reiss and Rhodes (1961). The descriptions shown in the case of very low status (for Phase 3) are based upon several years' experience with families of California Youth Authority wards.

6 DETAILS CONCERNING I-LEVEL THEORY AND PERSONALITY TYPES

I. Original Description of Maturity Levels 2, 3, and 4

In the original account of the interpersonal maturity theory, *level 2* was called the "integration of non-self differences." At this level,

> people are seen as kinds of means-objects to end-objects and, as such, only gradually acquire a new character and value in the eyes of the child. His dependency also assumes meaning in this phase. . . . He is faced with the fact that persons sometimes do not give him what he wants; and, because of his brief experience with persons and subsequent lack of information about them, he feels uncertain about his ability to predict what others will do. However, through trial and error procedures, he seeks answers to this, attempting to find particular people who can satisfy particular roles—for example, that of giver and supporter. (Sullivan, Grant, and Grant, 1957, p. 377)

In the original theory, *level 3* was called the "integration of rules." At this level the youngster discovers that

> not only must he be in contact with someone in order to get satisfactions, but that this necessary person must also be able to satisfy society's rules. . . . He is taught, both explicitly and implicitly, that definite rules govern the relationships between people and things, and that these rules seem to control "big" people. With this belief, he tends to transfer his feelings about the magic of people to the magic of rules. Rules are now seen as being the magic talismans of control. However, as yet, the child is unable to perceive the patterning of relationships which will later enable him to make generalizations about rules. Rules seem more or less arbitrary, black-and-white statements which are applicable only in specific situations. . . . Throughout this development one can see his concern with the problems of possible external control. He attempts to resolve the stresses in this phase by testing the limits of the rules and seeking concrete and unchanging formulae which will enable him to resolve all the problems that arise. (Sullivan, Grant, and Grant, 1957, p. 379)

Level 4 was called the "integration of conflict and response." Here,

> the child's behavior is [still] primarily influenced by his own needs, but he is also aware of the influence of others and their expectations upon him. At this point, social anxiety begins to emerge as a motivating force. He has accepted the impossibility of completely controlling or manipulating [others]. . . . [Instead,] he tries to see himself as others will see him, attempting to predict their reactions toward him. By introjecting into his own reaction system the responses of others to his behavior, he comes to experience himself as a social being. . . . This role-playing is a safe kind of practicing, leading to greater differentiation and social interaction. . . . However, as he shifts to many roles, he runs into conflict. In part this comes about because, while the

heroes he picks are related to his own needs, they are undoubtedly related to different needs [e.g., their own needs] as well. . . . Having thus globally accepted what others feel is right and wrong, the child is caught in the conflict of wanting to be liked by significant others and wanting to give expression to his own needs. Further, because of his own participation in the roles, some internalization has taken place, and when he fails to live up to these new standards, he feels guilty and critical of himself. (Sullivan, Grant, and Grant, 1957, p. 381)

II. Technical Details of I-Level Theory

The following points are basic to the theory of interpersonal maturity. All quotations are from Sullivan, Grant, and Grant (1957).

1. Personality development takes place almost entirely in the context of, and under the impetus of, interactions (exchanges) between individual and environment: "Communication and social interaction are crucial determinants in the development of [personality], helping to expand and elaborate the basic potential with which a person is born" (p. 373).
2. "Initially such interaction is relatively simple and is probably associated with reduction of *physiological tensions* in a primitive differentiation of self [from environment]." Later differentiation of self from environment occurs mainly on other grounds (pp. 373–374).
3. With increasing age, the child is exposed to, and interacts with, an increasing variety and range of social stimuli: "The normal pattern of emotional-social development follows a trend toward increasing involvement with persons, objects, and social institutions" (pp. 374–375). Interaction with these stimuli provides the basis for the child's increased awareness of (1) the complexities in his social environment, (2) the environment's expectations of him, and (3) the differences that exist between himself and others, and *among* others, as well. This increased awareness of the realities of his environment, and of the latter's expectations of him, "give[s] rise to new needs, demands and situations"

(p. 375): The individual now has a greater amount and variety of information and expectations to "integrate" (assimilate) into his already existing need system.
4. The child or youngster becomes increasingly aware of the differences and discrepancies that exist between some of this information and expectations, on the one hand, and his own, already existing needs and preferences, on the other.[1] These discrepancies and differentiations must somehow be responded to. The individual's response can occur at the perceptual/attitudinal level, and at the overt/behavioral level.
5. At any period in his life, the individual's responses are largely built upon previously established perceptions of, and attitudes toward, his social environment. (As indicated in item 2, the latter were originally built upon direct physical interactions with the immediate environment, during infancy.) The perceptions and attitudes in question are those which have played a major role in maintaining the individual's underlying need system, physiological and psychological aspects included. Because of their strategic role,[2] these perceptions and attitudes become relatively stable (consistent; predictable) at any point in time, and long-lasting as well. As to observable form and content, they are, in-the-main, mutually consistent and mutually reinforcing—that is, "integrated." They support and promote essentially the same objectives, though in somewhat different ways. This applies cross-sectionally (i.e., at any point in time) as well as longitudinally (across time).
6. Together, these perceptions and attitudes comprise the "core structure of personality" (p. 373). This core is not only the product of the individual's prior responses to the environment; it is, simultaneously, the primary basis of his present responses.
7. Broadly speaking, personality can be described as the pattern of an individual's commonly occurring attitudinal and behavioral responses to the stimuli, information, and expectations described in items 3 and 4 above. During any period of his life, an individual's personality

includes what might be called core and non-core features. Although the latter are largely an outgrowth or direct product of the former, both aspects are ultimately a product of all ideas, attitudes, and expectations to which an individual has been exposed. However, an individual is more than just a receiver and passive recorder of all such stimuli: "Cultural transmission . . . cannot by itself account for the character and style of what is transmitted, nor for the integrative character of the human mind [this would apply to core and non-core alike]" (p. 374). Instead, the individual *selects* from among the many stimuli to which he is exposed. He also groups and combines these selected items into a particular pattern: "A person builds within himself an integrative system of goals, values, and aspirations which are uniquely satisfying to him and manageable by him. Without such simplification and integration the complexity of stimuli impinging on him would be overwhelming"[3] (p. 374).

8. As indicated, the pattern in question is often described as "personality," or character. This would include core as well as non-core. Basically, core aspects of personality would include perceptions/attitudes/expectations. Non-core aspects would mainly include a larger number of derived, yet supportive, *perceptions/attitudes/expectations;* however, it would also include the individual's main response patterns, that is, his overt responses to, and modes of interacting with, the social environment.

9. In short, throughout any individual's life, the following general process occurs: Various stimuli are first discriminated (differentiated); later, some of these stimuli are selected, sorted out, and eventually assimilated (integrated).[4] This, in broad outline, is none other than the process of learning. However, when certain kinds of stimuli are assimilated (see below), it becomes possible to say, in a specific sense, that a "cognitive restructuring of experience and expectancy . . . takes place . . . [and] a new level of integration is achieved" (p. 375).

10. A new "level" of integration is achieved when the type and range of stimuli that have been discriminated and assimilated can be characterized as follows (here, the decisive feature is the third one, listed below): The new stimuli (1) are substantially different than, and/or broader than, those which were assimilated prior to that time, and which formed the basis of the individual's then current "core personality." The new stimuli (2) represent specified challenges (see levels 2–6, in item 11, below).[5] These challenges are sometimes described as "problems," or "developmental tasks." More specifically, the stimuli or challenges that must be assimilated are those which (3) bear on certain noteworthy and distinguishing features of the individual's *relationship* to his social environment. Each of the seven maturity levels is, in fact, differentiated from every other level on the basis of one such distinguishing feature. That is, every level of interpersonal maturity is organized around one such relationship feature. Therefore, by definition, it is these specific features or problems that the individual must come to terms with ("solve," or assimilate) before one can correctly say he is *progressing* within the maturity sequence.

11. Following are the distinguishing features in question, for maturity levels 2 through 6. Each feature represents a potential turning point in the individual's relationship to his social environment:

    Level 2: "Differentiation of the environment into persons and objects, with some appreciation of the characteristics of each" (p. 377).

    Level 3: "Perception of rules or formulae governing the relationships between people and objects, with a beginning awareness of potential for complex manipulation" (p. 378).

    Level 4: "Perception of the influence and psychological force of others" (p. 381).

    Level 5: "Perception of stable patterns in self and others" (p. 383).

    Level 6: "Perception of differences between one's self and the social roles which one may play [in certain types of situations]" (p. 384).

12. Each individual can deal with only one such feature at a time. Each higher-

numbered level of maturity is structurally more complex than the level which proceeds it; that is, the specific content of the former must, logically, have been preceded by that of the latter. As a result, all individuals must advance from lower maturity levels to higher levels in exactly the same sequence. However, few individuals progress beyond level 5.

13. The formal relationship that exists between differentiation that leads to subsequent integration of given relationship features, on the one hand, and the achievement of corresponding maturity levels, on the other, may be seen in the following illustrations. (These descriptions would apply to all remaining maturity levels as well.)

A. Movement beyond Level 1

The essential precondition for movement beyond level 1 is the "differentiation of the environment into persons and objects, with some appreciation of the characteristics of each." To the level 1 individual (i.e., the relatively advanced level 1 individual—someone who has begun to make the level 2 differentiation in question), this particular differentiation represents a new way of perceiving/experiencing the events in his environment, and a potentially new basis on which to respond to them. (This new way or new basis is not necessarily experienced, by the individual, as being easier or more satisfying.) However, technically speaking, level 2 is fully achieved only if, and when, these newly perceived "non-self differences"—that is, the level 2 challenge, or differentiation—become integrated with the core perceptions that existed at level 1.[6] This occurs when the level 2 perceptions have become dominant, that is, when the individual no longer interacts with his environment primarily on the basis of his level 1 perceptions.

The product of the earlier-mentioned integration—namely, the cognitive restructuring of former (level 1) perceptions on the basis of current (level 2) differentiations—is an expanded, partially new, qualitatively different set of core perceptions. These perceptions relate to self, environment, and potential as well as actual ways of interacting with that environment. The integrated perceptions that relate to "self" are referred to as the core personality of the level 2 individual.

To recapitulate: The end product of the individual's selections and rejections, arrangements and rearrangements, is a "relatively consistent set of expectations and attitudes." These function as "a kind of interpreting and working philosophy of life." As such, they comprise the central, and active, building blocks of his personality. "It is this nexus of gradually expanding experiences, expectations, hypotheses, and perceptions which make up the core of personality" (Sullivan, Grant, and Grant, 1957, p. 373). These building blocks, in turn, then help determine what shall be selected or rejected in the future. That is, they play an integral role in any subsequent movement toward the next higher level of maturity.

B. Movement beyond Level 2

The essential precondition for such movement is the "perception of rules or formulae governing the relationship between people and objects [etc.], . . ." (p. 378). From the standpoint of the level 2 individual, this recognition of "rules which govern" is a new way of perceiving, experiencing, and (in a broad sense of the term) understanding the environment. It provides a new basis for interacting with it, as well. Level 3 is fully attained when the rules or formulae in question become integrated with the core perceptions that existed at level 2. This involves a dominance of the former level over the latter, with regard to the individual's everyday interactions with his environment.

14. An inescapable, lifelong problem for all individuals is that of balancing (1) the internal tendency to change plus external pressure for change, with (2) the underlying need for emotional security and stability.[7] Involved, here, is the interaction between specific interests, personal ideals, and social expectations, on the one hand, and underlying needs for tension reduction and relative constancy, on the other. This interplay of often-divergent interests, expectations, and needs is dynamic in nature; its products (or ongoing/developing outputs/outcomes) are continuously shaped by the individual's core personality—that is, by his central perceptions and operating principles (the "interpreting or working philosophy of life") at any given stage of development. In this connection, core perceptions and

principles can play either a defensive/restrictive or an integrative role, depending largely on the type and level of stimulation that is involved.

15. Stimuli that are very stressful, anxiety-producing, or discrepant are likely to be actively resisted, misinterpreted, ignored, or denied. This may lead to a blocking-out or marked reduction of potentially useful information. It may also lead to a withdrawal from given social interactions, and a possible "fixation" at one's current level of maturity. Fixation may occur not only because of overly intense or long-continued stress and anxiety, but because of very low levels of stimulation and challenge. Stimuli that produce *moderate* amounts of stress, anxiety, challenge, or uncertainty are those most often associated with continued interpersonal growth.

III. Major Sources of I-Level Theory

The following writers and concepts have provided the background for I-level theory:

1. *G.H. Mead:* Interaction between self and society as the principal basis for the development of self; increasing importance of the individual's ability to assume the role of others, in later stages of social development; four main stages of development: impulsive, imitative (perceives and responds to behavior segments, not to roles), role-taking (responds—in turn—to role behavior of one individual after another), and "generalized other" or organization of roles (perceives and responds to the roles of "all the players").

2. *J. Piaget:* Four stages of cognitive, social, and moral development, ranging from less complex to more complex: motor, egocentric, incipient cooperation, and codification of rules.

3. *H.S. Sullivan:* The maturing capacity of an individual for complex experience is seen as a function of social opportunities, far more than biological make-up; his perception or interpretation of the environment is seen as both a product and an expression of the emergent "self-dynamism," the "integrative self," and "selective inattention"; relationship between (1) fixation/distortion of reality, and (2) excessive anxiety or stress.

4. *K. Lewin:* "Primitivization"; "de-differentiation."

5. *E. Erickson:* Fixed sequence of personal development, described in "eight stages of life"; problems at any one stage must be resolved before the individual can advance to the next level.[8]

6. *D. Bloch:* Delinquency as an "integration" designed to minimize the anxiety of real or imagined interpersonal relationships.

7. *R. Sarbin:* Relatively enduring cognitive structures, or "empirical selves," as "stages of refinement in the discrimination of stimuli"; higher stages of cognitive development are seen as products of the interaction between, and various subsequent integrations of, (1) the self and (2) those social roles that are perceived to be personally acceptable ["congruent"]. (Bloch, 1952; Erikson, 1950; Lewin, 1935; Mead, 1934; Piaget, 1926, 1929, 1969; Sarbin, 1952; Sullivan, 1940.)

One final, possible influence was Isaac's conceptualization of "relatability." Relatability was viewed as "a sequence of levels of increasing differentiation of the self from others and [as an] increasing affective appreciation of the delineation of others" (Isaacs, 1956, 12; Isaacs and Haggard, 1956). Other I-level sources include Adorno et al. (1950), Baldwin (1902), Tappan (1949), and Wolff (1950).

A few words might be said about early philosophical origins. Several basic features of I-level theory were strikingly anticipated—in some cases, paralleled—in the central tenets of the German idealist J. G. Fichte (1762–1814). In Fichte's (1792) system of philosophy, "complete self-consciousness is given in the form of self-knowledge, and is what the Ego ["Absolute Ego"] seeks to attain."[9] (See Fuller, 1955; the following quotations are from this source.) The development of self-knowledge proceeds by a succession of definite acts—called "Anstösse", or thrusts—"in which the Ego progressively organizes its experiences." As it does so, it "creates an experience in which *selves* are distinguished from one another, and from objects they assume to be external to themselves," that is, from objects of the external world. (The parallels between I-level theory and the Fichtean system are more evident if one substitutes the term "interpersonal awareness" for that of "self-knowledge," and "integration" or "cognitive restructuring" for that of "thrust.")

The organization of experience involves six distinct thrusts of progressively higher self-consciousness. The first thrust creates mere unreflective sensation, which is a step above consciousness. The subsequent ones are as follows:

2. The ego, in becoming aware of the fact that it is perceiving, differentiates itself from its perceptions and thus turns them into a non-ego other than itself. (Compare maturity level 1.)
3. The ego, by means of memory and imagination, turns its perceptions into a world of objects, and its awareness of them into a consciousness of things. (Compare maturity level 2.)
4. The ego reflects upon the subjective images in consciousness; it classifies them and thinks about them in general terms. (Compare maturity levels 3 and 4.)
5. The ego again reflects upon these concepts and, by exercising the faculty of judgment, arranges them in a logical relationship to each other. (Compare maturity level 5: The individual "begins to see patterns of relationships and significant symbols identifying these relationships. . . . He becomes aware of continuity in his own life and in the life of others, and senses a relationship in this continuity between responses in the past and responses in the present and future.")
6. The ego reflects upon its powers of judgment, recognizes itself to be the originator of the laws that govern its thinking, and knows itself to be the basis of its own knowledge. This represents the highest level of self-knowledge or self-consciousness. (Compare maturity levels 6 and 7: "The self, although it is [seen as] the integrated resultant of past experiences and interaction with others, can now [level 6] be perceived as separate and distinct from any specific relationship with others." At the highest level, level 7, the individual "begins to comprehend focusing or integrating processes in himself and others. . . . Along with increasing awareness of the process of integration within himself, he begins to get some perspective on previous modes of experiencing" (Sullivan, Grant, and Grant, 1957, pp. 384–385). He can see that an individual's behavior is both the result, and expression, of that person's particular processes of integration.)

IV. Factors and Developments Relating to Personality Types (Delinquent Subtypes)

Beginning in the middle 1950s, I-level theory was used in studies of military offenders and California Adult Corrections inmates. These investigations focused largely on maturity levels 2 through 5 and on major differences from one level to the next. During this research, substantial differences were noticed among individuals who fell within any one maturity level, for instance, level 3.

These within-level differences centered around the ways in which individuals often responded to their environment. They usually involved or reflected certain character traits or combinations of traits on the part of those individuals.[10] Many of these characteristics and behavioral differences (see "subtypes," in the text) had long been noted by scientists and nonscientists alike. Beginning in the early 1950s these characteristics were often called response styles or response sets (Cronbach, 1950, 1958; Gage and Cronbach, 1954; Guilford, 1959).

Maturity level had mainly focused on the individual's ways of perceiving and interpreting his "world." In contrast, response style or subtype placed main emphasis on his ways of overtly *responding to* those perceptions, and of interacting with others as a result of his interpretations.

Years of clinical research and experience suggested that these traits and patterns might often play a significant role in the development of delinquent behavior (Adams, 1961; Grant, 1961a; Grant and Grant, 1959; Gough and Peterson, 1952; Healy and Bronner, 1936; Jenkins and Hewitt, 1944; McCord, McCord, and Zola, 1959; Redl, 1969; Redl and Wineman, 1951; Sykes, 1958; Weeks, 1958). As a result, during 1960–1961, several of the above observations and hypotheses were brought together and organized, within the structure of the already existing maturity level system.

First and foremost, it was noted that the individual's response to his environment was closely related to his maturity level, since the latter itself reflected the way he interpreted that environment. However, the specific features of his response were not entirely determined by his particular level of maturity. In fact, the higher the I-level the greater were the number of readily observable response patterns. In a sense, higher I-levels seemed to allow for, or perhaps pave the way for, more freedom of response. Thus, as later described by Warren:

> An attempt was . . . made [in 1960–1961] to classify within each I-level according to *response set*. There appeared to be two major ways in which the integration Level 2 (I_2) individual responded to his perceptual frame of reference. Similarly, there appeared to be three typical response sets among delinquent I_3's, and four . . . among delinquent I_4's. In this manner . . . nine delinquent subtypes were identified.[11] (Warren, 1969, p. 52)

Among I_2's and I_3's, a broad and readily apparent distinction related to the factor of passivity versus activity. Among I_4's it related to that of personal disturbance versus *lack* of long-standing personal disturbance. Other factors could conceivably have been focused on as well, or instead. However, the former seemed to hold considerable promise with regard to the goal of developing treatment/control plans for delinquent offenders, plans which, hopefully, would reflect various factors that substantially and even decisively contributed to their delinquent behavior. Passivity, and long-standing personal disturbance, were thought to be among these factors.

Notes

1. He also becomes increasingly aware of differences between one set of information/expectations and other sets.
2. This also includes their reinforcement and satisfaction value.
3. "The word *integration,* as we use it here, refers to the usual or typical *process* by which various stimuli impinging on an organism are brought into relative harmony and stability with each other. [In other contexts the word is used] to describe modal patterns of cognitive organization" (Sullivan, Grant, and Grant, 1957, p. 374)—that is, a *product* rather than a process.
4. It is the individual's perception of, and response to, the stimuli that is assimilated, not the stimuli themselves.
5. And, often, temporary threats.
6. In effect, the differentiation → integration cycle must be rounded out.
7. Here, change, or growth, may be considered a product of ongoing interactions with the social environment. It includes and otherwise reflects all new information that may be acquired as a result of these interactions.
8. These problems may include, for example, overidentification with "the heroes of cliques and crowds," during the "identity" versus "role diffusion" stage.
9. To Fichte, consciousness is "an activity busied with realizing its own potentialities." Ego is "a process—not a substance—a striving toward a goal." Fichte's distinction between "Ego" and "Absolute Ego" is of no concern here.
10. During the 1940s and 1950s these combinations or blends were commonly referred to as personality configurations, or personality patterns. There is no distinct, widely agreed upon definition of "personality" within or across the fields of psychology, sociology, and psychiatry. This applies to the concept of personality "core," as well.
11. The term "set" has been used in two distinctly different ways, in I-level literature. In the present quotation it was used in connection with the individual's way of *responding to* his perceptual frame of reference, or perceived environment. In other contexts it was used in connection with his way of *perceiving* that environment. (The former relates to the individual's subtype; the latter relates to his maturity level alone.) For example, the following was written in 1959, prior to the delineation of any delinquent subtypes:

> Although this frame of reference [namely, the "theory of sequential I-Levels of interpersonal maturity"] suggests that delinquent behavior results from interactions between individuals, the emphasis has been put on delinquency proneness and [on] what it is within the individual that he takes with him into interpersonal relationships. This approach has recently received new emphasis from the methodological work of Cronbach. He has stated that we need to know much more about the "sets" that

people bring with them into interpersonal situations. More needs to be understood about the nature of delinquency proneness, in terms of interpersonal "sets," *before* we can study the effects of interpersonal interactions in determining delinquent behavior. The maturity levels theory maintains that these "sets" are extremely important. (Grant and Grant, 1959, p. 2; emphasis added)

The Cronbach 1958 article in question neither reviewed nor discussed any of the "response sets" that were widely recognized by the mid- to later 1950s—sets that related to the individual's ways of *responding* to given situations. (These included the sets of "acquiescence," "evasiveness," and "caution versus incaution." By chance, however, it was Cronbach who, several years earlier [1946, 1950], had first described these response sets.) Instead, the article focused on the individual's *perceptual* frame of reference itself, that is, on "the 'personality space' used by the perceiver" in his efforts to describe or understand other individuals. This space, or "map," consisted of explicit concepts ("con-

structs") and implicit assumptions in terms of which the individual "perceived" (i.e., differentiated, cognitively structured or organized, and then interpreted) his environment. If minimal differentiation were to occur, one result might be the "tendency to [erroneously] perceive others as [being] similar to oneself." Cronbach believed that the significance of the individual's perceptual map of others is illustrated by the recent theoretical work of George Kelly (1955), who considers the entire process of social learning as one of generating construct dimensions along which others are differentiated. He suggests that the individual and his social world may be revealed in the way he describes himself and significant others in his life with reference to these constructs. (Cronbach, 1958, pp. 355, 362, 364).

Here, the relationship to various descriptions of maturity level theory—as distinct from those of delinquent subtypes, or related response dimensions—is clear.

7 RARE TYPES OF YOUTHS

Asocial Youths

Passive-Asocial and Assertive-Asocial

From various perspectives, developmental ones included, these are the most childlike or immature offenders found in state as well as local correctional settings. Staff view most such youths as self-absorbed and as usually uninterested in other people—adults and peers alike—beyond what those individuals may be able to do *for* them or to them. Most peers often consider these youths blunderers, tagalongs, or "oddballs," and they frequently scapegoat such individuals, leave them "holding the bag," and otherwise exploit them.

To these youths, the social/interpersonal environment—especially that which centers around adults—-not only seems, but generally is, difficult to influence or to even communicate with successfully. In these and other ways, such everyday contexts and structures seem, to the youths, largely beyond their control.[1] Their relationships, for example, with individuals outside the home, often center on their own, following concern—one that frequently amounts to a preoccupation (though they do not conceptualize it in either such way): Will their needs and wishes—even for basics such as food, shelter (and related physical security/stability), and freedom from physical abuse—be met, that is, met by *others,* namely, adults. The frustrations and fears these individuals often experience because they feel little ability to personally meet their needs and wishes, to shape related events and potentially overwhelming conditions, or to avoid physically painful situations sometimes leads them to directly ask or even demand that those other individuals, in effect, take care (or much better care) of them, protect them, buy things for them, and so on.[2] Yet, they usually assume that few if any individuals *will* make much effort to respond, and that whatever responses may occur will probably be inconsistent, anyway.

With most asocial youths, a "no" response, by others, to those requests or demands often leads to the youths' sulking, pouting, verbal—and, less often, physical—lashing out, and/or to their marked withdrawal or perhaps even literal hiding. It sometimes leads, of course, to illegal behavior, for instance, to the youths' direct "taking" of what they feel they need or should have. Their upbringing was usually confusing to the point where they never came to understand the main reasons, such as the typical feelings, standards, and motivations, that would lead most people (i.e., the "others") to respond to those requests or demands in the way they do, and not just when the answer is "no." This lack of, or limitation in, basic understanding helps generate and then reinforce the following, long-standing feelings or implicit assumptions on the youths' part: It is *arbitrary* or *capricious* actions and reactions (a/r's) by parents and others—that is, a/r's concerning the youths—that are the main causes of their, the youths', frustrations, deprivations, fears, and overall unhappiness. Moreover, those a/r's are considered unjustified—or, of course, not even understandable.

It might be added that pets, toys, and/or various gadgets often provide these individuals stronger or more frequent feelings of comfort, relief, stability, and even emotional contact (including imaginary contact) than do most real-life adults. Apart from the youths' interest in various games and standard sports, it is those objects for which they show some of their few or clearest signs of enthusiasm and which, of course, they can partly or largely control. Finally, in most social situations, many such individuals find it difficult to sit still and focus on conversations for more than a few minutes (Grant, 1961c; Palmer, 1967b; Warren et al., 1966b).

The asocial youth category consists of three major "types." *Type A* (the "under-socialized") usually stems from one of the following: Long-term or even lifelong, general neglect (though not rejection per se) by parents or parent figures; lack of ongoing and/or varied social or interpersonal stimulation; active or passive parental reinforcement/encouragement of pre-latency or latency-age egocentricity, aggressivity, and related character traits often found in young children (frequently including preschoolers). This type includes (1) passive/conforming, (2) responsive/approval-seeking, and (3) aggressive/demanding individuals. The first two fall within the broader "passive-asocial" group; the third mainly belongs in the "assertive-asocial" group.

Type B individuals ("rejection-fear-confusion avoiders") were strongly affected by one or more of the following, again on a long-term basis: highly inconsistent or chaotic upbringing; overly controlling or inflexible environment; abusive, brutalizing, or bizarre parental handling; moderate to strong parental rejection, or intense parental ambivalence toward the youths (whether overt or covert). This type includes (1) anxious/acceptance-seeking, (2) withdrawn/constricted, (3) hostile/impulsive, and (4) erratic/autistic or schizoid/(pre)psychotic individuals. The first two best fit into the broader, passive-asocial grouping, whereas the third fits in the assertive-asocial group. Individuals comprising the fourth subgroup may be passive, assertive, or mixed.

Regarding *Type C* ("psycho-physically impaired, deficient, or disturbed"), clinical examination usually suggests or confirms the presence of one or more of the following, operating by themselves or in mutual interaction: (1) mild to severe organic brain impairment; (2) mild to moderate (or severe) mental deficiency; (3) major medical handicap(s) or sensory-motor impairment; and (4) chronic, progressive "childhood schizophrenia" (e.g., "process" schizophrenia). This applies whether the individuals'

social/interactional emphasis is on the more passive or more assertive side (Palmer, 1971b, 1971c).

Stress and Adjustment Reactions to Adolescence

The original situational-emotional (SE) reaction (Grant, 1961c; Warren et al., 1966b) was subsequently revised and refined by the present author, as two largely separable classifications: stress reactions and adjustment reactions. Together, these are called *stress and adjustment (SA) reactions to adolescence*. ("Stress reaction" is the one that corresponds most closely to Warren's SE.) SA reactions are considerably more common—in fact, they are not rare—at the local probation level. This is in considerable contrast to the state-agency population, in which repeat and/or chronic offenders are far more common, and are, in fact, the rule. At the local probation level, many or most offenders—its SA's included—are not repeaters, certainly not multiple repeaters.

A diagnosis of SA—particularly in contrast to one of *conflicted* (i.e., assertive-denier or anxious-confused)—presupposes the following (all subsequent material concerning SA's is quoted from Palmer [1971d, pp. 4–10]).

1. The childhood and preadolescent picture appears to be one of relative health or "normalcy." In any event, it contains little if anything by way of severe family strife and unusual or recurrent personal stress.

2. On balance, the self-image is positive, moderately positive, or, at least, not particularly negative.[3] This is in spite of the possible presence of a moderate to sizable amount of tension, anger, self-dissatisfaction, and/or felt guilt, primarily as a result of given events or pressures.

3. The events or pressures in question are predominantly post-pubertal, in terms of their temporal point of origin. That is, their emergence, and apparent impact, predate only slightly (if at all)—and then only seldom—the period of chronological adolescence.

There are three types of SA's—Types A, B, and C, as follows.

Type A: Situational—Trauma Reactions

This involves any of several responses to major structural changes or traumatic events within the family. It mainly includes (1) immediate and transitory reactions and/or (2) somewhat longer-term, progressive adaptations to one or more of the following external circumstances: death of one or both parents; sudden appearance-on-scene of "real" parent—with resulting change in the youth's guardianship; parental divorce/separation (actual or clearly imminent). Physical relocation of the family may or may not result from the above events. Subsequent changes in the nature of family demands, expectations, or overall interactions are directly traceable to external circumstances and events of this nature. . . . In general, it is these subsequent changes which pave the way for, and/or provide the more immediate stimulus for, socially unacceptable acting-out or eventual delinquent involvement per se. Some of these changes may include literal abandonment of the youth by one or both parents. . . .

Type A is comprised of two subgroups. These are Subgroup 1: "Reaction to New Types or Levels of Parental Control and Support" and Subgroup 2: "Reaction to Parental Abandonment or Open Rejection."

Type B: Role Adjustments— Integrity Strivings[4]

This refers to a number of reactions which may occur at any point during adolescence and which—in most instances—are quite counteractive in nature. They are usually directed at (1) neutralizing the effects of given parental stances or behavior, or (2) modifying or disproving the existence of given characteristics which the youth has observed within himself. Included are three main patterns:

1. Strivings for independence, "personal integrity," or identity. These strivings are largely focused upon specific features of the parental stance with regard to the youth. These features are felt to be personally detrimental and unacceptable, if not socially unjustified, by the youth. The "stances"—or general orientations on the part of one or both parents— would include: marked restrictiveness or over-protectiveness; highly patriarchal family structure, etc.
2. Rejection or counter-rejection of—or psychological/physical withdrawal from—one or both parents, or from the family as a whole. This would be in response to the presence of (a) increasingly apparent parental rejection of, or indifference toward, the youth,[5] and/or (b) sharp or pervasive inter-parental conflict.[6]
3. Rejection—by the youth—of the overly passive, compliant mode of interacting with parent-figures (and, to some extent, with peers) which has characterized the youth up to the point of pre-, early-, and/or middle-adolescence. The "rejection" may be forceful and direct or it may be relatively low-key yet equally pervasive.

The youth in question (especially if he falls within Subgroups 3 or 4 [listed next]) rather vigorously attempts to achieve or maintain what can be thought of as a sense of personal integrity. This is in spite of family pressures or conflicts which, in most cases, appear to operate in moderate if not strong opposition to the development and maintenance of such a feeling. . . .

Type B consists of three main subgroups. These are Subgroups 3: "Reaction to Parental Over-Restrictiveness, Over-Protectiveness, or Overly Patriarchal (Matriarchal) Structure," Subgroup 4: "Reaction to Inter-Parental Conflict and/or Parental Rejection/Insensitivity," and Subgroup 5: "Compensatory Role-Adjustments and Identity Strivings."

Type C: Characterological— Emotional Reactions

This involves any of several responses to specified types of situational stress or developmental crisis. Ordinarily, the stress or crisis cannot be handled by means of the youth's typical defenses and modes of adaptation. Instead, it activates—or "breaks through to"—given characterological "weak spots" or developmental/adaptational deficiencies, some of which are expressed in such forms as: "hypersensitivity," "inflexibility," etc. In some cases, the stress or crisis may instead (or in addition) reactivate given modes of interaction—or need-systems and ego-states[7]—most of which (1) ordinarily remain subordinate to other, more "age-appropriate" need-systems, etc., and (2) seldom play a sizable or direct role in the youth's everyday interactions.[8]

The *stress* in question may be sudden, and generally unexpected. It may involve: personal confrontation/direct-challenge by others; actual or perceived physical threat; etc. *Crisis* may be of a somewhat longer-term, developmental nature. It commonly involves a temporal conjunction of two or more major types of social readjustment, or impending choices—no one of which would appear to be easily reversed or "undone" (i.e., in the event that the youth would later wish to attempt this). Included are: moving away from home; either starting college or else beginning to work full-time, shortly after the completion (or [—in the case of work—] dropping out) of high school; joining the Armed Service; becoming engaged or married; etc. Thus, certain stimuli which are likely to engender the given reactions may be fairly sudden as to onset, and short-lived in terms of duration. Yet, in other cases, their emergence—and convergence—may take place gradually, and over a period of several months. The youth's reactions to the above stimuli may range from the more direct, uncomplicated, and transitory, on the one hand, to the indirect, complex, and fairly long-standing, on the other.

Characterological-emotional reactions are likely to occur in youths whose interactions and level of functioning are, under most conditions, at least moderately effective, efficient, or personally satisfying. However, [with] a minority of these individuals, the quality of adjustment in question can be characterized as borderline. These observations apply to the youths' level of conscious satisfactions as well. . . .

Type C contains three main subgroups. These are Subgroup 6: "Reaction to Situational Stress, Challenge, or Threat," Subgroup 7: "Reaction to Developmental Crisis or Impending Social Readjustment," and Subgroup 8: "Reaction to Direct Peer Influence, Pressure, or Manipulation."

Further Details Regarding Type C Youths

In one pattern, a somewhat isolated feature—a "weak spot," in one sense—within the personality system gets keyed-off by: a direct or sharp challenge to the individual's "ego" or pride; an impending major change in his life-circumstances; an unexpected physical threat; etc. From a developmental and/or adaptational framework, the "weak spot" would relate to—or be expressed in terms of—particular areas of hypersensitivity, insensitivity, "undercontrol," or cognitive distortion. Hypersensitivity and undercontrol may, e.g., be present with regard

to strivings for masculinity, autonomy, personal achievement, recognition, acceptance by specific individuals (including close friends of own or opposite sex), etc. Insensitivity and cognitive distortion may reflect lack of information, presence of specific misinformation, and/or generalized intolerance relative to given socio-political, ethnic, or racial issues. Factors such as hypersensitivity, cognitive distortion, etc., may sometimes interact with one another relative to the above areas or issues. Generally speaking, the individuals in question usually function and interact well within what are regarded as normal limits[9]—i.e., irrespective of the above areas of insensitivity, undercontrol, etc. In addition, they do not appear to be self-destructive in any ordinary sense of the term.

An equally common pattern relates to somewhat broader, or less "isolated," aspects of the individual's personality and mode of adaptation. Here, one or more of the following is likely to be present with regard to any given individual: frequent rigidity-of-functioning;[10] mild, yet moderately frequent feelings of insecurity, possibly combined with the presence of few areas of acknowledged competence[11] or felt personal accomplishments; fairly limited range of social-interactional skills. Factors such as these set the stage for the individual's inability and/or unwillingness to adequately, efficiently, or directly cope with (1) given challenges, (2) moderate or fairly high levels of stress, and/or (3) various social-developmental crises (role adjustments, etc.). The difficulties in question are expressed in terms of: temporary, or even somewhat longer-term regressive, evasive, or "time-binding" behavior;[12] hypersensitivity to criticism from others; decreased tolerance toward others; acquiescence to peer-pressure; etc. This may increase the individual's susceptibility to transitory delinquent acting-out. In addition, it may lower his level of intolerance toward somewhat more extensive "sprees."

(Each of the eight SA *subgroups* is described in detail, in Palmer [1971d].)

Prior to the above revisions and refinements, the complete description of "situational-emotional" offenders was as follows (Warren et al., 1966b, p. 43):

WAYS OF PERCEIVING THE WORLD

1. *Self-Definition.* Self-image is relatively positive (compared to Nx's and Na's) in terms of adequacy, pride, self-respect. May, however, judge his or her own

misbehavior severely and wish to make up for the difficulty he has caused others.

2. *Delinquency Ego-Alien.* Does not see himself as a delinquent. May characterize aspects of his present and past behavior as nonself, "not like him," incomprehensible to him.

WAYS OF RESPONDING TO THE WORLD

3. *Relationship Ability.* Relates with others in selective, non-compulsive way. May choose to be somewhat of a social isolate. Relationships, when present, are with specific other person and are personalized in nature, as opposed to being with anyone who in general happens to fill the friendship role.
4. *Causes of Delinquency.* Responds to emotional conflict in personal, family, or environmental situations by acting-out delinquen[tly].

PERCEIVED BY OTHERS AS

5. *Normal.* Personality development appears relatively normal. No evidence of long-term psychoneurosis or psychopathy. Shows distress or conflict about current problem, however.
6. *Goal Oriented.* Makes plans and follows through on them.

Delinquent Identifiers

During Phases 1 and 2 of the California experiment, delinquent identifiers (DI's)—then called cultural identifiers (CI's)—were described as follows (Warren et al., 1966b, pp. 46–47):

> Perceives himself as adequate, capable, independent, self-responsible. Sees himself or herself as more mature in action and attitude than others of the same age. Self-perceptions are typically realistic. Sees himself [as] able to function in both delinquent and nondelinquent worlds, depending upon his own wishes. He takes pride in living up to his own values and principles (which often include giving society and social agencies a bad time). . . .

Identification figures have been delinquent or criminal. Has internalized the value system of a deviant subculture. May take a strong stand against middle class values or may appear quite ambivalent about these values. . . .

Perceives inequalities and injustices along socioeconomic and racial lines and, as a result, has antipathy for the core culture. May initially distrust the motives of the worker. . . .

Does not feel anxious, does not perceive a need to change his view of the world or to improve himself personally. His problems [in his view] are typically conflicts between himself and society or his environment. . . .

Gives some evidence of being able to shift goals and behavior to fit changes in demands [by] the external world. Can assume new modes of behavior and find new solutions when the old ones are no longer successful. Flexibility is increased by CI's ability to play different roles or use different patterns of behavior in different situations. . . .

Delinquency is a more or less successful way of getting what he wants and can't afford, a way of expressing loyalty toward delinquent peers, or a way of attacking the core culture or the authority system. . . .

Responds to others primarily in terms of their integrity. Has contempt for hypocrites and phonies—those who violate what they appear to subscribe to. Respects individuals who live up to their ideals even when he disagrees with their values. . . .

Is interpersonally responsive [i.e., emotionally reactive]. Is able to express feelings freely. . . .

[Is] loyal to delinquent peers . . . even in their absence. [This occurs] not out of fear of retaliation, but rather because of [his] ability to maintain meaningful, long-term relationships. . . .

Is perceived by others as normal, having leadership qualities, goal-oriented, non-neurotic, non-psychopathic, interpersonally responsive.

In 1971, the present author distinguished three broad types within the above, generalized or global CI subtype, and also suggested that "DI" would be a better (e.g., less restrictive) label. The three types were as follows (Palmer, 1971d, pp. 33–34):

Type A: Pro-Delinquent Identifier and/or Anti-Core-Culture Adaptation

Individuals within this major category are likely to have developed a pro-delinquent outlook prior to the onset of adolescence. This outlook has ordinarily been actively supported by key parental figures or, at any rate, not especially opposed by them. The youths are likely to have been involved in considerable delinquency—of an official and/or unofficial nature—prior to the onset of adolescence. . . .

Subgroups within this type are: (1) Responsive, friendly, outgoing; (2) Distrustful, hostile, guarded; (3) Constricted, noncommittal, evasive; (4) Mixed or Other.[13]

Type B: Reactive Delinquent Identifier or Non-Neurotic Delinquent Adaptation

Relative to this major category, the identifications or adaptations in question are likely to have emerged during or shortly after the onset of adolescence. Key parental figures are ordinarily opposed to the youth's delinquent identifications or adjustment—irrespective of whether these are of a more transitory or more permanent nature. (The above comments—the latter in particular—apply more to subgroups 5 and 6 than to subgroup 7 [see next].) . . .

Subgroups within this type are: (5) Autonomy or acceptance-seeker;[14] (6) Subcultural rejector and/or minority-status rejector;[15] (7) Delinquency tolerant.[16]

Type C: Quasi-Neurotic Delinquent Identifier or Compensatory Delinquent Adaptation

The difficulties, disturbances (e.g., underlying sense of inadequacy), identifications, and adaptations in question are likely to have taken rather firm root well before the onset of adolescence. In most cases, however, their behavioral expressions do not emerge—at least in terms of clear-cut delinquent adjustments/accommodations—until the onset of adolescence. Key parental figures are generally nonsupportive of the youth's delinquency, although they may be protective of the youths themselves with reference to the attempted intervention of official social agencies.

The only subgroup that comprises this type is: (8) adequacy seeker and/or subculturally conflicted.[17]

In the 1971 document, the following was also indicated:

It now appears appropriate to refer to Cultural Identifiers as "Delinquent Identifiers" (DI's). The latter title would seem to more fully integrate the spectrum of facts at hand—i.e., it would represent or portray the data in a more inclusive and accurate manner. Thus, e.g., relative to many CI's, it has become apparent that, quite high on any list of crucial factors (with respect to the etiology of delinquent behavior), the following item would have to be included: An underlying rejection of—or, in any event, considerable disidentification with— (a) specified familial/subcultural *standards and expectations*,[18] and/or (b) the thought [of], or objective reality of, one's potential (or, [one's] actually emerging/impending) adult-centered social and economic "*status*"[19] within some given subculture.[20] Moreover, at (or close to) the time of their earliest recorded delinquent acting-out, many of these youths already appear to be partially identified with—or at least interested in and accepting of—several aspects of the dominant culture itself. The latter applies to other CI's as well.

At a theoretical as well as practical level, it would appear both meaningful and useful to classify many (here, 38%) of all Ci's (Di's) under the heading of "Adjustment Reaction." [See review of Stress and Adjustment Reactions, above.] In the case of these youths, the label of "Delinquent Identifier"—while of obvious relevance—would be used only secondarily. Here, the individuals' adolescent adjustment has come to include delinquent acting-out for reasons which, in and of themselves, not only partially distinguish [these youths] from most other Ci's, but which—more particularly—involve certain factors that have now been identified in connection with specific types of Se's [Sa's] as well: The *particular content* of the former individuals' delinquent identification or adaptation has been strongly conditioned by the various sources of personal satisfaction (perceived and/or actual satisfaction)—together with given social challenges/opportunities (again perceived and/or actual)—which prevailed, or appeared to be dominant,[21] within his immediate physical environment during the onset[22] of given, post-pubertal familial/developmental crises. However, the nature of the *underlying crises* per se was . . . similar in certain crucial respects to that which had initiated or set the stage for delinquent acting-out in the case of a number of Se's [Sa's]. (Palmer, 1971d, pp. vii–viii)

Notes

1. This even applies to the below-mentioned subgroups that are more responsive to other people or that often seek their approval, or even their basic acceptance.
2. This asking or demanding sometimes occurs in a state of panic, but seldom rage.
3. A "positive or moderately positive self-image" would mainly refer to the presence of a moderate to considerable degree of conscious and/or preconscious satisfaction with various features that the individual ordinarily associates with himself, his interactions with others, and/or his life circumstances in general. By itself, this type of self-image would not rule out the possible presence of "fairly low self-confidence" with respect to particular areas of challenge or pressure.
4. This type has considerable in common with the APA designation of "adjustment reaction of adolescence." However, as compared to the latter designation, the former is conceptually less inclusive and descriptively more specific.
5. This presumes an absence of familial structural changes, and major trauma, as described in connection with Type A.
6. Short of "imminent parental divorce," as referred to in connection with Type A.
7. For example, direct and barely modulated aggression, hostility, or rivalry; preadolescent dependency gratification; underlying egocentricity (including fear or survival-based selfishness and/or narcissistically oriented alterations of consciousness).
8. Thus, for example, the needs or drives in question ordinarily appear to be taken care of while the youth is meeting his more conscious, everyday needs or salient drives and interests.
9. That is, "normal" with respect to two or more of the following: everyday functioning (e.g., following through on role expectations; meeting basic job requirements); tangible accomplishments; adherence to fairly typical standards of conduct; presence of given interpersonal satisfactions.
10. For example: unwillingness to recognize the existence of newly emerging challenges, demands, or personal needs; difficulty in modifying or relinquishing current habit patterns, and/or unwillingness to consider alternative approaches; difficulty in "backing down," and/or unwillingness to admit that one may be unprepared to handle given tasks or challenges.
11. With respect to impersonal—as opposed to interpersonal—tasks or challenges.
12. For example: general withdrawal from usual (more independent, interdependent, or differentiated) forms of interaction; avoidance of given challenges; withdrawal from previous areas of interest or achievement.
13. Individuals who fall within subgroups 1 and 3 are often referred to—in APA terminology—as "dyssocial personalities" or "asocial personalities."
14. This refers to strivings for independence from the control of one's family, and/or strivings for peer acceptance/peer status. Individuals who fall within subgroup 5 may (collectively) be involved either in a compensatory and/or a transient—and somewhat less intense—form of delinquent identification.
15. This refers to the conscious *rejection* (also expressed in terms of delinquent/anti-middle-class adaptations) of familial subcultural standards, familial levels of social or economic status, and so on. Individuals who fall within subgroup 6 may (collectively) be involved either in sporadic and relatively rare delinquent acting-out or in a somewhat more permanent, and more often expressed, delinquent adaptation. (These two patterns appear to be about equally common.) The latter may or may not be accompanied by a definite internalization of delinquent values as representing a preferred, or even desirable, way of life.

16. Includes situations and conditions such as: (1) adaptation to long-standing or major economic difficulties, as, for example, in the case of nonneurotic (and I$_4$ level) prostitution; (2) opportunistic and/or libidinal behavior patterns or expressions of a socially unacceptable nature.

17. Most youths who fall within this category have been described in Neto and Palmer (1969).

18. The subculture in question would be that in which the individual had spent most of his childhood. The given system of "subcultural" values, expectations, and aspirations is likely to have been focused upon, and embodied within, the individual's core ("nuclear") family. However, it may have extended beyond the family in a number of respects, particularly as the youth approached and first entered chronological adolescence.

19. Here, the individual's "potential status" is often thought of as being closely linked with—or slowly acquired by virtue of—his particular minority-group membership, or ethnic background. This, in any event, is one of the "messages" that is also likely to be communicated to the individual himself—implicitly or explicitly—by, or through, the dominant culture and subculture that surrounds him.

20. That is, "status-in-life"—either in relation to (1) the standards and expectations of the given subculture itself and/or with reference to (2) those of the larger, more dominant cultural milieu.

21. For example, unavoidable, compelling, and/or "the only way to go" (i.e., to do things).

22. And for some time subsequent to.

NUMBER OF CONTACTS PER MONTH BETWEEN AGENT AND YOUTH DURING FIRST YEAR ON PAROLE

		Type of Youth	
Sample and Type of Contact	Conflicted	Power-Oriented	Passive-Conformist
I. Participants Only			
Counseling			
Individual	5.8	4.7	3.8
Group	2.1	2.0	3.5
Family	1.1	0.2	1.1
Pragmatically Oriented Interactions	1.1	0.8	1.1
Limit-Setting	1.2	2.3	1.5
Collateral Contacts	1.2	0.9	1.1
II. Typical Youths[a]			
Counseling			
Individual	3.1	3.2	2.1
Group	0.9	1.8	1.6
Family	0.4	0.1	0.4
Pragmatically Oriented Interactions	0.6	0.5	0.5
Limit-Setting	0.5	2.1	0.8
Collateral Contacts	0.4	0.5	0.6

[a]Includes participants and nonparticipants, that is, the total sample as defined in Chapter 3.

9 CRITERIA FOR FAVORABLE AND UNFAVORABLE DISCHARGE, USED THROUGHOUT THE YOUTH AUTHORITY DURING PHASES 1 AND 2[1]

317.1 Classification of Discharges

Discharges will be classified as follows:[2]

1. Honorable Discharge—Good record on parole
2. Discharge—Acceptable record on parole
3. Discharge—Borderline adjustment
4. Discharge—Expiration of commitment— whereabouts unknown
5. Discharge—Commitment to mental hospital
6. Discharge—Commitment to California Department of Corrections or other state or federal training school, reformatory or prison
7. Discharge—Commitment to probation and/or jail sentence
8. Discharge—Returned to state of legal residence
9. Discharge—Death
10. Discharge—Other

317.11 Honorable Discharge—Good Record on Parole

Within the last year while the ward has been on parole (or for the duration of the last period on parole, if shorter) the ward:

1. Has incurred no serious violations of law or of parole regulations; and
2. has demonstrated reasonable effort in ei- ther securing employment and/or in at- tendance at school; and
3. has had a reasonably satisfactory rela- tionship with his family; and
4. has made reasonable effort to comply with the rules and regulations of the Youth Authority and parole officer.

317.12 Discharge—Acceptable Record on Parole

At the time of discharge the ward was not in- volved in any difficulty. He was not under sus- pension or under investigation for a technical or a law violation. In the year prior to dis- charge (or for the duration of last period on parole, if shorter) there may have been minor infractions of the law and suspensions which resulted in restoration to parole, but ward ex- hibited fair adjustment regarding employ- ment, home or school and cooperation with the parole officer.

317.13 Discharge—Borderline Adjustment

At the time of discharge the ward may not have been in difficulty but during the year prior to discharge (or for the duration of last period on parole, if shorter) has consistently been in- volved in minor infractions of the law and of parole regulations. His adjustment regarding employment, home or school and his coopera- tion with the parole officer have been poor.

317.14 Discharge—Expiration of Commitment—Whereabouts Unknown

At the time of discharge the whereabouts of the ward was unknown. (No ward will be discharged with his or her whereabouts unknown prior to expiration of commitment.)

317.15 Discharge—Commitment to Mental Hospital

At the time of discharge the ward ha[d] been committed to a state mental hospital or similar institution.

317.16 Discharge—Commitment to California Department of Corrections or Other State or Federal Training School, Reformatory or Prison

At the time of discharge the ward had been committed to California Department of Corrections or other state or federal school, reformatory or prison, within or [outside] the State of California.

317.17 Discharge—Commitment to Probation and/or Jail Sentence

At the time of discharge the ward had been committed to a local jurisdiction (city or county) for a period of probation or for a jail sentence, or both.

317.18 Discharge—Returned to State of Legal Residence

This classification includes cases committed to the Youth Authority with a definite recommendation by the court for return to state of legal residence and such recommendation is carried out by the Youth Authority, or is returned in custody to an out-of-state agency that assumes jurisdiction of the ward. (Does not apply to wards being supervised for the Youth Authority in other states.)

317.19 Discharge—Death

The ward died prior to the expiration of his commitment to the Youth Authority.

317.191 Discharge—Other

This classification will be used for discharges that cannot be placed in one of the preceding nine categories. When used, a full explanation shall be made in the Board's Order of Discharge.

Notes

1. The following was excerpted from the Youth Authority Board Policy Manual (1961). All classifications of, and criteria for, discharge were established solely by the board.

2. Classifications 1 and 2, immediately below, were categorized by the research team as favorable ("good") discharges. Classifications 9 and 10—both very rare—were categorized as either favorable or unfavorable, depending on the individual's parole record. All remaining classifications were categorized as unfavorable ("poor") discharges.

10 Community Treatment Project Severity-of-Offense Scale

In 1957, a Severity of Parolee Violation Behavior Scale was developed by Martin Warren and Ernest Reimer of the California Department of Corrections. (For technical details, see: Warren, M., "Severity of Parolee Violation Behavior: An Instrument for Its Assessment," unpublished master's thesis, University of California, 1964.) Bertram Johnson, of the California Youth Authority, later revised this scale for use with a juvenile population by adding 14 items peculiar to youthful delinquency and by rewording two original items. During the next several years, more than 85 items were added by CTP staff. For further details, see Palmer (1968c, pp. 71–74).

Severity-of-Offense Scale

Severity	Offense
1	Medical
1	Protection
1	Preventive (ward's request)
1	Preventive (agent's request)
1	Uncooperative attitude
1	Missed group meeting
1	Home adjustment
1	Poor school adjustment
1	Simple runaway
1	Investigation
1	Traffic—parking violation
1	Traffic—signaling violation
1	Traffic—improperly equipped or defective vehicle
1	Traffic—turning violation
1	Traffic—passing or following violation
1	Traffic—light usage
1	Traffic—stopping or right-of-way violation
1	Traffic—no license
1	Forcible incest victim
1	Forcible rape victim
2	Loitering around a school
2	Curfew violation, loitering, trespassing
2	Runaway, whereabouts unknown
2	Fighting, no weapons
2	Drinking, possession of alcohol
2	Malicious mischief, disturbing the peace, etc.
2	Unlawful assembly
2	Begging
2	Causing traffic accident—property damage only
2	Speeding
2	Driving car with suspended/revoked license
3	Intoxication (alcohol, glue, etc.)
3	Riding in stolen car
3	Petty theft, unplanned
3	Missing, suspicious circumstances
3	Escape, no force
3	Parole revoked, suspicion of property theft
3	Receiving stolen property
3	Causing traffic accident—minor injuries
3	Possession of alcohol, transporting and consumption violation
3	Prowling
3	Vehicle tampering
3	Female partner, statutory rape
3	Arson—unintentional
3	Illegal or forcible entry
3	Possession of burglary tools

Severity	Offense
3	Interfering with peace officer
3	Possession of fictitious identification
3	False crime report
3	Contributing to delinquency of minor—alcohol
3	Contributing to delinquency of minor—obscene matter
3	Contributing to delinquency of minor—runaway
3	Child harassment
4	Auto theft, unplanned
4	Check passing, unplanned
4	Male partner, statutory rape
4	Unplanned theft other than petty or auto
4	Reckless driving, not intoxicated
4	Attempted felony offense, no threat or force
4	Alimony or child support payment failure
4	Participant in riot
4	Altering or counterfeiting documents for profit
4	Perjury
4	Sexual immorality or promiscuity
4	Causing traffic accident—major injury
4	Contributing to delinquency of minor—intercourse, mutual consent
4	Contributing to delinquency of minor—petty theft
4	Contributing to delinquency of minor—auto theft
4	Possession of illegal weapons
4	Possession of concealed weapons
4	Possession of narcotics paraphernalia
5	Petty theft, planned
5	Purse snatch, victim unharmed
5	Possession of marijuana
5	Hitting a teacher
5	Resisting arrest
5	Burglary, 2nd degree
5	Contributing to delinquency of minor—2nd degree burglary
5	Contributing to delinquency of minor—grand theft (excludes auto)
5	Pimping
5	Fraudulent solicitation of funds
5	Peeping Tom
5	Growing marijuana
5	Prostitution solicitation
5	Sale of altered or counterfeit documents
6	Homosexual act, same age partners
6	Narcotics addiction
6	Check passing, planned
6	Selling marijuana
6	Grand theft auto, planned
6	Battery
6	Suicide—attempted
6	Suicide—accidental
6	Prostitution
6	Extortion—no threat or force
6	Contributing to delinquency of minor—grand theft auto
6	Cough syrup addiction
6	Sexual act with animals
6	Pandering
6	Inciting riot
7	Male participant, group statutory rape—no force
7	Drunk driving
7	Abnormal sex act with minor, mutual consent
7	Negligent action causing death
7	Burglary, 1st degree, unplanned
7	Grand theft (not auto), planned
7	Contributing to delinquency of minor—marijuana
7	Contributing to delinquency of minor—1st degree burglary
7	Indecent exposure
7	Incest—willing participant
7	Incest act aggressor—no force
7	Arson, wilful
8	Possession of narcotics
8	Parole revoked, potential for violence
8	Selling narcotics to support own addiction
8	Burglary, 1st degree, planned
8	Sex act with minor, no threat or force
8	Escape, with force
8	Suicide, intentional
8	Contributing to delinquency of minor—narcotics
9	Purse snatch, victim harmed
9	Assault with deadly weapon, armed robbery

Severity	Offense
9	Assault to commit robbery, grand theft, rape, etc.
9	Attempted murder, administering poison
9	Selling narcotics, large scale
9	Forcible rape
9	Extortion with threat or force
9	Kidnapping—attempted
9	Kidnapping
9	Incest act, aggressor with force
10	Attempted murder while committing another felony
10	Sex act with minor, with force
10	Voluntary manslaughter
10	Murder, 2nd degree
10	Assault with caustic chemical
10	Murder, 1st degree
10	Train wrecking, attempted
10	Mayhem

11 COMPARISONS ON BACKGROUND CHARACTERISTICS OF EXPERIMENTAL AND CONTROL VALLEY MALES IN PHASE 1 AND 2 PAROLE AND POST-DISCHARGE FOLLOW-UPS

TABLE A11

Comparisons on Background Characteristics of Experimental and Control Valley Males in Phase 1 and 2 Parole and Post-Discharge Follow-ups[a]

I. Parole[b]

	BE		Age		IQ		Race				SES			Offense		
	M	σ	M	σ	M	σ	C	M	B	O	L	M	U	Pe	Pr	Ao
A. Total Group																
E	452	81	16.0	1.3	89.2	16.7	56	20	18	7	76	21	3	9	71	21
C	449	87	15.7	1.4	85.1	15.9	53	26	17	4	82	17	1	6	75	19
	NS[c]		(NS)[d]		(NS)		NS				NS			NS		
B. Na + Nx																
E	460	83	16.2	1.2	91.3	16.6	67	17	10	6	66	31	3	8	70	22
C	455	84	15.9	1.3	89.3	13.2	72	14	11	3	72	25	2	3	77	20
	NS		(NS)		NS		NS				NS			NS		
C. Cfc + Mp																
E	427	82	15.7	1.4	85.0	12.1	25	33	39	3	94	6	0	8	69	22
C	443	85	15.5	1.4	78.8	15.1	31	46	21	3	85	15	0	10	72	18
	NS		NS		(NS)		NS				NS			NS		
D. Cfm																
E	435	75	15.4	1.3	85.6	16.0	63	13	19	6	94	6	0	13	69	19
C	452	76	15.2	1.1	81.7	13.4	45	28	28	0	97	3	0	7	83	10
	NS		NS		NS		NS				NS			NS		

(continued on next page)

TABLE A11 (continued)

II. Post-discharge[e]

		BE		Age		IQ		Race				SES			Offense		
		M	σ	M	σ	M	σ	C	M	B	O	L	M	U	Pe	Pr	Ao
A.	Total Group																
	E	462	80	16.2	1.3	90.3	17.8	57	18	17	7	74	22	4	8	73	20
	C	459	85	15.9	1.2	85.1	15.7	52	28	16	4	82	17	1	6	75	18
		NS		NS		S[f]		NS				NS			NS		
B.	Na + Nx																
	E	474	76	16.4	1.1	92.6	18.3	67	16	10	7	63	34	4	11	71	19
	C	460	79	16.0	1.3	88.6	13.1	74	13	11	3	71	26	3	3	79	18
		(NS)		(NS)		(NS)		NS				NS			NS		
C.	Cfc + Mp																
	E	431	76	15.7	1.4	85.1	11.9	24	32	40	4	92	8	0	8	68	24
	C	462	77	15.6	1.4	79.7	14.0	30	48	18	3	85	15	0	9	73	18
		(NS)		NS		(NS)		NS				NS			NS		
D.	Cfm																
	E	430	79	15.5	1.2	87.2	18.0	75	8	8	8	92	8	0	0	83	17
	C	470	75	15.7	0.9	81.8	13.6	47	29	24	0	94	6	0	6	88	6
		(NS)		NS		NS		NS				NS			NS		

(continued on next page)

TABLE A11 (continued)

[a]The numbers shown for BE (base expectancy, aka level of parole risk), age, and IQ, are means and standard deviations (SDs). Those shown for race, SES, and offenses are percentages. See Appendix 12, note b, regarding the categories—within each of these last three factors—to which the respective percentages correspond. For these three factors the tests of statistical significances are based (computed), not on these percentages per se, but on the actual numbers of cases to which they correspond. (This also applies to comparable appendices and tables, e.g., Appendix 12 and Tables 21–1, 22–1, and 22–2, in which percentages are shown for these same factors.) Results of these chi square tests are indicated in terms of three categories: NS, (NS), and S. See notes c, d, and f, below, regarding these categories.

[b]See Table 8–1 for the sample-sizes of the total group, and of the conflicted, the power oriented, and the passive conformist youths, respectively.

[c]Not significant (p < .05). [d]Not significant, but a trend (p < .10 > .05). [e]See Table 8–2 regarding sample-sizes for the total group, the conflicted youths, and so on.

[f]Significant (p < .05).

COMPARISONS BETWEEN REGULAR CONTROLS AND DIRECTLY PAROLED CONTROLS ON SELECTED BACKGROUND VARIABLES[a]

Variable	Regular Controls				Directly Paroled Controls			
	Mean[b]			SD[b]	Mean[b]			SD[b]
Base Expectancy	446			84	464			95
Age	15.6			1.4	15.9			1.6
IQ	85.0			15.5	85.7			18.2
Race	52	28	17	4	54	21	1	11
SES	85	14		1	68	32		0
Offense	6	75		19	4	75		21

[a]Refers to Phase 1 and 2 Valley males. Sample-sizes: Regular—129; Direct—28. This is the "parole" sample (Table 8–1). Results also apply to the "postdischarge" and "parole + postdischarge" samples (Tables 8–2 and 8–3). Regular (R) controls and Directly Paroled (DP) controls are elsewhere called "long-term lockup" parolees—i.e., youths who were institutionalized prior to parole—and "direct and early parolees," respectively (Chapter 16: text and n. 13). Comparisons between the R and the DP controls yielded $p > .10$ results (statistically nonsignificant, i.e., $p > .05$) on base expectancy, age, IQ, race, and offense. For SES, $p < .10 > .05$ (statistical tendency).

[b]The means and SDs (standard deviations) refer to base expectancy, age, and IQ only. All figures shown for *race*, *SES*, and *offense* are *percentages*. Regarding race, the figures are for Caucasian, Mexican-American, Black, and all other, respectively. Regarding socioeconomic status they are for lower, middle, and upper, respectively. Concerning offense, they are for person, property, and all other, respectively.

13 PERFORMANCE OF VALLEY MALES IN AREAS OF SCHOOL AND PAID EMPLOYMENT

The following refers to the performance of Valley males during specified periods of their Youth Authority career.

Conflicted Youths

How did conflicted experimentals and controls compare in the areas of school and paid employment, with respect to various performance measures?

School

Thirty-three percent of the C's and 19 percent of the E's did *not* continue their formal education after they were first released to parole. In this connection, the following should be noted (the remainder of this paragraph applies to conflicted, passive-conformist, power-oriented, and rare types combined): Fifty-eight percent of all controls had attended school while they were institutionalized, prior to first release to parole. Because of this initial lockup, these individuals were, on the average, several months older than experimentals at point of first release. They were therefore more likely to have reached the age at which they were no longer legally required to remain in school. This age differential helps account for the E/C percentage difference on the item, "no further schooling during parole." In addition, the percentage difference in "average number of grades advanced during YA career" (see below) is partly accounted for by the fact that C's were more often revoked and reinstitutionalized than E's and that educational programming was readily available during periods of incarceration for those who were interested.

Now then, during their first year on parole, 22 percent of the remaining conflicted C's and 10 percent of the remaining conflicted E's (in both cases, it was these "remaining" youths who *did* continue their education) were *unfavorably removed* from school, by school authorities, on one or more occasions. Unfavorable removal referred to suspension, expulsion, and so on. Figures for the second year on parole were 9 percent (C) and 7 percent (E). (As indicated, this analysis focused on parole. Unfavorable removals and related experiences that occurred during *institutionalization* were not included.)

During their first year on parole, 16 percent of the C's and 18 percent of the E's *dropped out* of school and did not return during that year. Figures for the second year on parole were 14 percent (E) and 8 percent (C).

Forty-four percent of the conflicted C's and 57 percent of the E's *advanced* in school at least one grade during their YA career. However, C's advanced an average of 1.14 *grades* during their YA career, as compared with 0.99 for E's. Thus, although fewer controls progressed in school, those who did were likely to advance a little further than E's. As suggested, this probably reflected their greater amount of exposure to educational programming during lockup.

On balance, conflicted E's seem to have performed a little better than conflicted C's in the area of school adjustment.

Paid Employment

Included here are full-time, part-time, and odd jobs for which the individual was paid—by persons other than relatives, foster parents, and others with whom he was living.

Conflicted C's averaged 1.16 jobs per youth during their first year on parole; E's chalked up 1.33. Figures for the second year were 0.92 (C) and 1.34 (E). C's worked an average of 62 days during their first year on parole; E's worked 61 days. Figures for the second year were 35 (C) and 78 (E). Of employed youths, 11 percent of the C's and 18 percent of the E's were unfavorably dismissed—that is, fired—during their first year on parole; figures for the second year ("year two") were 13 percent (C) and 15 percent (E). (Firing was distinguished from being laid off, and quitting, for any of several reasons.)

All in all, conflicted E's and C's performed about equally well with respect to paid employment during their first year on parole. During year two, E's were somewhat ahead.

In sum, there were no sharp differences in the type or level of adjustment on the part of conflicted E's and C's in such areas as school and paid employment, during specified periods of their YA career. However, there was a fairly consistent, overall tendency for E's to perform somewhat better than C's.

Passive-Conformist Youths

How did passive-conformist C's and E's compare with respect to school and paid employment? As to *school,* 19 percent of the C's and 6 percent of the E's did not continue their education after being paroled. In their first year on parole, 43 percent of the remaining C's and 17 percent of the remaining E's were unfavorably removed from school, by school authorities, on one or more occasions. Figures for the second year were 11 percent (C) and 14 percent (E).

Ten percent of the passive-conformist C's and 17 percent of the E's dropped out during their first year on parole and did not return during that year; figures for year two were 15 percent and 14 percent, respectively. Sixty-seven percent of the C's and 57 percent of the E's advanced in school at least one grade during their YA career. Finally, C's advanced an average of 1.75 grades, as compared to 1.17 for E's, during that same period of time.

All in all, passive-conformists performed somewhat better in the traditional program than in CTP, with regard to school.

As to paid employment, passive-conformist controls averaged 1.19 jobs per youth during their first year on parole, as compared to 0.76 for experimentals. Figures for year two were 1.66 (C) and 1.28 (E). C's worked an average of 57 days during their

first year, as compared to 39 days for E's; figures for the second year were 121 and 67, respectively. Finally, 11 percent of the employed C's and 4 percent of the employed E's were fired at least once during their first year on parole; figures for year two were 15 percent and 16 percent.

In general, passive-conformist C's performed better than E's in the area of paid employment. This applied to their first as well as second year on parole.

In sum, passive-conformist controls definitely outperformed their experimental counterparts in the areas of school and paid employment, during their YA career.

Power-Oriented Youths

How did power-oriented C's and E's compare in the areas of school and paid employment? As to *school,* 12 percent of the C's and 5 percent of the E's did not continue their formal education after being paroled. During their first year on parole, 33 percent of the remaining C's and 19 percent of the remaining E's were unfavorably removed from school, by school authorities, at least once. Figures for the second year were 27 percent (C) and 13 percent (E).

Sixteen percent of the power-oriented C's and 9 percent of the E's dropped out during their first year on parole and did not return during that year; for year two the figures were 8 percent (C) and 6 percent (E). Seventy-six percent of the C's and 75 percent of the E's advanced at least one grade during their YA career. Finally, during that same period, C's advanced an average of 1.80 grades, as compared to 1.63 for E's.

On balance, power-oriented youths performed slightly worse in the traditional program than in CTP with regard to school.

In the area of paid employment, power-oriented controls averaged 1.15 jobs during their first year on parole, as compared to 0.83 for experimentals. Figures for the second year were 1.45 (C) and 0.95 (E). On the average, C's accumulated 44 workdays during their first year; E's chalked up 72. (Controls had a relatively high proportion of part-time and odd jobs.) Figures for year two were 55 (C) and 34 (E). Finally, 7 percent of the employed C's as compared to 0 percent of the employed E's were fired during their first year; for year two, the figures were 4 percent (C) and 12 percent (E).

In general, then, power-oriented C's were slightly ahead of E's in the area of paid employment.

The Total Group

How did the Total Group of C's and E's compare with regard to school and paid employment? In the area of *school*, 24 percent of the controls and 13 percent of the experimentals did not continue their education after they were first released to parole. During their first year on parole, 31 percent of the remaining C's and 12 percent of the remaining E's were unfavorably removed from school, by school authorities, at least once. During year two the figures were 18 percent (C) and 8 percent (E).

Fourteen percent of the C's and 15 percent of the E's dropped out during their first year on parole and did not return during that year; for year two, the figures were 12 percent and 9 percent, respectively. Fifty-nine percent of the C's and 61 percent of the E's advanced in school at least one grade during their Youth Authority career. Finally, C's advanced an average of 1.49 grades during their YA career, as compared to 1.19 for E's.

As to *paid employment*, controls averaged 1.15 jobs during their first year on parole, as compared to 1.12 for experimentals. Figures for the second year were 1.21 (C) and 1.27 (E). C's and E's both worked an average of 55 days during their first year; the figures for year two were 50 (C) and 57 (E). Finally, 11 percent of the employed C's and 7 percent of the employed E's were fired during their first year on parole; figures for year two were 8 percent and 14 percent.

In general, then, E's appeared to perform slightly better than C's in the area of school. However, no consistent or substantial differences were found with respect to paid employment.

14 MONTHLY RATE OF OFFENDING FOR FAVORABLE DISCHARGEES

Monthly rate of offending for favorable E and C dischargees will now be compared, for the post-discharge as well as the YA career *plus* post-discharge periods.

I. Post-Discharge Performance

As shown in Table A14–1, results on the post-discharge analysis of favorable dischargees are as follows:

Conflicted Youths

On four-year post-YA follow-up, conflicted experimentals were arrested 36 percent less often and convicted 37 percent less often than conflicted controls. The specific, monthly rates of offending were 0.030 (E) and 0.047 (C) for arrests, and 0.019 versus 0.030 for convictions. This refers to moderate plus severe offenses combined.

Results were much the same for severe offenses alone. E's were arrested 38 percent less often and were convicted 31 percent less often than C's. For violent offenses they were arrested half as often as C's; however, rates of conviction were identical for C's and E's.

These findings cannot be explained as a product of discretionary staff decisions (certainly not *differential* decisions), since the youths in question were no longer under YA jurisdiction. Nor can they be explained in terms of E/C differences in background characteristics, since the conflicted E's and C's who received a favorable discharge and were followed up for four years in the community were very similar on age, race, level of parole risk, and so on.

Passive-Conformist Youths

On four-year post-YA follow-up, passive-conformist E's were arrested 15 percent less often than passive-conformist C's; however, the latter individuals were *convicted* 24 percent less often than the former. For *severe* offenses, arrest and conviction rates clearly favored C's. Controls also outperformed experimentals on arrests for violent offenses; however, when it came to convictions, E and C rates were identical.

All in all, passive-conformist C's who received a favorable discharge had an edge over the E's subsequent to parole. However, given the findings on moderate plus severe arrests, the overall results can also be characterized as mixed.

Power-Oriented Youths

Power-oriented controls were arrested 46 percent less often and convicted 26 percent less often than power-oriented experimentals. The specific monthly rates were 0.039 (C) and 0.072 (E) for arrests, and 0.032 versus 0.043 for convictions. For severe offenses alone, the difference favored C's by 60 percent on arrests and 33 percent on convictions. In the case of violent offenses, E/C percentage differences were similar to those for all severe offenses combined, though not as sharp. In sum, power-oriented controls who received a favorable discharge clearly outperformed experimentals subsequent to parole.

The Total Group

When all youths are analyzed as a single group, experimentals were arrested 5 percent less often than controls and were convicted 19 percent less often, for moderate plus severe offenses combined. Except for the latter finding,

Number of Offenses per 1,000 Months at Risk for Favorably Discharged Valley Boys, Subsequent to Discharge from Youth Authority

Youth Type and Number of Offenses[a]

Type of Offense and Outcome Measure	Conflicted		Passive-Conformist		Power-Oriented		Total Group[b]	
	Exp.	Control	Exp.	Control	Exp.	Control	Exp.	Control
Moderate + Severe Offenses								
All arrests	30	47	23	27	72	39	36	38
Arrests with convictions	19	30	17	13	43	32	21	26
Severe Offenses								
All arrests	13	21	8	4	40	16	17	15
Arrests with convictions	9	13	2	1	15	10	9	9
Violent Offenses[c]								
All arrests	4	8	4	1	14	8	6	6
Arrests with convictions	3	3	0	0	4	3	3	3

[a]Sample sizes are as follows: Conflicted, E—61, C—20; Passive-Conformist, E—11, C—16; Power-Oriented, E—17, C—28; Total Group, E—105, C—79.
[b]See Table 8–1, note b.
[c]See Table 8–1, note c.

E/C differences in rate of offending were slight or nonexistent, regardless of severity level and the distinction between arrests and convictions. The reason for such minimal differences was the same as that described in connection with favorable plus unfavorable dischargees combined (Chapter 8).

II. YA Career (Parole) Plus Post-Discharge Performance Combined

When the parole and post-discharge periods are combined into one all-inclusive time period, the average follow-up for favorable dischargees is 6.8 years of community exposure. As shown in Table A14–2, results of this analysis are essentially as follows.

Conflicted E's clearly outperformed C's on arrests as well as convictions: The E/C *differences* were 43 percent (arrests) and 37 percent (convictions) for moderate plus severe offenses, and 47 percent and 36 percent for severe offenses. E's remained ahead on arrests for violent offenses.

Passive-conformist E's outperformed C's on arrests and especially convictions, for moderate plus severe offenses combined. However, results for severe and violent offenses were mixed.

Power-oriented C's outperformed E's on arrests as well as convictions, for moderate plus severe offenses combined: The E/C *differences* were 28 percent and 20 percent, respectively. There were no substantial differences for severe and violent offenses alone.

For the *total group,* favorably discharged E's outperformed favorably discharged C's on arrests and convictions alike: Monthly rates were 0.032 (E) and 0.041 (C) for arrests and 0.019 versus 0.027 for convictions. Results of this seven-year follow-up generally favored E's over C's in the case of severe and violent offenses as well; however, the differences in question were not at all striking. Moreover, they could have been accounted for by chance alone. At any rate, the following applied to the total group analysis as a whole, especially to moderate plus severe offenses combined. As with favorable plus unfavorable dischargees combined, the post-discharge performance of favorably discharged power-oriented C's no longer carried enough weight to completely counterbalance the post-YA *and parole* performance of favorably discharged, conflicted E's.

Number of Offenses per 1,000 Months at Risk for Favorably Discharged Valley Boys—Parole and Post-discharge Periods Combined[a]

Youth Type and Number of Offenses[b]

Type of Offense and Outcome Measure	Conflicted		Passive-Conformist		Power-Oriented		Total Group[c]	
	Exp.	Control	Exp.	Control	Exp.	Control	Exp.	Control
Moderate + Severe Offenses								
All arrests	26	46	31	38	57	41	32	41
Arrests with convictions	17	27	16	26	35	28	19	27
Severe Offenses								
All arrests	10	19	10	10	19	17	12	15
Arrests with convictions	7	11	3	6	10	9	7	9
Violent Offenses[d]								
All arrests	3	8	5	3	9	8	5	6
Arrests with convictions	4	5	1	2	3	3	2	3

[a]See Table 8–3, note a.

[b]Sample sizes are as follows: Conflicted, E—61, C—20; Passive-Conformist, E—11, C—16; Power-Oriented, E—17, C—28; Total Group, E—105, C—79.

[c]See Table 8–1, note b.

[d]See Table 8–1, note c.

15 METHOD FOR COMPUTING THE NUMBER OF ARRESTS PER 100 YOUTHS DURING A NINE-YEAR FOLLOW-UP

Shown in Table A15–1 are the steps used to compute the number of arrests per 100 experimentals and 100 controls during a nine-year YA (pre-discharge) plus post-YA (post-discharge) follow-up (see Figures 10–1 through 10–4). The "Total Arrests per 100 Youths," that is, the results of the main computations, are shown in Column N.

The following might be noted regarding the *supplementary* figures and computations shown in Columns P through S. If the "Extrapolated Extra Arrests" shown in Column L had been based on postdischarge performance alone (Columns P and Q), rather than pre-discharge and post-discharge combined (Columns A and B), the change in total arrests per 100 youths would have been negligible. Specifically, there would have been 302 rather than 303 arrests among conflicted E's, 307 rather than 305 among passive-conformist E's, and so on (compare Columns R and S with Columns L and N).

TABLE A15-1

Steps Used to Compute Total Arrests per 100 Experimentals and 100 Controls during a Nine-Year YA + Post-YA Follow-Up

Youth Group		Col. A Arrests per 1,000 Months at Risk (Table 8–3)	Col. B Months at Risk per Arrest[a]	Col. C Months at Risk during Follow-Up (Subtotal)[b]	Col. D Arrests per Youth during Follow-Up (Subtotal)[c]	Col. E Months of Lockup during Follow-Up[b]
Conflicted	E	33	30.3	79.1	2.61	13.6
	C	69	14.5	76.6	5.28	30.9
Passive-Conformist	E	33	30.3	79.8	2.63	13.3
	C	66	15.2	80.1	5.27	27.6
Power-Oriented	E	61	16.4	88.2	5.38	19.1
	C	53	18.9	76.2	4.03	24.1
Total Group	E	38	26.3	83.0	3.16	14.4
	C	61	16.4	77.1	4.70	28.6

[a]1,000 ÷ Col. A.
[b]Pre-discharge + post-discharge combined.
[c]Col. C ÷ Col. B.
E = Experimental.
C = Control.

(continued on next page)

TABLE A15-1 *(continued)*

Youth Group		Col. F Months at Risk Plus Lockup Time during Follow-Up (Subtotal)[d]	Col. G E/C Difference in Months of Follow-Up[e]	Col. H Months of Lockup during Post-Discharge	Col. I % of Post-Discharge Time in Lockup[f]	Col. J Extrapolated Extra Months of Lockup during Post-discharge[g]
Conflicted	E	92.7	14.8	7.4	0.134	2.0
	C	107.5	—	15.8	—	—
Passive-Conformist	E	93.1	14.6	7.2	0.130	1.9
	C	107.7	—	12.5	—	—
Power-Oriented	C	107.3	—	9.5	—	—
	E	100.3	7.0	11.3	0.191	1.3
Total Group	E	97.4	8.3	7.5	0.135	1.1
	C	105.7	—	13.8	—	—

[d]Col. C + Col. E.
[e]Smaller number subtracted from larger, in Col. F.
[f]Col. H ÷ Col. H + 48.
[g]Col. G × Col. I.

(continued on next page)

TABLE A15-1 (continued)

Youth Group		Col. K Extrapolated Extra Months at Risk during Post-discharge[h]	Col. L Extrapolated Extra Arrests per Youth during Post-discharge[i]	Col. M Total Arrests per Youth[j]	Col. N Total Arrests per 100 Youths[k]	Col. O Percentage Reduction or Increase in Arrests[l]
Conflicted	E	12.8	0.42	3.03	303	
	C	—	—	5.28	528	43% reduction
Passive-Conformist	E	12.7	0.42	3.05	305	
	C	—	—	5.27	527	42% reduction
Power-Oriented	E	—	—	5.38	538	
	C	5.7	0.30	4.33	433	24% increase
Total Group	E	7.2	0.27	3.43	343	
	C	—	—	4.70	470	27% reduction

[h] Col. G - Col. J.
[i] Col. K ÷ Col. B.
[j] Col. D + Col. L.
[k] Col. M × 100.
[l] For reductions: (C–E) ÷ C. For increases: (E–C) ÷ C. Thus, all reductions or increases are on the part of experimentals, in relation to controls.

(continued on next page)

TABLE A15–1 (continued)

Youth Group		Col. P Arrests per 1,000 Months at Risk during Post-Discharge (Table 8–2)	Col. Q Months at Risk per Arrest during Post-Discharge[m]	Col. R Extrapolated Extra Arrests per Youth[n]	Col. S Total Arrests per 100 Youths[o]
Conflicted	E	32	31.3	0.41	302
	C	58	17.2	—	528
Passive-Conformist	E	35	28.6	0.44	307
	C	38	26.3	—	527
Power-Oriented	C	68	14.7	—	538
	E	43	23.3	0.24	427
Total Group	E	39	25.6	0.28	344
	C	45	22.2	—	470

[m] 1,000 ÷ Col. P.

[n] Col. K ÷ Col. Q; that is, based on post-discharge performance only.

[o] (Col. D + Col. R) × 100; that is, based on post-discharge performance only.

RATE OF ARREST DURING EACH OF 11 YEARS PRIOR TO YOUTH AUTHORITY COMMITMENT, FOR VALLEY BOYS

I. Conflicted Youths

Type of Offense, and Study Group	Rate of Arrest[a]										
	Year Prior to Commitment										
	1	2	3	4	5	6	7	8	9	10	11
Moderate + Severe											
Experimentals	165	73	36	21	13	5	1	2	0	0	0
Controls	162	51	35	19	7	5	0	2	0	0	2
Severe Offenses											
Experimentals	30	15	2	2	1	0	0	1	0	0	0
Controls	32	7	7	5	0	0	0	0	0	0	0
Violent Offenses											
Experimentals	13	7	1	0	1	0	0	1	0	0	0
Controls	7	2	2	2	0	0	0	0	0	0	0

II. Passive-Conformist Youths

Type of Offense, and Study Group	Rate of Arrest[a]										
	Year Prior to Commitment										
	1	2	3	4	5	6	7	8	9	10	11
Moderate + Severe											
Experimentals	201	69	7	0	0	7	0	0	0	0	0
Controls	211	49	59	15	5	0	0	0	0	0	0
Severe Offenses											
Experimentals	21	0	0	0	0	0	0	0	0	0	0
Controls	34	0	10	0	0	0	0	0	0	0	0
Violent Offenses											
Experimentals	21	0	0	0	0	0	0	0	0	0	0
Controls	10	0	0	0	0	0	0	0	0	0	0

[a]Specifically, number of arrests per 1,000 months at risk—as in Tables 8–1 through 8–6.

III. Power-Oriented Youths

Type of Offense, and Study Group	Rate of Arrest[a]										
	Year Prior to Commitment										
	1	2	3	4	5	6	7	8	9	10	11
Moderate + Severe											
Experimentals	163	73	73	40	20	20	0	3	0	0	0
Controls	189	38	48	43	8	0	0	0	3	0	0
Severe Offenses											
Experimentals	17	17	13	3	0	0	0	0	0	0	0
Controls	38	3	10	8	0	0	0	0	3	0	0
Violent Offenses											
Experimentals	17	13	7	3	0	0	0	0	0	0	0
Controls	20	3	8	3	0	0	0	0	0	0	0

IV. Total Group

Type of Offense, and Study Group	Rate of Arrest[a]										
	Year Prior to Commitment										
	1	2	3	4	5	6	7	8	9	10	11
Moderate + Severe											
Experimentals	169	69	40	23	12	10	1	3	0	0	0
Controls	181	42	40	24	6	2	0	1	1	0	1
Severe Offenses											
Experimentals	27	14	4	2	1	0	0	1	0	0	0
Controls	32	3	7	4	0	0	0	0	1	0	0
Violent Offenses											
Experimentals	16	7	2	1	1	0	0	1	0	0	0
Controls	12	2	3	2	0	0	0	0	0	0	0

[a]Specifically, number of arrests per 1,000 months at risk—as in Tables 8–1 through 8–6.

17 RATE OF ARREST FOR MODERATE PLUS SEVERE OFFENSES DURING EACH OF 11 YEARS PRIOR TO YOUTH AUTHORITY COMMITMENT, FOR VALLEY BOYS— BY AGE

I. Under 16

Type of Offense, and Study Group	Rate of Arrest[a]										
	Year Prior to Commitment										
	1	2	3	4	5	6	7	8	9	10	11
Conflicted											
Experimentals	150	88	16	10	0	0	0	0	0	0	0
Controls	160	46	33	8	4	0	0	0	0	0	0
Passive-Conformist											
Experimentals	243	64	3	0	0	7	0	0	0	0	0
Controls	204	46	39	21	7	0	0	0	0	0	0
Power-Oriented											
Experimentals	192	68	53	26	0	0	0	0	0	0	0
Controls	257	37	45	23	9	0	0	0	0	0	0
Total Group											
Experimentals	186	75	29	18	0	6	2	3	0	0	0
Controls	205	37	34	16	5	0	0	0	0	0	0

(continued on next page)

(continued)

II. 16 and Over

Type of Offense, and Study Group	Rate of Arrest[a]										
	Year Prior to Commitment										
	1	2	3	4	5	6	7	8	9	10	11
Conflicted											
Experimentals	169	70	40	24	15	6	1	2	1	0	0
Controls	164	54	36	26	8	6	0	3	0	0	3
Passive-Conformist											
Experimentals	162	73	10	0	0	7	0	0	0	0	0
Controls	221	53	83	7	0	0	0	0	0	0	0
Power-Oriented											
Experimentals	138	76	90	51	39	39	0	6	0	0	0
Controls	135	38	50	59	7	0	0	0	5	0	0
Total Group											
Experimentals	161	67	44	25	17	11	1	3	1	0	0
Controls	161	46	46	31	8	6	0	3	3	0	3

[a]Specifically, number of arrests per 1,000 months at risk—as in Tables 8–1 through 8–6.

NUMBER OF OFFENSES PER 1,000 MONTHS AT RISK DURING THREE-YEAR PRECOMMITMENT AND THREE-YEAR POSTCOMMITMENT (PAROLE) PERIODS, FOR VALLEY MALES—BY AGE

I: Under 16

| | Youth Type and Number of Offenses[a] | | | | | | | |
| | Conflicted | | Passive-Conformist | | Power-Oriented | | Total Group | |
Offense Group and Follow-Up	Exp.	Control	Exp.	Control	Exp.	Control	Exp.	Control
Moderate + Severe Offenses								
Precommitment period	83	86	111	92	100	116	96	96
Parole period	23	82	15	85	57	98	32	86
% difference[b]	−72	−5	−86	−8	−43	−16	−67	−10
Severe Offenses								
Precommitment period	11	13	7	14	15	18	14	14
Parole period	9	33	6	27	23	56	13	34
% difference[b]	−18	+154	−14	+93	+53	+211	−7	+143
Violent Offenses								
Precommitment period	5	6	3	2	8	10	7	6
Parole period	2	16	6	14	16	25	7	17
% difference[b]	−60	+167	+100	+600	+100	+150	0	+183

[a]Includes all good and all poor dischargees.

[b]A minus sign signifies a reduction in rate of arrest from the precommitment to the postcommitment period. A plus sign signifies an increase in rate from precommitment to postcommitment.

II: 16 and Over

Offense Group and Follow-Up	Youth Type and Number of Offenses[a]							
	Conflicted		Passive-Conformist		Power-Oriented		Total Group	
	Exp.	Control	Exp.	Control	Exp.	Control	Exp.	Control
Moderate + Severe Offenses								
Precommitment period	91	91	94	113	98	77	91	88
Parole period	37	79	59	86	53	37	41	66
% difference[b]	–59	–13	–37	–24	–46	–52	–55	–25
Severe Offenses								
Precommitment period	16	18	7	23	13	11	14	15
Parole period	15	25	20	23	19	13	16	22
% difference[b]	–6	+39	+186	0	+46	+18	+14	+47
Violent Offenses								
Precommitment period	8	3	7	9	9	8	7	5
Parole period	7	11	10	4	6	7	7	9
% difference[b]	–13	+267	+43	–56	–33	–13	0	+80

[a]Includes all good and all poor dischargees.

[b]A minus sign signifies a reduction in rate of arrest from the precommitment to the postcommitment period. A plus sign signifies an increase in rate from precommitment to postcommitment.

19 NUMBER AND SEVERITY OF PRIOR ARRESTS AMONG VALLEY BOYS—BY AGE[a]

I. Under 16

Youth Type and Offense Group		Prior Arrests[b]			
		Average Number of Arrests		Average Severity of Arrests[c]	
		Exp.	Control	Exp.	Control
Conflicted	1–10[d]	4.53	4.40	3.23	3.00
	3–10	2.53	2.36		
	6–10	0.35	0.32		
	Violent	0.12	0.12		
Passive-Conformist	1–10[d]	4.88	4.07	3.15	3.66
	3–10	3.25	3.00		
	6–10	0.25	0.47		
	Violent	0.13	0.07		
Power-Oriented	1–10[d]	4.94	5.24	3.25	3.27
	3–10	3.12	3.59		
	6–10	0.53	0.53		
	Violent	0.29	0.29		
Total Group	1–10[d]	4.70	4.35	3.25	3.33
	3–10	3.04	2.86		
	6–10	0.40	0.38		
	Violent	0.21	0.15		

[a]Includes all good + poor dischargees.
[b]Includes all offenses prior to the commitment offense. Excludes all dependency-and-neglect contacts, all modification hearings (e.g., change of status or placement), and so on.
[c]Refers to all arrests—severities 1–10 inclusive. Average severity was not computed for the 3–10, 6–10, and violent offense groups, since these categories are range-restricted.
[d]Includes offenses of a relatively minor nature (severity levels 1–2), in addition to those of levels 3–10.

II. 16 and Over

Youth Type and Offense Group		Prior Arrests[b]			
		Average Number of Arrests		Average Severity of Arrests[c]	
		Exp.	Control	Exp.	Control
	1–10[d]	5.31	5.11	3.13	3.37
Conflicted	3–10	3.01	3.11		
	6–10	0.57	0.63		
	Violent	0.30	0.11		
	1–10[d]	4.88	4.69	3.03	3.39
Passive-Conformist	3–10	2.75	2.92		
	6–10	0.13	0.77		
	Violent	0.13	0.31		
	1–10[d]	6.53	5.09	3.19	3.10
Power-Oriented	3–10	4.11	2.64		
	6–10	0.63	0.50		
	Violent	0.47	0.23		
	1–10[d]	5.28	4.80	3.16	3.28
Total Group	3–10	3.08	2.78		
	6–10	0.54	0.54		
	Violent	0.30	0.16		

[a]Includes all good + poor dischargees.

[b]Includes all offenses prior to the commitment offense. Excludes all dependency-and-neglect contacts, all modification hearings (e.g., change of status or placement), and so on.

[c]Refers to all arrests—severities 1–10 inclusive. Average severity was not computed for the 3–10, 6–10, and violent offense groups, since these categories are range-restricted.

[d]Includes offenses of a relatively minor nature (severity levels 1–2), in addition to those of levels 3–10.

COMPUTATION OF YOUTH AUTHORITY CAREER COSTS

Career costs were derived in the following manner. First, per-month per-ward costs were obtained for each Youth Authority program component. These costs were obtained from the YA's (1) Annual Statistical Reports and (2) its Annual Program Description and Budget Report Series prepared for the Governor's Budget (Davis et al., 1961 through 1973; Governor's Budget, 1962–1963, 1963–1964, 1966–1967, 1971–1972). These per-month per-ward costs are shown in Table A20–1.

Using these figures (also shown in Table A20–2, Col. D), career costs were then computed separately for favorable and unfavorable dischargees, for each of the three price periods. Each such cost was computed separately for conflicted, passive-conformist, power-oriented, and all other youths,[1] based on actual figures for individuals who fell within the given price-period sample.[2] The entire procedure was carried out separately for E's and C's. Thus, as shown in Table A20–2, the following are illustrative, yet actual figures and results for conflicted youths who fell within the middle price-period sample (four groups of conflicted youths are shown: E favorable dischargees; E unfavorable dischargees; C favorable dischargees; C unfavorable dischargees):[3]

The next, and final, step was the computation of costs for the total group. This was done by weighting the costs for each youth group (favorable plus unfavorable dischargees combined) according to the extent of that group's representation within the given price-period sample (Table A20–3, Column B). Capital outlay costs were added at this point (Table A20–3, Column A_1). (YA computation of such costs included amortization, in equal amounts, over an average "bed life" of approximately 45, 45, and 35 years for the early, middle, and later price periods, respectively.) Figures and results are shown in Table A20–3.

TABLE A20–1

Monthly Costs per Ward for Three Price Periods, by Youth Authority Program Component

| | | Program Component | | |
| | | Institution | Regular | CTP |
Price Period	NRCC[a]	and Camp	Parole	Parole
Early[b]	$410	$313	$26	$134
Middle[c]	528	403	38	181
Later[d]	799	617	53	245

[a]Northern Reception Center and Clinic.
[b]1963 costs.
[c]1966–1967 costs.
[d]1971–1972 costs.
Sources: Davis et al., 1971, 1973; Governor's Budget, 1962–1963, 1963–1964, 1966–1967, 1971–1972.

TABLE A20–2

Computation of Career Costs for Conflicted Youths in Middle Price-Period Cohort

Discharge Group	Cost Element				
	Col. A	Col. B	Col. C	Col. D	Col. E
	No. of Wards	No. of Months in Program Component	No. of Ward Months in Program Component (Col. A × Col. B)	Cost per Ward Month in Program Component	Cost for All Wards (Col. C × Col. D)
Experimental Favorable Dischargees[a]					
Parole	80	32.2	2,576	$181	$466,256
Institution/Camp	80	3.4	272	403	109,616
NRCC	80	1.3	104	528	54,912
				Total	$630,784
Experimental Unfavorable Dischargees[b]					
Parole	20	30.1	602	$181	$108,962
Institution/Camp	20	9.0	180	403	72,540
NRCC	20	2.3	46	528	24,288
				Total	$205,790
Experimental Favorable + Unfavorable Dischargees		Career costs for 80 favorable experimental dischargees			$630,784[c]
		Career costs for 20 unfavorable experimental dischargees			205,790[d]
		Total career costs for 100 experimental dischargees			836,574
		Average career costs for each experimental dischargee			8,366

[a]All sample sizes are adjusted to a base of 100 (or 100%). Thus, in Col. A, 80 refers to the fact that a favorable discharge was received by 80 percent of all conflicted experimental dischargees to whom the middle price-period costs apply.

[b]In Col. A, 20 indicates that an unfavorable discharge was received by 20 percent of the conflicted experimental dischargees to whom the middle price-period costs apply.

[c]The average career cost for favorable dischargees (E's) was $7,885 ($630,784 ÷ 80).

[d]The average career cost for unfavorable dischargees (E's) was $10,290 ($205,790 ÷ 20).

(continued on next page)

TABLE A20-2 (continued)

		Cost Element		
	Col. A	Col. B	Col. C	Col. D	Col. E
Discharge Group	No. of Wards	No. of Months in Program Component	No. of Ward Months in Program Component (Col. A × Col. B)	Cost per Ward Month in Program Component	Cost for All Wards (Col. C × Col. D)
Control Favorable Dischargees[e]					
Parole	50	33.7	1,685	$ 38	$ 64,030
Institution/Camp	50	11.0	550	403	221,650
NRCC	50	2.1	105	528	55,440
				Total (excludes capital outlay)	$341,120
Control Unfavorable Dischargees[f]					
Parole	50	25.7	1,285	$ 38	$ 48,830
Institution/Camp	50	17.2	860	403	346,580
NRCC	50	3.6	180	528	95,040
				Total (excludes capital outlay)	$490,450
Control Favorable + Unfavorable Dischargees					
Career costs for 50 favorable control dischargees					$341,120[g]
Career costs for 50 unfavorable control dischargees					490,450[h]
Total career costs for 100 control dischargees					831,570
Average career costs for each control dischargee (excludes capital outlay)					8,316

[e]All sample sizes are adjusted to a base of 100 (or 100%). Thus, in Col. A, 50 refers to the fact that a favorable discharge was received by 50 percent of all conflicted control discharges to whom the middle price-period costs apply.

[f]In Col. A, 50 indicates that an unfavorable discharge was received by 50 percent of the conflicted control discharges to whom the middle price-period costs apply.

[g]The average career cost for favorable dischargees (C's) was $6,822 ($341,120 ÷ 50).

[h]The average career cost for unfavorable dischargees (C's) was $9,809 ($490,450 ÷ 50).

TABLE A20-3

Computation of Career Costs for Total Group of Youths, Separate for Early, Middle, and Later Price Periods

Cost Element

Price Period and Youth Type	Experimentals			Controls				
	Col. A	Col. B	Col. C	Col. A	Col. A$_1$	Col. A$_2$	Col. B	Col. C
	Career Cost per Youth	% of Youths in Cohort[a]	Total Cost (Col. A × Col. B)	Career Cost per Youth	Capital Outlay Cost[b]	Total Career Cost per Youth[c]	% of Youths in Cohort[d]	Total Cost (Col. A$_2$ × Col. B)
Early								
Conflicted	$ 6,180	48	$ 296,640	$ 5,876	$ 403	$ 6,279	43	$ 269,997
Passive-Conformist	6,231	13	81,003	5,820	403	6,223	18	112,014
Power-Oriented	8,676	24	208,224	5,257	403	5,660	24	135,840
All Others	8,011	15	120,165	5,419	403	5,822	15	87,330
Total Group		100	$ 706,032				100	$ 605,181
	Average career cost per experimental dischargee (Total Group)		$ 7,060			Average career cost per control dischargee (Total Group)		$ 6,052
Middle								
Conflicted	$ 8,366	57	$ 476,862	$ 8,316	$ 448	$ 8,764	41	$ 359,324
Passive-Conformist	8,595	9	77,355	8,912	448	9,360	18	168,480
Power-Oriented	11,803	21	247,863	7,169	448	7,617	25	190,425
All Others	9,755	13	126,815	7,530	448	7,978	16	127,648
Total Group		100	$ 928,895				100	$ 845,877
	Average career cost per experimental dischargee (Total Group)		$ 9,289			Average career cost per control dischargee (Total Group)		$ 8,459

(continued on next page)

TABLE A20–3 *(continued)*

	Cost Element							
	Experimentals			Controls				
Price Period and Youth Type Later	Col. A Career Cost per Youth	Col. B % of Youths in Cohort[a]	Col. C Total Cost (Col. A × Col. B)	Col. A Career Cost per Youth	Col. A₁ Capital Outlay Cost[b]	Col. A₂ Total Career Cost per Youth[c]	Col. B % of Youths in Cohort[d]	Col. C Total Cost (Col. A₂ × Col. B)
Conflicted	$12,377	65	$ 804,505	$13,371	$ 900	$14,271	49	$ 699,279
Passive-Conformist	12,107	10	121,070	13,912	900	14,812	21	311,052
Power-Oriented	16,889	18	304,002	12,280	900	13,180	22	289,960
All Others	10,453	7	73,171	12,513	900	13,413	8	107,304
Total Group		100	$1,302,748				100	$1,407,595
Average career cost per experimental discharge (Total Group)			$ 13,027			Average career cost per control discharge (Total Group)		$ 14,076

[a] All sample sizes are adjusted to a base of 100 (or 100%). Thus, for example, regarding the middle price-period cohort, conflicted youths accounted for 57 percent of all experimental dischargees—favorable + unfavorable. Passive-conformist, power-oriented, and all other groups accounted for the remaining 9 percent, 21 percent, and 13 percent, respectively.

[b] As shown in Col. A₁, capital outlay costs were computed at $403, $448, and $900 per youth for the early, middle, and later price periods, respectively. (Davis, C. CYA cost comparisons. Fiscal years 1963–1964 through 1972–1973. Information Systems Section, Division of Research, California Youth Authority. 1973.) Each stay refers to the initial period of institutionalization, one that was experienced by 83 percent of all male controls—prior to their first release to parole. (Experimentals were never institutionalized prior to initial parole. Only those who were later revoked experienced a Youth Authority incarceration at other than NRCC.) These capital outlay figures do not reflect periods of institutionalization that were experienced by C's and E's as a result of revocation, subsequent to initial parole. If the latter periods had been included, the difference in capital outlay costs between C's and E's would be somewhat greater than that reflected in the above figures. This is because C's were revoked and institutionalized at a substantially higher rate than E's. This factor—greater institutionalization of C's than E's—would be partly but not completely offset by the fact that 17 percent of all male C's had been directly paroled from NRCC, four to six weeks after their first commitment to the Youth Authority. (As seen in Table A20–2, NRCC costs are computed, for C's and E's alike, independent of capital outlay associated with incarceration in YA institutions.) (Youth Authority Information Systems Section, 1980, 1984)

[c] Col. A₂ = Col. A + Col. A₁.

[d] Based on the same approach described in note a.

Notes

1. "All other" refers to the four rare types combined.
2. These figures relate to (1) the proportion of favorable to unfavorable dischargees (see Table A20–2, Column A; also see notes a, b, e, and f of this table), and (2) the average number of months spent in each YA program component, during the youths' YA career (Table A20–2, Column B).
3. To simplify the illustration, capital outlay costs are not included at this point. These costs are included in Table A20–3.

COMPUTATION OF POST-DISCHARGE COSTS FOR OTHER CORRECTIONAL AND LAW ENFORCEMENT EXPERIENCES, SEPARATE FOR EXPERIMENTALS AND CONTROLS

	Cost Element			
	Col. A	Col. B	Col. C	Col. D
Discharge Group and Cost-Item	No. of Youths	No. of Months Exposure	Cost per Month of Exposure	Cost for All Youths (Cols. A × B × C)
Experimental Favorable Dischargees[a]				
Prison	86	2.3	$288	$ 59,966
Jail	86	1.0	450	38,700
Adult Parole	86	1.6	77	10,595
Probation	86	2.9	21	5,237
Experimental Unfavorable Dischargees[b]				
Prison	14	30.4	$288	$122,573
Jail	14	4.1	450	25,830
Adult Parole	14	19.5	77	21,021
Probation	14	6.7	21	1,970
Experimental Favorable + Unfavorable Dischargees	Post-YA costs per 86 favorable E dischargees			$111,498
	Post-YA costs per 14 unfavorable E dischargees			171,394
	Total post-YA costs per 100 E dischargees			282,892
	Average post-YA costs for each E dischargee			2,829

[a]All sample sizes are adjusted to a base of 100 (or 100%.) Thus, in Col. A, 86 refers to the fact that a favorable discharge was received by 86 percent of all experimental dischargees to whom the 1971-1972 price-period costs apply.

[b]In Col. A, *14* indicates that an unfavorable discharge was received by 14 percent of all experimental dischargees to whom the given price-period costs apply.

(continued on next page)

	Cost Element			
	Col. A	Col. B	Col. C	Col. D
Discharge Group and Cost-Item	No. of Youths	No. of Months Exposure	Cost per Month of Exposure	Cost for All Youths (Cols. A × B × C)
Control Favorable Dischargees[c]				
Prison	74	2.9	$288	$ 61,805
Jail	74	0.8	450	26,640
Adult Parole	74	1.4	77	7,977
Probation	74	2.6	21	4,040
Control Unfavorable Dischargees[d]				
Prison	26	36.0	$288	$269,568
Jail	26	7.2	450	84,240
Adult Parole	26	22.2	77	44,444
Probation	26	6.4	21	3,494
Control Favorable + Unfavorable Dischargees	Post-YA costs per 74 favorable C dischargees			$100,462
	Post-YA costs per 26 unfavorable C dischargees			401,746
	Total post-YA costs per 100 C dischargees			502,208
	Average post-YA costs for each C dischargee			5,022[e]

[c]All sample sizes are adjusted to a base of 100 (or 100%). Thus, in Col. A, 74 refers to the fact that a favorable discharge was received by 74 percent of all control dischargees to whom the 1971–1972 price-period costs apply.

[d]In Col. A, 26 indicates that an unfavorable discharge was received by 26 percent of all control dischargees to whom the given price-period costs apply.

[e]$5,022 minus $2,829 (i.e., the cost per C minus the cost per E) = $2,193. $2,193 minus $108 (the C/E cost difference for processing and adjudication) = $2,085.

The status and role of matching at the Community Treatment Project were somewhat, though not fundamentally, different during much of Phase 1 than during Phase 2. However, matching did not simply *change;* it grew in importance and expanded in scope, though its status and role were substantial from the start. In addition, the basis of matching changed somewhat from Phase 1 to Phase 2; and, by 1964, matching was conceptualized more broadly and systematically than before. These developments, and related issues, will be briefly described.

Phase 1

Until the closing months of Phase 1, the personality characteristics of prospective workers (candidates), while assumed to be fairly important with respect to offenders, were not given heavy weight in connection with the interviews that were used to select parole agents for CTP; in fact, a detailed formulation of worker characteristics did not exist during most of Phase 1. In contrast, the candidates' willingness and probable ability to utilize CTP's broadly defined, preestablished treatment/control approaches *was* given heavy weight with regard to worker selection.

These treatment/control approaches had been prescribed at the start of Phase 1 and were to be used with all members of specified subtypes; thus, they were called subtype prescriptions. They included not only broad treatment modalities such as Guided Group Interaction, but "lists of tentative treatment-suggestions . . . with regard to goals and techniques of treatment and strategies of control" (Adams and Grant, 1961, p. 6). The workers' willingness and ability to utilize vari-

ous modalities and techniques was viewed as part of a *professional orientations* factor (though that specific term was not used), one that included methods of working with youths, beliefs regarding delinquency causation, and so on. For reasons indicated below, this factor was considered very important throughout Phase 1.

Before continuing, two points should be kept in mind. (1) Each treatment/control plan (intervention plan) developed by CTP workers was to primarily reflect the diagnosed needs and environmental conditions of youths as *individuals,* not primarily the hypothesized, that is, theoretically formulated, needs of all youths who fell within their particular *subtype.* Nevertheless, subtype needs were to be taken quite seriously by CTP workers, and they were expected to play a major role in all intervention plans.[1] (2) Phase 1 was seen *primarily* as a hypothesis-development, not hypothesis-testing, effort (Adams and Grant, 1961, pp. 2–3, 6). The implications of these points will be apparent below.

The following should also be noted. CTP's broadly defined, preestablished approaches were "tentative" prescriptions only: They were viewed, from the beginning of Phase 1, as subject to revision and possible rejection (Adams and Grant, 1961, pp. 7–8). Nevertheless, they were regarded as probably the *best available* prescriptions and as having relevance to all members of specified subtypes.[2] As a result, they were to be given a fair test (though this itself was hard to define) before—if necessary—being discarded or greatly altered. Given this situation and given point (1), above, some type of integration or accommodation was required. Specifically, CTP workers, when developing intervention plans for individual youths, were expected to utilize given subtype prescriptions *in conjunction with* concrete plans that reflected the needs and circumstances of those particular youths. In any event, they were expected to utilize the preestablished modalities and techniques whenever possible.

Now then, the utilization of subtype prescriptions related to CTP's hypothesis-*testing* effort, whereas, in some contrast, the development of individualized plans was central to its hypothesis-*development* and prescription-refinement effort.[3] Meanwhile, the candidates' professional orientation was considered central to *both* efforts: (1) It was regarded as the main index of whether the candidates would be willing and able to utilize certain preestablished approaches; and (2) it was considered a good predictor (when combined with information about their prior training and experience) of how well they might develop individualized plans and might help conceptualize refinements in those approaches. Therefore, since both such efforts applied to all nine subtypes and, accordingly, to all worker/youth matches, they and the candidates' professional orientation were routinely evaluated with regard to the selection of CTP workers. This practice was continued during Phase 2.

Phase 2

Once the Phase 2 proposal had explicitly focused attention on the possible importance of worker characteristics and worker functions (see below), matching—now with added emphasis on worker/youth *relationships*—assumed a preeminent role in the selection of these individuals (Palmer, 1968b). This occurred despite the critical role that was played by professional orientations during Phase 1, and despite the anticipated continuation of this role during Phase 2. In short, matching, which already played an important role, largely in connection with professional orientations, now began to play a still more important role, in connection with that and other factors combined.

Like the Phase 2 proposal itself (early 1964), this role augmentation and broadening of scope reflected the following. In late 1963, numerous research findings had become available regarding the relationship between worker characteristics (e.g., traits and feelings) and worker functions (e.g., subgoals and roles), on the one hand, and the probable re-

sponses by given youths to each such factor, on the other (Palmer, 1963, 1965).[4] Before then, information and hypotheses concerning worker characteristics and worker functions was of a very general nature only, a point that partly applied to the professional orientations factor as well (Grant, 1961c; Grant, Warren, and Turner, 1963; Havel, 1963, 1965). In addition, by 1964, considerable practical experience had accumulated within CTP regarding not only the feasibility and apparent appropriateness of various subtype prescriptions or components thereof, but concerning the possible significance of worker characteristics in terms of effectively *implementing* those prescriptions (Grant, Warren, and Turner, 1963; Riggs, Underwood, and Warren, 1964; Palmer, 1965). These developments strengthened and consolidated the position of matching at CTP.

Despite this new information and added experience regarding various *types* of youth, the importance of individualized intervention did not decrease during Phase 2.[5] Its original priority was maintained even though, in accordance with the Phase 2 proposal, hypothesis *testing* (and, therefore, the utilization of subtype prescriptions) was considered even more important during Phase 2 than Phase 1 (Warren, Palmer, and Turner, 1964a, pp. 2–4, 8). Given this and other Phase 2 priorities—some unchanged from Phase 1, others moderately altered—the Phase 2 selection interviews focused on essentially the same issues as those which were considered during Phase 1. However, since somewhat different weight was now given to such factors as worker characteristics and worker functions, a wider range of information was requested and obtained.

Other Developments

Prior to Phase 2 the explicit framework for matching that is briefly reviewed in Chapter 11 was, in most respects, implicit only. That is, the underlying concepts of matching—though neither spelled out nor formally presented—were recognized in a general way by the experiment's researchers and CTP operations staff. As a result, these ideas helped establish a consistent policy with respect to worker selection and caseload assignment. This policy existed throughout Phase 1 despite the absence of (1) detailed information regarding worker characteristics and professional orientations and (2) written instruments (e.g., a formal interview schedule and rating checklists for use with candidates) for systematically implementing the concepts in question. Once these concepts had been made explicit and the preceding information became available, it was easier to develop the necessary instruments. These instruments were conceptualized and developed during 1964–1968 (Palmer, 1967a, 1968c, 1968d).

Notes

1. For this reason the candidates' recognition of these hypothesized needs was assessed during the selection interviews.

2. As indicated in the Phase 1 proposal, these prescriptions had been based on prior research (Adams, 1961; Grant, 1961b; Grant and Grant, 1959; Jenkins and Hewitt, 1944).

3. Though Phase 1 contained a set of varied and partly competing goals, for example, hypothesis testing and hypothesis development, the researchers hoped to achieve each such goal, at least to a substantial degree.

4. *Subgoals* included such items as the following: (1) change youth's image of authority figures; (2) exemplify successful adjustment and satisfaction to youth; (3) motivate youth to try out new standards and limits; (4) help youth express his feelings differently than before.

5. For one thing, with added experience numerous differences were becoming apparent within each subtype. This was apart from the basic priority regarding individualized intervention—one which, by design, remained unchanged from Phase 1.

23 Selected Questions Used with Candidates for CTP[1]

1. What basic goals, and what kind of intermediate or secondary goals, do you set for yourself when working with parolees? The concern here is with the majority of cases you have worked with, not so much with the more exceptional cases.

2. What aspects of your personal background, your academic training, and so on, do you see as having contributed the most to your work as a parole agent?

3. The next question deals with causes of delinquent behavior: What do you regard as the most crucial, most pervasive, or even most typical factor or set of factors involved in the development and persistence of most delinquent behavior—as defined legally?

4. In the case of most youngsters on parole, what do you regard as the key ingredient involved in bringing about casework movement, that is, in bringing about behavioral or attitudinal change in a positive direction? Another way of asking this might be: What do you believe to be the essential mechanism that underlies casework progress—the requisite condition or the basic reason(s) why most youngsters will begin to, and continue to, respond in a beneficial way?

5. What are the broad outlines of, and methods involved in, your treatment approach with most youngsters? That is, what general strategy or strategies do you usually prefer to follow, and what basic techniques do you find to be helpful in carrying this out?

6. This next question has two parts: What qualities and characteristics (personal,

educational, and so forth) do you feel are really *essential* for doing a good job as a parole officer? And, what qualities and characteristics would you ideally hope to find in a parole officer?

7. The next two or three questions will try to get at certain differences encountered by nearly everyone who works with youngsters. The first question is: What kind of youngsters do you find the easiest to work with? Why do you think they are easiest to work with? . . . and What, basically, do you do or not do with them—as a result of their being easier to work with—that you do differently with other individuals?

8. What kind of youngsters do you find the most difficult to work with? Again, why do you think this is so? and What, basically, do you do or not do with these youngsters—as a result of their being more difficult to work with—that you do differently with others?

9. What other groups or types of youngsters whom you have encountered in your work seem to require rather definite modifications so far as your general approach or goals are concerned?

10. In what main ways would you compare or contrast your own adolescence to that of the youngsters you usually work with? (Allow interviewee to respond fully; then add:) Do you think some of these similarities (and/or) differences that you mentioned have influenced the *way* you work with these individuals—the approaches you use or the goals you work toward?

11. What are the main satisfactions you find in your work? What are the main dissatisfactions?
12. What do you consider to be the chief factor—professional, personal, or other—that limits you in your work so far as your goals with youngsters are concerned? and How do you see this as actually influencing the work that you do?
13. What do you feel was the most difficult treatment decision you ever had to make, and what was it that made that decision especially difficult?

In the next question I'd like you to be thinking about youths in general, regardless of whether they might have gotten in trouble with the law:

14. What do you think youngsters really want and need?

Note

1. Excerpted from the 28-question "Open-Ended Interview Schedule for Use with Parole Agents" (Palmer, 1967a, pp. 60–63; Palmer and Warren, 1967, pp. 76–79). The present questions are numbers 1, 2, 6, 7, 8, 9, 11, 12, 13, 16, 17, 19, 20, and 26, respectively, on the original Schedule. For some interviewees (candidates with different work backgrounds), the words "youths," "clients," "probation," "probation officer," "group supervisor," and/or "social worker" were substituted for "parolees," "parole," and "parole officer." Seldom were all 28 questions asked during the assessment interview. For questions 7, 8, and 9, candidates were asked to give one or more specific examples—that is, actual cases—where possible. The following was also asked of each candidate: "I would like you to think of the best supervisor (parole or otherwise) you have ever had or known and, also, of the worst one you have ever had or known. Would you briefly describe what these individuals were like and also tell me why you think one was the best and the other the worst?"

24 FACTORS CONTRIBUTING TO "BRANCHING OUT" BY WORKERS

The factors that contributed to branching out across subtypes (youth groups) varied from worker to worker; and the relationships or interactions between these factors were not entirely known. However, the factors themselves were known, at least those which followed-up workers (agents) described as most important to them. These factors fell within two main groups or sets (listed below); and these sets interacted with each other along certain general lines, described on the following pages.

Specifically, the factors and interactions that agents considered most important were: factors #1, #2, and to a lesser extent #3, on the one hand, *combined with (i.e., in interaction with)* #4, #5, and/or #6, on the other (thus, factors from Set A, and especially Set B, did not seem sufficient in themselves; instead, when they described "branching out," agents mentioned one or more factors from both sets):

Set A
factor 1: agents' office and field exposure to other youth groups[1] (usually including personal contact with the youths)
factor 2: agents' observations of coworkers interacting with other youth groups (groups with which the coworkers were matched)
factor 3: agents' discussions with coworkers about other youth groups (those with which coworkers were matched).

Set B
factor 4: agents' casework supervision
factor 5: agents' sensitization to personal assets and blind spots (e.g., through

on-the-job peer interactions and formal group processes)
factor 6: agents' formal training in specific concepts and techniques.[2]

Of these factors, only #1 and #2 seemed essential (in the sense of a sine qua non) with regard to branching out. That is, both factors were always mentioned by agents; both were usually described as rather important; and neither ever seemed to be fully substituted for by others. Yet, however necessary they may have been, these factors did not seem quite sufficient by themselves. This situation will now be reviewed, together with the more frequently observed, and described, interactions.

In many respects, factors #1, #2, and #3 ("A-factors") set the stage for branching out: Together, they allowed workers to personally observe, determine, and vicariously experience *which* goals and subgoals could be worked toward with other youth groups, *how* those efforts might be implemented, *how* the youths usually responded to such efforts, and *how* other agents felt about the youths. Having made these observations and formed various impressions, many workers were then relatively receptive to further input and discussion regarding those youths; this input mainly involved factors #4, #5, and/or #6 ("B-factors"). Thus, for example, once these workers were in an actively interested or at least open frame of mind, casework supervision (factor #4) was in a good position to help them evaluate, better understand, or more fully accept the need for, or the possible/probable value of, various techniques and strategies for interacting with those youths. In effect, the casework supervisor was then able to reinforce and focus the agents' earlier observations, impressions, and experiences. (He usually did this by relating them not only to I-level concepts, but to the agents' underlying assumptions about youths, to their long-term professional interests, and to their areas of interpersonal strength.)

Thus, together, A- and B-factors helped—sometimes challenged—workers to seriously consider the possibility of using, or using more often, techniques and strategies (1) with which they frequently felt uncomfortable, (2) that they ordinarily preferred to avoid or downplay, (3) upon which they simply had placed little value, or (4) that they had regarded as inappropriate. For example, these factors sometimes helped increase their motivation to use either more *or* fewer controls (i.e., more or fewer than with youths on their current—original—caseload), to interact on either a more *or* less formal basis, and to focus on the youths' personal feelings and past experiences to a greater *or* lesser extent.

Sometimes the main issue was not motivation, or the overcoming of doubt; it was a lack of familiarity with specific concepts, or a relative inexperience with given approaches. In such cases, B-factors—such as factor #6—sometimes served to acquaint agents with specific concepts or with promising ways to achieve given goals. Yet whatever the key issue may have been, B-factors generally helped expand or modify the workers' understanding of, and/or evaluation of, various techniques and strategies. These were especially ones that research staff and CTP administrative personnel considered either essential or probably quite useful with respect to implementing prescribed approaches and to increasing the chances of obtaining constructive responses from given youths. In this connection, B-factors also helped or challenged many agents to focus on personal attributes that might otherwise have limited their interactions with those youths, and may have thus prevented them from achieving particular goals.

As implied earlier, similar contributions were made by A-factors, for instance, factor #3 (discussions with co-workers). Moreover, once the B-factors had supplied a certain amount of reinforcing-and-focusing input, *continued* input from A-factors then took on added significance to many agents. This was mainly because they were then more sensitive to particular meanings and to the implications of given events.

To briefly review: Given the "stage-setting" or activating input from various A-factors and given the "reinforcing" as well as focusing or directing input from one or more B-factors, subsequent—that is, continued—contributions from A- and B-factors (especially in combination) then helped many workers feel even more interested in or comfortable about modifying or expanding some of their current patterns of interaction and major areas of focus. For example, given the original (activating and focusing) inputs, continued input from factor #3—particularly when combined with input from #5 or #6—was often influential in further motivating workers to utilize new techniques or to focus on different areas.

To be sure, these inputs did not always occur in the specific sequence mentioned (A leading to B leading to A/B), or in the exact manner described. Moreover, they seldom occurred in sharply delineated steps. Thus, for example, A-factors sometimes prepared workers to use new or partly different techniques and strategies even *without* much reinforcement and specific direction from B-factors, simultaneously or otherwise. Also, "continued input" usually played a less important role when the central issue related to basic familiarization rather than to underlying motivation or to the overcoming of substantial doubt. Nevertheless, the sequence and interactions described earlier did represent the general thrust of developments with respect to branching out. In this regard they were quite common at CTP irrespective of the youth groups to which workers were originally assigned.

In sum, all six factors, particularly A-factors, helped workers become more knowledgeable about given youth groups—that is, more aware of their typical needs, expectations, preferences, strengths, or limits, and of their *range of responses* to various stimuli and demands. This gave them a concrete picture of what to expect from these youths, and, therefore, a point of reference against which to measure their own preferences, techniques, and assets. (A similar development occurred with workers who did not wish to branch out across subtypes, while at CTP.) In general, factors #4, #5, and #6—usually in that order of priority—often helped these workers confirm, question, or expand upon the information, experiences, and impressions associated with A-factors. In that respect, B-factors both helped and challenged them to increase their

996   APPENDIX 24

sensitivity to, and level of sophistication regarding, issues and needs that were relevant to the youth groups in question. Continued input from one or more A-factors, plus formal and informal training in specific concepts and techniques (B-factors), then gave many workers the final sense of direction or added measure of confidence they wanted or needed before "taking the plunge": asking their supervisor to add one or two youth groups to their caseload. Immediately prior to that point, peer support often played a major role in maintaining or increasing the individuals' resolve.[3]

Despite this frequently observed pattern—one that many workers shared, at least at a broad level—each worker was affected by the preceding factors in his own particular way, and responded at his own specific pace.

Two other factors were mentioned fairly often in connection with branching out; however, most workers attached less importance to them than did the researchers:

Set C
factor 7: positive experiences with individuals on workers' caseload[4]
factor 8: similarity in approach used with specific youths on workers' caseload and that used by other workers with individuals from other youth groups

Regarding factor #7, positive experiences with several youths on their caseload gave most agents an added feeling of confidence in their abilities. With some of these agents, this aroused a desire to "conquer new worlds" in terms of working with *additional* subtypes. That is, these individuals regarded new youth groups as an interesting and worthwhile challenge—partly a personal challenge—and/or a logical next step in their development as workers. With other agents, positive experiences heightened their interest in working with the *same* (originally assigned) youth groups—though perhaps modifying or expanding their approach. This response again reflected a sense of personal challenge and/or a desire for professional growth; however, it involved a different kind of branching out. (For related discussion, see Chapter 11, endnotes 17 and 18.)

Factor #8 was based on the existence of psychological and behavioral similarities between particular individuals with whom the agents were *presently* working (usually two to four such youths) and other individuals from youth groups with which they *wanted* to work. The existence of these similarities reflected the fact that (1) variations always exist within any group of individuals, and (2) among any *two* groups of individuals (e.g., the "presently" and "wanted" groups)—even those categorized as different from each other with respect to subtype—some members of the first group will have more (sometimes many more) features in common with members of the second group than will all remaining members of the first group. Since the earlier-mentioned similarities were sometimes rather numerous and were not of a superficial nature, they sometimes helped agents become familiar with common or critical needs, characteristics, and behaviors of youth groups with which they wanted to work. B-factors often provided support—reinforcing input—in this regard.

The presence of these similar or shared features was expressed in the agents' *particular approach* to the youths under consideration—individuals with whom they were currently working. This was the case because agents routinely tried to modify both the prescribed (preestablished) approach and their own typical (modal) approach to any given subtype in light of the needs, traits, and behaviors of each youth as an individual. To be sure, agents neither tried to nor succeeded in modifying *all* such techniques and strategies when working with the present youths—the approximately two to four individuals in question. Moreover, the changes they made were sometimes only moderate in degree. Nevertheless, the fact remained that, when working with their original caseload, many agents thus occasionally used techniques and strategies that were considered appropriate for youth groups that they wanted, or later wanted, to add to their caseload. Their use of these approaches made it more likely that administrative staff *would* eventually add those youth groups to their caseload.

Factor #8 also operated in connection with originally assigned youths who were fairly rapidly moving from one I-level to the next; at least, it operated when the latter I-level contained youth groups that the agents wished to add to their caseload. Specifically, as the former youths made major strides toward the next higher level—say, the I_4 level—agents working with those youths usually modified their approach in order to accommodate the individuals' changing preferences and needs. (This applied whether or not agents wished to add given youth groups to their caseload.) These modifications usually resulted in a set of techniques and strategies that seemed appropriate for the I-level toward which the youths were moving. To be sure, agents sometimes found it difficult to make these modifications—in a sense, to change their relationship with the youths.[5] However, once the modifications were made, most such agents became increasingly accepting of what, for them, was a new approach: a group of interrelated techniques and strategies that would probably be appropriate for many individuals who fell within the "higher-level" category from the *start*—more specifically, an approach that could probably be used with youth groups which most such agents also wished to eventually add to their caseload. The preceding events were most often observed with regard to passive-conformists who were fairly rapidly moving toward the I_4 level, whether or not they had been closer-than-average to it from the start.[6]

Other, less often mentioned factors were: *(#9) formal consultation received by workers* and *(#10) desire for professional advancement within, and greater scope of contribution to, the project, department, or field.* Factor #10 centered on the workers' desire to gain breadth of experience in order to increase their chances of eventually becoming supervisors or administrators who could serve as better resources or more knowledgeable policymakers than might otherwise be the case.

Notes

1. That is, youth groups other than those to which the agents were originally assigned. (Throughout this appendix, this will be the specific meaning of "other youth groups.")

2. This training usually centered on approaches or topics such as conjoint family therapy, psychodrama, transactional analysis, and specific aspects of I-level (Berne, 1961, 1964, 1966; Corsini, 1957; Harris, 1967; Haskell, 1961, 1975; Moreno, 1953, 1959; Satir, 1967). (Psychodrama focused on ways of helping youths understand a wider range of social situations, and of responding to these situations more appropriately and effectively than before.) By 1966—halfway through Phase 2—many agents had been substantially influenced by various principles of reality therapy (Glasser, 1965), though no formal training was given in this regard.

3. Regardless of the agents' interest in working with given youth groups, the casework supervisor and researchers made the final decision as to whether these individuals—given their personality characteristics and professional orientations, for the most part—would probably elicit positive responses from most such youths. Rarely did administrative staff—basically, the supervisor—try to discourage these agents from branching out across subtypes, or actually prevent them from doing so.

4. In this context, "positive experiences" usually meant at least two of the following: personally satisfying relationship with youth, usually including youth's satisfaction with agent as well; major improvement in youth's attitude toward others and in overall personal adjustment; little or no illegal behavior by youth; favorable discharge of youth from YA.

5. A-factors were often helpful to agents under these conditions. This also applied to B-factors—#4 in particular.

6. It was much easier for agents to modify their approach with I_2's who were relatively rapidly becoming I_3's—specifically passive-conformists—than with most I_3's who were fairly rapidly becoming I_4's. For one thing, the differences in techniques and the change in worker/youth relationship were smaller in the former case.

Number of Contacts between Matched Agents, Unmatched Agents, and Two Groups of Conflicted and Power-Oriented Youths throughout Youth Authority Career

Youth Sample and Type of Contact[a]	Type of Youth and Agent							
	Assertive-Denier		Anxious-Confused		Group Conformist		Manipulator	
	Matched	Unmatched	Matched	Unmatched	Matched	Unmatched	Matched	Unmatched
I. Participants Only								
Counseling								
Individual	4.5	5.6	8.0	6.1	4.5	4.3	5.9	3.1
Group	4.6	0.6	1.0	1.3	1.2	1.9	0.3	1.7
Family	0.2	0.7	1.1	0.4	0.6	0.3	0.0	0.0
Pragmatically Oriented								
Interactions	0.5	1.4	0.9	0.9	1.9	1.2	0.0	0.5
Limit-Setting	0.5	1.6	0.8	1.1	4.7	2.7	6.7	1.9
Collateral Contacts	0.7	0.6	1.2	0.6	1.0	0.7	0.0	0.8
II. Typical Youths[b]								
Counseling								
Individual	1.7	3.0	2.7	2.4	4.5	2.5	3.3	2.1
Group	1.5	0.4	0.4	0.6	1.2	1.7	0.3	1.4
Family	0.1	0.5	0.4	0.1	0.4	0.2	0.0	0.0
Pragmatically Oriented								
Interactions	0.1	0.8	0.4	0.4	1.8	0.7	0.0	0.3
Limit-Setting	0.2	0.9	0.4	0.4	4.6	1.4	6.7	1.2
Collateral Contacts	0.3	0.4	0.3	0.2	0.8	0.5	0.0	0.4

[a]Sample sizes are as follows: *Matched*: Group Conformist—6; Manipulator—5; Assertive-Denier—18; Anxious-Confused—29. *Unmatched*: Group Conformist—16; Manipulator—15; Assertive-Denier—29; Anxious-Confused—41.

[b]Includes participants and nonparticipants, that is, the total sample as defined in Chapter 3.

26 RATE OF OFFENDING DURING PAROLE FOR SPECIFIED YOUTH TYPES

As indicated in Chapters 4 and 5, the power-oriented group was composed of group conformists and manipulators, whereas the conflicted group consisted of assertive-deniers and anxious-confused youths. How did these four youth types (subgroups) perform during parole? More specifically: (1) How did the respective E and C subgroups compare with each other on rate of offending? (2) How did each "matched E" and "unmatched E" subgroup compare with its control subgroup? (3) How did specified matched (and unmatched) E subgroups compare with other matched (and unmatched) E subgroups? These questions are addressed, respectively, in sections I, II, and III below. (Matching is described in Chapter 11. Controls could not be subdivided into matched and unmatched groups.)

The method used to answer these questions was identical to that described in Chapter 8—and, for the matching analyses (sections II and III, below), that described in Chapter 11. Specifically, it was identical with regard to samples, definitions, data sources, criterion measures, statistical tests, and so on. As always, "more" and "fewer"—for example, more arrests and fewer convictions—refers to *rate* of offending per unit of time (viz., the standard "1,000" months at risk). Supplementary information regarding assertive-deniers and anxious-confused males from San Francisco is presented in section IV.

I. E's versus C's[1]
Group Conformists
As seen in Table A26–1, there were no significant differences between E and C group conformists on moderate plus severe arrests and

convictions. However, E's tended to have fewer severe arrests, and fewer violent arrests and convictions, than C's. ("Tendency" always means: p < .10 > .05. "Significant" means: p < .05 or < .01.)

Manipulators
Experimental manipulators (Mp's) had significantly fewer moderate plus severe arrests, and tended to have fewer severe arrests, than controls. However, no significant E/C differences or tendencies were found regarding convictions, for those same severity groupings. Nor were differences found for violent arrests and convictions. (Table A26–1.)

Although (1) experimental manipulators had fewer moderate plus severe arrests than their controls whereas (2) experimental group conformists (G-C's) did not, the former subgroup (E Mp's) performed no better than the latter (E G-C's) in this respect: 56 versus 55 moderate plus severe arrests per 1,000 months at risk. The difference in E versus C outcomes between (1) and (2), above, reflected the fact that *control* group conformists tended to outperform *control* manipulators relative to moderate plus severe arrests: 51 versus 84 per 1,000 months at risk. (No such C versus C difference existed with respect to violent arrests.)

Assertive-Deniers
Experimental assertive-deniers had strikingly fewer arrests and convictions than controls, with regard to all severity groupings (p < .01 or .05 in all cases). (Table A26–1.)

Anxious-Confused Youths
Experimental anxious-confused youths tended

TABLE A26-I

Number of Offenses per 1,000 Months at Risk during Parole, for Group Conformist, Manipulator, Assertive-Denier, and Anxious-Confused Valley Boys

Type of Offense and Outcome Measure	Youth Type and Number of Offenses[a]							
	Group Conformist		Manipulator		Assertive-Denier		Anxious-Confused	
	Exp.	Control	Exp.	Control	Exp.	Control	Exp.	Control
	M UM		M UM		M UM		M UM	
Moderate + Severe Offenses								
All arrests	55 (66, 50)	51	56 (33, 68)	84	35 (18, 47)	118	34 (45, 24)	50
Arrests with convictions	32 (41, 28)	27	44 (30, 52)	54	21 (8, 31)	69	22 (30, 15)	35
Severe Offenses								
All arrests	18 (26, 15)	20	24 (16, 28)	40	13 (6, 18)	48	15 (21, 9)	13
Arrests with convictions	8 (20, 2)	14	20 (16, 22)	29	7 (4, 9)	28	11 (16, 6)	9
Violent Offenses[b]								
All arrests	7 (5, 9)	18	17 (7, 22)	14	6 (2, 9)	22	6 (10, 3)	7
Arrests with convictions	2 (5, 0)	8	13 (7, 17)	12	3 (2, 5)	16	4 (8, 1)	6

[a]All figures shown in parentheses refer to matched (M) and unmatched (UM) youths, respectively. Sample sizes are: Group Conformist, E—18, (6, 12), C-20; Manipulator, E—18, (6, 12), C—19; Assertive-Denier, E—37, (16, 21), C—31; Anxious-Confused, E—62, (30, 32), C—33.

[b]Includes: armed robbery, rape (attempted or actual), assault with deadly weapon, aggravated assault, kidnapping, murder (attempted or actual), and so on. These offenses are part of the broader category labeled Severe Offenses (sale of narcotics, grand theft auto, 1st-degree burglary, drunk driving, etc.).

to have fewer moderate plus severe arrests, and they had significantly fewer such convictions, than controls. No E/C differences were observed relative to severe and violent offenses. (Table A26–1.)

Although (1) experimental assertive-deniers (A-D's) had far fewer severe and violent arrests and convictions than their *controls* whereas (2) experimental anxious-confused (A-C) youths did not, the former subgroup (E A-D's) did not perform significantly better than the *latter* (E A-C's) in these regards—for example, 13 versus 15 severe arrests and 6 versus 6 violent arrests per 1,000 months at risk, respectively. (Convictions for severe offenses were no exception to the above.) Thus, the difference in E versus C outcomes between (1) and (2), above, reflected the fact that *control* assertive-deniers performed markedly worse than *control* anxious-confused youths relative to severe and violent offenses. (Control A-D's performed much worse than control A-C's in relation to *moderate plus severe* offenses as well, whereas neither experimental subgroup outperformed the other in this respect.) This means that the E/C differences described in Chapter 8, for conflicted boys on parole, were almost exclusively due to the much poorer performance of control assertive-deniers than control anxious-confused youths, not to the performance of experimental A-D's versus that of experimental A-C's. In short, these E/C differences can be traced primarily to assertive-denier youths—controls in particular.

II. Matched E's and Unmatched E's, versus C's[2]
Group Conformists
Though there were no overall (matched plus unmatched) differences between experimental group conformists and their controls on moderate plus severe arrests and convictions (section I, above), matched G-C's tended to perform worse than controls: 41 versus 27 convictions per 1,000 months at risk. On the other hand, they tended to have fewer *violent* arrests than controls; and the UM group, which also tended to have fewer violent arrests, had fewer severe arrests and convictions as well: 15 versus 29 arrests and 2 versus 14 convictions. (Table A26–1.)

Manipulators
Although experimental manipulators had sig-

nificantly fewer moderate plus severe arrests than controls (section I, above), this difference was mainly accounted for by matched rather than unmatched Mp's. (Matched Mp's also tended to have fewer moderate plus severe convictions, and had fewer severe arrests, than C's. The difference between unmatched Mp's and controls was not significant, with respect to moderate plus severe arrests and convictions alike.) In addition, matched Mp's tended to have fewer violent arrests than controls, while *un*matched Mp's had neither significantly more nor fewer such arrests than controls. (Table A26–1.)

Assertive-Deniers
Matched and unmatched experimental assertive-deniers each had significantly fewer arrests and convictions than controls, with regard to moderate plus severe—and severe—offenses. These E/C differences were considerably sharper among matched than unmatched A-D's. Matched A-D's had significantly fewer violent arrests and convictions than controls; for unmatched youths, these same differences *tended* to be significant. (Table A26–1.)

Anxious-Confused Youths
Matched anxious-confused youths performed neither better nor worse than controls on moderate plus severe—and violent—arrests and convictions. However, they tended to perform *worse* than controls with regard to severe convictions. Unmatched A-C's performed significantly *better* than controls on moderate plus severe arrests and convictions, and tended to perform better relative to violent convictions. They performed neither better nor worse with respect to severe arrests and convictions, and on violent arrests as well. (Table A26–1.)

III. E's versus E's (across Subtypes)
Group Conformists versus Manipulators[3]
As shown in Table A26–1, *matched* group conformists tended to have *more* moderate plus severe arrests than matched manipulators: 66 versus 33 per 1,000 months at risk. (With a substantially larger sample size, a difference of this magnitude would have been significant.) No G-C/Mp differences were found regarding severe and violent offenses. *Unmatched* group conformists tended to have *fewer* moderate plus severe arrests, and had significantly fewer

moderate plus severe convictions, than unmatched manipulators: 50 versus 68, and 28 versus 52, respectively. They tended to have fewer severe and violent arrests and had significantly fewer such convictions. In short, matched group conformists performed somewhat worse than matched manipulators (except with respect to violent offenses), whereas unmatched G-C's performed substantially better than unmatched Mp's.

Assertive-Deniers versus Anxious-Confused Youths

Matched assertive-deniers had significantly *fewer* arrests and convictions for moderate plus severe, and severe, offenses than matched anxious-confused youths—for example, 18 versus 45 moderate plus severe arrests per 1,000 months at risk. They tended to have fewer violent arrests as well. *Unmatched* assertive-deniers had significantly *more* moderate plus severe arrests and convictions, and they tended to have more severe and violent arrests, than unmatched anxious-confused youths. Thus, matched assertive-deniers performed considerably better than matched anxious-confused youths, whereas unmatched A-D's performed worse than unmatched A-C's. (Table A26–1.)

General Observations

Within the power-oriented and conflicted groups, respectively, neither subgroup consistently outperformed the other. For example, manipulators did not always perform better than group conformists, and assertive-deniers did not always outperform anxious-confused youths. In this regard, the relative performance of each subgroup was differentially linked to the presence or absence of matching. Specifically, among power-oriented individuals matching was of greater benefit to manipulators than to group conformists; among conflicted youths it was more beneficial to assertive-deniers than to anxious-confused individuals. At the same time, the *absence* of matching—with matching defined as in Chapter 11—was more beneficial to group conformists than to manipulators, and to anxious-confused youths than to assertive-deniers.

Finally, when one compares all four subgroups (matched and unmatched youths included), matched assertive-deniers had the fewest arrests and convictions for moderate

plus severe, and severe, offenses: For matched and unmatched group conformists, manipulators, assertive-deniers, and anxious-confused youths, respectively, the rates for moderate plus severe arrests were 66, 50, 33, 68, *18*, 47, 45, and 24 per 1,000 months at risk. (Thus, for example, 66 and 50 refer to matched and unmatched G-C's, and *18* refers to matched A-D's.) Regarding these same youths, the rates for severe arrests were 26, 15, 16, 28, 6, 18, 21, and 9. In general, the rates for unmatched anxious-confused youths were second lowest. (Table A26–1.)

IV. Conflicted San Francisco Youths

The following results suggest that, as in the Valley, assertive-deniers from San Francisco performed particularly well in CTP, during parole. (In the interests of space, specific figures will not be presented.)

CTP versus Controls

Within San Francisco, assertive-deniers from CTP had significantly fewer moderate plus severe arrests, and fewer violent arrests, than A-D controls. They tended to have fewer severe arrests and convictions, and fewer moderate plus severe (and violent) convictions, as well. As to anxious-confused youths, too few controls were present to allow for meaningful statistical comparisons with CTP (and with GGI).

CTP versus GGI

When assertive-deniers from CTP were compared with those from GGI, the former had significantly fewer severe arrests than the latter; they tended to have fewer severe convictions and fewer violent arrests as well. Anxious-confused youths from CTP tended to have fewer severe and violent convictions than their counterparts from GGI; however, no significant CTP/GGI differences or statistical tendencies were found for *moderate plus severe* arrests and convictions, even though anxious-confused youths from CTP had 28 percent *more* such arrests than their counterparts in GGI.

CTP versus CTP

When assertive-deniers and anxious-confused youths from CTP were compared with each other, the former individuals had significantly fewer moderate plus severe arrests and tended to have fewer severe arrests than the latter. No statistically significant A-D/A-C differences were found with respect to convictions, even though assertive-deniers had substantially (33 percent) fewer moderate plus severe convictions than anxious-confused youths.

GGI versus Controls; GGI versus GGI

Finally, assertive-deniers from GGI tended to have fewer moderate plus severe arrests than A-D Controls; however, no other GGI/control differences were found—tendencies or otherwise. When A-D's and A-C's from GGI were compared with each other, no significant differences or statistical tendencies were found; nor were substantial percentage differences observed.

Notes

1. Results for the *post-discharge* and *parole plus post-discharge* periods are shown in Appendix 27.
2. *Matched* experimentals were similar to their controls on most background characteristics. More specifically, out of 24 analyses (six background characteristics for each of four youth groups), seven significant E/C differences or statistical tendencies were found: (1) matched group conformists (E's) were older than C's (by 14 months); (2) matched group conformists were more likely to be non-Caucasian than C's; (3) matched manipulators were more likely to be non-Caucasian than C's; (4) matched assertive-deniers were older than C's (by 12 months); (5) matched assertive-deniers were slightly worse parole risks than controls (13 points lower in Base Expectancy, an almost negligible difference); (6) matched anxious-confused youths tended to be older than C's (by six months); (7) matched anxious-confused youths tended to have a higher IQ than C's (by three points—essentially negligible). *Unmatched* experimentals were very similar to their controls, except as follows (again, 24 E/C comparisons were made): (1) unmatched group conformists had a higher IQ than C's (by six points); (2) the unmatched manipulator group tended to be comprised of more non-Caucasian youths than its control group; (3) unmatched assertive-deniers tended to be older than C's (by 11 months).
3. Out of 24 background-characteristics comparisons, four significant differences or statistical tendencies were found: (1) matched group conformists were better parole risks than matched manipulators (higher Base Expectancy by 138 points, a substantial difference); (2) unmatched group conformists tended to be older than unmatched manipulators (by 16 months, also a substantial difference); (3) unmatched group conformists had a higher IQ than unmatched manipulators (by 10 points, a moderate difference); (4) unmatched assertive-deniers were more likely to be non-Caucasian than unmatched anxious-confused youths (48% versus 22% of their respective groups).

27 RATE OF OFFENDING DURING POST-DISCHARGE AND DURING PAROLE PLUS POST-DISCHARGE PERIODS, FOR SPECIFIED YOUTH TYPES

In Appendix 26 (section I), rates of offending during *parole* were presented for experimentals versus controls—group conformists, manipulators, assertive-deniers, and anxious-confused youths, specifically. In the present appendix, rates are presented for these same E's and C's, with regard to the *post-parole* and *parole plus post-discharge* periods, respectively. (Post-parole is synonymous with "post-YA" and "post-discharge.") In effect, we asked: Was the parole performance of E's—compared to that of C's—the same or different after YA discharge? That is, did the parole performance of E's *hold up* relative to that of C's, for each such youth type? The method used to answer this question was the same as that in Chapter 8 and Appendix 26.[1] Results are as follows.

Group Conformists

As shown in Table A27–1, experimental group conformists tended to have more violent arrests (i.e., arrests for violent offenses) than their controls during the *post-discharge* period: 14 versus 7 per 1,000 months at risk. This was the opposite of that observed in connection with parole. No other significant E/C

differences or statistical tendencies were found with regard to post-discharge, for example, in connection with moderate plus severe offenses; and, in that respect, there were no changes in the performance of E's versus C's, from parole to post-discharge.

As shown in Table A27–2, no significant E/C differences or tendencies were observed relative to the *parole plus post-discharge* periods combined, for any severity grouping. This reflected the fact that, on some indices (moderate plus severe offenses), the parole performance of experimental group conformists remained the same as that of controls, subsequent to YA discharge; and, on other indices (violent offenses), it was counterbalanced and "canceled" subsequent to discharge.

Manipulators

As shown in Table A27–1, experimental manipulators had significantly more moderate plus severe—and severe—arrests and convictions than their controls, during post-discharge; for instance, there were 79(E) versus 33(C) moderate plus severe arrests per 1,000 months at risk. Thus, various differences that favored E's over

Number of Offenses per 1,000 Months at Risk Subsequent to Discharge from Youth Authority, for Group Conformist, Manipulator, Assertive-Denier, and Anxious-Confused Valley Boys

	Youth Type and Number of Offenses[a]							
	Group Conformist		Manipulator		Assertive-Denier		Anxious-Confused	
Type of Offense and Outcome Measure	Exp.	Control	Exp.	Control	Exp.	Control	Exp.	Control
Moderate + Severe Offenses								
All arrests	56	50	79	33	24	58	38	57
Arrests with convictions	38	41	48	22	17	31	21	31
Severe Offenses								
All arrests	17	20	54	13	13	21	15	24
Arrests with convictions	10	14	21	6	9	13	7	10
Violent Offenses[b]								
All arrests	14	7	13	9	3	5	6	12
Arrests with convictions	7	4	3	1	2	2	4	5

[a]Sample sizes are as follows: Group Conformist, E—12, C—19; Manipulator, E—13, C—14; Assertive-Denier, E—29, C—20; Anxious-Confused, E—41, C—18.
[b]See Table 8–1, note c.

TABLE A27–2

Number of Offenses per 1,000 Months at Risk during Parole and Post-Discharge Periods Combined, for Group Conformist, Manipulator, Assertive-Denier, and Anxious-Confused Valley Boys[a]

	Youth Type and Number of Offenses							
	Group Conformist		Manipulator		Assertive-Denier		Anxious-Confused	
Type of Offense and Outcome Measure	Exp.	Control	Exp.	Control	Exp.	Control	Exp.	Control
Moderate + Severe Offenses								
All arrests	55	51	65	55	29	86	36	53
Arrests with convictions	35	35	46	36	18	49	22	34
Severe Offenses								
All arrests	18	23	37	25	13	34	15	18
Arrests with convictions	9	14	20	16	8	20	9	10
Violent Offenses[b]								
All arrests	10	11	15	11	4	13	6	9
Arrests with convictions	4	6	9	6	3	8	4	5

[a]"Parole" refers to the entire Youth Authority career, as in Table 8–1. "Post-Discharge" refers to the four-year, post-YA follow-up, as in Table 8–2. Sample sizes are the same as in Table A27–1.
[b]See Table 8–1, note c.

C's during *parole*—some significant, and most of them substantial—were sharply reversed with respect to post-discharge. However, no significant E/C differences were found in connection with violent offenses, for the post-discharge period; and, no parole-to-post-discharge changes took place in this regard, again for E's versus C's.

For parole plus post-discharge combined, E's tended to perform worse than C's with respect to severe arrests; however, no other tendencies or reliable differences were found. Thus, with one exception, the post-discharge performance of experimental manipulators (relative to that of controls) did not clearly outweigh the *parole* performance of these youths (again, relative to controls), even though it was *counterbalanced* by the latter. (Table A27–2.)

Assertive-Deniers

As with parole, experimental assertive-deniers had significantly fewer moderate plus severe offenses than controls, during post-discharge: 24 versus 58 (arrests) and 17 versus 31 (convictions) per 1,000 months at risk. Though E's had 38 percent fewer severe arrests than C's, this difference was not reliable; and no significant E/C differences were found regarding violent arrests. In general, then, the parole performance of experimental A-D's held up, relative to that of controls. (Table A27–1.)

For parole plus post-discharge combined, E's had significantly fewer arrests than C's with respect to all severity groupings. They had fewer moderate plus severe convictions and tended to have fewer severe convictions as well. These outcomes, for those two periods combined, reflected the fact that parole and post-discharge findings had consistently supported—not diverged from, let alone opposed or counterbalanced—each other. (Table A27–2.)

Anxious-Confused Youths

As with parole, experimental anxious-confused youths—during post-discharge—had substantially fewer moderate plus severe offenses than their controls: 38 versus 57 (arrests) and 21 versus 31 (convictions) per 1,000 months at risk ($p < .10 > .05$ in both cases). Although E's had over 35 percent fewer severe arrests than C's, this difference was not reliable; however, E's had significantly fewer violent arrests than C's. At any rate, despite minor exceptions, the post-discharge performance of experimental A-C's (relative to that of controls) was similar to the *parole* performance of these individuals (again, relative to C's). It might be noted that, for E's versus *E's,* the absolute rates of offending were also very similar for parole as compared to post-discharge—for example, 34 versus 38 moderate plus severe arrests, respectively. (Table A27–1.)

For parole plus post-discharge combined, experimental A-C's tended to have fewer moderate plus severe arrests and convictions than controls: E/C differences were 32 percent and 35 percent, respectively. As with assertive-deniers, results for the parole and post-discharge periods supported—rather than diverged from, or opposed—each other, chiefly for moderate plus severe offenses. (Table A27–2.)

Summary

In sum, the parole performance of group conformists (G-C's) remained essentially the same subsequent to YA discharge, when E's and C's were compared with regard to moderate plus severe—and severe—offenses. However, the relative performance of experimental G-C's changed for the worse, in connection with arrests for violence. The performance of experimental manipulators changed considerably from parole to post-discharge: For moderate plus severe, and severe, offenses, it went from slightly better to clearly worse (relative to controls), from the former period to the latter. Finally, with assertive-deniers and anxious-confused youths, parole performance largely held up. Here, E's continued to outperform C's, at least on moderate plus severe offenses combined.

Note

1. Experimentals were similar to controls on the six background characteristics. Specifically, out of 24 E/C comparisons, only the following differences were found: (1) E group conformists tended to be older than C's (by four months); (2) E group conformists had a higher IQ than C's (by 10 points); (3) E manipulators were more likely to be non-Caucasian than C's; (4) E assertive-deniers tended to be older than C's (nine months); (5) E assertive-deniers tended to be committed to the YA for fewer property offenses and more "Other" offenses than controls (and also for more offenses against persons). No E/C differences or statistical tendencies were found regarding anxious-confused youths. ("Tendency" meant: $p < .10 > .05$.)

FIVE GROUPS OF STATUS 1 YOUTHS

In the Phase 3 proposal to NIMH, the five groups of Status 1 youths were described as follows.

Group A

Youngsters who, psychologically and interpersonally,

1. are quite disturbed and openly disorganized relative to overall, everyday functioning; and who
2. at times become highly agitated or even delusional when under the pressures of everyday life. These youths need to achieve a given level of functional stability or ego-strengthening prior to their return to the community proper, and to the pressures which they are likely to encounter within that setting.

Group B

Youngsters who have an intense drive to prevent other persons from exerting controls upon them or from substantially influencing the direction of their lives. These youths are prepared to use "everything" in their power, for example, runaway or violence, to avoid:

1. ongoing confrontation by concerned authority figures;
2. reality-testing their marked fear of secure adults; and
3. involvement in nonexploitive relationships with adults in general.

   Prior to return to the community, an institution-based treatment/control experience is needed in order to:

1. focus the attention of these youths on the parole agent;
2. allow for a large quantity of intensive therapeutic confrontation (e.g., exposure of youths' dysfunctional patterns of adjustment, and defense);
3. reduce the youths' intense fear of the parole agent; and
4. establish, in the youths' mind, the concern of the parole agent.

Group C

Youngsters who are unable to recognize, or who vigorously attempt to deny, the existence and influence of the unusually destructive relationships and loyalty-binds in which they are involved, at home and/or within the community. These youths need to have their principal problems and patterns of self-destruction inspected, or at least clearly outlined, prior to their being able to participate in the development of realistic, nondestructive plans with reference to their adaptation and growth within a community setting. Under present conditions it seems possible to accomplish this goal only when they are in a setting that can ensure them a period of rest or relief from those destructive relationships and binds, that is, from conditions which would otherwise:

1. undermine the youth/parole agent relationship at a time when this relationship was still in its formative stage;
2. maintain the youths' anxiety at a level that would preclude the development of any substantial degree of insight; and
3. operate so as to (a) lead the youths into delinquent behavior of a frequency or

magnitude sufficient to result in their early revocation and removal from the community setting, and to (b) maintain their status as the "sick" or "bad" boy.

Group D

Youngsters who are "nonneurotic" and of a relatively high level of maturity, but who need to be shown that their freedom will definitely be withdrawn if they persist in their delinquent patterns. With these youths, initial institutional placement would be designed to communicate just one essential message: that even apart from questions of "rightness" or "wrongness" and/or harm to other individuals, "crime just doesn't pay" in terms of the loss—associated with confinement—of the many personally satisfying activities in which these youths are usually capable of engaging.

Group E

Youngsters who—operating from underlying motives of a self-defeating nature—have become immersed in, and increasingly committed to, the use of drugs and/or a drug subculture, to the point of feeling very little interest in coping with long-range social expectations or pressures. These youngsters frequently feel that—other than drugs and experiences which center around involvement with drugs—"nothing really matters." They are, commonly, in the process of consciously devaluating or strongly rejecting their wishes or previously felt needs for personal involvement with others. Their relationships with others are often seen as taking on an increasingly exploitive tone. This stance is frequently defended by these youths on grounds that other people (peers or adults) are of little significance or value, whether as persons in their own right or in terms of what they appear—in the youths' eyes—to contribute to others.

In a setting which ensures that their attention will be drawn to the parole agent, Group E youths need to move in the direction of viewing the agent as an individual who not only seems genuine as a person, but who:

1. Appears both sensitive to and appreciative of many feelings and underlying issues with which the youths are concerned . . . yet who, at the same time,
2. Appears capable of considering these issues from a perspective which is new to

these youths—one which, in the eyes of the youths, seems to have some merit.

Prior to release to the community setting, these individuals should begin to:

1. Recognize the possibility that the parole agent (and/or a group of peers) may actually be an individual whose experiences have provided him with something that merits serious attention.

   There should also be an indication that the above interest in pursuing the possibility of establishing some type of nonexploitive relationship with the parole agent (or with new sets of peers) is working in the direction of the former's (i.e., the relationship's) becoming a vehicle through which the youth, specifically,
2. becomes motivated to seriously reassess his consciously adopted stance, commitments, and focal concerns. (Palmer, 1969a, pp. 6–8)

Method and Additional Comparisons
Method

The excellent match that was obtained among key comparison groups, such as RC's and RR's, was the result of a carefully monitored, stratified randomization: Throughout Phase 3, after every four months of case intake, the four experimental groups (RC, RR, CR, CC) were analyzed and compared with one another regarding each of the six background characteristics, especially age, parole risk, and race. If any group, say, RC's, was "out of line" on a given characteristic—that is, was substantially different than its key comparison group (RR's), and/or, secondarily, was somewhat different than all other groups combined—the following step was taken. The ratio that would ordinarily be applied to the Table of Random Numbers was adjusted to increase the chances that the characteristic in question would balance out (i.e., would be rather evenly distributed among the key comparison groups) by the time several more youths had entered the project. For example, to obtain a better balance among groups, the probability of obtaining a "qualifying" random number would be temporarily changed from 50/50 to 75/25, in connection with a particular group (RC's) that, at the time, was found to be insufficiently represented with respect to a given characteristic (say, Mexican American youths).

Additional Comparisons

(1) No significant differences or statistical tendencies were found on any of the six background characteristics when inappropriately placed youths (RC's plus CR's) were compared with appropriately placed youths and when Status 1 youths (RR's plus RC's) were compared with Status 2 youths (CC's plus CR's). (2) No significant differences or tendencies were found when RC's were compared with RR's on I-level (I_2, I_3, I_4), and on subtype grouping (passive-conformist, power-oriented, conflicted, all others). The same results, that is, no significant differences or tendencies, were obtained when CR's were compared with CC's, when "inappropriates" were compared with "appropriates," and when Status 1 youths were compared with Status 2 youths—in connection with these same dimensions.

29 COMPARISONS ON BACKGROUND CHARACTERISTICS OF SELECTED YOUTH GROUPINGS, FOR PHASE 3 MALES IN PAROLE FOLLOW-UP ANALYSIS

Background Characteristics

Sample and Youth Grouping	BE[a] $\bar{M}$	BE[a] σ	Age $\bar{M}$	Age σ	IQ $\bar{M}$	IQ σ	Race[b] C	Race[b] M	Race[b] B	Race[b] O	SES[c] LL	SES[c] L	SES[c] M	SES[c] U	Offense[d] Pe	Offense[d] Pr	Offense[d] O
Total Group																	
RC	462	86	16.2	1.5	90.4	17.0	80	10	10	0	40	25	30	5	35	45	20
vs.																	
RR	472	98	16.6	1.9	92.0	16.2	72	11	17	0	44	33	11	11	31	42	28
p-level:	70 > 50		70 > 50		70 > 50			80 > 70				50 > 30				90 > 80	
CR	528	103	16.6	1.6	90.2	17.0	67	14	19	0	39	33	28	0	25	56	19
vs.																	
CC	522	96	16.3	1.3	90.8	15.5	57	14	23	6	23	43	31	3	26	49	26
p-level:	70 > 50		50 > 30		90 > 80			50 > 30				50 > 30				80 > 70	
Conflicted Youths																	
RC	472	89	16.3	1.5	92.0	18.1	78	11	11	0	44	22	28	6	33	44	22
vs.																	
RR	461	102	16.6	1.5	94.3	15.5	88	4	8	0	40	32	16	12	32	36	32
p-level:	70 > 50		80 > 70		70 > 50			70 > 50				70 > 50				80 > 70	
CR	539	104	16.5	1.8	91.1	16.5	78	7	15	0	26	37	37	0	26	52	22
vs.																	
CC	525	130	16.6	1.2	92.9	15.2	64	12	16	8	20	36	40	4	32	40	28
p-level:	70 > 50		80 > 70		50 > 30			50 > 30				80 > 70				70 > 50	

[a] Base Expectancy scores are higher than in Phases 1 and 2 because a revised, five-factor formula was used in Phase 3 (Beverly, 1968; Palmer, 1970b, pp. 17, 69).

[b] C = Caucasian; M = Mexican American; B = Black; O = Other.

[c] In Phase 3, the Phase 1 and 2 category "lower SES" was subdivided into "lower, lower SES" (i.e., very low SES) and "lower SES." Thus, LL = lower, lower SES; L = lower SES; M = middle SES; and, U = upper SES (Palmer, 1970b, pp. 17, 68). The remaining categories were unchanged.

[d] Pe = Person; Pr = Property; O = Other.

NUMBER OF ARRESTS PER 1,000 MONTHS AT RISK DURING A FOUR-YEAR POST-DISCHARGE FOLLOW-UP, FOR PHASE 3 MALES

	Arrests, Youths, and Type of Arrests[a]					
Youth Status and Youth Group	Total Group			Conflicted Youths Only		
	Moderate + Severe	Severe	Violent[b]	Moderate + Severe	Severe	Violent[b]
Status 1 RC	36	16	5	36	16	5
RR	23	11	2	23	14	2
Status 2 CR	29	19	13	34	21	13
CC	27	10	4	21	12	6
RC + CR[c]	31	18	10	35	19	10
RR + CC[d]	25	11	3	22	13	4

[a]Sample sizes are as follows: Total Group: RC—4, RR—11, CR—10, CC—10. Conflicted youths: RC—4, RR—9, CR—8, CC—7. Included are all favorable plus unfavorable dischargees from CTP who were followed for 48 risk-months as of the data cutoff. *Total Group* was defined as in Table 13–2.

[b]Moderate + severe, severe, and violent offenses were defined, measured, and analyzed as in Chapters 8 through 11.

[c]RR + CR = Inappropriately assigned youths.

[d]RR + CC = Appropriately assigned youths.

31 APPROACHES USED TO IDENTIFY CTP'S KEY FACTORS

Limitations and Issues

CTP's study design did not make it possible to focus on each identified ("key") factor in a controlled, systematic way, within the context of the present experiment. For instance, given CTP's priorities and operational constraints, it was impossible to implement and maintain the following, wide-ranging variations across or even within agent caseloads:[1]

1. vary caseload size from, say, six to 20;
2. reduce length of contacts (total program duration) to 15, 12, and perhaps even 8 months; and
3. do *not* utilize preestablished guidelines, intensive contacts, or even moderately individualized intervention.

Such variations would have been needed in order to determine the specific impact, on youths, of *differing types or amounts of input* (e.g., smaller and larger caseloads, shorter and longer contacts, nonintensive and intensive contacts), and to then compare each such impact with that of the traditional program. This process would have made it possible to systematically estimate the importance of each identified factor, such as caseload size, with respect to reducing illegal behavior. The importance of each factor as compared to that of any remaining factor, for instance, length of contacts, could also have been determined, again with respect to rate of offending (r.o.o.). Such estimates would have been available in quantitative (relatively precise) rather than qualitative (broad categorical) terms alone.

To implement such input variations and to especially ensure that enough youths would be present regarding each type of input, sev-

eral experiments and parole units would have been required—either that or one extremely large, long-term effort. In the former strategy or design, one or possibly two factors would be varied at a time, within each experiment or unit. These factors might, for example, be caseload size and/or total length of contacts, or perhaps intensity of contacts and degree of individualized intervention. In the latter design, assuming one could overcome organizational and operational constraints, all factors would be varied simultaneously, according to a complex study plan. Here, ideally, the impact of each factor would be later sorted out statistically.[2]

In both designs, at least two conditions would exist: (1) Numerous, wide-ranging inputs (see [1] through [3] above) would be present with regard to each youth group, such as passive-conformists, and many youths would be involved with respect to each *combination* of input (say, caseload size of 20) and youth group. The youths would be distributed across more than one caseload. (2) The preceding inputs would be systematically introduced and strictly maintained for adequate periods of time, to ensure that the conditions of the experiment(s) were met in every instance. Again, these experiments and parole units would not be subject to certain operational constraints that existed in the present study.

Opportunities within CTP

Within the present study, the first and most essential condition did exist, albeit in a rather limited way: Though input variations existed regarding each of the first seven factors shown in Figure 15–1, and although a sufficient number of youths were present with respect to many combinations of input and group, these variations fell within much narrower limits than those suggested earlier, certainly for the first five factors. In short, the variations were not wide-ranging, whether within or across caseloads (and parole units as well). For instance, from the close of CTP's buildup stage (see Chapter 2) through the end of Phase 2, the following variations or differences were observed from one agent's caseload to the next (i.e., "across" caseloads), with regard to any given youth group:

1. caseload size not infrequently varied between 9 and 13, occasionally 14 (this mainly applied "within" agent caseloads);
2. some agents usually "moved" youths through the project 20 percent to 25 percent faster than did most agents;
3. some agents made more use of CTP's preestablished guidelines than did most agents, whereas others made considerably less use of them; and
4. some agents had less intensive contacts with youths (i.e., a substantially lower rate of contact) than did most agents; also, they or other agents were likely to utilize less extensive contacts or operate less flexibly with respect to programming.

This restricted range of variations essentially eliminated the possibility of making refined estimates regarding the impact of each individual factor; however, it did not prevent one from making those which were rather broad. The latter possibility derived from the presence of the earlier-mentioned input variations (condition #1), even though these were not *wide*-ranging. Moreover, this possibility was independent of the fact that, to obtain such estimates, the preceding inputs did not have to be systematically introduced and strictly maintained in every instance. In short, despite the absence of systematic "controls" (condition #2), many combinations of input and youth group nevertheless did appear at frequent points during Phases 1 and 2. These combinations remained present for substantial periods of time and they usually involved several youths each. Other combinations existed for insufficiently short time periods and/or involved very few youths (e.g., few youths across several agent caseloads, collectively).

Many variations from average or modal inputs were observed not just across caseloads, but within the individual agent's caseload, that is, relative to *his own* more typical approaches. The latter variations could have existed not only throughout any fairly lengthy time period (e.g., the agent's second six months at CTP, as compared to most or all other periods) but also across the years (e.g., during his third year as compared with previous years, with respect to many youths who were placed on his later caseload after most youths had left his original one). Finally, substantial short-term variations (one to three months) were also noted, mainly with factors and subfactors included in (1) and (4) above. Although many agents therefore varied *often,* most agents still did not vary a great deal. For this reason, the largest as well as longest-term variations or differences generally existed across, not within, caseloads.

Information regarding the existence, direction, and extent of changes in various inputs was essentially based on the following: (1) long-term, on-site observations by researchers, plus frequent informal discussions—also involving researchers—with operations staff and, to a lesser extent, with youths; (2) routine documentation, such as Quarterly Case Summaries, by each parole agent; (3) participation, by researchers, in follow-up staffings with operations personnel, (4) formal follow-up interviews between researchers and youths, and (5) similar, detailed follow-ups between researchers and staff. These information sources applied to *impacts* (performance) as well. Here, of course, while (1), (3), and (4) were the principal bases for detecting and evaluating short- and intermediate-term impacts, long-term, "official" behavioral impact was derived and analyzed from CI&I rapsheets alone. (At first—for many years—it was derived chiefly from YA case files. "Long-term" referred to the individual's YA career and to four-years post-discharge.) Information concerning the short- and intermediate-term impacts of factors #8 through #10—the Global Program Features—was likewise derived from (1) and (4) above; however, it was also based not only on intake interviews with youths and, to a lesser extent, on follow-up interviews with parole agents, but, in the case of factor #10, on (3) as well.

Inputs and Performance (Impact)
Via these research observations, follow-up interviews, and other specified sources/methods,

the earlier-mentioned *inputs* were repeatedly noted during Phases 1 and 2. Such inputs, which involved (1) "variations" and (2) average levels/modal approaches alike, were observed within as well as across caseloads. Also, within caseloads, numerous *performance changes* (improvements, plateaus, slowdowns, and setbacks) were noted in the youths' behavior and in other aspects of their adjustment; and, across caseloads, *performance differences* (better, equivalent, or worse behavior and adjustment) were observed. Like input changes themselves, for example, changes in frequency of youth/agent contacts, these within-caseload changes and across-caseload differences were of a short-, intermediate-, or longer-term nature.

Within caseloads, the existence, direction, and extent of *input changes* was determined in relation to the agents' average or modal approaches. As to performance changes, the standard of reference for determining their existence, direction, and extent was the youths' behavior and overall adjustment during a time period that immediately preceded those changes; this also applied to rate of change. In any event, within caseloads, youths were compared with themselves, with respect to given time periods.

Across caseloads, the existence and nature of *input differences,* that is, differing approaches from agent to agent, was determined by comparing the respective caseloads. This applied to performance differences as well, that is, to differing levels of behavior and adjustment. These across-caseload comparisons did not necessarily focus on the same time period for all agents involved, such as January through August of a particular year. Nor did they necessarily involve an identical time span, say, a six-month span, regardless of whether the identical time *period* (calendar span) was involved; instead, a time span could have been somewhat shorter or longer for one agent than for another. Finally, time spans that related to inputs did not have to precisely match those which concerned performance; this applied to within-caseload changes as well.

Given these research observations, distinctions, and analytic guidelines, how was it determined and estimated which inputs contributed—and contributed the most—to performance?

Often, *within* caseloads, distinct changes in behavior and in other aspects of adjustment were immediately preceded by specifiable changes in inputs, say, in intensity or extent of contacts. For instance, slowdowns and setbacks sometimes occurred when frequency of youth/agent contacts substantially decreased; and substantial improvements were sometimes observed soon after more extensive contacts, that is, wider-ranging intervention, had been undertaken. Similarly, *across* caseloads, youths who were generally exposed to more intensive or extensive contacts often showed higher levels of performance than comparable youths who were exposed to less. Also, youths whose agents followed CTP's preestablished guidelines more closely than other agents or who were more flexible in their approach than others sometimes showed better overall performance or perhaps more rapid improvement than comparable youths. However, as discussed below, the relationship between inputs and performance was not always simple; in fact, it was not always known. Moreover, with some youths, differing inputs did not seem to matter.

Usually, on any given occasion, it was impossible to unequivocally link each known input change to a given, subsequent performance change, that is, to do so in a definitive—or even a highly probable—cause-effect sense. This was often because the input changes had not occurred one at a time. For example, within a given caseload, two inputs, that is, specified types and amounts of given factors, were likely to have changed at about the same time, prior to an identified change in given youths' behavior and adjustment. In such an instance it was impossible to decide whether both factors had contributed to the performance change and, if they had, which one was more important. (As discussed below, a decision could be made only on the basis of *several* observations.) Similarly, across any two caseloads, two or three input differences often existed simultaneously, say, throughout the first six months of several passive-conformists' program exposure. That is, any two agents who were working with a given youth group often differed from each other on more than one factor alone, during a specified time period and/or intervention stage. Though these agents may have closely resembled each other on "all" or at least many remaining factors, these input differences complicated the explanation of any given performance difference that might have existed across their caseloads, during the period or stage in question.

In addition, within caseloads, (1) input change was not always accompanied by substantial, subsequent performance change. Moreover, (2) performance change was not always preceded by an identifiable *input* change from CTP. (Absence of performance change did not necessarily signify poor performance; and many important inputs did not come from CTP.) Finally, (3) when performance change did take place shortly after a given input change, the direction of relationship sometimes differed from that indicated earlier; for instance, slowdowns or setbacks occasionally occurred when frequency of contacts increased. Parallel sequences, for instance, *input difference leading to no substantial performance difference* (see [1] above), were observed *across* caseloads as well.

Despite such complications, certain input → performance (as output) sequences were repeatedly observed.[3] For example, among agents who had worked with a given youth group, say, passive-conformists, input changes that occurred in a given direction (e.g., *greater* intensity and/or *increased* flexibility) were more likely to be associated with particular types of performance change than were those which occurred in an opposite direction, or else those which were very minimal. More specifically, within caseloads, the former input changes were more likely than either of the latter to be soon followed by:

1. improved rather than worsened performance;
2. moderate or occasionally sizable improvements; and
3. relatively rapid, short- and intermediate-term improvements.

Moreover, within limits, performance changes (1) through (3) were sometimes preceded by input changes that had occurred not simply in a given direction, but to a greater degree than in the case of otherwise similar changes. As suggested, these input changes often involved more than one factor at a time.

(Parallel input → performance relationships were often observed *across* caseloads.[4] For example, passive-conformists on caseloads characterized by greater use of CTP's preestablished guidelines were more likely than those on the remaining caseloads to show performance changes (1) through (3). Such relationships were reflected in the findings for "matched" versus "unmatched" agents as well, in connection with these and other—though not all other—youth subtypes.)

Such input/performance sequences were more obvious with some factors than with others, for any given youth group. (These sequences were not considered "obvious" based on one or two instances alone; instead, they had been observed several times, within and/or across caseloads.) For example, the following was observed within caseloads, when other-than-minimal input changes occurred in a given direction regarding factor "x" (say, "individualization," or "extent of contact"): Such change was more likely to be associated with performance changes (1) through (3), above, than was comparable input change with respect to factor "y."[5] Similarly, when moderate to sizable input change occurred in connection with factor "x" as well as "y" or perhaps "z," the related performance changes were likely to be greater in *degree* or *rate* with regard to "x."[6] In such respects, some factors seemed more influential or catalytic than others.

As suggested, these sequences or relationships were not equally apparent with all factors. For instance, even when across-caseload comparisons (see below) were added to those mentioned earlier, and even though repeated observations were still involved, it was often impossible to form strong impressions as to whether a given factor was either more or less influential than each of several others; moreover, in such cases, the available evidence suggested that most "x"/"y" differences which did exist were probably small. At any rate, for various reasons other than default, of the first seven factors listed in Table 15–1, most seemed approximately as important as most remaining factors, relative to any given youth group. Still, as discussed in the text, certain factors (individually) usually stood out over two or more others (also individually), in the case of most youth groups.

The relative importance of one factor versus another sometimes became evident even though both factors (as inputs) had often changed, not just one at a time (as above), but together with one or more others.[7] More specifically, after many informal observations as well as subsequent comparisons had been made, the following became clear (collectively, these observations related to several caseloads in the case of each youth group; thus, they necessarily occurred over several years, even though each individual observation covered a much shorter time):

Certain combinations of factors were more likely than others to be associated with performance changes (1) through (3), above, particularly when given factors, such as factor "x," were included among the former combinations at a particular level or greater. That is, by first observing, and by then comparing and contrasting, numerous combinations (sets of input change with respect to specified dimensions), it became clear that, for various such combinations, better performance was more likely to occur whenever certain individual factors (say, factors "x" and "t") were present at a given level or greater—that is, at the level ("subsequent level") they had reached in connection with their input change. This performance difference applied almost regardless of various other factors with which "x" and "t" were each combined (say, "y" and "z"), that is, despite the changes or lack of changes in the input levels of "y" and "z"—and, thus, in the latter's subsequent level itself. These numerous observations, and so on—which related to within- as well as across-caseload combinations, that is, to sets of input change as well as input difference—thus helped sort out the influence of at least some factors as compared to others, albeit at a broad level and in nonquantitative terms only. In effect, this process—a kind of observational or qualitative "analysis of variance" and in some respects a "factor analysis"—slowly (i.e., over many years) helped tease-out, zero-in on, and otherwise identify input changes, and, thus, specific (key) factors, that seemed to make a greater and lesser difference with regard to given performance changes—positive as well as negative. Its results were informally integrated with—at any rate, added to—the already-mentioned impressions, those essentially based on single-factor changes and differences.

Review, Further Details, and Closing Remarks

Based on several types of information (direct observations, routine documentation, follow-up staffings, informal discussions, and formal interviews), short- and intermediate-term changes in youth behavior (performance) were often identified as resulting from specifi-

able types and levels of input, whether the latter were "variations" or "modal." Some inputs seemed more powerful than others with respect to producing/assisting/allowing these performance changes; and, whatever the former's power, several years of informal observations and comparisons were required in order to identify most input/performance sequences with a fair degree of confidence.

Together, these input/performance sequences—the more powerful combined with the less—helped researchers and operations staff form converging impressions regarding: (1) how much impact given factors had on youth behavior and other aspects of adjustment, and (2) the importance of given factors as compared to others. With the partial exception of key factors #6 and #7 (change-agent dimensions), these impressions were not the result of detailed, systematic statistical analyses; nevertheless, they were based on large amounts, and a broad range of, detailed information from key individuals who were actively involved with respect to the inputs and performance changes in question. (Short- and intermediate-term impacts often linked with long-term outcomes, including those derived from CI&I rapsheets. Long-term outcomes were used in the statistical analysis of change-agent dimensions.)

Converging impressions and detailed qualitative information notwithstanding, the lack of an experimental design that not only focused on, but that specifically centered on, key factors per se made it impossible to quantify the contribution of individual factors and to develop refined distinctions—including, for example, a complete ranking—as to their relative importance. Instead, such impressions centered on, in fact were limited to, three broad distinctions within each of two areas: (1) *overall level of impact* ("very important"; "important"; "of slight importance"); and, (2) *relative impact* ("more important than"; "about as important as"; "less important than"). Perhaps the most systematic observations—those which, in addition, *were* subject to statistical analyses concerning impact on youth behavior—related to factors #6 and #7. Results from these analyses—therefore, for these particular factors—served as external reference points against which the remaining factors were partly assessed regarding the earlier-mentioned distinctions, with respect to each of several youth groups.

In conclusion, the present approaches to assessing key factors were the outgrowth of a long-term "natural experiment" in which modest-sized, often-repeated, unplanned input variations occurred, together, of course, with the more typical inputs. While quite different from, and vastly better than, mere guesswork or speculation, these approaches were by no means a first-rate substitute for specifically focused and carefully controlled experimentation. Nevertheless, given CTP's study design, they were the only approaches available; and, in any event, they did seem able to support the distinctions in question. As a result, these approaches helped bridge the gap between empirically untested hypotheses, on the one hand, and refined experimental results, on the other.

Notes

1. In this appendix, "variations" will refer to substantial deviations from typical approaches, that is, from the most common type of approach or from the average amount of input (e.g., 11 or 12 youths per caseload, or about 7 face-to-face youth/staff contacts per month per typical youth [participants plus nonparticipants]). Thus, in the present context, "input" will refer to the entire range of available approaches—variations and typical approaches combined. Since "input variations" will be synonymous with "variations," it, too, will refer to substantially different approaches alone—those which differ noticeably from the mean or mode.

2. In the latter case, the interactions among these several variables might preclude a precise and unequivocal specification of the contribution, to youth behavior, of each individual factor. Nevertheless, good approximations could probably be obtained if extraneous factors could be controlled. Interaction issues aside, more youths would probably have to be studied than were involved in the present (CTP) investigation, however many experiments and parole units would be involved and however many factors would be varied simultaneously.

3. Here, "observe" is used in a broad sense, and it involves all information sources mentioned earlier.

4. Here, in contrast to within-caseload observations, a given time span was not compared with a preceding time span. Thus, the term "sequence" does not apply across caseloads and it has been specifically dropped.

5. The latter input change would have occurred at about the same time as—either earlier or later than—the former.

6. The likelihood of these performance differences between "x" and "y" seemed to partly depend on the absolute levels of each such factor to begin with, that is, prior to their respective input change. (This interacted with the degree of input change itself. For example, rather minimal changes in factors "x" and "y" seldom seemed to be associated with differences in performance change, regardless of the original "level" of each factor.) A parallel phenomenon was observed *across* caseloads, relative to any single factor.

7. These impressions or estimates resulted from observations that, collectively, involved various combinations of factors, many of which were repeated several times. In each combination, one or more such factors changed from a given input level to some other level, during an identified time span. It was this set of inputs that defined each "combination."

I-LEVEL DIAGNOSIS AND ETHNICITY ISSUES

As indicated, the causes of racial imbalance were centered not on I-level theory or on each youth's I-level per se, but on particular subtypes that fell within the I_3 and I_4 levels. These causes reflected not only diagnostic shortcomings and conceptual issues but local social-cultural realities. The shortcomings and issues will be described; but to better understand them, three background factors will first be reviewed.

Background, and Bases of Diagnoses
First, 1969–1971 was a time of considerable flux and variation regarding the diagnostic methods being used in the Youth Authority. This reflected several developments, including the fact that (1) CTP was not the YA's only I-level related program at the time, (2) relatively rapid ("mass") diagnosis—classification—was increasingly considered the only practical way to achieve large-scale, institutional assignment, and (3) YA administrators wished to encourage local initiative and to support local decision-making wherever possible (Andre and Mahan, 1972; Jesness et al., 1972; Pond, 1970; Pond and Davis, 1973; Pond et al., 1974). Given these developments and goals, alternative approaches to CTP's interview-only method were being actively explored, especially in connection with institutional program assignment.

Second, during the period under consideration (1969–1971), few youths had been assigned to the living units in question (those viewed as racially unbalanced), and to institutional programs in general, based on a Jesness Inventory (JI) diagnosis alone. (JI testing frequently occurred at NRCC, that is, before the

youth was sent to an institution;[1] however, quite often, it first—or also—occurred within the institution.[2]) For example, many youths were interviewed shortly after arriving at the institution, and the resulting, interview-based I-level diagnosis, which was usually made in combination with a case file review, occasionally overrode the JI-based diagnosis if and when the two disagreed. (Interviews conducted in institutions were often somewhat briefer than, and not as "deep" as, those conducted in the CTP experiment.)[3] In any event, whether or not such an interview had occurred, institution staff mainly relied on one or two weeks of behavioral observation (again, combined with case file material) to confirm the Jesness Inventory diagnosis—specifically, to either finalize or change it. Not infrequently, these observations, which centered on the youths' everyday interactions with staff and peers, did produce a change.

Finally, some diagnoses were based mainly or exclusively on a combination of interview, behavioral observation, and case file review, all of which occurred within the institution.[4] At any rate, the I-level and subtype diagnoses of institutionalized youths were usually based on more than one data source. Here, the combination of JI and behavioral observation (plus case records) generally received the most weight, with the latter usually playing a decisive role in finalizing each diagnosis and a major role in occasionally modifying it.

Diagnostic Shortcomings
When the Jesness Inventory or the clinic interview indicated that a youth was an I_3 or, in

some cases, an I_4, but institution staff felt uncomfortable about his specific subtype diagnosis, such as passive-conformist or manipulator, staff sometimes changed the subtype diagnosis after interviewing and/or further observing him and after further reviewing his case file. In so doing, they sometimes misdiagnosed Mexican American youths as "cultural conformists" (group conformists). They did so for one of two main reasons (in the following discussion, it is not necessary to assume that the original subtype diagnosis was always correct; also, all information sources—the possible bases for a diagnosis—other than the JI or the clinic interview will be called supplementary diagnostic sources, or SDSs):

1. Information that could have distinguished the individual from cultural conformists had *not* been obtained from any SDSs. That is, few if any key differentiating clues had been gathered by the earlier-mentioned staff, those who were unsure about the original—the JI-based or clinic-interview-based—subtype diagnosis. Such information, which would have centered not only on the youth's view of and responses to others, but especially on his view of himself and on his personal values, was not always elicited during the institution interview; and sometimes, it might not have been "heard" by the interviewer. More often, however, most such information was simply not easy to obtain via the *behavioral observations* that were made; nor was it routinely available, and clearcut, from the case file material. This information might, for instance, have shown that despite his occasionally "pat" or perhaps boastful remarks and his surface indifference or withdrawal, the youth, unlike most Cfc's, did not really consider himself tough or sly, had not largely rejected adults and numerous dominant-culture values, and seldom *liked* to view himself as a delinquent.

Given this relative absence of key information from any SDS, such items and thought sequences as the following often dominated staff's diagnostic considerations: (a) Since this (the hypothetical) youth *has* sometimes or often associated with delinquent peers in his community, (b) since this same youth *has* sometimes tried to gain acceptance or status from these peers and *was* probably involved in delinquency for, or partly for, this reason once or twice, (c) since he did often gravitate toward youths of his own ethnic group during his clinic stay or his first several days in the in-

stitution, (d) since many Mexican American YA commitments—certainly cultural conformists—have strong delinquent peer affiliations, and (e) since this youth *is* Mexican American—such information, taken together, indicates that he might be a Cfc. Certainly, items (a) through (c) were consistent with the (then-standard) summary statement regarding cultural conformists: A Cfc is one who "responds with conformity to [a] specific reference group, [i.e., to] delinquent peers" (Warren, 1967a, p. 3; 1969, p. 53). Relying mainly on such information, and given this consistency, it was concluded that the youth should probably be called a Cfc, whether or not this corresponded to his original diagnosis.

To be sure, cultural conformists had no monopoly on items (a) through (c); most other youth groups sometimes exhibited these same behaviors and motives. The difference was that, with non-Cfc's, items (a) and (c) seldom comprised the most salient behaviors and item (b), especially "acceptance," rarely provided the most influential or long-standing motives for their delinquency as a whole, especially among males. Nevertheless, since these and closely related items were almost universal among Cfc's, the fact remained that the hypothetical youth *had* shown certain behaviors that were characteristic of this group (subtype), and he *had* shared certain basic Cfc motives on given occasions. In addition, the fact that many Mexican American commitments who had strong peer affiliations were Cfc's and that *this* youth was Mexican American further associated him with this particular subtype; in many cases, this association was probably based on sheer analogy and/or related extrapolations.[5] Sometimes in combination with the youth's earlier-mentioned, for example, boastful, remarks and with various surface attitudes or adjustments, this association, which reflected items (d) and (e), helped staff feel more comfortable about inferring that the youth's *typical* behavior and/or *most influential* delinquency-producing motives were probably similar or identical to those of most Cfc's. Usually, it was this inference that led directly to their conclusion that the individual was a Cfc.

This inference, however, was weak, essentially because it was not mainly based on key diagnostic information. Specifically, it did not reflect evidence that, if present, would have borne directly on the *differences* among various youth groups, especially differences relating to their most influential motives. Instead, the inference seemed to mainly rest not only on items such as (a) through (c)—factors that were *similar* across Cfc's and other youth groups—but, most often, on those items in combination with (d) and (e). (As mentioned later, the "cultural conformist" label itself contributed to this inference.)

Basically, the influence of items (d) and (e) resulted from the racial correspondence between the individual youth, on the one hand, and a particular set of youths (Mexican American Cfc's), on the other: this correspondence between "individual" and "set" suggested a possible correspondence with respect to subtype. Since race was centrally involved, this suggestion may have partly reflected stereotypic thinking, one form of oversimplification.[6] At least, when staff associated the "individual" with Cfc's partly or largely because of race, they may not have done so based on a simplified if not oversimplified *logic* alone, for example, on reasoning by broad or loose analogy; in short, various connotations or preconceptions, in this case racial preconceptions, may have been involved as well, or instead. At any rate, although stereotyping—primarily a "content factor"—did seem common with respect to items (d) and (e), its degree of importance was unclear. For one thing, its contribution to the association in question could not be neatly separated from that of other possible content factors, such as nonstereotypic, published research information. Similarly, little was known with certainty about the joint contribution of these content factors (nonscientific preconceptions; empirical information), on the one hand, as compared to that of process or logical factors (ways of thinking), on the other; that is, the extent of their respective contributions to items (d) and (e) was unclear. Nevertheless, whatever its ingredients (stereotypic thinking, research data, etc.) may have been, and whatever *their* relative contributions may have been, the association in question seemed to have contributed significantly to the earlier-mentioned inference.

Given the weakness of this inference, the final conclusion (diagnosis: Cfc), while plausible, was not compelling. It was largely derived from evidence that, while consistent with a diagnosis of Cfc, did not point specifically to it. In effect, a thought sequence which was facilitated by the absence or near absence of key differentiating information had led to a diagnosis that was based on what was quite possibly the next best set of available information: items such as (a) through (c), plus other reflections of attitude and adjustment. Items (d) and (e), in turn, often seemed to be used to help interpret this "next-best" information, and thus relate it to specific issues.

For example, staff frequently used (d) and (e) to deal with the fact that items (a) through (c) were indeed shared by other youth groups. More specifically, they used the former items to help decide which one of those youth groups the individual was most likely to belong to; in this respect, (d) and (e) helped staff view that information from a particular perspective, or "sort it out" relative to a particular question. However, if key, differentiating information had been available from the start—information that related to different behaviors and, especially, to longer-standing motives than those reflected in the shared items—those shared items, items (a) through (c), might well have been seen from yet another (at any rate a different and possibly broader) perspective than that from which they *were* seen, that is, seen, in part, because of items (d) and (e). In fact, if differentiating information had been present, (d) and (e) might hardly have been used to interpret items (a) through (c) in the first place. In that event, the behavior and motives that were reflected in those shared items, and in closely related items, might not have been viewed as quite possibly the dominant or most significant facts concerning the youth's interactions with peers, and his delinquency overall. A misdiagnosis might then have been avoided.

2. Information that could have distinguished the individual from Cfc's *had* been obtained but was largely overridden by other types of information, especially by shared items such as those already reviewed.[7] More specifically, although key differentiating items had been obtained, for instance, during an interview, those items, collectively, received lower priority than shared items such as (a) through (c) or than other nondifferentiating reflections of attitude and adjustment. In effect, the differentiating items were inadequately integrated, by staff, with the remaining information—items (a) through (c), and so on. That is, the respective information sets—key items, shared items, and so forth—had not been carefully interrelated with each

other, for example, logically melded into a broader, albeit equally unified picture of the individual.[8]

"Overriding" seemed to center on two or three relatively independent factors. In some cases, for example, staff's tendency to stereotype youths appeared to be the decisive ingredient; here, in effect, irrelevant or minimally relevant information had received top priority. In most cases, however, staff seemed to rely heavily on certain combinations of *relevant* though once again (as with stereotyping) *non*differentiating information; included, for instance, were items such as group involvement in delinquency combined with youth's defiance toward adults. In effect, these combinations, when evaluated by themselves, had been interpreted by staff in a somewhat fixed or preset way: They were linked with the Cfc category more often than with each remaining category.

This interpretation was by no means unjustified; indeed, the link in question was ultimately based on prior observations of youths who *had* been accurately diagnosed as Cfc's. However, with the hypothetical youth, the problem was that staff had decided to retain this interpretation despite the presence of *differentiating* items which specifically contraindicated a Cfc diagnosis. Apparently, staff had viewed the above combinations as such strong indicators of a Cfc diagnosis that they—staff—felt justified in giving those indicators clear precedence over items which, in fact, contraindicated that diagnosis and which may even have suggested specific alternatives instead. Insofar as they gave those combinations a form of privileged status, staff, in a sense, had assessed them independently of generally recognized contraindicators. In this respect, they had not evaluated those particular indicators as one more part—a major part, to be sure—of a broader, presumably interrelated context.

Thus, regardless of the specific factors involved—such as stereotyping—staff had not adequately utilized available information that could otherwise have altered their interpretation of certain individual items and/or combinations of items, and that could have helped them view the youth more realistically.

Misdiagnosed Blacks

Before continuing our review of misassigned Mexican Americans, the following might be noted relative to blacks: The overrepresentation of blacks in institutional living units that were established for *manipulators* (Mp's) was almost entirely due to misdiagnoses. These errors, which usually involved Bay Area I_4's (higher maturity youths), resulted essentially from staff's overemphasis on traits and attitudes that these individuals shared with many Mp's (middle maturity youths—I_3's), regardless of the latter's race.

More specifically, staff seemed to be misled by the "external front of adequacy, coolness, hardness, and . . . 'rapping'" that often characterized higher maturity Bay Area blacks who did not clearly fall within any one subtype (Neto and Palmer, 1969, p. 31). These "mixed I_4's" were not uncommon, at least in the Bay Area. They were best described as a combination of two already-existing subtypes, mainly cultural identifier (now "delinquent identifier") and assertive-denier (then "neurotic, acting-out"). Their "front," or readily apparent surface features, usually included not only a "jiving," "sharp looking," "fast-living," "street-wise" component, but, quite often, a general evasiveness.[9] Individually and especially collectively, several such features paralleled and/or complemented those which the I-level manual had emphasized relative to Mp's only: "conning . . . outsmarting . . . and self-perception [as] cynical [and] smooth . . ." (Warren et al., 1966b, pp. 22–23). The mixed I_4's "distrust of the larger culture" further paralleled this and other accounts of Mp's.

(The earlier-mentioned features were observed by researchers [mainly Neto] and parole staff associated with the CTP experiment, particularly the San Francisco study. Though mixed I_4's had been briefly mentioned in late 1968, their specific features were not systematically described and formally documented until late 1969, that is, not until the existence of such youths seemed unmistakable and relatively common within the Bay Area (Neto and Palmer, 1969; Palmer et al., 1968, p. 75). Despite this documentation and its wide distribution, many institutional staff remained unfamiliar with these descriptions until the early 1970s. By then, many [possibly most] misdiagnoses and misassignments had already occurred.[10] It might be mentioned that males had never been assigned to institutional living units on an I-level basis in the YA's southern California institutions.)

In some respects, the features in question did reflect a partly manipulative, often exploitive, seemingly self-centered, and feeling-resistant stance. However, in contrast to these typical Mp features, or stance, such characteristics, especially manipulation and exploitation, did not reflect the mixed I_4's principal interpersonal approach.[11] More important, they reflected neither the upper range of these individuals' social perceptiveness nor the full spectrum of their personality and value system—personal concern for others, and nonexploitive beliefs, included.[12]

Rather than primarily representing a power-oriented, I_3 view of the environment, most such features were part of the individuals' often but not entirely satisfying adaptation to the following social realities: (1) dominant-culture pressures and opportunities, and, especially, (2) *sub*cultural (primarily ethnic-centered) expectations and related, externally imposed obstacles. These opportunities, obstacles, and other factors bore not only on the youths' material security and enjoyments, their delay versus nondelay of gratification, and their social roles in general, but on their educational advancement and their legitimate versus illegitimate employment in particular. Partly independent of this social-adaptation dimension, some such features also seemed to reflect a personal defense against internalized, I_4 conflicts that centered on long-standing interactions between family-based expectations, on the one hand, and cultural/subcultural opportunities and limitations, on the other (Neto and Palmer, 1969).

In an equally broad but perhaps more immediate context, their frequent "coolness, hardness, and . . . 'rapping'" seemed to have helped these youths gain a sense of *belonging*. This feeling, and its related reality, centered not just on a given subculture and ethnic grouping, but, especially, on a specific peer environment. Such features also seemed to have helped these individuals gain a particular *status* within that environment—a status, or power, that increased their ability to achieve desired ends; this was more than simply feeling "in," and "with it." At perhaps a more personal level, those features probably helped these individuals gain, and maintain, a feeling of self-worth and hope. In any event, they often served to remind or assure both the youths and their friends that they, the youths, were by no means a "loser," a "pushover," an

"Uncle Tom," and so forth. In this respect, these and related features comprised a declaration of strength, independence, masculinity, and ethnic pride.[13]

As suggested toward the end of Phase 2, the delinquent involvements of these individuals seemed to be "partly an expression of an adolescent identity struggle—one which is taking place in the context of, and in terms of, deviant versus dominant systems of cultural values, together with the respective pressures represented by each" (Palmer et al., 1968, p. 75). Yet, as indicated earlier, such involvements reflected more than an identity struggle alone. All in all, like the "front" itself, they represented a particular group of black youths' way of coping with a specific *combination* of pressures, opportunities, limitations, and conflicts that were seldom experienced by non-black youths.

In sum, surface appearances notwithstanding, the present individuals were I_4's, not I_3's—and not I_3 manipulators in particular. Descriptively, their "front" comprised a behavioral/interactional or trait/attitude pattern that was relatively infrequent among higher maturity, non-black commitments to the Youth Authority from nonhighly urbanized settings. In this respect, many if not most such features—important components of personality, by any standard—were largely subcultural in origin and subculturally (or at least peer-group) reinforced. Despite this origin and source of reinforcement, these particular features did not, in themselves, reveal the youths' "core perception" of their environment—that is, their specific I-level. (See Appendix 6 and Warren et al., 1966b, pp. 22–23, regarding core perceptions.)

Although mixed I_4's were usually content to initially show most institutional staff little more than their "front," the misdiagnoses in question could have been avoided. Basically, a standard, depth interview could almost always have provided converging evidence regarding the existence of I_4 concepts, attitudes, and/or values, and, where applicable, personal conflicts as well; theoretically, such information could, by itself, have ruled out an I_3 (thus, an Mp) diagnosis. However, even when a detailed interview had been conducted, the earlier-mentioned features were often so striking and consistent that staff sometimes decided to downplay and, in effect, override whatever I_4 evidence was obtained; a similar decision was often made regarding other evidence as well.[14] In such cases staff usually believed that (1) those and related features had revealed the "*true*" individual whereas (2) what may have "*seemed*" like internalized, I$_4$ concepts and values were in fact noninternalized catchphrases that the youths had acquired during their prior contacts with authority figures—phrases they had learned could sometimes gain them an advantage by impressing, satisfying, and generally misleading "the man" ("the power").

In other cases, the features in question were again so striking—that is, during initial staff/youth contacts—that staff therefore considered the diagnosis rather clear-cut. As a result, from those points forward, they made only minimal efforts to obtain additional—thus, possible counter—evidence. Given the absence or near-absence of specific I$_4$ indicators, the presence of such features, especially in combination, did indeed point toward an I$_3$—and, quite plausibly, an Mp—diagnosis. Like the preceding staff (those who sometimes downplayed available evidence), these individuals were essentially unaware of the specific diagnostic issues in question, namely, the possible misclassification of mixed I$_4$'s as Mp's; in fact, they were seldom aware of this group's existence in the first place. Nevertheless, as indicated, the information that was needed in order to rule out a diagnosis of I$_3$, Mp could have been obtained via standard interview techniques. Once obtained, this information could have been used whether or not staff had been alerted to, and were thoroughly familiar with, the specific issue at hand.

We will now return to our review of Mexican American youths who were misclassified as cultural conformists.

Descriptive Shortcoming (Conceptual Issues)

We will briefly review the descriptive shortcoming that contributed substantially to the misdiagnosis and resulting misassignment of various Cfc's in the Youth Authority institutions under consideration. This shortcoming—specifically, a somewhat unbalanced or inadequately focused picture of Cfc's—resulted from two factors that were, and one factor that was not, emphasized in three prominent I-level sources ("official inputs").

These official inputs were: the standard summary statement regarding Cfc's; the "cultural conformist" label itself; the I-level manual on diagnosis and treatment (Warren, 1966b, 1967a, 1969). The extent to which this shortcoming influenced institutional diagnoses during the later 1960s was largely unrecognized at the time.

Together, the preceding inputs strongly suggested that two factors were central to the diagnosis of "Cfc":

1. a delinquent reference group ("group influence") and
2. membership in a subculture ("subcultural influence").

However, individually and collectively, those inputs did not highlight or otherwise focus attention on the critical role of one additional factor:

3. a delinquent self-perception; an acceptance of one's delinquency ("self-perception/attitude").

This factor referred to the youth's conscious satisfaction with being a delinquent, or, at least, to his continued, though in some cases decreasing, acceptance of, or even interest in, delinquent involvement (e.g., "messing around, with the guys").[15] The relationship between each input and each factor will now be reviewed more specifically.

(1) The *standard summary statement* concerning cultural conformists focused solely on factor #1 (group influence): A Cfc is one who "responds with conformity to [a] specific reference group, delinquent peers." This statement—which is complete as shown—included no reference to factors #2 and #3 (Warren, 1967a, 1969).

(2) The subtype label, "cultural conformist," focused on factor #2 (subcultural influence). Given the fact that all subtype labels were partly designed to provide major clues regarding delinquency causation, the existence of this focus seemed clear from the following: (a) If any factor *other* than "culture" had been considered central to causation, that factor—say, a psychological factor—would presumably have been reflected in the label by a term other than "cultural"; in short, theoreticians responsible for subtype labels would have used a different, more appropriate term

when qualifying "conformist." (Note that the "culture" factor could have involved one or more of the following: a shared, intraclass, antisocial value system; interclass/intergroup value conflicts; reduced social opportunities; and so on.) This clue-to-causation approach to labeling was used, for example, with "*immature conformists*" (now "*passive-conformists*")—individuals whose combination of interpersonal deficiencies and specific psychological difficulties, that is, whose essentially non*cultural* problems, made them highly vulnerable to delinquent peers. (b) Within the broad area of "culture," some type of *sub*cultural setting—one that was delinquency-tolerant or non-law-abiding—was apparently implied in the Cfc label. This seemed to be the case because, if the youth had been conforming to the *dominant* culture—a setting that, by definition, was delinquency-rejecting or law-abiding—he would presumably not have been a delinquent in the first place (unless, of course, certain other factors were involved).[16] (Had the latter conformist been an I_4, he might, for instance, have conceivably been labeled "situational, emotional reaction.") The above implication was also reflected in such concepts as "delinquent subcultural belongingness" and "local subculture," both of which were used in connection with Cfc's and which appear under input (3), below. At any rate, the present label implied that the youth's illegal behavior largely centered on his connection with, and, in some sense, his membership in, a nondominant (subcultural)—quite possibly a non-"middle-class"—setting. This implication became rather strong in light of the third and most detailed input: the I-level manual.

(3) The *I-level manual*, which contained 14 diagnostic indices and numerous suggestions regarding intervention with Cfc's, specifically supported the earlier-mentioned emphasis on group and subcultural influence. For instance, it offered such diagnostic leads, intervention-centered suggestions, and related observations as the following:

"Antisocial behavior seen [by youth] simply as meeting one's own needs or the needs of one's own group, reacting appropriately to a rejecting society"; "Companions not chosen [by youth] for their personal characteristics but rather by juxtaposition and/or signs of delinquent subculture belongingness"; "To the extent

possible, [the parole agent] should aim at alleviating cultural deprivation"; "Agent needs community organization knowledge, as well as a working knowledge of local subculture"; "[Youth] behaviorally complies with authority power structure [e.g., "policeman and social worker"] when this is unavoidable"; "Reasons for delinquency [often include] defiance of adults"; and, "[Intervention should] help him accept the legitimacy of the adult authority system." (Warren et al., 1966b, pp. 17–20)

Clearly, such phrases and terms as "reacting . . . to a *rejecting society*," "*delinquent subculture belongingness*," "alleviating *cultural deprivation*," and "*local subculture*" (emphasis added) implied that, psychologically and otherwise, Cfc's typically, or perhaps preponderantly, were part of a setting that differed from the dominant culture in several major respects—specific values and material opportunities included. Together with the earlier-mentioned observations, these phrases and terms also suggested that (a) the dominant culture was thought, by Cfc's, to purposely oppose, exploit, or unfairly control major aspects of their environment, and (b) Cfc's, in turn, rejected or otherwise opposed the dominant culture and its agencies of control. At any rate, the social/cultural gaps and mutual opposition in question closely paralleled gaps and opposition that were strongly suggested in the I-level manual in connection with a *separate* group of youths—youths whose diagnostic label had, like that of Cfc's, also included the term "cultural." This separate group was called "cultural identifiers" (see "Ci's," Chapter 4, Appendix 7). Here, such diagnostic leads and intervention goals as the following were presented:

"[Youth] has internalized the value-system of a *deviant subculture*. May take a strong stand against *middle-class values*"; "Perceives inequalities and injustice along *socioeconomic and racial* lines and, as a result, has antipathy for the *core culture*"; "Delinquency [often represents] a way of attacking the core culture or the *authority system*." "[Parole agent should] teach Ci how to meet status and material needs in ways acceptable to the *larger culture*." (Warren et al., 1966b, pp. 46, 48; emphasis added)

Despite its clear emphasis on subculture and its direct reference to cultural deprivation, the I-level manual did not explicitly state that Cfc's were invariably or even typically members of a *racial minority;* in fact, it never mentioned ethnicity in relation to these youths. Nevertheless, staff (manual-users) found it easy to connect the preceding descriptive and intervention-centered items—thus, the Cfc diagnosis itself—with minority membership. They based this connection on (a) their knowledge of the socioeconomic status of racial minorities, particularly blacks and Mexican Americans, throughout the United States, (b) their awareness of long-standing social conflicts between those minorities and members of the "dominant" culture, mainly middle-class Caucasians, and (c) their belief that direct relationships often existed not only within and across the numerous diagnostic and intervention-centered items, but between socioeconomic status and/or long-standing social conflicts, on the one hand, and several of those items, on the other. In short, a combination of (1) widely acknowledged facts regarding racial minorities and (2) various beliefs and assumptions concerning "official" descriptions and observations regarding Cfc's made it especially plausible for staff to infer that most Cfc's were indeed members of a minority group. At least, it seemed quite likely—and in this probabilistic sense, reasonable—that they would be members. Given this apparent likelihood regarding Cfc's as a whole, it was easier for staff to view any *particular* I$_3$ minority youth as, ipso facto, at least a candidate for the Cfc category.

The I-level manual never explicitly stated that factor 3—the individual's perception-of-self-as-a-delinquent, or at least his acceptance of illegal behavior—was absolutely essential to the diagnosis of Cfc. Yet, for the basic reasons that follow, this particular factor was actually more critical than factors 1 and 2—group and subcultural influence, respectively: (1) No youth should have been called a Cfc unless he had the self-perception/attitude in question. (2) Given that perception or attitude, a youth, under specified conditions, *could* validly have been called a Cfc even if he rarely associated with a delinquent group, and regardless of both his social class and his minority/nonminority membership/self-identification.[17] Despite the diagnostic significance of this factor, these reasons were not made explicit in the manual; nor were they clearly implied. In-

stead, the self-perception/attitude item (i.e., the factor-3 item), around which those reasons centered, was presented as simply one more diagnostic index. That is, it was neither singled out nor otherwise emphasized among the 14 items listed; as a result, its special importance was essentially passed over. (The item was: "Anti-social behavior [is] not ego-alien. . . . Delinquent acts are an acceptable part of the self-image." (Warren et al., 1966b, p. 17). In contrast, items that reflected factors 1 and 2 did receive heavy emphasis; for one thing, there were several such items each. Given the socioeconomic status of particular minority groups within the United States and given the conflicts that often existed between those groups and the "dominant" culture, this set the stage for the following.

Because factor 3's special importance was not made clear, the resulting, de facto *overemphasis* on factors 1 and especially 2 made it fairly easy for staff, particularly the less experienced, to place undue weight on the individual's subcultural status—more specifically, on his minority group membership. This overemphasis, and the resulting unbalanced picture of Cfc's, had clear implications for the earlier-mentioned inference in which it was presumed that the "*typical* behavior and/or *most influential* delinquency-producing motives" of specific individuals who were viewed as possible Cfc's were probably similar or identical to various behaviors/motives of "officially" acknowledged Cfc's, that is, of those described in the I-level manual. In brief, it made this inference, which drew substantially from the individual youth's minority group membership, seem not only more plausible to staff than might otherwise have been the case, but more legitimate—that is, "official-input" based—as well. In this connection, the overemphasis on factors 1 and 2 also appeared to indirectly and inadvertently support the tendency of some staff to stereotype given youths; almost certainly, it neither weakened nor opposed that trend. These effects, and the related trend, would probably have been curtailed, though not entirely eliminated, if the manual had explicitly indicated that minority membership was neither a definitive nor even a necessarily "revealing" index, for example, one that correlated *especially highly* with the diagnosis of Cfc. Those same effects would probably have been further curtailed—in fact, reduced from the start—if factor 3's role had been clarified.

In sum, certain shortcomings and related difficulties might well have been reduced or largely avoided if the I-level manual had clearly indicated the following: (1) What mattered most, in the diagnosis of Cfc, was the combination of group membership and, above all, a particular type of self-perception and/or attitude toward delinquent behavior. (2) Subcultural membership—including, specifically, non-middle-class/non-Caucasian status—was neither essential to a diagnosis of Cfc nor even a special and excellent clue. Such information could have been particularly useful to staff who, for whatever reasons, were somewhat unfamiliar with, or uncomfortable about, the sizable variations, that is, the personality and background differences, that existed among youths who legitimately fell within any given subtype.

Sociocultural Realities

Among Valley youths, even correctly diagnosed cultural conformists *were* overrepresented by Mexican Americans (MA's). For instance, of all youths in the CTP experiment (all subtypes included), 23 percent were MA's; however, of all *Cfc* youths in that study, 62 percent were MA's. This imbalance reflected two main factors in combination:

Minority members—blacks and Mexican Americans alike—were over represented in the I_3 category as a whole. Four interrelated items from the CTP experiment provide the background for understanding this first main factor.

a. Minority members were more likely to fall within the lower socioeconomic status (SES) category than nonminority members. Specifically, of all minority youths, 93 percent were lower SES; however, of all nonminority youths, 67 percent were lower SES. (r = .29 between race and SES. Since the sample size was over 500, this and the remaining correlations were significant well beyond chance, even though they accounted for relatively little variance.)

b. I_3's were twice as likely to be minority members than were I_4's. That is, of all I_3's, 60 percent were minority members; but of all I_4's, 31 percent were minority members. (r = .27 between I-level and race.) Also in the CTP experiment, the ratio of *minorities* to *nonminorities* was 9 to 10 and that of I_3's to I_4's was 6 to 10; thus, item "b" did not just reflect various base rates.

c. I_3's were more likely to be slightly younger than I_4's. Thus, for I_3's, the average age at intake was 15.2; for I_4's it was 15.7. (For I_2's the figure was 14.1; r = .34 between I-level and age.)[18]

d. I_3's were more likely to fall within the lower SES category than were I_4's. Of all I_3's, 91 percent were lower SES; of all I_4's, 71 percent were lower SES. (r = .23 between I-level and SES.) (Palmer et al., 1968, pp. 5–8; Palmer, 1976.)

Now then, minority youths were more likely to fall within the lower SES category than were nonminority youths ("a" above) because of widely recognized sociohistorical conditions. However, minority youths were more likely to be I_3's than I_4's ("b" above) in particular, because of two additional relationships combined: (1) I_3's were younger than I_4's ("c" above), and, at the same time, (2) I_3's more often fell within the *lower SES* (thus, the *minority*-youth) category than did I_4's ("d" above).

The first such relationship (age/I-level) probably reflected straightforward social-learning and cognitive-developmental factors alone, factors that applied to all youths and all races equally; as such, it differed in origin from the sociohistorical-based finding. The second relationship (SES/I-level) reflected routine processing-decisions by law enforcement and probation. Because of those decisions, outlined below, these agencies and departments—without realizing it—ended up sending many lower socioeconomic-status youths to the next "step" in the formal justice system at a slightly younger age than middle SES youths whose recorded offense histories were essentially the same.[19] Combined with the fact that I_3's were slightly younger than I_4's and that lower SES youths were very likely to be minority members, this age differential led to the overrepresentation of minorities in the I_3 category as a whole. The processing decisions in question seemed to occur as follows.

Given the option of either dismissing, diverting, or further processing each of several first-time offenders—who, for purposes of illustration, can be considered identical in age (say, 13.0) when arrested—law enforcement was a little more likely to *further process* those whose backgrounds were lower rather than middle SES. For example, it was slightly more likely to send the former youths to probation intake than to dismiss them (i.e., to "reprimand" or "counsel and release" them), and, say, to speak with their parents informally. Probation, in turn, was slightly more likely to accept those youths than middle SES youths, that is, to formally supervise them rather than dismiss or divert them. A similar situation arose relative to those probationers who, having again offended, became candidates for either the (1) Youth Authority or (2) an extension of probation—together, perhaps, with several months in a probation-operated camp. Throughout this series of decisions by law enforcement and probation—more specifically, at each such choice point—the average age difference between lower and middle SES youths slowly but progressively increased. Thus, of all individuals who eventually ended up in the YA, say, between ages 15 and 16, those from middle SES backgrounds were slightly older than average even though their offense histories (arrest rates included) were essentially the same as—or perhaps just slightly different than—all remaining youths.

Such processing decisions, for instance, "either send youth 'x' to probation intake or dismiss him," and "either commit youth 'y' to the YA or continue him on probation," did not seem to be based on socioeconomic status or race per se. However, an indirect connection existed. For example, once such principal determinants as *type of offense* had been considered, those decisions, if still unsettled, often seemed to rest on two main beliefs or assessments. Specifically, if the primary determinants did not, by themselves, settle a given processing (choice-point) question, then the following beliefs—the "secondary determinants"—would generally tip the scale in favor of *further* processing (move youth to next step in the justice system):

1. The individual probably has (or may well have) inadequate or questionable supports, resources, or external controls at home and/or in his community; yet he remains under pressure—often external pressure—to continue his delinquency.
2. It therefore seems risky to "simply drop the whole matter" (rather than "send

youth to probation intake"), to "extend the term of probation and/or place in camp" (rather than "commit youth to YA"), and so on.

Thus, the connection was as follows. Youths to whom the preceding beliefs were thought to apply were more likely to have lower than middle socioeconomic backgrounds; that is, this is "simply" how it turned out. By the same token, though in contrast, the possibility of releasing given individuals to their parents or guardians, rather than formally supervising them, was more often considered realistic for those who turned out to have *middle* rather than lower SES backgrounds. The latter also applied with respect to the use of various early forms of diversion, for example, diversion to mental health clinics and private agencies, for individual or family counseling. (Most such diversion occurred, of course, during pre–Youth Service Bureau days. [Palmer and Lewis, 1980b, pp. 1–22]) At any rate, presumed (and perhaps actual) family and community resources did not seem to be as rapidly "exhausted" with middle as with lower SES youths; nor, for that matter, were they as often "nonexistent" in the first place, or at least presumed to be so.

In sum, though lower and middle SES youths may have had similar offense histories, the former individuals were more likely to be taken into, and subsequently moved through, the justice system at a slightly younger age. This reflected law enforcement's and probation's perception of an important difference among individuals with respect to home-and/or community-centered supports, resources, controls, and pressures for continued delinquency; as it turned out, this difference was often associated with SES. Since SES was closely linked to minority status and since I-level was generally related to age (among adolescents), this age difference—given its relationship to the other factors just mentioned—meant that the Youth Authority's I_3 population was likely to be overrepresented by minority members. That, at least, applied to geographic areas whose YA commitments were not overwhelmingly minority (or lower SES) in the first place—thus, necessarily minority across *all* major I-levels.

The preceding factors or relationships did not directly contribute to misclassification; nor, indeed, was there reason for them to do so. Nevertheless, their collective product—overrepresentation of minorities in the I_3 category—did help facilitate the earlier-mentioned stereotypic thinking, and this thinking *was* probably related to misclassification in many cases. With respect to Mexican American youths, such facilitation applied especially when overrepresentation was combined with the following.[20] (This comprises the second of the "main factors.")

Within the Valley, (a) "reinforcers" of delinquent involvement and of an eventual delinquent self-image operated more strongly in neighborhoods within which preadolescent and young adolescent *Mexican Americans* were much more common than same-aged blacks and Caucasians than did (b) reinforcers who operated in neighborhoods within which *blacks* and *Caucasians* predominated. As described below, these differing reinforcers were *individuals*—usually more experienced delinquents—not motivations or particular incentives; and the predominantly Mexican American or predominantly non-MA neighborhoods in which they operated will be called neighborhoods "A" and "B," respectively. The youngsters whom these individuals reinforced had already begun to engage in illegal activities;[21] and it was after this reinforcement had occurred—usually for two or three years—that some such youngsters ended up in the Youth Authority, accurately diagnosed as Cfc's. (Throughout the 1960s, racial mixing was quite common in Sacramento and Stockton as a whole. However, most neighborhoods within these cities—lower SES neighborhoods included—contained a preponderance of youths from one major racial group only.)

More specifically, given the earlier-mentioned difference in operating strength—discussed below—the following apparently applied more often among the preceding Mexican American youths (neighborhood A) than among same-aged, non-MA youths from other areas (neighborhood B):[22] Feelings of masculinity, of considerable independence from parental control, and of peer-group acceptance as well as status could be obtained by *continuing* to engage in illegal and fringe activities—among other activities—and by adopting anti-core-culture attitudes and beliefs. Regardless of race, those feelings, plus related "fun" and "excitement," were usually obtained through the youths' participation with, and feedback from, more experienced,

often slightly older, delinquents; also, they usually occurred in a peer-group context.

In effect, the following applied within the Valley. Compared to neighborhood-B settings, typical neighborhood-A settings were more likely to contain a pool of relatively experienced delinquents who—through repeated encouragement *and* pressure—often reinforced the already existing behavioral tendencies, that is, the illegal and borderline activities, of less-experienced youngsters. In so doing, the former individuals—the "reinforcers"—helped produce a new set or generation of local Cfc's, some of whom later ended up in the Youth Authority.[23] Most reinforcers had probably been produced—at least, partly shaped and channeled—under similar circumstances, and by similar means, themselves.[24]

The tendencies in question were mainly reinforced on occasions in which the less-experienced youngsters—the "novices"—obtained feelings of satisfaction or relief in connection with the earlier-mentioned masculinity, independence, acceptance, status, fun, or excitement; these occasions did not always involve illegal or fringe activities per se. With many Cfc's, reinforcement eventually became less dependent on the physical presence and immediate response of reinforcers; in this respect, it became increasingly internalized or self-sustaining. Nevertheless, most reinforcement originally occurred, and for a considerable time continued to occur, in the presence of one or more reinforcers; and it often *did* relate to illegal and fringe activities.

As implied, reinforcers were found in all settings and neighborhoods—Valley and non-Valley, Mexican American and non-MA; moreover, they were usually of the same race as most individuals within their neighborhood. These youngsters provided novices with more than general and specific incentives: They offered a clear path, and they represented concrete models, for them to follow. In both respects, reinforcers helped crystallize, augment, or at least maintain the novices' already active tendencies; in any event, they often diverted the latter's attention from, and focused various feelings against, core-culture involvements and values. Within the Valley, this process was usually accompanied by, but seldom primarily depended upon, the reinforcers' frequent emphasis on "macho" attitudes and beliefs.

Regardless of region, city, or neighborhood, the existence of anti-core-culture attitudes and beliefs predated any given generation of reinforcers and novices. It seemed to mainly spring from long-standing ideological, economic, and interracial pressures and conflicts; in this respect, it was sociohistorical in origin. In addition, though these pressures and conflicts varied somewhat from time to time and place to place, the basic direction of those attitudes, and the general content of those beliefs, remained unchanged. It might be added that—specific origins notwithstanding—those attitudes and beliefs were not the exclusive property of any one racial group, regardless of whether that group numerically dominated a given area. This, at least, applied throughout the 1960s.

Sociohistorical conditions also seemed to underlie the fact that, in Sacramento and Stockton, neighborhood-A reinforcers had more impact on the delinquent involvement and eventual delinquent self-perceptions of novices than did neighborhood-B reinforcers.[25] As a result, depending on the exact nature of those conditions—say, citywide and perhaps even regionwide conditions—an opposite impact might well have occurred. Specifically, given different sociohistorical circumstances within the setting as a whole, Caucasian and black reinforcers might each have had more impact than Mexican American reinforcers, with respect to various neighborhoods in question—this, despite the personality of each individual reinforcer and novice. This rather different impact might have resulted in more Caucasian and/or black Cfc's than Mexican American Cfc's being sent to the YA from the given cities, or from comparable cities.

The factors or conditions responsible for the difference between A-reinforcers and B-reinforcers seemed to be of a different nature, or at least level, than those responsible for anti-core-culture attitudes and beliefs. More specifically, the greater impact of "A"—than "B"—reinforcers may have largely reflected two main factors, neither of which was particularly simple, and both of which applied throughout the 1960s:

(1) Within Sacramento and Stockton as a whole, and in the specific, respective neighborhoods in question, there seemed to be more delinquency-oriented and fringe-delinquency-oriented Mexican American than non–Mexican American groups and gangs, and more MA than non-MA reinforcers as well. As indicated, under different sociohistorical circumstances, this situation, or "ratio," could clearly have differed in other cities, or even within Sacramento and Stockton at other points in time. This situation resulted in more opportunities, pressures, and incentives for delinquent involvement among MA than among non-MA "novices"; it meant more potential peer-group rewards as well. Delinquent groups and gangs were a more salient part of the former individuals' life; they had a larger potential role and influence. This, in turn, gave MA reinforcers more potential and actual power in the eyes of those novices; and that, in turn, made the earlier-mentioned reinforcement more likely to occur.

For example, the apparent power and ubiquitous presence of delinquent groups or gangs resulted in more opportunities for delinquency. It made it easier for novices to visualize themselves participating in fun and excitement, and gaining status and acceptance via nonconventional activities. The apparent power of these groups or gangs made it harder for many novices to resist continued delinquency—to go against "the guys"; it also made them feel more *secure* in their delinquency, that is, more protected overall. This situation may have made it easier for any one reinforcer to impact given novices, since it placed him in a more powerful position—that is, one which was peer-group supported and therein "legitimized." Thus, as individuals, these reinforcers may have had no more "skill" in promoting delinquency than did reinforcers from other neighborhoods and races; yet, because of the overall situation within the former's neighborhood, their influence may have been larger. This consideration interacted with the following factor.

(2) The content of the beliefs—the "macho" element included—may have added to this situation. For instance, within the Valley, the idea of "toughness" and of resisting various representatives of the core culture *may* have been stronger or more widely held among MA than non-MA youths; again, this would have reflected local sociohistorical conditions. Thus, the intensity with which certain beliefs were held may have also contributed; and the *extent* to which they were held—and were perhaps partly supported by various adults—may have contributed as well. Again, this situation could have differed in other cities, or even within Sacramento and

Stockton at other points in time. However, during the 1960s, it—together with factors 1 and 2—may have helped to produce a higher number of MA Cfc's than non-MA Cfc's from the particular settings in question.

Notes

1. Some youths who were not tested at NRCC nevertheless received an interview-based diagnosis while in that setting. Depending on which institution they were sent to—an assignment that was not based on their I-level and subtype—these and other individuals either were or were not automatically rediagnosed, at the institution, via the "sequential I-level" approach that was being used as part of an NIMH-funded project. (See endnote 2.) Institution staff—usually a "classification committee"—were free to change the NRCC diagnosis based on their own information concerning the youth; this information may have come from an interview, from behavioral observations, and/or from case files. Regardless of the institution involved and the particular data sources used, each youth's assignment to any given living unit reflected *institution* staff's finalized diagnosis, and decision.

2. In the latter cases, the Jesness Inventory was routinely supplemented by a sentence completion test and an approximately 15-minute interview (Jesness et al., 1972, 1973). Together, these approaches, when computer-scored, yielded a "sequential I-level diagnosis" (SID); this I-level and subtype diagnosis was based on information from instruments (the JI, etc.) that were administered on a successive-hurdles basis, that is, if and as the second—and then the third—instrument was needed. Since 90 percent of these diagnoses were predictable from the JI alone—in other words, since the sentence completion test and the brief interview seldom changed the diagnosis—our text review, in order to avoid complexity where possible, does not try to distinguish between SIDs and diagnoses based on the JI alone. This review, however, remains complicated by the fact that one institution did not routinely utilize the SID approach when assigning

youths to living units; in addition, this institution's I-level interviews were, on average, substantially longer and usually more influential than those mentioned earlier (though they were still shorter than CTP's).

3. The CTP I-level interviews were, of course, never part of the "sequential approach" (Jesness et al., 1972, 1973).

4. Here, the interviews were *seldom* those conducted as part of the sequential approach.

5. *Analogy:* "Inference that if two or more things agree with one another in some respects they will probably agree in others." *Extrapolation:* "To project, extend, or expand (known data or experience) into an area not known or experienced so as to arrive at a usually conjectural knowledge of the unknown area by inferences based on an assumed continuity, correspondence, or other parallelism between it and what is known" (Webster, 1965, pp. 32, 296).

6. *Stereotype:* "Something conforming to a fixed or general pattern; especially, a standardized mental picture held in common by members of a group and representing an oversimplified opinion, affective attitude, or uncritical judgment (as of a person, race, an issue, or an event)" (Webster, 1965, p. 860).

7. The former information seldom seemed to be explicitly, purposely, and specially, *ignored*—and devalued—per se.

8. In some cases, differentiating items had not been integrated with *each other.* This, itself, may have occasionally contributed to their being only partially integrated with the remaining information.

9. Regarding the former component, many such youths "wanted to be 'where the action is,' to 'know what's happening' (criminal activity typically included) in the district, or to 'live a fast life while you're young.'" In addition, most such youths indicated that one reason for their illegal behavior was their "need for money, usually to buy clothes and to maintain them at the cleaners. To a large extent, this reflect[ed] a peer-oriented status need to look 'sharp'" (Neto and Palmer, 1969, p. 25).

10. Since institutional staff relied primarily on the finalized I-level manual instead of

the Neto/Palmer document in question, the following might be noted. After being written in 1961 and updated beginning in 1964, the I-level manual underwent both a major expansion and its finalization in 1966. This was a few years *before* the Bay Area features—and their relative frequency within that setting—had become clear to the preceding researchers and parole staff. (Impressionistic reports from the earlier-mentioned special parole units had suggested—also in the later 1960s—that comparable features were not uncommon among Los Angeles area blacks; but, *systematic* information was not collected from those units in this regard.) During 1961–1966, similar features had occasionally been observed among higher maturity Valley blacks; however, because of their relative infrequency within that setting and because impressions from the Bay Area were still fairly new, those features were not presented in the 1966 manual. With few exceptions, this manual understandably reflected the Valley experiment only. One last point: In 1970, the training center began presenting information from the Neto/Palmer document; however, it did not highlight this material. Even if CTDT *had* emphasized this information at that time and had related it to Mp's, the misdiagnosis/misassignment issue would probably have remained largely unchanged; for one thing, relatively few institutional staff (in turn, potential trainers of *other* such staff) had been trained by the center after 1969.

11. As stated in the I-level manual, the Mp "does not manipulate or 'con' as *one of a variety* of alternative techniques (as with [i.e., in contrast to] higher maturity individuals); rather, it is his *only* formula for operation" (Warren et al., 1966b, p. 23).

12. In contrast, the typical Mp "does not accept the utility of feelings and values as a basis of human relationships" (Warren et al., 1966b, p. 23).

13. At a less often verbalized and perhaps less conscious level, some such features also comprised an indirect "statement" or message to the following effect: The individuals in question considered themselves, and wished that others would consider them, persons to be reckoned with and otherwise taken seriously—in any case, persons who wanted something from life and merited some attention.

14. For example, without a depth interview, staff observations regarding the youths' interactions within their living unit might still have produced useful I_4 evidence. (It usually took *all* I_3's and I_4's about two weeks to substantially lower their guard and—outside a nonpressured interview situation—to thereby allow various living-unit staff to see much more than their "front.") To be sure, most such evidence (other than certain specific statements by the youths) would have been less direct and less specific than interview-based information.

15. Some of the differences implied here (within the overall Cfc classification) are also reflected in the distinction between "insulated" and "accessible" Cfc's (Chapter 15).

16. Because the following combination of conditions did not exist, this subcultural-setting interpretation of the Cfc label was based not on the systematic elimination or exclusion of every alternative possibility, but on restricted definitions and a particular context alone: (1) Every plausible causation possibility is already reflected in all remaining—that is, non-Cfc—subtype categories, collectively; (2) the youth in question does not fall within any such category.

17. Among *manipulators,* the perception/attitude in question was largely shared with Cfc's, as were most of the remaining 13 diagnostic items listed in the manual. The "specified conditions" were: The manipulator and cultural-*identifier* categories had to be ruled out, as did all others; and, of course, the youth had to be an I_3 in the first place.

18. This correlation would have been somewhat smaller if the age range of the present sample had itself been smaller, for example, 13–17 rather than (as at present, with I_2's included) 10–19. The correlations presented in items (a) through (c), collectively—and the one in item (d), which immediately follows in the text—are for Phases 1 and 2 Valley males only (Palmer, 1976). When a somewhat larger Phase 1 and 2 Valley sample was

analyzed—one in which 18 percent were female (and 65 percent of these were I_4's)—the correlations between age and I-level (e.g., item [c]) were .20 and .15, depending on whether age was dichotomized at 17 and older or at 16 and up (Palmer et al., 1968).

19. "Upper" SES youths comprised a very small percentage of the total sample and did not have to be distinguished from "middle" SES youths in the present discussion.

20. Stereotypic thinking may, itself, have sometimes contributed to the above-mentioned beliefs, that is, to the secondary determinants.

21. Thus, we are not speaking of incentives to commit first-time illegal activities, but, rather, of reinforcers of illegal activities that had already occurred.

22. It is unclear whether this also applied to non–Mexican American youths who resided in "MA-dominant" neighborhoods (neighborhood A).

23. Cfc's were not the only product in question.

24. Reinforcers were usually of the same race or ethnicity as most individuals within the given neighborhood; in this instance, they were Mexican Americans. They usually belonged to a small group of delinquents and their direct influence on most novices occurred mainly in that context. Despite their substantial, long-term and cumulative influence on these individuals, most reinforcers were neither group leaders nor co-leaders; at any rate, many or most were probably Cfc's themselves. (As suggested, the group itself was not necessarily a formal "gang." All in all, there seemed to be more MA than non-MA *gangs*—though not necessarily *groups*—within large portions of the Valley.)

25. Before continuing it might be kept in mind that (1) whereas many *delinquently involved* youths had neither anti-core-culture attitudes and beliefs nor had developed a delinquent self-perception, (2) youths who had developed a *delinquent self-perception,* that is, who were not just delinquently involved, almost always had an anti-core-culture stance. At any rate, no individual who had developed a delinquent self-perception could continue to be called a novice.

Basic Features of Classification for Treatment: An Overview

Classification for treatment (CFT) deals with such questions as: What should be done with this individual? What specific areas should be focused on? What approaches might help implement these efforts? Implicit, here, is a further question: In what setting, say, community or institution, might treatment best occur? Usually, however, this question has already been settled, mainly on legal, offense-centered grounds. The question of *when* to first intervene with (treat) offenders will be touched on later; for now, we will assume that the decision to treat has been made and that a setting for treatment—at least an initial setting—has been determined.

CFT assumes that offenders differ from each other, that some such differences may produce significantly different responses to specified types of treatment, and that these differences among offenders should therefore be reflected in the type of treatment which is offered. Corresponding to these differences are similarities: Though each person is ultimately unique, some offenders resemble others in ways that have similar implications for each. Classification is a way of organizing and summarizing these differences and similarities so that their main implications for treatment—and control—become clear.

For instance, classification for treatment assumes that (1) offenders differ from each other with respect to one or more of the following: *primary causes of illegal behavior; present situation; future prospects,* particularly in the absence of treatment. Thus, regarding their present situation, offenders may differ as to adjustment techniques, interests and skills, and/or life circumstances. More specifically, regarding "adjustment techniques" they may differ from each other in their typi-cal or perhaps preferred ways of interacting with their immediate environment or with certain categories of individuals, such as authority figures. By the same token, however, many offenders are also *similar* to certain other offenders with respect to adjustment techniques and such features as personality characteristics. Together, such a "group" of similar offenders can be distinguished from still other offenders with respect to those same techniques and features, or patterns thereof. Thus, such techniques and features—or other attributes and conditions—can provide a basis for defining, characterizing, and formally establishing distinguishable groups of offenders.

Classification for treatment also assumes the following. (2) The preceding differences and similarities, for instance, regarding life circumstances or perhaps primary interests and skills, often bear on the ways in which and means by which socially centered and offender-centered goals may be efficiently and humanely accomplished. (See endnote 1 regarding definitions.) Thus, for example, the offender-centered goals may often be achieved by differing means for one offender group than for another. (3) Given assumption (2), and to help achieve those goals, such differences and similarities should be reflected in *planning decisions* regarding: (a) the principal tasks that should be accomplished with each particular group or "category" of offenders; (b) the personal and/or environmental areas that should be focused on; and (c) the approaches, such as techniques and program components, that may help treaters as well as offenders focus on those areas and accomplish those tasks. (Some classification systems try to address all three planning areas.)[2]

Thus, for any individual, a treatment classification should do more than summarize and describe; it should, in effect, predict and perhaps prescribe. For instance, it should not just reflect—in the form of a label, number, or brief phrase—the main results from one's diagnostic assessment of the offender's personality, of his present situation, and so on. Instead, it should indicate (again, perhaps, via a label or similar "code") the main implications that those personality characteristics, the offender's present situation, and so forth, have for planning areas (a) through (c) above.[3] In short, besides describing the individual and his situation—that is, in addition to summarizing or otherwise referring to them in a condensed form, one that also distinguishes him from other individuals—a treatment classification should suggest or perhaps prescribe *principal tasks* (e.g., "reduce external pressures"), *areas of focus* (e.g., "family relationships"), and/or *specified approaches* which seem appropriate or even essential with respect to achieving socially centered and offender-centered goals for that particular "category" or "type" of individual.[4] Together, this set of brief diagnostic and treatment-centered messages (labels, phrases, etc.) can thus comprise the core or basis of a detailed, step-by-step plan for achieving those goals. In this regard,

> treatment plans may be considered *rational* not just if and when their components, steps, and priorities are "unified" in the sense of being (1) internally consistent and mutually compatible, but when those steps, etc., are (2) consistent with goals which in turn make sense relative to one's diagnostic findings regarding the individual's present situation, his future prospects, etc. [CFT] assists in rational planning insofar as it focuses attention on goals and content which are meaningful with respect to the latter dimensions (present situation, etc.). Thus, it can help determine optimal resource allocation. In this context, treatment plans may be considered *practical* insofar as they relate the preceding goals, components, etc., to available resources and actual rather than ideal options. Therefore, not all rational plans, as defined above, are practical—at least not within all agencies or at all times. (Palmer, 1984b, p. 257)

Many classification systems (CS's) currently exist, and some are more complex than others. The simplest systems focus on *one or two dimensions* only, for example, personality type and/or principal task. For each such dimension these systems may, for instance, place a given offender into one and only one of *three or four categories,* such as (1) the "asocial," "conformist," "manipulator," or "neurotic" categories that may comprise the personality-type dimension, or (2) the "environmental restructuring," "external surveillance," or "reduction of personal conflict" categories that may comprise the principal task dimension; some such tasks may apply to more than one personality type. In this way, a CS, whether simple or complex, eventually distributes the entire offender population across the specific categories that comprise a given dimension (e.g., 10% asocial, 35% conformist, 20% manipulator, and 35% neurotic, with respect to personality type); it does so separately for each dimension on which it focuses. Relatively complex systems focus on additional dimensions—that is, not just one or two—such as causes of illegal behavior and, perhaps, one or two treatment-planning factors. Moreover, these or previously mentioned dimensions may consist of several categories each, for instance, *six* causes of illegal behavior or six personality types. Though the latter, somewhat complex systems (1) convey more information and (2) can more easily pave the way for, or otherwise contribute to, relatively individualized treatment plans than can the former, they are generally more difficult to implement, for example, more time-consuming and expensive with regard to diagnostic processing and staff training.

No CS yet exists that satisfactorily combines the respective advantages of relative simplicity and relative complexity. For this and related reasons, classification for treatment has been in a fluid state since the early 1980s, and no *widely agreed upon* "best" or even most promising system exists. Among those that—despite shortcomings—have nevertheless demonstrated considerable utility in specified contexts, or which have shown promise regarding socially centered and/or offender-centered goals are the I-level, the Jesness Inventory-based, the Conceptual level, the MMPI, the Quay, and the Wisconsin (subsequently the National Institute of Corrections [NIC]) systems (Arling and Lerner, 1981;

Hunt, 1971; Jesness and Wedge, 1983a; Lerner, Arling, and Baird, 1986; Megargee, Bohn, and Sink, 1979; National Institute of Corrections, 1981; Quay and Parsons, 1971; Warren et al., 1966b). Still, no all-purpose CFT system seems likely to soon emerge. Moreover, the preceding systems do not, by themselves, try to classify institutionalized offenders for custody/security purposes (e.g., general management; escape risk) and/or for possible violent or suicidal tendencies, per se; to be sure, some such CS's, and others as well, indirectly bear on one or more of these issues. (For a detailed, systematic discussion of such issues, and for an adult-centered [but not limited] typology that empirically synthesizes several others, see Van Voorhis [1994].)

Many structural and content differences (SCDs) that exist across treatment-classification systems reflect differing views, by the systems' respective originators, as to *how many* and *which* dimensions are crucial to, or even substantially contribute to, the socially centered goal of reduced recidivism. Research to date has only begun to resolve these differing views. Other SCDs probably reflect the originators' differing implicit or explicit priorities or emphases, particularly on offender-centered as compared to socially centered goals. Empirical studies, by themselves, will not resolve these largely philosophical differences.

Though classification systems can hardly begin to reflect an offender's full individuality, they—their categories, labels, and so on—can nevertheless highlight certain dimensions, such as treatment-planning dimensions, that are relevant to persons who, despite their ultimate uniqueness, share given features and conditions. Still, even when each category, and the like, is *supplemented* by brief text discussion, by appendices, or by other explanatory material that expands upon or perhaps outlines its main points and implications, the categories in question—even collectively—can neither uncover nor communicate all that one might usefully know about those individuals, their life situations, and the details of their possible treatment.[5]

At best, these categories and labels—especially collectively—provide (1) a reasonable base or point of departure for further examination and, in any event, for more individualized or at least more specific planning; yet, granting its limitations, this base can be quite valuable.[6] No less important, these categories

also provide (2) general direction and at least a set of guidelines plus "opening moves" that are likely to prove worthwhile for the type of individual in question. Such guidelines and moves, which may also include approaches to avoid, would often remain valid and useful even if further examination and greater individualization were to occur (and especially if they were not), for example, occur with respect to initial planning. Finally, and in any event, it is generally agreed that an individual's classification should, if possible, be reviewed—and, if necessary, updated—at approximately six-month intervals, and probably in the event of crises.[7] Thus, like the initial plan itself, an offender's initial classification (IC) should not, and certainly need not, determine almost the entire course and content of his treatment, particularly if treatment promises to be lengthy, complex, or both. Still, for many offenders, IC may determine a good deal, for instance, much of the central thrust of—or, a general outline of—treatment, even if reassessments and mid-course adjustments occur.

As to *where* treatment might best begin, if classification systems only abstractly addressed this question, their answers, even if in the right direction, would often have limited value. However, CS's *can* provide useful specific suggestions when they address that question, not abstractly, but in connection with real-life alternatives—as in the following: Would the treatment plan that seems appropriate for individuals of classification "X"— or even for individual offender "X_1"—best be supported/promoted in setting "A," in setting "B," or in some *other* specified setting whose actual resources are mostly known?[8] That is, would the given plan, or an acceptable alternative thereof, best be supported by the specific resources and conditions that exist, for instance, in "A," but not in "B" or "C"; in fact, would the plan probably be supported at all? (Settings "A" through "C" would exist in specified, that is, actual, jurisdictions or agencies, within which the offenders must be placed.) Clearly, some treatment plans are more likely to "best" be, or even only satisfactorily be, supported in some than in other settings and perhaps types of settings; and in this connection, model settings could doubtlessly be conceptualized for various treatment approaches, and lists of essential ingredients or conditions could be compiled. Nevertheless, *likelihoods* aside—and even though such models and lists might be theoretically correct—the following remains the case: What *specifically* comprises the best or even the only acceptable setting within one jurisdiction or agency (J/A) may differ substantially from what comprises it in another. In fact, the best available setting in which to implement, say, offender "X_1's" treatment plan may be institutional in one J/A and community-based in another, depending on the type and quality of the J/A's institutions and community programs. As a result, though the question of "where" can be asked abstractly and answered in general terms, it is best addressed with regard to the specific alternatives that exist within a given J/A.

As to *when* one should initially intervene (regardless of *where*), criminal justice researchers increasingly believe this should occur, not at point of first known arrest—unless the offense is quite serious or the offender requests assistance—but at either the second or third arrest. This belief, which began to crystallize in the mid-1970s, is largely based on the demonstrated, sizable likelihood of continued offending by the latter arrestees only. At any rate, it might be kept in mind that initial and even subsequent intervention need not occur within the justice system itself and that, wherever it occurs, it need not always be "full-blown." (For guidelines—albeit generalized and partly abstract ones—designed to simultaneously address the questions of "when," "where," and, very broadly, "how" to intervene with first-, second-, and third (or more)-time juvenile offenders, see [Palmer and Lewis, 1980a, 1980b]. These guidelines, which may partly apply to adults as well, address those questions in the context of common but often conflicting objectives [e.g., avoid negative labeling; reduce unnecessary social control; provide service and assistance; reduce recidivism; reduce justice system costs]. Most of these objectives exert simultaneous, but usually unequal and (across time) often varying influence within any given jurisdiction and agency. At any rate, they are only guidelines, not individualized prescriptions; and they are neither psychological nor sociological classification systems per se.)

A continuing challenge within corrections is that of making currently available settings flexible enough to support a broad range of treatment approaches (interventions) regardless of when and where one intervenes, initially or otherwise. Insofar as this challenge is met, or at least some broadening occurs, information from present and future treatment-classification systems might be increasingly used by sentencing authorities in connection with their placement decisions. Especially since the later 1970s, many such individuals have based those decisions (not without justification, from various perspectives) largely on information regarding the offenders' *current and prior arrests or convictions,* and on the minimum penalties or controls prescribed by law. This will probably remain true for many years, at least. Nevertheless, with improved treatment-centered CS's—and, especially, with greater flexibility in given settings (even if the total number of settings were to remain unchanged)—many such decision-makers might give increased weight, though perhaps still not equal weight, to information regarding optimal or at least acceptable settings for implementing specific *treatment plans,* within a given jurisdiction or agency. The relationship between treatment plans and classification systems has been outlined above.

Notes

1. Socially centered goals involve the increased protection of society. At the level of individual intervention, these goals are achieved when the offender's behavior is modified so that it conforms to the law. They are promoted but not in themselves achieved by modifying his or her attitudes, by strengthening him as a person, by reducing various external pressures and increasing given supports or opportunities, and/or by helping him become more satisfied and self-fulfilled within the context of society's values. Attitude change, increased coping ability, and so on, comprise the offender-centered goal of treatment. Though this goal has absolute value in itself, it is—given the justice system's main role in society—chiefly a "means" to the socially centered "end" of public protection (Palmer, 1983, 1992).

2. It is further assumed that—via (3), above—classification, in principle, can help achieve socially centered and offender-centered goals in an effective, efficient, and humane way, even though all three dimensions are not necessarily maximized in any given instance (system).

3. An individual's diagnosis can be considered identical to his classification if the diagnosis—rather than being (1) a collection or perhaps synthesis and interpretation of information or data items, and (2) presented in narrative form—is presented only via a label, category, or phrase that summarizes, condenses, or otherwise briefly represents key aspects of that information or information synthesis/interpretation.

4. They may seem appropriate or essential based on practical experience, research findings, and/or theory. Their immediate feasibility and practicality, which are largely determined by available resources and actual rather than ideal options, are often separate matters.

5. This also applies to compound or "higher-level" categories and labels, such as those which combine individual categories from two or more dimensions.

6. The degree of individualization that may seem desirable and feasible is determined not just by one's theoretical and philosophical positions but by available resources and external constraints.

7. An updated classification should primarily reflect what seem to be major changes in individuals and their situation, not relatively *transitory* fluctuations such as temporary anxieties, moods, and interests, however strong. This relates to what is sometimes called the "trait versus state" issue, and it applies to the original classification as well. (Proneness to transitory fluctuations may itself be reflected in a given classification or category, original or updated.)

8. Again, it is categories, labels, and so on, which comprise or represent the content of CS's, and in terms of which offenders are described. Thus, regarding the text discussion, one might think of certain implicit categories/labels—say, "a," "b," and "c"—not simply as being *included* in the general classification referred to as "X," but as necessarily retaining their separate *identities* within it.

34 OFFENSE-CENTERED JUSTICE, DIFFERENTIAL SENTENCING/ ASSIGNMENT, AND STRATEGY 2

As indicated, Strategy 2 would bar specified youths with respect to their personal/ interpersonal (p/i) features—characteristics that may be prominent and reliably assessed. However, this strategy might raise an objection based on the view that sentencing, including program assignment, should reflect the individuals' instant and perhaps prior *offenses* only, and that p/i features should not be considered in this context even if they bear on treatment/control planning and risk of future offending. This or related views might be held on "equal justice" (offense-centered justice) grounds, even if scientific evidence or practical experience suggest the following: (1) The excluded youth groups or youth types are less amenable than other youths to the given program. (2) The underlying justification for the youths' exclusion may therefore center not just on the program's minimal ability or relative inability to assist them personally, but on its related role of protecting society.

The equal justice or offense-centered view mainly aims at deserts and/or retribution for socially unacceptable behavior; these responses are often considered ends in themselves. In effect, the offense-centered view focuses on the offenders' past, and it places relatively little weight on the motives or personalities "behind" the unacceptable behavior—at least with respect to their implications for future offending. Accordingly, with regard to sentencing and assignment, *individualization* or *differentiation* should—in this view—be minimized or excluded insofar as it focuses not on deserts or retribution but on intervention with respect to the offenders' future and

their possible future offending. As a result, supporters of the offense-centered position would probably prefer that the following situation did not exist: *Differential* sentencing and assignment (DSA) is a long-standing, widely accepted, and very common practice within the justice system. This practice will now be briefly reviewed. (As will be seen, DSA—certainly differential assignment—can be closely associated with Strategy 2.)

DSA is directly observed when—although the offenses of given offenders may seem rather similar from one such individual to the next—the sentences and/or assignments that those offenders receive often differ from one individual to the next.[1] (As used here, "sentence" generally focuses on *length,* whereas "assignment" refers to *program* and/or *setting*. In this connection, sentencing and assignment have often been called term-setting and disposition, respectively. [Where specified, assignment will sometimes mean *approach*.])

This practice—differential sentencing and assignment—differs from that associated with *equal* sentencing for equal, or seemingly equal, offenses (ESEO), the latter being a direct expression of the offense-centered view. However, considerable overlap can exist between these practices, especially regarding sentence length; in fact, despite the relative individualization it allows and promotes, DSA operates within widely recognized and generally accepted limits. These limits—in effect, evolved practices (often legislation per se)—refer to specific sentences/assignments usually associated with particular offenses. At any rate, differential sentencing and assignment—especially assignment—is a major form of "individualized justice" (need- and public protection–centered justice). Yet, DSA is not incompatible with sentencing guidelines; it can generally coexist with this approach, provided the "lines"—or, in the case of ESEO, the limits—are not narrow.

DSA's existence reflects two main facts: (1) Factors *in addition to* offenses, say, personal/interpersonal features, are often considered relevant not only to the goal of changing/assisting offenders but to that of protecting society. (2) The preceding, interrelated goals—certainly public protection—are widely considered at least as important as deserts, retribution, and/or ESEO itself.[2] Thus, for example, in the differential-sentencing-and-assignment approach, youths and adults are often placed on standard rather than intensive probation or are sent to camps rather than closed institutions depending not just on their offenses but on the respective programs' or settings' (1) likely impact on them as individuals and (2) probable ability to provide immediate and/or longer-term public protection. To estimate (1) and (2), staff must assess the offenders as individuals. More precisely, they must evaluate personal/interpersonal and other factors both in terms of their need-centered implications—available programs and settings aside—*and* in light of the available, respective programs' strengths and limitations. In this regard, DSA's main focus is on assignment, not sentence length; this applies whether or not Strategy 2 is involved—in fact, it applies overall.

As implied, DSA's relative individualization with respect to assignment need not ignore offenses. In fact, offenses can play a decisive role—certainly at the intake or eligibility-determination stage—even if personal/interpersonal features are added. For instance, during Phases 1 through 3 of the California experiment, all youths who were referred to CTP as well as to the YA's standard programs, such as all 13- to 18-year-old first commitments from Sacramento, were either included in or excluded from those programs based primarily on their offenses (Chapter 2); personal/interpersonal (p/i) features played no role in this decision.[3] However, factors besides *offense* then emerged. For example, during Phase 3, *p/i features,* among others, were then used to determine the specific setting—thus,

the type of program—in which intervention would best begin for each offense-eligible (o-e) youth. Moreover, during all phases of CTP, such features—plus the o-e youths' life circumstances, and so on—played a crucial role in generating specific community-based intervention plans, that is, approaches to be used in the given setting. Specific plans aside, the assignment decision, that is, the *post-offense-centered assignment decision,* focused, in effect, on the offense-eligible youths' relative amenability to the available alternative "programs" or, in Phase 3, the settings. (During Phase 3 these alternatives, that is, initial treatment/control settings, were community and institution [Dorm 3]. Amenability or suitability was determined by matching the youth against preestablished guidelines that were derived from prior research and operational experience [Chapter 13].) In short, a two-stage or dual-level approach was used in which (1) offenses first helped determine eligibility and (2) personal/interpersonal features then helped determine *program*—and, in Phase 3, *setting.* P/i features played no role during the first stage, and offenses were no more than secondary or tertiary in the next.

In a somewhat modified, dual-stage-*and*-level approach, offenses and p/i features could both be used to determine *eligibility,* in that order of priority. That is, individuals who are not excluded on the basis of their offense, and perhaps the community's reaction, could still be excluded in connection with certain salient, significant personal/interpersonal features, such as power orientation. For individuals declared *eligible,* specific p/i features—and factors such as life circumstances—could then be used to help derive not only intervention plans but, if necessary and possible, the optimal *setting* (from among those available) in which to carry out those plans. By using this modified approach to implement Strategy 2—in effect, by *making* this approach Strategy 2—a program's least suitable candidates could either be excluded at the outset or, in any event, could have less chance than other individuals of being included. This strategy would thus allow staff to focus on offenders for whom the program seems best, or much better, suited.

Differential sentencing and assignment centers on relative amenability/suitability (RAS)—a concept that has probably long been implicitly recognized as making practical sense in numerous contexts. Moreover, in justice system contexts, RAS—again, implicitly—has probably been regarded as not "unfair" to offenders, specifically, to individuals who seem least or less suited to a program. This presumed absence (or near-absence) of unfairness, or at least of unreasonableness, may be reflected in the following: If administrators had just enough potential eligibles (suitable, *offense-eligible* candidates) referred to their program to fill their caseloads yet also had many potential ineligibles (unsuitable or least suitable, *offense-eligible* candidates) referred to it, an understandable objection might be raised regarding those administrators' possible inappropriate or inefficient use of program resources if they made no attempt to exclude, or at least give lower priority to, the potential ineligibles. This objection would therefore center on their allocation of resources to many offenders who would probably not use them or use them constructively, and on their resulting, de facto withholding of those resources from others who might well use them constructively. This objection could occur, and might seem reasonable, whether or not their program was originally designed for the latter individuals.

Though the offense-centered approach has sometimes been associated with unduly long or short sentences and sentencing-guidelines and with overly harsh or lenient assignments, this neither invalidates its goal or rationale of "equality" nor diminishes its past achievements (e.g., reduction of gross inequities) and the likelihood of future improvements. Similarly, though the amenability/suitability approach has sometimes been misused or poorly applied within corrections, this neither invalidates *its* rationale nor diminishes its results and prospects.

Notes

1. DSA is much less likely to occur among individuals with extremely serious offenses or offense histories.
2. In the following, case-management issues—for example, the relationship between specified types of caseloads and correspondingly different workloads—need not be considered.
3. Nor were p/i features—or, for that matter, CTP and standard-program staff—involved in the time-setting aspect of sentencing.

35 RELATIONSHIPS BETWEEN CLASSIFICATION SYSTEMS AND INTERVENTION-CENTERED FACTORS

Whether complex or somewhat simplified, youth-classification systems may focus on personality characteristics, developmental levels, and so on. As discussed below, such dimensions may be distinguished from factors that reflect specific details of an individual's adjustment and life situation. These facts bear on needed staff skills, and they will now be briefly reviewed.

Like a complex classification system (CCS), a less complex system (LCS)—such as a five- rather than eight- or ten-category system—may highlight psychological or other characteristics. Within the psychological arena both systems may, for example, include such characteristics or features as conformity, manipulativeness, impulsivity, and autonomy-seeking. However, since various *additional* characteristics, say, apathy/uninvolvement or confusion/uncertainty, may be found in a complex system that may *not* be included in a less complex one, the main difference between a given CCS and an LCS can simply be the number and/or type of characteristics used, that is, the classifications (categories) as presented. These differences, especially the former, are not necessarily substantive; moreover, they would exist whether or not the LCS was derived from the CCS.

(Within most systems, characteristics such as those mentioned earlier, or, alternatively, those which comprise the nine I-level classifications [e.g., assertive-denier], are presented either "as-is"—that is, *singly*—or else in terms of "higher-level"—that is, *combined* and/or common-factor—concepts. [In both cases, they or their underlying concepts are communicated via labels, that is, category headings, or via brief phrases. Each labeled characteristic may then be discussed at length.] Thus, a less complex classification system may simply *combine* various CCS categories and thereby end up with fewer but broader and/or higher-level groupings than the latter; for example, an LCS's "conflicted" category may combine a CCS's assertive-denier and anxious-confused. In addition, as suggested earlier, several categories may be similar or identical across the complex and less complex systems; for instance, both systems may contain a passive-conformist group.)

Instead of, or in conjunction with, such features, say, personality features, an LCS or CCS may highlight various "levels." Included, for example, may be the youth's typical or perhaps highest-measured level of interpersonal, cognitive, or moral development, as in the Warren, Hunt, and Kohlberg systems, respectively. However, whether a classification system highlights personality (e.g., traits and attitudes), level, or other general features, it may still not reflect—indeed, may never even examine—numerous factors and combinations of factors that relate to the individual's ongoing adjustment and specific life situation.

For instance, though many manipulative, impulsive—say, power-oriented—offenders are quite similar to each other in important ways, they may also *differ* from each other with regard to interests, grade level, family structure, and social conditions. In addition, they would commonly differ less on any *one* factor, such as grade level, than on various patterns or combinations of factors. Yet, these differing patterns, which can be no less important for intervention-planning than most single-factor differences, may hardly be reflected in a complex let alone a simplified classification system. Moreover, to remain manageable, even a highly complex system could probably include no more than one or two of the factors that would underlie any set of potential *patterns;* that is, it could do so only if it excluded all patterns or combinations themselves. More specifically, such a system could formally and routinely incorporate few such factors in addition to its several *basic*—say, personality-centered—categories. (The underlying factors mentioned above, such as family structure and social conditions, may be called "individualizing factors." Personality characteristics and developmental level also individualize, but in certain less concrete ways.)

Unlike personality characteristics and developmental level, individualizing factors may directly reflect not only the specific content and direction of the youth's life but the expectations and behavior of its other major participants, for example, family and friends. As a result, an absence of, or a disregarding of, information concerning such factors could, by itself, preclude the development of concrete, realistic plans, especially those involving the community. Ideally, *both* types of information—personality and/or developmental, plus adjustments and/or life situation—would be used if one wished to provide a well-rounded picture of the youth vis-à-vis his immediate environment.

Considerable staff skill is needed to carefully interrelate and organize the preceding information, even the adjustments/life situation data alone. This applies even though personality characteristics, but not developmental level, can be assessed on *their* own—specifically, without being organized and subsequently used (e.g., for intervention-planning) on the basis of a *classification* system, and even if no such system exists within one's agency in the first place.

36 ISSUES RELATING TO PRIVATELY OPERATED CTP PROGRAMS

Models at Issue

Regarding privately operated CTP programs, two main models will be reviewed. In Model 1, *all* program staff would be *private,* that is, nonstate or noncounty, employees. In Model 2, the *casework supervisor* would be a *justice system,* that is, state (parole) or county (probation), employee, and all remaining staff would be private employees. In both models, staff and their employers would be completely responsible for all major operations: (1) staff hiring, matching, case assignment, supervision, training, promotions, and so on; (2) diagnosis, intervention planning, implementation of all plans; (3) establishment or at least operation of most program components and facilities, such as school, recreation, and community center, but not necessarily out-of-home placement and almost certainly neither short- nor longer-term detention.

In *both* models, operations (1) through (3) would be implemented in accordance with minimum standards and, where possible and appropriate, consistent with intervention guidelines. These standards and guidelines would be preestablished and monitored by the state or county, that is, by the private agency's client source (the "source agency"), and they would be embodied or reflected in a contract between the public and private agencies. The casework supervisor's possible role in operations (1) through (3), and especially in related functions, is summarized later, with respect to Model 2.

Whatever the standards and guidelines may be, and whichever the model, questions and problems would arise in three main areas: *legal, operational,* and *contracts.* These will now be reviewed.

Legal Issues

Legal issues would be particularly crucial in Model 1, since all program staff would be private employees rather than justice system officials. These issues or potential problem areas would center on staff's official authority and responsibility—or actual and perceived lack thereof—with respect to youths, parents, significant others, agencies, and out-of-home placement. Critical questions would arise in these areas and would focus directly on the *nature, feasibility, adequacy,* and *socio-legal*—not necessarily or primarily intervention-centered—*appropriateness* of staff's role. ("Feasibility" would include both de facto and de jure power and ability.) These questions—thus, the possible and probable problem areas—are as follows.

Youths

Under what conditions, if any, could and should program staff arrest and detain program youths? When, if ever, could they withdraw or reduce youths' privileges, even for non–penal code (PC) behaviors such as infractions or technical violations? Could and should they determine length of detention, at least for non-PC behaviors? Could or should they ever add conditions or requirements, such as community service? Could or should staff have the principal or decisive—though not necessarily exclusive—voice in removing youths from the program, that is, in revoking, unfavorably discharging, or transferring them subsequent to serious illegal behavior(s)? (Could they have a similar voice in *favorably* discharging youths, or would their source agency—thus, the justice system—either make this decision on its own or at least have to concur?) Could and should they ever remove—either unilaterally or together with the source agency—uncooperative or especially difficult youths? (Included, for example, would be those who show "little major progress" except that they no longer break the law or else are misbehaving in relatively minor ways, and perhaps considerably less than before.) Could and should staff arrange, approve, and monitor leaves of absence—and search for missing youths? How would they approach due process issues, and what role would they play in youth grievances? By implication, what would be the *justice system's*—that is, the source agency's and/or the court's or board's—responsibilities and review powers regarding any of the above? When, if ever, would and should this system establish its own conditions or requirements for program youths, individually or collectively?

In short, how, and to what extent, could and should private employees implement various legal and control-related functions? Must they be deputized in order to adequately perform these roles? If so—and if this were done—would they no longer differ from parole or probation staff with respect to legal authority and responsibility? What would be the private agency's formal relationship and responsibility to the source agency, irrespective of the latter's role in, and possible approaches to, program monitoring? Regardless of what might be specified or implied in the earlier-mentioned standards and guidelines, what controls and responsibilities could and should the state or county retain over program staff and individual youths with respect to legal and authority-centered functions, whether or not staff are deputized?

Parents, Employers, Etc.[1]
Where, and to what extent, could program staff insist that parents and others either do or not do such-and-such with program youths? What could and should they do if noncompliance occurs? What actual and perceived authority and legitimacy would they have with employers and various professionals, say, teachers? Would staff be an arm of the court and, if so, to what extent would and should they replace or supplement parole/probation staff? For instance, what, if any, would be program staff's role in preparing and presenting investigation reports, social histories, and possible recommendations, and in implementing such court-ordered requirements as victim restitution and child support? If they were not a direct, official arm of the court, how would program staff—that is, private employees—obtain and handle confidential information, not just that which involves known or alleged offenses? More broadly, what arrangements would they have with public agencies other than their source agency, within and outside the county and perhaps the state? Whether deputized or not—especially if not—what, in effect, could and couldn't they legitimately expect and/or require from those justice and non–justice system agencies, and what could the latter ask of them? Should the respective agencies interact with each other directly or only via the former's source agency, for instance, county probation?

Placement
Could and should program staff be empowered to remove youths from, and/or return them to, the parents' home, or to transfer them from any one placement to another? Could and should they recruit and hire—possibly even contract with and handle various payments to—placement personnel? Whether or not they hire, and so on, should they be largely responsible for the placement setting's general activities and atmosphere?

Several, but far from all, such legal issues could be reduced or avoided via *Model 2*, that is, by having the casework supervisor (CWS) be a state or county employee: This full-time, on-site staff member could officially represent the source agency—and, thus, the justice system—not only in the earlier-mentioned legal matters but in program monitoring with respect to the minimum standards described below and in quality control with regard to intervention.[2] As in Model 1, the CWS could play a central role in both diagnosis and planning. However, as suggested, only in Model 2 could he or she officially represent the source agency while doing so. (Alternatively, a staff member could be deputized in that regard.)

Operational Issues
Operational issues would center around the following: (1) Ensuring that preestablished, minimum standards are followed with respect to key factors #1, #2, and #3 (Chapter 15), that is, caseload size, intensive intervention,[3] and long-term contacts, respectively.

(2) Ensuring that individualized intervention remains dominant even though preestablished techniques and strategies (individually

and collectively) may be selectively or partially used with most youths who share certain characteristics or who fall within given classifications. In effect, this would involve utilizing key factor #4 (explicit, detailed guidelines, i.e., preestablished approaches), while downplaying neither #5 (individualization; flexible programming) nor the extensive intervention component of #3, especially in combination.[4]

(3) Sticking with difficult cases, for instance, during crises and/or after the youths' first or second minor or perhaps even moderate offense. In effect, neither (a) "pulling back" (during crises or otherwise), (b) relinquishing one's goal of making substantial impact, nor (c) removing youths from the program essentially because "the going has gotten rough" or because one's (staff's) frustration has escalated. Beyond this, rejecting any tendency to intentionally retain or give extra attention to the easier, less risky, less time-consuming, and possibly even less expensive, cases.[5]

(4) Not skimping on expenditures for individual youths (e.g., food, clothing, travel) or for program components and physical plant (e.g., school or arts and crafts, recreation and cultural enrichment, collateral contacts and consultation, or building and maintenance), in order to reduce costs and increase profits.[6]

(5) Reduced cost-effectiveness and cost-efficiency due to *overhead* that would either not exist or be considerably less in a justice system operation (e.g., program monitoring by state or county; administrative liaison; payments to, and for, staff and others; contract development and negotiations; secure files and maintenance of official documents).

Contract Issues

Contract issues would center on salaries, wages, benefits, work hours, overtime, raises, bonuses, vacations, strikes or work actions, and so on. In Models 1 and 2 alike, staff or their representatives would almost certainly want to negotiate such issues. Affirmative action policies relate to some, though not all, aspects and phases of hiring and contracting, and they would probably be addressed—not negotiated in the above sense—in these or related contexts. Finally, contracts might specify the age, sex, and types of youth to be served. "Types" may include each of several dimen-

sions, such as court of commitment (juvenile; adult), commitment offenses, offense history, and/or specified personality features.

Discussion and Conclusions

A *privately* operated CTP might have several advantages over a justice system program. For instance, it could involve substantially reduced official labeling—a factor that, however, might be only moderately important to the present, often long-since-"labeled," and perhaps self-labeled, youths. In addition, depending on local conditions, a private program might have better access to various community groups and private employers;[7] also, it might, but again would not necessarily, attract a larger pool of appropriate and readily available candidates (potential staff). Moreover, depending not only on the quality and skill of candidates who are selected, but on the source agency's regulations and policies, the private program might generate more creative ideas and be more open to experimentation. (Under similar conditions, creativity and openness could also exist in a justice system program, even if—as in the private program—preestablished guidelines are selectively employed. Nevertheless, the private program's relative independence would constitute a unique—yet, again, only a potential—advantage in this regard.) If actualized—especially collectively—such advantages, in this case a combination of probable, potential, and hypothetical advantages, could be quite valuable in Models 1 and 2 alike.

Yet, major advantages could be associated with *justice system* programs; and some such advantages would be more likely to occur than those just mentioned. For example, if all staff, not just the casework supervisor, were state or county employees, many of the earlier-mentioned problems could doubtlessly be avoided or reduced; this would especially apply to problems involving legal authority/responsibility and to operational tasks and management issues, such as sticking with difficult cases, and cost-effectiveness/efficiency. In addition, though there is neither evidence nor counterevidence to suggest that program impact, say, rate of offending, would be better in private than in justice system programs,[8] there are, as suggested, relatively strong reasons for believing that the former programs would involve more problems—

often large problems—than the latter. If impact were indeed no better, the private programs (operations) would, in effect, fail to justify or largely compensate for these added problems. Moreover, and impact aside, private operations might often be characterized by less program continuity in the long run, not just because of the preceding problems. (Here, continuity is used in a positive sense and should connote stability with minimal attendant rigidity. It need not preclude creativity and experimentation, though—toward these ends—stability must combine with flexibility.)

Finally, in justice system programs, staff turnover might be substantially less than in private programs; this factor is presumably important where staff/youth relationships are involved. Other things being equal,[9] this and the existence of fewer problems might, in turn, help clear the way for a higher rate, and a greater degree, of program improvement, for example, during any given program year. Individually and collectively, the preceding advantages and comparisons apply to justice system programs in connection with Models 1 and 2 alike.

All in all, based on the above, it seems unlikely that the possible or even probable advantages of private programs would often outweigh those of justice system programs, or, stated differently, would often compensate enough for the relative disadvantages. As a result, under most foreseeable and likely circumstances, it would probably be more practical—and, from one perspective, it would involve less justice system effort—to have the state or county operate such programs entirely with its own staff. This would further seem appropriate if the system's actual or projected, per-ward costs for CTP-type *intervention* (e.g., for such operations' salaries and program components) were about the *same* as those for private programs, since the system's costs would probably be *less* for most remaining, that is, *nonintervention,* aspects (e.g., support services and overhead). In short, under most conditions, the justice system might "just as well" hire the earlier-mentioned candidates itself and assume full as well as direct responsibility for all operations, legal functions, and contracting—for two broad reasons: This approach would probably produce fewer substantial problems, such as legal problems, and considerably fewer "hassles." More specifically, it would probably produce

fewer such problems than if the state or county tried to support, intercede for, negotiate with, monitor, and otherwise help establish and maintain an adequate/appropriate Model 1 or 2 program. In addition, the justice system approach might involve no more expense and quite possibly somewhat less. To be sure, if things "went wrong" in a private operation—especially Model 1—the justice system would not invariably "take the heat" or the entire blame. In contrast, with a justice system approach, responsibility would be unshared.

Despite the above, circumstances doubtlessly exist in which private agency approaches would be practical and appropriate, and might well be tried. This is apart from the fact that only by "trying" or testing could one directly determine whether the earlier-mentioned problems, advantages, and disadvantages indeed existed, and, if so, what *type and degree* of influence they had. (Obviously, we believe they all exist or would exist.) Once those questions were addressed, one could probably gather useful clues as to how various problems and disadvantages might be reduced or eliminated, and how given advantages might be maintained or increased. This testing-and-clue-gathering process would not require strict scientific controls, for example, complex research designs.

At any rate, if at all possible, *a potential source agency should itself operate a CTP-type program or a closely related type of program before encouraging or allowing a private agency to do so under its auspices.* This would apply even if Model 2 were proposed and if private programs in other jurisdictions had not only shown promise but seemed no harder to operate than justice system programs. From this perspective, the highest—and present—priority would be for justice system agencies to obtain first-hand experience operating CTP-type programs. Private programs could then be tried, as circumstances allowed.

This discussion-and-conclusions section would probably apply to models other than 1 and 2 alone.

Notes
1. Also included are guardians, relatives, friends, peers, teachers, doctors, lawyers, public agencies (e.g., law enforcement, courts and probation, employment,

health, welfare), private agencies, and so on.

2. Intervention could extend beyond not only interactions with parents and others, but possible roles and responsibilities regarding placement.

3. For instance, number of monthly face-to-face contacts.

4. Whereas "minimum standards" focus on key factors #1 through #3, "guidelines" relate specifically to #4. Minimum standards refer to "conditions of intervention," whereas guidelines center on "approaches to intervention" (Chapter 15).

5. This tendency differs from purposely "giving up" on cases that, despite strenuous and often long-term staff efforts, have clearly proven to be presently unreachable, and/or detrimental to the overall program.

6. The following is related to, yet separable from, possible skimping: Payments to private agencies should not be based on the number of youths served. (For a discussion of this and related issues, see Shichor [1995].)

7. This might be particularly true in probation, that is, in local rather than state agency contexts.

8. Specifically, and unfortunately, there is no evidence either way, since the private programs in question either do not yet exist (as of about 1984) or, if recently implemented, have not been sufficiently researched. (As of 1995, research shows no clear advantage of one type of program over the other, with respect to reduced offending.)

9. For example, the factors of staff skill, program resources, creativity, and initial level of overall program adequacy.

37 Factors Responsible for Discrepancies between Suspension Documents and Rapsheets

After discovering a substantial discrepancy in the number of nonminor arrests reported on suspension documents as compared to those on rapsheets, the researchers, in 1973, reviewed field files and checked with parole staff to identify factors that probably contributed to this problem. Factors that emerged were as follows. (Before the review took place and, especially, prior to the staff discussions, the researchers neither realized that some such factors existed nor that the remaining factors were so influential; the following presentation is based on a document [Turner and Davis, 1973b] that summarized and discussed these factors. All quotations are from that document.)

I. Minor Factors

A. **Factors not related to CYA operations**
1. *CI&I error.* CI&I's notification slip ("Notice of Arrest") was, for whatever reason, not sent to CYA (Central Office).
2. *Mailing problem.* Notice was sent to CYA but was lost in the mail, particularly if routed to individual parole units through State Messenger Service.

Together, these factors probably accounted for 1 or 2 percent of all discrepancies—more specifically, omissions of nonminor arrests—in both the E and C programs.

B. **Factors related to CYA operations**
1. Caseloads that are temporarily uncovered or minimally covered due to vacant positions may be inadequately monitored during those time periods.

2. Changes in agents, especially rapid changes over brief time-periods, may cause arrest notices to be missed.
3. Temporary absence of agents due to vacation, illness, training, task force assignment, and so on, may lead to missed notices.
4. CI&I's arrest notice may be "lost in the shuffle, unintentionally overlooked, etc., because of various situational problems involving workload." For instance, several wards "simultaneously violating parole may overload an agent with paperwork [and investigations], and may cause him to miss some notifications" either entirely or until long after the arrest and, perhaps, the sentence.
5. Clerical error. For example, the Notice of Arrest is misplaced, misfiled, or destroyed before agent receives, reviews, or records it.
6. Agent is derelict in monitoring his or her caseload or in completing required paperwork for all, many, or only particular youths.

Together, these factors probably accounted for about 20 percent of all omissions within the E and C programs, respectively. Though most such factors probably had about equal influence across those programs, factor 4 was probably more influential in the C program due to the larger number of moderately serious and very serious offenses—and the resulting, larger volume of investigations and reports—that occurred there at any one (average) time. Factors 1, 5, and 6 were perhaps the largest of these relatively minor factors, and they probably carried about equal weight, perhaps even when interacting with others.

II. Major Factors

Regarding these factors, the following should be noted in connection with suspensions and reporting. Following a law arrest, the E or C agent and supervisor would decide (1) if suspension of parole was needed, and, if not needed, (2) exactly how the given arrest, that is, the basis of the possible suspension, should be documented (e.g., in a Special Incident Report or in a "chrono"). The factors were as follows.

1. Degree to which the offense shown on the Notice of Arrest could be substantiated in court.[1]
2. Extent to which the youth had already been held accountable by other authorities. If, for example, the youth had been arrested by law enforcement for petty theft, resisting arrest, or receiving stolen property, and if, say, he had served or was serving a 10- to 45-day jail term for that offense, the CYA agent might have decided that that particular incarceration period (together, perhaps, with a fine that may have been imposed) was itself "sufficient . . . punishment for violating the terms of parole." Under those conditions the agent may then have decided (1) not to suspend the individual's parole and (2) to document the arrest and incarceration not on a suspension report (since no suspension was to occur), but in a Special Incident Report and/or chrono. In addition, he or she may have imposed new or increased controls or parole conditions on the youth. All such decisions and actions could, of course, only have occurred after the CYA agent first learned of the law arrest, the sentence (if any), and so on. Not only was such knowledge often first obtained specifically via receipt of CI&I's Notice of Arrest (in short, that knowledge had not been first obtained by other means, e.g., directly from the youth or parents), but—again often—that notice had itself arrived only after the youth had been

sentenced, had served part or all of his sentence, and so forth. Such delays in the agent's initial awareness of given arrests and sentences occurred more often in the C than E program, where agents generally contacted youths (or vice versa) once a month—and parents, teachers, or employers less often. As indicated earlier and in endnote 1, these delays sometimes indirectly influenced the decision to suspend or not suspend parole, when a choice existed.

3. Time span between the youth's law enforcement arrest and his anticipated favorable discharge. This factor always seemed to operate together with others, especially with seriousness of the arrest offense and nature of any resulting court action and sentence. For instance, if (1) the individual had been arrested by law enforcement for, and was found guilty of, a non-minor-severity offense and had served a court-imposed jail sentence that the agent considered "sufficient . . . punishment" for that offense, if (2) the offense, though nonminor, was not of *major* seriousness (e.g., first-degree burglary, assault with a deadly weapon, and robbery *were* serious) and had occurred within a few months of the youth's anticipated favorable discharge,[2] and if (3) the youth seemed to be adjusting satisfactorily subsequent to his release from jail, the Youth Authority agent might have decided not to file a suspension report. That is, under this not uncommon *set* of conditions some agents might have chosen to not, in their view, unnecessarily disrupt or otherwise jeopardize the youth's still (again, in their view) impending discharge. If, of course, yet another law arrest soon occurred and the agent's view of the youth's adjustment therefore seemed questionable or mistaken, a suspension report would almost certainly be filed irrespective of the original and perhaps now-very-likley-revised expectations regarding discharge.[3]
4. Rapidly escalating, albeit temporary, workload pressures. Typical, here, was the occurrence of above-average numbers of parole violations (either law or CYA arrests) and resulting reports/investigations—not simply by *themselves,* but soon after an influx of new or

uncovered cases (whether or not these cases were, themselves, above average in number or difficulty). Such combinations and snowballing occurred more often, and may usually have lasted longer, in the C than E program.

5. Procedures that were preferred or required in one or both programs, that is, in E and/or C. For instance, during 1961–1969 most program administrators or unit supervisors, particularly in CTP, "required agents to file a suspension report when they placed a ward in custody." (Note that this refers to YA-initiated, not law-enforcement-initiated, arrests.) Others, for example, within the control program, did not regularly require this action during those same years; or, in some cases, they required or preferred it yet may have implemented or enforced it less vigorously or consistently than the first-mentioned individuals. (With this as background, see endnote 4 for further details and for related discussion of *law* arrests.)

6. Establishment of guilt or innocence, for adult cases, that is, for persons 18 or older at the time. "Some agents routinely suspended parole prior to the final outcome of cases heard in Adult Court, i.e., regardless of what that outcome might eventually be. Others took that action only [but not invariably] if guilt or, much less often, innocence had already been established." More particularly, regarding the latter agents, if the young adult was found innocent, some such individuals often filed no suspension report and instead documented the arrest and overall situation elsewhere.[5]

Together, these six factors probably accounted for about 80 percent of all nonminor, CI&I-reported law enforcement contacts that were not recorded on CYA suspension documents. Several such factors—certainly 2, 3, and 6—played a significant role in this regard, especially when interacting with factor 4 and others already mentioned.

Notes

1. Often, after having been arrested and detained by the police, a youth may have been released without sentence for the following reasons: Based on law enforcement's investigation, (1) he apparently was not involved in the offense, or, (2) though possibly implicated in, or perhaps even entirely responsible for, the offense, his involvement either was not or could not be provable in court. (Note: Neither police nor probation diversion existed for Youth Authority wards during 1961–1969.) Given this situation, all charges against the youth may have been dropped or dismissed. (Dismissal, and so on, would have occurred immediately before his release; moreover, it would have occurred either soon after or at least several weeks after his arrest, and either before or after a trial.) This situation, which applied to juveniles as well as adults, left the E or C agent with a choice of either conducting or not conducting his own investigation and of *suspending parole* in the meantime. (However, as described in endnote 4, E agents—throughout most of Phases 1 and 2—were expected to suspend parole following a "law arrest," that is, law enforcement arrest.) If he chose to investigate—say, without a concurrent suspension—he sometimes soon found that the only evidence which seemed to implicate the youth was hearsay or circumstantial. (Such a finding, of course, could also have occurred if he had decided to *suspend* the youth.) Whatever the alleged offense, the type of evidence was particularly relevant, since, during Phases 1 and 2, the *standards* of evidence admissible in court were stricter for adults than for juveniles (persons under 18). Given such circumstances, the agent—especially with adults—(during Phase 1 as well as 2)—may then have chosen to write a Special Incident Report and/or to describe the situation in his chronos. (Chronos were more often used to record such events than were Special Incident Reports.) That is, he may have done so unless he planned to *suspend* parole—and thereafter submit a suspension report when placing the youth in custody—and then resume or perhaps expand his investigation. Due to caseload pressures alone, some agents were often unlikely to pursue the latter route, that is, to continue an investigation under the

earlier-mentioned circumstances, and to suspend parole in the meantime.

2. Here, the youth's overall adjustment had presumably been fair to good during at least the 6 to 12 months preceding his or her moderate-severity offense (e.g., unplanned auto theft, possession of illegal weapon, soliciting for prostitution).

3. At any rate, the anticipated discharge would be reviewed and almost invariably postponed. Moreover, the youth could conceivably have ended up with an *unfavorable* discharge if the recent offense or offenses were sufficiently serious.

4. The fact that some supervisors did not require the given suspension was allowable under Youth Authority policy, basically for the following, interrelated reasons: When any agent placed a youth in custody he had 48 hours in which to issue a warrant and suspend parole. However, these actions were not legally required if he planned to release the ward within 48 hours—as was often the case with technical violations and certain minor-severity offenses. Nor did parole legally *have* to be suspended following an arrest by *law enforcement,* provided there was no reason to believe that the ward, when released, would flee Youth Authority jurisdiction and/or endanger himself or others. Nevertheless, throughout most (nearly all) of Phases 1 and 2, *CTP* administrators/supervisors required that parole be suspended *whenever* a youth was arrested by law enforcement (LE); this applied even though the youth may have quickly been released by LE—whether (1) in connection with a minor- or non-minor-severity arrest, and

(2) with or without having gone to court. This policy existed due to the in-lieu, then-innovative nature of the program, and to keep the board well apprised of the youth's behavior. It was enforced and followed within the framework and limits described in this appendix.

5. Two points might be noted. (1) "Legal controls could be imposed upon proof of a parole violation [e.g., an offense/infraction], and for adults a Court conviction was considered sufficient proof of violation." Since—throughout Phases 1 and 2—the Youth Authority needed firmer grounds for imposing legal controls (e.g., lockup and [re]institutionalization) on adults than on juveniles, and since stricter standards of evidence were required with the former than the latter (e.g., hearsay or presumptive evidence carried little weight in adult court), the YA adopted the practice of "leaving the determination of law violation to the court, in the case of adult wards." It was in this context that, although *some* YA agents routinely suspended parole prior to the final outcome of adult court cases, others delayed that action until after the trial (or never took it). (2) Even if the ward was not convicted and the agent—for whatever reasons—submitted no suspension report in connection with a given law contact, CI&I had already automatically recorded that law contact on its rapsheets, simply because an arrest *had* occurred. In short, the rapsheet entry occurred independently of court and YA actions (or non-actions)—each of which had taken place, of course, after the arrest itself.

38 FACTORS AND WEIGHTS USED IN COMPUTATION OF BASE EXPECTANCY SCORES

I. Used in Phases 1 and 2 of CTP

	Add
1. Age at first admission (as of last birthday)	
Other	0
17 (only)	55
2. Age at release (as of last birthday)	
18+	0
17	155
16	223
15–	286
3. Prior record	
None, 0–2 delinq. contacts	0
None, 3 or more delinq. contacts	73
One or more prior commitments	112
4. No. of offense partners	
Three or more	0
One or two	81
None	102
5. Current attitude toward school	
Other	0
Markedly dislikes (extreme only)	63
6. No. of foster home placements	
None	0
One or more	76
7. Truancy	
None	0
Other	51

(continued on next page)

(continued)

8. Self-respect of family
   Other   0
   Marked   −39

9. Race
   Other   0
   Negro [black]   56

                  Total =

886 − Total = Base Expectancy Score

II. Used in Phase 3 of CTP*

1. Constant		192.2	<u>192.2</u>
2. Age at first admission			
	19+	383.9	
	18	352.5	
	17	332.4	
	16	237.8	
	15	123.4	
	14	95.6	
	13−	0.0	_____
3. Number of prior commitments			
	None	96.2	
	1 or more	0.0	_____
4. School misbehavior (truancy, etc.)			
	None	66.6	
	Some	0.0	_____
5. Number of prior escapes			
	None	66.5	
	1 or more	0.0	_____
6. Number of offense partners			
	1 or more	32.4	
	None	0.0	_____
		Total BE score	_____

*Beverly, Robert F. 1968. *A comparative analysis of base expectancy tables for selected subpopulations of California Youth Authority wards.* Research report No. 55. Sacramento: California Youth Authority.

PAROLED-OUT-OF-AREA YOUTHS AND NON-INTERVIEWED CONTROLS

I. Paroled-Out-of-Area Youths

Rationale and Definition

The following account of POAs appeared in CTP's 7th, 8th, and 9th research reports; except for the 3/31/68 *date,* the statement was identical in each report (Warren et al., 1966a; Palmer and Warren, 1967; Palmer et al., 1968, pp. 106–107):

From 10/31/61 through 3/31/68, a number of Control wards have spent a substantial period of their particular, total parole careers residing *outside of* the immediate Sacramento and Stockton geographic areas. Information relating to the parole performance of these wards does not appear to be as complete as that for wards who, during parole, resided within the immediate vicinity of Sacramento and Stockton. Research does not, for example, feel as confident about having obtained as complete an account either of parole violations or of parole suspensions (without violation) in the case of wards who had been paroled to a different part of the State, or to a different State, as compared with those on local parole.

In addition, wards who had been paroled outside the local area may have been presented with (a) sets of environmental stimuli, as well as with (b) law enforcement policies, practices, or traditions, which differed substantially or systematically from those presented to the Experimental and Control wards who had been on local parole. Furthermore, selective factors of an undetermined nature might have been involved in the very process of getting and/or

remaining Paroled Out of Area." [Palmer et al., 1968]

("For reasons such as these, it was felt that—with regard to parole performance—Experimentals should only be compared with Controls who had been on local parole, as defined [in the next paragraph]." The 7th, 8th, and 9th research reports then continued, with the subsequent definition of *POA* status and with related discussion.) [Palmer, 1974a]

Wards who, while on parole, resided in any of the following towns or areas were regarded as falling *within* the geographic limits of the Sacramento-Stockton study [they were thus on local parole]: Sacramento Area, Florin, Perkins, Mills, Citrus Heights, Del Paso Heights, Elverta, North Highlands, Rio Linda, North Sacramento, West Sacramento, Broderick, Bryte, Stockton Area, French Camp. Determination of each ward's residence was made by means of a systematic check of his entire file.

Wards who, while on parole, resided outside of the general Sacramento and Stockton geographic limits were either included or excluded from analyses of parole data on the basis of the criteria indicated below. The statistical analysis of suspension data—as well as information relating specifically to revocation, recommitment, and unfavorable discharge—was carried out only for those wards who, as of 3/31/68, (1) had *never* been on Parole Out of Area status; or, (2) if they *had* [been on] POA status, were able to meet the following criteria:

a. Wards initially released to any of the previously mentioned *local* areas must have had at least four consecutive months on parole prior to their POA; or, if initially released to parole *outside* of the study boundries, they must have returned to the area in less than two months.

b. In addition to "a" above, of the first 15 months of parole exposure, a ward could have accumulated a total of no more than three months POA time. These three months could have been distributed between no more than two separate instances of POA.

In light of considerations "a" and "b," a total of 84 Control wards were classified as POA [for purposes of the 3/68, 15-month parole follow-up]; and no suspension of *any* type incurred by any of these wards was considered in the statistical analyses. [Several of these youths were female.]

For any ward who had at some time been POA, and who *also* had been able to meet the above-cited criteria, *no* suspension (including any offense—irrespective of whether it led to revocation, recommitment, or unfavorable discharge) was included in the statistical analyses if that suspension took place while the ward was on POA status. In the case of wards who either had remained within the study area throughout their first 15 months on parole or who (on the basis of their having met criteria "a" and "b" above) otherwise could have been regarded as having been on local parole for the equivalent of 15 months, but who nevertheless had gone POA *subsequent to* the actual 15-month point in time—only those suspensions (*including* those which led to revocation, recommitment, or unfavorable discharge) which had taken place *prior to* POA status were considered in the statistical analyses.

Revocation, recommitment, and unfavorable discharge information *was* always included in the case of any ward whose suspension took place *prior to* his ever having been placed on POA status. Thus, *all* revocations, recommitments, and unfavorable discharges which occurred while wards were on local parole were included; and *no* revocations, recommitments, and unfavorable discharges which occurred while wards were on POA status were included.

Use of such criteria was seen as a way of "bringing about a scientifically controlled, or 'fair,' E/C comparison—viz., by holding constant such factors as 'a' and 'b' above." In any event, the comparison "could be fairer than that which would have resulted from the *inclusion* of Control POA's" (Palmer, 1974a, p. 13).

Policies and Scenarios
The lengthy quotation (above) also appeared in Palmer's 1974 reply, where it was supplemented by the following discussion and information:

. . . the very nature of CTP's operation absolutely required that *Experimental* wards remain within the local area, to the extent possible. Basically, this was due to the fact that adequate implementation of the intensive, differential intervention concept[1] could only be "guaranteed" (or even made probable) within the context of a *particular* community—viz., that in which the CTP operation was being carried out—and not simply within "just any" California community. For better or worse, Experimentals were in a sense obliged [essentially, required] to deal with their problems—personal, family, and/or neighborhood—within their home community, where possible. In their attempts to do so, they were at least able to rely upon the resources of CTP. (p. 13)

Even the CYA Board lent its support to the Project, on this point. That is to say, it did look upon CTP as a program that literally was in lieu of *institutionalization,* and not simply in lieu of either (a) regular parole or (b) any other "intensive" parole program—local or otherwise. (p. 14)

By way of contrast, none of the above restrictions, specific policies, and obligations, were ever looked upon as being quite applicable with regard to *Controls.* . . . Thus, e.g., at any point in time, any given Control and/or his parent(s) could arrange for a conference with the youth's parole agent and, during the given conference, perhaps arrive at an understanding to the effect that (a) it might be better for the youth to, say, "start out fresh" in some other part of the State, and/or "get away" from certain local community pressures or possibly "temptations," or that (b) it would be in the family's best interest to move from the local area, and that the youth might just as well go along with them; etc.[2]

It was also rather common for, say, a given Control to simply leave the Sacramento/Stockton area and notify his parole agent of this fact a couple of weeks later—by phone or letter, and for the first time. On this same occasion, he would be likely to tell his agent that he was holding (or might be on the verge of obtaining) a new job, living with a parent or relative, feeling "less hassled" by peers and/or police, and so on. Faced with this fait accompli, together with a report such as the above, the parole agent—already laden with his caseload of approximately 70 youths—was often, though by no means always, willing to give the youth the benefit of the doubt, in addition to being cautiously supportive. At the same time he was very likely to insist that the youth quickly report to a parole office within the given area (e.g., Los Angeles). Soon afterward, the agent and his supervisor would initiate the action (phone calls and paperwork) that would result in an official transfer to the new area. (p. 14)

Related Conditions

It might be worthwhile to [now review] certain conditions that were found to be associated with the out-of-area move, on the part of Control POA's.[3] As discussed below, POAs have been divided into two broad categories.

1. The following applies to youths who were "paroled out of area" after having been released to parole. That is, the individuals in question went POA from their home community—the latter being either Sacramento or Stockton.[4]
    A. The first POA move was initiated by the following individual(s): parole agent (16 percent); parent(s) or relative(s) (35 percent); youth (48 percent).
    B. (1) In cases where the parole agent had initiated the POA placement,

the primary reason or reasons for the placement were given as follows:[5] youth wants to obtain work or work-related training elsewhere . . . or has a job lead[6] (43 percent); youth is disruptive/rejecting in own home (29 percent); youth is rejected/"banned" from home by parent(s) (14 percent); youth is to live independently (self, . . . or newly married) (14 percent).

    (2) When parents/relatives initiated the first POA placement, the reasons were: to seek work/training; job lead (13 percent); youth to remain with parents, who were moving (60 percent); moved to live with relatives (14 percent); all other reasons (14 percent).

    (3) When the youth himself initiated the placement, the reasons were: to seek work/training; job lead (48 percent); moved to live with relatives (14 percent); moved to live with other parent (14 percent);[7] rejected/"banned" from home by parent(s) (10 percent); to live independently (10 percent); all other reasons (five percent).

C. The youth's present, *non-POA* placement [i.e., "prior-to-POA placement"] was seen, by the parole agent, as being: not harmful (52 percent); somewhat harmful (26 percent); definitely or extremely harmful (23 percent).

D. The youth's present, *non-POA* placement was seen, by agent, as becoming: neither worse nor better (55 percent); slightly worse (32 percent); definitely or markedly worse (13 percent).

E. The proposed/actual *POA* placement was expected to be, or was seen (by the agent) as being: neutral or "50–50" (26 percent); somewhat helpful (41 percent); definitely or extremely helpful (32 percent).

2. The following applies to youths who were "paroled out of area" *directly from the CYA institution itself.*[8]
    A. The POA move was initiated by: parole agent (50 percent); parent(s) or relative(s) (23 percent); youth (28 percent).

B. (1) In cases where the parole agent had initiated the placement, the primary reason or reasons were: to live with parents (21 percent);[9] to live with relatives (21 percent); to live in group/foster/boarding home (18 percent); to seek work/training; job lead (three percent); all other reasons (13 percent); no information (24 percent).

    (2) When the parents or relatives initiated the placement, the reasons were: to live with parents (50 percent); to seek work/training; job lead (11 percent); to live with relatives (6 percent); all other reasons (22 percent); no information (11 percent).

    (3) When the youth himself initiated the placement, the reasons were: to live with parents (35 percent); to seek work/training; job lead (15 percent); to live with relatives (10 percent); to live in group/foster/boarding home (5 percent); all other reasons (20 percent); no information (15 percent).

C. The youth's preinstitutional, *non-POA* placement was seen, by the parole agent, as being: not harmful (55 percent); somewhat harmful (45 percent); definitely or extremely harmful (0 percent).

D. The youth's preinstitutional, *non-POA* placement was seen, by agent, as becoming: neither worse nor better (20 percent); slightly worse (43 percent); definitely or markedly worse (38 percent).[10]

E. The out-of-area *POA* placement was expected (by the agent) to be: neutral or 50-50 (65 percent); somewhat helpful (25 percent); definitely or markedly helpful (10 percent). (Palmer, 1974a, pp. 15–17)

II. Non-Interviewed Controls

Rationale and Definition

The following account of NIC's appeared in the 1974 reply (p. 19):

During 1966–1967, CTP's per-staff, research workload sharply increased. Among other things, this was due to the fact that the San Francisco experiment—by then in full swing—required more attention than had been anticipated [mainly for data collection]. To reduce the pressure on research staff it was decided, in mid-1966, that the following steps (among others) would be taken with regard to periods of especially heavy activity: A portion of the newly committed Valley cases—all of whom would already have randomly fallen Control—would, again on a random basis, simply *not* be interviewed, diagnosed-and-second-rated, etc. Nor would they be administered the California Psychological Inventory, the Jesness Inventory, and so on.[11] From an operational point of view, these individuals were to be (and they *were*) handled in the same manner as all other Controls, in every other respect.

As of the 7th Research Report (data-cutoff 3/31/66), all C's had been interviewed, diagnosed, etc. As a result, there did not yet exist any such category as 'NIC.' It was only [soon] after 3/31/66 that this category first came into being. . . .

CTP research nevertheless maintained an otherwise standard file on all NIC's; and originally, it was assumed that these individuals would probably be analyzed as a subgroup within the overall Control group, at least in connection with one or two criterion measures. However, it soon became evident that—because of their lack of any *I-level diagnosis*—there was, strictly speaking, no particular group into which they could be placed, for purposes of comparison. Under the circumstances—and also [because] the research team had already accumulated 270 rather well-matched [non-POA'd] C's—it was decided, when preparing for the subsequent (*8th*) Research Report, to simply set aside all NIC's (males and females). This decision was made even easier when it was found that there were no significant differences between NIC's and C's with respect to Age, I.Q., Race, SES, Offense, and Base Expectancy. (These early findings received further confirmation a few years after the 1961–1969 experiment ended. [See text—Chapter 21]) Thus, to all intents and purposes, the NIC's were looked upon as a special category of "analytic ineligibles."

Notes

1. "As defined in terms of CTP's particular intervention strategies. These, of course, generally called for some form of agent-youth matching, and often required a number of weekly, personal contacts between agent and youth" (p. 13).

2. "Within the E program, it was possible to take a rather close look at claims of this nature and to discuss them in considerable detail with the family and ward. The upshot was that the families in question typically decided that it was not, after all, so important for them to move 'just yet' ... or that (irrespective of whether they were to ... move) it might be at least as important for them to allow/encourage the youth to 'stay behind' in order to continue with his CTP program" (p. 14).

3. "The following is based upon a complete review of the research files of all male POA's. (N = 70) Of the earlier-mentioned 71 POA's, one had been erroneously classified as POA" (p. 15).

4. "In short, they were 'POA'd' after having first returned to their home community upon release from a CYA [YA] institution. This is in contrast to having been POA'd ... (directly upon release) from the *institution*, itself. Included within the present category are 44 percent of all POA's. These individuals spent an aver-

age of 5.2 months in their home community prior to being placed out of the local area for the first time" (p. 15).

5. "Not infrequently, *two* reasons were presented in the placement report. This applies throughout the present category" (p. 15).

6. "This category will be referred to as follows: 'to seek work/training; job lead'" (p. 15).

7. "That is, with a parent other than the one with whom he was previously living" (p. 15).

8. "This includes 56 percent of all POA's. These individuals spent an average of 8.9 months in their out-of-area placement, prior to either returning to Sacramento/ Stockton or else moving on to a second out-of-area placement; etc." (p. 16).

9. "Mainly to live with parents who had moved from the Sacramento/Stockton area while the youth was still in an institution" (p. 16).

10. "The seeming, and at least partial, discrepancy in the agents' reporting as between '(C)' ('definitely or extremely harmful' = zero percent) and '(D),' above, cannot be accounted for by means of the casefiles alone" (p. 17).

11. "Including travel, the overall savings for research was several hours per NIC" (p. 19).

INFORMATION BASES FOR DESCRIPTIONS AND CONCEPTS RELATING TO PRECOMMITMENT YEARS AND TO SELECTED DEVELOPMENTS AMONG NONOFFENDERS

Serious Multiple Offenders

Concerning serious multiple offenders' pre-CYA development, their pre-CYA relations with other youths, and so on, the *sources* of information that are used for the descriptions and concepts presented in this chapter first involve the following: detailed, cumulative case files regarding all experimental and control youths in the NIMH/CYA experiment (1961–1973)—Sacramento, Stockton, and San Francisco alike. Included in each individual's file were not only all probation and court documents—that is, official, pre-CYA information—concerning that youth's life and adjustment, but selected results from a researcher's taped initial interview with that individual and from a parole agent's initial interviews with the youth and his parents/guardians.[1] Later added to this file was pre-CYA information that sometimes emerged after the youth—particularly one in the Community Treatment Project—came to know his parole agent better.[2] Of further value, and partly incorporated into each Phase 3 youth's file, were additional types and/or levels of information regarding the pre-CYA period that research staff obtained from all youths. These were obtained during the initial interview,

as part of implementing the "Developmental-Adaptation" framework which was used throughout that phase of the experiment (1969–1973). (Regarding this framework, see Chapter 27.)

Second, material in the present chapter reflects the author's examination, throughout 1979–1992 (well after the NIMH/CYA experiment had ended), of the following: extensive case-file material—again containing CYA and all probation/court documents—that bore on the several "*types* of information" in question (see text), on approximately 750 to 800 additional male SMOs who were then in CYA institutions and camps or who had been released to parole.[3] Together, these individuals, who were usually first commitments to the Youth Authority from throughout the state and were mostly from juvenile courts, comprised the full spectrum of serious, young, multiple offenders. Among them were some 150 who would have been ineligible for the NIMH/CYA experiment (mainly in Phases 1 and 2) because of their commitment offense or their histories of unusual violence alone.[4]

Third, concepts and descriptions in this chapter, and several in Chapters 25, 29, and

30, also reflect the author's estimated 200 to 250 extensive discussions, regarding serious and less serious offenders, with CYA and non-CYA correctional personnel, from the mid-1970s to the early 1990s. Collectively, these individuals, who were mainly within but also from outside California, either were or had been engaged in one or more of the following: intake and classification; individual diagnosis; casework (including liaison with families and outside agencies); direct intervention with youths, that is, control plus treatment of them; management and administration; broad policy-making. In general, their work centered on standard, intensive, or specialized programs and/or operations, within parole, institutional, residential, or probation settings. Most such individuals had had years of direct, often personal, experience with hundreds, sometimes thousands, of delinquents, either on a onetime, short-term, or longer-term basis. Discussions also occurred with numerous researchers—co-workers and others—and with academicians as well, some of whom had been practitioners. Significant inputs also came, of course, from the correctional literature—books, articles, and reports.

Together, the above provided a large amount of strongly converging, mostly experience-based, objective and subjective evidence, opinion, and knowledge as to what made most SMOs "tick," and regarding major paths those youths had typically traveled in getting to where they now were. This information was essentially consistent over a long period of time, and it applied to urbanized as well as less urbanized settings. The extent to which it applies to very low population-density settings is unknown.

Regarding the SMOs taken individually, it should be noted that case-file information concerning the steps that collectively comprised the paths these youths had taken was, in many instances, sketchy or otherwise incomplete. (Together, these particular youths are called the "file-1" group.) More precisely, information about one or more steps was often absent, and in that sense a "gap" or—more often—"gaps" existed. (The nature of these gaps frequently varied from one such youth to the next. For instance, in some cases only an early step or two was missing; in many others, a middle or perhaps later step was involved. As can be seen, information existed regarding the early, middle, and later

steps for file-1 youths *collectively,* even though it was often missing individually. This was because of the collective overlap involved.)

This situation partly reflected the fact that the initial interview, especially but not only during Phases 1 and 2 of the experiment, had usually tried to elicit only a moderate amount of that particular pre-CYA information in the first place. At the same time, the probation/court material, and other available information, was itself only moderate in that respect, for most such youths.

Despite those gaps regarding file-1 individuals, and partly because the steps/paths information (from whatever sources) was more detailed in the case of many *other* youths ("file-2" individuals), a picture emerged that seemed clear for SMOs overall. This picture of the main steps that comprised the typical paths of SMOs-to-be was based on a combination of (1) the earlier-mentioned, sketchy files, (2) the many other, more detailed files, and (3) other information that occasionally supplemented the interview-and-probation/court material regarding file-1 and -2 youths alike. (Discussion-based input to the author, mainly concerning non-CYA individuals, also contributed.)

In short, when the lives of large numbers of individuals were reviewed and reflected upon collectively—these being processes that occurred *cumulatively,* over several years—(1) regularly repeated, mutually interrelated details, and (2) frequently repeated sequences of those details, stood out clearly, and, by that point, had a sizable base. (These "repeated . . . details, and . . . sequences" . . . are here called patterns and paths.) As that occurred, no major gaps seemed to remain with respect to *what* comprised SMOs' typical paths, that is, what main psychological and interpersonal steps they consisted of.

Basically, then, the information that *was* available regarding the file-1 and especially file-2 youths—each type of youth collectively, and both types jointly—had directly revealed the specific content of SMOs' paths. (In so doing, it had, in effect, also clarified the nature of, or at least the probable/usual content of, what might have existed in place of the gaps.) At any rate, it was essentially in and through the process of reviewing and reflecting upon large quantities of information that the major details and their sequences (1) emerged and "lined up," as it were, and

(2) became evident *as* common patterns or otherwise major paths. Those details and sequences were not infrequent in *absolute* terms, that is, even while being the most common ones; and, as indicated, they were neither obscure nor subtle.

In reality, this empirically derived plus conceptually synthesized picture of given paths had already been observed, albeit on a reduced scale, *along the way*—that is, in numerous individual youths, through the years. In particular, it had been seen—in most of its later-regarded essentials, such as several specific details—among many youths in the file-2 group. In this respect, the more or less finalized "picture [that eventually] emerged"— that is, the derived/synthesized (D/S) one, which reflected the totality of data—was partly an extension of what had already appeared in a sizable minority of case files even as of the NIMH/CYA experiment's middle years.[5] At any rate, and beyond its direct relationship to those numerous youths, the final— the D/S—picture that emerged substantially applied to, and in that sense represented, a large majority of SMOs. It was not an abstraction, statistical or other, that actually pertained to only a moderate or perhaps even smaller percentage of youths.

Nonoffenders and Other Youths

Descriptions and concepts regarding (1) nonoffenders, (2) never-arrested but self-admitted minor offenders, and (3) arrested—"known"— minor offenders, reflect not just statements by hundreds of CYA wards about their own pre-CYA interactions with these individuals. Instead, they also reflect the author's synthesis of the innumerable statements and accounts he has heard and read, continuing over several decades, mainly from and by individual nonoffenders themselves, and, to a lesser extent, from/by groups (2) and (3) as well. These statements and accounts related, for example, to the youths' self-concepts or self-image (together, their "self-perception"), their life situation, their interests and activities, and their interactions with peers as well as adults. They occurred, especially, in the various *media* (radio, television, large circulation newspapers—also magazines and student publications), exactly as they do today. They involved either current ("live") matters or else recollections; and, in both such cases, they mainly

took the form of casual observations and cursory remarks; terse, focused, sometimes soul-baring statements; solicited or unsolicited comments and opinions about other adolescents; informal writings or sketches; and, to a much lesser extent, lengthier, detailed, statements or writings.

Also contributing to the author's synthesis were results from many formal and informal surveys that were conducted—intermittently— over the past three decades, nationally, regionally, and locally. These were carried out by various researchers, pollsters, and so on, and their quality varied widely, to be sure. Collectively, they touched and often focused on youths' self-perceptions, values, wishes, interests, usual activities, role models, felt needs, issues and concerns, major likes and dislikes, personal problems, frustrations, fears, relationships with others, attitudes toward parents/authority figures in particular, views regarding the future, attitudes toward postadolescence roles, and involvements in risky or illegal behavior. The earlier-mentioned statements and accounts in the *media* usually related to one or more such areas themselves; and, with few exceptions, the descriptions found in this source or vehicle were quite similar to those appearing in the surveys.

Finally, various descriptions and concepts in the present chapter—not just those involving nonoffenders—also reflect books, journal articles, and other literature on childhood and adolescence.

Information from the media, the surveys, and the literature is also reflected in the "Theoretical Perspectives" section of Chapter 25. See, for example, that section's "Primary or Basic Goals," "Expectations in Adolescence," and "Salient Dimensions."

Notes

1. In the experiment's intensive, in-lieu program, namely, the Community Treatment Project, selected information from the research and agent interviews was discussed during the "initial staffing" and was then incorporated, in part or whole, into the combined "Background and Diagnosis" plus "Treatment/Intervention" Plan document that resulted from this staffing. These interviews, and related procedural *differences* between the CTP and standard programs, are described in Chapter 2.

2. Within CTP, that and other new information about the youth's early adjustment was often discussed in supervisory case conferences—"Quarterlies" and others (Chapter 19).

3. The files were reviewed mainly in connection with formal Research Division studies, substudies, and specific analyses, for example, in order to: (1) determine the percentage of CYA wards who had records of being abused by parents/ guardians in specified ways, or who had ever been placed out-of-home or been sent to a probation camp prior to their first CYA commitment; and, (2) identify wards whose offenses had escalated in defined ways during specified time periods, and whose offense histories included physical violence, had involved "gangs," and so on.

4. The author and other researchers occasionally examined probation files as well. This was done in connection with various studies or special-request analyses in which Youth Authority samples or subsamples were compared to those under local supervision, usually statewide.

5. If the interviews had focused more specifically and/or at greater length on the content areas in question, the derived/synthesized picture would perhaps have been directly observed in a clear majority of individuals. At any rate, it would—at least, it could—have then been more concretely and clearly reflected in those youths' respective files, with regard to amount and scope of detail.

TECHNICAL DETAILS CONCERNING THREE-LEVEL SERIES, AND PREDICTABILITY OF ILLEGAL BEHAVIOR

Five technical points will now be mentioned; an extensive discussion will then follow.

A. Using the present series as the basis of comparison, any other three-step series that contains one or more substantively different *features* in any of its *levels,* say, its first, is, strictly speaking, ipso facto a "different" series. This is because, in the present discussion, any and all series are differentiated *in terms of* their features (content), that is, are defined, individualized, and otherwise set apart on that particular basis. Moreover, unless otherwise specified, all three-level series are operationally distinguished from each other *only* in terms of, that is, only by, the specific substance—the features per se—of which they are comprised; this is the case even though other bases could have been used in addition or instead. Thus, for example, no three-level series is defined—here—as a distinct entity on the basis of, or in conjunction with, either or both of the following: (1) the *order* in which its features appear, when more than one such feature applies, to the given youths, within any one or more of the three-level series' respective levels, and/or (2) the type of *relationship* that exists between each such level, regardless of any feature's order per se.[1] (Cf. point 4 of the text [p. 26-5], regarding relationships.)

B. The particular *features* that comprise level one of the present series are, as indicated, very common among the present youths, that is, the SMOs-to-be, and those found in level two are common as well.[2] (This also applies to various features found in the numerically same level of certain other three-level series, ones not specified here.)[3] Nevertheless, even those features, and the overall levels as well (i.e., all their features combined), are usually

not *as* widespread as is much of the content found in the present level *three.* This heavily reflects the fact that level three—a broad way of coping with those earlier levels, especially the second—is mainly driven by, as well as directed at, personal dynamics, including their usual interpersonal manifestations, which are themselves widespread across the present youths.[4] Thus, the widespread nature of level three content does *not* simply result from or mainly reflect the following facts: Feelings of *relief and/or satisfaction* that are associated with given activities, attitudes, and stances (AASs) are qualitatively similar to each other across many of the present individuals. (This refers to similarity with respect to their consciously experienced nature, that is, to the particular feelings of relief/satisfaction themselves, whatever the *content* of the AASs, and of earlier difficulties/problems, may be.) Those qualitatively similar feelings are, in addition, quantitatively very common across the given youths. (The AASs in question are ones that have been reinforced mainly by other youths and which are major constituents of level three. See text section titled "Reinforcement by Nonoffenders.")

C. When any level *one* feature, such as "frustration" generated by difficulties/problems, evolves to level *two* (in this case, to "feelings of futility" concerning those same or closely related D/Ps), that first feature seldom entirely dissolves or otherwise vanishes even though it is now markedly altered. Specifically, it does not fully lose its original identity and entirely cease to affect youths on that particular basis. Again, however, that level-one identity is greatly changed, as is the feature's overall influence on the given D/Ps. The same applies—albeit in a different context—to any level two feature, if and when it substantially changes. That is, it, too, does not entirely disappear in the above respects, when level *three* features or elements emerge and help youths adapt to it.

D. Any two individuals can move from level one to level two and then on to level three—sometimes even directly from one to three—in terms of what might be called differing tracks. Each track can be described not just with regard to content per se, this being the particular set or group of features involved for those respective youths. Instead, it can also refer to the order—the *sequence*—in which those features appear, within and across the given levels. For instance, regarding sequence, any given track can be analytically described, that is, broken down, with respect to (1) where it begins, (2) where it ends, and (3) what specific route it involves, irrespective of exactly where it starts and ends.[5] Thus, concerning aspect (1), one youth may, for example, begin with level one's "frustration" rather than its "worry." Another, however, may start with "worry" and only later experience substantial, related "frustration" (same type of content, but different sequence); or he or she may begin with still a *different* level one feature, such as "self-doubt" or perhaps "anger." Similarly, regarding aspect (3), the first youth may, for instance, move from level one's "frustration" to its "worry" or perhaps its "self-doubt," and only after *that* to level two's ". . . futility," and so on. The second individual, however, might move directly from "frustration" to those "feelings of futility." At any rate, differing overall paths and differing specific routes—the latter being the sequences of features—can and often do occur, across the present youths.

Another type of difference centers on the overall amounts of terrain that differing youths may cover, especially the number of features that are involved before they reach level three. This factor—sheer number[6]—is separable from intensity and duration per se, for any particular feature and sequence. As might be expected, certain combinations of amount, particular features, sequence, and so on, have implications that are substantially different than others, with respect to the nature and onset of illegal behavior and concerning aspects of intervention itself. This applies (1) despite the many similarities that

are likely to exist, across respective youths, regarding the content and underlying dynamics of the youths' individual and collective level *three* features themselves; and it does so especially, but not only, when (2) the earlier-mentioned combinations of level one and two features involve considerably more intensity and/or duration than do the others.[7]

One additional matter will be mentioned. This centers on the *predictability of illegal behavior*—especially including multiple offending—based mainly on the features that exist at the three respective levels.

E. By itself, the occurrence of "frustration," "self-doubt," or any other level *one* feature does not necessarily presage illegal behavior, let alone multiple such behavior. In fact, each such feature is common among youths we have called *non*offenders (nonO's), though it is usually present to a much lesser degree in these individuals. ("NonO's" have been alternatively called "NO's." The terms are synonymous.) The nonO category includes not only many youths who do *not* have sizable, long-standing difficulties/problems (these being the majority of individuals) but others who do have such D/Ps—ones that sometimes lead to maladaptive and/or self-injurious activities and stances which, however, are not *illegal*. At any rate, the mere presence of a level one feature is, by itself, no more than a mediocre predictor of delinquency. More precisely, it is mediocre for any *group* or category of youths. (That is the case even though the following would apply to any *particular* youth who falls within the SMOs-to-be category. With that youth—in fact, with many such individuals—any one feature, for example, "anger," may contribute substantially to delinquent behavior. It may do so directly and immediately or else it may help pave the way indirectly. Moreover, in the former case, it may sometimes be a decisive factor—a trigger, even a "last straw"—with respect, say, to a rare, impulsive act.[8] Like substantial contributions in general, triggering is more likely to occur not only if, of course, various *preconditions* [e.g., opportunities] exist, but if certain *events* [e.g., threats or major personal challenges] are perceived, by the youth, as existent or imminent, and/or if certain other level one *features* [e.g., "frustration"] are or have recently been present.)

However, when a level one feature, say, "anger," is long-lasting and—especially—

when it evolves to level *two,* for instance, to "intensified, often-generalized . . . anger and hostility," the contribution of that evolved form to illegal behavior is larger than that of the previous one. In this respect the correlation between youth feature and behavioral outcome is higher; viewed longitudinally, it has accumulated. In addition, if and when youths move to level *three,* the correlation between feature and outcome increases still further. This is the case even though the earlier—the level one and two—features may hardly be recognizable at this time, and although certain *reactions* to them may now be prominent instead.

Still, even at the start of level three, the degree of accurate prediction is not high. In fact, although it is higher than at level one, it is no more than moderate—again, for the overall group of youths. (With any *one* individual, however, it may be a strong predictor, that is, a definite danger sign.) This situation refers to level three's starting features. Concerning these features, see items listed under Categories "A" and "B" in the text sections starting with "Types of Level-3 Effects."

This pertains not just to the prediction of (1) *any* illegal behavior other than the rare or very infrequent (say, first- and perhaps second-time, relatively minor such behavior), but, especially, to that of (2) *multiple* offending. In both cases the prediction period would cover at least several months, even one or two years. It is mainly when level three—most notably its Category B activities—*further* develops, and in some respects consolidates, that illegal behavior (again, for the youths collectively) becomes quite likely to occur (if it has not already done so once or twice), and that, in particular, *multiple* such activities become likely, and much more predictable. (This can apply within a shorter time frame than that just mentioned. Regarding this "*further* develop[ment]," see text section titled "Increased Investment in Risky/Trouble-Related Behavior: Phase C.")

Concerning levels *one* and *two,* respectively, the predictability of outcomes (1) and (2), above, is usually higher when two or more features, rather than any one, are active at the same or approximately same time.[9] Yet, even here, predictability is not high in absolute terms—not, once again, until a relatively advanced phase of level three is reached. This is the case, in other words, whether many or few features have been involved at those preceding levels, and despite the fact that the *more* such features are involved, the higher, in general, is the chance that level three will itself be reached.

Notes

1. "Order," which denotes sequence itself and which thus implies "series," would be a fully valid basis on which to distinguish any two or more series from each other. (Here, order refers to the particular sequence in which *features*—contents—appear within and across the *levels* that, collectively, comprise the respective series. Cf. point D, in this appendix.) However, for immediate as well as general purposes, *content* itself, rather than how it is arranged, is used as the formal basis of definition and differentiation, even though it is not the sole fulcrum of the discussion.

2. As mentioned in the text, no one feature—that is, no given content (e.g., "feelings of frustration")—can be present in level one *and* level two of any given series, except, of course, in an evolved form (e.g., as "feelings of futility") within the latter level.

3. The features that comprise these "other" series are each different than the four later listed, in the text, for level one and the four listed there for level two of the *present,* three-level series. As can be inferred from the text, any series, whether it is an "other" one or the present one, can involve several *sequences* in connection with its various *features.* (Cf. point D, in the appendix, regarding paths and routes.) For instance, focusing on the eight features referred to in connection with the present series' first two levels (collectively), one sequence of features, that is, one particular path, could begin with level one's "feelings of frustration" and might then move directly to level two's "feelings of futility." Another sequence, however, could start with level one's "worry" and might then move directly to level two's ". . . often stronger, feelings of anxiety and insecurity"; and so on, regarding the remaining features of those respective levels. Any one of these *sequences* of *features* can be involved

when the present, three-step series—that is, series of levels—is referred to.

4. These dynamics play major roles in generating, triggering, and maintaining not only the youths' difficulties/problems but many of their salient desires and fears, as such. Also, they reflect—are partly *effects,* not just causes of—various actual as well as felt needs. (Whereas first-generation D/Ps often play a central role in bringing about the level one and two reactions, the youths' *desires* and *fears* are often decisive in generating step *three* and in later triggering specific illegal actions, especially repeated ones. Initial "generating [and] triggering" aside, those D/Ps and desires/fears both play various maintenance roles, as well.)

5. In other words, "track" can involve and be described from two separable yet interwoven perspectives. In the first, it is thought of as the entire "terrain"—the overall path—that stretches from a starting point ("a") to an end point ("z"). It is viewed solely *as* that stretch or expanse, and not as an aggregate of particular features or contents. As a result, whether a track is short or long, it is not—in this perspective-one capacity as "entity-that-encompasses-a-particular-span"—described in terms of the features which are the sole constituents or substance *of* that path. This would apply to any other possible analytic subdivisions, that is, other constituents or contents, as well.

The second perspective does involve substantive and analytic matters, that is, content and subdivisions. Here, "track" is viewed and described as a *specific* route that is taken when a youth moves from content or feature "a" to that of "z," for example, via "b," "c," and so on. In other words, it is here, and in this way, that content is added to the perspective-one framework or shell, that is, to "track-as-overall-path-or-span." Thus, in perspective two, "track" is *differentiated,* is analytically subdivided rather than considered an undivided entity. In this regard its divisions, that is, delineated contents, consist of specific features (e.g., frustration; worry), and these are presented—arranged—so as to reflect their temporal sequence as well, e.g., across levels.

6. This number refers to the differing *types* of features. These features are essentially *feelings and emotions,* for example, frustrations, worries, anger, and futility—each a distinguishable type. More specifically, they are first and second level effects of, that is, "reactions" to, certain experiences the youths have had, ones that are often mutually related. Individually and collectively, these reactions—say, the level one feelings/emotions—often last a long time, not just weeks but months or more. Especially when they do, it is mainly because of the following: These feelings and emotions, in conjunction with aspects of the above experiences (which helped trigger them), reflect and express personal and interpersonal dynamics that involve needs (1) which are usually longstanding and remain largely unmet, (2) regarding which those youths feel recurring pressures and discomfort, and (3) that bear on many parts of the individuals' lives.

(When those experiences are not viewed as inputs alone, the earlier-mentioned "effects," that is, the feelings/emotions, can be considered later aspects of the given experiences themselves, not exterior to them. In this substantively and temporally expanded framework, the experiences, in toto, are thus viewed as sequences of events *and* reactions [effects]: Structurally, they are considered inputs and outputs [I&Os] jointly; and, in any given individual, these I&Os become associated with each other and, in that respect, consolidated functionally. "Expanded framework" is also reflected in the fact that even the individuals' *prior* experiences—those which then became the earlier-mentioned inputs—were I&O composites. That is, they themselves included and partly reflected still-earlier feelings and emotions, namely, reactions or effects that had been triggered and which were in that sense outputs.)

The above "frustrations, worries," and so on, usually differ to a large degree from identically named feelings and emotions that almost all adolescents sometimes experience in connection with relatively *immediate* personal matters and interpersonal interactions which are their—the feelings', and so forth—main generators and triggers. For one thing, the latter feelings/emotions, compared to the above, are more likely to be short-lived and less likely to have negative or portentous implications of a large-scale nature. (The earlier-mentioned feelings/emotions are the more unusual or uncommon ones, say, in terms of their main underlying dynamics. They will be called Type I in order to distinguish them from the more commonly occurring ones: Type II.) (Besides being fairly common *across* most youths, the "relatively immediate . . . matters and . . . interactions"—input experiences—are not infrequent *within* any given individual. In these respects, not only the feelings and emotions but their immediately preceding triggers [input experiences] are qualitatively and quantitatively "usual" in the sense of common or typical. At any rate, they do not mainly reflect major, usually long-standing needs that are largely unmet.)

It might be kept in mind that Type I feelings/emotions, for example, those at level one such as frustration, self-doubt, and anger, do not *invariably* have a substantial negative impact, let alone a major one. Nevertheless, as already indicated, those feelings/emotions often do negatively affect the youths, and they do so in a broad range of areas. Whether it is substantial or major, such impact is more likely to occur not just when, for instance, (1) the intensity of those feelings/emotions ("reactions") is considerable, but, more particularly, (2) if and when such level one reactions evolve to level *two* (whatever their intensity had been), and, still further, (3) if—once that level is reached—events transpire that help generate level three. At any rate, negative impacts can occur in connection with (1) through (3) not only with respect to delinquency but in areas separate from it. In addition, the chances of *serious, continued, and/or nonsporadic* delinquent activities, of substantial delinquent adjustment overall, and of sizable impact on social-psychological growth and development each increase considerably if level three is reached and maintained. (Cf. point E of this appendix.)

7. Level three involves the individuals' ways of coping with their first and especially second level experiences/reactions (E/Rs). As described later, these E/Rs usually predate, or else only moderately overlap, the establishment of relatively *firm* patterns of delinquency; and, of course, they reflect various difficulties/problems, needs, desires, fears, and so on, that helped generate, trigger, and sustain them (the E/Rs).

THE A/R CYCLE, LONG-STANDING DIFFICULTIES, AND MOTIVATION

The A/R Cycle and Unmet Emotional Needs: General Considerations

Despite the immediate and even longer-term relief and gratifications obtained via this action/reaction (a/r) cycle, many of the youths' long-standing needs for emotional security remain largely unmet. Partly for this reason and partly because the a/r cycle soon becomes somewhat self-reinforcing, this cycle does not eventually fade away on its own or even greatly diminish. More specifically, regarding the first reason, the cycle continues because the youths' unmet security needs still exert substantial force and those individuals have a drive to address them—even though they do not think of them in terms of "unmet security needs," per se. Concerning the second reason, the cycle continues because it provides significant immediate gains—relief and gratifications—*even though* long-standing needs remain unmet.

Positive or Potentially Positive Developments

Given this backdrop, three related developments might be noted: First, when various anxieties and feelings of overall unhappiness are at least being *reduced* via the a/r cycle, this, by itself, frequently helps the present youths *free up or "turn on" certain energies, interests, and motivations* that have been unavailable to them or withheld by them mainly for emotional reasons. This release occurs even though the individuals' long-standing needs—now somewhat reduced—are still largely unmet. Second, depending on which particular interests, and so on, are involved, on how they are directed and sustained once released, and on the overall external situation (e.g., no major new pres-

sures are occurring), that first development can soon set the stage for *improved everyday functioning (IEF)* in given areas, and can even actively lead toward it. Third, this improvement, in turn, can contribute to the *further reduction or alleviation of long-standing, unmet needs,* and to *potentially better long-term adaptation;* at least, the second development—IEF—can lay important groundwork for near-term and/or later progress in those regards. It can do so, for example, by (1) helping the youths feel increased confidence *in* some of their abilities, or *that* they have abilities, by (2) helping them feel somewhat more acceptable to selected individuals (even peers and/or others *apart* from risky-behavior contexts), and by (3) therein decreasing their routine defensiveness regarding various tasks and individuals, or at least increasing their interest in them.

Nevertheless, although the stage is set for the second and third developments, that is, for "improved everyday functioning" and for "further reduction . . . ," these often do *not* occur; and when they *do* materialize at this point, they are frequently small and/or short-lived. Such outcomes occur mainly because the same *negative* or problem-related process (specified next) that helped generate and trigger the earlier-mentioned series of *positive* or potentially positive developments not only remains in force while those three developments are first emerging and sometimes even after they are well underway, but because it substantially opposes, weakens, or unravels them. The process in question is the overall action/reaction cycle; and here, we will emphasize its risky activities, attitudes, and stances (AASs).

Negative Effects of AASs (Activities, Attitudes, and Stances)

More specifically, these risky, trouble-related activities/attitudes/stances often generate—by their very nature—various types and degrees of *difficulty* for those individuals, particularly with adults or the law. (As indicated earlier, these AASs do so in conjunction with the related peer attention/approval that subsequently contributes to the youths' near-term relief/gratifications, that is, to those individuals' felt gains or emotional boosts.) In turn, those external difficulties, with their frequent social/personal complications and repercussions, often make it hard for these youths to simultaneously do either or both of the following: (a) maintain the earlier-mentioned energy release and (b) advance, or want to advance, the given interests and motivations. In short, they make it hard to support and/or promote even the *first* of the three positive developments, not to mention the second, that is, given areas of subsequently improved everyday functioning. At any rate, the AASs and difficulties in question not only oppose and often constrict the given energy release in the first place; instead, they frequently retard, sidetrack, dilute, diminish, block, and/or entirely dismantle various everyday *gains—interpersonal and/or practical gains or nascent gains*. This applies to the potential longer-term benefits as well, that is, to the third development. In effect, then, the present "boosts"—the *peer-based emotional gains*—are often intertwined with various external difficulties. Because of the latter, the three positive developments are often forestalled, hampered, or undone. In this regard, the earlier-mentioned gain in self-confidence and in the feeling of being somewhat more acceptable to others—here called a "confidence and self-image boost," and originally associated with improved everyday functioning—may itself hardly evolve, or survive.

A Selected Implication for Intervention

One implication of this overall situation might be mentioned, one that may not always be readily drawn or perhaps self-evident: Intervention programs might often be in a better position than otherwise if they could start focusing on the present youths—the B-criticals—(1) *soon after* these individuals have received their peer-based emotional gains but (2) *before* those youths become overly dependent upon,

or otherwise bound to, the peers in question (or, more broadly, before they become bound to the action/reaction cycle itself—of which those peers, and the AASs, are integral parts).

(In general, the emotional gains ["boosts"] that relate directly to *peer approval* per se, and, thus, to the risky activities themselves, occur either prior to the programs or else—quite often—during their early stages, and in spite of their efforts. [Despite important similarities regarding positive emotional tone, these boosts, as implied, are substantively distinguishable from the "confidence and self-image boost" that is often and especially linked with the second positive development, that is, with improved everyday functioning.] At any rate, the preprogram and even early-program occurrence of peer-based emotional boosts is either entirely or largely beyond the intervention programs' control. Moreover, irrespective of when those boosts were to occur or begin, they would not be intentionally supported or otherwise reinforced by those programs. [Here, too, these peer-based boosts can be distinguished from the "confidence and self-image boost" or gain—which is linked mainly and most directly to IEF, and involves prosocial functioning: The latter boost *would* be programmatically supported.] More precisely, the peer-based emotional gains would not be supported in connection with their invariably related, *risky AASs,* since doing so could directly or indirectly reinforce the AASs themselves. Nevertheless, those emotional gains would *themselves* be utilized by given programs if, and insofar as, the gains were separated from those AASs.)

Utilization of peer-based emotional gains "if [they are] separated from those AASs" would occur in the context of the (1)–(2) focusing sequence mentioned earlier. This "*soon after . . . [but] before*" strategy is analogous to that in which a given planet—say, Jupiter [analogue: *the peers*—those who approve of given AASs and thereby reinforce them)—is used to provide a "gravity assist" (boost) to a spacecraft (analogue: *the youths*). That is, the planet's literal pull or attraction (analogue: *the peers' ability to reinforce and thereby boost*) is used to accelerate the approaching craft in order to give it the added momentum it will need to help it proceed with its larger journey—*past* the planet (analogue: *to prosocial contexts*). The critical event, of course, involves steering the craft away from the planet's (the peers') vicinity and attraction at just the right moment, that is, window of opportunity. This window occurs shortly after the craft has received its useful or optimal "boost" (analogue: *a sizable self-approval or self-acceptance boost*)—that is, has received a substantial acceleration *toward* the planet— but before it can become locked into a permanent orbit *around* it, or can even plunge directly into it (analogue: *become highly dependent upon, or even "done in by," given peers*). (With a spacecraft, the acceleration would have to involve the *needed* amount or more, not just a helpful but nonetheless possibly insufficient one. Acceleration, which would be caused by the planet's pull, would, as indicated, be used to boost the craft *away* from the planet—but now with a higher speed than it had when it first reached the planet's vicinity.)

Long-Standing Difficulties
LSDs and Everyday Functioning
The earlier-mentioned implication regarding intervention strategies applies irrespective of the following points concerning the youths' "everyday functioning."

A. With some B-criticals who manifest little or no improvement in everyday functioning, this situation does not mainly result from *AAS-generated difficulties,* that is, difficulties and repercussions springing from risky/trouble-related activities, attitudes, and/or stances. Instead, it is chiefly due to their having *long-standing difficulties (LSDs)* whose collective strength or pressure—"force"—is well above average for the total group of nonimproved B-criticals. These LSDs include family-, personal-, and/or environment-centered problems and challenges. Because their cumulative force is so large, these difficulties are hard to entirely or even largely suppress; as a result, they are usually active rather than fairly quiescent or largely held in abeyance. In addition, these long-standing difficulties are expressed in many contexts, not just a few; and their overall impact on the improvement of everyday functioning is usually considerable rather than slight or moderate. Relative quiescence, frequent "abeyance," and moderate influence on improvement are more characteristic of, or at least more common in, LSDs whose strength is average or less.[1]

(In many contexts, the LSDs' force operates as "momentum" or push; for example, it opposes or clashes with given factors, changes, or conditions, and it thereby actively disrupts or eliminates. In many other contexts these difficulties operate more as "inertia" or weight—stonewalling, forestalling, or otherwise impeding, but not necessarily dismantling or destroying. In both respects, however, the force is active and operative in the sense of having actual influence or impact on the youths' everyday adjustment—here, in particular, on its improvement or lack thereof. ["Well above average," "marked strength," and "unusually strong" are synonymous, as are "strength," "pressure," and "force."])

Often, the marked, collective strength of these long-standing difficulties entirely *predates* these B-criticals' AASs and, of course, the difficulties that those risky activities generate with adults, with the law, and in other respects. In this circumstance, it is these long-standing difficulties rather than the AAS-generated ones that can be the main or sole source of interference with the earlier-mentioned improvement in the youths' everyday functioning, not to mention interference with the functioning itself. However, even when some of that collective (overall) strength first develops or perhaps expands soon *after* those AAS-generated difficulties begin, *most* of that overall strength may still have preceded the AAS-generated difficulties and repercussions. (In this second case, the above strength may develop or expand because, for example, those AAS difficulties have either aroused or exacerbated certain already strong LSDs. For instance, the youths' parents, with whom relations may have long been poor, may have become agitated, oppositional, and/or increasingly rejecting when they learned about those individuals' risky or increasingly risky activities and of resulting encounters with school officials, with the law, and so on.) At any rate, the long-standing difficulties, whose collective strength is often well above average long before the AAS-generated difficulties begin and then *increase* those LSDs (not just add *to* them), can—even in this second case—be the main factor that blocks the occurrence of improved everyday functioning (IEF) or that substantially limits its scope, strength, and/or overall stability.

(Two items before continuing. [1] As implied earlier, when *average-strength* LSDs dominate, *AAS-generated* difficulties are usually the main blocking or limiting factor with respect to IEF. This applies whether or not the long-standing difficulties entirely precede the AAS-generated one. [2] With the *overall* group of B-criticals, not just those discussed here in point A, even *average*-strength LSDs are often strong in absolute terms. This is the case even though—as before—the overall influence of such LSDs on improved everyday functioning is usually less than that of AAS-generated difficulties.)

B. As indicated in A, the unusually strong, long-standing difficulties can curtail or eliminate the improved everyday functioning. They can do so by countering, weakening, or entirely undoing various effects that the earlier-mentioned, *peer-based emotional gains* have or would otherwise have in connection with generating and reinforcing that improvement. (The focus, here, is still on the B-criticals discussed in point A—those who "manifest little or no improvement in everyday functioning, . . . chiefly due to their having [well-above-average LSDs].") That is, regarding this improved or potentially improved functioning, the countering or weakening force—in this respect, the "negative" force—that is exerted collectively by those long-standing difficulties can be larger than the functionally opposite force that is released and promoted by those youths' emotional gains. As a result, the negative force can overcome, limit, or vitiate its opposite—the latter being the one with generative or supportive effects ("positive" effects) in connection with improved everyday functioning.

As will be recalled, the peer-based emotional gains are ordinarily accompanied by a reduction or alleviation of at least some long-standing difficulties. Following that reduction there is often a release of energies, interests, and motivations that can set the stage for improved functioning even when those interests and motivations coexist with risky activities, attitudes, and stances. With the present B-criticals, however, the overall strength of the long-standing difficulties (LSDs) is so large to begin with—namely, "well above average"— that considerable strength still exists even after the reduction/alleviation which accompanies those emotional gains. This remaining LSD strength is large enough to still keep much of those youths' energies bound and many of their interests as well as motivations withheld. At any rate, the *release* of energy/interest/ motivation that is associated with the youths'

emotional gains is less—often substantially less—than it would have been if the long-standing difficulties were smaller to begin with, or, in any event, if they had been *largely* reduced. Because of that lesser release, the degree of improvement in everyday functioning is itself less, as is the chance that such improvement will occur in the first place.

More specifically, because the overall strength of the long-standing difficulties is so large at the outset, the youths' individual LSDs (or parts thereof) that remain *un*reduced after the earlier-mentioned reduction/alleviation takes place are still considerably larger, that is, stronger, than the youths' *other* individual LSDs (or some of their parts). That is, they are larger/stronger than the LSDs (or their parts) which have been *reduced*. Under this circumstance—especially when the individual LSDs are aggregated and considered collectively, as an interacting whole—the energies, interests, and/or motivations that are *released* remain considerably less than those which are not. This situation, in turn, is reflected in the reduced level and likelihood of improved everyday functioning. In sum, even after various long-standing difficulties or parts thereof have been reduced, those which remain (viz., the "unreduced" LSDs, etc.) are usually strong enough— collectively—to still curtail much of the energy, interest, and motivation that exists. That energy continues to be bound up by the youths, or otherwise withheld by them. (All this is independent of the fact that even the *reduced*—not eliminated—LSDs can themselves help curtail some of that energy, interest, and motivation.)

Given this situation, and notwithstanding the fact that even though the emotional gains often lead to important areas of improvement (e.g., important regarding everyday adjustment), these improvements, collectively, do not often constitute large, let alone marked, changes and gains in *overall*, everyday functioning. Nor do they usually lead to them.[2]

LSDs and Movement toward the Future

To further elaborate, *tensions, frustrations, and anxieties (TFAs)* that are expressions and extensions of the still-remaining LSDs are among the main forces that retard or otherwise interfere with the emergence of various improvements.[3] Moreover, regarding the improvements that *do* emerge, those continued tensions, and so on, often make it difficult for these to then develop or further develop in certain important respects, for instance, to substantially stabilize and/or expand (individually), to functionally connect with each other and then consolidate (collectively) as well as gain momentum, and to otherwise grow stronger and potentially more influential. For this reason, among others, those tensions, frustrations, and anxieties, and the still-remaining LSDs with which they closely connect, can make it hard for the youths to move forward substantially, especially based on such individual and collective improvements. This is the case even though the present TFAs and long-standing difficulties are less than had originally existed (since some LSDs and their related TFAs were reduced), thereby making such movement at least easier and more likely than it would otherwise have been. (Since the tensions/frustrations/anxieties are major expressions and aspects of those difficulties themselves, only the latter—the LSDs—need now be focused on as such.)

More precisely, the still-remaining LSDs—particularly the unreduced ones—can seriously interfere with the individuals' substantially moving ahead in ways that can promote their longer-term, that is, post-adolescence, future. At any rate, those difficulties can markedly interfere with early and—no less—with subsequent movement in that direction; they can even block the latter movement for long periods of time, not just retard or weaken it briefly. Whether the interference centers on early or subsequent movement, the impact of those LSDs on that longer-term adjustment can be even larger if the individuals in question are no more than moderately *motivated* to seriously move in that direction. ("Longer-term" and "long-term" are equivalent, here.) This level of motivation is very common, from an early point on. Motivation, and two types of long-standing difficulties, are discussed shortly, under "Interactions between Long-Standing Difficulties and Motivation."

Long-standing difficulties can have a negative—interfering—effect on the youths' long-term adjustment even while the earlier-mentioned improvements are playing a key role in helping those individuals stay afloat or barely afloat in terms of meeting *immediate and near-term* social expectations and requirements.[4] Nevertheless, despite this near-term adjustment, the above interference—interference with the emergence and/or further development of various improvements—often results in those youths falling farther and far-

ther behind most other adolescents with respect to overall, *longer-term* social adjustment and related personal growth.[5] This is especially, but not only, the case when that LSD-based interference is combined with the individuals' lukewarm motivation.

Moreover, once these youths fall substantially behind with regard to long-term social adjustment and related growth, they often become increasingly vulnerable to added and unexpected social pressures and challenges of a *here-and-now* nature, not just those bearing on longer-term adjustment. This occurs despite the earlier-mentioned areas of improvement, even though these "positives" (e.g., new or stronger abilities, and new or better information) generally slow the process and soften the negative effects. At any rate, the youths' overall difficulties or problems sometimes escalate at that point, and, in a sense, seem to "pile on" or to "close in on" those individuals. This situation, in turn, often further arouses and reinforces the youths' interest in risky activities and in related, near-term relief as well as gratifications. (This concludes point B.)

Points A and B apply irrespective of the following circumstances and developments: (1) Even when long-standing difficulties are already well above average in strength and in level of activity, they can grow yet *stronger* and can become further activated or aroused. (2) Even if the youths' LSDs have been *reduced* in strength instead of having grown stronger, they can later *return* to their prereduction level. Each development—"grow . . . stronger" and "later *return*"—may center on self, family, school, and so on; it is particularly likely to begin during or soon after actual crises, or during impending crises and otherwise increasing tensions. Whatever its main context, such as family or school, each development can occur even if areas or pockets of improved functioning have already emerged in connection with that same context, and with others as well.

Development (2)—"later *return*" to the higher level of long-standing difficulties—often counterbalances or unravels that improved functioning. More specifically, it frequently ends up neutralizing or even undoing advances that had become emotionally and otherwise possible largely because those LSDs had been substantially reduced.[6] Both (1) and (2) are often generated and triggered by interactions between the youths' *un*reduced LSDs (plus their reduced but not eliminated LSDs), on the one hand, and their risky activities, on the other—with individuals such as adults and peers generally playing important parts in this process. More specifically, developments (1) and (2) are usually generated and triggered by crises and tensions that result from those interactions; and both developments can occur even if various areas of improved functioning or adjustment have begun to stabilize somewhat (individually) and to consolidate as well (collectively).

Thus, crises, growing tensions, and their related LSDs can often have large effects on the present youths' adjustment. For instance, they can seriously weaken and even functionally silence or eradicate emotional, cognitive, and other strengths these individuals have developed, ones they may have utilized in various contexts. These effects can often last not just for days or weeks, but for several months or more. During any such period, further complications and difficulties may arise that might not have otherwise emerged, or whose scope and impact might well have been less even if they had arisen. (All this is apart from the *gains* that can eventually result from given crises, under various conditions.)

Interactions between Long-Standing Difficulties and Motivation

Within limits, (A) high levels of long-standing difficulties are often accompanied by *low to moderate* degrees of motivation to seriously move in a future-oriented direction, and the former—the LSDs—are partly responsible for that motivation. Also within limits, (B) lower and lowered (cf. "reduced") levels of LSD are often accompanied by *higher and increased* motivation, and they are partly responsible for them.[7] Given part A of that overall—"AB"—relationship, and given that those "high levels of [LSD]" characterize the present B-criticals, these two factors, in combination, largely account for the fact that "no more than moderat[e]" motivation (M) to seriously address long-term, largely prosocial adjustment issues is very common among these individuals, at the developmental points under consideration.

In both parts of that AB relationship (basically: M = inverse (f) LSD), the *long-standing difficulties* are the determining or controlling force, whereas—within limits (see point 3, below)—level of "*motivation . . . , to seriously address*" is mainly the resultant, that is, the product. However, under certain conditions—

particularly when the youths have established a considerably stronger social and/or personal position for themselves and have substantial motivation "to seriously address . . ."—the emphasis can shift: That same motivation regarding future adjustment can increasingly *affect* the individuals' long-standing difficulties; and, beginning at some point, it can usually have more impact on those difficulties than the latter have on it. In that respect, the individuals' *motivation* can now function as the more active force or the main immediate input, whereas—within limits of its own—the *level of LSD* can mainly become the resultant or output. (Here: inverse of LSD = (f) M.) In particular, the youths' motivation can now help these individuals reduce or better contain various long-standing difficulties, or, at least, some of their effects.

Three points before continuing:

1. As indicated, that shift in emphasis from the AB relationship to what is called the "present" one requires a substantial degree of motivation, at least. This motivation, the object of which is to "seriously address long-term . . . adjustment issues," mainly reflects, and subsequently begins to accompany, new types and/or degrees of satisfaction and relief that those youths experience in connection with their "stronger social and/or personal position." As such, it is not largely based on the relief and gratifications associated with these individuals' *risky/trouble-related activities*. In this respect it differs from the motivation that is involved in, and helps reinforce, the individuals' earlier-mentioned, already existing, *action/reaction cycle*—of which those AASs are an integral part.[8]

2. In both the AB relationship and the present one—and, thus, in the shift of emphasis from the former to the latter—long-term-adjustment issues occupy center stage; that is, as indicated in point 1, the youths' motivation relates to them, in particular. To be sure, an identical type of shift from an AB relationship to a present one, that is, from one involving LSD-based dominance to one centering on motivation-based dominance, can occur in connection with the individuals' more *immediate* adjustment as well. That is, motivation which focuses on *here-and-now* issues, yet whose content does not

center on the a/r cycle, can itself grow stronger and can eventually reduce or better contain—can, in that sense, itself dominate—the long-standing difficulties. (In reality, it would usually do so not by itself but in conjunction with *long-term* motivation that might be active and substantial at the time.) Nevertheless, for present purposes, the remainder of this discussion need only focus on the long-term rather than here-and-now aspect and motivation, as it has thus far.

3. Here, "within limits" refers to any range of values that is other than full; for example, it might extend from "moderately low," on one end, to "sizable," on the other, but not extend outside either one. Thus, for instance, in an AB relationship, long-standing difficulties, as inputs, may affect (substantially or at all) a large portion of the motivation spectrum; yet they may rarely, if ever, so affect that spectrum's full or virtually full range—namely, from "absent or very low," on one end, to "marked or extremely high," on the other.

The earlier-mentioned shift from the AB relationship to that in which long-standing difficulties are dominated or partly controlled by the individuals' long-term motivation is often a major step or development in B-criticals' lives, as in those of others. It is major despite the following: (1) Rather than being a sudden event, and, in that respect, a "breakthrough," the shift is almost always preceded by back-and-forth fluctuations between those LSDs, on the one hand, and that motivation factor, on the other, as to which one dominates the other. (2) Even *after* it occurs, the shift is not an all-or-none matter; that is, the domination is never total. (3) Even when the M-factor eventually comes to dominate the LSDs most of the time, a rapid and other-than-transitory return to LSD dominance always remains a nonremote possibility under conditions of major, unexpected, or unusual stress. Also, the *initial* attainment of M-dominance, in particular, or even of M/LSD parity, is almost always a difficult, "bootstrap" operation for B-criticals. This applies especially, but not only, when (as during the time period under consideration) the youths lack assistance that might be provided by relevant correctional or other intervention, and/or by effective support systems in general. If anything, this difficulty

increases, not decreases, the significance of that shift.

In sum, the youths' present motivation, provided it is sizable and that certain other conditions exist, can help reduce or better contain various long-standing difficulties and/or their effects. (This reduction, etc. goes beyond simply ignoring or sidestepping those difficulties and their effects, even though it often includes it.) In such respects, the youths can dominate or partly control those LSDs, and/or their effects, rather than have certain important feelings and activities dominated—often markedly dominated—*by* them. This shift can occur even though the difficulties in question do continue to have an other-than-minor negative effect, for instance, a dampening effect, on the individuals' level of motivation to seriously address long-term adjustment issues. More broadly, the shift can and does occur even though the youths' difficulties and motivations interact with each other, and substantially influence each other, before, during, and after that shift; and they often do so simultaneously.

Type 1 and 2 LSDs—and "Breathing Room"

This discussion has centered on two generally distinguishable types of long-standing difficulties: ones that had been *moderately or considerably reduced* ("type 1") and ones that had *not been reduced or were hardly reduced,* and which thus constituted the harder-core LSDs ("type 2"). These types were part of what had been a broader, original group—a "total group"—of LSDs. Within this total, some difficulties had been essentially resolved, mooted, or otherwise eliminated as significant factors in the youths' recent months or years, through various means and circumstances (e.g., some youths' external situation had changed). Together, types 1 and 2 constituted all *remaining* difficulties in that total group; that is, they comprised the LSDs which had not been eliminated, even though some had been *reduced.*

Regarding the *type 1* LSDs (whether individually or collectively), these and/or their effects are first reduced or alleviated partly via (a) the *relief and/or gratifications associated with the action/reaction cycle,* and partly due to (b) *satisfactions associated with here-and-now (ongoing), prosocial activities* that coexist with (a). Later, they are alleviated, contained, partly sidestepped, or otherwise reduced when the individuals' (c) *future-oriented motivation* enters the picture and helps lead to changes that contribute to those results. This (c)-generated reduction of type 1 LSDs is over and beyond that produced by (a) and (b), even though one or both of the latter often help pave the way for (c). At any rate, (a) and (b) together, then followed by (c), is the typical sequence, whether or not the former two contribute little or much. (Future-oriented motivation is an integral part of the youths' longer-term adjustment efforts, not of their a/r cycle, and so on.)

(Three details before continuing: First, conditions (a) and (b) temporally overlap each other; and, during the overall time span under consideration, specific gratifications, and so forth, that are associated with those conditions are often other than sparse. Second, the (a)/(b) coexistence is usually awkward and unsteady, mainly due to inconsistencies and/or discordance between the two. Third, the "relief" component of condition (a), above, may, for example, involve the countering of anticipated rejection by peers. Such countering, when largely successful, sometimes helps relieve related aspects of the youths' long-standing difficulties.)

Cross-sectionally and through time, the extent and rate of the (c)-generated reduction of long-standing difficulties are limited partly by the continued influence of the type 1 LSDs themselves. More specifically, these aspects of the reduction are constrained by the influence of difficulties that remain *active* even though they have been *reduced* by any one or more of the above conditions, such as (a). No less important, the (c)-generated reduction is limited in those respects by the fact that the present individuals, like most other prospective multiple offenders, often have sizable reservations about trying to seriously move forward, in the first place. The youths maintain these reservations (1) despite various gratifications which they believe or implicitly assume are part of such movement and of its related involvements or resulting roles, and (2) irrespective of gratifications they may have actually, albeit briefly and only partially, *experienced,* not just anticipated or assumed. Together with their effects, these reservations—and the youths' overall ambivalence (discussed elsewhere)—also pertain to the following LSDs.

Concerning *type 2 LSDs* (again individually and collectively), these, and their main effects, are usually unreduced or only slightly reduced in power and scope by condition (a), above. When present, conditions (b) and/or (c) reduce those long-standing difficulties and/or effects more than does (a); yet even then, the reductions are seldom more than moderate, albeit still important.[9] Whether via (a), (b), or (c), or all three combined, the reduction of type 2 difficulties would seldom occur if these long-standing difficulties were highly active and forceful all or almost all of the time. What makes those reductions other than rare—makes them even possible—is the following (complementary and supplementary factors are omitted): Despite those LSDs' "harder-core" nature, they, or at least many of them, exert a *low to moderate* level of force often enough to allow the youths what might be called "breathing room." At any rate the LSDs, whether individually or in various combinations, are sufficiently and *sufficiently often* contained, or in abeyance; they are not "highly active and forceful" a high percentage of the time.

Being "allow[ed]" that breathing room means the youths are left with enough energy, emotional opportunities, and external opportunities or literal freedom of action—enough, for example, so that they can try to move forward if they wish. Absent such room or space, these individuals, like many or most others, would seldom sustain the level of motivation needed to keep moving forward, or—often—to even seriously keep trying. Here, and in the following, "moving forward" combines process, progress, and goal. Basically, it means engaging in activities, acquiring practical and interpersonal knowledge and skills, developing personal strengths, and so on, that can ordinarily help—or does help—lead to a constructive later-adolescent adjustment and, especially, to a similar post-adolescence.[10]

Commonalities and Interactions across Long-Range and Here-and-Now Issues

The youths' attempts to *move forward* regarding long-range issues have some content similarities to their efforts to address everyday, that is, *here-and-now,* issues, such as near-term expectations, challenges, and requirements. Some temporal overlap exists between those two types or areas of effort, as well. Partly because of this substantive and structural commonality, the earlier-mentioned breathing room is itself similar in various respects, across those two areas or contexts.

More specifically, the type and level of breathing room that is ordinarily available to youths in connection with their efforts to move forward in terms of addressing *long-range* issues (say, challenges), also exists with respect to various *near-term* issues; that is, it is found with here-and-now expectations, challenges, and requirements themselves. At least, considerable similarity and even some identity exists across the long-range and near-term contexts, regarding the nature of that breathing room.

(Substantive commonality exists not just in connection with long-range and near-term *efforts,* but with regard to the respective *outcomes* of those efforts, for example, regarding the youths' resulting progress in the former and latter areas. Specifically, long-range—that is, future-oriented—progress and closely related changes, when these indeed occur, often have some content similarity and identity to near-term changes, for instance, to results of the youths' efforts to address their here-and-now challenges, and so on. [The particular similarity that exists between long-range and near-term *progress*—and, for that matter, between long-range and near-term *efforts*—differs, of course, from the particular similarity/identity that exists in connection with *breathing room,* also across those long-range and near-term contexts.])

The similarity/identity that exists across those temporal contexts with respect to breathing room also partly reflects an often moderate to substantial *interdependence*—a give-and-take—between those two types or areas of effort. That is, it partly reflects an interaction or relationship, of significant but varying strength, between the existence and/or extent of the youths' *here-and-now* efforts (also, their resulting progress), on the one hand, and their *long-range* efforts (and—again—progress), on the other. Insofar as this relationship is causal, per se, the "here-and-now" area's influence on the "long-range" is usually stronger than the latter's is on the former. At any rate, efforts and outcomes within each area or context can influence those in the other.

Given the often sizable extent of the earlier-mentioned (1) content similarities and (2) interdependence and causal interactions, separately, and given the overall scope of conditions (1) and (2), together, the following applies: The similarity and partial identity that exists across the near-term and long-range contexts with regard to breathing room does

so even in spite of important content *differences* that exist across those same temporal contexts, and despite *often-far-from-strong* interactions, as well.

Breathing room is seldom extensive for the present youths, whether in the long-term context or in the here-and-now. In each situation its very existence largely reflects the fact that the youths are not faced with pressures and problems whose overall strength, frequency, and pace—that is, whose collective quantity and intensity—is enough to do the following, particularly the first: largely pre-empt, dilute, divert, or directly block those individuals' needed and otherwise obtainable *personal energy and attention,* and mostly block or otherwise disrupt the youths' actual, not just perceived, access to valuable *external resources and supports.* (Cf. factor #2 of the eight-factor sequence; also cf. secondary goals A_{2g} and B_{2g}—themselves in Chapter 25.)

Selected Motivations and Issues Involved in Modifying One's Life Situation

Whereas the "quantity and intensity" factor helps make forward movement even possible, that is, allows it to occur, one of the strong and common reasons the youths' actually *try* to move forward and to otherwise modify their life situation is their desire to reduce various tensions, frustrations, and anxieties associated with long-standing difficulties; these are TFAs that, unlike others, have *not* been largely contained or quiescent in recent months or years. That reason or incentive, and the following points, can apply to TFAs associated with *any* sizable difficulties, even those which are not long-standing and not of type 2. However, unless otherwise indicated, we will emphasize the long-standing and will specifically focus on type 2.

Often, the present youths implicitly assume that in order to improve their near-term as well as longer-range situation, or to at least reduce the unpleasantness associated with it, they will have to engage in and perhaps even center on *risky, trouble-related activities, attitudes, and stances* (AASs), including related adjustment patterns. However, most such youths also assume, or believe, that various *prosocial activities* can themselves contribute to those ends (even while helping to achieve yet others, especially those involving near-term satisfactions). For this reason, among others, those individuals usually then engage or further engage in the given activities, often even in parallel with certain trouble-related AASs. (Other such youths also engage in various prosocial activities, though with little or no interest in long-range goals.)

With given youths, those prosocial activities or efforts—especially efforts to move toward long-range goals—occur despite these individuals' ongoing, frequently *strong ambivalence* about so moving. More specifically, those activities occur—proportionately often (not in absolute numbers)—in the face of numerous reservations and mixed feelings about engaging in future-oriented activities that may result in changes they believe or implicitly assume might seriously clash with adjustment patterns they largely want to establish or maintain. Alternatively, though sometimes in addition, those prosocial activities or efforts may occur when, for various reasons, the individuals' ambivalence is temporarily *less focused, less salient, and/or less active than usual.* In either case, the youths' desire to reduce given tensions, frustrations, and anxieties, especially those stronger than average, is frequently part of the picture; it plays a large role in motivating them to modify various aspects of their lives. Other, more directly *positive* desires or incentives often contribute to that wish, as well.

This situation commonly sets the stage for certain binds (these do not center on the AAS-generated factor of "paying the price," mentioned earlier in Chapter 26): When the present individuals begin to reduce certain tensions, and so on, associated with long-standing difficulties—reduce them especially via prosocial activities/involvements—the changes that help bring about these reductions may, themselves, soon generate, arouse, or augment other tensions and concerns, namely, those which reflect the youths' ambivalence about *moving forward.* In response to this situation, most of the present individuals strike an ongoing balance—a running, shifting, often uncomfortable compromise, as it were—between the reduction of LSD tensions/frustrations/anxieties, on the one hand, and the generation/arousal/augmentation of future-oriented ones, on the other.

Negative Implications of Released and/or Intensified LSDs

A few closing points. Under conditions of unusual, unexpected, or otherwise major stress, it is especially the type 2 LSDs that—upon being triggered by such stress—sometimes become highly aroused or even exacerbated. More particularly, that stress may trigger either or both of the following: (1) a large-scale release of LSDs whose overt expression was previously *constrained* (CO); (2) an overall intensification, or perhaps an increased focusing, of LSDs that were already often *expressed (EX)*—and, in any event, were expressed more often, more fully, and more directly than the CO's.

(Prior to that triggering, CO's were ordinarily quiescent, held in abeyance, or otherwise constrained, to a moderate or larger degree. ["Ordinarily" emphasizes conditions of normal stress for the given youths.] Though thus constrained, these long-standing difficulties still retained much strength. Specifically, during that "prior" [pre-triggering] period, much of their strength existed as what might be considered "bound" or "stored"—thus, "potential," yet not entirely dormant—energy. During that same period, *EX's,* despite their frequency and level of *activity* and their readily apparent strength, themselves had some stored energy. However, this energy comprised a smaller portion of their total strength than did similar energy in the case of CO's.[11])

Once the earlier-mentioned release and/or intensification occurs, it can substantially weaken or block the individuals' near-term and future-oriented interests and efforts—together called "activities."[12] This disruption can occur especially if factors such as external support and assistance do not soon intervene to reduce or reverse the main triggering conditions—and related complications that subsequently help sustain or even worsen matters. Absent such factors, the given activities can be disrupted and even virtually eliminated, for long periods, whether the power of those released/intensified difficulties is exerted mainly as "momentum" or as "inertia."

At any rate, once the release/intensification of CO or EX difficulties occurs, the youths focus on personal stress more than before. Whether or not—as part of that focus—they also substantially increase their involvement in risky/trouble-related activities per se, these individuals soon give considerably *less* attention than before to the already-mentioned activities that can promote prosocial adjustment. At least, their attention in that respect may soon be less focused, largely *un*focused, regularly interrupted, and/or minimally sustained. For such reasons, those near-term and future-oriented interests and efforts may not develop solidly or very far.[13]

When the arousal or intensification of those long-standing difficulties is accompanied by *tensions, frustrations, and/or anxieties* already associated with given LSDs—and it often is—the disruption in question can be even larger than it might have been without those TFAs. As indicated, those *LSDs* are frequently, but not only, of the CO (constrained) type. As to the *TFAs,* these are ones that—in the pre-triggering period—were largely held in abeyance themselves (like the LSDs), or, in any event, had usually remained at fairly or barely manageable levels.

Finally, it might be noted that given types of feeling can help generate outcomes that greatly differ from each other in differing contexts. For instance, although some of the earlier-mentioned tensions had—in the *post-triggering* period—helped *disrupt* or further disrupt the youths' efforts and some of their already-achieved advances, those and/or other tensions had—during the *pre-*triggering period—often helped provide an incentive for *making* some of those very same efforts and advances, that is, those which were later disrupted.[14] Basically, this difference in outcomes reflects the differences in meaning that those feelings had to the given individuals, across the respective contexts. At any rate, although the *specific* tensions differed from each other across those contexts—in this case, the post- and pre-triggering situations—they nevertheless were tensions in each instance. This and the preceding points apply even though more than one major triggering event or crisis can occur for any given youth, and whatever their causes may be.

Notes

1. In this discussion we will not focus on the effects of *recently generated* (yet not AAS-generated) difficulties as opposed to *long-standing* ones, or on major interactions between the former and the latter. We will simply emphasize whichever LSDs have been continued to the present (whatever their average activity level), regardless of whether they were substantially modified by any recently generated difficulties (RGDs) and irrespective of their possible

role in generating and significantly shaping those RGDs. When the recently generated difficulties do modify long-standing ones, they usually do not change those LSDs for the better—not, for example, in the sense of decreasing their strength by substantially altering their nature per se. RGDs do, however, sometimes dilute and otherwise weaken LSDs' impact by changing their manner and frequency of expression and by shifting the contexts in which they ordinarily appear. This is independent of the fact that a resurgence of *long-standing difficulties* frequently exacerbates the recently generated ones.

2. Despite their often limited but far from negligible strength and/or scope with regard to everyday functioning, the improvements in question are also important because they can constitute critical preconditions for *further* possible improvements—intermediate-term and longer. In this connection, those improvements may be necessary, or often necessary, though seldom sufficient by themselves.

3. The youths often recognize these tensions, frustrations, and anxieties *as such.*

4. Two points might be noted. First, in preventing the above expansion, stabilization, and overall strengthening of improvements that have emerged, the tensions, frustrations, and anxieties are, in effect, often supported by various *desires and interests* on the youths' part. Such desires and interests can divert attention from, or can otherwise dilute and weaken (definitely not strengthen), the improvements in everyday functioning that have already emerged. Moreover, they can do this on their own, even if the TFAs are temporarily below their usual strength. At any rate, the youths' conscious wishes and interests, not just the feelings (TFAs) in question, frequently play a significant role in preventing the earlier-mentioned strengthening. These wishes and interests are sometimes pointed and recent. Second, the following applies to tensions, frustrations, and anxieties that remain associated with the individuals' collective difficulties—particularly with (1) long-standing difficulties that are not largely quiescent or in abeyance, and even after (2) the earlier-mentioned reduction takes place in those LSDs: These tensions, frustrations, and

anxieties constitute forces—in this case, internal pressures—that help lead the present B-criticals to *repeat* their risky activities, and so on, and to sustain the action/reaction cycle as a whole. Since these forces center on a need and/or desire to avoid or reduce continued or anticipated *negative* feelings and experiences per se (such as upset, anger, and hassles), their focus and function differs from that of the stimuli—also stimuli to repeat those risky activities—which center on *positive* reinforcement. The latter stimuli are associated with the youths' already obtained, relief aspect of that cycle, and, especially, with related gratifications. As can be inferred from the first point, above, the pressures to repeat risky activities, and so on, themselves reflect various desires and interests, as well, not just TFAs.

5. As these individuals fall behind, they generally engage in fewer conventional activities, and, hence, they obtain less actual and potential reinforcement for *continued,* let alone increased, prosocial involvement. Though "falling . . . behind" usually starts out slowly and fairly steadily, and then generally continues that way, its pace sometimes quickens later on.

6. If the youths' stress has been major—and especially if also long-standing—considerable counterbalancing or unraveling can sometimes occur even if these individuals have continued to improve their everyday functioning in selected areas. Be this as it may, the longer this improved functioning has continued, the less likely it is to be entirely or even largely neutralized or undone (briefly or otherwise), even given considerable acute stress. Nevertheless, the possibility of sizable to marked neutralization or undoing always remains.

7. Here, "within limits" thus means that the correlation between level of LSD and degree of motivation, while substantial (albeit inverse), is far from perfect.

8. Ways in which, and conditions under which, correctional intervention can sometimes help youths achieve a "stronger . . . position" are described elsewhere in this book.

9. Reductions generated by condition (a) differ, of course, from those which may occur during certain *interventions,* in connection with the "*soon after . . .* [but] *before*" strategy. That strategy, it might be added, would usually have a broader, but not necessarily more important, impact on type 1 LSDs.

10. As part of this movement, and often as a precondition, the present individuals, like many others, would have to reduce or eliminate various dysfunctional or problem-centered relationships and adjustment patterns.

11. As can be inferred from these and earlier points, EX's, compared to CO's, more often exerted sizable influence on the youths' near-term and long-range efforts, during the several months or the year or so that preceded the stress-based triggering.

12. This development is not limited to activities that have been only slightly or moderately established, for instance, ones that only recently emerged and/or are no more than casually pursued.

13. With most such youths, this withdrawal of attention is not completely or almost wholly "forced"; for instance, it is not the result of their facing entirely irresistible pressures or of their having or perceiving few if any viable and desired alternatives. In particular, that withdrawal is not just due to the initial and continuing effects of major external stress, on the one hand, combined, say, with insufficient or nonexistent support, on the other—influential those these are. Instead, the withdrawal in question may constitute a retrenchment or relinquishment that the youths partly *prefer,* for example, one they may even increasingly desire, and, in any event, may either actively help bring about or passively allow to happen. (Once the major external stress occurs, such retrenchment or relinquishment is not rare.)

14. This type of change—from an "incentive" to a source of "disruption"—would most often occur with those tensions that, during the pre-triggering period, would require the most effort to keep at manageable levels. In this regard they could be considered the least easy or the most difficult, depending on the reference points in question.

43 SKILL DEFICITS AND EXPERIENTIAL VERSUS GENETIC FACTORS

Here, as elsewhere, "problems" mainly refers to the individuals' ongoing internal and/or external conflicts, pressures, and other related or resulting difficulties. Because of these problems, and often independent of other factors such as skill deficits (see below) and/or constricted social opportunities, the youths' overall adjustment is often shaky or unstable and it involves, in effect, an unsteady and sensitive balance; this applies despite the individuals' not infrequent surface calm. Given its major fault lines or overall weakness, this adjustment is susceptible to types and levels of stress or challenge that most nonoffenders can largely handle; more specifically, it can be substantially disrupted by that stress and challenge.

(This is the case especially, but not only, if the following applies with respect to adult [A]-based and societal/community [S/C]-based external supports, during the time period under consideration [note: these supports can be largely distinguished from social *opportunities* per se]: The A-based supports and the S/C-based (institutional/agency) supports—such as interpersonal, organizational, and/or structural supports, none of which are peer-based—are literally few in number, low in quality, unusually hard to access (whatever their number or quality), underutilized (for emotional reasons), and/or largely unreliable. Among other things, adequately utilized supports can often help individuals connect up with, and/or remain involved with, various available *opportunities,* even in the face of negative external pressures. These opportunities, in turn, can be support*ive.*)

Such instability, weakness, and resulting vulnerability can also reflect the individuals' interpersonal and practical skill deficits. Partly because of these shortcomings, though also due to the earlier-mentioned "problems," the youths' adjustment can be erratic and vulnerable—even despite these individuals' *strengths.* Whether these strengths are slight or substantial in number and/or degree, they temporally coexist with the shortcomings. However, like various *external supports,* they may often be functionally unavailable or otherwise underutilized.

Regarding those *deficits,* these mainly appear to be breakdowns, slowdowns, or impairments in learning and development. They largely originate in contexts or settings such as the social-structural, the interpersonal, and the familial, and they usually continue to reflect them and their specific inputs or lacks thereof during subsequent months or years. *Within* those contexts or settings, yet operating partly independent of them, these same deficits often reflect motivational and/or emotional factors as well, or instead. The contexts or settings, and these factors, can be thought of as "experiential" or E-factors, as can supplementary ones such as the situational and level-of-opportunity. Individually and collectively, they can be distinguished from G-factors, described below.

In this as in previous discussions involving deficits—specifically, interpersonal and practical skill deficits on the part of serious multiple offenders (SMOs)—emphasis is on ones that are usually *sizable* and generally *long-lasting.* These quantitative features apply to those deficits in an absolute as well as comparative sense; to elaborate on them, we need only focus on the comparative: On average, these deficits or shortcomings are larger in degree, broader in scope, and longer in duration among (1) *SMOs* than among (2) *nonoffenders* and (3) *offenders other than SMOs.* That is, in groups (2) and (3), respectively, skill deficits, when present at all (and some almost always are), are generally smaller or more moderate in those respects than they are within group (1). As such, most deficits that are present in groups (2) and (3) are more typical or common than the more sizable/long-lasting ones found in (1).[1] In that respect they comprise what can be viewed as the average or normal shortcomings—learning-and-development slowdowns, arrests, and so on—on the part of any given youths, for any particular age group.

Two supplementary points, before turning to G-factors.

1. The earlier-mentioned, average differences in *extent*—specifically, in degree, scope, and duration—exist even though there is some content overlap across the three youth groups. That is, those quantitative differences exist despite the areas of substantive identity or at least similarity that are present across the shortcomings found among SMOs, on the one hand, and the nonoffenders, and so on, on the other.

2. As can be seen in connection with certain E-factors listed previously, such as the "interpersonal and . . . motivational," successful learning and development (L&D) would commonly draw from adequate *external supports,* for example, those which are now low in number and/or largely unreliable. At any rate, such supports could help preclude various L&D deficits and they could reduce the degree, scope, and/or duration of others.

Only seldom do the presently emphasized skill deficits seem to mainly stem from and rely on *constitutional* or any similarly inborn factors—in effect, on built-in structures, forces, and/or strong dispositions. In particular, these "usually *sizable . . .*" deficits seldom seem to mainly originate in, and then largely continue to reflect, what are widely termed "genetic" or G-factors. This applies even to those G's whose activation and general manner of expression are viewed as largely contingent upon certain external stimuli.

Contingent G-factors, specified below, are commonly distinguished from a second set. The latter, largely *self-activating and self-*

directing G's, are usually considered intrinsically strong enough and otherwise self-sufficient and preprogrammed enough to be internally activated (released, set off) under most conditions, and to be subsequently expressed in much the same way across various settings. In contrast, *contingent* G's are generally regarded as factors whose likelihood of being activated and whose manner and extent of expression when they *are* triggered can vary considerably, depending mainly on the presence, quality, and/or degree of given external stimuli. Collectively, both types of G's can include factors such as the morphological, neurological, hormonal, and so on.

As implied, the preceding does not mean that *no* inherent or at least partially predetermined factors ("inputs") exist that can significantly help generate and maintain given skill deficits within any group of offenders or nonoffenders (including, that is, any *individuals* in those groups). Nor does it mean there are no such input differences *across* the differing youth groups—say, no average differences in those G-factors—that can significantly contribute to various *output differences* between one such group and another. ("Factors," "G-factors," and "inputs" are used synonymously.)

(Note that, for any given youth group, it is the *inputs*—here, the G-factors—that can help generate and otherwise determine the deficits for that particular group; and, if those inputs *differ* from one such group to the next, the resulting deficits—as direct or indirect products or outputs of those varied inputs—can themselves differ *across* those corresponding groups. Thus, it is the presumed *differences* in inputs from one group to another—not any one input itself—that can help determine observed differences in the various outputs. Here, these outputs refer to observed differences in deficits from one youth group to another, and they are called the "across-group output differences." As before, the groups under consideration are the SMO, on the one hand, and the nonoffender as well as the other-than-SMO offender, on the other—that is, groups (1), (2), and (3), respectively. Thus, in the present case, the across-group outcome differences are the differences in degree, scope, and/or duration of deficits, for group (1) as compared to groups (2) and (3), respectively.)

More particularly, then, the preceding does not mean there are no such general or specific physical, intellectual, energy-level, and/or reactivity-level inputs and differences in inputs, respectively, among youths collectively, that can significantly contribute to, that is, can help produce, such effects. (These effects or outcomes are the deficits and the differences in deficits—again respectively, and also correspondingly—within and across the specified groups.) Instead, it means that those built-in or largely built-in factors (G-factors), collectively, almost always appear to make much *smaller* contributions to the sizable, usually long-standing deficits under consideration than do the essentially experiential factors (E-factors), themselves collectively.[2] This point regarding the smaller contributions of G-factors pertains not just to the *deficits* that exist within any one youth group but also to the *differences* in those deficits, that is, the differences that exist across the given youth groups.[3] (For present purposes, it is not necessary to focus on any *within*-group differences in the deficits.) Also, like all other points in the appendix, this one applies to serious multiple offenders overall, not just to the B-youths within that group.

Notes

1. Besides their "more sizable/long-lasting" deficits, many group (1) youths have some moderate deficits themselves, that is, some "more typical" shortcomings. At the same time, some group (2) and (3) individuals have certain *above*-average deficits (AADs)—though they have fewer of them than do group (1) youths. Also, among (2)'s and (3)'s, the *ratio* of AADs to moderate deficits is lower than it is among (1)'s: For example, using purely hypothetical numbers to express this comparison since the exact ratios are unknown, there would be about *1* above-average deficit and *2* moderate ones per youth in the nonoffender, and so on, groups, as compared to roughly *3* AADs and *3* moderates per individual in the

SMO—thus, a ratio of about 1 to 1 among the latter.

2. Here, "collectively" simply means that the given deficits can be partly determined—influenced—by any two or more factors, acting as inputs; in this regard, a collective or joint input is functionally identical to a combined one. Such influence or effect—that is, output—can occur "simultaneously" or "successively." Simultaneous influence can be based on slight, considerable, *or* almost complete temporal overlap on the part of the respective input factors. Successive influence can itself be based on either partial or essentially complete temporal overlap; or else, as distinct from the simultaneous, it can reflect *no* such overlap. In addition, it can occur in terms of small, moderate, or large accumulation (incremental changes), for example, within or across early, middle, or later childhood. All of the above pertains to E-factors, as well.

3. Further, this point applies whether the G-factors are thought of as largely or even entirely self-activating and self-directing, on the one hand, or as mainly triggered by external stimuli, on the other—for example, by physical injury/abuse, or else by unusually heavy pressures. This pertains whether or not most such factors are viewed as having first been substantially activated during infancy, early childhood, or well afterward, and whether most E-factors are seen as first coming into play somewhat later, on average, than most G's. (Sometimes, certain external stimuli or conditions are viewed as *preventing* these potentially negative G-factors from being fully or even substantially actuated or impelled, whether or not during their usual time periods. In any event, some such stimuli exert their influence by acting as pressures; others, by providing support.)

44 FACTORS BEARING ON THE CRYSTALLIZATION OF THE ILLEGAL-BEHAVIOR PATTERN

The following points might be useful regarding the crystallization of the illegal-behavior pattern, especially with respect to its second contributing feature—particularly 2(b). This feature, like (1) itself, relates to the behaviors' perceived "sufficiency" with regard to generating various reliefs/satisfactions. These R/S's, in turn, help reinforce the behaviors themselves. To facilitate the presentation, we will discuss "sufficient reliability" separate from "sufficient worth."

General Considerations: Nature of Processes and Products

A. The youths' view that illegal-behavior inputs are sufficiently reliable is usually, and largely, a preconscious integration of accumulated, personal experiences with those inputs, on the one hand, and the reliefs/satisfactions (R/S's) that soon follow them, on the other. More specifically, this youth view, which usually involves an intermingling of perceptions and feelings, reflects the *connections* they make between those illegal behaviors (IB's) and the subsequent R/S's.[1] A selected, albeit key quantitative aspect of this input/output relationship will be described in C and D, below.

Two points before further proceeding.

1. Having the just-mentioned "feelings" about this relationship is comparable to having a "sense" about it, often one to which the youths have attached few words. Such feelings, and various unformulated or only vaguely or globally formulated impressions, are often principal and prominent features of implicit assumptions. Though often part of the im-

plicit, such feelings, and global as well as undifferentiated impressions, often accompany explicit beliefs as well, even though they are generally less pronounced in this case. All in all, they are present among, and are otherwise part of, preconscious and conscious processes—and products—alike. (The earlier-mentioned "youth view" is a *product,* even though it is subject to later change under various conditions.)

2. As discussed in C and D, below, one important "quantitative" aspect of the input/output relationship in question centers on whether the youths consider *illegal behavior* sufficiently *reliable* in the sense of helping to generate the R/S's often enough—more precisely, proportionately often enough. Separately, in E, an important "qualitative" aspect focuses mainly on whether these individuals consider the *R/S's* that are generated sufficiently *worthwhile.* In particular, it centers on these relief/satisfactions' "felt emotional significance." (In this connection it does not focus *mainly* on the pragmatic adjustments and the practical/social requirements often associated with instrumental utility, even though such utility, itself, often is emotionally significant to these youths. Thus, it does not center largely on the means-to-ends value of these R/S's in the largely pragmatic domain—heavily future-oriented or not.)

In short, two separable aspects of "sufficiency" will be distinguished, even though they interact with each other to a sizable degree, and in mutually enhancing ways:[2] These aspects are *input relia-*

bility and *output value or worth.* The former is discussed together with "sufficient reliability," the latter with "sufficient worth." "Overall sufficiency" includes both of these combined, and other, largely undiscussed factors as well.

At any rate, the present individuals, like most other serious multiple offenders, seldom develop the earlier-mentioned view regarding sufficient reliability mainly via conscious *reflection, calculation, comparison, interrelating,* and/or similar thought processes and analytic as well as synthetic efforts. This applies even when such processes are carried out in a fairly *un*systematic, *un*focused, global, and/or casual as well as sporadic way. Again, these and related conscious processes and efforts are—individually and collectively—seldom the *chief* overall contributors to the youths' view that illegal behavior is a sufficiently reliable generator of relief/satisfactions. This is in spite of the fact that at least one of those processes often *is* part of the picture (together with preconscious ones), albeit—even here—usually on a more global or "intuitive" than differentiated, delineated, and/or word-centered basis. It is also the case despite the fact that, when the given processes *are* in the picture, their contribution to the youths' view is often substantial.

B. When the integration process occurs preconsciously or largely so, this is not just because of emotional—dynamic—reasons; instead, it can, and commonly does, reflect ways in which *structural* factors are used, as well. (See Appendix 45 regarding structural factors and their relationship to others called *emotional/dynamic.*) Moreover, even when the emotional component or factor does play a particularly strong role, as is often the case, the youths' view in question, that is, their integration or product of the essentially preconscious process, can readily become conscious at times. In any event, the emotional component does not—say, by virtue of its very nature (though necessarily in the context of other factors as well)—invariably exert a strong or steady pressure which thereby often forces the integration process to occur outside consciousness. Nor does it preclude a resulting, preconscious integration, that is, product or view, from later becoming conscious. (As implied, the emotional/dynamic component, not just the structural one, is itself usually part of *conscious* processes as well. At any rate,

this factor does not invariably lead to *pre*conscious activities, let alone generate or otherwise involve such activities only.)

Sufficient Reliability
C. What some youths consider sufficiently reliable, in the sense of "occurring often enough," others may not. To briefly describe this reliability and to illustrate the nature of this across-youth variation, we will focus on a particular quantitative factor, namely, the percentage-of-relief/satisfaction experiences. Specifically, this will center on the percentage of certain inputs—certain illegal behaviors—that are believed or implicitly assumed to generate or otherwise lead to that R/S. (Though this factor usually makes a sizable contribution to the youths' view of reliability, that is, to their eventual, perceived and felt likelihood of considering their illegal behaviors reliable, it does not, by itself, ensure that such a view will occur. Sufficient reliability does, however, *allow* it to occur.)

As implied, in order for a perception and feeling of reliability to develop, some youths seem to want—in a sense, need—a higher likelihood of relief/satisfaction than do others. For one thing, they want or need this R/S to occur on a higher percentage of occasions. As discussed next, "occasions" is defined by a particular denominator or base, one that determines the maximum possible number of such R/S experiences, insofar as these can be considered psychologically discrete or relatively complete. (When this base is focused on, the terms "occasion" and "event" are synonymous. However, only the first such term, or else that of "activity," will generally be used.)

Any given percentage, such as 60 or 30, can be thought of as the direct result of a specified "numerator" (N) and "denominator" (D). In the present case, this denominator—the base—is the *number of illegal behaviors (activities)* that occur during a given time period, and the numerator is the *number of relief/satisfaction experiences* that occur during a partly or largely overlapping period which begins after the first such IB.

(As indicated earlier, the youths implicitly or explicitly regard particular R/S's as products of given illegal behaviors; that is, they consider them their results or *outputs.* It is these and only these outputs or products—namely, relief/satisfactions—that are involved here, and which, as such, constitute the numerator. As to the illegal behaviors—the inputs—these, analytically, constitute and therein determine the maximum number of occasions or activities in response to which those relief/satisfactions [the N's] can occur.[3] That is, the IB's, collectively, comprise the number of inputs that *can* lead to the given outputs [these being the R/S's, i.e., the numerators or N's]—themselves collectively. Thus, the illegal behaviors—the inputs, that is, the base or D's—jointly set the analytic stage for what is quantitatively possible by way of directly related outputs [N's]. It is in this context that "percentage" refers to the ratio of N's to D's.[4])

The higher the N/D ratio—say, *two N's* (relief/satisfaction experiences) rather than *one* for every *three D's* (illegal behavior activities)—the higher, as indicated, is the percentage of those numerator (R/S) experiences. Some youths, in effect, require a ratio such as the former—two outputs for every three inputs—to help them consider those inputs reliable generators of the outputs. In contrast, other youths generally require, or at least accept, the one-versus-three range.[5] Again, satisfactory ratios do not, by themselves, guarantee that the youths *will* consider the illegal behaviors sufficiently reliable, let alone sufficient overall. (As indicated, "overall" involves not just the quantitative but the qualitative.) Nevertheless, those ratios are required as minimums, or preconditions, even for quantitative sufficiency alone.

D. Even if *few* illegal behaviors and few corresponding reliefs/satisfactions occur during a period of several months or more following the first such inputs, this, by itself, need not prevent the youths from considering those behaviors reliable enough with respect to generating such R/Ss. More precisely, the individuals may still come to view the IB's as sufficient in this regard, provided they are satisfied with the earlier-mentioned *ratio* of numerator to denominator, that is, are at least accepting or otherwise fairly comfortable with that relationship between reliefs/satisfactions and illegal behaviors. At any rate, small absolute numbers need not, by themselves, prevent the youths from considering those behaviors an adequate or better generator, since the dominant consideration is the *relationship*—as reflected in the ratio—that exists between the number of R/Ss and that of IBs.

Examples of such small but possibly acceptable, interrelated numbers—hence, ratios—are: 1 relief/satisfaction experience to 2 illegal behavior activities; 2 R/Ss to 2 IBs; 1 to 3; and 2 to 3—in each case, during the given time span.[6]

As implied, for the IB-generated reliefs/satisfactions to have considerable felt relevance to various needs, issues, and/or desires that behavior has to generate, or seem likely to generate, the given R/S's within a time frame with which the youths are able and largely willing to deal. In most cases, this mainly includes their near and intermediate future.[7] This situation pertains not just to the illegal behaviors and reliefs/satisfactions *collectively*, across that overall time frame—say, several months or more. Instead, for the most part, the *individual* IBs and their corresponding individual R/Ss should not be temporally far apart, especially if a small absolute number of these inputs and outputs occur during the period in question.

Sufficient Worth

E. Besides *ratio* per se, an added contributor to the youths' view of overall sufficiency is the felt *intensity* of their relief/satisfaction experiences. Still another contributor is the felt *emotional significance* (ES) of those R/S's, and of the illegal behaviors' content itself. It is ES on which we will now focus; and in this regard, "significance," "importance," "value," and "worth" will be used synonymously.[8]

The presence of felt emotional significance is integral to the youths' view that given illegal behaviors are sufficient overall. This reflects the following interrelationships, taken together: (1) Such emotional significance is an essential aspect of *satisfactoriness*; (2) satisfactoriness is a key component of that which the youths consider *acceptable* to themselves (or more than just acceptable);[9] (3) acceptability, in turn, is a baseline feature or ingredient of any feeling of *sufficient worth* (in effect, it is a minimum requirement of that worth); and (4) such worth is a critical part of *overall sufficiency* itself. (The latter applies even though that feeling of worth neither comprises nor can generate overall sufficiency entirely by itself.)

In other words (to restate those relationships in reverse order): First, *overall* sufficiency requires sufficient worth (among other things), and acceptability is a key feature of that worth. Next, when any acceptability exists, some degree of satisfactoriness—not just satisfaction—is also present (again, among other things). Finally, satisfactoriness is partly based on, always requires, and always includes some type and degree of *emotional significance*—some felt worth. That is, whenever satisfactoriness is found, such ES has shortly preceded it and also accompanies it; in addition, *only* when emotional significance or felt worth is present, or has recently existed, does a substantial amount of satisfactoriness itself exist—even though other factors may themselves have contributed to the latter and to satisfac*tion*.

In the following, it might be kept in mind that illegal behavior often or proportionately often leads to reliefs/satisfactions regarding the youths' personal needs, issues, and/or desires (NIDs). For instance, by eliciting given responses from some of those individuals' peers, IB helps generate feelings of relief, and so on, concerning the former's need for approval or their desire for acceptance. When, or soon after, that illegal behavior and relief/satisfaction thus address those NIDs, they become—individually and jointly—emotionally significant to the youths; that is, they are then felt to have personal value and meaning.

Basically, IBs and R/Ss can acquire emotional significance or importance because the given needs, issues, and/or desires are considered important themselves.[10] More specifically, it is these NIDs' already existing status (standing) with respect to *their* significance or value that opens up the possibility for those *behaviors and R/Ss* to become significant; that is, that status provides a specific opportunity and reason for this to occur, in the first place. Thus, if the NIDs did not already seem important to the youths, at least to a substantial degree, those individuals would not subsequently view the illegal behaviors and reliefs/satisfactions as particularly significant either—this, even if those IBs and R/Ss *were* to address those NIDs (for whatever reasons).

In summary, IBs and R/Ss that substantially address some of the youths' personal needs, issues, and/or desires can and often do become emotionally important. This occurs because those individuals view them as leading to, and otherwise involving, *benefits* with respect to those NIDs—NIDs that already feel and otherwise seem important and which the youths are usually motivated to address in one way, and by one means, or another. (The illegal behaviors serve largely as generators of or triggers for those benefits; the reliefs/satisfactions are a major reflection of the given benefits, and they reinforce the IB's themselves.) The preceding points apply whether those needs/issues/desires are general or specific, and long-standing or fairly new.

NIDs: Capacities and Range of Influence

F. Even before they are addressed, many of the previously mentioned NIDs generate considerable force and thereby underlie and otherwise influence given activities and attitudes. It is in regard to these influences—generative, supportive, and even shaping effects—that these needs/issues/desires can be viewed as key bases of "meaning" as well as importance. Beyond these foundational and shaping capacities, the NIDs sometimes comprise ingredients, that is, subject matter, of meaning itself. This, for instance, is reflected in the fact that (1) nothing which is *in*significant, or meaningless and unimportant, would be even *called* a "need," except, perhaps, a minor one. Similarly, (2) that which is "desired," at least frequently and/or intensely, would seldom be considered meaningless, especially but not only to most persons desiring it.[11]

In each such capacity or role, say, that of base or constituent, these needs, issues, and desires—-more precisely, their respective effects—usually span various aspects of the individuals' personal and social life. That is, first, the effects of these NIDs encompass a *range* of processes, activities, and content areas (PACs);[12] and, secondly, these PACs often involve or even center on the youths' personal emotional experiences, their interpersonal interactions, and/or their societal expectations. (They center on them individually, not just collectively.) In particular, in their relationship to those needs, issues, and/or desires, the illegal behaviors and the subsequent R/S's bear on dimensions and levels— "areas"—such as the following (these are major areas or portions of the just-mentioned range; and, the IBs and R/Ss in question can be emotionally significant in connection with both of them):

1. *Dynamics and feelings* associated with the given NIDs. This involves not only factors and forces that *underlie* the

needs, issues, and desires, but feelings that *result* from those NIDs.

2. *Conscious interests and efforts* that reflect and evolve from those NIDs. This involves not just conventional and relatively unconventional activities and opportunities that are available to most adolescents *as* adolescents, but experiences and challenges that can bear significantly on post-adolescent adjustment. Concerning both time periods, it includes but extends beyond educational, vocational, and other pragmatically oriented as well as skill-centered matters.[13]

Regarding each such area, felt emotional significance centers on what the youths believe or assume illegal behaviors have done, are doing, and/or can do *for* them, by way of providing reliefs/satisfactions in connection with the given NIDs. (These needs, issues, and desires, which are mutually related, involve, for example, such focal points as approval/acceptance, independence/autonomy, and enjoyment/excitement, respectively.)[14] Though emotional significance, as used here, thus emphasizes felt or anticipated gains, the youths do not entirely ignore actual or possible costs, that is, that which they believe the illegal behaviors and their subsequent R/S's may directly or indirectly do *to* them. These costs, which typically include "hassles," restrictions, and/or reduced support, are generally distinguishable from the earlier-mentioned "shortfalls" that are experienced, for instance, in relation to the desired frequency and intensity of given reliefs/satisfactions.[15]

Overall Sufficiency: Major Features and Components

As can be seen, felt emotional significance heavily involves personal meanings that center on content—on needs, issues, desires, adjustments, and so on—that the youths consider important. To distinguish this content or subject matter from quantitative features, say, from the *frequency* and *intensity* of any given content, it can be described as qualitative. Though the qualitative aspect of overall sufficiency interacts with the quantitative, these respective aspects or dimensions (e.g., worth, and reliability) are also separable from—can vary somewhat independently of—one another; in any event, they mainly complement each other regarding their respective contribu-

tions to such sufficiency. This interactive, complementary relationship applies, in particular, to the *emotional significance or worth* aspect of the qualitative dimension, on the one hand, and to the *reliability* aspect of the quantitative, on the other. Other applicable aspects of each dimension need not be detailed here.

Given the fact that overall sufficiency involves the qualitative and quantitative dimensions combined, that is, combined regarding their complementary contributions, and given that these dimensions, collectively, include among their aspects those of reliability and emotional significance or worth, the following is the case: When overall sufficiency exists, not only have the youths' reliability requirements already been satisfied (minimally or otherwise), but, on balance, their illegal behavior–generated reliefs/satisfactions have felt, and have otherwise seemed, emotionally worthwhile to at least a substantial degree. (As indicated, the felt-worth feature also applies to the given behaviors themselves.) Moreover, these reliefs/satisfactions have had that felt worth irrespective of their perceived shortfalls, for example, those concerning their desired intensity and perhaps even rate.

Viewed prospectively rather than retrospectively, the contribution that results from the combination of felt reliability and felt emotional worth often goes far, not only toward allowing for overall sufficiency, but toward actively facilitating it; at any rate, it often comprises the bulk of what is needed in both respects. (This, of course, applies increasingly if and as the *intensity* aspect is increased.)

Additional Observations

G. Even when the youths (1) feel their illegal behaviors are helping them obtain moderately or highly reliable reliefs/satisfactions within an acceptable time frame, and even when they (2) feel those benefits, on balance, outweigh the known drawbacks, many such individuals seek or maintain those (and other) R/Ss by differing means as well:[16] In both cases they seek those reliefs/satisfactions mainly via (a) the earlier-described, risky/trouble-related *AASs* and/or (b) relatively *conventional* activities or routes—these latter being less "risky/. . ." than (a), or even non-risky per se.[17]

Thus, for instance, in connection with point (b), the present youths do not entirely withdraw from their already existing prosocial and other non-illegal activities, efforts, and involvements (AEIs). This applies especially to AEIs in which they are most interested, those which they find intrinsically more manageable, and/or those for which they feel the most external support. (Not infrequently, it also, or alternatively, applies to AEIs that they feel the most adult-directed pressure to maintain.) Nevertheless, these individuals often substantially reduce the frequency and scope of prosocial/non-illegal AEIs even when difficulties do *not* seem great or unusual, when substantial external support *exists,* and so on. In such instances, they do so in order to better accommodate, and perhaps give increased prominence or priority to, certain illegal behaviors, related adjustment patterns, and sometimes various AASs themselves—particularly on a short-term basis.

Notes

1. Thus, one main product of these perceptions and feelings is an implicit expectation regarding the R/Ss' likelihood of occurring, subsequent to the given IBs. Though this expectation is, in effect, a prediction, and thus a form of judgment, it is not, in itself, an *evaluative* judgment—particularly an assessment concerning worth or goodness as such (an assessment that is mainly conscious).

2. Regarding this interaction, sufficient quantities can, for example, help the youths feel that greater *worth* exists; they can do so despite the fact that quantity, as such, cannot fully substitute for worth, which can be viewed as a quality. Similarly, when considerable perceived worth exists, less *quantity* is needed, even though a certain minimum always remains necessary. The youths do not explicitly make such connections and conceptualize "interaction" as such. Moreover, within the present context, they do not conceptualize quantity and quality as such, in the first place.

3. To simplify the presentation, this framework assumes there is only one relief and/or satisfaction experience—one such output—for any given illegal behavior (input). In reality, however, more than one R/S can occur, depending on exactly how that term, and illegal behavior, is defined and measured. Nevertheless, the outcome of the present discussion would not essentially change if a "*more than one*" framework were used. This is because the discussion centers on the differential *ratio* that exists between respective outputs (R/Ss), on the one hand, and their perceived respective inputs (IBs), on the other, regardless of what the R/Ss' exact, absolute *numbers* may be. Finally, and not unrelated to the implication just mentioned, it also suffices, in the present discussion, that the input/output relationship is considered more or less linear—that is, linear as the respective numbers rise, whatever their underlying, mutual ratio may be. (Linearity, here, partly reflects the particular range of values—the raw R/S and IB numbers—under consideration.)

4. Operationally, any such N or D is a rate, one that involves a frequency-of-occurrence divided by a period-of-time; and here, "percentage" is the ratio of that N-rate to that D-rate. To simplify the presentation, it is not necessary to explicitly reflect the time dimension and to present as well as discuss each rate *as* a rate. Instead, each time period is operationally subsumed within its N or D; and in this context, the meaning and analytic role of "rate" is self-evident.

5. Thus far, we have focused on the rate of illegal behaviors, not on their "type" or on other primarily qualitative matters (except perceived worth). The youths assume, usually implicitly, that only some types of behaviors will be acceptable to given peers and will then be able to elicit desired responses from them.

6. Though all such numbers are small as *numbers,* almost all adults consider them large—too large—in view of their nature. This judgment applies especially to the number of illegal behaviors; and its reference is to (1) the immediate physical/psychological effects of those behaviors on all parties concerned and to (2) their possible longer-term consequences for those individuals as well.

7. The quantitative meanings of "near" and "intermediate" can vary somewhat, across youths, depending, for example, on the intensity of the respective individuals' felt and/or actual pressures. These variations, which may also occur *within* any

youth (across time), can also reflect such factors as the following: level of felt support; level and rate of reliefs/satisfactions previously experienced and, in any event, presently experienced; also, life situation perceived as generally improving, as worsening, or as holding steady. Because such factors can bear on the individuals' sense of overall urgency and on the quality of their thinking and decision-making, they can have sizable implications for intervention. They can affect, for instance, the needed rate and/or overall frequency of initial staff/youth contacts and can help determine particular areas of focus—such as family, peers, practical skills, and decision-making processes themselves.

8. In Section E, "reliefs/satisfactions" can be thought of not just at the individual-event level, that is, in terms of each R/S experience singly, but as a collection of experiences or events, that is, as all R/Ss cumulatively; nevertheless, in order to simplify matters, it will be helpful to emphasize the collective level, and this applies to illegal behaviors as well. Other things being equal, the *intensity* (and related overall weight) of the youths' cumulative relief/satisfaction experiences partly reflects these R/Ss' absolute *number,* that is, their frequency. It does so even though that intensity—viewed collectively (as in an *average* of all intensities)—can also vary independently of that number. Though intensity is important in many situations, its specific nature and related aspects need not be further focused on here.

9. More specifically, some degree of satisfactoriness is always an essential aspect or ingredient of *any* degree of *acceptability;* it comprises an intrinsic part of, though not all of, the latter concept. Thus, absent at least some perception or feeling of satisfactoriness on the youths' part, no acceptability can exist.

10. As indicated and implied, illegal behaviors and reliefs/satisfactions can each be emotionally significant to the youths even when their absolute numbers are small. Also, their significance can increase as those numbers rise.

11. For any given youth, *needs, issues, and desires (NIDs)* each have (1) meaning—

specific and more general significance—and (2) an *amount* of felt importance as well (itself emotional, practical, or other). NIDs have these features even prior to the occurrence of *illegal behavior (IB)* and of any *reliefs/satisfactions (R/Ss)* those individuals come to associate with this IB. Together, the NIDs' meaning and amount of felt importance, each of which can be mainly personal or interpersonal in focus, will be called "overall significance." (Below, we will focus on the felt *positive* side or aspects of the NIDs' significance—recognizing, however, the following: Not infrequently, the present youths view given needs, issues, and even desires as having aspects and qualities that sometimes involve complications, frustrations, and the like, and which, as a result, seem other than straightforward and unalloyed with respect to their felt value or import.) Once the illegal behavior occurs and those NIDs and R/Ss become psychologically linked with each other in and through it (and sometimes also via its related attitudes and stances), those needs, issues, and desires often acquire a somewhat different overall significance.

(Note that the first-mentioned link or association was between IBs and R/Ss. The present one is between those R/Ss and the *NIDs—via* those IBs. Regarding the latter relationship, R/Ss and NIDs become associated with each other, and then continue to interact with one another, once the peers' apparent approval of certain IBs generates reliefs/satisfactions that subsequently help the youths deal with or otherwise relate to those needs, issues, and desires. [Here, in thus "relat[ing]," the individuals have partly addressed, adjusted to, and otherwise temporarily come to terms with those NIDs. In this regard the R/S's have occurred *prior to* the given adjustment, and so on, not mainly as an expression or result *of* it. However, see next.] In turn, this process—emphasis still being on positive aspects—often leads to further R/Ss, ones that are expressions of certain outcomes rather than facilitators of them. At any rate, some reliefs/satisfactions *precede* and make it easier to address given NIDs; they may even serve as preconditions for doing so. Other R/Ss follow—more specifically, they later result from—the addressing or partial addressing of those NIDs. As an ongoing process, the overall *action/reaction cycle* involves both aspects of R/S. Here, however, we need only emphasize the first.)

Nevertheless, even after that meaning and importance has been acquired, that is, once such change has occurred, the NIDs in question continue to reflect much of their earlier, *already* existing, overall significance—that is, their pre-IB, or "original," significance. In other words, this significance remains—qualitatively and quantitatively—at least partly different than and partially independent of that which developed in connection with the *illegal behavior* and some of that IB's effects. In this regard the NIDs' original meaning and importance—its pre-IB identity, as it were—could be described as having been later *modified,* not wholly transformed. (As implied earlier, the amount of importance that modified NIDs are felt to have is not always *more* than it had been, shortly before the IB began.) This partial independence can be further seen if and after the illegal behavior is later reduced or eliminated. At any rate, the meaning and amount of felt importance on the part of given NIDs can then change from what they were when they were linked or more closely linked with that IB.

Overall significance (OS), as defined earlier, does not exist in connection with needs, issues, and desires alone; instead, such "meaning and . . . felt importance," combined, also exists with respect to illegal behaviors and their associated reliefs/satisfactions, themselves. (With NIDs and such behaviors alike, OS reflects not just presently experienced and assumed benefits—and problems or tensions—but anticipated ones as well.) In addition, OS sometimes varies across time, and it may do so substantially. The nature and extent of this variation reflects not only qualitative and quantitative changes in those IBs and R/Ss themselves but such factors as (1) the type and amount of needs, issues, and desires which existed *before* that illegal behavior got underway, and (2) the over-

all significance of those and the subsequently modified NIDs.

12. For each NID category—need, issue, and desire, taken individually—this is *usually* the case. For any *two or more* such categories—if one is "desire"—it is *preponderantly* the case.

13. For any given youth, the degree of emphasis on area 1 and area 2—each individually—can vary through time; and, during that same period or other periods, there can be alternations in which of these areas dominates the other. Whichever area is dominant, and however much or little each area is emphasized (whether or not it dominates), the youths' *illegal behaviors* still have a means-to-ends relationship to those individuals' desired reliefs/satisfactions. In that and other respects, those IB's retain what can be described as a broad, cross-situational, and intrinsic instrumental utility or function.

14. These individuals do not *think* of this situation in terms such as "needs," "issues," "independence/autonomy," "reliefs/satisfactions," and so on. Nevertheless, most of them sense—have some awareness or recognition—that a connection exists between the first of the following items (or between one or more of its components), on the one hand, and one or more of the remaining items, on the other (they sense this with respect to specific, concrete experiences or events, not as an abstract matter): (1) their *tensions, emotions, or desires;* (2) certain attitudes they have toward other individuals and/or toward given situations/ expectations; (3) their illegal behaviors; and (4) their later, post-IB feelings of relief/satisfaction. More specifically, they implicitly assume ("sense. . . .") that the presence of the first sometimes contributes to that of others. Finally, many of the present youths also sense a connection not only between items (2) and (3) but—especially (and often more explicitly)—between (3) and (4).

15. A few points before continuing: (1) The "dynamics" involved in area 1, above, are those primarily relating to youths as separate individuals; they are not "universal," in the sense of being the same for everyone or almost everyone. In

particular, no single set of dynamics applies with enough accuracy, specificity, and scope to use—with all or even most individuals—as the primary basis for implementing the level of individualized intervention emphasized in this book. This is despite the following: (a) Many similarities *do* exist across most youths with respect to dynamics, especially regarding certain motives and drives taken one by one rather than as an integrated, interrelated package or set. This also applies to "feelings" (themselves in area 1) and to general as well as specific needs—dimensions that, of course, relate to dynamics itself. It pertains within and across the already-described youth subtypes (Chapters 4 and 5), as well. (b) By themselves, and especially when combined with the more individualized dynamics, these similarities can play an important, in fact major, role in the above as well as other interventions, particularly in helping them get underway. (Nevertheless, see Chapter 19 regarding major limitations, and potential problems.) At any rate, certain accounts of dynamics *can* help describe many youths as individuals, without, however, being *universally* descriptive and—for certain interventions—also without having sufficient applicability to, or even broad appropriateness for, *most* individuals.

(2) Reliefs/satisfactions, for instance, ones that often follow apparent peer acceptance, may be consciously experienced by the present youths not just for minutes, hours, or days, but often considerably longer—and, in the latter case, not necessarily at a below-average intensity. Whichever duration is involved, these R/Ss may overlap *previously* experienced R/S's temporally and substantively. (*Substantive* refers, for example, to the content or type of feelings and emotions involved.) When at least substantive overlap occurs, and especially when there is also the temporal, the respective reliefs/satisfactions can enhance each other and can often result in more reinforcement, say, of peer-approved behaviors, than would generally be provided by either R/S alone. This can occur especially if—as is usually the case—the *NIDs* (needs, issues, and/or desires) to

which the respective R/S's pertain are themselves largely the same, across those differing experiences.

(3) Emotional significance (ES) is often positively correlated with intensity of reliefs/satisfactions. Specifically, a greater amount of felt ES is frequently associated with a higher degree of R/S. This applies to major as well as less important NIDs. Also, the *relief* aspect of reliefs/satisfactions is often closely related to the "needs and issues" components of NIDs (i.e., it occurs in relation to them), and to their frequently associated, preexisting complications, frustrations, and/or tensions. The *satisfactions* aspect of R/S is closely related to the "desires" component of NIDs. However, these respective relationships are not mutually exclusive, partly because reliefs and satisfactions sometimes overlap and also because needs, issues, and desires themselves often intermingle.

(4) Emotional significance, like intensity, centers on or heavily involves feelings, and it is a fundamental component of *overall* significance. The latter—OS—reflects matters that bear on instrumental utility as well, for example, those involved in addressing and partly coming to terms (a) not only with personal needs, issues, and/or desires but with concrete, societal expectations or demands, and in doing so (b) in seemingly realistic or promising ways, in particular.

(5) When the individuals' view and concept of self enters the picture, this can involve actual, outwardly presented, and/or desired aspects. *Actual* encompasses and centers on the self-recognized or personally felt; it especially emphasizes that which the individual considers real (true; most common; and/or central), whether largely desired or not. *Presented-for-others,* or *outwardly-available,* centers on overall persona (as in Jung, 1923)—including, but not necessarily dominated by, any possible facade or front. Finally, given the preceding aspects, the focus of *desired* is self-evident; and, with any given individual, its scope may or may not include most of the *actual.*

16. Whichever means they use or emphasize, the following remains the case: When dealing with their personal needs, issues,

and desires, one of the youths' cardinal goals is that of obtaining relief and/or satisfaction. This is also true whether their "view" regarding the chances of obtaining such benefits mainly involves an implicit or perhaps global assumption rather than a more explicit and focused belief.

17. Regarding conventional routes, the youths commonly utilize these to some degree unless (1) their ambivalence about doing so is often unusually strong, or—if it is usually no more than *moderate,* or even strong—unless (2) the challenges themselves seem too large, the possible satisfactions are mostly unclear, or much of the known content is uninteresting or even distasteful to them.

A third, less common, but still far from rare route involves relatively unconventional (RU), though not illegal, activities. *These* activities need not include conspicuously problemed AASs; at any rate, this route need not be risky/trouble-related, particularly, but not only, in the manner associated with given activities, attitudes, and stances. Substantial involvement in RU activities commonly results in moderate disapproval and/or opposition from particular adults, not usually in the *strong* negative reactions frequently triggered in those individuals by various AASs and—especially—by illegal behaviors per se.

Finally, as with numerous *non*offenders, many of the present youths combine the conventional and the RU. With some of these latter individuals, this mixture may be further accompanied by some of the earlier-discussed *AASs*—and their particular risks.

45 STRUCTURAL FACTORS AND THEIR RELATIONSHIP TO EMOTIONAL/DYNAMIC FACTORS

We will briefly discuss the two main factors that enter into the earlier-mentioned "integration process," particularly when this process is largely preconscious, and when its product, in any event, helps determine whether the youths view "illegal behavior inputs [as] sufficiently reliable." The factors in question are the "structural" and the "emotional/dynamic." Partly because emotions and related dynamics—and vice versa—have already been described in various chapters and appendices, the descriptive emphasis, here, will be on the structural. At any rate, the main, relevant aspects of these two broad factors and their interrelationships will be presented.

Structural Factors and Their Aspects or Expressions

Structural factors, collectively, are general approaches by means of which and in terms of which youths interact with their external and internal environments and organize their experiences. These approaches involve such modalities or areas as *acting, feeling, and thinking;* and within *thinking,* there are dimensions or components such as "reflecting" and-the "use of words" (see A through C, below). ("Interact[ing] . . . and organiz[ing]" include, for example, the acquiring of, the processing of, and the further responding to sensory, emotional, and cognitive stimuli and information.)

The remarks in Appendix 44 concerning "the integration process" as being largely preconscious are centered not on those general approaches (e.g., "thinking") as such, but on some of their aspects or expressions, particularly on *ways* they are typically used. These ways—here called "styles"—reflect, among

other things, *preferences* that youths have for any one general approach over any other (see item A, below); they also reflect the degree of *attention or emphasis* those individuals give or do not give to any *single* approach or to any of its *components* (see B and C). Thus, in the present case, any serious multiple offender (SMO) may regularly utilize any or all of the following styles, dispositions, or strong inclinations (this list is not exhaustive; nor is it unique to preconscious integrations, though its items are very common among them):

A. quantitatively above-average emphasis on *acting* over *thinking,* or on acting first over thinking first;
B. quantitatively less-than-average *self-reflection,* especially, but not only, regarding personal issues; and
C. quantitatively less-than-average *use of words* per se, whether or not in comparison to direct "intuition," "instinct," and/or "feeling," as well.

Utilization of these styles does not reflect a level of physical, intellectual, and emotional capacity which differs fundamentally from that found in other individuals, among whom would be less serious offenders, and nonoffenders. While some of these individuals often use A, B, and/or C themselves, many others in these same categories (1) mainly have and mainly use styles that are somewhat different than A through C or that may even contrast with them; or (dominance—e.g., main usage—aside), the latter individuals may simply (2) utilize these other styles to a greater degree. (The following continues the emphasis on serious multiple offenders.)

For any given SMO, the present styles, such as A above, are commonly used in several contexts, not just a few; they are also relatively enduring, not highly transitory (cf. "traits" versus "states"). These styles, and various others, have usually developed over a long period, via common learning processes and reinforcement mechanisms. They have done so *mainly* in everyday settings and situations, such as school and leisure activities, in which almost all youths regularly participate. (Across these individuals, this participation—not just exposure—is usually similar in type, though sometimes very different in degree.) At any rate, for the youths collectively, these styles—structural factors—do not ordinarily spring from *highly charged* or otherwise unusually difficult *negative* emotional settings, situations, processes, and dynamics; and for most such SMOs individually, they do not *mainly* do so. ("Emotional settings," and so on—and the input they provide or involve—will be called "emotional/dynamic [E/D] factors." Strong *negative* E/Ds involve, for instance, particularly stressful social/environmental conditions, and/or unusually strained interpersonal interactions, especially when these are prolonged. They do not involve simply mild or moderate difficulties, moderate or even vigorous challenges and competition, and so on.)

To elaborate on the preceding points: Unless E/D factors are unusually difficult, styles such as A through C can and generally do spring from or develop on other bases. More specifically, they largely develop, and more or less gel, under long-term conditions, via common processes, and in relatively standard settings, such as those just referred to. Moreover, this development, and gelling, which pertains to youths individually and collectively, can occur with little more than modest input and reinforcement from typical *positive* E/Ds.

(Regarding "little more than modest": Positive E/Ds, which are supportive inputs, can, of course, substantially contribute to—can, for instance, *supplement* and even *complement*—the development and consolidation of those styles. More particularly, these emotional/dynamic factors can, and often do, help bring about [1] the existence of styles, that is, of structural factors, such as A through C above. In addition, they can help determine or enhance [2] the particular character or pattern—the nature—of those styles, together with

[3] the latter's quantitative aspects, and/or [4] their extent of stable functioning. Nevertheless, the existence of those *E/Ds*—specifically, the quantitatively more-than-*modest* presence and operation of those positive inputs—is not, by itself, usually a sine qua non with respect to promoting or producing the just-mentioned outcomes; this particularly applies to outcomes [1] and [4]: existence and stable functioning, respectively. That is, the positive emotional/dynamic factors in question are, usually, not absolutely essential beyond that point, even though increased amounts can further help, and can affect outcome [3] as well. At any rate, it is in this sense and to that extent that styles—structural factors—such as A through C can generally *develop,* and can more or less solidify, independently of those emotional/dynamic inputs.)

Also, once those styles have developed and are somewhat *consolidated,* they can be *maintained* with little specific positive emotional/dynamic input and reinforcement (I&R), or with little further I&R. In any case, once that developmental level is reached, the styles in question can be applied and maintained rather independently of input from most, though usually not from extreme, *negative* inputs, as well. Both points apply to most of the present youths.

A previously implicit point might now be made explicit. As already indicated, styles A through C, collectively, involve not just a substantially "below-average" emphasis on specified general approaches but a similarly "below-average" use of certain components thereof, for example, the self-reflection component of "thinking." However, neither that emphasis nor this usage is so extensive in degree or so unusual in any respect—besides not being extreme, in the first place—as to commonly render those approaches and components fairly ineffective. At any rate, neither that first nor that second quantitative departure from the norm largely curtails the ability of those approaches and components—more precisely, those *styles*—to help the youths adequately address commonly occurring challenges, requirements, opportunities, and desires, or to remain in a position to do so. Here, particular focus is on "challenges, . . . and desires" which are relatively *prosocial.* In addition, the styles in question are applied under conditions that are rather commonplace and which, as such, are seldom *"highly charged or . . . unusually difficult"* in negative respects. Though (1) this ability to help youths adequately address these prosocial challenges, tasks, and so on, under such ordinary conditions thus exists with respect to styles A through C above, and although (2) the same type of ability exists in connection with the counterparts or opposites of those styles (see next), the presence and operation of certain negative emotional/dynamic factors, particularly of *marked* negatives, can often reduce or otherwise hamper it—in both instances.

Though styles A, B, and C, in particular (especially B and C), may be adequate to the various challenges, requirements, and standard opportunities under those everyday conditions, this does not ipso facto mean they are *as* capable of addressing those same challenges, and so on, as are other styles—ones that the youths would utilize under similarly commonplace conditions. (The latter styles would include, for example, counterparts and opposites such as: *thinking* over acting; *above-average,* or even *average,* self-reflection; and *above* average use of words.) Nor, however, does the preceding imply that styles A through C are *not* as capable as those others, at least in various respects and circumstances. This is seen, for instance, when the youths utilize the first group of styles to address certain personal desires and/or rapidly emerging opportunities. Similarly, those styles would usually provide a more effective basis or context for the use of certain defense mechanisms (as distinct from other adjustment techniques), whereas their counterparts or opposites would be better suited to, or more consonant with, other types of defense.

Emotional/Dynamic, Structural, and Other Factors, in Relation to Preconscious Processes

When preconscious rather than conscious processes predominate during given time periods—often lengthy ones—this, in itself, does not necessarily mean that *negative emotional/ dynamic factors* are then stronger than *structural* ones, and that they dominate them in that regard. Instead, the structural factors can be primary, and this applies even when the negative E/Ds—especially collectively—*are* strong, as is very often the case. (Those and the following points still have reference to serious multiple offenders—SMOs, except where specified.) Negative E/D factors will

sometimes be called the "first group" of problems, difficulties, and/or conflicts; it is a group associated with SMOs. A second group of emotional/dynamic factors—not called "negatives" even though it, too, includes problems, and the like—will be distinguished below. This is a group associated with "nonoffenders" rather than with SMOs.

The following details, and the subsequent discussion, still focus on preconscious processes. (1) When emotional/dynamic factors, collectively, *are* stronger than the structural, they, the former, may or may not also be more *widespread, pervasive, and/or numerous* than the latter. To be sure, when those E/Ds are strong on *their own*—whether or not also comparatively, though in any event still collectively—they generally *are* widespread, and so on. Nevertheless, this positive correlation exists despite the fact that having one or more such features is neither a prerequisite to the E/Ds' becoming strong nor an essential ingredient of its remaining so.

(2) The negative E/Ds under discussion are, especially collectively, more than "simply mild or moderate." Instead, they are basically *strong*—"basically," in the sense of "very often," not just "most often" or modally, and not just "on average." If, rather than being strong, those E/Ds are *extreme* (including marked) and have perhaps long been extreme (conditions which are neither rare nor, however, very frequent), their chances of dominating the structural factors throughout the given time periods are substantially higher than if they had "only" been strong; in fact, their chances are then very high. Also, during *crises,* strong or even moderate E/D factors often grow temporarily extreme, individually and—again—collectively. At such times, they, too, almost always dominate the structural.[1]

The following applies aside from whether the emotional/dynamic factors or the structural factors are dominant, that is, regardless of which type is stronger than the other, during given time periods (here, "strength" emphasizes influence on preconscious processes, and "time" can extend to the present): When the E/Ds are strong in an absolute sense, that is, on their own (and even if they do often dominate), this does not invariably mean they are the main *reason* the given processes have become largely preconscious, in the first place. Instead, as already indicated, the structural factors can be, and often are, the principal generators and channelers of that development. Other aspects of causation are discussed later.

The immediately preceding points apply not just to *negative* E/Ds but to another group. This second group of emotional/dynamic factors is applicable and common to *most adolescents ("nonoffenders")*. Since this group of E/Ds is thus associated with this quantitatively preponderant population, it is more typical or common than the *first* group—the E/Ds associated with a much smaller population, namely, the serious multiple offenders. The second group of E/D factors is further described in technical point #2, below, and in the subsequent discussion as well; the first group is emphasized in #1 and #3, and also later on.[2] As will be seen, most problems, difficulties, and/or conflicts that comprise the first group can be characterized as "negative," especially but not only when they interact with each other and thereby escalate their respective strengths. Most problems, and so on, that comprise the second group need not be considered negative; at least, they are much less so, individually and even collectively.[3]

Technical Points
(1) Collectively, "negative" emotional/dynamic factors heavily involve personal *problems, difficulties, and/or conflicts (PDCs)* which, as indicated, are quite often *strong*. They are strong not just in their effect on preconscious processes but in their influence on the individuals' broader adjustment. At any rate, these E/D factors are more than just substantial (here, the equivalent of *moderate*) with regard to their effects/influence; instead, they and their given PDCs are often *severe* and otherwise major in that respect. In addition, these emotional/dynamic factors and PDCs often *feel* severe to many youths, and their implications or consequences regarding near- and longer-term adjustment can be large and/or numerous in any event. (As can be seen, "strong" and "severe" involve the same issues as well as interrelated contexts; and these terms, together with "major," have equivalent meanings.) Despite their strength, their severity, and so on, these emotional/dynamic factors are distinguished from the earlier-mentioned, smaller group of negative E/Ds referred to as *extreme*, or *unusually strong*, and sometimes thought of as "marked."[4]

The next point reflects the fact that although negative emotional/dynamic factors heavily involve strong PDCs, far from *all* E/D factors—still problems, difficulties, and/or conflicts—are strong, or even unusual. This applies especially, but not only, to the nonoffenders, as compared to SMOs.

(2) Strong, negative emotional/dynamic factors—especially collectively—can be distinguished from a second group of E/D factors—themselves involving problems, difficulties, and/or conflicts. The "first group" of PDCs differs from the second in average strength or severity and with respect to its consequences (see below regarding details); this reflects important differences in content and it exists despite the simultaneous presence of considerable *shared* content. The second group mainly involves a "typical" range and level of adolescent adjustment problems and challenges, ones that most adults associate with the preponderance of adolescents; they associate them with SMOs to a much lesser extent. For such reasons, among others, these are problems/difficulties/conflicts that those adults consider more "normal." At any rate, the PDCs in question, and the challenges as well, *are* quite salient among most nonoffenders; yet, many or most adults' perceptions in this regard notwithstanding, such relatively "normal" (typical, common) problems, and so on, are not highly uncommon among SMOs. Also, they exist together with these youths' other types and/or levels of PDCs.

The first group of problems, difficulties, and/or conflicts—the strong negatives—is usually more severe, and more often severe, than the second; these differences underlie its greater average strength. Also, these PDCs more often *feel* severe, and their negative consequences can be greater. Though the *second*—more typical—group of PDCs (individually and collectively) sometimes feels severe to nonoffenders, and although it can have serious consequences for these individuals, as well, the youths in question can usually handle them better than can most SMOs and can generally prevent the more serious consequences from occurring. Though many of these more common, second-group PDCs are *moderate* in strength, various other such PDCs are strong or else moderate to strong. Nevertheless, it is the "moderates" that qualitatively and quantitatively comprise the bulk of nonoffenders' problems, difficulties, and/or conflicts and which, as such, largely underlie that PDC group's "typical" or "common" nature.

As the preceding implies, serious multiple offenders themselves have various PDCs that fall within the more typical, that is, the mostly moderate, range. However, of all these SMOs' problems, difficulties, and conflicts—at any rate, of their PDCs that, collectively, encompass the categories of *moderate, strong,* and *extreme*—the percentage that consists of *strong* PDCs only is especially large. Also, this degree of representation is considerably larger among SMOs than among nonoffenders—the latter being youths for whom a high percentage of all problems/difficulties/conflicts consists of the *moderates* rather than the other two categories.

(3) Regarding serious multiple offenders, the following applies to the substantial or at least not inconsiderable percentage of problems, and so on, that fall within the *moderate* category: These PDCs usually interact not just with each other, but with the given youths' *strong* PDCs.[5] These interactions, especially in conjunction with those that occur among the strong PDCs themselves, produce the combined, major negative effect implied earlier. In particular, those problems, and so forth, collectively produce an effect—more precisely, effects—whose overall severity and potential consequences are well beyond the averages or medians seen in most adolescents; this is the case even though such effects reflect interactions themselves. It is this overall severity, together with those same PDCs' frequent chronicity, their often broad—collective—scope, and the extent of their interrelationships, that makes these problems, difficulties, and so on, potentially or actually harmful to self and/or others, and in that sense especially "negative."

Finally, the effects in question, for example, the negative consequences, are likely to be stronger if one or more serious, long-standing *skill deficits* or related shortcomings exists in addition to this mixture of moderate and strong PDCs. As indicated earlier, that type and degree of deficit or shortcoming is frequent among SMOs and less common in most other youths.

Causation and Negative E/Ds
Regarding causation, the following pertains to negative E/Ds in particular, especially but not only *collectively* (alternatively, one could say it applies to the major negative *effects* of the interactions among most or all of the offenders' problems, difficulties, and/or conflicts, even excluding any extreme PDCs):[6] Such emotional/dynamic factors (or effects) may or may not be "too much"—psychologically too hard, overall—for the youths to focus on and cope with consciously, during given time periods.[7] In particular, they may or may not be too difficult for these serious multiple offenders to consciously deal with—whether directly or not, and carefully or not—(1) other than infrequently, (2) other than on a sporadic, transitory, or even evanescent basis, and, in any event, (3) to more than a slight or moderate degree. Nevertheless, even when (a) those strong, personal problems, and so on, *are* too difficult to consciously address in other than those ways, as is often the case, and even when (b) those same problems, difficulties, and/or conflicts *do* then contribute significantly to the genesis and even maintenance of the preconscious processes, the overall contribution of these strong E/D factors to (a) and (b) is, at times, still quantitatively less than that of the structural factors—themselves operating "especially but not only *collectively.*" This applies even when the E/Ds' contribution is nonetheless essential.

At any rate, negative E/Ds, even without being extreme (individually or collectively), are sometimes too difficult for serious multiple offenders to consciously focus on and cope with, during given periods.[8] Though this situation can result from the above "problems, . . . and/or conflicts" alone, that is, operating by themselves, existing *skill deficits* can and often do add substantially to the picture, as can/do shortcomings and/or complications closely related to or resulting from them. Moreover, these inputs or contributions are often compounded by the moderate to strong ambivalence these individuals may have about trying to increase or add various skills. (Major reasons for such ambivalence have already been mentioned.) These mixed feelings are usually a major aspect and expression of the strong problems, difficulties, and/or conflicts themselves.

Negative E/Ds, and Conscious Processes
Though negative emotional/dynamic factors often make important contributions to preconscious processes, and although they may

sometimes be more important than structural factors in that regard, this does not ipso facto mean that those E/Ds are quantitatively and causally unimportant with respect to *conscious* processes, and that they are seldom if ever *more* important than the structural in that connection. This applies whether the conscious or preconscious are dominant at the time. Thus, for example, when conscious processes dominate, negative E/D factors—including given problems, difficulties, and/or conflicts—can still be important in themselves, and they can outweigh the structural as well. This applies especially, but not only, if those E/Ds are collectively strong (not necessarily extreme). At any rate, such factors do not just affect, or heavily and perhaps mainly affect, preconscious processes.

Notes

1. Extreme negative E/Ds do not occur only during crises, and shortly before as well as after them. Also, in the *absence* of crises, their duration is often other than brief.

2. Besides the "positive" E/D factors mentioned in the opening section of this appendix, "negative" E/Ds—here called the "first group"—are the main ones that have been focused on thus far.

3. To broaden the perspective, the following might be kept in mind: (1) Though problems, difficulties, and/or conflicts (PDCs) generally involve and often center on *needs, desires, and related interests (NDIs)*, (2) far from all NDIs involve, let alone center on, *PDCs.* Point (1) reflects the fact that PDCs' subject matter or scope—and, ipso facto, that of emotional/dynamic factors—is not limited to *NDIs,* even though these motivators frequently play a crucial role in that context. Point (2) reflects the fact that needs, desires, and related interests do not, in and of themselves, invariably generate or otherwise necessarily lead to *problems, difficulties, and conflicts.* Both points apply whether or not the problems, and so on, either are or are not mostly *negative,* as in the first and sec-

ond groups, respectively. (NDIs are equivalent to Appendix 44's "NIDs.")

4. E/Ds that are extreme or unusually strong—(E/Ds often produce personal problems, difficulties, and/or conflicts, whatever their strength)—would be *felt* as, and would often objectively be, *extremely severe* or *unusually severe.* E/Ds that are *strong,* but not extreme, would be mainly experienced as *severe.*

5. Though they can interact with each other whether or not their preexisting content involves substantial overlap, they can do so to a greater degree if it does.

6. What follows would apply even if the individual PDCs were only aggregated and did not, at any rate, *strongly interact* with each other—say, interact fairly intensively, broadly, and/or frequently. Nevertheless, even when their interactions are not *intense,* they are often broad and/or frequent. Such interactions commonly occur among "negative" personal problems, difficulties, and/or conflicts, especially, but not only, when these PDCs are individually strong and have preexisting content overlap.

7. This situation usually exists entirely apart from crises or related major threats or upheavals. It also, of course, often exists *during* crises, and when they are impending. (At such times the youths' *motivation* to focus—and, with it, their usual, overall ability to do so—often plummets.)

8. Some problems, difficulties, and/or conflicts—though seldom many at a time—can be indirectly addressed even if the youths do not consciously focus on them as such. This is the case whether or not, but especially if, those PDCs—individually—(1) are other than extreme and (2) have been, at least in part, functionally separated from certain other PDCs (ones that are themselves negative). Various persons can sometimes help these individuals make and retain this separation, and can then help them address given PDCs without their—the youths—directly and often consciously focusing on them.

46 COMMON CONTRIBUTORS TO RECIDIVISM IN SELECTED TYPES OF OFFENDERS

A number of common, underlying contributors to conflicted individuals' recidivism will now be mentioned, and others will be listed shortly.[1] Passive-conformist youths will be specified, as well. Though post-program behavior will be emphasized, the contributing factors are essentially the same as those involved in many pre-program offenses, except where specified. Also, some overlap exists among these factors.

Contributors and Broad Dynamics

Factors 1 and 2

By committing new offenses and by being locked up or otherwise externally punished for them, many conflicted youths—now sometimes young adults—are not only able to *express* one or both of the following, but to psychologically *punish themselves* for doing so:

1. Their long-standing feelings of anger or resentment toward others, mainly toward one or both parents, legal guardians, and so on.
2. Their opposition to various expectations, responses, wishes, and demands by parents or others, for example, (a) expectations or preferences regarding continued dependency/submissiveness, (b) responses of displeasure over expressions of independence/assertiveness, and (c) wishes or demands involving primary loyalty, such as to family over peers, or to one parent over another. This opposition is usually overt and behavioral rather than covert and only verbal.

Thus, regarding these factors, and some that follow, these youths have a largely underlying wish—one that is mixed with its opposite—to be *caught and externally punished* sooner or later. Even prior to being caught, they will generally begin to psychologically *punish themselves*, for instance, by increasing their level of unhappiness, frustration, or misery in various ways. (Depending on the individuals' further interactions with parents and others, and on other life events, these forms of self-punishment may—from the youth's standpoint—"suffice" for a long time, even if the youths have not been caught.) However, if they are not soon apprehended, as, for example, via direct, standard, law enforcement efforts or citizen actions, they sometimes "let the word get around" via friends/acquaintances, or else they turn themselves in. Once these individuals are sentenced, the ensuing external punishment itself becomes—psychologically—a part or extension of the earlier self-punishment.

Thus, regarding Factors 1 and 2, the external as well as internal punishment, and the sense of unhappiness, and so on, partly relieve feelings of guilt, distress, and anxiety that stem from, or are augmented by, the anger, resentment, or opposition that these youths have expressed, and which they may have continued to express. This relief, however, establishes only a partial *status quo ante* with others, and/or within oneself. For instance, the overall relationship with others is no longer quite the same as before; in fact, the preexisting problems will have sometimes been compounded. This is especially likely to occur if certain inputs from others—such as inputs 2a, 2b, and/or 2c, above—have been intensified rather than modified or reduced, in response to the individuals' original actions/expressions.

In short, full equilibrium is not established via the punishment and self-punishment. Instead, even apart from the compounding that may be based on intensified inputs from others (e.g., parents), the feelings of unhappiness, frustration, and misery mentioned earlier can sometimes generate complications of their own and can lead to further distress and anxiety. Thus, although recidivism may serve certain dynamic functions, it sometimes—in fact, often—creates more problems for the individuals than it relieves. It often triggers a downward spiral or escalates an already existing one; and this can also occur in connection with Factor 1, depending on how those youths express their anger.

Factor 3

Often, by recidivating, and by possibly returning to related adjustment patterns and perhaps even crime-oriented peers, many conflicted as well as passive-conformist individuals may directly escape from, delay, or otherwise avoid/reduce/divert the following:

3. Strong external and internal pressures that engender considerable anxiety and/or fear.

Regarding the external pressures, these can involve various life challenges, family demands/dynamics, and so on, ones that the individuals find psychologically and otherwise too difficult to handle or satisfy at the time. Not only are those pressures and demands often accompanied by external confrontations, for example, ones initiated by parents, but they generate internal pressures and conflicts that—like the external pressures themselves—result in anxiety and/or fear (though not necessarily guilt feelings). The latter two often reflect the youths' anticipated (1) failure to satisfy those and other individuals, and (2) a resulting disapproval/rejection—or even added pressure—by them. This sequence is directly based on past experiences and on extrapolations from them, not to mention any existing confrontations themselves.

Faced with such realities and expectations, these particular individuals find it easier to return to earlier behaviors and to more accepting but often delinquent friends—and to

avoid or give up on various challenges. In effect, they choose not to directly, strenuously, or often *oppose*—as do the Factor 1 and especially Factor 2 youths—but, rather, to *escape*, and so on. That is, they prefer "flight," or even withdrawal, to "fight," or to other fairly direct opposition.

Thus, in order to largely satisfy the general or overall goal of avoiding/reducing/diverting (a) those external pressures, (b) the subsequent internal pressures, and (c) the anxieties that arise from both (a) and (b), these youths, unlike those involved in Factors 1 and/or 2, have less "need," that is, psychological need, *for external punishment/control per se*, especially in order to relieve feelings of guilt, in order to "pay" for feelings of anger and/or resentment, and so on. Nevertheless, when the present individuals *are* caught or turn themselves in, and when they are subsequently punished in standard external ways (as they have been in the past), their specific wish to *escape/reduce* various pressures is more likely to be satisfied or satisfied to a greater degree. Thus, they, too, have some motivation to engage in behavior that can lead to such punishment—this, despite the possible longer-term *consequences*, which most of them do not focus on at the time.

At any rate, via external punishment—say, removal from the community, and, hence, from home, school, job training/seeking, and/or existing employment—these individuals may relieve or escape from strong, continued, post-program pressures, demands, and social realities. Though this relief is usually just temporary, and although the youths generally realize or assume this will be the case, such relief is not ipso facto less important to them.

Shared Issues, Dynamics, and Implications

Broadly speaking, during and shortly after adolescence, the social and personal issues involved in those Factor 3 pressures—and, extending into other social/personal levels, in Factor 2 as well—commonly center on the following questions: (1) "Should the individuals adopt new adjustment patterns and role relationships?" If so, (2) "Which ones should they be?" and (3) "How and when should the youths or young adults move forward or keep moving ahead in those respects?" The question of "Which role relationships?" and, especially, that of "How and when to move?" frequently dominates various phases of these youths' interactions with their parole agents, whether or not in rehabilitation-centered programs.

Contributing to the difficulties that issues (1), (2), and (3) create for the present individuals—and this applies to Factor 1, as well—are yet other issues or dynamics. These almost always predate adolescence and they are usually strong, largely unresolved, and beneath the surface. They generally involve the youths' unmet or largely unsatisfied need or desire for acceptance, affection, and sometimes even basic attention, on the one hand, and their perception of instead being only tolerated, minimally valued, or even taken for granted—or else actually disliked, "used," and/or specifically unwanted/rejected—on the other. Such dynamics and perceptions are often integral to these individuals' underlying feelings of inadequacy, of "badness," and/or of being unable to satisfy others (mainly but not only adults) in any event, and of then being—or once again being—(further) disapproved, rejected, or ignored by them.

Regarding all three factors, the following relates not only to the earlier-mentioned adjustment patterns but to the post-program illegal behavior in which these individuals engage (this is behavior which they know could lead not only to apprehension by the law, but—like the earlier adjustment patterns themselves—to immediate job loss or even to difficulty obtaining employment in the first place):[2] In effect, these patterns and behaviors often express the youths' willingness or even desire to *not* change or move forward—more specifically, to not move along fairly standard, socially and/or parentally accepted/desired channels. To be sure, by not changing or moving forward even moderately, they risk further pressure from or disapproval by parents, and/or a crisis in their dependency relationship with them. (This applies whether moderate or marked dependency is involved.)

Whether apart from or in addition to actual pressures, *felt* pressures—such as assumed and psychological ones—are more likely to occur if little forward movement takes place, or if it occurs along lines *disapproved* by the parents/guardians. In either case, increased external conflicts are then likely to occur, especially if the youths still live at home. Moreover, such conflicts, and possibly even a crisis in the overall youth/parent relationship, are more likely to occur if—despite

some movement—these youths or young adults (most noticeably the passive-conformists) still feel largely unprepared to take serious practical steps or further steps toward adulthood and physical emancipation. This would apply even if they already *are* somewhat interested in taking such steps, and are perhaps becoming more interested in doing so.

In this context, and especially if that interest is no more than mild, minor illegal acts, and/or various behaviors that could be characterized as "foot-dragging," passive aggression, or even direct defiance, sometimes serve to sidestep the given issues and pressures. Often, they simultaneously affirm—largely for the benefit of the parents, the youths themselves, and peers—some degree of autonomy, nondependency, and seeming strength, courage, or "manhood" (manhood insofar as the illegal, borderline, or other activities involve an expression of "willpower," determination, daring, and risk). However, despite the self-assertion that directly or indirectly characterizes such activities, and in spite of given features or qualities associated with manhood, those actions entail and imply little if any social-psychological movement toward—let alone tentative commitment to—more or less traditional, or at least socially accepted, forms of *adulthood,* or to increased responsibility per se. Instead, their immediate practical effect is to place, or maintain, those particular dimensions of change "on hold," or to even complicate their eventual attainment. Still, such actions do simultaneously serve notice that some degree of autonomy is possible and desired.

Given these as well as earlier-described activities and motives, it can be seen that the present youths' involvement in post-program illegal behavior, and with crime-oriented or crime-tolerant peers, often reflects—at a broader level—their *ambivalence* about substantially changing their long-standing adjustment patterns and main role relationships, for example, modifying them for perhaps the first time since a pre-program period. In other cases, however, it mainly reflects their ambivalence about *continuing* to change in ways that began during their program, or even about maintaining various changes and readjustments that occurred.

Together, the preceding events are not functionally limited to "escape from pressures," "relief of guilt feelings," and "*self-*punishment." Instead, these youths' (and here, emphasis is on conflicted youths') trouble with the law sometimes serves, that is, it also serves, to intentionally hurt one or both *parents,* or others. In particular, the persons toward whom this emotional hurt is directed are ones for whom the offenders still have strong negative feelings, individuals from whom they may even continue to receive, or feel they are receiving, "messages" of dislike, disapproval, or rejection—mixed with few compensating positive words and actions.[3]

Factors 4, 5, and 6

Further involved in the drive for self-punishment that contributes to some individuals' troubles are three other factors, ones that are usually, though not invariably, interwoven and which are no less pervasive than 1 through 3 (the following still focuses on the post-program period; also, although the conflicted group again dominates, the specific *youths* in question are often different than those associated with the earlier factors):

4. These youths or young adults continue to feel they are badly failing (a) themselves or (b) others, and hence deserve not just criticism or rebuke, but punishment, discomfort, or deprivation.[4]
5. These individuals still have various impulses, wishes, thoughts, or emotions that they sometimes want to express, or feel almost driven to express, but which they (a) consider "bad" or even "evil," (b) often think they should therefore "pay for" (e.g., psychologically), and/or (c) believe may have to be restrained by external means.[5] (Some such impulses, wishes, and so on, may already have been expressed illegally, though the offenders might not have been caught, externally punished, and thereby at least temporarily controlled.)[6]
6. Though they do want some form of happiness, these youths or young adults feel they (a) might not deserve much of it, and/or that they will, in any event, (b) probably experience less of it (and will perhaps have fewer direct pleasures in particular) than will most other persons, at least in typical situations or by usual means.

Factor 4b and, to a lesser extent, Factor 5, also contribute to the recidivism of many passive-conformists, some of whom have even made substantial progress in their programs; however, Factor 3 is usually a much larger contributor with these youths. Factor 6a often reduces conflicted (and passive-conformist) individuals' resistance to involving themselves in trouble-laden situations, and it makes them more likely to often engage in negative self-fulfilling prophecies. Simultaneously, 6b makes them more prone to involve themselves with—and often follow—peers who have access to quick and seemingly easy "payoffs" or pleasures, some of which are illegal or borderline. In general, Factor 6 partly results from a combination of 1, 2, 4, and 5, above, for instance, from the youths' feelings of guilt or inadequacy in connection with them. However, on a longer-term basis and in a more pervasive way, this factor—as well as 4 and 5 themselves—reflects those individuals' feelings of being disliked, unwanted, or at least minimally valued by key individuals (other than the earlier-mentioned peers).[7]

Selected Implications

In light of such factors, external punishments and external controls will often fail to prevent these individuals from recidivating, although they will generally reduce its chances. This is true even when these youths—partly because of their programs (SEC-oriented or not)—have essentially rejected crime-oriented peers, have obtained employment, have left a harmful home setting, and so on, and although such advances have further reduced the chances of recidivism.

Specifically, those punishments/controls, especially by themselves, will often fail to achieve the desired goal if the present individuals have not resolved or considerably reduced various internal psychological issues;[8] also, they will then often fail even when combined with the youths' rejection of delinquent peers, and so forth. In this respect the psychological issues in question thus involve factors which, if largely unresolved or unrelieved, will have done more than, say, contribute to the youths' *pre*-program and possible *in*-program difficulties and delinquency. In particular, they will have driven those individuals to express various feelings, emotions, and impulses which—while often providing the youths a temporary sense of autonomy/independence/power and pleasure (and while partly counteracting their opposites)—may nevertheless soon end up undermining or complicating their longer-term, *post*-program adjustment. This outcome often results not just from the direct interpersonal and practical consequences of the feelings, emotions, and impulses that have been expressed—for instance, consequences stemming from other persons' negative reactions to those expressions—but from the youths' related drive for external punishment and self-punishment themselves.

Regarding the self-punishment component, this discussion has emphasized such precursors and links as the following: self-expression → self-punishment; guilt feelings → self-punishment; self-expression → guilt feelings → self-punishment. In other respects it has centered on somewhat different links, ones that are, however, just as close and no less related to illegal behavior: pressures → escape-seeking → anxiety-reduction; inadequacy feelings → follow others (also: "give up" on challenges easily).

For the present individuals to greatly weaken or break from such links they need to learn new ways of expressing and satisfying given needs and wishes—less self-defeating, more self-enhancing, yet nondestructive, ways. This often means that—mainly during their program—they must recognize and address their often self-defeating or destructive relationships with parents and others, and must develop satisfying alternatives to their present behavioral reactions to those individuals and to various types of stress, guilt feelings, anxiety, and so on. They must develop, or sometimes increase, practical skills/capacities as well, not just for the more direct and obvious reasons but because this can put them in a stronger position vis-à-vis those relationships and various interactions with peers.

Experiential Learning

The earlier-mentioned *learning* includes but goes beyond the intellectual or cognitive; similarly, the *addressing* generally involves more than—sometimes even other than—counseling, pragmatically oriented discussions, following through on explicit contingency or other contract arrangements, and/or completing various structured-learning modules per se. Instead, to the extent feasible, most such individuals should directly and repeatedly see and feel that—through their own efforts, though with program assistance at various points—they

can have experiences and relationships that are quite different than the generally negative ones they have often had thus far. Moreover, these different, more positive, live experiences can give them a strong basis of comparison, one that can help them better *recognize* self-defeating or even wasteful relationships in the first place, particularly in their own lives. (The earlier, more negative experiences and relationships were mainly a combination of (1) ones they were allowed, encouraged, and, in some ways, forced to have, for example, by parents/guardians/peers, and of (2) others which they themselves more deliberately chose to have or pursue, often without realizing that different, more satisfying and constructive possibilities might be open to them under various conditions.) Also, these individuals need to see that they can enjoy other experiences at least as much as some which they have had with crime-oriented or crime-tolerant persons, of whatever age.

In any event, the present youths or young adults should have concrete experiences that can help them personally see and feel the following. (1) Such activities/interactions (a/i's) are not, somehow, "beyond them"; (2) they, themselves, can help generate and sustain such a/i's, (even though—with support from their parole agent and others—they may have to "try and try again"); and (3) such a/i's need not be short-lived and rare. The youths should also personally see that they can not only be strong and capable (in any event, be an equal) when interacting with others, and can experience satisfactions at the time, but that they can do so while being—in the broad sense of these terms—*good* and *genuine*. In the present context, these qualities or clusters would especially focus on, or at least include, being honest and helpful to others rather than, say, trying to fool them, taking advantage of them, often trying to "get around the rules" when interacting with them, and—in various other ways—disregarding their needs and feelings, not to mention their rights.[9] In general, these firsthand experiences would have to take place—particularly in the beginning—with persons other than those with whom their interactions have thus far been unhappy, unreliable, or destructive. This, at least, would be the case unless the latter individuals were willing and able to change in major ways and to do so fairly quickly—these changes being over and beyond, but also requiring, initial good faith efforts on their parts, and attempts to improve communications as well.

Even while these important inputs are occurring and the resulting experiential learning is taking place, something no less significant should occur, namely, inputs that can affect certain other parts of the self and self-image. Specifically, these individuals, like many others, should have experiences/interactions that can eventually help them realize and believe that they actually can be and are—or *probably* can be and probably are—accepted, valued, and liked, (1) even when they are not presenting a facade, and (2) even though the acceptance may be neither unlimited nor unconditional.

This basic realization/belief also involves *feelings,* and its strength can slowly increase in that respect as well. It is often fostered and reinforced not just by the previously mentioned interactions in general, but by factors such as the following in particular (usually in combination, and, in many respects, implicitly):

1. The consistent interest and frequent support they receive from others whom they feel are concerned with their well-being, and who "don't give up as soon as things get bad or rough."
2. Their, the youths', partial identification with individuals, such as concerned staff, whom they like or admire in various ways.
3. The accomplishments and progress which they, the youths, have made during the program, whether or not the preceding identification has occurred.
4. Positive feedback from, and other salient or enjoyable moments with, persons whose opinions they respect—
   (a) especially, but not only, if those individuals know a good deal about them, and (b) not just in relation to accomplishments/progress.

Together, such experiences/interactions, and the resulting realization/belief, would speak not just to the youths' desired self-image, and "ego" (seen as a coping element or force in mental activity), per se. Rather, they—and especially the *feeling* that goes with this realization/belief—would implicitly and explicitly touch on the youths' earlier-mentioned, unmet or insufficiently met need/desire for acceptance, affection, and/or basic attention. In any event, the individuals should come to feel this acceptance or even conditional acceptance, and so on, from individuals other than delinquent/criminal-oriented peers.

In contrast, (a) *absent* the learning, the relearning, the self-organizing, and the redirecting of the youths' motivations and "willpower" that can each result from the above experiences, interactions, realizations, and feelings, and—instead—(b) *given* these individuals' still-existing drive for self-punishment, for escape from pressures, and so on,[10] certain reactions may occur that would not be predicted from, say, current deterrence theory alone. For instance, in the absence of (a) but in the presence of (b), some conflicted individuals might think and act as follows:

1. If and as they realize that external punishment may be fairly certain and even relatively swift, this—other things being equal—could sometimes increase, not decrease, their interest in offending.[11]

   (This hypothesis or scenario implicitly requires that the offenders in question take it for granted, hope, or believe that the given punishment will probably be sufficient, on the one hand, but not excessive—for example, not too painful, too uncomfortable, or too disruptive—on the other. However, it does not require that offenders' estimates are always accurate.)

   This follows from the fact that, as indicated earlier, some conflicted individuals commit given offenses partly *in order to* get punished in certain ways and to thereby soon reduce various guilt feelings, pressures, fears, and the like (see, e.g., Factors 1 through 3).

2. Certainty, and especially swiftness, aside, if the offenders feel a need for *considerable* rather than slight punishment, or, perhaps, for stronger punishment/control than before, the following could take place:[12] Relatively severe offenses,[13] or else ones that are more severe than before, could have a greater attraction for these individuals than they otherwise would.[14] Under these conditions, offenses that are severe or more severe than those committed previously would be more likely to occur—provided that the offenders considered those behaviors likely to produce stronger punishments, though not ones that are extreme. Thus,

in the present scenario, punishments/ restrictions that—within limits—would be of greater average severity/duration than those which the justice system has used thus far could lead to an increase, not a decrease, in recidivism.

Obviously, key dimensions in points 1 and 2 center on the following questions: (a) To what degree do these individuals still "need" (psychologically need) to punish themselves, and so on—and, more specifically, need to do so via behaviors that are illegal or which lead in that rather than less harmful directions? (As implied earlier, some such youths punish themselves in legal ways, as well.) (b) What general type/severity of offenses do those individuals implicitly assume will be likely, or needed, in order to gain that objective? Some offenses that, in their view, are relatively minor, might not be seen as likely to produce the sufficiently strong or lengthy punishment/respite. This would apply even if that punishment—of whatever type—seemed almost inevitable, and also fairly swift. To be sure, many rapid and certain sanctions *would* help deter various individuals for given periods of time, whether or not the punishment were strong.

Notes

1. Factors that, in turn, contribute to all of *these* will be briefly mentioned.
2. Though younger, middle, and even many or most older adolescents recognize these possible near-term consequences of their illegal behavior, they seldom focus on the fact that such consequences, say, those involving employment, may continue well into the future. Young adults, however, do give this some thought.
3. With some youths, the following applies not only to their illegal behavior but to their ambivalence about substantially changing their long-standing adjustment patterns or about continuing to do so— and about generally moving forward (this ambivalence often results in resistance/reluctance): Among other things, the youths' resistance and/or reluctance is a way of expressing resentment over what they regard as one or both parents' or other key adults' general dislike or rejection of them. This is especially but not only the case if these youths believe those

individuals are nevertheless also expecting, or actively pressuring them for, substantial achievements and/or various other changes in the near future (whether or not those changes are to be accompanied by physical emancipation). Such reactions and possible beliefs by the youths need not necessarily or largely reflect a further belief that those parents or other adults have, in addition, compared them unfavorably with other individuals, such as siblings; however, they often partly do reflect that belief. All this is apart from the fact that—via given illegal behaviors, as well as the above resistance/reluctance —some youths implicitly try to let the parents or other adults know that they (the latter) are "right" about them (the youths) in certain ways, but that they are also "wrong" about them (and about how they may have treated them), in equally or more important ways.

4. This "hence deserve" is mainly rooted in emotion, not in strong or specific external conventions, let alone in firm logic. That is, it chiefly reflects the individuals' past experiences, personal thought associations, "life scripts," and so on—not, for instance, (1) widely agreed upon ethical principles and practices, or (2) various external or objective rules, requirements, and "if-x-then-y" relationships that involve mutual obligations.
5. The emotions in question are other than the anger and resentment of Factor 1, though some may relate to these.
6. Regarding hoped-for external control, some such expressions partly involve a "cry for help," as may others that are not illegal. This is true even though the youths—via those same expressions/ actions—allow those very same impulses, wishes, thoughts, and emotions (or else ones the youths consider less "bad") to be partly or largely *satisfied* or relieved.
7. Such feelings, especially if accompanied by those of inadequacy, by fear of eventually failing and thereby upsetting or angering others, or by both, partly account for these individuals' following tendencies (any or all of which may exist in the same youth): (1) Soon "giving up," that is, no longer trying, when faced with moderate to difficult challenges or with steady opposition, when given little

support, and sometimes when even given *substantial* support and encouragement. (2) Thinking "it's all useless anyway, so why even bother!" (3) Assuming that most people will be "against" them in any event, whether or not, but especially if, those individuals learn certain things about them, or get close to them. (Many such youths often implicitly assume those individuals would be *uninterested* in them, even if they did not learn various "bad" things about them.)

8. To be sure, even if those issues were resolved or considerably reduced, this, by itself, would not fully guarantee the short- and long-term elimination or marked reduction of illegal behavior. Nevertheless, with many youths, such resolution, and so on, would be an essential precondition, and the *non*attainment of those goals would be guaranteed or virtually guaranteed if little or no resolution occurred.

9. Some such individuals would be learning—for literally the first time, or else more clearly than before—(1) what nonexploitive and/or nondeceptive interactions are generally like, and (2) that neither they nor other persons must end up feeling hurt, confused, angry, or disappointed by their mutual interactions, whether these are quick, simple, and impersonal, or lengthy, complex, and personal. Among conflicted youths, both (1) and (2) apply not just to numerous assertive-deniers but to many anxious-confused as well.

10. These drives can each vary in degree, both within and across individuals.

11. Swiftness would have an increased importance here, if, for instance, the youths' main immediate drive involved such factors as the following (not necessarily in combination): (1) escape from external pressures (distinguished from self-punishment); and, (2) an attempt to obtain external/structural control over various personal impulses—some of which they fear they might express and which they consider "worse" than those they have already expressed.

12. This situation would arise with, but not be limited to, some individuals who have bizarre or very violent thoughts and/or impulses much more often than do the vast majority of offenders. More specifically, it would sometimes arise whether or not, but especially if, the following were also the case: (1) Some of those thoughts/impulses experienced by the given individuals have already been partly or largely acted-out (though the youths may not have been caught for that), and/or are felt, by those individuals, to be strong and perhaps growing stronger, in any event. (2) Whether or not they have been acted-out, many such thoughts/impulses sometimes frighten these youths or often make them quite anxious. Under such conditions, these individuals sometimes preemptively act-out in *relatively* severe ways, though generally not in the "bizarre or very violent" ways they know or believe are possible.

13. Again, these would not be the bizarre and/or very violent offenses mentioned in endnote 12, above.

14. With other offenders, relatively *minor* external punishments could suffice with respect to temporarily relieving their drive for self-punishment, to helping them escape from pressures and thereby relieve anxiety, and so on. In such instances, the offenses themselves could be, on average, less severe than before—though no less likely to occur.

47 ELEMENTS USED IN SEVEN PROGRAMS THAT FOCUSED ON VARIOUS TARGETS

The CTP, Winnipeg, and CREST operations each addressed a similar target: moderately serious to very serious delinquents in community settings. Their major elements were counseling, pragmatically oriented discussions, routine supervision or limit-setting, and other features if and as needed, such as academic or vocational training, collateral contacts, and material aid. Were these elements also observed in four programs that had various *other* targets?

To address this question we examined ("observed") the published program descriptions of the CTP, Winnipeg, and CREST operations ("Set 1" programs), and of the remaining four programs as well ("Set 2"). The Set 2 programs—specified below—were appropriate for the question at hand, since they were already known to have focused mainly or exclusively on targets which differed from that of Set 1. (Like CTP, and so on, they, too, were successful with their targets.) The basic elements used by the Set 1 programs were mentioned above. Regarding Set 2, the situation was as follows:

The Boston Program

As with all Set 1 programs, this was a community-based operation; here, however, clients were less seriously delinquent. The major program features were counseling (about personal issues), job placement plus job counseling, and, if necessary, remedial education. Pragmatically oriented discussions were integral to the job-centered components. Less supervision/surveillance/limit-setting occurred than in Set 1 programs, possibly because these youths were less delinquent.

The Canadian Volunteers in Corrections Program (CaVIC)

Like the Set 1 and Boston programs, this one took place in the community. Though it included no young and few middle adolescents, it had many older ones. However, it focused equally on young adults, and—regardless of age—it involved less serious offenders, as in the Boston operation but unlike Set 1. CaVIC's main program features were pragmatically oriented discussions, collateral contacts, counseling, and—mainly for non-adults—recreational activities. (Collaterals included, for example, general advocacy/brokerage and contact with families and friends.) Academic and vocational training were infrequent in themselves and less common than in Set 1 programs. This may have reflected a combination of the clients' higher average age, their relatively low delinquency—and, possibly, a view by program staff that other ingredients would be adequate or better, or that relatively few of these individuals had significant skill/capacity deficits in those areas.

Los Angeles Camps

Here, as in Winnipeg and CREST, most clients were moderately serious delinquents; but in contrast, L.A.'s setting was institutional. The more successful camps often combined academic training, counseling, work assignments within and outside camp, recreational and socializing experiences on-grounds and off-grounds, and contacts with community members. Since the youths were securely or semi-securely confined, supervision/surveillance/limit-setting—while present—was somewhat different than in community programs.

Likewise, pragmatically oriented discussions regarding issues of and arrangements for "everyday" community life (e.g., out-of-home placement, return to school, driver's license, job-seeking plans) were deemphasized until later in the youths' stay.

The Danish Program

Here, as in the Boston and CaVIC programs, less serious offenders were involved. However, in contrast to those programs and unlike all three in Set 1, this operation was institutional. Moreover, unlike all programs other than CaVIC, it addressed adults (here, only adults). Despite these differences, the Danish program's major ingredients were counseling, pragmatically oriented discussions, collateral contacts, and material aid—as in Set 1. (The categories other than "counseling" commonly involved concrete, post-institutional issues such as employment assistance, financial advice, residence placement, and monetary aid.) Not surprisingly, the type of supervision or limit-setting generally associated with *community* operations was essentially absent, since the present clients were incarcerated; in addition, little academic and vocational training took place—again unlike Set 1. The latter may have occurred partly because most offenders were apparently not seen as having substantial skill/capacity deficits in those areas (in fact, the opposite often applied), and, perhaps, also because they were adults. (CaVIC, which mainly addressed older adolescents and young adults, similarly deemphasized such training.)

Thus, several elements that were used in all three (Set 1) programs which focused on (1) serious juvenile offenders (SJOs) in the community were also utilized—with considerable regularity—in programs that, collectively, focused on four other targets. Those targets were: (2) less serious juvenile offenders in the community, (3) less serious adult offenders (LSAOs) in the community, (4) SJOs in an institution, and (5) LSAOs in an institution. Across those seven programs, the most common elements were counseling, pragmatically oriented discussions or staff activities, and some form of supervision or limit-setting. In effect, those elements—which were copresent in any given program and were, in that sense, mutually linked with each other—were the most widely relied upon combination, or the *core* combination for targets (1) through (5). They appeared in virtually all programs and were apparently used with almost all clients.

Often associated with that core were academic and/or vocational (a/v) training, and collateral contacts. However, unlike the core, these features were used—in four of the seven programs—with only some clients. (It was assumed they were not needed with everyone.) In that respect they were supplements or complements: used "as needed," to focus more on given individuals. Yet, in the three remaining programs, either a/v training (in one program) or collateral contacts (in two others) *were* used with almost all clients; in that regard, those features were not supplements/complements. As to material aid, this—in the programs in which it appeared—was used "as needed," not across-the-board.

At any rate, the seven programs not only had several major features in common, but those features had been applied, collectively and successfully, to a sizable range of targets.

48 GENERAL GUIDELINES AND SPECIFIC INFORMATION IN INTERVENTION PLANNING

If one wishes to work with a given client at the level of individualization emphasized in this book, that client's intervention should build upon an initial intervention plan whose content and scope should be primarily determined by the type of information described and illustrated below. It should not be mainly determined by preexisting, "general guidelines," though these can play an important role in shaping that plan.

Such guidelines, for example, those used in CTP (Warren et al., 1966b), can exist separately for each client type ("client group")—that is, one set per type—and they are presumed to apply to all members of that group (thus the term *general* guidelines). These guidelines focus, for one thing, on several core and as-needed program elements, and such elements are either recommended for use or else simply listed for the practitioner's consideration in connection with an intervention plan for any member of the client group. Usually, guidelines also list and recommend techniques which have often proven useful for working with that client group, and they may mention some that are generally counterproductive (see Chapter 6). In these and other respects they thus contain the major ingredients and aspects of what we have called the "overall approach" for those clients; that is, they contain ingredients/aspects that might be used with them (and some which should not be used). However, as indicated next, this guidelines approach to focusing on clients is not quite what we have in mind when we speak of a sufficiently individualized intervention plan. At least, it is not all we have in mind.

To reach the level of individualization that is needed for such a plan with regard to *any given client,* the thrust and details of that plan should be primarily determined by specific, maximally current information about that particular individual's needs, interests, abilities, overall life situation, relationship with parents, and so on.[1] To be sure, various needs, life circumstances, and so forth, that apply to him will be very similar to those found in other, though perhaps not all other, members of his client group; and some of these common factors and conditions may well be mentioned in the guidelines. (The way these needs, life circumstances, and other factors as well as conditions are *combined* with each other will be similar less often, across those members of the client group. At any rate, only a few combinations, if any, are likely to be focused upon in the guidelines. This is certainly the case with present-day guidelines, though future ones could conceivably be more comprehensive in this regard.) To develop the intervention plan, information about such factors/conditions would first be obtained at intake—from the youth, others, and various records.

The main differences and interrelationships between this individual-centered information, on the one hand, and that which can be usefully extracted from general guidelines, on the other, will now be illustrated in connection with three types of program elements (ingredients): academic and vocational training, out-of-home placement, and external controls. In these examples, we will assume the individual is a passive-conformist, though other client groups could have been used. Also, the examples, especially the last two, will emphasize community settings.

Individual-Centered and Guidelines-Based Information
Academic and Vocational Training
It is specific information about the individual's personal interests, abilities, age, grade level, and various other factors that should determine (1) whether he would initially receive either academic or vocational training (assuming availability), (2) which particular academic or vocational fields he might best pursue, (3) what level he should probably start at, and so on. More precisely, it is that type, range, and level of information—once it is integrated and its action implications become clear—that should be the main determinants. Preexisting, general guidelines that describe passive-conformists as a group would not provide an adequate information base for making the above determination—certainly not a base that is as broad as the above with respect to its range of factors, yet which is also specific and current.

Nevertheless, since the youth is not only a particular person but (when conceptualized by staff) a *type* of person, namely, a passive-conformist, those preexisting guidelines—since they focus on his type—could play a role. For instance, they could help implement the above decisions once they are made—help, say, by suggesting possibly useful strategies and techniques that could support the given decisions. More specifically, those guidelines could provide clues as to how staff might interest and involve the client in the above training, and how they might maintain his involvement. To be sure, clues may be obtained from other sources, as well.

Out-of-Home Placement
In a second example, such factors/conditions as a client's (1) relationship with parents or guardians, (2) own desires and preferences, and (3) overall life situation should be the main determinants of whether he should receive an out-of-home placement, and, if so, what kind would be realistic and perhaps best (independent/relatives/foster/group; temporary/long-term). The general guidelines for passive-conformists could not zero in on that individual's situation as pointedly and realistically as could such factors and conditions,

since the guidelines could not reflect his actual circumstances, available choices, particular feelings, and so on (let alone the feelings of parents, relatives, and others).

Nevertheless, though they could not provide the specific, converging evidence needed in order to make an optimal placement/no-placement decision, general guidelines could again play a role. For instance, they could help staff better understand certain long-term dynamics that underlie many or most passive-conformists' relationship with their parents. (Here, "dynamics" are distinguished from their effects, for example, from whether the youth/parent relationship is mainly supportive, abusive, or mutually rejecting. [Guidelines cannot indicate *which* of these applies to a specific client.])

(Though guidelines-based summaries of typical dynamics may only partly apply to any specific client and should not be accepted uncritically, they may still provide valuable—sometimes crucial—insight. As such, they may help staff *better* address various placement issues,[2] not to mention other issues and factors that can bear on the youth's feelings and behavior. [The preceding applies independent of the fact that staff's understanding of dynamics—whether these focus on youth/parent relationships or on other areas—need not come from guidelines alone.])

Also, if an out-of-home placement *is* needed, the following would be relevant, especially if any departure from home would likely generate problems and challenges of its own (not to mention opportunities): Guidelines, particularly when used with the more individualized information itself, could provide not only clues that might ease the client's departure from his parents'/guardians' home and that might facilitate a possible return later on; instead they could also offer suggestions regarding the types of foster or group homes—and their parents/operators—that might be particularly effective or ineffective. Again, however, the guidelines, by themselves, would not provide the specific, current details needed in order to make the most informed placement versus no-placement decision in the first instance regarding the given individual. This would be true even if the guidelines-based statement of *dynamics* applied closely to that youth.

External Controls
As a final example, the type and amount of

external controls (limit-setting) that would be necessary and preferred should mainly reflect the youth's recent adjustment patterns, principal defenses, and overall life situation. They should reflect various personality characteristics, as well—ones not limited to those common to his client type. Among these factors and conditions should be the immediate triggers of his illegal behavior; his known level of involvement with delinquency, delinquent peers, and so on; his level of impulsivity/evasiveness/frustration-tolerance; the type and level of likely supervision by parents/others; and the circumstances of any runaways (e.g., feelings of threat or rejection; bid for attention). Besides contributing to a risk score or to an overall, qualitative risk assessment, such factors and conditions could supply general and specific clues/directions regarding types, amounts, and areas of needed intervention, and they could comprise a baseline against which to later measure positive and negative change.

Though preexisting guidelines might well list such factors and conditions and may indicate that they should be evaluated, they could not—obviously—*perform* or contain that evaluation itself, with respect to any actual youth. As a result, they could not provide the specific information needed to make decisions that could instill the maximum feasible confidence regarding the appropriate types/amounts of limit-setting for any such youth. At any rate, they could not provide the best available and most specifically informed decisions about the individual, even if their recommendations for passive-conformists as a *group* were, on average, fairly close to the mark.[3]

Despite this significant limitation, general guidelines could often suggest types of external controls that are likely to be counterproductive or essentially unworkable—not simply *disliked* by the youths, or even moderately but often resisted by them. Yet even so, before staff accepts those suggestions, it is important for them to reflect on whether they do indeed seem largely applicable to the particular individual in question. In this regard, a related, underlying caution is in order: Since guidelines-based clues often can be valuable and can therein save time and effort, staff should resist any tendencies on their part to less often seek specific, current information from the individual youths and significant

others—say, to less often seek it, or to perhaps even seek less of it, on the belief that, given the guidelines, enough is already known, that most improvements over guidelines-based information will be marginal, or that certain probabilities are already high enough in any event. Moreover, by seeking and utilizing the more individualized information, time and effort will generally be saved in any event, in the long run.

General Issues

By utilizing and interrelating information about the given youth's motivations, needs, fears, defenses, overall life situation, and so on, the individualized approach could thus do more than help determine *which* program elements or variations should be used, for example, out-of-home placement, particular kinds of controls, either academic or vocational training, and so on. Instead, it could also provide converging evidence regarding the intensities, durations, starting points, and sequences that might be feasible, appropriate, and the most accurate with respect to the given youth. This, too, would apply to whichever program elements are to be used, whether "core" or "as-needed." Also, it would often pertain in major ways, not just at the level of fine-tuning. At any rate, as implied, the individualized approach would be appropriate, and should receive the heaviest weight, even if certain program elements, certain intensities of those elements (e.g., weekly group counseling), and so forth, have already been specified in the guidelines.[4] (See "Precedence," below.)

(In the case of guidelines, the elements, intensities, and so on, would not, of course, have been specified with respect to the particular youth in question. Rather, the reference—unless it had been explicitly delimited, that is, qualified—would presumably be to any member of the client group. This would be true even though, theoretically [and simultaneously], its main focus would be, or at least should be, on the more *typical* [average and/or modal] members of that group.)

If, for whatever reasons, specific or detailed information cannot be initially obtained regarding an individual client or a given area of his life, staff should certainly focus on the guidelines to a greater extent than otherwise. Such increased consideration, and possible utilization, would be particularly appropriate with respect to *techniques*. This is because not only substantial experience but careful research suggests that certain types of staff input and related staff/client interactions are very often more helpful than others, sometimes much more helpful, for instance, with passive-conformist as well as conflicted youths.

As is clear, preexisting guidelines can and already do contain a good deal of relevant and accurate material, whether in relation to techniques or other aspects of intervention. Moreover, this relevance and accuracy would apply across a large portion of the developmental-adaptation spectrum described in Chapter 27. In addition, this guidelines material—more specifically, the information, listings, and recommendations—is certainly more individualized than that which is ordinarily used in connection with *standard* programs.[5] However, when one compares the guidelines-based level of individualization with the substantially higher "level" emphasized in this book, a rather different picture emerges. (The higher level is used as the basis of comparison because it involves a type, scope, and detailing of information we consider necessary and sufficient with respect to the goal mentioned shortly, and it is thus a level toward which to strive.) Specifically, by using the latter level of individualization as the standard of comparison, one can see that the guidelines-based approach (GBA) to intervention planning is often unable to provide sufficiently specific and accurate information/ recommendations; at least, it does so less often than the more individualized approach. (Again, this global assessment of GBA is solely from the perspective of how often— compared to the more individualized approach—it can provide the type and amount of information we consider necessary and sufficient in order to help achieve the long-range, growth-centered goal associated with that higher degree of individualization itself. The guidelines-based approach *can* help achieve those goals, but not as often as can the more individualized approach.)

At any rate, although GBA has several important strong points, it cannot sufficiently individualize—and in that respect cover—certain important, intervention-relevant areas, dimensions, or situations, such as placement, unusual circumstances, crises, and changes through time (including growth and retrogression alike). With some such areas, this limitation centers on overall planning or strategic matters; it occurs especially because these tasks—in order to help achieve the long-range, growth-centered goal—call for an *integration* of considerable information about the given individual, more specifically, for an interrelating of certain types and levels of information (and a subsequent highlighting of central, emerging themes/factors). With other areas, the limitation focuses on more immediate, tactical, day-by-day decisions and challenges.

Nor would guidelines-based information (GBI) sufficiently individualize or otherwise adequately represent youths who, in other than minor or superficial ways, are somewhat atypical of their group with regard to their interests, abilities, and/or certain personality features.[6] At any rate GBI would not, on balance, represent those youths *as well as* would the more individualized approach, or represent them in an adequate way *as often*.[7] This applies to factors, conditions, and issues that have strategic and tactical implications alike.

Precedence

If one wished to develop an intervention plan that emphasized the more individualized approach, the following would apply in the case of any specific client, typical or not:[8] If (1) the apparent action implications of the specific, current information obtained regarding that client differ from those suggested in a set of preexisting guidelines that focus on his *type,* the former implications should be given precedence over the latter. Similarly, if (2) an either/ or decision is required, as in the case of placement, the implications drawn from that same individual-based information pool should again be favored. Yet, in both (1) and (2), the guidelines-based implications should be kept in mind. Moreover, they should be later reconsidered—together with relevant new information about the particular youth—if the existing intervention is definitely faltering (and assuming, of course, that the youth does fall within the given client type[9]).

Both (1) and (2) are independent of the important fact that guidelines can and almost certainly will expand and improve in the future—will encompass and reflect more and better knowledge through the years, and can then, accordingly, be given increased relative weight. In short, the *specific, maximally current information* about the individual client should even then remain central—should *not,* for instance, while continuing to be essential, become only secondary to the guidelines. This, at least, would be appropriate as long as staff, supervisors, and others have converging reasons to believe that the information which staff/others obtain about individual clients is of good quality with respect to the earlier-mentioned factors and conditions (viz., needs, interests, abilities, life situation, etc.), and that staff/others can integrate/interrelate that information well (internally and externally) when developing an intervention plan.

(Assuming the presence of good quality information and integration, on the one hand, and given fairly reliable classifications of intervention-relevant youth types, on the other, the overall utility of expanded and improved guidelines could ultimately approach and perhaps almost equal that of specific, current information in several respective areas [though not, e.g., with regard to crises, unusual circumstances, and various abrupt shifts]. On balance, however, the value of guidelines would neither surpass nor substitute for that of specific information when planning for any given individual and when making subsequent changes in strategies, techniques, and so on. Instead, the two types/levels of information would continue to complement each other.)

Even if intervention progresses rather than falters, and if and as the youth's life circumstances and/or outlook change in any event, some adjustments, improvements, and/or substitutions would probably be necessary or desirable with respect to various program elements, techniques, intensities, and other factors/approaches that have been used.[10] Where possible, such midcourse (though not necessarily onetime) changes should derive from information about the specific youth and from staff's overall experience with him. However, as implied, various changes could also reflect selected recommendations from the guidelines.

Notes

1. At the agency or total-caseload level, plans based on such information should be developed for at least a large majority of clients before that agency's interventions—

collectively—should be described as "individualized," in the sense used here.

2. For instance, applicable youth/parent dynamics could provide clues regarding the type of relationship the youth might anticipate, and tend to establish, with various foster or group home parents/operators, and with other adults as well.

3. This situation pertains to the *particular* youth and is essentially independent of the following: The average variation in what constitutes an appropriate and workable type and amount of limit-setting may well be larger for some youth *groups* than for others, for example, larger for the anxious-confused and assertive-deniers than for passive-conformists.

4. Here, "specified" means either listed for consideration or explicitly/implicitly recommended for use.

5. This applies to most of the discrete items, for instance, the separately listed or recommended elements and techniques, which comprise that material. Thus, it is not limited to those same items viewed in the aggregate, that is, collectively.

6. This would apply even if (1) the *life situations* of these individuals were fairly *typical,* and if (2) the guidelines provided *some,* perhaps considerable, understanding of such youths, whatever their life situations.

7. As indicated, adequacy or sufficiency is being judged with reference to the long-term, growth-centered intervention goal for serious multiple offenders. To achieve a less challenging goal, a different type of information and level of individualization would generally suffice—whether for typical or atypical youths.

8. As in the discussion thus far, this assumes that the information base—here, the pool of specific information about the client—encompasses its usual range of subjects and issues, and seems reliable in the sense of credible.

9. For instance, he displays several though not necessarily most of the key factors associated with that type (and few if any associated with each remaining type), especially its underlying dynamics. This applies whether or not he is generally atypical.

10. This would apply not only to each element, technique, and so on, individually, but to any two or more of them together, for example, in connection with their relative emphasis and priority. It would also apply whether or not those features were originally derived from individual-based sources (e.g., youths), from general guidelines, or from both.

FURTHER DISCUSSION AND NOTES TO CHAPTER 22

For the remaining discussions it would be useful to keep in mind the distinction between (1) *differential (unequal) opportunity for inclusion in a sample,* that is, DO across E's and their C's, and (2) *bias toward success,* again among E's compared to their C's: DO for inclusion may or may not exist whether or *not* E's or C's are biased toward success, that is, whether or not either one has a built-in advantage over the other. By the same token, bias toward (i.e., unequal likelihood of) success may exist—or, alternatively, may *not* exist—whether or not unequal opportunity for *inclusion* exists. All this applies irrespective of the degrees involved. (Bias toward success, of course, would be related to E/C differences in *background items,* if such differences did exist; and, as already indicated, differential opportunity for *inclusion in a sample* was linked, by Lerman, not only to the presence of such E/C differences in background items but to the presumed bias toward success.)

The present sample. As is evident from the above, experimentals who comprised the 1973 CI&I sample (109 E's, 90 C's) had no built-in advantage over their controls; nor did these controls have an edge over the experimentals. Instead, these groups—the E's and C's—were essentially equal to each other on background items traditionally considered useful for predicting success, and so described (absent BE) by Lerman as well. This follow-up sample, which Lerman discussed in his Note (1973 and 1975), was, as we mentioned earlier, the same type as that used in one of the present book's central follow-ups—one now called "the present sample" (see Table 8-1).[9] Both the 1973 and the present sample

consisted of favorable dischargees (FDs) and unfavorable dischargees (UDs) from the E and C programs, respectively, and of such individuals alone; they both focused on the parole period and they each drew from CI&I rapsheets alone, not from Youth Authority documents. However, compared to the 1973 follow-up, the present one (173 E's, 157 C's) was considerably expanded, since enough time had passed to allow 64 additional E's and 67 more C's to be included. (Note: In both samples, FD and UD were the statuses or achieved-conditions that defined and established the *sample:* For any given youth, one or the other was required for his inclusion in the sample. In the *analysis* of that sample, however, FD and UD were not used as measures of the sample's *success,* that is, of its E's and C's performance (P); to do so would have been circular. Instead, P was measured by the youth-behavior specified below. [In the terminology of Chapter 21, the present sample, like that of the 1973, was an "available" one, not an "eligible" one.])

As indicated in Chapter 8 and shown in Appendix 11 (Pt. I), E's and C's who comprised the present sample were similar to each other on BE, age, IQ, race, SES, and offense; in particular, no statistically significant difference existed between them on these respective items. This applied to the total group and to its conflicted, its power oriented, and its passive conformist youths alike—that is, to these last three groups (plus the rare types) combined, and to each of the three groups separately. (With one exception, it pertained to the book's post-discharge sample as well.[10] The exception, namely, IQ, was the same as that in the 1973 sample.) Nor did numerically *sizable* differences, such as substantial percentage differences, exist between E's and C's in this CI&I parole follow-up; here, the one exception involved the factor of race, in the case of power oriented and passive conformist youths,[11] though not in that of the conflicted and the total groups. Basically, the preceding findings, viewed collectively, mean that the youths who constituted this available sample were neither more nor less likely to outperform their C's. That is, their respective performance levels were likely to be essentially the same as each other. This conclusion can also be drawn when one focuses on (1) the key measure of risk, namely, base expectancy, *individually*, whether or not one *also* focuses on (2) one of BE's traditionally central components—namely, age.

In the follow-up analysis of this sample, "performance" referred to arrests—widely considered a reflection of youth-behavior—and to subsequent convictions—basically, a consequence of that behavior. It excluded other possible outcome measures, such as rate of favorable and unfavorable discharge, rate of revocation, and so on. With respect to this analysis, then, the present sample was not biased—specifically, as follows: (1) The *total group* of E's (N = 173) was no more likely to outperform the total group of C's (N = 157) with regard to rate of arrest and conviction than these C's were likely to outperform the E's on these measures. (2) The *conflicted* E's (N = 99) were no more likely to outperform their conflicted C's (N = 64) on these measures than these conflicted C's were likely to outperform the conflicted E's on them. And so on, for the *power oriented* E's and C's and, separately, for the *passive conformist* E's and C's. (The same applied to the post-discharge sample [Table 8-2; Appendix 11, Pt. II], again with respect to the total group and—separately—to its conflicted, power oriented, and passive conformist youths. As with the parole follow-up, rate of arrest and conviction was used. In this, the post-discharge context, actions such as revocation by the YA and favorable as well as unfavorable discharge from the YA no longer existed.) In sum, neither group had a built-in advantage over the other by virtue of its background features—an advantage with regard to its expected rate of arrest and conviction. When the E's and C's who comprise an available sample are essentially equal to each other, that is, are equal

regarding their expected performance levels, it is appropriate to utilize that sample as a basis for comparing their performance, such as their level of response to their respective programs.[12] This in fact was done in Chapter 8, using the present CI&I sample of E's and C's and utilizing these individuals' arrests as well as convictions as measures of their performance—and, with that, of their programs' comparative effectiveness: The total group of E's was compared to its "equal-expectations" total group of C's; the conflicted group of E's was compared to *its* equal-expectations *conflicted* group of C's; and so on, for the power-oriented E's and C's and, separately, for the passive-conformist E's and C's. Thus, each such comparison was between an E group and a C group whose levels of expected performance were essentially equal, based on the just-reviewed, risk-related, background features. (This also applied to the post-discharge analysis and, ipso facto, to the parole + post-discharge.) Finally, since E/C differences in background items were neither statistically significant nor numerically substantial (e.g., for the total group and for conflicted youths), these differences provided little support, let alone *strong* support or even broad suggestions, regarding the presence of differential organizational screening and of resulting or related unequal opportunity for the E's and their C's to be included in the CI&I parole follow-up samples—that is, the present one and the 1973.

Representativeness

To provide further context on the issue of opportunity for inclusion in the present follow-up sample (Table 8-1) and regarding the question of whether C's and E's differed in this respect, two sets of figures might be useful; the first also bears on this sample's representativeness. Here, representativeness will focus on *sample-composition*—specifically, on the degree to which power oriented, passive conformist, and conflicted individuals, respectively, were present in the CYA/NIMH experiment's overall sample. (Recall that these groups, which were the experiment's three main subtype-combinations or subtypes, together constituted the preponderance of the overall sample, that is, of the "total group.") The question of representativeness will center on whether the present sample's subtype-composition was similar to that of the experiment's *earlier* samples. These earlier samples included, but were not limited to, ones that described all diagnosed youths who had been randomly assigned to either the C or E program. This review will supplement information concerning specific *background characteristics* (BE, age, etc.) of the given youths.

Before presenting the two sets, a few words about these characteristics, which we distinguish from the youth-*subtype* aspect of sample-composition: Information already presented indicates that the present follow-up sample *is* representative of the experiment's earlier samples with respect to base expectancy, age, IQ, race, SES, and offense—that is, to individual features which bear on risk of offending. For instance, a comparison of (1) figures and related findings that are discussed in Chapter 21, together with (2) other material such as Table 21-1 and Appendix 11 (Pt. I), indicates the following: The March 31, 1966 sample, the March 31, 1968 sample, the "updated suspensions analysis" (UDSA) sample, and the present sample (the last one being this book's parole follow-up sample [Table 8-1]), are similar to each other; and in this connection, the present sample resembles the preceding three. More specifically, this information indicates that (1) the *control* youths are similar to one another across all samples, (2) the *experimental* youths are likewise similar to one another, and (3) these C's and E's are similar to *each other,* as well, within each sample. Depending on the particular sample involved, points (1) through (3) pertain to all or almost all six background items. They do so with respect to the total group, to that group's subtype-combinations, and, depending on the particular *item* involved, to all or almost all of its individual subtypes in the 1966 and 1968 samples. (Regarding these *individual* subtypes, *only* they appeared in the 1966 and 1968 samples, since the three-way categorization [subtype-combinations] was not used in the experiment's statistical analyses of background items until the early 1970s. A few years later, after the present follow-up sample had been determined, standard analyses and resulting comparisons indicated that the findings regarding across-samples similarity and within-sample similarity would apply when the three-way subtype categorization [power oriented, etc.] was used with the 1966 and 1968 samples as well. No analyses of the

six background characteristics were carried out separately for each of the *individual* subtypes [Ap, Cfm, Cfc, Mp, Na, etc.], *as* individual subtypes, in connection with the *present* sample as well as the *updated suspensions* sample.) At any rate, a direct comparison of the text figures, the tables, and so on, that appear in this book indicates that the present follow-up sample's C's and E's were representative of (1) the 1966 sample in connection with the several background characteristics, (2) the 1968 sample with respect to those features, and (3) the updated suspensions sample with regard to those features.

We next review the two sets of figures that focus on the three-way youth-classification: power-oriented (Cfc + Mp), passive-conformist, and conflicted (Na + Nx). The first set centers on the question of whether, or to what degree, the present follow-up sample's three-way classification—that is, its subtype-composition—resembled that of all youths who had been assigned to the experiment and, in this respect, represented those individuals. The set's figures are presented separately for C's and E's. The "present follow-up sample," which is also called the "present sample" (still Table 8-1), focuses—as does the overall review—on Phase 1 and 2 Valley males only.

Before proceeding, however, it might be kept in mind that representativeness can exist whether or not any or all of the following three factors themselves exist, that is, are present—in whatever degree; in addition, each of these *factors* can be present whether or not *representativeness* simultaneously exists: *differential processing/screening (DPS),* of youths, by an organization and/or its programs; *differential opportunity for inclusion (DOI),* of those youths, in a sample; and *bias toward success (BTS)*—in each instance, on the part of C's versus E's. This mutual independence, that is, this "whether or not" aspect, means that the following is the case (*note:* Although examples will be presented in terms of C's only, they apply equally to E's): If, say, C's—control youths—who are part of the present sample were found to be *unrepresentative* or largely unrepresentative of all or almost all C's (collectively) who had already been assigned to the experiment as of a given time (e.g., 1966 or 1968), this, by itself, would neither automatically nor necessarily support, let alone require, the conclusion that

DPS, DOI, and/or BTS *existed* with respect to the present sample. (Had this conclusion been drawn, [a] DPS and DOI might have been viewed as essential or, in any event, as likely causes of or contributors to that unrepresentativeness, and [b] BTS might have been considered an inevitable or at least a likely consequence of it.) Similarly, if these same C's from the present sample were, instead, *representative* or largely representative of those same earlier-assigned C's, this, by itself, would not necessitate the conclusion that differential processing/screening, differential opportunity for inclusion, and/or a built-in advantage with respect to success are *absent* from the present sample. In other words, this sample's C's may be (1) unrepresentative or largely unrepresentative of an earlier (and larger) sample's C's, or, alternatively, they may be (2) representative or largely representative of it—in *each* case, whether or not the present sample's C's have been differentially processed, and so on. At any rate, the presence of *DPS* and/or *DOI* does not necessarily lead to unrepresentativeness (*UR*), although, if present, it/they may sometimes contingently promote it. In addition, their absence does not guarantee or even necessarily support representativeness (*R*), and *UR* as well as *R*, respectively, can have causes other than those two factors or their absence. Nor is *BTS*, if and when it exists, necessarily, let alone exclusively, a product of unrepresentativeness; and when BTS does not exist, this does not automatically mean the present sample is *representative*.

Two further points might be mentioned. 1. *Representativeness*, in itself, plays a key role in determining the main areas in which, and the extent to which, given findings can be empirically (inductively) applied—that is, generalized on the basis of shared elements and conditions. In this respect, *R* has a direct and integral bearing on practical and theoretical utility. Regarding "elements," if, for instance, various *background characteristics* (e.g., age, IQ, and race) and the overall *subtype-composition* (see "proportionate representation," below) of the youths who comprise a follow-up sample, such as the present one (called sample "Y"), were comparable to those of the youths from an earlier sample (sample "X," i.e., one from which Y—here, all dischargees—was derived), the findings that would be obtained from Y could be considered applicable or at least potentially

applicable to the type and range of individuals who comprised X. (In the CYA/NIMH experiment, all youths who constituted Y—the present sample [Table 8-1]—had also been part of X, the earlier one, and part of *it* only. They were not a group of different *individuals,* even though their number was smaller.) In addition, findings concerning the sample-Y youths from any *one* subtype or subtype-group (e.g., the power-oriented) would apply or potentially apply to the sample-X youths from that same subtype/subtype-group if these particular X's and Y's were comparable to each other on most or all of the given background features. This individual-subtype/subtype-group-level comparability would exist even if the Y-sample's and the X-sample's respective *overall subtype-compositions* (which are reviewed in Set 1, below) were *not* comparable. "Overall . . . composition" refers to the proportionate representation of a sample's various subtypes/subtype-groups collectively. (*Note.* [a] In any given instance, all aspects of point 1 apply whether or not any relationship—specifically, a contingent association—exists between (1) a sample's representativeness or unrepresentativeness, on the one hand, and (2) differential processing/screening, differential opportunity for inclusion, and bias toward success [or an absence of these], on the other. This holds with respect to point 2, as well. [b] The comparability of various "conditions," such as external circumstances, can, of course, make a critical difference between potential and actual applicability.) 2. As indicated, *R* (representativeness) is a key dimension in assessing the applicability of given findings; involved, in the present context, is the *R* of youths to whom those findings pertain. In point 1's hypothetical example, the role of background characteristics and overall subtype-composition was highlighted in connection with the examination of these individuals' *R*. However, whether one focuses on these dimensions or on others, the assessment of *R*—that is, of representativeness on the part of a sample's C's, also its E's, and even its C's and E's combined—is different than an assessment of the appropriateness, and in this respect the *validity (V)*, of certain findings as such. For instance, regarding the *V* of findings that center on the comparative effectiveness of a control and an experimental program, a critical question is whether the C and E youths who are being compared are essentially equal to each other as to their expected level of performance (e.g., their rate of arrest), when they first enter their respective programs. This question is addressed in terms of variables such as base expectancy, age at intake, and others that are commonly used to predict such performance or at least comparative levels of risk. In any event, the question regarding validity is not addressed on the basis of those youths' *representativeness*. For example, it is not addressed in terms of (1) whether the C-group that helped constitute a given sample (say, the "Y") is comparable to the C-group that was part of the sample (say, the "X") from which it was *drawn*, (2) whether the E-group that completed sample Y is comparable to the E's in sample X—from which *it*, too, was drawn, and (3) whether this across-sample comparability also exists for the C's and E's combined. Instead, the validity question centers on the C's compared to the E's (or vice versa); more specifically, it focuses on this comparison in connection with the first sample (Y). ("Y," of course, is what we have called the "present sample.") That is, it focuses on whether the C's and E's who comprise the sample to which the *findings* apply—that is, focuses on whether the youths whose *performance* is mutually compared—have an equal or approximately equal chance of succeeding, prior to entering their respective programs. Involved, here, is a within-sample, E/C comparison, not an across-samples, C/C comparison, E/E comparison, and so on. At any rate, the appropriateness and significance of distinguishing between an assessment of representativeness and one that centers on validity—particularly on whether C/E comparisons, hence their resulting findings, are unbiased—is reflected in the following: (1) C's and, separately, E's, can each be representative of a sample or population from which they were each drawn even though they may differ from one another regarding their pre-program chances of success. (2) Alternatively, C's and E's can be essentially *equal* to each other regarding those chances, yet one or both groups may be *un*representative in the sense described. (Both (1) and (2) can apply even when—in examining whether sample Y is comparable to X—C's and E's are *combined* and analyzed together. In such analyses, however, sizable C/C as well as E/E differences that *may* each exist can largely counterbalance and cancel each other and

may thereby become statistically masked.) In case (1), the E/C outcome-results on comparative effectiveness may lack the already-mentioned type of validity even though their range of possible *applicability* could have been considerable if they *had* been valid. In case (2), the outcome-results may be *valid*, yet their scope of actual or potential applicability might be narrow or at least unclear.

Set 1: C and E representativeness in eligible and available samples. As of March 31, 1966, the *control* program's total group of Valley males consisted of 24% power oriented, 19% passive conformist, and 40% conflicted youths, respectively; the remainder were the rare types, collectively (Warren et al., 1966a, 32). These figures referred to all male C's who had been released to parole from 1961 to that point, and, as such, they involved what Lerman called an "eligible" sample. We review this 1966 sample partly because he considered it, and the background as well as individual subtypes data associated with it, particularly useful as (1) a benchmark for describing the CYA/NIMH experiment's C and E samples immediately prior to the formal introduction of the statewide Probation Subsidy program (which impacted the types of youth sent to the CYA) and as (2) a baseline or standard against which to assess the representativeness and appropriateness of the experiment's subsequent samples—that is, relative to youths who had been randomly assigned to it as of early 1966 (1975, 229–230).[13] Regarding the eligible sample of male Valley controls as of March 31, 1968 (another sample Lerman discussed in his Note), the figures—23%, 18%, and 44%, again for the power oriented, passive conformist, and conflicted C's, respectively—were very similar to those just shown (Palmer et al., 1968, 2). This somewhat later sample was considerably larger than that of 1966 and it constituted the preponderance of what were eventually all Phase 1 and 2 controls released to parole. (To simplify the following presentation, figures regarding the "updated suspensions" sample have been placed in endnotes.)[14]

In the *present sample* (Table 8-1)—which was a parole follow-up of all C's and E's who had been discharged (not simply released to parole, and perhaps still on it) as of a given cutoff date, and which was called an "available" sample (i.e., available for use as a cohort, say, in a follow-up of dischargees)—the figures for controls were *25%*, *18%*, and *41%*, still for the power oriented, passive conformist, and conflicted groups, respectively. Thus, this sample, which is the one used in the present book's parole follow-up of male, Phase 1 and 2 Valley C's, was almost identical, in its youth-group composition, to that of 3/31/66, and it was also very similar in this regard to the sample that existed as of 3/31/68, toward the end of Phase 2. In short, each of the eligible (the 1966 and 1968) C-samples, on the one hand, and the available (i.e., the present) C-sample just-described, on the other, were essentially the same as one another with respect to the proportionate representation of the three major youth-groups that, together, predominantly comprised these respective samples. In this regard, the present sample's C's (the availables) were representative of all C's (the eligibles) who had entered Phase 1 and 2 over the years. This was the case even though the just-mentioned, 1966 and 1968 eligible samples and figures also included and reflected all control youths who had been paroled-out-of-area (Chapter 21). As a result, they included/reflected all diagnosed Valley males (POAs + non-POAs) who had been randomly assigned to the CYA/NIMH experiment's C program. (Regarding non-diagnosed youths—individuals who were non-study cases—see "NICs," in Chapter 21.)

As of 3/31/66, the *experimental* program's total group of Valley males who had been released to parole from 1961 to that point consisted of *23%* power oriented, *14%* passive conformist, and *48%* conflicted youths, respectively—the rest again being rare types. By 3/31/68, the percentages for these E groups were *21, 11,* and *55*.[15] In the *present* sample (Table 8-1), they were *21, 9,* and *57*— these figures being fairly similar to those of 1966 and almost identical to those of 1968. Thus, as with the *available controls,* who were described in the preceding paragraphs, these available experimentals—that is, the present sample of E's—were representative of the 1966 and 1968 eligible samples. More specifically, they were representative, with respect to the three major youth-groups, of all males who had entered the Phase 1 and 2 E program over the years, by virtue of having been randomly assigned to it. In effect, the composition of male Valley E's, like that of male Valley C's, underwent little change in this regard from the "eligible" samples to the

present—that is, to this book's—"available" one. There was, however, a slight-to-moderate change among conflicted E's from the 1966 sample to that of 1968.

(Changes involving the *present* sample and the book's post-discharge.sample, will be discussed later. Meanwhile, the following might be noted regarding the increased representation of conflicted E's and, to a lesser extent, conflicted C's, from 1966 to 1968. The statewide Probation Subsidy program, which officially began in mid-1966, was operationally well underway in Sacramento and Stockton starting around the following January. By then, these local probation departments were, among other things, increasingly focusing various resources on youths with whom they believed they could make the largest difference, one they hoped would include these individuals' not being eventually sent to the Youth Authority. To help bring about this modified focus—one that involved their giving increased overall priority to youths they considered moderately problemed and/or only moderately involved in delinquency, rather than heavily enmeshed in it—these departments had increased the pace at which they sent certain *other* individuals to the Youth Authority; by doing so, they reserved a little more of their overall time and resources for working with the former, whom they also considered much more numerous than the latter. To subsequently maintain that focus, they essentially sustained that pace. These "others" were individuals they regarded as their more overtly disturbed/unstable and/or long-term problemed, as well as often very resistive, cases. In particular, they were youths for whom the departments believed their resources might not be most appropriately used and might be insufficient or least adequate in any event, even if somewhat augmented. Given all this, the following occurred. If these individuals committed a new offense—not always one that was relatively serious, and whether or not augmented resources and/or different approaches had been used—the departments were more likely than before to immediately send these youths to the YA rather than continue supervising them and otherwise trying to work with them. Regarding this decision-and-action, the following assumption regularly entered the picture; it was based on the departments' prior experience with, and their current information about, the CYA/NIMH experiment and the Youth Authority overall: There was about a 50 percent chance that any individual whom they committed to the YA in connection with a nonviolent offense, and who resided in a qualifying geographic area, would be (1) placed in the YA's "specialized," intensive, community-based program [CTP], and that if he were *not* so placed, he would be (2) sent to an institution that might well have an available specialized program itself. One such nearby institution was Preston, particularly until early 1968; others were Close and Holton, starting in early 1968. At any rate, local departments believed that the individual, once committed, might well receive a type and level of needed service and control that would be better than what they, themselves, would provide.

As it turned out, a large majority of these committed, "overtly disturbed/unstable and . . . often very resistive" youths were in the *conflicted* category. [It largely "turned out" this way, rather than being planned as such, in the sense that neither department explicitly utilized the I-Level classification system at the time, even though several staff members were generally familiar with it. Also, no Sacramento probation staff attended the Center for Training in Differential Treatment until early 1968, and none from Stockton (San Joaquin county) attended until almost the end of Phase 2 (Warren and the Staff of CTDT, 1972).] More specifically, between January, 1967 and the end of Phase 2, approximately three-fourths of all males who became either E's or diagnosed [i.e., non-NIC] C's were classified, within the experiment, as conflicted. This was a considerably higher percentage than before; and of these conflicted youths, close to two-thirds [C's = 68%; E's = 66%] were in the anxious-confused category rather than the assertive-denier. [It might be added that a higher percentage of conflicted and *non*conflicted individuals whom those departments sent to the YA during the given period and who became either C's or E's were younger than youths these departments had previously sent.] At any rate, chiefly because of the above, the representation of conflicted C's as well as E's increased somewhat, though not greatly, from 1966 to 1968. Note 16 reviews the fact that this increase was unequal, across the C and E programs.)

The preceding Set 1 figures, which were presented separately for C's and E's, indicate that the percentage of the 1966 sample of eligible C's that consisted of power oriented, passive conformist, and conflicted youths, respectively, was fairly similar to the percentage of the 1966 sample of eligible E's which consisted of these same groups, respectively: 24, 19, and 40, for the C's and 23, 14, and 48 for the E's. (The eight percentage-points difference between the conflicted C's and conflicted E's, and, to a lesser extent, the percentage-point difference between the passive conformist C's and E's, increased somewhat as of *1968*; here, the percentages of the total group—that is, the percents-of-representation—were 23, 18, and 44 for C's and 21, 11, and 55 for E's, with respect to the same three youth-groups. Regarding the main reasons for the changes among conflicted youths from 1966 to 1968, see the two preceding paragraphs in combination with n. 16.) In the *present* sample (Table 8-1), the percentages were 25, 18, and 41 among C's and 21, 9, and 57 for E's. Thus, although the *power oriented* individuals in this sample were still represented about equally across the control and experimental programs, the C and E *passive conformists* now noticeably differed from each other in this regard, as did the C and E *conflicted* youths. These differences (not so much the *increases* in the respective differences—increases which were each only modest), particularly that between the 41 percent for conflicted C's and the 57 percent for conflicted E's, were not entirely accounted for by the earlier-mentioned changes in commitments to the Youth Authority that were associated with Probation Subsidy (and with factors mentioned in n. 16), at least as implemented locally in the later 1960s and as continued to the end of Phase 2. Nor was the fact that the difference between conflicted C's and conflicted E's *further* increased in connection with the *post-discharge* sample (Table 8-2) entirely accounted for on that basis. (Here, the C's proportionate representation had decreased somewhat, from the present sample—that is, from the parole follow-up [Table 8-1]—to the post-discharge sample, whereas that of E's remained essentially the same as in the present sample. As a result, the C/E percentage-point difference increased—from 16, in the present sample, to 21, in the post-discharge. More on this shortly, and also on the substantial difference that emerged between C and E power oriented youths.)

Set 2: C and E performance and base expectancies. Neither the youths we have studied nor their levels of performance are all alike. We have described personal and interpersonal differences among these individuals—specifically, among the power-roiented, passive-conformist, and conflicted— in Chapters 4 and 5. Concerning C and E performance, we have detailed the parole, the post-discharge, and the combined parole + post-discharge outcomes in Chapter 8, for Phase 1 and 2 Valley males and females—in each case, separately for those three youth-groups. Regarding differences in outcome among the males, the following was observed concerning those groups, first for *C's* and then—separately—among *E's*. (To simplify the presentation we will focus mainly on findings regarding moderate + severe [m + s] arrests combined; as is indicated, however, fairly similar results were obtained for m + s convictions, though less so for C's than for E's. In addition, emphasis will be on parole [Table 8-1], though other periods are included.)

During parole, the monthly rate of offending (r.o.o.) among *controls (C's)* for m + s arrests was slightly lower for the power-oriented youths than for passive-conformists and conflicted: .066, .086, and .080, respectively. Regarding convictions, the rates were .039, .061, and .050. For arrests and, separately, convictions, these differences in r.o.o. between the *power-oriented* individuals, on the one hand, and the *passive-conformist* as well as the *conflicted,* on the other, all reached the .05 level of significance. (There were two r.o.o.-comparisons—hence, two r.o.o. differences—with respect to arrests, and two comparisons/differences regarding convictions.) Given the fact that the base expectancies (risk-levels) of these three youth-groups were very similar to each other (443, 452, and 455, respectively [Appendix 11, Pt. I]), those differences in r.o.o. suggest that the C-program had, or may have had, slightly more impact on the power-oriented youths than on each of the other two. This suggestion received slight or modest—and, in any event, partial—support from the arrest rates for the combined *parole + post-discharge* period: In this approximately seven-year follow-up, the monthly rates for the power-oriented, the passive-conformist, and the conflicted individuals were .053, .066, and .069, respectively, and the corresponding BEs for

these youths were again very similar to each other: 462, 470, and 460 (Table 8-3; Appendix 11, Pt. II). (For the power-oriented individuals versus the *passive-conformists,* the significance level reached only p < .20 > .10 in connection with the differences in r.o.o. [.053 vs. .066]. For the power-oriented versus the *conflicted* it reached .05 with respect to the r.o.o's [.053 vs. .069—with conflicted youths having twice the sample-size of the passive-conformists in the preceding finding].) Regarding convictions, however, the r.o.o's for this long-term follow-up were .035, .042, and .041—all chance-differences alone. (The three BEs were, of course, identical to those just mentioned, as they were for the following.) For the *post-discharge* period by itself, the results were mixed—with the power-oriented youths outperforming the *conflicted* only, and in connection with arrests alone. (Table 8-2.)

With respect to *experimentals (E's),* within-program performance-differences were again observed between power-oriented individuals, on the one hand, and passive-conformist as well as conflicted youths, on the other; this time, however, the differences between the power-oriented and these other two were sharper and more consistent. (In addition, this time the power-oriented individuals performed *worse* than each of the others rather than slightly better than them, or, at least, better than the conflicted youths.) For m + s arrests, the monthly rates of offending for the three youth-groups were .055, .032, and .034, respectively; regarding convictions they were .039, .015, and .022. For these arrests and convictions alike, the differences in r.o.o. between the power-oriented youths and each of the others were non-chance (p ≤ .05). (Again there were two comparisons-hence-differences regarding arrests, and a separate two for convictions. Non-chance differences—specified shortly—were found in connection with the four power-oriented- versus-other comparisons for the below-mentioned, combined *parole + post-discharge period* as well.) Given that the BEs of these youth-groups— certainly the first two of them—were fairly similar to each other (427, 435, and 460, for the power-oriented, passive-conformist, and conflicted, respectively), the preceding rates of offending suggest that the E-program definitely had a different level of impact on the power-oriented individuals than on the others. This suggestion received support in the combined parole + post-discharge analysis. Here, the rates of arrest were .061, .033, and .033, respectively; the corresponding BEs were 431, 430, and 474; and, the rates of conviction followed suit. In addition, the suggestion was largely supported by findings regarding the *post-discharge period* by itself—that is, the four-year, post Youth Authority follow-up alone. Here, the differences in rate of arrest reached .05 for the power-oriented versus the *passive-conformist* and also versus the *conflicted,* although, for rate of conviction, only the latter difference—the one for power-oriented versus conflicted—was non-chance. (All tests of statistical significance mentioned in "Set 2"—that is, all tests of the C versus C differences in r.o.o., and, separately, all tests of the E versus E differences—were based on the Mann-Whitney "U," corrected for ties.)

Opportunity for Inclusion

We will now focus on the question of whether C's and E's who entered their respective programs during 1961–1969 subsequently had an equal opportunity to be included in the parole follow-up sample—the "present sample"— that has been discussed thus far. Except for 41 C's and 39 E's who were purposely excluded when this sample was being constructed (see "Analytic Exclusions," below), every male, Phase 1 and 2 Valley C and E who had received a favorable or unfavorable discharge from the Youth Authority as of the mid-1970s and who was neither an "NIC" nor a "POA" was included in it. These were the sole analytic criteria for inclusion, and no distinctions or allowances were made with respect to (1) the youths' particular base expectancy, age, IQ, race, SES, offense, subtype (hence, subtype-group), I-Level, length of time on or after parole, and number of offenses during or after parole, and also regarding (2) any other feature, condition, circumstance, or status, including ones that predated the YA. At any rate, the sample involved dischargees only, and its analysis centered on their arrests and convictions during parole, to point of discharge. "NICs" were undiagnosed cases; "POAs" were youths paroled-out-of-area.

"Favorable discharge" (FD) and "unfavorable discharge" (UD) constituted legal statuses whose statewide, YA board-established criteria were presented in Appendix 9, and which have been otherwise described and

discussed in Chapters 4, 8, and 21, in endnotes 2, 5, and 7 of this chapter, and elsewhere. Implicit in these preestablished criteria but operating independently of them and focused beyond them, the following situation existed throughout Phase 1 and 2, and it pertained to all C's and E's from the start of their respective programs: No policies and accompanying practices existed at any level whose aim—primary or other—was to (1) increase the chances that any one group of youths, *compared to any or all others,* would receive a favorable discharge, and/or to (2) make it harder for any group, still compared to the others, to avoid an unfavorable one. This reflected the overall Department's, the YA board's, and the C- as well as E-program (i.e., operational) staffs' hope that all youths would receive a *favorable* discharge if possible—in that respect would succeed on parole, and succeed equally. In any event, neither formal nor informal advantages and/or hurdles that had the above and/or related aims were established for any youths as distinguished from any others, based on these individuals' background features, their particular subtypes, or anything else. In this regard all such youths had an equal chance to obtain a FD or, for that matter, a UD. Specifically, within each program, and regardless of its particular nature, content, location, and point in time (e.g., 1961, 1964, 1967), all C's and all E's had an equal opportunity to receive a *favorable* discharge if—as reflected in the broad, YA board criteria—they stayed out of trouble with the law (at least non-minor trouble), did not otherwise pose a serious problem to others (e.g., by acting disruptively toward them), adjusted or evidently tried to adjust satisfactorily in school or in connection with employment, and were not persistently uncooperative toward their parole agent. By the same token, they had an equal opportunity to receive an *unfavorable* discharge if they did *not* stay out of trouble with the law; and so on. In short, all C's, in comparison to all E's, had what can be called an "equal baseline opportunity" (EBO)—one that reflected broad policy and intent. This EBO, however, did not ensure that (1) the respective groups of C's (specifically, the power-oriented compared to the passive-conformist compared to the conflicted) had what can be called an "equal actual likelihood" (EAL) of receiving, say, a favorable discharge, that (2) the respective groups of E's (i.e., "the power-oriented compared to . . .") had a similar EAL, that (3) any given group of C's (e.g., the power-oriented) would have the same likelihood as its counterpart among the E's (the power-oriented), and that (4) all C's *combined* (i.e., all groups—subtypes—collectively) would have the same likelihood as all E's *combined*.

Regarding EAL, we will first discuss point (4)—the broadest one—and will then touch on others. As will be seen, the point-(4) C's and E's, despite their just-mentioned, equal *baseline opportunity*, were not, in fact, equally or almost equally likely to *end up with*, say, a favorable discharge. (The same applied, separately, concerning their likelihood of ending up with an unfavorable one.) Yet, even in this regard, the following itself applied: The fact that these collective C's and collective E's were not equally likely to receive a particular type of discharge, here, an FD, did not ipso facto mean they would have an unequal—say, a lower—chance of being *included in the present sample*. Instead, their chances were essentially the same, and this basically reflected the following: (1) Any of the earlier-specified (e.g., non-NIC, non-POA) youths could be included in it if, instead of receiving a *favorable* discharge, they received an *unfavorable* one; that is, either type would suffice for inclusion, and all youths could receive one or the other. (2) Almost all youths who had entered the experiment during Phase 1 and 2 had received either a FD or a UD as of the cutoff for sample construction. The few who were still not discharged had entered the experiment in the final years of Phase 2 and, unlike all *others* who had entered it during this period (i.e., unlike all others who had subsequently become *dischargees*—youths who, however, were themselves also non-NICs and non-POAs), these individuals were still either in an institution or on parole, for at least their second time.[17]

The fact that C's and E's—still all subtypes combined—were not equally likely to end up with favorable discharges sprang, in part, from the following C/E differential; this applied to non-NICs and non-POAs during Phases 1 and 2 combined, though more so in the first period: E-staff continued to work with the preponderance of youths who had committed a moderate-level offense (e.g.: auto theft; possession of concealed/illegal weapon; resisting arrest; 2nd degree burglary; posses-

sion of marijuana) at some point in their program, and they did so at essentially the same level as before that offense. In contrast, if those youths had been in the C-program when they committed that offense, about 20 percent (not percentage-points) fewer would have been worked with by their parole agent to the same degree as before—in contrast, especially, to being revoked and institutionalized at that point. (Involved, in both the E and C cases, was the individuals' first such offense. E-staff were able to keep working with these youths, rather than have them institutionalized, if the YA board accepted their recommendation that the individuals be "restored to parole" [following the "suspension of parole" that had automatically occurred, as a result of the offense]—subject to adoption of a revised treatment-control plan. C-staff, however, were less likely than E to recommend restoral, following the given, moderate-level offense [MLO]; and the board was equally likely to accept E and C recommendations, whether these were for or against restoral.) By helping these individuals (1) return to parole and (2) then remain on parole as long as an MLO did not recur (see exceptions, below), and/or as long as substantial *minor*-level offending did not occur, staff in effect gave these youths what they considered a further chance to work on their problems and issues within the community and to keep building—without a major break—on whatever progress the youths had already made and on supports that may have been established. In the E and C programs alike, most such restored youths made positive use of this opportunity and eventually received a favorable discharge (compare: Palmer, 1968a, 9, 24–25. *Note.* A large majority of what are termed MLOs in the present book were called "severe" offenses in the 1968a report. There [p. 5], "severe" was very broadly defined; this was done to contrast it with numerous offenses which, in this book and elsewhere, have been categorized as "minor-severity." Because there was no middle category in that report, the report's "severe" offenses included—in fact, consisted very largely of—this book's "moderate-severity" offenses). (In the E-program, approximately 15 percent of all youths who had been restored to parole following a MLO were later restored a second time in connection with a MLO; in the C-program the figure was 6 percent—again for Phases 1 and 2 combined. In both programs, however, restoral almost never occurred if the first and second moderate-level offense, collectively, were any combination of auto theft, possession of concealed/illegal weapon, and 2nd degree burglary. Thus, for instance, a second auto theft would rarely be followed by a restoration if it had been preceded by an auto theft or by a "possession of . . ."; and so on.)

To keep restorals-following-MLOs in perspective it should be noted that, of all the just-described non-NIC, non-POA Phase 1 and 2 males who received a *favorable* discharge, 36 percent of the E's and 24 percent of the C's had committed one or the other of the following (the second of these was much more common, in both programs): (1) *no* non-traffic/non-reporting/non-attendance offenses or infractions at all; (2) one or more minor-severity offense only (e.g.: runaway; incorrigibility; loitering; fighting, no weapons; drinking/possession of alcohol. See Appendix 10, severity-levels 1 and 2. The non-traffics also included injury accidents and drunken driving; "non-reporting" meant to the parole agent; "non-attendance" centered on group meetings and involved E's only.) In short, many favorable dischargees, E's and C's alike, had had no occasion on which to be either restored or not restored to parole, rather than be institutionalized, in connection with a moderate-level offense; this was because they had committed no such offense. The general background and rationale for E-staff's decisions to recommend restoral following any minor- or moderate-severity offense is reviewed in n. 18. An account of C-staff's decisions to do so must be presented in a separate format, due to a publication deadline. This account, which is necessarily quite complex, would have comprised the bulk of n. 19.

Additional discussion regarding "opportunity for inclusion" will itself appear in a separate format, for the same reason. This discussion will indicate that the E-*program* and, separately, the C-*program,* had differing degrees of appropriateness for and power with their differing groups of youth. These differences—e.g., differences in the program's *ability to address* the respective individuals' (groups') needs and defenses, and *to tap* their interests, motivations, and strengths or skills—led some youth-groups to be better able to successfully complete their program than others. This was reflected, for example,

in the much higher level of success (or lower *rate of offending*) among conflicted E's (especially the assertive-deniers) than among power oriented E's. It was also reflected in differing rates of success among various C-groups. Differences *across* programs with regard to appropriateness/power were reflected in the very different rates among conflicted E's than among conflicted C's, and so on. In effect, given youth-groups, utilizing the resources and approaches that were available to them in their respective programs, created their own particular likelihoods of success or nonsuccess—of *offending* or *not offending*. The fact that the differing groups' respective *risk-levels* were not a key contributor to the just-mentioned differences can be seen by comparing and contrasting the levels that appear in the book's several relevant appendices.

In addition, there were no E or C *policies* that operated so as to intentionally or otherwise give any one youth-group a better or worse chance of succeeding than any other—a better or worse chance of offending, of being recommended for restoral-to-parole, of being reinstitutionalized, and so on. Staff in the E as well as C programs tried equally hard with all their youths, that is, regardless of the kind or "type" of individuals involved; and the Youth Authority board made no distinctions based on youth-type, either. Finally, neither policies nor practices that related to restoral versus non-restoral, and so on, caused any individuals—regardless of type—to *offend, in the first place;* and, they made such illegal behavior neither more nor less likely to occur. In creating—via their offense or non-offense behavior—their greater or lesser likelihoods of being reinstitutionalized for long periods of time, *E's and C's* each thereby directly contributed to their relative likelihoods, not only of success or non-success per se, but of eventually becoming part of any given discharge sample—with its particular data-cutoff.

Notes

9. This and the 1973 CI&I sample differed from the updated suspensions analysis (UDSA) sample—(1) many of whose youths had not yet been favorably or unfavorably discharged and (2) which utilized Youth Authority documents rather than CI&I rapsheets.

10. As seen in Appendix 11 (Pt. II), the *total group* of E's and C's who comprised the post-discharge sample were similar to each other, in that no statistically significant (SS) difference existed between them on BE, age, race, SES, and offense, respectively. However, an SS difference did exist on IQ, one in which E's were 5 points higher than C's. No SS difference was found between E's and C's on any of these six items in the case of *conflicted, power oriented,* and *passive conformist* youths, respectively. Each of the preceding points fully applies to the parole + post-discharge (P + PD) sample as well, because the P + PD was literally identical to the post-discharge (PD) sample. That is, (1) all individuals who qualified for inclusion in the PD also qualified for inclusion in the P + PD; (2) *only* those who qualified for the former also did so for the latter; and (3) everyone who qualified for the P + PD was *included* in it.

11. Given the sample-sizes involved, these differences were not statistically significant.

12. When E's and C's are already as close to each other as these were (in the present case, on *background items*), covariance techniques need not be used to statistically fine-tune whatever differences do exist. Moreover, when each such E/C difference—a difference across any two items at a time, from among a group of several items (here, six)—is small or very small, as in the present case, not all of them may become *smaller* subsequent to covariance adjustment. (This especially applies if the intercorrelations among many of the items that have such differences are not particularly high.) More specifically, some differences may even increase a little.

13. Lerman indicated that one of this 1966 sample's "major advantage[s]" was that it "provided detailed evidence that the total eligible experimental and control samples were comparable [to each other] regarding sex, socioeconomic status, type of commitment offense, age, and IQ." Also, the C/E difference on race did not reach the ".05 level"—still for the total sample—though it did reach .10. Finally, although there were "a number of significant differences in population characteristics between the experimental and control group *diagnostic subtypes,* . . . the overall proportions appeared comparable" (1975, 229–230; emphasis added). "Population characteristics" referred to background features, such as age, and the "diagnostic subtypes" were the Ap, Cfm, Cfc, Mp, Na, and so on, analyzed individually. Given that the six above-listed features (base expectancy being unmentioned) were considered by Lerman with respect to each diagnostic subtype, there were 48 possible significant differences; that is, six could have existed for each of eight subtypes. (No C/E comparisons could be made for the Aa.) Seen in this context, the number of statistically significant (.05) differences that existed was relatively small: In the 1966 sample, a total of six were found—one each, for sex, offense, age, and IQ, and two for race. In the 1968 sample, three were found (Warren et al., 1966, 34–35; Palmer et al., 1968, 5–7).

14. Regarding the updated suspensions analysis (UDSA) sample—an available sample—the percentages were very similar to those for the 1968 eligible sample. The UDSA percentages were *24, 18,* and *46* for the power oriented, passive conformist, and conflicted C's, respectively. This sample, which was mainly used to examine rate of suspensions during the youths' first 16 months on parole, whether or not these individuals had been discharged, was discussed in Lerman's Note (1975, 232–234) and extensively reviewed in Chapter 21 of the present book. Also reviewed in 21 were the major shortcomings which were found, during 1972–1973, in the experiment's suspension documents, and, hence, in UDSA outcome analyses that centered on those documents. Nevertheless, information regarding the UDSA sample's youth-characteristics, which was separable from that regarding its outcome analyses, was useful for comparing the sample's subtype-composition with that of the 1966, 1968, and present samples, respectively.

15. In the UDSA sample the percentages were *18, 11,* and *60,* for the power oriented, passive conformist, and conflicted E's, respectively. These figures, for this

available sample, were similar to those for the 1968 eligible one.

16. From 3/31/66 to 3/31/68, there was a smaller increase in the proportionate representation of conflicted C's than of conflicted E's, although each group's increase was modest. Among C's, the change was from 40 percent of the total sample to 44 percent of the total; among E's, it was from 48 percent to 55. This C/E difference primarily resulted from the following: On the one hand, C's who were first committed to the Youth Authority starting in January, 1967 were, on average, released to parole from an institution beginning around mid-August, 1967—that is, about two-thirds through the two-year period from 3/31/66 to 3/31/68. In contrast, E's who were first committed starting at that same time were released almost immediately, that is, starting slightly over *one*-third of the way through that period. Thus, there was less time for "extra" youths—in particular, the Probation Subsidy-accelerated *conflicted* individuals—to accumulate in the C program than in the E, and to thereby raise the proportionate representation of the C-youths much beyond that in the 3/31/66 eligible sample. (This and the 3/31/68 sample consisted of all releasees to parole, as of those dates. The commitment rate from Sacramento and Stockton [combined] to the YA remained comparable between 1/67–8/67, on the one hand, and from that point through 3/68, on the other.)

A secondary factor centered on the random-assignment ratios (RARs) that were used at various points during the two-year period. These RARs determined the relative number of youths who, through time, were channeled into the C program as compared to the E—and, hence, who were reflected in the 3/31/68 eligible sample. A final, no less important factor was that of Non-Interviewed Controls (NICs)—a category that was first created in mid-1966. Starting at that point, these were individuals who had been randomly assigned to the C program but who, based on a further random drawing then made on these youths, were not interviewed and thereby diagnosed (i.e., classified in terms of I-Level/subtype). This factor, like the secondary one, reduced the rate at which youths who were, in fact, conflicted—in this case, however, undiagnosed as such—became part of the C (control) component of the 3/31/68 eligible sample. As with the primary factor, namely, differential time (and, in effect, opportunity), it thereby limited the extent to which "extra" conflicted youths could raise the percentage of this group's C-representation beyond that of the 1966 eligible sample. (It might be added that NICs accumulated at approximately the same rate prior to and subsequent to 3/31/68—the latter period extending to the end of Phase 2.) As explained in Chapter 21, there were no E NICs.

17. It might be mentioned that the number of male NICs which had accumulated as of 3/31/68 had doubled by the end of Phase 2, to a total of 51. (Among them was a male, whose first name was Gail, who had been mistakenly counted as a female NIC in the 3/31/67 sample.) Also, the number of male *POAs* that had accumulated as of 3/31/68 had increased by the end of Phase 2 (and it subsequently increased further, in connection with late-Phase 2-releasees), though at a lower rate and to a proportionately much lesser extent than among NICs.

18. In their efforts to help youths stay out of trouble with the law, make related personal and interpersonal changes when needed, and eventually receive a favorable discharge from parole (and, with this, automatically from the YA), C and E program staff each used approaches and available resources they considered not only appropriate but, in many cases, essential—at any rate, hopefully *sufficient*, collectively. Apart from these expected, global types of similarity, major substantive differences existed. For instance, the E-program, that is, the Community Treatment Project, (1) had a wider range of available resources than the C. More precisely, it had this feature in connection with the particular setting in which (the *community*), and the specific time during which (*parole*), two major realities prevailed: On the one hand, all youths—there and then—ran

their highest risk of engaging in illegal behavior that could eventually lead to an unfavorable discharge, and that could do so almost immediately if it were serious enough. On the other hand, it was also there and then that these individuals had their key opportunity to make personal and social adjustments and advances which, if accompanied by the youths' rejection or avoidance of illegal behavior, could fully satisfy the requirements for a *favorable* discharge. No youth could meet the FD requirements by making progress in an institution alone. Every one had to demonstrate certain adjustments within the community itself; and it was in this setting that the E-program could apply, and usually did apply, a wider range and even a larger overall quantity of resources per youth than could, and did, the C. In addition, the E-program (2) usually applied its resources, and its approaches, more intensively and flexibly than did the C, particularly with respect to the frequency and timing of agent/youth contacts and agent-efforts overall—including responses to crisis. Further, (3) E-staff, given their much smaller caseloads than C, usually got considerably closer to the youths and learned more about their views, needs, and feelings. They usually learned more about family members as well, and often about other sources of known or potential support and/or stress. Partly because of all this, E-staff were better able than C to observe the youths' strengths, skills, actual and felt limitations and vulnerabilities, and various factors that often triggered their fears, defenses, and acting-out. Together, the item-(2) and -(3) features helped E-staff focus more than the C on relevant specifics, current developments, recurring themes, and overall complexities in the individuals' lives. It also helped them (a) better tap various strengths, major motivations, interests, and desires (therein helping the youths become more personally involved), (b) more accurately determine when and to what extent to believe the youth, (c) see and support progress and genuine efforts when these had occurred or were just beginning, (d) recognize and respond more rapidly or at least relevantly to difficulties

and their effects, and (e) thus be considered more valuable by many youths.

Besides those E/C differences in resources, approaches, information, and responses, often-large differences existed with respect to *goals*—generally in emphasis, but often in direction. Regarding emphasis, most E-staff believed they should help youths work not only toward a favorable discharge per se but, simultaneously, toward long-term, positive post-discharge adjustment (PPDA); they believed they should place considerable weight on the latter goal. This PPDA, which most C-staff did not try to emphasize, was an expansion of the Youth Authority's broad aim of helping individuals satisfy the criteria for favorable discharge alone—an objective on which all C-staff did specifically and primarily focus and which E-staff themselves specifically addressed. Unlike the C, however, the latter believed they had the external working conditions needed to help most youths prepare and position themselves to eventually achieve or approach the expanded—the long-term—goal as well. Chief among these conditions, in their view, were program resources, supervisory assistance, and overall opportunity—the latter including low caseloads, considerable flexibility, and enough time.

Regarding the youth's preparation itself, E-staff believed this could almost always be best brought about (achieved)—and, with many youths, probably *only* achieved—via experiences, progress, and changes on the part of the youths that could occur and become consolidated especially in the community, not in an institution. More specifically, most E-staff believed this preparation for long-term PPDA could be best or only achieved if—preferably under conditions of relative environmental stability—the individuals experienced, and learned to adjust to or better adjust to, "real-life" (taken to mean *community-centered*) challenges, opportunities, and relationships (CORs), ones that were non-destructive and non-exploitive in nature. In particular, they believed or assumed that if the youths could (1) become motivated to seriously apply or further apply some of their abilities and potentials to these CORs, could (2) be actively and clearly supported in these efforts, by the agent and others, and could (3) then experience more and/or stronger satisfactions than dissatisfactions in connection with them for—very often—a year or more, the following would have a good chance of occurring: These and related satisfactions would cumulatively help those individuals—and, under some conditions, decisively help them—willingly reduce and then discontinue their delinquent activities and their often-harmful relationships as well as adjustment patterns. This curtailment, and termination, would usually take place at roughly the same time that these youths were experiencing ongoing or increased personal and/or social satisfactions with the new forms and aspects of adjustment, and were usually feeling less anxious about them. Seldom would these developments take place smoothly and steadily; instead, there would be various ups and downs, sometimes including illegal behavior and temporary or seeming regression. Concerning point (1), above, most staff believed or assumed that the "if" was a particularly large and central one. Regarding (2) and (3), they felt that they and the youth—sometimes separately, sometimes together—would have to overcome or neutralize various opposing or otherwise interfering factors and conditions as well—some external, others internal, and some long-standing, others more recent. At any rate, they felt that new satisfactions, by themselves, would seldom suffice, even if the youths were to closely associate them with the given CORs. Finally, most staff believed that the given satisfactions, plus a growing dissatisfaction with or disinterest in previous relationships and adjustments, would eventually help the youths develop a significantly different outer image—for example, a more desired persona—as well as self-image, or would at least add important positive dimensions to their present ones.

Bibliography

Abramson, R. (1957), "Youth Authority Training for Graduate Social Work Students," *Youth Authority Quarterly,* 10, 12–19.

Ackrill, J. (1987), *A New Aristotle Reader, (Poetics).* Princeton: Princeton University Press.

Adams, S. (1961), "Effectiveness of Interview Therapy with Older Youth Authority Wards: An Interim Evaluation of the PICO Project," Research Division Report no. 20. Sacramento: California Youth Authority.

—— (1966), "Development of a Program Research Service in Probation," Research Report no. 27. Los Angeles: Los Angeles County Probation Department.

—— (1974), "Evaluation Research in Corrections: Status and Prospects," *Federal Probation,* 38, 14–21.

—— (1975), "Evaluation Research in Corrections: A Practical Guide," Washington, DC: U.S. Department of Justice, Law Enforcement Assistance Administration.

—— (1977), "Evaluating Correctional Treatments: Toward a New Perspective," *Criminal Justice and Behavior,* 4, 323–339.

Adams, S. and M. Q. Grant (1961), "A Demonstration Project: An Evaluation of Community-Located Treatment for Delinquents. (Proposal for Phase 1.)" Sacramento: California Youth Authority.

Adams, S. and C. Hopkinson (1964), "Interim Evaluation of the Intensive Supervision Caseload Project," Research Report no. 12. Los Angeles: Los Angeles County Probation Department.

Adams, W., P. Chandler, and M. Neithercutt (1971), "The San Francisco Project: A Critique," *Federal Probation,* 35, 45–53.

Adlfinger, L. (1978), "Colorado's Differential Treatment Model and Population Characteristics," *The International Differential Treatment Association Newsletter,* 7, 25–27.

—— (1980), "Colorado Classification Study," *Journal of the International Differential Treatment Association,* 10, 68–74.

—— (1983), "Colorado's Division of Youth Services (I-Level)," *The International Differential Treatment Association Newsletter,* 13, 7.

—— (November 2, 1995), Personal Communication.

Adorno, T., E. Frenkel-Brunswick, D. Levinson, and N. Sanford (1950), *The Authoritarian Personality.* New York: Harper.

Agee, V. (1979), *Treatment of the Violent Incorrigible Adolescent.* Lexington, MA: Lexington.

—— (1982), "Expressives and Instrumentals: A Way of Analyzing Worker Style," *Journal of the International Differential Treatment Association,* 11, 32–39.

—— (1986), "Institutional Treatment Programs for the Violent Juvenile. (The Closed Adolescent Treatment Center)," in S. Apter and A. Goldstein (eds.), *Youth Violence: Program and Prospects.* New York: Pergamon, pp. 75–88.

Aichorn, A. (1931), *Wayward Youth.* New York: Viking Press.

—— (1964), "The Child Guidance Worker and the Child," in O. Fleischman, P. Kramer, and H. Ross (eds.), *Selected*

Papers of August Aichorn. New York: International Universities Press.

Akers, R. (1977), *Deviant Behavior: A Social Learning Perspective.* Belmont, CA: Wadsworth.

Alcock, S. (1979), "Differential Treatment in Residential Care—Fits and Misfits," *Journal of the International Differential Treatment Association,* 8, 9–16.

——— (1986), "Adolescent Situational Offenders—Some Further Remarks," *Journal of the International Differential Treatment Association,* 15, 7–20.

Alexander, J. and B. Parsons (1973), "Short-term Behavioral Intervention with Delinquent Families: Impact on Family Process and Recidivism," *Journal of Abnormal Psychology,* 81, 219–225.

Alexander, J., C. Barton, R. Schiavo, and B. Parsons (1976), "Systems-Behavioral Interventions with Families of Delinquents: Therapist Characteristics, Family Behavior, and Outcome," *Journal of Consulting and Clinical Psychology,* 44, 656–664.

Alexander, J. and B. Parsons (1982), *Functional Family Therapy.* Monterey, CA: Brooks/Cole.

Allen, F. (1981), *The Decline of the Rehabilitative Ideal: Penal Policy and Social Purpose.* New Haven: Yale University Press.

Allen, H., E. Carlson, E. Parks, and R. Seiter (1978), *Halfway Houses.* Washington, DC: U.S. Department of Justice. Law Enforcement Administration Agency.

Allinson, R. (1978), "Martinson Attacks His Own Earlier Work," *Criminal Justice Newsletter,* 9, 4.

——— (1979), "Current Trends in Community Corrections: Favored Strategies and Promising Projects," *Criminal Justice Newsletter,* 10, 1–3.

——— (1980), "Massachusetts Recidivism Drop Cited as Proof of Success of 'Reintegration' Model," *Criminal Justice Newsletter,* 11, 1–2.

Alschuler, A. (1978), "Sentencing Reform and Prosecutorial Power: A Critique of Recent Proposals for 'Fixed' and 'Presumptive' Sentencing," in *Determinate Sentencing: Proceedings of the Special Conference on Determinate Sentencing.* Washington, DC: National Institute of Law Enforcement and Criminal Justice. June 2–3, 1977.

Altschuler, D. and T. Armstrong (1990a), "Intensive Community-Based Aftercare Programs: Assessment Report." Baltimore: Johns Hopkins University, Institute for Policy Studies.

——— (1990b), "Intensive Community-Based Aftercare Programs: Assessment Report." Washington, DC: Office of Juvenile Justice and Delinquency Prevention.

——— (1991), "Intensive Aftercare for the High-Risk Juvenile Parolee: Issues and Approaches in Reintegration and Community Supervision," in T. Armstrong (ed.), *Intensive Interventions with High-Risk Youths: Promising Approaches in Juvenile Probation and Parole.* Monsey, NY: Willow Tree Press.

American Correctional Association (1981), "Corrections and Public Awareness," Series 2, no. 1. College Park, MD: ACA.

American Friends Service Committee (1971), *Struggle for Justice: A Report on Crime and Punishment in America.* New York: Hill and Wang.

American Probation and Parole Association (1988), "Intensive Supervision Probation and Parole (ISP). Program Brief." Washington, DC: U.S. Department of Justice. Bureau of Justice Assistance.

American Psychological Association (1954), "Technical Recommendations for Psychological Tests," Washington: D.C.

Andre, C. and J. Mahan (1972), "A Final Report on the Differential Education Project, Paso Robles School for Boys," Educational Research Series, no. 11. Sacramento: California Youth Authority.

Andrew, J. (1974), "Delinquency, the Wechsler P > V Sign, and the I-Level System," *Journal of Clinical Psychology,* 30, 331–335.

——— (1980), "Verbal I.Q. and the I-Level Classification for Delinquents," *Criminal Justice and Behavior,* 7, 193–202.

Andrews, D. and J. Bonta (1994), *The Psychology of Criminal Conduct.* Cincinnati, OH: Anderson Publishing Company.

Andrews, D., J. Bonta and R. Hoge (1990), "Classification for Effective Rehabilitation: Rediscovering Psychology," *Criminal Justice and Behavior,* 17, 19–52.

Andrews, D. and J. Kiessling (1980), "Program Structure and Effective Correctional Practices: A Summary of the CaVIC Research," in R. Ross and

P. Gendreau (eds.), *Effective Correctional Treatment.* Toronto: Butterworths.

Andrews, D. and J. Wormith (1989), "Personality and Crime: Knowledge Destruction and Construction in Criminology," *Justice Quarterly,* 6, 289–309.

Andrews, D., I. Zinger, R. Hoge, J. Bonta, P. Gendreau, and F. Cullen (1990), "Does Correctional Treatment Work? A Clinically Relevant and Psychologically Informed Meta-analysis," *Criminology,* 28, 369–404.

Angel, C. (1988), "Making a Difference—Not Just a Donation," *Los Angeles Daily Journal,* December 26, 1988, 1–2.

Annis, H. and D. Chan (1983), "The Differential Treatment Model: Empirical Evidence from a Personality Typology of Adult Offenders," *Criminal Justice and Behavior,* 10, 159–173.

Applegate, B., F. Cullen, and B. Fisher (1997), "Public Support for Correctional Treatment: The Continuing Appeal of the Rehabilitative Ideal," *The Prison Journal,* 74, 237–258.

A.R.A. Consultants, (1981), "Report on the Hard-to-Serve Child in Ontario," Ottawa: Ministry of Community and Social Services.

Argyle, M. (1961), "A New Approach to the Classification of Delinquents with Implications for Treatment," *California State Board of Corrections Monograph,* 2, 15–26.

Arling, G. and K. Lerner (1981), "CMC—Strategies for Case Planning and Supervision," Model Probation and Parole Management Project. Washington, DC: National Institute of Corrections.

Armstrong, T. (1988), "National Survey of Juvenile Intensive Probation Supervision, Parts I and II," *Criminal Justice Abstracts,* 20(2,3), 342–348, 497–523.

Austin, J. (1986), "Using Early Release to Relieve Prison Crowding: A Dilemma in Public Policy," *Crime and Delinquency,* 32, 404–502.

Austin, J. and B. Krisberg (1982), "The Unmet Promise of Alternatives to Incarceration," *Crime and Delinquency,* 28, 374–409.

Austin, R. (1975), "Construct Validity of I-Level Classification," *Criminal Justice and Behavior,* 2, 113–129.

—— (1977), "Differential Treatment in an Institution: Reexamining the Preston Study," *Journal of Research in Crime and Delinquency,* 14, 177–194.

Bailey, W. (1966), "Correctional Outcome: An Evaluation of 100 Reports," *Journal of Crime, Law, Criminology, and Police Science,* 57, 153–160.

Baird, C. (1982), "The Wisconsin Workload Determination Project—Two Year Followup," Washington, DC: National Institute of Corrections.

—— (1984), "Classification of Juveniles in Corrections: A Model System Approach." Washington, DC: Arthur D. Little, Inc.

Baird, C., R. Heinz, and B. James (1979), "The Wisconsin Case Classification/Staff Deployment Project. A Two-Year Followup Report," Project Report no. 14. Madison, WI: Department of Health and Social Services, Division of Corrections.

Baker, M. and J. Mahan (1973), "A Second Differential Education Model for I_4 Neurotic Anxious Students," Differential Education Project. Sacramento: California Youth Authority.

Baldwin, J. (1902), *Social and Ethical Interpretations in Mental Development.* New York: Macmillan.

Ball, R., C. R. Huff, and J. Lilly (1988), *House Arrest and Correctional Policy. Doing Time at Home.* Newbury Park, CA: Sage.

Ballard, K. (1963), "Interpersonal Personality Inventory Manual." Vacaville, CA: Institute for the Study of Crime and Delinquency and the California Department of Corrections.

Bandura, A. (1973), *Aggression: A Social Learning Analysis,* Englewood Cliffs, NJ: Prentice-Hall.

Banks, J., A. Porter, T. Silver, and V. Unger (1977), "Evaluation of Intensive Special Probation Projects. Phase 1 Report," National Evaluation Program, Washington, DC: U.S. Department of Justice. Law Enforcement Assistance Administration.

Barker, P. (1978), "The Impossible Child: Some Approaches to Treatment," *Canadian Psychiatric Association Journal,* 23, 1–21.

Barkwell, L. (1976), "Differential Treatment of Juveniles on Probation: An Evaluation," *Canadian Journal of Crime and Corrections,* 18, 363–378.

—— (1980), "Differential Probation Treatment and Delinquency," in R. Ross and

P. Gendreau (eds.), *Effective Correctional Treatment*. Toronto: Butterworths.

Barrett-Lennard, G. (1962), "Dimensions of Therapist Response As Casual Factors in Therapeutic Change," *Psychological Monographs,* 76 (Whole no. 43), 1–36.

Barton, W. and J. Butts (1990), "Viable Options: Intensive Supervision Programs for Juvenile Delinquents," *Crime and Delinquency,* 36, 238–256.

Bayer, R. (1981), "Crime, Punishment, and the Decline of Liberal Optimism," *Crime and Delinquency,* 27, 169–190.

Bazemore, G., T. Dicker, and R. Nylan (1994), "Juvenile Justice Reform and the Difference It Makes: An Exploratory Study of the Impact of Policy Change on Detention Worker Attitudes," *Crime and Delinquency,* 40, 37–53.

Beck, B. (1954), "What We Can Do About Juvenile Delinquency," *Child Welfare,* 33, 3–7.

Becker, H. (1963), *Outsiders: Studies in the Sociology of Deviance.* New York: Free Press.

Beker, J. and D. Heyman (June 9 and 27, 1970), Written Personal Communications.

Beker, J. and D. Heyman (1971), "A Critical Appraisal of the California Differential Treatment Typology of Adolescent Offenders." New York: Jewish Board of Guardians and the Fairfield University.

——— (1972), "A Critical Appraisal of the California Differential Treatment Typology of Adolescent Offenders." *Criminology,* 10, 3–50.

Benekos, P. (1990), "Beyond Reintegration: Community Corrections in a Retributive Era," *Federal Probation,* 54, 52–56.

Bennett, L., M. Cahn, E. Kaplan, J. Peters, Jr., A. Cardarelli, C. Smith, W. Cunningham, T. Taylor, M. Feeley, R. Parks, L. Sechrest, R. Redner, W. Skogan, J. Tiens, K. Colton, and R. Yin (eds.) (1979), *How Well Does It Work? Review of Criminal Justice Evaluation. 1978.* Washington, DC: U.S. Department of Justice. Law Enforcement Assistance Administration, pp. 63–106.

Bennett, L. and M. Ziegler (1975), "Early Discharge: A Suggested Approach to Increased Efficiency in Parole," *Federal Probation,* 39, 27–30.

Benoit, K. and T. Clear (1981), "Case Management Systems in Probation," Wash-ington, DC: U.S. Department of Justice, National Institute of Corrections.

Berne, E. (1961), *Transactional Analysis in Psychotherapy.* New York: Grove Press.

——— (1964), *Games People Play.* New York: Grove Press.

——— (1966), *Principles of Group Treatment.* New York: Grove Press.

Bernsten, K. and K. Christiansen (1965), "A Resocialization Experiment with Short-Term Offenders," *Scandanavian Studies in Criminology,* 1, 35–54.

Betz, B. (1963), "Validation of the Differential Treatment Success of 'A' and 'B' Therapists with Schizophrenic Patients," *American Journal of Psychiatry,* 119, 883–884.

Beverly, R. (1959), "A Method of Determination of Base Expectancies for Use in Assessment of Effectiveness of Correctional Treatment," Research Division Report no. 3. Sacramento: California Youth Authority.

——— (1964), "Base Expectancies and the Initial Home Visit Research Schedule," Research Division Report no. 37. Sacramento: California Youth Authority.

——— (1965), "The BGOS: An Attempt at the Objective Measurement of Levels of Interpersonal Maturity," Research Division Report no. 48. Sacramento: California Youth Authority.

——— (1968), "A Comparative Analysis of Base Expectancy Tables for Selected Sub-Populations of California Youth Authority Wards," Research Division Report no. 55. Sacramento: California Youth Authority.

Beyer, W. (1974), "Temporary Detention in the Community Treatment Project," *Youth Authority Quarterly,* 27, 16–24.

Binder, A., G. Geis, and D. Bruce (1988), *Juvenile Delinquency: Historical, Cultural, and Legal Perspectives.* New York: Macmillan.

Binder, A., M. Schumacher, G. Kurz, and L. Moulson (1985), "A Diversionary Approach for the 1980s," *Federal Probation,* 49, 4–12.

Blackmore, J., M. Brown, and B. Krisberg (1988), "Juvenile Justice Reform: The Bellwether States." Ann Arbor, MI: Center for the Study of Youth Policy and the University of Michigan.

Blakely, C., W. Davidson, C. Saylor, and M. Robinson (1980), "Kentfields Rehabilitation Program: Ten Years Later," in

R. Ross and P. Gendreau (eds.), *Effective Correctional Treatment*. Toronto: Buttersworth.

Blew, D., D. McGillis, and G. Bryant (1977), "An Exemplary Project. Project New Pride—Denver, Colorado." Washington, DC: U.S. Department of Justice. Law Enforcement Assistance Administration.

Bloch, D. (1952), "The Delinquent Integration," *Psychiatry*, 15, 297–303.

Blumstein, A., J. Cohen, S. Martin, and M. Tonry (eds.) (1983), "Research on Sentencing: The Search for Reform. Summary Report." Washington, DC: U.S. Department of Justice. National Institute of Justice.

Blumstein, A., J. Cohen, and D. Nagin (eds.) (1978), *Deterrence and Incapacitation: Estimating the Effects of Criminal Sanctions on Crime Rates*. Washington, DC: National Academy of Sciences.

Blumstein, A., J. Cohen, J. Roth, and C. Visher (1986), *Criminal Careers and Career Criminals. (Volumes I and II)*. Washington, DC: National Academy Press.

Bohnstedt, M. and R. Beverly (1960), "Initial Home Visit Research Schedule. A Preliminary Report," Research Division Report no. 16. Sacramento: California Youth Authority.

Bonner, D. and W. White (1970), "Toliver Community Center." Sacramento: California Youth Authority.

Bottcher, J. (1993), "Dimensions of Gender and Delinquent Behavior: An Analysis of Qualitative Data on Incarcerated Youths and Their Siblings in Greater Sacramento," Research Division. Sacramento: California Youth Authority.

——— (1995), "Gender As Social Control: Qualitative Study of Incarcerated Youths and Their Siblings in Greater Sacramento," *Justice Quarterly*, 12, 33–57.

Braithwaite, J. (1988), "Restorative Justice," in M. Tonry (ed.), *The Handbook of Crime and Punishment*. New York: Oxford University Press.

Braithwaite, J., R. Johnston, P. Wright, V. Wiita, and H. Johnson (1964), "Annual Statistical Report, 1964," Research Division. Sacramento: California Youth Authority.

Braithwaite, J., A. Taylor, V. Wiita, D. Brown, and H. Johnson (1962), "Annual Statistical Report, 1962," Research Division.

Sacramento: California Youth Authority.

Braithwaite, J., P. Wright, V. Wiita, and H. Johnson (1963), "Annual Statistical Report, 1963," Research Division. Sacramento: California Youth Authority.

Breed, A. (1973a), "In Defense of the State's Probation Subsidy Policy," *Los Angeles Times*, February 25.

——— (1973b), "Reply to National Institute of Mental Health (Saleem Shah) regarding Paul Lerman's Report, 'Community Treatment, Social Control, and Juvenile Delinquency: Issues in Correctional Policy,' (April 18, 1973)." Sacramento: California Youth Authority.

Bremner, R., J. Barnard, T. Hareven, and R. Mennel (eds.) (1971), *Children and Youth in America: A Documentary History*. Cambridge, MA: Harvard University Press.

Brennan, T. (1987), "Classification: An Overview of Selected Methodological Issues," In D. Gottfredson and M. Tonry (eds.), *Prediction and Classification: Criminal Justice Decision-making*. Chicago: University of Chicago Press.

Brice, D. (1976), "Differential Treatment Unit, New York City Probation Department," *The International Differential Treatment Association Newsletter*, 2, 13–17.

Brill, R. (1978), "Implications of the Conceptual Level Matching Model for Treatment of Delinquents," *Journal of Research in Crime and Delinquency*, 15, 229–246.

——— (1979), "Development of Milieus Facilitating Treatment. Final Report no. 4." Montreal: Universite De Montreal, Groupe De Recherche sur L'Inadaptation Juvénile.

Brill, R. and M. Reitsma (1980), "Comparison of the Effects of Matching Treaters to Delinquent Clients Using Conceptual Level and I-Level Theories," *Journal of the International Differential Treatment Association*, 9, 37–48.

Budnoff, I. (1963), "A Psychometric Typology of Delinquents. NIMH Research Report no. 1," Los Angeles: Los Angeles County Probation Department.

Bureau of Criminal Statistics and Special Services Staff (1985), Proceedings of the Attorney General's Crime Conference 85. Sacramento: Department of Justice. Division of Law Enforcement.

Bureau of Justice Statistics (1977), "An Introduction to the National Crime Survey." Washington, DC: U.S. Department of Justice.

——— (1982), "Criminal Victimization in the United States, 1973–80 Changes, 1973–80 Trends." Washington, DC: U.S. Department of Justice.

Burgess, A. (1965), *A Clockwork Orange*. New York: Ballantine Books.

Burnett, R. (October 25, 1982), Written Personal Communication.

Byrne, J. (1989), "Reintegrating the Concept of *Community* into Community-Based Corrections," *Crime and Delinquency*, 35, 471–499.

——— (1990), "The Future of Intensive Probation Supervision and the New Intermediate Sanctions," *Crime and Delinquency*, 36, 6–41.

Butler, E. (1965), "Personality Dimensions of Delinquent Girls," *Criminologica*, 3, 7–10.

Butler, E. and S. Adams (1966), "Typologies of Delinquent Girls: Some Alternative Approaches," *Social Forces*, 44, 401–407.

Byrne, J., A. Lurigio, and C. Baird (1989), "The Effectiveness of the New Intensive Supervision Programs," *Research in Corrections*, 2, 1–75.

California Department of Justice (1977), *Crime and Delinquency in California, Delinquency and Probation. 1967–1976.* Sacramento: Department of Justice. Bureau of Criminal Statistics.

Campbell, D. (1960), "Recommendations for APA Test Standards regarding Construct, Trait, or Discriminant Validity," *American Psychologist*, 15, 546–553.

Campbell, D. and D. Fiske (1959), "Convergent and Discriminant Validation by the Multitrait-multimethod Matrix," *Psychological Bulletin*, 56, 81–105.

Caplan, G. (1974), "An Exemplary Project: Providence Educational Center." Washington, DC: U.S. Department of Justice. Law Enforcement Assistance Administration.

——— (1975), "The Philadelphia Neighborhood Youth Resources Center: An Exemplary Project." Washington, DC: U.S. Department of Justice. Law Enforcement Assistance Administration.

Cavior, H. and A. Schmidt (1978), "A Test of the Effectiveness of a Differential Treatment Strategy at the Robert F. Kennedy Center," *Criminal Justice and Behavior*, 5, 131–139.

Center, A. and S. Cutlip (1978), *Effective Public Relations*. Englewood Cliffs, NJ: Prentice-Hall.

Chambliss, W. and R. Seidman (1971), *Law, Order, and Power*. Reading, MA: Addison-Wesley.

Chandler, M. (1973), "Egocentrism and Anti-social Behavior: The Assessment and Training of Social Perspective–Taking Skills," *Developmental Psychology*, 9, 326–333.

Chen, H. (1990), *Theory-Driven Evaluations*. Newbury Park, CA: Sage.

Chen, H. and P. Rossi (eds.) (1992), *Using Theory to Improve Programs and Policy Evaluations*. New York: Greenwood Press.

Chesley, F. (1976), "Baltimore City Intensive Probation Project," *The International Differential Treatment Association Newsletter*, 1, 3–6.

Chesney-Lind, M. (1993), *The Female Offender*. Thousand Oaks, CA: Sage.

Childers, F. (1964), "Cottage Counselors' Perceptions of Institutionalized High-Maturity Level Delinquent Girls," Los Angeles: University of Southern California, School of Social Work. Unpublished Masters Thesis.

Citizens Inquiry on Parole and Criminal Justice (1975), *Prisons without Walls*. New York: Praeger.

Clark, R. (1970), *Crime in America*. New York: Simon & Schuster.

Clear, T. (1994), *Harm in American Penology: Offenders, Victims, and Their Communities*. Albany, NY: State University of New York Press.

Clear, T. and K. Gallagher (1985), "Probation and Parole Supervision: A Review of Current Classification Practices," *Crime and Delinquency*, 31, 423–443.

Clear, T. and P. Hardyman (1990), "The New Intensive Supervision Movement," *Crime and Delinquency*, 36, 42–60.

Clements, C. (1981), "The Future of Offender Classification. Some Cautions and Prospects," *Criminal Justice and Behavior*, 8, 15–38.

——— (1986), "Offender Needs Assessment." College Park, MD: American Correctional Association.

—— (1987), "Assessing Offender Needs: Developments and Prospects," *Corrections Today*, 49, 112–119.

Clements, F. and M. Kleiman (1977), "Fear of Crime in the United States: A Multivariate Analysis," *Social Forces*, 56, 519–531.

Cloward, R. and L. Ohlin (1960), *Delinquency and Opportunity*. New York: Free Press.

Coates, R., A. Miller, and L. Ohlin (1978), *Diversity in a Youth Correctional System*. Cambridge, MA: Ballinger.

Cohen, A. (1955), *Delinquent Boys*. New York: Free Press.

—— (1966), *Deviance and Control*. Englewood Cliffs, NJ: Prentice-Hall.

Cohen, A. R. (1956), "Experimental Effects of Ego-Defense Preference on Interpersonal Relations," *Journal of Abnormal and Social Psychology*, 52, 19–27.

Cohen, J. (1988), *Statistical Power Analysis for the Behavioral Sciences*. Hillsdale, NJ: Lawrence Erlbaum Associates, pp. 179–213.

Cohen, S. and B. Conklin (eds.) (1985), "The Power of Public Support. A Handbook for Corrections." Sacramento: California Probation, Parole, and Correctional Association.

Cole, G. and C. Logan (1977), "Parole: The Consumer's Perspective," *Criminal Justice Review*, 2, 71–80.

Collingwood, T., A. Douds, and H. Williams (1976), "Juvenile Diversion: The Dallas Police Department Youth Services Program," *Federal Probation*, 43, 23–27.

Collingwood, T. and R. Genthner (1980), "Skills Training As Treatment for Juvenile Delinquents," *Professional Psychology*, 11, 591–598.

Commission Staff (1990), "Blue Ribbon Commission on Inmate Population Management. Final Report." Sacramento: California State Legislature.

Community Treatment Project Staff (1963), "Community Treatment Project. First Year Report of Action and Evaluation," CTP Research Report no. 2. Sacramento: California Youth Authority.

Conrad, J. (1965), "Annual Research Review, Division of Research." Sacramento: California Department of Corrections.

—— (1973), "Corrections and Simple Justice," *Journal of Criminal Law and Criminology*, 64, 208–217.

—— (1978), "Are You Really All Right, Jack?" Paper Presented at the Minnesota Corrections Association meeting, October 25, 1978. Columbus, OH: The Academy for Contemporary Problems.

—— (1982a), "Criminal Justice Research Is About People," *Crime and Delinquency*, 28, 618–626.

—— (1982b), "Research and Developments in Corrections: A Thought Experiment," *Federal Probation*, 46, 66–69.

Cook, T., H. Cooper, D. Cordray, H. Hartman, L. Hedges, R. Light, T. Louis, and F. Mosteller (eds.) (1992), *Meta-analysis for Explanation: A Casebook*. New York: Russell Sage Foundation.

Cook, W. and D. Johns (1965), "The Institutional Experience Summary: A Preliminary Presentation of Selected Data," Research Division Report no. 44. Sacramento: California Youth Authority.

Cook, W., J. Walters, and P. Logan (1960), "Annual Statistical Report, 1960," Research Division. Sacramento: California Youth Authority.

Cooley, C. (1902), *Human Nature and the Social Order*. New York: Scribner.

Corsini, R. (1957), *Methods of Group Psychodrama*. New York: Blankenship Division.

Croft, I. and T. Grygier (1956), "Social Relationships of Truants and Juvenile Delinquents," *Human Relations*, 9, 439–466.

Cronbach, L. (1946), "Response Sets and Test Validity," *Educational Psychology Measurement*, 6, 475–494.

—— (1950), "Further Evidence on Response Sets and Test Design," *Educational Psychology Measurement*, 10, 3–31.

—— (1958), "Proposals Leading to Analytic Treatment of Social Perception Scores," in R. Taguiri and L. Petrullo (eds.), *Person, Perception, and Interpersonal Behavior*. Stanford, CA: Stanford University Press, pp. 353–378.

Cronbach, L. and P. Meehl (1955), "Construct Validity in Psychological Tests," *Psychological Bulletin*, 52, 281–302.

Cross, H. (1966), "The Relation of Parental Training Conditions to Conceptual Level in Adolescent Boys," *Journal of Personality*, 34, 348–365.

Cross, H. and J. Tracy (1969), "A Study of

Delinquent Boys in Connecticut: Application of the Interpersonal Level Classification System and Its Relationship to Guilt." Storrs, CT: Connecticut Research Commission and the University of Connecticut.

———— (1971), "Personality Factors in Delinquent Boys: Differences between Blacks and Whites," *Journal of Research in Crime and Delinquency*, 8, 10–22.

Cullen, F. (1994), "Social Support As an Ongoing Concept for Criminology," Presidential Address to the Academy of Criminal Justice Sciences. Chicago, IL. March 9, 1994.

Cullen, F. and B. Applegate (1997), *Offender Rehabilitation: Effective Correctional Intervention.* Brookfield, VT: Ashgate.

Cullen, F. and K. Gilbert (1982), *Reaffirming Rehabilitation.* Cincinnati, OH: Anderson.

Cullen, F., S. Skovron, J. Scott, and V. Burton, Jr. (1990), "Public Support for Correctional Treatment, The Tenacity of Rehabilitative Ideology," *Criminal Justice and Behavior*, 17, 6–18.

Cullen, F. and J. Wright (1995), "The Future of Corrections," in B. Maguire and P. Radosh (eds.), *The Past, Present, and Future of American Criminal Justice.* New York: General Hall.

Cullen, F., J. Wright, and B. Applegate (1993), "Control in the Community: The Limits of Reform?" Paper Presented at the International Association of Residential and Community Alternatives Seventh Annual Meeting. Philadelphia, PA. November 3–6, 1993.

Currie, E. (1985), *Confronting Crime.* New York: Pantheon Books.

———— (1987), "What Kind of Future? Violence and Public Safety in the Year 2000." San Francisco: National Council on Crime and Delinquency.

Curry, D., C. Andre, and J. Mahan (1972), "Differential Education Model for I_3 Immature Conformists," Differential Education Project. Sacramento: California Youth Authority.

Curry, D., C. Daly, C. Andre, and J. Mahan (1973), "Differential Education Model for I_3 Immature Conformists," Differential Education Project. Sacramento: California Youth Authority.

Daly, C., C. Andre, and J. Mahan (1972),

"Differential Education Model for I_4 Neurotic Anxious Students," Differential Education Project. Sacramento: California Youth Authority.

Davidson, G. and R. Stuart (1975), "Behavior Therapy and Civil Liberties," *American Psychologist*, 30, 755–763.

Davidson, W., R. Gottschalk, L. Gensheimer, and J. Mayer (1984), "Interventions with Juvenile Delinquents: A Meta-analysis of Treatment Efficacy." Washington, DC: National Institute of Juvenile Justice and Delinquency Prevention.

Davidson, W. and M. Robinson (1975), "Community Psychology and Behavior Modification: A Community-Based Program for the Prevention of Delinquency," *Journal of Corrective Psychiatry and Behavior Therapy*, 21, 1–12.

Davidson, W., R. Redner, C. Blakely, C. Mitchell, and J. Emshoff (1987), "Diversion of Juvenile Offenders: An Experimental Comparison," *Journal of Consulting and Clinical Psychology*, 55, 68–75.

Davis, C. (1970), "Parole Agent Time-Reporting System Study," Research Division. Sacramento: California Youth Authority.

———— (1971), "Estimating the Long-Term Costs of a Youth Authority Commitment," Research Division. Sacramento: California Youth Authority.

Davis, G. (1973), "CYA Cost Comparisons. Fiscal Years 1963–1964 Through 1972–1973," Information Systems Section, Research Division. Sacramento: California Youth Authority.

Davis, G., D. Dreyer, P. Pike, H. Orsborn, and L. Wong (1971), "Annual Report. Program Description and Statistical Summary ('Annual Statistical Report, 1971')," Research Division. Sacramento: California Youth Authority.

Davis, G., T. Leahy, H. Orsborn, P. Pike, and L. Wong (1972), "Some Statistical Facts on the California Youth Authority," Research Division. Sacramento: California Youth Authority.

Davis, G., T. Leahy, P. Pike, H. Orsborn, and D. McDaniel (1971), "Institutional Experience Summary. 1968 Parole Releases," Research Division. Sacramento: California Youth Authority.

Davis, G., T. Leahy, P. Pike, H. Orsborn, L. Wong, and D. McDaniel (1970), "Annual Statistical Report, 1970," Research Division. Sacramento: California Youth Authority.

Davis, G., T. Leahy, P. Pike, H. Orsborn, L. Wong, and V. Wiita (1969), "Annual Statistical Report, 1969," Research Division. Sacramento: California Youth Authority.

Davis, G., T. Leahy, P. Wright, R. Johnston, R. Lai, and V. Wiita (1966), "Annual Statistical Report, 1966," Research Division. Sacramento: California Youth Authority.

Davis, G. and P. Pike (1969), "Institutional Experience Summary. 1967 Parole Releases," Research Division. Sacramento: California Youth Authority.

—— (1971), "Institutional Experience Summary. 1969 Parole Releases," Research Division. Sacramento: California Youth Authority.

—— (1983), "Follow-Up of Wards Discharged from Department of the Youth Authority in 1975," Research Division. Sacramento: California Youth Authority.

Davis, G., P. Pike, L. Guttman, H. Orsborn, and L. Wong (1973), "Some Statistical Facts on the California Youth Authority," Research Division. Sacramento: California Youth Authority.

Davis, G., P. Pike, L. Guttman, H. Orsborn, L. Wong, and M. Marus (1972), "Annual Statistical Report, 1972," Research Division. Sacramento: California Youth Authority.

—— (1973), "Annual Statistical Report, 1973," Research Division. Sacramento: California Youth Authority.

—— (1974), "Annual Statistical Report, 1974," Research Division. Sacramento: California Youth Authority.

—— (1975), "Annual Statistical Report, 1975," Research Division. Sacramento: California Youth Authority.

Davis, G., P. Pike, H. Orsborn, and L. Guttman (1973), "Follow-Up of Wards Discharged from CYA during 1965," Research Division Report no. 64. Sacramento: California Youth Authority.

Davis, G., P. Pike, H. Orsborn, L. Guttman, and L. Wong (1975), "Some Statistical Facts on the California Youth Authority," Research Division. Sacramento: California Youth Authority.

Davis, G., H. Sawusch, and L. Wong (1970), "Some Statistical Facts on the California Youth Authority," Research Division. Sacramento: California Youth Authority.

Davis, G., P. Wright, R. Johnston, R. Lai, and V. Wiite (1965), "Annual Statistical Report, 1965," Research Division. Sacramento: California Youth Authority.

Davis, J. and A. Cropley (1976), "Psychological Factors in Juvenile Delinquency," *Canadian Journal of Behavioral Science,* 8, 68–77.

Davis, R., A. Lurigio, and W. Skogan (eds) (1997), *Victims of Crime.* Thousand Oaks, CA: Sage.

Deichsel, W. (1987), *Die Offene Tur. Jugendberatungsstelen in der Bundesrepublik Deutschland, in Holland, und in den Vereinigten Staaten.* Munchen, Germany: Profil Verlag GribH.

DeJong, W. and C. Stewart (1980), "An Exemplary Project. Project CREST— Gainesville, Florida." Washington, DC: U.S. Department of Justice. National Institute of Justice.

Dent, J. and G. Furse (1978), "Exploring the Psycho-Social Therapies through the Personalities of Effective Therapists." Washington, DC: U.S. Department of Health, Education, and Welfare. Alcohol, Drug Abuse, and Mental Health Administration.

Deutsch, M. (1975), "Equity, Equality, and Need: What Determines Which Value Will Be Used As the Basis of Distributive Justice?" *Journal of Social Issues,* 31, 137–149.

Dibble, G. and G. Dabel (1978), *Successful Habilitation of Ex-Offenders.* Hayward, CA: M-2 Sponsors, Inc.

—— (1979), *Positive Impact on Recidivism. Evaluating M-2 by the Base Expectancy Method. Executive Summary.* Hayward, CA: M-2 Sponsors, Inc.

Dickover, R. (1970), "Annual Research Review," Division of Research. Sacramento: California Department of Corrections.

DiIulio, J. (1990), "Getting Prisons Straight," in G. Ingram (ed.), *Correctional Programs in the Year 2000. The June 9, 1989 Conference on Issues in Corrections. A Record of Proceedings.* Washington, DC: U.S. Department of Justice. Federal Bureau of Prisons.

Dillingham, D., A. Klaus, T. Wilson, and

L. Gonzales (1975), "Right to Be Heard: Evaluation of the Ward Grievance Procedure in the CYA," Research Division. Sacramento: California Youth Authority.

Dixon, M. and W. Wright (1974), "Juvenile Delinquency Prevention Programs. An Evaluation of Policy Related Research on the Effectiveness of Prevention Programs. Report on the Findings of an Evaluation of the Literature." Washington, DC: National Science Foundation.

Dolina, A. (November, 1995), Personal Communication.

Dowell, R. (1972), "Adolescents As Peer Counselors." Cambridge, MA: Harvard University. Unpublished doctoral dissertation.

Downes, D. and P. Rock (eds.) (1979), *Deviant Interpretations*. New York: Barnes and Noble.

Dreo, H. (1976), "Colorado's I-Level Training," *The International Differential Treatment Association Newsletter*, 2, 16–17.

Duffee, D. and E. McGarrell (1990), *Community Corrections: A Community Field Approach*. Cincinnati, OH: Anderson Publishing Company.

Dunford, F., W. Osgood, and H. Weichselbaum (1982), "National Evaluation of Diversion Projects. Executive Summary," Washington, DC: U.S. Department of Justice. Office of Juvenile Justice and Delinquency Prevention.

Eaks, D. (1972), "Interpersonal Maturity Level and Future Time Perspective of Delinquents." Berkeley: University of California. Unpublished doctoral dissertation.

Efron, K. (1983), "Use of Conceptual Level Matching Model at Craigwood (Ontario)," *The International Differential Treatment Association Newsletter*, 14, 5–6.

—— (1984), "Use of Conceptual Level Matching Model in Residential Programming," *The International Differential Treatment Association Newsletter*, 17, 6–7.

Ellickson, P. and J. Petersilia (1983), "Implementing New Ideas in Criminal Justice." Santa Monica, CA: RAND.

Elliott, D. (1979), "Recurring Issues in the Evaluation of Delinquency Prevention and Treatment Programs," Boulder, CO: Behavioral Research Institute.

—— (1980), "Recurring Issues in the Evaluation of Delinquency Prevention and Treatment Programs," in D. Shichor and D. Kelly (eds.), *Critical Issues in Juvenile Delinquency*. Lexington, MA: Lexington Books.

Elliott, D., S. Ageton, and R. Canter (1979), "An Integrated Theoretical Perspective on Delinquent Behavior," *Journal of Research in Crime and Delinquency*, 16, 3–27.

Elliott, D., D. Huizinga, and S. Menard (1989), *Multiple Problem Youth. Delinquency, Substance Use, and Mental Health Problems*. New York: Springer-Verlag.

Emmick, S. (1978), "Selection of I-Level Trainees," *Journal of the International Differential Treatment Association*, 7, 37–38.

Empey, L. (1967), "Alternatives to Incarceration." Washington, DC: U.S. Department of Health, Education, and Welfare. Office of Juvenile Delinquency and Youth Development.

—— (1978), *American Delinquency: Its Meaning and Construction*. 2nd ed. Homewood, IL: Dorsey.

Empey, L. and M. Erickson (1972), *The Provo Experiment: Evaluating Community Control of Delinquency*. Lexington, MA: Lexington Books.

Empey, L. and S. Lubeck (1971), *The Silverlake Experiment*. Chicago: Aldine.

Empey, L., G. Newland, and S. Lubeck (1965), "The Silverlake Experiment. Progress Report no. 2." Los Angeles: University of Southern California. Youth Studies Center.

Empey, L. and J. Rabow (1961), "The Provo Experiment in Delinquency Rehabilitation," *American Sociological Review*, 26, 679–695.

Empey, L. and M. Stafford (1991), *American Delinquency: Its Meaning and Construction*. 3rd ed. Belmont, CA: Wadsworth.

Erickson, E. (1950), *Childhood and Society*. New York: Norton.

Erwin, B. (1987), "Evaluation of Intensive Probation Supervision in Georgia." Atlanta, GA: Georgia Department of Corrections.

Eze, E. (1959), "Report on Parole Attitude Scale Administered to Nine Units in Los Angeles and Bay Areas," Division of Research. Sacramento: California Department of Corrections.

Fagan, J. (1990a), "Social and Legal Policy Dimensions of Violent Juvenile Crime," *Criminal Justice and Behavior,* 17, 93–133.

——— (1990b), "Treatment and Re-integration of Violent Delinquents: Experimental Results," *Justice Quarterly,* 7, 233–263.

Fagan, J., M. Forst, and T. Vivona (1988), "Treatment and Re-integration of Violent Juvenile Offenders: Experimental Results." San Francisco: The URSA Institute.

Fagan, J. and E. Hartstone (1986), "Innovation and Experimentation in Juvenile Corrections: Implementing a Community Reintegration Model for Violent Juvenile Offenders." San Francisco: The URSA Institute.

Feeney, F., T. Hirschi, and E. Lemert (1977), "An Evaluation of the California Probation Subsidy Program. Volume VI. A Summary," Davis: University of California. Center on Administration of Criminal Justice.

Ferdinand, T. (1966), *Typologies of Delinquents,* New York: Random House.

——— (1967), "Some Inherent Limitations in Rehabilitating Juvenile Delinquents in Training Schools," *Federal Probation,* 31, 30–36.

——— (1978), "Female Delinquency and Warren's Typology of Personality Patterns: An Evaluation," *Social Work Research and Abstracts,* 14, 32–41.

Fichte, J. (1792), *Theory of Science (Grundlage der Gesampter Wissenschaftsleher),* synopsis in B. Fuller, *A History of Philosophy* (1955). New York: Henry Holt.

Figueira-McDonough, J. and E. Selo (1980), "A Reformulation of the 'Equal Opportunity' Explanation of Female Delinquency," *Crime and Delinquency,* 26, 333–343.

Finckenauer, J. (1978), "Crime As a National Political Issue: 1964–1976," *Crime and Delinquency,* 24, 13–27.

——— (1982), *Scared Straight and the Panacea Phenomenon.* Englewood Cliffs, NJ: Prentice-Hall.

Fischer, C. (ed.) (1989), "Massachusetts Sheriffs Easing Jail Crowding with Day Centers," *Criminal Justice Newsletter,* 20, 4–5.

——— (1990a), "Florida Adopts New System Stressing Community Treatment," *Criminal Justice Newsletter,* 21, 1–2.

——— (1990b), "Nebraska Legislature Begins Shift to Community Sanctions," *Criminal Justice Newsletter,* 21, 4–5.

——— (1993), "30 Organizations Call for Shift in Criminal Justice Policy," *Criminal Justice Newsletter,* 24, 3–4.

Fishman, R. (1977), *Criminal Recidivism in New York City: An Evaluation of the Impact of Rehabilitation and Diversion Services.* New York: Praeger.

Flynn, E. (1974). "Environmental Variables: Their Impact on the Correctional Process," in A. Roberts (ed.), *Correctional Treatment of the Offender.* Springfield, IL: Charles R. Thomas.

——— (1978), "Classification Systems," in L. Hippchen (ed.), *Handbook on Correctional Classification.* Cincinnati, OH: Anderson Publishing Company.

Fogel, D. (1975), *We Are the Living Proof. The Justice Model for Corrections.* Cincinnati, OH: Anderson Publishing Company.

——— (1976), "The Case for Determinacy in Sentencing and the Justice Model in Corrections," *American Journal of Corrections,* 38, 25–28.

Folkard, M., A. Fowles, B. McWilliams, W. McWilliams, D. D. Smith, D. Smith, and G. Walmsley, (1974), "IMPACT: Intensive Matched Probation and After-Care Treatment. Volume I. The Design of the Probation Experiment and an Interim Evaluation," Home Office Research Study no. 24. London: Her Majesty's Stationery Office.

Folkard, M., D. Smith, and D. D. Smith (1976), "IMPACT: Intensive Matched Probation and After-Care Treatment. Volume II. The Results of the Experiment," Home Office Research Study no. 36. London: Her Majesty's Stationery Office.

Foote, C. (1978), "Deceptive Determinate Sentencing, Proceedings of the Special Conference on Determinate Sentencing." Washington, DC: U.S. Department of Justice. National Institute of Corrections.

Force, R. (1986), "Treatment Philosophy/Modality of a Residential Treatment Center," *The International Differential Treatment Association Newsletter,* 23, 9–13.

Fosen, R. and M. Q. Grant (1961), "Variations among Offenders in Perception of Norms: Implications for the Theory of Differential Opportunity Systems," Presented at the American Sociological Association Annual Meeting. St. Louis, MO. September 2, 1961.

France, S. (1968), "A Comparison of Integration Level Theory and Conceptual Level Theory Using a Delinquent Population." Syracuse, NY: Syracuse University. Unpublished master's thesis.

Frank, R. and D. Cohen (1979), "Psychosocial Concomitants of Biological Maturity in Preadolescence," *American Journal of Psychiatry*, 136, 1518–1524.

Frankel, M. (1973), *Criminal Sentences: Law without Order*. New York: Hill and Wang.

Freud, A. (1937), *The Ego and the Mechanisms of Defense*. London: Hogarth Press.

Freud, S. (1914), "On Narcissism: An Introduction," in E. Jones (ed.), *Collected Papers of Sigmund Freud. Vol. IV.* (1956), London: Hogarth Press and the Institute of Psychoanalysis.

———— (1917), "Mourning and Melancholia," in E. Jones (ed.), *Collected Papers of Sigmund Freud. Vol. IV.* (1956), London: Hogarth Press and the Institute of Psychoanalysis.

Freundlich, D. and L. Kohlberg (1972), "Moral Reasoning in Delinquent Youth." Harvard University. Unpublished manuscript.

Fuller, B. (1955), *A History of Philosophy*. New York: Henry Holt.

Gaensbauer, T. and J. Lazerwitz (1979, "Classification of Military Offenders," *Crime and Delinquency*, 25, 42–54.

Gage, N. and L. Cronbach (1954), "Conceptual and Methodological Problems in Interpersonal Perception: Studies in the Generality and Behavioral Correlates of Social Perception. Report no. 4." Urbana, IL: Bureau of Educational Research.

Galvin, J. and K. Polk (1982), "Any Truth You Want: The Use and Abuse of Crime and Criminal Justice Statistics," *Journal of Research in Crime and Delinquency*, 19, 135–165.

Garofalo, J. (1977), "Public Opinion about Crime: The Attitudes of Victims and Nonvictims in Selected Cities." Washington, DC: U.S. Department of Justice. Law Enforcement Assistance Administration.

———— (1979), "Victimization and the Fear of Crime," *Journal of Research in Crime and Delinquency*, 16, 80–97.

Garrett, C. (1985), "Effects of Residential Treatment on Adjudicated Delinquents: A Meta-analysis," *Journal of Research in Crime and Delinquency*, 22, 287–308.

Gendreau, P. (1993), "The Principles of Effective Intervention with Offenders," Paper presented at the "What Works in Community Corrections" Conference of the International Association of Residential and Community Alternatives. Philadelphia, PA. November 3–6, 1993. Seventh Annual Meeting.

———— (1994), "What Works in Community Corrections: Promising Approaches in Reducing Criminal Behavior," Paper Presented at the International Association of Residential and Community Alternatives. Seattle, WA. November 3, 1994. Eighth Annual Meeting

Gendreau, P. and D. Andrews (1989), "What the Meta-analysis of the Offender Treatment Literature Tells Us about 'What Works,'" Ottawa: University of Ottawa, Laboratory for Research on Assessment and Evaluation in the Human Services.

———— (1990), "Tertiary Prevention: What the Meta-analysis of the Offender Treatment Literature Tells Us about 'What Works,'" *Canadian Journal of Criminology*, 32, 173–184.

Gendreau, P., F. Cullen, and J. Bonta (1994), "Intensive Rehabilitation Supervision: The Next Generation in Community Corrections?" *Federal Probation*, 58, 72–78.

Gendreau, P. and R. Ross (1979), "Effective Correctional Treatment: Bibliotherapy for Cynics," *Crime and Delinquency*, 25, 463–489.

———— (1984), "Correctional Treatment: Some Recommendations for Successful Intervention," *Juvenile and Family Journal*, 34, 31–40.

———— (1987), "Revivification of Rehabilitation: Evidence from the 1980s," *Justice Quarterly*, 4, 349–407.

Gensheimer, L., J. Meyer, R. Gottschalk, and W. Davidson (1986), "Diverting Youth

from the Juvenile Justice System: A
Meta-analysis of Intervention Efficacy,"
in S. Apter and A. Goldstein (eds.),
Youth Violence: Program and Prospects.
New York: Pergamon.

Gerard, R. (1975), "Classification by Behav-
ioral Categories, and Its Implications for
Differential Treatment," in L. Hippchen
(ed.), *Corrrectional Classification and
Treatment: A Reader.* Cincinnati, OH:
Anderson Publishing Company.

Gibbons, D. (1965), *Changing the Law-
breaker: The Treatment of Delinquents
and Criminals.* Englewood Cliffs, NJ:
Prentice-Hall.

—— (1986), "Correctional Treatment and
Intervention Theory: Bringing Sociology
and Criminology Back In," *International
Journal of Offender Therapy and Comparative Criminology,* 30, 255–271.

Gibbons, D. and D. Garrity (1959), "Some
Suggestions for the Development of Etio-
logical and Treatment Theory in Criminology," *Social Forces,* 38, 51–58.

—— (1962), "Definitions and Analysis of
Certain Criminal Types," *Journal of
Criminal Law, Criminology, and Police
Science,* 53, 27–35.

Gilligan, C. (1979), "Woman's Place in Man's
Life Cycle," *Harvard Educational Review,* 49, 431–445.

Girard, S., E. Turner, C. Laurendeau, and
C. Renaud (1979), "Effective Case Management for Delinquents: Fact or Fic-
tion?" Montreal: University of Montreal.
Department of Criminology.

Glaser, D. (1973a), *Routinizing Evaluation:
Getting Feedback on Effectiveness of
Crime and Delinquency Programs.*
Washington, DC: Department of Health,
Education, and Welfare. National Insti-
tute of Mental Health.

—— (1973b), "The State of the Art of
Criminal Justice Evaluation," Paper Presented at the Second Annual Meeting of
the Association for Criminal Justice Research (California). Los Angeles: CA.
November 9, 1973.

—— (June 11, 1974), Written Personal
Communication.

—— (1975), "Achieving Better Questions:
A Half Century's Progress in Correctional Research," *Federal Probation,* 39,
3–9.

Glasser, W. (1965), *Reality Therapy: A New
Approach.* New York: Harper & Row.

Golan, N. (1980), "Using Situational Crises
to Ease Transitions in the Life Cycle,"
American Journal of Orthopsychiatry,
50, 542–550.

Golden, S. (1968), "A Guide to Treatment
Programs in the California Youth Au-
thority," Division of Rehabilitation.
Sacramento: California Youth Authority.

Goodman, G. (1972), *Companionship Therapy.* San Francisco: Jossey-Bass.

Goodwin, R. (1976), "Citizens in Correc-
tions. An Evaluation of 13 Correctional
Volunteer Programs," Research Division.
Sacramento: California Youth Authority.

Gottfredson, D. and K. Ballard, Jr. (1963),
"Interpersonal Maturity Measurement
by the California Psychological Inven-
tory," Vacaville, CA: Institute for the
Study of Crime and Delinquency and the
California Department of Corrections.

Gottfredson, D. M. and M. Tonry (1987),
"Prediction and Classification," in D. M.
Gottfredson and M. Tonry (eds.), *Crimi-
nal Justice Decision Making.* Chicago:
University of Chicago Press.

Gottfredson, M. (1979a), "Parole Guidelines
and the Reduction of Sentencing Disparity," *Journal of Research in Crime and
Delinquency,* 16, 218–231.

—— (1979b), "Treatment Destruction
Techniques," *Journal of Research in
Crime and Delinquency,* 16, 39–54.

—— (1980), "Response to Lerman," *Journal of Research in Crime and Delinquency,* 17, 130–133.

Gottfredson, M., S. Mitchell-Hersfeld, and
T. Flanagan (1982), "Another Look at
the Effectiveness of Parole Supervision,"
*Journal of Research in Crime and Delin-
quency,* 19, 277–298.

Gottfredson, S. and D. M. Gottfredson
(1986), "Accuracy of Prediction Models," in A. Blumstein, J. Cohen, J. Roth,
and C. Visher (eds.), *Criminal Careers
and Career Criminals. (Volume II).*
Washington, DC: National Academy
Press.

Gottfredson, S. and R. Taylor (1986), *Per-
son-Environment Interactions in the
Prediction of Recidivism: The Social
Ecology of Crime.* New York: Springer-
Verlag.

Gough, H. (1960), "Manual for the California Psychological Inventory." Palo Alto,

CA: Consulting Psychologists Press.

——— (1969), "California Psychological Inventory Manual," Palo Alto, CA: Consulting Psychological Press.

Gough, H. and D. Peterson (1952), "The Identification and Measurement of Predispositional Factors in Crime and Delinquency," *Journal of Consulting Psychology*, 16, 207–212.

Gould, D. and R. Beverly (1963), "The Initial Home Visit Research Schedule and Its Relationship to Parole Performance," Research Division Report no. 33. Sacramento: California Youth Authority.

Governor's Budget (1962–63 et al.), "Annual Program Description and Budget Report, Youth and Adult Corrections Agency," for Fiscal Years 1962–63, 1963–64, 1966–67, 1971–72, 1982–83, 1992–93. Sacramento.

Grant, J. and M. Q. Grant (1959), "A Group Dynamics Approach to the Treatment of Non-Conformists in the Navy," *Annals of the American Academy of Political and Social Sciences*, 322, 126–135.

Grant, M. Q. (1961a), "A Current Trend in Correctional Research. Interaction between Kinds of Treatments and Kinds of Delinquents," *California State Board of Corrections Monograph*, 2, 5–14. Sacramento.

——— (1961b), "A Study of Conformity in a Nonconformist Population," Berkeley: University of California. Unpublished dissertation.

——— (1961c), "Interpersonal Maturity Level Classification: Juvenile," Research Division. Sacramento: California Youth Authority.

——— (1962a), "Community Treatment Project. An Evaluation of Community Treatment for Delinquents," CTP Research Report no. 1. Sacramento: California Youth Authority.

——— (1962b), "Community Treatment Project. Second Progress Report," Sacramento: California Youth Authority. (Two-page Overview. February 1, 1962.)

——— (1963), "A Differential Treatment Approach to the Delinquent and His Family," Paper Presented at the California Conference for Health and Welfare. Los Angeles. March 25, 1963.

Grant, M. Q., M. Warren, and J. Turner (1963), "Community Treatment Project.

An Evaluation of Community Treatment for Delinquents," CTP Research Report no. 3. Sacramento: California Youth Authority.

Greenberg, D. (1977), "The Correctional Effects of Corrections: A Survey of Evaluations," in D. Greenberg (ed.), *Corrections and Punishment*. Beverly Hills: Sage.

Greenwood, P. and S. Turner (1993), "Evaluation of the Paint Creek Youth Center: A Residential Program for Serious Delinquents," *Criminology*, 31, 263–279.

Greenwood, P. and F. Zimring (1985), *One More Chance: The Pursuit of Promising Intervention Strategies for Chronic Juvenile Offenders*. Santa Monica, CA: RAND.

Grenny, G. (1971), "The Relationship of Treater Personality to Methods of Behavior Change: A Study of Differential Treatment in the California Youth Authority," Berkeley: University of California. Unpublished doctoral dissertation.

Griffiths, K. (1981), "The California Youth Authority: Its Beginnings, Modification, and Future," Research Division. Sacramento: California Youth Authority.

Gruenewald, P., S. Lawrence, and B. West (1985), "National Evaluation of the New Pride Replication Program." Walnut Creek, CA: Pacific Institute for Research and Evaluation.

Guilford, J. (1954), *Psychometric Methods*. New York: McGraw-Hill.

——— (1959), *Personality*. New York: McGraw-Hill.

Gullotta, T., G. Adams, and R. Montemayor (1997), *Delinquent Violent Youth*. Newbury Park/Thousand Oaks, CA: Sage.

Gunderson, E. (1956), "Group Testing Diagnostic Manual. First Revision," San Diego, CA: U.S. Naval Retraining Command, Camp Elliott.

Gunderson, E. and K. Ballard (1960), "Changes in Nonconformist Attitudes Induced in Closed Living Groups," Research Newsletter no. 5, 4–10. Sacramento: California Department of Corrections.

Gunderson, E., K. Ballard, and P. Huge (1958), "The Relationship of Delinquency Potential Scale-Scores of Naval Recruits to Later Military Performance," Ninth Technical Report on Rehabilitation Research. San Diego, CA: U.S. Naval Retraining Command, Camp Elliott.

Gunderson, K. (November, 1995), Personal Communication.

Gustitus, W. and F. Hebison (1986), "A Retrospective Analysis of Coping Outcome as Related to Interpersonal Maturity Level and Program Completion in a Differential Treatment Setting," *Journal of the International Differential Treatment Association,* 15, 37–51.

Haan, N. (1977), *Coping and Defending: Processes of Self-Environment Organization.* New York: Academic Press.

Haapanen, R. (1991), "Patterns of Violent Crime: A Longitudinal Investigation," Research Division. Sacramento: California Youth Authority.

Haapanen, R. and C. Jesness (1982), "Early Identification of the Chronic Offender. Executive Summary," Research Division. Sacramento: California Youth Authority.

Hahn, P. (1998), *Emerging Criminal Justice: Three Pillars of a Proactive Justice System.* Thousand Oaks, CA: Sage.

Haire, S. (1970), "Handbook for Foster Parents," Division of Rehabilitation. Sacramento: California Youth Authority.

Haire, S. and T. Palmer (1969), "An Overview of Issues General to the Use of Group Homes for Youthful Offenders," Group Homes Project Report. Sacramento: California Youth Authority.

Haley, H. (1982), "Differential Classification and Correctional Objectives," *Journal of the International Differential Treatment Association,* 11, 40–45.

Halleck, S. and A. Witte (1977), "Is Rehabilitation Dead?" *Crime and Delinquency,* 23, 372–382.

Haller, S. and F. Mullany (1988), "Marketing Community Corrections," Washington, DC: U.S. Department of Justice. National Institute of Corrections.

Hamparian, D., R. Shuster, S. Dinitz, and J. Conrad (1978), *The Violent Few.* Lexington, MA: Lexington Books.

Hanna, W. (1977), "Boys' Farm and Training School," *The International Differential Treatment Association Newsletter,* 3, 6–14.

——— (1978), "Organizations and Differential Treatment: A Blueprint for Action," *The International Differential Treatment Association Newsletter,* 6, 3–21.

Harland, A. and P. Harris (1984), "Develop-

ing and Implementing Alternatives to Incarceration: A Problem of Planned Change in Criminal Justice," *University of Illinois Law Review,* 2, 319–364.

Harlow, E., J. Weber, and L. Wilkins (1971), "Community-Based Correctional Programs. Models and Practices." Washington, DC: National Institute of Mental Health. Center for Studies of Crime and Delinquency.

Harlow, N. and E. Nelson (1982), "Management Strategies for Probation in an Era of Limits." Washington, DC: U.S. Department of Justice. National Institute of Corrections.

Harris, M. (1987), "Observations of a 'Friend of the Court' on the Future of Probation and Parole," *Federal Probation,* 51, 12–22.

Harris, P. (1977), "Delinquents, Nondelinquents, and I-Level. Part I," *The International Differential Treatment Association Newsletter,* 4, 26–42.

——— (1978), "Delinquents, Nondelinquents, and I-Level. Part II," *The International Differential Treatment Association Newsletter,* 5, 1–8.

——— (1979), "The Interpersonal Maturity of Delinquents and Nondelinquents," *Dissertation Abstracts International.* University Microfiles. Albany, NY: State University of New York at Albany.

——— (1980), "A Differential Approach to the Study of Personality and Delinquency," *Journal of the International Differential Treatment Association,* 8, 28–36.

——— (1983), "The Interpersonal Maturity of Delinquents and Nondelinquents," in W. Laufer and J. Day (eds.), *Personality Theory, Moral Development, and Criminal Behavior.* Lexington, MA: Lexington Books.

——— (1986a), "I-Level and Problems of Reliability and Validity," *Journal of the International Differential Treatment Association,* 15, 1–6.

——— (1986b), "Obstacles to Implementing Differential Treatment," *Journal of the International Differential Treatment Association,* 14, 1–7.

——— (1988), "The Interpersonal Maturity Level Classification System: I-Level," *Criminal Justice and Behavior,* 15, 58–77.

Harris, P. and S. Smith (1993), "Developing Community Corrections: An Implementation Perspective," Paper Presented at the International Association of Residential and Community Alternatives. Seventh Annual Meeting.

Harris, P. M., T. Clear, and C. Baird (1989), "Have Community Supervision Officers Changed Their Attitudes toward Their Work?" *Justice Quarterly,* 6, 233–246.

Harris, T. (1967), *I'm OK—You're OK. A Practical Guide to Transactional Analysis.* New York: Harper & Row.

Hartnagel, T. (1979), "The Perception and Fear of Crime: Implications for Neighborhood Cohesion, Social Activity, and Community Affect," *Social Forces,* 58, 176–193.

Harvey, O., D. Hunt, and H. Schroder (1961), *Conceptual Systems and Personality Organizations.* New York: Wiley.

Harvie, E. and R. Brill (1977), "Client Characteristics. Technical Report no. 3," Montreal: University of Montreal. Groupe de Recherche sur L'Inadaptation Juvénile.

——— (1978), "Client Characteristics. Final Report no. 3," Montreal: University of Montreal. Groupe de Recherche sur L'Inadaptation Juvénile.

Haskell, M. (1961), "An Alternative to More and Larger Prisons: A Role Training Program for Social Reconnection," *Group Psychotherapy,* 14, 30–38.

——— (1975), *Socioanalysis: Self-Direction via Sociometry and Psychodrama.* Los Angeles: Anderson, Ritchie, and Simon.

Havel, J. (1960), "Interactions between Treatment Method and Offender Type," *California State Board of Corrections Monograph,* 1, 27–30. Sacramento.

——— (1963), "Special Intensive Parole Unit. Phase IV," Division of Research Report no. 10. Sacramento: California Department of Corrections.

——— (1965), "Special Intensive Parole Unit. Phase 4: The Parole Outcome Study," Division of Research Report no. 13. Sacramento: Department of Corrections.

Havel, J. and E. Sulka (1962), "Special Intensive Parole Unit. Phase 3," Division of Research Report no. 3. Sacramento: Department of Corrections.

Hawkins, J., P. Pastor, M. Bell, and S. Morrison (1980), "A Typology of Cause-Focused Strategies of Delinquency Prevention," Washington, DC: U.S. Department of Justice. Office of Juvenile Justice and Delinquency Prevention.

Hayman, M. (1977), "One-Stop Rehabilitation in Cincinnati," *Target—Newsletter of Innovative Projects,* 6, 3–5. Washington, DC: International City Management Association.

Hayner, N. (1961), "Characteristics of Five Offender Types," *American Sociological Review,* 26, 96–102.

Healy, W. and A. Bronner (1936), *A New Light on Delinquency and Its Treatment.* New Haven: Yale University Press.

Hebison, F. (1986), "Differential Treatment: A Followup Study of Treatment Success," *Journal of the International Differential Treatment Association,* 14, 25–35.

Hebison, F. and W. Gustitus (1982), "Integration Level—Conceptual Level. Implementation Process at St. Francis Boys' Homes. A Historical Summary," Salina, KS: The St. Francis Boys' Homes, Inc. Presented at the Annual Meeting of the International Differential Treatment Association. Wayzata, MN. May 1982.

Heide, K. (1982), "Classification of Offenders Ordered to Make Restitution by Interpersonal Maturity and by Specific Personality Dimensions," *Dissertation Abstracts International.* University Microfiles. Albany, NY: State University of New York at Albany.

——— (1983), "An Empirical Assessment of the Value of Utilizing Personality Data in Restitution Outcome Prediction," in W. Laufer and J. Day (eds.), *Personality Theory, Moral Development, and Criminal Behavior.* Lexington, MA: Lexington Books.

Henggeler, S. (1989), *Delinquency in Adolescence.* Newbury Park, CA: Sage.

Higgins, T. (1977), "The Crime Cost of California Early Minor Offenders: Implications for Prevention," *Journal of Research in Crime and Delinquency,* 14, 195–205.

Hindelang, M., M. Gottfredson, and J. Garofalo (1978), *Victims of Personal Crime: An Empirical Foundation for a Theory of Personal Victimization,* Cambridge, MA: Ballinger.

Hirschi, T. (1969), *Causes of Delinquency.* Berkeley: University of California Press.

—— (1979), "Separate and Unequal Is Better," *Journal of Research in Crime and Delinquency,* 16, 34–38.

Hissong, J. (October and November, 1995), Personal Communications.

Hobbs, D., R. Auwaeter, M. Anderson, D. Sams, and G. Kistner (1969), "An Evaluation of One Segment of the I-Level Program at NRCC: The Diagnostic Interview," Division of Rehabilitation. Sacramento: California Youth Authority.

Hoffman, P. and J. Beck (1975), "Parole Decision-Making: A Salient Factor Score," *Journal of Criminal Justice,* 2, 195–206.

Hogan, K., T. Johnston, and L. Liehmann (1994), "Craigwood Youth Services. Program Services Manual." London: Ontario.

Hoghughi, M. (1988), *Treating Problem Children: Issues, Methods, and Practices.* Newbury Park: Sage.

Holland, J. and B. Skinner (1961), *The Analysis of Behavior.* New York: McGraw-Hill.

Holt, R. and L. Luborsky (1952), "Research in the Selection of Psychiatrists: A Second Interim Report," *Bulletin of the Menninger Clinic,* 16, 125–135.

Hompesch, R. and I. Hompesch-Cornetz (1979), *Jugendcriminalitat und Padagogisches Handeln. Eine Untersuchung an Resozialisierungsprogrammen der California Youth Authority. Band I.* Frankfurt, Germany: Bock and Herchen Verlag.

Horney, K. (1937), *The Neurotic Personality of Our Time.* New York: Norton.

Howard, G. (1974), "Center for Training in Differential Treatment. Phases I and II. Summary of Activities and Findings," Sacramento: Human Learning Systems and the California Youth Authority.

Howard, G., J. McHale, and M. Q. Warren (1974), "A Video-Tape Training Model for I-Level Classification," Sacramento: Center for Training in Differential Treatment, Human Learning Systems, and National Institute of Mental Health, in cooperation with the California Youth Authority.

Howell, J. (1997), *Juvenile Justice and Youth Violence.* Newbury Park/Thousand Oaks, CA: Sage.

Howell, J., B. Krisberg, J. Hawkins, and J. J. Wilson (1995), *A Sourcebook: Serious, Violent, and Chronic Juvenile Offenders.* Newbury Park, CA: Sage.

Huff, R., C. Andre, and J. Mahan (1972), "Differential Education Model for I_3 Manipulators and I_3 Cultural Conformists," Differential Education Project Report. Sacramento: California Youth Authority.

—— (1973), "Differential Education Model for I_3 Manipulator and I_3 Cultural Conformist Students," Differential Education Project Report (revised). Sacramento: California Youth Authority.

Hunt, D. (1965), "Indicators of Developmental Change in Lower Class Children," Washington, DC: United States Office of Education.

—— (1971), *Matching Models in Education.* Toronto: Ontario Institute for Studies in Education.

Hunt, D., L. Butler, J. Noy, and M. Rosser (1978), *Assessing Conceptual Level by the Paragraph Completion Method.* Toronto: Ontario Institute for Studies in Education.

Hunt, D. and R. Hardt (1965), "Developmental Stage, Delinquency, and Differential Treatment," *Journal of Research in Crime and Delinquency,* 2, 20–31.

Hunt, D. and J. McManus (1968), "Preliminary Investigation of Boys Known to Probation. Final Report," Washington, DC: U.S. Department of Justice. Office of Law Enforcement Assistance.

Hurwitz, J. (1965), "Three Delinquent Types: A Multivariate Analysis," *Journal of Criminal Law, Criminology, and Police Science,* 56, 328–334.

Information Systems Section (1978), "Statistical Fact Sheet no. 53 (June 20, 1978)," Research Division. Sacramento: California Youth Authority.

—— (1971), "Statistical Fact Sheet no. 31 (May 27, 1971)," Research Division. Sacramento: California Youth Authority.

—— (1974), "CYA Cost-Comparisons: Fiscal Years 1963–64 through 1972–73," Research Division. Sacramento: California Youth Authority.

—— (1979), "Statistical Fact Sheet no. 56 (June 8, 1979)," Research Division. Sacramento: California Youth Authority.

Ingram, G. (1970), "Matching Volunteers

and Juvenile Offenders," in P. Zelhart and J. Plummer (eds.), *Institute on Research with Volunteers in Juvenile Delinquency.* Fayetteville, AR: University of Arkansas, Arkansas Rehabilitation Research and Training Center.

―――― (ed.) (1990), "Correctional Programs in the Year 2000. The June 9, 1989 Conference on Issues in Corrections. A Record of Proceedings," Washington, DC: U.S. Department of Justice. Federal Bureau of Prisons.

Isaacs, K. (1956), "Relatability: A Proposed Construct and An Approach to its Validation," Chicago: University of Chicago. Unpublished Doctoral Dissertation.

Isaacs, K. and E. Haggard (1956), "Some Methods Used in the Study of Affect in Psychotherapy," In L. Gottschalk and S. Auerbach (eds.), *Methods of Research in Psychotherapy.* New York: Appleton-Century-Crofts.

Ives, V. and M. Q. Grant (1956), "Initial Steps in the Measurement of Interpersonal Maturity," Sixth Technical Report on Rehabilitation Research. Camp Elliott, San Diego: U.S. Naval Retraining Command.

Izzo, R. and R. Ross (1990), "Meta-analysis of Rehabilitation Programs for Juvenile Delinquents," *Criminal Justice and Behavior,* 17, 134–142.

Jackson, P. (1978), "The Bay Area Parole Study," Research Division Report. Sacramento: California Youth Authority.

―――― (1983), *The Paradox of Control. Parole Supervision of Youthful Offenders.* New York: Praeger.

Jamison, C., B. Johnson, and E. Guttman (1966), "An Analysis of Post-Discharge Criminal Behavior," Research Division Report no. 49. Sacramento: California Youth Authority.

Jenkins, R. (1980), "Similarities, Differences, and Translations between the Classification of Delinquents Used by the American Psychiatric Association (DSM-II) and the Quay System, and the I-Level System," *Journal of the International Differential Treatment Association,* 9, 48–53.

Jenkins, R. and L. Hewitt (1944), "Types of Personality Structure Encountered in Child Guidance Clinics," *American Journal of Orthopsychiatry,* 14, 84–94.

Jesness, C. (1962), "The Jesness Inventory: Development and Validation," Research Division Report no. 29. Sacramento: California Youth Authority.

―――― (1963), "Redevelopment and Revalidation of the Jesness Inventory," Research Division Report no. 35. Sacramento: California Youth Authority.

―――― (1965), "The Fricot Ranch Study: Outcomes with Small versus Large Living Groups in the Rehabilitation of Delinquents," Research Division Report no. 47. Sacramento: California Youth Authority.

―――― (1966), *The Jesness Inventory.* Palo Alto, CA: Consulting Psychologists Press.

―――― (1969), "The Preston Typology Study. Final Report," Sacramento: Institute for the Study of Crime and Delinquency and the California Youth Authority.

―――― (1971), "The Preston Typology Study: An Experiment with Differential Treatment in an Institution," *Journal of Research in Crime and Delinquency,* 8, 38–52.

―――― (1971–1972), "Comparative Effectiveness of Two Institutional Treatment Programs for Delinquents," *Child Care Quarterly,* 1, 119–139.

―――― (1974), "Sequential I-Level Classification Manual." Sacramento: American Justice Institute and the California Youth Authority.

―――― (1975a), "An Overview of the Youth Center Research Project," *Youth Authority Quarterly,* 28, 7–24.

―――― (1975b), "Comparative Effectiveness of Behavior Modification and Transactional Analysis Programs for Delinquents," *Journal of Consulting and Clinical Psychology,* 43, 758–779.

―――― (1975c), "The Impact of Behavior Modification and Transactional Analysis on Institution Social Climate," *Journal of Research in Crime and Delinquency,* 12, 79–91.

―――― (1978), "Small May Be Beautiful But Is It Cost Effective?" *Journal of Research in Crime and Delinquency,* 15, 25–30.

―――― (1980), "Matching Students with Teachers: An Interim Report," Research Division. Sacramento: California Youth Authority.

―――― (1983), *The Jesness Inventory (Revised).* Palo Alto, CA: Consulting Psychologists Press.

—— (1986), "Validity of Jesness Inventory Classification with Nondelinquents," *Educational Psychological Measurement,* 46, 447–461.

—— (1988), "The Jesness Inventory Classification System," *Criminal Justice and Behavior,* 15, 78–91.

—— (January 26 and September 22, 1999), Personal Communications.

Jesness, C., T. Allison, P. McCormick, R. Wedge, and M. Young (1975a), "An Evaluation of the Effectiveness of Contingency Contracting with Delinquents," Sacramento: California Youth Authority.

—— (1975b), "Cooperative Behavior Demonstration Project: Final Report." Sacramento: California State Office of Criminal Justice Planning.

Jesness, C., M. Bohnstedt, M. Molof, and R. Wedge (1973), "Sequential I-Level Classification." Sacramento: American Justice Institute and the California Youth Authority.

Jesness, C., W. DeRisi, P. McCormick, and R. Wedge (1972), "The Youth Center Research Project. Final Report." Sacramento: The American Justice Institute and the California Youth Authority.

Jesness, C. and R. Wedge (1970), "Sequential I-Level Classification Manual. (Provisional Sequential System)," Research Division. Sacramento: California Youth Authority.

—— (1983a), "Classifying Offenders: The Jesness Inventory Classification System. Technical Manual." Sacramento: California Youth Authority.

—— (1983b), "Manual for Youth Counselors." Sacramento: California Youth Authority.

—— (1984), "Validity of a Revised Jesness Inventory I-Level Classification with Delinquents," *Journal of Consulting and Clinical Psychology,* 52, 997–1010.

Johns, D. (1965), "A Pilot Time Study of Four Experimental Parole Units," Research Division Report. Sacramento: California Youth Authority.

—— (1967), "Institutional Program Patterns. Parole Prognosis and Outcome," Research Division Report no. 52. Sacramento: California Youth Authority.

—— (1977), "An Evaluation of Seven Selected Probation Subsidy Programs," Research Division Report. Sacramento: California Youth Authority.

Johns, D. and T. Palmer (1970), "Atmosphere and Activities in a Community Center Dayroom for Delinquent Adolescents," Community Treatment Project Report Series: 1970, no. 1. Sacramento: California Youth Authority.

Johns, D., P. White, and S. Berkowitz (1974), "California's Probation Subsidy Program: A Progress Report to the Legislature, 1966–1973." Sacramento: California Youth Authority.

Johnson, B. (1960), "Parole Agent Job Analysis. Parole Research Project," Research Division Report no. 19. Sacramento: California Youth Authority.

—— (1962), "Parole Performance of the First Year's Releases. Parole Research Project: Evaluation of Reduced Caseloads," Research Division Report no. 27. Sacramento: California Youth Authority.

Johnson, B. and R. Peters (1961), "Parole Agent Characteristics as of June, 1959," Research Division Report no. 24. Sacramento: California Youth Authority.

Johnson, G., T. Bird, J. Little, and S. Beville (1981), "Delinquency Prevention: Theories and Strategies." Washington, DC: U.S. Department of Justice. Office of Juvenile Justice and Delinquency Prevention.

Johnson, S. (1982), "Differential Classification and Treatment: The Case against Us," *Journal of the International Differential Treatment Association,* 11, 7–18.

Jung, C. (1923), *Psychological Types.* Harcourt, Brace.

Kegan, R. (1979), "The Evolving Self: A Process Conception for Ego Psychology," *The Counseling Psychologist,* 8, 5–34.

—— (1982), *The Evolving Self,* Cambridge, MA: Harvard University Press.

Keller, O. and B. Alper (1970), *Halfway Houses: Community-Centered Correction and Treatment.* Lexington, MA: Lexington Books.

Kelly, G. (1955), *The Psychology of Personal Constructs.* New York: Norton.

Kenney, R., G. Hopkins, A. Owyung, and M. Q. Warren (1965), "Community Treatment Project Progress Report, December 1965," Task Force Report to the Legislature. Sacramento: California Youth Authority.

Kenney, R., C. Kuhl, G. Avery, and G. Marriot (1970), "Community Treatment Project Evaluation, Task Force Report." Sacramento: California Youth Authority.

Kerr, D. (1978), "The Prediction of Recidivism in Juvenile Delinquents," Denver, CO: University of Denver. Unpublished paper.

Kilchenstein, J., P. Waldman, L. Ellard, T. Wright, and M. Barton (1977), "Community Treatment: The Baltimore City Intensive Probation Project. Final Program Report." Baltimore: Department of Juvenile Services, Court and Community Services Division.

—— (1979), "I-Level Theory in Baltimore City's Differential Treatment Program: Report on Study as of June 1978," Baltimore: Department of Juvenile Services, Court and Community Services Division.

Klein, M. (ed.) (1984), *Western Systems of Juvenile Justice*. Beverly Hills: Sage.

Klockers, C. (1975), "The True Limits of Correctional Effectiveness," *The Prison Journal*, 55, 53–64.

Knight, D. (1970), "The Marshall Program: Assessment of a Short-Term Institutional Treatment Program. Part II: Amenability to Confrontive Peer-Group Treatment," Research Division Report no. 59. Sacramento: California Youth Authority.

—— (1972), "Delinquency Causes and Remedies: The Working Assumptions of California Youth Authority Staff," Research Report no. 61. Sacramento: California Youth Authority.

Kobrin, S. and M. Klein (1982), "National Evaluation of the Deinstitutionalization of Status Offender Programs." Washington, DC: U.S. Department of Justice. Office of Juvenile Justice and Delinquency Prevention.

—— (1983), *Community Treatment of Juvenile Offenders: The D.S.O. Experiment*. Beverly Hills: Sage.

Kohlberg, L. (1964), *Stages in the Development of Moral Thought and Action*. New York: Holt, Rinehart, and Winston.

—— (1976), "Moral Stages and Moralization," in T. Lickona (ed.), *Development and Behavior*. New York: Holt, Rinehart, and Winston.

Kohlberg, L., K. Kauffman, P. Scharf, and J. Hickey (1973), *The Just Community Approach in Corrections: A Manual*. Niantic, CT: Connecticut Department of Corrections.

Kratcoski, P. (1985), "The Functions of Classification Models in Probation and Parole: Control or Treatment-Rehabilitation?" *Federal Probation*, 49, 49–56.

Kress, J. (1980), *Prescription for Justice. The Theory and Practice of Sentencing Guidelines*. Cambridge, MA: Ballinger.

Krisberg, B. (1980), "Utility of Process Evaluations: Crime and Delinquency Programs," in M. Klein and K. Tielman (eds.), *Handbook of Criminal Justice Evaluation*. Beverly Hills: Sage.

Krisberg, B. and J. Austin (1993), *Reinventing Juvenile Justice*. Newbury Park, CA: Sage.

Krisberg, B., J. Austin, and P. Steele (1989), "Unlocking Juvenile Corrections: Evaluating the Massachusetts Department of Youth Services." San Francisco: National Council on Crime and Delinquency.

Krisberg, B., A. Baake, D. Neuenfeldt, and P. Steele (1989), "Demonstration of Post-Adjudication, Non-Residential Intensive Supervision Programs: Selected Program Summaries." San Francisco: National Council on Crime and Delinquency.

Krisberg, B., D. Neuenfeldt, and A. Baake (1991), "Juvenile Intensive Supervision Programs: The State of the Art," San Francisco: National Council on Crime and Delinquency.

Krisberg, B., O. Rodriguez, A. Baake, D. Neuenfeldt, and P. Steele (1989), "Demonstration of Post-Adjudication, Non-Residential Intensive Supervision Programs: Assessment Report." San Francisco: National Council on Crime and Delinquency.

Krisberg, B. and I. Schwartz (1983), "Rethinking Juvenile Justice," *Crime and Delinquency*, 29, 333–364.

Krisberg, B., I. Schwartz, P. Litsky, and J. Austin (1986), "The Watershed of Juvenile Justice Reform," *Crime and Delinquency*, 32, 5–38.

Ku, R. (1975), "An Exemplary Project. The Volunteer Probation Counselor Program—Lincoln, Nebraska." Washington, DC: U.S. Department of Justice. Law Enforcement Assistance Administration.

Lab, S. and J. Whitehead (1988), "An Analysis of Juvenile Correctional Treatment," *Crime and Delinquency*, 34, 60–85.

Larivee, J. (1989), "Evaluation of the Hampden County Day Reporting Center." Boston: Crime and Justice Foundation.

Larson, R. (1979), "Interim Analysis of 200 Evaluations on Criminal Justice." Cambridge, MA: Massachusetts Institute of Technology, Operations Research Center.

Latessa, E. (1987), "The Effectiveness of Intensive Supervision with High-Risk Probationers," in B. McCarthy (ed.), *Intermediate Punishments: Intensive Supervision, Home Confinement, and Electronic Surveillance.* Monsey, NJ: Criminal Justice Press.

Laufer, W. and J. Day (eds.) (1983), *Personality Theory, Moral Development, and Criminal Behavior.* Lexington, MA: Lexington Books.

Leahy, T. (1970), "Estimating Career Costs of Selected Repeat Criminal Offenders," Research Division. Sacramento: California Youth Authority.

LeBlanc, M., W. Hanna, and R. Brill (1975), "An Evaluative Study Proposal for a Differential Treatment Program at the Boys' Farm Training School." Montreal: University of Montreal. Groupe de Recherche sur L'Inadaptation Juvénile.

LeBlanc, P. (1978), "The Family and Interpersonal Maturity," *The International Differential Treatment Association Newsletter,* 5, 9–16.

LeClair, D. (1979), "Community-Based Reintegration: Some Theoretical Implications of Positive Research Findings," Research Report no. 180. Boston: Massachusetts Department of Corrections.

——— (1985), "The Effect of Community Reintegration on Rates of Recidivism: A Statistical Overview of Data for the Years 1971 through 1982," Research Report no. 279. Boston: Massachusetts Department of Corrections.

Lee, R. and N. Haynes (1980), "Project CREST and the Dual-Treatment Approach to Delinquency: Methods and Research Summarized," in R. Ross and P. Gendreau (eds.), *Effective Correctional Treatment.* Toronto: Butterworths.

Lee, R. and S. Olejnik (1981), "Professional Outreach Counseling Can Help the Juvenile Probationer: A Two-Year Follow-Up Study," *The Personnel and Guidance Journal,* 59, 445–449.

Legendre, G. (1979), "Differential Treatment in a Girl's Unit," *Journal of the International Differential Treatment Association,* 8, 3–8.

Lemert, E. (1967), "The Juvenile Court— Quest and Realities," in President's Commission on Law Enforcement and Administration of Justice, Task Force on Juvenile Delinquency and Youth Crime. Washington, DC: Government Printing Office.

——— (1971), *Instead of Court: Diversion in Juvenile Justice.* Washington, DC: U.S. Department of Health, Education, and Welfare. National Institute of Mental Health.

——— (1972), *Human Deviance, Social Problems and Social Control.* Englewood Cliffs, NJ: Prentice-Hall.

Lerman, P. (1968), "Evaluative Studies of Institutions for Delinquents: Implications for Research and Social Policy," *Social Work,* 13, 55–64.

——— (1972), "Community Treatment, Social Control, and Juvenile Delinquency: Issues in Correctional Policy," Draft Report Presented to the National Institute of Mental Health. New Brunswick, NJ: Rutgers University.

——— (1973), "Appendix A. A Methodological Note on the CTP Analysis," (draft), for *Community Treatment and Social Control: A Critical Analysis of Juvenile Correctional Policy* (1975)—titled, in the 1972 draft: "Community Treatment, Social Control, and Juvenile Delinquency: Issues in Correctional Policy," Presented to the National Institute of Mental Health, Center for Studies in Crime and Delinquency.

——— (1975), *Community Treatment and Social Control: A Critical Analysis of Juvenile Correctional Policy.* Chicago: University of Chicago Press.

——— (1979), "American Concerns: Keeping Order versus Fighting Crime," in L. Empey (ed.), *Juvenile Justice: The Progressive Legacy and Current Reforms.* Charlottesville: University of Virginia Press.

——— (1980a), "M. Gottfredson's 'Treatment Destruction Techniques': A Comment," *Journal of Research in Crime and Delinquency,* 17, 126–129.

——— (1980b), "Trends and Issues in the Deinstitutionalization of Youths in Trouble,"

Crime and Delinquency, 26, 281–298.

Lerner, K.,G. Arling, and C. Baird (1986), "Client Management Classification Strategies for Case Supervision," *Crime and Delinquency,* 32, 254–271.

Leschied, A. and K. Thomas (1983), "Craigwood's Program for Hard-to-Serve Juvenile Offenders: A Three-Year Evaluation," Ailsa Craig, Ontario (Canada): Craigwood Youth Services.

Leventhal, G., J. Karuza Jr., and W. Fry (1980), "Beyond Fairness: A Theory of Allocation Preferences," in G. Mikula (ed.), *Justice and Social Interaction.* New York: Springer-Verlag.

Levinson, R. and R. Gerard (1973), "Functional Units: A Differential Correctional Approach," *Federal Probation,* 37, 8–16.

Levrant, S., F. Cullen, B. Fulton, and J. Woznaik (1999), "Reconsidering Restorative Justice: The Corruption of Benevolence Revisited?" *Crime and Delinquency,* 45, 3–27.

Lewin, K. (1935), *A Dynamic Theory of Personality.* New York: McGraw-Hill.

Lewis, H. (1954), *Deprived Childhood (The Mershal Experiment: A Social and Clinical Study).* London: Oxford University Press.

Lewis, R. (1976), "M-2 Project Evaluation: Final Parole Follow-Up of Wards in the M-2 Program," Research Division Report. Sacramento: California Youth Authority.

——— (1983), "Scared Straight—California Style: Evaluation of the San Quentin Squires Program," *Criminal Justice and Behavior,* 10, 209–226.

Lillyquist, M. (1980), *Understanding and Changing Criminal Behavior.* Englewood Cliffs, NJ: Prentice-Hall.

Lipsey, M. (1992), "Juvenile Delinquency Treatment: A Meta-analytic Inquiry into the Validity of Effects," in T. Cook, H. Cooper, D. Cordray, H. Hartman, L. Hedges, R. Light, T. Louis, and F. Mosteller (eds.), *Meta-analysis for Explanation: A Casebook.* New York: Russell Sage Foundation.

Lipsey, M. and J. Derzon (1998), "Predictors of Violent or Serious Delinquency in Adolescence and Early Adulthood: A Synthesis of Longitudinal Research," in R. Loeber and D. Farrington (eds.), *Serious and Violent Juvenile Offenders: Risk Factors and Successful Interventions.* Newbury Park/Thousand Oaks, CA: Sage.

Lipsey, M. and D. Wilson (1998), "Effective Intervention for Serious Juvenile Offenders: A Synthesis of Research," in R. Loeber and D. Farrington (eds.), *Serious and Violent Juvenile Offenders: Risk Factors and Successful Interventions.* Newbury Park/Thousand Oaks, CA: Sage.

Lipton, D., R. Martinson, and J. Wilks (1975), *The Effectiveness of Correctional Treatment: A Survey of Treatment Evaluation Studies.* New York: Praeger.

Loeber, R. and D. Farrington (eds.) (1998), *Serious and Violent Juvenile Offenders: Risk Factors and Successful Interventions.* Newbury Park/Thousand Oaks, CA: Sage.

Loevinger, J. (1966), "The Meaning and Measurement of Ego Development," *American Psychologist,* 21, 195–206.

——— (1976), *Ego Development.* San Francisco: Jossey-Bass.

Loevinger, J. and R. Wessler (1970), *Measuring Ego Development. I: Investigation and Use of a Sentence Completion Test.* San Francisco: Jossey-Bass.

Logan, C. (1972), "Evaluation Research in Crime and Delinquency: A Reappraisal," *Journal of Criminal Law, Criminology, and Police Science,* 63, 378–387.

Logan, C. and G. Gaes (1993), "Meta-analysis and the Rehabilitation of Punishment." Washington, DC: U.S. Department of Justice. Federal Bureau of Prisons.

Lohman, J., A. Wahl, R. Carter, and S. Lewis (1967), "The Intensive Supervision Caseload: A Preliminary Evaluation," the San Francisco Project, Research Report no. 11. Sacramento: California Department of Corrections.

Look, L. and M. Q. Warren (1965), "Use of Group Homes As an Element in Differential Treatment Planning for Delinquents," Proposal submitted to the National Institute of Mental Health. Sacramento: California Youth Authority.

Loughran E., R.Van Vleet, A. Rutherford, I. Schwartz, and T. Marshall (1987), "Reinvesting Youth Corrections Resources: A Tale of Three States." Ann Arbor, MI: University of Michigan, Center for the Study of Youth Policy.

Lovaas, O. and B. Bucher (eds.) (1974), *Perspectives in Behavior Modification with*

Deviant Children. Englewood Cliffs, NJ: Prentice-Hall.

Love, C. and J. Allgood (1987), "Butner Study: The Final Analysis," Washington, DC: U.S. Department of Justice. Federal Bureau of Prisons.

Lukin, P. (1981), "Recidivism and Changes Made by Delinquents during Residential Treatment," *Journal of Research in Crime and Delinquency,* 18, 101–112.

Lundman, R. (1984), *Prevention and Control of Juvenile Delinquency.* New York: Oxford University Press.

—— (1986), "Beyond Probation: Assessing the Generalizability of the Delinquency Suppression Effect Measures Reported by Murray and Cox," *Crime and Delinquency,* 32, 134–147.

Lundy, R. (1956), "Assimilative Projection and Accuracy of Prediction in Interpersonal Perception," *Journal of Abnormal and Social Psychology,* 52, 33–38.

Lyttle, W. (1979), "The KEY Program: Alternatives for Youth. Annual Report." Framington, MA: The KEY Program, Inc.

Macallair, D. (1991), "Reaffirming Rehabilitation in Juvenile Justice." San Francisco: Center on Juvenile and Criminal Justice.

—— (1994), "Disposition Case Advocacy in San Francisco's Juvenile Justice System: A New Approach to Deinstitutinalization," *Crime and Delinquency,* 40, 84–95.

MacKay, W. (1962), "Maturity of Interpersonal Perceptions and Persistence of Junior College Students." Berkeley: University of California. Unpublished doctoral dissertation.

MacKenzie, D., C. Posey, and K. Rapaport (1988), "A Theoretical Revolution in Corrections: Varied Purposes for Classification," *Criminal Justice and Behavior,* 15, 125–136.

Makkay, E. (1966), "Juvenile Delinquency Field Demonstration and Training Project: The Newton-Baker Project. Interim Report," Boston: The Judge Baker Guidance Clinic.

Maltz, M. (1980), "Beyond Suppression: More Sturm und Drang on the Correctional Front," *Crime and Delinquency,* 26, 389–397.

—— (1984), *Recidivism.* Orlando, FL: Academic Press.

Maltz, M., A. Gordon, D. McDowall, and R. McCleary (1980), "An Artifact in Pretest–Posttest Designs: How It Can Mistakenly Make Delinquency Programs Look Effective," *Evaluation Review,* 4, 225–240.

Mann, D. (1976), "Intevening with Convicted Serious Juvenile Offenders." Washington, DC: U.S. Department of Justice. Law Enforcement Assistance Administration.

Mannheim, H. and L. Wilkins (1955), *Prediction Methods in Relation to Borstal Training.* London: Her Majesty's Stationery Office.

Martin, J. (1959), "Academic Achievement and Interpersonal Relationships." Berkeley: University of California. Unpublished doctoral dissertation.

Martin, S., L. Sechrest, and R. Redner (1981), *New Directions in the Rehabilitation of Criminal Offenders.* Washington, DC: National Academy Press.

Martinson, R. (1974), "What Works—Questions and Answers about Prison Reform," *The Public Interest,* 35, 22–54.

—— (1976), "California Research at the Crossroads," *Crime and Delinquency,* 22, 180–191.

—— (1979), "Symposium on Sentencing, Part 2," *Hofstra Law Review,* 7, 243–258.

Martinson, R. and J. Wilks (1977), "Save Parole Supervision," *Federal Probation,* 41, 23–27.

Maskin, M. (1976), "The Differential Impact of Work-Oriented vs. Communication-Oriented Juvenile Correctional Programs upon Recidivism Rates in Delinquent Males," *Journal of Clinical Psychology,* 32, 432–433.

Massimo, J. and M. Shore (1963), "The Effectiveness of a Comprehensive Vocationally Oriented Psycho-therapeutic Program for Adolescent Delinquent Boys," *American Journal of Orthopsychiatry,* 33, 634–642.

Mathias, R., P. DeMuro, and R. Allinson (eds.) (1984), *Violent Juvenile Offenders: An Anthology.* San Francisco: National Council on Crime and Delinquency.

Matlin, M. (ed.) (1976), "Rehabilitation, Recidivism, and Research. (Robert Martinson, Ted Palmer, Stuart Adams)." Hackensack, NJ: National Council on Crime and Delinquency.

Matza, D. (1964), *Delinquency and Drift.* New York: Wiley.

Maugham, W. S. (1951), *The Summing Up.* New York: The New American Library of World Literature, Inc.

McCarthy, B. (ed.) (1987), *Intermediate Punishments: Intensive Supervision, Home Confinement, and Electronic Surveillance.* Monsey, NY: Criminal Justice Press.

McCarthy, B. and B. J. McCarthy (1991), *Community-Based Corrections.* Pacific Grove, CA: Brooks/Cole.

McCleary, R. (1975), "How Structural Variables Constrain the Parole Officer's Use of Discretionary Powers," *Social Problems,* 23, 209–225.

——— (1980), "Book Review of Murray and Cox's 'Beyond Probation: Juvenile Corrections and the Chronic Delinquent,'" *Crime and Delinquency,* 26, 387–389.

McConnell, J. (1970), "Criminals Can Be Brainwashed—Now," *Psychology Today,* 3, 14–18, 74.

McCord, J. (1978), "A Thirty-Year Follow-Up of Treatment Effects," *American Psychologist,* 33, 284–289.

McCord, W.M., J. McCord, and I. Zola (1959), *Origins of Crime.* New York: Columbia University Press.

McCorkle, L., A. Elias, and F. Bixby (1958), *The Highfields Story.* New York: Holt, Rinehart, and Winston.

McDonald, D. (1989), "The Cost of Corrections: In Search of the Bottom Line," *Research in Corrections,* 2, 1–40.

McDonald, J. (1965), "Current Status of the School Program," in M. Q. Warren and T. Palmer, "Community Treatment Project: An Evaluation of Community Treatment for Delinquents," CTP Research Report no. 6. Sacramento: California Youth Authority.

McDonald, W. (1976), "Criminal Justice and the Victim: An Introduction," in W. McDonald (ed.), *Criminal Justice and the Victim.* Beverly Hills: Sage, pp. 17–55.

McDowell, C. (1984), *Criminal Justice: A Community Relations Approach.* Cincinnati, OH: Pilgrimage Press.

McEachern, A., E. Taylor, J. Newman, and A. Ashford (1968), "The Juvenile Probation System. Simulation for Research and Decision-Making," *American Behavioral Scientist,* 11, 1–48.

McHale, J. (1977), "The Use of Video Package in I-Level Classification Training," *The International Differential Treatment Association Newsletter,* 3, 15–17.

——— (1978), "Treatment Strategies for I_4 Neurotic Clients," *The International Differential Treatment Association Newsletter,* 6, 22–27.

McKee, J. (1964), "The Draper Experiment: A Programmed Learning Project," in G. Ofiesh and W. Meierhenry (eds.), *Trends in Programmed Instruction.* Washington, DC: National Education Association.

——— (1970), "The Use of Programmed Instruction in Correctional Institutions," *Journal of Correctional Education,* 4, 8–12, 28.

McLachlan, J. (1972), "Patient and Therapist Correlates of Change During Psychotherapy," Toronto: University of Toronto and Ontario Institute for Studies in Education. Unpublished Doctoral Dissertation.

McLaren, K. (1992), "Reducing Reoffending: What Works Now." Wellington, New Zealand: Department of Justice. Penal Division.

McNair, D., D. Callahan, and M. Lorr (1962), "Therapist 'Type' and Patient Response to Psychotherapy," *Journal of Consulting Psychology,* 26, 425–429.

McNamara, D. (1977), "The Medical Model in Corrections: Requiescat in Pace," *Criminology,* 14, 439–448.

McShane, M. and F. Williams III (1989), "Running on Empty: Creativity and the Correctional Agenda," *Crime and Delinquency,* 35, 562–576.

Mead, G. (1934), *Mind, Self, and Society.* Chicago: University of Chicago Press.

Meeker, F. (1969), "Differential Treatment in the Correctional Institution Using I-Level Classification," *Youth Authority Quarterly,* 22, 18–21.

Megargee, E., M. Bohn, Jr., and F. Sink (1979), *Classifying Criminal Offenders: A New System Based on the MMPI.* Beverly Hills: Sage.

Merton, R. (1975), *Social Theory and Social Structure.* Glencoe, IL: Free Press.

Mertz, D. (1978), "Implementation of I-Level in the Colorado Youth Institutional System," *The International Differential Treatment Association Newsletter,* 7, 34–36.

Miller, D. (1972), "A Construct Validity Study of the Interpersonal Maturity Level Classification System for Youthful Offenders." Amherst: University of Massachusetts. Unpublished doctoral dissertation.

——— (1978), "Differential Treatment in the Division of Youth Services," *The International Differential Treatment Association Newsletter,* 7, 28–33.

——— (November 1, 1995), Personal Communication.

Miller, E. (1977), "Is Parole Necessary?" in E. Miller and M. Montilla (eds.), *Corrections in the Community.* Reston, VA: Reston Publishing Company, pp. 253–263.

Miller, W. (1958), "Lower Class Culture As a Generating Milieu of Gang Delinquency," *Journal of Social Issues,* 14, 5–19.

Minor, W. (1981), "Techniques of Neutralization: A Reconceptualization and Empirical Examination," *Journal of Research in Crime and Delinquency,* 18, 295–318.

Mitchell, J. and J. Pierce-Jones (1960), "A Factor Analysis of Gough's California Psychological Inventory," *Journal of Consulting Psychology,* 24, 453–456.

Mitford, J. (1971), "Kind and Usual Punishment in California," *The Atlantic Monthly,* 227, 45–52.

——— (August 1973), "The Torture Cure," *Harpers,* 16–30.

——— (1974), *Kind and Usual Punishment: The Prison Business.* New York: Random House.

Molof, M. (1965), "Prediction of Future Assaultive Behavior among Youthful Offenders," Research Division Report no. 41. Sacramento: California Youth Authority.

——— (1967), "Differences between Assaultive and Non-assaultive Juvenile Offenders in the California Youth Authority," Research Division Report no. 51. Sacramento: California Youth Authority.

——— (1969), "I-Level Classification at the California Youth Authority Clinics: An Interim and Technical Report," Research Division. Sacramento: California Youth Authority.

——— (1970), "Statistical Prediction of Recidivism among Female Parolees in the California Youth Authority," Research Division Report no. 57. Sacramento: California Youth Authority.

Molof, M. and C. Jesness (1972), "Project Sequil. The Development of a Sequential I-Level Classification System. Yearly Report: February 1971–January 1972," Sacramento: American Justice Institute and the California Youth Authority.

——— (1973), "Construct Validity of the Interpersonal Maturity Level (I-Level) Classification System for Delinquent Offenders." Sacramento: California Youth Authority and the American Justice Institute.

Monahan, J. (1976), "The Prevention of Violence," in J. Monahan (ed.), *Community Mental Health and the Criminal Justice System.* New York: Pergamon Press.

——— (1981), *Predicting Violent Behavior: An Assessment of Clinical Techniques.* Beverly Hills: Sage.

Montada, L. (1980), "Developmental Changes in Concepts of Justice," in G. Mikula (ed.), *Justice and Social Interaction.* New York: Springer-Verlag.

Moore, E. (1978), "An Empirical Study of Matching in Helping Relationships," *Canadian Journal of Social Work Education,* 4, 19–34.

Moore, R. (1976), "Nebraska Matches Volunteers and Probationers. (Project Target)," Washington, DC: *International City Management Association,* 5, 5.

Moos, R. (November 1973), "Community-Based Correctional Programs: A Critical Appraisal," Report to NIMH, Center for Studies in Crime and Delinquency. Stanford, CA: Social Ecology Laboratory.

——— (1975), *Evaluating Correctional and Community Settings.* New York: Wiley.

Moreno, J. (1953), *Who Shall Survive?* New York: Beacon House.

——— (1959), "Psychodrama," in S. Arieti (ed.), *American Handbook of Psychiatry (Vol. 2).* New York: Basic Books.

Moriarty, L. and R. Jerin (1998), *Current Issues in Victimology Research.* Durham, NC: Carolina Academic Press.

Morris, N. (1974), *The Future of Imprisonment.* Chicago: University of Chicago Press.

——— (1978), "Conceptual Overview and Commentary on the Movement toward Determinacy," in *Determinate Sentencing: Proceedings of the Special Conference on Determinate Sentencing.* Washington, DC: U.S. Department of Justice.

National Institute of Law Enforcement and Criminal Justice, pp. 1–11.

Morris, N. and M. Miller (1987), "Predictions of Dangerousness in the Criminal Law." Washington, DC: U.S. Department of Justice. National Institute of Justice. Research Brief.

Morris, N. and M. Tonry (1990), *Between Prison and Probation: Intermediate Punishments in a Rational Sentencing System*. Oxford, England: Oxford University Press.

Morris, N. and M. Wasserman (June 14, 1974), Written Personal Communication.

MSSD Policy Manual (1968), "Metropolitan Social Services Department Policy Manual, 1968." Louisville, KY: Metropolitan Social Services Department of Jefferson County.

——— (1971), "Metropolitan Social Services Department Policy Manual, 1971." Louisville, KY: Metropolitan Social Services Department of Jefferson County.

Mueller, P. (1960), "Success Rates As a Function of Treatment Assignment and Juvenile Delinquency Classification Interaction." *California State Board of Corrections Monograph*, 1, 7–14.

Mullen, J. (1985), "Corrections and the Private Sector." Washington, DC: U.S. Department of Justice. National Institute of Justice.

Mullen, J., K. Carlson, and B. Smith (1980), "American Prisons and Jails. Volume I: Summary Findings and Policy Implications of a National Survey." Washington, DC: U.S. Department of Justice. National Institute of Justice.

Munroe, R. (1955), *Schools of Psychoanalytic Thought: An Exposition, Critique, and Attempt at Integration*. New York: The Dryden Press.

Murray, C. (1980), "Reply to Michael Maltz," *Crime and Delinquency*, 26, 397–398.

Murray, C. and L. Cox (1979), *Beyond Probation: Juvenile Corrections and the Chronic Delinquent*. Beverly Hills: Sage.

Murray, C., D. Thomson, and C. Israel (1978a), "UDIS: Deinstitutionalizing the Chronic Juvenile Offender," Washington, DC: American Institutes for Research.

——— (1978b), "UDIS: Deinstitutionalizing the Chronic Juvenile Offender. Executive Summary." Washington, DC: American Institutes for Research.

Myers, G. (1962), "The Outcome of Probation Practice," Youth Studies Center Report. Los Angeles: University of Southern California.

National Advisory Commission on Criminal Justice Standards and Goals (1973a), "Corrections." Washington, DC: U.S. Department of Justice. Law Enforcement Assistance Administration.

——— (1973b), "Criminal Justice System." Washington, DC: U.S. Department of Justice. Law Enforcement Assistance Administration.

——— (1973c), "Victimization Surveying: Its History, Uses, and Limitations." Washington, DC: U.S. Department of Justice. Law Enforcement Assistance Administration.

——— (1976a), "Criminal Justice Research and Development." Washington, DC: U.S. Department of Justice. Law Enforcement Assistance Administration.

——— (1976b), "Juvenile Justice and Delinquency Prevention." Washington, DC: U.S. Department of Justice. Law Enforcement Assistance Administration.

National Council on Crime and Delinquency (1981), "Juvenile Justice: Tough Enough? The NCCD's Response to *Beyond Probation*." Hackensack, NJ: The National Council on Crime and Delinquency and the Office of Social Justice for Young People.

National Crime Justice Information and Statistics Service (1976), "Criminal Victimization in the United States: A Comparison of 1973 and 1974 Findings." Washington, DC: U.S. Department of Justice. Law Enforcement Assistance Administration.

National Crime Survey Report (1983), "Criminal Victimization in the United States, 1981." Washington, DC: U.S. Department of Justice. Bureau of Justice Statistics.

National Institute of Corrections (1981), "Model Probation and Parole Management Project." Washington, DC: U.S. Department of Justice, National Institute of Corrections.

——— (1982), "Classification: Principles, Models, and Guidelines." Washington, DC: U.S. Department of Justice.

National Institute of Justice (1985, September), "Introducing New Pride," NIJ Reports. Washington, DC: U.S. Department of Justice, pp. 9–12.

Neithercutt, M. and D. M. Gottfredson (1973), "Caseload Size Variations and Differences in Probation/Parole Performance." Pittsburgh: National Center for Juvenile Justice.

Nelson, E., R. Cushman, and N. Harlow (1980), "Program Models. Unification of Community Corrections." Washington, DC: U.S. Department of Justice. National Institute of Justice.

Nelson, E., H. Ohmart, and N. Harlow (1978), "Promising Strategies in Probation and Parole." Washington, DC: U.S. Department of Justice. National Institute of Law Enforcement and Criminal Justice.

Neto, V. (1972), "Alameda County Probation Department Differential Treatment Unit," Progress Report no. 3. Oakland, CA: Alameda County Probation Department.

—— (1973), "Differential Decision-Making and Probation Effectiveness." Davis: University of California, Center on Administration of Criminal Justice.

Neto, V. and T. Palmer (1969), "Patterns of Conflict among Higher Maturity Urban Negro Delinquents," Community Treatment Project Report Series: 1969, no. 3. Sacramento: California Youth Authority.

Nichols, R. and R. Schnell (1963), "Factor Scales for the California Psychological Inventory," Journal of Consulting Psychology, 27, 228–235.

Nugent, H. and T. McEwen (1988), "Judges and Trial Court Administrators Assess Nation's Criminal Justice Needs." Washington, DC: U.S. Department of Justice. National Institute of Justice.

Nunnally, J. (1967), Psychometric Theory. New York: McGraw-Hill.

Nydes, J. (1954), "Basic Premises for Therapeutic Practice," Symposium, 63rd Annual Meeting of the American Psychological Association, New York: September, 1954.

Nye, F. (1958), Family Relationships and Delinquent Behavior. New York: Wiley.

O'Donnell, C., T. Lydgate, and W. Fo (1979), "The Buddy System: Review and Follow-Up," Child Behavior Therapy, 1, 161–169.

Ohlin, L (ed.) (1973), Prisoners in America. Englewood Cliffs, NJ: Prentice-Hall.

Ohlin, L., R. Coates, and A. Miller (1974), "Radical Correctional Reform: A Case Study of the Massachusetts Youth Correctional System," Harvard Educational Review, 44, 74–111.

—— (1978), Reforming Juvenile Corrections: The Massachusetts Experience. Cambridge, MA: Ballinger.

Ohlin, L. and A. Miller (1985), Delinquency and Community. Beverly Hills: Sage.

O'Leary, V. and T. Clear (1984), "Directions for Community Corrections in the 1990s." Washington, DC: U.S. Department of Justice. National Institute of Corrections.

O'Leary, V. and K. Hanrahan (1976), Parole Systems in the United States. Hackensack, NJ: National Council on Crime and Delinquency.

Orsagh, T. and M. Marsden (1985), "What Works When: Rational-Choice Theory and Offender Rehabilitation," Journal of Criminal Justice, 13, 269–277.

O'Sullivan, M., J. Guilford, and R. de Mille (1965), "The Measurement of Social Intelligence," The Psychological Laboratory, Report no. 34. Los Angeles: University of Southern California.

OVTS Policy Manual (1968), "Ormsby Village Treatment Center Policy Manual, 1968." Louisville, KY: Metropolitan Social Services Department of Jefferson County.

Palk, C. (1964), "An Analysis of Cottage Staff's Perceptions of the Behavior of Girls Classified as I-3 Maturity Level at Las Palmas School for Girls," Los Angeles: University of Southern California, School of Social Work. Unpublished Masters Thesis.

Palmer, T. (1963), "Types of Probation Officers and Types of Youth on Probation: Their Views and Interactions," Youth Studies Center Report. Los Angeles: University of Southern California.

—— (1965), "Types of Treaters and Types of Juvenile Offenders," Youth Authority Quarterly, 18, 14–23.

—— (1967a), "Personality Characteristics and Professional Orientations of Five Groups of Community Treatment Project Workers: A Preliminary Report on Differences among Treaters," Community Treatment Project Report Series: 1967, no. 1. Sacramento: California Youth Authority.

—— (1967b), "Relationships between

Needs of Youngsters and Characteristics of Treaters: Illustrations of Factors Which Bear on Matching," Paper Presented at the National Meeting of the Big Brothers of America, Anaheim, CA. June 21, 1967.

—— (1968a), "An Evaluation of Community Treatment for Delinquents. Issues and Findings Relating to Differential and Rational Decision-Making in the Community Treatment Project." CTP Research Report no. 9, part 3. Sacramento: California Youth Authority.

—— (1968b), "An Overview of Matching in the Community Treatment Project," Paper Presented at the Annual Meeting of the Western Psychological Association, San Diego, CA. March 30, 1968.

—— (1968c), "Recent Findings and Long-Range Developments at the Community Treatment Project," CTP Research Report no. 9, part 2. Sacramento: California Youth Authority.

—— (1968d), "The Form 3 Rating Inventory for Matching Staff and Youth," Community Treatment Project Technical Material. Sacramento: California Youth Authority.

—— (1969a), "A Demonstration Project: An Evaluation of Differential Treatment for Delinquents: The Community Treatment Project Phase III Proposal." Sacramento: California Youth Authority.

—— (1969b), "A Developmental-Adaptation Theory of Youthful Personality," Community Treatment Project Report Series: 1969, no. 2. Sacramento: California Youth Authority.

—— (1969c), "California's Community Treatment Project in 1969: An Assessment of Its Relevance and Utility to the Field of Corrections," Prepared for the U.S. Joint Commission on Correctional Manpower and Training. Sacramento: California Youth Authority.

—— (1969d), "Stages of Psycho-social Development As Reflected in Two New Levels of Interpersonal Maturity," *Youth Authority Quarterly,* 22, 29–48 (Fall).

—— (1970a), "California's Community Treatment Project: A Brief Review of Phases I and II (1961–68) and an Overview of Phase III (1969–74)." Sacramento: California Youth Authority.

—— (1970b), "California's Community Treatment Project. The Phase I, II, and III Experiments: Developments and Progress," CTP Research Report no. 10. Sacramento: California Youth Authority.

—— (1970c), "Reply to Eight Questions Commonly Addressed to California's Community Treatment Project," Community Treatment Project Report Series: 1970, no. 2. Sacramento: California Youth Authority.

—— (1971a), "California's Community Treatment Program for Delinquent Adolescents," *Journal of Research in Crime and Delinquency,* 8, 74–92.

—— (1971b), "California's Community Treatment Project. The Phase III Experiment: Progress to Date," CTP Research Report no. 11. Sacramento: California Youth Authority.

—— (1971c), "I_2 Types and Subgroups. Overview and Background Data," Community Treatment Project Report Series: 1971, no. 4 (December). Sacramento: California Youth Authority.

—— (1971d), "Non-neurotic Higher Maturity Delinquent Adolescents," Community Treatment Project Report Series: 1971, no. 3 (Winter). Sacramento: California Youth Authority.

—— (1971e), "Patterns of Adjustment among Delinquent Adolescent Conformists," Community Treatment Project Report Series: 1971, no. 1 (Spring). Sacramento: California Youth Authority.

—— (1972a), "A Synopsis of California's Group Home Project Final Report ("Differential Placement of Delinquents in Group Homes")." Sacramento: California Youth Authority.

—— (1972b), "The Group Homes Project Final Report: Differential Placement of Delinquents in Group Homes." Sacramento: California Youth Authority.

—— (1973a), "Matching Worker and Client in Corrections," *Social Work,* 18, 95–103.

—— (1973b), "Relationships among Offender Classifications: Palmer and Warren; Spencer-Conrad and Warren; Makkay and Warren; Gibbons and Warren." Sacramento: California Youth Authority. (unpublished)

—— (1973c), "Response to Lerman's Draft of 'Social Control and Community Treatment of Juvenile Delinquents: Issues in Correctional Policy.'" Sacramento: California Youth Authority.

—— (1973d), "The Community Treatment Project in Perspective: 1961–1973," Community Treatment Project Report Series: 1973, no. 1. Sacramento: California Youth Authority.

—— (1973e), "The Community Treatment Project: Updated Analyses and Recent Findings," Paper presented at the American Correctional Association Annual Meeting. Seattle, WA: August 14–15, 1973.

—— (1974a), "Reply to Lerman's Draft of 'A Methodological Note on CTP' (in Final Draft of 'Social Control and Community Treatment of Juvenile Delinquents: Issues in Correctional Policy')." Sacramento: California Youth Authority.

—— (1974b), "The Youth Authority's Community Treatment Project," *Federal Probation,* 38, 3–14.

—— (1975a), "Guide for Coding CTP Parole Agents' Use of Program Elements." Sacramento: California Youth Authority. (unpublished)

—— (1975b), "Martinson Revisited," *Journal of Research in Crime and Delinquency,* 12, 133–152.

—— (1976), "Statistical Findings of the Community Treatment Project, Phases 1 through 3. Report to the National Institute of Mental Health," CTP Final Report. Sacramento: California Youth Authority.

—— (1978a), *Correctional Intervention and Research: Current Issues and Future Prospects.* Lexington, MA: Lexington Books.

—— (1978b), "Matching of Workers and Clients: Some Observations on Dynamics," *International Differential Treatment Association Newsletter,* 5, 25–32.

—— (1979), "Differential Placement of Delinquents in Group Homes," *Journal of the International Differential Treatment Association,* 8, 17–23.

—— (1983), "The 'Effectiveness' Issue Today: An Overview," *Federal Probation,* 47, 3–10.

—— (1984a), "The Nature and Effectiveness of Positive Treatment Programs," Report for 1983 and Resource Material Series no. 25. Fuchu, Tokyo, Japan: United Nations and Far East Institute for the Prevention of Crime and the Treatment of Offenders.

—— (1984b), "Treatment and the Role of Classification: A Review of Basics," *Crime and Delinquency,* 30, 245–267.

—— (1989), "California's Juvenile Probation Camps: Summary." Sacramento: California Youth Authority.

—— (1991a), "The Effectiveness of Intervention: Recent Trends and Current Issues," *Crime and Delinquency,* 37, 330–346.

—— (1991b), "The Habilitation/Developmental Perspective: A Missing Link in Corrections," *Federal Probation,* 55, 55–65.

—— (1992), *The Re-emergence of Correctional Intervention.* Newbury Park, CA: Sage.

—— (1993), "Programmatic and Non-programmatic Aspects of Successful Intervention," Paper Presented at the International Association of Residential and Community Alternatives. Seventh Annual Meeting. Philadelphia, PA. November 3–6, 1993.

—— (1994), *A Profile of Correctional Effectiveness and New Directions for Research.* Albany: State University of New York Press.

—— (1995a), "Issues in Growth-Centered Intervention with Serious Juvenile Offenders," *Legal Studies Forum,* 18, 263–298.

—— (1995b), "Programmatic and Non-programmatic Aspects of Successful Intervention: New Directions for Research," *Crime and Delinquency,* 41, 100–131.

Palmer, T. and J. Helm (1975), "Further Relationships among Offender Classifications: Hunt, Kohlberg, Loevinger, Palmer, Schroder, Van den Daele, and Warren," Sacramento: California Youth Authority. (Unpublished).

Palmer, T., M. Bohnstedt, and R. Lewis (1978), "The Evaluation of Juvenile Diversion Programs: Final Report." Sacramento: California Youth Authority and the California State Office of Criminal Justice Planning.

Palmer, T. and G. Grenny (1971), "Stance and Techniques of Matched Nx, Na, Mp-Cfc, Cfm, and I₂ Workers. A Self-Description of the Treatment Methods Used as Well as Rejected by Five Groups of Low

Caseload Parole Agents at California's Community Treatment Project," Community Treatment Project Report Series: 1971, no. 2 (Summer). Sacramento: California Youth Authority.

Palmer, T. and A. Herrera (1972a), "Community Treatment Project Post-Discharge Analysis: An Updating of the 1969 Analysis for Sacramento and Stockton Males," Community Treatment Project Briefing. Sacramento: California Youth Authority.

―――― (1972b), "CTP's San Francisco Experiment (1965–1969): Post-Discharge Behavior of Differential Treatment and Guided Group Interaction Subjects," Community Treatment Project Briefing. Sacramento: California Youth Authority.

Palmer, T. and R. Lewis (1980a), "A Differentiated Approach to Juvenile Diversion." *Journal of Research in Crime and Delinquency,* 17, 209–229.

―――― (1980b), *An Evaluation of Juvenile Diversion.* Cambridge, MA: Oelgeschlager, Gunn, and Hain.

Palmer, T., V. Neto, D. Johns, J. Turner, and J. Pearson (1968), "The Sacramento-Stockton and the San Francisco Experiments," CTP Research Report no. 9, part 1. Sacramento: California Youth Authority.

Palmer, T., J. Pearson, and S. Haire (1969), "Selected Instruments Used in the Group Home Project." Sacramento: California Youth Authority.

Palmer, T. and J. Turner (1970), "Community Treatment Project Post-Discharge Analysis: A Brief Review." Community Treatment Project Briefing. Sacramento: California Youth Authority.

Palmer, T. and M. Q. Warren (1967), "An Evaluation of Community Treatment for Delinquents. The Sacramento and Stockton Experiments," CTP Research Report no. 8, part 1. Sacramento: California Youth Authority.

Palmer, T. and R. Wedge (1989), "California's Juvenile Probation Camps: Findings and Implications," *Crime and Delinquency,* 35, 234–253.

Palmer, T. and E. Werner (1972a), "A Review of I-Level Reliability and Accuracy in the California Community Treatment Project," Community Treatment Project Report Series: 1972, no. 2. Sacramento: California Youth Authority.

―――― (1972b), "California's Community Treatment Project. The Phase III Experiment: Progress to Date," CTP Research Report no. 12. Sacramento: California Youth Authority.

―――― (1973), "California's Community Treatment Project. The Phase III Experiment: Progress to Date," CTP Research Report no. 13. Sacramento: California Youth Authority.

Panizzon, A., G. Olson-Raymer, and N. Guerra (1991), "Delinquency Prevention: What Works/What Doesn't." Sacramento: California State Office of Criminal Justice Planning.

Parent, D. (1990), "Day Reporting Centers for Criminal Offenders. A Descriptive Analysis of Existing Programs." Washington, DC: U.S. Department of Justice. National Institute of Justice.

Parker, L. (1986), *Parole and the Treatment of Offenders in Japan and the United States.* New Haven: University of New Haven Press.

Parloff, M. (1956), "Some Factors Affecting the Quality of Therapeutic Relationships," *Journal of Abnormal and Social Psychology,* 52, 5–10.

Pauker, J. and E. Hood (1979), "A Review of Four Systems for Classifying the 'Impossible' Child and Adolescent." Ottawa, Ontario: Ontario Ministry of Community and Social Service, Children's Services Division.

Pearson, F. (1988), "Evaluation of New Jersey's Intensive Supervision Program," *Crime and Delinquency,* 34, 437–448.

Pearson, J. (1970), "A Differential Use of Group Homes for Delinquent Boys," *Children,* 17, 143–148.

Persons, R. (1967), "Relationship between Psychotherapy with Institutionalized Boys and Subsequent Community Adjustment," *Journal of Consulting Psychology,* 31, 137–141.

Persons, R. and H. Pepinsky (1966), "Convergence in Psychotherapy with Delinquent Boys," *Journal of Consulting Psychology,* 13, 329–334.

Petersilia, J. (1987), "Expanding Options for Criminal Sentencing," Santa Monica, CA: RAND.

―――― (1990), "When Probation Becomes More Dreaded Than Prison," *Federal Probation,* 54, 23–27.

—— (1991), "The Value of Correctional Research: Learning What Works," *Federal Probation, 55,* 24–26.

Petersilia, J. and S. Turner, (1992), "An Evaluation of Intensive Probation in California," *Journal of Criminal Law and Criminology,* 82, 610–658.

Petersilia, J., S. Turner, and J. Kahan (1985), "Granting Felons Probation: Public Risks and Alternatives," Santa Monica, CA: RAND.

Petersilia, J., S. Turner, and J. Peterson (1987), "Prison versus Probation in California: Implications for Crime and Offender Recidivism," Santa Monica, CA: RAND.

Pettit, D. (1961), "A Classification System for Inmate Population in Saskatchewan Gaols Based on a Concept of Interpersonal Maturity." Saskatoon, Saskatchewan: University of Saskatchewan. Unpublished master's thesis.

Piaget, J. (1926), *The Language and Thought of the Child.* New York: Harcourt and Brace.

—— (1929), *The Child's Conception of the World.* New York: Harcourt and Brace.

—— (1969), *Psychology of the Child.* New York: Basic Books.

Pike, P. (1969), "Youth Authority Clinic Testing, 1968," Research Division. Sacramento: California Youth Authority.

—— (1971), "Youth Authority Clinic Testing, 1970," Research Division. Sacramento: California Youth Authority.

Pilnick, P., A. Elias, and N. Clapp (1966), "The Essexfield Concept: A New Approach to the Social Treatment of Juvenile Delinquents," *Journal of Applied Behavioral Sciences,* 2, 109–121.

Platt, A. (1969), *The Child Savers: The Invention of Delinquency.* Chicago: University of Chicago Press.

—— (1974), "The Triumph of Benevolence: The Origin of the Juvenile Justice System in the United States," in R. Quinney (ed.), *Criminal Justice in America: A Critical Understanding.* Boston: Little, Brown.

Platt, J. and M. Prout (1987), "Cognitive-Behavioral Theory and Interventions for Crime and Delinquency," in E. Morris and C. Braukman (eds.), *Behavioral Approaches to Crime and Delinquency.* New York: Plenum.

Pond, E. (1969), "Los Angeles Community Delinquency Control Project. Program Report no. 2," Research Division. Sacramento: California Youth Authority.

—— (1970), "The Los Angeles Community Delinquency Control Project: An Experiment in the Rehabilitation of Delinquents in an Urban Community," Research Division Report no. 60. Sacramento: California Youth Authority.

Pond, E. and C. Davis (1971), "Summary Report of the California Youth Authority's Community Parole Center Progress," Research Division. Sacramento: California Youth Authority.

—— (1973), "A Comparative Study of the Community Parole Center Program," Research Division Report no. 63. Sacramento: California Youth Authority.

Pond, E., C. Davis, J. Seckel, D. Haeberlin, and J. Holland (1974), "Increased Parole Effectiveness Program. Final Report," Research Division. Sacramento: The California Council on Criminal Justice and the California Youth Authority.

Pownall, G. (1963), "An Analysis of the Role of the Parole Supervision Officer." Urbana/Champaign: University of Illinois. Unpublished doctoral dissertation.

President's Commission on Law Enforcement and Administration of Justice (1967a), "Task Force Report: Corrections." Washington, DC: Government Printing Office.

—— (1967b), "Task Force Report: Juvenile Delinquency and Youth Crime." Washington, DC: Government Printing Office.

—— (1967c), "The Challenge of Crime in a Free Society," Washington, DC: Government Printing Office.

Pritchard, D. (1979), "Stable Predictors of Recidivism: A Summary," *Criminology,* 17, 15–21.

Pritchard, G. (1976), "I-Level in Manitoba," *The International Differential Treatment Association Newsletter,* 1, 6–8.

—— (December 1995), Personal Communication.

Quay, H. (1964), "Personality Dimensions in Delinquent Males as Inferred from the Factor Analysis of Behavior Ratings," *Journal of Research in Crime and Delinquency,* 1, 33–37.

—— (1977), "The Three Faces of Evaluation. What Can Be Expected to Work,"

Criminal Justice and Behavior, 4, 341–354.

——— (1984), "Managing Adult Inmates." Washington, DC: American Correctional Association.

——— (1987), "Institutional Treatment," in H. Quay (ed.), *Handbook of Juvenile Delinquency.* New York: Wiley.

Quay, H. and L. Parsons (1971), "The Differential Behavior Classification of the Juvenile Offender." Washington, DC: U.S. Department of Justice. Bureau of Prisons.

Quinney, R. (1970), *The Social Reality of Crime.* Boston: Little, Brown.

——— (1977), *Class, State, and Crime.* New York: Longman.

——— (ed.) (1974), *Criminal Justice in America.* Boston: Little, Brown.

Rabow, J. and J. Manos (1979), "Social Scientists' Contribution to the Demise of Delinquency Rehabilitation," *Crime Prevention Review,* 6, 23–30.

Rae-Grant, N. (1978), "Arresting the Vicious Cycle: Care and Treatment of Adolescents Displaying the Ovinnik Syndrome," *Canadian Psychiatric Association Journal,* 23, 22–40.

Rathbun, C. (November 1995), Personal Communication.

Rawls, J. (1971), *A Theory of Justice.* Cambridge, MA: Harvard University Press.

Reckless, W. (1967), *The Crime Problem.* New York: Appleton–Century–Croft.

Redl, F. (1969), "Adolescents—Just How Do They React?" in G. Caplan and S. Lebovici (eds.), *Adolescence: Psychosocial Perspectives.* New York: Basic Books.

Redl, F. and D. Wineman (1951), *Children Who Hate.* New York: Free Press.

Regnery, A. and C. Lauer (1984), "Evaluation of the Habitual Serious and Violent Juvenile Offender Program and Operation Hardcore Program. Notice of Issuance of Guidelines for a Program Evaluation," *Federal Register,* 49, 524.

Reiss, A. (1951), "Delinquency As a Failure of Personal and Social Controls," *American Sociological Review,* 15, 196–207.

——— (1952), "Social Correlates of Psychological Types of Delinquents," *American Sociological Review,* 17, 710–718.

Reiss, A. and A. Rhodes (1961), "The Distribution of Delinquency in the Social Class Structure," *American Sociological Review,* 26, 720–732.

Reitsma-Street, M. (1984), "Differential Treatment of Young Offenders: A Review of the Conceptual Level Matching Model," *Canadian Journal of Criminology,* 26, 199–216.

——— (1988), "The Conceptual Level Matching Model in Corrections," *Criminal Justice and Behavior,* 15, 92–107.

Reitsma, M. and R. Brill (1978b), "Staff Tasks. Technical Report no. 1." Montreal: University of Montreal. Groupe de Recherche sur L'Inadaptation Juvénile.

——— (1978b). "The Human Resource. A Description of the Treatment Staff of Shawbridge Youth Centers. Final Report no. 2," Montreal: Universite de Montreal. Groupe de Recherche sur L 'Inadaptation Juvénile.

Report on the Criminal Code Reform Act of 1977 (1978). Washington, DC: Senate Committee on the Judiciary, Senate Document no. 555. 95th Congress, First Session.

Rich, H. and A. Bush (1978), "The Effect of Congruent Teacher-Student Characteristics on Instructional Outcomes," *American Educational Research Journal,* 15, 451–457.

Riggs, J., W. Underwood, and M. Q. Warren (1964), "Interpersonal Maturity Level Classification: Juvenile. Diagnosis and Treatment of Low Maturity Delinquents," Community Treatment Project Research Report no. 4. Sacramento: California Youth Authority.

Robbins, I. (1986), "Privatization of Corrections. Defining the Issues," *Federal Probation,* 50, 24–30.

Roberts, C. (1970), "A Final Evaluation of the Narcotic Control Program for Youth Authority Parolees," Research Division Report no. 58. Sacramento: California Youth Authority.

Robinson, J., L. Wilkins, R. Carter, and A. Wahl (1969), "The San Francisco Project. A Study of Federal Probation and Parole. Final Report," Division of Research. Sacramento: California Department of Corrections.

Robison, J. and G. Smith (1971), "The Effectiveness of Correctional Programs," *Crime and Delinquency,* 17, 67–80.

Romig, D. (1978), *Justice for Our Children.*

Lexington, MA: Lexington Books.

Rose, R., R. Stokes, and R. Craft (1977), "Probation Subsidy Programs. 1976–1977." Sacramento: California Youth Authority.

Rosenbaum, J. (1989), "Family Dysfunction and Female Delinquency," *Crime and Delinquency,* 35, 31–44.

Rosenheim, M. (ed.) (1976), *Pursuing Justice for the Child*. Chicago: University of Chicago Press.

Ross, R. (1990), "Time to Think: A Cognitive Model of Offender Rehabilitation and Delinquency Prevention," Research Summary. Ottawa: University of Ottawa.

Ross, R. and E. Fabiano (1985), *Time to Think: A Cognitive Model of Delinquency Prevention and Offender Rehabilitation*. Johnson City, TN: Institute of Social Science and Art.

Ross, R., E. Fabiano, and C. Ewles (1988), "Reasoning and Rehabilitation," *International Journal of Offender Therapy and Comparative Criminology,* 32, 29–35.

Ross, R. and P. Gendreau (1980), *Effective Correctional Treatment*. Toronto: Butterworths.

Rothman, D. (1971), *The Discovery of the Asylum: Social Order and Disorder in the New Republic*. Boston: Little, Brown.

Rotter, J. (1966), "Generalized Expectancies for Internal versus External Control of Reinforcement," *Psychological Monographs,* 80 (1, Whole no. 609).

Rubenfeld, S. (1967), "Typological Approaches and Delinquency Control: Status Report." Washington, DC: U.S. Department of Health, Education, and Welfare, Public Health Service. National Institute of Mental Health.

Rubin, S. (1979), "New Sentencing Proposals and Laws in the 1970s," *Federal Probation,* 43, 3–8.

Rutter, M. and H. Giller (1983), *Juvenile Delinquency Trends and Perspectives*. New York: Pergamon.

Sacks, H. and C. Logan (1979), *Does Parole Make a Difference?* Storrs, CT: University of Connecticut School of Law Press.

Sarason, I. and V. Ganzer (1973), "Modeling and Group Discussion in the Rehabilitation of Juvenile Delinquents," *Journal of Counseling Psychology,* 20, 442–449.

Sarbin, R. (1952), "A Preface to a Psychological Analysis of the Self," *Psychological Review,* 59, 11–22.

Sasfy, J. (1975), "Assumptions Research in Probation and Parole: Initial Description of Client, Worker, and Project Variables," High Impact Anti-Crime Program Report. Washington, DC: U.S. Department of Justice. Law Enforcement Assistance Administration and the MITRE Corporation.

Satir, V. (1967), *Conjoint Family Therapy*. Palo Alto, CA: Science and Behavior Books.

Satten, J., E. Novotny, S. Ginsparg, and S. Averill (1970), "Ego Disorganization and Recidivism in Delinquent Boys," *Bulletin of the Menninger Clinic,* 34, 270–283.

Savage, E. and M. Weston (1975), "One-to-One Equals Hope," *Youth Authority Quarterly,* 28, 37–40.

Saylor, L. (1993), "Current Construction Costs: 1993. 30th Annual Edition," Los Angeles: Saylor Publications.

Schafer, S. (1976), "The Victim and Correctional Theory: Integrating Victim Reparation with Offender Rehabilitation," in W. McDonald (ed.), *Criminal Justice and the Victim*. Beverly Hills: Sage.

Scharf, P. (1978), *Moral Education*. Davis, CA: Responsible Action.

Scheuer, A. (1971), "The Relationship between Personal Attributes and Effectiveness in Teachers of the Emotionally Disturbed," *Exceptional Children,* 31, 723–731.

Schmidt, P. and A. Witte (1988), *Predicting Recidivism Using Survival Models*. New York: Springer-Verlag.

Schrag, C. (1944), "Social Types in a Prison Community." Seattle: University of Washington. Unpublished master's thesis.

——— (1954), "Leadership among Prison Inmates," *American Sociological Review,* 19, 37–42.

——— (1961), "A Preliminary Criminal Typology," *Pacific Sociological Review,* 4, 11–16.

——— (1971), *Crime and Justice: American Style*. Washington, DC: National Institute of Mental Health, Crime and Delinquency Issues.

Schroder, H., M. Driver, and S. Streufert (1967), *Human Information Processing*. New York: Rinehart and Winston.

Schur, E. (1971), *Labeling Deviant Behavior.* New York: Harper & Row.

———— (1973), *Radical Nonintervention: Rethinking the Delinquency Problem.* Englewood Cliffs, NJ: Prentice-Hall.

Schutz, W. (1960), *FIRO: A Three-Dimensional Theory of Interpersonal Behavior.* New York: Holt, Rinehart, and Winston.

Schwitzgebel, R. (1972), "Limitations on the Coercive Treatment of Offenders," *Criminal Law Bulletin,* 8, 267–320.

Scott, A., J. Albright, G. Hopkins, O. Imai, and M. Q. Warren (1966), "Temporary Detention: A Task Force Evaluation." Sacramento: California Youth Authority.

Scott, J. and J. Hissong (1973), "An Effective Structure and Program for Institutional Change," *Federal Probation,* 37, 42–52.

Sealy, A. and C. Banks (1971), "Social Maturity, Training, Experience, and Recidivism amongst British Borstal Boys," *British Journal of Criminology,* 11, 245–264.

Sechrest, D. and D. Shichor (1993), "Corrections Goes Public (and Private) in California," *Federal Probation,* 57, 3–8.

Sechrest, L. (1987), "Classification for Treatment," In D. Gottfredson and M. Tonry (eds.), *Prediction and Classification: Criminal Justice Decision-making.* Chicago: University of Chicago Press.

Sechrest, L., S. O. White, and E. Brown (1979), *The Rehabilitation of Criminal Offenders: Problems and Prospects.* Washington, DC: National Academy of Sciences.

Seckel, J. and C. Davis (1975), "1975 Parole Agent Time Study," Research Division. Sacramento: California Youth Authority.

Seckel, J. and J. Turner (1980), "Institutional Violence Reduction Project: The Impact of Changes in Living-Unit Size and Staffing," Research Division. Sacramento: California Youth Authority.

Seiter, R., E. Carlson, H. Bowman, J. Grandfield, and N. Beran (1977), "Halfway Houses. National Evaluation Program. Phase I Summary Report." Washington, DC: U.S. Department of Justice. National Institute of Law Enforcement and Criminal Justice.

Selman, R. (1977), "To Understand and to Help," in P. Scharf (ed.), *Readings in Moral Education.* Minneapolis, MN: Western Press.

Selman, R. D. Jaquette, and D. Lavin (1977),

"Interpersonal Awareness in Children: Toward an Integration of Developmental and Clinical Child Psychology," *American Journal of Orthopsychiatry,* 47, 264–274.

Serrill, M. (1975), "Is Rehabilitation Dead?" *Corrections Magazine,* 1, 3–12, 21–32.

———— (1976), "Critics of Corrections Speak Out," *Corrections Magazine,* 2, 3–8.

Shah, S. (1973a), March 13, May 3, and September 20, 1973; Written Personal Communications.

———— (1973b), "Perspectives and Directions in Juvenile Corrections, "*Psychiatric Quarterly,* 47, 1–25.

Shane-DuBow, S., A. Brown, and E. Olsen (1985), "Sentencing Reform in the United States: History, Content, and Effect." Washington, DC: U.S. Department of Justice. National Institute of Justice.

Shaw, C. and H. McKay (1972), *Juvenile Delinquency and Urban Areas.* Chicago: University of Chicago Press.

Shawver, L. and B. Sanders (1977), "A Look at Four Critical Premises in Correctional Views," *Crime and Delinquency,* 23, 427–434.

Sherman, L., D. C. Gottfredson, D. MacKenzie, J. Eck, P. Reuter, and S. Bushway (1997), *Preventing Crime: What Works, What Doesn't, What's Promising.* Washington, DC: U.S. Department of Justice. Office of Justice Programs.

Shichor, D. (1980), "The New Criminology: Some Critical issues," *British Journal of Criminology,* 20, 1–19.

———— (1992), "Following the Penological Pendulum: The Survival of Rehabilitation," *Federal Probation,* 56, 19–25.

———— (1995), *Punishment for Profit.* Newbury Park, CA: Sage.

Shore, M. and J. Massimo (1979), "Fifteen Years after Treatment: A Followup Study of Comprehensive Vocationally Oriented Psychotherapy," *American Journal of Orthopsychiatry,* 49, 240–245.

Siegal, L. and J. Senna (1981), *Juvenile Delinquency: Theory, Practice, and Law.* St. Paul, MN: West Publishing Company.

Sigler, M. (1975), "Abolish Parole?" *Federal Probation,* 39, 42–48.

Simon, F. (1971), "Prediction Methods in Criminology," Home Office Research Study no. 7. London: Her Majesty's Stationery Office.

Singer, M. (1969), "Experiment in a Small County," *Youth Authority Quarterly,* 22, 14–17.

——— (1971), "Yuba County: An I-Level Approach to Special Supervision," *Youth Authority Quarterly,* 24, 16–19.

Singer, R. (1979), *Just Deserts: Sentencing Based on Equity and Desert.* Cambridge, MA: Ballinger.

Skogan, W. and M. Maxfield (1981), *Coping with Crime: Individual and Neighborhood Reactions.* Beverly Hills: Sage.

Sluder, R. and R. Shearer (1992), "Personality Types of Probation Officers," *Federal Probation,* 56, 29–35.

Smith, C. and P. Alexander (1980), *A National Assessment of Serious Juvenile Crime and the Juvenile Justice System: The Need for a Rational Response. Volume I. Summary.* Washington, DC: U.S. Department of Justice. Law Enforcement Assistance Administration.

Smith, D. (1974), "Relationship between the Eysenck and Jesness Personality Inventories," *British Journal of Criminology,* 4, 376–384.

Smith, R. (1965), "Probation Subsidy: A Plan of Action," *Youth Authority Quarterly,* 18, 1–4.

——— (1968), "1969—A Year of Decision," *Youth Authority Quarterly,* 22, 3–6.

——— (1971), "A Quiet Revolution: Probation Subsidy." Washington, DC: U.S. Department of Health, Education, and Welfare. Youth Development and Delinquency Prevention Administration.

Spence, D. (1973), "Analog and Digital Descriptions of Behavior," *American Psychologist,* 28, 479–488.

Spencer, C. (1966), "A Typology of Violent Offenders," Division of Research Report no. 23. Sacramento: Department of Corrections.

Staff of the Boys' Farm and Training School (1971), "Treating Delinquent Youth. The Boys' Farm (Shawbridge) Develops an I-Level Program." Montreal: Ministry of Social Affairs, Government of Quebec.

Staff of the Computation Laboratory (1955), *Tables of the Cumulative Binomial Probability Distribution.* Cambridge, MA: Harvard University Press.

Stafford, M. and O. Galle (1984), "Victimization Rates, Exposure to Risk, and Fear of Crime," *Criminology,* 22, 173–185.

Stanley, D. (1976), *Prisoners among Us: The Problem of Parole.* Washington, DC: The Brookings Institute, pp. 81–103.

Stapleton, W. and L. Teitelbaum (1972), *In Defense of Youth.* New York: Russell Sage Foundation.

Star, D. (1979), "Summary Parole. A Six and Twelve Month Follow-Up Evaluation," Division of Research Report no. 60. Sacramento: California Department of Corrections.

Stephenson, R. and F. Scarpetti (1969), "Essexfields: A Non-residential Experiment in Group Centered Rehabilitation of Delinquents," *American Journal of Corrections,* 31, 12–18.

St. Francis Annual Report (1981), "1981 Annual Report of the St. Francis Boys' Homes." Salina, KS: The St. Francis Boys' Homes, Inc.

St. Francis Boys' Homes (1975), "Where We Are and How We Got Here." Salina, KS: The St. Francis Boys' Homes, Inc.

——— (1979), "Your Guide to the St. Francis Boys' Homes in Kansas." Salina, KS: The St. Francis Boys' Homes, Inc.

——— (1981), "Director's Report, Clinical Coordinator's Report, and Research Director's Report," in *St. Francis 1981 Annual Report.* Salina, KS: The St. Francis Boys' Homes, Inc.

——— (1981/1982), *Manual of Standard Operating Procedures.* Salina, KS: The St. Francis Boys' Homes, Inc.

Stoppard, J. and A. Miller (1981), "Cognitive Matching in Therapy Research," Paper Presented at the Forty-Second Annual Meeting of the Canadian Psychological Association. Toronto. June 1981.

——— (1985), "Conceptual Level Matching in Therapy: A Review," *Current Psychological Research and Reviews,* 4, 46–68.

Strasberg, P. (1978), *Violent Delinquents. A Report to the Ford Foundation from the Vera Institute of Justice.* New York: Monarch Press.

Strupp, H. (1960), "Nature of Psychotherapists' Contribution to the Treatment Process," *Archives of General Psychiatry,* 3, 219–231.

Studt, E. (1960), "Social Work in Corrections." New York: Russell Sage Foundation.

——— (1967), "The Reentry of the Offender

into the Community." Washington, DC: U.S. Department of Health, Education, and Welfare. Office of Juvenile Delinquency and Youth Development.

Stumphauser, J. (ed.) (1974), *Behavior Modification Therapy with Delinquents*. Springfield, IL: Charles C. Thomas.

Sullivan, C., M. Q. Grant, and J. Grant (1955), "Delinquency Integrations. First Revision of Second Technical Report." San Diego, CA: U.S. Naval Training Command, Camp Elliott.

—— (1957), "The Development of Interpersonal Maturity: Applications to Delinquency," *Psychiatry*, 20, 373–395.

Sullivan, E., G. McCullough, and M. Stager (1970), "A Developmental Study of the Relationship between Conceptual, Ego, and Moral Development," *Child Development*, 41, 399–411.

Sullivan, H. (1940), *Conceptions of Modern Psychiatry*. New York: Norton.

—— (1953), *The Interpersonal Theory of Psychiatry*. New York: Norton.

Sundland, R. and E. Barker (1962), "The Orientations of Psychotherapists," *Journal of Consulting Psychology*, 26, 201–212.

Sutherland, E. and D. Cressey (1970), *Principles of Criminology*. New York: Lippincott.

Sydiaha, D. (1964), "Criterion Reliability: A Study of Folkways and Mores of the Psychological Profession," *The Canadian Psychologist*, 5, 17–34.

Sykes, G. (1958), *The Society of Captives*. Princeton, NJ: Princeton University Press.

Tannenbaum, F. (1938), *Crime and the Community*. New York: Columbia University Press.

Tappan, P. (1949), *Juvenile Delinquency*. New York: McGraw-Hill.

Thomas, D. (1977), "Equity in Sentencing," Sixth Annual Pinkerton Lecture, School of Criminal Justice. Albany: State University of New York.

Thomas, K. (November and December 1995), Personal Communications.

Thornberry, T. (1987), "Toward an Interactional Theory of Delinquency," *Criminology*, 25, 863–891.

Toch, H. (1977), *Living in Prison*. New York: Free Press.

Tolhurst, G. (1966), "A Test of Russon's Clinical Classification System for Delinquency," Saskatoon, Saskatchewan: University of Saskatchewan. Unpublished master's thesis.

Tolhurst, G. and CTDT Staff (1970), "The Center for Training in Differential Treatment: Final Report of Phase I, Part 2." Sacramento: American Justice Institute and the California Youth Authority.

Tonry, M. (1990), "Stated and Latent Features of ISP," *Crime and Delinquency*, 36, 174–191.

Towberman, D. (1992), "National Survey of Juvenile Needs Assessment," *Crime and Delinquency*, 38, 230–238.

Tracy, H. (1969), "Interpersonal Maturity, Locus of Control, and Future Time Perspective in Delinquent Boys," Storrs: University of Connecticut. Unpublished Masters Thesis.

Tremper, C. (1982), "Major Issues in Juvenile Probation." Sacramento: American Justice Institute.

Truax, C. (1963), "Effective Ingredients in Psychotherapy: An Approach to Unraveling the Patient-Therapist Interaction," *Journal of Counseling Psychology*, 10, 256–263.

Truax, C., D. Wargo, and L. Silber (1966), "Effects of Group Psychotherapy with High Accurate Empathy and Nonpossessive Warmth upon Female Institutionalized Delinquents," *Journal of Abnormal Psychology*, 71, 267–274.

Truax, C., D. Wargo, and N. Volksdorf (1970), "Antecedents to Outcome in Group Counseling with Institutionalized Juvenile Delinquents," *Journal of Abnormal Psychology*, 76, 235–242.

Turiel, E. (1966), "An Experimental Analysis of Developmental Stages in the Child's Moral Judgment," *Journal of Personal and Social Psychology*, 3, 611–618.

Turner, E. (1969), "A Girl's Group Home: An Approach to Treating Delinquent Girls in the Community," Community Treatment Project Report Series: 1969, no. 1. Sacramento: California Youth Authority.

—— (1971), "Community Treatment's New Residential Component," *Youth Authority Quarterly*, 24, 25–33.

—— (1976), "Community Treatment Project. Phase III," *The International Differential Treatment Association Newsletter*, 2, 3–12.

—— (December 1995), Personal Communication.

Turner, E. and T. Palmer (1973), "The Utility of Community-Based Group Homes for Delinquent Adolescent Girls," *Journal of the American Academy of Child Psychiatry,* 12, 273–291.

Turner, J. and G. Davis (1973a), "Information Exchange between California Department of Justice (C.I.I. Bureau) and the Department of Youth Authority," Community Treatment Project and Research Division Technical Briefing. Sacramento: California Youth Authority.

―――― (1973b), "Reasons for Shortage of C.I.I-Reported Law Enforcement Contacts in CYA Parole Agents' Reports," Community Treatment Project and Research Division Technical Briefing. Sacramento: California Youth Authority.

Turner, J., V. Neto, T. Palmer, and M. Q. Warren (1967), "An Evaluation of Community Treatment for Delinquents. The San Francisco Experiment," CTP Research Report no. 8, part 2. Sacramento: California Youth Authority.

Turner, S., J. Petersilia, and E. Deschenes (1992), "Evaluating Intensive Supervision Probation/Parole (ISP) for Drug Offenders," *Crime and Delinquency,* 38, 539–556.

Twentieth Century Task Force (1978), "Confronting Youth Crime. Report of the Twentieth Century Fund Task Force on Sentencing Policy toward Young Offenders." New York: Holmes and Meier.

Uniform Crime Reports: 1975(1976), "Crime in the United States." Washington, DC: U.S. Department of Justice. Federal Bureau of Investigation.

U.S. Department of Justice (1975), "Criminal Victimization in 13 American Cities." Washington, DC: Law Enforcement Assistance Administration. National Criminal Justice Information and Statistics Service.

Van den Daele, L. (1968), "A Developmental Study of the Ego-Ideal," *Genetic Psychology Monographs,* 78, 191–256.

Van den Hagg, E. (1975), *Punishing Criminals.* New York: Basic Books.

Van Groningen, J., C. Andre, and J. Mahan (1972), "Differential Education Model for I$_4$ Neurotic Acting-Out Students," Differential Education Project. Sacramento: California Youth Authority.

―――― (1973), "Differential Education Model for I$_4$ Neurotic Acting-Out Students," Differential Education Project. Sacramento: California Youth Authority.

Van Krevelen, A. (1958), "Judgments of Personality Traits in Self and Others," *Journal of Clinical Psychology,* 13, 133–136.

Van Ness, D. and K. Strong (1998), *Restoring Justice.* Cincinnati, OH: Anderson Publishing Company.

Van Voorhis, P. (1983), "An Application of Kohlberg's Stages of Moral Development in a Restitution Field Setting," *Journal of the International Differential Treatment Association,* 13, 49–60.

―――― (1985), "Restitution Outcome and Probationers' Assessments of Restitution: The Effects of Moral Development," *Criminal Justice and Behavior,* 12, 259–287.

―――― (1986), "A Cross-Classification of Five Offender Typologies: Results of the Pilot Study," *Journal of the International Differential Treatment Association,* 15, 126–137.

―――― (1987), "Correctional Effectiveness: The High Cost of Ignoring Success," *Federal Probation,* 51, 56–62.

―――― (1988), "A Cross-Classification of Five Offender Typologies: Issues of Construct and Predictive Validity," *Criminal Justice and Behavior,* 15, 24–38.

―――― (1991), "Psychological Classification of the Adult Male Prison Inmate. Executive Summary," Cincinnati, OH: University of Cincinnati. Department of Criminal Justice.

―――― (1994), *Psychological Classification of the Adult, Male Prison Inmate.* Albany: State University of New York Press.

Vera Institute Programs in Criminal Justice Reform (1972), "Vera Institute of Justice, Ten-Year Report: 1961–1971," New York: Vera Institute of Justice.

Vito, G. (1986), "Felony Probation and Recidivism: Replication and Response," *Federal Probation,* 50, 17–25.

Vogel, J. (1959), "Authoritarianism in the Therapeutic Relationship." Chicago: University of Chicago. Unpublished doctoral dissertation.

Von Hirsch, A. (1976), *Doing Justice: The Choice of Punishments.* New York: Hill and Wang.

―――― (1984), "The Ethics of Selective

Incapacitation: Observations on the Contemporary Debate," *Crime and Delinquency,* 30, 175–194.

——— (1990), "The Ethics of Community-Based Sanctions," *Crime and Delinquency,* 36, 162–173.

Von Hirsch, A. and K. Hanrahan (1978), "Abolish Parole?" Washington, DC: U.S. Department of Justice. Law Enforcement Assistance Administration.

——— (1979), *The Question of Parole.* Cambridge, MA: Ballinger.

Von Wright, G. (1972), "Induction," in *Encyclopedia Brittanica,* Vol. 12, pp. 182–185. Chicago, London, Toronto, Geneva, Sydney, Tokyo, and Manila: Encyclopedia Britannica, Inc.

Waldman, P. (1977), "Community Treatment Project (Baltimore City Intensive Probation). Final Program Report," Baltimore, MD: Department of Juvenile Services.

——— (1979), "I-Level Theory in Baltimore City's Differential Treatment Project," Baltimore, MD: Department of Juvenile Services.

——— (1980), "I-Level Theory in Baltimore City's Differential Treatment Program: Report on Study as of June 1978," *Journal of the International Differential Treatment Association,* 10, 16–27.

Wall, J., J. Hawkins, D. Lishman, and M. Fraser (1981), "Juvenile Delinquency Prevention: A Compendium of 36 Program Models." Washington, DC: U.S. Department of Justice. Office of Juvenile Justice and Delinquency Prevention.

Walters, J., D. Brown, and P. Logan (1961), "Annual Statistical Report, 1961," Research Division. Sacramento: California Youth Authority.

Warnock, G. (1972), "Qualities," in *Encyclopedia Brittannica,* Vol. 18, pp. 914–916. Chicago, London, Toronto, Geneva, Sydney, Tokyo, and Manila: Encyclopedia Britannica, Inc.

Warren, M. Q. (1964), "Severity of Parolee Violation Behavior: An Instrument for Its Assessment." Berkeley: University of California. Unpublished master's thesis.

——— (1965a), "Implications of a Typology of Delinquents for Measures of Behavior Changes: A Plea for Complexity," *Youth Authority Quarterly,* 18, 6–13.

——— (1965b), "Community Treatment Project: An Integration of Theories of Cau-

sation and Correctional Practice," Paper Presented at the Annual Conference of the Illinois Academy of Criminology. Chicago, May 14, 1965.

——— (1966), "Classification of Offenders As an Aid to Efficient Management and Effective Treatment," Paper Prepared for the President's Commission on Law Enforcement and Administration of Justice, Task Force on Corrections. Sacramento: California Youth Authority.

——— (1967a), "The Community Treatment Project after Five Years," CTP Report. Sacramento: California Youth Authority.

——— (1967b), "The Community Treatment Project History and Prospects," Paper Presented at the First National Symposium of Law Enforcement Science and Technology, Illinois Institute of Technology. Chicago, March 8, 1967. Sacramento: California Youth Authority.

——— (1969), "The Case for Differential Treatment of Delinquents," *Annals of the American Academy of Political Social Sciences,* 381, 47–59.

——— (1970), "A Differential Intervention Model Aimed at Predelinquent and Other Vulnerable Children," Paper Presented at the Delinquency Prevention Strategy Conference, Santa Barbara, California, February 17–20, 1970. Sacramento: American Justice Institute and California Youth Authority.

——— (1971), "Classification of Offenders As an Aid to Efficient Management and Effective Treatment," *Journal of Crime, Law, Criminology, and Police Science,* 62, 239–258.

——— (1972a), "Classification for Treatment," Paper Presented at the National Institute of Law Enforcement and Criminal Justice Conference on the State of Research, Washington, D. C. May 4, 1972.

——— (1972b), "Correctional Treatment in Community Settings. A Report of Current Research," Prepared for the VI International Congress on Criminology, Madrid, Spain. September 21–27, 1970. Washington, DC: National Institute of Mental Health.

——— (1974), "Differential Intervention with Juvenile Delinquents," Paper Presented at the Juvenile Justice Standards Conference, American Bar Association, Berkeley, California. October 13–15, 1974.

——— (1977), "Correctional Treatment and Coercion: The Differential Effectiveness Perspective," *Criminal Justice and Behavior*, 4, 355–376.

——— (1982a), "A Follow-Up Study of Female Delinquents from the 1960s," *Journal of the International Differential Treatment Association*, 12, 59–68.

——— (1982b), "Delinquency Causation in Female Offenders," in N. Rafter and E. Stanko (eds.), *Judge, Lawyer, Victim, Thief: Women, Gender Roles, and Criminal Justice*. Boston: Northeastern University Press.

Warren, M. Q. and CTDT Staff (1972), "Center for Training in Differential Treatment: Final Report of Phase I (1967–1970). Part 1: Description and Evaluation of Training Project." Sacramento: American Justice Institute and the California Youth Authority.

Warren, M. Q., G. Howard, E. Thompson, and J. McHale: CTDT Staff (1974), "Center for Training in Differential Treatment: Final Report of Phase II (1970–1974). Description and Evaluation of Training Project." Sacramento: Human Learning Systems and the California Youth Authority.

Warren, M. Q. and T. Palmer (1965), "Community Treatment Project. An Evaluation of Community Treatment for Delinquents," CTP Research Report no. 6. Sacramento: California Youth Authority.

Warren, M. Q., T. Palmer, V. Neto, and J. Turner (1966a), "Community Treatment Project. An Evaluation of Community Treatment for Delinquents," CTP Research Report no. 7. Sacramento: California Youth Authority.

Warren, M. Q., T. Palmer, and J. Turner (1964a), "A Demonstration Project. An Evaluation of Community-Located Treatment for Delinquents. Proposal for Phase 2." Sacramento: California Youth Authority.

——— (1964b), "Community Treatment Project. An Evaluation of Community Treatment for Delinquents," CTP Research Report no. 5. Sacramento: California Youth Authority.

Warren, M. Q., T. Palmer, J. Turner, A. Dorsey, J. McHale, G. Howard, J. Riggs, J. Roberson, and W. Underwood (1966b), "*Interpersonal Maturity Level Classification: Juvenile Diagnosis and Treatment of Low, Middle, and High Maturity Delinquents*," Community Treatment Project. Sacramento: California Youth Authority.

Webster, N. (1965), *Webster's Seventh New Collegiate Dictionary*. Springfield, MA: Merriam.

——— (1974), *Webster's New World Dictionary of the American Language*. New York: The World Publishing Company.

Wedge, R. and T. Palmer (1989), "California's Juvenile Probation Camps: A Technical Analysis of Outcomes for a 1982 Release Cohort. Camps, Ranches, and Schools Study. Report no. 4." Sacramento: California Youth Authority.

——— (1994), "California's Juvenile Probation Camps: A Validation Study." Sacramento: California Youth Authority.

Wedge, R., R. White, and T. Palmer (1980), "I-Level and the Treatment of Delinquents," *Youth Authority Quarterly*, 33, 26–37.

Weeks, H. (1958), *Youthful Offenders at Highfields*. Ann Arbor: University of Michigan Press.

Weis, J. and J. Hawkins (1981), "Preventing Delinquency." Washington, DC: U.S. Department of Justice. Office of Juvenile Justice and Delinquency Prevention.

Wells, W. (1978), "I-Level Task Force Report." Sacramento: California Youth Authority, Institutions and Camps Branch.

Werner, E. (1972), "Relationships among Interpersonal Maturity, Personality Configurations, Intelligence, and Ethnic Status," Community Treatment Project Report Series: 1972, no. 1. Sacramento: California Youth Authority.

——— (1975), "Psychological and Ethnic Correlates of Interpersonal Maturity among Delinquents," *British Journal of Criminology*, 15, 51–68.

Werner, E. and T. Palmer (1975), "Psychological Characteristics of Successful and Unsuccessful Parolees: Implications of Heteroscedastic and Nonlinear Relationships," *Journal of Research in Crime and Delinquency*, 13, 165–178.

Werner, E. E. (1989), "Children of the Garden Island," *Scientific American*, 260, 106–111.

West, D. and D. Farrington (1977), *The Delinquent Way of Life*. London: Hienemann.

White, P. and D. Johns, (1973), "A Re-analysis of Lerman's Data As It Relates to Probation Subsidy," Research Division. Sacramento: California Youth Authority.

Whitehead, J. and S. Lab (1989), "A Meta-analysis of Juvenile Correctional Treatment," *Journal of Research in Crime and Delinquency,* 26, 276–295.

Whitehorn, J. and B. Betz (1954), "A Study of Psychotherapeutic Relationships between Physicians and Schizophrenic Patients," *American Journal of Psychiatry,* 111, 321–331.

—— (1960), "Further Studies of the Doctor as a Crucial Variable in the Outcome of Treatment with Schizophrenic Patients," *American Journal of Psychiatry,* 117, 215–223.

Whitesel, B. (1972), "An Assessment of Human Figure Drawings and Levels of Social Maturity." Sacramento: California State University. Unpublished master's thesis.

Wicker, T. (1975), *A Time to Die.* New York: Quadrangle/The New York Times Book Company.

—— (1976), Quoted in M. Serrill, "Critics of Corrections Speak Out," *Corrections Magazine,* 2, 3–8, 21–26.

Wier, C. (1975), "Summary of Closed Adolescent Treatment Center Evaluation. Final Report." Boulder, CO: Department of Institutions, Division of Youth Services and the Colorado Youth Services Institute.

Wilkins, L., J. Kress, D. Gottfredson, J. Calpen, and A. Gelman (1978), "Sentencing Guidelines: Structuring Judicial Discretion: Report on the Feasibility Study." Washington, DC: U.S. Department of Justice.

Wilks, J. and R. Martinson (1976), "Is the Treatment of Criminal Offenders Really Necessary?" *Federal Probation,* 40, 3–9.

Willman, H. and R. Chun (1973), "Homeward Bound. An Alternative to the Institutionalization of Adjucated Juvenile Offenders," *Federal Probation,* 37, 52–58.

Wilson, B. (1964), "The Behavior of the Delinquent Girl of Low Level Maturity as Perceived by Cottage Staff," Los Angeles: University of Southern California, School of Social Work. Unpublished masters thesis.

Wilson, J. (1975), *Thinking about Crime.* New York: Basic Books.

—— (1980), "'What Works' Revisited: New Findings on Criminal Rehabilitation," *The Public Interest,* 61, 3–17.

Wilson, J. and R. Herrnstein (1985), *Crime and Human Nature.* New York: Simon & Schuster.

Witkin, H., R. Dyk, H. Faterson, D. Goodenough, and S. Karp (1962), *Psychological Differentiation: Studies of Development.* New York: John Wiley and Sons.

Witkin, H., P. Oltman, E. Raskin, and S. Karp (1971), *Manual: Embedded Figures Test, Children's Embedded Figures Test, Group Embedded Figures Test.* Palo Alto, CA: Consulting Psychologists Press.

Wolf, F. (1986), *Meta-analysis. Quantitative Methods for Research Synthesis.* Beverly Hills: Sage.

Wolfe, L. (1978), "A Study of Organizational Compatibility." San Francisco: University of San Francisco. Unpublished doctoral dissertation.

Wolff, W. (1950), *The Threshold of the Abnormal.* New York: Hermitage House.

Wolfgang, M., R. Figlio, and T. Sellin (1972), *Delinquency in a Birth Cohort.* Chicago: University of Chicago Press.

Woodring, T. (1971), "Lorge-Thorndike and Wechsler I.Q. Comparisons among Youth Authority Wards," Research Division Report. Sacramento: California Youth Authority.

Wooldredge, J. (1988), "Differentiating the Effects of Juvenile Court Sentences on Eliminating Recidivism," *Journal of Research in Crime and Delinquency,* 25, 264–300.

Wright, K. (1988), "The Relationship of Risk, Needs, and Personality Classification Systems and Prison Adjustment," *Criminal Justice and Behavior,* 15, 454–471.

Wright, K., T. Clear, and P. Dickson (1984), "Universal Application of Probation Risk-Assessment Instruments: A Critique," *Criminology,* 22, 113–134.

Wright, K. and P. Meyer (1981), "A System Analysis of Crime Control Strategies," *Criminology,* 18, 531–547.

Wright, P., (1969), "A Comparison of Admission Characteristics of Youth Authority Wards, 1959–1968," Research Division, Information Systems Section. Sacramento: California Youth Authority.

Wright, W. and C. Jesness (1981), "Quality of Life, Problem Behavior, and Juvenile Delinquency," In J. Epstein (ed.), *The Quality of School Life*. Lexington, MA: D. C.: Heath.

Wright, W. and M. Dixon (1973), "Juvenile Delinquency Prevention. A Review of Evaluation Studies." *Journal of Research in Crime and Delinquency*, 14, 36–67.

Wylie, R. (1972), "An Alternative to Institutional Expansion," Montreal, Quebec: The Shawbridge Boys' Farm and Training School.

Wylie, R., W. Hanna, and P. Scully (1971), "Treating Delinquent Youth. The Boys' Farm (Shawbridge) Develops an I-Level Program," *Review of the Childhood and Youth Welfare Services*, 11, 1–40. Quebec: Department of Social Affairs.

Yochelson, S. and S. Samenow (1976), *The Criminal Personality. Volume 1: A Profile for Change*. New York: Jason Aronson.

——— (1977), *The Criminal Personality. Volume 2: The Change Process*. New York: Jason Aronson.

Yockey, W. and J. Kleine (1972), "Survey of Parole Reporting in Los Angeles County." Sacramento: California Youth Authority.

Youth Authority Board Policy Manual (1961 Revision). Sacramento: California Youth Authority.

——— (1974 Revision). Sacramento: California Youth Authority.

Youth Authority Budget Office (1982). "Operations Costs and Construction Cost Estimates," Sacramento: California Youth Authority.

——— (1994). "Construction Costs," Sacramento: California Youth Authority.

Youth Authority Facilities Planning Division (1995), "1995 Construction Cost Estimates," Sacramento: California Youth Authority.

Youth Authority Information Systems Section (1980), "Comparative Costs, Fiscal Years 1964-65 through 1978-79," Research Division Report. Sacramento: California Youth Authority.

——— (1984), "Comparative Costs, Fiscal Years 1964–65 through 1982–83," Research Division Report. Sacramento: California Youth Authority.

Youth Development and Delinquency Prevention Administration (1972), "National Strategy for Delinquency Prevention." Washington, DC: U.S. Department of Justice.

Zaidel, S. (1970), "Affect Awareness, Intelligence, and Interpersonal Maturity Classification." Los Angeles: University of California. Unpublished doctoral dissertation.

——— (1973), "Intelligence and Affect Awareness in Classifying Delinquents," *Journal of Research in Crime and Delinquency*, 10, 47–58.

Zedlewski, E. (1987), "Making Confinement Decisions." Washington, DC: U.S. Department of Justice.

Zimring, F. (1976), "A Consumer's Guide to Sentencing Reform: Making the Punishment Fit the Crime," Hastings Center Report no. 6. Hastings-on-Hudson, NY, pp. 13–17.